February 22–25, 2016
San Francisco, CA, USA

Association for Computing Machinery

Advancing Computing as a Science & Profession

wsdm 2016

WSDM'16

Proceedings of the Ninth ACM International Conference on
Web Search and Data Mining

Sponsored by:

ACM SIGIR, ACM SIGKDD, ACM SIGMOD, and ACM SIGWEB

Supported by:

Adobe, Baidu, Google, Microsoft, Yelp, A9, Facebook, LinkedIn, Netflix, Operator, Yahoo! Labs, Yandex, and Artificial Intelligence

Association for
Computing Machinery

Advancing Computing as a Science & Profession

The Association for Computing Machinery
2 Penn Plaza, Suite 701
New York, New York 10121-0701

Notice to Past Authors of ACM-Published Articles
ACM intends to create a complete electronic archive of all articles and/or other material previously published by ACM. If you have written a work that has been previously published by ACM in any journal or conference proceedings prior to 1978, or any SIG Newsletter at any time, and you do NOT want this work to appear in the ACM Digital Library, please inform permissions@acm.org, stating the title of the work, the author(s), and where and when published.

ISBN: 978-1-4503-3716-8 (Digital)

ISBN: 978-1-4503-4499-9 (Print)

Additional copies may be ordered prepaid from:

ACM Order Department
PO Box 30777
New York, NY 10087-0777, USA

Phone: 1-800-342-6626 (USA and Canada)
+1-212-626-0500 (Global)
Fax: +1-212-944-1318
E-mail: acmhelp@acm.org
Hours of Operation: 8:30 am – 4:30 pm ET

Printed in the USA

Preface by the General Chairs

Welcome to the Ninth ACM International Conference on Web Search and Data Mining (WSDM 2016) at the Mission Bay Conference Center in San Francisco from February 22nd to 25th of 2016. WSDM has gone a full circle around the globe and is back in the San Francisco Bay Area after 8 years. Since its beginnings in 2008 at the Stanford campus, WSDM has been established as one of the premier forums in the areas of search and data mining. The conference has also evolved, and today, the "Web" in its name encompasses a much wider set of technologies including the mobile eco-systems and representing how 3 billion users go online today worldwide.

This year the main technical program of WSDM preserves the format of the previous years and includes 3 days of single-track keynotes, practice and experience talks as well as research presentations. The program is well balanced between industry and academia which makes WSDM an opportunity for those two communities to connect and exchange ideas. The day preceding the main program includes the usual program of workshops, tutorials, and doctoral consortium, as well as two new events: VC & Industry Day; and the first official WSDM Cup data mining and prediction challenge workshop. The workshops allow for people with more specific interests to gather and discuss these in a smaller setting. In addition to the WSDM Cup workshop, which focuses on entity ranking in heterogeneous graphs, this year we also accepted four additional workshops on such diverse topics as query understanding, online ad targeting, ethics of online experimentation, and retrieval of X-rated information. The two accepted tutorials are on the topics of mining online data on politics, and click models for web search. This year the doctoral consortium provided a forum for 13 PhD students to get feedback on their dissertation work from some of the most prominent experts in the field of their study. Having WSDM in the San Francisco Bay Area provided a unique opportunity to connect the WSDM community with the venture capitalist and industrial community. The VC & Industry Day was added to take advantage of the high number of the VCs and relevant companies in the Bay Area and allow for these communities to meet and interact. The VC & Industry day presents a series of talks from prominent members of the VC community as well as industry leaders mixed with panels on topics ranging from the use of data science in startups to the sharing economy.

Our goal was to produce a well-rounded program that is technically strong, diverse, and relevant to today's state of the online world. We hope you find it enjoyable and inspiring. Foremost, we would like to thank the authors of all submitted papers as well as the speakers at the conference. The program was selected by the program committee and senior program committee members and we would like to thank them for ensuring a high quality program. We would like to thank the entire organizing committee and especially the PC chairs, Jennifer Neville and Filip Radlinski. Finally, special thanks goes to ACM and our sponsors that made the conference possible.

Welcome to WSDM 2016!

Paul Bennett
Microsoft Research

Vanja Josifovski
Pinterest

Preface by the Program Chairs

Welcome to WSDM, the 9th annual ACM International Conference on Web Search and Data Mining, held in San Francisco, USA. WSDM is one of the premier conferences on web inspired research involving search and data mining. We are pleased to present here the proceedings of the conference. The program reflects the breadth and diversity of research in the field and showcases the latest developments in the field.

The conference received a total of 368 submissions, out of which 67 were accepted for publication. As has been customary for the conference, we used a two-tier single-blind review process. In the first stage, three to four program committee members were assigned to every paper. The PC members provided ratings and comments while evaluating the papers according to the standard criteria of relevance, quality, reproducibility, clarity, and impact. In the second stage, every paper was assigned to a senior PC member. The senior PC member was tasked to oversee a discussion amongst the reviewers and attempt to reach a consensus recommendation for the paper. The final decisions were based on all of the above, as well as the senior PC member's recommendation. Ultimately 67 papers were selected for inclusion in the program.

The WSDM 2016 acceptance rate of 18.2% is comparable to the previous years. The accepted papers are from 90 institutions in 18 countries. The top technical areas covered by the accepted papers (as indicated by paper keywords) are machine learning (19%), social networks (16%), search (15%), social media (10%), and ranking (9%). This year, continuing with the WSDM tradition, oral presentation slots were allocated to all 67 accepted papers. Out of the 67 papers, 20 were assigned long presentation slots and 47 were assigned short presentation slots. This assignment was based on the topic and results in each paper, with the Program Chairs assigning long slots to papers more likely to appeal to a broader audience. In addition to the oral presentations, all papers will be presented as posters in interactive sessions.

We would like to acknowledge the tremendous work of the 41 senior program committee members, 243 program committee members, and 133 additional reviewers. Much of the credit for creating a high quality technical program goes to them. To recognize the hard work of the best reviewers, which is rarely publicized, we have awarded 21 Outstanding Reviewer Awards to members of the program committee, who were nominated by senior PC members as standing out amongst the reviewers.

The technical program this year also features keynotes by prominent researchers from academia and industry, Jeff Dean (Google), Yiling Chen (Harvard University), and Foster Provost (New York University). The program also features four invited Practice & Experience talks, which were introduced for the first time at WSDM 2014. These comprise Yoelle Maarek (Yahoo Labs), Jie Tang (Tsinghua University), Lars Backstrom (Facebook), and Mor Naaman (Cornell Tech/Seen.co). We would like to thank the keynote and P&E speakers for sharing their technical insights and research contributions with the conference attendees.

In addition, the program includes five workshops, two tutorials, and the WSDM Doctoral Consortium. We are happy to announce the first WSDM Cup Competition and expanded Industry Day that includes talks from venture capital investors and startups, taking advantage of the San Francisco location. The challenge in the inaugural 2016 WSDM CUP, organized by Microsoft and Elsevier, was to assess the query-independent importance of scholarly articles using data from the Microsoft Academic Graph. The VC & Industry Day includes four keynote and invited talks, three panels, and a poster session, discussing the role and application of data science in industry.

We are grateful to all those who submitted papers to the conference, as well as past and present attendees of the conference. Thanks to them WSDM has become a well-known international forum. We would also like to thank the general chairs, Paul Bennett and Vanja Josifovski, who were our partners in putting the conference program together, providing helpful feedback and advice along the way.

We hope you will find the WSDM program interesting and thought-provoking. Our goal was not only to give the authors the opportunity to share ideas with other researchers and practitioners from around the world, but also to foster new research and innovation in this fascinating Web era.

Jennifer Neville
Purdue University

Filip Radlinski
Microsoft

Table of Contents

Session: Search and Semantics

Session Chair: Vanessa Murdock *(Microsoft)*

Practice & Experience Track 1

Session Chair: Mounia Lalmas *(Yahoo Labs)*

Session: Observing Users

Session Chair: Mounia Lalmas *(Yahoo Labs)*

Keynote Address 2

Session: Leveraging Users

Session Chair: Yoelle Maarek *(Yahoo Labs)*

Session: Big Data Algorithms

Session Chair: Ronny Lempel *(Outbrain)*

Session: Entities and Structure

Session Chair: Lada Adamic *(Facebook)*

Practice & Experience Track 3

Session Chair: Brian Davison *(Lehigh University)*

Session: Social Events

Session Chair: Brian Davison *(Lehigh University)*

Tutorials

Workshop Summaries

Doctoral Consortium

WSDM 2016 Conference Organization

General Chairs: Paul N. Bennett (Microsoft Research)
Vanja Josifovski (Pinterest)

Program Chairs: Jennifer Neville (Purdue University)
Filip Radlinski (Microsoft)

Workshop Chairs: Eugene Agichtein (Emory University)
Dafna Shahaf (Hebrew University / Microsoft Research)

Tutorial Chairs: Sergei Vassilvitskii (Google)
Kira Radinsky (SalesPredict)

Doctoral Consortium Chairs: Kevyn Collins-Thompson (University of Michigan)
Andrew Tomkins (Google)

VC & Industry Day Chair: Lance Riedel (Pinterest)

WSDM Cup Chairs: Alex Wade (Microsoft Research)
Kuansan Wang (Microsoft Research)
Antonio Gulli (Elsevier B.V.)
Yizhou Sun (Northeastern University)

Best Paper Award Chair: Brian Davison (Lehigh University)

Treasurer: Milad Shokouhi (Microsoft)

Local Chair: Sandeep Tata (Google)

Media, Publicity, Web Chair: Polo Chau (Georgia Tech)

Sponsorship Chairs: James G. Shanahan (NativeX)
Rodrygo L.T. Santos (Federal University of Minas Gerais, Brazil)

Proceedings Chair: Anne Schuth (University of Amsterdam)

Webmaster and Web Designer: Minsuk (Brian) Kahng (Georgia Tech)

Steering Committee: Ricardo Baeza-Yates (Yahoo)
Paolo Boldi (University of Milano)
Andrei Broder (Google)
Brian D. Davison (Lehigh University)
Nick Koudas (University of Toronto)
Hang Li (Huawei Technologies)
Bing Liu (University of Illinois at Chicago)
Marc Najork (Google)

Senior Program Committee:

Lada Adamic (Facebook)
Deepak Agarwal (LinkedIn)
Eugene Agichtein (Yahoo Labs and Emory University)
Leman Akoglu (Stony Brook University)
Aris Anagnostopoulos (Sapienza University of Rome)
Ricardo Baeza-Yates (Yahoo Labs)
Ron Bekkerman (University of Haifa)
Ben Carterette (University of Delaware)
Deepayan Chakrabarti (University of Texas at Austin)
Kenneth Church (IBM)
Charles Clarke (University of Waterloo)
Kevyn Collins-Thompson (University of Michigan)
Nick Craswell (Microsoft)
Bruce Croft (University of Massachusetts Amherst)
Cristian Danescu-Niculescu-Mizil (Cornell University)
Ian Davidson (University of California, Davis)
Brian Davison (Lehigh University)
Maarten de Rijke (University of Amsterdam)
Fernando Diaz (Microsoft Research)
Ariel Fuxman (Google)
Evgeniy Gabrilovich (Google)
Ravi Kumar (Google)
Mounia Lalmas (Yahoo Labs)
Ronny Lempel (Outbrain)
Hang Li (Huawei Technologies)
Jimmy Lin (University of Waterloo)
Yan Liu (University of Southern California)
Yoelle Maarek (Yahoo Labs)
Vanessa Murdock (Microsoft)
Marc Najork (Google)
Alice Oh (KAIST)
B. Aditya Prakash (Virginia Tech)
Steffen Rendle (Google)
Pavel Serdyukov (Yandex)
Fabrizio Silvestri (Yahoo Labs)
Yaron Singer (Harvard University)
Evimaria Terzi (Boston University)
Ingmar Weber (Qatar Computing Research Institute)
Ryen W. White (Microsoft Research)
Emine Yilmaz (University College London)
Yisong Yue (California Institute of Technology)

WSDM 2016 Program Committee

Mikhail Ageev (Moscow State University)
Amr Ahmed (Google Research)
James Allan (University of Massachusetts Amherst)
Omar Alonso (Microsoft)
Tim Althoff (Stanford University)
Ashton Anderson (Stanford University)
Javed Aslam (Northeastern University)
Josh Attenberg (Etsy and NYU Stern School of Business)
Leif Azzopardi (University of Glasgow)
James Bagrow (University of Vermont)
Ashraf Bah Rabiou (University of Delaware)
Peter Bailey (Microsoft)
Leandro Balby Marinho (Federal University of Campina Grande)
Krisztian Balog (University of Stavanger)
Nicola Barbieri (Yahoo Labs)
Justin Basilico (Netflix)
Luca Becchetti (Sapienza University of Rome)
Andras A. Benczur (Institute for Computer Science and Control, Hungarian Academy of Sciences)
Michael Bendersky (Google)
Fabricio Benevenuto (Federal University of Minas Gerais (UFMG))
Klaus Berberich (Max Planck Institute for Informatics)
Smriti Bhagat (Facebook)
Albert Bifet (Télécom ParisTech)
Roi Blanco (Yahoo Labs)
Sebastian Blohm (Microsoft)
David Bodoff (University of Haifa)
Francesco Bonchi (ISI Foundation)
Ceren Budak (University of Michigan)
Suratna Budalakoti (Oracle Labs)
Jamie Callan (Carnegie Mellon University)
Carlos Castillo (Qatar Computing Research Institute)
James Caverlee (Texas A&M University)
Stefano Ceri (DEI, Politecnico di Milano)
Kaushik Chakrabarti (Microsoft)
Kevin Chen-Chuan Chang (University of Illinois at Urbana-Champaign)
Yi Chang (Yahoo Labs)
Laurent Charlin (Columbia University)
Duen Horng Chau (Georgia Institute of Technology)
Wei Chen (Microsoft Research)
Lu Chen (Wright State University)
Justin Cheng (Stanford University)
David Choi (Carnegie Mellon University)
Aleksandr Chuklin (University of Amsterdam)
Paul Clough (University of Sheffield)
Aron Culotta (Illinois Institute of Technology)
Jeffrey Dalton (Google)
Ovidiu Dan (Lehigh University)
Van Dang (Google)
Anirban Dasgupta (IIT Gandhinagar)
Mimno David (Cornell University)
Munmun De Choudhury (Georgia Institute of Technology)
Gianmarco De Francisci Morales (Aalto University)
Gerard de Melo (Tsinghua University)
Yves-Alexandre de Montjoye (Massachusetts Institute of Technology and Harvard University)
Pavel Dmitriev (Microsoft)
Peter Dolog (Aalborg University)
Debora Donato (StumbleUpon Inc)
Doug Downey (Northwestern University)
Alexey Drutsa (Yandex)
Susan Dumais (Microsoft Research)
Carsten Eickhoff (ETH Zurich)
Hoda Eldardiry (Palo Alto Research Center)
Alessandro Epasto (Brown University)
Alex Fabrikant (Google)
Xin Fan (Baidu)
Hui Fang (University of Delaware)
Henry Feild (Endicott College)
Paolo Ferragina (University of Pisa)
Dennis Fetterly (Microsoft Research)
Aram Galstyan (USC Information Sciences Institute)
Zeno Gantner (Nokia gate5 GmbH)
Luis Garcia Pueyo (Google)
Venkata Rama Kiran Garimella (Aalto University)
Aristides Gionis (Aalto University)
Nazli Goharian (Georgetown University)
Behzad Golshan (Boston University)
Manuel Gomez Rodriguez (MPI for Software Systems)
Siddharth Gopal (Carnegie Mellon University)

Antonino Gulli (Elsevier)
Krishna Gummadi (MPI for Software Systems)
Qi Guo (Microsoft)
Manish Gupta (Microsoft)
Gleb Gusev (Yandex)
Ido Guy (Yahoo Labs)
Hamed Haddadi (Queen Mary University of London)
Ahmed Hassan (Microsoft Research)
Claudia Hauff (Delft University of Technology)
Eshcar Hillel (Yahoo Labs)
Jake Hofman (Microsoft Research)
Katja Hofmann (Microsoft)
Petter Holme (Sungkyunkwan University)
Liangjie Hong (Yahoo Labs)
Xia Hu (Texas A&M University)
Xuanjing Huang (Fudan University)
Grace Hui Yang (Georgetown University)
Seung-Won Hwang (Yonsei University)
Stratis Ioannidis (Northeastern University)
Dietmar Jannach (TU Dortmund)
Xin Jiang (Huawei Noah's Ark Lab)
Jiepu Jiang (University of Massachusetts Amherst)
Xiaoming Jin (Tsinghua University)
Gareth Jones (Dublin City University)
Joemon Jose (University of Glasgow)
Jaap Kamps (University of Amsterdam)
Bhargav Kanagal (Google)
U Kang (Seoul National University)
Nattiya Kanhabua (Aalborg University)
Evangelos Kanoulas (University of Amsterdam)
Zohar Karnin (Yahoo Labs)
Makoto P. Kato (Kyoto University)
Emre Kıcıman (Microsoft Research)
Aleksander Kolcz (Twitter)
Arnd Christian König (Microsoft Research)
Nick Koudas (University of Toronto)
Ioannis Koutis (University of Puerto Rico-Rio Piedras)
Udo Kruschwitz (University of Essex)
Oren Kurland (Technion - Israel Institute of Technology)
Branislav Kveton (Adobe Research)
Wai Lam (The Chinese University of Hong Kong)
Renaud Lambiotte (University of Namur)
Theodoros Lappas (Stevens Institute of Technology)
Daniel Larremore (Santa Fe Institute)
Silvio Lattanzi (Google)
Joonseok Lee (Google Research)
Sune Lehmann (Technical University of Denmark)
Jochen Leidner (Thomson Reuters Corporation)
Kristina Lerman (University of Southern California)
Jure Leskovec (Stanford University)
Liane Lewin-Eytan (Yahoo Labs)
Cheng Li (University of Michigan)
Yingyu Liang (Princeton University)
David Liben-Nowell (Carleton College)
Dan Liebling (Microsoft Research)
Ee-Peng Lim (Singapore Management University)
Christina Lioma (University of Copenhagen)
Nelly Litvak (University of Twente)
Huan Liu (Arizona State University)
Yuanhua Lv (Microsoft Research)
Michael Lyu (The Chinese University of Hong Kong)
Craig Macdonald (University of Glasgow)
Debapriyo Majumdar (Indian Statistical Institute Kolkata)
Amin Mantrach (Yahoo Labs)
Winter Mason (Facebook)
Julian Mcauley (University of California, San Diego)
Richard Mccreadie (University of Glasgow)
Yelena Mejova (Qatar Computing Research Institute)
Peter Mika (Yahoo Labs)
Einat Minkov (University of Haifa)
Bhaskar Mitra (Microsoft)
Dunja Mladenic (Jozef Stefan Institute)
Franco Maria Nardini (ISTI-CNR)
Wolfgang Nejdl (L3S Research Center & University of Hannover)
Jian-Yun Nie (Universite de Montreal)
Alexandros Ntoulas (Samsung Research America)
Neil O'Hare (Yahoo Labs)
Joel Oren (University of Toronto)
Liudmila Ostroumova Prokhorenkova (Yandex)
Aditya Pal (IBM)
Sinno Jialin Pan (Nanyang Technological University, Singapore)
Rong Pan (Sun Yat-sen University)
Spiros Papadimitriou (Rutgers University)
Paolo Papotti (Qatar Computing Research Institute)
Virgil Pavlu (Northeastern University)
Leto Peel (Université catholique de Louvain)
Jian Pei (Simon Fraser University)

Barbara Poblete (University of Chile)
Daniele Quercia (Bell Labs)
Kira Radinsky (SalesPredict)
Hema Raghavan (IBM Research)
Fiana Raiber (Technion - Israel Institute of Technology)
Karthik Raman (Cornell University)
Sujith Ravi (Google)
Berthier Ribeiro-Neto (Google & UFMG)
Derek Ruths (McGill University)
Barna Saha (University of Massachusetts Amherst)
Rodrygo Santos (Universidade Federal de Minas Gerais)
Tamas Sarlos (Google)
Anne Schuth (University of Amsterdam)
Lior Seeman (Harvard University)
Erik Selberg (Amazon)
Dafna Shahaf (Stanford University)
James G. Shanahan (Independent Consultant, San Francisco)
Yue Shi (Yahoo Labs)
Milad Shokouhi (Microsoft)
Ambuj Singh (University of California, Santa Barbara)
Sameer Singh (University of Washington)
Steven Skiena (Stony Brook University)
Ian Soboroff (NIST)
Aya Soffer (IBM)
Oren Somekh (Yahoo Labs)
Daria Sorokina (A9 (Amazon))
Ramakrishnan Srikant (Google)
Isabelle Stanton (Google)
Bogdan State (Stanford University)
Harald Steck (Netflix)
Fabian M. Suchanek (Télécom ParisTech)
Torsten Suel (New York University)
Neel Sundaresan (Microsoft)
Marcin Sydow (PJIIT and ICS PAS, Warsaw)
Partha Talukdar (Indian Institute of Science)
Kunal Talwar (Google)
Chenhao Tan (Cornell University)
Lei Tang (Clari)
Jie Tang (Tsinghua University)
Sandeep Tata (Google)
Paul Thomas (CSIRO)
Hanghang Tong (Arizona State University)
Dolf Trieschnigg (Mydatafactory and University of Twente)
Panayiotis Tsaparas (University of Ioannina)
Charalampos Tsourakakis (Harvard University)
Oren Tsur (Harvard University & Northeastern University)
Yury Ustinovskiy (Yandex)
Sergei Vassilvitskii (Google)
Quan Wang (Chinese Academy of Sciences)
Ting Wang (Lehigh University)
Chi Wang (Microsoft Research)
Kuansan Wang (Microsoft Research)
Jun Wang (University College London)
Yue Wang (University of Michigan)
Hongning Wang (University of Virginia)
Gerhard Weikum (Max Planck Institute for Informatics)
Udi Weinsberg (Facebook)
Ji-Rong Wen (Renmin University of China)
Tim Weninger (University of Notre Dame)
Robert West (Stanford University)
Hua Wu (Baidu)
Wei Wu (Microsoft Research)
Rongjing Xiang (Google)
Jun Xu (Institute of Computing Technology, Chinese Academy of Sciences)
Tao Yang (Ask.com and UCSB)
Mi-Yen Yeh (Institute of Information Science, Academia Sinica)
Elad Yom-Tov (Microsoft Research)
Shuai Yuan (University College London)
Mustafa Zengin (University of Delaware)
Dan Zhang (Facebook)
Qi Zhang (Fudan University)
Weinan Zhang (University College London)
Shiqi Zhao (Baidu)
Bo Zhao (LinkedIn)
Jun Zhao (Institute of Automation, Chinese Academy of Sciences)
Zhe Zhao (University of Michigan)
Vincent W. Zheng (Advanced Digital Sciences Center)
Imed Zitouni (Microsoft)

WSDM 2016 Additional Reviewers

Daniel Agun (University of California, Santa Barbara)
Dyaa Albakour (Signal Media)
Victor Amelkin (University of California, Santa Barbara)
Oren Anava (Technion - Israel Institute of Technology)
Cigdem Aslay (University Pompeu Fabra)
Jordan Atlas (Microsoft)
Noa Avigdor-Elgrabli (Yahoo Labs)
Joel Barajas (University of California, Santa Cruz)
Christian Bauckhage (Fraunhofer IAIS)
Ghazaleh Beigi (Arizona State University)
Richard Berendsen (University of Amsterdam)
Edward Bortnikov (Yahoo Labs)
Janez Brank (Jozef Stefan Institute)
Marc Cartright (Google)
Andrea Ceroni (L3S Research Center)
Xixian Chen (The Chinese University of Hong Kong)
Shirley Zhe Chen (University of Michigan)
Tao Cheng (Microsoft)
Shay Cohen (University of Edinburgh)
Luis Cruz (University of Porto)
Andrea Cuttone (Technical University of Denmark)
Liang Dai (NativeX, University of California Santa Cruz)
Ron Daniel (Elsevier)
Shiri Dori-Hacohen (University of Massachusetts Amherst)
Tianming Du (University College London)
Yuan Fang (Institute for Infocomm Research, A*STAR)
Mehrdad Farajtabar (Georgia Institute of Technology)
Donatella Firmani (Sapienza University of Rome)
John Foley (University of Massachusetts Amherst)
Gaurang Gavai (Palo Alto Research Center)
Ricard Gavalda (Universitat Politècnica de Catalunya)
Phil Gooch (City University London)
Paul Groth (Elsevier)
Francesco Gullo (UniCredit)
Francisco J. Gutierrez (University of Chile)
Richard Guy (Microsoft)
John Hanley (Palo Alto Research Center)
Faegheh Hasibi (Norwegian University of Science and Technology)
Jose Miguel Herrera (Universidad de Chile)
Chaya Hiruncharoenvate (Georgia Institute of Technology)
Tao Hoang (Advanced Digital Sciences Center)
Tad Hogg (Institute for Molecular Manufacturing)
Maya Hristakeva (Mendeley)
Juhua Hu (Simon Fraser University)
Xin Jin (University of California, Santa Barbara)
Isaac Jones (Arizona State University)
Jaya Kawale (Adobe)
Blaž Kažič (Jozef Stefan Institute)
Dongwoo Kim (Microsoft)
Pigi Kouki (University of California, Santa Cruz)
Timothy La Fond (Purdue University)
Omer Lev (University of Toronto)
Jundong Li (Arizona State University)
Xin Li (Baidu)
Yongsub Lim (KAIST)
Nedim Lipka (Bauhaus University, Weimar)
Ahmad Mahmoody (Brown University)
Kleanthis Malialis (University College London)
Giuseppe Manco (ICAR-CNR)
Ilya Markov (University of Amsterdam)
Sourav Medya (University of California, Santa Barbara)
Qiaozhu Mei (University of Michigan)
Pavel Metrikov (Northeastern University)
Tom Minka (Microsoft Research)
Enys Mones (Technical University of Denmark)
Fred Morstatter (Arizona State University)
Tu Ngoc Nguyen (L3S Research Center)
Anh Van Dong Nguyen (University of California, Santa Barbara)
Inna Novalija (Jozef Stefan Institute)
Daan Odijk (University of Amsterdam)
Adi Omari (Technion - Israel Institute of Technology)
Sujit Pal (Elsevier)
Ha-Myung Park (KAIST)
Yuval Pinter (Yahoo Labs)
Dror Porat (IBM)
Mauricio Quezada (University of Chile)
Suhas Ranganath (Arizona State University)

Luis Rei (Jozef Stefan Institute)
Kan Ren (Shanghai Jiao Tong University)
Matteo Riondato (Two Sigma Labs)
Petar Ristoski (University of Mannheim)
Xin Rong (University of Michigan)
Yifei Rong (YOYI Inc.)
Michael Rowell (Microsoft)
Karankumar Sabhnani (University of Delaware)
Egor Samosvat (Yandex)
Justin Sampson (Arizona State University)
Aharon Satt (IBM)
Michal Shmueli-Scheuer (IBM)
Isaac Sijaranamual (University of Amsterdam)
Arlei Silva (University of California, Santa Barbara)
Jaspreet Singh (L3S Research Center)
Janez Starc (Jozef Stefan Institute)
Luka Stopar (Jozef Stefan Institute)
Arkadiusz Stopczynski (Technical University of Denmark)
Acar Tamersoy (Georgia Institute of Technology)
Xun Tang (University of California, Santa Barbara)
Fangbo Tao (University of Illinois at Urbana-Champaign)
Mohamad Ali Torkamani (University of Oregon)
Nam Khanh Tran (L3S Research Center)
Anh Tuan Tran (L3S Research Center)
Gareth Tyson (Queen Mary University of London)
Utkarsh Upadhyay (MPI for Software Systems)
Isabel Valera (MPI for Software Systems)
George Valkanas (Stevens Institute of Technology)
Pim van der Hoorn (University of Twente)
Christophe Van Gysel (University of Amsterdam)
Garnet Vaz (Microsoft)
Nikos Voskarides (University of Amsterdam)
Suhang Wang (Arizona State University)
Wenbo Wang (Wright State University)
Ran Wolff (Yahoo Labs)
Liang Wu (Arizona State University)
Yu Wu (Beihang University)
Liang Wu (Columbia University)
Xiaokui Xiao (Nanyang Technological University)
Chenyan Xiong (Carnegie Mellon University)
Hui Xu (The Chinese University of Hong Kong)
Amit Yadav (Indian Statistical Institute Kolkata)
Zi Yang (Carnegie Mellon University)
Yu Yang (Simon Fraser University)
Yang Yang (Beihang University)
Junjie Yao (East China Normal University)
Shanshan Ying (Advanced Digital Sciences Center)
Hongyuan You (University of California, Santa Barbara)
Qi Yu (University of Southern California)
Ruirong Zhang (Tsinghua University)
Zihan Zhang (Tsinghua University)
Yuting Zhang (Tsinghua University)
Hongyi Zhang (The Chinese University of Hong Kong)
Shenglin Zhao (The Chinese University of Hong Kong)
Lu Zheng (Facebook)
Bo Zong (University of California, Santa Barbara)

WSDM 2016 Sponsors & Supporters

Sponsors:

SIGIR Special Interest Group on Information Retrieval

ACM SIGMOD

KDD

sig web

Diamond Supporter:

Adobe

Platinum Supporters:

Baidu 百度

Google

Microsoft

yelp

A9

Gold Supporter:

facebook

Silver Supporters:

LinkedIn

NETFLIX

Operator

YAHOO! LABS

Bronze Supporter:

Yandex

Special Supporter:

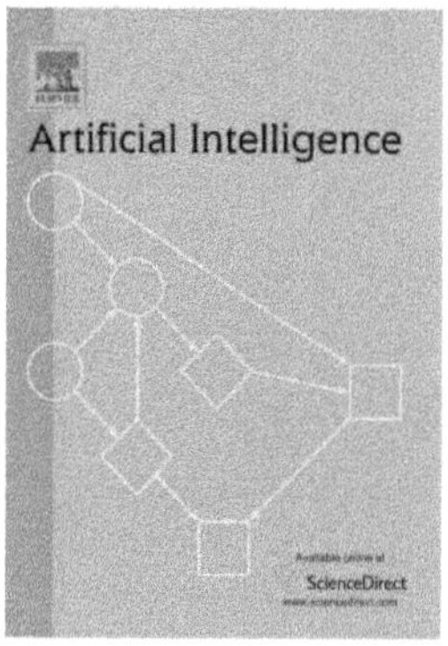

Friends:

KDnuggets™

SF DATA MINING

RESEARCH NEWS

You are what you read.

Large-Scale Deep Learning for Building Intelligent Computer Systems

Jeff Dean
Google
jeff@google.com

ABSTRACT

For the past five years, the Google Brain team has focused on conducting research in difficult problems in artificial intelligence, on building large-scale computer systems for machine learning research, and, in collaboration with many teams at Google, on applying our research and systems to dozens of Google products. Our group has recently open-sourced the TensorFlow system (tensorflow.org), a system designed to easily express machine ideas, and to quickly train, evaluate and deploy machine learning systems. In this talk, I'll highlight some of the design decisions we made in building TensorFlow, discuss research results produced within our group, and describe ways in which these ideas have been applied to a variety of problems in Google's products, usually in close collaboration with other teams.

This talk describes joint work with many people at Google.

Keywords

Neural networks; distributed systems; machine learning; deep learning; computer vision; speech recognition; language understanding

BIO

Jeff Dean joined Google in 1999 and is currently a Google Senior Fellow in Google's Research Group, where he leads the Google Brain team, Google's deep learning research team in Mountain View, working on systems for speech recognition, computer vision, language understanding, and various predictive tasks.

He has co-designed/implemented five generations of Google's crawling, indexing, and query serving systems, and co-designed/implemented major pieces of Google's initial advertising and AdSense for Content systems.

He is also a co-designer and co-implementor of Google's distributed computing infrastructure, including the MapReduce, BigTable and Spanner systems, protocol buffers, LevelDB, the recently open-sourced TensorFlow system for machine learning, systems infrastructure for statistical machine translation, and a variety of internal and external libraries and developer tools. He received a Ph.D. in Computer Science from the University of Washington in 1996. He is a Fellow of the ACM and the AAAS, a member of the U.S. National Academy of Engineering, and a recipient of the Mark Weiser Award and the ACM-Infosys Foundation Award in the Computing Sciences.

WSDM'16, February 22–25, 2016, San Francisco, CA, USA
ACM 978-1-4503-3716-8/16/02.
http://dx.doi.org/10.1145/2835776.2835844

Who Will Reply to/Retweet This Tweet? The Dynamics of Intimacy from Online Social Interactions

Nicholas Jing Yuan[†], Yuan Zhong[†‡], Fuzheng Zhang[†],
Xing Xie[†], Chin-Yew Lin[†], Yong Rui[†]
[†]Microsoft Research
[‡]Northeastern University, Boston, MA, USA
{nichy, fuzzhang, xingx, cyl, yongrui} at microsoft.com, zhong.yu at husky.neu.edu

ABSTRACT

Friendships are dynamic. Previous studies have converged to suggest that social interactions, in both online and offline social networks, are diagnostic reflections of friendship relations (also called social ties). However, most existing approaches consider a social tie as either a binary relation, or a fixed value (named *tie strength*). In this paper, we investigate the *dynamics* of dyadic friend relationships through online social interactions, in terms of a variety of aspects, such as *reciprocity*, *temporality*, and *contextuality*. In turn, we propose a model to predict *repliers* and *retweeters* given a particular tweet posted at a certain time in a microblog-based social network. More specifically, we have devised a learning-to-rank approach to train a ranker that considers elaborate user-level and tweet-level features (like sentiment, self-disclosure, and responsiveness) to address these dynamics. In the prediction phase, a tweet posted by a user is deemed a query and the predicted repliers/retweeters are retrieved using the learned ranker. We have collected a large dataset containing 73.3 million dyadic relationships with their interactions (replies and retweets). Extensive experimental results based on this dataset show that by incorporating the dynamics of friendship relations, our approach significantly outperforms state-of-the-art models in terms of multiple evaluation metrics, such as MAP, NDCG and Topmost Accuracy. In particular, the advantage of our model is even more promising in predicting the exact sequence of repliers/retweeters considering their orders. Furthermore, the proposed approach provides emerging implications for many high-value applications in online social networks.

Categories and Subject Descriptors

H.2.8 [**Database Management**]: Data mining; J.4 [**Social and Behavioral Science**]: Sociology

Keywords

dynamic tie strength, friendship relation, online social interaction

WSDM'16, February 22–25, 2016, San Francisco, CA, USA.

 ISBN 978-1-4503-3716-8/16/02...$15.00

DOI: http://dx.doi.org/2835776.2835800

1. INTRODUCTION

Social ties have been extensively studied in domains as varied as sociology [11], psychology [30], and biology [6]. It is well recognized that *proximity* [1, 27] and *homophily* [18, 23] play key roles in the formation of friendships: People tend to be friends with others who are close by, and/or similar to themselves in terms of age, ethnicity, education, and even genotypes [6].

However, not all friendships are equal. The concept of tie strength was introduced by Granovetter [11] as early as the 1970's, where the frequency of interaction was used as a diagnosis of the tie strength. Until recently, however, the rapidly increasing digitalization of communications provided the availability to estimate tie strength using large-scale communication data such as emails [28, 12] and mobile phone logs [26, 5]. During the past few years, the emergence of online social networks has profoundly changed the way people communicate and socialize: People interact with much lower communication cost and greater variety of modes, (e.g., on Twitter, a user can *reply* to a friend's tweet, or *retweet* a tweet so as to broadcast it to his/her followers). Social ties and tie strength in online social networks were also brought to attention of researchers. Several studies have exploited rich interaction data in online social networks to investigate the strength between dyadic ties [35, 8, 17, 29].

Nevertheless, most existing studies consider tie strength as static: either a category (strong/weak tie) or a fixed value. However, the dynamics of tie strength, which have rarely been addressed, play a non-negligible role in understanding friend relationships. First, the strength of a tie may not be reciprocal [25]. For example, Alice considers Bob her best friend, but Bob may consider Carol his best friend. Second, tie strength can evolve over time, e.g., your best friend during high school may not be your current best friend. Third, given different contexts such as location, emotion, and environment, people may perceive different feelings of closeness, i.e., tie strength. For instance, when you travel to another city, you may frequently interact with some local friends (e.g., alumni) who you have not been in touch with for a long time. Given the above dynamic characteristics, a static measurement of tie strength is usually coarse-grained, and sometimes unrealistic.

In this paper, we examine dynamics of tie strength through a microblog-based social network and on this basis we propose a general model to predict the repliers and retweeters of a particular tweet considering friendship dynamics. Specifically, given *a tweet posted by a particular user at a certain time*, we aim to predict *which friends of this user will reply to/retweet this tweet.* Note that for replying and retweeting, the results may be quite different. To tackle this problem, we convert the prediction task into an information retrieval task: Given the tweet posted by u as a query, we retrieve a ranked list of friends of u, according to their intentions of replying to/retweeting this tweet, where the ranking model is learned through a *learning-to-rank* framework.

Such prediction can enable a variety of promising applications in online social networks, e.g., people are more likely to adopt a product recommended by a close friend (after viewing his/her retweet talking about the product) than a casual acquaintance. Thus an accurate prediction of potential reactors can guide advertisers and marketers to design better incentive mechanisms. Our approach and findings can also help users create content to engage reactions and increase social impact, e.g., suggesting the best time of a day to post a tweet related to a certain topic that can trigger a discussion among the contacts in your social circle. Meanwhile, the proposed framework for analyzing friendship dynamics can also be applied to online communication platforms such as Skype and WhatsApp. For instance, creating and maintaining contact groups (or social circles) are usually tedious. However, given the precise estimation of dynamic tie strength, we can automatically provide a list of "local friends" a person would like to call when traveling to a given city.

To the best of our knowledge, this is the first work that predicts both repliers and retweeters at *tweet-level* (i.e., the prediction considers both the content of a tweet and the context of a user). Overall, this paper offers the following contributions:

- We exploit the dynamics of social interactions in terms of reciprocity, temporality, and contextuality, and craft a collection of features from online social networks to measure the interaction dynamics. In particular, we explicitly model the *responsiveness* of a user, which captures the availability, capacity, and tendency of a user's interaction behaviors.

- Based on a large dataset we have collected from Sina Weibo, we develop a learning-to-rank framework incorporating the above features, so as to predict both repliers and retweeters based on the content of a tweet and the context of a user. In addition, our model can predict the sequence of repliers and retweeters for a particular tweet, i.e., who replies/retweets the first, second, etc.

- We have conducted extensive experiments to validate the effectiveness of the proposed prediction model with multiple evaluation metrics. The results show that by considering the dynamics of tie strength, our approach significantly outperforms state-of-the-art models in terms of predictive power validated by multiple metrics such as MAP, NDCG, and Topmost Accuracy.

The rest of this paper is organized as follows: Sec. 2 explores the dynamics of social interactions in various aspects. Sec. 3 introduces the prediction model of online social interactions. Sec. 4 presents the experimental results based upon a large-scale dataset. Finally, related work is reviewed in Sec. 5 and the paper is briefly concluded in Sec. 6.

2. DYNAMICS OF SOCIAL INTERACTIONS

Given an online social network as a directed graph $G = (U, F)$, where U are users, and F are the following relations ($(u, v) \in F$ means a user $u \in U$ follows $v \in U$ on G), we define a *friend* and an *ego network* as follows.

DEFINITION 1 (FRIEND). *A user $u \in U$ is referred to as a* friend *of user $v \in U$ (or u and v have a friendship relation), denoted by $u \sim v$, if $(u, v) \in F$ and $(v, u) \in F$.*

DEFINITION 2 (EGO NETWORK). *The* neighbours *of a user $u \in V$ are defined as*

$$\mathring{E}_u = \{v | u \sim v, v \in U\}, \quad (1)$$

and the ego network *of u is $E_u = \mathring{E}_u \cup \{u\}$.*

Sutcliffe et al. [30] suggest that interaction frequency is one of the most reliable correlations of relationship strength in both humans and animals. In this section, exemplified with interaction data from Sina Weibo[1] (a microblog-based social network known as the Chinese Twitter), we introduce several key aspects of friendship dynamics. The dataset was crawled using open APIs (refer to Sec. 3.1 for the crawling procedure and Sec. 4.2.1 for the data description).

2.1 Reciprocity

From an economic perspective, social interaction can be considered an investment for maintaining tie strength and bringing benefit to the ego [30]. However, the investment will not necessarily equal the benefit.

To quantify the reciprocity between two users u and v, we first calculate the *percentile rank* of v in terms of outgoing interactions from u to v, which measures the percentage of users who have received more or as many interactions from u compared with v (the smaller PR is, the higher rank v has), denoted by $\text{PR}_u(v)$:

$$\text{PR}_u(v) = \frac{||\{w | f_{u \to w} > f_{u \to v}\}|| + 0.5||\{w | f_{u \to w} = f_{u \to v}\}||}{||\mathring{E}_u||}, \quad (2)$$

where $f_{u \to w}$ is the outgoing interaction frequency from u to w.

Then we define the Reciprocal Interaction Rank (RIR) from u to v as follows.

$$\text{RIR}_{u \to v} = (PR_u(v) - PR_v(u)) \times \mathfrak{D}. \quad (3)$$

Here, we scale the original difference between $PR_u(v)$ and $PR_v(u)$ with $\mathfrak{D} = 150$, which is the so called Dunbar's number. Dunbar [4] believed that the number of stable social ties in an ego network is approximated to be 150 on average, which is correlated with the relative neocortex size. This number was recently validated using Facebook and Twitter data [10]. Note that RIR is an asymmetric measurement, which shows the degree of inequality in terms of perceived tie strength to a certain extent.

We plot the distribution of reciprocal interaction ranks of 1 million randomly sampled social ties on Sina Weibo as shown in Figure 1(a), where we only present the distribution of positive values since the negative ones are mirror symmetric. As is shown, for a large portion of social ties, the reciprocal interaction rank deviates from zero, which indicates the asymmetry of tie strength.

2.2 Temporality

The tie strength between a dyadic relation may change over a certain period of time.

For example, if we consider the friend who we reply to/retweet the most often as the "best friend", we can identify whether the best friend changes over time. We randomly sampled 1 million users and identified their best friends for each month. Then we count the number of distinct best friends for each user during about 51 months (the range of our dataset). Figure 1(b) and Figure 1(c) present the distributions of the number of distinct best friends in terms of replies and retweets respectively. Apparently, almost all users have changed their best friends, and most users (64% for reply and 74%) have 3 distinct best friends during this period. We note that although the best friends based on different interaction types (e.g., replies and retweets) may vary for an individual, the distributions look similar.

2.3 Contextuality

Given different contexts, people may perceive different degrees of intimacy. Such contexts include locations, availability (to inter-

[1]http://weibo.com

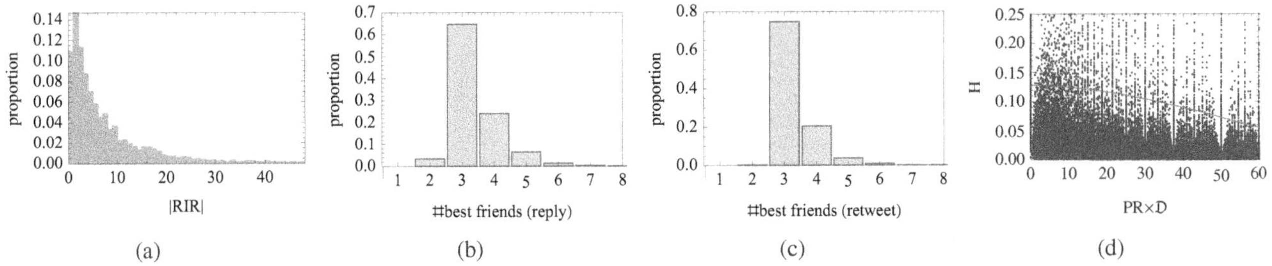

Figure 1: Dynamics of tie strength w.r.t different aspects based on Sina Weibo data

act), emotional states and other factors (we will detail them later in Sec. 3.3).

For example, emoticons are popular in many online social networks, where some emoticons, such as a smiling face, represent delightful emotions while some others convey unhappiness, which imply the emotion of a user when posting a tweet/reply. We randomly sampled 1 million users and computed the ratio of replies that contain happy emoticons sent from u to each of u's friends v, denoted as $\mathrm{H}_{u\to v}$, divided by all the replies sent from u to his/her friends (note that here we use the ratio for normalization over all users). Meanwhile, we calculated the percentile rank (PR) for each of the user pairs and scaled it with the Dunbar's Number introduced in Sec. 2.1. Then, we have a list: $\{(x_i, y_i)\}_{i=1}^{L}$, where x_i is the PR value scaled by $\mathfrak{D}$ and y_i is the ratio of happy-emoticon replies for the ith user pair. Figure 1(d) shows the scatter plot as well as a fitted curve of these pairs, which clearly indicates that when people reply to a friend's tweet, they are more likely to enclose an emoticon if the friend is ranked higher (in terms of the PR value).

3. LEARNING TO RANK FRIENDS

Given a tweet $\mathcal{T}$ posted on a microblog-based social network (such as Twitter or Sina Weibo) by user u, at time t, this section introduces a model to rank u's friends according to their intentions of replying and retweeting $\mathcal{T}$ respectively. We first provide an overview of the system in Sec. 3.1, and detail the key components later in Sec. 3.2, 3.3, and 3.4.

3.1 Overview

As illustrated in Figure 2 and Figure 3, our model works as a typical machine-learned search engine that includes three phases: the crawling phase, the offline training phase, and the online prediction phase, where the training and prediction phases are two core parts of our inference model.

• **Crawling.** In the crawling phase, we start from a seed user dataset obtained through the LifeSpec system [36]. By calling the APIs, we can retrieve all the friends of a user and recursively explore a large number of users, which is the *Expanding Step* of the crawler. Later on, in order to get all the tweets and replies of the users, we traverse their ego-networks and crawl all their tweets and their neighbours' tweets. This is the *Shrinking Step*. Note that Sina Weibo does not provide an API to crawl the replies posted by a user directly, so, we work around this by extracting a user's replies from each tweet posted by the user's friends (since there is an API to get the replies to a particular tweet). The Expanding Step and the Shrinking Step, as shown on the left side of Figure 2, are performed iteratively to achieve both the coverage (i.e., a large number of users) and the effectiveness (since we need all replies posted by these users to analyze their tie strength based on the online interaction histories). As a result, for each target user[2], we crawled profiles, tweets (including retweets), and replies of all the users in u's ego network E_u.

[2]A target user is the user whose friends will be ranked.

• **Training.** In the training phase shown on the right side of Figure 2, we construct a series of *user-level* and *tweet-level* features. Here, user-level features are comprised of reciprocal rank, profile affinity, topic affinity, and a responsiveness matrix, for each target user. The two categories of affinity capture the homophily between u and u's friends. For example, the similarity of educational background is one of the features in the profile affinity. For each affinity, we build a sorted list where each entry of the list is an affinity value calculated based on a social tie (u, v), where $v \in \mathring{E}_U$. Here, the topic affinity is computed based on the named-entities extracted from each tweet and reply posted by users in E_u. We note that for certain languages written without spaces (e.g., Chinese), text segmentation, which is a standard NLP task, should be pre-processed to segment the sentences into component words carrying meaningful units. All the affinity features are sorted in descending order of affinity value, which could also be considered the inverted indexes in a typical retrieval system. Through responsiveness analysis (detailed in Sec. 3.3), the responsiveness matrix is derived from u's historical interaction behaviors with $\mathring{E}_u$, which summarizes u's *tendency*, *availability*, and *capacity* to interact with his/her friends. In our model, all these indexes and the responsive matrix are periodically updated so as to keep track of users' temporal updates of their profile and topic affinity, as well as the responsiveness. Meanwhile, tweet-level features are extracted from each tweet and reply posted by users in E_u, which are derived from sentiment analysis and self-disclosure analysis. To learn a ranking model combining all the features, we sample a set of positive and negative instances to train the model. Given a tweet $\mathcal{T}$ posted by a user u at time t and the actual repliers/retweeters, we perform supervised learning to train a ranking model following the typical learning-to-rank framework.

• **Prediction.** In the prediction phase (detailed in Sec. 3.5), given a query, i.e., a tweet $\mathcal{T}$ posted by a user u at time t, we first perform query understanding to analyze the context (after named-entity recognition, segmentation, sentiment and self-disclosure analysis, as in the training phase), and feed the ranking model with all the extracted features to generate a score for each candidate, thus obtaining the final ranking list.

In summary, our model is designed to address the dynamics of tie strength and social interactions, where different components of models reflect various aspects of the dynamics as annotated in Figure 2.

Reciprocity. We model all interactions for each dyadic relationship as directed behaviors instead of undirected behaviors employed in many existing approaches [8], thus non-reciprocal patterns are explicitly measured, e.g., the responsiveness analysis reveals the relative tendency to interact with each friend in the ego network.

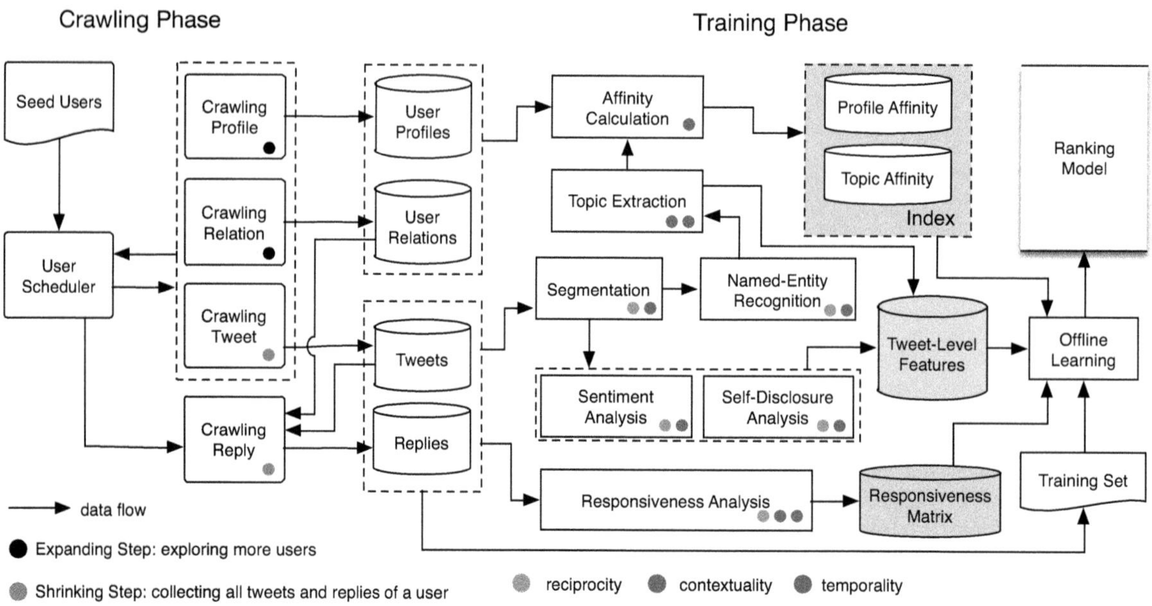

Figure 2: The crawling phase and training phase.

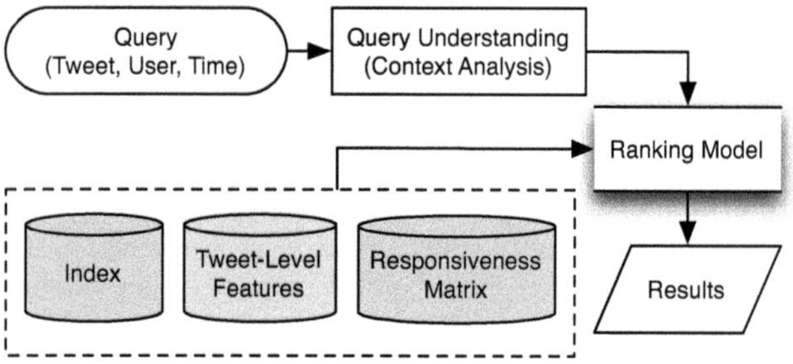

Figure 3: The prediction phase.

Temporality. Our prediction system works as a typical search engine, where the indexes and responsiveness matrices are updated periodically to ensure the freshness of the features. Meanwhile, the tweet-level features are streaming data that is updated in real-time to reflect the timely and subtle change in users' sentiment and degree of self-disclosure.

Contextuality. We extract rich contextual features from the tweets and replies, which diagnose a user's context when interacting with friends, such as mood, opinion, availability, and even physical environment.

3.2 Affinity Calculation

3.2.1 *Profile Affinity*

We use the following features to build indexes representing profile affinity: *Gender*, *Age*, *Education*, *City*, and *CommonFriends*. We build a sorted list for each feature to index u's friends $v_1, v_2, \ldots \in \mathring{E}_u$. Some features are binary, e.g., *Gender* and *City* respectively indicate whether a friend of u has the same gender and lives in the same city as u. Other features are real-valued features calculated using affinity functions. For *Education* and *CommonFriends*, we utilize Jaccard Similarity, e.g., given u's school list S_u (a user may publish several schools including high school, college, etc. on her profile page), and v's school list S_v, *Education* affinity is calculated by

$$\text{Affinity}(\textit{Education}) = \frac{|S_u \cap S_v|}{|S_u \cup S_v|}. \quad (4)$$

Similarly, *CommonFriends* is obtained by

$$\text{Affinity}(\textit{CommonFriends}) = \frac{|\mathring{E}_u \cap \mathring{E}_v|}{|\mathring{E}_u \cup \mathring{E}_v|}. \quad (5)$$

For *Age*, we use the following affinity measurement:

$$\text{Affinity}(\textit{Age}) = \frac{\min(A_u, A_v)}{\max(A_u, A_v)}, \quad (6)$$

where A_u and A_v are the ages of u and v.

We note that the above features are provided by most users in our target Sina Weibo dataset (described later in Sec. 4.2.1), mainly because the system guides users to input these attributes once a user registers the website, and as long as such information has not been provided, the system will redirect to the page asking the user to input these attributes every time the user logs in to the system. Nevertheless, for the users without such attributes, we assign -1 for the corresponding features.

3.2.2 *Topic Affinity*

To summarize and compare users' topics of interest, we first identify named-entities from users' tweets and replies, following the method proposed in [20] (segmentation of Chinese words is preprocessed). Next, we remove the non-named entities from the corpus, and perform topic discovery and topical keyword extraction for each user. The reason for using a filtered corpus is that unlike formal text such as news reports, tweets are very short text strings, with more diverse topics and many noisy or meaningless words. For the same reason, traditional topic discovery methods designed for formal long text such as Latent Dirichlet Allocation (LDA) does not perform well on tweets [38]. To tackle this challenge, we employ the topical keyphrase extraction approach introduced by Zhao et al. [37]. In this method, a Twitter-LDA model is leveraged to discover topics, where each word in a tweet is either assigned as a topical word or a background word according to a Bernoulli test, then a

Sentiment	Emoticons
Happy	
Sad	

Figure 4: Classifications of emoticons on Sina Weibo

PageRank-based method is utilized to identify important words in a topic as topical key phrases.

As a result, we obtain a topic distribution $\boldsymbol{\theta}_u = (\boldsymbol{\theta}_u^{(1)}, \boldsymbol{\theta}_u^{(2)} \ldots \boldsymbol{\theta}_u^{(K)})$ for each user u, where $\boldsymbol{\theta}_u^{(i)}$ is a distribution over words, $i = 1, 2, \ldots, K$. And for each topic i, we identify a list of important words through cTPR (context-aware topical PageRank) [38], as the topical keywords of user u. In many social networks, users self-tag several keywords as their interests. We merge the identified keywords and the self-tags, as the final keywords of the users, which will be used in the online prediction phase. In addition, we compute the topic affinity between u and $v \in \mathring{E}_u$ using cosine similarity as follows:

$$\text{Affinity}(Topic) = \frac{\boldsymbol{\theta}_u \cdot \boldsymbol{\theta}_v}{\|\boldsymbol{\theta}_u\| \|\boldsymbol{\theta}_v\|}, \qquad (7)$$

and index the affinity values with a sorted list, as in the profile affinity indexes.

3.3 Context Analysis

On microblog-based social networks, people may interact with both close friends and casual acquaintances. However, as discussed earlier, different contexts such as emotions, opinions, and level of self-disclosure capture the rich dynamics of tie strength. We perform sentiment analysis and self-disclosure analysis for each tweet (including retweets) and reply posted by users in $\mathring{E}_u$ to extract context features.

3.3.1 Sentiment

We perform sentiment analysis to mine both emotions (such as happy, sad) and polarity (positive/neutral/negative) from each tweet. On microblogs such as Twitter and Sina Weibo, people frequently use emoticons to express their emotions. These emoticons were also explicitly manually labeled to different classes as shown in Figure 4. To classify the tweets and replies according to polarity, we leverage the emoticons as noisy labels to train a SVM classifier using a linear kernel [9]. In addition to unigram and bigram features, we also adopt other contextual features such as punctuation, hashtags and several target-dependent features introduced by Jiang et al. [15] to train a classifier. For each tweet and reply, we obtain the polarity using the trained model and classify the emotion based on the emoticons (if no emoticons are used, we assign it a dummy class as the emotion).

3.3.2 Self-Disclosure Analysis

In social psychology, self-disclosure is found to be the key characteristic indicating the strength of social ties [24, 31]. However, canonical methods for measuring self-disclosure often require psychological assessments based on questionnaires. Nevertheless, some linguistic features reveal the degree of self-disclosure in online interactions. We measure self-disclosure for each tweet and reply with the following indicative linguistic features (only the first two features are applied to replies since the latter two are not available for replies in Sina Weibo):

- Length of tweets/replies. Although the length of tweets is limited (e.g., 140 words in Twitter and 140 Chinese characters in Sina Weibo), when users tend to self-expose by sharing personal information, feelings, or thoughts with others, they often use more words [14].

- Occurrence of first person words such as "I," "me," "my," "mine," etc. Several studies have suggested that this feature is indicative of self-disclosure in both online and offline social interactions [3].

- Geo-Tweets. On many social networks such as Twitter and Sina Weibo, users can post geo tweets, indicating their geo-locations of themselves when posting that tweet, which is considered a typical behavior of self-disclosure [2]

- Client Types. We have the information of the clients (desktop client/mobile client) when people post a tweet, which exposes (or indicates) users' physical status, e.g., if users tweet using mobile clients, it is more likely that they are on the move, otherwise, i.e., using web client, they are probably sitting in front of their PCs at home or at work.

3.3.3 Responsiveness Analysis

Existing methods for predicting repliers/retweeters usually assume that all u's friends have read the tweets posted by u and are equally available to interact with u [29], which is often an unrealistic assumption. In responsiveness analysis, we use historical interaction data to explicitly measure 1) the availability that a user has to reply to/retweet a tweet; 2) the capacity of a user to read tweets and interact with others; and 3) the tendency of a user to interact with a particular friend. All these factors are time-dependent variables.

Actually, given a time bin $\Delta = [t_1, t_2]$, we can "reconstruct" the timeline of a user by retrieving all the tweets and replies posted by E_u during Δ. Let $\mathcal{T}_u^{\Delta}$ denote the tweets posted by u within Δ (including retweets), and let $\mathcal{R}_{v,u}^{\Delta}$ denote the replies sent from v to u within Δ. Then a user u's cost of reading the tweets and replies within Δ could be estimated by

$$\sum_{v \in \mathring{E}_u} \left(\|\mathcal{T}_v^{\Delta}\| + \|\mathcal{R}_{v,u}^{\Delta}\| \right). \qquad (8)$$

In practice, we partition a day into discrete time bins and aggregate the above statistics over multiple days, to compute the average cost for each time bin of a day. Intuitively, the more cost u spends on reading these tweets and replies, the less available that u is to respond (reply to/retweet) a particular tweet posted within a given time period. Meanwhile, the capacity of u to reply to friends' tweets can be approximated by

$$\sum_{v \in \mathring{E}_u} \|\mathcal{R}_{u,v}^{\Delta}\|. \qquad (9)$$

Thus we formally define the *Responsiveness* of v in terms of replying to u's tweets within Δ as

$$r_{v \to u}^{\Delta}|_{reply} = \frac{\|\mathcal{R}_{v,u}^{\Delta}\| - \frac{1}{\|\mathring{E}_v\|} \sum_{w \in \mathring{E}_v} \|\mathcal{R}_{v,w}^{\Delta}\|}{\frac{1}{\|\mathring{E}_v\|} \sum_{w \in \mathring{E}_v} \left(\|\mathcal{T}_w^{\Delta}\| + \|\mathcal{R}_{w,v}^{\Delta}\| \right)}, \qquad (10)$$

where the numerator captures both the tendency of v to reply to u, as well as the capacity of v, and the inverse of the denominator captures the availability as discussed earlier. The responsiveness of v in terms of retweeting u can be similarly calculated by replacing $\mathcal{R}_{v,w}^{\Delta}$ in the numerator of Eq. (10) with $\mathcal{RT}_{v,w}^{\Delta}$, where $\mathcal{RT}$ represents retweets, i.e.,

$$r_{v \to u}^{\Delta}|_{retweet} = \frac{\|\mathcal{RT}_{v,u}^{\Delta}\| - \frac{1}{\|\mathring{E}_v\|} \sum_{w \in \mathring{E}_v} \|\mathcal{RT}_{v,w}^{\Delta}\|}{\frac{1}{\|\mathring{E}_v\|} \sum_{w \in \mathring{E}_v} \left(\|\mathcal{T}_w^{\Delta}\| + \|\mathcal{R}_{w,v}^{\Delta}\| \right)}. \qquad (11)$$

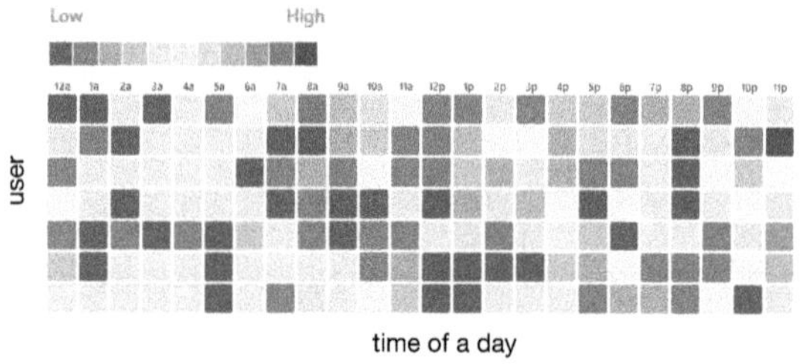

Figure 5: Responsiveness matrix of a user

As a result, for each target user u, we calculate the responsiveness with respect to each of u's friends, thus obtaining two responsive matrices (for replies and retweets), where each row of the matrix is associated with a user, and each column indicates a time bin as shown in Figure 5.

3.4 Learning the Ranking Model

Given a tweet q posted by user u as a query, and u's friends $\mathring{E}_u$ as candidate documents, a feature vector $\mathbf{x}(q, v)$ is generated for each query-document pair (q, v) where $v \in \mathring{E}_u$. Here $\mathbf{x}(q, v)$ consists of all the extracted user-level features associated with user u and v (e.g., the profile affinity between u and v), and tweet-level features associated with q. Suppose $Y = (1, 2, \ldots, m)$ is the label set for a query-document pair, where the label indicates the relevance, i.e., the intention to reply to/retweet a tweet. The training set is represented by $S = (\mathbf{x}_i, y_i)_{i=1}^{N}$, where $\mathbf{x}_i \in X$ is the feature vector of the ith query-document pair and $y_i \in Y$. We aim to train a ranking model $F(S) = f(\mathbf{x})$, which assigns a score for a feature vector $\mathbf{x}$, and can rank the documents for a given query.

The above setting follows the typical learning-to-rank framework for information retrieval. We note that by using the same learning framework, we can learn the ranking functions for different interaction types, such as replies and retweets. According to whether label set Y is binary, our prediction task has two sub-forms:

- Binary Relevance Judgment ($|Y|$=2). In this case, we neglect the orders of the repliers/retweeters given a particular tweet. Assume a tweet q posted by user u at time t. The users who reply to q are treated as relevant instances, and users who do not reply to q are regarded as irrelevant instances. Note that even though the label is binary, the ranking task is not equivalent to the typical classification/regression task since they have different optimization criteria (a perfect ranking does not necessarily mean a perfect classification/regression).

- Ordinal Relevance Scale ($|Y|$>2). In this case, we predict not only the repliers/retweeters of a tweet, but also their orders, i.e., who will reply/retweet first, second, etc. This is obviously harder than the first task, and requires finer-grained and more accurate understanding of the dynamic tie strength and users' interaction behavior patterns in the online social network.

Over the past decades, various algorithms have been proposed to learn the ranking functions, most of which convert the learning problem into an optimization problem by minimizing a defined loss function $L(F(S))$. These algorithms can be generally categorized to point-wise approaches, pair-wise approaches, and list-wise approaches, mainly in terms of the loss function [19]. We evaluated a number of well-adopted learning algorithms to learn the ranking functions separately and examined their performance in our framework (refer to Sec. 4.2.4 for more details). We note that the purpose of applying different learning algorithms is for demonstrating the applicability of our model, whereas a thorough comparison of these learning algorithms is beyond the focus of this paper.

Table 1: Percentage of users with profile information (%)

gender	city	education	age
100	92.9	35.03	31.89

3.5 Prediction

In the online prediction phase, given a query, i.e., tweet $\mathcal{T}$ posted by u at time t, we perform query understanding to generate contextual features from the query. We first extract topical keywords (refer to Sec. 3.2.2) after the pre-processing of segmentation and named-entity recognition. Next we perform sentiment analysis (Sec. 3.3.1) and self-disclosure analysis (Sec. 3.3.2) using the same approach as in the training phase. Then we feed the extracted tweet-level features as well as the user-level features from the candidates to the trained ranking models (different models for repliers and retweeters), and finally retrieve a ranking list by sorting the candidates according to the scores of the ranking function.

4. EVALUATION

4.1 Dataset

We collected a large dataset covering 1.116 billion tweets posted by 1.126 million users with all their replies and retweets to their friends, which range from Sep. 2009 to Dec. 2013. The covered users form 73.262 million dyadic friendship relations.

The percentage of users (among all the 1.1M users) who have different types of profile information on Sina Weibo is reported in Table 1. Such information is leveraged when we build the profile affinity index (Sec 3.2.1). For topic affinity calculation, we set the number of topics $K = 50$ and we retrieved the top 20 keywords for each topic. We chose these parameter settings because they generally gave coherent and meaningful topics for our dataset after our manual validation.

4.2 Settings

4.2.1 Preliminary

To evaluate the prediction models, we removed the tweets that had no replies/retweets) for replier/retweeter prediction, which resulted in two final datasets: 1) the tweet-reply dataset containing 215.165M tweets and 446.910M replies, 2) the tweet-retweet dataset containing 29.348M tweets and 38.152M retweets, which indicated that these users interacted with their friends more by replying than retweeting.

For both the replier prediction and retweeter prediction, we conducted a 10-fold cross validation for all the compared models. In each fold, we used 6 parts for training, 2 parts for validation, and the remaining 2 parts for testing. The validation set was used to tune the hyper-parameters of the learning algorithms, such as the combination coefficient in RankingSVM and the number of trees in LambdaMART, and then we fixed the parameters to train the models using the training set. The test set was used to evaluate the performance of the trained models. Note that all the reported results are the average performances over the 10 trials.

Furthermore, in order to evaluate the temporal effect on the performance, i.e., the temporality dynamics, we performed experiments using a batch training mode. We equally segmented the data according to the time that the tweet (i.e., query) was posted into 6 segments where each segment contains the data in a period of about 8.5 months. For each segment, we used the previous segment as the training (60%) and validation (40%) set, and the current segment as the test set (note that the first segment was only used for burning up).

4.2.2 *Baselines*

To the best of our knowledge, there is no existing model that can predict both repliers and retweeters for a given tweet. Nonetheless, we compared our method against the following related state-of-the-art approaches.

• Social, Topical, and Activity features based model (**STA**) [29]. In this approach, a logistic regression model is trained to determine whether a user will or will not reply to another user, using a set of social features (such as the common friends), topical features (such as the topical similarity of tweets), and activity features (such as the number of previous replies). "List" related features in this model were not available for our dataset because Sina Weibo does not have the "List" feature that Twitter does (the comparable function in Sina Weibo is the social "groups," which are only visible to the users themselves).

• Homophily-based Graphical model (**HG**) [35]. In this graphical model, the tie strength between dyadic users is a latent variable solely dependent on the similarity of user profiles. The interactions between users (such as replies, retweets, and tags) are impacted by the latent tie strength.

Since both STA and HG are binary classifiers that can not directly be used for prediction, we obtained their prediction results by ranking the output probabilities for each classified instance.

4.2.3 *Criteria*

Given a test set with m tweets $q_1, q_2, \ldots, q_m$ (as queries), the predicted result for q_i is represented by a ranked list π_i for $i = 1, 2, \ldots, m$. We evaluated the results for binary judgment, using the following criteria for all the compared methods:

• Topmost Accuracy (Acc). This measures the ratio of successfully predicted repliers/retweeters to the number of tweets, i.e.,

$$\text{Acc} = \frac{\| \sum_{i=1}^{m} \delta_{\{l_{\pi_i^{-1}(1)}=1\}} \|}{m}, \tag{12}$$

where $\delta_{\{\cdot\}}$ is the indicator function and $l.$ is the label of a user (replier/retweeter is labeled 1 and non-replier/non-retweeter is labeled 0).

• Mean Average Precision (MAP). The Average Precision for tweet q_i, denoted as AP_i, is calculated by

$$\text{AP}_i = \frac{\sum_{k=1}^{m} \text{P@}k \cdot \delta_{\{l_{\pi_i^{-1}(k)}=1\}}}{R_i}, \quad \text{P@}k = \frac{\sum_{t \le k} \delta_{\{l_{\pi_i^{-1}(t)}=1\}}}{k}$$

where R_i is the number of actual repliers/retweeters of the tweet q_i. MAP is the average over all AP_i for $i = 1, 2, \ldots, m$.

• Normalized Discounted Cumulative Gain (NDCG). This is a widely-adopted measurement for evaluating ranking quality. The Discounted Cumulative Gain (DCG) at position k for a query with ranked result π is given by

$$\text{DCG@}k = \frac{\sum_{j=1}^{k} G(l_{\pi^{-1}(j)})}{\log(1+j)}, \tag{13}$$

where $G(\cdot)$ is the gain function (we set $G(x) = 2^x - 1$ in our experiments). Then NDCG@k is calculated by normalizing DCG@k with its maximum value (i.e., replacing π with the ideal ranking in Eq. (13)).

For evaluating the sequence of repliers/retweeters (ordinal relevance scale), we also employed the NDCG metric, where we labeled the first replier/retweeter with 3, the second replier/retweeter with 2, the third and latter repliers/retweeters with 1, and non-repliers/non-retweeters were still labeled 0. Furthermore, we replace $l_{\pi_i^{-1}(1)} = 1$ in Eq. (12) with $l_{\pi_i^{-1}(1)} = 3$ (which is a stricter metric) to evaluate whether a model was able to identify the actual first replier/retweeter in Sec. 4.3.2.

4.2.4 *Ranking Functions*

We evaluated the following models for training the ranker (Sec. 3.4).

LogisticRegression is a widely used model for binary classification that can also be considered a pointwise approach in the learning-to-rank framework [19]. The ranking function is defined as follows:

$$f(\mathbf{x}) = \Pr(y = 1|\mathbf{x}) = \frac{1}{1 + e^{-c - \langle \mathbf{w}, \mathbf{x} \rangle}}, \tag{14}$$

where $\mathbf{w}$ is the weight vector for the feature vector $\mathbf{x}$, which is estimated using maximum likelihood estimation.

RankingSVM [16] is a pairwise approach that applies the SVM on pairwise training instances, so as to learn a linear ranking function $f(\mathbf{x}) = \langle \mathbf{w}, \mathbf{x} \rangle$, where the weight feature $\mathbf{w}$ is trained by minimizing the regularized hingle loss function, given by

$$\frac{1}{2}\|\mathbf{w}\|^2 + C \sum_{(i,j) \in \mathcal{P}} [\langle \mathbf{w}, \mathbf{x}_i - \mathbf{x}_j \rangle]_+, \tag{15}$$

where $[x]_+ = \max(0, 1 - x)$, and $(i, j) \in \mathcal{P}$ means candidate i is preferred over candidate j.

LambdaMART [34] is a listwise approach, which learns a combination of regression trees as the ranking function, denoted as

$$f(\mathbf{x}) = \sum_{i=1}^{T} \alpha_i f_i(\mathbf{x}), \tag{16}$$

where each $f_i(\mathbf{x})$ is a regression tree over the features. LambdaMart is trained by empirically optimizing IR measures such as NDCG directly, which has shown excellent performance on several real-world ranking problems including the 2010 Yahoo! Learning-to-Rank Challenge.

In the evaluation, we label the results of our model by considering the dynamic tie strength using the above ranking functions as **DTS1**, **DTS2**, and **DTS3**, respectively.

4.3 Results

4.3.1 *Predicting the Replier/Retweeter*

Figure 6 presents the NDCG over k for replier/retweeter predictions in terms of binary judgment, i.e., actual repliers and retweeters were all considered relevant documents regardless of their order. According to the evaluation results, our method significantly outperforms the baseline methods, with the STA method performing better than the HG method. For example, as depicted in Figure 6(a), even the worst ranking function of our method DTS1 improves the NDCG@1 of STA with 0.15. Note that both DTS1 and STA employ Logistic Regression. However, DTS1 considers more dynamic features such as reciprocal rank, sentiment, self-disclosure, and responsiveness. Furthermore, we found that the DTS3 model, which

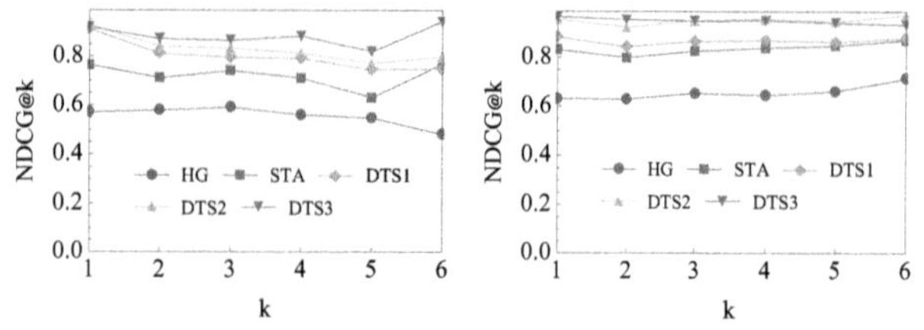

(a) replier prediction (b) retweeter prediction

Figure 6: NDCG@k in terms of binary judgment

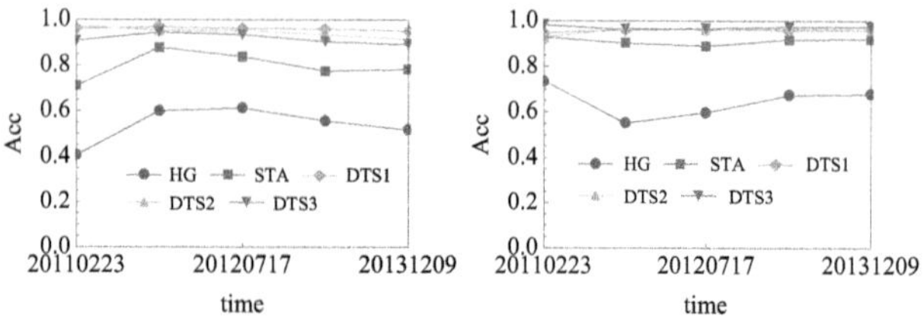

(a) replier prediction (b) retweeter prediction

Figure 7: Acc in terms of binary judgment

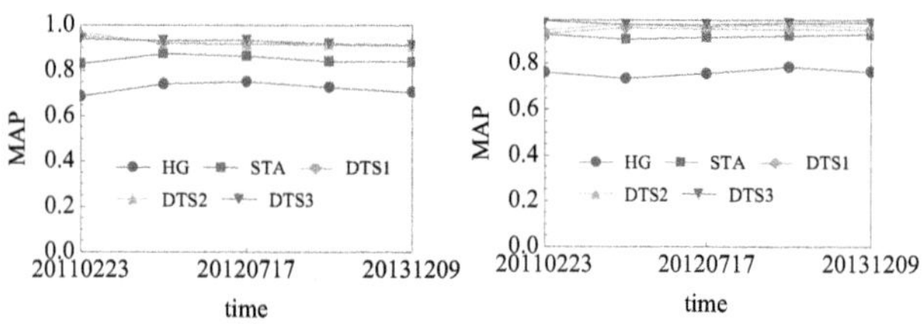

(a) replier prediciton (b) retweeter prediction

Figure 8: MAP in terms of binary judgment

is a listwise learning algorithm achieving the highest performance in terms of NDCG@k for $k = 1, 2, \ldots, 6$.

Figure 6(b) similarly presents the corresponding results for retweeter prediction. Overall, we observe that all algorithms show better performance compared with replier prediction, while the dynamic features demonstrate the advantage again. As mentioned earlier in Sec. 4.2.1, users retweet their friends less often than they reply. This finding is also in coherence with previous studies, which suggest that retweeting is more driven by the content while replying is more related to social relationships [21, 29].

Figure 7 and Figure 8 show the Topmost Accuracy and MAP in the batch training mode. The results show that our methods that consider the dynamic tie strength between dyadic relations reveal higher predictive power for both replier and retweeter. Furthermore, the results of our method (for all the ranking functions) are more stable than competing approaches. For ACC and MAP, the three ranking functions achieve similar performances.

We further conducted greedy forward selection to investigate the contribution of different features in our model using the best performer, DTS3. As presented in Table 2 (NDCG@1 and NDCG@3 are presented as examples while the results for $k = 1, 2, \ldots, 6$ show similar patters), every type of feature improves the NDCG measurement. The responsiveness shows critical improvement for replier prediction and topic affinity shows the most important improvement for retweeter prediction. As more and more dynamic features are incorporated, the NDCG is monotonically increased.

4.3.2 Predicting the Replier/Retweeter Sequence

Figure 9 shows the evaluation results of NDCG and Acc respectively in terms of ordinal relevance scale. It is clear that the NDCG

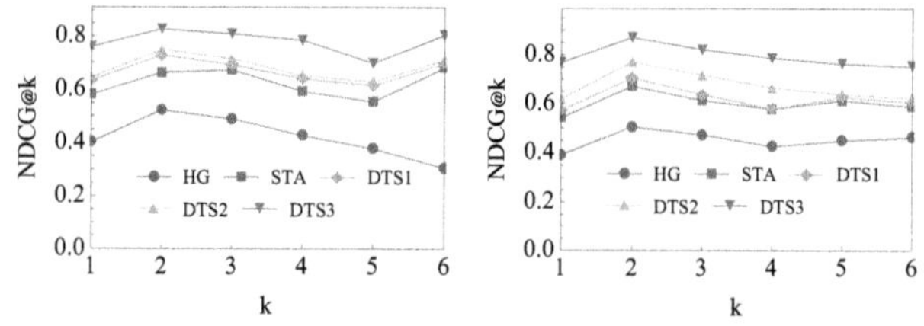

(a) replier prediction (b) retweeter prediction

Figure 9: NDCG@k in terms of ordinal relevance scale

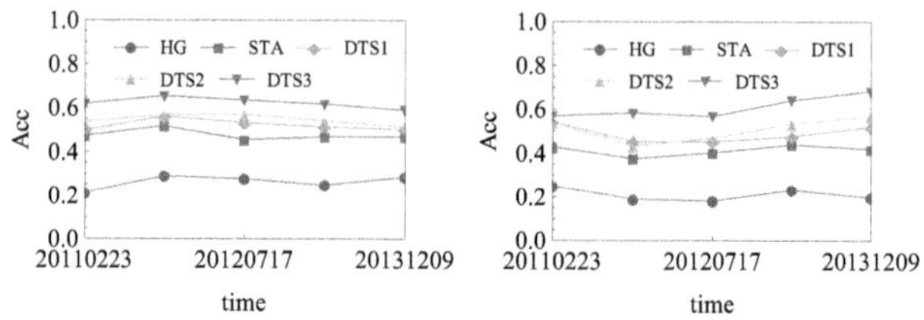

(a) replier prediction (b) retweeter prediction

Figure 10: Acc in terms of ordinal relevance scale

results of all the compared models are lower than the previous results, which indicates that predicting the order of repliers and retweeters is much more challenging. For example, NDCG@1 of both STA and DTS3 are about 0.15 lower than the binary judgment case. However, the dynamic models still perform better than the baselines, suggesting that the subtle dynamics of tie strength are faithfully reflected in users' online interaction behaviors. Besides this, we found that the advantage of DTS3 over the other two ranking functions is more significant when the order of replying/retweeting is considered. On average, DTS3 improves the NDCG with 0.16 gain for replier prediction and 0.19 gain for retweeter prediction over STA.

Figure 10 presents the Topmost Accuracy for replier and retweeter prediction. Note that, the Topmost Accuracy here is stricter than the previous Acc measurement, since the prediction for a query is considered correct only if a model output the actual first replier or retweeter, while the Acc in the binary judgment case considers all repliers as correct. According to the results, DTS3 model achieves the best performance with an Acc higher than 0.6, and the gap between DTS3 with other methods (including other ranking functions) are much more prominent than in the previous binary judgment setting. The contributions of different features were also studied using DTS3 and reported in Table 3. Similar patterns are shown as the previous for replier prediction, which suggest the difference between users' replying and retweeting behaviors and reveal the predictive power of tie strength dynamics on predicting repliers and retweeters.

5. RELATED WORK

5.1 Estimation of Tie Strength

The strength of social ties has been studied for decades in social science. In 1973, Granovetter [11] explicitly defined the tie strength as the "combination of amount of time, the emotional intensity, the intimacy, and the reciprocal services which characterize the tie," and suggested using the frequency of interaction to estimate tie strength, which was later adopted by many subsequent studies [30, 22].

The proliferation of digital communications brought the opportunity to estimate tie strength with large-scale communication data. For example, using mobile phone logs, Onnela et al. [26] studied

Table 2: NDCG w.r.t features in terms of binary relevance
P: profile affinity, T: topic affinity, R: reciprocity
r: responsiveness, S: sentiment, D: self-disclosure

replier			retweeter		
Method	NDCG@1	NDCG@3	Method	NDCG@1	NDCG@3
P	0.786	0.735	P	0.858	0.808
Pr	0.832	0.781	PT	0.908	0.881
PrR	0.854	0.819	PTR	0.934	0.921
PrRT	0.886	0.842	PTRr	0.948	0.933
PrRTD	0.905	0.855	PTRrD	0.960	0.945
PrRTDS	0.919	0.866	PTRrDS	0.969	0.950

Table 3: NDCG w.r.t features in terms of relevance scale
P: profile affinity, T: topic affinity, R: reciprocity
r: responsiveness, S: sentiment, D: self-disclosure

replier			retweeter		
Method	NDCG@1	NDCG@3	Method	NDCG@1	NDCG@3
P	0.623	0.693	P	0.626	0.677
Pr	0.664	0.740	PT	0.679	0.730
PrR	0.703	0.764	PTR	0.710	0.772
PrRT	0.736	0.785	PTRr	0.739	0.795
PrRTD	0.750	0.799	PTRrD	0.758	0.809
PrRTDS	0.761	0.808	PTRrDS	0.769	0.821

the local and global structure of a society-wide communication network and identified that social networks are robust to the removal of strong ties but fall apart after a phase transition if the weak ties are removed. Roth et al. [28] proposed a measurement termed "Interaction Rank" to model the group-level tie strength, where the interactions were weighted by recency to measure the tie strength, and outflowing interactions were considered to be more indicative than inflowing interactions.

Recently, online social networks has rapidly developed. There has been increasing interest in measuring the tie strength in online social networks [8, 35, 13, 17]. Gilbert and Karahalios [8] proposed a set of variables to classify strong ties and weak ties using Facebook data. Later, Gilbert [7] applied similar approaches to Twitter data and found that the Facebook tie strength model can generally be applied to Twitter. With Linkedin data, Xiang et al. [35] proposed a graphical model to learn the tie strength of a dyadic relationship. In this model, the tie strength is a latent variable directly determined by profile similarity and the interaction behaviors are conditionally independent given the tie strength. Wiese et al. [33] studied the sharing behaviors of online social networks and found that frequency of communication can predict both tie strength and willingness to share. Jones et al. [17] identified strong ties using Facebook interaction data, and compared with the ground truth obtained from users' self-reported data, where they found that interaction frequency is more indicative than profile attributes for estimating tie strength, regardless of whether the interactions are public or private.

Our work differs from existing approaches in the following ways: 1) We focus on mining the dynamics of tie strength from social interaction data in terms of various aspects such as temporality, contextuality, and reciprocity; 2) We have developed a learning-to-rank approach to predict interaction behaviors in online social networks by considering the dynamics of tie strength.

5.2 Prediction of Online Social Interactions

Wang and Huberman [32] addressed the predictability of online social interactions by measuring conditional entropy and mutual information with data from Epinions (a consumer review site) and Whrrl (a location-based social network), and suggested that strong deterministic components were embedded in social interactions.

Recently, a number of models have been proposed to predict various types of social interactions in online networks. Xiang et al. [35] proposed a generative model to estimate the occurrence of certain interactions such as posting on Facebook Walls. Macskassy and Michelson [21] investigated the motifs of users' retweeting behaviors on Twitter and proposed different models: general model, content model, homophily model, and recency model, where the content-based propagation was found to be better at explaining retweeting behavior. Replying behavior was also studied in several literatures [13, 29]. In contrast to retweeting behavior, replying is found to be more driven by tie strength and homophily, e.g., Schantl et al. [29] proposed a regression model combining a set of topical and social factors. Using this model, they found that social features are more indicative of user replying behavior. However, this model is only capable of classifying whether a user will reply to another user without considering the effect of current tweet, i.e., the prediction results are identical for different tweets posted by a user.

In this work, we aim to predict multiple types of interactions (reply/retweet) with a general framework, and we focus on the predictions at a finer granularity. First, a key difference between our model and previous ones (such as STA and HG) is that unlike existing ones which provide predictions at *user-level*, our model is at *tweet-level*, i.e., previous models will generate the same prediction for different tweets posted by a user while our model incorporates dynamic features such as the content of a tweet and the context of a user, which are crucial because users' replying and retweeting behaviors are typically affected by these factors.

Second, almost all existing models [35, 21, 29] assume that the user reads all tweets posted by her friends (shown on the user's own timeline) and is equally available to interact with others, which is unrealistic. Instead, by reconstructing users' timelines and analyzing their historical interaction behavior, we propose the responsiveness measure to explicitly consider a user's availability, tendencies and capacity to consume a tweet and respond to their friends. Finally, in contrast to previous approaches that consider only binary situations (replier/non-replier, retweeter/non-retweeter), our model is able to predict the order of repliers/retweeters by employing a learning-to-rank framework.

6. CONCLUSION

In this paper, we have addressed the dynamics of tie strength and social interactions from multiple aspects, and developed a comprehensive framework to predict repliers and retweeters given a tweet posted by a user at a certain time. Extensive evaluations were performed to validate the effectiveness of our method. As a result, the proposed model considering a variety of dynamic features significantly outperforms state-of-the-art methods. While the dynamics of tie strength show compelling predictive power for online social interactions, we have also been concerned with some potential limitations in this work, e.g., the sampling bias of the dataset. However, we believe that the friendship dynamics in online social networks will bring more and more attention in both industry and academia, and have a profound impact on many high-value applications, such as online communication, social recommendation, and viral marketing.

References

[1] R. Athanasiou and G. A. Yoshioka. The spatial character of friendship formation. *Environment and Behavior*, 1973.

[2] J. Y. Bak, S. Kim, and A. Oh. Self-disclosure and

relationship strength in twitter conversations. In *Proceedings of the 50th Annual Meeting of the Association for Computational Linguistics: Short Papers-Volume 2*, pages 60–64. Association for Computational Linguistics, 2012.
[3] A. Barak and O. Gluck-Ofri. Degree and reciprocity of self-disclosure in online forums. *CyberPsychology & Behavior*, 10(3):407–417, 2007.
[4] R. I. Dunbar. Neocortex size as a constraint on group size in primates. *Journal of Human Evolution*, 22(6):469–493, 1992.
[5] N. Eagle, A. S. Pentland, and D. Lazer. Inferring friendship network structure by using mobile phone data. *Proceedings of the National Academy of Sciences*, 106(36):15274–15278, 2009.
[6] J. H. Fowler, J. E. Settle, and N. A. Christakis. Correlated genotypes in friendship networks. *Proceedings of the National Academy of Sciences*, 108(5):1993–1997, 2011.
[7] E. Gilbert. Predicting tie strength in a new medium. In *Proceedings of the ACM 2012 Conference on Computer Supported Cooperative Work*, pages 1047–1056. ACM, 2012.
[8] E. Gilbert and K. Karahalios. Predicting tie strength with social media. In *Proceedings of the SIGCHI Conference on Human Factors in Computing Systems*, pages 211–220. ACM, 2009.
[9] A. Go, R. Bhayani, and L. Huang. Twitter sentiment classification using distant supervision. *CS224N Project Report, Stanford*, 2009.
[10] B. Gonçalves, N. Perra, and A. Vespignani. Modeling users' activity on twitter networks: Validation of dunbar's number. *PloS one*, 6(8):e22656, 2011.
[11] M. S. Granovetter. The strength of weak ties. *American journal of sociology*, pages 1360–1380, 1973.
[12] M. Gupte and T. Eliassi-Rad. Measuring tie strength in implicit social networks. In *Proceedings of the 3rd Annual ACM Web Science Conference*, pages 109–118. ACM, 2012.
[13] M. Gupte and T. Eliassi-Rad. Measuring tie strength in implicit social networks. In *Proceedings of the 3rd Annual ACM Web Science Conference*, pages 109–118. ACM, 2012.
[14] D. J. Houghton and A. N. Joinson. Linguistic markers of secrets and sensitive self-disclosure in twitter. In *Proceedings of the 2012 45th Hawaii International Conference on System Sciences*, pages 3480–3489. IEEE Computer Society, 2012.
[15] L. Jiang, M. Yu, M. Zhou, X. Liu, and T. Zhao. Target-dependent twitter sentiment classification. In *Proc. ACL*, pages 151–160, 2011.
[16] T. Joachims. Optimizing search engines using clickthrough data. In *Proc. SIGKDD*, pages 133–142. ACM, 2002.
[17] J. J. Jones, J. E. Settle, R. M. Bond, C. J. Fariss, C. Marlow, and J. H. Fowler. Inferring tie strength from online directed behavior. *PloS one*, 8(1):e52168, 2013.
[18] P. F. Lazarsfeld, R. K. Merton, et al. Friendship as a social process: A substantive and methodological analysis. *Freedom and control in modern society*, 18(1):18–66, 1954.
[19] T.-Y. Liu. *Learning to rank for information retrieval*. springer, 2011.
[20] X. Liu, S. Zhang, F. Wei, and M. Zhou. Recognizing named entities in tweets. In *Proc. ACL*, pages 359–367, 2011.
[21] S. A. Macskassy and M. Michelson. Why do people retweet? anti-homophily wins the day! In *Proc. ICWSM*, 2011.
[22] P. V. Marsden and K. E. Campbell. Measuring tie strength. *Social forces*, 63(2):482–501, 1984.
[23] M. McPherson, L. Smith-Lovin, and J. M. Cook. Birds of a feather: Homophily in social networks. *Annual review of sociology*, pages 415–444, 2001.
[24] D. G. Myers. *Social psychology*. McGraw-Hill New York, 2010.
[25] P. M. Olk and D. E. Gibbons. Dynamics of friendship reciprocity among professional adults. *Journal of Applied Social Psychology*, 40(5):1146–1171, 2010.
[26] J.-P. Onnela, J. Saramäki, J. Hyvönen, G. Szabó, D. Lazer, K. Kaski, J. Kertész, and A.-L. Barabási. Structure and tie strengths in mobile communication networks. *Proceedings of the National Academy of Sciences*, 104(18):7332–7336, 2007.
[27] P. Preciado, T. A. Snijders, W. J. Burk, H. Stattin, and M. Kerr. Does proximity matter? distance dependence of adolescent friendships. *Social networks*, 34(1):18–31, 2012.
[28] M. Roth, A. Ben-David, D. Deutscher, G. Flysher, I. Horn, A. Leichtberg, N. Leiser, Y. Matias, and R. Merom. Suggesting friends using the implicit social graph. In *Proc. SIGKDD*, pages 233–242. ACM, 2010.
[29] J. Schantl, C. Wagner, R. Kaiser, and M. Strohmaier. The utility of social and topical factors in anticipating repliers in twitter conversations. In *Proceedings of ACM Web Science*, 2013.
[30] A. Sutcliffe, R. Dunbar, J. Binder, and H. Arrow. Relationships and the social brain: Integrating psychological and evolutionary perspectives. *British journal of psychology*, 103(2):149–168, 2012.
[31] A. L. Vangelisti and D. Perlman. *The Cambridge handbook of personal relationships*. Cambridge University Press, 2006.
[32] C. Wang and B. A. Huberman. How random are online social interactions? *Scientific reports*, 2, 2012.
[33] J. Wiese, P. G. Kelley, L. F. Cranor, L. Dabbish, J. I. Hong, and J. Zimmerman. Are you close with me? are you nearby?: investigating social groups, closeness, and willingness to share. In *UbiComp*, pages 197–206, 2011.
[34] Q. Wu, C. J. Burges, K. M. Svore, and J. Gao. Adapting boosting for information retrieval measures. *Information Retrieval*, 13(3):254–270, 2010.
[35] R. Xiang, J. Neville, and M. Rogati. Modeling relationship strength in online social networks. In *Proceedings of the 19th international conference on World wide web*, pages 981–990. ACM, 2010.
[36] N. J. Yuan, F. Zhang, D. Lian, K. Zheng, S. Yu, and X. Xie. We know how you live: exploring the spectrum of urban lifestyles. In *Proceedings of the first ACM conference on Online social networks*, pages 3–14. ACM, 2013.
[37] W. X. Zhao, J. Jiang, J. He, Y. Song, P. Achananuparp, E.-P. Lim, and X. Li. Topical keyphrase extraction from twitter. In *Proceedings of the 49th Annual Meeting of the Association for Computational Linguistics: Human Language Technologies-Volume 1*, pages 379–388. Association for Computational Linguistics, 2011.
[38] W. X. Zhao, J. Jiang, J. Weng, J. He, E.-P. Lim, H. Yan, and X. Li. Comparing twitter and traditional media using topic models. In *Advances in Information Retrieval*, pages 338–349. Springer, 2011.

Cross-modality Consistent Regression for Joint Visual-Textual Sentiment Analysis of Social Multimedia

Quanzeng You and Jiebo Luo
University of Rochester
Rochester, NY 14623
{qyou, jluo}@cs.rochester.edu

Hailin Jin
Adobe Research
San Jose, CA 95110
hljin@adobe.com

Jianchao Yang
Snapchat Inc
Venice, CA 90291
jianchao.yang@snapchat.com

ABSTRACT

Sentiment analysis of online user generated content is important for many social media analytics tasks. Researchers have largely relied on textual sentiment analysis to develop systems to predict political elections, measure economic indicators, and so on. Recently, social media users are increasingly using additional images and videos to express their opinions and share their experiences. Sentiment analysis of such large-scale textual and visual content can help better extract user sentiments toward events or topics. Motivated by the needs to leverage large-scale social multimedia content for sentiment analysis, we propose a cross-modality consistent regression (CCR) model, which is able to utilize both the state-of-the-art visual and textual sentiment analysis techniques. We first fine-tune a convolutional neural network (CNN) for image sentiment analysis and train a paragraph vector model for textual sentiment analysis. On top of them, we train our multi-modality regression model. We use sentimental queries to obtain half a million training samples from Getty Images. We have conducted extensive experiments on both machine weakly labeled and manually labeled image tweets. The results show that the proposed model can achieve better performance than the state-of-the-art textual and visual sentiment analysis algorithms alone.

Categories and Subject Descriptors

I.2 [**Artificial Intelligence**]: Vision and Scene Understanding; I.5.4 [**Pattern Recognition**]: Applications—*Computer vision*

Keywords

sentiment analysis, cross-modality regression, multimodality analysis

1. INTRODUCTION

The increasing popularity of social networks attracts more and more people to share their experiences and to express their opinions on virtually all events and subjects in online social network platforms. Each day, billions of messages and posts are generated. In this study, we focus on deriving people's opinions or sentiments towards topics and events happening in real world. In other words, we are interested in automatical detection of sentiment from online user generated content.

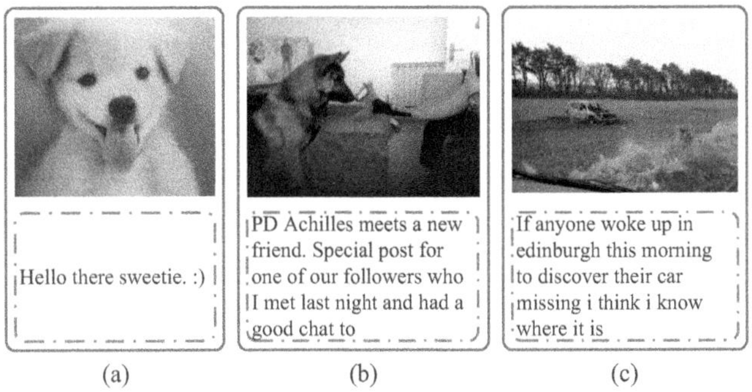

Figure 1: Examples of image tweets from Twitter.

Figure 1 shows several example image tweets from Twitter. Image tweets refer to those tweets that contain images. If we take a look at these three example image tweets, we can observe that in example (a), both image and the text indicate that this tweet carries a positive sentiment; in (b) while it is difficult to tell the sentiment from the image in the *middle* image tweet, however, we can tell that this tweet expresses positive sentiment from the text; in (c) on the contrary, it is hard to tell the sentiment from the text, however the worn-out car in the image suggest an overall negative sentiment. These examples explain the motivation for our work. We would like to learn people's overall sentiment over the same object from different modalities of the object provided by the user. In particular, we focus on inferring people's sentiment according to the available images and the short and informal text.

Many researchers have contributed to sentiment analysis. For instance, there are related works on detecting users' sentiment and applying sentiment analysis to predict box-office revenues for movies [1], political elections [23, 29] and economic indicators [3, 35]. In particular, recently published works started to focus on analyzing sentiment of informally user generated content from online social networks. However, current techniques are mostly based on the analysis of textual content to detect sentiment. On the other hand,

WSDM'16, February 22–25, 2016, San Francisco, CA, USA.
© 2016 ACM. ISBN 978-1-4503-3716-8/16/02...$15.00
DOI: http://dx.doi.org/10.1145/2835776.2835779

visual content, including both images and videos, are becoming increasingly popular in all mainstream online social network platforms. For example, Twitter's support of image tweets and Vine as well as Facebook's Instagram are all designed to support people to share and post more visual content. More interestingly, statistics show that the usage of image in a tweet is able to increase the popularity of this tweet in terms of clicks , retweets, and favorites[1]. This can encourage Twitter users to post more visual content. We cannot ignore the prevalently available visual content in analyzing online users' sentiment.

To the best of our knowledge, little attention has been paid to the sentiment analysis of visual content as well as multi-modality sentiment analysis. Only a few recent works attempted to predict visual sentiment using features from images [25, 5, 4, 34] and videos [21]. Visual sentiment analysis is extremely challenging, as image sentiment involves a much higher level of abstraction and subjectivity in the human recognition process [16], on top of a wide variety of visual recognition tasks including object, scene, action and event recognition. However, Convolutional Neural Networks [19, 7, 17] have been proved to be very powerful in solving computer vision related tasks. Due to the challenges of visual sentiment analysis, we propose a multi-modality framework to analyze sentiment on top of state-of-the-art techniques in both visual and textual analysis.

To that end, we address in this work two major challenges as follows: 1) we propose a novel multi-modality regression model, which can integrate different modality features for sentiment analysis, and 2) we demonstrate the feasibility of using weakly labelled data for multi-modal sentiment analysis and how to easily transfer models from one domain to another domain. The contributions of this paper include

- We employ the state-of-the-art machine learning algorithms to a solve a challenging novel problem, multi-modality sentiment analysis. In particular, we adopt Convolutional Neural Networks [17, 32] to visual sentiment analysis and employ the state-of-the-art distributed representation of documents [18] for textual sentiment analysis.

- We propose a novel multi-modality regression model, CCR, which tries to impose consistent constraints across related but different modalities. The formulation of the model is simple yet generalizable and can be easily implemented. The analysis and experimental results on sentiment analysis validate the effectiveness of the proposed model.

- Our model can be trained on a large scale data set in a mini-batch mode. In particular, we show that it is possible to employ *weakly* labeled data to learn models for highly abstract tasks, such as sentiment analysis and achieve satisfying performance.

- To evaluate our model against competing algorithms, we build a manually labeled sentiment data set using Amazon Mechanical Turk. This data set will be released to the research community to promote further investigations on both textual and visual sentiment.

[1]http://tinyurl.com/lb4xkak

2. RELATED WORK

For sentiment analysis of online user generated textual content, dictionaries based approaches [29, 2, 8, 13] have been widely used due to its efficiency and simplicity. Very recently, distributed representation of words started to attract research attention due to its ability in learning robust features for words [20]. Le and Mikolov [18] further proposed an approach to learn distributed representation for documents. They applied their document representations to sentiment analysis and achieve the best performance over existing competing algorithms.

There are also several recent works on visual sentiment analysis. The work in [25] is a machine learning algorithm to predict the sentiment of images using pixel-level color histogram and SIFT bag of words visual features. Motivated by the fact that sentiment involves high-level abstraction, which may be easier to explain by objects or attributes in images, both [4] and [34] proposed to employ visual entities or attributes as features for visual sentiment analysis. In [4], 1200 adjective noun pairs (ANP) are extracted to crawl images from Flickr. The responses of the trained 1200 ANP classifiers can be considered as mid-level features for visual sentiment analysis. The work in [34] employed a similar mechanism but using 102 scene attributes instead. More recently, You *et al.* [32] proposed a progressively trained Convolutional Neural Network for visual sentiment analysis. Compared with other approaches that employ low-level or mid-level features, CNN achieved the state-of-the-art performance in predicting image sentiments. A bench-marking analysis of CNN on emotion analysis is proposed in [33].

There are only a few publications on analyzing sentiment using multi-modalities, such as text and images. Both [30] and [6] employed both text and images for sentiment analysis, where late fusion is employed to combine the prediction results of using n-gram textual features and mid-level visual features [4]. In addition, researchers have investigated cross-modal issues in other multimedia retrieval related tasks. Rasiwasia *et al.* [24] employed canonical correlation analysis (CCA) to learn the correlations between visual features and textual features for image retrieval. Besides that, Feng *et al.* [10] further developed so-called correspondence autoencoder for cross-modal retrieval, where a code layer is shared between the visual and textual autoencoder for *unsupervised* learning of parameters. Ngiam *et al.* [22] also proposed a multimodal *unsupervised* deep learning model, which achieved the best published results in visual speech classification. Meanwhile, Nitish and Ruslan [28] employed multimodal deep Boltzmann machine to learn joint representation of images and text by the sharing of high-level abstract representation. On the other hand, learning semantic mappings between visual and textual feature spaces has become popular due to the success of deep learning. Socher *et al.* [26] learned the semantic mappings in order to classify unseen visual classes. Frome *et al.* [11] employed hinge loss instead of using squared loss in their objective function to learn the semantic mapping between words and deep visual features for image annotation. Socher *et al.* [27] tried to even learn the transformation between sentence descriptions and images by margin based loss function on Recursive Neural Network and Convolutional Neural Network. More recently, Gong *et al.* [12] employed largely weakly annotated images to help learn the visual and textual embedding in their proposed stacked auxiliary embedding.

Inspired by these works on learning joint visual and textual models, we also rely on the recently successful deep learning techniques to extract features from images and text. However, different from the previously mentioned works, all of which are intended for unsupervised learning of shared feature embedding space between images and short text for image annotation or retrieval, our work intends to use supervised learning to enforce the consistency between the prediction labels of different features for sentiment analysis.

3. CROSS-MODALITY CONSISTENT REGRESSION (CCR)

In this section, we describe the details of our proposed model. Our main motivation is that different modalities should be consistent in terms of depicting the same subject. In sentiment analysis, given multiple modalities, we expect the utilization of features extracted from different modalities, such as images and text, to achieve more accurate sentiment analysis results.

3.1 Cross-modality consistent regression

Our model accepts input from different modalities of the same subject. The penalties between the predicted label distributions of different modality features need to be taken into consideration. To measure the penalty between any two different predicted label distributions, we employ KL divergence. In particular, let p and q denote two probability distributions of the same length. We define $D(p \parallel q)$ as the sum of KL divergence between them.

$$D(p \parallel q) = D_{KL}(p \parallel q) + D_{KL}(q \parallel p) \quad (1)$$

Assume we have a total of M different modalities and a total of N training instances. If we consider a pair-wise penalty of the given M modalities, we have to solve a total of $\binom{M}{2}$ penalty terms between any pair of modalities, which may be too complicated for a relatively large M. Instead, we first concatenate all the features from the M modalities and add penalty terms between the M individual modality features and the concatenated features. In this way, only M penalty terms need to be added. Motivated by these observations, the objective function is formulated in Eqn. (2). We denote by x_i^m (for $m \in \{1, \cdots, M\}$) the m-th modality features of the i-th instance and by x_i^c the concatenated features from all the M modality features of the i-th instance. $\Theta = \{\theta^c, \theta^1, \cdots, \theta^M\}$ are the parameters that needs to be learned. λ and γs are the hyper parameters to control the weights of different components in the proposed model.

$$\begin{aligned} \min_{\Theta,\lambda,\gamma_1,\cdots,\gamma_M} J(\Theta) &= \frac{1}{N}\sum_{i=1}^{N} D(y_i \parallel p_{\theta^c}(x_i^c)) + \frac{\lambda}{2}\theta^{cT}\theta^c \\ &+ \frac{\lambda}{2}\sum_{m=1}^{M}\theta^{mT}\theta^m + \sum_{m=1}^{M}\frac{\gamma_m}{N}\sum_{i=1}^{N} D(p_{\theta^c}(x_i^c) \parallel p_{\theta^m}(x_i^m)) \end{aligned} \quad (2)$$

Let $p_\theta(x_i)$ be the prediction function for the label distribution of x_i given the parameter vector θ. We use softmax function to evaluate the probability distribution, which is defined as

$$p_\theta(x_i) = \frac{1}{\sum_{k=1}^{K} e^{\theta_k^T x_i}}[e^{(\theta_1^T x_i)}, e^{(\theta_2^T x_i)}, \cdots, e^{(\theta_K^T x_i)}]^T, \quad (3)$$

where K is the number of classes and θ_k is the parameter vector for the k-th class, *i.e.* θ_k is a sub-vector of θ and $\theta_k = \theta_{[(k-1)|x|, k|x|)}$ (we use $|x|$ to denote the length of the feature vector).

The first component of the objective function is the consistency constraint between the ground-truth label and the predicted label distribution using concatenated features. Next, regularization terms are added to the framework to prevent overfitting. The last component considers the predicted distribution consistency between each single modality features and the concatenated features. In this way, we hope that it is possible to propagate knowledge learned from different modalities to each other to improve the overall performance of the system.

3.2 Relation to softmax regression

The proposed model is closely related to softmax regression, where the objective is to minimize the loss function in Eqn. (4). Similarly, $\theta = [\theta_1; \theta_2; \ldots; \theta_K]$ is the parameter vector, $\delta(\cdot)$ is the indicator function and x_i is the feature vector for the i-th instance.

$$\min_\theta -\frac{1}{N}\left(\sum_{i=1}^{N}\sum_{k=1}^{K}\delta(y_i = k)\ln\frac{\exp(\theta_k^T x_i)}{\sum_{j=1}^{K}\exp(\theta_j^T x_i)}\right) \quad (4)$$

Indeed, softmax regression is a special case of the first component $\frac{1}{N}\sum_{i=1}^{N} D(y_i \parallel p_{\theta^c}(x_i^c))$ of our proposed model. Eqn. (5) shows more details of this loss term, where C_1 and C_2 are constants determined by y_i. We use $p_\theta(k|x_i)$ to represent the probability of assigning x_i to class k, *i.e.* the k-th element in Eqn. (3). If we are given a *hard* label for each instance, *i.e.* y_{ik} only has one and only one non-zero entry, then the term $-y_{ik}\ln p_{\theta^c}(k|x_i)$ in Eqn. (5) is the same with the loss objective of softmax regression.

$$\begin{aligned} D(y_i \parallel p_{\theta^c}(x_i^c)) &= \sum_{k=1}^{K} p_{\theta^c}(k|x_i^c)\ln p_{\theta^c}(k|x_i^c) \\ &- y_{ik}\ln p_{\theta^c}(k|x_i^c) + C_1 p_{\theta^c}(k|x_i^c) + C_2 \end{aligned} \quad (5)$$

In addition, there are two other terms related to $p_{\theta^c}(x_i)_k$ in Eqn. (5), which are related to cross entropy. This is the main reason to use KL divergence instead of softmax regression for the first component of our model, which is favorable for tasks with noisy and uncertain labels, such as sentiment analysis.

3.3 Parameter learning

Even though KL divergence is convex, the proposed objective function is not convex on its parameters Θ. In this section, we explain in detail how to learn the parameters in our model.

3.3.1 Gradient descent

We resort to gradient descent to optimize the objective function $J(\Theta)$ in Eqn. (2). The gradient of the $J(\Theta)$ with respect to θ^c is

$$\begin{aligned} \frac{\partial J(\Theta)}{\partial\theta^c} &= \frac{1}{N}\sum_{i=1}^{N}\frac{\partial D(y_i \parallel p_{\theta^c}(x_i^c))}{\partial\theta^c} + \lambda\theta^c \\ &+ \sum_{m=1}^{M}\frac{\gamma_m}{N}\sum_{i=1}^{N}\frac{\partial D(p_{\theta^c}(x_i^c) \parallel p_{\theta^m}(x_i^m))}{\partial\theta^c}. \end{aligned} \quad (6)$$

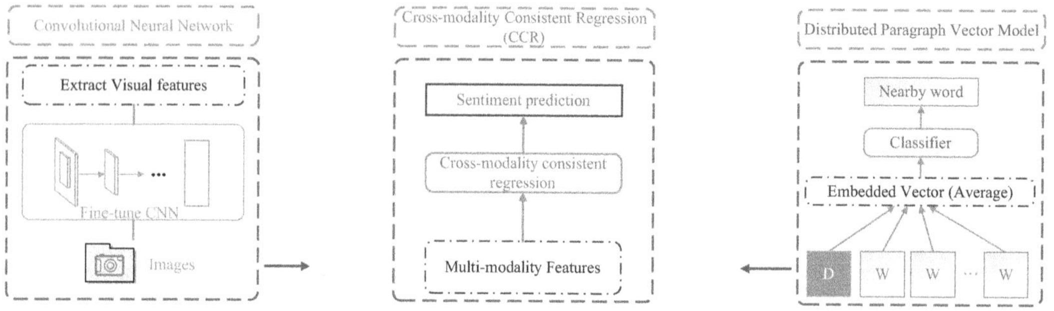

Figure 2: The framework for multi-modality sentiment analysis. ***Left:*** **We fine-tune a CNN visual sentiment analysis model, which is employed to extract visual features for testing images.** ***Right:*** **We train a distributed paragraph vector model on the related titles and descriptions of the images to learn textual features.** ***Middle:*** **The proposed cross-modality consistent regression model is trained on the visual and textual features to learn the final sentiment classifier.**

For last derivative term $\frac{\partial D(p_{\theta^c}(x_i^c) \| p_{\theta^m}(x_i^m))}{\partial \theta^c}$, we have[2]

$$\frac{\partial D_{KL}(p_{\theta^c}(x_i^c) \parallel p_{\theta^m}(x_i^m)) + D_{KL}(p_{\theta^m}(x_i^m) \parallel p_{\theta^c}(x_i^c))}{\partial \theta^c_{jl}} = \sum_{k=1}^{K}\left(1-\frac{p_{\theta^m}(k|x_i^m)}{p_{\theta^c}(k|x_i^c)} - \ln\frac{p_{\theta^m}(k|x_i^m)}{p_{\theta^c}(k|x_i^c)}\right)\frac{\partial p_{\theta^c}(k|x_i^c)}{\partial\theta^c_{jl}}. \quad (7)$$

where

$$\frac{\partial p_{\theta^c}(k|x_i^c)}{\partial \theta^c_{jl}} = \frac{\partial \frac{\exp(\theta_k^{c\,T} x_i^c)}{\sum_{k=1}^{K}\exp(\theta_k^{c\,T} x_i^c)}}{\partial \theta^c_{jl}} = (\delta(k=j) - p_{\theta^c}(k|x_i^c))\, p_{\theta^c}(j|x_i^c) x_{il}^c \quad (8)$$

We can also calculate the first derivative term $\frac{\partial D(y_i \| p_{\theta^c}(x_i^c))}{\partial \theta^c}$, which is similar to Eqn. (7).

The gradient of the objective function $J(\Theta)$ with respect to θ^m for $m \in \{1, 2, \ldots, M\}$ is

$$\frac{\partial J(\Theta)}{\partial \theta^m} = \lambda\theta^m + \sum_{m=1}^{M}\frac{\gamma_m}{N}\sum_{i=1}^{N}\frac{\partial D(p_{\theta^c}(x_i^c) \parallel p_{\theta^m}(x_i^m))}{\partial \theta^m}. \quad (9)$$

Since $D(p_{\theta^c}(x_i^c) \parallel p_{\theta^m}(x_i^m))$ is symmetric in terms of θ^m and θ^c, we can apply Eqn. (7) to calculate the derivatives of Eqn. (9).

3.3.2 Learning algorithm and convergence analysis

There are two groups of parameters in our model, namely θ^c and $\{\theta^1, \theta^2, \cdots, \theta^M\}$. In our implementation, we learn those two groups of parameters iteratively. Specifically, in each iteration, the learning algorithm will try to update the two groups of parameters sequentially. Since, we built a large data set for our experiments, we employ mini-batch L-BFGS to learn the parameters[3].

Algorithm 1 summarizes the main steps for **C**ross-modality **C**onsistent **R**egression (CCR). The proposed objective function is differentiable, thus the function is smooth in terms of Θ. Meanwhile, it is easy to prove that $J(\Theta) \geq 0$. The objective function is lower-bounded. During each iteration of the learning algorithm, we are trying to find a smaller

Algorithm 1 Cross-modality consistent regression (CCR)

Require: $X^1, X^2, \cdots, X^M$ a total of M different modality features on a collection of objects X.
$Y = \{y_1, y_2, \ldots, y_N\}$ sentiment labels of X

```
Randomly split the objects into mini-batches
Concatenate the M modality features to get X^c
Randomly initialize Θ = {θ^c, θ^1, ..., θ^M}
repeat
    Randomly select one mini-batch X_b
    Apply L-BFGS to update θ^c on X_b with derivative in
    Eqn. (6) and objective function in Eqn. (2)
    for m from 1 to M do
        Randomly select one mini-batch X_b
        Apply L-BFGS to update θ^m on X_b with derivative
        in Eqn. (9) and objective function in Eqn. (2)
    end for
until Convergent or reach the maximum numbers of
iterations
return Θ
```

$J(\Theta)$ using L-BFGS. It is possible that mini-batch training may lead to oscillations of the objective function between different batches. However, overall we are still able to conclude that the iterative learning algorithm in Algorithm 1 converges when there is enough number of iterations.

We will discuss in the experimental section on how to select the hyper-parameters of our model, *i.e.* λ and γs.

3.3.3 Prediction algorithm

We can employ the learned model for prediction of testing instances given their M modality features. Recall that our training objective is to enforce the consistency of prediction results using different sets of modality features. Similarly, in the prediction stage, we also intend to obtain the same objective. Let p denote the desired label distribution of the testing instances, then we have

$$\min_p J(p|p_{\theta^1}, p_{\theta^2}, \ldots, p_{\theta^M}) = \sum_{k=1}^{M}\sum_i p(i)\ln\frac{p(i)}{p_{\theta^k}(i)}$$
$$s.t. \sum_i p(i) = 1. \quad (10)$$

[2]Recall that θ_j^c is a sub-vector of θ^c, we use θ_{jl}^c to represent the l-th element of θ_j^c.

[3]When the whole data set can fit into the machine's memory, it is also possible to employ full-batch L-BFGS.

THEOREM 1. *The optimal solution to* $J(p|p_{\theta^1}, p_{\theta^2}, \ldots, p_{\theta^M})$ *is that* $p(i) = \frac{\sqrt[M]{\Pi_k p_{\theta^k}(i)}}{\sum_j \sqrt[M]{\Pi_k p_{\theta^k}(j)}}$.

PROOF. The Lagrange function for the above problem is

$$\Lambda(p, \lambda) = \sum_{k=1}^{M} \sum_{i} p(i) \ln \frac{p(i)}{p_{\theta^k}(i)} + \lambda(\sum_{i} p(i) - 1).$$

Derivative of Λ with respect to $p(i)$ is

$$\frac{\partial \Lambda}{\partial p(i)} = M \ln p(i) - \sum_{k=1}^{M} \ln p_{\theta^k}(i) + M + \lambda.$$

Let the derivative equal 0, we have

$$M \ln p(i) = \sum_{k=1}^{M} \ln p_{\theta^k}(i) - M - \lambda.$$

From the constraint $\sum_i p(i) = 1$, we conclude that

$$p(i) = \frac{\sqrt[M]{\Pi_k p_{\theta^k}(i)}}{\sum_j \sqrt[M]{\Pi_k p_{\theta^k}(j)}}$$

□

4. MULTI-MODALITY SENTIMENT ANALYSIS

In this section, we describe in details on how to apply the proposed model to multi-modality sentiment analysis. In particular, we focus on how to extract the state-of-the-art visual and textual features and apply them to the proposed model. Figure 2 shows the framework for multi-modality sentiment analysis. The recent developed Convolutional Neural Network (CNN) [17] has achieved the state-of-the-art performance on a wide range of vision tasks. You *et al.* [32] conducted experiments on deploying CNN for visual sentiment analysis and achieved better performance than both low-level [25] features and mid-level [4, 34] features. Inspired by their conclusion, we propose to use CNN for the extraction of visual features. In particular, we employ the pre-trained CNN model on imagenet [15] to fine-tune a CNN model for visual sentiment analysis. The details on fine-tuning the CNN model will be discussed in the experimental section. Next, the fine-tuned CNN model is employed to extract visual features from the second to the last layer of the neural network.

For textual features, Le and Mikolov [18] developed an unsupervised language model to learn distributed representations for documents. They applied the learned representations to analyze textual sentiment, which achieved the best performance compared with other existing state-of-the-art textual sentiment analysis models. We employed the proposed model to learn distributed representations for related text of each image. In particular, We use descriptions and titles of each image as the body of a document to learn the textual features of each image.

Given the visual and textual features, we are able to train a cross-modality consistent regression model for sentiment analysis. Meanwhile, the trained visual and textual model can extract visual and textual features for testing images and text individually, which next can be used to predict the sentiment distribution for the image and related text respectively.

5. EXPERIMENTS

In this section, we conduct experiments to evaluate the performance of the proposed cross-modality consistent regression model on sentiment analysis. To train the visual and textual model in Figure 2, we choose to crawl data from Getty Images[4]. The main reasons to use Getty Images are its relatively formal descriptions of images and its convenient and powerful query based searching system.

5.1 Training visual and textual models

To fine-tune the pre-trained CNN model for sentiment analysis, we need a relatively large labeled data set, which can cost huge human efforts. Meanwhile, different people may have somewhat different opinions on the sentiment of the same object, which makes it harder to have a well labeled training data set. In our implementation, we propose to use *weakly* labeled data to train our neural network. To be more specific, we use a list of keywords for both positive and negative sentiment.[5] We query Getty Images with these keywords and all the returned images are labeled using the sentiment labels of these keywords. In this way, we are able to collect a large weakly labeled data set consisting of both images and text, which is employed to fine-tune the CNN model and learn the paragraph vector for related text of each image. Table 1 summarizes the statistics of our collected data set from Getty Images. In total, there are 101 keywords. We collect a total of over half million weakly labeled images as well as their titles and descriptions.

Table 1: Summary of the dataset from Getty Image.

Sentiment	Num of Keywords	Num of Images
Positive	37	311,940
Negative	64	276,281
Sum	101	588,221

Given the above collected data set, we randomly split them into 80% for training and 20% for testing. We fine-tune the CNN model on the publicly available implementation Caffe [15]. We run the GPU accelerated version of Caffe implementation with a total iteration of $200,000$ on a Linux X86_64 machine with 32G RAM and two NVIDIA GTX Titan GPUs. The fine-tuned model is then employed to extract features for both training and testing images.

For textual model, the title and description of each image are concatenated as a single *document*. We use the algorithm in [31] to pre-process the textual data. First, numbers and special characters are removed. Then, we tokenize the text using the tokenizer model from NLTK (http://www.nltk.org). We also remove those words that appear less than 5 times in all the documents. The size of the paragraph vectors is 400 and the size of the nearby word window is 5, which are the default settings in [18].

We compare the performance of the proposed model with several baseline algorithms, including the following several different approaches. We also tried to use canonical correlation analysis (CCA) on this task. However, due to the scalability issue of CCA, we cannot fit all the training data into memory to learn the correlation using CCA. Table 2

[4]http://www.gettyimages.com
[5]http://www.sci.sdsu.edu/CAL/wordlist/origwordlist.html

Table 2: **Performance of CCA on different testing data (see following sections for detailed description of the data).**

Testing Data	Precision	Recall	F1	Accuracy
Getty	0.697	0.718	0.708	0.687
Twitter	0.769	0.698	0.731	0.727
AMT Twitter	0.66	0.52	0.559	0.526

summarizes the results of CCA on different sets of testing data using the same visual and textual features with other approaches using a single randomly selected mini-batch (10,240 instances). The results suggest poor performance compared with other approaches (see following details for details of the testing data and results of other approaches). Thus, we do not further compare the results of CCA with other approaches in the following experimental sections.

For all the following results of CCR, we run the algorithm 10 times with randomized initialization of the parameters. The averaged results are reported. The results of the following baselines are also reported and analyzed.

- **Single visual model.** We only use the visual features to build a logistic regression model, which outperforms models on both low-level and mid-level visual features [32].
- **Single textual model.** The paragraph feature vectors are also fed to a logistic classifier to predict the sentiment [18].
- **Early fusion.** We concatenate both visual and textual features and build a logistic regression model on these concatenated features.
- **Late fusion.** The average of the prediction sentiment score of visual and textual models is used as the prediction score of the late fusion model [30, 6].

5.2 Performance on Getty Images testing data set

We extract visual features for the 20% testing images given the fine-tuned CNN model. In this paper, we use the second to the last layer to extract features, which has a total of 4096 features for each image. For textual features, since the training is unsupervised, all documents are given to the model to learn their features [18].

Following the steps in Algorithm 1, we split the training data into mini-batches and train all visual, textual logistic regression model and CCR model on the same collection of mini-batches. In our implementation, we use a batch size of 10240, which is a trade-off between memory load and convergence rate.

Figure 3 shows the changes of the objective loss functions with the increase of mini-batch iteration numbers. The results show that the loss function value changes on some randomly chosen validation data set and training data set are comparable. Meanwhile, since we employ L-BFGS, the loss function converges after about 10 iterations, *i.e.* running on 10 mini-batches.

Since we have about 4,000 visual features and 4,00 textual features for each image, we try to balance the two modalities in selecting the hyper-parameters. In all of our experiments,

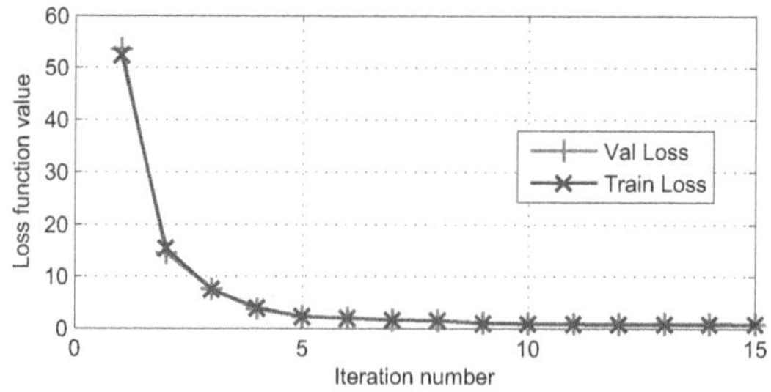

Figure 3: Changes of the objective loss function on both training and validating data set.

Table 3: Performance on the testing data set by different approaches.

Algorithm	Precision	Recall	F1	Accuracy
Textual	0.806	0.544	0.655	0.696
Visual	0.747	0.745	0.746	0.732
Early Fusion	0.778	0.769	0.774	0.763
Late Fusion	0.785	**0.775**	0.780	0.769
CCR	**0.846**	0.759	**0.800**	**0.800**

we set λ to be 1, γ_v for visual features also to be 1 and γ_t for textual features to be 5[6]. Table 3 shows the performance of different approaches on the 20% weakly labeled testing data from Getty Images. The results show that visual features may have comparable precision and recall on these data. Textual features can achieve higher precision but lower recall. Both early fusion and late fusion can produce improved results over single modalities. However, both fail to improve the performance of precision than the single textual model. On the other hand, the proposed CCR model can improve the performance of both precision and recall than the two single models. Meanwhile, CCR performs best among all the methods in terms of both F1 and accuracy score.

5.3 Performance on Twitter data set

We also build a new data set from image tweets. In particular, we employ the Twitter streaming API to collect a large number of Tweets. In total, we collected about 15 million Tweets. Next, we keep Tweets that contain both images and English text. In total, we collect 220,000 image tweets. In our implementation, we employ the recent proposed VADER [14] to weakly label these tweets, which is a rule based textual sentiment analysis and attuned to Twitter contexts. Next, we select the top ranked positive and negative image tweets according to the VADER score. We manually filter out duplicates, low-quality, porn and all-text images. In this way, we collect a total of 31,584 *weakly* labeled image tweets, 16,844 of them are positive tweets and the rest are negative.

Since images from Twitter are much more diverse and different from Getty Images and tweets are also much more informal, we could not directly apply the trained model from Getty Images to these image tweets. Instead, we randomly

[6]Indeed, there is no significant different when we set $\gamma_t \in [5, 10]$, which is close to the proportion of feature size $|x_v|$ and $|x_t|$.

Figure 4: Top confidently ranked examples by AMT workers. Top row (in blue rectangle) shows positive examples and bottom row (in red rectangle) shows negative examples.

Figure 5: Ambiguously ranked examples by AMT workers. Top row (in blue rectangle) shows positive examples and bottom row (in red rectangle) shows negative examples. See text for explanation.

split this data set into batches with the same size of 10240. We use the first batch the testing data set and the rest the training data set to fine-tune both CNN and paragraph vector model. In particular, we slightly fine-tune the CNN model previously trained on the Getty Images with 2,000 iterations with the learning rate set to 0.001. For paragraph vector model, we feed both the descriptions from Getty Images and the tweet text of the 31,584 image tweets to this model to learn the vector representation for each tweet. For the tweets, we preprocessed them by further replacing hashtags, url links and user ids with special string sequences. Table 4 shows the results on the randomly selected 10240 testing image tweets. It is interesting to find that the textual features works better than the visual features. This may be due to the fact that we obtain the weak labels from text based system VADER and an insufficient number of images for CNN to find a relatively good local optima. However, the proposed CCR are able to improve the performance on the same set of visual and textual features.

5.3.1 Performance on manually labeled tweets

Meanwhile, in order to have more accurate labels for these image tweets, we employed crowd intelligence, Amazon Mechanical Turk (AMT), to generate sentiment labels for selected image tweets, in a similar fashion to [5]. We recruited 5 AMT workers for each of the candidate image tweet. We

Table 4: Performance on the Twitter testing data set by different approaches.

Algorithm	Precision	Recall	F1	Accuracy
Textual	0.746	0.693	0.727	0.722
Visual	0.584	0.561	0.573	0.553
Early Fusion	0.730	0.744	0.737	0.717
Late Fusion	0.634	0.610	0.622	0.604
CCR	**0.831**	**0.805**	**0.818**	**0.809**

test the performance of different models on this manually labeled data using the previously fine-tuned models on the *weakly* labeled image tweets. We randomly select 2,000 image tweets and post them in AMT for sentiment annotation. After receiving the batch results from AMT, we keep those that have at least 4 agreements on the sentiment label and also exclude those that appears in the previously weakly labeled image tweets for fine-tuning. Eventually, we have 613 image tweets, of which 389 are labelled positive and 224 are labelled negative by 5 AMT workers.

Table 5 gives the performance of different approaches. CCR performs best in terms of precision, F1 and accuracy. However, it has a slightly lower recall. Compared with the results in Table 4, visual features show significant improve-

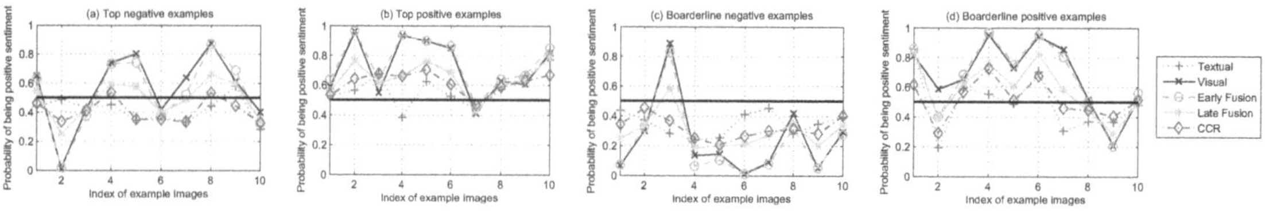

Figure 6: Machine performance on confident and uncertain examples labelled by AMT workers.

Table 5: Performance on the AMT manually labeled data set by different approaches.

Algorithm	Precision	Recall	F1	Accuracy
Textual	0.832	0.638	0.722	0.688
Visual	0.762	0.715	0.737	0.677
Early Fusion	0.776	**0.740**	0.758	0.700
Late Fusion	0.799	0.738	0.767	0.716
CCR	**0.886**	0.730	**0.800**	**0.769**

Table 6: Top 100 most confident sentiment prediction distribution of different algorithms.

Senti	Alg	5 Agree	4 Agree	4 Obj	5 Obj
Neg	Textual	22	52	7	19
	Visual	23	45	13	19
	Early	23	50	9	18
	Late	28	52	7	13
	CCR	**29**	**58**	**4**	**9**
Pos	Textual	61	**24**	12	3
	Visual	62	20	13	5
	Early	66	20	11	3
	Late	69	**24**	**6**	1
	CCR	**71**	22	7	**0**

ment, which may be due to the fact that AMT workers take both text and image to label the sentiment. Meanwhile, it is possible that the labels by AMT workers are biased compared with the weak labels given by VADER, causing relatively poor performance of both CCR and Early Fusion compared with the results in Table 4.

5.3.2 *Analysis of top ranked examples*

We also compare and analyze the top ranked examples of both AMT workers and machines. Since each image is labeled by 5 AMT workers into one of *strongly negative (-2)*, *negative (-1)*, *positive (1)* and *strongly positive (2)*, we rank images according to the sum of their scores by these 5 workers. Next, we select the top ranked positive and negative examples as well as some borderline examples. Figure 4 shows the top 10 ranked negative and positive examples by AMT workers. For negative examples, most of them are related to some bad experienced topics, such as car accident, environmental change and so on. Most of the positive examples are kind of cute, happy images along with some funny short descriptions. For comparison, ambiguously ranked examples are also selected and shown in Figure 5, where most of these examples also seem reasonable. It seems that the disagreement of these borderline examples may come from the inconsistency between the text and the visual content of an image tweet. Meanwhile, some of these image tweets may have celebrity related topic, which may also cause different opinions among different groups of fans.

Next, we conduct experiments on the performance of different machine approaches on these selected human labeled examples. Figure 6 shows the predicted results of different approaches on the two selected groups of example images in Figure 4 and Figure 5. It is interesting to note that for negative examples, machines seem to be uncertain on the confident examples given by AMT workers. However, they are confident on those uncertain examples. For positive examples, it seems that machine is kind of having similar recognition ability on both the confident and uncertain examples. These results demonstrate that the trained machine model and human beings may have different recognition ability towards the sentiment of the same group of images, which may be due to difference between the limited training samples for machines and the constantly learning process for human beings.

We also extract the top 100 positive and top 100 negative image tweets by AMT workers. The prediction results of different approaches are given in Table 6. Overall, CCR outperforms other approaches in both negative and positive categories in terms of accuracy. Meanwhile, all approaches seem to be more likely to agree with AMT workers on the positive category. This may be due to the biased nature of social networks, where users are more likely to post positive content than negative content.

In addition, we extract the most *confident* prediction examples of different approaches on the manually labeled image tweets by AMT workers. We rank the images by the prediction score of each model. Figure 7 shows the top ranked 5 images of each model on both positive and negative categories respectively (red circles indicate wrongly predicted samples). All the image tweets are ranked from left to right in a decreasing order. There are many common highly ranked examples between different approaches. However, different approaches have different ranking orders. In particular, highly ranked examples using textual features seems to have strong discriminative words than those using visual features, which explains the main reason of the two wrongly predicted examples. Similarly, only using visual features may also lead to wrong confident examples due to the lack of knowledge from the text data. Meanwhile, we note that there are no shared top ranked examples with that given by human beings in Figure 4. Again, these differences may come from different learning scenarios for both human beings and machines. Meanwhile, this also suggests the challenging nature of visual sentiment analysis.

6. CONCLUSIONS

Sentiment analysis, in particular visual sentiment analysis, is a challenging and interesting problem. In this work,

(a) Negative examples using textual features
(b) Positive examples using textual features
(c) Negative examples using visual features
(d) Positive examples using visual features
(e) Negative examples using early fusion
(f) Positive examples using early fusion
(g) Negative examples using late fusion
(h) Positive examples using late fusion
(i) Negative examples using CCR
(j) Positive examples using CCR

Figure 7: Examples of most confident image tweets of different approaches. *Left* column shows the most confident negative examples. *Right* column shows the most confident positive examples.

we aim to analyze sentiment via both visual and textual content. The recently developed machine learning algorithms lead to the availability of robust visual and textual features for abstract tasks, such as sentiment analysis. Due to the largely easily accessible weakly labeled data, we can train both visual and textual models to extract robust features for sentiment analysis. We develop a cross modality consistency regression model, which tries to enforce the agreement between sentiment labels predicted by different modality features. The experimental results suggest that the proposed multi-modality regression model outperforms both the state-of-the-art single textual and visual sentiment analysis models and two fusion models.

Meanwhile, the main advantage of using convolutional neural networks and unsupervised paragraph vector model is that we can transfer the knowledge to other domains using a much simpler fine-tuning technique than those in the literature *i.e.*, [9]. We also hope our sentiment analysis results can encourage further research on online user generated multimedia content.

Acknowledgements

This work was generously supported in part by Adobe Research, and New York State CoE IDS. Jianchao Yang performed related work while he was with Adobe Research.

7. REFERENCES

[1] S. Asur and B. A. Huberman. Predicting the future with social media. In *WI-IAT*, volume 1, pages 492–499. IEEE, 2010.

[2] J. Bollen, H. Mao, and A. Pepe. Modeling public mood and emotion: Twitter sentiment and socio-economic phenomena. In *ICWSM*, 2011.

[3] J. Bollen, H. Mao, and X. Zeng. Twitter mood predicts the stock market. *Journal of Computational Science*, 2(1):1–8, 2011.

[4] D. Borth, T. Chen, R. Ji, and S.-F. Chang. Sentibank: large-scale ontology and classifiers for detecting sentiment and emotions in visual content. In *ACM MM*, pages 459–460. ACM, 2013.

[5] D. Borth, R. Ji, T. Chen, T. Breuel, and S.-F. Chang. Large-scale visual sentiment ontology and detectors using adjective noun pairs. In *ACM MM*, pages 223–232. ACM, 2013.

[6] D. Cao, R. Ji, D. Lin, and S. Li. A cross-media public sentiment analysis system for microblog. *Multimedia Systems*, pages 1–8, 2014.

[7] D. C. Cireşan, U. Meier, J. Masci, L. M. Gambardella, and J. Schmidhuber. Flexible, high performance convolutional neural networks for image classification. In *IJCAI*, pages 1237–1242, 2011.

[8] D. Davidov, O. Tsur, and A. Rappoport. Enhanced sentiment learning using twitter hashtags and smileys. In *ICL*, pages 241–249, 2010.

[9] L. Duan, D. Xu, I.-H. Tsang, and J. Luo. Visual event recognition in videos by learning from web data. *IEEE PAMI*, 34(9):1667–1680, 2012.

[10] F. Feng, X. Wang, and R. Li. Cross-modal retrieval with correspondence autoencoder. In *ACM MM*, pages 7–16. ACM, 2014.

[11] A. Frome, G. S. Corrado, J. Shlens, S. Bengio, J. Dean, T. Mikolov, et al. Devise: A deep visual-semantic embedding model. In *NIPS*, pages 2121–2129, 2013.

[12] Y. Gong, L. Wang, M. Hodosh, J. Hockenmaier, and S. Lazebnik. Improving image-sentence embeddings using large weakly annotated photo collections. In *ECCV*, pages 529–545. Springer, 2014.

[13] X. Hu, J. Tang, H. Gao, and H. Liu. Unsupervised sentiment analysis with emotional signals. In *WWW*, pages 607–618, 2013.

[14] C. Hutto and E. Gilbert. Vader: A parsimonious rule-based model for sentiment analysis of social media text. In *ICWSM*, 2014.

[15] Y. Jia, E. Shelhamer, J. Donahue, S. Karayev, J. Long, R. Girshick, S. Guadarrama, and T. Darrell. Caffe: Convolutional architecture for fast feature embedding. *arXiv preprint arXiv:1408.5093*, 2014.

[16] D. Joshi, R. Datta, E. Fedorovskaya, Q.-T. Luong, J. Z. Wang, J. Li, and J. Luo. Aesthetics and emotions in images. *IEEE Signal Processing Magazine*, 28(5):94–115, 2011.

[17] A. Krizhevsky, I. Sutskever, and G. E. Hinton. Imagenet classification with deep convolutional neural networks. In *NIPS*, pages 1097–1105, 2012.

[18] Q. Le and T. Mikolov. Distributed representations of sentences and documents. In *ICML*, 2014.

[19] Y. LeCun, L. Bottou, Y. Bengio, and P. Haffner. Gradient-based learning applied to document recognition. *Proceedings of the IEEE*, 86(11):2278–2324, 1998.

[20] T. Mikolov, I. Sutskever, K. Chen, G. S. Corrado, and J. Dean. Distributed representations of words and phrases and their compositionality. In *NIPS*, pages 3111–3119, 2013.

[21] L.-P. Morency, R. Mihalcea, and P. Doshi. Towards multimodal sentiment analysis: Harvesting opinions from the web. In *ICMI*, pages 169–176, 2011.

[22] J. Ngiam, A. Khosla, M. Kim, J. Nam, H. Lee, and A. Y. Ng. Multimodal deep learning. In *ICML*, pages 689–696, 2011.

[23] B. O'Connor, R. Balasubramanyan, B. R. Routledge, and N. A. Smith. From tweets to polls: Linking text sentiment to public opinion time series. *ICWSM*, 11:122–129, 2010.

[24] N. Rasiwasia, J. Costa Pereira, E. Coviello, G. Doyle, G. R. Lanckriet, R. Levy, and N. Vasconcelos. A new approach to cross-modal multimedia retrieval. In *ACM MM*, pages 251–260. ACM, 2010.

[25] S. Siersdorfer, E. Minack, F. Deng, and J. Hare. Analyzing and predicting sentiment of images on the social web. In *ACM MM*, pages 715–718. ACM, 2010.

[26] R. Socher, M. Ganjoo, C. D. Manning, and A. Ng. Zero-shot learning through cross-modal transfer. In *NIPS*, pages 935–943, 2013.

[27] R. Socher, Q. Le, C. Manning, and A. Ng. Grounded compositional semantics for finding and describing images with sentences. In *NIPS Workshop*, 2013.

[28] N. Srivastava and R. Salakhutdinov. Multimodal learning with deep boltzmann machines. In *NIPS*, pages 2222–2230, 2012.

[29] A. Tumasjan, T. O. Sprenger, P. G. Sandner, and I. M. Welpe. Predicting elections with twitter: What 140 characters reveal about political sentiment. *ICWSM*, 10:178–185, 2010.

[30] M. Wang, D. Cao, L. Li, S. Li, and R. Ji. Microblog sentiment analysis based on cross-media bag-of-words model. In *ICIMCS*, pages 76:76–76:80. ACM, 2014.

[31] S. Wang and C. D. Manning. Baselines and bigrams: Simple, good sentiment and topic classification. In *ACL*, pages 90–94, 2012.

[32] Q. You, J. Luo, H. Jin, and J. Yang. Robust image sentiment analysis using progressively trained and domain transferred deep networks. In *The Twenty-Ninth AAAI Conference on Artificial Intelligence (AAAI)*, 2015.

[33] Q. You, J. Luo, H. Jin, and J. Yang. Building a large scale dataset for image emotion recognition: The fine print and the benchmark. In *The Thirtieth AAAI Conference on Artificial Intelligence (AAAI)*, 2016.

[34] J. Yuan, S. Mcdonough, Q. You, and J. Luo. Sentribute: image sentiment analysis from a mid-level perspective. In *WISDOM*, page 10, 2013.

[35] X. Zhang, H. Fuehres, and P. A. Gloor. Predicting stock market indicators through twitter "i hope it is not as bad as i fear". *Procedia-Social and Behavioral Sciences*, 26:55–62, 2011.

How Relevant is the Irrelevant Data: Leveraging the Tagging Data for a Learning-to-Rank Model

Noor Ifada[1,2], Richi Nayak[1]
[1]Queensland University of Technology (QUT), Australia
[2]University of Trunojoyo Madura (UTM), Indonesia
noor.ifada@{qut.edu.au, if.trunojoyo.ac.id}, r.nayak@qut.edu.au

ABSTRACT

For the task of tag-based item recommendations, the underlying tensor model faces several challenges such as high data sparsity and inferring latent factors effectively. To overcome the inherent sparsity issue of tensor models, we propose the *graded-relevance* interpretation scheme that leverages the tagging data effectively. Unlike the existing schemes, the *graded-relevance* scheme interprets the tagging data richly, differentiates the non-observed tagging data insightfully, and annotates each entry as one of the "relevant", "likely relevant", "irrelevant", or "indecisive" labels. To infer the latent factors of tensor models correctly to produce the high quality recommendation, we develop a novel learning-to-rank method, *Go-Rank*, that optimizes Graded Average Precision (GAP). Evaluating the proposed method on real-world datasets, we show that the proposed interpretation scheme produces a denser tensor model by revealing "relevant" entries from the previously assumed "irrelevant" entries. Optimizing GAP as the ranking metric, the quality of the recommendations generated by *Go-Rank* is found superior against the benchmarking methods.

Categories and Subject Descriptors

H.3.3 [**Information Search and Retrieval**]: Information Filtering

Keywords

Item recommendation, Tagging data, Graded-relevance scheme, Graded average precision

1. INTRODUCTION

In the websites that allow users to annotate items with tags, a ternary correlation is naturally formed. Over a period, the ternary data recording the users tagging activities can be accumulated that reflect the user profiles. This data includes complex relationships as users are allowed annotating the same item with different tags as well as annotating different items with the same tag. Analysis of this data enables discovering latent factors that govern the ternary correlations. A tag-based item recommendation system can utilize the captured correlation of tagging data and predict the list of items which may be of interest to a user. The success of such systems highly depends upon how those correlations are exploited [1].

WSDM'16, February 22-25, 2016, San Francisco, CA, USA
© 2016 ACM. ISBN 978-1-4503-3716-8/16/02…$15.00
DOI: http://dx.doi.org/10.1145/2835776.2835790

The multi-dimensional tagging data can naturally be modeled with a tensor model, and the latent correlations inherent in the data can be inferred [2-4]. However, generating recommendations using a tensor model is not a trivial task. It imposes several challenges including the following two that are the focus of this paper.

Data sparsity. Each user uses and annotates only a small number of tags and items respectively. This means that only a few entries are observed per user and, consequently, the tensor model becomes highly sparse [5-7]. The interpretation of tagging data is crucial in solving the sparsity problem in tensor models [5, 8]. Given that tagging data holds records of existing entries, the observed entries can be interpreted in a straightforward manner from the data. In contrast, interpreting the non-observed data is a non-trivial task. Currently, there exist two interpretation schemes. According to the *boolean* scheme, non-observed entries are labelled as "0" and the observed entries are labelled as "1" [4]. According to the *set-based* scheme, non-observed entries are interpreted as a mixture of "irrelevant" and "indecisive" entries, whereas the observed or "relevant" entries are given higher values than that of the "irrelevant" ones [5]. The "irrelevant" entries are entries that users do not like, while the "indecisive" are entries that users might like in the future, i.e. entries to be predicted by the recommender system. The *boolean* scheme certainly faces the sparsity problem as the non-observed data dominate a tensor model. The *set-based* scheme has shown to solve this problem; however, it over-generalizes the "irrelevant" entries. The scheme interprets that, on each observed $(user, tag)$ set, any items other than those appearing in observed entries are "irrelevant" [5]. We have recently shown that the *set-based* interpretation leads inaccurate results and presented that the "irrelevant" entries should only be interpreted from items which have not been annotated by the user using any tags, on each observed $(user, tag)$ set [8]. It is of critical importance that how such non-observed data entries, which should not simply be regarded as "irrelevant" entries, be interpreted. Those entries are certainly not the "indecisive" entries as the items of the entries have already been selected by the user in the past and, for that reason, we are not interested to predict them in the future. An efficient interpretation scheme that can further differentiate the non-observed data and overcome the sparsity problem is in sighted.

Learning from the latent factors. The task of a tag-based recommendation system is to generate the list of items, which may be of interest to a user, by learning the users' tagging history. The recommended items are ordered in descending order based on the predicted preference score which reflects the preference level of a user in selecting an item based on a tag. The score is calculated from the latent factors that govern the tagging data ternary correlations. In practice, users show more interest to the fewer items at the top of the list rather than the ones further down [9] and, therefore, the order of items in the list is crucial. In this case, the recommendation task can be considered as a ranking problem and can be approached as "learning-to-rank" for generating a quality top-N recommendation list [9-11]. For this reason, the latent factors of a tensor model can be learned so as to directly optimize ranking metric. The metrics such as Mean Average Precision (MAP) and Mean Reciprocal Rank (MRR) have been formulated to handle the binary relevance data [12, 13]. Unfortunately, these metrics are unsuitable for learning the latent factors of tensor model if the tagging data is interpreted as ordinal relevance data [10]. Though the NDCG (Normalized Discount Cumulative Gain) metric can handle ordinal relevance data [10], it is unsuitable to handle graded data with "transitional" entries, as described in the previous challenge. An alternative metric that can handle the aforementioned graded data is required as the object of optimization for learning the latent factors of the tensor model.

In this paper we address the above two challenges by proposing a *graded-relevance* interpretation scheme to effectively leverage the tagging data, and a novel learning-to-rank method that directly optimizes a graded evaluation metric to learn the latent factors of the tensor model. The proposed *graded-relevance* scheme interprets the tagging data with four distinct entries, i.e. "relevant", "likely relevant", "irrelevant", and "indecisive". The scheme sets the entries of non-observed data, which are not "irrelevant", as the transitional entries between the "relevant" and "irrelevant" entries. Each tagging data entry can then be graded with one of the ordinal relevance values of $\{2,1,0,-1\}$. The learning-to-rank method, called as *Go-Rank*, generates an optimal list of recommended items from the Graded Average Precision (GAP) [14] perspective for all users. GAP works as the generalization of Average Precision (AP) for ordinal relevance data. Using GAP as the optimized ranking metric allows the learning model to set up thresholds so that the "likely relevant" entries can be regarded as either "relevant" or "irrelevant" entries. Experimental results on real-world datasets show that *Go-Rank* outperforms state-of-the-art recommendation methods in recommendation quality. It ascertains that the efficient interpretation scheme solves the sparsity problem and assists the "learning-to-rank" method, which directly optimizes GAP as the appropriate ranking metric, to produce high quality recommendation.

To the best of our knowledge, this is the first work on tag-based item recommendation system that leverages the tagging data as graded relevance data. Our contributions can be summarized as follows: (1) a novel *graded-relevance* interpretation scheme to leverage the tagging data, (2) a novel tag-based item recommendation method, *Go-Rank*, that directly optimizes a (smoothed) GAP for learning the latent factors of tensor model built with data labelled using the *graded-relevance* scheme. This is the first time GAP has been proposed to optimize a learning-to-rank model for recommendation method using tagging data as implicit feedback.

The remainder of this paper is organized as follows. Section 2 presents the related works. Section 3 describes the proposed *graded-relevance* scheme. Section 4 details the *Go-Rank* learning method. Section 5 presents the experimental results based on real world datasets. Section 6 concludes the paper.

2. RELATED WORK

Tensor models have been successfully used to represent and analyze the latent relationships inherent in three-dimensional tagging data [3, 4, 6, 15]. The tensor model, used as a predictor function, maps the ternary latent correlations inherent in tagging data to a predicted preference score. These scores can then be used in ranking the recommendation items. The tensor based recommendation methods have shown improved results over the matrix based methods [4, 6]. The selection of tagging data interpretation scheme is crucial for tensor models as it determines how the user profiles are built based on the users past tagging histories. While the tagging data holds records of observed tagging entries, existing interpretation schemes vary in the way they interpret the non-observed entries.

The *boolean* scheme [4] simply labels the non-observed tagging entries as "0" and the observed ones as "1". The tensor model built with data labelled using this scheme results in highly sparse model as the non-observed data usually dominate the tensor entries. Moreover, this scheme overfits the mixed values that can be revealed from the non-observed entries, as using a one single value of "0" makes it difficult to predict the ranking list that might interest users in future [5]. The *set-based* scheme [5] was proposed to tackle the problems of *boolean* scheme and has shown more accurate interpretation of the tagging data. This scheme interprets non-observed data as a mixture of "irrelevant" and "indecisive" entries. The "irrelevant" entries are entries that users do not like, while the "indecisive" are entries that users might like in the future, i.e. entries to be predicted by the recommendation system. In this scheme, the rules of labelling are typically assigning higher values to the observed or "relevant" entries in comparison to "irrelevant" ones [5]. This scheme results in dense data. However, to generate quality recommendations, an efficient scheme is more important instead of just getting more entries [8].

Our recent study has shown that the *set-based* scheme over-generalizes the "irrelevant" entries [8] and can mislead the recommendation performance. According to this scheme, on each observed $(user, tag)$ set, any items other than those appearing in observed entries are labelled as "irrelevant" [5]. It disregards the fact that some of those items may have been annotated by the user using other tags. Principally, on each observed $(user, tag)$ set, only items, that have not been annotated by the user using any tags, should be interpreted as "irrelevant" [8, 16]. This opens up a new problem of how those entries of non-observed data, which should not simply be regarded as "irrelevant", are interpreted. Those entries cannot be regarded as "indecisive" entries since items of the entries have already been selected by the user in the past and therefore we are not interested to predict them in the future. In this paper, we propose a novel *graded-relevance* scheme that sets those entries as the transitional entries between the "relevant" and "irrelevant" entries, and label them as "likely relevant". As a result, our proposed interpretation scheme generates tagging data entries that are identical to explicit rating data.

Several Information Retrieval researches have listed that users show more interest to the fewer items at the top of the list than the ones further down the list [9]. This makes the "learning-to-rank" approach suitable for generating a quality top-N recommendation list [9-11]. In a tensor recommendation model, the latent factors of the ternary correlations can be learned so as to directly optimize ranking metric. In the last few years, researchers have proposed the recommendation models optimized based on MAP [12] and MRR [13], but these models can only deal with binary relevance data. Since the tag-based recommendation systems use the ordinal relevance data, these models are not suitable.

For ordinal relevance data, a well-known tag recommendation method is PITF [17]. The recommendation model is built by creating pairs of items as its focus is to get the ranking order within each items pair correctly, instead of getting the correct order of the entire items in recommendation list. The objective function is based on Area Under the ROC Curve (AUC) optimization that undesirably assigns equal penalty to all mistakes done in the recommendation list regardless of their positions, such as top or bottom [12]. PITF is based on the *set-based* scheme, consequently it overgeneralizes the "irrelevant" entries of the non-observed data. As a tag recommendation method, PITF generated the recommendations with two specified dimensions, i.e. user and item. In contrast, in our work, we generate item recommendations that are made with specified users only and, therefore, the item predicted preference scores must be calculated for the whole available tags before being sorted as a list of top-*N* recommendation.

We have recently proposed a tag-based item recommendation method, Do-Rank [16], that implemented a more efficient version of the *set-based* scheme to interpret the tagging data and used Discount Cumulative Gain (DCG) as the learning model optimization criterion. However, given the characteristic of entries generated from the *graded-relevance* scheme proposed in this paper, a recommendation method will need an optimization criterion that allows the learning model to control when to regard the "likely relevant" entries as "relevant" or 'irrelevant". Consequently, Do-Rank or using (N)DCG as the optimization criterion for learning model will be inappropriate.

Researchers have proposed recommendation methods based on optimized NDCG [18] and GAP [19] by using rating data as the explicit feedback. Our problem is considerably different and difficult in comparison to those works due to the nature of ordinal rating data generated in our model. A recommendation method with explicit rating data builds its model by collecting the rating values given on each $\langle user, item\rangle$ binary correlation. The list of recommendations is then generated from the ranked predicted preference scores inferred from the non-observed $\langle user, item\rangle$ correlations [18, 20]. In contrast, our model is built from the $\langle user, item, tag\rangle$ ternary correlations tagging data and the ordinal rating values are given on each $(user, tag)$ set. This means that there exist multiple rating values on each $(user, tag)$ set, instead of just one rating value like the one given for the explicit feedback data. Eventually, the recommendation list needs to be generated by ranking the predicted preference scores for all items, under all tags, which may be interest to a user.

In this paper, we propose a novel learning-to-rank method that optimizes GAP for the case of ordinal relevance data of implicit feedback, called as *Go-Rank*, and generates a list of recommended items from the GAP perspective to all users. Using GAP in our model allows us to set thresholds in the learning model so that the "likely relevant" entries can be regarded as either "relevant" or "irrelevant" entries.

3. LEVERAGING TAGGING DATA

Tagging data consists of observed entries which form the ternary correlations between users, items, and tags. The observed entries can be labelled as "relevant" in which users have expressed their interest to items explicitly by annotating those items using tags. Let $U = \{u_1, u_2, u_3, \dots, u_Q\}$ be the set of Q users, $I = \{i_1, i_2, i_3, \dots, i_R\}$ be the set of R items, and $T = \{t_1, t_2, t_3, \dots, t_S\}$ be the set of S tags. Tagging data can be denoted as $A \subseteq U \times I \times T$, where a vector of $(u, i, t) \in A$ represents the activity of user u to annotate item i using tag t.

The ternary correlation within tagging data can be naturally modelled as a three-dimensional tensor of $\mathcal{Y} \in \mathbb{R}^{Q\times R\times S}$ where each tensor entry, $y_{u,i,t}$, is given a numerical value that represents the relevance grade of tagging activity. Each slice of the tensor represents a user matrix which contains the user tag usage for each item. The tensor $\mathcal{Y}$ is then used as the ranking learning model.

In this paper, we propose an extended set of possible tensor entries and derive a corresponding optimization metric for learning the tensor model. In the remainder of this section, we first explain why previously proposed entry choices are not optimal (Section 3.1) and present a new set of possible entries based on the idea that, on each observed (u, t) set, the entries of non-observed data cannot simply be regarded as "irrelevant" entries. The proposed *graded-relevance* interpretation scheme for generating the optimal tensor entries is one of the main contributions of this paper.

3.1 Data Interpretation: Problem

We present a tensor toy example of $\mathcal{Y} \in \mathbb{R}^{3\times4\times5}$ in Figure 1 where $U = \{u_1, u_2, u_3\}$, $I = \{i_1, i_2, i_3, i_4\}$ and $T = \{t_1, t_2, t_3, t_4, t_5\}$. The "+" symbols represent the observed entries of tagging data. For instance, the first slice in Figure 1 shows that user u_1 has tagged item i_2 with tag t_1 and t_3. A typical tag-based item recommendation system interprets tagging data A using the *boolean* scheme, as illustrated in Figure 2(a), to build the tensor learning model $\mathcal{Y}$. This scheme uses the following rules for interpreting the data:

$$y_{u,i,t} := \begin{cases} 1 & if\ (u,i,t) \in A \\ 0 & otherwise \end{cases} \tag{1}$$

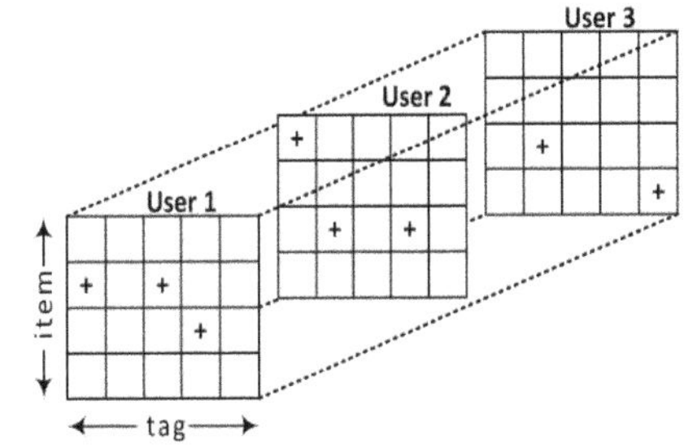

Figure 1. A tensor toy example of observed entries

Figure 2(a) reveals two shortcomings of *boolean* scheme: (1) the sparsity problem – 0 values dominate the data and (2) the overfitting problem – all non-observed entries are denoted as 0, however, other values can be revealed from them [5]. The *set-based* scheme [5] can overcome these drawbacks. Using the *set-based* scheme, the non-observed entries can be differentiated as "irrelevant" and "indecisive" according to each observed (u, t) set. The rules of labelling are as follows: higher ordinal values are assigned to the observed or "relevant" entries and labelled with "1" value, whereas "irrelevant" entries (i.e. users do not like) are labelled with "-1" value. The "0" value is used to label "indecisive" entries that can be predicted for generating recommendations. The *set-based* scheme uses the following rules:

$$y_{u,i,t} := \begin{cases} 1 & if\ (u,i,t) \in A \\ -1 & if\ (u,i,t) \notin A\ and\ (u,*,t) \in A \\ 0 & otherwise \end{cases} \tag{2}$$

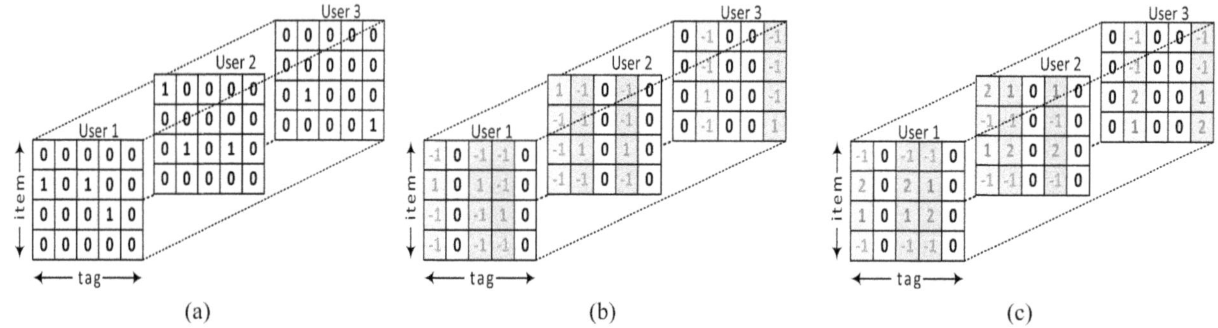

Figure 2: The entries of tensor $\mathcal{Y} \in \mathbb{R}^{3\times4\times5}$ generated from various interpretation schemes: (a) *boolean*, (b) *set-based*, and (c) *graded-relevance*

Our previous study [8] has shown that the *set-based* scheme is incorrect as it over-generalizes the "irrelevant" entries and results in inferior recommendation performance. On each observed (u,t) set, the scheme interprets any items other than those appearing in observed entries as "irrelevant" entries [5] and disregards the fact that some of those items have been annotated by the user using other tags. Actually, only the items, on each observed (u,t) set, that have not been annotated by user u using any tags should be interpreted as "irrelevant" entries [8]. Yet, how to interpret the entries of non-observed data that should not simply be regarded as "irrelevant" remains unsolved.

We use the entries of User 1 (u_1) in Figure 1 to better explain the issue. Using the *set-based* scheme as illustrated in Figure 2(b), we can list the observed and non-observed entries based on each (u,t) set of the user. The observed entries show that there exist (u_1,t_1), (u_1,t_3), and (u_1,t_4) sets that have been used to annotate $\{i_2\}$, $\{i_2\}$, and $\{i_3\}$, respectively. These observed entries are regarded as "relevant" entries while all non-observed entries of non-existed set, i.e. (u_1,t_2) and (u_1,t_5) on any items can easily be interpreted as "indecisive" entries. The problem becomes apparent when the "irrelevant" entries are to be interpreted. It can be seen that on all sets, both i_1 and i_4 have never been annotated by u_1 using any other tags, and therefore it makes sense to assume that the entries of (u_1,t_1), (u_1,t_3), and (u_1,t_4) with $\{i_1,i_4\}$ are "irrelevant". However, the entries of i_3 with (u_1,t_1) and (u_1,t_3) should not simply be interpreted as "irrelevant" as i_3 occurs as "relevant" on (u_1,t_4). Similarly, i_2 is "relevant" on (u_1,t_1) and (u_1,t_3), and therefore (u_1,t_4) with i_2 cannot be "irrelevant". Simply labelling those entries as "irrelevant" is improper and can result in inferior recommendation performance [8]. It can be noted that those entries definitely cannot be labelled "indecisive" as we do not want to predict them in the future.

3.2 Graded-Relevance Scheme

We propose the *graded-relevance* interpretation scheme to effectively leverage the tagging data for building the tensor ranking learning model $\mathcal{Y}$. Following the general rule, the observed entries are regarded as "relevant", indicating that users have shown their interest to the entries. From the observed entries, we extract the list of distinct items that have been annotated by user u using any tags. This list, denotes as C_u, is defined as follows:

$$C_u = \{i \mid (u,i,*) \in A\} \tag{3}$$

The item set C_u assists in distinguishing the non-observed data that do not belong to either the "irrelevant" or the "indecisive" category. On each observed (u,t) set, the entries which items have been annotated using other tags are labelled as "likely relevant" entries. As a result, the *graded-relevance* scheme insightfully differentiates the non-observed data and exposes them as a mixture of three entries: (1) "likely relevant" entries – user is probably interested to the entries, yet it is not explicitly revealed, (2) "irrelevant" entries – user is not interested with the entries, and (3) "indecisive" entries – user might be interested to the entries in the future. The "likely relevant" entries are revealed as entries that, even though they do not occur in the observed set, the items of the entries have actually been annotated by the user using other tags.

Having the four possible distinct values for each entry, we assign the entries with an ordinal value which is graded from the highest to the lowest ones, i.e. "relevant", "likely relevant", "indecisive", and "irrelevant". As illustrated in Figure 2(c), the *graded-relevance* scheme can generate entries labelled with $\{2,1,0,-1\}$ for the tensor model and make it comparable to explicit rating data. The *graded-relevance* scheme uses the following rules:

$$y_{u,i,t} \coloneqq \begin{cases} 2 & if\ (u,i,t) \in A \\ 1 & if\ (u,i,t) \notin A\ and\ i \in C_u\ and\ (u,*,t) \in A \\ -1 & if\ (u,i,t) \notin A\ and\ i \in I \backslash C_u and\ (u,*,t) \in A \\ 0 & otherwise \end{cases} \tag{4}$$

At the next stage, for learning the latent factors of the tensor model, we propose optimizing the ranking metric that can appropriately handle the ordinal relevance of tensor entries generated from the *graded-relevance* scheme.

4. LEARNING-TO-RANK WITH TENSOR MODEL

We first describe the tensor-based recommendation model in general and then present in detail how the tensor model can be learned by optimizing the GAP ranking metric.

4.1 Tensor-based Recommendation Model

The latent ternary correlation $\langle user, item, tag \rangle$ can be inferred after factorizing the tensor model in which entries are populated by implementing the proposed *graded-relevance* scheme to interpret the tagging data. In this paper, we use CP [2] as the factors model as well as the predictor function. CP is a well-known factorization technique that has shown to be less expensive in both memory and time consumption as compared to another popular factorization technique of Tucker [2].

As illustrated in Figure 3, CP factorizes a third-order tensor $\mathcal{Y} \in \mathbb{R}^{Q\times R\times S}$ into three latent factor matrices $\hat{U} \in \mathbb{R}^{Q\times F}$, $\hat{I} \in$

$\mathbb{R}^{R\times F}$, $\hat{T} \in \mathbb{R}^{S\times F}$ and a diagonal core tensor $\mathcal{C} \in \mathbb{R}^{F\times F\times F}$, where F is the column size of the corresponding latent factor matrices. These latent factor matrices are used in calculating the predicted score that reflects the preference level of a user in choosing an item for a tag. The predicted preference score is calculated as:

$$\hat{y}_{u,i,t} := \sum_{f=1}^{F} \hat{u}_{u,f} \cdot \hat{\imath}_{i,f} \cdot \hat{t}_{t,f} = [\![\hat{U}_u, \hat{I}_i, \hat{T}_t]\!] \quad (5)$$

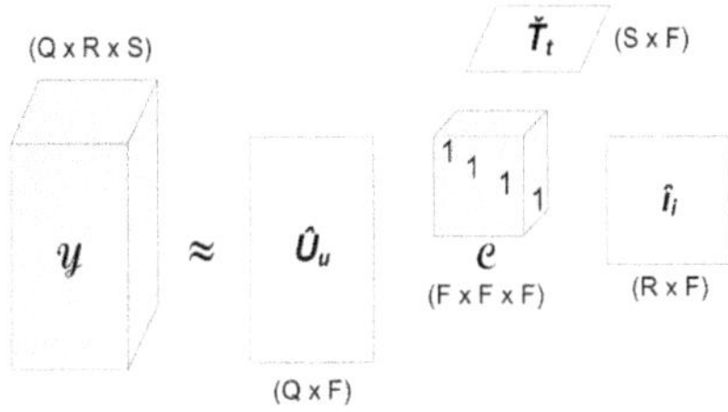

Figure 3. The CP factorization model for third-order tensor

Assuming that users show interest to a few top recommended items only [9], the factorized tensor model can be optimized with respect to the ranking metric during the learning procedure in order to generate quality item recommendations to users by exploiting their tag usage.

4.2 Learning to Rank with Tensor Model

The development of *Go-Rank*, the second main contributions of this paper, is presented in this section. *Go-Rank* directly optimizes the appropriate ranking metric for learning the latent factors of tensor model built with entries labelled using the *graded-relevance* scheme.

4.2.1 Optimization Criterion

The unique characteristic of the generated tensor entries, detailed in Section 3.2, requires an optimization criterion that allows the learning model to control when to regard the "likely relevant" entries as "relevant" or 'irrelevant". We propose to use Graded Average Precision (GAP) as the ranking metric to optimize the latent factors of tensor model. GAP is the generalization of Average Precision (AP) metric for ordinal relevance data [14]. Using GAP as the optimized ranking metric allows us to set up thresholds in the learning model so that the "likely relevant" entries can be regarded as either "relevant" or "irrelevant" entries. The task of recommendation can now be formulated as recommend an optimal (from the GAP perspective) items list to users using the latent factor matrices of tensor model. Based on the original definition of GAP [14], the score for a user u under tag t is formulated as:

$$GAP_{u,t} := \frac{\sum_{i\in I}\sum_{k=1}^{c}\sum_{j\neq i} g_k \mathbb{I}(y_{u,i,t}\geq 1)\mathbb{I}(y_{u,j,t}\geq \mu_k)\frac{\mathbb{I}(r_{u,j,t}\leq r_{u,i,t})}{r_{u,i,t}}}{\sum_{l=1}^{c} n_{u,l,t}\sum_{k=1}^{l} g_k} \quad (6)$$

where $c = max(y_{u,i,t})$ and $y_{u,i,t}$ is the relevance label assigned from the ordinal relevance set of $\{2,1,0,-1\}$ obtained from the initial tensor model. The $r_{u,i,t}$ is the ranking position of item i for user u with tag t and, is approximated using $\hat{y}_{u,i,t}$ (which is calculated from the latent factor matrices using Equation (5)). The g_k denotes the threshold probability that the user sets as a threshold of relevance at grade μ_k, i.e. regarding the entries with grades equal or larger than μ_k as "relevant" and the others as "irrelevant". In other words, g_k and μ_k are the parameters that control whether the "likely relevant" entries should be regarded as "relevant" or 'irrelevant". It is to be noted that the probability values must be exclusive and exhaustive probabilities [14]:

$$\sum_{k=1}^{c} g_k = 1 \quad (7)$$

The $\mathbb{I}(\cdot)$ is the indicator function which is equal to 1 if the condition is satisfied, and 0 otherwise. The $n_{u,l,t}$ is number of items labelled with grade l by user u using tag t. The GAP score for all users under all tags can be defined as:

$$GAP := \frac{1}{QS}\sum_{u\in U}\sum_{t\in T}\frac{\sum_{i\in I}\sum_{k=1}^{c}\sum_{j\neq i}\beta_{gy}\frac{\mathbb{I}(r_{u,j,t}\leq r_{u,i,t})}{r_{u,i,t}}}{\sum_{l=1}^{c} n_{u,l,t}\sum_{k=1}^{l} g_k} \quad (8)$$

Notice that for notational convenience, we perform the following substitution:

$$\beta_{gy} = g_k \mathbb{I}(y_{u,i,t} \geq 1)\mathbb{I}(y_{u,j,t} \geq \mu_k) \quad (9)$$

The list of recommended items is generated for user u by ranking all the items in descending order of the computed preference scores over all items under all tags.

4.2.2 Ranking Smoothing

From Equation (8), we can see that GAP is dependent to the ranking positions of items in the recommendation list as it is reliant on the values of $\mathbb{I}(r_{u,j,t} \leq r_{u,i,t})$ and $r_{u,i,t}$. Given that the ranking positions are determined via the predicted relevance scores calculated based on the model parameters (i.e. latent factor matrices), the GAP function becomes unsmooth. This condition makes it difficult to apply the standard optimization methods which require smoothness in the objective function, such as the gradient based approaches, in the learning procedure [10, 21]. We tackle this problem by implementing the smoothing function [10] to the ranking position with respect to the model parameters as follows:

$$\mathbb{I}(r_{u,j,t} \leq r_{u,i,t}) \approx \sigma(\Delta\hat{y}) \quad (10)$$

$$r_{u,i,t} \approx 1 + \sum_{j\neq i}\sigma(\Delta\hat{y}) \quad (11)$$

where σ is the logistic function $\sigma(x) = \frac{1}{1+e^{-x}}$ and $\Delta\hat{y} = \hat{y}_{u,i,t} - \hat{y}_{u,j,t}$. Substituting Equations (10) and (11) to Equation (8), we obtain the smoothed approximation of GAP:

$$sGAP := \frac{1}{QS}\sum_{u\in U}\sum_{t\in T}\frac{\sum_{i\in I}\sum_{k=1}^{c}\sum_{j\neq i}\beta_{gy}\frac{\sigma(\Delta\hat{y})}{1+\sum_{j\neq i}\sigma(\Delta\hat{y})}}{\sum_{l=1}^{c} n_{u,l,t}\sum_{k=1}^{l} g_k} \quad (12)$$

The resultant objective function with λ_Θ as regularization coefficient corresponds to σ_Θ for avoiding overfitting is formulated as:

$$L(\Theta) := \frac{1}{QS}\sum_{u\in U}\sum_{t\in T}\frac{\sum_{i\in I}\sum_{k=1}^{c}\sum_{j\neq i}\beta_{gy}\frac{\sigma(\Delta\hat{y})}{1+\sum_{j\neq i}\sigma(\Delta\hat{y})}}{\sum_{l=1}^{c} n_{u,l,t}\sum_{k=1}^{l} g_k} - \lambda_\Theta\|\Theta\|_F^2 \quad (13)$$

4.2.3 Learning Algorithm

We present the algorithm to optimize model parameters Θ of $\Delta\hat{y}$ formulated in Equation (13). We use gradient descent to minimize the objective function. We do not consider QS and $\sum_{l=1}^{c} n_{u,l,t}\sum_{k=1}^{l} g_k$ coefficients as they have no influence on the optimization. Given a case (u,i,j,t) with respect to model parameters $\{\hat{U}_u, \hat{I}_i, \hat{I}_j, \hat{T}_t\}$, the gradient of $sGAP$ can be computed as:

$$\frac{\partial L}{\partial \theta} = \frac{\partial}{\partial \theta}\left(\sum_{u\in U}\sum_{t\in T}\frac{\sum_{i\in I}\sum_{k=1}^{c}\sum_{j\neq i}\beta_{gy}\sigma(\Delta\hat{y})}{1+\sum_{j\neq i}\sigma(\Delta\hat{y})}\right) - \lambda_\theta\theta \quad (14)$$

By replacing $\sigma(\Delta\hat{y})$ as δ, for notational convenience, the derivation formulation can be rewritten as:

$$\frac{\partial L}{\partial \theta} = \sum_{u\in U}\sum_{t\in T}\frac{\sum_{i\in I}\sum_{k=1}^{c}\sum_{j\neq i}\left[\left(\frac{\partial}{\partial\theta}(\beta_{gy}\delta)\right)\left(1+\sum_{j\neq i}\delta\right)\right]-\left[(\beta_{gy}\delta)\left(\frac{\partial}{\partial\theta}\left(1+\sum_{j\neq i}\delta\right)\right)\right]}{\left[1+\sum_{j\neq i}\delta\right]^2} - \lambda_\theta\theta \quad (15)$$

The resulted gradient of $sGAP$ is obtained as:

$$\frac{\partial L}{\partial \theta} = \sum_{u \in U} \sum_{t \in T} \frac{\sum_{i \in I} \sum_{k=1}^{c} \sum_{j \neq i} \beta_{gy} \left(\left[(-\delta + \delta^2)(1 + \sum_{j \neq i} \delta) \frac{\partial}{\partial \theta} \Delta \hat{y} \right] - \left[\delta \left(\sum_{j \neq i} (-\delta + \delta^2) \frac{\partial}{\partial \theta} \Delta \hat{y} \right) \right] \right)}{\left[1 + \sum_{j \neq i} \delta \right]^2} - \lambda_\theta \theta \quad (16)$$

Since β_{gy} is determined by $\mathbb{I}(y_{u,i,t} \geq 1)\mathbb{I}(y_{u,j,t} \geq \mu_k)$, it ensures that the entries must not be "irrelevant", the grade of entries must be at least equal to the threshold μ_k, and, most importantly, users are not using the whole available tags. Knowing this, we can implement a sparsity-aware approach to make the learning algorithm more efficient and faster. Instead of calculating $sGAP$ for the entire item set across all tags, we can optimize $sGAP$ only across tags that have been used by user u, $V_u = \{t | (u, *, t) \in A\}$, for items which entries are labelled as "relevant" or "likely relevant" for the user, i.e. $Z_u = \{i | y_{u,i,t} = 2 \cup y_{u,i,t} = 1\}$. Other entries are not necessary to be included since their values are always less than any threshold graded values of μ, which means that $\mathbb{I}(y_{u,j,t} \geq \mu_k)$ will always be 0. As a result, the gradient of $sGAP$ given a case (u, i, j, t) with respect to the model parameter, $\{\hat{U}_u, \hat{I}_i, \hat{I}_j, \hat{T}_t\}$, becomes:

$$\frac{\partial L}{\partial \theta} = \sum_{u \in U} \sum_{t \in V_u} \frac{\sum_{i \in Z_u} \sum_{k=1}^{c} \sum_{j \neq i} \beta_{gy} \left(\left[(-\delta + \delta^2)(1 + \sum_{j \neq i} \delta) \frac{\partial}{\partial \theta} \Delta \hat{y} \right] - \left[\delta \left(\sum_{j \neq i} (-\delta + \delta^2) \frac{\partial}{\partial \theta} \Delta \hat{y} \right) \right] \right)}{\left[1 + \sum_{j \neq i} \delta \right]^2} - \lambda_\theta \theta \quad (17)$$

To apply the $sGAP$ optimization, we only have to compute the gradient of $\frac{\partial}{\partial \theta} \Delta \hat{y}$. The gradients for the model based on its parameters are: $\frac{\partial \Delta \hat{y}}{\partial \hat{U}_u} = (\hat{I}_i \odot \hat{T}_t - \hat{I}_j \odot \hat{T}_t)$, $\frac{\partial \Delta \hat{y}}{\partial \hat{I}_i} = (\hat{U}_u \odot \hat{T}_t)$, $\frac{\partial \Delta \hat{y}}{\partial \hat{I}_j} = -(\hat{U}_u \odot \hat{T}_t)$, $\frac{\partial \Delta \hat{y}}{\partial \hat{T}_t} = (\hat{U}_u \odot \hat{I}_i - \hat{U}_u \odot \hat{I}_j)$, where $\odot$ denotes element-wise product. The *Go-Rank* learning algorithm is outlined in Figure 4.

Algorithm: *Go-Rank* Learning
Input : Training set $D_{train} \subseteq U \times I \times T$, threshold probability $g \in \{g_1, g_2\}$, threshold grade $\mu \in \{\mu_1, \mu_2\}$, learning rate α, factor matrix column size F, regularization λ, maximal iteration $iterMax$
Output: Learned factor matrices $\hat{U}$, $\hat{I}$, $\hat{T}$
$Q = |U|$, $R = |I|$, $S = |T|$, $\mathcal{Y} \in \mathbb{R}^{Q \times R \times S}$, $y_{u,i,t} \in \{2, 1, 0, -1\}$
Populate $\mathcal{Y}$ using Equation (4)
$c = max(y_{u,i,t})$
$Z_u = \{i | y_{u,i,t} = 2 \cup y_{u,i,t} = 1\}$
$V_u = \{t | (u, *, t) \in A\}$
Initialize $\hat{U}^{(0)} \in \mathbb{R}^{Q \times F}, \hat{I}^{(0)} \in \mathbb{R}^{R \times F}, \hat{T}^{(0)} \in \mathbb{R}^{S \times F}, h = 0$
repeat
  for $u \in U$ **do**
    $\hat{U}_u \leftarrow \hat{U}_u + \alpha \frac{\partial L}{\partial \hat{U}_u}$ based on Equation (17)
  for $t \in T$ **do**
    $\hat{T}_t \leftarrow \hat{T}_t + \alpha \frac{\partial L}{\partial \hat{T}_t}$ based on Equation (17)
  for $u \in U$ **do**
    for $t \in V_u$ **do**
      for $i \in Z_u$ **do**
        for $k \leftarrow 1$ **to** c **do**
          for $j \neq i$ **do**
            $\hat{I}_i \leftarrow \hat{I}_i + \alpha \frac{\partial L}{\partial \hat{I}_i}$ based on Equation (17)
            $\hat{I}_j \leftarrow \hat{I}_j + \alpha \frac{\partial L}{\partial \hat{I}_j}$ based on Equation (17)
  $++h$
until $h \geq iterMax$

Figure 4. *Go-Rank* Learning Algorithm

4.2.4 *Complexity Analysis and Convergence*

We analyze the complexity of learning process for a single iteration. Complexity of the initial *Go-Rank* function (Equation 12) is $O(F(Q + S + QScR^2))$ where $c = max(y_{u,i,t})$. Given that $\mathcal{Y} \in \mathbb{R}^{Q \times R \times S}$, the total number of possible entries of the tensor model, i.e. the sum of "relevant", "likely relevant", irrelevant" and "indecisive" entries, is calculated as $|Y| = QRS$. Since $|Y| \gg Q, S, R, F, c$, the overall complexity of *Go-Rank* in one iteration can be regarded as $|Y|$. In other words, it is linear to the total number of possible entries of tensor model.

After the implementation of the proposed sparsity-aware approach for making the learning process to run efficiently and faster, complexity of the *Go-Rank* function (as summarized in Figure 4), becomes $O(F(Q + S + Q\tilde{v}\, c\tilde{n}^2))$ where $\tilde{v}$ and $\tilde{n}$ denote the average number of V_u and Z_u respectively. Since $\tilde{v} \ll S$ and $\tilde{n} \ll R$, the *Go-Rank* complexity now becomes $|\tilde{Y}|$, i.e. the sum of "relevant" and "likely relevant" entries of the tensor model, where $|\tilde{Y}| \ll |Y|$.

5. EMPIRICAL ANALYSIS

We use the MovieLens and LastFM datasets to evalaute the proposed *graded-relevance* interpretation scheme of tagging data and the proposed tag-based item recommendation method *Go-Rank*. These two datasets have been commonly used in recommendation techniques evaluation. MovieLens is obtained from the GroupLens Research Group corpus (http://ww.grouplens.org) and is an extension of MovieLens10M dataset published, while the LastFM corpus is retrieved from the Last.fm online music system (http://www.last.fm/) [22]. The MovieLens dataset consists of 47,957 observed entries from 2,113 users, 5,908 movies/items, and 9,079 tags. The LastFM dataset consists of 186,479 observed entries from 1,892 users, 12,523 artists/items, and 9,749 tags.

In this paper, we implemented a variety of p-cores to eliminate the noise and decrease sparsity [4]. Moreover, it avoids the non-stable results that tend to occur when only one choice of core size is used in experiments [23]. The p-core technique [24] is implemented by selecting users, items, and tags that have occurred in at least p number posts. Post is the set of distinct user-item sets in the observed tagging data. In the experiments, we investigated the variety of p for each dataset, i.e. 15-core and 20-core sets for the MovieLens dataset, and 50-core and 55-core sets for the LastFM dataset. It is to be noted that, the bigger the p-core is, the less sparse the commonly resulted set. Table 1 shows that, for the MovieLens dataset, the density of "relevant" entries of the 15-core is more sparse than that of the 20-core, i.e. $0.0283 < 0.0284$. However, implementing p-core technique on the LastFM dataset results into conflicting behavior as Table 1 shows that the density of "relevant" entries of the 50-core is less sparse than that of the 55-core, i.e. $0.2465 > 0.1479$.

Each core of each dataset was randomly divided, using 5-fold cross validation, into a training set D_{train} (80%) and a test set D_{test} (20%) based on the number of posts data. The D_{train} and D_{test} do not overlap in posts, i.e., there exist no triplets for a user-item combination in the training set if a triplet $(u, i, *)$ is present in the test set. The recommendation task is to predict and rank the top-N items for the users present in D_{test}. The performance is measured using AP and NDCG, and reported over the average values.

Following the initialization approach proposed for a ranking model [20], we randomly initialized the factor matrices of our model. For a tensor-based method, a latent factor matrix with size between 10-64 is usually acceptable for generating quality recommendation [5, 12, 13, 17, 19, 25]. Here, we set the size of latent factor matrix $F = 32$ for *Go-Rank* and other tensor-based benchmarking methods. In order to empirically tune the other parameters in *Go-Rank*, we used all the observed entries available in D_{train} of each dataset. The best performances were achieved using the following values: learning rate $\alpha = 0.01$ and regularization $\lambda = 1e^{-05}$.

5.1 Impact of *Graded-Relevance* Scheme

We first examine the impact of *graded-relevance* scheme on tensor density. We compare the density of tensor entries resulted from the *graded-relevance* scheme with those of the *boolean* and *set-based* schemes as listed in Table 1. The statistics are reported, as the average density over all 5-fold D_{train}, on each dataset.

Table 1 shows that the proposed *graded-relevance* interpretation scheme is able to generate more dense data representation than the *boolean* scheme, concurring with previous outcome [5], as well as the *set-based* scheme. Results show that the density of "indecisive" entries on both the *graded-relevance* and *set-based* schemes are same. However, as previously explained in Section 3.2, the *graded-relevance* scheme breaks down the "irrelevant" entries of *set-based* scheme into "likely relevant" and "irrelevant" entries.

From Table 1, we can also see that, compared to the very low number of "relevant" entries, the *graded-relevance* scheme revealed significant number of "likely relevant" entries. In this case, by using the threshold probability [14], as shown in the following section, portion of these entries can then be possibly regarded as "relevant" entries. Additionally, the comparison between the numbers of "irrelevant" entries of the *graded-relevant* scheme to those of the *set-based* scheme is also worthwhile to observe. We can see that only a small amount of the "irrelevant" entries of *set-based* scheme are revealed as "likely relevant" entries using the *graded-relevance* scheme.

Interpretation Scheme	Entries	Density (%)			
		MovieLens		LastFM	
		15-core	20-core	50-core	55-core
boolean	Relevant	0.0283	0.0284	0.2465	0.1479
	Irrel./ Indecisive	99.9717	99.9716	99.7535	99.8521
set-based	Relevant	0.0283	0.0284	0.2465	0.1479
	Irrelevant	2.0969	2.4147	4.5894	4.8249
	Indecisive	97.8748	97.5569	95.1641	95.0272
graded-relevance	Relevant	0.0283	0.0284	0.2465	0.1479
	Likely Relevant	0.2493	0.3729	0.6984	0.7917
	Irrelevant	1.8477	2.0418	3.8911	4.0332
	Indecisive	97.8748	97.5569	95.1641	95.0272

Table 1. The comparison of tensor entries densities generated from various interpretation schemes: *boolean*, *set-based*, and *graded-relevance*

5.2 Impact of Probability Values

This experiment is conducted to examine how "relevant" is the "likely relevant" data. The probabilities values, $g \in \{g_1, g_2\}$ where $g_1 + g_2 = 1$, are the probabilities that regulate whether the "likely relevant" entries should be regarded as "relevant" or "irrelevant". We used g_1 and g_2 to determine the percentage of considering the "likely relevant" entries as "relevant" and 'irrelevant" respectively. For example, $g_1 = 0.1$ indicates that 10% of "likely relevant" entries will be considered as "relevant" and the other 90% of those will be considered as "irrelevant". We experimented with a total grid of probability values between 0 and 1 with an interval of 0.1, resulting $g_1 \in \{0.0, 0.1, 0.2, 0.3, 0.4, 0.5, 0.6, 0.7, 0.8, 0.9, 1.0\}$. Figure 5 and Figure 6 show the results as the average values over all 5-fold D_{train}, on each dataset.

It is to be noted that the threshold of regarding the "likely relevant" entries as either "relevant" or 'irrelevant" entries is fixed as $\mu \in \{2,1\}$, following the grades of the "relevant" and "likely relevant" entries formulated in Equation (4). In this case, depending on which threshold value is used, $y_{u,j,t} \geq \mu$ will determine the entries as "relevant" and the others as "irrelevant".

For the MovieLens dataset, Figure 5(a) and Figure 5(b) present the impact of probability values on 15-core and 20-core sets, respectively. The results show that not all of the "likely relevant" entries are "irrelevant". For example, in Figure 5(a) and Figure 5(b), the highest AP@5 are achieved when $g_1 = 0.2$ and $g_1 = 0.3$ for the 15-core and 20-core sets, respectively. This means that, a total of 20% or 30% of the "likely relevant" entries are actually found "relevant".

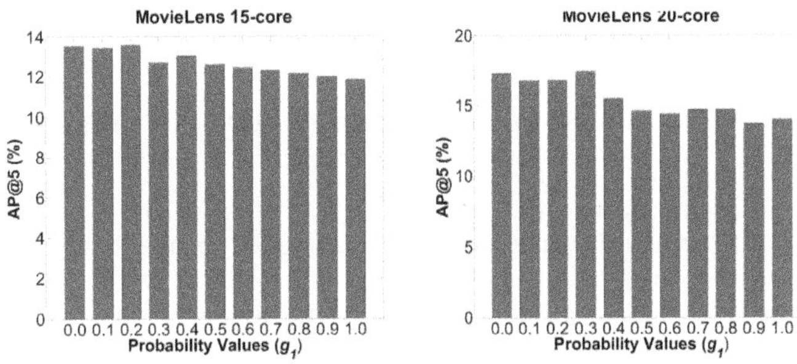

(a) (b)

Figure 5. Impact of probability values on the MovieLens dataset: (a) 15-core and (b) 20-core sets

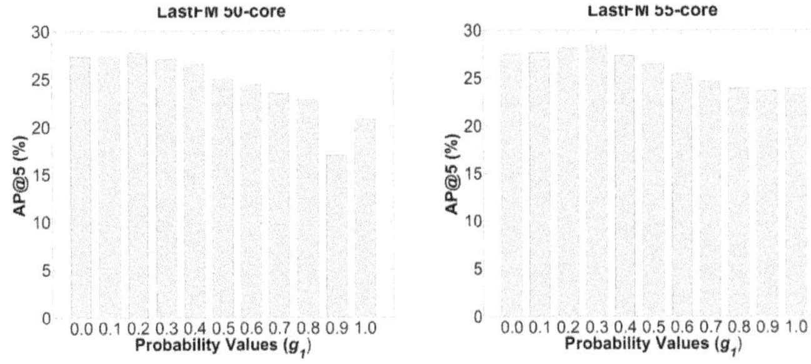

(a) (b)

Figure 6. Impact of probability values on the LastFM dataset: (a) 50-core and (b) 55-core sets

For the LastFM dataset, Figure 6(a) and Figure 6(b) present the impact of probability values on 50-core and 55-core sets, respectively. Complementing the results on the MovieLens dataset, those of the LastFM dataset also show that not all of the "likely relevant" entries are "irrelevant". For example, in Figure 6(a) and Figure 6(b), the highest AP@5 is achieved when $g_1 = 0.2$ and $g_1 = 0.3$ for the 50-core and 55-core sets, respectively. Hence, a total of 20% or 30% of the "likely relevant" entries of the sets can be regarded as "relevant".

All of these results establish that, on each observed (u, t) set, any items other than those appearing in the observed entries should not simply be regarded as "irrelevant" since some of them have been annotated by the user using other tags. In this case, the *graded-relevance* scheme is an efficient scheme as it sets the "transitional" entries as distinct entries positioned between the "relevant" and "irrelevant" entries.

5.3 Effectiveness of the Learning Algorithm

We examine the effectiveness of *Go-Rank* learning algorithm in terms of its learning time and convergence. We show the effectiveness of *Go-Rank* in Figure 7 using the MovieLens 20-core set. Implementation on other datasets gives similar results.

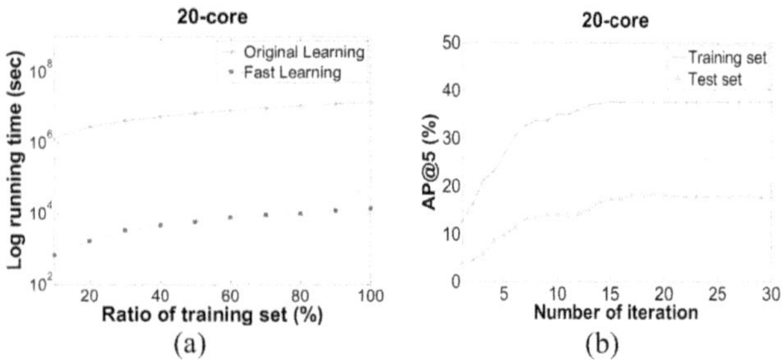

Figure 7. Effectiveness of *Go-Rank*: (a) Scalability and (b) Convergence

To investigate the impact of optimizing $sGAP$ using the fast learning approach (Equation (17)), we measure the running time for learning the model on a single iteration at different scales, i.e. 10% to 100% of one of the D_{train} resulted from the 5-fold cross validation split. Figure 7(a) shows that the fast learning approach time is extremely faster compared to that of the original learning model (Equation (16)). Figure 7(b) shows the evalution of AP@5 across iterations on the training and test sets. On both sets, AP score gradually increases along the iterations and converge after a few number of iterations. These results demonstrate that *Go-Rank* effectively optimizes GAP.

5.4 Performance Comparison

In this paper, we used the following benchmarking methods to be compared with the performance of the proposed *Go-Rank* method in terms of recommendation quality:

- **PITF** [17] is the pair-wise tensor model that was originally developed for tag recommendations. The method implements *set-based* scheme, to build *pair-wise ranking* on each user-item set, and AUC-based optimization. We have adapted the method to generate item recommendations based on the $(user, tag)$ sets. Note that the size of latent factor matrix is set as $F = 32$, the same as the setting for the proposed *Go-Rank* method. The other parameters are empirically tuned as $\alpha = 0.01$ and $\lambda = 5e^{-05}$.
- **CP-TRPR** [3] is the probabilistic ranking tensor-based method that implements *boolean* scheme and ranks the predicted preference scores by utilizing users past collaborative tagging data via probabilistic ranking approach. The ranking process is a subsequent stage following the tensor model learning process. The size of latent factor matrix is set as $F = 32$, and the other parameters are empirically tuned as $tolerance = 1e^{-04}$, $\lambda = 0$ and $voc\_size = 20$.
- **HOSVD-Max (MAX)** [4] is the conventional tensor-based method that implements *boolean* scheme and directly ranks the list of recommendations based on the maximum values of the predicted preferences scores. The size of latent factor matrix is set as $F = 32$, and the other parameters are empirically tuned as $tolerance = 1e^{-04}$ and $\lambda = 0$.
- **Graded-HOSVD-Max (Graded-MAX)** is the modification of the HOSVD-Max [4]. In this case, instead of using the *boolean* scheme, we implement our proposed *graded-relevance* scheme for building the tensor model.
- **CTS** [1] is the state-of-the-art matrix-based method that implements *boolean* scheme and ranks the recommendations by using the users past tagging activities in forming users' likelihood. The empirically tuned parameters are $neigborhood\_size = 50$ and $model\_size = 50$.

Table 2 and Table 3 show the performance comparison between the proposed *Go-Rank* with the benchmarking methods on the Movielens and LastFM datasets, respectively. Based on those results, we obtain the following three observations.

Methods	**15-core (Score in %)**						**20-core (Score in %)**					
	NDCG@1	**NDCG@5**	**NDCG@10**	**AP@1**	**AP@5**	**AP@10**	**NDCG@1**	**NDCG@5**	**NDCG@10**	**AP@1**	**AP@5**	**AP@10**
PITF	5.07	4.28	3.99	5.07	8.44	9.23	6.87	6.09	5.67	6.87	12.13	13.20
CP-TRPR	**9.74**	7.01	5.85	**9.74**	13.55	14.35	11.85	**8.91**	7.34	11.85	17.19	17.63
MAX	9.43	7.05	5.81	9.43	13.36	13.83	**12.77**	8.89	7.42	**12.77**	16.94	17.44
Graded-MAX	4.44	3.77	3.30	4.44	7.81	8.38	6.06	5.18	4.64	6.06	10.97	11.71
CTS	9.70	7.00	5.80	9.70	13.49	14.10	11.74	8.99	7.57	11.74	16.70	17.18
Go-Rank	**8.70**	**7.61**	**6.79**	**8.70**	**13.58**	**14.76**	**12.58**	**8.60**	**7.66**	**12.58**	**17.42**	**17.74**

Table 2. NDCG and AP at top-*N* position on MovieLens dataset

Methods	50-core (Score in %)						55-core (Score in %)					
	NDCG@1	NDCG@5	NDCG@10	AP@1	AP@5	AP@10	NDCG@1	NDCG@5	NDCG@10	AP@1	AP@5	AP@10
PITF	12.30	10.91	9.76	12.30	20.52	21.42	13.86	11.77	10.75	13.86	21.98	22.63
CP-TRPR	15.12	13.63	12.26	15.12	24.02	24.26	18.82	15.65	13.77	18.82	27.55	27.10
MAX	17.44	14.29	12.51	17.44	24.90	24.27	17.21	14.84	13.02	17.21	25.35	25.25
Graded-MAX	15.69	12.52	10.66	15.69	22.75	22.22	13.65	11.27	9.57	13.65	20.76	20.88
CTS	12.20	10.73	9.58	12.20	19.33	19.84	15.80	13.45	11.74	15.80	24.22	23.88
Go-Rank	**18.92**	**15.60**	**13.56**	**18.92**	**27.69**	**27.37**	**18.83**	**15.79**	**13.85**	**18.83**	**28.36**	**27.79**

Table 3. NDCG and AP at top-*N* position on LastFM dataset

First, the proposed *Go-Rank* outperforms all of benchmarking methods in terms of NDCG and AP (at most top-*N* positions) on both datasets. Note that, in contrast to AP, the higher the top-*N* position, the less the NDCG score is. The results confirm that *Go-Rank* is an effective approach for learning the tensor model built with data labelled using the proposed *graded-relevance* interpretation scheme. In this case, the GAP optimization of *Go-Rank* allows us to set up thresholds in the learning model so that the "likely relevant" entries can be regarded as either "relevant" or "irrelevant" entries. Previously described in Section 5.2, portion of "likely relevant" entries are found "relevant" that consequently assists *Go-Rank* to produce high quality recommendation. On the other hand, optimizing inappropriate objective function on a tensor model, built with data labelled using the *graded-relevance* scheme, results in inferior recommendation quality. This can be seen by comparing the results of Graded-MAX with those of MAX. It is to be noted that the objective function of both the Graded-MAX and MAX is minimizing the Mean Square Error (MSE), which is more suitable for solving a classification problem [3]. Their difference is in the interpretation scheme implemented for building the tensor model. Graded-MAX results a poorer recommendation quality compared to MAX, despite the fact that it implemented the *graded-relevance* scheme to build the tensor model, since it simply used the generated data as it is. In this case, Graded-MAX disregards the constraint that the "likely relevant" entries should be further regarded as either "relevant" or "irrelevant" in order to effectively learn the tensor model.

Second, we can see that the *Go-Rank* outperforms PITF. It is to be noted that both methods implements the non-*boolean* interpretation schemes to build the tensor models, i.e. *Go-Rank* uses the *graded-relevance* scheme while PITF uses the *set-based* schemes. *Go-Rank* attains great improvement over PITF, in both NDCG and AP, for two main reasons. *Go-Rank* build the learning model as a *list-wise* ranking model, i.e. aiming to get the order of all lists correctly. Whereas PITF builds the learning model as a *pair-wise* ranking model, which means that it attempts to get the correct ranking order within each pair only. Moreover, *Go-Rank* enhances the top-*N* recommendation performance by optimizing the top-biased measure GAP, i.e. the generalization of AP for ordinal relevance data. While PITF implements the equal-penalty measure AUC [12]. On the other hand, we can also see the outperformance of CP-TRPR over PITF, despite the fact that the former implements the *boolean* scheme to generate the tensor entries. The reason for this is because CP-TRPR implements a subsequent stage, the probabilistic ranking approach, following the MSE-based optimization learning process [3], for generating the recommendations. In this case, the second stage of the method probabilistically re-ranks the list of candidate items for each user, generated from the learned latent factors, as a *list-wise* ranking model in order to get the correct order of recommendations. Additionally, we also notice that CTS underperforms *Go-Rank*, especially on the LastFM dataset. This result indicates that projecting the ternary correlations of tagging data into two-dimensional model is impacting recommendation quality [4].

Third, by relating Table 1 with Table 2 and Table 3, we can see that the "relevant" tensor entries density, resulted from variety of p-cores on the same dataset, is impacting the *Go-Rank* performance improvement over other benchmarking methods. In this case, the less sparse the density is, the higher the performance improvement achieved, and vice versa. For example, the improvement comparison of *Go-Rank* over CP-TRPR can be observed as follows. As on the MovieLens dataset, the density of 15-core (i.e. 0.0283) is more sparse than that of the 20-core (i.e. 0.0284), the improvement of the former (e.g. $AP@5 = 0.22\%$) is lower than that of the latter (e.g. $AP@5 = 1.34\%$). On the other hand, on the LastFM dataset, the density of 50-core (i.e. 0.2465) is less sparse than that of the 55-core (i.e. 0.1479), therefore the improvement of the former (e.g. $AP@5 = 15.28\%$) is higher than that of the latter (e.g. $AP@5 = 2.94\%$). This result indicates that the *graded-relevance* scheme succeed to optimally generate entries from the observed tagging data for building the tensor model and to accommodate the GAP-based learning algorithm.

6. CONCLUSION AND FUTURE WORK

We have presented *Go-Rank*, a novel top-*N* tag-based item recommendation method that implements the proposed tagging data *graded-relevance* interpretation scheme and directly optimizes the (smoothed) GAP for generating ordered list of items that might interest the users. For improving the scalability of *GoRank*, we developed and implemented a fast learning approach that apply optimization only across tags that have been used by the user, and items of "relevant" and "likely relevant" entries. Experimental results on real-world datasets confirm that the *graded-relevance* is an efficient scheme as it leverages the tagging data more effectively. It establishes that, on each observed (u, t) set, any items other than those appearing in observed entries should not simply be all regarded as "irrelevant" entries, as considered in previous schemes.

Empirical analysis shows that *Go-Rank* is scalable and outperforms all benchmarking methods on the AP and NDCG measures. All of these ascertain that implementing the *graded-relevance* scheme and optimizing GAP for building the learning model improve the recommendation performance. For the future work, we would like to investigate the potential of implementing the *graded-relevance* scheme for optimizing other ranking metrics to generate tag-based item recommendations.

7. ACKNOWLEDGEMENT

This work is supported by the Directorate General of Higher Education (DGHE) Indonesia. Computational resources and services are provided by the HPC and Research Support Group, Queensland University of Technology, Brisbane, Australia.

8. REFERENCES

[1] Kim, H.-N., Ji, A.-T., Ha, I., and Jo, G.-S., Collaborative Filtering based on Collaborative Tagging for Enhancing the Quality of Recommendation. *Electronic Commerce Research and Applications*, 9(1): 73-83, 2010.

[2] Kolda, T. and Bader, B., Tensor Decompositions and Applications. *SIAM Review*, 51(3): 455-500, 2009.

[3] Ifada, N. and Nayak, R., *A Two-Stage Item Recommendation Method Using Probabilistic Ranking with Reconstructed Tensor Model.* In *User Modeling, Adaptation, and Personalization*, pages 98-110, Springer, 2014.

[4] Symeonidis, P., Nanopoulos, A., and Manolopoulos, Y., A Unified Framework for Providing Recommendations in Social Tagging Systems Based on Ternary Semantic Analysis. *IEEE Transactions on Knowledge and Data Engineering*, 22(2): 179-192, 2010.

[5] Rendle, S., Balby Marinho, L., Nanopoulos, A., and Schmidt-Thieme, L. Learning Optimal Ranking with Tensor Factorization for Tag Recommendation. In *Proceedings of The 15th ACM SIGKDD International Conference on Knowledge Discovery and Data Mining,* pages 727-736, Paris, France, 2009.

[6] Rafailidis, D. and Daras, P., The TFC Model: Tensor Factorization and Tag Clustering for Item Recommendation in Social Tagging Systems. *IEEE Transactions on Systems, Man and Cybernetics, Part A: Systems and Humans*, 43(3): 673-688, 2013.

[7] Leginus, M., Dolog, P., and Žemaitis, V., *Improving Tensor Based Recommenders with Clustering*. In *User Modeling, Adaptation, and Personalization*, pages 151-163, Springer Berlin Heidelberg, 2012.

[8] Ifada, N. and Nayak, R. An Efficient Tagging Data Interpretation and Representation Scheme for Item Recommendation. In *Proceedings of The 12th Australasian Data Mining Conference*, Brisbane, Australia, 2014.

[9] Cremonesi, P., Koren, Y., and Turrin, R. Performance of Recommender Algorithms on Top-N Recommendation Tasks. In *Proceedings of The 4th ACM Conference on Recommender Systems,* pages 39-46, Barcelona, Spain, 2010.

[10] Chapelle, O. and Wu, M., Gradient Descent Optimization of Smoothed Information Retrieval Metrics. *Information Retrieval*, 13(3): 216-235, 2010.

[11] Xu, J. and Li, H. AdaRank: A Boosting Algorithm for Information Retrieval. In *Proceedings of The 30th Annual International ACM SIGIR Conference on Research and Development in Information Retrieval,* pages 391-398, Amsterdam, The Netherlands, 2007.

[12] Shi, Y., Karatzoglou, A., Baltrunas, L., Larson, M., Hanjalic, A., and Oliver, N. TFMAP: Optimizing MAP for Top-N Context-Aware Recommendation. In *Proceedings of The 35th International ACM SIGIR Conference on Research and Development in Information Retrieval,* pages 155-164, Portland, Oregon, USA, 2012.

[13] Shi, Y., Karatzoglou, A., Baltrunas, L., Larson, M., Oliver, N., and Hanjalic, A. CLiMF: Learning to Maximize Reciprocal Rank with Collaborative Less-is-More Filtering. In *Proceedings of The 6th ACM Conference on Recommender Systems,* pages 139-146, Dublin, Ireland, 2012.

[14] Robertson, S.E., Kanoulas, E., and Yilmaz, E. Extending Average Precision to Graded Relevance Judgments. In *Proceedings of The 33rd International ACM SIGIR Conference on Research and Development in Information Retrieval,* pages 603-610, Geneva, Switzerland, 2010.

[15] Nanopoulos, A., Item Recommendation in Collaborative Tagging Systems. *IEEE Transactions on Systems, Man and Cybernetics, Part A: Systems and Humans*, 41(4): 760-771, 2011.

[16] Ifada, N. and Nayak, R., *Do-Rank: DCG Optimization for Learning-to-Rank in Tag-Based Item Recommendation Systems.* In *Advances in Knowledge Discovery and Data Mining*, pages 510-521, Springer, 2015.

[17] Rendle, S. and Schmidt-Thieme, L. Pairwise Interaction Tensor Factorization for Personalized Tag Recommendation. In *Proceedings of The 3rd ACM International Conference on Web Search and Data Mining,* pages 81-90, New York, USA, 2010.

[18] Weimer, M., Karatzoglou, A., Le, Q.V., and Smola, A., Maximum Margin Matrix Factorization for Collaborative Ranking. *Advances in Neural Information Processing Systems*, 2007.

[19] Shi, Y., Karatzoglou, A., Baltrunas, L., Larson, M., and Hanjalic, A. GAPfm: Optimal Top-N Recommendations for Graded Relevance Domains. In *Proceedings of The 22nd ACM International Conference on Information & Knowledge Management,* pages 2261-2266, San Francisco, California, USA, 2013.

[20] Balakrishnan, S. and Chopra, S. Collaborative Ranking. In *Proceedings of The 5th ACM International Conference on Web Search and Data Mining,* pages 143-152, Seattle, Washington, USA, 2012.

[21] Wu, M., Chang, Y., Zheng, Z., and Zha, H. Smoothing DCG for Learning to Rank: A Novel Approach using Smoothed Hinge Functions. In *Proceedings of The 18th ACM Conference on Information and Knowledge Management,* pages 1923-1926, Hong Kong, China, 2009.

[22] Cantador, I., Brusilovsky, P., and Kuflik, T. Second Workshop on Information Heterogeneity and Fusion in Recommender Systems (HetRec2011). In *Proceedings of The 5th ACM Conference on Recommender Systems,* pages 387-388, Chicago, Illinois, USA, 2011.

[23] Doerfel, S. and Jäschke, R. An Analysis of Tag-recommender Evaluation Procedures. In *Proceedings of The 7th ACM Conference on Recommender Systems,* pages 343-346, 2013.

[24] Batagelj, V. and Zaveršnik, M. *Generalized Cores*. arXiv preprint cs/0202039, 2002.

[25] Shi, Y., Karatzoglou, A., Baltrunas, L., Larson, M., and Hanjalic, A. xCLiMF: Optimizing Expected Reciprocal Rank for Data with Multiple Levels of Relevance. In *Proceedings of The 7th ACM conference on Recommender Systems,* pages 431-434, Hong Kong, China, 2013.

Quantifying Controversy in Social Media

Kiran Garimella
Aalto University
Helsinki, Finland
kiran.garimella@aalto.fi

Gianmarco De Francisci Morales
Aalto University
Helsinki, Finland
gdfm@acm.org

Aristides Gionis
Aalto University
Helsinki, Finland
aristides.gionis@aalto.fi

Michael Mathioudakis
HIIT, Aalto University
Helsinki, Finland
michael.mathioudakis@hiit.fi

ABSTRACT

Which topics spark the most heated debates in social media? Identifying these topics is a first step towards creating systems which pierce echo chambers. In this paper, we perform a systematic methodological study of controversy detection using social media network structure and content.

Unlike previous work, rather than identifying controversy in a single hand-picked topic and use domain-specific knowledge, we focus on *comparing topics in any domain.* Our approach to quantifying controversy is a graph-based three-stage pipeline, which involves (*i*) building a *conversation graph* about a topic, which represents alignment of opinion among users; (*ii*) partitioning the conversation graph to identify potential sides of the controversy; and (*iii*) measuring the amount of controversy from characteristics of the graph.

We perform an extensive comparison of controversy measures, as well as graph building approaches and data sources. We use both controversial and non-controversial topics on Twitter, as well as other external datasets. We find that our new random-walk-based measure outperforms existing ones in capturing the intuitive notion of controversy, and show that content features are vastly less helpful in this task.

1. INTRODUCTION

Given their widespread diffusion, online social media are becoming increasingly important in the study of social phenomena such as peer influence, framing, bias, and controversy. Ultimately, we would like to understand how users perceive the world through the lens of their social media feed. For instance, to offer users the possibility to balance their "news diet" [20, 21] on controversial topics by recommending contrarian content, which supports a view that differs from what they are mostly exposed to [25]. However, before addressing these advanced application scenarios, we first need to focus on the fundamental yet challenging task of distinguishing whether a topic of discussion is controversial, Our work is motivated by interest in observing controversies at societal level, monitoring their evolution, and possibly understanding which issues become controversial and why.

WSDM 2016, February 22–25, 2016, San Francisco, California, USA

ISBN ACM 978-1-4503-3716-8/16/02. DOI: 10.1145/1235

The study of controversy in social media is not new; there are many previous studies aimed at identifying and characterizing controversial issues, mostly around political debates [1, 7, 23, 24] but also for other topics [15]. And while most recent papers have focused on Twitter [7, 15, 23, 24], controversy in other social-media platforms, such as blogs [1] and opinion fora [2], have also been analyzed.

However, most previous papers have severe limitations. First, the majority of previous studies focus on controversy regarding political issues, and in particular, they are centered around long-lasting major events, such as elections [1, 7]. More crucially, most previous works can be characterized as *case studies*, where controversy is identified in a single carefully-curated dataset, collected using ample domain knowledge and auxiliary domain-specific sources (e.g., an extensive list of hashtags regarding a major political event, or a list of left-leaning and right-leaning blogs).

We aim to overcome those limitations. Our goal is to identify controversy regarding topics in any domain (e.g., political, economical, or cultural), and in a general setting, i.e., without prior domain-specific knowledge about the topic in question. In addition, we aim at comparing different topics, in order to find the most controversial ones. These properties allow to deploy a system in-the-wild, and are valuable for building real-world applications.

In order to enable such a versatile framework, we work with topics that are defined in a lightweight and domain-agnostic manner. Specifically, when focusing on Twitter, a topic can be specified as a text query. For example, "#beefban" is a special keyword (a "hashtag") that was employed by Twitter users to signal that their posts referred to a decision of the Indian government, in March 2015, about the consumption of beef meat in India. In this case, the query "#beefban" defines a topic of discussion, and the related activity consists of all posts that contain the query.

We represent a topic of discussion with a *conversation graph.* In such a graph, vertices represent people, and edges represent conversation activity and interactions, such as *posts*, *comments*, *mentions*, or *endorsements.* Our working hypothesis is that it is possible to analyze the conversation graph of a topic to reveal how controversial the topic is. In particular, we expect the conversation graph of a controversial topic to have a *clustered structure.* This hypothesis is based on the fact that a controversial topic entails different sides with opposing points of view, and individuals on the same side tend to endorse and amplify each other's arguments [1, 2, 7].

Our main contribution is to test this hypothesis. We achieve this by studying a large number of candidate features, based on the following *aspects* of activity: (*i*) *structure of endorsements*, i.e., who agrees with whom on the topic, (*ii*) *structure of the social network*, i.e., who is connected with whom among the participants in the conversation, (*iii*) *content*, i.e., the keywords used in the topic, (*iv*) *sentiment*, i.e., the tone (positive or negative) used to discuss the topic. Our study shows that, except from content-based features, all the other ones are useful in detecting controversial topics, to different extents. Particularly for Twitter, we find the endorsement features (i.e., retweets) to be the most useful.

The extracted features are then used to compute the *controversy score* of a topic. We offer a systematic definition and provide a thorough evaluation of measures to quantify controversy. We employ a broad range of topics, both controversial and non-controversial ones, on which we evaluate several measures, either defined in this paper or coming from the literature [15, 24]. We find that one of our newly-proposed measure, based on *random walks*, is able to discriminate controversial topics with great accuracy. In addition, it also generalizes well as it agrees with previously-defined measures when tested on datasets from existing work. We also find that the *variance* of the sentiment expressed on a topic is a reliable indication of controversy.

The approach to quantifying controversy presented in this paper can be condensed into a three-stage pipeline: (*i*) build a *conversation graph* among the users who contribute to a topic, where edges signify that two users are in agreement, (*ii*) identify the potential sides of the controversy from the graph structure or the textual content, and (*iii*) quantify the amount of controversy in the graph.

The rest of this paper is organized as follows. Section 2 discusses how this work fills gaps in the existing literature. Subsequently, Section 3 provides a high level description of the pipeline for quantifying controversy for a topic, while Sections 4, 5, and 6 detail each stage. We empirically evaluate the proposed measures of controversy in Section 7. Section 8 extends the evaluation to a few measures that do not fit the pipeline. We conclude in Section 9 with a discussion on possible improvements and directions for future work, as well as lessons learned from carrying out this study.

2. RELATED WORK

Analysis of controversy in online news and social media has attracted considerable attention, and a number of papers have provided very interesting case studies. In one of the first papers, Adamic and Glance [1] study the link patterns and discussion topics of political bloggers, focusing on blog posts on the U.S. presidential election of 2004. They measure the degree of interaction between liberal and conservative blogs, and provide evidence that conservative blogs are linking to each other more frequently and in a denser pattern. These findings are confirmed by the more recent study of Conover et al. [7], who also study controversy in political communication regarding congressional midterm elections. Using data from Twitter, Conover et al. identify a highly segregated partisan structure (present in the retweet graph, but not in the mention graph), with limited connectivity between left- and right-leaning users. In another recent work related to controversy analysis in political discussion, Mejova et al. [23] identify a significant correlation between controversial issues and the use of negative affect and biased language.

The papers mentioned so far study controversy in the political domain, and provide case studies centered around long-lasting major events, such as presidential elections. In this paper, we aim to identify and quantify controversy for any topic discussed in social media, including short-lived and ad-hoc ones. The problem we study has been considered by previous work, but the methods proposed so far are, to a large degree, domain-specific.

The work of Conover et al. [7], discussed above, employs the concept of modularity and graph partitioning in order to verify (but not quantify) controversy structure of graphs extracted from discussion of political issues on Twitter. In a similar setting, Guerra et al. [15] propose an alternative graph-structure measure. Their measure relies on the analysis of the boundary between two (potentially) polarized communities, and performs better than modularity. Differently from these studies, our contribution consists in providing an extensive study of a large number of measures, including the ones proposed earlier, and demonstrating clear improvement over those. We also aim at quantifying controversy in diverse and in-the-wild settings, rather than carefully-curated domain-specific datasets.

In a recent study, Morales et al. [24] quantify polarity via the propagation of opinions of influential users on Twitter. They validate their measure with a case study from Venezuelan politics. Again, our methods are not only more general and domain agnostic, but they provide more intuitive results. In a different approach, Akoglu proposes a polarization metric that uses signed bipartite opinion graphs [2]. The approach differs from ours as it relies on the availability of this particular type of data, which is not as readily available as social-interaction graphs.

Similarly to the papers discussed above, in our work we quantify controversy based on the graph structure of social interactions. In particular, we assume that controversial and polarized topics induce graphs with clustered structure, representing different opinions and points of view. This assumption relies on the concept of "echo chambers," which states that opinions or beliefs stay inside communities created by like-minded people, who reinforce and endorse the opinions of each other. This phenomenon has been quantified in many recent studies [3, 11, 14].

A different direction for quantifying controversy followed by Choi et al. [6] and Mejova et al. [23] relies on text and sentiment analysis. Both studies focus on language found on news articles. In our case, since we are mainly working with Twitter, where text is short and noisy, and since we are aiming at quantifying controversy in a domain-agnostic manner, text analysis has its limitations. Nevertheless, we experiment with incorporating content in our approach.

Finally, our findings on controversy have many potential applications on news-reading and public-debate scenarios. For instance, quantifying controversy can provide a basis for analyzing the "news diet" of readers [20, 21], offering the chance of better information by providing recommendations of contrarian views [25], or trying to deliberate debates [10] and connect people with opposing opinions [9, 13].

3. PIPELINE

Our approach to measuring controversy is based on a systematic way of characterizing social media activity. We employ a pipeline with three stages, namely *graph building*, *graph partitioning*, and *measuring controversy*. The final output of the pipeline is a value that measures how controversial a topic is, with higher values corresponding to higher degree of controversy. We provide a high-level description of each stage here and more details in the sections that follow.

3.1 Building the Graph

The purpose of this stage is to build a *conversation graph* that represents activity related to a single *topic* of discussion. In our pipeline, a topic is operationalized as a *query*, and the social media activity related to the topic consists of those items (e.g., posts) that match the given query. For example, in the context of Twitter, the query might simply consist of a keyword, such as "#ukraine", in which case the related activity consists of all tweets that contain that keyword. Even though we describe textual queries in standard document-retrieval form, in principle queries can take other forms, as long as they are able to induce a graph from the social media activity (e.g., RDF queries, or topic models).

Each item related to a topic is associated with one user who generated it, and we build a graph where each user who contributed to the topic is assigned to one vertex. In this graph, an edge between two vertices represents *endorsment*, *agreement*, or *shared point of view* between the corresponding users. Section 4 details several ways to build such a graph.

3.2 Partitioning the Graph

In the second stage, the resulting conversation graph is fed into a *graph partitioning* algorithm to extract *two* partitions (we defer considering multi-sided controversies to a further study). Intuitively, the two partitions correspond to two disjoint sets of users who possibly belong to different sides in the discussion. In other words, the output of this stage answers the following question: "assuming that users are split into two sides according to their point of view on the topic, which are these two sides?" Section 5 describes this stage in further detail. If indeed there are two sides which do not agree with each other –a controversy– then the two partitions should be loosely connected to each other, given the semantic of the edges. This property is captured by a measure computed in the third and final stage of the pipeline.

3.3 Measuring Controversy

The third and last stage takes as input the graph built by the first stage and partitioned by the second stage, and computes the value of a *controversy measure* that characterizes how controversial the topic is. Intuitively, a controversy measure aims to capture how separated the two partitions are. We test several such measures, including ones based on random walks, betweenness centrality, and low-dimensional embeddings. Details are provided in Section 6.

4. GRAPH BUILDING

This section provides details about the different approaches we follow to build graphs from raw data. We use posts on Twitter to create our datasets.[1] Twitter is a natural choice for the problem at hand, as it represents one of the main fora for public debate in online social media, and is often used to report news about current events. Following the procedure described in Section 3.1, we specify a set of queries, and build one graph for each query. The set of topics we choose is balanced between controversial and non-controversial ones, so as to test for both false positives and false negatives.

We use Twitter hashtags as queries. Users employ hashtags to indicate the topic of discussion their posts pertain to. Among the large number of hashtags that appear in the Twitter stream, we consider hashtags that were trending during the period from Feb 27 to Jun 15, 2015. By manual inspection we find that most trending hashtags are not related to controversial discussions.

We first manually pick a set of 10 hashtags that we know represent *controversial* topics of discussion. All topics in this set have been widely covered by mainstream media, and have generated ample discussion both online and offline. Moreover, to have a dataset that is balanced between controversial and non-controversial topics, we sample another set of 10 hashtags that represent *non-controversial* topics of discussion. These hashtags are related mostly to soft news and entertainment, but also to events that, while being impactful and dramatic, did not generate large controversies (e.g., #nepal and #germanwings). In addition to our intuition that these topics are non-controversial, we manually check a sample of tweets and, are unable to identify any controversy.[2]

For each hashtag, we retrieve all tweets that contain it and are generated during the observation window. We also ensure that the selected hashtags are associated with a large enough volume of activity. Table 1 presents the final set of hashtags, along with their description and the number of related tweets.[3] For each hashtag, we build a graph G where we assign a vertex to each user who employs it, and generate edges according to one of the following four approaches.

1. Retweet graph. Typically, retweets are used as endorsements. Users who retweet signal endorsement of the opinion expressed in the original tweet by propagating it further. Retweets are not constrained to occur only between users who are connected in Twitter's social network, but users are allowed to re-post tweets generated by any other user.

We select the edges for graph G based on the retweet activity in the topic: an edge exists between two users u and v if there are at least *two* ($\tau = 2$) retweets between them that use the hashtag, irrespective of direction. We remark that, in preliminary experimentation with this approach, building the retweet graph with a threshold $\tau = 1$ did not produce reliable results. We presume that a single retweet on a topic is not enough of a signal to infer endorsement. Using $\tau = 2$ retweets as threshold proves to be a good trade-off between high selectivity (which hinders analysis) and noise reduction. The resulting size for each retweet graph is listed in Table 1.

2. Follow graph. In this approach, we build the follow graph induced by a given hashtag. We select the edges for graph G based on the social connections between Twitter users *who employ the given hashtag*: an edge exists between users u and v if u follows v or vice-versa. We stress that the graph G built with this approach is topic-specific, as the edges in G are constrained to connections between users who discuss the topic that is specified as input to the pipeline.

The rationale for using this graph is based on an assumption of the presence of homophily in the social network, which is a common trait in this setting. To be more precise, we

[1]From the full Twitter firehose stream.

[2]Code and networks used in this work are available at http://github.com/gvrkiran/controversy-detection.

[3]We use a hashtag in Russian, #марш, which we refer to as #russia_march from here on, for convenience.

Table 1: Datasets statistics: hashtag, sizes of the follow and retweet graphs, and description of the event. The top group represent controversial topics, while the bottom one represent non-controversial ones.

Hashtag	# Tweets	Retweet graph		Follow graph		Description and collection period (2015)
		$\|V\|$	$\|E\|$	$\|V\|$	$\|E\|$	
#beefban	84 543	1610	1978	799	6026	Government of India bans beef, Mar 2–5
#nemtsov	183 477	6546	10 172	2156	46 529	Death of Boris Nemtsov, Feb 28–Mar 2
#netanyahuspeech	254 623	9434	14 476	4292	297 136	Netanyahu's speech at U.S. Congress, Mar 3–5
#russia_march	118 629	2134	2951	1189	16 471	Protests after death of Boris Nemtsov ("march"), Mar 1–2
#indiasdaughter	167 704	3659	4323	1542	9480	Controversial Indian documentary, Mar 1–5
#baltimoreriots	218 157	3902	4505	1441	28 291	Riots in Baltimore after police kills a black man, Apr 28–30
#indiana	116 379	2467	3143	946	24 328	Indiana pizzeria refuses to cater gay wedding, Apr 2–5
#ukraine	287 438	5495	9452	3383	84 035	Ukraine conflict, Feb 27–Mar 2
#gunsense	318 409	7106	11 483	1821	103 840	Gun violence in U.S., Jun 1–30
#leadersdebate	1 139 344	25 983	44 174	9566	344 088	Debate during the U.K. national elections, May 3
#sxsw	343 652	9304	11 003	4558	91 356	SXSW conference, Mar 13–22
#1dfamheretostay	501 960	15 292	26 819	3151	20 275	Last OneDirection concert, Mar 27–29
#germanwings	907 510	29 763	39 075	2111	7329	Germanwings flight crash, Mar 24–26
#mothersday	1 798 018	155 599	176 915	2225	14 160	Mother's day, May 8
#nepal	1 297 995	40 579	57 544	4242	42 833	Nepal earthquake, Apr 26–29
#ultralive	364 236	9261	15 544	2113	16 070	Ultra Music Festival, Mar 18–20
#FF	408 326	5401	7646	3899	63 672	Follow Friday, Jun 19
#jurassicworld	724 782	26 407	32 515	4395	31 802	Jurassic World movie, Jun 12-15
#wcw	156 243	10 674	11 809	3264	23 414	Women crush Wednesdays, Jun 17
#nationalkissingday	165 172	4638	4816	790	5927	National kissing day, Jun 19

expect that *on a given topic* people will agree more often than not with people they follow, and that for a controversial topic of discussion this phenomenon will be reflected in well-separated partitions of the resulting graph. Note that using the entire social graph would not necessarily produce well-separated partitions that correspond to single topics of discussion, as those partitions would be "blurred" by the existence of additional edges that are due to other reasons (e.g., offline social connections).

On the practical side, while the retweet information is readily available in the stream of tweets, the social network of Twitter is not. Collecting the follower graph thus requires an expensive crawling phase. The resulting graph size for each follow graph is listed in Table 1.

3. Content graph. We create the edges of graph G based on whether users post instances of the same content. Specifically, we experiment with the following three variants: create an edge between two vertices if the users (*i*) use the same hashtag, other than the one that defines the topic, (*ii*) share a link to the same URL, or (*iii*) share a link with the same URL domain (e.g., cnn.com is the domain for all pages on the website of CNN).

4. Hybrid content & retweet graph. We create edges for graph G according to a state-of-the-art process that blends content and graph information [26]. Concretely, we associate each user with a vector of frequencies of mentions for different hashtags. Subsequently, we create edges between pairs of users whose corresponding vectors have high cosine similarity, and combine them with edges from the retweet graph, built as described above. For details, we refer the interested reader to the original publication [26].

5. GRAPH PARTITIONING

As previously explained, we use a graph partitioning algorithm to produce two partitions on the conversation graph. To do so, we rely on a state-of-the-art off-the-shelf algorithm, METIS [19]. Figure 1 displays the two partitions returned for some of the topics on their corresponding retweet and follow graphs (Figures 1(a)-(d) and Figures 1(e)-(h), respectively).[4] The partitions are depicted in blue or red. The graph layout is produced by Gephi's ForceAtlas2 algorithm [16], and is based solely on the structure of the graph, not on the partitioning computed by METIS.

From an initial visual inspection of the partitions identified on retweet and follow graphs, we find that the partitions match well with our intuition of which topics are controversial (the partitions returned by METIS are well separated for controversial topics). To make sure that this initial assessment of the partitions is not an artifact of the visualization algorithm we use, we try other layouts offered by Gephi. In all cases we observe similar patterns. We also manually sample and check tweets from the partitions, to verify the presence of controversy. While this anecdotal evidence is hard to report, indeed the partitions seem to capture the spirit of the controversy.[5]

On the contrary, the partitions identified on content graphs fail to match our intuition. All three variants of the content-based approach lead to sparse graphs and highly overlapping partitions, even in cases of highly controversial issues. The same pattern applies for the hybrid approach, as shown in Figure 2. We also try a variant of the hybrid graph approach with vectors that represent the frequency of different URL domains mentioned by a user, with no better results. We thus do not consider these approaches to graph building any further in the remainder of this paper.

Finally, we try graph partitioning algorithms of other types. Besides METIS (cut based), we test spectral clustering, label propagation, and affiliation-graph-based models. The difference among these methods is not significant, however from visual inspection METIS generates the cleanest partitions.

[4] Other topics show similar trends, omitted for lack of space.
[5] For instance, of these two tweets for #netanyahuspeech from two users on either side, one is clearly supporting the speech https://t.co/OVeWB4XqIg, while the other highlights

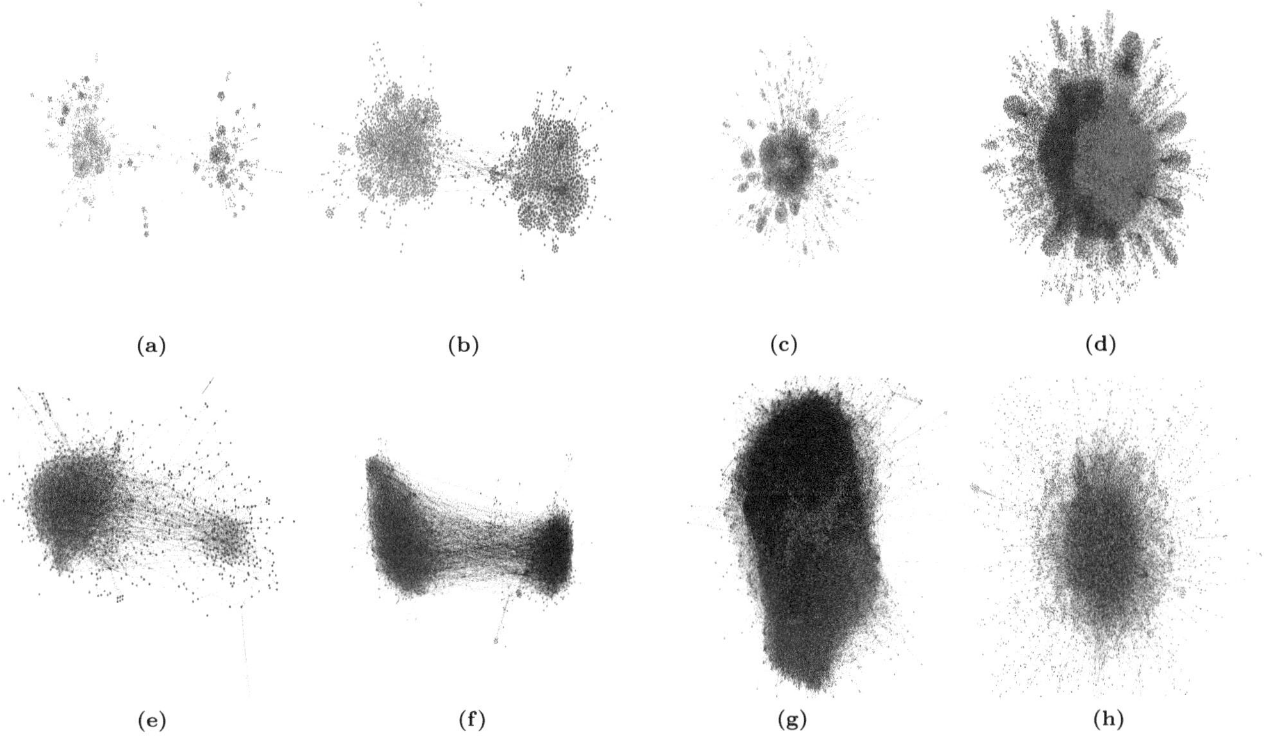

Figure 1: Sample conversation graphs with retweet (top) and follow (bottom) features (visualized using the force-directed layout algorithm in Gephi). The left side is controversial, (a,e) #beefban, (b,f) #russia_march, while the right side is non-controversial, (c,g) #sxsw, (d,h) #germanwings.

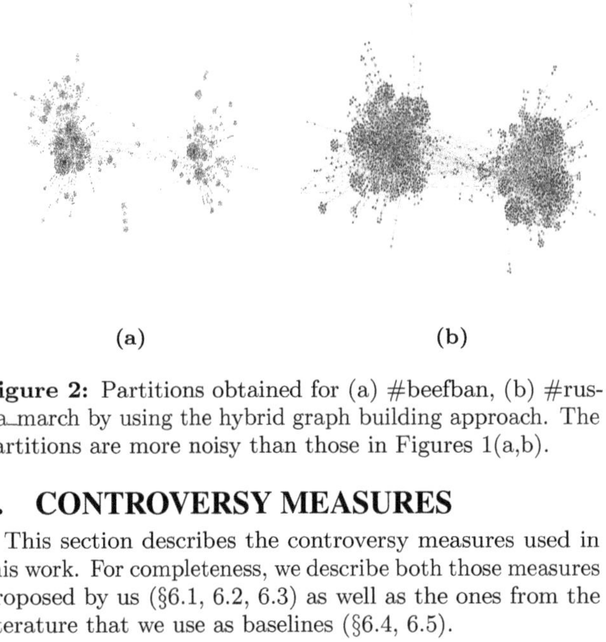

Figure 2: Partitions obtained for (a) #beefban, (b) #russia_march by using the hybrid graph building approach. The partitions are more noisy than those in Figures 1(a,b).

6. CONTROVERSY MEASURES

This section describes the controversy measures used in this work. For completeness, we describe both those measures proposed by us (§6.1, 6.2, 6.3) as well as the ones from the literature that we use as baselines (§6.4, 6.5).

6.1 Random walk

This measure uses the notion of random walks on graphs. It is based on the rationale that, in a controversial discussion, there are authoritative users on both sides, as evidenced by a large degree in the graph. The measure captures the intuition of how likely a random user on either side is to be exposed to authoritative content from the opposing side.

Let $G(V,E)$ be the graph built by the first stage and its two partitions X and Y, ($X \cup Y = V$, $X \cap Y = \emptyset$) identified by the second stage of the pipeline. We first distinguish the k *highest-degree vertices* from each partition. High-degree is a proxy for authoritativeness, as it means that a user has received a large number of endorsements on the specific topic. Subsequently, we select one partition at random (each with probability 0.5) and consider a random walk that starts from a random vertex in that partition. The walk terminates when it visits any high-degree vertex (from either side).

We define the `Random Walk Controversy` (*RWC*) measure as follows. *"Consider two random walks, one ending in partition X and one ending in partition Y, RWC is the difference of the probabilities of two events: (i) both random walks started from the partition they ended in and (ii) both random walks started in a partition other than the one they ended in."* The measure is quantified as

$$RWC = P_{XX}P_{YY} - P_{YX}P_{XY}, \tag{1}$$

where P_{AB}, $A, B \in \{X, Y\}$ is the conditional probability

$$P_{AB} = P(\text{start in partition } A \mid \text{end in partition } B).$$

The aforementioned probabilities have the following desirable properties: (*i*) they are not skewed by the size of each partition, as the random walk starts with equal probability from each partition, and (*ii*) they are not skewed by the total degree of vertices in each partition, as the probabilities are conditional on ending in either partition (i.e., the fraction of random walks ending in each partition is irrelevant). *RWC* is close to one when the probability of crossing sides is low, and close to zero when the probability of crossing sides is comparable to that of staying on the same side.

the negative reactions https://t.co/v9RdPudrrC.

6.2 Betweenness

Let us consider the set of edges $C \subseteq E$ in the cut defined by the two partitions X, Y. This measure uses the notion of edge betweenness and how the betweenness of the cut differs from that of the other edges. Recall that the betweenness centrality $bc(e)$ of an edge e is defined as

$$bc(e) = \sum_{s \neq t \in V} \frac{\sigma_{s,t}(e)}{\sigma_{s,t}}, \tag{2}$$

where $\sigma_{s,t}$ is the total number of shortest paths between vertices s, t in the graph and $\sigma_{s,t}(e)$ is the number of those shortest paths that include edge e.

The intuition here is that, if the two partitions are well-separated, then the cut will consist of edges that bridge *structural holes* [5]. In this case, the shortest paths that connect vertices of the two partitions will pass through the edges in the cut, leading to high betweenness values for edges in C. On the other hand, if the two partitions are not well separated, then the cut will consist of *strong ties*. In this case, the paths that connect vertices across the two partitions will pass through one of the many edges in the cut, leading to betweenness values for C similar to the rest of the graph.

Given the distributions of edge betweenness on the cut and the rest of the graph, we compute the KL divergence d_{KL} of the two distributions by using kernel density estimation to compute the PDF and sampling 10 000 points from each of these distributions (with replacement). We define the `Betweenness Centrality Controversy` (BCC) measure as

$$BCC = 1 - e^{-d_{KL}}, \tag{3}$$

which assumes values close to zero when the divergence is small, and close to one when the divergence is large.

6.3 Embedding

This measure is based on a low-dimensional embedding of graph G produced by Gephi's ForceAtlas2 algorithm [16] (the same algorithm used to produce the plots in Figures 1 and 2). We opt for this algorithm as it produces well-separated plots for controversial topics.

Let us consider the two-dimensional embedding $\phi(v)$ of vertices $v \in V$ produced by ForceAtlas2. Given the partition X, Y produced by the second stage of the pipeline, we calculate the following quantities:

- d_X and d_Y, the average embedded distance among pairs of vertices in the same partition, X and Y respectively,
- d_{XY}, the average embedded distance among pairs of vertices across the two partitions X and Y.

Inpsired by the Davies-Bouldin (DB) index [8], we define the `Embedding Controversy` measure EC as

$$EC = 1 - \frac{d_X + d_Y}{2d_{XY}}. \tag{4}$$

EC is close to one for controversial topics, corresponding to better-separated graphs and thus to higher degree of controversy, and close to zero for non-controversial topics.

6.4 Boundary Connectivity

This controversy measure was proposed by Guerra et al. [15], and is based on the notion of boundary and internal vertices. Let $u \in X$ be a vertex in partition X; u belongs to the *boundary* of X iff it is connected to at least one vertex of the other partition Y, and it is connected to at least one vertex in partition X that is not connected to any vertex of partition Y. Following this definition, let B_X, B_Y be the set of boundary vertices for each partition, and $B = B_X \cup B_Y$ the set of all boundary vertices. By contrast, vertices $I_X = X - B_X$ are said to be the *internal* vertices of partition X (similarly for I_Y). Let $I = I_X \cup I_Y$ be all internal vertices in either partition. The reasoning for this measure is that, if the two partitions represent two sides of a controversy, then boundary vertices will be more strongly connected to internal vertices than to other boundary vertices of either partition. This intuition is captured in the formula

$$GMCK = \frac{1}{|B|} \sum_{u \in B} \frac{d_i(u)}{d_b(u) + d_i(u)} - 0.5 \tag{5}$$

where $d_i(u)$ is the number of edges between vertex u and internal vertices I, while $d_b(u)$ is the number of edges between vertex u and boundary vertices B. Higher values of the measure correspond to higher degrees of controversy.

6.5 Dipole Moment

This controversy measure was presented by Morales et al. [24], and is based on the notion of *dipole moment* that has its origin in physics. Let $R(u) \in [-1, 1]$ be a polarization value assigned to vertex $u \in V$. Intuitively, extreme values of R (close to -1 or 1) correspond to users who belong most clearly to either side of the controversy. To set the values $R(u)$ we follow the process described in the original paper [24]: we set $R = \pm 1$ for the top-5% highest-degree vertices in each partition X and Y, and set the values for the rest of the vertices by label-propagation. Let n^+ and n^- be the number of vertices V with positive and negative polarization values, respectively, and ΔA the absolute difference of their normalized size $\Delta A = \left| \frac{n^+ - n^-}{|V|} \right|$. Moreover, let gc^+ (gc^-) be the average polarization value among vertices n^+ (n^-) and set d as half their absolute difference, $d = \frac{|gc^+ - gc^-|}{2}$. The dipole moment controversy measure is defined as

$$MBLB = (1 - \Delta A)d. \tag{6}$$

The rationale for this measure is that, if the two partitions X and Y are well separated, then label propagation will assign different extreme (± 1) R-values to the two partitions, leading to higher values of the $MBLB$ measure. Note also that larger differences in the size of the two partitions (reflected in the value of ΔA) lead to decreased values for the measure, which takes values between zero and one.

7. EXPERIMENTS

In this section we report the results of the various configurations of the pipeline proposed in this paper. As previously stated, we omit results for the content and hybrid graph building approaches presented in Section 4 as they do not perform well. We instead focus on the retweet and follow graphs, and test all the measures presented in Section 6 on the Twitter topics described in Table 1. In addition, we test all the measures on a set of external datasets used in previous studies [1, 7, 15] to validate the measures against a known ground truth. Finally, we use an evolving dataset from Twitter collected around the death of Venezuelan president Hugo Chavez [24] to show the *evolution* of the controversy measures in response to high-impact events.

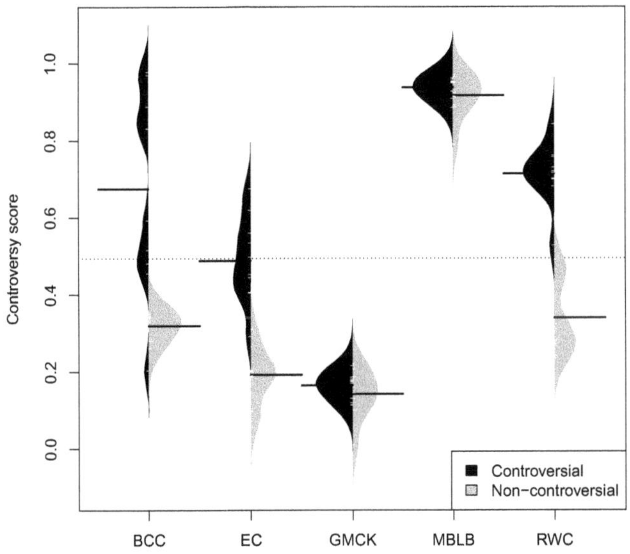

Figure 3: Controversy scores on *retweet* graphs of various controversial and non-controversial datasets

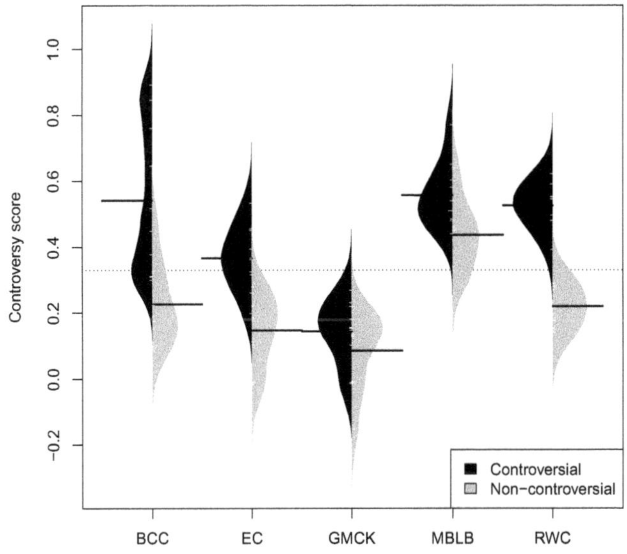

Figure 4: Controversy scores on *follow* graphs of various controversial and non-controversial datasets.

To avoid potential overfitting, we use only eight graphs as testbed during the development of the measures, half of them controversial (beefban, nemtsov, netanyahu, russia_march) and half non-controversial (sxsw, germanwings, onedirection, ultralive). This procedure resembles a 40/60% train/test split in traditional machine learning applications.[6]

Twitter hashtags. Figure 3 and Figure 4 report the scores computed by each measure for each of the 20 hashtags, on the retweet and follow graph, respectively. Each figure shows a set of beanplots,[7] one for each measure. Each beanplot shows the estimated probability density function for a measure computed on the topics, the individual observations are shown as small white lines in a one-dimensional scatter plot, and the median as a longer black line. The beanplot is divided into two groups, one for controversial topics (left/dark) and one for non-controversial ones (right/light). A larger separation of the two distributions indicates that the measure is better at capturing the characteristics of controversial topics. For instance, this separation is fundamental when using the controversy score as a feature in a classification algorithm.

Figures 3 and 4 clearly show that *RWC* is the best measure on our datasets. *BCC* and *EC* show varying degrees of separation and overlap, although *EC* performs slightly better as the distributions are more concentrated, while *BCC* has a very wide distribution. The two baselines *GMCK* and *MBLB* instead fail to separate the two groups. Especially on the retweet graph, the two groups are almost indistinguishable.

For all measures the median score of controversial topics is higher than for non-controversial ones. This result suggests that both graph building methods, retweet and follow, are able to capture the difference between controversial and non-controversial topics. Given the broad range of provenience of the topics covered by the dataset, and their different characteristics, the consistency of results is very encouraging.

External datasets. We have shown that our approach works well on a number of datasets extracted in-the-wild from Twitter [12]. However, how well does it generalize to datasets from different domains?

We obtain a comprehensive group of datasets kindly shared by authors of previous works: *Political blogs*, links between blogs discussing politics in the US [1]; *Twitter politics*, Twitter messages pertaining to the 2010 midterm election in US [7]; and the following five graphs used in the study that introduced *GMCK* [15], (a) *Gun control*, retweets about gun control after the shooting at the Sandy Hook school; (b) *Brazil soccer*, retweets about to two popular soccer teams in Brazil; (c) *Karate club*, the well-known social network by Zachary [28]; (d) *Facebook university*, a social graph among students and professors at a Brazilian university; (e) *NYC teams*, retweets about two New York City sports teams.

Table 2 shows a comparison of the controversy measures under study on the aforementioned datasets.[8] For each dataset we also report whether it was considered controversial in the original paper, which provides a sort of "ground truth" to evaluate the measures against.

All the measures are able to distinguish controversial graphs to some extent, in the sense that they return higher values for the controversial cases. The only exception is Karate club. Both *RWC* and *MBLB* report low controversy scores for this graph. It is possible that the graph is too small for such random-walk-based measures to function properly. Conversely, *BCC* is able to capture the desired behavior, which suggests that shortest-path and random-walk based measures might have a complementary function.

Interestingly, while the Political blogs datasets is often considered a gold standard for polarization and division in online political discussions, all the measures agree that it presents only a moderate level of controversy. On the other hand, the Twitter politics dataset is clearly one of the most

[6]A demo of our controversy measures can be found at https://users.ics.aalto.fi/kiran/controversy.

[7]A beanplot is an alternative to the boxplot for visual comparison of univariate data among groups.

[8]The datasets provided by Guerra et al. [15] are slightly different from the ones used in the original paper because of some irreproducible filtering used by the authors. We use the datasets provided to us verbatim.

Table 2: Results on external datasets. The 'C?' column indicates whether the previous study considered the dataset controversial (ground truth).

Dataset	$\|V\|$	$\|E\|$	C?	*RWC*	*BCC*	*EC*	*GMCK*	*MBLB*
Political blogs	1222	16 714	✓	0.42	0.53	0.49	0.18	0.45
Twitter politics	18 470	48 053	✓	0.77	0.79	0.62	0.28	0.34
Gun control	33 254	349 782	✓	0.70	0.68	0.55	0.24	0.81
Brazil soccer	20 594	82 421	✓	0.67	0.48	0.68	0.17	0.75
Karate club	34	78	✓	0.11	0.64	0.51	0.17	0.11
Facebook university	281	4389	✗	0.35	0.26	0.38	0.01	0.27
NYC teams	95 924	176 249	✗	0.34	0.24	0.17	0.01	0.19

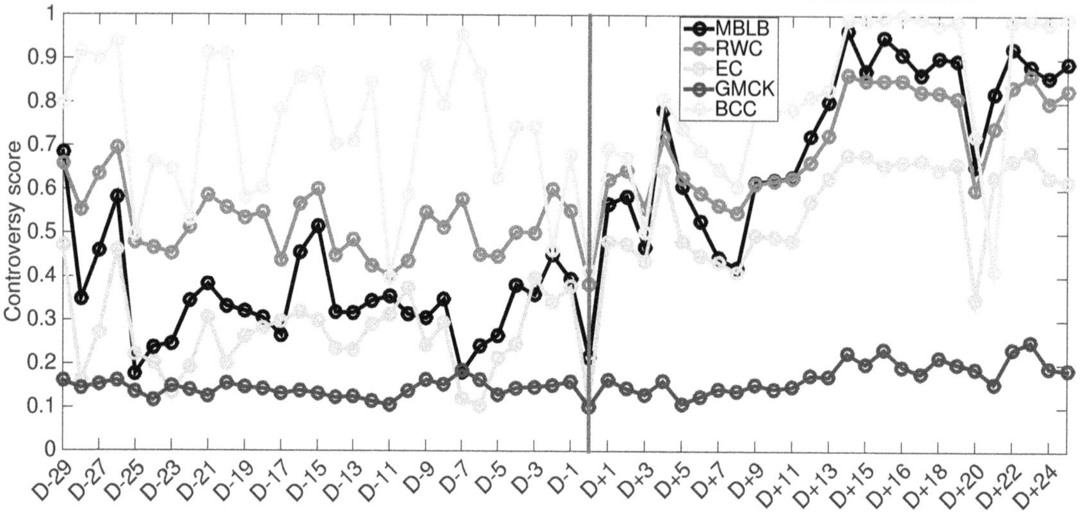

Figure 5: Controversy scores on 56 retweet graphs from Morales et al. Day 'D' (indicated by the blue vertical line) indicates the announcement of the death of president Hugo Chavez.

controversial one across all measures. This difference might suggest that the measures are more geared towards capturing the dynamics of controversy as it unfolds on social media, which might differ from more traditional blogs. For instance, one such difference is the *cost* of an endorsement: placing a link on a blog post arguably consumes more mental resources than clicking on the retweet button.

For the Gun control dataset, Guerra et al. needs to manually distinguish three different partitions in the graph: gun rights advocates, gun control supporters, and moderates. Our pipeline is able to find the two communities with opposing views (grouping together gun control supporters and moderates) without any external help. All measures agree with the conclusions drawn in the original paper that this topic is highly controversial.

Evolving controversy. We have shown that our approach also generalizes well to datasets from different domains. But in a real deployment the measures need to be computed continuously, as new data arrives. How well does our method work in such a setting? And how do the controversy measures evolve in response to high-impact events?

To answer these questions, we use a datasets from the study that introduced *MBLB* [24]. The dataset comprises Twitter messages pertaining to political events in Venezuela around the time of death of Hugo Chavez (Feb-May 2013). The authors built a retweet graph for each of the 56 days (one graph per day) around the day of the death.

Figure 5 shows how the intensity of controversy evolves according to the measures under study (which occurs on day 'D'). The measure proposed in the original paper, *MBLB*, which we use as 'ground truth', shows a clear decrease of controversy on the day of the death, followed by a progressive increase in the controversy of the conversation. The original interpretation states that on the day of the death a large amount of people, also from other countries, retweeted news of the event, creating a single global community that got together at the shock of the news. After the death, the ruling and opposition party entered in a fiery discussion over the next elections, which increased the controversy.

All the measures proposed in this work show the same trend as *MBLB*. Both *RWC* and *EC* follow very closely the original measure (Pearson correlation coefficients r of 0.944 and 0.949, respectively), while *BCC* shows a more jagged behavior in the first half of the plot ($r = 0.743$), due to the discrete nature of shortest paths. All measures however present a dip on day 'D', an increase in controversy in the second half, and another dip on day 'D+20'. Conversely, *GMCK* reports an almost constant moderate value of controversy during the whole period ($r = 0.542$), with barely noticeable peaks and dips. We conclude that our measures generalize well also to the case of evolving graphs, and behave as expected in response to high-impact events.

8. CONTENT

In this section we explore alternative approaches to measuring controversy that use only the content of the discussion rather than the structure of user interactions. As such, these methods do not fit in the pipeline described in Section 3. The question we address is "does content help in measuring the controversy of a topic?" In particular, we test two types of features extracted from the content. The first, is a typical IR-inspired bag-of-words representation. The second instead is based on NLP tools for sentiment analysis.

8.1 Content as bag of words

We take in input the raw content of the social media posts, in our case the Tweets containing a specific hashtag. We represent each tweet as a vector in a high-dimensional space composed of the words used in the whole topic, after standard preprocessing used in IR (lowercasing, stopword removal, stemming). Following the lines of our main pipeline, we group these vectors in two clusters by using CLUTO [18] with cosine distance.

The underlying assumption is that the two sides, while sharing the use of the hashtag for the topic, use different vocabularies in reference to the issue at hand. For example, for #beefban a side may be calling for "freedom" while the opposing one for "respect." We use KL divergence as a measure of distance between the vocabularies of the two clusters, and the I2 measure [22] of clustering heterogeneity.

We use an unpaired Wilcoxon rank-sum test at the $p = 0.05$ significance level, but we are unable to reject the null hypothesis that there is no difference in these measures between the controversial and non-controversial topics. Therefore, there is not enough signal in the content representation to discern between controversial and non-controversial topics with confidence. This result suggests that the bag-of-words representation of content is not a good basis for our task. It also agrees with our earlier attempts to use content to build the graph used in the pipeline (see Section 4) – which suggests that using content for the task of quantifying controversy might not be straightforward.

8.2 Sentiment Analysis

Next, we resort to NLP techniques for sentiment analysis to analyze the content of the discussion. We use SentiStrength [27] trained on tweets to give a sentiment score in $[-4, 4]$ to each tweet for a given topic. In this case we do not try to cluster tweets by their sentiment. Rather, we analyze the difference in distribution of sentiment between controversial and non-controversial topics.

While it is not possible to say that controversial topics are more positive or negative than non-controversial ones (results omitted due to space constraints), we can detect a difference in their variance. Indeed, controversial topics have a higher variance than non-controversial ones, as shown in Figure 6. Controversial ones have a variance of at least 2, while non-controversial ones have a variance of at most 1.5.

In practice, the "tones" with which controversial topics are debated are stronger, and sentiment analysis is able to detect this aspect. While this signal is clear, it is not straightforward to incorporate it into the measures based on graph structure. Moreover, this feature relies on technologies that do not work reliably for languages other than English and hence cannot be applied for topics such as #russia_march.

9. DISCUSSION

The task we tackle in this work is certainly not an easy one, and this study has some limitations, which we discuss in this section. We also report a set of negative results that we produced while coming up with the measures presented. We believe these results will be very useful in steering this research topic towards a fruitful direction.

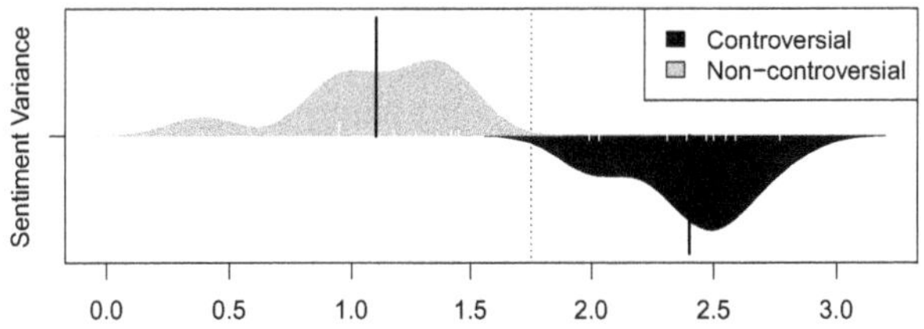

Figure 6: Sentiment variance controversy score for controversial and non-controversial topics.

9.1 Limitations

Twitter only. We present our findings mostly on datasets coming from Twitter. While this is certainly a limitation, Twitter is one of the main venues for online public discussion, and one of the few for which data is available. Hence, Twitter is a natural choice. In addition, our measures generalize well to datasets from other social media and the Web.

Choice of data. We manually pick the controversial topics in our dataset, which might introduce bias. In our choice we represent a broad set of typical controversial issues coming from religious, societal, racial, and political domains. Unfortunately, ground truths for controversial topics are hard to find, especially for ephemeral issues. However, the topics are unanimously judged controversial by the authors. Moreover, the hashtags represent the intuitive notion of controversy that we strive to capture, so human judgement is an important ingredient we want to use.

Overfitting. While this work presents the largest systematic study on controversy in social media so far, we use only 20 topics for our main experiment. Given the small number of examples, the risk of overfitting our measures to the dataset is real. We reduce this risk by using only 40% of the topics during the development of the measures. Additionally, our measures agree with previous independent results on external datasets, which further decreases the likelihood of overfitting.

Reliance on graph partitioning. Our pipeline relies on a graph partitioning stage, whose quality is fundamental for the proper functioning of the controversy measures. Given that graph partitioning is a hard but well studied problem, we rely on off-the-shelf techniques for this step. A measure that bypasses this step entirely is highly desirable, and we report a few unsuccessful attempts in the next subsection.

Multisided controversies. Not all controversies involve only two sides with opposing views. Some times discussions are multifaceted, or there are three or more competing views on the field. The principles behind our measures neatly generalize to multisided controversies. However, in this case the graph partitioning component needs to automatically find the optimal number of partitions. We defer experimental study of such cases to an extended version of this paper.

9.2 Negative Results

We briefly review a list of methods that failed to produce reliable results and were discarded early in the process of refining our controversy measures.

Mentions graph. Conover et al. [7] rely on the mention graph in Twitter to detect controversies. However, in our dataset the mention graphs are extremely sparse given that we focus on short-lived events. Merging the mentions into the retweet graph does not provide any noticeable improvement.

Previous studies have also shown that people retweet similar ideologies but mention across ideologies [4]. We exploit this intuition by using correlation clustering for graph partitioning, with negative edges for mentions. Alas, the results are qualitatively worse than those obtained by METIS.

Cuts. Simple measures such as size of the cut of the partitions do not generalize across different graphs. Conductance (in all its variants) also yields poor results. Prior work identifies controversies by comparing the structure of the graph with randomly permuted ones [7]. Unfortunately, we obtain equally poor results by using the difference in conductance with cuts obtained by METIS and by random partitions.

Community structure. Good community structure in the conversation graph is often understood as a sign that the graph is polarized or controversial. However, this is not always the case. We find that both assortativity and modularity (which have been previously used to identify controversy) do not correlate with the controversy scores, and are not good predictors for how controversial a topic is. The work by Guerra et al. [15] presents clear arguments and examples of why modularity should be avoided.

Partitioning. As already mentioned, bypassing the graph partitioning to compute the measure is desirable. We explore the use of the all pairs expected hitting time computed by using SimRank [17]. We compute the SPID (ratio of variance to mean) of this distribution, however results are mixed.

9.3 Conclusions

In this paper, we performed the first large-scale systematic study for quantifying controversy in social media. We have shown that previously-used measures are not reliable and demonstrated that controversy can be identified both in the retweet and topic-induced follow graph. We have also shown that simple content-based representations do not work in general, while sentiment analysis offers promising results.

Among the measures we studied, the random-walk-based *RWC* most neatly separates controversial topics from non-controversial ones. Besides, our measures gracefully generalize to datasets from other domains and previous studies.

This work opens several avenues for future research. First, it is worth exploring alternative approaches and testing additional features, such as, following a generative-model-based approach, or exploiting the temporal evolution of the discussion of a topic. From the application point of view, the controversy score can be used to generate recommendations that foster a healthier "news diet" on social media.

Acknowledgements This work is supported by the European Community's H2020 Program under the scheme "INFRAIA-1-2014-2015: Research Infrastructures," grant agreement #654024 "SoBigData: Social Mining & Big Data Ecosystem." We would like to thank Morales et al. [24] for providing the code and networks for the *MBLB* method.

10. REFERENCES

[1] L. A. Adamic and N. Glance. The political blogosphere and the 2004 us election: divided they blog. In *LinkKDD*, pages 36–43, 2005.

[2] L. Akoglu. Quantifying political polarity based on bipartite opinion networks. In *ICWSM*, 2014.

[3] J. An, D. Quercia, and J. Crowcroft. Partisan sharing: facebook evidence and societal consequences. In *COSN*, pages 13–24, 2014.

[4] A. Bessi, G. Caldarelli, M. Del Vicario, A. Scala, and W. Quattrociocchi. Social Determinants of Content Selection in the Age of (Mis)Information. In *Social Informatics*, pages 259–268, 2014.

[5] R. S. Burt. *Structural holes: The social structure of competition.* Harvard university press, 2009.

[6] Y. Choi, Y. Jung, and S.-H. Myaeng. Identifying controversial issues and their sub-topics in news articles. In *Intelligence and Security Informatics*, pages 140–153. Springer, 2010.

[7] M. Conover, J. Ratkiewicz, M. Francisco, B. Gonçalves, F. Menczer, and A. Flammini. Political Polarization on Twitter. In *ICWSM*, 2011.

[8] D. L. Davies and D. W. Bouldin. A cluster separation measure. *IEEE TPAMI*, 1(2):224–227, 1979.

[9] A. Doris-Down, H. Versee, and E. Gilbert. Political blend: an application designed to bring people together based on political differences. In *C&T*, pages 120–130, 2013.

[10] K. M. Esterling, A. Fung, and T. Lee. How Much Disagreement is Good for Democratic Deliberation? The CaliforniaSpeaks Health Care Reform Experiment. *SSRN*, 2010.

[11] S. R. Flaxman, S. Goel, and J. M. Rao. Filter bubbles, echo chambers, and online news consumption, 2015.

[12] K. Garimella, G. De Francisci Morales, A. Gionis, and M. Mathioudakis. Exploring Controversy in Twitter. In *CSCW [demo]*, 2016.

[13] E. Graells-Garrido, M. Lalmas, and D. Quercia. Data portraits: Connecting people of opposing views. *arXiv preprint arXiv:1311.4658*, 2013.

[14] C. Grevet, L. G. Terveen, and E. Gilbert. Managing political differences in social media. In *CSCW*, pages 1400–1408, 2014.

[15] P. H. C. Guerra, W. Meira Jr, C. Cardie, and R. Kleinberg. A measure of polarization on social media networks based on community boundaries. In *ICWSM*, 2013.

[16] M. Jacomy, T. Venturini, S. Heymann, and M. Bastian. ForceAtlas2, a continuous graph layout algorithm for handy network visualization designed for the Gephi software, 2014.

[17] G. Jeh and J. Widom. SimRank: A measure of structural-context similarity. In *KDD*, pages 538–543, 2002.

[18] G. Karypis. CLUTO - A clustering toolkit, 2002.

[19] G. Karypis and V. Kumar. METIS - Unstructured Graph Partitioning and Sparse Matrix Ordering System, 1995.

[20] J. Kulshrestha, M. B. Zafar, L. E. Noboa, K. P. Gummadi, and S. Ghosh. Characterizing information diets of social media users. In *ICWSM*, 2015.

[21] M. LaCour. A balanced news diet, not selective exposure: Evidence from a direct measure of media exposure. *SSRN*, 2012.

[22] U. Maulik and S. Bandyopadhyay. Performance evaluation of some clustering algorithms and validity indices. *IEEE TPAMI*, 24(12):1650–1654, 2002.

[23] Y. Mejova, A. X. Zhang, N. Diakopoulos, and C. Castillo. Controversy and sentiment in online news. *Symposium on Computation + Journalism*, 2014.

[24] A. Morales, J. Borondo, J. Losada, and R. Benito. Measuring political polarization: Twitter shows the two sides of Venezuela. *Chaos*, 25(3), 2015.

[25] S. A. Munson, S. Y. Lee, and P. Resnick. Encouraging reading of diverse political viewpoints with a browser widget. In *ICWSM*, 2013.

[26] Y. Ruan, D. Fuhry, and S. Parthasarathy. Efficient community detection in large networks using content and links. In *WWW*, pages 1089–1098, 2013.

[27] M. Thelwall. Heart and soul: Sentiment strength detection in the social web with sentistrength. In *CyberEmotions*, pages 1–14, 2013.

[28] W. Zachary. An information flow model for conflict and fission in small groups. *J. of Anthropological Research*, 33: 452–473, 1977.

Understanding and Identifying Advocates for Political Campaigns on Social Media

Suhas Ranganath†, Xia Hu⋆, Jiliang Tang‡, Huan Liu†
† Arizona State University, ⋆ Texas A&M University, ‡ Yahoo! Labs
{srangan8,huan.liu}@asu.edu, hu@cse.tamu.edu, jlt@yahoo-inc.com

ABSTRACT

Social media is increasingly being used to access and disseminate information on sociopolitical issues like gun rights and general elections. The popularity and openness of social media makes it conducive for some individuals, known as advocates, who use social media to push their agendas on these issues strategically. Identifying these advocates will caution social media users before reading their information and also enable campaign managers to identify advocates for their digital political campaigns. A significant challenge in identifying advocates is that they employ nuanced strategies to shape user opinion and increase the spread of their messages, making it difficult to distinguish them from random users posting on the campaign. In this paper, we draw from social movement theories and design a quantitative framework to study the nuanced message strategies, propagation strategies, and community structure adopted by advocates for political campaigns in social media. Based on observations of their social media activities manifesting from these strategies, we investigate how to model these strategies for identifying them. We evaluate the framework using two datasets from Twitter, and our experiments demonstrate its effectiveness in identifying advocates for political campaigns with ramifications of this work directed towards assisting users as they navigate through social media spaces.

Keywords

Advocacy; Political Campaigns; User Interactions

1. INTRODUCTION

Social media is emerging to be a popular information channel for sociopolitical issues of broad importance for e.g. elections and gun rights. It provides access to a wide range of perspectives on these issues, enabling users to form independent opinions. Owing to this, millions of people are using social media to seek information, gather perspectives, and participate in discussions on these important issues. The popularity of social media as an information channel for important issues has given rise to individuals who use it to try and push their agenda for political campaigns [16]. Media advocacy is defined in the the literature as "the strategic use of mass media to advance a social or public initiative" [18]. We are motivated by this to define advocates for political campaigns on social media as individuals who use social media to advance strategically their agenda for a given political campaign. During the 2014 Indian elections, for example, a set of individuals formed an organization called NaMo Brigade with the motto of "Mission: Narendra Modi as PM" and used social media platforms to advocate for the election of Narendra Modi as Prime Minister [26].

Although these campaigns have considerable social media presence [37], it is difficult to identify individual accounts of advocates. Designing algorithms to identify accounts of individual advocates can better inform users as they navigate through social media spaces. People accessing information about an issue, for e.g. an election, through social media can be notified whether a given account is an advocate before reading their messages. On the other hand, understanding and modeling the characteristics of social media advocates can help campaign managers in recruiting new advocates for their digital political campaigns.

This task faces several challenges. First, advocates employ nuanced message construction and propagation strategies to shape user opinion and increase the spread of their messages, making it difficult to distinguish them from random users posting on issues related to the campaign. Second, these strategies are very diverse, manifesting both in the activity patterns restricted to individual advocates like constructing persuasive messages, and multiple relational patterns like shared language and interactions, making it a challenge to study collectively them in a unified model.

Theoretical constructs of strategies for message construction, propagation, and community formation by advocates have been extensively studied in social sciences. Social movement theory records persuasive language and high degrees of emotion in the messages of advocates in their attempts to shape the opinion of people [28]. The literature on campaign communications [12] studies the widespread use of focused messaging for effective communication during political campaigns. Also, distinctive language patterns shared among people with similar affiliations foster easier communication of messages between them [32]. To increase the reach of messages during political campaigns, the utility of popular users for widespread propagation has been studied in [14]. Formation of social and interaction networks between advocates for

WSDM 2016 February 22-25, 2016, San Francisco, CA, USA
© 2016 ACM. ISBN 978-1-4503-3716-8/16/02...$15.00
DOI: http://dx.doi.org/10.1145/2835776.2835807

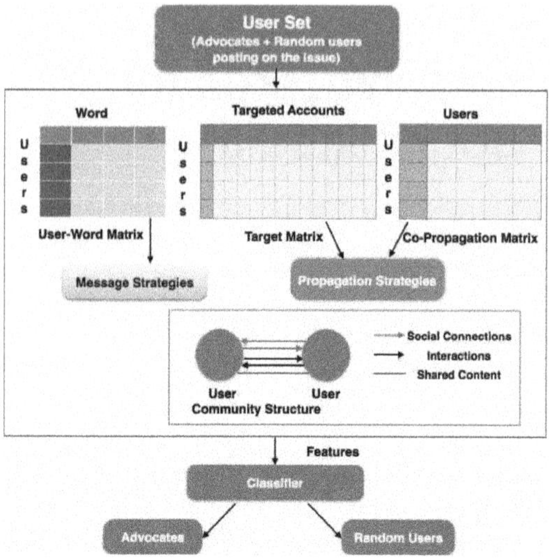

Figure 1: The proposed framework to identify advocates for political campaigns on social media

the purpose of easier coordination and communication has been investigated in social movement literature [28].

In this paper, we model the nuanced message strategies, propagation strategies, and community structure of advocates guided by sociological literature and integrate them to identify advocates for political campaigns on social media. We primarily focus on the following questions: How to model the nuanced strategies of advocates for political campaigns on social media? How to integrate them to design a unified framework for identifying advocates for political campaigns in social media?

The primary contributions of this work are:

- A definition of the problem of identifying advocates for political campaigns on social media,
- A computational framework to gain insights into the strategies of the advocates and identify them by collectively modeling their strategies, and
- Evaluation of the framework in identifying advocates of political campaigns in the social media platform Twitter using two real-world datasets.

2. PROBLEM STATEMENT

In this section, we introduce notations and terms used in the paper and formally define the problem statement. We first define some notations. Boldface uppercase letters (e.g $\mathbf{X}$) denote matrices and boldface lowercase letters (e.g. $\mathbf{x}$) vectors. $\mathbf{X}_{\mathrm{ij}}$ signifies the element in the ith row and j^{th} column of $\mathbf{X}$ and the ith column of $\mathbf{X}$ by $\mathbf{X}_i$. The Frebonius norm of $\mathbf{X}$ is denoted as $||\mathbf{X}||_{\mathrm{F}} = \sqrt{\sum_{\mathrm{i,j}} \mathbf{X}_{\mathrm{ij}}^2}$. The n mode vector product of a tensor $\mathcal{M} \in \mathbb{R}^{D_1 \times D_2 \times .. \times D_N}$ with $\mathbf{x} \in \mathbb{R}^{D_n}$ is given by $\mathcal{M} \times_n \mathbf{x}$ and results in a tensor of size $D_1 \times D_2 \times .. \times D_{n-1} \times D_{n+1} \times ... \times D_N$ whose each element is given by $(\mathcal{M} \times_n \mathbf{x})_{d_1 d_2 .. d_{n-1} d_{n+1} ... d_N} = \sum_{d_n=1}^{D_n} \mathcal{M}_{d_1 d_2 .. d_N} \mathbf{x}_{d_n}$. The set of advocates is denoted as $\mathbf{a}$ and the set of random users using keywords related to the issue as $\mathbf{v}$. The set of users is denoted as $\mathbf{u} = [\mathbf{a}, \mathbf{v}]$ and the total number of users as N.

We now define terms related to different kinds of strategies of advocates that can be characterized. Message strategies deal with the construction of status messages of advocates with the aim of shaping the opinions of people. We develop characterizations on four types of message strategies possibly present in the status messages of advocates: persuasive language, a high degree of emotion, topical focus and shared language patterns. We construct the user word matrix $\mathbf{S} \in \mathbb{R}^{\mathrm{N} \times \mathrm{l}}$ from the status messages with tf-idf weighting, where l is the total number of words. Shared language patterns between two users in $\mathbf{u}$ are modeled taking hashtags as instances of language patterns. For each user $\mathbf{u}_{\mathrm{i}} \in \mathbf{u}$, we construct a vector of hashtags $\mathbf{h}_{\mathbf{u}_{\mathrm{i}}}$ from his status messages. We define matrices capturing shared hashtag information as $\mathcal{Z}^1$, where $\mathcal{Z}_{\mathrm{ij}}^1 = \mathrm{jac\_sim}(\mathbf{h}_{\mathbf{u}_{\mathrm{i}}}, \mathbf{h}_{\mathbf{u}_{\mathrm{j}}})$. jac_sim($\mathbf{x}$,$\mathbf{y}$) indicates the Jaccard similarity between $\mathbf{x}$ and $\mathbf{y}$.

Propagation strategies comprise of the strategies employed by advocates to increase the spread of their messages. We model the propagation strategies of advocates from their targeting and co-propagation behavior. For each user in $\mathbf{u}_{\mathrm{i}} \in \mathbf{u}$, let $\mathbf{ta}_{\mathrm{u}}$ denote the set of people targeted by the user. We define the targeting matrix $\mathbf{T} \in \mathbb{R}^{\mathrm{N} \times \mathrm{R}}$ where $\mathbf{T}_{\mathrm{ij}}$ is equal to the number of times $\mathbf{u}_{\mathrm{i}}$ has targeted $\mathbf{r}_{\mathrm{j}}$ where $\mathbf{r} = \bigcup_{\mathrm{i} \in \mathbf{u}} \mathbf{ta}_{\mathrm{i}}$ and R is the total number of users in $\mathbf{r}$. We next define the co-propagation network as $\mathbf{P} \in \mathbb{R}^{\mathrm{N} \times \mathrm{N}}$, where $\mathbf{P}_{\mathrm{ij}}$ is the number of times $\mathbf{u}_{\mathrm{j}}$ has propagated a message of $\mathbf{u}_{\mathrm{i}}$.

Community structure deals with the patterns arising from the networks formed by advocates to facilitate easier communication and coordination. We model the community structures arising from social connections and interactions between advocates. The social connection matrix is defined as $\mathcal{Z}^2 \in \mathbb{R}^{\mathrm{N} \times \mathrm{N}}$. The value of $\mathcal{Z}_{\mathrm{ij}}^2$ is 1 if $\mathbf{u}_{\mathrm{i}}$ connects to $\mathbf{u}_{\mathrm{j}}$ and 0 otherwise. We also capture the interactions between the users in $\mathcal{Z}^3 \in \mathbb{R}^{\mathrm{N} \times \mathrm{N}}$ where $\mathcal{Z}_{\mathrm{ij}}^3$ is equal to the number of times $\mathbf{u}_{\mathrm{i}}$ interacts with $\mathbf{u}_{\mathrm{j}}$. In addition, we define the tensor $\mathcal{Z}$ to hold the information contained in the relational matrices $\mathcal{Z}^1, \mathcal{Z}^2$ and $\mathcal{Z}^3$, where $\mathcal{Z}_{\mathrm{ijt}} = \mathcal{Z}_{\mathrm{ij}}^{\mathrm{t}}$.

We model the message strategies, propagation strategies, and community structure and study them in a unified supervised learning framework to identify advocates for political campaigns on social media. The problem statement can then be stated as follows: *"Given a set of advocates for a given political campaign on social media* $\mathbf{a}$ *and a set of random users posting on the campaign* $\mathbf{v}$*, their status message matrix* $\mathbf{S}$*, the targeting matrix* $\mathbf{T}$*, the propagation network* $\mathbf{P}$*, and the relational tensor* $\mathcal{Z}$*, determine if a new user* x *is an advocate of the political campaign."*

3. QUANTIFYING STRATEGIES

In this section, we study the different nuanced strategies employed by advocates for political campaigns on social media drawing from theoretical constructs present in sociological literature and present ways to model them. We first study the employed strategies in terms of their message strategies, propagation strategies, and community structure. We explore each of them in detail, and then present ways to model them to derive characteristics possibly capable of distinguishing between advocates for political campaigns and random users posting on the campaign.

3.1 Quantifying Message Strategies

Message strategies deal with patterns from the construction of the status messages of advocates. Advocates can employ persuasive language in their status messages and attempt to sway opinions of other users. Parallels can be seen in the sociological literature which documents the high use of persuasive language during social movements [28]. The status messages of advocates can also contain a high degree of emotions both positive; when they try to generate positive feelings about their campaign, or negative; when they try to generate feelings of anger, fear, and anxiety [28].

Message strategies of advocates can also manifest across a set of status messages. For instance, advocates can concentrate their status messages around a small number of topics in their attempts at effective communication, resulting in high topical focus. Parallels can be seen in studies of campaign communications [12], which shows a widespread use of focused messaging. An advocate can also share distinctive language patterns with other advocates to support common issues and facilitate easier communication. Shared language patterns among people with similar affiliations have been shown in speech codes theory to foster easier communication [32]. Next, we present ways to model characteristics arising from persuasive language, emotions, focused messaging, and shared language patterns.

The use of persuasive language can be quantified by modeling theoretical principles of persuasion [10]. We consider two principles of reason and affinity [10] and model their occurrence. People employ reason as a rational justification for their views while persuading others. The number of words related to reason [13] in the status messages of a user is used to quantify reason. Expressions of affinity can also be used as a tool for persuasion by using words conveying liking, compliments, and association. We use social words in the LIWC corpus [31] to model expressions of affinity and count their occurrence in the messages of each user. We postulate that advocates in $\mathbf{a}$ use a higher number of words denoting persuasion than random users $\mathbf{v}$ posting on the campaign.

The emotional content in the posts of the users in $\mathbf{u}$ can be modeled using the positive and negative emotional words from the LIWC corpus [31]. We postulate that advocates in social media use a higher number of emotional words, both positive and negative than random users posting on an issue. A higher use of emotion can be an indication that advocates have a strong belief in their cause, which separates them from paid workers posting promotional comments for a campaign, who display fewer emotions in their posts [23].

To model the topical focus of a user in $\mathbf{u}$, we first compute the topic distribution using LDA [6] on the user word matrix $\mathbf{S}$. The topic model results in the user topic matrix $\mathbf{DT} \in \mathbb{R}^{n \times t}$, where $\mathbf{DT}_{ij}$ is the number of times a word of user $\mathbf{u}_i$ has been assigned to topic $\mathbf{t}_j$ and t is the number of topics. To obtain the topic probability distribution, the document-topic matrix can be normalized $\mathbf{DT}$ to obtain $\mathbf{DT}'$, where each row of $\mathbf{DT}'$ contains the probability distribution over topics of a user. The entropy of the topic distribution from the corresponding row of $\mathbf{DT}$ for each user i to construct a vector $\mathbf{e}_i$ where $\mathbf{e}_i = \sum_{j=1}^{j=t} -\mathbf{DT}'_{ij}\log(\mathbf{DT}'_{ij})$. It is evident that a lower value of entropy for a user implies greater concentration on fewer topics in his messages and a higher value implies distribution over a larger number of topics. Therefore, the higher the topical focus in the status messages of a user, the lower the value of his entropy. We postulate that advocates have a higher topical focus in their messages than random users posting on the campaign.

We next model the shared language patterns among users in $\mathbf{u}$ and use hashtags as instances of language patterns. For each advocate a $\in \mathbf{a}$, let $\mathcal{Z}^1_{ab}$ denote the amount of hashtags he shares with any other advocate $b \neq a \in \mathbf{a}$ measured by Jaccard similarity. Similarly, let $\mathcal{Z}^1_{av}$, where v $\in \mathbf{v}$ is a random user posting on issues related to the campaign. We postulate that an advocate for a political campaign shares a higher amount of hashtags with other advocates than with random users in $\mathbf{v}$ posting on the campaign. We evaluate these characteristics using the datasets in Section 4.2.1.

Until now, we characterized and modeled message strategies capable of distinguishing advocates for political campaigns from random users posting on the issue like persuasive language, emotion, topical focus and shared language patterns with other advocates. We next examine characteristics of propagation strategies employed by advocates to increase the reach of these messages.

3.2 Quantifying Propagation Strategies

We examine the propagation strategies of advocates for political campaigns on social media, focusing on their targeting and co-propagation behavior. Social media enables advocates to target specific users for propagating information. We propose that advocates target popular users more frequently than random users posting on the campaign as popular users help to get messages across to a wider audience [14]. We then investigate how advocates assist each other in spreading their messages.

We first model the targeting behavior of the users in $\mathbf{u}$. Let $\mathbf{r}$ is the set of people targeted by all users in $\mathbf{u}$ as defined in Section 2. Taking the number of users connecting to a user as a measure of his popularity, we construct the vector $\mathbf{c}$ where $\mathbf{c}_i$ is the number of people connecting to $\mathbf{r}_i$. We postulate that the attention of advocates is more skewed towards users with higher popularity than the attention of random users posting on the campaign. To model this postulate, we compute the vector $\mathbf{sta} = \mathbf{Tc}$, where $\mathbf{sta}_k$ is the sum of number of times a user k targets an user $\mathbf{r}_i$ weighted by $\mathbf{c}_i$, the number of users connecting to $\mathbf{ta}_i$. The value of $\mathbf{sta}_k$ is higher if the user k targets popular users a higher number of times. Therefore, our postulate is satisfied when advocates for a political campaign have a higher value of $\mathbf{sta}$ than random users posting on the campaign.

We next model the co-propagation behavior of users in $\mathbf{u}$. Advocates will be more interested in propagating messages of other advocates, and also, their messages will be more likely to be propagated by other advocates than random users posting on the campaign. Based on this, we characterize advocates by their hubs and authority scores [21] in the information propagation network $\mathbf{P}$. We compute hubs and authority scores of users in $\mathbf{u}$ using the information propagation network $\mathbf{P}$ and postulate that advocates have higher hub and authority scores than random users posting on the campaign. We evaluate these characteristics using the datasets in Section 4.2.2.

Until now, we proposed characteristics of advocates for political campaigns on social media from their message strategies and propagation strategies along with methods for modeling them. We next propose characteristics related to the community structure arising from their relationships with other advocates for the campaign.

3.3 Quantifying Community Structure

Community structure deals with the patterns arising from the networks formed by advocates to facilitate easier communication and coordination. Social media provides opportunities for advocates to connect to each other through many different types of relationships. Advocates can form social connections, interact with each other for coordination, and carry out conversations. The formation of networks of social connections and interactions between advocates for communication and coordination have been studied in theoretical studies of social movements [28]. Social connections and interactions between advocates can give rise to the similarity in community memberships. We now postulate a few underlying hypothesis to establish the similarity in community memberships between advocates in social media

We first present postulates underlying community structure arising from social connections and interactions of advocates. For each advocate $a \in \mathbf{a}$, let $\mathcal{Z}^2_{ab}$ be 1 if a connects to b and 0 otherwise, where b is another advocate $b \neq a \in \mathbf{a}$ and $\mathcal{Z}^2$ is defined in Section 2. Similarly, let $\mathcal{Z}^2_{av}$ be 1 if a connects to b and 0 otherwise, where $v \in \mathbf{v}$ is a random user posting on issues related to the campaign We then postulate that advocates are more likely to form social connections with other advocates than with random users posting on the campaign. We follow a similar procedure using $\mathcal{Z}^3$ to postulate that advocates are more likely to interact with each other than with random users posting on the campaign. These postulates underly that advocates have similar community memberships for different types of relationships. Are these community memberships of advocates are similar when measured across relationship types?

To model this, we first select the users with whom the advocates have at least one type of relation with. For each advocate, we construct a vector $\mathbf{co}_{ab}$, $b \neq a \in \mathbf{a}$, where each element is the number of types a pair of advocates have relations in. Similarly, we construct the vector $\mathbf{co}_{av}$, $v \in \mathbf{v}$, where each element is the number of types of relations between a pair of advocate and a random user posting on the campaign. We postulate that given an advocate has established one type of relation with a user, he has a significantly higher propensity to form more types of relation if the user is another advocate than if he is a random user posting on the campaign. The postulate, if verified, underlies that community memberships of advocates are shared across different relationship types, and hence, they can be jointly inferred by combining different relationship types in an efficient manner.

In this section, we draw from theoretical constructs in sociological literature to propose different characterizations of the nuanced message strategies, propagation strategies, and community structure of advocates for political campaigns on social media. Next, we are going to use two real-world datasets from Twitter to evaluate these characteristics in their ability to distinguish between advocates and random users posting on the issue.

4. EVALUATING STRATEGIES

In this section, we describe the datasets used to evaluate our characterizations of advocates of political campaigns in social media. We have two datasets from Twitter, each related to a political campaign carried out using Twitter. We then use these datasets to evaluate the ability of the proposed characterizations of strategies to distinguish between advocates for a given political campaign and random users posting on issues related to the campaign.

4.1 Datasets

We have two datasets related each related to a political campaign. The first dataset is focused on advocates for the Indian election campaign. The rise of around 200 million users of social media in India has made it an important platform for political discourse during elections [19]. Independent groups like NaMo Brigade [26] were formed to advocate for the political campaign of Narendra Modi. The second dataset is related to the issue of gun rights in the United States. This campaign is focused on preserving gun rights, which is being questioned in the wake of increasing gun-related violence. Organizations advocating to preserve gun rights as the National Rifles Association (NRA) have considerable social media presence [30].

Parameter	Elections	Gun Rights
Total # of Users	9390	7695
# of Tweets	20,362,442	19,275,481
# of Links	514,501	899,535
Users posting on the campaign	8500	7000
# of Advocates	890	695

Table 1: Statistics of the datasets of advocates.

Although these organizations have a considerable media presence, it is a challenge to obtain labels for individual users involved in advocacy. Previous literature proposes the use of publicly compiled lists as an effective alternative for inferring affiliations of social media users [20]. The authors in [5] have utilized lists in Twitter to characterize topical-identity based groups. Informed by this literature, we identified two public Twitter lists, titled "NaMo Brigade" [4], for advocates for the election campaign of Narendra Modi and "NRA" [35], for the advocates for gun rights.

To validate the datasets, we apply the mark and recapture technique, drawing from population estimation methodologies [8]. For each of the two lists, we draw two random samples and estimate the total number of errors in the list as follows. Let the probability of finding errors in the random samples r_1 and r_2 be p_{r_1} and p_{r_2}. The number of errors in both the samples will then be given by $e_{r_1} = p_{r_1} N_e$ and $e_{r_2} = p_{r_2} N_e$, where N_e is the total number of errors to be estimated. The number of errors in the intersection of the two samples is then $e_{r_1 r_2} = p_{r_1} p_{r_2} N_e$. The number of errors in the dataset N_e can then be estimated as $N_e = e_{r_1} e_{r_2} / e_{r_1 r_2}$ This is shown to overestimate the population, and hence we use a variation to estimate the number of errors as

$$N_e = \frac{(e_{r_1} + 1) \times (e_{r_2} + 1)}{e_{r_1 r_2} + 1} - 1 \quad (1)$$

A measure of uncertainty is given by the standard error, which estimates of the variability of N if the above experiment is conducted repeatedly. This is computed as follows

$$SE = \sqrt{\frac{(e_{r_1} + 1) \times (e_{r_2} + 1) \times (e_{r_2} - e_{r_1 r_2}) \times (e_{r_1} - e_{r_1 r_2})}{(e_{r_1 r_2} + 1)^2 \times (e_{r_1 r_2} + 2)}} \quad (2)$$

From the standard error, we then calculate the 95% confidence interval i.e. the range within which the number of errors lies with 95% certainty as $I_e = N_e \pm 1.96 \times SE$, where I_e is the 95% confidence interval of the error estimate.

We draw random samples of 10% of the size of the list and use external evaluators to verify them. The evaluators are asked to assess whether a user is an advocate of a given political campaign in social media. The definition of advocates is given to "individuals who use social media to advance strategically their agenda for a given political campaign", according to the definition provided in Section 1. The evaluators mark 1 if they think the member is an advo-

Factors	Features	Elections	Gun Rights
Message Strategy			
Persuasion	Reason	3.52*	6.52**
	Liking	1.717***	1.04***
Focus	Entropy	-3.63***	-0.21**
Emotion	+ve	0.5731**	0.3669**
	-ve	0.7782***	0.2621**
Shared Language		3.8571***	10.57***
Propagation Strategy	Targeting	2.15***	1.91*
	Hubs	2.91***	-.3185
	Authorities	6.39***	0.51*
Community Structure	Following	1.5625***	0.9086***
	Followers	2.045*	0.9554***
	Interactions	1.441***	0.0112**
	Multiple	.468***	4.08***

Table 2: Evaluating strategies using logistic regression coefficients with p-value from t test (*-$p < 0.05$,-$p < 0.01$,***-$p < 0.0001$)**

cate and 0 otherwise. We then estimate the total number of errors from Eq 1 and the confidence interval. The percentage accuracy of the two lists 'NaMo Brigade' and 'NRA' are 92.10%±5.29% and 90.07%±6.27% respectively. Validating the accuracy of the lists, we use their members as ground truths for the set of advocates **a**.

To construct the set **v**, we collect a set of random users who posted with hashtags related to the given campaigns. We obtain the related hashtags from [34] by giving the initial hashtag as "#modi" for the dataset related to the elections and "#progun" for the dataset related to gun rights and assign the set of users posting using the hashtags as **v**. We randomly sampled **v** and a very few number of users were ascertained as advocates, which we removed from the set. We collect the friends, followers, profile, and statuses of both advocates in **a** and random users in **v** for the two campaigns. Some statistics of the datasets is presented in Table 1.

4.2 Evaluation

We now evaluate the characterizations of advocates to distinguish between advocates and random users posting on the issue using the datasets. Characterizations restricted to individual advocates such as persuasion, focus, emotion and propagation strategies are evaluated using logistic regression. The positive class is given by the advocates from the set **a** and the negative class consists of the random users posting on the campaign from **v**. The regression coefficients for all the characterizations along with the significance values derived from the t-test are shown in Table 2.

Characterizations of pairwise relational patterns such as shared language and community structure are evaluated using paired t-test. We present the coefficients of the t-test along with its significance values in Table 2. We next evaluate the characterizations grouping them into message strategies, propagation strategies, and community structure.

4.2.1 Message Strategies

We first evaluate the ability of characterizations of message strategies to distinguish between advocates and random users posting on the campaign. From Table 2, we can see a strong evidence of the use of persuasive language by advocates in both the datasets, indicative of the attempts of advocates to sway the opinions of others. A significantly higher use of words denoting reason and affinity by advocates can be observed, demonstrating that the proposed model of persuasive language is effective. High positive and negative emotional content, which can be used to generate strong feelings about the campaign, is a strong characteristic in the tweets of advocates. This indicates that unlike workers who are paid to comment or post on a particular issue leading to a lack of emotion in their posts [23], advocates show a higher level of emotion in their messages.

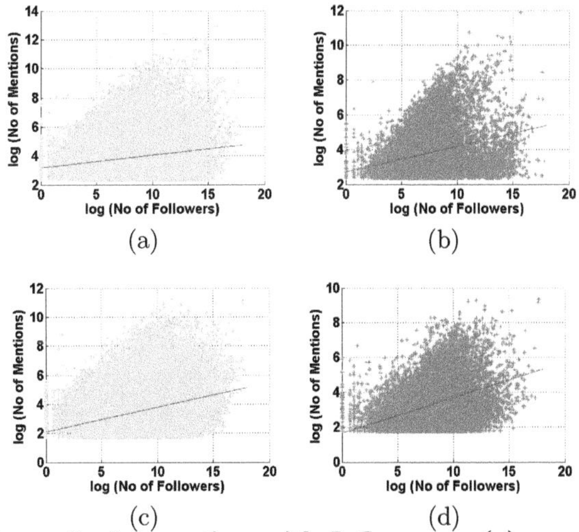

Figure 2: Interacting with Influencers (a) random users posting on the election campaign ($\rho = 0.08$) (b) advocates for election campaign ($\rho = 0.15$) (c) random users posting on gun rights ($\rho = 0.15$) (d) advocates for gun rights ($\rho = 0.20$)

A negative coefficient in the topical focus of advocates with high significance demonstrates that they concentrate their posts around fewer topics for effective messaging compared to random users posting on the campaign. In our experiments, we assign the number of topics t=20. The speech code theory states that users with common affiliations develop a common lingo to foster easier communication [32]. This is borne out by a significantly high coefficient of common hashtags, showing that advocates share higher amount of hashtags with other advocates than with random users posting on the campaign.

These observations indicate that the characterizations of message strategies drawn from theoretical constructs from sociological literature and the proposed approaches to modeling them are effective in distinguishing between advocates and random users posting on the campaign. We next evaluate the ability of the characterizations of the propagation strategies of advocates to distinguish between advocates and random users posting on the campaign.

4.2.2 Propagation Strategies

We first focus on the patterns arising from advocates targeting specific users, which can be performed in Twitter through the mention feature. The number of people who connect to the set of people targeted by the users in **u**, given by **c** in Section 3.2 can be measured by their follower count in Twitter. We first examine if the targeting patterns of advocates differ from those of normal users posting on the issue. We plot the targeting patterns of users in Fig 2 with

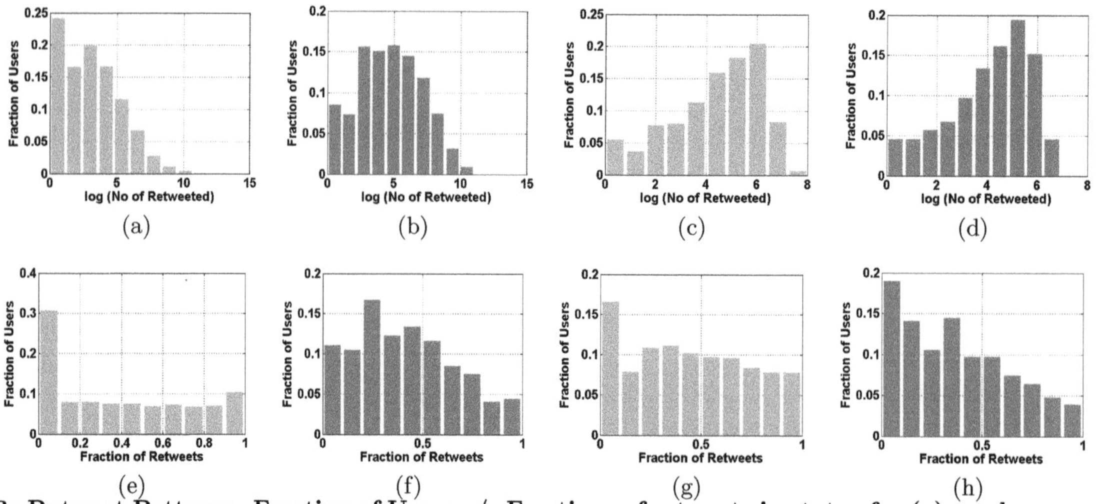

Figure 3: Retweet Patterns. Fraction of Users v/s Fractions of retweets in status for (a) random users posting on and (b) advocates for the election campaign, (c) random users posting on and (d) advocates related for gun rights. Fraction of users v/s no of times users are retweeted by (e) random users posting on and (f) advocates for election campaigns, (g) random users posting on, and (h) advocates for gun rights

the log of the number of mentions on the y-axis and the log of the number of followers on the x-axis. For each plot, we fit a line to the data that minimizes the least square error in the data and its slope, ρ, given in the caption. A higher value of ρ indicates that people with a higher number of followers are targeted more frequently.

We can see that mentioning patterns of advocates from Fig 2 that Fig 2(b) and 2(d) have a greater slope than that of random users posting on the campaign Fig 2(a) and 2(c). Advocates might target popular users as they have the potential to increase the reach of information. We model this notion in Section 3.2 and present the results in Table 2. We can say from a significantly high coefficient value of the targeting characteristic that the targeting patterns of advocates are more significantly skewed towards popular users than those of random users posting on the campaign.

We next evaluate the characterizations of co-propagation behavior of users in $\mathbf{u}$. Fig 3 (a), (b), (c), and (d) illustrates the number of times each user has been retweeted. The logarithm of the times the user is retweeted in shown in the x-axis and the fraction of users who have been retweeted the corresponding number of times, choosing users with more than 100 tweets, on the y-axis. A larger fraction of advocates is retweeted than random users posting on the campaign.

For each user in $\mathbf{u}$, we next compute the ratio of a number of their retweets to his total number of tweets. The retweet ratio is plotted on the x-axis and the fraction of users with the retweet ratio on the y-axis, choosing users with more than 100 tweets, in Fig 3 (e), (f), (g), and (h). A similar pattern can be observed, where the retweet ratio of random users posting on the campaign follows a power law distribution and those of advocates have a skewed distribution with a higher fraction of users actively involved in information propagation. These observations are reflected in Table 2, in the effectiveness of hubs and authority scores for distinguishing advocates and random users posting on the campaign.

These observations indicate that the proposed characterizations of propagation strategies drawn from sociological theories and approaches for modeling them can effectively distinguish between advocates and random users posting on the campaign. We next evaluate the ability of the characterizations of the community structure in their ability to distinguish between advocates for political campaigns and random users posting on the campaign.

4.2.3 Community Structure

We first evaluate the characteristics of social relationships of advocates. From Table 2, we can see that advocates tend to connect with each other significantly more than with random users posting on the topic. This indicates advocates are utilizing social media to build a strong network of connections with each other. Advocates interact significantly more with other advocates for the campaign than with random users posting on it, indicating that they maintain a high level of interactions with each other. These provide evidence of a community structure between advocates.

We next examine if advocates tend to establish multiple types of relationships with each other. From Table 2, we see that given that an advocate has established one type of relation with a user, he has a significantly higher propensity to form multiple types of relation if the user is another advocate than if he is a normal user posting on the campaign. These results indicate a strong network of social connections and interactions between advocates, verifying our postulates. This also provides a basis to infer jointly community membership of users across different relationship types.

Until now, we proposed a set of characteristics capable of effectively distinguishing between advocates and random users posting on the issue. The set of characterizations include both individual characteristics from their messages and propagation strategies and multiple relational patterns like social connections, shared content patterns, and interactions, forming a heterogeneous feature space. We next design a mathematical formulation to combine individual and multiple pairwise characteristics in a unified framework to identify advocates for a political campaign.

5. A UNIFIED MODEL

Integration of individual and relational characteristics in a unified homogenous space for classification can be performed by deriving latent variables from the relational matrix [36].

A difference here is that we have multiple types of pairwise relations between users, and we need to derive latent dimension memberships by jointly exploiting pairwise connections across multiple types of relations. Individual characteristics can be then be combined with the latent variables derived from the relational characteristics to construct features for classification.

Let the proposed individual characteristics be denoted as $\mathcal{I}$ and the relational characteristics be arranged in a tensor $\mathcal{Z}$ as defined in Section 2. Tensors have been used in literature to analyze jointly multi-modal relationships in applications such as community detection [25] and link prediction [11]. We first factorize the tensor $\mathcal{Z}$ to derive latent dimension memberships from the relational characteristics. Different types of connections between two users can be captured by their similarity in their memberships of latent dimensions. Two users who have pairwise relationships with each other across different types will have higher similarity in their latent dimension memberships than two users who do not have pairwise relationships with each other.

We factorize the tensor $\mathcal{Z}$ to obtain the user matrices $\mathbf{U} \in \mathbb{R}^{\mathrm{N\times K}}$ and $\mathbf{V} \in \mathbb{R}^{\mathrm{N\times K}}$, and the relationship type dimension matrix $\mathbf{T} \in \mathbb{R}^{\mathrm{T\times K}}$, where K is the number of latent dimensions, by solving the following optimization problem

$$\min_{\mathbf{U},\mathbf{V},\mathbf{T}} ||\mathcal{Z} - [\![\mathbf{U},\mathbf{V},\mathbf{T}]\!]||^2_{\mathrm{F}}, \tag{3}$$

where $[\![\mathbf{U},\mathbf{V},\mathbf{T}]\!] \in \mathbb{R}^{\mathrm{N\times N\times T}}$ is given by

$$[\![\mathbf{U},\mathbf{V},\mathbf{T}]\!] = \sum_{k=1}^{K} \mathbf{u}_k \circ \mathbf{v}_k \circ \mathbf{t}_k.$$

Here $\mathbf{u}_k$, $\mathbf{v}_k$, $\mathbf{t}_k$ are the $\mathrm{k^{th}}$ column vectors of $\mathbf{U}$, $\mathbf{V}$ and $\mathbf{T}$ respectively. The symbol $\circ$ represents the vector outer product such that if the tensor $\mathcal{Y} = \mathbf{u}_k \circ \mathbf{v}_k \circ \mathbf{t}_k$ then $\mathcal{Y}_{\mathrm{efg}} = (\mathbf{u}_k)_{\mathrm{e}}(\mathbf{v}_k)_{\mathrm{f}}(\mathbf{t}_k)_{\mathrm{g}}$. Substituting this in Eqn 3, we get

$$f = \min_{\mathbf{U},\mathbf{V},\mathbf{T}} ||\mathcal{Z} - \sum_{k=1}^{K} \mathbf{u}_k \circ \mathbf{v}_k \circ \mathbf{t}_k||^2_{\mathrm{F}}, \tag{4}$$

We optimize this function motivated by the conjugate linear optimization method [1]. We first arrange the vectors $\mathbf{u}$,$\mathbf{v}$ and $\mathbf{t}$ in a single vector $\mathbf{x} = [\mathbf{u},\mathbf{v},\mathbf{t}]$ and calculate the gradient of $\mathbf{f}(\mathbf{x})$ with respect to each $\mathbf{x}_k^n$ where $\mathbf{x}^1 = \mathbf{u}, \mathbf{x}^2 = \mathbf{v}, \mathbf{x}^3 = \mathbf{t}$. f can be rewritten as

$$f = \underbrace{\frac{1}{2}||\mathcal{Z}||^2}_{f_1} - \underbrace{\langle \mathcal{Z}, \sum_{k=1}^{K} \mathbf{x}_k^1 \circ \mathbf{x}_k^2 \circ \mathbf{x}_k^3 \rangle}_{f_2} + \underbrace{\frac{1}{2}||\sum_{k=1}^{K} \mathbf{x}_k^1 \circ \mathbf{x}_k^2 \circ \mathbf{x}_k^3||^2}_{f_3} \tag{5}$$

The gradient of f is obtained by computing its partial derivative with respect to each element in $\mathbf{x}$ denoted by $\mathbf{x}_k^m$. So

$$\frac{\partial f_1}{\partial \mathbf{x}_k^m} = 0 \tag{6}$$

as $\mathcal{Z}$ is a constant with respect to $\mathbf{x}_k^m$. The partial derivative of f_2 with respect to each element in $\mathbf{x}$ denoted by $\mathbf{x}_k^m$ can then be computed as follows.

$$\frac{\partial f_2}{\partial \mathbf{x}_k^1} = \mathcal{Z}\times_2\mathbf{x}_k^2\times_3\mathbf{x}_k^3,\ \frac{\partial f_2}{\partial \mathbf{x}_k^2} = \mathcal{Z}\times_1\mathbf{x}_k^1\times_3\mathbf{x}_k^3,\ \frac{\partial f_2}{\partial \mathbf{x}_k^3} = \mathcal{Z}\times_1\mathbf{x}_k^1\times_2\mathbf{x}_k^2, \tag{7}$$

where $\times_n$ is the n-mode multiplication operator as defined as Section 2. The partial derivative of f_3 with respect to each term in $\mathbf{x}$ denoted by $\mathbf{x}_k^m$ can be computed as

$$\frac{\partial f_3}{\partial \mathbf{x}_k^m} = \sum_{j=1}^{K}(\prod_{\substack{r=1 \\ r\neq m}} \mathbf{x}_k^{r\mathrm{T}}\mathbf{x}_j^r)\mathbf{x}_j^r \tag{8}$$

The overall gradient can then be computed as

$$\frac{\partial f}{\partial \mathbf{x}_k^m} = \frac{\partial f_1}{\partial \mathbf{x}_k^m} - \frac{\partial f_2}{\partial \mathbf{x}_k^m} + \frac{\partial f_3}{\partial \mathbf{x}_k^m} \tag{9}$$

where $\frac{\partial f_1}{\partial \mathbf{x}_k^m}$, $\frac{\partial f_2}{\partial \mathbf{x}_k^m}$, $\frac{\partial f_3}{\partial \mathbf{x}_k^m}$ are as described in Eqn 6, Eqn 7 and Eqn 8 respectively. The gradient descent step repeated for all values of m and k is continued until convergence. As the objective function in Eqn 4 is convex, the optimization is guaranteed to converge. The computational complexity of the iterations is low due to the high sparsity of $\mathcal{Z}$.

To give an intuitive understanding of the optimization term in Eqn 4, we rewrite it as follows

$$\min_{\mathbf{U},\mathbf{V},\mathbf{T}} ||\sum_{\mathrm{t}=0}^{\mathrm{T}} \mathcal{Z}_{\mathrm{t}} - \mathbf{U}\mathbf{D}_{\mathrm{t}}\mathbf{V}^{\mathbf{T}}||^2_F, \tag{10}$$

where $\mathcal{Z}_{\mathrm{t}}$ represents the user relations of type t and $\mathbf{D}_{\mathrm{t}} \in \mathbb{R}^{\mathrm{K\times K}}$ is a diagonal matrix whose diagonal elements are the $\mathrm{t^{th}}$ row of $\mathbf{T}$. The matrices $\mathbf{U}$ and $\mathbf{V}$ contains the latent dimension memberships of users jointly inferred across different relationship types. If $\mathcal{Z}_t \forall t$ is symmetric then $\mathbf{U} = \mathbf{V}$. The matrix $\mathbf{T}$ contains the contribution of each relation type to different dimensions. For example, a high value of $\mathbf{t_2}$ signifies that high-scoring users in $\mathbf{u_2}$ form connections with high-scoring users in $\mathbf{v_2}$ through relationship type 2. The latent features representing different kinds of pairwise relationships between users can be obtained from any linear combination of $\mathbf{U}$ and $\mathbf{V}$. For our experiments, we use $\mathbf{L} = \mathbf{U} + \mathbf{V}$ after column normalization as latent features. We combine the individual characteristics $\mathcal{I}$ and the latent features $\mathbf{L}$ to construct a feature set $F = \{\mathcal{I}, \mathbf{L}\}$ for identifying advocates for political campaigns in social media.

Method	Elections AUC	Elections F1	Gun Rights AUC	Gun Rights F1
Random	0.4983	0.1607	0.5053	0.1536
Retweet Ratio	0.5804	0.1797	0.5078	0.1118
Volume	0.6830	0.2406	0.6519	0.2332
Bag of Words	0.7379	0.3515	0.7305	0.2919
Combine	0.7599	0.3604	0.7460	0.3065
Our Method	**0.9301**	**0.6341**	**0.9431**	**0.6046**

Table 3: Comparison with different baselines.

6. IDENTIFYING ADVOCATES

In this section, we evaluate the performance of our framework by answering the following questions. How effective is our framework for identifying advocates for political campaigns on social media? How good are the characteristics group in identifying advocates? How robust is the proposed framework for variation in training sizes?

6.1 Performance Evaluation

We classify the feature set derived in Section 5 using Linear Discriminant Analysis and perform 10-fold cross validation to evaluate the performance of the framework in identifying advocates. We measure the performance using two metrics, AUC, and F1-measure and present the results in

Table 3. We have the following baselines to compare the performance of our framework.

- **Random :** We randomly assign labels to all the users.
- **Retweet Ratio [27]:** The fraction of retweets per overall tweets is used as a feature.
- **Activity :** The total number of tweets of the users, is used for as a feature.
- **Bag of Words :** We use all the words in the status messages of users as features after tf-idf weighting,
- **Combine:** We combine all the proposed baselines by concatenating all the features.

We compare the performance of the baselines and the proposed framework and illustrate the results in Table 3. Random assignment gives an AUC value of around 0.5 and the F1 measure is low for both the datasets indicating the difficulty of the problem. The retweet ratio is used to characterize the propagating behavior of biased users in [27]. We model a wider range of propagation strategies advocates employ in social media, and as we can see from Table 4, where our characterizations of propagation strategies outperform the retweet ratio. From Table 3, we see that advocates are more active than random users posting on the campaign. We model specific patterns in the messages based on the strategies of advocates and hence outperform this baseline that considers only the total number of messages.

The "Bag of Words" performs better than the other baselines, but the number of features here is high. We model specific strategies of advocates related to the message, propagation and community structure instead of using all the posted words, enabling us to outperform this baseline. Combining all the baselines gives a slight improvement in the performance, indicating the potential benefits of integrating heterogeneous information. The proposed framework outperforms the baselines demonstrating that it effectively models and integrates characteristics useful for identifying advocates for political campaigns. This signifies the ability of the framework in understanding the strategies and model them to effectively to identify advocates. We perform the t-test between the results of our framework and the baselines and find that the difference is significant.

In summary, we can say that our framework outperforms the baselines demonstrating that it effectively models and integrates strategies useful for identifying advocates for political campaigns. We next analyze the contributions of different characteristic groups in identifying advocates.

6.2 Contributions of Characteristic Groups

We separately select characteristics related to message strategies, propagation strategies, and community structure and present them to the classifier. We compare the performance of different characteristic groups in identifying advocates using AUC and F1 measure with 10-fold cross validation and illustrate the results in Table 4.

We first examine the performance of message strategies by combining individual characteristics and the latent features from shared content. From Table 4, we can see that the characterizations of message strategies like persuasion, emotion, focus, and shared linguistic patterns outperform random characteristics by a significant margin. This demonstrates that proposed characterizations of messages strategies contribute significantly in identifying advocates.

Method	Elections		Gun Rights	
	AUC	F1	AUC	F1
Random	0.4983	0.1607	0.5053	0.1536
Mess Strat	0.8240	0.4303	0.8517	0.4727
Prop Strat	0.8210	0.3689	0.5707	0.1904
Mess+ Prop Strat	0.8804	0.5152	0.8680	0.4934
Comm Struct	0.8918	0.5117	0.8859	0.4834
Overall	0.9301	0.6341	0.9431	0.6046

Table 4: Performance of different groups

The performance of characteristics related to propagation strategies is much higher in the dataset related to elections than in the dataset related to gun rights. This is an indication that advocates in election campaigns place more emphasis on information propagation. On combining characterizations from both message strategies with propagation strategies, we observe an improvement in performance. This demonstrates the contribution of characterizations of propagation strategies in identifying advocates.

The characteristics related to community structure perform well in both the datasets. This indicates that advocates in social media have strong relationships with other advocates of the issue and display strong interactions with each other. A combination of all the three characteristic groups performs significantly better than individual characteristic groups demonstrating the effectiveness of our framework for integrating these characterizations.

In summary, we can say that all the proposed characteristic groups contribute significantly to identifying advocates for political campaigns in social media. We next evaluate the robustness of the framework to variations of training data size and assess its effect on identifying advocates.

6.3 Performance with Varying Training Sizes

We now answer the following questions: How does the framework perform with varying proportions of training data? How effective is the framework when we use the labels of popular users, potentially more accessible, for training?

We vary the relative proportion of training and testing sizes from $\alpha = \{10\% - 90\%\}$ with increments of 10%. For each value of α, we take the mean performance of 100 random samples with $\alpha\%$ used for training and the rest for testing. We repeat the procedure for the different values of α and illustrate the results in Figure 4.

In many cases, the labels of popular users might be well known, and the labels might be therefore potentially easier to obtain. To evaluate the framework in this scenario, we take the number of followers of a user as an indication of his popularity and sort the users in decreasing number of their followers. For each value of α, we select the users in the top $\alpha\%$ of followers for training and the rest for testing and obtain the performance. We repeat the procedure for all the values of α and illustrate the results in Figure 4.We make the following observations from the figure.

The performance of the algorithm is significantly higher than the nearest baseline for all relative proportions of training data for both methods of sampling. The performance slightly increases for higher proportions of training data but is overall robust for varying size of training data. Finally, random selection of training data performs only slightly better than selecting users with a high number of followers. This demonstrates that labels of just the popular users, which are

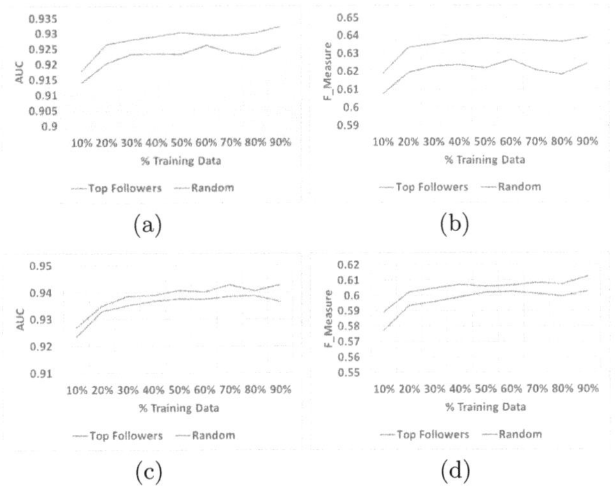

Figure 4: Effect of size of training data with training data randomly chosen and chosen ordered according to the number of followers for election dataset with (a) AUC (b) F1 measure and dataset on the gun rights with (c) AUC and (d) F1 Measure

potentially easier to obtain, can be effective in identifying advocates for political campaigns on social media.

In summary, the experiment demonstrates that the framework is robust to variation in training data size and can also effectively identify advocates for political campaigns even when only the labels of popular users are known.

7. RELATED WORK

We present the related work in three categories: the study of advocacy groups in social media, the use of social media to carry out campaigns and identification of attributes of social media users. We next survey each of them in detail.

Advocacy in social media has received considerable attention in the recent sociological literature. Obar et.al [29] surveyed advocacy organizations to analyze their social media use and stated that the ability of social media to facilitate civic engagement and foster collective action is the primary motivations. The Twitter use of nonprofit organizations was studied in [16]; communicating relevant information, building user communities and call for action were found to be their principal objectives. The behavior of advocacy groups during crises was investigated in [38], and the role of social media in organizing and distributing work related to rescue operations was discussed. The Facebook pages of advocacy groups were studied in [7], and they link behaviors such as network activity and query responses by advocacy groups to the extent and growth of their network. These works provide a qualitative understanding of the activities of advocacy organizations in social media, but do not propose models to identify individual advocates.

The use of social media to carry out campaigns has received considerable attention in literature [17, 22]. Extracting campaigns from social media using textual similarity has been studied in [22] and the authors here do not concentrate on identifying individual advocates. Crowdturfing, where paid crowdsourced workers are used to post advertisements for a product, has generated considerable interest [23, 9, 24]. Paid workers are detected by less use of emotion in their content [23], predominant use of URLs [24] and lack of interaction with other users [9]. We find that advocates in social media have high emotional and textual content in their messages and show strong communication among themselves. Substantial work has been done on the behavior of opinion leaders [3] in social media. Any social media user can try to advance an agenda on an issue without necessarily being an opinion leader.

Researchers have studied the spread of political misinformation [33] by identifying malicious links that spread through social networks. We are interested in individual users who are advocating for an issue, and they need not necessarily spread misinformation. The behavior of social media users with bias on a given political issue have been studied in [27]. The paper identifies users who consistently retweet messages from users with a particular viewpoint. We aim to identify users who actively try to advance an agenda that manifests in their distinct strategies.

Substantial efforts have been made to identify attributes of social media users to give an additional context to their posts. The properties of social relationships is shown to be beneficial in identifying user attributes across social media sites [40]. Researchers have worked on identifying political orientations of users from their retweets [39] and network connections [2]. The architecture of a web-based system to aggregate profile attributes of a user drawn from diverse social media platforms is described in [15]. These works focus on inferring different personality attributes of social media users but do not determine whether a user is an advocate for a political campaign on social media.

8. CONCLUSIONS

In this paper, we present a framework to identify advocates for political campaigns on social media. We characterize advocates through their message strategies, propagation strategies, and community structure and propose different characterizations based on them. We integrate heterogeneous information derived from these diverse characterizations and demonstrate that the framework can identify effectively advocates for political campaigns on social media. We analyze contributions of individual characteristic groups like message strategies, propagation strategies, and community structure in identifying advocates. Finally, we evaluate the performance of the framework for different proportions of training sizes and demonstrate that the framework is robust to variation in training data size. This research is in a step towards informing users before they imbibe information from these accounts and also enabling campaign managers to identify advocates to assist in digital political campaigns.

Future work can consider the detection of groups of people involved in advocacy in social media drawing from community detection methods. Advocates might use strategies other than those studied here, and investigation into the strategies will increase the understanding of their behavior. The impact of advocates on meme popularity in social media is an interesting area of future research and can give insight on the impact of their activities. Studying information seeking patterns among social media advocates of a particular political campaign can give interesting insights into interactions among members of social communities. Finally, studying the evolution of the behavior and interaction networks of advocates can provide information about the process of community formation in online social media.

9. ACKNOWLEDGEMENTS

This material is based upon work supported by, or in part by, Office of Naval Research (ONR) under grant number N000141010091.

10. REFERENCES

[1] E. Acar, D. M. Dunlavy, and T. G. Kolda. A scalable optimization approach for fitting canonical tensor decompositions. *J.Chemo*, 2011.

[2] L. Akoglu. Quantifying political polarity based on bipartite opinion networks. In *ICWSM*, 2014.

[3] S. Aral and D. Walker. Identifying influential and susceptible members of social networks. *Science*, 337(6092):337–341, 2012.

[4] A. Baruah. Namo Brigade. http://goo.gl/JKdmlP, 2014. [Online; accessed 7-May-2015].

[5] P. Bhattacharya, S. Ghosh, J. Kulshrestha, M. Mondal, M. B. Zafar, N. Ganguly, and K. P. Gummadi. Deep twitter diving: exploring topical groups in microblogs at scale. In *CSCW*. ACM, 2014.

[6] D. M. Blei, A. Y. Ng, and M. I. Jordan. Latent dirichlet allocation. *JMLR*, 2003.

[7] D. S. Bortree and T. Seltzer. Dialogic strategies and outcomes: An analysis of environmental advocacy groups' facebook profiles. *PRR*, 2009.

[8] J. E. Brower, J. H. Zar, and C. N. Von Ende. Field and laboratory methods for general ecology. 1998.

[9] C. Chen, K. Wu, V. Srinivasan, and X. Zhang. Battling the internet water army: Detection of hidden paid posters. In *ASONAM*, 2013.

[10] R. B. Cialdini. *Influence: The psychology of persuasion*. Quill New York, NY, 1993.

[11] D. M. Dunlavy, T. G. Kolda, and E. Acar. Temporal link prediction using matrix and tensor factorizations. *TKDD*, 2011.

[12] D. M. Farrell and P. Webb. Political parties as campaign organizations. 2006.

[13] I. Gilbert and T. Henry. Persuasion detection in conversation. Technical report, DTIC Document, 2010.

[14] S. González-Bailón, J. Borge-Holthoefer, and Y. Moreno. Broadcasters and hidden influentials in online protest diffusion. *American Behavioral Scientist*, page 0002764213479371, 2013.

[15] P. Gundecha, S. Ranganath, Z. Feng, and H. Liu. A tool for collecting provenance data in social media. In *KDD*, pages 1462–1465. ACM, 2013.

[16] C. Guo and G. D. Saxton. Tweeting social change: How social media are changing nonprofit advocacy. *NVS*, 2013.

[17] X. Hu, J. Tang, Y. Zhang, and H. Liu. Social spammer detection in microblogging. In *IJCAI*, 2013.

[18] D. H. Jernigan and P. A. Wright. Media advocacy: Lessons from community experiences. *JPHP*, 1996.

[19] A. Khullar and A. Haridasan. Politicians slug it out in India's first social media election. http://goo.gl/ZXZm3W, 2014. [Online; accessed 9-November-2014].

[20] D. Kim, Y. Jo, I.-C. Moon, and A. Oh. Analysis of twitter lists as a potential source for discovering latent characteristics of users. In *CHI Workshop on Microblogging*, 2010.

[21] J. M. Kleinberg. Authoritative sources in a hyperlinked environment. *JACM*, 1999.

[22] K. Lee, J. Caverlee, Z. Cheng, and D. Z. Sui. Campaign extraction from social media. *TIST*, 2014.

[23] K. Lee, P. Tamilarasan, and J. Caverlee. Crowdturfers, campaigns, and social media: Tracking and revealing crowdsourced manipulation of social media. In *ICWSM*, 2013.

[24] H. Li, A. Mukherjee, B. Liu, R. Kornfield, and S. Emery. Detecting campaign promoters on twitter using markov random fields. In *ICDM 2014*, pages 290–299, Dec 2014.

[25] Y.-R. Lin, J. Sun, H. Sundaram, A. Kelliher, P. Castro, and R. Konuru. Community discovery via metagraph factorization. *TKDD*, 2011.

[26] A. Lulla. Achtung! It's the NaMo Brigade! http://goo.gl/XeHEzf, 2014. [Online; accessed 14-December-2015].

[27] C. Lumezanu, N. Feamster, and H. Klein. # bias: Measuring the tweeting behavior of propagandists. In *ICWSM*, 2012.

[28] J. D. McCarthy and M. N. Zald. Resource mobilization and social movements: A partial theory. *AJS*, 1977.

[29] J. A. Obar, P. Zube, and C. Lampe. Advocacy 2.0: An analysis of how advocacy groups in the united states perceive and use social media as tools for facilitating civic engagement and collective action. *JIP*, 2012.

[30] A. Palmer. NRA campaign in high gear. http://goo.gl/PYBXDq, 2014. [Online; accessed 9-November-2014].

[31] J. W. Pennebaker, M. E. Francis, and R. J. Booth. Linguistic inquiry and word count: Liwc 2001. *Mahway: Lawrence Erlbaum Associates*, 2001.

[32] G. Philipsen, G. Philipsen, and T. Albrecht. A theory of speech codes. *Dev.CommTheo*, 6, 1997.

[33] J. Ratkiewicz, M. Conover, M. Meiss, B. Gonçalves, A. Flammini, and F. Menczer. Detecting and tracking political abuse in social media. In *ICWSM*, 2011.

[34] RiteTag. Twitter hashtags. http://goo.gl/X88aY7, 2014. [Online; accessed 7-August-2014].

[35] M. Robinson. NRA, PRO-GUN, GUN OWNER. http://goo.gl/OyDDGR, 2014. [Online; accessed 7-August-2014].

[36] L. Tang and H. Liu. Relational learning via latent social dimensions. In *KDD*, 2009.

[37] I. Today. Rise of the Cyber Hindu. http://goo.gl/NvxAw6, 2014. [Online; accessed 7-May-2015].

[38] J. I. White, L. Palen, and K. M. Anderson. Digital mobilization in disaster response: Self-organization of on-line pet advocates in response to hurricane sandy. In *CSCW*, 2014.

[39] F. M. F. Wong, C. W. Tan, S. Sen, and M. Chiang. Quantifying political leaning from tweets and retweets. In *ICWSM*, 2013.

[40] R. Zafarani and H. Liu. Users joining multiple sites: Friendship and popularity variations across sites. *Information Fusion*, 28:83 – 89, 2016.

Exploiting New Sentiment-Based Meta-level Features for Effective Sentiment Analysis

Sérgio Canuto
Federal University of Minas Gerais
Computer Science Department
Belo Horizonte, MG, Brazil
sergiodaniel@dcc.ufmg.br

Marcos André Gonçalves
Federal University of Minas Gerais
Computer Science Department
Belo Horizonte, MG, Brazil
mgoncalv@dcc.ufmg.br

Fabrício Benevenuto
Federal University of Minas Gerais
Computer Science Department
Belo Horizonte, MG, Brazil
fabricio@dcc.ufmg.br

ABSTRACT

In this paper we address the problem of automatically learning to classify the sentiment of short messages/reviews by exploiting information derived from meta-level features i.e., features derived primarily from the original bag-of-words representation. We propose new meta-level features especially designed for the sentiment analysis of short messages such as: (i) information derived from the sentiment distribution among the k nearest neighbors of a given short test document x, (ii) the distribution of distances of x to their neighbors and (iii) the document polarity of these neighbors given by unsupervised lexical-based methods. Our approach is also capable of exploiting information from the neighborhood of document x regarding (highly noisy) data obtained from 1.6 million Twitter messages with emoticons. The set of proposed features is capable of transforming the original feature space into a new one, potentially smaller and more informed. Experiments performed with a substantial number of datasets (nineteen) demonstrate that the effectiveness of the proposed sentiment-based meta-level features is not only superior to the traditional bag-of-word representation (by up to 16%) but is also superior in most cases to state-of-art meta-level features previously proposed in the literature for text classification tasks that do not take into account some idiosyncrasies of sentiment analysis. Our proposal is also largely superior to the best lexicon-based methods as well as to supervised combinations of them. In fact, the proposed approach is the only one to produce the best results in all tested datasets in all scenarios.

CCS Concepts

•Information systems → Document representation; •Computing methodologies → Machine learning approaches;

WSDM'16, February 22–25, 2016, San Francisco, CA, USA.
© 2016 ACM. ISBN 978-1-4503-3716-8/16/02 ...$15.00.
DOI: http://dx.doi.org/10.1145/2835776.2835821

Keywords

meta features, sentiment analysis

1. INTRODUCTION

The popularity of online forums, reviews and social networks has led numerous people to share their opinions on a wide range of subjects, including products, events, news and even daily experiences. Dealing with this massive amount of data, generated everyday on online platforms, can bring a number of new opportunities to businesses and markets. In particular, the sentiment analysis of such unstructured data can reveal how people feel about a particular product or service.

In this work, we focus on a supervised learning paradigm to deal with sentiment classification of short messages/(micro-)reviews, since it is one of the most effective and adaptable approaches for this task [18]. Given a set of training messages classified into one or more predefined sentiments/polarities, the task is to automatically learn how to classify new (unclassified) messages, using a combination of features of these messages that associate them with predefined sentiments or polarities. In particular, we focus on the supervised (binary) task of discriminating between positive and negative polarities of the messages. The reasons for this are threefold: (i) in several domains (e.g., reviews and micro-reviews), the basic motivation for people to write such messages is to provide positive or negative feedback on products, experiences and services that can be helpful to others; (ii) even in other domains in which "neutral" opinions can occur more frequently, many applications are interested in knowing only the most "polarized" opinions about certain topics (e.g., politicians, events, etc); and finally (iii), even if identifying neutral positions is important, some works (e.g., [4, 25, 33] have advocated doing this in a prior step (aka, subjectivity extraction) before determining the polarity of the message, which is our focus here.

A recent trend that has emerged in supervised approaches for text classification, that works in the data engineering level instead of in the algorithmic level, is the introduction of meta-level features[1] that can replace or work in conjunction with the the original set of (bag-of-words-based) features [7, 6, 21, 22, 27]. Such meta-level features, which are usually manually designed and extracted from other features, cap-

[1]In this paper, we will use the terms "meta-level features" and "meta-features" interchangeably.

ture intrinsic relationships among a pair (*document, class*) or a triple (*document, class, algorithm*). These meta-level features can capture insightful new information about the unknown underlying data distribution that relates the observed patterns to the associated category.

However, despite their potential, meta-level features have not been extensively studied in sentiment classification tasks. Specifically, they were not evaluated with any of the most common sentiment analysis benchmarks for this task (e.g. twitter, youtube, reviews, amazon, etc). In this paper we fulfill this gap. Moreover, inspired by recent work [6, 7, 17, 35] which takes into account the labels of training documents to generate meta-level features, we propose a new set of meta-level features based on the lazy classifier method kNN as well as freely available evidence towards the positivity or negativity of messages.

These new meta-level features exploit sentiment and distances distributions in a possibly noisy neighborhood considering the scarcity of information in short messages. In more details, we make use of BM25 [23] as similarity score in kNN, since it is an useful measure to rank documents with short messages as queries. We also exploit the neighborhood of a test example in both the training set and in a dataset containing 1.6 millions of tweets automatically labeled by its users with emoticons [14]. This methodology allow us to exploit discriminative information from different domains, even in noisy ones, like the large twitter dataset with emoticons. The last additional evidence we exploit is taken from the weighted sentiment polarity of the nearest neighbors by using recent lexicon-based methods to infer the message's polarity towards a sentiment [2, 19, 31]. In our experiments our approach outperformed by large margins all baselines which include: (i) the traditional Bag-of-word representation; (ii) the sets of meta-features proposed previously in the literature for general text classification tasks; (iii) the best lexicon-based methods; and (iv) supervised ensembles of lexicon-based methods. In fact, our approach was the sole one to win in all (nineteen) tested datasets.

In sum, the main contributions of this paper are: (i) the proposition and evaluation of new meta-level features especially designed for sentiment analysis of short messages; (ii) a comprehensive study on the use of ours and previously proposed kNN-based meta-level features in this context; (iii) a simple method to easily extract discriminative information from highly noisy external data.

This paper is organized as follows. In Section 2 we discuss related work. In Section 3 we introduce our proposed meta-level features and the state-of-art kNN-based meta-level features. In Section 4 we present the experimental setup and discuss the experimental results. Finally, in Section 5 we present our conclusions and highlight future work.

2. RELATED WORK

2.1 Sentiment Analysis

Current sentiment extraction tasks differ according to the types of classes predicted (positive or negative, subjective or objective), the classification techniques used, and the considered classification levels, which comprehend sentence, aspect or document level [12]. Each level depends on the granularity of the sentiment class, which may be predicted to whole documents (for document-level), to individual sentences (for sentence-level) or to specific aspects of entities (for aspect-level). In this work, we focus at the sentiment detection of messages composed of one or a few short sentences, such as tweets, comments and (micro-)reviews.

Regarding the document classes, there is an active research on subjectivity classification [5, 34, 29, 3], in which the goal is to discriminate objective messages from subjective ones. Some works separate subjective sentences from objective ones and then classify the polarity (positive or negative) of the opinions expressed in the subjective sentences [4, 25, 33]. These efforts present empirical evidence that performing a simultaneous classification between positive, negative and objective (neutral) messages is worst than a two-step approach that filters the objective messages first.

Regarding the classification techniques, most methods can be categorized into one of two main groups: supervised approaches [16], which use a wide range of features and labeled data for training sentiment classifiers, and lexicon-based approaches [2, 19, 31], which make use of pre-built lexicons of words weighted with their sentiment orientations to determine the overall sentiment of a given document. Specifically, recent methods such as Vader [19] and SentiStrength [31] rely on linguistic clues (e.g., punctuation and words that intensify or invert polarity) and on a dictionary of words provided with their sentiment scores, manually labeled [2]. Their dictionaries differ, since Vader's lexicons include most internet slag terms and SentiStrength rely on the combination of diverse available lexicon dictionaries. They also differ on their scoring scheme, since SentiStrength [31] weights the sentiment of a message by attributing to it the sentiment score of the most positively (or negatively) classified word in the message, and Vader sums the scores in of the words in the message. Instead of relying on a dictionary of lexicons, SentiWordNet [2] explores relationships between unambiguous polarized (or neutral) "concepts" in order to find the average polarity of close concepts associated to a message. Therefore, terms like dog and bite (both representing neutral concepts in SentiWordNet) appearing in the same message could eventually be expanded with a more emotional term like hurt, which holds a negative polarity. We choose to use these three lexicons as the basis to construct our meta-level features as they showed to be effective for sentiment detection in recent benchmark comparison studies [15, 1, 28].

Overall, unlike the above efforts, most supervised approaches are direct applications of the traditional classification techniques. Thus, to the best of our knowledge, our effort is the first to propose specific meta-level features for text classification in the sentiment analysis domain.

2.2 Meta-Level Features for Text Classification

Meta-features have been proposed to improve the effectiveness of text classification. They can be based on ensemble of classifiers [10, 32], derived from clustering methods [21, 27] or from the instance-based kNN method [17, 35].

Meta-features derived from ensembles exploit the probability distribution over all classes generated by each of the individual classifiers composing the ensemble [32]. In [10] other ensemble-based meta-features were also used, includ-

[2]the sentiment of each word was manually adjusted. In Vader, for example, each word was manually scored with 9 degrees of valence (between extremely positive to extremely negative).

ing: the entropies of the class probability distributions and the maximum probability returned by each classifier. This scheme was found to perform better than using only probability distributions. The most recent effort regarding sentiment analysis towards this kind of meta-feature uses only the scores of the first level classifier's output [18, 8].

Clustering techniques may also be used to derive meta-features. In this case, the feature space is augmented using clusters derived from a previous clustering step considering both the labeled and unlabeled data [27, 21]. The idea is that clusters represent higher level "concepts" in the feature space, and the features derived from the clusters indicate the similarity of each example to these concepts. In [27] the largest n clusters are chosen as representatives of the major concepts. Each cluster c contributes with a set o meta-features like, for instance, binary feature indicating if c is the closest of the n clusters to the example, the similarity of the example to the cluster's centroid, among others. In [21] the number of clusters is chosen to be equal to the predefined number of classes and each cluster corresponds to an additional meta-feature.

Recently, several works [6, 7, 17, 35] have been proposed to use kNN as the main tool to generate meta-features. Despite the fact that these meta-features are not created based on an ensemble of classifiers, they differ from the previously presented meta-features derived from clusters because they explicitly capture information from the labeled set. In more details, [17, 35] reported good results by designing meta-features that make a combined use of local information (through kNN-based features) and global information (through category centroids) in the training set. This work is extended in [7] by the use of meta-features derived from the class distribution, the entropy and the within-class cohesion observed in the k nearest neighbors of a given test document x. In order to make the meta-feature generation viable for huge data, [6] proposed a GPU-based kNN implementation for highly dimensional and sparse textual data.

The kNN-based meta features proposed in this work differ from the ones presented in previous works [17, 35] due to the fact that we focus on engineering meta-features for sentiment analysis in short messages. Besides using BM25 as similarity measure, we explore additional information from a large dataset containing 1.6 millions of emoticons [14] and from recently proposed lexicon-based methods [31, 19, 2] to infer the document's polarity.

In next section we describe in details previously proposed meta-level features for general text classification tasks, as well as our newly proposed kNN-based ones for sentiment analysis. As we shall see, our proposed meta-features are more effective then the previous ones in most datasets as they consider intrinsic aspects of the sentiment analysis of short messages.

3. META-LEVEL FEATURES

Let $\mathcal{X}$ and $\mathcal{C}$ denote the input (feature) and output (class) spaces, respectively. Let $\mathbb{D}_{train} = \{(x_i, c_i) \in \mathcal{X} \times \mathcal{C}\}|_{i=1}^{n}$ be the training set. Recall that the main goal of supervised classification is to learn a mapping function $h : \mathcal{X} \mapsto \mathcal{C}$ which is general enough to accurately classify examples $x' \notin \mathbb{D}_{train}$.

3.1 Gopal et al's Meta-Level Features

The kNN-based meta-level features proposed in [17], are designed to replace the original input space $\mathcal{X}$ with a new informative and compact input space $\mathcal{M}$. Therefore, each vector of meta-level features $m_f \in \mathcal{M}$ is expressed as the concatenation of the following sub-vectors, which are defined for each example $x_f \in \mathcal{X}$ and category $c_j \in \mathcal{C}$ for $j = 1, 2, \ldots, |\mathcal{C}|$.

- $\vec{v}_{\vec{x}_f}^{dist} = [dist(\vec{x}_{ij}, \vec{x}_f)]$ A k-dimensional vector whose elements $dist(\vec{x}_{ij}, \vec{x}_f)$ denote a distance score between $\vec{x}_f$ and the ith nearest class c_j neighbor of $\vec{x}_f$
- $\vec{v}_{\vec{x}_f}^{cent} = [dist(\vec{x}_j, \vec{x}_f)]$ A 1-dimensional vector where $\vec{x}_j$ is the c_j centroid (i.e., vector average of all training examples of the class c_j).

These sub-vectors are composed of distances (Euclidean, Manhattan and Cosine) that make a combined use of local information (through kNN-based features) and global information (through category centroids). More specifically, each test example is directly compared to a set of nearest labeled examples and category centroids, which are assumed to be enough to effectively characterize and discriminate categories. The intuition behind these meta-features consists in the assumption that if the distances between an example to the nearest neighbors belonging to the category c (and its corresponding centroid) are small, then the example is likely to belong to c.

Considering k neighbors and using three distance measures, the number of features in vector x_f is $(3k + 3)$ per category, and the total of $(3k + 3)|\mathcal{C}|$ for all categories. The size of this meta-level feature set is much smaller than that typically found in ATC tasks, while explicitly capturing class discriminative information from the labeled set.

3.2 Canuto et al's Meta-Level Features

Similarly to the meta-level features previously presented, the meta-features proposed in [7] are also based on nearest neighbor search. However, they go beyond by also exploiting discriminative information from the labeled set under several aspects, namely the class distribution in the neighborhood of the test example $\vec{x_f}$, the within-class cohesion and entropy.

In particular, the first key aspect of these meta-features is the fact that they exploit the continuity hypothesis which guarantees the kNN classifier's success: the existence of a mode in the class distribution of the neighborhood of $\vec{x_f}$ usually determines the category of $\vec{x_f}$. They also exploit a summarized version of the Gopal et al's meta-features through category distance quartiles instead of the full distance distribution, which reduces considerably the number of dimensions and prevents overfitting in small datasets.

Another key aspect exploited by these meta-features refers to proximities of the neighbors of $\vec{m_f}$ belonging to some class $c_i \neq c_j$ to the centroid of c_j. This directly evaluates the class cohesion in the neighborhood of $\vec{x_f}$, being an important information regarding the uncertainty level in such region of the input space. Finally, the entropy of the neighborhood and the correlation between neighbors from different classes provide additional evidence about the purity of the top ranked neighbors.

3.3 Proposed Meta-Level Features for Sentiment Analysis

Similarly to the baseline meta-level features, the proposed meta-features for sentiment analysis are based on nearest neighbor search. However, we focus on dealing with specific aspects of sentiment analysis of short messages. We use BM25 [23] for dealing with short texts as queries and exploit additional information from lexical-based methods as well as the inexpensive (though noisy) tweet messages labeled by Tweeter users with emoticons.

Given the examples in the original input space $\mathcal{X}$, the proposed vector of meta-level features $m_f \in \mathcal{M}$ is expressed as the concatenation of the following sub-vectors, which are defined for each example $x_f \in \mathcal{X}$ and category $c_j \in \mathcal{C}$ for $j = 1, 2, \ldots, |\mathcal{C}|$.

- $\vec{v}^{rawsim}_{\vec{x}_f} = [sim(\vec{x}_{ij}, \vec{x_f})]$ A k-dimensional vector produced by considering the k nearest neighbors of class c_j to the target vector x_f. More specifically, $\vec{x}_{ij}$ is the ith $(i \leq k)$ nearest neighbor to $\vec{x}_f$, and $sim(\vec{x}_{ij}, \vec{x_f})$ is the a similarity score (BM25 or cosine) between them. Thus, k meta-level features are generated to represent x_f.

- $\vec{v}^{cagglex}_{\vec{x}_f} = [\sum sim(\vec{x}_{ij}, \vec{x_f}) * p_{ij}]$ A 1-dimensional vector produced by considering the weighted polarity sum of the k nearest neighbors of x_f that belong to the class c_j. The similarity $sim(\vec{x}_{ij}, \vec{x_f})$ between $\vec{x}_f$ and its ith $(i \leq k)$ nearest neighbor $\vec{x}_{ij}$ is used to weight the polarity p_{ij} of the document x_{ij}. The polarity score p_{ij} (that represents the valence of a positive sentiment, for example) is given by a lexical-based method.

- $\vec{v}^{maxminlex}_{\vec{x}_f} = [max(sim(\vec{x}_{ij}, \vec{x_f}) * p_{ij}), min(sim(\vec{x}_{ij}, \vec{x_f}) * p_{ij})]$ A 2-dimensional vector produced by considering the maximum and minimum document weighted polarity of the k nearest neighbors of the target vector x_f that belong to the class c_j. The similarity $sim(\vec{x}_{ij}, \vec{x_f})$ between $\vec{x}_f$ and its ith $(i \leq k)$ nearest neighbor $\vec{x}_{ij}$ is used to weight the polarity p_{ij} of the document x_{ij}.

- $\vec{v}^{agglex}_{\vec{x}_f} = [\sum sim(\vec{t}_i, \vec{x_f}) * p_i)]$ A 1-dimensional vector with the weighted polarity sum of the k-nearest neighbor's polarities. The similarity $sim(\vec{t}_i, \vec{x_f})$ between $\vec{x}_f$ and its ith $(i \leq k)$ nearest neighbor $\vec{t}_i$ is used to weight the polarity p_i of the document t_i

- $\vec{v}^{rawlex}_{\vec{x}_f} = [p_f]$ A 1-dimensional vector produced by one of the (possibly many) outputs of a lexical-based method. The output p_f corresponds to the polarity score of the document represented by x_f.

With exception of $\vec{v}^{rawlex}_{\vec{x}_f}$, all remaining described vectors depend on a similarity measure in order to find the nearest neighbors. We generate our meta-features with two similarity scores: Cosine (i.e., $sim(\vec{x}, \vec{q}) = Cosine(\vec{x}, \vec{q})$) and BM25 (i.e., $sim(\vec{x}, \vec{q}) = BM25(\vec{x}, \vec{q})$). Cosine similarity is one of the most popular similarity measures applied to text documents in numerous information retrieval, text classification and clustering applications. Furthermore, it produced very good results when applied together with bag-of-words weighted with TF-IDF in previous meta-features studies [7]. We also compute the vectors using the BM25 similarity score due to its effectiveness on dealing with short queries in information retrieval, which is the case when dealing with short messages as queries for kNN. These two similarity scores are fundamentally different, since BM25 computes the similarity based on terms in a query document appearing in other documents, regardless the additional terms that are not in the query document. On the contrary, cosine similarity considers all terms from both compared documents, since it is symmetrical.

The vectors were grouped into 4 categories, considering whether they use only the polarity information (RAWLEX), only the neighborhood distance information (RAWSIM), the combination of distances with polarities (KNNLEX) and information generated from the external data containing tweet messages labeled with emoticons, instead of the original training data (TWEMOT). Table 1 summarizes the names we give to different groups of meta-features depending on the variations of these factors.

Group	Description
RAWSIM	Vector $\vec{v}^{rawsim}_{\vec{x}_f}$
RAWLEX	Vector $\vec{v}^{rawlex}_{\vec{x}_f}$
KNNLEX	Vectors $\vec{v}^{cagglex}_{\vec{x}_f}$, $\vec{v}^{maxminlex}_{\vec{x}_f}$ and $\vec{v}^{agglex}_{\vec{x}_f}$
TWEMOT	Vectors $\vec{v}^{cagglex}_{\vec{x}_f}$, $\vec{v}^{maxminlex}_{\vec{x}_f}$, $\vec{v}^{agglex}_{\vec{x}_f}$ and $\vec{v}^{rawsim}_{\vec{x}_f}$ computed using only the neighborhood from the tweet dataset with emoticons.

Table 1: Groups of proposed meta-features.

As described in Table 1, the proposed meta-features are able to capture discriminative information from the labeled set using different sources of information. We now further analyze the proposed groups of meta-features, describing which characteristics of the data each of them aim to exploit.

For the RAWSIM features, each test example $\vec{x}_f$ is directly compared to a set of nearest labeled examples. The intuition behind these meta-features consists in the assumption that if the distances between an example to the nearest neighbors belonging to a category c are small, then the example is likely to belong to c.

The RAWLEX features are the raw scores produced by outputs of the used lexicon-based methods. All used methods produce one score for positive polarity and another for negative polarity. Each one of these raw scores correspond to a one-dimensional vector $\vec{v}^{rawlex}_{\vec{x}_f}$.

The KNNLEX features also use the neighborhood distances, but they are only employed for finding and weighting the polarity of the nearest neighbors. More specifically, the meta-features $\vec{v}^{cagglex}_{\vec{x}_f}$ supply the agglomerated polarity of the category c's neighbors. This meta-feature obtains, for each neighbor, the polarity valence p towards a sentiment (e.g., negativity score) using a lexicon-based method (e.g., SentiStrength). The weighted sum of these polarities can be seen as the summarization of the distribution of the neighbor's polarities. If the neighbors of a test document $\vec{x}_f$ have very high values for the positive polarity p and they are also very close to $\vec{x}_f$, the sentiment of $\vec{x}_f$ is likely to be positive. This summarization can be useful, since the lexical-based approaches usually have a small coverage of words which often are not in a particular message. The exploitation of the neighborhood of this message aims at easing this coverage problem by looking at the words of the neighbors.

Another way to analyze the neighborhood polarity distribution is by looking at the maximum and minimum values. The meta-features $\vec{v}^{maxminlex}_{\vec{x}_f}$ extract this additional information to complement the agglomerated polarity previously described. The final meta-feature belonging to the KNNLEX group is the agglomeration $\vec{v}^{agglex}_{\vec{x}_f}$. It differs from the other meta-features because it does not use the labeled information, but just summarizes the polarity of the k nearest neighbors without looking at their categories. By ignoring the category of the neighbors, it is possible to exploit the existence of a mode in the polarity distribution of the neighborhood.

Most meta-features depend on a training set in which we find the k-nearest neighbors. We generate them using the traditional training set (that follows the same distribution of the test documents). Besides this traditional training set, we use an additional very large dataset with 1.6 million tweet messages with emoticons inserted by the users (which can be considered as noisy labels) as a training set. The group of meta-features TWEMOT comprises all the proposed kNN-based meta-features generated using this twitter training set. There are two factors that make possible the exploration of this highly noisy tweet dataset. First, we exclude all messages from the tweet dataset that are not in the neighborhood of a query document $\vec{x}_f$. By doing so, we ignore a huge volume of messages that are not close to the domain of interest in which $\vec{x}_f$ is inserted. The second factor is related to the fact that the neighborhood's information is summarized with similarity scores. This summarization with fewer features can be easily evaluated regarding its discriminative power.

Considering k_t neighbors from the tweet dataset, k_o neighbors from the original training data, the $|\mathcal{C}|$ sentiment categories, 2 similarity measures (cosine and BM25) and p polarity scores, the number of features generated will be $2|\mathcal{C}|(k_t + k_o) + p + 4(1 + 3|\mathcal{C}|)$. Specifically, k_t meta-features per category are generated by the vector $\vec{v}^{rawsim}_{\vec{x}_f}$ derived from the k_t nearest neighbors from the tweet dataset. Since we use two similarity measures, we will generate one vector for each similarity measure which gives us $2k_t$ meta-features per category, or $|\mathcal{C}|2k_t$. Similarly, we generate $2k_o$ meta-features driven by the original labeled data, which gives us $2|\mathcal{C}|(k_t + k_o)$ meta-features generated by $\vec{v}^{rawsim}_{\vec{x}_f}$. The equation also accounts for p polarity scores given by each single lexical-based method output, as described in $\vec{v}^{rawlex}_{\vec{x}_f}$.

The vectors $\vec{v}^{cagglex}_{\vec{x}_f}$ and $\vec{v}^{maxminlex}_{\vec{x}_f}$ provide three meta-features per category and $\vec{v}^{agglex}_{\vec{x}_f}$ provides only one meta-feature, generating the total of $1+3|\mathcal{C}|$ meta-features. Since they are generated using two similarity measures and two different datasets (original training dataset and tweets dataset), the final number of features driven from these vectors are $4(1+3|\mathcal{C}|)$.

In any case, the size of this meta-level feature set is much smaller than that typically found in bag-of-words representation, while explicitly capturing class discriminative information from the labeled set, polarity scores and external data.

4. EXPERIMENTAL EVALUATION

We start by presenting the experimental setup (Section 4.1) followed by the experimental results using distinct sets of meta-features (Section 4.2).

4.1 Experimental Setup

4.1.1 Textual Datasets

In order to evaluate the meta-feature strategies, we use a recent and publicly available benchmark [28] with nineteen real-world textual datasets gathered from different works. They are named aisopos_tw [13], debate [9], narr_tw [24], pappas_ted [26], pang_movie [25], sanders_tw[3], ss_bbc [30], ss_digg [30], ss_myspace [30], ss_rw [30], ss_twitter [30], ss-youtube [30], stanford_tw [14], semeval_tw[4], vader_amzn [19], vader_movie [19], vader_nyt [19], vader_tw [19] and yelp_review[5]. In addition to the previously described datasets, we also exploit the information of 1.6 millions of tweets automatically labeled by its emoticons [14]. All these datasets contain short texts as documents, which are distinct from documents usually found in text classification (e.g. news and web pages).

dataset	#msgs	#feat	density	#pos	#neg
aisopos_tw	278	1493	13.0	159	119
debate	1979	3360	11.5	730	1249
narr_tw	1227	3508	11.3	739	488
pappas_ted	727	1635	11.7	318	409
pang_movie	10662	12432	13.9	5331	5331
sanders_tw	1091	3102	13.5	519	572
ss_bbc	752	5655	40.3	99	653
ss_digg	782	4015	22.2	210	572
ss_myspace	834	2639	14.7	702	132
ss_rw	705	4595	43.3	484	221
ss_twitter	2289	7777	13.8	1340	949
ss_youtube	2432	6275	12.2	1665	767
stanford_tw	359	1620	12.0	182	177
semeval_tw	3060	9087	16.4	2223	837
vader_amzn	3610	3678	11.9	2128	1482
vader_movie	10568	11980	14.0	5242	5326
vader_nyt	4946	8756	13.0	2204	2742
vader_tw	4196	7346	11.2	2897	1299
yelp_review	5000	19398	71.5	2500	2500

Table 2: Dataset caracteristics

For all datasets, we performed a traditional preprocessing task: we removed stopwords, using the standard SMART list and the standard Term Frequency-Inverse Document Frequency (TF-IDF) weighting scheme for our Bag-of-Words (BoW) representation. As previously mentioned, we consider only messages with a clear polarity (positive or negative), since our focus is on this binary classification task.

Table 2 shows some of the characteristics of the datasets used to evaluate our meta-features. The first column indicates the name of the dataset used in our experiments, the second column is the number of messages in the dataset, the third shows the number of features (words) represented in the dataset, the fourth corresponds to the average number of words (density) of a message, and the last two columns show the number of positive and negative messages, respectively.

4.1.2 Evaluation, Algorithms and Procedures

The meta-level features were compared using the MicroF_1 score, which is a standard text categorization measure[6]. In order to compute this measure, the system-made decisions on test set $\mathcal{D}$ with respect to a specific category must be divided into three groups: True Positives (TP), False Positives (FP) and False Negatives (FN), respectively. The terms positive and negative refer to the classifier's prediction, and the terms true and false refer to whether that prediction corresponds to the external judgment. The measure

[3]http://www.sananalytics.com/lab/twitter-sentiment
[4]https://www.cs.york.ac.uk/semeval-2013/task2
[5]http://www.yelp.com/dataset_challenge
[6]Results with MacroF_1 are very similar and are omitted for space reasons.

is described as:

$$F_1 = \frac{2TP}{2TP + FP + FN}$$

All experiments were executed using a 5-fold cross-validation procedure. The parameters were set via cross-validation within the training set, and the effectiveness of the algorithms running with distinct types of features were measured in the test partition. In other words, all results correspond to the effectiveness average in the 5 test partitions.

In order to evaluate the performance of different groups of features, we adopted the LIBLINEAR [11] implementation of the SVM classifier. The regularization parameter was chosen among eleven values from 2^{-5} to 2^{15} by using 5-fold cross-validation within each training dataset. The other parameter necessary to execute the experiments is the size of neighborhood used in kNN-based meta-level features. The neighborhood size k was chosen among ten values from 10 to 100 by also using 5-fold cross-validation within each training dataset. The parameters b and k_1 of the BM25 similarity score used in kNN were set to the default values 0.75 and 2 [23], respectively.

We use three recent and freely available lexicon-based classifiers Vader [19], SentiStrength [31] and SentiWordnet [2] to estimate the sentiment value of each message. Specifically, we extract the positive and negative sentiment scores of each message using these methods, along with combined and neutral scores given by Vader.

All experiments were run on a Quad-Core Intel® Xeon® E5620, running at 2.4GHz, with 16Gb RAM. The meta-features were generated using our GPU-based implementation of kNN[7]. It took only a few hours to generate all kNN-based meta-features using the mid-range NVIDIA 740 GPU, with 2Gb RAM. To compare the average results on our 5-fold cross-validation experiments, we assess the statistical significance of our results by means of a paired t-test with 95% confidence and Bonferroni correction to account for multiple tests. This test assures that the best results, marked in **bold**, are statistically superior to others. The obtained results (and their 95% confidence intervals) are described in Section 4.2. We also count the number of datasets in which a particular group of features is among the best (win count). Specifically, if one approach is statistically superior or tied to others in one dataset, it will be considered a winning approach and will receive one additional win count point. If another approach is statistically tied to a winning approach, then it will also receive an additional win count point.

4.2 Experimental Results

In this section we present results for a series of experiments to evaluate the effectiveness of meta-features. Initially, we present results comparing the effectiveness of our solution with the traditional Bag of Words (BoW) representation. Next, we compare the proposed meta-features with the state-of-the-art meta-features for text classification. Then, we compare the results of the best lexicon-based methods and a supervised ensemble of lexicon-based methods with our meta-features. Finally, we present a study of each individual group of proposed meta-features.

[7]Source code is available under GNU Public License (GPL) at http://purl.oclc.org/NET/gtknn/.

4.2.1 Proposed Meta Features versus Bag-of-Words

We start by demonstrating the effectiveness of the proposed meta-features compared to the set of original features (BoW) when both are used to train SVM classifiers and when BoW is used to train the kNN classifier. As Table 3 shows, the proposed meta-features are consistently among the best in all the nineteen datasets, while BoW only achieves the best results on eight and six datasets using, respectively, the SVM and kNN classifiers. Surprisingly, the kNN classifier performs almost as good as the state-of-art SVM classifier, which indicates the importance of the neighborhood in the sentiment analysis context.

The proposed meta-features performed better than the BoW in eleven out of the nineteen datasets. The most significant gains were up to 16%, 14%, 9%, 7%, 6% and 5.7%, respectively obtained in vader_tw, ss_twitter, narr_tw, semeval_tw, ss_youtube and ss_digg. These results justify meta-features as a replacement for the original high dimensional feature space.

dataset	Proposed	BoW (SVM)	BoW (kNN)
aisopos_tw	**89.2 ± 5.4**	**89.6 ± 2.8**	**82.8 ± 7.0**
debate	**80.0 ± 2.9**	77.4 ± 1.3	76.7 ± 1.6
narr_tw	**88.8 ± 2.0**	81.4 ± 2.7	80.3 ± 3.0
pappas_ted	**72.8 ± 3.0**	**76.1 ± 5.8**	**77.8 ± 4.3**
pang_movie	**78.6 ± 1.0**	76.9 ± 1.3	76.9 ± 1.1
sanders_tw	**86.5 ± 2.4**	**84.5 ± 3.1**	**82.3 ± 4.8**
ss_bbc	**88.6 ± 3.8**	**87.4 ± 5.6**	**87.4 ± 6.0**
ss_digg	**82.1 ± 2.6**	77.6 ± 3.7	78.1 ± 2.6
ss_myspace	**88.4 ± 1.2**	**86.2 ± 2.8**	**85.5 ± 2.4**
ss_rw	**79.8 ± 5.0**	**76.0 ± 4.1**	71.8 ± 2.1
ss_twitter	**82.6 ± 1.1**	72.8 ± 2.8	71.0 ± 0.9
ss_youtube	**86.1 ± 1.6**	81.2 ± 2.5	77.5 ± 1.1
stanford_tw	**86.9 ± 3.5**	**84.7 ± 3.0**	**83.0 ± 4.9**
semeval_tw	**85.8 ± 1.9**	80.2 ± 1.6	76.0 ± 1.2
vader_amzn	**78.0 ± 1.0**	74.1 ± 1.4	72.0 ± 2.4
vader_movie	**79.9 ± 0.6**	78.2 ± 0.6	77.8 ± 1.0
vader_nyt	**71.2 ± 2.5**	67.1 ± 1.2	65.1 ± 3.4
vader_tw	**97.2 ± 0.6**	84.0 ± 1.1	81.8 ± 0.8
yelp_review	**93.4 ± 1.1**	**93.3 ± 0.4**	83.9 ± 2.0
win count	19	8	6

Table 3: Average F_1 with the proposed meta-features, and the bag-of-words performing with SVM and kNN classifiers.

4.2.2 Proposed versus State-of-art Meta-level Features

We now compare the relative effectiveness of our proposed meta-features regarding the state-of-art literature meta-level features for general text classification. As shown in Table 4, the set of proposed meta-features for sentiment analysis is consistently among the best in all nineteen compared datasets. The second best meta-feature group, was capable of being among the best in only six datasets. This is a strong evidence towards the robustness of the proposed meta-features for the specific task of sentiment analysis of short messages. Notice particularly, the significant improvements obtained by the proposed meta-features on vader_tw, ss_twitter, vader_nyt, narr_tw and aisopos_tw with gains ranging from 8% to 13% over the best baseline.

The reasons for the low competitiveness of the baseline meta-features are twofold: (i) most sentiment analysis datasets have only a few documents with very short messages and (ii) they do not exploit any specific characteristic of sentiment analysis. The proposed meta-features address these

dataset	Proposed	Gopal et al [17]	Canuto et al [7]
aisopos_tw	**89.2 ± 5.4**	71.2 ± 6.3	82.4 ± 4.6
debate	**80.0 ± 2.9**	**78.2 ± 1.7**	76.6 ± 1.6
narr_tw	**88.8 ± 2.0**	82.2 ± 1.0	81.0 ± 2.9
pappas_ted	**72.8 ± 3.0**	**67.0 ± 10.0**	**76.6 ± 3.8**
pang_movie	**78.6 ± 1.0**	77.3 ± 0.9	77.5 ± 1.4
sanders_tw	**86.5 ± 2.4**	83.2 ± 3.2	83.4 ± 1.7
ss_bbc	**88.6 ± 3.8**	**86.1 ± 5.3**	**86.3 ± 6.3**
ss_digg	**82.1 ± 2.6**	**76.3 ± 5.2**	**78.5 ± 3.8**
ss_myspace	**88.4 ± 1.2**	**86.2 ± 4.0**	**85.7 ± 3.2**
ss_rw	**79.8 ± 5.0**	**75.2 ± 2.3**	70.9 ± 1.0
ss_twitter	**82.6 ± 1.1**	73.4 ± 2.2	73.1 ± 1.4
ss_youtube	**86.1 ± 1.6**	79.8 ± 1.7	80.2 ± 1.9
stanford_tw	**86.9 ± 3.5**	80.5 ± 4.5	**84.4 ± 3.4**
semeval_tw	**85.8 ± 1.9**	79.1 ± 1.2	71.6 ± 1.1
vader_amzn	**78.0 ± 1.0**	74.2 ± 2.2	74.0 ± 1.6
vader_movie	**79.9 ± 0.6**	78.8 ± 1.0	78.8 ± 1.0
vader_nyt	**71.2 ± 2.5**	66.1 ± 1.9	66.4 ± 2.8
vader_tw	**97.2 ± 0.6**	85.6 ± 0.8	84.2 ± 1.1
yelp_review	**93.4 ± 1.1**	87.3 ± 1.5	90.0 ± 1.3
win count	19	6	5

Table 4: Average F_1 with different groups of meta-features. Canuto et al's MF are the state-of-art kNN based meta-features.

dataset	Proposed	Lex Ensem	Best Lex
aisopos_tw	**89.2 ± 5.4**	85.2 ± 5.9	83.4 ± 6.8
debate	**80.0 ± 2.9**	70.1 ± 1.2	67.4 ± 3.3
narr_tw	**88.8 ± 2.0**	85.8 ± 2.4	81.2 ± 1.9
pappas_ted	**72.8 ± 3.0**	**72.6 ± 7.0**	**72.8 ± 3.2**
pang_movie	**78.6 ± 1.0**	68.4 ± 1.3	63.7 ± 1.0
sanders_tw	**86.5 ± 2.4**	75.5 ± 2.2	73.1 ± 3.6
ss_bbc	**88.6 ± 3.8**	**88.6 ± 4.6**	84.7 ± 1.8
ss_digg	**82.1 ± 2.6**	80.5 ± 5.4	77.2 ± 3.4
ss_myspace	**88.4 ± 1.2**	87.3 ± 1.5	82.6 ± 1.8
ss_rw	**79.8 ± 5.0**	**78.2 ± 5.6**	**78.0 ± 3.8**
ss_twitter	**82.6 ± 1.1**	79.5 ± 2.6	75.8 ± 2.9
ss_youtube	**86.1 ± 1.6**	83.0 ± 3.4	78.6 ± 1.0
stanford_tw	**86.9 ± 3.5**	79.4 ± 6.9	78.5 ± 3.2
semeval_tw	**85.8 ± 1.9**	82.9 ± 1.5	77.9 ± 1.1
vader_amzn	**78.0 ± 1.0**	71.4 ± 2.2	68.5 ± 1.6
vader_movie	**79.9 ± 0.6**	68.8 ± 1.5	64.2 ± 1.0
vader_nyt	**71.2 ± 2.5**	67.5 ± 1.6	65.4 ± 2.1
vader_tw	**97.2 ± 0.6**	**97.3 ± 0.6**	95.0 ± 1.6
yelp_review	**93.4 ± 1.1**	88.8 ± 2.0	82.7 ± 0.9
win count	19	4	2

Table 5: Average F_1 with the proposed meta-features, a simplified ensemble of the lexical-based outputs and best result of an individual lexical method.

issues by: (i) using an external tweet dataset with 1.6 millions of documents; (ii) utilizing a specific similarity score for short queries (BM25), and (iii) by exploiting lexicon-based methods which deal with sentiment analysis specificities.

4.2.3 *Proposed versus Lexical Approaches*

We now compare the relative effectiveness of our proposed meta-features in comparison to a simplified ensemble using lexical-based methods [2, 19, 31] as first level classifiers, in which their outputs are combined with the SVM classifier. We also use the individual classification of the best unsupervised lexical method as baseline. As show in Table 5, our approach outperformed by large margins both, the lexical ensemble and the best unsupervised method, in various situations, with gains over the best baseline ranging from 9% to 16% in six datasets, namely vader_movie, pang_movie, debate, sanders_tw, stanford_tw and vader_amzn. The most significant gains were on our two biggest datasets vader_movie and pang_movie, with 16% and 15% respectively, which is an evidence that the proposed meta-features can extract more discriminative information from large training datasets.

The results of the best lexical unsupervised method (last column of Table 5) are tied to the supervised methods in only two datasets: pappas_ted and ss_rw, some of the smallest ones. However, the best unsupervised approach could achieve results superior to 75% of effectiveness in twelve of the nineteen datasets, a significant fact, as it does not use any domain-specific labeled information to classify messages. This demonstrates why and how this type of source can produce useful and supplementary information to be exploited in other approaches. Finally, exploiting the lexical approaches in a supervised manner (the Lexical ensemble) helped to improve results substantially in the most datasets, achieving gains about 7% on pang_movie, vader_movie, semeval_tw and yelp_review. This further justifies the use of such information in our meta-features.

4.2.4 *Similarity Measure for the Proposed Meta-level Features*

In this experiment, we investigate the role and the impact of the two used similarity functions – cosine and BM25 – in our results. Table 6 shows that using BM25 to deal with the similarity of short messages is in fact better than using the cosine similarity, since it is consistently better or tied with the cosine results. In all datasets, BM25 never performs worse than cosine, with small but statistically significant gains up to 2% in six datasets. It is important to point out that the these statistically significant gains are present only in datasets with relatively small density.

dataset	COSINE	BM25
aisopos_tw	**88.2 ± 6.5**	**90.0 ± 6.9**
debate	79.0 ± 2.8	**80.6 ± 2.6**
narr_tw	87.5 ± 2.7	**89.4 ± 2.1**
pappas_ted	**73.6 ± 5.7**	**74.8 ± 5.3**
pang_movie	**78.2 ± 1.1**	**78.1 ± 0.6**
sanders_tw	**86.4 ± 1.7**	**86.1 ± 3.3**
ss_bbc	**88.3 ± 4.7**	**87.4 ± 5.9**
ss_digg	**82.0 ± 2.5**	**81.0 ± 5.1**
ss_myspace	**88.7 ± 1.2**	**86.3 ± 4.3**
ss_rw	**80.4 ± 5.4**	**79.0 ± 3.5**
ss_twitter	82.1 ± 1.3	**83.0 ± 0.8**
ss_youtube	85.1 ± 1.6	**86.7 ± 1.3**
stanford_tw	**88.3 ± 6.5**	**87.5 ± 3.7**
semeval_tw	**85.8 ± 1.0**	**85.9 ± 2.4**
vader_amzn	77.3 ± 1.3	**78.2 ± 1.1**
vader_movie	**79.4 ± 1.1**	**79.5 ± 0.6**
vader_nyt	**71.6 ± 1.8**	**71.8 ± 1.7**
vader_tw	96.9 ± 0.7	**97.4 ± 0.6**
yelp_review	**92.6 ± 0.9**	**92.9 ± 0.9**
win count	13	19

Table 6: Average F_1 of the proposed meta-features generated using only cosine or BM25 as similarity scores.

4.2.5 *Analysis of the Proposed Groups of Meta Features*

In this section we investigate the quality of each proposed group of meta-level features in isolation as well as the supplementary information they bring to other groups. Table 7 shows the effectiveness of the SVM classifier trained with each group of the proposed meta-features in isolation. As can be seen, all groups achieved relatively good results in iso-

dataset	RAWLEX	RAWSIM	KNNLEX	TWEMOT
aisopos_tw	**85.2 ± 5.9**	**86.4 ± 2.4**	**83.9 ± 8.3**	**83.8 ± 5.7**
debate	70.1 ± 1.2	**79.0 ± 3.0**	**78.7 ± 2.0**	69.0 ± 1.4
narr_tw	**85.8 ± 2.4**	**82.2 ± 3.4**	**81.2 ± 2.8**	**85.3 ± 2.1**
pappas_ted	**72.6 ± 7.0**	**76.5 ± 2.5**	**65.5 ± 4.3**	**74.8 ± 6.0**
pang_movie	68.4 ± 1.3	**77.5 ± 0.7**	**77.1 ± 0.4**	65.5 ± 1.2
sanders_tw	75.5 ± 2.2	**82.7 ± 3.1**	**83.5 ± 3.5**	74.6 ± 2.8
ss_bbc	**88.6 ± 4.6**	**86.5 ± 6.1**	**86.7 ± 5.8**	**87.7 ± 5.9**
ss_digg	**80.5 ± 5.4**	**78.3 ± 2.4**	**74.9 ± 2.7**	**77.1 ± 1.8**
ss_myspace	**87.3 ± 1.5**	**85.6 ± 2.1**	**85.4 ± 3.5**	**87.2 ± 3.2**
ss_rw	**78.2 ± 5.6**	**72.6 ± 2.8**	**72.8 ± 2.4**	**71.4 ± 4.1**
ss_twitter	**79.5 ± 2.6**	73.7 ± 2.7	72.6 ± 2.0	**78.2 ± 2.6**
ss_youtube	**83.0 ± 3.4**	**78.8 ± 1.3**	**78.1 ± 2.0**	**81.2 ± 1.3**
stanford_tw	**79.4 ± 6.9**	**81.1 ± 3.9**	**83.3 ± 6.4**	**80.5 ± 8.0**
semeval_tw	**82.9 ± 1.5**	78.0 ± 1.3	77.3 ± 2.0	**80.8 ± 2.5**
vader_amzn	**71.4 ± 2.2**	**73.4 ± 1.3**	**75.0 ± 2.4**	66.3 ± 1.1
vader_movie	68.8 ± 1.5	**78.3 ± 0.6**	**78.6 ± 0.9**	66.7 ± 1.3
vader_nyt	**67.5 ± 1.6**	**66.9 ± 2.4**	**66.4 ± 2.8**	**66.0 ± 1.4**
vader_tw	**97.3 ± 0.6**	84.7 ± 1.5	84.1 ± 1.2	89.1 ± 0.7
yelp_review	88.8 ± 2.0	**91.1 ± 0.6**	87.9 ± 0.9	79.8 ± 1.3
win count	15	16	15	12

Table 7: Average F_1 of each proposed group of meta-features in isolation.

dataset	ALL	no RAWLEX	no RAWSIM	no KNNLEX	no TWEMOT
aisopos_tw	89.2 ± 5.4	86.4 ± 6.3	86.0 ± 6.4 ↓	88.9 ± 6.7	90.7 ± 3.6
debate	80.0 ± 2.9	78.8 ± 2.4 ↓	79.9 ± 2.9	79.5 ± 2.7	80.2 ± 2.9
narr_tw	88.8 ± 2.0	86.1 ± 1.3 ↓	88.8 ± 2.4	89.1 ± 2.2	88.0 ± 1.5
pappas_ted	72.8 ± 3.0	72.5 ± 1.6	76.6 ± 5.5	69.6 ± 6.8	72.9 ± 3.3
pang_movie	78.6 ± 1.0	78.0 ± 1.0 ↓	78.2 ± 0.8	78.3 ± 0.9	78.5 ± 1.0
sanders_tw	86.5 ± 2.4	84.7 ± 2.4 ↓	85.8 ± 2.3 ↓	85.6 ± 2.6	86.2 ± 3.1
ss_bbc	88.6 ± 3.8	88.3 ± 5.3	87.9 ± 4.1	88.6 ± 4.7	86.7 ± 4.7 ↓
ss_digg	82.1 ± 2.6	80.1 ± 1.3 ↓	81.5 ± 2.8	81.8 ± 3.0	81.6 ± 3.3
ss_myspace	88.4 ± 1.2	86.2 ± 1.4 ↓	88.7 ± 1.5	89.0 ± 1.5	87.9 ± 2.7
ss_rw	79.8 ± 5.0	74.8 ± 5.1 ↓	79.7 ± 5.6	80.2 ± 4.8	80.4 ± 4.4
ss_twitter	82.6 ± 1.1	77.8 ± 3.1 ↓	83.0 ± 1.5	82.7 ± 1.0	80.9 ± 2.2 ↓
ss_youtube	86.1 ± 1.6	83.0 ± 0.9 ↓	85.8 ± 2.0 ↓	86.4 ± 1.8	84.7 ± 1.9 ↓
stanford_tw	86.9 ± 3.5	83.9 ± 5.6	86.3 ± 4.0	86.1 ± 3.0 ↓	84.7 ± 5.1 ↓
semeval_tw	85.8 ± 1.9	82.0 ± 1.2 ↓	85.8 ± 1.7	85.6 ± 1.7	85.3 ± 0.5
vader_amzn	78.0 ± 1.0	75.3 ± 2.0 ↓	76.9 ± 1.4 ↓	77.3 ± 1.3	77.5 ± 2.8
vader_movie	79.9 ± 0.6	79.3 ± 0.9 ↓	79.1 ± 1.1 ↓	79.1 ± 1.0 ↓	79.8 ± 0.6
vader_nyt	71.2 ± 2.5	69.5 ± 1.3 ↓	71.4 ± 2.0	71.2 ± 2.1	70.9 ± 2.6
vader_tw	97.2 ± 0.6	89.6 ± 1.3 ↓	97.2 ± 0.7	97.2 ± 0.7	97.3 ± 0.5
yelp_review	93.4 ± 1.1	91.1 ± 0.7 ↓	93.0 ± 1.1 ↓	92.3 ± 1.0 ↓	93.0 ± 1.1

Table 8: Average F_1 removing one group of meta-features from the full set. ↓ indicates statistically significant losses due to the removal of a meta-feature group from the full set ALL.

lation. In fact, there are ten datasets in which all the groups are statistically tied. Despite this, there is no isolated group that is consistently among the best in all datasets, and there are only two datasets in which one specific group is better than all remaining ones.

TWEMOT achieves the worst performance among the four groups, being only twelve times among the best individual groups. This is expected, since TWEMOT exploits primarily the evidence from an external dataset of tweets, labeled with emoticons. It is interesting to notice how TWEMOT and RAWLEX have similar results in most datasets. Similarly, KNNLEX and RAWSIM also share some close results. This may be due the fact that both TWEMOT and RAWLEX try to exploit external sources of information to classify messages, but KNNLEX and RAWSIM are focused primarily on exploiting the neighborhood inside the training data.

In order to further analyze the effects of possibly noisy meta-features and the supplementary information provided by the groups, we performed a new set of experiments in which we removed one group of meta-features from the full set ALL before training the SVM classifier. Table 8 shows the effects of such procedure.

The first observation is that the removal of the meta-feature group RAWLEX produced significant losses with regards to the set with ALL meta-features in most datasets. This is an evidence supporting the supplementary discriminative evidence provided by the output scores of lexical methods. This was somewhat expected, since these methods provide specific additional information about lexical clues on the message.

The second most impacting group is RAWSIM, which provides the similarity information between a message and their neighborhood. The removal of this group causes statistically significant losses in six datasets, demonstrating the supplementary nature of pure similarity scores. In three datasets, KNNLEX is capable of providing supplementary information by combining similarity scores with lexical evidence in a message's neighborhood. Although it does not produce high improvements, since RAWLEX, RAWSIM and TWEMOT already provide some of this information, the statistical significant losses demonstrate that there is additional information that can be extracted from this group in some datasets.

The removal of the TWEMOT group also produces significant losses in four datasets. This is an evidence towards the importance of the additional information exploited by the large (and noisy) tweet dataset. As we can see, the remotion of this group does not improve the effectiveness in any dataset. This is surprising – TWEMOT is capable of capturing useful classification evidence from a highly noisy dataset for some datasets, without harming the remaining ones.

As we can see, the removal of any single group does have positive impacts on the effectiveness in several datasets. This is evidence that the proposed meta-features are not inserting noise and can be included in the pool of available evidence in order to exploit additional information from the data in the hard task of sentiment analysis of short messages.

4.2.6 Importance of Groups with using $2^k r$ Factorial Design

The best way to evaluate the interactions among our four groups of meta-features is by doing an analysis of all 2^k possible combinations of groups for each dataset[8]. By replicating the experiments with each possible combination (using 5-fold cross validation), we can also evaluate the effects of uncontrollable external factors. We follow the standard quantitative approach called $2^k r$ factorial design [20] to analyze the effects of the individual groups of meta-features, as well as the effectiveness improvements produced by their interactions.

The first step to perform a $2^k r$ factorial design is to define the binary factors that may affect a response variable (e.g., MicroF_1 score). In our case, each factor corresponds to the presence or absence of one group of meta-features. We name the presence of each group of features as follows:

- A – Presence of KNNLEX
- B – Presence of RAWSIM
- C – Presence of TWEMOT
- D – Presence of RAWLEX

In order to summarize the analysis of the nineteen datasets with the sixteen possible combinations of our four factors, we clustered our datasets into two groups, according to the importance and interaction of meta-features in each dataset. We hope to keep similar datasets in the same group in order to summarize the results of the group. We use a simple k-means algorithm to group close datasets according to their individual factorial design results. The found groups are:

- **Group 1 datasets:** debate, pang_movie, sanders_tw, vader_amzn, vader_movie and yelp_review.
- **Group 2 datasets:** aisopos_tw, narr_tw, pappas_ted, ss_bbc, ss_digg, ss_myspace, ss_rw, ss_twitter, ss_youtube, stanford_tw, semeval_tw, vader_nyt and vader_tw.

For each dataset, we compute the percentage of variation in the results that can be explained by each individual group of meta-features and by the interaction between groups of meta-features considering each possible combination. We summarize the effects of each combination[9] on different datasets by showing its average. Table 9 shows this summarization for the two groups of datasets. In addition to the mean value, we also show the lowest and the highest value among the datasets in each group.

[8]We consider the case without any group using a "random" classifier, which returns positive with a 50% chance.

[9]The 95% confidence interval on the effects of all combinations of the tested datasets are always inferior to 1%.

Factor/ Interaction	Group 1 datasets		Group 2 datasets	
	Mean	Range	Mean	Range
A	19.5	[14.4, 24.3]	6.1	[3.8, 10.1]
B	19.8	[10.9, 26.3]	5.7	[1.1, 9.3]
C	3.3	[2.2, 5.5]	9.5	[3.2, 16.2]
D	9.6	[4.6, 17.2]	20.7	[7.3, 39.5]
A:B	17.3	[10.3, 22.4]	5.6	[3.6, 9.1]
A:C	2.6	[1.6, 3.8]	4.8	[2.8, 7.4]
B:C	2.6	[1.8, 4.2]	4.0	[2.2, 6.2]
A:D	3.9	[2.4, 8.1]	4.5	[3.2, 8.0]
B:D	3.8	[2.8, 6.3]	3.6	[1.6, 5.3]
C:D	2.2	[1.4, 3.2]	6.8	[3.8, 9.4]
A:B:C	2.9	[1.9, 4.2]	4.6	[2.6, 10.0]
A:B:D	3.9	[2.6, 6.3]	3.8	[2.4, 5.6]
A:C:D	1.9	[1.4, 3.6]	4.0	[1.4, 6.0]
B:C:D	1.8	[1.2, 2.8]	3.3	[0.4, 6.2]
A:B:C:D	1.9	[1.3, 2.9]	3.0	[0.6, 5.6]
Residuals	2.8	[0.7, 5.7]	9.9	[0.6, 30.4]

Table 9: Explained percentage of result variation by individual meta-feature groups and interactions between them.

As we can see, the variation on results in the datasets of group 1 can mostly be explained by the presence of A (KNNLEX) and B (RAWSIM) in isolation. The inclusion of each one of these groups account for about 20% of all the variation in the observed results. The interaction between A:B is the third most important observed factor. In fact, the effects of A, B and A:B account for 60% of all the MicroF_1 variation. The fourth most important factor is the inclusion of D, which accounts for about 10% of the variation, showing the importance of the RAWLEX meta-features in isolation. The remaining effects, though small, account together for about 30% of the total variation in the results, which highlights the supplementarity among the proposed groups of meta-features.

Regarding the datasets in group 2, the presence of D (RAW-LEX) in isolation accounts for 20% of all the MicroF_1 variations in the experiments. The presence of C (TWEMOT) in isolation and the interaction C:D are the most important effects to explain the results. This means that the use of additional information from the lexical-based approaches and from the large tweet corpus are the most important factors for these datasets. It is important to notice that A, B and most of the interactions have a considerable participation to explain the results. The residuals (inexplicable fraction of the variation in the results) are quite high (about 10%) on the second group. This may be due the fact that most of the datasets on the second group are small, which leads to higher variability when classifying samples from them. Since they are more likely to suffer from overfitting due to shortage of training information, their dependence on external data (provided by RAWLEX and TWEMOT) is expected.

5. CONCLUSIONS AND FUTURE WORK

In this paper we proposed new meta-level features for sentiment analysis, especially for the case of short messages. We experimentally compared them with (i) the original features (bag-of-words); (ii) previously proposed state-of-the-art meta-features found in the literature for automatic text classification; (iii) state-of-the-art lexicon-based sentiment analysis methods; and (iV) supervised ensembles of lexicon-based methods.

Our controlled experiments with these new meta features on nineteen benchmark datasets showed significant effectiveness improvements in most datasets over all baselines. In fact, our proposed approach was the best one in all tested datasets and scenarios, with no other approach getting close to this result. This provides strong evidence towards the benefits of using the more compact and informative space of features proposed in this paper to replace highly dimensional bag-of-words representation. By introducing meta-level features that effectively and efficiently capture important information from highly noisy external domains while keeping the standard formulation of the automated classification problem, we enable our solution to be applied in a number of different sentiment analysis scenarios.

We hope this study provides useful insights into how to enhance the performance of sentiment analysis by improving the representation schemes for instances, categories and their relationships. A line of future research would be to explore our meta features with other classification algorithms and feature selection techniques in different sentiment analysis tasks, such as scoring movies or products according to their related reviews.

6. ACKNOWLEDGMENTS

This work was partially supported by the Brazilian government through CNPq, CAPES and FAPEMIG.

7. REFERENCES

[1] M. Araújo, P. Gonçalves, F. Benevenuto, and M. Cha. ifeel: A system that compares and combines sentiment analysis methods. In *WWW'14*, 2014.

[2] S. Baccianella, A. Esuli, and F. Sebastiani. Senti wordnet 3.0: An enhanced lexical resource for sentiment analysis and opinion mining. In *LREC'10*, 2010.

[3] C. Banea, R. Mihalcea, J. Wiebe, and S. Hassan. Multilingual subjectivity analysis using machine translation. In *EMNLP'08*, pages 127–135, Stroudsburg, PA, USA, 2008.

[4] L. Barbosa and J. Feng. Robust sentiment detection on twitter from biased and noisy data. In *COLING '10*, pages 36–44, Stroudsburg, PA, USA, 2010.

[5] P. Biyani, S. Bhatia, and C. Caragea. Using non-lexical features for identifying factual and opinionative threads in online forums. *Knowledge-Based Systems*, 69(0):170 – 178, 2014.

[6] S. Canuto, G. Marcos, W. Santos, T. Rosa, and M. Wellington. Efficient and scalable metafeature-based document classification using massively parallel computing. In *Proc. SIGIR*, 2015.

[7] S. Canuto, T. Salles, M. A. Gonçalves, L. Rocha, G. Ramos, L. Gonçalves, T. Rosa, and W. Martins. On efficient meta-level features for effective text classification. In *CIKM'14*, pages 1709–1718, 2014.

[8] N. F. da Silva, E. R. Hruschka, and E. R. H. Jr. Tweet sentiment analysis with classifier ensembles. *Decision Support Systems*, 66(0):170 – 179, 2014.

[9] N. A. Diakopoulos and D. A. Shamma. Characterizing debate performance via aggregated twitter sentiment. In *SIGCHI'10*, pages 1195–1198. ACM, 2010.

[10] S. Dzeroski and B. Zenko. Is combining classifiers with stacking better than selecting the best one? *Machine Learning*, 54(3):255–273, 2004.

[11] R.-E. Fan, K.-W. Chang, C.-J. Hsieh, X.-R. Wang, and C.-J. Lin. LIBLINEAR: A library for large linear classification. *Journal of Machine Learning Research*, 9:1871–1874, 2008.

[12] R. Feldman. Techniques and applications for sentiment analysis. *Commun. ACM*, 56(4):82–89, Apr. 2013.

[13] Fotis Aisopos. Manually annotated sentiment analysis twitter dataset ntua. www.grid.ece.ntua.gr, 2014.

[14] A. Go, R. Bhayani, and L. Huang. Twitter sentiment classification using distant supervision. Technical report, Stanford, December 2009.

[15] P. Gonçalves, M. Araújo, F. Benevenuto, and M. Cha. Comparing and combining sentiment analysis methods. In *COSN'13*, 2013.

[16] P. Gonçalves, D. H. Dalip, H. Costa, M. A. Gonçalves, and F. Benevenuto. On the combination of "off-the-shelf" sentiment analysis methods. In *SAC'16*. ACM, 2016.

[17] S. Gopal and Y. Yang. Multilabel classification with meta-level features. In *SIGIR'10*, 2010.

[18] A. Hassan, A. Abbasi, and D. Zeng. Twitter sentiment analysis: A bootstrap ensemble framework. In *SocialCom'13*, pages 357–364. IEEE, 2013.

[19] C. J. Hutto and E. Gilbert. VADER: A parsimonious rule-based model for sentiment analysis of social media text. In *ICWSM'14*, 2014.

[20] R. Jain. *The art of computer systems performance analysis - techniques for experimental design, measurement, simulation, and modeling.* Wiley professional computing. Wiley, 1991.

[21] A. Kyriakopoulou and T. Kalamboukis. Using clustering to enhance text classification. In *SIGIR'07*, pages 805–806, 2007.

[22] A. Kyriakopoulou and T. Kalamboukis. Combining Clustering with Classification for Spam Detection in Social Bookmarking Systems. RSDC '08, 2008.

[23] C. D. Manning, P. Raghavan, and H. Schütze. *Introduction to Information Retrieval.* Cambridge Press, NY, USA, 2008.

[24] S. Narr, M. Hulfenhaus, and S. Albayrak. Language-independent twitter sentiment analysis. *Knowledge Discovery and Machine Learning (KDML)*, pages 12–14, 2012.

[25] B. Pang and L. Lee. A sentimental education: Sentiment analysis using subjectivity summarization based on minimum cuts. In *ACL'04*, Stroudsburg, PA, USA, 2004.

[26] N. Pappas and A. Popescu-Belis. Sentiment analysis of user comments for one-class collaborative filtering over ted talks. In *SIGIR'13*, pages 773–776. ACM, 2013.

[27] B. Raskutti, H. L. Ferrá, and A. Kowalczyk. Using unlabelled data for text classification through addition of cluster parameters. In *ICML'02*, 2002.

[28] F. Ribeiro, M. Araújo, P. Gonçalves, F. Benevenuto, and M. A. Gonçalves. A benchmark comparison of state-of-the-practice sentiment analysis methods. *arXiv preprint arXiv:1512.01818*, 2015.

[29] F. Su and K. Markert. From words to senses: A case study of subjectivity recognition. In *COLING '08*, pages 825–832, Stroudsburg, PA, USA, 2008.

[30] M. Thelwall. Heart and soul: Sentiment strength detection in the social web with sentistrength. http://sentistrength.wlv.ac.uk/documentation/SentiStrengthChapter.pdf, 2013.

[31] M. Thelwall, K. Buckley, G. Paltoglou, D. Cai, and A. Kappas. Sentiment in short strength detection informal text. *J. Am. Soc. Inf. Sci. Technol.*, 61(12):2544–2558, Dec. 2010.

[32] K. M. Ting and I. H. Witten. Issues in stacked generalization. *J. Artif. Int. Res.*, 10(1):271–289, 1999.

[33] X. Wang, C. Zhang, and M. Wu. Sentiment classification analysis of chinese microblog network. In G. Mangioni, F. Simini, S. M. Uzzo, and D. Wang, editors, *Complex Networks VI*, volume 597 of *Studies in Computational Intelligence*, pages 123–129. Springer, 2015.

[34] J. Wiebe and E. Riloff. Creating subjective and objective sentence classifiers from unannotated texts. In *CICLing'05*, pages 486–497, Berlin, Heidelberg, 2005. Springer-Verlag.

[35] Y. Yang and S. Gopal. Multilabel classification with meta-level features in a learning-to-rank framework. *Mach. Learn.*, 88:47–68, 2012.

Mobile App Tagging*

Ning Chen*, Steven C. H. Hoi†, Shaohua Li‡, Xiaokui Xiao§
*Alibaba Group, Hang Zhou, P.R. China,
†School of Information Systems, Singapore Management University, Singapore,
‡Joint NTU-UBC Research Centre of Excellence in Active Living for the Elderly (LILY),
Nanyang Technological University, Singapore,
§School of Computer Engineering, Nanyang Technological University, Singapore
hzzjucn@gmail.com,†chhoi@smu.edu.sg,‡lishaohua@ntu.edu.sg,§xkxiao@ntu.edu.sg

ABSTRACT

Mobile app tagging aims to assign a list of keywords indicating core functionalities, main contents, key features or concepts of a mobile app. Mobile app tags can be potentially useful for app ecosystem stakeholders or other parties to improve app search, browsing, categorization, and advertising, etc. However, most mainstream app markets, e.g., Google Play, Apple App Store, etc., currently do not explicitly support such tags for apps. To address this problem, we propose a novel auto mobile app tagging framework for annotating a given mobile app automatically, which is based on a search-based annotation paradigm powered by machine learning techniques. Specifically, given a novel query app without tags, our proposed framework (i) first explores online kernel learning techniques to retrieve a set of top-N similar apps that are semantically most similar to the query app from a large app repository; and (ii) then mines the text data of both the query app and the top-N similar apps to discover the most relevant tags for annotating the query app. To evaluate the efficacy of our proposed framework, we conduct an extensive set of experiments on a large real-world dataset crawled from Google Play. The encouraging results demonstrate that our technique is effective and promising.

Keywords

Mobile app markets; app tagging; online kernel learning

1. INTRODUCTION

With the rocketing development of mobile applications (a.k.a "apps"), app market has drawn much more attention among researchers within data mining communities. App market is a new form of software repository which contains a wealth of multi-modal data associated with apps, e.g., text descriptions, screenshot images, user reviews, and so on. Such app market data is (i) large in volume; (ii) changing rapidly; and (iii) potentially useful for various stakeholders in the mobile app ecosystem. However, we discover that most mainstream app markets (e.g., Google Play, Apple App Store, Amazon Appstore, etc.) currently do not explicitly contain tags for apps. In this paper, an app tag is referred to as a keyword which indicates the core functionality, main content or key concept of an app.

App tagging can benefit different stakeholders of mobile app ecosystems. For users, app tags facilitate them browse and locate their desired apps. For developers, terse and concise tags help them elevate the possibility of their apps being discovered by users, which leads to more downloads and profits. For app platform providers, app tags are useful for various purposes, e.g., categorizing apps in a much finer granularity. App tags also help improve app search quality in practice, e.g., a recent WSDM talk [28] from Tencent MyApp (a China app market serving hundreds of millions of users) showed that mining tags can enrich query and app representations so as to improve app search engine quality. The huge potential value of app tags motivates this study.

App tagging is a nontrivial and very difficult problem. One naive way is to let humans assign tags for apps. However, it is extremely labour intensive and time-consuming to manually tag a huge number of apps (Google Play and Apple App Store have more than 1 million apps). Therefore, it has become a pressing need to develop an automatic app tagging approach. In this paper, we propose to tackle automated mobile app tagging by exploring a search-based annotation paradigm which has been proved effective for image and video tagging [22, 20, 26]. In general, our proposed search-based app tagging framework comprises two main stages. Given a novel query app without tags, the first stage goes looking for a set of apps that are semantically most similar to the query app by searching a large app database. To facilitate the similarity search process, we learn an effective app similarity function by using our proposed Averaged Adaptive Online Kernel Learning (AAOKL) algorithm which leverages multi-modal heterogeneous data in app markets. The second stage aims to automatically discover some relevant tags for the query app from the text data (e.g., "Description") of both the query app and its nearest neighbour apps. To achieve this goal, we formulate it as an automatic keywords extraction task [7], and propose an unsupervised App Tag Extraction (ATE) approach. Finally, the top-ranked tags obtained by ATE are recommended to annotate the query app.

To evaluate the efficacy of our proposed search-based app tagging framework, we conduct an extensive set of experi-

*This work was done while the first author was a PhD candidate at Nanyang Technological University, Singapore.

WSDM'16, February 22–25, 2016, San Francisco, CA, USA.
© 2016 ACM. ISBN 978-1-4503-3716-8/16/02...$15.00
DOI: http://dx.doi.org/10.1145/2835776.2835812

ments based on a real-world dataset crawled from Google Play. The encouraging results have demonstrated that our technique is effective and promising. For example, Figure 1 presents two app tagging results achieved by our proposed framework. The first row of Figure 1 shows the logos, names and categories (in Google Play) of these two apps: *Asphalt 7: Heat* and *Piano Melody Free*. The second row of Figure 1 shows top 10 tags annotated (correct ones are in red). Supplementary materials (including additional results, datasets, etc.) are publicly available at http://apptag.stevenhoi.org/.

Name: Asphalt 7: Heat **Category:** Racing	**Name:** Piano Melody Free **Category:** Education
race	songs
cars	music
car	song
races	piano music
drift	pianos
gameloft	kids
tracks	instruments
real racing	flute
racer	classical
racing experience	ear

Figure 1: Two examples showing the tagging results attained by our proposed framework (AAOKL + ATE). The correct tags are highlighted in red color.

In summary, this paper makes the following contributions:

- We investigate a new research problem of automated mobile app tagging by mining emerging mobile app market data. To the best of our knowledge, this is the first comprehensive work to address this problem;
- We propose a novel search-based app tagging framework by mining multi-modal app market data, comprising two key new techniques: (i) a new online kernel learning algorithm; and (ii) a new unsupervised app tag extraction approach;
- We conduct an extensive set of experiments to evaluate the performance of our proposed auto app tagging framework on a large real-world dataset.

The rest of the paper is organized as follows: Section 2 discusses some related work; Section 3 gives the problem formulation; Section 4 introduces the proposed search-based app tagging framework; Section 5 presents the dataset used in this work; Section 6 shows the empirical results; Section 7 discusses some limitations and threats to validity; finally Section 8 concludes this paper.

2. RELATED WORK

In this section, we group related studies into three categories, and survey the literature of each category in detail.

2.1 App Markets Mining and Analysis

App markets contain a wealth of multi-modal data associated with apps, which is potentially useful for different app ecosystem stakeholders. In recent years, there are emerging studies on mining app markets data to facilitate various applications, such as app reviews mining and analysis [4], app recommendation [27], and so on. Although the nature of data used in the above studies is similar to ours, the techniques used and research goals are very different. Our work aims to use the knowledge discovered from app markets data to automatically tag apps with suitable keywords.

To the best of our knowledge, there is one previous study which is closely related to our work. Chen et al. [3] studied the problem of modeling high-level mobile app similarity and presented a framework named *SimApp* to tackle this problem. Generally speaking, our work differs from their work mainly in that we improve the *SimApp* framework and further combine it with a novel app tag extraction approach to address a different task, i.e., automatic app tagging.

2.2 Search-based Annotation

In the last few years, search-based annotation paradigm has been applied to a variety of media types, e.g., images [19, 20, 22], faces [18, 17], videos [26], and so on. For example, Wu et al. [22] proposed an online learning framework to optimize distance metric for search-based image annotation by mining a mass of social images. Zhao et al. [26] presented a data-driven video annotation framework which (i) first retrieves visual duplicates; (ii) then recommends representative tags.

While similar in spirit, our work differs in three aspects: (i) for our search-based app tagging, the feature representation of an app is quite different from that of an image (or video); (ii) our work explores a very different technique, i.e., online kernel learning, to improve the similarity search process in our framework. (iii) we propose a more advanced tag extraction approach rather than a simple majority voting to resolve our unique and challenging app tagging task.

2.3 Online Learning

We propose to learn the app similarity function using online learning techniques [9], a family of efficient and scalable machine learning algorithms, which has found promising results for many large-scale applications, such as classification and regression [8], multimedia search [23], social media, cybersecurity, and so on. Our work differs from the existing studies in that (i) we formulate and solve a challenging problem in a new application domain with distinct features; (ii) unlike traditional classification tasks, our online kernel learning aims to learn an optimal combination of multiple kernel functions from multi-modal data in an online fashion.

This work is also related to our previous study in [3], which proposed an Online Kernel Weight Learning (OKWL) algorithm that follows the first-order optimization, i.e., online gradient descent, which may suffer slow convergence. In this paper, we present a new improved online kernel learning algorithm named "AAOKL" by exploring averaged stochastic gradient descent [24] and adaptive subgradient methods [6] to improve the convergence rate significantly.

3. PROBLEM FORMULATION

This section formally formulates the problem of automatic app tagging. We first define a mobile app a_i as follows:

DEFINITION 1 (MOBILE APP). Each mobile app a_i is represented by a set of n modalities: $a_i = [m_{i1}, m_{i2}, ..., m_{in}]$, where each $m_{ij} (1 \leq j \leq n)$ denotes one modality (feature type) of mobile app a_i.

In this work, we explore the multi-modal data representation in app markets to represent an app. For example, Figure 2 shows an example of 10 modalities associated with the "YouTube" app in Google Play.

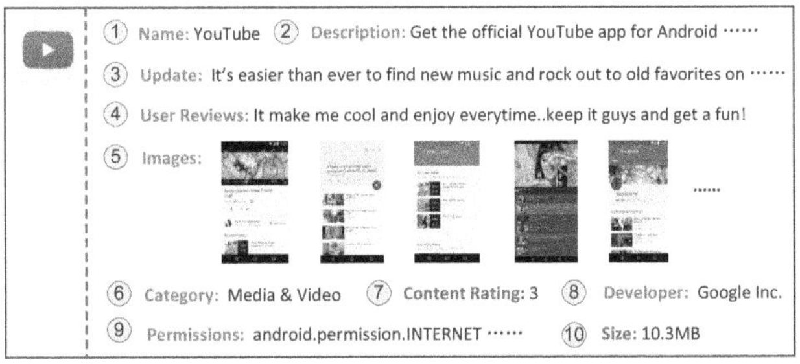

Figure 2: Example of the multi-modal information associated with the "YouTube" app in Google Play. The names of modalities are in red colour.

DEFINITION 2 (APP TAG). An app tag is a succinct and concise keyword or phrase that describes the core functionality, main content or key concept of the app.

According to Definition 2, an *app tag* should be terse and concise. Therefore, in this work, we restrict an *app tag* to be unigram or bigram ("term" in short). To better understand our definition of *app tag*, we use the tagging results shown in Figure 1 for illustration. For example, "songs", "music" and "piano music" are considered to be tags of the app *Piano Melody Free* in our problem, since they indicate the main content (and functionality) of this app, while "kids" and "flute" do not. Note that, some terms in the *Category* and *Name* attributes of an app can also be viewed as its tags, e.g., "racing" is a tag of the game *Asphalt 7: Heat*. However, in this work, we focus on automatically discover more semantic tags beyond *Category* and *Name* of apps.

DEFINITION 3 (AUTOMATIC APP TAGGING). Given an app a_i, the goal of automatic app tagging is to automatically assign a list of tags to a_i by exploiting the metadata of both app a_i and a set of its semantically similar apps $\mathcal{S}(a_i)$.

In our problem, we aim to use the metadata of (i) a target app a_i; and (ii) a set of nearest neighbour apps of a_i together to discover some tags to annotate app a_i. We adopt such scheme since (1) it is often difficult to automatically find meaningful tags only relying on an app's own metadata, especially when the metadata is limited; and (2) we hope that the metadata of those nearest neighbor apps can help provide more knowledge and clues to improve the quality of the target app's tags. In this work, the metadata used for extracting app tags refers to the "Description" and "Update" (changes of the latest version) text of apps.

Remark. This work focuses on automatically discovering app tags (as defined in Definition 2) by exploiting metadata of apps in app markets. We have noticed that other kinds of tags (e.g., tags based on users' searching intentions) can be mined from other data sources (e.g., users' searching logs), which however is out of the main scope of this work.

In general, the automatic app tagging problem faces two challenges. First, given a novel app, we require an effective app similarity function to find the query app's semantically similar apps. Second, we need an effective tag extraction scheme which can automatically discover high quality app tags from a bunch of text data. In Section 4, we will present our solutions to address both challenges in detail.

4. OUR APP TAGGING FRAMEWORK

In this section, we first give an overview of our proposed app tagging framework to address the problem stated in Definition 3, and then present each component in detail.

4.1 Overview

Figure 3 presents the architecture of our proposed framework for automatic app tagging. The framework depicted in Figure 3 is essentially a search-based app tagging approach. Solid arrows in Figure 3 present the main process of the proposed framework. Specifically, when a query app (without tags) is submitted (1), we first conduct a similarity search process (2) to find N apps that are most semantically similar to the query app from a large app database (3). Then, the "Description" and "Update" text of the query app and its' top-N similar apps (4) are utilized by our proposed App Tag Extraction (ATE) approach to automatically discover a list of terms for the query app (5). Finally, the top-ranked terms are recommended to tag the query app (6). Note that, in this work, we consider the most complex case, i.e., **no** apps in our app database contain any tags, since app tagging is currently not supported by most mainstream app markets. Dashed arrows in Figure 3 present the process for learning the app similarity function. Specifically, given the stream of training data generated from a subset of the app database (I), we develop an online kernel learning algorithm to incrementally learn the app similarity function which is then adopted in the similarity search process (II).

In general, there are two major challenges for the proposed auto mobile app tagging framework as shown in Figure 3. The first is to learn an effective app similarity function efficiently to facilitate the app similarity search. We attempt to tackle it by developing a new online kernel learning algorithm by learning from multi-modal data in app markets (see Section 4.2 and 4.3). The second challenge is to automatically extract relevant tags from a bunch of text data effectively. To solve this, we propose an unsupervised app tag extraction approach (see Section 4.4).

4.2 Measuring App Similarity by Kernels

A kernel function can be viewed as a pairwise similarity function. In this work, we follow the same set of 10 kernel functions as defined in [3], denoted as $K_k (1 \leq k \leq 10)$, to measure the app similarity in different modalities as shown in Figure 2 (For more details, please refer to [3]).

4.2.1 Name

Each app has a *name*, which is essentially a short string of characters. Therefore, we adopt the well-known string kernel [11] to measure the app similarity in this modality. Let n_i and n_j denote the names of apps a_i and a_j, respectively. We can then define the kernel on the name modality as follows:

$$K_1(a_i, a_j) = \sum_{u \in \Sigma^*} \phi_u(n_i)\phi_u(n_j)$$

where Σ^* denotes the set of all subsequences, u denotes a subsequence, and ϕ is a feature mapping function. For space limitation, please refer to [11] for more technical details.

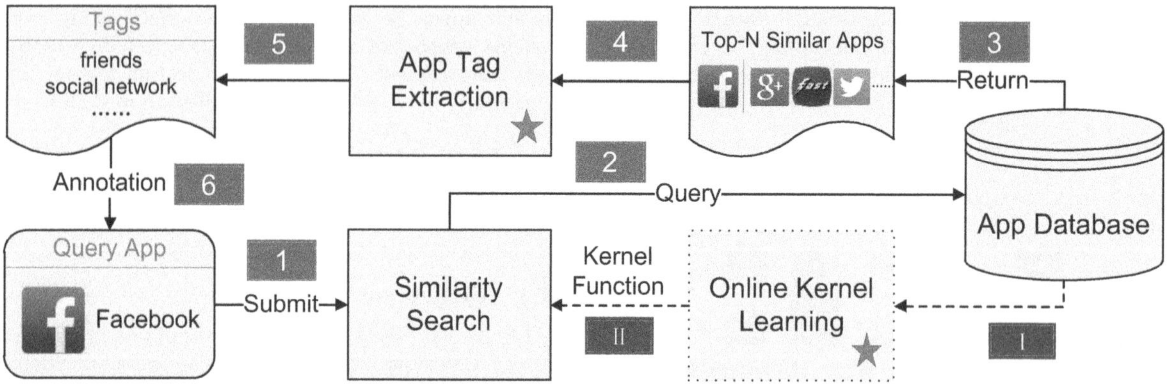

Figure 3: The system architecture of the proposed auto mobile app tagging framework. The key challenges we address in this work include (i) an online kernel learning algorithm; and (ii) an app tag extraction approach (see Figure 4 in Section 4.4).

4.2.2 Descriptions, Updates, and User Reviews

In this work, we exploit three types of **text** data, i.e., *descriptions*, *updates* and *user reviews*. We employ the same scheme used in [25] to measure the app similarity in these three modalities. Next, we use the text *description* modality as an example to illustrate the idea.

We collect all the apps' descriptions and treat them as documents. Then, we use LDA [1] to learn the topic distribution of each description. Thus, each app description can be represented as a fixed length vector $\mathbf{t} \in \mathbb{R}^{|T|}$, where $|T|$ denotes the number of description topics. Let $\mathbf{t}_i$ and $\mathbf{t}_j$ denote the description texts of a_i and a_j, respectively. We measure the app similarity in this modality by using the following normalized liner kernel:

$$K_2(a_i, a_j) = \frac{\mathbf{t}_i \cdot \mathbf{t}_j}{\|\mathbf{t}_i\| \, \|\mathbf{t}_j\|}$$

Following the same way, we denote $\mathbf{u}_i$ and $\mathbf{u}_j$ as the *update* text of apps a_i and a_j, respectively. The similarity between a_i and a_j in this modality is given by,

$$K_3(a_i, a_j) = \frac{\mathbf{u}_i \cdot \mathbf{u}_j}{\|\mathbf{u}_i\| \, \|\mathbf{u}_j\|}$$

It is slightly different for *user reviews*, i.e., we need to gather all the user reviews of an app together as a document. Let $\mathbf{r}_i$ denote the review topics distribution of app a_i, we have,

$$K_4(a_i, a_j) = \frac{\mathbf{r}_i \cdot \mathbf{r}_j}{\|\mathbf{r}_i\| \, \|\mathbf{r}_j\|}$$

4.2.3 Images

We apply the bag-of-(visual)-words (BoW) to represent an app in visual space. We extract SIFT features from images, cluster the SIFT features using the fast K-means algorithm, then quantize the SIFT descriptors of a given image into the set of $|V|$ "visual words" (clusters), and finally compute a compact BoW representation $\mathbf{v} \in \mathbb{R}^{|V|}$. Typically, an app a_i has more than one screenshot image, so we use the centroid of all screenshots belong to a_i to represent it in the visual space, i.e., $\overline{\mathbf{v}}_i = \sum_m \mathbf{v}_m / |a_i|$, where $\mathbf{v}_m$ denotes the visual representation of an image of a_i, and $|a_i|$ denotes the total number of images belong to a_i. We measure the visual similarity between a_i and a_j using the RBF kernel as:

$$K_5(a_i, a_j) = exp\left(-\frac{\|\overline{\mathbf{v}}_i - \overline{\mathbf{v}}_j\|^2}{2\sigma^2}\right)$$

where σ is the bandwidth parameter. By default, we set σ as the average Euclidean distance in this paper.

4.2.4 Category and Content Rating

We explore two types of **nominal** data, i.e., *category* and *content rating*. Let c_i and c_j denote the category lables of apps a_i and a_j, respectively, we have,

$$K_6(a_i, a_j) = \begin{cases} 1 & \text{if} \quad c_i = c_j \\ 0 & \text{if} \quad c_i \neq c_j \end{cases}$$

Let cr_i and cr_j denote the content ratings of app a_i and a_j, respectively. We measure the similarity between a_i and a_j in this modality as follows,

$$K_7(a_i, a_j) = \begin{cases} \beta^{|cr_i - cr_j|} & \text{if} \quad |cr_i - cr_j| < cr_{max} - cr_{min} \\ 0 & \text{if} \quad |cr_i - cr_j| = cr_{max} - cr_{min} \end{cases}$$

where cr_{max} and cr_{min} represent the maximum and minimum ratings in the app market's content rating system, respectively. β is a decay factor within the range of [0,1].

4.2.5 Developer

Every app is associated with a *developer*. Each developer usually has some specialized categories of apps. First, we collect all the category labels in the app market and build a category dictionary with size $|D|$. Then, the developer of each app is represented as a vector $\mathbf{d} \in \mathbb{R}^{|D|}$ following the *tf-idf* scheme. Let $\mathbf{d}_i$ and $\mathbf{d}_j$ denote the developers of apps a_i and a_j, respectively. We measure the app similarity in this modality by employing the RBF kernel, i.e.,

$$K_8(a_i, a_j) = exp\left(-\frac{\|\mathbf{d}_i - \mathbf{d}_j\|^2}{2\sigma^2}\right)$$

4.2.6 Permission

We use the bag-of-words model to represent the permissions required by an app. First, we collect all the permissions and compile a dictionary with size $|P|$. Then, the permissions of an app are converted into a vector in $\mathbb{R}^{|P|}$ using the *tf-idf* weighting scheme. In this way, an app a_i can be represented as a vector $\mathbf{p}_i \in \mathbb{R}^{|P|}$. We also apply the RBF kernel to measure the app similarity in the permission space, i.e.,

$$K_9(a_i, a_j) = exp\left(-\frac{\|\mathbf{p}_i - \mathbf{p}_j\|^2}{2\sigma^2}\right)$$

4.2.7 Size

Let s_i and s_j denote the size (storage space) of app a_i and a_j, respectively. We measure the similarity between a_i and a_j in this modality using the Laplacian Kernel, formally,

$$K_{10}(a_i, a_j) = exp\left(-\frac{|s_i - s_j|}{\gamma}\right)$$

where we set γ as the average absolute value of size difference (unit: MB) between two apps.

4.3 Learning Optimal Weights for Kernels

We propose to model the app similarity function f as a linear combination of multiple kernels, i.e.,

$$K(a_i, a_j; \mathbf{w}) = \sum_{k=1}^{n} w_k K_k(a_i, a_j)$$

where a_i and a_j are the i-th and j-th app, respectively. $K(a_i, a_j; \mathbf{w})$ is the target app similarity function f. K_k denotes the kernel function for the k-th modality of apps, n is the total number of kernels, and $\mathbf{w} \in \mathbb{R}^n$ is the weight vector with each w_k denotes the weight of the k-th kernel.

To learn the optimal combination weights $\mathbf{w}$, we follow the two key schemes adopted in [3], i.e., (i) online learning framework; and (ii) learning from side information of triple-wise app relationship. However, the Online Kernel Weight Learning algorithm, which follows the first order optimization framework, proposed in [3] suffers from the slow convergence issue. To address this limitation, in this work, we present a new online kernel learning algorithm by exploring (i) the adaptive subgradient method [6], which is a second order online optimization method; and (ii) averaged stochastic gradient descent [24, 15].

4.3.1 Averaged Adaptive Online Kernel Learning

In the training phase, we assume a collection of training data is given sequentially in the form of triplet [23], i.e.,

$$\mathcal{T} = \{(a_i, a_i^+, a_i^-), i = 1, ..., |\mathcal{T}|\}$$

where each triplet (a_i, a_i^+, a_i^-) indicates that app a_i is more semantically similar to app a_i^+ than a_i^-. Here, $|\mathcal{T}|$ denotes the total number of triplets in $\mathcal{T}$. Note that, such training triplets can be obtained by various ways in practice, e.g., using existing app search engines. Our goal is to learn a kernel function $K(a_i, a_j; \mathbf{w})$ such that all triplets in $\mathcal{T}$ satisfy,

$$K(a_i, a_i^+) > K(a_i, a_i^-) + \epsilon$$

where ϵ is a margin factor (we set as +1) to ensure a sufficiently large difference.

Algorithm 1 presents the core procedure of our proposed Averaged Adaptive Online Kernel Learning (AAOKL) algorithm. First of all, we introduce the inputs of AAOKL. $\mathcal{T}$ is a collection of training triplets given sequentially. λ is a regulization parameter, η_0 is a learning rate constant and t_0 specifies the start point (iteration) of the averaging process. Initially, we set $\mathbf{w}_1$ (non-averaged weights) and $\overline{\mathbf{w}}_1$ (averaged weights) to the vectors with all elements equal to $1/n$, where n is the number of base kernels, so each base kernel is assigned the same weight. $\mathbf{G}_0 \in \mathbb{R}^{n \times n}$ is the initial diagonal matrix which is used to store the historical gradients. The initial averaging rate u_1 is set to 1 (Line 1).

For each iteration t, we set the learning rate $\eta_t = \eta_0(1 + \lambda\eta_0 t)^{-3/4}$ [2] (Line 3). Then, for a triplet $(a_{i_t}, a_{i_t}^+, a_{i_t}^-)$ re-

Algorithm 1: Averaged Adaptive Online Kernel Learning

Input: $\mathcal{T}$, λ, η_0, t_0

1 Initialize: $\mathbf{w}_1 = \overline{\mathbf{w}}_1 = 1/n$, $\mathbf{G}_0 = 0$, $u_1 = 1$

2 **for** $t = 1, 2, ..., |\mathcal{T}|$ **do**

3 Set $\eta_t = \eta_0(1 + \lambda\eta_0 t)^{-3/4}$.

4 Receive one triplet $(a_{i_t}, a_{i_t}^+, a_{i_t}^-)$ from $\mathcal{T}$.

5 Compute $\mathbf{s}_{i_t}^+$ and $\mathbf{s}_{i_t}^-$.

6 Set hinge loss: $l(\mathbf{w}_t; (a_{i_t}, a_{i_t}^+, a_{i_t}^-)) = max\{0, \epsilon - \mathbf{w}_t \cdot \mathbf{s}_{i_t}^+ + \mathbf{w}_t \cdot \mathbf{s}_{i_t}^-\}$.

7 **if** $l(w_t; (a_{i_t}, a_{i_t}^+, a_{i_t}^-)) = 0$ **then**

8 $\mathbf{g}_t = \lambda\mathbf{w}_t$

9 **end**

10 **else if** $l(w_t; (a_{i_t}, a_{i_t}^+, a_{i_t}^-)) > 0$ **then**

11 $\mathbf{g}_t = \lambda\mathbf{w}_t + \mathbf{s}_{i_t}^- - \mathbf{s}_{i_t}^+$

12 **end**

13 **for** $j = 1, 2, ..., n$ **do**

14 $\mathbf{G}_{t,jj} = \sum_{\tau=1}^{t} \mathbf{g}_{\tau,j}^2$

15 $\mathbf{w}_{t+1,j} \leftarrow \mathbf{w}_{t,j} - \frac{\eta_t}{\sqrt{\mathbf{G}_{t,jj}}}\mathbf{g}_{t,j}$

16 **end**

17 Set $u_t = 1/max\{1, t - t_0\}$.

18 Update $\overline{\mathbf{w}}_{t+1} \leftarrow \overline{\mathbf{w}}_t + u_t(\mathbf{w}_{t+1} - \overline{\mathbf{w}}_t)$

19 **end**

Output: $\overline{\mathbf{w}}_{|\mathcal{T}|+1}$

ceived from $\mathcal{T}$, $i_t \in \{1, ..., |\mathcal{T}|\}$ (Line 4), we compute $\mathbf{s}_{i_t}^+$ and $\mathbf{s}_{i_t}^-$ (Line 5), respectively as follows:

$$\mathbf{s}_{i_t}^+ = [K_1(a_{i_t}, a_{i_t}^+), ..., K_k(a_{i_t}, a_{i_t}^+), ..., K_n(a_{i_t}, a_{i_t}^+)]^T$$
$$\mathbf{s}_{i_t}^- = [K_1(a_{i_t}, a_{i_t}^-), ..., K_k(a_{i_t}, a_{i_t}^-), ..., K_n(a_{i_t}, a_{i_t}^-)]^T$$

The objective function upon receiving the triplet $(a_{i_t}, a_{i_t}^+, a_{i_t}^-)$ at iteration t is formulated as:

$$\mathcal{L}(\mathbf{w}_t; i_t) = \frac{\lambda}{2}||\mathbf{w}_t||^2 + l(\mathbf{w}_t; (a_{i_t}, a_{i_t}^+, a_{i_t}^-))$$

where $l(\mathbf{w}_t; (a_{i_t}, a_{i_t}^+, a_{i_t}^-))$ is the hinge loss for $(a_{i_t}, a_{i_t}^+, a_{i_t}^-)$ which is defined as follows (Line 6):

$$\begin{aligned} l(\mathbf{w}_t; (a_{i_t}, a_{i_t}^+, a_{i_t}^-)) &= max\{0, \epsilon - K(a_{i_t}, a_{i_t}^+) + K(a_{i_t}, a_{i_t}^-)\} \\ &= max\{0, \epsilon - \mathbf{w}_t \cdot \mathbf{s}_{i_t}^+ + \mathbf{w}_t \cdot \mathbf{s}_{i_t}^-\} \end{aligned}$$

We consider sub-gradient of the objective $\mathcal{L}(\mathbf{w}_t; i_t)$ with respect to $\mathbf{w}_t$ (Line 7-12):

$$\mathbf{g}_t = \frac{\partial\mathcal{L}(\mathbf{w}_t; i_t)}{\partial\mathbf{w}_t} = \begin{cases} \lambda\mathbf{w}_t & l(\mathbf{w}_t; (a_{i_t}, a_{i_t}^+, a_{i_t}^-)) = 0 \\ \lambda\mathbf{w}_t + \mathbf{s}_{i_t}^- - \mathbf{s}_{i_t}^+ & l(\mathbf{w}_t; (a_{i_t}, a_{i_t}^+, a_{i_t}^-)) > 0 \end{cases}$$

Let $\mathbf{G}_t \in \mathbb{R}^{n \times n}$ denote the diagonal matrix at iteration t where the j-th diagonal element $\mathbf{G}_{t,jj}$ stores the sum of the squares of all past gradients of the j-th feature (kernel), i.e., $\sum_{\tau=1}^{t} \mathbf{g}_{\tau,j}^2$ (Line 14). Then, for the j-th feature, we update:

$$\mathbf{w}_{t+1,j} \leftarrow \mathbf{w}_{t,j} - \frac{\eta_t}{\sqrt{\mathbf{G}_{t,jj}}}\mathbf{g}_{t,j}$$

where $\frac{\eta_t}{\sqrt{\mathbf{G}_{t,jj}}}$ is the j-th feature's specific learning rate at iteration t (Line 15). In such a way, every feature has it's own learning rate that adapts to the data dynamically.

Except for normal weight updates, we start averaging weights at certain iteration t_0 (which can be tuned experimentally), the output $\overline{\mathbf{w}}_t$ is the average of all the weights from iteration t_0 to t, formally,

$$\overline{\mathbf{w}}_t = \begin{cases} \mathbf{w}_t & t < t_0 \\ \frac{1}{t-t_0+1}\sum_{l=t_0}^{t} \mathbf{w}_l & t \geqslant t_0 \end{cases}$$

We compute this average using a recursive formula [2], i.e.,

$$\overline{\mathbf{w}}_{t+1} \leftarrow \overline{\mathbf{w}}_t + u_t(\mathbf{w}_{t+1} - \overline{\mathbf{w}}_t)$$

where $u_t = 1/max\{1, t - t_0\}$ is the averaging rate (Line 17-18). Finally, after $|\mathcal{T}|$ iterations, we output the learned weight vector $\overline{\mathbf{w}}_{|\mathcal{T}|+1}$ as the optimal combination weights.

Remark. Learning the app similarity function $K(a_i, a_j; \mathbf{w})$ is necessary, as shown in two cases: (i) when an app similarity function is **not** available in mobile app ecosystem, our technique can build one from scratch; (ii) when an existing app similarity function is **not** effective enough, we can improve it significantly (see Section 5.5 in [3]).

4.4 App Tag Extraction Approach

Given a novel app a_0 (without tags) as a query, we first apply the learned app similarity function to find a set of N nearest neighbor apps for this app via searching a large app database. The novel app a_0 and its N nearest neighbor apps $\mathcal{S}(a_0) = \{a_1, a_2, ..., a_N\}$ form an app set which we denote as $A_0 = \{a_0, a_1, a_2, ..., a_N\}$. Our objective is to automatically discover a list of tags associated with a_0 by mining the "Description" and "Update" text of all the apps in A_0 ($A_0.text$ in short). In this study, we formulate it as an automatic keywords extraction task [7]. Specifically, we first extract valid terms (i.e., n-grams, $n \leq 2$) from $A_0.text$. Then, we apply a common stopword list to remove terms which begin or end with a stopword on the list. The remaining terms are considered as *candidate terms*, from which we aim to find the most appropriate ones as app a_0's tags.

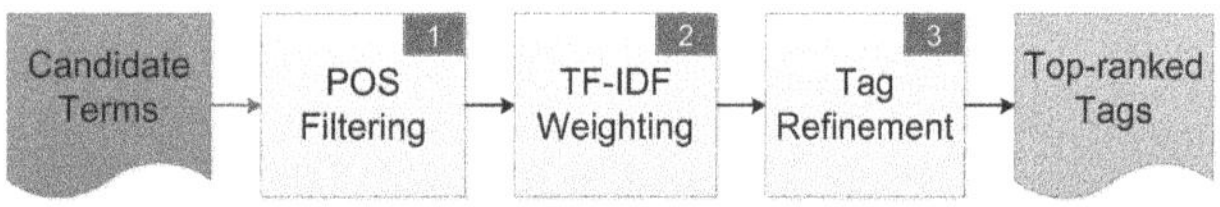

Figure 4: Overview of the App Tag Extraction approach.

To achieve this goal, we propose an unsupervised App Tag Extraction (ATE) approach. Figure 4 presents the overview of ATE, which consists of three steps. Specifically, the first step applies a list of pre-defined Part-of-Speech (POS) patterns to filter unlikely candidate terms. Then, the second step computes a TF-IDF score for each of the remaining terms. In the last step, we refine those terms with the highest TF-IDF scores by using a modified TextRank [13] algorithm. Finally, the top-ranked terms are recommended to tag the query app. Next, we present each step in detail.

4.4.1 Part-of-Speech Filtering

Syntactic properties of terms can be useful for identifying app tags. We use the Part-of-Speech (POS) info to remove unlikely candidate terms. Specifically, we first pre-define a list of POS patterns, and only those terms that match any of these patterns are kept. In this way, the number of candidate terms can be further reduced. Since nouns, verbs and adjectives are more likely to be tags, we define the POS patterns listed as follows for unigram and bigram, respectively (following the Penn Treebank tagset [12]):

- NN, JJ, NNS, VBP, VB, VBG, VBZ (unigram)
- NN NN, JJ NN, NN NNS, JJ NNS, NNS NN, VBG NN (bigram)

In particular, we use the Stanford POS tagger [16] to get the POS information of the candidate terms.

4.4.2 TF-IDF Weighting

Given a set of candidate terms for a query app a_0, it's not an easy task to identify which terms are more likely to be tags of a_0. In this study, we propose a measure to rank the possibility of terms to be app tags based on the following three intuitions: (1) a term appears more frequently in $A_0.text$ is more likely to be an app tag; (2) a very common term in the app domain is less likely to be an app tag; and (3) the terms from neighbor apps which are more similar to the query app a_0 is expected to have greater likelihood than those from neighbor apps which are less similar to a_0.

In particular, for each app, we combine its "Description" and "Update" texts together as one document. Let $T_0 = \{t_1, t_2, ..., t_i, ...\}$ denote the set of candidate terms extracted from the documents of all apps in A_0, where A_0 includes the query app a_0 and the top-N similar apps of a_0. The likelihood of a term t_i to be a tag of a_0 is defined as:

$$TFIDF(t_i) = IDF_i \sum_{j=0}^{N} TF_{ij} \times Sim(a_j, a_0) \quad (1)$$

where TF_{ij} denotes the number of times t_i appears in the document of app a_j and $Sim(a_j, a_0)$ is the similarity score between apps a_j and a_0. IDF_i denotes the Inverse Document Frequency of term t_i obtained from a large auxiliary corpus, i.e.,

$$IDF_i = log(D/D_i)$$

where D_i is the number of documents in the corpus that contain term t_i, and D is the total document size of the corpus. By using Equation (1), we can get a ranked list (in decreasing order) of candidate terms denoted as T_0' for tagging the query app a_0. Note that Equation (1) captures all the three intuitions summarized earlier.

4.4.3 Tag Refinement by Modified TextRank

Given the ranked list T_0' (in decreasing order of TF-IDF score), we add a refinement step with the aim of pushing terms that are more likely to be tags to the top of the list. To archive our goal, we propose a modified TextRank [13] algorithm. Next, we present our idea in detail.

Let $T_0'^{(1/N)}$ denote the top $\lfloor |T_0'|/N \rfloor$ ranked terms in T_0', where N is the number of similar apps retrieved from the app database, and $|T_0'|$ is the total number of terms in T_0'. We build an undirected graph $G = (V, E)$ from $T_0'^{(1/N)}$, where V is a set of vertices and E is a set of edges. Each node $v_i \in V$ corresponds to an unigram $u_i \in T_0'^{(1/N)}$, and an edge $e_{ij} \in E$ connects two nodes v_i and v_j. The weight w_{ij} of the edge e_{ij} is proportional to the semantic relevance between v_i (u_i) and v_j (u_j). Different from the original TextRank [13] algorithm which uses co-occurrence relation, we measure the semantic relevance between two unigrams (words) based on the word embedding technique.

Word embedding is an important technique in NLP where each word in the vocabulary is mapped to a dense, low-dimensional and real-valued vector. The embedded feature vector somewhat describe the semantic characteristics of the corresponding word. Given a large auxiliary corpus, we can learn the vector representations of words in an unsupervised manner by utilizing the *skip-gram* architecture proposed in [14] (detailed settings will be given in Section 6.2.3). We expect such representation of words is beneficial to measuring the semantic relevance between two words.

Let $\mathbf{u}_i$ and $\mathbf{u}_j$ denote the vector representations of unigrams u_i and u_j, respectively. We measure the semantic relevance $w_{i,j}$ between u_i and u_j using a polynomial kernel:

$$w_{i,j} = \left(\frac{\mathbf{u}_i \cdot \mathbf{u}_j}{\|\mathbf{u}_i\| \, \|\mathbf{u}_j\|} + c \right)^d$$

where $w_{i,j}$ is a non-negative value, and we set $c = 1$, $d = 2$.

The TextRank (TR) score of a node v_i (which represents u_i) is defined as follows:

$$TR(v_i) = (1-d) + d * \sum_{v_j \in (V - v_i)} \frac{w_{ij}}{\sum_{v_k \in (V - v_j)} w_{jk}} TR(v_j) \quad (2)$$

where $V - v_i$ denotes the set of all the nodes in V except v_i; and $d \in [0, 1]$ is a damping factor which we set to 0.85 (the same as in [13]) in our implementation. The larger value of $TR(v_i)$, the greater probability of u_i to be an app tag.

To get the TR scores of unigrams, initially, all nodes are assigned the same scores of 1.0. Then, Equation (2) is applied iteratively until convergence (we set threshold = 0.0001). For each bigram in $T_0^{'(1/N)}$, we set its TR score as the average value of TR scores of the two words of the bigram. After the TR scores of all the terms in $T_0^{'(1/N)}$ are obtained, for each term $t_i \in T_0^{'(1/N)}$, we define its final score as the product of TF-IDF score and the normalized TR score, formally,

$$F(t_i) = TFIDF(t_i) \times \tilde{TR}(t_i) \quad (3)$$

Finally, the top-ranked terms (in terms of final score) are selected as tags for the input query app.

5. DATASET

In this section, we introduce a real-world dataset crawled from Google Play for conducting our empirical evaluations. Table 1 presents some statistics of this dataset[1].

Global App Repository: We collected app data from Google Play at full stretch. For each app, we crawled all the metadata (associated with it) available on Google Play, including description text, permissions, user reviews, etc. This yielded a *global app repository* with 1,039,127 apps in 42 categories. The *global app repository* is used as an auxiliary repository to learn (obtain) the vector representations and IDF values of words. The *retrieval database*, *training set* and *query set* discussed below are all subsets of the *global app repository*. Note that, these subsets are mutually disjoint.

Training Set: The *training set* is used for learning the app similarity function. In particular, we randomly sample 15,000 apps from the *global app repository*, and use them to generate training triplets.

Query Set: Apps in Google Play do not have tags, making it difficult for evaluating the tagging performance of our technique. Fortunately, we found three alternative Android markets (i.e., SlideME[2], Samsung Galaxy Apps[3] and PandaApp[4]), in which some apps are tagged. Such information can be utilized to build our *query set*. Specifically, we first crawl apps' metadata and their associated tags as many as possible from these three markets, respectively. Second, for each Google Play app in our *global app repository*, we try to find its duplicates from the three markets by matching app *names* and *developers*. We use the tags associated with these duplicates as the ground truth tags for the corresponding Google Play app. Third, we manually check the ground truth tags and refine their quality by employing a list of rules. Specifically, we (i) remove tags that contain non-English characters; (ii) apply a list of carefully defined stopwords to eliminate clearly noisy tags; (iii) remove tags that contain more than two words, etc. Fourth, we select an app as a candidate query app if it contains at least four ground truth tags (after removing noisy tags). Finally, we randomly sample 1000 apps from the candidate query apps (<2000 apps) as the *query set* (see Section 7 for details.).

Retrieval Database: We randomly sampled 60,000 apps from the *global app repository* as the *retrieval database*, which is served as an app knolwedge DB for search-based tagging. Empirically such a scale is able to retrieve enough highly similar apps for most queries.

	Training	Query	Retrieval
#Apps	15,000	1,000	60,000
#Permissions	115,846	7,980	459,155
#Reviews	5,600,265	1,664,430	25,608,494
#Images	115,688	10,078	463,428

Table 1: Some statistics of the Google Play dataset used in this study. "#" denotes the number of some object.

6. EMPIRICAL EVALUATION

6.1 Evaluation Metrics

To evaluate the performance of different kernel functions for measuring app similarity, we follow the two metrics as introduced in [3], i.e., Precision@K and mean Average Precision (mAP). In addition, we adopt two metrics: AP@K and HIT@K, to evaluate the tagging accuracy as follows:

- **AP@K:** The Average Precision for top-K tags. For each query app, we compute the proportion of correct tags among the top-K ranked tags, and finally compute the average AP@K over the entire *query set*.
- **HIT@K:** For each query app in the *query set*, we follow the previous study [18] to compute the hit rate at top-K annotated results, which measures the likelihood of having at least one of the ground truth tags among the top-K results. When averaged across the entire *query set*, this yields the HIT@K measure.

6.2 Experimental Setup

6.2.1 Find App-App Relevance

Before applying our proposed AAOKL algorithm, we need to generate a set of training triplets from a set of training apps $\mathcal{A}$. To generate such triplets, for each app $a_i \in \mathcal{A}$, we need to find a list of apps belong to $\mathcal{A}$ that are somewhat relevant to a_i, denoted as $R(a_i)$.

[1]The dataset is available at http://apptag.stevenhoi.org.
[2]http://slideme.org/
[3]http://apps.samsung.com/
[4]http://android.pandaapp.com/

Google Play has a *"Similar"* feature which recommends users a list of similar apps for each app. We collected a set of p ($p = 530966$) such lists $L = \{l_1, l_2, ..., l_p\}$ from the web portal of Google Play, where $l_k (1 \le k \le p)$ represents the k-th list. Given two apps a_i and a_j ($a_i, a_j \in \mathcal{A}, i \neq j$), let $freq(a_i, a_j)$ denote the number of lists they both appear in. If $freq(a_i, a_j)$ exceeds a pre-defined threshold θ (which is used to reduce noise, we set it equal to 2), we consider a_j to be relevant to a_i, and add a_j into $R(a_i)$. In such a way, for each app $a_i \in \mathcal{A}$, we can obtain a list of relevant apps $R(a_i)$ and a list of irrelevant apps $\mathcal{A} - R(a_i)$.

6.2.2 Generation of Triplet Instances

After the app-app relevance of the *training set* $\mathcal{A}$ (as described in Section 5) is built, we sample the training triplets $\mathcal{T}' = \{(a_i, a_i^+, a_i^-), i = 1, ..., m\}$ as follows. First of all, we randomly sample an app a_i from $\mathcal{A}$. Then, we uniformly sample an app a_i^+ from the list of apps which are similar to a_i, i.e., $R(a_i)$. Finally, we uniformly sample an app a_i^- from the list of apps which are not similar to a_i, i.e., $\mathcal{A} - R(a_i)$. In this way, we generate a set of 50K training triplets $\mathcal{T}'$ which is used through our experiments.

6.2.3 Building Vector Representations of Words

In our experiments, we perform unsupervised learning of vector representations of words by using the skip-gram architecture of the *word2vec* tool in gensim[5]. We build the training corpus by using the "Description" and "Update" text of all the apps in the *global app repository* (excluding apps in the *query set*). The resulting vocabulary contains about 0.1 million words, and each word is associated with a 300-dimensional vector. The learned word vectors are then used to compute the semantic relevance between word pairs as described in Section 4.4.3.

6.3 Evaluation of Kernel Functions

6.3.1 Compared Methods

To evaluate the performance of our proposed AAOKL algorithm in modeling app similarity, we compared it with a variety of methods listed below:

- **Single:** three informative single kernels: K_1 (Name), K_2 (Description) and K_4 (User Reviews);
- **Uniform:** $K_1 \sim K_{10}$ are uniformly combined with each kernel function having the same weight;
- **OKWL[3]:** Online Kernel Weight Learning, an Online Gradient Descent algorithm for combining multiple kernels. We follow the same parameter settings used in [3], i.e., $\eta_0 = 0.01$ and $\lambda = 10^{-4}$;
- **AAOKL:** the proposed AAOKL algorithm for combining $K_1 \sim K_{10}$. We select the parameters using a small sample of training triplets, and set $\eta_0 = 1$, $\lambda = 10^{-4}$ and $t_0 = 10$.

Note that, since the proposed AAOKL algorithm follows the online learning framework, in this study, we did not compare it with batch learning methods, such as learning to rank or kernel alignment [5], etc. We may explore and compare more methods in future work.

[5]https://radimrehurek.com/gensim/

6.3.2 Results for Triplets Classification

In the **first** experiment, we compare AAOKL with OKWL based on a triplets classification task. First, we randomly sample a set of 5000 apps as the test set from the *retrieval database* as described in Section 5. Then, we generate a set of 20K test triplets from the test set by using the method described in Section 6.2.2. Given the training triplets $\mathcal{T}'$, we run AAOKL and OKWL and trace their test errors over the training triplets as they process during learning. Figure 5 summarizes the average results over 50 runs.

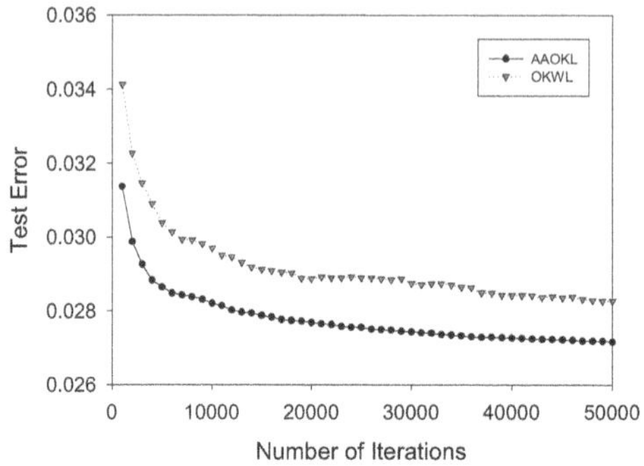

Figure 5: Test errors of AAOKL and OKWL as a function of the number of iterations (averaged over 50 runs).

We can draw some observations from Figure 5. First, AAOKL converges significantly faster than OKWL, indicating that the app similarity function learned by AAOKL can be more accurate given the same number of iterations. Second, AAOKL is more attractive since OKWL does not reach its asymptotic performance. Both observations validate that AAOKL is better than OKWL in learning app similarity.

6.3.3 Results for Similar App Recommendation

In the **second** experiment, we compare all the methods listed in Section 6.3.1 based on a similar app recommendation task. Specifically, for each query app in the test set used in the **first** experiment, we rank all other test apps according to their similarity scores to the query app, and then extract top ones as recommended apps. The ground truth (i.e., the app-app relevance of the test set) is obtained using the method described in Section 6.2.1. We measure the performance of all the compared methods in term of Precision@K and mAP. Since the largest K value in this experiment is 5, we only use test apps that have at least 5 similar apps as query apps. Table 2 shows the comparison results, from which we can draw some observations.

	mAP	K=1	K=3	K=5
AAOKL	**0.366** ±0.0007	**0.600** ±0.0012	**0.514** ±0.0010	**0.456** ±0.0012
OKWL	0.358 ±0.0013	0.592 ±0.0018	0.506 ±0.0021	0.448 ±0.0015
Uniform	0.273	0.514	0.427	0.367
Review	0.211	0.394	0.333	0.296
Desc.	0.166	0.327	0.275	0.245
Name	0.088	0.253	0.195	0.159

Table 2: mAP and Precision@K (K = 1, 3, 5) of all compared methods. The scores achieved by AAOKL and OKWL are averaged over 10 runs. "Desc." is short for "Description".

First, among the compared methods, AAOKL obtains the best results consistently in terms of both mAP and Precision@K (K=1,3,5) measures, which further validates its efficacy. Second, OKWL achieves worse mAP and Precision@K scores (with larger standard deviations) than AAOKL on this similar app recommendation task, which is consistent with the results for the triplets classification task shown in Figure 5. Third, the *Uniform* combination performs better than all the single kernels evaluated, but performs worse than AAOKL and OKWL. Such results indicate that the idea of combining different kernels is helpful, but this kind of simple strategy cannot yield the best results, thus learning the optimal combination weights of kernels in an effective way is required. Fourth, the *Review* kernel reports the best performance among all the single kernels evaluated, which indicates that user review is the most informative modality.

6.3.4 *Results for App Tagging*

In the **third** experiment, we fix the app tag extraction method, and evaluate the impact of app similarity functions in the search-based app tagging procedure. Specifically, for each query app in the *query set* (as described in Section 5), we apply different app similarity functions obtained (Uniform, OKWL and AAOKL) to search semantically similar apps from the *retrieval database* (as described in Section 5). In particular, a set of top $N = 10$ (the impact of varied N values will be examined in Section 6.5) similar apps are retrieved, then the proposed App Tag Extraction (ATE) approach is used to get the top-K tags for each query app. We also include "Query" as an important baseline method, which uses ATE to extract tags from the text data of the query app only, without leveraging any text data of its similar apps. The AP@K and HIT@K (K=1, 5, 10) are used as the evaluation metrics. The results are shown in Table 3, from which we can draw two observations.

Metric	Method	K=1	K=5	K=10
AP@K (%)	Query	18.70	11.78	8.58
	Uniform	22.80	13.44	10.01
	OKWL	24.70	14.76	11.12
	AAOKL	**26.60**	**15.34**	**11.33**
HIT@K (%)	Query	18.70	42.80	51.80
	Uniform	22.80	48.00	58.20
	OKWL	24.70	50.90	60.30
	AAOKL	**26.60**	**51.40**	**62.80**

Table 3: Evaluation of app similarity functions for automatic app tagging. ATE is used to extract tags. $N = 10$.

First of all, among all the methods, we found that AAOKL (+ATE) achieves the best results (in terms of both metrics) for the full range of K evaluated. For example, compared with OKWL (+ATE), AAOKL (+ATE) improves the AP@1 score by about 7.7%. This fact indicates that better learned kernel functions lead to better tagging performance.

Second, the baseline method Query (+ATE) performs much worse than the other three search-based methods in terms of both AP@K and HIT@K (K=1, 5, 10) scores. For example, AAOKL (+ATE) achieves 0.2660 while Query (+ATE) only achieves 0.1870 in terms of AP@1. Such results clearly demonstrate that (i) relying on an app's own metadata is not effective for app tagging; (ii) the effectiveness of retrieving similar apps for automatic app tagging. Due to space limitation, we give some qualitative tagging results on our website to further verify these findings.

6.4 Evaluation of Tag Extraction Methods

We also conduct an experiment to evaluate the performance of our proposed unsupervised App Tag Extraction (ATE) approach. In this experiment, we fix AAOKL as the kernel learning method and set the number of similar apps retrieved to 10 ($N = 10$). Then, three different schemes for extracting app tags are compared. Specifically, the first scheme is *TF-IDF* (the baseline), which only applies the Equation (1) (see Section 4.4.2) to rank tags. The second scheme *TF-IDF+POS* includes a Part-of-Speech (POS) filtering step (see Section 4.4.1) before applying Equation (1). Finally, ATE represents our proposed integrated approach shown in Figure 4. Table 4 summarizes the comparison results. From Table 4, we can draw two observations below.

Metric	Method	K=1	K=5	K=10
AP@K (%)	TF-IDF	23.90	14.10	10.37
	TF-IDF+POS	24.50	14.60	11.02
	ATE	**26.60**	**15.34**	**11.33**
HIT@K (%)	TF-IDF	23.90	49.60	59.60
	TF-IDF+POS	24.50	50.80	61.30
	ATE	**26.60**	**51.40**	**62.80**

Table 4: Evaluation of different tag extraction methods. AAOKL is adopted to learn the kernel function. $N = 10$.

First of all, we found that *TF-IDF+POS* performs slightly better than the baseline method *TF-IDF* in terms of both AP@K and HIT@K scores, which indicates that POS filtering is helpful in improving the tag extraction performance.

Second, with $K = 1, 5, 10$, our proposed ATE approach always achieves the best tagging performance, which shows that the tag refinement step is also be able to improve the tag extraction performance. By looking into the results, we found that, compared with *TF-IDF*, ATE improves the average precision scores by around 10%. Such fair results demonstrate the superiority of ATE in extracting app tags.

6.5 Evaluation of Varied N Values

We conduct an experiment to examine if the number of top retrieved similar apps, denoted as N, would affect the app tagging performance. Figure 6 presents the tagging performance of AAOKL+ATE (the best scheme) at top-K ($K = 1, 5, 10$) tags by varying N from 1 to 100.

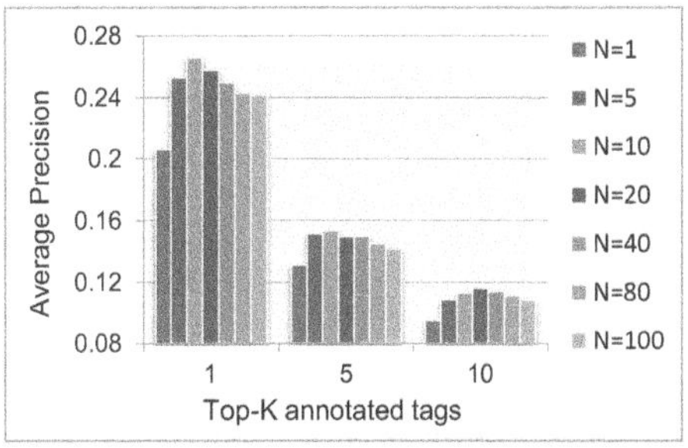

Figure 6: Comparisons of AP@K under different top-N similar apps retrieved. We apply the AAOKL + ATE scheme.

From the results shown in Figure 6, we can see that (i) when $N = 10$, AAOKL+ATE attains the best AP@1 and AP@5 scores; and (ii) when $N = 20$, AAOKL+ATE achieves the best AP@10 score. Another observation is that, when N is smaller than 10 or larger than 40, the average precision scores drop. The reason is straightforward: if N is too small, there are not enough similar apps retrieved, while if N is too large, some less relevant apps may be retrieved, which may result in introducing noisy tags. Therefore, the app tagging performance degrades. In practice, we need to tune N empirically to achieve the best tagging performance.

7. LIMITATION & THREAT TO VALIDITY

Despite the encouraging results, this work has some limitations. First of all, the size of the *retrieval database* (60K apps) in our current experiments is relatively small for the search-based tagging process. It is relatively easy for conducting the retrieval task with this scale. However, when the *retrieval database* is very large (e.g., 1-million apps), the efficiency of similarity search can be a great challenge. In our future work, we plan to address this challenge by exploring fast approximate similarity search and indexing techniques, e.g., Kernel LSH [10]. Besides, this work also has one potential threat to validity, which relates to the generality of our app tagging framework. We validate our framework based on 1000 apps (with ground truth tags) from Google Play. It is unclear that if our technique can attain similar good or even better results when being applied to other large number of apps in both Google Play and other app markets. We may examine this issue extensively in our future studies.

8. CONCLUSION AND FUTURE WORK

This paper presented a novel auto mobile app tagging framework which aims to annotate a novel mobile app automatically by mining large amounts of multi-modal data in app markets via search-based annotation paradigms. Encouraging results from the extensive experiments validate the efficacy of our technique. Future work can (i) explore more modalities of apps; (ii) develop more effective app similarity learning techniques by other multi-modal learning [21, 23]; (iii) conduct more extensive empirical studies on other larger-scale datasets; and (iv) explore potential applications for mobile app search, browsing, categorization and beyond.

9. ACKNOWLEDGMENTS

This work was supported in part by the National Research Foundation, Singapore under its IDM Futures Funding Initiative and administered by the Interactive and Digital Media Programme Office, and Singapore Ministry of Education Academic Research Fund Tier 1 Grant (14-C220-SMU-016). This work was also supported by a grant (ARC19/14) from MOE, Singapore and a gift from Microsoft Research Asia.

10. REFERENCES

[1] D. M. Blei, A. Y. Ng, and M. I. Jordan. Latent dirichlet allocation. *J. Mach. Learn. Res.*, 3:993–1022, Mar. 2003.

[2] L. Bottou. Stochastic gradient descent tricks. In *Neural Networks: Tricks of the Trade*, pages 421–436. 2012.

[3] N. Chen, S. C. Hoi, S. Li, and X. Xiao. Simapp: A framework for detecting similar mobile applications by online kernel learning. In *WSDM*, pages 305–314, 2015.

[4] N. Chen, J. Lin, S. C. H. Hoi, X. Xiao, and B. Zhang. Ar-miner: Mining informative reviews for developers from mobile app marketplace. In *ICSE*, pages 767–778, 2014.

[5] C. Cortes, M. Mohri, and A. Rostamizadeh. Two-stage learning kernel algorithms. In *ICML*, pages 239–246, 2010.

[6] J. Duchi, E. Hazan, and Y. Singer. Adaptive subgradient methods for online learning and stochastic optimization. *J. Mach. Learn. Res.*, 12:2121–2159, July 2011.

[7] S. K. Hasan and V. Ng. Automatic keyphrase extraction: A survey of the state of the art. In *ACL*, pages 1262–1273, 2014.

[8] S. C. Hoi, R. Jin, P. Zhao, and T. Yang. Online multiple kernel classification. *Machine Learning*, 90(2):289–316, 2013.

[9] S. C. Hoi, J. Wang, and P. Zhao. Libol: A library for online learning algorithms. *The Journal of Machine Learning Research*, 15(1):495–499, 2014.

[10] B. Kulis and K. Grauman. Kernelized locality-sensitive hashing for scalable image search. In *CVPR*, pages 2130–2137. IEEE, 2009.

[11] H. Lodhi, C. Saunders, J. Shawe-Taylor, N. Cristianini, and C. Watkins. Text classification using string kernels. *J. Mach. Learn. Res.*, 2:419–444, Mar. 2002.

[12] M. P. Marcus, M. A. Marcinkiewicz, and B. Santorini. Building a large annotated corpus of english: The penn treebank. *Comput. Linguist.*, 19(2):313–330, June 1993.

[13] R. Mihalcea and P. Tarau. Textrank: Bringing order into texts. In *EMNLP*, pages 404–411, July 2004.

[14] T. Mikolov, I. Sutskever, K. Chen, G. S. Corrado, and J. Dean. Distributed representations of words and phrases and their compositionality. In *NIPS*, pages 3111–3119, 2013.

[15] B. T. Polyak and A. B. Juditsky. Acceleration of stochastic approximation by averaging. *SIAM Journal on Control and Optimization*, 30(4):838–855, 1992.

[16] K. Toutanova and C. D. Manning. Enriching the knowledge sources used in a maximum entropy part-of-speech tagger. In *EMNLP/VLC*, pages 63–70, 2000.

[17] D. Wang, S. C. Hoi, Y. He, and J. Zhu. Mining weakly labeled web facial images for search-based face annotation. *IEEE TKDE*, 26(1):166–179, 2014.

[18] D. Wang, S. C. Hoi, Y. He, J. Zhu, T. Mei, and J. Luo. Retrieval-based face annotation by weak label regularized local coordinate coding. *TPAMI*, 36(3):550–563, 2014.

[19] X.-J. Wang, L. Zhang, F. Jing, and W.-Y. Ma. Annosearch: Image auto-annotation by search. In *CVPR*, volume 2, pages 1483–1490. IEEE, 2006.

[20] L. Wu, S. C. Hoi, R. Jin, J. Zhu, and N. Yu. Distance metric learning from uncertain side information with application to automated photo tagging. In *ACM MM*, pages 135–144, 2009.

[21] P. Wu, S. C. Hoi, H. Xia, P. Zhao, D. Wang, and C. Miao. Online multimodal deep similarity learning with application to image retrieval. In *ACM Multimedia*, pages 153–162, 2013.

[22] P. Wu, S. C.-H. Hoi, P. Zhao, and Y. He. Mining social images with distance metric learning for automated image tagging. In *WSDM*, pages 197–206, 2011.

[23] H. Xia, S. C. Hoi, R. Jin, and P. Zhao. Online multiple kernel similarity learning for visual search. *IEEE Trans. Pattern Anal. Mach. Intell.*, 36(3):536–549, 2014.

[24] W. Xu. Towards optimal one pass large scale learning with averaged stochastic gradient descent. *arXiv preprint arXiv:1107.2490*, 2011.

[25] P. Yin, P. Luo, W.-C. Lee, and M. Wang. App recommendation: A contest between satisfaction and temptation. In *WSDM*, pages 395–404, 2013.

[26] W.-L. Zhao, X. Wu, and C.-W. Ngo. On the annotation of web videos by efficient near-duplicate search. *IEEE TMM*, 12(5):448–461, Aug. 2010.

[27] H. Zhu, H. Xiong, Y. Ge, and E. Chen. Mobile app recommendations with security and privacy awareness. In *KDD*, pages 951–960, 2014.

[28] J. Zhuo. Semantic matching in app search. http://www.wsdm-conference.org/2015/practice-and-experience-talks/, Feb. 2015.

CCCF: Improving Collaborative Filtering via Scalable User-Item Co-Clustering

Yao Wu[†]*, Xudong Liu[‡]*, Min Xie[♯], Martin Ester[†], Qing Yang[‡]
[†]School of Computing Science, Simon Fraser University, Burnaby, BC, Canada
[‡]Institute of Automation, Chinese Academy of Sciences, Beijing, China
[♯]Walmart Labs, San Bruno, CA, USA
[†]{wuyaow, ester}@sfu.ca [‡]{xudong.liu, qyang}@nlpr.ia.ac.cn [♯]mxie@walmartlabs.com

ABSTRACT

Collaborative Filtering (CF) is the most popular method for recommender systems. The principal idea of CF is that users might be interested in items that are favorited by similar users, and most of the existing CF methods measure users' preferences by their behaviors over all the items. However, users might have different interests over different topics, thus might share similar preferences with different groups of users over different sets of items. In this paper, we propose a novel and scalable method CCCF which improves the performance of CF methods via user-item co-clustering. CCCF first clusters users and items into several subgroups, where each subgroup includes a set of like-minded users and a set of items in which these users share their interests. Then, traditional CF methods can be easily applied to each subgroup, and the recommendation results from all the subgroups can be easily aggregated. Compared with previous works, CCCF has several advantages including scalability, flexibility, interpretability and extensibility. Experimental results on four real world data sets demonstrate that the proposed method significantly improves the performance of several state-of-the-art recommendation algorithms.

Categories and Subject Descriptors

H.3.3 [**Information Search and Retrieval**]: Information Filtering

Keywords

Collaborative Filtering; Recommender Systems; Co-Clustering

1. INTRODUCTION

The goal of recommender systems is to deliver proper items to users in order to improve user engagement and merchant revenue. Collaborative Filtering (CF) is the most popular method for recommender systems [16]. The underlying assumption of CF is that if a user u has similar preferences with another user v on many items, it is more likely for them to share preferences over the remaining items than a randomly chosen pair of users.

*The first two authors contributed equally.

WSDM'16, February 22–25, 2016, San Francisco, CA, USA.

ISBN 978-1-4503-3716-8/16/02...$15.00

DOI: http://dx.doi.org/10.1145/2835776.2835836

Typical CF methods measure users' preferences by their historical behaviors over the entire item space. For example, the user-based nearest neighbors method measures the similarity between pairs of users by their preferences on all the items [16]; Matrix Factorization decomposes the whole user-item matrix into two low-rank sub-matrices where the collective intelligences are represented as latent factors in the model [8]. However, this assumption does not always hold, especially when the underlying system includes a large set of items of different types. For example, an Amazon user share similar tastes on books with a certain group of users, while having similar preferences with another group of users on movies.

It is more natural to model the users and the items using subgroups, where each subgroup includes a set of like-minded users and the subset of items that they are interested in, and each user/item can be assigned to multiple subgroups so that users can share their interests with different subsets of users on different subsets of items. Partitioning users and items into subgroups for CF has been studied by several previous works, where user clustering [26], item clustering [13] and user-item co-clustering [6] methods have been proposed to boost the performance of collaborative filtering. However, in these methods each user/item is only allowed to be assigned to a single subgroup, so that they are not able to model the case where users have multiple interests. To address this problem, several other papers [18, 20, 21] extend the Mixed Membership Stochastic Blockmodels (MMSB) [2] to allow mixed memberships. However, these methods optimize the accuracy of rating/link prediction instead of the practically important problem of top-N recommendation.

In [25], the authors propose a unified framework for improving collaborative filtering via overlapping co-clustering, which can be employed for top-N recommendation. It works as follows: 1) Users and items are first grouped into multiple overlapping subgroups with different weights. 2) After obtaining the subgroups, any traditional CF method can be applied to each subgroup separately to make the predictions for the users on their unrated items in the same subgroup. 3) The final recommendation list for a user is aggregated from the results in the subgroups that she/he is involved in. The authors of [31] adopt a similar framework, and propose to partition the user-item matrix by permuting the rows and columns of the user-item matrix to form (approximate) Bordered Block Diagonal matrices.

However, the co-clustering objective function of [25] is based on a weighted graph cut problem, which partitions the underlying graph into non-overlapping subgroups and minimizes the total costs associated with the cut edges. Therefore, [25] does not *intrinsically* learn overlapping subgroups. Also, solving the weighted graph cut problem has a high computational complexity. In [31], assignments of users and items to subgroups are deterministic and have equal weight, *i.e.*, users are forced to have equal amount of interest in each subgroup that they are assigned to, thus affiliation strengths are not modeled.

We argue that in order to model users' shared interests in different subsets of items, we have to resort to overlapping co-clustering methods which have the following three properties:

- The proposed method should be able to model the strength of affiliations between users, items and subgroups by assigning weights to each user and item for each subgroup. As we shall see later in this work, these weights are critical when aggregating the results from subgroups to make the final recommendation.
- The proposed method should be able to model a user's interest in an item through her/his affiliations with different subgroups.
- The proposed method should have the property that the more subgroups that a user u and an item i share, and the higher the affiliation strengths of u and i with the subgroups they share, the more likely u should be interested in i.

In this paper, we propose a novel co-clustering method, called CCCF (CO-CLUSTERING FOR COLLABORATIVE FILTERING). In CCCF, each user/item can belong to multiple subgroups, and we use an affiliation strength score to denote the strength of the relationship between the user/item and the corresponding subgroup. CCCF models the probability of a user liking an item as a function based on subgroup affiliation strengths between users, items and their shared subgroups. If a user and an item share multiple subgroups, we assume that each such shared subgroup has an independent chance to trigger the link[1] between them [27]. As will be discussed in Section 3, the resulting CCCF model satisfies the three desired properties stated above.

To estimate the parameters, such as the affiliation strengths, of the proposed model, we formulate the problem as a probabilistic model and leverage a scalable Markov Chain Monte Carlo method, of which the complexity is linear *w.r.t.*the size of the dataset, thus making the underlying algorithm scalable. After we get the subgroups and the affiliation strengths of the users and items, any traditional CF method can be applied to each subgroup to make the predictions for the users on the items within the same subgroup. Finally, we leverage the affiliation strengths to aggregate the results from all the subgroups to make the final recommendation.

CCCF has the following four benefits (see details in Section 3.5): 1) The structure of the obtained subgroups can be very flexible, and is not restricted to be of certain shapes as in previous works. 2) It is easy to interpret the relationships between user/item and the obtained subgroups through the affiliation strengths. 3) CCCF can be easily modified to leverage content features of users/items which is challenging for previous works. 4) The computational complexity of the proposed model is linear *w.r.t.*the number of data points, thus making CCCF scalable to large datasets.

We evaluate the proposed method on four real world data sets. Our experimental results demonstrate that the proposed method outperforms state-of-the-art methods on the Top-N recommendation task. A qualitative analysis also shows that the obtained subgroups are semantically meaningful.

In the rest of this paper, we first introduce the problem definition and some useful notations in Section 2. In Section 3, we describe the CCCF model and present a scalable inference method. Experimental results on four real world data sets are shown in Section 4. We finally discuss some related works in Section 5 and conclude this paper in Section 6.

[1] Here a link between a user and an item means the user likes the item. If there is no link between them, we treat it as missing.

Table 1: Mathematical Notations

Symbol	Value	Description
y_{ui}	$\{0,1\}$	user u's feedback on item i
ϕ_{uk}	$[0,1]$	latent membership of user u in subgroup k
ϕ_{ik}	$[0,1]$	latent membership of item i in subgroup k
θ_k	$[0,1]$	in-group preference strength of subgroup k
$z_{u\to i,k}$	$\{0,1\}$	membership indicator of user u in subgroup k when interacting with item i
$z_{i\to u,k}$	$\{0,1\}$	membership indicator of item i in subgroup k when interacting with user u

2. PROBLEM DEFINITION

Given a set of users $\mathcal{U} = \{u|u = 1, ..., U\}$, a set of items $\mathcal{I} = \{i|i = 1, ..., I\}$, as well as the log of users' historical preferences $\mathcal{O} = (u, i, y_{ui})$, the goal of recommender systems is to recommend to each user u a list of items that will maximize her/his satisfaction. Here, y_{ui} can be numeric ratings in the scale of, say, $[1, 5]$ or binary values $\{0, 1\}$.

In this paper, we mainly focus on the case of *implicit* feedback, namely, we only have a partial information of the items that users have viewed/liked, and users' feedback on other items is missing. This is the most common scenario in practice. However, the proposed method can also be applied to other cases with slight modifications. For implicit feedback, all y_{ui} in $\mathcal{O}$ are 1; and for those $(u', i', y_{u'i'})$ triples not belonging to $\mathcal{O}$, the corresponding $y_{u'i'}$'s are missing. We use $\mathcal{O}'$ to denote the set of missing triples. The goal of top-N recommendation is to recommend each user a list of N items that she/he is most likely to like, *i.e.*, to pick the list of missing $y_{u'i'}$-s for every user which are most likely to be 1.

Some important notations used in this paper are listed in Table 1. We use u to index a user, and i and j to index items, and use normal font symbol x to denote scalars and bold math symbols $\boldsymbol{x}$ to denote vectors. The k-th element of vector $\boldsymbol{x}_i$ is denoted by x_{ik}.

3. METHODOLOGY

3.1 Overview

The overall procedure of our method, also used by [25, 31], is as follows:

1. Cluster users and items into subgroups, where users and items can be assigned to multiple subgroups and each subgroup includes a group of like-minded users and a set of items that these users are particularly interested in. We present a scalable co-clustering method called CCCF in Section 3.2.

2. In each subgroup, we apply traditional collaborative filtering methods (*e.g.*, ITEMCF, MATRIX FACTORIZATION) to learn users' preferences over the items within this subgroup. Since the learning of CF models in each subgroup is independent from each other, this step can be easily done in parallel (See Section 3.3).

3. For each user, we aggregate the recommendation results from all the subgroups that she/he is involved in. We discuss several aggregation strategies in Section 3.4 and study their performance in Section 4.3.4.

The main differences from previous works [25, 31] lie in step 1 and 3, which will be explained in detail in Section 3.2 and 3.4, respectively. In Section 3.5, we elaborate the benefits of the proposed method compared to those related works.

3.2 Scalable Co-Clustering for CF

In this subsection, we present Co-Clustering for Collaborative Filtering (CCCF), a co-clustering model which assigns users and items into overlapping subgroups. As discussed in Section 1, our goal is to find several latent subgroups, where each subgroup includes a set of like-minded users and the subset of items they are interested in. We assume that each user/item has a latent membership vector over subgroups. The memberships reveal users' latent interests on different types of items and items' latent properties that would be consumed by users, respectively. The links between users and items are generated based on the interactions between users, items and subgroups, *i.e.*, a user has larger chance to like an item if they both have strong affiliations to the same subgroups.

The two principles of designing CCCF are:

- A user has multiple types of interests so that she/he should be assigned to multiple subgroups with different strengths. Analogously, items are also allowed to be affiliated to multiple subgroups.
- The reason that a user likes an item is explained by the subgroup affiliations, *i.e.*, a user is more likely to like an item *if and only if* they belong to same subgroups. And we assume that the probability of a user liking an item depends on two ingredients: 1) The more overlapping subgroups a user shares with an item, the higher the probability that the user likes the item is. 2) A link between a user and an item can be explained by a dominant reason, *i.e.*, if a user and an item both have large affiliation strengths with a single subgroup, it is sufficient to form the link between them.

We assume there are K subgroups and each user/item has a probability of belonging to each subgroup. We denote by $\phi_{uk} \in [0,1]$ the affiliation strength of user u to subgroup k, and $\phi_{ik} \in [0,1]$ the affiliation strength of item i to subgroup k. We sample ϕ_{uk} and ϕ_{ik} from Beta distributions parameterized by predefined constants α_{k1} and α_{k2}.

$$\begin{aligned} \phi_{uk} &\sim \text{Beta}\left(\alpha_{k1}, \alpha_{k2}\right) \\ \phi_{ik} &\sim \text{Beta}\left(\alpha_{k1}, \alpha_{k2}\right) \end{aligned} \tag{1}$$

Intuitively, ϕ_{uk} represents the probability that user u likes the items in subgroup k. Analogously, ϕ_{ik} is the probability that item i is liked by the users in subgroup k. Items having large memberships in subgroup k share some latent properties recognized by a group of like-minded users.

The reasons why we use Beta distribution for ϕ_{uk} and ϕ_{ik} are: 1) In our work, we define $\boldsymbol{\phi}$ as membership variables with values in $[0, 1]$, and we do not enforce $\boldsymbol{\phi}_u$ to form a probabilistic distribution over the set of all the subgroups as the Mixed Membership models (*e.g.*, [2, 18]) do. Instead, users and items can have large affiliation strengths with multiple subgroups, which has been shown to be more suitable for modeling overlapping subgroups [27, 28]. 2) Beta distribution is the conjugate prior of Bernoulli distribution, which we use for the indicator variable z later. This enables us to perform sampling steps more efficiently (see Section 3.2.1).

We assume that each subgroup k has an independent chance θ_k to trigger the link between user u and item i if both of them belong to this subgroup, and the overall probability relies on the rate that at least one of the K event succeeds.

Here θ_k acts as a parameter to model the strength of connectivity within each subgroup k, meaning that the larger θ_k is, the more likely it is to form links between users and items within this subgroup. This parameter can model the fact that in practice, some subgroups are more active than others. Also, if a user belongs to this subgroup, there is a large chance of her/him liking an item shared by users within this subgroup, whereas for the less active subgroups, the chance of her/him liking an item shared by users within the subgroup is lower.

We also place a Beta distribution as the prior of θ_k:

$$\theta_k \sim \text{Beta}\left(\beta_1, \beta_2\right). \tag{2}$$

Since our goal in this paper is to find several focused subgroups, we'd like all the learned θ_k-s being close to 1. This prior knowledge can be incorporated into the model by, *e.g.*, setting $\beta_1 = 10$ and $\beta_2 = 1$.

For a pair of user u and item i, we use a parameter $z_{u\to i,k}$[2] to denote whether user u belongs to subgroup k or not when forming the link with item i. $z_{u\to i,k}$ is an indicator parameter drawn from a Bernoulli distribution parameterized by user u's group affiliation weight ϕ_{uk}. The parameter $z_{i\to u,k}$ which represents item i's affiliation with subgroup k for the link with user u is defined analogously.

$$\begin{aligned} z_{u\to i,k} &\sim \text{Bernoulli}\left(\phi_{uk}\right) \\ z_{i\to u,k} &\sim \text{Bernoulli}\left(\phi_{ik}\right) \end{aligned} \tag{3}$$

Then, the probability p_{uik} that subgroup k triggers a link between user u and item i is defined as

$$p_{uik} = \begin{cases} \theta_k, & \text{if } z_{u\to i,k} = 1 \text{ and } z_{i\to u,k} = 1 \\ 0, & \text{otherwise.} \end{cases} \tag{4}$$

Note that, if either the user or the item do not belong to subgroup k, the probability of forming a link via this subgroup is 0.

The overall probability p_{ui} that user u likes item i is modeled as the overall success rate of the K independent events, each of which represents the probability of a subgroup k to trigger the link between u and i.

$$p_{ui} = 1 - \textstyle\prod_k (1 - p_{uik}) = 1 - \prod_k (1 - \theta_k)^{z_{u\to i,k} z_{i\to u,k}} \tag{5}$$

The link between user u and item i is sampled as follows:

$$y_{ui} \sim \text{Bernoulli}\left(p_{ui}\right), \tag{6}$$

where $y_{ui} = 1$ means user u has a link with item i and $y_{ui} = 0$ means the link between them is missing.

We show the generative process in Algorithm 1.

Note that in addition to using the subgroup affiliations to explain the observed links with $y_{ui} = 1$, the CCCF model also needs to consider the missing links (where $y_{ui} = 0$) properly to avoid non-meaningful subgroup affiliations. However, the number of missing links is usually almost as large as $U \cdot I$ due to the data sparsity, which makes it impractical for large data sets. To address this issue, we randomly sample a subset of the missing links during the inference, and alternate different subsets in different iterations. Specifically, we randomly select N_u missing links for each user u, where N_u is proportional to the number of u's observed links.

3.2.1 Parameter Estimation

Maximum likelihood estimation is intractable for this model due to the existence of hidden variables. We use a Markov Chain Monte

[2] Here the notation $u \to i$ is used to denote user u's assignment when forming the link with the item i. Similar notations are also used in, *e.g.*, [2].

Algorithm 1 Generative Process of CCCF.

Input: $\mathcal{O}$, $\mathcal{O}'$, $\boldsymbol{\alpha}$ and $\boldsymbol{\beta}$
for all $k \in \{1, ..., K\}$ **do**
  for all $u \in \mathcal{U}$ **do**
    Draw $\phi_{uk} \sim \text{Beta}(\alpha_{k1}, \alpha_{k2})$
  end for
  for all $i \in \mathcal{I}$ **do**
    Draw $\phi_{ik} \sim \text{Beta}(\alpha_{k1}, \alpha_{k2})$
  end for
  Draw $\theta_k \sim \text{Beta}(\beta_1, \beta_2)$
end for
for all $(u, i, y_{ui}) \in \mathcal{O} \cup \mathcal{O}'$ **do**
  for all $k \in \{1, ..., K\}$ **do**
    Draw $z_{u \to i,k} \sim \text{Bernoulli}(\phi_{uk})$
    Draw $z_{i \to u,k} \sim \text{Bernoulli}(\phi_{ik})$
    if $z_{u \to i,k} = 1$ and $z_{i \to u,k} = 1$ **then**
      Set $p_{uik} = \theta_k$
    else
      Set $p_{uik} = 0$
    end if
  end for
  Set $p_{ui} = 1 - \prod_k (1 - p_{uik})$
  Draw $y_{ui} \sim \text{Bernoulli}(p_{ui})$
end for

Carlo (MCMC) method to estimate the parameters where we iteratively sample unknown variables from their conditional distributions given all the observations and the other variables fixed.

Denoting the set of items that user u has links with in the training data (including the observed links and randomly sampled negative links) by $\mathcal{T}_u$, we have the following sampling equation for $z_{u \to i,k}$ (latent variables $\boldsymbol{\phi}$ have been integrated out):

$$\begin{aligned} & p(z_{u \to i,k} = 1 | z_{\neg(u \to i,k)}, \boldsymbol{y}, \boldsymbol{\theta}, \alpha_{k1}, \alpha_{k2}) \\ & \propto \left(n_{uk}^{\neg i} + \alpha_{k1}\right) p(y_{ui} | \boldsymbol{z}_{\neg(u \to i,k)}, z_{u \to i,k} = 1, \boldsymbol{\theta}), \\ & p(z_{u \to i,k} = 0 | z_{\neg(u \to i,k)}, \boldsymbol{y}, \boldsymbol{\theta}, \alpha_{k1}, \alpha_{k2}) \\ & \propto \left(n_u - 1 - n_{uk}^{\neg i} + \alpha_{k2}\right) p(y_{ui} | \boldsymbol{z}_{\neg(u \to i,k)}, z_{u \to i,k} = 0, \boldsymbol{\theta}), \end{aligned} \tag{7}$$

where $n_{uk}^{\neg i} = \sum_{j \in \mathcal{T}_u \setminus \{i\}} \mathbf{1}(z_{u \to j,k} = 1)$ and $n_u = |\mathcal{T}_u|$

Since we sample different subsets of missing links during different iterations, a missing link might be new at iteration t. In this case, we do not have previous statistics of $z_{u \to i,k}$ and $z_{i \to u,k}$ to sample their new values according to Equation 7. Inspired by the stochastic collapsed variational Bayesian inference method for Latent Dirichlet Allocation [5], we use some additional *burn-in* steps to update these statistics before doing the sampling.

Since it is intractable to directly sample the posterior of each θ_k, we update these parameters using Metropolis-Hasting steps, where in each iteration a candidate for the next sample is generated from a *"proposal"* distribution. The proposed sample is accepted with some probability, otherwise the previous sample is duplicated. To be specific, in each iteration we propose each θ_k's new value from $\theta_k \sim \text{Beta}\,(\beta_1, \beta_2)$ and accept this new value with probability

$$\min\left(1, \frac{P(\boldsymbol{y}|\boldsymbol{z}, \boldsymbol{\theta}^{(t)}) P(\boldsymbol{\theta}^{(t)}|\boldsymbol{\beta})}{P(\boldsymbol{y}|\boldsymbol{z}, \boldsymbol{\theta}^{(t-1)}) P(\boldsymbol{\theta}^{(t-1)}|\boldsymbol{\beta})}\right). \tag{8}$$

If the new value is rejected, the previous value is retained.

The overall inference procedure is shown in Algorithm 2. After we get the optimized parameters $\boldsymbol{\theta}$ and $\boldsymbol{z}$, the group memberships

Algorithm 2 Inference Procedure for CCCF

Input: Randomly initialize $\boldsymbol{z}$. Set each $\theta_k = 1$.
Output: $\boldsymbol{z}, \boldsymbol{\theta}, \boldsymbol{\phi}$
while not converged or maximum number of iterations **do**
  Randomly sample a subset of missing values $\mathcal{O}''$ and set the training set as $\mathcal{T} = \mathcal{O} \cup \mathcal{O}''$.
  for all $(u, i, y_{ui}) \in \mathcal{T}$ **do**
    for all $k \in \{1, ..., K\}$ **do**
      Sample $z_{u \to i,k}$ using Equation 7.
      Sample $z_{i \to u,k}$ similarly.
    end for
  end for
  while not converged **do**
    for all $k \in \{1, ..., K\}$ **do**
      Update θ_k using Equation 8
    end for
  end while
end while
Compute $\boldsymbol{\phi}_u$ and $\boldsymbol{\phi}_i$ for all u and i using Equation 9 and 10.

$\boldsymbol{\phi}$ can be computed by

$$\phi_{uk} = \frac{\sum_{i \in \mathcal{T}_u} z_{u \to i,k} + \alpha_{k1}}{n_u + \alpha_{k1} + \alpha_{k2}}, \tag{9}$$

$$\phi_{ik} = \frac{\sum_{i \in \mathcal{T}_i} z_{i \to u,k} + \alpha_{k1}}{n_i + \alpha_{k1} + \alpha_{k2}}. \tag{10}$$

3.3 Collaborative Filtering in Subgroups

After getting the group affiliation strengths, we assign to each subgroup k a threshold ϵ_k. If user u's (or item i's) affiliation strength ϕ_{uk} (ϕ_{ik}) is larger than ϵ_k, we assume that this user/item belongs to this subgroup. Then, *any* Collaborative Filtering algorithm can be applied to a subgroup to compute the prediction $\hat{y}_{ui}^k$, which represents user u's preference on item i based on subgroup k.

The choice of the underlying CF methods depends on a lot of factors, such as data sparsity, complexity, model interpretability and latency of recommendation. One benefit of the framework is that the method does not rely on a specific CF algorithm. Any CF method of interest can be used and the framework will likely improve their performances. In our experiments, we choose four most representative CF models as the base methods applied to the subgroups, and show that the framework improves their recommendation performances by a significant margin on four real world data sets.

To make this paper self-contained, here we discuss the four CF methods which we use in our experiments. The reason why we choose these methods is that they cover a diverse set of methods ranging from the simplest solution to state-of-the-art models.

Popularity (POP). Items are scored by the percentage of users who like them.

$$y_{ui} = \sum_{u'} \frac{y_{u'i}}{|\mathcal{U}|} \tag{11}$$

Though simple, POP is widely used in today's industry as it is extremely easy to implement. The disadvantage is that it is not a personalized method and all the users receive the same recommendations. This problem can be solved by the proposed framework. CCCF first partitions users and items into subgroups. The item popularity within a specific subgroup indicates the popularity among a small group of people. Using the recommendation method that we will discuss in Section 3.4, CCCF provides users personalized recommendations by aggregated ranking lists of items that are popular in the subgroups that users are particularly interested in.

ITEMCF [17]. We use Jaccard correlation as the similarity measure and set the number of nearest neighbors to 50.

$$\hat{y}_{ui} = \sum_{j \in \mathcal{O}_u} s(i, j), \tag{12}$$

where $s(i, j)$ is the Jaccard similarity between the set of users who have liked item i and j, respectively.

MF (with negative sampling) [8, 12]. Matrix Factorization, or Latent Factor Model is the most popular Collaborative Filtering method for recommender systems. The preference of user u on item i is the dot product of the latent feature vectors of the user and the item, with some bias terms.

$$\hat{y}_{ui} = \alpha + b_u + b_i + \boldsymbol{u}_u^\top \boldsymbol{v}_i \tag{13}$$

The model parameters, latent factors and bias term, are learned by optimizing the following objective function.

$$\sum_{(u,i) \in \mathcal{T}} \ell(y_{ui}, \hat{y}_{ui}) + \lambda \mathcal{R}(\boldsymbol{b}, \boldsymbol{u}, \boldsymbol{v}), \tag{14}$$

where $\mathcal{R}$ is the regularization term.

For implicit feedback, we sample a subset of missing values as negative samples, and re-sample the subset for each learning iteration.

WARP [22, 23]. Matrix factorization with the WARP loss [22] is the state-of-the-art method for top-n recommendation on implicit feedback data, which has been used by many recent works [7, 24]. The main difference between WARP and MF is the objective function. WARP models the relative orders between items, which is the goal of top-N recommendation.

Another way of making recommendation in the subgroup is just setting $\hat{y}_{ui}^k = \theta_k$. However, this makes a strong assumption that users in a subgroups have the same preferences for all the items within this subgroup, which will result in suboptimal recommendation results. We will discuss this case in Section 3.4 and compare it with other recommendation methods in Section 4.3.4.

3.4 Recommendation

The last but not the least question is to how to compute the final recommendation list for each user. In [25], the authors just keep several subgroups with the largest weights for each user and sum up the recommendation scores from the selected subgroups. In [31], the proposed algorithm gets the final prediction of user u on an item i by averaging the predicted scores of u on i in all subgroups they share.

However, users and items belong to the subgroups with different weights, and the final recommendation should not ignore the weights. In this paper, we propose to use an affiliation strength weighted aggregation function to compute the final recommendations:

$$\hat{y}_{ui} = \sum_k \phi_{uk} \cdot \phi_{ik} \cdot \theta_k \cdot \hat{y}_{ui}^k \tag{15}$$

This aggregation function matches our motivation of designing the co-clustering method: 1) The prediction $\hat{y}_{ui}^k$ has a large value if the user and the item both have large affiliation strengths with this subgroup; 2) The more subgroups the user and the item share, the larger their predicted score is. The comparison with other aggregation methods is discussed in Section 4.3.4.

We note that for some CF methods (*e.g.*, WARP [22], BPR [15]), the prediction score $\hat{y}_{ui}^k$ is only a relative measurement (*i.e.*, $\hat{y}_{ui} > \hat{y}_{uj}$ means user u prefers item i than j) and unbounded. Before aggregating the scores, we first scale all the predictions of a user to $[0, 1]$.

In this following we also present three other strategies to aggregate the results.

CCCF-PR. As discussed in Section 3.3, the most straightforward way is just using the in-group strength θ_k-s as the prediction scores for the subgroups and calculating the overall score as follows:

$$\hat{y}_{ui} = \sum_k \phi_{uk} \cdot \phi_{ik} \cdot \theta_k \tag{16}$$

Comparing with Equation 15, this strategy sets all $\hat{y}_{ui}^k$ to 1. From another point of view, it can be thought as applying the *random* prediction (all the items have the same prediction score 1) base method in the subgroups.

CCCF-AVG. This is the strategy used in [32], where the average predicted score is taken as the overall score, ignoring the affiliation strengths of users and items.

$$\hat{y}_{ui} = \sum_k \hat{y}_{ui}^k / K \tag{17}$$

CCCF-MAX. As discussed in Section 3.2, a user would like an item as long as the probability on one of the subgroup is large enough. Another strategies is to make the prediction using the maximum score among these subgroups.

$$\hat{y}_{ui} = \max_k \hat{y}_{ui}^k \tag{18}$$

3.5 Discussion

In this subsection, we discuss several properties of the proposed model.

- **Scalability.** The complexity of the proposed CCCF method is linear in the number of observed links. On the other side, the objective function of the method proposed in [25] is NP-hard, and their optimization method for the relaxed objective involves a step of solving the top eigenvectors of a squared matrix with size $M = U + I$. To our best knowledge, the computational complexity of the fastest eigenvalue decomposition solver is $O(M^{2.367})$ when the matrix has some special structures [14].
- **Flexibility.** The structure of the subgroups in CCCF is flexible to model any kind of overlapping subgroups where these subgroups can be densely overlapping, hierarchically nested or non-overlapping. The methods in [32] and [31] are not so flexible since they assume the subgroups to form (approximate) Bordered Block Diagonal matrices. The method proposed in [25] uses an objective function of a weighted graph cut problem, which is designed to partition the graph into non-overlapping parts, thus it does not intrinsically discover overlapping subgroups.
- **Interpretability.** CCCF is a probabilistic model where the resulting affiliation strengths have semantic meanings. The strengths are particularly important when aggregating the results from different subgroups to make final recommendation (see Section 3.4). Also, as shown in Section 4, we analyze the top items with the largest affiliation strengths of each subgroup and find that these items have similar properties (*e.g.*, locations, categories in the Yelp data).
- **Extensibility.** When we are able to get some useful features for users and items, it is easy for CCCF to leverage the fea-

Table 2: Data Statistics

	#users	#items	#dyads	#density(%)
Lastfm	1.8K	1.5K	50K	1.76
MovieLens	35K	5.6K	3.4M	1.73
Netflix	46K	13K	8M	1.33
Yelp	2.8K	2.8K	80K	1.02

tures in the learning procedure as prior knowledge or supervisions (*e.g.*, [1], [29]). On one hand, it makes the subgroups even more interpretable by enforcing that the users/items in the same subgroup share some common features. On the other hand, features can help dealing with the cold-start problem – some users/items may have too few connections to be assigned to the right subgroups. It is not straightforward for the methods of [25] and [31] to achieve this goal.

4. EXPERIMENTS

Our experiments are designed to answer the following two questions: 1) Can the proposed method improve the accuracy of recommendation? 2) How meaningful are the discovered subgroups?

4.1 Data Sets and Preprocessing

We use four publicly available data sets: Last.fm[3], MovieLens 10M[4], Netflix[5] and Yelp[6]. As discussed in Section 2, we are more interested in the *implicit* feedback case. We follow the preprocessing steps that have been used in many recent works (*e.g.*, [15, 30], *et al.*.). For the data sets with explicit ratings, we remove the ratings of less than 4 stars and convert the remaining ratings to 1. We remove users and items with less than 20 ratings. The statistics of the resulting data sets are shown in Table 2. For each user, we randomly hold 20% of her/his feedback in the test data and use the rest of her/his ratings as training data.

4.2 Evaluation Measures

In the case of top-N recommendation, we present each user with N items that have the highest predicted values and have not been adopted by the user in the training data. We evaluate different approaches based on which of the items are actually adopted by the user in the test data.

Precision and Recall. Given a top-N recommendation list $C_{N,\text{rec}}$, precision and recall are defined as

$$\begin{aligned} \text{P@}N &= \frac{|C_{N,\text{rec}} \bigcap C_{\text{adopted}}|}{N} \\ \text{R@}N &= \frac{|C_{N,\text{rec}} \bigcap C_{\text{adopted}}|}{|C_{\text{adopted}}|}, \end{aligned} \tag{19}$$

where C_{adopted} are the items that a user has adopted in the test data. The precision and recall for the entire recommender system are computed by averaging the precision and recall over all the users, respectively.

F-measure. The F-measure represents a trade-off between precision and recall. We consider the F_β metric, which is defined as

$$\text{F}_\beta\text{@}N = (1+\beta^2)\cdot\frac{\text{P@}N \times \text{R@}N}{\beta^2 \cdot \text{P@}N + \text{R@}N}. \tag{20}$$

where β is a weight to control the balance. In our experiments, we use $F1$ metric with $\beta = 1$. We also calculate the $F1$ score for each user and report the average score.

[3]https://grouplens.org/datasets/hetrec-2011/
[4]https://grouplens.org/datasets/movielens/
[5]http://www.netflixprize.com/
[6]http://www.yelp.com/dataset_challenge/

Mean Average Precision (MAP). Average precision (AP) is a ranked precision metric that gives larger credit to correctly recommended items in higher positions. AP@N is defined as the average of precisions computed at all positions with an adopted item, namely,

$$\text{AP@}N = \frac{\sum_{k=1}^{N} \text{P@}k \times \text{rel}(k)}{\min\{N, |C_{\text{adopted}}|\}}, \tag{21}$$

where $\text{Precision}(k)$ is the precision at cut-off k in the top-N list $C_{N,\text{rec}}$, and $\text{rel}(k)$ is an indicator function equaling 1 if the item at rank k is adopted, otherwise it equals zero. Finally, Mean Average Precision (MAP@N) is defined as the mean of the AP@N scores of all users.

4.3 Accuracy of Top-N Recommendation

4.3.1 *Implementation Details*

We choose 4 popular CF methods as the comparison partners, and these 4 methods also serve as the base methods applied to each subgroup (as discussed in Section 3.3). We first train CCCF on the training data, and then apply the above CF methods in each subgroup. At last, for each user, we predict her/his preferences on all the unrated items by aggregating the predictions from the subgroups the user is involved in, and pick the Top-N items with largest predicted values to form the recommendation list. We set the hyperparameters of CCCF by cross validation on the training data. We found that the performance is not so sensitive to the choices of α and β. We empirically set them as: $\alpha_{k1} = 1, \alpha_{k2} = 1, \beta_1 = 10$, $\beta_2 = 1$ and $\epsilon = 0.1$. We will study how the choice of K impacts the performance in Section 4.3.5.

4.3.2 *CCCF vs. No Co-Clustering*

We first study the performance of CCCF comparing with the CF methods that are directly applied on the training data without co-clustering.

The results are shown in Table 3, 4 and 5. The overall observation is that CCCF improves the base methods on most of the cases – the best scores on all the data sets are all from CCCF. For most of the cases, CCCF improves the corresponding base method by at least 10%. Especially, combining CCCF with simple recommendation methods like POP can produce fairly good results.

We note that the performance of these CF methods varies a lot on different data sets. For example, on the Yelp data set, we observe that ITEMCF performs better than MF and WARP; while WARP is the best method on the Netflix data set. This means that no single CF method can beat all others at all times. The advantage of the proposed framework that we do not rely on the underlying base method, and users of our method are free to configure their favorite predictors in order to adapt to different scenarios.

4.3.3 *CCCF vs. Other Co-Clustering Methods*

We compare CCCF against two other co-clustering based methods MCoC [25] and BBDF [31], which are the most recent co-clustering methods for recommender systems, and adopt the same three-step framework. For MCoC and BBDF, we carefully choose the best parameters (*e.g.*, the number of top eigenvectors for MCoC, the density level in BBDF) to ensure fair comparisons. For both CCCF and MCoC, we set the number of subgroups to 10. The number of subgroups in BBDF is determined by the density parameter, which is chosen by cross validation.

Figure 1 shows the results for F1@10 and MAP@10 on the four data sets. The general observation is that CCCF outperforms the other two co-clustering methods in most cases. The only exception is on the Yelp data set, where both MCoC and CCCF achieve a

Table 3: CCCF vs. No Co-Clustering on the Lastfm data

	POP		ITEMCF		MF		WARP	
	NONE	CCCF	NONE	CCCF	NONE	CCCF	NONE	CCCF
P@10	0.070	0.134	0.173	0.174	0.152	0.156	0.178	0.187
R@10	0.090	0.176	0.223	0.250	0.204	0.217	0.253	0.264
F1@10	0.078	0.149	0.189	0.198	0.170	0.177	0.203	0.213
MAP@10	0.182	0.355	0.446	0.456	0.399	0.402	0.428	0.442

Table 4: CCCF vs. No Co-Clustering on the Netflix data

	POP		ITEMCF		MF		WARP	
	NONE	CCCF	NONE	CCCF	NONE	CCCF	NONE	CCCF
P@10	0.189	0.283	0.308	0.312	0.330	0.354	0.347	0.364
R@10	0.047	0.075	0.085	0.085	0.091	0.098	0.095	0.100
F1@10	0.070	0.109	0.123	0.123	0.132	0.142	0.138	0.145
MAP@10	0.348	0.471	0.493	0.505	0.528	0.551	0.538	0.556

Table 5: CCCF vs. No Co-Clustering on the Yelp data

	POP		ITEMCF		MF		WARP	
	NONE	CCCF	NONE	CCCF	NONE	CCCF	NONE	CCCF
P@10	0.018	0.046	0.048	0.057	0.043	0.046	0.047	0.056
R@10	0.024	0.058	0.062	0.072	0.055	0.058	0.058	0.068
F1@10	0.018	0.046	0.048	0.058	0.044	0.046	0.047	0.055
MAP@10	0.050	0.124	0.142	0.159	0.124	0.131	0.137	0.152

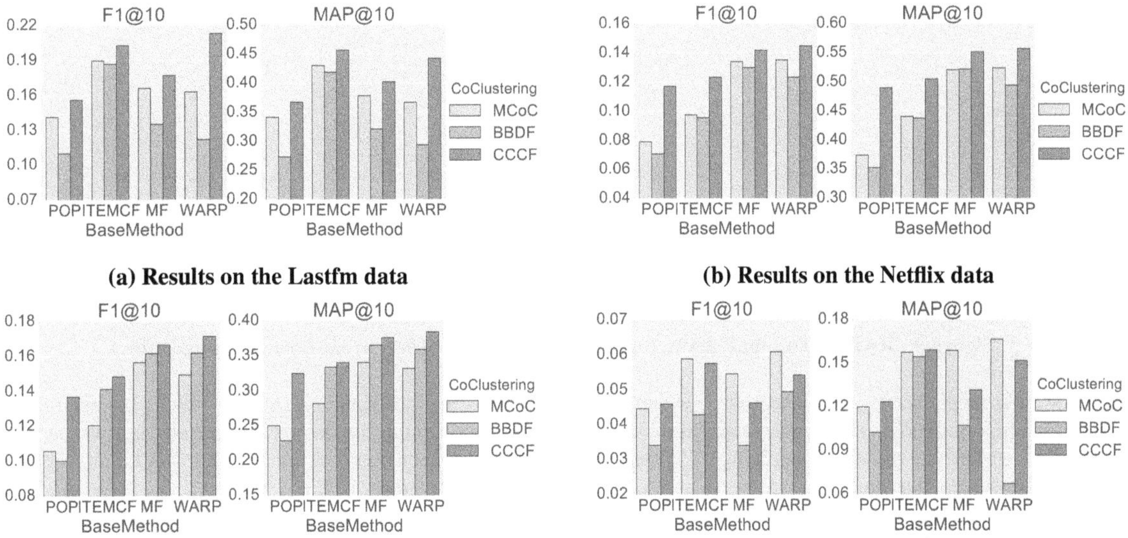

(a) Results on the Lastfm data **(b) Results on the Netflix data**

(c) Results on the MovieLens data **(d) Results on the Yelp data**

Figure 1: Comparison with other two co-clustering methods on the three data sets.

large performance gain compared to BBDF, and MCoC obtains the best results on this data set. This is likely due to the fact that the users and items of the Yelp data are isolated by the geographical distance, *i.e.*, they are more likely to form subgroups by the cities they are in.

Surprisingly, in some cases, MCoC and BBDF even decrease the performance of some of the base methods on the Lastfm, Netflix and MovieLens data. As discussed in Section 3.5, MCoC is actually optimizing a non-overlapping clustering objective function. So on the data sets that do not have obvious clustering structures, the clustering result of MCoC fails to boost recommendation accuracy. The performance of BBDF is not as good as expected on all the data sets except MovieLens. One reason may be that it assumes the user-item matrix follows some specific structure, and not all the data sets have this property. For example, for the Yelp data set, users and items are more likely to form non-overlapping clusters, due to the geographical separations of users and items. In this case, it is impossible for BBDF to find a reasonable bordered-block sub-matrix, which produces unsatisfactory results.

4.3.4 On the Choice of Aggregation Method

As discussed in Section 3.4, there are several alternative ways to aggregate recommendations from subgroups to make final recommendations: CCCF-PR, CCCF-MAX, CCCF-AVG. In this subsection, we compare these three alternatives with the method we proposed in Equation 15 (referred to as CCCF).

The MAP@10 results are shown in Figure 2. For the base method ITEMCF, CCCF-MAX can provide similar performance as CCCF,

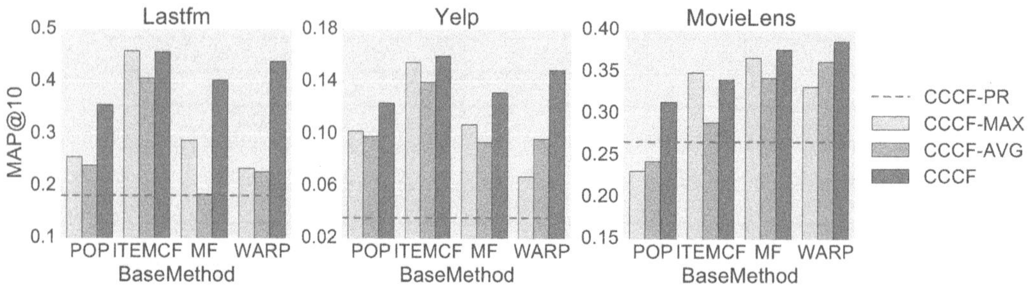

Figure 2: MAP@10 on the Lastfm and Yelp data with different strategies to aggregate the results from subgroups. Here we use the same co-clustering results and CF base methods. The only difference between the comparisons is the recommendation strategy. CCCF-PR does not need a base method and we plot it using the dashed line.

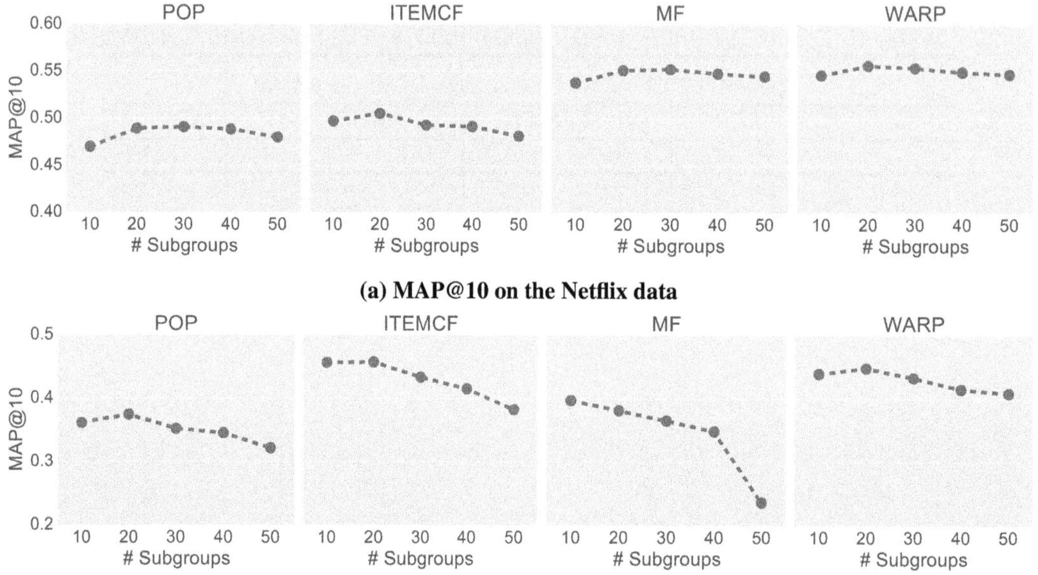

(a) MAP@10 on the Netflix data

(b) MAP@10 on the Lastfm data

Figure 3: MAP@10 on the Lastfm and Netflix data with different numbers of subgroups.

but its results for other methods are not competitive. For the Yelp data, CCCF-PR is outperformed by other aggregation methods by a large margin. This means that the step of applying a CF method in the subgroup is necessary. For almost all the cases, CCCF outperforms alternatives, which indicates that the steps of applying CF methods in each subgroup and considering the affiliation strengths are both essential when aggregating the results.

4.3.5 On the Number of Subgroups

In this subsection, we study how the choice of the number of subgroups K impacts the recommendation result. Due to space limits, we only show the results on the Lastfm and Netflix data. The results on MovieLens and Yelp data show similar trends. The results are shown in Figure 3.

We observe that for the Netflix data, setting K to 20 is a good choice where all the four base methods get best results. The Netflix data is not so sensitive to the number of subgroups. For the Lastfm data, 10 and 20 are the best choices. Increasing the number decreases the performance.

We note that increasing K would not necessarily increase the recommendation performance. The user-item matrix is very sparse, and increasing the number of subgroups would keep splitting large subgroups into several more focused small overlapping groups. Taking an extreme case for example, we might learn a lot of small subgroups that all of the users and items have links with each other. This case produces perfect co-clusters, but we do not have *new* items to recommend to users, which would hurt the recommendation performance.

4.4 Analysis of the Co-Clustering Results

In this section, we conduct a qualitative analysis of the co-clustering results to provide anecdotal evidence that the discovered subgroups are meaningful.

The goal of our method is to find focused subgroups, where the items in the same subgroup share some common latent properties that attract a group of like-minded users. Users' interests are usually not explicit, and we only have limited information about users in the data sets due to privacy issues. It is easier and more straightforward to study the item properties because we have more detailed information about items.

Table 6 shows the items with largest affiliation strengths from 3 sample subgroups from 10 total subgroups. We also present their locations and categories to study what these items are. We can see that the items from each subgroup share similar geographical and semantic properties. The top items from the first subgroups are all businesses from the city *Phoenix*, and most of them are restaurants. We can regard this subgroup as "Restaurants in *Phoenix*". Similarly, the top items from the second subgroup are also restaurants,

Table 6: **Items with largest affiliation strengths from 3 out of 10 subgroups on the Yelp data. We show their locations and the most representative categories that these items belong to.**

Sample Cluster 1			Sample Cluster 2			Sample Cluster 3		
Business Name	**City**	**Description**	**Business Name**	**City**	**Description**	**Business Name**	**City**	**Description**
Gallo Blanco	Phoenix	Restaurants	Bread and Butter	Henderson	Restaurants	Las Vegas North Premium Outlets	Las Vegas	Shopping
Lux	Phoenix	Restaurants	Snow Ono Shave Ice	Las Vegas	Restaurants	Orleans Hotel & Casino	Las Vegas	Casinos & Hotels
Postino Central	Phoenix	Restaurants	Buldogis Gourmet Hot Dogs	Las Vegas	Restaurants	Fremont Street Experience	Las Vegas	Entertainment
Maizie's Cafe & Bistro	Phoenix	Restaurants	Sweet Tomatoes	Las Vegas	Restaurants	Conservatory & Botanical Garden	Las Vegas	Entertainment
Cherryblossom Noodle Cafe	Phoenix	Restaurants	Strip N Dip Chicken Strips	Las Vegas	Restaurants	Planet Hollywood Las Vegas Resort & Casino	Las Vegas	Casinos & Hotels
Pizza a Metro	Phoenix	Restaurants	Patisserie Manon	Las Vegas	Restaurants	Flamingo Las Vegas Hotel & Casino	Las Vegas	Casinos & Hotels
SideBar	Phoenix	Bars	Island Flavor	Las Vegas	Restaurants	New York - New York	Las Vegas	Casinos & Hotels
Churn	Phoenix	Coffee & Tea	Japanese Curry Zen	Las Vegas	Restaurants	Miracle Mile Shops	Las Vegas	Shopping
Carly's Bistro	Phoenix	Restaurants	Slidin' Thru	Las Vegas	Restaurants	Palms Casino Resort	Las Vegas	Casinos & Hotels
Federal Pizza	Phoenix	Restaurants	Art of Flavors	Las Vegas	Food	The Forum Shops	Las Vegas	Shopping

but they are all in the greater Las Vegas area (*Henderson* is a city adjacent to *Las Vegas*). The third subgroup contains hotels, casinos or attractions in *Las Vegas*. The users from this subgroup are more likely to be tourists of *Las Vegas*, while the users of the second subgroup may also be the *Las Vegas* locals.

5. RELATED WORK

Using co-clustering based methods to improve CF has been studied by several previous works. [26] uses the K-means algorithm to cluster users into several subgroups and uses the subgroup assignments to smooth the unrated data for each individual user. [6] proposes a scalable CF framework based on a weighted co-clustering method.

Bayesian Co-Clustering (BCC) [18] adopts the Mixed Membership Stochastic Blockmodels (MMSB) [2] to the user-item bipartite graph. They assume that there are several latent user clusters and item clusters, and each user/item has mixed memberships to the latent clusters. The link between a user and an item is generated by the sum of the coefficient weights between the clusters they belong to. [20] proposes a collapsed Gibbs sampling and a collapsed variational Bayesian algorithm for BCC. [21] further extends BCC to a nonparametric model that can automatically learn the number of clusters from the data. In [4], the user and item latent factors are described by a nonparametric mixture of Gaussians based on their cluster allocations. [3] uses additive co-clustering to build concise model for matrix approximation. In these works, users and items are *separately* partitioned into user clusters and item clusters, which is totally different from co-clustering method used in this paper which groups users and items into the same clusters in a holistic manner. Also, these works optimize either the likelihood of the probabilistic mixed membership model on all the user-item links [18, 20, 21], or the accuracy of the point-wise rating prediction [4, 3], which can not guarantee good top-N recommendation results as they are optimizing a different goal [15, 19]. On the other hand, our method can utilize state-of-the-art top-N recommendation models as the base CF method in subgroups.

The idea of divide-and-conquer has also been used in other related works for collaborative filtering [11, 10, 9]. Divide Factor Combine (DFC) [11] divides a large-scale matrix factorization task into smaller subproblems by random row/column selections, solves each subproblem in parallel using an arbitrary base matrix factorization algorithm, and combines the subproblem solutions using techniques from randomized matrix approximation. The authors of [10] propose a model called Local Low-Rank Matrix Approximation (LLORMA), leading to a representation of the observed matrix as a weighted sum of several local low-rank matrices. They further extend LLORMA to the Local Collaborative Ranking (LCR) model [9] to consider the relative orders of items. The main differences from ours are: 1) They partition the user-item matrix by either random row/column sampling [11] or random anchor points [10, 9], while our goal is to find locally focused subgroups. 2) They focus on the rating prediction [11, 10] and collaborative ranking [9] problems on observed ratings[7] and ignore the fact that ratings are missing not at random. It leads to unsatisfactory top-N recommendation results [15, 19]. 3) They rely on the matrix factorization techniques, while ours can apply any CF method in the subgroups. This is important because matrix factorization is not always the best choice for all the cases, which has also been shown in our experiments (see Section 4.3.2).

The closest works are [25, 31, 32], which propose models that cluster users and items into the same subgroups. The authors of [25] propose an overlapping user-item co-clustering method based on a weighted graph-cut optimization problem. The objective function is NP-Hard, and they propose to optimize a relaxed problem. However, the learning involves solving the top eigenvectors of a large squared matrix so it cannot scale to large data sets. In [31] and [32], the authors permute rows and columns of the user-item rating matrix to form (approximate) Bordered Block Diagonal (BBD) matrices, and then apply traditional CF to each BBD matrix.

The framework used in our paper, as well as in [25, 31], has several benefits. 1) It partitions the matrix into several overlapping sub-matrices, which are denser than the original matrix, thus making the CF methods more feasible. 2) Any CF method can be used in each subgroup. Since the performance of different methods varies under different scenarios, this allows users to select their favorite CF base methods for the subgroups. 3) The training of the CF methods in subgroups can be trivially parallelized.

As discussed in Section 3.5, compared with previous works [25, 31], CCCF has various benefits including scalability, flexibility, interpretability and extensibility.

[7]Although LCR [9] models the orders of items, it still only considers the ranking between *observed* ratings.

6. CONCLUSION

In this paper, we proposed the scalable co-clustering method CCCF to improve the performance of CF-based methods for Top-N recommendation. The intuition of our model is that users may have different preferences over different subsets of items, where these subsets of items may overlap, and we explore subgroups of users who share interests over similar subsets of items through overlapping clustering. Experimental results on four real world data sets demonstrate that CCCF can improve four representative CF base methods (POP, ITMECF, MF, WARP) by co-clustering, and it also outperforms other co-clustering based methods (MCoC and BBDF). Qualitative analysis on the data sets also shows that the discovered subgroups are semantically meaningful.

A potential future work is to combine the idea of CCCF with Locally Collaborative Ranking (LCR) [9], where when applying the CF methods to the subgroups, the group affiliation strengths could also considered. Our model is complementary to LCR in the sense that it can replace the randomized anchor points selection and define the distance function using the joint user-item affiliation strengths. Also, it would be interesting to incorporate user and item features into the CCCF model in order to further improve the clustering results and to make them more interpretable. Besides, in this paper, the number of subgroups is a pre-defined hyperparameter. How to automatically determine the best number of subgroups using a Bayesian nonparametric method is also worth exploring.

7. REFERENCES

[1] D. Agarwal and B.-C. Chen. Regression-based latent factor models. In *Proceedings of the 15th ACM SIGKDD international conference on Knowledge discovery and data mining*, pages 19–28. ACM, 2009.

[2] E. M. Airoldi, D. M. Blei, S. E. Fienberg, and E. P. Xing. Mixed membership stochastic blockmodels. In *Advances in Neural Information Processing Systems*, pages 33–40, 2009.

[3] A. Beutel, A. Ahmed, and A. J. Smola. Accams: Additive co-clustering to approximate matrices succinctly. In *Proceedings of the 24th International Conference on World Wide Web*, pages 119–129, 2015.

[4] A. Beutel, K. Murray, C. Faloutsos, and A. J. Smola. Cobafi: collaborative bayesian filtering. In *Proceedings of the 23rd international conference on World wide web*, pages 97–108, 2014.

[5] J. Foulds, L. Boyles, C. DuBois, P. Smyth, and M. Welling. Stochastic collapsed variational bayesian inference for latent dirichlet allocation. In *Proceedings of the 19th ACM SIGKDD international conference on Knowledge discovery and data mining*, pages 446–454. ACM, 2013.

[6] T. George and S. Merugu. A scalable collaborative filtering framework based on co-clustering. In *ICDM'05*. IEEE, 2005.

[7] L. Hong, A. S. Doumith, and B. D. Davison. Co-factorization machines: modeling user interests and predicting individual decisions in twitter. In *Proceedings of the sixth ACM international conference on Web search and data mining*, pages 557–566. ACM, 2013.

[8] Y. Koren, R. Bell, and C. Volinsky. Matrix factorization techniques for recommender systems. *Computer*, (8):30–37, 2009.

[9] J. Lee, S. Bengio, S. Kim, G. Lebanon, and Y. Singer. Local collaborative ranking. In *Proceedings of the 23rd international conference on World wide web*, pages 85–96, 2014.

[10] J. Lee, S. Kim, G. Lebanon, and Y. Singer. Local low-rank matrix approximation. In *Proceedings of The 30th International Conference on Machine Learning*, pages 82–90, 2013.

[11] L. W. Mackey, M. I. Jordan, and A. Talwalkar. Divide-and-conquer matrix factorization. In *Advances in Neural Information Processing Systems*, pages 1134–1142, 2011.

[12] A. Mnih and R. Salakhutdinov. Probabilistic matrix factorization. In *Advances in neural information processing systems*, pages 1257–1264, 2007.

[13] M. O'Connor and J. Herlocker. Clustering items for collaborative filtering. In *Proceedings of the ACM SIGIR workshop on recommender systems*, volume 128, 1999.

[14] V. Y. Pan and Z. Q. Chen. The complexity of the matrix eigenproblem. In *Proceedings of the Thirty-first Annual ACM Symposium on Theory of Computing*, STOC '99, pages 507–516. ACM, 1999.

[15] S. Rendle, C. Freudenthaler, Z. Gantner, and L. Schmidt-Thieme. Bpr: Bayesian personalized ranking from implicit feedback. In *Proceedings of the Twenty-Fifth Conference on Uncertainty in Artificial Intelligence*, pages 452–461, 2009.

[16] F. Ricci, L. Rokach, and B. Shapira. *Introduction to recommender systems handbook*. Springer, 2011.

[17] B. Sarwar, G. Karypis, J. Konstan, and J. Riedl. Item-based collaborative filtering recommendation algorithms. In *Proceedings of the 10th International Conference on World Wide Web*, pages 285–295. ACM, 2001.

[18] H. Shan and A. Banerjee. Bayesian co-clustering. In *ICDM'08*, pages 530–539. IEEE, 2008.

[19] H. Steck. Training and testing of recommender systems on data missing not at random. In *Proceedings of the 16th ACM SIGKDD international conference on Knowledge discovery and data mining*, pages 713–722. ACM, 2010.

[20] P. Wang, C. Domeniconi, and K. B. Laskey. Latent dirichlet bayesian co-clustering. In *Machine Learning and Knowledge Discovery in Databases*, pages 522–537. Springer, 2009.

[21] P. Wang, K. B. Laskey, C. Domeniconi, and M. I. Jordan. Nonparametric bayesian co-clustering ensembles. In *SDM*. SIAM, 2011.

[22] J. Weston, S. Bengio, and N. Usunier. Wsabie: Scaling up to large vocabulary image annotation. In *IJCAI*, pages 2764–2770, 2011.

[23] J. Weston, C. Wang, R. Weiss, and A. Berenzweig. Latent collaborative retrieval. In *Proceedings of the 29th International Conference on Machine Learning*, pages 9–16, 2012.

[24] J. Weston, R. J. Weiss, and H. Yee. Nonlinear latent factorization by embedding multiple user interests. In *Proceedings of the 7th ACM conference on Recommender systems*, pages 65–68. ACM, 2013.

[25] B. Xu, J. Bu, C. Chen, and D. Cai. An exploration of improving collaborative recommender systems via user-item subgroups. In *Proceedings of the 21st International Conference on World Wide Web*, pages 21–30. ACM, 2012.

[26] G.-R. Xue, C. Lin, Q. Yang, W. Xi, H.-J. Zeng, Y. Yu, and Z. Chen. Scalable collaborative filtering using cluster-based smoothing. In *Proceedings of the 28th annual international ACM SIGIR conference on Research and development in information retrieval*, pages 114–121. ACM, 2005.

[27] J. Yang and J. Leskovec. Community-affiliation graph model for overlapping network community detection. In *ICDM'12*, pages 1170–1175. IEEE, 2012.

[28] J. Yang and J. Leskovec. Overlapping community detection at scale: A nonnegative matrix factorization approach. In *Proceedings of the Sixth ACM International Conference on Web Search and Data Mining*, pages 587–596. ACM, 2013.

[29] J. Yang, J. McAuley, and J. Leskovec. Community detection in networks with node attributes. In *ICDM'13*, pages 1151–1156. IEEE, 2013.

[30] S.-H. Yang, B. Long, A. J. Smola, H. Zha, and Z. Zheng. Collaborative competitive filtering: learning recommender using context of user choice. In *Proceedings of the 34th international ACM SIGIR conference on Research and development in Information Retrieval*, pages 295–304. ACM, 2011.

[31] Y. Zhang, M. Zhang, Y. Liu, and S. Ma. Improve collaborative filtering through bordered block diagonal form matrices. In *Proceedings of the 36th international ACM SIGIR conference on Research and development in information retrieval*, pages 313–322. ACM, 2013.

[32] Y. Zhang, M. Zhang, Y. Liu, S. Ma, and S. Feng. Localized matrix factorization for recommendation based on matrix block diagonal forms. In *Proceedings of the 22Nd International Conference on World Wide Web*, pages 1511–1520. ACM, 2013.

On the Efficiency of the Information Networks in Social Media

Mahmoudreza Babaei
MPI-SWS, Germany

Przemyslaw Grabowicz
MPI-SWS, Germany

Isabel Valera
MPI-SWS, Germany

Krishna P. Gummadi
MPI-SWS, Germany

Manuel Gomez-Rodriguez
MPI-SWS, Germany

ABSTRACT

Social media sites are information marketplaces, where users produce and consume a wide variety of information and ideas. In these sites, users typically choose their *information sources*, which in turn determine what specific information they receive, how much information they receive and how quickly this information is shown to them. In this context, a natural question that arises is how *efficient* are social media users at selecting their information sources.

In this work, we propose a computational framework to quantify users' efficiency at selecting information sources. Our framework is based on the assumption that the goal of users is to acquire a set of unique pieces of information. To quantify user's efficiency, we ask if the user could have acquired the same pieces of information from another set of sources *more efficiently*. We define three different notions of efficiency – link, in-flow, and delay – corresponding to the number of sources the user *follows*, the amount of (redundant) information she acquires and the delay with which she receives the information. Our definitions of efficiency are general and applicable to any social media system with an underlying information network, in which every user follows others to receive the information they produce.

In our experiments, we measure the efficiency of Twitter users at acquiring different types of information. We find that Twitter users exhibit sub-optimal efficiency across the three notions of efficiency, although they tend to be more efficient at acquiring non-popular pieces of information than they are at acquiring popular pieces of information. We then show that this lack of efficiency is a consequence of the triadic closure mechanism by which users typically discover and follow other users in social media. Thus, our study reveals a tradeoff between the efficiency and discoverability of information sources. Finally, we develop a heuristic algorithm that enables users to be significantly more efficient at acquiring the same unique pieces of information.

Categories and Subject Descriptors: H.1.2 [**Information Systems**]: Models and Principles – *Human information processing*

WSDM'16, February 22–25, 2016, San Francisco, CA, USA.

DOI: http://dx.doi.org/10.1145/2835776.2835826

General Terms: Human Factors; Measurement; Performance.
Keywords: Efficiency; information network; social media; information; cover set; rewiring algorithm; optimization; lossless.

1. INTRODUCTION

Over the last decade, the advent of social media has profoundly changed the way people produce and consume information online. A characteristic feature of many social media sites (e.g., Twitter or Pinterest) that distinguishes them from mainstream news media sites (e.g., CNN.com or NYTimes.com) is the *information network* created by consumers *following* their preferred producers of information [6, 18, 10]. However, the task of selecting information sources from potentially tens to hundreds of millions of users poses serious challenges and raises important questions that have not yet been addressed. For example, recent studies have observed that out of fear of missing out on important information, users tend to follow too many other users [14]. In the process, they receive a lot of redundant information [4], become overloaded, and effectively miss the information they are interested in [12, 19]. Moreover, it is very hard to ascertain the quality, relevance, and credibility of information produced by social media users [2, 8, 11]. Also, many users rely on their network neighborhood for discovering new sources of information, as observed by the large number of triadic closures [26, 13, 24] in link creation.

The motivation behind this work originates from two fundamental questions: 1) How *efficient* are the users of a social media site at selecting which other users to follow to acquire information of their interest? and, 2) can we propose methods to enable a user to acquire the same pieces of information from another set of users in the social media site *more efficiently*? To answer these intertwined questions, we view the structure of the information networks in social media sites as the outcome of a network formation game [17], where a node (*i.e.*, user) links to other nodes to solve a specific task (*i.e.*, acquire information relevant to the user). In this work, we propose a general computational framework to quantify and optimize the efficiency of links created by users to acquire information.

With such a framework in place, we analyze the efficiency of information networks of social media users, addressing several important additional questions. For instance, a user might aim to receive pieces of information of different popularity. However, can popular information be covered as efficiently as non-popular information? Additionally, previous studies have identified triadic closure [26, 13, 24] and information diffusion [28, 23, 3] as salient mechanisms that trigger new link creation in social networks. However, how efficient are information networks created with these mechanisms? Similarly, it has been observed that in information systems such as Wikipedia [29, 30], links are primarily established to make related content more easily discoverable, rather than for some nuanced notion of efficiency. Is the link creation in user-generated information networks such as Twitter driven by a similar goal, *i.e.*, discovering users in the network neighborhood, rather than for efficiency in acquiring information?

Our computational framework is based on the following key concept: given a set of unique ideas, pieces of information, or more generally, *memes* $\mathcal{I}$ spreading through an information network, there is an *optimal* set of nodes that, if followed, would enable us to get to know $\mathcal{I}$. Naturally, this concept relies on defining what is an optimal set. Here, we consider three notions of optimality, which lead to three types of efficiencies:

I. **Link efficiency.** The optimal set $\mathcal{U}^l(\mathcal{I})$ is the one that contains the smallest number of users. Then, we compute link efficiency by comparing the number of people a user follows, i.e., the number of *followees*, with the size of the optimal set $\mathcal{U}^l(\mathcal{I})$. Finding the optimal set reduces to a minimum set cover problem, which can be solved using a well-known and efficient greedy algorithm with provable guarantees [15].

II. **In-flow efficiency.** The optimal set $\mathcal{U}^f(\mathcal{I})$ is the one that provides the least amount of tweets per time unit. Then, we compute in-flow efficiency by comparing the amount of tweets per time unit a user receives from the people she follows with the amount of tweets per time unit she would have received by following the users in the optimal set $\mathcal{U}^f(\mathcal{I})$. Finding the optimal set reduces to a minimum weighted set cover problem, which again can be solved efficiently with provable guarantees [15].

III. **Delay efficiency.** The optimal set $\mathcal{U}^t(\mathcal{I})$ is the one that provides the memes as early as possible. Then, we compute delay efficiency by comparing the average delay per meme that the user achieves through the people she follows with the average delay she would achieve by following the users in the optimal set. Here, we define the delay at acquiring a meme in a social media system as the difference between the time when the user received the meme in her timeline and the time when the meme was first mentioned by a user in the social media system. Finding the optimal set reduces to finding the set of users who made the first mention of each of the memes in the social media system.

Although the concept of link efficiency has been previously introduced by us in [4], here we extend it to account for other definitions of efficiency, i.e., in-flow and delay efficiency. Another study related to ours uses set covers for efficient detection of outbreaks [21]. However, that related work does not compare the optimal sets to the sets encountered in reality.

In this study, we apply the three notions of efficiency to the information network of Twitter users. Our analysis does not only show how efficient users are at acquiring information, but also helps us in understanding the influence of different factors on efficiency:

1. We find that users acquire information sub-optimally with respect to the three notions of efficiency. However, the higher is the coverage of information that they want to acquire, the higher is the efficiency.

2. While the popular pieces of information are acquired inefficiently, less popular pieces of information are acquired more efficiently.

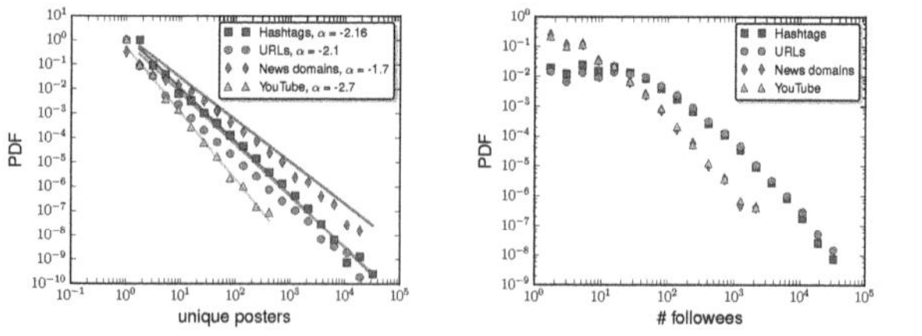

(A) Users per meme (B) The number of followees

Figure 1: The distributions of (A) the number of users posting a unique meme and (B) the number of followees posting a specific type of meme at least once. For (A), a power-law is fitted (solid lines) and the exponent α is given.

3. Users trade followees' discoverability for information efficiency. While, for a typical Twitter user, many people in her original ego-network may be discovered by triadic closure, very few people in the optimized efficient ego-networks can be discovered in that way.

4. We introduce a heuristic algorithm that considerably increases both user's inflow and delay efficiencies and delivers to her the same unique pieces of information, by rewiring user's information network.

Our empirical findings also shed light on how our notion of efficiency relates to user's ego-network structure (*e.g.*, triangle closure, clustering coefficient).

2. DATASET

We use a large Twitter dataset, as reported in previous work [9], which comprises the following three types of information: profiles of 52 million users, 1.9 billion directed follow links among these users, and 1.7 billion public tweets posted by the collected users. The link information of the network is based on a snapshot taken at the time of data collection, in September 2009. In our work, we limit ourselves to tweets published during one week, from July 1, 2009 to July 7, 2009, and filter out users that did not tweet before July 1, in order to be able to consider the social graph to be *approximately* static. After this filtering, we have 395,093 active users, 39,382,666 directed edges, and 78,202,668 tweets.

Then, we sample 10,000 users at random out of the 395,093 active users and reconstruct their timelines by collecting all tweets published by the (active) people they follow (among all the 395,093 users), build their ego-networks (i.e., who follows whom among the people they follow), and track all the unique memes they were exposed to during the observation period. We consider four different types of memes:

I. **Hashtags.** Hashtags are words or phrases inside a tweet which are prefixed with the symbol "#". They provide a way for a user to generate searchable metadata, keywords or tags, in order to describe her tweet, associate the tweet to a (trending) topic, or express an idea. Hashtags have become ubiquitous and are an integral aspect of the social Web nowadays [25].

II. **URLs.** We extract all URLs mentioned inside tweets [22]. Since most of URLs in Twitter are shortened, we unwrap them by calling the API of the corresponding shortening service. Here, we considered seven popular URL shorteners:

bit.ly, tinyurl.com, is.gd, twurl.nl, snurl.com, doiop.com and eweri.com, and discard any URL that could not be unwrapped. In general, URLs correspond to online articles, posts, links, or websites.

III. **News domains.** We extract all domain names mentioned inside tweets that correspond to mainstream media sites indexed by Google News [20]. News domains correspond to media outlets, which may be specializing in the coverage of some topics or perspectives.

IV. **YouTube videos.** We extract all URLs mentioned inside tweets that match the pattern `www.youtube.com/watch`. Here, each of these URLs corresponds to a different YouTube video.

The above memes provide different levels of granularity. For example, news domains are very generic, while YouTube videos are fairly specific. In more detail, the set of active users mention $286,219$ unique hashtags, $379,424$ URLs, 18,616 news domains, and $19,998$ YouTube videos. Figure 1A shows the distribution of the number of unique posters for different types of memes, which follows a power-law distribution. The tail of the distribution, as expected, is the heaviest for news domains, while the lightest for YouTube videos. Moreover, as shown in Figure 1B, the tail of the distribution of the number of followees tweeting at least one of the memes is also a power-law. In the remainder, we consider only such followees.[1] Also, we focus on users whose information network is fairly developed by filtering out any user following less than 20 followees.

Note that, although our methodology does not depend on the particular choice of meme, it does make two key assumptions. First, it assumes we can distinguish whether two memes are equal or differ. Distinguishing certain memes such as hashtags may be trivial but distinguishing others, such as ideas, may be very difficult. Second, it assumes that receiving several copies of the same meme from different users does not provide additional information, even if different users express different opinions about the meme. It would be interesting to relax the second assumption in future work.

Importantly, in 2009 Twitter did not have features such as "Lists" and "Personalized Suggestions", so the main way users received and processed information was through their feed, for which we have complete data. The drawback of using older data is smaller number of users and social activity.

3. DEFINITIONS OF EFFICIENCY

In this section, we introduce three different notions of efficiency, namely, link, in-flow and delay efficiency. For each type of efficiency, we provide a formal definition and propose a method to approximately compute it with provable guarantees.[2] Then, we use the methods to investigate the efficiency of Twitter users at acquiring information.

3.1 Link efficiency

Definition: Our definition of link efficiency follows from our prior definition [4]. Consider a user u and the set of unique memes $\mathcal{I}_u$ she is exposed to through her feed in a given time period, by following $|\mathcal{U}_u|$ users. Then, we define the optimal set $\mathcal{U}^l(\mathcal{I}_u)$ as the minimal set of users that, if followed, would expose the user to at least $\mathcal{I}_u$, and define the link efficiency of a user u at acquiring memes as

$$E_u^l = \frac{|\mathcal{U}^l(\mathcal{I}_u)|}{|\mathcal{U}_u|}, \quad (1)$$

where $0 \leq E_u^l \leq 1$. If the number of users she follows coincides with the number of users in the minimal set, then her efficiency value is $E_u^l = 1$. The larger the original number of followees in comparison with the size of the minimal set, the smaller the link efficiency. Figure 2 illustrates our definition of link efficiency.

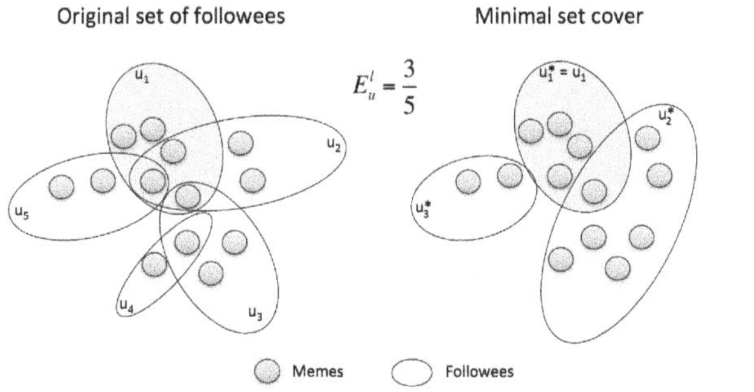

Figure 2: Our notion of link efficiency, E_u^l. We define link efficiency as $E_u^l = |\mathcal{U}^l(\mathcal{I}_u)|/|\mathcal{U}_u|$, where $\mathcal{I}_u$ is the set of (unique) memes (blue circles) a user u receives in her timeline by following a set of followees $\mathcal{U}_u = \{u_1, \ldots, u_5\}$ (left), and $\mathcal{U}^l(\mathcal{I}_u) = \{u_1^*, u_2^*, u_3^*\}$ (right) is the minimal set cover (of users) that, if followed, would provide the same set of memes $\mathcal{I}_u$. In the illustration, each user u_i posts the memes within the associated ellipsoid. Hence, in this example, the link efficiency value is $E_u^l = 3/5$.

Algorithm 1: Greedy set cover for estimating link efficiency

Input: set of all users $\mathcal{U}$; set of unique memes $\mathcal{I}_u$; followee set $\mathcal{U}_u$; set of memes $\mathcal{I}^v$ posted by user v
Set $\mathcal{U}^l = \emptyset$;
Set $\mathcal{X} = \mathcal{I}_u$;
while $\mathcal{X} \neq \emptyset$ **do**
  Set $v^* = \text{argmin}_{v \in \mathcal{U} \setminus \mathcal{U}^l} \frac{1}{|\mathcal{X} \cap \mathcal{I}^v|}$;
  Set $\mathcal{U}^l = \mathcal{U}^l \cup \{v^*\}$;
  Set $\mathcal{X} = \mathcal{X} \setminus \mathcal{I}^{v^*}$;
end
Output: $\mathcal{U}^l$

Examples of link inefficiency: Our definition captures two types of link inefficiency, which we illustrate by two extreme examples. If a user u follows $|\mathcal{U}_u|$ other users, each of them mentioning different (disjoint) sets of memes, and there is another user $v \notin \mathcal{U}_u$ that cover all the memes the followees cover, then the user's efficiency will be $E_u^l = 1/|\mathcal{U}_u|$. If a user u follows $|\mathcal{U}_u|$ other users and all these users mention exactly the same memes, then the user's efficiency will be $E_u^l = 1/|\mathcal{U}_u|$ and $\lim_{|\mathcal{U}_u| \to \infty} E_u^l = 0$. The former type of link inefficiency is due to following users that individually post too few memes, while the latter is due to following users that collectively produce too many redundant memes.

Computing link efficiency: In practice, computing E_u^l, as defined by Eq. 1, reduces to finding the minimal set of users $\mathcal{U}^l(\mathcal{I}_u)$, which can be cast as the classical minimum set cover problem [16]. Although the minimum set cover problem is NP-hard, we can approximate $\mathcal{U}^l(\mathcal{I}_u)$ using a well-known and efficient greedy algorithm [15], which returns an $O(\log d)$ approximation of the min-

[1]Considering all followees leads to qualitatively similar results, but lower absolute values of efficiency.

[2]Delay efficiency, unlike link and in-flow efficiencies, can be computed exactly.

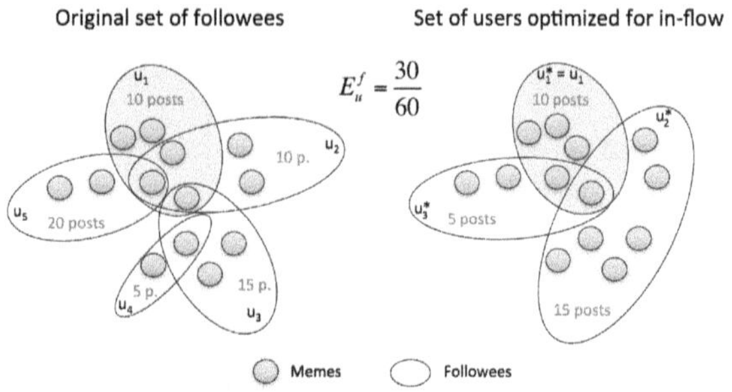

Figure 3: Our notion of in-flow efficiency, E_u^f. We define in-flow efficiency as $E_u^f = f(\mathcal{U}^f(\mathcal{I}_u))/f(\mathcal{U}_u)$, where $\mathcal{I}_u$ is the set of (unique) memes (blue circles) a user receives in her timeline by following a set of followees $\mathcal{U}_u = \{u_1, \ldots, u_5\}$ (left), and $\mathcal{U}^f(\mathcal{I}_u) = \{u_1^*, u_2^*, u_3^*\}$ (right) is the set cover (of users) with the smallest associated in-flow $f(\mathcal{U}^f(\mathcal{I}_u))$ that, if followed, would provide the same set of memes $\mathcal{I}_u$. In the illustration, each user u_i posts the memes within the associated ellipsoid and the red values in the ellipsoid represent the in-flow of each user. Hence, in this case, the in-flow efficiency value is $E_u^{\mathrm{f}} = 30/60 = 0.5$.

Algorithm 2: Greedy set cover for estimating in-flow efficiency

Input: set of all users $\mathcal{U}$; set of unique memes $\mathcal{I}_u$; number of tweets N^v posted by user v; set of memes $\mathcal{I}^v$ posted by user v
Set $\mathcal{U}^{\mathrm{f}} = \emptyset$;
Set $\mathcal{X} = \mathcal{I}_u$;
while $\mathcal{X} \neq \emptyset$ **do**
  Set $v^* = \arg\min_{v \in \mathcal{U} \setminus \mathcal{U}^{\mathrm{f}}} \frac{N^v}{|\mathcal{I}^v \cap \mathcal{X}|}$;
  Set $\mathcal{U}^{\mathrm{f}} = \mathcal{U}^{\mathrm{f}} \cup \{v^*\}$;
  Set $\mathcal{X} = \mathcal{X} \setminus \mathcal{I}^{v^*}$
end
Output: $\mathcal{U}^{\mathrm{f}}$

imum size set cover, where $d = \max_{v \in \mathcal{U}} |\mathcal{I}^v|$ is the maximum number of memes posted by any user. Refer to Algorithm 1 for a full description of our procedure to approximate link efficiency.

3.2 In-flow efficiency

Definition: Consider a user u and the set of unique memes $\mathcal{I}_u$ she is exposed to through her feed in a given time period, by following $|\mathcal{U}_u|$ users. Then, we define the optimal set $\mathcal{U}^{\mathrm{f}}(\mathcal{I}_u)$ as the set of users that, if followed, would expose the user to, at least, $\mathcal{I}_u$, while providing the least amount of tweets per time unit, *i.e.*, the minimum tweet in-flow. In particular, we define the in-flow efficiency of a user u at acquiring memes as

$$E_u^{\mathrm{f}} = \frac{f(\mathcal{U}^{\mathrm{f}}(\mathcal{I}_u))}{f(\mathcal{U}_u)}, \tag{2}$$

where $f(\mathcal{U}_u)$ denotes the amount of tweets produced by the set of users $\mathcal{U}_u$ per time unit (user u's in-flow) and $0 \leq E_u^{\mathrm{f}} \leq 1$. The in-flow efficiency $E_u^{\mathrm{f}} = 1$ if user u's in-flow coincides with the amount of tweets per time unit posted by the users in the optimal set $\mathcal{U}^{\mathrm{f}}(\mathcal{I}_u)$. Here, the larger is user u's in-flow in comparison with the amount of tweets per time unit posted by the users in the optimal set, the lower is her in-flow efficiency. Figure 3 illustrates our definition of in-flow efficiency using an example.

Examples of in-flow inefficiency: As in the case of link inefficiency, this definition captures several types of in-flow inefficiency.

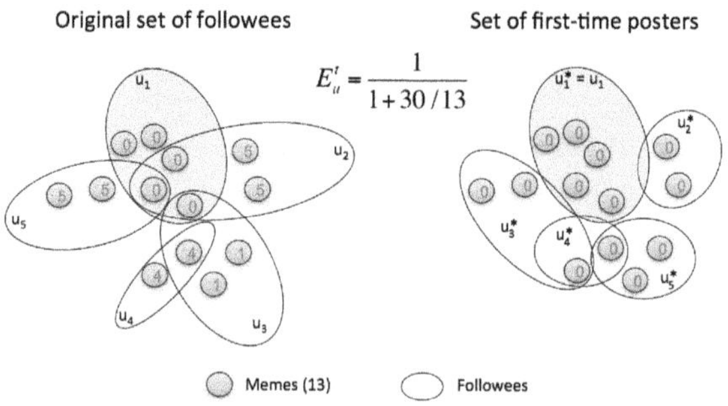

Figure 4: Our notion of delay efficiency, E_u^t. We define delay efficiency as $E_u^t = 1/(1 + \langle t_i - t_i^0 \rangle_{i \in \mathcal{I}_u})$, where t_i is the time in which a user receives meme i in her timeline, t_i^0 is the time when the meme is first mentioned by a user in the whole social media system, $\mathcal{I}_u$ is the set of (unique) memes (blue circles) a user receives in her timeline by following a set of followees $\mathcal{U}_u = \{u_1, \ldots, u_5\}$ (left), and $\mathcal{U}^t(\mathcal{I}_u) = \{u_1^*, \ldots, u_5^*\}$ (right) is the set cover (of users) that, if followed, would provide the same set of memes $\mathcal{I}_u$ as early as possible. In the illustration, each user u_i adopts the memes within the associated ellipsoid for the first time after a delay indicated by the red number. Hence, the delay efficiency is $E_u^t = 1/(1 + 30/13)$.

First, it is easy to see that the example of extreme link inefficiency due to following users posting exactly the same memes, also leads to in-flow inefficiency.

Second, there is another type of in-flow inefficiency, which we illustrate by an additional extreme example. Consider user u that follows $|\mathcal{U}_u|$ other users and the amount of tweets produced by these followees has a divergent mean, *e.g.*, it has a Pareto distribution (a power law) with exponent $\alpha \leq 1$. Then, if there exists another set of $|\mathcal{U}_u|$ users mentioning the same unique memes and the amount of tweets produced by them has a non-divergent mean, *e.g.*, it is a Pareto distribution with exponent $\alpha > 1$, the user's efficiency will converge to zero as $|\mathcal{U}_u|$ increases, *i.e.*, $\lim_{|\mathcal{U}_u| \to \infty} E_u^{\mathrm{l}} = 0$. Asymptotically, an infinite in-flow could be replaced with a finite in-flow that include the same set of unique memes.

Computing in-flow efficiency: In practice, computing the optimal set of users $\mathcal{U}^{\mathrm{f}}(\mathcal{I}_u)$ reduces to solving the weighted set cover problem, which is also NP-hard. Analogously, we can find an approximate solution to $\mathcal{U}^{\mathrm{f}}(\mathcal{I}_u)$ using a greedy algorithm [15], which returns an $O(\log d)$ approximation to the set cover with minimum in-flow, where $d = \max_{v \in \mathcal{U}} |\mathcal{I}^v|$ is the maximum number of memes posted by any user. Refer to Algorithm 2 for a full description of our procedure to approximate in-flow efficiency with an approximation factor $O(\log d)$.

3.3 Delay efficiency

Definition: Consider a user u and the set of unique memes $\mathcal{I}_u$ she is exposed to through her feed in a given time period, by following $|\mathcal{U}_u|$ users. Then, we define the optimal set $\mathcal{U}^{\mathrm{t}}(\mathcal{I}_u)$ as the set of users that, if followed, would expose the user to, at least, $\mathcal{I}_u$, with the smallest time delay. Here, we define the delay at acquiring a meme provided by a set $\mathcal{U}_u$ as the difference between the time when a user in $\mathcal{U}_u$ first mentions the meme and the time when the meme was first mentioned during the given time period by any user in the whole social media system. We then define the delay efficiency of a user u at acquiring memes as

$$E_u^{\mathrm{t}} = \frac{1}{1 + \langle t_i - t_i^0 \rangle_{i \in \mathcal{I}_u}}, \tag{3}$$

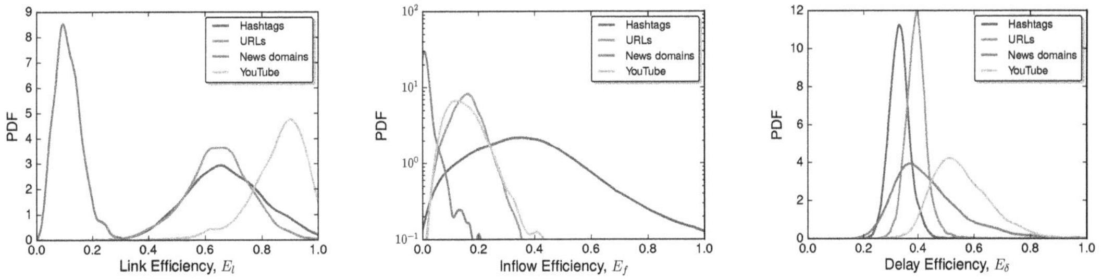

(A) Link efficiency (B) In-flow efficiency (C) Delay efficiency

Figure 5: The distributions of link, in-flow, and delay efficiencies for the four types of memes.

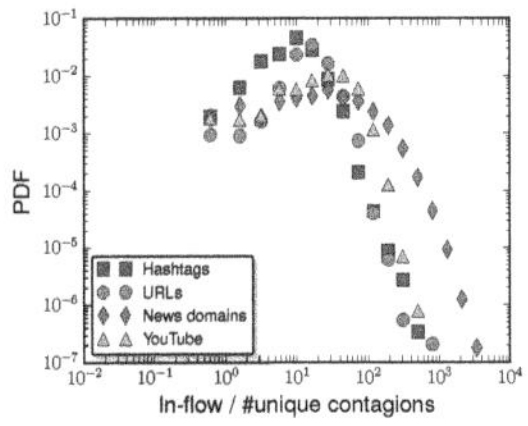

Figure 6: The distribution of the ratio between the number of received tweets and unique memes.

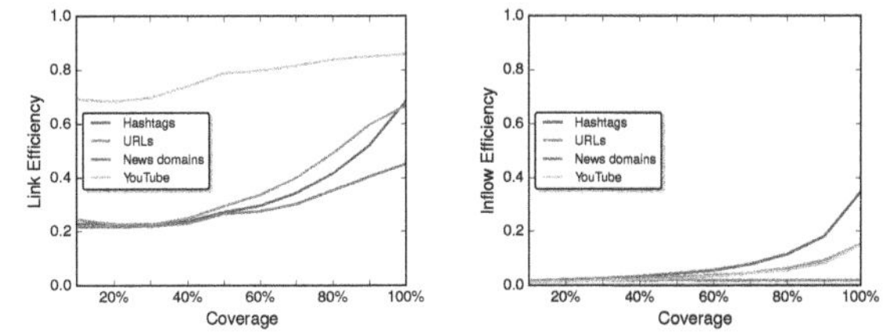

(A) Link efficiency (B) Inflow efficiency

Figure 7: The average link and in-flow efficiencies versus the percentage of covered memes.

where t_i is the time a user in $\mathcal{U}_u$ first mentions meme i, t_i^0 is the time when the meme is first mentioned by a user in the whole social media system, and $\langle t_i - t_i^0 \rangle_{i \in \mathcal{I}_u}$ is an average delay over all memes received by user u, measured in days. The delay efficiency $E_u^{\mathbf{t}} = 1$ if the followees of the user u are the first to post the set of memes $\mathcal{I}_u$ in the whole system. The delay efficiency becomes lower than 1 when the user is exposed to the memes at later times than their time of birth. The larger is the average delay of received memes, the smaller is the delay efficiency. Figure 4 illustrates our definition of delay efficiency using an example.

Computing delay efficiency: In this case, we can compute the delay efficiency directly by finding when each of the memes appeared for the first time in the system, without resorting to approximation algorithms, as in the case of link and in-flow efficiencies. One can query the first time of appearance for each meme in $O(1)$ by building a mapping between memes and their first time of appearance in a hashtable.

3.4 Efficiency of Twitter users

Once we have the three definitions of users' efficiency defined by Eqs. 1-3, we use them to investigate how efficient Twitter users are at acquiring four different types of memes: hashtags, URLs, news domains and YouTube videos.

First, we estimate the empirical probability density function[3] (PDF) for each type of efficiency and meme. We show the results in Figure 5, in which we find several interesting patterns. First, all PDFs resemble a normal distribution, however, their peaks (modes) and widths (standard deviations) differ across efficiencies and type of memes. For most users and most types of memes, the efficiency value is significantly below one, giving empirical evidence that users are typically sub-optimal. Second, while the PDFs for link (Figure 5A) and delay (Figure 5C) efficiencies look quite similar, the in-flow efficiency differs significantly (Figure 5B). Third, users are most efficient at acquiring YouTube videos, followed by URLs and hashtags, and news domains. This order coincides with the ordering of the exponents of the corresponding power-law distribution of memes' popularity (Figure 1A), *i.e.*, the exponent of the power-law (its absolute value) is the highest for YouTube links, followed by URLs and hashtags, and finally for news domains. Note that the higher the exponent is, the higher the proportion of non-popular memes with respect to the popular ones, and thus one can conclude that users are more efficient at acquiring non-popular memes than popular memes. A plausible explanation is that users posting non-popular memes are likely to be included in the optimal set, since there is nobody else who posts these memes and, as a consequence, the optimal set differs less from the original set of followees. Moreover, note that in Figure 5B, the in-flow efficiency of both news domains and YouTube videos is shifted to the left (*i.e.*, presents much lower efficiency values) compared to the link efficiency in Figure 5A. This shift is due to the fact that, as shown in Figure 6, ratio between the total number of received tweets and unique memes is much larger for unique news domains and YouTube video memes than for hashtags and URLs, which in turn, translates into a lower in-flow efficiency.

In the above measurements, we estimated the probability density functions of user's efficiency considering full coverage of the received memes. Importantly, it is straightforward to extend our definitions of link and in-flow efficiencies to account for partial coverage, by simply considering a set of users that, if followed, would expose the user to, at least, a percentage of the unique memes $\mathcal{I}_u$, by stopping the greedy algorithm whenever the given percentage is reached. Note, however, that computing the efficiency for a partial coverage based on the full set of followees would be unfair, since

[3]The PDFs have been empirically estimated using kernel density estimation [7].

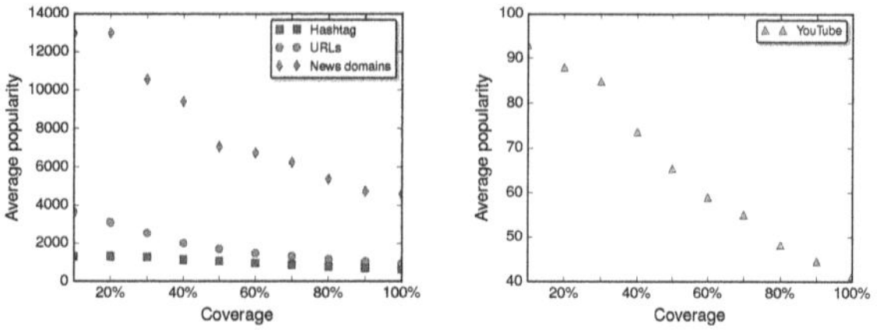

(A) Hashtags, URLs, news (B) YouTube videos

Figure 8: The average popularity of covered memes as a function of the percentage of covered memes.

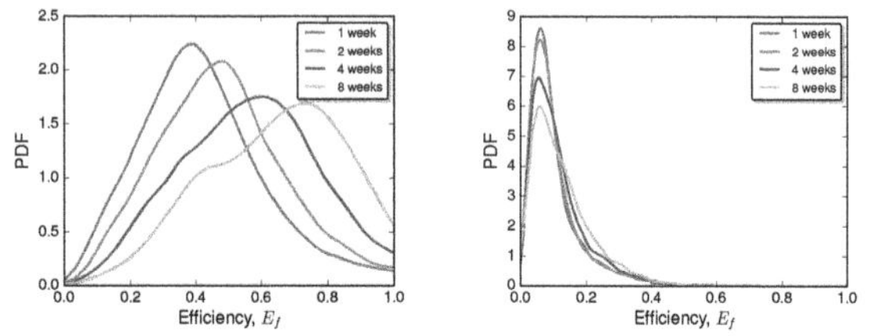

(A) 100% Coverage (B) 80% Coverage

Figure 9: In-flow efficiency measured for hashtags appearing in the time periods of different lengths. The results for other efficiencies and meme types are qualitatively the same.

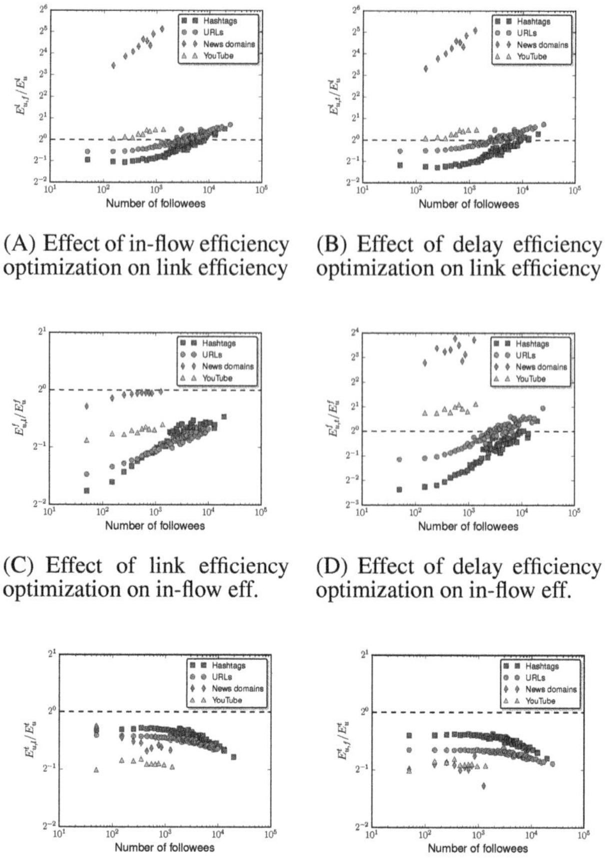

(A) Effect of in-flow efficiency optimization on link efficiency (B) Effect of delay efficiency optimization on link efficiency

(C) Effect of link efficiency optimization on in-flow eff. (D) Effect of delay efficiency optimization on in-flow eff.

(E) Effect of link efficiency optimization on delay eff. (F) Effect of in-flow efficiency optimization on delay eff.

Figure 10: The effect of optimization of one of the efficiencies on another efficiency, plotted as the ratio of the efficiency in the optimized network and the original network against the number of followees. The dashed line marks the ratio equal to 1, which corresponds to the lack of change in the efficiency due to the respective optimization.

some of the followees in $\mathcal{U}_u$ may be not tweeting any of the covered memes. Thus, for the purpose of computing the efficiencies for partial coverage, we take into account only the users in $\mathcal{U}_u$ who tweet at least one of the covered memes. Figure 7 shows the average link and in-flow efficiencies against coverage for the same four memes. As one may have expected, the higher the coverage, the higher the link and in-flow efficiency, since the memes that are covered first by the greedy algorithm are the popular ones, as shown in Figure 8. This result confirms that users are more efficient at acquiring less popular information, but less so at acquiring more popular information. A plausible explanation is that less popular information is produced by only a handful of users and so the optimization is limited to this set of users.

Finally, we investigate if our results are consistent across different time periods. In particular, we measure user efficiency based on time periods of different lengths: one, two, four and eight weeks. In Figure 9A, we can observe that as we increase the period, there are more unique memes there to cover, which results in an increase in the efficiency. However, the distribution of efficiency is nearly unchanged for 80% coverage (Figure 9B). Thus, the findings presented in this study are qualitatively robust to the choice of time period. Additionally, we find that the choice of the week does not influence the distributions of efficiency, however, these results are not shown due to space limitation.

4. CROSS-EFFICIENCY

In our definitions of efficiency, the optimal set for a given user is the set of users that minimizes the number of links, in-flow or delay, while covering the same set of unique memes. However, this naturally raises the question as to how efficient the optimal sets for a given definition of efficiency are in terms of the other definitions. For example, how efficient is the link-optimal set with respect to in-flow or delay efficiency? In this section, we first address this question, then introduce the idea of finding sets of users that jointly optimize multiple notions of efficiency, and finally develop a heuristic algorithm that simultaneously improves both in-flow and delay efficiency of users.

4.1 Cross-efficiency of optimal sets

Given a user u and the set of unique memes $\mathcal{I}_u$ she is exposed to in a given time period, our definitions of efficiency compare the original set of followees with the optimal sets $\mathcal{U}^{\mathrm{l}}(\mathcal{I}_u)$, $\mathcal{U}^{\mathrm{f}}(\mathcal{I}_u)$ and $\mathcal{U}^{t}(\mathcal{I}_u)$ in terms of number of links, in-flow and average delay, respectively. Here, we assess the efficiency of the optimal sets for each definition of efficiency in terms of the other definitions, which we call *cross-efficiencies*. More specifically, we compute the link efficiency of the optimal sets for in-flow and delay efficiency, *i.e.*,

$$E^{\mathrm{l}}_{u,\mathrm{f}} = \frac{|\mathcal{U}^{\mathrm{l}}(\mathcal{I}_u)|}{|\mathcal{U}^{\mathrm{f}}(\mathcal{I}_u)|} \quad \text{and} \quad E^{\mathrm{l}}_{u,\mathrm{t}} = \frac{|\mathcal{U}^{\mathrm{l}}(\mathcal{I}_u)|}{|\mathcal{U}^{\mathrm{t}}(\mathcal{I}_u)|},$$

the in-flow efficiency of the optimal sets for link and delay efficiency, *i.e.*,

$$E^{\mathrm{f}}_{u,\mathrm{l}} = \frac{f(\mathcal{U}^{\mathrm{f}}(\mathcal{I}_u))}{f(\mathcal{U}^{\mathrm{l}}(\mathcal{I}_u))} \quad \text{and} \quad E^{\mathrm{f}}_{u,\mathrm{t}} = \frac{f(\mathcal{U}^{\mathrm{f}}(\mathcal{I}_u))}{f(\mathcal{U}^{\mathrm{t}}(\mathcal{I}_u))},$$

and the delay efficiency of the optimal sets for link and in-flow efficiency, *i.e.*,

$$E^{\mathrm{t}}_{u,\mathrm{l}} = \frac{1}{1 + \langle t^{\mathrm{l}}_i - t^0_i \rangle_{i \in \mathcal{I}_u}} \quad \text{and} \quad E^{\mathrm{t}}_{u,\mathrm{f}} = \frac{1}{1 + \langle t^{\mathrm{f}}_i - t^0_i \rangle_{i \in \mathcal{I}_u}},$$

where t^{l}_i is the time a user in $\mathcal{U}^{\mathrm{l}}(\mathcal{I}_u)$ first mentions meme i and t^{f}_i is the time a user in $\mathcal{U}^{\mathrm{f}}(\mathcal{I}_u)$ first mentions meme i.

Typically, we would like to know if an efficiency of an optimized information network is increased in comparison with the efficiency of the original network. Thus, in the reminder of this section we focus on measuring the ratio of an efficiency of the optimized and original networks. If the ratio is higher than one for the given optimization algorithm, then the corresponding efficiency is improved by that algorithm with respect to the original set of followees. If the ratio is below one then the respective efficiency is decreased by the optimization algorithm.

We measure the ratio between the efficiency of the optimal sets and the original set of followees for the three definitions of efficiency (see Figure 10). The ratio tends to be below one or close to one for most meme types, which indicates that optimizing for one definition of efficiency generally results in decreased efficiency with respect to the other two definitions.

However, there are a few exceptions. For example, in terms of link and in-flow efficiency, the optimal sets for news domains are more efficient than the original sets (diamonds in Figures 10A, 10B, and 10D). This observation may happen due to the following reason: news domains tend to be more popular than the other types of memes (as shown in Figure 1). As a consequence, a user may receive multiple copies of the same news domain from various followees, and it is very easy to find efficient sets in terms of in-flow; it is enough to simply remove some of their followees from the network to improve both link and in-flow efficiencies.[4]

Finally, in Figures 10A-10D, we note that the improvement in the link and in-flow efficiencies tends to grow with the number of followees due to the increased number of redundant (non-unique) information received by the users who follow many other people. However, in Figures 10E-10F, the improvement in the delay efficiency tends to drop with the number of followees because it is likely that users who receive many copies of the same meme receive it early on. Thus, for users with many followees, it is harder to improve the delay efficiency.

4.2 Joint-optimization of efficiencies

So far, we have looked for optimal sets of users in terms of a single efficiency (be it link, in-flow or delay). Moreover, in the previous section, we have shown that optimal sets in terms of a single efficiency typically decrease the other efficiencies. Therefore, one could imagine developing an algorithm a looking for sets of users that are optimized with respect to several efficiencies; in other words, a multi-objective algorithm. Given such an algorithm a, we could compute the efficiency of the optimal set $\mathcal{U}_a(\mathcal{I}_u)$ with respect to single quantities, *i.e.*,

$$E^{\mathrm{l}}_{u,\mathrm{a}} = \frac{|\mathcal{U}^{\mathrm{l}}(\mathcal{I}_u)|}{|\mathcal{U}^{\mathrm{a}}(\mathcal{I}_u)|}, \; E^{\mathrm{f}}_{u,\mathrm{a}} = \frac{f(\mathcal{U}^{\mathrm{f}}(\mathcal{I}_u))}{f(\mathcal{U}^{\mathrm{a}}(\mathcal{I}_u))} \text{ and}$$
$$E^{\mathrm{t}}_{u,\mathrm{a}} = \frac{1}{1 + \langle t^{\mathrm{a}}_i - t^0_i \rangle_{i \in \mathcal{I}_u}}$$

where t^{a}_i is the time a user in $\mathcal{U}^{\mathrm{a}}(\mathcal{I}_u)$ first mentions meme i. Ideally, we would like to find optimal sets that are efficient with respect to the considered quantities. Here, as a proof of concept, we next develop a heuristic method to find sets of users optimized with respect to both in-flow and delay.

Algorithm 3: Greedy set cover for jointly optimizing in-flow and delay efficiencies

Input: set of all users $\mathcal{U}$; set of unique memes $\mathcal{I}_u$; set of memes $\mathcal{I}^v$ posted by user v
Set $\mathcal{U}^* = \emptyset$;
Set $\mathcal{X} = \mathcal{I}_u$;
while $\mathcal{X} \neq \emptyset$ **do**
  Set $v^* = \arg\min_{v \in \mathcal{U} \setminus \mathcal{U}^{\mathrm{f}}} \frac{N^{\alpha}_v T^{\beta}_v}{|\mathcal{I}^v \cap \mathcal{X}|}$;
  Set $\mathcal{U}^* = \mathcal{U}^* \cup \{v^*\}$;
  Set $\mathcal{X} = \mathcal{X} \setminus \mathcal{I}^{v^*}$
end
Output: $\mathcal{U}^*$

Joint optimization of in-flow and delay efficiency

We leverage the greedy algorithm from the weighted set cover problem to design a heuristic method that finds sets of users with high in-flow and delay efficiencies, while delivering the same unique memes to the user (refer to Algorithm 3). In particular, in the heuristic method, the weights are powers of tweets in-flow N^{α}_v and average delay T^{β}_v over all unique memes produced by the user v. The exponents α and β can be readily adjusted to induce higher or lower in-flow efficiency and delay efficiency, respectively. Here, we experiment with $\alpha = 1$ and $\beta = 0.5$, which achieves a good balance between in-flow and delay efficiency.

We summarize the ratio of link, in-flow and delay efficiency of the set of users provided by our heuristic method and the original set of followees in Figure 11. We discus several interesting observations. First, since the algorithm does not optimize with respect to the number of links, the link efficiency is not improved by this algorithm, *i.e.*, the ratio between the link efficiency of the set provided by the heuristic method and the link efficiency of the original set of followees ratio is around or below 1 for three out of four meme types. Second, we find that both in-flow and delay efficiencies are significantly increased over the efficiency of the original set of followees for all types of memes. The in-flow efficiency is, on average, 7.4-times higher for news domains, 1.8-times higher for hashtags, 1.3-times higher for URLs, 1.2-times higher for YouTube videos. The delay efficiency is, on average, 1.8-times higher for news domains, 1.4-times higher for hashtags, 1.4-times higher for URLs, 1.2-times higher for YouTube videos. There is always an increase in in-flow and delay efficiencies independently of the number of followees that the users have originally. However, while the improvement in the in-flow efficiency tends to be larger for users with many followees, the improvement in the delay efficiency is larger for users with fewer followees. Thus, we conclude that our algorithm increases both in-flow and delay efficiency of users.

[4]In fact, over 85% of users receive less unique news domains than they have followees.

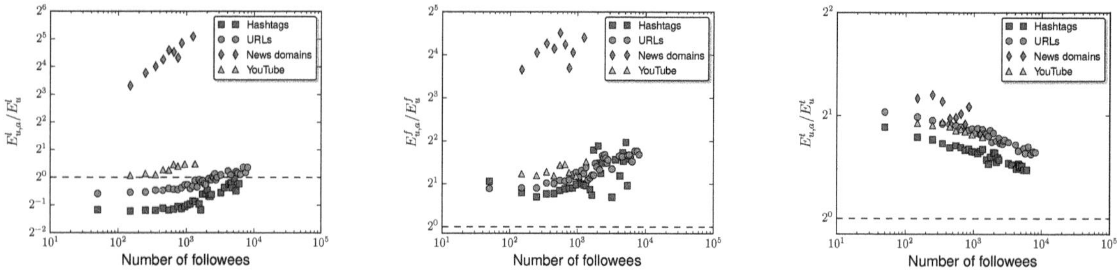

(A) Effect on link efficiency

(B) Effect on in-flow efficiency

(C) Effect on delay efficiency

Figure 11: The effect of optimization of both in-flow and delay efficiencies on different types of efficiencies, plotted as the ratio of the affected efficiency of the optimized network and the original network against the number followees.

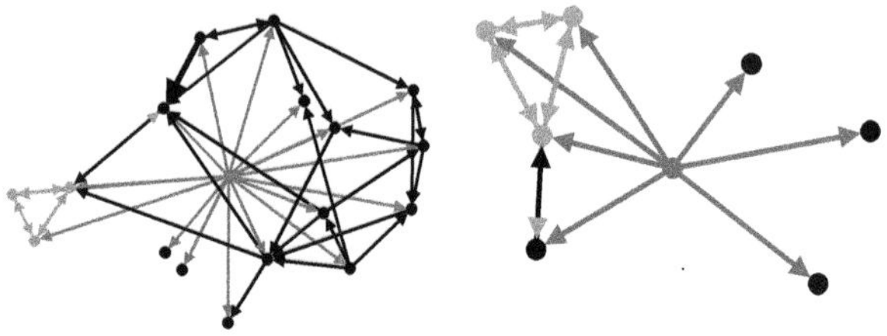

(A) Original

(B) Minimal set cover

Figure 12: Ego-networks for a Twitter user (red node). Some users (black nodes) only belong to one of the ego-networks while others (gray nodes) belong to both. The original ego-network contains more triangles than the ego-network induced by the minimal set cover, whose structure is closer to a star.

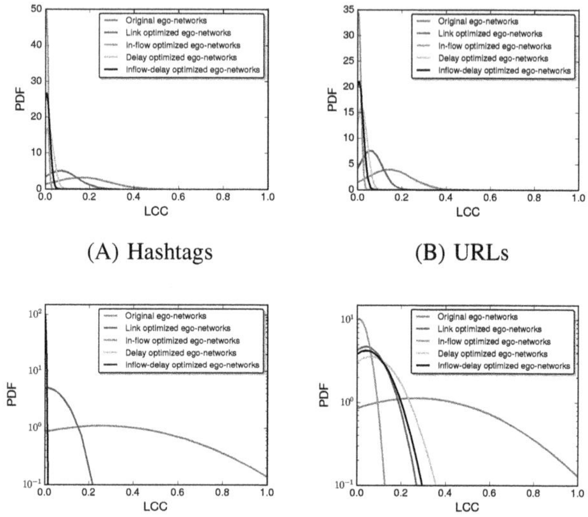

(A) Hashtags

(B) URLs

(C) News domains

(D) YouTube videos

Figure 13: The distributions of local clustering coefficient (LCC) of the original ego-network (green circles) and the ego-networks optimized for link (blue circles), in-flow (red circles), delay (teal circles), and inflow-delay efficiency (black circles) for: (A) hashtags, (B) URLs, (C) news domains, (D) and YouTube videos.

5. STRUCTURE OF EGO NETWORKS: ORIGINAL VS. OPTIMIZED

In the previous sections, we have introduced three meaningful definitions of efficiency and applied them to show that Twitter users tend to choose their information sources inefficiently. In this section, we investigate the rationale behind this sub-optimal behavior by comparing the structure of the user's ego-networks associated with both the original set of followees and the sets optimized for efficiency. Here, we define a user's ego-network as the network of connections (who-follows-whom) between the ego user and her followees.

First, as an example, we take one particular user and illustrate the structure of her original ego-network and the ego-network of an optimal set in terms of link efficiency (Figure 12). By visual comparison of both ego-networks, we can see that while the ego-network induced by the optimal set displays a structure much closer to a star, the original ego-network contains many more triangles and higher clustering coefficient. Due to its proportionally lower number of triangles, the optimal set is not *discoverable* by triadic closure [26, 13, 24] or information diffusion [5], which have been recently shown to be two major driving forces for link creation in social networks [28, 23, 3].

Remarkably, this phenomenon happens systematically across all users, efficiency definitions, and types of memes, as displayed in Figure 13, which shows the distribution of local clustering coefficient (LCC) for the users' original ego-networks and the ego-networks induced by different optimized sets. We find that while the LCC distribution for the original ego-networks is well spread and centered at $0.15 - 0.30$, the LCC distributions for the ego-networks induced by the optimal sets are skewed towards zero.[5] One could still think that this is simply a consequence of differences in the number of followees, *i.e.*, the size of the ego-network. However, Figure 14 rules out this possibility by showing a striking difference of several orders of magnitude between the LCC of the original ego-networks and the ego-networks induced by the optimal sets across a wide range of number of followees. These findings suggest that the way in which social media users discover new people to follow (*e.g.*, triadic closure or information diffusion) or receive recommendations (*e.g.*, pick people in a 2-hop neighbor-

[5]Note that the distribution of clustering coefficient of inflow-delay optimized network is located between distributions of in-flow optimized and delay optimized ego-networks.

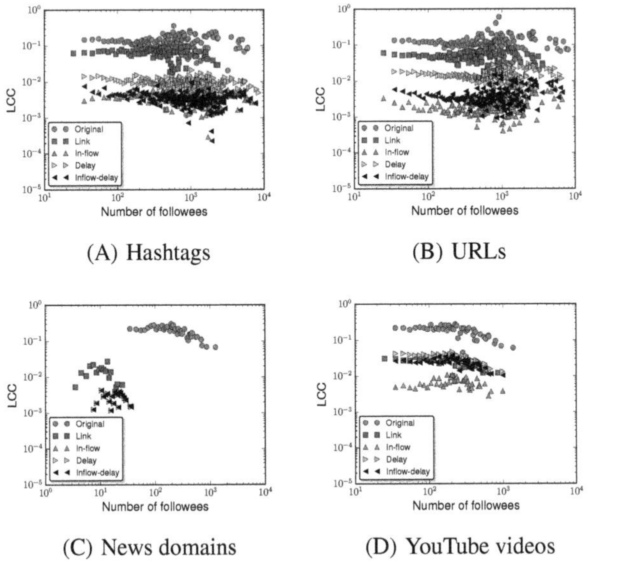

(A) Hashtags (B) URLs

(C) News domains (D) YouTube videos

Figure 14: Average local clustering coefficient versus the number of followees in the original ego-network (green circles) and the ego-networks optimized for link (blue squares), in-flow (red triangles), delay (teal triangles), and inflow-delay efficiency (black triangles).

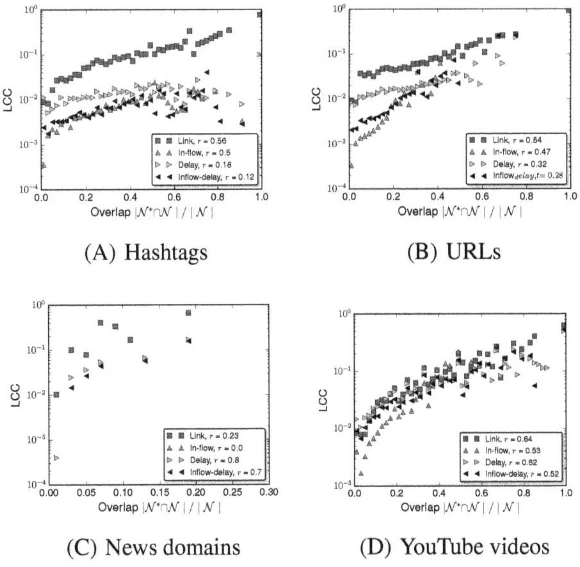

(A) Hashtags (B) URLs

(C) News domains (D) YouTube videos

Figure 15: Local clustering coefficient of the optimized ego-networks versus the overlap between the original ego-network and the ego-networks optimized for link (blue squares), in-flow (red triangles), delay (teal triangles), and inflow-delay efficiency (black triangles).

hood [1]) can lead to sub-optimal information networks in terms of (link, in-flow and delay) efficiency.

We have argued that optimal sets typically differ from the original set of followees due to their low number of triangles in the associated ego-networks, and thus lack of discoverability. However, are optimal sets with higher number of triangles in efficient ego-networks easier to discover for users? Figure 15 answers this question positively by showing the average local clustering coefficient in the ego-network induced by the optimal set against the overlap between the users in the optimal set and the original set of followees. Here, by overlap we mean the fraction of users in the optimal set that are also in the original set of followees. In particular, we find a positive correlation (Pearson's $0.07 < r < 0.55$, $p < 10^{-10}$) between the local clustering coefficient and the overlap, which indicates that if the nodes in the optimal set are *discoverable* through triadic closure, the user may be more likely to find them and decide to follow them.

6. DISCUSSION

We have defined three intuitive notions of user's efficiency in social media – link, in-flow and delay efficiency – to assess how *good* users are at selecting who to follow within the social media system to acquire information. Our framework is general and applicable to any social media system where every user *follows* others within the system to receive the information they produce. We have then leveraged our notions of efficiency to help us in understanding the relationship between different factors, such as the popularity of received information and the users' ego-networks structure.

Here, we have focused on three definitions of efficiency (link, in-flow, and delay). However, we could leverage this idea to define more complex notions of efficiency. For example, we could define efficiency in terms of diversity, *i.e.*, it would be interesting to find the set of users that, if followed, would cover the same unique memes while maximizing the diversity of topics or perspectives that are delivered with the memes, and then compare this set with the original set of followees in terms of diversity. This would provide a framework to mitigate the effects of the filtering bubble and echo chamber present in current social media systems. Moreover, some of the memes could be treated preferentially over other memes. This could be achieved by means of covering a list of non-unique memes favoring repetitions of a preferential subset of memes, *e.g.*, memes matching the user's interests should be delivered to the user more often. Remarkably, these more complex notions of efficiency can often be expressed as integer linear programs, similarly to the minimal set cover problem, which can be solved using relaxation methods with provable guarantees [27].

Additionally, we have introduced a heuristic method that improves both in-flow and delay efficiency of users, while still delivering them the same unique memes. Similar heuristics can be naturally designed to optimize efficiency with respect to multiple quantities (be it link, in-flow, delay, or diversity). In this context, it would be very interesting to design methods with provable guarantees to find sets of users that are optimal with respect to multiple quantities.

Our work also opens other interesting venues for future work. For example, we have defined and computed a measure of efficiency for each user independently. However, one could also think on global notions of efficiency for the Twitter information network as a whole, perhaps using a multi set cover approach. Finally, since we have applied our framework to study information efficiency only on Twitter, it would be interesting to study information efficiency of other microblogging services (Weibo, Pinterest, Tumblr) and social networking sites (Facebook, Google+).

7. REFERENCES

[1] L. A. Adamic and E. Adar. Friends and neighbors on the web. *Social networks*, 25(3):211–230, 2003.

[2] E. Agichtein, C. Castillo, D. Donato, A. Gionis, and

G. Mishne. Finding high-quality content in social media. In *Proceedings of the 1st International Conference on Web Search and Data Mining*, pages 183–194, 2008.
[3] D. Antoniades and C. Dovrolis. Co-evolutionary dynamics in social networks: A case study of twitter. *arXiv preprint arXiv:1309.6001*, 2013.
[4] M. Babaei, P. Grabowicz, I. Valera, and M. Gomez-Rodriguez. On the users' efficiency in the twitter information network. In *Proceedings of the 9th International AAAI Conference on Weblogs and Social Media*, 2015.
[5] E. Bakshy, I. Rosenn, C. Marlow, and L. Adamic. The role of social networks in information diffusion. In *Proceedings of the 21st international conference on World Wide Web*, pages 519–528, 2012.
[6] R. Bosagh Zadeh, A. Goel, K. Munagala, and A. Sharma. On the precision of social and information networks. In *Proceedings of the first ACM conference on Online social networks*, pages 63–74. ACM, 2013.
[7] A. W. Bowman and A. Azzalini. *Applied smoothing techniques for data analysis*. Clarendon Press, 2004.
[8] C. Castillo, M. Mendoza, and B. Poblete. Information credibility on twitter. In *Proceedings of the 20th International Conference on World Wide Web*, pages 675–684, 2011.
[9] M. Cha, H. Haddadi, F. Benevenuto, and P. K. Gummadi. Measuring User Influence in Twitter: The Million Follower Fallacy. In *Proceedings of the 4th International AAAI Conference on Weblogs and Social Media*, pages 10–17, 2010.
[10] N. A. Christakis and J. H. Fowler. Social network sensors for early detection of contagious outbreaks. *PloS one*, 5(9):e12948, 2010.
[11] M. Farajtabar, M. Gomez-Rodriguez, N. Du, M. Zamani, H. Zha, and L. Song. Back to the past: Source identification in diffusion networks from partially observed cascades. In *Proceedings of the 18th International Conference on Artificial Intelligence and Statistics*, 2015.
[12] M. Gomez-Rodriguez, K. Gummadi, and B. Schoelkopf. Quantifying Information Overload in Social Media and its Impact on Social Contagions. In *Proceedings of the 8th International AAAI Conference on Weblogs and Social Media*, pages 170–179, 2014.
[13] M. S. Granovetter. The strength of weak ties. *American journal of sociology*, pages 1360–1380, 1973.
[14] N. Hodas and K. Lerman. How visibility and divided attention constrain social contagion. In *Proceedings of the 2012 ASE/IEEE International Conference on Social Computing*, pages 249–257, 2012.
[15] D. S. Johnson. Approximation algorithms for combinatorial problems. In *Proceedings of the fifth annual ACM symposium on Theory of computing*, pages 38–49. ACM, 1973.
[16] R. M. Karp. *Reducibility among combinatorial problems*. Springer, 1972.
[17] M. Kearns. Experiments in social computation. *Communications of the ACM*, 55(10):56–67, 2012.
[18] H. Kwak, C. Lee, H. Park, and S. Moon. What is twitter, a social network or a news media? In *Proceedings of the 19th International Conference on World Wide Web*, pages 591–600, 2010.
[19] K. Lerman and T. Hogg. Leveraging position bias to improve peer recommendation. *PLoS One*, 9(6), 2014.
[20] J. Leskovec, L. Backstrom, and J. Kleinberg. Meme-tracking and the dynamics of the news cycle. In *Proceedings of the 15th ACM SIGKDD international conference on Knowledge discovery and data mining*, pages 497–506, 2009.
[21] J. Leskovec, A. Krause, C. Guestrin, C. Faloutsos, J. VanBriesen, and N. Glance. Cost-effective outbreak detection in networks. In *Proceedings of the 13th ACM SIGKDD international conference on Knowledge discovery and data mining*, pages 420–429. ACM, 2007.
[22] A. Mislove, M. Marcon, K. P. Gummadi, P. Druschel, and B. Bhattacharjee. Measurement and analysis of online social networks. In *Proceedings of the 7th ACM SIGCOMM conference on Internet measurement*, pages 29–42, 2007.
[23] S. A. Myers and J. Leskovec. The bursty dynamics of the twitter information network. In *Proceedings of the 23rd International Conference on World Wide Web*, pages 913–924, 2014.
[24] D. M. Romero and J. Kleinberg. The directed closure process in hybrid social-information networks, with an analysis of link formation on twitter. In *Proceedings of the 4th International AAAI Conference on Weblogs and Social Media*, 2010.
[25] D. M. Romero, B. Meeder, and J. Kleinberg. Differences in the mechanics of information diffusion across topics: idioms, political hashtags, and complex contagion on twitter. In *Proceedings of the 20th International Conference on World Wide Web*, pages 695–704, 2011.
[26] G. Simmel. *The Sociology of Georg Simmel*. Free Press of Glencoe, 1950.
[27] V. V. Vazirani. *Approximation algorithms*. Springer, 2001.
[28] L. Weng, J. Ratkiewicz, N. Perra, B. Gonçalves, C. Castillo, F. Bonchi, R. Schifanella, F. Menczer, and A. Flammini. The role of information diffusion in the evolution of social networks. In *Proceedings of the 19th ACM SIGKDD international conference on Knowledge discovery and data mining*, pages 356–364, 2013.
[29] R. West and J. Leskovec. Automatic versus human navigation in information networks. In *Proceedings of the 6th International AAAI Conference on Weblogs and Social Media*, 2012.
[30] R. West and J. Leskovec. Human wayfinding in information networks. In *Proceedings of the 21st International Conference on World Wide Web*, pages 619–628, 2012.

Modeling and Predicting Learning Behavior in MOOCs

Jiezhong Qiu[†], Jie Tang[†♯], Tracy Xiao Liu[‡], Jie Gong[⋆],
Chenhui Zhang[†], Qian Zhang[†], and Yufei Xue[†]
[†]Department of Computer Science and Technology, Tsinghua University
[♯]Tsinghua National Laboratory for Information Science and Technology (TNList)
[‡]Department of Economics, School of Economics and Management, Tsinghua University
[⋆]NUS Business School, National University of Singapore
qjz12@mails.tsinghua.edu.cn, jietang@tsinghua.edu.cn, liuxiao@sem.tsinghua.edu.cn, gong@nus.edu.sg

ABSTRACT

Massive Open Online Courses (MOOCs), which collect complete records of all student interactions in an online learning environment, offer us an unprecedented opportunity to analyze students' learning behavior at a very fine granularity than ever before.

Using dataset from xuetangX, one of the largest MOOCs from China, we analyze key factors that influence students' engagement in MOOCs and study to what extent we could infer a student's learning effectiveness. We observe significant behavioral heterogeneity in students' course selection as well as their learning patterns. For example, students who exert higher effort and ask more questions are not necessarily more likely to get certificates. Additionally, the probability that a student obtains the course certificate increases dramatically (3× higher) when she has one or more "certificate friends".

Moreover, we develop a unified model to predict students' learning effectiveness, by incorporating user demographics, forum activities, and learning behavior. We demonstrate that the proposed model significantly outperforms (+2.03-9.03% by F1-score) several alternative methods in predicting students' performance on assignments and course certificates. The model is flexible and can be applied to various settings. For example, we are deploying a new feature into xuetangX to help teachers dynamically optimize the teaching process.

Keywords

MOOCs; Predictive model; User behavior; Online engagement

1. INTRODUCTION

Massive open online courses (MOOCs) have become increasingly popular and offered students around the world the opportunity to take online courses from prestigious universities. Three pioneer MOOC platforms—Coursera, edX, and Udacity—offer hundreds of courses and draw more than 100,000 registrants per course [25]. 2012 was called "The Year of the MOOC" by New York Times [23]. Following the three pioneers, many other platforms have also been developed quickly around the world, such as Khan Academy in North America, Miriada and Spanish MOOC in Spain, Iversity in German, FutureLearn in England, Open2Study in Australia, Fun in France, Veduca in Brazil, Schoo in Japan, and xuetangX in China. MOOCs are without doubt leading a revolution of education, by gathering global education resources and restructuring the learning environment, e.g., providing online forums to geographically-dispersed students. Furthermore, as all students' learning behavior occurs online, it enables us to evaluate students' performance in a more objective and quantitative way. For example, KDD CUP 2015 used the MOOC data to offer a challenge of predicting students' dropout rate among a number of courses.[1]

MOOC platforms collect complete records of students' online activities, which enables us to take a closer look at students' learning behavior than ever before. However, new challenges have also emerged. For example, the low completion rates of MOOC participants—preliminary statistics show that less than 5% of the participants have completed a course—has been a central criticism [16, 25]. Moreover, MOOC is not just a place for teaching or learning. It also provides an interactive platform to support group-level interactions among students, lecturers, and teaching assistants. Students with various motivations to study MOOCs [2] have very different learning behavioral patterns, and these online learning behavior may also deviate from those in traditional learning environments. Therefore, there is a clear need to understand user behavior in MOOCs, and more importantly, to design effective mechanisms to motivate more participation in both courses learning and social interaction.

In this paper, we focus on studying how students engage in MOOCs and to what extent we can predict their learning behavior. Understanding the complex and subtle forces underlying the learning process can significantly help design better courses and improve the learning effectiveness. More specifically, how to retain students in a course? How to estimate the completion rate of a course? How to evaluate the learning performance of different students? Despite several relevant studies, such as course completion analysis [16], learning behavior analysis [25], and student classification and engagement analysis [2], there are few systematical studies on modeling students' learning behavior for different categories of courses.

Employing xuetangX,[2] one of the largest MOOC platform from China, as the basis of our study, we systematically investigate the aforementioned problem. We first conduct an in-depth analysis to understand the degree to which user demographics (gender, age, and education background) influence students' forum activities and learning behavior including watching videos and working on assignments. Moreover, we estimate each of the three factors' im-

WSDM'16, February 22–25, 2016, San Francisco, CA, USA.
© 2016 ACM. ISBN 978-1-4503-3716-8/16/02 ...$15.00.
DOI: http://dx.doi.org/10.1145/2835776.2835842.

[1]http://kddcup2015.com
[2]http://www.xuetangx.com

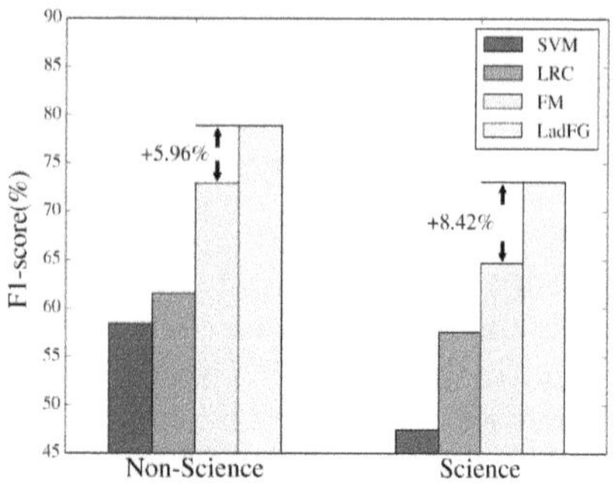

(a) Assignment Grade Prediction

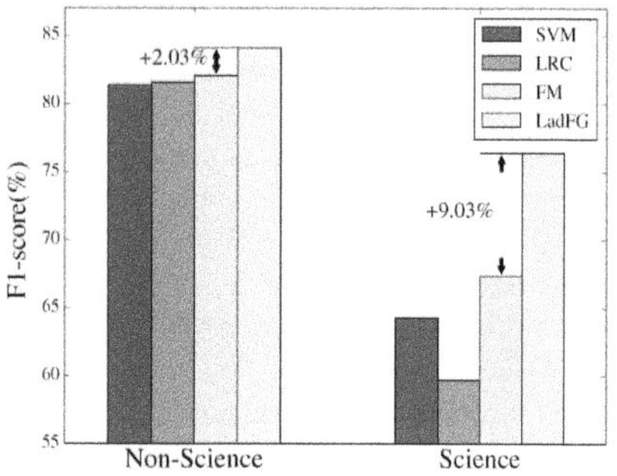

(b) Certificate Earner Prediction

Figure 1: Performance of Learning Behavior Prediction by Different Methods. (a) Assignment grade prediction, and (b) Certificate earner prediction. Please refer to § 4 for definitions of the comparative methods.

portance on students' learning performance, e.g., the likelihood of getting certificates. We have several intriguing discoveries. First, hard working and frequent questioning do not necessarily imply high learning performance. Second, engaging in the course forum is a significant indicator for students' learning performance. Third, homophily [18] — the idea that similarity and connection tend to co-occur, or "birds of a feather flock together" [20] — plays an important role for predicting students' learning behavior. The probability that a student obtains the course certificate increases dramatically (3× higher) when she has one or more "certificate friends".

We then propose a latent dynamic factor graph (LadFG) to model and predict learning behavior in MOOCs. The model incorporates students' demographics, forum activities, and learning behavior into a unified framework. It captures the dynamic information and homophily correlations between students, and projects students' learning behavior into a latent continuous space. Although the model is general enough to be applied to various settings, we particularly consider two prediction tasks: assignment grade prediction and certificate earner prediction. The former predicts students' performance on assignment, while the latter predicts which students could get the certificates after a course ends. Figure 1 shows the performance of different comparison methods for the two prediction tasks on both science courses and non-science courses. Clearly, the proposed method improves the prediction accuracy by up to 9.03% over the alternative methods. Based on the results of the proposed model, we are deploying a new feature into the xuetangX system to help lecturers optimize their teaching process.

Table 1: The Description of the Dataset.

Category	Type	Number
Course	All	11
Science	CS	3
	EE	2
Non-Science	Economics	2
	History	3
	Sports	1
User	Total #	88,112
	Max #students/course	31,120
	Min #students/course	2,631
Forum	# new posts	13,021
	# replies	16,367
Activity	Activity types	21
	# Activity logs	56,800,000

Note: the data spans from Oct 10, 2013 to Jun 26, 2014.

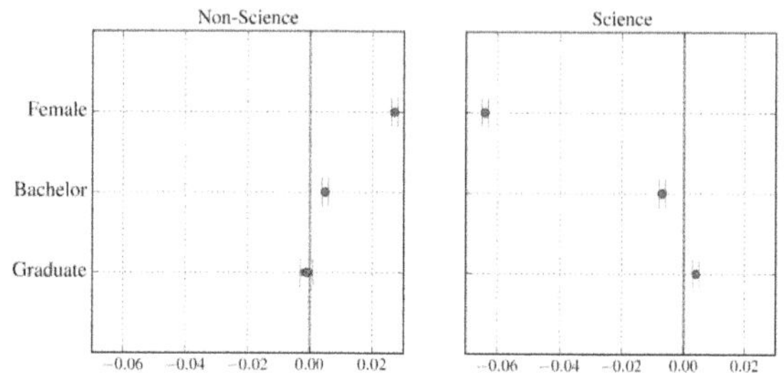

Figure 2: Regression Analysis for Course Selection by the Linear Probability Model.

Data. Our data comes from xuetangX, a partner of edX. The system was launched in October 2013 and up to November 2015, it has offered 670 courses (including courses from Tsinghua University, Peking University, and edX courses from MIT, Stanford, UC Berkeley, etc.) and attracted 1,700,000 registered users. The dataset used in this paper consists of 11 completed courses in the Fall 2013 and Spring 2014 semesters. We categorize the courses into two types: science (Computer Science and Electronic Engineering) vs. non-science (Economics, History, and Sports) courses. The average number of registered users for the science courses is lower than that of the non-science courses, though the difference is not statistically significant (5,911 vs. 12,959, $p = 0.247$, two-sided t-tests). Each course has a discussion forum for students to post/reply questions and to interact with each other. The dataset also consists of multiple types of students' activities such as watching videos, working on assignments, downloading resources and etc. In total, there are 56,800,000 time-stamped activity logs. Table 1 reports summary statistics of the dataset.

We first conduct a regression analysis to examine correlation between student demographics and course selection. Regarding demographics, we consider gender, education (graduate degree including master and PhD, bachelor, and those with degree below bachelor), and age. As age and education are significantly and positively correlated ($p = 0.000$, chi-square test), we focus on education here. Figure 2 shows regression results from a linear probability model of course enrollment.[3] The dependent variable is whether user v_i registers a course. The independent variables are (1) female dummy and (2) education level dummies including

[3]We present the linear probability model as it is easier for results interpretation. All results are robust when probit or logit models are used.

bachelor, graduate, and the omitted variable is bachelor below. Additionally, we control for age and course characteristics by including course category and estimated weekly hours in learning. From the results, we observe that compared to male students, females are significantly more likely to take non-science courses ($p < 0.01$), and less likely to choose science courses ($p < 0.01$). Moreover, compared to users with low education (<bachelor), bachelors are significantly more likely to take non-science courses ($p < 0.01$), and significantly less likely to choose science courses ($p < 0.01$). In contrast, graduate students are significantly more likely to take science courses ($p < 0.05$).

Organization. Section 2 presents pattern analysis for student activities; Section 3 formulates the problem and presents the proposed model; Section 4 presents the experimental results; Section 5 discusses related work and Section 6 concludes the work.

2. PATTERNS OF STUDENT ACTIVITY

In this section, we investigate students' learning activities including forum activities and time spent on videos and assignments. Moreover, we examine how each of these factors affects a user's likelihood of getting certificates, i.e., a student's final grade in a course is at least 60 out of 100.

Several common features apply throughout our regression analysis. First, robust standard errors are reported in parentheses. Second, two-sided p-values are reported and significant at: * 10%; ** 5%; *** 1%. Third, age and course type dummies are controlled in all regressions. Finally, in all regression analyses, we consider ordinary least squares (OLS) models.

2.1 Learning Activity Patterns

We first study users' participation pattern of forum activities including posting new threads and replying to questions. Second, we study their learning behavior for watching videos and doing assignments.

Engagement patterns of forum activity. In course forums, students can post new questions and answer existing questions. Overall, the level of forum activities is very low: 94% users in our sample never participate in posting or replying to questions. Additionally, among active users, their forum activities decrease with time ($p < 0.05$) for all but new post in science courses ($p > 0.1$), suggesting that users' participation enthusiasm in courses decays over time. This observation is consistent with that in previous studies [2, 25].

We present ordinary least squares (OLS) estimates of the relationship between student characteristics and the number of forum activities in Table 2. The dependent variable is the number of new posts (Columns 1 and 3) or replies (Columns 2 and 4) per student, and the independent variables include gender, education level, and the required effort level for a course (specified by the teacher). It is interesting that women are only more active in asking questions in non-science courses, while they are much more quiet in science courses. Within non-science courses (Columns 1 and 2), women post significantly more questions than men ($p < 0.01$), though they reply marginally significantly fewer questions ($p < 0.1$). In contrast, their amount of new post in science courses is significantly less than male students (Column 3, $p < 0.05$).

Pertaining to forum activities between students with different education levels, we find that bachelors post significantly more questions in non-science courses (Column 1). In contrast, graduate students do not ask many questions while their amount of replies in science courses is marginally significantly higher than those with degrees below bachelor (Column 4, $p < 0.1$). The effect size is also

Table 2: Regression Analysis for Forum Activities.

	Non-Science		Science	
	New Post	Reply	New Post	Reply
	(1)	(2)	(3)	(4)
Female	0.089***	-0.024*	-0.026**	-0.053
	(0.013)	(0.013)	(0.011)	(0.145)
Bachelor	0.029***	0.007	0.015	0.074*
	(0.011)	(0.010)	(0.010)	(0.045)
Graduate	0.001	0.007	0.016	0.306*
	(0.016)	(0.030)	(0.013)	(0.156)
Effort	0.277***	-0.053***		
	(0.058)	(0.017)		
Constant	-0.534***	0.228***	0.050**	0.092
	(0.122)	(0.054)	(0.022)	(0.059)
Obs.	74,480	74,480	19,269	19,269
R^2	0.013	0.001	0.001	0.002

Note: Constant—the learned offset by the regression model; Obs.—the number of observations in each category; and R^2 — the proportion of variance in the criterion that is explained by the estimated regression model.

Table 3: Regression Analysis for Effective Learning Time.

	Non-Science		Science	
	Video	Assignment	Video	Assignment
	(1)	(2)	(3)	(4)
Female	8.588***	3.985***	-7.890***	-4.793**
	(1.181)	(0.400)	(2.281)	(2.277)
Bachelor	1.019	1.123**	8.032***	8.946***
	(1.389)	(0.454)	(1.876)	(1.898)
Graduate	-5.618***	-1.918***	6.945***	4.817**
	(1.774)	(0.567)	(2.585)	(2.247)
Effort	-29.489***	1.895***		
	(1.345)	(0.521)		
Constant	101.258***	-4.246***	26.746***	22.566***
	(4.970)	(1.538)	(4.241)	(6.293)
Obs.	74,480	74,480	19,269	19,269
R^2	0.035	0.021	0.002	0.002

higher than that for bachelors (0.306 vs. 0.074, $p = 0.105$), which indicates that people with different education levels may play different roles in forums. In addition, within non-science courses, users post more questions when a course requires more working hours (Column 1, $p < 0.01$). However, the amount of replies is significantly negatively correlated with course effort requirements (Column 2, $p < 0.01$). One explanation is that more difficult courses may induce more questions, while these questions may be more challenging for users to answer.

Engagement patterns of videos and assignments. First, we define user v_i's effective learning time below.

Definition 1. **Effective learning time.** It represents the actual (or valid) time that a student spends on watching videos and working on assignments.

In practice, it is difficult to accurately measure students' study time [8]. For example, after a student clicks a video, she may leave and work on something else. Therefore, we design an algorithm based on deterministic finite automaton to approximate effective learning time. Specifically, we define three states: *idle*, *video*, and *assignment*, in the state automaton. The automaton starts with idle, and changes states when it receives certain activities triggered by students. For example, when the student triggers a "play video" activity, the state changes from idle to video. While a "pause" activity changes the state back to idle. Altogether, the duration between two activities will be counted as the effective learning time. In addition, there is threshold-triggered transition from any states to idle. The idea is that if a student stays in a state, e.g., video, for a long time (longer than a threshold),[4] the automaton moves back to idle.

Applying the algorithm described above, we estimate each user's effective learning time on a certain course. Similar to forum activities, time spent on videos and assignments is extremely few. Specifically, the median time for watching videos is 4.53 minutes per course and 0 for working on assignments. In fact, 36% users never watch videos, and 52% of them never do assignments, suggesting that doing assignments requires more effort from users. In addition, for users who have active learning records, the amount of video and assignment related activities increases in time ($p < 0.01$) for all but assignments in non-science courses ($p > 0.1$). We suspect that students may only spend time on learning when the deadline approaches.

We report regression results of users' effective learning time in Table 3. First, compared to male students, female students spend significantly more time on both videos and assignments in non-science courses (Columns 1-2), while they spend significantly less time on both activities in science courses (Columns 3-4). Again, this echoes our prior findings on gender differences in both course selection and forum activities. Second, for both science and non-science courses, bachelors work hardest among all education groups, and the effect size is significantly stronger for science courses than non-science course (video: 8.032 vs. 1.019, $p = 0.003$; assignment: 8.946 vs. 1.123, $p = 0.000$). Graduate students spend least time on study in non-science courses (Columns 1-2). In science courses, though their effort is higher than those with degrees below bachelors, it is still lower than that for bachelors (video: 6.945 vs. 8.032, $p = 0.648$; assignment: 4.817 vs. 8.946, $p = 0.076$). Additionally, when the course requires higher effort, students spend significantly more time on assignments (Column 2). Surprisingly, they spend significantly less time on videos (Column 1). One possibility is that the time spent on videos is also correlated with unobserved course characteristics, e.g., the length of videos.

2.2 Certificate Rate

Now, we examine whether the likelihood of getting the certificate is correlated with user demographics, forum activities and effective learning time. Overall, among 11 courses in our data, the certification rate lies between 0.84% and 14.95%. The average certification rate for science courses is lower than that in non-science courses, though the difference is not statistically significant (1.11% vs. 4.68%, $p = 0.178$, two-sided t-tests).

Table 4 summarizes results from linear probability models. In the first model specification (Columns 1-2), we only include demographic information used in prior regressions, and we control for forum activities and effective learning time in the second model (Columns 3-4). First, we find that compared to male students, females are significantly more likely to get the certificate in non-science courses (Column 1 of Model 1); however, the size of the gender difference decreases significantly after we control for forum activities and effective learning time in Model 2 (0.014 vs. 0.002, $p = 0.000$, chi-square test). This suggests that the superiority of women's performance in non-science courses is mainly driven by their effort in forum and learning activities.

[4]In our implementation, we set the threshold to 20 minutes based on human feedback.

Table 4: Regression Analysis for Certificate Rate: All Users.

	Model 1		Model 2	
	Non-Science	Science	Non-Science	Science
	(1)	(2)	(3)	(4)
Female	0.014***	-0.003	0.002*	0.001
	(0.002)	(0.002)	(0.001)	(0.002)
New Post	—	—	0.004***	0.038***
			(0.001)	(0.008)
Reply	—	—	0.004**	0.001*
			(0.002)	(0.001)
Video	—	—	0.000***	-0.000
			(0.000)	(0.000)
Assignment	—	—	0.003***	0.000***
			(0.000)	(0.000)
Bachelor	0.014***	0.003*	0.011***	-0.001
	(0.002)	(0.002)	(0.001)	(0.001)
Graduate	0.007***	0.004	0.013***	0.001
	(0.002)	(0.002)	(0.002)	(0.002)
Effort	-0.072***		-0.072***	
	(0.003)		(0.003)	
Constant	0.286***	0.018***	0.280***	0.006
	(0.013)	(0.006)	(0.011)	(0.004)
Obs.	74,480	19,269	74,480	19,269
R^2	0.024	0.001	0.462	0.363

Second, compared to students with degrees below bachelors, bachelors are significantly more likely to get the certificate in non-science courses and the result is robust in both models (Columns 1 and 3, $p < 0.01$), while their high effort on science courses does not transform to significantly higher certificate rate.[5] Surprisingly, graduate students are also significantly more likely to get the certificate in non-science courses (Column 1: 0.007, $p < 0.01$), although their effective learning time is significantly lower than others. Moreover, after controlling for effort, the size of the effect is almost doubled (Column 3: 0.013, $p < 0.01$). This implies that the certificate rate is not only related to effort, but also ability and existing knowledge level. In particular, for graduate students who may have higher learning ability, once they exert effort, they have a higher chance to get certificates. Additionally, the required effort level for a course is significantly and negatively correlated with the likelihood of getting certificates (Columns 1 and 3).

Last but not least, we discuss effect of forum activities and effective learning time on certificate rate. Specifically, both forum activities are good predictors for getting certificates. In non-science courses, the size of the effect between posting and replying questions is about the same (0.004 vs. 0.004, $p = 0.837$, F-test). In contrast, in science courses, posting questions matters more than answering them (0.038 vs. 0.001, $p = 0.000$, F-test), suggesting that students who ask questions are more likely to get certificates than those who answer questions. Moreover, in both two types of courses, the amount of time spent on videos and assignments are significantly positively correlated with certificate rates,[6] although the magnitude of the effect is very small.

[5]The effect is positive and marginally significant in Model 1 and it becomes negative and insignificant in Model 2.

[6]The only insignificance is the effect of video time in science courses.

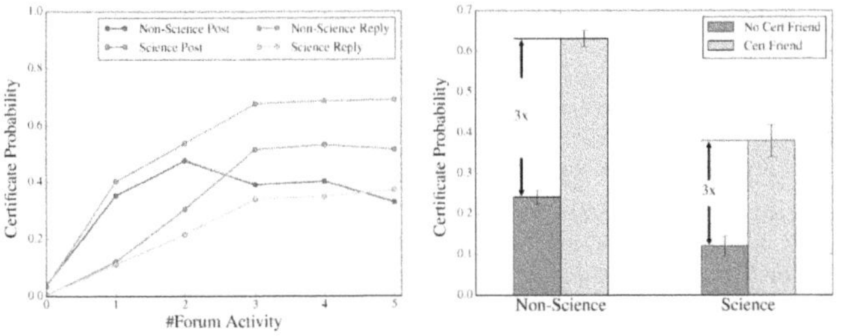

(a) Forum Activity (b) Certificate Rate

Figure 3: Forum Activity and Certificate Rate for Active Users.

As the distribution of forum activities is highly skewed, our findings might be contaminated by the large number of inactive users. As a robustness check, we focus on the active users, e.g., those who have posted at least one thread in the forum. Overall, the relationship between forum activities and certificate rate is still positive and significant, with a slight decline in magnitude. It implies that to improve the likelihood of getting certificates, it is more important to be present and participate, while the intensity of participation, for instance posting another thread, matters less. This is supported by Figure 3(a), in which we plot the percentage of students obtaining a certificate by the number of forum threads they post. Clearly, the certificate rate increases sharply with the first few posts, but the benefit from further incremental activities becomes smaller. Another empirical finding is the spillover effect. We define a "certificate friends" dummy which is coded as 1 if a user interacts with other students who finally get certificates, and it is significantly positively correlated with users' likelihood of getting certificates, suggesting the importance of homophily correlation and positive learning spillover from well-performed students.

Summary. In summary, we have the following observations:

- Female students are more likely to ask questions in non-science course forums, though not necessarily reply more questions. They also spend more time on watching videos and working on assignments for non-science courses.
- Bachelors ask more questions, especially in non-science courses. Interestingly, graduate students are not as active as bachelors in terms of asking questions, but they are quite active in answering questions, especially in science courses.
- Both forum activities and effective learning are significant predictors for certificate rate, suggesting the importance of encouraging students to participate in forum discussions.

3. MODEL FRAMEWORK

Now, we turn to discuss how to model the learning behavioral data. We propose a latent dynamic factor graph (LadFG) model to address the problem. The model incorporates observed learning activities, including forum activities, watching videos, and doing assignments, into a unified framework. Different from previous research on factor graph model [26], in LadFG, we use a latent learning state to model students' learning state. Based on the modeling results, we will introduce how to apply the model to predict students' learning behavior.

3.1 Formulation

To present the model precisely, we introduce some necessary notations. Let V denote a set of $|V| = N$ students. We first define students' observed learning activities as follows:

Definition 2. **Learning Activity**: Let $Y \in \{0,1\}^{T\times N\times n}$ be a tensor, with each element $Y_{t,i,j}$ representing the jth activity by student $v_i \in V$ at time t, where T is the number of time stamps and n is the number of activities.

The activity space includes all activities (e.g., doing assignments and getting certificates) that we are interested in. We use a $n-$dimensional vector $Y^t(i) = [Y_{t,i,0}, Y_{t,i,1}, \ldots, Y_{t,i,n-1}]^{\mathrm{T}}$ to represent all activities performed by student v_i at time t. Moreover, we introduce the definition of latent learning state.

Definition 3. **Latent Learning State**: For each student v_i at time t, we define a $m-$dimensional vector of continuous latent states $Z^t(i) = [Z_{t,i,0}, Z_{t,i,1}, \ldots, Z_{t,i,m-1}]^{\mathrm{T}}$, with $Z_{t,i,j} \in [0,1]$. Latent states of all students at all time stamps are recorded in a tensor $Z \in [0,1]^{T\times N\times m}$.

To facilitate model description, we define $\mathbf{Z}_{t-p}^{t-1}(i) = \left[Z^{t-1}(i)^{\mathrm{T}}, Z^{t-2}(i)^{\mathrm{T}}, \ldots, Z^{t-p}(i)^{\mathrm{T}}\right]^{\mathrm{T}} \in [0,1]^{m\times p}$ as the vector of latent states of student v_i in the previous p time stamps. Finally, for modeling student behavior, we define attributes (features) for students in different time stamps as follows.

Definition 4. **Time-varying Attribute Tensor**: Let $X \in \mathbb{R}^{T\times N\times d}$ be a tensor in which $X_{t,i,j}$ represents the jth attribute of student v_i at time t, and d is the number of defined attributes (features). We use a d-dimensional vector $X^t(i) = [X_{t,i,0}, X_{t,i,1}, \ldots, X_{t,i,d-1}]^{\mathrm{T}}$ to represent the attribute values of student v_i at time t.

The attribute tensor includes all possible attributes associated to students at different time stamps, e.g., demographics and all behavior except the defined learning activities.[7] The attributes may not change over time, e.g., gender. In this case, we have $X^0(i) = X^1(i) = \cdots = X^{(T-1)}(i)$.

Our goal for modeling learning behavior is to find a mapping from students' attribute tensor to the observed learning activities. Instead of directly learning the mapping, we use latent learning states as the bridge to connect the two sets of observation variables. Based on this idea, we propose a latent dynamic factor graph (LadFG) model.

3.2 Latent Dynamic Factor Graph Model

Figure 4 shows the graphical representation of the LadFG model. Each student is associated with a feature vector $X^t(i)$ and a set of activities $Y^t(i)$ for time t. We use latent states $Z^t(i)$ to model students' activities and features. In Figure 4, each group of circles stands for a student's latent learning states $Z^t(i) = [Z_{t,i,0}, \cdots, Z_{t,i,m-1}]$ at time t, which is used to characterize the intention of the student to perform different activities. Each group of latent states is associated with an activity vector $Y^t(i)$, a vector of attributes $X^t(i)$, and it depends on the student's historic learning states $\mathbf{Z}_{t-p}^{t-1}(i)$ in previous p time stamps. Furthermore, $f(W_d S^t(i) + b_d)$ denotes a factor function to capture the dynamic dependency. The method of modeling students' activities using latent states is similar to the assumption in Dynamic Factor Graph (DFG) [21], Markov Decision Process (MDP) [14], and Deep Learning [13]. Activity correlations between students are also modeled in the latent state space using function $f(.)$. Different from traditional models, we also model a long-distance

[7] In different prediction applications, the defined learning activities and attribute tensor may be different.

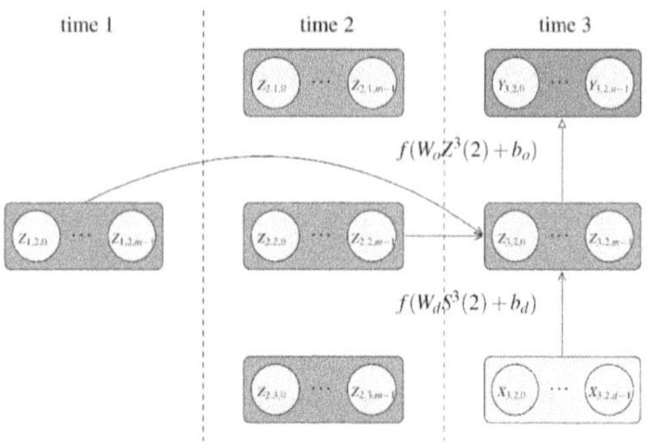

Figure 4: Graphical Representation of the LadFG Model. Each group of circles stands for a student's latent learning states $Z^t(i)$ at time t, which is used to characterize the intention of the student to perform activities $Y^t(i)$; each group of latent states is associated with an activity vector $Y^t(i)$, a vector of attributes $X^t(i)$, and depends on the student's historic learning states $\mathbf{Z}_{t-p}^{t-1}(i)$ in previous p time stamps; $f(W_dS^t(i)+b_d)$ and $f(W_oZ^t(i)+b_o)$ denote two factors to capture the latent learning states and dynamic dependency, respectively.

dependency—a student's latent state can depend on her states in previous p time stamps.

In the LadFG model, we use function $f(.)$ to capture correlations between different (observed or latent) variables. For simplicity, we use logistic regressions to model the dependency, although it can be replaced by any other functions. Specifically, we define f as a sigmoid function

$$f(z) = \frac{1}{1+e^{-z}}.$$

Moreover, for latent state $Z^t(i)$, LadFG models the observed learning activities $Y^t(i)$ by:

$$Y^t(i)^* = f(W_oZ^t(i) + b_o) \tag{1}$$

where $W_o \in \mathbb{R}^{n\times m}$, $b_o \in \mathbb{R}^n$ are observation model parameters.

The dynamic model establishes a time-dependent correlation between a sequence of p past latent state $\mathbf{Z}_{t-p}^{t-1}(i)$, attributes $X^t(i)$ and latent state $Z^t(i)$. For easy explanation, we define inputs of dynamic model as:

$$S^t(i) = \left[\mathbf{Z}_{t-p}^{t-1}(i)^{\mathrm{T}}, X^t(i)^{\mathrm{T}}\right]^{\mathrm{T}} \tag{2}$$

Then the latent states can be obtained by :

$$Z^t(i)^* = f(W_dS^t(i) + b_d) \tag{3}$$

where $W_d \in \mathbb{R}^{m\times(mp+d)}$ and $b_d \in \mathbb{R}^m$ are model parameters.

Based on all parameters above, we define the objective function of the LadFG model as follows.

$$\mathcal{O}(\Theta) = \sum_{i=0}^{N-1}\sum_{t=0}^{T-1}\left\|Z^t(i) - Z^t(i)^*\right\|^2 + \sum_{i=0}^{N-1}\sum_{t=0}^{T-1}\left\|Y^t(i) - Y^t(i)^*\right\|^2 + \lambda_w\left(\|W_o\|^2 + \|W_d\|^2\right) + \lambda_z\sum_{i=0}^{N-1}\sum_{t=0}^{T-2}\|Z^t(i) - Z^{t+1}(i)\|^2 \tag{4}$$

Input: number of epochs L;
number of batches in each epoch in M Step B;
latent states dimension m;
E Step learning rate η_z and M Step learning rate η_Θ;
weight decay parameters λ_z and λ_w
Output: learned parameters $\Theta = \{W_d, W_o, b_d, b_o\}$, latent states Z;
Initialize model parameters Θ;
Initialize latent states Z;
for $l = 1$ **to** L **do**
  E Step:% fix Θ, update Z
  Compute gradient $\nabla Z_{t,i,j}$;
  Update $Z_{t,i,j} \leftarrow Z_{t,i,j} + \eta_z\nabla Z_{t,i,j}$;
  M Step:% fix Z, update Θ
  for $b = 1$ **to** B **do**
    Generate random integer $t_\alpha < t_\beta$ from $[0, T)$
    Calculate the gradient of all parameters and update according to X, Y, Z in time span $[t_\alpha, t_\beta]$:
    Update $W_o \leftarrow W_o + \eta_\Theta\nabla W_o$;
    Update $b_o \leftarrow b_o + \eta_\Theta\nabla b_o$;
    Update $W_d \leftarrow W_d + \eta_\Theta\nabla W_d$;
    Update $b_d \leftarrow b_d + \eta_\Theta\nabla b_d$;
  end
end
return Θ and Z;

Algorithm 1: Learning and Inference by LadFG.

where λ_w is a parameter that controls the regularization value; and λ_z controls the degree of smoothness between learning states of consecutive time stamps. Here, we use square loss as the loss function and apply L-2 regularization on model parameters to overcome overfitting problems.

Learning an LadFG model is to estimate a configuration of parameters $\Theta = \{W_o, b_o, W_d, b_d\}$ and latent states Z from a given historic behavior log that minimizes the objective function Eq.(4). As the objective function has a closed form solution, it can be learned efficiently by the gradient descent method, e.g. stochastic gradient descent (SGD).

3.3 Model Learning

We have two sets of learning variables: model parameters Θ and latent states Z. To learn these parameters, we use an EM-style algorithm to achieve the minimization of the objective function (Eq. 4) iteratively. The learning algorithm is summarized in Algorithm 1. Specifically, there are two major steps:

1. **E-step:** fix all model parameters Θ and update Z, by using a gradient descent method.
2. **M-step:** fix all latent states Z and update each model parameter in Θ.

Each parameter is updated by $\theta_i \leftarrow \theta_i + \eta\frac{\partial\mathcal{O}}{\partial\theta_i}$, where η is the learning step. The gradient of each parameter w.r.t the objective function can be derived in the following ways. We use $Z_{t,i,j}$ and $W_{d u,v}$ as the example to explain the gradient, and omitted others due to space limitation.

$$\frac{\partial\mathcal{O}}{\partial Z_{t,i,j}} = 2(Z_{t,i,j} - Z^*_{t,i,j}) - 2\sum_{k=1}^{p}\sum_{l=0}^{m-1}(Z_{t+k,i,l} - Z^*_{t+k,i,l})Z^*_{t+k,i,l}(1 - Z^*_{t+k,i,l})W_{dl,(k-1)m+j} - 2\sum_{l=0}^{n-1}(Y_{t,i,l} - Y^*_{t,i,l})Y^*_{t,i,l}(1 - Y^*_{t,i,l})W_{ol,j} + 2\lambda_z(Z_{t,i,j} - Z_{t+1,i,j}) - 2\lambda_z(Z_{t-1,i,j} - Z_{t,i,j})$$

$$\frac{\partial \mathcal{O}}{\partial W_{du,v}} = -2\sum_{i=0}^{N-1}\sum_{t=0}^{T-1}(Z_{t,i,u} - Z^*_{t,i,u})Z^*_{t,i,u}(1 - Z^*_{t,i,u})S_{t,i,v} + 2\lambda_w W_{du,v}$$

Finally, according to our definition, we have:

$$S_{t,i,v} = \begin{cases} Z_{t-\lfloor \frac{v}{m} \rfloor -1, i, v \bmod m}, & \text{if } v < m \times p \\ X_{t,i,v-mp}, & \text{if } v \geq m \times p \end{cases} \quad (5)$$

Feature Definition and Implementations. Our implementation of learning algorithm is based on the machine learning framework Theano [3, 5]. To train the LadFG model, we mainly define three categories of features.

- **Demographics:** These features are derived from students attributes including: gender, age, education. We consider binary features for each discrete value of every attribute, and in total we have eighteen demographics-based features.
- **Forum:** These features are derived from forum activities, respectively representing the number of different forum activities, the number of replies received from other students, etc. We also consider some homophily correlation features such as the number of replies received from well-performed students. There are six forum activity-based features.
- **Learning Behavior:** These features include a list of statistical features such as the number of chapters a student browses, the number of deadlines she completes and the total time she spends on watching videos and doing assignments. In total, there are ten features defined in this category.

4. EXPERIMENTAL RESULTS

The proposed method for modeling students' learning behavior is very general and can be applied to different settings in MOOCs. Furthermore, using data from xuetangX, we present various experiments in this section to evaluate the effectiveness and efficiency of the proposed method. All datasets and codes will be publicly available.

4.1 Experimental Setup

Evaluation Aspects. To quantitatively evaluate the proposed model, we consider the following performance measurements:

- **Assignment Grade Prediction.** We apply our methods to the MOOC data to predict students' grades on assignments and compare different methods. Specifically, each course has multiple assignments and a student will get a grade after completing an assignment. Our goal is to predict students' grade for each assignment. We cast the prediction task as a binary classification problem, e.g., for non-science courses, "Yes", if a student's grade is ranked top 30% of all students. Otherwise, it is "No".[8]
- **Certificate Earner Prediction.** We use our methods to model and predict whether a student will get the certificate after completing a course.

[8]We use 30% as the cutoff for non-science courses because on average, 30% of students who completed at least one assignment eventually earned the course certificate. The cutoff for science courses is 10%.

Table 5: Performance of Assignment Grade Prediction with Different Methods (%).

Category	Method	AUC	Precision	Recall	F1-score
Science	LRC	80.96	50.65	68.02	57.57
	SVM	70.99	50.44	45.93	47.42
	FM	90.39	61.48	70.35	64.67
	LadFG	**96.26**	**66.52**	**81.40**	**73.09**
Non-Science	LRC	73.10	75.59	53.45	61.54
	SVM	71.45	**77.01**	48.94	58.41
	FM	85.73	67.36	81.69	72.95
	LadFG	**90.47**	73.28	**85.68**	**78.91**

- **Parameter Sensitivity Analysis.** We analyze the sensitivity of different parameters in our methods: latent dimension m, the parameter p, and model convergence.

Finally, we present results of error analysis for our method. In all experiments, we remove the "register-only" students in our experiments.[9]

Comparison Methods and Evaluation Metrics. We compare our model with several alternative predictive models:

- **Logistic Regression (LRC) [19]:** It uses logistic regressions to train a classification model and employs the classification model to make the prediction.
- **SVM [10]:** It uses SVM to train the classification model and employs it to make the prediction. For SVM, we employ LIBLINEAR [10].
- **Factorization Machines [1, 17]:** Factorization models have been proposed and successfully applied to recommendation and prediction tasks. As the factorization model projects the input feature space onto a latent space, it enables us to learn more complex interactions between features.

Altogether, we try to use the same set of features in all comparison methods. Regarding tunable parameters m, p, η_Θ, η_z, λ_w and λ_z in LadFG, we find the best configuration using cross validation (i.e., $m = 5$, $p = 2$, $\eta_z = 0.5$, $\eta_\Theta = 0.1$, $\lambda_w = 0.01$ and $\lambda_z = 0.01$). Moreover, we evaluate the performance of comparison methods in terms of Area Under Curve (AUC), Precision (Prec.), Recall (Rec.), and F1-Measure (F1) [7]. Additionally, all algorithms are implemented in Python, and all experiments are performed on an x64 machine with 2.9GHz intel Core i7 CPU and 8GB RAM.

4.2 Assignment Grade Prediction

We conduct assignment grade prediction for the 11 courses in our dataset. In each course, we use the first half (before the mid-term) of the data for training and the second half (after the mid-term) for testing the prediction performance. Table 5 presents the average prediction performance of different methods and the largest performance numbers under each index are bolded. Overall, the proposed LadFG model clearly outperforms all alternative methods. In terms of F1-score, LadFG achieves a 16.0-25.6% improvement compared

[9]It refers to students who only register a course, but never actually engage in any course activities.

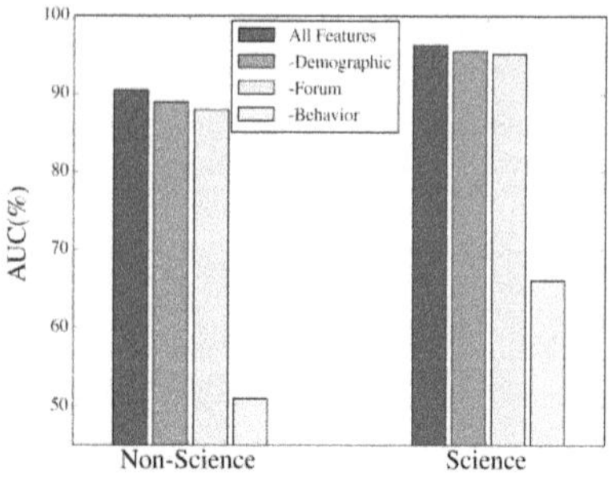

Figure 5: Feature Contribution Analysis for Assignment Grade Prediction.

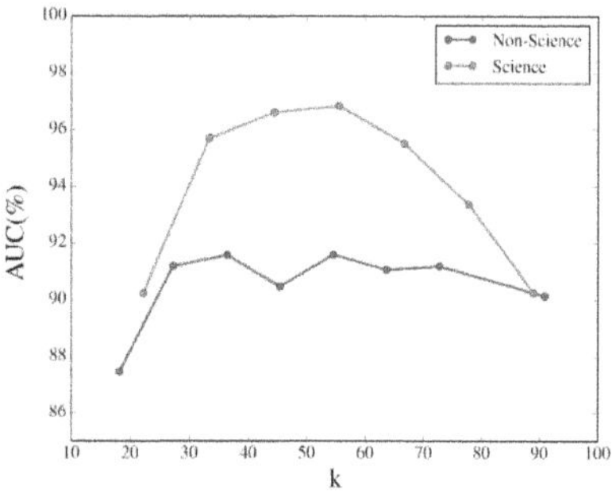

Figure 6: Average Prediction Performance by Varying the Percentage of Data for Training.

to SVM and LRC, neither of which considers the latent interactions between variables. Although FM which also considers the interactions between variables outperforms SVM and LRC, it cannot effectively leverage the temporal information and correlations between students. Consequently, it still underperforms LadFG. We perform two sided t-tests and all the p-values are < 0.01, which indicates that the improvements of our proposed models over the comparison methods are statistically significant.

Feature Contribution Analysis. We study how different categories of features (demographics, forum activities, and learning behavior) help the prediction task. The learning behavior includes all activities related to watching videos and doing assignments. Specifically, each time, we respectively remove demographics, forum activities, and learning behavior when training our proposed model, and compare performance of assignment grade prediction based on the trained models. Figure 5 shows the AUC performances for each type of courses. "All Features" stands for the LadFG model considering all features defined in our method. "-Demographic", "-Forum", and "-Behavior" indicate results from removing demographics, forum activities, and learning behavior, respectively. Apparently, the learning behavior features contribute significantly to the results for both types of courses. It is also worthwhile to note that learning behavior seems to be more important for modeling the non-science courses. Without learning behavior-based features, the performance of assignment grade prediction in non-science courses is worse than that in science courses.

Effect of the percentage of the training data. We investigate the performance of assignment grade prediction by varying the percentage of the training data. Figure 6 shows the average prediction performance. The x-axis ($k = 20 - 90$) indicates the percentage of data we use for training. It is very interesting that non-science

Table 6: Performance of Certificate Earner Prediction with Different Methods (%).

Category	Method	AUC	Precision	Recall	F1-score
Science	LRC	92.13	**83.33**	46.51	59.70
	SVM	92.67	52.17	83.72	64.29
	FM	94.48	61.54	74.42	67.37
	LadFG	**95.73**	73.91	**79.07**	**76.40**
Non-Science	LRC	94.16	76.93	89.20	82.57
	SVM	93.94	76.96	88.60	82.37
	FM	94.87	**80.22**	86.23	83.07
	LadFG	**95.54**	79.76	**89.01**	**84.10**

Table 7: Efficiency Performance of Different Methods.

Category	LRC	SVM	FM	LadFG
Science	0.07sec	2.35sec	2.7min	1.4min
Non-Science	1.46sec	9.8min	4.1min	8.6min

courses seem to be more *predictable*. LadFG achieves a stable performance for non-science courses using only 30% of data for training. For science courses, the prediction performances vary a lot and they depend on the amount of data used for training. Additionally, it seems difficult to predict grades of the last assignments in science courses.

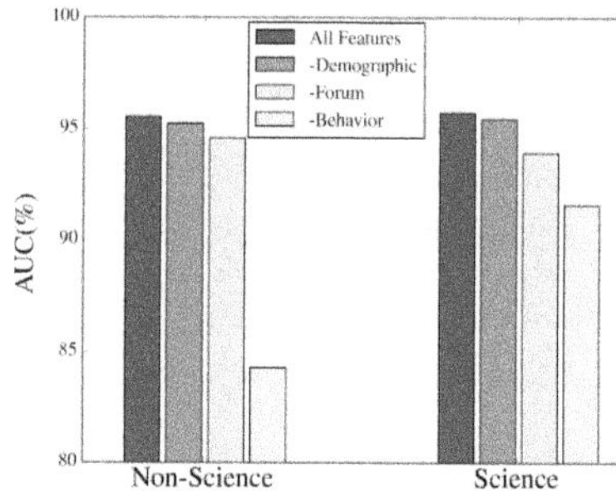

Figure 7: Feature Contribution Analysis for Certificate Earner Prediction.

4.3 Certificate Earner Prediction

Moreover, we use certificate earner prediction to evaluate the effectiveness of the proposed model. Again, we use the first half of the data (before the mid-term) for training each method, and apply the learned model to predict whether a student would get the course certificate. Table 6 summarizes the performance of different methods for predicting certificate earners. Consistently, LadFG performs better than alternative methods. In addition, we conduct a similar feature contribution analysis for certificate earner prediction. Figure 7 shows the prediction performance of the proposed model by considering different categories of features and we have similar results as those for assignment grade prediction.

4.4 Parameter Sensitivity Analysis

We now discuss how different parameters influence the performance of our methods, as well as presenting the efficiency perfor-

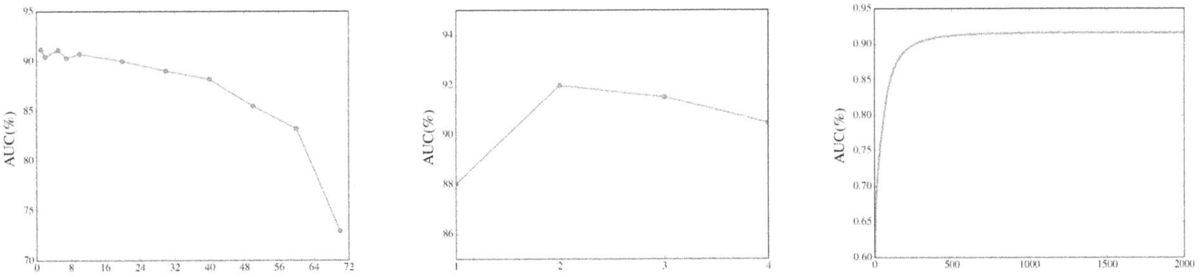

(a) Latent dimension m (b) Parameter p (c) Convergence analysis

Figure 8: Parameter Analysis. (a) Performance of LadFG model by varying the latent dimension m; (b) Performance of LadFG model by varying the parameter p; (c) Convergence analysis of LadFG.

mance. In all the analyses, we use the assignment grade prediction as the example, and report the average performance on non-science and science courses respectively.

Effect of Latent Dimension m. We evaluate how the latent dimension m affects the quality of the models learned by LadFG. We perform an analysis by varying the dimension of latent space in the proposed LadFG method. Figure 8(a) shows its AUC performance with different numbers of topics. We find that LadFG results in a better performance when the latent dimension is smaller than 20. In addition, increasing the dimension results in a performance drop and this might be due to the data sparsity.

Effect of Parameter p. Pertaining to the parameter p, Figure 8(b) shows the performance of LadFG with different p (other parameters are fixed, e.g., $m = 5$). Although the performance changes when we vary the value of p, the best performance is obtained when $p = 2$ (by considering latent states of two previous time stamps).

Convergence analysis. We further investigate the convergence of the learning algorithm for LadFG. Figure 8(c) presents the convergence analysis of the algorithm. The algorithm converges within 500 iterations. Furthermore, this rapid convergence enables us to do efficient training of the model on large scale datasets.

Efficiency. We compare the efficiency of the different methods. Table 7 lists the average running time of the comparison algorithms for training the prediction models. Overall, all methods have good efficiency performance, and the running time of different methods ranges from seconds to minutes. LadFG results in a slightly lower efficiency compared with FM.

4.5 Error Analysis

In the end, we conduct an error analysis on the results of our approach and observe three major types of errors.

(1) *Unpredictable negative cases.* The proposed LadFG model fails in the following scenario in which a substantial proportion is credited to final exams in certain courses. Some active learners, who engage in forums and lectures enthusiastically, may not take tests due to personal reasons, e.g., scheduling conflicts, and they would be misclassified into certificated group.

(2) *Unpredictable positive cases.* In contrast, some inactive students never participate in forums and have very few learning activities. However, they still complete assignments (or pass the final exams) with extremely high scores, and they are incorrectly grouped to be low grade in the assignment grade prediction (or uncertificated in the certificate earner prediction). We randomly choose several of those students and conduct interviews with them. We find that a substantial proportion of them are very skillful undergraduate or graduate students who have taken similar courses offline. Therefore, they are capable of taking online tests without spending much effort.

(3) *Swing cases.* LadFG would become ineffective for certificate earner prediction on "swing" cases as well. Each course has a minimum passing score, above which the student would be certificated. Swing cases are those students whose scores are hovering around the minimum score. Our model would misclassify these swing cases and draw a wrong conclusion.

5. RELATED WORK

MOOCs boom swiftly in recent years and have attracted millions of users worldwide. Experiences in offline education which predict dropouts and school failures do not fully satisfy the need in MOOCs. Analyzing and mining the big data from online courses becomes an important topic to understand students' behavior. We review related literature in three topics: attribute analysis, engagement analysis and time-related feature analysis.

Attribute analysis: This line of researches mainly focuses on studying the relationship between user demographic attributes and their behavioral patterns in online courses. For example, Guo et al.[11] investigated how navigation strategies vary by demographics. Based on demographic results, Wilkowski et al.[27] found no correlation between prior skills and course completion rates. Furthermore, their study showed that students who completed course activities were more likely to earn certificates than those who did not. Moreover, Seaton et al.[25] examined activities that help students get certificates.

Engagement analysis: More and more researchers start to analyze students' engagement in courses. For online open courses, Anderson et al.[2] developed a taxonomy of individual engagement style, and there was a further discussion between student engagement and their grades. Since student dropouts in MOOCs have gathered widespread attention, Ramesh et al.[24] proposed a latent representation model which could be applied to abstract student engagement types and to predict dropouts. Additionally, for traditional courses, Bayer et al.[4] predicted dropouts and school failures when student data has been enriched with data derived from students' social behavior. Related studies can be also found in [12, 22]. However, most existing research on engagement shared similarities with Champaign et al.'s work[8]. They estimated time spent on different resources and examined correlations between time and students' performance.

Forum analysis: Several interesting work examines MOOC forums, which plays an important role in online learning. Chaturvedi et al.[9] predicted instructor's intervention in forums. Brinton et al.[6] investigated factors correlated with the decline of forum activities, and found strategies to classify and rank thread relevance. Additionally, Huang[15] explored super-posters on forums and studied their engagement patterns. They found that super-posters display above-average engagement, enroll in more courses, and obtain better grades than the average forum participants. However, these studies might isolate and overstate the importance of forum performance.

To the best of our knowledge, there was little work utilizing temporal correlations between demographics, forum behaviors, and learning activity patterns to model and predict assignment grade performance and certificate earners.

6. CONCLUSION

In this paper, we study a novel problem of modeling and predicting learning behavior in MOOCs. We conduct in-depth analysis for student demographics, and learning activity patterns in course forums, videos and assignments. We propose a latent dynamic factor graph (LadFG) to incorporates students' demographics, forum activities, and learning behavior into a unified framework. Our experimental results on two prediction tasks: assignment performance prediction and certificate earner prediction, validate the effectiveness of the proposed model.

The general idea in this paper, to model and predict learning behavior in MOOCs, represents an interesting and new research direction. There are many potential future directions for this work. A straightforward task would be to incorporate human feedback into the proposed model. Other courses and more information on users would also be worth exploring. Looking further ahead, we believe that different models and semi-supervised learning algorithms for exploring social network structures should be beneficial. Finally, building a theory of why and how students join and quit different courses is an intriguing direction for future research.

Acknowledgements. The work is supported in-part by the National High-tech R&D Program (2014AA015103), Natural Science Foundation of China (61222212), National Social Science Foundation of China (13&ZD190), Tsinghua University Initiative Scientific Research Program (20141081231) and a research fund supported by Huawei Inc.

7. REFERENCES

[1] D. Agarwal and B.-C. Chen. Regression-based latent factor models. In *KDD'09*, pages 19–28, 2009.

[2] A. Anderson, D. Huttenlocher, J. Kleinberg, and J. Leskovec. Engaging with massive online courses. In *WWW'14*, pages 687–698, 2014.

[3] F. Bastien, P. Lamblin, R. Pascanu, J. Bergstra, I. Goodfellow, A. Bergeron, N. Bouchard, D. Warde-Farley, and Y. Bengio. Theano: new features and speed improvements. In *Deep Learning and Unsupervised Feature Learning NIPS 2012 Workshop*, 2012.

[4] J. Bayer, H. Bydzovská, J. Géryk, T. Obsivac, and L. Popelinsky. Predicting drop-out from social behaviour of students. In *EDM'12*, pages 103–109, 2012.

[5] J. Bergstra, O. Breuleux, F. Bastien, P. Lamblin, R. Pascanu, G. Desjardins, J. Turian, D. Warde-Farley, and Y. Bengio. Theano: a cpu and gpu math expression compiler. In *SciPy'10*, volume 4, page 3, 2010.

[6] C. G. Brinton, M. Chiang, S. Jain, H. Lam, Z. Liu, and F. M. F. Wong. Learning about social learning in moocs: From statistical analysis to generative model. *IEEE Transactions on Learning Technologies*, 7(4):346–359, 2014.

[7] C. Buckley and E. M. Voorhees. Retrieval evaluation with incomplete information. In *SIGIR'04*, pages 25–32, 2004.

[8] J. Champaign, K. F. Colvin, A. Liu, C. Fredericks, D. Seaton, and D. E. Pritchard. Correlating skill and improvement in 2 MOOCs with a student's time on tasks. In *L@S'14*, pages 11–20, 2014.

[9] S. Chaturvedi, D. Goldwasser, and H. Daumé III. Predicting instructor's intervention in MOOC forums. *ACL'14*, pages 1501–1511, 2014.

[10] R.-E. Fan, K.-W. Chang, C.-J. Hsieh, X.-R. Wang, and C.-J. Lin. LIBLINEAR: A library for large linear classification. *JMLR*, 9:1871–1874, 2008.

[11] P. J. Guo and K. Reinecke. Demographic differences in how students navigate through MOOCs. In *L@S'14*, pages 21–30, 2014.

[12] A. Hershkovitz, R. S. Baker, S. M. Gowda, and A. T. Corbett. Predicting future learning better using quantitative analysis of moment-by-moment learning. In *EDM'13*, pages 74–81, 2013.

[13] G. E. Hinton, S. Osindero, and Y.-W. Teh. A fast learning algorithm for deep belief nets. *Neural Computation*, 18:1527–1554, 2006.

[14] R. A. Howard. *Dynamic Programming and Markov Processes*. The M.I.T. Press, 1960.

[15] J. Huang, A. Dasgupta, A. Ghosh, J. Manning, and M. Sanders. Superposter behavior in MOOC forums. In *L@S'14*, pages 117–126, 2014.

[16] R. F. Kizilcec, C. Piech, and E. Schneider. Deconstructing disengagement: analyzing learner subpopulations in massive open online courses. In *LAK'13*, pages 170–179, 2013.

[17] Y. Koren. Factorization meets the neighborhood: a multifaceted collaborative filtering model. In *KDD'08*, pages 426–434, 2008.

[18] P. F. Lazarsfeld and R. K. Merton. Friendship as a social process: A substantive and methodological analysis. *M. Berger, T. Abel, and C. H. Page, editors, Freedom and control in modern society, New York: Van Nostrand*, pages 18–66, 1954.

[19] J. Leskovec, D. Huttenlocher, and J. Kleinberg. Predicting positive and negative links in online social networks. In *WWW'10*, pages 641–650, 2010.

[20] M. McPherson, L. Smith-Lovin, and J. Cook. Birds of a feather: Homophily in social networks. *Annual review of sociology*, pages 415–444, 2001.

[21] P. Mirowski and Y. LeCun. Dynamic factor graphs for time series modeling. In *ECML/PKDD'09*, pages 128–143, 2009.

[22] S. O. Nesterko, D. Seaton, J. Reich, J. McIntyre, Q. Han, I. Chuang, and A. Ho. Due dates in MOOCs: does stricter mean better? In *L@S'14*, pages 193–194, 2014.

[23] L. Pappano. The year of the MOOC. *The New York Times*, 2(12):2012, 2012.

[24] A. Ramesh, D. Goldwasser, B. Huang, H. Daume III, and L. Getoor. Learning latent engagement patterns of students in online courses. In *AAAI'14*, pages 1272–1278, 2014.

[25] D. T. Seaton, Y. Bergner, I. Chuang, P. Mitros, and D. E. Pritchard. Who does what in a massive open online course? *Communications of the ACM*, 57(4):58–65, 2014.

[26] W. Tang, H. Zhuang, and J. Tang. Learning to infer social ties in large networks. In *ECML/PKDD'11*, pages 381–397, 2011.

[27] J. Wilkowski, A. Deutsch, and D. M. Russell. Student skill and goal achievement in the mapping with google MOOC. In *L@S'14*, pages 3–10, 2014.

Beyond Ranking: Optimizing Whole-Page Presentation

Yue Wang[1]*, Dawei Yin[2], Luo Jie[3]†, Pengyuan Wang[2], Makoto Yamada[2,4], Yi Chang[2], Qiaozhu Mei[1,5]
[1]Department of EECS, University of Michigan, Ann Arbor, MI, USA
[2]Yahoo Labs, 701 First Avenue, Sunnyvale, CA, USA
[3]Snapchat, Inc., 64 Market St, Venice, CA, USA
[4]Bioinformatics Center, Institute for Chemical Research, Kyoto University, Uji, Kyoto, Japan
[5]School of Information, University of Michigan, Ann Arbor, MI, USA
[1,5]{raywang, qmei}@umich.edu
[2]{daweiy, pengyuan, yichang}@yahoo-inc.com
[3]luoj.roger@gmail.com [2,4]myamada@kuicr.kyoto-u.ac.jp

ABSTRACT

Modern search engines aggregate results from different *verticals*: webpages, news, images, video, shopping, knowledge cards, local maps, etc. Unlike "ten blue links", these search results are heterogeneous in nature and not even arranged in a list on the page. This revolution directly challenges the conventional "ranked list" formulation in ad hoc search. Therefore, finding proper *presentation* for a gallery of heterogeneous results is critical for modern search engines.

We propose a novel framework that learns the optimal *page presentation* to render heterogeneous results onto search result page (SERP). Page presentation is broadly defined as the strategy to present a set of items on SERP, much more expressive than a ranked list. It can specify item positions, image sizes, text fonts, and any other styles as long as variations are within business and design constraints. The learned presentation is content-aware, i.e. tailored to specific queries and returned results. Simulation experiments show that the framework automatically learns eye-catchy presentations for relevant results. Experiments on real data show that simple instantiations of the framework already outperform leading algorithm in federated search result presentation. It means the framework can *learn* its own result presentation strategy purely from data, without even knowing the "probability ranking principle".

Categories and Subject Descriptors

H.3.3 [**Information Systems**]: Information Search and Retrieval; I.5.1 [**Pattern Recognition**]: Model

*This work was done when the first author was on an internship at Yahoo! Labs.

†This work was done when the third author was working at Yahoo Labs.

WSDM'16, February 22–25, 2016, San Francisco, CA, USA.

DOI: http://dx.doi.org/10.1145/2835776.2835824

1. INTRODUCTION

A decade ago, search engines returned "ten blue links". Result presentation was straightforward: ranking webpages by estimated relevance. It naturally saves user effort as she scans down the list, hopefully hitting the desired information at top ranks. This "probability ranking principle" was long envisioned in the 1970s [36], and later confirmed by eye-tracking studies [20, 19] and search log analysis [24, 15].

Today's search engines return far richer results than "ten blue links". Aside from webpages, results can also include news, images, video, shopping, structured knowledge, and local business maps. Each specific corpus is indexed by a *vertical* search engine; they are *federated* to serve the user's information need. Unlike "ten blue links", vertical search results have different visual appearance, layouts and sizes. They span across multiple columns on the page, not restricted in the mainline list (Figure 1).

Federated search results have been transforming user interaction patterns on search result pages (SERPs). Human eyeballs are spontaneously attracted by graphical results, causing a significant attention bias known as the *vertical bias* [12, 26, 31]. More interestingly, blue links surrounding a vertical result are also examined with increased probability [12]. In the presence of vertical results, user satisfaction towards an entire SERP cannot be reliably inferred from preference judgments for pairs of results [6].

These observations indicate that users do *not* sequentially scan results returned by federated search. Although the conventional "ranked list" formulation can still be used for federated search result presentation [5, 4], it is essentially a first-order approximation of the problem.

In this paper, we propose a novel framework that learns the optimal presentation for heterogeneous search results on SERP. Page presentation is broadly defined as the strategy to present a set of heterogeneous items on SERP, much more expressive than a ranked list. It can specify item positions, image sizes, text fonts, or any other styles as long as changes of these elements are allowed by business constraints [1] and page design templates. The goodness of a presentation is measured by user satisfaction metric: better presentation will make the user happier. The framework first learns a scoring function that maps search results and their presen-

[1]For example, sponsored results must be placed on the top.

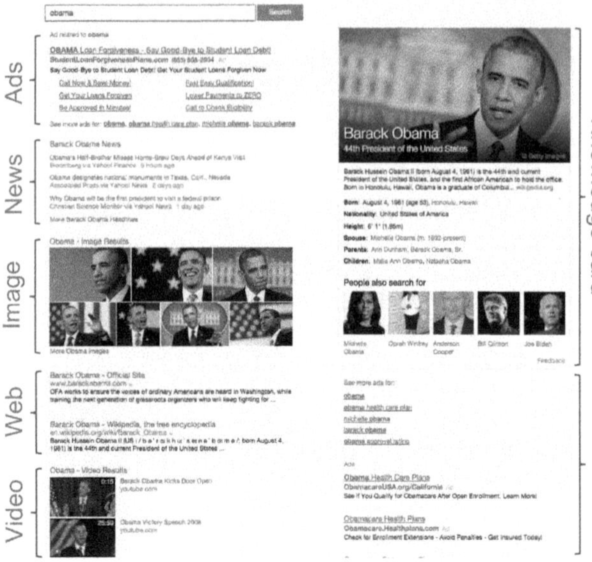

Figure 1: Modern search engine result page.

tation on SERP to user satisfaction metric. Then, given search results of a new query, the framework computes a presentation that maximizes user satisfaction.

The framework is quite general. First, practitioners can flexibly define the scope of page presentation. It can encode item positions (both horizontal and vertical) as well as element styles, such as image sizes and text fonts. It naturally encompasses ranked list as a special case. Second, different application scenarios can adopt different user satisfaction metric. It is not limited to click-based metric, but can also take other interactive behaviors into account, such as dwelling time and time-to-first-click. Lastly, the framework can potentially be instantiated in other interactive search scenarios, such as presenting search results on mobile and tablet devices, displaying multimedia feeds in online social networks, and arranging items on retailing websites.

We conduct experiments on both synthetic and real data to demonstrate the potential power of the proposed framework. Simulation experiments show that the framework can adapt to different types of attention bias and learn to present relevant results to catch user's eyeballs. This means our approach directly targets the new challenge brought by federated search, where users may not scan the results sequentially, and results are not in a ranked list. In real data experiments, simple instantiations of the framework outperform the leading algorithm in federated search result ranking. This is encouraging, because ranking algorithms use the probability ranking principle in its result presentation, while our framework does not even know the existence of it. Nevertheless, it *learns* its own result presentation principle purely from data and is able to deliver the state-of-the-art performance.

Our main contribution is summarized as follows:

- We formulate a new problem, *whole-page presentation optimization*, which extends the homogeneous document ranking in ad hoc search;
- We propose a general framework that computes the optimal presentation for federated search results.
- Experiments on synthetic and real data demonstrate that the proposed framework is promising in solving the new problem.

2. PROBLEM FORMULATION

The problem statement of page presentation optimization is as follows: "given search results to be displayed on a page, to find the optimal presentation that maximizes user satisfaction". We assume the following setting: search engine returns a set of results upon receiving a query, and renders the items on SERP according to some presentation strategy. As the SERP is shown to the user, she interacts with it and get certain degree of satisfaction. Now let us define some important concepts in our setting:

Definition 1 (Page Content): Page content is the set of search results to be displayed on a page. Each search result is an **item**. Upon receiving user's query, search engine backend returns a set of k items. Each item is represented as a vector $\mathbf{x}_i$ [2]. Note that different users and different queries will produce different sets of items, so $\mathbf{x}_i$ also encodes information from actual users and queries. Page content is represented as concatenation of k item vectors: $\mathbf{x}^\top = (\mathbf{x}_1^\top, \cdots, \mathbf{x}_i^\top, \cdots, \mathbf{x}_k^\top)$. The domain of $\mathbf{x}$ is defined by all possible page content returned by the backend, denoted as $\mathcal{X}$.

Definition 2 (Page Presentation): Page presentation defines the way in which page content $\mathbf{x}$ is displayed, such as position, vertical type, size, and color. It is encoded as a vector $\mathbf{p}$. The domain of $\mathbf{p}$ is defined by all possible page presentations permitted by business and design constraints, denoted as $\mathcal{P}$.

Definition 3 (Search Result Page, SERP): When page content $\mathbf{x}$ is put on page according to presentation strategy $\mathbf{p}$, a search result page (SERP) is generated. In other words, content $\mathbf{x}$ and presentation $\mathbf{p}$ uniquely determine a SERP. It is represented as a tuple $(\mathbf{x}, \mathbf{p}) \in \mathcal{X} \times \mathcal{P}$.

Definition 4 (User Response): User response includes her actions on SERP, such as number of clicks, positions of clicks, dwell time of clicks, and time to first click. This information is encoded in a vector $\mathbf{y}$. The domain of $\mathbf{y}$ is defined by all possible user responses, denoted as $\mathcal{Y}$.

Definition 5 (User Satisfaction): The user experiences certain degree of satisfaction as she interacts with the SERP. We assume that user satisfaction can be calibrated as a real value $s \in \mathbb{R}$: larger value of s means higher satisfaction.

The user response is a strong indicator for satisfaction. Intuitively, if a user opened the SERP, clicked on the top result right away, then spent long time dwelling on that result, she was highly likely to be happy with the result. With definitions above, we formulate our problem:

Page Presentation Optimization is to find the presentation $\mathbf{p} \in \mathcal{P}$ for a given page content $\mathbf{x} \in \mathcal{X}$, such that when the SERP $(\mathbf{x}, \mathbf{p})$ is presented to the user, her satisfaction score s is maximized.

[2]Throughout the paper we use bold lowercase letters for *column* vectors.

If we assume that there exists a scoring function $F : \mathcal{X} \times \mathcal{P} \to \mathbb{R}$ that maps SERP $(\mathbf{x}, \mathbf{p})$ to user satisfaction score s, then page presentation optimization problem can be formally written as

$$\max_{\mathbf{p} \in \mathcal{P}} F(\mathbf{x}, \mathbf{p}),$$
$$\text{subject to constraints on presentation } \mathbf{p}.$$

The problem of page presentation optimization is both new and challenging. It is new because page presentation can be flexibly defined, which opens up possibility to learn brand-new ways to display information. Retrieval and recommender systems typically use a ranked list for displaying homogeneous content. As heterogeneous results are weaved onto webpages, it is critical to present them in a proper manner to maximize user's utility. The problem is challenging because it is rather unclear how to find the scoring function that maps the *entire* SERP (content and presentation) to user satisfaction. We propose our solution framework in the next section.

3. PRESENTATION OPTIMIZATION FRAMEWORK

We propose to solve page presentation optimization using a supervised learning approach. This section sets up a general framework for our approach, including data collection methodology, design of scoring function $F(\cdot, \cdot)$, the learning and optimization stages. In the next section, we describe actual instantiations of the framework.

3.1 Data Collection Through Exploration

Supervised machine learning needs labelled training data. The caveat in data collection here is that normal search traffic cannot be used as the training data to learn the scoring function $F(\mathbf{x}, \mathbf{p})$. This is because in normal search traffic, search engine has a deterministic policy to present page content $\mathbf{x}$, which is controlled by existing model/rules within the system. In other words, page presentation $\mathbf{p}$ is uniquely determined given page content $\mathbf{x}$. However, we expect the model F to tell us user satisfaction as we search through *different* page presentations. Confounding between $\mathbf{x}$ and $\mathbf{p}$ will bias the learned model, which will be a serious problem.

To eliminate confounding, we allocate "presentation exploration bucket" to do randomized experiments. For each request in the bucket, we organize page content with random page presentation. Here "random" means to uniformly draw presentation strategies within business and design constraints, such that user experience is not hurt too much. Further, the presentation exploration traffic is controlled within a very small amount so as not to affect overall quality of the search service. Data collected in this way allow unbiased estimation of the scoring function.

In cases that showing random exploration results to the users is not desired, it would also be possible to either hire human annotators to label the page, or collect data from multiple buckets with different fixed presentation strategy as every Internet company is doing for testing their UI changes. Since we have already developed a good data collection through exploration framework in our production system, we choose to take this approach for data collection.

3.2 Learning Stage

The core of page presentation optimization is to estimate the scoring function $s = F(\mathbf{x}, \mathbf{p})$. We might consider two approaches:

(I) ***Direct approach:*** Collect page-wise user satisfaction ratings and directly model the dependency between SERP and user satisfaction. The dependency path is "$(\mathbf{x}, \mathbf{p}) - s$".

(II) ***Factorized approach:*** First predict user response $\mathbf{y}$ on SERP, then find a function that measure user satisfaction from these responses. The dependency path is "$(\mathbf{x}, \mathbf{p}) - \mathbf{y} - s$".

Approach (I) is straightforward. However it is very difficult, particularly at a large scale, to obtain explicit user rating s towards the *entire* SERP. To construct such data set, we would have needed substantial amount of observations and human annotation to overcome training data sparseness.

Approach (II) takes two steps. The first step is to predict user responses on a given page; the second step is to measure user satisfaction based on her page-wise response. Introducing user response variable $\mathbf{y}$ permits a separation of concerns. On the one hand, user response on a page is a direct consequence of interacting with the page. On the other hand, user satisfaction is typically estimated from user responses *only*, e.g. using total number of clicks, or long dwell time. In Approach (II), the complex dependency in $F(\cdot, \cdot)$ is decomposed into two relatively independent factors. Furthermore, on a practical note, Approach (II) is more realistic for current Web technology because user response on SERP can be easily collected via Javascript, whereas explicitly asking the users to evaluate the whole page is very uncommon. Therefore, we adopt the ***factorized approach***.

In factorized approach, the first step is to learn a *user response model*

$$\mathbf{y} = f(\mathbf{x}, \mathbf{p}), \ \forall\, \mathbf{x} \in \mathcal{X}, \mathbf{p} \in \mathcal{P}.$$

This is a supervised learning task; the actual form of $f(\mathbf{x}, \mathbf{p})$ can be chosen flexibly. We can simply build one model for each component y_i in $\mathbf{y}$, or we can jointly predict all components of $\mathbf{y}$ using structured output prediction [10]. In any case, user's responses on the page depends on both the content (whether it is relevant, diverse, or attractive) and the presentation (whether it is close to the top, around a graphical block, or shown in big size).

The second step is a utility funciton which defines a *user satisfaction metric*

$$s = g(\mathbf{y}), \forall\, \mathbf{y} \in \mathcal{Y}.$$

Finding the right user satisfaction metric based on page-wise user responses is not the focus of this paper, and can itself be a substantial research topic in interactive information systems [21, 30, 38]. Indeed, practitioners often heuristically define the metric as aggregation of fine-grained user responses, such as click-through rates, long-dwell-time clicks, time-to-first-click.

Finally, our scoring function for the entire SERP is

$$s = F(\mathbf{x}, \mathbf{p}) = (g \circ f)(\mathbf{x}, \mathbf{p}) = g(f(\mathbf{x}, \mathbf{p})).$$

3.3 Optimization Stage

We compute the optimal presentation $\mathbf{p}^*$ given content $\mathbf{x}$ by solving the following optimization problem:

$$\max_{\mathbf{p}\in\mathcal{P}} g(f(\mathbf{x},\mathbf{p})),$$

subject to constraints on presentation $\mathbf{p}$.

Computational cost of this optimization problem depends on actual form of the objective function $F = g \circ f$ and the constraints on presentation $\mathbf{p}$. In the next section we show that for certain instantiations of f and g, $\mathbf{p}^*$ can be computed quite efficiently.

4. INSTANTIATIONS OF PRESENTATION OPTIMIZATION FRAMEWORK

This section describes instantiations of the framework, including feature representation, user satisfaction metric, two user response models and their learning and optimization stages. We conclude this section by showing that the framework encompasses learning to rank.

4.1 Features

Both content and presentation on a SERP are represented in a feature vector, which will be the input to user response models.

Content Features

Content features contain information of the query and corresponding search results, similar to those used in learning to rank. We adopt the same content features as used in [23] to facilitate direct comparison in experiments (Section 6):

- **Global result set features**: features derived from all returned results. They indicate the content availability of each vertical.
- **Query features**: lexical features such as the query unigrams, bigrams and co-occurrence statistics. We also use outputs of query classifiers, and historical session based query features, etc.
- **Corpus level features**: query-independent features derived for each vertical and web document such as historical click-through rates, user preferences, etc.
- **Search result features**: extracted from each search result. A list of statistical summary features such as relevance scores and ranking features of individual results. For some verticals, we also extract some domain specific meta features, such as if the movie is on-screen and if the movie poster is available in the movie vertical, and the number of hits for the news articles from the news vertical in the last few hours.

Presentation Features

Presentation features encode the way in which search results are displayed on SERP, which are novel features in our framework. Concrete examples include:

- **Binary indicators**: whether to show an item on a position. The scheme can encode positions in a wireframe, such as a list or multi-column panels. Let there be k positions in the frame, and k items to be displayed. Let i be the index of items, j be the index of positions, $1 \le i, j \le k$. The presentation of item i, $\mathbf{p}_i$, is a 1-of-k binary encoding vector. If document i is placed at position j, then the j-th component of $\mathbf{p}_i$ is 1 and all others are 0. In this case we denote the value of $\mathbf{p}_i$ as $p_{ij} = 1$. The page presentation $\mathbf{p}^\top = (\mathbf{p}_1^\top, \cdots, \mathbf{p}_k^\top)$ consists of $k \times k$ binary indicator variables, essentially encoding the permutation of k objects.
- **Categorical features**: discrete properties of page items, e.g., multimedia type of an item (shown as text or image), typeface of a textual item;
- **Numerical features**: continuous properties of page items, e.g. brightness and contrast of a graphical item.
- **Other features**: e.g. certain interactions between page content and presentation may affect user response, such as "a textual item immediately above a graphical item".

We use two types of presentation features in real data experiments. We encode positions of items with binary indicators. For the local search results, we encode presentation size as a categorical feature ("single" vs. "multiple" entries).

4.2 User Satisfaction Metric

We assume that user satisfaction metric $g(\mathbf{y})$ is in the form of weighted sum of components in $\mathbf{y}$:

$$g(\mathbf{y}) = \mathbf{c}^\top \mathbf{y}.$$

In experiments, we use the click-skip metric for k items [23]:

$$g(\mathbf{y}) = \sum_{i=1}^{k} y_i,$$

where $y_i = 1$ if item i is clicked, and $y_i = -1$ if item i is skipped *and* some item below is clicked. A skip often indicates wasted inspection, so we set it to be a unit of negative utility. This metric strongly prefers adjacent clicks at top positions.

4.3 User Response Models

We use two models for predicting page-wise user response. The first model takes as features quadratic interaction between content and presentation. It permits an efficient optimization stage. The second model uses gradient boosted decision trees to capture more complex, nonlinear interaction between content and presentation. We expect it to generate improved performance.

Quadratic Feature Model

First, let us consider a simple instantiation of user response model that has efficient solution in the optimization stage. Since it uses quadratic interaction features between $\mathbf{x}$ and $\mathbf{p}$, we call it *Quadratic Feature Model.*

Assume there are k positions for k items. Page content $\mathbf{x}$ is the concatenation of k item vectors; page presentation is encoded using binary indicators, $\mathbf{p} \in \{0,1\}^{k\times k}$, as defined in Section 4.1. The model also contains fully interaction between $\mathbf{x}$ and $\mathbf{p}$ as features. Let vec($\mathbf{A}$) denote the row vector containing all elements in matrix $\mathbf{A}$, taken column by column, left to right. The augmented feature vector $\boldsymbol{\phi}$ for Quadratic Feature Model is:

$$\boldsymbol{\phi}^\top = (\mathbf{x}^\top, \mathbf{p}^\top, \text{vec}(\mathbf{x}\mathbf{p}^\top)).$$

Let $\mathbf{y} \in \mathbb{R}^k$ be the user response vector; each component y_i is a user response (e.g. click or skip) on item i. A linear model f_i is used to predict each y_i in $\mathbf{y}$:

$$y_i = f_i(\phi) = \mathbf{w}_i^\top \phi = \mathbf{u}_i^\top \mathbf{x} + \mathbf{v}_i^\top \mathbf{p} + \mathbf{x}^\top \mathbf{Q}_i \mathbf{p}. \quad (1)$$

$\mathbf{u}_i$, $\mathbf{v}_i$, and $\mathbf{Q}_i$ are coefficients for content-only, presentation-only, and content-presentation quadratic interaction features, respectively. The coefficients $\mathbf{w}_i = \{\mathbf{u}_i, \mathbf{v}_i, \mathbf{Q}_i\}$ can be estimated using regularized linear regression. To avoid overfitting, we regularize the L_2 norm of $\mathbf{u}_i$ and $\mathbf{v}_i$, and further impose low-rank regularization on $\mathbf{Q}_i$ to handle the sparsity issue of quadratic features.

In total, we will have k such models, each predicting one y_i in $\mathbf{y}$. To group the k models in notation, let us write coefficients as $\mathbf{U} = (\mathbf{u}_1, \cdots, \mathbf{u}_k)^\top, \mathbf{V} = (\mathbf{v}_1, \cdots, \mathbf{v}_k)^\top, \mathbf{Q} = \text{diag}(\mathbf{Q}_1, \cdots, \mathbf{Q}_k)$, and "copy" $\mathbf{x}$ and $\mathbf{p}$ k times to get the matrix $\mathbf{X} = \text{diag}(\mathbf{x}^\top, \cdots, \mathbf{x}^\top)$ and the vector $\mathbf{t}^\top = (\mathbf{p}^\top, \cdots, \mathbf{p}^\top)$. To clarify dimensionality, if $\mathbf{x} \in \mathbb{R}^n$, $\mathbf{p} \in \mathbb{R}^m$, then $\mathbf{U} \in \mathbb{R}^{k \times n}$, $\mathbf{V} \in \mathbb{R}^{k \times m}$, $\mathbf{X} \in \mathbb{R}^{k \times nk}$, $\mathbf{Q} \in \mathbb{R}^{nk \times mk}$, and $\mathbf{t} \in \mathbb{R}^{mk}$. The user response model can be written as

$$\mathbf{y} = f(\mathbf{x}, \mathbf{p}) = \mathbf{U}\mathbf{x} + \mathbf{V}\mathbf{p} + \mathbf{X}\mathbf{Q}\mathbf{t}.$$

Denote user satisfaction metric as $g(\mathbf{y}) = \mathbf{c}^\top \mathbf{y}$. Then the scoring function $F = g \circ f$ is

$$\begin{aligned} F(\mathbf{x}, \mathbf{p}) &= g(f(\mathbf{x}, \mathbf{p})) \\ &= \mathbf{c}^\top \mathbf{U}\mathbf{x} + \mathbf{c}^\top \mathbf{V}\mathbf{p} + \mathbf{c}^\top \mathbf{X}\mathbf{Q}\mathbf{t} \\ &= \mathbf{c}^\top \mathbf{U}\mathbf{x} + \mathbf{a}^\top \mathbf{p} \end{aligned} \quad (2)$$

where $\mathbf{a} = \mathbf{V}^\top \mathbf{c} + \sum_{i=1}^k c_i \mathbf{Q}_i^\top \mathbf{x}$ is a known vector.

To this end, the optimization stage is to find the $\mathbf{p}$ that maximizes (2) subject to the constraints on $\mathbf{p}$. Since page content $\mathbf{x}$ is given, the first term in (2) is a constant and can be dropped. The second term $\mathbf{a}^\top \mathbf{p}$ is a linear term of $\mathbf{p}$. Since $\mathbf{p} \in \{0,1\}^{k \times k}$ encodes a k-permutation, Each component in $\mathbf{a} \in \mathbb{R}^{k \times k}$ represents the gain of user satisfaction if item i is placed in position j, $1 \le i, j \le k$. Therefore, the optimization problem reduces to *maximum bipartite matching*, a special case of linear assignment problem. It can be efficiently solved by Hungarian algorithm [25] with time complexity $O(|\mathbf{p}|^3) = O(k^6)$. On a single-core computer with 2GHz CPU, the problem can be solved within 10 milliseconds for $k = 50$ items.

Gradient Boosted Decision Tree Model

In order to capture more complex, nonlinear interaction between content $\mathbf{x}$ and presentation $\mathbf{p}$, we replace the quadratic feature model f_i in previous section with a gradient boosted decision trees model h_i^{GBDT}. Gradient boosted decision trees (GBDT) is a very effective method for learning nonlinear functions [18].

Our feature vector is

$$\phi^\top = (\mathbf{x}^\top, \mathbf{p}^\top),$$

and each user response y_i in $\mathbf{y}$ is predicted by a GBDT model:

$$y_i = h_i^{\text{GBDT}}(\mathbf{x}, \mathbf{p}).$$

The user satisfaction metric is $g(\mathbf{y}) = \mathbf{c}^\top \mathbf{y} = \sum_{i=1}^k c_i y_i$.

In optimization stage, since each h_i is now a nonparametric model, we cannot get the analytical form of $F(\mathbf{x}, \mathbf{p}) = \sum_{i=1}^k c_i h_i^{\text{GBDT}}(\mathbf{x}, \mathbf{p})$ in terms of $\mathbf{p}$. That is, the optimization over $\mathbf{p}$ is intractable. Nevertheless, in realistic settings, the search space of $\mathbf{p}$ is usually pruned down to tens of possible values by business and design constraints. We implement parallel enumeration to quickly find the optimal presentation that maximizes user satisfaction.

4.4 Special Case: Learning to Rank

When we restrict page presentation to be a ranked list, and assume that users are more satisfied if more relevant results are placed at top ranks, then presentation optimization reduces to the traditional ranking problem. We point out this connection to demonstrate the generality of the proposed framework.

The instantiation is as follows. We use binary indicators in Section 4.1 to represent the ranked list. Let user response $\mathbf{y}$ decompose into k components, each representing the user's utility of seeing result i at rank j_i. Let user response model $f(\mathbf{x}, \mathbf{p})$ decompose into k real-valued component, each only taking as input $\mathbf{x}_i$ and its rank j_i. So we have

$$\begin{aligned} f(\mathbf{x}, \mathbf{p}) &= f(\mathbf{x}_1, \cdots, \mathbf{x}_k, \mathbf{p}_1, \cdots, \mathbf{p}_k) \\ &= (f_1(\mathbf{x}_1, \mathbf{p}_1), \cdots, f_k(\mathbf{x}_k, \mathbf{p}_k))^\top \\ &= (f_1(\mathbf{x}_1, p_{1j_1} = 1), \cdots, f_k(\mathbf{x}_k, p_{kj_k} = 1))^\top. \end{aligned} \quad (3)$$

Typically, the ranking function $h(\mathbf{x}_i)$ of result i is position-independent. It can also be interpreted as the score of result i seen on the top rank ($j_i = 1$). That means

$$h(\mathbf{x}_i) = f_i(\mathbf{x}_i, p_{i1} = 1).$$

Furthermore, traditional ranking problem assumes that the utility of a result is discounted by a factor w_j if it is ranked at position j. $w_j > 0$ is a decreasing function of j. E.g. in discounted cumulative gain (DCG),

$$w_j = \frac{1}{\log_2(1+j)}.$$

The discounting assumption implies:

$$\begin{aligned} f_i(\mathbf{x}_i, p_{ij} = 1) &= w_j f_i(\mathbf{x}_i, p_{i1} = 1) \\ &= w_j h(\mathbf{x}_i). \end{aligned} \quad (4)$$

Combining (3) and (4), user response model is realized as

$$f(\mathbf{x}, \mathbf{p}) = (w_{j_1} h(\mathbf{x}_1), \cdots, w_{j_k} h(\mathbf{x}_k))^\top,$$

where $h(\cdot)$ is the ranking function. User satisfaction is measured by the quality of ranked list, which *accumulate* the gain at each position:

$$g(\mathbf{y}) = \sum_{i=1}^k y_i = \sum_{i=1}^k w_{j_i} h(\mathbf{x}_i).$$

Clearly, maximum user satisfaction $g(\mathbf{y})$ is always achieved by *sorting the results by descending relevance scores.* This is the default presentation strategy of learning to rank.

5. SIMULATION STUDY

We demonstrate potential capability of presentation optimization framework by simulation. We use synthetic dataset so that we know the "ground truth" mechanism to maximize user satisfaction, and we can easily check whether the algorithm can indeed learn the optimal page presentation to maximize user satisfaction. We have two goals in this study:

(1) We show that the framework enables general definition of page presentation.

(2) We use both position bias and item-specific bias to show that the framework can automatically adapt to user interaction habits.

5.1 Overview

We first give a brief overview of simulation workflow. The simulated "presentation exploration bucket" will generate a page containing a set items with random presentation. Every time a new page is generated, each item is assigned some amount of reward (e.g. relevant information) drawn from an underlying distribution. The simulated "user" will have a certain type of attention bias: (1) position bias, in which more attention is paid to certain region of the page than elsewhere (Figure 2a); (2) vertical bias, or item-specific bias, in which more attention is attracted by a specific type of item and its surrounding area (Figure 2b).

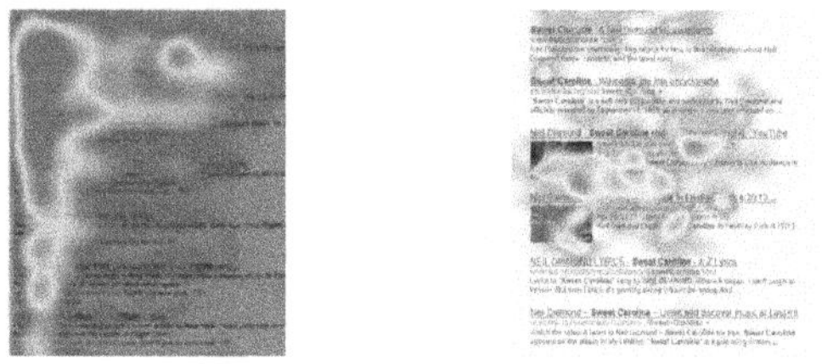

(a) Position bias [2] (b) Vertical bias [1]

Figure 2: Different types of user attention bias.

An "interaction" happens when the "presentation exploration bucket" generates a page and the "user" examines it with attention bias. When the user examines an item, she receives the corresponding reward. User satisfaction towards the page is the sum of rewards. The page content, presentation, as well as the examined items and positions (user responses), become data that the framework learns from. Finally, we test if the framework successfully learned user's attention bias. Given a new set of items, we expect to see that the framework will place items with higher rewards to positions with more concentrated attention to achieve maximum user satisfaction. Therefore, to visualize the model's current belief in user attention bias, we can plot the distribution of item rewards on the page.

5.2 Data Generating Process

On the "search engine" side, a page (either 1-D list or 2-D grid) contains k positions. The page content $\mathbf{x} = (x_1, \cdots, x_k)^\top$, $x_i \sim \mathcal{N}(\mu_i, \sigma)$ represents intrinsic rewards of k items. We set $k = 10$ for 1-D list and $k = 7 \times 7$ for 2-D grid. μ_i's are random numbers drawn from in $[0, 1]$, $\sigma = 0.1$. The page presentation $\mathbf{p}$ is drawn from length-k permutations uniformly at random. The whole page is represented as $(\mathbf{x}, \mathbf{p})$.

On the "user" side, attention bias is simulated as follows:

Position bias: whether to examine position j is a Bernoulli random variable with parameter p_j. A real-life example is the top-down position bias, commonly observed when the user interacts with a ranked list.

Item-specific bias: whether to examine item i is a Bernoulli random variable with parameter p_i. A real-life example is the vertical bias, commonly observed when the user interacts with a page that contains vertical search results (images, videos, maps, etc).

Then, the "user" will "interact" with the page $(\mathbf{x}, \mathbf{p})$: k binary values are drawn from k Bernoulli distributions, and recorded as a user response vector $\mathbf{y} \in \{0, 1\}^k$. if item i is examined, $y_i = 1$, the user receives a reward x_i. The user satisfaction equals the sum of reward of examined items. We generate 100,000 pages to train the Quadratic Feature Model described in Section 4.3.

5.3 Discussion

To visualize the learned optimal presentation, we pick a random $\mathbf{x}$ and compute the corresponding optimal presentation $\mathbf{p}^*$, then arrange the x_i's according to $\mathbf{p}^*$. A page is visualized as a heat map of x_i's rewards. Ideally, the items with higher reward ("better content") should be placed onto the position with higher probability of user attention.

(a) Position bias (b) Ideal presentation (c) Learned presentation

Figure 3: Top position bias and presentation on 1-D list.

(a) Position bias (b) Ideal presentation (c) Learned presentation

Figure 4: Top-left position bias and presentation on 2-D canvas.

(a) Position bias (b) Ideal presentation (c) Learned presentation

Figure 5: Two-end position bias and presentation on 2-D canvas.

Figure 3, 4, and 5 visualize the presentation results under various position biases. We can see that the algorithm indeed learns to put "better content" to positions with more user attention. Because the definition of page presentation is general, it is able to handle both 1-D list and 2-D grid. Furthermore, it can capture complicated distribution of position bias on a 2-D canvas: the top-left position bias in Figure 4, and the top-bottom position bias in Figure 5.

Figure 6 visualizes the result under item-specific bias. This is an interesting case where an item on the page is very eye-catchy, and it also attracts user's attention to its surrounding items (e.g., an image attracts user's eyeballs on itself as well as its caption and description text). Also, suppose that for items farther away from that eye-catchy item, the user's

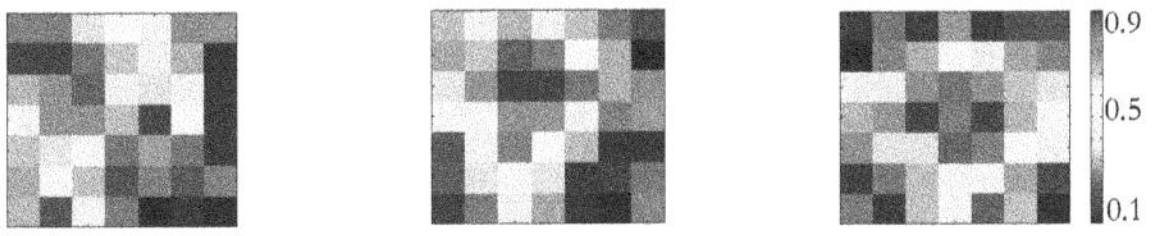

(a) $s = 4.07$ (b) $s = 4.92$ (c) $s = 5.41$

Figure 6: Item-specific bias. s: page-wise user satisfaction. When a specific item (e.g. image) attracts user attention to not only itself but also its surrounding results, then the page-wise reward is highest when the vertical is placed at the center of the page.

attention drops further down. Then the optimal presentation strategy is to place the item on the *center* of the page, so that the whole page delivers the most reward. In Figure 6, we see that user satisfaction value s is highest when the item (the dark red region) is centered on the page.

6. REAL DATA EXPERIMENTS

We demonstrate the effectiveness of page presentation optimization framework by conducting experiments on the real-world data set collected via a commercial search engine.

6.1 Data Collection

We use a very small fraction of search traffic as the presentation exploration buckets. The data was collected through the year 2013. Vertical search results whose presentation are explored include *news*, *shopping*, and *local listings*. In the exploration buckets, the order of Web results are kept untouched and verticals are randomly slotted into allowed positions with uniform probability. Randomly generated SERPs are not influenced by any ranking algorithm in the system. As pointed out in Section 3.1, this is required to eliminate page content confounding when training models. The exploration SERP is then presented to the user who interacts with it in a normal fashion. Users response on the SERP, along with page-wise content information like the query, document features from backends, are logged.

6.2 Methods

We use two pointwise ranking models as baseline method. They are trained using the content features as described in Section 4.1. The first baseline method has been adopted in production (LOGIT-RANK) [23]. It estimates a logistic regression model for each vertical result (including web result):

$$y_i = \sigma(\mathbf{w}_i^\top \mathbf{x}_i),$$

where y_i is a binary target variable that indicates whether the result is clicked ($y_i = +1$) or skipped ($y_i = -1$) as described in Section 4.2, and $\sigma(\cdot)$ is the sigmoid link function rescaled to $[-1, 1]$.

The second baseline method uses gradient boosted decision trees to learn a pointwise ranking function (GBDT-RANK). This is essentially replacing the logistic regressor in LOGIT-RANK with a GBDT regressor:

$$y_i = h_i^{\text{GBDT}}(\mathbf{x}_i).$$

We evaluate the two instantiations of presentation optimization framework described in Section 4.3: the Quadratic

Table 1: Match rate between random exploration presentation p and predicted optimal presentation p*. "Until Web$_1$ " means that p and p* encode the same presentation above the 1st webpage result.

	Until WEB$_1$	Until WEB$_2$	Until WEB$_3$
LOGIT-RANK	68.68%	46.76%	30.85%
QUAD-PRES	71.63%	50.68%	33.42%

Feature Model (QUAD-PRES) and the GBDT Model (GBDT-PRES). They use page-wise information $(\mathbf{x}, \mathbf{p})$ to predict the user response *vector*, i.e. the vector of clicks and skips.

In implementation, we use Vowpal Wabbit [27] to learn logistic regression models, and XGBoost [13] to learn the gradient boosted decision tree models. The hyperparameters of the models are tuned on a small holdout data set.

6.3 Evaluation

We use half of the exploration SERP as training set (January – June), the rest as test set. It contains hundreds of millions of pageviews and was collected from real search traffic. Compared to standard supervised learning setup, it is difficult to do an unbiased offline performance evaluation because of the interactive nature of the task (see Section 4.3 in [23]). This is because the offline data $(\mathbf{x}^{(n)}, \mathbf{p}^{(n)}, \mathbf{y}^{(n)})$ is collected using a particular logging policy, so we only observe user response $\mathbf{y}^{(n)}$ for a specific page presentation $\mathbf{p}^{(n)}$. In offline evaluation, when the algorithm is given page content $\mathbf{x}^{(n)}$, it may output a presentation $\mathbf{p}^{*(n)} \neq \mathbf{p}^{(n)}$, for which we do not observe user response, hence cannot evaluate its goodness. To address this problem, we use an offline policy evaluation method proposed by Li et al. [28] for evaluating online recommendation systems. It is simple to implement and provides an unbiased performance estimate, thanks to data collected through random exploration. Given a stream of events $(\mathbf{x}^{(n)}, \mathbf{p}^{(n)}, \Pr(\mathbf{p}^{(n)}), \mathbf{y}^{(n)})$ collected through random exploration, where $\Pr(\mathbf{p}^{(n)})$ is the probability for the SERP $(\mathbf{x}^{(n)}, \mathbf{p}^{(n)})$ to be generated from uniform random exploration, the average user satisfaction for N offline events can be computed as

$$\bar{s} = \frac{1}{N} \sum_{n=1}^{N} \frac{g(\mathbf{y}^{(n)}) \mathbf{1}_{\{\mathbf{p}^{*(n)} == \mathbf{p}^{(n)}\}}}{\Pr(\mathbf{p}^{(n)})},$$

where $\mathbf{1}_{\{\cdot\}}$ is the indicator function, and $g(\mathbf{y}^{(n)})$ is user satisfaction towards SERP n. This means the algorithm is evaluated on those exploration SERPs whose presentation *matches* what is chosen by the algorithm; otherwise the SERP is discarded in offline evaluation.

As the match goes deeper down the page, the match rate decreases (Table 1). If we require *exact match* between predicted $\mathbf{p}^{*(n)}$ and actual $\mathbf{p}^{(n)}$, a large fraction of test set will be discarded and the performance estimates tend to have large variance hence unreliable. Our evaluation only focuses on vertical results shown above the first, second, and third webpage result. Note that the first webpage result is *not* always on top rank; the top rank is frequently occupied by the vertical results.

6.4 Results

Table 2 shows the average page-wise user satisfaction. It is encouraging to see that whole-page optimization methods outperform ranking methods, because ranking methods utilize probability ranking principle to rank results by relevance, which assumes a top-down position bias. QUAD-PRES and GBDT-PRES do not make this assumption, but *learns* its own result presentation principle purely from data. The reason that GBDT models work better than logistic regression models, mainly because logistic regression assumes linear decision boundary, while GBDT is capable of modeling non-linear decision boundary.

Table 2: Average user satisfaction ($\times 10^{-3}$).

	Until Web_1	Until Web_2	Until Web_3
LOGIT-RANK	-0.25	1.79	1.89
GBDT-RANK	2.18	3.68	2.22
QUAD-PRES	0.62	6.39	5.37
GBDT-PRES	**2.68**	**6.72**	**8.24**

Note that in our definition of user satisfaction metric $g(\mathbf{y})$, a skip causes negative utility ($y_i = -1$). The fact that QUAD-PRES and GBDT-PRES generally work better than the baseline methods is because they take into consideration the retrieved items, the page presentation, and their interaction on the entire SERP, not just a single result. The presentation-blind models LOGIT-RANK and GBDT-RANK always want to put on top the results that will most probably gets clicked. However, for certain queries people might intentionally skip the graphical results (e.g., when shopping ads are shown when the search intent is in fact informational). In such cases, a click tends to happen *below* the top rank. In contrast, presentation optimization methods will consider both the result and its position on the page. That leads to more sensible arrangement of results. We see that GBDT-PRES attracts more clicks and has less skips when we evaluate deeper down the SERP.

Table 3, 4, and 5 shows the click-through rate (CTR) above Web_1, Web_2, and Web_3, respectively. "S. Local" means a single entry of local business result (such as restaurants); "M. Local" means multiple entries of local business results. They are the same vertical/genre results presented in different sizes. In terms of CTR, ranking methods have very strong performance because they are directly optimized for high CTR. However, whole-page optimization methods still achieve competitive or sometimes better CTR by taking into account page-wise information.

It is interesting to see that for News vertical, there is not much help to know about other results on the SERP, neither their presentation. In contrast, knowing page-wise results helps improve the CTR of top-ranked local listings by a large margin. A possible explanation is that news, more like general webpages, contain rich text information and their content relevance can be readily modeled by standard ranking functions. On the other hand, local listings are in drastically different nature compared to webpages and news, therefore knowing the complementary information from other webpage results helps predicting the click/skip patterns. We can also observe small improvements in CTR of the shopping results. Since the shopping results shown on the top are most likely to be skipped, the algorithm learns to become extremely conservative in showing shopping verticals on top. This leads to a much smaller coverage of shopping results in the entire traffic.

As the match goes deeper down the page, the local ranking algorithms show decreased performance in terms of CTR. This is because the local ranking methods tend to greedily put the high CTR items on top of the page, but ignores the content on the entire page. In contrast, the page presentation algorithms, especially GBDT-PRES, still get good CTR on News and Multi-local verticals, which takes larger coverage. This is attributed to the fact that they model user response over the entire page.

Table 3: CTR, match until Web_1

	News	Shopping	S. Local	M. Local
Coverage	0.46%	0.02%	0.02%	0.71%
LOGIT-RANK	21.05%	40.79%	11.58%	30.02%
GBDT-RANK	23.28%	53.32%	38.26%	52.27%
QUAD-PRES	21.97%	49.85%	47.16%	39.93%
GBDT-PRES	22.34%	46.15%	48.12%	49.18%

Table 4: CTR, match until Web_2

	News	Shopping	S. Local	M. Local
Coverage	2.0%	0.11%	0.03%	2.3%
LOGIT-RANK	16.44%	23.71%	18.51%	8.92%
GBDT-RANK	16.31%	30.39%	36.73%	23.11%
QUAD-PRES	14.78%	13.57%	23.39%	27.53%
GBDT-PRES	16.21%	40.83%	33.18%	35.23%

Table 5: CTR, match until Web_3

	News	Shopping	S. Local	M. Local
Coverage	3.8%	0.18%	0.11%	3.4%
LOGIT-RANK	14.52%	21.48%	13.80%	9.65%
GBDT-RANK	12.51%	42.96%	24.93%	22.42%
QUAD-PRES	11.45%	12.88%	15.47%	24.38%
GBDT-PRES	14.11%	36.00%	24.72%	30.66%

7. RELATED WORK

As a general framework for search result presentation, this work draws on various aspects in IR research. It is inspired by the task of federated search result presentation. It extends traditional "ranked list" formulation to more a general notion of "presentation". Finally, it delivers optimal presentation by learning from interactive search logs.

7.1 Document Ranking in Retrieval

Document ranking has long been the core problem of ad hoc retrieval. Given a query, the retrieval system returns a list of documents ranked by decreasing probability of relevance. The presentation is optimal with respect to the user's effort when she sequentially and independently examines results from top to bottom [36]. Design and evaluation of document ranking functions are at the central stage of IR research, dating from vector space models [37] and language modeling ranking functions [40] to more recent machine learning ranking [29] and top document reranking [11, 22, 35].

Our framework extends homogeneous document ranking to heterogeneous content presentation. Document ranking is a special case when presentation is a ranked list. From an algorithmic perspective, we use *all* documents on SERP to determine the optimal presentation, which is in the same spirit of reranking/global ranking [35, 22]. The difference is that our framework allows much more general notion of presentation than a list. In fact, global ranking algorithms, and more broadly, structured prediction algorithms in machine learning literature [10], can be readily plugged into our framework as the user response model.

7.2 Federated Search

Federated search (or aggregated search) refers to searching through a collection of specialized search engines, *verticals*, and aggregating the results on SERP. Usually, contents from different verticals are heterogeneous and visually rich. Federated search has two sub-tasks: vertical selection and result presentation [32, 3]. Given a query, the task of vertical selection is to accurately determine which candidate verticals provide potentially relevant results [7, 8]. After getting results from candidate verticals, the task of result presentation is to merge vertical results with general webpage results on the same page [5].

This paper is concerned with result presentation. Previous approaches formulate it as a ranking problem [5, 34, 23]. Specifically, [5, 23] employ pointwise ranking functions to rank results and blocks, while [5, 34] also construct pairwise preference judgments to train a ranking function. [14] considers 2-D grid presentation for image and shopping results. Our framework allows more flexible definition of presentation than ranked list and 2-D grid, e.g. arbitrary frames, image sizes, and text fonts.

Federated search results significantly change the landscape of SERP, which in turn calls for changes in evaluation methodology. Bailey et al. [9] propose the notion of *whole-page relevance*. They argue that the Cranfield-style evaluation is inadequate to quantify user's holistic experience on modern SERP, such as overall presentation and coherence. It proposes to evaluate whole-page relevance by assigning grades to various SERP elements. Our framework incorporates this idea by defining an appropriate user satisfaction metric that guides the search of optimal presentation.

Our work is related to the whole-page optimization for sponsored search [16] or online ads bidding [33], where the focus is to optimize revenue of the search service provider. Our framework is more general and can be applied in these problems by changing the optimization objective.

7.3 Search Behavior Modeling

To deliver good search experience, understanding user behavior on SERP is critical. Eye-tracking experiments [20, 19] and click log analyses [24, 15] observe that users follow sequential order in browsing blue-link-only SERPs. Lower-ranked results are examined with lower probability. On the one hand, these results confirm the probability ranking principle, encouraging search engines to put more relevant results on top. On the other hand, the position bias has to be handled with care when using click-through data as relevance judgments to train ranking functions [24].

As heterogeneous results appear on modern SERP, users do not necessarily follow sequential order in browsing search results. Studies observe more interesting user interaction patterns, notably vertical bias [12, 26, 31] and presentation bias [39]. These patterns not only make it questionable to stick to the probability ranking principle, but also complicates the inference of relevance judgments from click-through data. As a result, global ranking that takes into account relations between documents is developed [32], and click modeling of federated search becomes even more elaborate [12, 17].

Instead of building click models, our framework uses randomized experiments to understand user's presentation preference. Using presentation exploration buckets, we collect user responses on almost identical contents rendered with different presentations. Interaction logs collected in this way are almost free from presentational bias and can be used to estimate user response to a specific presentation given the search content[3]. This enables automatic generation of presentations for different contents, which is more scalable than hand-crafted presentation rules.

8. CONCLUSION

This paper proposes a new problem in web search: *whole-page presentation optimization*. Modern retrieval systems return a collection of heterogeneous results, calling for more flexible presentation strategies than the conventional ranked list. This paper formulates the problem as a mathematical optimization problem, and proposes a framework that solves the problem in a data-driven fashion. This general framework is instantiated to enable more flexible and expressive definition of page presentation than ranked list. Simple instantiations of the framework are shown to outperform ranking-based methods in satisfying federated search users.

This study opens up many interesting avenues for the future work. We can instantiate the general presentation optimization framework properly on other heterogeneous content presentation scenarios, such as mobile and tablet search, where user's attention bias may be different from that on large screens. User response models can be instantiated in more sophisticated ways, e.g., modeling cursor position as conditional random fields over the SERP canvas. Finally, defining a proper quantitative metric for user satisfaction based on SERP-level, fine-grained user behaviors can be explored in human computer interaction research.

9. ACKNOWLEDGEMENTS

We sincerely thank the anonymous reviewers for their useful comments. This work is partially supported by the National Science Foundation under grant number IIS-1054199.

10. REFERENCES

[1] Eye tracking study: Google results with videos. https://www.looktracker.com/blog/eye-tracking-case-study/google-results-with-videos-eye-tracking-study.

[2] Google ads in second position get more attention. http://miratech.com/blog/eye-tracking-google.html.

[3] Trec federated web search track. https://sites.google.com/site/trecfedweb.

[4] J. Arguello and F. Diaz. Vertical selection and aggregation. In B. Long and Y. Chang, editors, *Relevance Ranking for Vertical Search Engines*. Elsevier, 2013.

[5] J. Arguello, F. Diaz, and J. Callan. Learning to aggregate vertical results into web search results. In *Proceedings of the 20th ACM conference on Information and knowledge management*, pages 201–210, 2011.

[6] J. Arguello, F. Diaz, J. Callan, and B. Carterette. A methodology for evaluating aggregated search results. In

[3]The presentation can never be completely random due to constraints of business and SERP template itself.

Advances in information retrieval, pages 141–152. Springer, 2011.

[7] J. Arguello, F. Diaz, J. Callan, and J.-F. Crespo. Sources of evidence for vertical selection. In *Proceedings of the 32nd ACM SIGIR conference on Research and development in information retrieval*, pages 315–322, 2009.

[8] J. Arguello, F. Diaz, and J.-F. Paiement. Vertical selection in the presence of unlabeled verticals. In *Proceedings of the 33rd ACM SIGIR conference on Research and development in information retrieval*, pages 691–698, 2010.

[9] P. Bailey, N. Craswell, R. W. White, L. Chen, A. Satyanarayana, and S. M. Tahaghoghi. Evaluating whole-page relevance. In *Proceedings of the 33rd ACM SIGIR conference on Research and development in information retrieval*, pages 767–768, 2010.

[10] G. Bakir, T. Hofmann, B. Schölkopf, A. Smola, B. Taskar, and S. Vishwanathan. Predicting structured data. 2007.

[11] J. Carbonell and J. Goldstein. The use of mmr, diversity-based reranking for reordering documents and producing summaries. In *Proceedings of the 21st ACM SIGIR conference on Research and development in information retrieval*, pages 335–336, 1998.

[12] D. Chen, W. Chen, H. Wang, Z. Chen, and Q. Yang. Beyond ten blue links: enabling user click modeling in federated web search. In *Proceedings of the fifth ACM conference on Web search and data mining*, pages 463–472, 2012.

[13] T. Chen. extreme gradient boosting library. https://github.com/tqchen/xgboost.

[14] F. Chierichetti, R. Kumar, and P. Raghavan. Optimizing two-dimensional search results presentation. In *Proceedings of the fourth ACM conference on Web search and data mining*, pages 257–266, 2011.

[15] N. Craswell, O. Zoeter, M. Taylor, and B. Ramsey. An experimental comparison of click position-bias models. In *Proceedings of the 2008 Conference on Web search and data mining*, pages 87–94, 2008.

[16] N. R. Devanur, Z. Huang, N. Korula, V. S. Mirrokni, and Q. Yan. Whole-page optimization and submodular welfare maximization with online bidders. In *Proceedings of the fourteenth ACM conference on Electronic commerce*, pages 305–322, 2013.

[17] F. Diaz, R. W. White, G. Buscher, and D. Liebling. Robust models of mouse movement on dynamic web search results pages. In *Proceedings of the 22nd ACM conference on information and knowledge management*, pages 1451–1460, 2013.

[18] J. H. Friedman. Stochastic gradient boosting. *Computational Statistics & Data Analysis*, 38(4):367–378, 2002.

[19] H. Gord. Eye tracking on universal and personalized search. http://searchengineland.com/eye-tracking-on-universal-and-personalized-search-12233. Technical report, Enquiro Research.

[20] L. A. Granka, T. Joachims, and G. Gay. Eye-tracking analysis of user behavior in www search. In *Proceedings of the 27th ACM SIGIR conference on Research and development in information retrieval*, pages 478–479, 2004.

[21] M. Hearst. The evaluation of search user interfaces. In *Search User Interfaces.* Cambridge University Press, 2019.

[22] S. Ji, K. Zhou, C. Liao, Z. Zheng, G.-R. Xue, O. Chapelle, G. Sun, and H. Zha. Global ranking by exploiting user clicks. In *Proceedings of the 32nd ACM SIGIR conference on Research and development in information retrieval*, pages 35–42, 2009.

[23] L. Jie, S. Lamkhede, R. Sapra, E. Hsu, H. Song, and Y. Chang. A unified search federation system based on online user feedback. In *Proceedings of the 19th ACM SIGKDD conference on Knowledge discovery and data mining*, pages 1195–1203. ACM, 2013.

[24] T. Joachims, L. Granka, B. Pan, H. Hembrooke, and G. Gay. Accurately interpreting clickthrough data as implicit feedback. In *Proceedings of the 28th ACM SIGIR conference on Research and development in information retrieval*, pages 154–161, 2005.

[25] H. W. Kuhn. The hungarian method for the assignment problem. *Naval Research Logistics Quarterly*, 2(1-2):83–97, 1955.

[26] D. Lagun and E. Agichtein. Effects of task and domain on searcher attention. In *Proceedings of the 37th ACM SIGIR conference on Research and development in information retrieval*, pages 1087–1090, 2014.

[27] J. Langford. Vowpal wabbit. http://hunch.net/ vw.

[28] L. Li, W. Chu, J. Langford, and R. E. Schapire. A contextual-bandit approach to personalized news article recommendation. In *Proceedings of the 19th conference on World Wide Web*, pages 661–670, 2010.

[29] T.-Y. Liu. Learning to rank for information retrieval. *Foundations and Trends in Information Retrieval*, 3(3):225–331, 2009.

[30] Y. Liu, Y. Chen, J. Tang, J. Sun, M. Zhang, S. Ma, and X. Zhu. Different users, different opinions: Predicting search satisfaction with mouse movement information. In *Proceedings of the 38th ACM SIGIR conference on Research and development in information retrieval*, 2015.

[31] Z. Liu, Y. Liu, K. Zhou, M. Zhang, and S. Ma. Influence of vertical result in web search examination. In *Proceedings of the 38th ACM SIGIR conference on Research and development in information retrieval*, 2015.

[32] B. Long and Y. Chang. *Relevance Ranking for Vertical Search Engines.* Elsevier, 2014.

[33] P. Metrikov, F. Diaz, S. Lahaie, and J. Rao. Whole page optimization: how page elements interact with the position auction. In *Proceedings of the fifteenth ACM conference on Economics and computation*, pages 583–600, 2014.

[34] A. K. Ponnuswami, K. Pattabiraman, Q. Wu, R. Gilad-Bachrach, and T. Kanungo. On composition of a federated web search result page: using online users to provide pairwise preference for heterogeneous verticals. In *Proceedings of the fourth ACM conference on Web search and data mining*, pages 715–724, 2011.

[35] T. Qin, T.-Y. Liu, X.-D. Zhang, D.-S. Wang, and H. Li. Global ranking using continuous conditional random fields. In *Advances in neural information processing systems*, pages 1281–1288, 2009.

[36] S. E. Robertson. The probability ranking principle in ir. In *Journal of Documentation*, pages 294–304, 1977.

[37] G. Salton and C. Buckley. Term-weighting approaches in automatic text retrieval. *Information processing & management*, 24(5):513–523, 1988.

[38] A. Schuth, K. Hofmann, and F. Radlinski. Predicting search satisfaction metrics with interleaved comparisons. In *Proceedings of the 38th ACM SIGIR conference on Research and development in information retrieval*, 2015.

[39] Y. Yue, R. Patel, and H. Roehrig. Beyond position bias: Examining result attractiveness as a source of presentation bias in clickthrough data. In *Proceedings of the 19th conference on World Wide Web*, pages 1011–1018, 2010.

[40] C. Zhai and J. Lafferty. A study of smoothing methods for language models applied to ad hoc information retrieval. In *Proceedings of the 24th ACM SIGIR conference on Research and development in information retrieval*, pages 334–342, 2001.

Understanding and Measuring User Engagement and Attention in Online News Reading

Dmitry Lagun*
Google
dlagun@google.com

Mounia Lalmas
Yahoo Labs
mounia@acm.org

ABSTRACT

Prior work on user engagement with online news sites identified dwell time as a key engagement metric. Whereas on average, dwell time gives a reasonable estimate of user engagement with a news article, it does not capture user engagement with the news article at *sub-document* level nor it allows to measure the proportion of article read by the user.

In this paper, we analyze online news reading patterns using large-scale viewport data collected from 267,210 page views on 1,971 news articles on a major online news website. We propose four engagement metrics that, unlike dwell time, more accurately reflect how users engage with *and* attend to the news content. The four metrics capture different levels of engagement, ranging from bounce to complete, providing clear and interpretable characterizations of user engagement with online news. Furthermore, we develop a probabilistic model that combines both an article textual content and level of user engagement information in a joint model. In our experiments we show that our model, called TUNE, is able to predict future level of user engagement based on textual content alone and outperform currently available methods.

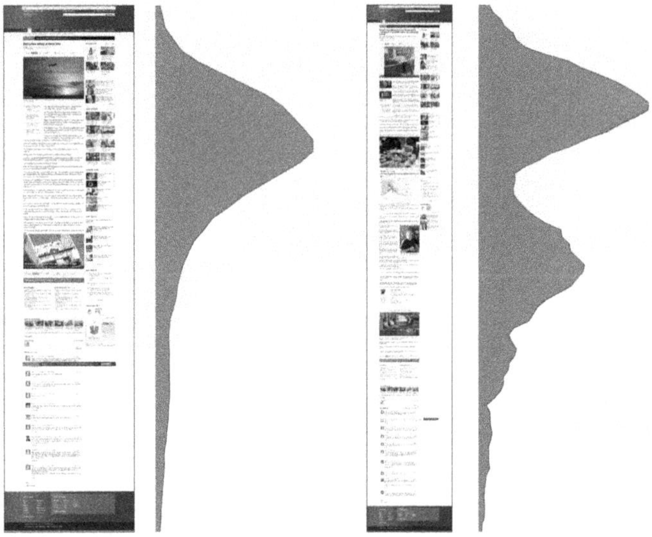

(a) Most common (b) Less common

Figure 1: Two example pages showing different patterns of user attention: (a) shows the most common pattern when reader's attention decays monotonically towards the bottom of the article; (b) shows unusual distribution of attention indicating that content positioned closer to the end of the article attracts significant portion of user attention. The blue densities on the right side indicate the average amount of time users spent viewing a particular part of the article.

1. INTRODUCTION

User engagement has been coined as the "emotional, cognitive and behavioral connection that exists between a user and a resource" [5]. Online content providers such as news portals constantly seek to attract large shares of online attention by keeping their users engaged. A common challenge is to identify which aspects of the online interaction influence user engagement the most. We focus on one component of engagement with online content, "stickiness", concerned with users "spending time" on a content provider site.

This component of engagement is usually described as a combination of cognitive processes such as focused attention, affect and interest, traditionally measured using surveys [29]. It is also measured through large-scale analytical metrics that assess users' depth of interaction with the site. *Dwell time*, the time spent on a resource (e.g., a webpage) is one such metric, and has proven to be a meaningful and robust metric of user engagement in the context of web search [2, 6] and recommendation tasks [34].

However, dwell time has limitations. For example, consider Figure 1 which shows examples of two webpages (news articles) of a major news portal, with associated distribution of time users spend at each vertical position of the article. We see two patterns. In (a) users spend most of their time towards the top of the page, whereas in (b) users spend significant amount of time further down the page, likely reading and contributing comments to the news articles. Although the dwell time for (b) is likely to be higher (the data shows this), it does not tell us much about user attention on the page, neither it allows us to differentiate between consump-

*Work done while a student at Emory University, and as part of a Yahoo Faculty Research and Engagement Program.

WSDM'16, February 22 - 25, 2016, San Francisco, CA, USA

ISBN 978-1-4503-3716-8/16/02...$15.00

DOI: http://dx.doi.org/10.1145/2835776.2835833

tion patterns with similar dwell time values. Using *viewport time* allows us to do exactly this.

In this work we build upon this observation and analyze patterns in online news reading using *viewport* data. Viewport is defined as the position of the webpage that is visible at any given time to the user. Such data allows us to measure aspects of user engagement with news articles that are *not measurable with dwell time*, such as the proportion of article read by the user or the amount of time spent at each part of the article. Furthermore, we employ viewport data to develop user engagement metrics that can measure to what extent the user interaction with a news article follows the signature of positive user engagement, i.e., users read most of the article and read/post/reply to a comment. Unlike dwell time, our metrics do not depend on the amount of textual content in the article but, instead, on the proportion of article read by users making it easier to compare articles with different amount of content.

We take one step further and develop a probabilistic model that accounts for both the extent of the engagement *and* the textual topic of the article. In contrast with previously explored text-only approaches, our model utilizes the viewport behavioral data, that enables the model to learn a joint mapping between textual topic and user engagement level. Through our experiments we demonstrate that such model is able to predict future level of user engagement with a news article significantly better than currently available methods. In addition, our model can be used, e.g. by the news editors, as an exploratory tool to investigate which textual topics correspond to higher engagement levels.

Our paper makes the following contributions:

- an analysis of large-scale viewport data in news reading, including the description of typical patterns of news reading by the online users of a large news portal;
- a family of user engagement levels that reflects user attention during news article reading; and
- a joint model of news article textual content and level of user engagement.

2. BACKGROUND AND MOTIVATION

Several works looked at the relationship between dwell time and properties of webpages. A study [27] asking participants to provide explicit feedback about the interestingness of news articles they read revealed a strong tendency to spend more time on interesting articles rather than on uninteresting ones, similarly to that reported in [10, 14]. However, only a very weak correlation between the length of articles and associated reading times was found, indicating that most articles were only read in parts, not in their entirety. Recently, [34] showed that article length correlated with dwell time, but only to some extent. They observed a large variance for articles longer than 1,000 words, suggesting that users may have a maximum "time-budget" to consume an article. The presence of videos and photos, and the article genre (e.g. politics versus food) had an effect on dwell time [34]. Works looking at webpage aesthetics showed that layout and textual features [33], and that a combination of content and dynamic features (e.g. page size or time to download all URLs) [22] had an effect on page dwell time. Finally, [18] successfully incorporated webpage readability level and search query topic into predicting dwell time.

The above and other works showed dwell time to be strong signal of user interest, an important component of user engagement [3, 4, 24]. Their aim was also to identify aspects of the webpage that make users spend time on it. However, dwell time does not capture where on the page users are focusing, namely the *user attention*. It just tells us that users spend time on it and this may be caused by the page properties such as its length, its genre, etc. Hence the suggestion of using other measurements to study user attention, an important component of user engagement [5].

Studies of user attention using eye-tracking provided numerous insights about typical content examination strategies, such as top to bottom scanning of web search results [23]. In the context of news reading, [4] showed gaze to be reliable indicator of interestingness and to correlate with self-reported engagement metrics, such as focused attention and affect. However, due to the high cost of eye-tracking studies, a considerable amount of research was devoted to finding more scalable methods of attention measurement, which would allow monitoring attention of online users at large scale. Mouse cursor tracking was proposed as a cheap alternative to eye-tracking, and the relationship between cursor and gaze was studied [28]. Mouse cursor position was shown to be aligned with gaze position, when users performed a click or a pointing action in many search contexts.

Mouse cursor movement has been studied to inform various types of user engagement with web content, in particular to infer user interests in webpages [15]. For instance, [31] found that the ratio of mouse cursor movement to time spent on a webpage was a good indicator of how interested users were in the webpage content, and explored the extent to which cursor tracking can inform about whether users are attentive to certain content when reading it, and what their experience was. Recently, [3] recorded the mouse cursor movements from users reading interesting versus non-interesting news articles, from which they generated cursor gesture patterns through unsupervised learning. They identified several significant correlations between cursor behaviour and the focused attention and affect engagement metrics, and could predict with high accuracy user interests on the news articles based on the cursor gestures. Finally, [16, 19] showed that mouse cursor movements outperform dwell time in their ability to predict relevance ratings.

However, despite promising results on using mouse cursor for measurement of user attention [28] in web search, it has been shown that the extent of coordination between gaze and mouse cursor depends on the user task [9], e.g. text highlighting, pointing or clicking. Moreover, it was found [9] that eye and cursor are poorly coordinated during cursor inactivity, hence limiting the utility of mouse cursor as an attention measurement tool in a news reading task, where minimal pointing is required. Thus, we propose to use instead *viewport time* to study user attention.

Using viewport to measure the amount of time users spend on each portion of the webpage is not new. It was used as an implicit feedback information to improve search result ranking for subsequent search queries [8], to help eliminating position bias in search result examination, detecting bad snippets and improving search result ranking [20] and in document summarization [1]. Viewport time was successfully used on mobile devices to infer user interest at the sub-document level [17]. More recently, it was used for accurate measurement of search result examination on a mobile phone and was helpful for the evaluation of rich informational results that may lack active user interaction, such as click [21]. Our work adds to this body of works, and explores viewport time, as a coarse, but more robust instrument to measure user attention during news reading.

3. VIEWPORT DATA

Information about the amount of time online users spend reading a particular portion of a news article can be measured by tracking the position of user *viewport*. Similarly to [21], we define *viewport* as the position of the webpage portion visible to the user at any given time.

To collect viewport data for our study, we used JavaScript tracking instrumentation that allowed us to track user scroll positions, the size of the user browser viewport (width and height), as well as the position of key page elements, such as article header, body and comment blocks. This information allowed us to reconstruct the scrolling actions and calculate the amount of time users spend at given portion of the news article. Similar instrumentation was used in [1, 17, 20, 21].

We calculate the time a user spent viewing an article at a vertical position y, or simply viewport time, as:

$$ViewportTime(y) = \sum_{i=1}^{\#scrolls} t_i \cdot \mathcal{I}(y \in V_i)$$

where t_i is the time the user spent at the i-th scroll position, V_i is the viewport defined by the scroll offset and the size of the user browser window and $\mathcal{I}(\cdot)$ is an indicator function that evaluates to one if y falls inside of V_i, otherwise it evaluates to zero.

We analyze the *viewport* of a sample of data collected during one calendar month in 2013. We collected viewport data for 267,210 page views on an online news website from Yahoo!. These page views include visits to 1,971 unique news articles. We ensured that each individual news article received at least 10 page visits. Approximately 60% of the articles in our dataset have user comments.

4. NEWS READING BEHAVIOR

We take a holistic approach to analyze how users read online news. First, we analyze the overall pattern of news article examination represented by a distribution of the time users spend at each portion of the article. Then, we describe our findings on the effect of the article media components on the attention of a news reader. Finally, to analyze sequence of user actions (e.g., scroll), we apply a mixture of Markov chains model that enables us to identify common news article reading patterns from the viewport data.

4.1 Overall Pattern of User Attention

First, we analyze the overall pattern of news article examination measured with viewport time. Figure 2 shows the viewport time distribution computed from all page views in our data. It has a bi-modal shape with the first peak occurring at approximately 1000 px and the second, less pronounced peak at 5000 px. This suggests that most page views have the viewport profile that falls between cases (a) and (b) of Figure 1. This also shows that on average user spends significantly smaller amount of time at lower scroll positions – the viewport time decays towards the bottom of the page. The fact that users spend substantially less

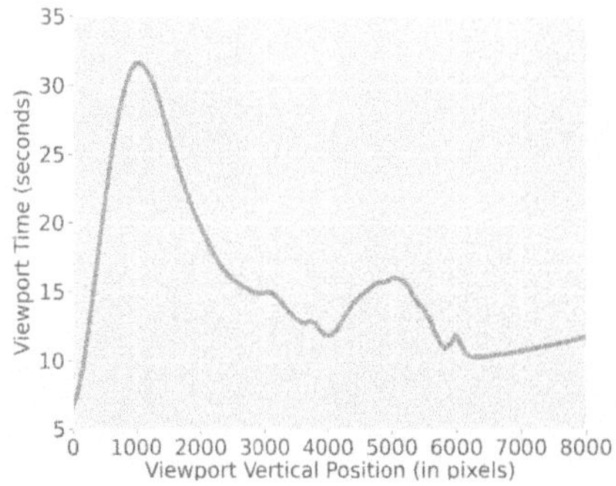

Figure 2: Distribution of viewport time averaged across all page views.

time reading seemingly equivalent amount of text (top versus bottom of the article) may also explain the weak correlation between article length and the dwell time reported in several works [22, 27, 34].

Figure 2 provides us with an overall picture on *how* users consume the news articles; however, it tells us nothing about article reading dynamics, i.e., "how often do users skip portion of the article". In Section 4.3, we attempt to answer such questions, and analyze how users navigate through the news article until they decide to leave the page.

4.2 Effect of Media Elements

We now analyze the possible impact of image and video on viewport time. We use non-parametric methods to estimate the distributions of *viewport* time conditioned on the presence of image or video element on the page. Using a Gaussian kernel density estimator we estimate the joint distribution of four variables: *viewport* time T, *viewport* vertical position Y, presence of image element I and presence of video element V. By fixing the values for some of the variables and ensuring proper normalization (by numerical integration) we can derive a conditional distribution of the other variable(s). For example, if we are interested in the effect of article images on viewport time at the same position, we can analyze the differences between the conditional distributions $P(T|Y = y, I = 0, V = 0)$ and $P(T|Y = y, I = 1, V = 0)$.

When expected viewport times are different across different conditions (e.g., video presence versus absence), we perform the Kolmogorov-Smirnov (KS) test to establish statistical significance of the observed difference $D = \sup_x |F_1(x) - F_2(x)|$, where D is the test statistic, $F_1(x)$ and $F_2(x)$ are cumulative distributions under comparison. We compute the empirical distribution of viewport time by evaluating the appropriate condition distribution at fixed number of points ($N = 200$) that reasonably covers the support of viewport time distribution ([0, 300] seconds).

Figure 3a shows the expected *viewport* time at various vertical positions of the viewport conditioned on the presence of an image. Two solid curves represent conditional means, i.e. expected values, of the viewport time given the presence of images. We also show the probability of an image displayed at each vertical position $P(I = 1|Y = y, V = 0)$. We see large difference in the expected *viewport* time at the very beginning of the page – users tend to stay almost twice longer at the first screen when the article starts with an image, compared to articles without an image on top. Due to

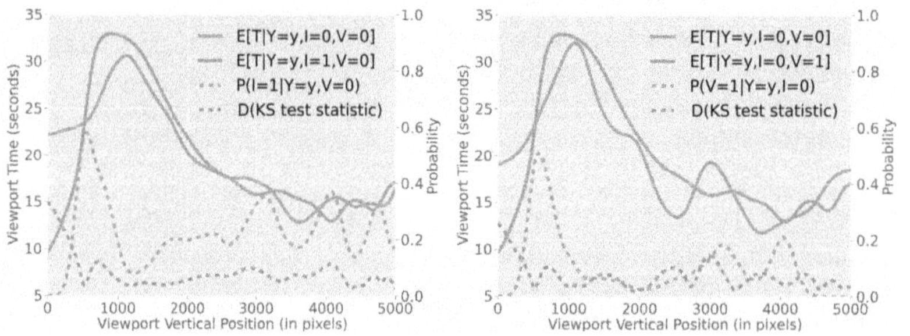

(a) Image (b) Video

Figure 3: Effect of media elements on viewport time.

the large sample size, the KS-test shows significant differences (p<0.001) at all vertical offsets. However, the peak value of the KS test statistic D is found near the article's top, which is consistent with the difference in distribution means. Figure 3b shows the same as above, but with respect to video. Overall, the presence of image or video significantly affects viewport time in initial viewport.

4.3 Markovian Analysis of News Reading

The *viewport time* analysis identified a strong positional bias in news article reading. However, it left unanswered several important questions, e.g. "How do users navigate (consume) the article during the page visit?", "Do users always read from top to bottom or are there deviations from this pattern?". To address these questions, we analyze article reading behavior through Markov chains.

Data Pre-processing: For this analysis we represent the user scrolling actions as states in a Markov chain. Specifically, using the position of the viewport and the article layout information we determine the portion of the article visible to a user during a given point in time. We divide an article into four areas of interest (AOI): *Top*, *Middle*, *Bottom* and *Comment*. The *Top-Bottom* AOIs are located in the beginning, middle (50%) and in the end of the article main content; the vertical dimension of each of the AOIs (except *Comment*) is equal to the height of the user viewport.[1] Then, given the page view and the associated sequence of viewport positions $\{y_i\}_{i=1}^{n}$ ordered by time, we construct a sequence of $\{v_i\}_{i=1}^{n^*}$ encoding portions of the article viewed by a user. To reduce noise in the viewport movement data we ignore viewport positions that lasted less than one second. Each viewport position is transformed into the Markov chain state by finding the closest AOI and making sure the recorded viewport position lays within one screen from the AOI margin (making sure the AOI was visible to the user). If no AOI meets this criteria, we discard this viewport position. Furthermore, as we are interested in studying the within article reading patterns, we eliminate self-transitions by collapsing adjacent states that correspond to the same portion of the article, hence the number of viewport positions n and the length of the Markov chain n^* might not always match. Finally, we augment the viewing sequences with initial *Start* and terminal *Leave* states, so our set of possible states becomes $\mathcal{O}$ ={*Top*, *Middle*, *Bottom*, *Comment*, *Start*, *Leave*}.

Identifying Reading Patterns: The Markov chain models the article reading behavior using the following probabilistic distribution:

$$P(\mathbf{V_{1:n}}) = P(V_1 = v_1) \prod_{i=2}^{n} P(V_i = v_i | V_{i-1} = v_{i-1})$$

where V_i is a random variable representing the portion of the article (an AOI) viewed at the i-th time, v_i is the observed AOI viewed at the i-th time, and n is the number of times user transitioned from one portion of the article to another. The probabilities $P(V = v_i)$ and $P(V_i = v_i | V_{i-1} = v_j)$ can be directly estimated from the data, e.g., by counting the number of transitions from v_j to v_i and ensuring proper normalization ($\sum_{v \in \mathcal{O}} P(V = v | V_j) = 1$).

However, such approach will only allow us to analyze the *average* reading behavior, potentially ignoring the variability in article examination found in the data. Thus, we model the article reading behavior using a discrete mixture of Markov chains (MMC), which is able to account for different reading patterns present in the data. We choose MMC over more standard Hidden Markov Model (HMM [30]) on purpose, since our goal is to cluster entire page views, rather than state observations. The MMC models the data using the following distribution:

$$P(\mathbf{V_{1:n}}) = \sum_{k=1}^{K} \alpha_k P_k(V_1 = v_1) \prod_{i=2}^{n} P_k(V_i = v_i | V_{i-1} = v_{i-1})$$

where $P_k(V_1)$ and $P_k(V_i|V_{i-1})$ are mixture specific probability distributions, α_k is a mixture weight and k indexes the mixture component. Unlike the Markov chain model, MCC requires inference that could be done using the Expectation Maximization algorithm (EM [12]). The following equations are used to optimize the log-likelihood:

$$P^{(t)}(z_{j,k} = 1) = \frac{\alpha_k P_k^{(t)}(V_{j,1}) \prod_{i=2}^{n_j} P_k^{(t)}(V_{j,i}|V_{j,i-1})}{\sum_{k=1}^{K} \alpha_k P_k^{(t)}(V_{j,1}) \prod_{i=2}^{n_j} P_k^{(t)}(V_{j,i}|V_{j,i-1})}$$

$$\alpha_k^{(t+1)} = \frac{1}{N} \sum_{j=1}^{N} P^{(t)}(z_{j,k} = 1)$$

$$P_k^{(t+1)}(V_i = o_m | V_{i-1} = o_l) = \\ = \frac{\sum_{j=1}^{N} P^{(t)}(z_{j,k} = 1) \sum_{i=2}^{n_j} \mathbf{I}(v_i = o_m) \mathbf{I}(v_j = o_l)}{\sum_{j=1}^{N} P^{(t)}(z_{j,k} = 1) \sum_{i=2}^{n_j} \mathbf{I}(v_j = o_l)}$$

[1]Alternative AOI definitions are possible. In this paper, we favor simplicity over other concerns.

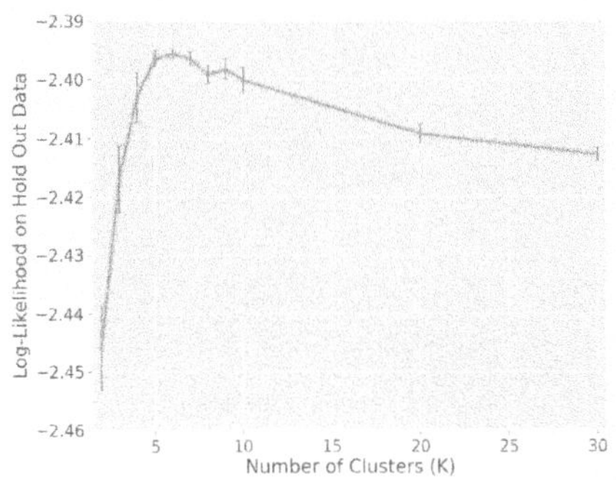

Figure 4: Log-Likelihood for different numbers of clusters (**k**). The optimal is achieved when **k**=6. The error bars shows the standard deviation of the mean (averaged over 24 random restarts).

where $z_{j,k}$ is a binary variable indicating whether j-th page view belongs to cluster k.

Choosing the Optimal Number of Mixture Components: To determine the optimal optimal number of clusters **K**, we experiment with different values of **K** and choose the one that maximizes the model generalization ability on a held-out data. That is, we split our data set in equal proportions, and use the first half of the data for training, while the second half of the data is used for assessing the model performance on an out of sample data. Due to the non-convex nature of the optimization problem, the EM algorithm is not guaranteed to find the globally optimal solution. Hence, we perform multiple restarts for the same value of **K** and report the average log-likelihood across all random restarts. In our experiments, the number of random restarts was equal to 24. Figure 4 shows the log-likelihood on the held-out data for different values of **K**. The log-likelihood is maximized at **K**=6, and the model starts to overfit with **K** larger than six, which negatively impacts its generalization ability.

Identified Reading Patterns: The reading patterns identified after running the Markov mixture model with **K=6** on the entire data set are summarized in Figure 5. We focus on the four largest clusters (ordered by their size), which account for the majority of the data.

Figure 5a shows the most probable sequences generated from the model together with their probabilities (shown on top). A considerable number of users with this pattern leave the page after viewing the article *Top* part. Although the transition diagram does not give us information on how much time users spend in the "Top" state, it clearly shows that users following this pattern are unlikely to scroll down the page. Interestingly, the second most probable sequence shows a different pattern, when users are starting reading the article at the *Top*, then transition to the *Middle*, then return back to the *Top*, followed by a page *Leave*. The third cluster (Figure 5c) is very similar to this cluster, except for the fact that users are more likely to return to the Top position from *Middle*, *Bottom* and *Comment.*

The second and fourth clusters are shown in Figures 5b and 5d. They both describe users that read the article entirely from *Top* to *Bottom* (*Top*, *Middle*, *Bottom*), and even likely to transition to *Comment* upon reaching the *Bottom* part of the article. Although these reading patterns are the most desirable goal for a news website, and are likely to be associated with high level of user engagement, to the best of our knowledge, they have not been used to study and optimize user engagement with online news. The second most probable sequence shows a shallower reading, i.e., when users leave the page upon reaching the article midpoint, which is more akin to the cascade examination of web search results [11].

Our results show that most users are likely to read article from top to bottom, and some are likely to scroll up before leaving the page. We found that the reading depth differs greatly ranging from deep engagement, when the entire article is read, to relatively short reading, when users leave after examining the first screen of the article. While some of these may seem obvious, in terms of the identified news reading patterns, to the best of our knowledge, this work is the first to validate them on a large-scale data using unsupervised sequence clustering. Clearly, by analyzig the dwell time alone we would not be able to distinguish between such patterns. More importantly, these results warrant a revision of user engagement metrics beyond *high* and *low* user engagement levels dictated by dwell time.

5. ENGAGEMENT LEVEL METRICS

Motivated by the reading patterns identified in the previous section, we propose a set of user engagement levels that more accurately reflect user engagement *and* attention with a news article, compared to current approaches using dwell time. Given the availability of viewport data, our proposed taxonomy classifies each individual page view into one of the four *level* categories: *Bounce*, *Shallow* engagement, *Deep* engagement and *Complete* engagement.

A *Bounce* indicates that users do not engage with the article and leave the page relatively quickly. We adopt 10 seconds dwell time threshold to determine a *Bounce*. Other thresholds can be used, for example accounting for genre (politics versus sport); we leave this for future work.

If the user decides to stay and read the article but reads less than 50% of it, we categorize such a page view as *Shallow* engagement, since the user has not fully consumed the content. The percentage of article read is defined as the proportion of the article body (main article text) having a *viewport* time longer than 5 seconds. Using 50% is rather arbitrary and used only to distinguish between extreme cases of shallow reading and consumption of the entire article. It is sufficient to demonstrate the insights brought with our proposed four levels of engagement.

On the other hand, if the user decides to read more than 50% of the article content, we refer to this as *Deep* engagement, since the user most likely needs to scroll down the article, indicating greater interest in the article content.

Finally, if after reading most of the article the user decides to interact (post or reply) with comments, we call such experience *Complete* engagement. The users are fully engaged with the article content to the point of interacting with its associated comments.

To understand what insights these engagement levels can bring, in particular in terms of modeling user attention, we group our data according to the proposed taxonomy, and compare each group with three sets of measures. Table 1 presents a summary of this comparison. We start with dwell time, *viewport* time broken down for the proposed engagement levels. We then report *viewport* time for article header

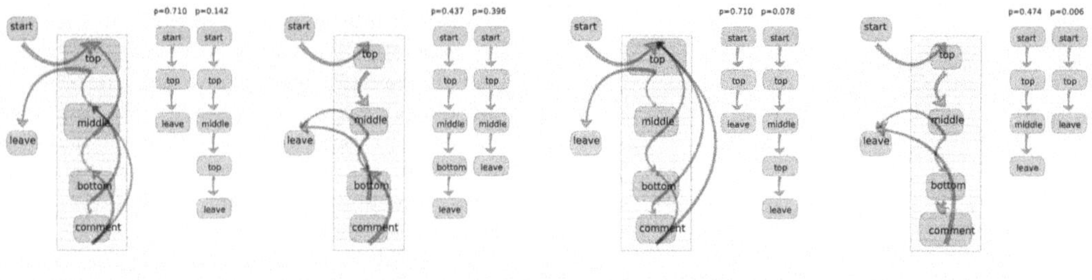

(a) Cluster 1 (b) Cluster 2 (c) Cluster 3 (d) Cluster 4

Figure 5: Top four reading patterns identified with a mixture of Markov chain models.

Metric	*Bounce* (N=26542)	*Shallow* (N=63982)	*Deep* (N=164197)	*Complete* (N=12489)	p-value (ANOVA)
dwell	6.17 (0.02)	63.75 (0.37)	99.02 (0.22)	228.35 (1.48)	<0.001 (F=16091.6)
header time	2.99 (0.03)	15.39 (0.14)	18.48 (0.08)	17.41 (0.25)	<0.001 (F=1369.6)
body time	5.06 (0.02)	35.13 (0.21)	86.24 (0.20)	85.00 (0.70)	<0.001 (F=12229.3)
comment time	0.56 (0.01)	17.27 (0.23)	9.72 (0.07)	110.90 (0.89)	<0.001 (F=24012.4)
% header time	0.31 (0.00)	0.23 (0.00)	0.17 (0.00)	0.09 (0.00)	<0.001 (F=4784.3)
% body time	0.62 (0.00)	0.58 (0.00)	0.76 (0.00)	0.40 (0.00)	<0.001 (F=16377.2)
% comment time	0.07 (0.00)	0.20 (0.00)	0.07 (0.00)	0.51 (0.00)	<0.001 (F=20180.4)
% article read	0.12 (0.00)	0.23 (0.00)	0.83 (0.00)	0.84 (0.00)	<0.001 (F=318141.1)
# comment clicks	0.01 (0.00)	0.43 (0.01)	0.00 (0.00)	3.14 (0.03)	<0.001 (F=25351.6)

Table 1: Means and standard errors of the fine grained engagement measures for *Bounce*, *Shallow*, *Deep* and *Complete* engagement levels.

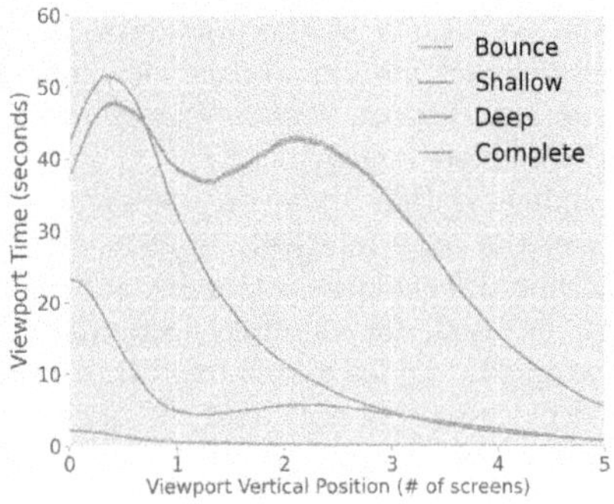

Figure 6: Mean viewport time at different viewport positions for each of the engagement levels: *Bounce*, *Shallow*, *Deep* and *Complete*. The thickness of a line corresponds to the standard error of the mean.

(usually a title which may include small image thumbnail), body (main body of the article), and comment block. We report the percentage of the total *viewport* time spent viewing one of these regions. The percentage of article read is defined according to the above definition. The comment clicks shows the number of clicks on the comment block.

For each measure, we report the mean and standard errors. The last column of the table shows the p-value and test statistics for the one way analysis of variance (ANOVA), allowing us to establish statistical differences in measured quantities among the four engagement levels. All of the ANOVA tests showed significant differences (p<0.001). Due to lack of space we omit the pos-hoc analysis of the pairwise differences between the four groups.

While we find that dwell time and *viewport* time on head, body and comment increase from *Bounce* to *Complete*, we note that the distribution of the percentage of time among these blocks changes in an interesting manner. The *viewport* time on head steadily decreases from 0.31 for *Bounce* to 0.09 for *Complete* indicating that users spend an increasing amount of time reading content deeper in the article. The percentage of article read steadily increases from *Bounce* to *Complete*, as expected. With respect to this measure, *Bounce* (12%) and *Shallow* (23%) clearly represent low levels of engagement with the article, since less than 25% of the article was read. On the other hand, *Deep* and *Complete* correspond to the situations when the majority (83%) of the article was read. The number of comment clicks is highest for the *Complete* class (3.14), followed by *Shallow* (0.43),[2] suggesting that users may engage with comments even if they do not read a large proportion of the article.

To complement this analysis, we show the average *viewport* time computed at varying vertical position in Figure 6. Each of the four curves corresponds to one of the engagement levels. The thickness of the line shows the standard error (only visible for *Complete*). We see that for the page views in the *Bounce* case, users rarely scroll down the page, whereas many users in the *Shallow* case spend approximately another 5 seconds of *viewport* time at lower scroll positions. *Deep* engagement is characterized by significant time spent on the entire article (peak at the first screen amounts to about 50 seconds) with a steady position decay of the *viewport* time towards the bottom. Interestingly, the *viewport* time profile for *Complete* engagement no longer monotonically decays with the position; instead it has a bi-modal shape. We believe this is due to a significant time users spend viewing and interacting with comments which are normally placed right after the main article content.

[2]The number of clicks for *Deep* is zero due to the definition of the *Deep* engagement class.

Symbol	Description
T	number of topics
D	number of articles
V	number of unique words
N_d	number of word tokens in article d
θ_d	the multinomial distribution of topics for article d
ϕ_z	multinomial distribution of words for topic z
ψ_z	dirichlet distribution of engagement rates for topic z
z_{di}	topic assignment for i-th word token in article d
w_{id}	i-th word token in article d
ε_d	user engagement profile for article d (multinomial)

Table 2: Notation used in TUNE model.

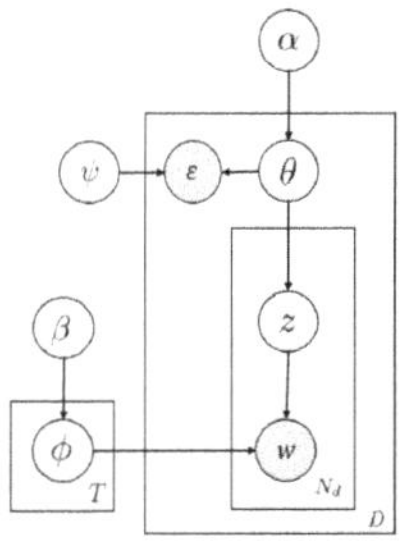

Figure 7: Topics of User Engagement (TUNE) model.

We put forward four user engagement levels that characterize how users *attend* to articles they have decided to read, as they landed on the article page. We recall that we are not attempting to capture scrolling behaviors, but to exploit these to understand which parts of a news article users engaged with, and to map these to the four proposed engagement levels. Our analysis shows that these levels are intuitive, and bring more refined insights about how user engage with articles, than using dwell time alone. The engagement levels were derived using the viewport time information, which can be computed through scalable and non-intrusive instrumentation. Next, we study how viewport time can be used to predict these levels of engagement based on the textual topics of a news article.

6. MODELING ARTICLE CONTENT AND LEVEL OF USER ENGAGEMENT

The four user engagement level metrics derived in the previous section provide clear criteria for measuring user engagement in the context of news reading at sub-document level, thus accounting for user attention. In this section we investigate whether we can model the distribution of user engagement levels with an article purely from the article textual content. If we are able to do this, this would allow us (and news content providers) to optimize online news content more effectively, compared to current methods.

The primary source of information that online users interact during news reading is the actual article text. Thus, we choose to model article text in conjunction with engagement levels observed with viewport data. To this end, we adopt a topic modeling approach, because of its intuitive structure and great ability to model textual data. Among many latent topic models, Latent Dirichlet Allocation (LDA) [7] gained significant popularity due to its relative simplicity and good empirical results. Hence, we adopt LDA for our task. Unlike the original LDA model, which uses word co-occurrence within a document to form topics, we design a model that uses both sources of information – word co-occurrence and level of user engagement – to define the topics. We call our model TUNE for Topics of User Engagement with News.

We briefly review the basic LDA model. The notation is summarized in Table 2 and the plate diagram is shown in Figure 7. LDA is a Bayesian network that generates a document (a news article in our context) using a mixture of topics [7]. In its generative process, for each document d, a multinomial distribution θ_d over the topics is sampled from a Dirichlet distribution with parameter α. Then, to generate each word a topic z_{di} is chosen from this topic distribution, and a word w_{di} is chosen by random sampling from a topic multinomial distribution $\phi_{z_{di}}$. An efficient inference allows to greatly improve the robustness of the model by "integrating out" nuance parameters θ and ϕ.

To represent a user level of engagement with the article we adopt the taxonomy introduced in Section 5. The fact that some popular articles in our dataset may have large number of page views will make the proposed model to focus on modeling of such popular articles. To avoid this, we normalize for article popularity by computing an article user engagement profile – a multinomial distribution over the four engagement levels calculated over all page views for the article. More specifically, using the engagement levels introduced earlier, we classify each individual page view into the engagement level and calculate the article user engagement profile as follows:

$$\varepsilon = \left(\frac{\#Bounce}{N}, \frac{\#Shallow}{N}, \frac{\#Deep}{N}, \frac{\#Complete}{N} \right)$$

where N is total number of page views for the article.

There are several ways user engagement information can be incorporated into the LDA model. Since its introduction, LDA model has been extended to include document author information [13], the time the document was generated [32] and many other types of information (e.g. [25]). Generalization of these was introduced in [25] allowing conditioning topics on arbitrary features of the document. As our goal is to predict future user engagement level based on an article text, we want to be able to derive tractable inference for ε. The Topic over Time (TOT) model in [32] meets this criterion, thus, we adopt its structure to incorporate the user engagement levels into the LDA model. The graphical structure of our model is summarized in Figure 7 and its generative process is described as follows:

1. Draw T multinomial distributions ϕ_z from Dirichlet prior β, one for each topic z
2. For each article d, draw a multinomial distribution θ_d from Dirichlet prior α. Then for each word w_{di} in article d:
   (a) Draw a topic z_{di} from multinomial θ_d
   (b) Draw a word w_{di} from multinomial $\phi_{z_{di}}$
   (c) Draw a user engagement level ε_{di} from Dirichlet $\psi_{z_{di}}$

This generative process follows an alternative view of TOT model, which is more suitable for performing Gibbs inference. In this view, a user engagement profile is generated for each word, while in practice it is only measured once per entire article. In our experiments, we assign the same profile of user engagement to all words within the same article. As shown in the process, the posterior distribution over topics depends on both the text and the level of user engagement. More precisely, the conditional distributions in the TUNE model are defined as follows:

$$\theta_d|\alpha \sim Dirichlet(\alpha)$$
$$\phi_z|\beta \sim Dirichlet(\alpha)$$
$$z_{di}|\theta_d \sim Multinomial(\theta_d)$$
$$w_{di}|z_{di} \sim Multinomial(\phi_{z_{di}})$$
$$\varepsilon_{di}|\psi_{z_{di}} \sim Multinomial(\psi_{z_{di}})$$

An exact inference is intractable in the TUNE model, as in other LDA like models. We therefore employ collapsed Gibbs sampling to perform approximate inference. Using conjugate priors (Dirichlet) for the multinomial distributions allows us to "integrate out" nuance parameters θ and ϕ and not sample them during the inference. For simplicity and speed we estimate the parameters of the Dirichlet distribution $\psi_{z_{di}}$ using fixed point iterations proposed in [26]. Instead of estimating hyper-parameters we employ commonly used heuristics and set $\alpha = 50/T$ and $\beta = 0.1$.

In the Gibbs sampling procedure above, we need to compute the conditional distribution:

$$P(z_{di}|\mathbf{w}, \varepsilon, \mathbf{z}_{\text{-}di}, \alpha, \beta, \Psi) \propto (m_{dz_{di}} + \alpha_{z_{di}} - 1)$$
$$\times \frac{n_{z_{di}w_{di}} + \beta - 1}{\sum_{v=1}^{V} n_{z_{di}} + \beta - 1} \frac{\Gamma(\sum_{j=1}^{4} \psi_{z_{di},j})}{\prod_{j=1}^{4} \Gamma(\psi_{z_{di},j})} \prod_{j=1}^{4} \varepsilon_j^{\psi_{z_{di},j}-1}$$

where n_{zv} is the number of tokens of word v that are assigned to topic z, m_{dz} represents the number of tokens in article d that were assigned to topic z, ε_j refers to the j-th component of the article engagement profile. The last factor in this conditional probability distribution corresponds to the user engagement model captured with the Dirichlet distribution over the engagement levels. We omit the detailed derivations for the rest of the formula and the Gibbs sampling procedure, since they are identical to the TOT model and can be found in the original paper [32].

Using this model and the Gibbs sampling procedure we can predict the future level of user engagement with an article. Given the trained model (estimated collection of probabilities) and a test article, we infer simultaneously the topic assignment for the words in this article together with the level of user engagement by running Gibbs sampling until the topic assignment and ε converge. Note that at the test stage we sample topic assignments and engagement levels for words in the test article, and that the same quantities for words in the training data remain unchanged, allowing the model to condition its prediction on the training data.

Our model goes beyond an ordinary LDA and extends it by incorporating viewport based user engagement information into the model. Such approach allows us to learn a joint mapping between text content and user engagement, which can be used to either predict future level of user engagement or to better understand which topics attract user interest and lead to higher level of engagement. To the best of our knowledge, this is the first attempt to combine these types of data into a joint model. While the model extension presented in this paper is a relatively simple one, it provides a clean way to combined both sources of information. We nonetheless plan to investigate more sophisticated ways to combine textual and viewport data in future work.

7. PREDICTING ENGAGEMENT LEVELS

To investigate whether our approach (TUNE) is able to model user level of user engagement from article text we experiment with the prediction of the engagement levels (*%Bounce*, *%Shallow*, *%Complete* and *%Deep*) for held-out articles. Our experiments are based on the set of articles described in Section 3. Since the engagement rates are numeric, we use the Pearson correlation coefficient to evaluate the quality of the prediction. To ensure that our estimates of the model performance are not over-optimistic, we perform a ten-fold cross validation over our data. Thus, we repeatedly train ten models and use them to obtain the predictions for each of the held-out set among the ten folds. We report the Pearson correlation computed from the ten test folds combined.

We compare our approach to several baseline variants. All models in our experiments perform a linear regression from a set of features to one of the engagement levels, and differ only in the exact features used to train linear regression. We also report the results for predicting dwell time.

The *NumWords* feature encodes the number of words in the article. The features in the *Media* group (9 in total) include dimensions and vertical position of the largest image/video element on the page, as these were shown to have some effect in Section 4.2 in viewport bias and in the work of [34] for predicting dwell time. It also includes the number of media (image or video) elements on the page. Other features such as article genre, text sentimentality are left for future work.

The features in the *LDA* group represent the article topic probabilities computed using the standard LDA model that does not account for the level of engagement, where T denotes the number of topics. Finally, the features in the TUNE group represent the predicted engagement levels (four values). Note that these features are obtained by training/testing ten TUNE models in order to not leak the label data between the cross validation folds. Table 3 reports the performance of the regression models with the various feature sets.

The baseline model using the number of words in the article is able to predict *%Shallow* with 0.494 and *%Deep* with 0.37 correlation, but fails to predict *%Bounce* or *%Complete*. This suggests that the length of an article text has no effect on user decision to either bounce (to hardly read the article) nor to fully engage with the article, such as reading and/or posting comments. The number of words provides some indications on how long users will spend on the article (as shown with *Dwell*, which is not new) but when *they decide* to actually read the article.

Adding the article media features improves the performance for *Dwell* and all engagement levels, except *%Bounce*. This confirms, as already reported in [34], that media elements entice users to spend time on an article (e.g. watching the video in addition to reading the text). However, they have little effect on users deciding to read an article, suggesting that it is not the presence/absence of media elements that makes users bounce.

The features extracted with the original LDA model substantially improve the prediction quality and achieve almost two-fold improvement in *%Bounce* rate. This shows that the topic of the article has a clear effect in enticing the users to start reading the article. It should be noted that users who landed on the article, thus leading to a page view, in principle intended to read the article. However, when landing on the article page, they decided to not read it. There can be many reasons for this, for instance the way the story was

Feature Set	Dwell	%Bounce	%Shallow	%Deep	%Complete
NumWords	0.420	0.063	0.494	0.370	0.017
NumWords + Media	0.465	0.071	0.571	0.410	0.185
NumWords + Media + LDA (T=5)	0.528	0.119	0.597	0.466	0.328
NumWords + Media + LDA (T=10)	0.528	0.110	0.606	0.497	0.379
NumWords + Media + LDA (T=20)	0.543	0.15	0.626	0.531	0.402
NumWords + Media + LDA (T=50)	0.547	0.143	0.629	0.538	0.405
NumWords + Media + TUNE (T=5)	0.476	0.079	0.648	0.544	0.282
NumWords + Media + TUNE (T=10)	0.526	0.311	0.713	0.660	0.400
NumWords + Media + TUNE (T=20)	0.537	0.349	0.724	0.682	0.409
NumWords + Media + TUNE (T=50)	0.545	0.333	**0.742**	**0.697**	0.428
NumWords + Media + LDA + TUNE (T=50)	**0.572**	0.334	0.730	0.696	**0.442**
Dwell	1.000	**0.392**	0.203	0.128	0.351

Table 3: Comparison of regression models with different feature sets. The table reports Pearson correlation coefficient between predicted engagement rates and the actual levels.

presented, i.e. its scope and the topics covered. It is for the editors to understand what causes this behavior.

Not surprisingly, the TUNE features enable even higher performance lift. This clearly suggests that it is possible to predict the level of engagement with respect to the topics of the article (how much of the article will be consumed and also as a consequence the time spent on it). Note that as T increases, the predictions get better, with the exception of *%Bounce* for which TUNE with T=20 performs slightly better than TUNE with T=50, although the difference is not statistically significant (p-value>0.1, two tailed t-test). On *%Bounce*, *%Shallow* and *%Deep* TUNE (T=50) performs significantly better (p-value<0.01, two tailed t-test) than a baseline approach denoted as NumWords + Media + LDA(T=50); the performance of TUNE with T=50 is not significantly different from the baseline (p-values>0.1) for *Dwell* and *Complete* rate predictions.

Finally, the model that combines all the feature groups performs best on Dwell time and *%Complete* rate. It achieves 0.334 for *%Bounce*, 0.73 for *%Shallow*, 0.696 for *%Deep* and 0.442 *%Complete* engagement levels prediction. The TUNE model with T=50 performs reasonably well showing highest correlation with ground truth values for *%Shallow* and *%Deep* engagement levels.

Our results would have been incomplete, if we would not try to use dwell time to predict the engagement classes. Some may argue that our four engagement classes can be distinguished by setting appropriate thresholds for dwell time. However, this is not the case. The last row of Table 3 shows to what extent average dwell time is able to predict specific class of user engagement. We find that dwell time provides a strong signal for identifying *%Bounce*, which is reasonable, given our definition of *Bounce*.[3] However, dwell time does not match the performance of other approaches for the rest of the classes. This is likely due to the inability of dwell time to capture how users attend to the articles they are engaging with, e.g., amount of content read, etc. It is possible that combining dwell time with other content or behavioral features could lead to higher predictive performance. However, doing so would undermine the purpose of our work – *using content only features to predict level of user engagement.*

These results show that combining user engagement *and* article text information into a joint model clearly benefits the quality of future user engagement prediction. Our proposed *joint model* is able to provide accurate predictions about future user engagement levels for a news article, which can be used by news editors to fine tune the article content and optimize the user experience with it more effectively.

[3]Note that Bounce rate and average dwell time are different quantities; hence, accuracy of prediction using average dwell time is far from perfect.

8. CONCLUSIONS AND FUTURE WORK

This paper proposes a novel way to measure user engagement in the context of online news reading. We focus on *viewport* time, which is the time a user spends viewing an article at a given position and which can be instrumented at large scale, to derive measurement of engagement that accounts for how users *attend* to the content they are reading. We analyzed the viewport data of a sample of 267,210 page views on a total of 1,971 news articles from a major online news website from Yahoo.

First, the viewport time analysis, which to our best knowledge is the first large scale analysis of the kind, identified a strong positional bias in news article reading, which by itself is not new. However, although users often remain in the upper part of an article, some users do find the article interesting enough to spend significant amount of time at the lower part of the article, and even to interact with the comments. Thus, some articles entice users to deeply engage with their content.

Second, we carry out an analysis of viewport data, employing a mixture of Markov chains, to identify how users read articles, and accounting for the depth of the article consumption. We identified four main patterns, clearly showing that most users read article from top to bottom, and some users scroll up before leaving the page. We found that the reading depth differs greatly ranging from deep engagement, when the entire article is read, to relatively short reading, when users leave after examining the first screen of the article. These patterns inspired us to propose a taxonomy for user engagement, with four levels, namely *Bounce*, *Shallow* engagement, *Deep* engagement and *Complete* engagement. Our analysis shows that these levels are intuitive, and bring more refined insights about how user engage with articles, than using dwell time alone.

Third, we described a probabilistic approach that allowed us to incorporate these four levels of engagement in the modeling of the topics covered by a news article. We do this by employing LDA, and develop what we call Topics of User Engagement with News (TUNE). We show that the level of user engagement could be successfully incorporated in the topic modeling using the LDA approach. We carried out experiments to investigate how article features such as their length and the presence of media elements affect the prediction of our proposed metrics of engagement levels. We found that TUNE, compared to two baselines (using article length only and using the original LDA) leads to improved performance not only with respect to the proposed metrics of engagement levels, but also dwell time.

We also obtained several interesting insights. The presence of media elements, although enticing users to dwell longer on the page, has little effect on users deciding whether to actually read the article (i.e. the effect on *Bounce* was small). The same was observed with respect to article length. This indicates that what matters most is the actual content of the article *and* the way the story it is covering is presented. Although, in itself, this statement may be obvious, we could demonstrate this effect by incorporating the four engagement levels within the LDA topic modeling approach.

In the future, we want to experiment further with TUNE, and look at more features of articles, including with respect to aspects related to their genre, layout, and the presence of advertisements on the article page. This will bring more extensive insights into user engagement with online content, that are usually only possible through small-scale experimentation using surveys and eye-tracking. Furthermore, in this paper, the engagement patterns and the resulting modeling were with respect to article pages, and not users. It is very likely that users engage in different ways with online content, and whether this has an effect on our proposed four engagement levels should be investigated. Finally, this work was applied in the context of news reading on desktop. The next step would be to deploy the same instrumentation and corresponding measurement methodology in the context of tablet and smartphone.

9. REFERENCES

[1] M. Ageev, D. Lagun, and E. Agichtein. Improving search result summaries by using searcher behavior data. In *Proc. of SIGIR*, pages 13–22. ACM, 2013.

[2] E. Agichtein, E. Brill, and S. Dumais. Improving web search ranking by incorporating user behavior information. In *Proc. of SIGIR*, pages 19–26. ACM, 2006.

[3] I. Arapakis, B. Cambazoglu, and M. Lalmas. Understanding within-content engagement through pattern analysis of mouse gestures. In *Proc. of CIKM*. ACM, 2014.

[4] I. Arapakis, M. Lalmas, B. B. Cambazoglu, M.-C. Marcos, and J. M. Jose. User engagement in online news: Under the scope of sentiment, interest, affect, and gaze. *JAIST*, 2014.

[5] S. Attfield, G. Kazai, M. Lalmas, and B. Piwowarski. Towards a science of user engagement (position paper). In *WSDM Workshop on UMWA, year=2011*.

[6] M. Bilenko and R. W. White. Mining the search trails of surfing crowds: identifying relevant websites from user activity. In *Proc. of WWW*, pages 51–60, 2008.

[7] D. M. Blei, A. Y. Ng, and M. I. Jordan. Latent dirichlet allocation. *JMLR*, 3:993–1022, 2003.

[8] G. Buscher, L. van Elst, and A. Dengel. Segment-level display time as implicit feedback: a comparison to eye tracking. In *Proc. of SIGIR*, pages 67–74, 2009.

[9] M. C. Chen, J. R. Anderson, and M. H. Sohn. What can a mouse cursor tell us more?: correlation of eye/mouse movements on web browsing. In *CHI extended abstracts*, pages 281–282. ACM, 2001.

[10] M. Claypool, P. Le, M. Wased, and D. Brown. Implicit interest indicators. In *Proc. of IUI*. ACM, 2001.

[11] N. Craswell, O. Zoeter, M. Taylor, and B. Ramsey. An experimental comparison of click position-bias models. In *Proc. WSDM*, pages 87–94. ACM, 2008.

[12] A. P. Dempster, N. M. Laird, and D. B. Rubin. Maximum likelihood from incomplete data via the em algorithm. *Journal of the Royal Statistical Society*, pages 1–38, 1977.

[13] E. Erosheva, S. Fienberg, and J. Lafferty. Mixed-membership models of scientific publications. *In Proc. of PNAS*, 101:5220–5227, 2004.

[14] S. Fox, K. Karnawat, M. Mydland, S. Dumais, and T. White. Evaluating implicit measures to improve web search. *TOIS*, 23(2):147–168, 2005.

[15] J. Goecks and J. Shavlik. Learning users' interests by unobtrusively observing their normal behavior. In *Proc. of IUI*, pages 129–132.

[16] Q. Guo and E. Agichtein. Beyond dwell time: estimating document relevance from cursor movements and other post-click searcher behavior. In *Proc. of WWW*, pages 569–578. ACM, 2012.

[17] J. Huang and A. Diriye. Web user interaction mining from touch-enabled mobile devices, 2012.

[18] Y. Kim, A. Hassan, R. W. White, and I. Zitouni. Modeling dwell time to predict click-level satisfaction. In *Proc. of WSDM*, pages 193–202. ACM, 2014.

[19] D. Lagun, M. Ageev, Q. Guo, and E. Agichtein. Discovering common motifs in cursor movement data for improving web search. In *Proc. of WSDM*, pages 183–192. ACM, 2014.

[20] D. Lagun and E. Agichtein. Viewser: enabling large-scale remote user studies of web search examination and interaction. In *Proc. of SIGIR*, 2011.

[21] D. Lagun, C. Hsieh, D. Webster, and V. Navalpakkam. Towards better measurement of attention and satisfaction in mobile search. In *Proc. of SIGIR*. ACM, 2014.

[22] C. Liu, R. W. White, and S. Dumais. Understanding web browsing behaviors through weibull analysis of dwell time. In *Proc. of SIGIR*, pages 379–386, 2010.

[23] L. Lorigo, M. Haridasan, H. Brynjarsdóttir, L. Xia, T. Joachims, G. Gay, L. Granka, F. Pellacini, and B. Pan. Eye tracking and online search: Lessons learned and challenges ahead. *JASIST*, 59(7):1041–1052, 2008.

[24] L. McCay-Peet, M. Lalmas, and V. Navalpakkam. On saliency, affect and focused attention. In *Proc. of CHI*, pages 541–550, 2012.

[25] D. Mimno and A. McCallum. Topic models conditioned on arbitrary features with dirichlet-multinomial regression. *arXiv preprint arXiv:1206.3278*, 2012.

[26] T. Minka. Estimating a dirichlet distribution, 2000.

[27] M. Morita and Y. Shinoda. Information filtering based on user behavior analysis and best match text retrieval. In *Proc. of SIGIR*, pages 272–281, 1994.

[28] V. Navalpakkam, L. Jentzsch, R. Sayres, S. Ravi, A. Ahmed, and A. Smola. Measurement and modeling of eye-mouse behavior in the presence of nonlinear page layouts. In *Proc. of WWW*, pages 953–964, 2013.

[29] H. L. O'Brien and E. G. Toms. The development and evaluation of a survey to measure user engagement. *JASIST*, 61(1):50–69, January 2010.

[30] L. Rabiner and B.-H. Juang. An introduction to hidden markov models. *ASSP Magazine, IEEE*, 3(1):4–16, 1986.

[31] B. Shapira, M. Taieb-Maimon, and A. Moskowitz. Study of the usefulness of known and new implicit indicators and their optimal combination for accurate inference of users interests. In *Proc. SAC*, pages 1118–1119, 2006.

[32] X. Wang and A. McCallum. Topics over time: a non-markov continuous-time model of topical trends. In *Proce. of KDD*, pages 424–433. ACM, 2006.

[33] O. Wu, Y. Chen, B. Li, and W. Hu. Evaluating the visual quality of web pages using a computational aesthetic approach. In *Proc. of WSDM*, pages 337–346, 2011.

[34] X. Yi, L. Hong, E. Zhong, N. N. Liu, and S. Rajan. Beyond clicks: dwell time for personalization. In *Proc. of RecSys*, pages 113–120, 2014.

Publication Date Prediction through Reverse Engineering of the Web

Liudmila Ostroumova Prokhorenkova, Petr Prokhorenkov,
Egor Samosvat, Pavel Serdyukov
Yandex
Leo Tolstoy st. 16, Moscow, Russia
{ostroumova-la, eeight, sameg, pavser} @yandex-team.ru

ABSTRACT

In this paper, we focus on one of the most challenging tasks in temporal information retrieval: detection of a web page *publication date*. The natural approach to this problem is to find the publication date in the HTML body of a page. However, there are two fundamental problems with this approach. First, not all web pages contain the publication dates in their texts. Second, it is hard to distinguish the publication date among all the dates found in the page's text.

The approach we suggest in this paper supplements methods of date extraction from the page's text with novel link-based methods of dating. Some of our link-based methods are based on a probabilistic model of the Web graph structure evolution, which relies on the publication dates of web pages as on its parameters. We use this model to estimate the publication dates of web pages: based only on the link structure currently observed, we perform a "reverse engineering" to reveal the whole process of the Web's evolution.

Categories and Subject Descriptors

H.3.3 [**Information Storage and Retrieval**]: Information Search and Retrieval

Keywords

Publication dates; web pages; link-based method; likelihood optimization

1. INTRODUCTION

In recent years, time dimension has been gaining increasing importance for search engines, leading to a new research area known as temporal information retrieval [3]. In this paper, we focus on one of its most challenging tasks: detection of a document *publication date*. Web page publication dates constitute an extremely valuable piece of knowledge for a variety of search tasks. For example, this information is essential for computing features for recency-sensitive ranking of web documents [4, 5]. Page publication dates can also be used in crawling policies [15]: links found on recently created pages usually lead to recently created pages with up-to-date content, therefore the corresponding pages should be crawled in priority.

Unfortunately, the publication dates of a large share of web pages cannot be easily and reliably determined. The most common way to determine the publication date of a web page is *content-based*, i.e., to find this date in the HTML body of this page. For example, some specific categories of web pages, like news articles, usually contain their publication dates within their content. Yet, even in this case, there are several difficulties: such pages may contain several candidate dates to choose from, these dates can be written in different formats and for different time zones, etc. Needless to say, the content-based approaches cannot detect publication dates for web documents that do not contain any text, e.g., images or videos. In this paper we suggest an algorithm which estimates the dates of web pages regardless of the presence of the exact publication date in their HTML bodies.

In some other cases, a web page's publication date can be considered equal to the date of the first crawl of that page. However, due to resource constraints, not all web-sites are re-crawled frequently enough to make it possible to detect new pages immediately after their publication. In addition, we may consider the scenario when a search engine plans to start operating in a new country. Since that country has not been considered as the search engine's target market until this moment, it is very unlikely that it has been investing a lot of resources into crawling and re-crawling the pages interesting mostly to the users of that country, therefore we cannot count on the first crawl dates to recover the publication dates of most pages. Similar situation arises when a search engine plans to expand its index in the same country (e.g., by deeper crawls).

The algorithm we suggest in this paper combines content-based methods of date extraction with novel *link-based methods*. We mostly focus on the publication date detection for pages which are not likely to contain the correct publication date in their HTML bodies. For such pages, we use the link structure in order to estimate their publication dates. We propose a group of multi-step *date propagation* methods, which iteratively estimate the dates of pages using the already known dates of their neighbors. Our approach generalizes and extends several one-step link-based methods proposed in the literature [14, 16]. We also propose a theoretically grounded approach which is based on a realistic model of the Web [10]. It was shown in [11] that the popularity of almost all new pages decays exponentially with time. Based on this observation, a realistic model of link

WSDM'16, February 22–25, 2016, San Francisco, CA, USA.
© 2015 ACM. ISBN 978-1-4503-3716-8/16/02 ...$15.00.
DOI: http://dx.doi.org/10.1145/2835776.2835796.

evolution was proposed in [10]. In this model, the publication dates of web pages are used to predict the evolution of the Web link structure. Here we do the reverse operation, i.e., we use this model to estimate the publication dates of web pages. Given only the currently observed link structure, we apply "reverse engineering" to reveal the whole process of the Web's evolution. Namely, we find such publication dates which maximize the probability that the Web graph observed in reality is produced by this model. To the best of our knowledge, we are the first to propose a model-based probabilistic method for document dating. To sum up, the contributions of this paper are the following:

- We suggest an algorithm for publication date detection which combines content-based methods of date extraction with link-based methods.
- As link-based methods, we propose a general approach to date propagation as well as a more sophisticated algorithm based on a realistic model of the Web.
- We suggest a method which allows us to reduce the computational complexity of our algorithms. As a result, the proposed algorithms run in linear time.
- We also propose a novel data-driven parameter selection method which adapts the algorithms to each host individually. The motivation behind this is that different parts of the Web may evolve by different rules, therefore, we should adapt our methods and parameters to these rules.

We perform the experiments on two different datasets: one dataset consists of about 4M web pages located on 70 different hosts, another one is MemeTracker dataset [1].

The rest of the paper is organized as follows. In the next section, we discuss different existing approaches to web documents' dating. In Section 3, we present our approaches and the model on which some of them are based. Section 4 describes the data used to analyze the performance of our algorithm. The experimental results are presented in Section 5. Finally, we conclude the paper and outline directions for future research.

2. RELATED WORK

The problem of publication date detection was analyzed in a variety of studies. In this section, we briefly describe the state-of-the-art approaches.

Extraction of publication date. The most widely used approaches to dating web documents are based on the recognition of temporal expressions in their texts [2, 7]. However, the problem of choosing the correct publication date from among the recognized candidates, which is central to document dating, is not discussed in these papers. A more complete solution to content-based dating is suggested in [13]. Here all three necessary steps are made: date extraction, normalization of candidate dates, choosing the correct publication date. However, this method can be applied only to pages which contain the publication dates in their texts or URLs.

Link-based methods. Link structure of a graph can also be used in order to estimate publication dates. For example, in [14] a link-based method was used to solve a different but related problem: they estimate the last update time, i.e., the moment when the content of a page was updated, while we are interested in the moment when the page was initially created. The following assumption is used in [14]: connected web resources tend to have similar update patterns. In order to estimate a document's Last-Modified value, the authors consider several types of neighbors, like documents containing links to the given document or documents pointed to by the given document. They observed a positive correlation between a document's Last-Modified value and the Last-Modified average over its neighbors. The strongest correlation occurs with a document's out-links. We use these methods as our baselines in this paper.

Both the publication date and the last modified date are useful for a search engine. For some pages, like the main pages of news sites, the last modified date shows whether the news articles referred by them are up-to-date. On the other hand, for the majority of web pages, their publication date is the date when their main content was created, while the Last-Modified value often corresponds to some minor layout changes. For example, the main content of news pages usually stays stable, while surrounding ads and dynamic links are constantly changing. Therefore, publication dates are often used as features in web search ranking [4].

In [16] backlinks are used to estimate the publication date of URI. Authors take the earliest timestamp out of the following: the first time someone shortened the URI, the first time someone tweeted the URI, the first time it appeared in a public web archive, etc. The method based on the same principle (taking the earliest of the publication dates of the pages linking the given one) we also use as our baseline.

In this paper, we generalize the notion of aggregation and consider different functions for aggregating the information over the neighbors of a page. We also generalize the notion of propagation: in [14] and [16], only one-step propagation is considered (i.e., only the nearest neighbors are used to predict the date of a page), while we assume that the propagation can be done in multiple steps.

Language models. Language models are also often applied to dating web documents [6, 8, 9]. Such models are useful when there is no explicit publication date in the body of a document. However, the problem is that the date detection granularity is too coarse for such approaches: their error rates are often measured in years, decades or even centuries.

In this paper, we suggest a new link-based method which, as any link-based method, has to be combined with a text-based date extraction approach: the reliable candidate publication dates extracted from documents' texts are used to detect the publication dates of documents that have no reliable (or any) candidate dates found in their content.

3. ALGORITHM

3.1 General scheme

In this section, we describe our algorithm for publication date detection. Obviously, at the beginning of the dating process no dates are known. In this situation, only a text (or metadata) based date extraction method can help to date some documents. Further, we can use link-based methods in order to approximate the publication dates of the rest of the documents, for which the content-based method could not determine their publication dates with sufficient certainty. It is important to note that the first stage of the dating process is unavoidable, since any link-based dating method requires some reliable publication dates ("anchor" dates) to be fixed for a fraction of documents, as it needs to be guided toward some specific time period the correct publication dates of the other documents most probably belong to. The general description of our algorithm is the following.

Stage 1: content-based extraction of anchor and seed dates. As we discussed, the first stage of our algorithm is to extract candidate dates from the URL and the HTML body of each page and choose the most probable publication date from among the candidates. Our content-based method of dates extraction is described in Section 3.2. For some pages it is possible to detect highly reliable *anchor dates*, which will be fixed for the rest of the algorithm. For some other pages, candidates dates can also be extracted, but they are less reliable and their estimates can be improved at Stage 3, such dates are called *seed dates*. For the rest of the pages, content-based date extraction is simply impossible.

Stage 2: anchor and seed dates propagation. Obviously, some pages may not have any dates in their texts. Therefore, at the second stage of our algorithm, we choose some approximations of dates for all such pages, i.e., for the pages without the seed or anchor dates. These estimates can be improved at Stage 3. We use and compare several *date propagation* methods. The description of these methods is given in Section 3.3. In our experiments, if some pages have no dates even after the date propagation, then we set some *constant* value for them.

Stage 3: likelihood optimization. Seed dates, propagated dates, and constant dates together form *initial dates* which can be improved at this stage by our *likelihood optimization* method. Our method is based on the model of the Web evolution, which is described in Section 3.4. We find the dates which maximize the probability that the observed graph is produced by this model. This stage is described in Section 3.5.

Let us sum up the notation. *Anchor dates* are trusted dates which are extracted from URLs or HTML bodies of pages and they cannot be changed during the link-based dating process. *Seed dates* are not such reliable dates extracted from the texts. *Propagated dates* are dates obtained as a result of the date propagation procedure. *Constant dates* are set for all other pages.

3.2 Anchor and seed dates extraction

Our research focuses on link-based dating methods, and such methods always work on the top of content-based approaches, though are not specific to any of them. In this paper, we use a state-of-the-art content-based method to extract dates. This method relies on several rules (regular expressions) in order to extract dates. The rules are similar to the ones described in [13], but they are adapted to Russian language. Several problems analyzed in [13] do not occur in our case: almost all pages are in one language, belong to one time zone, and most dates have only one interpretation (e.g., 03/04/05 usually means 3 April, 2005). In contrast to [13], we can extract dates not only from the URL, title, or snippet, but also from the HTML body of a page.

First, using our rules, we extract dates from the URL and the HTML body of a page. Then, as in [13], we remove apparently corrupted dates such as dates referring to a very old time or some time in the future. Then, in order to choose the best date, we look at where each candidate date was found: in the document's URL, title, main content, etc. We have a larger number of page components than [13], since we consider the entire page contents, not their summaries. We utilize the segmentator currently used by Yandex, the most popular search engine in Russia, which allows us to split document into zones/locations, such as title and main content of a document. We consider the following locations:

1. URL
2. Title
3. Just before main content
4. Just after main content
5. Main content of a document
6. All other locations

In Section 5, we analyze the reliability of dates found in different parts of a document. Based on these experimental results, we use the following method of choosing the anchor date. If there is a date found in the URL of a document, then we take this date. Otherwise, we take the date from the title. If there is no such date, then we take the date from before the main content of a document. If all three locations contain no candidate dates, then this page has no anchor date. The dates found at the other locations are less reliable, but they can be used as seed dates. In Section 5, we show that dates found after the main content are more reliable than the dates found in the main content, while the dates found in the main content are more reliable than the dates found in other locations (category 6 above).

3.3 Date propagation

Several date propagation methods were proposed in [14] and [16]. The idea of these approaches is to take the dates of a web page's immediate neighbors and use some function of them in order to estimate the date of the page. In [14], the authors propose estimating the last update time as the average of the last update times over either the documents containing links to the given document or the documents outlinked by the given document. In [16], the earliest date of the web pages containing links to a given page is used as the estimate for its publication date. We generalize and extend these approaches in two ways:

- We propose and compare various aggregation functions;
- We compare two propagation schemes: one-step propagation, as used in [14, 16], and multi-step propagation that we propose in this paper.

Let us first define several aggregation functions we consider in this paper. The three of them were already discussed: *in-avg* propagation takes the average over the dates of the documents containing links to the selected document, *out-avg* propagation takes the average over the dates of the documents pointed to by the selected document, *in-min* takes the minimum of the dates of the documents containing links to the selected document. We also propose *all-avg* propagation, which takes the average over all neighbors' dates, *out-max*, which takes the maximum over the out-neighbors dates, and *out-max-in-min*, which is the middle between *in-min* and *out-max*. The latter method is motivated by the assumption that a page p is usually created later than the pages pointed by p and earlier than the pages which contain links to p. Finally, one more aggregation method called *model-q* (q is a parameter, $0 \leq q \leq 1$) is discussed in Section 3.6.

We consider the seed and anchor date propagation not necessarily as a one-step, but also as a multi-step process. At each step, we consider all pages which have at least one already dated neighbor, i.e., a neighbor with an anchor date, a seed date, or a date assigned at the previous steps of the propagation process. For these pages we approximate their publication dates by taking a function of the dates of their neighbors (we consider both incoming and outgoing links). Note that, at the first propagation step, as in [14, 16], we take a function of anchor and seed dates (obtained at Stage 1), while, at the next steps, we take a function of only the dates that had been obtained by the propagation at the previous steps. We continue this procedure until we cannot date more pages. Note that after applying any method or combination of methods from Sections 3.2 and 3.3 we may have pages that are not dated. In this case we set their dates to a predefined constant value (see Section 5.1).

3.4 Model description

In addition to the previously described propagation methods, we also propose a more sophisticated link-based approach which is motivated by the realistic probabilistic model of the Web [10]. The general approach from [10] models the behavior (in terms of links creation) of pages that may belong to different hosts. In this paper we mostly work with intra-site links, therefore here we describe the model with only one host[1]. If one needs to apply the method for many hosts and inter-links, it is just necessary to regard all hosts as one host in this case (and we do this for one of our datasets). Our model differs from the model [10] in several respects and further in this section we describe these differences and the reasons for them.

The model under consideration has several parameters. For each page p, we have the number of outgoing links m_p, its intrinsic quality q_p, and the publication time t_p. Besides these page-specific parameters, we also have the rate of attractiveness decay λ, an auxiliary constant c ($c > \lambda$), and the number of pages n. Note that the parameters n and m_p are completely defined by the link structure of the host. On the contrary, the parameters t_p (for pages without anchor dates), q_p, λ, and c are hidden, and will therefore be tuned during the optimization procedure (see Section 3.5).

The model can be described as follows. At the beginning we have n pages and no links between them. Each page p has its publication time t_p. Then, for each page p we generate m_p outgoing links. All links are modeled as mutually independent random variables that determine their target pages. The probability of a page r to be chosen as a target page for a link from a page p is proportional to the relative attractiveness of r according to p, which is a function of q_r (intrinsic quality of r) and the age difference $a_{p,r}$ for the pages p and r, that is, $t_p - t_r$. Note that in the model the difference $a_{p,r}$ can be negative, i.e., there is a possibility of an edge between p and r with $t_p < t_r$. In a real web graph such a link can be added at a moment $t > t_r$ if p was updated at t. The attractiveness function is defined as follows:

$$\mathrm{attr}(q_r, a_{p,r}) = \begin{cases} q_r \cdot e^{-\lambda a_{p,r}} \cdot \left(1 - \frac{e^{-c a_{p,r}}}{2}\right) & \text{if } a_{p,r} \geq 0\,, \\ q_r \cdot e^{-\lambda a_{p,r}} \cdot \frac{e^{c a_{p,r}}}{2} & \text{if } a_{p,r} < 0\,. \end{cases} \tag{1}$$

Let us discuss the case of $a_{p,r} \geq 0$. First of all, the attractiveness of r is proportional to its quality. Second, the attractiveness decreases with the age of r, i.e., older pages are less popular. These two multipliers are proposed and motivated in [10]. The third multiplier is explained further in this section. In the case of $a_{p,r} < 0$, as we also discuss further, the probability of a link is small and decreases exponentially with $a_{p,r}$.

We use this model in order to estimate the publication dates of web documents. Namely, we are given an oriented graph (nodes are the web documents and edges are the links between them) and we assume that this graph is constructed according to the procedure described above. We are given the observed values of some parameters (the numbers of outgoing links m_p and some anchor publication dates t_p) and want to find the rest of the unknown values to maximize the probability that the observed graph is constructed under the described model. The parameters with unknown values are: the rate of attractiveness decay λ, the constant c, the qualities of all pages q_p, the publication times for non-anchor pages t_p. The detailed description of our method of likelihood maximization is given in Section 3.5.

As we discussed earlier, the model we use in this paper slightly differs from the model described in [10]. The differences are the following.

- The number of outgoing links for each page is not a random variable, but a fixed number. We assume this since we know the number of outgoing links for each page from the real data.
- Pages appear at specific times t_p, which are not set randomly according to a Poisson process. In other words, in our case, t_p are the model parameters, this allows us to use a maximum-likelihood estimation method and estimate t_p from the real data. For the same reason, q_p are not random variables but parameters, also to be estimated from the real data.
- We change the attractiveness function a little. In [10] the attractiveness function is defined as $\mathrm{attr}(q_r, a_{p,r}) = q_r \cdot e^{-\lambda a_{p,r}} \cdot I(a_{p,r} > 0)$. As a result, edges going from older pages to newer ones are prohibited in [10]. We replace the indicator $I(x > 0)$ (the Heaviside step function) by the following sigmoid function:

$$f(x) = \begin{cases} 1 - \frac{e^{-cx}}{2} & \text{for } x \geq 0\,, \\ \frac{e^{cx}}{2} & \text{for } x < 0\,. \end{cases} \tag{2}$$

  Sigmoid functions are often used to smooth the step function. The larger the value c in (2), the closer the sigmoid function to the step function.

The latter modification helps us solve the following two problems.

1. In the original model [10], the probabilities of edges are not differentiable. On the other hand, our method of finding the optimum parameters requires continuously differentiable probabilities and here the sigmoid function helps.
2. Although, it was shown in [10] that in real data almost all links go from newer pages to older ones, there are always some edges which go conversely (e.g., a page can be updated and a link to some newer page can be added). In this case, according to the original model [10], the probabilities of some edges are equal to 0 and, regardless of the tuning of all the parameters, the probability of getting the observed graph is equal to 0. Therefore, we would not be able to find the optimum parameters in this case. We avoid this problem by using a sigmoid function, so that in our case this probability is always greater than 0.

Note that the above-mentioned problems can be solved by using any sigmoid function, for example, the well-known

[1]Although inter-site links can be successfully used in some applications, for example when a website mainly links to other websites rather than to its own pages, in our dateset (see Section 4.1) there are less than 1% of links which are inter-site (including those pointing outside the dataset).

logistic function. We choose the sigmoid function $f(x)$ defined in Equation (2) since it allows us to find the optimal parameters with an algorithm of lower complexity (see Appendix for details). We require $c > \lambda$ since we want to have $\text{attr}(r) \to 0$ as $a_{p,r} \to -\infty$, i.e., we want the probabilities of edges which go from older pages to newer ones to be exponentially small. We do this since usually in real networks almost all links go from newer pages to older ones [10].

3.5 Likelihood optimization

Now we present our optimization algorithm which is based on the model described above. For each host, the algorithm consists of the following steps.

1. Fix c and λ.
2. Find initial approximations of t_i, and q_i for all pages.
3. Take several optimization steps for improving the initial estimates of t_i and q_i. While the estimates of q_i are improved for all pages, we do not change t_i for the pages with the anchor dates.
4. Select the appropriate stopping time.

Initial approximations. First, we fix c and λ. We choose the optimal values for each host according to the *data-driven parameter selection method* (see Section 3.7).

Then, we find the initial approximations of t_i, and q_i (for all pages i). Several methods of choosing the initial approximations of publication dates are described in Sections 3.3 and 3.6, namely, anchor dates, seed dates, propagated dates, and constant dates. Recall that anchor dates are reliable and we do not change them, while other dates can be corrected.

It was shown in [10] that a good model for the real data can be obtained if (1) the attractiveness of a page is proportional to its quality and decreases exponentially with its age, (2) the quality of a page is proportional to the number of its incoming links. Based on this observation, initially, we consider the quality q_i of a page i to be equal to the number of incoming links to this page.

Optimization steps. This is the most important part of the likelihood optimization algorithm. Recall that our primary goal is to improve the initial publication dates for the web pages without anchor dates. Since we assume that the model described in Section 3.4 is realistic, we want to find the values of the parameters which maximize the probability that a random graph G_{model} constructed according to the model coincides with the link graph G_{real} observed in the reality. We want to maximize the likelihood, that is (disregarding the constant multiplier $\prod_p m_p!$)

$$L(\bar{t},\bar{q}) = \prod_{ij \in G_{real}} \mathrm{P}(ij \in G_{model}). \tag{3}$$

By i and j we denote nodes of a graph and the notation $ij \in G$ means that the oriented edge from i to j belongs to the graph G. Further in the paper we assume that the nodes are ordered according to their publication times, i.e., $i \leq j$ if and only if $t_i \leq t_j$. Edges are generated independently, therefore we can just consider their product in Equation (3). According to the model, the likelihood function $L(\bar{t},\bar{q})$ is the following:

$$L(\bar{t},\bar{q}) = \prod_{ij \in G_{real}, i \geq j} \frac{q_j e^{-\lambda(t_i - t_j)}\left(1 - \frac{e^{-c(t_i-t_j)}}{2}\right)}{W(t_i)} \cdot \prod_{ij \in G_{real}, i<j} \frac{q_j e^{-\lambda(t_i-t_j)} \frac{e^{c(t_i-t_j)}}{2}}{W(t_i)},$$

where $W(t_i)$ is the total weight of all pages at time t_i:

$$W(t_i) = \sum_{j \leq i} q_j e^{-\lambda(t_i-t_j)}\left(1 - \frac{e^{-c(t_i-t_j)}}{2}\right) + \sum_{j>i} q_j e^{-\lambda(t_i-t_j)} \frac{e^{c(t_i-t_j)}}{2}. \tag{4}$$

The weight $W(t_i)$ appears in the denominator since we have to normalize attractiveness in order to obtain a probability.

The idea of the optimization algorithm is the following. For each page p (without an anchor date) we want to improve our guess about its publication time t_p. It means that we want to find t_p and q_p that maximize $L(t_p, q_p)$ in the two-dimensional space. Our method of finding all such optimal points simultaneously is based on the gradient descent method[2]. This method requires the computation of all partial derivatives of the function $\log L(\bar{t},\bar{q})$ with respect to t_i and q_i. These derivatives we compute in Appendix. For each page p we make one step in the quality dimension (in the right direction according to the corresponding derivative, see Equation (6)). And for all pages without the anchor dates we make one step in the time dimension (see Equation (5)). At each step we change quality and time by ± 1 (i.e., one day for the time dimension and one unit for the quality dimension). In Appendix, we describe an efficient algorithm for computing *all* the derivatives *in linear time*. Finally, the complexity of the likelihood optimization algorithm is $O(N\,e)$, where e is the number of edges and N is the number of optimization steps. Note that the complexity of one step of any date propagation method is $O(e)$.

Stopping criteria. From the beginning, we suspected that our optimization algorithm works better for some hosts, while for others it can be less useful. We apply a data-driven parameter selection algorithm (see Section 3.7) in order to find the optimal number of steps of the optimization procedure for each host and, in particular, to decide whether we should use this optimization for this host or not.

3.6 Simplification of likelihood optimization

In this section, we answer the following question: is there any similarity between the date propagation strategies and the likelihood optimization? In particular, we show that the likelihood optimization algorithm (implicitly and approximately) uses an aggregation function. At the end of this section, we propose new aggregation functions which are based on the probabilistic model described above.

It was shown in [10] that $W(t_i)$ is asymptotically a constant. So, we can replace $W(t_i)$ in the likelihood function $L(\bar{t},\bar{q})$ by a constant W. Because of this approximation, the qualities of individual pages become just multipliers in the likelihood function $L(\bar{t},\bar{q})$, so we further assume $q_i = 1$ for all i. These assumptions substantially simplify all the above reasonings (see Section 3.5). Let us now try to find the optimal date for a page p given the dates of all its neighbors. The function we want to maximize depends only on the probabilities of incoming and outgoing links for p:

$$\prod_{pi \in G_{real}} \mathrm{P}(pi \in G_{model}) \cdot \prod_{jp \in G_{real}} \mathrm{P}(jp \in G_{model})$$

$$= \prod_{pi \in G_{real}} \frac{e^{-\lambda(t_p - t_i)} f(t_p - t_i)}{W} \cdot \prod_{jp \in G_{real}} \frac{e^{-\lambda(t_j - t_p)} f(t_j - t_p)}{W}.$$

[2] *http://en.wikipedia.org/wiki/Gradient_descent*

Now, if we take a logarithm of this function and approximate $f(x)$ by

$$\tilde{f}(x) = \begin{cases} 1 & \text{for } x \geq 0\,, \\ \frac{e^{cx}}{2} & \text{for } x < 0\,, \end{cases}$$

then the function we have to maximize is

$$F(t_p) = -\lambda \sum_{pi \in G_{real}} (t_p - t_i) - \lambda \sum_{jp \in G_{real}} (t_j - t_p)$$

$$+c \sum_{pi \in G_{real}, t_p < t_i} (t_p - t_i) + c \sum_{jp \in G_{real}, t_j < t_p} (t_j - t_p)\,.$$

Let us find the solution to this maximization problem. Let $deg_{in}(p)$ be the number of incoming links to p, $deg_{out}(p)$ be the number of outgoing links from p, and $deg(p) = deg_{in}(p) + deg_{out}(p)$ be the total number of links. Consider all neighbors of p (both incoming and outgoing) and sort their publication times: $T_1 \leq \ldots \leq T_{deg(p)}$. Clearly, $F(t_p)$ is continuous on $(-\infty; +\infty)$ and differentiable on $(-\infty; +\infty)$ except at the points T_i, $1 \leq i \leq deg(p)$. The derivative $F'(t_p)$ is equal to

$$F'(t_p) = \lambda(\deg_{in}(p) - deg_{out}(p))$$

$$+c\left(|\{pi \in G_{real}, t_p < t_i\}| - |\{jp \in G_{real}, t_j < t_p\}|\right)\,.$$

Therefore, $\text{argmax}(F(t_p)) = T_k$, where

$$k = \lceil deg_{out}(p) - \frac{\lambda}{c}(deg_{out}(p) - deg_{in}(p)) \rceil\,.$$

However, if the value $deg_{out}(p) - \frac{\lambda}{c}(deg_{out}(p) - deg_{in}(p))$ is integer, then $F'(t_p) = 0$ on the interval $[T_k; T_{k+1}]$, and $\text{argmax}(F(t_p))$ is the whole interval $[T_k; T_{k+1}]$, so, in this case, we choose $t_p = \frac{T_k + T_{k+1}}{2}$.

Interestingly, the solution to this simplified problem depends only on the ratio λ/c, not on both of them. We denote this ratio by q, $0 \leq q \leq 1$. Note that if $c = 2\lambda$ ($q = 0.5$), then the optimal t_p is the median of its neighbors' dates.

The obtained result gives us a group of date propagation methods which we call *model-q* propagation, $0 \leq q \leq 1$. We use the obtained aggregation function with the multi-step propagation principle. The optimal q can be chosen by the data-driven parameter selection method, described in the next section.

3.7 Data-driven parameter selection

Our motivation for this approach is that different hosts obviously have different properties, therefore different methods/parameters can be optimal for them. We propose a data-driven parameter selection method in order to answer three questions:

- How many steps of the likelihood optimization should be applied?
- Which λ and c are optimal?
- Which date propagation method is the best for a host?

In order to find the best parameters we do the following. We take all host's pages with anchor dates and divide them into 5 equal disjoint subsets (buckets). Then, for each bucket B, we "forget" all anchor dates for the pages from this bucket. After this, we apply the set of algorithms we want to compare and measure the mean absolute error on pages in B (we compare the estimated dates with the actual anchor dates). Then we average the errors over all 5 buckets and choose the best combination of parameters, i.e., the one which gives the minimum average error.

4. DATA

In order to measure the performance of our algorithms we use two different datasets. The first dataset is a large sample of the web pages crawled by Yandex over a period of 17 months. Another dataset is the publicly available MemeTracker dataset [1].

4.1 Crawled dataset

Data sources. In this section, we describe the data sources we use in order to obtain the first dataset.

The first data source is the collection of documents crawled by Yandex. For each crawled page p we know the date when it was crawled t_p^{crawl}, the page's text, and its outgoing links. The second data source is the logs of Yandex.Metrica (*https://metrica.yandex.com/*) — a special tool for a site owner which allows to analyze user activity on the site (this tool is distributed by Yandex and is similar to, e.g., Google Analytics). In these logs, all anonymized user visits to the web pages of sites with the tool installed are recorded.

For our experiments we need both data sources. Further on we explain how we use them in order to get the ground truth dates.

Dataset. First, we sampled 10 random hosts H_i from one week (in December 2012) logs of Yandex.Metrica. We consider the set of all pages P_i on the host H_i which were crawled by the search engine during the period from January 2013 to May 2014. This dataset (D_1) is used for our preliminary experiments (see Section 5.1).

We also collected the additional data for 60 random hosts sampled in the same way. We use this dataset (D_2) for the final validation of our algorithms on the crawled data.

Overall, our crawled dataset consists of 4M pages from 70 hosts, the smallest host is of size 5K pages, the largest one is of size 1.2M pages. For each page p in the dataset we collected the following data: URL, document's text, the time of the first crawl t_p^{crawl}, outgoing links, and the first user visit recorded in the logs of Yandex.Metrica t_p^{visit}.

Ground truth dates. In order to compare our algorithm with the baseline strategies, we need to obtain the true publication dates for a set of web pages. It is a typical problem for link-based methods and methods based on language models. If some pages have real publication dates in their URL or HTML body, then some sample can be manually annotated. If there is no publication date anywhere on a web page, then it is impossible to even manually annotate a date. However, in this paper we mostly focus on the web pages without explicit dates in their body. Therefore, we have to somehow determine the actual publication dates for many such web pages somehow.

In order to determine dates we use two sources of information: the date t_p^{crawl} when a page p was first crawled by the search engine and the date t_p^{visit} when p was first visited by a user. The dates t_p^{crawl} and t_p^{visit} may coincide with the date of creation or they may be later. Finally, we use the following approximation of the ground truth: if for a page p we have $|t_p^{crawl} - t_p^{visit}| \leq 24$ hours, then this page is created at $t_p^{credible} = min\{t_p^{crawl}, t_p^{visit}\}$. We choose a 24 hours threshold since we measure error in days in this paper. Only 93K pages (~3%) in our dataset D_1 have $t_p^{credible}$ time.

Admittedly, $t_p^{credible}$ is not 100% correct publication date, but we argue that this is the best approximation that a search engine can get for such pages. In order to verify the quality of the obtained dataset we take a random sample of

1K pages (100 per host for dataset D_1) which have $t_p^{credible}$ times and manually annotate dates for them. There are three possible situations for each such page:

- If the publication date can be found in the text of a document and it coincides with $t_p^{credible}$ date, then we say that $t_p^{credible}$ is correct.
- If the publication date can be found in the text of a document and it differs from $t_p^{credible}$ date, then we say that $t_p^{credible}$ is incorrect.
- If the publication date cannot be found in the text of a document, then we cannot say anything about the correctness of $t_p^{credible}$.

We get the following result. Out of 1K manually annotated dates only 19 have incorrect seed dates. On the other hand, 398 pages have no publication dates in their texts or URLs. These pages are not uniformly distributed over the hosts, namely, there are 3 hosts where almost all pages have unknown dates. This means that any method which extracts dates from the text is useless for such hosts. Remaining 583 pages have publication dates in their texts or URLs and these dates coincide with $t_p^{credible}$ date. Based on the above observations, further we validate all the algorithms on pages with $t_p^{credible}$ date.

4.2 Memetracker dataset

We also use MemeTracker public dataset [1], which covers about 96M blog posts and news articles published during 9 months from August, 2008 to April, 2009, and 418M links between them. See [12] for the details on how this data was collected. Our primary reason for using this additional dataset is to put aside the problem of date extraction from the page's text and to focus on the main problem — link-based date estimation. The pages in this dataset have publication timestamps. For our experiments we kept only links pointing to the documents also in the dataset, i.e., links with known timestamps both for the source and the destination. We finally obtained a dataset of about 29M links and 12M documents that we use in the following experiments. Since we know the time when each document was posted on the Web, in this dateset we have the ground truth dates for all the pages. For this dataset we do not analyze date extraction algorithms and focus only on link-based methods.

Our dataset consists of the pages belonging to about 250K different hosts. This means that a lot of hosts are represented by a very small number of pages: e.g., about 65K hosts are represented by only one page. Therefore, analyzing the hosts individually will not be effective. Further, we treat MemeTracker dataset as one host.

5. EXPERIMENTS

In this section, we compare several algorithms of publication dates estimation. All algorithms assign publication dates to all the pages in a dataset and then we compare their precision. As the measures of precision we use the mean absolute error, the median of the absolute errors, which is more resistant to outliers, and the *mean weighted absolute error*: $\sum_p \frac{deg_{in}(p)\cdot \text{AbsErr}(p)}{\sum_i deg_{in}(i)}$, i.e., for each page p the error AbsErr(p) is weighted by the normalized number of incoming links $deg_{in}(p)$. The latter measure reflects how precisely we can estimate dates for more important pages. All metrics are measured in days.

We compare the following algorithms. First, we consider the 1-step propagation algorithms: *1-step in-avg*, *1-step out-avg*, *1-step all-avg*, *1-step in-min*, *1-step out-max*, *1-step out-max-in-min* (see Section 3.3). Note that our baselines are *1-step in-avg*, *1-step out-avg* from [14], and *1-step in-min* from [16]. Second, we consider the multi-step propagation algorithms: *in-avg*, *out-avg*, *all-avg*, *in-min*, *out-max*, *out-max-in-min*, *model-q* (the last one is defined in Section 3.6). Finally, we consider the likelihood optimization algorithm (see Section 3.5).

Location	mean / median / weighted err.	coverage (by non-constant)
Constant date	124 / 113 / 159	0%
+ URL	95.5 / 94.2 / 145	19.6%
+ before main content	87.3 / 92.1 / 103	20.1%
+ title	80.0 / 76.3 / 95.7	20.6%
+ after main content	79.1 / 75.4 / 95.2	20.8%
+ main content	78.8 / 74.0 / 87.7	21.3%
+ other	59.1 / 35.2 / 72.7	47.2%

Table 1: Errors for different seed dates on D_1

5.1 Experiments on crawled dataset D_1

In this section, we analyze the reliability of dates extracted from different parts of a document (see Section 3.2). Based on the results of these experiments, we choose seed dates for our optimization algorithm. All the experiments here are performed on dataset D_1.

We consider all pages in dataset D_1 and the dates extracted from their URLs and HTML bodies. First, we measure the precision of each location separately in order to find the most reliable locations. We noticed that the most reliable location is *URL* (the mean absolute error is 1.0 day) followed by *before main content* location (4.3 days) and *title* (4.8 days). If a date was found in one of these three locations on the page, then we say that this page has an anchor date (see Section 3.1). The other locations are less reliable: *after main content* (34 days), *main content* (74 days), *other* (88 days). If a date was found in one of these three locations, then we say that this date is the seed date. Finally, about a half of the pages in dataset D_1 have dates in their texts (i.e., they have a seed or an anchor date assigned) and 20% of the pages have an anchor date.

Now we want to compare several strategies which assign dates to *all* web pages based only on their URLs and HTML bodies. The first very basic strategy assigns constant dates to all web pages. As expected, the best constant date is the middle of the considered time interval, i.e., the middle of September, 2013. If we assigned this date to all the pages in our dataset, then the mean absolute error would be equal to 124 days (see Table 1)[3]. Then, we order the locations according to their mean errors and analyze different combinations of locations. First, we add the dates found in URLs, i.e., if a document has a date in its URL, then we assign this date, otherwise we assign the constant date. We further add more and more locations and measure the mean, the median and the mean weighted absolute errors (see Table 1). The last column in this table shows the fraction of non-constant dates for a given combination of locations. However recall that we average errors over *all* web pages.

[3]In practice, we may not have any "considered time interval", especially if a search engine comes to a new market. In these cases, a practitioner may choose to assign no date instead of a constant date or assign the date to be the date of the first crawl. We use the constant dates in order to fairly compare the precision of all algorithms given the full coverage.

	Method	mean/median/ weighted err	coverage
baselines	seed and anchor dates	57.1/30.2/70.0	47.7%
	1-step in-avg	55.9/29.8/56.9	49.3%
	1-step out-avg	56.3/27.6/68.2	64.1%
	1-step in-min	58.0/29.8/66.0	49.3%
proposed methods	1-step all-avg	55.5/27.7/57.0	64.4%
	1-step out-max	56.9/28.1/67.5	64.1%
	1-step out-max-in-min	56.7/30.3/70.0	49.0%
	in-avg	55.5/29.7/56.5	49.7%
	out-avg	58.0/25.0/70.1	68.6%
	all-avg	52.4/22.3/55.6	69.7%
	in-min	57.8/29.7/65.8	49.7%
	out-max	57.1/22.3/72.7	68.6%
	out-max-in-min	56.6/30.0/70.2	49.4%
	model-0.5	51.9/19.7/53.9	69.7%
	model-0.6	**51.2**/19.7/**53.6**	69.7%
	model-0.7	51.4/**19.5**/53.7	69.7%
	likelihood optimization	**49.9/19.1/51.2**	69.7%

Table 2: Comparison of the algorithms on D_2

5.2 Experiments on crawled dataset D_2

In this section, we analyze the performance of our methods and compare them with the baseline approaches on dataset D_2.

Date propagation. We analyze and compare different date propagation methods. First, we extract seed and anchor dates as described in the previous section. Then, we compare several date propagation functions (see Sections 3.3 and 3.6). The results of this comparison are presented in Table 2. We compared several values of q in model-q propagation ($q = 0.0, 0.1 \ldots, 1.0$) on dataset D_1 also. The best results were obtained with $q = 0.6$. In Table 2 we present the results for $q \in \{0.5, 0.6, 0.7\}$ on dataset D_2. Note that the optimal value for each host can be tuned by our data-driven parameter selection method. In Table 2, we are mostly interested in the second column, which shows the mean/median/weighted errors measured on all pages. Model-q propagation shows the best results according to all metrics. Note that we set constant dates to the pages which are not dated, so the third column demonstrates the coverage of the dating method (i.e., the fraction of non-constant dates after the dating procedure) and the second column shows the average errors over all pages, including those which were assigned with the constant date. Usually, the multi-step propagation has a smaller error than one-step propagation because of the higher coverage.

We also applied our data-driven parameter selection approach in order to choose the best propagation strategy for each host. This allowed us to improve the mean absolute error up to 50.5 days, although, median absolute error and mean weighted absolute error slightly increased to 19.9 and 54.0 respectively. Note that the parameter selection method minimizes mean absolute error, so there is no guarantee that any other measures will improve (if one were to consider another measure as the most important, that measure should be used as the target of minimization).

Likelihood optimization. First, for each host we choose the best method among all propagation methods with our data-driven parameter selection approach. The dates obtained by this propagation are used as initial dates for the likelihood optimization. Second, we use the parameter selection method to find out if the likelihood method is better (according to the mean absolute error) with any settings of its parameters (we fix the maximum number of steps $N = 100$). We noticed that our data-driven parameter selection approach chooses zero number of steps to about 40% of hosts, which means that for other 60% the likelihood optimization is predicted to be useful with some values λ, c, $N_0 > 0$. Likelihood optimization allowed us to get better results according to all measures. Finally, we get 11%, 31%, and 10% improvements of mean, median, and weighted errors respectively over the best (according to the corresponding metric) of the baselines.

	Method	mean/median/ weighted err	coverage
baselines	anchor dates	77.6/79.7/89.6	50.0%
	1-step in-avg	71.0/73.3/39.7	57.9%
	1-step out-avg	66.8/66.6/41.7	65.5%
	1-step in-min	71.5/73.6/77.8	57.9%
proposed methods	1-step all-avg	64.1/62.3/38.6	68.6%
	1-step out-max	67.4/67.0/50.0	65.5%
	1-step out-max-in-min	73.5/75.8/58.0	54.8%
	in-avg	70.2/72.5/39.0	58.9%
	out-avg	64.5/62.4/39.6	69.0%
	in-min	70.9/73.0/77.2	58.9%
	all-avg	**58.0**/52.6/37.9	75.3%
	out-max	65.5/63.1/48.1	69.0%
	out-max-in-min	72.7/75.2/56.3	55.8%
	model-0.3	58.3/52.3/43.0	75.3%
	model-0.4	**58.0/52.0**/38.1	75.3%
	model-0.5	58.2/52.2/**35.7**	75.3%
	likelihood optimization	**57.4/51.3/33.4**	75.3%

Table 3: Comparison of the algorithms on MemeTracker

Note that, for instance, in the case of web search ranking [4], even small improvements in the publication date estimates may affect the quality of ranking. Since the quality is of the highest priority in such applications (used by hundreds of millions of people daily), it should be preferred to periodically apply the best method, i.e., the likelihood optimization. For some other applications, where the complexity can be an issue, it might be preferred to use our multi-step date propagation methods of lower complexity, which demonstrate slightly worse but still sufficiently good results (see Appendix for the discussion of complexity).

5.3 Experiments on MemeTracker

Recall that this dataset consists of about 12 million web pages with known dates. In order to measure the performance of the algorithms we take x% random web pages and "forget" their dates. We consider all dates that are left as anchor ones. Then, we find initial approximations for the forgotten dates by using the date propagation methods. After that, we apply the likelihood optimization procedure. In this section, we measure the average errors only using the pages with forgotten dates. Mean errors measured over *all* pages would be two times smaller (since half of the pages have zero errors). We take 15th of December as the constant date since it is the middle of the considered time interval.

The results for $x = 50\%$ are presented in Table 3. The value $x = 50\%$ is chosen according to our observations on the crawled dataset, where we observe that about half of the pages have no seed or anchor dates (see the coverage for seed dates in Table 2). We applied our data-driven parameter selection algorithm to choose the propagation method and it chose *model-0.4*. Then, we apply the likelihood optimization algorithm. The data-driven parameter selection method predicts the likelihood optimization to be useful in this case (with 80 steps). Note that the obtained likelihood optimization algorithm is the best according to all three measures.

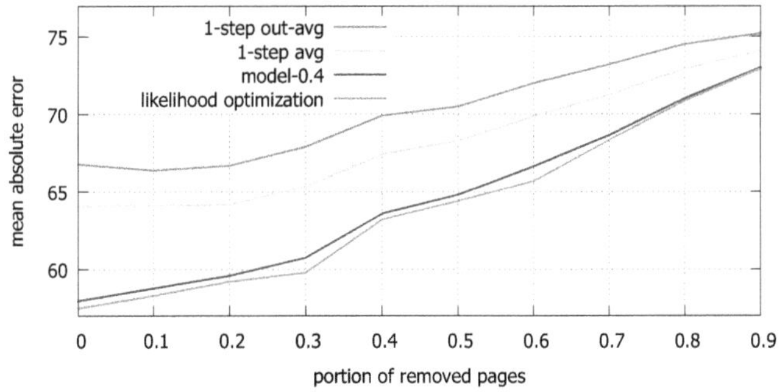

Figure 1: Influence of sparsity in data: mean absolute error

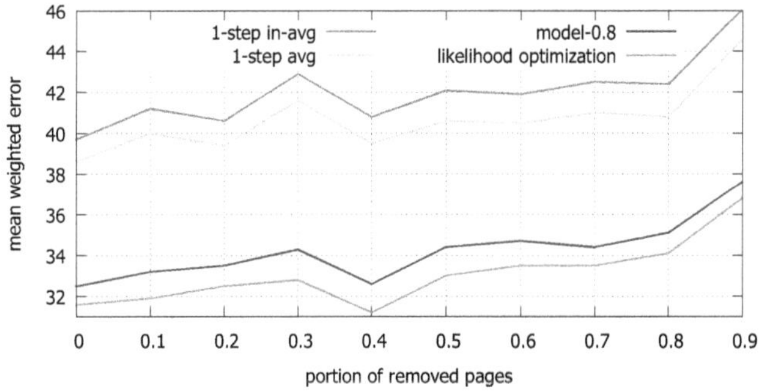

Figure 2: Influence of sparsity in data: mean weighted error

Performance on reachable pages only. Recall that we average errors over all web pages with forgotten dates, although about a half of these pages do not have any date even after the multi-step date propagation; these pages are assigned the constant date and all link-based methods are useless for such pages (they are not connected by any path to any dated page). If we exclude these pages from the evaluation and measure the error on the remaining pages, then we obtain more distinguishable results: e.g., the mean error of the best baseline *1-step out-avg* is **56.3** days, of *model-0.4* is **38.9** days (**-31%**), of the likelihood optimization is **37.7** days (**-33%**). On the crawled dataset we can make similar observations.

Dataset size influence. In addition, we analyze the influence of the dataset size on the quality of our algorithms. In order to do this, we thin out the data: we progressively remove a bigger fraction of web pages, and then, as before, we assume that for the half of the remaining pages the dates are not known and we estimate these dates with our methods. The obtained mean absolute error is shown on Figure 1. Here we present the following methods: the best of the baselines *1-step out-avg*, the best one-step method *1-step avg*, the best multi-step method *model-0.4*, and the likelihood optimization method. As expected, a sparser link structure leads to worse performance of the algorithms. We also demonstrate that it is possible to improve the weighted error measure much more if our parameter selection approach directly optimizes this measure. Figure 2 is analogous to Figure 1, but it presents the mean weighted error for all the algorithms. Here the best baseline is *1-step in-avg* and the best multi-step algorithm is *model-0.8*. The parameters of the likelihood optimization algorithm are chosen according to the data-driven parameter selection approach which optimizes the mean weighted error. It turns out that the weighted error is much less sensitive to the sparsity in data than the mean absolute error.

Finally, it is worth mentioning that all the improvements obtained on both datasets are statistically significant according to the paired t-test at less than 0.001 level.

6. CONCLUSION AND FUTURE WORK

In this paper, we suggested and compared several methods for publication dates estimation. We primarily focused on link-based methods: we systematized and generalized several simple date propagation methods previously proposed in the literature and we also suggested a more sophisticated likelihood optimization based method. In addition, we proposed the data-driven parameter selection approach which allows to tune our algorithms individually for each host. We demonstrated the improvements over the baseline approaches on two large Web samples: the first one consists of pages crawled by a major commercial search engine and the second one is MemeTracker public dataset. For example, the mean error is improved by 10% and 14% on the crawled and MemeTracker datasets respectively. If we exclude isolated pages from the evaluation, we get up to 33% improvements.

The most promising direction for the future research is to deeper analyze the hosts for which the likelihood optimization is predicted not to be useful. The link structure can evolve by some other rules in such cases, therefore it is reasonable to develop and apply a more suitable model for these hosts.

7. REFERENCES

[1] http://www.memetracker.org/data.html.

[2] D. Ahn, J. Rantwijk, and M. Rijke. A cascaded machine learning approach to interpreting temporal expressions. *Proc. of NAACL-HLT Conference*, 2007.

[3] R. Campos, G. Dias, A. M. Jorge, and A. Jatowt. Survey of temporal information retrieval and related applications. *ACM Computing Surveys*, 47, 2014.

[4] A. Dong, Y. Chang, Z. Zheng, G. Mishne, J. Bai, R. Zhang, K. Buchner, C. Liao, and F. Diaz. Towards recency ranking in web search. *Proc. WSDM*, pages 11–20, 2010.

[5] A. Dong, R. Zhang, P. Kolari, and J. Bai. Time is of the essence: Improving recency ranking using twitter data. *Proc. WWW*, pages 331–340, 2010.

[6] N. Kanhabua and K. Nørvåg. Using temporal language models for document dating. *Proc ECML PKDD*, 2009.

[7] O. Kolomiyets and M.-F. Moens. Comparing two approaches for the recognition of temporal expressions. *KI 2009: Advances in Artificial Intelligence*, 2009.

[8] A. Kumar, J. Baldridge, M. Lease, and J. Ghosh. Dating texts without explicit temporal cues. *arXiv preprint arXiv:1211.2290*, 2012.

[9] A. Kumar, M. Lease, and J. Baldridge. Supervised language modeling for temporal resolution of texts. *Proc. of CIKM*, pages 2069–2072, 2011.

[10] D. Lefortier, L. Ostroumova, and E. Samosvat. Evolution of the media web. *Proc. of WAW, LNCS*, 8305:80–92, 2013.

[11] D. Lefortier, L. Ostroumova, and E. Samosvat. Timely crawling of high-quality ephemeral new content. *Proc. CIKM*, pages 745–750, 2013.

[12] J. Leskovec, L. Backstrom, and J. Kleinberg. Meme-tracking and the dynamics of the news cycle. *KDD*, 2009.

[13] Y. Lu, W. Meng, W. Zhang, K.-L. Liu, and C. Yu. Automatic extraction of publication time from news search results. *Proc. ICDE Workshops*, 2006.

[14] S. Nunes, C. Ribeiro, and G. David. Using neighbors to date web documents. *Proc. WIDM*, 2007.

[15] C. Olston and M. Najork. Web crawling. *Foundations and Trends in Information Retrieval*, 4(3):175–246, 2010.

[16] H. M. Salah and M. L. Nelson. Carbon dating the web: estimating the age of web resources. *Proc. WWW*, 2013.

APPENDIX

Complexity reduction. Let us discuss the complexity of the likelihood optimization algorithm which optimizes q_p for all pages and t_p for all pages without anchor dates. Let n and e be the number of nodes and the number of edges in the graph G_{real}, respectively. The naïve straightforward method allows to compute $W(t_i)$ for all i in $O(n^2)$. After this, $L(\bar{t}, \bar{q})$ can be computed in $O(n^2+ne)$. If we want to use the gradient descent method for each node, then one step of the gradient descent for only one node can be made in $O(n^2+ne)$. Making one optimization step for all nodes would take $O(n^3+n^2e)$. Since we have hundreds of thousands pages on one host, this complexity is far too high. That is why we propose an efficient method which allows to simultaneously optimize qualities and dates for *all* pages and allows to make one optimization step for all pages with $O(n+e)$ complexity.

We assume that nodes are sorted according to the current estimates of their publication times, i.e., $t_1 \leq \ldots \leq t_n$. First, we compute $W(t_i)$ for all i in $O(n)$:

$$W(t_i) = \sum_{j \leq i} q_j e^{-\lambda(t_i - t_j)} \left(1 - \frac{e^{-c(t_i - t_j)}}{2}\right)$$
$$+ \sum_{j>i} q_j e^{-\lambda(t_i - t_j)} \frac{e^{c(t_i - t_j)}}{2} = e^{-\lambda t_i} \sum_{j \leq i} q_j e^{\lambda t_j}$$
$$- \frac{e^{-(\lambda+c)t_i}}{2} \sum_{j \leq i} q_j e^{(\lambda+c)t_j} + \frac{e^{(c-\lambda)t_i}}{2} \sum_{j>i} q_j e^{-(c-\lambda)t_j}.$$

We can precompute all partial sums in the last equality in $O(n)$. After that, the values $W(t_i)$ for all i can be computed in $O(n)$. And the value $L(\bar{t}, \bar{q})$ can be computed in $O(n+e)$.

Now we can compute the partial derivatives of $L(\bar{t}, \bar{q})$ with respect to t_i for all i in $O(n+e)$. Let us start with some auxiliary observations

$$g(x) = \frac{\partial}{\partial x} f(x) = \begin{cases} \frac{ce^{-cx}}{2} & \text{for } x \geq 0, \\ \frac{ce^{cx}}{2} & \text{for } x < 0, \end{cases}$$

$$\frac{\partial}{\partial t_k} f(t_i - t_j) = (\delta_{ik} - \delta_{jk}) g(t_i - t_j),$$

$$\frac{\partial}{\partial t_k} e^{-\lambda(t_i - t_j)} = -\lambda(\delta_{ik} - \delta_{jk}) e^{-\lambda(t_i - t_j)}.$$

Recall that $W(t_i) = \sum_j q_j e^{-\lambda(t_i - t_j)} f(t_i - t_j)$. Now we calculate partial derivatives of $W(t_i)$ with respect to t_k:

$$\frac{\partial W(t_i)}{\partial t_k} = \sum_j q_j e^{-\lambda(t_i - t_j)} (\delta_{ik} - \delta_{jk}) \left(g(t_i - t_j) - \lambda f(t_i - t_j)\right)$$
$$= \delta_{ik} \sum_j q_j e^{-\lambda(t_i - t_j)} \left(-\lambda f(t_i - t_j) + g(t_i - t_j)\right)$$
$$- \sum_j q_j e^{-\lambda(t_i - t_j)} \delta_{jk} \left(-\lambda f(t_i - t_j) + g(t_i - t_j)\right)$$
$$= \delta_{ik} \left(V(t_i) - \lambda W(t_i)\right) - q_k e^{-\lambda(t_i - t_k)} \left(g(t_i - t_k) - \lambda f(t_i - t_k)\right)$$
$$= \delta_{ik} \left(-\lambda W(t_i) + V(t_i)\right) - q_k h(t_i - t_k),$$

where $h(x) = e^{-\lambda x} \left(g(x) - \lambda f(x)\right)$ and

$$V(t_i) = \sum_j q_j e^{-\lambda(t_i - t_j)} g(t_i - t_j).$$

Similar to $W(t_i)$, all $V(t_i)$ can be computed in $O(n)$.

Recall that

$$L(\bar{t}, \bar{q}) = \prod_{ij \in G_{real}} \frac{q_j e^{-\lambda(t_i - t_j)} f(t_i - t_j)}{W(t_i)}.$$

Now we calculate

$$\frac{\partial}{\partial t_k} \log L(\bar{t}, \bar{q})$$
$$= \frac{\partial}{\partial t_k} \sum_{ij \in G_{real}} \left(\log q_j - \lambda(t_i - t_j) + \log f(t_i - t_j) - \log W(t_i)\right)$$
$$= \sum_{ij \in G_{real}} -\lambda(\delta_{ik} - \delta_{jk}) + \sum_{ij \in G_{real}} \frac{(\delta_{ik} - \delta_{jk}) g(t_i - t_j)}{f(t_i - t_j)}$$
$$- \sum_{ij \in G_{real}} \frac{\delta_{ik} \left(-\lambda W(t_i) + V(t_i)\right) - q_k h(t_i - t_k)}{W(t_i)}$$
$$= -\lambda(deg_{out}(k) - deg_{in}(k)) + \sum_{kj \in G_{real}} \frac{g(t_k - t_j)}{f(t_k - t_j)}$$
$$- \sum_{ik \in G_{real}} \frac{g(t_i - t_k)}{f(t_i - t_k)} - \left(\frac{deg_{out}(k) \left(-\lambda W(t_k) + V(t_k)\right)}{W(t_k)}\right)$$
$$+ q_k \sum_i \frac{deg_{out}(i) h(t_i - t_k)}{W(t_i)}$$
$$= -\frac{V(t_k)}{W(t_k)} deg_{out}(k) + \lambda\, deg_{in}(k) + \sum_{kj \in G_{real}} \frac{g(t_k - t_j)}{f(t_k - t_j)}$$
$$- \sum_{ik \in G_{real}} \frac{g(t_i - t_k)}{f(t_i - t_k)} + q_k \sum_i \frac{deg_{out}(i) h(t_i - t_k)}{W(t_i)}. \quad (5)$$

The first four terms in the last equation can be computed in $O(n+e)$. It remains to compute

$$q_k \sum_i \frac{deg_{out}(i) h(t_i - t_k)}{W(t_i)} = q_k \sum_{i \geq k} \frac{deg_{out}(i) h(t_i - t_k)}{W(t_i)}$$
$$+ q_k \sum_{i<k} \frac{deg_{out}(i) h(t_i - t_k)}{W(t_i)} = -\lambda q_k e^{\lambda t_k} \sum_{i \geq k} \frac{deg_{out}(i) e^{-\lambda t_i}}{W(t_i)}$$
$$+ \frac{(\lambda + c) q_k e^{(\lambda+c)t_k}}{2} \sum_{i \geq k} \frac{deg_{out}(i) e^{-(\lambda+c)t_i}}{W(t_i)}$$
$$+ \frac{(c - \lambda) q_k e^{(\lambda-c)t_k}}{2} \sum_{i<k} \frac{deg_{out}(i) e^{(c-\lambda)t_i}}{W(t_i)}.$$

This expression for all k can be computed in $O(n)$.

The partial derivatives with respect to q_k can be computed in a similar way:

$$\frac{\partial}{\partial q_k} \log L(\bar{t}, \bar{q}) = \frac{deg_{in}(k)}{q_k} - e^{\lambda t_k} \sum_{i \geq k} \frac{deg_{out}(i) e^{-\lambda t_i}}{W(t_i)}$$
$$- \frac{e^{(\lambda+c)t_k}}{2} \sum_{i \geq k} \frac{deg_{out}(i) e^{-(\lambda+c)t_i}}{W(t_i)}$$
$$- \frac{e^{(\lambda-c)t_k}}{2} \sum_{i<k} \frac{deg_{out}(i) e^{(c-\lambda)t_i}}{W(t_i)}. \quad (6)$$

Finally, the complexity of the likelihood optimization algorithm is $O(N e)$, where N is the number of optimization steps. Recall that the complexity of one step of any date propagation method is $O(e)$.

Note that during the computation of the partial derivatives we have to calculate the sum of exponents e^{t_i} several times and a lot of such exponents are too large to fit the double or long double types what makes the computation infeasible. The solution to this problem is to operate with the logarithms of numbers (see *http://blog.smola.org/post/987977550/log-probabilities-semirings-and-floating-point*).

To Suggest, or Not to Suggest for Queries with Diverse Intents: Optimizing Search Result Presentation

Makoto P. Kato
kato@dl.kuis.kyoto-u.ac.jp

Katsumi Tanaka
tanaka@dl.kuis.kyoto-u.ac.jp

Kyoto University
Yoshida Honmachi, Sakyo, Kyoto, Japan 6068501

ABSTRACT

We propose a method of optimizing search result presentation for queries with diverse intents, by selectively presenting query suggestions for leading users to more relevant search results. The optimization is based on a probabilistic model of users who click on query suggestions in accordance with their intents, and modified versions of intent-aware evaluation metrics that take into account the co-occurrence between intents. Showing many query suggestions simply increases a chance to satisfy users with diverse intents in this model, while it in fact requires users to spend additional time for scanning and selecting suggestions, and may result in low satisfaction for some users. Therefore, we measured the loss of time caused by query suggestion presentation by conducting a user study in different settings, and included its *negative* effects in our optimization problem. Our experiments revealed that the optimization of search result presentation significantly improved that of a single ranked list, and was beneficial especially for patient users. Moreover, experimental results showed that our optimization was effective particularly when intents of a query often co-occur with a small subset of intents.

Categories and Subject Descriptors

H.3.3. [**Information Search and Retrieval**]

Keywords

search result diversification; query suggestion; optimization

1. INTRODUCTION

Web search queries are often *ambiguous* and/or *underspecified*, as indicated by their word lengths: 3.1 for desktop searches and 2.9 for typed mobile searches [13]. This problem of Web search queries will not be resolved in the near future, since the number of mobile users is still increasing as of December 2014 [1], and so the average length of Web search queries is accordingly expected to decrease. Therefore, search result diversification has been considered as an important challenge for Web search engines, and extensively studied to satisfy as many intents as possible behind an ambiguous or underspecified query.

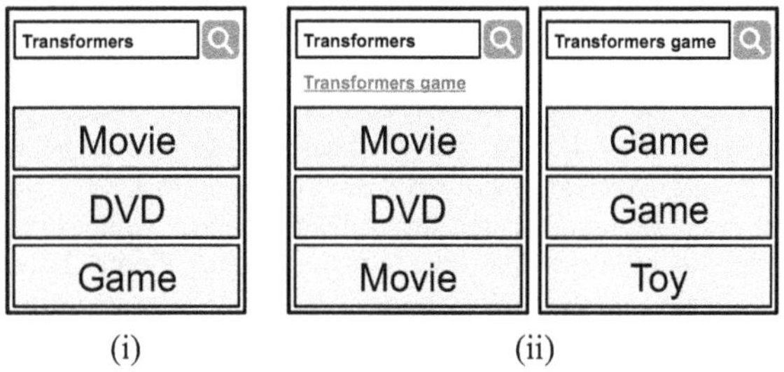

Figure 1: Search result diversification (i) without query suggestions, and (ii) with query suggestions.

Although most of the existing work has focused on diversification in a single ranked list, *query response paradigm* is not always satisfactory for diverse intents. Figure 1 (i) shows an example of a search engine result page (SERP) for query "Transformers". Assume that all the documents are relevant to a single intent at the same level. Despite high diversity in SERP (i), this SERP cannot present many relevant search results in the top three for any intent behind this query: only a relevant result for movie, DVD, and game intents, and no relevant one for the others. In addition, users interested in games have to skip two irrelevant search results for reaching a relevant search result. Therefore, diversification on a single ranked list cannot fully satisfy many users, especially when a given query has a lot of ambiguity. In fact, the average number of intents is 7.92 in the NTCIR INTENT tasks [26, 29], and may overabound for a single SERP including ten search results.

We can overcome the limitation by taking into account the interaction between searchers and search engines. Figure 1 (ii) shows a SERP for query "Transformers" presenting query suggestion "Transformers game", and one for this query suggestion. Users interested in movies may browse the SERP returned in response to the original query and find two relevant results, while users interested in games may click on the query suggestion and find two relevant results. As seen in this example, presenting query suggestions can lead users to their desired search results and increase the chance to satisfy many users at a high level. Whereas, it in fact requires users to spend additional time for scanning and selecting suggestions, and may result in lower satisfaction for some users. To suggest, or not to suggest: that is the question.

The goal of this paper is to develop a method of optimizing search result presentation, *i.e.* selecting a set of query suggestions to be presented, and ranked list of documents for each of the input query and suggestions. There are three main challenges in this problem. First, search results have been usually optimized by max-

WSDM'16, February 22–25, 2016, San Francisco, CA, USA.

ISBN 978-1-4503-3716-8/16/02...$15.00
DOI: http://dx.doi.org/10.1145/2835776.2835805

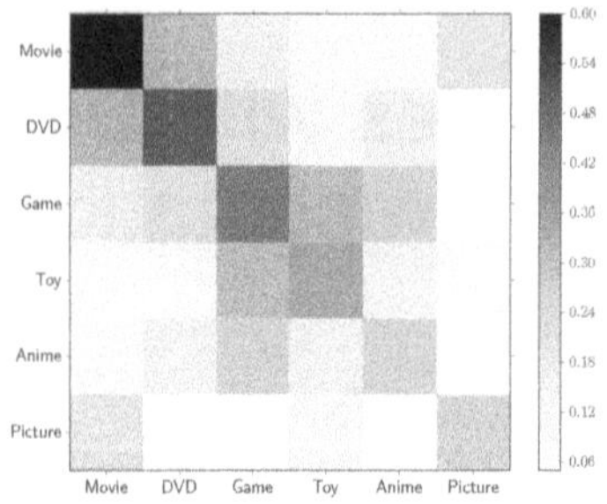

Figure 2: Joint intent probability for query "Transformers".

imizing a certain evaluation metric, while our problem includes uncertain factors such as intent and query suggestion click probabilities. In this paper, we formalize the optimization of search result presentation as a maximization problem of expected utility of users who click on query suggestions in accordance with their intents. Second, users have been assumed to have a single intent in conventional search result diversification, while, in reality, they do have multiple intents in a session. Figure 2 shows intents behind query "Transformers", and their *joint* intent probability $P(x, y \in X|q)$, the probability of users who input query q and have intents including both x and y. For example, (Movie, DVD) cells represent the probability of users interested in topics including "Movie" and "DVD". Appropriate search result presentation highly relies on the co-occurrence of intents, as search results relevant to tightly coupled intents should not be included in different SERPs (*e.g.* "Movie" and "DVD"). Therefore, we propose *joint-intent-aware* evaluation metrics to measure the expected utility of users with multiple intents. Third, effects of query suggestions on user search behaviors need to be calibrated. Although the query suggestion effects on search behaviors have been studied in the literature (*e.g.* [20]), it is still unclear how much time users have to spend for scanning and selecting from query suggestions. To answer the question, we conducted a user study in desktop and mobile environments, and incorporated findings into the optimization of search result presentation.

Experiments were carried out to demonstrate the effectiveness of the search result presentation optimization. We utilized two test collections developed in the NTCIR INTENT tasks [26, 29], and found that our optimization could significantly improve that of a single ranked list. Our contributions can be summarized as follows: (1) we proposed a searcher model interacting with query suggestions in accordance with their multiple intents, and a method of optimizing search result presentation for an ambiguous or underspecified query; (2) we conducted a user study to examine the effects of query suggestions on search behaviors, and calibrated some parameters used in the searcher model; and (3) we demonstrated the effectiveness of the search result presentation optimization, and confirmed that our optimization was effective especially for patient users and queries with a limited number of intents.

The rest of the paper is organized as follows. Section 2 surveys related work on search result diversification. Section 3 introduces our model for optimizing search result presentation. Section 4 describes a user study we conducted for calibrating effects of query suggestions. Section 5 presents experimental results. Finally, Section 6 concludes by outlining future work.

2. RELATED WORK

The literature contains many studies on search result diversification, which can be classified into implicit and explicit approaches.

Implicit approaches are based on an assumption that similar documents are likely to be redundant as they cover similar interest. One early work on search result diversification was an implicit approach presented by Carbonell and Goldstein [7]. They balanced the relevance of documents to a query and dissimilarity among retrieved documents by maximal marginal relevance. Zhai, Cohen, and Lafferty proposed some evaluation metrics for taking into account the redundancy of documents that generalizes the precision and recall [31]. They also extended the MRR-based approach by using several types of novelty measures. Chen and Karger proposed an implicit approach for search result diversification based on optimizing objective functions, which are defined as the probability of at least k relevant documents for all users [12]. Radlinski, Kleinberg, and Joachims proposed methods of learning diverse rankings based on multi-armed bandits [25]. Their algorithms maximize the expected total reward based on feedback by users with different interests. As a result, their algorithm produces diverse search results to satisfy different types of users.

In contrast, explicit approaches directly model user intents, and try to maximize the coverage of documents relevant to each intent. Agrawal *et al.* proposed IA-select algorithm for search result diversification and intent-aware evaluation metrics [3]. They took an explicit approach that modeled intents of a given query, and formalized a search result diversification problem as a maximization of the probability of at least one relevant document for all the intents. Carterette and Chandar proposed a probabilistic model for faceted topic retrieval, and methods of retrieving a set of documents that maximizes the probability of including all facets for a given query [8]. Their problem is slightly different from the search result diversification problem, while their approach can be regarded as an explicit one for search result diversification. Santos, Macdonald, and Ounis proposed a probabilistic model for search result diversification called xQuAD, which explicitly models an ambiguous or underspecified query as a set of subqueries [27]. While their model was similar to Agrawal *et al.*'s IA-select, they also proposed methods of generating subqueries and estimating their importance, and established a practical approach to search result diversification. Dou *et al.* proposed a method of mining intents from various types of sources such as anchor texts, query logs, clusters of search results [14]. Recent search result diversification methods were developed on the basis of the combination of implicit and explicit approaches [16], learning to rank [32], rank aggregation [23], and multiple knapsack problem [30]. We also take an explicit approach in our search result presentation optimization.

Although, to the best of our knowledge, our work is the first trial to optimize search results including query suggestions, some closely related work exists outside the search result diversification. One is dynamic ranked retrieval proposed by Brandt *et al.* [6]. Their dynamic rankings provide search results that can change based on user feedback (*e.g.* clicks on search results). Their approach is to optimize the expected utility of users with different interests, and similar to ours expect that i) we allow users to have multiple intents, ii) we take into account the effects of user interaction on their satisfaction, and iii) we do not only rank search results but also select the optimal query suggestion set. Another closely related work is query suggestion optimization proposed by Anagnostopoulos *et al.* [4]. Their approach is based on optimization of the expected utility of query reformulations, while search result optimization and diverse intents of a query have not been considered together with query suggestions.

Some work modeled user effort for measuring the utility of search results, or developing a new evaluation metric. Dunlop proposed time-to-view graphs that measure the time to find a given number of relevant documents [15]. Järvelin *et al.* proposed an extension to the discounted cumulated gain for evaluating multiple query sessions, by including a discount factor for query reformulations [18]. Baskaya, Keskustalo, and Järvelin conducted a simulation-based experiment to compare search strategies, by taking into account time constraints [5]. Smucker and Clarke calibrated a discount factor in an evaluation metric based on the time spent reaching a certain rank [28]. Our user study gives an insight into the cost of query suggestions in this line of work.

3. METHODOLOGY

This section describes our model for optimizing search result presentation, *i.e.* selecting a set of query suggestions and ranked lists of documents. First, we propose a probabilistic model of users interacting with query suggestions, and formalize the problem of search result presentation optimization. Second, we introduce joint-intent-aware evaluation metrics for measuring the search result utility with multiple intents. Third, we propose methods of estimating probabilities used in the optimization problem. Finally, we describe an algorithm for the optimization problem.

3.1 User Model

We propose a probabilistic model of users interacting with query suggestions, and then formalize the problem of search result presentation optimization as maximization of the expected utility of users following the probabilistic model.

Our user model is described as follows:

1. A user inputs query q and receives a SERP $\mathbf{d}^{(a_q)}$ presenting query suggestions S;
2. The user decides either to continue to browse the SERP or to click a presented query suggestion following probability $P(a|q, S)$, where $a \in A$, a set of user actions such as browsing the presented SERP (denoted by a_q), and selecting a query suggestion $s \in S$ (denoted by a_s), *i.e.* $A = \{a_q\} \cup A_S$ and $A_S = \{a_s\}_{s \in S}$;
3. If the user continues to browse $\mathbf{d}^{(a_q)}$, s/he can obtain utility u with probability $P(u|q, S, a_q, \mathbf{d}^{(a_q)})$;
4. If the user clicks on query suggestion s, s/he can browse another SERP $\mathbf{d}^{(a_s)}$ and obtain utility u with $P(u|q, S, a_s, \mathbf{d}^{(s)})$.

This probabilistic model enables us to formalize the expected utility of search results with query suggestions as shown below:

$$E[u|q, S, \mathbf{D}] = \sum_{a \in A} P(a|q, S) E[u|q, S, a, \mathbf{d}^{(a)}], \quad (1)$$

where $\mathbf{D}$ is a set of SERPs (*i.e.* $\mathbf{D} = \{\mathbf{d}^{(a)}\}_{a \in A}$).

The problem of optimizing search result presentation can be formalized as maximization of the expected utility of search results with query suggestions:

$$(S^*, \mathbf{D}^*) = \underset{(S, \mathbf{D})}{\operatorname{argmax}} \, E[u|q, S, \mathbf{D}]. \quad (2)$$

In other words, we assume that search result presentation is optimal if its expected utility is maximized.

The expected utility $E[u|q, S, a, \mathbf{d}^{(a)}]$ in Equation 1 can be approximated by the value of a joint-intent-aware evaluation metric for users who take a particular action. In the following subsections, we introduce the joint-intent-aware evaluation metric, and methods of estimating some probabilities in Equation 1.

3.2 Joint-intent-aware Evaluation Metrics

Agrawal *et al.* proposed intent-aware metrics for diversity-aware evaluation [3], and their general form is shown below:

$$\mathrm{IA}(\mathbf{d}) \ = \ \sum_{i \in I} P(i|q) M_i(\mathbf{d}), \quad (3)$$

where $\mathbf{d} = (d_1, \ldots, d_r, \ldots)$ is a ranked list of documents, I is a set of intents for a given query q, $P(i|q)$ is the probability of intent i of users inputting query q, and $M_i(\mathbf{d})$ is an evaluation metric for a particular intent i. Note that we use an intent as a user interest in a certain subtopic of a query (*i.e. topical search intents* [21]), and assume that there is a one-to-one relationship between intents and subtopics. The evaluation metric $M_i(\mathbf{d})$ can be instantiated by discounted cumulative gain (DCG) [17], expected reciprocal rank (ERR) [11], and even a recently proposed metric such as time-biased gain (TBG) [28].

As we mentioned earlier, we introduce joint-intent-aware versions to take into account the co-occurrence of multiple intents. In Agrawal *et al.*'s intent-aware metrics, they modeled the intent probability by a multinomial distribution over a set of intents I, and assumed that each user has a single intent. In contrast, we assume that each user can have multiple intents in a search session, and model the intent probability as a probability over a power set of intents 2^I. By letting $P(X|q)$ be a probability of joint intent $X \subset I$ given query q, a joint-intent-aware metric is defined as follows:

$$\mathrm{JIA}_{P(X|q)}(\mathbf{d}) = \sum_{X \in 2^I} P(X|q) M_X(\mathbf{d}), \quad (4)$$

where $M_X(\mathbf{d})$ is an evaluation metric for a particular *intent set* X. We can naturally define join-intent-aware versions of intent-aware evaluation metrics by defining $M_X(\mathbf{d})$ as the sum of $M_i(\mathbf{d})$ for $i \in X$, *i.e.* $M_X(\mathbf{d}) = \sum_{i \in X} M_i(\mathbf{d})$. The reason why we use the sum of $M_i(\mathbf{d})$ is that we assume users can obtain gains based on each of their intents, which are accumulated.

Although the computation of a joint-intent-aware evaluation metric by a naïve method requires $2^{|I|}$ computations of $P(X|q)$ and $M_X(\mathbf{d})$, we can save on the computational cost by using a basic theorem: $E[Y] = \sum_i \omega_i E[X_i]$ where $Y = \sum_i \omega_i X_i$. By using $M_X(\mathbf{d}) = \sum_{i \in I} \mathbf{1}(i \in X) M_i(\mathbf{d})$ ($\mathbf{1}(x)$ is an indicator function), a joint-intent-aware evaluation metric can be computed by the following equation:

$$\mathrm{JIA}_{P(X|q)}(\mathbf{d}) = \sum_{i \in I} P(i \in X|q) M_i(\mathbf{d}), \quad (5)$$

where $P(i \in X|q)$ is the probability of X including i given query q. Formally, $P(i \in X|q) = \sum_{X \in 2^I} \mathbf{1}(i \in X) P(X|q)$. Thus, we only need to estimate $P(i \in X|q)$ for computing a joint-intent-aware evaluation metric.

The joint-intent-aware evaluation metric is utilized to approximate the expected utility $E[u|q, S, a, \mathbf{d}^{(a)}]$ in Equation 1:

$$\begin{aligned} E[u|q, S, a, \mathbf{d}^{(a)}] &= \mathrm{JIA}_{P(X|q,S,a)}(\mathbf{d}^{(a)}) \quad (6) \\ &= \sum_{X \in 2^I} P(X|q, S, a) M_X(\mathbf{d}^{(a)}), \quad (7) \end{aligned}$$

where $P(X|q)$ is replaced with $P(X|q, S, a)$ (a probability of intent set X for a user who issues q and takes action a for query suggestions S), since the distribution of intent sets can be different after taking a particular action a for query suggestions S.

Furthermore, we take into account the *negative* effect of query suggestions in the expected utility. Presented query suggestions may interrupt browsing of SERPs and cause time loss, probably because of the viewport narrowed by the query suggestion space or time spent assessing query suggestions. Selecting query suggestions also requires some time from the users, which accordingly reduces the utility of SERPs returned in response to clicked query suggestions. Both effects can possibly increase as the number of query suggestions increases, and can be represented by time $t_{n,a}$, where n is the number of query suggestions (*i.e.* $|S|$), and a is an action taken by the user.

TBG is a time-based evaluation metric proposed by Smucker and Clarke [28], and discounts the gain at each rank by the expected time to reach the rank. Thus, TBG can naturally include the time loss $t_{n,a}$ as follows:

$$M_i^{\mathrm{TBG}}(\mathbf{d}) = \sum_{r=1}^{N} G_i(r) \exp\left(-\frac{\ln 2}{h}(T_i(r) + t_{n,a})\right), \quad (8)$$

where $G_i(r)$ is the gain at rank r in terms of intent i, $T_i(r)$ is the time to reach rank r, and h is the *half-life* of users ($h = 224$ unless otherwise noted). Although the original version of TBG does not include cutoff parameter N, we include it since we can only evaluate a limited number of search results in reality. DCG [17] and ERR [11] can also include the time loss by converting it to *rank loss* $R(t_{n,a})$, which is the rank that users can reach in time $t_{n,a}$:

$$M_i^{\mathrm{DCG}}(\mathbf{d}) = \sum_{r=1}^{N} \frac{g_i(r)}{\log_\beta(1 + r + R(t_{n,a}))}, \quad (9)$$

$$M_i^{\mathrm{ERR}}(\mathbf{d}) = \sum_{r=1}^{N} \frac{1}{r + R(t_{n,a})} h_i(r) \prod_{r'=1}^{r-1} (1 - h_i(r')), \quad (10)$$

where $g_i(r)$ is a relevance grade for the r-th document in terms of intent i, β is the base of the logarithm ($\beta = 2$ in this paper), and $h_i(r) = (2^{g_i(r)} - 1)/2^{g_{\max}}$, the probability of relevance of the r-th document to intent i ($g_{\max}$ is the maximum relevance grade). In this way, the time loss $t_{n,a}$ and rank loss $R(t_{n,a})$ penalize the score of an evaluation metric. Their calibration is explained in Section 4.

3.3 Estimation of Probabilities

In this subsection, we propose methods of estimating two probabilities in the maximization problem in Equation 2: the probability of taking action a for a given query q and query suggestions S (*i.e.* $P(a|q, S)$), and the probability of joint intents for query q and taking action a for query suggestions S (*i.e.* $P(X|q, S, a)$).

We assume the following settings for the estimations. First, we assume that intents for a query are used as query suggestions, *i.e.* $S \subset I$. This is not a strong limitation as intents (or subtopics) provided by the NTCIR INTENT tasks are quite similar to ordinary query suggestions [26, 29]. The task organizers in fact explicitly mentioned that intents (or subtopics) can be used for query suggestions. Second, we assume that the frequency of intent sets is available for each query. If a search engine query log is available, one can obtain it by extracting all the sessions including a query, and regarding co-occurring queries within a session as an intent set. In our experiments, we obtained the frequency of intent sets by using a crowd-sourcing service and asking workers to vote for intents assuming that they were users who issued a particular query.

Estimation of $P(a|q, S)$.

Directly estimating the probability $P(a|q, S)$ is not practical since this probability depends on presented query suggestions S, and we may not be able to obtain training data for an arbitrary set of query suggestions. Therefore, we first decompose the probability $P(a|q, S)$ by marginalizing intent set X:

$$P(a|q, S) = \sum_{X \in 2^I} P(a|X, S)P(X|q). \quad (11)$$

It is still hard to estimate $P(a|X, S)$ (the probability of taking action a for users with intent set X given query suggestions S), while we can naturally approximate it for the case of $a \in A_S$ as follows:

$$P(a_s|X, S) \simeq p_{\mathrm{QS}} \frac{\mathbf{1}(s \in X)}{|X \cap S|}. \quad (12)$$

This approximation indicates that users select query suggestions relevant to their intents with the same probability determined by parameter p_{QS}. For example, users click on a query suggestion with a probability $p_{\mathrm{QS}}/2$ if two query suggestions relevant to their intents are presented in a SERP.

The assumption above simplifies Equation 11 as follows:

$$P(a_s|q, S) = p_{\mathrm{QS}} \sum_{k=1}^{|S|} \frac{1}{k} P(s \in X, |S \cap X| = k|q), \quad (13)$$

where $P(s \in X, |S \cap X| = k|q)$ is the probability of X including s and k elements of S given query q. By letting $f_{q,s,k}$ be the frequency of intent sets for query q including s and k elements of S, and f_q be the frequency of intent sets for query q, $P(s \in X, |S \cap X| = k|q)$ can be estimated as $f_{q,s,k}/f_q$.

Having estimated $P(a_s|q, S)$, we can obtain $P(a_q|q, S)$ as follows: $P(a_q|q, S) = 1 - \sum_{s \in S} P(a_s|q, S)$.

Estimation of $P(X|q, S, a)$.

As we showed in Equation 5, we do not necessarily estimate $P(X|q, S, a)$ for all possible X but do estimate $P(i \in X|q, S, a)$ for each intent i. The probability of $P(i \in X|q, S, a)$ is also hard to directly estimate due to the lack of training data, while this probability can be obtained with Bayes' rule:

$$P(i \in X|q, S, a) = \frac{P(a|i \in X, S)P(i \in X|q)}{P(a|q, S)}. \quad (14)$$

The estimate of $P(i \in X|q)$ is $f_{q,i}/f_q$ where $f_{q,i}$ is the frequency of intent set X including i for query q. The probability $P(a|i \in X, S)$ can be transformed into the following:

$$P(a|i \in X, S) = \sum_{X \in 2^I} P(a|X, S)P(X|i \in X), \quad (15)$$

where $P(X|i \in X)$ is the probability of X when the user is known to have intent i. By using the approximation in Equation 12, we can obtain the following solution for $P(a_s|i \in X, S)$:

$$P(a_s|i \in X, S) = p_{\mathrm{QS}} \sum_{k=1}^{|S|} \frac{1}{k} P(s \in X, |S \cap X| = k|i \in X), \quad (16)$$

where $P(s \in X, |S \cap X| = k|i \in X)$ is the probability of X including s and k elements of S conditioned by $i \in X$, which is estimated as $f_{q,i \wedge s,k}/f_{q,i}$ where $f_{q,i \wedge s,k}$ is the frequency of intent sets for query q including i, s, and k elements of S.

In the same way as $P(a|q, S)$, we can obtain$P(a_q|i \in X, S)$ as follows: $P(a_q|i \in X, S) = 1 - \sum_{s \in S} P(a_s|i \in X, S)$.

3.4 Optimization

We describe a method of selecting the optimal query suggestions and retrieving the optimal ranked lists of documents for a given query and each query suggestion. The optimization algorithm is described in Algorithm 1.

The input of this algorithm includes a query q, a set of query suggestion candidates $\mathcal{S}$, and a set of documents $\mathcal{D}$. The algorithm outputs the optimal query suggestions S^* and ranked lists of documents for a given query and each query suggestion $\mathbf{D}^*$. This algorithm iteratively selects a query suggestion that maximizes the expected utility $E[u|q, S, \mathbf{D}]$ when it is added to the query suggestion set. When no query suggestion can improve the expected utility, this algorithm stops and returns the optimal query suggestions that have been selected.

If we can obtain the optimal query suggestions, the optimization problem can be reduced to a problem of finding the optimal ranked list of documents for each action. The greedy algorithm in lines 5-7 can provide the optimal result for DCG. The theoretical lower-bound of a greedy algorithm for ERR-IA, which is $(1 - 1/e)$ times the optimal value, was suggested by Chapelle *et al.* [10]. They used a real dataset to demonstrate that a greedy algorithm can yield results almost equivalent to the optimal results for many cases. This property is also inherited by the joint-intent-aware version of ERR, as both have the same form.

Algorithm 1 Optimization of query suggestions and ranked list of documents

Input: A query q, a set of query suggestion candidates $\mathcal{S}$, and a set of documents $\mathcal{D}$.
Output: Query suggestions S^*, and ranked lists of documents $\mathbf{D}^*$.

1: $E_{\max} = \max_{\mathbf{d}^{(a_q)}} E[u|q, \emptyset, a_q, \mathbf{d}^{(a_q)}]$
2: **for** $k = 1$ to $|\mathcal{S}|$ **do**
3:   **for each** $s \in \mathcal{S}/S^*$ **do**
4:     $S = S^* \cup \{s\}$
5:     $A = \{a_q\} \cup A_S$
6:     **for each** $a \in A$ **do**
7:       /* a greedy algorithm for ranking documents */
8:       **for** $r = 1$ to N **do**
9:         $D = \mathcal{D}/\mathbf{d}^{(a)}$
10:         $d_r^{(a)} = \mathrm{argmax}_{d \in D} E[u|q, S, a, (d_1^{(a)}, \ldots, d_{r-1}^{(a)}, d)]$
11:       **end for**
12:       $\mathbf{d}^{(a)} = (d_1^{(a)}, \ldots, d_{N-1}^{(a)}, d_N^{(a)})$
13:     **end for**
14:     $\mathbf{D} = \{\mathbf{d}^{(a)}\}_{a \in A}$
15:     **if** $E[u|q, S, \mathbf{D}] > E_{\max}$ **then**
16:       $\mathbf{D}^* = \mathbf{D}$
17:       $S^* = S$
18:       $E_{\max} = E[u|q, S^*, \mathbf{D}^*]$
19:     **end if**
20:   **end for**
21:   /* break if none of query suggestion candidates is added */
22:   **if** $k < |S^*|$ **then**
23:     **break**
24:   **end if**
25: **end for**

The complexity of the optimization problem in Equation 2 is at least NP-hard if ERR is used for $E[u|q, S, a, \mathbf{d}^{(a)}]$, since the optimization of ERR-IA is NP-hard [10]. Although the greedy algorithm does not guarantee the optimal solution, the worst case bound of our algorithm is $\max_{\mathbf{d}^{(a_q)}} E[u|q, \emptyset, a_q, \mathbf{d}^{(a_q)}]$, which is the maximum of the expected utility of a single ranked list. Thus, one can use our algorithm ensuring that resultant SERPs including query suggestions are at least better than the optimized SERP without query suggestions. The time complexity of our algorithm is $O(|\mathcal{S}|^3 N |\mathcal{D}| T_{\mathrm{JIA}})$, where T_{JIA} is the number of computations for JIA($\mathbf{d}$). The computation for estimating probabilities $P(a|q, S)$ and $P(X|q, S, a)$ is assumed to be smaller than that for selecting N documents, *i.e.* $|\mathcal{S}|^2 < N|\mathcal{D}|T_{\mathrm{JIA}}$ and $|\mathcal{S}||I| < N|\mathcal{D}|T_{\mathrm{JIA}}$. The time complexity can be reduced by setting the maximum number of query suggestions to be presented in a SERP. By letting M be the maximum number of query suggestions ($M = 5$ in our experiment), the reduced time complexity is $O(|\mathcal{S}|M^2 N|\mathcal{D}|T_{\mathrm{JIA}})$. In our experiments, there are few cases where more than four query suggestions are estimated to be optimal.

4. USER STUDY

We conducted a user study to calibrate the time loss $t_{n,a}$ and rank loss $R(t_{n,a})$ used in joint-intent-aware evaluation metrics. Questions we address here are summarized as follows:

1. When n query suggestions are presented in a SERP, how much additional time do users have to spend to click on the first search result in the SERP?
2. When n query suggestions are presented in a SERP, how much additional time do users have to spend to click on the first search result in another SERP returned in response to a query suggestion?
3. Which rank could users reach in time equivalent to the estimated time loss?

The first question corresponds to calibrating t_{n,a_q}, *i.e.* the time loss for browsing the SERP for the input query when n query suggestions are presented, while the second question corresponds to calibrating t_{n,a_s}, *i.e.* the time loss for browsing a SERP for a query suggestion $s \in S$ when n query suggestions are presented. The last question corresponds to calibrating the rank loss $R(t_{n,a_q})$.

4.1 Settings

We developed a search system that resembles modern commercial search engines, asked experimental participants to complete given tasks, and measured task completion time in different situations. As devices used for searching might affect search completion time, this study was carried out in both *desktop* and *mobile* environments. Figures 3(a) and 3(b) show screenshots of our search systems for different device types. They are conventional ten-blue-link SERPs including a search box, titles, URLs and summaries of Web pages. Query suggestions were placed under the search box and links to verticals. The font size of query suggestions was the same for more than one query suggestion, while a single query suggestion was presented in a similar way as the "Did you mean?" suggestion, and slightly bigger than multiple query suggestions as can be seen in Figure 3(a). Participants were allowed to click on titles of Web pages and query suggestions, but not to type queries or use the other vertical during a task. To measure time spent in SERPs and monitor actions taken during the search, we used a Javascript code used in a study on Web search success prediction [2][1].

Tasks given to participants were to click on a title of a Web page relevant to a specific topic. Eight topics (ID: 105, 108, 116, 137, 377, 303, 338, and 312) were selected from queries used in the NTCIR INTENT-1 and -2 Japanese subtasks [26, 29]. Our topic selection criteria were i) the topic is famous enough to be known by most ordinary users, and ii) the topic is ambiguous or underspecified enough to include at least five subtopics. In addition to the topics, we selected one of the subtopics for each topic, and created an information need for each subtopic. For example, the information need "a recipe using red wine and apples" was created for topic 105 ("red wine") and its subtopic ("red wine cooking"). As another example, the information need "a toy dinosaur museum" was created for topic 312 ("dinosaur") and its subtopic ("dinosaur

[1]http://ir-ub.mathcs.emory.edu/uFindIt/

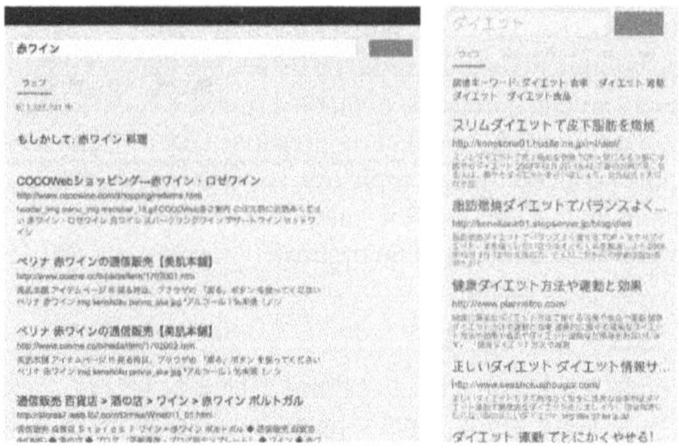

(a) Desktop (b) Mobile

Figure 3: Screenshots of the search system.

museum"). We used information needs so specific that there is only one relevant document in the document collection.

The participants were given an instruction "Please search with search keywords (topic) and find a document that you expect to contain information on (information need) as fast as possible from search results for (topic) or suggested search keywords", where variables (*e.g.* (topic)) were replaced with specific phrases we had prepared. After reading the instruction for a topic, participants could start the search task by clicking on a search button next to a text form containing a topic as a search query. Participants were then shown a SERP for the topic (*e.g.* "red wine") as well as query suggestions including a selected subtopic for the topic (*e.g.* "red wine cooking"). Query suggestions were randomly selected from subtopics of a topic, and always included a subtopic used for creating an information need for the topic. When participants clicked on one of the search results and pressed "OK" for a confirmation dialog box, they could read the instruction for the next topic.

Variables we considered in the user study are i) the number of query suggestions (0, 1, 3, and 5), ii) topics (eight topics explained earlier), and iii) position of relevant documents. We placed relevant documents within one of the four types of positions: **top-top** (the top three ranks in the SERP for a topic as well as the top three ranks in the SERP for the subtopic relevant to a presented information need), **bottom-top** (the bottom three ranks in the SERP for a topic as well as the top three ranks in the SERP for the subtopic relevant to a presented information need), **nowhere-top** (only the top three ranks in the SERP for the subtopic relevant to a presented information need), and **nowhere-bottom** (only the bottom three ranks in the SERP for the subtopic relevant to a presented information need). Note that we did not include top-bottom and bottom-bottom cases simply because a more specific subtopic relevant to a document is unlikely to give a lower score to the relevant document than its topic. Ranks of a relevant document were randomized within a specified rank range (*i.e.* the top three or bottom three ranks) so that participants did not learn the exact position of relevant documents.

We used a within-subject design for the user study, and every participant was subjected to every treatment for each variable. The combinations of treatments were counterbalanced by the Graeco-Latin square. Thus, all the combinations were examined exactly the same number of times, and the number of required participants were $4 \times 8 \times 4 = 128$ for four query suggestions, eight topics, and four types of relevant document positions.

We recruited experiment participants through Lancers[2], one of the most popular crowd-sourcing services in Japan. Each participant was required to complete eight search tasks for eight topics in different settings, and paid 100 JPY for the tasks. As we could monitor their search task accuracy by checking whether they clicked on a relevant document, we rejected participants who clicked on more than two irrelevant documents. Having excluded participants on the basis of their search task accuracy and lack of Javascript support, we obtained user behavior data of 128 participants for each device type (256 in total)[3].

[2]http://www.lancers.jp/

4.2 Calibration

This subsection describes our model of time spent reaching a certain rank in a SERP, and calibration of the time and rank loss.

We assumed that there were two factors affected by the number of query suggestions. One is the time spent assessing query suggestions, *scan time*, while the other is the time spent clicking on one of the query suggestions, *click time*. Thus, we used the following models of time spent before reaching the top ranked search result after taking action a when n query suggestions are presented:

$$t_{n,a} = \begin{cases} T_{\mathrm{scan}}(n) + T_{a_q} & (a = a_q) \\ T_{\mathrm{scan}}(n) + T_{\mathrm{click}}(n) + T_{a_q} + T_{a_s} & (a \in A_S) \end{cases}, \quad (17)$$

where $T_{\mathrm{scan}}(n)$ is the scan time for n query suggestions, $T_{\mathrm{click}}(n)$ is the click time for n query suggestions, T_{a_q} is constant time before reaching the top ranked document in the first SERP, and T_{a_s} is constant time before reaching the top ranked document in a SERP returned in response to a query suggestion. We explored the shape of the functions $T_{\mathrm{scan}}(n)$ and $T_{\mathrm{click}}(n)$ in our preliminary analysis, and found that a linear function ($T_{\mathrm{scan}}(n) = \alpha n$) or an exponential function ($T_{\mathrm{scan}}(n) = \alpha \exp(n)$) fitted the observed data well.

To calibrate each parameter in the models of time spent before reaching the top ranked search result, we also modeled the time spent in a search task in our user study. One possible approach is similar to that used in Smucker and Clarke's work, where *ranks of clicked search results* are included in Equation 17 [28]. We compared several alternatives to their approach and found that ranks of clicked search results could not explain a large amount of the variance in the spent time, while *the length of page scrolls* could explain it far better. Below, we show rank-based and scroll-based models for the time spent doing the search tasks:

$$T_{\mathrm{rank}}(n, a, r) = t_{n,a} + T_r r, \quad (18)$$

$$T_{\mathrm{scroll}}(n, a, l) = t_{n,a} + T_l l, \quad (19)$$

where r is the clicked rank, T_r is the time spent per search result, l is the length of page scrolls, and T_l is the time per scroll length.

Table 1 shows the R-squared of least squares fittings. R-squared is a metric indicating how much variance of an objective variable can be explained by independent variables. The scroll-based models are more appropriate for both desktop and mobile devices than the ranked-based models. In addition, exponential functions for scan and click times were slightly better than linear functions in terms of R-squared. Figure 4 shows the average time spent on the first SERP as a function of the number of query suggestions presented, and also supports that exponential functions are suitable at least for five or fewer query suggestions. Therefore, we employed exponential functions for modeling the scan and click times.

Parameters estimated by using the scroll-based model are listed in Table 2. The estimated coefficient for the scan time was higher than that for the click time in desktop, while the estimated coefficient for the scan time was lower than that for the click time in mobile. These results indicate that presenting query suggestions gives a smaller effect on SERP browsing for mobile users than desktop ones, while clicking on a query suggestion requires more time from

[3]Data available at http://www.mpkato.net/projects/optimizing-search-result-presentation/

Table 1: **R-squared of least squares fittings for different models.**

Model (Eq. No.)	Scan / Click time	R-squared	
		Desktop	Mobile
Rank-based (18)	αn	0.130	0.126
	$\alpha \exp(n)$	0.133	0.126
Scroll-based (19)	αn	0.445	0.440
	$\alpha \exp(n)$	**0.448**	**0.442**

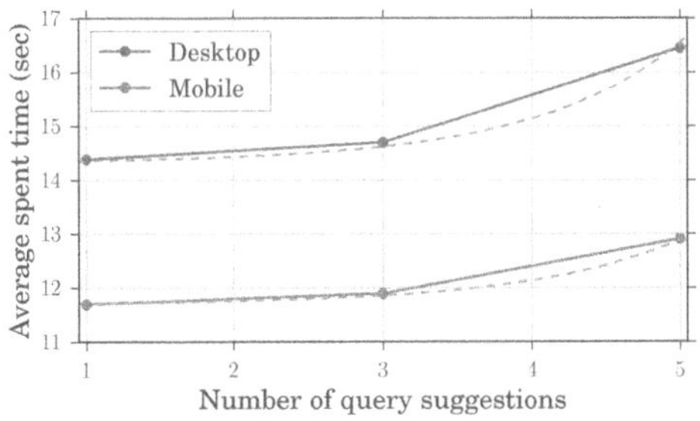

Figure 4: Average time spent at the first SERP as a function of the number of query suggestions presented.

mobile users than desktop ones. They could be explained by studies on desktop and mobile searchers by using eye-tracking devices. Joachims, Granka, and Pan showed that the fixation ratio on summaries of search results decreased in ascending order of ranks [19]. In contrast, Lagun *et al.* reported that mobile users gazed at the second and third search results for a significantly longer time than the first search result [22]. Based on their findings, we could hypothesize that mobile users are more tolerant to query suggestions presented at the top of SERPs than desktop users.

Finally, we calibrate the rank loss $R(t_{n,a})$ by using estimated time spent before reaching the top ranked search result after taking an action, and estimated time spent for reaching a search result at a certain rank without query suggestions presented. The former time could be estimated by using Equation 17, while the latter time could be estimated by using the rank-based model in Equation 18. Figures 5(a) and 5(b) show the estimated time for reaching the top ranked search result after taking actions a_q and a_s as a function of the number of presented query suggestions in desktop and mobile environments, respectively. The horizontal dotted lines represent the estimated time for reaching a certain rank r without query suggestions presented. For desktop users, for example, the time spent for reaching the top ranked search result in the first SERP with four query suggestions presented equals to that for reaching the third search result in the first SERP without query suggestions. We could see large effect of query suggestions on the first SERP browsing (a_q) for desktop users, but little effect for mobile users. We determined the rank loss so that the decay by $R(t_{n,a})$ at the first rank in evaluation metrics became equivalent to that requiring the same time without query suggestions, *i.e.* $t_{n,a} = T_{\text{rank}}(0, a_q, R(t_{n,a}))$. Table 3 summarizes the time and rank loss estimated on the basis of the user study.

5. EXPERIMENTS

In this section, we answer the following research questions based on our experimental results:

RQ1 In which search scenario can the optimization of search result presentation achieve significant improvement?

RQ2 Can the optimization of search result presentation make steady improvement in a practical setting?

RQ3 What kind of queries can benefit from the optimization of search result presentation?

Table 2: Parameters estimated by using the scroll-based model. Note that α_{scan} and α_{click} are parameters in $T_{\text{scan}}(n) = \alpha_{\text{scan}} \exp(n)$ and $T_{\text{click}}(n) = \alpha_{\text{click}} \exp(n)$.

Parameter	Desktop	Mobile
α_{scan}	0.0238 ± 0.0132	0.00191 ± 0.0120
α_{click}	0.0190 ± 0.0180	0.0284 ± 0.0158
T_{a_q}	8.34 ± 1.03	5.95 ± 0.908
T_{a_s}	1.54 ± 1.43	2.47 ± 1.25
T_l	0.00936 ± 0.000385	0.0101 ± 0.000406

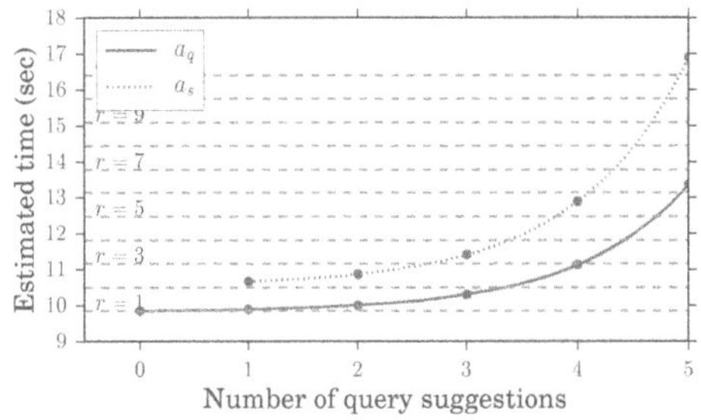

(a) Desktop

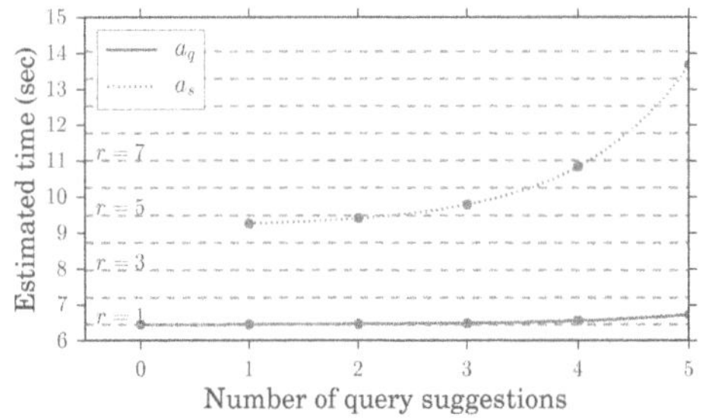

(b) Mobile

Figure 5: Estimated time for reaching the top ranked search result after taking actions a_q and a_s as a function of the number of presented query suggestions. The horizontal dotted lines represent the estimated time for reaching a certain rank r.

5.1 Settings

We utilized two test collections developed in the NTCIR INTENT-1 and -2 Japanese tasks [26, 29]. The NTCIR INTENT-1 Japanese test collection includes 100 ambiguous or underspecified queries, while the INTENT-2 Japanese test collection includes 66 ambiguous or underspecified queries. These test collections also contain subtopics for each query, and per-subtopic graded relevance for a subset of ClueWeb09-JA.

Although the intent probability for each subtopic was available in both of the test collections, we could not obtain the frequency of *intent sets* from each assessor in these two test collections. Thus, we used the crowd-sourcing service, Lancers, to obtain the frequency of intent sets. We showed workers a topic and its subtopics in random order, and asked them to vote for multiple subtopics assuming that they input the topic as a query to a search engine. We gave the workers an instruction "Please vote for multiple topics you would be especially interested in if you input (query) as

Table 3: Time and rank loss for each action with n query suggestions.

	Time t_{n,a_q} (Rank $R(t_{n,a_q})$)		Time t_{n,a_s} (Rank $R(t_{n,a_s})$)	
n	Desktop	Mobile	Desktop	Mobile
1	8.41 (0.0624)	5.95 (0.00431)	10.0 (2.50)	8.50 (3.35)
2	8.51 (0.232)	5.96 (0.0160)	10.2 (2.81)	8.64 (3.53)
3	8.82 (0.693)	5.99 (0.0479)	10.8 (3.64)	9.03 (4.05)
4	9.64 (1.95)	6.05 (0.135)	12.2 (5.89)	10.1 (5.41)
5	11.9 (5.36)	6.23 (0.370)	16.2 (12.0)	12.9 (9.15)

a search keyword", where "(query)" was replaced with an actual query in the test collections. We assigned 20 workers for each topic, and used resultant data for estimating probabilities $P(a|q, S)$ and $P(X|q, S, a)$ as we explained in Section 3[3]. The only parameter that we have in our optimization method but did not estimate from the user study was p_{QS}, a probability of clicking on a query suggestion when it is only an intent relevant to the user. Thus, we tested our method with different values for p_{QS} in our experiments.

We used DCG, ERR, and TBG with cutoff parameter $N = 10$ for the optimization and evaluation. The expected time used in TBG is defined as follows:

$$T_i(r) = \sum_{r'=1}^{r-1} T_S + T_D(r')P(C = 1|R = g_i(r')). \quad (20)$$

Time to evaluate the snippet of a search result, $T_S = 4.4$, and time to judge document at rank r, $T_D(r) = 0.018 \cdot \mathrm{len}(r) + 7.8$ ($\mathrm{len}(r)$ is the number of words in the document), were calibrated on the basis of desktop search tasks in English [28]. As we used Japanese documents in our experiments, $T_D(r)$ was slightly modified by reference to statistics that the average reading speed is 300 words per minute in English and 500 words per minute in Japanese. Therefore, we used the following settings in a desktop environment, *i.e.* $T_S = 4.4$ and $T_D(r) = 0.011 \cdot \mathrm{len}(r) + 7.8$. We changed the settings in a mobile environment based on the time spent per search result in the user study: $T_r = 0.66$ for desktop and $T_r = 0.76$ for mobile. We simply multiplied the time parameters by the ratio 0.76/0.66, *i.e.* $T_S = 5.1$ and $T_D(r) = 0.013 \cdot \mathrm{len}(r) + 9.1$. The document length $\mathrm{len}(r)$ was set to 1,500 for convenience, which was the average document length in the test collections. We also made small changes in TBG to deal with graded relevance. The gain in TBG was defined as $G_i(r) = 0.493 g_i(r)$, and probability of click on a relevant snippet, $P(C = 1|R = g_i(r))$, was set to 0.64 if $g_i(r) > 0$; otherwise, 0.39. Thus, we assumed that the gain is proportional to the relevance grade, and probability of click on a snippet is constant for non-zero relevance grades.

The three evaluation metrics, DCG, ERR, and TBG, have different characteristics, and may be suitable for evaluation in different scenarios. When we use $\beta = 2$ for DCG (the base of the logarithm) and $h = 224$ for TBG (the half-life of users), ERR exhibits the highest top-heaviness, while TBG exhibits the lowest top-heaviness. The top-heaviness is possibly measured by the rank at which the evaluation metric reduces the gain to half in the case where no relevant search results appears: 2 for ERR, 3 for DCG, and approximately 18/15 in desktop/mobile scenarios for TBG. Thus, ERR may reflect very impatient users, while TBG may represent patient users who can continue search for a long time. In our experiments, we report results with these three evaluation metrics, and discuss scenarios where the optimization of search result presentation was effective.

We tested our optimization algorithm with two systems. One is *oracle* system in which we utilized the ground truth of joint intent probability and per-subtopic graded relevance for demonstrating the characteristics of our optimization method. Another is *practical* system where we estimated the joint intent probability and per-subtopic graded relevance. To estimate the joint intent probability, we used Bing Search API[4] to retrieve top 100 Web documents returned in response to each query, regarded the appearance of a term included in a subtopic as a *vote*, and obtained an intent set from each document. The rest of the estimation was the same as that based on a crowd-sourcing service. We trained a regressor by using the per-subtopic graded relevance of 66 queries used in NTCIR INTENT-2, and predicted the per-subtopic graded relevance of 100 queries used in NTCIR INTENT-1. Thus, only 100 queries were used in the experiments with the practical system. We used gradient boosted regression trees (GBRT) as a regressor, since it has been shown to be reasonably effective in a learning to rank challenge [9]. We extracted seven types of features that have been frequently used for learning to rank [24], from each pair of (subtopic, title), (subtopic, body), and (subtopic, title and body). The features included the length of text, number of subtopic terms included, sum of the frequency of subtopic terms, TF-IDF score, BM25 score, and language model scores with Dirichlet and Jelinek-Mercer smoothing methods. The details of the features are described in our dataset[3]. The best parameters for GBRT were determined by 3-fold cross validation with the NTCIR INTENT-2 test collection. We regarded subtopics as queries and evaluated the accuracy of the predicted per-subtopic relevance grades by normalized DCG. The best single feature, a TF-IDF score for the subtopic-body pair, achieve 0.189, while GBRT achieved 0.297.

5.2 Experimental Results

RQ1 In which search scenario can the optimization of search result presentation achieve significant improvement?

Table 4 shows the improvement by the optimization of search result presentation with the oracle system, and percentage of queries for which n query suggestions were estimated to be the best. The improvement was defined as the percent increase from the optimized single ranked list to those with query suggestions in terms of a certain evaluation metric, *i.e.* $100 \cdot (E[u|q, S^*, \mathbf{D}^*] - E[u|q, \emptyset, a_q, \mathbf{d}^{(a_q)*}]) / E[u|q, \emptyset, a_q, \mathbf{d}^{(a_q)*}]$, where asterisks indicate that the search results and query suggestions were optimized by Algorithm 1. Note that the improvement was averaged over queries for which our optimization algorithm decided to present query suggestions. When we used DCG or TBG as an evaluation metric, our optimization could achieve significant improvement in both of the devices, and even with a small probability of clicking on a query suggestion (*e.g.* $P_{\mathrm{QS}} = 0.25$). While one or two query suggestions were estimated to be the best for DCG, two or more query suggestions were the best for TBG. Moreover, query suggestions were presented for many queries when TBG was used. On the other hand, presenting query suggestions was estimated to be ineffective when ERR was used: very small or no improvement can be seen in any settings. As we discussed earlier, ERR is suitable for measuring the satisfaction of impatient users, while TBG is suitable for patient, careful users. Therefore, we can hypothesize that the optimization of search result presentation was helpful for users who want to carefully gather information and can spend a long time, while it might be disrupting for users who want to quickly find a single answer.

Figure 6 shows the effect of the half-life in TBG with $p_{\mathrm{QS}} = 1$. The x-axis indicates ranks at which the gain was reduced to half by used half-life parameters when no relevant result appears, and y-axis indicates the improvement by the search result presentation

[4]https://datamarket.azure.com/dataset/bing/search

Table 4: Improvement by the optimization of search result presentation for different values for p_{QS}. Significant differences at $\alpha = 0.05$ are indicated by bold font and asterisks (*).

Device (Metric)	p_{QS}	Gain (%)	Cohen's d	% of queries for which n QSs were the best				
				1	2	3	4	5
Desktop (ERR)	0.25	N/A	N/A	0	0	0	0	0
	0.50	N/A	N/A	0	0	0	0	0
	0.75	0.21	N/A	0.60	0	0	0	0
	1.00	2.51	N/A	0.60	0	0	0	0
Desktop (DCG)	0.25	**1.18***	2.44	4.20	0	0	0	0
	0.50	**2.02***	0.97	13.3	0	0	0	0
	0.75	**3.77***	1.21	15.1	0	0	0	0
	1.00	**4.66***	1.11	18.7	1.20	0	0	0
Desktop (TBG)	0.25	**1.84***	1.34	7.20	39.8	38.6	7.80	0
	0.50	**3.81***	1.37	8.40	34.3	36.1	14.5	0.60
	0.75	**5.95***	1.39	10.8	33.1	32.5	17.5	0.60
	1.00	**9.23***	1.51	12.7	30.1	36.1	15.7	0.60
Mobile (ERR)	0.25	0.33	3.20	1.20	0	0	0	0
	0.50	1.18	2.96	1.20	0	0	0	0
	0.75	0.49	0.90	3.60	0	0	0	0
	1.00	**0.56***	0.79	6.60	0	0	0	0
Mobile (DCG)	0.25	**0.77***	0.88	21.1	3.00	0	0	0
	0.50	**1.66***	0.92	21.7	4.20	0	0	0
	0.75	**2.72***	0.99	21.1	4.80	0.60	0	0
	1.00	**3.84***	1.02	21.7	5.40	0.60	0	0
Mobile (TBG)	0.25	**1.90***	1.36	6.60	20.5	39.8	24.1	2.40
	0.50	**3.86***	1.38	6.60	23.5	37.3	22.9	3.00
	0.75	**5.91***	1.38	11.4	28.3	29.5	23.5	1.80
	1.00	**9.19***	1.50	12.0	26.5	33.1	21.1	1.80

optimization with 95% confidence intervals. For example, $x = 3$ indicates $h = 27.5$ (desktop) and 31.7 (mobile), by which the gain at the third rank was reduced to half. As we expected, the improvement decreased as the half-life decreased, yet it was still large even at $x = 3$. This suggests that our optimization is effective in desktop or mobile environments even if we assume that half of the users stop reading a SERP after 27.5 or 31.7 (sec).

In summary, our optimization could achieve significant improvement when we assume that users are moderately patient (*i.e.* ones expected in DCG and TBG). The more patient users are, the more effectively search engines can improve the expected utility of such users by several query suggestions.

RQ2 Can the optimization of search result presentation make steady improvement in a practical setting?

Figure 6 shows the improvement by the oracle and practical systems. Each of six areas in the figure shows results with different metrics and devices. Significant improvement by the practical system was indicated by an asterisk ($\alpha = 0.05$). While the optimization with ERR (left) failed to improve the expected utility, the optimization with DCG (center) and TBG (right) could achieve steady improvement. Although the TBG-based optimization could achieve limited improvement, the DCG-based optimization seems robust to the error in the intent probability and per-subtopic relevance grades. One possible explanation is the risk of presenting search results relevant to a specific intent. The relevance estimation possibly failed for a certain type of intents. For example, documents relevant to a certain type of intents may not include terms in their subtopic, and *vice versa*. The risk of presenting many irrelevant search results in a SERP, therefore, can increase as the number of presented query suggestions increases. Thus, it is possible that a method likely to suggest many queries, *i.e.* the TBG-based optimization, shows lower performance when the estimation of intent probability and relevance grades is not accurate.

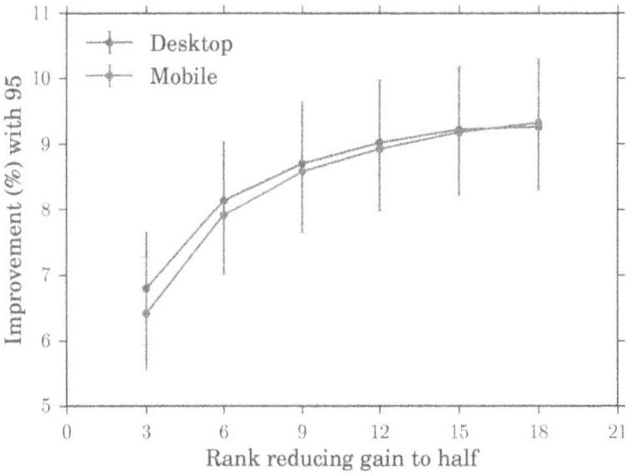

Figure 6: Improvement by the optimization with TBG as a function of the rank at which the gain is reduced to half.

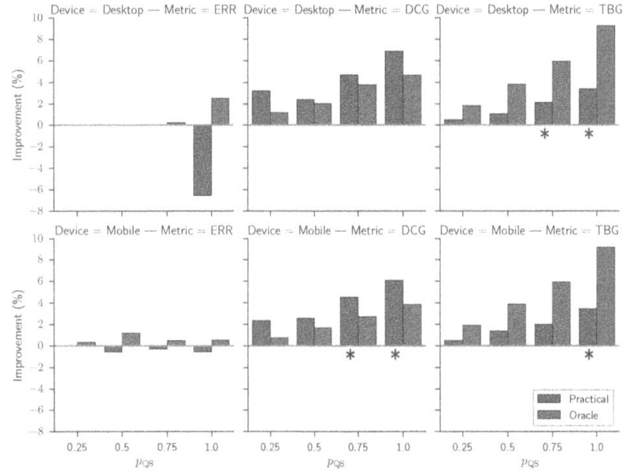

Figure 7: Improvement by the oracle and practical systems. Significant improvement by the practical system was indicated by asterisks ($\alpha = 0.05$).

RQ3 What kind of queries can benefit from the optimization of search result presentation?

Intuitively, the optimization with query suggestions should work effectively if we could decrease the uncertainty of intents by presenting query suggestions. To investigate this intuition, we measured *expected relative entropy* of intents, and examined the correlation between the improvement and entropy.

Figure 8 shows the improvement by the oracle system using TBG and $p_{QS} = 1$ in the desktop setting as a function of the expected relative entropy, which was computed as follows:

$$E[H] = \sum_{i \in I} P(i \in X|q)(H[X] - H[X|i \in X]) \qquad (21)$$

where $H[X] = -\sum_{i \in I} P(i \in X) \log P(i \in X)$ and $H[X|i \in X] = -\sum_{j \in I} P(j \in X|i \in X) \log P(j \in X|i \in X)$. The expected relative entropy reflects the expectation of the amount of information that can be obtained when one knows a user has an intent. Thus, high expected relative entropy indicates that an intent often co-occurs with not all, but a small subset of intents. We can see medium positive correlation between the performance improvement and expected relative entropy ($r = 0.528$, $p < 0.01$). Some of the most improved topics were indicated in Figure 8:

ID: 159 "Iseya" a popular and traditional name for kabuki actors, restaurants, or confectionery shops including 18 diverse subtopics.

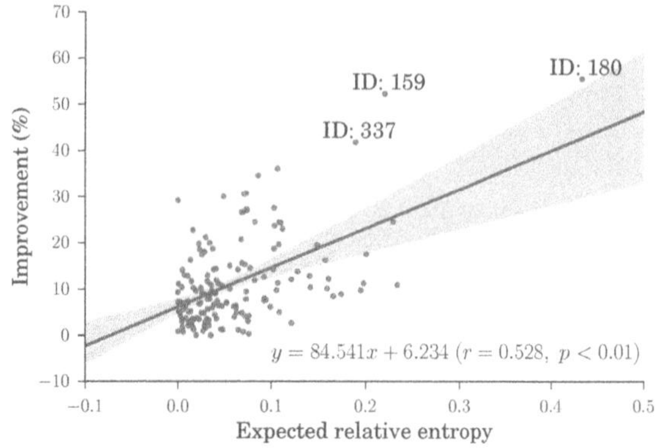

Figure 8: Improvement by the optimization with TBG as a function of the expected relative entropy.

ID: 180 "Tachibana high school" a name for totally different high schools in Japan.

ID: 337 "kiwi" an underspecified query including "lose weight", "buy", "cultivation", and "alcohol" intents, all of which do not often co-occur with the others.

As indicated by the correlation coefficient and examples, our optimization can improve the expected utility especially for queries whose intents do not often co-occur with the others, or co-occur with a small subset of intents.

6. CONCLUSIONS

We proposed a method of optimizing search result presentation for an ambiguous or underspecified query. We developed a searcher model interacting with query suggestions in accordance with their multiple intents, conducted a user study to examine the effects of query suggestions on search behaviors, and calibrated parameters used in the searcher model. Our experiments demonstrated the effectiveness of the search result presentation optimization, and showed that the optimization was effective especially for patient users and queries with a limited number of intents. Our future work includes experiments with real users, and integration of query suggestion generation and search result presentation optimization.

7. ACKNOWLEDGEMENTS

This work was supported in part by the following projects: Grants-in-Aid for Scientific Research (Nos. 25240050, 15H01718, and 26700009) from MEXT of Japan, and Microsoft Research CORE Project.

8. REFERENCES

[1] Statcounter global stats. Retrieved January 14, 2015, from http://gs.statcounter.com/#desktop+mobile-comparison-ww-monthly-201312-201412.

[2] M. Ageev, Q. Guo, D. Lagun, and E. Agichtein. Find it if you can: a game for modeling different types of web search success using interaction data. In *SIGIR*, pages 345–354, 2011.

[3] R. Agrawal, S. Gollapudi, A. Halverson, and S. Ieong. Diversifying search results. In *WSDM*, pages 5–14, 2009.

[4] A. Anagnostopoulos, L. Becchetti, C. Castillo, and A. Gionis. An optimization framework for query recommendation. In *WSDM*, pages 161–170, 2010.

[5] F. Baskaya, H. Keskustalo, and K. Järvelin. Time drives interaction: simulating sessions in diverse searching environments. In *SIGIR*, pages 105–114, 2012.

[6] C. Brandt, T. Joachims, Y. Yue, and J. Bank. Dynamic ranked retrieval. In *WSDM*, pages 247–256, 2011.

[7] J. Carbonell and J. Goldstein. The use of mmr, diversity-based reranking for reordering documents and producing summaries. In *SIGIR*, pages 335–336, 1998.

[8] B. Carterette and P. Chandar. Probabilistic models of ranking novel documents for faceted topic retrieval. In *CIKM*, pages 1287–1296, 2009.

[9] O. Chapelle and Y. Chang. Yahoo! learning to rank challenge overview. In *Yahoo! Learning to Rank Challenge*, pages 1–24, 2011.

[10] O. Chapelle, S. Ji, C. Liao, E. Velipasaoglu, L. Lai, and S.-L. Wu. Intent-based diversification of web search results: metrics and algorithms. *Information Retrieval*, 14(6):572–592, 2011.

[11] O. Chapelle, D. Metlzer, Y. Zhang, and P. Grinspan. Expected reciprocal rank for graded relevance. In *CIKM*, pages 621–630, 2009.

[12] H. Chen and D. R. Karger. Less is more: probabilistic models for retrieving fewer relevant documents. In *SIGIR*, pages 429–436, 2006.

[13] H. Cui, J.-R. Wen, J.-Y. Nie, and W.-Y. Ma. Query expansion by mining user logs. *IEEE TKDE*, 15(4):829–839, 2003.

[14] Z. Dou, S. Hu, K. Chen, R. Song, and J.-R. Wen. Multi-dimensional search result diversification. In *WSDM*, pages 475–484, 2011.

[15] M. D. Dunlop. Time, relevance and interaction modelling for information retrieval. In *SIGIR Forum*, volume 31, pages 206–213, 1997.

[16] J. He, V. Hollink, and A. de Vries. Combining implicit and explicit topic representations for result diversification. In *SIGIR*, pages 851–860, 2012.

[17] K. Järvelin and J. Kekäläinen. Cumulated gain-based evaluation of ir techniques. *ACM TOIS*, 20(4):422–446, 2002.

[18] K. Järvelin, S. L. Price, L. M. L. Delcambre, and M. L. Nielsen. Discounted cumulated gain based evaluation of multiple-query ir sessions. In *ECIR*, pages 4–15, 2008.

[19] T. Joachims, L. Granka, B. Pan, H. Hembrooke, and G. Gay. Accurately interpreting clickthrough data as implicit feedback. In *SIGIR*, pages 154–161, 2005.

[20] M. P. Kato, T. Sakai, and K. Tanaka. Structured query suggestion for specialization and parallel movement: effect on search behaviors. In *WWW*, pages 389–398, 2012.

[21] M. P. Kato, T. Yamamoto, H. Ohshima, and K. Tanaka. Investigating users' query formulations for cognitive search intents. In *SIGIR*, pages 577–586, 2014.

[22] D. Lagun, C.-H. Hsieh, D. Webster, and V. Navalpakkam. Towards better measurement of attention and satisfaction in mobile search. In *SIGIR*, pages 113–122, 2014.

[23] S. Liang, Z. Ren, and M. de Rijke. Fusion helps diversification. In *SIGIR*, pages 303–312, 2014.

[24] T.-Y. Liu, J. Xu, T. Qin, W. Xiong, and H. Li. Letor: Benchmark dataset for research on learning to rank for information retrieval. In *SIGIR 2007 workshop on learning to rank for information retrieval*, pages 3–10, 2007.

[25] F. Radlinski, R. Kleinberg, and T. Joachims. Learning diverse rankings with multi-armed bandits. In *ICML*, pages 784–791, 2008.

[26] T. Sakai, Z. Dou, T. Yamamoto, Y. Liu, M. Zhang, R. Song, M. P. Kato, and M. Iwata. Overview of the NTCIR-10 INTENT-2 Task. In *NTCIR-10*, 2013.

[27] R. L. Santos, C. Macdonald, and I. Ounis. Exploiting query reformulations for web search result diversification. In *WWW*, pages 881–890, 2010.

[28] M. D. Smucker and C. L. Clarke. Time-based calibration of effectiveness measures. In *SIGIR*, pages 95–104, 2012.

[29] R. Song, M. Zhang, T. Sakai, M. P. Kato, Y. Liu, M. Sugimoto, Q. Wang, and N. Orii. Overview of the NTCIR-9 INTENT Task. In *the 9th NTCIR Workshop Meeting on Evaluation of Information Access Technologies (NTCIR-9)*, pages 82–105, 2011.

[30] H.-T. Yu and F. Ren. Search result diversification via filling up multiple knapsacks. In *CIKM*, pages 609–618, 2014.

[31] C. X. Zhai, W. W. Cohen, and J. Lafferty. Beyond independent relevance: methods and evaluation metrics for subtopic retrieval. In *SIGIR*, pages 10–17, 2003.

[32] Y. Zhu, Y. Lan, J. Guo, X. Cheng, and S. Niu. Learning for search result diversification. In *SIGIR*, pages 293–302, 2014.

Term-by-Term Query Auto-Completion for Mobile Search

Saúl Vargas*
University of Glasgow
Glasgow, UK
saul.vargas@glasgow.ac.uk

Roi Blanco
Yahoo Labs
London, UK
roi@yahoo-inc.com

Peter Mika
Yahoo Labs
London, UK
pmika@yahoo-inc.com

ABSTRACT

With the ever increasing usage of mobile search, where text input is typically slow and error-prone, assisting users to formulate their queries contributes to a more satisfactory search experience. Query auto-completion (QAC) techniques, which predict possible completions for user queries, are the archetypal example of query assistance and are present in most search engines. We argue, however, that classic QAC, which operates by suggesting whole-query completions, may be sub-optimal for the case of mobile search as the available screen real estate to show suggestions is limited and editing is typically slower than in desktop search. In this paper we propose the idea of term-by-term QAC, which is a new technique inspired by predictive keyboards that suggests to the user one term at a time, instead of whole-query completions. We describe an efficient mechanism to implement this technique and an adaptation of a prior user model to evaluate the effectiveness of both standard and term-by-term QAC approaches using query log data. Our experiments with a mobile query log from a commercial search engine show the validity of our approach according to this user model with respect to saved characters, saved terms and examination effort. Finally, a user study provides further insights about our term-by-term technique compared with standard QAC with respect to the variables analyzed in the query log-based evaluation and additional variables related to the successfulness, the speed of the interactions and the properties of the submitted queries.

Categories and Subject Descriptors: H.3.3 [Information Storage & Retrieval]: Query Formulation

Keywords: query auto completion, word prediction, user models, query logs

1. INTRODUCTION

Query Auto-Completion (QAC) is a widely known and deployed mechanism that facilitates the task of formulating queries in search engines. In its basic version, a QAC mechanism presents to the user possible completions for the query the user is entering. In more elaborated cases, QAC techniques can also rephrase and correct some parts of the query that the user has already typed. Completions for queries are typically based on previous queries that have been submitted to the search engine, although some QAC systems are capable of constructing new queries that are adapted to the search context of the user [4, 22]. QAC has attracted an increasing level of interest from the research community with proposals that take into account personalization, context, time-awareness and user behavior in QAC systems.

Assisting users to formulate their queries becomes fundamental in the context of mobile search. The use of search engines in mobile devices such as smartphones and tablets has experienced a rapid growth in the last years [13]. Text input in mobile devices is generally much slower and clumsier than in traditional desktop environments. Therefore, QAC can be considered, in principle, even more useful in the context of mobile search. We argue however that classical QAC mechanisms give sub-optimal results in such context, as their direct adaptation to mobile search disregards problems related to the smaller screen real estate and the slower and clumsier text input and editing in mobile devices.

In this paper we propose a novel QAC mechanism in which the system suggests to the user one term at a time, rather than whole-query completions. We believe that this method is more suited to mobile search as it allows a faster exploration of suggestions and it adapts better to the particularities of text editing in mobile devices. This idea is inspired by the word prediction mechanisms present in predictive keyboards available in major mobile operating systems. Based on this, we describe a term-by-term QAC system implemented using a query-term graph, a data structure that allows the efficient storage and exploitation of query log data. We also adapt a prior user model for QAC to design effectiveness metrics for both standard and term-by-term QAC in offline evaluations.

Our proposal is tested under two different experimental settings. In the first setting, metrics based on a user model for QAC are used to evaluate data from the mobile query log of a commercial search engine following standard evaluation methodologies. In the second, we conduct a user study which compares our approach with standard QAC for the formulation of queries for a series of search tasks and provides insights into the validity of our proposal in terms of different user-engagement measures.

The rest of the paper is structured as follows. Section 2 reviews the related work on mobile search, query auto-

*Currently in Mendeley Ltd., London, UK.

WSDM 2016, February 22 - 25, 2016, San Francisco, CA, USA

ACM 978-1-4503-3716-8/16/02 ...$15.00.
DOI: http://dx.doi.org/10.1145/2835776.2835813

completion and word prediction. In Section 3 we provide a discussion of the inconveniences of standard QAC in mobile search and the advantages that a term-by-term QAC mechanism might bring. A system for term-by-term QAC based on a structure called query-term graph is presented in Section 4. Metrics to measure the effectiveness with respect to saved terms and examination effort of the standard and our new QAC methods are provided in Section 5. In Section 6 we present and discuss two different experimental settings that have been carried out to validate our idea. Finally, Section 7 offers the conclusions and future work.

2. RELATED WORK

This Section presents prior research related to our proposal. First, we comment on studies that have analyzed the characteristics of queries submitted from mobile devices. We review then the literature on QAC, for which we present a new technique. Finally, we briefly discuss the literature on word prediction, which inspired part of our work.

2.1 Mobile Search

In the last decade, a number of studies have been dedicated to understanding the trends and search behavior in mobile search, focusing particularly on the differences between desktop and mobile search regarding topics and characteristics of search sessions and queries.

For example, the work of Kamvar and Baluja [16] presents the analysis of Google search logs from 2005 in the US. Their study shows, among other interesting results, that better text input capabilities in mobile devices result in longer queries and that search sessions are sensibly shorter (1.6 queries per session) than in desktop search (>2 queries per session). In a more recent study, Kamvar and Baluja [17] show the evolution of search behavior over time by analyzing search logs from 2007. This study indicates an increase in the length of queries (from 2.3 mean terms per query in 2005 to 2.7 in 2007) and in the percentage of queries with one accepted result (from 10% to 50%). In both studies, adult content is the most popular content category for mobile searchers.

Baeza-Yates et al. [2] compared the characteristics of mobile and desktop queries submitted to the Yahoo Japan search engine in 2006. Among other observations, the authors found a close correspondence between the number of terms of queries in both scenarios, but a larger discrepancy between the number of characters per query (7.9 in desktop and 9.6 in mobile). They also showed that online shopping, health and sports are the most popular search topics in that market.

Church et al. [8] analyzed the search habits of European users in 2005, revealing several specific details about their search patterns. For example, they report that 23% of the queries are modifications of previously submitted queries, of which half of them correspond to single term substitutions. Later on, the same authors extended in [7] their study by including a much larger sample of queries and an analysis of click-through data from Google mobile search.

Studying the particular nuances of mobile user behavior might yield improvements in mobile search. For instance, Song et al. [26] introduced a study performed on the Bing mobile search engine in 2012. Based on their results regarding the search behavior in terms of time distribution, search locality, query categories and other characteristics, the authors proposed a new framework to improve ranking on mobile search by incorporating mobile-specific features and transferring knowledge from desktop search relevance to mobile search.

2.2 Query Auto-Completion

Query auto-completion systems have attracted an increasing level of interest by both the research community and industry. Data for such systems comes from past user queries. In its simplest variant, QAC algorithms rank completions by their popularity in the past, an algorithm which we refer to as most-popular completion [3] throughout this work. However, recent research has focused on going beyond such basic mechanisms and taking into account the search context and the preferences of users. For example, Bar-Yossef and Kraus [3] proposed a context-sensitive QAC algorithm that considers the current browsing session in order to suggest completions related to the topics of the session. Shokouhi and Radinsky [25] presented a time-sensitive approach in which query suggestions are ranked by *forecasted* frequency adapted to the moment the query is formulated, instead of being ranked by their past frequency. In a similar direction, Whiting and Jose [27] have proposed a QAC method that takes into account query recency and emergence as improvements over plain time-independent query frequency. Additionally, user demographics have been considered by Shokouhi [24] to personalize the ranking of query suggestions. In our proposal, we take a different research direction in which, instead of improving QAC in terms of personalization, context and time-awareness, we propose a novel manner of suggesting query predictions that is better adapted to the characteristics of mobile devices.

Following a different research direction, other authors have studied how users interact with QAC systems as a way to provide better measurements of the effectiveness of such systems. For example, Kamvar and Baluja [18] studied how users interact with QAC systems in mobile search and, as a result, reported interesting usage patterns. Kharitonov et al. [19] proposed a user model for QAC based on cascade-based metrics [6]. By learning the model parameters from a query log of Yandex, the authors derive two different metrics for the evaluation of QAC effectiveness that show a higher correlation with success rate than prior metrics proposed for the task. Li et al. [20] proposed a two-dimensional click model that, instead of being used to evaluate the effectiveness of QAC systems, is used to improve the ranking of suggestions. The query log-based evaluation of our proposal is based on these two previous papers. Finally, Mitra et al. [21] and Hofmann et al. [14] studied user interactions with the QAC system of Bing. Our user study adapts some of the metrics for query formulation analyzed in [14].

2.3 Word Prediction

Word prediction technologies focus on the tasks of completing or predicting the next word in general text input. Darragh et al. [9] described an early proposal of this technology based on a new interface that partially automates typed input and increases the speed and ease of text input. Research on word prediction has typically been oriented towards assisting users with disabilities [12]. However, with the widespread adoption of mobile devices, this technology has experimented a massive adoption with the so-called predictive keyboards, present nowadays in modern mobile operating systems [23], where word prediction is one of the most relevant features. The success of predictive keyboards is the main motivation for our proposal for term-by-term QAC.

3. APPLYING NEXT-TERM PREDICTION TO QUERY AUTO-COMPLETION

Mobile search, despite its ever increasing usage, is limited by the characteristics of text input and display of mobile platforms. Specifically, text input in mobile devices such as smartphones and tablets is generally much slower and clumsier than in personal computers, as users have to rely on smaller, on-screen keyboards. Moreover, text display is also limited by the comparably smaller screen real estate of mobile devices, which further complicates text input and editing especially in single-line search boxes as long queries may not be displayed completely and text selection is, by our own experience, a difficult task in such devices. In order to facilitate the task of query formulation in such scenario, we identify two types of technologies that help users formulate queries in mobile search.

On the one hand, QAC techniques are the archetypal system for query formulation assistance, which, in principle, could be considered even more useful in mobile search than in the case of desktop search given the previously described limitations for entering text in smartphones and tablets. We find however that suggesting to the users completions for whole queries may be sub-optimal in this case, as we identify a number of problems related with the described characteristics of text input and display in mobile devices after having tested the mobile versions of several commercial web search engines, such as Bing, Yahoo and Google. These problems can be summarized as follows:

- Given the limited screen real estate (notably in the case of smartphones), QAC systems are restricted to show a small set of query completions and, moreover, when a completion does not fit in a single line, the explored interfaces of web search engines take one the following sub-optimal approaches: showing a fragment of the completions (thus making more difficult its reading) or display them in several lines (so that less different completions are shown at the same time).
- Text reading in mobile devices is cumbersome as well, so one can expect that users would have to spend some time to evaluate whole-query suggestions, which ultimately leads to ignoring the suggestions.
- The user may not be interested in the exact whole completion, but a fraction or a variation of it. However, as previously pointed out, text editing in mobile interfaces (especially in the general case of touchscreens) is generally a clumsy process and users may be reluctant to accept partially relevant suggestions that would require editing.

On the other hand, term prediction systems, which are a related but different technology that is applied to generic text input in mobile devices, have been found to be a useful feature implemented by predictive keyboards to cope with the aforementioned problems for general text input in mobile devices. Such systems provide two types of predictions: current term prediction, in which the keyboard shows completions for the term that the user is typing, and next term prediction, in which a small number of suggested terms (typically three) are presented to the user as possible next terms after the last term entered by the user. In this work, we are interested specifically in the second type of prediction. Next term predictions, as found in predictive keyboards, are typically based on common sequences of words that may take into account the writing patterns of the users and other data such as address books, thus not being specifically crafted for the purpose of query formulation. The success of next term prediction technologies in predictive keyboards is manifested by their inclusion as default input methods in all major mobile operative systems and also in the app markets of these, where the number of installations of alternative predictive keyboard apps are counted by millions.

We propose in this work a method for query formulation assistance that lies at the intersection of QAC and next term prediction. The idea is to re-define QAC by suggesting, rather than whole completions, one term at a time to formulate the intended query. Note that we do not propose to replace QAC by predictive keyboards, but to re-purpose algorithms for standard QAC algorithms to provide completions based on single terms. We believe that this approach, that we refer to as term-by-term QAC, solves the limitations found for standard QAC for the following reasons:

- As only single terms are suggested to the users, space limitations are drastically reduced.
- The time required to read suggested terms is significantly smaller than in the case of whole completions, which should increase the usage of such technologies and shorter interaction times.
- As only one term at a time is presented to the user, problems related with editing suggestions are also partly solved, as the need of editing the suggestion will be generally smaller and, even in that case, editing the suggestion will require less effort than editing whole completions.

As already pointed out, a term prediction mechanism deals with two closely related but different prediction tasks: completing the current term and predicting the next one. In order to simplify our analysis, in this study we focus exclusively on the second case. Focusing on the second case is reasonable as prior studies have found that QAC systems have a higher chance of being used after complete terms have been entered [20, 21]. Moreover, current term completion can also be seen as a special case of next term prediction, meaning that the conclusions of focusing on one type of prediction can be generalized to the other.

4. THE QUERY-TERM GRAPH

We now propose an efficient method to implement a term-by-term QAC system based on previous queries submitted to a search engine. Relying on previous queries is a standard way of implementing QAC by major search engines [3] and most proposals from the state of the art follow this approach [15, 24, 25, 27]. In particular, our solution makes use of queries gathered from a commercial search engine and stores them in a graph structure that we refer to as query-term graph, which allows an efficient way of storing and retrieving millions of queries. We describe next our query-term graph, a procedure to build it from previously submitted queries and two algorithms for suggesting the most popular completion in standard and term-by-term QAC.

4.1 Definition

The query-term graph is a directed, weighted graph that stores millions of queries in a compact way. It is composed of three types of nodes: a unique root node with no incoming edges that represents the start of every query, intermediate nodes that contain query terms and end-of-query nodes with no outgoing edges that mark the end of a query. All the paths of the query-term graph starting from the root node

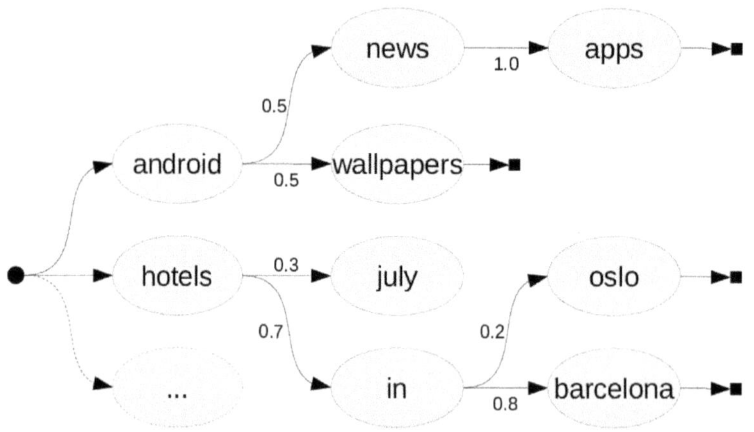

Figure 1: Example of a query-term graph. The root node (circle) is located on the left, the query terms occupy intermediate positions and the leaf nodes (squares) mark the end of queries.

and ending in a leaf node represent queries that the QAC system can provide as completions. Each edge has a weight that represents the probability of the paths that contain it to be the completions of the sub-path that starts from the root node and ends in the source node of the edge. See Figure 1 for an example of a query-term graph. In this example, we can see that queries such as `android news apps` and `hotels in oslo` are stored in the graph as paths from the root to leaf nodes.

Although the query-term graph has some resemblance with the well-known tries [11], it has significant differences nonetheless. First, the intermediate nodes of our graph store terms rather than characters. Second, ours is a weighted graph as we need weights to calculate the likelihood of completions. Third, our query-term graph is not necessarily restricted to a tree-like structure since we may allow intermediate nodes to share branches. That can be useful, for instance, when different starting terms share many suffixes, such as the case of synonyms or entities of the same category. See Figure 2 for an example of two nodes having common branches. In this case, both `android` and `iphone` share suffixes such as `apps` or `wallpapers`.

4.2 Construction

The construction of a query-term graph using a query log can be costly since millions of queries need to be processed and added to this structure. We briefly detail here the steps involved in an efficient procedure for building a query-term graph for millions of queries submitted to a commercial search engine. To illustrate the process, we consider the small example of a query log in Table 1 that generates the query-term graph of Figure 1.

In its most simple configuration, such as to implement algorithms to provide the most-popular completion that we detail in the next section, only the set of submitted queries in the query log is required. After an initial pre-processing to discard anomalous queries and queries composed of only one term – which our term-by-term mechanism has no use for –, a first step involves counting the number of times each unique query has been repeated. After that, we determine the structure of the query-term graph by identifying all the different paths starting from the root node together with the aggregated frequency of each of them. We do this by splitting every query by its terms and extracting all the different prefixes, that is, the possible paths of the graph starting from the root node. In this step we also assign an unique id to every unique path, including the zero-length path of the root node, with id 0. For instance, for the queries of the query-term graph of Figure 1, we would have generated the list of sub-paths with their respective aggregated frequencies and ids of Table 2.

Once the paths of the query log have been determined, the next step consists in determining the nodes and edges of the graph based on the extracted sub-paths. The nodes are determined by the id and last term of every sub-path extracted in the previous step. The edges are in turn extracted by finding for each path its immediate sub-path (the longest path which is a sub-sequence of the target one), a process that can be efficiently performed by having the list of paths in lexicographical order. In our example, the resulting edges together with their weights would be, following the format `(src, dest; count)`, the following: `(0, 1; 10)`, `(1, 2; 5)`, `(2, 3; 5)`, `(1, 4; 5)`, `(0, 5; 100)`, `(5, 6; 70)`, `(6, 7; 56)`, `(6, 8; 14)` and `(5, 9; 30)`. A normalization of the weights of the outgoing edges of each nodes so that they sum 1 may also be performed for convenience. Note that all the previous steps can be carried out by means of scalable, distributed programming models such as MapReduce [10]. Finally, the resulting sets of nodes and edges that form our query-term graph can be efficiently stored with help of compression graph techniques such as the Webgraph framework [5].

As mentioned, the previous steps describe the construction of a simple query-term graph – more precisely in this case, a directed tree – based on previous queries with weights derived from the popularity of each query. However, additional steps could be considered to enrich the construction of the graph. For instance, other indicators for the quality of the queries such as the number of clicked results for each query, could be easily incorporated to provide better completions. Also, identifying common suffix patterns between queries could be used not only to reduce the size of the graph (see Figure 2), but also to infer previously unseen query completions.

4.3 Usage

The standard and more direct approach for QAC consists in suggesting for a given query prefix its most popular completions [3]. Many of the state-of-the-art proposals build on this idea and refine it to make personalized, context-aware recommendations. We now describe how most popular com-

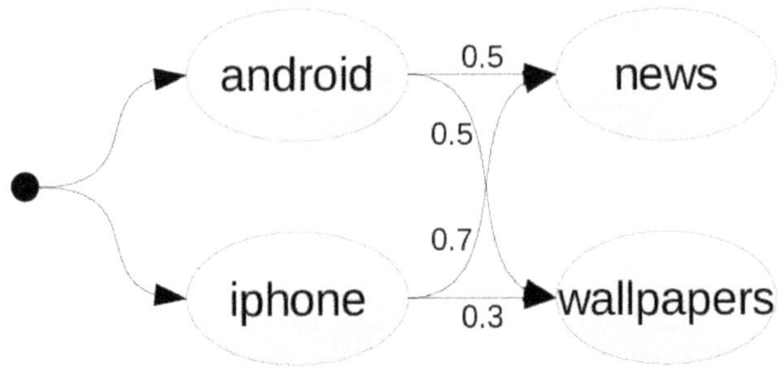

Figure 2: Example of the of common branches of nodes in the query-term graph.

pletions, either in standard or term-by-term QAC, can be implemented using our query-term graph.

On the one hand, the term-by-term most popular completion using the query-term graph basically consists in keeping track of the path followed by the user when submitting a query, as defined by the current terms of it, and presenting suggestions in the form of the N terms of the destination nodes of the outgoing edges with higher weights, possibly including the special end-of-query leaf nodes to indicate to the user that the current state of the query may be sufficient.

On the other hand, despite not being its intended purpose, the query-term graph can also be used to implement a standard most-popular completion mechanism suggesting entire queries. As in the term-by-term case, the algorithm needs to trace the path followed by the current state of the query. For a given query prefix, the suggestions in the form of whole-query completions are extracted by searching in the graph the continuing paths to leaf nodes whose probabilities – as product of the probabilities of their edges – are among the N highest. Note that this procedure can be efficiently implemented by means of a pruned depth-first search in which candidate branches whose maximum probability is lower than the current candidate completions are discarded.

By comparing the two previous algorithms, it is clear that the algorithm for standard most-popular completion – even with optimizations – is costlier than its term-by-term counterpart, in which the search is reduced to select the immediate edges with highest probabilities. Although standard QAC is generally implemented by means of alternative data structures and algorithms, possibly more optimal for that task, we claim that the computational cost of our term-by-term QAC is generally smaller than the standard whole-query approach given its simplicity. Therefore, even though computational efficiency of QAC mechanisms is not a goal of this paper, we believe our approach is appealing also in this respect.

5. A USER MODEL FOR TERM-BY-TERM QUERY AUTO-COMPLETION

The differences between the standard and term-by-term QAC methods can be further explained by means of a user model that explains how users examine and select the suggestions provided by each method. In this section we provide such user model for both alternatives and present three derived metrics, namely saved characters, saved terms and effort, to evaluate QAC using query log data. As stated in Section 3, in this paper we take the simplification of only dealing with the problem of providing suggestions after the user has finished entering a whole term of the query. This decision is reflected in the formulation of the user model we describe,

count	path
5	android news apps
5	android wallpapers
56	hotels in barcelona
14	hotels in oslo
30	hotels july

Table 1: Example of a really small query log.

id	count	path
1	10	android
2	5	android news
3	5	android news apps
4	5	android wallpapers
5	100	hotels
6	70	hotels in
7	56	hotels in barcelona
8	14	hotels in oslo
9	30	hotels july

Table 2: Possible sub-paths of the queries in Table 1.

although a generalized version that takes into account the current term completion case can be easily included.

Recently, Kharitonov et al. [19] proposed a user model for the evaluation of QAC in which the probability of a user examining a suggestion depends on two dimensions, namely the position of the suggestion in a given list of suggestions and the length of the current formulated query. In a similar manner, the work of Li at al. [20] explores these two-dimensions in a click model for QAC. These models build on two basic assumptions. First, they assume that a user, while typing a query, examines every completion suggested by the QAC mechanism with a probability that depends on the current state the entered query (e.g. the user might examine more suggestions at the beginning of the formulation process) and the position of the completion in the list of suggestions (typically with decreasing probability with the position) but does not depend on the suggestions for previous prefixes (i.e. even if the previous suggestions were not satisfactory, they do not influence the examination probability of the next suggestions). Second, it is assumed that only completions that match the query that the user has in mind may be accepted.

Following these assumptions, we consider the random variable E_i^j that models if the j-th suggestion provided after the i-th term of the query is examined. By denoting as $j = m(i)$ the position of the suggestion that matches the intended query after the i-th term (in the case that none of the suggestions matches the intended query, then $m(i) = \infty$), we consider then the probability $p(E_i^{m(i)})$ of providing a satisfying suggestion after i terms of the intended query have been entered. This probability plays however different roles depending on the method for QAC. In the case of standard QAC, where suggestions are whole-query completions, the probability of examination of a given suggestion after i terms have been entered has to take into account the fact that the matching completion may have been shown in previous suggestions. In case the matching completion was shown and selected, the suggestions at query position i are not examined. This way, in standard QAC the probability $p(M_{STD}^i)$ of matching the intended query after i terms have been entered is determined by the following equation:

$$p(M_{STD}^i) = p(E_i^{m(i)}) \prod_{i'<i} \left(1 - p(E_{i'}^{m(i')})\right) \tag{1}$$

In the case of term-by-term QAC, suggestions only consist

of predictions for the next term of the query. Therefore, the fact that previous suggestions have been accepted does not affect, as assumed by our model, the examination probability at position i, so the matching probability $p(M^i_{TBT})$ at query position i is simply given by the probability of examination:

$$p(M^i_{TBT}) = p(E_i^{m(i)}) \quad (2)$$

In prior work [19, 20] the probability distribution of examination $p(E_i^j)$ for standard QAC was estimated with query log data. As data for term-by-term QAC is not available to date, we rely in this work on a fixed probability $P(E_i^j) = 1/(j+1)$ which is reciprocal to the position of each completion of the suggestion list for both standard and term-by-term QAC. While not taking into account the horizontal dimension, i.e. the state of the entered prefix of the query, the experiments of [19] show that this reciprocal estimation is only moderately worse than models learned from user interactions and, moreover, is in line with the commonly considered MRR metric used to evaluate QAC algorithms found in many offline experiments of prior work [3, 15, 20, 24, 25, 27]. Note that we assume the same probability of examination for both methods, although we could consider higher probabilities for the term-by-term completions as they are shorter than their whole-query counterparts.

Similarly to [19], we measure with our model the effectiveness in terms of the number of characters, as well as terms, that the QAC methods save the user to enter. Given our previous assumptions, the proportion of characters or terms that a standard QAC saves entering are given, respectively, by the following equations:

$$CS_{STD} = \frac{1}{c(q) - c(q_1)} \sum_{i=1}^{t(q)-1} (c(q) - c(q_i))\, p(M^i_{STD}) \quad (3)$$

$$TS_{STD} = \frac{1}{t(q) - 1} \sum_{i=1}^{t(q)-1} (t(q) - i)\, p(M^i_{STD}) \quad (4)$$

where $t(q)$ is the number of terms of the intended query q, $c(q)$ is the number of characters and q_i is the sub-query until the i-th term. The same magnitudes for term-by-term QAC are in turn given by the following equations:

$$CS_{TBT} = \frac{1}{c(q) - c(q_1)} \sum_{i=1}^{t(q)-1} (c(q_{i+1}) - c(q_i))\, p(M^i_{TBT}) \quad (5)$$

$$TS_{TBT} = \frac{1}{t(q) - 1} \sum_{i=1}^{t(q)-1} p(M^i_{TBT}) \quad (6)$$

Another variable of interest, related but different to the number of saved terms would be the effort involved in examining the suggestions provided. We define it as the expected number of suggestions examined by the user normalized by the query length. In the case of standard QAC this quantity is given by:

$$EF_{STD} = \frac{1}{t(q) - 1} \sum_{i=1}^{t(q)-1} \sum_{j \leq m(i)} p(E_i^j) \prod_{i' < i} \left(1 - p(E_{i'}^{m(i')})\right) \quad (7)$$

while for term-by-term QAC is determined by:

$$EF_{TBT} = \frac{1}{t(q) - 1} \sum_{i=1}^{t(q)-1} \sum_{j \leq m(i)} p(E_i^j) \quad (8)$$

These three metrics and their formulation for both QAC mechanisms are used in the query log-based experiments in the next section. Additionally, we will provide equivalent measurements with real user data.

6. EXPERIMENTS

The observations made in Section 3 suggest that a term-by-term approach to QAC might benefit the formulation of queries in mobile search. To test the validity of this proposal, we have conducted two different experiments. The first one is a query log-based experiment in which one month data from a commercial search engine is evaluated following standard practices in the related work [3, 19, 20, 27] in which both standard (STD) and term-by-term (TBT) most-popular completion algorithms are evaluated with the metrics defined in Section 5. The second experiment consists in a user study in which a set of users was asked to perform a series of query formulation tasks with the assistance of both methods in their mobile devices.

6.1 Mobile Query Log-Based Evaluation

6.1.1 Setup

We have performed an evaluation of the compared QAC methods using a query log from a commercial search engine. In particular, our query log for this evaluation consists of queries submitted from mobile devices to Yahoo, a major US search engine. We collected a set of queries submitted from mobile devices in one month period. For efficiency reasons, we have discarded queries having more than 8 terms. The data from the first 20 days was taken as training to build the query-term graph, while a random sample of 41 million queries from the remaining period has been used for test.

We have created two implementations of the systems detailed in Section 4, namely the most-popular completion for both standard and term-by-term QAC, using the data from the training subset. Although more complex QAC mechanisms have been proposed in the state of the art (see Section 2), many experimental evaluations acknowledge that the simpler most-popular completion approach offers competitive performance at the smallest implementation cost [3, 15, 20, 24]. Indeed, we believe that, for the purpose of our work, the improvements of more elaborate QAC techniques do not alter the comparison between the standard and our term-by-term QAC variants.

For testing purposes, an alternative implementation of the term-by-term QAC in which terms are picked from whole-query completions in the order determined by the rank of the latter was also considered. Even when this approach outperforms the standard QAC with respect to the considered metrics, it performs worse than our proposed, more efficient term-by-term QAC from Section 4. Thus, we do not include the results for this alternative system.

The evaluation of the remaining two systems is based on common assumptions found in prior work [3, 19, 20, 27]. In particular, each query in the test both serves as simulation of user behavior – our simulated user enters sequentially the terms of the query to activate the QAC mechanism – and as gold standard – only suggestions matching the rest of the query are considered as satisfactory. In this setting, the suggestion lists are composed of $N = 10$ completions each. As previously stated in Section 5, we assume that the probability of examining a suggested completion is reciprocal to its position (more precisely, $p(E_i^j) = 1/(j+1)$) for both standard and term-by-term QAC.

6.1.2 Results

The outcomes of our evaluation are found in Tables 3 and 4. Since our two compared most-popular completion

		N	CS		TS		EF	
			STD	TBT	STD	TBT	STD	TBT
		17,853,330	0.1759	0.2111	0.1761	0.2216	1.5206	1.3225
t(q)	2	3,573,019	0.0641	0.0745	0.0641	0.0745	1.8143	1.7833
	3	5,081,503	0.1414	0.1859	0.1416	0.1939	1.5825	1.4066
	4	4,542,236	0.2021	0.2504	0.2057	0.2657	1.4311	1.1837
	5	2,657,039	0.2510	0.2913	0.2518	0.3073	1.3444	1.0566
	6	1,227,555	0.2858	0.3147	0.2804	0.3329	1.3014	0.9787
	7	517,222	0.3189	0.3312	0.3068	0.3490	1.2609	0.9298
	8	254,756	0.3633	0.3475	0.3481	0.3639	1.1857	0.8850
⌈log10 f(q)⌉	0	9,838,824	0.1672	0.2047	0.1677	0.2158	1.5457	1.3409
	1	7,100,953	0.1787	0.2138	0.1789	0.2243	1.5110	1.3141
	2	833,071	0.2393	0.2523	0.2353	0.2577	1.3507	1.2092
	3	75,054	0.3292	0.3168	0.3262	0.3205	1.0822	1.0096
	4	5,149	0.4286	0.3926	0.4278	0.3960	0.7754	0.7760
	5	265	0.4671	0.4371	0.4672	0.4397	0.6497	0.6463
	6	14	0.4838	0.4595	0.4810	0.4613	0.6065	0.5774

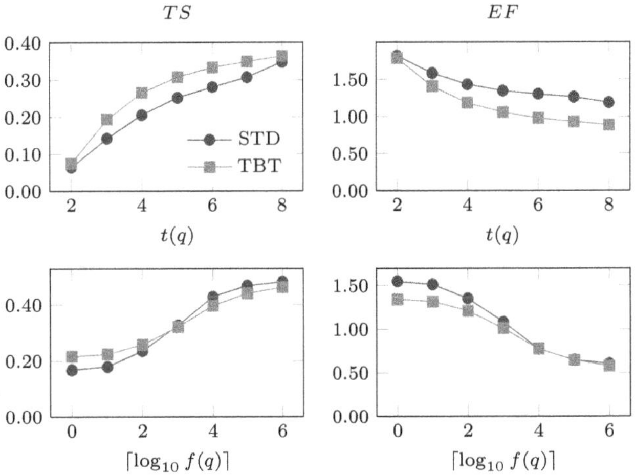

Table 3: Results for the set of previously seen queries in the mobile query log-based evaluation. Corresponding plots (for TS and EF) on the right.

		N	CS_{TBT}	TS_{TBT}	EF_{TBT}
		24,311,303	0.0517	0.0618	1.0757
t(q)	2	2,852,182	0.0031	0.0031	1.6524
	3	5,172,474	0.0306	0.0365	1.3235
	4	5,781,961	0.0549	0.0648	1.0679
	5	4,583,313	0.0703	0.0828	0.8961
	6	2,962,515	0.0766	0.0918	0.7802
	7	1,819,564	0.0766	0.0941	0.6993
	8	1,139,294	0.0743	0.0930	0.6377
⌈log10 f(q)⌉	0	22,761,496	0.0507	0.0607	1.0683
	1	1,542,835	0.0672	0.0772	1.1828
	2	6,718	0.0666	0.0753	1.3203
	3	245	0.0671	0.0768	1.3680
	4	9	0.0784	0.0741	1.3415

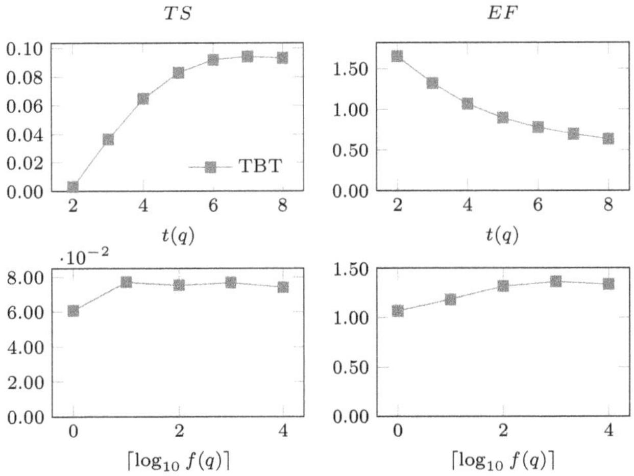

Table 4: Results for the set of previously unseen queries in the mobile query log-based evaluation. Corresponding plots (for TS and EF) on the right.

systems cannot suggest queries that are not present in the training set [22], we first divide the random sample of the test set into queries that appeared in the training set (Table 3) and new queries (Table 4). In particular, as the standard most-popular completion algorithm is not able to provide successful suggestions according to our evaluation methodology, Table 4 does not include its outcomes, as they are, as expected, completely unsatisfactory. For the remaining outcomes, we show the results of the characters saved (CS), terms saved (TS) and effort (EF) metrics according to the global average for unique queries and, also, detailed according to two different criteria: the number of terms of the final queries $t(q)$ and the frequency of them $f(q)$.

The results for previously seen queries in Table 3 show some of the advantages of our term-by-term approach, namely an average higher number of saved characters and terms with a smaller effort in terms of the number of suggestions explored. This can be already observed in the average over the almost 18 million queries in our test subset. A more detailed analysis can be done with respect to the number of terms and frequency of the queries.

Regarding the number of terms of the queries, we can first observe that the normalized number of saved characters and terms increases with the length of the final query for both compared approaches, while the relative effort decreases. This is expected as the longer the query is, the more specific it is so that popular existing completions match it. When comparing between approaches, the global trend shows that the term-by-term approach provides in general more saved characters and terms with less effort. Regarding CS and TS, we see that both methods have a similar performance for queries of size 2, although the gap between them is larger for longer queries with the exception of the queries with 8 terms, in which the performance is again similar. This is not the case of the effort metric, in which the relative improvements of our method over the standard QAC increase along with the length of the queries.

When we analyze our results in terms of the frequency of the queries, these illustrate the performance of both compared approaches for different levels of query popularity, showing in particular that our method works better than the standard one for long-tail queries and similarly for more popular ones. A common trend for both methods is that, the more popular the query is, the better both systems work in terms of the considered metrics. This outcome is expected as both systems are based on providing the most popular completions in the past. When comparing between systems by query frequency by saved characters and terms, the results indicate that our term-by-term method is better that the standard most-popular completion for not so popular queries (frequency

Figure 3: Examples of the search interface for the user study for the same search task with standard (left) and term-by-term (right) QAC.

less than or equal to 100 times), while for highly popular (and easier to predict) queries the standard most-popular completion method is slightly better. In any case, the effort involved in the term-by-term method is always smaller than in the standard approach, although the differences are smaller the more frequent the query is.

Finally, in Table 4 we show the results of our term-by-term most-popular completion approach for queries in the test subset that did not appear in the previous training subset. As previously explained, the results for the standard most-popular completion are not included here as this method, according to this offline evaluation methodology, is unable to provide satisfactory suggestions, given that their suggestions never match completely the intended query. However, our term-by-term method is able to assist the user even in such unfavorable scenario as it is still able to suggest terms that matches prefixes of unseen queries. As the results show, the number of saved characters and terms in this setting is much smaller than the values obtained from the evaluation previously seen queries. For instance, for unseen queries of two terms our system is practically incapable of providing any valid suggestion, although the success ratio improves for longer queries. In fact, for longer queries, our term-by-term system seems to be of some help as it successfully suggest terms in the beginning of longer queries. In terms of effort, we see smaller values than that of the case of seen queries. This is expected, since as soon as the system reaches a sub-query outside the query-term graph it stops providing suggestions. Contrary to the results in the previously seen queries, the frequency of the queries does not seem to affect significantly the number of saved characters and terms of them, although it has an influence on the effort, which increases for more popular queries.

6.2 User Study

6.2.1 Setup

We provide an additional perspective of the performance of our term-by-term approach in terms of a controlled user study. Based on data from the same query log for a longer period of three months, we have built another query-term graph and implemented a web-based QAC interface adapted to mobile browsers. It implements both standard and term-by-term most-popular completion algorithms showing $N = 5$ possible completions after a whole term has been entered. The interface logs every relevant interaction of the users with the system: when suggestions were shown, if they were rejected or accepted (and the position of the accepted completion) and when the user submitted the resulting query. In the case of standard most-popular completion, we allowed the users to keep formulating their queries even if they accepted a whole-query completion. See Figure 3 for examples of the query formulation interface. Users were asked to access the interface with their mobile devices and complete a series of query formulations for the 20 tasks in Table 5. The formulations were shuffled to counter-balance any order effect. Users were not aware of which completion mechanisms were being tested, and they had freedom to ignore query assistance if they wanted to. Each task was repeated for each QAC method. In total, we recruited a total of 25 evaluators who performed a total of 968 query formulations (some users did not complete all the formulations). From these formulations, we discarded one term queries and formulations that were not performed using both methods for the same search tasks, resulting in 350 pairs of formulations where both compared methods have been used by the same user to complete the same task. Despite its small scale, this study allows us to measure certain variables of interest of QAC systems that cannot be otherwise estimated by a query log-based evaluation.

#	description
1	Should I buy and iPad or a Samsung tablet?
2	Buy the "Breaking Bad" series in DVD.
3	Recipe for strawberry cupcakes.
4	What to see in Barcelona.
5	Upcoming Taylor Swift concerts in Europe.
6	When does the fifth season of Game of Thrones start?
7	Price of the tickets of The Lion King musical in Broadway.
8	Will Hillary Clinton run for president in 2016?
9	Cast of The Expendables 3.
10	What is the migration route of the monarch butterfly?
11	The weather forecast in Los Angeles for the next week.
12	Price of Tesla Motor cars.
13	Last news about the Ukraine crisis in the last month.
14	Which countries are affected by the ebola outbreak?
15	Find funny pictures of cute cats.
16	How to take a screenshot on Android phones.
17	Find a cheap laser print.
18	Resources for learning arabic language.
19	What is the highest mountain in California?
20	How many Starbucks are there in San Francisco?

Table 5: Search tasks of the user study.

From the recorded interactions of our test users we have measured a series of variables related to the effectiveness of both QAC completion approaches. First, we took some measurements related to the operation of the QAC methods themselves, namely the number of times they were activated (`suggestions`), the average ratio of accepted suggestions (`accepted`) and the average position of the accepted com-

	t	event	query
STD	0	suggest	ipad
	1,571	reject	ipad vs
	1,890	suggest	ipad vs
	10,353	reject	ipad vs samsung
	10,355	suggest	ipad vs samsung
	15,432	accept (3)	ipad vs samsung galaxy tablet
	15,444	suggest	ipad vs samsung galaxy tablet
	17,475	submit	ipad vs samsung galaxy tablet
TBT	0	suggest	ipad
	2,048	reject	ipad vs
	2,050	suggest	ipad vs
	6,969	accept (2)	ipad vs samsung
	6,977	suggest	ipad vs samsung
	8,853	accept (1)	ipad vs samsung galaxy
	8,860	suggest	ipad vs samsung galaxy
	10,213	accept (2)	ipad vs samsung galaxy tablet
	10,235	suggest	ipad vs samsung galaxy tablet
	11,366	submit	ipad vs samsung galaxy tablet

Table 6: Example of a query formulation task with both methods for a same user. For each formulation process, we indicate the sequence of events starting from the first activation of the QAC mechanism with the elapsed time and the state of the query. For acceptance of suggestions, the position of the accepted completion is indicated.

pletion (`accept_pos`). The second block of measurements is related to the benefits perceived by the user which were measured by our query log-based evaluation, namely the number of saved terms (`terms_saved`), the average number of completions examined for each suggestion assuming that users examined sequentially all listed completions until finding the right one (`effort`) and, also, the number of saved characters (`chars_saved`). The third set of measurements considers the time (in seconds) spent for formulating queries, including the total time of query formulation (`total_time`) and the average time taken to accept or reject suggestions (`accept_time` and `reject_time`, respectively). Finally, the last set of measurements evaluates the properties of the resulting queries in terms of the number of characters of the submitted queries (`query_chars`) and their number of terms (`query_terms`).

6.2.2 *Example*

Before providing a detailed discussion of the results of the user study, we show in Table 6 a selected example that illustrates the differences of the standard and term-by-term QAC methods for assisting the same user in formulating the search task number 1 in Table 5. As we can see, in this particular example the user ends up formulating the same query when using either mechanisms. However, in the process of formulating the final query we see significant differences between one method and the other.

On the one hand, in the formulation process assisted with the standard QAC method, we see that the user rejects the two first suggestions shown and only accepts the third one which completes the last two terms of the query that is submitted. We also observe how the user takes considerable time exploring the list of suggestions and is forced to go to the third position of the accepted suggestion to find the desired completion. In this case, the system is able to save the user entering two out for four terms of the query (not including the first term).

One the other hand, the formulation with help of the term-by-term QAC mechanism shows the advantages of our method for this particular user and search task. As we can see, the QAC system is activated a total of five times (one more than in the standard method), for which the completions shown are accepted in three cases. The position of the accepted completions is, moreover, very low (first and second positions only), which accounts for a faster decision time. In the end, the user is able to save typing three terms of the intended query.

property	STD	TBT	
`suggestions`	2.9514	3.1486	**6.68%**
`accepted`	0.3661	0.4029	**10.06%**
`accept_pos`	2.0908	1.9601	-6.25%
`chars_saved`	0.2386	0.2551	6.91%
`terms_saved`	0.2753	0.2838	3.08%
`effort`	3.9221	3.7924	**-3.31%**
`total_time`	12.6345	12.6133	-0.17%
`accept_time`	3.3058	2.8943	**-12.45%**
`reject_time`	4.8333	4.4531	**-7.87%**
`query_chars`	22.9686	22.6200	-1.52%
`query_terms`	3.4600	3.3914	-1.98%

Table 7: Results of the user study. Statistically significant relative improvements of the term-by-term method (Wilcoxon signed-rank test with $p < 0.05$) are marked in bold.

6.2.3 *Results*

The global results of the user study can be found in Table 7. As it can be seen, a number of statistically significant differences are observed between methods (Wilcoxon signed-rank test with $p < 0.05$). In the first block of results, which deal with the success of the QAC method under testing, we see that the term-by-term method is activated a 6.68% more times than the standard one. This is expected as the standard mechanism, by providing longer completions, is expected to be used less for an average task. Regarding the success of the suggestions, we see that completions provided by our term-by-term method have a higher ratio of acceptance. Also, the average position of the accepted completions is lower (i.e. appears higher in the list of suggestions) than in the standard method, although the difference is not found statistically significant.

The second block of results relates to the direct measurement of the metrics defined by the user model in Section 5, together with the number of characters saved. In general these results provide a weak confirmation of our claims and observations from the query log-based evaluation, showing that more terms are saved with a smaller effort, but with a much smaller relative difference than in the previous evaluation and with significant differences found only in the effort metric.

A third category of results measure the amount of time involved in exploring suggestions and the total time involved in query formulation. The outcomes indicate that users tend to spend a similar amount of time to formulate the queries in both methods, although the time required to accept or reject suggestions is smaller in the term-by-term approach. The latter observations can be explained by the fact that the suggestions are typically much shorter than in the standard case, which facilitates a faster exploration of the suggestions.

Finally, a last set of observations comprises the properties of the submitted queries, in terms of the number of characters and terms. As the results show, queries formulated with the assistance of the standard QAC method seem to be slightly longer (both in characters and terms) than the queries with help of the term-by-term method, although the difference does not seem to be statistically significant. By taking a closer look at the submitted queries between methods, we see that in 37% of the cases the pairs of queries for a same user in a search tasks were identical for both methods and, for the pairs of different queries, the normalized Levenshtein distance was in average 0.38, which indicates that the queries were indeed different but shared similar terms.

7. CONCLUSIONS AND FUTURE WORK

In this paper we tackled the problem of using query auto-completion mechanisms in mobile search. We identified a series of inconveniences of standard whole-query completions caused by the limitations of text input and display in mobile devices such as smartphones and tables. In order to alleviate these issues, we proposed a term-by-term QAC mechanism that suggests, rather than whole-query completions, one term at a time. We described an implementation of this term-by-term QAC system that uses a structure called query-term graph, which allows an efficient storage and retrieval of query completions. We also proposed a user model for the interaction with QAC systems based on prior work from which we derive metrics to asses the efficiency of QAC in query log-based evaluations. An experiment with a query log from a commercial search engine demonstrated that our QAC mechanism significantly outperforms well-established state-of-the-art standard auto-completion mechanisms. Furthermore, a small user study provided insights about and confirmed the benefits of our system throughout a wide number of evaluation metrics.

We envision two main directions for future work. First, we want to enhance our term-by-term QAC method by incorporating additional sources of information. On one hand, we believe that most of the ideas of more recent proposals for standard QAC – such as those described in Section 2 – can be easily adapted to our approach. On the other hand, we will explore enhancements specific to our query-term graph. In particular, the detection and merging of sub-paths of the graph [1] (as shown in Figure 2) could be a way not only to reduce the size of the structure, but also to discover unseen query formulations that ultimately improve the prediction capabilities of our system. Also, we will extend our method to provide suggestions that may also include short phrases.

As a second research direction, we want to study the online user behavior of our auto-completion paradigm in the context of a commercial mobile search engine, observing real traffic and a large number of user interactions, to shed light on the particularities of different auto-completion methods in a live setting. Furthermore, we want to study the characteristics of queries formulated with the assistance of both standard and term-by-term QAC methods in terms of the quality of the retrieved search results.

8. REFERENCES

[1] P. Anchuri, M. J. Zaki, O. Barkol, S. Golan, and M. Shamy. Approximate graph mining with label costs. In *19th ACM Conference on Knowledge Discovery and Data Mining*, KDD '13, pages 518–526, 2013.

[2] R. Baeza-Yates, G. Dupret, and J. Velasco. A study of mobile search queries in Japan. In *16th International World Wide Web Conference*, WWW '07, 2007.

[3] Z. Bar-Yossef and N. Kraus. Context-sensitive query auto-completion. In *20th International World Wide Web Conference*, WWW '11, pages 107–116, 2011.

[4] S. Bhatia, D. Majumdar Debapriyo and P. Mitra. Query suggestions in the absence of query logs. In *34th ACM Conference on Research and Development in Information Retrieval*, SIGIR '11, pages 795–804, 2011.

[5] P. Boldi and S. Vigna. The Webgraph framework I: Compression techniques. In *13th International World Wide Web Conference*, WWW '04, pages 595–602, 2004.

[6] O. Chapelle, D. Metlzer, Y. Zhang, and P. Grinspan. Expected reciprocal rank for graded relevance. In *18th ACM Conference on Information and Knowledge Management*, CIKM '09, pages 621–630, 2009.

[7] K. Church, B. Smyth, K. Bradley, and P. Cotter. A large scale study of european mobile search behaviour. In *10th Conference on Human Computer Interaction with Mobile Devices and Services*, MobileHCI '08, pages 13–22, 2008.

[8] K. Church, B. Smyth, P. Cotter, and K. Bradley. Mobile information access: A study of emerging search behavior on the mobile internet. *ACM Transactions on the Web*, 1(1), May 2007.

[9] J. Darragh, I. H. Witten, and M. James. The reactive keyboard: a predictive typing aid. *Computer*, 23(11):41–49, Nov 1990.

[10] J. Dean and S. Ghemawat. Mapreduce: Simplified data processing on large clusters. *Communications of the ACM*, 51(1):107–113, Jan. 2008.

[11] E. Fredkin. Trie memory. *Communications of the ACM*, 3(9):490–499, Sept. 1960.

[12] N. Garay-Vitoria and J. González-Abascal. Intelligent word-prediction to enhance text input rate. In *2nd Conference on Intelligent User Interfaces*, IUI '97, pages 241–244, 1997.

[13] J.-L. Gomez-Barroso, R. Compano, C. Feijoo, M. Bacigalupo, O. Westlund, S. Ramos, A. Jaokar, F. Alvarez, R. De Waele, G. Mateos-Barrado, and C. Garcia-Jimenez. *Prospects of Mobile Search*. Publications Office of the European Union, 2010.

[14] K. Hofmann, B. Mitra, F. Radlinski, M. Shokouhi. An eye-tracking study of user interactions with query auto completion. In *23rd ACM Conference on Information and Knowledge Management*, CIKM '14, pages 549–558, 2014.

[15] J.-Y. Jiang, Y.-Y. Ke, P.-Y. Chien, and P.-J. Cheng. Learning user reformulation behavior for query auto-completion. In *37th ACM Conference on Research and Development in Information Retrieval*, SIGIR '14, pages 445–454, 2014.

[16] M. Kamvar and S. Baluja. A large scale study of wireless search behavior: Google mobile search. In *ACM Conference on Human Factors in Computing Systems*, CHI '06, pages 701–709, 2006.

[17] M. Kamvar and S. Baluja. Deciphering trends in mobile search. *Computer*, 40(8):58–62, Aug. 2007.

[18] M. Kamvar and S. Baluja. Query suggestions for mobile search: understanding usage patterns. In *ACM Conference on Human Factors in Computing Systems*, CHI '08, pages 1013–1016, 2008.

[19] E. Kharitonov, C. Macdonald, P. Serdyukov, and I. Ounis. User model-based metrics for offline query suggestion evaluation. In *36th ACM Conference on Research and Development in Information Retrieval*, SIGIR '13, pages 633–642, 2013.

[20] Y. Li, A. Dong, H. Wang, H. Deng, Y. Chang, and C. Zhai. A two-dimensional click model for query auto-completion. In *37th ACM Conference on Research and Development in Information Retrieval*, SIGIR '14, pages 455–464, 2014.

[21] B. Mitra, M. Shokouhi, F. Radlinski, and K. Hofmann. On user interactions with query auto-completion. In *37th ACM Conference on Research and Development in Information Retrieval*, SIGIR '14, pages 1055–1058, 2014.

[22] B. Mitra, and N. Craswell. Query auto-Completion for rare prefixes. In *24th ACM Conference on Information and Knowledge Management* , CIKM '15, pages 1755–1758, 2015.

[23] J. Pasquero, J. Griffin, and D. Mckenzie. Method and apparatus for word prediction selection, Sept. 17 2014. EP Patent App. EP20,130,159,459.

[24] M. Shokouhi. Learning to personalize query auto-completion. In *36th ACM Conference on Research and Development in Information Retrieval*, SIGIR '13, pages 103–112, 2013.

[25] M. Shokouhi and K. Radinsky. Time-sensitive query auto-completion. In *35th ACM Conference on Research and Development in Information Retrieval*, SIGIR '12, pages 601–610, 2012.

[26] Y. Song, H. Ma, H. Wang, and K. Wang. Exploring and exploiting user search behavior on mobile and tablet devices to improve search relevance. In *22nd International World Wide Web Conference*, WWW '13, pages 1201–1212, 2013.

[27] S. Whiting and J. M. Jose. Recent and robust query auto-completion. In *23rd International World Wide Web Conference*, WWW '14, pages 971–982, 2014.

Collaborative Denoising Auto-Encoders for Top-N Recommender Systems

Yao Wu
Simon Fraser University
Burnaby, BC, Canada
wuyaow@sfu.ca

Christopher DuBois
Dato Inc.
Seattle, WA, USA
chris@dato.com

Alice X. Zheng
Dato Inc.
Seattle, WA, USA
alicez@dato.com

Martin Ester
Simon Fraser University
Burnaby, BC, Canada
ester@cs.sfu.ca

ABSTRACT

Most real-world recommender services measure their performance based on the top-N results shown to the end users. Thus, advances in top-N recommendation have far-ranging consequences in practical applications. In this paper, we present a novel method, called Collaborative Denoising Auto-Encoder (CDAE), for top-N recommendation that utilizes the idea of Denoising Auto-Encoders. We demonstrate that the proposed model is a generalization of several well-known collaborative filtering models but with more flexible components. Thorough experiments are conducted to understand the performance of CDAE under various component settings. Furthermore, experimental results on several public datasets demonstrate that CDAE consistently outperforms state-of-the-art top-N recommendation methods on a variety of common evaluation metrics.

Categories and Subject Descriptors

H.3.3 [**Information Search and Retrieval**]: Information Filtering

Keywords

Recommender Systems; Collaborative Filtering; Denoising Auto-Encoders

1. INTRODUCTION

In recent years, recommender systems have become widely utilized by businesses across industries. Given a set of users, items, and observed user-item interactions, these systems can recommend other items that the users might like. Personalized recommendation is one of the key applications of machine learning in e-commerce and beyond. Many recommendation systems use *Collaborative Filtering* (CF) methods to make recommendations. In production, recommender systems are often evaluated based on the performance of the top-N recommendations, since typically only a few recommendations are shown to the user each time. Thus, top-N recommendation methods are of particular interest.

In this paper, we present a new model-based collaborative filtering (CF) method for top-N recommendation called Collaborative Denoising Auto-Encoder (CDAE). CDAE assumes that whatever user-item interactions are observed are a *corrupted* version of the user's full preference set. The model learns latent representations of corrupted user-item preferences that can best reconstruct the full input.[1] In other words, during training, we feed the model a subset of a user's item set and train the model to recover the whole item set; at prediction time, the model recommends new items to the user given the existing preference set as input. Training on corrupted data effectively recovers co-preference patterns. We show that this is an effective approach for collaborative filtering.

Learning from intentionally corrupted input has been widely studied. For instance, Denoising Auto-Encoders [24] train a one-hidden-layer neural network to reconstruct a data point from the latent representation of its partially corrupted version. However, to our best knowledge, no previous work has explored applying the idea to recommender systems.

CDAE generalizes several previously proposed, state-of-the-art collaborative filtering models (see Section 3.2). But its structure is much more flexible. For instance, it is easy to incorporate non-linearities into the model to achieves better top-N recommendation results. We investigate the effects of various choices for model components and compare their performance against prior approaches on three real world data sets. Experimental results show that CDAE consistently outperforms state-of-the-art top-N recommendation methods by a significant margin on a number of common evaluation metrics.

Our contributions can be summarized as follows:

- We propose a new model CDAE, which formulates the top-N recommendation problem using the Auto-Encoder framework and learns from corrupted inputs. Compared to related methods, CDAE is novel in both model definition and objective function.
- We demonstrate that CDAE is a generalization of several state-of-the-art methods but with a more flexible structure.
- We conduct thorough experiments studying the impact of the choices of different components in CDAE, and show that CDAE outperforms state-of-the-art methods on three real world data sets.

The rest of the paper is organized as follows. Section 2 provides the problem definition, background, and useful notations. Section 3 describes our proposed model and learning algorithm in detail. We

[1] We follow the typical top-N recommendation setup and consider only user-item interaction data in this paper. Handling of additional data, such as user/item features and contextual information, is left as future work.

WSDM'16, February 22–25, 2016, San Francisco, CA, USA.

ISBN 978-1-4503-3716-8/16/02...$15.00

DOI: http://dx.doi.org/10.1145/2835776.2835837

discuss related work on applying neural network methods to recommender systems in Section 4. Experimental results for the components analysis and performance comparisons are presented in Section 5. We conclude with a summary of this work and discussion of future work in Section 6.

2. PROBLEM DEFINITION

Given a set of users $\mathcal{U} = \{u = 1, ..., U\}$, a set of items $\mathcal{I} = \{i = 1, ..., I\}$, and a log of the users' past preferences of items $\mathcal{O} = (u, i, y_{ui})$, our goal is to recommend to each user u a list of items that will maximize her/his satisfaction. In many cases, the log contains only *implicit* feedback where all the y_{ui} are 1; the rest of the triples are assumed missing. We use $\bar{\mathcal{O}}$ to denote the set of unobserved, missing triples, and $\mathcal{O}'$ an augmented user-item pairs dataset that includes some data sampled from $\bar{\mathcal{O}}$. (We discuss $\mathcal{O}'$ in more detail in the subsection on objective functions.) Let $\mathcal{O}_u$ denote the set of item preferences in the training set for a particular user u, and $\bar{\mathcal{O}}_u$ the unobserved preferences of user u. Items in $\bar{\mathcal{O}}_u$ are the candidates to be recommended to user u. The goal of the recommender is to pick for each user u a subset of items from the candidate set, the predicted values of which are most likely to be 1.

In some cases, y_{ui} are numeric ratings in the range of, say, $[1, 5]$ or binary values $\{0, 1\}$. For simplicity, we only consider the case of implicit feedback in this paper. Numeric ratings can be handled with slight modifications to our method.

In the rest of the paper, we use u to index a user, and i and j to index items. Vectors and matrices are denoted by bold symbols, where symbols in lower case (*e.g.*, $\boldsymbol{x}$) represent vectors and symbols in upper case (e.g., $\boldsymbol{X}$) represent matrices. Unless stated differently, $\boldsymbol{x}_i$ also represents a vector where i is used to distinguish different vectors. We denote the i-th row of matrix $\boldsymbol{X}$ by $\boldsymbol{X}_i$ and its (i, j)-th element by $\boldsymbol{X}_{ij}$.

2.1 Overview of Model-based Recommenders

Most machine learning models can be specified through two components: **model definition** and **objective function** during training. The model definition formulates the relationship between the input (*e.g.*, user ids, item ids, interactions, other features, etc.) and output (ratings or implicit feedback of items). The objective function is what the training process optimizes to find the best model parameters.

Recommender Models

In general, recommender models are defined as

$$\hat{y}_{ui} = \mathcal{F}_{\boldsymbol{\theta}}(u, i), \tag{1}$$

where $\hat{y}_{ui}$ is the predicted preference of user u on item i, and $\boldsymbol{\theta}$ denotes the model parameters we need to learn from training data.

Different choices of the function $\mathcal{F}_{\boldsymbol{\theta}}$ correspond to different assumptions about how the output depends on the input. Here we review 4 common recommender models.

Latent Factor Model (LFM). LFM models the preference $\hat{y}_{ui}$ as the dot product of latent factor vectors $\boldsymbol{v}_u$ and $\boldsymbol{v}_i$, representing the user and the item, respectively [9, 17]. [2]

$$\hat{y}_{ui} = \mathcal{F}^{LFM}_{\boldsymbol{v}}(u, i) = \boldsymbol{v}_u^\top \boldsymbol{v}_i \tag{2}$$

In addition, hierarchical latent factor models [1, 32] and the factorization machine [14] can model interactions between user or item side features.

[2] To simplify notation, we assume that the latent factors are padded with a constant to model the bias.

Similarity Model (SM). The Similarity model [8] models the user's preference for item i as a weighted combination of the user's preference for item j and the item similarity between i and j. It is a natural extension of an item-based nearest neighbor model. The difference is that SM does not use predefined forms of item similarity (*e.g.*, *Jaccard*, *Cosine*). Instead, it learns a similarity matrix from data [12].

$$\hat{y}_{ui} = \mathcal{F}^{SM}_{\boldsymbol{S}}(u, i) = \sum_{j \in \mathcal{O}_u \setminus \{i\}} y_{uj} \cdot \boldsymbol{S}_{ji} \tag{3}$$

Factorized Similarity Model (FSM). The problem with the Similarity Model is that the number of parameters is quadratic in the number of items, which is usually impractical. A straightforward solution is to factorize the similarity matrix into two low rank matrices [8, 7].

$$\hat{y}_{ui} = \mathcal{F}^{FSM}_{\boldsymbol{p},\boldsymbol{q}}(u, i) = \left(\sum_{j \in \mathcal{O}_u \setminus \{i\}} y_{uj} \cdot \boldsymbol{p}_j \right)^\top \boldsymbol{q}_i \tag{4}$$

LFSM (LFM+FSM). The above models can also be combined. For example, combining LFM and FSM results in the model SVD++ [8], which proved to be one of the best single models for the Netflix Prize.

$$\hat{y}_{ui} = \mathcal{F}^{LFSM}_{\boldsymbol{p},\boldsymbol{q}}(u, i) = \left(\sum_{j \in \mathcal{O}_u \setminus \{i\}} y_{uj} \cdot \boldsymbol{p}_j + \boldsymbol{p}_u \right)^\top \boldsymbol{q}_i \tag{5}$$

Objective Functions for Recommenders

Objective functions for training recommender models can be roughly grouped into two groups: point-wise and pair-wise.[3] Pair-wise objectives approximates ranking loss by considering the relative order of the predictions for pairs of items. Point-wise objectives, on the other hand, only depend on the accuracy of the prediction of individual preferences. Pair-wise functions are usually considered to be more suitable for optimizing top-N recommendation performance. However, as we demonstrate in our experiments, this is not necessarily the case for all data sets.

Regardless of the choice of a pair-wise or point-wise objective function, it is critical to properly take into account unobserved feedback within the model. Models that only consider the observed feedback fail to account for the fact that ratings are *not* missing at random. These models are not suitable for top-N recommenders [13, 23].

Let $\ell(\cdot)$ denote a loss function and $\Omega(\boldsymbol{\theta})$ a regularization term that controls model complexity and encodes any prior information such as *sparsity*, *non-negativity*, or *graph regularization*. We can write the general forms of objective functions for recommender training as follows.

Point-wise objective function.

$$\sum_{(u,i) \in \mathcal{O}'} \ell_{point}(y_{ui}, \hat{y}_{ui}) + \lambda \Omega(\boldsymbol{\theta}). \tag{6}$$

Here $\mathcal{O}'$ denotes an augmented dataset that includes unobserved user-item pairs. The problem with using only observed user-item pairs is that, when users provide only implicit "like"s without explicit ratings, all the observed values y_{ui} are equal to 1. In this case, directly optimizing the point-wise objective function over $\mathcal{O}$ leads

[3] Some models use list-wise objective functions [28, 22], but they are not as widely adopted as point-wise and pair-wise objectives.

Table 1: Overview of related model-based recommenders.

Name	Model	Objective Function
MF [9] / PMF [17]	LFM	ℓ^{SL}_{point}
SVD++ [8]	LFSM	ℓ^{SL}_{point}
MMMF [16]	LFM	ℓ^{HL}_{point}
WSABIE [29]	LFM	ℓ^{HL}_{pair}
BPR-MF [15]	LFM	ℓ^{LL}_{pair}
SLIM [12]	SM	ℓ^{SL}_{point}
FISM [7]	FSM	ℓ^{SL}_{point}, ℓ^{SL}_{pair}
WRMF [6]	LFM	*weighted* ℓ^{SL}_{point}
COFI [28]	LFM	NDCG loss
CLIMF [21]	LFM	MRR loss

to a trivial model that predicts all the ratings as 1.[4] A common solution is to augment $\mathcal{O}$ with a subset of *negative* user-item pairs[5] from the unobserved set $\bar{\mathcal{O}} = \{\mathcal{U} \times \mathcal{I}\} \setminus \mathcal{O}$, and train the model on the augmented set $\mathcal{O}'$. Several strategies for sampling negative user-item pairs are discussed in [13]. $\mathcal{O}'$ can also include duplicate samples to simulate weighted feedback (*e.g.*, [6]).

Pair-wise objective function.

$$\sum_{(u,i,j)\in\mathcal{P}} \ell_{pair}(y_{uij}, \hat{y}_{uij}) + \lambda\Omega(\boldsymbol{\theta}), \tag{7}$$

where $y_{uij} = y_{ui} - y_{uj}$, $\hat{y}_{uij} = \hat{y}_{ui} - \hat{y}_{uj}$, and $\mathcal{P}$ is a set of triplets sampled from $\mathcal{O}'$, each of which includes a user u and a pair of items i and j, where usually i is a positive item and j is a negative item.

For both pair-wise and point-wise objective functions, the choice of the loss function $\ell(\cdot)$ is important. Here we list a few commonly used loss functions for both point-wise and pair-wise objectives:

- SQUARE LOSS: $\ell^{SL}(y, \hat{y}) = \frac{1}{2}(y - \hat{y})^2$;
- LOG LOSS: $\ell^{LL}(y, \hat{y}) = \log(1 + \exp(-y \cdot \hat{y}))$;
- HINGE LOSS: $\ell^{HL}(y, \hat{y}) = \max(0, 1 - y \cdot \hat{y})$;
- CROSS ENTROPY LOSS: $\ell^{CE}(y, \hat{y}) = -y\log(p) - (1 - y)\log(1 - p)$, where $p = \sigma(\hat{y}) = 1/(1 + \exp(-\hat{y}))$.

Note that, for LOG and HINGE losses, the value y for the negative examples should be -1 instead of 0.

Table 1 summarizes recent models for top-n recommendation that fit this framework. For explicit feedback, the loss function can be slightly different (*e.g.*,[11]). Also, several recent papers study position-aware pair-wise loss functions (*e.g.*, WARP [29, 30], CLiMF [21]). For this paper, we do not propose any new objective functions. Any objective function that fits the described framework can be used with our model.

To summarize, the two key components of designing model-based recommenders are: 1) a suitable way to represent the relations between inputs and outputs. 2) a proper objective function and a proper way to deal with the relationship between observed and unobserved feedback.

2.2 Denoising Auto-Encoders

A classical auto-encoder [2] is typically implemented as a one-hidden-layer neural network that takes a vector $\boldsymbol{x} \in \mathbb{R}^D$ as input and maps it to a hidden representation $\boldsymbol{z} \in \mathbb{R}^K$ through a mapping function

$$\boldsymbol{z} = h(\boldsymbol{x}) = \sigma\left(\boldsymbol{W}^\top \boldsymbol{x} + \boldsymbol{b}\right),$$

where $\boldsymbol{W}$ is a $D \times K$ weight matrix and $\boldsymbol{b} \in \mathbb{K}$ is an offset vector. The resulting latent representation is then mapped back to a reconstructed vector $\hat{\boldsymbol{x}} \in \mathbb{R}^D$ through

$$\hat{\boldsymbol{x}} = \sigma\left(\boldsymbol{W}'\boldsymbol{z} + \boldsymbol{b}'\right).$$

The reverse mapping may optionally be constrained by *tied weights*, where $\boldsymbol{W}' = \boldsymbol{W}$.

The parameters of this model are trained to minimize the average reconstruction error:

$$\underset{\boldsymbol{W},\boldsymbol{W}',\boldsymbol{b},\boldsymbol{b}'}{\arg\min} \frac{1}{n}\sum_{i=1}^{n} \ell(\boldsymbol{x}_i, \hat{\boldsymbol{x}}_i), \tag{8}$$

where ℓ is a loss function such as the *square loss* or the *cross entropy loss* mentioned in the previous subsection.

The Denoising Auto-encoder (DAE) [24] extends the classical auto-encoder by training to reconstruct each data point $\boldsymbol{x}$ from its (partially) corrupted version $\tilde{\boldsymbol{x}}$. The goal of DAE is to force the hidden layer to discover more robust features and to prevent it from simply learning the identity function [24]. The corrupted input $\tilde{x}$ is typically drawn from a conditional distribution $p(\tilde{\boldsymbol{x}}|\boldsymbol{x})$. Common corruption choices are the additive Gaussian noise and the multiplicative mask-out/drop-out noise. Under mask-out/drop-out corruption, one randomly overwrites each of the dimensions of $\boldsymbol{x}$ with 0 with a probability of q:

$$\begin{aligned} P(\tilde{\boldsymbol{x}}_d = \delta\boldsymbol{x}_d) &= 1 - q \\ P(\tilde{\boldsymbol{x}}_d = 0) &= q \end{aligned} \tag{9}$$

To make the corruption unbiased, one sets the uncorrupted values to $\delta = 1/(1 - q)$ times their original value.

3. PROPOSED METHODOLOGY

In this section, we introduce a new model–Collaborative Denoising Auto-Encoder (CDAE). The model learns correlations between the user's item preference by training on a corrupted version of the known preference set. A preference set is binary, *i.e.*, containing only information about whether an item is preferred or not. Therefore, as we will see, CDAE is uniquely suitable for top-N preference recommendations.

3.1 Collaborative Denoising Auto-Encoder

Similar to the standard Denoising Auto-Encoder, CDAE is also represented as a one-hidden-layer neural network. The key difference is that the input also encodes a latent vector for the user, which allows CDAE to be a much better recommender model, as we see in section 5. Figure 1 shows a sample structure of CDAE. CDAE consists of 3 layers, including the input layer, the hidden layer and the output layer.

In the input layer, there are in total $I + 1$ nodes, where each of the first I nodes corresponds to an item, and the last node is a user-specific node (the red node in the figure), which means the node and its associated weights are unique for each user $u \in \mathcal{U}$ in the data. We refer to the first I nodes as *item input nodes*, and the last node as *user input node*. Given the historical feedback $\mathcal{O}$ by users on the item set $\mathcal{I}$, we can transform $\mathcal{O}$ into the training set containing U instances $\{\boldsymbol{y}_1, \boldsymbol{y}_2, ..., \boldsymbol{y}_U\}$, where $\boldsymbol{y}_u = \{y_{u1}, y_{u2}, ..., y_{uI}\}$ is the I-dimensional feedback vector of user u on all the item in $\mathcal{I}$. $\boldsymbol{y}_u$ is a sparse binary vector that only has $|\mathcal{O}_u|$ non-zero values: $y_{ui} = 1$ if i is in the set $\mathcal{O}_u$, otherwise, $y_{ui} = 0$.

[4]For explicit feedback data, only modeling observed feedback is also insufficient to make good top-N recommendations [13, 23].
[5]Here we use the term *negative* to denote missing feedback.

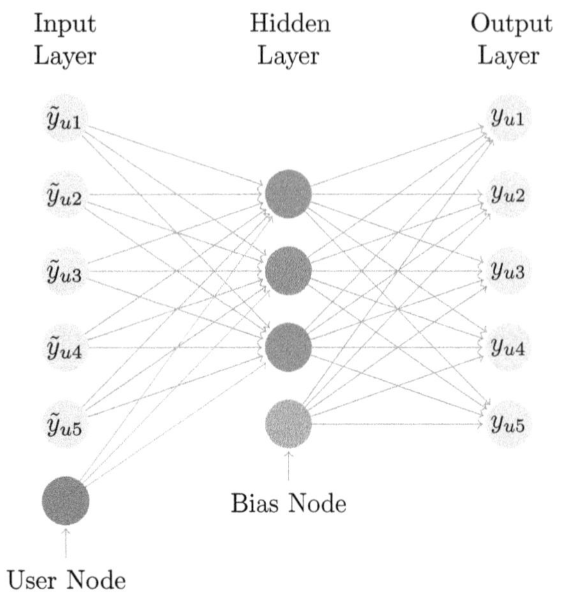

Figure 1: A sample CDAE illustration for a user u. The links between nodes are associated with different weights. The links with *red* color are user specific. Other weights are shared across all the users.

There are K nodes in the hidden layer and these nodes are fully connected to the nodes of the input layer. Here K is a predefined constant which is usually much smaller than the size of the input vectors. The hidden layer also has an additional node to model the bias effects (the pink node in the figure). We use $\boldsymbol{W} \in \mathbb{R}^{I \times K}$ to denote the weight matrix between the *item input nodes* and the nodes in the hidden layer, and $\boldsymbol{V}_u \in \mathbb{R}^K$ to denote the weight vector for the *user input node*. Note that $\boldsymbol{V}_u$ is a user-specific vector, *i.e.*, for each of the users we have one unique vector. From another point of view, $\boldsymbol{W}_i$ and $\boldsymbol{V}_u$ can be seen as the distributed representations of item i and user u respectively.

In the output layer, there are I nodes representing reconstructions of the input vector $\boldsymbol{y}_u$. The nodes in the output layer are fully connected with nodes in the hidden layer. The weight matrix is denoted by $\boldsymbol{W}' \in \mathbb{R}^{I \times K}$. We denote the weight vector for the bias node in the hidden layer by $\boldsymbol{b} \in \mathcal{R}^I$.

Formally, the inputs of CDAE are the corrupted feedback vector $\tilde{\boldsymbol{y}}_u$ which is generated from $p(\tilde{\boldsymbol{y}}_u|\boldsymbol{y}_u)$ as stated in Equation 9. Intuitively, the non-zero values in $\boldsymbol{y}_u$ are randomly dropped out independently with probability q. The resulting vector $\tilde{\boldsymbol{y}}_u$ is still a sparse vector, where the indexes of the non-zero values are a subset of those of the original vector.

CDAE first maps the input to a latent representations $\boldsymbol{z}_u$, which is computed as follows:[6]

$$\boldsymbol{z}_u = h\left(\boldsymbol{W}^\top \tilde{\boldsymbol{y}}_u + \boldsymbol{V}_u + \boldsymbol{b}\right), \tag{10}$$

where $h(\cdot)$ is an *element-wise* mapping function (e.g., *identity function* $h(\boldsymbol{x}) = \boldsymbol{x}$ or *sigmoid function* $h(\boldsymbol{x}) = \sigma(\boldsymbol{x}) = 1/(1+e^{-\boldsymbol{x}})$), and $\boldsymbol{b} \in \mathbb{R}^K$ is the offset vector.

At the output layer, the latent representation is then mapped back to the original input space to reconstruct the input vector. The output value $\hat{y}_{ui}$ for node i is computed as follows:

$$\hat{y}_{ui} = f\left(\boldsymbol{W}_i'^\top \boldsymbol{z}_u + b_i'\right), \tag{11}$$

where $\boldsymbol{W}' \in \mathbb{R}^{I \times K}$ and $\boldsymbol{b}'$ are the weight matrix and the offset vector for the output layer, respectively. $f(\cdot)$ is also a mapping function.

We learn the parameters of CDAE by minimizing the average reconstruction error:

$$\underset{\boldsymbol{W},\boldsymbol{W}',\boldsymbol{V},\boldsymbol{b},\boldsymbol{b}'}{\arg\min} \frac{1}{U}\sum_{u=1}^{U} \mathbb{E}_{p(\tilde{\boldsymbol{y}}_u|\boldsymbol{y}_u)} \left[\ell\left(\tilde{\boldsymbol{y}}_u, \hat{\boldsymbol{y}}_u\right)\right] + \mathcal{R}\left(\boldsymbol{W}, \boldsymbol{W}', \boldsymbol{V}, \boldsymbol{b}, \boldsymbol{b}'\right), \tag{12}$$

where $\mathcal{R}$ is the regularization term to control the model complexity. In this paper we use the squared $L2$ Norm.

$$\mathcal{R}(\cdot) = \frac{\lambda}{2}\left(\|\boldsymbol{W}\|_2^2 + \|\boldsymbol{W}'\|_2^2 + \|\boldsymbol{V}\|_2^2 + \|\boldsymbol{b}\|_2^2 + \|\boldsymbol{b}'\|_2^2\right) \tag{13}$$

We apply Stochastic Gradient Descent (SGD) to learn the parameters. Algorithm 1 provides the detailed procedure. Because the number of output nodes equals the number of items, the time complexity of one iteration over all users is $O(UIK)$, which is impractical when the number of users and the number of items are large. Instead of computing the gradients on all the outputs, we only sample a subset of the negative items $\mathcal{S}_u$ from $\bar{\mathcal{O}}_u$ and compute the gradients on the items in $\mathcal{O}_u \cup \mathcal{S}_u$. The size of $\mathcal{S}_u$ is proportional to the size of $\mathcal{O}_u$. So the overall complexity of the learning algorithm is linear in the size of $\mathcal{O}$ and the number of latent dimensions K. A similar method has been discussed in [5]. An alternative solution is to build a *Hierarchical Softmax* tree on the output layer [10], but it requires the loss function on the output layer to be softmax loss.

Algorithm 1 Learning algorithm for CDAE

```
Initialize parameters with random values.
iter ← 0
while iter < maxIter or error on validation set decreases do
    for all u ∈ U do
        Sample ỹ_u ~ p(ỹ_u|y_u) using Equation 9.
        Compute z_u using Equation 10.
        Sample negative samples S_u ⊂ Ō_u.
        for all i ∈ O_u ∪ S_u do
            Update W'_i and b'_i using Equation 14, 15 and 20.
        end for
        Compute ∂ℓ/∂z_u using Equation 16.
        for all j ∈ {j | j ∈ I and ỹ_uj > 0} do
            Update W_j using Equation 17 and 20.
        end for
        Update V_u using Equation 18 and 20.
        Update b using Equation 19 and 20.
    end for
    iter ← iter + 1
end while
```

The gradients for the parameters are as follows:

$$\frac{\partial \ell}{\partial \boldsymbol{W}_i'} = \frac{\partial \ell}{\partial \hat{y}_{ui}} \frac{\partial \hat{y}_{ui}}{\partial \boldsymbol{W}_i'} + \lambda \boldsymbol{W}_i' \tag{14}$$

$$\frac{\partial \ell}{\partial b_i'} = \frac{\partial \ell}{\partial \hat{y}_{ui}} \frac{\partial \hat{y}_{ui}}{\partial b_i'} + \lambda b_i' \tag{15}$$

$$\frac{\partial \ell}{\partial \boldsymbol{z}_u} = \sum_{i \in \mathcal{O}_u \cup \mathcal{S}_u} \frac{\partial \ell}{\partial \hat{y}_{ui}} \frac{\partial \hat{y}_{ui}}{\partial \boldsymbol{z}_u} + \lambda \boldsymbol{z}_u \tag{16}$$

[6] Here we compute the hidden representation using the sum of the weight vectors. Other choices such as concatenation and max pooling are also possible.

Table 2: **Sample Mapping Functions. Note that all the operations in this table are element-wise.**

	$h(\boldsymbol{x})$	Gradient $\frac{\partial h}{\partial \boldsymbol{x}}$
Identity	$\boldsymbol{x}$	$\mathbf{1}$
Sigmoid	$\sigma(\boldsymbol{x})$	$\sigma(\boldsymbol{x})(\mathbf{1}-\sigma(\boldsymbol{x}))$
Tanh	$\tanh(\boldsymbol{x})$	$\mathbf{1}-\tanh^2(\boldsymbol{x})$

$$\frac{\partial \ell}{\partial \boldsymbol{W}_j} = \frac{\partial \ell}{\partial \boldsymbol{z}_u}\frac{\partial \boldsymbol{z}_u}{\partial \boldsymbol{W}_j} + \lambda \boldsymbol{W}_j \tag{17}$$

$$\frac{\partial \ell}{\partial \boldsymbol{V}_u} = \frac{\partial \ell}{\partial \boldsymbol{z}_u}\frac{\partial \boldsymbol{z}_u}{\partial \boldsymbol{V}_u} + \lambda \boldsymbol{V}_u \tag{18}$$

$$\frac{\partial \ell}{\partial \boldsymbol{b}} = \frac{\partial \ell}{\partial \boldsymbol{z}_u}\frac{\partial \boldsymbol{z}_u}{\partial \boldsymbol{b}} + \lambda \boldsymbol{b} \tag{19}$$

We apply AdaGrad [4] to automatically adapt the step size during the learning procedure. The update formula is as follows:

$$\boldsymbol{\theta}^{(t+1)} = \boldsymbol{\theta}^{(t)} - \frac{\eta \boldsymbol{g}_\theta^{(t)}}{\sqrt{\beta + \sum_{s=1}^{t} \boldsymbol{g}_\theta^{(s)}}}, \tag{20}$$

where $\boldsymbol{\theta}^{(t)}$ is the value of the parameter $\boldsymbol{\theta}$ at the t-th SGD step and $\boldsymbol{g}_\theta^{(t)}$ is its gradient at step t.

Recommendation. At prediction time, CDAE takes user u's existing reference set (without corruption) as input, and the items from the candidate set $\bar{\mathcal{O}}_u$ that have largest prediction values on the output layer are recommended to him/her.

3.2 Discussion

Components. CDAE is very flexible in that the mapping function $h(\cdot)$, point-wise or pair-wise objectives, the loss function $\ell(\cdot)$, and the corruption probability q can all be chosen to suit the application. Table 2 lists mapping function choices explored in this paper. As for the loss function, all the choices discussed in Section 2.1, both *point-wise* and *pair-wise*, can be used. Different choices of these functions result in different variants of the model with different representation capabilities. Our experiments show that no single variant always produces the best results. One benefit of the proposed general framework is that one can try several variants and find the one that best fits the task.

It's worth noting that pair-wise objective does not perform much better than point-wise objective for CDAE, at least in our experiments. Similar results have also been reported in [7]. This may be a characteristic of implicit feedback data. See section 5.4 for more details.

Generalization of other models. CDAE is a generalization of latent factor models. The representations mentioned in Section 2.1 can all be interpreted as special cases of this framework.

Specifically, if we choose the *identity* mapping function for both $h(x)$ and $f(x)$ and not add noise to the inputs, the output value of $\hat{y}_{ui}$ in Equation 11 becomes:

$$\begin{aligned} \hat{y}_{ui} &= f\left(\boldsymbol{W}_i'^{\top} \boldsymbol{z}_u + b_i'\right) \\ &= \boldsymbol{W}_i'^{\top} h\left(\boldsymbol{W}^{\top}\tilde{\boldsymbol{y}}_u + \boldsymbol{V}_u + \boldsymbol{b}\right) + b_i' \\ &\cong \boldsymbol{W}_i'^{\top}\left(\sum_{j\in\mathcal{O}_u} \tilde{y}_{ui}\boldsymbol{W}_j + \boldsymbol{V}_u\right). \end{aligned} \tag{21}$$

In the last step we omit the bias term to make the comparison clearer. We can see that the representation in Equation 21 is equivalent to that in Equation 5, *i.e.*, the **LFSM** model.

If we set the corruption level q to 1, all the non-zero values in the input vector would be dropped out. We get the following prediction:

$$\hat{y}_{ui} = \boldsymbol{W}_i'^{\top}\boldsymbol{V}_u, \tag{22}$$

which is equivalent to the representation in Equation 2, *i.e.*, the LFM model. Alternatively, if we remove the *user input node* and its associated weights, the resulting model is equivalent to **FSM** in Equation 4:

$$\hat{y}_{ui} = \boldsymbol{W}_i'^{\top}\left(\sum_{j\in\mathcal{O}_u} \tilde{y}_{ui}\boldsymbol{W}_j\right). \tag{23}$$

Another possible mapping function is the *linear* function $h(\boldsymbol{x}) = \boldsymbol{U}^\top \boldsymbol{x}$, where $\boldsymbol{U}$ is a $K \times K$ transform matrix. If we use a user-specific matrix $\boldsymbol{U}_u \in \mathbb{R}^{K\times K}$ on the hidden layer, the representation becomes

$$\hat{y}_{ui} = \boldsymbol{W}_i'^{\top}\left(\boldsymbol{U}_u^{\top}\left(\sum_{j\in\mathcal{O}_u} \tilde{y}_{ui}\boldsymbol{W}_j\right)\right), \tag{24}$$

which is related to the Latent Collaborative Retrieval model proposed in [30].

We tried the *linear* mapping function in our experiments, but found that its performance is not as good as others. One reason is likely that it has many more parameters to estimate, which can easily lead to overfitting. We also experimented with setting $\boldsymbol{U}_u$ to be a diagonal matrix to reduce the number of parameters, but the improvements over the identity were still not significant. With this in mind, we do not include the linear mapping function in Table 2, nor report the results in the rest of this paper.

Summary. CDAE is a flexible framework for top-N recommendation. It generalizes several very popular existing methods. The proposed framework is naturally compatible with the denoising trick, which can further improve the results of recommendation, as shown in the next section.

4. RELATED WORK

An overview of the model-based collaborative filter methods has been discussed in Section 2.1. In this section, we discuss the few related works on neural networks for recommender systems.

Restricted Boltzmann Machines (RBM) [18] is the first work that applies neural network models to recommender systems. However, RBM targets rating prediction, not top-N recommendation, and its loss function considers only the observed ratings. It is technically challenging to incorporate negative sampling, which would be required for top-N recommendation, into the training of RBM. For this reason, we do not compare with RBM in our experiments, but test several other neural network baselines that work for top-N recommendation (see Section 5.4).

We are aware of a concurrent proposal called AutoRec [20], which uses the Auto-Encoder for rating prediction. The main differences are as follows: 1) AutoRec only considers the observed ratings in the loss function, which does not guarantee the performance for top-N recommendation. 2) They use the vanilla Auto-Encoder structure, while we prove that introducing user factors in the model can greatly improve performance. 3) AutoRec does not employ the denoising technique, which is a major part of our work.

Another related work is [27], which also uses the Auto-Encoder for recommender systems. This work studies the particular problem of article recommendation, and improves the well-known model Collaborative Topic Regression [26] by replacing its Topic Model component by a Bayesian Auto-Encoder, which is used for learning the latent feature representations for the articles. Different from

Table 3: Dataset Statistics

	#users	#items	#dyads	density(%)
ML	69K	8.8K	5M	0.82
Netflix	37K	11K	4.8M	1.18
Yelp	9.6K	7K	243K	0.36

this model, our model is a generic model and addresses the general top-N recommendation problem, and the inputs are user behaviors instead of item/article features.

5. EXPERIMENTAL RESULTS

Our experimental evaluation consists of two parts. First, we study the effects of various choices of the components of CDAE. Second, we compare CDAE against other state-of-the-art top-N recommendation methods. The source code of CDAE will be available from https://github.com/jasonyaw/CDAE.

5.1 Data Sets and Experimental Setup

We use 3 popular data sets: MovieLens 10M (ML)[7], Netflix[8] and Yelp (from Yelp Dataset Challenge[9] in 2014). For each data set, we keep those with ratings no less than 4 stars and treat all other ratings as missing entries. Those ratings that are retained are converted to a y_{ui} score of 1. This processing method is widely used in previous work on recommendation with implicit feedback (e.g., [15, 31, 7]). We iteratively remove users and items with fewer than 5 ratings. For each user, we randomly hold 20% of the ratings in the test set, and put the other ratings in the training set. The statistics of the resulting data sets are shown in Table 3.

5.2 Implementation Details

We perform 5-fold cross validation on the training data sets to select the best hyperparameters for all the models, and then use the best hyperparameters to train models on the whole training data sets.

We use Stochastic Gradient Decent (SGD) to learn the parameters for both the proposed method and comparison partners. AdaGrad [4] is used to automatically adapt the step size during the learning procedures. We set $\beta = 1$ and try different step sizes $\eta \in \{1, 0.1, 0.01, 0.001\}$ and report the best result for each model.

For negative sampling, we experiment with different numbers of negative samples and find that $NS = 5$ consistently produces good results. This means that, for each user, the number of negative samples is 5 times the number of observed ratings of this user.

5.3 Evaluation Metrics

In the case of top-N recommender systems, we present each user with N items that have the highest predicted values but are not adopted by the user in the training data. We evaluate different approaches based on which of the items are actually adopted by the user in the test data.

Precision and Recall. Given a top-N recommendation list $C_{N,\text{rec}}$, precision and recall are defined as

$$\text{Precision@}N = \frac{|C_{N,\text{rec}} \bigcap C_{\text{adopted}}|}{N}$$
$$\text{Recall@}N = \frac{|C_{N,\text{rec}} \bigcap C_{\text{adopted}}|}{|C_{\text{adopted}}|}, \quad (25)$$

[7]http://grouplens.org/datasets/movielens

[8]http://www.netflixprize.com

[9]http://www.yelp.com/dataset_challenge

where C_{adopted} are the items that a user has adopted in the test data. The precision and recall for the entire recommender system are computed by averaging the precision and recall over all the users, respectively.

Mean Average Precision (MAP). Average precision (AP) is a ranked precision metric that gives larger credit to correctly recommended items in top ranks. AP@N is defined as the average of precisions computed at all positions with an adopted item, namely,

$$\text{AP@}N = \frac{\sum_{k=1}^{N} \text{Precision@}k \times \text{rel}(k)}{\min\{N, |C_{\text{adopted}}|\}}, \quad (26)$$

where Precision(k) is the precision at cut-off k in the top-N list $C_{N,\text{rec}}$, and rel(k) is an indicator function equaling 1 if the item at rank k is adopted, otherwise zero. Finally, Mean Average Precision (MAP@N) is defined as the mean of the AP scores for all users.

Usually, these metrics are consistent with each other, *i.e.*, if a model performs better than another model on one metric, it is more likely that it will also produce better results on another metric. Due to space limits, we mainly show the results of MAP@N with $N = \{1, 5, 10\}$ on several evaluation tasks since it takes the positions into consideration.

5.4 Analysis of CDAE Components

The main components of the proposed CDAE model include the types of the mapping functions, the loss function and the level of corruption. Different choices of these components result in different variants of the model that make different top-N recommendations. In this subsection, we study these variants on the 3 data sets.

For the mapping function, we show results for the *identity* function and *sigmoid* function on the hidden layer and the output layer. (Results for the *tanh* function are similar to those of the *sigmoid* function and hence omitted.) There are $2^3 = 8$ total combinations of choices for the mapping functions (on both layers) and the loss function. Among them, the logistic loss function requires $\hat{y}$ to be a value between 0 and 1, so it must be associated with a sigmoid function on the output layer. Note that the combination of the sigmoid function and the logistic loss is equivalent to the cross entropy loss discussed in Section 2.1. Therefore, we study 4 variants[10] of our model in this subsection. Table 4 describes the function choices for each variant.

Table 4: Four sample variants of the CDAE model.

	Hidden Layer	Output Layer	Loss Function
M1	Identity	Identity	Square
M2	Identity	Sigmoid	Logistic
M3	Sigmoid	Identity	Square
M4	Sigmoid	Sigmoid	Logistic

In our extensive experiments, we observed that the pair-wise objective function did not perform much better than point-wise objectives for CDAE. One possible cause is that for the implicit feedback with binary ratings, point-wise loss functions are sufficient for separating those items preferred by the user and those not preferred. In other words, a well-designed point-wise loss can be discriminating enough to model the user's preference in these datasets, and the pair-wise loss is not needed. For this reason, results on pair-wise objective functions are omitted in the rest of this paper. On a related note, as we show in section 5.5, the BPR model, which uses pair-wise loss, does not perform better than MF, which uses point-wise

[10]We omit the results of another 2 variants (replacing the loss functions of M2 and M4 with square loss) since their performances are similar to those of M2 and M4 respectively.

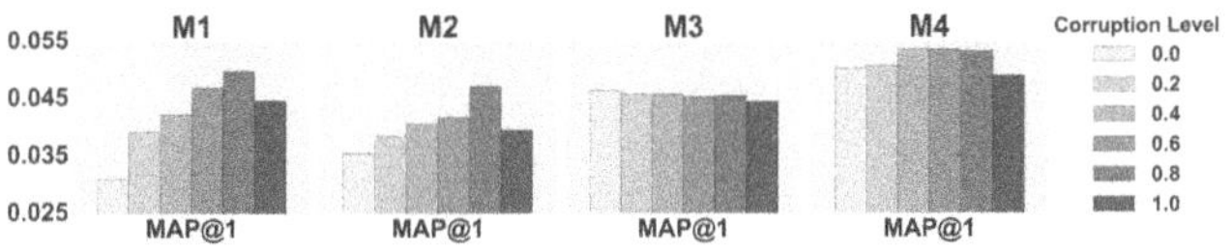

(a) MAP@1

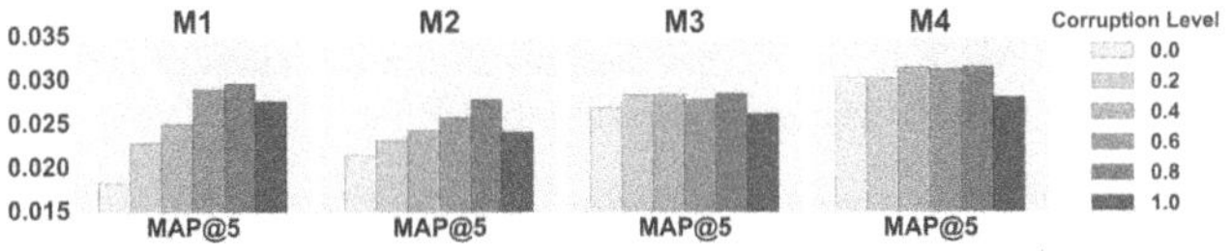

(b) MAP@5

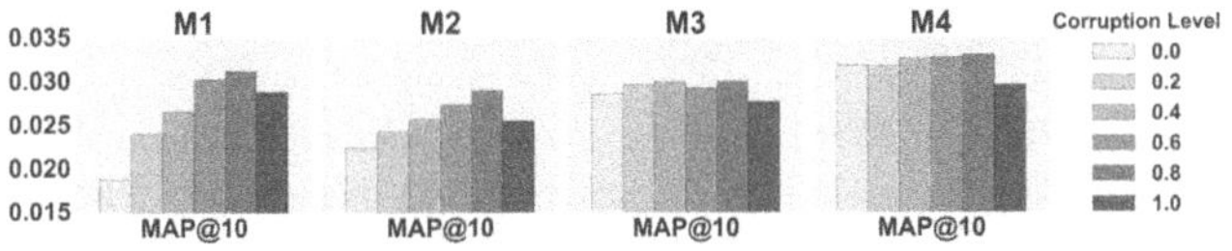

(c) MAP@10

Figure 2: Model performance comparison on Yelp data.

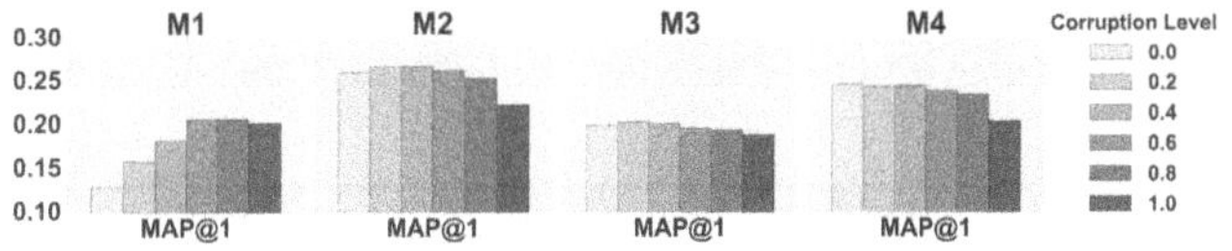

(a) MAP@1

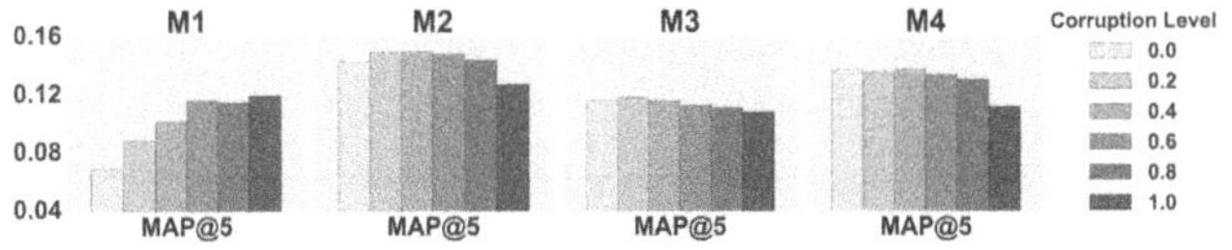

(b) MAP@5

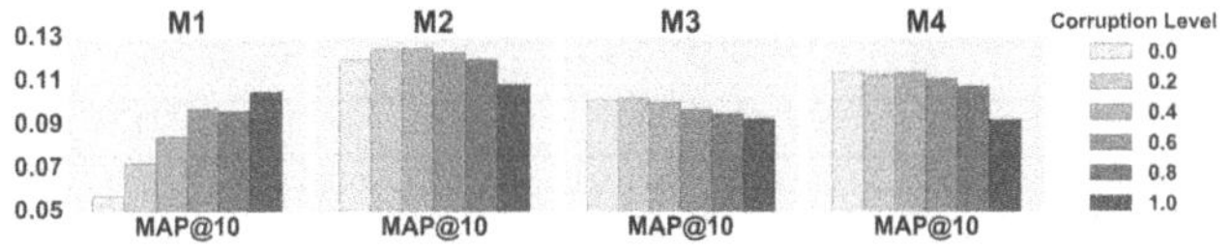

(c) MAP@10

Figure 3: Model performance comparison on Netflix data.

loss. Similar results have also been reported in [7]. This might be due to the same reason as for CDAE. Moreover, BPR is designed to optimize for the AUC, not top-N metrics such as precision, recall, or MAP. Hence, for multiple models for top-N recommendation, pair-wise loss functions may not be necessary for all data sets.

We train each of the four variants under varying corruption levels (q in Equation 9) from $\{0, 0.2, 0.4, 0.6, 0.8, 1\}$. The number of latent dimensions K is set to 50 unless otherwise stated. The results on the three data sets are shown in Figure 2, 3 and 4 respectively.

The general observation is that the best model depends on the data set. No single variant of CDAE always produces the best results. So one should choose the components (mapping function, objective function, loss function, and corruption level) depending on the data. Consider the two different extremes of corruption level: $q = 0$ (no input corruption) and $q = 1$ (complete input corruption). For variant M1, the results of $q = 0$ are much worse than those of $q = 1$. This indicates that simply summing up all the input vectors ($q = 0$) is insufficient for learning good representations, and is in fact worse than dropping out all of them ($q = 1$). Note that introducing non-linear functions can largely alleviate the problem, as evidenced in the results for the other three variants with $q = 0$. Adding noise on the input can also prevent this problem (see the results of M1 with various corruption levels), which means that the denoising technique can help with learning more robust representations.

The denoising technique appears beneficial especially for variants M1 and M2. On the Yelp data set, all four variants can be improved by adding relatively higher levels of noise (e.g., $q = 0.8$). Variant M2 is the best model for the Netflix data set, and setting $q = 0.2$ and $q = 0.4$ can slightly improve the results. On MovieLens data, setting $q = 0.8$ makes M2 almost as good as M4, the best model. However, in some cases, the best results are those without any input corruption ($q = 0$).

In general, M4 produces relatively better results on all three data sets. In particular, it achieves the best MAP scores on Yelp and MovieLens. This indicates that non-linear functions help to increase the representation capability of the model, thus improving the recommendations.

Comparison with DAE. A main difference between CDAE and classical DAE is the user-specific input between the input layer and the hidden layer, namely, the vector $\boldsymbol{V}_u$. We study two cases here – with the user-specific vectors (CDAE) and without the user-specific vectors (DAE). We conduct experiments on the three data

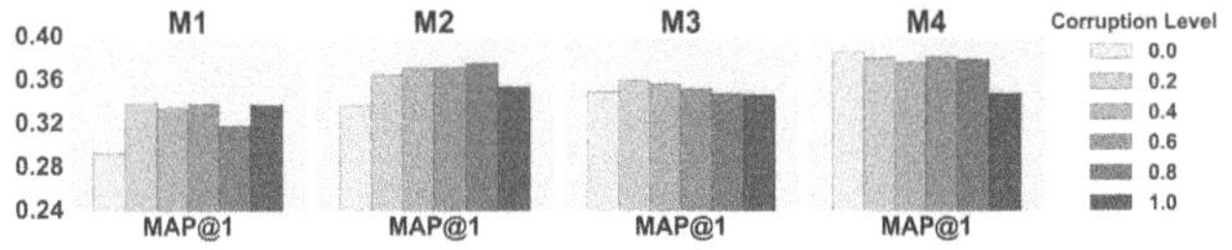

(a) MAP@1

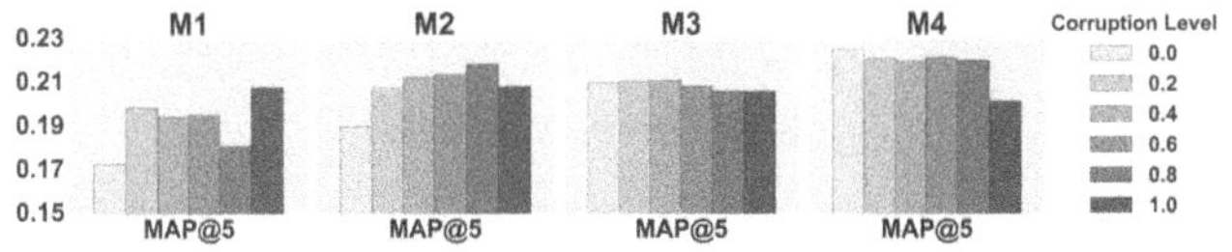

(b) MAP@5

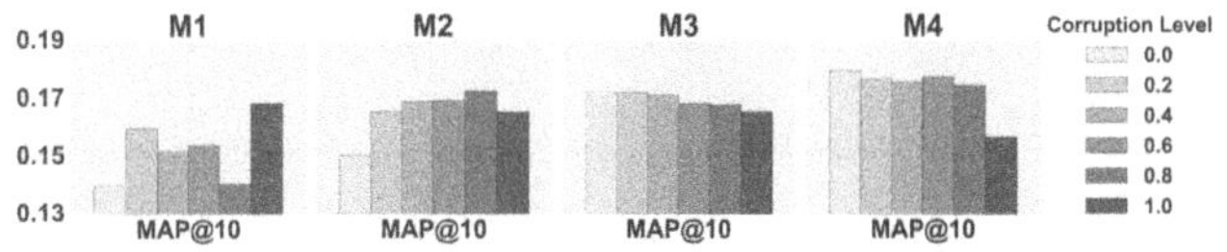

(c) MAP@10

Figure 4: Model performance comparison on MovieLens data.

Table 5: Comparison with DAE on the Yelp data.

	MAP@1		MAP@5		MAP@10	
Model	**DAE**	**CDAE**	**DAE**	**CDAE**	**DAE**	**CDAE**
M1	0.0275	0.0327	0.0164	0.0201	0.0172	0.0210
M2	0.0369	0.0420	0.0225	0.0241	0.0236	0.0254
M3	0.0443	0.0460	0.0270	0.0285	0.0289	0.0303
M4	0.0529	0.0528	0.0315	0.0319	0.0329	0.0334

Table 6: Comparison with DAE on the MovieLens data.

	MAP@1		MAP@5		MAP@10	
Model	**DAE**	**CDAE**	**DAE**	**CDAE**	**DAE**	**CDAE**
M1	0.2807	0.2933	0.1619	0.1730	0.1278	0.1402
M2	0.3134	0.3368	0.1785	0.1900	0.1408	0.1509
M3	0.3270	0.3494	0.1953	0.2099	0.1579	0.1722
M4	0.3625	0.3860	0.2123	0.2252	0.1684	0.1797

sets, and get relatively similar results. We show the results on the Yelp data and on the MovieLens data in Table 5 and 6 respectively. We can see that for models M1 and M2, using user-specific vectors greatly improves the results on the Yelp data. As the performances of the models get better for M3 and M4, the gain becomes relatively smaller. For the MovieLens data, using user-specific vectors consistently outperforms the alternative choice.

Table 7: Effects of using tied weights on MovieLens data. "TW" means using tied weights, while "NTW" means no tied weights.

	MAP@1		MAP@5		MAP@10	
Model	TW	NTW	TW	NTW	TW	NTW
M1	0.1739	0.2933	0.0983	0.1730	0.0763	0.1402
M2	0.3707	0.3368	0.2086	0.1901	0.1643	0.1509
M3	0.3482	0.3494	0.2044	0.2099	0.1669	0.1722
M4	0.3530	0.3860	0.2007	0.2252	0.1609	0.1797

Table 8: Effects of using tied weights on Netflix data. "TW" means using tied weights, while "NTW" means no tied weights.

	MAP@1		MAP@5		MAP@10	
Model	TW	NTW	TW	NTW	TW	NTW
M1	0.1172	0.1301	0.0551	0.0695	0.0428	0.0571
M2	0.2567	0.2608	0.1418	0.1431	0.1177	0.1199
M3	0.1172	0.2000	0.0551	0.1162	0.0428	0.1011
M4	0.2287	0.2474	0.1260	0.1370	0.1066	0.1143

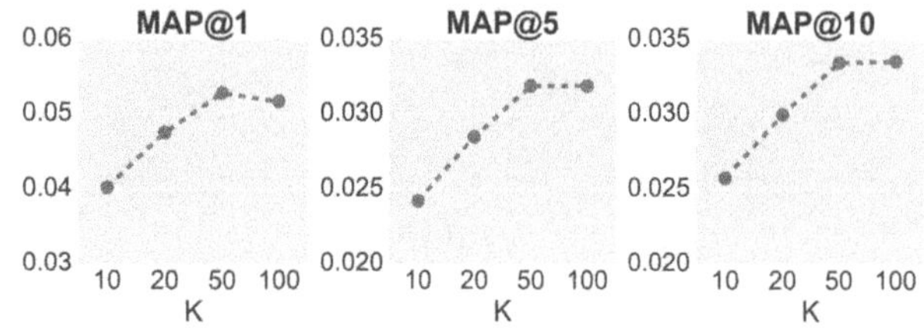

(a) Results on Yelp data.

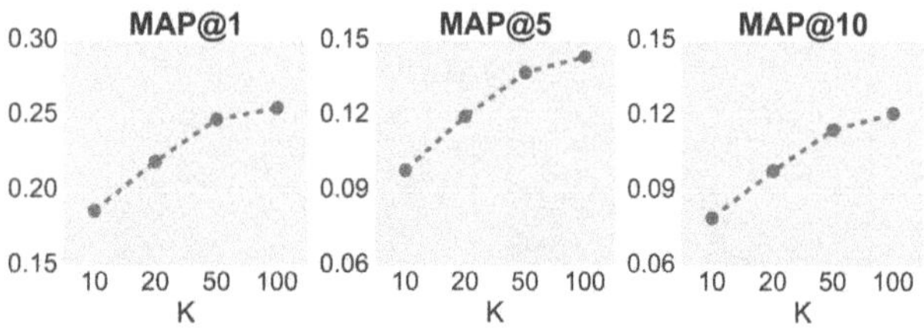

(b) Results on Netflix data.

Figure 5: The effects of the number of latent dimensions.

Tied weights. We study the effects of using tied weights (TW) for the weight matrices, where we force $\boldsymbol{W} = \boldsymbol{W}'$. Results on MovieLens and Netflix data sets are shown in Table 7 and 8, respectively. We refer to the cases of "no tied weights" as NTW. The results on Yelp data are similar to those on Netflix data, so we omit them here. Other than variant M2 on MovieLens data, the results of NTW are much better than TW. On Netflix data, NTW consistently outperforms TW by at least 10%. On both data sets, the best MAP scores are from models with NTW (M4+NTW in Table 7 and M2+NTW in Table 8, respectively). Thus we do not recommended using tied weights for CDAE.

The number of latent dimensions. We study the effects of the number of latent dimensions K. Results on Yelp data and Netflix data are shown in Figure 5. From the figures, we can see that the performance increases with larger K, but only up to a point. When K becomes large enough, the performance no longer improves and can in fact decrease due to overfitting.

5.5 Experimental Comparisons with Previous Models

In this section, we compare CDAE with a number of popular top-N recommendation methods. Note that comparisons against Denoising Auto-Encoder (DAE) and its non-denoising variant (when $q = 0$) are already discussed in Section 5.4.

These baseline methods are:

- **POP**: Items are recommended based on how many users have rated them.
- **ITEMCF** [19]: We use Jaccard similarity measure and set the number of nearest neighbor to 50.
- **MF (with negative sampling)** [9]: We train the Latent Factor Model with point-wise objective functions (with square, log, hinge and cross entropy losses) and negative sampling[11], and report the best results.
- **BPR** [15]: BPR is the state-of-the-art method for recommendation based on implicit feedback. As discussed in Section 2.1, BPR-MF is a Latent Factor Model with the pair-wise log loss function. In addition to the log loss used in the original paper [15], we also experiment with square and hinge loss functions and report the best results.
- **FISM** [7]: FISM is a variant of FSM with point-wise square loss function[12]. We also test log loss and hinge loss and report the best results.

For all the baseline methods, we carefully choose the hyperparameters by cross validation to ensure fair comparisons. We train the 4 variants of CDAE discussed in Table 4 with different corruption levels, and report the best results. For all the latent factor models (including MF, BPR, FISM and CDAE), we set the number of latent dimensions to 50 and use an additional dimension to model the bias. Other implementation details are as discussed in Section 5.2.

Figure 6, 7 and 8 show the MAP@N scores of all models on Yelp, MovieLens and Netflix, respectively. Since Recall is another widely used metric for comparing top-N recommendation models, we also include plots of the Recall scores on the three data sets in Figure 9, 10 and 11.

In general, the results of MAP and Recall are consistent, *i.e.*, the performance orderings of models are almost the same. One exception is on the Yelp data, where MF gets better MAP@N scores than BPR, but BPR has better Recall@N scores.

According to the results of MAP@10 and Recall@10, CDAE consistently outperforms other compared methods. On the Yelp data, CDAE outperforms the other methods with a large margin on all the evaluation metrics. The MAP@10 score and Recall@10 score of CDAE are at least 15% better than those of the second best model MF. For the Netflix data set, ITEMCF achieves much better results than other methods such as MF, BPR and FISM, particularly on the metrics MAP@1 and Recall@1. CDAE is the only model that can beat ITEMCF on metrics MAP@10 and Recall@10, where CDAE outperforms ITEMCF by around 10%.

It is surprising to see that BPR and FISM achieve lower MAP scores than MF on Yelp and Netflix data sets. The only data set on which they achieve better results is MovieLens, but the performance gains are not significant.

[11]We note that, for implicit feedback data, MF with negative sampling has the same objective function with WRMF [6] – both of them assign high confidence on the observed/positive feedback and low cofidence on the missing/negative feedback. We do not compare with WRMF because its computational speedup trick for ALS only works with squared loss.

[12]We also tried the pair-wise loss functions, but the results are not as good as for the point-wise functions. The same observation is reported in the original paper.

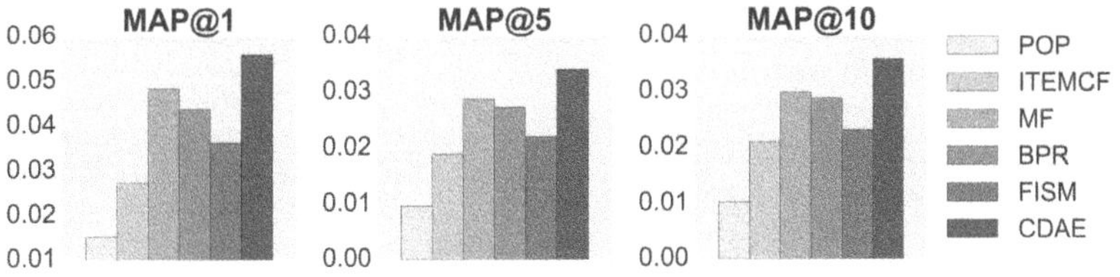

Figure 6: MAP scores with different N on the Yelp data set.

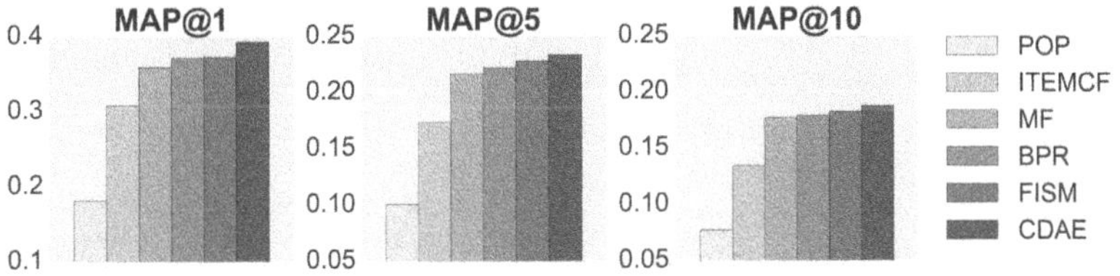

Figure 7: MAP scores with different N on the MovieLens data set.

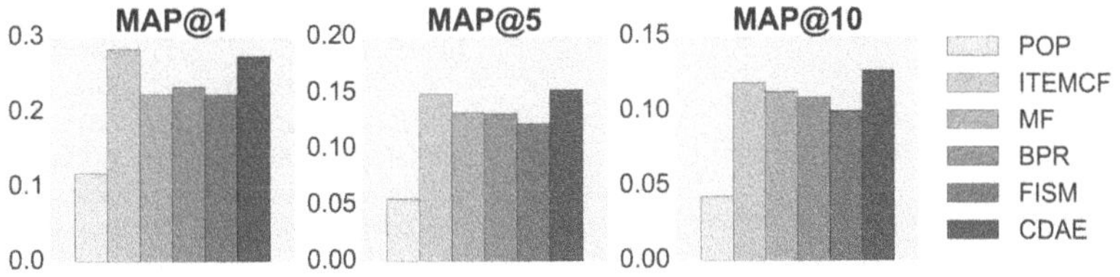

Figure 8: MAP scores with different N on the Netflix data set.

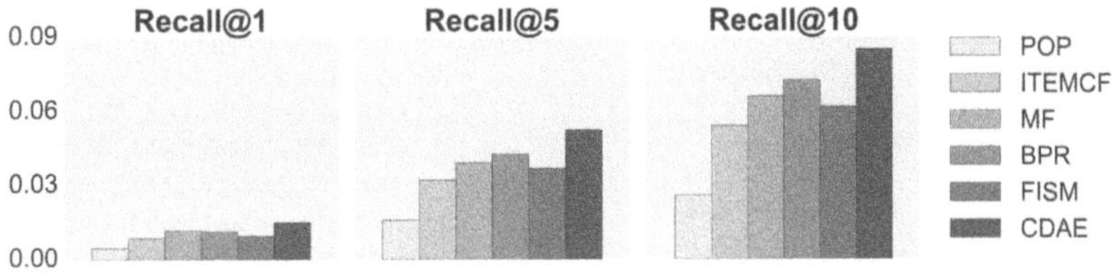

Figure 9: The Recall scores with different N on the Yelp data set.

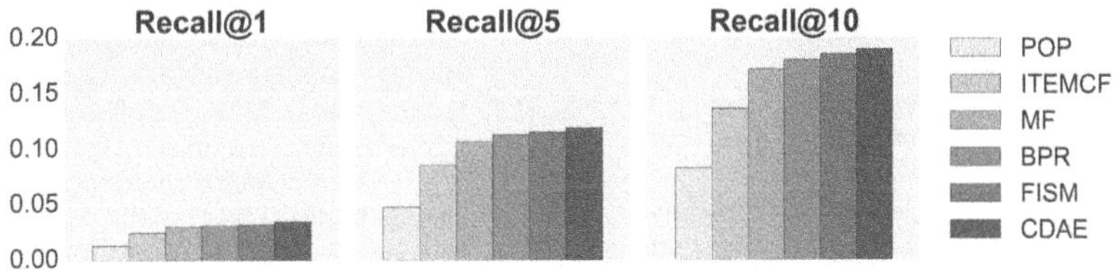

Figure 10: The Recall scores with different N on the MovieLens data set.

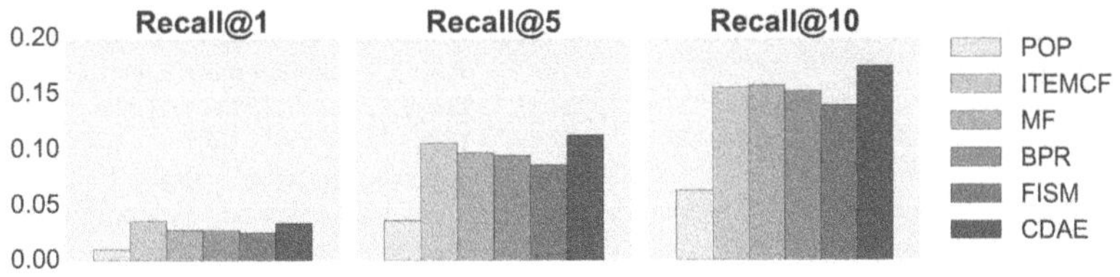

Figure 11: The Recall scores with different N on the Netflix data set.

6. CONCLUSION

In this paper, we presented the Collaborative Denoising Auto-Encoder (CDAE) for the top-N recommendation problem. CDAE learns distributed representations of the users and items via formulating the user-item feedback data using a Denoising Auto-Encoder structure. Several previous works can be seen as special cases of the proposed model. We conducted a comprehensive set of experiments on three data sets to study how the choice of the model components impacts the performance. We also compared CDAE against several other state-of-the-art top-N recommendation methods and the results show that CDAE outperforms the rest of the methods by a large margin.

The proposed model enables a wide range of future works on applying neural networks to recommender systems. Here we list some potential directions.

Deep Neural Network. The neural network structure used in our paper is shallow. A straightforward extension is to stack the model as done in the stacked DAE [25]. Our preliminary experiments on the stacked CDAE do not show significant improvement over CDAE. We plan to investigate the reason and try to improve it. Also, the idea of marginalized DAE [3] might be able to speed up the training and improve the performance. It would also be interesting to consider applying other neural network structures such as Convolutional Neural Networks and Recurrent Neural Networks to this framework.

Feature-aware Recommendation. User and item features can be important for producing semantically meaningful models and dealing with the *cold-start* problem. It is worth exploring how to incorporate user and item features to improve the proposed model.

Context-aware Recommendation. In many applications, one might benefit from incorporating contextual information (such as time, location, browser session, etc.) into the recommendation process in order to recommend items to users in certain circumstances. We leave such extensions as future work.

7. REFERENCES

[1] D. Agarwal and B. Chen. Regression-based latent factor models. In *Proceedings of the 15th ACM SIGKDD International Conference on Knowledge Discovery and Data Mining*, pages 19–28, 2009.

[2] Y. Bengio, P. Lamblin, D. Popovici, and H. Larochelle. Greedy layer-wise training of deep networks. In *Advances in Neural Information Processing Systems*, pages 153–160, 2006.

[3] M. Chen, K. Q. Weinberger, F. Sha, and Y. Bengio. Marginalized denoising auto-encoders for nonlinear representations. In *Proceedings of the 31st International Conference on Machine Learning (ICML-14)*, pages 1476–1484, 2014.

[4] J. Duchi, E. Hazan, and Y. Singer. Adaptive subgradient methods for online learning and stochastic optimization. *The Journal of Machine Learning Research*, 12:2121–2159, 2011.

[5] X. Glorot, Y. Bengio, and Y. N. Dauphin. Large-scale learning of embeddings with reconstruction sampling. In *Proceedings of the 28th International Conference on Machine Learning (ICML-11)*, pages 945–952, 201.

[6] Y. Hu, Y. Koren, and C. Volinsky. Collaborative filtering for implicit feedback datasets. In *Proceedings of the Eighth IEEE International Conference on Data Mining*, pages 263–272, 2008.

[7] S. Kabbur, X. Ning, and G. Karypis. FISM: factored item similarity models for top-n recommender systems. In *Proceedings of the 19th ACM SIGKDD international conference on Knowledge discovery and data mining*, pages 659–667. ACM, 2013.

[8] Y. Koren. Factorization meets the neighborhood: a multifaceted collaborative filtering model. In *Proceedings of the 14th ACM SIGKDD International Conference on Knowledge Discovery and Data Mining*, pages 426–434. ACM, 2008.

[9] Y. Koren, R. Bell, and C. Volinsky. Matrix factorization techniques for recommender systems. *Computer*, 42(8):30–37, 2009.

[10] S. Lauly, H. Larochelle, M. Khapra, B. Ravindran, V. C. Raykar, and A. Saha. An autoencoder approach to learning bilingual word representations. In *Advances in Neural Information Processing Systems*, pages 1853–1861, 2014.

[11] J. Lee, S. Bengio, S. Kim, G. Lebanon, and Y. Singer. Local collaborative ranking. In *Proceedings of the 23rd International Conference on World Wide Web*, pages 85–96. ACM, 2014.

[12] X. Ning and G. Karypis. SLIM: Sparse linear methods for top-N recommender systems. In *Proceedings of the 11th IEEE International Conference on Data Mining*, pages 497–506, 2011.

[13] R. Pan, Y. Zhou, B. Cao, N. N. Liu, R. Lukose, M. Scholz, and Q. Yang. One-class collaborative filtering. In *Proceedings of the Eighth IEEE International Conference on Data Mining*, pages 502–511, 2008.

[14] S. Rendle. Factorization machines with libfm. *ACM Transactions on Intelligent Systems and Technology (TIST)*, 3(3):57, 2012.

[15] S. Rendle, C. Freudenthaler, Z. Gantner, and L. Schmidt-Thieme. Bpr: Bayesian personalized ranking from implicit feedback. In *Proceedings of the Twenty-Fifth Conference on Uncertainty in Artificial Intelligence (UAI)*, pages 452–461, 2009.

[16] J. D. Rennie and N. Srebro. Fast maximum margin matrix factorization for collaborative prediction. In *Proceedings of the 22nd international conference on Machine learning*, pages 713–719. ACM, 2005.

[17] R. Salakhutdinov and A. Mnih. Probabilistic matrix factorization. In *Advances in neural information processing systems*, pages 1257–1264, 2007.

[18] R. Salakhutdinov, A. Mnih, and G. Hinton. Restricted boltzmann machines for collaborative filtering. In *Proceedings of the 24th international conference on Machine learning*, pages 791–798. ACM, 2007.

[19] B. Sarwar, G. Karypis, J. Konstan, and J. Riedl. Item-based collaborative filtering recommendation algorithms. In *Proceedings of the 10th international conference on World Wide Web*, pages 285–295. ACM, 2001.

[20] S. Sedhain, A. K. Menon, S. Sanner, and L. Xie. Autorec: Autoencoders meet collaborative filtering. In *Proceedings of the 24th International Conference on World Wide Web Companion*, WWW'15 Companion, pages 111–112, 2015.

[21] Y. Shi, A. Karatzoglou, L. Baltrunas, M. Larson, N. Oliver, and A. Hanjalic. Climf: learning to maximize reciprocal rank with collaborative less-is-more filtering. In *Proceedings of the sixth ACM conference on Recommender systems*, pages 139–146. ACM, 2012.

[22] Y. Shi, M. Larson, and A. Hanjalic. List-wise learning to rank with matrix factorization for collaborative filtering. In *Proceedings of the fourth ACM conference on Recommender systems*, pages 269–272. ACM, 2010.

[23] H. Steck. Training and testing of recommender systems on data missing not at random. In *Proceedings of the 16th ACM SIGKDD international conference on Knowledge discovery and data mining*, pages 713–722. ACM, 2010.

[24] P. Vincent, H. Larochelle, Y. Bengio, and P.-A. Manzagol. Extracting and composing robust features with denoising autoencoders. In *Proceedings of the 25th international conference on Machine learning*, pages 1096–1103. ACM, 2008.

[25] P. Vincent, H. Larochelle, I. Lajoie, Y. Bengio, and P.-A. Manzagol. Stacked denoising autoencoders: Learning useful representations in a deep network with a local denoising criterion. *The Journal of Machine Learning Research*, 11:3371–3408, 2010.

[26] C. Wang and D. M. Blei. Collaborative topic modeling for recommending scientific articles. In *Proceedings of the 17th ACM SIGKDD international conference on Knowledge discovery and data mining*, KDD '11, pages 448–456. ACM, 2011.

[27] H. Wang, N. Wang, and D.-Y. Yeung. Collaborative deep learning for recommender systems. In *Proceedings of the 21th ACM SIGKDD International Conference on Knowledge Discovery and Data Mining*, KDD '15, pages 1235–1244. ACM, 2015.

[28] M. Weimer, A. Karatzoglou, Q. V. Le, and A. J. Smola. COFI RANK-maximum margin matrix factorization for collaborative ranking. In *Advances in Neural Information Processing Systems*, pages 1593–1600, 2007.

[29] J. Weston, S. Bengio, and N. Usunier. WSABIE: scaling up to large vocabulary image annotation. In *Proceedings of the 22nd International Joint Conference on Artificial Intelligence (IJCAI'11)*, pages 2764–2770, 2011.

[30] J. Weston, C. Wang, R. Weiss, and A. Berenzweig. Latent collaborative retrieval. In *Proceedings of the 29th International Conference on Machine Learning (ICML-12)*, pages 9–16, 2012.

[31] S.-H. Yang, B. Long, A. J. Smola, H. Zha, and Z. Zheng. Collaborative competitive filtering: learning recommender using context of user choice. In *Proceedings of the 34th international ACM SIGIR conference on Research and development in Information Retrieval*, pages 295–304. ACM, 2011.

[32] L. Zhang, D. Agarwal, and B.-C. Chen. Generalizing matrix factorization through flexible regression priors. In *Proceedings of the Fifth ACM Conference on Recommender Systems*, RecSys '11, pages 13–20. ACM, 2011.

Personalized PageRank Estimation and Search: A Bidirectional Approach

Peter Lofgren
Department of CS
Stanford University
plofgren@cs.stanford.edu

Siddhartha Banerjee
School of ORIE
Cornell University
sbanerjee@cornell.edu

Ashish Goel
Department of MS&E
Stanford University
ashishg@stanford.edu

ABSTRACT

We present new algorithms for Personalized PageRank estimation and Personalized PageRank search. First, for the problem of estimating Personalized PageRank (PPR) from a source distribution to a target node, we present a new bidirectional estimator with simple yet strong guarantees on correctness and performance, and 3x to 8x speedup over existing estimators in experiments on a diverse set of networks. Moreover, it has a clean algebraic structure which enables it to be used as a primitive for the Personalized PageRank Search problem: Given a network like Facebook, a query like "people named John," and a searching user, return the top nodes in the network ranked by PPR from the perspective of the searching user. Previous solutions either score all nodes or score candidate nodes one at a time, which is prohibitively slow for large candidate sets. We develop a new algorithm based on our bidirectional PPR estimator which identifies the most relevant results by sampling candidates based on their PPR; this is the first solution to PPR search that can find the best results without iterating through the set of all candidate results. Finally, by combining PPR sampling with sequential PPR estimation and Monte Carlo, we develop practical algorithms for PPR search, and we show via experiments that our algorithms are efficient on networks with billions of edges.

Categories and Subject Descriptors

H.3.3 [**Information Search and Retrieval**]: Search process; G.2.2 [**Graph Theory**]: Graph Algorithms

Keywords

Personalized Search; Personalized PageRank; Social Network Analysis

1. INTRODUCTION

On social networks, personalization is necessary for returning relevant results for a query. For example, if a user searches for a common name like John on a social network like Facebook, the results should depend on who is doing the search and who their friends are. A good personalized model for measuring the importance of a node t to a searcher s is Personalized PageRank $\pi_s(t)$ [20, 13, 12] – this motivates a natural *Personalized PageRank Search Problem*: Given

- a network with nodes V (each associated with a set of keywords) and edges E (possibly weighted and directed),
- a keyword inducing a set of targets:
  $T = \{t \in V : t \text{ is relevant to the keyword}\}$
- a searching user $s \in V$ (or more generally, a distribution over starting nodes),

return the top-k targets $t_1, \ldots, t_k \in T$ ranked by Personalized PageRank $\pi_s(t_i)$.

The importance of personalized search extends beyond social networks. For example, personalized PageRank can be used to rank items in a bi-partite user-item graph, in which there is an edge from a user to an item if the user has liked that item. This has proven useful on YouTube when recommending videos [5] and on Twitter for suggested users [3, 12]. On the web graph there is a large body of work on using Personalized PageRank to rank web pages (e.g. [14, 13]). The most clear-cut motivation for our work is for the social network name-search application discussed above, which we use as a running example in this paper.

The personalized search problem is difficult because every searching user has a different ranking on the target nodes. One naive solution would be to precompute the ranking for every searching user, but if our network has n users this requires $\Theta(n^2)$ storage, which is clearly infeasible. Another naive baseline would be to use power iteration [20] at query time, but that would take $\Theta(m)$ computation between the search query and response, where m is the number edges, which is also clearly infeasible. The challenge we face is to create a data structure much smaller than $O(n^2)$ which allows us to rank $|T|$ targets in response to a query in less than $O(|T|)$ time.

Previous work has considered the problem of personalized search on social networks. For example Vieira et. al. [24] consider this problem and provide excellent motivation for why results to a name-search query should be ranked based the friendships of the searching user and the candidate results. They and others (e.g. [4]) propose to rank results by shortest path length. However, this metric doesn't take into account the number of paths between two users: If the searcher and two results John A and John B are distance 3 apart, but the searcher and John A are connected by 100 length-3 paths while the searcher and John B are connected

WSDM'16, February 22–25, 2016, San Francisco, CA, USA.

ISBN 978-1-4503-3716-8/16/02...$15.00
DOI: http://dx.doi.org/10.1145/2835776.2835823

by a single length-3 path, than John A should be ranked above John B, yet the shortest distance can't distinguish the two. To the best of our knowledge, no prior work has solved the Personalized PageRank search problem using less than $O(n^2)$ storage and $O(|T|)$ query time. The reason we are able to solve this is by exploiting a new bidirectional method of PageRank, introduced in [19] and improved in this work.

Our search algorithm is based on two key ideas. The first is that we can find the top target nodes without having to consider each separately by *sampling a target $t_i \in T$ in proportion to its Personalized PageRank $\pi_s(t_i)$*. Because the top results typically have a much higher personalized PageRank than an average result, by sampling we can find the top results without iterating over all the results. The second idea is that the probability of a random walk exactly reaching an element in T is often very small, but by pre-computing an expanded set of nodes around each target, we can efficiently sample random walks until they get close to a target node, and then use the pre-computed data to sample targets t_i in proportion to $\pi_s(t_i)$.

There are currently two main limitations to our work. First, because we do pre-computation on the set of nodes relevant to a query, we need the set of queries to be known in advance, although in the case of name search we can simply let the space of queries be the set of all first or last names. Second, the pre-computed storage is significant; for name-search it is $O\left(n\sqrt{m}\right)$ to achieve query running time $O(\sqrt{m})$, where n is the number of nodes and m is the number of edges. However, large graphs tend to be sparse, so this is still much smaller than $O\left(n^2\right)$ and is less storage than any prior solution to the Personalized PageRank Search problem. Also, pre-computation doesn't need to be done for all queries: for queries with small or very large target sets we describe alternative algorithms which do not require pre-computation. These alternatives also overcome the limitation on queries being known in advance.

Contributions: To summarize, in this work we present:

- A new bidirectional PageRank estimator, `Bidirectional-PPR` (section 3), which has the following features:
  - *Simple analysis*: We combine a simple linear-algebraic invariant with standard concentration bounds. The new analysis also allows generalizations to arbitrary Markov Chains, as done in [6].
  - *Easy to implement*: The complete algorithm is only 18 lines of pseudo-code.
  - *Significant empirical speedup*: For a given accuracy, it executes 3x-8x faster than the fastest previous algorithm, `FAST-PPR` [19], on a diverse set of networks.
  - *Simple linear structure:* As shown in section 4.1, the estimates are a simple dot-product between a forward vector x^s and a reverse vector y^t – this enables the development of PPR samplers.
  - *Parallelizability:* Because the estimate is a dot-product, the precomputed vectors can be sharded across many servers, and the estimation algorithm can be naturally distributed, as shown in [11].
- Two new solutions to the Personalized PageRank Search problem – `BiPPR-Grouped` and `BiPPR-Sampling`. Given any set of targets T:
  - `BiPPR-Precomp-Grouped` precomputes and stores the reverse vectors $y^t, t \in T$ after grouping them by their coordinates. This exploits the natural sparsity of these vectors to speed-up the computation of the PPR estimates at runtime.
  - `BiPPR-Precomp-Sampling` samples nodes $t \in T$ proportional to their PPR $\pi_s(t)$. Now since PPR values are usually highly skewed, this serves as a good proxy for finding the top k search results.
- Extensive simulations on the Twitter-2010 network to test the scalability of our algorithms for PPR-search. Our experiments demonstrate the trade-off between storage and runtime, and suggest that we should use a combination of methods, depending on the size of the set of targets T induced by the keyword.

2. PRELIMINARIES

We are given a graph $G = (V, E)$ with n nodes and m edges. Define the out-neighbors of a node u by $\mathcal{N}^{out}(u) = \{v : (u, v) \in E\}$ and let $d^{out}(u) = |\mathcal{N}^{out}(u)|$; define $\mathcal{N}^{in}(u)$ and $d^{in}(u)$ similarly. Define the average degree of nodes $\bar{d} = \frac{m}{n}$. If the graph is weighted, for each $(u, v) \in E$ there is some positive weight $w_{u,v}$; otherwise we define $w_{u,v} = \frac{1}{d^{out}(u)}$ for all $(u, v) \in E$. For simplicity we assume the weights are normalized such that for all u, $\sum_v w_{u,v} = 1$.

The personalized PageRank from source distribution σ to target node t can be defined using linear algebra as the solution to the equation $\pi_\sigma = \pi_\sigma(\alpha\sigma + (1-\alpha)W)$, or equivalently defined using random walks

$$\pi_\sigma(t) = \Pr[\text{a random walk starting from } s \sim \sigma \text{ of length} \sim \text{geometric}(\alpha) \text{ stops at } t]$$

as shown in [2]. For concreteness, in this paper we often assume $\sigma = e_s$ for some single node s (meaning the random walks always start at a single node s), but all results extend in a straightforward manner to any starting distribution σ.

Personalized PageRank was first defined in the original PageRank paper [20]. For more on the motivation of Personalized PageRank, see [13] and the survey [10].

3. PAGERANK ESTIMATION

In this section, we present our new bidirectional algorithm for PageRank estimation. We first develop the basic algorithm along with its theoretical performance guarantees; next, we outline some extensions of the basic algorithm; finally, we conclude the section with simulations demonstrating the efficiency of our technique.

The `Bidirectional-PPR` Algorithm

At a high level, our algorithm estimates $\pi_s(t)$ by first working backwards from t to find a set of intermediate nodes 'near' t and then generating random walks forwards from s to detect this set.

The reverse work from t is done via the `Approx-Contributions` algorithm (see Algorithm 1) of Andersen et. al. [1], that, given a target t and a desired *additive error-bound* $r_{\max}$, produces estimates $p^t(s)$ of the PPR $\pi_s(t)$ for every start node s. More specifically, the `Approx-Contributions` algorithm produces two non-negative vectors $p^t \in \mathbb{R}^n$ and $r^t \in \mathbb{R}^n$ which satisfy the following invariant (Lemma 1 in [1])

$$\pi_s(t) = p^t(s) + \sum_{v \in V} \pi_s(v) r^t(v). \tag{1}$$

`Approx-Contributions` terminates once each residual value $r^t(v) < r_{\max}$; now, viewing $\sum_{v \in V} \pi_s(v) r^t(v)$ as an error term, Andersen et al. observe that $p^t(s)$ estimates $\pi_s(t)$ up to a maximum additive error of $r_{\max}$.

Our `Bidirectional-PPR` algorithm is based on the observation that in order to estimate $\pi_s(t)$ for a *particular* (s,t) pair, we can boost the accuracy by sampling and adding the residual values $r^t(v)$ from nodes v which are sampled from π_s. To see this, we first interpret Equation (1) as an expectation:

$$\pi_s(t) = p^t(s) + \mathbb{E}_{v\sim\pi_s}[r^t(v)].$$

Now, since $\max_v r^t(v) < r_{\max}$, the expectation $\mathbb{E}_{v\sim\pi_s(v)}[r^t(v)]$ can be efficiently estimated using Monte Carlo. To do so, we generate $w = c\frac{r_{\max}}{\delta}$ random walks of length $Geometric(\alpha)$ from start node s; here c is a parameter which depends on the desired accuracy, $r_{\max}$ is the maximum residual after running `Approx-Contributions`, and δ is the minimum PPR value we want to accurately estimate. Let V_i be the final node of the ith random walk; note that $\Pr[V_i = v] = \pi_s(v)$. Let $X_i = r^t(V_i)$ denote the residual from the final node of the ith random walk, and $\bar{X} = \frac{1}{w}\sum_{i=1}^{w} X_i$. Then `Bidirectional-PPR` returns as an estimate of $\pi_s(t)$:

$$\widehat{\pi}_s(t) = p^t(s) + \bar{X}$$

The complete pseudocode is given in Algorithm 2.

Algorithm 1 `Approx-Contributions`$(G, \alpha, t, r_{\max})$ [1]

Inputs: graph G with edge weights $w_{u,v}$, teleport probability α, target node t, maximum residual $r_{\max}$

```
Initialize (sparse) estimate-vector p_t = 0⃗ and (sparse) residual-vector r_t = e_t (i.e. r_t(v) = 1 if v = t; else 0)
while ∃v ∈ V s.t. r_t(v) > r_max do
    for u ∈ N^in(v) do
        r_t(u) += (1 − α) w_{u,v} r_t(v)
    end for
    p_t(v) += α r_t(v)
    r_t(v) = 0
end while
return (p_t, r_t)
```

Algorithm 2 `Bidirectional-PPR`(s, t, δ)

Inputs: graph G, teleport probability α, start node s, target node t, minimum probability δ, accuracy parameter c (in our experiments we use $c = 7$)

```
Choose r_max = c_balance/√m, where c_balance is tuned to balance forward and reverse work. (For greater efficiency, use the balanced version described in Section 3.)

(p_t, r_t) = Approx-Contributions(t, r_max, α)
Set number of walks w = c r_max/δ   (cf. Theorem 1)
for index i ∈ [w] do
    Sample a random walk starting from s (sampling a start from s if s is a distribution), stopping after each step with probability α; let v_i be the endpoint
    Set X_i = r_t(v_i)
end for
return π̂_s(t) = p_t(s) + (1/w) Σ_{i∈[w]} X_i
```

Accuracy Analysis

We first prove that `Bidirectional-PPR` returns an estimate with the desired accuracy with high probability:

THEOREM 1. *Given start node s (or source distribution σ), target t, minimum PPR δ, maximum residual $r_{max} > \frac{2e\delta}{\alpha\epsilon}$, relative error $\epsilon \leq 1$, and failure probability p_{fail},* `Bidirectional-PPR` *outputs an estimate $\widehat{\pi}_s(t)$ such that with probability at least $1 - p_{fail}$ the following hold:*
- *If $\pi_s(t) \geq \delta$:* $\quad |\pi_s(t) - \hat{\pi}_s(t)| \leq \epsilon\pi_s(t)$.
- *If $\pi_s(t) \leq \delta$:* $\quad |\pi_s(t) - \hat{\pi}_s(t)| \leq 2e\delta$.

The above result shows that the estimate $\hat{\pi}_s(t)$ can be used to distinguish between 'significant' and 'insignificant' PPR pairs: for pair (s,t), Theorem 1 guarantees that if $\pi_s(t) \geq \frac{(1+2e)\delta}{(1-\epsilon)}$, then the estimate is greater than $(1+2e)\delta$, whereas if $\pi_s(t) < \delta$, then the estimate is less than $(1+2e)\delta$. The assumption $r_{\max} > \frac{2e\delta}{\alpha\epsilon}$ is easily satisfied, as typically $\delta = O\left(\frac{1}{n}\right)$ and $r_{\max} = \Omega\left(\frac{1}{\sqrt{m}}\right)$. The proof is a straightforward application of Chernoff bounds and appears in the full version of this paper.

Running Time Analysis

The runtime of `Bidirectional-PPR` depends on the target t: if t has many in-neighbors and/or large global PageRank $\pi(t)$, then the running time will be slower than for a random t. Theorem 1 of [1] states that `Approx-Contributions` $(G, \alpha, t, r_{\max})$ performs $\frac{n\pi(t)}{\alpha r_{\max}}$ pushback operations, and the exact running time is proportional to the sum of the in-degrees of all the nodes where we pushback from. In the worst case, we might have $d^{in}(t) = \Theta(n)$ and `Bidirectional-PPR` takes $\Theta(n)$ time. However, for *a uniformly chosen target node*, we can prove the following:

THEOREM 2. *For any start node s (or source distribution σ), minimum PPR δ, maximum residual r_{max}, relative error ϵ, and failure probability p_{fail}, if the target t is chosen uniformly at random, then* `Bidirectional-PPR` *has expected running time*

$$O\left(\sqrt{\frac{\bar{d}}{\delta}}\frac{\sqrt{\log(1/p_{fail})}}{\alpha\epsilon}\right).$$

In contrast, the running time for `Monte-Carlo` to achieve the same accuracy guarantee is $O\left(\frac{1}{\delta}\frac{\log(1/p_{\text{fail}})}{\alpha\epsilon^2}\right)$, and the running time for `Approx-Contributions` is $O\left(\frac{\bar{d}}{\delta\alpha}\right)$. The fastest previous algorithm for this problem, the `FAST-PPR` algorithm of [19], has an average running time bound of $O\left(\frac{1}{\alpha\epsilon^2}\sqrt{\frac{\bar{d}}{\delta}}\sqrt{\frac{\log(1/p_{\text{fail}})\log(1/\delta)}{\log(1/(1-\alpha))}}\right)$ for uniformly chosen targets. The running time bound of `Bidirectional-PPR` is thus asymptotically better than `FAST-PPR`, and in experiments the constants required for the same accuracy are smaller, making `Bidirectional-PPR` is 3 to 8 times faster on a diverse set of graphs.

PROOF. In [18], it is proven that for a uniform random t, Approx-Contributions runs in average time $\frac{\bar{d}}{\alpha r_{\max}}$ where $\bar{d}$ is the average degree of a node. On the other hand, from Theorem 1, we know that we need to generate $O\left(\frac{r_{\max}}{\delta\epsilon^2}\ln(1/p_{\text{fail}})\right)$ random walks, each of which can be sampled in average time $1/\alpha$. Finally, we choose $r_{\max} = \frac{\epsilon}{\alpha}\sqrt{\frac{\bar{d}}{\ln(2/p_{\text{fail}})}}$ to minimize our running time bound and get the claimed result. □

Extensions Bidirectional-PageRank extends naturally to generalized PageRank using a source distribution σ rather than a single start node – we simply sample an independent starting node for each walk, and replace $p_t(s)$ with the expected value of $p_t(s)$ when s is sampled from the starting distribution.

The dynamic runtime-balancing method proposed in [19] can improve the running time of Bidirectional-PageRank in practice. In this technique, $r_{\max}$ is chosen dynamically in order to balance the amount of time spent by `Approx-Contributions` and the amount of time spent generating random walks. To implement this, we modify `Approx-Contributions` to use a priority queue in order to always push from the node v with the largest value of $r_t(v)$. We also change the while loop so that it terminates when the amount of time spent achieving the current value of $r_{\max}$ first exceeds the predicted amount of time required for sampling random walks, $c_{\text{walk}} \cdot c \cdot \frac{r_{\max}}{\delta}$, where c_{walk} is the average time it takes to sample a random walk. For full pseudocode, see [17].

Experimental Validation

We now compare `Bidirectional-PPR` to its predecessor algorithms (namely: `FAST-PPR` [18], `Monte Carlo` [2, 9] and `Approx-Contributions` [1]). The experimental setup is identical to that in [18]; for convenience, we describe it here in brief. We perform experiments on 6 diverse, real-world networks: two directed social networks (Pokec (31M edges) and Twitter-2010 (1.5 billion edges)), two undirected social network (Live-Journal (69M edges) and Orkut (117M edges)), a collaboration network (dblp (6.7M edges)), and a web-graph (UK-2007-05 (3.7 billion edges)). Since all algorithms have parameters that enable a trade-off between running time and accuracy, we first choose parameters such that the mean relative error of each algorithm is approximately 10%. For bidirectional-PPR, we find that setting $c = 7$ (i.e., generating $7 \cdot \frac{r_{\max}}{\delta}$ random walks) results in a mean relative error less than 8% on all graphs; for the other algorithms, we use the settings determined in [18]. We then repeatedly sample a uniformly-random start node $s \in V$, and a random target $t \in T$ sampled either uniformly or from PageRank (to emphasize more important targets). For both `Bidirectional-PPR` and `FAST-PPR`, we used the dynamic-balancing heuristic described above. The results are shown in Figure 1.

Note that `Bidirectional-PPR` is 3 to 8 times faster than `FAST-PPR` across all graphs. In particuar, `Bidirectional-PPR` only needs to sample $7\frac{r_{\max}}{\delta}$ random walks, while FAST-PPR needs $350\frac{r_{\max}}{\delta}$ walks to achieve the same mean relative error. This is because `Bidirectional-PPR` is unbiased, while `FAST-PPR` has a bias from `Approx-Contributions`.

4. PERSONALIZED PAGERANK SEARCH

We now turn from Personalized PageRank estimation to the Personalized PageRank search problem:

Given a start node s (or distribution σ) and a query q which filters the set of all targets to some list $T = \{t_i\} \subseteq V$, return the top-k targets ranked by $\pi_s[t_i]$.

We consider as baselines two algorithms which require no pre-computation. They are efficient for certain ranges of $|T|$, but our experiments show they are too slow for real-time search across most values of $|T|$:

- `Monte-Carlo` [2, 9]: Sample random walks from s, and filter out any walk whose endpoint is not in T. If we desire n_s samples, this takes time $O(n_s/\pi_s[T])$, where $\pi_s[T] := \sum_{t \in T} \pi_s[t]$ is the probability that a random walk terminates in T. This method works well if T is large, but in our experiments on Twitter-2010 it takes minutes per query for $|T| = 1000$ (and hours per query for $|T| = 10$).
- `Bidirectional-PPR`: On the other hand, we can estimate $\pi_s[t]$ to each $t \in T$ separately using `Bidirectional-PPR`. This has an average-case running time $O\left(|T|\sqrt{\bar{d}/\delta_k}\right)$ where δ_k is the PPR of the kth best target. This method works well if T is small, but is too slow for large T; in our experiments, it takes on the order of seconds for $|T| \leq 100$, but more than a minute for $|T| = 1000$.

If we are allowed pre-computation, then we can improve upon `Bidirectional-PPR` by precomputing and storing a reverse vector from all target nodes. To this end, we first observe that the estimate $\hat{\pi}_s[t]$ can be written as a dot-product. Let $\tilde{\pi}_s$ be the empirical distribution over terminal nodes due to w random walks from s (with w chosen as in Theorem 1); we define the *forward vector* $x_s \in \mathbb{R}^{2n}$ to be the concatenation of the basis vector e_s and the random-walk terminal node distribution. On the other hand, we define the *reverse vector* $y^t \in \mathbb{R}^{2n}$, to be the concatenation of the estimates p^t and the residuals r^t. Formally, define

$$x_s = (e_s, \tilde{\pi}_s) \in \mathbb{R}^{2n}, \qquad y^t = (p^t, r^t) \in \mathbb{R}^{2n}. \tag{2}$$

Now, from Algorithm 2, we have

$$\hat{\pi}_s[t] = \langle x_s, y^t \rangle. \tag{3}$$

The above observation motivates the following algorithm:

- `BiPPR-Precomp`: In this approach, we first use `Approx-Contributions` to pre-compute and store a reverse vector y^t for each $t \in V$. At query time, we generate random walks to form the forward vector x_s; now, given any set of targets T, we compute $|T|$ dot-products $\langle x_s, y^t \rangle$, and use these to rank the targets. This method now has an *worst-case* running time $O\left(|T|\sqrt{\bar{d}/\delta_k}\right)$. In practice, it works well if T is small, but is too slow for large T. In our experiments (doing 100,000 random walks at runtime) this approach takes around a second for $|T| \leq 30$, but this climbs to a minute for $|T| = 10,000$.

The `BiPPR-Precomp` approach is faster than `Bidirectional-PPR` (at the cost of additional precomputation and storage), and also faster than `Monte-Carlo` for small sets T, but it is still not efficient enough for real-time personalized search. This motivates us to find a more efficient algorithm that scales better than `Bidirectional-PPR` for large T, yet is fast for small $|T|$. In the following sections, we propose two different approaches for this – the first based on pre-grouping the precomputed reverse-vectors, and the second based on sampling target nodes from T according to PPR. For convenience, we first summarize the two approaches:

- `BiPPR-Precomp-Grouped`: Here, as in `BiPPR-Precomp`, we compute an estimate to each $t \in T$ using `Bidirectional-PPR`. However, we leverage the sparsity of the reverse vectors $y^t = (p^t, r^t)$ by first grouping them in a way we will describe. This makes the dot-product more efficient. This method has a *worst-case* running time of $O\left(|T|\sqrt{\bar{d}/\delta_k}\right)$, and in experiments we find it is much faster than `BiPPR-Precomp`. For our parameter choices its running time is less than 250ms across the range of $|T|$ we tried.
- `BiPPR-Precomp-Sampling`: We again first pre-compute the reverse vectors y^t. Next, for a given target t, we define the *expanded target-set* $T_t = \{v \in [2n] | y^t[v] \neq 0\}$, i.e., the set of nodes with non-zero reverse vectors from t. At

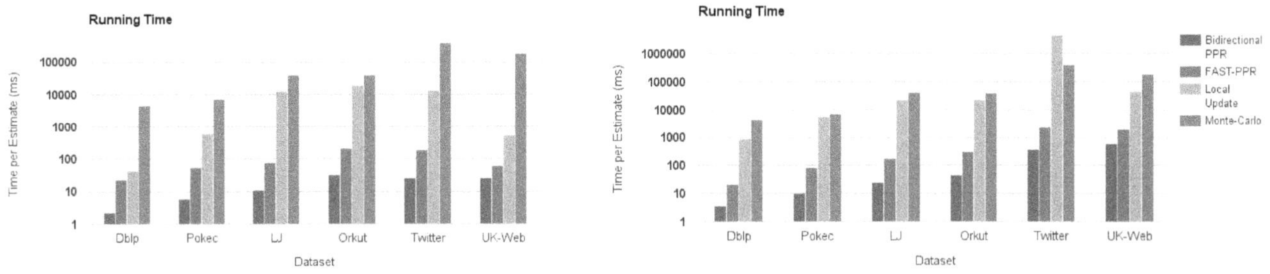

(a) Sampling targets uniformly

(b) Sampling targets from PageRank distribution

Figure 1: Average running-time (on log-scale) for different networks. We measure the time required for estimating PPR values $\pi_s(t)$ with threshold $\delta = \frac{4}{n}$ for 1000 (s,t) pairs. For each pair, the start node is sampled uniformly, while the target node is sampled uniformly in Figure 1(a), or from the global PageRank distribution in Figure 1(b). In this plot we use teleport probability $\alpha = 0.2$.

run-time, we now sample random walks forward from s to nodes in the expanded target sets. Using these, we create a sampler in average time $O(r_{\max}/\delta_k)$ (where as before δ_k is the kth largest PPR value $\pi_s[t_k]$), which samples nodes $t \in T$ with probability proportional to the PPR $\pi_s[t]$. We describe this in detail in Section 4.2. Once the sampler has been created, it can be sampled in $O(1)$ time per sample. The algorithm works well for any size of T, and has the unique property that in can identify the top-k target nodes without computing a score for all $|T|$ of them. For our parameter choice its running time is less than 250ms across the range of $|T|$ we tried.

We note here that the case $k = 1$ (i.e., for finding the top PPR node) corresponds to solving a Maximum Inner Product Problem. In a recent line of work, Shrivastava and Li [21, 22] propose a sublinear time algorithm for this problem based on Locality Sensitive Hashing; however, their method assumes that there is some bound U on $\|y^t\|_2$ and that $\max_t \langle x_s, y^t \rangle$ is a large fraction of U. In personalized search, we usually encounter small values of $\max_t \langle x_s, y^t \rangle$ relative to $\max \|y^t\|_2$ – finding an LSH for Maximum Inner Product Search in this regime is an interesting open problem for future research. Our two approaches bypass this by exploiting particular structural features of the problem – `BiPPR-Precomp-Grouped` exploits the sparsity of the reverse vectors to speed up the dot-product, and `BiPPR-Precomp-Sampling` exploits the skewed distribution of PPR scores to find the top targets without even computing full dot-products.

4.1 Bidirectional-PPR with Grouping

In this method we improve the running-time of `BiPPR-Precomp` by pre-grouping the reverse vectors corresponding to each target set T. Recall that in `BiPPR-Precomp`, we first pre-compute reverse vectors $y^t = (p^t, r^t) \in \mathbb{R}^{2n}$ using `Approx-Contributions` for each t. At run-time, given s, we compute forward vector $x_s = (e_s, \tilde{\pi}_s)$ by generating sufficient random-walks, and then compute the scores $\langle x_s, y^t \rangle$ for $t \in T$. Our main observation is that *we can decrease the running time of the dot-products by pre-grouping the vectors y^t by coordinate.* The intuition behind this is that in each dot product $\sum_v x_s[v] y^t[v]$, the nodes v where $x_s[v] \neq 0$ often don't have $y^t[v] \neq 0$, and most of the product terms are 0. Hence, we can improve the running time by grouping the vectors y^t in advance by coordinate v. Now, at run-time, for each v such that $x_s[v] \neq 0$, we can efficiently iterate over the set of targets t such that $y^t[v] \neq 0$.

An alternative way to think about this is as a sparse matrix-vector multiplication $Y^T x_s$ after we form a matrix Y^T whose rows are y^t for $t \in T$. This optimization can then be seen as a sparse column representation of that matrix.

Algorithm 3 BiPPRGroupedPrecomputation$(T, r_{\max})$

Inputs: Graph G, teleport probability α, target nodes T, maximum residual $r_{\max}$

$z \leftarrow$ empty hash map of vectors such that for any v, $z[v]$ defaults to an empty (sparse) vector in $\mathbb{R}^{2|V|}$
for $t \in T$ **do**
  Compute $y^t = (p_t, r_t) \in \mathbb{R}^{2|V|}$ via `Approx-Contributions`$(G, \alpha, t, r_{\max})$
  for $v \in [2|V|]$ such that $y_t[v] > 0$ **do**
    $z[v][t] = y^t[v]$
  end for
end for
return z

Algorithm 4 BiPPRGroupedRankTargets$(s, r_{\max}, z)$

Inputs: Graph G, teleport probability α, start node s, maximum residual $r_{\max}$, z: hash map of reverse vectors grouped by coordinate

Set number of walks $w = c\frac{r_{\max}}{\delta}$ (In experiments we found $c = 20$ achieved precision@3 above 90%.)
Sample w random-walks of length $Geometric(\alpha)$ from s; compute $\tilde{\pi}_s[v]$ = fraction of walks ending at node v
Compute $x_s = (e_s, \tilde{\pi}_s) \in \mathbb{R}^{2|V|}$
Initialize empty map score from V to $\mathbb{R}$
for v such that $x_s[v] > 0$ **do**
  for t such that $z[v][t] > 0$ **do**
    score(t) += $x_s[v] z_v[t]$
  end for
end for
Return T sorted in decreasing order of score

We refer to this method as `BiPPR-Precomp-Grouped`; the complete pseudo-code is given in Algorithm 4. The correctness of this method follows again from Theorem 1. In experiments, this method is efficient for T across all the sizes of T we tried, taking less than 250 ms even for $|T| = 10,000$. The improved running time of `BiPPR-Precomp-Grouped` comes at the cost of more storage compared to `BiPPR-Precomp`. In the case of name search, where each target typically only has a first and last name, each vector y^t only appears in two of these pre-grouped structures, so the storage is only twice the storage of `BiPPR-Precomp`. On the other hand if a target t contains many keywords, y^t will be included in many of these pre-grouped data structures, and storage cost will be significantly greater than for `BiPPR-Precomp`.

4.2 Sampling from Targets Matching a Query

The key idea behind this alternate method for PPR-search is that by sampling a target t in proportion to its PageRank we can quickly find the top targets without iterating over all of them. After drawing many samples, the targets can be ranked according to the number of times they are sampled. Alternatively a full `Bidirectional-PPR` query can be issued for some subset of the targets before ranking. This approach exploits the skewed distribution of PPR scores in order to find the top targets. In particular, prior empirical work has shown that on the Twitter graph, for each fixed s, the values $\pi_s[t]$ follow a power law [3].

We define the PPR-Search Sampling Problem as follows:

Given a source distribution s and a query q which filters the set of all targets to some list $T = \{t_i\} \subseteq V$, sample a target t_i with probability $p[t_i] = \frac{\pi_s[t_i]}{\sum_{t \in T} \pi_s[t]}$.

We develop two solutions to this sampling problem. The first, in $O(w) = O(r_{\max}/\delta_k)$ time, generates a data structure which can generate an arbitrary number of independent samples from a distribution which approximates the correct distribution. The second can generate samples from the exact distribution $\pi_s[t_i]$, and generates complete paths from s to some $t \in T$, but requires time $O(r_{\max}/\pi_s[T])$ per sample. Because the approximate sampler is more efficient, we present that here and defer the exact sampler to [17].

The `BiPPR-Precomp-Sampling` Algorithm

The high level idea behind our method is *hierarchical sampling*. Recall that the start node s has an associated forward vector $x_s = (e_s, \pi_s)$, and from each target t we have a reverse vector y^t; the PPR-estimate is given by $\pi_s[t] \approx \langle x_s, y^t \rangle$. Thus we want to sample $t \in T$ with probability:

$$p[t] = \frac{\langle x_s, y^t \rangle}{\sum_{j \in T} \langle x_s, y^j \rangle}.$$

We will sample t in two stages: first we sample an intermediate node $v \in V$ with probability:

$$p'_s[v] = \frac{x_s[v] \sum_{j \in T} y^j[v]}{\sum_{j \in T} \langle x_s, y^j \rangle}.$$

Following this, we sample $t \in T$ with probability:

$$p''_v[t] = \frac{y^t[v]}{\sum_{j \in T} y^j[v]}.$$

It is easy to verify that $p[t] = \sum_{v \in V} p'_s[v] p''_v[t]$. Figure 2 shows how the sampling algorithm works on an example graph. The pseudo-code is given in Algorithm 5 and Algorithm 6.

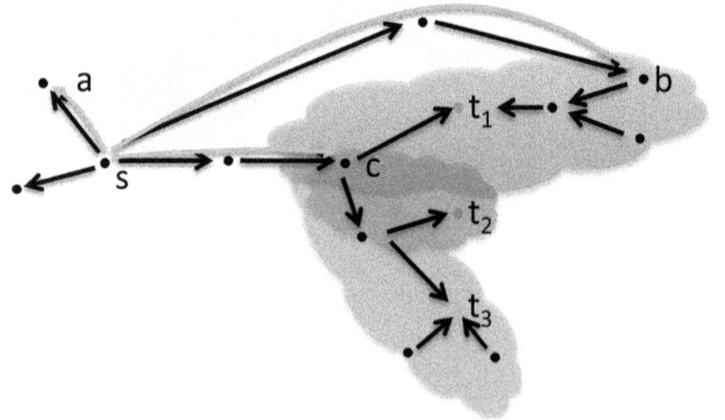

Figure 2: Search Example: Given target set $T = \{t_1, t_2, t_3\}$, for each target t_i we have drawn the expanded target-set, i.e., nodes v with positive residual $y^{t_i}[v]$. From source s, we sample three random walks, ending at nodes a, b, and c. Now suppose $y^{t_1}(b) = 0.64, y^{t_1}(c) = 0.4, y^{t_2}(c) = 0.16$, and $y^{t_3}(c) = 0.16$ – note that the remaining residuals are 0. Then we have $y^T(a) = 0, y^T(b) = 0.64$ and $y^T(c) = 0.72$, and consequently, the sampling weights of (a, b, c) are $(0, 0.213, 0.24)$. Now, to sample a target, we first sample from $\{a, b, c\}$ in proportion to its weight. Then if we sample b, we always return t_1; if we sample c, we sample (t_1, t_2, t_3) with probability $(5/9, 2/9, 2/9)$.

Note that we assume that some set of supported queries is known in advance, and we first pre-compute and store a separate data-structure for each query Q (i.e., for each target-set $T = \{t \in V : t \text{ is relevant to } Q\}$). In addition, we can optionally pre-compute w random walks from each start-node s, and store the forward vector x_s, or we can compute x_s at query time by sampling random walks.

Algorithm 5 SamplerPrecomputationForSet($T, r_{\max}$)

Inputs: Graph G, teleport probability α, target-set T, maximum residual $r_{\max}$

1: **for** $t \in T$ **do**
2: Compute $y^t = (p^t, r^t) \in \mathbb{R}^{2|V|}$ via `Approx-Contributions`$(G, \alpha, t, r_{\max})$
3: **end for**
4: Compute $y^T = \sum_{t \in T} y^t$
5: **for** $v \in V$ such that $y^T[v] > 0$ **do**
6: Create sampler$_v$ which samples t with probability $p''_v[t]$ (For example, using the alias sampling method [25], [15, section 3.4.1]).
7: **end for**
8: **return** $(y^T, \{\text{sampler}_v\})$

Running Time: For a small relative error for targets with $\pi_s[t] > \delta$, we use $w = cr_{\max}/\delta$ walks, where c is chosen as in Theorem 1. The support of our forward sampler is at most w so its construction time is $O(w)$ using the alias method of sampling from a discrete distribution [25], [15, section 3.4.1]. Once constructed, we can get independent samples in $O(1)$ time. Thus the query time to generate n_s samples is $O(cr_{\max}/\delta + n_s)$.

Accuracy: `BiPPR-Precomp-Sampling` does not sample exactly in proportion to π_s; instead, the sample probabilities

Algorithm 6 SampleAndRankTargets($s, r_{\max}, y^T, \{\text{sampler}_v\}$)

Inputs: Graph G, teleport probability α, start node s, maximum residual $r_{\max}$, reverse vectors y^T, intermediate-node-to-target samplers $\{\text{sampler}_v\}$.

Set number of walks $w = c\frac{r_{\max}}{\delta}$. In experiments we found $c = 20$ achieved precision@5 above 90% on Twitter-2010.
Set number of samples n_s (We use $n_s = w$)
Sample w random walks from s and let $\tilde{\pi}_s$ be the empirical distribution of their endpoints; compute forward vector $x_s = (e_s, \tilde{\pi}_s) \in \mathbb{R}^{2|V|}$
Create sampler$_s$ to sample $v \in [2|V|]$ with probability $p'_s[v]$, i.e., proportional to $x_s[v]y^T[v]$
Initialize empty map score from V to $\mathbb{N}$
for $j \in [0, n_s - 1]$ **do**
    Sample v from sampler$_s$
    Sample t from sampler$_v$
    Increment score(t)
end for
Return T sorted in decreasing order of score

are proportional to a distribution $\hat{\pi}_s$ satisfying the guarantee of Theorem 1. In particular, for all targets t with $\pi_s[t] \geq \delta$, this will have a small relative error ϵ, while targets with $\pi_s[t] < \delta$ will likely be sampled rarely enough that they won't appear in the set of top-k most sampled nodes.

Storage Required: The storage requirements for `BiPPR-Precomp-Sampling` (and for `BiPPR-Precomp-Grouped`) depends on the distribution of keywords and how $r_{\max}$ is chosen for each target set. For simplicity, here we assume a single maximum residual $r_{\max}$ across all target sets, and assume each target is relevant to at most γ keywords. For example, in the case of name search, each user typically has a first and last name, so $\gamma = 2$.

THEOREM 3. *Let graph G, minimum-PPR value δ and time-space trade-off parameter r_{max} be given, and suppose every node contains at most γ keywords. Then the total storage needed for BiPPR-Precomp-Sampling to construct a sampler for any source node (or distribution) s and any set of targets T corresponding to a single keyword is $O\left(\frac{\gamma m}{\alpha r_{max}}\right)$.*

We can choose $r_{\max}$ to trade-off this storage requirement with the running time requirement of $O(cr_{\max}/\delta)$ – for example, we can set both the query running-time and per-node storage to $\sqrt{c\gamma\bar{d}/\delta}$ where $\bar{d} = m/n$ is the average degree. Now for name search $\gamma = 2$, and if we choose $\delta = \frac{1}{n}$ and $\alpha = \Theta(1)$, the per-query running time and per-node storage is $O(\sqrt{m})$.

PROOF. For each set T corresponding to a keyword, and each $t \in T$, we push from nodes v until for each v, $r^t[v] < r_{\max}$. Each time we push from a node v, we add an entry to the residual vector of each node $u \in \mathcal{N}^{in}(v)$, so the space cost is $d^{in}(v)$. Each time we push from a node v, we increase the estimate $p^t[v]$ by $\alpha r^t[v] \geq \alpha r_{\max}$, and $\sum_{t\in T} p^t[v] \leq \sum_{t\in T} \pi_v[t] = \pi_v[T]$ so v can be pushed from at most $\frac{\pi_v[t]}{\alpha r_{\max}}$ times. Thus the total storage required is

$$\sum_{v\in V} d^{in}(v)(\#\text{ of times } v \text{ pushed}) \leq \sum_{v\in V} d^{in}(v)\frac{\pi_v[T]}{\alpha r_{\max}} \quad (4)$$

Let $\mathcal{T}$ be the set of all target sets (one target set per keyword). Then the total storage over all keywords is

$$\sum_{T\in\mathcal{T}}\sum_{t\in T}\sum_{v\in V} d^{in}(v)\frac{\pi_v[t]}{\alpha r_{\max}} \leq \gamma\sum_{v\in V}\sum_{t\in V} d^{in}(v)\frac{\pi_v[t]}{\alpha r_{\max}} \leq \gamma\sum_{v\in V} d^{in}(v)\frac{1}{\alpha r_{\max}} \leq \gamma\frac{m}{\alpha r_{\max}}.$$

□

Adaptive Maximum Residual: One way to improve the storage requirement is by using larger values of $r_{\max}$ for target sets T with larger global PageRank. Intuitively, if T is large, then it's easier for random walks to get close to T, so we don't need to push back from T as much as we would for a small T. We now formalize this scheme, and outline the savings in storage via a heuristic analysis, based on a model of personalized PageRank values introduced by Bahmani et al. [3].

For a fixed s, we assume the values $\pi_s[v]$ for all $v \in V$ approximately follow a power law with exponent β. Empirically, this is known to be an accurate model for the Twitter graph – Bahmani et al. [3] find that the mean exponent for a user is $\beta = 0.77$ with standard deviation 0.08. To analyze our algorithm, we further assume that π_s restricted to T also follows a power law, i.e.:

$$\pi_s[t_i] = \frac{1-\beta}{|T|^{1-\beta}} i^{-\beta}\pi_s[T]. \quad (5)$$

Suppose we want an accurate estimate of $\pi_s[t_i]$ for the top-k results within T, so we set $\delta_k = \pi_s[t_k]$. From Theorem 1, the number of walks required is:

$$w = c\frac{r_{\max}}{\delta_k} = c_2\frac{r_{\max}|T|^{1-\beta}}{\pi_s[T]}$$

where $c_2 = k^\beta c/(1-\beta)$. If we fix the number of walks as w, then we must set $r_{\max} = w\pi_s[T]/(c_2|T|^{1-\beta})$. Also, for a uniformly random start node s, we have $\mathbb{E}[\pi_s[T]] = \pi[T]$ (the global PageRank of T). This suggests we choose $r_{\max}(T)$ for set T as:

$$r_{\max}(T) = \frac{w\pi[T]}{c_2|T|^{1-\beta}} \quad (6)$$

Going back to equation (4), suppose for simplicity that the average $d^{in}(v)$ encountered is $\bar{d}$. Then the storage required for this keyword is bounded by:

$$\sum_{v\in V} d^{in}(v)\frac{\pi_v[T]}{r_{\max}} = \bar{d}\frac{n\pi[T]}{r_{\max}} = \frac{mc_2|T|^{1-\beta}}{w}.$$

Note that this is independent of $\pi[T]$. There is still a dependence on $|T|$, which is natural since for larger T there are more nodes which make it harder to find the top-k. For $\beta = 0.77$, the rate of growth, $|T|^{0.23}$ is fairly small, and in particular is sublinear in $|T|$.

Dynamic Graphs: So far we have assumed that the graph and keywords are static, but in practice they change over time. When a keyword is added to some node T, the node's reverse vector y^t needs to be added to the sampling data structure for that keyword. When an edge is added, the residual values need to be updated. We leave the extension to dynamic graphs to future work.

4.3 Experiments

We conduct experiments to test the efficiency of these personalized search algorithms as the size of the target set varies. We use one of the largest publicly available social networks, Twitter-2010 [16] with 40 million nodes and 1.5 billion edges. For various values of $|T|$, we select a target set T uniformly among all sets with that size, and compare the running times of the four algorithms we propose in this work, as well as the `Monte Carlo` algorithm. We repeat this using 10 random target sets and 10 random sources s per target set, and report the median running time for all algorithms. We use the same target sets and sources for all algorithms.

Parameter Choices: Because all five algorithms have parameters that trade-off running time and accuracy, we choose parameters such that the accuracy is comparable so we can compare running time on a level playing field. To choose a concrete benchmark, we chose parameters such that the precision@3 of the four algorithms we propose are consistently greater than 90% for the range of $|T|$ we used in experiment. We chose parameters for `Monte-Carlo` so that our algorithms are consistently more accurate than it, and its precision@3 is greater than 85%. In the full version we plot the precision@3 of the algorithms for the parameters we use when comparing running time.

We used $\delta = \pi_s(t_k)$ where $\pi_s(t_k)$ is estimated using Eqn. 5, using $k = 3$, power law exponent $\beta = 0.77$ (the mean value found empirically on Twitter), and assuming $\pi_s(T) = \frac{|T|}{n}$ (the expected value of $\pi_s(T)$ since T is chosen uniformly at random). Then we use Equation 6 to set $r_{\max}$, using $c = 20$ and two values of w, 10,000 and 100,000. We used the same value of $r_{\max}$ for `BiPPR-Precomp`, `BiPPR-Precomp-Grouped`, and `BiPPR-Precomp-Sampling`. For `Monte-Carlo`, we sampled $\frac{40}{\delta}$ walks[1].

Results: Figure 3 shows the running time of the five algorithms as $|T|$ varies for two different parameter settings in the trade-off between running time and precomputed storage requirement. Notice that `Monte-Carlo` is very slow on this large graph for small target set sizes, but gets faster as the size of the target set increases. For example when $|T| = 10$ Monte Carlo takes half an hour, and even for $|T| = 1000$ it takes more than a minute. `Bidirectional-PPR` is fast for small T, but slow for larger T, taking more than a second when $|T| \geq 100$. In contrast, `BiPPR-Precomp-Grouped` and `BiPPR-Precomp-Sampling` are both fast for all sizes of T, taking less than 250 ms when $w = 10,000$ and less than 25 ms when $w = 100,000$.

The improved running time of `BiPPR-Precomp-Grouped` and `BiPPR-Precomp-Sampling`, however, comes at the cost of pre-computation and storage. With these parameter choices, for $w = 10,000$ the pre-computation size per target set in our experiments ranged from 8 MB (for $|T| = 10$) to 200MB (for $|T| = 1000$) per keyword. For $w = 100,000$, the storage per keyword ranges from 3 MB (for $|T| = 10$) to 30MB (for $|T| = 10,000$).

[1]Note that `Monte-Carlo` was too slow to finish in a reasonable amount of time, so we measured the average time required to take 10 million walks, then multiplied by the number of walks needed. When measuring precision, we simulated the target weights `Monte-Carlo` would generate, by sampling t_i with probability $\pi_s(t_i)$; this produces exactly the same distribution of weights as `Monte-Carlo` would.

To get a larger range of $|T|$ relative to $|V|$, we also perform experiments on the Pokec graph [23] which has 1.6 million nodes and 30 million edges. Figure 4 shows the results on Pokec for $w = 100,000$. Here we clearly see the cross-over point where `Monte-Carlo` becomes more efficient than `Bidirectional-PPR`, while `BiPPR-Precomp-Grouped` and `BiPPR-Precomp-Sampling` consistently take less than 250 milliseconds. On Pokec, the storage used ranges from 800KB for $|T| = 10$ to 3MB for $|T| = 10,000$.

We implement our algorithms in Scala and report running times for Scala, but in preliminary experiments `BiPPR-Precomp-Grouped` is 3x faster when re-implemented in C++, we expect the running time would improve comparably for all five algorithms. Also, we ran each experiment on a single thread, but the algorithms parallelize naturally, so the latency could be improved by a multi-threaded implementation. We ran our experiments on a machine with a 3.33 GHz 12-core Intel Xeon X5680 processor, 12MB cache, and 192 GB of 1066 MHz Registered ECC DDR3 RAM. We measured the running time of the tread running each experiment to exclude garbage collector time. We loaded the graph used into memory and completed any pre-computation in RAM before measuring the running time of the algorithms.

5. RELATED WORK

Prior work on PPR Estimation The `Bidirectional-PPR` algorithm introduced in the first half of this work builds on the `FAST-PPR` algorithm presented in [19] – for details of prior work on Personalized PageRank estimation, see the section on existing approaches in [19]. Although `FAST-PPR` was the first algorithm for PPR estimation with sublinear running-time guarantees, it has several drawbacks which are improved upon by our new `Bidirectional-PPR` algorithm:

- `Bidirectional-PPR` has a simple linear structure which enables searching; Eqn. 3 shows that the estimates are a dot-produce between a forward vector x^s and a reverse vector y^t. In contrast, estimates in [19] require monitoring each walk to detect collisions with a "frontier" set.
- `Bidirectional-PPR` is 3x-8x faster than `FAST-PPR` for the same accuracy in experiments on diverse networks.
- `Bidirectional-PPR` is cleaner and more elegant, leading to simpler correctness proofs and performance analysis. This also makes it easier to generalize to arbitrary Markov Chains, as done in [6].

Comparison to Partitioned Multi-Indexing For personalized search, our indexing scheme is partially inspired by the Partitioned Multi-Indexing (PMI) scheme of Bahmani et al. [4]. Similar to our methods, PMI uses a bidirectional approach to rank search results according to shortest path distance from the searching user. Shortest path is easier to estimate than PPR, due to the fact that shortest path is a metric; moreover, shortest path is believed to be a less effective way of ranking search results than PPR. From a technical point of view, PMI is based on 'sweeping' from closer to more distant targets based on a distance oracle; in contrast, we use sampling to find the most relevant targets.

Prior work on Personalized PageRank Search In [7], Berkhin builds upon the previous work [14] and proposes efficient ways to compute the personalized PageRank vector π_s at runtime by combining pre-computed PPR vectors in a query-specific way. In particular, they identify "hub" nodes in advance, using heuristics such as global PageRank, and precompute approximate PPR vectors $\hat{\pi}_h$ for each hub

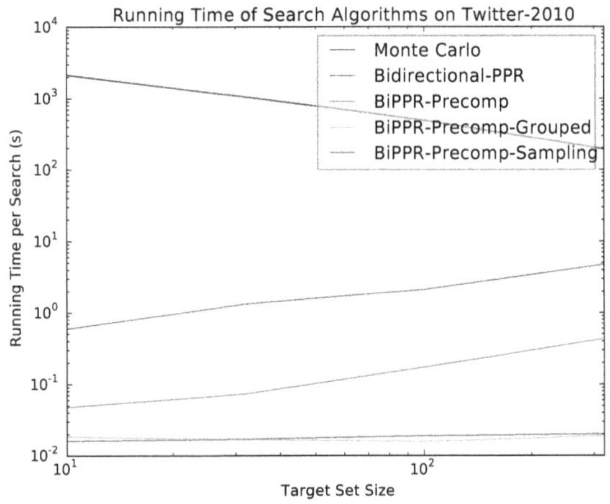

(a) Running Time, More Precomputation

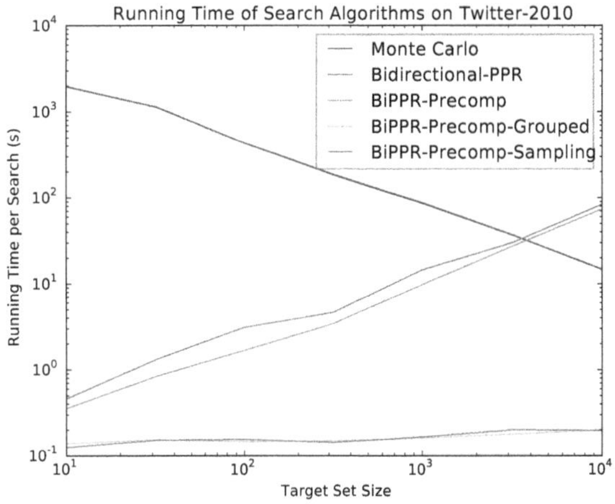

(b) Running Time, Less Precomputation

Figure 3: Running time on Twitter-2010 (1.5 billion edges) on log-scale, with parameters chosen such that the Precision@3 of our algorithms exceeds 90% and exceeds the precision@3 of `Monte-Carlo`. The two plots demonstrate the storage-runtime tradeoff: Figure 3(a) (which performs $10K$ walks at runtime) uses more pre-computation and storage compared to Figure 3(b) (with $100K$ walks).

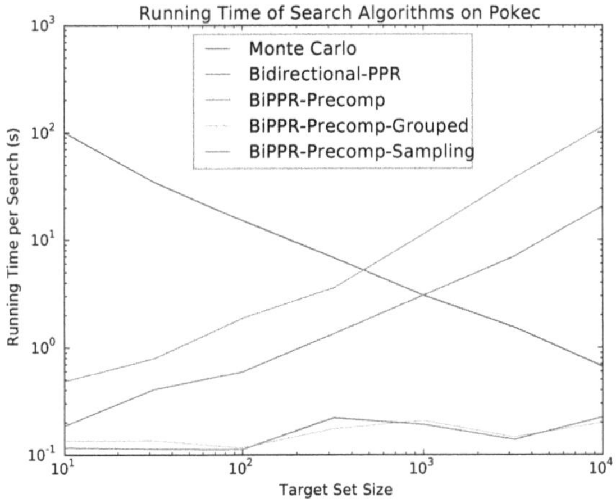

Figure 4: Running time on Pokec (30 million edges) performing 100K walks at runtime. Notice that `Monte-Carlo` is slow for small $|T|$, `Bidirectional-PPR` is slow for large $|T|$, and `BiPPR-Precomp-Grouped` and `BiPPR-Precomp-Sampling` are fast across the entire range of $|T|$.

node using a local forward-push algorithm called the Bookmark Coloring Algorithm (BCA). Chakrabarti [8] proposes a variant of this approach, where Monte-Carlo is used to pre-compute the hub vectors $\hat{\pi}_h$ rather than BCA.

Both approaches differ from our work in that they construct complete approximations to π_s, then pick out entries relevant to the query. This requires a high-accuracy estimate for π_s even though only a few entries are important. In contrast, our bidirectional approach allows us compute only the entries $\pi_s(t_i)$ relevant to the query.

6. ACKNOWLEDGMENTS

Research supported by the DARPA GRAPHS program via grant FA9550-12-1-0411, and by NSF grant 1447697. One author was supported by an NPSC fellowship.

7. REFERENCES

[1] R. Andersen, C. Borgs, J. Chayes, J. Hopcraft, V. S. Mirrokni, and S.-H. Teng. Local computation of pagerank contributions. In *Algorithms and Models for the Web-Graph*. Springer, 2007.

[2] K. Avrachenkov, N. Litvak, D. Nemirovsky, and N. Osipova. Monte carlo methods in pagerank computation: When one iteration is sufficient. *SIAM Journal on Numerical Analysis*, 2007.

[3] B. Bahmani, A. Chowdhury, and A. Goel. Fast incremental and personalized pagerank. *Proceedings of the VLDB Endowment*, 2010.

[4] B. Bahmani and A. Goel. Partitioned multi-indexing: bringing order to social search. In *Proceedings of the 21st international conference on World Wide Web*. ACM, 2012.

[5] S. Baluja, R. Seth, D. Sivakumar, Y. Jing, J. Yagnik, S. Kumar, D. Ravichandran, and M. Aly. Video suggestion and discovery for youtube: taking random walks through the view graph. In *Proceedings of the*

17th international conference on World Wide Web, pages 895–904. ACM, 2008.

[6] S. Banerjee and P. Lofgren. Fast bidirectional probability estimation in markov models. In *Advances in Neural Information Processing Systems*, pages 1423–1431, 2015.

[7] P. Berkhin. Bookmark-coloring algorithm for personalized pagerank computing. *Internet Mathematics*, 3(1):41–62, 2006.

[8] S. Chakrabarti. Dynamic personalized pagerank in entity-relation graphs. In *Proceedings of the 16th international conference on World Wide Web*, pages 571–580. ACM, 2007.

[9] D. Fogaras, B. Rácz, K. Csalogány, and T. Sarlós. Towards scaling fully personalized pagerank: Algorithms, lower bounds, and experiments. *Internet Mathematics*, 2005.

[10] D. F. Gleich. PageRank beyond the web. *arXiv*, cs.SI:1407.5107, 2014. Accepted for publication in SIAM Review.

[11] A. Goel, P. Gupta, and P. Lofgren. In preparation: Cross partitioning: Realtime computation of cosine similarity, personalized pagerank, and more. Technical report, Stanford University, 2015. available at http://www.stanford.edu/~plofgren/.

[12] P. Gupta, A. Goel, J. Lin, A. Sharma, D. Wang, and R. Zadeh. Wtf: The who to follow service at twitter. In *Proceedings of the 22nd international conference on World Wide Web*. International World Wide Web Conferences Steering Committee, 2013.

[13] T. H. Haveliwala. Topic-sensitive pagerank. In *Proceedings of the 11th international conference on World Wide Web*, pages 517–526. ACM, 2002.

[14] G. Jeh and J. Widom. Scaling personalized web search. In *Proceedings of the 12th international conference on World Wide Web*. ACM, 2003.

[15] D. E. Knuth. *The Art of Computer Programming, Vol. 2: Seminumerical Algorithms, 3rd Edition*. Reading, Mass.: Addison-Wesley, 1998.

[16] Laboratory for web algorithmics. http://law.di.unimi.it/datasets.php. Accessed: 2014-02-11.

[17] P. Lofgren. *Efficient Algorithms for Personalized PageRank*. PhD thesis, Stanford University, 2015. available at http://cs.stanford.edu/people/plofgren/.

[18] P. Lofgren and A. Goel. Personalized pagerank to a target node. *arXiv preprint arXiv:1304.4658*, 2013.

[19] P. A. Lofgren, S. Banerjee, A. Goel, and C. Seshadhri. Fast-ppr: Scaling personalized pagerank estimation for large graphs. In *Proceedings of the 20th ACM SIGKDD International Conference on Knowledge Discovery and Data Mining*, KDD '14, pages 1436–1445, New York, NY, USA, 2014. ACM.

[20] L. Page, S. Brin, R. Motwani, and T. Winograd. The pagerank citation ranking: bringing order to the web. 1999.

[21] A. Shrivastava and P. Li. Asymmetric lsh (alsh) for sublinear time maximum inner product search (mips). In *Advances in Neural Information Processing Systems*, pages 2321–2329, 2014.

[22] A. Shrivastava and P. Li. Improved asymmetric locality sensitive hashing (alsh) for maximum inner product search (mips). *stat*, 1050:13, 2014.

[23] Stanford network analysis platform (snap). http://http://snap.stanford.edu/. Accessed: 2014-02-11.

[24] M. V. Vieira, B. M. Fonseca, R. Damazio, P. B. Golgher, D. d. C. Reis, and B. Ribeiro-Neto. Efficient search ranking in social networks. In *Proceedings of the sixteenth ACM conference on Conference on information and knowledge management*. ACM, 2007.

[25] A. J. Walker. An efficient method for generating discrete random variables with general distributions. *ACM Trans. Math. Softw.*, 3(3):253–256, Sept. 1977.

Your Cart tells You: Inferring Demographic Attributes from Purchase Data

Pengfei Wang, Jiafeng Guo, Yanyan Lan, Jun Xu, Xueqi Cheng
CAS Key Lab of Network Data Science and Technology
Institute of Computing Technology, Chinese Academy of Sciences
wangpengfei@software.ict.ac.cn
{guojiafeng,lanyanyan,junxu,cxq}@ict.ac.cn

ABSTRACT

Demographic attributes play an important role in retail market to characterize different types of users. Such signals however are often only available for a small fraction of users in practice due to the difficulty in manual collection process by retailers. In this paper, we aim to harness the power of big data to automatically infer users' demographic attributes based on their purchase data. Typically, demographic prediction can be formalized as a multi-task multi-class prediction problem, i.e., multiple demographic attributes (e.g., gender, age and income) are to be inferred for each user where each attribute may belong to one of N possible classes (N≥2). Most previous work on this problem explores different types of features and usually predicts different attributes independently. However, modeling the tasks separately may lose the ability to leverage the correlations among different attributes. Meanwhile, manually defined features require professional knowledge and often suffer from under specification. To address these problems, we propose a novel Structured Neural Embedding (SNE) model to automatically learn the representations from users' purchase data for predicting multiple demographic attributes simultaneously. Experiments are conducted on a real-world retail dataset where five attributes (gender, marital status, income, age, and education level) are to be predicted. The empirical results show that our SNE model can improve the performance significantly compared with state-of-the-art baselines.

Categories and Subject Descriptors

H.2.8 [**Database Applications**]: Data mining

General Terms

Algorithm, Theory, Experimentation, Performance

Keywords

Demographic attribute, Structured Neural Embedding, multi-task multi-class prediction

WSDM2016, February 22-25, 2016, San Francisco, CA, USA.
@2016 ACM. ISBN 978-1-4503-3716-8/16/02$15.00
DOI: http://dx.doi.org/10.1145/2835776.2835783 .

1. INTRODUCTION

Obtaining users' demographic attributes is crucial for retailers to conduct market basket analysis [21], adjust marketing strategy [11], and provide personalized recommendations [23, 27]. However, in practice, it is usually not easy to obtain this kind of personal data such as age, gender, and income, etc. This is particularly true for traditional offline retailers[1], who collect users' demographic information mostly in a manual way (e.g. requiring costumers to provide demographic information for registering some shopping cards). Most users are reluctant to provide detailed information or even refuse to register their demographics due to privacy and other reasons. Through our analysis on a large scale real-world retail dataset over shopping-cards where five demographic attributes (i.e., gender, marital status, income, age, and education level) are considered, as shown in Figure 1, more than 85% users only have partial attributes and 5% users have no attributes at all.

The difficulty in collecting demographic attributes in retail scenario thus raises an interesting research question: Can we inference users' demographic attributes automatically based on their purchase behaviors? Although some recent studies suggest that demographic attributes are predictable from different behavioral data, such as linguistics writing [6], web browsing [17], electronic communications [9, 13], social media [15, 29], and mobile data [4, 28, 29] to our best knowledge, seldom practice has been conducted on purchase behaviors in retail scenario.

In general, demographic prediction can be formalized as a multi-task multi-class problem, i.e., multiple demographic attributes (e.g., gender, age and income) are to be inferred for each user based on their behavioral data where each attribute may belong to one of N possible classes, $N \geq 2$ (e.g., age may refer to young, adult, or old). In the retail scenario, the behavioral data refer to users' purchase history typically recorded by the POS terminals. The prediction task may take two forms: 1) Given a set of users with partial demographic attributes, how to predict the unknown attributes? (referred to as Partial-Label prediction) 2) Given a set of users with partially/fully labeled attributes, how to predict the demographic attributes for new users? (referred to as New-User prediction)

[1]In this work, we mainly focus on traditional retailers in offline business rather than those in online e-commerce, where no additional behavioral data rather than transactions is available for analysis. Hereafter we will use retail/retailer for simplicity when there is no ambiguity.

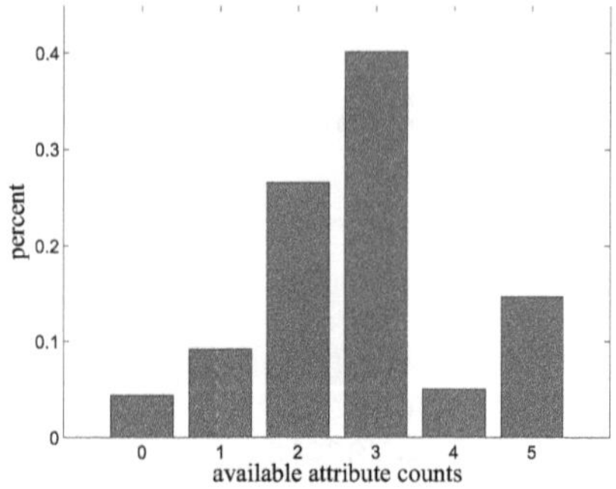

Figure 1: Distribution of demographic attribute count over users with shopping card. X axis stands for the number of available attributes per user, y axis indicates the proportion of users.

Previous work on demographic prediction usually predicts different attributes independently based on manually defined features [4, 19, 22, 28, 29]. For example, Zhong et al. [29] tried to predict six demographic attributes (i.e., gender, age, education background, sexual orientation, marital status, blood type and zodiac sign) separately using spatial, temporal and location knowledge features. However, manually defined features usually require professional knowledge and often suffer from under specification. Meanwhile, by predicting each attribute independently, one may not be able to leverage the potential correlations between different attributes (e.g., correlation between age and marital status). Some recent studies proposed to take the relations between different attributes into account [4, 28]. For example, Dong et al. [4] employed a Double Dependent-Variable Factor Graph model to predict gender and age simultaneously. Zhong et al. [28] attempted to capture pairwise relations between different tasks when predicting six demographic attributes from mobile data. However, these methods still rely on various human-defined features which are often costly to obtain.

To tackle the above problems, in this paper we propose a novel Structured Neural Embedding (SNE) model to automatically learn the representations (i.e., features) from users' purchase data for predicting multiple demographic attributes simultaneously in retail scenario. Specifically, we characterize each user by his/her purchase history using the bag-of-item representations. We then map each item to a vector in a continuous space, aggregate all the item vectors to form the user representation, and further feed this representation to a log-bilinear model for structured prediction. As compared with previous methods, the proposed SNE model enjoys the following two merits: 1) The features of users are automatically learned towards the goal of the prediction tasks. 2) By employing a structured prediction model, we can fully leverage the potential correlations between different attributes to improve the prediction accuracy. The proposed SNE model can be learned efficiently using the stochastic gradient descent (SGD) method.

We conduct extensive experiments on a real-world retail dataset to demonstrate the effectiveness of the proposed method. Some state-of-the-art baseline methods on demographic prediction and multi-task learning are taken into comparison. We tested different methods on both the Partial-Label and New-User prediction problems. The empirical results demonstrated that our approach is more effective than all the baseline methods.

Overall, the major contributions of our work are as follows:

- We make the first attempt to investigate the prediction power of users' purchase data for demographic prediction in retail scenario.
- We propose a novel SNE model for the multi-task multi-class prediction problem which can not only learn the data representations automatically but also capture the relations between different attributes in a structured way.
- We conduct extensive experiments on a real-world retail dataset to demonstrate the effectiveness of the proposed SNE model as compared with different baseline methods.

The rest of the paper is organized as follows. After a summary of related work in Section 2, we describe the problem formalization of demographic prediction in retail scenario in Section 3. In section 4 we present our proposed model in detail. Section 5 concludes this paper and gives the future work.

2. RELATED WORK

In this section we briefly review three research areas related to our work: demographic prediction, multi-task & multi-class prediction, and representation learning.

2.1 Demographic Prediction

Demographic prediction has been studied in different scenarios in academia. Early work on demographic prediction attempted to predict demographic attributes based on the linguistics writing and speaking. For example, Schler et al. [22] found that there are significant differences in both writing style and content between male and female bloggers as well as among authors of different ages. Otterbacher [19] used logistic regression model to infer users' gender based on content of reviews.

Later, the digital communication and Internet offered new opportunities for inferring demographic attributes. Different approaches have been proposed to infer demographic attributes based on users' browsing history [9, 17]. Torres [5] found that the clicked pages were correlated with the demographic characteristics of users. Hu et al. [9] calculated demographic tendency of web pages, and modeled users' demographic attributes through a discriminative model. In [2], Bi et al. infers the demographic attributes of search users based on the models training on the independent social datasets. They demonstrated that by leveraging social and search data in a common representation, they can achieve better accuracy in demographic prediction.

Recently, the fast development of online social networks and mobile computing technologies accumulated large scale of user data, making it possible and also valuable to infer users' demographic attributes in these scenarios. Mislove [15] found that users with common profiles were more likely to be friends and often formed a dense community. Zhong et al. [28] proposed a supervised learning framework to predict users' demographic attributes based on mobile data. Dong et al. [4] focused on micro-level analysis of the mobile networks to infer users' demographic attributes. Culotta et al. [3] fitted a regression model to predict users' demographic attributes using information on followers of each website on Twitter.

As we can see, most existing work on demographic prediction focused on designing different features for the prediction tasks. Besides, to the best of our knowledge, seldom practice has been conducted on demographic prediction based on purchase behaviors in retail scenario.

2.2 Multi-task & Multi-class Prediction

The idea of learning multiple tasks together is to improve the generalization performance by leveraging the information contained in the related tasks. A typical way for this purpose is to learn tasks in parallel while using a shared representation [4, 10, 28]. Many algorithms have been proposed to solve multi-task learning with various kernels and regularizers to address the correlation between tasks. For example, Micchelli et al. [14] discussed how different kernels can be used to model relations between tasks and presented linear multi-task learning algorithms. Evgeniou et al. [7] presented an approach to multi-task learning based on the minimization of regularization functions.

Meanwhile, multi-class classification is the problem of classifying instances into one of the more than two classes. Usually two ways are used to solve this kind of problem: 1) one-against-one [1], which builds a classification for each pair of classes; and 2) one-against-all [25], which creates one binary problem for each of classes.

In this paper, we formalize the demographic prediction in retail scenario as a multi-task multi-class problem, where we propose to solve it by using structured prediction based on automatic representation learning.

2.3 Representation Learning

Learning representations of the data makes it easier to extract useful information when building classifiers or other predictors. That is why representation learning has attracted more and more attention and become a field in itself in the machine learning community.

Many remarkable empirical successes have been achieved based on representation learning in various applications in both academia and industry. For example, in speech recognition and signal processing, Alex Graves et al. [8] designed a deep recurrent neural network for speech recognition and obtain the best score on benchmark. In object recognition, Krizhevsky et al. [12] proposed to use convolutional neural network to classify image and achieved the record-breaking results. In natural language processing, Mnih [16] proposed three graphical models to define the distribution of next word in a sequence by using distributed representations.

In this work, we propose to use representation learning for demographic prediction in retail scenario, a new application area where representation learning might be helpful.

3. OUR APPROACH

In this section, we first introduce the formalization of demographic prediction problem in retail scenario. We then talk about the key idea of our approach. After that , we describe the proposed SNE in detail. Finally, we present the learning and prediction procedure of SNE and give some discussions on the model.

Table 1: List of demographic attributes used in this work

Attributes	Values
gender	male, female
age	young(14-24), adult(25-34), middle-age(35-49), old(>50)
marital status	single, married
income	ultra-low(<2k/month), low(2k-4k/month) medium(4k-6k/month), high(>6k/month)
education level	doctor, master, bachelor, college, high school, middle school

3.1 Problem Formalization

In our work, we aim to predict multiple demographic attributes based on users' behavioral data in retail scenario. Specifically, each user can be characterized by his/her purchase history, i.e., a set of items. The demographic attributes we are interested in include gender, age, marital status, income, and education level, which are useful signals for market basket analysis. The values each attribute may take are listed in Table 1, and for each attribute the possible values are exclusive. For each user, given part/none of his/her attributes, we want to predict all the unknown attributes.

Obviously, the above prediction task can be formalized as a multi-task multi-class problem. Specifically, let $T = \{T_1, T_2, \ldots, T_K\}$ be a set of multi-class prediction tasks (i.e., predicting demographic attributes), where each task $T_k \in T$ is associated with C_k classes (i.e., multiple attribute values), $C_k \geq 2, k = 1, 2, \ldots, K$. The total class number across all the tasks is $C = \sum_{k=1}^{K} C_k$. Let U be a set of $|U| = M$ users and I be a set of $|I| = N$ items. Each user is represented by $(x^{(i)}, y^{(i)}), i = 1, 2, \ldots, M$, where $x^{(i)}$ denotes the purchase history of the i-th user, and $y^{(i)} = \{y_1^{(i)}, y_2^{(i)}, \ldots, y_K^{(i)}\}$ denotes the set of attribute labels of the i-th user. Note here $y_k^{(i)}$ denotes the attribute label under the k-th task $T_k \in T$ for the i-th user, which takes value from $\{1, 2, \ldots, C_k\}$.

Given the notations defined above, we define the following two prediction problems:

- **Partial-Label prediction:** Given a set of users X with partial demographic attributes Y^L, the objective is to learn a function to predict the remaining unknown attributes

$$f : X \to Y^U$$

  where Y^U denotes the observed attributes and that to be predicted over the same set of users X respectively.

- **New-User prediction:** Given a set of users X^L with partially/fully labeled attributes Y^L, the objective is to learn a function to predict the demographic attributes for new users

$$f : X^N \to Y^N$$

  where X^N and Y^N denote the purchase history and the attributes of the new users. Note that here $X^L \cap X^N = \emptyset$.

We can see that the first problem focuses on predicting the missing attributes for the same users used in training, while

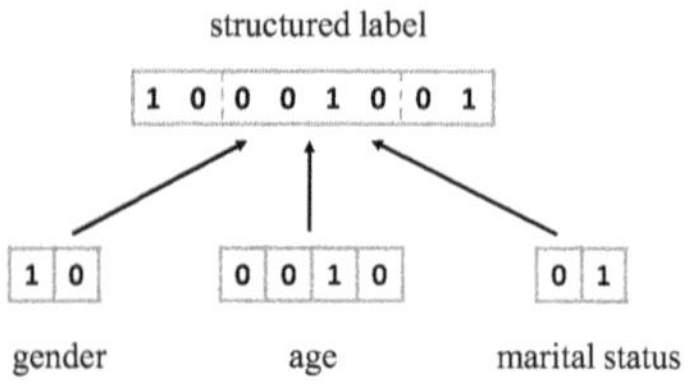

Figure 2: Structured representation of multi-task multi-class predictions.

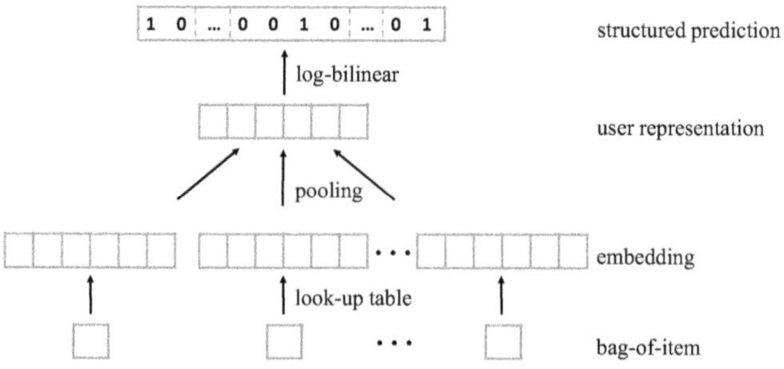

Figure 3: Architecture of SNE model.

the second one emphasizes the generalization ability of the prediction model to new users.

3.2 Key Idea

In our work, we introduce a novel structured prediction method based on representation learning to solve the above demographic prediction problems. The key motivation of this model comes from the following two folds.

Firstly, a fundamental problem in demographic prediction based on users' behavior data is how to represent users. Many existing work investigated different types of human defined features [4, 19, 28]. However, it is usually costly to define features manually since expertise knowledge is required and one has to do the same job task by task. Moreover, human defined features may often suffer from under specification since it is difficult to identify those hidden complicated factors for prediction tasks. Some recent work employs unsupervised feature learning methods [9, 13, 29], like Singular Vector Decomposition (SVD), to automatically extract low-dimension features from the raw data. However, the features learned in an unsupervised manner may not be optimal for the prediction tasks. Therefore, in this work we proposed to automatically learn representations of users for demographic prediction in a supervised way.

Secondly, as demographic prediction can be viewed as a multi-task problem, there might be correlations among different tasks that can be leveraged to improve the prediction accuracy. For example, users' marital statuses are more likely to be single if they are young, and a better educated person may have more chance to have higher income. However, most previous work treated different attributes as separate prediction tasks [3, 13, 29], thus ignored the correlations among these attributes (detailed discussion please refer to Section 3.4). In our work, we try to explicitly model the correlation information between different tasks by turning the multiple multi-class prediction tasks into a single structured prediction task.

Here we take the attributes gender, age, and marital status in our problem as an example. These three prediction tasks are 2-class, 4-class, and 2-class classification problems respectively. To turn them into a structured problem, we encode each task's label by a one-hot representation, and concatenate these labels to generate a single structured label, as shown in Figure 2. The benefit of this structured formalization is obvious, as the correlation among tasks can now be explicitly encoded in this label vector, e.g. label vector referring to young and single is much more popular than that referring to young and married. Therefore, by learning based on such structured labels, we can directly learn the features that are useful for revealing the correlation between multiple prediction tasks.

3.3 Structured Neural Embedding Model

Based on the above two ideas, we now present the proposed Structured Neural Embedding (SNE) model in detail. In retail scenario, each user is characterized by his/her purchase history, i.e., a set of items. In SNE, we take the bag-of-item representation as the user input, and map each item to a vector in a continuous space. We then aggregate all the item vectors using some operator to form the user representation, and feed this representation to a log-bilinear model for the structured prediction. The architecture of our model is shown in Figure 3.

More formally, let $\mathbf{V}^I = \{\vec{v}_j^I \in \mathbb{R}^{D_v} | j = 1, \ldots, N\}$ denote all the item vectors in a D_v-dimension continuous space. For the i-th user with purchase history $x^{(i)}$ (i.e., a set of purchased items), we aggregate the item vectors to form the user representation by

$$\vec{v}^{(i)} = g(\vec{v}_j^I : j \in x^{(i)})$$

where $g(\cdot)$ denotes the aggregation function. In our work, we investigate three types of pooling functions as the aggregation operator for computational efficiency.

- *unique pooling*:

$$\vec{v}^{(i)} = g_{uniq}(\vec{v}_j^I : j \in x^{(i)}) = \frac{1}{|uniq(x^{(i)})|} \sum_{j \in uniq(x^{(i)})} \vec{v}_j^I$$

  where $uniq(x^{(i)})$ represents the set of unique items purchased by i-th user.

- *average pooling*:

$$\vec{v}^{(i)} = g_{avg}(\vec{v}_j^I : j \in x^{(i)}) = \frac{1}{|x^{(i)}|} \sum_{j=1}^{|x^{(i)}|} \vec{v}_j^I$$

- *max pooling*:

$$\vec{v}^{(i)} = g_{max}(\vec{v}_j^I : j \in x^{(i)}) = \begin{bmatrix} max(\vec{v}_1^I[1], \ldots, \vec{v}_{|x^{(i)}|}^I[1]) \\ max(\vec{v}_1^I[2], \ldots, \vec{v}_{|x^{(i)}|}^I[2]) \\ \vdots \\ max(\vec{v}_1^I[D_v], \ldots, \vec{v}_{|x^{(i)}|}^I[D_v]) \end{bmatrix}$$

  Where $\vec{v}_j^I[l]$ denotes the l-th dimension in $\vec{v}_j^I$.

Based on the aggregated vector of the i-th user, SNE defines the probability of assigning demographic attributes $y^{(i)}$ to the user via a log-bilinear model:

$$p(y^{(i)}|x^{(i)}) = \frac{exp(\vec{v}^{(i)\top} \mathbf{W} \vec{y}^{(i)})}{\sum_{\vec{y} \in \mathcal{Y}} exp(\vec{v}^{(i)\top} \mathbf{W} \vec{y})} \quad (1)$$

where $\vec{y}^{(i)} \in \{0,1\}^C$ denotes the structured vector of $y^{(i)}$, $\mathcal{Y}$ denotes all the possible structured vectors of different combinations of attributes, and $W = \mathbb{R}^{D_v \times C}$ denotes the interaction matrix. Note that since each task is a multi-class problem (i.e., only one class can be assigned to each task), the total size of $\mathcal{Y}$ is $|\mathcal{Y}| = \prod_{k=1}^{K} C_k$.

It is worth noting that when $y^{(i)}$ only contains partial attributes, we will construct a set of structured vectors $\vec{y}^{(i)}$ corresponding to the same $y^{(i)}$ by fixing the values for the known attributes and enumerating all the possible values for the missing attributes. Let $\mathcal{Y}^{(i)}_{partial}$ denote the set of corresponding vectors, the computation of $p(y^{(i)}|x^{(i)})$ becomes

$$p(y^{(i)}|x^{(i)}) = \frac{\sum_{\vec{y}^{(i)} \in \mathcal{Y}^{(i)}_{partial}} exp(\vec{v}^{(i)\top} \mathbf{W} \vec{y}^{(i)})}{\sum_{\vec{y} \in \mathcal{Y}} exp(\vec{v}^{(i)\top} \mathbf{W} \vec{y})} \quad (2)$$

Since the enumeration of all the possible values of missing attributes will appear in both numerator and denominator in Equation (2), they can be eliminated for computation simplicity. Therefore, we can obtain a general version of Equation (1) handling both partial and full attributes

$$p(y^{(i)}|x^{(i)}) = \frac{exp(\vec{v}^{(i)\top} \mathbf{W}_c \vec{y}^{(i)}_c)}{\sum_{\vec{y}_c \in \mathcal{Y}_c} exp(\vec{v}^{(i)\top} \mathbf{W}_c \vec{y}_c)} \quad (3)$$

Where the subscript c denotes a *compact* version of the variable. A compact structured vector $\vec{y}^{(i)}_c$ is a concatenation of one-hot representations of known attributes in $y^{(i)}$, while a compact interaction matrix $\mathbf{W}_c$ is formed by removing the columns corresponding to the missing attributes from the original $\mathbf{W}$.

The objective function of SNE is then defined as the log likelihood over all the users as follows:

$$\ell_{SNE} = \sum_{i=1}^{M} \log p(y^{(i)}|x^{(i)}) - \lambda \|\Theta\|_F^2 \quad (4)$$

where λ is the regularization constant and Θ are the model parameters (i.e. $\Theta = \{\mathbf{W}, \mathbf{V}^I\}$).

3.4 Learning and Prediction

Learning SNE model involves maximize the objective function defined in Equation (4). However, the direct optimization is intractable due to the high computational cost of the normalization term which is proportional to $|\mathcal{Y}|$. Therefore, we adopt the negative sampling technique [20, 24] for efficient optimization, which approximates the original objective ℓ_{SNE} with the following objective function:

$$\ell_{NEG} = \sum_{i=1}^{M} \Big(\log \sigma(\vec{v}^{(i)\top} \mathbf{W} \vec{y}^{(i)}) + k_{neg} \cdot \mathbb{E}_{\vec{y}^{neg} \sim P_{\mathcal{Y}}} [\log \sigma(-\vec{v}^{(i)\top} \mathbf{W} \vec{y}^{neg}))] \Big) - \lambda \|\Theta\|_F^2$$

where $\sigma(x)$ is the logistic function $\sigma(x) = 1/(1+e^{-x})$, k_{neg} is the number of "negative" samples, and $\vec{y}^{neg}$ is the sampled structured vector, drawn according to the noise distribution $P_{\mathcal{Y}}$ which is modeled by empirical distribution over all possible attribute combinations. As we can see, the objective of SNE with negative sampling aims to differentiate the ground truth from noise by increasing the probability of the correct label combination given the user input and deceasing that of any wrong combinations.

We then apply stochastic gradient descent algorithm to maximize the new objective function for learning the model. The updating algorithm is shown in Algorithm 1.

Algorithm 1 Learning algorithm of SNE model

Initialize model Θ: $\{\mathbf{W}, \mathbf{V}^I\}$ randomly
t=0
repeat
    $t \leftarrow t+1$;
    for i=1,...,|U| **do**
        $\vec{v}^{(i)} = f(\vec{v}^I_j : j \in x^{(i)})$
        for each $\vec{w}$ in $\mathbf{W}_c \vec{y}^{(i)}_c$ **do**
            $\vec{w} \leftarrow \vec{v}^{(i)} \sigma(-\vec{v}^{(i)} \sum_{\vec{w}} \vec{w})$
        end for
        for k=1,...,n **do**
            for each $\vec{w}$ in $\mathbf{W}_c \vec{y}^{neg}_c$ **do**
                $\vec{w} \leftarrow -\vec{v}^{(i)} \sigma(\vec{v}^{(i)} \sum_{\vec{w}} \vec{w})$
            end for
        end for
        $W_{neg} \leftarrow \mathbf{W}_c \vec{y}^{neg}_c$, $W_{pos} \leftarrow \mathbf{W}_c \vec{y}^{(i)}_c$
        for each $j \in x^{(i)}$ **do**
            $\vec{v}^{(i)}_j \leftarrow \sum_{\vec{w} \in W_{pos}} \vec{w} \sigma(-\vec{v}^{(i)} \sum_{\vec{w} \in W_{pos}} \vec{w}) - \sum_k^n \sum_{\vec{w} \in W_{neg}} \vec{w} \sigma(\vec{v}^{(i)} \sum_{\vec{w} \in W_{neg}} \vec{w})$
        end for
    end for
until converge or t> num
return $\mathbf{W}, \mathbf{V}^I$

With the learned item representations $\mathbf{V}^I$ and interaction matrix $\mathbf{W}$, the prediction process is to find the best attributes for a given user according to

$$y* = arg \max_{y \in \mathcal{Y}} p(y|x)$$

For Partial-Label prediction problem, part of the attributes are fixed and we want to decide the rest; For New-User prediction problem, we need to predict the whole set of attributes. These two problems can be solved similarly in an efficient way. We first re-write the log-bilinear model as follows

$$\begin{aligned} p(y|x) &= \frac{exp(\vec{v}^\top \mathbf{W} \vec{y})}{\sum_{\vec{y} \in \mathcal{Y}} exp(\vec{v}^\top \mathbf{W} \vec{y})} \propto exp(\vec{v}^\top \mathbf{W} \vec{y}) \\ &= \sum_{j: I(\vec{y}[j]=1)} v^\top \mathbf{W}_{*j} \end{aligned} \quad (5)$$

Where $\vec{y}[j]$ denotes the j-th entry in $\vec{y}$, $\mathbf{W}_{*j}$ denotes the j-th column of the interaction matrix, and $I(\cdot)$ denotes the indicator function.

The Equation (5) shows that the probability of an attribute set is proportional to the sum of scores (i.e.,$v^\top \mathbf{W}_{*j}$) corresponding to the attribute assignments (i.e., $\vec{y}[j]$ set as 1). Since in our work each task is a multi-class problem where only one class can be assigned, the best attribute set is then a combination of assignments with the highest score from each task given the input. In this way, for each user input, we only need to conduct a forward computation to generate the scores for each attribute entry, and select the highest one for each task as the final prediction. For Partial-Label problem, we simply select for those missing attributes while leaving the known attributes fixed.

3.5 Discussion

In this section we try to compare the difference between our structure learning model and conventional multi-task learning methods.

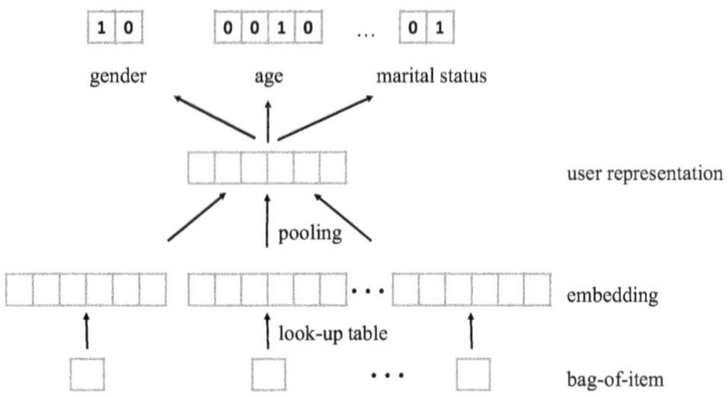

Figure 4: Architecture of joint model for multi-task multi-class prediction.

In conventional multi-task learning, a joint model is typically employed to learn several related tasks at the same time by using a shared representation, as shown in Figure 4. In this model, each task is viewed as a separate prediction problem and the objective function is a sum over these tasks:

$$\ell_{JOINT} = \sum_{i=1}^{M}\sum_{k=1}^{K} \log p(y_k^{(i)}|x^{(i)}) - \lambda\|\Theta\|_F^2$$

Where $y_k^{(i)}$ denotes the k-th attribute of the user.

The joint model can improve the prediction performance by learning the commonality among multiple tasks through the shared representation. This is the same as our SNE model. The major difference lies in how we model the prediction tasks. In joint model, each attribute is modeled as a separate prediction task, thus the correlation between attributes (like seeing one attribute makes it more likely to see another simultaneously) is ignored. Some multi-task learning methods try to consider the correlation among tasks by kernels or regularizers [7, 30], but they usually rely on explicit knowledge of relationships among tasks. While in our structured model, we turn the multiple prediction tasks into a single structured prediction task. Therefore, we can see that in the objective function of the SNE model (Equation (4)), there is no summation over the tasks. The learning over the structured label vector makes us be able to learn the important patterns revealing the correlation among multiple tasks.

One may argue that the structured formalization makes the prediction task more difficult than original separate tasks since the output space becomes much larger. However, with the large scale user behavioral data, this sparse problem can somehow be alleviated and our experimental results show that we can indeed improve the prediction performance by our structured formalization.

4. EXPERIMENTS

In this section, we conduct empirical experiments to demonstrate the effectiveness of our proposed SNE model on demographic attribute prediction in retail scenario. We first introduce the experimental settings. Then we analyze the effect of different aggregation operators and negative sampling strategies to our SNE model. Finally, we compare our SNE model to the baseline methods to demonstrate the effectiveness in both Partial-Label prediction and New-User prediction scenarios.

Table 2: Distribution of demographic attributes on BeiRen dataset.

Attributes	Value	Percentage
gender	male	28.5%
	female	71.5%
age	young	7.4%
	adult	39.4%
	middle age	41.6%
	old	11.6%
martial status	single	39.9%
	married	60.1%
income	ultra-low	16.6%
	low	50.3%
	medium	19.3%
	high	13.8%
education level	doctor	0.4%
	master	8.0%
	bachelor	48.7%
	college	2.9%
	high school	12.2%
	middle school	27.8%

4.1 Experimental Settings

Here we introduce the experimental settings including the dataset, baseline methods, and evaluation metrics.

4.1.1 Dataset

We conduct our empirical experiments over a real world large scale retail dataset, namely BeiRen dataset[2]. This dataset comes from a large retailer[3] in China, which records its supermarket purchase histories during the period from 2012 to 2013. It contains 49, 290, 149 transactions over 220, 828 items belonging to 1, 206, 379 users. For research purpose, the dataset has been anonymized with all the users and items denoted by randomly assigned IDs for the privacy issue. We first conduct some pre-process on the BeiRen dataset. We only keep the users who have all the five demographic attributes (i.e., gender, age, marital status, income, and education level) provided. We then extract all the transactions related to these users to form their purchase histories, and remove all the items bought by less than 5 times. After preprocessing, the dataset contains 61, 097 distinct items and 57, 693 distinct users with full attributes. In average, each user has bought about 110.6 distinct items. The detailed distribution of different attributes are listed in Table 2.

For experiments on Partial-Label prediction, we randomly set the observed ratio of users' demographic attributes from 10% to 90% with the step length as 10%. All the users' with their partially observed attributes and purchase histories are taken as training data, and the task is to predict the hidden attributes of these users.

For experiments on New-User prediction, we split the dataset into two non overlapping set, i.e. a training set and a testing set, with the ratio 9 : 1. The resulting training set contains 51, 923 users, and the test set contains 5, 770 users.

4.1.2 Baseline Methods

We evaluate our model by comparing with several state-of-the-art methods on the demographic attribute prediction task:

- POP: The most popular combination of demographic attributes in the training set is taken as prediction. Obviously this heuristic baseline ignores users' pur-

[2]http://www.bigdatalab.ac.cn/benchmark/bm/dd?data=Beiren
[3]http://www.brjt.cn/

Table 3: Comparison of different aggregation operators in SNE with varied observed attribute ratio from 10% to 90%

ratio	wPrecision			wRecall			wF1			Hamming Loss		
	SNE_{uniq}	SNE_{max}	SNE_{avg}	SNE_{uniq}	SNE_{max}	SNE_{avg}	SNE_{uniq}	SNE_{max}	SNE_{avg}	SNE_{uniq}	SNE_{max}	SNE_{avg}
10	0.071	0.163	**0.166**	0.034	0.072	**0.079**	0.047	0.106	**0.115**	0.543	0.455	**0.445**
20	0.169	0.228	**0.239**	0.096	0.108	**0.121**	0.123	0.147	**0.161**	0.492	0.452	**0.433**
30	0.214	0.294	**0.310**	0.129	0.138	**0.168**	0.161	0.188	**0.221**	0.487	0.455	**0.431**
40	0.247	0.318	**0.320**	0.181	0.214	**0.224**	0.208	0.256	**0.264**	0.488	0.441	**0.428**
50	0.338	0.368	**0.376**	0.247	0.275	**0.283**	0.302	**0.321**	0.319	0.455	**0.427**	0.429
60	0.419	0.407	**0.410**	0.307	0.339	**0.343**	0.354	0.370	**0.372**	0.457	**0.427**	0.428
70	0.451	0.448	**0.481**	0.370	0.402	**0.403**	0.407	0.424	**0.431**	0.457	0.428	**0.425**
80	0.485	0.503	**0.514**	0.428	0.462	**0.471**	0.455	0.482	**0.491**	0.451	0.431	**0.423**
90	0.528	0.534	**0.556**	0.491	0.511	**0.530**	0.511	0.522	**0.543**	0.451	0.432	**0.421**

chase history, and only relies on the correlations among demographic attributes for prediction.

- SVD-Single: A singular value decomposition (SVD)[4] is first conducted over the user-item matrix to obtain low dimensional representations of users. Then a logistic model is learned over the low dimensional representation to predict each demographic attribute separately. This method has been widely used in demographic attribute prediction [9, 17, 29].

- SVD-Structured: Different from SVD-Single, a structured learning model (i.e., log-bilinear model) is used to predict multiple demographic attributes based on the low dimensional representations obtained by SVD decomposition.

- JNE: The joint neural embedding (JNE) model is a typical multi-task learning method as discussed in Section 3.5. All the tasks are assumed to share the same latent representation of the user, and a joint model is employed to predict multiple attributes in parallel.

For both SVD and neural embedding based methods, we run several times with random initialization by setting the dimensionality as 100. We compare the average results of different methods and demonstrate the results in the following sections.

4.1.3 Evaluation Metrics

We employ the following evaluation metrics to evaluate the performance of demographic prediction methods against the groundtruth.

- Hamming Loss: the hamming loss is a wildly used metric [18, 26], which calculates how many times an instance-label pair is misclassified. The metric is calculated as follows:

$$\text{Hamming Loss} = \frac{1}{|U|}\sum_i \frac{|y^{*(i)} \triangle y_{test}^{(i)}|}{|y_{test}^{(i)}|}$$

Where $\triangle$ stands for the symmetric difference between two sets, $y_{test}^{(i)}$ denotes the set of attributes to be predicted for the i-th user, and $y^{*(i)}$ denotes the set of predicted attributes. Note that Hamming Loss is an attribute level metric, which takes each demographic attribute independently for evaluation. As we can see, The smaller the value of Hamming Loss is, the better performance the model obtains.

[4]http://tedlab.mit.edu/~dr/SVDLIBC/

- Weighted F1: we follow the idea in [4] to use weighted F1 as an evaluation metric since we consider each class is as important as each other. The weighted F1 is computed as follows:

$$\text{wPrecision} = \frac{1}{|\mathcal{Y}|}\sum_{y\in\mathcal{Y}} \frac{\sum_i I(y^{*(i)} = y_{test}^{(i)})}{\sum_i I(y = y_{test}^{(i)})}$$

$$\text{wRecall} = \frac{1}{|U|}\sum_i I(y^{*(i)} = y_{test}^{(i)})$$

$$\text{wF1} = \frac{2 \times \text{wPrecision} \times \text{wRecall}}{\text{wPrecision} + \text{wRecall}}$$

where $I(\cdot)$ is an indicator function. Note that these weighted metrics are more strict than Hamming Loss in that the prediction for a user is correct only when the set of attributes are all correctly predicted. As we can see, the weighted precision is the prediction accuracy in the label combination view while the weighted recall is the prediction accuracy in the user view.

4.2 Study of the SNE Variations

We first analyze the multiple variations of the proposed SNE model, including the aggregation operators and negative sampling strategies.

4.2.1 Effect of Aggregation Operators

In SNE model, we can employ different aggregation operators to obtain users' representations from item vectors. In this work, we introduced three types of pooling functions, namely unique pooling, average pooling, and max pooling. Here we study which kind of operator works better with respect to the demographic prediction. We denote the corresponding SNE model as SNE_{uniq}, SNE_{avg}, and SNE_{max}, and show the performance results over the Partial-Label prediction problem in Table 3.

As we can see, among all the three variations of SNE model, SNE_{avg} performs better than both SNE_{uniq} and SNE_{max} in terms of different measures in most cases. The results indicate that the frequency information of items is important for demographic prediction, which is ignored in both SNE_{uniq} and SNE_{max}. This is reasonable since someone who frequently buys wine and cigarette is more likely to be an adult man than someone happens to buy these items.

4.2.2 The Impact of Negative Sampling

To learn the proposed SNE model, we employ negative sampling procedure for optimization. One parameter in this procedure is the number of negative samples we draw each time, denoted by k_{neg}. Here we investigate the impact of the

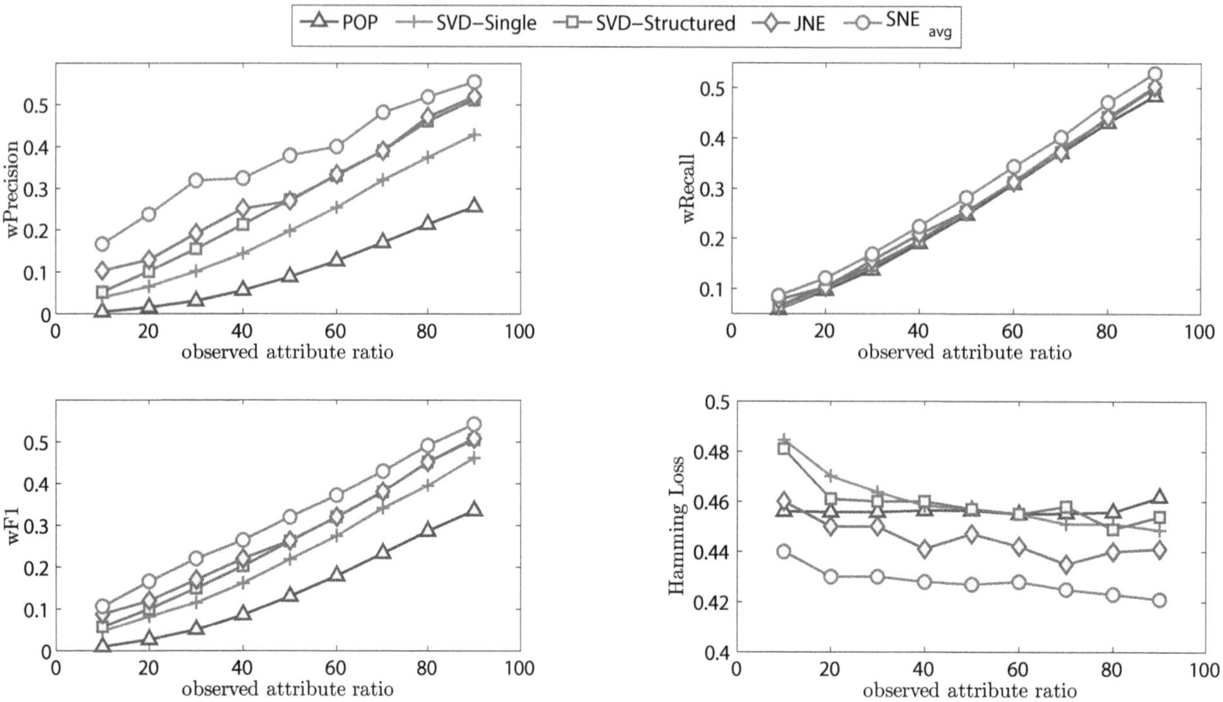

Figure 5: Performance comparison over different methods on Partial-Label prediction in terms of wPrecision, wRecall, wF1 and Hamming Loss.

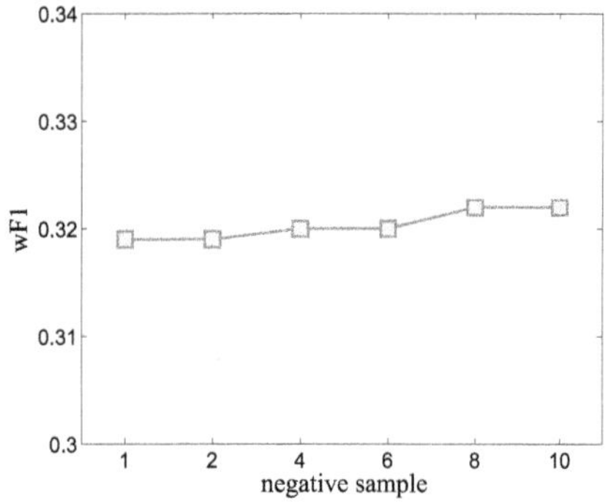

Figure 6: Performance of wF1 with the increase of negative samples with the observed attribute ratio set as 50%.

sampling number k_{neg} to the performance of Partial-Label prediction. Specifically, we tried $k_{neg} \in \{1, 2, 4, 6, 8, 10\}$, and depict the test performance of SNE$_{avg}$ in terms of wF1 against k_{neg} in Figure 6, where the observed attribute ratio is set as 50%.

As we can see, the test performance is quite stable with the increase of the negative sampling number. We have also tried other observed attribute ratios, and find similar stable results. Therefore, the results demonstrate that the optimization of the SNE model is not sensitive to the negative sampling number. We set $k_{neg} = 1$ in our learning procedure for efficiency.

4.3 Performance Comparison on Demographic Prediction

Now we compare our SNE model with the state-of-the-art baseline methods on demographic predictions, including both Partial-Label prediction and New-User prediction. Here we choose SNE$_{avg}$ as the representative of our model for clear comparison.

4.3.1 Partial-Label Prediction

The results of different methods on Partial-Label prediction are shown in Figure 5. We have the following observations:

(1) It is unsurprising to see that with the increase of the observed label ratio (i.e., more observed attributes in learning), all the methods can obtain better performances in prediction.

(2) By simply using the most popular combination of attributes as prediction, the POP method can achieve reasonably good performance especially in terms of wRecall and Hamming Loss. This is due to the fact that the attribute distribution is extremely skewed with the most popular combination (female, adult, married, medium income, high school) takes up to 5.6% of users. Not surprisingly, POP is the worst in terms of wPrecision and wF1, since it cannot predict other combinations of attributes.

(3) Using SVD to obtain low dimensional representations of users can obtain better performance than POP. For example, the relative improvement of SVD-Single over POP is 10.2%, and by SVD-Structured over POP is 18.5%, in terms of wPrecision when observed label ratio is 50%.

(4) The structured learning methods can improve the performances over the single models, by considering the correlation among multiple prediction tasks. For example, the relative improvement of SVD-Structured over SVD-Single is about 10.1% in terms of wF1 when the observed label ratio is 50%, and that of SNE over JNE is about 14.0%.

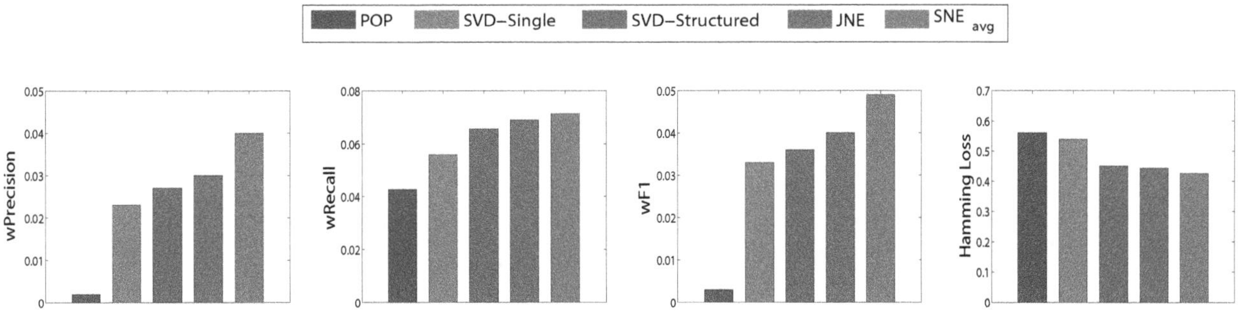

Figure 7: Performance comparison over different methods on New-User prediction .

Table 4: Performance comparison on Partial-Label prediction over different user groups.

user activeness	method	wPrecision	wRecall	wF1	Hamming Loss
Inactive	POP	0.083	0.238	0.122	0.467
	SVD-Single	0.182	0.234	0.211	0.476
	SVD-Structured	0.259	0.242	0.251	0.466
	JNE	0.304	0.269	0.286	0.452
	SNE_{avg}	**0.350**	**0.281**	**0.312**	**0.431**
medium	POP	0.093	0.259	0.138	0.445
	SVD-Single	0.200	0.278	0.232	0.426
	SVD-Structured	0.324	0.285	0.304	0.422
	JNE	0.334	0.289	0.310	0.414
	SNE_{avg}	**0.371**	**0.289**	**0.324**	**0.411**
active	POP	0.102	0.271	0.148	0.438
	SVD-Single	0.189	0.289	0.229	0.412
	SVD-Structured	0.327	0.286	0.305	0.417
	JNE	0.339	0.297	0.318	0.411
	SNE_{avg}	**0.361**	**0.299**	**0.327**	**0.410**

(5) By learning representations towards the end task, we can achieve better performances than methods based on representations learned in an unsupervised way (i.e., SVD). For example, the relative improvement of JNE over SVD-Single is 11.1% in terms of wF1 when the observed label ratio is 50%.
(6) Finally, by learning the representations to predict multiple tasks in a structured way, our SNE can achieve the best performance in terms of all the evaluation measures under different observed label ratios. The improvement of SNE over the second best method (JNE) is significant (p-value<0.01) in terms of all the evaluation metrics.

4.3.2 *New-User Prediction*

We further compare the performance of SNE against baseline methods on predicting new users' demographic attributes. Results of different methods on new user prediction are shown in Figure 7.

From the results we can obtain similar conclusions as in Partial-Label prediction. Both SVD decomposition and structured learning can improve the performance, while supervised representation learning can work better than unsupervised one. The proposed SNE model can achieve the best performance in New-User prediction, and the improvement of SNE over the second best method (JNE) is significant (p-value<0.01) in terms of all the evaluation metrics.

4.3.3 *Performance on Different User Group*

To further investigate the performance of different methods, we split the users into three groups (i.e., inactive, medium and active) based on their activeness. A user is taken as inactive if there are less than 100 items in his/her purchase history, and active if there are more than 500 items in the purchase history. The remaining users are taken as medium. In this way, the proportions of inactive, medium and active are 62.6%, 31.3%, and 6.1% respectively. The results of Partial-Label prediction when observed ratio is 50% are shown in Table 4. As we can see, the relative performance improvement of SNE over JNE is about 2.6%, 1.4%, 0.9% in terms of wF1 on inactive, medium and active users respectively. In other words, the performance gain of SNE is larger on inactive users than medium and active users. The results indicate that structured prediction can work better by leveraging the correlation between tasks to compensate the limited input information, as compared with joint prediction.

5. CONCLUSION

In this paper,we address the problem of demographic prediction based on users' purchase behaviors. We propose a novel SNE model which can automatically learn the representations to predict a set of demographic attributes simultaneously. Experiments on the real-world purchase dataset demonstrate that our model can outperform the state-of-the-art baselines consistently under different evaluation metrics.

Although the SNE model is proposed in this retail scenario, it is in fact a general model which can be applied on other multi-task multi-class problems. In the future, we would like to extend the usage of our SNE model to other applications to verify its effectiveness. Moreover, the proposed SNE model is still a *shallow* model. Therefore, it would also be interesting to try some deeper architectures to extract more expressive representations for demographic prediction.

6. ACKNOWLEDGE

This research work was funded by 973 Program of China award number under Grant 2014CB340401, 863 Program of

China award number under Grant 2014AA015204, 973 Program of China award number under Grant 2012CB316303, National Natural Science Foundation of China award numbers under Grant 61472401, 61433014, 61203298, 61425016, and Key Research Program of the Chinese Academy of Sciences under Grant NO.KGZD-EW-T03-2, and the Youth Innovation Promotion Association CAS, Grant no.20144310, and the Technology Innovation and Transformation Program of Shandong (Grant No.2014CGZH1103).

7. REFERENCES

[1] E. L. Allwein, R. E. Schapire, and Y. Singer. Reducing multiclass to binary: A unifying approach for margin classifiers. *J. Mach. Learn. Res.*, 1:113–141, Sept. 2001.

[2] B. Bi, M. Shokouhi, M. Kosinski, and T. Graepel. Inferring the demographics of search users: Social data meets search queries. In *Proceedings of the 22Nd International Conference on World Wide Web*, WWW '13, pages 131–140, Republic and Canton of Geneva, Switzerland, 2013. International World Wide Web Conferences Steering Committee.

[3] A. Culotta, N. R. Kumar, and J. Cutler. Predicting the demographics of twitter users from website traffic data. In *Twenty-ninth National Conference on Artificial Intelligence (AAAI)*, 2015.

[4] Y. Dong, Y. Yang, J. Tang, Y. Yang, and N. V. Chawla. Inferring user demographics and social strategies in mobile social networks. In *Proceedings of the 20th ACM SIGKDD International Conference on Knowledge Discovery and Data Mining*, KDD '14, pages 15–24, New York, NY, USA, 2014. ACM.

[5] S. Duarte Torres and I. Weber. What and how children search on the web. In *Proceedings of the 20th ACM International Conference on Information and Knowledge Management*, CIKM '11, pages 393–402, New York, NY, USA, 2011. ACM.

[6] P. Eckert. Gender and sociolinguistic variation. *Readings in Language and Gender*, 1997.

[7] T. Evgeniou and M. Pontil. Regularized multi–task learning. In *Proceedings of the Tenth ACM SIGKDD International Conference on Knowledge Discovery and Data Mining*, KDD '04, pages 109–117, New York, NY, USA, 2004. ACM.

[8] A. Graves, A. Mohamed, and G. E. Hinton. Speech recognition with deep recurrent neural networks. *CoRR*, abs/1303.5778, 2013.

[9] J. Hu, H.-J. Zeng, H. Li, C. Niu, and Z. Chen. Demographic prediction based on user's browsing behavior. In *Proceedings of the 16th International Conference on World Wide Web*, WWW '07, pages 151–160, New York, NY, USA, 2007. ACM.

[10] Y. Ji and S. Sun. Multitask multiclass support vector machines: Model and experiments. *Pattern Recogn.*, 46(3):914–924, Mar. 2013.

[11] K. Kalyanam and D. S. Putler. Incorporating demographic variables in brand choice models: An indivisible alternatives framework. *Marketing Science*, 16(2):166–181, May 1997.

[12] A. Krizhevsky, I. Sutskever, and G. E. Hinton. Imagenet classification with deep convolutional neural networks. In F. Pereira, C. Burges, L. Bottou, and K. Weinberger, editors, *Advances in Neural Information Processing Systems 25*, pages 1097–1105. Curran Associates, Inc., 2012.

[13] D. S. M. Kosinski and T. Graepel. Private traits and attributes are predictable from digital records of human behavior. *Proceedings of the National Academy of Sciences*, 2013.

[14] C. Micchelli and M. Pontil. Kernels for multi-task learning. *NIPS*, 2005.

[15] A. Mislove, B. Viswanath, K. P. Gummadi, and P. Druschel. You are who you know: Inferring user profiles in online social networks. In *Proceedings of the Third ACM International Conference on Web Search and Data Mining*, WSDM '10, pages 251–260, New York, NY, USA, 2010. ACM.

[16] A. Mnih and G. Hinton. Three new graphical models for statistical language modelling. In *Proceedings of the 24th International Conference on Machine Learning*, ICML '07, pages 641–648, New York, NY, USA, 2007. ACM.

[17] D. Murray and K. Durrell. Inferring demographic attributes of anonymus internet users. In *Revised Papers from the International Workshop on Web Usage Analysis and User Profiling*, WEBKDD '99, pages 7–20, London, UK, UK, 2000. Springer-Verlag.

[18] S. Nowozin and C. H. Lampert. Structured learning and prediction in computer vision. *Found. Trends. Comput. Graph. Vis.*, 6(3–4):185–365, Mar. 2011.

[19] J. Otterbacher. Inferring gender of movie reviewers: Exploiting writing style, content and metadata. In *Proceedings of the 19th ACM International Conference on Information and Knowledge Management*, CIKM '10, pages 369–378, New York, NY, USA, 2010. ACM.

[20] T. M. Quoc V. Le. distributed representations of sentences and documents. *The 31st International Conference on Machine Learning*, 2014.

[21] I. S. C. Rick L. Andrews. Identifying segments with identical choice behaviors across product categories: An intercategory logit mixture model. *International Journal of Research in Marketing*, 2002.

[22] J. Schler, M. Koppel, S. Argamon, and J. W. Pennebaker. Effects of age and gender on blogging. In *AAAI*, 2006.

[23] S. Sedhain, S. Sanner, D. Braziunas, L. Xie, and J. Christensen. Social collaborative filtering for cold-start recommendations. In *Proceedings of the 8th ACM Conference on Recommender Systems*, RecSys '14, pages 345–348, New York, NY, USA, 2014. ACM.

[24] K. C. G. C. J. D. Tomas Mikolov, Ilya Sutskever. Distributed representations of words and phrases and their compositionality. *Conference on Neural Information Processing Systems 2013. Proceedings*, pages 3111–3119, 2013.

[25] Y. Yi Liu, Zheng. One-against-all multi-class svm classification using reliability measures. *IEEE International Joint Conference on Neural Networks*, 2005.

[26] M.-L. Zhang and K. Zhang. Multi-label learning by exploiting label dependency. In *Proceedings of the 16th ACM SIGKDD International Conference on Knowledge Discovery and Data Mining*, KDD '10, pages 999–1008, New York, NY, USA, 2010. ACM.

[27] X. W. Zhao, Y. Guo, Y. He, H. Jiang, Y. Wu, and X. Li. We know what you want to buy: A demographic-based system for product recommendation on microblogs. In *Proceedings of the 20th ACM SIGKDD International Conference on Knowledge Discovery and Data Mining*, KDD '14, pages 1935–1944, New York, NY, USA, 2014. ACM.

[28] E. Zhong, B. Tan, K. Mo, and Q. Yang. User demographics prediction based on mobile data. *Pervasive Mob. Comput.*, 9(6):823–837, Dec. 2013.

[29] Y. Zhong, N. J. Yuan, W. Zhong, F. Zhang, and X. Xie. You are where you go: Inferring demographic attributes from location check-ins. In *Proceedings of the Eighth ACM International Conference on Web Search and Data Mining*, WSDM '15, pages 295–304, New York, NY, USA, 2015. ACM.

[30] Y. J. Zhou J, Chen J. Clustered multi-task learning via alternating structure optimization. *Advances in neural information processing systems.*, 2011.

Reducing Click and Skip Errors in Search Result Ranking

Jiepu Jiang
Center for Intelligent Information Retrieval
College of Information and Computer Sciences
University of Massachusetts Amherst
jpjiang@cs.umass.edu

James Allan
Center for Intelligent Information Retrieval
College of Information and Computer Sciences
University of Massachusetts Amherst
allan@cs.umass.edu

ABSTRACT

Search engines provide result summaries to help users quickly identify whether or not it is worthwhile to click on a result and read in detail. However, users may visit non-relevant results and/or skip relevant ones. These actions are usually harmful to the user experience, but few considered this problem in search result ranking. This paper optimizes relevance of results and user click and skip activities at the same time. Comparing two equally relevant results, our approach learns to rank the one that users are more likely to click on at a higher position. Similarly, it demotes non-relevant web pages with high click probabilities. Experimental results show this approach reduces about 10%–20% of the click and skip errors with a trade off of 2.1% decline in nDCG@10.

Keywords

Click; interactive search; web search; search result ranking

1. INTRODUCTION

The "10 blue links" paradigm has been ruling search engines for decades. It is an interaction mode where systems deliver results through a search engine result page (SERP), filled with a ranked list of summaries. These summaries are previews of result web pages, usually customized to queries, such that users can spend a small effort assessing whether it is worthwhile or not to click on a link and read in detail. Almost all current search engines adopt this mode.

The accuracy of this interaction mode greatly affects user experience. Although sometimes searchers learn relevant information solely from the SERP (e.g., "good abandonment" [5, 11, 23]), usually they need to read the result documents to satisfy their information needs. In such a case, it helps little to rank a relevant result at the top if users would not click on it. Skipping a relevant result may even have a slight adverse effect, because it requires effort to examine the summary. Similarly, clicking a non-relevant result costs the searchers' effort and may cause frustration, which seems even more harmful than skipping a non-relevant one.

WSDM'16, February 22–25, 2016, San Francisco, CA, USA.
© 2016 ACM. ISBN 978-1-4503-3716-8/16/02. . . $15.00
DOI: http://dx.doi.org/10.1145/2835776.2835838

One straightforward solution to the problem is to generate better search result summaries, such that searchers can make more accurate click and skip decisions. Much work has been done in this direction [29, 32], but reported click accuracy is not satisfying. For example, Yilmaz et al. [33] reported that in a commercial search engine query log, the probability of clicking on results judged as *Perfect*, *Excellent*, *Good*, *Fair*, and *Bad* are 0.94, 0.71, 0.55, 0.45, and 0.49, respectively.

Another solution is to provide answers to queries directly [6, 10]. For example, nowadays many search engines can answer "Sunday, June 21" for the query "2015 father's day". Search engines usually display direct answers on the top area of the SERP, followed by the conventional "10-blue links". Correct answers free users from reading results. However, it remains unclear how many queries can be satisfied by direct answers. For example, it seems difficult to generate answers for queries such as "new Macbook vs. Surface".

In this paper, we look into the problem from a new angle—we demote results with high risks of click and skip errors in search result ranking to optimize users' click behavior. Comparing two equally relevant results, our approach learns to rank the one searchers are more likely to click on at a higher position. This reduces the chances of skipping relevant results. Similarly, we rank non-relevant results with high click probabilities to lower positions to reduce click errors. Similar to existing approaches, we also rank more relevant results on top of less relevant and non-relevant ones in order to maintain high relevance of the ranked lists.

This approach is complementary to existing solutions. For example, one can employ a new snippet generation algorithm to produce better summaries, but these summaries will still vary in risks of click and skip errors. In such case, our approach can further assist the new snippet generation algorithm by optimizing click and skip interaction. Similarly, while showing direct answers, search engines can still apply our approach to the conventional "10-blue links" as a back-up. In addition, our approach is the only known solution for situations where search providers do not have direct control over result summaries (e.g., metasearch engines).

Our approach assumes the existence of two types of ground truths—result relevance and click probability. In this paper, we rely on editorial relevance judgments for the former, and we estimate the latter from search logs. We design a metric, click-sensitive nDCG, to measure the quality of a ranked list taking into account both relevance and click and skip errors. We train ranking models to optimize this metric. Our approaches use features such as the characteristics of summaries and past user activities in the session. Experimental results on the TREC session track dataset show our approach can reduce about 10% to 20% of the click and skip errors with a trade off of 2.1% decline in nDCG@10.

2. RELATED WORK

Our study is related to previous work in three areas. The first area is approaches for estimating unbiased click probability of results from search logs. Previous studies modeled click probability as depending on the result's rank (position-based models [4, 25]) and the quality of other results on the same SERP (cascade models [9, 14, 17, 19]). The estimated click probability is usually referred to as *attractiveness* [17]. It has been widely used as surrogates for editorial relevance judgments to train ranking models [4], or as features to rank search results [3]. We use similar approaches to estimate the click probability ground truth. But our ranking models do not use past clicks of results as features due to the lack of a secondary click probability ground truth for evaluation.

Our ranking approach differentiates click probability (attractiveness) and result relevance. This is also related to previous work that estimates both click probability and post-click satisfaction from search logs [9, 16, 19, 36]. Chapelle et al. [9] introduced the product of result click probability and post-click satisfaction probability as a measure of result relevance. They found that using this measure to train ranking models can improve the relevance of results (evaluated using editorial relevance judgments) compared with those trained using only click probability. Our ranking models are trained to optimize a similar metric, but are different in that, 1) we use the product of click probability and editorial relevance judgments for the gain of relevant results, 2) we further apply a penalty to non-relevant results, weighted by click probabilities, and 3) we evaluate by looking into both relevance of results and the risks of click and skip errors.

Another related area is studies of the influence of result summary characteristics on user click behavior. Tombros et al. [29] applied query-biased summaries to search systems, which improved users' accuracies and speed of clicking results. White et al. [32] came to a similar conclusion. Cutrell et al. [15] found that summaries of different lengths can lead to different click accuracies. Yue et al. [34] found that clicks are significantly biased towards results with more attractive titles. White et al. [31] found that when searching medical-related issues, users are significantly more likely to click on captions containing potentially alarming medical terminology such as "heart attack" and "medical emergency". A few previous works also predicted click behavior based on summary characteristics. For example: Clarke et al. [12] used features related to results' title, snippets, and URLs to predict click behavior; Hofmann et al. [20] used result summary features to correct attractiveness bias in online experiments. Our work is related to these previous studies in that we also rely on result summary characteristics as ranking features.

In addition, click behavior is also affected by context factors. For example: Cutrell et al. [15] found that users have different click behavior patterns in navigational and informational search tasks; Shokouhi et al. [27] studied how repeated results in different queries of a session were clicked by users; Jiang et al. [21] reported different browsing and clicking patterns between the first query and follow up queries in a session. This suggests that our task may benefit from the large body of work on contextual search [1]. Specifically, our ranking models use features related to past user activities in a search session, which is similar to previous work of contextual search using local session search history [18, 24, 26], although we deal with a different task. Here we only consider recent search context in a search sessions due to the lack of large scale real search logs. But the task may also benefit from longer-term search contexts, as suggested by previous work on revisiting behavior [2, 28].

3. CLICK AND SKIP ERRORS

3.1 Definition and Goal

We study the problem in the de facto standard search result page (SERP) setting. The search engine shows a ranked list of summaries linking to the result documents. Searchers first examine the summaries and then make decisions about whether or not to click on the links and read the web pages in detail. A result's summary usually consists of its title, URL, and a query-biased snippet [29, 32].

We consider two related, but different notions: *relevance* is the actual usefulness of a result document, and we assume it can only be acquired after users click on the result and read its content; *attractiveness* is how useful the result summary appears to users before they actually read its content. We quantify the attractiveness of a result by its click probability given that users examined its summary. This is similar to previous work [9, 17]. Relevance and attractiveness are correlated, but do not fully agree with each other.

We define *click error* as clicks on non-relevant results, and *skip error* as users skipping relevant results without clicking after viewing summaries. Let p be the probability of clicking on a result. If the result is not relevant, p quantifies the risk of the click error. For a relevant result, $1-p$ measures the risk of the skip error. Click and skip errors happen when relevance and attractiveness conflict with each other.

Most existing work ranks search results by relevance. Attractiveness is usually adopted as a cheap surrogate for relevance to substitute or complement editorial relevance judgments [9]. In contrast, we do not use attractiveness as a surrogate for relevance, but as an indicator for whether or not users can effectively interact with the summary (e.g., making correct click and skip decisions). We believe that the discrepancy between relevance and attractiveness is harmful and should be avoided in search result ranking. This is a key difference between our approach and previous work.

We perform search result ranking that satisfy rules R_1–R_3. To facilitate discussion, we further introduce a few notations: D_i refers to a document; g_i is a monotonic increasing function of r_i for the gain of reading a document D_i with relevance r_i; s is the cost to examine a summary; c is the cost to click on and read a result document. Here we assume s and c are constants for all documents for simplicity.

[$\boldsymbol{R_1}$] If $p_1 \geq p_2$ and $r_1 \geq r_2 > 0$, rank D_1 over D_2.

R_1 is the case that both relevance and attractiveness prefers D_1 over D_2. In this case, it ensures optimized search efficiency (here it is intuitively defined as the ratio between gain and cost) to rank D_1 over D_2. Let g_1 and g_2 denote the gain of reading D_1 and D_2, and $g_1 \geq g_2$ because $r_1 \geq r_2$. The expected gain on D_1 and D_2 are $p_1 g_1$ and $p_1 g_2$, respectively, and $p_1 g_1 \geq p_1 g_2$. The expected cost of users on D_1 and D_2 are $s + cp_1$ and $s + cp_2$, including both the cost of examining summaries (s) and the expected cost to click on and read the documents (cp_1 and cp_2). It is easy to prove the following inequation, where the left and the right sides are search efficiency on D_1 and D_2, respectively. It suggests that ranking D_1 over D_2 can ensure better search efficiency at higher ranks. Similar to existing approach, R_1 ranks more relevant results over less relevant and non-relevant ones. In addition, R_1 reduces skip errors—D_1 has a smaller risk of skip error comparing to D_2, because $1 - p_1 \leq 1 - p_2$.

$$\frac{p_1 g_1}{s + cp_1} \geq \frac{p_2 g_1}{s + cp_2} \geq \frac{p_2 g_2}{s + cp_2}$$

[***R*$_2$**] If $r_1 > 0$ and $r_2 = 0$, rank D_1 over D_2.

R_2 is straightforward—ranking relevant results over non-relevant ones regardless of attractiveness. It is because users cannot benefit from D_2, but they have the chance to benefit from D_1, although the chance varies by click probability.

[***R*$_3$**] If $r_1 = r_2 = 0$ and $p_1 < p_2$, rank D_1 over D_2.

R_3 ensures that non-relevant results with lower click probabilities will be ranked at a higher position than those with higher click probabilities. This reduces the chances of click error and users' costs. In this case, users benefit from neither documents, but would have a higher expected cost on D_2 (because $s + cp_2 > s + cp_1$).

These rules summarize the main idea of our ranking approach. As we discussed, with mild assumptions, these rules reduce click and skip errors and maintain optimized search efficiency (gain/cost ratio). Similar to existing approaches, R_1 and R_2 also prefer more relevant results over less relevant and non-relevant ones. Yet the rules are not comprehensive enough for ranking any pairs of results.

For the rest of the cases (i.e., $r_1 > r_2 > 0$ and $p_1 < p_2$, the cases that relevance does not agree with attractiveness), we heuristically rank the result with a greater expected gain (gp) at a higher position. For example, we rank D_2 over D_1 if $g_2 p_2 > g_1 p_1$. This is reasonable to some degree, because (under our assumptions) it requires both relevance and click to acquire useful information. Whereas this sometimes conflicts with conventional ranking approaches that prefer more relevant results over less relevant ones. For example, it may prefer a marginally relevant result with a high click probability over a highly relevant one with a low click probability. In addition, it may rank results with greater risks of skip errors (lower click probability) at higher positions if they are relevant enough. Due to these reasons, we do not summarize this heuristic as a rule. We feel it requires further discussion, but we left it for future work, because in our dataset only a small fraction of results fall into this condition.

3.2 Dataset

To perform such ranking of search results, we need ground truth for result relevance and click probabilities. We use the TREC 2014 session track dataset [8], because it provides the largest publicly accessible non-anonymous query logs with relevance judgments at the time of our study. We estimate the click probability ground truth from the search logs.

The TREC 2014 session track dataset [8] collected 1,257 search sessions and 4,666 queries on 60 different search tasks. A search session includes a sequence of queries for the search task, the results and summaries shown on the SERPs, and users' search activities (e.g., clicks). Users of these sessions are paid workers from Amazon Mechanical Turk. They were shown the task descriptions and were requested to work on the tasks using an experimental search system for at least 3 minutes. Their search interaction was recorded. The session track removes the SERP and searcher interaction information for the last query of each session, because the goal was to evaluate techniques of retrieving results for the last query.

Table 1: Features for predicting $P_{view}(D, S)$.

$rank$	Rank of the result D.
$\log(rank) + 1$	Rank of the result in log base.
$P_{view}(rank)$	Probability of viewing results at the rank.
$P_{view}(rank, k)$	Probability of viewing results at the rank, given the lowest clicked rank on S is k.
$c(rank)$	Clicked on the result D?.
$c(rank{\pm}n)$	Clicked on the result at n higher or lower ranks of D? $n = 1, 2$.
$c(rank{+})$	Clicked on any results at a lower rank?

The experimental search system was built on Indri[1] and worked on a full index of the ClueWeb12 dataset[2]. The system ranks results by matching query terms and phrases to web pages' contents, titles, URLs, and anchor texts linking to the web pages. Due to the large size of the ClueWeb12 dataset (about 733 million web pages), a result caching strategy was adopted to ensure that the system could respond requests in at most 6 seconds [8]. Result snippets are generated using Indri's built-in functions. According to its source code[3], Indri constructs result snippets by selecting document fragments with the highest coverage of query terms, with a bias to the beginning of documents. This is similar to many other approaches [29]. Result relevance was judged by assessors from NIST. The pool of judgment involved all results displayed to the searchers, as well as the top-ranked results from participants' runs. Due to its large volume, only parts of the sessions were included into the judgment pool.

Carterette et al. [8] introduced more details of the dataset.

3.3 Estimating Click Probabilities

This section describes the approach of estimating results' click probabilities in the TREC dataset. For a query q and a result D, the goal is to estimate the likelihood that users, when searching for q, would click on D after viewing its summary. This probability, $P_{click}(D)$ is estimated as Equation 1, where: S_i is the collection of q's SERPs containing D; $P_{view}(D, S_i)$ is the probability that users viewed D's summary on S_i; $c(D, S_i)$ equals to 1 if users clicked on D on S_i, or 0 otherwise. The numerator counts the expected number of times D has both been viewed and clicked. The denominator is the expected number of times D has been viewed.

$$P_{click}(D) = \frac{\sum_{S_i} P_{view}(D, S_i) c(D, S_i)}{\sum_{S_i} P_{view}(D, S_i)} \quad (1)$$

$P_{view}(D, S_i)$ comes from a logistic regression model trained to predict result fixation obtained using eye-tracking devices. The training data comes from Jiang et al.'s study [21]. We label D as viewed on S_i if there is an observed eye fixation longer than 100ms on the result's area. The logistic regression model makes use of the 10 features described in Table 1. We do not use characteristics of the result for prediction to avoid overlap with the ranking features in Section 4.

We evaluate the accuracy of the $P_{view}(D, S_i)$ model using a 10-fold cross validation setting. The dataset involves eye

[1] http://www.lemurproject.org/

[2] http://www.lemurproject.org/clueweb12.php/

[3] See src/SnippetBuilder.cpp (line 146-197) in Indri 5.8.

Table 2: A summary of all ranking features in four different categories.

Query independent features	
Length	Length of summary title/snippet, with or without stop words.
Length_URL	Length of the URL (by characters/by levels of directories).
#unique_words	Number of unique words in title/snippet.
%stopwords	Percent of stop words in title/snippet.
%wordstag	Percent of words in <a>, <p>, <li>, <td>, heading tags, and emphasis tags (e.g., <b>, <em>).
TF/IDF	Average/max/min values of TF/IDF/TF×IDF for words in result summary title/snippet.
#fragment	Number of document fragments in the snippet.
pagerank	Pagerank for the web page (in percentile).
spamrank	Waterloo spam rank scores [13] for the webpage (in percentile).
Features using the current query	
%qterm	Percent of query terms in title/snippet/URL.
#qtermtag	Frequency of query terms in different HTML tags.
%qtermtag	Percent of query terms in different HTML tags.
QLscore	Normalized query likelihood score of the summary/web page.
#window(k)	Number of windows of size k in web page covering all terms, any bigrams, or any trigrams in query.
minwindow	Minimum window size in web page covering all terms, any bigrams, or any trigrams in queries.
Features using the past queries within the same session	
%past qterm	Percent of past query terms in title/snippet/URL. Separately consider ADD/KEEP/RMV terms.
%past qterm by Q	%past qterm considering two specific types of queries: 1) past queries w/ user clicks; 2) past query reformulations whose second query has clicks.
%past SERP term	Coverage of words from past clicked/skipped SERP titles in the summary's title/snippet.
QLscore past clicks	Normalized query likelihood score of past queries, past queries with clicks, past clicked results.
Repeated Result	Whether the same URL was clicked or skipped by the searcher on previous SERPs.
Situational features	
#previous clicks	The number of past clicks in the session. Separately consider SAT (>30s) and DSAT clicks (<15s).
#previous queries	The number of previous queries. We separately consider queries with clicks and without clicks.

fixation evidence for 3,492 results, where 52% have at least one fixation (have been viewed) and 32% were clicked. The logistic regression model can achieve 0.74 average accuracy on the 10 folds ($SD = 0.024$). We use this dataset to train $P_{view}(D, S_i)$ models mainly because the search tasks performed in the user study also come from the TREC session track. We expect the $P_{view}(D, S_i)$ model to be generalizable to the TREC session track dataset.

The accuracy of the click probability estimation in Equation (1) depends on both the accuracy of $P_{view}(D, S_i)$ and the size of S_i. In the TREC session track dataset, on average D has 2.76 impressions. To handle the limited observations in the dataset, we further smooth the estimation as Equation 2, where $P_{click}(R)$ is the probability to click on results with D's relevance label (R). The values of $P_{click}(R)$ comes from those reported by Yilmaz et al. [33], where they also labeled results using five levels of relevance. The probabilities to click on results with relevance labels from 4 to 0 are 0.94, 0.71, 0.55, 0.45, and 0.49, respectively. We set μ to 1.

$$P_{click}(D) = \frac{\sum_{S_i} P_{view}(D, S_i) c(D, S_i) + \mu P_{click}(R)}{\sum_{S_i} P_{view}(D, S_i) + \mu} \quad (2)$$

Note that many click models can also serve the purpose—estimating click probabilities. Here we do not mean to compare with them or claim superiority of any approach. We adopt the described approach mainly because the limited number of repeated observations in the dataset makes it difficult to train and evaluate click models. Our approach is probably a better one for this very specific situation, because at least $P_{view}(D, S_i)$ can be trained and evaluated using another reliable dataset with similar search settings. This is not a limitation of our approach, but a compromise to the data we have. We suggest readers to adopt large-scale and real search logs and the state-of-the-art click models [9, 16, 19, 30] to estimate click probability ground truth.

4. FEATURES

This section introduces features for ranking search results. We focus on features using information such as textual and structural characteristics of summaries. We do not use past clicks for the query-result pair outside the scope of the current session. This ensures that our approach can be applied to new queries and tail queries, for which past click information is not available in large scale. But it should be noted that for many popular queries and results, such information is available and can be adopted as ranking features as well.

Table 2 lists four categories of features adopted in our study. We analyze features by correlating with click probabilities among relevant and non-relevant results separately. We measure correlations using Pearson's r. Dark and light shadings stand for $p < 0.01$ and $p < 0.05$, respectively.

4.1 Query-independent Features

Table 3 reports correlations between query-independent features and click probabilities. Results show users are more likely to click on result summaries with shorter titles and URLs, but we did not find any significant correlations between click probabilities and snippet length.

Click probability also correlates with web page structure. Results show that searchers are more likely to click on relevant results with a high proportion of actual content (e.g., texts in <p> tags) and a low percentage of navigational

Table 3: Correlation: query-independent features and P_{click}.

Features	Pearson's r with P_{click}	
	Relevant	Non-relevant
length title	−0.120	−0.067
length URL directory	−0.106	−0.036
%word <a>	−0.105	0.080
%word emphasis	0.049	−0.080
%word heading	−0.045	−0.077
%word <li>	0.055	0.088
%word <p>	0.136	0.020
max TF×IDF snippet	0.099	−0.028
pagerank	0.143	−0.067
spamrank	−0.092	−0.009

Table 4: Correlation: current query features and P_{click}.

Features	Pearson's r with P_{click}	
	Relevant	Non-relevant
%qterm title	0.266	0.119
%qterm snippet	0.197	0.140
%qterm URL	0.208	0.069
min window all qterms	0.076	−0.021
min window bigrams	0.116	−0.103
min window trigrams	0.122	−0.011
#win k=10 all qterms	0.319	0.143
#win k=10 bigrams	0.187	−0.040
#win k=10 trigrams	0.135	−0.009

texts (e.g., <a> tags), but click errors often happen in web pages with a high proportion of navigational texts.

Click probability also correlates with the informativeness of words in summaries (e.g., as measured by the TF×IDF value of words). Web page authority (by page rank) is also positively correlated with click probability for relevant results, but negatively correlated for non-relevant ones.

4.2 Features Using Current Query

Table 4 reports correlations between click probability and features using information of the current query.

We adopt features measuring the similarity between query and result summary or web page, including coverage of query terms in summary title, snippet, and URL, and the query likelihood (QL) scores [35]. When matching terms in URLs, we count term occurrence by whether or not it is a subsequence of the URL. The original QL scores are not comparable between different queries. Therefore we normalize QL scores by query length, i.e., each query term is assigned a weight $1/|Q|$, where $|Q|$ is the length of the query. We found that all these features are positively correlated with click probabilities, regardless of among relevant or non-relevant results. Yet the correlations are consistently stronger in relevant results. Similar to the web page structure features in Section 4.1, the proportion of query terms in different HTML tags are also correlated with results' click probability.

We also use features matching query term phrases in web pages, including the number of windows of size k covering all query terms, and the minimum window size covering all query terms. We set the minimum window size to the document length when not all query terms occur in the web page. Most of these features are useful, as suggested by Table 4.

4.3 Features Using Session Information

We use the coverage of past query terms in summary title, snippet, and URL as features. We compute the coverage of terms for each past query and use the mean value as features. Following Guan et al.'s work [18], we also separately consider three types of terms in past query reformulations. For a query q_1 and its reformulation q_2, ADD terms are those in q_2 but not in q_1, KEEP terms are those in both queries, and RMV terms are those in q_1 but not in q_2. We compute the coverage of ADD, KEEP, and RMV terms for each past query reformulation and use their mean values as features. When calculating these features, we also consider different types of query reformulations, e.g., from a query without click to another with clicks (noclick-click). Table 5 shows that most past query similarity features are correlated with click probability of non-relevant results, while only a small number of them have significant correlations with click probability for relevant results. Results in Table 4 and Table 5 suggest that current query features are more correlated with click activity in relevant results, but past query features are more predictive of those in non-relevant results.

Table 5: Correlation: past query features and P_{click}.

Features	Pearson's r with P_{click}	
	Relevant	Non-relevant
%past q	0.030	0.028
%past q clicked	0.037	0.125
%past q ADD	0.234	0.205
%past q ADD click-click	0.190	0.188
%past q ADD noclick-click	0.098	0.100
%past q RMV	0.129	0.106
%past q RMV click-noclick	0.026	0.108
%past q RMV click-click	0.055	0.098
QL pastq	0.018	0.075
QL pastq w/ click	−0.022	0.164
QL clicked snippet	−0.030	0.156

4.4 Situational Features

We also suspect searchers' click and skip decisions are related to situational factors that are independent of any specific results, i.e., in a certain period of a session, searchers are more likely to click on or skip results. Situational features include: the number of past clicks, SAT clicks (dwell time > 30s), and DSAT clicks (dwell time < 15s); the number of previous queries and those with clicks. Both features are correlated with click probabilities in non-relevant results, while the correlations are not significant in relevant results.

5. RANKING

We rank search results considering both relevance and the risks of click and skip errors. The task would be easy if we can make perfect predictions on relevance and click probabilities. In such case, we can simply apply rules in section 3 and rank results by predicted relevance and click probabilities. Unfortunately, making such perfect predictions seems beyond the ability of current technology.

We tackle this challenge by training LambdaMART rankers [7] to optimize an nDCG style metric. This metric encodes the ranking rules in Section 3. It also applies position-based discounts to put an emphasis on top-ranked results.

5.1 Click Sensitive nDCG (cs-nDCG)

Let $L = D_1, D_2, \ldots, D_n$ be a ranked list of n results. We measure D_i's contribution to the quality of the ranked list by $g(D_i)$, as in Equation 3, where: r_i is the relevance grade for D_i; p_i is the probability to click on D_i after viewing its summary, as we described in Section 3.3; g_p is the penalty to click on a non-relevant result.

$$g(D_i) = \begin{cases} (2^{r_i} - 1)p_i & r_i > 0 \\ -g_p p_i & r_i = 0 \end{cases} \quad (3)$$

Equation 3 weights the gain of a relevant result by its click probability. It uses the same gain function as in nDCG. In addition, Equation 3 sets an adverse effect for a clicked non-relevant results, which can set off the positive contribution (gain) of relevant results. The scale of the adverse effect is controlled by a parameter g_p, and we weight the adverse effect of a result by its click probability as well.

Similar to nDCG, we sum up the contribution of results at each rank, with a position-based discount function. We refer to the sum as cs-DCG for the ranked list, as in Equation (4). The position-based discount function is the same as the one used in nDCG, which ensures top-ranked results have a greater impact on the quality of the ranked list.

$$\text{cs-DCG}(L) = \sum_{i=1}^{n} \frac{g(D_i)}{\log_2(i+1)} \quad (4)$$

Click sensitive nDCG (cs-nDCG) for a ranked list is calculated by normalizing its cs-DCG to the range $[0, 1]$. Unlike DCG, cs-DCG may take negative values due to the penalty of clicking non-relevant results. Thus, we normalize cs-DCG by both its lower and upper bounds, as in Equation 5. The ideal ranked list (L_{best}) and the worst ranked list (L_{worst}) can be constructed by sorting documents by descending and ascending order of $g(D_i)$.

$$\text{cs-nDCG}(L) = \frac{\text{cs-DCG}(L) - \text{cs-DCG}(L_{worst})}{\text{cs-DCG}(L_{best}) - \text{cs-DCG}(L_{worst})} \quad (5)$$

When training LambdaMART models using cs-nDCG, we update using the following λ-gradients, where Δcs-nDCG is the cs-nDCG value gained by swapping a pair of results D_i and D_j in the ranked list.

$$\lambda_{ij} = S_{ij} \left| \Delta\text{cs-nDCG} \frac{\partial C_{ij}}{\partial o_{ij}} \right| \quad (6)$$

5.2 Properties of cs-nDCG

The gain function of the cs-nDCG metric, as described in Equation 3, ensures that the metric prefers search ranking conforming to the rules discussed in Section 3.1.

The metric satisfies R_1. When $p_1 \geq p_2$ and $r_1 \geq r_2 > 0$:

$$g(D_1) - g(D_2) = (2^{r_1} - 1)p_1 - (2^{r_2} - 1)p_2 > 0$$

Therefore, replacing D_2 by D_1 can increase the value of the metric. The metric also satisfies R_2, because when $r_1 > 0$ and $r_2 = 0$:

$$g(D_1) - g(D_2) = (2^{r_1} - 1)p_1 + g_p p_2 > 0$$

The metric also satisfies R_3, because when $r_1 = r_2 = 0$ and $p_1 < p_2$:

$$g(D_1) - g(D_2) = g_p(p_2 - p_1) > 0$$

Now we discuss the cases that are not included in R_1–R_3, i.e., $r_1 > r_2 > 0$ and $p_1 < p_2$. We analyze the chances that the metric will rank a less relevant result over a more relevant one, which is conflicting with existing relevance ranking of search results. In order to make the metric prefer D_2 over D_1, we should have:

$$\frac{p_2}{p_1} > \frac{2^{r_1} - 1}{2^{r_2} - 1}$$

Practically, when $r_1 = r_2 + 1$, the ratio p_2/p_1 needs to be at least as high as 15/7 (the case when $r_2 = 3$ and $r_1 = 4$) to make the metric prefer D_2 over D_1 in ranking. The click probability ratio has to be even higher when $r_2 = 2$ (7/3) and $r_2 = 1$ (3/1).

The following table shows the mean, maximum, minimum, and standard deviation of estimated P_{click} for results in our dataset. According to the table, the largest possible p_2/p_1 between documents with $r = 3$ and those with $r = 4$ is $0.82/0.64 = 1.28$, which is smaller than the minimum required ratio to rank $r = 3$ over $r = 4$ (15/7). Therefore, the metric would not rank $r = 3$ over $r = 4$ in our dataset. Similarly, the metric will not rank $r = 2$ over $r = 3$, because $0.69/0.32 < 7/3$. A small proportion of results with $r = 1$ may be preferred over those with $r = 2$. In order to be ranked over $r = 2$, a document with $r = 1$ requires at least 0.54 click probability. Only 5.8% of all results with $r = 1$ have a click probability higher than that value.

Relevance	Mean P_{click}	Min–Max P_{click}	SD P_{click}
4	0.74	0.64–0.87	0.089
3	0.59	0.32–0.82	0.133
2	0.44	0.18–0.69	0.110
1	0.36	0.11–0.65	0.101
0	0.39	0.08–0.74	0.091

Our analysis suggests that, in most cases, our approach will not conflict with conventional relevance ranking of search results. Of course, the chances vary by the estimated click probability in the dataset. However, considering it requires at least about 2 to 3 times greater click probability to rank a less relevant result over a more relevant one, it seems safe to conclude that in any reasonable dataset, there is only a slight chance that our approach will conflict with existing relevance ranking of results. This quality ensures that after introducing click probability into ranking, our approach will not radically decline relevance of results.

5.3 Incorporating Partly Judged Queries

In a practical search engine, relevance judgments are costly to scale up, but search logs are cheap and increasing all the time. Once we have relevance judgments for a set of queries, we may have more and more incoming queries providing new clicks. We can reuse the old relevance judgments for the new queries with the same topic, but these queries may have unjudged results. It is risky to simply assume that all unjudged results as non-relevant and put them into training. Instead, we simply set Δcs-nDCG to 0 if either or both results of a swapping pair has not been judged—we skip updating model in case of unjudged results. Similarly, when training using regular nDCG as the target metric, we can also incorporate partly judged queries by setting ΔnDCG and λ-gradients to 0 if either or both results of the swapping pair are unjudged.

The TREC 2014 session track dataset offers opportunities for studying whether it is helpful to use partly judged queries for training. Among the 1,257 sessions in the dataset, only results for queries in the first 120 sessions were fully judged. The rest of the sessions have overlap with the fully judged 120 sessions in topics. We reuse the relevance judgments for the 120 fully judged sessions to other sessions with the same topics in the dataset. The other sessions include unjudged results, and we only use these sessions for training.

6. EXPERIMENT

We use our approaches to re-rank the top 10 results for queries in the TREC 2014 session track dataset. We only re-rank the top 10 results because the dataset only provides the top 10 results. We evaluate results by both the relevance of the re-ranked list and the chances of click and skip errors (based on the estimated click probability ground truth).

We select queries which have full relevance judgments and at least one click on the top 10 results. In order to calculate features using past user interaction information, we do not select the first query of each session. This selects 145 queries. These queries are used for evaluation. To make use of partly judged queries, we further select other queries (excluding the first query of each session) with at least 2 results being judged and at least one click in the top 10 results. This selects 222 partly judged queries. We use 10-fold cross validation in all experiments: each fold uses 70% of the 145 fully judged queries for training, 20% for validation, and 10% for testing. We also use the 222 partly judged queries for training using the approach described in Section 5.3.

We do not evaluate results using cs-nDCG since this metric has not yet been validated as an evaluation metric. Instead, we evaluate results using regular nDCG@10 and metrics measuring click and skip errors in search result ranking.

One of the metric is discounted cumulated click & skip errors at rank k (DCE@k). Similar to discounted cumulated gain (DCG), we can measure the cumulated number of click and skip errors at rank k with a position-based discount, as in Equation 7 and 8. $[r_i = 0]$ and $[r_i > 0]$ are two binary variables that take the value 1 if their statements are true, or the value 0 otherwise. The overall DCE is defined as the sum of DCE_{click} and DCE_{skip}.

$$\text{DCE}_{click}@k = \sum_{i=1}^{k} \frac{p_i[r_i = 0]}{\log_2(i+1)} \quad (7)$$

$$\text{DCE}_{skip}@k = \sum_{i=1}^{k} \frac{(1-p_i)[r_i > 0]}{\log_2(i+1)} \quad (8)$$

Another metric is the number of pairwise ranking errors. We count the following types of pairwise ranking errors in the re-ranked results:

- $R_{skip>click}$ is the cases that, for two equally relevant results, the one with a lower click probability (a higher chance of skip error) is at a higher rank. We separately count $R_{skip>click}$ for different levels of relevance as well ($r = 1, 2, 3, 4$).
- $NR_{click>skip}$ is the cases that, for two non-relevant results, the one with a higher click probability (a higher chance of click error) is at a higher rank.
- $NR{>}R$ is the cases that a non-relevant result is at a higher rank than a relevant one.
- $LowR{>}HighR$ is the cases that a less relevant result is at a higher rank than a more relevant one (but both results are relevant with $r > 0$). Note that this is not necessarily an error, but it can indicate how well search result ranking conforms to the conventional relevance ranking of search results (which requires $HighR{>}LowR$).

Table 7: Ranking models using different features.

Runs	nDCG@10	DCE@5 All	DCE@5 click	DCE@5 skip
All Features	0.278	1.388	0.241	1.148
Web page	0.279	1.404	0.248	1.156
Title	0.272	1.369	0.285	1.083
Snippet	0.265	1.334	0.310	1.024
URL	0.255	1.340	0.342	0.998
Current Query	0.275	1.373	0.299	1.074
Past Queries	0.238	1.368	0.371	0.997
Q Independent	0.273	1.395	0.244	1.151

Dark and light shadings indicate significant differences with "All Features" at $p < 0.01$ and $p < 0.05$, respectively.

We compare our approach (the LambdaMART ranking model trained for cs-nDCG) with a few baselines. Little previous work targets this problem. Therefore, we compare with the LambdaMART ranking model trained for the regular nDCG. We also compare with the state-of-the-art ad hoc search models and contextual search approaches in a session with strong reported performance on the TREC session track datasets, including:

- Query likelihood with Dirichlet smoothing (QL) [35].
- Context sensitive relevance feedback (CSRF) [26]. CSRF is a relevance feedback approach considering past search queries and contents of clicked results within the same session. Variants of CSRF were ranked at the top in the TREC 2011 and 2012 session tracks [22].
- We also compare with the original ranking of results in the search log, and the perfect and worst possible rankings of results by nDCG and by cs-nDCG.

We report mean values of the evaluation metrics on the 145 fully judged queries in following sections. We test significant difference of results using a paired t-test.

7. EVALUATION

7.1 Click-Sensitive Ranking Models

Table 6 shows re-ranking effectiveness of our approaches and the baseline approaches using both fully judged and partly judged queries for training in each fold. We set $g_p = 1$ when using cs-nDCG for training.

Results show that our approach can significantly reduce the chances of click and skip errors with a slight decline in the relevance of the ranked list. As Table 6 shows, our ranking model trained for cs-nDCG@10 ("All Features (cs-nDCG)") significantly reduced the overall DCE@5 by 9.6% (1.388 vs. 1.535, smaller values are better) comparing to the baseline model using the same features but trained for the regular nDCG@10 ("All Features (nDCG)"). DCE@5 for the click error alone fell by 19.1% (0.241 vs. 0.298), and that for the skip error alone was reduced by 7.1% (1.148 vs. 1.236). All the differences are significant at $p < 0.01$.

The effectiveness of our approach for reducing click and skip errors can also be verified by looking into $R_{skip>click}$

Table 6: Comparison of ranking models (using all features) optimized for nDCG and cs-nDCG, and other baseline approaches.

Runs	nDCG@10	DCE@5			$R_{skip>click}$					*NR click>skip*	*NR>R*	*LowR >HighR*
		All	click	skip	All	$r=4$	$r=3$	$r=2$	$r=1$			
Original	0.210	1.284	0.399	0.885	2.77	0.01	0.08	0.43	2.26	8.83	6.32	1.96
Perfect (Relevance)	0.296	-	-	-	-	-	-	-	-	-	0	0
Worst (Relevance)	0.144	-	-	-	-	-	-	-	-	-	14.77	3.90
Perfect (cs-nDCG)	0.295	1.418	0.132	1.286	0	0	0	0	0	0	0	0.03
Worst (cs-nDCG)	0.144	1.078	0.752	0.326	6.35	0.02	0.32	0.94	5.07	19.86	14.77	3.87
QL (nDCG)	0.250	1.445	0.353	1.092	3.14	0.01	0.10	0.44	2.55	11.01	3.74	1.79
QL (cs-nDCG)	0.249	1.440	0.356	**1.084**	3.18	0.01	0.08	0.46	2.62	11.21	3.63	1.79
CSRF (nDCG)	0.255	1.454	0.364	1.089	2.98	0.01	0.04	0.43	2.48	11.07	3.53	1.61
CSRF (cs-nDCG)	0.254	1.451	0.364	1.087	2.98	0.01	0.08	0.46	2.27	10.11	4.33	1.68
All Features (nDCG)	**0.284**	1.535	0.298	1.236	3.10	0	0.08	0.53	2.50	11.48	**1.61**	**0.13**
All Features (cs-nDCG)	0.278	**1.388**	**0.241**	1.148	**1.95**	0	0.03	**0.29**	**1.63**	**6.51**	2.33	0.50

Bold font indicates the best results in its column (excluding the oracle runs). Dark and light shadings stand for $p < 0.01$ and $p < 0.05$.

pairwise errors. This refers to the cases where results with higher chance of skip errors are ranked over equally relevant results with lower chance of skip errors. The total number of $R_{skip>click}$ pairwise errors fell by 37% (1.95 vs. 3.10). Such pairwise error is not common among $r = 4$ and $r = 3$, because only a very small fraction of relevant results have relevance grades 3 or 4 in the dataset. Most relevant results have relevance grades 2 or 1, for which the chances of $R_{skip>click}$ errors decreased by 45% and 35%, respectively. In addition, $NR_{click>skip}$ error also fell by 43%. This is the cases that non-relevant results with greater risks of click errors are ranked over those with fewer risks. Thus, both metrics agree that our approach can successfully reduce click and skip errors in search result ranking. Note that the number of pairwise ranking errors is an $O(n^2)$ measure regarding the number of results n. This is why the improvements seem greater than those for DCE@5.

While reducing click and skip errors by about 10%–20%, the relevance of the ranked lists only slightly declined—nDCG@10 fell by 2.1% (0.278 vs. 0.284, $p < 0.01$). The number of pairwise ranking errors between relevant and non-relevant results (*NR>R*) increased by 45% (2.33 vs. 1.61), and that between more relevant and less relevant results increased by 284% (0.50 vs 0.13). It should be noted that the large relative scale of the differences come from the small number of these errors in the baseline approach ("All Features (nDCG)"). The actual increase in the number of pairwise ranking errors is small, as suggested by the small differences in nDCG@10 between the two approaches.

Comparing to other ad hoc search and session search baselines (e.g., QL and CSRF), our approach consistently outperforms all of them in both relevance of results and the overall chances of click and skip errors. All the ad hoc search and session search baselines have smaller DCE@5 for skip errors, but this is in fact because these approaches achieved limited relevance. Since less relevant results were ranked at the top, the chances of having skip errors is naturally smaller (since non-relevant results always have zero skip error). The advantage of our approach over these baselines is not surprising considering much more information is adopted into our ranking features comparing to the baselines. This also suggests our feature set is very effective for solving both relevance-based ranking and click-sensitive ranking.

"Worst (Relevance)" and "Worst (cs-nDCG)" provide upper bounds for different types of errors in the dataset. *NR>R* and *LowR>HighR* are pairwise ranking errors related to the relevance of search results, which sum up to a total of 18.87 in our dataset. $R_{skip>click}$ and $NR_{click>skip}$ are those related to click and skip errors, which sum up to 26.21. Our approach "All Features (nDCG)" reduced the relevance-based pairwise ranking errors to 1.74 ($1.61 + 0.13$), about 10% of the total possible errors. In contrast, "All Features (cs-nDCG)" reduced the click and skip error related ranking errors to 8.46 ($1.95 + 6.51$), about 1/3 of the total possible errors. This suggests that existing approaches can already solve over 90% of the ranking errors related to result relevance, but they can handle only about 2/3 of all possible click and skip errors, leaving large room for improvements.

7.2 Effectiveness of Features

We further analyze the effectiveness of different feature sets in this section. Table 7 shows results for models trained using cs-nDCG ($g_p = 1$) with different sets of features.

We first compare features using web page full content ("Web page") with those using different elements of result summaries ("Title", "Snippet", and "URL"). As Table 7 shows, models using web page content can achieve better relevance of results, but significantly more skip errors ("DCE@5 skip"). Actually, features using only result snippet information can achieve the best overall DCE@5—even less errors than using the combination of all other features, but it achieved limited relevance of results. This indicates that result summary characteristics are important features for reducing click and skip errors in search result ranking, which is not surprising because searchers mainly made their click and skip decisions based on web page summaries. This result also suggests that it is important to include information of result summaries into ranking. Conventional approaches only use result web pages for ranking, while our experiments show it is beneficial to further incorporate information from result summaries to reduce the chances of click and skip errors. As Table 7 also suggests, combining title, snippet, and URL features with web page content features can lead to a slight decline of overall DCE@5, but no significant change in nDCG@10.

Note that our experiment setting inflated the effectiveness of result summaries in ranking relevant and non-relevant results. This is because all ranking candidates come from the top 10 results of a moderately effective system (the original system has 0.210 nDCG@10). Therefore, results in Table 7 do not mean that, by sorely using information from result summaries, we can achieve nDCG@10 close to those using full web page content.

Comparing features using different query information, we found that features using past query information ("Past Queries")

Table 8: Ranking models using different training data.

Runs	nDCG@10	DCE@5		
		All	click	skip
nDCG both	0.284	1.535	0.298	1.236
cs-nDCG both	0.278	1.388	0.241	1.148
nDCG full	0.280	1.521	0.307	1.213
cs-nDCG full	0.276	1.429	0.256	1.173

Shadings indicate significant differences between "* both" and "* full" at 0.01 or 0.05 levels.

is the least useful. In contrast, features using the current query information alone ("Current Query") achieved similar performance to the full model ("All Features"), with only a slightly worse nDCG. This suggests that the inclusion of within-session user interaction features provide limited contribution to the problem in our dataset. It also suggests that our approach can be effectively generalized to cases where the local session context information is not available (e.g., the first query of a session).

7.3 Training Using Partly Judged Queries

We further evaluate whether incorporating partly judged queries into training can improve the effectiveness of the ranking models. We compare models using both fully judged and partly judged queries for training (labeled with "both") with those using only fully judged queries (labeled with "full")—each fold only used 70% of the 145 fully judged queries for training. We train ranking models using all features. Table 8 shows the results.

After incorporating partly judged queries ("cs-nDCG both"), we observed significant improvements in both relevance of results and declines in the chances of click and skip errors. Comparing to models trained using only fully judged queries ("cs-nDCG full"), we observed considerable declines in overall DCE@5 (1.388 vs. 1.429, $p < 0.01$) and click errors (0.241 vs. 0.256, $p < 0.05$). This suggests that using partly judged queries can significantly improve the effectiveness of search result ranking, achieving both higher relevance of results and fewer click and skip errors. After using partly judged queries, we also observed similar improvements for models trained using regular nDCG.

Results in this section suggest that, in a practical situation (e.g., a large search engine with abundant search logs), the effectiveness of our approach will not be restricted by the size of relevance judgments (which is usually small in scale comparing to query logs). Our study suggests that we can complement limited editorial relevance judgments using new click and skip observations on queries of similar topics, even when these new queries do not have full relevance judgments.

To conclude, results in section 7 demonstrate that the proposed approach can effectively reduce the chances of click and skip errors with a small decline in result relevance. Our analysis also suggests that existing approaches work relatively well enough in ranking relevant and non-relevant results, but have limited performance in ranking results with risks of click and skip errors. This leaves opportunity for future work.

8. DISCUSSION AND CONCLUSION

In this paper, we explored the instantiation of a new ranking paradigm of search systems—ranking results by not only relevance, but also how likely searchers may commit an error when viewing result summaries displayed on the SERP, i.e., clicking on a non-relevant result and/or skipping a relevant one. This ranking paradigm provides a more practical view of search engine result ranking comparing to existing approaches—purely ranking relevant results over non-relevant ones.

We instantiate the new ranking paradigm based on two parts: a set of features predictive of both result relevance and searchers' click and skip behavior; a metric measuring the quality of a ranked list considering both factors, which can be used to optimize ranking models. Results in section 7 suggest that using the cs-nDCG metric, we can train ranking models that can effectively reduce the chances of click and skip errors comparing to existing methods (the same ranker with same features optimized for regular nDCG). The cost for reducing click and skip errors is about a 2.1% decline in nDCG@10. It remains unclear whether or not it is worthwhile to trade 2.1% of nDCG@10 for optimized click and skip interaction. We leave this for future work. But we believe it is at least reasonable to question whether nDCG (as well as other metrics that purely consider relevance of the ranked list) is comprehensive enough to give insights to potential users' experience after they interact with the ranked list, because it requires both relevant results and correct interaction to deliver the useful information to the searchers. Failing to achieve either may fail to satisfy searchers.

Our study also stands for a new interactive search mode in which the system ranks results by not only results themselves, but also the possible ways of presenting results to the searchers (e.g., summaries). This is essentially a key advantage of our approach. Results in Section 7.2 also demonstrate improvements after incorporating result summary information into ranking. It may potentially be generalized to the form of search result ranking in which we have multiple candidate summaries for each result, and the task is to select not only the best ranking of results, but also the best presentations of results to be displayed on the SERP. The best ranking of results may also depend on the appropriate presentations of results as well. This stands for an end-to-end task of solving search result ranking and result snippet generation at the same time, while currently the two tasks are processed by separate procedures. Here we did not explore this possibility because our dataset provides only one summary for each result.

In addition, our approach does not rely on past click information from search logs or extensive contextual features to achieve its effectiveness. As Section 7.2 suggests, using only features related to the current search query, the ranking model can achieve effectiveness that is comparable to the full model (using all features). This shows that the approach can be generalized to cases where users' search history are not available.

Admittedly, there are also a few limitations in our study. Among which, the representativeness of the dataset is probably the most apparent and arguable one. The TREC session track dealt with relatively more complex search tasks [23] than those normally submitted to the search engines (e.g., navigational search). In addition, the search log provides limited impressions for each query-URL pair comparing to real web search logs, which makes the estimated click probability ground truth less reliable. Therefore, we believe it is necessary to re-evaluate this technique using a large scale dataset and real search logs.

To conclude, despite a few limitations, our study demonstrated the possibility and benefits of ranking search results considering both relevance of results and searcher click and skip errors. As Section 7 shows, existing IR approaches can already achieve strong performance when ranking relevant and non-relevant results, but they are not equally effective in ranking results with different risks of click and skip errors. This leaves us great opportunity and large room for improvements in the future.

9. ACKNOWLEDGMENT

This work was supported in part by the Center for Intelligent Information Retrieval and in part by NSF grant #IIS-0910884. Any opinions, findings and conclusions or recommendations expressed in this material are those of the authors and do not necessarily reflect those of the sponsor. We thank the anonymous reviewers for their thoughtful and constructive comments.

10. REFERENCES

[1] Overview of the special issue on contextual search and recommendation. *ACM Trans. Inf. Syst.*, 33(1), 2015.
[2] E. Adar, J. Teevan, and S. T. Dumais. Large scale analysis of web revisitation patterns. In *CHI '08*, 2008.
[3] E. Agichtein, E. Brill, and S. Dumais. Improving web search ranking by incorporating user behavior information. In *SIGIR '06*, 2006.
[4] E. Agichtein, E. Brill, S. Dumais, and R. Ragno. Learning user interaction models for predicting web search result preferences. In *SIGIR '06*, 2006.
[5] O. Arkhipova and L. Grauer. Evaluating mobile web search performance by taking good abandonment into account. In *SIGIR '14*, 2014.
[6] M. S. Bernstein, J. Teevan, S. Dumais, D. Liebling, and E. Horvitz. Direct answers for search queries in the long tail. In *CHI '12*, 2012.
[7] C. J. Burges. From RankNet to LambdaRank to LambdaMART: An overview. Technical Report MSR-TR-2010-82, Microsoft Research, 2010.
[8] B. Carterette, E. Kanoulas, M. Hall, and P. Clough. Overview of the TREC 2014 session track. In *TREC 2014*, 2014.
[9] O. Chapelle and Y. Zhang. A dynamic bayesian network click model for web search ranking. In *WWW '09*, 2009.
[10] L. B. Chilton and J. Teevan. Addressing people's information needs directly in a web search result page. In *WWW '11*, 2011.
[11] A. Chuklin and P. Serdyukov. Good abandonments in factoid queries. In *WWW '12 Companion*, 2012.
[12] C. L. A. Clarke, E. Agichtein, S. Dumais, and R. W. White. The influence of caption features on clickthrough patterns in web search. In *SIGIR '07*.
[13] G. V. Cormack, M. D. Smucker, and C. L. Clarke. Efficient and effective spam filtering and re-ranking for large web datasets. *Inf. Retr.*, 14(5):441–465, 2011.
[14] N. Craswell, O. Zoeter, M. Taylor, and B. Ramsey. An experimental comparison of click position-bias models. In *WSDM '08*, 2008.
[15] E. Cutrell and Z. Guan. What are you looking for?: An eye-tracking study of information usage in web search. In *CHI '07*, 2007.
[16] G. Dupret and C. Liao. A model to estimate intrinsic document relevance from the clickthrough logs of a web search engine. In *WSDM '10*, 2010.
[17] G. E. Dupret and B. Piwowarski. A user browsing model to predict search engine click data from past observations. In *SIGIR '08*, 2008.
[18] D. Guan, S. Zhang, and H. Yang. Utilizing query change for session search. In *SIGIR '13*, 2013.
[19] F. Guo, C. Liu, A. Kannan, T. Minka, M. Taylor, Y.-M. Wang, and C. Faloutsos. Click chain model in web search. In *WWW '09*, 2009.
[20] K. Hofmann, F. Behr, and F. Radlinski. On caption bias in interleaving experiments. In *CIKM '12*, 2012.
[21] J. Jiang, D. He, and J. Allan. Searching, browsing, and clicking in a search session: Changes in user behavior by task and over time. In *SIGIR '14*, 2014.
[22] J. Jiang, D. He, and S. Han. On duplicate results in a search session. In *TREC 2012*, 2012.
[23] J. Li, S. Huffman, and A. Tokuda. Good abandonment in mobile and PC internet search. In *SIGIR '09*, 2009.
[24] J. Luo, S. Zhang, and H. Yang. Win-win search: Dual-agent stochastic game in session search. In *SIGIR '14*, 2014.
[25] M. Richardson, E. Dominowska, and R. Ragno. Predicting clicks: Estimating the click-through rate for new ads. In *WWW '07*, 2007.
[26] X. Shen, B. Tan, and C. Zhai. Context-sensitive information retrieval using implicit feedback. In *SIGIR '05*, 2005.
[27] M. Shokouhi, R. W. White, P. Bennett, and F. Radlinski. Fighting search engine amnesia: Reranking repeated results. In *SIGIR '13*, 2013.
[28] J. Teevan, E. Adar, R. Jones, and M. A. S. Potts. Information re-retrieval: Repeat queries in yahoo's logs. In *SIGIR '07*, 2007.
[29] A. Tombros and M. Sanderson. Advantages of query biased summaries in information retrieval. In *SIGIR '98*, 1998.
[30] C. Wang, Y. Liu, M. Wang, K. Zhou, J.-y. Nie, and S. Ma. Incorporating non-sequential behavior into click models. In *SIGIR '15*, 2015.
[31] R. W. White and E. Horvitz. Captions and biases in diagnostic search. *ACM Trans. Web*, 7(4), 2013.
[32] R. W. White, J. M. Jose, and I. Ruthven. A task-oriented study on the influencing effects of query-biased summarisation in web searching. *Inf. Process. Manage.*, 39(5), 2003.
[33] E. Yilmaz, M. Shokouhi, N. Craswell, and S. Robertson. Expected browsing utility for web search evaluation. In *CIKM '10*, 2010.
[34] Y. Yue, R. Patel, and H. Roehrig. Beyond position bias: Examining result attractiveness as a source of presentation bias in clickthrough data. In *WWW '10*, 2010.
[35] C. Zhai and J. Lafferty. A study of smoothing methods for language models applied to ad hoc information retrieval. In *SIGIR '01*, 2001.
[36] F. Zhong, D. Wang, G. Wang, W. Chen, Y. Zhang, Z. Chen, and H. Wang. Incorporating post-click behaviors into a click model. In *SIGIR '10*, 2010.

Hierarchical Semi-supervised Classification with Incomplete Class Hierarchies

Bhavana Dalvi *
Allen Institute for AI
Seattle, WA, 98103
bhavanad@allenai.org

Aditya Mishra
Seattle University
Seattle, WA 98122
mishraa@seattleu.edu

William W. Cohen
Carnegie Mellon University
Pittsburgh, PA 15213
wcohen@cs.cmu.edu

ABSTRACT

In an entity classification task, topic or concept hierarchies are often incomplete. Previous work by Dalvi et al. [12] has showed that in non-hierarchical semi-supervised classification tasks, the presence of such unanticipated classes can cause semantic drift for seeded classes. The Exploratory learning [12] method was proposed to solve this problem; however it is limited to the flat classification task. This paper builds such exploratory learning methods for hierarchical classification tasks.

We experimented with subsets of the NELL [8] ontology and text, and HTML table datasets derived from the ClueWeb09 corpus. Our method (OptDAC-ExploreEM) outperforms the existing Exploratory EM method, and its naive extension (DAC-ExploreEM), in terms of seed class F1 on average by 10% and 7% respectively.

Categories and Subject Descriptors: I.2.6[Artificial Intelligence]: Learning - Knowledge acquisition.

Keywords: Semi-supervised Learning; Hierarchical Classification; Ontology Extension; Concept Discovery.

1. INTRODUCTION

A common way to organize information is by classification into a concept or topic hierarchy. For example, the Open Directory Project and the Yahoo! Directory are examples of topic hierarchies developed to organize pages on the Web, and Wordnet, NELL and Freebase are examples of large knowledge bases that organize entities into concept hierarchies. However, in an open-domain task, hierarchies are often incomplete, in the sense that there is meaningful structure in the data not captured by the existing hierarchy. E.g., consider a hierarchical entity classification task, with class hierarchy 'onto-1' shown in Figure 1 (left). There are 2 types of locations defined in it: 'State' and 'Country'. However, the unlabeled data about entities on the Web can include location entities of type 'City', 'Museum', etc., that are absent in this ontology, hence called 'unanticipated classes'.

Dalvi et al. [12] showed that in a non-hierarchical semi-supervised classification task, the presence of such unanticipated classes hidden in the unlabeled data can cause semantic drift for seeded classes. They also proposed an approach to solve this semantic drift problem by employing exploratory learning. This algorithm is an extension of the semi-supervised EM algorithm that can create new classes for datapoints that do not belong to the classes known upfront. It explores different numbers of classes while learning. In this paper we first summarize a naive extension of this approach (DAC-ExploreEM method), that applies exploratory learning in a top-down divide and conquer (DAC) manner. However, we notice that DAC-ExploreEM improves over flat ExploreEM in only some cases. Finally we present an optimized version of it (OptDAC-ExploreEM method [11]) that gives more significant improvements over the baseline.

Our proposed OptDAC-ExploreEM method traverses the class hierarchy in top-down fashion to detect whether and where to add a new class for the given datapoint. It also uses a systematic optimization strategy to find the best set of labels for a datapoint given ontological constraints in the form of subset and mutual exclusion constraints.

We demonstrate OptDAC-ExploreEM's effectiveness through extensive experiments on datasets constructed with subsets of the NELL ontology (shown in Figure 1) and text and semi-structured HTML table datasets derived from the ClueWeb09 corpus. In particular, OptDAC-ExploreEM improves seed class F1 on average by 13% when compared to its semi-supervised counterpart (OptDAC). It also outperforms both previously proposed exploratory learning approaches FLAT-ExploreEM and DAC-ExploreEM [11] in terms of seed class F1 on average by 10% and 7% respectively.

Contributions:

Our contributions are as follows:

- We present a method that can do hierarchical semi-supervised classification in the presence of incomplete class hierarchies. It enriches existing knowledge base in two ways: first, by adding new instances to the existing classes; and second, by discovering new classes and adding them at appropriate places in the ontology. Our earlier work [12] had proposed similar approach in the context of flat classification (or clustering) setting, i.e., no hierarchical constraints between classes. As opposed to this, the current work does classification (or clustering) in the presence of class hierarchies.

- Our proposed method, named OptDAC-ExploreEM uses divide and conquer style approach to add a new class and mixed integer programming based optimization to find the best set of labels for a datapoint given the ontological constraints.

*Work done while at Carnegie Mellon University.

WSDM'16, February 22–25, 2016, San Francisco, CA, USA.

DOI: http://dx.doi.org/10.1145/2835776.2835810.

Figure 1: Subsets of NELL [8] ontology used in our hierarchical classification experiments. Some nodes in onto-1 are bold-faced, they are used as seeded classes in the experiments described in Section 5.

- We demonstrate the effectiveness of our method through extensive experiments on four hierarchical entity classification datasets constructed with subsets of the NELL ontology (shown in Figure 1) and text, semi-structured HTML table datasets derived from ClueWeb09 [7].
- To facilitate further research on this topic, we have made the hierarchical entity classification datasets publicly available [1].

Outline:

Rest of the paper is organized as follows: In Section 2, we define the problem formally and then present a generic version of the "Hierarchical Exploratory EM" algorithm. Section 3 describes different variants of this algorithm. Overview of the datasets is covered in Section 4 followed by experimental findings in Section 5. We discuss the related work in Section 6, and conclude in Section 7.

2. OUR APPROACH

Our method is derived from the Exploratory EM algorithm proposed by Dalvi et al. [12]. Exploratory learning takes the same inputs as traditional Semi-Supervised Learning (SSL) methods, i.e. a set of classes $C_1, C_2, \ldots C_k$, a few labeled datapoints X^l and a large number of unlabeled datapoints X^u. X^l contains a (usually small) set of "seed" examples of each class, the task is to learn a model from X^l and use it to label datapoints in X^u. Every example x may be predicted to be in either a known class $C_i \in C_1 \ldots C_k$, or a newly discovered class $C_i \in C_{k+1} \ldots C_m$.

There are two main differences between the Exploratory EM algorithm (ExploreEM) and standard classification-EM (SemisupEM) approaches to SSL. First, in the E step, each of the unlabeled datapoint x is either assigned to one of the existing classes, or to a newly-created class. A new class is introduced when the probabilities of x belonging to existing classes are close to uniform. This suggests that x is not a good fit to any of the existing classes, and that adding x to any existing class will lower the total data likelihood substantially. Second, in the M-step of iteration t, we choose either the model proposed by ExploreEM method which might have more classes than the previous iteration $t-1$, or the baseline model with same number of classes as iteration $t-1$. This choice is based on whether exploratory model satisfies a model selection criterion in terms of increased data likelihood and model complexity. This intuition is derived from the Structural EM approach [14].

As per the experimental results presented in [12], the ExploreEM method is comparable or better than "Gibbs sampling with Chinese Restaurant Process (CRP) approach" and does not involve tuning the concentration parameter for CRP. However, ExploreEM is limited to flat class hierarchies. In this paper we propose the Hierarchical Exploratory EM algorithm which can work with incomplete class hierarchies and small amount of seed labels.

2.1 Problem Definition

Given a set of class constraints Z_k, a small set of labeled data points X^l, their labels Y^l, and a large set of unlabeled data points X^u; the task is to label data points from X^u, adding m new classes if needed and extending the class constraints to Z_{k+m}. Here, each point from X^l can have multiple labels at different levels of the hierarchy satisfying constraints Z_k, and Z_{k+m} defines the class constraints on k seed and m newly added classes, $Z_k \subseteq Z_{k+m}$ and the labels Y^u of X^u satisfy Z_{k+m}. Next let us see different methods proposed to solve this problem.

2.2 Flat Exploratory EM

One simple way to use ExploreEM algorithm [12] for our purpose will be to run it as it is at each level of hierarchy. Henceforth, we refer to this approach as FLAT-ExploreEM and consider it as a baseline for our proposed Hierarchical Exploratory EM approach. At each level, it selects one of the existing classes or creates a new class in case the datapoint doesn't clearly belong to one of the known classes. This algorithm does not make explicit use of class constraints while making class assignments at each step. Hence the assignments done by this algorithm might not be consistent, since assignments at level 3 are not influenced by assignment at level 2.

2.3 Hierarchical Exploratory EM

We summarize a generic Hierarchical exploratory learning algorithm that can take a set of class constraints in terms of sub-

[1]Datasets used in this paper are available to download at `http://rtw.ml.cmu.edu/wk/WebSets/hierarchical_ExploratoryLearning_WSDM2016/index.html`

Algorithm 1 Generic Hierarchical Exploratory EM

1: **function Hierarchical-ExploreEM** (X^l, Y^l, X^u, Z_k): θ_{k+m}, Z_{k+m}, Y^u
2: **Input**: X^l labeled data points; Y^l labels of X^l;
X^u unlabeled data points;
Z_k manually input constraints on k seed classes $\Longleftarrow$
3: **Output:** $\{\theta_1, \dots, \theta_{k+m}\}$ parameters for k seed and m newly added classes; Y^u labels for X^u;
Z_{k+m} Set of class constraints between $k+m$ classes; $\Longleftarrow$
{Initialize classifiers θ_j for class C_j using seeds provided for C_j}
4: $\theta_1^0 \dots \theta_k^0 = argmax_\theta L(X^l, Y^l)$
5: **while** class assignments AND #classes not converged **do**
6: k_{old} is #classes before E step. Log-likelihood *BaseLL* $= logP(X|\theta^{(t)}_{k_{old}}, Z^{(t)}_{k_{old}})$
{E step: (Iteration t) Classify each datapoint at each level}
7: **for** i=1 to $|X|$ **do**
8: Find $P(C_j|X_i)$ for all classes C_j
{Assign a bit vector of labels for each unlabeled datapoint. A new class gets created for a datapoint that does not fit into existing classes.}
9: $Y_i^{(t)}$ = **ConsistentAssignment**($P(C_j|X_i)$, h, $Z^{(t)}$) $\Longleftarrow$
{If a new class is created, then class constraints are updated accordingly.}
10: $Z^{(t)}$ = **UpdateConstraints**($X^l, Y^l, X^u, Y^u, Z^{(t)}$) $\Longleftarrow$
11: **end for**
12: k_{new} is #classes after E step. Log-likelihood *ExploreLL* $= logP(X|\theta^{(t)}_{k_{new}}, Z^{(t)}_{k_{new}})$
{M step: Recompute model parameters based on $Y^{(t)}$ }
13: **if** Model selection criterion(k_{old}, *BaseLL*, k_{new}, *ExploreLL*) selects exploratory model **then**
{Adopt the new model with k_{new} classes}
14: $\theta^{(t+1)}_{k_{new}} = argmax_\theta L(X^l, Y^l, X^u, Y^{u(t)}|\theta^{(t)}_{k_{new}}, Z^{(t)}_{k_{new}})$
15: $Z^{(t+1)} = Z^{(t)}_{k_{new}}$
16: **else**
{Keep the old model with k_{old} classes}
17: $\theta^{(t+1)}_{k_{old}} = argmax_\theta L(X^l, Y^l, X^u, Y^{u(t)}|\theta^{(t)}_{k_{old}}, Z^{(t)}_{k_{old}})$
18: $Z^{(t+1)} = Z^{(t)}_{k_{old}}$
19: **end if**
20: **end while**
21: **end function**

class or mutual exclusion constraints (proposed in our preliminary work [11]). This algorithm, in each iteration, assigns a bit vector to each data point with one bit per class. Class constraints decide whether a bit vector is consistent or not, e.g. if class constraints include "Car is of type Machine", then for consistency, when the bit for "Car" is set, the bit for "Machine" should also be set. Further new classes can be added during each iteration, hence the length of these bit vectors changes dynamically and the algorithm maintains class constraints containing old as well as newly added classes. The generic Hierarchical Exploratory EM algorithm is described in Algorithm 1. The important differences from the FLAT-ExploreEM algorithm are marked using $\Longleftarrow$. There can be multiple ways to implement functions "ConsistentAssignment" and "UpdateConstraints", which we will discuss below.

Lines 13-19 of Algorithm 1 does model selection. Similar to Exploratory EM [12], at the end of every E step, we evaluate two models, one with and one without adding extra classes. These two models are scored using a model selection criterion like AIC, BIC or AICc, and the model with best penalized data likelihood score is selected in each iteration. The extended Akaike information criterion (AICc) suited best for our experiments since our datasets have large number of features and small number of data points.

Algorithm 2 MinMax criterion for new class creation

1: **function Is Nearly Uniform**($[P(C_1|x) \dots P(C_k|x)]$):
2: **Input**: $[P(C_1|x) \dots P(C_k|x)]$: probability distribution of existing classes given a data point x
3: **Output:** *decision* : **true** iff new class needs to be created
4: k : current number of classes
5: $maxProb$ = max($P(C_j|x)$)
6: $minProb$ = min($P(C_j|x)$)
7: **if** $maxProb/minProb < 2$ AND $maxProb < 2/k$ **then**
8: *decision* = true
9: **else**
10: *decision* = false
11: **end if**
12: **end function**

Computing Probability of Classes given a Datapoint (Algorithm 1: Line 8)

This step computes probabilities $P(C_j|x_i;\theta_j)$, where θ_j is the current estimate of model parameters for class C_j. A variety of techniques may be used for this estimation, we briefly describe one such choice here: the seeded version of K-Means, proposed by Basu and Mooney [3]. In this model $P(C_j|x) \propto P(x|C_j)*P(C_j)$, and we define $P(x|C_j) \propto x \cdot C_j$, i.e., the inner product of a vector representing x and a vector representing the centroid of cluster j. Specifically, x and C_j both can be represented as L_1 normalized feature vectors. The centroid of a new cluster is initialized using feature counts from x. Since the EM algorithm can be used for both classification and clustering tasks, we will use the terms "class" and "cluster" interchangeably.

Modeling Class Constraints

Consider a toy example of ontological class constraints in Figure 2. Here, we can see two kinds of class constraints imposed by the ontology. Following are example constraints:
(1) The "Subset" constraint between "Fruit" and "Food" categories suggests that if a datapoint is classified as "Fruit", then it should also be classified as "Food". (2) The "Mutual Exclusion" constraint between "Food" and "Organization" says if a datapoint is classified as "Food", then it should not be classified as "Organization", and vice versa.

Let $\{C_1, \dots C_K\}$ be the Knowledge Base (KB) categories. Let *Subset_k* be the set of all subset or inclusion constraints, and *Mutex_k* be the set of all mutual exclusion constraints. In other words, *Subset_k* $= \{\langle i,k\rangle \mid C_i \subseteq C_k\}$ and *Mutex_k* $= \{(i,k) \mid C_i \cap C_k = \phi\}$. The class constraints referred to as Z_k in Algorithm 1 can be defined as $Z_k = \{$*Subset_k*, *Mutex_k*$\}$.

3. VARIANTS OF HIERARCHICAL EXPLORATORY EM

Hierarchical Exploratory EM (described in Algorithm 1) is a generic algorithm that can be instantiated in different ways, by changing the functions "ConsistentAssignment" and "UpdateConstraints". Next we describe two such variants namely, DAC-ExploreEM and OptDAC-ExploreEM.

3.1 Divide and Conquer (DAC-ExploreEM)

One simple instantiation of Algorithm 1 can be done by using Divide-and-Conquer (DAC) strategy introduced in [11]. Here we assume that classes are arranged in a tree hierarchy, and classes at any one level are mutually exclusive. To do class assignments for

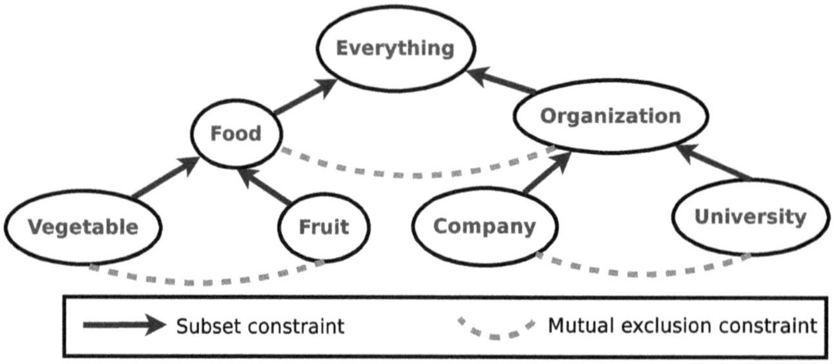

Figure 2: An example of ontological class constraints.

any unlabeled datapoint, we traverse the class ontology from root to leaf level. Every data point belongs to the root node. Then at each level we chose the best label at that level and consider only its children as candidates at the next level.

Further we check whether the probability distribution among the candidate classes at each level is nearly uniform (using heuristic described in Algorithm 2) to decide whether to create a new class at that level. We do not describe the "ConsistentAssignment" and "UpdateConstraints" functions formally, however they can be easily derived by setting parameter $q = 1$ in the OptDAC-ExploreEM algorithm that we present next.

Also, note that the example ontologies in Figure 1 have tree structure. However, in practice, class constraints can be more complicated (e.g., overlapping classes can exist). The DAC-ExploreEM algorithm is limited to a tree structured ontology and assumes mutual exclusion of classes at any level of hierarchy. Next we present the OptDAC-ExploreEM algorithm that can work with more complicated class constraints.

3.2 Optimized Divide and Conquer (OptDAC-ExploreEM)

DAC-ExploreEM can do semi-supervised learning in the presence of unanticipated classes. However, we will see in the experimental evaluation (refer to Section 5.2) that DAC-ExploreEM could provide marginal improvements over the baseline (ExploreEM). During the error analysis we found that the classification at higher levels of hierarchy is not perfect, and once we make a decision at level i of the ontology, there is no way to change the decision once we move on to level $i + 1$. Here we present a softer version of this method, that keeps track of top-q labels at each level instead of keeping only the best label.

Algorithm 3 describes how the "ConsistentAssignment" and "UpdateConstraints" functions are implemented for this approach. It is similar to DAC-ExploreEM method in the sense that we traverse the classes in top down fashion, and check whether new class needs to be created at each level of the hierarchy. However, at each level l of the class hierarchy, a mixed-integer program is run to get optimal class assignments for the active classes from levels 1 to l. Further instead of considering only the best classes in previous levels, the top-q classes from each level are selected to be added into the set of active classes, which are used in turn to select the candidate classes at the next level of hierarchy.

This method combines the Divide-and-Conquer strategy to detect/place new classes and the mixed integer programming based optimization strategy to assign an optimal set of labels to a datapoint given the ontological constraints. The optimal label assignment method is generic enough to support any set of subset and mutual exclusion class constraints. The new class detection based on Divide and Conquer can be extended for non-tree hierarchies using a breadth first search strategy that can be applied to any graph. Hence the OptDAC-ExploreEM method can be extended easily for non-tree structured ontologies.

Note that like DAC-ExploreEM, it makes greedy decisions about new cluster creation. However, it performs overall optimization of label assignments while satisfying the ontological constraints. This lets us correct any sub-optimal decisions made by the greedy heuristic at higher levels of the class hierarchy. Generally as we increase the value of q, we may get some improvement in accuracy at the cost of increased runtime. Since the value of q directly decides the size of active nodes set used while taking the decision at each level of the hierarchy, there is a trade-off between time complexity and solution optimality. For all the experiments in this paper, we added the top two classes per level to the set of selected classes (i.e. $q = 2$) in Line 21 of Algorithm 3. This approach is referred to as OptDAC-ExploreEM below.

Optimal Label Assignment given Class Constraints (Algorithm 3: Line 20)

Let $X = \{x_1, \dots x_N\}$ be the datapoints, and $\{C_1, \dots C_K\}$ be the KB categories. Let $y_{ji} \in \{0, 1\}$ be an indicator variable specifying whether x_i belongs to C_j. Let θ_j denote the centroid for category C_j. Using the model parameters θ_j for class C_j, we can estimate $P(C_j|x_i)$, the probability of x_i belonging to C_j. Given the category membership probabilities $\{P(C_j|x_i)\}$ estimated in the E step, this step computes the category membership variables $\{y_{ji},\ \forall\ 1 \le i \le N,\ 1 \le j \le K\}$. We solve a Mixed-Integer Program (MIP) to estimate y_{ji}'s. One such problem is solved for each datapoint. This MIP takes the scores $\{P(C_j|x_i)\}$, and class constraints Z_k as input and produces a bit vector of labels y_{ji}'s as output.

$$\underset{\{y_{ji}\},\zeta_{jk},\delta_{jk}}{\text{maximize}} \left(\sum_{\mathrm{j}} \mathrm{y_{ji}} * \mathrm{P(C_j|x_i)} - \sum_{\langle \mathrm{i,k} \rangle \in \mathrm{Subset}} \zeta_{\mathrm{ik}} - \sum_{\langle i,k \rangle \in Mutex} \delta_{ik} \right) \quad (1)$$

subject to,

$$y_{ji} \ge y_{ki} - \zeta_{jk}, \quad \forall \langle j,k \rangle \in \mathit{Subset\_k}$$
$$y_{ji} + y_{ki} \le 1 + \delta_{jk}, \quad \forall \langle j,k \rangle \in \mathit{Mutex\_k}$$
$$\zeta_{jk}, \delta_{jk} \ge 0,\ y_{ji} \in \{0,1\}, \quad \forall j,k$$

Algorithm 3 OptDAC-ExploreEM

function ConsistentAssignment-OptDAC ($P(C_j|x)$, $Z_k\}$): Y_x, Z_{k+m}
Input: $P(C_j|x)$ probability distribution of classes given a datapoint x; Z_k class constraints on k seed classes.
Output: $label(x)$ assignment of x to classes satisfying Z_k; Z_{k+m} extended set of class constraints on $k+m$ classes.
h is the height of the class ontology.
for l = 1 to h **do**
  if x has seed label at level l **then**
    label(x, $level_l$) = seed label;
  else
    $candidateC$ = children of active classes
    if $candidateC$ is not empty **then**
      Let P_{cand} = probability distribution over $candidateC$
      if Is Nearly Uniform (P_{cand}) (using Algorithm 2) **then**
        Create a new class C_{new} at level l
        Initialize parameters for class C_{new} using x
        Set parent(C_{new}) = class choice at level $l-1$
        Add C_{new} to active classes
      end if
      P_{active} = probability distribution over active classes
      Z_{active} = class constraints between active classes
      Choose $label(x, level_l)$ by computing optimal label assignment considering (P_{active}, Z_{active}) (using Eq. 1)
      Add top-q classes to the set of active classes using P_{active} as scores
    end if
  end if
end for
end function
function UpdateConstraints-OptDAC (X, Y, Z^{old}): Z^{new}
Input: X: Dataset; Y: Class assignments for each point in X; Z^{old}: Old constraints on the existing set of classes.
Output: Z^{new}: Updated set of class constraints,
Each newly created class is assigned a single parent at the time of creation
Add each parent, child relationship as a constraint in $Z_{k'}$
end function

The MIP formulation for a datapoint x_i is presented in Equation 1. For each datapoint, this method tries to maximize the sum of scores of selected labels, after penalizing for violation of class constraints. Let ζ_{jk} be the slack variables for *Subset_k* constraints, and δ_{jk} be the slack variables for *Mutex_k* constraints. To solve these mixed integer linear programs we used the MOSEK solver [2].

Such optimization techniques have been shown to be effective for the task of semi-supervised learning in the presence of multiple data views and hierarchical class constraints [9, 13]. Here we use this formulation for the task of hierarchical exploratory learning.

4. DATASETS AND EXPERIMENTAL METHODOLOGY

In this section we present the experimental results of our Hierarchical Exploratory EM approach. Figure 1 shows two ontologies that we used in this paper, each being a subset of NELL's ontology at different point in NELL's development.

4.1 Datasets

Our task includes discovering new classes that are not present in the input class ontology. To make the evaluation easier, we created datasets that have ground truth labels for all entities in them, i.e. the entire class hierarchy is known. However, only part of that hierarchy and corresponding training data is given as input to the algorithm. Rest of the classes and corresponding labels are unknown to the algorithm, and used only during evaluation. Thus we are simulating the scenarios where some classes are known while others are unanticipated. To achieve this, we derived four datasets using the two ontologies (shown in Figure 1) and two feature sets extracted from the ClueWeb09 corpus. The first ontology, named onto-1 in Figure 1 (left), has 3 levels and 11 classes. The second ontology, named onto-2 in Figure 1 (right), has 4 levels and 39 classes.

We created our datasets using the two corpora: *Text-Patterns* and *HTML-Tables*, both derived from ClueWeb09 data [7]. *Text-Patterns* corpus contains frequency counts of text context patterns that occurred with each entity w.r.t. text sentences that appeared in ClueWeb09 dataset. *HTML-Tables* corpus contains frequency counts of table columns in which entities occurred, derived from HTML tables that appeared in ClueWeb09 dataset. E.g. an entity "Pittsburgh" having a *Text-Patterns* feature, value being ("lives in _arg1", 1000) means that the entity "Pittsburgh" appeared in arg1 position of the context "lives in _arg1" for 1000 times in the sentences from ClueWeb09 dataset. Similarly, an entity "Pittsburgh" having a *HTML-Tables* feature, value being ("clueweb09-en0011-94-04::2:1", 1) means that the entity "Pittsburgh" appeared once in HTML table 2, column 1 from ClueWeb09 document id "clueweb09-en0011-94-04".

To create a dataset from an ontology, we took all entities that are labeled with at least one of the classes under consideration, and retrieved their feature representation in terms of occurrences with text patterns or HTML table columns. Thus we created four datasets Text-Small to Table-Medium, using combinations of two ontologies and two corpora. Table 1 describes the statistics about these four datasets. These datasets are made publicly available [2].

4.2 Methods

We experimented with three different methods for the entity clustering task: FLAT, DAC, and OptDAC. Each of them have SemisupEM and ExploreEM variants. The SemisupEM variant performs semisupervised learning with the seeded classes, whereas ExploreEM variant can add extra classes discovered from unlabeled data. SemisupEM and ExploreEM variants of the FLAT method are the baselines proposed in [12]. DAC and OptDAC methods are new contributions of this paper.

- FLAT: This method performs flat entity classification at each level of the class hierarchy. Decisions made at each level are independent.
- DAC: This is a greedy method for hierarchical classification described in Section 3.1.
- OptDAC: This is the hierarchical classification method described in Section 3.2.

Further we used seeded K-Means algorithm for clustering (as described in Section 2.3) and the MinMax criterion [12] for new class creation (described in Algorithm 2).

4.3 Methodology

For the experiments in this paper, we feed a part of the ontology (seed classes) to the algorithm and rest of the part (unanticipated classes) is hidden from the algorithm. SemisupEM variant of each method learns classifiers only for seed classes. Along with this, ExploreEM variant of each method can add new classes. To make the semi-supervised and exploratory variants of each method comparable, we use "macro-averaged seed class F1" as the evaluation metric. It is computed by macro averaging F1 values of seed classes

[2]Datasets used in this paper can be download from `http://rtw.ml.cmu.edu/wk/WebSets/hierarchical_ExploratoryLearning_WSDM2016/index.html`

Dataset	Feature Type	Ontology	#Classes	#Levels	#Classes per level	#Entities	#Contexts	#(Entity, context) pairs	#(Entity, label) pairs
Text-Small	Text	onto-1	11	3	1, 3, 7	2.5K	3.4M	8.8M	7.2K
Text-Medium		onto-2	39	4	1, 4, 24, 10	12.9K	6.7M	25.8M	42.2K
Table-Small	Tables	onto-1	11	3	1, 3, 7	4.3K	0.96M	6.3M	12.2K
Table-Medium		onto-2	39	4	1, 4, 24, 10	33.4K	2.2M	21.4M	126.1K

Table 1: Statistics of the hierarchical entity classification datasets used in this paper. Refer to Section 4.1 for more details.

Dataset	Level	Macro-avg. Seed Class F1		
		W/o constraints	W constraints	
		FLAT SemisupEM	**DAC** SemisupEM	**OptDAC** SemisupEM
Text-Small	2	46.6	47.1	**52.0**
	3	23.5	**26.1**	25.8 △
Text-Medium	2	53.2	**53.7**	53.3
	3	27.9	33.4 ▲	**33.9** ▲
	4	17.4	24.5	**26.8** △
Table-Small	2	69.5	74.6 ▲	**74.8** ▲
	3	36.8	38.8 △	**38.9** ▲
Table-Medium	2	62.7	**64.8**	62.2
	3	43.7	46.4 ▲	**48.0** ▲
	4	47.3	**57.7** ▲	57.1 ▲

Table 2: Comparison of FLAT, DAC, and OptDAC methods in the semi-supervised setting. ▲ (and △) indicates that improvements of the DAC and OptDAC methods are statistically significant compared to the FLAT method with 0.05 (and 0.1) significance level. Please refer to Section 5.1 for details.

only. Further, if ExploreEM variant improves the seed class F1 over SemisupEM variant, it indicates that adding extra classes helped towards keeping the seed classes pure (i.e. reducing semantic drift).

This "macro-averaged seed class F1" metric is further averaged for 10 runs of each algorithm. Each run's input consists of different seed ontologies and randomly sampled 10% of relevant datapoints as seed examples. The same set of inputs is given to all algorithms being compared. Note that, for a given dataset with a choice of of seed classes and training percentage, there are many ways to generate a train-test partition. We report results using 10 random train-test partitions of each dataset. The same partitions are used to run all the algorithms being compared and to compute the statistical significance of results.

For Text-Small and Table-Small, we generated 10 sets of seed examples, for the same seed ontology. The chosen seed ontology is bold-faced in Figure 1 (left). Here seed ontology always contains the same 7 out of 11 classes. For Text-Medium and Table-Medium, seed ontology also varies across runs. In each run, we randomly chose 10 leaf nodes according to their class frequency (i.e. popular class is more likely to be chosen in each run). After sampling 10 leaf nodes (sampling without replacement), we included all their ancestors to create the seed ontology for that run. The average ontology size generated using this method was 16.7. Table 3 column 2 shows avg. number of seed classes chosen at each level of the hierarchy. 10% of the datapoints from leaf classes are them randomly sampled, and hierarchical labels of this datapoints are used as training data for the run.

5. EXPERIMENTAL RESULTS

In this section we will compare semi-supervised and exploratory variants of FLAT, DAC and OptDAC methods, in order to answer certain research questions.

5.1 Do ontological constraints help?

Table 2 shows the comparison between semi-supervised versions of all three methods. The best values in each row (per dataset per level in the hierarchy) are bold-faced. We can see that for every row, the best performance was given by a method that uses ontological constraints while clustering. Hence we can conclude that using ontological constraints do help.

We also did statistical significance tests with 0.05 (and 0.1) significance level denoted by ▲ (and △) in Table 2. Results show that in 5 out of 10 cases the gains of DAC over FLAT are statistically significant, whereas OptDAC method proved to be better by producing statistically significant gains over FLAT in 7 out of 10 cases.

5.2 Is Exploratory learning better than semi-supervised learning for seed classes?

We present the comparison of Semi-supervised vs. Exploratory versions of all three methods in Table 3. The best performance in each row is bold-faced. From Table 3 we can see that, ExploreEM version of each algorithm improves seed class F1 when compared to SemisupEM for all three methods in 24/30 cases. Our proposed approach OptDAC-ExploreEM improves seed class F1 on average by 13% when compared to its semi-supervised counterpart.

While comparing among the ExploreEM approaches, OptDAC method independently beats previously proposed FLAT and DAC methods in 8/10 cases each. Empirically, OptDAC-ExploreEM outperforms FLAT-ExploreEM and DAC-ExploreEM in terms of seed class F1 on average by 10% and 7% respectively.

Further we did statistical significance tests for performance improvements of DAC-ExploreEM and OptDAC-ExploreEM over FLAT-ExploreEM, with 0.05 (and 0.1) significance level denoted by ▲ (and △) in Table 3. It shows that improvements of DAC-ExploreEM are statistically significant in 2/10 cases, whereas im-

Dataset	#Seed /#Ideal classes	Level	FLAT SemisupEM	FLAT ExploreEM	DAC SemisupEM	DAC ExploreEM	OptDAC SemisupEM	OptDAC ExploreEM
			Macro-avg. Seed Class F1					
Text-Small	2/3	2	46.6	**64.4**	47.1	61.8	52.0	62.6
	4/7	3	23.5	32.7	26.1	36.3	25.8	**42.3** ▲
Text-Medium	3.9/4	2	53.2	50.2	**53.7**	47.2	53.3	52.5
	9.4/24	3	27.9	27.0	33.4	26.8	33.9	**34.9** ▲
	2.4/10	4	17.4	25.8	24.5	29.4	26.8	**31.6** ▲
Table-Small	2/3	2	69.5	75.8	74.6	76.2	74.8	**80.0** ▲
	4/7	3	36.8	**43.9**	38.8	40.9 ▽	38.9	41.5
Table-Medium	3.9/4	2	62.7	61.3	64.8	**65.0** ▲	62.2	**65.0** ▲
	9.4/24	3	43.7	49.1	46.4	48.6	48.0	**50.1**
	2.4/10	4	47.3	52.2	57.7	**59.9** ▲	57.1	58.4 ▲

Table 3: Comparison of FLAT, DAC, and OptDAC methods using KM representation on Text-Small to Table-Medium. ▲ (and △) indicates that improvements of the DAC-ExploreEM and OptDAC-ExploreEM methods are statistically significant when compared to the FLAT-ExploreEM method with 0.05 (and 0.1) significance level. Please refer to Section 5.1 for more details.

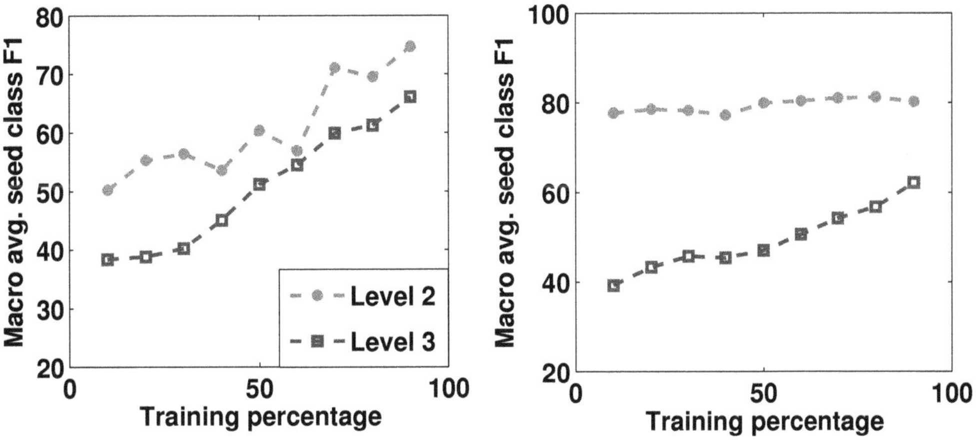

Figure 3: Comparison of OptDAC-ExploreEM method with different training percentage on datasets Text-Small (left) and Table-Small (right).

provements of OptDAC-ExploreEM are significant in 6/10 cases. Thus OptDAC-ExploreEM turns out to be the best method being compared.

Note that the results presented in Table 2 are subset of results presented in Table 3, however the statistical significance is computed against different baselines. In Table 2, statistical significance is computed against FLAT SemisupEM method, whereas in Table 3, it is computed against FLAT ExploreEM method, hence represented in separate tables.

5.3 What is the effect of varying the number of labeled examples?

We ran OptDAC-ExploreEM method on datasets Text-Small and Table-Small with different values of training percentage averaged over 10 random train/test partitions of our data.

In Figure 3, we can see that as the training percentage increases the performance of OptDAC-ExploreEM method improves. Also note that as we go down the hierarchy relative improvements are more larger. For example, there are larger relative improvements at Level 3 compared to Level 2 of the hierarchy.

5.4 How do the methods compare in terms of runtime?

Here we compare runtimes of all methods averaged over all the runs with different seed ontologies and seed training data. In our MATLAB implementation, the running time of Exploratory EM is much longer. Table 4 shows that the increase in runtime of ExploreEM variants compared to their SemisupEM counterparts is by the factor 3.2 on average across all methods and datasets. Further the exploratory methods take on average 10.3 times the time of SemisupEM variant of the FLAT method.

In particular, OptDAC-ExploreEM method is on average twice as expensive as DAC-ExploreEM. This is due to the fact that DAC-ExploreEM takes greedy decisions at each level of the hierarchy, whereas OptDAC-ExploreEM keeps track of the top-q active nodes. We set $q = 2$ in these experiments. Thus the value of q results in a trade-off between improvement in seed class F1 and increased runtime of the algorithm.

5.5 Evaluation of extended cluster hierarchies

In this section, we present the evaluation of extra clusters added by our Hierarchical Exploratory EM algorithm to the incomplete

Dataset	Avg. runtime in sec.	Average run-time in multiple of FLAT-SemisupEM				
	FLAT	FLAT	DAC		OptDAC	
	SemisupEM	ExploreEM	SemisupEM	ExploreEM	SemisupEM	ExploreEM
Text-Small	53.5	8	1	6	7	17
Table-Small	50.7	3	3	6	10	21
Text-Medium	524.7	5	7	11	11	25
Table-Medium	5932.4	4	6	7	7	10

Table 4: Comparison of average runtimes of all methods. Please refer to Section 5.4 for more details.

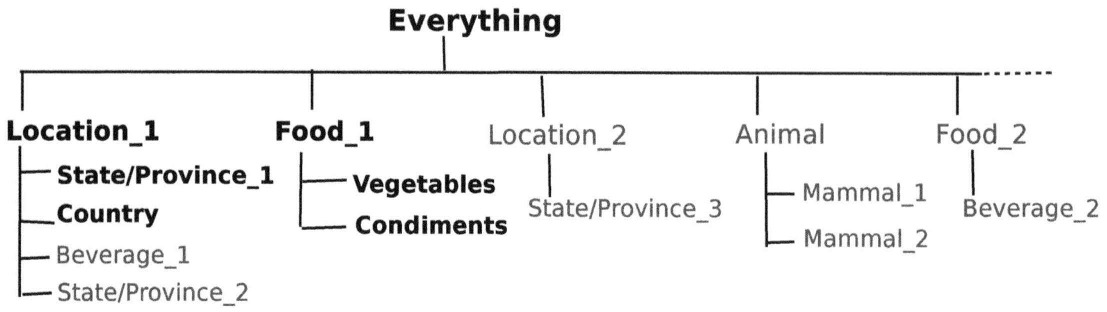

Figure 4: An example extended ontology applying our OptDAC-ExploreEM method on the Table-Small dataset. The seeded classes are bold-faced, whereas the newly added classes are in Blue and are not bold-faced. Please refer to Section 5.5 for details.

class ontology given as input. If it started with k classes, and produced $k + m$ classes as output, we first need to label these m extra classes. Since our datasets are completely labeled, each new class can be assigned a majority label based on entities assigned to that class and level of the class in the hierarchy. E.g. if the class is at level 2 in the hierarchy then we choose the best label at level 2 of the class hierarchy.

Figure 4 shows an example of an extended class hierarchy generated by OptDAC-ExploreEM algorithm on Table-Small starting with 7 seed classes from onto-1. The bold-faced nodes are from seed ontology, and nodes in blue (non bold-faced) are the ones added by our proposed exploratory learning methods. It is labeled using the above described majority label approach. (Note that there are multiple clusters with same label, to differentiate them we have labeled them as "Food_1", "Food_2" etc.)

Once this labeling is done, we can measure the precision of labels across (parent, child) links in the cluster hierarchy. E.g. in Figure 4, parent-child link between (Food_2, Beverage_2) is correct, however the link between (Location, Beverage) is incorrect. These links can be classified into seed or extra links based on whether the child cluster was one of the seed clusters or introduced by the Hierarchical Exploratory EM algorithm.

Dataset	Fraction of unanticipated classes	%Precision of (parent, child) edges		
		Seed	Extra	All
Text-Small	0.36	88.3	84.5	85.5
Table-Small	0.36	100.0	90.4	92.4
Text-Medium	0.62	80.7	22.6	46.8
Table-Medium	0.62	95.7	36.1	63.9

Table 5: Precision of child, parent edges created by OptDAC-ExploreEM. Please refer to Section 5.5 for details.

Table 5 shows the link precision values for OptDAC-ExploreEM algorithm when run on all four datasets. We can see that for seed clusters, accuracy numbers are high (81 - 100%) for all four datasets. In terms extra clusters, for the Text-Small and Table-Small datasets with smaller ontology (onto-1), and unanticipated class fraction being low, the precision of edges for extra clusters is very high in around 85%.

However for the Text-Medium and Table-Medium datasets, with a medium sized ontology (onto-2), and with higher fraction of unanticipated classes, the precision for extra clusters is quite low around 30%. This indicates that the task of detecting new classes and adding them at right positions in the ontology is a challenging task, and it gets even more challenging with the complexity and degree of incompleteness of the input ontology.

Even though the newly created clusters are not perfect, we observed that these hierarchical exploratory learning methods improve seed class F1 on all four entity classification datasets (refer to Table 3). Thus, these techniques help reduce semantic drift of seeded classes by filtering out those datapoints that do not belong to any of the existing classes.

6. RELATED WORK

Here we propose a novel hierarchical SSL method that is robust when the unlabeled data contains unanticipated classes i.e. classes other than those present in the class hierarchy given as input. To the best of our knowledge this specific problem is relatively less explored, even though in real-world settings, there can be unanticipated (and hence unseeded) classes in any large-scale hierarchical SSL task.

There has also been some work in unsupervised hierarchical clustering [17, 23, 5] that can discover cluster/topic hierarchies given a large unlabeled dataset, however they do not make use of any supervision that might be available. Exploratory learning differs in that we learn the number of clusters as well as centroids for those clusters jointly in a single run of the EM algorithm, while using the available supervision for seed clusters. Apart from standard K-Means, our EM framework can also be used with other clustering/classification algorithms like Naive Bayes and von Mises-

Fisher, and we specifically evaluate the performance difference on the seeded classes.

There has been a lot of research done in the area of supervised hierarchical classification [6, 16, 24]. These methods assume that the class hierarchy is complete and there is enough training data to learn classifiers for each node in the class hierarchy. On the other hand we considered the situation where only part of the ontology is known upfront with very few seed examples for each of the seed class. Further our method can be easily extended to cases where class constraints are more complicated than the examples considered in this chapter, e.g. overlapping classes and mutual exclusion constraints.

Another related research area is constructing web-scale knowledge bases [8, 1] by doing information extraction from various data-sources. NELL internally uses Coupled semi-supervised learning [8] that takes into account subclass and mutual exclusion constraints among classes to filter extraction patterns and instances at the end of each bootstrapping iteration. The ontology (class hierarchy) is not explicitly used in the prediction process. I.e. it does flat classification with class constraints applied as post-processing in between two iterations of bootstrapping. Our approach on the other hand does collective hierarchical classification.

There has also been some work to extend existing ontologies. Mohamed et al. [19] propose a co-clustering based two step approach to discover new relations between two already existing classes in the knowledge base. These new relations are named using centroid features of the intermediate clusters. This method is focused on relation discovery between known classes. Snow et al. [22] discover new WordNet synsets by using evidence from multiple sources, however their approach is focused on discovering new isA relations, and not meant for building hierarchical classifiers for the learnt hierarchy. Pal et al. [20] proposed a technique based on Indian Buffet Process that could learn with existing feature hierarchies as well as extend them based on structure discovered from unlabeled data. Their method relies only on the containment relationships and the hierarchies they experimented with are domain specific e.g. restaurants domain.

Reisinger and Paşca [21] addressed the same problem as ours, working with the Wordnet hierarchy. Their fixed-structure and sense selective approaches use the Wordnet hierarchy directly and annotate existing concepts with generic property fields (attributes). On the other hand, Nested Chinese Restaurant Process (nCRP) approach is hierarchical extension of LDA to infer arbitrary fixed-depth tree structures from data. nCRP generates its own annotated hierarchy whose concept nodes do not necessarily correspond to Wordnet concepts. Our method is in the middle of these two approaches, as it uses the existing class hierarchy with small amount of training data and extends it dynamically as new clusters of datapoints are discovered.

Another set of techniques focus on completely unsupervised information extraction and ontology discovery [15, 4, 21, 10]. Though very effective, these approaches are not making use of the valuable information hidden in the existing knowledge bases. Our approach is relatively novel in the sense that it is in between semi-supervised and unsupervised learning, where some part of ontology is known, and this knowledge is used to discover the missing parts of the ontology along with populating it with new data instances.

To define the similarity among two entities we use bag of word features about co-occurrences of text patterns with the noun-phrases. There can be more effective approaches of document representation like the lower dimensional continuous Skip-gram features, proposed by Mikolov et al. [18]. Their technique learns low dimensional vectors that potentially embed semantics of noun-phrases.

Acknowledgments:

This work is supported in part by the Google PhD fellowship in Information Extraction, and NSF grant No. IIS1250956-NSF-COHEN. The views and conclusions contained herein are those of the authors and should not be interpreted as necessarily representing the official policies or endorsements, either expressed or implied, of Google, or NSF.

7. CONCLUSIONS AND FUTURE WORK

In this paper, we propose the Hierarchical Exploratory EM approach that can take an incomplete class ontology as input, along with a few seed examples of each class, to populate new instances of seeded classes and extend the ontology with newly discovered classes. Experiments with subsets of NELL ontology and and text, semi-structured HTML table datasets derived from the ClueWeb09 corpus show encouraging results in terms of seed class F1 scores. We will make our hierarchical entity classification datasets publicly available to encourage future research in this area.

Our proposed hierarchical exploratory EM method, named OptDAC-ExploreEM performs better than flat classification and hierarchical semi-supervised EM methods at all levels of hierarchy, especially as we go further down the hierarchy. Experiments show that OptDAC-ExploreEM outperforms its semi-supervised variant on average by 13% in terms of seed class F1 scores. It also outperforms both previously proposed exploratory learning approaches FLAT-ExploreEM and DAC-ExploreEM in terms of seed class F1 on average by 10% and 7% respectively.

In future, we would like to apply our method on datasets with non-tree structured class hierarchies. We briefly discussed how our proposed OptDAC-ExploreEM method can be used for this task. Further, our experiments focused on an information extraction task of classifying entities into a knowledge base class hierarchy. However, our techniques can also be applied to other tasks like document classification into topic hierarchies on datasets like Reuters, and classifying images into a class hierarchy for datasets like ImageNet.

References

[1] Freebase. *http://freebase.com.*

[2] AIMMS. The MOSEK toolkit.

[3] S. Basu, A. Banerjee, and R. Mooney. Semi-supervised clustering by seeding. In *In Proceedings of 19th International Conference on Machine Learning (ICML-2002.* Citeseer, 2002.

[4] D. M. Blei, T. L. Griffiths, and M. I. Jordan. The nested chinese restaurant process and bayesian nonparametric inference of topic hierarchies. *Journal of the ACM (JACM)*, 57(2):7, 2010.

[5] D. M. Blei, T. L. Griffiths, M. I. Jordan, and J. B. Tenenbaum. Hierarchical topic models and the nested chinese restaurant process. *Advances in neural information processing systems*, 16:17, 2004.

[6] L. Cai and T. Hofmann. Hierarchical document categorization with support vector machines. In *Proceedings of the thirteenth ACM international conference on Information and knowledge management*, pages 78–87. ACM, 2004.

[7] J. Callan. The clueweb09 dataset. `http://boston.lti.cs.cmu.edu/Data/clueweb09/`.

[8] A. Carlson, J. Betteridge, R. C. Wang, E. R. Hruschka Jr, and T. M. Mitchell. Coupled semi-supervised learning for information extraction. In *Proceedings of the third ACM international conference on Web search and data mining*, pages 101–110. ACM, 2010.

[9] B. Dalvi and W. W. Cohen. Multi-view hierarchical semi-supervised learning by optimal assignment of sets of labels to instances. 2014.

[10] B. Dalvi, W. W. Cohen, and J. Callan. Websets: Extracting sets of entities from the web using unsupervised information extraction. In *Proceedings of the Fifth ACM International Conference on Web Search and Data Mining*, WSDM '12, pages 243–252, New York, NY, USA, 2012. ACM.

[11] B. Dalvi, W. W. Cohen, and J. Callan. Classifying entities into an incomplete ontology. In *Proceedings of the 2013 workshop on Automated knowledge base construction*, pages 31–36. ACM, 2013.

[12] B. Dalvi, W. W. Cohen, and J. Callan. Exploratory learning. In *Machine Learning and Knowledge Discovery in Databases*, pages 128–143. Springer, 2013.

[13] B. Dalvi, E. Minkov, P. P. Talukdar, and W. W. Cohen. Automatic gloss finding for a knowledge base using ontological constraints. In *Proceedings of the Eighth ACM International Conference on Web Search and Data Mining*, WSDM '15, pages 369–378, New York, NY, USA, 2015. ACM.

[14] N. Friedman. The bayesian structural em algorithm. In *Proceedings of the Fourteenth conference on Uncertainty in artificial intelligence*, pages 129–138. Morgan Kaufmann Publishers Inc., 1998.

[15] Z. Ghahramani, M. I. Jordan, and R. P. Adams. Tree-structured stick breaking for hierarchical data. In *Advances in Neural Information Processing Systems*, pages 19–27, 2010.

[16] S. Gopal, Y. Yang, B. Bai, and A. Niculescu-Mizil. Bayesian models for large-scale hierarchical classification. In *Advances in Neural Information Processing Systems*, pages 2411–2419, 2012.

[17] C. D. Manning, P. Raghavan, and H. Schtze. Introduction to information retrieval. In *Cambridge University Press*, 2008.

[18] T. Mikolov, I. Sutskever, K. Chen, G. S. Corrado, and J. Dean. Distributed representations of words and phrases and their compositionality. In *Advances in Neural Information Processing Systems*, pages 3111–3119, 2013.

[19] T. P. Mohamed, E. R. Hruschka, Jr., and T. M. Mitchell. Discovering relations between noun categories. In *Proceedings of the Conference on Empirical Methods in Natural Language Processing*, EMNLP '11, pages 1447–1455, Stroudsburg, PA, USA, 2011. Association for Computational Linguistics.

[20] A. Pal, N. Dalvi, and K. Bellare. Discovering hierarchical structure for sources and entities. In *Twenty-Seventh AAAI Conference on Artificial Intelligence*, 2013.

[21] J. Reisinger and M. Paşca. Latent variable models of concept-attribute attachment. In *Proceedings of the Joint Conference of the 47th Annual Meeting of the ACL and the 4th International Joint Conference on Natural Language Processing of the AFNLP: Volume 2-Volume 2*, pages 620–628. Association for Computational Linguistics, 2009.

[22] R. Snow, D. Jurafsky, and A. Y. Ng. Semantic taxonomy induction from heterogenous evidence. In *Proceedings of the 21st International Conference on Computational Linguistics and the 44th annual meeting of the Association for Computational Linguistics*, pages 801–808. Association for Computational Linguistics, 2006.

[23] P. Willett. Recent trends in hierarchic document clustering: a critical review. *Information Processing & Management*, 24(5):577–597, 1988.

[24] L. Xiao, D. Zhou, and M. Wu. Hierarchical classification via orthogonal transfer. In *Proceedings of the 28th international conference on machine learning (ICML-11)*, pages 801–808, 2011.

Is Mail The Next Frontier In Search And Data Mining?

Yoelle Maarek
Yahoo Labs
MATAM Park, Haifa 31905, Israel
yoelle@ymail.com

1. ABSTRACT

The nature of Web mail traffic has significantly evolved in the last two decades, and consequently the behavior of Web mail users has also changed. For instance a recent study conducted by Yahoo Labs showed that today 90% of Web mail traffic is machine-generated [1] This partly explains why email traffic continues to grow even if a significant amount of personal communications has moved towards social media. Most users today are receiving in their inbox important invoices, receipts, and travel itineraries, together with non-malicious junk mail such as hotel newsletters or shopping promotions that could safely ignore. This is one of the reasons that a majority of messages remain unread, and many are deleted without being read [3]. In that sense, Web mail has become quite similar to traditional snail mail. In spite of this drastic change in nature, many mail features remain unchanged. While 70% of mail users do not define even a single folder [5], folders are still predominant in the left trail of many Web mail clients. Mail search results are still mostly ranked by date [2], which makes the retrieving of older messages extremely challenging. This is even more painful to users, as unlike in Web search, they will know when a relevant previously read message has not been returned.

In this talk, I present the results of multiple large-scale studies that have been conducted at Yahoo Labs in the last few years. I highlight the inherent challenges associated with such studies, especially around privacy concerns [4]. I will discuss the new nature of consumer Web mail, which is dominated by machine-generated messages of highly heterogeneous forms and value. I will show how the change has not been fully recognized yet by my most email clients. As an example, why should there still be a reply option associated with a message coming from a "do-not-reply@" address?. I will introduce some approaches for large-scale mail mining specifically tailored to machine-generated email. I will conclude by discussing possible applications and research directions.

WSDM 2016 February 22-25, 2016, San Francisco, CA, USA

ACM ISBN 978-1-4503-3716-8/16/02.
DOI: http://dx.doi.org/10.1145/2835776.2835847

2. BIOGRAPHY

Yoelle Maarek is VP Research at Yahoo heading the Yahoo Labs teams in Israel and UK, which conduct research around mail, search and native ads. Prior to this, Yoelle was the Director of Google Haifa Engineering Center, which she opened in 2006. There, she led the team that launched "Google Suggest". From 1989 to 2006, Yoelle was with IBM Research, first in the US, and then in Israel. She received her PhD in Computer Science from the Technion, in Haifa, Israel. She graduated from the Ecole Nationale des Ponts et Chaussées in Paris, France, and received a graduate degree in Computer Science from Paris VI University, both in 1985. Yoelle currently serves as Vice Chair of the SIGIR Executive committee and is an elected member of IW3C2. She became an ACM Fellow in 2013.

3. ACKNOWLEDGEMENTS

A huge thanks to all my fellow researchers at Yahoo Labs and to our incredible mail engineering partners at Yahoo without whom none of this work could have been conducted. And of course we are grateful to the hundreds of millions of Yahoo mail users, whose behavior we have extensively studied, without infringing their privacy.

4. REFERENCES

[1] N. Ailon, Z. Karnin, E. Liberty, and Y. Maarek. Threading machine generated email. In *Proceedings of WSDM'2013*, New York, NY, USA, 2013.

[2] David Carmel, Guy Halawi, Liane Lewin-Eytan, Yoelle Maarek, and Ariel Raviv. Rank by time of by relevance? revisiting email search. In *Proceedings of CIKM'2015*, November 2015.

[3] Dotan DiCastro, Liane Lewin-Eytan, Yoelle Maarek, and Zohar Karnin. You've got mail, and here is what you could do with it! analyzing and predicting actions on email messages. In *Proceedings of WSDM'2016*, San-Francisco, CA, Feb 2016.

[4] Dotan DiCastro, Liane Lewin-Eytan, Yoelle Maarek, Ran Wolff, and Eyal Zohar. Enforcing k-anonymity in web mail auditing. In *Proceedings of WSDM'2016*, San-Francisco, CA, Feb 2016.

[5] Y. Koren, E. Liberty, Y. Maarek, and R. Sandler. Automatically tagging email by leveraging other users' folders. In *Proceedings of KDD'2011*, San Diego, CA, Aug 2011.

Portrait of an Online Shopper: Understanding and Predicting Consumer Behavior

Farshad Kooti, Kristina Lerman
USC Information Sciences Institute
Marina del Rey, CA
{kooti, lerman}@isi.edu

Luca Maria Aiello
Yahoo Labs
London, UK
alucca@yahoo-inc.com

Mihajlo Grbovic, Nemanja Djuric, Vladan Radosavljevic
Yahoo Labs
Sunnyvale, CA
{mihajlo, nemanja, vladan}@yahoo-inc.com

ABSTRACT

Consumer spending accounts for a large fraction of economic footprint of modern countries. Increasingly, consumer activity is moving to the web, where digital receipts of online purchases provide valuable data sources detailing consumer behavior. We consider such data extracted from emails and combined with with consumers' demographic information, which we use to characterize, model, and predict purchasing behavior. We analyze such behavior of consumers in different age and gender groups, and find interesting, actionable patterns that can be used to improve ad targeting systems. For example, we found that the amount of money spent on online purchases grows sharply with age, peaking in the late 30s, while shoppers from wealthy areas tend to purchase more expensive items and buy them more frequently. Furthermore, we look at the influence of social connections on purchasing habits, as well as at the temporal dynamics of online shopping where we discovered daily and weekly behavioral patterns. Finally, we build a model to predict when shoppers are most likely to make a purchase and how much will they spend, showing improvement over baseline approaches. The presented results paint a clear picture of a modern online shopper, and allow better understanding of consumer behavior that can help improve marketing efforts and make shopping more pleasant and efficient experience for online customers.

Categories and Subject Descriptors

H.4.3 [**Information Systems**]: Information systems applications

Keywords

Online shopping, demographics, prediction

1. INTRODUCTION

Consumer spending is an integral component of economic activity. In 2013, it accounted for 71% of the US gross domestic product (GDP)[1], a measure often used to quantify economic output and general prosperity of a country. Given its importance, many studies focused on understanding and characterizing consumer behavior. Researchers examined gender differences and motivations in shopping [10, 22], as well as spending patterns across urban areas [37].

In recent years, shopping has increasingly transitioned from in-store to an online experience. Consumers use internet to research product features, compare prices, and then purchase products from online merchants, such as Amazon or Walmart. Moreover, platforms like eBay allow people to directly sell products to one another. While there exist concerns about the risks and security of online shopping [7, 32, 42], large numbers of people, especially younger and wealthier [23, 39], choose online shopping even when similar products can be purchased offline [15]. The new habits of customers have had a tremendous economic impact on online market, with an estimated $1,471 billion dollars spent by 191 million shoppers in 2014 in the United States alone[2].

Most of the online purchases result in a confirmation or shipment email sent to the shopper by the merchant. These emails provide a rich source of evidence to study online consumer behavior across different shopping websites. Unlike previous studies [31], which were based on surveys and thus limited to relatively small populations, we used large-scale email data to perform an in-depth study of online shopping. More specifically, we extracted online receipts from 20.1M Yahoo Mail users, amounting to 121 million purchases worth 5.1B dollars. The extracted information included names of purchased products, their prices, and purchase timestamps. We used email user profile to link this information to demographic and geolocation data, such as gender, age, and zip code. This information enabled us to characterize patterns of online shopping activity and their dependence on demographic and socio-economic factors. We found that, for example, men on average make more purchases and spend more money on online purchases. Moreover, online shopping appears to be widely adopted by all ages and economic classes, although shoppers from high-income areas buy more expensive products than less wealthy shoppers.

Looking at temporal factors affecting online shopping, we found patterns common to other online activities as well [26]. Not surprisingly, online shopping has daily and weekly cycles showing that people fit online shopping routines into their everyday life. Furthermore, purchasing decisions appear to be correlated. The more expensive a previous purchase was, the longer the shopper has to wait until the next purchase. This can be explained by the fact that

[1]https://research.stlouisfed.org/fred2/series/PCE/
[2]http://www.statista.com/topics/871/online-shopping/

WSDM'16, February 22–25, 2016, San Francisco, CA, USA.
© 2016 ACM. ISBN 978-1-4503-3716-8/16/02...$15.00
DOI: http://dx.doi.org/10.1145/2835776.2835831

most shoppers have a finite budget and need to wait longer between purchases to buy more expensive items.

In addition to temporal and demographic factors, social networks are believed to play an important role in shaping consumer behavior (e.g., by spreading information about products through the word-of-mouth [33]). Previous studies examined how consumers use their online social networks to gather product information and recommendations [19, 20], although the direct effect of recommendations on purchases was found to be weak [27]. In addition, people who are socially connected are generally more similar to one another than unconnected people [29], and hence are more likely to be interested in similar products. Our analysis confirmed that shoppers who are socially connected and e-mail each other tend to purchase more similar products than unconnected shoppers.

Once we understand the factors affecting consumer behavior, we can use this knowledge to predict future purchases. Given users' purchase history and demographic data, we address a problem of predicting the time and price of their next purchase. Our method attains a relative improvement of 108.7% over the random baseline for predicting the price of the next purchase, and 36.4% relative improvement over the random baseline for predicting the time of the next purchase. Interestingly, demographic features were shown to be the least useful in these prediction tasks, while temporal features carried the most discriminative information.

The contributions of the paper are summarized below:

- In-depth analysis of a unique and very rich data set describing consumer behavior, extracted from purchase confirmations merchants send to shoppers (Section 2);
- A quantitative analysis of an impact of demographic, temporal, and social factors on consumer behavior (Section 3);
- Prediction of consumer behavior, where we predict the time of the next purchase and how much money will be spent (Section 4).

Better understanding of consumer behavior can benefit both consumers and advertisers. Knowing when consumers are ready to make a purchase and how much they are willing to spend can improve the effectiveness of advertising campaigns, in terms of optimizing ad impressions and budget spend. Understanding these patterns can also make online shopping experience more efficient for consumers. Considering that consumer spending presents such a large portion of the economy, even a small efficiency gain can have significant impact on the overall economic activity.

2. DATA SET

Most online purchases result in a confirmation email being sent by the merchant to the shopper. These emails provide a unique opportunity to study the shopping behavior of people across different online retail stores, such as Amazon, eBay, or Walmart.

Yahoo Mail is one of the world's largest email providers with more than 300M users[3], and many online shoppers use this email service for receiving purchase confirmations. We selected these emails by using a precompiled list of email addresses of popular merchants. Applying a set of manually specified extraction rules to the email body, we extracted the list of purchased *item names* and the *price* of each item. In case of multiple items purchased in a single order, we considered them as individual purchases occurring at the same time. Therefore, throughout the paper the expression "purchase" will refer to a purchase of a single item. In order to be able to analyze purchases by category (e.g., electronics, books,

[3]**http://www.comscore.com/**

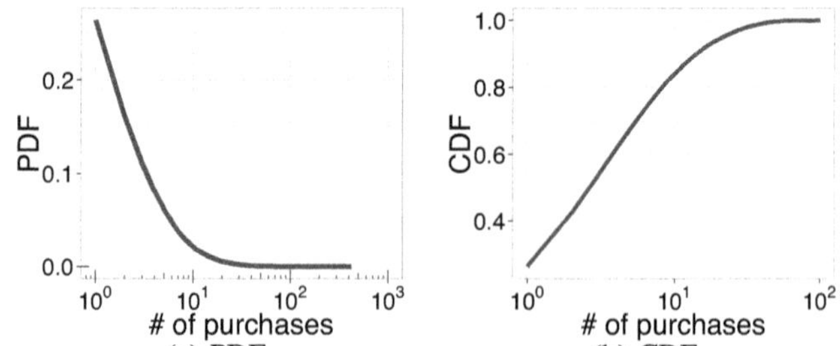

(a) PDF (b) CDF

Figure 1: Distribution of number of purchases made by users

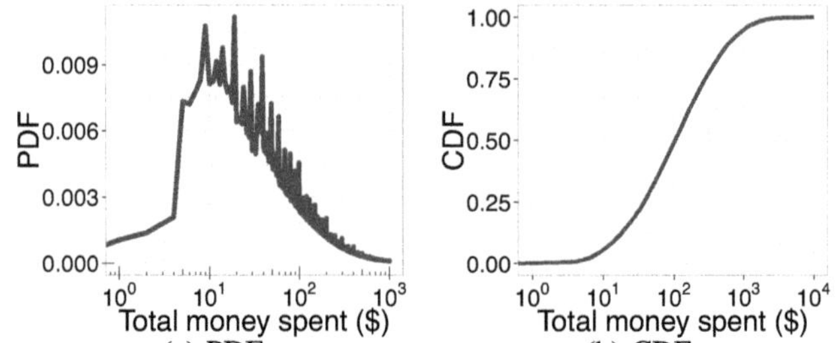

(a) PDF (b) CDF

Figure 2: Distribution of total money spent by users

handbags), we developed a categorization module based on the purchased item names. Specifically, an item name was used as an input to a classifier that predicts the *item category*. We used a three levels deep, 1,733 node Pricegrabber taxonomy[4] to categorize the items. The details of categorization are beyond the scope of this paper.

We limited our study to a random subset of Yahoo Mail users in the US. Our data set contains information on 20.1M users, who collectively made 121M purchases from several top retailers between February and September 2014, amounting to total spending of 5.1B dollars. For each user we extracted *age*, *gender*, and *zip code* information from the Yahoo user database. We excluded users who made more than 1,000 purchases (amounting to less than 0.01% of the sample), as these accounts are likely to belong to stores and not individual users. The analysis of the data set was performed in aggregate and on anonymized data.

In order to examine social aspects of the shopping behavior, we used the Yahoo email network data set in addition to the data set of purchases. The email network can be represented as a directed graph $\mathcal{G}$, with edges denoted by (i, j, N_{ij}) signifying that user i sent N_{ij} emails to user j. For our analysis we retained only edges with a minimum of 5 exchanged messages, and considered only a subgraph $\mathcal{C}$ of $\mathcal{G}$ induced by the two-hop neighborhood of the users who made purchases (i.e., their immediate contacts and contacts of their contacts). The subgraph $\mathcal{C}$ was used to construct a list of 1st-level contacts and 2nd-level contacts for each online shopper.

Let us take a closer look at the data set characteristics. In Figure 1(a) we show the distribution of number of purchases per user, which reveals the expected heavy-tailed characteristic. Figure 1(b) shows that only 5% of the users made more than 20 purchases. In contrast, the distribution of total money spent per user peaks at around 10 dollars, sharply decreasing for smaller amounts (Figure 2(a)). Also, there is a non-negligible minority of people who spend a substantial amount of money for online shopping, such as 5% of the users spent more than 1,000 dollars (Figure 2(b)).

Items being purchased also have drastically different levels of popularity, as shown by the distribution in Figure 3. Disney's Frozen

[4]**http://www.pricegrabber.com**

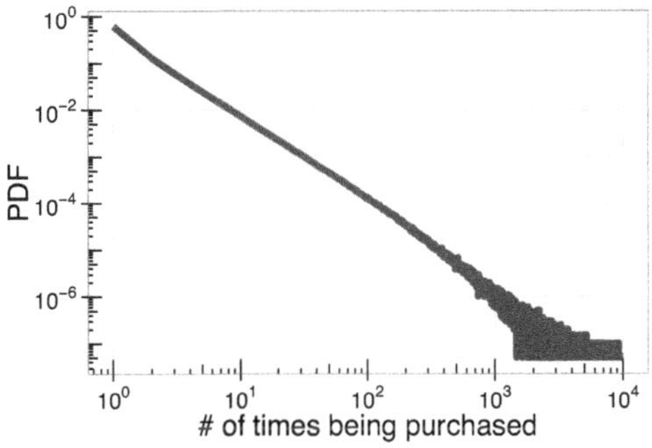

Figure 3: Number of times different items have been purchased

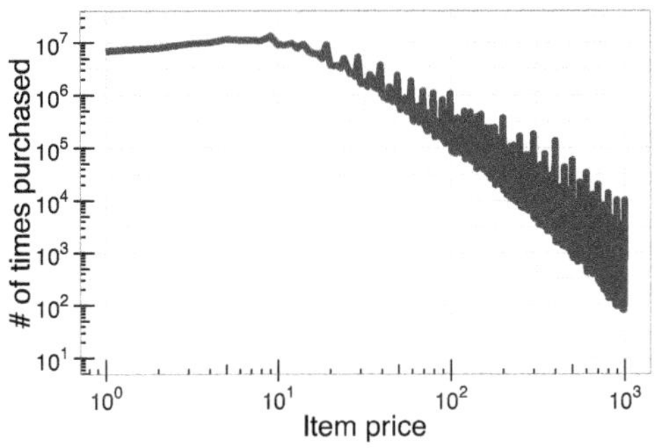

Figure 4: Number of item purchases as a function of price

Table 1: Top 5 most purchased products

Rank	Product name	# of purchases
1	Frozen (DVD)	202,103
2	Cards Against Humanity (Cards)	110,032
3	Google Chromecast	59,548
4	HDMI cable	54,402
5	Pampers	51,044

Table 2: Top 5 products with the most money spent on them

Rank	Product name	Money spent on product
1	Play Station 4	$ 7.0M
2	Frozen (DVD)	$ 3.8M
3	Kindle	$ 3.2M
4	Samsung Galaxy Tab	$ 2.7M
5	Cards Against Humanity	$ 2.5M

Table 3: Top product categories purchased by women and men

Rank	Top categories	Distinctive women	Distinctive men
1	Android	Books	Games
2	Accessories	Dresses	Flash memory
3	Books	Diapering	Light bulbs
4	Vitamins	Wallets	Accessories
5	Shirts	Bracelets	Batteries

DVD, the most popular item in the data set, has been purchased more than 200,000 times, whereas the vast majority of the items has been purchased less than 10 times. Table 1 lists the top 5 most frequently purchased items. Intuitively, the set of items that users have spent the most money on is a different set, because a single purchase of an expensive item would account for the same amount of money of several purchases of cheaper items (Table 2). In fact, the number of times an item is purchased negatively correlates with the price of that item (Figure 4). This is in line with previous survey-based studies [7] that found the vast majority of items purchased online are worth at most few tens of dollars.

3. PURCHASE PATTERN ANALYSIS

In this section we present a quantitative analysis of factors affecting online purchases. We examine the role of demographic, temporal, and social factors that include gender and age, daily and weekly patterns, frequency of shopping, tendency towards recurring purchases, and budget constraints.

3.1 Demographic Factors

Let us consider how gender, age, and location (i.e., zip code) affect purchasing behavior of customers. First, we measured fraction of all email users that made an online purchase. We found that higher fraction of women make online purchases compared to men (Figure 5(a)), albeit men make slightly more purchases (Figure 5(b)) and spend more money on average (Figure 5(c)). It is interesting that, as a result, men spend much more money in total (Figure 5(d)). The same patterns hold across different age groups. The presented results back up findings from earlier consumer surveys which revealed that man have a higher perceived advantage of online shopping [2], while women havie a higher concern for negative consequences of online purchasing [17], resulting in a higher number of purchases made by men.

With respect to the age, spending ability increases as people get older, peaking for the population between age 30 to 50 and then declining afterwards. The same pattern holds for number of purchases made, average item price, and total money spent (Figures 5(b), 5(d), 5(c)). Different generations also purchase different types of products online (Table 5). Younger shoppers (18-22 years old) purchase more phone accessories and games, whereas older shoppers (60-70 years old) are much more interested in buying TV shows. Also, blood sugar medicine is purchased more by the older users, which is expected.

Differences exist across genders as well. Table 3 shows the top five categories of purchased products for male and female customers. Even though the ranking of the top products is the same, each product accounts for different fraction of all purchases within the same gender. To find the most distinctive categories, we compare the fraction of all the items bought by both genders, and consider the categories that have the largest differences. Books, dresses, and diapering are the categories that were more disproportionately bought by women, whereas games, flash memory sticks, and accessories (e.g., headphones) are the categories purchased more by men. The largest differences range from only 0.5% to 1%, but are statistically significant. This result is aligned with previous research on offline shopping that found men more keen in buying electronics and entertainment products, while women more inclined to buy clothes [11, 22]. We repeated the same gender analysis at a product level (Table 4). Consistently, there is a high overlap between most purchased products.

In the following, we measure the impact of economic factors on online shopping behavior. We use the US census data to retrieve median income associated with each zip code, making an inferred income for a user an aggregated estimate. Nevertheless, given the large size of this data set this coarse approach was enough to observe clear trends. The number of purchases, average product

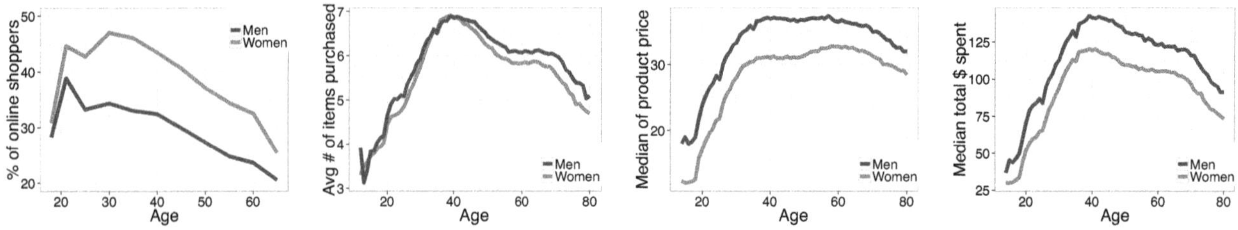

(a) Percentage of online shoppers (b) Number of purchases (c) Average price (d) Total money spent

Figure 5: Demographic analysis broken down by age: (a) Percentage of online shoppers; (b) number of items purchased; (c) average price of products purchased; and (d) total spent by men and women

Table 4: Top products purchased by women and men

Rank	Top women	Top men	Distinctive women	Distinctive men
1	Frozen	Frozen	Frozen	Chromecast
2	iPhone screen protector	Game of Thrones	iPhone screen protector	Game of Thrones
3	Cards Against Humanity	Chromecast	iPhone screen protector	Titanfall Xbox One
4	iPhone screen protector (another brand)	Cards Against Humanity	iPhone case	Playstation 4
5	Game of Thrones	iPhone screen protector	iPhone case	Godfather collection

Table 5: Differences in the products purchased by younger (18-22 yo) and older (60-70 yo) users

Rank	Top younger users	Top older users	Distinctive younger users	Distinctive older users
1	iPhone screen protector	Frozen	iPhone screen protector	Frozen
2	iPhone screen protector	Game of Thrones	iPhone screen protector (another brand)	Game of Thrones
3	Cards Against Humanity	Chromecast	Cards Against Humanity	Downton Abbey
4	iPhone case	Downton Abbey	iPhone case	Blood sugar medicine
5	Frozen	Hunger Games	iPhone case	TurboTax Package

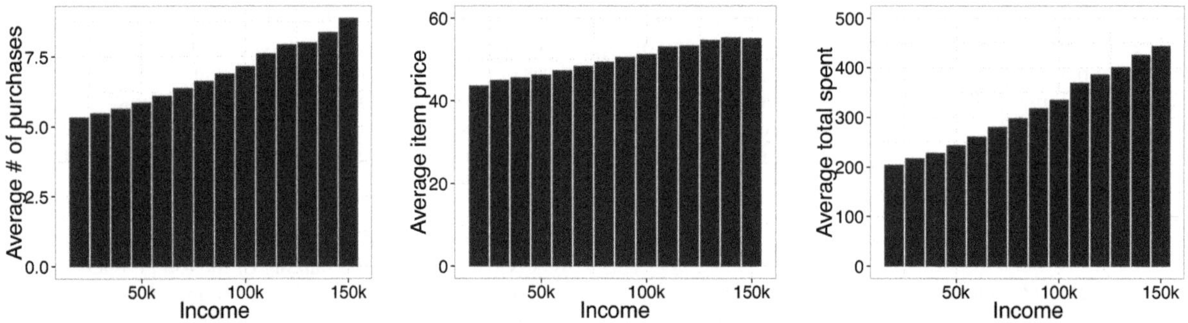

(a) Number of purchases (b) Average item price (c) Total money spent

Figure 6: Effect of income on purchasing behavior

price, and total money spent are all positively correlated with income (Figures 6(a), 6(b), and 6(c) respectively). While users living in high-income zip codes do not buy substantially more expensive products, they do make more purchases, spending more money in total than users from lower-income zip codes. Although the factors that lead to lower-income households spending less online are multiple and complex, part of this effect can be explained by the reluctance of people who are concerned with their financial safety to trust and make full use of online shopping, as pointed out by previous studies [23].

3.2 Temporal Factors

Our data set spans a period of eight months, giving us opportunity to investigate temporal dynamics of purchasing behavior and factors affecting it. Besides daily and weekly cycles and periodic purchasing, we observed temporal variations that we associate with financial depletion: users wait longer to buy more expensive items, waiting for the budget to recover from the previous purchases.

3.2.1 Daily and Weekly Cycles

Figure 7 shows the daily number of purchases over a period of two months. The figure indicates a clear weekly shopping pattern with more purchases taking place in the first days of the week and fewer purchases on the weekends. On average there are 32.6% more purchases on Mondays than Sundays. There also exists strong diurnal patterns in shopping behavior (Figure 8). Interestingly, most of the purchases occur during the working hours (i.e., in the morning and early afternoon). Note that for this analysis we in-

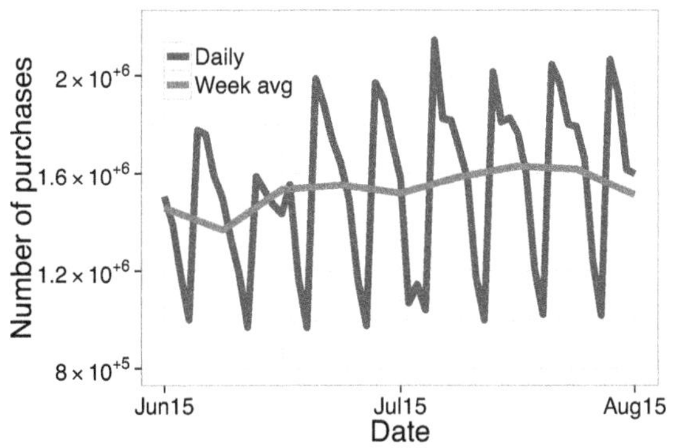

Figure 7: Number of purchases in a day and average weekly

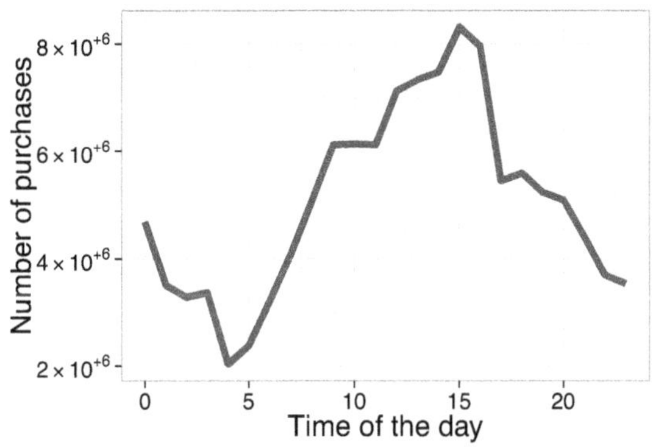

Figure 8: Number of purchases in each hour of the day

Table 6: Top 5 items with the most number of repurchases

Rank	Item name	Median purchase delay
1	Pampers 448 count	42
2	Bath tissue	62
3	Pampers 162 count	30
4	Pampers 152 count	31
5	Frozen	12

ferred the time zone from the user's zip code, which might be different from a shipping zip code for a purchase.

Researchers have also reported monthly effects, where people spend more money at the beginning of the month when they receive their paychecks, compared to the end of the month [14]. To test the *first-of-the-month* phenomenon, we compared spending in the first Monday of the month with the last Monday of the month. We considered the first and the last Mondays and not the first and the last days, because the strong weekly patterns would result in an unfair comparison if the first and the last day of the month are not the same day of the week. Our data does not support the earlier findings and there are months in which the last Monday of the month includes more activity compared to the first Monday of the month.

3.2.2 *Recurring Purchases*

Some products are purchased periodically, such as printer cartridges, water filters, or toilet paper. Finding these items and their typical cycle would help predicting purchasing behavior. We do this by counting the number of times each item has been purchased by each user, then from each user's count we eliminate those products purchased only once, and lastly we aggregate the number of

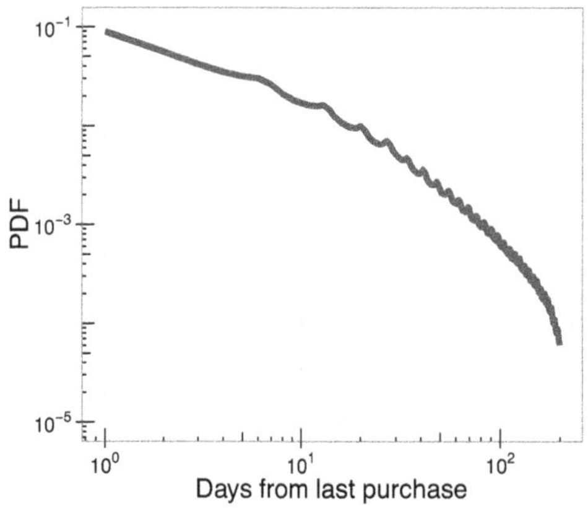

Figure 9: Distribution of number of days between purchases

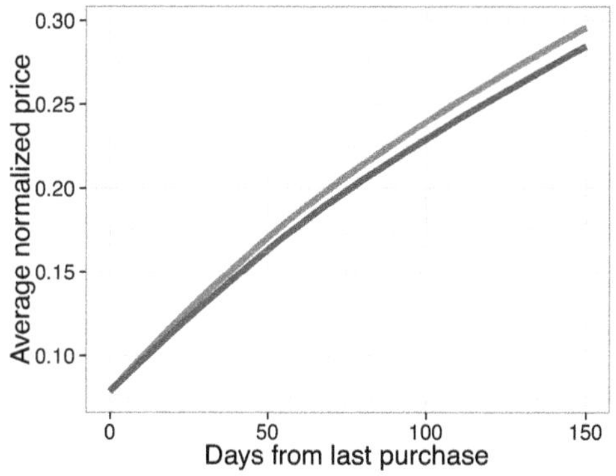

Figure 10: Relationship between purchase price and time to next purchase (0.95 confidence interval are shown yet too small to be observed)

purchases per each item. Table 6 shows the top five such products, along with the median number of days between purchases. Out of the top 20 products only four are neither toilet paper nor tissue (Frozen, Amazon gift card, chocolate chip cookie dough, and single serve coffees). In the top 20 list, the only unexpected item is the Frozen DVD, which probably made the list due to users buying additional copies as gifts or due to purchases by small stores that were not eliminated by our removal criterion of maximum 1,000 purchases. Interestingly, the number of days between purchases for most of the top 20 items is close to 1 or 2 months, which might be due to automatic purchasing that users can set up.

3.2.3 *Finite Budget Effects*

Finally, we study the dynamics of individual purchasing behavior. Figure 9 shows the distribution of number of days between purchases. The distribution is heavy-tailed, indicating bursty dynamics. The most likely time between purchases is one day and there are local maxima around multiples of 7 days, consistent with weekly cycles we observed.

An individual's purchasing decisions are not independent, but constrained by their finances. Budgetary constraints introduce temporal dependencies between purchases made by the user: After buying a product, the user has to wait some time to accumulate money to make another purchase. Previous work in economics studied models of budget allocation of households across different types of goods to maximize an utility function [13] and analyzed

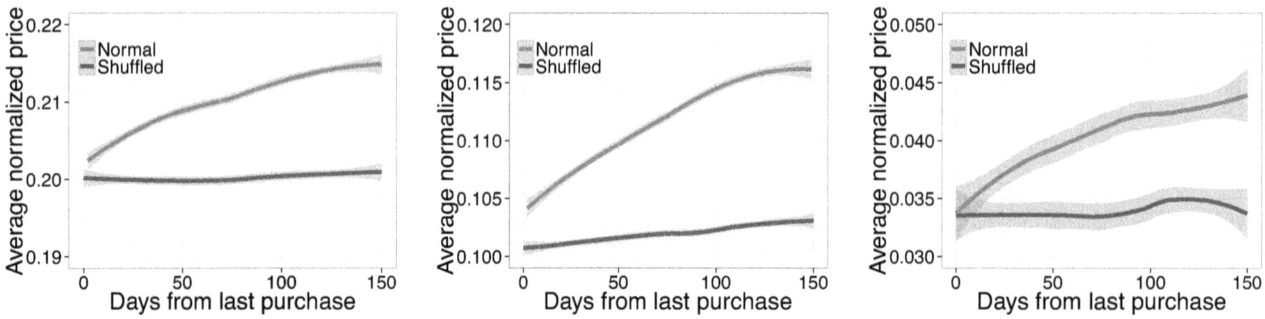

(a) Users with 5 purchases (b) Users with 9-11 purchases (c) Users with 28-32 purchases

Figure 11: Relationship between purchase price and time to next purchase with 0.95 confidence interval

conditions under which people are willing to break their budget cap [8]. However, we are not aware of any study aimed to support the hypothesis of the time of purchase being partly driven by an underlying cyclic process of budget depletion and replenishment.

To test this hypothesis, we examined the relationship between purchase price and the time period since last purchase. Since different users have different spending power, we considered the normalized change in the price given the number of days from the last purchase. In other words, we computed how users divide their personal spending across different purchases, given the time delay between purchases. We then averaged the normalized values for all users, and report the change for each time delay. Figure 10 shows that as the time delay gets longer, users spend higher fraction of their budgets, which supports our hypothesis. To test that our analysis does not have any bias in the way the users are grouped, we perform a shuffle test by randomly swapping the prices of products purchased by users. This destroys the correlation between the time delay and product price. We then do the same analysis with the shuffled data and expect to see a flat line. However, the same increase also exists in the shuffled data, indicating a bias in the methodology. This is due to the heterogeneity of the underlying population: we are mixing users with different number of purchases. Users making more purchases have lower normalized prices and also shorter time delays, and are systematically overrepresented in the left side of the plot, even in the shuffled data.

To partially account for heterogeneity, we grouped users by the number of purchases (i.e., those who made exactly 5 purchases, those with 9-11 purchases, and 28-32 purchases). Even within each group there is variation as the total spending differs significantly across users, which we address by normalizing the product price by the total amount of money spent by the user, as explained above. If our hypothesis is correct, there should be a refractory period after a purchase, with users waiting longer to make a larger purchase. We clearly observe a positive relationship between (normalized) purchase price and the time (in days) since last purchase (Figure 11), but not in the shuffled data, which produces a horizontal line. We conclude that the relationship between time delay and purchase price arises due to behavioral factors, stemming from the limited budget of customers.

3.3 Social Factors

An individual's behavior is often correlated with that of his or her social contacts (or friends). In online shopping, this would result in users purchasing products that are similar to those purchased by their friends. Distinct social mechanisms give rise to this correlation [5]. First, a friend could influence the user to buy the same product by highly recommending it. This is the basis for social contagions in general, and "word-of-mouth" marketing in particular, although empirical evidence suggests that influence has a limited effect on shopping behavior [27]. Alternatively, users could have bought the same product as their friends purchased, because people tend to be similar to their friends, and therefore, have similar needs. The tendency of socially connected individuals to be similar is called homophily, and it is a strong organizing principle of social networks. Studies have found that people tend to interact with others who belong to a similar socio-economic class [16, 29] or share similar interests [25, 4]. Finally, a user's and their friend's behavior may be spuriously correlated because both depend on some other external factor, such as geographic proximity. In reality, all these effects are interconnected [9, 3] and are difficult to disentangle from observational data [35]. For example, homophily often results in selective exposure that may amplify social influence and word-of-mouth effects.

We investigate whether social correlations exist, although we do not resolve the source of the correlation. Specifically, we study whether users who are connected to each other via email interactions tend to purchase similar products in contrast to users who are not connected. To measure similarity of purchases between two users, we first describe the purchases made by each user with a vector of products, each entry containing the frequency of purchase. This approach results in large and sparse vectors due to the large number of unique products in our data set. To address this challenge, we use vectors of product categories, instead of product names. There are three levels of product categories, and we perform our experiments at all levels.

We compare similarity of category vectors of pairs of users who are directly connected in the email network (104K pairs of users) with the same number of pairs of randomly chosen users (who are not directly connected). We use cosine similarity to measure similarity of two vectors. Using top-level categories to describe user purchases gives average similarity of 0.420 between connected pairs of users, whereas random pairs have similarity of 0.377 on average (+11% relative change as compared to connected pairs). Using the more detailed level-2 categories to describe purchases gives average similarity of 0.215 for connected versus 0.170 for random pairs of users (+26% relative increase). Finally using the most detailed, level 3, categories results in average similarity of 0.188 for connected vs. 0.145 for random pairs of users (+30% relative increase). Although the absolute similarity decreases as a more detailed product vector is used, shoppers who communicate by email are always more similar than random shoppers who are not directly connected.

Gender also plays an important role when measuring purchase similarity between user pairs. To quantify this effect, we calculate the cosine similarity between the vectors of number of purchases from the detailed category (level 3), and take the average of the cosine similarity. Instead of taking the average for all the connected pairs, we separate the pairs based on the gender of the users in the pair: woman-woman, man-man, and woman-man. The woman-woman pairs have the highest average cosine similarity with 0.192, next followed by man-man pairs with average similarity of 0.186. Heterogeneous pairs are the least similar ones, with average cosine similarity of 0.182. The similarity measures are still greater than measures for random pairs of users, which have similarity of 0.145. Woman-man pair having the smallest similarity primarily supports our earlier finding about a sensible difference in the type of goods that attract interests of the two genders. Previous work also found that receiving a shopping recommendation from a friend will have a greater positive effect on willingness to purchase online among women than among men [17]. The highest similarity of female-female pairs might be partly explained by that effect.

4. PREDICTING PURCHASES

Predicting the behavior of online shoppers can help e-commerce sites to improve the shopping experience by the means of personalized recommendations on one hand, and on the other to better meet merchants' needs by delivering targeted advertisements. In a recent study, Grbovic et al. addressed the problem of predicting the next item a user is going to purchase using a variety of features [50]. In this work, we consider the complementary problems of predicting *i)* the *time* of the next purchase, and *ii)* the *amount* that will be spent on that purchase.

Predicting the exact time and price of a purchase (e.g., using regression) is a hard problem, therefore we focused on the simpler classification task of predicting the class of the purchase among a finite number of predefined price or time intervals. We experimented with different classification algorithms and Bayesian Network Classification yielded the highest accuracy. To estimate the conditional probability distributions we used direct estimates of the conditional probability with $\alpha = 0.5$. The classifier was trained on the first six months of purchase data and evaluated on the last two. From each entry we extracted 55 features belonging to a variety of categories:

- *Demographics of online shoppers* (4 features): Gender, age, location (zip code), and income (based on zip code).
- *Purchase price history* (19 features): Price of the last three purchases, price category of the last three purchases, number of purchases, mean price of purchased item, median price of purchased items, total amount of money spent, standard deviation in item prices, number of earlier purchases in each price group (5 groups), price group with the most number of purchases and the count for it, and total number of purchases until that point.
- *Purchase time history* (13 features): Time of last three purchases, mean time between purchases, median time between purchased, standard deviation in times between purchases, number of earlier purchases in each time group, and time group with the most number of purchases and the count for it.
- *Purchase history of products* (4): Last three categories of products purchased, most purchased category.
- *Time or price of the next purchase* (1 feature): We also assume that we know when the next purchase is going to happen. This seems unrealistic at first, but we include this feature because the system is going to make recommendations at a given time, and we assume that the shopper is going to make the decision at that time. For having a symmetrical problem we also consider the price of the next purchase, which would be similar as knowing the budget of the user.
- *Contacts* (14 features): Mean, median, standard deviation, minimum, maximum, and 10th and 90th percentile of price and time of the purchases of the contacts of the users.

Table 7: Top predictive features for prediction of the price of the next item and their χ^2 values

Rank	Feature	χ^2 value
1	Most used class earlier	214,996
2	Number of under $6 purchases	115,560
3	Median price of earlier purchases	106,876
4	Mean price of earlier purchases	91,409
5	Number of over $40 purchases	84,743

For the aggregated features such as average price of item purchased, we used only purchases in the training period and did not consider future information. To evaluate the proposed approach, we compared results of our classifier to three baselines:

- Random prediction;
- Price or purchase delay of the previous purchase;
- Most popular price or purchase delay of the purchases a target user made in the past.

4.1 Price of the Next Purchase

We partition prices in five classes using $6, $12, $20, and $40 as price thresholds to obtain equally-sized partitions. These thresholds represent (a) very cheap products that cost less than $6 (20.7% of the data); (b) cheap products between $6 and $12 (20.3%); (c) medium-priced products between $12 and $20 (19.3%); (d) expensive products that cost more than $20, but less than $40 (19.9%); and finally (e) very expensive products worth more than $40 (19.8%). Our classifier achieves an accuracy of 43.2% with a +108.7% relative improvement over the 20.7% accuracy of the random classifier (i.e., relative size of the largest class).

A category of the last purchase and the most frequent purchase category turn out to be quite strong predictors, achieving accuracy of 29.3% and 29.8% by themselves, respectively. The supervised approach outperforms them with a +47.4% and +45.0% relative improvement, respectively. When measuring the predictive power of the features with the χ^2 statistics (Table 7) we find that the highest predictive power is the most frequent class of earlier purchases, by far. This suggests that users tend to buy mostly items in the same price bracket. The second feature in the ranking is the number of purchases from the very cheap category, followed by median and mean of earlier prices. In general, all the top 16 most informative features are related to the price of earlier purchases. After those, median time between purchases and time delay before the last purchase are the most predictive features. The relatively high position of the last time delay in the feature rank suggests that the recommender system should consider the time that has passed from the last purchase of the user, and change the suggestions dynamically. In other words, if the user has made a purchase recently, cheaper products should be favored over more expensive products to the user, whereas if a long period of time has passed since the last purchase, more expensive products should be advertised to the user, as they are more likely to be purchased. All of the demographics features have limited predictive power and are ranked last (though the demographics might affect the purchase history), with income being the most important among them.

Table 8: Top predictive features for prediction of time of next purchase and their χ^2 values

Rank	Feature	χ^2 value
1	Number of earlier purchases	48,719
2	Median time between purchases	35,558
3	Time since the first purchase	30,741
4	Previous time delay	30,692
5	Class of previous time delay	22,710

4.2 Time of the Next Purchase

Similarly to purchase price, prediction of purchase time could be leveraged to make a better use of the advertisement space. If the user is likely not to purchase anything for a certain period of time, ads can be momentarily suspended or replaced with ads that are not related to consumer goods.

For creating the categories, we choose thresholds of 1, 5, 14, and 33 days. Very short delays are within a day (22.8% of our data), short delays between 1 and 5 days (20.9%), medium delays between 5 and 14 (19.6%), long delays between 14 and 33 (18.2%) and the very long delays exceed 33 days (18.5%). Training a Bayesian Network on all the features yields an accuracy of 31.1%, a +36.4% relative improvement over the 22.8% accuracy of the random prediction baseline. The accuracy of our classifier is also +24.9% relatively higher than the baseline of predicting as the last purchase delay, which has accuracy of 24.9%. Finally, the most occurred purchase has an accuracy of 22.2%, which is outperformed by our classifier by +40.1% relatively.

Ranking features by their χ^2 (Table 8), we find that the most informative feature is the number of earlier purchases that the user has made so far, followed by median time delay, previous purchase delay, time since the first purchase, and the class of the previous purchase delay.

To summarize, we trained two classifiers for predicting the price and the time of the next purchase. Our algorithm outperformed the baselines in both prediction tasks, by a higher margin in case of predicting the price. Table 9 summarizes all of our results showing a relative improvement of 108.7% for predicting the price of the next item purchased and 36.4% for predicting the time of the next purchase over the majority vote baseline. Interestingly, user demographics were not particularly helpful for making any prediction, and the observed correlations in earlier sections of the paper are masked by other features such as the history of prior purchases.

5. RELATED WORK

Most of previous research on shopping behavior and characterization of shoppers has been conducted through interviews and questionnaires administered to groups of volunteers composed by at most few hundred members.

Offline shopping in physical stores has been studied in terms of the role of demographic factors on the attitude towards shopping. The customer's gender predicts to some extent the type of purchased goods, with men shopping more for groceries and electronics, while women more for clothing [11, 22]. Gender is also a discriminant factor with respect to the attitude towards financial practices, financial stress, and credit, and it can be a quite good predictor of spending [22]. Many shoppers express the need of alternating the experience of online and offline shopping [46, 41], and it has been found that there is an engagement spiral between online and offline shopping: searching for products online positively affects the frequency of shopping trips, which in its turn positively influences buying online [15].

Online shopping has been investigated since the early stages of the Web. Many studies tried to draw the profile of the typical online shopper. Online shoppers are younger, wealthier, more educated than the average Internet user. In addition, they tend to be computer literate and to live in the urban areas [47, 39, 40, 15]. Their trust of e-commerce sites and their understanding of the security risks associated with online payments positively correlate with their household income and education level [23, 24], and it tends to be stronger in males [17]. The perception of risk of online transactions influences shoppers to purchase small, cheap items rather than expensive objects [7]. Customers of online stores tend to value the convenience of online shopping in terms of ease of use, usefulness, enjoyment, and saving of time and effort [32]. Their shopping experience is deeply influenced by their personal traits (e.g., previous online shopping experiences, trust in online shopping) as well as other exogenous factors such as situational factors or product characteristics [32].

Demographic factors can influence the shopping behavior and the perception of the shopping experience online. Men value the practical advantages of online shopping more and consider a detailed product description and fair pricing significantly more important than women do. In contrast, some surveys have found that women, despite the ease of use of e-commerce sites, dislike more than men the lack of a physical experience of the shop and value more the visibility of wide selections of items rather than accurate product specifications [45, 2, 43, 24]. Unlike gender, the effect of age on the purchase behavior seems to be minor, with older people searching less for online items to buy but not exhibiting lower purchase frequency [38]. With extensive evidence from a large-scale dataset we find that age greatly impacts the amount of money spent online and the number of items purchased.

The role of the social network is also a crucial factor that steers customer behavior during online shopping. Often, social media is used to communicate purchase intents, which can be automatically detected with text analysis [20]. Also, social ties allow for the propagation of information about effective shopping practices, such as finding the most convenient store to buy from [19] or recommending what to buy next [27]. Survey-based studies have found that shopping recommendations can increase the willingness of buying among women rather than men [17].

Factors leading to purchases in offline stores have been extensively investigated as they have direct consequences on the revenue potential of retailers and advertisers. Survey-based studies attempted to isolate the factors that lead a customer to buy an item or, in other words, to understand what the strongest predictors of a purchase are. Although the mere amount of online activity of a customer can predict to some extent the occurrence of a future purchase [6], multifaceted predictive models have been proposed in the past. Features related to the phase of information gathering (access to search features, prior trust of the website) and to the purchase potential (monetary resources, product value) can often predict whether a given item will be purchased or not [21, 31].

Prediction of purchases in online shopping is a task that has been addressed through data-driven studies, mostly on click and activity logs. User purchase history is extensively used by e-commerce websites to recommend relevant products to their users [28]. Features derived from user events collected by publishers and shopping sites are often used in predicting the user's propensity to click or purchase [12]. For example, clickstream data have been used to predict the next purchased item [44, 34]; click models predict online buying by linking the purchase decision to what users are exposed to while on the site and what actions they perform while on the site [30, 36]. Besides user click and purchase events, one can

Table 9: **Summary of the prediction results. Accuracy: percentage of correctly classified samples. Majority vote: always predicting the largest group, or predicting randomly. Most used: the group the user had the most in earlier purchases. AUC: Weighted average of Area Under the Curve for classes. RMSE: Root Mean Square Error. The improvements are reported over the majority vote.**

Prediction	Majority vote (random classifier)	Last used	Most used	Our classifier	Absolute improvement	Relative improvement	AUC	RMSE
Item price	20.7%	29.3%	29.8%	43.2%	22.5%	108.7%	0.676	0.3806
Purchase time	22.8%	24.9%	22.2%	31.1%	8.3%	36.4%	0.634	0.4272

leverage product reviews and ratings to find relationships between different products [49]. Email is also a valuable source of information to analyze and predict user shopping behavior [50]. Click and browsing features represent only a weak proxy of user's purchase intent, while email purchase receipts convey a much stronger intent signal that can enable advertisers to reach their audience. The value of commercial email data has been recently explored for the task of clustering commercial domains [18]. Signals to predict purchases can be strengthened by demographic features [1]. Also, information extracted from customers' profiles in social media, in combination with the information of their social circles, can help with predicting the product category that will be purchased next [48].

6. CONCLUSION

Studying the online consumer behavior as recorded by email traces allows to overcome the limitations of previous studies that focused either on small-scale surveys or on purchases' logs from individual vendors. In this work, we provide the first very large scale analysis of user shopping profiles across several vendors and over a long time span. We measured the effect of age and gender, finding that the spending ability goes up with age till the age of 30, stabilizes in the early 60s, and then starts dropping afterwards. Regarding the gender, a female email user is more likely to be an online shopper than an average male email user. On the other hand, men make more purchases, buy more expensive products on average, and spend more money. Younger users tend to buy more phone accessories compared to older users, whereas older users buy TV shows and vitamins & supplements more frequently. Using the user location, we show clear correlation between income and the number of purchases users make, average price of products purchased, and total money spent. Moreover, we study the cyclic behavior of users, finding weekly patters where purchases are more likely to occur early in the week and much less frequently in the weekends. Also, most of the purchases happen during the work hours, morning till early afternoon.

We complement the purchase activity with the network of email communication between users. Using the network, we test if users that communicate with each other have more similar purchases compared to a random set of users, and we find indeed that is the case. We also consider gender of the users and find that woman-woman pairs are more similar than man-man pairs that are also more similar to each other than the woman-man pairs. Finally, we use our findings to build a classifier to predict the price and the time of the next purchase. Our classifier outperforms the baselines, especially for the prediction of the price of the next purchase. This classifier can be used to make better recommendations to the users.

Our study comes with a few limitations. First, we can only capture purchases for which a confirmation email has been delivered. We believe this is the case for most of online purchases nowadays. Second, if users use different email addresses for their purchases, we would not have their full purchase history. Similarly, people can share a purchasing account to enjoy some benefits (e.g., an Amazon Prime account between multiple people). However, as suggested by the fact that less than 0.01% of the users have goods shipped to more than one zip-code, that occurs rarely in our data set. Third, the social network that we considered, albeit big, is not complete. However, the network is large enough to observe statistically significant results. Lastly, we considered the items that were purchased together as separate purchases; it would be interesting to see which items are usually bought together in the same transaction.

Acknowledgements

This work was supported in part by AFOSR under contract FA9550-10-1-0569, and by DARPA under contract W911NF-12-1-0034.

7. REFERENCES

[1] Combination of multiple classifiers for the customer's purchase behavior prediction. *Decision Support Systems*, 34(2):167 – 175, 2003.

[2] Understanding gender-based differences in consumer e-commerce adoption. *Commun. Association for Information Systems*, 26, 2005.

[3] L. M. Aiello, A. Barrat, C. Cattuto, G. Ruffo, and R. Schifanella. Link creation and profile alignment in the aNobii social network. In *SocialCom*, 2010.

[4] L. M. Aiello, A. Barrat, R. Schifanella, C. Cattuto, B. Markines, and F. Menczer. Friendship prediction and homophily in social media. *ACM Trans. Web*, 6(2):9:1–9:33, Jun 2012.

[5] A. Anagnostopoulos, R. Kumar, and M. Mahdian. Influence and correlation in social networks. In *KDD*, pp. 7–15, 2008.

[6] S. Bellman, G. L. Lohse, and E. J. Johnson. Predictors of online buying behavior. *Commun. ACM*, 42(12):32–38, 1999.

[7] A. Bhatnagar, S. Misra, and H. R. Rao. On risk, convenience, and internet shopping behavior. *Commun. ACM*, 43(11):98–105, Nov. 2000.

[8] J.-S. Chiou and C.-C. Ting. Will you spend more money and time on internet shopping when the product and situation are right? *Computers in Human Behavior*, 27(1):203 – 208, 2011.

[9] D. Crandall, D. Cosley, D. Huttenlocher, J. Kleinberg, and S. Suri. Feedback effects between similarity and social influence in online communities. In *KDD'08*, pp. 160–168, 2008.

[10] R. R. Dholakia. Going shopping: key determinants of shopping behaviors and motivations. *Int. J. Retail & Distribution Management*, 27(4):154–165, 1999.

[11] R. R. Dholakia. Going shopping: key determinants of shopping behaviors and motivations. *Int. J. Retail and Distribution Management*, 27:154–165, 1999.

[12] N. Djuric, V. Radosavljevic, M. Grbovic, and N. Bhamidipati. Hidden conditional random fields with deep user embeddings for ad targeting. In *ICDM*, pp. 779–784, 2014.

[13] R. Y. Du and W. A. Kamakura. Where did all that money go?

understanding how consumers allocate their consumption budget. *J. Marketing*, 72(6):109–131, 2008.

[14] W. N. Evans and T. J. Moore. Liquidity, economic activity, and mortality. *Review of Economics and Statistics*, 94(2):400–418, Jan. 2011.

[15] S. Farag, T. Schwanen, M. Dijst, and J. Faber. Shopping online and/or in-store? a structural equation model of the relationships between e-shopping and in-store shopping. *Transportation Research Part A: Policy and Practice*, 41(2):125–141, 2007.

[16] S. L. Feld. The focused organization of social ties. *The American Journal of Sociology*, 86(5):1015–1035, 1981.

[17] E. Garbarino and M. Strahilevitz. Gender differences in the perceived risk of buying online and the effects of receiving a site recommendation. *J. Business Research*, 57(7):768 – 775, 2004.

[18] M. Grbovic and S. Vucetic. Generating ad targeting rules using sparse principal component analysis with constraints. In *WWW Companion*, pp. 283–284, 2014.

[19] S. Guo, M. Wang, and J. Leskovec. The role of social networks in online shopping: Information passing, price of trust, and consumer choice. In *EC*, pp. 157–166, 2011.

[20] V. Gupta, D. Varshney, H. Jhamtani, D. Kedia, and S. Karwa. Identifying purchase intent from social posts. In *ICWSM*, 2014.

[21] T. Hansen, J. Moller Jensen, and H. Stubbe Solgaard. Predicting online grocery buying intention: a comparison of the theory of reasoned action and the theory of planned behavior. *Int. J. Information Management*, 24(6):539–550, 2004.

[22] C. R. Hayhoe, L. J. Leach, P. R. Turner, M. J. Bruin, and F. C. Lawrence. Differences in spending habits and credit use of college students. *J. Consumer Affairs*, 34(1):113–133, 2000.

[23] J. A. Horrigan. Online shopping. *Pew Internet & American Life Project Report*, 36, 2008.

[24] T.-K. Hui and D. Wan. Factors affecting internet shopping behaviour in singapore: gender and educational issues. *Int. J. Consumer Studies*, 31(3):310–316, 2007.

[25] J.-H. Kang and K. Lerman. Using lists to measure homophily on twitter. In *AAAI workshop on Intelligent Techniques for Web Personalization and Recommendation*, July 2012.

[26] F. Kooti, L. M. Aiello, M. Grbovic, K. Lerman, and A. Mantrach. Evolution of conversations in the age of email overload. In *WWW*, pp. 603–613, 2015.

[27] J. Leskovec, L. A. Adamic, and B. A. Huberman. The dynamics of viral marketing. *ACM Trans. Web*, 1(1), May 2007.

[28] G. Linden, B. Smith, and J. York. Amazon.com recommendations: Item-to-item collaborative filtering. *IEEE Internet Computing*, 7(1):76–80, Jan. 2003.

[29] M. McPherson, L. Smith-Lovin, and J. M. Cook. Birds of a feather: Homophily in social networks. *Annual Review of Sociology*, 27(1):415–444, 2001.

[30] A. L. Montgomery, S. Li, K. Srinivasan, and J. C. Liechty. Predicting online purchase conversion using web path analysis. Technical report, 2002.

[31] P. A. Pavlou and M. Fygenson. Understanding and predicting electronic commerce adoption: An extension of the theory of planned behavior. *MIS quarterly*, pp. 115–143, 2006.

[32] T. Perea y Monsuwé, B. G. Dellaert, and K. De Ruyter. What drives consumers to shop online? a literature review. *Int. J. Service Industry Management*, 15(1):102–121, 2004.

[33] T. Rodrigues, F. Benevenuto, M. Cha, K. Gummadi, and V. Almeida. On word-of-mouth based discovery of the web. In *IMC*, pp. 381–396, 2011.

[34] S. Senecal, P. J. Kalczynski, and J. Nantel. Consumers' decision-making process and their online shopping behavior: a clickstream analysis. *J. Business Research*, 58(11):1599–1608, 2005.

[35] C. R. Shalizi and A. C. Thomas. Homophily and contagion are generically confounded in observational social network studies. *Sociological Methods and Research*, 40(2):211–239, 2011.

[36] C. Sismeiro and R. E. Bucklin. Modeling purchase behavior at an e-commerce web site: A task-completion approach. *J. Marketing Research*, 41(3):306–323, 2004.

[37] S. Sobolevsky, I. Sitko, R. Tachet des Combes, B. Hawelka, J. Murillo Arias, and C. Ratti. Cities through the prism of people's spending behavior. *arXiv*, 2015.

[38] P. Sorce, V. Perotti, and S. Widrick. Attitude and age differences in online buying. *Int. J. Retail & Distribution Management*, 33(2):122–132, 2005.

[39] W. R. Swinyard and S. M. Smith. Why people (don't) shop online: A lifestyle study of the internet consumer. *Psychology & Marketing*, 20(7):567, 2003.

[40] W. R. Swinyard and S. M. Smith. Activities, interests, and opinions of online shoppers and non-shoppers. *International Business and Economics Research Journal*, 3(4):37–48, 2011.

[41] M. Tabatabaei. Online shopping perceptions of offline shoppers. *Issues in Information Systems*, 10(2):22–26, 2009.

[42] T. S. Teo. Attitudes toward online shopping and the internet. *Behaviour & Information Technology*, 21(4):259–271, 2002.

[43] F. Ulbrich, T. Christensen, and L. Stankus. Gender-specific on-line shopping preferences. *Electronic Commerce Research*, 11(2):181–199, 2011.

[44] D. Van den Poel and W. Buckinx. Predicting online-purchasing behaviour. *European Journal of Operational Research*, 166(2):557 – 575, 2005.

[45] C. Van Slyke, C. L. Comunale, and F. Belanger. Gender differences in perceptions of web-based shopping. *Commun. ACM*, 45(8):82–86, Aug. 2002.

[46] M. Wolfinbarger and M. C. Gilly. Shopping online for freedom, control, and fun. *California Management Review*, 43(2):34–55, 2001.

[47] M. Zaman and M. Y. W. Meng. Internet shopping adoption: A comparative study on city and regional consumers. In *ANZMAC*, pp. 2421–2428. Deakin University, 2002.

[48] Y. Zhang and M. Pennacchiotti. Predicting purchase behaviors from social media. In *WWW*, pp. 1521–1532, 2013.

[49] J. McAuley, R. Pandey, J. Leskovec. Inferring networks of substitutable and complementary products. In *ACM SIGKDD*, pp. 785–794, 2015.

[50] M. Grbovic, V. Radosavljevic, N. Djuric, N. Bhamidipati, J. Savla, V. Bhagwan, and D. Sharp E-commerce in Your Inbox: Product Recommendations at Scale. In *ACM SIGKDD*, pp. 1809–1818, 2015.

Evolution of Privacy Loss in Wikipedia

Marian-Andrei Rizoiu*
NICTA, ANU

Lexing Xie
ANU, NICTA
Canberra, Australia

Tiberio Caetano
Ambiata, ANU, UNSW
Sydney, Australia

Manuel Cebrian
NICTA
Melbourne, Australia

ABSTRACT

The cumulative effect of collective online participation has an important and adverse impact on individual privacy. As an online system evolves over time, new digital traces of individual behavior may uncover previously hidden statistical links between an individual's past actions and her private traits. To quantify this effect, we analyze the evolution of individual privacy loss by studying the edit history of Wikipedia over 13 years, including more than 117,523 different users performing 188,805,088 edits. We trace each Wikipedia's contributor using apparently harmless features, such as the number of edits performed on predefined broad categories in a given time period (*e.g.* Mathematics, Culture or Nature). We show that even at this unspecific level of behavior description, it is possible to use off-the-shelf machine learning algorithms to uncover usually undisclosed personal traits, such as gender, religion or education. We provide empirical evidence that the prediction accuracy for almost all private traits consistently improves over time. Surprisingly, the prediction performance for users who stopped editing after a given time still improves. The activities performed by new users seem to have contributed more to this effect than additional activities from existing (but still active) users. Insights from this work should help users, system designers, and policy makers understand and make long-term design choices in online content creation systems.

Keywords online privacy, de-anonymization, temporal loss of privacy.

1. INTRODUCTION

Privacy is a relatively new concern of modern society [14]. Historically, compromising one's privacy was a difficult task, being mainly achieved by using constant physical surveillance, costly by nature, and easy to thwart. The advent of the online environment has changed the privacy landscape: users of social network, blogging, microblogging platforms willingly or unwillingly share information with the public and with organizations. The general public are already aware [4, 16] that information inadvertently left online can hurt privacy, and researchers showed that [12] personal attributes can be predicted from these online behavioral traces. However, the longitudinal change of privacy loss is not well understood – namely, how information collected over several years can compromise privacy, and how the predictability of private attributes evolve. In this paper, we set out to answer such challenging questions by curating a novel large-scale behavioral trace dataset, and by measuring the predictability of personal traits in a number of ways.

We construct a new dataset from all editing activities in and around Wikipedia – the largest encyclopedia to date collaboratively constructed by hundreds of thousands of users. We use as input each user aggregated editing activities in a number of broadly defined content and community categories, and the target output are personal traits from Wikipedia *badges*, i.e., what users choose to disclose on their personal pages. This problem and system setting allows us to make several key observations: (1) We show that Wikipedia editors' private traits can be inferred using off-the-shelf machine learning algorithms, and that the prediction performance consistently improves over our prediction period from 2007 to 2013. In particular, our results include predicting an individual's gender, educational status and religious views. Among the different personal attributes, a subset of showed high prediction accuracy as measured by the equal-precision-recall metric – namely, the editors' gender at 0.79, practicing muslim religion at 0.9 or being jewish at 0.91. (2) We quantify the effect of different features using a temporal measure called information transfer. We observe that while the marginal utility of newer features decreases over time, the new users consistently add additional information for the prediction tasks. (3) We show that the prediction of private attributes continues to improve for users who exited the system – or stopped editing after 2007. The continued loss of privacy for these users seems to be associated with two quantifiable factors: the information learned from a user's own activity (or *online breadcrumbs*) and the activity of other editors.

To the best of our knowledge, this is the first work to quantify longitudinal change in privacy loss, carried out on a large dataset and over more than 13 years. Not only do we show that private traits can be predicted increasingly well with time, we also provide several methods to quantify the value of new information over time, and the different source of information loss - from more activity or more users. Our

*Corresponding author: marian-andrei@rizoiu.eu

WSDM'16, February 22–25, 2016, San Francisco, CA, USA.

ACM ISBN 978-1-4503-3716-8/16/02..
DOI: http://dx.doi.org/10.1145/2835776.2835798

findings suggest privacy continues to erode for all users, even after one stops publishing data online. Our findings also can help design data storage and retention policies, can make users aware of the implications of seemingly harmless online activities, and adds to the very lively research topic about online privacy.

2. RELATED WORK

The value of privacy. Social scientists have been interested in how individuals perceive and values their privacy. Acquisiti et al. [2] revealed that the perceived value of privacy, while not entirely arbitrary, is highly malleable. For example, there is a large gap between the amount of money that individuals would accept to disclose private information and the amount of money they would pay to protect it. Furthermore, certain categories seem particularly vulnerable to the online privacy issue. Young adults have been shown [5] to be as worried about their privacy as older adults, especially in what concerns giving personal information to businesses, having photos of them uploaded to the internet or the legislation protecting privacy. On the contrary, Hoofnagle et al. [10] found that young adults tend to expose themselves more, especially on popular social networks, because they are less aware of the risks, less informed about the protection given by law and more prone to social peer pressure. Our work can contribute to the public understanding of privacy risks, by studying on public open data and with quantifiable outcomes.

Privacy Loss and inferring private traits. One definition of Personal Identifiable Information (PII) is private information relating to a person, which can be deductively identified, based on the person's public profile [19]. This is a source of concern particularly in the context of the Open Data effort of governments, in which anonymous datasets are released publicly, after removing private attributes such as name and contact information. The literature shows many applications in which private information, which was never intended to be publicly released, can be inferred from apparently harmless data. In one notorious example, the medical condition of an American politician was inferred starting from anonymized medical records released to the public [23]. Researchers found that de-anonymization can be carried out in large-scale. The 2011 IJCNN Social Network Challenge was won by de-anonymizing the identity of the Flikr users, including those in the test set [18]. More recently, De Montjoye et al. [7] showed that only four spatio-temporal points are enough to identify 95% of individual trajectories using mobile carrier's antenna information, while the same group [17] show that 90% of individuals can be re-identified using their credit card transactions trajectory.

Another salient source of private informations are patterns of online behavior. Kosinski, Stillwell and Graepel showed [12] how private traits like gender, sexual orientation, ethnic origin and even the fact that a user's parents have divorced before her twenty-first birthday can be accurately inferred from apparently harmless, naturally revealed public data, such as Facebook likes. In another data domain, the pattern of an individual's online or phone activity have been shown [21] to reveal precious information about her habits and preferences. Furthermore, computer-based evaluations of human personality have been shown more accurate than those of close friends [27].

We show that private information can be extracted not only from structured anonymized datasets (such as [23]) or datasets rich in social information (such as [12, 21]), but even from data traces left for the public good, such as Wikipedia. Ramachandran and Chaintreau [20] recently studies how the structure of locally connected individuals affects privacy loss. Our focus is in the time dimension – in quantifying the temporal evolution of privacy loss.

Editing behavior in Wikipedia. Wikipedia is the largest online collaborative encyclopedia. In its early years, Wikipedia showed rapid growth. Initial studies [3] explained the growth as driven by the rapidly increasing user base. The growth of the English Wikipedia slowed after 2007, with fewer new editors joining, and fewer new articles created. A few studies [8, 22] explain this dynamic as Wikipedia editors face increasingly limited opportunities to make novel contributions, with the *easy* articles already been created, leaving only more difficult topics to write about. To make useful contributions to the site, editors must also meet an increasingly high bar of expertise in their field. In addition, Halfaker and McNeil [9] consider that Wikipedia's mechanisms for managing quality and consistency deterred newcomers.

In our profile of Wikipedia's growth and decline (Sect. 5), we were surprised to see that the changes of activity over time are not uniform across content and personal demographic attributes. There is a rise in site maintenance, and some user groups showed slower decline (*PhD*), or even a rise (self-identified *muslism* users) in editing activities. Finally, while social interactions in Wikipedia have been studied before [6, 26], to the best of our knowledge, this is the first study of private traits that can be inferred from editing activities.

3. WIKIPEDIA ACTIVITIES AND USER TRAITS

Why Wikipedia? Wikipedia is an ideal data source for studying longitudinal predictability of private traits, due to the following three reasons. Firstly, it is an apparently harmless dataset, whose purpose is to be a reservoir of knowledge, with little or no focus on personal or social information. Unlike online social networks centered on users' profiles, Wikipedia is not intended to record any individual contributor's personal and social interactions. Secondly, Wikipedia's entire edit history is publicly accessible. Wikipedia provides the longitudinal editing history for individuals, spanning over a decade – 2001–2013 at the time of our snapshot. Such a unique long temporal extent allows the study of the effect of time in online privacy. Finally, Wikipedia contributors are from many geographic locations and numerous social, religious, educational and political backgrounds – providing a rich and diverse sample for activities and candidate personal traits. We show that as Wikipedia accumulates user data and editing activity, increasing amounts of private information can be inferred (see Sect. 6).

The Wikipedia dataset. Our dataset contains 13 years of edit history, from the beginning of Wikipedia in January 2001 to July 2013. 188,805,088 revisions are performed by 117,523 editors to 22,172,813 pages. A revision is a Wikipedia term referring to an atomic edit of a page by a user with an associated timestamp. All data used in this study are obtained from July 2013 public Wikipedia dump, more details about data processing are in the supplemental material (SI) [1]. For predicting private traits (Sect. 4 and 6.1) we limit the studied period between 01/2007 and 07/2013 in order to have sufficient numbers of users.

Table 1: Features to describe user editing patterns. (A) The *basic* feature set quantifying the number of edits to all Wikipedia articles and various community and user pages. (B) additional features in the *extended* feature set, encoding edits to the thematic categories within Wikipedia CONTENT.

A.	Feature name	Wikipedia namespace codes	Feature description
Basic feature set	CONTENT	0, 6	Revisions made to the body of the Wikipedia articles. Corresponds to the actual creation of information.
	TALK-C	1, 7	Discussions on the talk pages of the Wikipedia articles. Corresponds to the overhead around the creation of encyclopeadic information.
	USER	2	Revisions made to user pages, including a user's own page or another user's page. Similar to profile edits and posts in online social networks.
	TALK-U	3	Revisions on the talk page corresponding to user pages. This is similar to social discussions, e.g., writing to a user's wall in a social network.
	WIKI	4, 5	Revisions on community pages, help desk, village pump, and related talk pages.
	INFRA	8, 9, 10, 11, 12, 13, 14, 15, 100, 101	Revisions on pages that provide infrastructure for other tasks in Wikipedia; template, categories and portals.

B.	***Extended* feature set: the 26 thematic features added to the *basic* set**
AGRICULTURE, APPLIED-SCIENCES, ARTS, BELIEF, BUSINESS, CHRONOLOGY, CULTURE, EDUCATION, ENVIRONMENT, GEOGRAPHY, HEALTH, HISTORY, HUMANITIES, LANGUAGE, LAW, LIFE, MATHEMATICS, NATURE, PEOPLE, POLITICS, SCIENCE, SOCIETY, TECHNOLOGY	

User activity profiles. We encode a user's activity using two sets of features. In the *basic* set, we count the number of revisions performed in a given period of time, over six predefined categories of the edited pages. The intuition behind these features is to capture the intent of a user's editing effort. For example, the CONTENT feature captures edits made to main Wikipedia articles and can be associated with the knowledge creation effort. Similarly, the WIKI and INFRA features quantify the effort put into organizing the editing effort (*i.e.*, community pages, help desks), while USER and TALK-U captures the social components, such as constructing a personal page and talking to other users. Features in the *basic* set are based on the Wikipedia namespaces and a summary of their respective meanings is in Table 1. Wikipedia namespaces are organizational categories, to encode the intended purpose of a page (details in SI [1]). The second set of features, *i.e.* the *extended* set, is constructed by adding to the *basic* set 26 new categories based on Wikipedia's top-level category hierarchy. A Wikipedia page can be assigned by its editors to one or more of the 26 thematic categories such as History, Geography, *etc.* The *extended* set provides a more detailed profiling of a users' activity, by capturing their editing interests. Details of feature construction are described in Sect. 4.

The editors' personal information. Many Wikipedia users keep a user page (resembling a social network profile), on which they distribute information about themselves, their interests or the causes they support. Some distribute information typically considered as private, such as their gender, ethnic origin, religion, education, or even sexual preferences. We retrieve these records using public APIs[1], and use them as target personal traits. For the purpose of this study, we selected three private traits with sufficient user bases: gender (declared by 6936 users), education (*undergrads*, *grads* and *Phd*, declared by 9224 users) and religion (*christian*, *muslim*, *atheist* or *jewish*, declared by 7685 users).

4. MEASURING PRIVACY LOSS

We study the loss of privacy by modeling it as a prediction problem: how well can we predict a given a class variable Y (*i.e.*, gender, education or religion) using descriptive features X in the *basic* or *extended* set. By following a set of users through time, we observe the dynamics of the predictive performance. We define the temporal loss of privacy as better explaining a variable linked to a private trait, as we observe editing behaviors for longer periods of time. In this work we use two sets of tools. The first is a predictive approach: we predict the private traits of a hold-out set of users on increasingly longer activity history on Wikipedia, and we observe the change in prediction accuracy. The second approach uses *information transfer*, a measure from physics and economics, to quantify the uncertainty in Y explained by feature X over time.

4.1 Encoding activities over time

We denote a feature X_i^u as computed in the timeframe i for user u, with $X \in \{$CONTENT, TALK-C, USER, TALK-U, WIKI, INFRA$\}$ for the *basic* set, and encoded similarly for the *extended* set. We construct a series of temporal datasets, each having a 3-month period in addition to the previous. A user appears in a temporal dataset if she/he has performed at least one revision during or before the last 3-months. We construct two kinds of features over time, the instantaneous features f_i^u for user u in the ith 3-month period alone, and the longitudinal feature $F_i^u = [f_{1:i}^u]$ for user u – containing the series up to (and including) timeframe i. Features are constructed by counting the number of revisions performed by u during the given timeframe, over the predefined categories, *e.g.*, f_i^u = (CONTENT$_i^u$, TALK-C$_i^u$, USER$_i^u$, TALK-U$_i^u$, WIKI$_i^u$, INFRA$_i^u$) for the *basic* set. Naturally, features F_i^u describe both the past and the current activities, and contain temporally increasing quantities of information. In addition, for newly joined editors, we explicitly encode the missing values in previous timeframes. This is done by including a binary missing feature flags for each activity category, a value of 0 means an editor has joined Wikipedia (even if she is on a pause during timeframe i), and 1 means the editor has not joined Wikipedia, i.e. missing. For the *basic* set, this results in additional six binary features, i.e., f_i^u = (CONTENT$_i^u$, p_C$_i^u$, TALK-C$_i^u$, p_TC$_i^u$, USER$_i^u$, p_U$_i^u$, TALK-U$_i^u$, p_TU$_i^u$, WIKI$_i^u$,

[1] https://www.mediawiki.org/wiki/API:Users

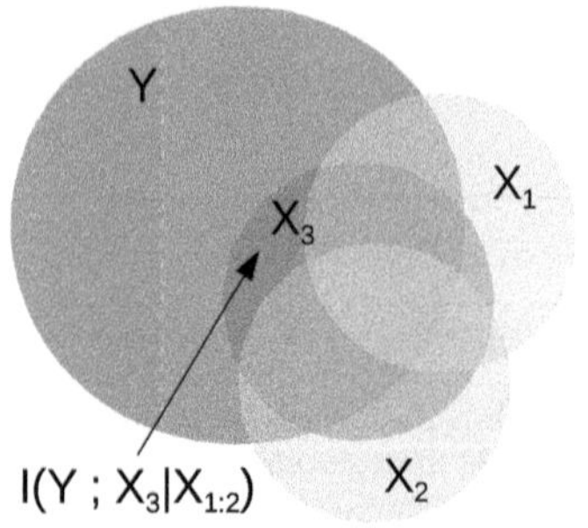

Figure 1: Venn diagram illustration of the Information Transfer measure between target variable Y and feature X, over three successive time points X_1, X_2 and X_3. Even if X_3 explains a large portion of the information in Y, most of Y was already explained by X_1 and X_2, and the new informationX_3 brings is given by the conditional mutual information $I(Y; X_3|X_{1:2})$.

$\texttt{p\_W}_i^u$, $\texttt{INFRA}_i^u$, $\texttt{p\_W}_i^u$), where features prefixed with `p_` are the missing flags of the preceding feature. For the *extended* set, additional features for the 26 categories are constructed in the same manner and appended to each f_i^u. We tried other schemes to encode user activity, such as cumulative features to encode activities from the beginning of until timeframe i, and found them to have lower performance. Therefore the rest of the paper presents only the incremental scheme.

4.2 Predicting personal attributes

We evaluate how well a private trait can be predicted by setting up a set of binary classification tasks. Multi-class target variables (*i.e.*, religion and education) are transformed to binary prediction tasks in a one-vs.-all fashion (*e.g.*, *christian* vs. non-*christian*). We use 2:1 stratified splits to construct the training and test user subsets – 66% of the editors are randomly selected to be part of the training set, and the remaining 33% are used for testing, with the random sampling preserving class priors. One model is learned for each class and each time period, using logistic regression classifier with L1 regularization that favors sparse feature weights, with the hyperparameter obtained by cross-validation [11]. We also tried the L2 regularizer and observed lower performances. The performance is evaluated using the AUC metric (the area under the ROC curve) [11], intuitively random guess classifiers have an AUC of 0.5, and perfect classification has 1.0. Accuracy and F-score for predicting each private trait are given in the SI [1]. We independently sample the train/test split 10 times, and record the mean and standard deviation of the AUC. While other classifiers can be used, we have not tried them in our experiments since our interest lies in the evolution of prediction performance and not its absolute value.

4.3 Information transfer over time

Information theory measures are useful for capturing feature relevance in prediction tasks [13]. One particular measure, Information Transfer, was recently used [24] to uncover hidden links in social media. Intuitively, we capture the uncertainty of private information with the entropy of the target variable Y. The quantity of private information explained by feature X is then given by the mutual information $I(Y; X)$. Since feature X takes different values for each 3-months timeframe, it is useful to quantify the additional information contained in time period X_t that were not already contained by earlier features $X_{1:t-1}$. The *Information Transfer* measure, $I(Y; X_t|X_{1:t-1})$, is designed for this purpose. Fig. 1 illustrated the intuition behind $I(Y; X_t|X_{1:t-1})$ using a Venn diagram. In this example, X_3 contains quite a lot of information about Y – expressed as the mutual information $I(Y; X_3)$, or the large intersection between red and blue circles. However, the *new* information that X_3 provides, in addition to $X_{1:2}$, is much smaller – expressed as $I(Y; X_3|X_{1:2})$, as $I(Y; X_3)$ minus the part already covered by $I(Y; X_1)$ and $I(Y; X_2)$. Intuitively, information transfer is the Conditional Mutual Information of Y and X_t given $X_{1:t-1}$, or the amount of uncertainty that will be reduced after observing X_t:

$$I(Y; X_t|X_{1:t-1}) = H(Y|X_{1:t-1}) - H(Y|X_{1:t}) \ .$$

The relationship above follows from the definition of mutual information and conditional entropy [13]. We implemented information transfer using the `infotheo` toolbox in R [15], which computes conditional entropies and in high-dimensional input spaces by quantizing the input. We use Information Transfer $I(Y; X_t|X_{1:t-1})$ and conditional entropies $H(Y|X_t)$ and $H(Y|X_{1:t})$ to answer two key questions: which features are most important in the disclosure of private information, and which time periods are critical to privacy loss.

5. EDITING BEHAVIOUR OVER TIME

In this section, we present a profile of wikipedia editing behaviour over time. While our profile concur with the slowdown of Wikipedia [8, 9, 22], our analysis detects the rise of maintenance effort and shows that different user groups contribute differently to various functional and topical sections of the encyclopedia.

The decline of editorship and rise of maintenance. It has been observed [8, 9, 22] that Wikipedia's growth slowed since 2007, with fewer new editors joining, and fewer new articles created. Our profiling shows the same phenomenon. Fig. 2 shows the number of active editors, new editors, and number of edits over time. A user is considered active in a time interval if she has submitted at least one revision in the given period. A user is considered a new users (or a newcomer) if she made her first revision in the given time interval. We can see that the slowdown started in 2007, with both the active population, and the total number of revisions decreasing steadily – as seen in the volume of `CONTENT` revisions in Fig. 2a, and revisions to the `Nature` section in Fig. 2b. We can also see that while the overall growth rate is slowing, the increasing amounts of accumulated information require an increasing effort to organize. Fig. 2c shows that the number of infrastructure-related revisions (`INFRA`) continues to increase, made by a decreasing number of users. To the best of our knowledge, this is the first work to detect and quantify this *rise of maintenance*.

Different growth trends across editor demographics. One explanation [8] for the slowdown of Wikipedia is that the easy articles have already been created. This means that in order to make a novel, useful contribution to the site, editors must meet an increasingly high bar of expertise in the field. Fig. 3a plots the active population size for users with a declared education level. The three curves corresponding to *undergrads*, *graduates* and *PhD* have been scaled in [0, 1] to

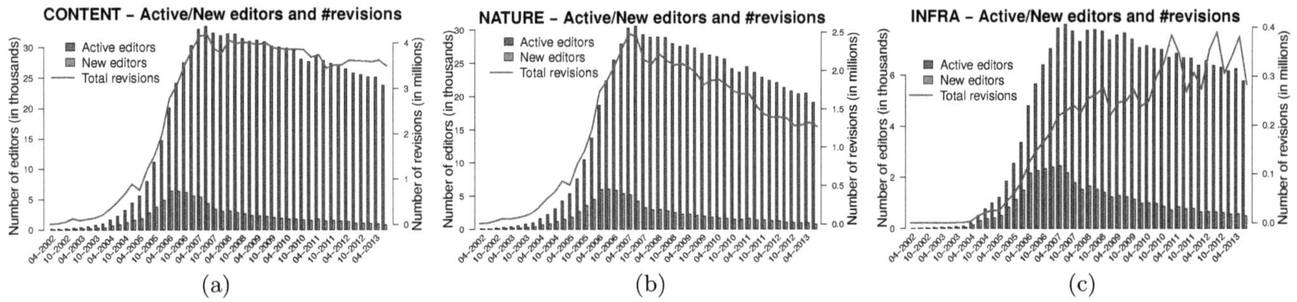

Figure 2: Wikipedia growth slowing down. (a) The decrease of the number of active editors, new editors and the total number of revisions for CONTENT (a) and thematic features (shown here NATURE, others in the SI [1]) (b). (c) The maintenance effort (INFRA revisions) needed to internally handle the bulk of Wikipedia is increasing.

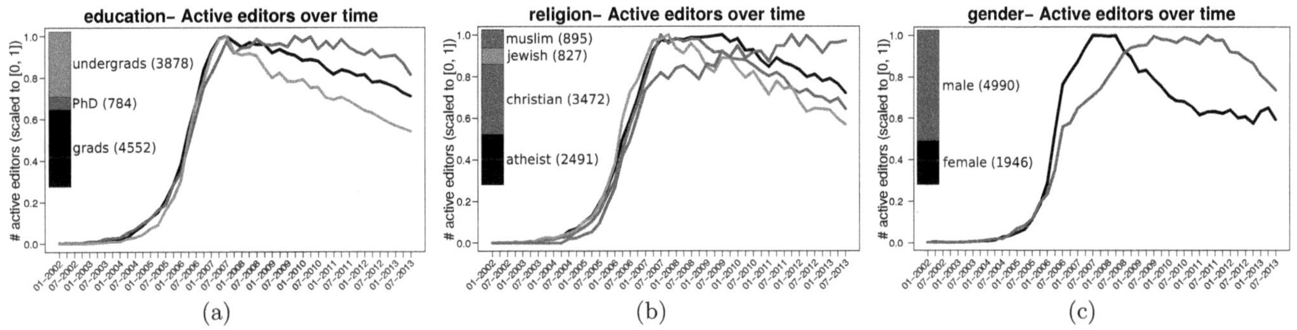

Figure 3: The population of active editors over time, broken down by (a) gender, (b) education and (c) religion. Magnitudes for all classes are scaled from 0 to 1. Barplots show the relative effectives of classes, absolute effectives are given in parenthesis.

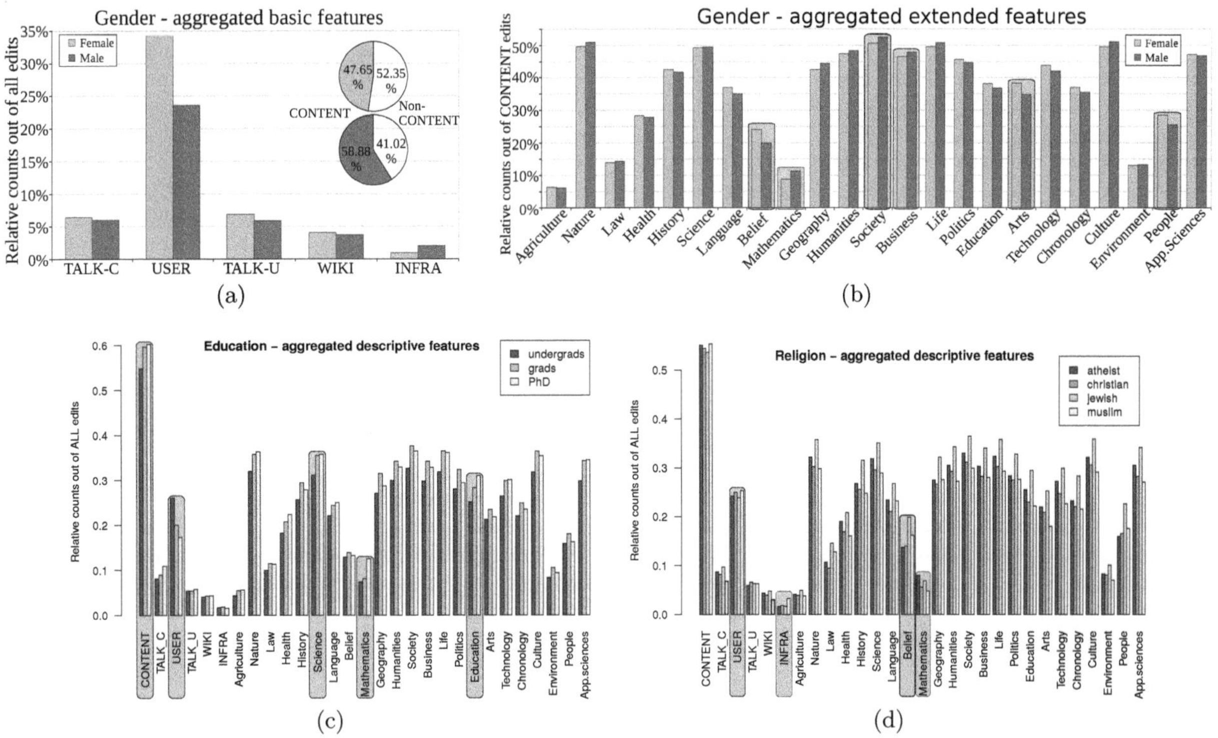

Figure 4: Aggregated descriptive features show differences in editing patterns, when tabulated per gender (a) and (b), education (c) and religion (d). Features were computed as percentages out of the total revision count Particularly interesting features (*i.e.*, features on which the separation is clearer or some patterns are inverted) are highlighted.

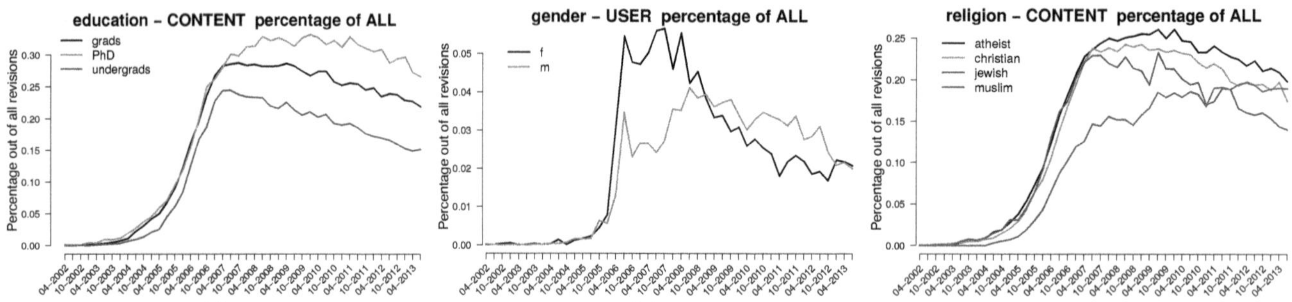

(a) (b) (c)

Figure 5: Temporal evolution of mean values of features, broken down by classes in each private trait. We present three selected examples of pairs (feature, trait), other graphics are in the SI [1]: (a) (`CONTENT`, education), (b) (`USER`, gender) and (c) (`CONTENT`, religion). All values are computed as the number of revisions on the given category during a timeframe and expressed as percentages of the total number of revisions. The mean value over all users is presented.

render them comparable. All three population show the expected initial rapid increase. The *undergrads* and *graduates* reach maximum at the same time as the general population The more specialized *PhD* population seems to peak much later, in early 2010, which seems to confirm the hypothesis that the required increase in the specialization of editors is one of the factors responsible for the slowdown of Wikipedia. We can also see differing demographic trends across different groups in editors' religion and gender. In Fig. 3b, the number of *christian, jewish* and *atheist* editors start to decrease around 2007. On the other hand, the self-declared *muslim* population seems to continuously increase, at a slower pace than during Wikipedia's initial growth 2001-2007. Fig. 3c plots the number of active editors by gender, we can see that the number of active female editors started decreasing earlier than that of male editors. While gender imbalance in Wikipedia has been previously studied [9], no other discussion of the evolution across time of gender, religion and education is present in prior literature.

Aggregated edit counts correlate with private traits. We describe a user's editing activity by aggregating her revision counts over a number of predefined categories. We conduct a exploratory analysis by presenting the averages of the features, with consideration for each of the private traits. Fig. 4a shows differences between the average male and female behavior: 59% of all the revisions performed by males are `CONTENT`, compared to 48% for females. Females tend to socially relate more, by writing more on `USER` pages (35% of all revisions for females, less than 25% for males). Similarly, Fig. 4b presents average male (highlighted in blue) and female (highlighted in red) behavior, over features in the *extended* set. Females edit more subjects like **`Agriculture`**, **`Health`**, **`History`**, **`Language`**, **`Belief`**, **`Arts`** and **`People`**, while males edit more **`Mathematics`**, **`Society`**, **`Business`**, **`Geography`** and **`Culture`**. While the absolute differences between average behavior on gender tend to be rather small, they indicate a separability of the two classes. We perform a similar analysis for education (Fig. 4c) and religion (Fig. 4d): *undergrads* create less `CONTENT` revisions and more `USER` revisions. *graduates* and *PhD* populations both dedicate a higher percentage of revisions to `CONTENT`. The *PhD* are more active on technical categories, such as **`Science`**, **`Mathematics`**, **`Education`**, **`Technology`**, **`Health`** and **`Applied Sciences`**, and the *graduates* edit more subjects like **`People`**, **`Environment`**, **`Culture`**, **`Society`** and **`Life`**. When aggregating per religion, Fig. 4d shows that the *jewish* editors are the most prolific in all thematic sections (the *extended* feature set), except **`Mathematics`**. *muslim* editors dedicate higher attention to **`Belief`**, **`Language`**, **`Law`** and **`INFRA`**, and lower attention to **`Arts`**, **`Education`** and **`Society`**. *Atheist* users dedicate more time editing **`Mathematics`**, **`Science`**, **`Nature`** and **`Culture`**, and less time to **`People`** and **`Law`**. This static analysis of mean behavior suggests that there are regularities in the editing patterns for each population. These could be exploited for training a classifier and predicting weather a new user belongs to any of these classes.

Evolution of editing patterns. We further study how editing patterns evolve over time. For each feature, we compute the mean number of revisions over each timeframe, broken down by class. This value is still an aggregate measure over an entire subpopulation, but it evolves temporally, therefore hinting changes in editing patterns. Fig. 5 shows examples of temporal evolution for three selected pairs (feature, private trait). More examples are presented in the SI [1]. Fig. 5a shows the feature `CONTENT` differentiated over levels of education. The static pattern shown in Fig. 4c is a result of change in editing patterns over time: editors with a PhD edit `CONTENT` more as Wikipedia matures, as also shown in the editor population breakdown in Figure 3a. For other features the editing pattern evolves over time. Contrasting Fig 5b and Fig 4a, we can see the differentiation of edits to the USER section by gender – female users edit more overall than male users, but this is only true until 2009. **`TALK-C`** and **`BELIEF`** also present the same temporal pattern shift, as shown in the SI [1]. Finally, some features present unexpected trends. Fig. 5c unveils that, unlike the general trend of decreasing number of contributions, `CONTENT` related edits increase for *muslim* editors. This temporal analysis reinforces the hypothesis that user editing patterns, as well as their evolution, are differentiated along different user traits.

6. PREDICTION RESULTS

We predict personal traits of editors using behavioral features described in Sec. 4.1. We report the prediction performance over time using different features. We also perform feature relevance analysis using the information trans-

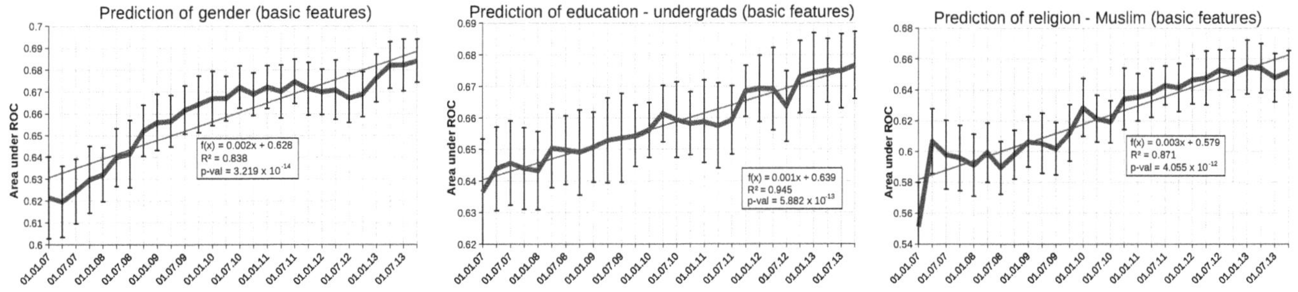

(a) (b) (c)

Figure 6: Temporal evolution of privacy loss, measure using mean AUC value over 20 executions (error bars denote standard deviation). Result of inferring, using binary predictors on the *basic* feature set, of gender (a), education/*undergrads* (b) and religion/*muslim* (c). The results for all the other binary predictors are given in the SI [1].

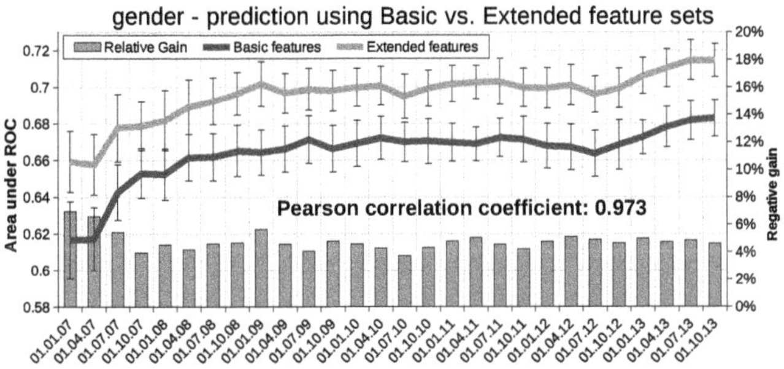

Figure 7: Comparison of the temporal evolution for the privacy loss on gender for the *basic* and *extended* feature sets. The *extended* feature set consistently provides better performances, while the AUC series of the predictors trained on the two feature sets are highly correlated and present the same trends.

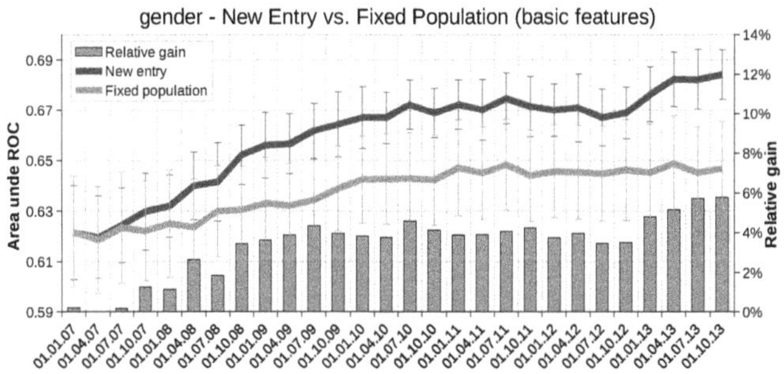

Figure 8: Evolution of privacy loss for the population fixed to its component in the first quarter of 2007 (*i.e.*, no newcomers) and a population in which new users can enter. We quantify the privacy loss due to newcomers as the relative gain of learning performance for the two populations.

fer metric to pin point the source of performance gain over time.

6.1 Predicting personal attributes over time

Predictability of private traits improves over time. We train binary predictors for every class of every private trait in our study, on datasets with increasing amounts of history (as shown in Sec. 4.2). The editors' activity is described using the *basic* feature set. Fig. 6 shows the AUC over time for three selected examples of private traits (all remaining classes are in the SI [1]). The graphics show the performance of predicting the gender of editors (Fig. 6a), whether they are *undergrads* (Fig. 6b) or of *muslim* religion (Fig. 6c). The AUC measure increases over time, roughly following a linear trend (coefficient of determination $R^2 > 0.83$ for all three examples). The AUC differences between the first and the last timeframes are statistically highly significant (t test $p < 0.001$, details and results in the SI [1]). We interpret this steady increase of performance over time as *loss of privacy*: as more historical information is available, the learning algorithm infers more accurately user traits which are potentially private.

We also report the model performance on an intuitive measure called *equal Precision and Recall* (ePR), defined as where a 45 degree line from the origin intersect with the precision-recall curve. For the three classes in Fig. 6, in the last timeframe, we obtain a mean ePR of 0.791 (for gender), 0.535 (for education/*undergrads*) and 0.9 (for religion/*muslim*). All the other classes and the evolution of ePR over time are found in the the SI [1]). The ePR measure allows to quantify how accurate are the predictions of certain private traits. We find that certain religious attributes have notably high prediction performance (*muslim* $ePR = 0.9$ and *jewish* $ePR = 0.913$) from behavioral features.

In a similar setup, we predict user gender using the *extended* feature set and we plot the AUC over time in Fig. 7. Alongside, we produce the results for the *basic* feature set and the relative gain between the two, for each timeframe. Predictions using the *extended* features consistently outperform those using the *basic* features, showing that knowledge about thematic editing patterns is informative about user private traits. The AUC over time series for the two types of features sets are highly correlated (Pearson correlation of 0.973). This shows that, while adding the thematic information improves the absolute value of the prediction accuracy, it seems to have little influence on the evolution of the privacy loss. We speculate that the evolution of privacy loss is not linked to the way the data is described, but it is rather intrinsic to the online social environment. To the best of our knowledge, this is the first study to highlight and quantify this *intrinsic cumulative effect* of time over privacy.

Sources of privacy loss: the *online breadcrumbs* and newcomers. We hypothesize that the temporal pri-

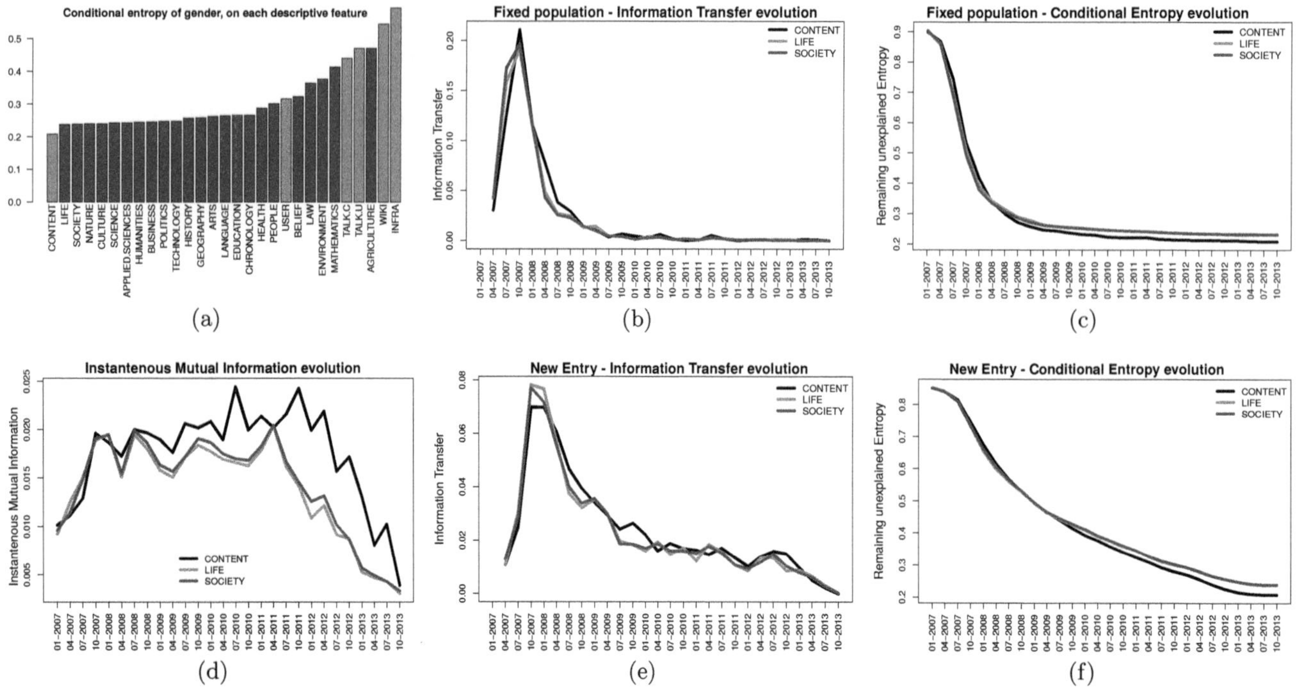

Figure 9: (a) Conditional entropy after conditioning on each feature (with New Entry NE). Feature are ordered by the conditional entropy $H(Y|X)$, here $Y = 0/1$ is the gender attribute, X is each feature. Lower is better. *Basic* features are shown in red, *extended* features in blue. (d) Mutual Information between each feature at time t and gender (on NE). *Information Transfer* on Fixed Population FP (b) and NE (e). Conditional entropy evolution on FP (c) and NE (f). We can see that while later edits contains just as much information about a user's privacy as the earlier edits, they contribute less to prediction gain, since most of the information they bring was already known.

vacy loss is caused by a joint effect of two factors: i) the information learned from new users who enter the population and ii) online breadcrumbs – a more accurate estimate of how the behavioral features correspond to personal traits. To separate these factors, we study two scenarios defined by subsets of the editor population: the *"New Entry"* (NE) in which new users can enter freely throughout time and *"Fixed population"* (FP), which is limited only to users active in the first timeframe (*i.e.*, first quarter of 2007). In Fig. 8, we plot the AUC over time when studied on FP and we compare it to NE. The curve corresponding to FP increases over time, though slower in later timeframes. The difference between the first and last timeframe is statistically very significant – t test $p < 0.01$. Intuitively, only the online breadcrumbs could cause this privacy decay for FP. By comparison, predictions on NE are constantly more accurate and continue to notably improve beyond the initial burst detected for FP. We attribute this additional improvement to information relating to new users entering the system.

Are later edits less harmful to one's privacy? Intuitively, the longer a user edits, the more she discloses about herself. We approach this issue using the Temporal Information Theory measure detailed in Sec. 4, on both FP and NE populations. Let T be the number of timeframes. Fig. 9a shows the conditional entropy of the class variable Y (here gender), after conditioning on all the temporal instantiations of a given feature X (*i.e.* $H(Y|X_{1:T})$), on the NE dataset. We can see which features which give out the most information about a user's gender. Consistent with the data profile in Sec. 5, CONTENT differentiates the most *males* from *females*. The thematic features, like **Life**, **Society**, **Nature** or **Culture** follow, having very similar scores. Surprisingly, USER distinguishes gender less than seen from the profiling analysis. An almost identical ordering of importance of features is obtained on FP. Fig. 9d presents the instantaneous mutual information over time between the gender variable and the three most important features. All three present very similar dynamics (both on NE and on FP). The information overlap between the temporal instantiation of features and the private trait remains almost constant until close to the end of the studied period. This answers the questions whether later edits are less harmful, by showing that later activity hurts privacy as much as the initial activity, as it discloses similar quantities of information. We further study the amount of *new* information introduced features in later timeframes. Fig. 9b and 9e show that the *Information Transfer* over time on respectively FP and NE, for the same three features. All series present an initial burst, after which they drop quickly. Note that, due to differences in the effectives of the FP and NE populations, the absolute values are not directly comparable and only their evolutions are meaningful. We can see that later features X_t bring few *new* information not already disclosed by the earlier features $X_{t-1}, X_{t-2} \ldots$. The take-home message for this subsection is: *While later edits contain just as much information about a user's privacy as the earlier edits, they tend to be less harmful since most of the information they bring has already been learned.*

The continuous impact of newcomers on privacy loss. Information Theory measures provide means for separately quantifying the privacy loss due "online breadcrumbs" and newcomers. For FP (Fig. 9b), the utility of later edits drops to virtually zero, whereas for NE (Fig. 9e) they decrease to a non-negligible score. The information inferred from newcomers seems to be moderate, but constant in time. This information is also responsible for the continuous increase of prediction performance detected in Fig. 8 for the NE population. Similar conclusions can be drawn by studying the conditional entropy over time for the two populations. For FP (Fig. 9c) it decreases rapidly and remains constant afterwards, showing that virtually no new information is learned after the initial burst. For NE (Fig. 9f), it continues to decay even after the initial burst, though at a slower pace.

6.2 Predicting the attributes of exited users

Privacy continues to erode even for retired users. We further analyze what happens to the privacy of users who left the system. After their retirement, no more user-originating information ("online breadcrumbs") is available to disclose private traits. We quantify the prediction performance on a user population who have edited prior to 01.01.2008, but stopped after this date. Therefore, any information introduced in the system by the users themselves is restricted to the timeframes before 2008. In Fig. 10a, we plot the AUC over time for the education/*undergrads* binary classifier. We observe an constant increase of prediction performance, even though it shows a saturation in later timeframes. An increase of prediction performance for for retired users is also observable for religion/*christian* (see the SI [1]), but not for any of the other binary classifiers. No longer being in activity, the loss of privacy after 01.2008 is not the result of the users' actions. A Temporal Information Theory analysis performed on this exited population shows *Information Transfer* values of zero after 01.2008 – i.e. no information originating with "online breadcrumbs". As far as we know, these are the first results to show that certain private traits could be predicted increasingly better even after the users exited the system.

Why does privacy degrade for exited users? Intuitively, user originating information is available only until the exit of the users, afterwards the source of new information are in the actions of other users. Predictions about unseen retired users can be made only using features relating to their period of activity (here 01/2007 - 12/2007). In the logistic regression models learned at each timeframe, the strength of the links between features and the class variable are given by the corresponding coefficients. We study the coefficients of features which encode the activity of users prior to their retirement (i.e. $X^u_{1:4}$). We show the coefficients relating to CONTENT (in Fig. 10b) and to USER (in Fig. 10c), in models learned for education/*undergrads* in each timeframe. In later timeframes, CONTENT features observe an increase in importance, with both $\mathrm{CONTENT}_2$ (number of CONTENT revisions in the 2nd quarter of 2007) and $\mathrm{CONTENT}_3$ steadily increasing from being completely absent in the initial models. $\mathrm{CONTENT}_4$ remains absent for all timeframes. Simultaneously, USER features decrease in importance, with USER_4 disappearing completely. We hypothesize that the AUC increase observed after 01.2008 originates with the currently active users *whose activity overlapped with the exited users*: classifier learns from users active both before and after 01.2008, by modifying the weights of features, including those before 01.2008. In this case, they learn that CONTENT features should have more importance, while USER features should have less. In summary, predicting of personal traits increase even for retired users, and the key factor for this improvement is better estimates on a subset of important features such as CONTENT.

7. DISCUSSION

We present a first study to quantify the extent of gradual privacy erosion over six years. First, we set up a large scale evaluation using Wikipedia editing behavior to predict private traits over time. We analyze a 13 year history of Wikipedia edits made by more than 117 thousand users. Our descriptive analysis showed that as Wikipedia evolves, editors of different personal traits shows distinct patterns in their volume of edits and topical preferences. Second, we provide experimental evidence that time has an adverse effect on privacy. We show that prediction performance on private traits, such as gender, education and religion, increases with longer Wikipedia editing history. Third, we show that prediction of private traits improves even for users who have stopped editing Wikipedia. We further quantify the effect of predictability, and found that the improved performance can be attributed to two factors: new editors of Wikipedia, and better estimate of feature relevance - with the first having a larger effect. To the best of our knowledge, this is the first study to quantify the change of private traits over time, using Wikipedia, an open online dataset containing behavior breadcrumbs. This work shall raise awareness in the public on the privacy implications of online activity over long periods of time. The fact that the information of newcomers can be used to learn more about existing members has profound implications: users do not have complete control over the consequences of the information they release. Reflecting on this work, we would like to discuss a few of its limitations, practical implications and connections to other areas of research.

What does it really mean for Wikipedia users, should they be worried? To the best of our knowledge, no studies have shown that the real identity of Wikipedia users can be revealed based on their editing activity. However, this may not the case for other social networks.

User disclosure bias. This work uses self-disclosed personal traits on users' public profile. It is well-known that such a data source is prone to users' disclosure biase. The set of users who voluntarily disclose private information might be biased towards users less concerned with their privacy, who in turn has a distinct behavioral pattern. Validating the effect of such a bias would require an alternative source of groundtruth and maybe even behavioral data, and is beyond the scope of this study.

What about other online platforms? Although we predict predict private traits from Wikipedia, similar prediction results (on a static snapshop) was reported for other platforms such as Facebook [12]. Being a collaborative encyclopedia, Wikipedia records relatively small amount of information about its users. More detailed longitudinal analyses could be performed on platforms such as Facebook, and it is likely to also see an increasing trend for predicting personal traits.

A natural law of evolution of privacy loss. This study provides empirical analysis about privacy loss. A longer-term open challenge is a physical model for privacy loss, i.e., predict the de-anonymization rate of a given anonymized dataset.

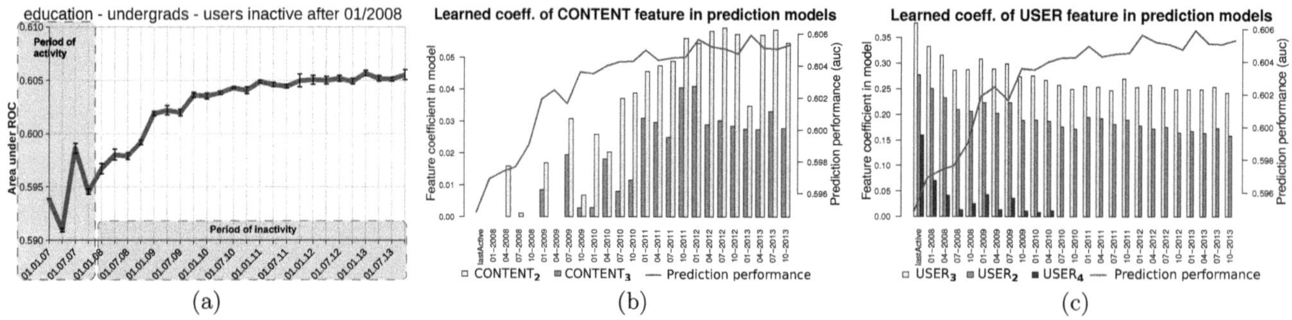

Figure 10: (a) Increase of prediction performance for for users retired after 01.2008 – education/*undergrads* (other in SI [1]). Coefficients one model per timeframe: (b) `CONTENT` coefficient (absent in the model corresponding to the dataset where users were last active) increase in importance. (c) `USER` relating features decrease in importance.

Effective conditions for preserving privacy? There is a growing literature on characterizing which privacy guarantees can be obtained under a given information release protocol [25]. We hope our findings invite new empirical and theoretical investigation into the case in which data release is spatio-temporal and heterogeneous across different entities. In light of this study, we advocate that new means should be found to tackle the issue of online privacy. We argue one feasible means to preserving privacy is to construct laws which would enable erasing the recorded activity in the online environment.

Acknowledgments NICTA is funded by the Australian Government through the Department of Communications and the Australian Research Council through the ICT Centre of Excellence Program. This material is based on research sponsored by the Air Force Research Laboratory, under agreement number FA2386-15-1-4018.

8. REFERENCES

[1] Supplementary material: Evolution of privacy loss in Wikipedia, 2015. http://goo.gl/JT6WK7.

[2] A. Acquisti, L. K. John, and G. Loewenstein. What is privacy worth? *The Journal of Legal Studies*, 42(2):249–274, June 2013.

[3] R. Almeida, B. Mozafari, and J. Cho. On the evolution of Wikipedia. In *ICWSM '07*, 2007.

[4] D. Barth-Jones, K. E. Emam, J. Bambauer, a. Cavoukian, and B. Malin. Assessing data intrusion threats. *Science*, 348(6231):194–195, Apr. 2015.

[5] d. boyd and A. E. Marwick. Social Privacy in Networked Publics: Teens' Attitudes, Practices, and Strategies. *A Decade in Internet Time: Symposium on the Dynamics of the Internet and Society*, sep 2011.

[6] C. Danescu-Niculescu-Mizil, L. Lee, B. Pang, and J. Kleinberg. Echoes of power: Language effects and power differences in social interaction. In *WWW*, page 699, 2012.

[7] Y.-A. de Montjoye, C. A. Hidalgo, M. Verleysen, and V. D. Blondel. Unique in the crowd: The privacy bounds of human mobility. *Scientific Reports*, 3, 2013.

[8] A. Gibbons, D. Vetrano, and S. Biancani. Wikipedia: Nowhere to grow. Tech. report, Standford, 2012.

[9] A. Halfaker, R. S. Geiger, J. T. Morgan, and J. Riedl. The Rise and Decline of an Open Collaboration System: How Wikipedia's Reaction to Popularity Is Causing Its Decline. *American Behavioral Scientist*, 57(5):664–688, Dec. 2012.

[10] C. J. Hoofnagle, J. King, S. Li, and J. Turow. How Different are Young Adults from Older Adults When it Comes to Information Privacy Attitudes and Policies? Ssrn scholarly paper, Apr. 2010.

[11] G. James, D. Witten, T. Hastie, and R. Tibshirani. *An Introduction to Statistical Learning*, volume 103 of *Springer Texts in Statistics*. Springer New York, 2013.

[12] M. Kosinski, D. Stillwell, and T. Graepel. Private traits and attributes are predictable from digital records of human behavior. *PNAS*, 110(15):5802–5805, 2013.

[13] D. J. MacKay. *Information theory, inference and learning algorithms*. Cambridge university press, 2003.

[14] A.-M. Meyer and D. Gotz. A new privacy debate. *Science*, 348(6231):194–194, Apr. 2015.

[15] P. E. Meyer. R package 'infotheo', 2014.

[16] Y.-a. D. Montjoye and a. S. Pentland. Assessing data intrusion threats–Response. *Science*, 348(6231):195–195, Apr. 2015.

[17] Y.-a. D. Montjoye, L. Radaelli, V. K. Singh, and a. S. Pentland. Unique in the shopping mall: On the reidentifiability of credit card metadata. *Science*, 347(6221):536–539, Jan. 2015.

[18] A. Narayanan, E. Shi, and B. I. P. Rubinstein. Link prediction by de-anonymization: How we won the kaggle social network challenge. In *IJCNN*, pages 1825–1834, 2011.

[19] A. Narayanan and V. Shmatikov. Myths and fallacies of personally identifiable information. *Comm. of the ACM*, 53(6):24–26, June 2010.

[20] A. Ramachandran and A. Chaintreau. The Network Effect of Privacy Choices. In *Workshop EcoNet*, pages 1–4, 2015.

[21] J. Saramaki, E. A. Leicht, E. Lopez, S. G. B. Roberts, F. Reed-Tsochas, and R. I. M. Dunbar. The persistence of social signatures in human communication. *PNAS*, 2014.

[22] B. Suh, G. Convertino, E. H. Chi, and P. Pirolli. The Singularity is Not Near: Slowing Growth of Wikipedia. In *WikiSym '09*, pages 8:1–8:10. ACM, Oct. 2009.

[23] L. Sweeney. k-anonymity: A model for protecting privacy. *International Journal of Uncertainty, Fuzziness and Knowledge-Based Systems*, 10(05):557–570, 2002.

[24] G. Ver Steeg and A. Galstyan. Information transfer in social media. In *WWW '12*, page 509, 2012.

[25] L. Wasserman and S. Zhou. A statistical framework for differential privacy. *Jour. of American Stat. Assoc.*, 105(489):375–389, 2010.

[26] H. T. Welser, D. Cosley, G. Kossinets, A. Lin, F. Dokshin, G. Gay, and M. Smith. Finding social roles in wikipedia. In *iConference*, pages 122–129. ACM, 2011.

[27] W. Youyou, M. Kosinski, and D. Stillwell. Computer-based personality judgments are more accurate than those made by humans. *PNAS*, 2014.

Keynote Speaker Bio

Yiling Chen
Gordan McKay Professor of Computer Science, Harvard University

BIO

Yiling Chen's research lies at the intersection of computer science and economics, encompassing algorithms, complexity, mechanism design, game theory, optimization, multi-agent systems, and machine learning.

She is interested in designing and analyzing social and organizational systems such as markets, information aggregation instruments, advertising mechanisms, and online communities, according to both computational and economic objectives.

Chen received a Ph.D. in Information Sciences and Technology from Pennsylvania State University, University Park; a Master of Economics from Tsinghua University, Beijing, China; and a Bachelor of Economics from Renmin University, Beijing, China.

Prior to Chen's appointment at Harvard, she was a Postdoctoral Research Scientist at Yahoo! Research, and served as a Teaching/Research Assistant at various institutions, including Pennsylvania State University, Iowa State University, and Tsinghua University.

Chen has served as the Tutorial Chair of the ACM Conference on Electronic Commerce (EC), 2008, and on the Program Committee for the International World Wide Web Conference (WWW), 2008, and the International Workshop on Internet and Network Economics (WINE), 2008. She has co-organized the 2nd and the 3rd Workshops on Prediction Markets, 2007-2008. She has also been a reviewer for Management Science, Information Systems Research, Decision Support Systems, Information Systems and e-Business Management, and various conferences.

Chen's awards include Outstanding Paper Award, ACM Conference on Electronic Commerce (EC), 2008; Honorable Mention, Decision Science Institute Doctoral Dissertation Competition, 2006; and eBRC Doctoral Support Award, eBusiness Research Center at Penn State University, 2004.

Modeling Intransitivity in Matchup and Comparison Data

Shuo Chen
Department of Computer Science
Cornell University
Ithaca, NY, USA
shuochen@cs.cornell.edu

Thorsten Joachims
Department of Computer Science
Cornell University
Ithaca, NY, USA
tj@cs.cornell.edu

ABSTRACT

We present a method for learning potentially intransitive preference relations from pairwise comparison and matchup data. Unlike standard preference-learning models that represent the properties of each item/player as a single number, our method infers a multi-dimensional representation for the different aspects of each item/player's strength. We show that our model can represent any pairwise stochastic preference relation and provide a comprehensive evaluation of its predictive performance on a wide range of pairwise comparison tasks and matchup problems from online video games and sports, to peer grading and election. We find that several of these task – especially matchups in online video games – show substantial intransitivity that our method can model effectively.

Keywords

Matchup, Pairwise Comparison, Representation Learning, Ranking, Sports, Games

1. INTRODUCTION

The modeling of pairwise comparison/two-player matches has seen a wide range of applications. To name some examples, it is used in sports [8] to predict which player/team is more likely to win in a given league or tournament. In matchmaking for online video games, it is used to pair players of equal strength to create a fun and fair gaming experience [20, 29]. It is also used in recommendation systems to learn rankings of items (e.g. movies) from pairwise preference statement [15].

The seminal work of [35], which later led to the well-known Bradley-Terry model [6, 27], is the basis for much of the research in this area [7]. The goal of many of these works is to learn a scalar parameter for each of the player/item from historic pairwise comparison data. These parameters usually represent the ranks or strengths of individuals, with higher ranks favored for the win over lower ranks in future comparisons.

However, using a single number to represent a player/item can be an oversimplification. For example, consider the game of rock-paper-scissors. It is impossible to assign one number to each item to correctly model the intransitive relations among them. More generally, in many real-world scenarios, there could be multiple attributes of each object. A tennis player could have different strengths in forehand, backhand, serve, return, lob, volley and so on. A soccer team could have players of different capability in each positions. A movie could have different facets, such as the genre or subgenre (a sci-fi movie that has romantic elements, or thriller packed with actions), or aspects of filmmaking (writing, performing, directing, editing, music, costume, visual effects, etc.). Given this multi-dimensional nature of ability, a tennis player with a strong serve may beat a player with a weak return, who in turn may beat another player with his strong lop, who in turn may beat the first player due to his strong return. This creates intransitive relations that a single number cannot represent.

In this paper, we propose a method for learning a multi-dimensional representation for each players from pairwise comparisons[1], which can model intransitive relations. We empirically evaluate the model on a variety of real-world datasets including sports, online competitive video games, movie preference, peer grading and elections. In particular, we investigate how much intransitivity our model detects in these applications, and in how far our model improves predictive accuracy.

WSDM'16, February 22–25, 2016, San Francisco, CA, USA.

ISBN 978-1-4503-3716-8/16/02...$15.00

DOI: http://dx.doi.org/10.1145/2835776.2835787

2. RELATED WORK

The fundamentals of pairwise comparison were established in [35, 6, 27]. [7] gives a survey of following works. In addition, learning to rank each player's strength has also been studied in the context of matchmaking system for online video games [16, 12, 22, 29]. These works all follow the principle of using a single scalar to measure the player's strength.

Although mentioned many times in the literature, intransitivity is not closely examined in most of the works. To the best of our knowledge, the only work that explicitly models intransitivity in matchup data is [9]. It uses a 2-dimensional[2] vector to model each player, and uses a ± 1 variable to record who is favored between any pair of players. However, it was only tested on very small datasets without any quantitative investigation into whether modeling intransitivity improves model fidelity[3]. The idea of multi-dimensional representation also appears in [24, 7], although no intransitivity related issues are addressed.

As ubiquitous as pairwise comparison is, pairwise models have attracted attention from a wide variety of research communities.

[1] We are going to use the terms pairwise comparison and matchup interchangeably in the rest of this paper.

[2] Theoretically it can be extended to higher-dimensional space.

[3] The ± 1 variables are decided by which player wins more in a matchup in the training dataset. We initially have this method implemented. However, its performance is generally below the baselines, so we did not include it in the experiments in Section 4.

In animal behavior studies, [33] suggested that the three types of male side-blotched lizards exhibit the rock-paper-scissors relation in their mating strategy. [3] and [37] looked at the dominance within groups of wild woodland caribou, and examined how pairs of caribou interacted with each other to compete for food, water or females. The statistical model proposed in [37] can actually handle intransitivity, but it relies on getting explicit additional features like age, gender and antler size, and can only handle two of those features at a time.

In economics, [28] is one of the earliest papers that touches on the topic of intransitivity. It suggested that a single utility function is not enough to model intransitivity, and a multi-dimensional vector of utility functions is needed. This coincides with our intuition. The following [14] mathematically analyzed how likely intransitivity occurs given the model proposed in [28]. [26] designed an experiment that collects pairwise preference from about 20 people. The results suggest that when aggregated, intransitivity does exist in these opinions.

In contrast to the aforementioned works, this paper proposes a method based on the multi-dimensional representation idea that explicitly models the intransitivity using only the boolean results of pairwise comparisons, i.e. without using any features of the items themselves. The trained model is aimed at predicting any future comparisons as correctly as possible. We use this method to examine a wide range of real-world applications to see whether modeling intransitivity helps or not.

Tangentially related, pairwise comparison also arises as a subroutine of multi-class classification problems [23, 4]. The goal here is to assign one or more best classes to each instance given the pairwise comparisons among all the classes. It differs from ours, as our focus is about any individual comparison for prediction.

The idea of learning multi-dimensional representations in a semantically meaningful latent space has also become a popular and effective method in many applications, including language modeling [30, 34], playlist generation [10, 31, 11], co-occurrence data modeling [17], recommendation system [19, 41] and image/social media tagging [39, 40].

Also related is the work [1], in which the authors use matrix factorization to predict scores of professional basketball games. The idea of using different feature functions for offense and defense is analogous to the model we propose. The major difference lies in three aspects. First, it does not explicitly studies the intransitive behavior. Second, the input differs, as our models takes simple binary win or lose results and theirs needs detailed scores. Lastly, we go beyond the specific basketball result prediction in their work, and empirically test on a collection of vastly different applications.

3. MODEL

3.1 Bradley-Terry model

In this paper, we focus on modeling matches/comparisons between two players/items, where we assume the outcome cannot be a draw (either the first player or the second player wins). Let us first review the Bradley-Terry model [6, 27] for pairwise comparison, upon which we build our model. In one of the most common forms of the Bradley-Terry model, each player's strength is represented by a single real number γ. The probability of player a beating player b is modeled as

$$\begin{aligned}\Pr(a \text{ beats } b) &= \frac{\exp(\gamma_a)}{\exp(\gamma_a)+\exp(\gamma_b)} \\ &= \frac{1}{1+\exp(-(\gamma_a-\gamma_b))} \\ &= S(M(a,b)). \qquad (1)\end{aligned}$$

Here $S(x) = 1/(1+\exp(-x))$ is the sigmoid/logistic function. $M(a,b)$ is what we call the matchup function of player a and player b in this paper. It measures the edge given to player a when matched up against player b. In Bradley-Terry model, it is simply modeled as $M(a,b) = \gamma_a - \gamma_b$, the difference of strengths between two players. Some properties of the Bradley-Terry model are:

1. The range of $M(a,b)$ is $\mathbb{R}$, with positive/negative meaning player a/b has more than 50% chance of winning, and 0 meaning it is an even matchup.
2. When $M(a,b) \to +\infty$, $\Pr(a \text{ beats } b) \to 1$. Similarly when $M(a,b) \to -\infty$, $\Pr(a \text{ beats } b) \to 0$.
3. $M(a,b) = -M(b,a)$. This makes sure that we always have $\Pr(a \text{ beats } b) = 1 - \Pr(b \text{ beats } a)$ satisfied.

Note that these three properties follow the properties of the sigmoid function. In fact, any real-valued function $M(a,b)$ that takes two players as arguments and satisfies property 3 can be plugged in and give us a Bradley-Terry-like model.

It is convenient to write down matchup relations among all players in a matrix, which we call the matchup matrix.

DEFINITION 1 (MATCHUP MATRIX). *For n players, an n by n real skew-symmetric matrix $\mathcal{M}$ is called a matchup matrix if for any two players a and b*[4]*, we have*

$$\mathcal{M}_{ab} = S^{-1}(\Pr(a \textit{ beats } b)) = \log\left(\frac{\Pr(a \textit{ beats } b)}{1-\Pr(a \textit{ beats } b)}\right).$$

3.2 Intransitivity model

The notion of stochastic intransitivity we are interested in modeling in this paper can be defined as follows.

DEFINITION 2 (INTRANSITIVITY). *Matchup relations of n players contain (stochastic) intransitivity if there exist three players a, b and c such that $\Pr(a \textit{ beats } b) > 0.5$, $\Pr(b \textit{ beats } c) > 0.5$ and $\Pr(c \textit{ beats } a) > 0.5$.*

Since using single number to represent how good a player is cannot effectively model the intransitivity in the data, we need a more expressive model. Our idea is to learn a multi-dimensional representation for each player. Building upon the Bradley-Terry model in Eq. (1), in the following we design a gadget for the matchup function $M(a,b)$ so that it makes use of the multi-dimensional representations and can model intransitivity.

Before explaining the gadget mathematically, we would like to describe it using a metaphor. Imagine two players a and b facing each other in a sword duel (depicted in Figure 1). Each player has two important spots: his blade, which he uses to attack his opponent, and his chest, which he does not want his opponent to attack. If a player's blade is closer to his opponent's chest than his opponent's blade to his chest, he is more likely to win. In Figure 1, the player on the left has the advantage, as given by the difference between the two distances shown in blue dashed lines.

[4]Without loss of generality, we assume the players are represented by integers here.

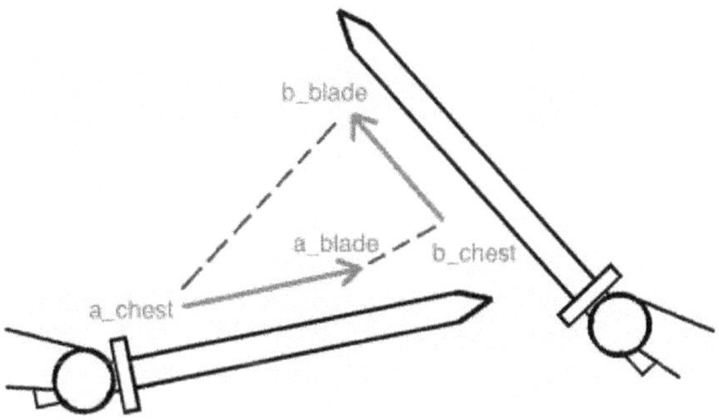

Figure 1: A metaphorical illustration of the gadget we use to model intransitivity. Player a and player b are in a sword duel. Player a's blade is closer to player b's chest than vice versa, as shown by the two blue dashed lines. This illustrates how, in our model, player a has a better chance of winning than player b.

Formally, we represent each player a with two d-dimensional vectors $\mathbf{a}_{\text{blade}}$ and $\mathbf{a}_{\text{chest}}$. Our matchup function is then defined as

$$M(a, b) = ||\mathbf{b}_{\text{blade}} - \mathbf{a}_{\text{chest}}||_2^2 - ||\mathbf{a}_{\text{blade}} - \mathbf{b}_{\text{chest}}||_2^2. \quad (2)$$

Note that this new matchup function is a real-valued function that satisfies property 3 discussed in Section 3.1, so we can just plug it in the sigmoid function to model $\Pr(a \text{ beats } b)$. We now have a multi-dimensional representation for each player, where the blade and chest vectors are used to capture different styles (strength or vulnerability) in their offense and defense. These styles have different effects when matched up against different opponents. We will refer to this model as the *blade-chest-dist* model. Later in Section 4, we will show that this gadget can capture intransitivity in synthetic and real datasets.

In many real-life games/sports, the absolute strength of a player is likely to still be a very important factor in wining or losing. Thus we also add bias terms to our new matchup function that are similar to the strength scalar in the original Bradley-Terry model. Then our *blade-chest-dist* model becomes

$$M(a, b) = ||\mathbf{b}_{\text{blade}} - \mathbf{a}_{\text{chest}}||_2^2 - ||\mathbf{a}_{\text{blade}} - \mathbf{b}_{\text{chest}}||_2^2 + \gamma_a - \gamma_b. \quad (3)$$

In this way, our model strictly generalizes the Bradley-Terry model.

In the discussion so far, we use the squared Euclidean distance to model the interaction between the representations of two players. This follows what has been successfully experimented in [10, 17, 38]. On the other hand, there are many works in the literature that favor an inner product as the interaction function [30, 39, 2]. Therefore, we also introduce our *blade-chest-inner* model

$$M(a, b) = \mathbf{a}_{\text{blade}} \cdot \mathbf{b}_{\text{chest}} - \mathbf{b}_{\text{blade}} \cdot \mathbf{a}_{\text{chest}} + \gamma_a - \gamma_b, \quad (4)$$

again with optional bias terms. We empirically evaluate and compare both of these models in Section 4.

How expressive are these models in their ability to capture intransitive relations? The following theorem states that any paiwise relation can be represented, if the dimensionality of the representation space is large enough.

THEOREM 1 (EXPRESSIVENESS). *The* blade-chest-inner *and* blade-chest-dist *models without the bias term can represent any matchup matrix $\mathcal{M}$ given a representation space of dimensionality d that is at least as large as the number of items n.*

PROOF. For the *blade-chest-inner* model, we choose $d = n$, and construct the blade and chest vectors as following: $\mathbf{a}_{\text{chest}}$ is unit vector with the ath element being 1 and others being 0. $\mathbf{a}_{\text{blade}} = \frac{1}{2}[\mathcal{M}_{a1}, \mathcal{M}_{a2}, \ldots, \mathcal{M}_{an}]$. According to the model, we have

$$M(a, b) = \mathbf{a}_{\text{blade}} \cdot \mathbf{b}_{\text{chest}} - \mathbf{b}_{\text{blade}} \cdot \mathbf{a}_{\text{chest}}$$
$$= \frac{1}{2}\mathcal{M}_{ab} - \frac{1}{2}\mathcal{M}_{ba} = \mathcal{M}_{ab}.$$

For the *blade-chest-dist* model, we choose $d = n + 1$. $\mathbf{a}_{\text{chest}}$ is similarly constructed as for the *blade-chest-inner* case. Note that now the last element of any chest vector is 0. Also $||\mathbf{a}_{\text{chest}}||_2^2 = 1$. For blade vectors, we do $\mathbf{a}_{\text{blade}} = \frac{1}{4}[\mathcal{M}_{a1}, \mathcal{M}_{a2}, \ldots, \mathcal{M}_{an}, C_a]$, where C_a is a padding number that makes sure $||\mathbf{a}_{\text{blade}}||_2^2$ equals to some positive constant C for any player a. Then,

$$M(a, b) = ||\mathbf{b}_{\text{blade}} - \mathbf{a}_{\text{chest}}||_2^2 - ||\mathbf{a}_{\text{blade}} - \mathbf{b}_{\text{chest}}||_2^2$$
$$= ||\mathbf{b}_{\text{blade}}||_2^2 + ||\mathbf{a}_{\text{chest}}||_2^2 - ||\mathbf{a}_{\text{blade}}||_2^2 - ||\mathbf{b}_{\text{chest}}||_2^2$$
$$+ 2(\mathbf{a}_{\text{blade}} \cdot \mathbf{b}_{\text{chest}} - \mathbf{b}_{\text{blade}} \cdot \mathbf{a}_{\text{chest}})$$
$$= C + 1 - C - 1 + 2\left(\frac{1}{4}\mathcal{M}_{ab} - \frac{1}{4}\mathcal{M}_{ba}\right) = \mathcal{M}_{ab}.$$

□

It is worth discussing the relations between the *blade-chest-dist* and *blade-chest-inner* models. Following the proof above, the matchup function of the *blade-chest-dist* model can be rewritten as

$$M(a, b) = 2(\mathbf{a}_{\text{blade}} \cdot \mathbf{b}_{\text{chest}} - \mathbf{b}_{\text{blade}} \cdot \mathbf{a}_{\text{chest}} + \gamma'_a - \gamma'_b), \quad (5)$$

where $\gamma'_a = (||\mathbf{a}_{\text{chest}}||_2^2 - ||\mathbf{a}_{\text{blade}}||_2^2)/2$ and $\gamma'_b = (||\mathbf{b}_{\text{chest}}||_2^2 - ||\mathbf{b}_{\text{blade}}||_2^2)/2$. This formulation is very similar to the matchup function of the *blade-chest-inner* model with bias term in Eq. (4). The difference is that now γ' depends on the blade and chest vectors instead of being a free parameter. As a result, although the two models are closely related, neither one generalizes the other, and their performance differences are investigated in Section 4.

3.3 Training

Given observed outcomes of pairwise comparisons, we would like to estimate a representation (consisting of a blade vector, a chest vector and an optional strength γ) for each player in order to be able to accurately predict the outcome of future matchups. In the following, we propose to do the training via maximum likelihood estimation. More specifically, suppose D is our training dataset, which contains all the match results among all players P used for training. Instead of having and individual record for each of the different comparisons, we collapse the matches between each pair of players into 4-tuples (a, b, n_a, n_b), where a and b ($\in P$) are the two players and n_a and n_b are the numbers of times each player wins against the other. The overall likelihood on the training dataset becomes

$$\prod_{(a,b,n_a,n_b) \in D} S\big(M(a, b)\big)^{n_a} \cdot \big(1 - S(M(a, b))\big)^{n_b}. \quad (6)$$

The log-likelihood is

$$L(D|\Theta) \triangleq \sum_{(a,b,n_a,n_b) \in D} l(a, b, n_a, n_b|\Theta)$$
$$= \sum_{(a,b,n_a,n_b) \in D} \Big(- n_a \log\big(1 + \exp(-M(a, b))\big)$$
$$- n_b \log\big(1 + \exp(M(a, b))\big)\Big), \quad (7)$$

where Θ contains all the parameters (blade, chest and γ). The term $l(a, b, n_a, n_b|\Theta)$ is the local log-likelihood on each of the 4-tuples.

To train the models, we used the stochastic gradient method [5]. Specifically, we repeatedly sampled 4-tuples from the training dataset, computed the sub-gradients of the local log-likelihood over the parameters, and updated the parameters until convergence.

3.4 Regularization

We also experimented with different regularization terms to prevent overfitting. The one we ended up using is $R(\Theta) = \sum_{a \in P} ||\mathbf{a}_{\text{blade}} - \mathbf{a}_{\text{chest}}||^2$. It pushes the blade and chest vectors for the same player together. Under heavy regularization, it tends to make our gadget degenerate to the original Bradley-Terry model. The regularized objective function becomes $L(D|\Theta) - \lambda R(\Theta)$, with λ being a regularization parameter that is tuned on a validation set.

3.5 Software

We implemented the training software in C with the various options mentioned above. The source code and the datasets used for testing in the following section are available at http://www.cs.cornell.edu/~shuochen/.

4. EXPERIMENTS

In this section, we first demonstrate that our model does capture intransitivity in synthetic datasets. We then explore a wide range of real-world datasets to evaluate in how far they exhibit intransitive behavior that can be captured by our models.

4.1 Synthetic datasets

To demonstrate that our proposed model can capture intransitivity on synthetic datasets, we begin by looking at the classic rock-paper-scissors game. The training dataset is generated as follows: there are three players, namely rock, paper and scissors. We generate $3,000$ games among them, with rock beating scissors $1,000$ times, scissors beating paper $1,000$ times, and paper beating rock $1,000$ times. We trained our *blade-chest-dist* model without the bias term, and we set the dimensionality of the vectors to be $d = 2$. We then visualize the learned model in the left panel of Figure 2. Each player is represented by an arrow, with the head being its blade vector, and the tail being its chest vector. The interlocking pattern in the visualization is evidence that our model captures the intransitive rule between the rock, paper and scissors.

There is also an interesting extension of the original rock-paper-scissors game in popular culture called rock-paper-scissors-lizard-Spock[5]. In addition to the three-way intransitivity between rock, paper and scissors, new rules for the other two players are added, and a graphical demonstration of the rules can be found here[6]. We generated $1,000$ matches for each matchup, and then do the training and visualization analogous to the classic rock-paper-scissors game. The results are shown in the right panel of Figure 2. Here we observe the similar interlocking pattern, with each of the 10 matchups correctly demonstrated.

4.2 General experiment setup on real-world datasets

The results on synthetic datasets demonstrate that our models can represent complex intransitive relations in low dimensional space. Now we move on to real-world datasets. Unless specified otherwise, the setup for the experiments is as follows: Given a dataset that contains all the 1 vs. 1 matches we collected, we randomly split it into 50% matches for training, 20% matches for validation, and 30% matches for testing. We vary models, dimensionality d for the representation and regularization parameter λ[7] for training, and validate them based on the average log-likelihood for each match on the validation partition. Then we evaluate the performance on the test partition. For each dataset, we do this random training-validation-testing split 10 times, and report the mean and standard deviation of the performance measures on the test partition.

We use two different measures: average test log-likelihood and test accuracy. The average test log-likelihood is defined similarly to the training log-likelihood. For the test partition D',

$$L(D'|\Theta) = \frac{1}{N'} \sum_{(a,b,n_a,n_b) \in D'} \Big(n_a \cdot \log(\Pr(a \text{ beats } b|\Theta)) + n_b \cdot \log(\Pr(b \text{ beats } a|\Theta))\Big), \quad (8)$$

where $N' = \sum_{(a,b,n_a,n_b) \in D'} (n_a + n_b)$ is the total number of games in the testing partition. Log-likelihood is always a negative value. The higher the value is, the better the model performs. The test accuracy is defined as

$$A(D'|\Theta) = \frac{1}{N'} \sum_{(a,b,n_a,n_b) \in D'} \Big(n_a \cdot \mathbb{1}^{\{\Pr(a \text{ beats } b|\Theta) \geq 0.5\}} + n_b \cdot \mathbb{1}^{\{\Pr(b \text{ beats } a|\Theta) > 0.5\}}\Big). \quad (9)$$

$\mathbb{1}^{\{\cdot\}}$ is the indicator function. This measure is a real number in $[0, 1]$, representing the percentage of matches whose (binary) outcome can be correctly predicted according to the model. The higher the value is, the better the model performs.

Unless noted otherwise, we only show results of models that include the bias terms. We will discuss the effects of removing the bias term in Section 4.7.

We compare our model against two baselines: the original Bradley-Terry model defined in Eq. (1) and what we call the naive baseline. The naive baseline separately estimates the chance of winning of each player based on their previous matches: $\Pr(a \text{ beats } b) = (n_a + 1)/(n_a + n_b + 2)$. We add 1 to both n_a and n_b to avoid negative infinite test log-likelihood. One should also note that if the winning probability returned by the naive model is exactly 0.5, Eq. (9) will predict the first player to be the winner when computing the accuracy, who is randomly chosen from the two.

4.3 How does modeling intransitivity affect the prediction in online competitive video games?

The first real-world application we would like to examine here is online competitive video games (a.k.a esports). We picked two of the most popular games in the esports scene: *Starcraft II* and *Defense of the Ancients 2*.

4.3.1 Starcraft II

Starcraft II is a military science fiction real-time strategy game developed and published by Blizzard Entertainment[8]. In the most common competitive setting, two players face off against each other. Each of them collects resources to build an army and fight his opponents, until one player's force is completely wiped out. Each player has options to build a variety of different combat units with different attributes such as building cost, building time, movement speed,

[5] http://en.wikipedia.org/wiki/Rock-paper-scissors-lizard-Spock
[6] http://www.recidivistsw.com/developer-notes/rock-paper-scissors-lizard.html

[7] For λ, we do grid search over powers of 10 from 1E-3 to 1E5.
[8] http://us.battle.net/sc2/en/

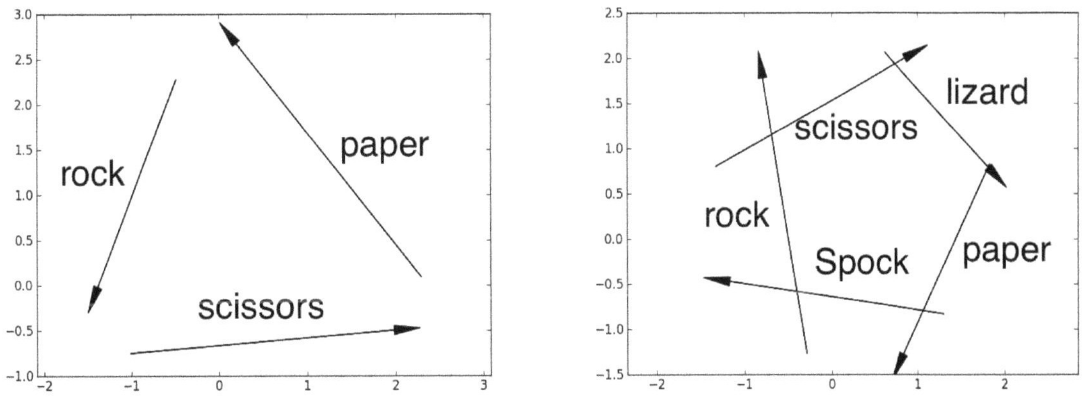

Figure 2: The visualization of our model trained on rock-paper-scissors (left panel) and rock-paper-scissors-lizard-Spock (right panel) datasets without bias terms and d set to 2. Each player is represented by an arrow, with the head being the blade vector and the tail being the chest vector.

attack range, toughness, etc. The choice of what and when to build based on scouting information from the enemy is an essential part of the strategy of *Starcraft II*.

We collected all the match results of professional *Starcraft II* players from the website aligulac.com up until February 20, 2014 (the day we did the crawling). There are two phases of *Starcraft II*: the original game *StarCraft II: Wings of Liberty* (WoL), and the later released expansion *StarCraft II: Heart of the Swarm* (HotS), which adds more options for the players and is often considered as a different game. We treat them separately. For of WoL, we have 4,381 players with 61,657 games, and 2,287 players with 28,582 games for HotS. Note that these games are from various competitions with different formats (single elimination, double elimination, group stage, round robin etc.), and for many competitions, the matching is decided by random draw without any seeding.

The results are plotted in Figure 3 and Figure 4. The improvement here stands out. On both datasets and for both average test log-likelihood and test accuracy, our models show clear superiority over the baselines once d is high enough, and our best model boosts the test accuracy by about 5%.

There are also some other interesting findings. First, the *blade-chest-inner* model tends to perform better than the *blade-chest-dist* model. Second, a substantially higher dimension is needed to accurately model this game than the two-dimensional model that is sufficient for rock-paper-scissors. We conjecture that this is due to the complexity of the rules governing this game.

The reason why intransitivity exists in *Starcraft II* can be explained from game design principles. At a low level, video game designers like to include elements of intransitivity in their games. One typical example in many war games is: cavalry is good against archer, archer is good against pikeman, and pikeman is good against cavalry. This keeps the game balanced, as players always have tools to counter any particular strategy or play style in the game.

At a high level, games that feature power buildup over time (including many trading card games and real-time strategy games such as *Starcraft II*) usually induce a set of strategies that are characterized by the stages of the game they focus on, with mid-game centric strategy beating early-game centric strategy, late-game centric strategy beating mid-game centric strategy and again early-game centric strategy beating late-game centric strategy. In the scenario of real-time strategy game in particular, there are also three main types of strategies called rush, boom and turtle[13], with rush (early aggression) beating boom (economy first), boom beating turtle (pure defensive), and turtle beating rush[9]. We believe that the relations between different types of general strategies that are associated with the nature of the game could also give rise to the captured intransitivity in the *Starcraft II* data.

4.3.2 Defense of the Ancients 2

Defense of the Ancients 2 (*DotA 2*)[10] is a multi-player online battle arena (MOBA) game developed by Valve Corporation. In contrast to *Starcraft II*, where each player commands a whole army, in *DotA 2* each player picks a single hero (in-game avatar) with teams of five players each facing off against each other. Each individual hero has its own strengths and weaknesses, so a particular one may be good against some others and bad against some others. The keys to victory usually include forming an overall balanced team and working together with teammates to cover each other's weaknesses. We crawled the match results of professional *DotA 2* teams from http://www.datdota.com/. The date range is from April 1st, 2012 to September 11th, 2014 (the start of their database until the day we did the crawling). The dataset contains 10,442 matches of 757 teams. These matches are from all kinds of competitive formats similar to *Starcraft II*.

The empirical results are shown in Figure 5. In terms of log-likelihood, we observed some limited but significant boost, especially from *blade-chest-inner*. However, there is little improvement in test accuracy over Bradley-Terry. These results suggest that, despite the existence of low-level intransitive elements, the team format seems to smooth out their effect, making the team's overall strength (single scalar from Bradley-Terry model) the deciding factor in determining match results. As a result, the high-level explanation (general set of strategies induced by the nature of the game that has intransitivity) seems to be a more reasonable one for the success on the *Starcraft II* datasets.

4.4 Does intransitivity exist in professional sports?

We examine tennis as an example of a single-player real-world professional sport[11]. We crawled or the tennis tournament matches

[9]Refer to Chapter 4 of [13] for more details.

[10]http://blog.dota2.com/

[11]Team-based competition are presumably more complicated as

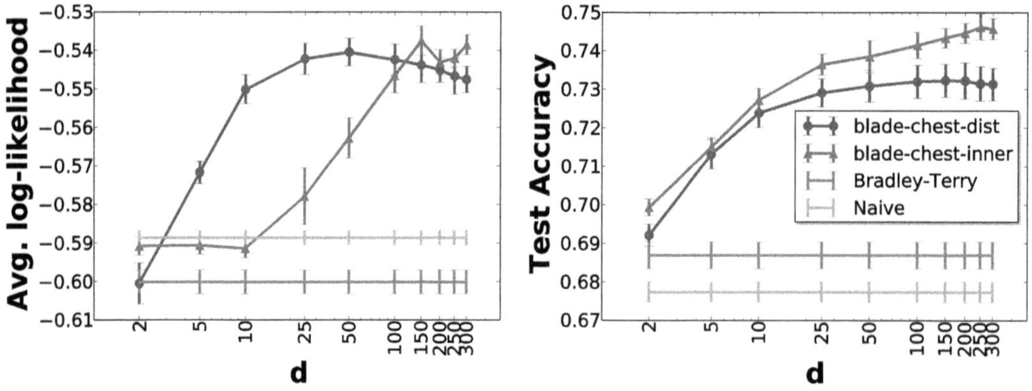

Figure 3: Average log-likelihood (left panel) and test accuracy (right panel) on *Starcraft II:WoL* dataset.

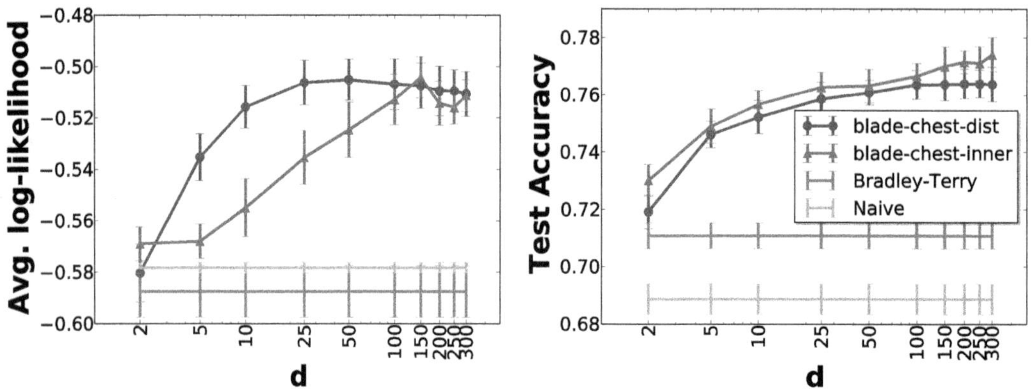

Figure 4: Average log-likelihood (left panel) and test accuracy (right panel) on *Starcraft II:HotS* dataset.

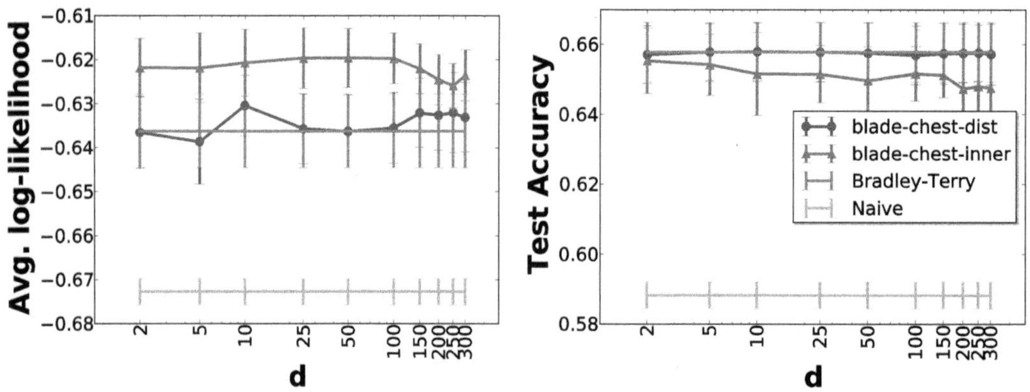

Figure 5: Average log-likelihood (left panel) and test accuracy (right panel) on *DotA 2* dataset.

organized by Association of Tennis Professionals (ATP)[12] from 2005 to 2012 using a Scala API [13]. These matches were played by the top male tennis players of the time, with 742 players and 23,806 games involved. The results are plotted in Figure 6. Similar to the *DotA 2* case, we observe a small boost over the Bradley-Terry baseline from our best model on log-likelihood, but no boost in terms of test accuracy.

There are at least two explanations. First, this could be just the way professional sports works. To become the best in the world, one needs to be an all-around excellent player without any substantial weakness. Therefore the rock-paper-scissors relations do not exist among top players due to selection effects. The second explanation is about how these players are matched up. The data results from tournaments matches, where single elimination bracket

things like team chemistry could be very crucial factor that affect a team's strength and yet hard to model at the same time. Also in professional leagues (like NBA and MLB), teams keep changing by signing/trading players.

[12] http://www.atpworldtour.com/

[13] https://github.com/danielkorzekwa/atpworldtour-api

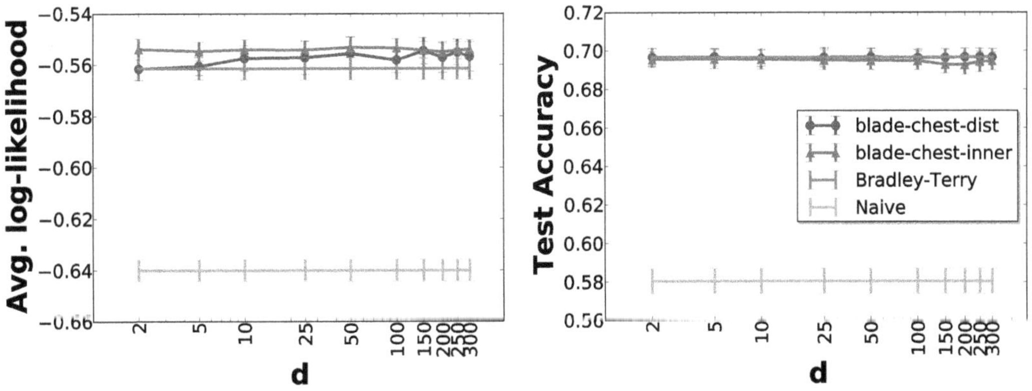

Figure 6: Average Log-likelihood (left panel) and test accuracy (right panel) on ATP tennis dataset.

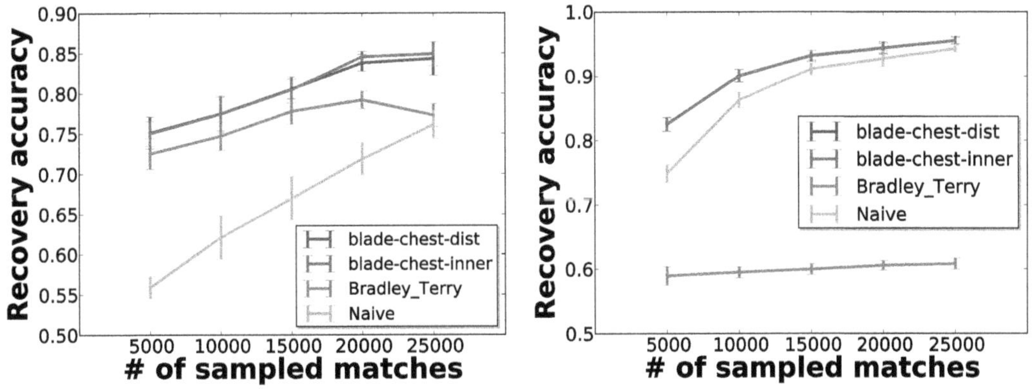

Figure 7: Recovery accuracy on *Street Fighter IV* (left panel) and randomized (right panel) matchup tables of 35 characters.

is the most common format. To form the bracket, some ranking-based[14] seeding is applied. As a result, in the first few rounds, there are a lot of matches of which the two participants have a large ranking discrepancy. Note that half of the matches of the tournament are already played after the first round of a single elimination bracket. The large difference in overall strength of the players in these matches may drown out any intransitivity that is present.

4.5 How does our method perform in matchup matrix recovery?

A possible explanation for the apparent lack of intransitivity in some of our experiments could be that there are not enough matchups in the test set for a significant amount of intransitivity to appear — analogous to a rock-paper-scissors test set where there are no paper-scissors matchups, leading to a single scalar parameter being enough to represent all comparisons. To amend this, we want to set up an experiment that tests all the matchups equally.

We accomplish this by examining our model's ability in recovering a matchup matrix. The example we use can be found on this webpage[15]. It is a 35-by-35 table. The numbers in it are integers in $[1, 9]$, and they measure the matchup relations among 35 selectable characters in *Super Street Fighter VI*[16], a 1 vs. 1 fighting game. These number were compiled by experts according to their knowledge of the game. We apply $S^{-1}(x/10)$ on those numbers to convert the table into a matchup matrix $\mathcal{M}$ as defined in Section 3.1. Our goal here is to uniformly sample matches from the matchup matrix, generate results according to the numbers, learn the representation of each character from the sample, and see how well we can recovery the matchup matrix according to the learned model.

We uniformly sampled from $5,000$ to $25,000$ matches. We evaluate the performance by accuracy on uneven matchups. To be more specific, after learning from the sampled matches, we can compute the recovered matchup matrix $\mathcal{M}'$, with $\mathcal{M}'_{ab} = M(a, b|\Theta)$. Let $U = \{(a, b)|\mathcal{M}_{ab} \neq 0\}$ be the set of uneven matchups. Our test recovery accuracy is defined as

$$R(\Theta) = \frac{1}{|U|} \sum_{(a,b)\in U} \mathbb{1}^{\{\mathcal{M}_{ab}\mathcal{M}'_{ab}>0\}}. \qquad (10)$$

One can think of this metric as being closely related to the test accuracy from the previous experiments.

The results are in the left panel of Figure 7. While there is not much difference between *blade-chest-dist* and *blade-chest-inner*, the superiority of our models over the baselines is clearly shown here.

We also ran a randomized version of this experiment. We generated a matchup matrix for 35 players, and each entry of the matrix was a uniformly selected integer value in $[1, 9]$, and then it was applied to by $S^{-1}(x/10)$. We made sure that $\mathcal{M}_{ab} = -\mathcal{M}_{ba}$. Clearly, there is no notion of intrinsic strength or play style at all.We used the same sampling strategy as above to generate the

[14] e.g. http://www.atpworldtour.com/Rankings/Singles.aspx

[15] http://iplaywinner.com/news/2011/1/5/super-street-fighter-4-tier-list-january-2011.html

[16] http://www.streetfighter.com/us/ssfiv

Table 1: Test log-likelihood on rank aggregation datasets.

DATASET	NAIVE	B-T	OUR BEST
PEER POSTER	−0.6256 ± 0.0001	−0.5920 ± 0.0004	**−0.5826 ± 0.0001**
PEER FINAL	−0.5426 ± 0.0001	−0.5923 ± 0.0020	**−0.4887 ± 0.0008**
MOVIELENS	−0.6886 ± 0.0002	−0.6152 ± 0.0005	**−0.5982 ± 0.0001**
JESTER	−0.6557 ± 0.0001	**−0.6474 ± 0.0001**	**−0.6474 ± 0.0001**
SUSHI_A	−0.6186 ± 0.0001	−0.6215 ± 0.0001	**−0.6181 ± 0.0002**
SUSHI_B	−0.6784 ± 0.0001	**−0.6203 ± 0.0001**	−0.6205 ± 0.0002
ELECTION_A5	−0.6271 ± 0.0001	**−0.6258 ± 0.0001**	**−0.6258 ± 0.0001**
ELECTION_A9	−0.6552 ± 0.0001	−0.6561 ± 0.0001	**−0.6548 ± 0.0001**
ELECTION_A17	−0.6971 ± 0.0001	−0.6971 ± 0.0001	**−0.6908 ± 0.0002**
ELECTION_A48	−0.6646 ± 0.0001	−0.6649 ± 0.0001	**−0.6643 ± 0.0002**
ELECTION_A81	−0.6617 ± 0.0001	−0.6629 ± 0.0001	**−0.6607 ± 0.0001**
ELECTION_SF07	**−0.5388 ± 0.023**	−0.5469 ± 0.0023	**−0.5388 ± 0.0021**
ELECTION_CM	**−0.5005 ± 0.0005**	−0.5028 ± 0.0004	**−0.5005 ± 0.0005**
ELECTION_DW	−0.4752 ± 0.0008	−0.4769 ± 0.0008	**−0.4751 ± 0.0010**
ELECTION_DN	**−0.4949 ± 0.0006**	−0.4968 ± 0.0006	**−0.4949 ± 0.0005**

Table 2: Test accuracy on rank aggregation datasets.

DATASET	NAIVE	B-T	OUR BEST
PEER POSTER	0.6570 ± 0.0001	0.7088 ± 0.0008	**0.7094 ± 0.0009**
PEER FINAL	0.6353 ± 0.0003	0.7545 ± 0.0014	**0.7588 ± 0.0060**
MOVIELENS	0.5870 ± 0.0001	0.6794 ± 0.0002	**0.6798 ± 0.0002**
JESTER	0.6142 ± 0.0001	**0.6236 ± 0.0001**	**0.6236 ± 0.0001**
SUSHI_A	0.6529 ± 0.0001	0.6529 ± 0.0001	**0.6535 ± 0.0005**
SUSHI_B	0.6123 ± 0.0001	0.6582 ± 0.0001	**0.6591 ± 0.0005**
ELECTION_A5	0.6531 ± 0.0001	**0.6587 ± 0.0001**	**0.6587 ± 0.0001**
ELECTION_A9	0.6123 ± 0.0001	0.6088 ± 0.0001	**0.6125 ± 0.0002**
ELECTION_A17	0.5311 ± 0.0001	0.5262 ± 0.0001	**0.5318 ± 0.0009**
ELECTION_A48	0.5996 ± 0.0001	0.6001 ± 0.0001	**0.6002 ± 0.0001**
ELECTION_A81	0.5998 ± 0.0001	**0.6037 ± 0.0001**	**0.6037 ± 0.0001**
ELECTION_SF	0.7420 ± 0.0018	0.7401 ± 0.0021	**0.7423 ± 0.0022**
ELECTION_CM	0.7093 ± 0.0006	0.7081 ± 0.0005	**0.7094 ± 0.0004**
ELECTION_DW	0.7226 ± 0.0008	**0.7228 ± 0.0011**	0.7227 ± 0.0011
ELECTION_DN	**0.7094 ± 0.0008**	0.7091 ± 0.0008	**0.7094 ± 0.0008**

Table 3: The effects of the bias term on test log-likelihood (top) and accuracy (bottom).

DATASET	*blade-chest-dist* W/O	*blade-chest-dist* W/	*blade-chest-inner* W/O	*blade-chest-inner* W/
WoL	−0.5507 ± 0.0032	**−0.5405 ± 0.0035**	−0.5385 ± 0.0027	**−0.5375 ± 0.0037**
HotS	−0.5190 ± 0.0082	**−0.5051 ± 0.0080**	−0.5085 ± 0.0058	**−0.5042 ± 0.0080**
DotA 2	−0.6635 ± 0.0056	**−0.6304 ± 0.0069**	−0.6196 ± 0.0067	**−0.6194 ± 0.0062**
TENNIS	−0.5790 ± 0.0055	**−0.5546 ± 0.0051**	−0.5544 ± 0.0034	**−0.5533 ± 0.0040**
DATASET	*blade-chest-dist* W/O	*blade-chest-dist* W/	*blade-chest-inner* W/O	*blade-chest-inner* W/
WoL	0.7139 ± 0.0048	**0.7323 ± 0.0043**	**0.7468 ± 0.0037**	0.7462 ± 0.0034
HotS	0.7429 ± 0.0057	**0.7639 ± 0.0052**	0.7740 ± 0.0058	**0.7742 ± 0.0059**
DotA 2	0.6360 ± 0.0058	**0.6579 ± 0.0082**	0.6519 ± 0.0089	**0.6553 ± 0.0093**
TENNIS	0.6804 ± 0.0047	**0.6968 ± 0.0043**	0.6941 ± 0.0048	**0.6956 ± 0.0049**

training set. The results are in the right panel of Figure 7. The dominance of our methods remains the same (the two lines almost completely overlap). The role of two baselines get switched: the naive baseline that simply memorizes what happened in the training matches approaches the accuracy of our models as the size of the training set increases, while Bradley-Terry is almost unusable because its assumption does not match how the data is generated.

4.6 Do we see significant intransitivity in rank aggregation data?

In the previous experiments we used direct matchup data. Now we will use data in the form of rankings. The setup is as follows: we have a set of items/candidates, a subsets of which judges are asked to rank from most favored to least favored. The usual task is to aggregate these individual preferences in order to form an global ranking of all items. Here, however, we are more interested in predicting pairwise comparisons. Of particular interest is whether there are multi-dimensional aspects of the items that result in intransitivity.

Note that it is possible to have intransitivity in rank aggregation data. Imagine an example that bears a resemblance to the rock-paper-scissors scenario: We have three candidates A, B and C. The votes from three judges are $A > B > C$, $B > C > A$ and $C > A > B$. Breaking these votes into pairwise comparisons, we have A wins over B by $2:1$, B wins over C by $2:1$ and C wins over A by $2:1$. Could similar behaviors also make significant appearance in real-world data?

We tested it on a wide range of datasets, including (a) peer grading data for both poster presentation and final project from [32]; (b) the movielens 100k dataset [21]; (c) the Jester joke rating dataset [18]; (d) the sushi preference dataset on both granularities of ingredients [25]; and (e) several top election datasets from [36] in terms of size: A5, A9, A17, A48, A81, San Francisco 2007 Mayoral, County Meath, Dublin North and Dublin West. If the number of items assigned to each judge is very large, we subsampled randomly.

We follow the experiment setting in Section 4.2, except that we partition the data into training, validation and testing sets by judges rather than by individual comparisons. The (best validated) results are in Table 1 and Table 2. On most of the datasets, our method outperforms the baselines. However, the improvements are typically small, especially in terms of test accuracy. The results suggest that there is some, but not much intransitivity in these rank aggregation applications that can be captured by our model.

There could be two explanations for this. For one, most of the data we tested on contains a close to perfect ranking. Some intransitivity may exist for candidates of similar ranking, but it only accounts for a small part. Suppose we have N candidates, n of which have intransitivity among them. n is small compared to N, and when broken into pairwise comparisons, its effect gets further diluted to n^2 against N^2. The second explanation is about how the data is generated. They are not in natural pairwise comparison form. When each judge is asked to construct a ranking for all or a subset of the candidates, he or she is likely to have a global utility function in mind or in subconsciousness to help, which eliminates the space for intransitivities due to behavioral biases (e.g. framing).

4.7 How does the bias term affect the performance of our model?

We only showed the results of our model with the bias term so far. It is worth checking how much effect the added bias term has on our model. Here we take the previous 1 vs. 1 competition datasets, and list the best log-likelihood and accuracy we get from both models with and without the bias terms. As one can see in Table 3, adding the bias term is almost always beneficial (the only exception being test accuracy on WoL for *blade-chest-inner*). Another interesting observation is that *blade-chest-dist* seems to benefit more from the bias term than *blade-chest-inner*.

5. CONCLUSIONS

We presented a method for learning preference relations from pairwise comparison data. By modeling each item/player in a multi-dimensional space, the model can represent intransitive relations. We explore datasets ranging from online video games and sports to peer grading and election, finding that the new model provides improved prediction accuracy on several tasks, especially in the domain of online video games.

6. ACKNOWLEDGMENTS

We would like to thank Song Cao, Brad Gulko, Arzoo Katiyar, Albert Liu, Karthik Raman, Adith Swaminathan, Chenhao Tan, Wenlei Xie, Yexiang Xue, Johanna Ye, Yisong Yue for their constructive discussions and feedback. This work was supported in part through NSF Awards IIS-1247637, IIS-1217686, and IIS-1513692.

7. REFERENCES

[1] R. P. Adams, G. E. Dahl, and I. Murray. Incorporating side information in probabilistic matrix factorization with gaussian processes. *arXiv preprint arXiv:1003.4944*, 2010.

[2] N. Aizenberg, Y. Koren, and O. Somekh. Build your own music recommender by modeling internet radio streams. In *Proceedings of the 21st international conference on World Wide Web*, pages 1–10. ACM, 2012.

[3] C. Barrette and D. Vandal. Social rank, dominance, antler size, and access to food in snow-bound wild woodland caribou. *Behaviour*, pages 118–146, 1986.

[4] J. Bilmes, G. Ji, and M. Meila. Intransitive likelihood-ratio classifiers. In *NIPS*, pages 1141–1148, 2001.

[5] L. Bottou. Large-scale machine learning with stochastic gradient descent. In *Proceedings of COMPSTAT'2010*, pages 177–186. Springer, 2010.

[6] R. A. Bradley and M. E. Terry. Rank analysis of incomplete block designs: I. the method of paired comparisons. *Biometrika*, pages 324–345, 1952.

[7] M. Cattelan et al. Models for paired comparison data: A review with emphasis on dependent data. *Statistical Science*, 27(3):412–433, 2012.

[8] M. Cattelan, C. Varin, and D. Firth. Dynamic bradley–terry modelling of sports tournaments. *Journal of the Royal Statistical Society: Series C (Applied Statistics)*, 62(1):135–150, 2013.

[9] D. Causeur and F. Husson. A 2-dimensional extension of the bradley–terry model for paired comparisons. *Journal of statistical planning and inference*, 135(2):245–259, 2005.

[10] S. Chen, J. L. Moore, D. Turnbull, and T. Joachims. Playlist prediction via metric embedding. In *Proceedings of the 18th ACM SIGKDD international conference on Knowledge discovery and data mining*, pages 714–722. ACM, 2012.

[11] S. Chen, J. Xu, and T. Joachims. Multi-space probabilistic sequence modeling. In *Proceedings of the 19th ACM SIGKDD international conference on Knowledge discovery and data mining*, pages 865–873. ACM, 2013.

[12] P. Dangauthier, R. Herbrich, T. Minka, T. Graepel, et al. Trueskill through time: Revisiting the history of chess. In *NIPS*, 2007.

[13] G. S. Elias, R. Garfield, and K. R. Gutschera. *Characteristics of games*. MIT Press, 2012.

[14] W. V. Gehrlein. The probability of intransitivity of pairwise comparisons in individual preference. *Mathematical social sciences*, 17(1):67–75, 1989.

[15] D. F. Gleich and L.-h. Lim. Rank aggregation via nuclear norm minimization. In *Proceedings of the 17th ACM SIGKDD international conference on Knowledge discovery and data mining*, pages 60–68. ACM, 2011.

[16] M. E. Glickman. A comprehensive guide to chess ratings. *American Chess Journal*, 3:59–102, 1995.

[17] A. Globerson, G. Chechik, F. Pereira, and N. Tishby. Euclidean embedding of co-occurrence data. *Journal of Machine Learning Research*, 8(10), 2007.

[18] K. Goldberg, T. Roeder, D. Gupta, and C. Perkins. Eigentaste: A constant time collaborative filtering algorithm. *Information Retrieval*, 4(2):133–151, 2001.

[19] P. Gopalan, J. M. Hofman, and D. M. Blei. Scalable recommendation with poisson factorization. *arXiv preprint arXiv:1311.1704*, 2013.

[20] R. Herbrich, T. Minka, and T. Graepel. TrueskillâĎć: A

bayesian skill rating system. In *Advances in Neural Information Processing Systems*, pages 569–576, 2006.

[21] J. L. Herlocker, J. A. Konstan, A. Borchers, and J. Riedl. An algorithmic framework for performing collaborative filtering. In *Proceedings of the 22nd annual international ACM SIGIR conference on Research and development in information retrieval*, pages 230–237. ACM, 1999.

[22] T.-K. Huang, C.-J. Lin, and R. C. Weng. Ranking individuals by group comparisons. In *Proceedings of the 23rd international conference on Machine learning*, pages 425–432. ACM, 2006.

[23] T.-K. Huang, R. C. Weng, and C.-J. Lin. Generalized bradley-terry models and multi-class probability estimates. *The Journal of Machine Learning Research*, 7:85–115, 2006.

[24] D. R. Hunter. Mm algorithms for generalized bradley-terry models. *Annals of Statistics*, pages 384–406, 2004.

[25] T. Kamishima. Nantonac collaborative filtering: recommendation based on order responses. In *Proceedings of the ninth ACM SIGKDD international conference on Knowledge discovery and data mining*, pages 583–588. ACM, 2003.

[26] P. Linares. Are inconsistent decisions better? an experiment with pairwise comparisons. *European Journal of Operational Research*, 193(2):492–498, 2009.

[27] R. D. Luce. *Individual Choice Behavior a Theoretical Analysis*. john Wiley and Sons, 1959.

[28] K. O. May. Intransitivity, utility, and the aggregation of preference patterns. *Econometrica: Journal of the Econometric Society*, pages 1–13, 1954.

[29] J. E. Menke and T. R. Martinez. A bradley–terry artificial neural network model for individual ratings in group competitions. *Neural computing and Applications*, 17(2):175–186, 2008.

[30] T. Mikolov, I. Sutskever, K. Chen, G. S. Corrado, and J. Dean. Distributed representations of words and phrases and their compositionality. In *Advances in Neural Information Processing Systems*, pages 3111–3119, 2013.

[31] J. L. Moore, S. Chen, T. Joachims, and D. Turnbull. Learning to embed songs and tags for playlist prediction. In *ISMIR*, pages 349–354, 2012.

[32] K. Raman and T. Joachims. Methods for ordinal peer grading. In *Proceedings of the 20th ACM SIGKDD international conference on Knowledge discovery and data mining*, pages 1037–1046. ACM, 2014.

[33] B. Sinervo and C. M. Lively. The rock-paper-scissors game and the evolution of alternative male strategies. *Nature*, 380(6571):240–243, 1996.

[34] R. Socher, B. Huval, C. D. Manning, and A. Y. Ng. Semantic compositionality through recursive matrix-vector spaces. In *Proceedings of the 2012 Joint Conference on Empirical Methods in Natural Language Processing and Computational Natural Language Learning*, pages 1201–1211. Association for Computational Linguistics, 2012.

[35] L. L. Thurstone. A law of comparative judgment. *Psychological review*, 34(4):273, 1927.

[36] N. Tideman. *Collective decisions and voting*. Ashgate Burlington, 2006.

[37] J. Tufto, E. J. Solberg, and T.-H. Ringsby. Statistical models of transitive and intransitive dominance structures. *Animal behaviour*, 55(6):1489–1498, 1998.

[38] L. Van der Maaten and G. Hinton. Visualizing data using t-sne. *Journal of Machine Learning Research*, 9(2579-2605):85, 2008.

[39] J. Weston, S. Bengio, and N. Usunier. Wsabie: Scaling up to large vocabulary image annotation. In *Proceedings of the Twenty-Second international joint conference on Artificial Intelligence-Volume Volume Three*, pages 2764–2770. AAAI Press, 2011.

[40] J. Weston, S. Chopra, and K. Adams. #tagspace: Semantic embeddings from hashtags. In *EMNLP*, 2014.

[41] D. Zhou, S. Zhu, K. Yu, X. Song, B. L. Tseng, H. Zha, and C. L. Giles. Learning multiple graphs for document recommendations. In *Proceedings of the 17th international conference on World Wide Web*, pages 141–150. ACM, 2008.

Crowdsourcing High Quality Labels with a Tight Budget

Qi Li[1], Fenglong Ma[1], Jing Gao[1], Lu Su[1], Christopher J. Quinn[2]
[1]SUNY Buffalo, Buffalo, NY USA
[2]Purdue University, West Lafayette, IN USA
{qli22,fenglong,jing,lusu}@buffalo.edu , cjquinn@purdue.edu

ABSTRACT

In the past decade, commercial crowdsourcing platforms have revolutionized the ways of classifying and annotating data, especially for large datasets. Obtaining labels for a single instance can be inexpensive, but for large datasets, it is important to allocate budgets wisely. With limited budgets, requesters must trade-off between the quantity of labeled instances and the quality of the final results. Existing budget allocation methods can achieve good quantity but cannot guarantee high quality of individual instances under a tight budget. However, in some scenarios, requesters may be willing to label fewer instances but of higher quality. Moreover, they may have different requirements on quality for different tasks. To address these challenges, we propose a flexible budget allocation framework called Requallo. Requallo allows requesters to set their specific requirements on the labeling quality and maximizes the number of labeled instances that achieve the quality requirement under a tight budget. The budget allocation problem is modeled as a Markov decision process and a sequential labeling policy is produced. The proposed policy greedily searches for the instance to query next as the one that can provide the maximum reward for the goal. The Requallo framework is further extended to consider worker reliability so that the budget can be better allocated. Experiments on two real-world crowdsourcing tasks as well as a simulated task demonstrate that when the budget is tight, the proposed Requallo framework outperforms existing state-of-the-art budget allocation methods from both quantity and quality aspects.

1. INTRODUCTION

In the Internet age, the thriving growth of crowdsourcing platforms unleashes the astonishing power of crowd wisdom, which makes it more convenient and efficient to obtain labels. On commercial crowdsourcing platforms such as Amazon Mechanical Turk[1] (mTurk) and CrowdFlower[2], requesters design and post their tasks (also known as human intelligence tasks, HITs). Each HIT may contain one or several instances (such as images) to be labeled. Workers can view available HITs and choose whichever they want to work on. After the workers finish their jobs, requesters adjudicate the final results and pay the workers. As individual workers may make mistakes, requesters can ask multiple workers for each instance. This "repeated labeling" is commonly used and recommended by mTurk[3] to get more accurate labels. Although crowdsourcing is known to be a cheap source for individual labels, with the repeated labeling and a big pool of instances, it is important to use the budget wisely, especially when the budget is tight comparing with the size of instance pool. For example, ten thousand dollars may still be tight to label all inappropriate videos on YouTube. With a tight budget, the requesters can only afford a limited amount of labels and they need to decide which instances should get labels and how many on them.

One of the major dilemma the requester faces is the trade-off between **quantity** of labeled instances and **quality** of the final results. Intuitively, if we want more instances to be labeled (high quantity), each instance will receive less labels, resulting in a lower quality of the final results; on the other hand, if we want high quality results, we may end up with fewer questions being labeled (low quantity) so each instance can get more labels. This trade-off is even more noticeable under a tight budget. The preference of this trade-off may vary for different tasks. For some tasks, quantity is more important, but for others, quality is preferred. Under a tight budget, most existing budget allocation work [4, 11, 19, 24, 25, 30, 31, 38], though being able to achieve good quantity, cannot guarantee high quality for individual instances. Consider a case that a requester has N instances and can only afford N labels. Then these budget allocation methods will give exactly one label to each instance, and the final results are inadequate to justify. However, in some scenarios, requesters may prefer quality over quantity. They may be willing to label less instances, i.e., sacrifice quantity to some extent, but require what they get is of high quality. In that case, the existing methods cannot meet the requesters' needs. Therefore, a method is badly needed if requesters have a preference of quality over quantity under a tight budget.

To achieve this, the major challenge is how a requester can measure the quality of the labels, a problem often overlooked in the crowdsourcing literature. Most crowdsourcing algorithms use accuracy rate to measure the quality of fi-

[1]https://www.mturk.com/mturk/
[2]http://www.crowdflower.com/
[3]mturkpublic.s3.amazonaws.com/docs/MTURK_BP.pdf

WSDM'16, February 22–25, 2016, San Francisco, CA, USA.
© 2016 ACM. ISBN 978-1-4503-3716-8/16/02...$15.00
DOI: http://dx.doi.org/10.1145/2835776.2835797

nal results. It can be a nice measurement for an algorithm, but usually is impractical for requesters because the ground truths are often unknown, which is the reason requesters post the HITs in the first place. In this case, it is impossible to judge whether an instance is correctly labeled, and it is hard to tell how many labels are enough.

To address this challenge, we propose to use **confidence**, a user-specified measurement, to measure quality. Instead of judging a result as correct or incorrect, the requester can judge a result as confident or unconfident based on his "requirement," such as a minimum ratio between two classes' vote counts. If the results have high confidence under a strict requirement, it is likely that the results also have high accuracy. We use the following example to illustrate how confidence is decided under a requirement.

EXAMPLE 1. *Suppose a requester sets a requirement as a minimum ratio of* 4 *between two classes' vote counts. Then an instance with results of one vote for class* $+1$ *and two votes for class* -1 *is unconfident, while another instance with results of one versus four is confident. Comparing these two, the latter one is more likely to obtain the correct label.*

Using this measurement, the requesters can specify a concrete and detailed requirement to reflect their needs for quality. Another benefit of using confidence is that it can help requesters identify hard instances so that further actions can be taken. A challenging instance might remain unconfident after many rounds of labeling process. Then the requesters may not want to waste their precious budgets on that instance and should consider asking experts for labels.

In this paper, we develop a **Requ**irement based budget **allo**cation (Requallo) framework, which can adjust the allocation policy according to requesters' needs on quality in the form of a confidence requirement. No matter the size of a budget, the proposed Requallo framework can guarantee the requesters' desired quality while trying to maximize quantity (i.e., number of confident instances) and staying within the budget. Formally, the objective of the framework is stated as maximizing the overall expected completeness of the tasks subject to the budget, where completeness for an instance reflects how much confidence it gets under the requirement. To solve this optimization problem, we formulate it as a Markov decision process and use a one-step look-ahead greedy algorithm to search for the instance with the maximum reward in completeness to label next.

We further extend the basic model to incorporate workers' reliabilities. Instead of using vote counts when calculating expected completeness, we use the weighted vote counts derived via MLE estimation, where the weights are determined by the corresponding workers' reliability. Standard ways of inferring reliability for crowdsourcing include qualification, spammer detection, and EM based aggregation. Extensions on labeling in parallel and multi-class cases are also discussed.

In summary, we make the following contributions in this paper:

- We identify the trade-off between quantity and quality in crowdsourcing tasks under a tight budget. Requesters can specify a measure of quality.
- We build a flexible framework to allocate the budget for instances according to requesters' needs on quality. Examples of various quality requirements are discussed and demonstrated.
- We formulate the budget allocation problem as a Markov decision process and produce a sequential labeling policy. It maximizes the number of labeled instances that achieve the quality requirement while staying under the budget.
- We test the proposed framework on two real-world crowdsourcing tasks and a simulated task. The real-world tasks include one benchmark NLP task conducted on mTurk and one trivia game conducted via an app. The results clearly demonstrate the advantages of the framework when the budget is tight.

In the following section, we give a brief overview on the related work in crowdsourcing and budget allocation problem. Then in Section 3 we formulate the problem and derive the proposed Requallo framework. In Section 4, the behavior of different policies is examined and analyzed via experiments conducted on two real-world crowdsourcing tasks and a simulated task. Finally, we conclude the paper in Section 5.

2. RELATED WORK

Recent years have witnessed the growing importance and popularity of crowdsourcing applications in real life, and thus many research efforts have been contributed to the development of new algorithms and designs for crowdsourcing tasks. Quality is one of the biggest concern in crowdsourcing tasks [28]. Research topics for this concern include how to aggregate crowd labels [3, 5, 6, 21, 29, 33–35, 40], how to select which crowd workers to work for a instance/task [7, 9, 12, 37, 41], and how to better design the crowdsourcing questions/tasks [8, 22, 26, 32, 36, 39]. Either by better task design or targeting a small group of informative workers, fewer labels may be needed for each instance, so they can potentially save the costs. However, in those work, budget constraints are not explicitly considered.

Motivated by the label cost concern, the budget allocation problem in crowdsourcing has attracted considerable attention [4, 10, 11, 19, 24, 25, 30, 31, 38]. Methods in [25, 27, 30, 38] focus on pricing tasks given a budget. The platforms designed in [25, 27] use flexible prices for different workers. However, this work does not consider the quality of the results. Work in [10, 30, 38] takes quality into consideration. However, different from our problem setting, interdependent tasks are considered in [30] and negotiation between requesters and workers is required and modeled by game theory in [10, 38]. The method proposed in [11] provides a minimum number of labels in order to achieve target reliability ϵ. This work is built upon the assumption that instances have the same level of difficulty, which is different from ours. The work [31] further improves the theoretical guarantee from the PAC (probably approximately correct) perspective. All of these methods are all inapplicable when the budget is lower than supporting one label per instance.

Among the budget allocation work, [4, 19, 24] are the most related to ours. They all sequentially select instances to label. In [24], label uncertainty is estimated as the tail probability of a Beta distribution and the instances with the highest label uncertainties are selected for more labels. This work assumes that data quality is the same on all instances, whereas we assume the quality would be higher for easy instances. Both [4] and [19] model the sequential labeling problem as a Markov decision process, though they have different goals from ours: the goal in [4] is to maximize overall accuracy, while the goal in [19] is to maximize a utility function with consideration of pull market (i.e., workers may not accept jobs from requesters). Under our problem setting, [19] can be considered as a special case of the proposed Requallo framework (see Section 4.1). Under a tight budget (such as affording N labels for N instances), methods in [4, 24] tend to allocate the budget uniformly among the instances since querying on an unlabeled instance would be optimal. As a result, though a large quantity of instances may be labeled, very few of them could achieve the quality requirement. To the best of our knowledge, we are the first to address the trade-off between quantity and quality under the tight budget. The proposed Requallo framework takes requesters' specific needs for quality into account and works nicely even with very tight budgets.

3. METHODOLOGY

In this section, we introduce the proposed **Requ**irement based budget **allo**cation (Requallo) framework. We start with the basic framework, and then extend it to incorporate workers' reliability. Finally, some practical issues are discussed.

3.1 Basic Requallo Framework

Problem Setting and Formulation

Suppose a requester has N instances. Each instance is a binary labeling problem and they are independent of each other. The true label for the i-th instance Z_i is either $+1$ or -1. Adopting the idea from probabilistic classification, we model Z_i as a random variable. $P(Z_i = +1)$, which can be interpreted as the relative frequency that $+1$ appears when the number of workers approaches infinity, indicates the difficulty level of the i-th instance. If $P(Z_i = +1)$ is close to 0.5, it implies that the i-th instance is difficult, because even when the requester asks a large number of workers, there is still no predominant answer. On the other hand, if $P(Z_i = +1)$ is close to 1 (or 0), the instance is relatively easy. Here we assume that instances are not misleading, that is, $P(Z_i = +1) \gg 0.5$ (or $P(Z_i = +1) \ll 0.5$) implies that the true label Z_i is $+1$ (or -1).

Here, we assume all the workers are noiseless and independent, i.e., $P(y_{ij} = +1) = P(Z_i = +1)$ where y_{ij} is worker j's label on the i-th instance. In other words, the labels provided by the workers only depend on the true label of the instance and its difficulty level.[4] Based on this assumption, all labels for the i-th instance are essentially i.i.d. samples drawn from a Bernoulli distribution with $P_i = P(Z_i = +1)$. Majority voting can be used when conducting the final results since individual labels are equivalent. The cases that workers have different levels of reliability will be discussed in Section 3.2.

The proposed framework has two inputs. The requester specifies a confidence requirement and the budget. As mentioned in the introduction, different tasks may have different requirements. Therefore, the proposed framework can incorporate a variety of requirements as part of input. In this paper, the cost of a single label is assumed to be the same over all instances and all workers, so the budget works as a constraint that the requesters can only afford a certain amount of labels. We use T to denote the maximum amount. Note that we do not have to exhaust the budget. If all instances achieve the requirement before the budget is exhausted, the labeling process will be stopped and the remaining budget will be saved.

The goal of the proposed Requallo framework is to have as many instances as possible achieve the requirement under the budget, i.e., to maximize quantity while maintaining desired quality. Since the quantity can only be an integer, this goal will inevitably lead to an integer programming, an NP-hard problem. Therefore, we relax this integer constraint by maximizing the overall completeness subject to the budget, where completeness of an instance is a ratio in $[0, 1]$. The concrete definition of completeness will be introduced later.

Table 1 summarizes the frequently used notations in this paper; some will be introduced later.

Table 1: Notations

Notation	Definition
$\{1, 2, \ldots N\}$	index set of instances
$\{1, 2, \ldots M\}$	index set of workers
Z_i	true label of the i-th instance
$P(Z_i = +1), P_i$	difficulty level of the i-th instance
$y_{i,j}$	worker j's label on the i-th instance
T	maximum number of labels under the budget
a_i	vote count of $+1$ labels
b_i	vote count of -1 labels
$V_i(a_i, b_i)$	expected completeness of the i-th instance
$R(S^t, i^t)$	reward for the i-th instance at stage t
θ_j	reliability of worker j

Requirement Examples

Before formally introducing the proposed framework, we want to provide some examples of the requirements that requesters may be interested in. We denote the vote count for $+1$ class as a_i, and vote count for -1 class as b_i for the i-th instance. The requester expresses his quality needs for the final results using a specific requirement. A strict requirement will ask for a big difference between a_i and b_i (i.e., big $|a_i - b_i|$). If a requester needs high confidence on the results, then he can set a strict requirement.

One example of requirements is to set a minimum ratio between two classes' vote counts, i.e., to label the i-th instance as $+1$ if $a_i : b_i \geqslant c$ and as -1 if $b_i : a_i \geqslant c$, where the constant $c > 1$. If we estimate $P(Z_i = +1)$ with $\frac{a_i}{a_i+b_i}$, then this requirement is equivalent to setting a threshold on entropy, which is a commonly used measurement for information uncertainty. A larger c means a stricter requirement on the confidence.

Another possible requirement is to conduct a hypothesis test and approve the result when the observed labels are statistically significant. For example, Fisher exact test can be used [1], where the null hypothesis is that the observed labels are from a random guess and the alternative hypothesis is that they are not randomly guessed. Based on the null hypothesis, we can calculate the p-value, the probability that the observed labels and more extreme vote counts happen given that the workers provide random labels. When the null hypothesis is rejected with significance level of α, i.e., p-value $< \alpha$, we approve the result and determine the final label by majority voting. The significance level α is often set as a small value, usually 0.05, 0.1, or 0.2. A smaller α

[4] Note that in our definition a worker being noiseless does not mean that he provides correct labels for every instance, which is different from some literature.

gives a stricter requirement. We use the following example to illustrate how the Fisher exact test can be conducted.

Example 2. *Suppose we set $\alpha = 0.1$, and the observed vote counts are $a_i = 1$ and $b_i = 4$. To calculate the p-value, we find the more extreme case, with $a_i = 0$ and $b_i = 5$. Therefore, the p-value $= \binom{5}{1}0.5^1 0.5^4 + \binom{5}{0}0.5^0 0.5^5 = 0.1875$, which is greater than α. Then the null hypothesis cannot be rejected, that is, there is no strong evidence that the observed labels are not randomly guessed. For this observed labeling result, it does not achieve the requirement yet.*

The aforementioned requirements can also be combined with other simple requirements such as minimum count of labels per instance $a_i + b_i > \delta_{min}$ and maximum count of labels per instance $a_i + b_i < \delta_{max}$.

Calculating Completeness

An instance is completed once it is confident based on the requirement. We define the completeness of the i-th instance as the ratio between the observed total vote counts $a_i + b_i$ and the minimum count of labels it needs to achieve the requirement, where the latter is denoted as $r(a_i, b_i|Z_i)$. At the beginning of labeling process, an instance has no labels, so its completeness is 0. Then it gradually gets more and more labels. Once the instance achieves the requirement, then the ratio becomes 1, which means the labeling process on that instance is completed and it needs no more labels (therefore, $a_i + b_i$ will not increase any more). Note that the completeness depends on not only the current vote counts and the requirement, but also on Z_i. We use the following example to illustrate how to calculate completeness.

Example 3. *Suppose we have $a_i = 3$ and $b_i = 1$, and the requirement is the minimum ratio of 4. In the case that $Z_i = +1$, we can achieve the requirement if $a_i = 4$ and $b_i = 1$. Therefore, we need at least five labels to pass the requirement, i.e., $r(3, 1|Z_i = +1) = 4 + 1 = 5$. The completeness in this case is 4/5. However, if $Z_i = -1$, then we need at least $b = 12$ to achieve the requirement, which means minimum count of labels it needs is $r(3, 1|Z_i = -1) = 3 + 12 = 15$ labels, and the completeness is 4/15.*

From Example 3, it is clear that the denominator in the completeness $r(a_i, b_i|Z_i)$ is calculated based on the vote count of the opposite class of Z_i. That is, given $Z_i = +1$, the completeness is only determined by the vote count for -1(i.e. b_i) and vice versa. Therefore, we abbreviate $r(a_i, b_i|Z_i = +1) = r(b_i)$ and $r(a_i, b_i|Z_i = -1) = r(a_i)$. Table 2 shows examples of function $r(\cdot)$ with different input x' for several aforementioned requirements. These examples present that with x votes for the wrong class, how many total vote counts the i-th instance needs to achieve the corresponding requirement.

Expected Completeness

Since the completeness of the i-th instance depends on Z_i, which is a random variable, from a decision theory perspective we want to take an action that maximizes the expected completeness defined as follows:

$$\begin{aligned} V_i(a_i, b_i) &= \mathbb{E}(Completeness_i|a_i, b_i) \\ &= P(Z_i = +1|a_i, b_i)\frac{a_i + b_i}{r(b_i)} \\ &\quad + P(Z_i = -1|a_i, b_i)\frac{a_i + b_i}{r(a_i)}. \end{aligned} \quad (1)$$

Table 2: Some examples of $r(x)$ with different x'.

Requirement	x = 1	2	3	4	5
minimum ratio $c = 4$	5	10	15	20	25
minimum ratio $c = 5$	6	12	18	24	30
Fisher $p = 0.2$	5	8	10	12	15
Fisher $p = 0.1$	7	9	12	14	17
Fisher $p = 0.05$	8	11	13	16	18

If $P(Z_i = +1|a_i, b_i)$ is estimated based on empirical relative frequency $\frac{a_i}{a_i+b_i}$ (which is also the MLE estimator for Bernoulli(P_i)), then $V_i = \frac{a_i}{r(b_i)} + \frac{b_i}{r(a_i)} \leqslant 1$ and "=" can be satisfied only when the requirement is absolute consensus. This conflicts with our intuition, however, as the expected completeness should fall into the range of $[0, 1]$, and reach 1 when the labeling process is considered to be completed, i.e., when it meets the requirement $a_i + b_i = r(b_i)$ or $a_i + b_i = r(a_i)$.

In order to solve this problem, we propose to modify the estimation of $P(Z_i = +1)$ as following:

$$P(Z_i = +1|a_i, b_i) = \begin{cases} \frac{a_i}{a_i+b_i} + \frac{b_i}{r(b_i)} & \text{if } a_i > b_i, \\ 0.5 & \text{if } a_i = b_i, \\ \frac{a_i}{a_i+b_i} - \frac{a_i}{r(a_i)} & \text{if } a_i < b_i. \end{cases} \quad (2)$$

When the i-th instance achieves the requirement and $a_i > b_i$, the requester is confident about the result, so he will stop collecting labels for this instance and use $+1$ as the final class label. In such a case, a_i is usually much bigger than b_i and Z_i is believed to be $+1$ with confidence, so assigning $P(Z_i = +1|a_i, b_i) = 1$ is reasonable. In the case that the i-th instance is far from completed, $P(Z_i = +1|a_i, b_i)$ would still be close to $\frac{a_i}{a_i+b_i}$.

With the expected completeness defined in Eq. (1), the goal of achieving the requirement for as many instances as possible, while staying within the budget, is modeled as the following optimization problem:

$$\begin{aligned} \sup_{\pi} \quad & \mathbb{E}_\pi(\textstyle\sum_{i=1}^N V_i(a_i, b_i)) \\ s.t. \quad & \textstyle\sum_{i=1}^N a_i + b_i \leqslant T, \end{aligned} \quad (3)$$

where π is the policy to choose instances for labeling and $\mathbb{E}_\pi$ means the expectation taken over all the potential outcomes of the policy.

Markov Decision Process

A Markov decision process (MDP) is a natural framework for the optimization problem in Eq. (3). A MDP contains a set of states $\mathcal{S}$, a set of actions $\mathcal{A}$, transition probabilities from one state to another $\mathcal{P}$ and a real valued reward function $\mathcal{R}(\mathcal{S}, \mathcal{A})$.

In our problem setting, the set of states $\mathcal{S}$ consists of all the possible labeling observations that can be achieved under the budget. Since the budget is finite, $\mathcal{S}$ is also a finite set. At time t, we get exactly t labels, so the state is then:

$$\begin{aligned} \mathcal{S}^t = \{(a_i^t, b_i^t)_{i=1}^N | \quad & a_i^t, b_i^t \geqslant 0, \textstyle\sum_{i=1}^N a_i^t + b_i^t = t, \\ & a_i^t + b_i^t \leqslant \min(r(a_i^t), r(b_i^t))\}, \end{aligned} \quad (4)$$

where a_i^t and b_i^t are the vote counts at stage t.

The set of actions consists of the potential instances to be queried next, that is, the instances that do not achieve the requirement yet. If we only obtain one label on one instance at each time, the transition probability is essentially $P(Z_{i^t}|S^t, i^t)$, where i^t is the chosen instance to label at stage t. As the state of the i-th instance at time t is directly determined by (a_{i^t}, b_{i^t}), it is identical with $P(Z_{i^t}|a_{i^t}, b_{i^t})$ defined in Eq. (2).

For the reward function $R(S, i)$, we use the result from [4] and define the stage-wise expected reward as:

$$R(S^t, i^t) = \mathbb{E}(V_{i^t}(a_{i^t}^{t+1}, b_{i^t}^{t+1}) - V_{i^t}(a_{i^t}^t, b_{i^t}^t)|S^t, i^t), \quad (5)$$

and the optimization becomes:

$$\sup_{\pi} \mathbb{E}_{\pi}(\sum_{t=0}^{T-1} R(S^t, i^t)). \quad (6)$$

This stage-wise reward function is to evaluate how much difference an extra label can make prior to the decision. There are basically two cases to consider: the next label y_{i^t} is $+1$ or -1. Correspondingly, the differences it may make are:

$$R_{i^t}^{+1} = V_{i^t}(a_{i^t}^t + 1, b_{i^t}^t) - V_{i^t}(a_{i^t}^t, b_{i^t}^t),$$
$$R_{i^t}^{-1} = V_{i^t}(a_{i^t}^t, b_{i^t}^t + 1) - V_{i^t}(a_{i^t}^t, b_{i^t}^t).$$

Then $R(S^t, i^t)$ can be calculated as:

$$R(S^t, i^t) = P(y_{i^t} = +1)R_{i^t}^{+1} + P(y_{i^t} = -1)R_{i^t}^{-1}. \quad (7)$$

With the defined MDP model, there are well-developed algorithms to compute the optimal policy, such as dynamic programming [18] and linear programming [23]. However, the state space defined in Eq. (4) is exponential with respect to the budget. The computation complexity in such a case is intractable. Therefore, we use a one-step look-ahead greedy strategy instead to approximate the optimal policy. Motivated by [4], we also change the immediate reward function $R(S^t, i^t) = \max(R_{i^t}^{+1}, R_{i^t}^{-1})$ for better performance. The greedy strategy will provide a sequential policy and choose the instance that has the maximum immediate reward, the one with the most optimistic outcome for completeness in our setting. A similar strategy to build a policy for a MDP problem is also applied in [4,19]. Using the greedy strategy, the framework will label instances with the highest priority to easy ones that are also nearly complete.

Summary of the Basic Requallo Framework

So far, we have introduced the basic Requallo framework for a simple problem setting. The requester inputs his budget (or the maximum number of labels he can afford T) and his specific quality requirement. Based on the inputs, a sequential policy is provided to maximize the number of instances that achieve the requester's quality requirement. The framework is summarized in Algorithm 1.

3.2 Model Workers' Reliability

In the basic Requallo framework, we consider noiseless workers, that is, their labels only depend on the instances' true labels and difficulty levels. However, the assumption may be too strong in real-world crowdsourcing scenarios. If workers' varying reliabilities are considered, we may further save the budget in the labeling process by eliminating labels from unreliable workers or adjusting labels' weights based on the workers' reliability.

Suppose there are M workers, and the labels they provide on the i-th instance are $\{y_{i1}, \dots, y_{iM}\}$. Each worker has

Algorithm 1 Basic Requallo framework

Input: instances, maximum number of labels T, requester's requirement.
Output: labeling result for instances.

1: **while** $t \leqslant T$ and $\max_i R(S^t, i^t) > 0$ **do**
2: Based on the requirement, select an instance to label: $i_t = \arg\max_{i \in \{1,\dots,N\}} R(S^t, i^t)$.
3: Receive label $y_{i^t} \in \{+1, -1\}$
4: Update $a_{i^t}^{t+1}$ and $b_{i^t}^{t+1}$ according to y_{i^t}
5: Update $a_i^{t+1} = a_i^t$ and $b_i^{t+1} = b_i^t$ for all $i \neq i^t$
6: $t = t + 1$
7: **end while**
8: **return** Labeling results for instances.

a reliability degree denoted by θ_j, where j is the worker's index. θ_j is defined as $P(y_{ij} = Z_i|Z_i)$, i.e., the probability that worker j provides the same label as the one provided by the noiseless worker. If $\theta_j = 1$, it indicates worker j is noiseless. The label from a worker can be viewed as an output from two layers of Bernoulli sampling. First y_{ij} is drawn from Bernoulli($P_i = P(Z_i = +1)$), and then with probability of $1 - \theta_j$, y_{ij} flips its sign. As a result, we have:

$$P(y_{ij} = +1) = \theta_j P_i + (1 - \theta_j)(1 - P_i),$$
$$P(y_{ij} = -1) = \theta_j(1 - P_i) + (1 - \theta_j)P_i.$$

Here we assume that $\theta_j \geqslant 0.5$. Otherwise we can flip the sign of his labels so that $\theta_j \geqslant 0.5$.

In the following, we discuss how to incorporate workers' reliability under different types of requirements.

Fisher Exact Test Based Requirements

In the Fisher exact test, the p-value is calculated based on the worst case scenario: everyone is random guessing. Unfortunately, the hypothesis already assumes $P(y_{ij} = +1) = 0.5$, so workers' reliability cannot be explicitly applied. However, if we find anyone is indeed random guessing, that worker is considered as a spammer[5] and his labels can be removed. By doing so, the completeness of the task will increase with a high probability.

Example 4. *Let's revisit Example 2. Suppose the worker who answers $+1$ is a spammer. After remove his label, we get a result of $a_i = 0$ and $b_i = 4$. Therefore, p-value $= \binom{4}{0}0.5^0 0.5^4 = 0.0625$, which is smaller than α. The null hypothesis is rejected and this instance achieves the requirement. Its completeness is 1, so it needs no more labels.*

A simple way to detect spammers is to test if $\theta \approx 0.5$ based on the labeled instances that achieve the requirement and his labels on those instances. Note that for those instances, $P(Z_i = +1|a_i, b_i)$ is either 0 or 1 based on Eq. (2) and Z_i is provided by majority voting. In order to estimate θ_j more accurately, we only consider worker j when he provides a certain amount of labels on the labeled instances. Then we can either conduct a Fisher exact test or calculate the confidence interval of θ_j. If the observed labels from him cannot reject the hypothesis or 0.5 falls into the confidence interval, this worker is considered as a spammer and will be blocked for

[5]It should be noted that in some literature spammer has a different meaning. In this work, a spammer refers to a worker whose $\theta = 0.5$.

further labeling process. Some existing techniques [11,20,34] can also be applied.

Minimum Ratio Requirements

When using the minimum ratio requirement for vote counts between two classes, the key idea in the basic Requallo framework can still be applied, but we can readjust labels' weights based on the workers' reliability. By doing so, the expected completeness is then computed according to weighted vote counts instead of observed vote counts. Similarly, weighted voting can be used to obtain the final labels.

Given the labels from workers and their reliabilities $\{\theta_j\}$, we can estimate $P_i = P(Z_i = +1)$ based on the likelihood function:

$$\begin{aligned} f(y_{i1}, \ldots, y_{iM} | P_i, \{\theta_j\}_{j=1}^{M}) \\ = \prod_{j=1}^{M} \{(\theta_j P_i + (1-\theta_j)(1-P_i))^{\mathbb{1}(y_{ij}=+1)} \\ \times (\theta_j(1-P_i) + (1-\theta_j)P_i)^{\mathbb{1}(y_{ij}=-1)}\}, \quad (8) \end{aligned}$$

where $\mathbb{1}(y_{ij} = +1) = 1$ if $y_{ij} = +1$, and $\mathbb{1}(y_{ij} = +1) = 0$ if $y_{ij} = -1$. Then the MLE estimator for P_i is

$$\begin{aligned} P_i &= \arg\max f(y_{i1}, \ldots, y_{iM} | P_i, \{\theta_j\}_{j=1}^{M}) \\ s.t. &\quad P_i \in [0,1]. \end{aligned} \quad (9)$$

Although the closed-form solution is not easy to derive, there are many numerical ways to solve this optimization problem. Note that P_i may be 1 or 0 if some of the workers are unreliable. To prevent this, pseudo-labels can be added and more discussions can be found in Section 3.3.

Based on P_i, we can readjust the vote counts that satisfy:

$$\tilde{a}_i + \tilde{b}_i = a_i + b_i,$$
$$\tilde{a}_i : \tilde{b}_i = P_i : (1 - P_i).$$

Here $\tilde{a}_i$ and $\tilde{b}_i$ can be viewed as weighted vote counts, and they are derived as follows:

$$\tilde{a}_i = P_i(a_i + b_i),$$
$$\tilde{b}_i = (1 - P_i)(a_i + b_i).$$

The vote counts a_i and b_i in Eq. (1) then can be replaced by the $\tilde{a}_i$ and $\tilde{b}_i$. Similar to Eq. (2), we modify the MLE estimator as:

$$P(Z_i = +1 | \tilde{a}_i, \tilde{b}_i) = \begin{cases} \frac{\tilde{a}_i}{\tilde{a}_i + \tilde{b}_i} + \frac{\tilde{b}_i}{r(\tilde{b}_i)} & \text{if } \tilde{a}_i > \tilde{b}_i, \\ 0.5 & \text{if } \tilde{a}_i = \tilde{b}_i, \\ \frac{\tilde{a}_i}{\tilde{a}_i + \tilde{b}_i} - \frac{\tilde{a}_i}{r(\tilde{a}_i)} & \text{if } \tilde{a}_i < \tilde{b}_i. \end{cases} \quad (10)$$

When calculating the reward function Eq. (5), due to the limitation of crowdsourcing platforms, we cannot assign instances to specific workers and cannot forecast who will label the next instance. The worst case is considered then, i.e., the worker who currently has the lowest reliability degree (i.e. the θ_j that is closest to 0.5) will label the next instance.

Note that in Eq. (9) we assume θ_j is known. If the requester uses qualification exams or control questions among the instances, it can be easily inferred by the workers' performance on those tasks [15]. In the case that θ_j is unknown a priori, there are some existing techniques that can be used to estimate it under different crowdsourcing scenarios [3, 6, 14, 16, 17, 33–35, 40]. Many of them are aggregation algorithms that model worker reliability and conduct weighted vote to improve label accuracy. In the Requallo framework, they are also helpful to estimate labels' weighted vote counts. If a worker is likely to be a spammer, i.e., $\theta_j \approx 0.5$, we can also eliminate/block him from the labeling process.

3.3 Discussion and Practice Issues

Here we discuss several techniques to make the proposed framework more general and practical.

Multi-class Case

Multi-class labeling problems can be converted into binary classification problems as follows. The class with the highest votes is converted to +1 class, and the class with the second highest votes is converted to −1 class. If the most popular and the second most popular classes get similar votes, it still implies that the instance is hard to classify. On the other hand, if the most popular class predominates the votes, then we can regard it as an easy instance. This conversion is straightforward and the proposed Requallo framework can be applied to the corresponding binary problem.

Adding Pseudo-labels

At the early stage of the labeling process, the estimation of P_i may be unreasonable when either $a_i = 0$ or $b_i = 0$. The easiest solution to this problem is to give each instance pseudo-labels. For the model that incorporates workers' reliability, the pseudo-labels are considered to be from noiseless workers. The pseudo-labels can also be interpreted as prior knowledge from Bayesian point of view. In the experiments, we use one pseudo-label for each class as the initial label.

Choosing a Proper Requirement

If the requirement is not set properly, it is possible that no instances can achieve the requirement when the budget is exhausted. The requester need to keep in mind that crowd workers are usually non-experts, and normally do not receive any special training. Therefore, the requirement should be reasonable for the task difficulty as well as the budget. If the requester does not have a good estimate of task difficulty, we suggest to start with a small sample of instances and set a low requirement. If the instances can easily achieve the requirement, then gradually raise the bar. When the requirement is settled, all the instances can be tested.

4. EXPERIMENTS

In this section, we test the proposed Requallo framework to solve the budget allocation problems on two real-world crowdsourcing tasks and one simulated task. The results clearly demonstrate the advantages of Requallo framework when the budget is tight. We also provide some guidelines to requesters with different size of budgets and different needs.

4.1 Experiment Setup

In the experiments, we assume the basic setting as described in Section 3.1. We use one unit of the budget for one label.

Compared Methods

There are existing methods that consider budgets as discussed in Section 2, but some of them are not applicable when the budget is tight and need major modifications to fit our settings. Thus, the following budget allocation policies are compared. All of them are sequential labeling strategies.

- *Random.* This policy will randomly choose an instance and ask for one label.
- *Looping.* This strategy will pick the instances sequentially and ask for one label each time. Once the last instances is reached, it returns back to the first.
- *Opt-KG.* This budget allocation policy is proposed in [4]. The optimization goal for this policy is to maximize the overall accuracy and an MDP is formulated. It greedily chooses the next instance which has the largest possible reward. The prior distribution is set as Beta(1, 1) as suggested in the original paper.
- *LU.* This policy is proposed in [24]. As the full version of this method is designed for active learning, which is different from our problem setting, we only adopt the label uncertainty component (Eq. (4) in [24]) as the baseline and disregard the model uncertainty estimation. LU will choose the instance that has the highest label uncertainty in each iteration.
- *Requallo-c4.* This budget allocation policy is created by the proposed Requallo framework based on the minimum ratio of 4. We find that it is essentially the same policy as seq-lindley with a threshold of -0.73, which is proposed in [19][6]. That is, Requallo-c4 and seq-lindley will choose the same instance to label next. Although using different value functions, seq-lindley also adopts an MDP framework and a greedy algorithm to approximate the optimum policy. However, seq-lindley cannot take requirements other than the minimum ratio, while Requallo is more general. Thus, we can view seq-lindley as a special case of the proposed Requallo framework.
- *Requallo-p0.2.* This budget allocation policy is created by Requallo framework based on the requirement of Fisher exact test with a significant level of 0.2. In addition, we also add a maximum label count requirement as neither class can receive more than 14 labels.

As the proposed Requallo method can provide flexible budget allocation policies according to different requirements, we mainly use Requallo-p0.2 to compare with the baseline methods because the requirement is moderate and suitable for many tasks. Other Requallo policies are compared to provide a guideline for choosing proper requirements.

Performance Measures

We measure the performance from two aspects: quantity and quality. Due to the fact that baseline policies and the proposed Requallo policies have quite different goals, it is unfair to the baseline policies to measure quantity and quality only on the instances that achieve the requirements. It is also unfair to the Requallo policies to measure the performance without considering the requirements. Therefore, we choose a compromise and measure the performance with the minimum label count requirement, i.e., one instance needs to get at least three labels in order to be considered as labeled. The label count requirement is one of the most widely used requirements in crowdsourcing tasks. With the minimum requirement of 3, it is also one of the mildest in practice.

[6]Note that their problem setting is different from ours. Some modifications on the original method are necessary to fit our setting.

Under the minimum label count requirement, quantity is measured as the total number of labeled instances, i.e., the number of instances that have at least three labels. Quality is measured from two aspects: absolute count and accuracy. The former is defined as the number of correctly labeled instances. The latter is the percentage of correctly labeled instances in all labeled instances.

4.2 Real-World Crowdsourcing Tasks

In this section, we show the experimental results on two real-world datasets: the RTE dataset and the Game dataset. Comparing with the baselines, the Requallo framework shows a better balance for the trade-off between quantity and quality under a tight budget.

RTE Dataset [28]. This crowdsourcing task is conducted on mTurk for recognizing textual entailment (RTE). The dataset is publicly available[7] and considered to be a benchmark for crowdsourcing tasks. It contains 800 instances, and each one is queried to 10 different workers for a binary label. Ground truth for every instance is also provided, and 700 out of 800 instances can get correct labels from majority voting. More detailed descriptions about this dataset can be found in the original paper [28].

Game Dataset [2, 13]. This crowdsourcing task is conducted using an Android app based on a TV game show "Who Wants to Be a Millionaire". When a question is displayed on the show, the Android app simultaneously sends the question and the four candidate answers to the app users, and then users send their answers back voluntarily. Ground truth information is also recorded as revealed by the anchor of the show. The original dataset contains 2169 questions and 221653 answers from 38196 users. Here, a question can be viewed as an instance and a user's answer can be viewed as a label from a worker. The following preprocessing steps are applied on this dataset: 1) Instances with fewer than 20 labels are removed. By doing so, the policies can fully demonstrate their characteristics when the budget increases. 2) Misleading instances are removed, i.e., the instances on which majority voting gives incorrect answers. Due to the nature of the game show, it contains some tricky questions that are intended to trap people, and most people would choose the wrong answer. This kind of design is highly discouraged in regular crowdsourcing tasks. Therefore, removing those instances is more reasonable for crowdsourcing tasks. 3) Since the original questions are multiple-choice, we convert them into binary problems using the technique discussed in Section 3.3. After the preprocessing, Game dataset contains 1709 instances and 158385 labels.

To test the behavior of different budget allocation policies, we start from a very tight budget which is not enough to label all instances once, and then gradually increase the budget. In the RTE dataset, each instance has only 10 labels, so we focus more on the tight budget and stop increasing the budget when it reaches 4000, i.e., each instance has five labels on average. In the Game data, since more labels are available for each instance, we explore the policies until the budget reaches 15000, i.e., each instance has about nine labels on average. Figures 1 and 2 demonstrate the performance of different budget allocation policies on the two real-world crowdsourcing tasks respectively.

[7]http://sites.google.com/site/nlpannotations/

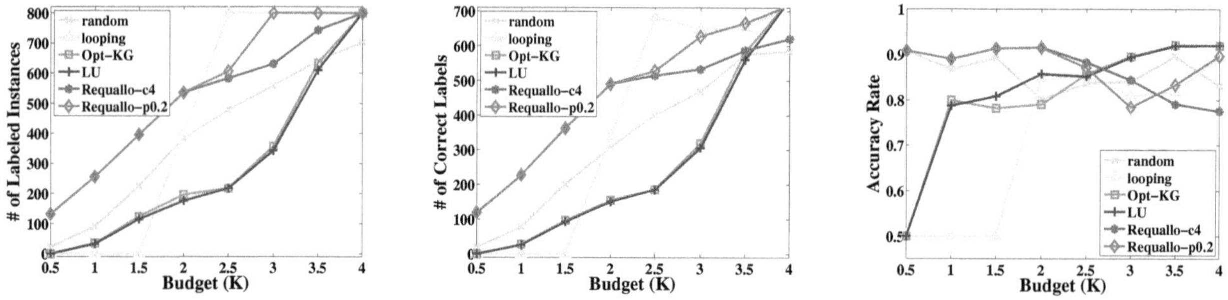

(a) Quantity (b) Absolute Count (c) Accuracy

Figure 1: Comparison of Budget Allocation on RTE Dataset

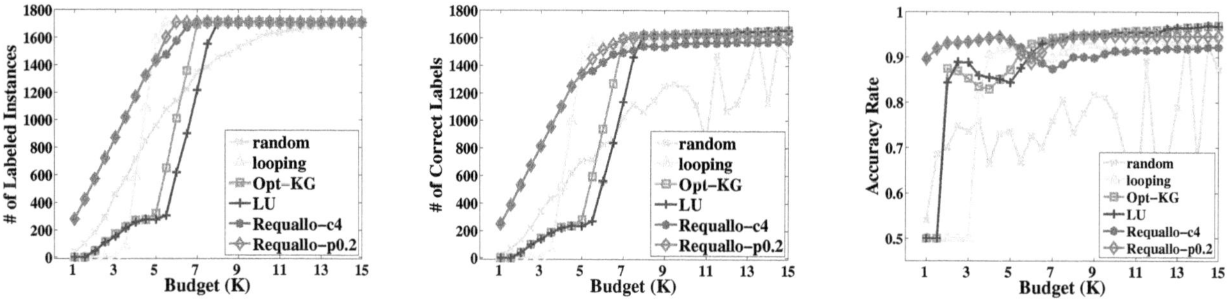

(a) Quantity (b) Absolute Count (c) Accuracy

Figure 2: Comparison of Budget Allocation on Game Dataset

In Figures 1a and 2a, the quantity of labeled instances is compared. The looping policy has no labeled instance until the budget reaches $2N$ (N is the number of instances), when every instance has exactly two labels. Then the quantity linearly increases to N as the budget increases from $2N$ to $3N$, when every instance has exactly three labels. If the budget is $3N$, then looping provides the best quantity. Random can get some instances labeled under a tight budget, but needs a big budget to reach the maximum quantity. Note that Opt-KG and LU have no instances labeled until the budget is greater than N. This is because both Opt-KG and LU will query one label for each instance at the initial stage. The quantity increases fast when the budget is higher than $3N$. Comparing with baseline policies, the proposed Requallo-p0.2 and Requallo-c4 can provide a remarkable amount of labeled instances even with a budget tighter than $2N$. When the budget is around $3N$, only looping can provide a slightly higher quantity.

Absolute counts of correctly labeled instances are compared in Figures 1b and 2b. The pattern is similar to the ones presented in quantity comparison. When the budget is tight, Requallo-p0.2 and Requallo-c4 show a big advantage. When the budget is sufficient, Requallo-p0.2 still demonstrates a competitive performance, even though the quality requirement is not strict. Note that when the budget is small, Requallo-p0.2 and Requallo-c4 have the same performance. The reason is that due to the overlap of their corresponding requirements, these two policies will choose the same instance to label at next step when all instances have less than three labels. However, when some instances have more labels, these two policies will choose different instances because the requirements differ then. On the Game dataset, Requallo-p0.2 stops labeling process after spending a cost of 7715 because all instances achieve the requirement. If the budget is higher than 7715, the extras will be saved.

Figures 1c and 2c presents the change of accuracy. As looping, Opt-KG and LU have no labeled instance at the initial stage, we use 0.5 to indicate that the result is uninformative. The looping policy gives a wavy but slightly increasing accuracy rate once every instance is labeled. The accuracy rate of the random policy fluctuates widely. Opt-KG and LU perform similarly. Both policies improve the accuracy when the budget increases and can achieve good results when the budget is sufficient. However, when the budget is tight, their accuracy is unsatisfactory.

Requallo-p0.2 provides a high accuracy except a low ebb when the budget is around $3.5N$. This pattern is subtle in Figure 1c because the budget limit is low, but it is clear in Figure 2c. This is because when the budget is tight, Requallo-p0.2 gives easy instances priority so that the completeness can be maximized. It also leads to a high accuracy rate as shown in the figures. When the budget increases, easy instances are all labeled, and Requallo-p0.2 starts to work on harder instances. At that time, however, there is still not enough budget for sufficient labels on those hard questions. As the evaluation is not conducted with the original requirement, there are some labeled instances that do not achieve the requirement yet. Therefore, the increasing speed of quantity is faster than the increasing speed of correctly labeled instances. This leads to the low ebb on accuracy. As the budget keeps increasing, Requallo-p0.2 can allocate sufficient labels on hard questions, so the accuracy raises back. A similar pattern happens to Requallo-c4. The low ebb occurs when the budget is around $4.5N$. The minimum ratio requirement is stricter than the Fisher exact test requirement on moderately hard questions, so once the easy instances are completed, Requallo-c4 intensively puts more effect on some hard questions. This slows down the increase of quantity, which causes the delay of low ebb on accuracy. The accuracy also raises back, but is slower.

In order to give some guidelines for requesters with different sizes of budgets and quality needs, other Requallo policies based on various requirements are also compared on Game dataset. Requallo-p0.2, Requallo-p0.1, and Requallo-p0.05 are the policies created based on Fisher exact test with different significance levels. The lower the p-value, the stricter the requirement. Requallo-c4 and Requallo-c5 are the policies created base on minimum ratio of 4 and 5 respectively. For these policies, we also adopt the same maximum label count requirements as mentioned in Section 4.1 as additional requirements. In addition, we show Requallo-m3, the policy with only minimum label count requirement, as a reference. Compared with the minimum ratio requirement, Fisher exact test based requirements are stricter at the initial stage, but looser when number of labels is relatively big. To better illustrate the effect of different requirements, we let the policies keep choosing instances until they are completed based on the requirement. The final labeling results are examined and Table 3 summarizes the performance.

Table 3: Comparison of Different Requallo Policies

Method	Cost	# Instances	# Correct	Accuracy
Requallo-p0.2	7715	1662	1587	0.9549
Requallo-p0.1	11191	1597	1558	0.9756
Requallo-p0.05	13878	1517	1493	0.9842
Requallo-c4	8689	1567	1518	0.9687
Requallo-c5	11266	1489	1464	0.9832
Requallo-m3	5127	1709	1580	0.9245

In Table 3, "Cost" is the total number of labels that each policy uses to finish labeling process. "# Instances" is the number of instances that achieve the corresponding requirement except for the maximum label count requirement. "# Correct" shows the number of correctly labeled instances among those who achieve the requirement. "Accuracy" is # Correct divided by # Instances. This table confirms our intuition of the trade-off between quantity and quality of the results, and the effect of different requirements. If a requester wants high quality results, he can set a strict requirement, but should expect a lower quantity of labeled instances or a higher cost. If the requester has a tight budget and no strong preference on quality, Requallo-p0.2 is a decent choice.

4.3 Simulated Crowdsourcing Task

As many crowdsourcing tasks are conducted to obtain training labels for machine learning problems, a simulation of such a scenario is created in this section, from crowdsourced labeling to training and finally testing. The Splice dataset from LIBSVM[8] is used as the target machine learning task. The original dataset contains 1000 training instances and 2175 testing instances. For each instance, there are 60 features and a binary label.

We first simulate the labels provided by crowd workers. A linear SVM classifier is learned on the training set and it provides a probability of being in class +1 for each training instance, which is used as $P(Z_i = +1)$. Random samples are drawn from Bernoulli($P_i = P(Z_i = +1)$) as the labels provided by noiseless workers for instance i. Under the same budget (from 500 to 5000), we then apply each policy and form a new training set by replacing the original labels with the labels given by the policy for all training instances. The same minimum label count requirement is used as in previous experiments. If a policy does not provide a label for an instance, it will be eliminated from the training set. Finally, new linear SVM classifiers are learned on the new training sets and applied to the test set.

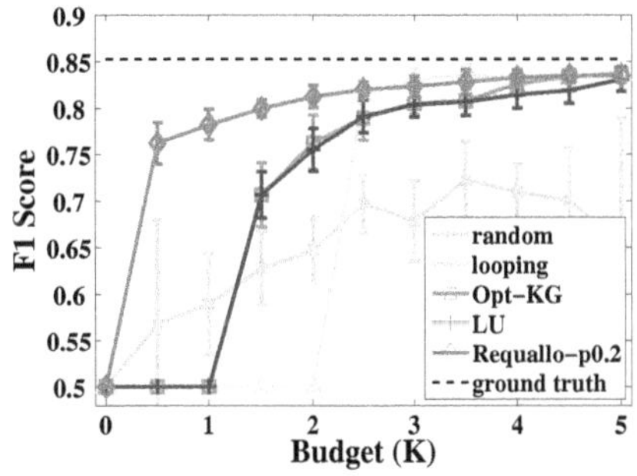

Figure 3: F1 Score on Test Data.

Due to the randomness in generating workers' labels, we run the simulation for 10 times and report the errorbar (standard deviation) of the results. The performance is evaluated as F1 score on testing data. A higher F1 score means a better performance. Figure 3 summarizes the results. Here we omit the results for Requallo-c4 because Requallo-p0.2 has almost the same performance. The black dash line represents the performance if the classifier is trained on the original training data, which is 0.853. Generally speaking, quantity and quality of training data are two of the most important factors for a good classifier. When the budget is tight, Requallo-p0.2 shows great advantages over baseline policies because of its excellent performance on both quantity and quality, which is also shown on the real-world crowdsourcing tasks. On the other hand, baseline policies need more labels to build up a good training set.

5. CONCLUSIONS

Crowdsourcing under a tight budget brings new unique challenges. Most existing budget allocation methods, which assume a sufficient budget is available, cannot achieve desired labeling quality if the budget is tight. As different requesters and tasks may have different needs on label quality, we proposed a framework that allows requesters specify their quality requirement on the results. The proposed framework can guarantee the requesters' desired quality while trying to maximize quantity under the budget. A Markov decision process is used to model the labeling process. To tackle the computational challenge, an approximate policy is built via a one-step look-ahead greedy algorithm. The policy sequentially chooses the next instance which can provide the highest reward on task completeness. The framework is further

[8]http://www.csie.ntu.edu.tw/~cjlin/libsvmtools/datasets/

extended to consider workers' reliability, so that unreliable workers can be eliminated from labeling process and reliable workers can have a higher weight in the vote counts. Experiments on both real-world and simulated crowdsourcing tasks demonstrate remarkable advantages of the proposed framework under a tight budget.

6. REFERENCES

[1] A. Agresti. A survey of exact inference for contingency tables. *Statistical Science*, pages 131–153, 1992.

[2] B. I. Aydin, Y. S. Yilmaz, Y. Li, Q. Li, J. Gao, and M. Demirbas. Crowdsourcing for multiple-choice question answering. In *Proc. of IAAI*, 2014.

[3] Y. Bachrach, T. Graepel, T. Minka, and J. Guiver. How to grade a test without knowing the answers—a Bayesian graphical model for adaptive crowdsourcing and aptitude testing. In *Proc. of ICML*, pages 1183–1190, 2012.

[4] X. Chen, Q. Lin, and D. Zhou. Optimistic knowledge gradient policy for optimal budget allocation in crowdsourcing. In *Proc. of ICML*, pages 64–72, 2013.

[5] N. Dalvi, A. Dasgupta, R. Kumar, and V. Rastogi. Aggregating crowdsourced binary ratings. In *Proc. of WWW*, pages 285–294, 2013.

[6] A. P. Dawid and A. M. Skene. Maximum likelihood estimation of observer error-rates using the EM algorithm. *Applied Statistics*, pages 20–28, 1979.

[7] P. Donmez, J. G. Carbonell, and J. G. Schneider. A probabilistic framework to learn from multiple annotators with time-varying accuracy. In *Proc. of SDM*, pages 826–837, 2010.

[8] S. Faradani, B. Hartmann, and P. G. Ipeirotis. What's the right price? Pricing tasks for finishing on time. *Proc. of HCOMP*, 2011.

[9] P. G. Ipeirotis and E. Gabrilovich. Quizz: Targeted crowdsourcing with a billion (potential) users. In *Proc. of WWW*, pages 143–154, 2014.

[10] H. Jin, L. Su, D. Chen, K. Nahrstedt, and J. Xu. Quality of information aware incentive mechanisms for mobile crowd sensing systems. In *MobiHoc*, pages 167–176, 2015.

[11] D. R. Karger, S. Oh, and D. Shah. Budget-optimal task allocation for reliable crowdsourcing systems. *Operations Research*, 62(1):1–24, 2014.

[12] H. Li, B. Zhao, and A. Fuxman. The wisdom of minority: Discovering and targeting the right group of workers for crowdsourcing. In *Proc. of WWW*, pages 165–176, 2014.

[13] Q. Li, Y. Li, J. Gao, L. Su, B. Zhao, M. Demirbas, W. Fan, and J. Han. A confidence-aware approach for truth discovery on long-tail data. *PVLDB*, 8(4), 2014.

[14] Q. Li, Y. Li, J. Gao, B. Zhao, W. Fan, and J. Han. Resolving conflicts in heterogeneous data by truth discovery and source reliability estimation. In *Proc. of SIGMOD*, pages 1187–1198, 2014.

[15] Q. Liu, A. Ihler, and M. Steyvers. Scoring workers in crowdsourcing: How many control questions are enough? In *NIPS*, pages 1914–1922, 2013.

[16] F. Ma, Y. Li, Q. Li, M. Qiu, J. Gao, S. Zhi, L. Su, B. Zhao, H. Ji, and J. Han. Faitcrowd: Fine grained truth discovery for crowdsourced data aggregation. In *Proc. of KDD*, pages 745–754, 2015.

[17] C. Meng, W. Jiang, Y. Li, J. Gao, L. Su, H. Ding, and Y. Cheng. Truth discovery on crowd sensing of correlated entities. In *Proc. of SenSys*, pages 169–182, 2015.

[18] M. L. Puterman. *Markov Decision Processes: Discrete Stochastic Dynamic Programming.* John Wiley & Sons, 2014.

[19] V. Raykar and P. Agrawal. Sequential crowdsourced labeling as an epsilon-greedy exploration in a markov decision process. In *Proc. of AISTATS*, pages 832–840, 2014.

[20] V. C. Raykar and S. Yu. Ranking annotators for crowdsourced labeling tasks. In *NIPS*, pages 1809–1817, 2011.

[21] V. C. Raykar, S. Yu, L. H. Zhao, G. H. Valadez, C. Florin, L. Bogoni, and L. Moy. Learning from crowds. *The Journal of Machine Learning Research*, 11:1297–1322, 2010.

[22] J. Redi and I. Povoa. Crowdsourcing for rating image aesthetic appeal: Better a paid or a volunteer crowd? In *Proc. of the International ACM Workshop on Crowdsourcing for Multimedia*, pages 25–30, 2014.

[23] S. Russell and P. Norvig. *Artificial Intelligence: A Modern Approach.* Prentice-Hall, Egnlewood Cliffs, 1995.

[24] V. S. Sheng, F. Provost, and P. G. Ipeirotis. Get another label? Improving data quality and data mining using multiple, noisy labelers. In *Proc. of SIGKDD*, pages 614–622, 2008.

[25] Y. Singer and M. Mittal. Pricing mechanisms for crowdsourcing markets. In *Proc. of WWW*, pages 1157–1166, 2013.

[26] A. Singla, I. Bogunovic, G. Bartók, A. Karbasi, and A. Krause. Near-optimally teaching the crowd to classify. In *Proc. of ICML*, pages 154–162, 2014.

[27] A. Singla and A. Krause. Truthful incentives in crowdsourcing tasks using regret minimization mechanisms. In *Proc. of WWW*, pages 1167–1178, 2013.

[28] R. Snow, B. O'Connor, D. Jurafsky, and A. Y. Ng. Cheap and fast — but is it good? Evaluating non-expert annotations for natural language tasks. In *Proc. of EMNLP*, pages 254–263, 2008.

[29] Y. Tian and J. Zhu. Learning from crowds in the presence of schools of thought. In *Proc. of SIGKDD*, pages 226–234, 2012.

[30] L. Tran-Thanh, T. D. Huynh, A. Rosenfeld, S. D. Ramchurn, and N. R. Jennings. Budgetfix: Budget limited crowdsourcing for interdependent task allocation with quality guarantees. In *Proc. of AAMAS*, pages 477–484, 2014.

[31] L. Tran-Thanh, M. Venanzi, A. Rogers, and N. R. Jennings. Efficient budget allocation with accuracy guarantees for crowdsourcing classification tasks. In *Proc. of AAMAS*, pages 901–908, 2013.

[32] L. Von Ahn and L. Dabbish. Labeling images with a computer game. In *Proc. of CHI*, pages 319–326, 2004.

[33] P. Welinder, S. Branson, P. Perona, and S. J. Belongie. The multidimensional wisdom of crowds. In *NIPS*, pages 2424–2432, 2010.

[34] P. Welinder and P. Perona. Online crowdsourcing: Rating annotators and obtaining cost-effective labels. In *CVPRW*, pages 25–32, 2010.

[35] J. Whitehill, T.-f. Wu, J. Bergsma, J. R. Movellan, and P. L. Ruvolo. Whose vote should count more: Optimal integration of labels from labelers of unknown expertise. In *NIPS*, pages 2035–2043, 2009.

[36] H. Wu, J. Corney, and M. Grant. Relationship between quality and payment in crowdsourced design. In *Proc. of CSCWD*, pages 499–504, 2014.

[37] Y. Xiao, Y. Zhang, and M. van der Schaar. Socially-optimal design of crowdsourcing platforms with reputation update errors. In *ICASSP*, pages 5263–5267, 2013.

[38] Q. Zhang, Y. Wen, X. Tian, X. Gan, and X. Wang. Incentivize crowd labeling under budget constraint. In *Proc. of IEEE Infocom*, 2015.

[39] H. Zheng, D. Li, and W. Hou. Task design, motivation, and participation in crowdsourcing contests. *International Journal of Electronic Commerce*, 15(4):57–88, 2011.

[40] D. Zhou, S. Basu, Y. Mao, and J. C. Platt. Learning from the wisdom of crowds by minimax entropy. In *NIPS*, pages 2195–2203, 2012.

[41] Y. Zhou, X. Chen, and J. Li. Optimal PAC multiple arm identification with applications to crowdsourcing. In *Proc. ICML*, pages 217–225, 2014.

Project Success Prediction in Crowdfunding Environments

Yan Li
Dept. of Computer Science
Wayne State University
Detroit, MI - 48202.
rock_liyan@wayne.edu

Vineeth Rakesh
Dept. of Computer Science
Wayne State University
Detroit, MI - 48202.
vineethrakesh@wayne.edu

Chandan K. Reddy
Dept. of Computer Science
Wayne State University
Detroit, MI - 48202.
reddy@cs.wayne.edu

ABSTRACT

Crowdfunding has gained widespread attention in recent years. Despite the huge success of crowdfunding platforms, the percentage of projects that succeed in achieving their desired goal amount is only around 40%. Moreover, many of these crowdfunding platforms follow "all-or-nothing" policy which means the pledged amount is collected only if the goal is reached within a certain predefined time duration. Hence, estimating the probability of success for a project is one of the most important research challenges in the crowdfunding domain. To predict the project success, there is a need for new prediction models that can potentially combine the power of both classification (which incorporate both successful and failed projects) and regression (for estimating the time for success). In this paper, we formulate the project success prediction as a survival analysis problem and apply the censored regression approach where one can perform regression in the presence of partial information. We rigorously study the project success time distribution of crowdfunding data and show that the logistic and log-logistic distributions are a natural choice for learning from such data. We investigate various censored regression models using comprehensive data of 18K Kickstarter (a popular crowdfunding platform) projects and 116K corresponding tweets collected from Twitter. We show that the models that take complete advantage of both the successful and failed projects during the training phase will perform significantly better at predicting the success of future projects compared to the ones that only use the successful projects. We provide a rigorous evaluation on many sets of relevant features and show that adding few temporal features that are obtained at the project's early stages can dramatically improve the performance.

Categories and Subject Descriptors

H.2.8 [**Database Management**]: Database applications-Data Mining; I.2.6 [**Artificial Intelligence**]: Learning; H.3.3 [**Information Search and Retrieval**]: Information filtering

WSDM'16, February 22–25, 2016, San Francisco, CA, USA.

 ISBN 978-1-4503-3716-8/16/02...$15.00
DOI: http://dx.doi.org/10.1145/2835776.2835791

Keywords

Prediction, project success, survival analysis, regression, crowdfunding.

1. INTRODUCTION

Crowdfunding has emerged as "the next big thing" in entrepreneurial financing. It aims at providing the seed capital for many start-up companies, creating job opportunities and reviving lost business ventures. Crowdfunding websites helped companies and individuals worldwide raise $89 million from the public in 2010 and explosively grown to $5.1 billion in 2013. The concept of crowdfunding is similar to micro-financing where the required funds are collected by pooling relatively small amounts of money from several individuals instead of a single venture capitalist. Over the past few years, crowdfunding platforms have raised several billion dollars worldwide, thereby becoming a viable alternative for people seeking the help of banks, brokers, and other financial intermediaries to jump-start their business ventures.

In spite of the tremendous success in crowdfunding, statistics show that only around 40% of the projects succeed in reaching their pledged goal (KickStarterStats) [15]. Even small amounts of improvement in the projects' success can bring potentially millions of dollars in the overall revenue for the creators. This can potentially lead to better innovation and provide more job opportunities since most of these projects will not receive any funding from other sources at such early stages of product development.

Project success is an extremely vital component of crowdfunding which, if correctly estimated, can provide some guideline to the project creators and backers about the progress and potential of the project. In addition, this information can guide future algorithms for recommending projects that are more likely to succeed for the backers. In other words, having a good prediction model can aid the individuals to invest in projects that are more likely to succeed in the future. Since many of the crowdfunding domains follow an "all-or-nothing" policy (which means the pledged money is collected only if the goal amount is reached in a certain predefined time duration), it becomes annoying to the users who invest in the projects that eventually do not succeed because if the investors fund projects that eventually fail, then it will waste their time (with no returns) and increase the "opportunity cost".

However, merely estimating whether a project will be successful or not using its corresponding goal date cannot provide a proper guideline to the backers who want to invest in popular projects. To illustrate the weakness of the classification based approaches to solve this problem and motivate our work, let us consider the following real-world example shown in Figure 1. If we just build a model to predict whether a project will succeed or not, then projects 1, 4, and 5 will be labeled as "failed", and projects 2, 3, and 6 will be labeled as "successful". Project 1 absorbed almost $40K during 30 days period and might have the potential to attract a lot of attention in few more days, while project 4 only absorbed $2K during 60 days. It obviously states that project 1 is much more attractive and valuable to investigate comparing to project 4, so that it is unfair for project 1 to put these two projects in one class which will mislead the investigators. Thus, classification methods are not suitable for project recommendation in the crowdfunding domain.

Typically, investors would like to invest in projects which can succeed as soon as possible. Our goal in this paper is to rank the projects based on their expected success date, and thus the investors can choose some interesting projects from the pool of highly-ranked projects. If the investor's behavior is influenced by our ranking result, then they will fund those highly-ranked projects (such as project 1 in the above example) which will then help the projects become successful eventually. It can also help the project creators to have an idea about where they stand with respect to other projects in terms of achieving the goal amount even before the project begins. Hence, a good success prediction model can help both investors (to choose some valuable and potentially successful projects) and creators (by providing some guidelines on the chance of success).

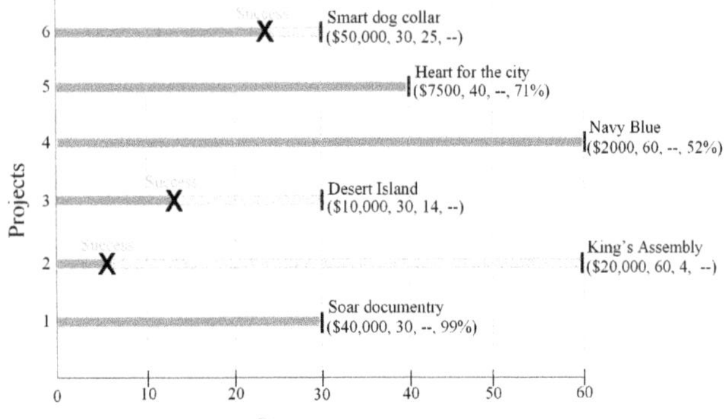

Figure 1: An example of 6 projects from the crowdfunding data. X-axis represents the project duration (in days). The projects with complete solid lines correspond to the failed projects (1,4, and 5 in this example). The remaining projects (2,3, and 6) are successful since they achieved the project goal amount within the goal date (which is marked by '**X**' in the figure). Each project is indicated in the following format: project title (w, x, y, z), where w indicates the project goal amount, x indicates the project duration, y indicates the number of days taken to achieve success, and z indicates the percentage of amount received by the goal date. It should be noted that while w and x are available for all the projects, y is available only for the successful projects and z is available only for the failed projects.

Due to the dynamic nature of the projects and the fact that the data contains information about both success and failed projects, it becomes non-trivial to build a prediction model for this crowdfunding data. Especially, the presence of both successful and failed projects in the training data along with the time information presents a complex environment for the prediction task. For the projects that are successful (projects 2,3, and 6 in Figure 1), the true value of the time taken for achieving success is exactly known. However, for the failed projects (projects 1,4, and 5 in Figure 1), the only information available is the amount they received until the project goal date and there will be no information about when those projects can receive the entire goal amount (become successful).

Standard regression and ranking models ignore the data about failed projects since the failed ones do not have the information about the actual success date. Hence, these standard regression approaches can only consider the successful projects (for which the number of days to achieve success is known and is a positive integer value). However, the failed projects carry important piece of information that they are not successful until a certain time point (project goal date). This information is vital and ignoring such information will reduce the model performance. Hence, *in this crowdfunding domain, there is a need for regression or ranking models that can potentially combine the information of both successful and failed projects.* In spite of the importance of the problem, this area of research is relatively unexplored in the data mining and machine learning communities.

In this paper, we will demonstrate that using the failed projects in the prediction model can provide significantly better results compared to the model that will only use successful projects for training. It should be noted that standard regression models suffer from two drawbacks when applied on this data. Since time can only be a positive number, the model should output only positive values. In addition, the model should accommodate the failed projects for which there is only partial information available. To effectively solve these challenges, we formulate the project success prediction task as a suvival analysis problem, where the failed projects can be viewed as the censored instances and successful projects as the uncensored instances, and utilize the censored regression approaches to slove the prediction task.

The main contributions of our work are summarized as follows:

- We formulate the project success prediction task as a survival analysis problem and show that the censored regression models that take complete advantage of both successful and failed projects during the training phase will perform significantly better at predicting the success of future projects compared to the ones that use only the successful project information.
- Show that the logistic and log-logistic distributions are a natural choice for fitting the parametric models for crowdfunding (Kickstarter) data and rigorously evaluate and compare these two models with various other censored regression models available in the literature.
- Evaluate the most optimal set of features that need to be extracted from the real crowdfunding domain (Kickstarter dataset) for predicting the project success.
- Demonstrate that adding few temporal features that are obtained after the project begins (at the early stages such as first 3 days) can dramatically improve the prediction performance.

The rest of this paper is organized as follows: Section 2 provides the related work in crowdfunding and prediction problems. The Kickstarter dataset and the formal definition of the prediction problem are described in Section 3; our analysis and solution of the prediction problem are given in Section 4. A detailed discussion of the experimental results is provided in Section 5 and Section 6 concludes our discussion.

2. RELATED WORK

2.1 Crowdfunding and Kickstarter

Since crowdfunding is still an emerging platform, most works in this domain are relatively new. The most popular form of crowdfunding is the reward-based, where the individuals fund a project in exchange for a variety of rewards. Kickstarter has become one of the most popular reward-based crowdfunding platforms. Raising a whopping $529 million in pledged amount and 22,252 successfully funded projects, the year 2014 was extremely successful for projects in the Kickstarter domain. Kickstarter terms the investors as backers, and the founders of a project as creators. The creators project their ideas by posting a detailed description about their projects. Usually, the description contains videos, images and textual information that explains the novelty of the project. In addition to this, the creators provide a detailed timeline, funding goal, and the rewards for different pledge levels. Even though the progress of the Kickstarter domain has been outstanding, the success rate of projects has not been very impressive. Recent statistics report a success rate of less than 50%. Being relatively new, very few studies have explored this domain from a data mining perspective [32, 10, 27].

In [20], the authors examine the dynamics of the Kickstarter domain. To understand the factors that motivate users to invest in crowdfunding projects, [12] and [17] perform the real-world analysis on crowdfunding platforms. The work in [22] delineates the impact of social network on Kickstarter projects. In their work, the authors leverage social network based features such as: promotional activity in Twitter, effect of weakly connected components, network diameter, triadic closures, etc. to predict the number of backers and funding amount that will be accrued by a project. The authors of [7] propose a Maximum-entropy distribution model and show the impact of team behaviors in the *Kiva.org* domain. There were also some prior efforts in exploring the effects of the internet on micro-financing, and peer-to-peer lending transactions [4, 2]. Studies on microfinance decision-making have discovered that lenders favor lending opportunities not only to the entities that are similar to themselves but also to individuals in situations that trigger an emotional reaction [1, 11]. While the domain is interesting and can potentially bring huge financial impact, it is surprising to see that most of the computational techniques proposed are relatively naive. To solve the problem described in the previous section, we need to have more sophisticated approaches that can provide insightful information about the prediction of project success.

2.2 Background on Prediction Methods

Before describing the work related to our approach, we will first highlight the drawbacks of the standard classification and regression models for solving the success prediction problem stated previously.

- Modeling crowdfunding data poses a new challenge in terms of incorporating the projects where we know the success date and the projects where we have only partial information that they did not succeed until a certain project goal date. Such projects are termed as *censored* ones. In traditional regression/classification setting, these projects are simply treated as missing data and they do not contribute any information unless one makes quite stringent assumptions followed by heavy computation (e.g. multiple imputation). However, using censored regression models, a likelihood function is constructed using the partial information.
- In regression problems, the outcome variable is continuous and will be any real number, while time by it's very nature will strictly be non-negative. The standard machine learning methods such as linear and logistic regression cannot be used to predict survival times. This is due to the fact that one cannot enforce linear and logistic regression algorithms to *predict non-negative outcomes*. The censored regression models can inherently handle this non-negative constraint and build models that predict only non-negative outcome variables.

It is clear from the above discussion that the censored regression models have some critical advantages compared to standard regression/classification. Albeit it is not to be seen as a competitor to the standard regression analysis, rather, such censored models are applicable to more specialized and complex modeling scenarios, namely, modeling Time-to-Event data. In this paper, we consider the event of interest to be the project success and the goal is to predict when a project can potentially become successful compared to the other ones that are available. Hence, in such problems, one will have complete information about the events for successful projects only. The failed projects will not have the event occurred and will be observed only until the project goal date. *The critical difference between our formulation and the standard regression approaches is the fact that our work incorporates both successful and failed projects simultaneously as opposed to using only the successful projects as done in regression based formulations.*

We will now introduce more details about the censored regression models that will be used in this paper. They mainly contain two components: (i) Time-to-event, i.e. time taken for a specific event of interest (project success) to occur and (ii) Censoring, i.e. partial information of projects where success did not occur. The form of censoring that is seen in our problem is the right censoring where the survival time is known to be longer than a certain value but its precise value is unknown. Additionally, there are also features that one needs to relate with time to explain time-to-event phenomenon (such as project success time). Such models test for differences in success times for two or more projects of interest, while allowing to adjust for the project features. More recently, few problems in computational advertising have been effectively tackled using such survival models [6]. In order to model the censored data, some of these approaches use an approximation of the likelihood function called the partial log likelihood, to train the survival model [8, 23].

3. DATASET AND PROBLEM

3.1 Dataset Description

(i) **Data sources:** For our experiments, we collected data from three different sources namely: Kickstarter, Twitter and Facebook. Our dataset was prepared using a two step approach. First, we obtained the Kickstarter projects and removed irrelevant projects. Second, we used these filtered set of projects to fetch their promotional activities from Twitter and Facebook. We describe this process in detail in this section.

Kickstarter Database: We obtained six months of Kickstarter data from *kickspy.*[1] Our dataset spans from 12/15/13 to 06/15/14, which consists of 27,270 projects. We removed projects that were canceled or suspended as well as those with less than one backer and $100 as pledged amount. In this manner, we obtained 18,093 projects.

Table 1: Basic statistics of our Kickstarter data consisting of 18,093 projects collected from Dec 2013 - Jun 2014.

Attribute	Mean	Min	Max	StdDev
Goal Amt	26,531.2	100	100,000,000	758,366.5
Pledged Amt	11,023.6	100	6,224,955	78,550.8
Duration(days)	31	1	60	10.05

Promotions from Twitter: Social media sites such as Twitter and Facebook are often used as means to promote Kickstarter projects. Researchers have shown that such promotional activities have a very strong impact on the success of Kickstarter projects [26, 22]. Therefore, in this paper, we built our database by retrieving tweets that contain the term *http://kck.st* in their URL field [2]. By expanding these short URLs, we eliminated tweets that did not map to our project database. Using this method, we obtained 106,738 unique tweets, which covered 55% of our projects. The remaining 45% were never promoted using Twitter.

Promotions from Facebook: Since Facebook does not allow us to fetch the data using their API, we simply scraped the following information from the Kickstarter website: *number of facebook shares for a project*, and *facebook friends of creators.*

(ii) **Feature extraction:** The various kinds of extracted features were successfully used in our recent work [26], which can be summarized as follows:

Project based features: We extracted 15 different features for every project in our database. The numerical features include the duration of project, the goal amount, the number of images, the presence of videos and the number of comments about the project. The duration of a project ranges anywhere between 1-60 days with an average of 30 days and the comments in Kickstarter are posted by those who are interested in the status of the ongoing projects; for every project, we count the number of comments posted by these users. The textual features such as project description, risks and challenges, and FAQs were converted into numerical values by counting the number of words in the respective feature. The categorical feature for a project is based on the topic of the project and it's geo-location. Kickstarter classifies the topical category of a project into 15 different groups such as art, comics, music, technology, publishing etc. For a detailed description of these features, the readers are encouraged to go through [26, 22].

Features from the project creators: This includes the number of projects created, projects backed by the creator, success ratio of the creator, and features obtained from creator's facebook profile (7 features).

Social network features (obtained from Twitter): These are network-based measures that were created using Twitter users who promoted the projects in our database. The features include tie-strength between the promoters of projects, number of bi-connected components, and the PageRank scores of Twitter users who promoted the projects in the first three days of the project duration (3 features). The details about the creation of these features can be found in our recent work [26].

Temporal features: The accumulation over the first three days in terms of the number of backers, the funding amount, the number of Twitter promotions and the number of Facebook shares (12 features).

(iii) **Distribution of Projects:** The maximum time period a project can last is 60 days. In other words, the creator can choose anywhere between 1 and 60 days for the project duration. In this crowdfunding problem, for each project, its starting day is considered to be the first day of our study time scale; thus, in the study time scale, the maximum value of the actual observed successful or failed day is 60. Figure 2 shows the overall statistics of all the 18,093 Kickstarter projects where the X-axis is the actual number of observed days and Y-axis is the logarithm (base 10) of the number of projects. We can observe that the successes and failures of projects occur at every possible day, and a relatively large amount of project creators choose 30 days as their project duration.

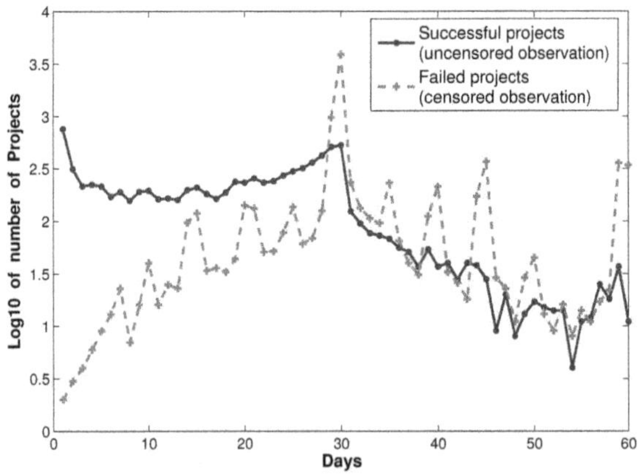

Figure 2: Distribution of the successful (in blue) and failed projects (in red) during the 60 days time window.

3.2 Problem Formulation

We formulate the problem of estimating project success and ranking in crowdfunding as a survival analysis problem and employ censored regression models which can simultaneously leverage both successful and failed projects. Survival analysis is one of the most important methods in the field of statistics [19, 25] which aims at modeling the time to a particular event of interest (project success in our

[1]www.kickspy.com

[2]we used the query API available at www.topsy.com

case). In such longitudinal studies, the observation starts from a certain starting timepoint and will continue until the occurrence of project success or the predefined project duration is reached (in which case the project success is not observed). This notion of having only partial information available about the project behaviour is also known as censoring [19, 28] and those failed projects are considered as censored observations. Given the historical database of successful and failed projects, the goal here is to estimate the time taken for the project success for a new project and recommend the project based on the result of our prediction. The problem can be formulated as follows:

Problem Statement:

For the ith project, let us consider its predefined project duration to be U_i and it takes T_i days to reach the project goal amount. It should be noted that T_i *is a latent value for failed projects because it did not reach its goal amount during the predefined project duration.* Each project can be represented by a triplet (X_i, y_i, δ_i), where X_i is $1 \times m$ project feature vector, and δ_i is the project failure indicator ($\delta_i = 1$ for a successful project and $\delta_i = 0$ for a failed project). The *observed time* y_i for a project is then defined as follows:

$$y_i = \begin{cases} T_i & \text{if } \textit{project is successful } (\delta_i = 1) \\ U_i & \text{if } \textit{project is failed } (\delta_i = 0) \end{cases} \quad (1)$$

The final goal of our work is to estimate T_j for a new (j^{th}) project whose feature descriptors are represented by X_j. It should be noted that T_j will be a non-negative continuous value in this case.

4. CENSORED REGRESSION FOR ESTIMATING PROJECT SUCCESS

4.1 Notations and Definitions

Let us first introduce some important probability functions in survival analysis and provide a connection between those functions and the prediction problem in the crowdfunding domain. The *survival function* $S(t) = Pr(T \geq t)$ is the probability that the time to the event of interest is no earlier than certain specified time t. In our case, the project success is the event of interest and T is the success date; hence, $S(t)$ is the probability that the project does not succeed after t days from the project starting date and we call it as the *unsuccessful probability* in short. The *cumulative death distribution function* $F(t) = 1 - S(t)$ can be renamed as the *cumulative successful probability* which represents the probability that the project achieves its goal amount within t days. The *density function* $f(t)$ is defined as $f(t) = \frac{dF(t)}{dt} = \frac{F(t+\Delta t)-F(t)}{\Delta t}$, where $\Delta t \to 0$ is a short time interval, represents the probability that a project achieves its goal amount at day t. To describe the characteristics of the crowdfunding data, both unsuccessful (survival) probability function and the density function are needed.

Let us consider a set of N projects out of which there are c failed projects and $(N-c)$ successful projects. As described earlier, the jth project is represented by (X_j, y_j, δ_j). For convenience, we use the general notation $\mathbf{b} = (b_1, b_2, \cdots, b_p)$ to represent a set of parameters and assume that the project success times follow a theoretical distribution with the unsuccessful probability function $S(t, \mathbf{b})$ and density function $f(t, \mathbf{b})$. If a project j is failed, then it is not possible to obtain the actual number of days that are needed to achieve its goal; however, it will be known that the project does not reach its goal amount until the last day of the predefined project duration U_j, so $S(U_j, \mathbf{b})$ should be a probability value that is close to 1. On the contrary, if project j is a successful project which is succeeded at T_j, then $f(T_j, \mathbf{b})$ should be a high probability.

4.2 Objective Function

Using these notations, we can now use $\prod_{\delta_j=1} f(y_j, \mathbf{b})$ to represent the joint probability of $(N-c)$ successful projects and $\prod_{\delta_j=0} S(y_j, \mathbf{b})$ to represent the joint probability of c failed projects. Hence, the complete likelihood function for all the N projects is given by

$$\begin{aligned} L(\mathbf{b}) &= \prod_{\delta_j=1} f(y_j, \mathbf{b}) \prod_{\delta_j=0} S(y_j, \mathbf{b}) \\ &= \prod_{\delta_j=1} f(y_j, \mathbf{b}) \prod_{\delta_j=0} (1 - F(y_j, \mathbf{b})) \end{aligned} \quad (2)$$

Note that $\mathbf{b}$ will not only contain the feature coefficient vector but also includes the parameters of the chosen theoretical distribution. Now, one of the problems that arise here is the determination of $f(t, \mathbf{b})$ which consists of two parts: functional form and parameter estimation. To make an efficient and accurate prediction, first an appropriate theoretical distribution has to be selected to describe the characteristic of the Kickstarter dataset.

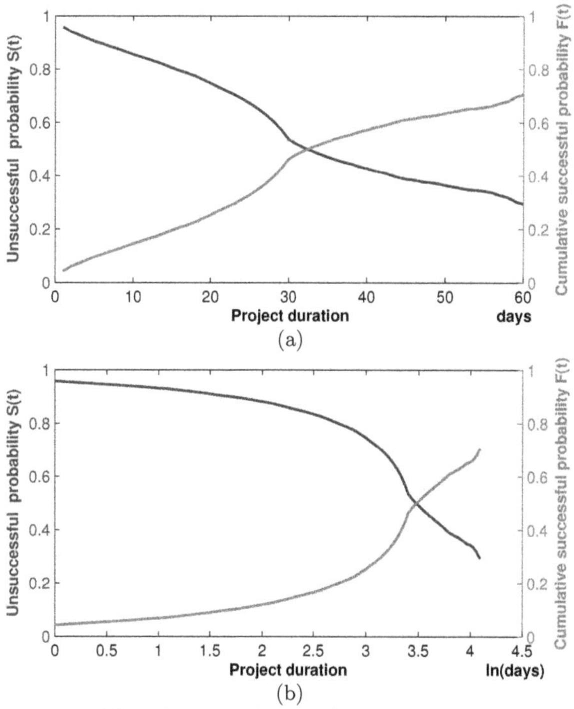

Figure 3: Plot showing the Kaplan-Meier Curves for the Kickstarter dataset. The Y-axis represents unsuccessful (survival) probability $S(t)$ and cumulative successful (death) probability $F(t)$. X-axis corresponds to the number of days in (a) and Logarithm of number of days in (b). The unsuccessful probability (in blue) and the cumulative successful probability (in red) are plotted.

We observed an interesting phenomenon that the $F(t)$ for

Kickstarter projects closely follows the cumulative distribution function (CDF) of a logistic distribution. Figure 3 shows the Kaplan-Meier curves for the Kickstarter data under two different scales on X-axis: (a) the project duration in days and (b) the logarithm of the project duration. Kaplan-Meier curve [18] is a popular non-parametric method which can be used to provide a general view of the overall distributions of $S(t)$ and $F(t)$ for a dataset with censored instances. In both figures 3(a) and 3(b), the blue curves correspond to the $S(t)$ and the red curves correspond to the $F(t)$. We see that the red curves have a shape approximately close to the CDF of a logistic function. These two figures show that *the logistic and log-logistic distributions are appropriate in modeling the probability of project success in the crowdfunding domain and hence these two distributions will be incorporated into the objective function given by Eq.(2).*

4.3 Model Learning

In this section, we will elaborate on the likelihood function by fitting both logistic and log-logistic distributions in Eq.(2). The Parameters for the objective function can be estimated using maximum likelihood estimation (MLE) [21].

Logistic distribution: The censored parametric regression with logistic distribution assumes that there exists a linear relationship between the observed time y_j and the feature vector X_j which is modeled as follows:

$$y_j = X_i\beta + \sigma\varepsilon_j \tag{3}$$

where $\beta = (\beta_1, \cdots, \beta_m)^T$ is the coefficient vector, σ is an adjusted parameter, and ε_j follows a logistic distribution. Thus, the observed time y_j follows the logistic distribution. Based on Eq.(3), the ε can be calculated as $\varepsilon = \frac{y-X\beta}{\sigma}$, and the cumulative successful function is defined as:

$$F(y,\beta,\sigma) = \frac{exp(\frac{y-X\beta}{\sigma})}{1+exp(\frac{y-X\beta}{\sigma})} \tag{4}$$

and the density function will be

$$f(y,\beta,\sigma) = \frac{F(y)}{dy} = \frac{\frac{1}{\sigma}exp(\frac{y-X\beta}{\sigma})}{\left[1+exp(\frac{y-X\beta}{\sigma})\right]^2} \tag{5}$$

Substituting Eq.(4) and Eq.(5) in Eq.(2), we obtain the likelihood function for logistic distribution

$$L(\beta,\sigma) = \prod_{\delta_j=1} \frac{\frac{1}{\sigma}exp(\frac{y_j-X_j\beta}{\sigma})}{\left[1+exp(\frac{y_j-X_j\beta}{\sigma})\right]^2} \prod_{\delta_j=0} \frac{1}{1+exp(\frac{y_j-X_j\beta}{\sigma})} \tag{6}$$

and the coefficient vector β and model parameter σ can be estimated by minimizing the negative log-likelihood

$$\begin{aligned} l(\beta,\sigma) = &\sum_{\delta_j=1} \left\{ \frac{y_j - X_j\beta}{\sigma} - \log\sigma - 2\log\left[1+exp(\frac{y_j-X_j\beta}{\sigma})\right]\right\} \\ &- \sum_{\delta_j=0} \log\left[1+exp(\frac{y_j-X_j\beta}{\sigma})\right] \end{aligned} \tag{7}$$

Log-logistic distribution: The parametric methods for censored regression with log-logistic distributions can be viewed as a special case of the accelerated failure-time (AFT) model where the logarithm of the observed time y_j is linearly related to the feature vector X_j [3]:

$$\log y_j = X_i\beta + \sigma\varepsilon_j \tag{8}$$

Similar to the logistic distribution case described above, ε_j follows a logistic distribution and can be calculated as $\varepsilon = \frac{\log y - X\beta}{\sigma}$, using Eq.(8); thus, we have

$$\begin{aligned} S(y,\beta,\sigma) &= \frac{1}{1+exp(\frac{-X\beta}{\sigma})y^{\frac{1}{\sigma}}} \\ f(y,\beta,\sigma) &= \frac{\frac{1}{\sigma}exp(\frac{-X\beta}{\sigma})y^{\frac{1}{\sigma}-1}}{\left[1+exp(\frac{-X\beta}{\sigma})y^{\frac{1}{\sigma}}\right]^2} \end{aligned} \tag{9}$$

and based on the same procedure described in the logistic distribution case, the log-likelihood function is given by

$$\begin{aligned} l(\beta,\sigma) = &\sum_{\delta_j=1} \left\{ \frac{-X_j\beta}{\sigma} + \frac{1-\sigma}{\sigma}\log y_i \right. \\ &\left. - \log\sigma - 2\log\left[1+exp(\frac{-X_j\beta}{\sigma})y_j^{\frac{1}{\sigma}}\right]\right\} \\ &- \sum_{\delta_j=0} \log\left[1+exp(\frac{-X_j\beta}{\sigma})y_j^{\frac{1}{\sigma}}\right] \end{aligned} \tag{10}$$

The coefficient vector β and model parameter σ of logistic and log-logistic distributions can be estimated by minimizing the negative of Eq.(7) and Eq.(10), respectively. These minimization problems can be solved using standard Newton-Raphson method and the gradients of the negative log-likelihood with respect to β and σ can be calculated using the chain-rule, and more details of solving it are available at [21].

5. EXPERIMENTAL RESULTS

We will now describe our experimental results including the evaluation metrics and implementation details of the methods used for experimental analysis.

5.1 Experiment setup

We evaluate the censored regression with logistic distribution and log-logistic distribution using Kickstarter data and compare these two models with other popular prediction methods that are available in the literature for handling censored observations. We used the following state-of-the-art methods for our comparison.

- **Cox proportional hazards model**: The Cox model [8] is the most commonly used semi-parametric model in survival analysis. The hazard function has the form $\lambda(t, X_i) = \lambda_0(t)exp(X_i\beta)$, where the $\lambda_0(t)$ is the common *baseline hazard function* for all individuals and β is the coefficient vector which can be estimated by minimizing the negative *log-partial likelihood* function.
- **Tobit regression**: Tobit model [30] is an extension of the linear regression $y_j = X_j\beta + \varepsilon_j, \varepsilon_j \sim N(0, \sigma^2)$, but the parameter is estimated by the maximum likelihood method rather than using the least square error. It uses the parametric method framework discussed in section 4.2 with the probability density function and the cumulative distribution function of the standard normal distribution.
- **Buckley-James estimation**: Buckley-James regression [5] is also a AFT model which uses Kaplan-Meier estimation to approximate the survival time of the censored observations as the target value, and then builds a linear model based on both the true survival times of uncensored observations and these approximated survival times.

- **Boosting concordance index**: Boosting concordance index (BoostCI) [24] is an approach where the concordance index metric (also known as the 'survival AUC' which is described in the next section) is modified into an equivalent smoothed criterion using the sigmoid function and the resulting optimization problem is solved using a gradient boosting algorithm.

The experiments in this work are performed in R programming environment. The Cox model, Tobit model, and the censored regression models with Logistic and Log-logistic distributions are implemented using the *survival* package [29]. In the survival package, the *coxph* function is employed to train the cox model and the Efron's method [9] is used to handle the tied observations. The Buckley-James Regression is fitted using the *bujar* package [31], and the BoostCI is trained based on the supporting information of [24] and the *mboost* package [16].

5.2 Evaluation metrics

Survival AUC, or the *concordance probability*, is used to measure the performance of regression and ranking models [14, 13]. Consider a pair of projects $(T_1, \hat{T}_1)$ and $(T_2, \hat{T}_2)$, where T_i is the actual observed day of success, and $\hat{T}_i$ is the predicted one. The concordance probability is defined as:

$$c = Pr(\hat{T}_1 > \hat{T}_2 | T_1 \geq T_2) \tag{11}$$

A high survival AUC value indicates a high concordance between predicted and observed time values. If T_i only has two possible values, then the regression models reduce to classification and the survival AUC will be the same as the standard Receiver operating characteristic (ROC) AUC. The survival AUC has the same scale as AUC, where 0.5 corresponds to random guessing and 1 indicates a perfect prediction. Survival AUC of standard regression model can be directly calculated using Eq.(11). In the Cox model, the output is related to the hazard rate and the project with a larger hazard rate should succeed earlier; the survival AUC of Cox model can be calculated by:

$$c = \frac{1}{num} \sum_{i \in \{1 \cdots N\} \delta_i = 1} \sum_{y_j > y_i} I(X_i \hat{\beta} > X_j \hat{\beta}) \tag{12}$$

where num denotes the number of comparable pairs and $I(\cdot)$ is the indicator function. The survival AUC for other methods, which directly target the time of success, should be calculated as:

$$c = \frac{1}{num} \sum_{i \in \{1 \cdots N\} \delta_i = 1} \sum_{y_j > y_i} I[S(\hat{y}_j | X_j) > S(\hat{y}_i | X_i)] \tag{13}$$

where $S(\hat{y}_i | X_i)$ is the predicted target value.

5.3 Results and Discussion

In this section we will discuss our experimental results of various censored prediction methods using different sets of features.

We performed experiments using different feature subsets: "Static" corresponds to the basic (static) statistical features obtained form the project description and the project creator; "Static+Social" corresponds to the basic (static) features along with the social network features obtained from Twitter; "Static+3days" denotes the basic (static) features along with the temporal features obtained at the beginning stages (first 3 days) of each project; "Static+Social+3days" denotes the complete set of features (union of all the previous three categories). In addition, for each feature set, we also generated two variants of the training data: "with censored", which includes both the successful and failed projects, and "without censored" which includes only the successful projects. Note that in the "without censored" version, the Tobit regression will become ordinary least squares (OLS) linear regression, and the other parametric censored regression models will become the corresponding uncensored regression models.

Table 2 provides the survival AUC (concordance index) values of each model on the Kickstarter data using 10-fold cross validation. For all the methods across all the feature set combinations, our results evidently show that adding the failed projects (censored observations) to the successful ones will provide significantly better prediction results compared to the corresponding data which contains only the successful projects ("without failed" version). By incorporating the failed projects, the survival AUC of all the methods was improved by 4.3% on an average. This result clearly indicates that *incorporating the failed projects (censored informations) will significantly help in building an accurate prediction model.*

In Figure 4, we show the concordance probability matrices (**C**) for four different methods using only the success projects and adding failed projects to the successful ones (containing all the features). The index of each element of the matrix plot corresponds to the actual observed days of a pair of comparable projects; in other words, $\mathbf{C}_{ij}$ is the concordance probability of all comparable project pairs whose actual observed days are represented by i and j, respectively. The term "actual observed days" used here corresponds to the number of days taken for obtaining the goal amount for successful projects and the total project time period (days until the goal date) for the failed projects. Note that this matrix is symmetric, and since we cannot calculate the concordance probability of two projects when their actual observed days are same, we had to set the value of diagonal elements to be 0. We can observe that there exists one common phenomenon among all the plots shown in Figure 4. The concordance probability of elements close to the diagonal are usually lower compared to the ones away from the diagonal.

This phenomenon reflects the fact that it is hard to predict the correct ordering when the two projects take similar number of days to succeed. In the top row, the four sub-figures are generated without using the failed projects for all features, and the four sub-figures in the bottom row are generated using both the successful and failed projects. The two sub-figures within the same column are generated using the same prediction method. The plot shows the distribution across all possible pairwise combinations and hence it will help us in visualizing and understanding the regions where the improvements are significant when using the failed projects. We can evidently see that, within same prediction method, the concordance probability is higher in the case of using the failed projects compared to the one where they are not being used.

From Table 2, we also observe that, compared to the features extracted from social network, the temporal (dynamic) features are more useful in prediction. *Significant improvements on prediction can be made if we can obtain the information from the first 3 days of the project progress.* This

Table 2: Performance comparison of various sets of features of Kickstarter projects with or without failed projects (censored observations) using Survival AUC values (along with their standard deviation).

	Static		Static+Social		Static+3days		Static+Social+3days	
	without failed	with failed	without failed	with failed	without failed	with failed	without failed	with failed
Cox	0.7322 (0.0104)	0.7727 (0.0092)	0.7463 (0.0098)	0.7942 (0.0089)	0.7667 (0.0126)	0.7965 (0.0093)	0.7724 (0.0121)	0.8098 (0.0087)
Tobit	0.7281 (0.0108)	0.7755 (0.0100)	0.7381 (0.0099)	0.7960 (0.0082)	0.7833 (0.0124)	0.8226 (0.0096)	0.7841 (0.0121)	0.8309 (0.0084)
BJ	0.7097 (0.0130)	0.7313 (0.0114)	0.7235 (0.0128)	0.7587 (0.0080)	0.8016 (0.0127)	0.8157 (0.0102)	0.8016 (0.0127)	0.8201 (0.0089)
BoostCI	0.5919 (0.0140)	0.6649 (0.0288)	0.6128 (0.0380)	0.6796 (0.0212)	0.8135 (0.0430)	0.8668 (0.0229)	0.8141 (0.0421)	0.8671 (0.0231)
Logistic	**0.7354 (0.0106)**	0.7815 (0.0095)	**0.7457 (0.0095)**	0.8009 (0.0086)	0.8332 (0.0097)	0.8659 (0.0075)	0.8331 (0.0094)	0.8695 (0.0067)
Log-logistic	0.7277 (0.0111)	**0.7826 (0.0099)**	0.7411 (0.0096)	**0.8029 (0.0081)**	**0.8800 (0.0057)**	**0.9010 (0.0056)**	**0.8774 (0.0060)**	**0.9030 (0.0057)**

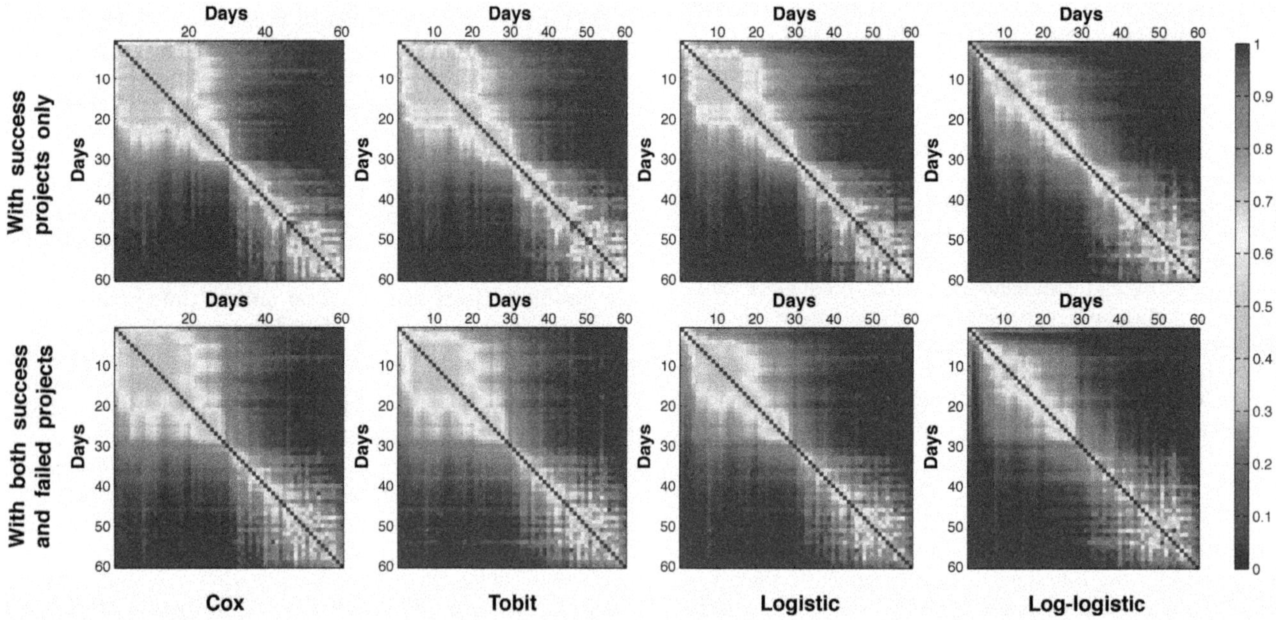

Figure 4: Concordance probability matrices for four different methods (Cox, Tobit, Logistic, and Log-logistic) using "with success projects only" (top row) and "with both success and failed projects" (bottom row). These results are based on all the features that are being studied.

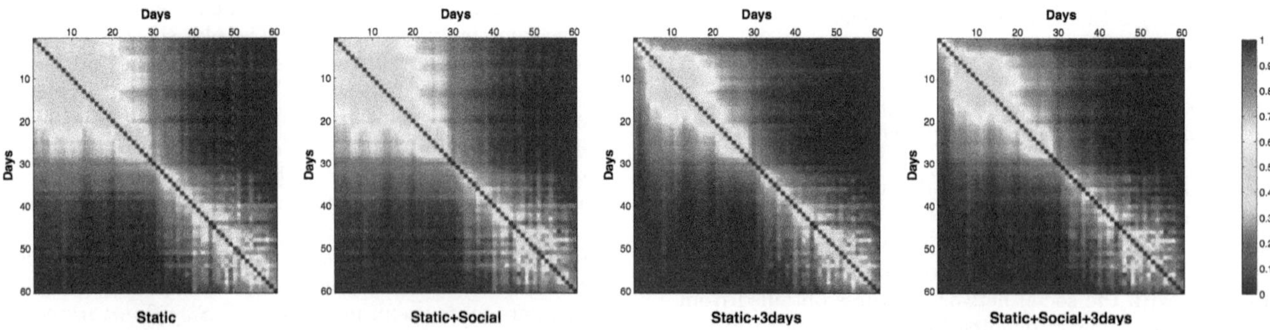

Figure 5: Concordance probability matrices obtained by the parametric censored regression with Logistic distribution using different feature subsets.

is a very useful characteristic in practice since it can guide the backers in deciding whether to invest in a particular project or not. Potentially this information can also be used in recommending projects to the backers. In Figure 5, we demonstrate the performance of the censored regression with Logistic distributions with different subset of features (using both failed and successful projects). We can clearly see that the model performance cannot be dramatically improved if we only combine the social network features with the static ones. However, adding the temporal features that are obtained at the beginning stages (first 3 days) of the project progress can dramatically help in improving the prediction performance. Overall, we can conclude that all the features obtained are useful for training the models, and the more appropriate features we collect the better the performance will become. From both Figures 4 and 5, we can also observe that all the methods show good prediction results when the actual observed days is large (greater than 20-30 days).

One of the main objectives of this paper is to demonstrate that, in the crowdfunding domain, when the goal is to predict project success, using only the successful projects will provide inferior prediction results compared to the case where failed projects are also being added. In other words, more value is added to the prediction when partial (censored) information from the failed projects is added to the successful projects (where the complete information on success is available). The partial information here refers to the fact that, in the failed projects, the information which is available is that the project did not receive success until the goal date and the information which is missing is that one does not know when the project will become successful.

While the above observations unanimously conclude that adding the failed projects is extremely useful in practice, we performed even more thorough analysis on the effects of adding such failed projects. The failed projects are censored (incomplete) observations; the data distribution of such censored observations have some correlations with the data distribution of the successful projects. The prediction result can be improved when we incorporate only a portion of the failed projects. In Figure 6, we present the prediction performance of different methods by varying the percentage of failed projects included in the model. It should be noted that the x-axis corresponds to the percentage of failed projects that are incorporated within the successful projects while building the prediction models. Hence, 0% corresponds to the case where only the successful projects were used and 100% corresponds to using all the projects (both successful and failed together). The results reported here are the average (of 10 different runs) improvements made by adding a random set of certain percentage of failed projects. From these four sub-figures we can see that the survival AUC can be improved dramatically even if only a relatively smaller portion (around 20%-30%) of the failed projects are incorporated, but the curve becomes close to a flat one when the failed projects added exceeds a certain limit.

6. CONCLUSION AND FUTURE WORK

In this paper, we solve the problem of predicting project success in a crowdfunding environment combined with innovative introduction of survival analysis based approaches. While the day of success is considered to be the time to reach an event, the failed projects are considered to be censored since the day of success is not known. We performed rigorous analysis of the Kickstarter crowdfunding domain to reveal unique insights about factors that impact the success of projects. Our experimental results show that incorporation of failed projects (censored information) can significantly help in building a robust prediction model and such censored models can perform better than standard prediction models that are available in the literature. Additionally, we also created several Twitter-based features to study the impact of social network on the crowdfunding domain. Our study shows that these social network-based features can help in improving the prediction performance. Most importantly, we found that the temporal features obtained at the beginning stage (first 3 days) of each project will significantly improve the prediction performance. In the future, we plan to implement a system which is able to rank the Kickstarter projects dynamically and help the project backers make a better decision on their investments in a real-time environment.

Acknowledgments

This work was supported in part by the US NSF grants IIS-1231742, IIS-1242304, and IIS-1527827.

7. REFERENCES

[1] J. Andreoni. Impure altruism and donations to public goods: a theory of warm-glow giving. *The economic journal*, pages 464–477, 1990.

[2] A. Ashta and D. Assadi. Do social cause and social technology meet? impact of web 2.0 technologies on peer-to-peer lending transactions. *Cahiers du CEREN*, 29:177–192, 2009.

[3] S. Bennett. Log-logistic regression models for survival data. *Applied Statistics*, pages 165–171, 1983.

[4] T. Bruett. Cows, kiva, and prosper. com: How disintermediation and the internet are changing microfinance. *Community Development Investment Review*, 3(2):44–50, 2007.

[5] J. Buckley and I. James. Linear regression with censored data. *Biometrika*, 66(3):429–436, 1979.

[6] O. Chapelle. Modeling delayed feedback in display advertising. In *Proceedings of the 20th ACM SIGKDD international conference on Knowledge discovery and data mining*, pages 1097–1105. ACM, 2014.

[7] J. Choo, D. Lee, B. Dilkina, H. Zha, and H. Park. To gather together for a better world: understanding and leveraging communities in micro-lending recommendation. In *Proceedings of the 23rd international conference on World wide web*, pages 249–260, 2014.

[8] D. R. Cox. Regression models and life-tables. *Journal of the Royal Statistical Society. Series B (Methodological)*, pages 187–220, 1972.

[9] B. Efron. The efficiency of cox's likelihood function for censored data. *Journal of the American Statistical Association*, 72(359):557–565, 1977.

[10] V. Etter, M. Grossglauser, and P. Thiran. Launch hard or go home!: predicting the success of kickstarter campaigns. In *Proceedings of the first ACM conference on Online social networks*, pages 177–182, 2013.

[11] J. Galak, D. Small, and A. T. Stephen. Microfinance decision making: A field study of prosocial lending. *Journal of Marketing Research*, 48(SPL):S130–S137, 2011.

[12] E. M. Gerber, J. S. Hui, and P.-Y. Kuo. Crowdfunding: Why people are motivated to post and fund projects on crowdfunding platforms. In *CSCW Workshop*, 2012.

[13] F. E. Harrell, R. M. Califf, D. B. Pryor, K. L. Lee, and R. A. Rosati. Evaluating the yield of medical tests. *JAMA*, 247(18):2543–2546, 1982.

[14] F. E. Harrell, K. L. Lee, R. M. Califf, D. B. Pryor, and R. A. Rosati. Regression modelling strategies for improved prognostic prediction. *Statistics in medicine*, 3(2):143–152, 1984.

[15] S. Heyman. Keeping up with kickstarter. *The New York Times, URL http://www.nytimes.com/2015/01/15/arts/international/keeping-up-with-kickstarter.html*, 2015.

[16] T. Hothorn, P. Buehlmann, T. Kneib, M. Schmid, and B. Hofner. Model-based boosting 2.0. *Journal of Machine Learning Research*, 11:2109–2113, 2010.

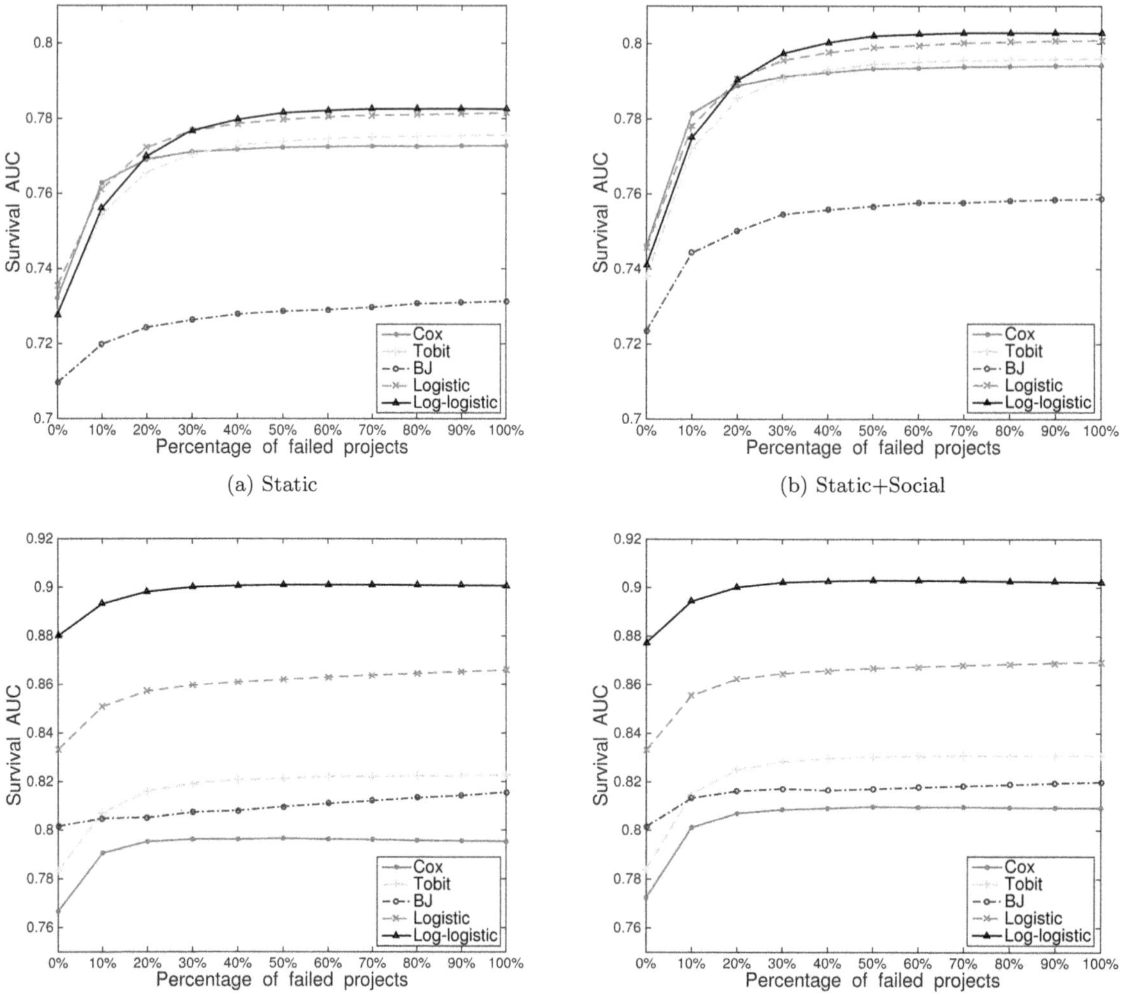

(a) Static (b) Static+Social

(c) Static+3days (d) Static+Social+3days

Figure 6: Survival AUC curves for different methods obtained by varying the percentage of failed projects included along with the successful ones.

[17] J. S. Hui, M. D. Greenberg, and E. M. Gerber. Understanding the role of community in crowdfunding work. In *Proceedings of the 17th ACM conference on Computer supported cooperative work & social computing*, pages 62–74. ACM, 2014.

[18] E. L. Kaplan and P. Meier. Nonparametric estimation from incomplete observations. *Journal of the American statistical association*, 53(282):457–481, 1958.

[19] J. P. Klein and M.-J. Zhang. *Survival analysis, software.* Wiley Online Library, 2005.

[20] V. Kuppuswamy and B. L. Bayus. Crowdfunding creative ideas: The dynamics of project backers in kickstarter. *SSRN Electronic Journal*, 2013.

[21] E. T. Lee and J. Wang. *Statistical methods for survival data analysis*, volume 476. Wiley. com, 2003.

[22] C.-T. Lu, S. Xie, X. Kong, and P. S. Yu. Inferring the impacts of social media on crowdfunding. In *Proceedings of the 7th ACM international conference on Web search and data mining*, pages 573–582, 2014.

[23] M. Lunn and D. McNeil. Applying cox regression to competing risks. *Biometrics*, pages 524–532, 1995.

[24] A. Mayr and M. Schmid. Boosting the concordance index for survival data–a unified framework to derive and evaluate biomarker combinations. 2014.

[25] R. G. Miller Jr. *Survival analysis*, volume 66. John Wiley & Sons, 2011.

[26] V. Rakesh, J. Choo, and C. K. Reddy. Project recommendation using heterogeneous traits in crowdfunding. In *Ninth International AAAI Conference on Web and Social Media*, 2015.

[27] V. Rakesh, W.-C. Lee, and C. K. Reddy. Probabilistic group recommendation model for crowdfunding domains. In *Proceedings of the ACM International Conference on Web Search and Data Mining (WSDM)*. ACM, 2016.

[28] C. K. Reddy and Y. Li. A review of clinical prediction models. In C. K. Reddy and C. C. Aggarwal, editors, *Healthcare Data Analytics*. Chapman and Hall/CRC Press, 2015.

[29] T. Therneau. A package for survival analysis in s. r package version 2.37-4. *URL http://CRAN. R-project. org/package= survival. Box*, 980032:23298–0032, 2013.

[30] J. Tobin. Estimation of relationships for limited dependent variables. *Econometrica: journal of the Econometric Society*, pages 24–36, 1958.

[31] Z. Wang and C. Wang. Buckley-james boosting for survival analysis with high-dimensional biomarker data. *Statistical Applications in Genetics and Molecular Biology*, 9(1), 2010.

[32] A. Xu, X. Yang, H. Rao, W.-T. Fu, S.-W. Huang, and B. P. Bailey. Show me the money!: an analysis of project updates during crowdfunding campaigns. In *Proceedings of the 32nd annual ACM conference on Human factors in computing systems*, pages 591–600, 2014.

Probabilistic Group Recommendation Model for Crowdfunding Domains

Vineeth Rakesh
Wayne State University
Detroit, MI - 48202
vineethrakesh@wayne.edu

Wang-Chien Lee
Pennsylvania State University
State College, PA - 16801
wlee@cse.psu.edu

Chandan K. Reddy
Wayne State University
Detroit, MI - 48202
reddy@cs.wayne.edu

ABSTRACT

Crowdfunding has gained a widespread popularity by fueling the creative minds of entrepreneurs. Not only has it democratized the funding of startups, it has also bridged the gap between the venture capitalists and the entrepreneurs by providing a plethora of opportunities for people seeking to invest in new business ventures. Nonetheless, despite the huge success of the crowdfunding platforms, not every project reaches its funding goal. One of the main reasons for a project's failure is the difficulty in establishing a linkage between it's founders and those investors who are interested in funding such projects. A potential solution to this problem is to develop recommendation systems that suggest suitable projects to crowdfunding investors by capturing their interests. In this paper, we explore Kickstarter, a popular reward-based crowdfunding platform. Being a highly heterogeneous platform, Kickstarter is fuelled by a dynamic community of people who constantly interact with each other before investing in projects. Therefore, the decision to invest in a project depends not only on the preference of individuals, but also on the influence of groups that a person belongs and the on-going status of the projects. In this paper, we propose a probabilistic recommendation model, called *CrowdRec*, that recommends Kickstarter projects to a group of investors by incorporating the on-going status of projects, the personal preference of individual members, and the collective preference of the group . Using a comprehensive dataset of over 40K crowdfunding groups and 5K projects, we show that our model is effective in recommending projects to groups of Kickstarter users.

Categories and Subject Descriptors

H.2.8 [**Database Management**]: Database applications-Data Mining; I.2.6 [**Artificial Intelligence**]: Learning; H.3.3 [**Information Search and Retrieval**]: Information filtering

WSDM'16, February 22–25, 2016, San Francisco, CA, USA.
 ISBN 978-1-4503-3716-8/16/02...$15.00
DOI: http://dx.doi.org/10.1145/2835776.2835793

Keywords

Recommendation; crowdfunding; probabilistic models; topic models; group recommendation.

1. INTRODUCTION

Crowdfunding has emerged as "the next big thing" in entrepreneurial financing. By providing the much-needed seed capital for new business ventures, it has created plenty of new job opportunities and revived lost business ventures. In 2014 alone, the crowdfunding platforms raised over $16.2 billions of dollars worldwide, thereby becoming a viable alternative to banks, brokers, and other financial intermediaries for people seeking funding to jump-start their business ventures. The concept of crowdfunding is analogous to micro-financing where the required funds are collected by pooling small amounts of money from several individuals. Since its launch in April 2009, Kickstarter has grown to become one of the most popular crowdfunding platforms. Kickstarter terms the founders of a project as *creators* and the investors as *backers*. The creators express their ideas by posting a detailed description about their project. Usually, the description contains videos, images and textual information that explains the novelty of the project. In addition, the creators provide a detailed timeline, funding goal, and the rewards for different pledge levels.

The need for recommender systems in crowdfunding platforms. Although the interest in using Kickstarter for crowdfunding has been outstanding, the success rate of projects is not very impressive. Statistical reports show that only about 37% of the projects succeeded in reaching their funding goal [19], which means over 60% of the crowdfunding projects in Kickstarter have failed. One of the main reasons for these failures is the lack of publicity [17]. We argue that recommendation systems that suggest suitable projects to crowdfunding investors can address this problem. Thus, in this paper, we propose a probabilistic recommendation model, called *CrowdRec*, that recommends projects to a *group* of potential backers. To the best of our knowledge, very few studies have explored the crowdfunding domain from a data mining perspective [3, 13, 23, 34].

Recommendation challenges in crowdfunding. Recommendation in crowdfunding poses a number of challenges. Based on our preliminary study on analyzing Kickstarter user behaviors [28], we found that a diverse set of factors collectively influence the users' decision to back a project. Hence, recommendation cannot be based on some simple set of straightforward features that are directly available from the projects. Consider the decision making of a

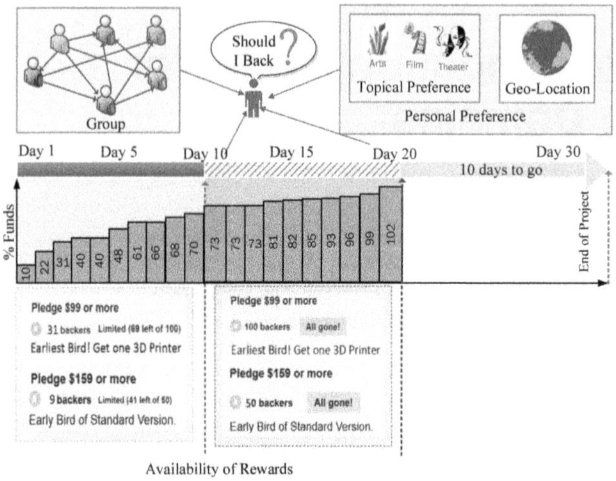

Figure 1: Impact of project, personal, and social network based features on Kickstarter users.

Kickstarter investor, as illustrated in Figure 1; we can see that the user is influenced by (1) his own personal interest, (2) the group (or community) that the user is associated with, and (3) the real-time status of the project. The personal interest of a backer is attributed to his preferences over the topic or the geo-location of the project. The group's influence on the other hand is amplified by the pervasive growth of social media such as Twitter and Facebook, where users' decision to back a project depends not only on their personal interests, but also on their relationship to a social-group of peer investors they communicate with. Therefore, when designing a recommender system for crowdfunding, it is important to incorporate the group's influence. Finally, due to the *transient* nature of crowdfunding projects, the real-time status of the project plays a critical role in determining the backing habits of a user. Notice that, in conventional recommendation such as movies or books, it is reasonable to apply collaborative filtering techniques since the recommended items usually can serve many users for several years. This is not the case in crowdfunding; in Kickstarter, once the project expires after its posting period, we cannot recommend the project to any user any more. For instance, as shown in Figure 1, the project has a duration of 30 days. Recommending it after expiration makes no sense. This transient nature of projects gives rise to some interesting real-time properties such as (a) *the popularity of projects* and (b) *the availability of rewards.* In Kickstarter, the popularity of a project could be measured based on the percentage of funds collected at a specific time. In Figure 1, we see that, on Day 10 the project has already collected over 70% of it's goal amount, indicating high popularity. Therefore, there is a high chance for a user to fund such popular projects. Nonetheless, the popularity is not the sole deciding factor. In the same figure, we can also see that, on Day 20, although the project remains popular, most of the rewards are already sold out (denoted by the phrase "All Gone") due to the demand. This in-turn means that people might not be interested in backing such projects (with no availability of certain type of rewards), despite it's popularity.

Overview of the proposed approach. To create a personalized recommendation system for crowdfunding, we propose a *group recommendation* model called *C*rowdRec. Using a probabilistic generative framework, we incorporate various heterogeneous features related to the project, users, and their social groups to precisely model the interests of investors. Notice that in the crowdfunding scenario, projects are like *living entities that survive for a finite duration, and are affected by real-time actions such as popularity and reward availability.* Therefore, we need to leverage the information about the dynamic on-going status of a project when recommending it to the users.

Research Contributions. The major contributions of this paper are summarized as follows:

1. We propose a group-recommendation model for crowdfunding domains, which incorporates the dynamic-status of the on-going projects to recommend Kickstarter projects for a group of investors.
2. We use a diverse set of features about the projects. These features include (1) topical preference (2) geo-location preference (3) social-network links of backers and (4) various temporal information about the projects to incorporate rich prior information into our probabilistic model.
3. Using comprehensive evaluation techniques, we show that our model outperforms a number of baselines and a state-of-the-art group-recommendation model to provide effective and meaningful recommendations for backer groups in Kickstarter.

The rest of this paper is organized as follows. We review the related work on crowdfunding and group recommendation models in Section 2. In Section 3, we discuss the notion of groups in Kickstarter and the challenges associated with group recommendation. The CrowdRec model and it's generative process are introduced in Section 4, followed by the derivation of the model parameters. In Section 5, we show the different ways of incorporating various prior information. In Section 6, we explain the data collection methodology and report the experimental results for performance evaluation. Finally, we conclude the paper in Section 7.

2. RELATED WORKS

In this section, we review two lines of related research namely, crowdfunding and recommender systems.

2.1 Crowdfunding Litrature

Crowdfunding and Kickstarter. Since crowdfunding is still an emerging research domain, most works in this area are relatively new. The dynamics of Kickstarter are examined in a recent survey [20], while various types of crowdfunding platforms are compared in [26]. In [14, 17], the authors analyze the crowdfunding platforms to learn the motivation behind the users who create and invest in crowdfunding projects. Moreover, the effect of frequent updates over the success rate of projects is explored in [34]; and the impact of social network on Kickstarter projects is delineated in [23].

Recommendation in Crowdfunding Platforms. So far, there are very few studies on developing recommendation models for crowdfunding platforms. In [11], a personalized loan recommendation system for a micro-financial platform called *Kiva.org* is proposed. Recently, an SVM classifier is trained using updates, comments, Facebook friends and other features from Kickstarter to recommend investors to Kickstarter projects [3]. In our previous work on Kickstarter [28], a variety of traits based on backer personality, geo-location, project quality, and social network have been analyzed and incorporated into a gradient boosting tree model to recommend backers to Kickstarter projects. Finally, in our recent work [21], we formulate a survival analysis problem to predict the success of Kickstarter projects.

2.2 Recommender Systems

Basic Recommendation Techniques. The core of all recommender systems is to obtain a utility function that estimates the preference of a user towards an item. Essentially, recommender systems can be divided into two main categories: collaborative filtering methods and content-based methods. Collaborative filtering-based techniques utilize the user rating of items to derive the similarity between the users (or items) to recommend relevant items to users. Content-based approaches, on the other hand, utilize the content features of the users (or items) to make the recommendation. These features might include user's topical interest, age, gender, etc. For a comprehensive summary of collaborative filtering techniques, the readers are referred to survey articles [1, 30]. In the context of crowdfunding, the heterogeneity in Kickstarter crowdfunding suggests hybrid recommendation techniques, which are gaining a lot of attention in recent years. A naive way of using hybrid recommendation is to use collaborative and content-based methods in parallel [5, 12, 31]; nonetheless, these approaches do not incorporate the influence of social groups to model the interests of users. In this work, we adopt probabilistic latent modeling (discussed below) to seamlessly integrate the collaborative and content-based filtering approaches into a unified group recommendation model.

Probabilistic Models for Recommendation. The original aspect model is proposed by Hofmann for Probabilistic Latent Semantic Analysis (PLSA) [15, 16]. Since then, more complex machine learning models have been proposed, including multinomial mixture models, latent dirichlet allocation (LDA), markov models and latent factor models [8, 24, 29]. The PLSA aspect model has been widely used in information retrieval and data mining applications [27]. For example, in [10], the aspect model is used for recommending communities, while in [35], an additional latent variable has been added to the aspect model to capture the influence of friends on a user's topical interest.

Group Recommendation. Different from conventional recommendation which typically recommends an item to a user, the group recommendation aims to either (a) recommend a group (or community) to a user or (b) recommend an item to a group of users. In type (a), one usually recommends a set of groups (i.e., communities) to a user based on various measures such as (1) topical similarity between the community and the user, (2) popularity of the community at a given time, (3) proximity of geo-location between the user and the members of the community, etc., [9, 10, 32, 33, 37]. Our definition of the group recommendation in this paper belongs to type (b), which is new to the data mining research and thus very few studies have explored this research direction [22, 25, 36]. In [35], a probabilistic aspect model is proposed to learn the interests of users using both their personal preference and the influence from their social network. Using score aggregation strategies such as average and least-misery techniques [4], recommendation of items is made for a targeted group of users. In [22], a unified group recommendation model is proposed and later extended by incorporating a group-topic distribution [36] to provide an improved recommendation. The group recommendation model proposed in this paper is uniquely different from the aforementioned works as we incorporate the "live-status" of projects along with user preference and group influence in the model.

3. GROUPS IN CROWDFUNDING

To elucidate the need for group recommendation in Kickstarter, we obtain backers who have their Twitter profiles and retrieve their friends and followers from Twitter search API. We then create communities of these backers to analyze *whether the backing habits of these investors are influenced by their relationship to a community*[1]. The process of community creation is detailed in our previous work [28]. To measure the influence of a group over the backer, we calculate their *Affinity* score as follows:

$$\mathit{Affinity}(b, g) = |F(b) \cap F(g)| \quad (1)$$

where $F(b)$ and $F(g)$ denote the set of all the followers and followees of a backer b and a community g, respectively; $|F(b) \cap F(g)|$ indicates the number of mutual friends between this backer and the members of the community. Figure 2(a) shows the outcome of this analysis, where $p(M(b,v)|M(g,v))$ indicates the probability of a user b backing a project v, given that v is backed by the members of the group g. In this notation, $M(b,v)$ denotes the action of a backer investing in project v and $M(g,v)$ denotes the same by a community g. From this figure, one can see that the stronger *affinity* of a user towards a group leads to a greater chance for this user to back the same project that was backed by the group. Therefore, given a project, the goal of our CrowdRec recommendation model is to *identify a group of users who may potentially back this project.*

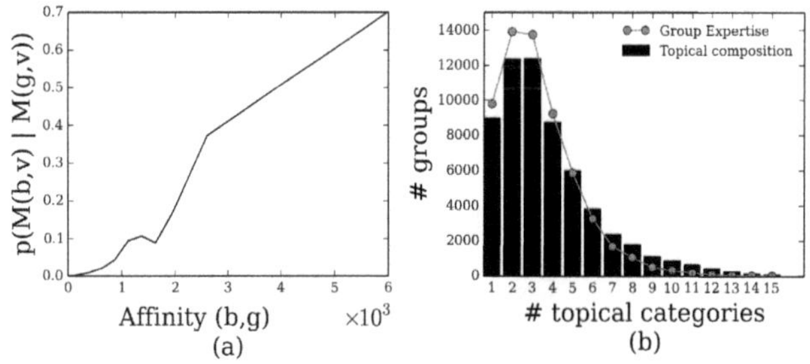

Figure 2: Characteristics of groups in Kickstarter. (a) shows the influence of communities (groups) over the backing habits of users and (b) shows the topical composition in groups.

Next, we analyze the preferences of individual members in a group. To proceed, for every group in our dataset, we calculate the number of unique topical categories of projects backed by the members of the group. As shown in Figure 2(b), although there are groups consisting of members who are interested in just one single topic, *a majority of them have diverse interests, i.e., the members have backed projects*

[1]In this paper, we also refer these communities as *groups*, so these two terms are used interchangeably.

from multiple topical categories. In addition, we analyze the expertise of individual group members by calculating the number of backers who are experts in a specific topical category of projects. We say a backer to be an expert in a topic if she has backed at least 3 projects from the same category and has over 15 backings in total. As depicted in Figure 2(b), a *majority of groups consist of backers who are experts in multiple topical categories.* We aim to exploit these observations in the proposed CrowdRec model.

4. CROWDREC: A PROBABILISTIC GENERATIVE MODEL

In this section, we introduce CrowdRec, a probabilistic generative model for recommending crowdfunding projects to groups of users. The recommendation model aims to capture the following observations: (1) A crowdfunding group may support projects from multiple topical categories, (2) A user's backing decision is based not only on her personal preference but also on the collective preferences of her groups; (3) A group's collective preference to support a project is strongly correlated with the personal preferences of topically authoritative users (i.e., users expertise) within the group, (4) The dynamic status of a project impacts both the individual investor's personal preferences and the group's collective preferences in backing crowdfunding projects.

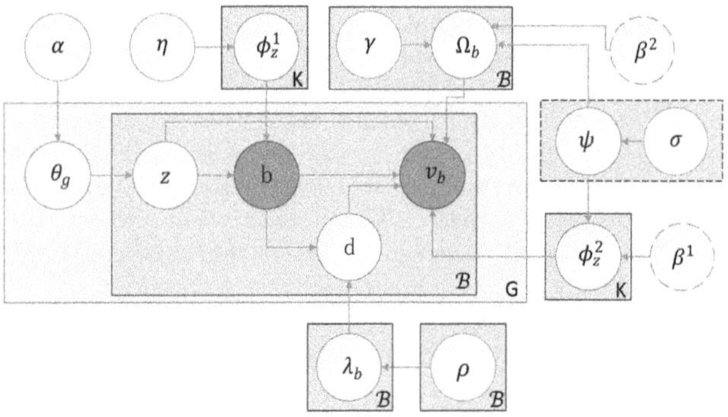

Figure 3: Graphical representation of the CrowdRec model.

In this section, we first formulate the modeling problem and then present the generative process captured in our CrowdRec model. Next, we show how the dynamic status of projects is incorporated into the model. Finally, we derive the parameters of the model to facilitate model learning via Gibbs sampling.

Problem Statement: Given a set of *projects* $V = \{v_1, v_2, ..., v_{|V|}\}$, a set of *backers* $B = \{b_1, b_2, ..., b_{|B|}\}$, and a set of *groups* $G = \{g_1, g_2, ..., g_{|G|}\}$, let $B^g \subset B$ denote a group of backers in group g, i.e., $B^g = \{b_1^g, b_2^g, ..., b_{|B^g|}^g\}$. The action of a group g backing a project v is denoted by $M(B^g, v) = \{(b, v)|b \in B^g\}$, where (b, v) refers to an individual b from a group g choosing to back a project v. The goal of our CrowdRec model is to recommend a ranked list of V projects to a target (or new) group $\widetilde{g}$.

4.1 Generative Process

The Graphical representation of the CrowdRec model is shown in Figure 3. We describe the generative process in our model as follows.

- Each group $g \in G$ is composed of members who are interested in certain particular project categories. Therefore, the collective preference of the group is captured by θ_g, which is represented as a distribution over a universal set of latent topics in projects. Here, θ_g follows a symmetric Dirichlet distribution, i.e., $\theta_g \sim Dirichlet(\alpha)$.
- Based on θ_g, the group g chooses a single topic z and nominates a user b to decide whether to back a project v. The distribution ϕ_z^1 captures the expertise of this backer over the topic z.
- To decide whether to back a project v, the nominated user relies on either her own personal interest or the collective preference of the group. This decision is governed by the random variable D, which takes the binary value 0 or 1. Thus, we model d using a binomial distribution with beta prior.
- If d is 0:
  - The user picks the project based on (1) *the group's influence* (i.e., collective preference), which is a multinomial over the distribution ϕ_z^2 and (2) *the current status of the project.* The current status of the project (in the dotted box) is denoted by a ψ, $\psi \sim Dirichlet(\sigma)$.
- If d is 1:
  - The user picks the project based on (1) *her own topical interest* (personal preference), which is a multinomial over the distribution Ω_b and (2) *the current status of the project.*

Incorporating Dynamic Status of Projects. Notice that the status of a project plays a key role in the generative process described above. It is an external factor determined by the progression of the project over time. In Figure 3, this is indicated by the *project-status* distribution ψ, which is constrained by a dirichlet prior σ. ψ in-turn affects the *project-topic* distribution ϕ^2 and *user-project* distribution Ω. When the user relies on the group's influence to back a project v, the project-topic distribution ϕ^2 (i.e. $V \times K$ matrix) is multiplied by the project-status distribution ψ (i.e. $1 \times V$ matrix). In other words, ψ becomes a prior for ϕ^2. Alternatively, if the user backs a project based on her own preference, Ω (i.e. $B \times V$ matrix) is multiplied by ψ.

In the CrowdRec model, β^1 and β^2 are concentration scalars that affects the extent to which a group (or a user) relies on project status to make the backing decision. When β^1 is high, the group strongly relies on the on-going status to back the project, which means ϕ^2 becomes similar to ψ. Alternatively, if β^1 is low, the group's decision to back a project is independent of the on-going status of the project. Same applies for the scalar β^2, which affects the variable Ω. In the literature, this type of formulation is known as the *hierarchical Polya-Urn model*, which has been used to model the global and local topic distributions in LDA [6, 2, 7]. Algorithm 1 summarizes the complete generative process and Table 1 provides the list of symbols used in this paper.

4.2 Parameter Estimation

To learn the parameters in the CrowdRec model, the eastimation of the posterior is given by:

$$p(z, d|b, v, \alpha, \eta, \gamma, \sigma, \rho) = \frac{p(z, d, b, v|.)}{p(b, v|.)} \quad (2)$$

Table 1: List of notations used in this paper.

Symbol	Description
$\mathcal{B} = \{b_i\}$	set of backers, b_i indicates a single backer
$\mathcal{V} = \{v_i\}$	project set, v_i indicates a single project
$G = \{g_j\}$	crowdfunding groups, g_j indicates a single group
D	a binary decision variable, representing d=1 or d=0
$Z = \{z_i\}$	latent topics assigned to projects in Z
K	number of topics specified as parameter
$i = (b, v)$	a tuple that indicates backer b picks project v
θ_g	topic distribution of a group g
ϕ_z^1	$B \times K$ latent matrix for a backer b
ϕ_z^2	$G \times K$ latent matrix for a group g
Ω_b	$B \times V$ matrix for a backer b
λ_b	prior for the binary decision variable D
ψ	dynamic status distribution of a project v
$\alpha, \eta, \gamma, \sigma, \rho$	parameters of $\theta, \phi^1, \Omega, \psi, \lambda$
β_1, β_2	concentration scalars for ϕ^2, Ω
$c_{k,g,i}$	# times i is assigned to topic k in group g
$c_{k,g,b}$	# times backer b is assigned to topic k in group g
$c_{k,g,v}$	# times project v is assigned to topic k in group g
$c_{b,g,v}$	# times project v is assigned to backer b in group g
$c_{b,g,d}$	# times choice d chosen by a backer b in group g

Algorithm 1: Generative process of `CrowdRec` model

for *each project* $v \in \mathcal{V}$ **do**
  Draw $\psi_v \sim Dirichlet(\sigma)$
end
for *each topic* $z_k, k \in \mathcal{K}$ **do**
  Draw $\phi_z^1 \sim Dirichlet(\eta)$
  Draw $\phi_z^2 \sim Dirichlet(\psi\beta^1)$
end
for *each backer* $b \in \mathcal{B}$ **do**
  Draw $\Omega_b \sim Dirichlet(\psi\beta^2\gamma)$
  Draw $\lambda \sim Beta(\rho)$
end
for *each group* $g \in G$ **do**
  Draw $\theta_g \sim Dirichlet(\alpha)$
  for *each backer,b in group g* **do**
    Draw $z \sim Multinomial(\theta_g)$
    Draw $b \sim Multinomial(\phi_z^1)$
    Draw the *decision* $d \sim Bernoulli(\lambda_b)$
    if $d = 0$ **then**
      Draw $v \sim Multinomial(\phi_z^2)$
    end
    if $d = 1$ **then**
      Draw $v \sim Multinomial(\Omega_b)$
    end
  end
end

The likelihood of the above equation is expanded as follows:

$$p(z, d, b, v|.) = \underbrace{\int p(z|\theta)p(\theta|\alpha)d\theta}_{(A1)} . \underbrace{\int p(b|z, \phi^1)p(\phi^1|\eta)d\phi^1}_{(A2)} . \underbrace{\int p(d|\lambda)p(\lambda|\rho)d\lambda}_{(A3)} . \underbrace{\int\int\int p(v|b, d, z, \Omega, \phi^2)p(\Omega|\gamma, \psi, \beta^2).p(\phi^2|\psi, \beta^1)p(\psi|\sigma)d\Omega d\phi^2 d\psi}_{(A4)} \quad (3)$$

To infer the parameters $\phi^1, \Omega, \psi, \phi^2$ and λ, we obtain samples from this high-dimensional distribution using collapsed Gibbs sampling-based approach. It is important to note that there are complex relationships between the latent-topic variable Z and the latent-decision variable D. To overcome this problem, we adopt the two-step Gibbs sampling method proposed by Yuan et. al. [36] by decomposing the expression $(A4)$ of Equation (3) as follows:

$$\int\int\int p(v|b, d, z, \Omega, \phi^2).p(\Omega|\gamma, \psi, \beta^2).p(\phi^2|\psi, \beta^1).p(\psi|\sigma)d\Omega d\phi^2 d\psi = \underbrace{\int\int p(v^0|z, d^0, \phi^2)p(\phi^2|\psi, \beta^1)p(\psi|\sigma)d\phi^2 d\psi}_{(B1)} \underbrace{\int\int p(v^1|b, d^1, \Omega)p(\Omega|\gamma, \psi, \beta^2)p(\psi|\sigma)d\Omega d\psi}_{(B2)} \quad (4)$$

where expression $(B1)$ corresponds to the decision variable $d = 0$; in other words, when a user chooses to back a project v^0 based on his group's interest and expression $(B2)$ corresponds to the decision $d = 1$ i.e., when a user chooses a project v^1 based on her own interest. Therefore, using Gibbs sampling, we sample the latent variable d for two different cases: (a) when $d = 0$ and (b) when $d = 1$. Similarly, we sample the latent variable z when (a) project v^0 is chosen and (b) when project v^1 is chosen.

The derivation of the collapsed Gibbs sampling equation for the topic-latent variable z and the decision-latent variable d is similar to [36]. The probability of a tuple $i = (b, v)$ belonging to a latent topic z is derived as follows:

$$p(z_{g,i} = k|Z^{-(g,i)}, v^0, b) \propto \frac{c_{k,g,i^*}^{-(g,i)} + \alpha_k}{c_{k^*,g,i^*}^{-(g,i)} + \alpha_{k^*}} \cdot \frac{c_{k,g^*,b}^{-(g,i)} + \eta_b}{c_{k,g^*,b^*}^{-(g,i)} + \eta_{b^*}} \cdot \left(\frac{c_{k,g^*,v}^{-(g,i)}}{c_{k,g^*,v^*}^{-(g,i)}} + \beta^1 \frac{c_{k^*,g^*,v}^{-(g,i)} + \sigma_v}{c_{k^*,g^*,v^*}^{-(g,i)} + \sigma_{v^*}}\right) \quad (5)$$

$$p(z_{g,i} = k|Z^{-(g,i)}, v^1, b) \propto \frac{c_{k,g,i^*}^{-(g,i)} + \alpha_k}{c_{k^*,g,i^*}^{-(g,i)} + \alpha_{k^*}} \cdot \frac{c_{k,g^*,b}^{-(g,i)} + \eta_b}{c_{k,g^*,b^*}^{-(g,i)} + \eta_{b^*}} \quad (6)$$

In the above, the variable of type $c_{x,y,z}$ indicates a count as described in Table 1, and the symbol $*$ over the subscript variables denotes the summation over the respective subscript variables. For example, $c_{k,g,v}$ indicates the number of times the project v is assigned to topic k in group g and $c_{k,g*,v}$ is the same variable that is summed across all the groups $g \in G$. The superscript symbol $-(g, i)$ means that we exclude the ith tuple for group g when sampling. The probability of a tuple $i = (b, v)$ choosing a decision d is derived as follows:

$$p(d_{g,i} = 0|D^{-(g,i)}, Z, v, b) \propto \frac{c_{b,g^*,d_0}^{-(g,i)} + \rho_0}{c_{b,g^*,d_1}^{-(g,i)} + c_{b,g^*,d_0}^{-(g,i)} + \rho_0 + \rho_1} \cdot \left(\frac{c_{k,g^*,v}^{-(g,i)}}{c_{k,g^*,v^*}^{-(g,i)}} + \beta^1 \frac{c_{k^*,g^*,v}^{-(g,i)} + \sigma_v}{c_{k^*,g^*,v^*}^{-(g,i)} + \sigma_{v^*}}\right) \quad (7)$$

$$p(d_{g,i} = 1|D^{-(g,i)}, Z, v, b) \propto$$

$$\frac{c^{-(g,i)}_{b,g^*,d_1} + \rho_1}{c^{-(g,i)}_{b,g^*,d_1} + c^{-(g,i)}_{b,g^*,d_0} + \rho_0 + \rho_1} \cdot \left(\frac{c^{-(g,i)}_{g^*,b,v} + \gamma_v}{c^{-(g,i)}_{g^*,b,v^*} + \gamma_{v^*}} + \beta^2 \frac{c^{-(g,i)}_{k^*,g^*,v} + \sigma_v}{c^{-(g,i)}_{k^*,g^*,v^*} + \sigma_{v^*}} \right) \quad (8)$$

After obtaining sufficient number of samples using the above Gibbs update rules, we can finally infer the parameters $\phi^1_z, \Omega_b, \psi, \phi^2_z$ and λ_b as follows:

$$\phi^1_{z,b} = \frac{c_{k,g^*,b} + \eta_b}{c_{k,g^*,b^*} + \eta_{b^*}} \quad (9a)$$

$$\Omega_{b,v} = \frac{c_{g^*,b,v} + \gamma_v}{c_{g^*,b,v^*} + \gamma_{v^*}} + \beta^2 \frac{c_{k^*,g^*,v} + \sigma_v}{c_{k^*,g^*,v^*} + \sigma_{v^*}} \quad (9b)$$

$$\psi_v = \frac{c_{k^*,g^*,v} + \sigma_v}{c_{k^*,g^*,v^*} + \sigma_{v^*}} \quad (9c)$$

$$\phi^2_{z,v} = \frac{c_{k,g^*,v}}{c_{k,g^*,v^*}} + \beta^1 \frac{c^{-(g,i)}_{k^*,g^*,v} + \sigma_v}{c^{-(g,i)}_{k^*,g^*,v^*} + \sigma_{v^*}} \quad (9d)$$

$$\lambda_b = \frac{c_{b,g^*,d_1} + \rho_1}{c_{b,g^*,d_1} + c_{b,g^*,d_0} + \rho_0 + \rho_1} \quad (9e)$$

Recommending projects: To recommend a set of projects to a new group $\widetilde{g}$, we need to learn the group-topic distribution $\theta_{\widetilde{g}}$. This is done by estimating the posterior distribution of topics $\widetilde{z}$, given the backers $\widetilde{b}$ and the estimated backer-topic distribution ϕ^1_z and the hyperparameter α_k that was obtained from our CrowdRec model $\mathcal{M}$.

$$p(\widetilde{z}_{\widetilde{g},j} = k|\mathcal{B}_j = b_j, \widetilde{Z}^{-(\widetilde{g},b)}, \mathcal{B}^{-(j)}; \mathcal{M}) \propto \phi^1_{k,b}(c^{-(\widetilde{g},i)}_{k,\widetilde{g},i^*}) \quad (10)$$

Once we sample the topics for this new group $\widetilde{g}$, we recommend a new project based on the following equation.

$$p(v|\widetilde{g}) = \prod_{b \in \mathcal{B}^{\widetilde{g}}} \psi_v \sum_{z \in Z} \theta_{\widetilde{g},z}.(\lambda_b.\Omega_{b,v} + (1 - \lambda_b).\phi^2_{z,v}) \quad (11)$$

The above equation captures the following components when recommending a project to a group: (1) the individual's personal preference over a project Ω, (2) the influence of the group over a backer is captured by ϕ^2, (3) the topical preference of the group and the users are captured by θ and Ω, and (4) finally, the dynamic status (or popularity) of the project ψ.

5. PRIOR INFORMATION

In this section, we discuss the approaches we adopt to estimate the priors incorporated in CrowdRec. Notice that we have priors for two different distributions: (1) a static prior γ for the distribution Ω_b, which is a $B \times V$ matrix indicating the preferences of backers towards the Kickstarter projects; (2) a dynamic prior σ for distribution ψ, which is a $1 \times V$ row matrix indicating the on-going status of the project.

For the first case, we estimate the static prior γ by exploiting the backing history of all the users $b \in B$. This backing history, denoted by $\mathcal{H}_b$, contains the details such as a project's topical category, the geo-location of project, and the person who created the project.[2] For most part, this information remains static. Since it is extracted from the backing history of users, we call γ as *user-specific* prior. On the contrary, in the second case, the prior information σ is not static due to the transient nature of the projects (as explained in Section 1). As σ is changed at regular time intervals, we term it as *dynamic-status* prior. The calculation of these priors are detailed in the following sections.

[2]In our experiments, we consider city and state as the geo-location of the projects.

5.1 User-Specific Priors

In this paper, we incorporate three features from the users' backing history to create the user-specific prior γ, namely: (a) topical preference (b) creator preference, and (c) geo-location preference.

Topical Preference: In our previous work [28], we observed that Kickstarter users have a strong topical preference in their decisions to back a project. We assume users have a tendency to continuously back projects in the same topical category. This tendency can be modelled as a conditional probability of a user b to back a project in topic t, given t is present in the backing history of this user, denoted by $P((b,t)|t \in \mathcal{H}_b)$. Using Bayes' theorem, it is derived as follows:

$$P((b,t)|t \in \mathcal{H}_b) = \frac{P(t \in \mathcal{H}_b|(b,t))\, P(b,t)}{P(t \in \mathcal{H}_b)} \quad (12)$$

Creator Preference: Users tend to develop an inclination towards creators whom they have backed in the past. We represent this as the conditional probability of a user b to back a creator e, given that e is in the backing history of this user, denoted by $P((b,e)|e \in \mathcal{H}_b)$. It is calculated in a similar way as that of Equation (12).

Geo-location Preference: Geo-location has a strong impact on the success of projects, and the level of impact depends on the topical category of the project [28]. For instance, we find that projects based on technology are relatively less dependent on their geo-location, while projects on theatrical arts are highly dependent. Therefore, we incorporate this information as prior by calculating the probability of a user b to back a project v, given b and v are from the same geo-location. This probability is represented by $p((b,v)|Loc(b,v) = \ell,\ \tau(v) = t)$, where $Loc(b,v)$ indicates the geo-location of the backer and project, $\tau(v)$ is the topic of the project v. This probability is calculated using Bayes' theorem by expanding the likelihood using the chain rule of probability.

Finally, the interest of a user b towards a project v is obtained as a linear combination of topic-, creator-, and geo-location-based preferences as follows:

$$\gamma_{b,v} = p((b,t)|.) + p((b,e)|.) + p((b,v)|.) \quad (13)$$

5.2 Dynamic-Status Priors

We incorporate two factors in the prior σ for the project status ψ, namely, (1) the popularity of the project, and (2) the availability of popular rewards at specific time t.

Popularity of project: The popularity of a project at time t is derived as follows:

$$\mathcal{P}o_t(v) = \frac{\#\text{ pledged amount of project } v \text{ at time } t}{\text{Goal amount of the project } v} \quad (14)$$

where $\mathcal{P}o_t(v)$ is the *popularity score* of project v at time t.

Availability of rewards: As explained earlier in Figure 1, the status of the project cannot be expressed purely based on it's popularity, but the availability of rewards should also be considered. To verify our claim, we extract the top 3 popular reward categories of projects and obtain the additional percentage of backers backing the project on the day when the rewards are sold out. The result of this analysis is given in Figure 4, which shows that the interest of users in backing a project decays with the depletion of popular reward categories. Therefore, we calculate this prior information as follows:

$$\mathcal{R}_t(v) = \frac{\#\text{ rewards sold out at time } t}{\#\text{ limited rewards}} \tag{15}$$

where $\mathcal{R}_t(v)$ is the *reward score* of the project v at time t. Using Equations (14) and (15), we define the dynamic-status prior for a project v as follows:

$$\sigma_{(v,t)} = \mathcal{R}_t(v) \times \mathcal{P}o_t(v) \tag{16}$$

The score $\sigma_{(v,t)}$ is constantly updated at different time intervals $\{t1, t2..., tn\}$ until the project expires.

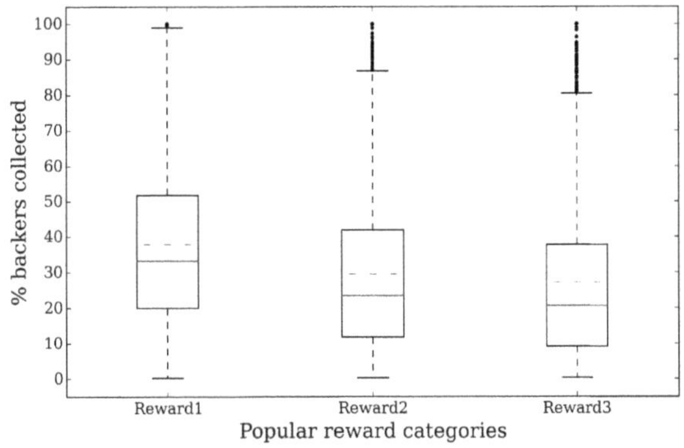

Figure 4: Decay of user interest with the depletion of popular reward categories.

6. EXPERIMENTS

In this section, we conduct comprehensive experiments to evaluate the performance of the CrowdRec model in comparison with state-of-the-art models. In the following, we first describe the datasets used in our experiments and then report the experimental results.

6.1 Dataset Description

For our experiments, we obtain six months of Kickstarter data (12/15/13 to 06/15/14) from *kickspy*, which consists of 27,270 projects. We remove projects that were canceled or suspended, with less than one backer, or with less than $100 of pledged amount. Next, we build a web-crawler to fetch backers from this filtered set of projects. As such, we obtain over 1 million backers for the remaining 18,143 projects after the removal process.

In our previous study [28], we show that backers in Kickstarter are distinguished by two important features: (a) the presence of social network profile,[3] and (b) the backing frequency. Therefore, in this paper, we leverage this information to categorize the backers $b \in \mathcal{B}$ into two types: (i) those who have linked their Kickstarter profiles to Twitter, and (ii) those without a Twitter profile. We denote these two types by Twt and Kck, respectively. In addition, we classify the backers into *occasional* backers who have backed 2-10 projects (denoted by *Occ*) and *experienced* backers who have backed over 10 projects (denoted by *Exp*). Thus, we have four different datasets: (1) **Twt-Occ** $= \{b|b \in \text{Twt} \cap (2 < \textit{Backings}(b) < 10)\}$; (2) **Twt-Exp** $= \{b|b \in \text{Twt} \cap (\textit{Backings}(b) > 10)\}$; (3) **Kck-Occ** $= \{b|b \in \text{Kck} \cap (2 < \textit{Backings}(b) < 10)\}$ and (4) **Kck-Exp** $= \{b|b \in \text{Kck} \cap (\textit{Backings}(b) > 10)\}$

Group Creation. A group consists of backers who have backed the same project. For the four datasets described above, we create groups of Kickstarter users using the methodology described in [4], i.e., in our group creation process, we calculate the inner group similarity between the group members using Pearson correlation co-efficient (PCC) and filter out groups which have PCC less than 0.2. The statistics of our backer-group datasets are shown in Table 2.

Table 2: Statistics of Kickstarter groups formed by frequent and occasional backers.

Dataset	#Bkrs/Grp	#Grps	Avg. #Prjs/Grp	#Prjs
Kck-Occ	10	30,100	2	1,609
Kck-Exp	10	20,675	4	1,397
Twt-Exp	5	3,373	3	959
Twt-Occ	5	3,513	2	1,104

6.2 Performance Evaluation

In the following, we first discuss the performance metrics employed in our evaluation and a number of recommendation models examined for comparison. Our evaluation is performed over all the four datasets *Twt-Occ*, *Twt-Exp*, *Kck-Exp*, and *Kck-Occ* by randomly holding-off 20% of the ground truth for testing. For most of our experiments we set the parameters β_1 and β_2 to be 0.5, the topic parameter K to 200 and the dynamic-status prior $\sigma_{(p,t)}$ is calculated using the 50% of the total project duration. The CrowdRec model and all other baselines are implemented using python's numpy numerical module, and scikits machine learning module.[4] The codes of our model are publicly hosted in the Github page.[5]

6.2.1 Evaluation Metrics

To evaluate the performance of ranking, we use the standard information retrieval measures. For every project, we compute: 1) P@N: *precision at rank N* is defined as the fraction of rankings in which the true backers are ranked in the *top-N* positions, 2) MRR: The *mean reciprocal rank* is the inverse of the position of the first true backer in the ranked set of backers produced by a recommendation model, 3) S@N: The *success at rank N* is the probability of finding at least one true backer in the *top-n* ranked set, and 4) DCG: The *discounted cumulative gain* [18] is based on the fact that highly relevant backers are more important than marginally relevant ones.

6.2.2 Baseline Methods for Comparison

We compare the performance of our model with a simple collaborative filtering-based approach that uses various aggregation strategies for group recommendation and other

[3]we only consider Twitter profiles since Facebook data is not publicly available.

[4]http://scikit-learn.org

[5]https://github.com/magnetpest2k5/Crec

state-of-the-art group recommendation models as described below:

- **Collaborative Filtering with averaging (*CFA*)**: First we learn user-project preference using user-based collaborative filtering. We then take the average of the recommended scores for a group and rank the preference scores to recommend a project to the group.
- **Collaborative Filtering with least-misery strategy (*CFL*)**: First we learn the user-project preference using user-based collaborative filtering. We then take the least scores as the recommended scores for a group and rank the preference scores to recommend a project to the group.
- **Collaborative Filtering with relevance disagreement (*CFR*)**: First we learn user-project preference using user-based collaborative filtering, and then takes the relevance score as CFA and the disagreement is calculated as the difference between the preference scores of individuals within a group.
- **COM Model:** The state-of-the-art group recommendation model that does not include the dynamic-status component [36].

6.2.3 *Experimental Results*

Overall Performance: Figure 5 shows that the performance of CrowdRec and COM are distinctly better than the collaborative filtering-based group recommendation techniques. Although, the collaborative filtering with averaging technique (CFA) produces better results than CFL and CFR, the approaches that heuristically aggregate the individual scores of backers to determine the groups' preference towards projects do not produce reasonable results.[6] It is also clear that the CrowdRec performs better than COM model in terms of both precision and recall. This shows that users strongly rely on the on-going status information of projects to make backing decisions.

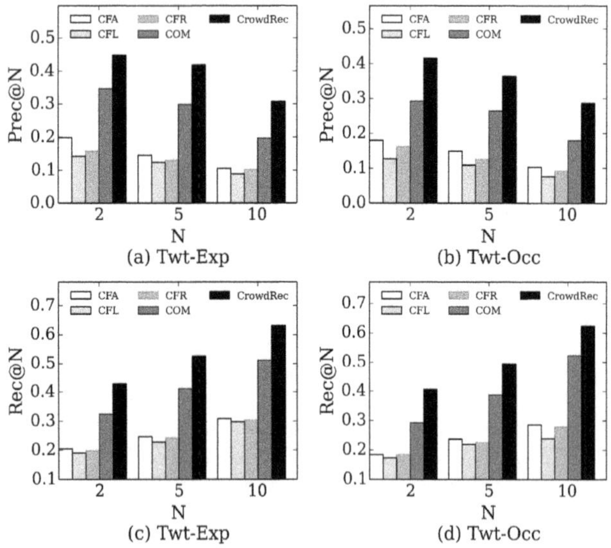

Figure 5: The precision and recall performance over experienced and occasional backers with Twitter profiles.

We also observe that the performance of CrowdRec over experienced backers (Figures 5(a) and 5(c)) is better than occasional backers (Figures 5(b) and 5(d)), because the former have a higher backing count, which provides a richer set of prior information about the backer's preference over topics, creators and geo-location compared to the occasional backers. Figure 6 shows similar set of results for the Kck dataset. In comparison to results shown in Figure 5, we see that the performance of our model slightly decreases in the dataset Kck. This is because the backers with Twitter profiles (i.e. dataset Twt) constantly receive Tweets about Kickstarter projects from their friends and followees, which leads to a better communication with their group members. Since one of the key components of our model is to effectively incorporate the groups' influence, it has a stronger impact over these type of users. Finally, in Table 3, we show the superior performance of CrowdRec over all other models by averaging the Success@N measure over all four datasets.

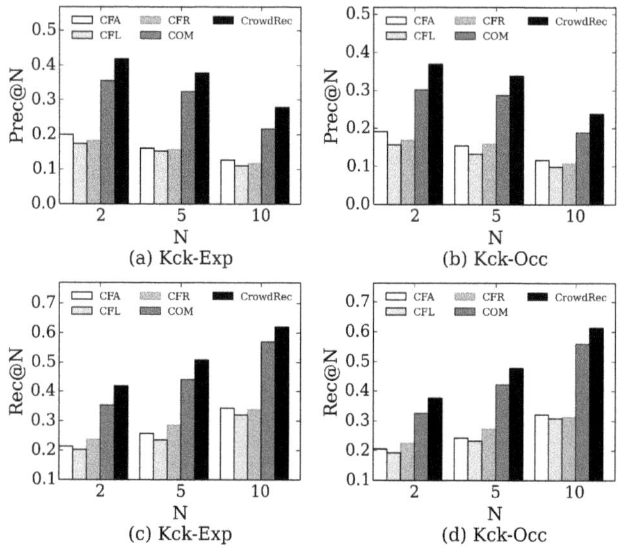

Figure 6: The precision and recall performance over experienced and occasional backers without Twitter profiles.

Table 3: The Average Performance over all datasets using Success @ N.

Model	Success@2	Success@5	Success@10
CFA	0.2638	0.3014	0.3352
CFR	0.2518	0.2857	0.3017
CFL	0.2698	0.3138	0.3369
COM	0.6347	0.7143	0.7584
CrowdRec	**0.6926**	**0.7436**	**0.7832**

Impact of Group Size: Depending on the number of backers in a group, a group can become more diverse or conservative in terms of their topical-preference. Therefore, we show the impact of group size on the performance of our model in Figure 7. Due to space constraints, we only show the recall performance for top 10 recommended projects. We again observe that CrowdRec performs better than COM and all other models irrespective of the group sizes. The performance of CrowdRec increases as we move from group size 2 to group size 5. However, this improvement becomes insignificant as the group size further increases. In fact, we observe that the performance slightly reduces for group sizes of 15 and above, mainly due to the sparsity of the data.[7]

[6]In [36] the authors report similar observations.

[7]Groups greater than 15 members are extremely few in num-

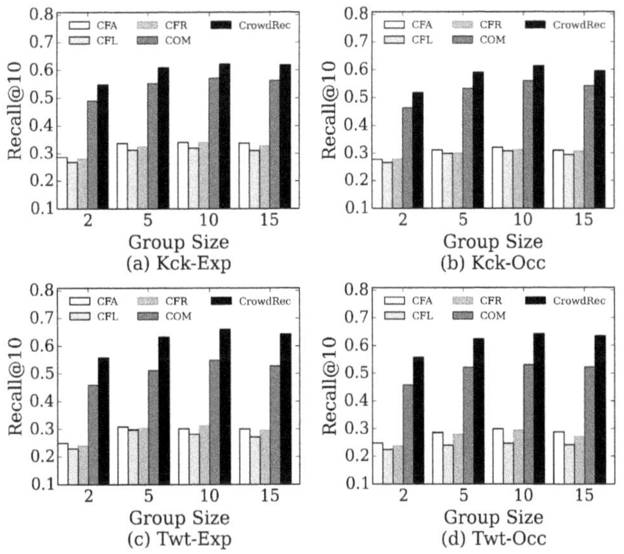

Figure 7: Effect of group sizes of Kickstarter users over the recall performance for all datasets.

Effect of Topic Size: To study the effect of topic size K over the performance of our model, in Figure 8, we plot the DCG scores of the top 10 recommended projects by varying K from 25 to 300. Similar to our prior observations, we see that the CrowdRec outperforms COM and all other models. Additionally, both CrowdRec and COM performs better on the backers with Twitter profiles (i.e. Twt-Exp and Twt-Occ) when compared to backers without Twitter profile (i.e. Kck-Exp and Kck-Occ). It is also important to note that the DCG values for experienced backers (Figure 8(a)) are higher than the occasional backers (Figure 8(b)), mainly because experienced backers have a much higher backing count (and thus richer prior information) than the occasional backers. Finally, we observe that the increase in the number of topics does not necessarily translate to a better performance. Although the DCG scores improves with the increase in topic count, the performance becomes static at about 200 topics. In fact, there is a slight decrease in the DCG scores when the topic count goes past 200.

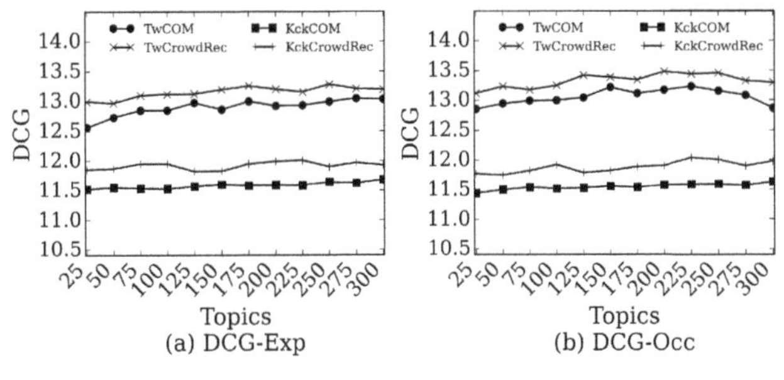

Figure 8: Effect of topics on the DCG measure.

Effect of Prior Information: Figure 9 shows the effect of various user- and project-based features that were used as priors in our model. In this figure, the y-axis denotes the priors and the x-axis indicates the MRR scores of the top 10 recommended projects. We begin with a symmetric prior (*s-prior*) and gradually add other features to the prior distribution, which is indicated by the + symbol. For instance, Topic$^+$ implies that we are including the topical-preference of users, which was calculated in Equation (12); similarly, Cr$^+$ implies we add creator preference into the prior information. We observe that simply by including the topic prior provides a significant boost to the MRR scores indicating that backers strongly depend on their topical interest to fund a project. Although, the addition of creator (*Cr*) and geo-location (*Geo*) preferences of backer improves the performance of the model, though it is not as significant as the topical-preference. Finally, the inclusion of the popularity prior (*Pop*) provides a significant boost yet again, which shows the importance of the information about the on-going status of the Kickstarter projects.

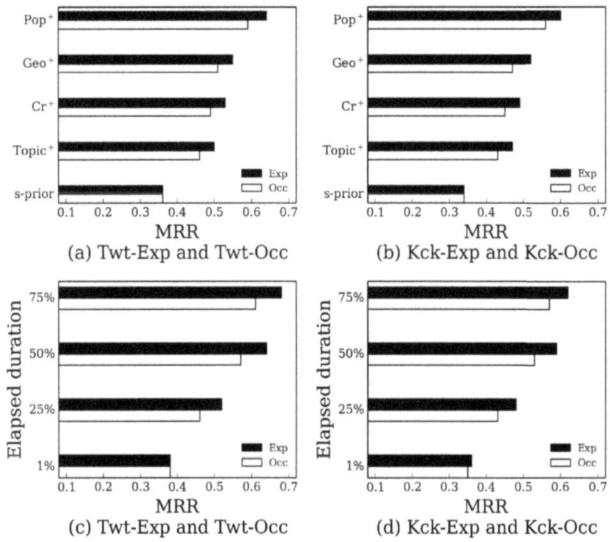

Figure 9: Effect of prior information ((a) and (b)) and project duration ((c) and (d)) on the recommendation performance. The terms *Topic*, *Cr*, *Geo* and *Pop* indicates the topical, creator, geolocation and popularity based priors, respectively.

Effect of Dynamic Status: Lastly, we show the effect of dynamically varying prior information in Figures 9(c) and 9(d). We calculate the status prior $\mathcal{R}_t$ using the Equation (14) at various intervals of the projects' duration ranging from 1% to 75% of the total project duration, which is indicated by the y-axis of this figure. It can be seen that, in general, the recommendation performance increases with the progression of the project. This is because, as the project progresses, we can obtain a much accurate estimation about it's status both in-terms of popularity and the availability of rewards.

7. CONCLUSION

In this paper, we introduced a recommendation framework for a popular crowdfunding platform, i.e., Kickstarter. We point out the challenges arising in Kickstarter, where the backing habits of its users depend on a diverse set of features, including topical, geo-location, temporal, and social traits. By exploiting the notion of groups, we proposed a recommendation model that effectively incorporates all these features when recommending projects to groups of Kickstarter

ber.

Quality Management in Crowdsourcing using Gold Judges Behavior

Gabriella Kaza [*]
Lumi
London, UK
gabs@lumi.do

Imed Zitouni
Microsoft
Bellevue, US
izitouni@microsoft.com

ABSTRACT

Crowdsourcing relevance labels has become an accepted practice for the evaluation of IR systems, where the task of constructing a test collection is distributed over large populations of unknown users with widely varied skills and motivations. Typical methods to check and ensure the quality of the crowd's output is to inject work tasks with known answers (gold tasks) on which workers' performance can be measured. However, gold tasks are expensive to create and have limited application. A more recent trend is to monitor the workers' interactions during a task and estimate their work quality based on their behavior. In this paper, we show that without gold behavior signals that reflect trusted interaction patterns, classifiers can perform poorly, especially for complex tasks, which can lead to high quality crowd workers getting blocked while poorly performing workers remain undetected. Through a series of crowdsourcing experiments, we compare the behaviors of trained professional judges and crowd workers and then use the trained judges' behavior signals as gold behavior to train a classifier to detect poorly performing crowd workers. Our experiments show that classification accuracy almost doubles in some tasks with the use of gold behavior data.

Categories and Subject Descriptors

H.3.4 [**Information Storage and Retrieval**]: Systems and Software—*performance evaluation (efficiency and effectiveness)*

Keywords

Experimentation, Measurement

1. INTRODUCTION

Recent years have seen a rapid adoption of crowdsourcing methods [12, 24, 20] in order to acquire annotations at large-scale in various contexts, from relevance judgments [9, 22, 1] to image labels [23] and semantic labels in knowledge corpora [30, 16]. With the appearance of crowdsourcing platforms, such as Amazon's Mechanical Turk (AMT)[1], crowdsourcing has become broadly accessible, enabling anyone to post jobs in the form of Human Intelligence Tasks (HITs) and engage a large population of workers within a short space of time at a relatively low cost. However, obtaining annotations from anonymous online workers can be challenging. Crowd workers are rarely trained and have diverse backgrounds and motivations for engaging in crowdsourcing tasks. Some workers may also display random behavior, cheating, and adversarial conduct [15, 14]. Consequently, the resulting data may be of varied quality.

Various methods of quality control have been developed as a result, aiming to enforce correct behavior during task completion or to enable the identification and removal of noise or spam from the crowdsourced data [22, 1]. The most established techniques rely on tasks with known answers (gold standard data) to estimate work quality [30, 9, 21, 13].

However, there are several issues with relying on gold data for quality control: 1) gold data is expensive to create and each administered gold test has an associated cost, 2) in a crowdsourcing scenario, the distribution of gold tests over workers is likely to be non-uniform, with most workers completing only very few tests, if any, while a few active workers may get frequently tested, and 3) gold tests may be of varying difficulty, e.g., lucky sloppy workers may pass easy tests while unlucky diligent workers may fail on difficult tests. Consensus methods overcome some of these issues, but they can greatly inflate costs due to the needed redundancy.

Recognizing these issues, there is recent interest in developing quality control mechanisms that do not rely on gold data. One such method is to observe crowd workers during task completion, for example, by logging their interactions with a HIT and using their behavior to detect the undesired among them [27, 10]. This is a promising research direction that holds the potential for greatly scaling and improving quality control in crowdsourcing. However, this line of research is still in its infancy and there is yet very little known about what behavioral signals are useful in detecting spamming or sloppy behavior across different tasks. It is also questionable how such a method may perform when most of the workers are of poor quality. For example, it is possible that a classifier trained on behavioral signals learnt mostly from sloppy or spam workers could lead to the rejection of high quality workers. At the same time, there is no previous

[*]Work carried out while Gabriella Kazai @ Microsoft, Cambridge, UK.

WSDM'16, February 22–25, 2016, San Francisco, CA, USA.
© 2016 ACM. ISBN 978-1-4503-3716-8/16/02...$15.00
DOI: http://dx.doi.org/10.1145/2835776.2835835

[1]https://www.mturk.com/

work on investigating the differences between the behaviors of trained professional judges vs crowd workers and how the behavior of one group of judges may be exploited to guide the detection of undesired behavior in the other group.

In this paper, we study the behaviors of both professional assessors and crowd workers in the context of three relevance assessing tasks, involving a total of nearly 50k relevance judgments for 12,302 HITs by 548 judges. The tasks vary in their complexity from judging the relevance of a single web search result, to a pair of search results and two lists of search results. We employ crowd workers through Clickworker, a crowdsourcing platform similar to Mechanical Turk, and trained judges via an in-house system and present them with the same HITs. We instrument the UIs using Javascript, so that the judges' interactions, e.g., mouse movements and clicks, are captured for analysis. Our goal is to compare the collected interaction data and derived behavioral statistics across the two groups of judges for the three tasks and establish if they are indicative of the judges' quality estimates. We then investigate the use of the trained judges' behavior as "gold behavior" to improve the detection of poorly performing crowd workers. To this end, we build and evaluate a classifier to detect poorly performing workers in our three judging tasks, based on behaviors features alone. We experiment with adding ideal behavior samples to the training set and with normalizing crowd workers behavior statistics by the ideal behavior signals obtained from trained judges. Our aim is to answer the following questions:

1. What differences can be observed in the behaviors of trained judges and crowd workers on the same tasks?
2. Are behavioral signals related to judge quality?
3. Can we use trained judges' behavioral signals to improve the accuracy of a classifier to detect poorly performing crowd workers?

The paper is organized as follows. Next, we review related work. We detail our experiment setup in section 3. The results of our analysis are presented in section 4. Our worker classification experiments are described in section 5. We close with conclusions and thoughts on future work.

2. RELATED WORK

A significant challenge in crowdsourcing is the detection of undesired workers, who, due to lack of expertise or motivation, contribute poor quality data, leading to noisy or incorrect datasets. Typical methods to combat this issue rely on gold data sets or redundancy [1]. However, these methods can be expensive and have limited application. Gold data based solutions, for example, rely on HITs with known answers to estimate worker quality and extrapolate this to the rest of the inputs. Redundancy based approaches rely on aggregation methods, such as majority voting [31], to filter out noise given multiple inputs. More sophisticated, probabilistic aggregation methods take worker reliability into account, e.g., [2, 14, 26, 11, 25]. However, these models need to observe a large number of inputs from each worker, which can be challenging since most workers typically only complete very few HITs.

A more recent approach is to focus on the way workers work, rather than on the output they produce [27, 10]. For example, the approach in [27], referred to as task fingerprinting, captures the process that workers use to complete a task, as embodied by their interactions with a HIT. Using small-scale experiments on a word classification, image tagging and text comprehension task with contributions from 21, 52 and 45 workers, they showed that behavioral features could be used to detect possible spam workers. Utilizing the number of clicks, the number of checkboxes accessed, and the difference between the Mechanical Turk reported task time and the log-based task time, their spam worker classifier achieved 83.2% accuracy in the word classification task. They also show some evidence that cross-task learning is feasible. Similarly, Hirth et al. in [10] propose an application layer monitoring approach that records detailed interactions. They demonstrate the method's potential on a language test task with 215 workers and show strong correlations between the amount of time workers spent interacting with parts of the UI and whether they qualified for the task. Our work is closely related to these works, but we study both crowd workers and trained judges and we investigate the use of ideal behavioral signals, as encoded by the behaviors of trained judges, to detect poorly performing crowd workers. We show that without gold behavior signals, we cannot reliably detect poor quality workers in complex tasks. We also conduct a much larger study involving nearly 550 workers and three different tasks, and investigate the cross-task use of both crowd and trained judges' behavior data.

Related work that analyzed workers' behavior and extracted spammer identification features include [32]. Related are also behavior based quality control methods that aim to enforce correct behavior during task completion, such as time control mechanisms to focus workers' attention [15] and designs that increase the effort of cheating [19]. Other techniques enable the discovery of dishonest workers through qualifying and trap questions [5]. Unlike these, we focus explicitly on detailed interaction data, examine the differences observed between crowd and trained judges and build a poorly performing worker detection system that does not rely on gold labels, but work on behavior signals alone.

Other aspects of crowd worker behavior have also been studied in the literature. Grady and Lease [9] investigated how varying certain aspects of the HIT design, e.g., title, terminology, and pay, affected annotation accuracy. Shaw et al. [29] looked at the effects of different social and financial incentive schemes but found that results were mainly dependent on the task difficulty. Kazai et al. [17] studied the effects of task design parameters, including the offered pay, the required effort, or the document ordering methods used had on label accuracy. Studying the 'human' characteristics of the crowds, the work in [18] investigated the relationship between properties of the HITs and that of the crowds attracted to the task, including their motivations, interests and knowledge. Attempting to categorize workers based on personality traits or behavioral aspects, works like [18, 6] showed differences between, e.g., diligent or sloppy and competent or incompetent workers. This work is similar to these only in the sense that it adds to a deeper understanding of the behaviors of crowd workers in the context of different work tasks.

Relatively little has been done so far in comparing different groups of workers. Researchers studied the quality of relevance label based evaluation and various aspects of assessors. For example, [28] looked at the variation and the consistency of judgments across different assessors and the resulting quality of system-level evaluation. Bailey et al. [3] compared the quality of judgments between expert and crowd judges, concluding that expert and non-expert judges provide different trade-offs in terms of judging quality and cost. More recently, the quality of judgments between trained and crowd judges have been compared in [4, 1], where crowd judges with reasonable quality control produced comparable output to expert judges.

In this paper, we extend these prior art by analyzing the behavioral characteristics of crowd and trained judges in various relevance judging tasks. We then show how the data from trained judges can be used to distinguish between high and low quality workers among the crowd. This is similar in goal to [25, 11], but instead of judgment or label patterns, we focus on behavior patterns, and more specifically, whether gold behavior signals can improve worker classification.

3. STUDY METHODOLOGY

Our ultimate goal is to study the performance of a supervised classifier to detect poorly performing crowd workers based only on their behavior and on the behavior of professional judges. The intuition is that the behavior of the trusted judges, who have been trained and are constantly monitored, may provide an oracle gold standard behavior, which can be used to separate poorly and well performing crowd workers. Toward this goal, we run a series of crowdsourcing experiments, both with crowd workers and trained judges, using three relevance assessing tasks of varying complexity, collecting relevance labels for: 1) a single web search result (S task), 2) a pair of web search results (P task), and 3) a pair of search result lists (L task). We instrument all three UIs to log user interactions and we collect data from crowd workers (C) via Clickworker and from trained judges (T) via an in-house platform. For each HIT in each combination of tasks and judge groups, i.e., $\{S, P, L\} \times \{C, T\}$, we collect labels from 3 different judges (redundancy). From the collected interaction logs, we generate 160 behavioral features for each worker. Features include statistics such as the average time a judge spent familiarizing themselves with a HIT before their first click. We detail each aspect of our experimental setup in this section. In the next section, we then compare the workers' and the trained judges' behaviors (section 4.1) and study how their behavior correlates with their work quality (section 4.2). Finally, we investigate the use of trusted judges' behavior signals in the detection of poorly performing crowd workers without the use of gold data (section 5).

3.1 Relevance Judging Tasks and HIT Designs

We collect relevance labels using three different HIT designs, corresponding to the following tasks:

*Single Web Page Judging Task (***S task***).*
In this task, judges were asked to indicate the relevance of a single web page to a query, using a 5 point scale. They also had the option to provide additional ratings or comments, e.g., rate the web page's trustworthiness and content quality.

*Pairwise Judging Task (***P task***).*
This task asked judges to provide two separate relevance labels for two web pages for a given query, shown side by side. The UI was the same as in the S task, but with two web pages and two sets of judging controls, see Figure 1.

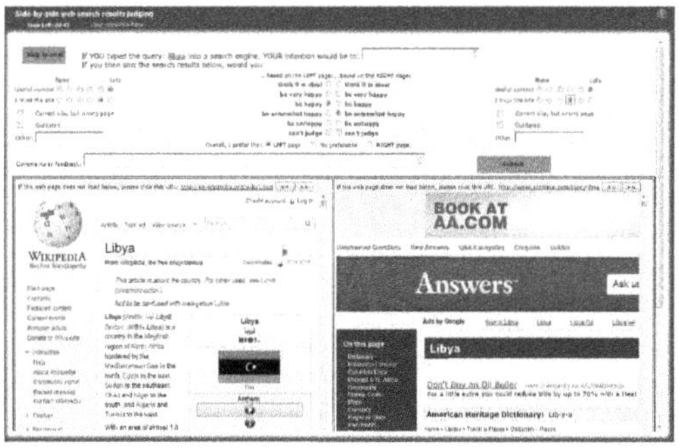

Figure 1: Pairwise HIT design: used to collect relevance labels for pairs of URLs for a given query

*Result Lists Judging Task (***L task***).*
This task showed two search result lists side by side, with 10 results in each list for a given query, and asked judges to provide a preference judgment on a 7 point scale, reflecting varying levels of preference for the left/right side or no preference. For each search result, the title, the URL and a snippet were shown. Judges also had the option to rate any of the 20 individual search results and to leave a comment.

3.2 Experiment Data

For all our tasks, we randomly sampled queries from the search logs of a commercial search engine. For the S and P tasks, for each query, we sampled a pair of search results. This yielded a total of 1,689 query-URL-URL tuples. In the P task, we then collected a total of $2 \times 10,134$ (i.e., 1,689 queries $\times 2$ judge groups $\times 3$ redundancy) relevance labels. For the S task, we separated the 1,689 query-URL-URL tuples into 2,946 unique query-URL pairs and collected a total of 17,676 (i.e., 2,946 queries $\times 2$ judge groups $\times 3$ redundancy) relevance labels. For the L task, we randomly sampled queries along with the top 10 search results from different search engines (or versions of the same engine). This sample contains 1,516 queries, for which we obtained a total of 9,096 (i.e., 1,516 queries $\times 2$ judge groups $\times 3$ redundancy) preference judgments.

Table 1 summarizes the collected data. In all tasks, we set a maximum for the number of labels a worker could contribute to avoid some workers dominating the dataset. Note that, out of the total 548 judges in our study, 7 contributed to both the SC and PC experiments, 3 to both SC and LC, and 8 to both PC and LC. There are 2 judges common to SE and PE, and 1 to SE and LE. No crowd or trained judges contributed to all three tasks. There are 64 common queries between the S/P and the L sets, but no common URLs.

3.3 Ground Truth

To evaluate the classifier's ability to detect poorly performing workers based on their behavior, we created gold data sets for all three tasks on which we can measure worker quality. We will refer to this as task-based or local worker quality. On average, crowd workers completed 31, 14 and 32 gold tasks in the S, P and L tasks, respectively, but with high variance and some only did one test. In addition, we calculate a global (marketplace based) quality score for each of our 548 judges based on gold data sets for all the various tasks they completed during a 6 months period, either on Clickworker or on the internal platform. This covers a total

Table 1: Number of HITs, judges, collected relevance labels, interaction log instances, interassessor agreement (Fleiss kappa) and pay per HIT in our single (S), pairwise (P) and list (L) judging tasks with crowd workers (C) or trained judges (T)

Set	Description	HITs	Judges	Rel. labels	Log inst.	Kappa	HIT Pay
SC	Single page UI (S), Crowd workers (C)	2,946	169	8,838	8,838	0.24	$0.05
ST	Single page UI (S), Trained judges (T)	2,946	9	8,838	8,838	0.46	-
PC	Pairwise UI (P), Crowd workers (C)	1,689	96	10,134	5,067	0.25	$0.08
PT	Pairwise UI (P), Trained judges (T)	1,689	15	10,130	5,065	0.54	-
LC	Lists UI (L), Crowd workers (C)	1,516	149	4,548	4,548	0.14	$0.20
LT	Lists UI (L), Trained judges (T)	1,516	131	4,548	4,548	0.24	-
	Total	12,302	548	47,036	36,904	-	-

of 377,084 gold judgments across 268 different tasks (average of 688.11 gold judgments and 11.77 tasks per worker). Figure 2a shows the relationship between judges' global and local performance scores.

We consider poorly performing crowd workers to be those whose local/global quality score falls below the average local/global quality calculated across all the workers and judges. We will measure the accuracy of the classifier's output against this ground truth.

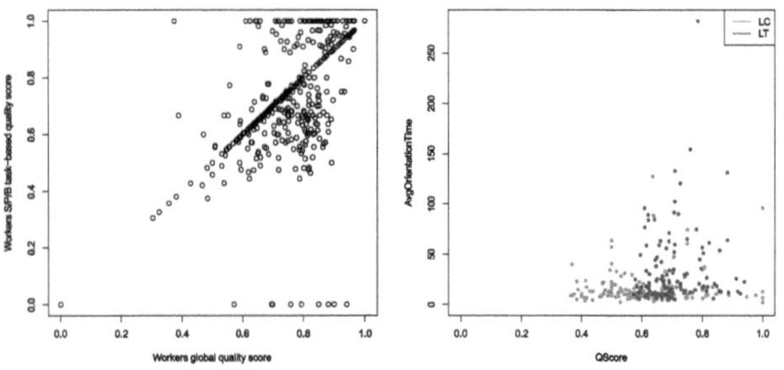

a) b)

Figure 2: a) Relationship between workers' global and local (S/P/L task based) quality scores, b) Crowd workers (red) and trained judges (blue) average orientation time and their global quality score

3.4 Behavioral Features

All three HIT designs were instrumented, using Javascript, to log mouse movement and click information as well as scrolling, window resizing, copy-paste events and when the window lost or got focus. Mouse movements were logged at every 0.25 seconds, unless the position of the mouse did not change at least 10 pixels. All mouse clicks on all the judging controls and search results were logged.

From the logs, we generate a total of 160 different behavioral features, such as the number of mouse movements or the period of time elapsed before the first click is observed, see Table 2. All behavioral features are calculated per judge over all the HITs the judge completed in a given task, e.g., in SC. All features marked with an * represent a set of statistics: Total (Tot), standard deviation (SD), Shannon's entropy (SE), minimum (Min), maximum (Max), average (Avg) and median (Med) over the per HIT values for a given judge in a given experiment. For example, TimeSpent* includes AvgTimeSpent, which is the number of seconds a judge spent on a HIT, averaged across all their HITs in an experiment, and SDevTimeSpent, which is the standard deviation of the per-HIT times over all their HITs in an experiment.

In our worker classification experiments, we will use these behavioral statistics to predict local/global poor-performers among the crowd, using only data obtained from the crowd or data both from the crowd and from trained judges, representing gold behavior. Before that, we study the differences between crowd and trained judges' behaviors.

4. RESULTS AND FINDINGS

In this section, we compare crowd workers and trained judges interactions with the same task and then examine whether behavioral signals correlate with worker quality.

4.1 Crowd vs Editorial Judge Behavior

Our aim is to answer our research question: Can we observe differences in the behaviors of crowd and trained judges on the same task?

Table 3 shows examples of per-experiment averages (and standard deviations) over the workers' average (Avg) behavioral features for the S, P and L tasks. We see a number of clear differences between crowd and trained judges that are consistent across all three tasks. Trained judges consistently spend longer on a HIT (AvgTimeSpent), even almost double that of crowd workers, regardless of the task, e.g., 64 seconds in SC, on average, compared with 110 seconds in ST. Crowd workers, on the other hand, are consistently busier, moving their mouse, clicking and shifting their attention on the UI more rapidly than trained judges (AvgMouseNormActivity and AvgClickNormActivity), e.g., crowd workers average 0.15 clicks per second in the L task, compared with 0.09 clicks per second observed for trained judges. This is also reflected in the smaller dwell times: crowd workers spent an average of 6.05 seconds between clicks in the P task, compared with 10.64 seconds for trained judges. The same trend is observed for the average time that judges spend viewing a web page after clicking its URL in a HIT (AvgURLViewClickDwellTime): trained judges spend almost twice as long examining a web page than crowd workers, e.g., 6.45 seconds in SC compared with 11.34 seconds in ST. In addition to spending more time looking at landing pages, trained judges also tend to view more of them, e.g., on average, 2.52 web pages are visited in LC compared with 5.98 pages in LT. Finally, we also see that trained judges consistently spend longer familiarizing themselves with a HIT before making their first click (AvgOrientationTime), e.g., crowd workers spend on average 12.53 seconds in LC while trained judges spend 17.63 seconds in LT, see Figure 2b.

Table 2: **Behavioral features used to characterize judges, generated from the logs for the Single (S), Pairwise (P) and List (L) judging tasks. The * means a set of features: Total (Tot), standard deviation (SD), Shannon's entropy (SE), minimum (Min), maximum (Max), average (Avg) and Median (Med). Time is in seconds.**

ID	Description
HITs	Total number of HITs completed by judge
Days	Total number of days when judge worked
AvgRPH	Average rate of judgment per hour
JudgmentsMade*	Number of relevance or preference judgments per HIT (e.g., changed their minds)
OptionalRatingsRatio*	Ratio of optional judgments completed per HIT
CmtLen*	Number of characters in comment field per HIT
HITsWithNoCmtRatio	Proportion of judge's HITs with no comment
HitsWithoutURLViewClickRatio	Proportion of judge's HITs when no URLs were clicked
HITsWithOptionalRatingsRatio	Proportion of judge's HITs where judge provided additional optional judgments
TimeSpent*	Number of seconds spent per HIT
SpamTime*	Time spent outside the HIT (excludes time spent on viewing clicked URLs) per HIT
ActiveRatio*	(TimeSpent - SpamTime) / TimeSpent
MouseActivity*	Number of logged mouse move events per HIT
MouseNormActivity*	Number of logged mouse move events per second and per HIT
MouseDwellTime*	Dwell times between mouse move events per HIT
MouseNormDwellTime*	Dwell times between mouse move events per second and per HIT
MicroMouseDwellTime*	Mouse move dwell times over all mouse move events in a judge's HITs (not per HIT)
ClickActivity*	Number of logged mouse clicks per HIT
ClickNormActivity*	Number of logged mouse clicks per second and per HIT
ClickDwellTime*	Dwell times between clicks per HIT
ClickNormDwellTime*	Dwell times between clicks per second and per HIT
MicroClickDwellTime*	Click dwell times over full set of clicks in judge's HITs (not per HIT)
OrientationTime*	Time elapsed before first click per HIT
URLViewClicks*	Number of URLs clicked per HIT
URLViewClickDwellTime*	Time spent on viewing a web page after clicking on its URL per HIT
CopyEvents*	Number of copy-paste events per HIT, e.g., into comment field
ScrollEvents*	Number of scrolling events per HIT
ResizeEvents*	Number of window resize events per HIT

Trained judges thus appear more thorough than crowd workers, spending more time studying the whole task and each web page to be judged. However, trained judges are paid by the hour while crowd workers are paid per HIT. Thus, crowd workers are incentivized to work faster, while there is less pressure on trained judges to do so (although their throughput rate is part of their quality evaluation – slow judges are re-trained, which is unpaid time).

A glance through the standard deviation scores (shown in brackets in Table 3) reveals that trained judges behaviors is more varied from one judge to another, while crowd judges seemed to work in a more homogeneous manner, see also Figure 2b. This is somewhat expected due to the smaller number of interactions that crowd workers accumulate during their shorter time on a HIT.

In summary, we see distinct differences between the behaviors of crowd and trained judges, working on the same task. However, the differences are consistent across all of our three judging tasks. It is reasonable to infer that the observed differences are a result of factors, such as the different pay structures, differences in the judges' aptitudes for due diligence or the obtained training (or lack thereof). While this is an important research question in itself, it is of less relevance to our current investigation, where we study whether behavior is predictive of quality and if it is possible to predict the quality of crowd workers with the help of behavioral signals from trained judges (representing gold behavior), despite the differences in their interaction patterns.

4.2 Judge Behavior and Quality

We saw that crowd and trained judges behave differently whilst working on the same tasks. However, we do not yet know if spending longer on a HIT, viewing more landing pages, leaving longer comments or contributing more optional judgments is a sign of a good or a poor quality judge. In this section, we focus on our second research question and study the relationship between behavior and quality.

To answer this question, in Table 4, we report the number of behavioral features that are statistically significantly ($p < 0.01$) correlated (either positively or negatively) with either the local or global quality scores of the judges. We also list the three most correlated features as examples. As we can see, many of the behavioral statistics are indicative of the workers' local/global quality scores. For example, the average comment length across a workers' HITs (AvgCmtLen) is positively correlated with their local quality score in the SC experiments, i.e., better performing crowd workers tend to leave longer comments in this task. The same feature may be positively or negatively correlated with quality across different tasks. For example, OrientationTime is generally positively related to work quality, while fast paced clicking (NormClickActivity) signals poor quality workers. on the other hand, higher average ratios of optional judgments provided by a judge (AvgOptionalRatingsRatio, not in the table) in the S task indicates better quality judge, while, in the L task, the more URLs a judge rated, the more likely that they are poor quality workers. This is reasonable

Table 3: Average (and standard deviation) of selected worker behavior statistics for the different experiments (tasks: (S, P, L) × judge groups: (C, T)).

	S task		P task		L task	
Behavioral feature	C	T	C	T	C	T
AvgTimeSpent	64 (32)	110 (55)	83 (30)	122 (53)	130 (47)	173 (41)
AvgMouseActivity	32 (10)	37 (15)	51 (14)	59 (21)	110 (27)	128 (40)
AvgClickActivity	5 (1)	6 (2)	8 (1)	9 (2)	14 (3)	15 (4)
AvgMouseNormActivity	0.73 (0.25)	0.40 (0.19)	0.90 (0.43)	0.72 (0.51)	0.99 (0.24)	0.75 (0.21)
AvgClickNormActivity	0.13 (0.05)	0.07 (0.04)	0.16 (0.07)	0.11 (0.08)	0.15 (0.04)	0.09 (0.03)
AvgMouseDwellTime	1.82 (1.28)	3.64 (3.77)	1.94 (0.94)	2.62 (1.91)	1.47 (0.66)	2.55 (1.69)
AvgClickDwellTime	7.43 (4.53)	13.19 (7.72)	6.05 (2.51)	10.64 (5.48)	7.03 (2.69)	10.93 (4.67)
AvgURLViewClicks	0.55 (0.40)	0.67 (0.69)	0.16 (0.14)	0.23 (0.41)	2.60 (1.27)	4.32 (2.19)
AvgURLViewClickDwellTime	6.45 (7.48)	11.34 (17.36)	2.35 (3.18)	3.54 (9.85)	2.52 (2.44)	5.98 (5.12)
AvgOrientationTime	12.53 (16.67)	17.63 (23.48)	16.78 (15.34)	18.65 (23.79)	15.90 (14.43)	32.82 (18.90)

as workers who rate a lot of landing pages, without necessarily visiting them, are less likely to be diligent and more likely to make erroneous judgments in the L task. Such differences in correlation patterns are not surprising since the different UIs and the different nature of the various tasks leads to different patterns of user interactions, which may be indicative of diligent workers in one task and sloppy workers in another. Looking at the worker's global quality, we also find a few behavioral features that correlate positively with task level performance but negatively with global performance. This is again not surprising as different task based behaviors generalize differently across tasks and when compared to workers' performance across many tasks.

However, the key point here is that a significant number of the behavioral features are indeed significantly correlated with workers' local and global quality scores. This confirms the potential of using user behavior to predict worker performance. Moreover, when we look at the crowd and trained judges' behaviors together, e.g., S/P/L rows in the table, we see an increase in the number of features that significantly correlate with judge quality. This suggests that adding data that represents ideal behavior by trusted judges increases our ability to predict crowd workers' quality. We explore this in the next section.

5. DETECTING UNDER-PERFORMERS

To answer our final research question, whether we can benefit from the use of trained judges' behavioral signals to detect poorly performing crowd workers, we use a machine learning framework to classify workers based on their behavior alone. We then study the impact that 1) adding trained judges' behavior data to the training set, and 2) using normalized behavior statistics has on the classifiers' accuracy. In the latter experiments, we represent crowd workers in terms of how different they behave from the average trained judge. We run several experiments on our three judging tasks and compare the classifiers' accuracy to a baseline when only crowd workers' behavior signals are used to detect under-performers. This baseline was chosen as our question focuses on the usefulness of ideal behavior. We leave the study of combining behavior based classifiers with other sources of worker quality, e.g., gold label based, to future work. As described in section 3.3, we use the worker classes we derived based on performance measured on gold tasks as our ground truth.

5.1 Gradient Boosted Decision Trees

We use Gradient Boosted Decision Trees (GBDT) to predict whether a judge's quality is below the average, using the ground-truth labels for training and evaluation. GBDT produces a prediction model in the form of an ensemble of decision trees serving as weak prediction models [8]. It builds the model in a stage-wise fashion and it generalizes them by allowing optimization of an arbitrary differentiable loss function. At every training step, a single regression tree is built to predict an antigradient vector. Step length is computed corresponding to the loss function and separately for every region determined by the tree leaf.

Let x be input variables and y an output variable that are connected via a joint probability distribution $P(x, y)$. In our experiments, a variable x_i of x is a judge with its corresponding behavioral feature set, and y_i of y is the label whether the judge performs below the overall average or not. Using a training set $(x_1, y_1), \ldots, (x_n, y_n)$, the goal is to find an approximation $\hat{F}(x)$ to a function $F^*(x)$ that minimizes the expected value of a loss function $L(y, F(x))$:

$$F^* = \arg\min E_{x,y} L(y, F(x))$$

The gradient boosting method assumes a real-valued y and seeks an approximation $\hat{F}(x)$ in the form of a weighted sum of functions $h_i(x)$ from class H:

$$F(x) = \sum_{i=1}^{M} \gamma_i h_i(x) + const$$

Starting with a model, consisting of a constant function $F_0(x)$, GBDT incrementally expands F in a greedy fashion:

$$F_0(x) = \arg\min_{\gamma} \sum_{i=1}^{n} L(y_i, \gamma)$$

,

$$F_m(x) = F_{m-1}(x) + \arg\min_{f \in H} \sum_{i=1}^{n} L(y_i, F_{m-1}(x_i) + f(x_i))$$

We choose $f \in H$ that most closely approximates the gradient of L and γ is then selected using line search [7]. Generic gradient boosting at the m-th step would fit a decision tree $h_m(x)$ to pseudo-residuals. Let J be the number of its leaves. The tree partitions the input J space into disjoint regions and predicts a constant value in each region. To get the GBDT model prediction, we need to compute the sum of responses of all the trees in the ensemble, then calculate

Table 4: Number of statistically significant (+/-) Spearman correlations between workers' behavioral features and their local/global quality scores and three most correlated behavior features (DwellTime was shortened to DT and HitsWithoutURLViewClickRatio to HitsWoURLClickR.

	Local (task based) worker quality				Global worker quality			
Set	+	Examples	-	Examples	+	Examples	-	Examples
SC	14	AvgOrientationTime	11	AvgActiveRatio	16	AvgOrientationTime	6	AvgActiveRatio
		MedMouseDT		AvgNormClickActivity		SDCmtLen		MinActiveRatio
		AvgCmtLen		SDOptionalRatingsRatio		SDOrientationTime		HITsWithNoCmtRatio
S	30	AvgCmtLen	29	AvgCopyEvents	24	MinMouseDT	6	MedJudgmentsMade
		AvgOpt.RatingsRatio		AvgNormClickActivity		MinClickDT		HITsWithNoCmtRatio
		AvgOrientationTime		AvgActiveRatio		AvgOrientationTime		AvgActiveRatio
PC	16	MedMouseActivity	12	MedMouseNormDT	12	MedMouseActivity	3	MedMouseNormDT
		MedMicroClickDT		AvgNormClickActivity		AvgSpamTime		AvgActiveRatio
		MedTimeSpent		SDNormClickActivity		AvgURLViewClicks		HitsWoURLClickR
P	20	AVgActiveRatio	91	AvgCmtLen	14	MinMouseActivity	66	Days
		AvgOpt.RatingsRatio		AvgMouseDwellTime		MinMicroClickDT		TotMouseNormDT
		SDTimeSpent		AvgClickNormDwellTime		MinOrientationTime		SENormClickDT
LC	7	MedSpamTime	5	HitsWoURLClickR	51	SEURLViewClicks	9	MinMicroClickDT
		AvgURLViewClicks		MedActiveRatio		TotURLViewClickDT		MedOrientationTime
		MedJudgmentsMade		MinResizeEvents		Days		MinClickDT
L	45	AvgTimeSpent	24	AvgOpt.RatingsRatio	57	SDMicroClickDT	29	MedActiveRatio
		AvgMouseDwellTime		AvgActiveRatio		MedSpamTime		AvgNormClickActivity
		AvgOrientationTime		AvgClickNormActivity		AvgClickDT		AvgActiveRatio

$\arg\max_{i=1..K}(f_i(x))$ to obtain our classification result. We use 10 fold cross validation.

5.2 Classifier Results

Table 5 gives the classification accuracy scores (accuracy and area under the TPR and FPR curve (AUC)) for our classifiers, applied separately in each of our three tasks and over all data. For each experiment, we report four sets of scores: 1) baseline (C), which only uses the crowd workers' behavior data, 2) combined (C+T), when the classifier is trained on both crowd and trained judges behaviors, 3) normalized crowd behavior (Cd), which only uses crowd workers data, where the behavior statistics reflect how differently crowd workers behave compared to the average trained judge, and 4) combined normalized (Cd+T), which is 2) and 3) applied at the same time. We perform predictions to detect underperforming crowd workers and evaluate the accuracy of the classifier against our ground truth labels, both in the context of a task (local) and across all tasks (global).

5.2.1 Predicting Local Quality

Looking at the Local columns in Table 5, we see improvements across the board when trained judges' behavior is taken into account compared to the baselines that only rely on crowd workers' behavior data, although the rate of improvement varies across tasks. One of the reasons for this is the varying number of trained judges in the different experiments. In the S and P tasks, we have 9 trained judges, and adding them to the training set (C+T) only leads to a small gain in accuracy and AUC. However, even with such a small number of judges, we see that the combined normalized (Cd+T) method leads to significant accuracy improvements over just using crowd behavior alone (C), both in local (for S) and in global (for S and P) (Chi-square test, two-tailed, $p < 0.05$). When there are plenty of trained judges, e.g., 131 in the L task, the normalization step alone only gives small improvement, e.g., Cd in L task, but again the combined normalized (Cd+T) method leads to the highest classification accuracy and AUC levels (Chi-square test, two-tailed, $p < 0.05$). We note that the high levels of accuracy in the P task is due to the fact that only a relatively small proportion of the crowd workers are labeled as 'below average', but this is reflected in the AUC scores.

Table 5: Poorly performing worker classification performance for detecting crowd workers whose local or global quality is below average across all judges

Experiment		Local		Global	
		Acc	AUC	Acc	AUC
S	C	69.62	0.63	67.67	0.62
	C+T	70.84	0.61	74.23	0.61
	Cd	72.10	0.62	76.18	0.63
	Cd+T	75.77	0.62	77.28	0.61
P	C	90.12	0.63	70.02	0.42
	C+T	92.06	0.64	79.24	0.56
	Cd	92.85	0.64	75.86	0.45
	Cd+T	93.80	0.65	80.15	0.64
L	C	60.40	0.52	43.04	0.45
	C+T	78.21	0.80	73.42	0.78
	Cd	64.36	0.63	53.60	0.48
	Cd+T	81.43	0.80	73.87	0.80
All	C	-	-	63.99	0.57
	C+T	-	-	73.44	0.66
	Cd	-	-	67.44	0.59
	Cd+T	-	-	76.62	0.69

5.2.2 Predicting Global Quality

Looking at the global columns in Table 5, we can see that predicting workers' global, marketplace-wide quality based on behavior observed in a single task is a harder ask. This is of course expected since the behavior observed in one task does not necessarily generalize to all the other tasks that workers may contribute to, after all, not all mathe-

Table 6: Worker classification accuracy over all our data and judges for detecting crowd workers for a given task whose local quality is below average across all judges

Experiment		Accuracy	AUC
S	C	88.44	0.86
	C+E	91.78	0.91
	Cd	87.46	0.88
	Cd+E	91.61	0.90
P	C	97.83	0.91
	C+E	98.24	0.94
	Cd	97.60	0.93
	Cd+E	98.24	0.95
L	C	84.16	0.82
	C+E	87.51	0.87
	Cd	84.11	0.86
	Cd+E	88.72	0.90

maticians are good musicians. However, in all our cases, adding trained judges' behavior improves the classification accuracy and the AUC scores. This is especially notable for the L task, where the accuracy and AUC scores nearly double when gold behavior data is incorporated. This means that using only the crowd behavior to infer the workers' marketplace-wide global quality is really unreliable without the presence of gold behavior signals. On the other hand, it is interesting to note that in simpler tasks, e.g., S task, a reasonable level of accuracy in predicting workers' general abilities can be obtained with just crowd behavior data in that one task. A possible explanation to this is that simpler tasks may provide more generalizable signals. It is easy to see that if workers do badly on the simplest tasks, they are more likely to also not do well on more complex tasks. In complex tasks, however, crowd behavior alone leads to poor classification performance.

5.2.3 *Cross-Task Quality Prediction*

To examine the use of behavior data across different tasks to detect under-achievers in a single task, we also run experiments to predict task based worker quality based on our merged dataset. The results are shown in Table 6. We see significant improvements in classification accuracy compared to the baselines (C) in Table 5. This suggests that other workers' behavior data from other tasks is actually helpful in detecting poor quality workers in the context of a given task. This suggests that both trusted judges and crowd workers' behavior data from a different task could be reused and exploited in other tasks. Since all our three tasks are relevance judging tasks, we can only confirm this in the case of related tasks. Investigation of the usefulness of cross-task behavior data is left for future work.

5.2.4 *Top Features*

Table 7 shows the top 10 features by our classifier in the three tasks and over all tasks when the classifier is trained with normalized crowd worker and trained judge behavior features. What is of particular interest is the high contributions of some standard deviation and entropy statistics, which capture the differences in a given judge's behavior from one HIT to another. We see that, in general, behavioral signals that are good indicators of poor quality workers include orientation time, optional ratings, mouse move and click dwell times and comment length. All these aspects can be thought of as reflecting workers attitudes towards due care and diligence. When trusted judges' behavorial signals, whom are assumed to be more diligent (and do appear that way based on their observed engagement levels), are added to the training data, the classifier is able to better separate out the less diligent workers than when only crowd data is available.

Table 7: Top 10 features for our classifier over workers in the different tasks when trained with normalized crowd worker and trained judge behavior features

S task Cd+E	P task Cd+E
MaxCmtLen	MedMouseNormDwellTime
AvgClickActivity	AvgScrollEvents
SDMouseNormActivity	SDMouseActivity
AvgMouseActivity	AvgSpamTime
SDMouseActivity	MedOrientationTime
SDTimeSpent	MedSpamTime
MedMouseDwellTime	AvgCmtLen
SDClickDwellTime	MaxNormClickActivity
MaxURLViewClickDwellT.	MaxTimeSpent
Days	SESpamTime
L task Cd+E	**All Cd+E**
SEURLViewClicks	AvgURLViewClicks
MaxTimeSpent	SDURLViewClicks
AvgMicroClickDwellTime	MaxTimeSpent
TotClickNormActivity	AvgHitsPerDay
SDMouseActivity	AvgOrientationTime
MedMouseNormDwellTime	SESpamTime
AvgCmtLen	AvgMouseDwellTime
MaxClickNormActivity	MinScrollEvents
MedOrientationTime	SDMouseActivity
MinMouseNormActivity	SDActiveRatio

5.3 Trained Judges

Trained judges may be a scarce resource, so in this section, we study how the number of trained judges impacts the accuracy of our classifier. We focus on the L task as it has the most number of trained judges. We gradually remove trained judges by random selection and report the re-calculated accuracy of the classifier in Figure 3. Clearly, removing trained judges does impact the classifier's performance negatively. On the flip side though, adding gold behavior data is an improvement over not having any. Furthermore, as we saw earlier, it is possible to re-use trained judges behavior data from other tasks. It may also be possible to generate noisy versions of a few trained judges' data (e.g., semi-supervised methods). The latter remains for future work for now.

5.4 Comparison to Gold Data Methods

We started off by using gold judgments to create our ground truth of worker quality, against which we evaluated our behaviour based classifiers. In this section, we examine how the accuracy of the resulting labels is affected when we remove workers classified as poor quality and their labels. We use the majority vote label derived from the trained judges as the true label and measure the accuracy of the

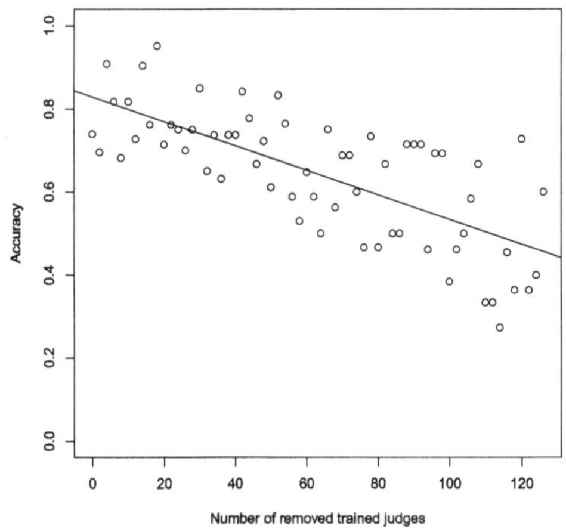

Figure 3: Impact on the classifier's accuracy when removing trained judges from the L task

crowd's majority vote label against that. A removed label is replaced with the correct label, thus assuming that the worker was blocked, the HIT re-published and another worker provided the correct label. Since this method is sensitive to the number of labels being replaced, we use the probability score of the classifier to rank workers and remove the poorest quality workers first till we reach the same number of replaced labels as our baseline, where we removed workers based on their gold judgments. we can see comparable results across the task, suggesting that behaviour based worker quality detection is a viable replacement to gold label based methods. In this case it could have also saved over $1.3k that was paid for the workers to complete gold labels.

Table 8: Label quality (accuracy) after removing poor quality workers, based on gold judgments, crowd behaviour alone, crowd and trained judge behaviour, normalised crowd behaviour and normalised crowd and trained judge behaviour

Task	All data	Gold	C	C+E	Cd	Cd+E
S	0.88	0.91	0.89	0.91	0.90	0.90
P	0.68	0.69	0.70	0.76	0.74	0.77
L	0.25	0.73	0.70	0.69	0.75	0.76

6. CONCLUSIONS

Despite significant interests and rapid adoption for crowdsourced evaluation, ensuring high quality output remains a key challenge. In this work, we investigated the possibility of using the behavior of trusted trained judges to detect poor-performing workers among the crowd. Looking at the behavioral differences between trained and crowd judges, we found that trained judges show many characteristics hinting at higher levels of focus and engagement. We then showed that behavior is indicative of judge quality. Finally, we built a classifier to detect workers who perform below average (across all judges). We demonstrated that the signals from trained judges do help to improve the classification accuracy, almost doubling it in some cases, compared to when only crowd behavior data is used. It is possible that this could be further improved when trained-judges pay incentives match those offered to the crowd. However, this work has showed that even despite these differences in pay incentives, gold behavior data by trained judges is beneficial, and for complex tasks it is even necessary for the accurate detection of poorly performing crowd workers. This is especially significant as gold labels are much more expensive to obtain for complex tasks and have limited use like all gold labels. On the other hand, gold behavior signals are reusable.

We note that our methods are not restricted to trained judges' behavior data, requesters could easily generate trusted 'ideal' behavior samples themselves for their own tasks and use that data to help identify poor quality workers among the crowd. Such a method of detecting undesired workers offers a more scalable solution than gold data based approaches and can be observed without having to pay for extra work that only contributes known labels. We found that only with a few tens of trained judges to solve a sample set of HITs for one or more tasks, poor performing workers can be detected, on the same or across different tasks, with high accuracy based only on their behavior. This method can of course be combined with gold label based filters as part of an overall crowdsourcing strategy. In such a case, the behavior of trained judges who provide the gold labels can be used as gold behavior signals, both in the current and similar tasks. Furthermore, while gold labels can become obsolete, e.g., the test becomes too old or compromised, behavior labels are more robust and generic. Our future work will investigate various cost based approaches to combine gold label and gold behavior signals as well as evaluating results across more diverse sets of tasks and worker pools, employing additional features such as mouse movement to improve performance.

7. REFERENCES

[1] O. Alonso. Implementing crowdsourcing-based relevance experimentation: an industrial perspective. *Information Retrieval*, 16(2):101–120, Apr. 2013.

[2] Y. Bachrach, T. Graepel, T. Minka, and J. Guiver. How to grade a test without knowing the answers—a bayesian graphical model for adaptive crowdsourcing and aptitude testing. In *Proc. of the 29th International Conference on Machine Learning (ICML-12)*, pages 1183–1190, 2012.

[3] P. Bailey, N. Craswell, I. Soboroff, P. Thomas, A. P. de Vries, and E. Yilmaz. Relevance assessment: are judges exchangeable and does it matter. In *Proc. of the 31st ACM SIGIR conf. on Research and development in IR*, SIGIR '08, pages 667–674, New York, NY, USA, 2008. ACM.

[4] R. Blanco, H. Halpin, D. M. Herzig, P. Mika, J. Pound, H. S. Thompson, and D. T. Tran. Repeatable and reliable search system evaluation using crowdsourcing. In W.-Y. Ma, J.-Y. Nie, R. A. Baeza-Yates, T.-S. Chua, and W. B. Croft, editors, *SIGIR*, pages 923–932. ACM, 2011.

[5] J. S. Downs, M. B. Holbrook, S. Sheng, and L. F. Cranor. Are your participants gaming the system?: screening Mechanical Turk workers. In E. D. Mynatt, D. Schoner, G. Fitzpatrick, S. E. Hudson, W. K. Edwards, and T. Rodden, editors, *CHI*, pages 2399–2402. ACM, 2010.

[6] C. Eickhoff and A. P. de Vries. How crowdsourcable is your task? In *Proc. of the Workshop on*

Crowdsourcing for Search and Data Mining (CSDM 2011), pages 11–14. ACM, 2011.

[7] J. Friedman. Greedy function approximation: A gradient boosting machine. *The Annals of Statistics*, 29(5):1189–1232, 2001.

[8] J. Friedman, T. Hastie, and R. Tibshirani. Additive logistic regression: a statistical view of boosting. *The Annals of Statistics*, 28(2):337–407, 2000.

[9] C. Grady and M. Lease. Crowdsourcing document relevance assessment with mechanical turk. In *Proc. of the NAACL HLT 2010 Workshop on Creating Speech and Language Data with Amazon's Mechanical Turk*, CSLDAMT '10, pages 172–179, 2010.

[10] M. Hirth, S. Scheuring, T. Hoßfeld, C. Schwartz, and P. Tran-Gia. Predicting Result Quality in Crowdsourcing Using Application Layer Monitoring. In *5th International Conference on Communications and Electronics (ICCE 2014)*, Da Nang, Vietnam, July 2014.

[11] D. Hovy, T. Berg-Kirkpatrick, A. Vaswani, and E. Hovy. Learning whom to trust with mace. In *Proceedings of NAACL-HLT*, pages 1120–1130, 2013.

[12] J. Howe. *Crowdsourcing: Why the Power of the Crowd Is Driving the Future of Business*. Crown Publishing Group, New York, NY, USA, 1 edition, 2008.

[13] P. G. Ipeirotis, F. Provost, and J. Wang. Quality management on Amazon Mechanical Turk. In *Proc. of the ACM SIGKDD Workshop on Human Computation*, HCOMP '10, pages 64–67, New York, NY, USA, 2010. ACM.

[14] E. Kamar, S. Hacker, and E. Horvitz. Combining human and machine intelligence in large-scale crowdsourcing. In *Proc. of the 11th International Conference on Autonomous Agents and Multiagent Systems-Volume 1*, pages 467–474. International Foundation for Autonomous Agents and Multiagent Systems, 2012.

[15] A. Kapelner and D. Chandler. Preventing satisficing in online surveys: A 'kapcha' to ensure higher quality data. In *The World's First Conference on the Future of Distributed Work (CrowdConf2010)*, 2010.

[16] G. Kasneci, J. Van Gael, R. Herbrich, and T. Graepel. Bayesian knowledge corroboration with logical rules and user feedback. In *Proc. of the 2010 European Conference on Machine learning and knowledge Discovery in Databases: Part II*, ECML PKDD'10, pages 1–18, Berlin, Heidelberg, 2010. Springer-Verlag.

[17] G. Kazai. In search of quality in crowdsourcing for search engine evaluation. In *Advances in Information Retrieval - 33rd European Conference on IR Research (ECIR 2011)*, volume 6611 of *LNCS*, pages 165–176. Springer, 2011.

[18] G. Kazai, J. Kamps, and N. Milic-Frayling. An analysis of human factors and label accuracy in crowdsourcing relevance judgments. *Inf. Retr.*, 16(2):138–178, 2013.

[19] A. Kittur, E. H. Chi, and B. Suh. Crowdsourcing user studies with mechanical turk. In *Proceeding of the 26th SIGCHI Conference on Human factors in computing systems*, CHI '08, pages 453–456, New York, NY, USA, 2008. ACM.

[20] A. Kittur, J. V. Nickerson, M. Bernstein, E. Gerber, A. Shaw, J. Zimmerman, M. Lease, and J. Horton. The future of crowd work. In *Proceedings of the 2013 conference on Computer supported cooperative work*, pages 1301–1318. ACM, 2013.

[21] J. Le, A. Edmonds, V. Hester, and L. Biewald. Ensuring quality in crowdsourced search relevance evaluation: The effects of training question distribution. In *SIGIR Workshop on Crowdsourcing for Search Evaluation*, pages 21–26, 2010.

[22] M. Lease and G. Kazai. Overview of the TREC 2011 crowdsourcing track. In *Proceedings of TREC*, 2011.

[23] S. Nowak and S. Rüger. How reliable are annotations via crowdsourcing: a study about inter-annotator agreement for multi-label image annotation. In *Proc. of the International Conference on Multimedia Information Retrieval*, MIR '10, pages 557–566, New York, NY, USA, 2010. ACM.

[24] A. J. Quinn and B. B. Bederson. Human computation: a survey and taxonomy of a growing field. In *Proc. of the 2011 Annual Conference on Human factors in computing systems*, CHI '11, pages 1403–1412, New York, NY, USA, 2011. ACM.

[25] V. C. Raykar and S. Yu. Ranking annotators for crowdsourced labeling tasks. In *NIPS*, pages 1809–1817, 2011.

[26] V. C. Raykar, S. Yu, L. H. Zhao, G. H. Valadez, C. Florin, L. Bogoni, and L. Moy. Learning from crowds. *The Journal of Machine Learning Research*, 99:1297–1322, 2010.

[27] J. Rzeszotarski and A. Kittur. Crowdscape: interactively visualizing user behavior and output. In *Proc. of the 25th annual ACM symposium on User interface software and technology*, UIST '12, pages 55–62, New York, NY, USA, 2012. ACM.

[28] F. Scholer, A. Turpin, and M. Sanderson. Quantifying test collection quality based on the consistency of relevance judgements. In *Proc. of the 34th ACM SIGIR conf. on Research and development in IR*, SIGIR '11, pages 1063–1072, New York, NY, USA, 2011. ACM.

[29] A. Shaw, J. Horton, and D. Chen. Designing incentives for inexpert human raters. In *Proc. of the ACM Conference on Computer Supported Cooperative Work*, CSCW '11, 2011.

[30] R. Snow, B. O'Connor, D. Jurafsky, and A. Y. Ng. Cheap and fast—but is it good?: evaluating non-expert annotations for natural language tasks. In *Proc. of the Conference on Empirical Methods in Natural Language Processing*, EMNLP '08, pages 254–263, Stroudsburg, PA, USA, 2008. Association for Computational Linguistics.

[31] L. Tran-Thanh, M. Venanzi, A. Rogers, and N. R. Jennings. Efficient budget allocation with accuracy guarantees for crowdsourcing classification tasks. In *Proc. of the 2013 international conference on Autonomous agents and multi-agent systems*, pages 901–908. International Foundation for Autonomous Agents and Multiagent Systems, 2013.

[32] D. Zhu and B. Carterette. An analysis of assessor behavior in crowdsourced preference judgments. In *SIGIR 2010 Workshop on Crowdsourcing for Search Evaluation*, pages 17–20, 2010.

On Obtaining Effort Based Judgements for Information Retrieval

Manisha Verma
University College London
m.verma@cs.ucl.ac.uk

Emine Yilmaz
University College London
emine.yilmaz@ucl.ac.uk

Nick Craswell
Microsoft
nickcr@microsoft.com

ABSTRACT

Document relevance has been the primary focus in the design, optimization and evaluation of retrieval systems. Traditional test collections are constructed by asking judges the relevance grade for a document with respect to an input query. Recent work [44] found an evidence that *effort* is another important factor in determining document utility, suggesting that more thought should be given into incorporating effort into information retrieval. However, that work did not ask judges to directly assess the level of effort required to consume a document or analyse how effort judgements relate to traditional relevance judgements.

In this work, focusing on three aspects associated with effort, we show that it is possible to get judgements of effort from the assessors. We further show that given documents of the *same* relevance grade, effort needed to find the portion of the document relevant to the query is a significant factor in determining user satisfaction as well as user preference between these documents. Our results suggest that if the end goal is to build retrieval systems that optimize user satisfaction, effort should be included as an additional factor to relevance in building and evaluating retrieval systems. We further show that new retrieval features are needed if the goal is to build retrieval systems that jointly optimize relevance and effort and propose a set of such features. Finally, we focus on the evaluation of retrieval systems and show that incorporating effort into retrieval evaluation could lead to significant differences regarding the performance of retrieval systems.

Keywords

Information retrieval; evaluation; effort; judgements

1. INTRODUCTION

Relevance is a fundamental concept in information retrieval. Human relevance assessments are collected to form test collections. These test collections are then used for relevance-focused evaluation of retrieval systems and relevance-focused optimization of the free parameters of such systems.

Based on the assumption that relevance is the primary factor that affects user satisfaction [20, 21], evaluation using relevance judgements should be predictive of overall satisfaction of real users who are interacting with a search system. Yet, research has shown that test collection and user based evaluation may not completely agree with each other [19, 39], or agree only when there is a significant gap in terms of quality of the systems compared [1, 2].

One potential reason for this mismatch is that there are factors other than relevance which contribute to user satisfaction. Such factors would not be captured by judging scheme focussed on topical relevance. By comparing implicit feedback obtained from real users and the judgements obtained from relevance assessors, Yilmaz *et al.* [44] recently showed that the utility of a document with respect to an actual user can be different from relevance of a document. In particular, they showed that *effort* required to find or consume relevant information within a document is a significant factor that can affect user satisfaction, and can lead to a real user abandoning a document, perhaps to find another relevant document that requires less effort. This abandonment of documents was correlated with documents that are long or have a relatively high reading level. Though this work detected and analysed abandonment of some relevant documents, it did not elaborate on what constitutes effort. In particular, it did not gather human judgements of factors other than relevance, that may contribute to effort or overall satisfaction. Such judgements could be used to evaluate and optimize retrieval systems that take into account both effort and relevance.

In this work, we build on the findings of Yilmaz *et al.* [44] by first identifying factors that characterize user effort, where effort can be defined as the amount of cognitive effort it takes user to find, read and understand information in a document. Mainly, we focus on three factors that might affect the effort required to find and consume relevant information 1) easiness to find relevant information in a document, 2) readability level of the document, and 3) easiness to understand the contents of the document. We conduct experiments to obtain explicit judgements for these factors and finally analyse which of these factors are significant for user satisfaction. We show that 1) it is possible to obtain judgements from assessors with respect to all these aspects, and 2) given documents of the same relevance grade, some of these effort related factors can have a direct impact on user satisfaction. In particular, we observe that easiness to find

WSDM'16, February 22–25, 2016, San Francisco, CA, USA.

DOI: http://dx.doi.org/10.1145/2835776.2835840

relevant information in the document is a significant factor that can affect user satisfaction.

Given the evidence that effort in document consumption can impact user satisfaction, retrieval systems should be optimized for effort together with relevance, and evaluation mechanisms should incorporate effort together with relevance. For this purpose we propose a set of features that could be used in an effort-aware ranking system. Analysis shows that some of the features which are significant for retrieving low effort documents are not captured when focusing solely on relevance. This suggests that part of the work in incorporating effort in retrieval optimization is to add new features. We also analyse the effect of incorporating effort into retrieval evaluation. We analyse systems submitted to TREC Web Track Adhoc task 2012-2014, and show that even though the top systems show similar performance in terms of relevance, these systems tend to perform quite differently when effort is considered.

We begin by explaining related work on relevance estimation and effort in information retrieval in Section 2. We elaborate on effort parameters and related user studies in Sections 3, 4 and 5 respectively. Our experiments and findings are reported in Section 6. Evaluation of TREC web track submissions is described in Section 7. We conclude with our findings and future work in Section 8.

2. RELATED WORK

There is a large body of work characterizing relevance and effort. We briefly discuss how effort is defined, measured and incorporated in information retrieval. Since we also study what factors are associated with effort, we briefly cover factors used to assess document relevance. Finally, we cover literature from other areas that highlight the importance of parameters we choose to capture effort.

Effort definitions and measurement

Existing literature defines and studies effort differently during various stages of information searching and gathering. For example, Gwizdka *et al.* [16] study user search effort where effort is only defined as number of documents visited while searching. However, in this work we study what factors best capture effort while consuming a *single* document. Similarly, Carterette *et al.* [6] study existing evaluation measures on basis of user model which estimates the effort a user must put forth to achieve a certain utility from ranked list. Smucker *et al.* [35] propose to evaluate search effectiveness on the basis of time spent and information gained (TBG) as user scans ranked document list. While TBG uses time spent on a document to implicitly measure effort, we collect explicit judgements of effort for a document. Recently, Ferro *et al.* [14] proposed a measure that evaluates the effectiveness of a system based on the effort it takes to retrieve desired information. They compare and contrast gain versus effort required to scan search results. While existing effort-based evaluation mechanisms [6, 14, 16, 35] account for user's interaction with a list of documents, we explicitly capture effort per *relevant document* regardless of its *position* in search results.

Some work has also studied user effort in searching or judging a document. Villa *et al.* [40] conducted a study that looked at the relationship between document length and both judging effort and accuracy. They concluded that accuracy is not affected by document size but judging longer documents required more effort. In this work, we use document length not as definition of effort but one of the features to predict effort. They also found that relevant documents require most effort to judge (significant differences were found for mental demand, physical demand, and effort). Our work would be useful in identifying and labelling such documents. Judging effort has also been studied for images, in [17] authors found that while image size did not affect judging accuracy, it significantly impacted the judging time.

Factors characterizing relevance

Since document relevance is of prime importance in evaluation, significant amount of work investigates what factors are important in assessing relevance and whether they remain constant or evolve with user's interaction with search results. Schamber *et al.* [33] concluded that relevance is a multidimensional concept that is affected by several factors.

Xu *et al.* [43] conducted a study to investigate criterion that users employ to make relevance judgements. They proposed that topicality, novelty, reliability, understandability, and scope characterize relevance. They found that topicality and novelty are the most important relevance criteria for the users, followed by understandability and reliability. Zhang *et al.* [45] also showed that understandability and reliability did not affect relevance. They also found understandability did not explain relevance judgements as completely as novelty and topicality did. Some work also studies what factors are important for judging relevance when search task and session are taken into account. Borlund [4] studied how user's notion of relevance changes with session time. Taylor's work [37] with two longitudinal studies investigated association between the search process and 15 different relevance criterion. They found both structure and understandability became more important to subjects during later search stages and are pre-requisite to positive relevance judgements. We use web page oriented features to capture structure and language specific readability measures to capture understandability in our experiments. Above mentioned work [4, 12, 31, 33, 43, 45] states that relevance has several components and factors like structure, reliability and topicality affect relevance judgements. Given that these parameters determine relevance, with this work, we conduct further analysis of factors that distinguish two *relevant* documents. We investigate whether factors such as understandability, findability etc. can be useful in distinguishing two documents of *equal* relevance grade. Importance of such factors will greatly differ when a relevant document is compared with irrelevant document, which is not the focus of this work.

Factors characterizing effort

We investigate three factors that may be associated with effort: ease of finding information in a document, ease of reading and understanding its content. Existing work does not study the role of these factors in judging effort, however, one or more of these factors have been used to improve quality of search results for end users. For instance, readability has been used to filter [10, 25] or personalize [11, 24, 36] search results according to user's language proficiency. It has been shown that webpage readability levels impact users understanding of the document. Chandar *et al.* [8] have also shown that readability affects assessor disagreement.

It has also been shown that users actively *find* relevant or interesting information on a page [13, 27, 26] and may not sequentially read entire webpages. Guo *et al.* [15] studied cursor movements and found that users read relevant documents at length *after* scanning them. Scanning indicates that user is actively looking for required information on the page.

Understanding or consuming document is important in satisfying an information need. Information foraging theory [28, 29] has been used to show that users actively seek, filter, read, and extract information to satisfy information need. Thus, while previous research uses above parameters independently to tailor search results for end users, it is not known which parameter is more important for differentiating two *equally relevant* documents. We aim to obtain explicit judgements for all these parameters to identify which factor is highly associated with judging effort for a relevant document.

3. METHODOLOGY

By comparing relevance judgements with implicit signals of user satisfaction obtained via click logs, recent work by Yilmaz *et al.* [44] shows that 1) there can be significant mismatches between the utility of a document to an actual user and relevance of the document, and 2) some of these mismatches can be explained by factors related to the effort needed to find and process relevant information. These findings were based on relevance judgements and the behaviour of real users, but did not involve direct judgements of effort or analysis of how such judgements could be incorporated into the overall evaluation of information retrieval systems. Our primary purpose in this work is to show that it is possible to get reliable judgements of effort from relevance assessors and that incorporating these judgements into retrieval evaluation could lead to differences in system rankings. For this purpose, we first identify factors associated with effort. We design a judging interface and get judgements associated with these factors. We then analyse which of these effort related factors tend to be important for user satisfaction.

3.1 Factors Associated with Effort

We base our selection of effort related factors on previous work [15, 26, 27, 42] and the user model proposed in Yilmaz *et al.* [44] where a user does not read an entire web page sequentially. These studies suggest following model: when users first access a web page, they quickly scan it to determine portions of the document relevant to the query (*findability*). This is followed by reading these parts (*readability*) and finally understanding these nuggets of information (*understandability*). Based on this behaviour, given an information need, we hypothesize that the effort needed to satisfy the information need is affected by three primary factors:

- **Findability**: Effort needed to find the relevant information in a document.
- **Readability**: Effort required to read a document.
- **Understandability**: Effort required to understand a document to satisfy the information need.

Findability

Given an information need, the first step required to satisfy the need is to find relevant part(s) of the document. It has been shown [15, 27, 42] that users do not read entire webpages but first scan them for relevant parts. Effort needed to find the relevant portion of the document could have a significant effect on user satisfaction. Even if the document is highly relevant, the user may give up and end up being unsatisfied if it takes her too long to find required information in the document.

Readability

Once a part of the text that is relevant to the information need has been found, the user then has to read it to extract useful information. Reading a verbose document containing long sentences and difficult vocabulary may take a lot of effort for the user and may cause the user to be less satisfied, all other things being equal. Readability of a document can be quite subjective as it depends on the reading ability of the user: A fairly advanced reader will navigate difficult documents with relative ease as compared to a non-native speaker who struggles with the language. In this work we only focus on readability of document text, we shall study variance in effort due to user's readability level in future.

Understandability

Given that user may read only parts of the document, she has to process and understand the content in order to satisfy the desired information need. Even if document text is readable, if the information is not presented in a coherent manner, there are flaws in the description or the information is spread throughout the document, it can be difficult to understand. Such factors, which can lead to the user being unsatisfied, we denote as problems of understandability. Understandability can also be affected by the layout of the page. For example, pages with a lot of outlinks or advertisements distract users [13, 30] and make it difficult to extract the relevant information from the page.

It is worth noting that there may be other user specific factors that attribute to effort such as language proficiency or expertise in search topic that can be investigated in future. With this work, we aim to identify which of the three factors are important representatives of user effort in determining document relevance. We posit that given two documents of *same* relevance grade, users will prefer a low effort document over high effort document. We also determine how these factors correlate with user preferences. The user study investigating these questions and our findings are presented in the following sections.

4. EFFORT BASED JUDGING

We use crowdsourcing mechanisms in order to get explicit judgements of effort. We judge each of our hypothesized factors separately: the effort needed to find information (Findability), the readability of the document (Readability), and the understandability of the document (Understandability). Each of these effort-related aspects is measured on four point scale: *'very easy'*, *'easy'*, *'somewhat difficult'* and *'very difficult'*. We also ask judges to provide judgements about how satisfied they are with the document, and the relevance of the document. A sample HIT is shown in Figure 1.

For this study, we use data from Kazai et al. [22], which

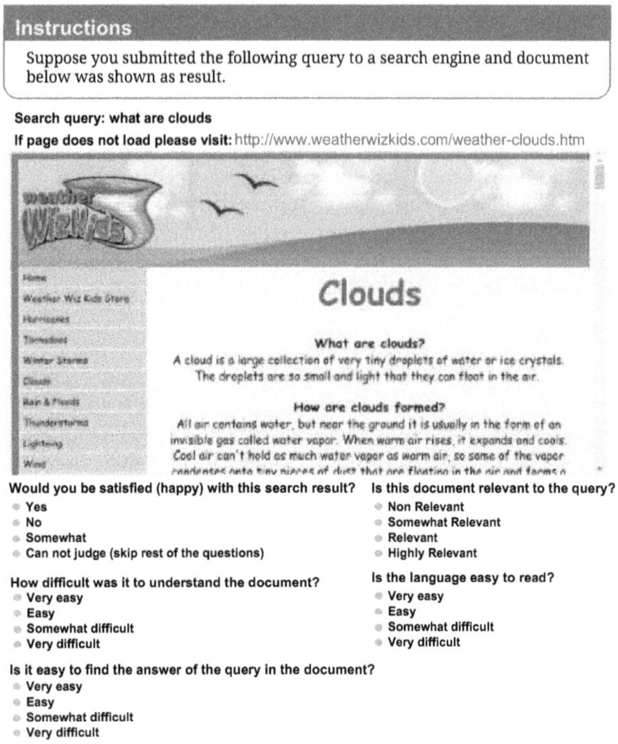

Figure 1: Sample Effort Judging HIT

consists of queries from TREC Web Track Ad Hoc task in 2009 and 2010. The full dataset contains 1603 URLs and 100 queries, where each query URL pair is judged on 5 grades of relevance by expert judges. Our main focus in this paper is to analyse how and whether effort affects user satisfaction for a relevant document. In this study, we control for relevance by excluding any non-relevant documents from our analysis, eliminating the lowest of the 5 grades. We also exclude inactive URLs from our analysis. Since effort is a factor that can affect user satisfaction only when a document is relevant,

Our goal with new crowd judgements is to eliminate differences due to relevance, and focus on effort-related differences identified in [44]. We therefore obtain our new judgements on pairs of documents with variation in effort but equal relevance. The signs of high and low effort are taken from [44]. Specifically, the number of words in a document (i.e., document length) and the readability level of the document measured by the readability measure LIX [5] are signals that can be associated with the effort needed to satisfy the information need in a document. We control for relevance by choosing documents with the same expert relevance grade (of the 4 remaining expert labels) and also eliminating one-word queries since such queries are ambiguous to untrained crowd judges. Hence, for each query in our dataset, from documents of same relevance grade, we include documents that have the maximum difference in terms of number of words and LIX. This way we ensure that both high and low effort documents are covered in our analysis, and can see which of our three hypothesized factors are seem to vary according to crowd judges.

Table 1: Effort Label Distribution

	very easy	**easy**	**somewhat difficult**	**very difficult**
Findability	89	41	17	19
Readability	96	46	13	11
Understandability	78	55	23	10

Table 2: Inter-annotator Agreement

Feature	**Alpha (α)**
Findability	0.35
Readability	0.22
Understandability	0.27
Satisfaction	0.38
Relevance	0.38

We used Amazon Mechanical Turk[1] (Mturk) to obtain preference labels where each tuple *(query, url)* in a HIT was judged for $0.04 by three labellers. We use the majority vote to determine final grade of each document. After removing spurious labels (determined by time spent on task) and 'can't-judge' cases, our dataset consists of 80 queries and 166 documents. Ground truth relevance labels from TREC collection has following distribution: 114, 29, 11, 12 marked 'highly relevant', 'relevant', 'somewhat relevant' and 'non relevant' respectively. Table 1 summarizes data collected from this experiment. Relevance labels obtained from Mturk has following distribution: 76, 52, 22 and 16 documents have been marked 'highly relevant', 'relevant', 'somewhat relevant' and 'non relevant' respectively. We obtain following judgement for satisfaction: 143, 15 and 8 documents have been marked 'yes', 'somewhat', 'no' respectively. The median and standard deviation of time spent on task was 36 seconds and 141 seconds respectively.

In order to measure the reliability of the judgements obtained and the inter-annotator agreement, we use Krippendorff's alpha (α) [18]. As shown in Table 2, Alpha values of effort judgements lie in range of 0.22 and 0.38, which is comparable or even higher than the alpha values observed in previous work that measures the inter-annotator agreement between assessors that judge document relevance [3, 23, 32].

The inter-annotator agreement appears to be the highest for relevance and satisfaction (*0.38*). In terms of effort based judgements, findability has the highest inter-annotator agreement (*0.35*), which is comparable to that of relevance and satisfaction. On the other hand, inter-annotator agreement between understandability and readability seems to be lower (*0.27* and *0.22*, respectively). One explanation for this is that ease of finding information is an objective question, while understandability and readability are subjective. They depend on the judge's background knowledge, reading level, intellectual capacity, etc. Therefore, judgements associated with findability seem to be more reliable than the other two judgements. However, the inter-annotator agreement for understandability and readability is still comparable and even higher than the agreement values reported for relevance judgements in the previous work [3].

Given that retrieval evaluation aims at predicting user satisfaction, the primary focus in retrieval evaluation has been

[1]https://www.mturk.com/

on getting judgements of relevance and assuming that user satisfaction is a direct function of relevance. If we were to analyse the correlations of the judgements for each pair of factors using Spearman correlation coefficient, satisfaction seems to be significantly correlated with two factors: relevance and findability (with Spearman correlation coefficient of 0.375 and 0.24, respectively). Both of these correlations are statistically significant with $p \leq 0.05$. High correlation between relevance and satisfaction is inline with previous work [20] which shows that they are correlated for higher relevance grades. The other two factors associated with effort, understandability and readability do not seem to be significantly correlated with satisfaction based on Spearman correlation. Our results confirm that in contrast to the common assumption, user satisfaction is not just a function of relevance but effort to find relevant information is also a significant factor that affects user satisfaction. Even though readability and understandability do not seem as significant factors in effort, we believe that one reason for this is due to the highly subjective nature of these judgements. Hence, these aspects associated with effort should be investigated on a personal basis and they should be considered in context of personalized retrieval and personalized evaluation of retrieval systems, which is outside of the scope of this study.

In order to confirm our analysis, we further use ordinal logistic regression to predict satisfaction of a document given the three effort based factors and relevance. The analysis is shown in Table 3. Using the aforementioned four features, we were able to predict satisfaction with Adjusted R^2 coefficient of 0.32. The table shows feature used in the regression study, together with the associated p values. It can be seen that while relevance, findability and understandability tend to get positive weight when predicting satisfaction, readability coefficient is negative but not significant. Similar to the conclusions of the correlation analysis, our regression results confirm that relevance and findability are significant factors in predicting user satisfaction. Thus, effort based judgements associated with findability should be incorporated into retrieval evaluation if the goal is to evaluate user satisfaction.

Overall, our study supports following hypothesis:

- Effort based factors are significant for user satisfaction.
- Findability is an important factor to characterize effort.

The aforementioned study assumes that judgements based on user satisfaction should be the gold standard used in evaluation and aims at identifying factors that are significant factors for predicting satisfaction. However, these findings are still subject to the reliability and validity of the judgements associated with satisfaction. In order to further validate the findings based on satisfaction analysis, we conducted a follow up study on agreement of user preferences with effort factors. With preference based judging, judges tend to have freedom to decide between documents and are not restricted to evaluate them with respect to some predefined factors. Hence, preference based judgements are useful in getting unbiased decisions about what users prefer to see in a document without making the judges think about particular aspects associated with a document (such as relevance). Therefore, we collect preference based judgements between two documents and study the correlation between the three effort based factors with user preferences,

Table 3: Factor importance for Satisfaction

Feature	p-value
Findablity$^+$	0.003
Readability$^-$	0.364
Understandability$^+$	0.054
Relevance$^+$	0

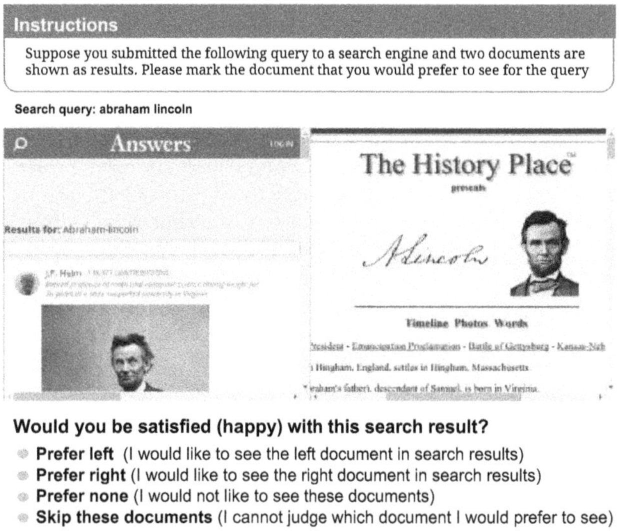

Figure 2: Sample Preference Judging HIT

analysing whether any of the effort related factors are significantly correlated with user preferences. The study and analysis are presented in the following section.

5. EFFORT-PREFERENCE CORRELATION

Primary aim of this experiment is to study and analyse preference correlation with effort factors defined in previous section. Preference judgements have been previously shown to be more reliable with better inter-annotator agreement than absolute judgements. For instance, Carterette *et al.* [7], studied assessor agreement and compared time spent on pairwise preference judgements and graded judgements. We use very similar guidelines and judging interface to the one used in that study. The judging interface used can be seen in Figure 2. Here two documents are shown side by side in separate frames to enable independent scrolling of either page. One important aspect associated with our judging interface is that we do not ask the judges to pick the document that is *more* relevant (which would bias them to think about relevance as opposed to what is really important for them). Instead, we provide judges with minimal instructions and just ask the judges to pick the document they would prefer.

Our main focus in this study is to analyse whether any of the effort related factors are important for user preferences. For this purpose, we use the same dataset as the one used in the effort based judging study (Section 4). We obtain preference based judgements on the documents of the same relevance grade. Thus, for each query, we show a pair of documents that are of the same relevance grade side by side to each user. We then analyse whether the users tend to prefer one document over the other, and whether any of the effort related factors are correlated with user preferences.

Table 4: Preference and Effort Factors Agreement

Factor	Percentage
Findability	0.607*
Readability	0.512
Understandability	0.511
Satisfaction	0.727*

We used Mturk to obtain preference labels where each triplet *(query, url1, url2)* in a HIT was judged for $0.04 by three workers. The total cost of the experiment was $23.5. We use the majority vote between three judges as the final judgement. After removing pairs with no clear preference (i.e., pairs which had 3 judges label 'Prefer left', 'Prefer right' and 'Both irrelevant') and the hits that were skipped by judges, we obtain a total of 81 triplets for our analysis. The median and standard deviation of time spent on preference interface are 17 seconds and 47 seconds respectively.

The average pairwise percentage agreement for the set of judgements obtained from this study is *0.60*, which is higher than random agreement of 0.5 ($p \leq 0.05$). Given that the judges are only shown same relevance grade documents, the fact that there is significantly higher agreement than random between the judges indicates that there are some additional factors that affect user satisfaction. When compared to the inter-annotator agreement values reported by Carterette *et al.* [7] (which focus on getting judgements associated with relevance, and asking judges to rate documents that could be of different relevance grades), the inter-annotator agreement in our study is comparable but slightly lower (approximately 0.7 versus 0.6). This is because our judging task is much harder since we focus on getting preference judgements on documents that are of *same* relevance grade.

Given the preference based judgements from the judges, we further analyse whether any of the effort related factors are significantly correlated with user preferences, i.e., whether the users tend to prefer low versus high effort documents and whether these preferences are statistically significant. Table 4 shows percentage agreement between preference and an effort factor. Basically it captures the percentage of pairs where if judges prefer one document over the other, the effort statistic also prefers that document, i.e. effort value of preferred document is lower than the other document. We also analyse the agreement of satisfaction based judgements (obtained via the effort based judging interface in the previous section) with user preferences.

It can be seen that satisfaction and findability are highly correlated with user preferences and these correlations are statistically significant ($p \leq 0.05$). The high correlation of satisfaction based judgements with user preferences further confirm the reliability of the satisfaction based judgements from the effort based judging study. Furthermore, our results here confirm that out of the three effort based factors, findability is the primary factor that can significantly affect user preferences and satisfaction. Given that the inter-annotator agreement between the preference judgements is 0.60, the agreement of 0.607 between findability and user preferences (obtained via the majority vote) is comparable with agreement between two random judges in terms of the documents they prefer.

Overall, our analysis shows that findability is an important factor that can affect user satisfaction and preferences, suggesting that retrieval systems should be built to optimize for findability together with relevance if the goal is to optimize user satisfaction. Our results further show that findability is another factor that should be considered together with relevance for evaluating user satisfaction. In the following sections, we focus on analysing how incorporating findability in building and evaluating retrieval systems could change the design of retrieval systems.

6. PREDICTING EFFORT VERSUS RELEVANCE

In this section, we focus on predicting the most important effort related factor: findability and analyse how building systems that optimize for this factor would require different types of features. In particular, we propose and investigate some features and their accuracy in predicting findability. We also use these features to predict relevance and compare and contrast features that are useful in predicting relevance and findability. Our hypothesis is that the features that are important for predicting findability are not necessarily correlated with features that are important for predicting relevance. This would suggest that in order to optimize for effort (or findability) together with relevance, search systems should include additional features (such as the ones proposed in this paper) that are designed to capture findability or effort to find relevant information.

First, we propose and describe several features that can capture the easiness of finding information in a document, then show the importance of these features for both predicting findability and relevance of a document.

6.1 Features

We propose several features that incorporate different dimensions of effort. The first set is text based features that are related to the content of the document and second is html oriented features that are related to the layout of the page.

6.1.1 *Text features*

We construct features from entire document text and from summary (part of the document that contains the query terms). Since a user may not always read the entire document if she has little time, often, the quickest way to judge a document is to search for the query terms and read the neighbouring paragraphs (i.e., the summary). We create document summary using sentences that contain query terms along with one sentence that appears before and after them. Similar features have been used previously in [44]. The features are summarized in Table 5.

- Typically, lengthier documents may require more effort than shorter documents. Hence, we use features that capture the length of document. They mainly cover number of words and sentences in a document. Similar values are also calculated for summary.

- Secondly, to assess the difficulty of the documents and corresponding summaries, we use three readability indices, namely Coleman Liau index (CLI) [9], Automated Readability Index (ARI) [34] and LIX [5]. These metrics are calculated by counting number of words, sentences and are used as a rough estimate for a document's difficulty. These features are calculated both

Table 5: Text features used for predicting findability and relevance

Summary and Document Specific Features			
avgSumChar	Avg #characters in summary	avgDocChar	Avg #characters in document
sumWords	#words in summary	docWords	#words in document
sumPunct	#punctuations in summary	docPunct	#punctuations in document
sumSent	#sentences in summary	docSent	#sentences in document
sumSentQT	#summary sentences with query terms	docSentQT	#document sentences with query terms
Readability Features			
sumARI	ARI Index of summary	docARI	ARI Index of document
sumCLI	CLI Index of summary	docCLI	CLI Index of document
sumLIX	LIX Index of summary	docLIX	LIX Index of document
Other Features			
queryFreq	#query appears in page	minQPos	Min pos of query term in document
qTermstInTitle	#query terms in title	maxQPos	Max pos of query term in document
qWinB	Fraction of bold text with all query terms	tRatio	Fraction of #words and #tags in html

for entire document and summary containing query terms.

- Finally, query term specific features are used to capture relevance of document with respect to input query. These features include number of query terms in text and title, as well as their min, max and median frequencies in both document and summary. We also use min, max and median positions of query terms in both document and summary.

6.1.2 Html Features

Users interact more with rich and responsive web pages and their layout or structure can be instrumental in finding useful information. We use some features that leverage underlying information in html markup. These structure oriented features are given in Table 6.

- The first set of features are associated with tag distribution in a document. We posit that tag distribution captures how well information is organized in a web page. For instance, users may find it difficult to navigate pages with a lot of outlinks or images. Thus, we extract percentage of tables, images, headings, paragraphs, lists and outlinks from the web page.

- Outlink distribution of a page is useful because too many outlinks can be distracting and hinder readability of the document. We consider fraction of words in hyperlinks and words in text as feature. We also use fraction of links within a page, to same domain and other sites as features.

- Some parts of webpage tend to be more important and attract more attention [30] than others. For instance, headings are useful for skimming content. We use number of headings that contain query terms, their min, max and average position as features. Similar features are extracted from outlinks.

- A user may look for information by searching for query terms in a webpage. Hence, we also extract features from span (window) of text that contains all query terms. We use number of such spans in a document, their min, max and average positions, their average length and spans that cover headings as features.

Table 7: Findability Features

Feature	p-val	Feature	p-val
$fTable^-$	0.00	$minWinPos^+$	0.00
$avgSumChar^-$	0.01	$meanPosOut^+$	0.01
$docCLI^-$	0.02	$sumWords^+$	0.02
$maxWinPos^-$	0.04	$fImg^+$	0.02

We would like to emphasize that the features proposed above are by no means exhaustive. This is a first step in the direction of identifying features that could be significant for effort and more features can be used to capture different aspects of effort.

6.2 Predicting Findability

Given the aforementioned features, we focus on predicting effort through these features and analyse which features are significant for predicting effort. Since findability seems to be the most important factor for user satisfaction, we focus on predicting findability and compare and contrast the features that are important for predicting findability with features that are important for predicting relevance.

We use Ordinal Logistic Regression with normalized feature values ($\mu = 0$, $\sigma^2 = 1$) to predict Findability labels obtained from effort judging (described in Section 4), and report Root Mean Squared Error (RMSE) to measure the quality of predictions. For validation of regression analysis in predicting labels, along the same lines of the analysis done in Table 4, we compare the agreement of predicted Findability labels with preference judgements obtained from assessors by computing the fraction of documents preferred by the users that are predicted to be of high findability according to the regression model. To summarize, preference agreement is calculated as follows: given predicted grade of two documents, what is direction of preference (document with higher findability grade will be preferred over a document with a lower findability grade).

RMSE for the predictions is 0.37. We also compute preference agreement between predicted Findability grades. Preference agreement for predicted Findability grades is 0.587, which is comparable to agreement of 0.6 between Findability and preference judgements if actual judgements of Findabil-

Table 6: Html features used for predicting findability and relevance

Dom Oriented Features			
fHead	Fraction of headings (h1,h2..h6)	fBoldItalics	Fraction of bold, italics and strong
fTable	Fraction of tables	fOutlinks	Fraction of outlinks
fDiv	Fraction of Divs	fImg	Fraction of images
fPara	Fraction of paragraphs	fList	Fraction of Lists
Outlink Oriented Features			
fSameDomain	Fraction of hrefs to same domain	aRatio	Normalized #words in hyperlinks
fDiffDomain	Fraction of hrefs to different domain	aTxtRatio	Fraction of words in hyperlinks and text tags
fOutPage	Fraction of hrefs to same page		
Query Term Window Specific Features			
qWinH	Fraction of headings with all query terms	minWinPos	Min window pos with all query terms
qWinO	Fraction of outlinks with all query terms	maxWinPos	Max window pos with all query terms
qWinB	Fraction of bold text with all query terms	meanWinPos	Mean window pos with all query terms
Query Specific Features			
minPosH	Min pos of heading with query terms	minPosOut	Min pos of outlink with query terms
maxPosH	Max pos of heading with query terms	maxPosOut	Max pos of outlink with query terms
meanPosH	Mean pos of heading with query terms	meanPosOut	Mean pos of outlink with query terms
countH	#Headings with query terms	countOut	#Outlinks with query terms

ity were used in the analysis (in Table 4). These results suggest that the model can reliably predict Findability.

Table 7 contains statistically significant features (p-val < 0.05) and direction of correlation coefficient. We posit that features that can help users find information quickly would be more important for Findability. We observe that both html and text features proposed above are important. Given that images and tables are useful in spotting information on a webpage, they (fImg and fTable) are significant in predicting Findability. While too many tables may make it difficult to find information, documents with more images have higher Findability grade. As expected, features such as minimum position of query terms in summary (minWinPos) and number of words (sumWords) in summary are also significant since these are directly correlated with the amount of effort needed to find the relevant information in the page. These results emphasize that position of query specific information on the page is important for reading/skimming entire document.

Our hypothesis is that if one solely focuses on predicting relevance, the features that are important for that purpose are likely to be different than the features that are important for findability, suggesting that retrieval systems need to use additional features such as the ones proposed in this paper in order to optimize for effort together with relevance. In order to validate our hypothesis, in next section, we use the aforementioned features to predict relevance and analyse the importance of features and how they differ from Findability features.

6.3 Relevance Prediction

Similar to the model for predicting Findability, we use our proposed features for predicting judgements of relevance obtained via the effort based judging interface. We use Ordinal Logistic Regression with normalized feature values ($\mu = 0$, $\sigma^2 = 1$) to predict relevance which results in 0.41 RMSE. Confusion matrix for the model is given in Table 8, where each cell is fraction of documents with actual label x_i and predicted label y_i. Table 9 shows features that are statistically significant (p-val < 0.05) for predicting relevance, together with the direction of correlations.

Table 8: Actual vs. Predicted Relevance Labels

		Predicted		
		1	**2**	**3**
Actual	**1**	0	0.8	0.2
	2	0.05	0.59	0.34
	3	0	0.13	0.86

Table 9: Relevance Feature Importance

Feature	p-val	Feature	p-val
$tRatio^-$	0.01	$termsInTitle^+$	0.01
$countH^-$	0.02	$qWinO^+$	0.01
$maxWinPos^-$	0.04	$fBoldItalics^+$	0.02
$docWords^-$	0.04	$fImg^+$	0.04

As shown in previous work [38], document content features impact relevance most followed by query and structure specific features. While features related to document length (docWords and maxWinPos) have negative coefficients (suggesting user preference for documents with fewer terms and sentences), query and summary specific features (qWinO, sumWords and termsInTitle) have positive coefficients. Documents with higher text to tag ratio (tRatio) have lower relevance suggesting that verbose documents which lack structure are not preferred by users. At the same time, it is interesting to note that users do not prefer documents that contain a lot of headings as documents with more headings (countH) have lower relevance grade.

Table 9 also suggests that important features for predicting relevance are different than features that are significant for predicting Findability.

Overall, our results confirm our hypothesis that 1) retrieval systems that are optimized for relevance are not necessarily optimizing for effort, 2) in order to build retrieval systems that optimize for user satisfaction, systems should

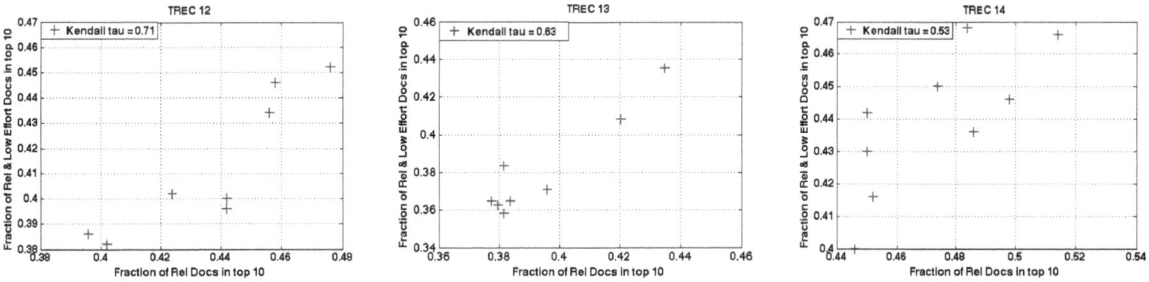

(a) Top 10 systems of 2012 (b) Top 10 systems of 2013 (c) Top 10 systems of 2014

Figure 3: Comparison of systems based on #relevant documents vs #low effort relevant documents ($p@10$)

be optimized for Findability together with relevance, and 3) additional features that capture ease of finding information in the page (such as the ones proposed in this paper) should be used in building and optimizing retrieval systems.

In the following section, we focus on evaluating the quality of retrieval systems and show how incorporating effort into retrieval evaluation could lead to very different conclusions in terms of the quality of retrieval systems.

7. EFFECT OF EFFORT ON RETRIEVAL EVALUATION

Until now, we have focused on getting relevance judgements associated with effort and have shown that user satisfaction and preferences can be significantly affected by effort related factors, in particular, by ease of finding information in a document. Since the primary goal in retrieval evaluation is to measure user satisfaction, our results suggest that effort should be incorporated into retrieval evaluation.

Previous work [41] has shown that variations in relevance assessments does not necessarily lead to significant differences in retrieval evaluation. Given this finding, we further analyse whether incorporating effort as a factor in retrieval evaluation could lead to significant differences in the evaluation of systems. For this purpose, we use data from TREC Adhoc task 2012 to 2014. Getting effort based judgements for these years would be very costly and time consuming. Since our results suggest that findability information is a primary factor that affects user satisfaction and that it is possible to predict findability with a good accuracy, we used the regressor designed in the previous section in order to predict the easiness of finding information in a document. Focusing on the top systems submitted to these years, we then analyse how their performance would change if easiness of finding information in a document was incorporated into retrieval evaluation. For this purpose, we first evaluated the fraction of relevant documents retrieved by these top performing systems in top 10 (i.e., precision at 10 value). We then compared this value with the fraction of relevant documents retrieved in top 10 that are also low effort (i.e., findability). Figure 3 shows the result of this experiment for TREC 2012 (left plot), 2013 (middle plot) and 2014 (right plot). The plots also show the Kendall's tau correlation between the ranking of systems obtained when the systems are ranked based on number of relevant documents versus number of low effort relevant documents retrieved in top 10.

It can be seen that top performing retrieval systems tend to vary significantly in terms of effort needed to find relevant information and that even if two systems may retrieve identical number of relevant documents in top 10, their performance may be very different from each other when ease of finding information in the document is considered. For example, for TREC 2012, the fourth and fifth best performing systems in terms of fraction of relevant documents retrieved in top 10 seem to have retrieved almost identical number of relevant documents in top 10, whereas when the effort to find relevant information is also considered as a factor, their performance seems to be different from each other. The same behaviour can be seen in TREC 2014 for the third and fourth best systems according to the number of relevant documents retrieved in top 10. In this case, there is a big gap in the performance of these systems when effort to find relevant information is considered. Given the importance of findability in a document for user satisfaction, the satisfaction of the users of these two search systems would be very different from each other even though they retrieved similar number of relevant documents in top 10.

Overall, our results suggest that when effort to find relevant information is considered, performance of retrieval systems could be quite different as opposed to just focusing on relevance. Therefore, new evaluation metrics that incorporate effort together with relevance are needed for building retrieval methodologies that are better aligned with user satisfaction.

8. CONCLUSION

Extensive research has been carried out in the past on characterizing relevance. If the underlying assumption is that user satisfaction is impacted by relevance then outcome of highly ranked systems on basis of relevance judgements, should align with satisfaction of real users. However, it has been shown that relevance and user satisfaction do not always agree, and users may still be dissatisfied with their search despite being served relevant documents. Recent work [44] showed that the utility of a document with respect to an actual user can be different than its relevance, which in turn impacts user satisfaction. Their work leaves room for further research as they do not explain what constitutes effort or how can effort judgements be obtained and incorporated in evaluation. With this work, we attempted to answer all these questions.

We proposed three characteristics that could be useful in measuring effort, mainly – Findability, Readability and Understandability. To evaluate these factors we conducted two user studies – an effort based study where we asked for explicit grades for these parameters and a follow-up preference study to validate whether effort parameters align with user preference. Our analysis indicates findability correlates well with user satisfaction among three parameters.

Having shown that findability is a reasonable predictor of user satisfaction, we compare important features for predicting findability with those useful for predicting relevance. Again, we observe useful predictors for findability and relevance capture different aspects. Towards the end, we analyse whether incorporating effort as a factor in retrieval evaluation could lead to significant differences in the evaluation of systems. Comparison of top performing runs on TREC Web track datasets of 2012-2014 suggests that performance of retrieval systems could be quite different when effort (in our experiments findability) is taken into account.

Our analysis suggests that effort based judgements can be explicitly collected from end users and can also be used to evaluate retrieval systems. There are several directions in which this work could progress. It would be interesting to analyse different label aggregation strategies to incorporate all the effort parameters. We would also look into incorporating effort into existing evaluation metrics or proposing new effort based metrics for retrieval evaluation.

9. REFERENCES

[1] A. Al-Maskari, M. Sanderson, P. Clough, and E. Airio. The good and the bad system: Does the test collection predict users' effectiveness? In *Proc. SIGIR*, 2008.

[2] J. Allan, B. Carterette, and J. Lewis. When will information retrieval be "good enough"? In *Proc. SIGIR*, 2005.

[3] O. Alonso and S. Mizzaro. Using crowdsourcing for {TREC} relevance assessment. *Inf. Process. Manage.*, 2012.

[4] P. Borlund. The concept of relevance in ir. *J. Assoc. Inf. Sci. Technol.*, 54(10):913–925, 2003.

[5] J. Brown and M. Eskenazi. Student, text and curriculum modeling for reader-specific document retrieval. In *Proceedings of the IASTED International Conference on Human-Computer Interaction. Phoenix, AZ*, 2005.

[6] B. Carterette. System effectiveness, user models, and user utility: A conceptual framework for investigation. In *Proc. SIGIR*. ACM, 2011.

[7] B. Carterette, P. N. Bennett, D. M. Chickering, and S. T. Dumais. Here or there: Preference judgments for relevance. In *Proc. ECIR*, 2008.

[8] P. Chandar, W. Webber, and B. Carterette. Document features predicting assessor disagreement. In *Proc. SIGIR*, 2013.

[9] M. Coleman and T. L. Liau. A computer readability formula designed for machine scoring. *J. Appl. Psychol.*, 1975.

[10] K. Collins-Thompson. Enriching the web by modeling reading difficulty. In *Proc. ESAIR*, ESAIR '13.

[11] K. Collins-Thompson, P. N. Bennett, R. W. White, S. de la Chica, and D. Sontag. Personalizing web search results by reading level. In *Proc. CIKM*, 2011.

[12] C. da Costa Pereira, M. Dragoni, and G. Pasi. Multidimensional relevance: Prioritized aggregation in a personalized information retrieval setting. *Inf. Process. Manage.*, 2012.

[13] D. DeStefano and J.-A. LeFevre. Cognitive load in hypertext reading: A review. *Computers in Human Behavior*, 2007.

[14] N. Ferro, G. Silvello, H. Keskustalo, A. Pirkola, and K. JÃd'rvelin. The twist measure for ir evaluation: Taking user's effort into account. *J. Assoc. Inf. Sci. Technol.*, 2015.

[15] Q. Guo and E. Agichtein. Beyond dwell time: Estimating document relevance from cursor movements and other post-click searcher behavior. In *Proc. WWW*, 2012.

[16] J. Gwizdka and I. Lopatovska. The role of subjective factors in the information search process. *Journal of the American Society for Information Science and Technology*, 2009.

[17] M. Halvey and R. Villa. Evaluating the effort involved in relevance assessments for images. In *Proc. SIGIR*, 2014.

[18] A. F. Hayes and K. Krippendorff. Answering the call for a standard reliability measure for coding data. *Communication Methods and Measures*, 2007.

[19] W. Hersh, A. Turpin, S. Price, B. Chan, D. Kramer, L. Sacherek, and D. Olson. Do batch and user evaluations give the same results? In *Proc. SIGIR*, 2000.

[20] S. B. Huffman and M. Hochster. How well does result relevance predict session satisfaction? In *Proc. SIGIR*, 2007.

[21] F. C. Johnson, J. R. Griffiths, and R. J. Hartley. Task dimensions of user evaluation of information retrieval systems. *Information research*, 2003.

[22] G. Kazai, N. Craswell, E. Yilmaz, and S. Tahaghoghi. An analysis of systematic judging errors in information retrieval. In *Proc. CIKM*, 2012.

[23] G. Kazai, J. Kamps, and N. Milic-Frayling. An analysis of human factors and label accuracy in crowdsourcing relevance judgments. *Inf. Retr.*, 2013.

[24] P. Kidwell, G. Lebanon, and K. Collins-Thompson. Statistical estimation of word acquisition with application to readability prediction. *JASA*, 2011.

[25] J. Y. Kim, K. Collins-Thompson, P. N. Bennett, and S. T. Dumais. Characterizing web content, user interests, and search behavior by reading level and topic. In *Proc. WSDM*, 2012.

[26] M. Morita and Y. Shinoda. Information filtering based on user behavior analysis and best match text retrieval. In *Proc. SIGIR*, 1994.

[27] M. Mosconi, M. Porta, and A. Ravarelli. On-line newspapers and multimedia content: An eye tracking study. In *Proc. SIGDOC*, 2008.

[28] P. Pirolli and S. Card. The sensemaking process and leverage points for analyst technology as identified through cognitive task analysis. In *Proceedings of international conference on intelligence analysis*, 2005.

[29] P. L. T. Pirolli. *Information Foraging Theory: Adaptive Interaction with Information.* 2007.

[30] O. Rokhlenko, N. Golbandi, R. Lempel, and L. Leibovich. Engagement-based user attention distribution on web article pages. In *Proc. HT*, 2013.

[31] T. Saracevic. Relevance: A review of the literature and a framework for thinking on the notion in information science. part ii: nature and manifestations of relevance. *J. Assoc. Inf. Sci. Technol.*, 58(13), 2007.

[32] P. Schaer. Better than their reputation? on the reliability of relevance assessments with students. In *Information Access Evaluation. Multilinguality, Multimodality, and Visual Analytics*, Lecture Notes in Computer Science. 2012.

[33] L. Schamber and M. Eisenberg. Relevance: The search for a definition. 1988.

[34] R. Senter and E. Smith. Automated readability index. Technical report, DTIC Document, 1967.

[35] M. D. Smucker and C. L. Clarke. Time-based calibration of effectiveness measures. In *Proc. SIGIR*, 2012.

[36] C. Tan, E. Gabrilovich, and B. Pang. To each his own: Personalized content selection based on text comprehensibility. In *Proceedings of WSDM*, 2012.

[37] A. Taylor. User relevance criteria choices and the information search process. *Inf. Process. Manage.*, 48, 2012.

[38] A. Tombros, I. Ruthven, and J. M. Jose. How users assess web pages for information seeking. *J. Assoc. Inf. Sci. Technol.*, 2005.

[39] A. H. Turpin and W. Hersh. Why batch and user evaluations do not give the same results? In *Proc. SIGIR*, 2001.

[40] R. Villa and M. Halvey. Is relevance hard work?: evaluating the effort of making relevant assessments. In *Proc. SIGIR*, 2013.

[41] E. M. Voorhees. Variations in relevance judgments and the measurement of retrieval effectiveness. *Inf. Process. Manage.*, 36(5), 2000.

[42] H. Weinreich, H. Obendorf, E. Herder, and M. Mayer. Not quite the average: An empirical study of web use. *ACM Trans. Web*, 2(1):5:1–5:31, Mar. 2008.

[43] Y. C. Xu and Z. Chen. Relevance judgment: What do information users consider beyond topicality? *J. Assoc. Inf. Sci. Technol.*, 57(7), 2006.

[44] E. Yilmaz, M. Verma, N. Craswell, F. Radlinski, and P. Bailey. Relevance and effort: An analysis of document utility. In *Proc. CIKM*, 2014.

[45] Y. Zhang, J. Zhang, M. Lease, and J. Gwizdka. Multidimensional relevance modeling via psychometrics and crowdsourcing. In *Proc. SIGIR*, 2014.

A Semantic Graph based Topic Model for Question Retrieval in Community Question Answering

Long Chen
School of Computing Science
University of Glasgow
Glasgow, UK
long.chen@glasgow.ac.uk

Joemon M Jose
School of Computing Science
University of Glasgow
Glasgow, UK
joemon.jose@glasgow.ac.uk

Haitao Yu
Faculty of Library, Information and Media Science
University of Tsukuba
Tsukuba, Japan
yuhaitao@slis.tsukuba.ac.jp

Fajie Yuan
School of Computing Science
University of Glasgow
Glasgow, UK
fajie.yuan@glasgow.ac.uk

Dell Zhang
DCSIS
Birkbeck, University of London
London, UK
dell.z@ieee.org

ABSTRACT

Community Question Answering (CQA) services, such as Yahoo! Answers and WikiAnswers, have become popular with users as one of the central paradigms for satisfying users' information needs. The task of question retrieval aims to resolve one's query directly by finding the most relevant questions (together with their answers) from an archive of past questions. However, as the text of each question is short, there is usually a lexical gap between the queried question and the past questions. To alleviate this problem, we present a hybrid approach that blends several language modelling techniques for question retrieval, namely, the classic (query-likelihood) language model, the state-of-the-art translation-based language model, and our proposed semantics-based language model. The semantics of each candidate question is given by a probabilistic topic model which makes use of local and global semantic graphs for capturing the hidden interactions among entities (e.g., people, places, and concepts) in question-answer pairs. Experiments on two real-world datasets show that our approach can significantly outperform existing ones.

Categories and Subject Descriptors

H.3.3 [**Information Storage and Retrieval**]: Information Search and Retrieval–Clustering; H.2.8 [**Information Systems Applications**]: Database Applications–Data mininglgorithm, Experimentation

Keywords

Community Question Answering; Question Retrieval; Knowledge Repository; Topic Modelling; Language Modelling

WSDM'16, February 22–25, 2016, San Francisco, CA, USA.

DOI: http://dx.doi.org/10.1145/2835776.2835809

1. INTRODUCTION

In recent years, Community Question Answering (CQA) services, such as Yahoo! Answers, WikiAnswers, Quora, Stack Overflow, and Baidu Zhidao, have become popular knowledge sources for Internet users to access useful information online. When a user submits a new question (i.e., *query*) in CQA, the system would usually check whether similar questions have already been asked and answered before. If so, the user's query could be resolved directly by returning those archive questions (i.e., *documents*) with their corresponding answers.

Identifying relevant questions in CQA repositories is a difficult task, since the questions asked by users are always short texts which would lead to a lexical gap between the queried question and the past questions. In addition, the limited length of questions causes the sparsity of word features. To address the above limitations, researchers have proposed the use of translation models [16,33] to capture the semantic relations between words. While useful in general, the effectiveness of such models largely depends on the availability of high-quality parallel corpora (e.g., *question-answer pairs* in this context). Furthermore, simple word-level analysis model cannot handle cases where entities (e.g., *people, places,* and *concepts*) are expressed by multi-word phrases.

To go beyond the mere word-level analysis, this paper proposes a question retrieval framework on the basis of semantic graphs which makes use of an *external* resource (namely *DBpedia*) as the background knowledge to overcome the problem of the lexical gap between the queried question and the past questions. As a simple illustration, Figure 1 displays a piece of global semantic graph produced by our proposed knowledge-rich approach [1] (cf. Section 4.2.1) from two questions: "Why Kobe is better than Jordan?" and "Who is better Kobe Bryant or Lebron James?". From this graph, one can easily see that "Basketball" and "BasketballPlayer" are the central entities (i.e., *concepts* in *DBPedia*) of these two questions, even though these entities didn't appear in the original questions. Furthermore, the rich semantic connections among entities could be exploited to help inferring the

[1] https://github.com/long4glasgow/Semantics-based-Question-Retrieval

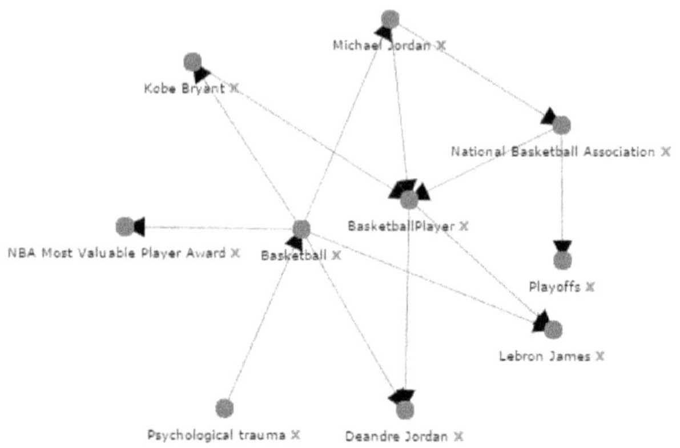

Figure 1: A piece of global semantic graph generated from two questions in Yahoo! Answers

latent topics of each question. Therefore, we would like to learn the interrelationships between entities in the global semantic graph, would allow effective information sharing among all questions in the archive. In addition to the global semantic graph, the inference of a question's latent topics could benefit from examining its similar questions according to their individual semantic graphs. In other words, if two questions have a large degree of overlap in terms of their semantic entities and relations, they probably bear a close topical resemblance to each other. Therefore, we also construct local semantic graphs for each question-answer pair in the archive with the hope to utilize their semantic similarities.

Given the semantic graphs, a novel topic modelling framework is proposed, namely, Semantic Graph based Topic Model (**SGTM**), which can seamlessly incorporate entities and relations from the semantic graphs into topic modelling. We then present a hybrid approach that blends several language modelling techniques for question retrieval, namely, the classic (query-likelihood) language model, the state-of-the-art translation-based language model, and our proposed semantics-based language model. Experiments on two real-world datasets show that the hybrid approach to question retrieval outperforms existing approaches significantly.

The rest of this paper is organized as follows. We firstly introduce the related work in Section 2. Section 3 formally defines the problem of topic modelling with semantic graph. Section 4 and 5 systematically present the proposed SGTM framework and the mixture language model. The experimental results of question clustering and question retrieval are reported in Section 6. Finally, we present our conclusion and future work in Section 7.

2. RELATED WORK

2.1 Topic Model with Network Analysis

The techniques of topic modelling, such as PLSA [12] and LDA [31], provide an elegant mathematical way to analyze large volumes of unlabelled text. Recently, a large number of studies, such as Author-Topic Model (ATM) [28] and Contextual Focused Topic Model (CFTM) [9], try to integrate some side information of network structure with topic modelling, but they mostly focus on homogeneous networks rather than heterogeneous networks. Entity-Topic Model (ETM) [18] combined LDA with entity-document relations, which is somewhat similar to our idea. However it assumes that an edge (entity-document)created in exactly the same way as a word, whereas our approach directly takes into account several types of relations (entity-document and entity-entity relations) through regularized propagation.

In Mei's seminal work [24], a homogeneous network was employed as a biased regularizer to overcome the overfitting problem of topic modelling. Deng et al. [10] later on combined Probabilistic Latent Semantic Analysis (PLSA) [12] (see Section 4.1) with the regularizer learned from a heterogeneous network. However, it was originally designed for academic networks, and thus didn't utilize the contextual information from any knowledge repositories. In addition, their framework only incorporates the heterogeneous network (i.e., relations among entities), while the homogeneous network (i.e., relations between entity pairs with weight) is completely ignored, whereas we consider both of them in our proposed framework.

2.2 Knowledge Rich Approaches

The recent advances in knowledge-rich approaches (e.g., DBPedia[2] and Knowledge Graph[3]) provide new techniques to gain insight into the semantic structure of a question archive. While enormous success has been made in several NLP tasks such as document similarity [26], topic labelling [15], and question answering [5], the feasibility and effectiveness of such knowledge-rich approaches in topic modelling and question retrieval are mostly unknown. Hulpus et al. [15] reported a framework that extracts sub-graphs from DBpedia to label the topics obtained from a topic model. However, they consider topic model and graph labelling as two separate processes, which may result in the loss of rich semantics. On the contrary, our framework discovers the latent topics and semantic network simultaneously, reinforcing the topic model performance with multi-typed relations. In addition, their graph construction process relies on a small set of manually selected DBpedia relations, which does not scale and needs to be tuned each time given a different knowledge repository. Instead, we pruned our semantic graphs by filtering and weighting the edges (see Section 4.2.2). This may look similar to [26], but their work attempts to produce graph-representation of documents for the task of document ranking, while we aim to construct semantic graphs for the task of topic modelling and question retrieval.

2.3 Question Retrieval

The technique of language modelling has proved to be effective for question retrieval in CQA. The state-of-the-art approach utilized the classic (query-likelihood) language model [34] (see Section 5.1) together with the translation-based language model [16,33] (see Section 5.2). Ji et al. [17] have recently reported an approach to question retrieval based on the question-answer topic model which uses LDA to learn the latent topics underlying the surface text of question-answer pairs. However, the semantic level of their work is substantially different from ours: their topic model is designed at word level, whereas ours relies on the external knowledge repository at the concept level, and thereby the topics in our model are more general and expressive.

[2]http://wiki.dbpedia.org/

[3]https://developers.google.com/freebase/

Cao et al. have proposed a category-based language model [6, 7] for question retrieval, but it requires users to manually assign one topic category to each of their query questions, which is not always feasible. Instead of using the manually labelled categories, Zhou et al. [36] later on improved Cao's framework using category-based entries extracted from Wikipedia, but their category-based model cannot be applied straightforwardly to incorporate topics into question retrieval, because it assumes that a question belongs to one and only one topic, while we believe that a question can have multiple topics (each to a certain degree).

3. PRELIMINARIES

In this section, we formally introduce several concepts and notations.

Definition 1 (Question): A ***question*** d in a archive D is a sequence of words $w_1 w2....w_{|d|}$, where w_i is a word from a fixed vocabulary. Following a common simplification in most work in information retrieval [12], we consider each question (i.e., document) as a bag of words, and use $n(d, w)$ to denote the number of occurrence of word w in d.

Definition 2 (Entity): An entity e in our system, given that we are using DBPedia resource URIs, can be either an instance or a concept in DBPedia. The former are concrete entries of DBPedia (e.g. *dbpedia : Barrack_Obama*), while the latter are the classes found within the DBPedia Ontology (i.e., the types of instances such as people, places, organizations).

Definition 3 (Semantic Graph): A semantic graph G consists of V the set of entities in the text data and E the set of edges representing the relations between entities. For instance, an edge $< u, v >$ is a binary directed relation from entity u to entity v, where we use $w(u, v)$ to denote the weight of $< u, v >$.

We call the semantic graph built from the entire corpus (the archive of past questions) the *global* semantic graph, and those built from individual documents (i.e., questions) *local* semantic graphs

Now we can formulate our problem of SGTM as follows. Given a question archive D and its corresponding semantic graph $G = (V, E)$, we would like to extract K major topics $Z = \{z_1, z_2, \ldots, z_K\}$ from D, where z_k is a probability distribution of words, and the probability of a word w is denoted as $P(w|z)$. What SGTM essentially does is to group similar or related questions into semantic clusters according to not only their textual similarity but also the underlying semantic graphs.

4. TOPIC MODELS

In this section, we propose a propagation algorithm to combine semantic graphs with the textual information for topic modelling, namely **Regularized Propagation**. The goal of this algorithm is to estimate the probabilities of topics for documents as well as other associated entities, in order to improve the performance of topic modelling.

4.1 Probabilistic Topic Models

In Probabilistic Latent Semantic Analysis (PLSA) [12], an unobserved topic variable $z_k \in \{z_1, ..., z_K\}$ is inferred from the occurrences of different words $w_j \in \{w_1, ..., w_M\}$ in a particular document $d_i \in \{d_1, ..., d_N\}$. The joint probability of an observed pair (d, w) can be expressed as

$$P(d_i, w_j) = P(d_i) \sum_{k=1}^{K} P(w_j|z_k) P(z_k|d_i) \quad (1)$$

where $P(w_j|z_k)$ is the probability of word w_j occurring in topic z_k, and $P(z_k|d_j)$ is the probability of topic z_k for document d_i. The model parameters can be estimated by maximizing the log likelihood of the document collection D

$$L(D) = \sum_{i=1}^{N} \sum_{j=1}^{M} n(d_i, w_j) \log \sum_{k=1}^{K} P(w_j|z_k) P(z_k|d_i) \quad (2)$$

through Expectation-Maximization (EM) [12].

PLSA provides a simplistic solution to find topics of documents. There is no guarantee that documents are associated with similar topics. Furthermore, in PLSA there is no constraint on the parameters $\theta_{ki} = P(z_k|d_i)$, the number of which grows linearly with the data. Therefore, the model tends to overfit the data. Latent Dirichlet Allocation (LDA) [31] which is essentially the Bayesian version of PLSA, can alleviate the overfitting problem, but it still ignores the semantic relationships among documents. In this paper, we propose to use the semantic graphs of the document collection to enhance PLSA topic modelling.

4.2 Semantic Graph based Topic Model

Generally speaking, an entity $e \in V$ is likely to be relevant to a specific topic of a question if its adjacent entities in the semantic graph are largely relevant to that topic. Following this intuition, we define a regularization term for the learning of topic model:

$$R_V(G) = (1-\mu) \sum_{i=1}^{|D|} \sum_{k=1}^{K} (P(z_k|d_i) - \sum_{e_i \in V_l} \sum_{e_u \in V_{d_i}} P(z_k|e_i) w(e_i|e_u))^2$$
$$+ \mu \sum_{i=1}^{|D|} \sum_{k=1}^{K} (P(z_k|d_i) - \sum_{e_j \in V_g} \sum_{e_u \in V_{d_i}} P(z_k|e_j) w(e_j|e_u))^2 \quad (3)$$

where μ is a bias parameter which strikes the optimal balance between the local semantic graph and the global semantic graph. V_l and V_g are two set of entities derived by local semantic graph and global semantic graph (see Section 4.2.1), respectively. $P(z_k|e_i)$ and $P(z_k|e_j)$ are estimated in the same way as $P(z_k|d_i)$ by using the EM algorithm (see Section 5.4.1). $w(e_i|e_u)$ is the weight between entity e_i and e_u in local semantic graph, $w(e_j|e_u)$ is the weight between entity e_j and e_u in global semantic graph (see Section 4.2.2).

To incorporate both the textual information and the semantic graph into the topic model, we define a **regularized propagation** framework by adding the regularization term with weight λ to the log-likelihood as follows:

$$L'_{rp}(D) = -(1-\lambda) L(D) + \lambda R_V(G_D) \quad (4)$$

where R_V is defined in equation (3). By minimizing R_V, we will smooth the topic distribution on the semantic graphs, where adjacent entities would have similar topic distributions. On the other hand, by minimizing $-L(C)$, we will find $P(z_i|d)$ and $P(w|z_i)$ which fit the text as much as possible. The parameter $\lambda \in [0, 1]$ is set to control the balance between the log-likelihood and the smoothness of topic distributions over the semantic graphs. When $\lambda = 0$, the

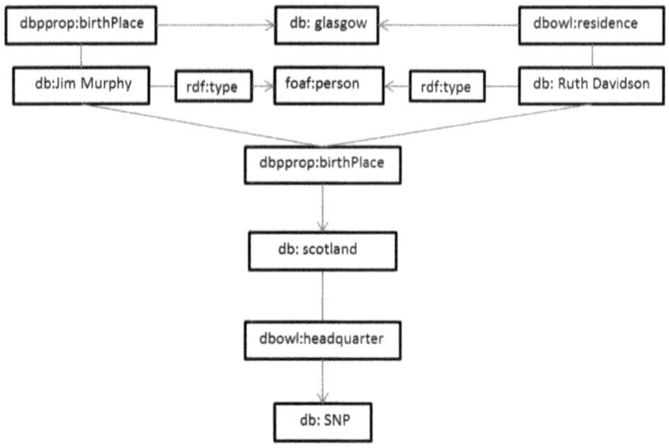

Figure 2: A sample semantic graph

objective function backs off to the standard PLSA. Minimizing $L'_{rp}(D)$ would only give us the topics which best fit the content of the document collection D. When $\lambda = 1$, the objective function backs off to R_V, which can be deemed as a "loss function" to measure how well the topic distributions on the semantic graph are consistent with the topic distribution on the documents. This is related to the objective of spectral clustering (e.g., ratio cut [8]). By minimizing $L'_{rp}(D)$, we can extract question clusters that making use of not only the text content of documents but also the structure of semantic graphs.

4.2.1 Mapping Questions into Semantic Graphs

When computing $P(e_j|e_u)$ in the above SGTM model, the method of [26] is adopted to construct the semantic graph. We start with a set of input entities C, which is found by using the off-the-shelf entity recognition tool DBpedia Spotlight[4].

We then create a directed graph G as follows: 1) we define the set of entities V of G to be made up of all input entities, i.e., we set $V := C$; 2) we connect the entities in V based on the directed paths found between them in DBpedia. Specifically, the set of entities in V are expanded into a graph by conducting a depth-first search along the DBpedia graph and adding all the visited relations and entities, to a certain limit. So the finally constructed semantic graph consists of all the "seed" entities identified from the documents together with all the edges found along the paths up to maximal length L that connect them. In this work, we set $L = 2$, as we find that the model with $L > 2$ tends to produce very large graphs and introduce lots of noise.

Figure 2 illustrates an example of a semantic graph generated from the set of entities { **db:Jim Mruphy, db:Ruth Davidson, db:SNP** }, which are found in the question "Have Jim Murphy and Ruth Davidson won SNP's general election?" Starting from these seed entities, we conduct a depth-first search to add relevant intermediate entities and relations to G (e.g., **db:scotland** and **foaf:person**). As a result, we obtain a semantic graph with additional entities and edges which provide us with rich knowledge about the original entities. Please note that we create two kinds of semantic graphs, namely, local semantic graph and global semantic graph. A local semantic graph is built for an individual question (associated with its answers) in order to detect its pairwise contextual similarities with other questions. The global semantic graph is constructed from the entities in the entire question archive, in order to capture the global contextual information of all existing questions.

[4]https://github.com/dbpedia-spotlight/dbpedia-spotlight

4.2.2 Semantic Relation Weighting

So far, we simply traverse a set of input entities from DBpedia graph. However, DBpedia ontology contains semantic relations at different levels which may not be equally informative. For example, in Figure 2, the seed entities **db:Jim Murphy** and **db:Ruth Davidson** can be connected through both **rdf:type foaf:person** and **dbpprop:birthPla**
but the former is less informative since it can apply to a large number of entities (i.e., all people in DBpedia). We can use real-valued weights to describe the degree of correlation between entities in the graph, and the core idea underlying our weighting scheme is to reward those edges that are most specific to the entities connected by them. Therefore we define the weighting function as

$$W = -\log(P(W_{Pred})) \tag{5}$$

where W is the weight of an edge, $P(W_{Pred})$ is the probability that the predicate W_{Pred} (such as **rdf:type**) is describing the specific semantic relation. This measure is based on the hypothesis that specificity is a good estimator for relevance. We can compute the document frequency for each type of predicates, as we have the whole DBpedia database available and are able to query for all possible realizations of the variable X_{Pred}. $P(W_{Pred})$ is then defined in a similar way as the tf-idf [23] representation of W_{Pred}. In our example, an edge labelled with **rdf:type** will accordingly get a weight W which is considerably lower than those labelled with **dbpprop:birthplace**.

There are often multiple relations between two entities, so the relation with the highest weight will be selected as the final edge. For instance, in the above example, **db:Jim Murphy** and **db:Ruth Davidson** can be connected by **db:glasgow**, **foaf:person**, and **db:scotland**. The path to **db:glasgow** will be selected since **dbowl:residence** has a higher weight than **dbpprop:birthPlace** and **rdf:type**.

5. RETRIEVAL MODELS

5.1 Classic Language Model

Using the classic (query-likelihood) language model [34] for information retrieval, we can measure the relevance of an archive question d with respect to the query question q as:

$$P_{cla}(q|d) = \prod_{w \in q} P_{cla}(w|d) \tag{6}$$

assuming that each term w in the query q is generated independently by the unigram model of document d. The probabilities $P_{cla}(w|d)$ are estimated from the bag of words in document d with Dirichlet prior smoothing.

5.2 Translation-based Language Model

There are often lexical gaps between a query question and archive questions in CQA. For example, "Where can I see movies for free online" and "Anyone share me a DVD streaming link?" probably have the same meaning but are expressed in quite different words. It has been demonstrated that this issue could be addressed by the translation-based language model [16,33]:

$$P_{tra}(q|d) = \prod_{w \in q} P_{tra}(w|d) \quad (7)$$

$$P_{tra}(w|d) = \sum_{t \in d} P(w|t)P(t|d) \quad (8)$$

where $P(w|t)$ represents the probability of a document term t being translated into a query term w. As in [33], we estimate such word-to-word translation probabilities $P(w|t)$ on a parallel corpus that consists of 200,000 archived question-answer pairs from Yahoo! Answers.

5.3 Topic-based Language Model

There could be different topics underlying different questions. In this paper, we propose to take the latent topics into account for question retrieval in the language modelling framework:

$$P_{top}(q|d) = \prod_{w \in q} P_{top}(w|d) \quad (9)$$

$$P_{top}(w|d) = \sum_{k=1}^{N} P(w|z_k)P(z_k|d) \quad (10)$$

where z_k represents a latent topics learned from the TMBP model [10], $P(w|z_k)$ is the unigram language model of topic z_k, and $P(z_k|d)$ is the probability that document d belongs to topic z_k. In this model, topics are captured at the concept level since an entity network is incorporated into the topic modelling framework. However, instead of exploiting external knowledge, such as DBpedia, the topic distribution of each entity is learned indirectly from its corresponding documents.

5.4 Semantics-based Language Model

The semantics-based language model proposed by us aims to capture the latent topics in a better way via exploiting the hidden interactions among different entities in the SGTM. It can be descried formally as follows:

$$P_{sem}(q|d) = \prod_{w \in q} P_{sem}(w|d) \quad (11)$$

$$P_{sem}(w|d) = \sum_{k'=1}^{N} P(w|z'_k)P_E(z'_k|d) \quad (12)$$

where z'_k represents a latent topics, $P(w|z'_k)$ is its corresponding unigram language model and $P_E(z'_k|d)$ is the probability that the question d belongs to that topic (cf. Section 5.4.1).

Compared to the topic-based language model of [17], the semantics-based language model presented above is more general and more robust, because instead of learning topics solely from the document collection at the word-level, it utilizes the SGTM topics which are at multiple semantic levels, namely words, entities, and the entity relations extracted from the knowledge repository, DBpedia.

5.4.1 *Model Fitting with the EM Algorithm*

To estimate $P(w|z_k)$ and $P(z_k|d)$ in the above model, we use the Expectation Maximization (EM) algorithm, which alternates two steps, E-step and M-step. The unobserved latent variables in our model include $\phi = P(w_j|z_k)$, $\theta = P(z_k|d_i)$, and $\varphi = P(z_k|e_l)$.

Let us first consider the parameter estimation in PLSA. In E-step, we calculate the posterior probabilities $P(z_k|d_i, w_j, e_l)$:

$$P(z_k|d_i, w_j) = \frac{P(w_j|z_k)P(z_k|d_i)}{\sum_{k'=1}^{K} P(w_j|z_{k'})P(z_{k'}|d_i)} \quad (13)$$

$$P(z_k|d_i, e_l) = \frac{P(z_k|e_l)P(e_l|d_i)}{\sum_{k'=1}^{K} P(z_{k'}|e_l)P(e_l|d_i)} \quad (14)$$

In the M-step, we maximize the expected complete data log-likelihood for PLSA:

$$Q_D = \sum_{i=1}^{N}\sum_{j=1}^{M} n(d_i, w_j) \sum_{k=1}^{K} P(z_k|d_i, w_j) \log \sum_{k=1}^{K} P(w_j|z_k)P(z_k|d_i) \quad (15)$$

There is a closed-form solution [10] to maximize Q_D, which are listed in Equation 16, 17, and 18.

$$P(w_j|z_k) = \frac{\sum_{i=1}^{N} n(d_i, w_j)P(z_k|d_i, w_j)}{\sum_{j'=1}^{M}\sum_{i=1}^{N} n(d_i, w_{j'})P(z_k|d_i, w_{j'})} \quad (16)$$

$$P(z_k|d_i) = \frac{\sum_{j=1}^{M} n(d_i, w_j)P(z_k|d_i, w_j)}{\sum_{j'=1}^{M} n(d_i, w_{j'})} \quad (17)$$

$$P(z_k|e_l) = \frac{\sum_{s=1}^{S} n(e_l, w_s)P(z_k|d_i, e_l)}{\sum_{s'=1}^{S} n(e_l, w_{s'})} \quad (18)$$

Thus the model parameters in PLSA could be estimated efficiently using the standard EM algorithm. However, due to the introduction of the regularizer $R_V(G)$, there is no such closed form solutions for parameter estimation in SGTM (Equation 4). Fortunately, we can use the generalized EM algorithm [25] to maximize the log-likelihood of $L'_{rp}(D)$. In the following, we will explain the model fitting procedure for $L'_{rp}(D)$.

It is easy to see that $L'_{rp}(D)$ and $L(D)$ share the same hidden variables z_k, and therefore could have the same E-step. Since the regularization $R_V(G)$ doesn't involve the parameter $P(w_j|z_k)$, we can still use the same M-step estimation for $P(w_j|z_k)$ as in Equation 16. Now the problem is how to estimate the parameter values $\phi = P(z_k|d_i)$ and $\theta = P(z_k|e_l)$. Instead of maximizing $P(z_k|d_i)$ and $P(z_k|e_l)$ directly, the generalized EM algorithm tires to improve the expected $P(z_k|d_i)$ as follows. First, we find $\theta_{t+1}^{(1)}$ using Equation 13 and 14, which maximizes Q_D instead of $L'_{rp}(D)$. Then, we start from $\theta_{t+1}^{(1)}$ and try to minimize $R_V(G)$, which can be done through the Newton-Raphson method [4]. Given a function $f(x)$ and the initial value x_t, the Newton-Raphson updating formula to decrease $f(x)$ is $x_{t+1} = x_t - \xi \frac{f'(x)}{f''(x)}$, where $0 \le \xi \le 1$ is the step parameter. With $\theta_{t+1}^{(1)}$, we can decrease $R(G)$ by updating $P(z_k|d_i)$ in each step.

$$P_E(z_k|d)_{t+1}^{(n+1)} = \xi P(z_k|d)_{t+1}^{(n)} + (1-\xi) \sum_{e \in V_d} \frac{P(z_k|e)}{|V_d|} \quad (19)$$

where $P(z_k|d_i, e_l)$ is obtained from the initial E-step, the step parameter ξ can be interpreted as a controlling factor of smoothing the topic distribution among the adjacent entities. It repeatedly updates $P_E(z_k|d)^n_{t+1}$ until $P_E(z_k|d)^{n+1}_{t+1} \leq P_E(z_k|d)^n_{t+1}$. We summarize the generalised EM algorithm for parameter estimation in this regularized propagation framework by using generalized EM algorithm in Algorithm 1.

5.5 Mixture Model

Since the classic language model, the translation-based language model and the semantics-based language model cover different grained semantic levels, it would be beneficial to combine their strengths for question retrieval. So we can mix the above language models via linear combination:

$$P_{mix}(q|d) = \alpha P_{cla}(q|d) + \beta P_{tra}(q|d) + \gamma P_{sem}(q|d) \quad (20)$$

where α, β, and γ are three non-negative weight parameters satisfying $\alpha + \beta + \gamma = 1$. When $\gamma = 0$, the complete mixture model backs off to the current state-of-the-art approach, i.e., the combination of the classic language model and the translation-based language model [33].

Algorithm 1: Model fitting for regularized propagation

Input : Input data, which includes: $G = (V, E)$ with word occurrences $n(d_i, w_j)$. The number of topics K, Newton step parameter γ, regularization parameter λ.

Output: $\phi = P(w_j|z_k)$, $\theta = P(z_k|d_i)$, and $\varphi = P(z_k|e_l)$

1: Random initialize the probability distribution ϕ_0 and θ_0
2: $t \leftarrow 0$;
while $t < MaxIteration$ **do**
  E-step: Calculate $P(z_k|d_i, w_j)$ and $P(z_k|d_i, e_l)$ as in Eq. 13 and 14
  M-step:
  Re-estimate $P(w_j|z_k)$ as in Eq. 16
  Re-estimate $P(z_k|d_i)$ as in Eq. 17
  Re-estimate $P(z_k|e_l)$ as in Eq. 18
  $P(z_k|d_i)^1_{t+1} \leftarrow P(z_k|d_i)_{t+1}$
  Calculate $P(z_k|d_i)^2_{t+1}$ as in Eq. 19
  while $L'_{rp}(C)^2_{t+1} > L'_{rp}(C)^1_{t+1}$ **do**
    $P(z_k|d_i)^1_{t+1} \leftarrow P(z_k|d_i)^2_{t+1}$
    Calculate θ^2_{t+1}, update $P(z_k|e)_{t+1}$
  end
  if $L'_{rp}(C)(\theta^{(1)}_{t+1}) \geq L'_{rp}(C)(\theta_t)$ **then**
    $P(z_k|d_i)_{t+1} \leftarrow P(z_k|d_i)^1_{t+1}$
    update $P(z_k|e)_{t+1}$
  end
  else
    Keep current θ, ϕ
  end
  $t \leftarrow t + 1$
end

6. EXPERIMENTS

6.1 Experimental Setup

We conducted experiments on two real-world CQA datasets. The first dataset, YA, comes from Yahoo! Answers. It is part of Yahoo! Labs' Webscope[5] L6 dataset that consists of 4,483,032 questions with their answers from 1 January 2006 to 1 January 2007. The second dataset, WA, comes from WikiAnswers. It contains 824,320 questions with their answers collected from WikiAnswers[6] from 1 January 2012 to 1 June 2012.

[5]http://webscope.sandbox.yahoo.com/

Table 1: Statistics of the YA and WA datasets

	YA	WA
# of questions	40,000	40,000
# of entities (local)	123,263	83,541
# of entities (global)	27,324	24,750
# of relations (local)	142,454	159,492
# of relations (global)	71,719	69,713

In order to produce the semantic graphs, we first apply DBpedia Spotlight on each question-answer pair of these two datasets. We use the *subject* field as question part and the *bestanswer* field as the answer part. The text of questions and answers have been preprocessed by case-folding and stopword-removal (using a standard list of 418 common words). Given the disambiguated entities (see Section 4.2.1), we create local and global entity collections, respectively, for constructing local and global semantic graphs. The creation process of entity collections is organized as a pipeline of filtering operations:

1. The isolated entities, which have no connections with the other members of the entity collection in the DBpedia repository, would be removed, since are almost useless in the topic propagation process.
2. The infrequent entities, which appear in less than five documents when constructing the global entity collection, would be discarded.
3. Similar to the previous step, we discard entities that appear less than twice in the question archive when constructing the local entity collections.

6.2 Experiments with Topic Modelling

We first experimented with topic modelling on 40,000 questions that are randomly sampled from the top ten categories of YA and WA dataset, respectively. The statistics of these two datasets along with their corresponding entities and relations are shown in Table 1. The top ten categories distributions in these two datasets are shown in Figure 3.

We randomly split each of the dataset into a training set, a validation set, and a test set with the ratio 2:1:1. We learned the parameters of the Semantic Graph based Topic Model (SGTM) as well as several other representative topic models from the training set, tuned the parameters of each model on the validation set, and evaluated the performance of each model on the test set. To demonstrate the effectiveness of our SGTM method, we compare it with the following topic modelling techniques:

- **PLSA:** The baseline approach which only employs the classic Probabilistic Latent Semantic Analysis [12].
- **ATM:** Author Topic Model, which combines LDA with authorship network [28]. In our experiments, authors are replaced with entities.

[6]http://wiki.answers.com/

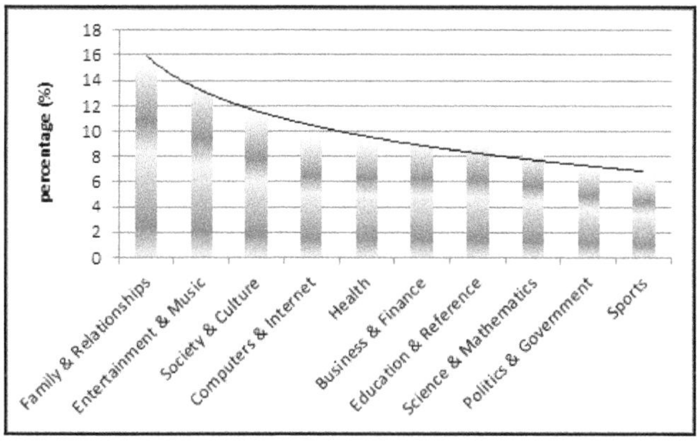

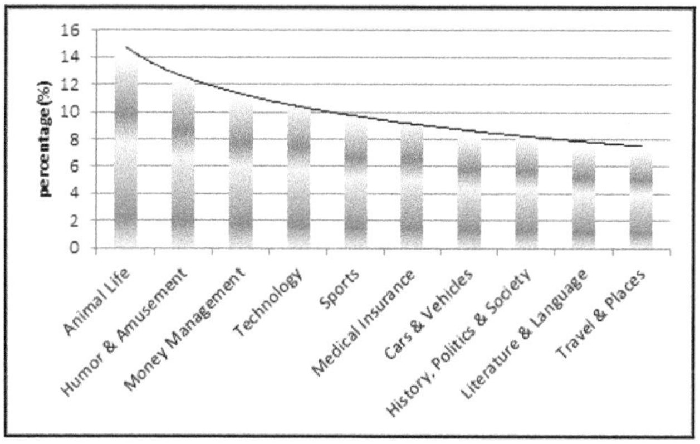

Figure 3: (a) and (b) show the category distribution of YA and WA datasets respectively

- **TMBP:** The state-of-the-art approach, Topic Model with Biased Propagation [10], which combines PLSA with an entity network (without using any external knowledge, such as DBpedia).

- **SGTM:** Our proposed Semantic Graph based Topic Model (See Section 4.2).

In order to evaluate our proposed topic model and compare it to existing ones, we use two metrics, accuracy (AC) and normalized mutual information (NMI), which are popular for evaluating the effectiveness of clustering methods. The accuracy is defined as $AC = \frac{\sum_1^n \delta(a_i, map(l_i))}{n}$ [32], where n denotes the total number of questions, $\delta(x, y)$ is the delta function that equals one if $x = y$ and zero otherwise, and $map(l_i)$ is the mapping function that maps each cluster label l_i to the corresponding label from the data corpus. Given two sets of document clusters, C and C', their mutual information is defined as: $MI(C, C') = \sum_{c_i \in C, c'_j \in C'} p(c_i, c'_j) \cdot \log_2 \frac{p(c_i, c'_j)}{p(c_i) \cdot p(c'_j)}$ [32], where $p(c_i)$ and $p(c'_j)$ are the probabilities that a randomly chosen document belongs to the clusters c_i and c'_j, respectively, and $p(c_i, c'_j)$ is the joint probability that a randomly chosen document belongs to the cluster c_i and c'_j at the same time.

Parameter Setting: For PLSA, we only use question-answer pairs for question clustering with no additional entity information. For ATM, we use symmetric Dirichlet priors in the LDA estimation with $\alpha = 50/K$ and $\beta = 0.01$, which are common settings in the literature. For TMBP, an entity-based heterogeneous network is constructed, and its parameter settings were set to be identical to those in [10].

Consistent to our previous setting of top 10 categories, we set the number of topics (K) to be 10 for both YA and WA. Figure 4 shows how the SGTM clustering performance varies with the different parameter values. The essential parameters in the SGTM framework are λ and μ. As mentioned in Section 4.2, λ controls the relative importance of the inherent textual information against the semantic graph information, and μ controls the balance between the local semantic graph and the global semantic graph. When $\lambda = 0$, it is the baseline PLSA model. When $\lambda = 1$, is is entirely determined by the graph regulation term R_V (cf. Equation 3). The performance of question clustering were tuned on the validation set and evaluated on the training set through 5-fold validation. The results reported in Figure 4 are those averaged over the five trials. It can be seen that SGTM with global semantic graphs generally performs better than SGTM with local semantic graphs, which possibly suggests that the global context is more important than the local context for the purpose of question clustering. Furthermore, the best performance is achieved when combining these two with the parameter setting: $\lambda = 0.4$ and $\mu = 0.5$.

Table 2 depicts the question clustering performances of different topic modelling methods. For each method, 20 test runs are conducted on the test set, and the final performance scores were calculated by averaging the scores from those runs. It can be seen that ATM outperforms the baseline PLSA with additional entity network information. As expected, TMBP outperforms ATM since it directly incorporates the heterogeneous network of entities. Our proposed SGTM improves accuracy by 9.1% over the classical PLSA baseline, and 2.9% over the state-of-the-art TMBP on YA dataset. A comparison using the paired t-test clearly shows that SGTM outperforms all the other methods PLSA, ATM, and TMBP significantly. This indicates that exploiting the semantic graph knowledge greatly improve the performance of topic modelling.

6.3 Experiments with Question Retrieval

We then experimented with question retrieval with a similar setup in [33]: 50 questions were randomly sampled from the YA and WA datasets respectively for testing, and the top archive questions (i.e., search results) returned for each test query question were manually labelled as either relevant or not.

In our question retrieval experiments, we compare the following four approaches:

- the baseline approach which only employs the classic language model (C);

- the state-of-the-art approach which combines the classic language model and the translation-based language model (C+T) [33];

- the proposed hybrid approach which blends the classic language model, the translation-based language model, and the topic-based language model (C+T+T) [10];

- a hybrid approach which combines the classic language model, the translation-based language model, and the semantics-based language model (C+T+S).

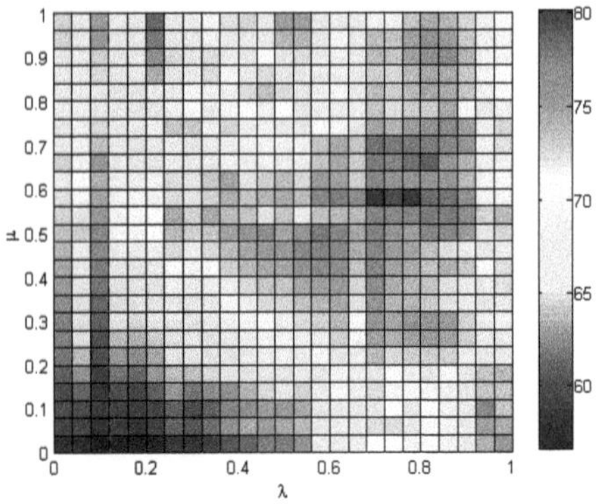

(a) YA

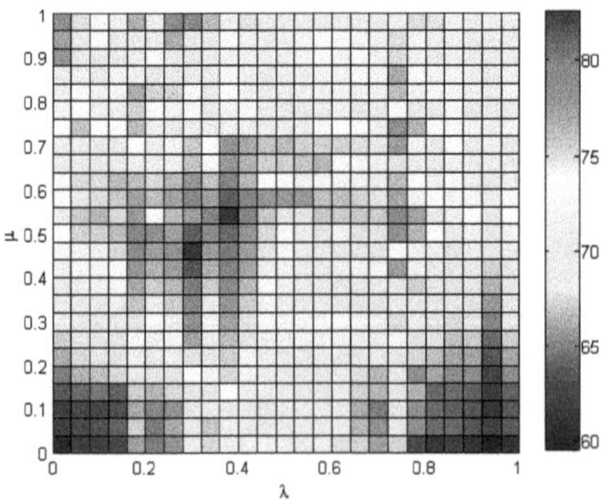

(b) WA

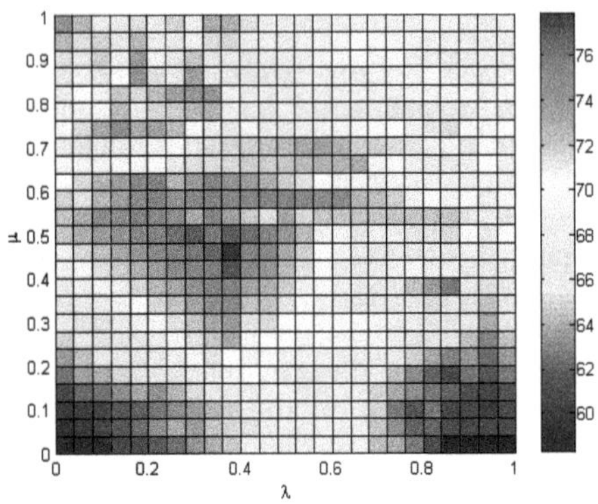

(c) YA

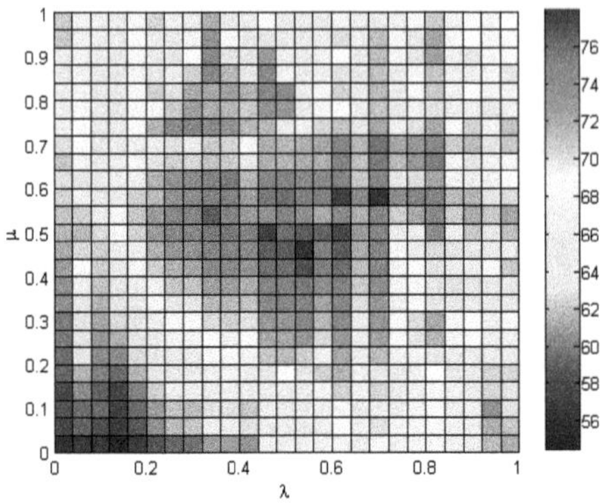

(d) WA

Figure 4: (a) and (b) show the accuracy (%) of SGTM framework with varying parameters λ and μ; (c) and (d) show the NMI (%) of SGTM framework with varying parameters λ and μ.

Table 2: The clustering performance of different methods on (a) YA and (b) WA datasets (-*-* and -* indicate the statistical significance of performance decrease from that of SGTM with p-value <0.01 and p-value < 0.05, respectively).

(a) YA

	PLSA	**ATM**	**TMBP**	**SGTM**
AC	0.662-*-*	0.685-*	0.724-*	0.753
NMI	0.657-*-*	0.732-*	0.765-*	0.819

(b) WA

	PLSA	**ATM**	**TMBP**	**SGTM**
AC	0.636-*-*	0.649-*-*	0.652-*	0.694
NMI	0.654-*-*	0.689-*-*	0.717-*	0.734

Parameter Setting: All parameter values of these approaches to question retrieval were tuned according to Precision at 10 (P@10) [22] or Mean Average Precision (MAP) [22]. The mixture coefficients in Equation 20 were tuned on the training data to achieve optimal results, as shown in Table 3. In the mixture models (C+T) and (C+T+S), the ratio between parameter values α and β was set as same as those in [33]. All the other parameters were set to their optimal values that have been found in Section 6.2.

Previously the number of topics K were set a priori as 10 (the number of categories) as we need the category label for calculating the accuracy. However, using only 10 topics is not necessarily the optimal value for the question retrieval task. Furthermore, it is well known that in general we need to use more topics for larger datasets to achieve the best topic modelling effect. Hence, we tried the mixture language model with different values of K. As shown in Figure 5, it is clear that the semantics-based approach (C+T+S) achieves the best result when $K = 40$, and the topic-based approach (C+T+T) achieves the optimal result when $K = 50$. These numbers are much smaller than the corresponding optimal K value (200) reported in the question-answer topic model [17]. As we explained in Section 5.4, in the topic-based language model, the topics were solely learned from the question-answer pairs at word-level, whereas in the semantics-based language model model, the topics are obtained from the question-answer pairs and also the external knowledge repository at both the word-level and the concept-level. Such *semantic* topics for each question are more powerful and expressive in SGTM, and thereby a much smaller number of topics is needed.

Given the optimal parameter values, the retrieval performances of those approaches on the test set, measured by $P@10$ and MAP, are reported in Table 4. Consistent to the observation in [33], adding the translation-based language model (C+T) brings substantial performance improvement

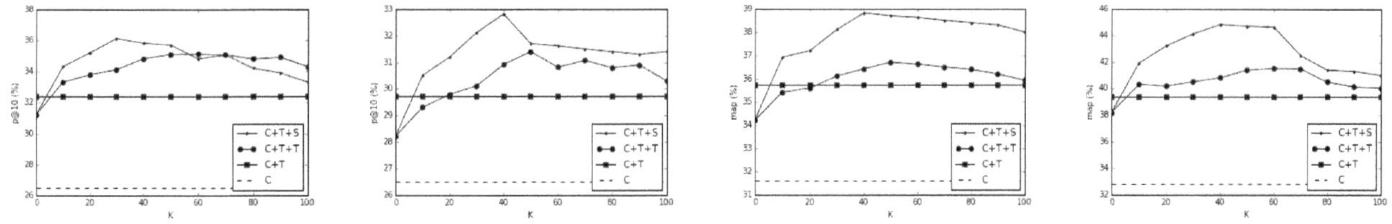

(a) YA (b) WA (c) YA (d) WA

Figure 5: (a) and (b) show the P@10 (%) of retrieval models with varying number of topics K; (c) and (d) show the NMI (%) of retrieval models with varying number of topics K.

Table 3: The mixture coefficients for different question retrieval approaches.

	C	C+T	C+T+T	C+T+S
α	1	0.3	0.18	0.18
β	0	0.7	0.42	0.42
γ	0	0.0	0.40	0.40

to the classic language model (C). More importantly, it is clear that our proposed hybrid approach incorporating the semantics-based language model (C+T+S) outperforms the state-of-the-art approaches (C+T) and also (C+T+T) significantly, according to both P@10 and MAP on YA and WA.

Table 4: The experimental results (statistical significance using t-test: ** indicates p-value < 0.01 while * indicates p-value < 0.05).

	C	C+T	C+T+T	C+T+S
P@10 (YA)	0.265	0.324	0.336	**0.341***
MAP (YA)	0.316	0.358	0.392	**0.433****
P@10 (WA)	0.263	0.297	0.315	**0.335***
MAP (WA)	0.328	0.394	0.421	**0.453***

7. CONCLUSION

In this paper, we propose a novel semantic graph based topic model (SGTM) for question retrieval. The new model supersedes the existing category-based language models because (i) question topics are more fine-grained than question categories; (ii) a question resides in only one category but could belong to multiple topics; and (iii) the integration of semantic graphs enables our topic model to capture the hidden contextual information of questions.

There are several interesting and promising directions in which this work could be extended. First, when learning the latent topics of questions, we could also include some metadata features such as the questions' categories (which have recently been shown to be useful for question retrieval [7]). Second, SGTM in the current form relies on one of the simplest topic models (PLSA), which makes sense as a first step towards integrating semantic graphs into topic models, but of course we could consider using more sophisticated topic models like LDA. Finally, besides question retrieval, SGTM could be applied to many other important tasks facing the lexical gap problem within CQA (such as question recommendation) and beyond (such as sentiment analysis on Twitter).

8. ACKNOWLEDGEMENTS

We thank the anonymous reviewer for their helpful comments. We acknowledge support from the EPSRC funded project named **A Situation Aware Information Infrastructure Project** (EP/L026015) and the **Integrated Multimedia City Data** (IMCD), a project within the ESRC-funded **Urban Big Data Centre** (ES/L011921/1). This work was also partly supported by NSF grant #61572223. Any opinions, findings and conclusions or recommendations expressed in this material are those of the author(s) and do not necessarily reflect the view of the sponsor.

9. REFERENCES

[1] Yang Bao, Nigel Collier, and Anindya Datta. A partially supervised cross-collection topic model for cross-domain text classification. CIKM '13, pages 239–248.

[2] Christian Bizer, Jens Lehmann, Kobilarov, Christian Becker, Richard Cyganiak, and Sebastian Hellmann. Dbpedia - a crystallization point for the web of data. volume 7, pages 154–165.

[3] David M. Blei, Andrew Y. Ng, Michael I. Jordan, and John Lafferty. Latent dirichlet allocation. volume 3, pages 459–565.

[4] Deng Cai, Qiaozhu Mei, Jiawei Han, and Chengxiang Zhai. Modeling hidden topics on document manifold. CIKM '08, pages 911–920.

[5] Li Cai, Guangyou Zhou, Kang Liu, and Jun Zhao. Large-scale question classification in cqa by leveraging wikipedia semantic knowledge. CIKM '11, pages 1321–1330.

[6] Xin Cao, Gao Cong, Bin Cui, and Christian S. Jensen. A generalized framework of exploring category information for question retrieval in community question answer archives. WWW '2010.

[7] Xin Cao, Gao Cong, Bin Cui, Christian Søndergaard Jensen, and Ce Zhang. The use of categorization information in language models for question retrieval. CIKM'2009.

[8] Pak K. Chan, Martine D. F. Schlag, and Jason Y. Zien. Spectral k-way ratio-cut partitioning and clustering. DAC '93, pages 749–754.

[9] Xu Chen, Mingyuan Zhou, and Lawrence Carin. The contextual focused topic model. KDD '12, pages 96–104.
[10] Hongbo Deng, Jiawei Han, Bo Zhao, Yintao Yu, and Cindy Xide Lin. Probabilistic topic models with biased propagation on heterogeneous information networks. KDD '11, pages 1271–1279.
[11] Weiwei Guo and Mona Diab. Semantic topic models: Combining word distributional statistics and dictionary definitions. EMNLP '11, pages 552–561.
[12] Thomas Hofmann. Unsupervised learning by probabilistic latent semantic analysis. In *Machine Learning*, volume 45, pages 256–269.
[13] Liangjie Hong, Byron Dom, Siva Gurumurthy, and Kostas Tsioutsiouliklis. A time-dependent topic model for multiple text streams. KDD '11, pages 832–840.
[14] Eva Hörster, Rainer Lienhart, and Malcolm Slaney. Image retrieval on large-scale image databases. CIVR '07, pages 17–24.
[15] Ioana Hulpus, Conor Hayes, Marcel Karnstedt, and Derek Greene. Unsupervised graph-based topic labelling using dbpedia. WSDM '13, pages 465–474.
[16] Jiwoon Jeon, W. Bruce Croft, and Joon Ho Lee. Finding similar questions in large question and answer archives. pages 84–90, Bremen, Germany, 2005.
[17] Zongcheng Ji, Fei Xu, Bin Wang, and Ben He. Question-answer topic model for question retrieval in community question answering. CIKM '12, pages 2471–2474, 2012.
[18] Hyungsul Kim, Yizhou Sun, Julia Hockenmaier, and Jiawei Han. Etm: Entity topic models for mining documents associated with entities. ICDM '12, pages 349–358.
[19] Fang Li, Tingting He, Xinhui Tu, and Xiaohua Hu. Incorporating word correlation into tag-topic model for semantic knowledge acquisition. CIKM '12, pages 1622–1626.
[20] Huajing Li, Zhisheng Li, Wang-Chien Lee, and Dik Lun Lee. A probabilistic topic-based ranking framework for location-sensitive domain information retrieval. SIGIR '09, pages 331–338.
[21] Linlin Li, Benjamin Roth, and Caroline Sporleder. Topic models for word sense disambiguation and token-based idiom detection. ACL '10, pages 1138–1147.
[22] Christopher D. Manning, Prabhakar Raghavan, and Hinrich Schtze. *Introduction to Information Retrieval*. Cambridge University Press, 2008.
[23] Christopher D. Manning, Prabhakar Raghavan, and Hinrich Schütze. *Introduction to Information Retrieval*. Cambridge University Press, New York, NY, USA, 2008.
[24] Qiaozhu Mei, Deng Cai, Duo Zhang, and ChengXiang Zhai. Topic modeling with network regularization. WWW '08, pages 101–110.
[25] Qiaozhu Mei, Deng Cai, Duo Zhang, and Chengxiang Zhai. Topic modeling with network regularization. WWW '08, pages 342–351.
[26] Michael Schuhmacher and Simone Paolo Ponzetto. Knowledge-based graph document modeling. WSDM '14, pages 543–552.
[27] Mark Steyvers, Padhraic Smyth, Michal Rosen-Zvi, and Thomas Griffiths. Probabilistic author-topic models for information discovery. KDD '04, pages 306–315.
[28] Jie Tang, Jing Zhang, Limin Yao, Juanzi Li, Li Zhang, and Zhong Su. Arnetminer: Extraction and mining of academic social networks. KDD '08, pages 428–437.
[29] Ivan Titov and Ryan McDonald. Modeling online reviews with multi-grain topic models. WWW '08, pages 111–120.
[30] Hongning Wang, Yue Lu, and Chengxiang Zhai. Latent aspect rating analysis on review text data: A rating regression approach. KDD '10, pages 783–792.
[31] Xing Wei and W. Bruce Croft. Lda-based document models for ad-hoc retrieval. SIGIR '06, pages 326–335.
[32] Wei Xu, Xin Liu, and Yihong Gong. Document clustering based on non-negative matrix factorization. SIGIR '03, pages 267–273.
[33] Xiaobing Xue, Jiwoon Jeon, and W. Bruce Croft. Retrieval models for question and answer archives. SIGIR '08.
[34] ChengXiang Zhai. *Statistical Language Models for Information Retrieval*. Morgan & Claypool Publishers, 2008.
[35] ChengXiang Zhai, Atulya Velivelli, and Bei Yu. A cross-collection mixture model for comparative text mining. KDD '04, pages 743–748.
[36] Guangyou Zhou, Yang Liu, Fang Liu, Daojian Zeng, and Jun Zhao. Improving question retrieval in community question answering using world knowledge. IJCAI '13, pages 2239–2245, 2013.
[37] Xiaojin Zhu, Zoubin Ghahramani, and John Lafferty. Semi-supervised learning using gaussian fields and harmonic functions. ICML '03, pages 912–919.

Modeling Check-in Preferences with Multidimensional Knowledge: A Minimax Entropy Approach

Jingjing Wang, Min Li, Jiawei Han and Xiaolong Wang
Department of Computer Science
University of Illinois at Urbana - Champaign
Urbana, IL 61801
{jwang112, minli3, hanj, xwang95}@illinois.edu

ABSTRACT

We propose a single unified minimax entropy approach for user preference modeling with multidimensional knowledge. Our approach provides a discriminative learning protocol which is able to simultaneously a) leverage explicit human knowledge, which are encoded as explicit features, and b) model the more ambiguous hidden intent, which are encoded as latent features. A latent feature can be carved by any parametric form, which allows it to accommodate arbitrary underlying assumptions. We present our approach in the scenario of check-in preference learning and demonstrate it is capable of modeling user preference in an optimized manner.

Check-in preference is a fundamental component of Point-of-Interest (POI) prediction and recommendation. A user's check-in can be affected at multiple dimensions, such as the particular time, popularity of the place, his/her category and geographic preference, etc. With the geographic preferences modeled as latent features and the rest as explicit features, our approach provides an in-depth understanding of users' time-varying preferences over different POIs, as well as a reasonable representation of the hidden geographic clusters in a joint manner. Experimental results based on the task of POI prediction/recommendation with two real-world check-in datasets demonstrate that our approach can accurately model the check-in preferences and significantly outperforms the state-of-art models.

1. INTRODUCTION

As the check-in feature becomes increasingly popular in major social network services (SNS) such as Foursquare, Facebook, etc., numerous research efforts have been aimed at mining users' check-in behaviors. In this paper, we consider the problem of modeling users' time-aware check-in preferences. Formally, our goal is to learn a time-aware distribution over POIs for each user: $p(l|u,t)$, where u denotes a user, t denotes a time point, l denotes a POI and $p(l|u,t)$ denotes the conditional probability that l is checked in given that the user is u and the time point is t. This distribution allows us to predict what are the top places a user would like to check in at a given time, which can be of great interest to both business owners and advertisement providers.

WSDM'16, February 22–25, 2016, San Francisco, CA, USA.

ISBN 978-1-4503-3716-8/16/02...$15.00

DOI: http://dx.doi.org/10.1145/2835776.2835839

To approach this problem, we propose a discriminative learning framework which allows a subset of the features to be latent under the *minimax entropy* principle. In contrast to the standard discriminative learning protocol (e.g. SVM, logistic regression) where features are readily available before training, we introduce the concept of *latent features*. The value of a latent feature is not known before training, but is specified by a parametric form with unknown parameters. The parametric form can capture arbitrary underlying assumptions to describe the feature. For example, if a set of latent features are cluster indicators, the parameters can specify the underlying clustering structure. During the training process, the latent parameters are jointly learned with the classification task. We illustrate in the following paragraphs why this is the desired strategy.

Why maximum entropy?

A naive way to estimate $p(l|u,t)$ is simple counting. For each user u at time t, we can get the histogram of POIs (l's) and view it as the objective distribution. While this distribution perfectly fits the seen data, it is not generalizable, *i.e.*, it can never predict unvisited POIs for users and will fail to generate outputs for unseen time points.

We prefer a model which *explains the seen data well and meanwhile has good generalizability*. To this end, instead of exactly matching $p(l|u,t)$ to the empirical distribution, it is natural to extract features from the `user-time-POI` $\langle utl \rangle$ tuples and impose the constraints that $p(l|u,t)$ match the empirical statistics in the feature space. Among these qualified distributions, we select the distribution with the maximum entropy as the optimal distribution, as it assumes least bias on the model beyond the constraints we specify [11].

Why minimax entropy? (Why latent features? Why should they be jointly learned?)

User preferences over POIs can be affected by explicit features such as the category of a POI, the day of a week, etc., meanwhile it can also be affected by the more ambiguous features such as the geographic region, which is less clear how to encode as features effectively. For example, it is not straightforward to draw the boundary for "downtown Manhattan" or to classify if a POI belongs to it. Therefore, we introduce latent features to model this kind of ambiguity. Taking the geographic feature as an example, we can assume there exist geographic clusters, each of which is specified by latent parameters: a center (coordinates of latitude and longitude) and a radius (a positive real number). Given a POI, we define a weight vector over different clusters as a *latent* feature vector, where the weight on each cluster is determined by a parametric function which takes the latitude-longitude of the POI as input. With both explicit and latent features, we propose a minimax entropy approach to jointly learn the latent parameters together with the check-in preferences ($p(l|u,t)$). The joint learning approach is motivated by the fact that *the clustering structure is not only determined by geographic proximity, but also affected by how well it explains user check-ins.* For example, even if two POIs are very close to each other geographically, if they have never been visited by the same user, it may not be appropriate to put them into the same cluster. In sum, the jointly learned geographic clusters are specially tailored to boost the learning task's performance rather than just provide a standalone clustering results.

Contributions

- We propose a single unified minimax entropy approach which elegantly leverages explicit features and latent features for user preference modeling. It boosts the flexibility and expressiveness of the standard discriminative learning models significantly.
- Flexible as the way latent features are defined by parametric forms, the parameters governing the latent features are recovered jointly with the learning task in a principled way, which serve to explain the inherent structure of the learning task.
- We demonstrate the effectiveness of our approach in the context of check-in preference learning with its rich types of information. It opens up a promising direction for preference learning with multidimensional heterogeneous knowledge.

The rest of the paper is organized as follows. Section 2 first details the modeling of users, POIs and the way we specify the geographic clusters; and then formally defines the problem. We introduce our framework for check-in preference modeling in Section 3 and discuss related work in Section 4. We analyze the connections of our approach to other standard approaches in Section 5, report our experimental results on real-world data in Section 6 and conclude our study in Section 7.

2. PROBLEM FORMULATION

In this section, we define the POI profiles and user profiles with both explicit knowledge and the latent geographic clustering structure governed by latent parameters. Then we give the formal definition of check-in preference modeling. The notations used in this paper are summarized in Table 1.

Let U, T, L, C be the user set, time set, POI set and category set respectively. Our data contains the histories of user check-ins.

DEFINITION 1 (CHECK-IN). *A check-in is denoted by a user-time-POI tuple $\langle utl \rangle$, where $u \in U, t \in T$ and $l \in L$. Each POI l is associated with its category, latitude and longitude. The time is represented by the day of week and hour of day*[1].

[1]There are 7x24 unique values in T under this setting. However, one can index time with finer or coarser granularity as well. Overlapped time intervals are also allowed.

Table 1: Summary of Notations

Symbol	Description
u, U	a user, user set
t, T	a time index, time index set; $day(t)$ and $hour(t)$ denote the day index and hour index of t, respectively
l, L	a POI, POI set; $cat(l)$ denotes the category of l
C	category set
$\mathbf{o} = (o_1, o_2, ..., o_R)$	the centers of the geographic clusters
$\mathbf{r} = (r_1, r_2, ..., r_R)$	the radiuses of the geographic clusters
$\mathbf{c}^u = (c_1^u, c_2^u, ..., c_C^u)$	u's category preference
$\mathbf{g}^u = (g_1^u, g_2^u, ..., g_R^u)$	u's geographic preference
$\mathbf{c}^l$	l's one-hot encoding of its category
$\mathbf{g}^l = (g_1^l, g_2^l, ..., g_R^l)$	l's weights on different regions
p^l	l's global popularity
$\mathbf{d}^l = (d_1^l, d_2^l, ..., d_7^l)$	l's daily popularity profile
$\mathbf{h}^l = (h_1^l, h_2^l, ..., d_{24}^l)$	l's hourly popularity profile
$\pi_{utl} = p(l\|u,t)$	the conditional probability of checking in at POI l given a user u and time t
$\tilde{\pi}_{ut} = \tilde{p}(u,t), \tilde{\pi}_{utl} = \tilde{p}(l\|u,t)$	the empirical distributions estimated from data
Π	the true check-in preference distribution

DEFINITION 2 (REGION). *A region is a geographic cluster defined by the latitude and longitude of the center $o = (o_{lat}, o_{lon})$ and a radius $r > 0$. The (o, r)'s are the latent parameters.*

DEFINITION 3 (POI PROFILE). *A POI l is represented by a profile*[2] $\rho(l) = [\mathbf{c}^l, \mathbf{g}^l(\mathbf{o}, \mathbf{r}), \mathbf{d}^l, \mathbf{h}^l, p^l]$.

- $\mathbf{c}^l$ (a one-hot encoding of l's category): $\mathbf{c}^l$ has $c_i^l = 1$ if the i-th category in C is the category of l and 0 otherwise.
- $\mathbf{g}^l$ (the geographic profile of l): The geographic profile of a POI is modeled by a weight vector over different regions. The weight is determined by the POI's distance to the center of a region and the radius of the region:

$$g_i^l = \exp(-\frac{dist(l, o_i)}{r_i}) \tag{1}$$

where $dist(\cdot,\cdot)$ is the Euclidean distance[3].

When $dist(l, o) = 0$, the weight reaches its maximum 1; as $dist(l, o)$ becomes larger, the weight decreases towards 0. The radius r controls the decreasing speed w.r.t $dist(l, o)$. A smaller r indicates a more concentrated cluster, *i.e.*, the weight decreases drastically as the distance increases. Note that the weight function does not necessarily have to be defined in this way. A function that can satisfy the desired properties suffices.

- p^l (global popularity of l): The global popularity of a POI is defined as the total number of check-ins at this POI.
- $\mathbf{d}^l, \mathbf{h}^l$ (the daily popularity profile and hourly popularity profile of l): POIs have time varying popularity as

[2]We use bold letters to denote column vectors. The comma between column vectors indicates a vertical stack of the vectors.
[3]Other distance measures apply as well.

well. For example, a nightclub has its rush hours at night but is either closed or rarely visited before sunset. We compute the time varying popularity based on the aggregate statistics from all users. d_i^l is the proportion of check-ins at l that happen on the ith day of a week and h_i^l is the proportion of check-ins at l that happen on the ith hour of a day.

DEFINITION 4 (USER PROFILE). *A user u is represented by a profile $\rho(u) = [\mathbf{c}^u, \mathbf{g}^u(\mathbf{o}, \mathbf{r})]$.*

- $\mathbf{c}^u$ (user u's preference over categories): We define user u's preference of category i (*i.e.*, c_i^u) to be the proportion of his/her check-ins that fall into category i.
- $\mathbf{g}^u$ (user u's preference over regions): In addition to the category preference, users are also characterized by their geographic preferences over different regions. We define user u's geographic preference of a region i (*i.e.*, g_i^u) to be the aggregate weights at region i of all his/her check-ins .

We are now able to formulate the check-in preferences modeling problem as follows.

PROBLEM 1 (CHECK-IN PREFERENCES MODELING). *Given a training set of user check-in tuples, where each tuple $\langle utl \rangle$ is associated with a user profile $\rho(u)$ and a POI profile $\rho(l)$, jointly learn the conditional probability of checking in at POI l given a user u and time t, denoted by $\pi_{utl} = p(l|u,t), \forall u,t,l$; and the geographic clustering structure governed by latent parameters $\mathbf{o}$ and $\mathbf{r}$.*

3. A MINIMAX ENTROPY APPROACH FOR MODELING CHECK-IN PREFERENCES

In this section, we first assume the latent parameters are given, *i.e.*, all the features are explicit, and present the maximum entropy (MaxEnt) model for learning the check-in preferences. Then we present the proposed minimax entropy model which estimates the latent parameters jointly with the preference learning.

3.1 A Maximum Entropy Model

The most aggressive way to model the check-in preferences is just to let π_{utl} equal the empirical distribution[4] $\tilde{\pi}_{utl} = \dfrac{\#\langle utl \rangle}{\sum_l \#\langle utl \rangle}$. However, this will overfit the data and is not generalizable. We want to construct a model which explains the seen data well, and meanwhile has good generalizability. To this end, we adopt the maximum entropy principle to specify $\{\pi_{utl}\}$, *i.e.*, we choose the most "uniform" distribution with carefully chosen constraints instantiated by features. These constraints should guarantee that our model accords with the data statistics we feel essential in modeling the check-in preferences.

[4]In this paper, we use $\#\langle utl \rangle$ to denote the number of appearances of the check-in tuple $\langle utl \rangle$ in the data, and $\#$ to denote the total number of check-ins. We use " $\tilde{}$ " to denote the empirical distribution. Later we will also see $\tilde{p}(u,t) = \tilde{\pi}_{ut} = \dfrac{\sum_l \#\langle utl \rangle}{\#}$

3.1.1 Features Based on Multidimensional Preferences

We consider the following factors to model check-in preferences: temporal preference, category preference, geographic preference and the popularity of the POI. Consider the following scenario: on a Friday evening, Alice just finished yet another week of hard work; she would like to have a great dinner at a seafood restaurant and then she figures a popular Boiling Crab branch is just nearby. Then it is very likely she checks in at this place. We design the following features to instantiate the constraints which will be used to specify our model $\{\pi_{utl}\}$.

- **Category Preference**. The extent to which a POI l matches a user u's category preference is estimated by $f_c(\langle utl \rangle) = {\mathbf{c}^u}^T \mathbf{c}^l$.
- **Geographic Preference**. The extent to which a POI l matches a user u's geographic preference is estimated by $f_g(\langle utl \rangle) = {\mathbf{g}^u}^T \mathbf{g}^l$.
- **Temporal Preference**. If we represent each time index t with two one-hot encodings: $\mathbf{d}^t$, $\mathbf{h}^t$ for the day and hour respectively, the extent to which a POI l's daily popularity matches a time t is estimated by $f_d(\langle utl \rangle) = {\mathbf{d}^l}^T \mathbf{d}^t$, and hourly popularity by $f_h(\langle utl \rangle) = {\mathbf{h}^l}^T \mathbf{h}^t$.
- **Popularity Preference**. As more popular POIs usually would expect more check-ins, we assign a popularity preference for each POI without distinguishing users. $f_p(\langle utl \rangle) = p^l$.

Let $\mathbf{f} = [f_c, f_g, f_d, f_h, f_p]^T$. It[5] measures how a POI matches a user's preference at a particular time. We employ constraints that require our model to accord with the data at each dimension of the preferences, *i.e.*, the model distribution matches the empirical distribution at the feature space:

$$\mathbb{E}_\pi(\mathbf{f}) = \mathbb{E}_{\tilde{\pi}}(\mathbf{f})$$

$$\text{i.e.,} \quad \sum_{u,t,l} \tilde{p}(u,t) p(l|u,t) \mathbf{f} = \sum_{u,t,l} \tilde{p}(u,t) \tilde{p}(l|u,t) \mathbf{f}$$

$$\text{i.e.,} \quad \sum_{u,t,l} \tilde{\pi}_{ut} \pi_{utl} \mathbf{f} = \sum_{u,t,l} \tilde{\pi}_{ut} \tilde{\pi}_{utl} \mathbf{f}$$

where $\mathbb{E}$ denotes expectation. Note that we do not model the joint distribution of u and t (*i.e.*, $p(u,t)$) since the goal is to predict l given u and t. We let $p(u,t) = \tilde{p}(u,t) = \tilde{\pi}_{u,t}$. The model parameters[6] here contain $\{\pi_{utl}, \forall u,t,l\}$ only. This also classifies our problem as a discriminative learning task (as opposed to generative learning).

3.1.2 A Maximum Entropy Model with Fixed Latent Parameters

With the constraints defined above, we formulate our MaxEnt model in this section.

[5]A complete notation should be $\mathbf{f}(\langle utl \rangle) = (f_c(\langle utl \rangle), f_g(\langle utl \rangle), f_d(\langle utl \rangle), f_h(\langle utl \rangle), f_p(\langle utl \rangle))^T$, in the following of the paper, we omit $(\langle utl \rangle)$ for brevity and readability.

[6]We slightly abuse the terminology *parameter*. Model parameters refer to π_{utl} and latent parameters refer to $(\mathbf{o}, \mathbf{r})$.

The conditional entropy of π_{utl} is given by

$$H(\pi) = -\sum_{u,t,l} \tilde{\pi}_{ut}\pi_{utl} \ln \pi_{utl} = -\mathbb{E}_{\pi}(\ln \pi_{utl})$$

As discussed in the previous section, we constrain the distribution π to a set $\mathcal{C}$ of allowed probability distributions:

$$\mathcal{C} = \{\pi | \sum_{u,t,l} \tilde{\pi}_{ut}\pi_{utl}\mathbf{f} = \sum_{u,t,l} \tilde{\pi}_{ut}\tilde{\pi}_{utl}\mathbf{f}\}$$

By the MaxEnt principle, we should select a model from $\mathcal{C}$ with maximum $H(\pi)$:

$$\pi^* = \arg\max_{\pi \in \mathcal{C}} H(\pi)$$

Therefore we have the following MaxEnt model for π:

$$\max_{\pi} -\sum_{u,t,l} \tilde{\pi}_{ut}\pi_{utl} \ln \pi_{utl} \quad (2)$$

$$s.t. \sum_{u,t,l} \tilde{\pi}_{ut}\pi_{utl}\mathbf{f} = \sum_{u,t,l} \tilde{\pi}_{ut}\tilde{\pi}_{utl}\mathbf{f} \quad (3)$$

$$\sum_{l} \pi_{utl} = 1 \quad \forall u,t \quad (4)$$

$$\pi_{utl} > 0 \quad \forall u,t,l \quad (5)$$

Note that equation (3) is a vector form of $|\mathbf{f}| = 5$ constraints, corresponding to the 5 dimensional preferences.

We solve the constrained optimization problem in the dual space (see Appendix A), which gives the following form of π_{utl}:

$$\pi_{utl} = \frac{\exp(\mathbf{w}^T\mathbf{f}(\langle utl \rangle))}{\sum_l \exp(\mathbf{w}^T\mathbf{f}(\langle utl \rangle))} \quad \forall u,t,l \quad (6)$$

where $\mathbf{w}$ is the Lagrange coefficients. Solving the primal problem turns out to be maximizing the log likelihood of the data with π_{utl} specified by Equation (6). Therefore we obtain the optimal $\mathbf{w}^*$ from the maximum likelihood estimation:

$$\mathbf{w}^* = \arg\max_{\mathbf{w}} LL \quad (7)$$

$$LL = \sum_{utl} \tilde{\pi}_{ut}\tilde{\pi}_{utl} \ln \pi_{utl} \quad (8)$$

Finally, the solution for the primal problem is given by:

$$\pi^*_{utl} = \frac{\exp(\mathbf{w^*}^T\mathbf{f})}{Z_{ut}}, \quad Z_{ut} = \sum_l \exp(\mathbf{w^*}^T\mathbf{f}) \quad \forall u,t,l$$

where $\mathbf{w}^*$ is the optimal Lagrange coefficients, each element of which corresponds to a constraint in Equation (3).

3.2 Recovering Latent Parameters via Minimax Entropy

In the previous section, we have completed the discussion for the case where we assume the latent parameters are given so that all the features are explicit. Now let us bring the latent features back. We have f_g as a *latent feature* which is parameterized by $(\mathbf{o}, \mathbf{r})$. Therefore $\mathbf{w}^*$ is also parameterized by $(\mathbf{o}, \mathbf{r})$. The optimal solution is thus $\pi^*(\mathbf{o}, \mathbf{r})$:

$$\pi^*_{utl}(\mathbf{o}, \mathbf{r}) = \frac{\exp(\mathbf{w}^*(\mathbf{o}, \mathbf{r})^T\mathbf{f}(\langle utl \rangle)(\mathbf{o}, \mathbf{r}))}{\sum_l \exp(\mathbf{w}^*(\mathbf{o}, \mathbf{r})^T\mathbf{f}(\langle utl \rangle)(\mathbf{o}, \mathbf{r}))} \quad \forall u,t,l$$

We propose that ***the optimal*** $(\mathbf{o}, \mathbf{r})$ ***should be chosen such that*** $\pi^*(\mathbf{o}, \mathbf{r})$ ***is minimized*** and justify this statement in this section.

To measure the quality of the check-in preference distribution, we use the standard Kullback-Leibler (KL) divergence [12] from $\pi^*(\mathbf{o}, \mathbf{r})$ to the true user check-in preference Π. Π is the true conditional distribution: $\Pi_{utl} = p_{true}(l|u,t)$[7]. The optimal $(\mathbf{o}, \mathbf{r})$ should give the smallest KL divergence:

$$(\mathbf{o}^*, \mathbf{r}^*) = \arg\min_{\mathbf{r}>0, \mathbf{o}} KL(\Pi, \pi^*(\mathbf{o}, \mathbf{r}))$$

where

$$\begin{aligned} KL(\Pi, \pi^*(\mathbf{o}, \mathbf{r})) &= \mathbb{E}_{\Pi}(\ln \Pi_{utl}) - \mathbb{E}_{\Pi}(\ln \pi^*_{utl}) \\ &= -\mathbb{E}_{\Pi}(\ln \pi^*_{utl}) - H(\Pi) \end{aligned}$$

The difficulty here is that the true distribution Π is unknown, thus we cannot directly evaluate the first term. However, under the assumption that our sample size is reasonably large, which means the expected feature statistics $\mathbb{E}_{\Pi}(\mathbf{f})$ can be approximated exactly by neglecting the estimation errors in the observed statistics $\mathbb{E}_{\tilde{\pi}}(\mathbf{f})$, we obtain the following theorem.

THEOREM 1. *The KL divergence from* $\pi^*(\mathbf{o}, \mathbf{r})$[8] *to the true distribution* Π *is given by* $KL(\Pi, \pi^*) = H(\pi^*) - H(\Pi)$

PROOF. We need to prove $\mathbb{E}_{\Pi}(\ln \pi^*_{utl}) = -H(\pi^*)$. As shown before, π^* has the following form:

$$\pi^*_{utl} = \frac{\exp(\mathbf{w^*}^T\mathbf{f})}{Z_{ut}}, Z_{ut} = \sum_l \exp(\mathbf{w^*}^T\mathbf{f}) \quad \forall u,t,l$$

where $\mathbf{w}^*$ is the optimal Lagrange coefficients. Hence we have

$$\begin{aligned} \mathbb{E}_{\Pi}(\ln \pi^*_{utl}) &= \mathbb{E}_{\Pi}(\mathbf{w^*}^T\mathbf{f}) - \mathbb{E}_{\Pi}(\ln Z_{ut}) \\ &= \mathbb{E}_{\tilde{\pi}}(\mathbf{w^*}^T\mathbf{f}) - \mathbb{E}_{\tilde{\pi}}(\ln Z_{ut}) \\ &\qquad \text{by } \mathbb{E}_{\tilde{\pi}}(\mathbf{f}) = \mathbb{E}_{\Pi}(\mathbf{f}) \\ &= \mathbb{E}_{\pi^*}(\mathbf{w^*}^T\mathbf{f}) - \mathbb{E}_{\pi^*}(\ln Z_{ut}) \\ &\qquad \text{by Equation (3)} \\ &= \mathbb{E}_{\pi^*}(\ln \pi^*_{utl}) = -H(\pi^*) \end{aligned}$$

and the result follows. □

As the entropy of Π is fixed, and the entropy of π^* is parameterized by $(\mathbf{o}, \mathbf{r})$, in order to minimize $KL(\Pi, \pi^*(\mathbf{o}, \mathbf{r}))$, we conclude that the latent variables should be estimated by minimizing the maximized entropy:

$$(\mathbf{o}^*, \mathbf{r}^*) = \arg\min_{\mathbf{o}, \mathbf{r}} \sum_{u,t,l} -\tilde{\pi}_{ut}\pi^*_{utl}(\mathbf{o}, \mathbf{r}) \ln \pi^*_{utl}(\mathbf{o}, \mathbf{r}) \quad (9)$$

Therefore, we obtain our entire minimax entropy framework

[7]As before, we do not model $\Pi_{ut} = p_{true}(u,t)$ and let $\Pi_{ut} = \tilde{\pi}_{ut}$.

[8]For brevity, we use π^* short for $\pi^*(\mathbf{o}, \mathbf{r})$ in this proof

as summarized in the following program:

$$\min_{\mathbf{o},\mathbf{r}} \max_{\pi} - \sum_{u,t,l} \tilde{\pi}_{ut}\pi_{utl} \ln \pi_{utl} \tag{10}$$

$$s.t. \sum_{u,t,l} \tilde{\pi}_{ut}\pi_{utl}\mathbf{f} = \sum_{u,t,l} \tilde{\pi}_{ut}\tilde{\pi}_{utl}\mathbf{f} \tag{11}$$

$$\sum_{l} \pi_{utl} = 1 \quad \forall u,t \tag{12}$$

$$\pi_{utl} > 0 \quad \forall u,t,l \tag{13}$$

$$r_i > 0 \quad \forall i \tag{14}$$

3.3 The Learning Algorithm

Algorithm 1: The learning Algorithm for the Minimax Entropy Approach of Check-in Preferences Modeling

Input: A user check-in database $\{\langle utl \rangle\}$
Output: Check-in preference $\{\pi_{utl}\}, \forall u,t,l$; geographic clustering parameters $(\mathbf{o},\mathbf{r})$

1 Do a K-means clustering on the latitude-longitude coordinates of the POIs. Initialize $\mathbf{o}^*$ and $\mathbf{r}^*$ to be centers and average distances to the centers.
2 **for** *iter = 1:Maxiter* **do**
3 **MaxEnt step.** With $(\mathbf{o},\mathbf{r})$ fixed to $(\mathbf{o}^*,\mathbf{r}^*)$, solve the MaxEnt problem to obtain $\mathbf{w}^*$.

$$\mathbf{w}^* = \arg\max_{\mathbf{w}} LL$$

$$\text{where } LL(\mathbf{w},\mathbf{o}^*,\mathbf{r}^*) = \sum_{utl} \tilde{\pi}_{ut}\tilde{\pi}_{utl} \ln \pi_{utl},$$

$$\pi_{utl} = \frac{\exp(\mathbf{w}^T\mathbf{f}(\mathbf{o}^*,\mathbf{r}^*))}{\sum_l \exp(\mathbf{w}^T\mathbf{f}(\mathbf{o}^*,\mathbf{r}^*))}$$

MinEnt step. With $\mathbf{w}$ fixed to $\mathbf{w}^*$, estimate the latent parameters $(\mathbf{o},\mathbf{r})$.

$$(\mathbf{o}^*,\mathbf{r}^*) = \arg\min_{\mathbf{r}>0,\mathbf{o}} -LL$$

$$\text{where } LL(\mathbf{w}^*,\mathbf{o},\mathbf{r}) = \sum_{utl} \tilde{\pi}_{ut}\tilde{\pi}_{utl} \ln \pi_{utl},$$

$$\pi_{utl} = \frac{\exp(\mathbf{w}^{*T}\mathbf{f}(\mathbf{o},\mathbf{r}))}{\sum_l \exp(\mathbf{w}^{*T}\mathbf{f}(\mathbf{o},\mathbf{r}))}$$

4 **end**

While it is hard to obtain a close form solution, we propose a neat coordinate descent learning procedure to solve the optimization problem.

We convert the inherent MaxEnt part to the dual space (see details in Appendix A) which reduces the problem to the following form:

$$\min_{\mathbf{r}>0,\mathbf{o}} \min_{\mathbf{w}} -LL \quad i.e., \quad \min_{\mathbf{r}>0,\mathbf{o},\mathbf{w}} -LL \tag{15}$$

where LL is given by Equation (8).

The objective now is to find the set of $(\mathbf{w},\mathbf{o},\mathbf{r})$ which minimizes the minus log likelihood LL of the data. This is divided to solving a MaxEnt problem (finding $\mathbf{w}^*$ with $(\mathbf{o},\mathbf{r})$ fixed) and a MinEnt problem (finding $(\mathbf{o}^*,\mathbf{r}^*)$ with $\mathbf{w}$ fixed).

Algorithm 1 sketches the learning algorithm. First, the geographic centers are initialized by a K-means clustering; the radius for each cluster is initialized by the average distance to the center. After initialization, we solve the MaxEnt and MinEnt problems alternately to get the optimal $(\mathbf{w},\mathbf{o},\mathbf{r})$. Both sides of optimization are solved by the L-BFGS [17] algorithm. See Appendix B for the optimization details.

4. RELATED WORK

Modeling the time aware check-in preference of users is the fundamental component of location[9] prediction and location recommendation. We review previous study on location prediction/recommendation tasks. Then we review the background of related discriminative models.

4.1 Location Prediction/Recommendation

There has been a substantial amount of research on location prediction/recommendation ever since the GPS devices became widely available. The prediction and recommendation tasks are closely related since they both predict a list of locations which are evaluated by the prediction accuracy. There are several subtle differences though. Location prediction usually focuses more on the places which have been already visited by a user and largely depends on the time point. Therefore, spatio-temporal regularity usually plays an important role in the task. On the contrary, location recommendation task focuses more on the unvisited locations based on collaborative filtering. The recommendation may or may not be time aware as well. Unlike movie recommendations where one may not want to watch a movie he/she has already watched before, a location can be checked in repeatedly by a user. Therefore it is desirable to include the places which have been visited before in the recommendation. In this paper, we do not distinguish between visited locations and new locations but output a distribution over all locations, where the most probable ones can be used for both prediction and recommendation.

One line of research [24, 25, 26, 27] focus on the study of GPS trajectories collected from human movements. Location prediction/recommendation on the trajectory data is a simpler task compared to the check-in data since trajectories contain consecutive movements of users which are very dense. The Nokia Research Center collected GPS data from 200 smartphone volunteers in the course of 1 year and launched a next place prediction challenge [14] in 2012. The best entries achieved prediction accuracies of above 50%.

However, location prediction/recommendation with the check-in data from LBSN is much more challenging due to the sparseness. Cheng *et al.* [4] propose a mixed hidden Markov model to predict the category of a user's next move and then predict the location given the category. However, while human movements may be Markovian, people usually do not check in at every POI they visit. Gao *et al.* [9, 10] explore the Hierarchical Pitman-Yor process [19] and view the check-in sequences as a language model to encode the historical effects. This method works much better for GPS trajectories [10] than check-in data [9] because the model also assumes dependencies between consecutive check-ins. Cho *et al.* [5], Yuan *et al.* [23] and Gao *et al.* [8, 7] highlight the daily periodicity of check-ins and show that temporal effects have significant influence on capturing users' check-in behaviors. Ye *et al.* [9] incorporate geographic influence to a collaborative filtering model by assuming a power-law distribution of the pairwise check-in distances. Cheng *et*

[9]In this paper, we use "location" and "POI" interchangeably as long as there is no ambiguity.

al. [3] extend this work to multi-center geographic distributions and combine it with a matrix factorization model. Yin *et al.* [21], Kurashima *et al.* [13] and Liu *et al.* [15, 16] propose generative models which introduce the concept of user/location profiles. Our approach is able to incorporate the various factors from the previous work and model them in a unified way.

4.2 Related Discriminative Models

The maximum entropy principle was first proposed by E.T. Jaynes [11] in 1957. It provides a very general rationale why we should select the model with the maximum entropy. It has seen widescale applications to real world problems recently especially within the natural language processing field [2]. Introducing latent variables to discriminative models is not new. The minimax entropy principle is first proposed in the computer vision community by Zhu *et al.* [30] for feature selection within the MaxEnt framework, which has motivated various methods of statistical estimation and pattern recognition. Lately Zhou *et al.* [28] adopted this methodology to study a crowdsourcing problem and demonstrated substantial performance improvement over existing methods. Previous work [20, 29, 22, 18] have introduced hidden variables to other discriminative models such as SVMs and CRFs in various forms as well. However, allowing features to be governed by a parametric form is innovative, which directly corresponds to the generative assumptions of the features. This makes our approach especially suited to user preference modeling where multidimensional heterogeneous information need to be modeled. The optimization of the parameters is naturally guided by the MinEnt principle, which not only makes it theoretically elegant but also leads to a handy coordinate descent solution.

5. DISCUSSIONS

In this section, we analyze the connections from our approach to several standard approaches. We also explain how various additional information can be incorporated and how cold start issue is naturally handled by our approach.

5.1 Connection to Maximum Likelihood Estimation

Our model has the intuitive interpretation of a discriminative maximum likelihood estimation (MLE). We have already seen that the final objective is to seek a maximum likelihood estimator $(\mathbf{w}^*, \mathbf{o}^*, \mathbf{r}^*)$ for the objective function LL, with the conditional probability defined as $p(l|u,t) = \pi_{utl} = \frac{\exp(\mathbf{w}^T\mathbf{f})}{\sum_l \exp(\mathbf{w}^T\mathbf{f})}$.

5.2 Connection to Matrix Factorization based Collaborative Filtering

Our model is a linear model in the sense that the prediction score is determined by $\mathbf{w}^T\mathbf{f}(\langle utl \rangle)$, and $\mathbf{w}$ is determined not only by the user check-in data, but also on the features $\mathbf{f}(\langle utl \rangle)$. In the standard matrix factorization (MF) model for recommendation where the access to meaningful information such as category, latitude and longitude is limited, it is still possible to perform prediction via purely utilizing the factorization of the user-item rating matrix R as approximated by the product of two low-rank matrices. Specifically, by carefully selecting a reasonable dimension parameter K which is much smaller than the number of users M and items N, MF approximates $R \approx U^T V$ where $U^{M\times K}$ is a user matrix and $V^{K\times N}$ is an item matrix. An interesting analogy is that the columns of U (or V) can be viewed as profiles of users (or items). However, unlike in our model where parameter estimation ($\mathbf{w}$) is performed and latent geographic clusters are learned jointly, this approach computes the prediction score in a rather simplified manner as $u^T v$ where u is the corresponding column in U for a user and v is the column in V for an item.

5.3 Incorporate Various Information

To make our model concrete, we defined every detail of how the features are generated. Nevertheless, the features do not necessarily have to be defined as we did in the previous sections. In this paper, we follow a natural thought that the category, geographic, temporal and popularity preferences are influential factors for a check-in. However, we can model other types of information into our learning framework as well in the forms of both explicit and latent features. For example, if the description and reviews of POIs are available, we can incorporate text features as explicit features. If social network information is available, we can incorporate friend clusters as latent features. With both explicit and latent features, our approach models ambiguous knowledge together with explicit knowledge in a unified manner to find the best possible way to utilize them.

5.4 Cold Start

As in most recommendation problems, cold start is an important issue in preference learning. If we have little historical data for a user, predicting her preference typically falls back to an appropriate way of utilizing "independent" features that do not reply on histories, such as gender, age, hometown, etc. Our model can elegantly handle such cases by just taking care of these information as additional features. They can be both explicit or latent. In this study, we do not have those demographic information available thus we do not define them in the profiles. However, these features can be utilized exactly the same way as the defined ones. We don't even need to worry about how to distinguish cold start users from the heavy users since the automatically learned weights help us to do the trade-off. In the extreme case where a user has no history at all, the prediction will fall back to a regression on those "independent" features. This treatment of cold start scenarios is of the similar style as in [1], with better expressiveness, reduced model complexity and simpler optimization procedure.

6. EXPERIMENTS

We introduce our datasets and report our experimental results in this section. We evaluate our proposed method on the location prediction/recommendation task.

First we evaluate the effectiveness of our method by accuracy of prediction under various settings. Then we zoom in to see the benefits from optimizing the latent parameters. At the end we conduct an efficiency study and analyze the scalability of our method.

6.1 Data

We conduct our experiments on two public real world datasets [6] obtained from Foursquare[10]. The first dataset (**CA**) contains 483,813 check-in records of 4,163 users in

[10]https://foursquare.com

California USA ranging from December 2009 to June 2013. The second dataset (**World**) contains 2,290,996 check-in records of 11,326 users around the world ranging from January 2011 to December 2011. We preprocess the datasets by removing the users and POIs with check-ins fewer than 20. Each check-in record consists of a user ID, a POI ID, a check-in timestamp, and the latitude and longitude of the POI. The first dataset has the category information of each POI while the second one does not.

We sort each user's check-ins chronologically and assign the first 80% of the check-ins to the training set and the remaining 20% to the test set.

6.2 Implementation

6.2.1 Smoothing the Category and Temporal Preference

Smoothing is a common practice to avoid overfitting and mitigate the effect from noise when estimating categorical distributions. It assigns a tiny probability to the categories that are not seen in the data. In our model, we do a simple add-one smoothing to the category preference and temporal preference of users.

6.2.2 Parameter Regularization

We incorporate a standard L_2 regularization on $\mathbf{w}$ in the MaxEnt step to avoid overfitting and numerical problems. The objective function becomes $-LL + \frac{1}{2}\beta||\mathbf{w}||_2^2$ where β is the regularization parameter. From our experiments, we found that our model is insensitive to parameter regularization. We set β to 0.2.

6.2.3 Number of Geographic Clusters

The number of clusters affect the granularity of the geographic regions. It can be empirically set by cross validation or specified by human knowledge of how fine grained regions we want to achieve. In this paper, we set the cluster number to 30 for the CA dataset and 200 for the World dataset.

6.2.4 Number of Iterations

We set the global iteration number $Maxiter$ to 20 and run 10 iterations within each L-BFGS step based on the empirical study of the convergence rate.

6.3 Effectiveness Study

6.3.1 Methods for Comparison

Existing models on location prediction/recommendation are usually specifically designed emphasizing a particular set of factors. Unlike our model, most of them cannot be generalized to take arbitrary features. In this study, we consider category, time, popularity and geographic coordinates. Thus we compare our method (the basic **MaxEnt** model with K-means initialization, and the full **Minimax** model) with the following three state-of-art models which can accept the same set of features.

- **PMM**. A spatial-temporal location *prediction* model proposed in [5], which studies the spatial-temporal regularity of user mobilities and builds a generative model for check-ins.
- **HMM**. A mixed hidden Markov location *prediction* model proposed in [4], which first predicts the category of user activity at the next step and then predict the most likely location given the estimated category distribution. This model is compared to only for the CA dataset because the category information is not available for the World dataset.
- **TGM**. A time-aware location *recommendation* model proposed in [23], which employs a user-based collaborative filtering framework with geographic influence incorporated by a linear combination. For the CA dataset, we enhance this model by a further linear combination with the category distribution at the prediction time for fair comparison.

6.3.2 Evaluation on Accuracy

Evaluation Metrics. We compute the accuracy of both location and category prediction on the test set for the CA dataset and the accuracy of location prediction for the World dataset. For each $\langle utl \rangle$ in the test data, we return the top-k locations predicted by each model for (u, t). As long as the true location l lies in the top-k set, we consider it as a correct prediction. For categories, we obtain the category list associated with the top-k predictions and evaluate the accuracy in the same way.

Performance. As shown in Figure 1, our method significantly outperforms the three baselines w.r.t both POI and category prediction at all position k's. TGM is not working well because 1) it takes a binary user-location matrix as the input for collaborative filtering which completely ignores the preference over different visited POIs; 2) it involves geographic and temporal influences in an ad-hoc manner which is difficult to coordinate in the optimal way; 3) the way it encodes the geographic knowledge is to do a power-law fitting of consecutive check-in distances, which is sensitive to outliers and cannot capture the clustering effect of check-ins. HMM relies a lot on the Markovian assumption of user activity. If a user's check-ins are not so dense (which is usually the case since people do not check-in at every POI they visit), the dependency between consecutive check-ins are weakened. Once the Markovian assumption does not hold, good performance would not be guaranteed. PMM gives the worst performance. The generative assumption that movements are governed by Gaussian spatial-temporal clusters is too strict and limits the model's expressiveness and generalizability. Another interesting phenomenon we can observe is that despite the lack of category information for the World dataset, the location prediction accuracy is higher than the CA dataset for all the models. In fact, the World dataset has comparative number of POIs with the CA dataset but has substantially large number of checkin records. This makes the learning task easier for all the models. The performance difference is more significant on the CA dataset, which concludes that when we have limited number of observations for training, our MiniMax model generalizes better than the baseline models.

6.3.3 The Influence of Latent Features

Performance. We plot the accuracy@top-5 of our model as the latent parameters are optimized with 20 iterations in Figure 2. The accuracy continues to improve as the latent parameters are optimized. It is also worth noting that the convergence is very fast.

A Visualization of the Geographic Clusters. To illustrate the intuition behind optimizing the latent parameters, we show a snapshot of the San Francisco Bay Area

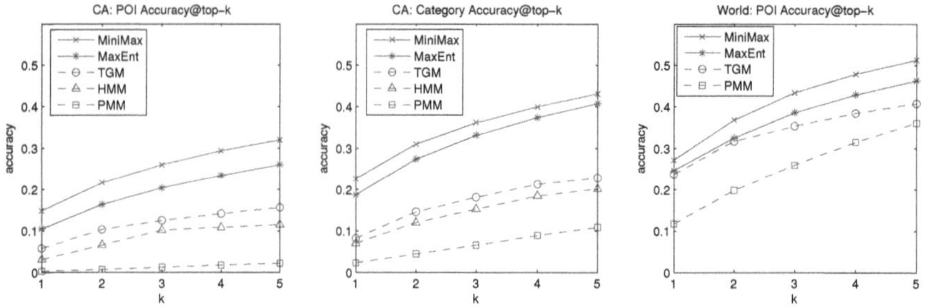

Figure 1: Prediction Accuracy @ top-k

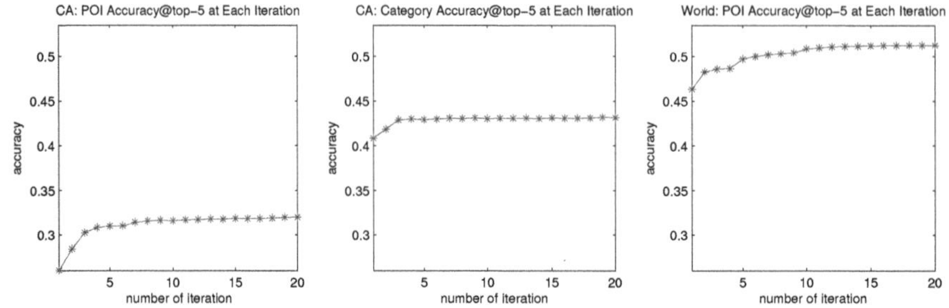

Figure 2: Prediction Accuracy @ top-5 as we optimize the latent parameters. The prediction becomes more accurate and the convergence is very fast.

Figure 3: Geographic Clusters

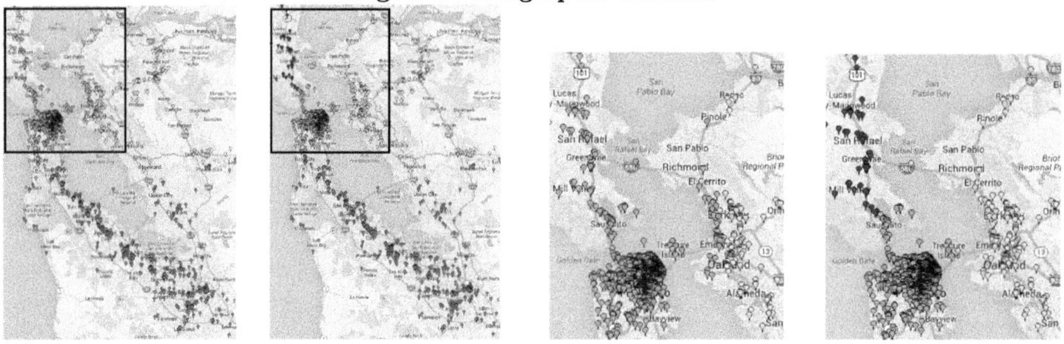

(a) SF k-means (b) SF (c) SF k-means (d) SF

geographic clusters obtained from our algorithm for the CA dataset in Figure 3(b). We assign each POI l to a cluster by selecting the largest weight of $\mathbf{g}^l$. Figure 3(a) shows the initial k-means clustering results.

The optimal clustering structure is refined from the K-means clustering via the interaction with the check-in preferences modeling. We can observe interesting refinements. As shown in Figure 3(d) and Figure 3(c), we zoom in to San Francisco (SF) city. As K-means clustering blindly clusters the POIs by geographic latitudes and longitudes, the cluster centered at SF (yellow) stretched to San Rafael, Oakland and Berkeley; while in the refined clusters, SF corresponds to a concentrated cluster. The SF cluster extends north right to the vicinity of the Golden Gate Bridge as tourists to SF would always like to explore the Golden Gate Bridge.

6.4 Efficiency Study

In this section, we first analyze the complexity of our algorithm and then present experimental results on the execution time.

6.4.1 Complexity Analysis

The coordinate descent algorithm contains a MaxEnt step and a MinEnt step. Within each step, the space and time consuming part lies in the evaluation of the function value and the gradient (see Appendix B), which determines the complexity of our algorithm. We show that both space and time complexity are linear w.r.t the number of users, time indices and POIs.

Space. At each iteration of both steps, we need to store π_{utl} for all (u, t) pairs that appear in the training set and any $l \in L$, which requires at most $O(|U||T||L|)$ space. Computation of the feature values are done at the beginning of each step and requires at most two components of (u, t, l), therefore does not affect the order of space complexity. The space required to store the current estimate of the solution in the MaxEnt step is the dimension of the features $\mathbf{f}$. In the

MinEnt step it is 3 times the number of geographic clusters, which is also not contributing to the order of complexity. Thus the overall space complexity is $O(|U||T||L|)$.

Time. At each iteration, to evaluate the function and gradient values, we need to compute π_{utl} for all (u,t) pairs that appear in the training set and any $l \in L$. Let the total iteration number be M and let the maximum function evaluation number be M_1 at one MaxEnt step and M_2 at one MinEnt step. The overall time complexity is $O(M(M_1 + M_2)|U||T||L|)$.

6.4.2 *Execution Time Evaluation*

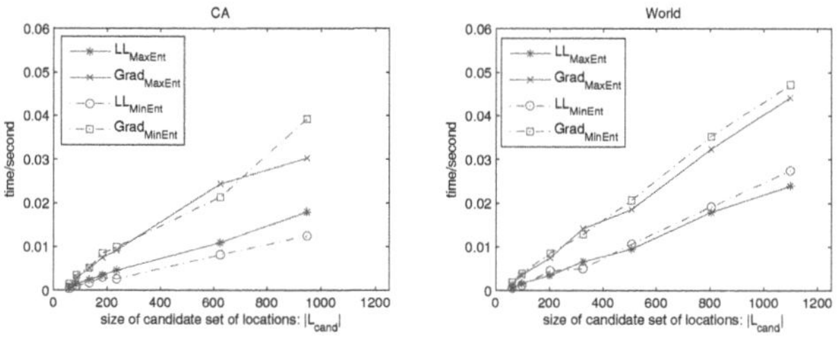

Figure 4: Average Execution Time of A Function/Gradient Evaluation

To examine the efficiency of our algorithm, we illustrate the execution time of a function/gradient evaluation for both the MaxEnt step and the MinEnt step. The time consuming computation of π_{utl} can be computed in parallel since $\{\pi_{utl}|l \in L\}$ can be computed for each (u,t) pair simultaneously. Therefore we examine the average execution time of a function/gradient evaluation over all (u,t) pairs. We vary the pruning threshold δ_α and obtain the *time - candidate set size* curves shown in Figure 4. They all exhibits a linear trend in $|L|$ while the gradient evaluation is more expensive than the function value evaluation. $|L_{cand}|$ is the average size of the candidate set over all (u,t) pairs. In the ideal case, the overall time complexity can be reduced to $O(M(M_1 + M_2)|L_{cand}|)$.

7. CONCLUSIONS

In this paper, we develop a novel minimax approach for modeling time-aware check-in preferences. Specifically, our approach has the advantage of investigating the multidimensional knowledge of entities (users, locations) as well as jointly learning the latent geographic clustering. The proposed discriminative model can strike a good balance between explaining seen data and generalizing to unseen data by requiring the model to satisfy meaningful relaxed constraints. Going beyond check-in preference modeling, the proposed minimax entropy model also provides a general guidance to model ambiguous features with arbitrary parametric forms, which significantly boosts the flexibility and expressiveness of the standard discriminative learning models.

Acknowledgment

Research was sponsored in part by the U.S. Army Research Lab. under Cooperative Agreement No. W911NF-09-2-0053 (NSCTA), National Science Foundation IIS-1017362, IIS-1320617, and IIS-1354329, HDTRA1-10-1-0120, and grant 1U54GM114838 awarded by NIGMS through funds provided by the trans-NIH Big Data to Knowledge (BD2K) initiative (www.bd2k.nih.gov), and MIAS, a DHS-IDS Center for Multimodal Information Access and Synthesis at UIUC.

8. REFERENCES

[1] D. Agarwal and B.-C. Chen. Regression-based latent factor models. KDD '09, New York, NY, USA. ACM.

[2] A. L. Berger, V. J. D. Pietra, and S. A. D. Pietra. A maximum entropy approach to natural language processing. *Computational linguistics*, 22(1):39–71, 1996.

[3] C. Cheng, H. Yang, I. King, and M. R. Lyu. Fused matrix factorization with geographical and social influence in location-based social networks. In *AAAI*, 2012.

[4] H. Cheng, J. Ye, and Z. Zhu. What's your next move: User activity prediction in location-based social networks. In *SDM*, pages 171–179, 2013.

[5] E. Cho, S. A. Myers, and J. Leskovec. Friendship and mobility: user movement in location-based social networks. In *KDD*, pages 1082–1090, 2011.

[6] H. Gao and H. Liu. Location-based social network data repository, 2014.

[7] H. Gao, J. Tang, X. Hu, and H. Liu. Exploring temporal effects for location recommendation on location-based social networks. In *RecSys*, pages 93–100, 2013.

[8] H. Gao, J. Tang, X. Hu, and H. Liu. Modeling temporal effects of human mobile behavior on location-based social networks. In *CIKM*, pages 1673–1678, 2013.

[9] H. Gao, J. Tang, and H. Liu. Exploring social-historical ties on location-based social networks. In *ICWSM*, 2012.

[10] H. Gao, J. Tang, and H. Liu. Mobile Location Prediction in Spatio-Temporal Context. *the Procedings of Mobile Data Challenge by Nokia Workshop at the Tenth International Conference on Pervasive Computing*, June 2012.

[11] E. T. Jaynes. Information theory and statistical mechanics. *Physical review*, 106(4):620, 1957.

[12] S. Kullback and R. A. Leibler. On information and sufficiency. *The Annals of Mathematical Statistics*, pages 79–86, 1951.

[13] T. Kurashima, T. Iwata, T. Hoshide, N. Takaya, and K. Fujimura. Geo topic model: Joint modeling of user's activity area and interests for location recommendation. WSDM '13, pages 375–384, New York, NY, USA, 2013. ACM.

[14] J. K. Laurila, D. Gatica-Perez, I. Aad, J. Blom, O. Bornet, T. M. T. Do, O. Dousse, J. Eberle, and M. Miettinen. From big smartphone data to worldwide research: The mobile data challenge. *Pervasive and Mobile Computing*, 9(6):752–771, 2013.

[15] B. Liu, Y. Fu, Z. Yao, and H. Xiong. Learning geographical preferences for point-of-interest recommendation. In *KDD*, pages 1043–1051, 2013.

[16] B. Liu and H. Xiong. Point-of-interest recommendation in location based social networks with topic and location awareness. In *SDM*, pages 396–404, 2013.

[17] D. C. Liu and J. Nocedal. On the limited memory bfgs

method for large scale optimization. *Mathematical programming*, 45(1-3):503–528, 1989.
[18] A. Quattoni, S. Wang, L.-P. Morency, M. Collins, and T. Darrell. Hidden conditional random fields. *IEEE transactions on pattern analysis and machine intelligence*, 29(10):1848, 2007.
[19] Y. W. Teh. A hierarchical bayesian language model based on pitman-yor processes. In *Proceedings of the 21st International Conference on Computational Linguistics and the 44th annual meeting of the Association for Computational Linguistics*, pages 985–992. Association for Computational Linguistics, 2006.
[20] S. Wang, D. Schuurmans, and Y. Zhao. The latent maximum entropy principle. *ACM Trans. Knowl. Discov. Data*, 6(2):8:1–8:42, July 2012.
[21] H. Yin, Y. Sun, B. Cui, Z. Hu, and L. Chen. Lcars: a location-content-aware recommender system. In *SIGKDD*, pages 221–229. ACM, 2013.
[22] C.-N. J. Yu and T. Joachims. Learning structural svms with latent variables. In *ICML*. ACM, 2009.
[23] Q. Yuan, G. Cong, Z. Ma, A. Sun, and N. Magnenat-Thalmann. Time-aware point-of-interest recommendation. In *SIGIR*, pages 363–372, 2013.
[24] V. W. Zheng, Y. Zheng, X. Xie, and Q. Yang. Collaborative location and activity recommendations with gps history data. In *WWW*, pages 1029–1038, 2010.
[25] Y. Zheng and X. Xie. Learning location correlation from gps trajectories. In *Mobile Data Management*, pages 27–32, 2010.
[26] Y. Zheng, L. Zhang, Z. Ma, X. Xie, and W.-Y. Ma. Recommending friends and locations based on individual location history. *TWEB*, 5(1):5, 2011.
[27] Y. Zheng, L. Zhang, X. Xie, and W.-Y. Ma. Mining correlation between locations using human location history. In *GIS*, pages 472–475, 2009.
[28] D. Zhou, J. C. Platt, S. Basu, and Y. Mao. Learning from the wisdom of crowds by minimax entropy. In *NIPS*, pages 2204–2212, 2012.
[29] J. Zhu, E. P. Xing, and B. Zhang. Partially observed maximum entropy discrimination markov networks. In D. Koller, D. Schuurmans, Y. Bengio, and L. Bottou, editors, *NIPS*. Curran Associates, Inc., 2009.
[30] S. C. Zhu, Y. N. Wu, and D. Mumford. Minimax entropy principle and its application to texture modeling. *Neural Computation*, 9(8):1627–1660, 1997.

APPENDIX

A. PRIMAL DUAL CONVERSION

The Lagrangian of the MaxEnt problem is

$$\begin{aligned}\mathcal{L} = &- \sum_{u,t,l} \tilde{\pi}_{ut}\pi_{utl} \ln \pi_{utl} \\ &+ \sum_{\alpha} w_\alpha \Big(\sum_{u,t,l} \tilde{\pi}_{ut}\pi_{utl} f_\alpha - \sum_{u,t,l} \tilde{\pi}_{ut}\tilde{\pi}_{utl} f_\alpha\Big) \\ &+ \sum_{u,t} \eta_{u,t}\Big(\sum_{l} \pi_{utl} - 1\Big)\end{aligned}$$

where $\{w_\alpha\}$ and $\{\eta_{u,t}\}$ are the Lagrange multipliers.

Let $\dfrac{\partial \mathcal{L}}{\partial \pi_{utl}} = 0$, we have

$$-\tilde{\pi}_{ut}(1 + \ln \pi_{utl}) + \sum_{\alpha} w_\alpha(\tilde{\pi}_{ut} f_\alpha) + \eta_{u,t} = 0$$

$$\Longleftrightarrow \ln \pi_{utl} = \sum_{\alpha} w_\alpha f_\alpha + \frac{\eta_{u,t}}{\tilde{\pi}_{ut}} - 1$$

Apply the constraint $\sum_l \pi_{utl} = 1 \quad \forall u, t$, we can get

$$\pi_{utl} = \frac{\exp(\sum_\alpha w_\alpha f_\alpha)}{\sum_l \exp(\sum_\alpha w_\alpha f_\alpha)} \forall u, t, l \tag{16}$$

Plugging Equation (16) into $\mathcal{L}$ gives that $\mathcal{L}$ is the minus log likelihood of the data. Maximizing the primal problem becomes minimizing the dual problem, which turns out to be maximizing the log likelihood of the data with π_{utl} specified by Equation (16). Therefore $\mathbf{w}^*$ is the maximum likelihood estimation:

$$LL = \sum_{utl} \tilde{\pi}_{ut}\tilde{\pi}_{utl} \ln \pi_{utl}, \quad \mathbf{w}^* = \arg\min_{\mathbf{w}} -LL$$

where π_{utl} is of the form given in Equation (16).

B. OPTIMIZATION DETAILS

We derive the gradients required by L-BFGS for both MaxEnt and MinEnt steps.

- The MaxEnt problem is an unconstrained optimization problem in the dual space. The gradient w.r.t $\mathbf{w}$ is given by

$$\frac{\partial LL}{\partial w_\alpha} = \sum_{u,t,l} \tilde{\pi}_{ut}\tilde{\pi}_{utl} f_\alpha - \sum_{u,t,l} \tilde{\pi}_{ut}\pi_{utl} f_\alpha$$

  where π_{utl} is given by Equation (16). This is the difference between the expectations of the feature f_α from the model and the empirical mean.
  The Hessian matrix is given by

$$\begin{aligned}\frac{\partial^2 LL}{\partial w_\alpha \partial w_\beta} =& \mathbb{E}_\pi\Big[\Big(\sum_{u,t,l} \tilde{\pi}_{ut}\tilde{\pi}_{utl} f_\alpha - \sum_{u,t,l} \tilde{\pi}_{ut}\pi_{utl} f_\alpha\Big) \\ & \Big(\sum_{u,t,l} \tilde{\pi}_{ut}\tilde{\pi}_{utl} f_\beta - \sum_{u,t,l} \tilde{\pi}_{ut}\pi_{utl} f_\beta\Big)\Big]\end{aligned}$$

  which is the covariance matrix of the features, and is thus positive definite[11]. This indicates that the MaxEnt problem is strictly convex and has a unique solution.
- The optimization over the latent parameters may or may not be convex, depending on the form of the chosen geographic weight function. In this paper, the problem is not convex and L-BFGS will converge to the local minimum. We take several trials of the iteration process to approach the global minimum.
  The gradient w.r.t $(\mathbf{o}, \mathbf{r})$ is given by

$$\frac{\partial LL}{\partial z_i} = \sum_{u,t,l} \tilde{\pi}_{ut}\tilde{\pi}_{utl} w_g \frac{\partial f_g}{\partial z_i} - \sum_{u,t,l} \tilde{\pi}_{ut}\pi_{utl} w_g \frac{\partial f_g}{\partial z_i}$$

  where z_i can be o_{ilat}, o_{ilon} or r_i, w_g is the weight corresponding to the geographic feature f_g and

$$\frac{\partial f_g}{\partial z_i} = g_i^u \frac{\partial g_i^l}{\partial z_i} + \frac{\partial g_i^u}{\partial z_i} g_i^l$$

  with g_i^l given by Equation (1).

[11] only in rare cases it may be positive semi-definite

You've got Mail, and Here is What you Could do With It! Analyzing and Predicting Actions on Email Messages

Dotan Di Castro
Yahoo Labs
Haifa 31905, Israel
dot@yahoo-inc.com

Zohar Karnin
Yahoo Labs
Haifa 31905, Israel
zkarnin@ymail.com

Liane Lewin-Eytan
Yahoo Labs
Haifa 31905, Israel
liane.leytan@yahoo.com

Yoelle Maarek
Yahoo Labs
Haifa 31905, Israel
yoelle@ymail.com

ABSTRACT

With email traffic increasing, leading Web mail services have started to offer features that assist users in reading and processing their inboxes. One approach is to identify "important" messages, while a complementary one is to bundle messages, especially machine-generated ones, in pre-defined categories. We rather propose here to go back to the task at hand and consider what actions the users might conduct on received messages. We thoroughly studied, in a privacy-preserving manner, the actions of a large number of users in Yahoo mail, and found out that the most frequent actions are typically *read, reply, delete* and a sub-type of delete, *delete-without-read*. We devised a learning framework for predicting these four actions, for users with various levels of activity per action. Our framework leverages both vertical learning for personalization and horizontal learning for regularization purposes. In order to verify the quality of our predictions, we conducted a large-scale experiment involving users who had previously agreed to participate in such research studies. Our results show that, for recall values of 90%, we can predict important actions such as read or reply at precision levels up to 40% for active users, which we consider pretty encouraging for an assistance task. For less active users, we show that our regularization achieves an increase in AUC of close to 50%. To the best of our knowledge, our work is the first to provide a unified framework of this scale for predicting multiple actions on Web email, which hopefully provides a new ground for inventing new user experiences to help users process their inboxes.

1. INTRODUCTION

The nature of email traffic has greatly changed in the last decade. Some recent studies have shown that more than 90% of non-spam Web email is now machine-generated, with messages of various importance, from critical etickets or invoices, to hotel newsletters, [2, 18]. Several mail clients have identified this evolution and have started to offer some organizational means to help users process their constantly growing inboxes. Thus AOL mail was one of the first mail services to provide high level *stacks* such as *Daily Deals, Social Notifications* or *Photos* and *Attachments*, [25]. Yahoo mail offers *Smart views*, which provide search facets for messages, such as *People, Social, Travel, Shopping and Finance*, as detailed in [18]. Gmail has also been offering various ways for users to scan their inboxes, first with its *Priority Inbox* [1], then with its *Smart Labels* and *Inbox Tabs*[1] and more recently with its *Inbox for Gmail* [15] experience, which supports automatic sorting into four semantic *Bundles* (*Travel, Purchases, Finance* and *Social.*)

All of these systems apply some classification scheme on messages, but typically ignore the end game, namely what action the user will take on them. In this paper, our goal is to study mail actions in details and explore a novel approach to predict them. More specifically, we first propose to conduct a large scale study of the actions conducted by real users in Yahoo mail, identify the most popular actions, such as *read, reply, delete*, and *forward*, and verify how predictable they are. Other actions, such as moving messages into folders, are of less interest since they are quite rare. Indeed, it has been shown that 70% of Web mail users never ever defined a single folder, [23]. The *delete* action is given special consideration. We distinguish between two *delete* behaviors. The first, referred to as *delete-with-read*, covers the case in which the message is first open, and we assume read even if not in depth, and then deleted. The second, *delete-without-read*, covers the case in which the message header, typically including the sender, subject line and possibly a short snippet of the body, are sufficient for the user to decide that s/he does not need to open it, let alone read it. We believe that these two actions are conceptually very different. The first carries some level of interest: its header is intriguing enough for the user to open (and most probably read) it. The second indicates a lesser level of interest: either the header brings sufficient information that the user does not need to read more, or more frequently, the header is sufficient for the user to decide that s/he has no interest whatsoever in the message, which is quite common with mass mailing. Note that we do not claim here is that a message that is only read is less important in essence that a message that was replied to or forwarded. It could be that by the simple nature of the message (an answer to a critical question for instance in personal communication, or a confirmation of shipment delivery in a machine-generated message), it does not require further action. This is one of the reasons for which we do not attempt to predict the importance of the email, which we believe is not only difficult but probably not useful per se, but prefer to try predicting each action independently.

[1]https://support.google.com/mail/answer/3055016?hl=en&p=inboxtabs&rd=1

WSDM'16, February 22–25, 2016, San Francisco, CA, USA.

DOI: http://dx.doi.org/10.1145/2835776.2835811

Some messages should by their simple nature only be read, as for instance Direct Answers or OneBoxes such as Weather or Stock Prices in Web Search, while others will demand further action.

Our task is thus to predict the most probable actions, from the list of sufficiently frequent actions, for any user and any incoming message. This task is inherently difficult, since as we will show, most Web mail users, unlike enterprise mail users who are out of the scope of this work, are quite passive. One major challenge is thus to support all Web mail users, across all levels of usage. To do so, we examine case-specific methods of regularization aimed to apply data learned vertically, from the collective of users, on a single user with a low usage level.

As mentioned earlier, in our context of Web email, with its huge amount of machine-generated messages, it is to be expected that a majority of messages will remain action-less. One simple but key result of our study is that we have verified that over 85% of the messages in an average inbox are never read. Consequently, identifying messages that have a non-negligible chance to be acted upon should already bring value to the user. The task is obviously challenging due to the diversity of messages, users and users' behaviors. However, like in any suggestion framework, the user will always have a choice of ignoring the suggestion. Our goal here is to offer a decent level of precision and a high level of recall for reasonably active users.

An additional motivation for this work, is to hopefully offer novel assistance features to mail users beyond suggestions. While discussing them is out of the scope of this paper, one can easily imagine various user experiences for ranking suggested actions in Smart phones mail clients, or dedicating a special view to messages that will probably be deleted without being fully opened. Note that this would be significantly different from some Gmail tabs such as "Social" or "Promotions", which still require the user to isolate the rare actionable message (for instance an interesting promotion that the user would wish to forward to a friend) in a long list of messages that will most probably be deleted without being read. Another direct application of our framework is mail search or alerting systems. For instance, a message that has little chance to be read should not be returned at a high rank in search results, as users will typically search only for "stuff they have seen" to paraphrase the work by Dumais et al. [16].

The contributions of our paper are three-fold:

1. We provide, to the best of our knowledge, the first large scale study of users' actions in a major Web mail service.
2. We formalize the task of "actionable email prediction", leveraging both local features representing an individual inbox, and global features representing the overall mail traffic, as well as introduce a novel learning method that supports all types of users, according to their levels of activity per action. We apply "vertical" learning for personalization over a single inbox and "horizontal" learning for regularization, especially needed for action-specific light users.
3. We describe a full system that was implemented and evaluated on Yahoo mail and detail a large scale experiment that was done on users who had agreed to participate in such studies.

The paper is organized as follows. Section 2 provides some key insights on how Web mail users act today on their messages, reporting results of a large scale study we conducted on Yahoo mail. Section 3 formalizes the task of predicting users' actions on delivered messages. Section 4 provides an exhaustive list of the mail-specific features we use. Section 5 describes in details our learning methodology, that relies on "vertical" learning for personalization and "horizontal" learning for regularization. Section 6 reports on the large scale experiments we conducted. We review related work in Section 7 and present our conclusions in Section 8.

2. STUDYING USERS' ACTIONS

2.1 Popular Actions

One important validation exercise before we address the task of predicting actions, is to verify whether users do act on their inbox. We examined the log of the actions performed by Yahoo mail users, and considered the number of users who performed at least one action over a period of two months, thus ignoring "dormant" users.

We observed that about 35% of the entire non-dormant population perform at least one action on a daily basis, which we believe is sufficient for motivating the task of predicting actions. Table 1 lists the most common actions over a period of two months. One interesting observation is that while read is obviously the most frequent action, conducted by 98% of users, for 44% of users it is, maybe surprisingly, the *only* action. This type of behavior reflects the evolution of Web mail traffic and a recent trend in Web mail usage. For more and more users, Web mail becomes more often used for bookkeeping of important messages (such as purchase receipts, or itineraries) of for getting updates from subscribed mailing lists, rather than communicating with friends or family. In that sense, Web mail becomes more and more similar in nature to traditional snail mail.

Action	Percentage of Users
read	98%
reply	29%
forward	28%
delete	18%

Table 1: Percentage of users performing an action at least once over two months

We further explored the reply action. While reply is intuitively a popular action, its coverage over the total volume of messages is very low. Indeed, we verified that it is performed on only 2% of incoming messages. For each message, we counted the number of users it was sent to. Note that we counted only once a single message that was sent separately to multiple users. This pattern is mostly observed in machine-generated email as human senders will typically use the CC field instead. The count of recipients per message was then aggregated by sender to compute the average number of users receiving an email from each sender during a period of two weeks. As it turns out, most of the senders do not send messages to many different users. However, the vast majority of email traffic is sent as expected by mass-senders, that send messages to many different users. This result is again consistent with our previous observations that Web mail is used less and less for personal communications and that, 90% of Web mail messages are now machine-generated, and as such do not expect a reply.

The graphs shown in Figure 1 provide more details on these counts. The lower graph gives the ratio of the messages triggering a reply action, with respect to their number of recipients. Clearly, the ratio is higher when the number of recipients is smaller (indicating a personal correspondence), thus explaining the overall low reply ratio, when considering the overall traffic.

Note that all other actions, such as moving into a folder, report as spam (or ham), starring a message etc. are significantly less frequent. Consequently we did not consider them in this work, as they are too rare to be of interest.

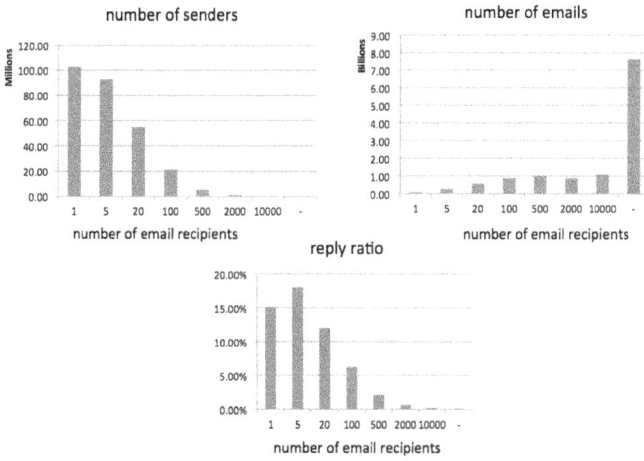

Figure 1: Senders, Messages and Reply Stats

2.2 Analyzing the Actions of Active Users

Following the global analysis on non-dormant users described above, we conducted a more thorough analysis of the actions of more active users. To this effect, we defined as active any user who performed at least one spam vote during a time period of 120 days. Since spam vote is a rare action, this is a convenient proxy for identifying regularly active users. Given this definition, we generated a dataset covering the actions of more than $110,000$ of such active users over this time period of 120 days. This dataset includes over $500M$ inbound messages and over $10M$ outbound messages, as well as their associated actions. More specifically, we considered the *read, reply, forward* and *delete* actions previously mentioned, as well as two specific sub-types of *delete*, namely *delete-with-read* and *delete-without-read.* Note that we did not access any data pertaining to an individual message or user, and considered only aggregated data over actions, for obvious privacy reasons. The same dataset was used for our action prediction experiments as reported in Section 6.

Figure 2 presents for each action, the percentage of users performing the action at least x times a day, on average. The plots are presented in log-scale to account for the wide range of values. Clearly, the *read* action (top blue curve) is the most frequent one, performed on a daily basis by most users. The next two actions are *delete-without-read* and *reply*, that are performed daily by over 30% and 10% of active users, respectively.

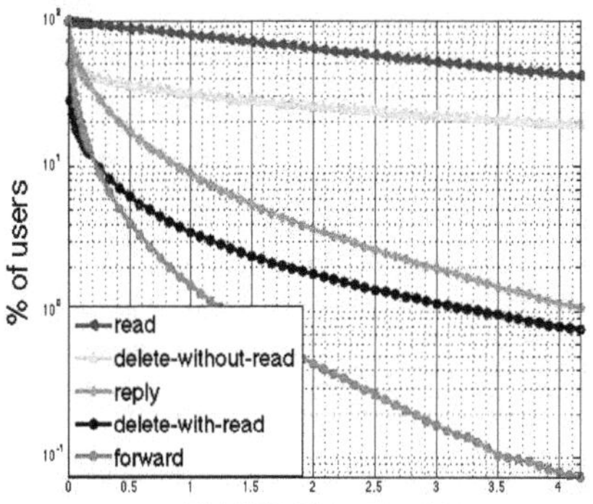

Figure 2: Daily Actions, taken over 120 days

Table 2 provides additional information on action coverage for messages according to the users' levels of activity. For each action a, we consider three sets of users, depending on their levels of activity represented by the number of actions of type a that they performed over our 120 days period. Users performing at least one action, users performing more than 70 actions, and users performing more than 200 actions. For each user set and each action, we computed the percentage of messages on which the action was performed, averaged over all users in the set. Note that as the total count of actions increases, so does the percentage per message. This means that users who perform many actions of a certain type do not do so simply because they receive more mail but rather because they are more active: they act more often on each message. This phenomenon is stronger in the actions of *forward, reply* and *delete-with-read*, where the percentage per message demonstrates a huge increases when considering active vs. non-active users. The varying percentage rates motivate a personalized approach to the action prediction task as it indicates that different recipients exhibit different behavior patterns.

Action # actions	*Read*	*Reply*	*Fwd*	*Delete-with-Read*	*Delete-without-Read*
> 0	15.3%	1.27%	0.36%	0.76%	10.43%
> 70	17.5%	5.54%	3.98%	3.15%	16.47%
> 200	20.2%	9.52%	7.32%	4.94%	19.76%

Table 2: Percentages of messages on which an action was performed according to various users' activity levels

We continue our analysis of the selected five actions, while pivoting our focus on the percentage of users rather than on the percentage of messages. Specifically, for each action a, Table 3 presents the percentage of users who perform an action of type a over at least $x\%$ of the messages in their inbox, for various values of x.

Action msg ratio	*Read*	*Reply*	*Fwd*	*Delete-with-Read*	*Delete-without-Read*
$\geq 0.5\%$	94.3%	30.2%	9.53%	9.77%	40.3%
$\geq 1\%$	91%	19.1%	4.31%	6.2%	36.61%
$\geq 2\%$	83.8%	10.1%	1.58%	3.48%	32.6%
$\geq 5\%$	63.3%	2.9%	0.25%	1.12%	25.71%
$\geq 10\%$	39.8%	0.58%	0.04%	0.29%	19.35%
$\geq 25\%$	11.7%	0%	0%	0%	8.66%

Table 3: Percentages of users performing an action over different ratios of their messages

After analyzing the *delete* operations in our dataset, we discovered that 89.5% of the *delete* actions are not preceded by any *read* operation, which confirms our intuition that *delete-without-read* is a common behavior that was worth isolating. This is also sustained by the statistics presented in Table 2, where one can observe the large gap between the percentages of messages that are associated with a *delete-with-read* action and those associated with a *delete-without-read* action. The difference between these two actions is also demonstrated in Figure 2 and Table 3, where the relative infrequency of *delete-with-read* is shown this time in terms of percentage of users who apply this action. We have verified that, as expected, the *delete-without-read* actions are in a huge majority conducted on machine-generated messages as opposed to personal communications. Note that this does not imply that all machine-generated messages will immediately be deleted by users, as it is clear that some of them are highly valuable and will be kept for future reference.

From both Tables 2 and 3, *read* naturally emerges as the most popular action, with *delete-without-read* as an intriguing runner-up. After our initial surprise, we realized that this behavior does make sense, given the new nature of Web mail traffic that we previously discussed. One the other end of the spectrum *forward* and *delete-with-read* are clearly much less frequent actions. As seen in Figure 2, even our active users do not perform either of these actions on daily basis. They are not only of limited interest to active users but will also be significantly more difficult to predict considering the sparsity of data. Consequently in our prediction task, we will deliberately ignore *forward* among the top four atomic actions and focus on *read, reply* and *delete*. In addition, given the high popularity of *delete-without-read*, we will also give it dedicated attention and attempt to predict it.

3. PREDICTING USER'S ACTIONS

We motivate and define below some of the concepts that are key to our task of predicting actions on any given message received by any given user.

3.1 Model & Features

Given a user i, we note $m_j^i \in M^i$ a message received by user i in his/her inbox M^i. The function $y(i,j,a)$ takes as value 1, if user i conducted action a on message m_j^i, and 0 otherwise. We define the task of *actionable email prediction* as predicting the value of $\hat{y}(i,j,a)$, for any new message m_j^i and for any action a, with a value 1 for predicting action a, and a value of 0 for a non-action. As discussed in Section 2, the actions we consider further are *read, reply, delete* and *delete-without-read*.

Each message m_j^i within the inbox is translated into a vector of features. We abuse notations and denote by m_j^i both the message and its associated feature vector. The extracted features range from "local" features, that is, features computed locally over a specific inbox, to "global" features computed over the entire mail dataset. Local features cover both features derived from the message content and header and features that reflect the behavioral pattern of the specific user over similar past messages. In contrast, global features refer to the entire dataset, typically referring to large senders. Examples include the overall number of messages sent by this specific sender, or the number of actions triggered by the sender across all users, etc. The exhaustive list of features we are using is detailed in Section 4. We regularly update our model as follows. When a user i performs an action a on message m_j^i, or does not perform this action on m_j^i over the predefined time period, we record the corresponding value of $y(i,j,a)$, and feed it as a labelled example to our model, the example being respectively positive or negative.

3.2 Horizontal vs Vertical Learning

Following [23], we propose to use a "vertical" view of email data, which focuses on each user's individual inbox and supports personalization, as well as a "horizontal" view of email across a very large number of email recipients, which leverages some type of "wisdom of crowds". In our *vertical learning* process, we learn from the historical data derived from a given inbox, considering both local and global features in order to predict actions on a new message. The quality of the prediction is therefore highly dependent on the availability of historical inbox data. However, we have observed in Section 2, that many users, even with large inboxes, are mostly passive and take very few actions. Even active users might focus on one type of action only. It is therefore critical to compensate for this lack of information by extrapolating from other users. To this effect we apply a complementary *horizontal learning* approach and apply regularization techniques as described next. We pause to mention that the concept of integrating between *horizontal* and *vertical* learning is not new and has been done in the past for tasks involving several types of data, including email (see e.g. [1]). Our novelty is the exact method for incorporating the horizontal learning, specially tailored for the task at hand (see also Section 5.3).

We consider two methods of regularization depending on the availability of historical data for a given user. The first method is applied to users who exhibit a very small amount of actions of a specific type in their inbox, and for whom the vertical learning model will probably perform poorly due to lack of data. In order to compensate for such sparse data, we compute, for each action, an *average user* model. We then add a specialized regularization term pulling the personalized model towards it, as detailed in Section 5.2, equation 2.

The second method is reserved to more active users, with respect to a given action. These users are defined as exhibiting a sufficient (above some action-specific threshold) number of positive examples. Our intuition here is that these users could benefit from the information derived from other users who somehow resemble them with respect to this action. It is clear that users exhibit various types of behavior on their email, yet the differences in behavior can be quite fine grained. Note that we are not trying to infer high-level type of inboxes (e.g., work-from-home, family, bookkeeping, etc.), but rather focus on behavioral patterns for each action. To this effect, we propose to identify *latent user* types with respect to each action. The rationale here is that each sufficiently active user will be somehow close to one of these latent types and could benefit from data learned on users who exhibit similar behavior for this action. To this effect we consider users with a rich dataset for a given action, and derive from them a relatively small number of latent user types. Note that, like in traditional collaborative filtering, we do not attempt to label or interpret these latent types as our goal is to exploit them solely for regularization. We explain in Section 5.2 how we identify a set of latent user types for each action, and how we leverage them for regularization purposes. We mention that this form of regularization, to the best of our knowledge, has not been suggested in the past, possibly due to its unique setting where the task involves learning multiple regressors (per user) that are assumed to have an underlying cluster-like structure (each cluster corresponds to a latent user type).

4. MAIL FEATURES

Given a user's inbox, we generate for each message a feature vector. Then for each possible action on a message, we assign to the corresponding feature vector a binary label that indicates whether the message triggered the respective action or not. We detail below how these feature vectors are generated.

The naive feature space of the predictor is quite large, given the numerous fields of the current Internet Message Format [28]. These features are derived from the message header (covering header fields such as `sender` including domain and associated IP, `cc`, "subject", etc.), from the message body and also additional meta-data fields provided by the mail service such as URLs included in the body. Potentially, the number of feature values that can be derived, especially from textual fields such as subject or body, can be quite large. One method to handle this, is to limit the scope of feature values as described later. For each message m, we denote the set of fields associated with m by $\mathcal{F} = \{f_1, \ldots, f_k\}$, where k is the total number of fields. We define a function $\phi(\cdot)$ that maps the set of fields $\mathcal{F}$ into features $x_1, \ldots, x_n$, where n is the total number of features.

As mentioned in Section 3, we distinguish between local features and global features. Local features represent the messages forming an individual user's inbox as well as the way the user reacted to similar messages in the past. In this context, similarity is defined with respect to the different fields from which the features are generated. Global features relate to the message sender, and characterize the way by which all users, as a collective, react to messages sent by the same sender.

Local features pertain to the different fields of a message m, and can be divided into the two following types:

- **Action independent:** Each such feature is based on a specific field $f_j \in m$, and indicates whether the user previously received messages with a similar (identical) value of f_j. We keep both a binary and scalar version of this feature. The binary feature holds a $0/1$ value that reflects whether or not the user received such a message in the past, while the value of the scalar feature holds the count of messages (received over a certain period of time) that have a similar field value for f_j. For example, consider the sender field, and assume message m_t^i was sent to user i from `info@twitter.com`. Then, the binary feature associated with the sender field for m_t^i indicates whether messages from `info@twitter.com` were received by user i in the past, while the scalar feature reflects the count of messages received from this sender. Table 4 details the different fields on which this type of features are based.
- **Action dependent:** Each such feature is based on a specific field $f_j \in m$ and a given action $a_z \in \mathcal{A}$ that might be performed on m. Consider a message m_t^i received at time t by user i, and sent by a sender s. Then, for each action $a_z \in \mathcal{A}$, we generate a feature that indicates whether user i ever performed this specific action a_z over messages sent by the same sender. Like in the previous case, we keep both binary and scalar versions of these features. Note that the total number of this type of features is a cross product of the number of fields we consider (namely k) and the number of actions considered

Global features pertain to senders over the entire mail dataset and are also divided into types, as detailed below:

- **General traffic sender features:** These features cover absolute and relative counts of messages exchanged between a given sender and the recipient population in our dataset. They include:
  - **Traffic features:** These features provide absolute and relative counts of messages both sent and received by the sender.
  - **Reply traffic features:** These features provide relative counts (expressed as percentages) of messages sent as reply messages, either *by* or *to* the sender. We also keep a feature indicating the ratio between the number of messages that the sender sent to users, and the number of messages it received from the mail users of our service.
- **Conditioned sender traffic features:** These features represent various types of sender traffic information, conditioned by certain attributes. They include:
  - **Sender traffic, conditioned by action:** Given a sender, this feature provides the total and relative counts (across the entire dataset) of sent messages that triggered a specific action.
  - **Sender traffic, conditioned by textual content:** Given a sender, this feature provides the total and relative counts of sent messages that include some specific words in their body. Examples of such words are "unsubscribe", "free", "delivered", etc, which are with high probability indicators of message types such as newsletters, promotions, purchases etc. These terms were manually chosen as the 50 most frequent words in the sender's messages (stop-words not included).
  - **Sender mass traffic:** Given a sender, this feature provides the total and relative counts of the messages sent by the sender to more than one recipient.
  - **Sender burst traffic:** Given a sender, this feature provides the relative count of messages sent by the sender in a burst. A burst corresponds to messages with identical subject, send over a small time interval. We have observed that bursts are quite frequent among mass senders of machine-generated email (for promotion campaigns for instance).

Finally, we add for every sender a global semantic feature, that we refer to as the **sender latent category feature**. This feature builds upon the work of Grbovic et al. [18], which identifies for any message or sender a high-level category out of the 6 latent categories that were identified on a large mail dataset. These 6 latent categories are: finance, shopping, social, travel, career, and personal communication. We compute for each sender the latent category using the classification approach described in this work, and associate either one the 6 values or a nil value, if the category cannot be inferred.

5. VERTICAL-HORIZONTAL LEARNING

In Sections 3,4, we described how we generate for each message a vector of features, which later becomes a labelled example, referred to as a *sample*, with respect to each action. More specifically, for each message m_j received by user i, and each monitored action a, we generate either a new positive sample for an observed value $y(i,j,a) = 1$ or a negative one for an observed valued $y(i,j,a) = 0$, as per the formalism introduced in Section 3.

Thus, the stream of messages received by the user is transformed into a stream of samples, ordered by time, each sample being created after some time interval. In order to run the learning process efficiently, we divide the stream of samples into small *batches*, the latest batch comprising the most recent samples. Upon creation of a new batch (e.g., a batch of samples aggregated on a daily basis), the learning model is retrained, based on the whole set of samples (including the samples of the latest batch). In the most extreme case, a batch consists of a single message only. This mechanism allows us to support an *online learning* process (see [30] and references therein). We build 4 types of predictors, one for each of the actions considered: *read, reply, delete*, and *delete-without-read.* We describe next the vertical and horizontal learning processes, that we have introduced and motivated in Section 3.

5.1 Vertical Learning

Vertical learning is by definition highly personalized and provides the best results, when enough historical data is available. For each user, the available data varies between the different actions. For example, a user with a heavy personal correspondence performs many replies, but might delete rarely. We thus define the level of activity of each user with respect to each action. Specifically, for a user i and action a, we define $n_{i,a}$ as the number of observed actions of type a performed by the user during the training period. We later demonstrate that unsurprisingly, for users with a large $n_{i,a}$ value, the vertical-learning based model performs well and does not have much to gain from the horizontal learning techniques mentioned below. We define "active users" for action a, as

Field	*Sender s*	*Sender Domain/IP*	*Recipients*	*Subject*	*Body*
Local, Action-Independent	# of inbox msg from similar sender s	# of inbox msg from similar domain/IP	# of inbox msg w/ similar recipients	# of inbox msg w/ similar subject	# of inbox msg w/ similar body words
Local, Action-Dependent	as above, cross action	as above, cross action	as above, cross action	as above, cross action	as above, cross action
Global, Action-Independent	-traffic sent/received by s -reply traffic sent to/from s -ratio between traffic sent & received by s -sender latent category	–	sender traffic with similar # of recipients	-sender traffic with similar subject words -sender traffic sent as burst	sender traffic with similar body words
Global, Action-Dependent	cross action: sender traffic triggering a specific action	–	–	–	–

Table 4: Global & Local Features

users whose $n_{i,a}$ value is above some action-specific threshold, as detailed in Section 5.2.

Vertical learning is performed as follows. For each inbox the model is trained solely based on messages and actions performed by the particular user. Formally, the vertical learning of the model for user i is done by training only on samples associated with the training set of user i. We note that this process is not purely vertical as some of the features (such as the rate of reply to message sent by a sender) are global and contain data obtained from different inboxes. For each user and action, we train a *personal predictor*, by using both positive and negative examples for action a from the user train set. We note that in this model, the labels of the examples corresponding to an action are skewed, since applying an action on a message is much less frequent than not applying the action. One way to address this is to take into consideration the frequency of the action. For each user and action, we use standard logistic regression to train our model, and conduct *cross validation* [19] on the models for users with at least 10 positive and 10 negative examples, optimizing for the AUC measure [24].

Although vertical learning may suffice for users with sufficient observed history, there will always be a non-negligible number of less active users with only a few actions. These include new users with small inboxes, more passive users with a usage rate below the required usage rate mentioned above, and also more active users, who do not equally favor all actions as mentioned in Section 3. In order to properly handle such users, we introduce a "horizontal" learning method.

5.2 Horizontal Learning

The horizontal learning approach is critical to our ability to predict actions for "all" users, including those with few samples. We refer to these users as "light users", that is, users with a $n_{i,a}$ value below some threshold. We described below how we derive information horizontally from all users across all inboxes.

"Average User" Horizontal Model.

For each action, we train a model with samples from many different inboxes, so as to be able to model an "average user". Using the entire set of message across these multiple users, we create for each action an *average inbox* based on a set of examples. Each such inbox is created using a set of samples counting about $10,000$ positive and $10,000$ negative examples, respectively representing messages that did or did not trigger the action. The examples are created by first applying a uniform sampling over the users, and then applying a uniform sampling over their messages. An *average user predictor* is then trained for each action, based on the average inbox of the considered action.

"Latent User-type" Horizontal Model.

The idea here to cluster users into a small number of latent types. This is done by computing the personal predictors of all users having a rich dataset for the considered action, and clustering these predictors according to their coefficient vectors. More specifically, for each action a, we choose about $2,500$ users who have more than 100 positive and 100 negative examples in their dataset (see Section 2.2). We train a personal predictor for each user i and each action a using vertical learning, getting as output the coefficient vector w^i_a. Then, we cluster these coefficient vectors using the k-means++ implementation [4], with standard methods for model selection, resulting in 8 clusters. For each cluster, a *latent type predictor* is computed, with a coefficient vector equal to the center of the corresponding cluster. The assumption is that the personal predictor of a user will typically be close to the predictor of its corresponding latent type. This way, a prior is learned for each type of user, later to be used in the regularization process.

Regularization.

A classic regularization process in the context of linear classifiers can be described as follows: We learn a coefficient vector w while minimizing

$$\mathbb{E}_{x,y}\left[\text{Loss}(w,x,y)\right] + \lambda\|w\|$$

Here, $\text{Loss}(w,x,y)$ describes the loss inferred by choosing a vector w for example x with label y, $\|w\|$ describes the norm of w (can be set to L1 or L2) and λ is a regularization parameter. In the specific case of Logistic regression we have (for $y \in \{-1,1\}$) $\text{Loss}(w,x,y) = \log\left(1 + e^{y\langle w,x\rangle}\right)$.

We apply two types of regularization depending on the type of users.

1. A user i is said to be active with respect to action a if $n_{i,a}$, the number of observed examples of the action in the corresponding training set not less than some threshold τ. A global optimization using a grid search over the user pool led us to set $\tau = 23$. For active users, we define their latent type according to the cluster to which they belong with respect to k-means (determined by the minimum distance between the coefficient vector of their personal predictor and the coefficient vector of the latent type predictor). The regularization is performed using their distance from the latent type predictor. That is, the optimization function in the training process is set to
$$\mathbb{E}_{x,y}\left[\text{Loss}(w,x,y)\right] + \min_{w_0 \in C} \lambda(n_{i,a})\|w - w_0\|. \quad (1)$$
Here, C is the set of coefficient vectors corresponding to latent predictors, and the norm used is the L2 norm. The regularization coefficient λ was set as $\lambda(n_{i,a}) = \alpha \cdot n_{i,a}^{-\beta}$ where α, β are hyper parameters. An optimization for α, β via a grid-search over the training data yielded $\alpha = 5, \beta = -0.4$. Notice that the weight of the regularization term decreases with the number of positive examples in the training set.

2. For light users, i.e. users with $n_{i,a} < \tau$, we do not have enough data to compute their latent types, thus regularization

is performed using the average user predictor only. Specifically, the optimization target in the training phase is defined as

$$\mathbb{E}_{x,y}\left[\mathrm{Loss}(w,x,y)\right] + \lambda'(n_{i,a})\|w - w_{\text{Avg}}\|, \quad (2)$$

where w_{Avg} is the coefficient vector of the average user predictor. For the regularization coefficient λ', we use the same technique of setting $\lambda(n_{i,a}) = \alpha' \cdot n_{i,a}^{-\beta'}$. The optimization of α', β' yielded $\alpha' = 6, \beta' = -0.5$.

5.3 Relation with Transfer Learning

There are several pieces of work that relate to the learning framework we suggest, mainly with respect to horizontal learning, which transfers actions behavior across users. The umbrella area is called *transfer learning* [27], and focuses on problems, for which a solution in one domain can be exploited in another domain. More precisely, a *source* dataset X_S, y_S and a *target* dataset X_T, y_T are being considered. The sets X_S and X_T contain feature vectors drawn from distribution $\mathcal{D}_S, \mathcal{D}_T$, respectively. The labels distribution of y_S and y_T are assumed to be dominated by $p(y|x, \lambda_S)$ and $p(y|x, \lambda_T)$ respectively, where some connection between λ_T, λ_S exists.

Several subproblems are defined in the context of transfer learning. In the *covariate shift* problem [31], it is assumed that $\lambda_T = \lambda_S$ but the distributions generating X_S and X_T are different. This is not a reasonable assumption in our case as it translates to the assumption that all users demonstrate the same behavior for the same inbox. The works of [10, 17] discuss cases in which $\lambda_T \neq \lambda_S$. The assumptions we are familiar with can be split into two types. The first type assumes that λ_S and λ_T are sufficiently close, hence using a regularization that pulls towards λ_S can benefit the learning process in the target data[2]. The second type assumes that despite the different distributions, there exists a single classifier achieving a sufficiently good performance on both the source and destination datasets.

Our application can be considered as an extension to the first type of assumption. We do not have a single source dataset, but rather many (e.g., all the users other than the one being handled), and we assume that all of the λ's are close in the sense that they are all drawn i.i.d from a distribution of distributions. Our assumption regarding the process for generating the different λ coefficients is the following. First, since we use a linear model, we assume that for each user i and sample x, y is a Bernoulli random variable (assuming labels in $\{0, 1\}$) whose expected value is determined by $\langle w_i, x\rangle$, where w_i is some unknown vector associated with user i. The i.i.d assumption regarding the λ_i's translates to assuming that all w_i are drawn i.i.d according to some unknown distribution $\mathcal{D}$. Our assumption of having a handful of *latent user types* translates into assuming that $\mathcal{D}$ is (close to) a mixed gaussian distribution. Keeping this assumption in mind, one can imagine two possible scenarios when learning a model for user i. In one setting, user i has a light activity level and it is not possible to predict, with sufficiently high confidence, the component of the mixture distribution from which it is derived. In this case, we perform a regularization using the average user predictor. On the other hand, when user i has a sufficient number of observed examples, it is possible to determine its associated component with high probability, hence we regularize the learning process with the latent user predictor.

The benefits of this approach is demonstrated in Figure 3. The figure depicts two examples of users i and k. User i is a light user, for whom we do not have many examples. Therefore, for user i, our

[2]We note that using a custom made regularization is not the only method to exploit the fact that λ_S, λ_T are close

Figure 3: Average User & Latent User-type Regularizations

estimation w_i of w_i^* (the true linear function associated with user i) is too far in order to determine its latent type (i.e., component in the mixture distribution). For that reason, a regularization according to the average predictor, i.e. using $\hat{w}_i$, yields better results then those obtained by performing a regularization using the latent type. For user k however, the number of observed examples is larger, and our approximation w_k of w_k^* is more precise. We are able to determine the latent type of user k, and use it for regularization in order to yield better results, as will be verified in our experiments.

6. EXPERIMENTS

In this section we describe the large scale experiments we carried on Yahoo mail data. The dataset we used for the experiments is described in Section 2, and we describe here the models we ran, as well as the results we achieved.

As described in Section 5, we divided each inbox in our dataset into a *train* and a *test* dataset, based on time. We evaluated 4 action predictors introduced in Section 5: *read, reply, delete*, and *delete-without-read*, separately. For every user i, and action a we learned 3 different predictors: (1) a *personal predictor*, (2) an *average user predictor*, and (3) a *latent type predictor*. Predictor (1) ignores the horizontal learning part and is trained solely based on the samples of user i. Predictor (2) uses regularization according to the average user model. Predictor (3) is built from the model described in Section 5, choosing the regularization method according to the number of observed samples for user i and action a.

For each predictor, action and user, we computed precision and recall values, using as ground truth the actual actions taken by the user in the test set. We then averaged them over all users. Formally, for user i, predictor type t (with t indicating the previously defined predictor type), action a, and recall value R ($R \in [0, \ldots, 100]$), we compute the precision at R for the predictor of type t, action a and user i, and denote it as $P(R, t, a, i)$. We set the precision at R score of predictor type t and action type a as $\mathbb{E}_i[P(R, t, a, i)]$, the expected value over all users. The area under the curve (AUC) score associated to an action type a and predictor t is formally defined the average (over recall values) precision of the action w.r.t the predictor ($\mathbb{E}_{i,R}[P(R, t, a, i)]$).

In order to best demonstrate the effectiveness of the regularization methods, for each action we consider only users with a low activity level. Specifically, users with fewer than 70 actions observed in the training period. We recall here that users with such low activity are not at all rare, even for the more common actions (see Section 2, Figure 2). The reason is that with over 70 actions, all 3 predictors performed similarly; this is due to the (somewhat unsurprising) fact that with a rich training set the regularization has a smaller impact. A comparison of the prediction types is given in Table 5. It lists the AUC score associated with every pair of predictor t and action a, where the users being considered are those with the above defined low activity level.

For these users, we can see the benefit of the regularization techniques (average-user based, latent user-type based). Although the regularizations did not provide a substantial improvement for all action types (for example, the *delete* and *delete-without-read* are insignificant), we see that for some actions the improvement is quite significant. For the reply action, we observe a lift of 32% using the average-user based regularization, and a lift of 48% for the latent user-type regularization (such an improvement could have a significant impact on these users specifically, pointing out their small set of "actionable" messages). For the read action, the lift is not as substantial but is significant nevertheless.

Action	*Read*	*Reply*	*Delete*	*Delete-without-Read*
Vertical	0.228	0.204	0.121	0.104
Avg. User	0.236	0.269	0.127	0.103
Latent Type	0.248	0.302	0.13	0.104

Table 5: AUC values per operation per model, averaged over users with a low activity level

To realize the effect of the activity level of a user on the performance of the prediction task we measured the AUC value for different levels of high activity; the results are given in Figure 4. For every action type, we measured the AUC score for users with at least X observed actions in the training period for X taking several possible values. Since we focused on relatively large values for X ($X \geq 70$) we do not present 3 different predictors as they all demonstrate practically the same performance. One can see that at $X = 200$, all action AUC score are (almost) completely stabilized.

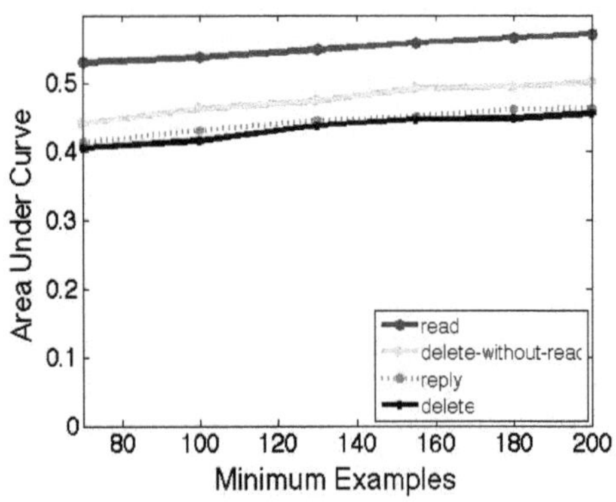

Figure 4: Area Under the Curve vs. minimum observed samples in the training set. The x axis is a minimum threshold for the number of observed positive samples in the training set. The y axis is the AUC score for each action, averaged over all users with at least x observed positive samples in their training set.

We paid special attention to highly active users, with more than 200 observed positive samples in the training set ($n_{i,a} \geq 200$), since they would benefit most from predicting actions. Figure 5 shows several precision/recall plots for them. As stated before, we are interested in the case of high recall. We see that for the reply action, we achieve a precision score of roughly 36% at recall 90%. As mentioned in Section 1, given the inherent difficulty of the task, this result is quite encouraging. Indeed, one could imagine a new mail feature that would put in a same view messages that should be replied to. In such a view, the reply link would achieve a CTR value of 30%, as compared to the 9.52% CTR that can be observed in an average inbox of such users today, as reported in Table 2. This shows an improvement of 200% for the reply action for users with more than 200 actions. In any case, we stress that CTR or other types of measures should be applied in accordance to the specific use case and user experience considered. We provide here the "backend system" for analyzing and predicting users' actions, which would enable the support of such experiences.

The full list of precision values for a recall of 90% is reported in Table 6. We use as baseline the average success of a constant predictor, predicting that the action will always be performed (100% recall). This is in fact a naive baseline when targeting a high recall, which corresponds to Table 2. Using this baseline over users with more than 200 actions, the increase achieved for our actions can be seen in Table 6. For *read*, which is another notable action, we demonstrated an increase from 20.2% to 37.9%.

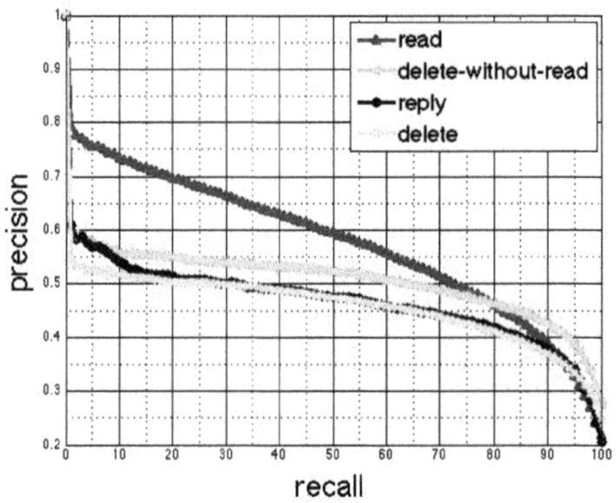

Figure 5: Precision-Recall - active users. For each action, the precision recall curve is averaged over users with more than 200 observed positive samples

Action	*Read*	*Reply*	*Delete*	*Delete-without-Read*
Baseline	20.2%	9.52%	20.29%	19.76%
Prec@90%	37.9%	37%	36.3%	41.6%

Table 6: Comparison with baseline for users with more than 200 actions

7. RELATED WORK

The problem of studying user's actions on messages is not new. It was traditionally conducted in a relative small scope, either leveraging the Enron corpus [21], a small set of monitored users, or users' studies, surveys, etc. The Enron corpus was used by numerous researchers as the basis for learning and predicting reply actions, by leveraging various email exchange features [11, 5, 26, 29]. Another approach was to track the actions of a small number of users. Thus in [9], the inboxes of 6 enterprise mail users were monitored in order to investigate the characteristics of an email message likely to be discarded. Dabbish et al. [8] investigated the more general task of predicting actions, as we do here, but their work was solely based on data obtained from the answers of a survey they conducted over 124 college students. The latter voluntarily reported data pertaining to message content, sender characteristics, communication frequency, etc. Using the same approach of considering few inboxes but focusing on different features (e.g., user profile, identity of recipients and sender, different natures of content), Dredze et al. [13, 14] developed a predictor for reply action, evaluating their results on 2-4 inboxes of graduate students. Tyler et al. [33] identified several factors that may influence the likelihood of response using an empirical study generally based on interviews. The replying behavior of users was investigated by Kooti et al. [22]. They focused on the various factors affecting reply time and length, on the influence of email overload, as well as on the synchronization of these reply characteristics in threads. The work presented in [22] is specific to the reply behavior only, which is deeply investigated. Users however are not differed with respect to their activity level, nor are other operations considered. To the best of our knowledge, the only piece of work that studied a wide range of actions over Web mail, as we do, is the work by Aberdeen et al. [1] on Gmail priority inbox. The distinction between enterprise or small-organization email prediction and Web email is critical since, as mentioned before, they drastically differ, not only in size, but in nature of traffic and behavior. In Gmail priority inbox, the notion of importance is based on the probability that a user will perform an action on a message, where the set of actions include actions such as reply, open, forward etc. We significantly differ from this work, as we intentionally ignore inferred importance and focus on predicting actions as the task at hand. Another distinction between our work and that of [1] is in the mix of the vertical and horizontal learning. In [1], a standard approach in which the vertical learning learns the difference between the user's model from the global model, learned separately in a horizontal learning phase. Here we use a problem specific approach, exploiting a hidden cluster-like structure of the users' behavioral patterns in order to best incorporate the weights learned horizontally to those learned vertically, as detailed in Section 5.

Less directly related to our work here is the large amount of literature around spam classification, such as [6, 34, 32]) or email organization, tagging or classification. In the area of spam classification, two pieces of work are worth noting. One is the early work by Taylor [32], who described how sender reputation has been leveraged in Gmail antispam filter. Like in our case, Taylor described methods that that are highly scalable and deal with mass senders. Another is the work by Bickel et al. [6], who applied as we do transfer learning on email, but for a different task namely spam filtering. The authors assume that each user's inbox is parameterized by a single (numeric) parameter coming from a different distribution. Given this parameter, the model of the label (i.e., $p(y|x)$ where $x \in X$ represents the message and y represents the label namely, spam or ham) is common to all inboxes.

In the area of mail organization, various classification methods have been proposed in different contexts. Klimt et al. [21] learned from individual inboxes in order to automatically assign messages to user-defined folders. Other methods for organizing a user's inbox, too numerous to exhaustively cite here, leveraged rule-based, information retrieval or machine learning methods, see as examples [3, 7, 12, 20]. Two pieces of work (co-authored by some of the authors on this paper) worth noting in this area, are the studies by Koren et al. [23], and Grbovic et al. [18] on Yahoo mail data. The first [23], proposed a classification method based on learning the most popular folders from the entire set of users, and introduced the notion of horizontal and vertical learning for email, which we endorse her. The other [18], described an approach for distinguishing between personal and machine-generated email, and for classifying messages into latent categories, which also influenced this work.

8. CONCLUSION

Based on a thorough study of users actions in Yahoo mail, we presented here a novel approach for predicting users' actions on newly received messages. Unlike some recent work that attempted to infer the message importance from user's activities, we intentionally decided to go back to the basics and focus on the actions themselves. We considered the most frequent actions, namely *read, reply, delete*, and a sub-type of delete, *delete-without-read*. We formalized the task of "actionable email prediction", and defined a learning framework that takes advantage of the size and nature of large-scale Web mail. More specifically we introduced both local (i.e., inbox-specific) and global (i.e., at the mail population level) features to represent messages, and devised "vertical" and "horizontal" methods to train and predict actions for all types of users. We verified that the quality of our vertical learning for action prediction on an individual inbox was highly dependent on the level of activity of the user for this action. Consequently, we complemented our vertical learning with horizontal learning for regularization purposes. To this effect, we defined two majors action-specific types of users according to their activity level for this action, namely "light" and "active" users. For light users, we applied a regularization method based on an "average user" horizontal model for each action. For more active users, our regularization method leveraged a "latent user-type" horizontal model, which allows to model the behavior of a representative user of the same latent-type. One clear benefit of this hybrid approach is that it allows to predict actions for all types of users, across numerous types of behavior, i.e, users who read and delete a lot but don't reply much, or users who reply a lot but never delete, etc.

We conducted a large scale experiment on data from Yahoo mail, building predictors for each type of action. Each predictor was trained both for active and light users. As expected the best performance was obtained on more active users, yet we showed that horizontal learning could compensate for the lack of data. For users with a high level of activity, we showed that for recall values of 90% we can predict important actions such as read or reply at precision levels of close to 40%. A possible exploitation of our results would be to offer for instance a view of the messages a user should reply to. In this view, the reply link would achieve a CTR value of 30%, as compared to the 9.52% CTR that can be observed in an average inbox of such users today, leading to an improvement of 200%. For users with a low activity level, we showed that our horizontal-based regularization methods achieve a significant increase in the AUC measure for most types of operations: the reply operation for example reached a lift of up to 48%.

To the best of our knowledge, our work is the first to provide a unified framework of this scale for predicting multiple actions on Web email, which hopefully provides a new ground for inventing new user experiences to help users process their inboxes.

9. REFERENCES

[1] D. Aberdeen, O. Pacovsky, and A. Slater. The learning behind gmail priority inbox. In *LCCC: NIPS 2010 Workshop on Learning on Cores, Clusters and Clouds*. Elsevier, 2010.

[2] N. Ailon, Z. Karnin, E. Liberty, and Y. Maarek. Threading machine generated email. In *Proceedings of WSDM'2013*, pages 405–414, New York, NY, USA, 2013.

[3] I. Alberts and D. Forest. Email pragmatics and automatic classification: A study in the organizational context. *JASIST*, 63(5):904–922, 2012.

[4] D. Arthur and S. Vassilvitskii. k-means++: The advantages of careful seeding. In *Proceedings of SODA'2007*, New Orleans, LA, Jan 2007.

[5] T. Ayodele and S. Zhou. Applying machine learning techniques for e-mail management: solution with intelligent e-mail reply prediction. *Journal of Engineering and Technology Research*, 1(7):143–151, 2009.

[6] S. Bickel and T. Scheffer. Dirichlet-enhanced spam filtering based on biased samples. *Advances in neural information processing systems*, 19:161, 2007.

[7] W. Cohen. Learning rules that classify e-mail. In *AAAI Spring Symposium on Machine Learning in Information Access*, pages 18–25, 1996.

[8] L. Dabbish, R. Kraut, S. Fussell, and S. Kiesler. Understanding email use: predicting action on a message. In *Proceedings of CHI'2005*, Portland,OR, Apr 2005.

[9] L. A. Dabbish, G. Venolia, and J.J. Cadiz. Marked for deletion: An analysis of email data. In *Proceedings of CHI'2003*, Fort Lauderdale, FL, Apr 2003.

[10] H. Daumé III. Frustratingly easy domain adaptation. *arXiv preprint arXiv:0907.1815*, 2009.

[11] P. Deepak, D. Garg, and V. Varshney. Analysis of enron email threads and quantification of employee responsiveness. In *Workshop on Text Mining and Link Analysis*, 2007.

[12] Y. Diao, H. Lu, and D. Wu. A comparative study of classification based personal e-mail filtering. In *Proceedings of PAKDD'2000*, Kyoto, Japan, Apr 2000.

[13] M. Dredze, J. Blitzer, and F. Pereira. Reply expectation prediction for email management. In *Proceedings of CEAS'2005*, Stanford, CA, Jul 2005.

[14] M. Dredze, T. Brooks, J. Carroll, J. Magarick, J. Blitzer, and F. Pereira. Intelligent email: Reply and attachment prediction. In *Proceedings of IUI'2008*, Canary Islands, Spain, Jan 2008.

[15] J. Duffy. Google inbox for gmail (for iphone). *PC Magazine*, Oct 2014.

[16] S. Dumais, E. Cutrell, JJ. Cadiz, G. Jancke, R. Sarin, and DC. Robbins. Stuff I've seen: A system for personal information retrieval and re-use. In *Proceedings of SIGIR*, pages 72–79, Toronto, Canada, 2003.

[17] T. Evgeniou and M. Pontil. Regularized multi–task learning. In *Proceedings of KDD'2004*, Seattle, WA, Aug 2004.

[18] M. Grbovic, G. Halawi, Z. Karnin, and Y. Maarek. How many folders do you really need? classifying email into a handful of categories. In *Proceedings of CIKM'2014*, 2014.

[19] T. Hastie, J. Friedman, and R. Tibshirani. *The elements of statistical learning: Data Mining, Inference, Prediction*, volume 2. Springer, 2009.

[20] S. Kiritchenko and S. Matwin. Email classification with co-training. In *Proceedings of the 2011 Conference of the Center for Advanced Studies on Collaborative Research*, pages 301–312, 2011.

[21] B. Klimt and Y. Yang. The enron corpus: A new dataset for email classification research. In *Proceedings of ECML'2004*, Pisa, Italy, Sep 2004.

[22] F. Kooti, L.M. Aiello, M. Grbovic, K. Lerman, and A. Mantrach. Evolution of conversations in the age of email overload. In *Proceedings of the 24th International Conference on World Wide Web*, WWW '15, pages 603–613, 2015.

[23] Y. Koren, E. Liberty, Y. Maarek, and R. Sandler. Automatically tagging email by leveraging other users' folders. In *Proceedings of KDD'2011*, San Diego, CA, Aug 2011.

[24] C.D. Manning, P. Raghavan, and H. Schütze. *Introduction to information retrieval*, volume 1. Cambridge university press Cambridge, 2008.

[25] Derek Mead. Aol's new alto client is visual email, and you don't need a new address. *MotherBoard*, Oct 2012.

[26] B. On, E. Lim, A. Purandare, and L. Teow. Mining interaction behaviors for email reply order prediction. In *Proceedings of ASONAM'2010*, pages 306–310, 2010.

[27] S.J. Pan and Q. Yang. A survey on transfer learning. *IEEE Transactions on Knowledge and Data Engineering*, 22(10):1345–1359, 2010.

[28] P. Resnick. Internet message format, rfc 5322, October 2008.

[29] M. Sappelli, S. Verberne, and W. Kraaij. Combining textual and non-textual features for e-mail importance estimation. In *Proceedings of the 25th Benelux Conference on Artificial Intelligence*, 2013.

[30] S. Shalev-Shwartz. Online learning and online convex optimization. *Foundations and Trends in Machine Learning*, 4(2):107–194, 2011.

[31] H. Shimodaira. Improving predictive inference under covariate shift by weighting the log-likelihood function. *Journal of statistical planning and inference*, 90(2), 2000.

[32] B. Taylor. Sender reputation in a large webmail service. In *Proceedings of CEAS'2006*, Mountain View, CA, Jul 2006.

[33] J. Tyler and J. Tang. When can i expect an email response? a study of rhythms in email usage. In *Proceedings of ECSCW'2003*, pages 239–258, Helsinki, Finland, Sep 2003.

[34] W.T. Yih, R. McCann, and A. Kolcz. Improving spam filtering by detecting gray mail. In *Proceedings of CEAS'2007*, Mountain View, CA, Aug 2007.

Hierarchical Label Propagation and Discovery for Machine Generated Email

James B. Wendt† Michael Bendersky† Lluis Garcia-Pueyo† Vanja Josifovski‡*
Balint Miklos† Ivo Krka† Amitabh Saikia† Jie Yang† Marc-Allen Cartright† Sujith Ravi†
†Google, Mountain View, CA, USA ‡Pinterest, San Francisco, CA, USA
†{jwendt, bemike, lgpueyo, bal, krka, amitabh, yangjie, mcartright, sravi}@google.com
‡vanja@pinterest.com

ABSTRACT

Machine-generated documents such as email or dynamic web pages are single instantiations of a pre-defined structural template. As such, they can be viewed as a hierarchy of template and document specific content. This hierarchical template representation has several important advantages for document clustering and classification. First, templates capture common topics among the documents, while filtering out the potentially noisy variabilities such as personal information. Second, template representations scale far better than document representations since a single template captures numerous documents. Finally, since templates group together structurally similar documents, they can propagate properties between all the documents that match the template. In this paper, we use these advantages for document classification by formulating an efficient and effective hierarchical label propagation and discovery algorithm. The labels are propagated first over a template graph (constructed based on either term-based or topic-based similarities), and then to the matching documents. We evaluate the performance of the proposed algorithm using a large donated email corpus and show that the resulting template graph is significantly more compact than the corresponding document graph and the hierarchical label propagation is both efficient and effective in increasing the coverage of the baseline document classification algorithm. We demonstrate that the template label propagation achieves more than 91% precision and 93% recall, while increasing the label coverage by more than 11%.

Categories and Subject Descriptors

H.4.3 [**Information Systems Applications**]: Communications Applications — *Electronic mail*

*Work done while at Google.

WSDM 2016 February 22-25, 2016, San Francisco, CA, USA

ACM ISBN 978-1-4503-3716-8/16/02.
DOI: http://dx.doi.org/10.1145/2835776.2835780

Keywords

Machine-generated email, structural template, hierarchical label propagation.

1. INTRODUCTION

Email is one of the most popular and frequently used web applications. Even with the more recent advent and widespread adoption of social networks, email continues to be the most pervasive form of online communication. Furthermore, it remains inextricably tied to user online identity. For example, the vast majority of account-based online services require an email address for validation purposes. This practice has effectively designated the inbox as a central and personal hub for the majority of online user activity, and will continue to act so for the foreseeable future.

According to the Radicati group [23], there are just over 2.5 billion email users in the world. This number is predicted to increase by 12% in four years time. The average consumer currently sends and receives an average of about 61 emails per day while business users send and receive an average of about 121. All together, about 196 billion emails are sent and received per day and is predicted to increase to 228 billion by 2018. This proliferation of email has led to the notion of *email overload*, in which users become overwhelmed when they can no longer organize, manage, and process their emails as quickly as they receive them [10].

The most widely adopted tools employed to manage this influx of emails—filters and labels—have not changed in years. Typical filters allow the user to sort mail based on a combination of header information and search terms. An example filter might automatically move all incoming emails received from "auto-confirm@amazon.com" to a *Shopping* folder. While filters can be powerful tools for managing emails from specific senders or sender domains, this is also largely the extent to which they are practical. For example, if a user wishes to label all incoming order confirmation emails to a *Shopping* folder, the user would need to manually generate filters for each potential sender. Given the vast number of e-commerce sites accessible on the web today, creating filters for each potential sender would require an insurmountable effort of creating relevant filters.

It is also important to note that email is no longer used solely for communication. It is used for information archiving and task management as well [11]. Automated machine-learned categorization of email can be an exceptionally powerful tool to improve user efficiency in inbox management by

Figure 1: Fictional example of two documents that were generated from the same structural template.

categorizing the email by logical folders or labels and reducing the inbox overload.

Categorization also produces an additional layer of semantic information that can be used to benefit the user experience. For example, consider an email that is automatically categorized as a flight itinerary. In this case, it would be beneficial to the user that the email service highlights this document and brings it to the forefront or alert the user of its importance near the relevant time of departure. On the other hand, a document labeled as a sales promotion might be skipped past the inbox altogether and archived for potential lookup later. Furthermore, email categorization can be used to help extract data from the email that is most relevant for a particular category.

In this paper, we present a novel technique for the categorization of machine-generated emails. We use *structural template* representations to create a scalable, robust, and accurate classifier that increases labeling coverage over a high-precision baseline classifier that does not employ structural template information.

We specifically target machine-generated emails for the following reasons: (a) they constitute a majority percentage of all emails [2], (b) machine-generated emails are very often instantiations of pre-defined structural templates. Figure 1 demonstrates a simple example of a structural template from a fictional *Dr. Seuss* store that is used to generate multiple documents by instantiating the template with the user-specific information (user name, purchased items, prices and order number).

Structural templates provide two important advantages for clustering and categorization. The first is that they scale better than emails since one template represents numerous emails. The second is that since templates represent structurally similar documents, they effectively capture common topics between documents while filtering out potential noise, such as personal information.

We use these advantages to formulate and explore three techniques for efficient and effective categorization. The first technique labels emails based on the majority label among the underlying emails that their corresponding template was inferred from. This simple classifier is a first step towards utilizing templates for email classification and does not take into consideration similarities or relationships between different templates.

The second technique utilizes inter-template similarities to build a centroid-based classifier. Templates are represented using either term-frequencies extracted from their fixed text or as a distribution of topics as inferred by Latent Dirichlet Allocation [8]. Fixed centroids are calculated for each label and are comprised of only those templates whose underlying email samples all correspond to a single label. Templates consisting of two or more labels in their underlying emails are labeled according to their closest centroid.

However, single centroids are often too coarse to adequately classify templates, which belong to the same label but may be vastly different from one another. Thus, we present a third technique which naturally follows the centroid approach, classifying templates using graph-based label propagation [24, 27]. Again, templates are represented using either bag-of-words or topic distributions, and distances or edges between templates are measured in terms of the similarity between their representations. Seed nodes are assigned from the same set used to calculate the centroids in the previous technique. These nodes are the first to emit their labels to their neighbors, then those neighbors emit them to their neighbors, and so on until the entire graph is labeled.

Once the label propagation process over the template graph is complete we propagate the label distributions of the templates to their underlying emails. We refer to this process as *hierarchical label propagation*.

Note that while the template-based categorization techniques discussed in this paper are focused on email data, they are general enough to be applied to any machine-generated documents including web pages, call data records, or government forms, among many others. To the best of knowledge, this is the first publicly available study on leveraging structural templates for the purpose of improving categorization of machine-generated documents in general, and specifically, machine-generated emails.

2. MODEL

In this section, we present the formal description of the hierarchical label propagation algorithm over a given machine-generated corpus. The algorithm operates in three main stages.

First, documents in the corpus are grouped by their underlying structural templates. Second, we construct a partially labeled graph over the template representations. Finally, we run a hierarchical label propagation algorithm over the template graph, which propagates the derived template labels to the individual document level.

The remainder of this section is organized as follows. In Section 2.1 we describe template representation methods for a machine-generated email corpus. In Section 2.2 we describe how these template representations can be organized as a graph. Finally, in Section 2.3, we describe several methods for label assignment and propagation over this template graph.

While in this section we focus on templatization and label propagation over an email corpus, the presented algorithms are general enough to be applied to any templatizable machine-generated document collection. Therefore, henceforth, we use the terms *document* and *email* interchangeably.

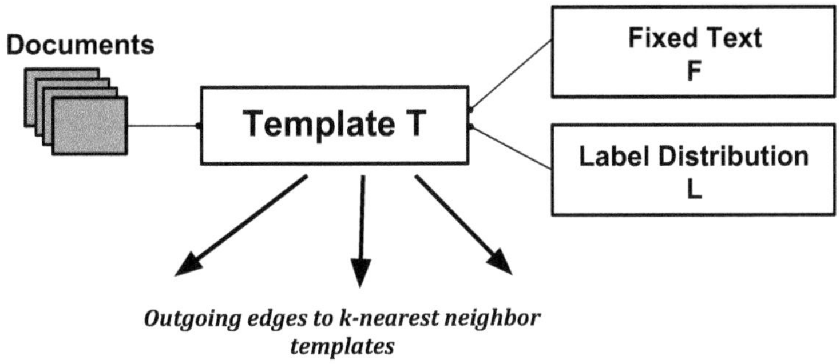

Figure 2: Template representation for graph construction.

2.1 Template Representations

There are multiple ways to derive structural templates from a stream of machine-generated documents. In smaller, specialized collections, the relation between the generating template and the document may be given a priori. For larger, web scale collections, techniques like locality sensitive hashing of document header text have been recently proposed [16].

There has been some previous work on template representation of machine-generated documents for email collections as well. Specifically relevant to this paper is work by Ailon et al. [2]. We use the approach proposed in their work, and map each incoming email document to a *template* that is uniquely identified by a

<*sender, subject-regexp*>

tuple. Subject regular expressions are obtained by mining frequent patterns and removing unique identifiers and personalized information, like names, from email subjects, as described by Ailon et al. [2].

In contrast to Ailon et al. [2], our approach goes beyond associating an email with a subject regular expression. For the purpose of template representation, we are interested in deriving (a) a textual representation of a template based on the content of the documents matching the template, and (b) a label distribution of the template.

This dual representation is then used to construct a template graph. Figure 2 summarizes this representation process, which is formally described next.

2.1.1 Textual Template Representation

Formally, we define template $\mathbf{T}$ as a set of documents $\mathbf{D^T} = \{D_1, \ldots, D_n\}$ matching a template identifier, as expressed by the <*sender, subject-regexp*> tuple.

To derive a textual representation of a template, we tokenize the set of documents $\mathbf{D^T}$, and derive a set of unique terms per template. Generally, this corresponds to a bag-of-words textual representation of the template.

Given a template term x, we define its *support* S_x as a number of documents in $\mathbf{D^T}$ that contain the term, or formally:

$$S_x^{\mathbf{T}} = |\{D | D \in \mathbf{D^T} \wedge x \in D\}| \tag{1}$$

We define the template *fixed text* as a set of terms for which the support is greater than some (large) fraction of the number of template documents, or formally:

$$\mathbf{F^T} = \{x | \frac{S_x^{\mathbf{T}}}{|\mathbf{D^T}|} \geq \tau\}, \tag{2}$$

where $0 < \tau < 1$ is set to a large fraction to remove personal information from the resulting template fixed text representation.

We then use the template fixed text representation $\mathbf{F^T}$, as a representation of a single node in a template graph. Note that this template representation addresses several important issues.

First, we only keep the fixed text of the template underlying any of the documents in the set $\mathbf{D^T}$. We remove noise and variabilities that are a result of introducing personal information into the documents. In this way, the template graph represents the true aspects of the underlying collection, and not those of its particular instantiations.

Second, note that Equation 2 ignores the actual number of documents used to construct the template. Therefore, each template is given the same weight, with no regard to the number of documents that were used to construct the template. This is beneficial for document collections that follow power law distributions. For instance, for email collections, document representation would be dominated by emails from more popular email senders, while template representation avoids this problem.

Finally, the resulting representation is significantly more compact than document representation, since a single template may cover hundreds or thousands of documents.

2.1.2 Topic Models for Template Representation

In addition to using single terms for template representation, we experiment with modeling templates using topic models [8]. We run a standard Latent Dirichlet Allocation topic modeling over the fixed text of the templates (see Equation 2). We then use the resulting topics along with their weights as template representations instead of the bag-of-words template representation.

2.1.3 Label Distribution

Each document associated with a template may be labeled by some classifier. Given some labeling scheme with m distinct labels, we associate each template with a label distribution:

$$\mathbf{L^T} = \{p(L_1|\mathbf{T}), \ldots, p(L_m|\mathbf{T})\}, \tag{3}$$

where the probability of a label given a template is simply a fraction of documents in the set $\mathbf{D^T}$ containing the label. As

Method	Similarity Metric	Edge Type
Cosine Similarity	$\frac{\sum_{x \in \mathbf{F}^{\mathbf{T}_i}, \mathbf{F}^{\mathbf{T}_j}} w(x,\mathbf{T}_i) w(x,\mathbf{T}_j)}{\sqrt{\sum_{x \in \mathbf{F}^{\mathbf{T}_i}} w(x,\mathbf{T}_i)^2} \sqrt{\sum_{x \in \mathbf{F}^{\mathbf{T}_j}} w(x,\mathbf{T}_j)^2}}$	Undirected
KL Divergence	$\exp(-\sum_{x \in \mathbf{F}^{\mathbf{T}_i} \cap \mathbf{F}^{\mathbf{T}_j}} p(x\|\mathbf{T}_i) \log \frac{p(x\|\mathbf{T}_i)}{\widetilde{p}(x\|\mathbf{T}_j)})$	Directed

Table 1: Template graph construction methods. We use either cosine similarity or KL divergence to define a weighted edge between a pair of templates $(\mathbf{T}_i, \mathbf{T}_j)$.

document labeling may be incomplete, we assign an empty label $L_\emptyset$ to documents that were not assigned any labels by the classifier.

2.2 Template Graph Construction

In this section we explain how the template graph is constructed given the fixed text representation described in the previous section.

Graph edges are constructed by selecting the k-nearest neighbors per node by similarity. We calculate edge weights using two metrics, cosine similarity and KL divergence. The two metrics used for graph construction are widely used for text similarity in information retrieval literature. In particular, KL divergence has been shown to be useful for graph construction over textual corpora [17]. The final edge weights are then computed by normalizing the weights of all outgoing edges from a node to sum up to one.

The weight of term x in template $\mathbf{T}$ is denoted by $w(x, \mathbf{T})$. For bag-of-words terms, this is a binary weight, which avoids over-weighting repeated fixed terms in the template (e.g., repetitions of the word *price* in receipts). For LDA topic representations, this is a topic weight assignment.

For further derivations we also define term probability

$$p(x|\mathbf{T}) = \frac{w(x, \mathbf{T})}{\sum_{x \in \mathbf{F}^{\mathbf{T}}} w(x, \mathbf{T})}, \quad (4)$$

and its smoothed version

$$\widetilde{p}(x|\mathbf{T}) = \frac{w(x, \mathbf{T}) + \epsilon}{\sum_{x \in \mathbf{F}^{\mathbf{T}}} w(x, \mathbf{T}) + |\mathbf{F}^{\mathbf{T}}|\epsilon}, \quad (5)$$

where ϵ is a small constant used for Laplacian smoothing.

Table 1 provides details on both the cosine similarity and the KL divergence metrics for graph construction.

2.3 Label Assignment and Propagation

Recall, from Section 2.1 that we associate a label distribution with a template. In this paper, we assume an existence of an underlying high-precision / low-recall classifier that assigns a single label to each document. Template label distribution is based on these document-level labels. The description of the document-level classifier is out of the scope of this paper, and for the remainder of this section, we assume that this classifier may be based on either hand-written rules or a supervised model that is specifically optimized for document-level precision. Such classifiers are common in critical user-facing tasks, where the cost of false positives is very high. An example of such a task is email spam detection, where marking something as spam may prevent a user from ever seeing an email.

In such high-precision scenarios, the classifier will err on the side of caution. Our approach enables grouping classifier decisions by a structural template, and improving the classifier recall, without sacrificing precision. Therefore, in the models described in the next sections we develop methods to assign a single optimal label $L^{\mathbf{T}}_{OPT}$ to a template based on the label distribution of its documents and the label distribution of its neighboring templates in the template graph.

Given that all the documents come from the same underlying template, the classifier decision should be unanimous for the template, which is the property we leverage in the *majority label* approach described in Section 2.3.1.

In addition, similar templates should have similar labels, which is addressed by the *centroid similarity* and the *hierarchical label propagation* approaches described in Section 2.3.2 and Section 2.3.3, respectively.

2.3.1 Majority Label

The majority labeling classifier is our most direct method for labeling documents by way of their corresponding templates. We use this classifier as a baseline for comparison against more advanced graph-based techniques.

As explained in Section 2.1, a template is assoicated with a label distribution $\mathbf{L}^{\mathbf{T}}$. The majority label classifier thus labels a template according to the label which is assigned to more than 50% of the documents in the template. Formally, the assigned label for template $\mathbf{T}$ is determined as:

$$L^{\mathbf{T}}_{OPT} = \begin{cases} L_i & \text{if exists } L_i \text{ s.t. } p(L_i|\mathbf{T}) > 0.5 \\ L_\emptyset & \text{otherwise} \end{cases}$$

For instance, if template $\mathbf{T}$ is comprised of 100 emails, 80 of which are labeled *Receipt* and 20 of which are labeled *Finance* by the baseline document classifier, then $L^{\mathbf{T}}_{OPT} =$ *Receipt* and all 100 emails in $\mathbf{D}^{\mathbf{T}}$ will be relabeled as *Receipt*.

On the other hand, if template $\mathbf{T}$ is comprised of 100 emails, with ten labels and ten emails assigned to each label, $L^{\mathbf{T}}_{OPT} = L_\emptyset$, and the emails in $\mathbf{D}^{\mathbf{T}}$ will not be relabeled.

Note that the majority label approach utilizes solely intra-template information for classification. It thus ignores the template graph structure, which is addressed by the approaches discussed in the next sections.

2.3.2 Centroid Similarity

The centroid similarity approach takes advantage of inter-template relationships for template label assignment. Templates are represented using their fixed text $\mathbf{F}^{\mathbf{T}}$, as discussed in Section 2.1. We then derive a set of *seed templates* for each label L_i (excluding the empty label) such that

$$\mathbb{S}^{L_i} = \{\mathbf{T}|p(L_i|\mathbf{T}) = 1\}. \quad (6)$$

In other words, seed templates are templates for which label assignment is already provided with 100% confidence by the underlying high-precision document classifier.

For each seed template set $\mathbb{S}^{L_i}$, we compute its centroid vector by averaging the fixed text vectors $\mathbf{F}^{\mathbf{T}}$ of its templates. Then, for every non-seed template $\mathbf{T}$ with label distribution $\mathbf{L}^{\mathbf{T}}$, we compute its similarity to the centroids of the labels in $\mathbf{L}^{\mathbf{T}}$. Similarity is computed using either one of the metrics shown in Table 1. We then assign the label of the *closest* centroid to template $\mathbf{T}$ and relabel all the documents in the template accordingly.

For instance, for a template comprised of 20 *Receipt* emails, 20 *Finance* emails emails, and 20 unlabeled emails, we will compute its distance to the *Receipt* and *Finance* centroids. If the *Receipt* centroid is the closest to the template, we will relabel all the 60 emails in the template as *Receipt*.

Note that unlike the majority labeling approach, the centroid similarity approach can assign labels to templates with uniform label distributions. It can even assign labels to templates in which the majority of the emails are unlabeled.

Centroid similarity leverages to some degree the structure of the template graph, however it only considers template aggregates (centroids) and not individual templates. If centroids represent clusters that are very broad, this could lead to a loss of precision in labeling, which we address by introducing the *hierarchical label propagation* approach.

2.3.3 Hierarchical Label Propagation

While the centroid similarity technique generally improves over majority labeling, it is built on the very broad assumption that a label has a single global centroid from which all templates of that label can be derived. However, this may not be the case for all labels.

Consider for example a *Travel* label which is comprised of subcategories such as flight itineraries, hotel reservations, and car rental information. While the intra-subcategory templates may be closely clustered together (i.e. have high similarities between one another in terms of shared vocabulary), it is not clear if the same holds for the inter-subcategory templates as well. Hence, we must consider the possibility that a single label will in fact have multiple clustering centers and cannot be represented by a single centroid.

Label propagation [27, 26] is a well known graph algorithm which propagates labels between neighboring nodes weighted by similarity. In our case, nodes are represented by templates and the graph is constructed as described previously in Section 2.2.

The label propagation algorithm that we use in this work is simple, yet effective. It operates in a hierarchical two-stage fashion. At the first stage, we run the label propagation on the template graph. At the second stage we propagate the labels derived on the template level to the individual documents.

Template propagation stage. We first construct a graph $G = (V, E, W)$ as described in Section 2.2. Here, $V = \{\mathbf{T}\}$ refers to the set of template nodes, E is the set of edges (between a template node and its k-nearest neighbors) and W is the edge weight matrix computed using KL divergence or cosine similarity. We use a set of labeled seed nodes $\mathbb{S} \subset V$ as defined in Equation 6 and provide this as input to the algorithm. The label set is L, where the size $|L| = m$. The goal of the template label propagation algorithm is a soft assignment of labels $\mathbf{L}^{\mathbf{T}}$ to each template node $\mathbf{T}$ in the graph [7, 26, 27, 24].

Our method uses the EXPANDER [24] framework and algorithm for propagation and learning label distributions. The propagation procedure utilizes an efficient iterative algorithm which defines an approximate solution at the $(i+1)th$ iteration, given the solution of the $(i)th$ iteration. In the first iteration of template propagation, seed nodes broadcast their labels to their k-nearest neighbors. Each node that receives an incoming broadcast from at least one neighboring node updates its existing label distribution according to the weights of the incoming message and the transmitted label distribution. In subsequent iterations, all nodes which have some label distribution participate in broadcasting their label distributions, and the procedure repeats until the propagated label distributions converge. In practice, the algorithm converges within a few ($k = 10$) iterations.

Document propagation stage. After convergence of the template propagation stage, we further propagate the labels from the templates to their documents. For this stage, we simply propagate the most likely label of the template to all of its constituent documents. Formally,

$$L^{\mathbf{T}}_{OPT} = \arg\max_{L_i} \hat{p}(L_i|\mathbf{T}),$$

where $\hat{p}(L_i|\mathbf{T})$ denotes the probability of label L_i according to distribution $\hat{\mathbf{L}}$, *after* the template propagation stage.

The two-stage hierarchical label propagation has two main advantages over the previously discussed methods. First, unlike the centroid similarity approach, it leverages the initial template label distribution as a *prior distribution* in the template propagation stage. Second, it iteratively updates this prior distribution based on the evidence from the neighboring nodes in the template graph, and propagates the updates to the template constituent documents. In Section 4 we show that these advantages lead to the superior performance of the hierarchical label propagation method compared to the other baselines.

3. RELATED WORK

In this section we discuss the state of the art techniques for email classification, including threading, foldering, and ranking, as well as techniques for template induction and label propagation.

3.1 Email Organization

Popular email management techniques include threading, foldering, and ranking.

Text classification has been one of the more popular machine learning applications over the last couple decades. Applications include language identification [19], genre analysis [13], and sentiment classification [20]. Automated email management methods include email categorization, which often employ text classification techniques. Bekkerman et al. explicitly explore the challenges of applying traditional document classification techniques, such as maximum entropy classifiers, naive bayes classifiers, and support vector machines, to email foldering [6]. They present a new formulation of the winnow algorithm and conclude with a discussion on the remaining challenges and difficulties that exist in email foldering.

Email threading is a technique in widespread use today that visually groups related emails together. Specifically, emails are threaded by header information, such as sender email addresses, subject string, and reply and forward prefixes. This technique is predominantly used to thread personal communications. However related machine-generated emails are often left unthreaded. For example, an e-commerce site might send multiple emails to a single user in response to a purchase. The first email might be a receipt or confirmation, followed by a shipment notification email, and followed finally by a delivery announcement or survey. Oftentimes each email in this correspondence has different subject lines and even different sender aliases which correspond to the specific notification type of the email. Current systems cannot thread these emails accurately due to their misaligned header information. Ailon et al. have presented techniques to thread these machine-generated emails through "causal threading" which leverages templates, learns causal relationships between emails from similar senders, and automatically threads incoming emails with distinct headers [2].

Automated email ranking is a relatively new technique which aims to assist in email management by classifying emails into important and unimportant categories. The goal is to reduce the amount of overhead required by the user in manually sorting through emails to find those with the highest importance. Possibly the most popular automated email ranking system in widespread use today is Google's Gmail priority inbox. This system ranks emails by the probability that a user will interact with an email in a meaningful way (e.g. open, reply, correct importance level) and within some amount of time from delivery [1]. They also go one step further by attempting to rank emails without explicit labeling from the user, although they do account for explicit labeling in their linear logistic regression models, which were explicitly chosen due to their ability to scale.

Along with the increased popularity of email over the last few decades, came the proliferation of spam. Unfortunately, the Simple Mail Transfer Protocol (SMTP), which is a standard protocol for electronic mail transmissions, has a number of limitations that spammers are able to capitalize on, and thus it is somewhat of a self-crippling system. While proposals exist to change SMTP in order to migrate the cost of spam from SMTP receiving servers to the spammers themselves (i.e. transition from a sender-push to a receiver-pull model) [12], changes to the underlying core email infrastructure would require a worldwide overhaul. As a result of these complexities, greylists and machine learning techniques have become the default methods for spam detection, many of which utilize textual analysis methods [21, 3, 25]. Caruana and Maozhen present a brief survey on current machine learning techniques for spam filtering, exploring both text classification methods as well as emerging approaches in peer-to-peer, social networking, and ontology-based semantic spam detection [9].

Other classification techniques have also been presented with the goal of assisting in email management. Bar-Yossef et al. present a new cluster ranking technique on mailbox networks—user-centric networks consisting of contacts with whom an individual exchanges email—to discover and identify communities [5]. They assert that their framework can be applied to generic clustering tasks as well. Grbovic et al. present methods for distinguishing between personal and machine-generated email and classifying messages into a few latent categories [14].

Most of the previously proposed classification, filtering, and ranking techniques rely on individual emails. In this paper, we demonstrate that they can be further improved for machine-generated email by applying them on a structural template level.

3.2 Template Induction

Data on the web is generally formatted in such a way that a machine can render it—thus presenting the data in a human-readable format—but not necessarily extract the pertinent information from it. For example, consider an itinerary sent from an airline company to its customer via email. The body of the message might contain images and text. A number of HTML tables and cells organize the images, boilerplate text, and pertinent information (i.e. date, flight number, airport codes) in such a way that when the message is rendered the important information is presented in a visually appealing manner to the user. However, it remains a difficult task for the machine to automatically locate among the HTML and text what is actually the central and important information in the document.

It has been estimated that over 60% of overall email traffic is comprised of machine-generated email [2], some of which contain personal and important information (e.g. purchases, tracking numbers, events, flights, hotel reservations). Techniques for template or wrapper induction have been extensively studied in an effort to enable the extraction of this structured data from web pages [4, 16, 18]. However, there is very little published work on using such structural templates for processing commercial email data.

3.3 Label Propagation

Label propagation operates on a geometric framework consisting of a set of labeled and unlabeled points. The goal is to predict the labels of unlabeled data using labeled data [27, 26, 7, 24]. Edge weights correspond to the relative similarities between points. In each iteration the label distributions of labeled points are propagated to each of their neighbors. In turn, data points that receive label distributions from one or more of their neighbors update their own label distributions according to a weighted sum of distributions proportional to the incoming edge weights.

This semi-supervised technique is especially useful in the age of big data considering that labeled data often come in very small quantities while unlabeled data can be orders of magnitude larger. A nice characteristic of this algorithm is that labels naturally cluster together based on their similarity metrics which enables multiple clusters per label to emerge. Gregory presents an extension of label propagation which enables multi-labeling for communities that might overlap one another [15]. In this paper, we use EXPANDER, the scalable label propagation framework presented by Ravi and Diao [24].

4. EVALUATION

4.1 Experimental Setup

We explore the use of two template representations in the experiments in the remainder of this section: bag-of-words and topic distributions. In both cases we only use terms found in the template's fixed text, as described in Section 2.1. For both representations, we discard 100 most frequent terms that appear over the entire template corpus, terms which appear fewer than 11 times in the entire template corpus, and terms which appear in fewer than 6 unique sender domains. Additionally, we stem words using

Label	Example of email types	# Labeled Templates
Finance	Financial statements, stock reports, bank account updates.	262
Receipt	Purchase receipts, order confirmations, shipping notices.	432
Travel	Travel itineraries, hotel reservations, car rentals.	201

Table 2: Experimental labels.

	Majority Label		Centroid Similarity		Label Propagation		
	Precision	Recall	Precision	Recall	Precision	Recall	
Finance	55.00	83.97	60.73	89.30	91.49	98.47	m, c
Receipt	89.35	79.63	85.05	95.87	97.82	93.52	c
Travel	86.57	86.57	86.62	95.33	95.00	94.53	m, c

Table 3: Label propagation vs. baselines: majority label, centroid (bag of words). Significant differences with Majority Label and Centroid Similarity are marked by m and c, respectively (statistical significance measured using McNemar's test with $p < 0.05$).

the Porter stemming algorithm [22] and only consider English templates for the purposes of evaluation. While we only investigate and evaluate English templates, since our techniques are unsupervised and do not take into account any language-specific features, we expect that they should generalize to other languages without substantial loss in effectiveness.

As a corpus, we generate templates over mailboxes of company employees who voluntarily signed up in the evaluation and agreed to participate in our experiment. We use several thousands such mailboxes with a total of close to a million machine generated emails. This data was treated with utmost care: for our evaluation, we examine only the generated templates, and not any individual emails.

We manually label the templates into three predefined categories in Table 2 for evaluation purposes. In order to limit the space of labeled templates, in the majority of our experiments, we only label templates for which the existing classification system (which is outside the scope of this paper) labels at least one email in a template.

Each template is labeled by two human annotators. During evaluation we found that inter-annotator agreement was above 90%. Templates for which no agreement was established are disregarded for evaluation. Templates that did not belong to any of these predefined categories were marked as "unlabeled".

4.2 Template Classification Experiments

4.2.1 Baselines

As baselines, we compare the precision and recall for majority label and centroid similarity label assignment techniques (described in Section 2.3.1 and Section 2.3.2, respectively) to the precision and recall of the hierarchical label propagation approach (described in Section 2.3.3). In this section, we use cosine similarity and bag-of-words template representations for template graph construction.

These baseline comparisons are shown in Table 3. The comparisons show that, for most labels, centroid similarity improves both precision and recall over the simple majority label approach. In particular, recall is significantly increased, which is not surprising, given that we make use of the inter-template information.

Overall, hierarchical label propagation outperforms both of these approaches to a statistically significant degree. For instance, for the *Finance* label, it increases the recall by more than 10%, and precision by more than 50% compared to the centroid similarity approach. This demonstrates that using local template similarities is more beneficial than the global centroid similarity alone.

Due to its superior performance, in the next section, we focus on the performance of the hierarchical label propagation model. We analyze its performance with different similarity metrics and template representations.

4.2.2 Hierarchical Label Propagation

We explore four different instantiations of the template graph consisting of the combinations of topic and bag-of-words models and using cosine similarity and KL divergence as similarity metrics. Table 4 compares these combinations of similarity metrics and template representations for the hierarchical label propagation.

We find that while the hierarchical label propagation with topics representation performs better than majority label and is consistent across all labels, the technique effectively suffers from a loss of resolution due to the use of Latent Dirichlet Allocation, a form of dimensionality reduction, and cannot improve much beyond about 90% for both precision and recall regardless of the underlying similarity metric and graph fan-out.

Overall, the bag-of-words fixed text term representation has the most consistent performance across all labels[1]. Both KL divergence and cosine similarity yield very similar results, and in both cases, both precision and recall are above 95%, which empirically validates the effectiveness of the hierarchical label propagation approach.

We also investigate the impact of graph connectivity on the precision and recall of the hierarchical label propagation in Figure 3. We find that precision and recall is the highest when each node is connected to its nearest 10 neighbors. While Figure 3 depicts the bag-of-words and cosine similarity case, we observe similar results for the other instantiations of the hierarchical label propagation as well. The intuition behind this result is the iterativeness of the label propagation algorithm, due to which graph connectivity plays a central role in label propagation accuracy. For sparsely connected graphs, it becomes more difficult for the correct label to propagate to and affect the label distribution of distant

[1]However, we should note that the changes compared to topic representation are in all but one case not statistically significant.

	Topics [KL]		Topics [CS]		BoW [KL]		BoW [CS]	
	Precision	Recall	Precision	Recall	Precision	Recall	Precision	Recall
Finance	80.44	83.21	83.09	86.26	93.13	93.13	91.49	98.47
Receipt	88.40	82.87	89.78	85.42	93.47	96.06	97.82	93.52
Travel	88.61	89.05	86.79	91.54	95.24	89.55	95.00	94.53 t_{cs}

Table 4: Comparison of algorithms for template label propagation: precision/recall per label. Template graph fan-out $k = 10$. Significant differences with Topics [CS] is marked by t_{cs} (statistical significance is measured using McNemara's test with $p < 0.05$).

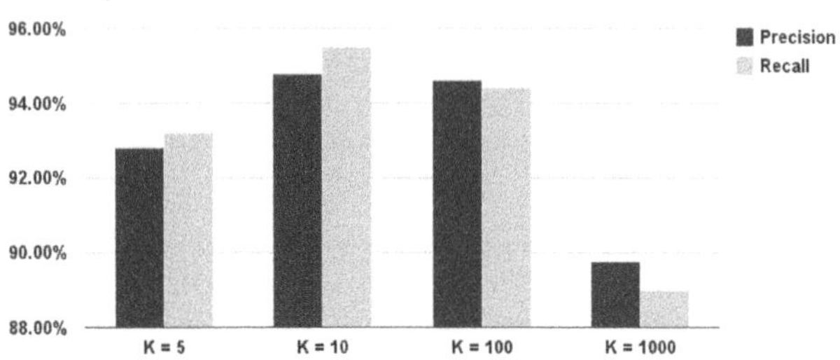

Figure 3: Precision/recall as a function of label propagation graph fan-out.

	Precision	Recall	Email coverage
Finance	93.08	99.64	+9.7%
Receipt	99.13	91.39	+16.8%
Travel	95.93	93.52	+5.7%

Table 5: Coverage increase per label.

nodes. On the other hand, densely connected graphs may have many weakly weighted edges that ultimately introduce noise to the propagated label distributions.

4.3 Coverage

One of the primary goals of this work is to increase the coverage of the existing labels using the structural template graph, compared to a high-precision email-based classifier. In our first coverage experiment, we run the bag-of-words cosine similarity hierarchical label propagation on all the templates that have at least one underlying sample labeled with either of the three aforementioned labels. In this way, we can use the sample email labels as a prior distribution for the label propagation algorithm.

The coverage results of this run are shown in Table 5. Precision and recall numbers in Table 5 are computed for only the non-seed templates. Email coverage numbers demonstrate the increase in the number of emails covered by the labels when applying the propagated template labels to their constituent documents. These results show that we can achieve, on average across labels, 11% increase in email coverage, while maintaining precision and recall well above the 90% mark.

Note however that while all the templates in this experiment have some hint of being labeled by one of the three aforementioned categories, there exists a large unlabeled template set. Therefore, in our second coverage experiment we instantiate a template graph consisting of all the templates, including those which do not have emails labeled as *Finance*, *Receipt*, or *Travel*. The newly added unlabeled

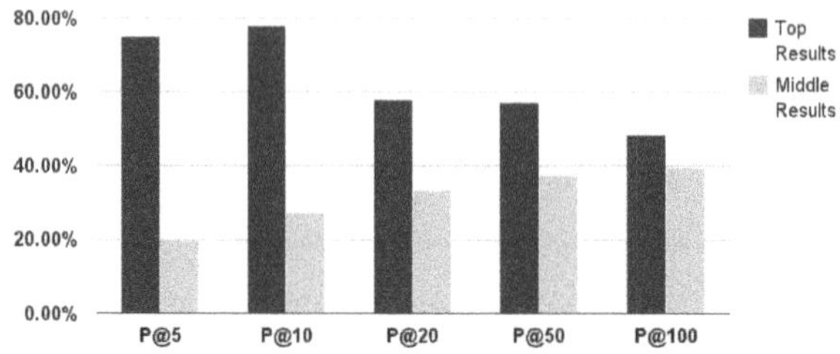

Figure 4: Precision@{1-100} for unlabeled templates. Results reported for both top ranked templates, and mid-ranked templates as comparison. P@X corresponds to the measured precision over X templates beginning at either the top or middle of the unlabelled set when sorted in descending order by most likely label weight.

templates outnumber the previous set of templates 7 to 1. Again, we represent templates using bag-of-words, calculate edge weights using cosine similarity, and connect each node to the nearest 10 neighbors.

After running label propagation we order all previously unlabeled templates by the weight of their most likely label $L^{\mathbf{T}}_{OPT}$. We then conduct two evaluations on this list. First, we measure precision at x top ranks (P@x) for the first 100 templates in the list. These precision numbers are represented by the dark-grey bars in Figure 4. Note that the top 10 templates are labeled with a total precision (over all three labels) of about 75% while after the top 20 templates precision drops to below 60%. Second, we measure P@x starting at the middle of the template list sorted by the most likely label. The light-grey bars in Figure 4 represent these precision numbers, which hover around 40%.

Overall, the comparison between the dark and light grey bars in Figure 4 demonstrates that there is a correlation between the label weights assigned by the hierarchical label propagation, and their correctness. Higher weighted labels are more likely to be correct than the lower weighted labels.

The biggest factor contributing to low measures of precision in Figure 4 is the fact that the hierarchical label propagation attempts to label the entire graph using only the labels it is provided (i.e. *Finance*, *Receipt*, *Travel*), when in fact, there are potentially a number of new labels that must be introduced to cover the newly added set. We discuss the prospect of label discovery in Section 4.5.

4.4 Scalability

As previously mentioned, one of our major motivations for using templates to classify emails is their scalability. According to Figure 5a, nearly 80% of emails in our corpus can be

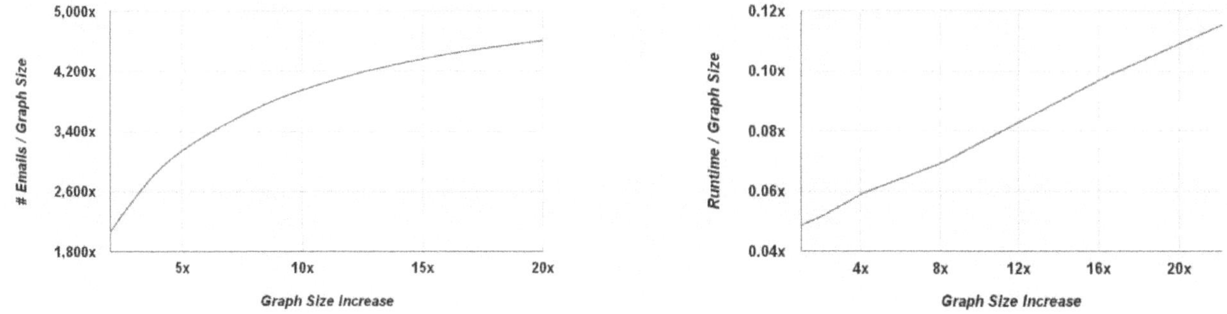

(a) Email coverage. (b) Label propagation runtime.

Figure 5: Email coverage and label propagation runtime as a function of the template graph size, as measured by the number of templates included in the graph.

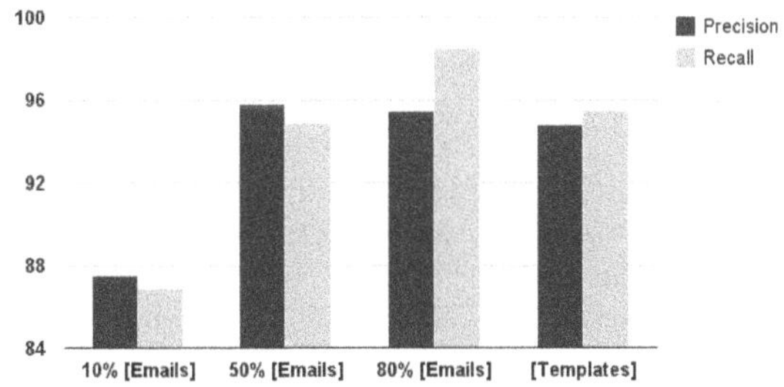

Figure 6: Comparison of sender/template level precision/recall for label propagation over email/template graphs.

covered using only 50% of the templates. Furthermore, the absolute number of templates required is up to three orders of magnitude less than the number of emails covered, since a single template generally represents 100 to 1,000 emails, as seen in Figure 5a. Since the runtime of the label propagation algorithm is approximately proportional to the size of the graph, as seen in Figure 5b, by using templates for classification instead of emails we can reduce runtime by orders of magnitude.

While templates scale better than emails, it is important to also consider the trade-offs in terms of the classifier performance. In Figure 6 we compare the effectiveness of the two approaches. Since emails do not have an equivalent label distribution that is characteristic to templates, and is used for seed selection, we cannot select seed nodes for the email graph using the same techniques used for the template graph. In place of the seed selection procedure, we experiment by randomly selecting some percentage of labeled emails as seed nodes (this percentage is labeled in Figure 6). We find that the template-based hierrarchical label propagation precision is comparable to using emails in the underlying graph structure, when we use either 50% or 80% of the emails as seed nodes for label propagation, and its recall is comparable to the 50% case.

4.5 Label Discovery

Table 6 demonstrates top topics for templates to which no existing labels were propagated. As such, these templates potentially belong to new undiscovered labels. Recall that each topic x, has a certain weight $w(x, \mathbf{T})$ for template $\mathbf{T}$. Topics are ranked for each label L (including an empty label $L_\emptyset$ for unlabeled templates) as:

$$\frac{\sum_{\mathbf{T} \in L} w(x, \mathbf{T})}{\sum_{\mathbf{T}} w(x, \mathbf{T})}.$$

Intuitively, top topics per label are the topics that are more likely to be associated to the label (including the empty label), compared to the entire collection.

The top topics for the unlabeled emails reveal interesting potential common themes for the unlabeled set. For instance, there are topics for live music shows, fashion promotions or newsletters, and business-related announcements.

These preliminary results indicate that our label propagation technique, in conjunction with template-based topic models, is useful not only for improving coverage for a prespecified label set, but also for discovering new emerging labels from the data.

5. CONCLUSION

In this paper, we have presented three new algorithms for classification of machine-generated emails using structural templates: majority label, centroid similarity, and hierarchical label propagation. We explored a number of underlying template representations including bag-of-words and topic distributions, different similarity metrics in template graph construction, and varying degrees of graph connectivity.

Our empirical evaluation demonstrates the superior effectiveness of the hierarchical label propagation technique using a template graph. Not only does it scale far better than email-based label propagation, but it is also comparable to it in terms of precision and recall. Hierarchical label propagation achieves above 90% precision and recall for all labels, while increasing the labeling coverage by more than 11%. Our experiments also demonstrate that hierarchical label propagation, along with template topic modeling, can be used for discovery of new labels in the corpus.

Unlabeled						
Business & Tech	*Music*		*Social*	*Fashion*	*Politics*	
develop	music	music	story	fashion	say	thank
technolog	world	ticket	her	deal	govern	contribut
job	love	show	his	sale	american	support
learn	artist	live	video	design	polit	campaign
compani	star	band	friend	brand	obama	donat

Table 6: Top topics for unlabeled templates. Each column shows top 5 stems per topics. Headers in italics represent a human-assigned topic label.

6. REFERENCES

[1] D. Aberdeen, O. Pacovsky, and A. Slater. The learning behind gmail priority inbox. In *NIPS Workshop on Learning on Cores, Clusters and Clouds*, 2010.

[2] N. Ailon, Z. S. Karnin, E. Liberty, and Y. Maarek. Threading machine generated email. In *Proceedings of WSDM*, pages 405–414, 2013.

[3] I. Androutsopoulos, J. Koutsias, K. V. Chandrinos, and C. D. Spyropoulos. An experimental comparison of naive bayesian and keyword-based anti-spam filtering with personal e-mail messages. In *Proceedings of SIGIR*, pages 160–167, 2000.

[4] A. Arasu and H. Garcia-Molina. Extracting structured data from web pages. In *Proceedings of SIGMOD*, pages 337–348, 2003.

[5] Z. Bar-Yossef, I. Guy, R. Lempel, Y. Maarek, and V. Soroka. Cluster ranking with an application to mining mailbox networks. *Knowledge and Information Systems*, 14(1):101–139, 2008.

[6] R. Bekkerman, A. McCallum, and G. Huang. Automatic categorization of email into folders: Benchmark experiments on Enron and SRI corpora. *Computer Science Department Faculty Publication Series*, page 218, 2004.

[7] Y. Bengio, O. Delalleau, and N. Le Roux. Label propagation and quadratic criterion. In O. Chapelle, B. Schölkopf, and A. Zien, editors, *Semi-Supervised Learning*, pages 193–216. MIT Press, 2006.

[8] D. M. Blei, A. Y. Ng, and M. I. Jordan. Latent dirichlet allocation. *Journal of Machine Learning Research*, 3:993–1022, 2003.

[9] G. Caruana and M. Li. A survey of emerging approaches to spam filtering. *ACM Computing Surveys (CSUR)*, 44(2):9, 2012.

[10] L. A. Dabbish and R. E. Kraut. Email overload at work: an analysis of factors associated with email strain. In *Proceedings of the Conference on Computer Supported Cooperative Work*, pages 431–440, 2006.

[11] L. A. Dabbish, R. E. Kraut, S. Fussell, and S. Kiesler. Understanding email use: predicting action on a message. In *Proceedings of SIGCHI*, pages 691–700, 2005.

[12] Z. Duan, Y. Dong, and K. Gopalan. DMTP: Controlling spam through message delivery differentiation. *Computer Networks*, 51(10):2616–2630, 2007.

[13] A. Finn, N. Kushmerick, and B. Smyth. Genre classification and domain transfer for information filtering. In *Proceedings of ECIR*, pages 353–362. 2002.

[14] M. Grbovic, G. Halawi, Z. Karnin, and Y. Maarek. How many folders do you really need?: Classifying email into a handful of categories. In *Proceedings of CIKM*, pages 869–878, 2014.

[15] S. Gregory. Finding overlapping communities in networks by label propagation. *New Journal of Physics*, 12(10):103018, 2010.

[16] C. Hachenberg and T. Gottron. Locality sensitive hashing for scalable structural classification and clustering of web documents. In *Proceedings of CIKM*, pages 359–368, 2013.

[17] O. Kurland and L. Lee. Pagerank without hyperlinks: Structural re-ranking using links induced by language models. In *Proceedings of SIGIR*, pages 306–313, New York, NY, USA, 2005. ACM.

[18] N. Kushmerick. *Wrapper Induction for Information Extraction.* PhD thesis, 1997. AAI9819266.

[19] B. Martins and M. J. Silva. Language identification in web pages. In *Proceedings of SAC*, pages 764–768, 2005.

[20] B. Pang, L. Lee, and S. Vaithyanathan. Thumbs up?: sentiment classification using machine learning techniques. In *Proceedings of EMNLP*, pages 79–86, 2002.

[21] P. Pantel et al. SpamCop: A spam classification & organization program. In *Proceedings of AAAI-98 Workshop on Learning for Text Categorization*, pages 95–98, 1998.

[22] M. Porter. The porter stemming algorithm, 2009. http://tartarus.org/~martin/PorterStemmer/.

[23] S. Radicati. Email statistics report, 2014-2018, 2014. http://www.radicati.com/wp/wp-content/uploads/2014/01/Email-Statistics-Report-2014-2018-Executive-Summary.pdf.

[24] S. Ravi and Q. Diao. Large scale distributed semi-supervised learning using streaming approximation. *arXiv preprint arXiv:1512.01752*, 2015.

[25] L. Zhang, J. Zhu, and T. Yao. An evaluation of statistical spam filtering techniques. *ACM Transactions on Asian Language Information Processing (TALIP)*, 3(4):243–269, 2004.

[26] D. Zhou, O. Bousquet, T. N. Lal, J. Weston, and B. Schölkopf. Learning with local and global consistency. In *Proceedings of NIPS*, pages 321–328, 2004.

[27] X. Zhu and Z. Ghahramani. Learning from labeled and unlabeled data with label propagation. Technical report, CMU-CALD-02-107, Carnegie Mellon University, 2002.

Enforcing k-anonymity in Web Mail Auditing

Dotan Di Castro
Yahoo Labs
MATAM, Haifa 31905, Israel
dot@yahoo-inc.com

Liane Lewin-Eytan
Yahoo Labs
MATAM, Haifa 31905, Israel
liane@yahoo-inc.com

Yoelle Maarek
Yahoo Labs
MATAM, Haifa 31905, Israel
yoelle@ymail.com

Ran Wolff
Yahoo Labs
MATAM, Haifa 31905, Israel
ranw@yahoo-inc.com

Eyal Zohar
Yahoo Labs
MATAM, Haifa 31905, Israel
eyalzo@gmail.com

ABSTRACT

We study the problem of k-anonymization of mail messages in the realistic scenario of auditing mail traffic in a major commercial Web mail service. Mail auditing is necessary in various Web mail debugging and quality assurance activities, such as anti-spam or the qualitative evaluation of novel mail features. It is conducted by trained professionals, often referred to as "auditors", who are shown messages that could expose personally identifiable information. We address here the challenge of k-anonymizing such messages, focusing on machine generated mail messages that represent more than 90% of today's mail traffic. We introduce a novel message signature *Mail-Hash*, specifically tailored to identifying structurally-similar messages, which allows us to put such messages in a same equivalence class. We then define a process that generates, for each class, masked mail samples that can be shown to auditors, while guaranteeing the k-anonymity of users. The productivity of auditors is measured by the amount of non-hidden mail content they can see every day, while considering normal working conditions, which set a limit to the number of mail samples they can review. In addition, we consider k-anonymity over time since, by definition of k-anonymity, every new release places additional constraints on the assignment of samples. We describe in details the results we obtained over actual Yahoo mail traffic, and thus demonstrate that our methods are feasible at Web mail scale. Given the constantly growing concern of users over their email being scanned by others, we argue that it is critical to devise such algorithms that guarantee k-anonymity, and implement associated processes in order to restore the trust of mail users.

1. INTRODUCTION

In the last decade, Web mail traffic has evolved, very much like regular snail mail, into being dominated by machine-generated messages. Some recent studies have verified that more than 90% of non-spam Web email is indeed generated by automated scripts, [1, 10]. These messages vary in importance: some represent highly valuable information (and often include sensitive personal details), such as shipment notifications, flight itineraries, social events, monthly bank statements, etc., while others are almost junk mail such as promotions or newsletters, from which users have forgotten to unsubscribe. Two common characteristics of these machine-generated messages is that most of them are highly structured documents, with rich HTML formatting, and they are repeated over and over, modulo minor variations, in the global mail corpus. These characteristics clearly facilitate the application of automated data extraction and learning methods at a very large scale, in order to offer users new mail features and applications including "customized search results, tailored advertising, and spam and malware detection" [9].

As much as these methods are, by design, automated, they still require from time to time some human intervention for quality assurance or evaluation purposes, or during the research phase of their development. Major Web mail services allow only a restricted group of trained employees, that we refer to as *auditors*[1], to access personal information under strict contractual confidentiality obligations, [16, 26, 9]. We argue here that there is a need to add automated mechanisms for preserving user privacy during the auditing process. Consider for example a supervised learning application that requires a training test. The auditors, should be shown only "anonymized" samples of mail messages, before they can be reviewed, annotated, classified, etc.

As we focus on machine-generated messages, each such sample is in fact the representative of a much larger set of messages, typically originating from the same sender, and having a similar HTML structure. Determining whether a message is human or machine-generated is out of the scope of this paper. We refer the reader to previous work, as proposed by some of the authors of this paper in [10], for a possible solution to this task. More generally, it is nowadays quite feasible to devise simple methods for capturing (non-malicious) machine-generated messages by leveraging signals such as the "burstiness" (i.e., large number of messages sent at once) of the traffic originating from a sender, its volume, the structure of the messages etc. Note that a

WSDM'16, February 22–25, 2016, San Francisco, CA, USA.

DOI: http://dx.doi.org/10.1145/2835776.2835803

[1]Note that these professionals are typically not developers as they purely focus on the qualitative aspect of the data. Some also refer to them as QA professionals or "editors".

perfect distinction between human and machine-generated messages is not a pre-requisite of this work, as we will see that our methods naturally eliminate rare messages. Note also that we exclusively consider the privacy concerns of *human recipients* and ignore those of mass-senders (typically machines), for whom personal information is not exposed in any case. More specifically, we consider machine-generated messages that might expose personal information of a given recipient, for instance the recipient's home address or telephone, or movies that she rented. We investigate how to preserve the recipient's privacy when auditors review one of her messages.

We propose a mail-specific anonymization mechanism, based on a novel function operating on a single mail message, which we coin *"Mail-Hash"* by analogy to Broder et al. *Min-Hash* technique [4]. This Mail-Hash function leverages the rich DOM structure most machine-generated messages have and computes a signature, in the hope of identifying messages that seem to have been generated by the same script. Given this signature, we then generate equivalence classes of messages. Grouping messages into equivalence classes should then be performed daily, while being able to efficiently cover billions of messages in any Web scale mail service.

Intuitively, message anonymization can be achieved by simply masking the variable content of these messages. Consider as a simplifying example, two order confirmation messages sent by the same online seller to two different recipients. These messages will likely have the same structure as well as a significant amount of common data. One message body consists of *"Hello Jessie, thank you for shopping with us. We have received your order of Green Mountain Coffee, and are preparing it for shipment, etc."*, while the other reads *"Hello Sergio, thank you for shopping with us. We have received your order of Bleu de Chanel, and are preparing it for shipment, etc."*. It is quite straightforward to hide the delta between these two messages, using for instance the notion of mail template suggested in [1]. Both messages would be mapped into the same mail template consisting of a tuple formed by the sender of the mail and the common body strings namely *" Hello *, thank you for shopping with us. We have received your order of *, and are preparing it for shipment, etc."*. Personal information, such as names (Jessie and Sergio in our example), addresses, or purchased products (Green Mountain coffee and Bleu de Chanel perfume in our example), which are necessarily variable across multiple recipients, would be automatically hidden. In reality, messages are more complex and include a great deal of HTML-formatting that we will discuss in details, but the intuition remains the same. We will also explain how to group messages in the same equivalence classes covering more than k recipients, so that k-anonymity can formally be verified. Once k-anonymity is achieved, since the masking process transforms all messages within a class into the same template, one can easily generate from the latter a nicely formatted mail sample that masks all the parts of the message that might break k-anonymity. We note that the privacy regulations and k-anonymity firm restrictions pose strict requirements on the process of equivalence classes and template generation, as will be presented in this work. These are inherently different from the application-driven requirements which typify template definition and computation as described in [1, 10].

In order to verify the benefits of our approach, we consider the *productivity of auditors* for every sample they are shown. Clearly, the more content an auditor can see, the more effective their reviewing or annotating task can be. Consider our previous example. While being short, auditors will easily be able to infer from it that the template refers to a purchase confirmation. A longer template that would indicate for instance a product category would even be more informative. Thus, we use the simple measure of *content coverage*, representing the amount of non-hidden mail content that the auditors can see. Our goal is thus to maximize content coverage in order for auditors to be highly effective, while enforcing k-anonymity. Note that there is a trade-off between these two: while an equivalence class should be large enough so as to cover at least k recipients (to enforce k-anonymization), it should be small enough to include only messages that are quite similar so as not to hide too much content, which would reduce content coverage.

Another challenge inherent to professional auditing is that auditors continue to be exposed to more and more mail samples over their tenure. Consequently k-anonymity needs to be considered not in isolation, but over time. Fortunately, professional auditing exhibits an additional property, which does not exist in usual anonymized release settings, it is tightly controlled: auditors are employed by the mail service and, as such, can be strictly governed in terms of their access not only to the current but also to future and auxiliary datasets. Taking advantage of this property, we consider the objective of releasing samples to be shown to an auditor on a daily basis, while retaining the k-anonymity of all releases over time. In addition, we take into account the capacity of auditors, and ensure the number of samples that they can be daily assigned does not go beyond some threshold representing their daily capacity. Our problem thus converges to an online mail auditing k-anonymization problem, whose objective is to release a bounded amount of samples to an auditor on a daily basis, while retaining the k-anonymity of all releases over time, and maximizing visible content. We propose an online mechanism for this problem, proving its scalability and evaluating it via experiments conducted over actual Yahoo mail traffic.

The contributions of our paper are threefold:

1. We provide, to the best of our knowledge, the first definition of k-anonymity for human auditing of mail messages.

2. We introduce a surprisingly simple yet efficient Mail-Hash function specifically tailored to identifying similarly structured mail messages.

3. We define a mail auditing process that is guaranteed to preserve the k-anonymity of mail users over time, while maximizing the productivity of mail auditors. We also demonstrate its feasibility at Web mail scale by providing detailed results of a full system we implemented over Yahoo mail.

The paper is organized as follows. Section 2 gives the problem definitions for the k-anonymization of mail messages in the auditing scenario. Section 3 presents our Mail-Hash function. Section 4 describes the complete k-anonymization process, from computation of equivalence classes based on Mail-Hash, through masking, and up to the online daily assignment of anonymized samples to the auditor. Section 5 reports on the large scale experiments we conducted. Finally, we review related work in Section 6 and present our conclusions in Section 7.

2. MAIL K-ANONYMIZATION

We first provide some general definitions for k-anonymity for mail releases in general. Then, we discuss the transformation actions, such as filtering and masking, that need to be applied in order to generate mail data releases that can make users indistinguishable and thus enforce k-anonymity. Finally, we present the realistic scenario of mail auditing, considering releases over time.

2.1 Definitions

Given a data table T in which each row contains the information of a single and unique individual, the table is k-anonymous if and only if each row repeats k or more times. An algorithm which accepts every table T, k-anonymous or not, and outputs a table T' which is guaranteed to be k-anonymous is called a k-anonymization algorithm. A table in which every row may include details of several individuals, which are denoted senders and recipients, is k-recipient anonymous if it is k-anonymous with respect to message recipients.

We represent a mail dataset D_t as a set of incoming mail messages $m_t[1], m_t[2], \dots, m_t[n]$ received by the entire set of users during a time interval t. For the sake of simplicity, we will consider as our default time interval a single day, which fits a common process of daily data release. Another simplifying assumption is to abstract any incoming mail message into a list of entities, where an entity can be a sender, or any character string in the subject or body of the message. A release R_t is then defined as a transformation of D_t into a set of uniquely identifiable users (mail recipients) and associated entities. We then refer to the tuple of all entities associated with a same message $m_t[i]$, as a *template*, reusing the terminology introduced by Ailon et al. in [1]. Like in their work, a template is defined as a tuple of a sender and a character string, which can be altered for abstraction as discussed later. One difference with their notion of templates however is that this string can be derived not only from the subject but most frequently from the body of the message.

A release R_t^u consists of the list of templates associated with user u in R_t (a template is associated with u if u received a message corresponding to this template). For any user u, we define the set of users $[u]_t$ as the set of all users v such that $R_t^v = R_t^u$. A single release R_t fulfills the requirement of k-anonymity, if for any user u in R_t, it holds that $|[u]_t| \geq k$. In other words, user u is indistinguishable from at least $k-1$ other users in the release as it maps to exactly the same list of templates. Figure 1 depicts a release, with two user groups examples. Each group is of size at least k, and includes users with exactly the same list of templates.

In the same spirit, a sequence of releases R_1 through R_t is k-anonymous if, for every user u, the intersection of all $[u]_i$ has more than k users, $\left|\bigcap_{i=1}^{t} [u]_i\right| \geq k$. In other words, user u is indistinguishable from at least $k-1$ other users over all releases, as they are associated with exactly the same list of templates over $R_1, \dots, R_t$.

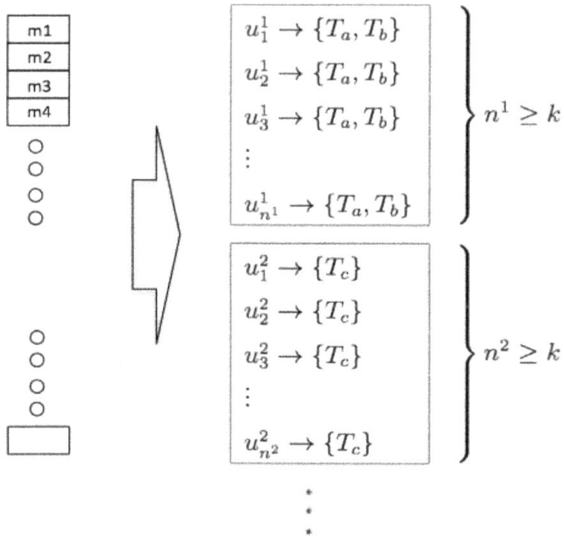

Figure 1: Two exemplary groups of users in a release. In group $\{u_1^1, \dots, u_{n^1}^1\}$ each user is associated with two templates T_a, T_b, and in group $\{u_1^2, \dots, u_{n^1}^2\}$ each user is associated with template T_c. The left side are the messages m_i included in the mail dataset.

2.2 From Dataset to Release

Intuitively, the transformation process consists of generating a list of templates for any given user u, so as to make the data informational enough to auditors and at the same time make u indistinguishable from others. Each template is an abstraction of a message sent by a given sender to u and obtained by deleting terms or sequence of terms (replacing them by a deletion marker $*$). Ailon et al. [1] showed that this abstraction of a message is particularly convenient for representing machine-generated messages generated by a same script on the sender side. In our context, we do not necessarily attempt to match a mail template to an unknown script, but still use the same type of abstraction in order to reduce variability between messages. We refer to this task as *masking*. In addition, we can remove users or messages altogether if they cannot be $k-$ *anonymized*. We refer to this task as *filtering*.

In order to support masking and filtering, we need first to identify mail messages that are similar enough so that k-anonymization can be enforced while allowing a maximum portion of content to remain unmasked. We explain in Section 3 how we have devised a novel "mail-hash" function that associates highly similar messages with a same signature. We can then group messages originating from the same sender, and having the same signature, into equivalence classes. Then, for all messages in a class, variables parts are masked so as to produce a unique template for the class [2]. In order to guarantee k-anonymization, each such class needs to cover at least k users. After the masking process, all messages in an equivalence class have in fact been reduced to the same template. Once this process is conducted, we associate with each user in the release, one or

[2]In the paper, we will use interchangeably the terms template and (equivalence) classes as they are associated in a 1-to-1 mapping.

several such templates, which drive the generation of *mail samples* that can be reviewed by the auditor. Each template is by definition derived from messages sent to at least k different users and as such preserves k-anonymity with respect to this data set.

One could imagine multiple ways to generate templates, as well as conducting masking and filtering. In order to select the most adequate method, we go back to the task at hand, namely assigning mail samples to auditors and maximizing their productivity, while maintaining the k-anonymity of every sample of mail they will be shown. It is obvious that the more unmasked data the auditor can see in a sample, the more effective she can be. Therefore, we propose to evaluate the usefulness of a sample via a raw quantitative measure of *content coverage*. More specifically, we define the content coverage of a sample, or rather of its underlying template and associated class, as the amount of data left in the template after masking, relative to the original source. We then derive the usefulness of a given release R_t, noted $CC[R_t]$, as the average content coverage of the templates in the release. In addition, it is clear that each auditor can review only a limited number of mail samples per work day, so we also need to ensure the number of daily samples that are assigned to an auditor is limited to some threshold Γ.

2.3 Online k-Anonymization

Optimizing R_t for content coverage, while not going over Γ samples, is however not sufficient. Indeed, as auditors get assigned new samples day after day, they are exposed to more data, and k-anonymization needs to be preserved over time. Therefore we need to generalize our problem to a new online problem, where our goal is to generate every day a new release R_t, taking into consideration both the current dataset D_t and previous releases $R_1, \ldots, R_{t-1}$, while retaining the k-anonymity of all releases. This new release should be generated so that the overall content coverage, denoted by CC, averaged over all releases, is maximized, and the number of samples assigned daily to an auditor is at most Γ. Note that we do consider the assignment of samples to multiple auditors, as auditors are obligated not to share or discuss sample data with each other, and thus these are independent tasks. Verifying whether the assignment process can be made more efficient by considering a pool of auditors, and optimizing over a pool rather than independently for each auditor, is out of the scope of this work.

3. THE MAIL-HASH SIGNATURE

In order to increase the chances of having enough users sharing the same templates in any mail release, we need to be able to detect structurally similar messages, in an extremely fast and scalable manner as we are dealing with Web mail. We introduce here Mail-Hash, a novel mail message signature specifically designed to address this requirement. This new technique is fast and simple, yet provides superior results when dealing with the special case of anonymizing machine generated email, as demonstrated in Section 5.

3.1 Motivation

Document similarity in the context of online information has been widely explored. Note that we intentionally ignore here the traditional measures of similarity used in Information Retrieval such as cosine or Jaccard, or their associated clustering techniques, such as complete-link or k-nearest neighbor. This is, not only for reasons of performance, (indeed computing pair-wise similarity between all messages might be prohibitive at Web mail scale) but also because of the task that requires stricter message similarity.

Therefore we elected to follow the school of work, pioneered by Manber [15], Heintze [11] and Broder[3] *et al.* [2, 3, 4, 5] for fingerprinting documents. Their methods use a small fixed-size sketch, which can be computed extremely fast for each document. Documents are usually reduced to a canonical sequence of tokens, considering the text and/or the surrounding HTML tags, and forming sub-sequences of terms called *shingles*, upon which the document sketch is computed. One of the main use cases of this approach is deduplication of Web pages for search or detecting plagiarism.

The Mail-Hash method we introduce here belongs to the same school of work but is tailored both to machine-generated mail messages that contain a great deal of HTML formatting common to numerous messages, and to our specific task at hand, namely enforcing k-anonymization. Note that personal messages that contain much less formatting and are in essence private are ignored by design and will never be shown to auditors.

3.2 The Algorithm

The goal of the Mail-Hash algorithm is to generate a single hash value, referred to as Mail-Hash, for each mail message. The idea is to prune the DOM tree [24] so as to leave only the XPath expressions [23] (or XPaths for short), that lead to "textual leaves", where textual leaves are non-empty alphanumerical strings. We then sign only the pruned DOM tree[4] of the mail, while ignoring the textual leaves and being resilient to some minor changes in the HTML formatting.

In order to sign the pruned DOM tree, we use the widely used MD5 [19] over the ordered list of all XPath expressions. We chose MD5 as it is considered a collision-free (although not collision-safe) hash algorithm that takes into account every character of the input, and is sensitive to position of characters, which in our case translates to the order of XPath entries. Although MD5 has 128-bits, we use only the lower 64-bits due to the fact that it is largely sufficient for a collision-free operation when the number of inputs is in the order of billions.

Algorithm 1 Mail-Hash

1: **Input**: mail message
2: **Output**: 64-bit signature
3: Parse the mail message to DOM tree
4: **For** each non-empty text element e_i in the DOM tree, generate a simple XPath t_i that leads from root to the text node, with all the elements along the path and necessary proximity positions
5: Concatenate all the XPath items t_i into a single string T, by their DFS order in the DOM tree
6: The Mail-Hash is the lower 64-bits of the MD5 of the string T

[3]See [12] for a large scale evaluation of Broder *et al.*'s algorithm).

[4]For simplicity, we will refer to the pruned DOM tree as the DOM tree from now on.

Messages that have the same DOM structure but differ by their textual leaves, will get the same Mail-Hash score. Note that an unwanted result might occur if messages have exactly the same DOM structure but their textual leaves differ. Another problem may arise if many messages have a unique DOM structure, resulting in a wide range of Mail-Hash values. We claim that both phenomena are rare in reality, making Mail-Hash an excellent choice in practice, as shown in Section 5. The details of the Mail-Hash generation algorithm are given in Algorithm 1. Figure 2 presents two examples of HTML mail messages and the detailed calculation of their Mail-Hash signatures. Figure 2a displays a short message with two non-empty textual leaves e_{a1}, e_{a2}. Therefore it has two XPath expressions t_{a1}, t_{a2} that form the concatenated string T_a.

Figure 2b presents a similar message sent to another receiver, with exactly the same HTML structure but slightly different textual leaves due to the receiver's first name. Although $e_{b1} \neq e_{a1}$, the identical structure results in $\forall_i t_{ai} = t_{bi}$ and therefore the signatures of the two messages are identical.

```
<html><body><p>Dear Ava,</p><p><b>Thank you for
contacting us.</b></p></body></html>
```

t_{a1} =/html/body/p[1], t_{a2} =/html/body/p[2]/b

T_a =/html/body/p[1] /html/body/p[2]/b

Mail-Hash(a) = $MD5_{64-bit}(T_a)$

(a) Mail message "a"

```
<html><body><p>Dear Bill,</p><p><b>Thank you for
contacting us.</b></p></body></html>
```

$t_{b1} = t_{a1}$, $t_{b2} = t_{a2}$

$T_b = T_a$

Mail-Hash(b)=Mail-Hash(a)

(b) Mail message "b"

Figure 2: Identical Mail-Hash values for two similar messages

Figure 3 also presents a similar message, but this time the signature is different because the structure is not completely identical. To be more precise, message c's structure contains the structure of message a, which infers they have a high resemblance. However, for being able to apply k-anonymization in the most efficient way, we must put message c in a different class, where it may or may not be joined with other similar messages. This last example shows the biggest difference between Mail-Hash and existing fingerprinting techniques that measure resemblance. The latter techniques tend to capture both resemblance and containment, while Mail-Hash captures all structural differences and does not group containers along with the contained documents (containment is not a desirable attribute between messages in the same equivalence class, but rather precise structural similarity).

3.3 Grouping by Mail-Hash Value

The Mail-Hash value of each message can be computed in the most efficient manner in a single pass over the entire mail dataset, resulting in $O(n)$ running time where n is the

```
<html><body><p>Dear Cathy,</p><p><b>Thank you for
contacting us.</b></p><p>Please call us to renew
your membership.</p></body></html>
```

$t_{c1} = t_{a1}$, $t_{c2} = t_{a2}$, t_{c3} =/html/body/p[3]

T_c =/html/body/p[1] /html/body/p[2]/b /html/body/p[3]

Mail-Hash(c) = $MD5_{64-bit}(T_c)$

Figure 3: Mail-Hash value for mail message "c"

number of mail messages in the dataset. This is the lower bound on the running time of any algorithm that needs to explore the entire corpus. We consider that all messages that share the same Mail-Hash value are *equivalent* and assign them to the same equivalence class. This process generates a large number of classes of various sizes, which can also cover the long-tail of mass senders, which send hundreds as opposed to thousands of daily messages. We detail in the next section how these classes are processed to generate masked samples that preserve k-anonymity and can be safely shown to auditors.

4. THE k-anonymity PROCESS

4.1 Outline

We describe the overall process of enforcing k-anonymity in the mail auditing process. Our process consists of three stages:

1. Grouping similar messages in equivalence classes, based on the Mail-Hash function.

2. Masking entities in messages belonging to a same class so as to enforce k-anonymity. The output of this process is a list of templates, where each template represents an equivalence class.

3. The assignment of templates to an auditor, note that this is an online process where templates to be shown to a given auditor are selected on a daily basis, while preserving the k-anonymity of the entire process.

Using the Mail-Hash algorithm described in Section 3, a Mail-Hash signature is computed for each message, and equivalence classes are formed. Each class contains messages that were sent from the same sender and have the same Mail-Hash signature. In order to ensure k-anonymization, classes with less than k users are filtered. Note that a user is counted only once per class, even if she received several messages belonging to the same class.

4.2 Masking

We consider each message as a set of textual entities, where each entity is a character string that consists of all the characters appearing between two subsequent HTML tags. An individual entity is retained if it contains at least one alphanumeric character. For each equivalence class, entities are deleted from the messages in the class, up to the point where all messages are identical, and thus k-anonymization is preserved at the class level. The deleted entities represent these variable term sequences that are not common to *all* messages in the class. As our objective is to maximize the content that is shown to the auditor, the masking operation is stopped when all messages are mapped into a same identical template, as defined in Section 2. The template consists of a sequence of terms, delimited by a $*$ deletion marker, which are common to all messages in the class. The template then allows to generate a masked mail sample (preserving mail formatting) that can be shown to auditors. We note that in some cases HTML tags might contain personal attribute values. Our solution is then applied by considering these values as textual entities.

Figure 4 shows a mail sample generated from a template representing a large set of equivalent mail messages sent by an ecommerce[5] site to a large number of users as order confirmation. All sensitive personal information has automatically disappeared, such as the name of recipient following the "Dear" greetings or his address in the "Ship to" field, without necessitating any deep parsing or semantic analysis. Yet some common qualifiers, such as the prefix `TSOT` in the order number, have been preserved.

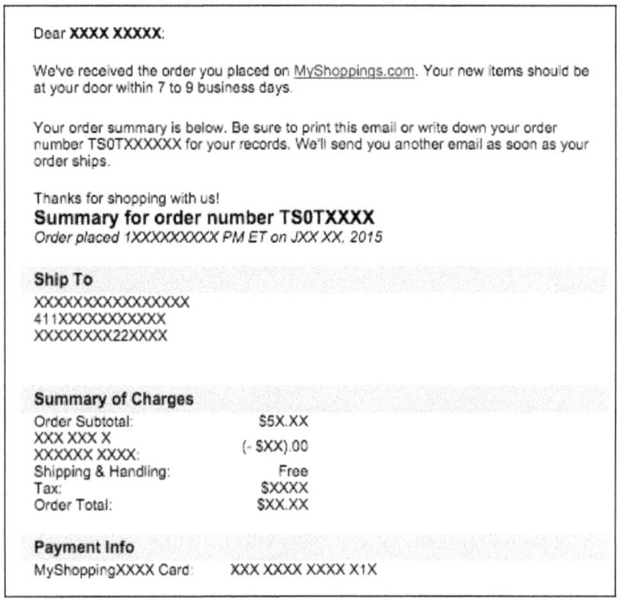

Dear **XXXX XXXXX**:

We've received the order you placed on MyShoppings.com. Your new items should be at your door within 7 to 9 business days.

Your order summary is below. Be sure to print this email or write down your order number TS0TXXXXXX for your records. We'll send you another email as soon as your order ships.

Thanks for shopping with us!

Summary for order number TS0TXXXX

Order placed 1XXXXXXXXX PM ET on JXX XX, 2015

Ship To

XXXXXXXXXXXXXXXX
411XXXXXXXXXXX
XXXXXXXX22XXXX

Summary of Charges

Order Subtotal:	$5X.XX
XXX XXX X XXXXXX XXXX:	(- $XX).00
Shipping & Handling:	Free
Tax:	$XXXX
Order Total:	$XX.XX

Payment Info

MyShoppingXXXX Card: XXX XXXX XXXX X1X

Figure 4: A masked email sample of a shopping receipt.

Another example is shown in Figure 5 with an itinerary confirmation for an airline (renamed here `FlighAirWays` for the same reason as before). Interestingly, more data is revealed here like the destination "ATLANTA", which is frequent enough to become part of the template (precisely, appears as destination for at least k users associated with the template), while the departing city remains masked. Note that fixing the time frame of a given release in our anonymization settings, bears a great deal of influence on the eventual amount of information that will be shown. It could very well be the case that with a shorter time frame, the departing city or the flight number might be exposed. For instance an application that would analyze the users' inboxes, in order to remind them of their departure details, might require auditors to verify that the automated script properly extracts the departure city. On the other hand, if the departing city is not a frequent hub and is not listed in at least k itineraries on a single day release, one option might be to adjust the process so as to generate multi-day releases for less frequent entities. We reserve to future work this type of improvements, which will be needed for specific tasks that demand more details.

[5]Note that we have renamed here this site `MyShoppings.com` in order to respect Yahoo mail terms of conditions of not sharing mail data externally.

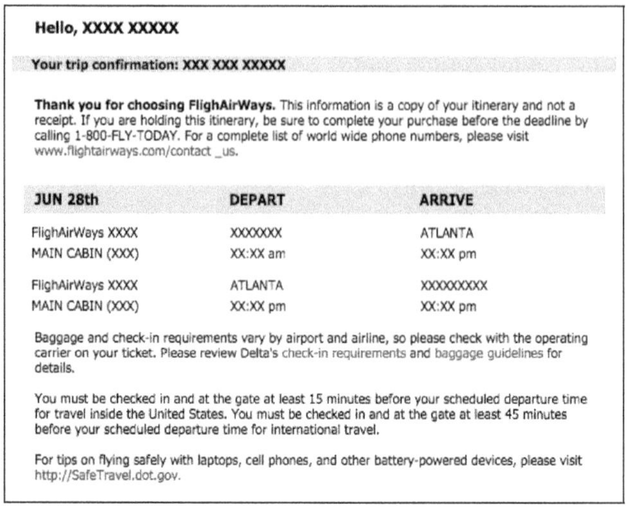

Hello, XXXX XXXXX

Your trip confirmation: XXX XXX XXXXX

Thank you for choosing FlighAirWays. This information is a copy of your itinerary and not a receipt. If you are holding this itinerary, be sure to complete your purchase before the deadline by calling 1-800-FLY-TODAY. For a complete list of world wide phone numbers, please visit www.flightairways.com/contact _us.

JUN 28th	DEPART	ARRIVE
FlighAirWays XXXX MAIN CABIN (XXX)	XXXXXXX XX:XX am	ATLANTA XX:XX pm
FlighAirWays XXXX MAIN CABIN (XXX)	ATLANTA XX:XX pm	XXXXXXXXX XX:XX pm

Baggage and check-in requirements vary by airport and airline, so please check with the operating carrier on your ticket. Please review Delta's check-in requirements and baggage guidelines for details.

You must be checked in and at the gate at least 15 minutes before your scheduled departure time for travel inside the United States. You must be checked in and at the gate at least 45 minutes before your scheduled departure time for international travel.

For tips on flying safely with laptops, cell phones, and other battery-powered devices, please visit http://SafeTravel.dot.gov.

Figure 5: A masked email sample of a travel itinerary.

4.3 Templates Assignment

After the generation of the list of daily templates (where k-anonymity is guaranteed for a user with respect to a single template), the goal is now to generate a daily release globally preserving k-anonymity. The release consists of the templates that will be assigned to an auditor.

Considering a single day, our goal is thus to show at most Γ templates to the auditor while preserving k-anonymity. For each message template m obtained from an equivalence class c, we denote by U_m the set of the recipients of the messages in c. We want to avoid the worst case scenario in which presenting two different templates associated with the same user might violate k-anonymization due to the connection between their content. Note that this is clearly a worst case scenario, yet it is beyond the scope of this paper to verify whether or not the combination of different contents breaks k-anonymity. Consequently, to remain on the safe side, once a user is associated with a template shown to the auditor, the same user cannot be associated with any future template that will be shown to the same auditor.

The daily assignment process of templates to the auditor is described by Algorithm 2. The algorithm is a simple greedy algorithm, which chooses the templates at random. For each chosen template m, it chooses k random users from U_m. These will be the users *associated* with template m. Then, these users are deleted from the sets of users $U_{m'}$ of all other templates. This step ensures that during the assignment, each user will be associated with at most one template assigned to the auditor.

Algorithm 2 can be naturally extended to operate online over a sequence of days. For each day t, we remove users who were previously chosen (i.e., users chosen during days $1, \ldots, t-1$) from the user sets of all templates created during

t. During this process, templates with a remaining set of less than k users are filtered out.

While the number of templates that can be shown to an auditor could be increased by using a different heuristic, we will show in Section 5 that this is not needed. Indeed, in our context of extremely large scale traffic covering millions of users, Algorithm 2 allows the daily assignment of templates to an auditor over a lifetime, while adhering to the constraint of assigning at most Γ templates per day.

Algorithm 2 Daily Release

```
Input: Set of templates M, parameters k ≥ 2, Γ ≤ |M|
Output: A set Q ≤ Γ of templates to display
while M is non-empty and |Q| < Γ do
    Choose at random a template m ∈ M
    Remove m from M
    if |m| ≥ k then
        Add m to Q
        Choose at random a set u_m(k) of k users from U_m
        Remove the k chosen users from the user set of every
          template m' ∈ M, update U_m' = U_m' \ u_m(k)
    end if
end while
```

Finally, we are ready to establish the following claim.

CLAIM 1. *k-anonymity holds for the online mail audition k-anonymization problem by applying our three-phase process.*

PROOF. By construction, k-anonymity holds for each user at the template level. This follows the fact that a template represents identical masked samples associated with at least k users. Furthermore, k-anonymity holds for each daily release following the fact that a user is associated with only a single template assigned to the auditor. Finally, k-anonymity holds for the entire online process of continuous daily assignments due to the fact that this constraint is kept for the entire lifetime period: once a user has been been associated with an assigned template, she/he will never be associated with any future template. □

5. EXPERIMENTS

5.1 Dataset

We use as dataset the actual Yahoo mail traffic, consisting of billions of incoming messages received in several subsequent days, after filtering out several large domains such as facebook or yahoogroups. Indeed, these domains lack interest in our context, as although being machine generated, they mostly include personal unstructured information. For the deep analysis of the hashing and grouping techniques, we focus on a random subset of over a billion messages received in a single day.

5.2 Mail-Hash vs. Min-Hash

In order to verify the benefits of Mail-Hash, we conducted an experiment comparing our proposed technique with the well-known Min-Hash function as our baseline. We use Min-Hash with a single hash function over the mail message, even if it can use a set of hash functions, as this is not needed when using our approach. We applied both functions to the entire message, excluding only URLs, which tend to contain long random strings, and obtained a single signature for each mail message. We then grouped all messages according to their signature, and measured the content coverage of each equivalence class, as defined in Section 2, derived from either Mail-Hash or Min-Hash values.

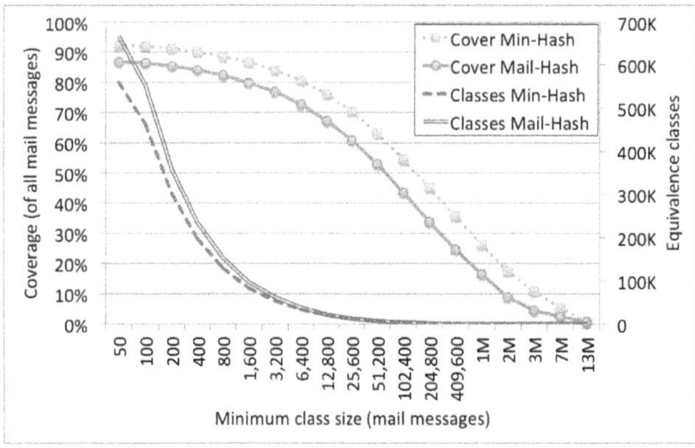

Figure 6: Mail-Hash vs. Min-Hash: compare coverage and number of equivalence classes.

Figure 6 presents the coverage and number of classes obtained, as a function of the minimal number of messages in a class. It shows that Min-Hash's coverage is slightly higher while the number of classes it generates is slightly lower. In other words, Min-Hash classes tend to be somewhat larger than Mail-Hash classes. The reason is that Min-Hash often treats containment[6] and resemblance in a similar way, putting the contained and container in the same group, while Mail-Hash usually generates two distinct signatures, one for each, thus putting them in two different equivalence classes.

5.3 Template/Class Content Coverage

We measured the content coverage of templates (and their associated classes) induced by Min-Hash and Mail-Hash. As per the definition given in Section 2, we considered the amount of data that can be revealed to auditors, relative to the overall original amount of data, if each template was the only template ever exposed.

Figure 7 depicts the content coverage of an equivalence class induced by a template, as a function of the class size. It separates the results according to class size so as not to bias the results towards the larger ones that might just be a kind of "garbage can". Naturally, larger classes are less useful in practice as they will expose fewer amount of shared data. The largest templates are a result of collisions that group together messages that were not necessarily generated by the same script (e.g., very short messages that are likely to have the same DOM tree but totally different textual values) and/or vary in a way that requires more masking due to the high variability of the data. The chart shows that Mail-Hash performs clearly better than Min-Hash, as it reveals a larger portion of common information.

In the experiment presented by Figure 7, we chose for our k anonymization parameter a value of $k = 25$. The same experiment was also run with values of $\{50, 75, 100\}$ leading to similar results. The reason is that this parameter influences only the minimal size of an equivalence class, but not its content coverage. This can also be seen from looking at the

[6]Containment refers to the case where a significant part of one document is contained in another, typically larger one.

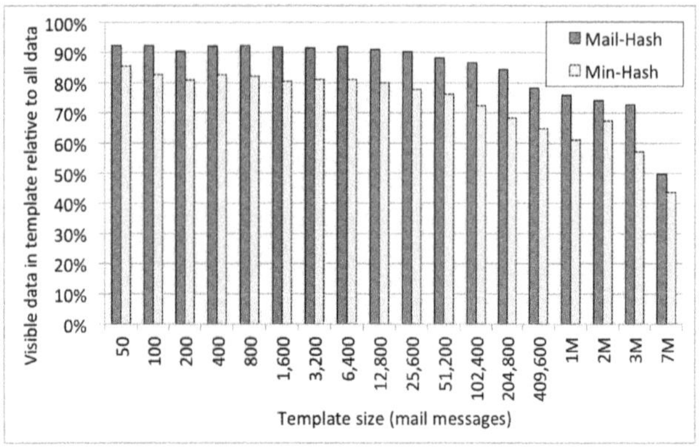

Figure 7: Mail-Hash vs. Min-Hash: the k-anonymity experiment with $k = 25$, comparing the coverage of templates as a function of the template size.

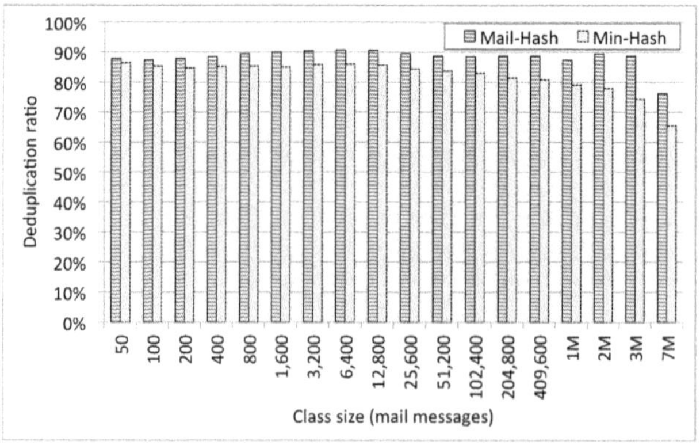

Figure 8: Mail-Hash vs. Min-Hash: compare deduplication ratio as a function of the equivalence-class size.

different classes in the left side of the graph that corresponds to the smaller sizes, all leading to a similar coverage of above 90%. In fact, a content coverage close to 90% is achieved for almost all classes (except the largest ones, which as explained before are valueless classes of high variability that do not contribute to our process). Consequently, the content coverage achieved for the daily release is close to 90% as well.

5.4 Deduplication in Equivalence Classes

This section presents an experiment we conducted to measure the average message similarity within each equivalence class, as an indicator for how "equivalent" our equivalence classes are.

We express the average message similarity in each class by measuring the deduplication level of k random messages in the class. For deduplication we use PACK chunking [28] which converts each message to a list of variable-size chunks. The deduplication level is calculated by initiating a pool of chunks using a random pivot message, and then adding the other $k-1$ messages from the class to the pool, one by one. Whenever a message is added, we measure the number of distinct chunks belonging to the added message, which also belong to at least one message that was already in the chunk pool. We then average over the $k-1$ add operations to get the total deduplication level.

Figure 8 shows the deduplication ratio as a function of the class size. Surprisingly, the average similarity achieved by Mail-Hash is always higher than Min-Hash, even though Mail-Hash covers only the DOM structure while Min-Hash covers the entire message. This indicates that Mail-Hash is able to infer chunk-level similarity without looking at the content of the chunks. In fact, it performs even better than a technique that looks into chunks and chooses some of them, as done by Min-Hash, which chooses a subset of the chunks for generating its signature.

This result also explains the higher content coverage achieved by Mail-Hash, as the more similar the messages within a class, the larger the amount of shared information that can be revealed.

5.5 Daily Releases

The last stage of our evaluation consists of demonstrating that it is feasible to generate daily releases, while preserving k-anonymity over time, and ensuring that auditors can safely continue review samples during their entire tenure. In addition, we demonstrate the scalability of our process by running Algorithm 2 over the actual Yahoo daily traffic during three consecutive days. Using $k = 100$ for k-anonymity, we measured the daily number of equivalence classes that were created, as well as their accumulative number, counting the same class that was created during different days only once. We used a threshold of $\Gamma = 1000$ on the number of samples that can be shown to an editor per day. Thus, due to the fact we restrict a user to be associated with a template only once (see Section 4.3), it follows that the daily number of users becoming "invalid" per day is 100,000 (that is, users that cannot be associated with a template in the future).

According to our online algorithm, such users are removed from future templates, potentially causing the filtering of templates with a remaining set of less than k users (see Algorithm 2). However, as can be observed in Table 1, the number of templates filtered per day is negligible ($\sim 250 - 630$) compared to the total number of accumulated templates ($> 720K$). Note that while the accumulated number of templates grows during the first days, it is expected to increase at a much slower pace after a while, when most of the stable equivalence classes have been identified in the system.

The ratio between the daily filtered templates and the overall number of templates (along new templates as well as new users entering the system over time) demonstrates that, in a realistic scenario over a traffic of such scale, $k-$ *anonymization* can be enforced online practically "forever" over the full tenure of an auditor.

Day	day 1	day 2	day 3
# accumulated templates	$466K$	$597K$	$727K$
# daily templates filtered	252	352	626

Table 1: Results for experiments conducted over Yahoo traffic during three consecutive days.

6. RELATED WORK

Using k-anonymization as a method for protecting individual privacy has first been suggested by Samarati and Sweeney [20]. It was then greatly popularized and adopted into key privacy related legislation such as HIPAA [22] and the EU Data Protection Directive [6]. k-Anonymity continues to be the single most practical tool for protecting individuals against inadvertent intrusion into their privacy. This is, in many ways, because it is simple and well understood. This same simplicity is the source of some of k-anonymity falls back.

As many have noticed (see [18]), k-anonymity breaks when there is lax control of auxiliary releases of information. In our work we claim that the exposure of internal auditors to such auxiliary releases can be limited via internal regulation. Additionally, it was noticed [14] that if data subjects are not sufficiently diverse then k-anonymity becomes ineffective. In the context of mail users this can occur with alias accounts and with inactive accounts and both those cases are evident to the Web-mail provider and can be filtered with no adverse effect on the application. Last, it was argued that the protection provided by k-anonymous releases can be de-anonymized [17] and that stronger models such as differential privacy [7] may be needed. While this is true in the general case, our concern is not protection against an adversary who invests effort in de-anonymization but rather protection against inadvertent exposure. Therefore we argue that k-anonymization provides sufficient protection for our application.

Optimal k-anonymization with respect to any non-trivial optimization criteria is NP-Hard [13]. Consequently, most k-anonymization techniques are heuristic. Our k-anonymization algorithm, like Mondarian's [13], is a multi dimensional technique: every template represents a different dimension and different equivalence classes of messages are anonymized using different combinations of dimensions. The unique aspect of our algorithm is the choice of classes of messages that will be co-anonymized. This choice relies on a deep domain understanding (mail traffic, and mail documents characteristics), which is atypical for general purpose anonymization algorithms.

The issue of multiple sequential releases have been studied by Wang, Fung et al. [25, 8] and by Shmueli et al. [21]. Their focus, however, is on the efficiency of computing the current release given all previous releases in terms of both computation and limited disclosure. Another work is that of *multi-release publishing* [27], where the data owner needs to release the data to different recipients, each seeing a different projection of the data. The challenge in this case is to preserve the k-anonymity of previous releases when a new projection is needed.

To the best of our knowledge this work is the first to consider sequential releases in a large scale data environment. Considering billions of new daily (mail) documents, we provide a complete solution enforcing k-anonymity over time, demonstrating through experiments at Web scale that our algorithm can be applied over a lifetime period of years, while producing daily a k-anonymized release that maximizes content coverage as we defined it.

7. CONCLUSIONS AND FUTURE WORK

We have defined here the novel problem of k-anomymization for human auditing of mail messages, which we believe is timely given the growing concerns of users over the privacy of their inboxes. We focus on the specific problem of enforcing the k-anonymity of recipients of machine-generated messages, when their messages are reviewed by human auditors for various quality assurance tasks. We proposed a mechanism that guarantees k-anonymization by grouping structurally-similar messages into a same equivalence class, and by generating for such classes masked mail samples that can be safely shown to auditors. To this effect, we introduced a highly efficient, yet surprisingly simple, message signature function, *Mail-Hash*, that allows to identify these structurally-similar messages, most probably generated by a same script. We also proposed a mail sample assignment process that guarantees k-anonymity of users while maximizing the auditors' productivity, according to a generic quantitative measure of content coverage. We demonstrated over real Yahoo mail traffic that our approach is feasible and presents detailed results of our experiments.

This work represents only a first step in the direction of improving the auditing process in most large Web mail companies. We sincerely hope it will trigger more efforts and alternate solutions towards devising more automated and more sophisticated methods for protecting users' privacy. We intend to continue exploring this venue along different directions. First, we would like to devise more qualitative measures of auditors' productivity, as opposed to our quantitative generic measure of raw content coverage. Such measures should probably be tailored to the specific task that required auditing in the first place. We also believe that some specific tasks will demand more control of the timeframe of a release, in order to reveal specific entities in mail samples, as in our example of flight itinerary in Figure 5.

One effect of our solution is the large number of classes potentially created per domain, sometimes fragmenting the same "logical template" into multiple equivalence classes due to slights changes in their structure. While for masking and anonymization purposes, it does not represent a limitation, it could pose a problem depending on the auditorial task at hand. Aggregating such classes together within the same logical component is left for future work.

In addition, it will be interesting to verify whether productivity can be improved by considering auditors not independently but as a pool, for which sample assignment need to be globally optimized. Finally, the next big challenge will be to tackle the much harder task of considering k-anonymization of highly variable human-generated messages.

Acknowledgements

We are grateful to our colleague Doug Sharp who motivated this problem and convinced us of the urgency of proposing principled methods for safe mail auditing. We owe a lot to Zohar Karnin for his constant insights. We also cannot thank enough our friends and colleagues in the Mail research and engineering teams at Yahoo, without whom this work would not have been possible.

8. REFERENCES

[1] Nir Ailon, Zohar S. Karnin, Edo Liberty, and Yoelle Maarek. Threading machine generated email. In *Proceedings of WSDM'2013*, pages 405–414, New York, NY, USA, 2013.

[2] Andrei Z Broder. On the resemblance and containment of documents. In *Compression and Complexity of Sequences 1997. Proceedings*, pages 21–29. IEEE, 1997.

[3] Andrei Z. Broder. Identifying and filtering near-duplicate documents. In *Proceedings of the 11th Annual Symposium on Combinatorial Pattern Matching*, COM '00, pages 1–10. Springer-Verlag, 2000.

[4] Andrei Z Broder, Moses Charikar, Alan M Frieze, and Michael Mitzenmacher. Min-wise independent permutations. *Journal of Computer and System Sciences*, 60(3):630–659, 2000.

[5] Andrei Z Broder, Steven C Glassman, Mark S Manasse, and Geoffrey Zweig. Syntactic clustering of the web. *Computer Networks and ISDN Systems*, 29(8):1157–1166, 1997.

[6] EU Directive. 95/46/ec of the european parliament and of the council of 24 october 1995 on the protection of individuals with regard to the processing of personal data and on the free movement of such data. *Official Journal of the EC*, 23(6), 1995.

[7] Cynthia Dwork. Differential privacy. In Michele Bugliesi, Bart Preneel, Vladimiro Sassone, and Ingo Wegener, editors, *Automata, Languages and Programming*, volume 4052 of *Lecture Notes in Computer Science*, pages 1–12. Springer Berlin Heidelberg, 2006.

[8] Benjamin Fung, Ke Wang, Ada Wai-Chee Fu, and Jian Pei. Anonymity for continuous data publishing. In *Proceedings of the 11th international conference on Extending database technology: Advances in database technology*, pages 264–275. ACM, 2008.

[9] Google. Privacy policy, Jun 2015. http://www.google.com/intl/en/policies/privacy/.

[10] Mihajlo Grbovic, Guy Halawi, Zohar Karnin, and Yoelle Maarek. How many folders do you really need? classifying email into a handful of categories. In *Proceedings of CIKM'2014*, 2014.

[11] Nevin Heintze. Scalable document fingerprinting. In *Proceedings of the USENIX Workhop on Electronic Commerce*, 1996.

[12] Monika Henzinger. Finding near-duplicate web pages: a large-scale evaluation of algorithms. In *Proceedings of the 29th annual international ACM SIGIR conference on Research and development in information retrieval*, pages 284–291. ACM, 2006.

[13] Kristen LeFevre, David J. DeWitt, and Raghu Ramakrishnan. Mondrian multidimensional k-anonymity. In *Proceedings of the 22Nd International Conference on Data Engineering*, ICDE '06, pages 25–50. IEEE Computer Society, 2006.

[14] Ashwin Machanavajjhala, Daniel Kifer, Johannes Gehrke, and Muthuramakrishnan Venkitasubramaniam. L-diversity: Privacy beyond k-anonymity. *ACM Transactions on Knowledge Discovery from Data*, 1(1):3, 2007.

[15] Udi Manber. Finding similar files in a large file system. In *Proc. of the USENIX winter technical conference*, pages 1–10, 1994.

[16] Microsoft. Services agreement, Jun 2014. http://windows.microsoft.com/en-us/windows/microsoft-services-agreement.

[17] Arvind Narayanan and Vitaly Shmatikov. Robust de-anonymization of large sparse datasets. In *Security and Privacy, 2008. SP 2008. IEEE Symposium on*, pages 111–125. IEEE, 2008.

[18] Paul Ohm. Broken Promises of Privacy: Responding to the Surprising Failure of Anonymization. *UCLA Law Review*, 57:1701–1777, 2010.

[19] R. Rivest. The MD5 Message-Digest Algorithm. *RFC 1321*, April 1992.

[20] Pierangela Samarati and Latanya Sweeney. Protecting Privacy when Disclosing Information: k-Anonymity and Its Enforcement through Generalization and Suppression. Technical Report SRI-CSL-98-04, 1998.

[21] Erez Shmueli, Tamir Tassa, Raz Wasserstein, Bracha Shapira, and Lior Rokach. Limiting disclosure of sensitive data in sequential releases of databases. *Information Sciences*, 191:98–127, 2012.

[22] US Dept. of HHS. Standards for privacy of individually identifiable health information; final rule, August 2002.

[23] W3C. XML Path Language (XPath) Version 1.0. *http://www.w3.org/TR/xpath/*, November 1999.

[24] W3C. Document Object Model (DOM) Level 3. *http://www.w3.org/DOM/DOMTR#dom3*, April 2004.

[25] Ke Wang and Benjamin Fung. Anonymizing sequential releases. In *Proceedings of the 12th ACM SIGKDD international conference on Knowledge discovery and data mining*, pages 414–423. ACM, 2006.

[26] Yahoo. Privacy center, Sept 2014. https://policies.yahoo.com/us/en/yahoo/privacy/index.htm.

[27] Chao Yao, X Sean Wang, and Sushil Jajodia. Checking for k-anonymity violation by views. In *Proceedings of the 31st international conference on Very large data bases*, pages 910–921. VLDB Endowment, 2005.

[28] Eyal Zohar, Israel Cidon, and Osnat Mokryn. The Power of Prediction: Cloud Bandwidth and Cost Reduction. In *Proc. of SIGCOMM*, 2011.

An Information-Theoretic Approach to Individual Sequential Data Sanitization

Luca Bonomi
University of California, San Diego
La Jolla, CA
lbonomi@ucsd.edu

Liyue Fan
University of Southern California
Los Angeles, CA
liyuefan@usc.edu

Hongxia Jin
Samsung Research America
San Jose, CA
hongxia.jin@samsung.com

ABSTRACT

Fine-grained, personal data has been largely, continuously generated nowadays, such as location check-ins, web histories, physical activities, etc. Those data sequences are typically shared with untrusted parties for data analysis and promotional services. However, the individually-generated sequential data contains behavior patterns and may disclose sensitive information if not properly sanitized. Furthermore, the utility of the released sequence can be adversely affected by sanitization techniques. In this paper, we study the problem of individual sequence data sanitization with minimum utility loss, given user-specified sensitive patterns. We propose a privacy notion based on information theory and sanitize sequence data via generalization. We show the optimization problem is hard and develop two efficient heuristic solutions. Extensive experimental evaluations are conducted on real-world datasets and the results demonstrate the efficiency and effectiveness of our solutions.

CCS Concepts

•Information systems → Data mining; •Security and privacy → Data anonymization and sanitization;

Keywords

Data Sanitization; Sequential Patterns; Mutual Information

1. INTRODUCTION

The increasing popularity of GPS-enabled mobile devices, apps, and wearable sensors greatly facilitates the vast generation of *sequential data* of various types. For example, such sequential data generated by a particular user might be a sequence of locations he visited, a sequence of physical activities he performed, or a series of purchase orders he made over time. Clearly, sharing these data sequences with untrusted parties would enable them to perform aggregation and mine patterns over a larger number of individuals, and ultimately to aid business decision-making. In return, individual data contributors will benefit from the outcome of such analysis, such as fitness ranking among the user community, restaurant recommendation based on location visited, and coupons based on items bought before.

However, individually generated data sequences contain *sequential patterns*, i.e., a set of atomic actions in a particular order, which may disclose sensitive information if not properly sanitized. Consider the following scenarios,

Scenario 1. A female customer who buys unscented lotions and zinc/magnesium supplements *first*, and unscented soaps and cotton balls in extra-large bags *later*, is probably pregnant and very close to her delivery date [7].

Scenario 2. A doctor leaves a patient's room and immediately enters a psychiatrist's office [29], might indicate that the patient is experiencing psychiatric problems.

Scenario 3. Sensitive physical activities can be inferred by a sequence of simple activities [20]. For example, going to toilet can be recognized by the following sequence: hand motions, sit, stand, hand motions.

To prevent the privacy breaches caused by such patterns, rather than single events or actions, data sequences must be sanitized to *hide* those sequential patterns prior to release.

A plethora of works have been developed to hide association rules [28, 3], frequent itemsets [25], or individual event [13]. However, they cannot be applied to sequential patterns which contain multiple atomic actions in a specific order within certain duration. A few works have been proposed to "hide" sequential patterns in a sequence database [1, 11, 14] or individual sequences [29], by reducing the occurrences of each sensitive pattern to a given threshold in the sanitized data. Among them, works in [1, 11, 29] adopt a *suppression* approach by removing individual symbols, e.g., events, when a sensitive pattern occurs. The authors of [14] adopt a *permutation* approach which re-arranges the ordering of symbols in each sensitive pattern in the released sequence. The drawback of suppression-based approaches is the data loss inflicted by deleting symbols in the released data, especially when sensitive patterns are frequent patterns. The permutation-based approaches break the inherent ordering in the sequential data and create "ghost" patterns that do not exist in the original database.

In this paper, we propose to sanitize individual sequence data for user-specified sequential patterns via *generalization*, which has been extensively applied to publishing and mining non-sequential data [26, 16, 15]. The key idea is to replace the fine-grained symbols, e.g. items, in the sensitive patterns with coarser data, e.g. categories, in order to

WSDM'16, February 22–25, 2016, San Francisco, CA, USA.
 ISBN 978-1-4503-3716-8/16/02...$15.00
DOI: http://dx.doi.org/10.1145/2835776.2835828

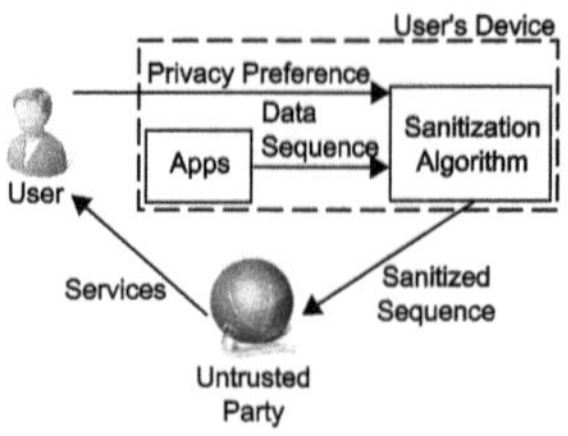

Figure 1: Setting

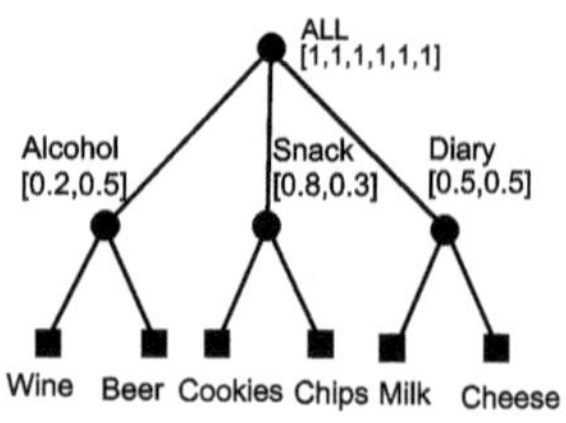

Figure 2: Taxonomy

guarantee privacy and to preserve the utility of the sanitized sequence. We propose a novel privacy model which measures the amount of information that an adversary could learn by observing the sanitized sequence. Our framework allows the data owners to specify sensitive patterns, privacy levels, and customized utility metrics. By enabling individuals to have full control over their data, we believe that our solutions could greatly improve current data sharing paradigm. The proposed sanitization algorithms can be easily embedded on mobile devices, as in Figure 1, where the sequence data generated from various apps is sanitized as specified by the user, prior to release to untrusted parties. Specifically, our major **contributions** are:

- We propose a novel notion, i.e., ϵ-mutual information privacy for hiding *sequential patterns* and sanitize individual sequences via *generalization*. Our privacy model based on information theory does not impose constraints on the adversary's prior knowledge, and provides privacy guarantee without deleting data or creating "ghost" patterns.
- We formally define an optimization problem for sequence sanitization, which satisfies the user-defined privacy constraint while minimizing the utility loss caused by generalization. We identify four variants of the problem: *global* vs. *local* generalization, and *offline* vs. *online* scenario. In this paper, we focus on the global generalization strategy and show that the problem is hard even in the offline case.
- We propose two algorithmic solutions to the proposed problem. The former exploits the monotonicity property of the privacy notion and adopts a top-down approach to refine the symbols generalization. The latter exploits the similarity between sensitive patterns and produces a generalization by clustering them in a bottom-up fashion.
- We perform an extensive experimental evaluation with real-world datasets. It shows that the bottom-up algorithm is more efficient, while the top-down approach provides better utility in the released data. We demonstrate the usability of our techniques in various settings and we believe our solutions can enable a wide range of sequential data sharing applications.

In the remaining of the paper, Section 2 reviews recent related works; Section 3 formally defines the sanitization problem and provides hardness results. Our proposed solutions are described in Section 4 and Section 5. Section 6 provides experimental results. Section 7 concludes the paper and states future research directions.

2. RELATED WORKS

Hiding Set Patterns. Here we use the term "set pattern" to represent static, non-sequential patterns. A plethora of works have been proposed to hide association rules [28, 3] and frequent itemsets [25, 12] from transaction data. Given a set of sensitive itemsets or rules, the goal is to reduce the *support* of itemsets or the *confidence* of rules in the released datasets. Recently, several approaches have been developed to anonymize set-valued data [18, 27] using a taxonomy tree. Although extensively studied, solutions for these problems are not applicable in our setting, as set patterns do not consider the sequential order between symbols.

Hiding Sequential Patterns. Existing techniques for sequential pattern hiding fall into two categories, *suppression* as in [1, 11, 29] and *permutation* as in [14]. Essentially, sequential patterns are "hidden" in the sanitized data by reducing the occurrences of each sensitive pattern to a given threshold. Suppression-based techniques [1, 11, 29] remove symbols from the sequence in order to reduce the exact matching of sensitive patterns. The drawback of those techniques is the data loss inflicted by deletion, especially when sensitive patterns are *frequent* patterns. To avoid data deletion, the permutation-based technique [14] re-arranges the ordering of symbols when a sensitive pattern occurs, thus reducing the matchings. However, permutation breaks the inherent ordering in the sequence data and creates "ghost" patterns that do not exist originally. From the *privacy* aspect, the support-based notion [1, 11, 14] is ad-hoc and only applicable to releasing sequence databases. Furthermore, it adopts a weaker adversary model where the sensitive patterns are unknown to the adversary. The work of [29] investigated the trade-off between public patterns and private (sensitive) patterns in a event stream, and allowed the disclosure of private patterns to preserve high-utility public patterns. As a result, the utility-oriented mechanism does not provide a privacy guarantee. The work in [13] hides sensitive contexts, i.e., individual events, in individual sequence data and guarantees privacy by bounding the difference between the adversary's *prior* and *posterior* belief, assuming that the adversary has background knowledge of a user's mobility patterns. While this work provides a nice privacy guarantee, its solution cannot be applied in our setting where sensitive patterns contain multiple events.

Privacy for Data Sequences. Numerous privacy notions have been adopted to sanitize data sequences. Previously k-anonymity and l-diversity have been adopted in [21, 24] for sanitizing sequence databases. When applied to protect patterns, k-anonymity and l-diversity treat each sensitive pattern equally, without considering frequent patterns are more susceptible for privacy breach. The rigorous notion of *differential privacy* [8] has been widely adopted for releasing *aggregate* queries [10] and for mining sequential patterns [2, 4]. Recently *local* differential privacy [6] has been proposed when the data aggregator is untrusted. However, it is not straightforward to apply to individual sequence sanitization. On the other hand, *mutual information* has been widely used to quantify information leakage in literature [5, 22, 23]. In particular, Calmon and Fawaz [5] adopted mutual information to introduce the information privacy notion which has been shown to provide stronger guarantee in term of information leakage than differential privacy. Based on these considerations, we adopt the mutual information notion to protect user-specified sensitive patterns.

3. PRELIMINARIES

3.1 Definitions

An *alphabet* Σ is a finite set of literals, i.e. symbols, where each literal represents an atomic event. A user-generated *sequence* $S = \{S[1], S[2], \ldots, S[n]\}$ of length n, i.e. $|S| = n$, is a set of events taken place in a sequential order, where $S[i] \in \Sigma$ for $i = 1, \ldots, n$. A *sequential pattern* contains multiple symbols in a specific order. Formally, we define a sequential pattern p of length m as $p = \langle a_1, a_2, \ldots, a_m \rangle$, where $a_i \in \Sigma$ for $i = 1, \ldots, m$.

DEFINITION 1 (PATTERN OCCURRENCE). *Given an input sequence S and a time window w, we said that a pattern $p = \langle a_1, a_2, \ldots, a_m \rangle$ occurs at position i_1 in S if there exists a subsequence of S with indices $i_1 < i_2 < \cdots < i_m$ such that: (1) $i_m - i_1 \leq w$ and (2) $S[i_k] = a_k$, for $k = 1, \ldots, m$.*

Furthermore, we define the *frequency* of a pattern p in S, denoted with $f_S(p)$, the number of occurrences of p in a user sequence S. For example, if $S = \{a, a, b\}$ and $p = \langle a, b \rangle$ and $w = 2$, $f_S(p) = 2$ because there are two subsequences of S, i.e. $\langle S[1], S[3] \rangle$ and $\langle S[2], S[3] \rangle$, that match p.

Taxonomy Tree-Based Generalization. Similar to [18, 27], we consult a *taxonomy tree* for generalizing the symbols to sanitize the input sequence. The benefit of using a taxonomy tree is that the generalized symbols, i.e. intermediate nodes, preserve the semantic meaning of the original data, i.e. leaf nodes, providing a trade-off between privacy and utility. Formally, let Σ_g be the alphabet of generalized symbols in the data domain, such as categories and sub-categories of products. A taxonomy tree $\mathcal{T}$ is a hierarchical structure between the most fine-grained events, i.e. symbols in Σ, and more general events, i.e. symbols in Σ_g. Intuitively, original data symbols in the input sequence appear in the leaves of $\mathcal{T}$, while the internal nodes are potential options for generalization. As in Figure 2, *Wine* is a fine-grained symbol and *Alcohol* is a general symbol. Let $\Sigma_e = \Sigma \bigcup \Sigma_g$ denote the *extended alphabet* induced by $\mathcal{T}$. Therefore, a generalization strategy can be defined as a function $h : \Sigma \mapsto \Sigma_e$ that maps a fine-grained symbol to its generalized form. A sequential pattern is transformed to a *generalized pattern* after one or more symbols in it have been generalized. In our work, we aim to design a sequence sanitization strategy to hide user-specified sensitive patterns by generalizing individual symbols.

Privacy Definition. In our problem setting, a user specifies a set of sensitive patterns $\mathcal{S}$ (i.e., patterns to hide) in a input sequence S and wants to release a sanitized sequence $\hat{S}$, to receive some services. We denote $\mathcal{G}$ as the set of generalized patterns observed in $\hat{S}$. Assuming an adversary has *prior knowledge* about the frequency distributions of the sensitive patterns, he aims to discover the *positions* of those patterns in S by observing $\hat{S}$. The rationale of this adversary model is two-fold: 1) The content of sensitive patterns are usually public, as in Scenario 1-3, and even the expected frequencies of sensitive patterns are publicly available statistics. For example, the frequency information can be derived by domain knowledge, e.g., how many times one goes to toilet per day, or released by mining aggregated data [2, 4]. 2) We consider the context of a pattern as sensitive information and thus should be protected. For example, the pattern ⟨*leave work, go to liqueur store*⟩ is not surprising at night. However, if the same pattern occurs frequently during the day, it might indicate an addiction problem.

Given a generalized pattern, the adversary can identify a set of sensitive patterns mapped to it using the publicly available taxonomy tree.

EXAMPLE 1. *Assume a user specifies three sensitive patterns, $p_1 = \langle Beer, Chips \rangle$, $p_2 = \langle Wine, Cheese \rangle$, and $p_3 = \langle Cookies, Milk \rangle$. Upon observing an occurrence of generalized pattern $\hat{p} = \langle Alcohol, All \rangle$, an adversary can infer a possible occurrence of p_1 or p_2, according to the taxonomy tree in Figure 2.*

Therefore, the positions of a generalized pattern $\hat{p}$ in $\hat{S}$ may enable the adversary to infer where the sensitive patterns mapped to it occur in the original sequence. Our goal is to bound the inference gain of the adversary by observing $\hat{S}$. We consider the standard statistical inference threat model in [5], where the inference gain is measured using *mutual information*, which has been widely used to quantify information leakage/privacy risk in literature [22, 23].

Let $\mathbb{S}$ denote the frequency distributions of sensitive patterns in S, which may be known to the adversary. Let $\mathbb{G}$ denote the frequency distributions of generalized patters in $\hat{S}$. As shown in [5], the average statistical information gain of the adversary by observing $\hat{S}$ is the mutual information between $\mathbb{S}$ and $\mathbb{G}$:

$$I(\mathbb{S}; \mathbb{G}) = H(\mathbb{S}) - H(\mathbb{S}|\mathbb{G}), \tag{1}$$

where H denotes the Shannon entropy. $I(\mathbb{S}; \mathbb{G})$ is bounded between 0 and $H(\mathbb{S})$. Using the mutual information, we define the following privacy notion for sequence sanitization:

DEFINITION 2 (ϵ-MUTUAL INFORMATION PRIVACY). *Given an input sequence S, a set of sensitive patterns $\mathcal{S}$, and $\epsilon \geq 0$, a sanitized sequence $\hat{S}$ satisfies ϵ-mutual information privacy if and only if $I(\mathbb{S}; \mathbb{G}) \leq \epsilon$.*

By upper-bounding the mutual information, our privacy notion imposes a lower bound on the conditional entropy $H(\mathbb{S}|\mathbb{G})$ in Equation 1. Intuitively, given a generalized pattern $\hat{p}$, a sanitization strategy yields higher conditional entropy by mapping a *diverse* set of sensitive patterns to $\hat{p}$, thus providing higher privacy. This observation also inspires us when designing our algorithmic solutions. The privacy parameter ϵ can be specified by individual data providers. A lower ϵ value indicates a higher privacy level, where perfect privacy is achieved by setting $\epsilon = 0$. Note that ϵ-mutual information privacy ($\forall \epsilon$) is always feasible, by generalizing all symbols to "*All*", i.e., root of taxonomy tree, where the released sequence is independent of the input, i.e., no additional information is gained by the adversary.

In our approaches, we use an empirical form of Equation 1. For each $p \in \mathcal{S}$ and $\hat{p} \in \mathcal{G}$, $\tilde{P}[p]$, $\tilde{P}[\hat{p}]$, and $\tilde{P}[p, \hat{p}]$ denote the empirical distributions of p and $\hat{p}$ and their joint distribution, respectively. These distributions are computed by counting the frequency of the patterns in the data sequences. Thus, the empirical form of Equation 1 is:

$$\begin{aligned} \tilde{I}(\mathbb{S}; \mathbb{G}) &= \sum_{p \in \mathcal{S}} \tilde{P}[p] \log \frac{1}{\tilde{P}[p]} - \sum_{p \in \mathcal{S}, \hat{p} \in \mathcal{G}} \tilde{P}[p, \hat{p}] \log \frac{\tilde{P}[\hat{p}]}{\tilde{P}[p, \hat{p}]} \\ &= \sum_{p \in \mathcal{S}, \hat{p} \in \mathcal{G}} \tilde{P}[p, \hat{p}] \log \frac{\tilde{P}[p, \hat{p}]}{\tilde{P}[p]\tilde{P}[\hat{p}]} \end{aligned} \tag{2}$$

In general, mutual information bounds the average information leakage; therefore, when ϵ value is high, not all sensitive patterns need to be generalized. To ensure that each sensitive pattern $p \in \mathcal{S}$ is sanitized, a lower ϵ value must be specified by the data provider, i.e., $\epsilon < \min_{p \in \mathcal{S}} \tilde{P}[p] \log \frac{1}{\tilde{P}[p]}$. However, we notice in our empirical evaluation that when the alphabet is small, each sensitive pattern will be sanitized even with higher ϵ values, e.g., 90% of $\tilde{H}(\mathbb{S})$.

Utility Metric. To quantify the utility loss inflicted by generalizing the original data symbols, we define a cost function $c : \Sigma \times \Sigma_e \mapsto \Re^+$, such that for a pair of symbols $(a, \hat{a})$, $c(a, \hat{a})$ returns the cost of generalizing a to $\hat{a}$. Note that prior to the generalization process, each user could specify or customize the cost for any particular symbol, according to its importance or the user's preferences. A formal definition for the cost function is as follows.

DEFINITION 3 (COST FUNCTION). *For any $a \in \Sigma$, let $\pi_a = \hat{a}_1, \ldots, \hat{a}_k$ be the root-to-leaf path in $\mathcal{T}$, i.e. $\hat{a}_1 = root$ and $\hat{a}_k = a$. A function $c : \Sigma \times \Sigma_e \mapsto \Re^+$ is a generalization cost function over $\mathcal{T}$, if $\forall a \in \Sigma$ the following properties hold:*

1. $c(a, \hat{a}_i) \geq c(a, \hat{a}_{i-1})$, *for* $i = 1, \ldots, k$
2. $c(a, \hat{a}) = \infty$ *if* $\hat{a} \notin \pi_a$
3. $c(a, \hat{a}) = 0 \Longleftrightarrow a = \hat{a}$

These properties guarantee: the cost monotonically increases when generalizing a leaf node to a higher-level node; the cost of generalizing a leaf node to its non-ancestor is prohibitive; and there's no cost of generalizing a leaf node to itself.

EXAMPLE 2. *Consider the taxonomy tree in Figure 2. Each internal node ν is associated with an array where each entry represents the cost of replacing a leaf node with ν. Suppose the scale of cost is $[0, 1]$, replacing any product with the root "All" incurs cost 1, while the cost of replacing "Cookies" with "Snack" is 0.8.*

In practice, the release of each data symbol, generalized or original, allows the user to receive certain services, such as fitness analysis or a grocery item coupon. Intuitively, sharing a generalized symbol would receive less utility than the original symbol. We define the overall utility loss for a generalized sequence as follows.

DEFINITION 4 (UTILITY LOSS). *The utility loss for a generalized sequence $\hat{S}$ obtained from a sequence S is:*

$$UL(S, \hat{S}) = \sum_{i=1}^{|S|} c(S[i], \hat{S}[i]) \tag{3}$$

The overall utility loss sums up the user-specified cost of generalizing each symbol in the input sequence. In future works, a *weight* can be introduced to indicate the importance of *event-time*, i.e. i, which is out of the scope of this paper.

3.2 Problem Variants

Based on the notions above, we formally define the Minimum Utility Loss Generalization problem (MULG) to sanitize individual sequence data.

PROBLEM 1 (MINIMUM UTILITY LOSS GENERALIZATION). *Given an input sequence S, a set of sensitive patterns $\mathcal{S}$, a cost function c, and $\epsilon \geq 0$, construct a sanitized version $\hat{S}$ such that (1) $\hat{S}$ satisfies ϵ-mutual information privacy, and (2) $\hat{S}$ incurs minimum utility loss.*

We identify several variants of the sequence sanitization problem and provide a brief discussion below.

Global vs. Local. The **global** variant generalizes all occurrences of one symbol in the same way, irrespective of when they occur in the sequence. On the other hand, the **local** generalization problem treats each occurrence of a symbol differently based on its context, i.e. the neighboring symbols in the sequence. In comparison, the local variant offers more flexibility in generalization options and more opportunities for utility optimization. However, it also presents a harder optimization problem than the global variant [29]. Furthermore, the highly locally customized generalization solutions may open up opportunities for adversary to make inference attacks, as discussed in [30].

Offline vs. Online. The **offline** variant makes generalization decisions after the entire sequence is generated, while in the **online** variant, decisions have to be made in real-time as each symbol is generated without knowledge of the future. Despite the importance of online sanitization in many real scenarios, achieving minimum utility loss in this setting is particulary hard due to the uncertainty for the future patterns. For this reason, we focus our study on the offline variant where the knowledge about the entire user sequence can be used to reach the optimality.

Based on the above considerations, we will focus on the *offline* sequence sanitization problem with *global* generalization solutions, i.e. g-MULG, in the rest of the paper. In particular, our goal is to identify a generalization function $h : \Sigma \mapsto \Sigma_e$ that maps each $a \in \Sigma$ into a unique symbol $\hat{a} \in \Sigma_e$ (i.e. $h(a) = \hat{a}$). Note that due to the unique solution for each symbol, the joint distribution $\tilde{P}[p, \hat{p}]$ is simplified to $\tilde{P}[p]$ in Equation 2.

Hardness Results. The following theorem states the hardness of the sanitization problem.

THEOREM 1. *The g-MULG problem where all the sensitive patterns are generalized is NP-hard.*

The result follows from similar arguments as in [1, 29, 17], and due to the limited space the proof is omitted. We observe that g-MULG problem does not enforce the generalization of all sensitive patterns to achieve ϵ-mutual information privacy. It is possible that some patterns are preserved while others are generalized. However, this does not change the hardness of the problem. In fact, we can always construct a solution for plain g-MULG by preserving some patterns and generalizing the rest as long as privacy is achieved.

4. TOP-DOWN APPROACH

Our first approach proceeds in a top-down fashion by progressively improving the utility of the symbols generalization without breaching privacy. The intuition is to start from the highest level of generalization for all the symbols, i.e., *root*, and then refine each symbol to enhance the utility as much as possible. A taxonomy tree constructed in the data domain is used to refine the symbol generalization. Among all the possible levels of generalization for a symbol, we choose the one that achieves highest utility while satisfying the privacy constraint. Before describing the proposed algorithm in detail, we first present some useful concepts and the monotonicity property of the solution space.

Refinement Process. The top-down approach starts with the highest level of generalization possible $g_f = [h(a_1) = \hat{a}_1, \ldots, h(a_{|\Sigma|}) = \hat{a}_{|\Sigma|}]$, where each symbol a_j is mapped to the root node of the taxonomy tree (i.e. $\hat{a}_j = root$). At each iteration i, the current generalization g_i is refined to improve the utility of the released sequence. This process is guided by the taxonomy tree $\mathcal{T}$, where given $g_i = [\hat{a}^i_1, \ldots, \hat{a}^i_{|\Sigma|}]$ for a symbol a_j, its current representation $\hat{a}^i_j$ is refined to $\hat{a}^{i+1}_j$ by selecting the successive node in $\mathcal{T}$ on the path from the root to a_j. Furthermore, symbols at the leaves of the subtree rooted by $\hat{a}^i_j$ other than a_j will be also refined to this new representation, $\hat{a}^{i+1}_j$.

EXAMPLE 3. *Consider the tree in Figure 2 and a generalization* $g = [Wine = All, Beer = All, Cookies = All, Chips = All, Milk = All, Cheese = All]$. *Furthermore, let Cookies be the symbol chosen to refine in the next iteration. Then the resulting generalization is* $g' = [Wine = All, Beer = All, Cookies = Snack, Chips = Snack, Milk = All, Cheese = All]$, *where both Cookies and Chips are refined to Snack since are leaves of the same subtree.*

As we progressively refine the symbol generalization to lower-level nodes in $\mathcal{T}$, the mutual information for the generalized sequence will never decreases. The following lemma states this important monotonicity property.

LEMMA 1 (MONOTONICITY). *Let g_i be the current generalization for the symbols in Σ. Consider g_{i+1} be the generalization obtained from g_i by further refining any symbols in Σ by using the taxonomy tree $\mathcal{T}$, then the following result holds* $\tilde{I}(\mathbb{S};\mathbb{G}_{i+1}) \geq \tilde{I}(\mathbb{S};\mathbb{G}_i)$.

PROOF. *Let a_j be the symbol in the current generalization $g_i = [\hat{a}^i_1, \ldots, \hat{a}^i_{|\Sigma|}]$ chosen to be refined from $\hat{a}^i_j$ to $\hat{a}^{i+1}_j$. Furthermore, let $L_\mathcal{T}(\hat{a}^{i+1}_j) = \{a_{i_1}, \ldots, a_{i_k}\}$ be the set of leaves refined to $\hat{a}^{i+1}_j$ according the taxonomy tree $\mathcal{T}$ and let $\hat{p} = h_i(p)$ be the generalized pattern obtained from any $p \in \mathcal{S}$ applying g_i. Then we observe that for each $p \in \mathcal{S}$, the following inequality holds: $P[h_i(p)] \geq P[h_{i+1}(p)]$. In fact, let assume that there exists a pattern $p \in \mathcal{S}$ such that $P[h_i(p)] < P[h_{i+1}(p)]$. Thus, there exists at least one occurrences of the symbols in $L_\mathcal{T}(\hat{a}^{i+1}_j)$ that is not generalized. However, this is not possible since $L_\mathcal{T}(\hat{a}^{i+1}_j)$ are mapped to $\hat{a}_j$ only with the generalization g_{i+1}, hence this proves that $P[h_i(p)] \geq P[h_{i+1}(p)]$. We use this fact to prove the monotonicity property as follows:*

$$\tilde{I}(\mathbb{S};\mathbb{G}_{i+1}) - \tilde{I}(\mathbb{S};\mathbb{G}_i) = \sum_{p \in \mathcal{S}} \tilde{P}[p] \log \frac{\tilde{P}[h_i(p)]}{\tilde{P}[h_{i+1}(p)]} \quad (4)$$

Since $P[h_i(p)] \geq P[h_{i+1}(p)]$, from the last equality we have that $\tilde{I}(\mathbb{S};\mathbb{G}_{i+1}) \geq \tilde{I}(\mathbb{S};\mathbb{G}_i)$. □

It is important to notice that such monotonicity property does not hold in general but it is a consequence of using a refinement procedure based on subtrees. Although in this way, we pay an additional cost in utility loss with respect to the optimal solution, the use of the monotonicity property allows us to greatly speed up our algorithm. In fact, if a generalization g violates the privacy level ϵ, then all the generalizations that can be obtained refining g will also violate the privacy. Hence, all these possible generalizations can be discarded in our process. This allows us to use the information in early steps of the algorithm to prune a large number of generalizations in the later steps. In particular, if a refinement operation on a symbol $a_i \in \Sigma$ fails at an early stage of the algorithm (i.e. violates the privacy) then such operation will also fail on any generalizations in later stages of the algorithm. This result is formalized below.

COROLLARY 1 (PRUNING). *Let g_i be the current generalization which satisfies privacy and g_{i+1} refine g_i by considering symbol a_j from $\hat{a}^i_j$ to $\hat{a}^{i+1}_j$. If g_{i+1} violates privacy, a_j as well as other symbols at leaf nodes in the subtree rooted by $\hat{a}^{i+1}_j$ can be pruned for further refinement.*

Algorithm 1 Top-Down Algorithm

1: **procedure** TOP-DOWN($\mathcal{S}, S, \epsilon, \mathcal{T}$)
  Input: sensitive patterns $\mathcal{S}$, user's input sequence S, privacy level ϵ, taxonomy tree $\mathcal{T}$;
  Output: sanitized sequence $\hat{S}$
2: $\Sigma' \leftarrow$ sort by freq. the symbols in Σ
3: $g_f = [\hat{a}_1, \ldots, \hat{a}_{|\Sigma'|}]$ with $\hat{a}_i \leftarrow \mathcal{T}.root$ for all i.
4: **while** (Σ' is not empty) **do**
5: $UL \leftarrow \infty$
6: **for** ($a_i \in \Sigma'$) **do**
7: $l_i \leftarrow$ current level of generalization for a_i in $\mathcal{T}$
8: $\hat{a}'_i \leftarrow$ refined symbol at level $l_i + 1$
9: $g \leftarrow g_f$
10: $L_\mathcal{T}(\hat{a}'_i) \leftarrow$ leaves of the subtree rooted by $\hat{a}'_i$
11: replace in g the generalization of $a_j \in L_\mathcal{T}(\hat{a}'_i)$ with $\hat{a}'_i$
12: **if** ($UL_S(g) > UL$) **then**
13: continue
14: **end if**
15: $\tilde{I}(\mathbb{S};\mathbb{G}) \leftarrow$ mutual information using g
16: **if** ($\tilde{I}(\mathbb{S};\mathbb{G}) \leq \epsilon$) **then**
17: $UL \leftarrow UL_S(g)$
18: $g' \leftarrow g$
19: **else**
20: remove $a_j \in L_\mathcal{T}(\hat{a}'_i)$ from Σ'
21: **end if**
22: **end for**
23: $g_f \leftarrow g'$
24: **end while**
25: $\hat{S} \leftarrow$ sanitize S using g_f
26: **return** $\hat{S}$
27: **end procedure**

PROOF. *It follows directly from the result in Lemma 1. In fact, since g_{i+1} fails to meet the privacy requirement, any refinement of g_{i+1} would also violate privacy. Furthermore, refinement of g_i at any leaf-node symbol in the subtree rooted by $\hat{a}^{i+1}_j$ will yield g_{i+1} or refinement of g_{i+1}, which would violate privacy and can be safely pruned.* □

These observations allows us to greatly reduce the number of generalizations considered. In fact, given h_{max} the maximum height of the taxonomy tree, we reduce the number of possible generalizations from $O(|\Sigma|^{h_{max}})$ to only a small polynomial function of $|\Sigma|$ and h_{max}.

Algorithm Description. Our procedure is reported in Algorithm 1. We start with a generalization g_f, where each symbol is generalized to the root node (i.e. maximum generalization level) and we sort all the symbols in Σ by decreasing order of frequency. In this way, we select first those symbols that potentially increase more the utility during our refinement process. Although the procedure in Algorithm 1 is defined on the entire alphabet Σ, we note that: 1) symbols that never occur in the input sequence can be discarded; 2) in some cases it is sufficient to generalize only the symbols in the sensitive patterns $\Sigma_\mathcal{S}$ to achieve the desired level of privacy. In fact, if the generalization g_f, where only the symbols in $\Sigma_\mathcal{S}$ are generalized to the root, achieves privacy, then we run our refinement process on $\Sigma_\mathcal{S}$ rather than consider the entire alphabet.

In the main loop (lines 4-24), we iteratively refine the current generalization. In particular, given the current generalized symbol $\hat{a}_i$ for a_i associated with a node ν at level l_i in the taxonomy tree, we select $\hat{a}'_i$ as the symbol represented by its corresponding child node at level $l_i + 1$ (lines 7-8). We then retrieve the leaves $L_\mathcal{T}(\hat{a}'_i)$ of the subtree rooted by ν and we refine the representation for the symbols in $L_\mathcal{T}(\hat{a}'_i)$ with $\hat{a}'_i$ (lines 9-10). At line 11, we compute the utility $UL_S(g)$ for the generalization g and at line 15 we test its privacy level. If the privacy is violated, the selected symbols in $L_{\mathcal{T}}(\hat{a}'_i)$ are discarded for further refinement according to our pruning criteria. After iterating among all the possible symbols, we pick the generalization option with minimum utility loss (line 23). The while loop terminates either when the possible refinement operations violate the privacy or the maximum level of refinement for each symbol is achieved. Finally, using the final generalization g_f we produce the sanitized sequence $\hat{S}$ which is returned as result.

Algorithm Analysis. In our implementation, we compute the frequency of all the symbols in the pre-processing step so that evaluating $UL_S(g)$ requires only $O(|\Sigma|)$. The privacy evaluation associated with $\tilde{I}(\mathbb{S};\mathbb{G})$ requires to compute the frequency information about the current set of generalized patterns. In principle, we can use any mining algorithm as a black box to compute such information. In our implementation, we use the mining algorithm in [11] which requires $O(|S| \times w \times m)$ time, where $|S|$ is the length of the sequence, w is the windows length, and m is the pattern length. Both the utility loss computation and privacy evaluation are performed in the most inner loop. Such loop is executed a number of time proportional to the number of internal nodes in the taxonomy tree. Given a taxonomy tree $\mathcal{T}$, where each internal node has at least two children, then we have that the number of internal nodes is $O(|\Sigma| - 1)$. Therefore, the worst case computational complexity for Algorithm 1 is $O(|\Sigma|^3 \times |S| \times w \times m)$. However, we note that individually generated sequences in practice contain a very small portion of the alphabet Σ and our solution is shown to be very efficient in the experiments.

5. BOTTOM-UP APPROACH

The previous solution greedily picks the symbol which yields minimum utility loss to refine and proceeds until privacy is breached. While designed to minimize the utility loss, the computational cost could be very high for large alphabets. Therefore, we propose an alternative algorithm that produces a generalization by directly exploiting the similarity between sensitive patterns. The key idea is to *cluster* sensitive patterns together and hide them with a generalization that inflicts minimum utility loss.

This algorithm takes a bottom-up approach and follows the idea of hierarchical clustering: starting from each sensitive pattern being in its own cluster, we iteratively merge the closest pair of clusters. In this way, we associate a group sensitive patterns to a common generalized pattern representing the centroid of the cluster. Intuitively, in each iteration we construct a generalization function $h(\cdot)$ that maps all the sensitive patterns within the same cluster to the same generalized pattern (i.e. centroid of the cluster). Initially, each pattern p is a cluster $\mathcal{C}(p)$ on its own and each symbol is represented with the finest granularity. Then, when pairs of clusters are merged a new generalization is produced. In our solution, we select the clusters to be merged in a way that minimizes the utility loss of the new generalization. This process ends when the specified privacy level is achieved. Before presenting our algorithm in details, we illustrate the key steps of our clustering process. We first show how to select a new representative when clusters are merged and define a distance metric that achieves minimum utility loss.

Cluster Representative. In principle, there are several ways to merge two clusters and define a common representative for their patterns. For example, one could define a generalization function that sets the non-matching symbols to the root. Although this map produces a new representative, it may not be optimal. Therefore, we are interested in finding a valid generalization function $h(\cdot)$ that leads to minimum utility loss in merging two clusters of patterns.

Algorithm 2 Least Common Generalized Pattern

procedure LCGP($p_1, p_2, \mathcal{T}$)
  Input: patterns $p_1 = \langle a_1, a_2, \dots, a_m \rangle$, $p_2 = \langle b_1, b_2, \dots, b_m \rangle$; taxonomy tree $\mathcal{T}$;
  Output: least common generalized pattern $LCGP(p_1, p_2)$

  For each unique symbol a in p_1, p_2 set $h_0(a) \leftarrow a$
  $j \leftarrow 1$
  for $j \leq m$ **do**
    $i \leftarrow 1$
    for $i \leq m$ **do**
      (a_i, b_i) symbols appearing at same position i
      $h_j(a_i) = h_j(b_i) \leftarrow lca(h_j(a_i), h_j(b_i))$
      $i \leftarrow i + 1$
    end for
    $j \leftarrow j + 1$
    $h_j(a) \leftarrow h_{j-1}(a)$ for every unique symbol a in p_1 and p_2
  end for
  $LCGP(p_1, p_2) \leftarrow \langle h_m(a_1), h_m(a_2), \dots, h_m(a_m) \rangle$
  return $LCGP(p_1, p_2)$
end procedure

PROBLEM 2 (MINIMUM GENERALIZATION). *Given two generalized patterns p_1 and p_2 representing the centroids for the clusters $\mathcal{C}(p_1)$ and $\mathcal{C}(p_2)$ respectively. Let $\Sigma(p_1, p_2)$ be the set of unique symbols for the sensitive patterns in the clusters and $f_S(a)$ denote the frequency of $a \in \Sigma$ in S, then the new representative for the patterns in the union of these clusters is $p = h^*(p_1) = h^*(p_2)$, where $h^*(\cdot)$ is computed as follows.*

$$h^*(\cdot) := \arg\min_{h(\cdot)} \sum_{a \in \Sigma(p_1,p_2)} c(a, h(a)) f_S(a)$$

such that $h(\cdot)$ is a valid generalization

To solve this problem, we introduce the notion of *least common generalized pattern* which defines $h^*(\cdot)$ exploiting the taxonomy tree structure.

DEFINITION 5 (LEAST COMMON GENERALIZED PATTERN). *Given two patterns $p_1 = \langle a_1, a_2, \dots, a_m \rangle$ and $p_2 = \langle b_1, b_2, \dots, b_m \rangle$ defined over Σ_e. Their least common generalized pattern $LCGP(p_1, p_2) = \langle c_1, c_2, \dots, c_m \rangle$ is determined by generalizing each unique symbol a both in p_1 and p_2 to $c = LCA_{p_1,p_2}(a)$. Where $LCA_{p_1,p_2}(a)$ represents the highest generalization of a among the least common ancestor of a and the symbols related to it, both in p_1 and p_2.*

The *LCGP* aims to find a generalization hierarchy between symbols. Since we are looking for a valid generalization $h(\cdot)$, we need to take into consideration the symbol-to-symbol dependency. In principle, a generalization of a symbol may have implications on others. For example, consider $p_1 = \langle Beer, Chips \rangle$ and $p_2 = \langle Wine, Beer \rangle$. Even though $p_1[1]$ ="*Beer*" and $p_2[1]$ ="*Wine*" have least common ancestor "*Alcohol*", due to the generalization of $p_1[2]$ ="*Chips*" and $p_2[2]$ ="*Beer*" to "*All*", also the symbol "*Wine*" is generalized to "*All*".

Algorithm 2 illustrates the computation of the Least Common Generalized Pattern for two patterns. We compute $LCGP(p_1, p_2)$ by iteratively generalizing each symbol in both p_1 and p_2. We observe that such computation can be performed efficiently by only processing each symbol $O(m)$ times, where m is the length of the patterns. At each iteration j, for each unique symbol a we construct a map $h_j(a)$. We start by setting $h_0(a) = a$ and at the end of the algorithm $h_m(a)$ will represent the value $LCA_{p_1,p_2}(a)$. In the inner loop at lines 7-10, we update the map iteratively as follows. For each position i, we select the pair of symbols (a_i, b_i) appearing in both p_1 and p_2 (i.e. $a_i = p_1[i]$ and $b_i = p_2[i]$) and we update their current map as $h_j(a_i) = h_j(b_i) = lca(h_j(a_i), h_j(b_i))$, where lca is the *least common ancestor* between the two symbols in the taxonomy tree $\mathcal{T}$. Since the computation of lca requires $O(h_{max})$ time, the overall complexity for Algorithm 2 is $O(h_{max} \times m^2)$. Below, we illustrate a running example for our algorithm.

EXAMPLE 4. *Consider the taxonomy tree in Figure 2, where each leaf represents a product, and let* $p_1 = \langle Beer, Chips\rangle$ *and* $p_2 = \langle Milk, Cookies\rangle$ *be two patterns. Then their least common generalized pattern is* $LCGP(p_1,p_2) = \langle All, Snack\rangle$. *Since* $lca(Beer, Milk) = All$ *and* $lca(Chips, Cookies) = Snack$, *at the end of the first iteration we have:* $h_1(Beer) = h_1(Milk) = All$ *and* $h_1(Chips) = h_1(Cereal) = Snack$, *where "All" is the highest among all the least common ancestors. In the successive iteration there are no updates, and therefore* $LCGP(p_1,p_2) = \langle All, Snack\rangle$. *Consider now the pattern* $p_3 = \langle Wine, Beer\rangle$. *In this case the least common generalized pattern for* p_1 *and* p_3 *is* $LCGP(p_1,p_3) = \langle All, All\rangle$. *At the end of the first iteration, we have that* $h_1(Wine) = Alcohol$ *and* $h_1(Beer) = h_1(Chips) = All$, *where "All" is the highest among all the least common ancestors. In the next iteration, the procedure updates the map for "Wine" leading to* $h_2(Wine) = lca(Alcohol, All) = All$, *while there is no updates for the other symbols.*

In our complete solution, given two clusters $\mathcal{C}(p_1)$ and $\mathcal{C}(p_2)$, we define the new representative pattern for their union as $p = LCGP(p_1, p_2)$. As we showed above, the selection of such a new representative for the clusters induces a new generalization map on each individual symbol a, where $\hat{a} = h_m(a) = LCA_{p_1,p_2}(a)$. Due to the nature of the least common ancestor we can show that such generalization is optimal according to Problem 2.

THEOREM 2. *Given two patterns* p_1 *and* p_2 *associated with the clusters* $\mathcal{C}(p_1)$ *and* $\mathcal{C}(p_2)$ *respectively. Then the* $LCGP(p_1,p_2)$ *minimizes the utility loss for representing the patterns both in* $\mathcal{C}(p_1)$ *and* $\mathcal{C}(p_2)$.

PROOF. *The proof proceeds by induction on the number of different symbols* k *in* $p_1 = \langle a_1, a_2 \ldots, a_m\rangle$ *and* $p_2 = \langle b_1, b_2 \ldots, b_m\rangle$.

Base Case. *Consider* $k = 1$, *then there exists* i *such that* $a_i \neq b_i$. *Therefore, the minimum utility loss is achieved by generalizing both* a_i *and* b_i *to their least common ancestor.*

Inductive Step. *We assume that the statement holds for* $k-1$ *and we prove it for* k. *Let* (a_i, b_i) *be the pair of symbols in* p_1 *and* p_2 *with the highest least common ancestor. Then any generalization function* $h(\cdot)$ *that generalizes both* p_1 *and* p_2 *has* $h(a_i) = h(b_i) = lca(a_i, b_i)$. *Therefore the utility loss is at least* $c(a_i, lca(a_i,b_i))f_S(a_i) + c(b_i, lca(a_i,b_i))f_S(b_i)$ *plus the generalization cost for the remaining* $k-1$ *different symbols. Among them, some may be replaced with* $lca(a_i,b_i)$ *if they are equal either to* a_i *or* b_i. *Then, let* $\{(a_{i_j}, b_{i_j})\}_{j=1}^{k-1}$ *be the set of these different symbols left to be generalized. By the induction hypothesis on these* $k-1$ *symbols, we have that the*

Algorithm 3 Bottom-Up Algorithm

1: **procedure** CLUSTERING($\mathcal{S}, S, \epsilon, \mathcal{T}$)
Input: sensitive patterns $\mathcal{S}$, user's input sequence S, privacy level ϵ, taxonomy tree $\mathcal{T}$;
Output: sanitized sequence $\hat{S}$
2: $\mathcal{C} \leftarrow$ set of centroids (one for each sensitive pattern)
3: $g_f = [\hat{a}_1, \ldots, \hat{a}_{|\Sigma|}]$ with $\hat{a}_i = a_i$ for all i.
4: **repeat**
5: **if** ($|\mathcal{C}| == 1$) **then**
6: Greedily generalize the symbols in g_f
7: **end if**
8: Compute distance between pair of centroids
9: $(p_1, p_2) \leftarrow$ the closest pair of centroids
10: $\mathcal{C} \leftarrow \mathcal{C} - \{p_1, p_2\}$
11: $p_3 \leftarrow$ LCGP($p_1, p_2, \mathcal{T}$)
12: $\mathcal{C}(p_3) \leftarrow \mathcal{C}(p_1) \bigcup \mathcal{C}(p_2)$
13: Add p_3 to the set $\mathcal{C}$
14: Update g_f according to $LCGP(p_1,p_2)$ ▷ Updates the centroids accordingly
15: **until** ($\tilde{I}(\mathbb{S} : \mathbb{G}_f) \leq \epsilon$)
16: $\hat{S} \leftarrow$ sanitized S using g_f
17: **return** $\hat{S}$
18: **end procedure**

map induced by the least common generalized patterns provides minimum utility loss. Then the final map produced by this procedure is the same as $LCGP(p_1,p_2)$ *and it achieves minimum utility loss for all the k different symbols.* ☐

Cluster Distance. Given two clusters, the least common generalized pattern defines a new representative which incurs minimum utility loss. To minimize the utility loss at each iteration, we select the pair of clusters that are closest to their least common generalized pattern. Formally, the distance between a pair of clusters $d_g(\cdot,\cdot)$ is defined below.

DEFINITION 6 (GENERALIZATION DISTANCE). *Given two centroids* p_1 *and* p_2 *associated with the clusters* $\mathcal{C}(p_1)$ *and* $\mathcal{C}(p_2)$ *respectively. The generalization distance between* p_1 *and* p_2 *is defined as:*

$$d_g(p_1,p_2) := \sum_{a \in \Sigma(p_1,p_2)} c(a, LCA_{p_1,p_2}(a)) f_S(a) \qquad (5)$$

Due to the taxonomy tree structure, we can show that the proposed generalization distance function is also metric.

Algorithm Description. Algorithm 3 iteratively constructs a generalization by merging clusters of patterns. The procedure starts with singleton clusters, one for each sensitive pattern. In the main loop (lines 4-15), at each iteration the closest pair of centroids (p_1, p_2) is merged. The new centroid is defined using the procedure in Algorithm 2, by computing $LCGP(p_1,p_2)$ (lines 11-12). Then, the current generalization for the symbols is updated according to the map induced by $LCGP(p_1,p_2)$. Since our generalization is a global generalization, this step requires also to update the other centroids to guarantee consistency. Finally, if the current generalization achieves the desired level of privacy we terminate the loop and return the corresponding sanitized sequence. Since the entire algorithm merges clusters of patterns, it may terminate with a single cluster which may not satisfy the privacy constraint. In such situation, we greedily further generalize the current symbols using the taxonomy tree till the privacy is achieved (lines 5-7).

Algorithm Analysis. Since we start with singleton clusters containing a sensitive pattern each, the total number of merging operations is $O(|\mathcal{S}|)$. In the merging step, we have to compute the new representative for the selected clusters.

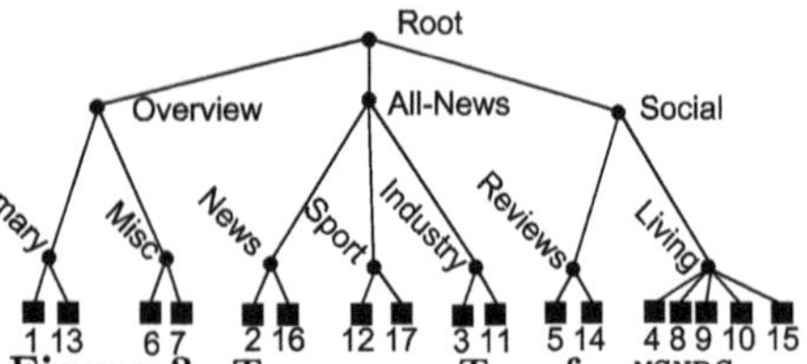

Figure 3: Taxonomy Tree for MSNBC

Table 1: Default Parameter Setting

Parameter	Description	Value
m	Pattern Length	2
w	Pattern Window	10
f_{min}	Patterns Minimum Frequency	10
$\|\mathcal{S}\|$	Number of Sensitive Patterns	4
ϵ	(Relative) Privacy Level	0.5

Such operation requires $O(h_{max} \times m^2)$ using Algorithm 2. The distance computation for the pairs of clusters requires the evaluation of the utility loss for the merged clusters, which can be performed in $O(|\Sigma_{\mathcal{S}}|)$. The privacy evaluation for the current generalization g_f is computed as in Algorithm 1. Since these operations are performed at each iteration of our solution, the total running time of our algorithm is $O(|\mathcal{S}|^3 \times h_{max} \times |S| \times w \times m^3 \times |\Sigma_{\mathcal{S}}|)$.

6. EXPERIMENTS

Here, we present a set of empirical evaluations for our solutions. Due to limited space and exponential run time, we omit the results obtained by the brute-force approach for finding the optimal solution.

6.1 Settings

Datasets. We consider two real-world sequence datasets: MSNBC[1] and RM[2] . MSNBC contains nearly 1 million sequences with maximum sequence length of almost 15,000 symbols, each of which corresponds to web pages visited by a user within 24-hour period. The alphabet size is 17, where each symbol represents a page category, such as "frontpage". An example taxonomy tree constructed for this dataset in Figure 3 is used in the evaluation. We discard those user sequences that contain less than 500 symbols and 36 users are preserved. RM dataset contains daily activities of 100 individuals and each user has a sequence of locations recorded by a smartphone over a year [9]. For evaluation, we keep the locations at area-id level and the alphabet size is 69. Since the spatial information about each area-id is absent, we construct a taxonomy tree by Equi Width Binning where each bin contains 10 consecutive area-id's. We preserve 32 users in this data set where the maximum sequence length is 20,000 symbols. Note that since the computation complexity of both our solutions is linear with the sequence length and the patterns are defined within a time window, increasing the length of input sequence does not necessarily make the problem more difficult.

Algorithm Setup. The default parameter values are presented in Table 1 unless specified otherwise. Since users behave differently and their sequences exhibit high variance, we specify a relative privacy level, ϵ as a percentage of the entropy of input sequence, instead of an absolute value. For instance, when $\epsilon = 0.5$, we bound the final mutual information for the released sequence to be at most 50% of the entropy the input sequence. Assuming the maximum generalization cost, i.e., leaf-to-root, is 1, we consider two customized cost functions based on the taxonomy tree: *linear* and *exponential*. In the former, the cost for generalizing a leaf node is uniformly divided among all levels of the tree, while in the latter the cost decay is exponential. In addition, a standard cost function based on the *information loss*, as defined in [19], is also evaluated. In this case, we measure the cost of generalizing a leaf node to an internal node ν as the ratio between the number of leaves in the subtree rooted by ν and the total number of leaves in $\mathcal{T}$. We observe that all three cost functions satisfy Definition 3.

[1]https://archive.ics.uci.edu/ml/machine-learning-databases/msnbc-mld/msnbc.data.html

[2]http://realitycommons.media.mit.edu/realitymining.html

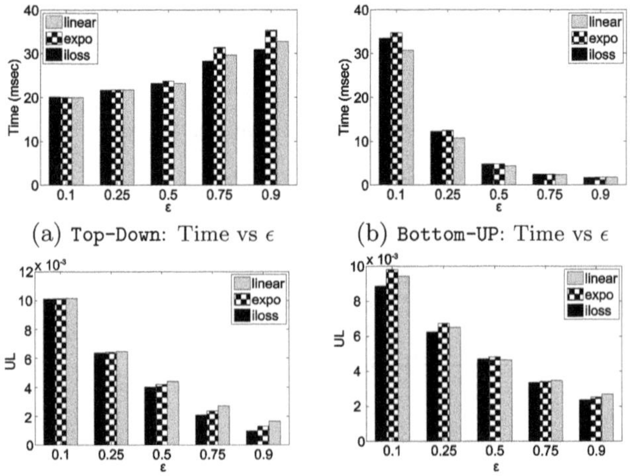

(a) Top-Down: Time vs ϵ (b) Bottom-UP: Time vs ϵ

(c) Top-Down: UL vs ϵ (d) Bottom-Up: UL vs ϵ

Figure 4: Privacy and Cost evaluation on MSNBC

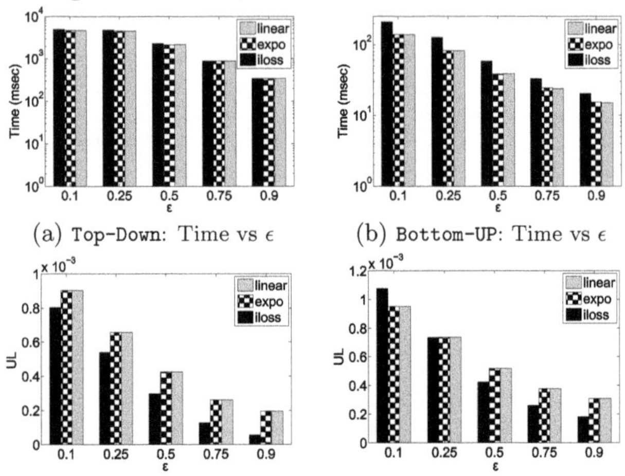

(a) Top-Down: Time vs ϵ (b) Bottom-UP: Time vs ϵ

(c) Top-Down: UL vs ϵ (d) Bottom-Up: UL vs ϵ

Figure 5: Privacy and Cost evaluation on RM

Evaluation Metrics. We evaluate the utility loss and the run time of our proposed solutions. In particular, for each user in the datasets, we randomly sample a pool of sensitive patterns of frequency at least f_{min} which are used as a input for our algorithms. For consistency, 25 runs are performed for each user and the average result is used. Since each user's sequence has different length, we normalize the utility loss with respect to the sequence length. Finally, we report the average among all the users in each dataset.

6.2 Results

Impact of Privacy Level ϵ and Cost Functions. Figure 4 and 5 present the run time and utility results for the MSNBC and RM dataset respectively. Small ϵ value in-

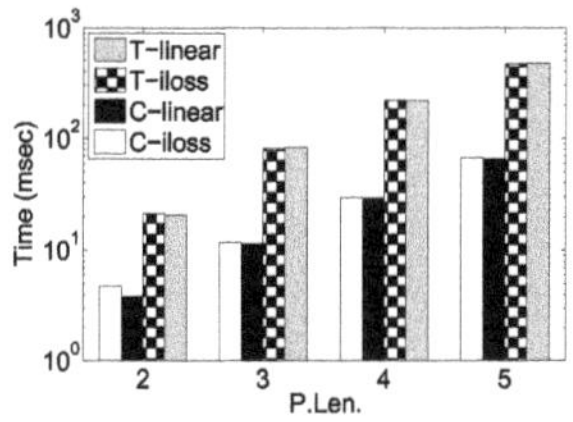

(a) MSNBC: Time vs P. Len.

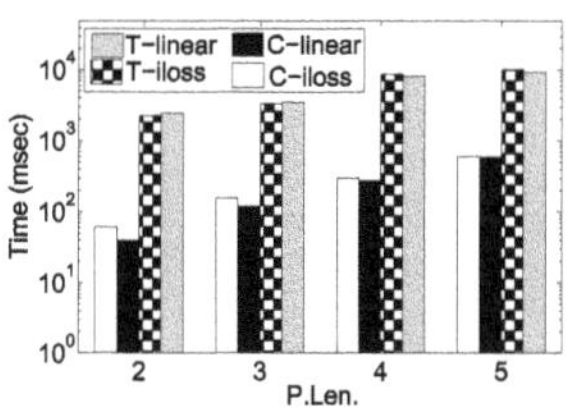

(b) RM: Time vs P. Len.

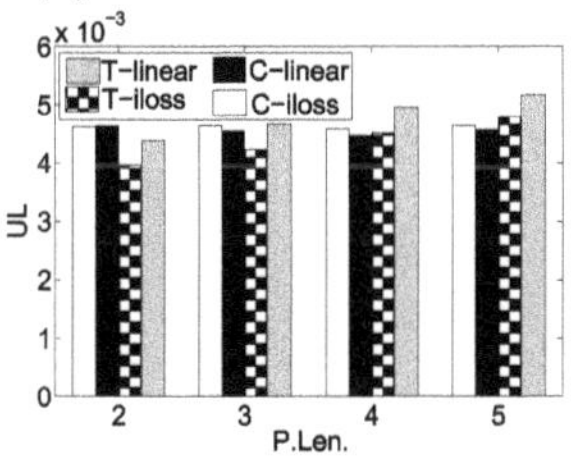

(c) MSNBC: UL vs P. Len.

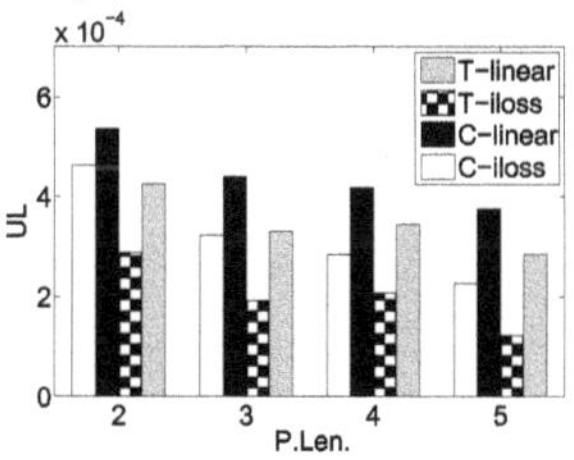

(d) RM: UL vs P. Len.

Figure 6: Impact of the Length of Sensitive Patterns

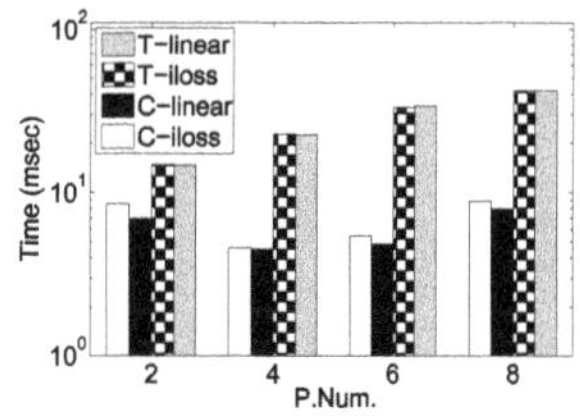

(a) MSNBC: Time vs P. Num.

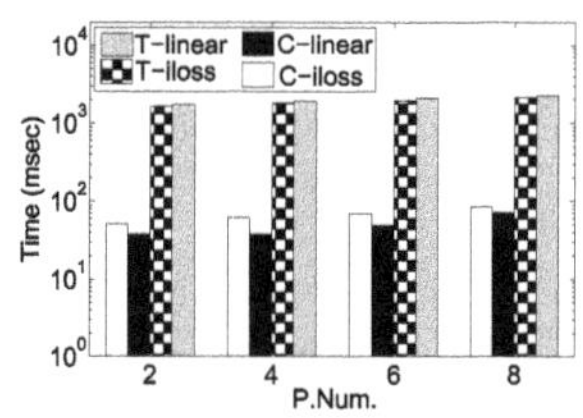

(b) RM: Time vs P. Num.

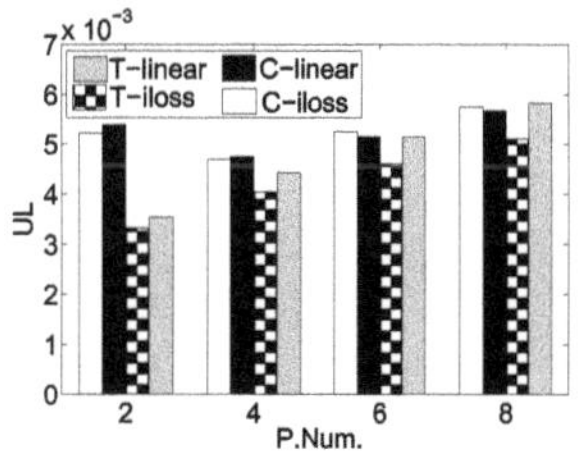

(c) MSNBC: UL vs P. Num.

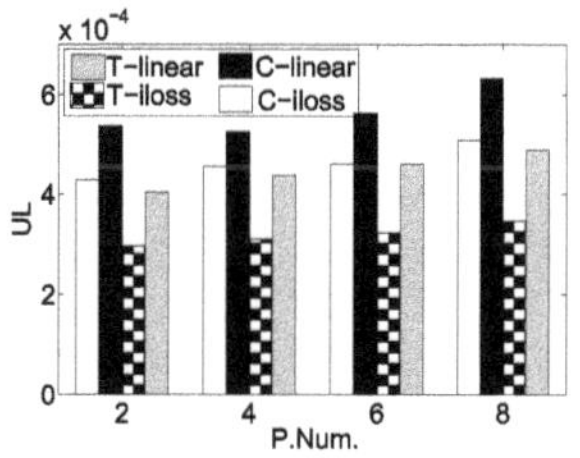

(d) RM: UL vs P. Num.

Figure 7: Impact of the Number of Sensitive Patterns

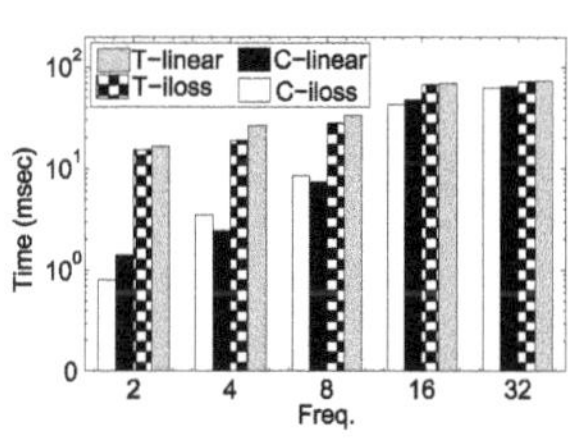

(a) Time vs Freq. (α)

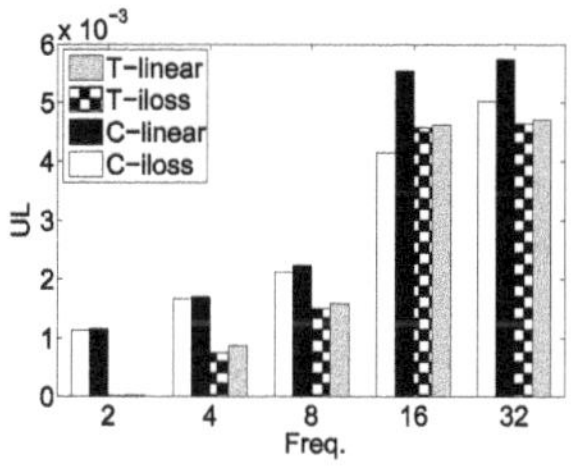

(b) UL vs Freq. (α)

Figure 8: Impact of the Frequency of Sensitive Patterns

dicates a high level of privacy and as ϵ increases, the privacy level becomes lower. When decreasing the privacy level, the `Bottom-Up` approach results in less run time in both datasets (Figure 4(b), 5(b)), as the algorithm may achieve the privacy level sooner by merging clusters. As the `Top-Down` approach starts with a feasible solution and performs refinement, its run time should increase as the privacy level decreases (Figure 4(a)). However, for `RM` dataset (Figure 5(a)), it shows a decreasing trend when $\epsilon \geq 0.5$. The reason is `RM` has a relatively large alphabet but a taxonomy tree with 3 levels only. When the privacy level is high, the entire alphabet are explored to satisfy the privacy constraint, although many symbols may be pruned at early stages. When decreasing the privacy level, only the symbols in sensitive patterns need to be generalized and the extra refinement allowed by the privacy relaxation is limited due to the height of the tree. As a result, we can only observe the dominant decrease caused by alphabet size in the overall run time. Comparing the two approaches, `Bottom-Up` is typically faster than `Top-Down`. Especially for the `RM` dataset we observe one order of magnitude speedup. From the utility perspective (Figure 4(c),4(d),5(c), 5(d)), as the privacy level decreases both solutions are able to reduce the utility loss for the released sequence. `Top-Down` preserves the utility better due to the independent generalization of symbols. Regarding the cost functions, we observe that the information loss, i.e. *iloss*, provides the least utility loss in both datasets and *linear* and *exponential* decay functions have similar performance. Therefore, for the rest of the experiments we only present results for *iloss* and *linear* as cost function.

Impact of the Length of Sensitive Patterns m. For simplicity, we denote the top-down approach and the bottom-up approach as `T` and `C` respectively. In Figure 6, we report the performance of our solutions when varying the length of sensitive patterns, i.e. the number of symbols in each pattern. As the pattern length increases, the run time for our solutions increases simultaneously because more symbols need to be considered and the matching of patterns for privacy evaluation becomes more expensive. We can observe that our approaches provide robust utility results with respect to m, since in both datasets (Figure 6(c), 6(d)) the utility loss for the released sequence does not present substantial changes.

Impact of the Number of Sensitive Patterns. Figure 7 reports the impact of the number of sensitive patterns. We observe that the run time for our top-down approaches in `MSNBC` increases with the number of sensitive patterns (Figure 7(a)), while in `RM` the run time tends to be stable (Figure 7(b)). We believe that this phenomenon is due to the nature of these datasets. In general, we could expect that an increment of the number of sensitive patterns increases the number sensitive symbols in Σ_S. For the `RM` dataset, our strategies may take advantage of the patterns distribution by limiting the generalization only on Σ_S rather than considering the entire Σ, leading to more stable performance on `RM`. The utility loss increases with the number of sensitive patterns since more symbols need to be generalized. The utility results for the two datasets are reported in Figure 7(c),7(d).

Impact of the Frequency of Sensitive Patterns. Figure 8 illustrates the impact of the frequency of sensitive patterns on the proposed solutions. To illustrate this dependency, we consider an absolute value of mutual information privacy $\epsilon = 0.1$. We select a single user sequence in the `MSNBC` dataset and we sample two sensitive patterns p_1, p_2 such that $f(p_1)/f(p_2) \geq \alpha$ where $\alpha \in \{2, 4, 8, 16, 32\}$. Intuitively, for small values of α the sensitive patterns have similar frequency and therefore are easy to protect. On the other hand, when α increases the patterns' frequency largely differs and the sanitization becomes hard. As expected, the run time for our solutions increases with α (Figure 8(a)), as well as the utility loss (Figure 8(b)), since more symbols are generalized in order to guarantee privacy.

Side Effects of Hiding Patterns. Figure 9 illustrates the side effects on the frequent patterns for a randomly selected user's sequence in the `MSNBC` dataset when the sensitive patterns are generalized. Comparing the original top-10 frequent patterns against those mined from the sanitized

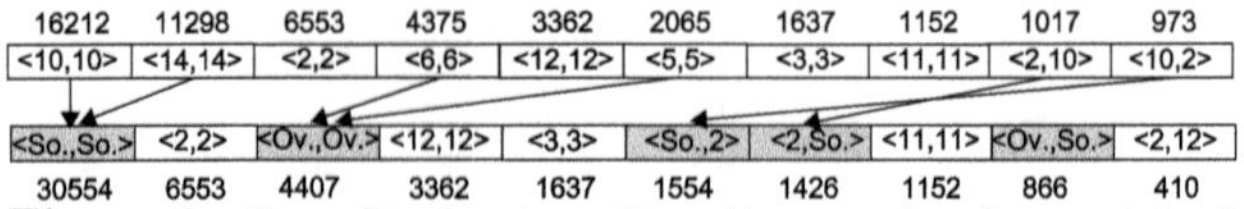

Figure 9: Case Study: top-10 patterns mined on original sequence (Top) and sanitized sequence (Bottom).

sequence, we observe that a large number of patterns are preserved and the two frequency distributions are very similar. The sanitization produced by the top-down approach generalizes the web-pages in subtrees associated with the categories *Social* (*So.*) and *Overview* (*Ov.*). This leads to an increment of the absolute frequency value for some patterns in the released sequence. For example, the patterns $\langle 10, 10\rangle$ and $\langle 14, 14\rangle$ are both generalized to $\langle So., So.\rangle$, which amplifies its occurrences. Furthermore, we notice that the semantic meaning of the frequent patterns is preserved at a coarser granularity enabling data mining applications to privately extract information about user's specific patterns. In this example, we can still infer that this user is interested in web-pages under the social and overview categories.

7. CONCLUSIONS

In this paper, we studied the problem of sanitizing individual data sequence to protect user-specified sensitive patterns. We introduced the notion of ϵ-mutual information privacy and proposed to generalize data symbols in the input sequence to satisfy the privacy definition. We showed that the problem of minimum utility loss sequence sanitization is hard and we designed two efficient solutions. The top-down approach constructs a generalization by refining each symbol according to the taxonomy tree. The bottom-up approach clusters sensitive patterns by exploiting pattern similarity. Our experiment results on real-world datasets showed that the bottom-up approach achieves similar utility results as the top-down approach while incurring considerably lower running time. Future research directions include the study of the utility guarantees of our solutions and the extension of the privacy model to provide worst-case guarantees.

8. REFERENCES

[1] O. Abul, F. Bonchi, and F. Giannotti. Hiding sequential and spatiotemporal patterns. *IEEE Trans. on Knowl. and Data Eng.*, 22(12):1709–1723, Dec. 2010.

[2] L. Bonomi and L. Xiong. A two-phase algorithm for mining sequential patterns with differential privacy. In *CIKM '13*, pages 269–278, New York, NY, USA, 2013. ACM.

[3] J. Cao, P. Karras, C. Raïssi, and K.-L. Tan. ρ-uncertaintyy: Inference-proof transaction anonymization. *Proc. VLDB Endow.*, 3(1-2):1033–1044, Sept. 2010.

[4] R. Chen, B. C. Fung, B. C. Desai, and N. M. Sossou. Differentially private transit data publication: A case study on the montreal transportation system. In *KDD '12*, pages 213–221, New York, NY, USA, 2012. ACM.

[5] F. du Pin Calmon and N. Fawaz. Privacy against statistical inference. In *Communication, Control, and Computing (Allerton), 2012 50th Annual Allerton Conference on*, pages 1401–1408, Oct 2012.

[6] J. Duchi, M. Jordan, and M. Wainwright. Local privacy and statistical minimax rates. In *Foundations of Computer Science (FOCS), 2013 IEEE 54th Annual Symposium on*, pages 429–438, Oct 2013.

[7] C. Duhigg. How companies learn your secrets. *The New York Times*, 2012.

[8] C. Dwork. Differential privacy. In M. Bugliesi, B. Preneel, V. Sassone, and I. Wegener, editors, *Automata, Languages and Programming*, volume 4052 of *Lecture Notes in Computer Science*, pages 1–12. Springer Berlin Heidelberg, 2006.

[9] N. Eagle and A. (Sandy) Pentland. Reality mining: Sensing complex social systems. *Personal Ubiquitous Comput.*, 10(4):255–268, Mar. 2006.

[10] L. Fan and H. Jin. A practical framework for privacy-preserving data analytics. In *WWW '15*, pages 311–321, Republic and Canton of Geneva, Switzerland, 2015. International World Wide Web Conferences Steering Committee.

[11] A. Gkoulalas-Divanis and G. Loukides. Revisiting sequential pattern hiding to enhance utility. In *KDD '11*, pages 1316–1324, New York, NY, USA, 2011. ACM.

[12] A. Gkoulalas-Divanis and V. S. Verykios. An integer programming approach for frequent itemset hiding. In *Proceedings of the 15th ACM International Conference on Information and Knowledge Management*, CIKM '06, pages 748–757, New York, NY, USA, 2006. ACM.

[13] M. Götz, S. Nath, and J. Gehrke. Maskit: Privately releasing user context streams for personalized mobile applications. In *SIGMOD '12*, pages 289–300, New York, NY, USA, 2012. ACM.

[14] R. Gwadera, A. Gkoulalas-Divanis, and G. Loukides. Permutation-based sequential pattern hiding. *2013 IEEE 13th International Conference on Data Mining*, 0:241–250, 2013.

[15] S. Hajian, J. Domingo-Ferrer, and O. FarrÃăs. Generalization-based privacy preservation and discrimination prevention in data publishing and mining. *Data Mining and Knowledge Discovery*, 28(5-6):1158–1188, 2014.

[16] X. He, Y. Xiao, Y. Li, Q. Wang, W. Wang, and B. Shi. Permutation anonymization: Improving anatomy for privacy preservation in data publication. In L. Cao, J. Huang, J. Bailey, Y. Koh, and J. Luo, editors, *New Frontiers in Applied Data Mining*, volume 7104 of *Lecture Notes in Computer Science*, pages 111–123. Springer Berlin Heidelberg, 2012.

[17] Y. He, S. Barman, D. Wang, and J. F. Naughton. On the complexity of privacy-preserving complex event processing. In *Proceedings of the 30th ACM SIGMOD-SIGACT-SIGART Symposium on Principles of Database Systems, PODS 2011, June 12-16, 2011, Athens, Greece*, pages 165–174, 2011.

[18] Y. He and J. F. Naughton. Anonymization of set-valued data via top-down, local generalization. *Proc. VLDB Endow.*, 2(1):934–945, Aug. 2009.

[19] V. S. Iyengar. Transforming data to satisfy privacy constraints. In *KDD '02*, pages 279–288, New York, NY, USA, 2002. ACM.

[20] O. Lara and M. Labrador. A survey on human activity recognition using wearable sensors. *Communications Surveys Tutorials, IEEE*, 15(3):1192–1209, Third 2013.

[21] B. Malin. *Protecting dna sequence anonymity with generalization lattices.* Carnegie Mellon University, School of Computer Science, 2004.

[22] A. McGregor, I. Mironov, T. Pitassi, O. Reingold, K. Talwar, and S. Vadhan. The limits of two-party differential privacy. In *Foundations of Computer Science (FOCS), 2010 51st Annual IEEE Symposium on*, pages 81–90, Oct 2010.

[23] L. Sankar, S. Rajagopalan, and H. Poor. Utility-privacy tradeoffs in databases: An information-theoretic approach. *Information Forensics and Security, IEEE Transactions on*, 8(6):838–852, June 2013.

[24] R. Sherkat, J. Li, and N. Mamoulis. Efficient time-stamped event sequence anonymization. *ACM Trans. Web*, 8(1):4:1–4:53, Dec. 2013.

[25] X. Sun and P. S. Yu. A border-based approach for hiding sensitive frequent itemsets. In *Proceedings of the Fifth IEEE International Conference on Data Mining*, ICDM '05, pages 426–433, Washington, DC, USA, 2005. IEEE Computer Society.

[26] Y. Tao, H. Chen, X. Xiao, S. Zhou, and D. Zhang. Angel: Enhancing the utility of generalization for privacy preserving publication. *Knowledge and Data Engineering, IEEE Transactions on*, 21(7):1073–1087, July 2009.

[27] M. Terrovitis, N. Mamoulis, and P. Kalnis. Local and global recoding methods for anonymizing set-valued data. *The VLDB Journal*, 20(1):83–106, Feb. 2011.

[28] V. Verykios, A. Elmagarmid, E. Bertino, Y. Saygin, and E. Dasseni. Association rule hiding. *Knowledge and Data Engineering, IEEE Transactions on*, 16(4):434–447, April 2004.

[29] D. Wang, Y. He, E. Rundensteiner, and J. F. Naughton. Utility-maximizing event stream suppression. In *SIGMOD '13*, pages 589–600, New York, NY, USA, 2013. ACM.

[30] R. C.-W. Wong, A. W.-C. Fu, K. Wang, and J. Pei. Minimality attack in privacy preserving data publishing. In *Proceedings of the 33rd International Conference on Very Large Data Bases*, VLDB '07, pages 543–554. VLDB Endowment, 2007.

Improving IP Geolocation using Query Logs

Ovidiu Dan[1,2], Vaibhav Parikh[2] and Brian D. Davison[1]

[1]Lehigh University, Bethlehem, PA, USA, {ovd209,davison}@cse.lehigh.edu
[2]Microsoft Bing, Redmond, WA, USA, vparikh@microsoft.com

ABSTRACT

IP geolocation databases map IP addresses to their geographical locations. These databases are important for several applications such as local search engine relevance, credit card fraud protection, geotargetted advertising, and online content delivery. While they are the most popular method of geolocation, they can have low accuracy at the city level. In this paper we evaluate and improve IP geolocation databases using data collected from search engine logs. We generate a large ground-truth dataset using real time global positioning data extracted from search engine logs. We show that incorrect geolocation information can have a negative impact on implicit user metrics. Using the dataset we measure the accuracy of three state-of-the-art commercial IP geolocation databases. We then introduce a technique to improve existing geolocation databases by mining explicit locations from query logs. We show significant accuracy gains in 44 to 49 out of the top 50 countries, depending on the IP geolocation database. Finally, we validate the approach with a large scale A/B experiment that shows improvements in several user metrics.

Categories and Subject Descriptors

H.3.m [**Information Search and Retrieval**]: Miscellaneous

General Terms

Measurement, Experimentation, Algorithms

Keywords

IP geolocation; geographic targeting; geotargeting; local search; contextual relevance; geographic personalization

1. INTRODUCTION

IP geolocation databases are widely used in online services to determine the location of users when real time location information is not available. Web search engines are an example of services which rely on this type of information. Search engines use the geographical location of users to personalize the results shown on the page. For instance, for the query "weather" search engines may display a page block with the local weather forecast based on the location of the user. Outside of the realm of search engines, IP geolocation databases are used for applications such as:

- **Content Delivery Networks** [21]: IP geolocation databases help direct users to the closest server, improving latency, throughput, and bandwidth costs.
- **Credit card fraud protection** [9]: Financial institutions use the location of online users in their fraud detection algorithms.
- **Advertising networks** [24]: IP geolocation of users can lead to better ad targeting and higher revenue.
- **Law enforcement** [27]: Locating IP addresses can help law enforcement in cybercrime investigations.
- **Location based content licensing** [25]: Streaming services such as Spotify and Netflix make use of IP geolocation to enforce geographic content restrictions.
- **E-commerce** [28]: Shopping Websites can use geolocation to apply correct taxes and shipping charges.
- **Organizations with regional offices** can use IP geolocation to direct users to their closest facility.

Although IP geolocation databases have much higher real-life coverage than methods such as Wi-Fi localization [11], they can still suffer from inaccurate information and low coverage in certain parts of the world. Accurate IP geolocation can make the difference between satisfied and dissatisfied customers. In the case of search engines, incorrect location data can lead to abandoned searches and engine switches. In other cases, such as credit card fraud protection, imprecise location information can lead to loss of revenue. In this paper, we present methods for measuring IP geolocation databases and improving their accuracy **at the city level** using query logs. More specifically, our contributions are:

1. **We describe a technique to generate IP geolocation ground truth data using real time location information.** We construct a dataset of 8.4 million IP addresses with known geographical location. The dataset is derived from a subset of search engine logs that contain real time global positioning information obtained from mobile devices. To the best of our knowledge this dataset is the largest ever reported in literature. *(Section 4)*
2. **We determine the impact of incorrect IP geolocation information on implicit user behavior.** We show that inaccurate geolocation information has a negative effect on users of search engines. Metrics such as click through rate, click success, and ad revenue are impacted. *(Section 5)*
3. **We evaluate the accuracy of three IP geolocation databases.** We measure the accuracy and the distance error of three major commercial IP geolocation databases. There are considerable differences between databases, with the best database having an

WSDM'16, February 22–25, 2016, San Francisco, CA, USA.

ACM 978-1-4503-3716-8/16/02 ...$15.00.
DOI: http://dx.doi.org/10.1145/2835776.2835820.

accuracy of 55% at the city level in the U.S., and the worst having an accuracy of 32.9%. *(Section 6)*

4. **We propose a preliminary method to improve IP geolocation databases using information extracted from user queries.** We show that user queries are a good source of location information. We use this information to improve an IP geolocation database by modifying the locations of certain IP ranges. The improved database can be used in a variety of other applications outside of search engines. We discuss privacy implications and steps we take to remove personally identifiable information. *(Section 7)*
5. **Finally, we run a large scale online experiment to validate our improvements to an IP geolocation database.** We conduct an A/B experiment on 1.7 million distinct search engine users and 3.2 million queries over the course of seven days, in the Mexico market. We observe improvements in several user metrics. *(Section 8)*

2. IP GEOLOCATION DATABASES

The most precise way to determine the location of an online service user is to use positioning systems such as GPS, Galileo, GLONASS and BeiDou [19, 13, 20]. Unfortunately, this information is only available on devices that have location capabilities. Other location detection methods include Wi-Fi positioning systems, as well as requesting users to self-report their location. In the former case, the location of the user is determined by comparing the list of wireless access points visible from the device to a list of access points with known locations. These databases suffer from lack of coverage, especially in rural areas [11]. In the latter case, having users self-report their location might be accurate in the short term, but such information can become stale in the long run if users move without updating their location.

IP geolocation databases are an alternative with higher coverage. They are typically provided by commercial vendors such as MaxMind, IP2Location, Neustar, IPligence, and Digital Element. These databases are compiled by combining data from different sources. The primary data sources are the five regional Internet registries, which manage how IP ranges and network autonomous system numbers are assigned to organizations around the world [22]. These registries maintain databases with mappings of IP ranges to the geographical location of the organizations that use these IPs. However, there are cases where large ISPs or multinational companies are assigned large IP ranges. Since these organizations deploy infrastructure over large areas, the geographic information contained in the registry databases is insufficient to obtain accurate locations from any IP address in the range. Secondary data sources can include more granular data collected from ISPs or from websites which collect user location data. In the former case, large ISPs maintain internal records of how they geographically subdivide large IP ranges provided by the Internet registries. In the latter case, the information is obtained from the logs of websites, such as weather websites, which ask the user to self-report their location.

Commercial IP geolocation providers offer their databases in a format similar to the example in Table 1. The IP ranges are specified as integers instead of the typical dotted-quad notation to make lookups faster. While most ranges cover IPv4 addresses, providers have more recently started to provide information on the IPv6 address space. However, since IPv6 adoption is currently low, we restrict our discussion to IPv4 ranges.

3. RELATED WORK

We divide previous research into two categories, based on the methods employed to generate IP geolocation: network delay and topology, and web mining.

Table 1: Rows from an IP geolocation database.

StartIP	EndIP	Country	State	City
16781312	16781567	JP	tokyo	tokyo
16789504	16789759	CN	guangdong	guangzhou
3147413504	3147413759	MX	quintana roo	cancun

3.1 Network Delay and Topology

The line of research on Network Delay relies on the observation that the delay experienced by network packets as they travel between two Internet hosts is proportional to the geographical distance between the hosts. Early work on IP geolocation by Padmanabhan and Subramanian discusses *GeoPing* [26], which uses delay measurements made from geographically distributed locations using ICMP packets to infer the coordinates of the target IP. The method has an error distance of 150 kilometers at the 25th percentile when locating 256 servers hosted in universities across the United States. *CBG* [17] is a method that uses a geometric approach using multilateration to estimate the location of a given target IP. Experimental results on 95 IP addresses in the U.S. and 42 addresses in Western Europe produce a median error distance of below 100 kilometers for the first dataset and below 25 kilometers for the second dataset, respectively. Youn et al. [33] develop a statistical method for IP geolocation based on applying kernel density estimation to delay measurements. On a dataset of 85 IP addresses, the method achieves a median error of 53 kilometers.

Network Topology Geolocation methods also use knowledge of the network structure to achieve increased accuracy. *GeoCluster*, also proposed by Padmanabhan and Subramanian [26], combines BGP routing information with sparse IPs of known locations to assign geographical locations to whole address prefixes. On a set of 256 target IPs located at universities in the United States, *GeoCluster* achieves a median error of 28 kilometers. This approach performs well with hosts located on university campuses, but it performs much worse on a larger and more realistic dataset, with errors of hundreds of kilometers. *TBG* [23], which stands for Topology-Based Geolocation, uses the *traceroute* tool to collect both the intermediate routers located between the fixed probes and target IP address, and the network round trip measurements along each intermediate link. *TBG* achieves higher accuracy than *CBG*, with a median error of 67 kilometers on a dataset consisting of hosts located at U.S. universities. *Octant* [32] is a framework where the location of the intermediate routers and target IP are constrained to specific regions based on their delays from landmarks and intermediate routers. It achieves a median accuracy of 22 miles on a set of 51 machines. *GeoTrack* [26] tries to infer the location of IP addresses from the DNS names of the routers along the *traceroute* path. It yields a median error distance of 590 km on a test dataset of 2,830 IPs.

Both Network Delay and Network Topology methods have significant limitations. First, all such methods require access to nodes spread throughout the globe to perform measurements. Second, geolocating a large number of IP addresses using network measurements can run into scalability issues, as each target IP address or range requires separate measurements. Third, not all networks allow ICMP pings or fully disclose their network topology. Fourth, routes on the Internet do not necessarily map to geographic distances. Fifth, previously reported mean and median errors of tens to hundreds of kilometers show that these methods cannot be used for practical applications at the city granularity. Sixth, the ground truth data for work in this area is usually limited to a few tens of IP addresses, typically located in the United States.

Our work addresses several of these limitations. We mine search engine logs by extracting explicit locations mentioned in user queries. This approach bypasses the limitations of delay measurements and network topology methods. We also use the logs to generate a ground truth dataset of 8.4 million IP addresses with known location, as determined by realtime GPS location. Our ground truth dataset is several orders of magnitude larger than the ones used in previous work. The three baselines we use generally outperform the median and mean distance error of approaches proposed in previous work. For instance, in the case of the United States, one of our baselines has a median error of only 6.9 kilometers. Finally, we show that our method improves accuracy across tens of countries, compared to prior work which usually evaluates locations in the United States, or a handful of large countries in Europe and Asia.

3.2 Web Mining

Web mining approaches use diverse information mined from the web. Guo et al. [18] extract locations mentioned in web pages and assign the locations to the IPs which host the content. Using an IP geolocation database as ground truth they report an agreement on the city level for 87% of the IPs. This work has two obvious problems: first, an IP geolocation database with unknown accuracy is used as ground truth; and second, the method focuses on geolocating IP addresses of servers, not of end users. Endo and Sadok [14] propose using *whois* information. Unfortunately, the evaluation section lacks a comparison against ground truth. Wang et al. [30] combine the *CBG* approach with extracting the location of web servers from the web pages that they host. Using the web servers as landmarks they are able to achieve good results, with a median error of 0.69 kilometers for the best data set, which contains 88 target IP addresses. The approach suffers from the same scalability limitations as network delay based methods. The results also depend on the density of servers in a geographical area.

Backstrom et al. [6] propose an interesting approach which relies on a user's social graph to determine their location. They derive the location of target users based on the locations of friends. Using self-reported location as ground truth they show an improvement over an unnamed IP geolocation database. For an error distance of less than 25 km, the amount of correctly classified IPs increases from 57.2% for the baseline to 67.5% for the proposed method. The authors state that this method works so long as an individual has a sufficient number of friends whose location is known, preferably more than 16.

4. GROUND TRUTH

Limited ground truth information has been a significant limitation in previous IP geolocation research, as discussed in Section 3. Previous work has typically used tens of IP addresses with known geographical location, mainly located in the U.S. We propose a method to generate a large scale evaluation set by aggregating real time location information from search engine logs. Using our method we have generated a ground truth set of more than 8.4 million IP addresses from across the world.

Mobile devices contain sensors for global positioning systems. Mobile applications can request access to real time location information in order to provide better results. While not all users are comfortable with sharing their location, a representative set of users agree to provide this information. We use this information from search engine logs to generate the ground truth set.

Although we collect most of the ground truth data from mobile devices, **we perform several filtering steps to ensure that most IP addresses in the ground truth set are from fixed broadband connections**. The main reason for retaining only fixed IP addresses is that here we aim to improve existing IP geolocation databases, which assume each IP address has a single location. Since here we are computing a ground truth set, it is reasonable to eliminate IP addresses which appear in multiple cities in the dataset. Second, obtaining the real location of fixed broadband connections is arguably more difficult than obtaining the location of mobile network connections, as most most wired devices such as desktop PCs do not contain sensors capable of determining real time location, while mobile devices do.

First, after aggregating all reported locations per IP address, we restrict the IP addresses to the ones where the location readings stay within a 1.6 kilometer (1 mile) radius. We then assign each IP address a centroid computed by combining these location readings in time. While this constraint does filter out some valid IP addresses, it ensures that the remaining addresses are located in a relatively fixed position. Consider a user who commutes to work in a close-by city. Although the heuristic will likely filter out their mobile IP address as cell phone tower coverage spans large geographical regions, it will retain their fixed broadband IP address, if the user connects the device to both networks. When the user reaches their home and switches to a fixed Wi-Fi connection, their device will still broadcast the real time location to the search engine, thus linking the fixed broadband connection to a fixed location which stays within a small radius. Second, we retain only the IP addresses which appear in the logs on at least three different days, with at least three different location readings. This step ensures that we filter out the devices which are only turned on for a short period of time or that broadcast the same identical stale location.

We have obtained 8.4 million IP addresses and their corresponding location by mining logs from the Bing search engine for a period of 180 days ending on October 10th, 2014. To the best of our knowledge, this is the largest ground truth set ever used in IP geolocation research. The set spans 220 countries, with a maximum of 2 million IP addresses in the United States. The top 50 countries by IP density have a mean and median size of 163,000 and 45,000 IP addresses, respectively.

5. IMPACT OF INCORRECT IP GEOLOCATION

We now use the ground truth dataset to analyze the impact of impressions where the location information is incorrect. These cases are nuanced as we expect the effect of incorrect information to become more apparent as the error increases. For instance, for the query *"restaurants"* a user might still click the results even if the search returns businesses from a close-by city.

We extract the impressions issued on the Bing search engine in a seven day period, across all devices. We intersect this set with our ground truth set and then we compute the distance between the ground truth location and the location from the IP geolocation database used by Bing. We compare the set of impressions where the distance between the real location and the assumed location is more than 15 km, to the impressions where the error distance is less than 15 km. We further partition the data based on queries with local intent versus all queries. By a query with local intent we mean queries with local context, such as "plumbers".

Table 2 shows the change in metrics for the queries issued from the U.S. market. Both overall and ad click through rates decrease when the location is incorrect. Prior research has shown that this metric is positively correlated with user satisfaction [16]. However, we observe that Algorithmic CTR increases for the "All queries"

Table 2: Change in metrics between queries where distance error is more than 15 km, versus when the error is less than 15 km. **Note that both result columns show the impact of incorrect locations.** The difference between the columns is that they show two subsets of the data. See text for an explanation of the two positive metrics.

Metrics	Local Intent	All Queries
Overall CTR	-4.3%	-12.8%
Algorithmic CTR	-1.1%	+2.4%
Algorithmic Click Success	-6.1%	+0.2%
Ads CTR	-17.9%	-6.1%
Ads Click Success	-15.2%	-7.0%
Ad Revenue	-40.3%	-6.0%

Results statistically significant using a two-sample t-test at 1%.

set. This increase can be attributed to users who avoid clicking on the answers which contain incorrect local content, and instead choose to click on algorithmic search results, which might be more general.

The table also indicates that ads click success is negatively affected. Click success occurs when the click results in a dwell time greater than or equal to 30 seconds [16]. This metric has also been correlated with user satisfaction. Therefore, since in our case the metric goes down, user satisfaction might suffer. However, in the case of algorithmic clicks we observe that there is an increase in success when the location is incorrect. This change can be caused by users that click on general algorithmic results because the local answer shows incorrect results. Finally, we can observe ad revenue decreases dramatically in both cases. Therefore, improving IP geolocation accuracy could lead to higher revenue.

Other geographic markets yield similar results, but we do not show them here due to space constraints. We conclude that when the IP geolocation data is incorrect there is a significant drop in metrics. These results reinforce our hypothesis that incorrect IP geolocation information can lead to lower user satisfaction.

6. EVALUATING IP GEOLOCATION DATABASES

We use the ground truth dataset described in Section 4 to evaluate three commercial IP geolocation databases, chosen based on their high self-reported accuracy. These databases represent the state of the art in the industry and, as we will show here, have higher coverage and better accuracy than most previously published research. Due to legal reasons we will use the generic names Vendor *A*, Vendor *B*, and Vendor *C* to denote them. The providers were chosen from among the companies listed in Section 2. Nevertheless, the findings are still valuable.

Table 3 presents basic statistics about these databases, generated on data available on October 10th, 2014. The IPv4 address space is 4.29 billion IP addresses, which includes 592 million addresses yet to be distributed to organizations, or reserved for other uses. Vendor *C* has the highest IP coverage at 3.6 billion, followed by the other two vendors each at 3.48 billion. The databases report countries using the ISO 3166-1 standard, which yields a maximum of 249 possible countries. Vendors *A* and *B* cover all possible countries, while Vendor *C* covers 247 of them. The last column in the table shows city level coverage. The difference between the vendors with highest and lowest city coverage is 36,357 cities. The databases have very high coverage at the IP and country level, but varying degrees of coverage at the city level.

We now turn to the ground truth data to evaluate the accuracy and error distance of the databases. Since the data is provided

Table 3: Basic statistics on the the IP geolocation databases used in this work.

Provider	IP Coverage	Countries	Cities
Vendor **A**	3.48B (~94.1%)	249 (100%)	87,842
Vendor **B**	3.48B (~94.1%)	249 (100%)	66,480
Vendor **C**	3.6B (~97.3%)	247 (99.2%)	102,837

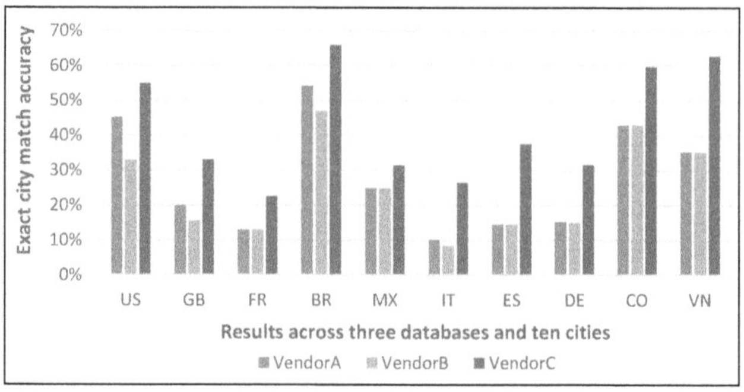

Figure 1: Accuracy at the city level for the three IP geolocation databases, across ten countries. Data points show exact city match accuracy.

by different companies, it is possible that the names of locations are not consistent. To solve this problem we have used the public Bing reverse geocoding API [2], which maps coordinates to street addresses. The reverse geocoder is aware of the boundaries of cities. This reverse geocoder is the same one that we have used while generating the ground truth dataset in Section 4. Since we are interested in geolocation at the city level, we discard the street addresses. We normalize the locations in each database by assigning a unique identifier to each distinct city. Using the same reverse geocoding method on the databases and on the ground truth data ensures a level playing field in terms of location names and identifiers. One important side effect to note is that all ground truth locations within the limits of a city are converted to the coordinates of the center of that city.

We compute the accuracy of exact city matches by counting how often the location of ground truth IPs matches the location given by the databases. In Figure 1 we show the accuracy for the three databases across the top ten countries by ground truth IP density. There are two interesting findings. First, none of the databases achieve an accuracy above 70% at the city level, and in some cases have an accuracy below 10%. Second, Vendor *C* outperforms the other two providers, often significantly, across all ten countries. The same findings hold for all countries. This finding is particularly interesting as in 37.4% of the database from Vendor *C* there is no city level information. This suggests that Vendor *C* has a high accuracy but low city-level IP coverage, while the converse is true for the other two vendors. We have also found that country-level accuracy is significantly better than city level accuracy, with a median of 95.3%, 96.7%, and 89.2% in the top 50 countries for the three vendors, respectively.

Exact city level matches might not present a complete picture of the performance of IP geolocation databases. Therefore, we also compute the error distance between the cities from the ground truth IPs, and the cities returned by the geolocation databases for these IPs. The error distance is given by the distance between the centers of the cities. For a given ground truth IP, if the ground truth and IP geolocation cities are the same, the distance is zero. Figure 2 shows the cumulative error distance for the three databases, in the United

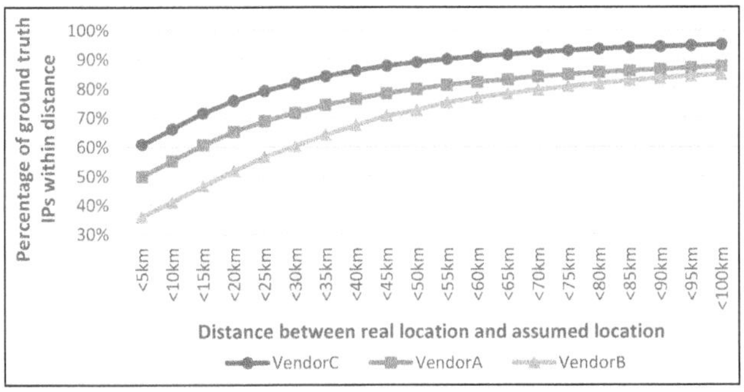

Figure 2: Cumulative error distance for the three IP geolocation databases in the United States. Data points show percentage of ground truth IPs where the real location and the IP geolocation assumed location fall within a certain distance. The distance interval on the X-axis is five kilometers.

States. The shape of the curves is similar in the other countries. The X axis shows the error distance at an interval of five kilometers and the Y axis shows the percentage of ground truth IPs with that error distance. For example, consider the three data points above the X-axis label titled *<10km*. The numbers show that the real location of 66.2%, 55.3%, and 41.1% of ground truth IPs is within 10 kilometers of the location provided by Vendors C, A, and B, respectively. The closer the curve is to the upper left corner, the smaller the error distance, and the better the results.

We have also performed a comparison of the accuracy and error distance results between our ground truth method, and the self-reported data provided by Vendor C for the United States. We have found that the exact city accuracy difference is within two percentage points, while the error distance at 10 kilometers is within seven percentage points. For the exact city match accuracy their results are within 10 percentage points of the results we have obtained in Figure 1.

7. IMPROVING IP GEOLOCATION

We investigate the feasibility of using location information extracted from search queries to improve IP geolocation databases **at the city level**. We define important terms used in the section, present the problem statement, go over challenges, discuss the approach we have taken, and evaluate it against the ground truth dataset.

The aim of the preliminary method presented here is not to optimize the model but rather to determine the predictive value of user queries in determining the location of IP addresses.

7.1 Definitions

We start by defining some terms used in this section.

- *Explicit location queries* are search engine user queries which contain locations. Examples include "weather in bellevue" and "movie showtimes in kirkland wa".
- A *target geolocation database* is a baseline IP geolocation database that we are starting from and which we are aiming to improve by combining it with locations extracted from user queries.
- *Reverse geocoding* is the process of converting a latitude and longitude pair to the corresponding readable address (continent, country, state, county, city, street, etc.). In this paper we reverse geocode locations down to the city level.
- *Primate cities* are cities which dominate the surrounding populated places economically and culturally due to their size [8].

7.2 Problem Statement

The examined commercial IP geolocation databases have higher accuracy, higher coverage, and lower error distance than previous research. For instance Vendor B, which had the worst results out of all commercial databases, has a median distance of 18 kilometers in the US, as measured by our ground truth set, while past research presented in Section 3 has a median error of 25 kilometers or more. So even the worst performing commercial database has a much better median distance than most published work. Furthermore, both total IP coverage and ground truth IP coverage are very low in previous research with only tens and up to thousands of IP addresses. Comparatively, Vendor B has a worldwide coverage of 3.48 billion IP addresses, and in this work we use a ground truth set of 8.4 million IP addresses.

Nevertheless, the accuracy of these commercial databases is still lacking for some practical applications and needs improvement. For example, Figure 2 shows that the database provided by Vendor A geolocates only 60% of the ground truth IPs within 15 kilometers of their actual location in the United States. If we were to use this database in a search engine setting, it might return incorrect location information for roughly 40% of real user IP addresses. In other countries the error distance can be even higher. If a search engine shows businesses, weather, or news for an incorrect location for 40% of the time, users might switch to a competitor.

To augment existing IP geolocation databases we must introduce new sources of information. One possible solution is to use real time location information, as we did for the ground truth data. While this approach has potential, in this work we focus instead on explicit location information extracted from user queries. **The reason why we use locations extracted from queries instead of directly using the ground truth set is the difference in IP coverage**. While our ground truth set covers 8.4 million IP addresses, the location information extracted from queries has a coverage several orders of magnitude higher. In our experiments we extract billions of location data points from queries. In future work we will investigate creating a hybrid approach which uses both methods, but in this paper we have decided to use the entirety of the ground truth dataset for testing.

Given a search engine log which includes IP addresses and user queries, and given an IP geolocation database, our task is to improve the accuracy of the geolocation database using the information in the log by correcting some of the locations in the database at the city level. The implication of starting from an existing database is that we are relying on the existing IP ranges already present in the database. The *maximum* IP range size in the three commercial databases we use is 256 addresses per range, which is a reasonably fine granularity. Furthermore, the coverage of the starting databases is very high, at more than 3.48 billion addresses each.

We are improving existing databases instead of creating a new database from scratch for several reasons. First, we aim to improve the existing state of the art, not replace it. Second, while the coverage of the locations we extract from user queries is high at 360 million distinct IP addresses, it is still not enough to cover all of the used IP range space. Third, as a practical manner it would be more efficient to make use of a single geolocation database which combines location information from different types of data sources. Creating an independent geolocation database from signals from GPS-equipped devices, locations extracted from queries, and other behavioral signals remains potential future work.

7.3 Technical Challenges

In order to extract locations from queries and combine them with an existing geolocation database, we had to overcome several technical challenges:

1. **We must extract locations from queries**. Given a query log, we must extract the explicit locations mentioned in the queries.
2. **Query logs have a large size and extracting locations from queries is computationally expensive at scale.** Our query logs contain billions of data points, which makes it difficult or impossible to store and process the data on a single machine. A secondary problem is that extracting locations from queries is computationally expensive. Therefore, we must extract queries which are most likely to contain locations.
3. **The locations in the database and the locations extracted from queries are not normalized.** We must normalize locations to bring them into a common space before we can combine and compare them directly. For instance the query "plumbers in nyc" contains the location "nyc", which cannot be matched directly with the location "40.7141667, -74.0063889" stored in the geolocation database.
4. **For a given IP range there can be multiple candidate locations extracted from the query log.** Users within a certain IP range are likely to search for a variety of different locations. We must rank these locations in order to pick the most likely candidate for the IP range.
5. **We need to compensate for the effect that primate cities have on surrounding towns.** Primate cities can skew results due to their overall popularity. Consider the example in Figure 3. Here we plot all the locations mentioned in user queries issued from a single IP range, within one month. In this example the radius of the circles depicts the number of times each location was mentioned by users. We can observe that London and Reading are both popular, but London is mentioned more often. The actual number of mentions is 2,159 for London and 1,254 for Reading. In reality, the correct location of users in this IP range is Reading. Here we observe that primate cities can skew the number of mentions due to their global popularity. Therefore, in our approach we must correct for this effect.
6. **We must combine the locations extracted from query logs with the pre-existing IP geolocation database**. For a given IP range, whenever a location extracted from queries does not match the location in the geolocation database, we must find a scoring system to choose whether to keep the original location or change it to the one extracted from user queries.
7. **The resulting combined database needs to be evaluated on a ground truth dataset and ideally tested on a production application**. Here the challenge is devising the ground truth set and determining which metrics to use. Note we have already partially covered this in Section 4. It is also worthwhile to obtain more proof of the improvements using a real production application. The challenge in this second case is determining objective measures of user satisfaction.

Since we are focused on the feasibility of using query logs to improve geolocation, wherever possible we have tried to reuse existing state-of-the-art technologies, allowing us to focus on the novel contributions instead of re-implementing solutions to already solved problems. More specifically, our contributions are focused on challenges *4*, *5*, *6*, *7*, and the second part of challenge *2*.

7.4 Datasets

Below is a list of the datasets we use in this section:

- **Main query log**: It contains 180 days of Bing query logs, ending on October 9th, 2014. This dataset spans hundreds of billions of queries.
- **Validation query log**: For parameter tuning we use 30 days of Bing query logs collected prior to the main query log. There is no overlap between the main query log and the validation log.
- **Baselines**: We use the three IP geolocation databases we previously described in Section 6 as baselines. We consider these databases to be the state of the art in the industry.
- **Ground truth**: The ground truth, which we described in Section 4, contains 8.4 million IP addresses with known location.

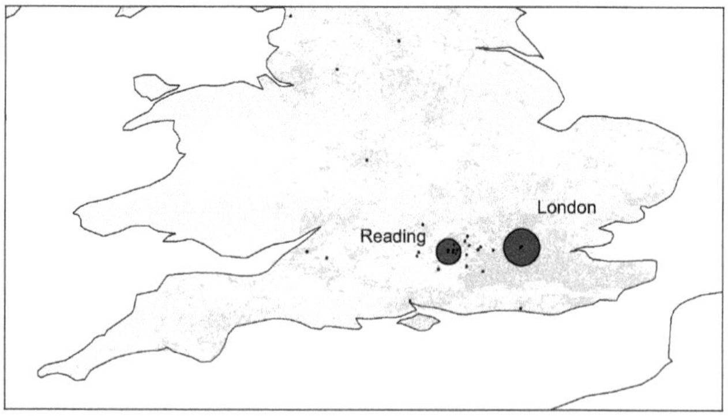

Figure 3: An example of the effect of *primate cities*. If we were to choose the location based solely on number of mentions, we would choose London. In reality, the correct location is Reading.

7.5 Approach

We propose improving IP geolocation databases by correcting the location of certain IP ranges using cities extracted from user queries. We begin from the assumption that when search engine users use explicit locations in their queries, in aggregate these queries reveal the users' location. This assumption may not be true at an individual user level. For example, a person might live in New York City, but they might be planning a vacation in Italy. Queries such as "restaurants in venice" might lead to the incorrect conclusion that the user lives in Italy. However, our hypothesis is that if we aggregate queries from users within the same IP range, the locations which are most mentioned will be geographically close to the users in the range. Furthermore, even at the individual level users do not search for the same non-local locations for extended periods of time. In our example, once the user has completed their research on Venice, they might resume searching for locations closer to home.

Users include explicit locations in their queries for several reasons. First, it is possible they do this because of habit or because they do not realize that search engines know their general location. Second, they might have noticed that the search engine returns incorrect location for their searches, and they are correcting it by explicitly specifying the location. For example, if for the query "weather" the answer shows the weather forecast in an incorrect city, the user is likely to click on a search result instead, switch engines, or requery using the explicit location, such as "weather in seattle". Third, they might be searching for information in a location other than their own city. The first two cases yield the true location of the user, while the last case can lead to false positives.

Figure 4 illustrates the intuition behind our approach with two examples. In each of the examples we plot the locations mentioned in queries issued from one IP range in a one month interval. The blue dots represent the distinct locations mentioned in the queries, while the shading around them shows how often each location was mentioned. The white dot reveals the real location of users in the IP range, as given by GPS information. The correct cities are Morelia in Mexico, and Florence in Italy, respectively. In both cases the city with most query mentions is also the correct one.

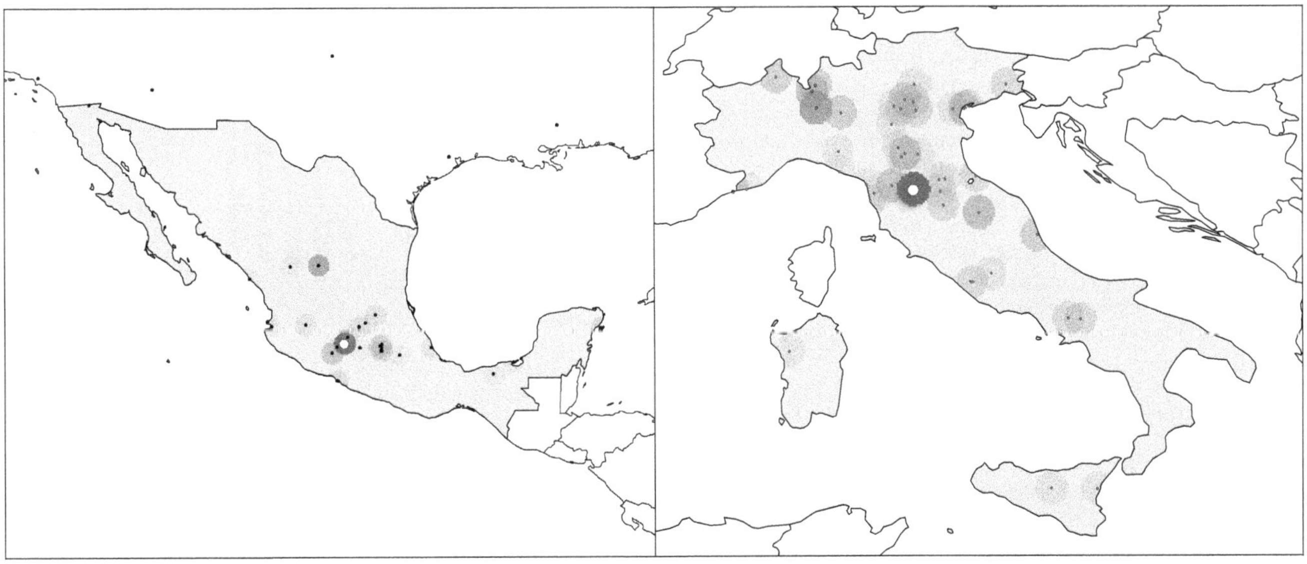

Figure 4: Examples of locations extracted from user queries. Each map shows data from a separate IP range. The individual points show the distinct geographical locations mentioned in user queries issued from the IP range. The amount of shading around them shows the frequency at which these locations were mentioned. The larger white dot shows the actual location of users in the IP range as given by realtime GPS data. The maps show that in both cases the location most frequently mentioned in user queries is also the real location of the users. The figure shows Morelia, Mexico on the left, and Florence, Italy on the right. The size of the IP ranges is 60 and 11 IP addresses, respectively.

Given search engine query logs and an IP geolocation database, our goal is to improve the accuracy of the database. Below is a summary of the steps we have taken to solve this problem.

1. **Extract queries** and corresponding IP addresses from query logs.
2. **Filter impressions**, keeping the ones likely to contain locations.
3. **Extract locations** from the queries that remain.
4. **Reverse geocode locations** extracted from queries and locations extracted from the target geolocation database.
5. **Aggregate locations** first on IP address, then on the IP ranges in the target IP geolocation database.
6. **Compute the popularity of each distinct location** to be used as a proxy for determining *primate cities*.
7. **Score the location candidates** in each IP range.
8. For each IP range where there are candidates, and where the top query location is different than the original location in the IP range, **decide whether to keep the original location** or modify it based on queries.
9. **Test the modified geolocation database** against the ground truth.

We will now provide details for each of the steps. We first extract the queries and IP addresses from the query log. We have performed this step using an implementation of SCOPE, which is a language for processing massive datasets in parallel across a distributed cluster of machines. Please refer to the work by Chaiken et al. for more details [10]. Due to the capabilities of SCOPE, this step is trivial to implement. The result is a smaller but still sizable dataset where we have removed unwanted extra metadata.

Second, we filter the impressions in the log obtained in the first step to retain only the queries which are most likely to contain explicit locations. This filtering step is required in order to reduce the number of queries we need to pass to the location extraction phase. We keep the impressions where the query has local intent, such as "plumbers in chicago", using the production Bing query classifier.

Next, we extract explicit locations from queries. To achieve this we use a method similar to the query dominant location extraction algorithm presented in Wang et al. [29]. We use the user query as input. The output contains the detected location, including the country, city, and coordinates. When no location is detected in the query, the output is empty. This results in several billion explicit location queries, issued from 360 million distinct IP addresses. Please refer to Subsection 7.8 for a discussion on reproducing these experiments using publicly available resources.

We then normalize both the locations extracted from user queries and the locations contained in the target IP geolocation database through reverse geocoding using the publicly available Bing reverse geocoding API. Given a latitude and longitude pair as input, the output is a normalized location at the city level which contains the country, state and city. Each city is assigned a unique identifier. Distinct cities with the same name receive different identifiers. Since the geocoding is performed at the city level the public Bing API achieves an excellent reverse geocoding accuracy in all 50 countries we test in this paper. We perform this step to ensure that the locations extracted from queries and the locations in the target database can be directly compared.

We aggregate the candidate locations per IP address. For each IP address where we have extracted at least one location from user queries, we count the occurrences of each distinct location. We then map these IP addresses on the IP ranges of the target geolocation database, and further aggregate locations per IP range. These two related tasks are performed in a distributed fashion. The result is a list of candidate locations for each IP range, along with their counts.

We then compute the popularity of each distinct city across all IP addresses. We use these counts as a proxy for determining *primate cities*. We name these counts *GlobalMentions*.

Next, we rank the candidate locations in each IP range to determine the top one for that range. For each location mentioned in an IP range we compute *MentionsNorm*, which stands for *normalized mentions* and is shown in Equation 1. For each IP range the candidate cities are ranked in descending order by *MentionsNorm* and the top location is retained. In the equation, *LocalMentions* is given by the number of times the current location was mentioned by users in the current IP range. *GlobalMentions* is the number of times the current location was mentioned across all IP addresses. *IPInst* counts the number of distinct IP addresses in the current IP range that have mentioned the location. Exponents x and y can increase or decrease the importance of *LocalMentions* over *GlobalMentions*. Using a local parameter search on the separate validation dataset we have set x to be 1.5 and y to be 0.5. The parameter search was performed using a step size of 0.1 and limits of 0.0 to 3.0. The exponents can account for *primate cities* by promoting smaller cities and demoting larges ones. In the previous example from Figure 3 London will now have a lower score than Reading, which is the correct choice.

$$MentionsNorm = \frac{LocalMentions^x}{GlobalMentions^y} \cdot IPInst \quad (1)$$

In the last step, for each IP range where the city in the database does not match the location extracted from user queries, we have to decide if we have to modify the location in the database. To achieve this we introduce Equation 2. *IPInstPercentage* in the equation is the percentage of IP addresses in the IP range which mentioned the current location, where *IPInst* is defined as in the previous equation and *EndIP* and *StartIP* are the last and first IP address in the range, respectively.

$$IPInstPercentage = \frac{IPInst}{EndIP - StartIP + 1} \quad (2)$$

To determine if we have to perform the replacement we use both equations 1 and 2. Using the same validation dataset we determine the cutoff thresholds for each equations. That is, we perform the replacement only if the top location in the IP range has *MentionsNorm* of at least 0.3 and *IPInstPercentage* of at least 5%. We have determined these thresholds using a local parameter search with a step size of 0.05 and 0.5%, respectively, a minimum of 0, and a maximum of 1 and 25%, respectively.

7.6 Ground Truth Evaluation

We compared the accuracy and distance error of the three commercial IP geolocation databases to the equivalent databases modified using our approach based on user queries. Figure 5 shows the improvements in exact city match accuracy for five high-traffic countries. We observe the best improvement for Vendor *B*, where for countries such as Germany, Italy, and Spain, the accuracy increases by more than 100%. Table 4 shows an evaluation summary for the top 50 countries by IP density. For Vendors *A* and *B*, the accuracy improves in 49 out of 50 countries, while for Vendor *B* the accuracy improves in 44 countries. In the few cases where accuracy decreases, it does so by less than 0.4%: in Israel for the first two vendors, and Colombia for the last one. Median and mean accuracy computed across all 50 countries show significant gains, especially for the first two vendors. For Vendor *C* the improvement is more modest, as this baseline had the highest initial accuracy. Nevertheless, for several countries such as India, Belgium, Netherlands, and Mexico the improvements are higher than 5% for Vendor *C*, with Taiwan seeing the best improvement at +74.2%.

The improvements are also apparent when we plot the cumulative error for the distance between correct and assumed locations. In Figure 6 we show the cumulative error for Vendor *B* in the United States. We do not superimpose the results for the other two vendors here to make the figure easy to understand. The shapes of the curves for the other two vendors are similar, but the improvements are less pronounced. The results for Vendor *B* show a remarkable improvement, as the percentage of ground truth IP addresses where the error is less than 5 kilometers increases from 36.1% to 58.7%.

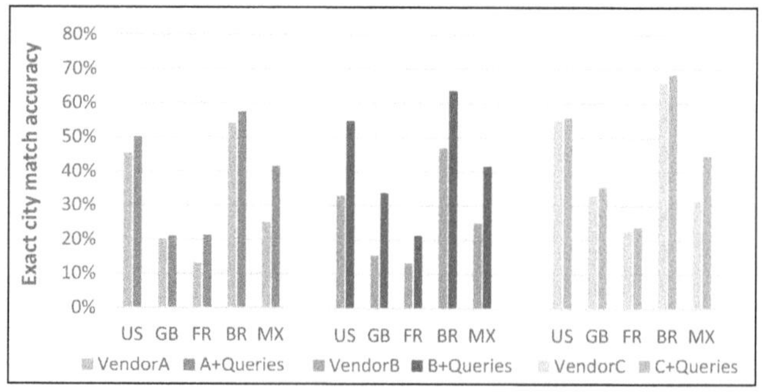

Figure 5: Improvement in accuracy for five high-traffic countries between the original IP geolocation databases and the databases modified using locations extracted from user queries.

Table 4: Summary of evaluation results across three IP geolocation databases and the top 50 countries by IP density. The results are for city level accuracy.

Vendor:	A	B	C
Countries Accuracy Improved	49	49	44
Countries Accuracy Decreased	1	1	6
Median Accuracy Change	+20.7%	+32.2%	+1%
Mean Accuracy Change	+114.8%	+121.1%	+3.4%
Worst Accuracy Change	-0.2%	-0.2%	-0.4%

7.7 Privacy Considerations

Our approach protects the privacy of search engine users, as query logs contain sensitive personal information. First, our method extracts locations from user queries, discarding other words in the queries. Second, all extracted locations are normalized using reverse geocoding. We retain location information only at city level granularity, although some queries initially contain locations which are precise up to the street level. Third, the location information is further aggregated at the IP range level, which combines data from individual users in that IP range into a single set of location counts. Aggregating data across a range of IP addresses makes the data less granular. These steps provide strong privacy safeguards as the output data is coarse and contains no personally identifiable information.

7.8 Reproducing Experiments

Most of the steps in our approach can be reproduced using public techniques and APIs. The IP geolocation databases can be obtained

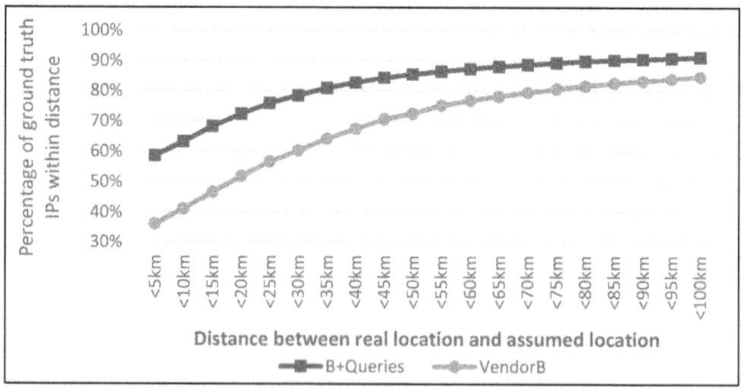

Figure 6: Cumulative error distance from ground truth to Vendor*B*'s IP geolocation database and the same database modified using locations extracted from user queries.

Table 5: Statistically significant changes in metrics for the A/B experiment carried out on the Mexico market.

Metrics	Change	P-Value
Overall Click Success	+0.8%	0.03
Answer Click Success	+1.67%	0.04
Ads CTR	+1.57%	0.03
Ads Click Success	+1.57%	0.03
Entity Pane CTR	+1.58%	0.03

from the companies previously listed in Section 2. Locations can be extracted from queries using publicly available alternatives such as Yahoo! PlaceSpotter [5] and OpenCalais [4]. Another substitute is a Named Entity Recognizer such as Stanford NER [15] or GATE ANNIE [12], combined with a geocoder such as the ones from Bing [1] or Google [3]. The same geocoders also provide functions for reverse geocoding, which would allow normalizing locations. Finally, all distributed aggregation steps can be implemented on an open source implementation of MapReduce, such as Hadoop [31].

8. VALIDATING IMPROVEMENTS

In order to validate our IP geolocation improvements, we have carried out an A/B experiment on the Bing search engine during the seven day period ending on November 1st, 2014. The treatment and control variants each spanned approximately 850,000 unique users and 1.6 million queries from the Mexico market, which represents a sizable percentage of that market. For the control we have used a proprietary IP geolocation database obtained by combining the databases from Vendors *A*, *B*, and *C*, and by adding other sources of information. The resulting database has higher accuracy at the city granularity than any of the individual databases from the three vendors. The geolocation database used in the treatment was generated by modifying the location of some of the IP ranges in the proprietary database, using the same data and methodology as described in Section 7. Comparing the two databases using the ground truth and methodology explained in Section 6 shows that the treatment database has 10% higher accuracy in the Mexico market than the control database. We have purposely chosen to conduct the experiment in a country where our observed improvement is neither the highest nor the lowest.

Table 5 contains the statistically significant changes in user metrics computed at the conclusion of the experiment. The first two rows show that both the overall and the answer success clicks have improved, with 0.8% and 1.67%, respectively. By answers we mean the special page blocks, such as restaurant and cinema listings, which are visually different than the algorithmic results. An improvement in the success metrics indicates that users are more likely to be satisfied with the results once they click on a link. The table also shows an improvement in advertising click through rate and click success. These changes can lead to higher advertising revenue. Finally, the metrics show that the click through rate on the Entity Pane has increased by 1.58%. By Entity Pane we mean the right side of the screen, also known as a Knowledge Graph in the context of the Google search engine, which presents rich contextual information such as details about businesses and maps with close-by restaurants. Since a large percentage of such contextual information is based on the location of the user, the increase in engagement could have been caused by displaying more relevant local information.

Finally, we studied the impact of the experiment on the local answer by focusing on the subset of page views from the IP ranges modified by our method. Compared to the control we see that the overall local answer coverage has decreased by 1.65%, but the click through rate on individual items has increased by 75.5%. These results, which are are statistically significant with P-value at 0.04 and 0.03 respectively, show that while the local answer is shown slightly less often, the engagement with the answer is much higher. The improvement in engagement suggests that the local results might be more accurate in the treatment due to higher geolocation accuracy.

9. DISCUSSION AND IMPLICATIONS

Our work is the first to propose improving IP geolocation databases using search engine logs. We claim that mining search engine logs is a natural choice for this task, as these logs centralize a great deal of location information from diverse and geographically dispersed users. This approach has several advantages: it does not rely on network delay measurements as previous research, it can scale to cover any country, and it generally leads to accuracy measurements which are higher than previous work. Furthermore, real time GPS location extracted from the logs can be used to generate large scale ground truth data.

Bennett et al. [7] demonstrated that search results can be improved by incorporating location-based features into the ranking function. Here we have shown that incorrect location can impact user experience negatively. Therefore, IP geolocation databases with higher accuracy can result in improvements in location-based personalization. Outside the realm of search engines our work has implications in fields such as credit card fraud protection. We have shown that IP geolocation databases have relatively high accuracy and low error distance in large countries, such as the United States. However, we have also seen that the accuracy is lower in smaller countries or countries with lower Internet penetration. Increasing the accuracy of IP geolocation is crucial to combating credit card fraud in countries such as Ukraine, and Malaysia [9].

10. CONCLUSIONS AND FUTURE WORK

In this paper we have generated a large scale ground truth IP geolocation dataset, we have studied the impact that incorrect IP geolocation has on search engine user metrics, and we have proposed a scalable approach to improving IP geolocation at the city level, using search engine logs. We have generated a large ground truth dataset, containing millions of IP addresses with known location, by mining GPS locations from search engine logs. Our ground truth dataset is the largest and most geographically diverse in the open literature, and the first to use GPS location from devices. We have demonstrated that IP geolocation information is vital to search engines by showing how user metrics degrade when the user location is incorrect. We have evaluated three state-of-the-art commercial IP geolocation databases, showing that their accuracy is generally higher than most previously published research efforts. Starting from the three baselines, we have demonstrated an approach to improve IP geolocation databases using explicit locations extracted from query logs. We have validated the IP geolocation improvement process by carrying out a large scale A/B test on the Bing search engine. The results are promising, with statistically significant improvements in several user metrics, such as click success and ads click through rate.

There are several directions for future work. One possible improvement could result from combining data from different sources. For instance, instead of strictly using locations from user queries one could combine them with the real time location we have used for our ground truth, or with social network information as proposed by Backstrom et al. [6]. Another promising approach would be to analyze the implicit behavior of users. Mining search result clicks in search engine logs or toolbar logs could reveal preferences towards local websites, such as *The Kirkland Reporter*. It could also be worthwhile to study the intent of local queries at a finer granularity. For example, we might want to see if queries for airplane tickets leaving from a certain location are more likely to show the real location of a user, compared to vacation related queries, such as "points of interest in vienna".

11. REFERENCES

[1] Bing Geocoding API. `http://msdn.microsoft.com/en-us/library/ff701711.aspx`, (accessed July 17, 2015).

[2] Bing Reverse Geocoding API. `http://msdn.microsoft.com/en-us/library/ff701710.aspx`, (accessed July 17, 2015).

[3] Google Geocoding API. `https://developers.google.com/maps/documentation/geocoding/`, (accessed July 17, 2015).

[4] OpenCalais. `http://www.opencalais.com/`, (accessed July 17, 2015).

[5] Yahoo! PlaceSpotter. `https://developer.yahoo.com/boss/geo/docs/key-concepts.html`, (accessed July 17, 2015).

[6] L. Backstrom, E. Sun, and C. Marlow. Find Me if You Can: Improving Geographical Prediction with Social and Spatial Proximity. In *WWW 2010*, pages 61–70, Raleigh, North Carolina, USA, 2010. ACM.

[7] P. N. Bennett, F. Radlinski, R. W. White, and E. Yilmaz. Inferring and Using Location Metadata to Personalize Web Search. In *SIGIR 2011*, pages 135–144, Beijing, China, 2011. ACM.

[8] B. J. L. Berry. City Size Distributions and Economic Development. *Economic Development and Cultural Change*, 9(4):573–588, 1961.

[9] T. P. Bhatla, V. Prabhu, and A. Dua. Understanding credit card frauds. *Cards business review*, 1(6), 2003.

[10] R. Chaiken, B. Jenkins, P.-A. Larson, B. Ramsey, D. Shakib, S. Weaver, and J. Zhou. Scope: Easy and efficient parallel processing of massive data sets. *Proc. VLDB Endow.*, 1(2):1265–1276, Aug. 2008.

[11] Y.-C. Cheng, Y. Chawathe, A. LaMarca, and J. Krumm. Accuracy Characterization for Metropolitan-scale Wi-Fi Localization. In *MobiSys 2005*, pages 233–245, Seattle, Washington, 2005. ACM.

[12] H. Cunningham, D. Maynard, K. Bontcheva, and V. Tablan. GATE: A Framework and Graphical Development Environment for Robust NLP Tools and Applications. In *ACL 2002*, pages 168–175, 2002.

[13] A. El-Rabbany. *Introduction to GPS: The Global Positioning System*. Artech House mobile communications series. Artech House, 2002.

[14] P. Endo and D. Sadok. Whois Based Geolocation: A Strategy to Geolocate Internet Hosts. In *AINA 2010*, pages 408–413, April 2010.

[15] J. R. Finkel, T. Grenager, and C. Manning. Incorporating Non-local Information into Information Extraction Systems by Gibbs Sampling. In *ACL 2005*, pages 363–370, Ann Arbor, Michigan, 2005.

[16] S. Fox, K. Karnawat, M. Mydland, S. Dumais, and T. White. Evaluating Implicit Measures to Improve Web Search. *ACM Transactions on Information Systems*, 23(2):147–168, Apr. 2005.

[17] B. Gueye, A. Ziviani, M. Crovella, and S. Fdida. Constraint-Based Geolocation of Internet Hosts. *IEEE/ACM Transactions on Networking*, 14(6):1219–1232, Dec 2006.

[18] C. Guo, Y. Liu, W. Shen, H. Wang, Q. Yu, and Y. Zhang. Mining the Web and the Internet for Accurate IP Address Geolocations. In *INFOCOM 2009*, pages 2841–2845, April 2009.

[19] B. Hofmann-Wellenhof, H. Lichtenegger, and J. Collins. *Global Positioning System: Theory and Practice*. Springer, 1993.

[20] B. Hofmann-Wellenhof, H. Lichtenegger, and E. Wasle. *GNSS – Global Navigation Satellite Systems: GPS, GLONASS, Galileo, and more*. Springer, 2007.

[21] C. Huang, D. Maltz, J. Li, and A. Greenberg. Public DNS system and Global Traffic Management. In *INFOCOM 2011*, pages 2615–2623, April 2011.

[22] K. Hubbard, M. Kosters, D. Conrad, D. Karrenberg, and J. Postel. Internet Registry IP Allocation Guidelines. Technical report, United States, 1996.

[23] E. Katz-Bassett, J. P. John, A. Krishnamurthy, D. Wetherall, T. Anderson, and Y. Chawathe. Towards IP Geolocation Using Delay and Topology Measurements. In *IMC 2006*, pages 71–84, Rio de Janeriro, Brazil, 2006. ACM.

[24] B. Kölmel and S. Alexakis. Location based advertising. In *First International Conference on Mobile Business*, Athens, Greece, 2002.

[25] L. MacVittie. Geolocation and Application Delivery. `https://f5.com/resources/white-papers/geolocation-and-application-delivery`, 2012 (accessed November 28, 2015).

[26] V. N. Padmanabhan and L. Subramanian. An Investigation of Geographic Mapping Techniques for Internet Hosts. In *SIGCOMM 2001*, pages 173–185, San Diego, California, USA, 2001. ACM.

[27] C. A. Shue, N. Paul, and C. R. Taylor. From an IP Address to a Street Address: Using Wireless Signals to Locate a Target. In *WOOT 2013*, Washington, D.C., 2013. USENIX.

[28] D. J. B. Svantesson. E-Commerce Tax: How The Taxman Brought Geography To The 'Borderless' Internet. *Revenue Law Journal*, 17(1):11, 2007.

[29] L. Wang, C. Wang, X. Xie, J. Forman, Y. Lu, W.-Y. Ma, and Y. Li. Detecting Dominant Locations from Search Queries. In *SIGIR 2015*, pages 424–431, Salvador, Brazil, 2005. ACM.

[30] Y. Wang, D. Burgener, M. Flores, A. Kuzmanovic, and C. Huang. Towards Street-level Client-independent IP Geolocation. In *NSDI 2011*, pages 365–379, Berkeley, CA, USA, 2011. USENIX.

[31] T. White. *Hadoop: The Definitive Guide*. O'Reilly and Associates Series. O'Reilly, 2012.

[32] B. Wong, I. Stoyanov, and E. G. Sirer. Octant: A Comprehensive Framework for the Geolocalization of Internet Hosts. In *NSDI 2007*, pages 23–23, Berkeley, CA, USA, 2007. USENIX Association.

[33] I. Youn, B. Mark, and D. Richards. Statistical Geolocation of Internet Hosts. In *ICCCN 2009*, pages 1–6, Aug 2009.

Geographic Segmentation via Latent Poisson Factor Model

Rose Yu[1,*]
qiyu@usc.edu

Andrew Gelfand [2]
agelfand@yahoo-inc.com

Suju Rajan [2]
suju@yahoo-inc.com

Cyrus Shahabi [1]
shahabi@usc.edu

Yan Liu [1]
yanliu.cs@usc.edu

[1]Department of Computer Science
University of Southern California

[2] Personalization Sciences
Yahoo Labs

ABSTRACT

Discovering latent structures in spatial data is of critical importance to understanding the user behavior of location-based services. In this paper, we study the problem of geographic segmentation of spatial data, which involves dividing a collection of observations into distinct geo-spatial regions and uncovering abstract correlation structures in the data. We introduce a novel, Latent Poisson Factor (LPF) model to describe spatial count data. The model describes the spatial counts as a Poisson distribution with a mean that factors over a joint item-location latent space. The latent factors are constrained with weak labels to help uncover interesting spatial dependencies. We study the LPF model on a mobile app usage data set and a news article readership data set. We empirically demonstrate its effectiveness on a variety of prediction tasks on these two data sets.

Categories and Subject Descriptors

H.2.8 [**Database Applications**]: Data Mining

Keywords

geographic segmentation, spatial data, mobile app usage

1. INTRODUCTION

The proliferation of in-vehicle navigation systems and GPS-equipped mobile devices over the last decade has resulted in a dramatic increase in the collection of spatial data. Understanding latent structures in such data is crucial to user behavior modeling and other prediction tasks including targeted advertising, personalization and location-based recommender system. Due to privacy concerns or limitations in the spatial resolution of the collection devices, spatial data are often available in an aggregated form, where spatial observations from distinct users are combined into counts occurring at coarse spatial locations.

This paper deals with the geographic segmentation of spatial count data. *Geographic segmentation* refers to the task of dividing observations into distinct geographical regions and identifying abstract structures in these observations [9]. Spatial clustering, e.g. [3, 16] is a common approach to tackle the problem. However, it usually relies on the spatial auto-correlation of actual geography of locations. Our interest in geographic segmentation is motivated primarily by our desire to understand how mobile app usage behavior for different categories of mobile users varies spatially. Our goal in this case is to describe a joint distribution of the number of uses of an app at a particular spatial location using data aggregated from many devices. By doing so we hope to answer some important questions of interest to mobile app developers, marketing researchers and many others. For instance, do people tend to use one app or one type of app when at a particular location? Which locations are likely to result in the use of a particular type of app?

In our setting, geographic segmentation is challenging because our observations have no correlation with the actual geography of the location, but the type of the location. For example, the fact that someone is interested in running a Yelp app, is not because she is at a specific geo-coordinate but because she is nearby a restaurant. Therefore, we need to capture the implicit relationship between a specific geographical area and the type of interest in that area, which is data dependent. Second, the density of the user population varies drastically across different locations. For instance, the number of observed uses of an app in San Francisco will be much larger than the number of uses of that app in Sunnyvale. As a result, aggregate spatial counts data would easily violate the spatial stationarity assumptions of many standard statistical methods. Finally, while aggregate statistics can mitigate the variability in individual usage data, it can also result in the accumulation of additive noise. This requires the model to take into account the intrinsic uncertainties in the data and automatically learn the underlying correlation.

To collectively address all these challenges, we develop a novel hierarchical Bayesian model, called the Labeled Poisson Model (LPF), to describe spatial count data. As the name suggests, the model describes the counts at a spatial location as a Poisson distribution with a mean that factors over a joint item-location latent space. The LPF model is

*Part of the work done while the author was interning at Yahoo Labs

WSDM'16, February 22–25, 2016, San Francisco, CA, USA.

ISBN 978-1-4503-3716-8/16/02...$15.00

DOI: http://dx.doi.org/10.1145/2835776.2835806

also semi-supervised and uses weak labels on the geographic observations to help uncover underlying spatial dependencies. We study this model on two different data sets. One is a data set of mobile app usage collected by Yahoo Aviate, an intelligent launcher for Android devices; the other is a data set of the Yahoo news articles that were clicked on in different regions of the US. We use the LPF model to predict the number of uses of an app or clicks of a news article at a particular location and evaluate its efficacy by holding out the observed item counts at a set of locations (the test set) and observing how well the model can recover these held out values.

We observe that the semantics of a location, rather than its spatial coordinates (e.g. longitude, latitude), play a key role in the task of geographic segmentation. For mobile app usage, the types of business venues near a location influence the distribution of app activation at that location. For news data, demographic information such as the population, median age and income are important factors in determining the number of clicks in a location. Our proposed LPF model is able to utilize such information to infer the underlying spatial correlations and more accurately estimate the counts at a location. Moreover, our model is privacy preserving as it exploits the aggregate statistics rather than individual data. Our work provides some insight into the design of a general-purpose geographic segmentation strategy.

2. RELATED WORK

The use of aggregate statistics for behavior profiling is a fairly common practice in the data mining community. The early work of [18, 15] discovered web usage patterns by clustering page views and navigation paths across all users to a particular site. More recently, the authors in [10] use an aggregated set of page views and user transactions to generate a set of overlapping usage profiles. These usage profiles are then employed in a "personalization engine" to tailor the set of pages shown to a user when they first visit a site. The authors in [12] studied the reliability of crowd-sourced information, where the information (e.g. an entry in *Wikipedia*) from one source can be influenced by other sources. They propose a probabilistic model to tease out the dependency between sources and uncover the true information.

Geographic segmentation is of particular interest in marketing research, where the goal is to divide a market into distinct geographical regions (e.g. countries, cities or neighborhoods), so that a company or organization can use the market segmentation to, for example, decide how to market or promote a product in a region (see e.g., [9] for an overview of the geographic segmentation problem). Geographic segmentation has also seen successful applications in detecting crime hot spots [9] and geographical annotations[23]. Spatial clustering is a common approach in geographic segmentation. Many methods for finding clusters in spatial data exist (see e.g., [11]), and density-based methods that divide the spatial observations into distinct groups are particularly popular. DBSCAN [3] is one such density-based algorithm that works by first clustering points that lie in close spatial proximity to each other, and then removing outliers whose nearest neighbor is farther than some pre-specified threshold.

To our knowledge, geographic segmentation of mobile app usage has not yet been studied. Existing work [1, 8] has shown that time of day, location (e.g., whether at home, work, or out at a restaurant), activity (e.g., whether walking, running, or driving), and even social setting drive app usage behavior. However, this work did not consider location in a systematic way, instead mapping location to a small set of categories (e.g., at home, at work, or other). Location semantics has been studied in geographic topic modeling literature [21, 5, 22]. However, location semantics for mobile app usage stays under-explored. Yet other work [20, 6] has focused on location-based recommendation, which is somewhat different from our problem. In there, the goal is to find a set of spatially relevant items (e.g. nearby restaurants, local events or even mobile apps) for a particular user.

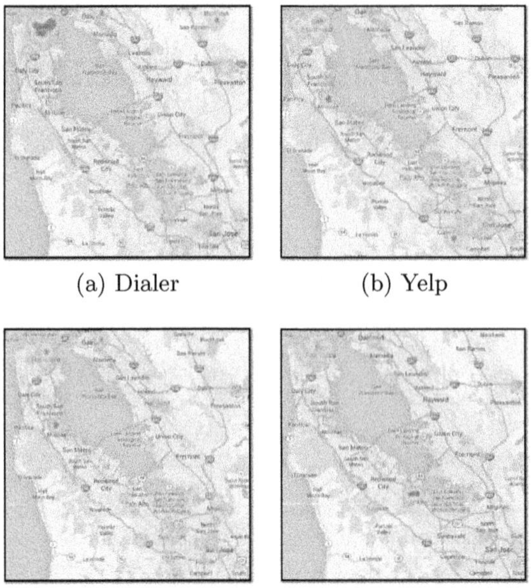

(a) Dialer (b) Yelp

(c) FlappyBird (d) Snapchat

Figure 1: Heatmap of the number of open events for the Dialer, Yelp, Flappy Bird and Snapchat apps. Opens are aggregated for 100 active devices over a 7 month period in the San Francisco Bay area. Red denotes a higher frequency of open events.

3. EXPLORATORY ANALYSIS

We conduct an exploratory analysis of spatial counts for two different application areas - namely, mobile app usage and news article click data. After introducing each of these data sets, we study the distribution of their spatial counts and check for the existence of spatial correlation. We also identify important characteristics of the geographic distribution in these settings.

3.1 App Usage Data

We collected app usage data from 14,836 mobile devices on which Yahoo Aviate [1] was installed. As mentioned, Yahoo Aviate is a mobile launcher for Android devices. The Android operating systems reports every time a user opens an app or brings an app to the foreground. For each such app open event, Yahoo Aviate records the name of the app that was opened, the time at which it was opened and the approximate location (latitude, longitude) of the device when

[1]https://play.google.com/store/apps/details?id=com.tul.aviate

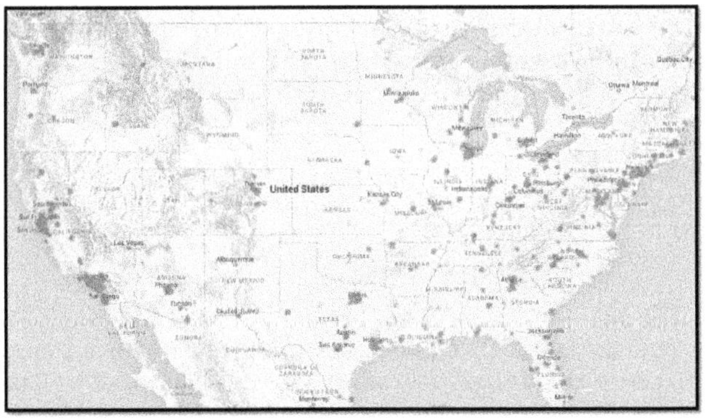

Figure 2: Heatmap of the number of articles read in different locations in the United States.

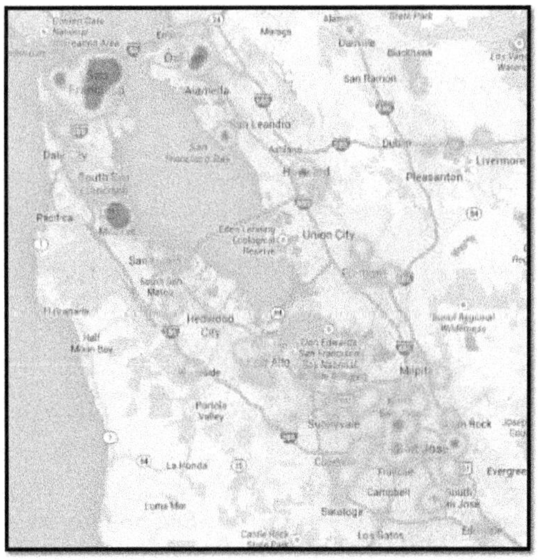

Figure 3: Heatmap of the number of open events for the 100 most popular apps. Opens are aggregated for 100 active devices over a 7 month period and red denotes a higher frequency of opens.

the app was opened [2]. App open events were recorded over a 7-month period for devices in the San Francisco Bay area.

Figure 1 is a heat map visualizing the number of opens of four popular apps - namely, Dialer, Yelp, Flappy Bird and Snapchat. The numbers of opens of each app are aggregated across the 100 devices with the most total open events. Areas where an app was frequently opened are shown in red and areas of infrequent app opens are uncolored. Interestingly, from this figure it appears that how frequently an app is opened at a location can be explained (at least in part) by looking at both the type of venues near that location and the intended functionality of the app. For example, Dialer, which is a communication app, is frequently used by the San Francisco Pier 39, a popular tourist destination. Yelp, which is a travel & local recommendations app is popular in Santana Row, an area with many shops, restaurants and bars. Flappy Bird, which is an arcade game, has a similar distribution to Yelp, which suggests that games may be popular in areas of commerce as well. Finally, Snapchat, a communication and social networking app, is highly concentrated near Stanford, a university area.

The results in Figure 1 suggest that mobile app usage at a location may be influenced by the types of business nearby. In order to understand how the frequency of all app opens varies spatially, we next aggregate the open events of the active users across the 100 most popular apps. Figure 3 displays the counts after this additional level of aggregation. Note that while the app opens are spread over the entire bay area, apps are opened with the highest frequency near the bay area's three major airports - SFO in Millbrae, SJC in San Jose and OAK in Oakland. One possible explanation for the phenomena is that people tend to open apps with increased frequency while waiting for flights.

3.2 Yahoo News Data

We also collected data from the interaction of 182,355 users with the news stream on the Yahoo homepage. The Yahoo stream shows a personalized list of news articles to each user visiting the page. Every article in the stream that a user clicks on is recorded. For each such article, we also record a set of categorical labels describing what that article is about, as well as the zip code from which the user's click originated. The categorical labels are topical in nature, such as 'Sports', 'Art', and 'Education', and an article can be labeled with multiple categories. The categories associated with an article are obtained by classifying the news article via a multi-labeled topical classifier.

We collect the click records per article and map each postal code to a longitude and latitude point [3]. Figure 2 is a heat map showing the counts of clicks in each postal area. For ease of plotting, we uniformly sampled 1,000 locations. Unlike the app usage data, the article click data are spread across the entire US. Big cities like San Francisco, Los Angeles and New York, which have large populations experience the largest number of clicks, while clicks are far more sparse in less densely populated areas. In addition, the spatial resolution for the article click records is at the postal code level. Since a zip code is likely to contain many types of businesses, using business categories to provide semantics for a location (as we did for the app usage data) will be of little help. For this reason, we choose postal code level population and demographic information to provide semantics for a location.

3.3 Distribution of Spatial Events

We analyze the distribution of app open and article click counts across all locations. Figure 4 is a log-log plot that tabulates the number of location cells at which a given event occurred. For Aviate app usage data, we use a $10^3 \times 10^3$ grid. For article click data, we use a $10^2 \times 10^2$ grid. The results of Aviate app usage data are shown in the top row and the news article results are shown on the bottom row. The left

[2]Note that an open event does not necessarily correspond to actual usage. Some apps, such as music players, run in the background. Nonetheless, we use the number of opens as a proxy for app usage.

[3]This was done using the Geocoding library: https://developers.google.com/maps-engine/documentation/geocode

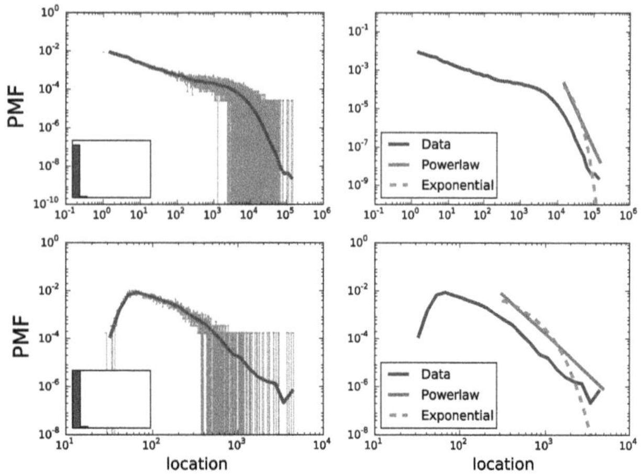

Figure 4: Plot of the number of locations at which a given event count occurred for Aviate app open events (upper row) and Yahoo! news article click events (bottom row). Left column is the raw probabilistic mass function. The right column shows the fit of the power-law and exponential distributions to this count data.

column contains plots of the empirical distributions of each data set. Interestingly, we see that while the count data are generally sparse, they closely follow the power law distributions. The right column shows the fit of the power law distribution to these empirical distributions. For comparison, we also fit the exponential distribution. For both data sets, we observe a good fit for the power law distribution, which is aligned with the findings in [19] on spatial event frequency over distances. The fact that aggregated spatial count data is power-law distributed suggests that we need a heavy-tailed distribution to model frequency counts. This finding motivates our choice of the Poisson distribution in the LPF model.

3.4 Study of Spatial Variation

The analysis in the previous two subsections show the existence of spatial auto-correlations in the aggregate counts of mobile app usage and news article click records. However, the counts do not seem to vary smoothly over space, meaning that the counts in one location do not seem similar to the counts in nearby locations. Local smoothness can be quantified by computing the correlation between the differences in observed counts and geographical distance. We evaluate the spatial smoothness of the app usage data by drawing a grid over the bay area and binning the app open events at different locations into each of the grid cells. We compute the Pearson correlation coefficient between differences in app usage and the distance between cell centers. Table 1 displays the correlation between app usage and inter cell distance for several differently sized grids. Note that spatial correlation can also be evaluated using variogram or auto-variogram with different covariance functions, here we use Euclidean distance as a simple example. We observe that almost no-correlation exists between app usage and the distance between location centers. As a result, we cannot assume that people living in a neighborhood tend to use similar mobile applications.

Table 1: Pearson correlation coefficient between the difference in the distribution over opens of popular apps in two cells i and j and the euclidean distance between cells i and j.

Grid Size	100	400	900	1600	2500
Pearson	-0.0406	-0.0327	-0.0158	-0.0221	-0.0167

The key insight we draw from the exploratory analysis in this section is that a location's semantics, either venue categories or demography, affect the distribution of counts in that location. In the app usage data set, the types of venues near a location can provide a hint as to the users' intent when opening an app. For example, when a user is in an area with many bars and restaurants and they open a restaurant review app, such as Yelp, their intent is probably to eat. Or, if they are in a university or high school area and they open SnapChat, their intent is probably to communicate with their friends. For the news article click data, we have noticed that zip code level demographic information, such as the median household income, median age and even total population can affect the types of articles clicked. These observations suggest that the semantics provided by categorical labels of a location, rather than simply the spatial coordinates, are needed when describing correlations in the observed spatial count data.

In the next section, we propose a model that uses the correlation between different location semantics and item types to model the intensity of aggregate spatial events. Often times, an app may be opened (or an article may be clicked on) for different reasons and the semantics associated with a location may also be uncertain. For instance, the number of opens of the Yelp app at a location can be explained by the fact that Yelp is an app used to recommend local restaurants, shops and services and also by the presence of restaurants, shops and services near that location. Therefore, we adopt a hierarchical Bayesian approach that models the uncertainty in the categorical labels assigned to each location and each item. Our approach borrows from the Labeled LDA model [13] and marries the multi-label supervision common in document classification with co-occurrence preference indicators commonly used in collaborative filtering models.

4. LABELED POISSON FACTOR MODEL

In this section, we formally introduce the Labeled Poisson Factor (LPF) model. The LPF model is a probabilistic graphical model that describes a process for generating aggregate spatial count data. Much like the probabilistic factor model of [14], the frequency of events at a location are due to the interaction of latent factors - in this case an item latent factor and a location latent factor. However, we associate labels to the dimensions of the latent space and use supervision to constrain the set of latent factors that can be used to explain the count at a particular location. In the remainder of this section, we elaborate on the generative process of our model and describe a collapsed Gibbs sampler used for learning and inference. The tedious derivations of the sampler are omitted for clarity of presentation.

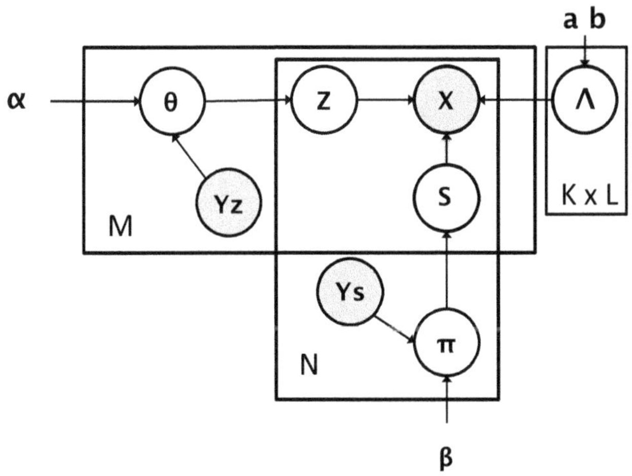

Figure 5: Graphical model of Labeled Poisson Factor model. Shaded circles are observations, blank circles are latent variables and the variables without a circle are model parameters.

Table 2: Latent Poisson Factor Model Notation

Symbols	Semantics
α	Dirichlet prior for item category
β	Dirichlet prior for location category
θ	Item category distribution parameter
π	Location category distribution parameter
Z	Item category indicator
S	Location category indicator
Yz	Item category labels
Ys	Location category labels
X	Spatial activity frequencies
Λ	Intensity distribution parameter
a, b	Shape, scale for Gamma prior distribution

The LPF model can be represented by the graphical model in Figure 5. Let X be an M by N data matrix describing the aggregated counts for the M items at N different locations, where X_{ij} is the aggregated count of item i at location j. In our setting, the item counts are either the number of opens of an app or the number of clicks on a news article. Yz is an M by K binary label matrix for each item, where $Yz_{ik} \in \{0, 1\}$ is 1 if item i has label k and there are a total of K possible labels. Ys is an N by L binary label matrix for the N different locations, where $Ys_{jl} \in \{0, 1\}$ is 1 if location j has label l and there are a total of L possible labels. In the app usage setting, the L different labels for a location come from Foursquare, which describe the types of business venues near that location. For example, a location may be considered a 'Food' and 'Nightlife' area, but not a 'Residential' area. In the news article setting, labels are derived from demographic data, such as median household income and age.

Since our count data exhibits power-law properties, we choose to model every count X_{ij} in X using a Poisson distribution. Since we also observed a co-occurrence of certain types of apps or news articles with specific types of locations, we further assume that the Poisson distribution for item i

Algorithm 1 Generative Process of the LPF model

```
Input: hyper-parameter α, β, a, b
for i = 1 to M do
    α_i = SHRINK(α, Yz_i)
    Draw θ_i ~ Dir(α_i)
    for j = 1 to N do
        Draw Z_ij ~ Categorical(θ_i)
    end for
end for
for j = 1 to N do
    β_j = SHRINK(β, Ys_j)
    Draw π_i ~ Dir(β_j)
    for i = 1 to M do
        Draw S_ij ~ Categorical(π_i)
    end for
end for
for k = 1 to K do
    for l = 1 to L do
        Draw Λ_kl ~ Gamma(a, b)
    end for
end for
for j = 1 to N do
    for i = 1 to M do
        Draw X_ij ~ Poisson(Λ_{z_ij, s_ij})
    end for
end for
function SHRINK(u, v)
    u' = u
    Squeeze out entries in u' where v = 0
return u'
end function
```

at location j has an intensity (mean) that factorizes over an items latent factor and a locations latent factor. Each item i is modeled as a multinomial mixture of item categories θ_i. However, rather than being a multinomial with K outcomes, the distribution of categories for item i, θ_i, is restricted so that it is only defined over the categorical labels assigned to item i in the matrix Yz. Each location j is also modeled as multinomial mixture distribution of categories π_j, that is similarly restricted to the categorical labels for location j given in matrix Ys. When no positive labels are observed for item i or location j, we assume that θ_i and π_j have all K and L possible outcomes, respectively.

Most existing Poisson factorization approaches model the Poisson intensity parameter for element X_{ij} as the inner product of two latent vectors: $X_{ij} \sim \text{Poisson}(\theta_i^T \pi_j)$. In our setting, this would imply an independence of the location factors and the item factors. We relax this assumption by imposing a joint latent space, Λ, and allow each item to pick a category based on location and vice versa. This modification describes the spatial data more accurately and introduces more flexibility into the model. The binary labels in Yz and Ys can only provide weak guidance to the actual categories contributing to an observed count because of the mutual dependence of item and location categories in the joint latent space. The binary labels nonetheless constrain the priors on latent factors: the category of an item or a location is constrained to belong to the categories indexed by the non-zero entries of the labels in Yz and Ys, respectively.

Our model is a variation of the Bayesian Poisson factorization model [24], which replaces the usual Gaussian likelihood

Algorithm 2 Collapsed Gibbs Sampler for the LPF model.

Input: data X, Yz, Ys, training mask I, Dirichlet hyper-parameters α, β, Gamma shape, scale hyper-parameters a, b

```
repeat
  Randomly initialize Z, S, Λ.
  Initialize category counts nZ, nS as zero matrices
  for i = 1 to M do
    α_i = SHRINK(α, Yz_i)
  end for
  for j = 1 to N do
    β_j = SHRINK(β, Ys_j)
  end for
  for i = 1 to M do
    for j = 1 to N do
      nZ_{Z_ij,i} = nZ_{Z_ij,i} + I_ij, nS_{S_ij,j} = nS_{S_ij,j} + I_ij
    end for
  end for
  for i = 1 to M do
    for j = 1 to N do
      if I_ij then
        Sample Z_ij ~ Multi(1, [α_i + nZ^{¬ij}_{:,i}] ∘ Yz_i)
        Sample S_ij ~ Multi(1, [β_j + nS^{¬ij}_{:,j}] ∘ Ys_j)
        Update nZ, nS
      end if
    end for
  end for
  for k = 1 to K do
    for l = 1 to L do
      Count activity nI_kl = Σ_{ij:Z_ij=k,S_ij=l} I_ij
      a' = a + Σ_{i,j} X_ij ∘ I_ij, b' = b/(1 + nI_kl * b)
      Sample Λ_kl ~ Gamma(a', b')
    end for
  end for
until Converge
```

and real-valued representations in probabilistic matrix factorization with a Poisson likelihood and non-negative representations. As pointed out by [4], Poisson factorization is better at handling sparse data and enjoys more efficient inference.

Algorithm 1 describes the generative process of the LPF model in detail. For each item i, we sample a multinomial distribution θ_i over item categories from a truncated Dirichlet prior α_i. The truncated Dirichlet prior α_i is found by using Yz to retain only the parameters in α corresponding to positively labeled categories. In particular, α_i is formed from α by setting the concentration parameters for the unlabeled categories to zero. For each location j, we then sample an independent item factor indicator Z_{ij} from the categorical distribution parameterized by θ_i. In a similar fashion, we generate location factor indicators S_{ij} by first sampling π_j from a Dirchlet prior β_j constrained using the location labels in the matrix Ys and then sampling S_{ij} from π_j for each item i. Finally, we generate the aggregate spatial count X_{ij} according to Poisson distribution with intensity $\Lambda_{Z_{ij},S_{ij}}$. For convenience, we put a conjugate Gamma prior on the joint latent space Λ. We use a Gibbs sampler for inference and learning. For efficiency, we collapse the latent variables of type $\{\theta_i\}$ and space $\{\pi_i\}$. The update steps of the collapsed Gibbs sampler are described in Algorithm 2.

5. EXPERIMENTS

We conduct several experiments to evaluate the capability of the LPF model to accurately capture spatial correlations and predict the number of spatial counts at a particular location, or for a particular item.

5.1 Setup

Our overall experimental setup is shown in Figure 6. In the first stage, we extract labels for each of the M items. In the second stage, we identify the N locations and assign labels to each. In the case of the app usage data, we discretize the geographical area into N equally sized cells; for the news article data, the number of locations N is equal to the number of distinct postal codes. Details on how the labels are extracted follow below. In the final stage, we evaluate the LPF model by holding out the observed counts at some of the locations and assess how well the model can recover those values.

Table 3: Characteristics of the Aviate app usage and Yahoo news article click data sets.

Aviate App Usage		
Time Period	# of Devices	# of Records
7 month	14,836	51,765,517
# of AppOpen	# of LocUpdate	# of Apps
33,896,214	17,869,303	46,248

News Article Click	
# number of users	# number of records
182,355	1,034,615
# of articles	# of locations
30,544	5,907
# of article category	# of location category
21	40

We now describe how the categorical labels were identified for app usage data. The Yahoo Aviate launcher provides a mapping of each app to 24 named collection types, such as 'Productivity', 'News', 'Restaurants', etc. These collection types provide a natural labeling for each app. We discretize the San Francisco Bay Area into equally sized cells and use the Foursquare API to identify the set of business venues in each cell. Each business is associated with one of 10 categorical tags, such as 'Restaurant', 'Nightlife Spot', or 'College or University'. We use these categorical tags to label each cell.

For the Yahoo news article data, we gather demographic information for each zip code area, including the median income, age, number of households and the population density. We then compute the national percentile of each demographic feature and map them to values 0-9. For example, '0' in income indicates the median income at that locale is in the bottom 10% nationally and 1 indicates the median income is in the 10-20% percentile nationally. The key statistics of these two data sets are shown in Table 3.

(a) Item Labeling (b) Location Labeling (c) Matrix Completion

Figure 6: Set up of the LPF model experiments. (a): categorical labeling for items (b): categorical labeling for locations (c): hold out assessment of the aggregated counts.

5.2 Baseline

We compare the LPF model with the following baselines.

- LPF-Loc: the LPF model using only location labels
- LPF-Item: the LPF model using only item labels
- BPF : Bayesian Poisson Factor Analysis [24]
- MFSI: Matrix Factorization with Side Information [7]
- NMF: Non-negative Matrix Factorization [2]
- PM: Poisson Mixture model
- Global Mean: Mean of all training data
- Loc Mean: Mean of each location
- Item Mean: Mean of each item
- All Zero: Always predict zero

We mainly compare the LPF model with other latent factor models. We include LPF-Loc, which is the LPF model with supervision only on the labels of the locations, LPF-Item, which is the LPF model with supervision only on the labels of the items, and BPF to evaluate the benefits of incorporating both item and location semantics for the geographic segmentation task. We also include MFSI and NMF as non-Bayesian factorization methods. The comparison between latent factor models and other density-based spatial clustering techniques such as DBSCAN is not within the scope of the study in this paper. For NMF, we use the source code in http://www.csie.ntu.edu.tw/~cjlin/nmf/others/nmf.py. For MFSI, we use the GraphLab Create.

5.3 Mobile App Usage

We evaluate the predictive performance of the LPF model in three different settings: 1) A static setting; 2) A dynamic setting; and 3) While varying grid size.

Static Setting.

In this section, we evaluate the LPF model in a static setting by aggregating the app usage across all 7 months. We select the 100 most popular apps and bin the San Francisco Bay area into 100 equally sized grid cells. We aggregate the number of opens of each app in each cell across all 14,836 devices. We normalize the counts by the total number of devices and randomly remove 20% of the entries in the 100 by 100 data matrix X. These are the missing values that we try to recover. We repeat the process 10 times and report the average prediction RMSE with respect to the ground truth frequencies.

Table 4: RMSE of the LPF model and several baseline approaches on the Aviate app usage data. App opens are aggregated across 14,836 devices at 100 locations. The results are averaged over 10 random 80% - 20% training-test splits.

Algorithm	Mean	Variance
Labeled Poisson Factor	**1.1293**	0.1569
LPF-Item	1.2200	0.1780
LPF-Loc	1.1484	0.1989
Bayesian Poisson Factor Analysis	1.1927	0.2508
MFSI	1.4111	0.0085
Poisson Mixture	1.3159	0.2270
Non-negative Matrix Factorization	1.2096	0.2513
Global Mean	1.2841	0.2238
Loc Mean	1.2670	0.1870
Item Mean	1.2347	0.2024
All Zero	1.4488	0.2210

Table 4 shows the RMSE comparison of the LPF model and the baselines. Notice that the LPF model achieves the lowest RMSE in this setting. By comparing LPF with LPF-Item and LPF-Loc we can begin to understand the importance of the supervision provided by the item and location labels. When aggregating across the devices, we see that location semantics have a bigger impact on performance (RMSE of 1.22 for LPF-Item vs RMSE of 1.14 for LPF-Loc). On the other hand, LPF has relatively low variance in terms of prediction. This is mainly due to the inherent sparsity in the data, which is alleviated by Bayesian priors and the supervision from labels.

Figure 7 shows the geographic segmentation for a set of cells centered in Palo Alto with grid size 100. This plot is generated by first estimating the location category distribution, π_j, at each location j and then assigning the most probable category $l_j = \arg\max \pi_j$ to each location. We use different colors to denote different categories. Three ma-

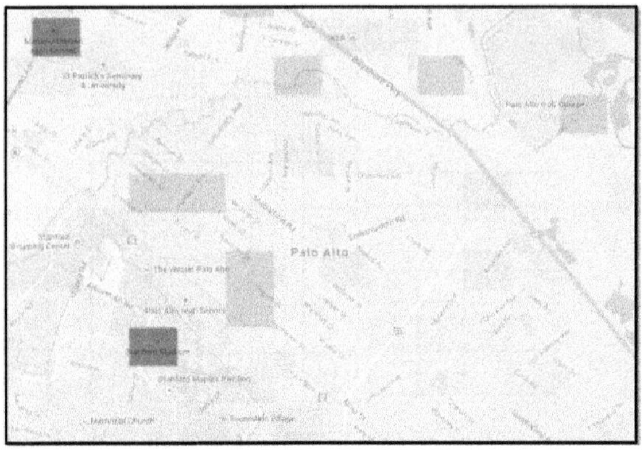

Figure 7: Color-coded segmentation of Palo Alto area learned by LPF. The segment type are decided by assigning the most probable category with respect to the location category distribution π.

jor segments are identified in the plot. The brown color highlights the 'school' areas, including Stanford university on the bottom left and Menlo-Atherton High School on the top left. The yellow color represents shopping areas, including Escondido Village, Stanford Shopping Center and Ikea in the top middle. Finally, the orange color denotes hotels that appear near the Palo Alto Golf Course and The Westin Palo Alto. We note that these segments (learned by LPF) are discriminated by their categories rather than their actual geographic coordinates. The results suggest that LPF model can capture latent semantics in spatial count data.

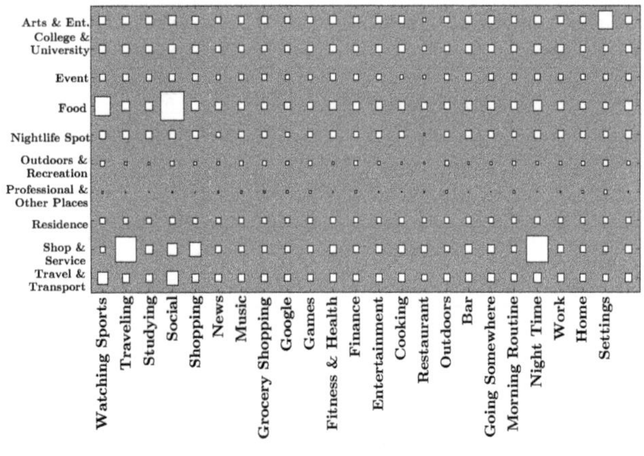

Figure 8: Hinton diagram of the joint latent space intensity, Λ of the LPF model. The area occupied by a square in this matrix is proportional to the magnitude of the intensity of that item-location category pair. So for example, 'Social' apps and 'Food' locations have a very strong intensity, while 'Music' apps and 'Food' locaitons have a much weaker intensity.

Figure 8 shows the Hinton diagram of the intensity of co-occurrence of app and location labels from the matrix Λ learned by LPF. We observe several interesting phenomenon in this learned joint latent space that are supported by our intutition. For example, night time apps are popular in food locations. Shopping apps are popular in shopping and services locations. Such results show that our model can correctly capture the underlying correlation between an app's category and a location's semantics.

Dynamic Setting.

In the dynamic setting, we make a sequence of predictions. Since the Aviate data set spans roughly 7 months, we split the data into 7, one month chunks. We train all methods using the data from month t and predict the number of opens for all apps at all locations in month $t+1$. We normalize the counts with respect to the total number of devices and the number of days in each month. We repeat the training and testing procedure 6 times and report the prediction RMSE for all methods in Table 5 for all time stamps.

In the dynamic setting, the counts in a single time stamp become quite sparse. As a result, the LPF model significantly outperforms the other baseline methods in all 6 of the evaluation periods. Notice that in the static setting, BPF and PM perform pretty well, while in the dynamic setting, the accuracy of both methods degrades. This demonstrates how the joint latent space and the supervision of the LPF can help alleviate the sparsity issue.

Varying Grid Size.

In our experimental setup, we discretize the San Francisco Bay area into evenly sized cells and binned the opens of each app into a cell. A major difficulty with binning in this fashion is choosing the right size for each cell. The size of a grid cell plays an important role as it not only affects the number of observed opens in a cell, but also the categorical labels associated with a cell. Small sized cells would lead to sparse observations. However, when a cell is too large, it will include business from a wide range of categories, which will consequently reduce the effectiveness of the location supervision.

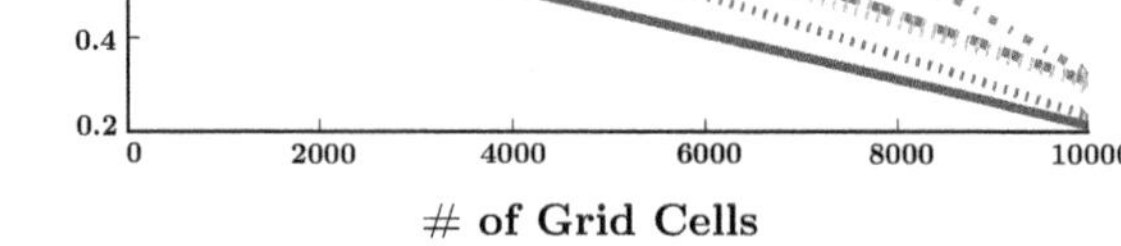

Figure 9: RMSE error bar for the LPF and baselines with respect to grid size over 10 random runs. The number of grid cells increases from 50 to 10,000.

In this subsection, we investigate the impact of differently sized grids on prediction accuracy. Each method is run on a grid ranging in size from 50 to 10,000 cells. For each grid size setting, we make API calls to Foursquare to obtain a finer-grained set of location categories. Figure 9 shows the prediction RMSE error bar with respect to the number of

Table 5: **RMSE comparison of the LPF model and several baseline approaches in the dynamic setting, where the app opens in month $t+1$ are predicted using the app open observations in month t. App opens were aggregated over 14,856 devices and 100 locations.**

TIME STAMP	LPF	BPF	PM	NMF	ZERO	GLOBAL	LOC-MEAN	ITEM -MEAN	MFSI
TS 1	**0.2986**	0.6128	0.5271	5.4878	0.6812	0.5265	0.3240	0.5120	1.2331
TS 2	**0.2838**	0.6103	0.5292	5.4912	0.6847	0.5292	0.3167	0.5118	1.2142
TS 3	**0.3150**	0.6461	0.5560	5.4767	0.7159	0.5555	0.3509	0.5363	1.2885
TS 4	**0.3347**	0.6359	0.5663	5.4643	0.7321	0.5661	0.3695	0.5462	1.2473
TS 5	**0.3306**	0.6297	0.5667	5.4715	0.7276	0.5667	0.3700	0.5474	1.2364
TS 6	**0.3112**	0.5139	0.4916	5.5575	0.6019	0.4911	0.3379	0.4730	1.3740

number of grid cells. LPF outperforms the other baselines[4]. As expected, the mean RMSE goes down for all methods as we increase the number of grid cells. This decrease is due to two things: first, as we increase the number of cells in a fixed area, we obtain finer-grained location information. Therefore, the supervision from location tags becomes increasingly sharp. Second, finer-grid binning results in more sparse observed counts. Thus, the absolute values of the frequency counts decreases.

5.4 News Article Clicks

To demonstrate the applicability of the LPF model to other types of spatial count data, we also evaluate on the Yahoo news articles data.

Table 6: RMSE comparison of the LPF model and baseline approaches on the Yahoo news article data. The results are averaged over 10 random split of the dataset using 80% - 20% training-test split.

ALGORITHM	MEAN	VARIANCE
LABELED POISSON FACTOR	**1.7956**	0.04476
LPF-ITEM	1.8004	0.04607
LPF-LOC	1.7998	0.04014
BAYESIAN POISSON FACTOR ANALYSIS	2.9659	0.04857
POISSON MIXTURE	2.4134	0.04829
NON-NEGATIVE MATRIX FACTORIZATION	3.7669	**0.02345**
GLOBAL MEAN	2.3753	0.04453
LOC MEAN	1.8049	0.04510
ITEM MEAN	2.3001	0.04364
ALL ZERO	3.3315	0.04639

We aggregate the article counts for 182,355 users and 30,544 articles. We randomly select 80% of the entries as training data and repeat this procedure 10 times. Table 6 shows the mean and variance of the prediction RMSE of LPF and the baselines. The LPF model achieves the lowest prediction RMSE in this setting too. Note that the gain from adding the supervision via location category labels is more significant than article category labels. This suggests that the density of news article clicks is more strongly related to location demographics than the topic of an article.

We also visualize the joint latent space intensity, Λ, in Figure 10. The size of a square represents the relative magnitude of the intensity for an item category - location category pair. Four different colors are used to differentiate the four types of demographic information. Though the model assigns almost equal weights for all location categories, there exists strong correlation of articles in Art & Entertainment, Technology & Electronics with the top 10% populations. The consumption of the news article category shows very weak dependencies with income. However, Society & Culture and Art & Entertainment articles tend to appeal more to zip codes with middle aged people.

[4]We omit the results for NMF and MFSI as their performance was significantly worse than the other methods

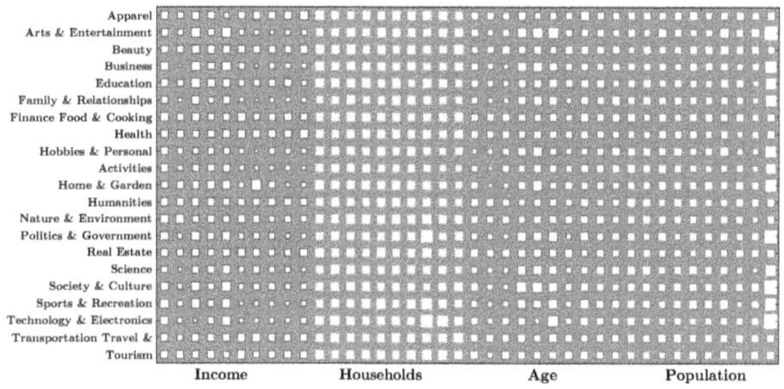

Figure 10: Hinton diagram of the joint latent space intensity on Yahoo news article data learned by LPF model. Colors correspond to different type of category tags: income, households, age and population.

6. CONCLUSIONS

In this paper, we studied the task of geographic segmentation on spatial count data, with applications in mobile application usage and news article readership. Through an exploratory analysis we found that the categories of locations, rather than the geographic coordinates, are more important in those applications. We developed a Bayesian hierarchical model, the Latent Poisson Factor (LPF) model, to capitalize on this observation and demonstrated the efficacy of LPF model at capturing rich spatial correlation structures and predicting aggregate counts on two data sets: Aviate app usage and Yahoo! news article clicks. Experiment results showed that our method can learn sensible spatial latent semantics as well as produce more accurate predictions.

7. ACKNOWLEDGMENTS

This work is supported in part by the U. S. Army Research Office under grant number W911NF-15-1-0491, NSF IIS-1254206 and USC Integrated Media System Center (IMSC). The views and conclusions are those of the authors and should not be interpreted as representing the official policies of the funding agency, or the U.S. Government.

8. REFERENCES

[1] M. Böhmer, B. Hecht, J. Schöning, A. Krüger, and G. Bauer. Falling asleep with angry birds, facebook and kindle: a large scale study on mobile application usage. In *Proceedings of the 13th International Conference on Human Computer Interaction with Mobile Devices and Services*, pages 47–56. ACM, 2011.

[2] A. T. Cemgil. Bayesian inference for nonnegative matrix factorisation models. *Computational Intelligence and Neuroscience*, 2009, 2009.

[3] M. Ester, H.-P. Kriegel, J. Sander, and X. Xu. A density-based algorithm for discovering clusters in large spatial databases with noise. In *Kdd*, volume 96, pages 226–231, 1996.

[4] P. K. Gopalan, L. Charlin, and D. Blei. Content-based recommendations with poisson factorization. In *Advances in Neural Information Processing Systems*, pages 3176–3184, 2014.

[5] L. Hong, A. Ahmed, S. Gurumurthy, A. J. Smola, and K. Tsioutsiouliklis. Discovering geographical topics in the twitter stream. In *Proceedings of the 21st international conference on World Wide Web*, pages 769–778. ACM, 2012.

[6] A. Karatzoglou, L. Baltrunas, K. Church, and M. Böhmer. Climbing the app wall: enabling mobile app discovery through context-aware recommendations. In *Proceedings of the 21st ACM international conference on Information and knowledge management*, CIKM '12, New York, NY, USA, 2012. ACM.

[7] Y. Koren, R. Bell, and C. Volinsky. Matrix factorization techniques for recommender systems. *Computer*, 42(8):30–37, 2009.

[8] J. J. Levandoski, M. Sarwat, A. Eldawy, and M. F. Mokbel. Lars: A location-aware recommender system. In *Proceedings of the 2012 IEEE 28th International Conference on Data Engineering*, ICDE '12, pages 450–461, Washington, DC, USA, 2012. IEEE Computer Society.

[9] H. J. Miller and J. Han. *Geographic data mining and knowledge discovery*. CRC Press, 2009.

[10] B. Mobasher, H. Dai, T. Luo, and M. Nakagawa. Discovery and evaluation of aggregate usage profiles for web personalization. *Data mining and knowledge discovery*, 6(1):61–82, 2002.

[11] R. T. Ng and J. Han. E cient and e ective clustering methods for spatial data mining. In *Proc. of*, pages 144–155, 1994.

[12] G.-J. Qi, C. C. Aggarwal, J. Han, and T. Huang. Mining collective intelligence in diverse groups. In *Proceedings of the 22nd international conference on World Wide Web*, pages 1041–1052. International World Wide Web Conferences Steering Committee, 2013.

[13] D. Ramage, D. Hall, R. Nallapati, and C. D. Manning. Labeled lda: A supervised topic model for credit attribution in multi-labeled corpora. In *Proceedings of the 2009 Conference on Empirical Methods in Natural Language Processing: Volume 1-Volume 1*, pages 248–256. Association for Computational Linguistics, 2009.

[14] R. Salakhutdinov and A. Mnih. Probabilistic matrix factorization. In *Advances in Neural Information Processing Systems*, volume 20, 2008.

[15] C. Shahabi, A. M. Zarkesh, J. Adibi, and V. Shah. Knowledge discovery from users Web-page navigation. In *Research Issues in Data Engineering, 1997. Proceedings. Seventh International Workshop on*, 1997.

[16] J. Shi, N. Mamoulis, D. Wu, and D. W. Cheung. Density-based place clustering in geo-social networks. In *Proceedings of the 2014 ACM SIGMOD international conference on Management of data*, pages 99–110. ACM, 2014.

[17] S. Xie, G. Wang, S. Lin, and P. S. Yu. Review spam detection via time series pattern discovery. In *Proceedings of the 21st international conference companion on World Wide Web*, pages 635–636. ACM, 2012.

[18] T. W. Yan, M. Jacobsen, H. Garcia-Molina, and U. Dayal. From user access patterns to dynamic hypertext linking. In *Proceedings of the Fifth International World Wide Web Conference on Computer Networks and ISDN Systems*, pages 1007–1014, 1996.

[19] M. Ye, D. Shou, W.-C. Lee, P. Yin, and K. Janowicz. On the semantic annotation of places in location-based social networks. In *Proceedings of the 17th ACM SIGKDD international conference on Knowledge discovery and data mining*, pages 520–528. ACM, 2011.

[20] H. Yin, B. Cui, L. Chen, Z. Hu, and C. Zhang. Modeling location-based user rating profiles for personalized recommendation. *ACM Trans. Knowl. Discov. Data*, 38, 2014.

[21] Z. Yin, L. Cao, J. Han, C. Zhai, and T. Huang. Geographical topic discovery and comparison. In *Proceedings of the 20th international conference on World wide web*, pages 247–256. ACM, 2011.

[22] Q. Yuan, G. Cong, Z. Ma, A. Sun, and N. M. Thalmann. Who, where, when and what: discover spatio-temporal topics for twitter users. In *Proceedings of the 19th ACM SIGKDD international conference on Knowledge discovery and data mining*, pages 605–613. ACM, 2013.

[23] H. Zhang, M. Korayem, E. You, and D. J. Crandall. Beyond co-occurrence: discovering and visualizing tag relationships from geo-spatial and temporal similarities. In *Proceedings of the fifth ACM international conference on Web search and data mining*, pages 33–42. ACM, 2012.

[24] M. Zhou, L. Hannah, D. Dunson, and L. Carin. Beta-negative binomial process and poisson factor analysis. *arXiv preprint arXiv:1112.3605*, 2011.

Scaling up Link Prediction with Ensembles

Liang Duan[1] Charu Aggarwal[2] Shuai Ma[1,*] Renjun Hu[1] Jinpeng Huai[1]

[1]SKLSDE Lab, Beihang University, China [2]IBM T. J. Watson Research Center, USA
{duanliang, mashuai, hurenjun, huaijp}@buaa.edu.cn charu@us.ibm.com

ABSTRACT

A network with n nodes contains O n^2 possible links. Even for networks of modest size, it is often difficult to evaluate all pairwise possibilities for links in a meaningful way. Furthermore, even though link prediction is closely related to missing value estimation problems, such as collaborative filtering, it is often difficult to use sophisticated models such as latent factor methods because of their computational complexity over very large networks. Due to this computational complexity, most known link prediction methods are designed for *evaluating* the link propensity over a *specified* subset of links, rather than for performing a global search over the entire networks. In practice, however, it is essential to perform an exhaustive search over the entire networks. In this paper, we propose an ensemble enabled approach to scaling up link prediction, which is able to decompose traditional link prediction problems into subproblems of smaller size. These subproblems are each solved with the use of latent factor models, which can be effectively implemented over networks of modest size. Furthermore, the ensemble enabled approach has several advantages in terms of performance. We show the advantage of using ensemble-based latent factor models with experiments on very large networks. Experimental results demonstrate the effectiveness and scalability of our approach.

Categories and Subject Descriptors

H.2.8 [**Database Management**]: Database Applications

Keywords

Link Prediction; Ensembles; Networks; Big Data

1. INTRODUCTION

The problem of *link prediction* or *link inference* is that of predicting the formation of future links in a dynamic and evolving network (see [7, 35, 36] for surveys). The link prediction problem has numerous applications, such as the recommendation of friends in a social network, the recommendation of images in a multimedia network, or the recommendation of collaborators in a scientific

WSDM'16, February 22–25, 2016, San Francisco, CA, USA.
© 2016 ACM. ISBN 978-1-4503-3716-8/16/02 ...$15.00.
DOI: http://dx.doi.org/10.1145/2835776.2835815.

Network Sizes	1 GHz	3 GHz	10 GHz
10^6 nodes	1000 sec.	333 sec.	100 sec.
10^7 nodes	27.8 hrs	9.3 hrs	2.78 hrs
10^8 nodes	$>$ 100 days	$>$ 35 days	$>$ 10 days
10^9 nodes	$>$ 10000 days	$>$ 3500 days	$>$ 1000 days

Table 1: The O n^2 problem in link prediction: Time required to allocate a *single machine cycle* to every node-pair possibility in networks of varying sizes and processors of various speeds.

network, and, therefore, link prediction methods have been studied extensively because of their numerous applications in various network-centered domains.

Link prediction methods are often applied to very large networks, which are also sparse. The massive sizes of such networks can create challenges for the prediction process in spite of their sparsity. This is because the *search space* for the link prediction problem is of the size O n^2 , where n is the number of nodes. Quadratic scalability can rapidly become untenable for larger networks. In fact, an often overlooked fact is that most *current link prediction algorithms evaluate the link propensities only over a subset of possibilities rather than exhaustively search for link propensities over the entire network, e.g., [23, 29].* In order to understand why this is the case, consider a network with ^{6} nodes. Note that a size such as ^{6} is not large at all by modern standards, and even common bibliographic networks such as DBLP now exceed this size. Even for this modest network, the number of *possibilities* for links is of the order of ^{12}. Therefore, a 1GHz processor would require at least ^{3} seconds just to allocate one *machine cycle* to every pair of nodes. This implies that in order to determine the top-ranked link predictions over the *entire network*, the running time will be much larger than ^{3} seconds. It is instructive, therefore, to examine how this (lower bound on) running time scales with increasing network size. Table 1 shows the time requirements for allocating a single machine cycle to each pair-wise possibility. The running times in this table represent very optimistic lower bounds on the required times because link prediction algorithms are complex and require far more than a single machine cycle for processing a node-pair. Note that for larger networks, even the presented lower bounds on the running times are impractical.

It is noteworthy that most link prediction algorithms in the literature are not designed to search over the entire space of O n^2 possibilities. A closer examination of the relevant publications shows that even for networks of modest size, these algorithms perform benchmarking only by evaluating over a *sample of the possibilities* for links. This is only to be expected in light of the lower bounds shown in Table 1. In other words, the *complete ranking problem* for link prediction in very large networks remains largely unsolved at least from a computational point of view. It is evident from the presented lower bounds in Table 1 that any ranking-based link prediction algorithm *must integrate search space pruning* within the prediction algorithm in order to even have any hope of exploring the $O\ n^2$ search space in a reasonable amount of time. The algorithmic design of most link prediction algorithms largely overlooks this basic requirement [7, 15].

The link prediction algorithms are classified into unsupervised and supervised methods. Unsupervised methods [13] typically use neighborhood measures such as the Adamic-Adar [1], and the Jaccard coefficient. Supervised methods [15] treat link prediction as a classification problem in which each node pair is treated as a test instance. Supervised methods are the state-of-the-art and generally provide more accurate results than unsupervised methods [15]. It is also noteworthy that most supervised methods evaluate link prediction algorithms by using only *a sample* of test links because of computational consideration. In real-world applications, it is often desirable to determine the *top-k* most relevant links for prediction *over all possibilities for test links*. This problem remains largely unsolved even for networks of any reasonable size.

The link prediction problem is also closely related to the missing value estimation problem, which is commonly used in collaborative filtering [3]. Just as collaborative filtering attempts to predict missing entries in a matrix of users and items, the link prediction problem attempts to predict missing entries in a node-node adjacency matrix. In fact, the missing value estimation framework seems to be a more compact and relevant model for the link prediction problem, as compared with the vanilla classification problem. Many of the modern methods for collaborative filtering use latent factor models [2, 17] such as SVD and NMF for predicting missing entries. These methods have been shown to be wildly successful at least within the domain of collaborative filtering [17]. In spite of the obvious similarity between link prediction and collaborative filtering and the obvious effectiveness of latent factor models, there are only a few methods [9] which attempt to use these models.

One of the reasons that latent factor models are rarely used in the link prediction domain is simply because of their complexity. In collaborative filtering applications, the item dimension is of the order of a few hundred thousand, whereas even the smallest networks in real-world settings contain more than a million nodes. Furthermore, collaborative filtering methods often perform the recommendation on a per-user basis rather than try to determine the top-k user-item pairs. The latter is particularly important in the context of link prediction. The factorization of a matrix of size $O\ n^2$ is not only computationally expensive, but also memory-intensive. As we will see later in this paper, one advantage of latent-factor models is that they are able to transform the adjacency matrix to a multidimensional space which can be searched efficiently *by pruning* large portions of the $O\ n^2$ search space in order to recommend the top-k possibilities. This is essential in such settings.

Contributions. In this paper, we explore an *ensemble-enabled approach* to achieving the aforementioned goals.

We show how to make latent factor models practical for link prediction by decomposing the search space into a set of smaller matrices. As a result, large parts of the $O\ n^2$ search space can be pruned without even having to evaluate the relevant node pairs. This provides an efficient approach for the top-k problem in link prediction. Furthermore, our problem decomposition method is an ensemble approach enabled with three structural bagging methods with performance guarantees, which has obvious *effectiveness* advantages. Note that the same bias-variance tradeoffs apply to the link-prediction problem, as they apply to the standard classification problem. Therefore, the use of an ensemble approach has obvious effectiveness advantages as well.

Using real-life datasets, we show that our ensemble-enabled approach for link prediction is both effective and efficient. For instance, (1) on Friendster with million nodes and billion edges, our approach could finish in an hour, while direct NMF, AA [1] and BIGCLAM [33] could not finish in a day, and (2) our approach improves the accuracy by , , (resp. , , and , ,) over direct NMF, AA and BIGCLAM on YouTube, Flickr and Wikipedia, respectively.

Organization. This paper is organized as follows. In the next section, we provide the basic framework for the approach and describe the efficient use of latent factor models for link prediction. Section 3 discusses how latent factor models can be augmented with ensembles to provide more effective and efficient results. Section 4 presents and discusses the experimental results, followed by related work in Section 5 and conclusions in Section 6.

2. LATENT FACTOR MODEL FOR SCALABLE LINK PREDICTION

We assume that $G\quad N, A$ is an undirected network containing node set N and edge set A. The node set N contains n nodes and the edge set A contains m edges. Furthermore, the $n \times n$ weight matrix $W\quad w_{ij}\ _{n \times n}$ contains the weights of the edges in A. The weight matrix is useful in representing the strengths of network connections in many real-world settings such as the number of publications between a pair of co-authors in a bibliographic network. The matrix is sparse, and many its entries are 0, which could be interpreted either as absence of links or as missing entries. While we assume that an undirected network is available, the approach can also be generalized to directed networks. The ranking problem for link prediction is formally stated as follows:

DEFINITION 1. *Given a network $G\quad N, A$ with node set N and edge set A, the ranking problem for link prediction is to determine the top-k node-pair recommendations such that these node pairs are not included in A.*

Note that this problem definition requires us to consider the entire search space of $O\ n^2$ possibilities, rather than a sample of the node pairs in the network.

Latent factor models work by associating a low dimensional factor with each row and column of the network. However, since link prediction is (predominantly) studied only for undirected networks, which have symmetric weight matrices, it suffices to associate an r-dimensional latent factor $\overline{F_i}$ with the ith node in the network. The value of r is the *rank* of the factorization. This is an issue, which we will discuss slightly later. The weight of a link between nodes i and j is defined by the use of the dot product between the factors of nodes i and j. In other words, for the weight matrix $W\quad w_{ij}\ _{n \times n}$, we would like to achieve the following:

$$w_{ij} \approx \overline{F_i} \cdot \overline{F_j}, \ \forall i, j \in \{\ , \ldots, n\}. \tag{1}$$

This condition can be directly written in matrix form. Let F be an $n \times r$ matrix, in which the ith row is the row vector $\overline{F_i}$. Then, the aforementioned condition of Equation (1) can be written as follows:

$$W \approx FF^T. \tag{2}$$

An important question arises as to whether entries in the matrix W corresponding to the absence of links should be treated as incomplete entries or whether they should be treated as zero, with the possibility of being incorrect. When latent factor models are used in collaborative filtering, such entries are typically treated as missing entries. However, unlike the absence of a rating, the absence of a link is indeed useful information *in the aggregate*, even though some node pairs have the propensity to form links *in the future*. Therefore, we argue that, unlike collaborative filtering, W should be treated as a completely specified matrix, but with noisy entries. Therefore, in the link prediction problem, latent factor models should be viewed as a way of *correcting* noisy entries with zero values, rather than strictly as a missing value estimation problem. Such assumptions also simplify the algorithmic development of latent factor models for link prediction. The idea here is that when we approximately factorize W into the form FF^T, the positive values of entries in FF^T can be viewed as the *predictions* of noisy 0-entries in W.

A second important question arises as to the choice of the latent factor model that must be used for prediction. There are many choices available for factorizing an adjacency matrix, especially when it is symmetric. Even a straightforward diagonalization of the matrix provides a reasonable factorization. We choose *non-negative* matrix factorization not only because of its interpretability advantages but also because it facilitates the $O\ n^2$ search phase of the prediction by providing a non-negative and sparse representation for each node.

We would like to determine the matrix F such that the Frobenius norm of $W - FF^T$ is minimized. This problem is referred to as symmetric NMF, and an efficient solution is proposed in [14], where F can be determined by starting with random nonnegative entries in , , and using the following multiplicative update rule:

$$F_{ij} \leftarrow F_{ij} \quad - \beta \quad \beta \frac{WF_{\ ij}}{FF^T F_{\ ij}}\ , \tag{3}$$

in which β is a constant in , [28].

Discussions. Let us examine the computational complexity of the update Equation (3). The matrix FF^TF can be fully materialized with $O\ r^2 \cdot n$ matrix multiplications, and the matrix WF can be computed in $O\ m \cdot r$ multiplications by observing that the sparse matrix W has only m non-zero entries corresponding to the number of edges. Therefore, each update takes $O\ n \cdot r^2 \quad m \cdot r$ time.

This remains quite high for large networks, which motivates us to develop fast searching techniques to speed up the process.

2.1 Efficient Top-K Prediction Searching

An advantage of the nonnegative factorization approach is that it enables an efficient search phase, which is generally not possible with most other link prediction methods. The value of $\overline{F_i} \cdot \overline{F_j}$ in Equation (1) provides a prediction value for the links. The goal of the search phase is to return the top-k links with the largest prediction values. In real-world settings, the matrix F is often nonnegative and sparse. This non-negativity and sparsity are particularly useful in enabling an efficient approach. In order to speed up the search, we define the notion of ϵ-approximate top-k predictions, denoted as top- ϵ, k predictions.

DEFINITION 2 (TOP- ϵ, k PREDICTIONS). *A set L of predicted links is a top- ϵ, k prediction, if the cardinality of L is k, and the k-th best value of $\overline{F_i} \cdot \overline{F_j}$ for a link $i, j \in L$ is at most ϵ less than the k-th best value of $\overline{F_h} \cdot \overline{F_l}$ over any link h, l in the network.*

Intuitively, this definition allows a qualitative tolerance of ϵ in the top-k returned links. Allowing such a tolerance significantly helps in speeding up the search process by pruning large portions of the search space, which is particularly important in an $O\ n^2$ search space of link predictions.

The first step is to create a new $n \times r$ matrix S, which is obtained by sorting the columns of F in a descending order. An inverted list is associated with each of the r latent variables containing the node identifiers of F arranged according to the sorted order of S. The r inverted lists can also be represented as an $n \times r$ matrix R. Let the number of rows in the p-th column of S ($p \in \ , r$), for which the value of S_{ip} is greater than $\sqrt{\epsilon/r}$ be f_p, and for which the value of S_{ip} is greater than 0 be f'_p, respectively.

Then the following nested loop is executed for each (say p-th) column of S:

> **for** each i to f_p **do**
>   **for** each j i to f'_p **do**
>   **if** $S_{ip} \cdot S_{jp} < \epsilon/r$ **then**
>   break inner loop;
>   **else** increase the score of node-pair R_{ip}, R_{jp} by
>   an amount of $S_{ip} \cdot S_{jp}$
>   **endfor**
> **endfor**

This nested loop is designed to track the relevant subset of node pairs from which one can determine the top- ϵ, k predictions. The nested loop typically requires much less time than $O\ n^2$ time because large portions of the search space are pruned. First, depending on the value of ϵ, the value of f_p is much less than n. This is particularly true if many entries of the factorized matrix F are close to 0. Furthermore, the inner loop is often terminated early. The value of ϵ therefore provides the user a way to set the trade-off between accuracy and efficiency. A hash-table is maintained which tracks all the pairs R_{ip}, R_{jp} encountered so far in the nested loop. Because of the pruning, the hash table usually needs to track a miniscule set of the $O\ n^2$ node-pairs in order to determine the ones that truly satisfy the top- ϵ, k requirement. In the process, we exclude the links which have already been represented with non-zero entries in W because such links are always likely to have the largest prediction values, which further reduces the searching space.

It remains to show that this procedure truly does find a valid set of top- ϵ, k link predictions. The reason that the procedure works correctly and efficiently is because of nonnegativity and sparsity.

PROPOSITION 1. *The nested loop method finds a valid set of top- ϵ, k predictions.*

PROOF. The main part of the proof is to show that any dot product is underestimated by at most ϵ. The aforementioned pseudocode containing the nested loop is executed r times, once for each latent component. Therefore, it suffices to show that the contribution of each nested loop is underestimated by at most ϵ/r. There are two sources of underestimation:

1. The outer loop does not consider rows i for which $S_{ip} < \sqrt{\epsilon/r}$. This effectively prunes the products between pairs i, j for which both S_{ip} and S_{jp} are less than $\sqrt{\epsilon/r}$. Therefore, the underestimation because of the ignoring of this pair is at most $\sqrt{\epsilon/r} \times \sqrt{\epsilon/r} \quad \epsilon/r$.
2. The second case is when the inner loop is terminated early. The early termination condition in this case is that the product is at most ϵ/r.

Therefore, in both these mutually exclusive cases, the underestimation is at most ϵ/r. Therefore, over all latent components the aggregate underestimation is at most $\epsilon/r \ \times r \quad \epsilon$.

This completes the proof. □

Discussions. While the basic matrix factorization method is able to allow us to provide efficiency and pruning to the search process, it is still not quite as fast as one may need for large networks. The main problem arises as a result of the factorization process itself, which can require as much as $O\ r\cdot\ m\quad n\cdot r$. Typically, the number r of latent factors varies from the orders of a few ten to a few hundred [30, 31]. For sparse networks, in which the node degree is less than r, the $O\ nr^2$ term might be the bottleneck. The required number of latent components r is often expected to increase with network size. In order to handle this computational problem, we propose the method of *ensemble decomposition*, which provides both efficiency *and* effectiveness advantages.

3. STRUCTURAL BAGGING METHODS

Since the link prediction problem scales worse than linearly with the network size, it is generally more efficient to solve smaller problems multiple times rather than solve a single large problem. The structural bagging approach provides an effective method to decompose the link prediction problem into smaller pieces that are solved independently. Furthermore, the aggregated results from multiple models often provide a robustness to the decomposition process [38]. In the following, we introduce three different ways for the bagging decomposition.

3.1 Random Node Bagging

Random node bagging is the simplest form of structural bagging. The basic idea of random node bagging is to iteratively apply the following three steps:

(1) Select a random set of nodes N_r from the graph G corresponding to a fraction f of the nodes in the network. Determine the node set $N_s \supseteq N_r$, corresponding to all nodes adjacent to N_r.

(2) Construct a reduced adjacency matrix W_s from the node set N_s by using the subgraph induced on N_s of G, referred to as an ensemble component or simply an ensemble, to select the relevant $|N_s|$ rows and columns of W.

(3) Apply the symmetric NMF method in Section 2 to the reduced matrix W_s. Use the pruning search process in Section 2.1 to determine the predictions of all pairs of nodes of N_s.

The main efficiency advantage of this approach is because of the smaller sizes of the matrices in the factorization. Furthermore, because of the smaller size of the induced subgraph in each ensemble component, the number of latent factors r, which is required, is also smaller. This will generally translate into efficiency advantages. In many cases, when the number of nodes is very large, it may be impractical to solve the entire problem in main memory. In such cases, the use of ensemble approach decomposes the problem into smaller memory-resident components.

The main problem with random node sampling is that it does not attempt to sample more *relevant* regions of the network which are more likely to contain possible links. Other forms of sampling are likely to be more effective in this context.

3.2 Edge Bagging

Edge bagging is designed to sample more *relevant* regions of the graph. After all, real-world networks are sparse and most of the $O\ n^2$ possibilities for edges are usually not populated. By sampling densely populated regions of the network, many node pairs will not be considered at all, but these node pairs are often not relevant to begin with.

The edge bagging approach proceeds as follows:

(1) Let N_s be a node set containing a single randomly chosen node. Nodes which are adjacent to N_s are randomly selected and added to N_s. In the event that no node is adjacent to N_s, a randomly chosen node from a different connected component is added to N_s. The procedure is repeated until N_s contains at least a fraction f of the total number of nodes.

(2) Construct a reduced adjacency matrix W_s from the node set N_s by using the subgraph induced on N_s of G, i.e., an ensemble, to select the relevant $|N_s|$ rows and columns of W.

(3) Apply the symmetric NMF method in Section 2 to the reduced matrix W_s. Use the pruning search process in Section 2.1 to determine the predictions of all pairs of nodes.

This method of growing the sampled node set with edge sampling is likely to select dense components from the network. Such dense components are more likely to contain random node pairs. Unlike the previous case where every node pair is considered with high probability, many node pairs will not be considered at all. However, such node pairs will typically not be present in the same dense component. Therefore, such node pairs are likely to be irrelevant, and in this way the approach already prunes unimportant node pairs during the process of ensemble construction.

3.3 Biased Edge Bagging

While the edge bagging procedure is effective at discovering dense components, it does have a drawback. Its main drawback is that it selectively includes nodes with high degrees within the resulting components. Therefore, the same high-degree nodes are very likely to be included in all the ensemble components. As a result, it often becomes more difficult to make robust predictions between low-degree nodes.

In biased edge bagging, exactly the same procedure is used as the case of edge bagging. The only difference is that when the node set N_s is grown, a random adjacent node is not selected. Rather, an adjacent node, which was selected the least number of times in previous ensemble components, is used. Ties are broken randomly.

This approach ensures that each node is selected with an approximately similar number of times across various ensemble components, and it prevents the repeated selection of high-degree nodes. Note that the bias in the edge bagging process makes that the vast majority node pairs will not be considered. However, such node pairs will usually be in components that are not as well connected. Therefore, such nodes are far less likely to form links. In most practical applications, one only needs to recommend a small number of node pairs for prediction. Therefore, it is reasonable to ignore such node pairs in the prediction process.

3.4 Using Link Prediction Characteristics

Different from existing sampling methods [32], our bagging methods should be designed in particular for link prediction. Motivated by the observation that most of all new links in social networks span within very short distances, typically closing triangles, which has been justified in [37], we develop three structural bagging approaches such that *a node is always sampled together with all its neighbors, which guarantees the possibility of forming triangles.* To achieve this, we revise the previous bagging methods as follows.

(1) For random node bagging, when a node is selected uniformly at random from the network G, the node together with all of its neighbors are put into the node set N_s.

(2) For edge and biased edge bagging, when a node adjacent to N_s is selected and added to N_s, all of its neighbors are put into the node set N_s together.

3.5 Bound of Node Bagging Ensembles

Observe that even each ensemble component is much smaller, multiple samples are required. To meaningfully rank the various node pairs, each node pair needs to be included in the ensemble components with performance guarantees. What is the required number of samples to ensure that each node pair is included at least μ times? Clearly, this number depends on the sampling fraction f. We next present a probabilistic bound on the expected number of times that a node pair is included as follows.

PROPOSITION 2. *The expected times of each node pair included in μ/f^2 ensemble components is at least μ.*

PROOF. Since each ensemble component includes a node with probability at least f, it follows that each node pair is included with probability f^2. Furthermore, all ensemble component are independent of each other. Let X be the times of each node pair is included in all ensemble components, and the expected value $E\ X$ of X is equal to $b \times f^2$, where b is the number of ensemble components. For $E\ X \ \geq \mu$, we have $b \geq \mu/f^2$. □

Note that the above bound holds only for the original random node bagging method, and it provides a theoretical guarantee. Indeed, we could do much better in practice. For instance, the setting of μ . and f . already achieves a pretty good result, as shown by our experimental study in Section 4.

3.6 Ensemble Enabled Top-K Predictions

We now explain the complete framework for top-k predictions enabled with ensembles, shown as follows.

given network $G\ N, A$ and parameters μ and f.
let Γ be empty;
repeat μ/f^2 times **do**
  let N_s be a sampled ensemble of G with at least $f \cdot n$ nodes;
  Compute $W_s \approx F_s \cdot F_s^T$ using NMF;
  let Γ' be top-k largest value node pairs i, j in $\{\overline{F_{s,i}} \cdot \overline{F_{s,j}}\}$;
  let Γ be top-k largest value node pairs i, j in $\Gamma' \cup \Gamma$;
return the top-k node pairs Γ not included in A.

To ensure that a node pair appears in the ensemble components at least μ expected times, μ/f^2 ensemble components are considered in total. For each time, an ensemble component N_s is sampled by one of the above node, edge and biased edge bagging methods, the symmetric NMF method in Section 2 is used to the reduced matrix W_s, and the aforementioned pruning search process in Section 2.1 is used to determine the predictions of all pairs of nodes. If a node pair appears in multiple ensemble components and has multiple predicted values, the maximum predicted value is considered. And, hence, only the top-k predicted links are maintained for each ensemble component. At the end of the process, the top-k predictions in all μ/f^2 ensemble components are returned.

4. EXPERIMENTAL STUDY

We next present an extensive experimental study of our ensemble-enabled approach for link prediction. Using real-life datasets, we conducted two sets of experiments to evaluate: (1) the effectiveness and efficiency of our approach vs. conventional methods AA [1] and BIGCLAM [33] and (2) the impacts of various factors.

4.1 Experimental settings

We first present our experimental settings.

Datasets. We used the following real-life network datasets, which are from the Koblenz Network Collection [1].

[1]http://konect.uni-koblenz.de/

Datasets	Date	Nodes	Edges
YouTube	2006-12-09 — 2007-02-22	1,503,841	3,691,893
	2007-02-23 — 2007-07-22	1,503,841	806,213
Flickr	2006-11-01 — 2006-11-30	1,580,291	13,341,698
	2006-12-01 — 2007-05-17	1,580,291	3,942,599
Wikipedia	2001-02-19 — 2006-10-31	1,682,759	28,100,011
	2006-11-01 — 2007-04-05	1,682,759	5,856,896

Table 2: Training and ground truth data. The data in the first time slot is the training data and the remaining is the ground truth data.

Parameters	Descriptions	Default Values
β	Coefficient in NMF update rule	0.5
$iter$	Number of iterations for NMF	50
r	Number of latent factors	10
ϵ	Tolerance of top-(ϵ, k) prediction	1
k	Number of links returned by top-(ϵ, k) prediction	1×10^5 / 1×10^6
μ	Expected appearing times of each node pair in ensemble components	0.1
f	Fraction of the number of nodes to be selected for an ensemble component	0.1
n	Number of nodes	See Table 2

Table 3: Parameters used in the experiments. Note that we set k $\times$ ^{5} for YouTube and k $\times$ ^{6} for other datasets.

(1) YouTube is a 7 month friendship network of YouTube users with , , nodes and , , undirected edges.
(2) Flickr is a 6 month friendship connections of Flickr users with , , nodes and , , directed edges.
(3) Wikipedia is a 6 year hyperlink network of the English Wikipedia with , , nodes and , , directed edges.
(4) Twitter is the follower network from Twitter with , , nodes and , , , directed edges.
(5) Friendster is the friendship network of the Friendster with , , nodes and , , , directed edges.

(1) YouTube, Flickr and Wikipedia contain timestamps of edge arrivals. For each of these datasets, the latest five month part is treated as its ground truth data for testing the accuracy, and the remaining part is treated as its training data, shown in Table 2. To test the scalability, we further generated five subnetworks with increasing sizes for each dataset, using the breadth first search started from the node with the largest degree. (2) Twitter and Friendster do not have timestamps, and are only used for the scalability test. (3) It does not make much sense to predict links for users who appear in the ground truth data, but not in the training data. Hence, we removed these users from the ground truth data. Moreover, since our link prediction methods focus on predicting links on undirected graphs, we ignored the direction of edges in the directed graphs.

Algorithms for comparison. We have carefully chosen a couple of algorithms to compare with our ensemble-enabled approach.
(1) Adamic/Adar (AA) [1]: AA is a popular neighborhood based method that produces a score for each link u, v , defined as below:

$$score\ u, v \qquad \sum_{z \in N(u) \cap N(v)} \frac{}{log|N\ z\ |},$$

where $N\ u$ is the set of neighbors of node u. Lu [35] showed that AA performs well on a range of networks because it only concerns 2-hop neighbors and reduces much of search space. Therefore, we implemented a top-k link prediction method by searching the k largest AA score links. The complexity of this method is $O\ nd^2log\ k$, where d is the average degree of networks. Another popular link prediction method is Katz [34], which is based on the ensemble of all paths. However, its complexity is $O\ n^3$,

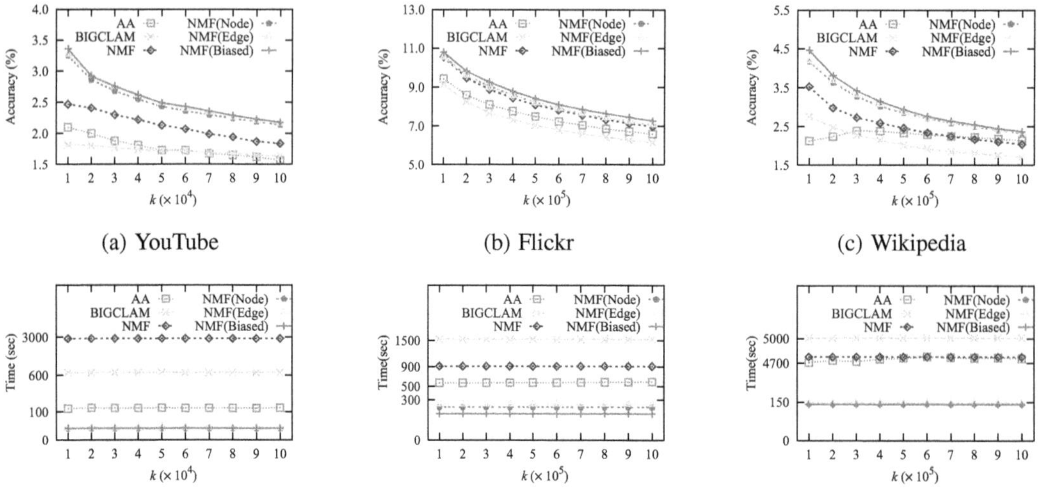

(a) YouTube (b) Flickr (c) Wikipedia

(d) YouTube (e) Flickr (f) Wikipedia

Figure 1: Accuracy and efficiency comparison: with respect to the number k of predicted links.

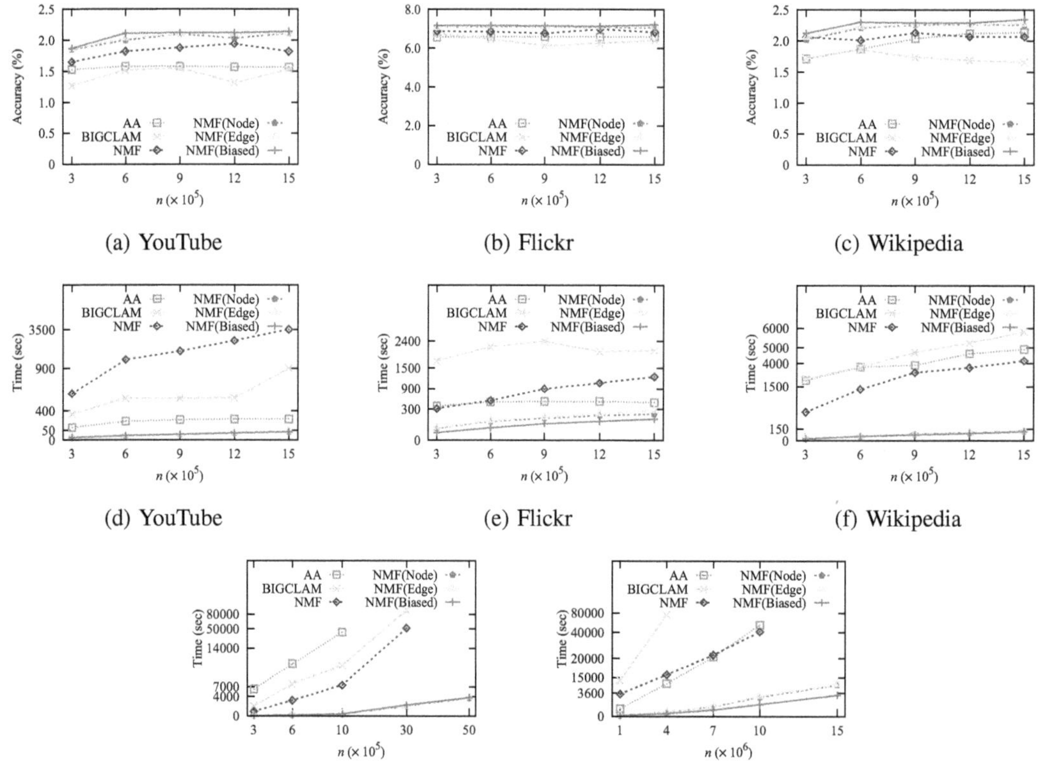

(a) YouTube (b) Flickr (c) Wikipedia

(d) YouTube (e) Flickr (f) Wikipedia

(g) Twitter (h) Friendster

Figure 2: Accuracy and efficiency comparison: with respect to the network sizes.

and does not work on large networks with millions of nodes. Thus, we did not choose Katz for comparison in the experiments.

(2) Cluster Affiliation Model for Big Networks (BIGCLAM) [33]: Yang and Leskovec developed this probabilistic generative model for networks based on community affiliations. An ingredient of BIGCLAM is based on the fact that, when people share multiple affiliations, the links between them stem for one dominant reason. This means that more communities a node pair shares, the higher the probability of the node pair being connected is. Let F be a nonnegative matrix where F_{uc} is the degree of the node u belongs to the community c. Give F, the BIGCLAM generates a graph $G\ N, A$ by creating edge u, v between a pair of nodes $u, v \in N$ with the probability

$$p\ u,v \qquad - exp\ -F_u \cdot F_v\ ,$$

where F_u is a weight vector for node u. Viewing the probability $p\ u,v$ as a score for the link u,v, it is reasonable to predict links based on BIGCLAM. The complexity of BIGCLAM is $O\ nd\ r$ d, where d is the average degree of networks. In addition, this model is not designed to search the entire space of O n^2 , and we revised it by our top-(ϵ, k) method to predict links.

Implementation. We implemented all algorithms including AA, BIGCLAM, link prediction method in Section 2 (NMF), NMF with random node bagging (NMF(Node)), NMF with edge bagging (NMF(Edge)) and NMF with biased edge bagging (NMF(Biased)) using C/C++ with no parallelization.

All experiments were conducted on a machine with 2 Intel Xeon E5–2630 2.4GHz CPUs and 64 GB of Memory, running 64 bit Windows 7 professional system. Each experiment was repeated 5 times, and the average is reported here.

4.2 Experimental Results

We next present our findings. In all the experiments, we fixed r to , , (resp. , ,) for NMF (resp. BIGCLAM) on YouTube, Flickr and Wikipedia, respectively. For three bagging methods, we fixed r by default (See Exp-2.3 for more details about the setting of r). The other parameters with their descriptions and default values are presented in Table 3.

4.2.1 *Comparison with* AA *and* BIGCLAM

In the first set of tests, we evaluated the effectiveness and efficiency of our methods compared with AA and BIGCLAM. Given one of top-k link prediction methods, denoted by x, its effectiveness of link prediction is evaluated with the following measure:

$$accuracy\ x \quad \frac{\#\text{ of correctly predicted links}}{\text{the number } k \text{ of predicted links}}.$$

Exp-1.1: Impacts of k. To evaluate the impacts of the number k of predicted links, we varied k from $\times$ ^{4} to $\times$ ^{5} on YouTube (resp. from $\times$ ^{5} to $\times$ ^{6} on Flickr and Wikipedia) and fixed other parameters to their default values. The results of accuracy and running time are reported in Figure 1(a), 1(b) and 1(c) and Figure 1(d), 1(e) and 1(f), respectively.

The accuracy results tell us that (a) NMF(Biased) outperforms other methods on all datasets, (b) three bagging methods always have higher accuracy than NMF, AA and BIGCLAM, (c) NMF is more accurate than AA and BIGCLAM, and (d) the accuracy of all methods decreases with the increment of k. Indeed, NMF(Biased) improves the accuracy by , , (resp. , , and , ,) over NMF, AA and BIGCLAM on YouTube, Flickr and Wikipedia, respectively. This verifies the effectiveness of our bagging methods.

The running time results tell us that (a) three bagging methods are much faster than NMF, AA and BIGCLAM, (b) the running time of all methods is insensitive to the increase of k, except AA whose complexity is O $nd^2 log$ k . Indeed, the three bagging methods finished the prediction in 300 seconds on the three datasets. Furthermore, NMF(Biased) is , . , (resp. . , . , and , ,) times faster than NMF, AA and BIGCLAM on YouTube, Flickr and Wikipedia, respectively. This verifies the efficiency of our bagging methods.

Note that the accuracy of all methods is not high, even the best accuracy (NMF(Biased) on Flickr when k $\times$ ^{5}) is less than . The reason is that there are more than $\times$ ^{12} possible links in the search space of each dataset, but less than $\times$ ^{7} links in the ground truth. In addition, NMF is slower than AA on three datasets because r is fixed to at least , which is consistent to the O nr^2 complexity of NMF. The running time of AA is about 100 seconds on YouTube, while more than 500 seconds on Flickr and 4700 seconds on Wikipedia. This is because that the average degree of these datasets are 5, 17 and 33, and AA takes more time with the increase of the degree of networks. The running time of BIGCLAM is also sensitive to the degree of networks because its complexity is O nd r d . As a result, it runs faster than NMF on YouTube when the degree is 5, while it takes more time on Flickr and Wikipedia when the degree is increased.

Exp-1.2: Impacts of network sizes. To evaluate the impacts of network sizes, we varied the number of nodes n from $\times$ ^{5} to . $\times$ ^{6} on YouTube, Flickr and Wikipedia (resp. from $\times$ ^{5} to $\times$ ^{6} on Twitter and from $\times$ ^{6} to . $\times$ ^{7} on Friendster). Since Twitter and Friendster do not contain ground truth for choosing the value of r, we fixed r on these datasets to the average value of its default values. Hence, on these two datasets, we fixed r for NMF (resp. r for BIGCLAM and r for bagging methods). The other parameters are fixed to their default values. The results of accuracy and running time are reported in Figure 2(a), 2(b) and 2(c) and Figure 2(d), 2(e), 2(f), 2(g) and 2(h), respectively. Note that there are *some missing plots* for NMF, AA and BIGCLAM in the Figure 2(g) and 2(h) because their running time is beyond 24 hours.

The accuracy results tell us that (a) NMF(Biased) obtains the highest accuracy on all datasets, (b) the three bagging methods perform better than NMF, AA and BIGCLAM, and (c) NMF has higher accuracy than AA and BIGCLAM. This means that our methods are accurate and robust with the increase of network sizes.

The running time results tell us that (a) bagging methods are much faster than other methods, (b) the running time of all methods increase nearly linearly with the increase of n. For instance, NMF(Biased) speeds up NMF, AA and BIGCLAM for around , , (resp. , ,) times on Twitter (resp. Friendster) and is thus essential for making our bagging methods scalable to large networks. Note that NMF is slower than BIGCLAM on YouTube but faster on other datasets because BIGCLAM requires more time with the increase of the degree of networks, which is consistent with the complexity analysis. In addition, the running time of BIGCLAM fluctuates when n between $\times$ ^{5} and . $\times$ ^{6} on YouTube and Flickr because the number of the iterations for its nonnegative matrix factorization method is not fixed.

4.2.2 *Impacts of Various Parameters*

In the second set of tests, we evaluated the impacts of parameters on the accuracy and running time of NMF, NMF(Node), NMF(Edge), NMF(Biased) and BIGCLAM. We first tested the impacts of μ and f in bagging methods. We then tested the impacts of r and ϵ.

Exp-2.1: Impacts of μ. To evaluate the impacts of μ, we varied μ from . to . and fixed other parameters to their default values. The accuracy and running time results are reported in Figure 3(a), 3(b) and 3(c) and Figure 3(d), 3(e) and 3(f), respectively. We also plotted the accuracy and running time of NMF for comparison.

The results tell us that (a) bagging methods have higher accuracy than NMF when μ is large enough, (b) the accuracy of bagging methods increases with the increment of μ and becomes stable when μ is greater than . . This means that the accuracy of bagging methods would increase and become stable with the increase of the number of ensemble components. Furthermore, (c) the running time of bagging methods increases linearly with the increase of μ since μ/f^2 ensemble components had been generated in each bagging method. Note that, when μ . , the accuracy of bagging methods is becoming stable and the running time of them is less than NMF. Therefore, we fixed μ . by default.

Exp-2.2: Impacts of f. To evaluate the impacts of f, we varied f from . to . and fixed other parameters to their default values. The accuracy and running time results are reported in Figure 4(a), 4(b) and 4(c) and Figure 4(d), 4(e) and 4(f), respectively.

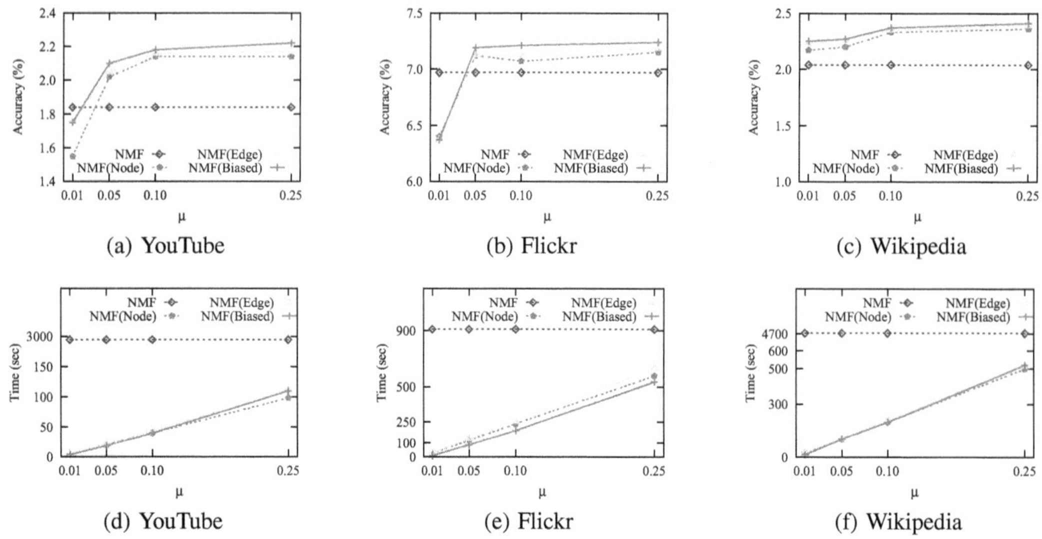

(a) YouTube (b) Flickr (c) Wikipedia

(d) YouTube (e) Flickr (f) Wikipedia

Figure 3: Accuracy and efficiency comparison: with respect to the expected appearing times μ.

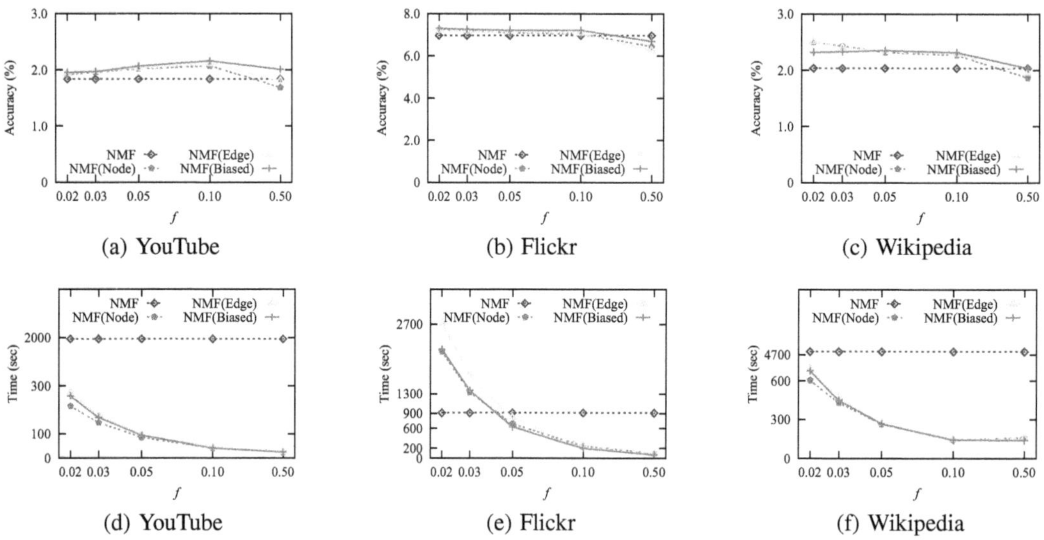

(a) YouTube (b) Flickr (c) Wikipedia

(d) YouTube (e) Flickr (f) Wikipedia

Figure 4: Accuracy and efficiency comparison: with respect to the fraction f

The results tell us that (a) bagging methods have higher accuracy than NMF when f between 0.02 and 0.1, (b) the accuracy of bagging methods decreases with the increase of f, and (c) the running time of bagging methods increases nearly linearly with the decrease of f. Note that the complexity of bagging methods is $O\ \ n_1r^2\ \ \ n_1d_1r\ \ *\mu/f^2$, where $n_1\ \ \ \ nf$ and d_1 is the average degree of each ensemble component. Since bagging methods are likely to select dense components, d_1 may be greater than r and the complexity is $O\ \ nd_1r\mu/f$. Thus, the running time of bagging methods increases with the decrease of f. Keeping the accuracy of bagging methods better than that of NMF, we fixed f . by default to achieve a better efficiency.

Exp-2.3: Impacts of r. To evaluate the impacts of r, we varied r from to and fixed other parameters to their default values. The accuracy and running time results are reported in Figure 5(a), 5(b) and 5(c) and Figure 5(d), 5(e) and 5(f), respectively.

The results tell us that (a) NMF(Biased) obtains the best accuracy compared with other methods, (b) bagging methods have higher accuracy than NMF and BIGCLAM, (c) the accuracy of NMF increases slightly with the increase of r and is always greater than that of BIGCLAM, and (d) the running time of NMF is increased quadratically with the increase of r since its complexity is $O\ \ nr^2$. A similar trend of running time is also found for bagging methods. To obtain the highest accuracy, we fixed r to , , (resp. , ,) for NMF (resp. BIGCLAM) on YouTube, Flickr and Wikipedia, respectively. Note that, when r , the accuracy of bagging methods is greater than the best accuracy of NMF. Hence, we fixed r by default for bagging methods.

Exp-2.4: Impacts of ϵ. To evaluate the impacts of ϵ, we varied ϵ from . to . and fixed other parameters to their default values. The accuracy and running time results are reported in Figure 6(a), 6(b) and 6(c) and Figure 6(d), 6(e) and 6(f), respectively.

The results tell us that (a) the accuracy of all methods is stable with the increase of ϵ, which means that the accuracy of our methods is insensitive to ϵ, and (b) the running time of all methods is decreased with the increase of ϵ because the larger ϵ reduces more search space. Thus, our top-(ϵ, k) method is reasonable for link prediction. Since the accuracy is insensitive to ϵ, we fixed ϵ by default to achieve a better efficiency.

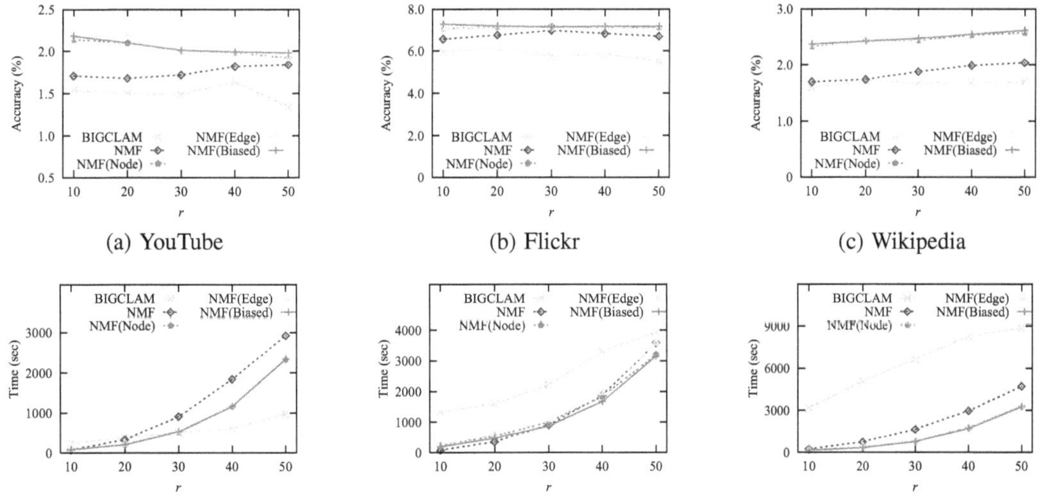

(a) YouTube (b) Flickr (c) Wikipedia

(d) YouTube (e) Flickr (f) Wikipedia

Figure 5: Accuracy and efficiency comparison: with respect to the number r of latent factors.

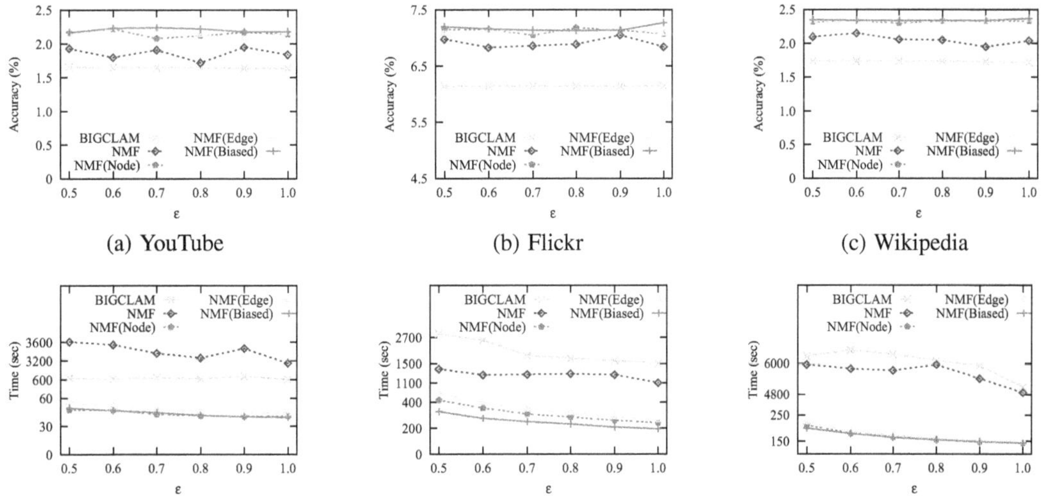

(a) YouTube (b) Flickr (c) Wikipedia

(d) YouTube (e) Flickr (f) Wikipedia

Figure 6: Accuracy and efficiency comparison: with respect to the tolerance ϵ of top-(ϵ, k) prediction.

Summary. From these experimental results on real-life social network datasets, we find the following. (1) NMF is able to predict links and can be sped up by the top-(ϵ, k) process to explore the $O\ n^2$ search space. It is more accurate than AA and BIGCLAM, which verifies the effectiveness of NMF. Moreover, NMF runs faster than BIGCLAM on dense networks, e.g., Flickr and Wikipedia, which is consistent with the complexity analysis that BIGCLAM is sensitive to the degree of networks. (2) However, the running time of NMF is increased quadratically with the increase of r. This might be a bottleneck for large networks. By decomposing the link prediction problem into smaller pieces and solving them independently, our bagging methods are more efficient and scale well with the size and density of large networks, e.g., NMF(Biased) finished in an hour on Friendster with . × ^{7} nodes and . × ^{9} edges, while NMF, AA and BIGCLAM could not finish in a day. Further, NMF(Biased) speeds up NMF, AA and BIGCLAM for around , , (resp. , ,) times on Twitter (resp. Friendster). (3) Combining link prediction characteristics, our bagging methods also provide the accuracy advantages for link prediction, e.g., NMF(Biased) is faster than the other methods, and improves the accuracy by , , (resp. , , and , ,) over NMF, AA and BIGCLAM on YouTube, Flickr and Wikipedia, respectively.

5. RELATED WORK

The link prediction problem has been studied extensively in the data mining and machine learning community [13, 35], which falls into unsupervised and supervised methods [15]. Unsupervised methods often assign scores to potential links based on the topology of the given graphs: (a) Adamic/Adar [1] is a common neighbor based method; (b) Katz [34] is a path based method which sums over all paths between two nodes, and there are also other path based methods, such as Local Path and Random Walk with Restart [35]; And (c) [12, 13] investigates the low rank approximation methods by generating a small rank matrix to approximate the initial adjacency matrix. Supervised methods [8, 15, 16] typically treat link prediction as a classification problem, e.g., supervised matrix factorization and random walk based approaches [5, 9]

Recently, several models for link prediction have been proposed, such as community affiliation models [25,33], stochastic topic models [39], negative link prediction models [40], statistical relational models [6, 10, 11, 22, 26] and Markov models [27]. Moreover, link prediction has also been studied for mining missing hyperlinks [4,41]. While some recent work has focused on the heterogeneous [18–21,24] and temporal [5,23] scenarios, these methods are not essentially designed to search the entire space of $O\ n^2$ possibilities. Indeed, they are often not able to prune the search space of possibilities, and are mostly designed to evaluate the link prediction propensities of a subset of node pairs.

Our method is related to NMF proposed in [30], which has been successfully used for collaborative filtering [17]. Since the adjacency matrix in our approach is symmetric, we adopt the symmetric NMF method [28]. Our work is also related to bagging predictor [38] that generates an aggregated predictor based on multiple bootstrap samples. Different from the bootstrap sampling methods, we focus on sampling subgraphs from large networks. Although a variety of graph sampling techniques were introduced in [32], our approach combines link prediction characteristics [37] with graph sampling methods to achieve high link prediction accuracy.

6. CONCLUSIONS AND FUTURE WORK

We have proposed an ensemble-enabled approach for top-k link prediction, which scales up link prediction on very large social networks. By decomposing a large network into smaller pieces, the bagging methods are more scalable to large networks with over 15 million nodes and 1 billion edges. We develop three bagging methods that are designed in particular for link prediction, and our bagging methods also provide better accuracy and scalability. Finally, we have experimentally verified that our ensemble-enabled approach is much more accurate and scalable than existing methods AA [1] and BIGCLAM [33].

A couple of topics need further investigation. First, we are to develop distributed approaches scalable on networks with billions of nodes, in a way similar to [31]. Second, we are to study personalized recommendations using our link prediction approach.

Acknowledgments. This work is supported in part by 973 program (No. 2014CB340300), NSFC (No. 61322207) and Special Funds of Beijing Municipal Science & Technology Commission. For any correspondence, please refer to Shuai Ma.

7. REFERENCES

[1] L. Adamic and E. Adar. Friends and neighbors on the web. *Social Networks*, 25, pp. 211–230, 2001.

[2] C. Aggarwal and S. Parthasarathy. Mining massively incomplete data sets by conceptual reconstruction. *KDD*, 2001.

[3] G. Adomavicius, and A. Tuzhilin. Toward the next generation of recommender systems: A survey of the state-of-the-art and possible extensions. *IEEE Transactions on Knowledge and Data Engineering (TKDE)*, 17(6), pp. 734–749, 2005.

[4] S. F. Adafre and M. Rijke. Discovering missing links in Wikipedia. *KDD Workshop on Link Discovery*, 2005.

[5] L. Backstrom, and J. Leskovec. Supervised random walks: predicting and recommending links in social networks. *WSDM*, 2011.

[6] M. Bilgic, G. Namata and L. Getoor. Combining collective classification and link prediction. *ICDM Workshop on Mining Graphs and Complex Structures*, 2007.

[7] L. Getoor and C. Diehl. Link mining: A survey. *SIGKDD Exploration*, pp. 3–12, 2005.

[8] J. R. Doppa, J. Yu, P. Tadepalli and L. Getoor. Chance constrained programs for link prediction. *NIPS Workshop on Analyzing Networks and Learning with Graphs*, 2009.

[9] A. K. Menon, and C. Elkan. Link prediction via matrix factorization. *Machine Learning and Knowledge Discovery in Databases*, pp. 437–452, 2011.

[10] L. Getoor, N. Friedman, D. Koller and B. Taskar. Learning probabilistic models of relational structure. *ICML*, 2001.

[11] L. Getoor, N. Friedman, D. Koller and B. Taskar. Learning probabilistic models of link structure. *Journal of Machine Learning Research*, 3, pp. 679–707, 2002.

[12] J. Kunegis and A. Lommatzsch. Learning Spectral Graph Transformations for Link Prediction. *ICML*, 2009.

[13] D. Liben-Nowell and J. Kleinberg. The link prediction problem for social networks. *Journal of the American society for information science and technology*, 58(7), pp. 1019–1031, 2007.

[14] B. Long, Z. Zhang, and P. Yu. Co-clustering by block value decomposition. *KDD*, 2005.

[15] R. Lichtenwalter, J. Lussier, and N. Chawla. New perspectives and methods in link prediction. *KDD*, 2010.

[16] R. Lichenwater and N. Chawla. Vertex Collocation Profiles: Subgraph Counting for Link Analysis and Prediction. *WWW*, 2012.

[17] B. Liu. Web Data Mining. *Springer*, 2010.

[18] G. Qi, C. Aggarwal, and T. Huang. Link Prediction across Networks by Cross-Network Biased Sampling. *ICDE*, 2013.

[19] Y. Sun, R. Barber, M. Gupta, C. Aggarwal, J. Han. Co-author Relationship Prediction in Heterogeneous Bibliographic Networks. *ASONAM*, 2011.

[20] Y. Sun, J. Han, C. Aggarwal, N. Chawla. When will it happen – Relationship Prediction in Heterogeneous Information Networks. *WSDM*, 2012.

[21] J. Tang, T. Lou, and J. Kleinberg. Inferring social ties across heterogenous networks. *WSDM*, 2012.

[22] B. Taskar, M. F. Wong, P. Abbeel and D. Koller. Link prediction in relational data. *NIPS*, 2003.

[23] D. Wang, D. Pedreschi, C. Song, F. Giannotti, and A.-L. Barabasi. Human mobility, social ties, and link prediction. *KDD*, 2011.

[24] Y. Yang, N. Chawla, Y. Sun, and J. Han. Predicting Links in Multi-Relational and Heterogeneous Networks. *ICDM*, 2012.

[25] T. Yang, R. Jin, Y. Chi, and S. Zhu. Combining link and content for community detection: a discriminative approach. *KDD*, 2009.

[26] K. Yu, W. Chu, S. Yu, V. Tresp and Z. Xu. Stochastic relational models for discriminative link prediction. *NIPS*, 2006.

[27] J. Zhu, J. Hong and G. Hughes. Using Markov models for web site link prediction. *HyperText*, 2002.

[28] C. Ding, X. He and H. D. Simon. On the Equivalence of Nonnegative Matrix Factorization and Spectral Clustering. *SDM*, 2005.

[29] C. Lee, M. Pham, N. Kim, M. K. Jeong, D. K. J. Lin and W. Art. A Novel Link Prediction Approach for Scale-free Networks. *WWW*, 2014.

[30] Lee, Daniel D. and Seung, H. Sebastian. Learning the parts of objects by non-negative matrix factorization. *Nature*, 401, pp. 788–791, 1999.

[31] Chao Liu, Hung-chih Yang, Jinliang Fan, Li-Wei He and Yi-Min Wang. Distributed Nonnegative Matrix Factorization for Web-Scale Dyadic Data Analysis on MapReduce. *WWW*, 2010.

[32] Ahmed, Nesreen K. and Neville, Jennifer and Kompella, Ramana. Network Sampling: From Static to Streaming Graphs. *Transactions on Knowledge Discovery from Data (TKDD)*, 8(2), pp. 7:1–7:56 2014.

[33] Jaewon Yang and Jure Leskovec. Overlapping Community Detection at Scale: A Nonnegative Matrix Factorization Approach. *WSDM*, 2013.

[34] L. Katz. A New Status Index Derived from Sociometric Analysis. *Psychometrika*, 18(1), pp. 39–43, 1953.

[35] Linyuan Lu and Tao Zhou. Link Prediction in Complex Networks: A Survey. *Physica A*, pp. 1150–1170, 2011.

[36] Mohammad Al Hasan and Mohammed J. Zaki. A survey of link prediction in social networks. *Social Network Data Analytics*, 2011.

[37] J. Leskovec, L. Backstrom, R. Kumar and A. Tomkins. Microscopic Evolution of Social Networks. *KDD*, 2008.

[38] Leo Breiman. Bagging Predictors. *Machine Learning*, 24(2), pp. 123–140, 1996.

[39] N. Barbieri, F. Bonchi and G. Manco. Who to Follow and Why: Link Prediction with Explanations. *KDD*, 2014.

[40] J. Tang, S. Chang, C. Aggarwal and H. Liu. Negative Link Prediction in Social Media. *WSDM*, 2015.

[41] R. West, A. Paranjape and J. Leskovec. Mining Missing Hyperlinks from Human Navigation Traces: A Case Study of Wikipedia. *WWW*, 2015.

DiFacto — Distributed Factorization Machines

Mu Li
Computer Science, Carnegie Mellon University
Marianas Labs Inc., Pittsburgh, PA
muli@cs.cmu.edu

Ziqi Liu
MOEKLINNS Lab, Computer Science
Xi'an Jiaotong University, Xi'an, China
ziqilau@gmail.com

Alexander J. Smola
Machine Learning, Carnegie Mellon University
Marianas Labs Inc., Pittsburgh, PA
alex@smola.org

Yu-Xiang Wang
Machine Learning Department
Carnegie Mellon University, Pittsburgh, PA
yuxiangw@cs.cmu.edu

ABSTRACT

Factorization Machines offer good performance and useful embeddings of data. However, they are costly to scale to large amounts of data and large numbers of features. In this paper we describe DiFacto, which uses a refined Factorization Machine model with *sparse memory adaptive constraints* and *frequency adaptive regularization.* We show how to distribute DiFacto over multiple machines using the Parameter Server framework by computing distributed subgradients on minibatches *asynchronously*. We analyze its convergence and demonstrate its efficiency in computational advertising datasets with billions examples and features.

1. INTRODUCTION

Nonlinear models for recommendation and estimation have experienced significant interest in recent years. The growing body in deep learning [3], kernels [7], and decision trees [22] bears witness of this development. For recommender systems and polynomial generalized linear models Factorization Machines (FM) [15, 16] offer a computationally efficient and powerful alternative. They achieve excellent results by using a low-rank expansion of the higher degree polynomial terms. Moreover, they offer a principled framework for a number of feature space heuristics in recommender systems, such as bias, features, cold-start strategies, and temporal models. This makes them a very attractive target for statistical modeling of high-dimensional sparse data occurring in many settings such as computational advertising, personalization, user profiling, recommendation, and search.

Unfortunately, despite low-rank expansions the memory cost remains tremendous for real-world settings. This occurs since each feature, each user, and each object need to be embedded into a low-dimensional space. A quick calculation shows that even on modest datasets such as Criteo's CTR estimation contest [6] we have up to 10^9 features. Realistic problems can have up to 10^{11} terms [8]. Even a modest 100 dimensional representation would require in the order of 1TB of data (parameters, preconditioners, auxiliary key storage). Even worse, the latter may be too simplistic for frequently occurring attributes. This makes the problem unsolvable on a single machine, when tackling industrial scale problems. Moreover, even multiple machines are heavily taxed by the large memory footprint. In order to address the above problems, we need:

1. A compact model with low computation and communication cost that nonetheless offers high-quality embeddings of the features.
2. An efficient mechanism for distributed optimization. This includes problem partitioning, optimization, and high performance communications protocols.

One key observation we made is that the importance of features in real datasets is not uniform, which deserves adaptive model capacities. In this paper, we propose a refined FM model, called DiFacto, which adaptively chooses the effective embedding dimension and regularization for each feature according to the importance, which is based on the feature frequency count and sparse regularization. The resulted model is up to 100x more compact than conventional FM and even provides better generalization accuracy.

We propose a fast distributed optimization algorithm based on the asynchronous stochastic gradient descent, with explicit modeling of the possibly non-uniform sparsity patterns in the training data and guarantee of satisfied sparse models. We prove that the proposed algorithm converges for this highly challenging nonconvex objective function even under asynchronous updates.

We describe a *Di*stributed *Facto*rization code (DiFacto) based on the Parameter Server framework [8, 17]. Experiments show that DiFacto scales to sparse data with billions of examples and features. To the best of our knowledge, our results describe one of the largest statistical model ever computed (using up to $1.2 \cdot 10^{11}$ features) over [1] by at least one order of magnitude. Our algorithms require only modest resources on a per-machine basis.

Outline. In section 2 we begin with an overview of Factorization Machines and of the Parameter Server framework. This is followed in Section 3 by a description of the statistical model employed in this paper, since it differs in a number of key parts from a simple Factorization Machine. Section 4 has details on the distributed optimization and convergence aspects of the problem. Experimental results are provided in Section 5. We conclude with a summary and discussion.

WSDM'16, February 22–25, 2016, San Francisco, CA, USA.

ISBN 978-1-4503-3716-8/16/02...$15.00
DOI: http://dx.doi.org/10.1145/2835776.2835781

2. BACKGROUND

2.1 Objectives

In this paper we address two related goals — recommendation and prediction. The distinction between those problems is partly due to different notation conventions, and partly due to slightly different objectives. In recommender systems [2] one is typically given *pairs* of entities, say users u and movies m for which a rating $y(u, m)$ needs to be estimated. The quality of an estimate $f(u, m)$ is evaluated, e.g. by the squared discrepancy between rating and estimate $\frac{1}{2}(y(u, m) - f(u, m))^2$, or by the quality of the relative ordering of ratings, or by per-session ordering of preferences. For an exhaustive summary of different such objectives see e.g. [13]. In short, we are interested in the performance of $f(u, m)$ relative to $y(u, m)$. Whenever we have additional features z_u, z_m regarding u and m respectively and context c, they form part of the estimate via $f(u, z_u, m, z_m, c)$. In the following we use the shorthand

$$x := (u, z_u, m, z_m, c) \text{ and } f(x) := f(u, z_u, m, z_m, c) \quad (1)$$

to indicate that we are interested in obtaining a *function* that consumes x as an argument to generate $f(x)$.

In prediction we are interested in the slightly more mundane goal of obtaining $f(x)$, given pairs of *features* x and *labels* y. Typical goals are to minimize the squared deviation $\frac{1}{2}(y - f(x))^2$ or the log-likelihood of a particular label $\log(1 + e^{-yf(x)})$. Note that y and $f(x)$ need not be of the same datatype. This was exploited substantially in structured estimation [19].

In the following we will not make major distinctions between both problems above. Instead, we will simply assume that x is either a set of covariates, such as the words occurring in a document for which the click through rate (CTR) of an advertisement is sought, or a set of recommendation and rating parameters. The quality will be evaluated via a loss function $l(x, y, f(x))$, yielding the risk functional

$$R[f, X, Y] := \frac{1}{|X|} \sum_{(x_i, y_i) \in (X, Y)} l(x_i, y_i, f(x_i)). \quad (2)$$

It is our goal to find some f such that, given a training set $X_{\text{train}}, Y_{\text{train}}$, the expected risk (or the risk on an unseen test set) is minimized.

2.2 Factorization Machine

The typical setting in our context is that of a very high d-dimensional (and sparse) $x \in \mathbb{R}^d$. For instance, in recommender systems x might only contain two nonzero terms — an indicator for the user, and one for the movie respectively, i.e. $x_u = 1$ and $x_m = 1$. The consequence is that linear models are of limited use. For instance, in a recommender system this would amount to

$$f(x) = \langle w, x \rangle = w_u + w_m. \quad (3)$$

This is the trivial model where recommendations are simply the sum of user and movie biases. Nonetheless, in CTR estimation problems [12], such assumptions are quite popular, due to the very high dimensionality of the model and the associated uncertainty in determining even just linear parameters. In particular, even a quadratic model is too expensive to estimate, since this would require $O(d^2)$ rather than $O(d)$ parameters. This is invariably too large since typically the number of observations $n \ll d^2$.

Rendle et al. [15, 16] introduced a principled strategy for alleviating this problem via a low-rank expansion instead of a general high-dimensional expansion. They propose

$$f(x) = \langle w, x \rangle + \sum_{i<j} x_i x_j \operatorname{tr}\left(V_i^{(2)} \otimes V_j^{(2)}\right) + \quad (4)$$

$$\sum_{i<j<k} x_i x_j x_k \operatorname{tr}\left(V_i^{(3)} \otimes V_j^{(3)} \otimes V_k\right) + \ldots$$

In other words, FM use a low-dimensional embedding of the (typically very sparse set of) features in x to a much smaller k_i-dimensional space via the embedding matrices $V^{(i)} \in \mathbb{R}^{d \times k_i}$. For the purpose of the current paper we limit ourselves to expansions up to second order (this is not a technical limitation of our algorithm but a mere convenience). This simplifies the exposition and it is sufficient, given the sparsity of the problem as we will discuss subsequently. Hence we may rewrite (4) via

$$f(x) = \langle w, x \rangle + \frac{1}{2} \|Vx\|_2^2 - \sum_{i=1}^{d} x_i^2 \|V_i\|_2^2 \quad (5)$$

Here we used the shorthand $V := V^{(2)}$ and $k_2 = k$, the polarization equality to rewrite the ordered sum, and the fact that $\operatorname{tr}(a \otimes b) = \langle a, b \rangle$. Moreover, V_i is the i-th column in V. Note also that (5) can be computed efficiently in $O(dk)$ time, requiring $O(dk)$ storage. This also illustrates a shortcoming of Factorization Machines.

Lemma 1 *Assume that we estimate (5) with an embedding dimension rank k. Then for features i for which $x_i \neq 0$ for less than $k + 1$ times, the problem of estimating (w_i, V_i) is underdetermined.*

PROOF. This follows directly from linear algebra: whenever $x_i = 0$ the terms v_i, V_i do not occur in (5). To solve a linear system of $k + 1$ variables we need at least the same number of constraints. □

Even worse, we need to store $O(k)$ memory even for variables that hardly ever occur. Given the power-law nature of many natural feature distributions, this is clearly undesirable. Lastly, large numbers of variables are not just hard to estimate and hard to store, they are also cumbersome in terms of optimization purposes, since they slow down convergence and need to be addressed, e.g. via additional stabilizers (regularization).

However, even in those cases the problem size remains formidable and we need tools for distributed inference: quite often the number of parameters significantly exceeds the amount of available memory on a computer. This calls for distributed *representations* and *optimization algorithms*.

2.3 Parameter Server

The underlying computational engine for the algorithm is the Parameter Server [8, 17]. In it, computation is performed by two separate groups of computers — workers and servers. The servers act as a generalized version of a (key,value) store which manages and updates the model parameters, while the workers process the training data that has been sharded (typically at random). The diagram below illustrates the machine layout.

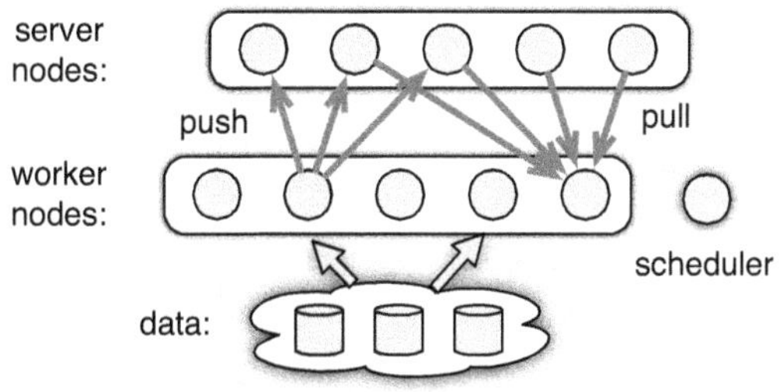

Task schedulers and resource manager allow for a controlled data flow. Moreover, they manage fault tolerance, e.g. to cope with failure of individual nodes. The pertinent aspects of this setup are that each one of the workers processes a distinct (random) block of data. w and V are stored in a distributed fashion on the server. Retrieval and updates are achieved by the following two operations:

push(key, value) sends a vector of (key, value) pairs in combination to the recipient (e.g. a group of servers holding parts of the data). To be more specific — in a distributed gradient update procedure, the workers might send the locally computed gradients to the servers. Due to the data sparsity, only a part of the gradients is nonzero, denoted by $(g_{i_1}, \ldots, g_{i_n})$ and $n \ll d$. Often it is desirable to present the gradients as a list of (key, value) pairs, namely $\{(i_j, g_{i_j})\}_{j=1}^{n}$, where the feature index is the key and the according gradient item is the value.

pull(key) requests the values associated with a list of keys. This is particularly useful whenever the amount of memory available is insufficient to hold a full model. Instead, workers prefetch the model entries relevant for solving the model only when needed.

The parameter server provides flexible data consistency model via a dependency graph (a DAG). It allows for a many algorithms ranging from bulk-synchronous processing to fully asynchronous algorithms and sketching services. See e.g. [8] for details on a range of related strategies. It also supports various filters to reduce the data communication costs. For the purpose of the present paper we ignore detailed systems considerations and focus mostly on the algorithm, the statistical model, and its application to a number of datasets.

3. STATISTICAL MODEL

3.1 Memory Adaptive Constraints

The first step in making factorization machines tractable is to modify (4) in line with Lemma 1. That is, whenever we have insufficient evidence of a feature occurring, it makes no sense to allocate much capacity to it. More to the point, instead of allocating a *fixed* number of dimensions k to *each* feature i, regardless of how frequently the i-th feature of example x, denoted by x_i, not equal to 0, we make this number dependent on n_i, the number of times $x_i \neq 0$ on the training set, i.e. more formally

$$n_i := |\{x : x_i \neq 0\}| . \quad (6)$$

Given a set of dimensionalities $\{k_i\}$ we modify the mapping $x_i \to x_i V_i$ such as to require that $V_{ij} = 0$ for all $j > k_i$. This forces infrequently occurring features to assume a rather lower-dimensional embedding using only k_i dimensions rather than the full set $k > k_i$, e.g. via

$$k_i = \begin{cases} k & \text{if } n_i > r \\ 0 & \text{otherwise} \end{cases} \quad (7)$$

where the threshold r could be simply $r = k$. This would effectively allow only for sufficiently frequent terms to be considered in the Factorization Machine embedding. We can also allocate small embeddings for these infrequent features:

$$k_i = \begin{cases} k & \text{if } n_i > r \\ \min(n_i, k) & \text{otherwise} \end{cases} \quad (8)$$

More refined choices use more than one level, e.g.

$$k_i = \begin{cases} k^{(1)} & \text{if } n_i > r^{(1)} \\ k^{(2)} & \text{if } r^{(1)} \geq n_i > r^{(2)} \\ 0 & \text{otherwise} \end{cases} \quad (9)$$

For instance set $k^{(1)} = r^{(1)} = 1000$ and $k^{(2)} = r^{(2)} = 100$, yielding a larger embedding for the most frequent keys.

3.2 Sparse Regularization

While the above strategy of variable elimination is entirely independent of the actual problem we solve, we also need a data adaptive capacity control mechanism that depends on the predictive power of features relative to the labels y_i. A popular choice is ℓ_1 regularization [20], which has been widely used in linear models for high dimensional data such as computational advertising [12]. We pick the penalty

$$\Omega[w] := \lambda_1 \|w\|_1$$

Here λ_1 controls the degree of sparsity. The sparse model induced by the ℓ_1 regularization not only penalizes complex model, it also reduces the computation cost of the gradient and saves the communication traffic. It results in a smaller final model which further makes deploying this model on an online service easier.

We can also apply a similar structured sparsity [14] on V to obtain sparse solution, such as

$$\Omega[w, V] = \sum_i \left[w_i^2 + \|V_i\|_2^2\right]^{\frac{1}{2}} + \|V_i\|_2 \quad (10)$$

Recall that in this case the derivative of the penalty vanishes at $w_i = 0$, provided that $V_i \neq 0$. Unfortunately, this penalty is harder to handle from the system perspective. Hence we replace it by a rather straightforward approximation that *directly* implements what (10) aims to accomplish — we require that $V_i = 0$ whenever $w_i = 0$. As experiments show, this is by no means detrimental to the overall outcome of the estimation. This also resembles most closely the ANOVA decomposition hierarchy proposed e.g. by [21].

3.3 Frequency Adaptive Regularization

It is well known that penalizing terms occurring at different frequency adaptively can lead to improved generalization performance [18]. For instance, in collaborative filtering the strategy to penalize frequent terms *more aggressively*, e.g. by performing shrinkage only whenever a user (or a movie) is being updated, has proven successful.

In DiFacto we use a slightly more general and flexible method for capacity control — to shrink only whenever an feature occurs in a minibatch. The consequence of this is that parameters associated with frequent features are less overregularized. The penalty can be presented as

$$\Omega[w, V] = \frac{1}{2} \sum_i \left[\lambda_i w_i^2 + \mu_i \|V_i\|_2^2\right] \text{ with } \lambda_i \propto \mu_i. \quad (11)$$

As we shall see, this approach can be implemented extremely conveniently, simply by adjusting the minibatch size.

Lemma 2 (Dynamic Regularization) *Assume that we solve a factorization machines problem with the following updates in a minibatch update setting: for each feature i,*

$$I_i \longleftarrow I\{[x_j]_i \neq 0 \text{ for some } (x_j, y_j) \in B\} \quad (12)$$

$$w_i \longleftarrow w_i - \frac{\eta_t}{b} \sum_{(x_j,y_j)\in B} \partial_{w_i} l(f(x_j), y_j) - \eta_t \lambda w_i I_i \quad (13)$$

$$V_i \longleftarrow V_i - \frac{\eta_t}{b} \sum_{(x_j,y_j)\in B} \partial_{V_i} l(f(x_j), y_j) - \eta_t \mu V_i I_i \quad (14)$$

Here B denotes the minibatch and b the according size, and I_i denotes whether or not feature i appears in this minibatch. Then effective regularization is given by

$$\lambda_i = \lambda\rho_i \text{ and } \mu_i = \mu\rho_i \text{ where } \rho_i = 1 - (1 - n_i/m)^b \approx \frac{n_i b}{m}$$

PROOF. The probability that a particular feature occurs in a random minibatch is $\rho_i = 1 - (1 - n_i/m)^b$. Observe that while the amount of regularization on the minibatches is not independent, it is additive (and exchangeable). Hence the expected amount of regularizations are $\rho_i\lambda$ and $\rho_i\mu$, respectively. Expanding the Taylor series in ρ_i yields the approximation. □

Note that for $b = 1$ we obtain the conventional frequency dependent regularization, whereas in the batch setting $b = m$ we obtain the Frobenius regularization. That is, choosing the minibatch size conveniently allows us to interpolate between both extremes efficiently.

3.4 Putting All Things Together

We obtain the following model and optimization problem:

$$\underset{w,V}{\text{minimize}} \ \frac{1}{|X|} \sum_{(x,y)} l(f(x), y) + \lambda_1 \|w\|_1 + \frac{1}{2} \sum_i \left[\lambda_i w_i^2 + \mu_i \|V_i\|_2^2\right] \quad (15)$$

$$\text{subject to } V_{ij} = 0 \text{ for } j > k_i$$

where the choice of constants λ_1, λ_i, μ_i and k_i are as discussed above. This model differs in two key parts from standard FM models: We add frequency adaptive regularization to better model the possible nonuniform sparsity pattern in the data. Secondly, we use sparsity regularization and memory adaptive constraints to control the model size, which benefits both the statistical model and system performance.

4. DISTRIBUTED OPTIMIZATION

Minimizing (15) is challenging since the potentially large model brings large communication cost. We focus on asynchronous optimization, which hides synchronization cost by communicating and computing in parallel. It has been shown that asynchronous block subspace descent can effectively solve nonconvex objective functions with a nonsmooth ℓ_1 regularizer [9]. However, it requires expensive data preprocessing. In this paper, we consider asynchronous stochastic gradient descent (SGD) [9] for optimization.

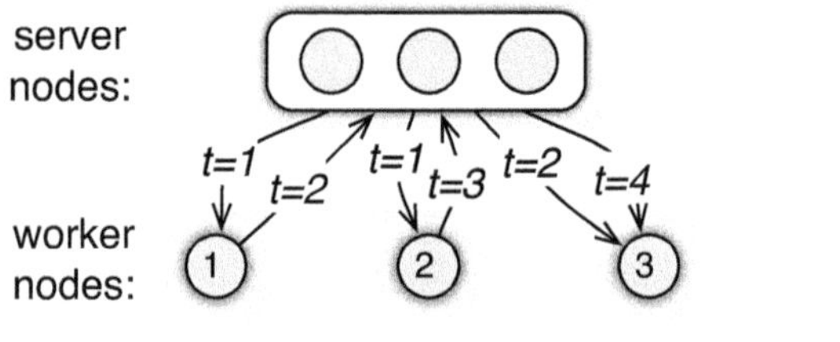

Figure 1: An illustration of asynchronous SGD. Workers W_1 and W_2 first pull weights from the servers at time 1. Next W_1 pushes the gradient back and therefore increase the timestamp at the servers. Worker W_3 pulls the weight immediately after that. Then W_2 and W_3 push the gradient back. The delays for W_1, W_2, and W_3 are 0, 1, and 1.

4.1 Asynchronous Stochastic Gradient Descent

For simplicity we assume that there is a single (virtual) server node, which maintains the model w and V (the parameter server framework provides for a clean abstraction for multiple servers). Multiple workers run SGD independently of each other. Each worker repeatedly reads data, pulls the recent model from the server, computes a gradient, and then pushes the gradient back. Due to the network delay, the received gradient the server used to update the model may be not computed based on the most recent model. An example is illustrated in Figure 1.

A worker can calculate the gradient of the loss in the standard way [15]. We first compute the partial gradient of f

$$\partial_{w_i} f(x, w, V) = x_i \quad (16)$$

$$\partial_{V_{ij}} f(x, w, V) = x_i [Vx]_j - x_i^2 V_{ij}, \quad (17)$$

Note that the term Vx can be pre-computed. Invoking the chain rule yields the gradient of l. Denote by $w(t)$ and $V(t)$ the model stored at the server on time t. Assume that at time t the server received gradient pushed from one worker

$$g^\theta(t) \leftarrow \partial_\theta l(f(x, w(t-\tau), V(t-\tau)), y) \quad (18)$$

where θ can be either w or V. τ is the delay, indicating that the gradient was computed using the model at time $t - \tau$.

As mentioned in Section 3.3, we use frequency adaptive regularization for w and V and the sparse induce ℓ_1 norm for w. In addition, we use AdaGrad [4] for a better model of the possible nonuniform sparsity in the data. In other words, assuming scalars λ in (14) and scalars η_V and β_V, the server updates V_{ij} by

$$n_{ij} \longleftarrow n_{ij} + \left[g_{ij}^V(t)\right]^2$$

$$V_{ij}(t+1) \longleftarrow V_{ij}(t) - \frac{\eta_V}{\beta_V + \sqrt{n_{ij}}} \left(g_{ij}^V(t) + \mu V_{ij}(t)\right) \quad (19)$$

where n_{ij} is initialized to 0. Updating w is slightly different to V due to the nonsmooth ℓ_1 regularizer. We adopted FTRL [11], which solves a "smoothed" proximal operator based on AdaGrad. Similarly denote by η_w and β_w the global learning rate. Updates in w_i are given by

$$\begin{aligned}
\sigma_i &\leftarrow \frac{1}{\eta_w}\left(\sqrt{n_i + [g_i^w(t)]^2} - \sqrt{n_i}\right) \\
z_i &\leftarrow z_i - g_i^w(t) + \sigma_i w_i(t) \\
n_i &\leftarrow n_i + [g_i^w(t)]^2 \qquad (20) \\
w_i(t+1) &\leftarrow \begin{cases} 0 & \text{if } |z_i| \le \lambda_1 \\ \left(\frac{\beta_w + \sqrt{n_i}}{\eta_w} + \lambda_2\right)^{-1}(z_i - \text{sgn}(z_i)\lambda_1) & \text{otherwise} \end{cases}
\end{aligned}$$

where both n_i and z_i is set to 0 at the beginning.

4.2 Convergence Analysis

The objective (15) is a challenging non-convex and non-smooth optimization problem and its convergence analysis is non-trivial, especially in the face of asynchronous updates. Here we provide a preliminary analysis of Algorithm 1 on a special case with $\lambda_1 = 0$. For notation simplicity we assume a fixed learning rate. It is straightforward to extend the results to handle the adaptive learning rate by assuming n_{ij} in (19) is bounded, see [illegible] for more details.

We will show that the simplified algorithm has an $O(1/\sqrt{t})$ ergodic convergence rate [illegible]. Due to the non-convexity, our results do not imply convergence to a KKT point. However, it is stronger than typical non-convex analysis in that there is an explicit convergence rate. Our results are based on a generic result in [illegible]. By carefully incorporating the specific properties of our problem, we arrive at a convergence bound that explicitly reveals the intuitive dependency on the sparsity of the data and the size of the minibatch in addition to the more typical maximum delay parameter for the asynchronous update. First we show Algorithm 1 reduces to simple asynchronous SGD.

Lemma 3 *Let η be the fixed learning rate for both parameter w and V, and in addition, $\lambda_1 = 0$, then the update equations (19) and (20) for solving the problem (15) becomes plain asynchronous SGD.*

PROOF. First of all, we note that despite the memory adaptive constraints $V_{ij} = 0$ for some i, j, we are essentially solving an *unconstrained* smooth optimization problem in a pre-defined coordinate subspace, which admits a simple (non-projected) SGD algorithm.

It remains to show that the stochastic gradient is unbiased. Since the minibatch is picked randomly, the expectation of the loss-function half of the partial stochastic gradient with respect to V is just the gradient. Since λ_i is frequency adaptively chosen, it does not affect the expectation of the gradient at all. Now we turn to the partial gradient with respect to w. Under the assumption that $\lambda_1 = 0$ and without AdaGrad it follows that $n_i = 0$. Hence for every $t \in \{1, \ldots T\}$ the update equation (16) becomes

$$w_i(t+1) \leftarrow \frac{\eta_w}{\beta_w} z_i(t+1) \text{ where } z_i(t+1) \leftarrow z_i(t) - g_i^w(t).$$

Substituting in $z_i(1) = \frac{\beta_w}{\eta_w} w_i(1)$, this recursion is essentially the SGD update equation

$$w_i(t+1) \leftarrow w_i(t) - \frac{\eta_w}{\beta_w} g_i^w(t)$$

with learning rate $\eta = \frac{\eta_w}{\beta_w}$. To show that the approximation is unbiased is again trivial since the data points are picked uniformly at random and the regularization weights μ_i are frequency adaptive. □

Theorem 4 (Lian et al. [illegible, Corollary 2]) *Assume that the stochastic gradient is unbiased and has variance bounded by σ^2 and that the gradient functional $\nabla f(\cdot)$ is L-Lipschitz. Also, assume that the global optimal solution x^* exists and $f^* > -\infty$. Moreover, assume the delay at time t τ_t is upper bounded by τ, then if we use a constant stepsize*

$$\eta := \sqrt{\frac{f(x_1) - f(x^*)}{L\tau\sigma^2}}.$$

then for every integer $T \ge \frac{4L(f(x_1) - f(x^*))}{\sigma}(\tau + 1)^2$, we have the output of the SGD obeying

$$\frac{1}{T}\sum_{t=1}^{T} \mathbb{E}(\|\nabla f(x_t)\|^2) \le 4\sqrt{\frac{(f(\theta_1) - f(\theta^*))L\sigma^2}{T}} \qquad (21)$$

Simplifying it further in our problem results in the following corollary, where the constants explicitly depend on the average sparsity of the data and size of the minibatch we use.

Corollary 1 *Denote by $\theta = \{w, V\}$ the parameters of the model and let $\phi_i(\theta) = l(f(x_i), y_i)$ be the objective function. Moreover, decompose the objective via*

$$\Phi(\theta) = \frac{1}{|X|}\sum_i \phi_i(\theta) + \sum_j [\lambda_j w_j^2 + \mu_j \|V_j\|^2].$$

Let the delay of the asynchronous gradient $\tau_t \le \tau$ for any update t and the minibatch size be b. Assume that the data X is bounded. More specifically, assume that it obeys the following property $s_i := \|x_i\|_0$, $\|X\|_\infty \le 1$ and $s_i \le s$.

In addition, assume that we work within a sublevel set of the problem such that $\|[w_{\text{supp}(x_i)}, V_{\text{supp}(x_i \otimes x_i)}]\| \le B_i$. Furthermore, assume that the regularization parameter is sufficiently small so that the regularization term does not weight more than the data term in the gradient.

Then there is a universal constant C and a data (sparsity) dependent constant

$$K := \frac{1}{|X|b}\max_i (s_i B_i)^2 \sum_{i=1}^{|X|}(s_i B_i)$$

such that setting stepsize $\eta = \sqrt{\frac{C\phi(\theta_1)}{\tau K}}$ results in a stochastic sequence of parameters that satisfies

$$\min_{t \in \{1,\ldots,T\}} \mathbb{E}\|\nabla\phi(\theta_t)\|^2 \le \frac{1}{T}\sum_{t=1}^{T}\mathbb{E}\|\nabla\phi(\theta_t)\|^2 \le 4\sqrt{\frac{\phi(\theta_1)\tau K}{T}}.$$

We first interpret the result before stating the proof.

1. The expected magnitude of the gradient on the LHS is an intuitive measure of the distance from the stationarity condition. While it is weaker than typical measures in convex optimization (e.g., primal suboptimality, mean square distance from the optimal solution), it should be in the same ball park for "nice" loss functions, as can be seen e.g. in discussions in [illegible, illegible].
2. When the data is sparser or the minibatch size is bigger, we can afford to use a larger learning rate and hence get faster convergence. Note that the results

captures the average sparsity so the quantity remains small even when a small number of data points are dense. This is especially important in face of the practical power law distributions.

PROOF OF COROLLARY 1. This is a simple specialization of Theorem 4 to our specific problem, which involves calculating the Lipschitz constant of the gradient and the variance of the stochastic gradient and upper bounding them using the intuitive quantities of interests. By the chain rule

$$\partial_\theta \phi_i(\theta) = \frac{\partial}{\partial f(x_i)} l(f(x_i), y_i) \frac{\partial}{\partial \theta} f(x_i).$$

Since l is the logistic loss, its Lipschitz constant is bounded by 1. Hence it follows from (16) and (17) that

$$\begin{aligned}\|\partial_\theta \phi_i(\theta)\| &\le 1 \cdot \sqrt{\sum_j (\partial_{w_j} f(x_i))^2 + \sum_{j,\ell} (\partial_{V_{j\ell}} f(x_i))^2} \\ &= \sqrt{\sum_j x_i^2 + \sum_{j,\ell} (x_j [Vx]_\ell - x_j^2 V_{j\ell})^2} \\ &\le \sqrt{s_i} \|x_i\|_\infty + s_i \|x_i [V x_i]^T\|_{2,\infty} \le s_i B_i\end{aligned}$$

Since the objective is differentiable, the Lipschitz constant can be obtained by upper bounding the gradient

$$\begin{aligned}\|\partial_\theta \phi(\theta)\| &\le \left\| \frac{1}{|X|} \sum_{i=1}^{|X|} \partial_\theta \phi_i(\theta) + 2\Lambda\theta \right\| \\ &\le \frac{1}{|X|} \sum_{i=1}^{|X|} s_i B_i + \|\Lambda \theta\|_2 \le \frac{2}{|X|} \sum_{i=1}^{|X|} s_i B_i\end{aligned}$$

where Λ is a big diagonal matrix that contains the frequency adaptive regularization weights λ_j and μ_j and the last inequality holds whne these weights are small.

The variance of the stochastic gradient is taken over an iid minibatch of size b, and it can be trivially bounded using the boundedness of the gradient

$$\sigma^2 \le \frac{\max_i \|\partial_\theta \phi_i(\theta)\|^2}{b} \le \frac{\max_i (s_i B_i + B)^2}{b} \le \frac{4 \max_i (s_i B_i)^2}{b}.$$

The last inequality can again be simplified under the assumptions that the regularization terms are small. Finally, we note that $\phi(\theta) \ge 0$ for any θ, so $\phi(\theta^*) \ge 0$. We arrive at the claim by substituting these bounds into (21) in Theorem 4. The proof is complete by noting that the minimum is always smaller than the mean in a sequence of numbers. □

4.3 Implementation

The sketch of DiFacto is shown in Algorithm 1. It is divided into three parts: the scheduler node runs the control logic, server nodes update the model, and the worker nodes compute the gradient.

Scheduler node issues commands, such as *process file i* or *save the model* to worker and server nodes. It also monitors the progress of workers. Once a straggler or a dead node is detected, the scheduler will re-issue the command which was sent to this node to another available node. Furthermore, the scheduler decides whether the stopping criteria have been reached. For example, we may terminate once the objective value on an additional validation set stops decreasing.

Algorithm 1 Implement DiFacto in the parameter server

Start: Create one scheduler node, m worker nodes and n server nodes over multiple machines.

Scheduler Node:

```
Assume the data is partitioned into s parts p_1, ..., p_s,
for t = 1 to T do
    Work packages P = {p_1, ..., p_s}
    Accomplished packages A = ∅
    while P ≠ ∅ do
        switch detected event from worker i do
            case idle
                Pick p ∈ P \ A and assign p to worker i
                A = A ∪ {p},
            case finished p
                P = P \ {p}
            case dead or timeout
                A = A \ {p},
    end while
end for
```

Worker i:

```
Receive command "processing p" from the scheduler
while read a minibatch from p do
    Pull w_i and V_i from server nodes for all features i
  that appear in this minibatch
    Compute the gradient based on (16) and (17)
    Push gradient back to servers
end while
```

Server i:

```
if received gradient from a worker then
    update w and V by using (20) and (19)
end if
```

Server nodes maintain and update the model w and V. Due to the adaptive memory constraints, the elements of V_i could be partly (or entirely) zeros. Therefore a server node only needs to allocate physical memory to a nonzero element V_i to reduce the memory footprint. This also saves bandwidth when handling model pull requests from the worker nodes. Conversely, when receiving gradients from a worker node, the server node updates the model using the steps discussed above.

Worker nodes perform most of the computation. After receiving a *process data p* command from the scheduler, a worker repeatedly reads minibatches from p, which is often a file stored in a distributed filesystem. For each minibatch B, the worker first finds the supporting feature indices $\mathcal{I} = \{i : x_i \neq 0 \text{ for some } x \in B\}$. Then it pulls (prefetches) the working set of the model from server nodes, namely $\{w_i, V_i : i \in \mathcal{I}\}$. Next the worker calculates the gradient of this minibatch and then pushes them to the servers.

Note that a worker node only needs to cache the minibatches being processed and the associated working sets to minimize the memory consumption. It also parallelizes data IO, computation, and communication (in particular prefetching) to hide IO cost. Besides, a worker node uses various filters to reduce the amount of data that need to be communicated. We adopt standard filters provided by the parameter server [8] including key caching (caching the keys in both sender and receiver to avoid duplicated communica-

name	# examples	# features	# entries
Criteo1 [1]	4.6×10^7	3.4×10^7	1.5×10^9
CTR1	2.9×10^5	1.4×10^7	3.5×10^7
Criteo2 [2]	1.5×10^9	3.6×10^8	5.0×10^{10}
CTR2 [3]	1.1×10^8	1.9×10^9	1.3×10^{10}

Table 1: A collection of click-through rate datasets.

tion) and lossless data compression. In addition, we use fixed-point encoding. Namely we convert the floating-point weight and gradient into shorter fixed-point integers during communication.

The codes are publicly available as part of the DMLC project http://dmlc.github.io/.

5. EXPERIMENTS

Quite clearly Factorization Machines are useful for many problems *beyond* computational advertising. That said, we feel that CTR estimation offers the most difficult challenges, both in terms of data set size and dimensionality.

5.1 Setup

Datasets: We collected several click-through rate datasets at various scales, as shown in Table 1. Criteo1 and Criteo2 are display advertising datasets from Criteo. The former is used in a recent Kaggle competition, for which we used the first 80% examples for training and the rest for test. The latter is by far the largest public released click-through rate dataset. We used the first 10 days data for training, and the 11-th day data for test. In both Criteo1 and Criteo2, each example has 13 integer features and 26 category features. We extracted sparse binary features via the widely-used one-hot encoding.

CTR2 is another advertising dataset sampled from a one month period from an anonymous Internet company. We used the on-production feature extraction module to obtain sparse binary anonymized features. Compared to the Criteo datasets, CTR2 has more 3 times more features per example due to the extensive feature engineering. We sampled a smaller dataset CTR1 from CTR2 for comparison with other systems which cannot scale to CTR2.

Machines: All experiments with performance numbers were run on Amazon EC2 c4.8xlarge instances. Each instance is equipped with dual Intel E5-2666 V3 2.8 GHz CPUs, 60 GB memory, and 10 Gigabit Ethernet. Auxiliary experiments, such as tuning the hyperparameters were carried out on a local cluster with 10 machines, with dual Intel E5-2680 v2 2.80GHz CPUs, 128 GB memory, and 40 GbE.

Hyperparameters: Unless stated otherwise, we choose the hyperparameters as follows: We run DiFacto with 100 workers and 100 servers on 10 physical machines. We fixed the dimension $k = 16$ and the minibatch size 10^4 for Criteo2 and 10^3 for CTR2. While the smaller dataset Criteo1 and CTR1, we decrease the minibatch sizes by 10 times respectively. We used a fixed regularizer for w with $\lambda_1 = 4$ and $\lambda = 0$, while choosing the constant μ for V within the range of $\{0, 10^{-5}, 10^{-4}, 10^{-3}\}$ based on an additional validation set.

[1] https://www.kaggle.com/c/criteo-display-ad-challenge
[2] http://labs.criteo.com/downloads/download-terabyte-click-logs
[3] https://github.com/mli/data

The elements in V were initialized uniformly at random in the range $[-0.01, 0.01]$. The fast learning rate η_w is selected between 0.001 and 0.1 with $\eta_V = \eta_w$ and $\beta_w = \beta_V = 1$. Finally, we stop the algorithm when the objective value on the validation set stops decreasing.

5.2 Adaptive memory

We first study the effectiveness of adaptive memory. We compare the following three setups which use different memory adaptive constraints in (15):

No memory adaption No constraint is applied, i.e. we do not force elements in V_i to 0.

Frequency threshold Only the constraint $V_i = 0$ for infrequent keys $n_i < k$ is used, where n_i is the occurrence of feature i in the data.

Frequency threshold + ℓ_1 shrinkage We add the constraint $V_i = 0$ if $w_i = 0$. That is, we mark V_i as inactive if w_i is set to 0 by the sparse induction ℓ_1 regularization.

We use the same hyper-parameters for all three setups and vary the dimension k from 1 to 64. The results are shown in Figure 2.

As can be seen, these memory adaptive constraints effectively reduce the model size. The reduction is about 100x for Criteo2 and 300x for CTR2 when $k = 64$. Therefore these constraints significantly decrease the server node memory consumption and network traffic. It also brings about a 20% reduction in the runtime. Especially when k is large, the resulted amount of communication may overwhelm the system. Being able to reduce the model size benefits the system performance a lot.

A more interesting observation is that these memory adaptive constraints do not affect the test accuracy. To the contrary, we even see a slight improvement when the dimension k is greater than 8 for CTR2. The reason could be that the model capacity control is of great importance when the dimension k is large. And these memory adaptive constraints can provide additional capacity control besides the ℓ_2 and ℓ_1 regularizers.

5.3 Fixed-point Compression

We evaluate lossy fixed-point compression for data communication. By default, both the model and gradient entries are represented as 32 bit floats. In this experiment, we compress these values to lower precision integers. More specifically, given a bin size b and number of bits n, we represent x by the following n-bit integer

$$z := \left\lfloor \frac{x}{b} \times 2^n \right\rfloor + \sigma, \qquad (22)$$

where σ is a Bernoulli random variable chosen such as to ensure that $\mathbf{E}[z] = 2^n \frac{x}{b}$.

We implemented the fixed-point compression as a user-defined filter in the parameter server framework. Since multiple numbers are communicated in each round, we choose b to be the absolute maximum value of these numbers. In addition, we used the key caching and lossless data compression (via LZ4) filters.

The results for $n = 8, 16, 24$ are shown in Figure 3. As expected, fixed-point compression linearly reduces the network traffic volume, since the traffic is dominated by communicating the model and gradient. A more interesting observation is that we obtained a 4.2x compression rate from 32-bit

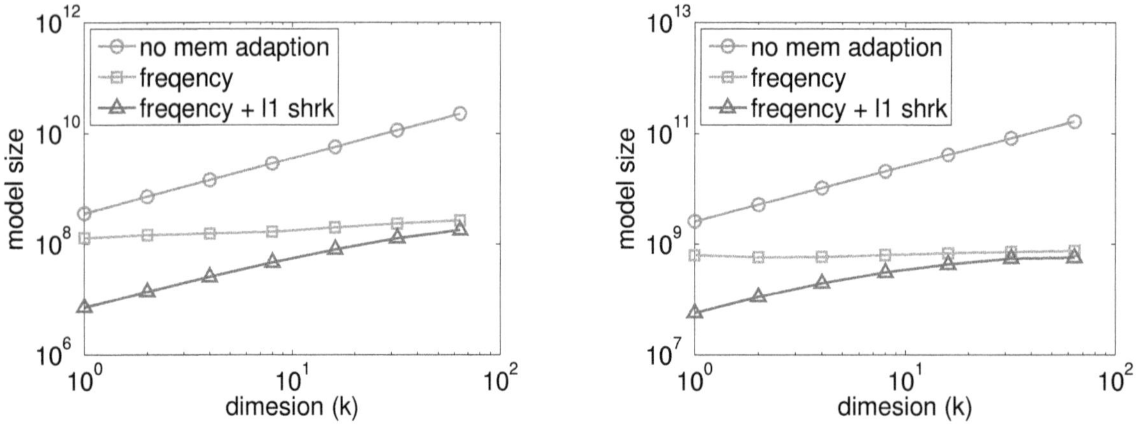

(a) Number of non-zero entries in V.

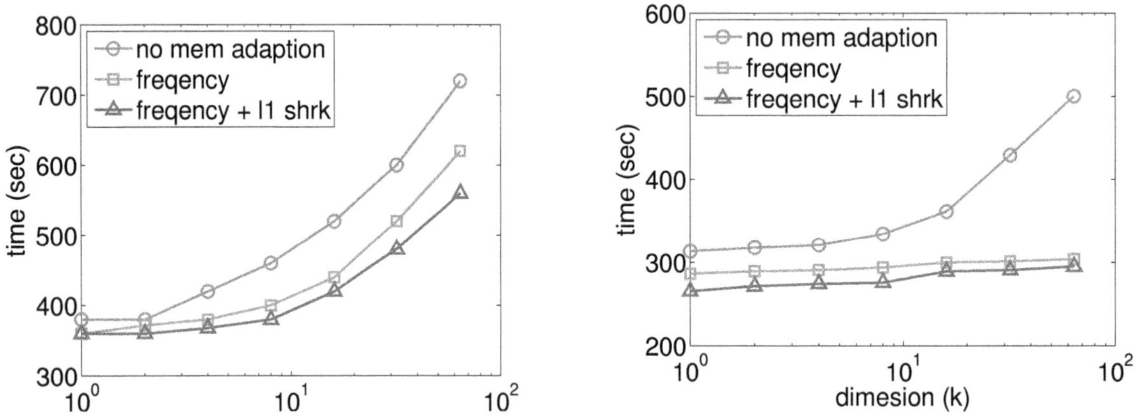

(b) Runtime for one iteration.

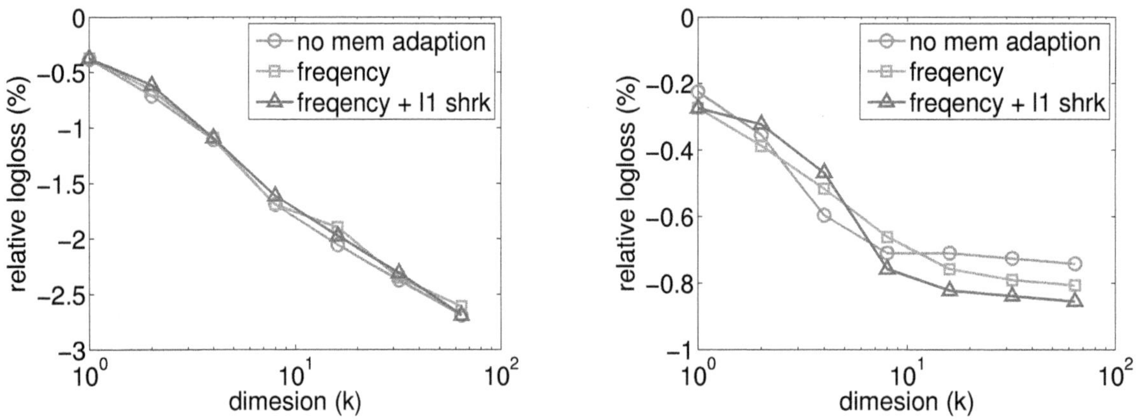

(c) Relative test logloss comparing to logistic regression ($k = 0$ and 0 relative loss).

Figure 2: Using different adaptive memory constraints when varying the embedding dimension. Left: Criteo2. Right: CTR2.

floating-point to 8-bit fixed-point on Criteo2. The reason is the latter improves the compression rate for the following lossless LZ4 compression.

We observed different effects of accuracy on these two datasets: CTR2 is robust to the number precision, while Criteo2 has a 6% increase of logloss if only using 1-byte presentation. However, a medium compression rate even improves the model accuracy. This might be because the lossy compression acts as regularizer to the objective function.

5.4 Comparison with LibFM

To our best knowledge, there is no publicly released distributed FM solver. Hence we only compare DiFacto to the popular single machine package LibFM developed by Rendle [15]. We only report results on Criteo1 and CTR1 on a single machine, since LibFM fails on the other two larger datasets. We perform a similar grid search of the hyper-parameters as we did for DiFacto. As LibFM only uses single thread, we run DiFacto with 1 worker and 1 server

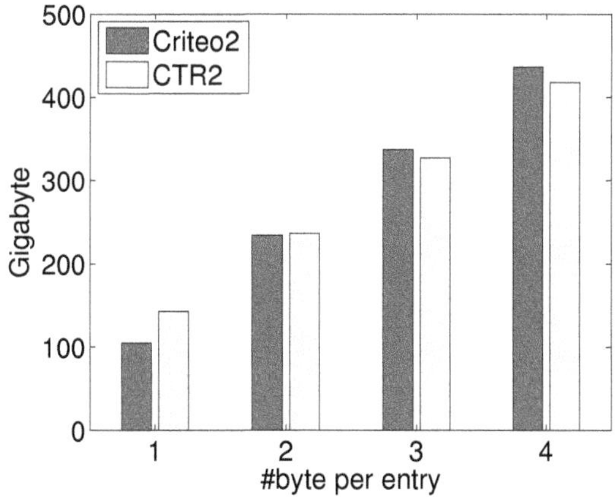

(a) Total data sent by workers in one iteration. The compression rates from 4-byte to 1-byte are 4.2x and 2.9x for Criteo2 and CTR2, respectively.

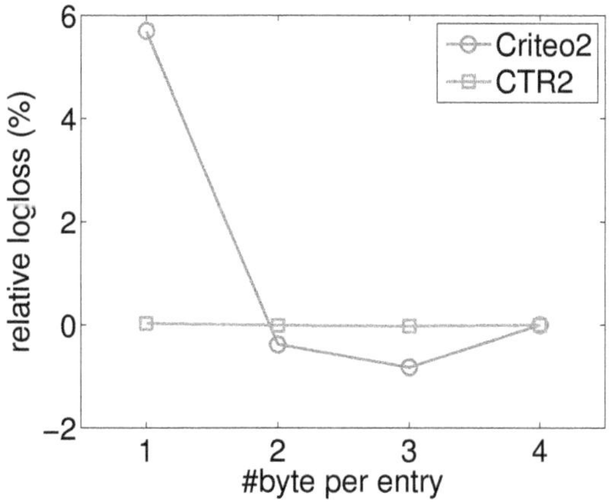

(b) The relative test logloss comparing to no fixed-point compression.

Figure 3: Compressing model and gradient using the fixed-point compression, where 4-byte means using the default 32-bit floating-point format.

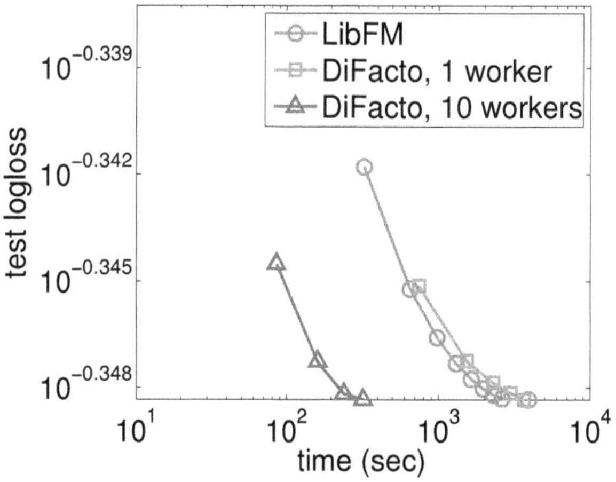

(a) Criteo1

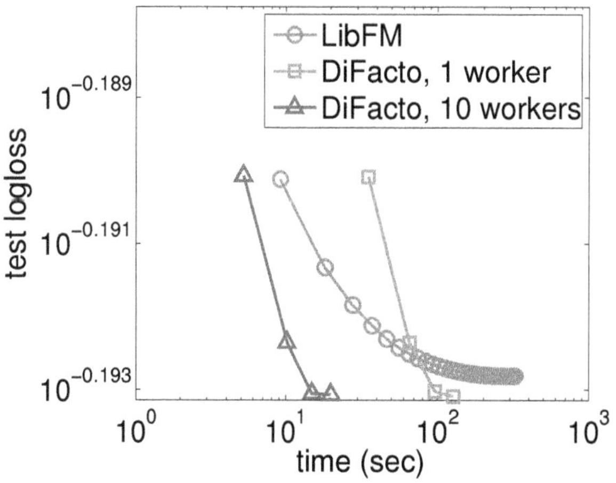

(b) CTR1

Figure 4: Comparison with LibFM on a single machine. The data preprocessing time for LibFM is omitted.

in sequential execution order. We also report the performance using 10 workers and 10 servers on a single machine for reference.

The results are shown in Figure 4. As can been seen, DiFacto converges significantly faster than LibFM, it uses 2 times fewer iterations to reach the best model. This is because the adaptive learning rate used in DiFacto better models the data sparsity and the adaptive regularization and constraints can further accelerate the convergence. In particular, the latter results in a lower test logloss on the CTR1 dataset, where the number of features exceeds the number of examples, requiring improved capacity control.

Also note that DiFacto with a single worker is twice slower than LibFM per iteration. This is because the data communication overhead between the worker and the server cannot be ignored in the sequential execution. More importantly, DiFacto does not require any data preprocessing to map arbitrary 64-bit integer and string feature indices, which are used in both Criteo1 and CTR2, to continuous integer indices. The cost of this data preprocessing step, required by LibFM but not shown in Figure 4, even exceeds the cost of training (1,400 seconds for Criteo1). Nevertheless, DiFacto with a single worker still outperforms LibFM thanks to the faster convergence. In addition, it is 10 times faster than LibFM when using 10 workers on the same machine.

5.5 Scalability

Finally, we study the scalability of DiFacto by varying the number of physical machines used in training. We run 10 workers and 10 servers in each machine, and increase the number of machines from 1 to 16. Both the time for each iteration and the logloss on the test dataset are recorded and shown in Figure 5.

We observe an 8x speedup from 1 machine to 16 machines on both Criteo2 and CTR2. The reason for the satisfactory performance is twofold. First, asynchronous SGD eliminates the need for synchronization between workers and it is tolerant to stragglers. Even though we used dedicated machines for the job, they still share network bandwidth with others. In particular, we observed a large variation of read speed when streaming data from Amazon's S3 service, despite using the IO optimized c4.8xlarge series of machines. This ensures that we actually take advantage of parallelization relative to LibFM, which is single core.

Second, DiFacto uses several filters which effectively re-

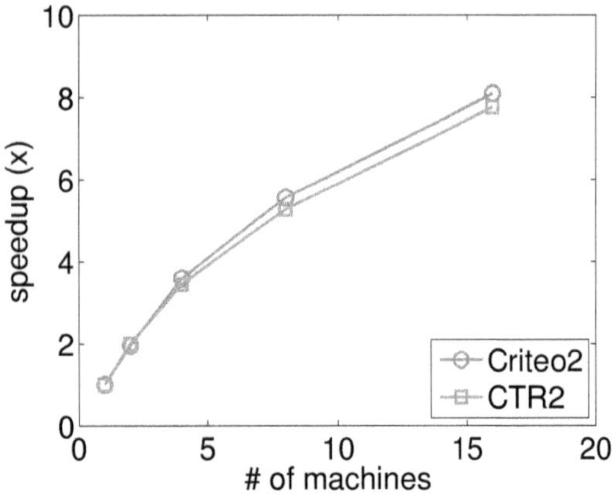

Figure 5: The speedup from 1 machine to 16 machines, where each machine runs 10 workers and 10 servers. The difference between the test logloss is within 0.5%, which is omitted in the figure.

duce the amount of network traffic. Even though CTR2 produces 10 times more network traffic than Criteo2, they have similar speedup performance.

There is a longstanding suspicion that the convergence of asynchronous SGD slows down when increasing the number of workers. Nonetheless, we did not observe a substantial difference in model accuracy. In other words, the relative difference of the objective logloss on test datasets is below 0.5% when increasing the number of workers from 10 to 160. This might be because the datasets we used are highly sparse and the features are not extremely correlated. Hence inconsistency due to concurrently updating by multiple workers may not have a major effect. These observations correspond well with what we predict in the convergence analysis.

6. CONCLUSION

In this paper we presented DiFacto, a high performance distributed factorization machine. DiFacto uses a refined factorization machine model with adaptive memory constraints and frequency adaptive regularization, which perform fine-grained capacity control based on both data and model statistics. DiFacto uses asynchronous stochastic gradient descent. We give theoretical convergence analysis and implement it in the parameter server framework. We evaluated DiFacto thoroughly on two real computational advertising datasets with up to billions of examples and features. We showed that DiFacto produces a very compact model, yet it retains similar generalization accuracy. We also demonstrated that DiFacto converges faster than the state-of-the-art package LibFM. Furthermore, DiFacto is able to solve TB scale problems on modest machines within hours.

References

[1] A. Ahmed, N. Shervashidze, S. Narayanamurthy, V. Josifovski, and A. J. Smola. Distributed large-scale natural graph factorization. In *World Wide Web Conference*, Rio de Janeiro, 2013.

[2] R. M. Bell and Y. Koren. Lessons from the netflix prize challenge. *SIGKDD Explorations*, 9(2):75–79, 2007. URL http://doi.acm.org/10.1145/1345448.1345465.

[3] J. Dean, G. Corrado, R. Monga, K. Chen, M. Devin, Q. Le, M. Mao, M. Ranzato, A. Senior, P. Tucker, K. Yang, and A. Ng. Large scale distributed deep networks. In *Neural Information Processing Systems*, 2012.

[4] J. Duchi, E. Hazan, and Y. Singer. Adaptive subgradient methods for online learning and stochastic optimization. *Journal of Machine Learning Research*, 12:2121–2159, 2010.

[5] S. Ghadimi and G. Lan. Stochastic first-and zeroth-order methods for nonconvex stochastic programming. *SIAM Journal on Optimization*, 23(4):2341–2368, 2013.

[6] Criteo Labs. Criteo terabyte click logs, 2014. http://labs.criteo.com/downloads/download-terabyte-click-logs.

[7] Q.V. Le, T. Sarlos, and A. J. Smola. Fastfood — computing hilbert space expansions in loglinear time. In *International Conference on Machine Learning*, 2013.

[8] M. Li, D. G. Andersen, J. Park, A. J. Smola, A. Amhed, V. Josifovski, J. Long, E. Shekita, and B. Y. Su. Scaling distributed machine learning with the parameter server. In *OSDI*, 2014.

[9] M. Li, D. G. Andersen, A. J. Smola, and K. Yu. Communication efficient distributed machine learning with the parameter server. In *Neural Information Processing Systems*, 2014.

[10] X. Lian, Y. Huang, Y. Li, and J. Liu. Asynchronous parallel stochastic gradient for nonconvex optimization. *arXiv preprint arXiv:1506.08272*, 2015.

[11] B. McMahan. Follow-the-regularized-leader and mirror descent: Equivalence theorems and l1 regularization. In *International Conference on Artificial Intelligence and Statistics*, pages 525–533, 2011.

[12] B. McMahan, G. Holt, D. Sculley, M. Young, D. Ebner, J. Grady, L. Nie, T. Phillips, E. Davydov, and D. Golovin. Ad click prediction: a view from the trenches. In *KDD*, 2013.

[13] T. Moon, A. J. Smola, Y. Chang, and Z. Zheng. Intervalrank: isotonic regression with listwise and pairwise constraints. In B.D. Davison, T. Suel, N. Craswell, and B. Liu, editors, *Proceedings of the Third International Conference on Web Search and Web Data Mining, WSDM*, pages 151–160. ACM, 2010.

[14] S. Negahban, P. Ravikumar, M.J. Wainwright, and B. Yu. A unified framework for high-dimensional analysis of m-estimators with decomposable regularizers. *arXiv preprint arXiv:1010.2731*, 2010.

[15] S. Rendle and L. Schmidt-Thieme. Pairwise interaction tensor factorization for personalized tag recommendation. In *Web search and data mining*, pages 81–90. ACM, 2010.

[16] S. Rendle. Time-Variant Factorization Models Context-Aware Ranking with Factorization Models. volume 330 of *Studies in Computational Intelligence*, chapter 9, pages 137–153. 2011. ISBN 978-3-642-16897-0.

[17] A. J. Smola and S. Narayanamurthy. An architecture for parallel topic models. In *Very Large Databases (VLDB)*, 2010.

[18] N. Srebro, N. Alon, and T. Jaakkola. Generalization error bounds for collaborative prediction with low-rank matrices. In L. K. Saul, Y. Weiss, and L. Bottou, editors, *Advances in Neural Information Processing Systems 17*, Cambridge, MA, 2005. MIT Press.

[19] B. Taskar, C. Guestrin, and D. Koller. Max-margin Markov networks. In S. Thrun, L. Saul, and B. Schölkopf, editors, *Advances in Neural Information Processing Systems 16*, pages 25–32, Cambridge, MA, 2004. MIT Press.

[20] R. Tibshirani. Regression shrinkage and selection via the lasso. *J. R. Stat. Soc. Ser. B Stat. Methodol.*, 58:267–288, 1996.

[21] G. Wahba. *Spline Models for Observational Data*, volume 59 of *CBMS-NSF Regional Conference Series in Applied Mathematics*. SIAM, Philadelphia, 1990.

[22] J. Ye, J.-H. Chow, J. Chen, and Z. Zheng. Stochastic gradient boosted distributed decision trees. In D. W.-L. Cheung, I.-Y. Song, W.W. Chu, X. Hu, and J.J. Lin, editors, *Conference on Information and Knowledge Management, CIKM*, pages 2061–2064. ACM, 2009.

Distributed Balanced Partitioning via Linear Embedding*

Kevin Aydin, MohammadHossein Bateni, Vahab Mirrokni
Google Research
New York, NY, USA
{kaydin,bateni,mirrokni}@google.com

ABSTRACT

Balanced partitioning is often a crucial first step in solving large-scale graph optimization problems: in some cases, a big graph is chopped into pieces that fit on one machine to be processed independently before stitching the results together, leading to certain suboptimality from the interaction among different pieces. In other cases, links between different parts may show up in the running time and/or network communications cost, hence the desire to have small cut size.

We study a distributed balanced partitioning problem where the goal is to partition the vertices of a given graph into k pieces, minimizing the total cut size. Our algorithm is composed of a few steps that are easily implementable in distributed computation frameworks, e.g., MapReduce. The algorithm first embeds nodes of the graph onto a line, and then processes nodes in a distributed manner guided by the linear embedding order. We examine various ways to find the first embedding, e.g., via a hierarchical clustering or Hilbert curves. Then we apply four different techniques such as local swaps, minimum cuts on partition boundaries, as well as contraction and dynamic programming.

Our empirical study compares the above techniques with each other, and to previous work in distributed algorithms, e.g., a label propagation method [34], FENNEL [32] and Spinner [23]. We report our results both on a private map graph and several public social networks, and show that our results beat previous distributed algorithms: we notice, e.g., 15-25% reduction in cut size over [34]. We also observe that our algorithms allow for scalable distributed implementation for any number of partitions. Finally, we apply our techniques for the Google Maps Driving Directions to minimize the number of multi-shard queries with the goal of saving in CPU usage. During live experiments, we observe an ≈ 40% drop in the number of multi-shard queries when comparing our method with a standard geography-based method.

*Certain additional discussions are left out due to space constraints. Refer to the full version [3] for details.

WSDM 2016 February 22-25, 2016, San Francisco, CA, USA

ACM ISBN 978-1-4503-3716-8/16/02.

DOI: http://dx.doi.org/10.1145/2835776.2835829

Keywords

Cut minimization; embedding to line; imbalance; local improvement; MapReduce; maps; partitioning; social networks

1. INTRODUCTION

Graph partitioning is a crucial first step in developing a tool for mining big graphs or solving large-scale optimization problems. In many applications, the partition sizes have to be balanced or almost balanced so that each part can be handled by a single machine to ensure the speedup of parallel computing over different parts. Such a balanced graph partitioning tool is applicable throughout scientific computation for dealing with distributed computations over massive data sets, and serves as a tradeoff between local computation and total communication amongst machines. In several applications, a graph serves as a substitute for the computational domain [11]. Each vertex denotes a piece of information and edges denote their dependencies. Usually, the goal is to partition the vertices where no part is too large, and the number of edges across parts is small, implying that most of the work is within a part and only minimal work takes place between parts. In these applications, links between different parts may show up in the running time and/or network communications cost. Thus, a good partitioning minimizes the amount of communication during a distributed computation. In other applications, a big graph is carefully chopped into parts that fit on one machine to be processed independently before finally stitching the individual results together, leading to certain suboptimality arising from the interaction between different parts. To formally capture these situations, we study a balanced partitioning problem where the goal is to partition the vertices of a given graph into k parts so as to minimize the total cut size.[1]

This is a challenging problem that is computationally hard even for medium-size graphs [2] as it captures the graph bisection [15], hence all attempts at tackling it necessarily relies on heuristics. While the topic of large-scale balanced graph partitioning has attracted significant attention in the literature [9, 10, 32, 34], the large body of previ-

[1]We emphasize that our main focus is on the size of the resulting cut and not the resource consumption of our algorithm, although it is fully distributable, uses linear space and runs for all the relevant experiments in reasonable amount of time (more or less comparable to the state of the art). Unfortunately, we cannot reveal the exact running times due to corporate restrictions. Nevertheless, we report in Section 6.4 relative running times of our algorithm on synthetic data of varying sizes to prove its scalability.

ous work study large-scale but non-distributed solutions to this problem. Several motivations necessitate the quest for a distributed algorithm for these problems: (i) first of all, huge graphs with hundreds of billions of edges that do not fit in memory are becoming increasingly common [32, 34]; (ii) in many distributed graph processing frameworks such as Pregel [22], Apache Giraph [7], and PEGASUS [18], we need to partition the graph into different pieces, since the underlying graph does not fit on a single machine, and therefore for the same reason, we need to partition the graph in a distributed manner; (iii) the ability to run a distributed algorithm using a common framework such as MapReduce on a platform consisting of commodity hardware makes an algorithm much more widely applicable in practice; and (iv) even if the graph fits in memory of a super-computer, implementing some algorithms requires superlinear memory which is not feasible on a single machine. The need for distributed algorithms has been observed by several practical and theoretical research papers [34, 32].

For streaming and some distributed optimization models, Stanton [29] has recently shown that achieving formal approximation guarantees is information theoretically impossible, say, for a class of random graphs. Given the hardness of this problem, we explore several distributed heuristic algorithms. Our algorithm is composed of a few logical, simple steps, which can be implemented in various distributed computation frameworks, e.g., MapReduce [8].

An application in Google Maps driving directions. As one application of our balanced partitioning algorithm, we turn to the Google Maps Driving Directions. This system computes the optimal driving route for any given *source-destination query* (pairs of points on the map). A plausible approach is to obtain a suitable partitioning of the graph beforehand so that each server handles its own section of the graph. Ideally we seek to minimize the number of cross-shard queries, since handling these is much more costly and entails extra communication and coordination across multiple servers. To reduce the cross-shard query traffic we aim to minimize the cut size between partitions, expecting that less directions will be produced with source and destination in different partitions. Reducing the cut size in practice results in denser regions in each partition, therefore most queries will be contained within one shard. We confirm this observation with extensive studies using historical query data and live experiments (details in 6.5). Conveniently, a linear embedding provides a very simple way of specifying partitions by merely providing two numbers for each shard's boundaries. Therefore it is straightforward and fast to identify the shard a given query point belongs to. As discussed later, our study of linear embedding of graphs while minimizing the cut size is partly motivated by these reasons.

Our Contributions. Our contributions in this paper can be divided into five categories.

1) We introduce a multi-stage distributed optimization framework for balanced partitioning based on first embedding the graph into a line and then optimizing the clusters guided by the order of nodes on the line.[2] This framework is not only suitable for distributed partitioning of a large-scale graph, but also it is directly applicable to balanced partitioning applications like those in Google Maps Driving Directions described above.

2) As for the initialization stage, we examine several ways to find the first embedding[3]: (i) by naïvely using a random ordering, (ii) for map graphs by the Hilbert-curve embedding, and (iii) for general graphs by applying hierarchical clustering on an edge-weighted graph where the edge weights are based either on the number of common neighbors of the nodes in the graph, or on the inverse of the distance of the nodes on the map. Whereas the Hilbert-curve embedding and our hierarchical clustering based on node distances may only be applied to maps graphs, the hierarchical clustering based on the number of common neighbors is applicable to all graphs. While all these methods prove useful, to our surprise, the latter (most general) initial embedding technique is the best initialization technique even for maps. We later explain that all these methods have very efficient and scalable distributed implementations.

3) As a next step, we apply four methods to postprocess the initial ordering and produce an improved cut. The methods include a metric ordering optimization method, a local improvement method based on random swaps, another based on minimum cuts in the partition boundaries, and finally a technique based on contracting the min-cut-based clusters, and applying dynamic programming to compute optimal cluster boundaries. Our final algorithm (called `Combination`) combines the best of our initialization methods, and iterates on the various postprocessing methods until it converges. The resulting algorithm is quite scalable: it runs smoothly on graphs with hundreds of millions of nodes and billions of edges.

4) As our empirical study, we compare the above techniques with each other, and more importantly with previous work. In particular, we compare our results to recent work in (distributed) balanced graph partitioning, including a recent label propagation-based algorithm [34], FENNEL [32], Spinner [23] and METIS [19].[4] We report our results on both a large private map graph, and also on several public social networks studied in previous work [34, 32, 23, 35]. First, we show that our distributed algorithm consistently beats the label propagation algorithm by Ugander and Backstrom [34] (on `LiveJournal`) by a reasonable margin for all values of k, e.g., for $k = 20$, we improve the cut by 25% (from 37% to 27.5% of total edge weight), and for $k = 100$, we improve the cut by 15% (from 49% to 41.5%). The clustering outputs can be found in [1]. In addition, for $k > 2$ partitions, we show that our algorithm beats METIS and FENNEL (on `Twitter`) by a reasonable factor. For $k = 2$, the results that we obtain beats the output of METIS, but it is slightly worse than the result reported by FENNEL. For both graphs, our results are consistently superior to that of Spinner [23] with a wide margin. We also note that our algorithms allow for scalable distributed implementation for small or large number of partitions. More specifically, changing k from 2 to tens of thousands does not change the running time significantly. As for comparing various initialization methods, we

[2]Embedding into a line is also essential in graph compression; see, e.g., [4, 6].

[3]It might be worth studying spectral embedding methods or standard embedding techniques into ℓ_1, but we did not try them due to not having a scalable distributed implementation, and also since the hierarchical clustering-based embedding worked pretty well in practice. We leave this for future research.

[4]Some works are indirectly compared to, and others (e.g., [35]) did not report cut sizes. We relied for these comaprisons on available cut results for a host of large public graphs.

observe that while geographic Hilbert-curve techniques outperform the random ordering, the methods based on the hierarchical clustering using the number of common neighbors as the similarity measure between nodes[5] outperform the geography-based initial embeddings, even for map graphs. As for comparing other techniques, we observe the random swap techniques are effective on `Twitter`, and the min-cut-based or contract and dynamic program techniques are very effective for the map graphs. Overall, we realize that these techniques complement each other, and combining them in a `Combination` algorithm is the most effective method.

5) As mentioned earlier, we apply our results to the Google Maps Driving Directions application, and deploy two linear-embedding-based algorithms on the World's Map graph. We first examine the best imbalance factor for our cut-optimization technique, and observe that we can reduce 21% of cross-shard queries by increasing the imbalance factor from 0% to 10%. The two methods that we examined via live experiments were (i) a baseline approach based on the Hilbert-curve embedding, and (ii) one method based on applying our cut-optimization post-processing techniques. By running live experiments on the real traffic, we observe the number of multi-shard queries from our cut-optimization techniques is 40% less compared to the baseline Hilbert embedding technique. This, in turn, results in less CPU usage in response to queries[6].

Other Related Work. Balanced partitioning is a challenging problem to approximate within a constant factor [16, 2, 12], or to approximate within any factor in several distributed or steaming models [29]. As for heuristic algorithms for this problem in the distributed or streaming models, a number of recent papers have been written about this topic [30, 34, 32]. Our algorithms are different from the ones studied in these papers. The most similar related work are the label propagation-based methods of Ugander and Backstrom [34] and Martella et al. (Spinner) [23] which develop a scalable distributed algorithm for balanced partitioning. Our random swap technique is similar in spirit to the label propagation algorithm studied by [34], however, we also examine three other methods as a postprocessing stage and find out that these methods work well in combination. Moreover, [34] studied two different methods for their initialization, a random initialization, and a geographic initialization. We also examine random ordering, and a Hilbert-curve ordering which is similar to the geographic initialization by [34], however we examine two other initialization techniques and observe that even for map-based geographic graphs, the initialization methods based on hierarchical clustering outperform the geography-based initial ordering. Overall, we compare our algorithm directly on a `LiveJournal` public graph (the only public graph reported in [34]), and improve the cut values achieved in [34, 23] by a large margin for all values of k. In addition, algorithms developed in [30, 32] are suitable for the streaming model, but one can implement variants of those algorithms in a distributed manner. We also compare our algorithm directly to the numbers reported on the large-scale `Twitter` graph by FENNEL [32], demonstrating the performance of our algorithm.

The reader is referred to the full version of the paper [1] to see the omitted proofs and discussions as well as additional related work.

[5]This is needed only once to obtain the initial graph, and the new edge weights in the subsequent rounds are computed via aggregation. Further note that approximate triangle counting can be done efficiently in MapReduce; see, e.g., [33].

[6]The exact decrease in CPU usage depends on the underlying serving infrastructure which is not our focus and is not revealed due to company policies. We note that there are several other algorithmic techniques and system tricks that are involved in setting up the distributed serving infrastructure for Google Maps driving directions. This system is handled by the Maps engineering team, and is not discussed here as it is not the focus of this paper.

2. PRELIMINARIES

For an integer n, we define $[n] = \{1, 2, \dots, n\}$. We also slightly abuse the notation and, for a function $f : A \mapsto \mathbb{R}$, define $f(A') = \sum_{a \in A'} f(a)$ if $A' \subseteq A$. For a function $f : S \mapsto T$, we let $f^{-1}(t)$ for $t \in T$ denote the set of elements in S mapped to t via f. For a permutation π, let π_i denote, for $i \in [n]$, the element in position i of π. Moreover, let $\pi(i \to j) = \{\pi_i, \pi_{i+1}, \dots, \pi_j\}$ for $i \in [n], j \in [n] \cup \{0\}$. Note that, in particular, $\pi(i \to j) = \emptyset$ if $j < i$.

2.1 Problem definition

Given is a graph $G(V, E)$ of n vertices with edge lengths and node weights, as well as an integer k, and a real number $\alpha \geq 0$. Let us denote the edge lengths by $d : E \mapsto \mathbb{R}$, and the vertex weights by $w : V \mapsto \mathbb{R}$. A partition of vertices of G into k parts $\{V_i : i \in [k]\}$ is said to be α-balanced if and only if $(1 - \alpha)w(V)/k \leq w(V_i) \leq (1 + \alpha)w(V)/k$. In particular, a zero-balanced (or fully balanced) partition is one where all partitions have the same weight. The cut length of the partition is the total sum of all edges whose endpoints fall in different parts: Our goal is to find an α-balanced partition whose cut size is (approximately) minimized.

The problem is NP-hard (the case of $\alpha = 0, k = 2$ is the minimum bisection problem). For arbitrary k, α, we get the minimum balanced k-cut problem, that is known to be inapproximable within any finite factor [2]; the best approximation factor for it is $O(\log^{1.5} n)$ (if $\alpha > 0$ is constant).

2.2 Our algorithm

Our algorithm consists of three main parts: (i) We first find a suitable mapping of the vertices to a line. This gives us an ordering of the vertices that presumably places (most) neighbors close to each other, therefore somewhat reduces the minimum-cut partitioning problem to an almost local optimization; (ii) then, we attempt to improve the ordering mainly by swapping vertices in a semilocal manner. These moves are done so as to improve certain metrics (perhaps, the cut size of a fully balanced partition), and finally, (iii) we use local postprocessing optimization in the "split windows" (i.e., a small interval around the equal-size partitions cut points taking into account permissible imbalance) to improve the partition's cut size.

Note that one implementation may use only some of the above, and clearly any implementation will pick one method to perform each task above and mix them to get a final almost balanced partition. Indeed, we report some of our results (specially those in comparison to the previous work) based on `Combination`, which uses `AffCommNeigh` to get the initial ordering and then iteratively applies techniques from the second and third stages above (e.g., `Metric`, `Swap`, `MinCut`) until the result converges. (The convergence in our experiments happens in two/three rounds.)

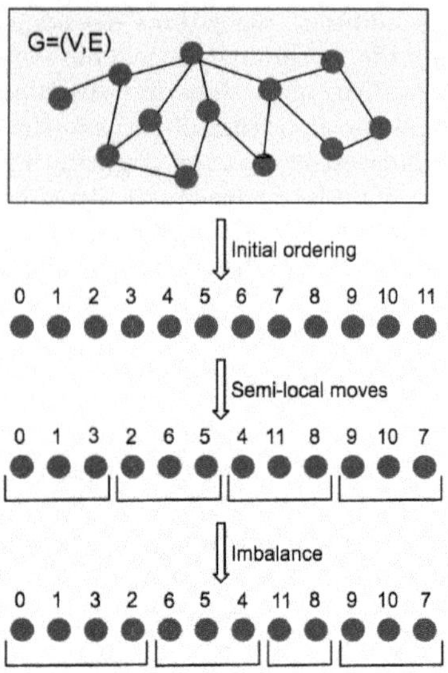

Figure 1: A natural flow for our algorithm. The vertices of G are first embedded on a line, then the embedding is improved via swaps, and finally imbalanced clusters are created according to the ordering of vertices. As we explain later on, iterating on these steps yields better results.

Algorithm 1 `Combination`(G, k, α)

Input: Graph G, number of parts k, imbalance param. α
Output: A partition of $V(G)$ into k parts

for all $(u, v) \in E(G)$ **do**
  $w(u, v) \leftarrow$ number of common neighbors of u, v
$\pi \leftarrow$ `AffinityOrdering`(G, w)
for $i = 0$ **to** k **do**
  $q(i) \leftarrow \lfloor \frac{in}{k} \rfloor$ {fully balanced split points}
repeat
  $(\pi', q') \leftarrow (\pi, q)$
  Use any (semilocal or imbalance-inducing) postprocessing technique on (G, π', q') to obtain (π, q)
until $\pi = \pi'$ **and** $q = q'$
for all $i \in [k]$ **do**
  $V_i \leftarrow \pi(q(i) + 1 \rightarrow q(i + 1))$
return $\{V_1, V_2, \ldots, V_k\}$

---

3. INITIAL MAPPING TO LINE

3.1 Random mapping

The easiest method to produce an ordering for the vertices is to randomly permute them. Though very fast, this method does not seem to lead to much progress towards our goal of finding good cuts. In particular, if we then turn this ordering into a partition by cutting contiguous pieces of equal size, we end up with a random partitiong of the input (into equal parts) which is almost surely a bad cut: a standard probablistic argument shows that the cut has expected ratio $1 - \frac{1}{k}$. Nevertheless, the next stage of the algorithm (i.e., the semilocal optimization by swapping) can generate a relatively good ordering with this naïve starting point.

3.2 Hilbert curve mapping

For certain graphs, geographic/geometric information is available for each vertex. It is fairly easy, then, to construct an ordering using a space-filling curve—prime examples are Peano, Morton and Hilbert curves, but we focus on the latter in this work. These methods are known to capture proximity well: nodes that are close in the space are expected to be placed nearby on the line.

There has been extensive study of the applicability of these methods in solving largescale optimization problems in parallel; see, e.g., [31, 24].

Not only can this algorithm be used on its own without any cut guarantees, but it can also be employed to break a big instance down into smaller ones that we can afford to run more intensive computations on. Both applications were known previously.

The previous works do not offer any theoretical guarantees on the quality of the cut generated from Hilbert curves. However, certain assumptions on the distributions of edge lengths and node positions let us bound the resulting cut ratio, and show that it is significantly less than the result of random ordering [17, 25, 14]. This is observed in our experiments, too.

3.3 Affinity-based mapping

One drawback of the Hilbert curve cover (even when coordinates are available) is that it ignores the actual edges in the graph. For an illustration, consider using the Hilbert curve to map certain points in an archipalego (or just a small number of islands or peninsulas). The Hilbert curve, unaware of the connectivities, traverses the vertices in a semirandom order, therefore, it may jump from island to island without covering the entire island first.

To address this issue, we use an agglomerative hierarchical clustering method, usually called average-linkage clustering[7]. We call the method "affinity clustering" since it takes into account the affinity of vertices. Informally, every node starts in a singleton cluster of its own, and then in several stages we group vertices that are closely connected, hence building a tree of these connections. More precisely, at every stage, each node turns on the connection to its closest neighbor, after which the connected components form clusters. The similarities used in the next level between constructed clusters are computed via some function of the similarities between the elements forming the clusters; in particular, we take the average function for this purpose.

The final ordering is produced by sorting the vertex labels produced as follows. Let the label for each vertex be the concatenation of vertex ID strings from the root to the corresponding leaf. Sorting the constructed labels places the vertices under each branch in a contiguous piece on the line. The same guarantee holds recursively, hence the (edge) proximity is preserved well. A pseudocode for this procedure is given in Algorithm 2: Line 15 uses notation $a\#b$ to denote the concatenation of labels for a and b. Notice that this pseudocode explains a sequential algorithm, however, the procedure can be efficiently implemented in a few rounds of

[7]Typically attributed to [28], this is reminiscent of a parallel version of Borůvka's algorithm for minimum spanning tree where the min operation is replaced by average.

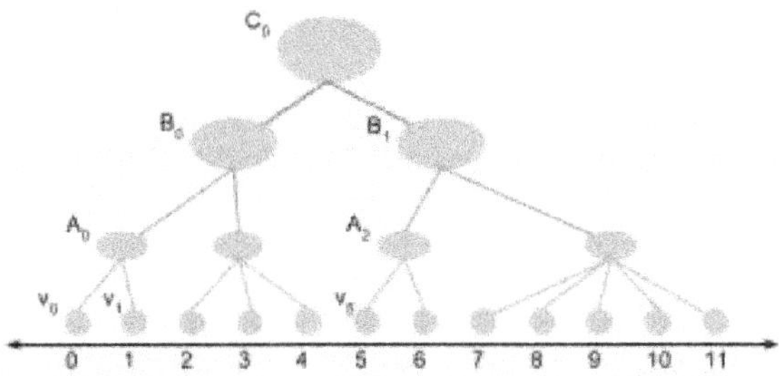

Figure 2: Illustration of Affinity tree ordering. The nodes at the bottom row correspond to the vertices of the graph, and the nodes at the higher levels are formed by merging nodes from lower levels. The vertices are finally sorted in the picture according to their labels. For instance, the label for v_0 is $C_0\#B_0\#A_0\#v_0$ whereas v_5 is labeled $C_0\#B_1\#A_2\#v_5$.

MapReduce. In fact, our algorithm is very similar to [27] but uses Distributed Hash Tables as explained in [20].[8]

Algorithm 2 `AffinityOrdering`(G, w)

Input: Graph G, (partial) similarity function w
Output: A permutation of vertices

$\mathcal{C}^0 \leftarrow \{\{v\} | v \in V(G)\}$
for $v \in V(G)$ **do**
  $\ell(v) \leftarrow v$
$i \leftarrow 0$
repeat
  for $s \in \mathcal{C}^i$ **do**
    $p(s) \leftarrow \arg\max_{t \in \mathcal{C}^i} w(s, t)$
  $\mathcal{C}^{i+1} \leftarrow \emptyset$
  for $t \in \{p(s) | s \in \mathcal{C}^i\}$ **do**
    $S \leftarrow p^{-1}(t)$
    $S' \leftarrow \bigcup_{s \in S} s$
    $\mathcal{C}^{i+1} \leftarrow \mathcal{C}^{i+1} \cup S'$
    $r \leftarrow \arg\min_{r' \in S'} s$
    for $s' \in S'$ **do**
      $\ell(s') \leftarrow r\#\ell(s')$
  $i \leftarrow i + 1$
until $|\mathcal{C}^i| = |\mathcal{C}^{i-1}|$
$\pi \leftarrow$ permutation of vertices sorted according to ℓ
return π

Intuitively, we expect vertices connected in lower levels (farther from the root) to be closer than those connected in later stages. (See Figure 2 for illustration.) In particular, we observed that a graph with several connected components gives an advantage to affinity tree ordering over the ordering produced by Hilbert curve.

For this approach to work, we require meaningful distances/similarities between vertices of the graph. Conveniently it does not matter whether we have access to distances or similarity values. However, though theoretically possible to run the affinity clustering algorithm on an unweighted graph with distances 1 and ∞ for edges and non-edges respectively, this leads to a lot of arbitrary tie-breaks that makes the result irrelevant.[9]

Fortunately, there are standard ways to impose a metric on an unweighted graph: e.g., common neighbors ratio or personalized page rank. We focus on the former metric and compute for every pair of neighbors the ratio of the number of their common neighbors over the total number of their distinct neighbors. Computing the number of common neighbors can be implemented using standard techniques in MapReduce, however, one can use sampling when dealing with high-degree vertices to improve the running time and memory footprint (leading to an approximate result).[10]

4. IMPROVE ORDERING USING SEMI-LOCAL MOVES

Given an initial ordering of vertices for example by `AffinityOrdering`, we can further improve the cut size by applying semilocal moves. The motivation here is that these simple techniques provide us with highly parallelizable algorithms that can be iteratively applied (e.g., by a MapReduce pipeline) so the result converges to high-quality partitions. In the following we discuss two such approaches.

4.1 Minimum Linear Arrangement

Minimum Linear Arrangement (MinLA) is a well studied NP-hard optimization problem [15].[11] Given an undirected graph $G = (V, E)$ (with edge weights w_{uv}) we seek a one-to-one function $\phi : V \to \{0, 1, \ldots, n-1\}$ that minimizes

$$\sum_{(u,v) \in E} |\phi(v) - \phi(u)| w_{uv}. \qquad (1)$$

Optimizing the sum above results in a linear ordering of vertices along a line such that neighbor nodes are nearby each other. The end result is that dense regions of the graph will be isolated into clusters and therefore makes it easier to identify cut boundaries on the line.

We have implemented a very simple distributed algorithm (in MapReduce) that directly optimizes MinLA. The algorithm simply iterates on the following MapReduce phases until it converges (or runs up to a specified number of steps):

- **MR Phase 1:** Each node computes its optimal rank as the weighted median[12] of its neighbors and outputs its new rank.
- **MR Phase 2:** Assigns final ranks to each node (i.e., handles duplicate resolution, for example, by simple ID-based ordering).

Note that since Phase 1 is done in parallel for each node and independently of other moves, there will be side effects, hence it is an optimistic algorithm with the hope that it will converge to a stable state after few rounds. Our experimental results show that in practice this algorithm indeed

[8]In fact, as mentioned therein, an implementation of the connected components algorithm within the same framework and using the same techniques provides a 20-40 times improvement in running time compared to best previously known algorithms.

[9]Practically the worse outcome is a highly unbalanced hierarchical partitioning because arbitrary tie-breaks favor the "first" cluster.

[10]As alluded earlier in the text, there are very fast distributed algorithms for computing this metric; see, e.g., [33].

[11]In fact, the problem admits $O(\log\log n)$ approximation on planar metrics [26] and $O(\sqrt{\log n}\log\log n)$ on general graph metrics [13, 5].

[12]All else fixed, moving a node to the weighted median of its neighbors—a standard computation in MapReduce—optimizes Equation 1.

converges for all the graph types that we tried, although the number of rounds depends on the underlying graph.

4.2 Rank Swap

Given an existing linear ordering of vertices in a graph we can further improve the cut size (of the fully balanced partition based on it) via semilocal swaps. Note that unlike MinLA heuristic discussed in Section 4.1, this process depends on the prechosen cut boundaries, i.e., the number of final partitions k. Notice that one expects that the semilocal swap operations will be effective once a good initial ordering provided by either the Affinity-based mapping and/or MinLA. Indeed our experimental results show that this procedure is extremely effective and produces cut sizes better than the competition on some public social graphs we tried.

`RankSwap` can be implemented in a straightforward way on a distributed (for example, MapReduce) framework as outlined by Algorithm 3.

Algorithm 3 `RankSwap`(G, k, r)

Input: Graph G, number of partitions k, number of intervals per partition r
Output: A partition of $V(G)$ into k parts
Controller:
Pair nearby partitions
Split each partition into r intervals $I_0, \ldots, I_{r-1}$ and randomly pair intervals between paired partitions
Map $\langle I_i; I_j \rangle$:
repeat
Pick node pair $u \in I_i$, $v \in I_j$ with the best cut improvement
Swap u and v
until no pair improves the cut
for all $u \in I_i \cup I_j$ **do**
Emit $\langle u; r_u \rangle$. {r_u is the new rank of u}
Reduce $\langle u; r_u \rangle$:
Emit $\langle u; r_u \rangle$. {Identity Reducer}

Subdividing each partition into intervals is important, especially for small number of partitions k, to achieve parallelism, and allowing possibly more time- and memory-consuming swap operations. Pairing the intervals between two partitions can be done in various ways. One simple example is random pairing. Our experiments showed that this is almost as effective as more complicated ones, hence we do not discuss the other methods in detail here.

The swap operation between two intervals (handled by each Mapper task) can be done in various ways. We have experimented with several methods each with increasing complexity and settled on the following one: 1) Sort the nodes in each interval in descending order by their cut size reduction. 2) Starting from the top node in the first interval find a best pair (if one exist) from the second interval. 3) If a pair is found swap the nodes and update all their neighbors and iterate.

Our extensive studies with this method confirmed that it gives the best results in terms of quality at the expense of an acceptable additional cost. It runs fast in practice due to the relatively small sizes of the intervals because of the parallelism we achieve. We can also afford an additional cost in the swap method because each interval pair is handled by a separate Mapper task.

5. IMBALANCE-INDUCING POSTPROCESSING

Here we several postprocessing techniques that allow us to take advantage of the permissible imbalance and produce better cuts.

First we sketch how the problem can be solved optimally if the number of vertices is not too large. This approach is based on dynamic programming and requires the entire graph to live in memory, which is a barrier for using this technique even if the running time were almost linear.[13] However, this algorithm is still usable with the caveat that one first needs to group together blocks of contiguous vertices and contract them into supernodes, such that the graph of supernodes fits in memory and is small enough for the algorithm to handle. The fact that nearby vertices are similar to each other implies that this sort of contraction should not hurt the subsequent optimization significantly. Indeed trying two different block sizes (resulting in 1000 and 5000 blocks) produced similar cuts.

The other two approaches work on the concept of "windows" and perform only local optimizations within each. Let π denote the permutation of vertices at the start of the local optimization, and let π_i be the i-th vertex in the permutation for $1 \leq i \leq n$. Given that we want to get k parts of (almost) the same size, we consider the ideal split points $q_j = \lfloor \frac{jn}{k} \rfloor$ for $1 \leq j < k$. Though there are only $k-1$ real split points, we define two dummy split points at either end to make the notation cleaner: $q_0 = 0$ and $q_k = n$. Then, the ideal partitions, in terms of size, will be formed of $\pi(q_j + 1 \rightarrow q_{j+1})$ for different $0 \leq j < k$. Given a permissible imbalance $\alpha > 0$, a window is defined around each (real) split point allowing for $\alpha/2$ imbalance on either side. More precisely, $W_j = \pi(\pi_{q_j - \alpha'} \rightarrow \pi_{q_j + \alpha'})$ for $\alpha' = \lceil \frac{\alpha n}{2k} \rceil$. Essentially we are free to shift the boundaries of partitions within each window without violating the balance requirements. We propose two methods to take advantage of this opportunity. One finds the optimal boundaries within windows, while the other also permutes the vertices in each window arbitrarily to find a better solution.

5.1 Dynamic program to optimize cuts

The partitioning problem becomes more tractable if we fix an ordering π of vertices and insist on each partition consisting of consecutive vertices (perhaps, with wrap-around). Here we focus on the case with no wrap-around.

Let $A_{i,j,q}$ for $1 \leq i, j \leq n, 1 \leq q \leq k, j \geq i-1$ denote the smallest cut size, using exactly q partitions, achievable for the subgraph induced by vertices $\pi(i \rightarrow j)$. Once all these entries are computed, $A_{1,n,k}$ yields the solution to the original problem. As is customary in dynamic programs, we only discuss how to find the "cost"—here, the cut size—of the optimal solution; augmenting the DP to find the actual solution—here, the partition—is then standard.

We fill in the table $A_{i,j,q}$ in the order of increasing q. For the case of $q = 1$, we clearly have $A_{i,j,q} = 0$ if and only if $w(\pi(i \rightarrow j)) \leq (1+\alpha)w(V)/k$,i.e., vertices $\pi(i \rightarrow j)$ fit in one part. Otherwise, it is defined as infinity.

We use a recurisve formula to compute $A_{i,j,q}$ for $q > 1$. The formula depends on $A_{i',j',q'}$ entries where $q' < q$, hence already computed. Let us introduce some notation before

[13]The procedure proposed here runs in time $O(n^3 \log k)$ but the running time can be improved to almost linear.

presenting the recurrence. We define $C(i,j,k)$ as the total length of edges going from $\pi(i \to j)$ to $\pi(j+1 \to k)$. We now present the recursive formula for computing $A_{i,j,q}$ as

$$A_{i,j,q} = \min_{i-1 \le k \le j} \left[A_{i,k,1} + A_{k+1,j,q-1} + C(i,k,j)\right]. \quad (2)$$

LEMMA 1. *Equation (2) is a valid recursion for $A_{i,j,q}$, which coupled with the initialization step given above yields a sound computation for all entries in the DP table.*

The above procedure can be implemented to run in time $O(n^3 k)$ and consume space $O(n^2 k)$. The key idea for improving the running time is to avoid computing $A_{i,j,q}$ for all values $1 \le q \le k$. Rather we focus on a limited subset of such q's of size $O(\log k)$. Recurrence (2) can be rewritten as

$$A_{i,j,q} = \min_{i-1 \le k < j} \left[A_{i,k,\lfloor \frac{q}{2} \rfloor} + A_{k+1,j,\lceil \frac{q}{2} \rceil} + C(i,k,j)\right]. \quad (3)$$

Then, it suffices to compute $A_{i,j,q}$ when $q \in \{\lfloor \frac{k}{2^l} \rfloor, \lceil \frac{k}{2^l} \rceil : l \ge 0\}$, reducing the running time to $O(n^3 \log k)$, where a bottom-up DP computation needs no more than three different values for q, hence an $O(n^2)$ memory usage.

5.2 Scalable linear boundary optimization

We now focus on a window $W = W_j$. (See the definition at the beginning of the section.) Note that all information on this window (including its vertices V_W and all their edges E_W) fit in memory (of one Mapper or Reducer). The linear optimization postprocessing finds a new split point in each window to minimize the total weight of edges crossing it.

Let B and A denote the set of vertices appearing before and after W, respectively, in the ordering π. The edges going from B to A are irrelevant to this step since they are cut regardless of the split point. The other edges have at least one endpoint in W. Then, there is a simple $O(|V_W| \cdot |E_W|)$-time algorithm to find the best split point in W: look at each candidate split point and go over all relevant edges to determine the weight of the associated cut.

This can be done more efficiently to run in time $O(|V_W| + |E_W|)$, too. Let s_v for $v \in W$ be the cut value (ignoring the effect of the edges between B and A). We scan the candidate split points from left to right, and compute $s_v - s_0$ where $s_0 = s_{\pi_{q_j - \alpha'}}$ (i.e., the cut value for the first split point in W).[14] For each vertex v following u, start with $s_u - s_0$, remove the edges between v and the vertices to its left (these already showed up in the cut value) and add up the edges between u and the vertices to its right to obtain $s_v - s_0$.

Since the windows are relatively small compared to the entire graph, and their corresponding subproblems can be solved independently, there is a very efficient MapReduce implementation for window-based postprocessing methods.

5.3 Scalable minimum-cut optimization

Once again we focus on a window $W = W_j$. Unlike the boundary optimization, the minimum-cut optimization is not bound to the ordering of vertices, and finds the best way to partition W into two pieces W_L and W_R so that the total weight of edges going from $B \cup W_L$ to $A \cup W_R$ is minimized where A, B were defined above.

[14]Clearly, s_0 is the total weight of edges between B and W and itself can be computed in time $O(|V_W| + |E_W|)$ (without hurting the overall runtime guarantee), however, the additive term $-s_0$ does not matter in comparing the different split point candidates.

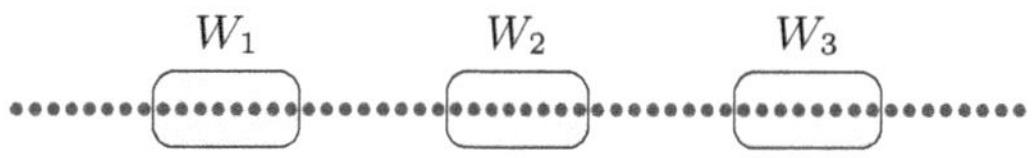

(a) The ordering of vertices on the line prior to `MinCut` procedure for an instance with k where the three windows are marked. The edges are not shown.

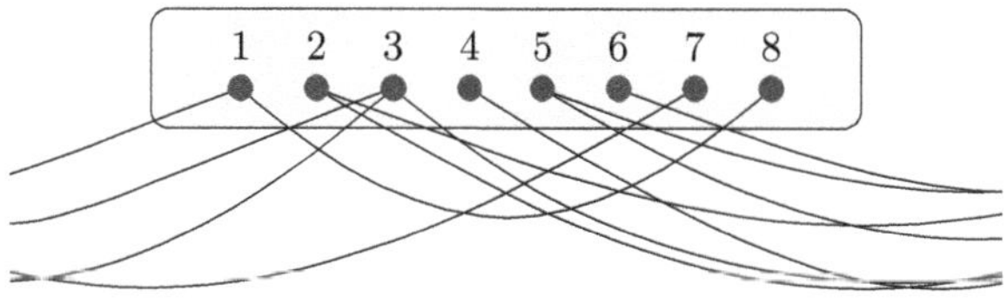

(b) Minimum cut instance for window W_2. The diagram only shows edges with one endpoint in the window (and excludes any edges coming from beyond the neighboring windows since those are not affected by the choice of the cut). The source node, to which all edges going to the left are attached, and the sink node, to which all edges going to the right are attached, are not shown.

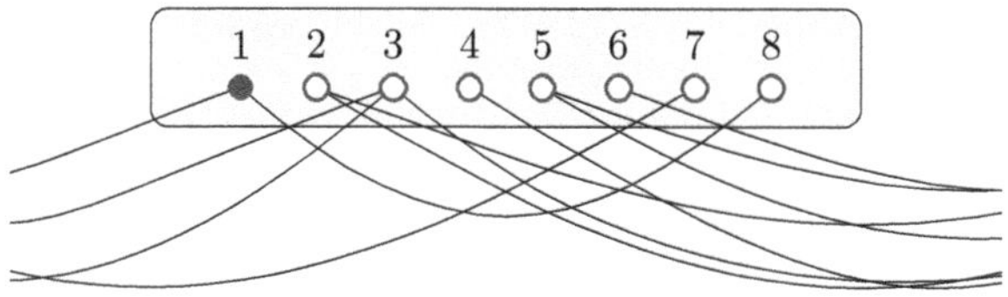

(c) The solution from `LinOpt`, which respects the ordering within the window and only optimizes for the split point. Solid and empty nodes are the two sides of the cut. The value of the cut is 4.

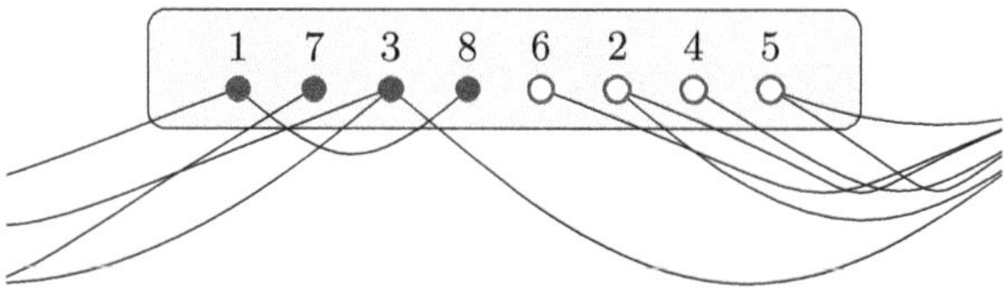

(d) The solution from `MinCut`, which tampers with the ordering within the window. The value of the cut is 1.

Figure 3: Illustration of `MinCut` postprocessing.

6. EMPIRICAL STUDIES

First we describe the different datasets that we use in our experiments. Next we compare our results to previous work, and we finally compare our different methods to each other: i.e., we demonstrate through experiments how much value each ingredient of the algorithm adds to the solution.

6.1 Datasets

We present our results on three datasets: `World-roads`, `Twitter` and `LiveJournal` (as well as publish our output on `Friendster`). As the names suggest, the first one is a geographic dataset while the last three are social graphs. All are big graphs, representatives of maps and social networks, and we test the quality and scalability of our algorithm on them.

`World-roads` A subset of the entire world road network with hundreds of millions of vertices and over a billion edges. (Due to near-planarity, the averagre degree is small.) The graph is unweighted, but vertices have longitude/latitude tags. Our algorithms run smoothly on this graph in reasonable time using a small number of machines, demonstrating their scalability.

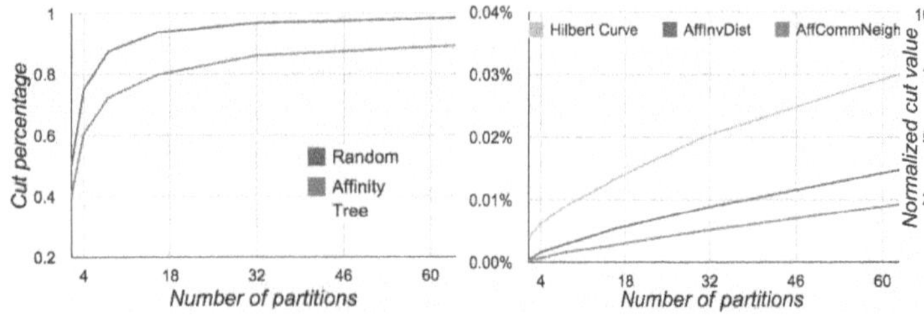

Figure 4: Comparison of the (fully balanced) cut size for `RandInit` and `AffCommNeigh` on `Twitter` (left) and `Hilbert`, `AffInvDist` and `AffCommNeigh` on `World-roads` (right).

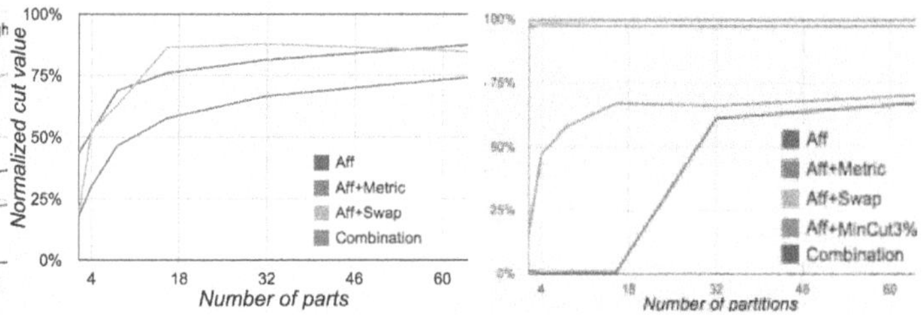

Figure 5: Comparison of the (fully balanced) cut size for some semilocal operations on `Twitter` (left) and fully balanced and 5%-imbalance cuts for `World-roads` (right). The results are compared to `AffComm-Neigh`, set as 100%.

`Twitter` The public graph of tweets[15], with about 41 million vertices (twitter accounts) and 2.4 billion (directed) edges (denoting followership) [21]. This graph is unweighted, too. We run all our algorithms on the undirected underlying graph.

`LiveJournal` The undirected version of this public social graph (snapshot from 2006) has 4.8 million vertices and 42.9 million edges [34].

6.2 Comparison of different Techniques

6.2.1 Initial ordering

We have four methods to obtain an initial ordering for the geographic graphs and two for non-geographic graphs. Here we compare these methods to each other based on the value of the cut obtained by chopping the resulting order into equal contiguous pieces. In order to make this meaningful, we report all the cut sizes as the fraction of cut edges to the total number of edges in the graph.

Figure 4 compares the results of two methods: `RandInit` produces a random permutation of the vertices, hence, as we observed prevously, gets a cut size of approximately $1 - \frac{1}{k}$; `AffCommNeigh` (using the `AffinityOrdering` with the similarity oracle based on the number of common neighbors) clearly produces better solutions with improvements ranging from 20% to 10% (more improvement for smaller number of parts). The `AffCommNeigh` tree in this case was pretty shallow (much lower than $\log n$) with only four levels. Whenever we report numbers for different number of partitions in one chart, $k = 2, 4, 8, 16, 32, 64$ are used for experiments.

Figure 4 also compares the results of three methods, each producing a cut of size at most 3% and significantly improving upon the $1 - \frac{1}{k}$ result of `RandInit`: Compared to `Hilbert`, the two other methods `AffInvDist` (using the inverse of geographic distance as the similarity oracle) and `AffCommNeigh`, respectively, obtain 90% to 50% and 95% to 70% improvement; once again the easier instances are those with smaller k. The corresponding trees, with 13 and 11 levels, respectively, are not as shallow as the one for `Twitter`. The quality of the cuts correlates with the runtime complexity of the algorithms: `RandInit` (fastest, but worst), `Hilbert`, `AffInvDist`, and `AffCommNeigh` (best, but slowest). Note that although the implementation of `Hilbert` seems more complicated, it is significantly faster in practice.

For the following experiments, we focus on `AffCommNeigh` since it consistently gives better results for different values of k (both for `Twitter` and `World-roads`). Specially in diagram legends, this initialization step may be abbreviated as `Aff`.

[15]Other graphs in [32] were either small or not public.

6.2.2 Improvements and imbalance

The performance of the semilocal improvement methods, `Aff+Metric` and `Aff+Swap`, as well as our main algorithm, `Combination`, on `Twitter` is reported in Figure 5. The diagram shows the percentage of improvement of each over the baseline `AffCommNeigh` for different values of $k = 2, \ldots 64$. Except for $k = 16, 32$, `Aff+Swap` outperforms `Aff+Metric`; their performance varies from 7% to 75%, with best performance for smaller k. Combining the two methods with the imbalance-inducing techniques to get `Combination` yields results significantly better than every single ingredient, with the relative improvement sometimes as large as 50%. The final results have very little imbalance, and indeed cuts of comparable quality can be obtained without any imbalance.

Figure 5 also sets the results of various postprocessing methods against one another and depicts their improvements compared to the baseline of `AffCommNeigh` when run on `World-roads`. The first two consists of semilocal optimization methods, `Aff+Metric` and `Aff+Swap`, which also appeared in the discussion for `Twitter`. These do not yield significant improvement over their `AffCommNeigh` starting point: the results compared to the starting point (baseline) ranges from 95% to 98%. The other two algorithms use imbalance-inducing ideas, and yield significantly better results. Our main algorithm, `Combination`, clearly outperforms all the others specially for small values of k.

All the experiments assume 3% imbalance in partition sizes—each partition may have size within range $(1 \pm 0.03)\frac{n}{k}$. However, only `Aff+MinCut` and `Combination` use this to improve the quality of the partition.

6.2.3 Convergence analysis

Next we consider the convergence rate of the two semilocal improvement methods on two graphs. For `Twitter`, the rate of convergence for metric optimization is the same whether we start with `AffCommNeigh` or `RandInit`. (See Figure 6.) The convergence happens essentially in three or four rounds.

The convergence for the rank swap methods happens in 10-15 steps for `Twitter` and in 5-10 steps for `World-roads`; more steps required for larger values of k.

The convergence for the metric optimization on `Twitter` happens in 3-4 steps if the starting point is `AffCommNeigh`. However, if we start with a random ordering, it may take up to 20 steps for the metric to converge.

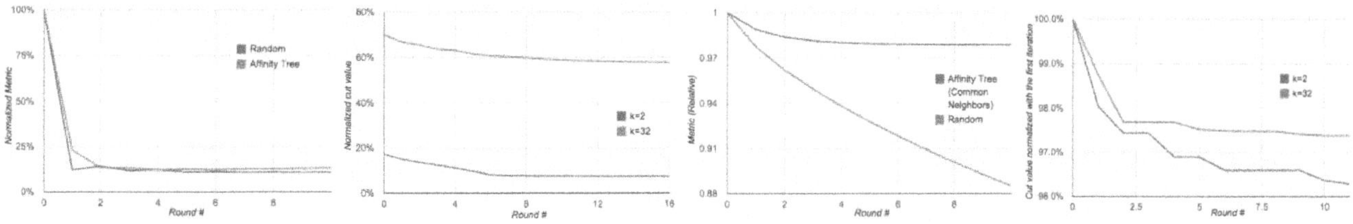

Figure 6: Convergence rate of `Aff+Metric` (first) and `Aff+Swap` (second) on `Twitter`, and then convergence rate of `Aff+Metric` (third) and `Aff+Swap` (fourth) on `World-roads`.

6.3 Comparison to Previous Work

The most relevant previous work are the scalable label propagation-based algorithms of Ugander and Backstrom [34] and Martella et al. [23]. The former reports results on an internal graph (for Facebook) and a public social graph, `LiveJournal`, while the latter reports results on `LiveJournal` and `Twitter`. The maximum partition imbalance is given in parentheses, and the cut sizes are reported as fractions of total number of edges in the graph.

k	[34] (5%)	`Spinner` (5%)	`Aff` (0%)	`Combination` (0%)
20	37%	38%	35.71%	**27.50%**
40	43%	40%	40.83%	**33.71%**
60	46%	43%	43.03%	**36.65%**
80	47.5%	44%	43.27%	**38.65%**
100	49%	46%	45.05%	**41.53%**

Even our initial linear embedding (obtained by constructing the hierarchical clustering based on a weighted version of the input, where edge weights denote the number of common neighbors between two vertices) is consistently better than the best previous result. Our algorithm with the post-processing obtains 15% to 25% improvement over the previous results (better for smaller k), and it only requires a couple of post-processing rounds to converge. We take note that the results of [34] allow 5% imbalance whereas our results produce almost perfectly balanced partitions.

`Twitter` is another public graph, for which the results of state-of-the-art minimum-cut partitioning is available. We report and compare the results of our main algorithm, `Combination`, for this graph to the best previous methods.

k	[30] (4−15%)	`Spinner` (5%)	`FENNEL` (10%)	`METIS` (3%)	`Combination` (3%)
2	34%	15%	**6.8%**	11.98%	7.43%
4	55%	31%	29%	24.39%	**18.16%**
8	66%	49%	48%	35.96%	**33.55%**
16	76%	61%	59%	N/A	**46.18%**
32	80%	69%	67%	N/A	**57.67%**

Algorithms developed in [30, 32] are suitable for the streaming model, but one can implement variants of those algorithms in a distributed manner. Our implementation of a natural distributed version of the FENNEL algorithm does not achieve the same results as those reported for the streaming implementation reported in [32]. However, we compare our algorithm directly to the numbers reported on `Twitter` by FENNEL [32].

Finally we report the cut sizes for `Friendster`, so others can compare their results with it. The running time of our algorithms are not affected with large k; the running time difference for $k = 2$ and tens of thousands is less than 1%, well within the noise associated with the distributed system. In fact, construction of the initial ordering is independent of k, and the post-processing steps may only take advantage of the increased parallelism possible for large k.

k	2	10	10^2
Cut size	11.9%	41.4%	59.8%

We also make our partitions for `Twitter`, `LiveJournal` and `Friendster` publicly available [1].

6.4 Scalability

We noted above that the choice of k does not affect the running time of the algorithm significantly: the running time for two and tens of thousands of partitions differed less than 1% for `Friendster`.

As another measure of its scalability, we run the algorithm with $k = 2$ on a series of random graphs (that are similar in nature) of varying sizes. In particular, we use RMAT graphs with parameter 20, 22, 24, 26 and 28, whose node and edge count is given in the table below. In addition, the last column gives the normalized running time of our algorithm on these graphs. Note that the size of the graph almost quadruples from one graph to the next.

graph	$\lvert V \rvert$	$\lvert E \rvert$	max degree	running time
RMAT 20	650K	31M	65K	100%
RMAT 22	2.4M	130M	160K	110%
RMAT 24	8.9M	525M	400K	133%
RMAT 26	32.8M	2.1B	1M	160%
RMAT 28	120M	8.5B	2.5M	402%

6.5 Google Maps Driving Directions

As discussed in Section 1, we apply our results to the Google Maps Driving Directions application. Note that the evaluation metric for balanced partitioning of the world graph is the expected percentage of cross-shard queries over the total number of queries. More specifically, this objective function can be captured as follows: we first estimate the number of times each edge of graph may be part of the shortest path (or the driving direction) from the source to destination across all the query traffic. This produces an edge-weighted graph in which the weight of each edge is proportional to the number of times we expect this edge appearing in a driving direction, and our goal is to partition the graph into a small number of pieces and minimize the total weight of the edges cut. We can estimate each weight based on historical data and use it as a proxy for the number of times the edge appears on a driving direction on the real data. This objective is aligned with minimizing the weighted cut, and we can apply our algorithms to solve this problem.

Before deciding about our live experiments, we realized it might be suitable to use an imbalance factor in dividing the graph, and as a result, we first examined the best imbalance factor for our cut-optimization technique. In particular, we observe that we can reduce cross-shard queries by 21% when increasing the imbalance factor from 0% to 10%.

The two methods that we examined via live experiments were (i) a baseline approach based on the Hilbert-curve embedding, and (ii) one method based on applying our cut-optimization postprocessing techniques. Note that both these algorithms first compute an embedding of nodes into a line, which results in a much simpler system to identify the corresponding shards for the source and destination of each query at serving time. Finally, by running live experiments on the real traffic, we observe the number of multi-sharded queries from our cut-optimization techniques is almost 40% less than the number of multi-sharded queries compared to the naïve Hilbert embedding technique.

7. CONCLUSION

We develop a scalable algorithm for balanced partitioning of geographic and general graphs. The algorithm is based on embedding the vertices onto a line before chopping the sequence of vertices into almost equal pieces. The initial ordering obtained from hierarchical agglomerative clustering using the number of common neighbors as similarity measure outperforms the Hilbert cover-based partitioning even for geographic graphs. While the most effective postprocessing techniques are random-swap local improvements and minimum cut-based boundary optimization, iterative use of different techniques until convergence gives best overall results. Our algorithms improves upon the previously developed distributed balanced partitioning algorithms [34, 32, 23]. In addition, live experiments for the Google Maps Driving Direction shows significant advantage of our algorithm over a standard Hilbert curve-based partitioning.

Acknowledgements. The authors wish to thank Aaron Archer and Raimondas Kiveris for fruitful discussions.

References

[1] Public data for balanced partioning paper. http://goo.gl/okvwpa, 2015.

[2] Andreev, K., and Räcke, H. Balanced graph partitioning. *Theory Comput. Syst. 39*, 6 (2006), 929–939.

[3] Aydin, K., Bateni, M., and Mirrokni, V. Distributed balanced partitioning via linear embedding. *CoRR abs/1512.02727* (2015).

[4] Boldi, P., Rosa, M., Santini, M., and Vigna, S. Layered label propagation: a multiresolution coordinate-free ordering for compressing social networks. In *WWW* (2011), pp. 587–596.

[5] Charikar, M., Hajiaghayi, M. T., Karloff, H. J., and Rao, S. l_2^2 spreading metrics for vertex ordering problems. *Algorithmica 56*, 4 (2010), 577–604.

[6] Chierichetti, F., Kumar, R., Lattanzi, S., Mitzenmacher, M., Panconesi, A., and Raghavan, P. On compressing social networks. In *KDD* (2009), pp. 219–228.

[7] Ching, A., and Kunz, C. Giraph : Large-scale graph processing on hadoop. In *Hadoop Summit* (2010).

[8] Dean, J., and Ghemawat, S. Mapreduce: Simplified data processing on large clusters. In *OSDI* (2004), pp. 137–150.

[9] Delling, D., Goldberg, A. V., Razenshteyn, I., and Werneck, R. F. F. Graph partitioning with natural cuts. In *IPDPS* (2011), pp. 1135–1146.

[10] Delling, D., Goldberg, A. V., Razenshteyn, I., and Werneck, R. F. F. Exact combinatorial branch-and-bound for graph bisection. In *ALENEX* (2012), pp. 30–44.

[11] Dongarra, J., Foster, I., Fox, G., Gropp, W., Kennedy, K., Torczon, L., and White, A. *The Sourcebook of Parallel Computing*. Morgan Kaufmann Publishers Inc., 2003.

[12] Feige, U., and Krauthgamer, R. A polylogarithmic approximation of the minimum bisection. *SIAM J. Comput. 31*, 4 (2002), 1090–1118.

[13] Feige, U., and Lee, J. R. An improved approximation ratio for the minimum linear arrangement problem. *Inf. Process. Lett. 101*, 1 (2007), 26–29.

[14] Fishburn, P. C., Tetali, P., and Winkler, P. Optimal linear arrangement of a rectangular grid. *Discrete Mathematics 213*, 1-3 (2000), 123–139.

[15] Garey, M. R., and Johnson, D. S. *Computers and Intractability: A Guide to the Theory of NP-Completeness*. W. H. Freeman, 1979.

[16] Goldschmidt, O., and Hochbaum, D. S. Polynomial algorithm for the k-cut problem. In *FOCS* (1988), pp. 444–451.

[17] Gotsman, C., and Lindenbaum, M. On the metric properties of discrete space-filling curves. *IEEE Transactions on Image Processing 5*, 5 (1996), 794–797.

[18] Kang, U., Tsourakakis, C. E., and Faloutsos, C. PEGASUS: A Peta-Scale Graph Mining System- Implementation and Observations.

[19] Karypis, G., and Kumar, V. A fast and high quality multilevel scheme for partitioning irregular graphs. *SIAM J. Sci. Comput. 20*, 1 (1998), 359–392.

[20] Kiveris, R., Lattanzi, S., Mirrokni, V., Rastogi, V., and Vassilvitskii, S. Connected components in mapreduce and beyond. In *SOCC* (2014).

[21] Kwak, H., Lee, C., Park, H., and Moon, S. What is Twitter, a social network or a news media? In *WWW* (2010), pp. 591–600.

[22] Malewicz, G., Austern, M. H., Bik, A. J., Dehnert, J. C., Horn, I., Leiser, N., and Czajkowski, G. Pregel: a system for large-scale graph processing. In *SIGMOD* (2010).

[23] Martella, C., Logothetis, D., and Siganos, G. Spinner: Scalable graph partitioning for the cloud. *CoRR abs/1404.3861* (2014).

[24] Moon, B., Jagadish, H. V., Faloutsos, C., and Saltz, J. H. Analysis of the clustering properties of the hilbert space-filling curve. *IEEE TKDE 13* (2001).

[25] Niedermeier, R., Reinhardt, K., and Sanders, P. Towards optimal locality in mesh-indexings. *Discrete Applied Mathematics 117*, 1-3 (2002), 211–237.

[26] Rao, S., and Richa, A. W. New approximation techniques for some linear ordering problems. *SIAM J. Comput. 34*, 2 (2004), 388–404.

[27] Rastogi, V., Machanavajjhala, A., Chitnis, L., and Sarma, A. D. Finding connected components in map-reduce in logarithmic rounds. In *ICDE* (2013), pp. 50–61.

[28] Sokal, R. R., and Michener, C. D. A statistical method for evaluating systematic relationships. *U. Kansas Science Bulletin 38* (1958), 1409–1438.

[29] Stanton, I. Streaming balanced graph partitioning algorithms for random graphs. In *SODA* (2014), pp. 1287–1301.

[30] Stanton, I., and Kliot, G. Streaming graph partitioning for large distributed graphs. In *KDD* (2012), pp. 1222–1230.

[31] Strongin, R. G., and Sergeyev, Y. D. *Global optimization with non-convex constraints: sequential and parallel algorithms*. Nonconvex Optimization and Its Applications. Kluwer academic publishers, 2000.

[32] Tsourakakis, C. E., Gkantsidis, C., Radunovic, B., and Vojnovic, M. FENNEL: streaming graph partitioning for massive scale graphs. In *WSDM* (2014), pp. 333–342.

[33] Tsourakakis, C. E., Kolountzakis, M. N., and Miller, G. L. Approximate triangle counting. *CoRR abs/0904.3761* (2009).

[34] Ugander, J., and Backstrom, L. Balanced label propagation for partitioning massive graphs. In *WSDM* (2013), pp. 507–516.

[35] Yan, D., Cheng, J., Lu, Y., and Ng, W. Blogel: A block-centric framework for distributed computation on real-world graphs. *PVLDB 7*, 14 (2014), 1981–1992.

Kangaroo: Workload-Aware Processing of Range Data and Range Queries in Hadoop*

Ahmed M. Aly†
Google Inc.
Mountain View, CA, USA
aaly@google.com

Hazem Elmeleegy
Turn Inc.
Redwood City, CA, USA
hazem.elmeleegy@turn.com

Yan Qi
Turn Inc.
Redwood City, CA, USA
yan.qi@turn.com

Walid Aref
Purdue University
West Lafayette, IN, USA
aref@cs.purdue.edu

ABSTRACT

Despite the importance and widespread use of range data, e.g., time intervals, spatial ranges, etc., little attention has been devoted to study the processing and querying of range data in the context of *big data*. The main challenge relies in the nature of the traditional index structures e.g., B-Tree and R-Tree, being *centralized* by nature, and hence are almost crippled when deployed in a distributed environment. To address this challenge, this paper presents *Kangaroo*, a system built on top of Hadoop to optimize the execution of range queries over range data. The main idea behind Kangaroo is to split the data into non-overlapping partitions in a way that minimizes the query execution time. *Kangaroo* is query workload-aware, i.e., results in partitioning layouts that minimize the query processing time of given query patterns. In this paper, we study the design challenges Kangaroo addresses in order to be deployed on top of a distributed file system, i.e., HDFS. We also study four different partitioning schemes that Kangaroo can support. With extensive experiments using real range data of more than one billion records and real query workload of more than 30,000 queries, we show that the partitioning schemes of Kangaroo can significantly reduce the I/O of range queries on range data.

1. INTRODUCTION

Hadoop has become a standard platform for big data analytics. Many businesses are increasingly becoming dependent on it, and this is especially true for the Internet companies. Moreover, the tools built on top of Hadoop such as Pig [25], Hive [28], Cheetah [6], etc make it easier for users to engage with Hadoop and run queries using friendly high-level languages.

*This research was supported in part by National Science Foundation under Grant IIS 1117766.

†All of the research conducted by the first author was done while being an intern at Turn Inc., and a PhD student at Purdue University.

WSDM'16, February 22–25, 2016, San Francisco, CA, USA.

 ISBN 978-1-4503-3716-8/16/02... $15.00

DOI: http://dx.doi.org/10.1145/2835776.2835841

One of the main issues with Hadoop is that executing a query usually involves scanning very large amounts of data to perform filtering, grouping, and aggregation, which can lead to high response times. Most prior work attempting to reduce the amount of data scanned during query processing has been considering either introducing traditional database indexing at the record-level or on filtering out entire partitions in case the query has some filtering criteria defined on the partition key. Moreover, except for very little work, such as [11], not enough attention has been given to addressing those concerns in the context of big *range* data, as opposed to the regular point data records.

To appreciate the significance of range data types and how they are central to many large-scale data-intensive industries, consider the following few examples:

- **Digital Advertising:** The goal in companies for digital advertising is to accurately and efficiently deliver the advertiser's message to the target audience in the online world, which is simply known as executing ad campaigns. For instance, Turn Inc. maintains anonymized profiles (based on cookie ids) for online users., which will help in deciding whether a given user is a good match for a certain advertiser. Obviously, running such campaigns results in an enormous amount of data generation. This data is later analyzed to try to glean insights related to how different users and user segments respond to the different marketing stimuli. Hence, in this context, we can consider each user profile as a range data record, whose range is defined by its lifetime; i.e. from the time the profile was created until the time of its last activity. Similarly, queries typically have time ranges, e.g., the duration of the campaign being analyzed. The need for this type of analysis also extends to other online players like big publishers, e.g., popular social networks or mobile apps, where they need to better understand the way the users interact with their websites or apps either for advertising purposes or for improving the user experience. In this case, they may want to track individual user sessions, which can also be regarded as range data records.
- **Television:** The television industry has some similarities to the online world. Specifically, the set-top boxes installed in homes by the TV service provider keep track of the viewed channels (and for how long). All those range data records are sent back to the service provider to be normally used for warehousing and analytics. Some of the common queries

against this type of data is to try to get a break down of the viewership for a certain TV program or TV ad. Clearly, those queries are range queries.

- **Telecom:** Calls made via cell phones can normally span multiple locations, i.e., multiple cell towers. Wireless telecom companies need to keep track of those call records, which also have associated time ranges, for billing purposes as well as for load-monitoring and capacity planning. Examples of analysis queries on this type of data can include a query returning a breakdown of call traffic by cell tower and customer demographics within a given period of time.
- **Customer Support:** Customer support tickets normally take some time before they are closed, and they are usually the subject of a lot of analysis – for example to understand the average response types to customers in certain classes of issues or by certain call agents. Also, those analyses would typically be limited to a certain time period.

In this paper, we present *Kangaroo*, a system built on top of Hadoop and designed especially to handle range data and range queries. Its key strength is centered around its ability to effectively partition the range data in such a way that maximizes the amount of data that can be skipped due to the irrelevance to the query. In other words, queries can "jump" over many irrelevant partitions, and hence the system name. The partitioning approach used by Kangaroo has many desirable and novel features, e.g., being workload-aware.

Our extensive experimental study on real data of more than one billion records and real query workload of more than 30,000 queries clearly demonstrates the effectiveness of Kangaroo.

The rest of this paper proceeds as follows. Section 2 motivates the problem, and describes the key requirements in a Hadoop-based system for processing range data and range queries. Section 3 overviews Kangaroo. Sections 4 and 5 explain the different algorithms employed by Kangaroo to perform the data partitioning. The experimental results are given in Section 6, and the related work is discussed in Section 7. Section 8 concludes the paper.

2. PROBLEM DEFINITION

We consider a set, R, of N_R records. Each record, r, is defined by a record id, $r.id$, some range data, say $r.start$ and $r.end$, and any other arbitrary attributes. A workload, Q, of N_Q queries is imposed on R. Each query, q, is also defined by a range, $q.start$ and $q.end$, such that a record, r, is only relevant to q if their ranges overlap. Also, every query, q, has a submission time, $q.submit\_time$. Our goal is to partition R such that the amount of data scanned by Q is minimized, and hence the cost of executing Q is minimized as well. As we motivate below, six main properties are desired in our partitioning scheme:

- **Workload Awareness:** Unlike traditional spatial indexing methods that focus on the data distribution irrespective of the query workload, we found that taking the workload into account can be very helpful. In particular, regions of data that are queried with high frequency need to be aggressively partitioned compared to the other less popular regions. This fine-grained partitioning of the in-high-demand data can result in significant savings in query processing time.
- **No Data Duplication:** Some existing spatial indexing methods, particularly space-partitioning trees, can cause data records to be duplicated in multiple partitions if those records happen to cross partition boundaries. This duplication is not desirable, especially in the context of very large datasets because of the potentially large storage overhead and the additional processing time required to de-duplicate the results.
- **No Data Splitting:** In big-data analytics, it is common that records have a nested structure. For instance, consider online user profiles, where each profile contains the user's different online events that define her interval of online activity. In this case, one possible solution to avoid data duplication across multiple partitions is to *split* those nested records across the partitions such that if two partitions cover two different time ranges, and the same user spans both ranges, then the profile can be split into two parts, such that each partition will only contain the part with events occurring within the partition's time range. Unfortunately, this solution is problematic because whenever we need to analyze the complete profiles, we will have to perform an expensive join across the different parts of each profile. In fact, this defeats the whole purpose of building user profiles, which is supposed to group the data that would normally to be analyzed together ahead of time, so that joins can be avoided.
- **No Partition Overlap:** Another alternative that is offered by other types of spatial indexes, e.g., R-tree and its variants, is to ensure that each data record belongs to one and only one partition, which eliminates the need for data duplication or splitting. However, this comes at the expense of allowing the partitions to *overlap*. When a query's range touches a region that belongs to the overlap of multiple partitions, all those partitions will have to be scanned, and hence the processing overhead can substantially increase.
- **Bounded Partition Size:** It is important for a partitioning scheme, especially when it operates in the Hadoop environment, to provide a means of control on the amount of skew in partition sizes. The key reason is that we want to avoid big skews across the reduce tasks of the map-reduce job performing data partitioning, as each output partition will be handled by one of those reducers. For this purpose, we define two configuration parameters, $min\_partition\_size$ and $max\_partition\_size$, that the user can set to control the lower and upper bounds of the partition sizes respectively.
- **Bounded Number of Partitions:** Another important feature of a partitioning scheme running on Hadoop is the ability to control the number of partitions. Allowing too many small partitions can be very harmful to the overall health of the Hadoop cluster (e.g., see [22, 18, 29]). In particular, the NameNode in charge of the Hadoop File System (HDFS) keeps track of the individual *blocks* comprising the HDFS files. This is a central shared resource in the cluster, and when it gets overloaded, it slows down the whole cluster. Therefore, it is a common practice in Hadoop to use large block sizes – in the order of hundreds of MBs – and also to avoid files that are much smaller than the block size. To this end, our partitioning scheme has the parameter, K_t, representing the *target* number of partitions. While K_t is used to guide the partitioning algorithm, the *actual* number of partitions, K_a, may end up being different from K_t. The reason for this discrepancy is that the setting of $min\_partition\_size$ and $max\_partition\_size$ will normally impact the final number of partitions. However, we still require K_a to be bounded w.r.t. K_t, precisely: $K_t \leq K_a \leq \quad \times K_t$.

3. THE KANGAROO SYSTEM

The Kangaroo system is built to address the above challenges. It can efficiently process Web-scale range data given a workload of range queries in a Hadoop environment. As described in Section 2,

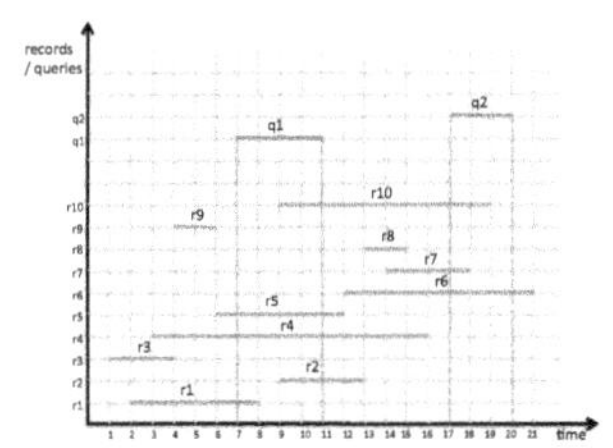

(a) Sample range data and range queries in the raw format (1D)

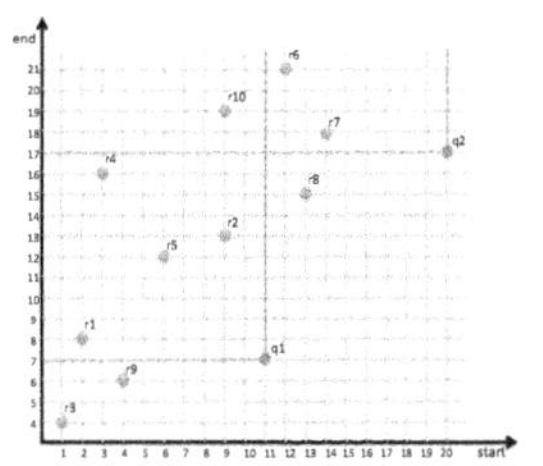

(b) Sample range data and range queries in the transformed format (2D)

it takes the historical query workload into account, ensures that data is neither duplicated nor split, that partitions do not overlap, and that the number and size of partitions are both bounded.

Note that point data and point queries are special cases of range data and range queries respectively, where each point can be thought of as a range whose start and end are identical. So they can be easily handled by Kangaroo.

3.1 Main Approach

Space Transformation: The main idea behind Kangaroo is that it begins by transforming the problem into a different space where the requirements of no duplication, no splitting, and no overlap can be easily met. Consider Figures 1(a) and 1(b). They both represent a scenario where we have 10 different range data records, $r_1 \ldots r_{10}$, and two range queries, q_1 and q_2. The ranges for both data records and queries are considered to be time intervals in this scenario. In Figure 1(a), they are plotted in the regular 1D space. It can be observed from the figure that it is impossible in this 1D space to partition this data into two or more non-overlapping partitions, with no data duplication or splitting. There does not exist any single partitioning point that would cleanly separate the data records into two different groups – let alone a bigger number of groups. The only solution is to drop one of our constraints by allowing partitions to overlap or data records to duplicate or split.

However, by transforming the problem into the 2D space, as shown in Figure 1(b), we can find valid partitioning schemes that satisfy all of our constraints. The transformation is performed as follows. For data records, their start and end values will correspond to the first and second dimensions in the new space respectively. This way, every range data record in the 1D space will now become a data point in the 2D space. On the other hand, queries will be transformed to rectangular ranges. The idea is that any overlapping record in the 1D space should now be a data point falling inside the query's rectangular range. Note that a record's range will only overlap with the query's range when both its start value is less than or equal to the query's end value, and its end value is greater than or equal to the query's start value. Thus, in the 2D space, the width of the query rectangle should span all possible start values from the minimum such value to the query's end value. Similarly, the height of the query rectangle should span all the possible end values from query start value to the maximum possible end value.

For example, in Figure 1(b), q_1's range is [7,11] in the 1D space. This is transformed into the rectangle whose top left corner is (1, 21) and whose bottom right corner is (11,7). Similarly, q_2's range in the 1D space is [17,20], while its rectangle in the 2D space has (1,21) as its top left corner and (20,17) as its bottom right corner. We can see that in Figure 1(a), q_1 overlaps with r_1, r_2, r_5, and r_{10}, whose corresponding data points in Figure 1(b) are enclosed inside q_1's rectangle. The same relationship applies between q_2 and records r_6, r_7, and r_{10}.

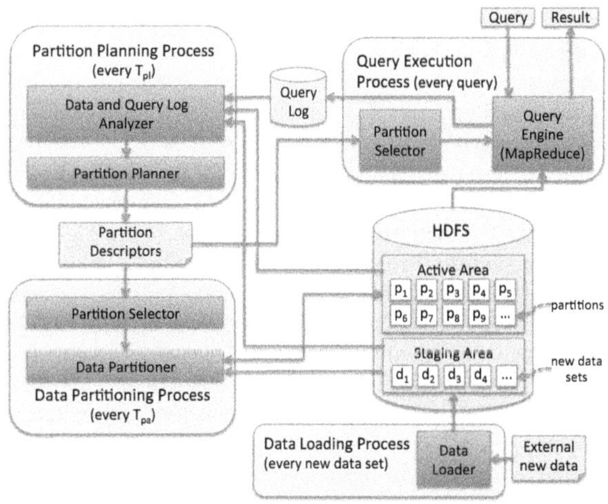

Figure 1: Architecture of Kangaroo

It is now clear that all queries will always share the same top left corner, which is the top left corner of the entire 2D space. Therefore, each query can be uniquely identified by its bottom right corner, which is the data point corresponding to its range's end and start values (the boundaries in reverse order).

Cost Model: In Kangaroo, the cost of executing a query is estimated by the number of records it has to read. Thus, the main optimization goal is to partition the data in a way that minimizes the number of retrieved records for a given query workload. We estimate the cost, i.e., quality, of a partitioning layout by the amount of records the queries of the workload will have to retrieve. More formally, given a partitioning layout, say L, the cost is:

$$Cost\ L \quad \sum_{\forall p \in L} O_q\ p\ \times C_r\ p\ , \tag{1}$$

where $O_q\ p$ is the number of queries that overlap Partition p, and C_r is the count of records in p. In Section 5, we show how the above cost function is efficiently evaluated for any given partitioning layout.

3.2 System Architecture

The overall architecture of Kangaroo is given in Figure 1. At the heart of the system is the data store maintained within HDFS. The data store has two main areas: a *staging* area, which only serves as a transient location for incoming new datasets, and an *active* area, into which the new datasets are ultimately loaded and made available to answer user queries.

As shown in Figure 1, Kangaroo has four main processes, each running on its own schedule independently from the other processes. However, they do interact through their inputs and outputs.

Partition Planning Process: This is the key process distinguishing Kangaroo from other Hadoop-based data processing systems. The *partition planning* process is responsible for identifying the (near) optimal partitioning scheme (according to the cost model in Equation 1) to be later used for partitioning the data and serving the query load. It has a *data and query analyzer* component, which aggregates and maps the active and new data records residing in HDFS, along with the historical queries from the query log – onto the 2D space. The data and queries in their new format are then passed to the *partition planner* to run the partitioning algorithm that would find the best partitioning scheme to minimize the useless data scanning while satisfying all the required constraints. The output partitioning scheme is then written to disk (typically on HDFS) to be available for other Kangaroo processes. This process runs every given time, T_{pl}. Depending on the anticipated rate of change in the workload patterns, T_{pl} can be configured to have different values, e.g, weekly, monthly, etc. It can also be dynamically triggered by a continuous monitoring system for the workload pattern changes. In Section 4, we describe in detail the different algorithms considered for the partition planner component.

Data Partitioning Process: This process runs at a higher frequency (every T_{pa}) than the partition planning process, e.g., daily. It is responsible for using the partitioning scheme derived by the planning process to actually construct the new partitions out of both the active (previously-partitioned) and the newly arriving (never-partitioned) data. There are two components used during the *data partitioning* process. The first component is the *partition selector*, which first loads the most recent partition descriptors from disk to memory, and then given an input data record, it can find the matching partition descriptor. This component is used by the second component, the *data partitioner*, to properly assign each scanned data record to its new partition. The data partitioner is implemented as a map-reduce job, where the mappers read different chunks of records and then send each record to the appropriate reducer, which will ultimately write the corresponding partition file to HDFS. Data partitioning is treated as an atomic transaction in the sense that all output partition files are first written to a temporary directory, and then only when partitioning is complete, the old active directory is deleted and the temporary directory is renamed to replace it. If any failures occur during partitioning, the temporary directory is deleted and the process can be repeated.

Query Execution Process: This process is continuously running as long as queries are being served by the system. It also has two components, where the first component is also an instance of the partition selector. It has a slightly different role in this context, where it is given a query as input and in return it provides all the partitions overlapping with the query range. The second component, which is the *query engine*, uses the partition selector to decide which partitions need to be scanned to answer a given query. The query engine is based on the Cheetah system [6], the data warehousing component used in Turn Data Management Platform (DMP) [12]. In addition to answering incoming queries, the query engine also logs all those queries, so that they can be later used by the partition planning process.

Data Loading Process: The *data loading* process is triggered by the arrival of a new dataset. The *data loader* would ingest the new data, perform any necessary sanity checking and transformations, and finally load the data into the staging area in HDFS. The new dataset waits in the staging area until the next run of the data partitioning process. Afterwards, the data partitions are moved to the active area to be ready for query answering. The data loading process is described in more detail in the context of Turn DMP [12].

4. PARTITIONING ALGORITHMS

4.1 Types of Partitioning Schemes

We consider two types of partitioning schemes that the partitioning algorithms can return: *grid-based* and *tree-based*. An example of grid-based partitioning schemes is given in Figure 2. In this type, the partitions form a coarse-grained grid structure that is overlaid on top of the original fine-grained grid of the 2D space. Hence the partitioning scheme can be represented using a pair of bit strings, B_1 and B_2, with lengths $(N_1 - \;)$ and $(N_2 - \;)$ for the first and second dimensions respectively. Each bit will denote either a row or a column in the original grid. A set bit indicates that the cor-

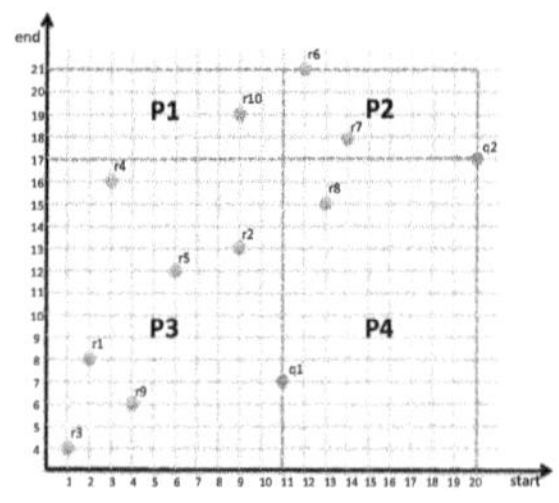

(a) Partitons layout

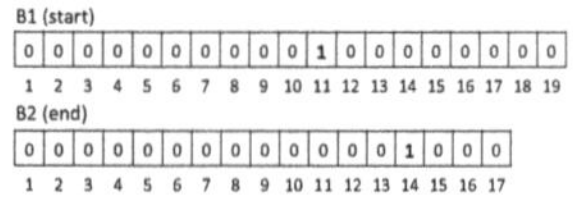

(b) Bit strings for the partitions in (a)

Figure 2: Grid-based partitioning

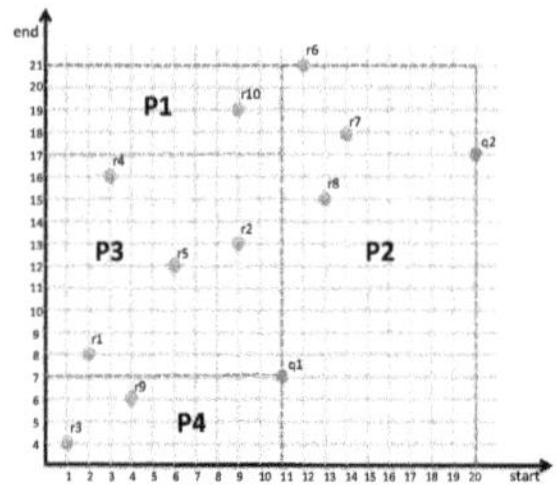

(a) Partitons layout

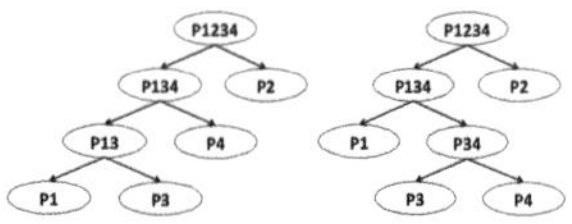

(b) Possible tree structures for the partitions in (a)

Figure 3: Tree-based partitioning

responding row or column acts as a borderline between partitions. For example, in Figure 2, B_1 and B_2 , indicating the two borderlines in the 4-partitions scheme depicted in the figure. (Note that the indexes below the bits in Figure 2(b) denote the positions of the first and second dimensions.)

Figure 3 shows an example of the more general tree-based partitioning scheme. The example also has four partitions, but they do not conform to a grid structure anymore. Instead, they can be represented by any of the two binary trees shown in Figure 3(b). In these trees, the root node represents a large partition covering the entire 2D space. Then, it is split into two smaller partitions captured by its two child nodes. Similarly, the children of each internal node are the outcome of splitting the partition it represents into two partitions, and so on. Note that with the grid-based partitioning scheme in Figure 2(a), q_1 will have to scan 7 records (Partitions P_1 and P_3) even though only 5 are relevant, while q_2 will only scan its 3 relevant records (Partitions P_1 and P_2). This gives a total of 10 scanned records for both q_1 and q_2. On the other hand, when the tree-based partitioning scheme in Figure 3(a) is used, q_1 will scan the 5 records it needs, while q_2 will scan an extra record beyond it 3 relevant records, resulting in a total of 9 scanned records for both queries, which is a lower cost.

Because of the large search space involved in both types of partitioning schemes, we considered multiple approximate algorithms to find the (near) optimal solution that minimizes the total cost. These schemes are described in the following subsections.

4.2 Grid-Based Algorithms

4.2.1 Genetic

The grid-based genetic algorithm has the same general outline common to all genetic algorithms (see Algorithm 1). It starts by generating an *initial random population* of partitioning schemes. Then, it iterates a given number of iterations. In each iteration, random pairs in the population go through *crossovers* to generate new offspring. A percentage of this offspring will further undergo *mutations*. The new generation consisting of all the offspring following the crossovers and mutations is then merged with the current population, and only the *most fit* partitioning schemes (the ones with the least costs) will survive until the next iteration, and so on. After all the iterations are over, the minimum cost partitioning scheme in the final population is selected as the answer.

To complete the description of this algorithm, some important details need to be covered, e.g., how the partitioning schemes are represented? how are the random partitioning schemes generated in the initial population? how are the crossovers and mutations performed? and how are the constraints on the partition size and number of partitions enforced?

Representation: As described in Section 4.1, grid-based partitioning schemes can be represented using a pair of bit strings, B_1 and B_2. The same representation is used by the genetic algorithm.

Algorithm 1 GridGenetic(R, Q, N_1, N_2, K_t, $min\_partition\_size$, $max\_partition\_size$)

```
1: //generate initial population of partitioning schemes
2: population = { }
3: for i = 1 to population_size do
4:    repeat
5:       ps = GridRandomPS(N1, N2, Kt)
6:    until IsFeasible(ps, min_partition_size)
7:    ps.cost = PSCost(ps, R, Q)
8:    insert ps into population, such that population remains sorted by
      cost.
9: end for
10: for i = 1 to n_iterations do
11:    //generate offspring
12:    offspring = { }
13:    for i = 1 to offspring_size do
14:       repeat
15:          pick two random parent partitioning schemes, ps1 and ps2
             from population.
16:          ps_child = GridCrossover(ps1, ps2)
17:          rand = a random number between 0 and 1
18:          if rand < mutation_prob then
19:             ps_child = GridMutation(ps_child)
20:          end if
21:       until IsFeasible(ps_child, min_partition_size)
22:       add ps_child to offspring.
23:    end for
24:    //merge offspring with population
25:    for each ps in offspring do
26:       ps.cost = PSCost(ps, R, Q)
27:       insert ps into population, such that population remains sorted
          by cost.
28:       if population.length > population_size then
29:          remove population[population_size + 1].
30:       end if
31:    end for
32: end for
33: ps* = population[1]
34: SplitLargePartititons(ps*, max_partition_size)
35: return ps*.
```

Random partitioning schemes: Given the target number of partitions along with the cardinalities of the two dimensions in the 2D space, GridRandomPS creates the two bit strings of a new random partitioning scheme as follows. First, we pick a random pair of values, K_1 and K_2, such that $K_1 \times K_2$ K_t. Then B_1 and B_2 are randomly generated as bit strings with a total number of bits equal to N_1 and N_2, of which (K_1-1) and (K_2-1) are set respectively.

Crossovers: Given a pair of partitioning schemes, we decide on a pair of (K_1, K_2) values, such that it is the closest to the midpoint of the two pairs corresponding to the two parents. We experimentally verified that this strategy is more effective than just randomly picking any valid pair for the child. In the next step, we construct B_1 and B_2 for the child by first *OR*-ing the B_1's of the parents and the B_2's of the parents respectively. Finally, a sufficient number of random bits is either set of reset to ensure that B_1 and B_2 for the child have exactly (K_1-1) and (K_2-1) set bits.

Mutations: The mutation operation is performed simply by swapping a random 0-bit and a random 1-bit in each of B_1 and B_2 of the input partitioning scheme.

Partition size and count constraints: Recall that all our algorithms have to conform with the constraint that the size of each partition in the output partitioning scheme should fall between $min\_partition\_size$ and $max\_partition\_size$. Additionally, the actual number of partitions should not exceed double the target number of partitions. The minimum size constraint is enforced using the **IsFeasible()** function (Lines 6, 21 in Algorithm 1), which will only allow a partitioning scheme to be considered if all of its partitions satisfy this constraint.

The maximum size constrain is satisfied through a post-processing step using the **SplitLargePartitions()** function. If the size of a large partition in the final partitioning scheme exceeds $max\_partition\_size$, it gets further partitioned, uniformly, into a number of sub-partitions given by the ratio of its size to $max\_partition\_size$. The partitioning key in this case is the record id, rather than the record range, to ensure that uniform partitioning can always be achieved.

Note that the worst case in terms of partitions imbalance in the output partitioning scheme (prior to splitting large partitions) will happen when all partitions are virtually empty except for one very large partition that almost has all of the data records. In this case, that large partition will be further split a maximum of K_t times, leading to an actual number of partitions, K_a $\times K_t$. We study the tradeoff in setting K_t, $min\_partition\_size$, and $max\_partition\_size$, and their impact on K_a in Section 6.

4.2.2 *Genetic with Dynamic Programming*

We also considered a variant of the grid-based genetic algorithm that uses dynamic programming along one of the dimensions. In particular, it uses the exact same framework captured by Algorithm 1. However, whenever any of these algorithms attempt to compute the second bit string, B_2, for a given partitioning scheme, it is not randomly generated. Instead, it is computed using a dynamic programming algorithm. The intuition here is that along one dimension, it is possible to compute the optimal 1D partitioning scheme somewhat efficiently without approximation.

Algorithm 2 shows how the optimal B_2 is computed. Let us first explain the need for dynamic programming. If B_2 can only have K_2 set bits, then the last set bit can have several valid positions. Going in the backward direction, those valid positions start from the last bit in B_2 back to position K_2 (where all the previous bits will have to be set too). Out of those alternative positions, to find the one leading to the optimal B_2, we first need to solve a smaller subproblem for each one of them. In the subproblem corresponding to position *pos*, we want to find the optimal positioning of (K_2-1) 1-bits in the substring of B_2 preceding *pos*. Once all the subproblems are solved, the optimal position, pos^*, for the last set bit in B_2 will be the one with the minimum sum of costs for (1) its corresponding subproblem occurring *before* pos^*, and (2) the K_1 individual partitions occurring *after* pos^*.

Note that those individual partitions are completely defined by B_1 along the first dimension and pos^* along the second dimension.

For example, in Figure 2, if B_1 is as shown and pos^*=14, then the individual partitions will be P_1 and P_2.

The above discussion shows how the problem has an optimal substructure, and hence can be solved using dynamic programming. At a high level, Algorithm 2 builds the dynamic programming matrix, M, where one axis represents the cardinality of the second dimension in our 2D space (i varied from 1 to N_2), and the second axis represents the target number of partitions we wish to have for that dimension (j varied from 1 to K_2). The matrix is built by incrementally computing the costs for all valid combinations across the two axes. During initialization, no partitioning is considered (j=1). Then, computing the cost for each subsequent cell in the matrix will be by finding the minimum across multiple sums of costs, as described above. Finally, when the entire matrix is computed, the minimum cost for the whole problem can be found in M N_2, K_2 . The optimal B_2 can then be derived by retracing the computation from M N_2, K_2 back to M , .

To compute the time complexity for this algorithm, note that there are O($N_2 \times K_2$) valid cels in the matrix. Moreover, the number of smaller subproblems required to compute each cell is O(N_2). Thus, the total time complexity is O($N_2^2 \times K_2$). Considering that this algorithm can be called a fairly large number of times by the genetic algorithm, it can potentially slow it down compared to the pure genetic approach in Section 4.2.1.

Algorithm 2 PartitionDP(R, Q, B_1, N_2, K_2)

//initialization
for i = 1 to N_2 **do**
  $M[i, 1] = 0$
  p_list = list of partitions of the form $p(x_1, 1, x_2, i)$, such that (a) x_1=1 or $B_1[x_1 - 1]$=1, (b) x_2=N_1 or $B_1[x_2]$=1, and (c) $B_1[x]$=0 for $x_1 \leq x < x_2$
  for each p in *p_list* **do**
    $M[i, 1]$ += **PCost**(p, R, Q)
  end for
end for
//main loop
for i = 2 to N_2 **do**
  for j = 2 to min(i, K_2) **do**
    $M[i, j] = \infty$
    for $h = j - 1$ to $i - 1$ **do**
      temp_cost = $M[h, j - 1]$
      p_list = list of partitions of the form $p(x_1, h + 1, x_2, i)$, such that (a) x_1=1 or $B_1[x_1 - 1]$=1, (b) x_2=N_1 or $B_1[x_2]$=1, and (c) $B_1[x]$=0 for $x_1 \leq x < x_2$
      for each p in *p_list* **do**
        temp_cost += **PCost**(p, R, Q)
      end for
      if *temp_cost* $< M[i, j]$ **then**
        $M[i, j]$ = *temp_cost*
      end if
    end for
  end for
end for
return B_2 resulting in partitioning scheme with minimum cost, $M[N_2, K_2]$, by retracing the computation of $M[N_2, K_2]$ back to $M[1, 1]$.

4.3 Tree-Based Algorithms

4.3.1 *Genetic*

The tree-based genetic algorithm uses exactly the same outline of Algorithm 1. The main difference, however, is in the way the partitioning schemes are represented, and consequently the related operations of generating new random partitioning schemes, crossovers, and mutations. The mechanisms used to enforce the partition size and count constraints are the same as the ones described for the grid-based algorithms in Section 4.2.1.

Representation: As explained in Section 4.1, tree-based partitioning schemes are represented as binary trees, where the leaf nodes capture the final partitions, while the internal nodes capture the parent enclosing partitions.

Random partitioning schemes: The random partitioning scheme for the tree-based genetic algorithm starts with a single-node tree that covers the entire space. Then, a random leaf node is picked, and randomly split into two partitions to form its two children. This process repeats until K leaf partitions are created.

Crossovers: The crossover operation is described in Algorithm 3. It is performed by splitting the two input parents using the same random split line. If, for example, the selected split line was vertical, then the right part of the first parent will be trimmed, keeping only the left part to be covered by its tree. Conversely, the second parent's tree will only keep the right part, while the left part will be trimmed. Then, a new root node is created for the child's tree that covers the entire 2D space. Subsequently, the roots of the two trimmed parent trees are added to the child's root as its two children. At this point, the child's tree may contain more or less leaf nodes than K_t. To correct this situation, existing leaf nodes are either randomly split or randomly merged with their siblings – until the total number of leaf nodes equals K_t.

The functions of trimming a tree given a split line and of merging a leaf node with its sibling are both more complex than the simple function of splitting a leaf node. The **TrimTree()** function operates recursively starting from the root. The root node is first trimmed using the split line. Then, if the split line goes through one of the child nodes, that child is properly trimmed too. If the child node was completely on the *to-keep* side of the split line, it remains unchanged. Otherwise, if it is on the *to-trim* side of the split line, then it is completely removed from the tree along with all of its descendants. For nodes that get partially trimmed, all their children will be examined and processed in the same way.

The **MergeRandomLeaf()** function is also recursive in the sense that it first finds a random leaf node to be merged, and then identifies its sibling. The sibling is precessed recursively as follows. Initially, the sibling node is expanded towards the neighboring to-be-merged node up until the border opposite to their shared border. Then, for each child of the sibling node, if the child shares a border with the to-be-merged node, then it is also expanded in the same direction until the opposite border of the to-be-merged node is reached. Otherwise, if the child does not share a border with the to-be-merged node, then it remains unchanged. By the end of processing the sibling node and its descendants, the randomly selected leaf node would have been completely merged with its neighbors and the total number of leaf nodes is decreased by one.

Mutations: The mutation operation for an input tree-based partitioning scheme is as simple as randomly splitting a leaf node in the tree to increase the leaf nodes by one, and then randomly merging a leaf node to bring the total number back to K_t.

4.3.2 *Greedy*

Similarly to the random partitioning scheme, the tree-based greedy algorithm, Algorithm 4, starts by creating a root node covering the entire space, and keeps splitting leaf nodes until the total number of leaf nodes is K_t. However, the main difference is in the way the next leaf node to split is chosen. It applies a greedy strategy rather than a random strategy. In particular, for each leaf node and for each feasible split for that node, that would not violate the minimum partition size requirement, the leaf node split resulting in the maximum gain in terms of cost reduction is chosen.

Algorithm 3 TreeCrossover(ps_1, ps_2)

K_t = number of leaf nodes in ps_1
randomly set $orientation$ to either "horizontal" or "vertical".
based on $orientation$, randomly pick a horizontal line, $y = s$, or a vertical line, $x = s$, where $1 \leq s \leq N_2$ or $1 \leq s \leq N_1$ resp.
TrimTree($ps_1.pt$, s, $orientation$, "after_trim_line")
TrimTree($ps_2.pt$, s, $orientation$, "before_trim_line")
construct a partitioning scheme, ps, such that $ps.pt.left = ps_1.pt$ and $ps.pt.right = ps_2.pt$.
k = number of leaf nodes in $ps.pt$
while $k < K_t$ **do**
  SplitRandomLeaf($ps.pt$)
  k += 1
end while
while $k > K_t$ **do**
  MergeRandomLeaf($ps.pt$)
  k -= 1
end while
return ps.

We denote the tree generated by the greedy algorithm as the *KNGR-tree* (pronounced "Kangaroo-tree"). This is because, as will be discussed in Section 6, it was shown to have superior properties compared to the other competing algorithms, and as a result, it is the default partitioning algorithm used by Kangaroo.

It is also worth noting that the greedy choice in the KNGR-tree is comparable to the one used for the KD-tree. Some of the key differences however, are that the KD-tree is not aware of the query load, and it normally does not provide any guarantees on the size or count of partitions (data records in leaf nodes).

Algorithm 4 TreeGreedy(R, Q, N_1, N_2, K_t, $min\_partition\_size$, $max\_partition\_size$)

construct a partition of the form $p(1, 1, N_1, N_2)$, and make it the root of a new partition tree, pt.
k = 1 //number of leaf nodes in pt
while $k < K_t$ **do**
  max_gain = 0, max_n = null, max_n_1=null, max_n_2 = null
  for each leaf node, n, in pt **do**
    for each possible split of n resulting in two new leaf nodes, n_1 and n_2, **do**
      if IsFeasible(n_1, $min\_partition\_size$) and **IsFeasible**(n_2, $min\_partition\_size$) **then**
        $gain$ = **PCost**(n, R, Q) - **PCost**(n_1, R, Q) - **PCost**(n_2, R, Q)
        if $gain > max\_gain$ **then**
          $max\_gain = gain$, $max\_n = n$, max_n_1=n_1, $max\_n_2 = n_2$
        end if
      end if
    end for
  end for
  split max_n into max_n_1 and max_n_2.
  k += 1
end while
construct partitioning scheme, ps^*, corresponding to pt.
SplitLargePartititons(ps^*, $max\_partition\_size$)
return ps^*.

5. COMPUTING THE COST

According to Equation 1 discussed in Section 3.1, the cost corresponding to a partition can be modeled as the number of queries that overlap the partition multiplied by the number of records inside the partition. This cost model would result into partitions of good quality if all the records have the same size (number of bytes). However, a more precise estimate of the cost corresponding to a partition would consider the size of each record in the cost formula. More formally, the cost of a certain partition, say p is:

$$Cost\ p \quad O_q\ p \times \sum_{\forall r \in p} Size\ r\ , \qquad (2)$$

where $O_q\ p$ is the number of queries that overlap with p and $Size\ r$ is the size of record r.

A basic operation in each of our proposed algorithms is to compute the cost corresponding to a given partition according to the above equation. For instance, in the tree-based greedy algorithm, we determine for each leaf node the best split that would achieve the maximum gain in terms of cost reduction. In particular, we try all the possible horizontal and vertical splits and for each pair of emerging partitions, we compute the cost. Thus, the computation of the cost of a certain partition has to be extremely efficient because it will have a direct impact on the overall running time of all the partitioning algorithms.

Given a partition, say p, the cost corresponding to p contains two components: 1) the size total data size in p and 2) the number of queries overlapping with p.

Because the raw data is not partitioned, one can have a complete scan of the data in order to determine the number of points in a given partition (i.e., the first component of the cost of a partition). Obviously, this is not practical to perform. Because we are interested in aggregates, i.e., count of points in a rectangle, scanning the individual points involves redundancy. [17] presents the idea of maintaining *prefix sums* in a grid in order to answer range-sum queries of the number of points in a window, in constant time, irrespective of the size of the window of the query or the size of the data. Hence, we preprocess the raw data in a way that enables quick lookup (in O time) of the count corresponding to a given rectangle. We maintain a two-dimensional grid that has a very fine granularity. The grid does not contain the data points, but rather maintains aggregate information. In particular, we divide the space into a grid, say G, of n rows and m columns. Each grid cell, say $G\ i,\ j$, initially contains the total number of points that are inside the boundaries of $G\ i,\ j$. This is achieved through a single MapReduce job that reads the entire data and determines the count for each grid cell. Afterwards, we aggregate the data corresponding to each cell in G using prefix-sums as in [17]. As we explain in [1] in more detail, to compute the number of points corresponding to any given partition, only four values need to be added/subtracted. Thus, in Kangaroo, the process of finding the number of points for any given partition is performed in O .

Extending the idea of prefix sums in a grid for counting the number of rectangles (i.e., queries) that overlap a partition is a bit challenging due to the problem of duplicate counting of rectangles. One way to address this challenge is to insert all the queries into an R-tree, and then given a partition, find the number of overlapping queries from the R-tree. However, this is inefficient because redundancy is involved as we are interested in aggregates. Euler histograms [4] were proposed to efficiently find the number of rectangles that intersect a given region without duplicates. Kangaroo employs a variant of the Euler histogram in [4] to efficiently compute the number of queries that overlap any given partition (without duplicates). Grid G is piggybacked with additional counters that enable Kangaroo to find the number of overlapping queries in O . For more details, the reader is referred to [1].

Note that the above techniques of grid-based pre-aggregation are key for the efficiency of our partitioning algorithms. Without pre-aggregation, e.g., using a straightforward approach of successive data scans or R-Tree-based computation, our proposed partitioning algorithms would be impractical (would take hours or even days for high values of K_t). With the O counting mechanisms, most of our partitioning algorithms are able to complete execution within one or two seconds as we demonstrate in Section 6.

6. EXPERIMENTS AND RESULTS

The Kangaroo system is implemented at Turn Inc to serve as part of its Data Management Platform (DMP) [12]. Turn DMP is a cloud-based service, particularly built for digital marketers. It already has a query execution process similar to the one shown in Figure 1. It translates a SQL-like language (Cheetah Query Language, or CQL) into map-reduce jobs. In this section, we focus on measuring the effectiveness of the partition planning process (in Figure 1), which plays the central role in the effectiveness of the entire system. In other words, we evaluate the partitioning algorithms proposed in Section 4. Note that this process runs periodically on a single node (i.e., it is not distributed).

We have also independently verified the positive impact of highly effective partitioning on the query speedup, which was expected because of the reduction in the amount of data scanned by each query. It is worth noting, however, that the actual gains in query processing are dependent on the CPU cost for each query, which can widely vary from one workload to another – for example, queries evaluating UDFs can be much more CPU-intensive than simple filtering-and-aggregation queries. For this reason we decided to focus our reported experiments on evaluating the partitioning algorithms.

Our performance measures are: 1) the running time of the algorithms, and 2) the I/O reduction percentage achieved by the partitioning algorithms for a given query-load. To measure the latter, we determine the number of unnecessary I/Os that a no-partitioning scheme would make for a given query-load and compare it to the number of unnecessary I/Os that our proposed algorithms would make for the same query-load. The less the number of unnecessary I/Os our proposed partitioning algorithms would make, the higher the I/O reduction percentage is.

As a baseline, we compare our proposed algorithms to what we refer to as the Random partitioning scheme that for a given K_t, uniformly splits the data by equally distant horizontal lines and equally distant vertical lines, i.e., performs uniform grid partitioning, such that the total number of partitions (i.e., grid cells) is K_t. We also tried to compare Kangaroo to an existing system, particularly SpatialHadoop [11] , which focuses on processing spatial data in Hadoop. Unfortunately, it expected a more recent Hadoop version than the one running on the test cluster we have access to. And since it was a shared cluster, we were not able to upgrade the Hadoop version and compare against SpatialHadoop. As an alternative, we ran an experiment (described in Section 6.3) that shows the effect of workload awareness, which is one of the key differentiators between Kangaroo and SpatialHadoop.

It is important to note that for the genetic algorithms we propose, we examined different values for the parameters: population size, number of offspring, and mutation probability. We preset these parameters to values that achieve the best. Precisely, our best configuration of these parameters is population size = 100, number of offsprings per iteration = 10, and mutation probability = 0.05. It is also worth noting that for all the experiments, to realize exactly K_t by the partitioning algorithms, we set the maximum partition size to ∞ and the minimum partition size to 0. These are the default values of these parameters, unless stated otherwise.

In the rest of this section, we study: 1) the effect of the number of partitions (K_t) on our performance metrics, 2) the effect of query load awareness on the I/O reduction percentage, 3) the effect of the query selectivity on the I/O reduction percentage, 4) the effect of the scale of the search space on the running time of the partitioning algorithms, and 5) the effect of the max-partition-size parameter on the number of actual partitions (i.e., K_a).

In the figures, we refer to the tree-based algorithms as **TB** and the grid-based algorithms as **GB**. For instance, 'Greedy TB' refers to the the tree-based greedy algorithm, while 'Genetic GB' refers to the grid-based genetic algorithm.

6.1 Experimental Setup

To evaluate Kangaroo, we use real datasets and real query workload that we have available at Turn. Our data is a sample of over one billion user profiles (each defined by a cookie id). Each user profile contains the user's history of impressions, clicks, and actions. It also has start and end timestamps defining the user's activity lifespan. Our workload is a sample of 30,000 queries collected from the logs of Turn DMP over a period of six months. Each query specifies a time range of interest, where only the users who were active during that time range are to be processed by the query. Since each query has a submission time, we shift the interval of each query in the workload by the number of days since the submission time. The rationale behind this interval-adjustment step is that we expect future queries to have a similar behavior to that of historical queries, except that the time ranges they specify will likely be relative to their (future) submission times. Therefore, a good approximation for those future queries is to consider them to be identical to the historical queries after having their time ranges properly shifted.

6.2 Effect of the Number of Partitions

In this experiment, we study the effect of the number of partitions (K_t) on our performance metrics. At different values of K_t (in log-scale), Figure 4(a) shows the percentage of I/O reduction each of our proposed partitioning algorithms can achieve in addition to that of the random partitioning scheme. As the figure demonstrates, the performance of all the proposed algorithms is better than that of the random partitioning scheme. Furthermore, our proposed algorithms tend to achieve maximal (100%) reduction percentages especially for high values of K_t. Notice that the Greedy TB algorithm achieves the best performance, reaching almost 100% reduction for only 512 partitions. Observe that the amount of reduction of the Genetic GB algorithm seems consistently proportional to the value of K_t. However, the three algorithms, the curves are not showing consistent proportions of reduction for the different values of K_t because of the fuzziness of the genetic algorithms.

Figure 4(b) shows the running time of our proposed algorithms at different values of K_t (in log-scale). As the figure demonstrates, the performance of the Genetic with Dynamic algorithm is the worst. The reason is due to the high cost of the Dynamic programming evaluation step. For high values of K_t, e.g., 2048, the algorithm can take more than a day to execute. However, the running time of the three other algorithms is relatively low (below one second). Interestingly, the Greedy TB algorithm has the lowest running time while achieving the highest I/O reduction percentage.

6.3 Effect of Workload Awareness

In this experiment, we study the effect of the workload awareness on the I/O reduction percentage that the partitioning algorithms can achieve. For simplicity, we choose the Genetic TB algorithm as it achieves the best performance as demonstrated in Section 6.2. In the experiment, we examine two costing models, one that considers both the number of points and the workload in computing the partitions, and the other considers only the number of points. One might view the latter model as a way to generate a two-dimensional k-d tree to partition the data according to the number of points.

Figure 4(c) gives the performance of the two models. It is clear from the figure that the workload-awareness results in better I/O reduction. Observe that the improvement is higher with small K_t values because when a small number of partitions is specified, the algorithm has less flexibility and this is where the usefulness of workload-awareness is pronounced the most.

6.4 Effect of Query Selectivity

In this experiment, we study the effect of the query selectivity on the I/O reduction percentage that the partitioning algorithms can achieve. We fix the value of K_t to 256. We categorize the queries of the workload according to the query selectivity. Intuitively, the higher the selectivity of the query is, the higher the chance of the partitioning algorithm to achieve high reduction percentages, and vice versa. For instance, when the query selectivity is low, e.g., 0%, i.e., the query has to scan all the data anyway, then, there is no room for reducing the I/O cost, i.e., the expected I/O reduction percentage is 0. In other words, an optimal curve for this experiment when the values of the x-axis are the query selectivities from 0% to 100% should be a straight line with slope = 1.

Figure 4(d) demonstrates the performance of the different partitioning algorithms for different query-selectivity values. It is clear from the figure that the Greedy TB algorithm tends to achieve the best performance, with consistent reduction percentages according to the query-selectivity. Furthermore, it's curve is close to a being a line with slope = 1, i.e., optimal performance as explained above.

6.5 Effect of the Scale of Search Space

In this experiment, we study the effect of the scale of the search space on the running time of the partitioning algorithms. Our original search space is defined by a grid of $\times$ lines. We fix the value of K_t to 100 and vary the scale of the grid by a scale factor that represents the portion of the grid the should be considered. For instance, if the scale factor is 0.5, it means that we consider half the size of the search space in the partitioning process.

Figure 4(e) demonstrates the performance of the partitioning algorithms for different scale factors. It is clear from the figure that the running time of the algorithms is directly proportional to the search space size. Observe that the running time of all the algorithms except the Genetic with Dynamic is below one second, which means that they are practical for even higher scale factors.

6.6 Effect of Skew in Partition Size

In this experiment, we study the effect of the parameter maximum partition-size on the number of actual partitioning K_1. We examine such effect in the Greedy TB algorithm as similar results can be obtained for the other three partitioning strategies. We fix the value of K_t to 100 and vary the value of the maximum partition size as follows. We define the ideal partition size as the total size of the whole space divided by K_t. We set the maximum partition-size as multiple of the ideal size. Figure 4(f) demonstrates the ratio between the actual number of partitions to the target number of partitions, i.e., $\frac{K_a}{K_t}$, for different values of the maximum partition-size. It is clear from the figure that the ratio $\frac{K_a}{K_t}$ always varies between 1 and 2. The worst case happens when the maximum partition size equals the ideal size. In this case, it is possible that the partitioning algorithm keeps fine-tuning a small region of space with K_t splits while leaving the rest of the space unpartitioned. In this case, the unpartitioned region requires at most another K_t additional splits, and hence the overall number of partitions K_a is K_t. Observe that when the maximum partition-size is sufficiently large, the ratio $\frac{K_a}{K_t}$ tends to 1 because in this case, the size of each of the K_t initial partitions is most probably less than the maximum partition-size, and hence no further splitting is needed.

7. RELATED WORK

Work related to Kangaroo can be categorized into three main categories: 1) centralized data indexing, 2) data indexing in distributed platforms, and 3) workload-aware query processing.

In centralized indexing, e.g., B-Tree [7], R-Tree [3, 16, 20], Quad-Tree [27], Interval Tree [9], k-d Tree [5], the goal is to split the data in a centralized index that should reside on one machine. Most of the indexes in this category aim at distributing the size of the data among a set of files, where in most cases, there is no restriction on the number of files that can be used. Consequently, in these indexes, the structure of the index can have unbounded decomposed until the finest granularity of data is reached in each split (e.g., file). For instance, the R-Tree recursively keeps splitting the space into rectangles until the number of points in each rectangle is less/greater than a certain threshold. This model of unbounded decomposition plays well for any query workload distribution; the very fine granularity of the splits (e.g., files) enables any query to retrieve its required data by scanning the minimal (or close to minimal) amount of data with very little redundancy.

In distributed indexing, e.g., (see [10, 19, 2, 11, 13, 14, 15, 21, 23, 24]), the goal is to split the data in a distributed file system in a way that optimizes the distributed query processing by minimizing the I/O overhead. Unlike the centralized indexes, indexes in this category are usually geared towards fulfilling the requirements of the distributed file system, e.g., keeping the number of input splits (in Hadoop) within a certain bound. For instance the Eagle-Eyed Elephant (E3) framework [13] was proposed to avoid accesses of data splits that are irrelevant to the query at hand. However, E3 considers only one-dimensional point data, and hence is not suited for interval-based data/queries. [11] presents SpatialHadoop; a system that can index spatial two-dimensional data using two-dimensional Grids or R-Trees. A similar effort in [21] addresses how to build R-Tree-like indexes in Hadoop for spatial data. However, none of these efforts is workload-aware.

Several research efforts try to leverage the skeweness of the query-workload to optimize the overall query execution. [1, 8, 26] present query-workload-aware systems and data partitioning mechanisms in distributed platforms. However, these systems cannot support range data and range queries. For instance, in [1], we consider only two-dimensional point (i.e., non-interval) data.

To the best of our knowledge, Kangaroo is the first effort to consider the problem of multi-dimensional range data/query indexing in a distributed system while being query-load aware.

8. CONCLUSIONS

In this paper, we have introduced *Kangaroo*, a system built on top of Hadoop and designed especially to handle range data and range queries. Its key strength is centered around its ability to effectively partition the range data in such a way that maximizes the number of partitions that queries can skip for not having any relevant data. In other words, queries can "jump" over many irrelevant partitions, and hence the system name. The partitioning approach used by Kangaroo also has many desirable and novel features: it (1) is workload-aware, (2) allows no data duplication across partitions, (3) allows no data splitting across partitions, (4) allows no partition overlap, (5) guarantees bounded partition sizes, and (6) guarantees bounded number of partitions. We also described four different partitioning algorithms to be used by Kangaroo and showed experimentally how one of them, tree-based greedy, outper-

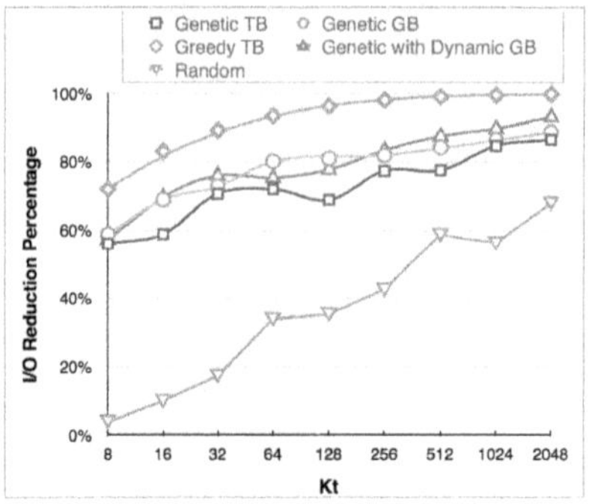

(a) I/O reduction percentage achieved at a given K_t.

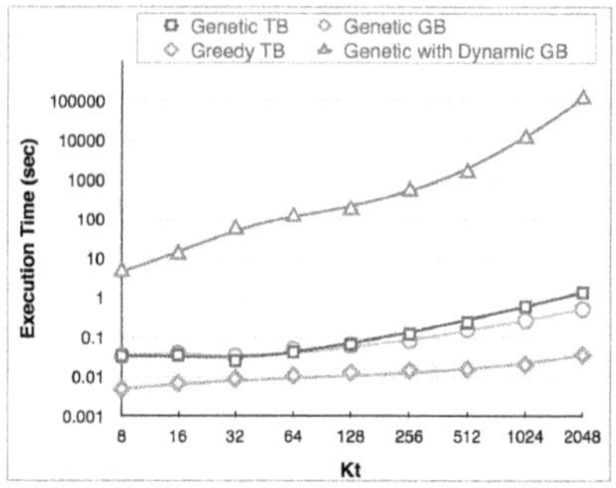

(b) Execution time of the partitioning algorithms at a given K_t.

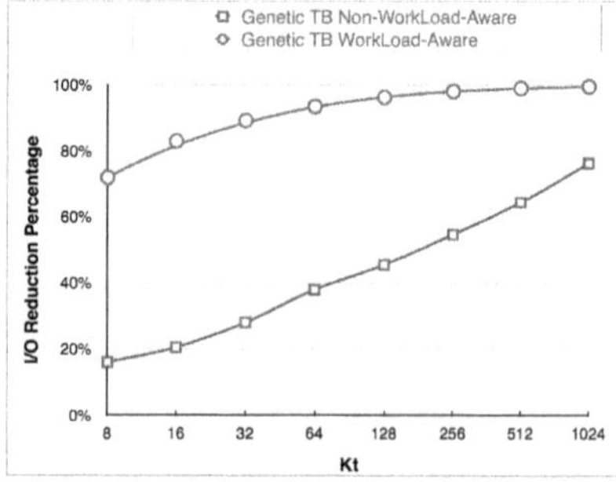

(c) Effect of query-load awareness.

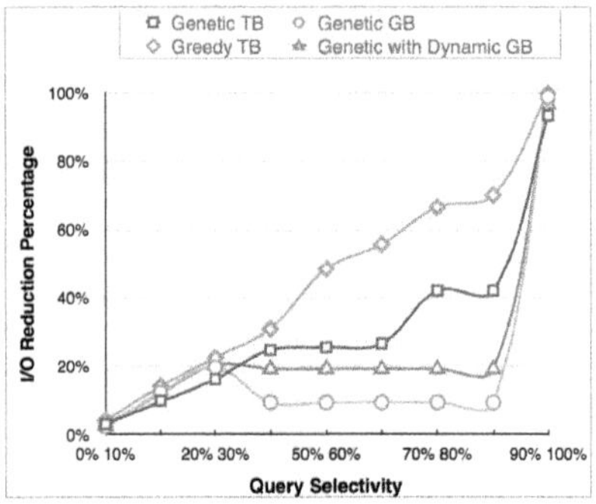

(d) I/O reduction percentage achieved given the query selectivity. K_t .

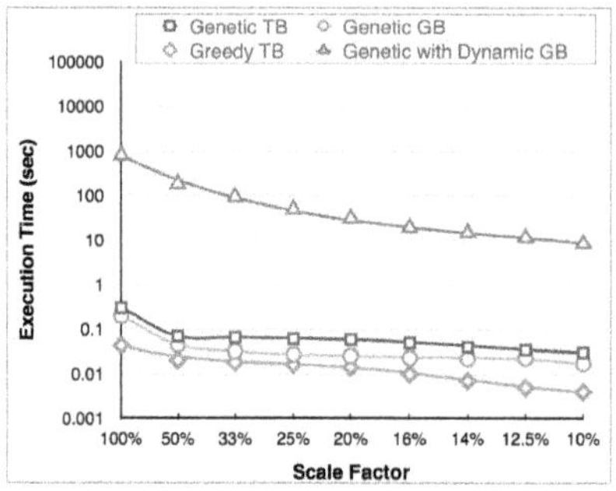

(e) Effect of the scale of the search space on the running time of the algorithms.

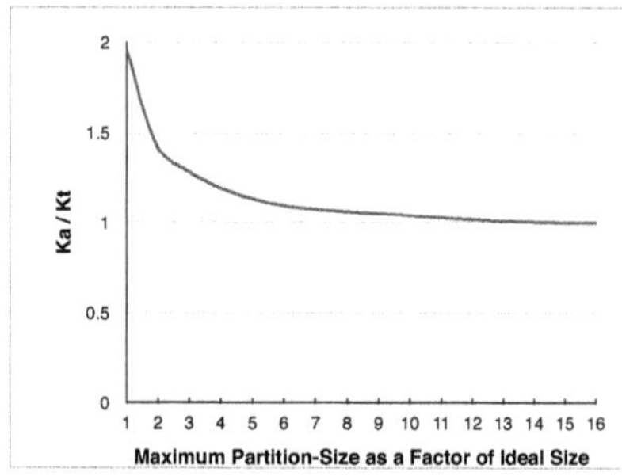

(f) Effect of *maximum partition size* on K_a. The ratio $\frac{K_a}{K_t}$ is always between 1 and 2.

Figure 4: Experimental Results

forms all the others. Our experimental study was based on a real datasets of over one billion data records and 30,000 queries. The study showed clearly the effectiveness of Kangaroo in processing range data and queries in big distributed systems.

9. REFERENCES

[1] A. M. Aly, A. R. Mahmood, M. S. Hassan, W. G. Aref, M. Ouzzani, H. Elmeleegy, and T. Qadah. AQWA: adaptive query-workload-aware partitioning of big spatial data. *PVLDB*, 8(13):2062–2073, 2015.

[2] J. Baker, C. Bond, J. C. Corbett, J. Furman, A. Khorlin, J. Larson, J.-M. Leon, Y. Li, A. Lloyd, and V. Yushprakh. Megastore: Providing scalable, highly available storage for interactive services. In *CIDR*, pages 223–234, 2011.

[3] N. Beckmann, H.-P. Kriegel, R. Schneider, and B. Seeger. The R*-tree: An efficient and robust access method for points and rectangles. In *SIGMOD*, pages 322–331, 1990.

[4] R. Beigel and E. Tanin. The geometry of browsing. In *LATIN*, pages 331–340, 1998.

[5] J. L. Bentley. Multidimensional binary search trees used for associative searching. *Commun. ACM*, 18(9):509–517, Sept. 1975.

[6] S. Chen. Cheetah: A high performance, custom data warehouse on top of mapreduce. *PVLDB*, 3(2):1459–1468, 2010.

[7] D. Comer. The ubiquitous B-tree. *ACM Comput. Surv.*, 11(2):121–137, 1979.

[8] C. Curino, Y. Zhang, E. P. C. Jones, and S. Madden. Schism: A workload-driven approach to database replication and partitioning. *PVLDB*, 3(1):48–57, 2010.

[9] M. de Berg, M. van Kreveld, M. Overmars, and O. Schwarzkopf. *Computational Geometry: Algorithms and Applications*. Springer-Verlag, 978-3-540-77973-5.

[10] J. Dittrich, J. Quiané-Ruiz, S. Richter, S. Schuh, A. Jindal, and J. Schad. Only aggressive elephants are fast elephants. *PVLDB*, 5(11):1591–1602, 2012.

[11] A. Eldawy and M. F. Mokbel. Spatialhadoop: A mapreduce framework for spatial data. In *ICDE*, pages 1352–1363, 2015.

[12] H. Elmeleegy, Y. Li, Y. Qi, P. Wilmot, M. Wu, S. Kolay, A. Dasdan, and S. Chen. Overview of turn data management platform for digital advertising. *PVLDB*, 6(11):1138–1149, 2013.

[13] M. Y. Eltabakh, F. Özcan, Y. Sismanis, P. J. Haas, H. Pirahesh, and J. Vondrák. Eagle-eyed elephant: split-oriented indexing in hadoop. In *EDBT*, pages 89–100, 2013.

[14] M. Y. Eltabakh, Y. Tian, F. Özcan, R. Gemulla, A. Krettek, and J. McPherson. Cohadoop: Flexible data placement and its exploitation in hadoop. *PVLDB*, 4(9):575–585, 2011.

[15] A. Floratou, J. M. Patel, E. J. Shekita, and S. Tata. Column-oriented storage techniques for mapreduce. *PVLDB*, 4(7):419–429, 2011.

[16] A. Guttman. R-trees: A dynamic index structure for spatial searching. In *SIGMOD*, pages 47–57, 1984.

[17] C. Ho, R. Agrawal, N. Megiddo, and R. Srikant. Range queries in OLAP data cubes. In *SIGMOD*, pages 73–88, 1997.

[18] L. Jiang, B. Li, and M. Song. The optimization of HDFS based on small files. In *IC-BNMT*, pages 912–915, 2010.

[19] A. Jindal, J. Quiané-Ruiz, and S. Madden. CARTILAGE: Adding flexibility to the hadoop skeleton. In *SIGMOD*, pages 1057–1060, 2013.

[20] H.-P. Kriegel, P. Kunath, and M. Renz. R*-tree. In *Encyclopedia of GIS*, pages 987–992. 2008.

[21] H. Liao, J. Han, and J. Fang. Multi-dimensional index on hadoop distributed file system. In *NAS*, pages 240–249, 2010.

[22] G. Mackey, S. Sehrish, and J. Wang. Improving metadata management for small files in HDFS. In *CLUSTER*, pages 1–4, 2009.

[23] S. Melnik, A. Gubarev, J. J. Long, G. Romer, S. Shivakumar, M. Tolton, and T. Vassilakis. Dremel: Interactive analysis of web-scale datasets. *PVLDB*, 3(1):330–339, 2010.

[24] G. Moerkotte. Small materialized aggregates: A light weight index structure for data warehousing. In *VLDB*, pages 476–487, 1998.

[25] C. Olston, B. Reed, U. Srivastava, R. Kumar, and A. Tomkins. Pig latin: a not-so-foreign language for data processing. In *SIGMOD*, pages 1099–1110, 2008.

[26] A. Pavlo, C. Curino, and S. B. Zdonik. Skew-aware automatic database partitioning in shared-nothing, parallel OLTP systems. In *SIGMOD*, pages 61–72, 2012.

[27] H. Samet. *Foundations of Multidimensional and Metric Data Structures*. Morgan Kaufmann Publishers Inc., 2006.

[28] A. Thusoo, J. S. Sarma, N. Jain, Z. Shao, P. Chakka, S. Anthony, H. Liu, P. Wyckoff, and R. Murthy. Hive - a warehousing solution over a map-reduce framework. *PVLDB*, 2(2):1626–1629, 2009.

[29] S. Zhang, L. Miao, D. Zhang, and Y. Wang. A strategy to deal with mass small files in HDFS. In *IHMSC*, volume 1, pages 331–334, 2014.

Feedback Control of Real-Time Display Advertising

Weinan Zhang[1], Yifei Rong[2,1], Jun Wang[1], Tianchi Zhu[3], Xiaofan Wang[4]
[1]University College London, [2]YOYI Inc., [3]Big Tree Times Co., [4]Shanghai Jiao Tong University
[1]{w.zhang, j.wang}@cs.ucl.ac.uk, [2]yifei.rong@yoyi.com.cn
[3]tc@bigtree.mobi, [4]xfwang@sjtu.edu.cn

ABSTRACT

Real-Time Bidding (RTB) is revolutionising display advertising by facilitating per-impression auctions to buy ad impressions as they are being generated. Being able to use impression-level data, such as user cookies, encourages user behaviour targeting, and hence has significantly improved the effectiveness of ad campaigns. However, a fundamental drawback of RTB is its instability because the bid decision is made per impression and there are enormous fluctuations in campaigns' key performance indicators (KPIs). As such, advertisers face great difficulty in controlling their campaign performance against the associated costs. In this paper, we propose a feedback control mechanism for RTB which helps advertisers dynamically adjust the bids to effectively control the KPIs, e.g., the auction winning ratio and the effective cost per click. We further formulate an optimisation framework to show that the proposed feedback control mechanism also has the ability of optimising campaign performance. By settling the effective cost per click at an optimal reference value, the number of campaign's ad clicks can be maximised with the budget constraint. Our empirical study based on real-world data verifies the effectiveness and robustness of our RTB control system in various situations. The proposed feedback control mechanism has also been deployed on a commercial RTB platform and the online test has shown its success in generating controllable advertising performance.

Keywords

Feedback Control, Demand-Side Platform, Real-Time Bidding, Display Advertising

1. INTRODUCTION

Emerged in 2009, Real-Time Bidding (RTB) has become a new paradigm in display advertising [22, 12]. Different from the conventional human negotiation or pre-setting a fixed price for impressions, RTB creates an impression-level auction and enables advertisers to bid for individual impression through computer algorithms served by demand-side platforms (DSPs) [33]. The bid decision could depend on the evaluation of both the utility (e.g., the likelihood and economic value of an impression for generating click or conversion) and the cost (e.g., the actual paid price) of each ad impression. More importantly, real-time information such as the specific user demographics, interest segments and various context information is leveraged to help the bidding algorithms evaluate each ad impression. With the real-time decision making mechanism, it is reported that RTB yields significantly higher return-on-investment (ROI) than other online advertising forms [31].

WSDM 2016, February 22-25, 2016, San Francisco, CA, USA.
 ISBN 978-1-4503-3716-8/16/02 ...$15.00.
DOI: http://dx.doi.org/10.1145/2835776.2835843.

Despite the ability of delivering performance-driven advertising, RTB, unfortunately, results in high volatilities, measured by major Key Performance Indicators (KPIs), such as CPM (cost per mille), AWR (auction winning ratio), eCPC (effective cost per click) and CTR (click-through rate). To illustrate this, Figure 1 plots the four major KPIs over time for two example campaigns in a real-world RTB dataset. All four KPIs fluctuate heavily across the time under a widely-used bidding strategy [25]. Such instability causes advertisers ample difficulty in optimising and controlling the KPIs against their cost.

In this paper, we propose to employ feedback control theory [2] to solve the instability problem in RTB. Feedback controllers are widely used in various applications for maintaining dynamically changing variables at the predefined reference values. The application scenarios range from the plane direction control [23] to the robot artificial intelligence [26]. In our RTB scenario, the specific KPI value, depending on the requirements from the advertisers, is regarded as the variable we want to control with a pre-specified reference value. Our study focuses on two use cases. (i) For performance-driven advertising, we concern with the feedback control of the average cost on acquiring a click, measured by effective cost per click (eCPC). (ii) For branding based advertising, to ensure a certain high exposure of a campaign, we focus on the control of the ratio of winning the auctions for the targeted impressions, measured by auction winning ratio (AWR). More specifically, we take each of them as the control input signal and consider the gain (the adjustment value) of bid price as the control output signal for each incoming ad display opportunity (the bid request). We develop two controllers to test: the widely used proportional-integral-derivative (PID) controller [6] and the waterlevel-based (WL) controller [10]. We conduct large-scale experiments to test the feedback control performance with different settings of reference value and reference dynamics. Through the empirical study, we find that the PID and WL controllers are capable of controlling eCPC and AWR, while PID further provides a better control accuracy and robustness than WL.

Furthermore, we investigate whether the proposed feedback control can be employed for controllable bid optimisation. It is common that the performance of an ad campaign (e.g., eCPC) varies from different channels (e.g., ad exchanges, user geographic regions and PC/mobile devices)

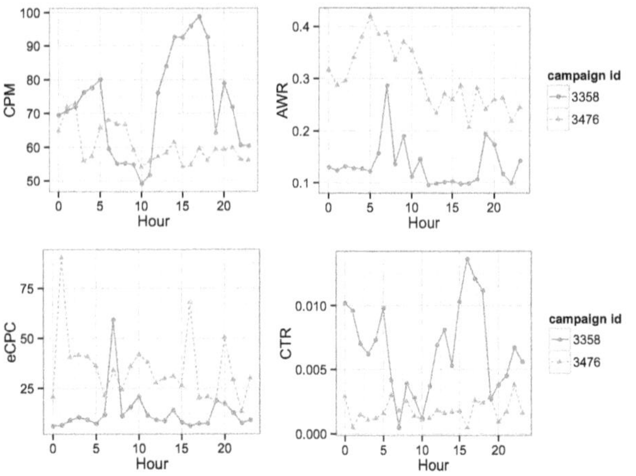

Figure 1: The instability of CPM (cost per mille), AWR (auction winning ratio), eCPC (effective cost per click), and CTR (click-through rate) for two sample campaigns without a controller. Dataset: iPinYou.

[34]. If one can reallocate some budget from less cost-effective channels to more cost-effective ones, the campaign-level performance would improve [35]. In this paper, we formulate the multi-channel bid optimisation problem and propose a model to calculate the optimal reference eCPC for each channel. Our experiments show that the campaign-level click number and eCPC achieve significant improvements with the same budget.

Moreover, the proposed feedback control mechanism has been implemented and integrated in a commercial DSP. The conducted live test shows that in a real and noisy setting the proposed feedback mechanism has the ability to produce controllable advertising performance.

To sum up, the contributions of our work are as follows. (i) We study the instability problem in RTB and investigate its solution by leveraging the feedback control mechanism. (ii) Comprehensive offline and online experiments show that PID controller is better than other alternatives and finds the optimal way to settle the variable in almost all studied cases. (iii) We further discover that feedback controllers are of great potential to perform bid optimisation through settling the eCPC at the reference value calculated by our proposed mathematical click maximisation framework.

The rest of this paper is organised as follows. Section 2 provides preliminaries for RTB and feedback control. Our solution is formally presented in Section 3. The empirical study is reported in Section 4, while the online deployment and live test are given in Section 5. Section 6 discusses the related work and we finally conclude this paper in Section 7.

2. PRELIMINARIES

To make the paper self-contained, in this section, we take a brief review on the RTB eco-system, bidding strategies, and some basics of feedback control theory.

2.1 RTB Flow Steps

The interaction process among the main components of the RTB eco-system is summarised into the following steps: (0) when a user visits an ad-supported site (e.g., web pages, streaming videos and mobile apps), each ad placement will trigger a call for ad (ad request) to the ad exchange. (1) The ad exchange sends the bid requests for this particular ad impression to each advertiser's DSP bidding agent, along with the available information such as the user and context information. (2) With the information of the bid request and each of its qualified ads, the bidding agent calculates a bid price. Then the bid response (ad, bid price) is sent back to the exchange. (3) Having received the bid responses from the advertisers, the ad exchange hosts an auction and picks the ad with the highest bid as the auction winner. (4) Then the winner is notified of the auction winning from the ad exchange. (5) Finally, the winner's ad will be shown to the visitor along with the regular content of the publisher's site. It is commonly known that a long time page-loading would greatly reduce users' satisfactory [22]. Thus, advertiser bidding agents are usually required to return a bid in a very short time frame (e.g., 100 ms). (6) The user's feedback (e.g., click and conversion) on the displayed ad is tracked and finally sent back to the winner advertiser. For a detailed discussion about RTB eco-systems, we refer to [34, 31]. The above interaction steps have the corresponding positions in Figure 2, as we will discuss later.

2.2 Bidding Strategies

A basic problem for DSP bidding agents is to figure out how much to bid for an incoming bid request. The bid decision depends on two factors for each ad impression: the utility (e.g., CTR, expected revenue) and cost (i.e., expected charged price) [33]. In a widely adopted bidding strategy [25], the utility is evaluated by CTR estimation while the base bid price is tuned based on the bid landscape [9] for the cost evaluation. The generalised bidding strategy in [25] is

$$b(t) = b_0 \frac{\theta_t}{\theta_0}, \tag{1}$$

where θ_t is the estimated CTR for the bid request at moment t; θ_0 is the average CTR under a target condition (e.g., a user interest segment); and b_0 is the tuned base bid price for the target condition. In this work, we adopt this widely used bidding strategy and adopt a logistic CTR estimator [27].

2.3 Feedback Control Theory

Feedback control theory deals with the reaction and control of dynamic systems from feedback and outside noise [2]. The usual objective of feedback control theory is to control a dynamic system so that the system output follows a desired control signal, called the reference, which may be a fixed or changing value. To attain this objective, a controller is designed to monitors the output and compares it with the reference. The difference between actual and desired output, called the error factor, is applied as feedback from the dynamic system to the control system. With the specific control function, the controller outputs the control signal, which is then transformed by the actuator into the system input signal sent back to the dynamic system. These processes form a feedback control loop between the dynamic system and the controller. Control techniques are widely used in various engineering applications for maintaining some signals at the predefined or changing reference values, such as plane navigation [23] and water distribution control [10].

3. RTB FEEDBACK CONTROL SYSTEM

Figure 2 presents the diagram of the proposed RTB feedback control system. The traditional bidding strategy is represented as the *bid calculator* module in the DSP bidding agent. The controller plays as a role which adjusts the bid price from the bid calculator.

Specifically, the *monitor* receives the auction win notice from the ad exchange and the user click feedback from the ad tracking system, which as a whole we regard as the dynamic system. Then the current KPI values, such as AWR

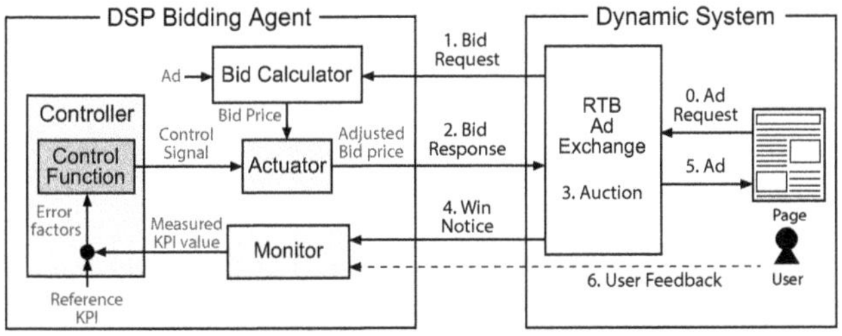

Figure 2: Feedback controller integrated in the RTB system.

and eCPC can be calculated. If the task is to control the eCPC with the reference value, the error factor between the reference eCPC and the measured eCPC is calculated then sent into the control function. The output control signal is sent to the *actuator*, which uses the control signal to adjust the original bid price from the bid calculator. The adjusted bid price is packaged with the qualified ad into the bid response and sent back to the ad exchange for auction.

3.1 Actuator

For the bid request at the moment t, the actuator takes into the current control signal $\phi(t)$ to adjust the bid price from $b(t)$ (Eq. (1)) to a new value $b_a(t)$. In our model, the control signal, which will be mathematically defined in the next subsections, is a gain on the bid price. Generally, when the control signal $\phi(t)$ is zero, there should be no bid adjustment. There could be different actuator models, and in our work we choose to use

$$b_a(t) = b(t)\exp\{\phi(t)\}, \tag{2}$$

where the model satisfies $b_a(t) = b(t)$ when $\phi(t) = 0$. Other models such as the linear model $b_a(t) \equiv b(t)(1 + \phi(t))$ are also investigated in our study but it performs poorly in the situations when a big negative control signal is sent to the actuator, where the linear actuator will usually respond a negative or a zero bid, which is meaningless in our scenario. By contrast, the exponential model is a suitable solution to addressing the above drawback because it naturally avoids generating a negative bid. In the later empirical study we mainly report the analysis based on the exponential-form actuator model.

3.2 PID Controller

The first controller we investigate is the classic PID controller [6]. As its name implies, a PID controller produces the control signal from a linear combination of the proportional factor, the integral factor and the derivative factor based on the error factor:

$$e(t_k) = x_r - x(t_k), \tag{3}$$

$$\phi(t_{k+1}) \leftarrow \lambda_P e(t_k) + \lambda_I \sum_{j=1}^{k} e(t_j)\Delta t_j + \lambda_D \frac{\Delta e(t_k)}{\Delta t_k}, \tag{4}$$

where the error factor $e(t_k)$ is the reference value x_r minus the current controlled variable value $x(t_k)$, the update time interval is given as $\Delta t_j = t_j - t_{j-1}$, the change of error factors is $\Delta e(t_k) = e(t_k) - e(t_{k-1})$, and λ_P, λ_I, λ_D are the weight parameters for each control factor. Note that here the control factors are all in discrete time $(t_1, t_2, \ldots)$ because bidding events are discrete and it is practical to periodically update the control factors. All control factors $(\phi(t), e(t_k), \lambda_P, \lambda_I, \lambda_D)$ remain the same between two updates. Thus for all time t between t_k and t_{k+1}, the control signal $\phi(t)$ in Eq. (2) equals $\phi(t_k)$.We see that P factor tends to push the current variable value to the reference value; I factor reduces the accumulative error from the beginning to the current time; D factor controls the fluctuation of the variable.

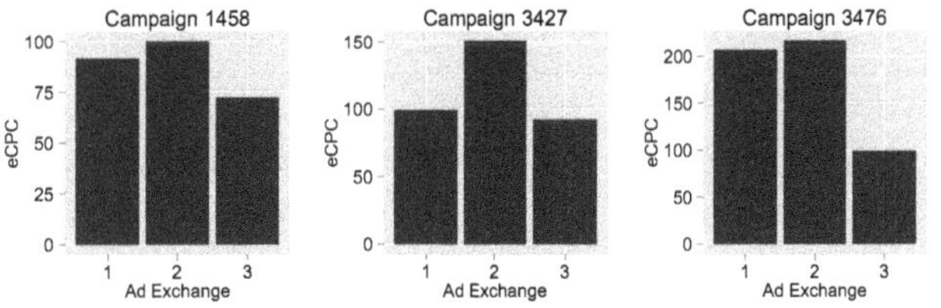

Figure 3: Different eCPCs across different ad exchanges. Dataset: iPinYou.

3.3 Waterlevel-based Controller

The Waterlevel-based (WL) controller is another feedback control model which was originally used to switching devices controlled by water level [10]:

$$\phi(t_{k+1}) \leftarrow \phi(t_k) + \gamma(x_r - x(t_k)), \tag{5}$$

where γ is the step size parameter for $\phi(t_k)$ update in exponential scale.

Compared to PID, the WL controller only takes the difference between the variable value and the reference value into consideration. Moreover, it provides a sequential control signal. That is, the next control signal is an adjustment based on the previous one.

3.4 Setting References for Click Maximisation

Given that the feedback controller is an effective tool to deliver advertisers' KPI goal, in this subsection, we demonstrate that the feedback control mechanism can be leveraged as a model-free click maximisation framework embedded with any bidding strategies [25, 33] and performs automatic budget allocation [17] across different *channels* via setting smart reference values.

When an advertiser specifies the targeted audience (usually also combined with ad impression contextual categories) for their specific campaign, the impressions that fit the target rules may come from separate channels such as different ad exchanges, user regions, users' PC/mobile devices etc. It is common that the DSP integrates with several ad exchanges and delivers the required ad impressions from all those ad exchanges (as long as the impressions fit the target rule), although the market prices [1] may be significantly different. Figure 3 illustrates that, for the same campaign, there is a difference in terms of eCPC across different ad exchanges. As pointed out in [34], the differences are also found in other channels such as user regions and devices.

The cost differences provide advertisers a further opportunity to optimise their campaign performance based on eCPCs. To see this, suppose a DSP is integrated to two ad exchanges A and B. For a campaign in this DSP, if its eCPC from exchange A is higher than that from exchange B, which means the inventories from exchange B is more cost effective than those from exchange A, then by reallocating some budget from exchange A to B will *potentially* reduce the overall eCPC of this campaign. Practically the budget reallocation can be done by reducing the bids for exchange A while increasing the bids for exchange B. Here we formally propose a model of calculating the equilibrium eCPC of each ad exchange, which will be used as the optimal reference eCPC for the feedback control that leads to a maximum number of clicks given the budget constraint.

Mathematically, suppose for a given ad campaign, there are n ad exchanges (could be other channels), i.e., $1, 2, \ldots, n$, that have the ad volume for a target rule. In our formula-

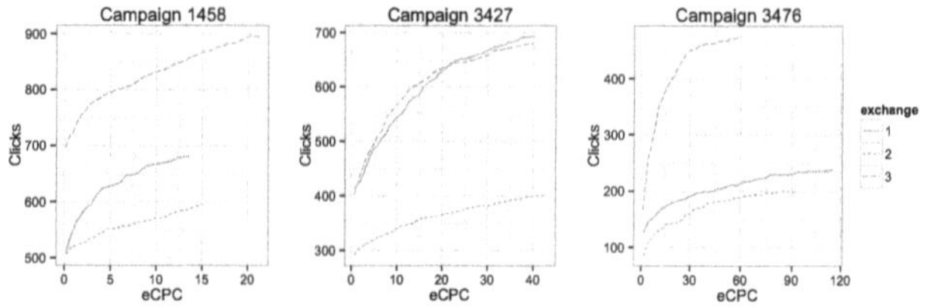

Figure 4: Number of Clicks against eCPC. Clicks and eCPC are calculated across the whole iPinYou training dataset of each campaign by tuning b_0 in Eq. (1).

tion we focus on optimising clicks, while the formulation of conversions can be obtained similarly. Let ξ_i be the eCPC on ad exchange i, and $c_i(\xi_i)$ be the click number that the campaign acquires in the campaign's lifetime if we tune the bid price to make its eCPC be ξ_i for ad exchange i. For advertisers, they want to maximise the campaign-level click number given the campaign budget B [33]:

$$\max_{\xi_1,\dots,\xi_n} \sum_i c_i(\xi_i) \tag{6}$$

$$\text{s.t.} \sum_i c_i(\xi_i)\xi_i = B. \tag{7}$$

Its Lagrangian is

$$\mathcal{L}(\xi_1,\dots,\xi_n,\alpha) = \sum_i c_i(\xi_i) - \alpha(\sum_i c_i(\xi_i)\xi_i - B), \tag{8}$$

where α is the Lagrangian multiplier. Then we take its gradient on ξ_i and let it be 0:

$$\frac{\partial \mathcal{L}(\xi_1,\dots,\xi_n,\alpha)}{\partial \xi_i} = c_i'(\xi_i) - \alpha(c_i'(\xi_i)\xi_i + c_i(\xi_i)) = 0, \tag{9}$$

$$\frac{1}{\alpha} = \frac{c_i'(\xi_i)\xi_i + c_i(\xi_i)}{c_i'(\xi_i)} = \xi_i + \frac{c_i(\xi_i)}{c_i'(\xi_i)}, \tag{10}$$

where the equation holds for each ad exchange i. As such, we can use α to bridge the equations for any two ad exchanges i and j:

$$\frac{1}{\alpha} = \xi_i + \frac{c_i(\xi_i)}{c_i'(\xi_i)} = \xi_j + \frac{c_j(\xi_j)}{c_j'(\xi_j)}. \tag{11}$$

So the optimal solution condition is given as follows:

$$\frac{1}{\alpha} = \xi_1 + \frac{c_1(\xi_1)}{c_1'(\xi_1)} = \xi_2 + \frac{c_2(\xi_2)}{c_2'(\xi_2)} = \cdots = \xi_n + \frac{c_n(\xi_n)}{c_n'(\xi_n)}, \tag{12}$$

$$\sum_i c_i(\xi_i)\xi_i = B. \tag{13}$$

With sufficient data instances, we find that $c_i(\xi_i)$ is usually a concave and smooth function. Some examples are given in Figure 4. Based on the observation, it is reasonable to define a general polynomial form of the $c_i(\xi_i)$ functions:

$$c_i(\xi_i) = c_i^* a_i \Big(\frac{\xi_i}{\xi_i^*}\Big)^{b_i}, \tag{14}$$

where ξ_i^* is the campaign's historic average eCPC on the ad inventories from ad exchange i during the training data period, and c_i^* is the corresponding click number. These two factors are directly obtained from the training data. Parameters a_i and b_i are to be tuned to fit the training data.

Substituting Eq. (14) into Eq. (12) gives

$$\frac{1}{\alpha} = \xi_i + \frac{c_i(\xi_i)}{c_i'(\xi_i)} = \xi_i + \frac{\frac{c_i^* a_i}{\xi_i^{*b_i}} \xi_i^{b_i}}{\frac{c_i^* a_i}{\xi_i^{*b_i}} b_i \xi_i^{b_i-1}} = \Big(1 + \frac{1}{b_i}\Big)\xi_i. \tag{15}$$

We can then rewrite Eq. (12) as

$$\frac{1}{\alpha} = \Big(1 + \frac{1}{b_1}\Big)\xi_1 = \Big(1 + \frac{1}{b_2}\Big)\xi_2 = \cdots = \Big(1 + \frac{1}{b_n}\Big)\xi_n. \tag{16}$$

$$\text{Thus } \xi_i = \frac{b_i}{\alpha(b_i+1)}. \tag{17}$$

Interestingly, from Eq. (17) we find that the equilibrium is *not* in the state that the eCPCs from the exchanges are the same. Instead, it is when any amount of budget reallocated among the exchanges does not make any more total clicks; for instance, in a two-exchange case, the equilibrium reaches when the increase of the clicks from one exchange equals the decrease from the other (Eq. (9)). More specifically, from Eq. (17) we observe that for ad exchange i, if its click function $c_i(\xi_i)$ is quite flat, i.e., the click number increases much slowly as its eCPC increases in a certain area, then its learned b_i should be small. This means the factor $\frac{b_i}{b_i+1}$ is small as well; then from Eq. (17) we can see the optimal eCPC in ad exchange i should be relatively small.

Substituting Eqs. (14) and (17) into Eq. (7) gives

$$\sum_i \frac{c_i^* a_i}{\xi_i^{*b_i}} \Big(\frac{b_i}{b_i+1}\Big)^{b_i+1} \Big(\frac{1}{\alpha}\Big)^{b_i+1} = B, \tag{18}$$

where for simplicity, we denote for each ad exchange i, its parameter $\frac{c_i^* a_i}{\xi_i^{*b_i}} \big(\frac{b_i}{b_i+1}\big)^{b_i+1}$ as δ_i. This give us a simpler form as:

$$\sum_i \delta_i \Big(\frac{1}{\alpha}\Big)^{b_i+1} = B. \tag{19}$$

There is no closed form to solve Eq. (19) for α. However, as b_i cannot be negative and $\sum_i \delta_i (\frac{1}{\alpha})^{b_i+1}$ monotonically increases against $\frac{1}{\alpha}$, one can easily obtain the solution for α by using a numeric solution such as the stochastic gradient decent or the Newton method [5]. Finally, based on the solved α, we can find the optimal eCPC ξ_i for each ad exchange i using Eq. (17). In fact, these eCPCs are the reference value we want the campaign to achieve for the corresponding ad exchanges. We can use PID controllers, by setting x_r in Eq. (3) as ξ_i for each ad exchange i, to achieve these reference eCPCs so as to achieve the maximum number of clicks on the campaign level.

As a special case, if we regard the whole volume of the campaign as one channel, this method can be directly used as a general bid optimisation tool. It makes use of the campaign's historic data to decide the optimal eCPC and then the click optimisation is performed by control the eCPC to settle at the optimal eCPC as reference. Note that this multi-channel click maximisation framework is flexible to incorporate any bidding strategies.

4. EMPIRICAL STUDY

We conduct comprehensive experiments to study the proposed RTB feedback control mechanism. Our focus in this section is on offline evaluation using a publicly-available real-world dataset. To make our experiment repeatable, we have published the experiment code[1]. The online deployment and test on a commercial DSP will be reported in Section 5.

4.1 Evaluation Setup

Dataset. We test our system on a publicly available dataset collected from iPinYou DSP [19]. It contains the ad log data from 9 campaigns during 10 days in 2013, which consists of 64.75M bid records, 19.50M impressions, 14.79K

[1]`https://github.com/wnzhang/rtbcontrol`

clicks and 16K Chinese Yuan (CNY) expense. According to the data publisher [19], the last three-day data of each campaign is split as the test data and the rest as the training data. The dataset disk size is 35GB. More statistics and analysis of the dataset is available in [34]. The dataset is in a record-per-row format, where each row consists of three parts: (i) The features for this auction, e.g., the time, location, IP address, the URL/domain of the publisher, ad slot size, user interest segments etc. The features of each record are indexed as a 0.7M-dimension sparse binary vector which is fed into a logistic regression CTR estimator of the bidding strategy in Eq. (1); (ii) The auction winning price, which is the threshold of the bid to win this auction; (iii) The user feedback on the ad impression, i.e., click or not.

Evaluation Protocol. We follow the evaluation protocol from previous studies on bid optimisation [33, 34] and an RTB contest [19] to run our experiment. Specifically, for each data record, we pass the feature information to our bidding agent. Our bidding agent generates a new bid based on the CTR prediction and other parameters in Eq. (1). We then compare the generated bid with the logged actual auction winning price. If the bid is higher than the auction winning price, we know the bidding agent has won this auction, paid the winning price, and obtained the ad impression. If from the ad impression record there is a click, then the placement has generated a positive outcome (one click) with a cost equal to the winning price. If there is no click, the placement has resulted in a negative outcome and wasted the money. The control parameters are updated every 2 hours (as one round).

It is worth mentioning that historical user feedback has been widely used for evaluating information retrieval systems [29] and recommender systems [13]. All of them used historic clicks as a proxy for relevancy to train the prediction model as well as to form the ground truth. Similarly, our evaluation protocol keeps the user contexts, displayed ads (creatives etc.), bid requests, and auction environment unchanged. We intend to answer that under the same context if the advertiser were given a different or better bidding strategy or employed a feedback loop, whether they would be able to get more clicks with the budget limitation. The click would stay the same as nothing has been changed for the users. This methodology works well for evaluating bid optimisation [1, 33] and has been adopted in the display advertising industry [19].

Evaluation Measures. We adopt several commonly used measures in feedback control systems [3]. We define the *error band* as the ±10% interval around the reference value. If the controlled variable settles within this area, we consider that the variable is successfully controlled. The **speed** of convergence (to the reference value) is also important. Specifically, we evaluate the *rise time* to check how fast the controlled variable will get into the error band. We also use the *settling time* to evaluate how fast the controlled variable will be successfully restricted into the error band. However, fast convergence may bring the problem of inaccurate control. Thus, two control **accuracy** measures are introduced. We use the *overshoot* to measure the percentage of value that the controlled variable passes over the reference value. After the settling (called the steady state), we use the *RMSE-SS* to evaluate the root mean square error between the controlled variable value and the reference value. At last, we measure the control **stability** by calculating the standard deviation of the variable value after the settling, named as *SD-SS*.

For bid optimisation performance, we use the campaign's total achieved click number and eCPC as the prime evaluation measures. We also monitor the impression related performance such as impression number, AWR and CPM.

Table 1: Overall control performance on eCPC.

Cpg.	Cntr	Rise	Settling	Overshoot	RMSE-SS	SD-SS
1458	PID	1	5	7.73	0.0325	0.0313
	WL	6	36	0	0.0845	0.0103
2259	PID	7	7	8.03	0.0449	0.0411
	WL	6	-	0	-	-
2261	PID	3	23	17.66	0.0299	0.0294
	WL	5	-	0	-	-
2821	PID	17	22	14.47	0.0242	0.0216
	WL	-	-	0	-	-
2997	PID	17	17	0.75	0.0361	0.026
	WL	-	-	0	-	-
3358	PID	3	7	23.89	0.0337	0.0287
	WL	-	-	0	-	-
3386	PID	9	13	7.90	0.0341	0.0341
	WL	-	-	0	-	-
3427	PID	1	12	29.03	0.0396	0.0332
	WL	-	-	0	-	-
3476	PID	1	5	7.64	0.0327	0.031
	WL	1	-	17.11	-	-

Table 2: Overall control performance on AWR.

Cpg.	Cntr	Rise	Settling	Overshoot	RMSE-SS	SD-SS
1458	PID	4	10	16.86	0.0153	0.0093
	WL	3	7	0.00	0.0448	0.0231
2259	PID	4	6	17.08	0.0076	0.0072
	WL	1	13	3.91	0.0833	0.0113
2261	PID	1	4	16.39	0.0205	0.0203
	WL	1	-	2.02	-	-
2821	PID	6	8	16.44	0.0086	0.0086
	WL	1	3	5.77	0.0501	0.0332
2997	PID	1	8	13.68	0.0151	0.0151
	WL	1	-	0.00	-	-
3358	PID	2	8	22.08	0.0250	0.0213
	WL	1	7	0.13	0.0332	0.0211
3386	PID	4	8	18.85	0.0133	0.0118
	WL	1	5	2.95	0.0300	0.0291
3427	PID	2	6	26.63	0.0200	0.0179
	WL	3	13	0.24	0.0482	0.0257
3476	PID	2	6	27.15	0.0175	0.0161
	WL	1	7	1.49	0.0308	0.0271

Empirical Study Organisation. Our empirical study consists of five parts with the focus on controlling two KPIs: eCPC and AWR. (i) In Section 4.2, we answer whether the proposed feedback control systems are practically capable of controlling the KPIs. (ii) In Section 4.3, we study the control difficulty with different reference value settings. (iii) In Section 4.4, we focus on the PID controller and investigate its attributes on settling the target variable. (iv) In Section 4.5, we leverage the PID controllers as a bid optimisation tool and study their performance on optimising the campaign's clicks and eCPC across multiple ad exchanges. (v) Finally, more discussions about PID parameter tuning and online update will be given in Section 4.6.

4.2 Control Capability

For each campaign, we check the performance of the two controllers on two KPIs. We first tune the control parameters on the training data to minimise the settling time. Then we adopt the controllers over the test data and observe the performance. The detailed control performance on each campaign is provided in Table 1 for eCPC[2] and Table 2 for AWR. Figure 5 shows the controlled KPI curves against the timesteps (i.e., round). The dashed horizontal line means the reference.

We see from the results that (i) all the PID controllers can settle both KPIs within the error band (with the settling time less than 40 rounds), which indicates that the PID control is capable of settling both KPIs at the given reference value. (ii) The WL controller on eCPC does not work that well on test data, even though we could find good parameters on training data. This is due to the fact that WL controller tries to affect the average system behaviour through transient performance feedbacks while facing the

[2] "-" cells mean invalid because of the failure to rise or settle.

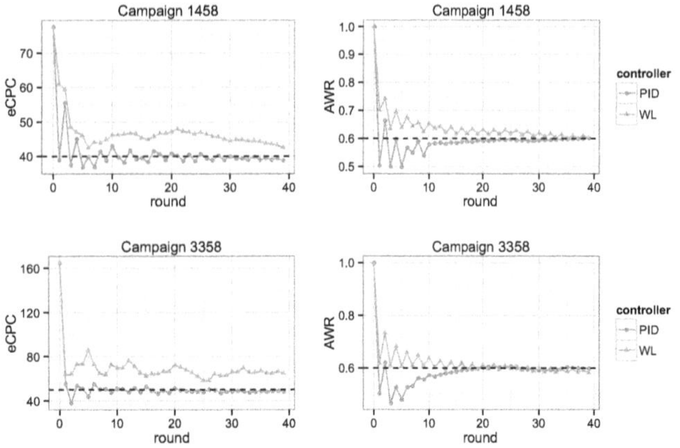

Figure 5: Control performance on eCPC and AWR.

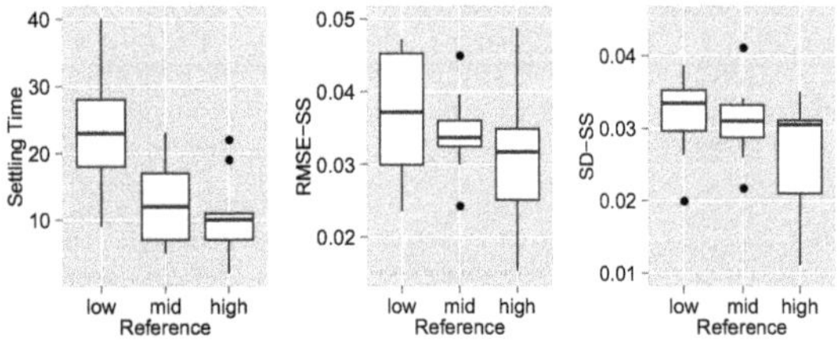

(a) PID on eCPC

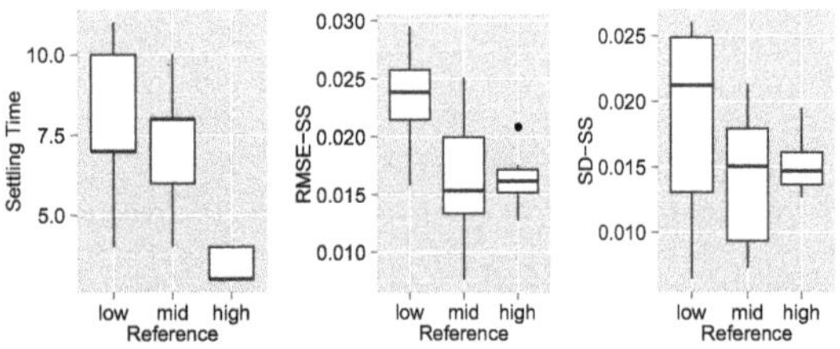

(b) PID on AWR

Figure 6: Control difficulty comparison with PID.

huge dynamics of RTB. (iii) For WL on AWR, most campaigns are controllable while there are still two campaigns that fail to settle at the reference value. (iv) Compared to PID on AWR, WL always results in higher RMSE-SS and SD-SS values but lower overshoot percentage. Those control settings with a fairly short rise time usually face a higher overshoot. (v) In addition, we observe that the campaigns with higher CTR estimator AUC performance (referring [34]) normally get shorter settling time.

According to above results, PID controller outperforms the WL controller in the tested RTB cases. We believe this is due to the fact that the integral factor in PID controller helps reduce the accumulative error (i.e., RMSE-SS) and the derivative factor helps reduce the variable fluctuation (i.e., SD-SS). And it is easier to settle the AWR than the eCPC. This is mainly because AWR only depends on the market price distribution while eCPC additionally involves the user feedback, i.e., CTR, where the prediction is associated with significant uncertainty.

4.3 Control Difficulty

In this section, we extend our control capability experiments further by adding higher and lower reference values in comparison. Our goal is to investigate the impact of different levels of reference values on control difficulty. We follow the same scheme to train and test the controllers as Section 4.2. However, instead of showing the exact performance value, our focus here is on the performance comparison with different reference settings.

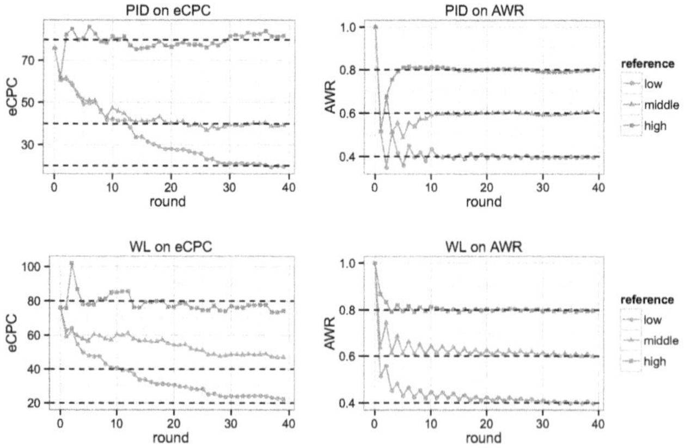

Figure 7: Control performance for campaign 3386 on eCPC and AWR with different reference values.

The distribution of achieved settling time, RMSE-SS and SD-SS, with the setting of three reference levels, i.e., low, middle and high, are shown in the form of box plot [20] in the Figure 6(a) and 6(b) for the eCPC and AWR control with PID. We observe that the average settling time, RMSE-SS and SD-SS, are reduced as the reference values get higher. This shows that generally the control tasks with higher reference eCPC and AWR are easier to achieve because one can simply bid higher to win more and spend more. Also as the higher reference is closer to the initial performance value, the control signal does not bring serious bias or volatility, which leads to the lower RMSE-SS and SD-SS. For the page limit, the control performance with WL is not presented here. The results are similar with PID.

Figure 7 gives the specific control curves of the two controllers with three reference levels on a sample campaign 3386. We find that the reference value which is farthest away from the initial value of the controlled variable brings the largest difficulty for settling, both on eCPC and AWR. This suggests that advertisers setting an ambitious control target will introduce the risk of unsettling or large volatility. The advertisers should try to find a best trade-off between the target value and the practical control performance.

4.4 PID Settling: Static vs. Dynamic References

The combination of proportional, integral and derivative factors enables the PID feedback to automatically adjust the settling progress during the control lifetime with high efficiency [7]. Alternatively, one can empirically adjust the reference value in order to achieve the desired reference value. For example of eCPC control, if the campaign's achieved eCPC is higher than the initial reference value right after exhausting the first half budget, the advertiser might want to lower the reference value in order to accelerate the downward adjustment and finally reach its initial eCPC target before running out of the budget. PID feedback controller implicitly handles such problem via its integration factor [7, 28]. In this section, we investigate with our RTB feedback control mechanism whether it is still necessary for advertisers to intentionally adjust the reference value according to the campaign's real-time performance.

Dynamic Reference Adjustment Model. To simulate the advertisers' strategies to adaptively change the reference value of eCPC and AWR under the budget constraint, we propose a dynamic reference adjustment model to calculate the new reference $x_r(t_{k+1})$ after t_k:

$$x_r(t_{k+1}) = \frac{(B - s(t_k))x_r x(t_k)}{Bx(t_k) - s(t_k)x_r}, \tag{20}$$

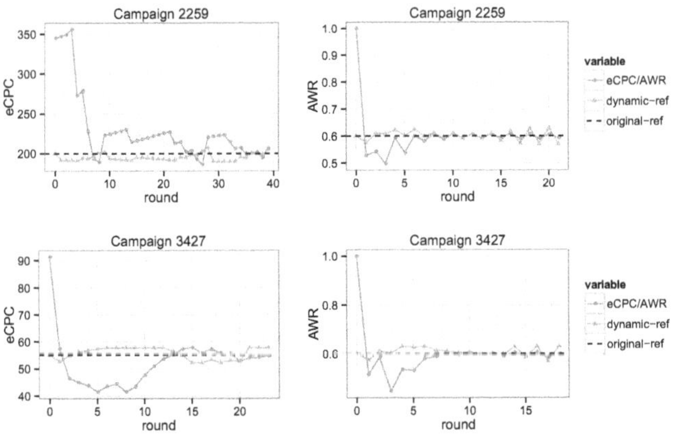

Figure 8: Dynamic reference control with PID.

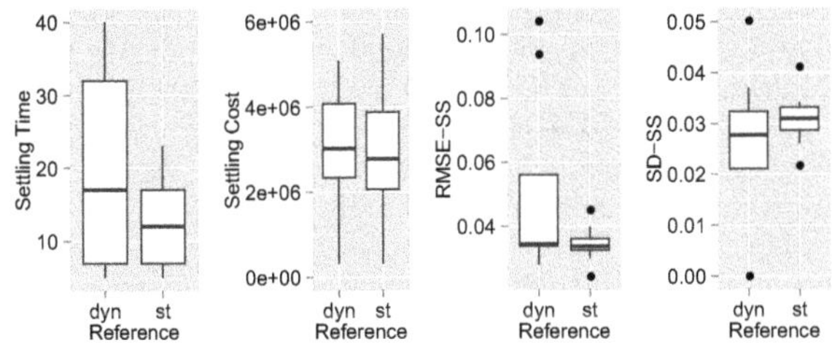

(a) PID on eCPC

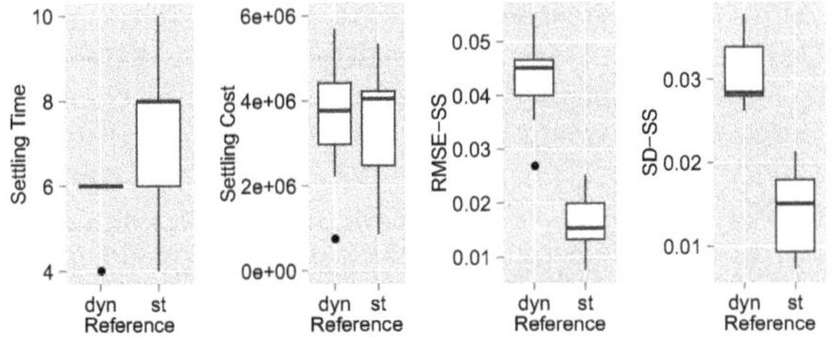

(b) PID on AWR

Figure 9: Dynamic v.s. static reference with PID.

where x_r is the initial reference value, $x(t_k)$ is the achieved KPI (eCPC or AWR) at timestep t_k, B is the campaign budget, $s(t_k)$ is the cost so far. We can see from Eq. (20) that when $x_r(t_k) = x_r$, $x_r(t_{k+1})$ will be set the same as x_r; when $x_r(t_k) > x_r$, $x_r(t_{k+1})$ will be set lower than x_r and vice versa. For readability, we leave the detailed derivation in appendix. Using Eq. (20) we calculate the new reference eCPC/AWR $x_r(t_{k+1})$ and use it to substitute x_r in Eq. (3) to calculated the error factor so as to make the dynamic-reference control.

Results and Discussions. Figure 8 shows the PID control performance with dynamic reference calculated based on Eq. (20). The campaign performance gets stopped at the point where the budget is exhausted. From the figure, we see that for both eCPC and AWR control, the dynamic reference takes an aggressive approach and pushes the eCPC or AWR across the original reference value (dashed line). This actually simulates some advertisers' strategy: when the performance is lower than the reference, then higher the dynamic reference to push the total performance to the initial reference more quickly. Furthermore, for AWR control, we can see the dynamic reference fluctuates seriously when the budget is to be exhausted soon. This is because when there is insufficient budget left, the reference value will be set much high or low by Eq. (20) in order to push the performance back to the initial target. Apparently this is an ineffective solution.

Table 3: Control performance on multi-exchanges with the reference eCPC set for click maximisation.

Cpg.	AdEx	Rise	Settling	Cpg.	AdEx	Rise	Settling
	1	13	26		1	9	20
1458	2	15	18	3358	2	14	39
	3	13	13		3	26	26
	1	10	38		1	6	18
2259	2	3	14	3386	2	12	12
	3	3	29		3	1	1
	1	3	30		1	16	16
2261	2	7	38	3427	2	35	35
	3	0	35		3	23	23
	1	6	17		1	18	29
2821	2	3	10	3476	2	22	28
	3	15	15		3	19	22
	4	4	38				

Furthermore, we directly compare the quantitative control performance between dynamic-reference controllers (dyn) with the standard static-reference ones (st) using PID. Besides the settling time, we also compare the settling cost, which is the spent budget before settling. The overall performance across all the campaigns is shown in Figure 9(a) for eCPC control and Figure 9(b) for AWR control. The results show that (i) for eCPC control, the dynamic-reference controllers do *not* perform better than the static-reference ones; (ii) for AWR control, the dynamic-reference controllers could reduce the settling time and cost, but the accuracy (RMSE-SS) and stability (SD-SS) is much worse than the static-reference controllers. This is because the dynamic reference itself brings volatility (see Figure 8). These results demonstrate that PID controller does perform a good enough way to settling the variable towards the pre-specified reference without the need of dynamically adjusting the reference to accelerate using our methods. Other dynamic reference models might be somewhat effective but this is not the focus of this paper.

4.5 Reference Setting for Click Maximisation

We now study how the proposed feedback control could be used for click optimisation purpose. As we have discussed in Section 3.4, bid requests usually come from different ad exchanges where the market power and thus the CPM prices are disparate. We have shown that given a budget constraint, the number of clicks is maximised if one can control the eCPC in each ad exchange by settling it at an optimal eCPC reference for each of them, respectively.

In this experiment, we build a PID feedback controller for each of its integrated ad exchanges, where their reference eCPCs are calculated via Eqs. (17) and (19). We train the PID parameters on the training data of each campaign, and then test the bidding performance on the test data. As shown in Table 3, the eCPC on all the ad exchanges for all tested campaigns get settled at the reference values[3] (settling time less than 40). We denote our multi-exchange eCPC feedback control method as multiple. Besides multiple, we also test a baseline method which assigns a single optimal uniform eCPC reference across all the ad exchanges, denoted as uniform. We also use the linear bidding strategy without feedback control [25] as a baseline, denoted as none[4].

The comparisons over various evaluation measures are reported in Figure 10. We observe that (i) the feedback-control-enabled bidding strategies uniform and multiple significantly outperform the non-controlled bidding strategy none in terms of the number of achieved clicks and eCPC. This suggests that properly controlling eCPCs would lead to an optimal solution for maximising clicks. (ii) By reallo-

[3]Campaign 2997 is only integrated with one ad exchange, thus not compared here.

[4]Other bidding strategies [33, 17] are also investigated. Producing similar results, they are omitted here for clarity.

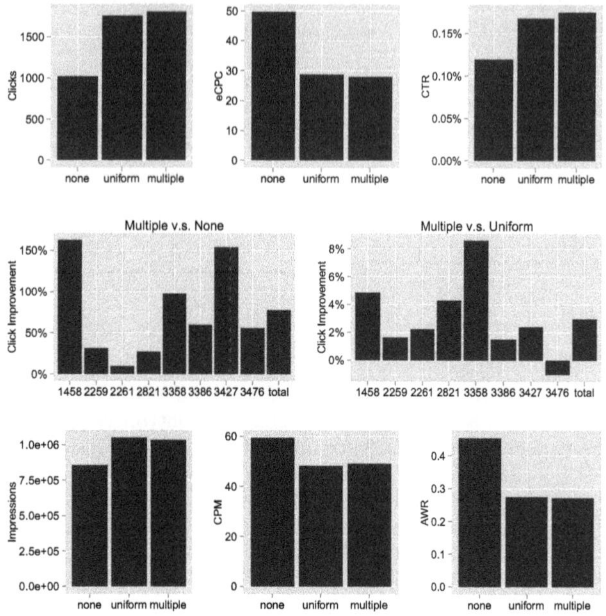

Figure 10: Bid optimisation performance.

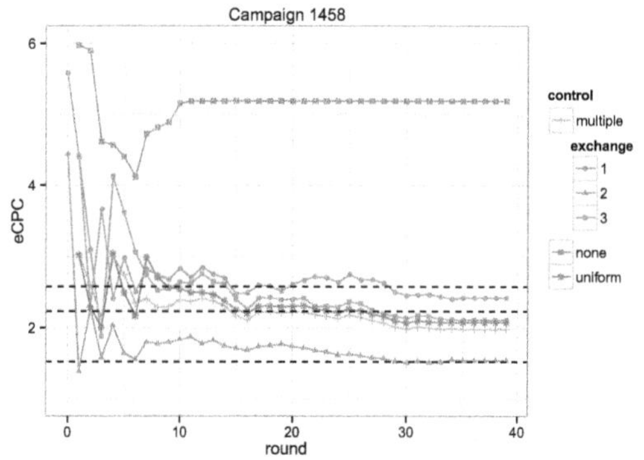

Figure 11: Settlement of multi-exchange feedback control.

cating the budget via setting different reference eCPCs on different ad exchanges, multiple further outperforms uniform on 7 out of 8 tested campaigns. (iii) On the impression related measures, the feedback-control-enabled bidding strategies earn more impressions than the non-controlled bidding strategy by actively lowering their bids (CPM) and thus AWR, but achieving more bid volumes. This suggests that by allocating more budget to the lower valued impressions, one could potentially generate more clicks. As a by-product, this confirms the theoretical finding reported in [33].

As a case study, Figure 11 plots the settling performance of the three methods on campaign 1458. The three dashed horizontal lines are the reference eCPCs on three ad exchanges. We see that the eCPCs on the three ad exchanges successfully settle at the reference eCPCs. At the same time, the campaign-level eCPC (multiple) settles at a lower value than uniform and none.

4.6 PID Parameter Tuning

In this subsection, we share some lessons learned about PID controller parameter tuning and online update.

Parameter Search. Empirically, λ_D does not change the control performance significantly. Just a small valued λ_D, e.g., 1×10^{-5}, will reduce the overshoot and slightly shorten the settling time. Thus the parameter search is focused on

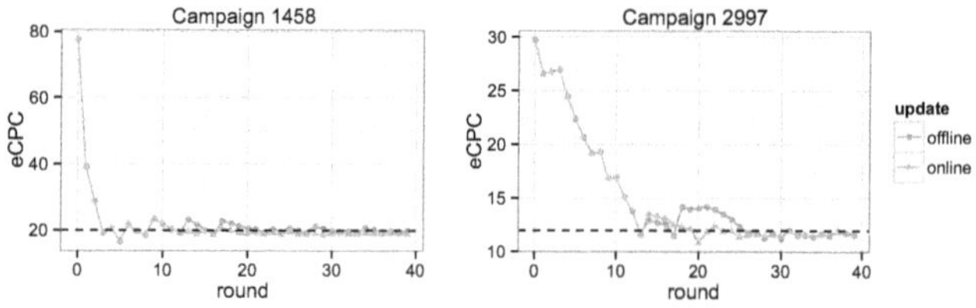

Figure 12: Control with online/offline parameter updating.

λ_P and λ_I. Instead of using the computationally expensive grid search, we perform an adaptive coordinate search. For every update, we fix one parameter and shoot another one to seek for the optimal value leading shortest settling time, and the line searching step length shrinks exponentially for each shooting. Normally after 3 or 4 iterations, the local optima is reached and we find such solution is highly comparable with the expensive grid search.

Setting $\phi(t)$ Bounds. We also find that setting up upper/lower bounds of control signal $\phi(t)$ is important to make KPIs controllable. Due to the dynamics in RTB, it is common that user CTR drops during a period, which makes eCPC much higher. The corresponding feedback would probably result in a large negative gain on the bids, leading extremely low bid price and thus no win, no click and no additional cost at all for remaining rounds. In such case, a proper lower bound (-2) of $\phi(t)$ aims to eliminate above extreme effects by preventing from a seriously negative control signal. In addition, an upper bound (5) is used in order to avoid excessive variable growth beyond the reference value.

Online Parameter Updating. As the DSP running with feedback control, the collected data can be immediately utilised for training a new PID controller and updating the older one. We investigate the possibility of the online updating of PID parameters with the recent data. Specifically, after initialising the PID parameters using training data, we re-train the controller for every 10 rounds (i.e., before round 10, 20 and 30) in the test stage using all previous data with the same parameter searching method as in the training stage. The parameter searching in re-training takes about 10 minutes for each controller, which is far shorter than the round period (2 hours). Figure 12 shows the control performance with PID parameters tuned online and offline respectively. As we can see after the 10th round (i.e., the first online tuning point), the online-tuned PIDs manage to control the eCPC around the reference value more effectively than the offline-tuned one, resulting shorter settling time and lower overshoot. In addition, no obvious disturbance or instability occurs when we switch parameters. With the online parameter updating, we can start to train the controllers based on several-hour training data and adaptively update the parameters from the new data to improve the control performance.

5. ONLINE DEPLOYMENT AND TEST

The proposed RTB feedback control system has been deployed and tested in live on BigTree DSP[5], a performance-driven mobile advertising DSP in China. BigTree DSP focuses on the programmatic buying for optimal advertising performance on mobile devices, which makes it an ideal place to test our proposed solution.

The deployment environment is based on Aliyun elastic cloud computing servers. A three-node cluster is deployed for the DSP bidding agent, where each node is in Ubuntu 12.04, with 8 core Intel Xeon CPU E5-2630 (2.30GHz) and

[5] `http://www.bigtree.mobi/`

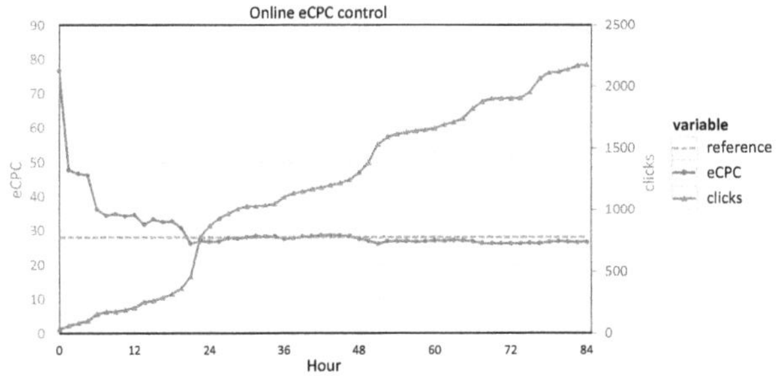

Figure 13: The online eCPC control performance and the accumulative click numbers of a mobile game campaign on BigTree DSP.

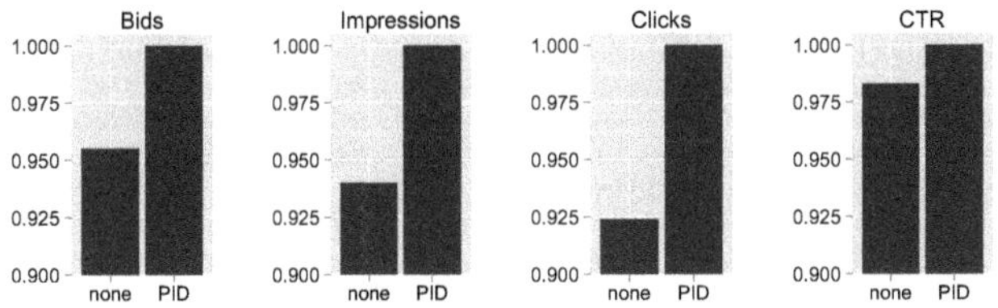

Figure 14: Relative performance for online test.

8GB RAM. The controller module is implemented in Python with uWSGI and Nginx.

For BigTree DSP controller module, we deploy the PID control function and tune its parameters. Specifically, we use the last 6-week bidding log data in 2014 as the training data for tuning PID parameters. A three-fold validation process is performed to evaluate the generalisation of the PID control performance, where the previous week data is used as the training data while the later week data is used for validation. The control factors ($\phi(t), e(t_k)$ in Eq. (4)) are updated for every 90 minutes. After acquiring a set of robust and effective PID parameters, we launch the controller module, including the monitor and actuator submodules, on BigTree DSP.

Figure 13 shows the online eCPC control performance on one of the iOS mobile game campaigns during 84 hours from 7 Jan. 2015 to 10 Jan. 2015. The reference eCPC is set as 28 RMB cent by the advertiser, which is about 0.8 times the average eCPC value of the previous week where there was no control. Following the same training process described in the previous section, we update the online control factors for every 90 minutes. From the result we can see the eCPC value dropped from the beginning 79 cent to 30 during the first day and then settled closed to the reference afterwards.

In the meantime, A/B testing is used to compare with the non-controlled bidding agent (with the same sampling rate but disjoint bid requests). Figure 14 shows the corresponding advertising performance comparison between a non-controlled bidding agent and the PID-control bidding agent during the test period with the same budget. As we can see, by settling the eCPC value around the lower reference eCPC, the PID-control bidding agent acquires more bid volume and win more (higher-CTR) impressions and clicks, which demonstrates its ability of optimising the performance.

Compared with the offline empirical study, the online running is more challenging: (i) all pipeline steps including the update of the CTR estimator, the KPI monitor linked to the database and the PID controller should operate smoothly against the market turbulence; (ii) the real market competition is highly dynamic during the new year period when we launched our test; (iii) other competitors might tune their bidding strategies independently or according to any changes of their performance after we employed the controlled bidding strategy. In sum, the successful eCPC control on an online commercial DSP verifies the effectiveness of our proposed feedback control RTB system.

6. RELATED WORK

Enabling the impression-level evaluation and bidding, much research work has been done on RTB display advertising, including bidding strategy optimisation [25, 33], reserve price optimisation [30], ad exchange auction design [4], and ad tracking [11].

In order to perform the optimal bidding, the DSP bidding agent should estimate both utility and cost of a given ad impression. The impression-level utility evaluation, including CTR and conversion rate (CVR) estimation, is the essential part for each bidding agent in DSPs. In [18] the sparsity problem of CVR estimation is handled by modelling the conversions at different hierarchical levels. The user click behaviour on mobile RTB ads is studied in [24]. On the cost evaluation side, bid landscape modelling and forecasting is much important to inform the bidding agent about the competitiveness of the market. The authors in [9] break down the campaign-level bid landscape forecasting problem into "samples" by targeting rules and then employ a mixture model of log-normal distributions to build the campaign-level bid landscape. The authors in [16] try to reduce the bid landscape forecasting error through frequently re-building the landscape models. Based on the utility and cost evaluation of the ad inventory, bid optimisation is performed to improve the advertising performance under the campaign budget constraint. Given the estimated CTR/CVR, the authors in [25, 18] employ linear bidding functions based on truth-telling attributes of second price auctions. However, given the budget constraint, the advertisers' bidding behaviour is not truth-telling. The authors in [33] propose a general bid optimisation framework to maximise the desired advertising KPI (e.g., total click number) under the budget constraint. Besides the general bid optimisation, the explicit bidding rules such as frequency and recency capping are studied in [31]. Moreover, the budget pacing [17] which refers to smoothly delivering the campaign budget is another important problem for DSPs.

There are a few research papers on recommender systems leveraging feedback controllers for performance maintenance and improvement. In [21], a rating updating algorithm based on the PID controller is developed to exclude unfair ratings in order to build a robust reputation system. The authors in [32] apply a self-monitoring and self-adaptive approach to perform a dynamic update of the training data fed into the recommender system to automatically balance the computational cost and the prediction accuracy. Furthermore, the authors in [14] adopt the more effective and well-studied PID controller to the data-feeding scheme of recommender systems, which is proved to be practically effective in their studied training task.

Compared to the work of controlling the recommender system performance by changing the number of training cases, our control task in RTB is more challenging, with much various dynamics from advertising environment such as the fluctuation of market price, auction volume and user behaviour. In [8], the authors discuss multiple aspects in a performance-driven RTB system, where the impression volume control is one of discussed aspects. Specifically, WL and a model-based controller are implemented to control the impression volume during each time interval. In [15], feedback control is used to perform budget pacing in order to stablise the conversion volume. Compared to [8, 15], our work is a more comprehensive study focused on the feedback control techniques to address the instability problem in RTB. Besides

WL, we intensively investigate the PID controller, which takes more factors into consideration than WL. For the controlled KPIs, we look into the control tasks on both eCPC and AWR, which are crucial KPIs for performance-driven campaigns and branding-based campaigns, respectively. In addition, we proposed an effective model to calculate the optimal eCPC reference to maximise the campaign's clicks using feedback controllers.

7. CONCLUSIONS

In this paper, we have proposed a feedback control mechanism for RTB display advertising, with the aim of improving its robustness of achieving the advertiser's KPI goal. We mainly studied PID and WL controllers for controlling the eCPC and AWR KPIs. Through our comprehensive empirical study, we have the following discoveries. (i) Despite of the high dynamics in RTB, the KPI variables are controllable using our feedback control mechanism. (ii) Different reference values bring different control difficulties, which are reflected in the control speed, accuracy and stability. (iii) PID controller naturally finds its best way to settle the variable, and there is no necessity to adjust the reference value for accelerating the PID settling. (iv) By settling the eCPCs to the optimised reference values, the feedback controller is capable of making bid optimisation. Deployed on a commercial DSP, the online test demonstrates the effectiveness of the feedback control mechanism in generating controllable advertising performance. In the future work, we will further study the applications based on feedback controllers in RTB, such as budget pacing and retargeting frequency capping.

8. REFERENCES

[1] K. Amin, M. Kearns, P. Key, and A. Schwaighofer. Budget optimization for sponsored search: Censored learning in mdps. *UAI*, 2012.

[2] K. J. Åström and P. Kumar. Control: A perspective. *Automatica*, 50(1):3–43, 2014.

[3] K. J. Åström and R. M. Murray. *Feedback systems: an introduction for scientists and engineers*. Princeton university press, 2010.

[4] S. Balseiro, O. Besbes, and G. Y. Weintraub. Repeated auctions with budgets in ad exchanges: Approximations and design. *Columbia Business School Research Paper*, (12/55), 2014.

[5] R. Battiti. First-and second-order methods for learning: between steepest descent and newton's method. *Neural computation*, 4(2):141–166, 1992.

[6] S. Bennett. Development of the pid controller. *Control Systems*, 13(6):58–62, 1993.

[7] S. P. Bhattacharyya, H. Chapellat, and L. H. Keel. Robust control. *The Parametric Approach, by Prentice Hall PTR*, 1995.

[8] Y. Chen, P. Berkhin, B. Anderson, and N. R. Devanur. Real-time bidding algorithms for performance-based display ad allocation. *KDD*, 2011.

[9] Y. Cui, R. Zhang, W. Li, and J. Mao. Bid landscape forecasting in online ad exchange marketplace. In *KDD*, pages 265–273. ACM, 2011.

[10] B. W. Dezotell. Water level controller, June 9 1936. US Patent 2,043,530.

[11] R. Gomer, E. M. Rodrigues, N. Milic-Frayling, and M. Schraefel. Network analysis of third party tracking: User exposure to tracking cookies through search. In *WI*, 2013.

[12] Google. The arrival of real-time bidding. Technical report, 2011.

[13] Y. Hu, Y. Koren, and C. Volinsky. Collaborative filtering for implicit feedback datasets. In *ICDM*, 2008.

[14] T. Jambor, J. Wang, and N. Lathia. Using control theory for stable and efficient recommender systems. In *WWW*, 2012.

[15] N. Karlsson and J. Zhang. Applications of feedback control in online advertising. In *American Control Conference*, 2013.

[16] K. J. Lang, B. Moseley, and S. Vassilvitskii. Handling forecast errors while bidding for display advertising. In *WWW*, 2012.

[17] K.-C. Lee, A. Jalali, and A. Dasdan. Real time bid optimization with smooth budget delivery in online advertising. In *ADKDD*, 2013.

[18] K.-C. Lee, B. Orten, A. Dasdan, and W. Li. Estimating conversion rate in display advertising from past performance data. In *KDD*, 2012.

[19] H. Liao, L. Peng, Z. Liu, and X. Shen. ipinyou global rtb bidding algorithm competition dataset. In *ADKDD*, 2014.

[20] R. McGill, J. W. Tukey, and W. A. Larsen. Variations of box plots. *The American Statistician*, 32(1):12–16, 1978.

[21] K. Meng, Y. Wang, X. Zhang, X.-c. Xiao, et al. Control theory based rating recommendation for reputation systems. In *ICNSC*, 2006.

[22] S. Muthukrishnan. Ad exchanges: Research issues. In *Internet and network economics*, pages 1–12. Springer, 2009.

[23] R. C. Nelson. *Flight stability and automatic control*, volume 2. WCB/McGraw Hill, 1998.

[24] R. J. Oentaryo, E. P. Lim, D. J. W. Low, D. Lo, and M. Finegold. Predicting response in mobile advertising with hierarchical importance-aware factorization machine. In *WSDM*, 2014.

[25] C. Perlich, B. Dalessandro, R. Hook, O. Stitelman, T. Raeder, and F. Provost. Bid optimizing and inventory scoring in targeted online advertising. In *KDD*, pages 804–812, 2012.

[26] G. Peterson and D. J. Cook. Decision-theoretic layered robotic control architecture. In *AAAI/IAAI*, page 976, 1999.

[27] M. Richardson, E. Dominowska, and R. Ragno. Predicting clicks: estimating the click-through rate for new ads. In *WWW*, pages 521–530. ACM, 2007.

[28] D. E. Rivera, M. Morari, and S. Skogestad. Internal model control: Pid controller design. *Industrial & engineering chemistry process design and development*, 25(1), 1986.

[29] J. Xu, C. Chen, G. Xu, H. Li, and E. R. T. Abib. Improving quality of training data for learning to rank using click-through data. In *WSDM*, 2010.

[30] S. Yuan, B. Chen, J. Wang, P. Mason, and S. Seljan. An Empirical Study of Reserve Price Optimisation in Real-Time Bidding. In *KDD*, 2014.

[31] S. Yuan, J. Wang, and X. Zhao. Real-time bidding for online advertising: measurement and analysis. In *ADKDD*, 2013.

[32] V. Zanardi and L. Capra. Dynamic updating of online recommender systems via feed-forward controllers. In *SEAMS*, 2011.

[33] W. Zhang, S. Yuan, and J. Wang. Optimal real-time bidding for display advertising. In *KDD*, 2014.

[34] W. Zhang, S. Yuan, J. Wang, and X. Shen. Real-time bidding benchmarking with ipinyou dataset. *arXiv*, 2014.

[35] W. Zhang, Y. Zhang, B. Gao, Y. Yu, X. Yuan, and T.-Y. Liu. Joint optimization of bid and budget allocation in sponsored search. In *KDD*, 2012.

APPENDIX

Reference Adjust Models. Here we provide the detailed derivation of the proposed dynamic-reference model Eq. (20) in Section 4.4. We mainly introduce the derivation of reference eCPC adjustment, while the derivation of reference AWR adjustment can be obtained similarly.

Let ξ_r be the initial eCPC target, $\xi(t_k)$ be the achieved eCPC before the moment t_k, $s(t_k)$ be the total cost so far, and B be the campaign budget. In such setting, the current achieved click number is $s(t_k)/\xi(t_k)$ and the target click number is B/ξ_r. In order to push the overall eCPC to ξ_r, i.e., push the total click number B/ξ_r with the budget B, the reference eCPC for the remaining time $\xi_r(t_{k+1})$ should satisfy

$$\frac{s(t_k)}{\xi(t_k)} + \frac{B - s(t_k)}{\xi_r(t_{k+1})} = \frac{B}{\xi_r}. \tag{21}$$

Solving the equation we have

$$\xi_r(t_{k+1}) = \frac{(B - s(t_k))\xi_r\xi(t_k)}{B\xi(t_k) - s(t_k)\xi_r}. \tag{22}$$

The derivation of reference AWR adjustment is much similar but with an extra winning function which links between the bid price and winning probability [33]. The result formula is just the same as Eq. (22). Using x as a general notation for eCPC and AWR variables results in Eq. (20) in Section 4.4.

Multi-Score Position Auctions

Denis Charles
Microsoft
1 Microsoft Way, Redmond, WA, USA
cdx@microsoft.com

Nikhil R. Devanur
Microsoft Research
1 Microsoft Way, Redmond, WA, USA
nikdev@microsoft.com

Balasubramanian Sivan
Microsoft Research
1 Microsoft Way, Redmond, WA, USA
balu2901@gmail.com

ABSTRACT

In this paper we propose a general family of position auctions used in paid search, which we call multi-score position auctions. These auctions contain the GSP auction and the GSP auction with squashing as special cases. We show experimentally that these auctions contain special cases that perform better than the GSP auction with squashing, in terms of revenue, and the number of clicks on ads. In particular, we study in detail the special case that squashes the first slot alone and show that this beats pure squashing (which squashes all slots uniformly). We study the equilibria that arise in this special case to examine both the first order and the second order effect of moving from the squashing-all-slots auction to the squash-only-the-top-slot auction. For studying the second order effect, we simulate auctions using the value-relevance correlated distribution suggested in Lahaie and Pennock [2007]. Since this distribution is derived from a study of value and relevance distributions in Yahoo! we believe the insights derived from this simulation to be valuable. For measuring the first order effect, in addition to the said simulation, we also conduct experiments using auction data from Bing over several weeks that includes a random sample of all auctions.

Categories and Subject Descriptors

F.0 [**Theory of Computation**]: General; J.4 [**Social and Behavioral Sciences**]: Economics

Keywords

Generalized Second Price Auction, Squashing

1. INTRODUCTION

Sponsored search auctions have been the "killer app" for algorithmic game theory, due to the enormity of the scale (with 10s of billions of dollars in annual revenue) and the automated nature of these auctions. On the one hand, the basic design of this auction, referred to as the Generalized Second Price (GSP) auction has been the gold standard and has remained constant in the academic community, while on the other hand several extensions have been incorporated into this basic design in practice. These extensions seek better trade-offs between various objectives and are held as trade secrets. The aim of this paper is to systematically consider a general family of auctions and identify specific instances that perform better than GSP and its variants that are used in practice.

One such widely adopted extension of the GSP auction is *squashing*, and was introduced in the widely cited paper of Lahaie and Pennock [13]. While the usual GSP auction ranks the ads by the product of their bids and click probabilities, squashing allows the click probability (or more generally a *relevance* score, denoted by e) to be raised to some fixed exponent (i.e., the ranking is by $b \times e^{\alpha}$, $\alpha \geq 0$, here b is the bid and e the click probability). This generalizes GSP to a single parameter family of auctions, thus giving more freedom in auction design.

In this paper we propose a general family of auctions, which we call multi-score position auctions (MSPA), and experimentally evaluate a particular sub-family of these auctions, which we term dual score auctions (DSA). The basic idea of an MSPA is that each slot has its own scoring function, along with an initial score to select the unordered set of ads to be shown. The payment rule is in the spirit of GSP: each ad must pay the minimum bid required to retain its slot. This generalizes GSP with squashing (and hence GSP), where the scoring function is the same for all slots, namely, the squashed score. There is a particularly attractive special case of DSA that only applies squashing to the first slot and does not squash the other slots. This special case seems appealing since it does not increase the number of auction parameters over the squashed-GSP auction and seems to be the simplest non-trivial example of a DSA auction. To our knowledge, all previous modifications to GSP consist of a single scoring function for the auction. We study this special case of DSA empirically in detail and also study the nature of its equilibria.

We examine both the first-order and second-order effect of going from the auction where we squash all slots uniformly with exponent α to the one where we squash only the top slot at α. In this context, first-order effect refers to a comparison of the two auctions' revenue and clicks based on existing bids. Second-order effect refers to making the same comparison, but using the respective equilibrium bids for each auction.

WSDM'16, February 22–25, 2016, San Francisco, CA, USA.

 ISBN 978-1-4503-3716-8/16/02...$15.00
DOI: http://dx.doi.org/10.1145/2835776.2835822

Our experimental setup to measure first-order effect.

Our experimental setup uses actual search queries and click responses to compute revenue and clicks, so it captures all the complex dependence of clicks on the entire context of the search results page. This avoids pitfalls of assumptions such as that the click-through rates are a product of a slot dependent factor and an advertisement dependent factor. We achieve this by using certain experimental traffic on Bing for which the order of the ads was randomized. Due to this randomness the order of the ads for some of these search results pages coincides with the order given by any specific DSA auction which we would like to measure. Furthermore, the randomization ensures that this happens sufficiently often and is a representative sample of all search queries. We use data from several weeks so that we have a sufficient volume of instances. Thus, we can evaluate the performance of a DSA auction for any choice of exponents.

Our simulation setup to measure second order effect.

With experiments on actual search engine traffic as described in the previous paragraph, it is very difficult to measure second order effects. This is because a typical A/B test is allotted a small fraction of *search engine traffic*. On the other hand, what we need to measure second order effect is a small set of *advertisers* to respond to the new auction format. This requires changing the auction format for all the queries relevant to all the advertisers in the concerned set, which often demands a large portion of traffic to be segregated for this experiment since each advertiser bids on numerous keywords. Given this difficulty, we measure second order effects using simulations à la Lahaie and Pennock [13]. They generate values and click-probabilities from a particular (joint) distribution which fits well a popular keyword in Yahoo! search. We use the same distribution as theirs. For any auction, given the values, we compute the bids that form an equilibrium and evaluate the auction at these bids to measure second-order effect. (Further, we use the same distribution to measure first-order effect too, for comparison with the experimental results from Bing traffic.)

A random sample of all queries.

This combination of simulations to measure advertiser reaction and real data to only measure first order effects has also been used in other recent papers such as Bachrach et al. [6] and Roberts et al. [17]. However, there is a significant difference in the nature of real data used by them and by us. The real data used by these papers, as well as the data used by Lahaie and Pennock [13] to derive their distributions are for a few popular keywords, keywords that are searched many times. However, it is known that a significant fraction of the revenue comes from the "tail queries", queries that are seen only a few times. Thus any insight obtained from such data may not necessarily be broadly applicable. The way we get our auction data is truly a random sample of all queries over several weeks and is therefore representative of the entire market. We provide more details of our experimental design in Section 3.

Findings from our first-order experiments.

Our main finding regarding first-order-effect based on Bing traffic is that *squashing only the top slot is better than squashing all the slots, both in terms of revenue, and the number of clicks (which is a proxy for user relevance/user satisfaction*, i.e., the DSA auction with exponent α for the top slot and exponent 1 for the remaining slots does better than the squashed GSP auction with exponent α. More details on the exact numbers are in Section 3. Furthermore, the first-order results measured from our experiments with actual Bing traffic are broadly in agreement with the first-order effect measured from simulations using the value and click-probabilities distribution from [13].

Findings from our second-order simulations.

The main task in measuring second order effects is computing the equilibrium of the squash-all-slots auction and squash-only-the-top-slot aucton. For computing the equilibrium of the squash-all-slots auction, we use standard, "lowest revenue fetching envy-free equilibrium" suggested independently by Edelman et al. [9] and Varian [19]. In his paper, Varian [19] gives empirical evidence for advertiser bids coinciding with the predictions of this envy-free equilibrium. For the squash-only-the-top-slot auction, equilibrium computation is more intricate, since there could be multiple equilibria (even after placing the envy-free restriction) and the equilibrium selection has a significant impact. But the overall trend is still positive, with a strong trend that shows that if the equilibrium prefers bidders with higher relevance, then the improvements are significant, and somewhat surprisingly, even more than what we get for the first order! This suggests that the search engine should try to steer the bids towards an equilibrium that favors more relevant advertisers, which is a good idea anyway. The search engine could do this, for instance, via bidding agents that can adjust bids, (under some constraints provided by the advertiser) or by influencing the matching of candidates to auctions. Equilibrium derivation is described in Section 4 and the results from simulations using these equilibria are described in Section 5.

Intuitive explanation.

Both the first-order and second-order effects point towards squash-only-the-top-slot auction being superior to squash-all-slots auction. While this fact acts as an empirical justification for using the former, here we provide an intuitive explanation for this phenomenon. The effect of squashing, which changes the rank-score from $b \cdot e$ to $b \cdot e^{\alpha}$ for $0 \leq \alpha \leq 1$, is to undermine the contribution of click probability in deciding the ordering of ads. (To see this, consider the extreme case of $\alpha = 0$, where the bids alone decide the ordering of ads.) When does squashing have a positive effect on revenue? Consider an arbitrary slot, and 2 competing ads for that slot. Fixing the ads in the other slots, let e_1, e_2 be the click probabilities of ads 1 and 2 for this slot under consideration; let b_1 and b_2 be the bids of these two ads. There are three natural rankings possible here: GSP ranks these ads according to their rank score of $b \cdot e$, squashed-GSP ranks these ads according to their rank-score $b \cdot e^{\alpha}$, and finally there is also the natural ranking of ads according to relevance (click probabilities). We analyze three different cases that come out of how these three different rankings compare, and argue that *only in one case can squashing improve revenue. Further, we argue that this case is likely to occur only for the first slot.* As a convention, let 1 be the ad that wins the slot under consideration when using GSP ranking, i.e., let $b_1 e_1 \geq b_2 e_2$. Note that GSP's revenue from this slot is $\frac{b_2 e_2}{e_1} e_1 = b_2 p_2$. Also, recall that $0 \leq \alpha \leq 1$.

1. *GSP order = Squashed-GSP order = Click-probability order.* Mathematically, this case translates to $\{b_1e_1 \geq b_2e_2;\ b_1e_1^\alpha \geq b_2e_2^\alpha; e_1 \geq e_2\}$. This is the only case where squashing improves revenue. GSP's revenue is b_2e_2 from this slot, while squashed-GSP's revenue is $\frac{b_2e_2^\alpha}{e_1^\alpha}e_1 = b_2e_2^\alpha e_1^{1-\alpha}$. The latter is at least b_2e_2 whenever $e_1 \geq e_2$ which is true in this case.

2. *GSP order = Squashed-GSP order ≠ Click-probability order.* Mathematically, this is $\{b_1e_1 \geq b_2e_2;\ b_1e_1^\alpha \geq b_2e_2^\alpha; e_1 \leq e_2\}$. In this case, squashed GSP's revenue is $\frac{b_2e_2^\alpha}{e_1^\alpha}e_1 = b_2e_2^\alpha e_1^{1-\alpha}$. The latter is at most b_2e_2 because we have $e_1 \leq e_2$ in this case. Thus squashing hurts revenue.

3. *GSP order = Click-probability order ≠ Squashed-GSP order.* Mathematically, this is $\{b_1e_1 \geq b_2e_2;\ b_1e_1^\alpha \leq b_2e_2^\alpha; e_1 \geq e_2\}$. In this case, squashed GSP's revenue is $\frac{b_1e_1^\alpha}{e_2^\alpha}e_2 = b_1e_1^\alpha e_2^{1-\alpha}$. The latter is at most b_2e_2 because we have $b_1e_1^\alpha \leq b_2e_2^\alpha$. Thus in this case squashing hurts revenue. Further, squashing also hurts the number of clicks, because in GSP the number of clicks is proportional to e_1, whrere as in squashed-GSP, due to a change in the ordering, the number of clicks is proportional to e_2, which is at most e_1.

The question now is, given that squashing hurts in 2 out of 3 cases, whether one should squash or not. Given that the above analysis is on a per-slot basis, a more refined question would be to identify which slots are likely to fall in case 1 and therefore should be squashed (as squashing increases revenue in case 1), and which slots are likely to fall under cases 2, 3 and therefore should not be squashed (as squashing decreases revenue in cases 2, 3, and sometimes also decreases clicks). We claim that slot 1 is more likely to fall in case 1 than any other slot. The reason is that often the GSP winner of the first slot wins not only in terms of $b \times e$ but also in the individual dimensions of b and e. In this case, it is immediate that we fall in case 1. Even if the first slot winner wins only in terms of e, but not in b, often the margin of victory in e is high enough that even if one alters the GSP rank-score a bit by introducing a squashing exponent, it is not very likely to alter GSP's order, and therefore GSP order = Squashed-GSP order = Click-probability order, putting us in case 1 where one gets higher revenue. But as one goes down to larger slot numbers (lower positions), the GSP winner is not so pronounced as the first slot winner: i.e., either the GSP winner of that slot doesn't always win in terms of click-probability e (putting us in case 2), or, the margin of victory in terms of click-probability e is not high enough that a tiny change in rank-score by squashing changes the squahsed-GSP order from GSP order puttting us in case 3. Thus the likelihood of being in case 1 decreases as we increase the slot numbers. Intuitively this explains why it is better not to squash the lower slots, and squash only the top slot.

Another implication of our results is that the revenue benefits of squashing accrue mostly from the top slot.

Generality of the results.

A natural question at this point is to assess the generality of our findings. For instance, will squash-only-the-top-slot be found superior in other search engines' data too? What are some properties in the dataset to look for to get a sense of whether this result will hold? The 3-case analysis in the previous paragraphs shows that for any dataset where the first slot winner wins "more comfortably" (i.e., the victory margin in terms of click-probability is sufficiently high) while the click-probability victory margin is not that large for the remaining slots, squash-only-the-top-slot auction is very likely to do better. This property is true in Bing data set, even after one excludes navigational queries and other "dominant advertiser queries" like Verizon bidding on "Verizon" keyword (although we are not allowed to release specific numbers like the bid decay rate, click probability decay rate, etc.). We believe that while the ratios may be different for different search engines, this general fact that the first slot winner wins "more" than the other slot winners should hold in most datasets.

Related Work: Apart from the foundational work of Aggarwal et al. [3], Edelman et al. [9], Varian [19], the work that is most closely related to ours is that of Lahaie and Pennock [13]. They propose a variant of the GSP auction, namely squashed GSP auctions, where the ranking uses a squashed score and contains as special cases both the rank-by-bid and usual GSP. They show that GSP with squashing allows the auctioneer to optimize revenue at equilibrium and justify their results with simulations. In later work Lahaie and McAfee [12] show that the squashed auction can, under certain circumstances, also produce an efficient ranking. Our work presents a further generalization of the auction mechanisms of these works. Our simulations closely match the ones done in Lahaie and Pennock [13]. We use counterfactual analysis to study the first-order effects and to analyze the revenue-relevance trade-offs for the auction on actual ad auction data. This methodology is expounded in Bottou et al. [7], however, in a machine learning rather than an auction design setting.

Other papers have proposed modifications to the basic mechanism. Aggarwal et al. [4] propose a truthful auction based on Gale-Shapley stable matching theory that can incorporate bidder and position specific minimum and maximum prices. Roberts et al. [17] propose an auction that ranks using the difference between the bid and the reserve price. In other words, the reserve price affects the ranking beyond just filtering out advertisers with low bids. They too use simulations and real data to show this could raise more revenue. Another example of an empirical evaluation of variants of the GSP auction is by Thompson and Leyton-Brown [18]. They too run simulations, similar to Lahaie and Pennock [13], using data generated from distributions believed to mimic the actual bid distribution. They compare the revenue guarantee at equilibrium with different quality-weighted reserve prices and un-weighted reserve prices, and conclude that un-weighted prices perform consistently better. They also show that squashing improves the revenue of quality-weighted reserve prices, which otherwise fall much behind un-weighted reserves. Bachrach et al. [6] also evaluate different ways of setting reserve prices, with an emphasis on the tradeoffs obtainable between different objectives, once again using a combination of simulations and real data.

GSP Auctions have been studied from many different angles [5, 1, 14, 16, 10], such as questioning the separability assumption about the click-through rates, which are observed to not hold in practice [8, 2, 11]. Ostrovsky and Schwarz [15] analyze how using reserve prices derived from Myerson's theory can help increase revenue. A more complete summary of these results is beyond the scope of this paper. However, we are not aware of any other papers suggesting modifications of the basic auction format itself.

2. MODEL

2.1 Position Auctions

Position Auctions refer to auctioning of ad slots alongside "organic search" results in response to a user query in a search engine. Abstractly, a set of ads, A, compete for a set of k slots numbered 1 through k, with $k < |A|$. The slots at the top of the page (which correspond to lower numbered slots in our notation) are more desirable to all the advertisers. The slots are allocated through an auction. The advertisers place bids that are used in the auction.

An important feature of this mechanism is that it is pay-per-click: while the search engine assigns slots, it gets paid only if the user clicks on the ad. Whether an ad gets clicked or not depends on the allocation of ads to slots, the most general view being that the click probability of any ad depends on the entire slate of ads being shown. A common assumption is the, so-called, rank-1 assumption: that the click probability is a product of an advertiser factor and the slot-factor. Opinions about the accuracy of this assumption are mostly divided. In any case, an important consideration in the auction is the inherent clickability of an ad, which we simply call as the click probability. This is estimated by the search engine/auctioneer using sophisticated machine learning algorithms. For the purpose of auction design these can be thought of as the input.

To complete the abstract auction design problem, the auction assigns each slot to an ad, and charges payments. We represent the assignment by $\sigma : [k] \to A$, $\sigma(j)$ is the identity of the ad that is assigned slot j.[1] Let v_j be the value of the ad in slot j for getting a click and let π_j be the payment made by the ad in slot j, on getting a click. Let $c(j, \sigma)$ be the probability that the ad in slot j is clicked, given the allocation σ.

Important objectives in these auctions are

1. Revenue: the expected revenue of an allocation σ and payment π is

$$\sum_{j=1}^{k} \pi_j c(j, \sigma).$$

Revenue is clearly of interest to the search engine.

2. Number of clicks: The expected number of clicks given an allocation σ is

$$\sum_{j=1}^{k} c(j, \sigma).$$

The number of clicks is an indication of ad relevance and engagement with the user, and is considered very important. More relevant ads and better engagement with the user bring back more users and, in the long run, benefit the search engine and the advertisers.

[1] In practice k is not fixed, but this is a minor and distracting feature that we ignore for the sake of discussion here.

2.2 Multi-score auctions

A multi-score auction is given by a set of $k+1$ functions, s_0 and s_j for $j = 1, \cdots, k$, from a pair of bid and click probability, (b, c), to a non-negative real number. Each s_j for $j = 0, \cdots, k$ is strictly monotonically increasing in each of its arguments. Let s_j^{-1} denote the inverse of s_j in the first argument, i.e., $s_j^{-1}(b', p)$ is the unique number b such that $s_j(b, p) = b'$.

The auction proceeds as follows, it first selects the top k ads according to s_0. Then it goes down the slots from 1 to k and for each $j = 1, \cdots, k$ picks the ad with the highest score according to s_j (from the ads not already picked for a higher slot) to be assigned slot j. The payments are set similar to the GSP rule: each advertiser pays the lowest amount he would have to bid in order to retain his slot. The auction is summarized in Algorithm 1.

All of our auctions can be extended to include reserve prices, but we ignore reserve prices to keep the exposition simple.

ALGORITHM 1: Multi-Score Position Auctions

Input: A set of candidate ads, A, and for each ad $i \in A$, its bid b_i and its click probability c_i.
Output: A selection and ranking of top k ads given by $\sigma : [k] \to A$. Their payments given by π_j, for $j = 1, \cdots, k$.
$S \leftarrow \arg k \max\{s_0(b_i, c_i) : i \in A\}$, the top k ads from A, ranked by $s_0(b_i, c_i), i \in A$;
$r_0 \leftarrow \arg\max\{s_0(b_i, c_i) : i \in A \setminus S\}$;
for $j = 1, \cdots, k$ **do**
  $\sigma(j) \leftarrow \arg\max\{s_j(b_i, c_i) : i \in S\}$;
  $S \leftarrow S \setminus \sigma(j)$;
  $\pi_j \leftarrow$
  $\max\left(\{s_j^{-1}(s_j(b_i, c_i), c_{\sigma(j)}) : i \in S\} \cup \{s_0^{-1}(r_0, c_{\sigma(j)})\}\right)$;
end

The multi-score auction is a generalization of standard auctions used in practice: the GSP auction corresponds to the scoring functions $s_j = bc$ for all j. Another common variant is GSP with *squashing*, which corresponds to $s_j = bc^\alpha$ for some α (we restrict to $\alpha \in [0, 1]$). Variants considered previously fall into the "single score" framework, where s_j is the same for all j. Extending it to possibly different scores for each slot gives more freedom to the auction designer.

2.3 Dual score auctions (DSA)

We consider a special case of the above general family of auctions. The class is parameterized by a pair of real numbers, (α, β). In the first step, the top k ads are picked according to bc^β. From among them, the ad in the first slot is picked according to bc^α, and the rest of the slots are filled with the remaining ads ranked by bc^β. In other words, these are multi-score auctions with $s_1(b, c) = bc^\alpha$ and $s_j(b, c) = bc^\beta$ for all $j \neq 1$.

We rename the ads so that σ is the identity function. Then advertiser 1 is charged

$$\max\left(\left\{\frac{b_j c_j^\alpha}{c_1^\alpha} : j \geq 2\right\} \cup \left\{\frac{b_j c_j^\beta}{c_1^\beta} : j > k\right\}\right).$$

Advertiser j for $j = 2, \cdots, k$ is charged $b_{j+1} c_{j+1}^\beta / c_j^\beta$. We refer to this auction as DSA(α, β).

There are also other ways to get sub-families of MSPAs with few parameters. For instance, one can consider a separate scoring function for candidate *selection* (s_0) and a different one for *ranking* (s_j for all $j \geq 1$). The space of MSPAs is quite huge and it is possible that there are several other interesting auctions in this framework.

3. EXPERIMENTS

We run experiments on actual data from Bing. These experiments measure first order effects, which measures the change in the performance metrics keeping the bids unchanged. It is almost impossible to effectively measure second order effects from real data. The reason is that such experiments are required to run only on a small sample of auctions. However, in order to measure the second order effects, all of the auctions an advertiser participates in must be included in the experiment. This creates a dependency which often forces to include a large part, if not all, of the auctions, contradicting the requirement that the experiment be only performed on a small fraction of auctions.

3.1 Experimental Design

For our empirical evaluation, we use data from existing randomized experiments in Bing. One of the existing experiments in Bing places the ads in an order that is chosen *uniformly at random from all permutations* from the set of auction candidates. This experiment itself runs on a random sample of actual search traffic. Given any value of (α, β), there is a non-trivial fraction of auctions for which the (random) order of the ads in this experiment matches the order of ads according to the auction $\text{DSA}(\alpha, \beta)$. This is a random sample of all auctions (since the randomization of the ad slate is independent of the auction) and given sufficiently many auctions, we get a representative sample of all search traffic. We use the bid data and the *actual user click reponses* from logged information for this experiment. We used logs from a duration of several weeks for the analysis. This lets us compare DSAs with different α, β parameters for a number of variants. As noted earlier, this is a significant departure from earlier papers which use data from a few popular keywords only. Moreover, our method allows us to evaluate the auctions with respect to actual clicks, which is also absent in previous work. Here are some key facts about our experimental design:

1. The data for the experiment was collected for a duration of 41 days.
2. The experiment performs a filtering that excludes navigational intent queries and other queries where there is a dominant advertiser, like Verizon bidding on the "Verizon" keyword.
3. Barring the dominant advertiser filter, and other sanitizations to remove nonbillable queries, etc., the experimental traffic represents a true random sample of the entire traffic to Bing.
4. For each value of α and β we report, the sample size, which is the number of samples in our data set that matched the order of $\text{DSA}(\alpha, \beta)$, was between 11 million and 13 million. Thus, there are no small sample issues.

Even though the order of the ads is randomized, it may not be perfect. A sanity check is to see whether for a given (α, β) there were sufficiently many queries for which the ads were ranked as per $\text{DSA}(\alpha, \beta)$. Due to confidentiality reasons, we present a slightly different statistic, for each β we present the average (over different αs) of the ratio of the number of queries matching $\text{DSA}(\alpha, \beta)$ to the number of queries matching $\text{DSA}(1, 1)$, i.e.,

$$\sum_{\alpha \in \Lambda} \frac{1}{|\Lambda|} \frac{\text{number of queries matching DSA}(\alpha, \beta)}{\text{number of queries matching DSA}(1, 1)}. \quad (1)$$

One caveat of our setup is that we cannot change the criteria used to select the *set* of ads, alternatively s_0 is the criterion that Bing used for selecting auction candidates during the time period of our data collection. We only capture effects that are due to re-ranking of candidate ads.

3.2 Experimental Results

The main chart is in Figure 1, which compares $\text{DSA}(\alpha, 1)$ with $\text{DSA}(\alpha, \alpha)$. This shows that $\text{DSA}(\alpha, 1)$ always pareto-dominates $\text{DSA}(\alpha, \alpha)$, with substantial improvements in *both* RPS and CTR. This is in agreeement with the simulation results presented in Figure 3. This is the most interesting conclusion of these experiments, indicating that squashing only the top slot is better than complete squashing.

Why restrict α to $[0, 1]$?

The optimal value of α is keyword specific, and depends on the correlation between bids and click-through-rates for that keyword. While theoretically the optimal α could lie anywhere in $(-\infty, +\infty)$, the kinds of correlation necessary to make the optimal α negative or too large are not realistic. Further, even if a negative α could afford the search engine large revenue in the short run, it results in very poor relevance, affecting user satisfaction. Consequently, we present results for $0 \leq \alpha \leq 1$ which seems to be the range of α's that give the right trade-off between revenue and relevance. Remarkably, Figure 1 shows that squashing only the top slot is better than squashing for *all* slots for all αs in $[0, 1]$. While we omit results for $\alpha \in [-1, 0]$, the trend of simultaneous increase in revenue and CTR continues to remain there too.

Next, we present a chart (Figure 2) showing that the number of queries is pretty evenly distributed, by giving for each β, the ratio of the number of queries matching $\text{DSA}(\alpha, \beta)$ to the number of queries matching $\text{DSA}(1, 1)$ as mentioned in Equation (1). Note that the value for $\beta = 1$ is less than 1, since this is an average over all αs.

4. EQUILIBRIA OF DSA

Unlike our experiments, where $c(j, \sigma)$ could be an arbitrary function of j and σ, measuring second-order effects of DSA requires computing DSA's equilibrium and hence some structure is necessary on $c(j, \sigma)$. We make the standard assumption that the ckick-through-rate of bidder s in position t is $e_s x_t$, for $e_s, x_t \in [0, 1]$. In our previous section's notation, $c(j, \sigma) = e_{\sigma(j)} x_j$. The quantity e_s is often referred to as the relevance of bidder s's ad and x_t is called as the position effect.

With the above separable click-through-rate assumption Varian [19] and Edelman et al. [9] characterize the set of envy-free equlibria or "symmetric Nash equilibria" (SNE) of the GSP auction and Lahaie and Pennock [13] do the same for GSP with squashing. These are a subset of pure Nash

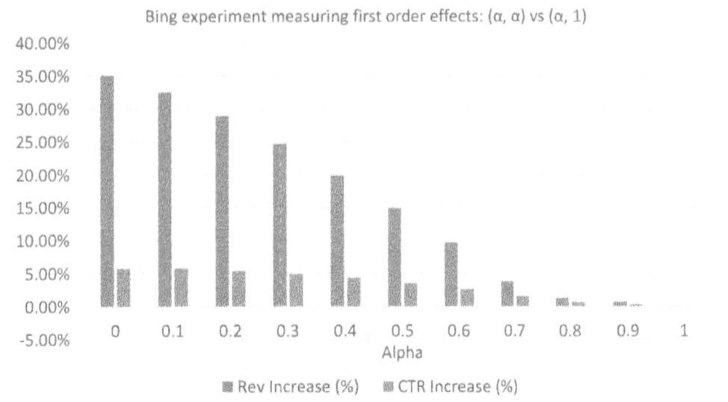

Figure 1: Impact on revenue and click-throughs for DSA(α,α) **vs.** DSA$(\alpha, 1)$**.**

Figure 2: Number of queries as a function of β.

equilibria, obtained by strengthening some of the Nash equilibrium constraints to make them symmetric for deviations that take the bidder above and below his current slot. The characterization says that such an equilibrium always exists, there is only one order of bidders that can result in an SNE and gives a closed form formula for the bids at the lowest price equilibrium (which is uniquely defined).

Unfortunately, there isn't such a simple characterization for the SNE of DSA, and a SNE may not exist. When they exist, there may be multiple orderings of bidders which support equilibria. The first fact is not problematic: our simulations show that equilibrium exists for more than 91% of queries[2] for all $\alpha \geq 0$. The second poses an interesting conundrum, and our simulations show that the choice of equilibrium order results in significant difference to the performance metrics. Before we detail the results of our simulations, we detail the equilibrium constraints. Fix a particular ordering of bidders, say bidder s is in slot s for $s \in [n]$. Then the SNE conditions are as follows. For DSA(α, β), let $w_s = e_s^\beta$ and $\widehat{w}_s = e_s^\alpha$. Let b_s be the bid of advertiser s.

We first write envy-free constraints for bidders in slots $s > 1$ to not envy each other:

[2]Note that as α gets closer to 1, the percentage of queries that have a SNE increases and hits 100% at $\alpha = 1$ since that corresponds to pure GSP.

$$\forall s \neq 1, t \neq 1, \quad \left(v_s - \frac{b_{s+1}w_{s+1}}{w_s}\right) e_s x_s \geq \left(v_s - \frac{b_{t+1}w_{t+1}}{w_s}\right) e_s x_t \tag{2}$$

Let $\widehat{p}_1 = \max_{s \geq 2} b_s \widehat{w}_s$. We now write constraints for bidders in slots $s > 1$ to not envy bidder in slot 1.

$$\forall s \neq 1, \qquad \left(v_s - \frac{b_{s+1}w_{s+1}}{w_s}\right) e_s x_s \geq \left(v_s - \frac{\widehat{p}_1}{w_s}\right) e_s x_1 \tag{3}$$

Finally, we write the constraints for bidder in slot 1 not to envy any bidder in slot $s \geq 2$.

$$\forall s \neq 1, \qquad \left(v_1 - \frac{\widehat{p}_1}{\widehat{w}_1}\right) e_1 x_1 \geq \left(v_1 - \frac{b_{s+1}w_{s+1}}{w_1}\right) e_1 x_s \tag{4}$$

Given an ordering of the bidders, we can check if equilibrium exists using conditions (2),(3),(4). Once we know equilibrium exists for a given order, we can also find the *lowest* price equilibrium bids as follows. While all kinds of complicated allocations and bids could satisfy conditions (2),(3),(4), note that once the bidder in the first slot is fixed, the remaining $k-1$ slots should necessarily satisfy mutual envy-free conditions among themselves, and therefore, by Edelman et al. [9] and Varian [19], there is a unique ordering among them, namely, the order of $v_s w_s = v_s e_s^\beta$. The lowest SNE bids for slots $3, \ldots, k$ is uniquely determined, and is given by (see Varian [19] and Lahaie and Pennock [13]):

$$b_{s+1}w_{s+1}x_s = \sum_{t=s}^{k}(x_t - x_{t+1})v_{t+1}w_{t+1}. \tag{5}$$

Fixing the above bids for slots $3, \ldots, k$ (bidders $s > k$ have $b_s = v_s$) determines the payments for all slots except 1 . The only quantity to be determined to compute revenue is $\widehat{p}_1$. We compute the smallest $\widehat{p}_1$ that satisfies conditions (3),(4). This determines the revenue to be $\frac{\widehat{p}_1}{\widehat{w}_1}x_1e_1 + \sum_{s=2}^{k}\frac{b_{s+1}w_{s+1}}{w_s}x_se_s$.

Remark 1. *It could be possible that an equilibrium for DSA(α,β) may exist satisfying conditions (2),(3),(4), but may not satisfy the lowest bids specified in (5). For our simulation purposes, we call such instances as no-equilibrium instances, and even with this restriction, the number of instances with equilbrium is at least 91% in the relevant regime of $\alpha \geq 0.4$. More precisely, we only look for equilibria that satisfy the lowest bid constraints for slots $3, \ldots, k$ in (5).*

Remark 2. *Note that since $\widehat{p}_1 = \max_{s\geq 2} b_s\widehat{w}_s$, bidder 2 is not necessarily the price setter for bidder 1.*

5. SIMULATIONS

We do simulations to compare the performance of DSA and GSP with squashing. The goal of doing simulations is to measure the second order effects, i.e., if we change the auction format, then we expect the advertisers to adjust their bids to the new format, with respect to which we should measure the performance metrics. How do advertisers bid? The standard assumption is that they bid at an SNE. Therefore we measure the percentage change in the performance metrics betweeen an SNE of GSP with squashing and an SNE of DSA. This is the same methodology used by Lahaie and Pennock [13] to compare GSP with squashing with pure GSP. For our simulations we use the same distribution as they did to generate the instances.

As in Lahaie and Pennock [13] we use a joint distribution for determining the bidders' value relevance pairs. The marginal distribution for values is a lognormal distribution with parameters $\mu = 0.35$ and $\sigma = 0.71$. The marginal distribution for relevance is a beta distribution with parameters $a = 2.71$ and $b = 25.43$. We use a Gaussian copula to create a joint distribution from these two marginal distributions, with differing levels of correlation. We report results for Spearman correlation levels that Lahaie and Pennock report fit well with the keyword for which they performed their simulations: namely, correlations of $0.3, 0.4, 0.5$.

We focus on the two most important objectives, revenue and click-throughs. We present relative impact on these two objectives as we move from $\text{DSA}(\alpha, \alpha)$ to $\text{DSA}(\alpha, 1)$. The percentage *increase* in revenue and the percent *increase* in clickthroughs are respectively

$$\left(\frac{\text{REV}(\alpha,1)}{\text{REV}(\alpha,\alpha)} - 1\right) \cdot 100 \text{ and } \left(\frac{\text{CTR}(\alpha,1)}{\text{CTR}(\alpha,\alpha)} - 1\right) \cdot 100.$$

Before we do the second order analysis, we do a first order analysis: how do the performance metrics change if we retain the SNE bids for the original auction. We do this as a sanity check to test whether this agrees with the first order analysis we perform on real data (see Section 3). These results are presented in Figure 3. The first order effects show a consistent improvement in both RPS and CTR for $\text{DSA}(\alpha, 1)$ vs. $\text{DSA}(\alpha, \alpha)$, in agreement with our analysis on real data. We emphasize that while simulation is for a single keyword's distribution, our real experiment is over a random selection of all queries for several weeks.

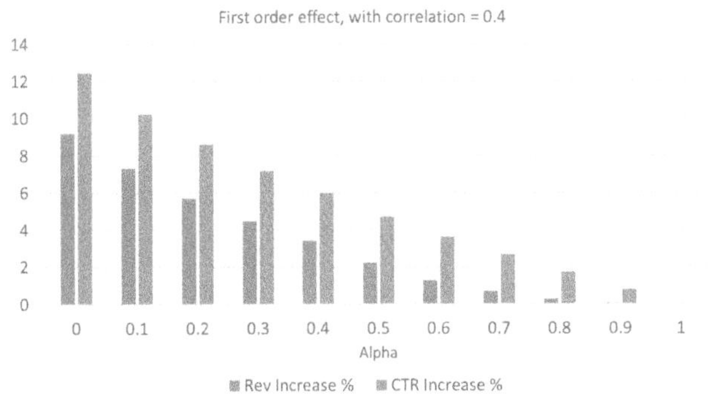

Figure 3: Impact on revenue and click-throughs for $\text{DSA}(\alpha, \alpha)$ vs. $\text{DSA}(\alpha, 1)$.

As mentioned before, there may not be an SNE at all in $\text{DSA}(\alpha, \beta)$ or there may be many orders of bidders for which equilibria exist. Observe that the possible number of such orders is at most n, since once you fix the bidder in the top slot, the rest of the bidders are ordered according to $b_j e_j^{\beta}$. Therefore it is computationally easy to just try all n choices for the first slot and check for equilibrium. This gives rise to the problem of equilibrium selection; if many of these choices lead to an equilibrium, which one do we choose?[3] We break ties according to the following 3 criteria, the relevance e_j, the α-score for true values $v_j e_j^{\alpha}$ and the β-score for true values $v_j e_j^{\beta}$. These orderings give successively lesser importance to relevance (the e_j's) and our simulations show that they perform successively worse.

The results of the second-order analysis are presented in Figure 4 for samples with a Spearman correlation of 0.4.

We also do simulations for samples with a Spearman correlation of 0.3 and 0.5. The results are in Tables 1, 2, 3 and 4, and the trends are consistent with what we get for correlation of 0.4.

The simulations suggest that the performance metrics depend significantly on the choice of equilibrium. As can be seen from Figure 4, there is a strong trend that shows that preferring advertisers with higher relevance can lead to a significant increase in all the desired peformance metrics. Perhaps surprisingly, when we simply use the relevance score (e_j) to break ties, this increase is even more than the first order increase. The search engine could steer the bids towards an equilibrium that prefers advertisers with higher relevance via, for example, bidding agents. Our simulations show that such a strategy could result in a significant improvement in the performance metrics.

References

[1] Abrams, Z. and Ghosh, A. 2007. Auctions with revenue guarantees for sponsored search. In *Internet and Network Economics, Third International Workshop, WINE 2007, San Diego, CA, USA, December 12-14, 2007, Proceedings*. 143–154.

[2] Aggarwal, G., Feldman, J., Muthukrishnan, S., and Pál, M. 2008. Sponsored search auctions with markovian users. In *Internet and Network Economics, 4th International Workshop, WINE 2008, Shanghai, China, December 17-20, 2008. Proceedings*. 621–628.

[3] Aggarwal, G., Goel, A., and Motwani, R. 2006. Truthful auctions for pricing search keywords. In *Proceedings 7th ACM Conference on Electronic Commerce (EC-2006), Ann Arbor, Michigan, USA, June 11-15, 2006*. 1–7.

[4] Aggarwal, G., Muthukrishnan, S., Pál, D., and Pál, M. 2009. General auction mechanism for search advertising. In *Proceedings of the 18th International Conference on World Wide Web, WWW 2009, Madrid, Spain, April 20-24, 2009*. 241–250.

[5] Athey, S. and Nekipelov, D. 2012. A structural model of sponsored search advertising auctions. Working paper.

[6] Bachrach, Y., Ceppi, S., Kash, I. A., Key, P., and Kurokawa, D. 2014. Optimising trade-offs among stakeholders in ad auctions. In *ACM Conference on Economics and Computation, EC '14, Stanford , CA, USA, June 8-12, 2014*. 75–92.

[7] Bottou, L., Peters, J., Quiñonero-Candela, J., Charles, D. X., Chickering, D. M., Portugaly, E.,

[3]Note that while there are multiple possible equilibria, all of these equilibria converge to the lowest revenue SNE when $\alpha = \beta$.

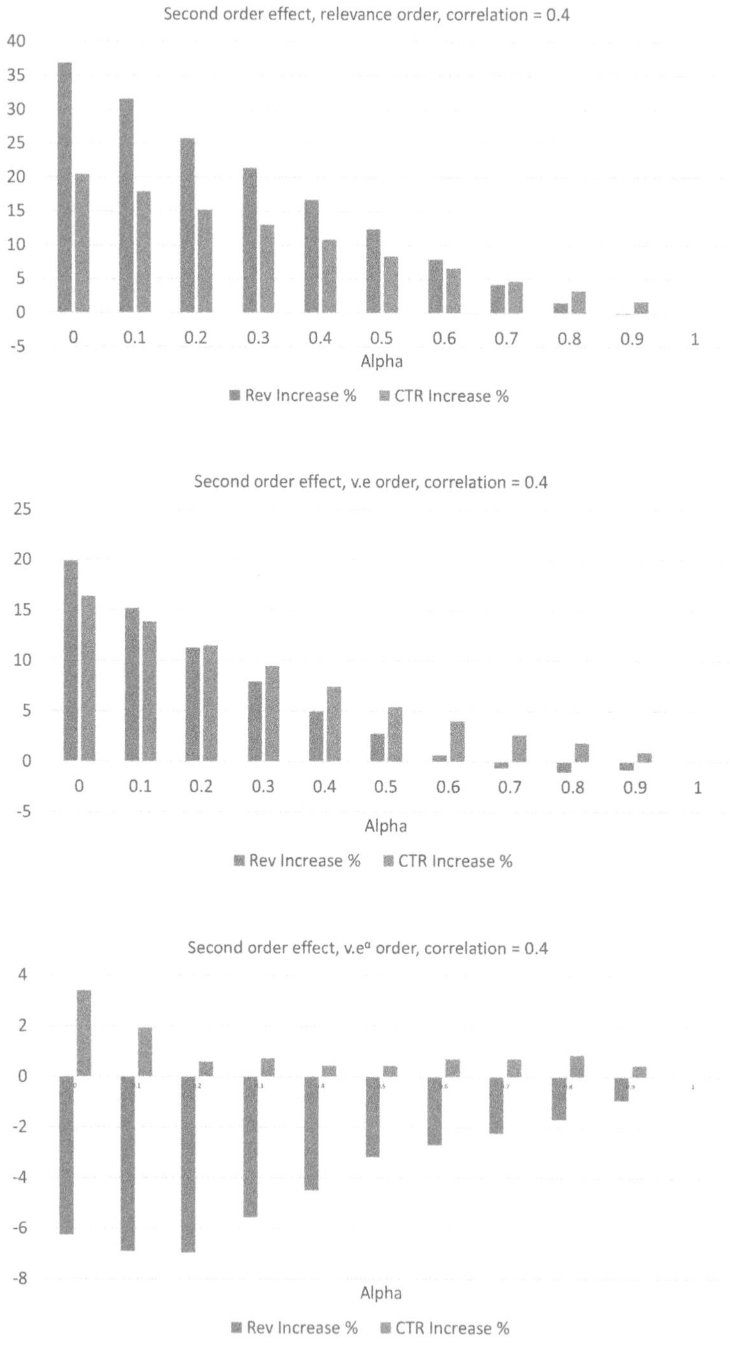

Figure 4: Impact on revenue and click-throughs for $\text{DSA}(\alpha, \alpha)$ **vs.** $\text{DSA}(\alpha, 1)$ **for correlation** $= 0.4$.

α	0	0.2	0.4	0.6	0.8	1
First-order ΔRev %	7.43	4.55	2.36	0.97	0.17	0
Second-order (Relevance) ΔRev %	28.06	21.63	14.36	6.62	1.19	0
Second-order ($v_j e_j$) ΔRev %	13.43	8.43	3.03	-0.36	-1.16	0
Second-order ($v_j e_j^\alpha$) ΔRev %	-9.23	-6.58	-4.45	-3.31	-1.9	0

Table 1: Impact on revenue for $\text{DSA}(\alpha, \alpha)$ **vs.** $\text{DSA}(\alpha, 1)$ **with a correlation of** 0.5.

α	0	0.2	0.4	0.6	0.8	1
First-order ΔCTR %	9.82	6.68	4.48	2.70	1.29	0
Second-order (Relevance) ΔCTR %	16.34	12.38	8.73	5.74	3.14	0
Second-order ($v_j \cdot e_j$) ΔCTR %	12.94	9.25	5.73	3.37	1.71	0
Second-order ($v_j \cdot e_j^\alpha$) ΔCTR %	1.61	0.79	0.58	0.68	0.69	0

Table 2: Impact on click-throughs for $\text{DSA}(\alpha, \alpha)$ **vs.** $\text{DSA}(\alpha, 1)$ **with a correlation of** 0.5.

α	0	0.2	0.4	0.6	0.8	1
First-order ΔRev %	10.98	7.11	3.95	1.71	0.35	0
Second-order (Relevance) ΔRev %	38.78	29.17	19.71	9.39	2.21	0
Second-order ($v_j \cdot e_j$) ΔRev %	21.43	13.91	7.56	1.88	-0.69	0
Second-order ($v_j \cdot e_j^\alpha$) ΔRev %	-8.81	-5.15	-3.01	-2.19	-1.6	0

Table 3: Impact on revenue for $\text{DSA}(\alpha, \alpha)$ **vs.** $\text{DSA}(\alpha, 1)$ **with a correlation of** 0.3.

α	0	0.2	0.4	0.6	0.8	1
First-order ΔCTR %	15.01	10.59	7.16	4.49	2.06	0
Second-order (Relevance) ΔCTR %	22.42	16.8	11.77	7.55	4.1	0
Second-order ($v_j \cdot e_j$) ΔCTR %	17.79	12.4	7.9	4.6	2.3	0
Second-order ($v_j \cdot e_j^\alpha$) ΔCTR %	2.85	1.41	0.37	0.67	0.83	0

Table 4: Impact on click-throughs for $\text{DSA}(\alpha, \alpha)$ **vs.** $\text{DSA}(\alpha, 1)$ **with a correlation of** 0.3.

RAY, D., SIMARD, P., AND SNELSON, E. 2013. Counterfactual reasoning and learning systems: The example of computational advertising. *Journal of Machine Learning Research 14*, 3207–3260.

[8] CAVALLO, R. AND WILKENS, C. A. 2014. GSP with general independent click-through-rates. In *Web and Internet Economics - 10th International Conference, WINE 2014, Beijing, China, December 14-17, 2014. Proceedings.* 400–416.

[9] EDELMAN, B., OSTROVSKY, M., AND SCHWARZ, M. 2007. Internet advertising and the generalized second-price auction: Selling billions of dollars worth of keywords. *The American Economic Review 97,* 1, pp. 242–259.

[10] GOMES, R. D. AND SWEENEY, K. S. 2009. Bayes-nash equilibria of the generalized second price auction. In *Proceedings of the 10th ACM Conference on Electronic Commerce.* EC '09. ACM, New York, NY, USA, 107–108.

[11] KEMPE, D. AND MAHDIAN, M. 2008. A cascade model for externalities in sponsored search. In *Internet and Network Economics, 4th International Workshop, WINE 2008, Shanghai, China, December 17-20, 2008. Proceedings.* 585–596.

[12] LAHAIE, S. AND MCAFEE, R. P. 2011. Efficient ranking in sponsored search. In *WINE.* 254–265.

[13] LAHAIE, S. AND PENNOCK, D. 2007. Revenue analysis of a family of ranking rules for keyword auctions. In *ACM Conference on Electronic Commerce.* 13–16.

[14] LIKHODEDOV, A. AND SANDHOLM, T. 2003. Auction mechanism for optimally trading off revenue and efficiency. In *Proceedings of the 4th ACM Conference on Electronic Commerce.* EC '03. ACM, New York, NY, USA, 212–213.

[15] OSTROVSKY, M. AND SCHWARZ, M. 2011. Reserve prices in internet advertising auctions: A field experiment. In *Proceedings of the 12th ACM conference on Electronic commerce.* ACM, 59–60.

[16] PIN, F. AND KEY, P. 2011. Stochastic variability in sponsored search auctions: observations and models. In *Proceedings 12th ACM Conference on Electronic Commerce (EC-2011), San Jose, CA, USA, June 5-9, 2011.* 61–70.

[17] ROBERTS, B., GUNAWARDENA, D., KASH, I. A., AND KEY, P. 2013. Ranking and tradeoffs in sponsored search auctions. In *ACM Conference on Electronic Commerce, EC '13, Philadelphia, PA, USA, June 16-20, 2013.* 751–766.

[18] THOMPSON, D. R. AND LEYTON-BROWN, K. 2013. Revenue optimization in the generalized second-price auction. In *Proceedings of the Fourteenth ACM Conference on Electronic Commerce.* EC '13. ACM, New York, NY, USA, 837–852.

[19] VARIAN, H. 2006. Position auctions. *International Journal of Industrial Organization 26,* 6, 1163–1178.

Multi-view Machines

Bokai Cao[1*], Hucheng Zhou[2], Guoqiang Li[3†] and Philip S. Yu[1,4]
[1]Department of Computer Science, University of Illinois at Chicago, IL, USA
[2]Microsoft Research, Beijing, China
[3]Huawei Technologies, Shenzhen, China
[4]Institute for Data Science, Tsinghua University, Beijing, China
caobokai@uic.edu, huzho@microsoft.com, liguoqiang9@huawei.com, psyu@cs.uic.edu

ABSTRACT

With rapidly growing amount of data available on the web, it becomes increasingly likely to obtain data from different perspectives for multi-view learning. Some successive examples of web applications include recommendation and target advertising. Specifically, to predict whether a user will click an ad in a query context, there are available features extracted from user profile, ad information and query description, and each of them can only capture part of the task signals from a particular aspect/view. Different views provide complementary information to learn a practical model for these applications. Therefore, an effective integration of the multi-view information is critical to facilitate the learning performance.

In this paper, we propose a general predictor, named multi-view machines (MVMs), that can effectively explore the full-order interactions between features from multiple views. A joint factorization is applied for the interaction parameters which makes parameter estimation more accurate under sparsity and renders the model with the capacity to avoid overfitting. Moreover, MVMs can work in conjunction with different loss functions for a variety of machine learning tasks. The advantages of MVMs are illustrated through comparison with other methods for multi-view prediction, including support vector machines (SVMs), support tensor machines (STMs) and factorization machines (FMs).

A stochastic gradient descent method and a distributed implementation on Spark are presented to learn the MVM model. Through empirical studies on two real-world web application datasets, we demonstrate the effectiveness of MVMs on modeling feature interactions in multi-view data. A 3.51% accuracy improvement is shown on MVMs over FMs for the problem of movie rating prediction, and 0.57% for ad click prediction.

*This work was done while the author was doing internship at Microsoft Research.
†This work was done before the author joins Huawei.

WSDM'16, February 22–25, 2016, San Francisco, CA, USA.
© 2016 ACM. ISBN 978-1-4503-3716-8/16/02...$15.00
DOI: http://dx.doi.org/10.1145/2835776.2835777

CCS Concepts

•Information systems → Data mining; •Computing methodologies → Machine learning; Factorization methods;

Keywords

multi-view learning, feature interaction, factorization

1. INTRODUCTION

Web data is available not only in great volume but also in multiple representations/views from a variety of sources or feature subsets. Generally, different views provide complementary information to learn an effective model for web-scale applications. Thus, multi-view learning can facilitate the learning performance and is prevalent in a wide range of application domains. For example, for the business on the web, it is critical to estimate the probability that the display of an ad to a specific user when s/he searches for a query will lead to a click. This process involves three entities: users, ads, and queries. An effective integration of features describing these different entities is directly related to precise targeting of an advertising system.

One of the key challenges of multi-view learning is to model the interactions/correlations between different views, wherein complementary information is contained. Conventionally, multi-kernel learning algorithms combine kernels associated with respective views to improve the learning performance [9]. Basically, coefficients are learned based on the usefulness/informativeness of the corresponding views, and thus inter-view correlations are only considered at the view-level. These approaches, however, fail to explore the explicit correlations between features across multiple views.

In contrast to modeling on views, another direction for modeling multi-view data is to directly consider the abundant correlations between features from different views. Feature interactions with different orders can reflect different but complementary insights. Assume that we have obtained a latent factor representing wealth/price-related attributes for each entity (*i.e.*, users, ads and queries) in the advertising system of a search engine, as illustrated in Table 1. For example, users who have high purchase power (*i.e.*, a positive latent factor, $a_{user} > 0$) may have interests in luxury products ($a_{ad} > 0$). However, a thoughtful recommender system should not always recommend luxury products to these users regardless of the query context. In Table 1, it is unreasonable to recommend a luxury bag ($a_{ad} > 0$) to the user when s/he searches for a disease ($a_{query} < 0$), in which case some

Table 1: An example showing the discrepancy between feature interactions with different orders. $\#1 = user + ad + query$, $\#2 = user \times ad + user \times query + ad \times query$, $\#3 = user \times ad \times query$.

User	Ad	Query	#1	#2	#3
1.20 (+)	1.80 (+)	0.50 (+)	3.50 (+)	3.66 (+)	1.08 (+)
1.20 (+)	1.80 (+)	-0.50 (-)	2.50 (+)	0.66 (+)	-1.08 (-)
1.20 (+)	-1.80 (-)	-0.50 (-)	-1.10 (-)	-1.86 (-)	1.08 (+)

relevant medicines or medical books ($a_{ad} < 0$) would seem better choices. We can observe that, in such scenarios, only the third-order interactions contribute positively to the recommendation of medicines and negatively to that of luxury bags, while the first-order and the second-order interactions insist to recommend something inappropriate in the specific context. Note here that we do not claim the higher order interactions can work as the best indicator by their own in all problems. Nevertheless, integrating their contributions into the decision function in an efficient manner is critical.

S. Rendle pioneers the concept of factorization machines (FMs) [10] which are now the state-of-the-art approach to model feature interactions and inspire this work. However, the practical implementations of FMs are usually limited to the second-order interactions, *i.e.*, pairwise correlations. This is partially due to the fact that a separate set of latent factors (parameters to be learned) is introduced for each order of interactions in FMs. That is to say, a feature has a latent representation when it is considered for the second-order interactions, while the same feature has a different representation for the third-order interactions. Moreover, the global bias and the first-order interaction terms in FMs are not factorized and independent from the latent factors for higher order interactions. These bias terms and latent factors for different orders altogether compose inconsistent representations of input features and thus compromise the model interpretability. In addition, independent factorization of interactions with different orders results in a large set of model parameters to be learned which makes the training process challenging.

The major challenge of including higher order interactions is that observations with such interactions become sparser with higher orders. Therefore, parameters representing higher order interactions can hardly be learned from their limited observations, especially from the extremely sparse data, *e.g.*, recommender systems. We suggest a common latent subspace for all features that is shared by different orders of interactions. In this manner, the full-order interactions observed in the data can collectively be used to learn a consistent representation in the latent feature space.

In this paper, we propose a novel model for multi-view prediction, called multi-view machines (MVMs). The main advantages of MVMs are outlined as follows:

- MVMs include the global bias and the full-order interactions between features from multiple views, ranging from the first-order interactions (*i.e.*, contributions of single features) to the highest-order interactions (*i.e.*, contributions of combinations of features from each view).
- MVMs jointly factorize the interaction parameters for different orders to allow accurate parameter estimation under sparsity and avoid overfitting via the effect of bias factors.
- MVMs are a general predictor that can work with different loss functions (*e.g.*, square error, hinge loss, logit loss) for a variety of machine learning tasks.

Table 2: Symbols.

Symbol	Definition and description
s	each lowercase letter represents a scale
$\mathbf{v}$	each boldface lowercase letter represents a vector
$\mathbf{M}$	each boldface capital letter represents a matrix
$\mathcal{T}$	each calligraphic letter represents a tensor, set or space
$\langle \cdot, \cdot \rangle$	denotes inner product
$\circ$	denotes tensor product or outer product
$\times_k$	denotes mode-k product
$\lvert \cdot \rvert$	denotes absolute value
$\lVert \cdot \rVert_F$	denotes (Frobenius) norm of vector, matrix or tensor

To empirically analyze and understand these advantages, we have the MVM model and other baselines implemented in a distributed environment, GraphX [4], which is a component of Spark [17]. Extensive experiments are conducted on real-world web application datasets, for regression and classification tasks, respectively. A 3.51% accuracy improvement is shown on MVMs over FMs for the problem of movie rating prediction, and 0.57% for ad click prediction.

2. BACKGROUND

In this section, we first state the problem of multi-view prediction and briefly review the adaptation of existing methods for multi-view prediction, including support vector machines (SVMs), support tensor machines (STMs) and factorization machines (FMs).

2.1 Multi-view Prediction

Suppose each instance has representations in m different views, *i.e.*, $\mathbf{x}^T = \left(\mathbf{x}^{(1)^T}, ..., \mathbf{x}^{(m)^T}\right)$, where $\mathbf{x}^{(p)} \in \mathbb{R}^{I_p}$, I_p is the dimensionality of the p-th view. Let $d = \sum_{p=1}^{m} I_p$, so $\mathbf{x} \in \mathbb{R}^d$. Considering the problem of click through rate (CTR) prediction for advertising display, for example, an instance corresponds to an *impression* which involves a user, an ad, and a query. Therefore, suppose $\mathbf{x}^T = \left(\mathbf{x}^{(1)^T}, \mathbf{x}^{(2)^T}, \mathbf{x}^{(3)^T}\right)$ is an impression, $\mathbf{x}^{(1)}$ contains information of the user profile, $\mathbf{x}^{(2)}$ is associated with the ad information, and $\mathbf{x}^{(3)}$ is the description from the query aspect. The result of an impression is *click* or *non-click*.

Given a training set with n labeled instances represented from m views: $\mathcal{D} = \{(\mathbf{x}_i, y_i) \mid i = 1, ..., n\}$, in which $\mathbf{x}_i^T = \left(\mathbf{x}_i^{(1)^T}, ..., \mathbf{x}_i^{(m)^T}\right)$ and $y_i \in \{-1, 1\}$ is the class label of the i-th instance. For CTR prediction problem, $y = 1$ denotes *click* and $y = -1$ denotes *non-click* in an impression. The task of multi-view classification is to learn a function $f : \mathbb{R}^{I_1} \times \cdots \times \mathbb{R}^{I_m} \to \{-1, 1\}$ that correctly predicts the label of a test instance. Alternatively, if $y_i \in \mathbb{R}$, it is a multi-view regression problem, *e.g.*, rating prediction.

Table 2 lists some basic symbols that will be used throughout the paper. In addition, we introduce the concept of tensors which are higher order arrays that generalize the notions of vectors (the first-order tensors) and matrices (the second-order tensors), whose elements are indexed by more than two indexes. Definitions of tensor product and mode-k product are given which will be used to formulate our proposed model.

DEFINITION 2.1 (TENSOR PRODUCT OR OUTER PRODUCT). *The tensor product* $\mathcal{X} \circ \mathcal{Y}$ *of a tensor* $\mathcal{X} \in \mathbb{R}^{I_1 \times \cdots \times I_m}$ *and another tensor* $\mathcal{Y} \in \mathbb{R}^{I'_1 \times \cdots \times I'_{m'}}$ *is defined by*

$$(\mathcal{X} \circ \mathcal{Y})_{i_1,\dots,i_m,i'_1,\dots,i'_{m'}} = x_{i_1,\dots,i_m} y_{i'_1,\dots,i'_{m'}} \quad (1)$$

for all index values.

DEFINITION 2.2 (MODE-k PRODUCT). *The mode-k product* $\mathcal{X} \times_k \mathbf{M}$ *of a tensor* $\mathcal{X} \in \mathbb{R}^{I_1 \times \cdots \times I_m}$ *and a matrix* $\mathbf{M} \in \mathbb{R}^{I'_k \times I_k}$ *is defined by*

$$(\mathcal{X} \times_k \mathbf{M})_{i_1,\dots,i_{k-1},j,i_{k+1},\dots,i_m} = \sum_{i_k=1}^{I_k} x_{i_1,\dots,i_m} m_{j,i_k} \quad (2)$$

for all index values.

Basically, through the mode-k matrix product, a new tensor of the same order is obtained by applying the matrix to each mode-k fiber of the tensor.

2.2 SVM Model

Vapnik introduced support vector machines (SVMs) [14] based on the maximum-margin principle. Essentially, SVMs integrate the hinge loss and the L2-norm regularization. The decision function with a linear kernel is as follows[1]:

$$\hat{y} = w_0 + \sum_{i=1}^{d} w_i x_i = w_0 + \sum_{p=1}^{m} \sum_{i_p=1}^{I_p} w_{i_p}^{(p)} x_{i_p}^{(p)} \quad (3)$$

where $\mathbf{x}$ is simply a concatenation of features from different views in the multi-view setting, *i.e.*, $\mathbf{x}^T = \left(\mathbf{x}^{(1)^T}, \dots, \mathbf{x}^{(m)^T}\right)$, as shown in Figure 1.

Obviously, no interactions between views are explored in Eq. (3). Through the employment of a nonlinear kernel, SVMs can implicitly project data from the feature space into a more complex high-dimensional space, which allows SVMs to model higher order interactions between features. However, as discussed in [10], all interaction parameters of nonlinear SVMs are completely independent.

For nonlinear SVMs, there must be enough instances $\mathbf{x} \in \mathcal{D}$ where $x_{i_p}^{(p)} \neq 0$ and $x_{i_q}^{(q)} \neq 0$ to reliably estimate the second-order interaction parameter $w_{i_p,i_q}^{(p,q)}$. The instances with either $x_{i_p}^{(p)} = 0$ or $x_{i_q}^{(q)} = 0$ cannot be used for estimating $w_{i_p,i_q}^{(p,q)}$. That is to say, on a sparse dataset where there are too few or even no cases for some higher order interactions, nonlinear SVMs are likely to degenerate into linear SVMs. Therefore, factorizing and projecting higher order interactions into a consistent latent space would facilitate parameter estimation under sparsity.

2.3 STM Model

Cao et al. investigated multi-view classification by modeling features interactions across views as a tensor, *i.e.*, $\mathcal{X} = \mathbf{x}^{(1)} \circ \cdots \circ \mathbf{x}^{(m)} \in \mathbb{R}^{I_1 \times \cdots \times I_m}$ [2] and solved the problem in the framework of support tensor machines (STMs) [13]. Basically, as shown in Figure 1, only the highest-order interactions are explored:

[1]The sign function is omitted, because the analysis and conclusions can easily extend to other generalized linear models, *e.g.*, logistic regression.

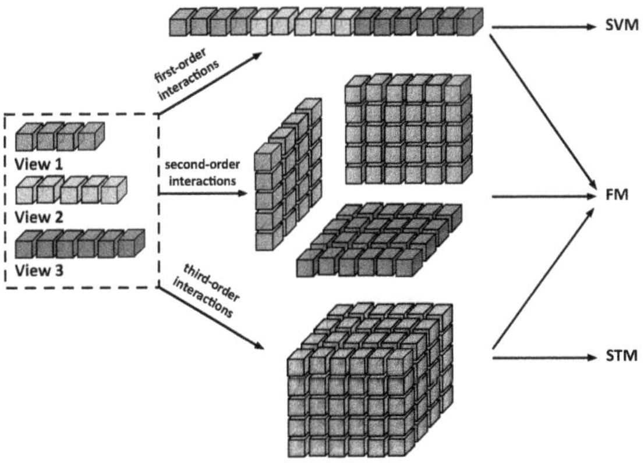

Figure 1: Related work (and variations) on modeling feature interactions in multi-view data.

$$\hat{y} = \sum_{i_1=1}^{I_1} \cdots \sum_{i_m=1}^{I_m} w_{i_1,\dots,i_m} \left(\prod_{p=1}^{m} x_{i_p}^{(p)} \right) \quad (4)$$

where $w_{i_1,\dots,i_m} = \prod_{p=1}^{m} w_{i_p}^{(p)}$, *i.e.*, a rank-one decomposition of the weight tensor $\mathcal{W} \in \mathbb{R}^{I_1 \times \cdots \times I_m}$ [2].

However, estimating a lower order interaction (*e.g.*, a pairwise one) reliably is easier than estimating a higher order one, and lower order interactions can usually explain the data sufficiently [12, 1]. Thus, it motivates us to include the lower order interactions into the model. Moreover, instead of a rank-one decomposition, it is desirable to apply a higher rank decomposition of the weight tensor to capture more latent factors and thereby achieving a better approximation to the original interaction parameters.

2.4 FM Model

Rendle introduced factorization machines (FMs) [10] that combine the advantages of SVMs with factorization models. The model equation of a 2-way FM is as follows:

$$\hat{y} = w_0 + \sum_{i=1}^{d} w_i x_i + \sum_{i=1}^{d} \sum_{j=i+1}^{d} \langle \mathbf{v}_i, \mathbf{v}_j \rangle x_i x_j \quad (5)$$

where $d = \sum_{p=1}^{m} I_p$ and $\langle \mathbf{v}_i, \mathbf{v}_j \rangle = \sum_{f=1}^{k} v_{i,f} v_{j,f}$.

Note that pairwise interactions between all features are included in FMs without consideration of the view segmentation. In the multi-view setting, there can be redundant correlations between features within the same view, *i.e.*, intra-view correlations, which are thereby unworthy of consideration. Field-aware FMs [6] integrate the field/view concept into the FM model where the extension is limited to the second-order feature interactions. The coupled group lasso model [16] is essentially an application of the 2-way FMs in multi-view classification. Let MVFM denote the multi-view variation of FMs with a decision function as follows:

$$\hat{y} = w_0 + \sum_{p=1}^{m}\sum_{i_p=1}^{I_p} w_{i_p}^{(p)} x_{i_p}^{(p)} + \sum_{i_1=1}^{I_1}\sum_{i_2=1}^{I_2} \left\langle \mathbf{v}_{i_1}^{(1)}, \mathbf{v}_{i_2}^{(2)} \right\rangle x_{i_1}^{(1)} x_{i_2}^{(2)}$$
$$+ \cdots + \sum_{i_{m-1}=1}^{I_{m-1}}\sum_{i_m=1}^{I_m} \left\langle \mathbf{v}_{i_{m-1}}^{(m-1)}, \mathbf{v}_{i_m}^{(m)} \right\rangle x_{i_{m-1}}^{(m-1)} x_{i_m}^{(m)} \tag{6}$$

The pairwise interaction parameter $w_{i_p,i_q}^{(p,q)} = \left\langle \mathbf{v}_{i_p}^{(p)}, \mathbf{v}_{i_q}^{(q)} \right\rangle$ in Eq. (6) indicates that $w_{i_p,i_q}^{(p,q)}$ can be learned from instances with $x_{i_p}^{(p)} \neq 0$ and some $x_{i_{q'}}^{(q')} \neq 0$ (sharing $\mathbf{v}_p$), or $x_{i_q}^{(q)} \neq 0$ and some $x_{i_{p'}}^{(p')} \neq 0$ (sharing $\mathbf{v}_q$). It makes MVFM (and FMs) more effective under sparsity than SVMs where only instances with $x_{i_p}^{(p)} \neq 0$ and $x_{i_q}^{(q)} \neq 0$ can be used to learn the second-order feature interaction $w_{i_p,i_q}^{(p,q)}$.

However, the interaction parameters for different orders are completely independent in MVFM (and FMs), *e.g.*, the first-order interaction parameter, $w_{i_p}^{(p)}$, and the second-order interaction parameter, $\mathbf{v}_{i_p}^{(p)}$, in Eq. (6). Furthermore, as illustrated in Figure 1, additional sets of model parameters will be introduced when we consider higher order feature interactions in MVFM (and FMs) which makes the learning process harder. A more effective strategy is needed when including the higher order interactions.

3. MULTI-VIEW MACHINE MODEL

3.1 Model Formulation

The key challenge of multi-view prediction is to model the interactions between features from different views, wherein complementary information is contained. Here, we consider nesting all interactions up to the mth-order between m views:

$$\hat{y} = \underbrace{\beta_0}_{\text{global bias}} + \underbrace{\sum_{p=1}^{m}\sum_{i_p=1}^{I_p} \beta_{i_p}^{(p)} x_{i_p}^{(p)}}_{\text{first-order interactions}}$$
$$+ \underbrace{\sum_{i_1=1}^{I_1}\sum_{i_2=1}^{I_2} \beta_{i_1,i_2}^{(1,2)} x_{i_i}^{(1)} x_{i_2}^{(2)} + \cdots + \sum_{i_{m-1}=1}^{I_{m-1}}\sum_{i_m=1}^{I_m} \beta_{i_{m-1},i_m}^{(m-1,m)} x_{i_{m-1}}^{(m-1)} x_{i_m}^{(m)}}_{\text{second-order interactions}}$$
$$+ \cdots + \underbrace{\sum_{i_1=1}^{I_1}\cdots\sum_{i_m=1}^{I_m} \beta_{i_1,\ldots,i_m}\left(\prod_{p=1}^{m} x_{i_p}^{(p)}\right)}_{m\text{th-order interactions}} \tag{7}$$

Let us add an extra feature with constant value 1 to the feature vector $\mathbf{x}^{(p)}$, *i.e.*, $\mathbf{z}^{(p)^T} = (\mathbf{x}^{(p)^T}, 1) \in \mathbb{R}^{I_p+1}, \forall p = 1, ..., m$. Then, Eq. (7) can be compactly rewritten as:

$$\hat{y} = \sum_{i_1=1}^{I_1+1}\cdots\sum_{i_m=1}^{I_m+1} w_{i_1,\ldots,i_m}\left(\prod_{p=1}^{m} z_{i_p}^{(p)}\right) \tag{8}$$

where $w_{I_1+1,\ldots,I_m+1} = \beta_0$ and $w_{i_1,\ldots,i_m} = \beta_{i_1,\ldots,i_m}, \forall i_p \leq I_p$. For $w_{i_1,\ldots,i_m}$ with some indexes satisfying $i_p = I_p + 1$, it encodes lower order interaction between views whose $i_p \leq I_p$. Hereinafter, let $w_{i_p}^{(p)}$ denote $w_{i_1,\ldots,i_m}$ where only $i_p \leq I_p$ and $i_q = I_q + 1, q \neq p$, and let $w_{i_p,i_q}^{(p,q)}$ denote $w_{i_1,\ldots,i_m}$ where $i_p \leq I_p$, $i_q \leq I_q$ and $i_r = I_r + 1, r \notin \{p, q\}$, *etc.*

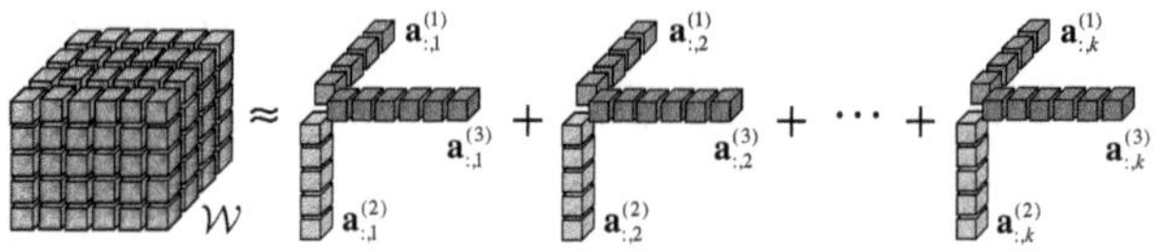

Figure 2: CP factorization. The third-order ($m = 3$) tensor $\mathcal{W}$ is approximated by k rank-one tensors. The f-th factor tensor is the tensor product of three vectors, *i.e.*, $\mathbf{a}_{:,f}^{(1)} \circ \mathbf{a}_{:,f}^{(2)} \circ \mathbf{a}_{:,f}^{(3)}$.

The number of parameters in Eq. (8) is $\prod_{p=1}^{m}(I_p + 1)$, which can make the model prone to overfitting and ineffective on sparse data. Therefore, we assume that the effect of interactions has a low rank and the mth-order weight tensor $\mathcal{W} = \{w_{i_1,\ldots,i_m}\} \in \mathbb{R}^{(I_1+1)\times\cdots\times(I_m+1)}$ can be factorized into k factors:

$$\mathcal{W} = \mathbf{C} \times_1 \mathbf{A}^{(1)} \times_2 \cdots \times_m \mathbf{A}^{(m)} \tag{9}$$

where $\mathbf{A}^{(p)} \in \mathbb{R}^{(I_p+1)\times k}$, and $\mathbf{C} \in \mathbb{R}^{k\times\cdots\times k}$ is the identity tensor, *i.e.*, $c_{i_1,\ldots,i_m} = \delta(i_1 = \cdots = i_m)$. Basically, Eq. (9) is a CANDECOMP/PARAFAC (CP) factorization [7] as shown in Figure 2, with element-wise notation $w_{i_1,\ldots,i_m} = \sum_{f=1}^{k}\prod_{p=1}^{m} a_{i_p,f}^{(p)}$. The number of model parameters is reduced to $k\sum_{p=1}^{m}(I_p + 1) = k(m + d)$. It transforms Eq. (8) into:

$$\hat{y} = \sum_{i_1=1}^{I_1+1}\cdots\sum_{i_m=1}^{I_m+1}\left(\prod_{p=1}^{m} z_{i_p}^{(p)}\right)\left(\sum_{f=1}^{k}\prod_{p=1}^{m} a_{i_p,f}^{(p)}\right) \tag{10}$$

We name this model in Eq. (10) as multi-view machines (MVMs). As shown in Figure 3, the full-order interactions between multiple views are modeled in a tensor, and they are factorized collectively. The model parameters that have to be estimated are:

$$\mathbf{A}^{(p)} \in \mathbb{R}^{(I_p+1)\times k},\ p = 1, ..., m \tag{11}$$

where the i_p-th row $\mathbf{a}_{i_p}^{(p)^T} = (a_{i_p,1}^{(p)}, ..., a_{i_p,k}^{(p)})$ within $\mathbf{A}^{(p)}$ describes the i_p-th feature in the p-the view with k factors.

DEFINITION 3.1 (BIAS FACTOR). *The bias factor is a collection of bias from each factor. In MVMs, the last row of $\mathbf{A}^{(p)}$, i.e., $\mathbf{a}_{I_p+1}^{(p)^T}$, represents the bias factor of the p-th view, and it is always associated with $z_{I_p+1}^{(p)} = 1$ in Eq. (10).*

Hence,

$$w_{I_1+1,\ldots,I_m+1} = \sum_{f=1}^{k}\prod_{p=1}^{m} a_{I_p+1,f}^{(p)} \tag{12}$$

is the *global bias*, denoted as w_0 hereinafter.

3.2 Time Complexity

Next, we show how to compute the decision function of MVMs efficiently. The straightforward time complexity of Eq. (10) is $O(k\prod_{p=1}^{m}(I_p + 1))$. However, we observe that there is no model parameter which directly depends on feature interactions, due to the joint factorization. Therefore, the time complexity can be largely reduced.

LEMMA 3.1. *The model equation of MVMs can be computed in $O(k(m + d))$.*

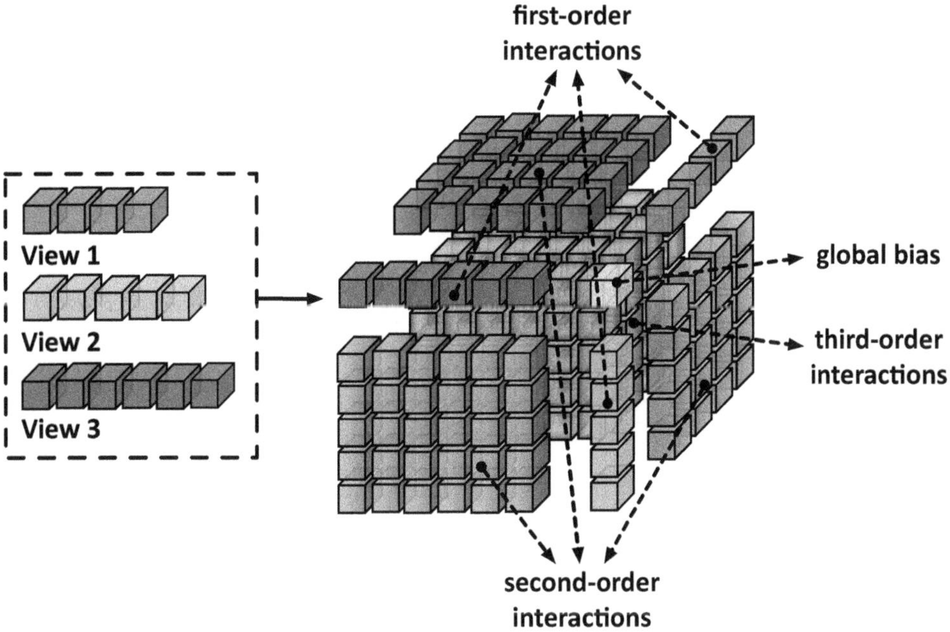

Figure 3: Multi-view machines. The full-order feature interactions in multi-view data are modeled in a tensor and jointly factorized into a common latent subspace.

PROOF. The feature interactions in Eq. (10) can be reformulated as:

$$\begin{aligned}&\sum_{i_1=1}^{I_1+1}\cdots\sum_{i_m=1}^{I_m+1}\left(\prod_{p=1}^{m} z_{i_p}^{(p)}\right)\left(\sum_{f=1}^{k}\prod_{p=1}^{m} a_{i_p,f}^{(p)}\right)\\ =&\sum_{f=1}^{k}\sum_{i_1=1}^{I_1+1}\cdots\sum_{i_m=1}^{I_m+1}\left(\prod_{p=1}^{m} z_{i_p}^{(p)} a_{i_p,f}^{(p)}\right)\\ =&\sum_{f=1}^{k}\left(\sum_{i_1=1}^{I_1+1} z_{i_1}^{(1)} a_{i_1,f}^{(1)}\right)\cdots\left(\sum_{i_m=1}^{I_m+1} z_{i_m}^{(m)} a_{i_m,f}^{(m)}\right)\end{aligned} \quad (13)$$

This equation has only linear complexity in both k and I_p. Thus, its time complexity is $O(k(m+d))$, which is in the same order of the number of model parameters. □

3.3 Discussion

The joint factorization of the global bias and the full-order interactions is important for MVMs. Thus, dependencies exist when interactions share the same feature. It benefits MVMs for parameter estimation under sparsity, since the latent factor $\mathbf{a}_{i_p}^{(p)}$ can be learned from any instances whose $x_{i_p}^{(p)} \neq 0$, which allows the second-order interaction $w_{i_p,i_q}^{(p,q)}$ can be approximated from instances whose $x_{i_p}^{(p)} \neq 0$ *or* $x_{i_q}^{(q)} \neq 0$ rather than instances whose $x_{i_p}^{(p)} \neq 0$ *and* $x_{i_q}^{(q)} \neq 0$ as in nonlinear SVMs. Therefore, the interaction parameters in MVMs can be effectively learned without direct observations of such interactions in a training set of sparse data.

The main difference between FMs and MVMs is that the interaction parameters for different orders are completely independent in FMs, *e.g.*, the first-order interaction $w_{i_p}^{(p)}$ and the second-order interaction $\mathbf{v}_{i_p}^{(p)}$ in Eq. (6). On the contrary, in MVMs, all orders of interactions share the same set of latent factors $\mathbf{a}_{i_p}^{(p)}$ in Eq. (10). For example, the combination of $\mathbf{a}_{i_p}^{(p)}$ and the bias factors from other $m-1$ views, *i.e.*, $\mathbf{a}_{I_1+1}^{(1)}, ..., \mathbf{a}_{I_{p-1}+1}^{(p-1)}, \mathbf{a}_{I_{p+1}+1}^{(p+1)}, ..., \mathbf{a}_{I_m+1}^{(m)}$, approximates the first-order interaction $w_{i_p}^{(p)}$. Similarly, we can obtain the second-order interaction $w_{i_p,i_q}^{(p,q)}$ by combining $\mathbf{a}_{i_p}^{(p)}$, $\mathbf{a}_{i_q}^{(q)}$ and other $m-2$ bias factors. Therefore, compared to MVMs, FMs are partially and independently factorized. Such difference is more significant for higher order FMs. As summarized in Table 3, assuming the same number of factors for different orders of interactions, the model complexity of an m-way FM is $O(kmd)$ which can be much larger than $O(k(m+d))$ of MVMs.

3.4 Extensions

MVMs are flexible in the interactions of interests. That is to say, when there are too many views available for a learning task and interactions between some of them may obviously be physically meaningless, or sometimes the very high order interactions may not be intuitively interpretable, it is not desirable to include these potentially redundant interactions in the model. In such scenarios, one can (1) partition (overlapping) groups of views, (2) construct multiple MVMs on these view groups where the full-order interactions within each group are included, and (3) implement a coupled matrix/tensor factorization [5]. This strategy excludes the inter-group feature interactions.

On the other hand, in scenarios where the view segmentation is not given, one may be aggressive to consider interactions between all features, which becomes the problem setting of the original FMs. To achieve this purpose, we can simply repeat the same feature set in multiple views. Overall, MVMs are applicable with either conservative or radical strategies. Although MVMs can be easily adapted

Table 3: Summary of related work. Model complexity refers to both the number of parameters in the model and the time complexity to compute the decision function.

Method	Model complexity	Feature interactions	Parameter factorization
Support vector machines (SVMs) [14]	$O(d)$	first-order	none
Support tensor machines (STMs) [13]	$O(kd)$	highest-order	factorized ($k = 1$ [2])
Factorization machines (FMs) [10]	$O(kmd)$	up to full-order	partially and independently factorized
Multi-view machines (MVMs)	$O(k(m+d))$	full-order	fully and jointly factorized

to include/exclude interactions between any features, that is outside the scope of this paper; our focus is on investigating how to effectively explore the full-order feature interactions from a given set of views.

4. LEARNING MULTI-VIEW MACHINES

To learn model parameters in MVMs, we consider the following regularization framework:

$$\underset{\Theta}{\operatorname{argmin}} \sum_{(\mathbf{x},y)\in\mathcal{D}} \mathcal{L}(\hat{y}(\mathbf{x}|\Theta), y) + \lambda\Omega(\Theta) \tag{14}$$

where $\Theta = \{\mathbf{A}^{(p)} | \ p = 1, ..., m\}$ represents all model parameters, $\mathcal{L}(\cdot)$ is the loss function, $\Omega(\cdot)$ is the regularization term, and λ is the trade-off between the empirical loss and the risk of overfitting.

Importantly, MVMs can be used to perform a variety of machine learning tasks, depending on the choices of the loss function. For example, to conduct regression, one can use the square error:

$$\mathcal{L}^S(\hat{y}(\mathbf{x}|\Theta), y) = (\hat{y}(\mathbf{x}|\Theta) - y)^2 \tag{15}$$

and for classification problems, the logit loss can be used:

$$\mathcal{L}^L(\hat{y}(\mathbf{x}|\Theta), y) = \log(1 + \exp(-y \cdot \hat{y}(\mathbf{x}|\Theta))) \tag{16}$$

or the hinge loss. The regularization term is chosen based on our prior knowledge about the model parameters. Typically, we can apply L2-norm.

4.1 Gradient Descent

The model can be learned efficiently by alternating least square (ALS), stochastic gradient descent (SGD), L-BFGS, *etc.* From Eq. (13), the gradient of the MVM model is:

$$\frac{\partial \hat{y}(\mathbf{x}|\Theta)}{\partial \theta} = z_{i_p}^{(p)} \left(\sum_{i_1=1}^{I_1+1} z_{i_1}^{(1)} a_{i_1,f}^{(1)} \right) \cdots \left(\sum_{i_{p-1}=1}^{I_{p-1}+1} z_{i_{p-1}}^{(p-1)} a_{i_{p-1},f}^{(p-1)} \right) \left(\sum_{i_{p+1}=1}^{I_{p+1}+1} z_{i_{p+1}}^{(p+1)} a_{i_{p+1},f}^{(p+1)} \right) \cdots \left(\sum_{i_m=1}^{I_m+1} z_{i_m}^{(m)} a_{i_m,f}^{(m)} \right) \tag{17}$$

where $\theta = a_{i_p,f}^{(p)}$, and $z_{i_p}^{(p)} = 1$ if $i_p = I_p + 1$, otherwise $z_{i_p}^{(p)} = x_{i_p}^{(p)}$. It validates that MVMs possess the multilinearity property [11], because the gradient along θ is independent of the value of θ itself.

Note that in Eq. (17), the sum $\sum_{i_p=1}^{I_p+1} z_{i_p}^{(p)} a_{i_p,f}^{(p)}$ and their product can be precomputed for updating the f-th factor of all features. Hence, each gradient can be computed in constant time $O(1)$. In an iteration, including the precomputation time, all parameters can be updated in $O(k(m+d))$. It can be even reduced under sparsity, where most of the elements in $\mathbf{x}$ (or $\mathbf{z}$) are 0 and thus, the sums have only to be computed over the non-zero elements, and only non-zero parameters need to be updated according to Eq. (17).

It is straightforward to embed Eq. (17) into the gradient of the loss functions *e.g.*, Eqs. (15)-(16), for direct optimization, as follows:

$$\frac{\partial \mathcal{L}^S(\hat{y}(\mathbf{x}|\Theta), y)}{\partial \theta} = 2(\hat{y}(\mathbf{x}|\Theta) - y) \cdot \frac{\partial \hat{y}(\mathbf{x}|\Theta)}{\partial \theta} \tag{18}$$

$$\frac{\partial \mathcal{L}^L(\hat{y}(\mathbf{x}|\Theta), y)}{\partial \theta} = \frac{-y}{1 + \exp(y \cdot \hat{y}(\mathbf{x}|\Theta))} \cdot \frac{\partial \hat{y}(\mathbf{x}|\Theta)}{\partial \theta} \tag{19}$$

4.2 Distributed Implementation

Web-scale applications in the real world always contain a huge number of entities represented in multiple views, *e.g.*, users, movies, ads, queries, with millions of instances, *e.g.*, ratings, impressions. In this section, we introduce a design for scalable learning and its implementation on top of GraphX [4], which is a component of Spark [17] for graphs and graph-parallel computation and provides high performance, scalability and fault-tolerance for the learning process.

The training data is represented as a graph that contains two types of vertices, *i.e.*, instance vertices and feature vertices. A directed edge from a feature vertex to an instance vertex exists if the feature is non-zero in the instance. The graph representation is efficient due to the inherent sparsity of the training data. The factor vector (or weight coefficient that is not factorized in some baselines) of a feature is represented as attributes of the corresponding feature vertex, the label information of an instance is represented as the attribute of the corresponding instance vertex, and the feature value is represented as the edge attribute. For distributed learning, the graph is partitioned and scheduled to different computing nodes for execution by the underlying distributed graph framework. In this manner, both data parallelism and model parallelism are achieved.

Each iteration in the gradient descent algorithm consists of two major steps, *i.e.*, feed-forward and back-propagation. In the feed-forward process, messages are sent from feature vertices to instance vertices following the edges which are arrays $\mathbf{b} = \mathbb{R}^k$ where $b_f = z_{i_p}^{(p)} * a_{i_p,f}^{(p)}$. An instance vertex receives all messages from its connected feature vertices and sums them in view-wise. The predicted value is then computed accordingly based on Eq. (13). In the back-propagation process, messages are sent from instance vertices to feature vertices which are arrays $\mathbf{c} = \mathbb{R}^k$ where each element represents a gradient. A feature vertex averages the gradients received from its connected instance vertices and updates the factor vector accordingly based on Eqs. (18)-(19).

5. EXPERIMENTS

5.1 Experimental Setup

Data collections. To evaluate the performance of multi-view prediction, we conduct extensive experiments on the MovieLens dataset for movie rating prediction (regression) and the BingAds dataset for CTR prediction (classification), respectively.

- **MovieLens dataset**[2]. A regression task for rating prediction is studied on the public dataset, MovieLens. Ratings are made on a 5-star scale, with half-star increments. Each rating in this dataset has three views, *i.e.*, users, movies and implicit user feedback. The user view consists of binary feature vectors for user ids, and thus for each rating there is only one non-zero feature in the user view, *i.e.*, the associated user id; the same for the movie view. The implicit feedback view is constructed following SVD++ [8] to capture users' history information. Specifically, it consists of all movies the user has ever rated and it is normalized. Hence, this view makes use of implicit feedback information and indicates users' preference. For this problem, the performance is measured by root mean square error (RMSE).

- **BingAds dataset**[3]. A classification task for CTR prediction is investigated on a dataset collected from ad impression logs of Bing, comprising three views: queries, ad URLs and impression information. Each instance is labeled as 1 if the impression is clicked and -1 otherwise. The query view consists of unigrams of user query words[4]. The ad URL view includes URLs corresponding to the shown ads. The impression view is composed of impression locations and matched types. All features are hashed as integer ids and represented by binary values. There are multiple non-zero features in the query view, only one non-zero feature in the ad URL view, and 2 non-zero features in the impression view. Area under the curve (AUC) is used as the evaluation metric.

See Table 4 for more information about the statistics and parameters used for each dataset.

Table 4: The statistics and parameters for each dataset. The number in braces indicates the dimensionality of the corresponding view.

Dataset	MovieLens	BingAds
Views	users (138,493) movies (27,278) impl. (27,278)	queries (958,426) ad URLs (1,935,510) impressions (18)
n	20,000,263	28,622,281
η	0.1	0.1
λ	0.01	0.01
k	20	20
#iterations	200	200

Compared models. In order to demonstrate the effectiveness of modeling feature interactions in multi-view data, we compare the following models:

- **Linear regression/logistic regression (LR).** We implement linear regression for regression tasks, *e.g.*, rating prediction, and logistic regression for classification tasks, *e.g.*, CTR prediction. They are essentially representative linear models (including linear SVMs), but with different loss functions, *e.g.*, the square error and the logit loss, respectively. It is discussed in the form of SVMs in detail in Section 2.2.

- **Tensor factorization (TF)** is a generalization of matrix factorization to higher orders. We can directly use tensors to model the multi-view data and factorize the weight tensor [2]. When the hinge loss is used, it can be solved in the framework of support tensor machines (STMs) [13]. When there are two views with categorical features, TF is reduced to conventional matrix factorization without bias terms. It is introduced as the STM model in Section 2.3.

- **Factorization machine (FM)** explores pairwise interactions between all features without consideration of the view segmentation [10]. Its adaptation in the multi-view setting, denoted as mvFM, considers feature interactions across views with the decision function in Eq. (6). This FM variation is specifically reviewed in Section 2.4. In addition to the popular 2-way FM model, we also implemented 3-way FMs to include higher order interactions, denoted as mvFM-3d, where feature interactions with different orders are modeled but with separate sets of parameters[5]. Moreover, we regularized the second-order and the third-order interactions sharing the same latent factors and assigned the global bias and the first-order interactions with independent weights that are not factorized, denoted as mvFM-reg.

- **Multi-view machine (MVM)** is our proposed model to explore the full-order interactions embedded within multi-view data, where feature interactions with different orders are jointly factorized and thereby sharing the same set of latent factors.

Configuration. All compared models are implemented on top of GraphX in Spark and trained with iterative forward and backward steps as in introduced in Section 4.2. The stochastic gradient descent with adaptive (sub)gradient [3] is used as the optimization method. The code has been made available at GitHub[6].

For a fair comparison, the same parameter setting in Table 4 is used for all compared models. A deterministic data sampling is applied on both datasets so that 80% data is used for training and the other 20% for test. All models are trained with the same hardware configuration, where 10 homogeneous computing nodes are connected via 40Gbps

[2]http://grouplens.org/datasets/movielens

[3]The dataset is used internally in the Bing Ads team for model experiments rather than training product models.

[4]Stemming, lemmatization, removing stop-words, *etc.*, are handled beforehand.

[5]In experiments, the rank k in mvFM-3d is set to 10 for both the second-order and the third-order interactions, so that the number of model parameters stays the same as other factorization baselines.

[6]https://github.com/cloudml/zen/tree/mvm_opt/ml/src/main/scala/com/github/cloudml/zen/ml/recommendation

Table 5: Prediction accuracy. ↓ indicates the smaller the value the better the performance; ↑ indicates the larger the value the better the performance.

Dataset	MOVIELENS (RMSE) ↓	BINGADS (AUC) ↑
MVM	0.8376	0.7917
FM	0.8681	0.7872
MVFM	0.8447	0.7729
MVFM-3D	0.9060	0.7201
MVFM-REG	0.9807	0.6947
TF	0.8572	0.6645
LR	1.0017	0.7450

Infiniband network and each node has 16 2.40GHz Intel(R) Xeon(R) CPU E5-2665 cores and 128GB memory. There are 1 driver configured with 25GB memory and 10 workers configured with 100GB memory. The data is partitioned into 160 partitions based on node degree [15] to balance the load in each core and reduce the communication among cores.

5.2 Multi-view Prediction Accuracy

The experimental results are shown in Table 5. On the MOVIELENS dataset, the smaller RMSE, the better an algorithm. We can observe that LR is a simple baseline because as a conventional linear model, it neglects any interactions between features. However, such feature interactions can be critical in the sparse data, which explains much better performance achieved by FM through including pairwise feature interactions. We further find that MVFM is able to outperform FM by excluding intra-view correlations. In our case of movie rating prediction on SVD++ data [8], intra-view correlations indicate interactions between movies the user has rated before which do not have direct influence on the user's preference of the current movie. However, inter-view correlations include interactions between the current movie and those movies rated by the user which are critical by matching the latent factor of the current movie and that of rated movies in the past. It validates the importance of introducing the view concept to learn an effective model in many problems.

The two variations of MVFM, MVFM-3D and MVFM-REG, add the third-order feature interactions in addition to the 2-way MVFM. The difference is that MVFM-REG uses the same set of latent factors for the second-order and the third-order interactions, while MVFM-3D introduces different parameters for interactions with different orders. It seems that the inclusion of higher order interactions fails to bring us any accuracy improvement, but TF manages to perform well by solely relying on the highest-order interactions. It might imply that the consensus and complementary information between lower order and higher order interactions need to be better taken care of, which leads to our MVM model. Overall, we can observe from Table 5 that MVM achieves the best performance through joint factorization of feature interactions with different orders.

On the BINGADS dataset, FM shows better performance than MVFM implying intra-view correlations might be important for this problem. Consider the impression view comprising 2 non-zero features for each instance, *i.e.*, impression location and matched type. Feature interactions between impression locations and matched types are not included in MVFM, whose variations and TF are even defeated by the linear model, LR.

5.3 Convergence Efficiency

In this section, we show more details about the training procedure of compared models. Figure 4(a) illustrates the training loss on the MOVIELENS dataset where results are plotted in a log scale for better resolution on final convergence in the late stage. We observe that several compared models can fit themselves very well on the training data. For example, the final converged training RMSE of MVFM-REG is as small as 0.5879; however, its test RMSE turns out to be 0.9807. It is clear that these models are easily prone to overfitting. On the contrary, our MVM model fits the training data with a moderate training RMSE = 0.7855, and achieves the best test RMSE = 0.8376, as shown in Table 5.

Figure 5(a) shows similar observations on the BINGADS dataset where the overfitting problem is more significant. There is a possible reasoning about the capacity of MVMs to avoid overfitting. The joint factorization of the global bias, the first-order interactions, the second-order and higher order interactions plays a key role through the effect of bias factors $\mathbf{a}^{(p)}_{I_p+1}$. The bias factor of each view will be updated by all instances, since it is always associated with a non-zero feature. Considering lower order interactions, other factor vectors contribute to the decision function by combining with bias factors of other views, as shown in Eq. (10). Therefore, bias factors are frequently retrieved and updated, making themselves relatively sensitive among model parameters. Our initial experiments found that the MVM model would suffer an unstable convergence process without the use of adaptive gradient [3]. Fortunately, this problem can be greatly alleviated by adaptively choosing an appropriate learning rate, as illustrated by the monotonic convergence process shown in Figure 4(a) and Figure 5(a). With this problem solved, bias factors bring MVMs with the capacity to avoid overfitting by storing and providing the *global knowledge*, because each training instance will update them and each test instance will be predicted based on them. Such global knowledge is critical to model the bias information per view per factor and thus makes MVMs a robust model. In contrast, other compared methods (*e.g.*, LR, FM) use a single model parameter, *i.e.*, the global bias, for the purpose of the global knowledge, which is insufficient.

Figure 4(b) and Figure 5(b) compare the time cost of each model on the MOVIELENS dataset and the BINGADS dataset, respectively. We find that our MVM model has the best system performance among models that consider high order feature interactions without bringing too much system overhead than the linear model, LR. The steep rise of LR and TF in Figure 5(b) appears because of fault occurrence during training and automatic recovery by Spark.

5.4 Hyperparameter Sensitivity

In all experiments, the parameter η is heuristically set to 0.1 for MVMs and other baseline models, since the performance is insensitive to the initial learning rate by using the adaptive gradient [3]. In this section, we study the influence of the other two key hyperparameters, k and λ, in our MVM model. Due to the space limit, only results on MOVIELENS dataset are presented.

Experiments are conducted for different k and the results are shown in Figure 6(a). In contrast to findings in other

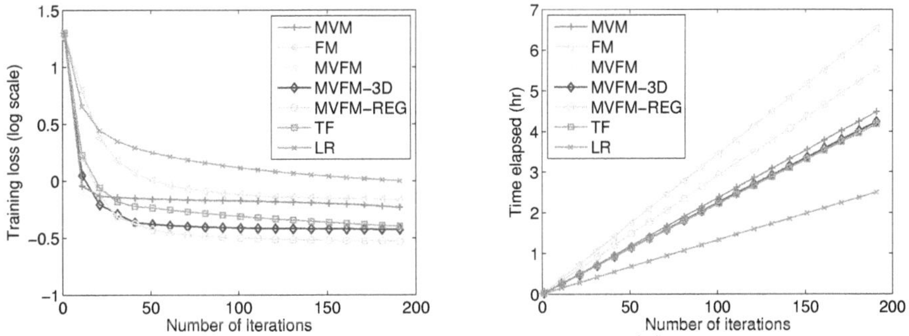

(a) Training loss. (b) Time cost.

Figure 4: The training procedure on the MovieLens dataset.

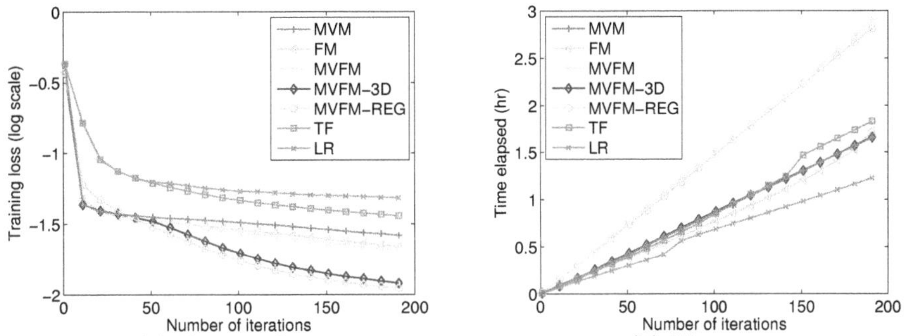

(a) Training loss. (b) Time cost.

Figure 5: The training procedure on the BingAds dataset.

related models based on latent factors [16, 11] where accuracy can steadily get improved with larger k, we observe that both the converged training loss and test loss turn out to be better with the increasing of k and reach a peak at $k = 40$, after which the accuracy will obviously decrease. It is reasonable in a general sense, because larger k renders the model with greater expressiveness which also leads to higher risk of overfitting. When the expressiveness of the model exceeds the information embedded in data, it is likely that the model will fit the training data very well yet fail on the test data. On the other hand, larger k leads to more model parameters which make it harder to learn an effective model within limited iterations. In general, Figure 6(a) indicates that the performance of our MVM model in Table 5 can be further improved with $k = 40$ at the cost of a linear increase in both runtime and memory.

Moreover, we investigate the influence of the regularization parameter λ and present the results in Figure 6(b). We observe that our MVM model is insensitive to λ in a relatively large range and performs well and steadily when $\lambda \leq 0.1$. It makes sense because large λ will let the regularization term override the effect of the loss function and thus dominate the objective.

5.5 Scalability

To investigate the scalability of our distributed learning framework introduced in Section 4.2, we compute the speedup factor relative to the time cost with 4 nodes by varying the number of computing nodes from 4 to 10. The number of training data partitions is always configured to be the number of cores. Experiments are repeated 10 iterations, and the average speedup factors with standard deviations are reported in Figure 6(c). We can observe that the speedup appears to be close to linear and close to the ideal speedup factors. Therefore, our distributed implementation of the MVM model is very scalable for web-scale applications.

The gap between the real and ideal speedup may result from the increasing communication cost with the increasing number of computing nodes, since copies of instance and feature vertices would be distributed in more computing nodes which leads to larger state synchronization cost of each instance and feature vertice. We will consider using the parameter server to alleviate such problem.

6. CONCLUSION AND FUTURE WORK

In this paper, we have proposed a multi-view machine (MVM) model and presented a stochastic gradient descent (SGD) learning method with a distributed implementation on Spark. In general, the model is particularly designed for data that is composed of features from multiple views, between which the full-order interactions are effectively explored. In contrast to other models that include only partial feature interactions or factorize different orders of interactions separately, MVMs jointly factorize the full-order feature interactions and thereby benefiting parameter estimation under sparsity and rendering the model with the capacity to avoid overfitting. Moreover, MVMs can be applied to a variety of supervised machine learning tasks, including classification and regression. Empirical studies on real-world

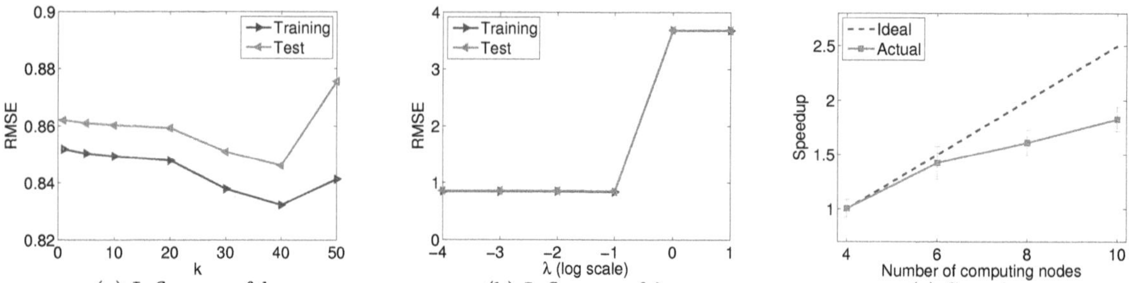

(a) Influence of k. (b) Influence of λ. (c) Speedup.

Figure 6: Sensitivity analysis of hyperparameters and the speedup of the distributed learning framework.

web application datasets demonstrate the effectiveness of MVMs on modeling feature interactions in multi-view data, which outperform baseline models for multi-view prediction.

The MVM model can be further investigated in several directions for future work. For example, in addition to SGD, we are interested in implementation of other learning algorithms in a distributed environment to facilitate convergence efficiency, *e.g.*, alternating least square (ALS) and Markov Chain Monte Carlo (MCMC) for MVMs. It is also interesting to have our model applied to other multi-view prediction problems. Moreover, defining an evaluation metric for an effective view segmentation would be critical for the subsequent multi-view learning.

7. ACKNOWLEDGEMENTS

We would like to thank the anonymous reviewers for their comments. We also thank Dinggang Shen for his discussions, Chunhui Zhang from the Bing Ads team for providing the dataset and Bo Zhao for helping with the experiments.

8. REFERENCES

[1] Yuanzhe Cai, Miao Zhang, Dijun Luo, Chris Ding, and Sharma Chakravarthy. Low-order tensor decompositions for social tagging recommendation. In *WSDM*, pages 695–704. ACM, 2011.

[2] Bokai Cao, Lifang He, Xiangnan Kong, Philip S. Yu, Zhifeng Hao, and Ann B. Ragin. Tensor-based multi-view feature selection with applications to brain diseases. In *ICDM*, pages 40–49. IEEE, 2014.

[3] John Duchi, Elad Hazan, and Yoram Singer. Adaptive subgradient methods for online learning and stochastic optimization. *The Journal of Machine Learning Research*, 12:2121–2159, 2011.

[4] Joseph E Gonzalez, Reynold S Xin, Ankur Dave, Daniel Crankshaw, Michael J Franklin, and Ion Stoica. GraphX: Graph processing in a distributed dataflow framework. In *OSDI*, pages 599–613. USENIX, 2014.

[5] Liangjie Hong, Aziz S Doumith, and Brian D Davison. Co-factorization machines: modeling user interests and predicting individual decisions in twitter. In *WSDM*, pages 557–566. ACM, 2013.

[6] Yu-Chin Juan, Yong Zhuang, and Wei-Sheng Chin. *LIBFFM: A Library for Field-aware Factorization Machines*, 2015. Software available at http://www.csie.ntu.edu.tw/~cjlin/libffm.

[7] Tamara G Kolda and Brett W Bader. Tensor decompositions and applications. *SIAM review*, 51(3):455–500, 2009.

[8] Yehuda Koren. Factorization meets the neighborhood: a multifaceted collaborative filtering model. In *KDD*, pages 426–434. ACM, 2008.

[9] Gert RG Lanckriet, Nello Cristianini, Peter Bartlett, Laurent El Ghaoui, and Michael I Jordan. Learning the kernel matrix with semidefinite programming. *The Journal of Machine Learning Research*, 5:27–72, 2004.

[10] Steffen Rendle. Factorization machines. In *ICDM*, pages 995–1000. IEEE, 2010.

[11] Steffen Rendle. Factorization machines with libFM. *Intelligent Systems and Technology*, 3(3):57, 2012.

[12] Steffen Rendle and Lars Schmidt-Thieme. Pairwise interaction tensor factorization for personalized tag recommendation. In *WSDM*, pages 81–90. ACM, 2010.

[13] Dacheng Tao, Xuelong Li, Weiming Hu, Stephen Maybank, and Xindong Wu. Supervised tensor learning. In *ICDM*, pages 8–pp. IEEE, 2005.

[14] Vladimir Vapnik. *The nature of statistical learning theory*. Springer Science & Business Media, 2000.

[15] Cong Xie, Ling Yan, Wu-Jun Li, and Zhihua Zhang. Distributed power-law graph computing: Theoretical and empirical analysis. In *NIPS*, pages 1673–1681, 2014.

[16] Ling Yan, Wu-jun Li, Gui-Rong Xue, and Dingyi Han. Coupled group lasso for web-scale CTR prediction in display advertising. In *ICML*, pages 802–810, 2014.

[17] Matei Zaharia, Mosharaf Chowdhury, Tathagata Das, Ankur Dave, Justin Ma, Murphy McCauley, Michael J Franklin, Scott Shenker, and Ion Stoica. Resilient distributed datasets: A fault-tolerant abstraction for in-memory cluster computing. In *NSDI*, pages 2–2. USENIX, 2012.

Transductive Classification on Heterogeneous Information Networks with Edge Betweenness-based Normalization

Phiradet Bangcharoensap
Tokyo Institute of Technology
phiradet.b@ai.cs.titech.ac.jp

Tsuyoshi Murata
Tokyo Institute of Technology
murata@cs.titech.ac.jp

Hayato Kobayashi
Yahoo Japan Corporation
hakobaya@yahoo-corp.jp

Nobuyuki Shimizu
Yahoo Japan Corporation
nobushim@yahoo-corp.jp

ABSTRACT

This paper proposes a novel method for transductive classification on heterogeneous information networks composed of multiple types of vertices. Such networks naturally represent many real-world Web data such as DBLP data (author, paper, and conference). Given a network where some vertices are labeled, the classifier aims to predict labels for the remaining vertices by propagating the labels to the entire network. In the label propagation process, many studies reduce the importance of edges connecting to a high-degree vertex. The assumption is unsatisfactory when reliability of a label of a vertex cannot be implied from its degree. On the basis of our intuition that edges bridging across communities are less trustworthy, we adapt edge betweenness to imply the importance of edges. Since directly applying the conventional edge betweenness is inefficient on heterogeneous networks, we propose two additional refinements. First, the centrality utilizes the fact that networks contain multiple types of vertices. Second, the centrality ignores flows originating from endpoints of considering edges. The experimental results on real-world datasets show our proposed method is more effective than a state-of-the-art method, GNetMine. On average, our method yields 92.79 ± 1.25% accuracy on a DBLP network even if only 1.92% of vertices are labeled. Our simple weighting scheme results in more than 5 percentage points increase in accuracy compared with GNetMine.

Categories and Subject Descriptors

I.2.6 [**Artificial Intelligence**]: Learning; E.1 [**Data**]: Data Structures—*Graphs and networks*

Keywords

Transductive Classification, Heterogeneous Information Network, Edge Betweenness Centrality

WSDM'16, February 22–25, 2016, San Francisco, CA, USA.

ISBN 978-1-4503-3716-8/16/02...$15.00

DOI: http://dx.doi.org/10.1145/2835776.2835799

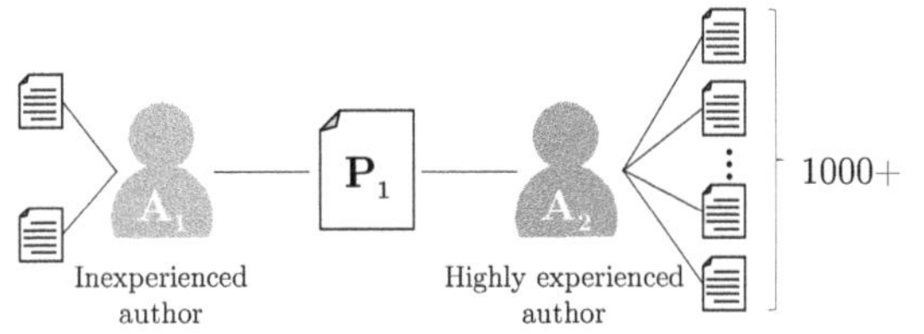

Figure 1: Bibliographic network countering the degree-based normalization. The research theme of the paper P_1 should conform to that of the highly experienced author A_2 rather than that of the inexperienced author A_1 because the research theme of A_2 is more well-established than A_1

1. INTRODUCTION

In machine learning, supervised learning has been a prominent paradigm. It makes predictions on the basis of a limited amount of data samples and their expected outputs. In many cases, manually labeling all data in a given dataset is a great burden as it is hard to scale, expensive, and prone to human-error. In contrast, a huge pool of unlabeled data always exists with lower cost, especially in this era of big data. *Semi-supervised learning* (SSL) that makes use of such unlabeled data has been gaining more attention.

Many Web data can be described as a network, where vertices represent entities of the system, and edges encode interactions or relationships between the entities. Networks can consist of multiple types of vertices such as bibliographic networks (author, paper, and conference), social networks (user, content, and page), and e-commerce purchasing logs (buyer, product, and seller). These kinds of networks are generally referred to as *heterogeneous information networks*.

We bring the two lines of research together by proposing a novel method for transductive semi-supervised classification on heterogeneous information networks. Given a network where a limited number of vertices hold initial labels, the classifier generally propagates the initial label information to the whole network. The classifier does not produce any decision functions or general rules to serve further unseen data. This paradigm is generally called *transductive* classification. The propagation process of many graph-based classifiers is based on the *smoothness* assumption — if two vertices are linked by a strong tie, then their outputs are likely to be close [5]. Several studies reduce influence of edges in accordance with the degrees of their endpoints to suppress

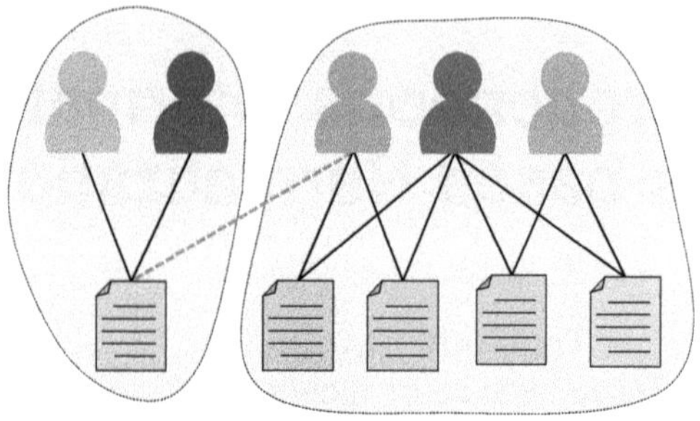

Figure 2: Network with an inter-community edge denoted by the red dashed line. The reliabilities of labels propagating through such inter-community edge should be discounted.

popular vertices from dominating the propagation process [16, 15, 17]. While edge weight normalization seems like a simple heuristic, it is one of the deciding factors for boosting the predictive performance. We observe significant improvement in accuracy by changing the normalization method to our proposed one.

We argue that the degree-based method is not effective when reliability of a label of a vertex cannot be implied from its degree. Figure 1 illustrates a bibliographic network consisting of two authors and their papers. Author A_1 tends to be inexperienced. In contrast, author A_2 is a top author who has published thousands of papers. Suppose we aim to infer the research theme of the paper P_1 from its neighbors, A_1 and A_2, on the basis of the smoothness assumption. Following the degree-based normalization, the label of P_1 tends to conform with present label of A_1, rather than the high profile author A_2, especially when the confidences of labels from A_1 and A_2 are comparable. We argue that this is not always reasonable. An author publishing many papers tends to have more well-established research interests than a young author. Thus, the research theme of the paper P_1 should conform to the research theme of A_2. This example shows that the degree-based method is not always effective.

This paper provides a new insight into the edge weight normalization. Instead of edges originating from high degree vertices, we propose that edges bridging across communities, called *inter-community edges*, are less reliable for making label inference. Generally, the term community means a set of vertices that are densely connected internally and loosely connected with vertices outside. Figure 2 illustrates an example of an inter-community edge denoted by the red dashed line. The most well-known measure capturing the characteristic is *edge betweenness centrality*. It has been applied in many applications, for example community detection [11], biological function investigation in protein interaction networks [8], and topology-controlling for wireless sensor networks [7]. We discover that naïvely applying the conventional edge betweenness in heterogeneous networks is ineffective because it is defined on the basis of an assumption that networks are homogeneous. We enhance the centrality by considering that networks contain multiple types of vertices.

The main contribution of this paper is twofold: (1) this paper sheds new light on employing the concept of the edge betweenness centrality in the edge weight normalization (2) we further improve the centrality to make it suitable for heterogeneous networks. With the proposed normalization, we gain more than 5 percentage points increase in accuracy from a state-of-the-art method, GNetMine [16], on dense networks derived from the DBLP dataset. It highlights that the edge weight normalization has a serious effect on accuracy of graph-based classification.

This paper first gives an overview of transductive learning in Section 2. It then details the proposed method in Section 3. Section 4 presents experiment results of the proposed method in comparison with existing state-of-the-art research on various datasets and settings. Finally, Section 5 concludes this paper and provides potential extensions.

2. RELATED WORK

In 2003, Zhu et al. proposed a SSL method based on a Gaussian random field model, popularly known as *label propagation* (LP) [27]. It tries to maintain smoothness of labels over the given graph and strictly preserve the initial labels by optimizing a cost function. In practical cases, some initial labels are possibly inaccurate because of human errors in a dataset preparation process. Zhou et al. proposed *local and global consistency* (LGC) [26] which allows initial labels to be slightly changed. Another contribution is that it is the very first method to normalize edge weights in accordance with the degree of their endpoints, while previous research did not normalize the weights [23, 27, 3]. This degree-based normalization has been exploited in *spectral clustering* before [6, 20]. *Adsorption* [2] and *modified adsorption* [24] have been proposed. They reduce the importance of vertices with respect to the Shannon entropy of their edges, which becomes inversely proportional to their degrees in unweighted networks. In 2014, Gong et al. proposed a new concept of smoothness called *local smoothness* via ReLISH [12]. It regularizes labels of vertices weakly connected to neighbors to prevent erroneous label propagation.

The methods presented above assume that an input network contains a single type of vertices called *homogeneous information network*. Researchers have recently become increasingly interested in mining heterogeneous networks. In 2010, Ji et al. proposed GNetMine [16], which generalizes LGC to heterogeneous networks. GNetMine inherits the degree-based edge weight normalization from LGC. However, GNetMine considers the types of edges when it measures degrees of vertices. In 2011, Ji et al. proposed RankClass [15], which combines ranking and classification in order to analyze more accurately. RankClass normalizes edge weights in two ways: the degree-based and the confidence-based method. In 2014, Luo et al. proposed HetPathMine [17], which extends GNetMine by incorporating the concept of *meta-path* [22]. The term meta-path means a path composed of a sequence of relations defined between different vertex types. The method measures the significance of meta-paths and utilizes them for classification. It inherits the degree-based normalization as well. Jacob et al. proposed to compute a latent representation of vertices in a space that is common to all types of vertices, and deduce labels from the representation [13]. Their method does not normalize the influence of edges.

Overall, some previous works do not normalize edge weights, and some normalize them in accordance with the degrees of their endpoints. We originally propose to penalize inter-community edge. The proposed normalization can be easily plugged into the mentioned methods.

3. PROPOSED METHOD

3.1 Problem Definition

This section begins by formally defining heterogeneous information networks. Next, it will specify the transductive classification problem on heterogeneous networks. We use capital bold letters for matrices (e.g. $\mathbf{A}$), and lower case bold letters for column vectors (e.g. $\mathbf{a}$). Capital bold letters with subscripts represent elements of the matrix (e.g. $\mathbf{A}_{ij}$ is the element at the ith row and j^{th} of column of $\mathbf{A}$). Functions are denoted by capital non-bold letters (e.g. F). Sets are denoted by capital non-bold italic letters (e.g. S).

Definition 1. Heterogeneous information network. A heterogeneous information network, in this work, is defined as an unweighted undirected network $G = (V, E, W)$. V is a set of n vertices. The set is composed of t types of vertices denoted by $V_1 = \{v_{11}, \cdots, v_{1n_1}\}, \cdots, V_t = \{v_{t1}, \cdots, v_{tn_t}\}$, where $n_i = |V_i|$ and $n = \sum_{i=1}^{t} n_i$. When $t = 1$, the network G becomes a homogeneous information network. One vertex belongs to exactly one type, in other words, $\forall i, j : i \neq j \rightarrow V_i \cap V_j = \emptyset$. E is a set of m edges, composed of $e = (v_{ip}, v_{jq}) \in V \times V$. $W = \{\mathbf{W}_{11}, \cdots, \mathbf{W}_{tt}\}$ is a set of adjacency matrices denoted by $\mathbf{W}_{ij} \in \{0,1\}^{n_i \times n_j}$, where $i, j \in \{1, \cdots, t\}$. An element $\mathbf{W}_{ij,pq} = 1$ if two vertices $v_{ip} \in V_i$ and $v_{jq} \in V_j$ are linked together, otherwise zero. We say a network has r types of relationships when $|\{\mathbf{W}_{ij} \mid \mathbf{W}_{ij} \in W \wedge \mathbf{W}_{ij} \neq \mathbf{0}\}| = 2r$.

Definition 2. Transductive classification on heterogeneous networks. The inputs of the problem are a heterogeneous information network $G = (V, E, W)$ and a set of initial label information L. V_L is a set of labeled vertices. $\mathcal{C}$ is a set of possible labels, typically $|V_L| \ll |V|$. Without loss of generality, we assume that the possible labels are $\mathcal{C} = \{1, \cdots, |\mathcal{C}|\}$. The existence of a tuple (v, c) in L means the vertex v is initially labeled with the label c. In other words, c is an initial label of v. The set $V_U = V - V_L$ is the set of unlabeled vertices. This study assumes the given network contains no self-loops. The goal of the transductive classification task is to predict the labels of all unlabeled vertices V_U. First, the classifier computes soft label column vectors $\mathbf{f}_i^c \in \mathbb{R}^{n_i}$, for all $i \in \{1, \cdots, t\}$ and $c \in \mathcal{C}$. A column vector $\mathbf{f}_i^c = [f_{i1}^c, \cdots, f_{in_i}^c]^\top$ represents the confidence that each vertex in V_i should belong to a label c. A high value of f_{ip}^c shows that the classifier believes that a vertex v_{ip} tends to belong to the class c.

3.2 Basic Framework

The input of our proposed method is a heterogeneous information network $G = (V, E, W)$ and a set of labeled vertices L. First, the label information from L is represented as initial label column vectors $\mathbf{y}_i^c \in \{0,1\}^{n_i}$, for $i \in \{1, \cdots, t\}$ and $c \in \mathcal{C}$. A column vector $\mathbf{y}_i^c = [y_{i1}^c, \cdots, y_{in_i}^c]^\top$ encodes the label information of all vertices $v_{ip} \in V_i$ regarding a label $c \in \mathcal{C}$. If a vertex v_{ip} is labeled to a class c, $(v_{ip}, c) \in L$, then $y_{ip}^c = 1$, otherwise zero. The proposed method propagates label information from the labeled vertices V_L to the entire network. Our proposed method has a trade-off between the two following constraints. First, the initial labels of seed vertices should be retained, called *fitting constraint*. Second, similar labels should be assigned to neighboring vertices, called *smoothness constraint*. To this end, the proposed method seeks the set of soft label matrix vectors that minimizes the cost function

$$\mathrm{J}(\mathbf{f}_1^c, \cdots, \mathbf{f}_t^c) = \sum_{i=1}^{t} \mathrm{E}(\mathbf{f}_i^c) \tag{1}$$

$$\begin{aligned}\mathrm{E}(\mathbf{f}_i^c) =& \alpha_i \sum_{p=1}^{n_i} \left(f_{ip}^c - y_{ip}^c\right)^2 \\ &+ \sum_{j=1}^{t} \lambda_{ij} \sum_{p=1}^{n_i} \sum_{q=1}^{n_j} \bar{\mathbf{W}}_{ij,pq} \left(f_{ip}^c - f_{jq}^c\right)^2,\end{aligned} \tag{2}$$

where α_i and λ_{ij} are non-negative parameters balancing between the fitting and smoothness constraints, and $\bar{\mathbf{W}}_{ij,pq}$ is a normalized weight of an edge between vertices $v_{ip} \in V_i$ and $v_{jq} \in V_j$. For all i, j, the parameter λ_{ij} is equal to λ_{ji}. The edge weight normalization process is described in further detail in Section 3.3. A higher value of a normalized edge weight $\bar{\mathbf{W}}_{ij,pq}$ indicates that the soft labels of v_{ip} and v_{jq} tend to be more similar. The term *global cost function* will be used when referring to J(.), and *local cost function* for E(.). After the optimal $\mathbf{f}_i^{c*} = [f_{i1}^{c*}, \cdots, f_{in_i}^{c*}]^\top$ is found, for $i \in \{1, \cdots, t\}$ and $c \in \mathcal{C}$, the final predicted label of a vertex v_{ip} can be simply determined as

$$c_{ip} = \underset{c \in \mathcal{C}}{\operatorname{argmax}}\ f_{ip}^{c*}. \tag{3}$$

The first term of the right hand side of Eq.(2) corresponds to the fitting constraint. A parameter α_i indicates trustworthiness of initial labels of seed vertices in a vertex type V_i. Suppose there is a bibliographic network containing vertices representing author, papers, and conferences such that some vertices are labeled with their research theme. Suppose we want to infer the research theme of every vertex. Generally, a research theme of an author is more ambiguous than that of a conference, so determining the initial labels of an author is prone to errors. Therefore, the parameter α_i of conference vertices should be higher than that of the authors. The second term enforces the smoothness constraint. The parameter λ_{ij} controls the degree of reliability of relations between vertices in V_i and V_j. A large λ_{ij} means labels of vertices in V_i can be faithfully inferred from labels of their neighbors in V_j. A user may set the parameter λ_{ij} of relationships between papers and conferences to be higher than that between papers and authors. These two parameters allow the method to treat each type of relationship uniquely, which is an advantage of learning on heterogeneous networks.

3.3 Edge Weight Normalization

We normalize the weight of an edge $e = (v_{ip}, v_{jq}) \in E$ as

$$\bar{\mathbf{W}}_{ij,pq} = \frac{1}{\mathrm{C}(e)} \mathbf{W}_{ij,pq}, \tag{4}$$

where C(.) is a *normalizing function*. By plugging Eq.(4) into Eq.(2), we obtain the complete definition of E(.). Our cost function is different from that of GNetMine, particularly the second term of E(.). The second term of E(.) of GNetMine is

$$\sum_{j=1}^{t} \lambda_{ij} \sum_{p=1}^{n_i} \sum_{q=1}^{n_j} \mathbf{W}_{ij,pq} \left(\frac{f_{ip}^c}{\sqrt{d_{ij,p}}} - \frac{f_{jq}^c}{\sqrt{d_{ji,q}}} \right)^2,$$

where $d_{ij,p}$ is the summation of the pth row of $\mathbf{W}_{ij}$. GNetMine aims to reduce the impact of popular vertices. Hence, the normalizing terms, $d_{ij,p}$ and $d_{ji,q}$, are located below f_{ip}^c

and f_{jq}^c of vertices. In contrast, we aim to reduce the impact of inter-community edges. Therefore, our normalizing function C(.) is located below the weight of edges as Eq.(4).

Ideally, C(e) is expected to be high if the edge e is an inter-community edge. We hypothesize that labels propagating through such edge are less reliable for making inference. The normalization help us decrease erroneous flows propagating through inter-community edges.

The inter-community characteristic can be captured by *edge betweenness centrality* [11, 19]. It measures the influence of an edge over flows of information between vertices, assuming that the flows follow the shortest paths. Originally, the edge betweenness centrality is defined as

$$\mathrm{C_{B0}}(e) = \sum_{s,t \in V} \frac{\sigma(s,t|e)}{\sigma(s,t)}, \tag{5}$$

where $\sigma(s,t|e)$ is the number of the shortest paths from vertex s to vertex t passing through an edge e, and $\sigma(s,t)$ is the number of the shortest paths from s to t. By convention, let $\frac{0}{0} = 0$ in this equation. From now on, the edge centrality $\mathrm{C_{B0}}(.)$ is called *homogeneous edge betweenness centrality* because the centrality is defined on the basis of an assumption that the given network contains single type of vertices. The fact that some networks contain multiple types of vertices is not considered. In contrast, we propose an edge betweenness centrality for heterogeneous networks, called *heterogeneous edge betweenness centrality.* It has two important properties: excluding flows from endpoints and ignoring irrelevant flows, which means flows from vertices of non-target types. The proposed heterogeneous edge betweenness of an edge $e = (v_{ip}, v_{jq})$, where $v_{ip} \in V_i$ and $v_{jq} \in V_j$, is defined as

$$\mathrm{C_{B1}}(e) = 1 + \sum_{s \in V_i \setminus \mathrm{EP}(e)} \sum_{t \in V_j \setminus \mathrm{EP}(e)} \frac{\sigma(s,t|e)}{\sigma(s,t)}, \tag{6}$$

where $\mathrm{EP}(e)$ indicates the set of endpoints of the edge e, which is $\{v_{ip}, v_{jq}\}$.

The idea of excluding flows from endpoints is motivated by Freeman's vertex betweenness [9]. He defined the betweenness of a vertex u as

$$\mathrm{VB}(u) = \sum_{s,u,t \in V : s \neq u \neq t} \frac{\sigma(s,t|u)}{\sigma(s,t)}, \tag{7}$$

where $\sigma(s,t|u)$ is the number of the shortest paths from a vertex s to a vertex t passing through a vertex u. We observed that one important property of vertex betweenness is missing from edge betweenness — flows originating from the vertex u are not counted. Therefore, when calculating the edge betweenness of an edge, we propose to ignore flows originating from its endpoints. The experimental results presented in Section 4.2 ensure the benefit of this refinement.

The homogeneous edge betweenness, defined in Eq.(5), does not differentiate multiple types of vertices. Figure 3 shows an example of a heterogeneous network where the homogeneous edge betweenness exhibits an irrational result. The vertices with the prefixes A, P, and C represent author, paper, and conference vertices, respectively. Let us start by calculating $\mathrm{C_{B0}}(e_4)$ and $\mathrm{C_{B0}}(e_5)$ as

$$\mathrm{C_{B0}}(e_4) = 2\left[\sum_{s \in \{A_1,A_2,A_3,P_1\}} \sum_{t \in \{A_4,P_2,C_1\}} \frac{\sigma(s,t|e)}{\sigma(s,t)}\right] = 24,$$

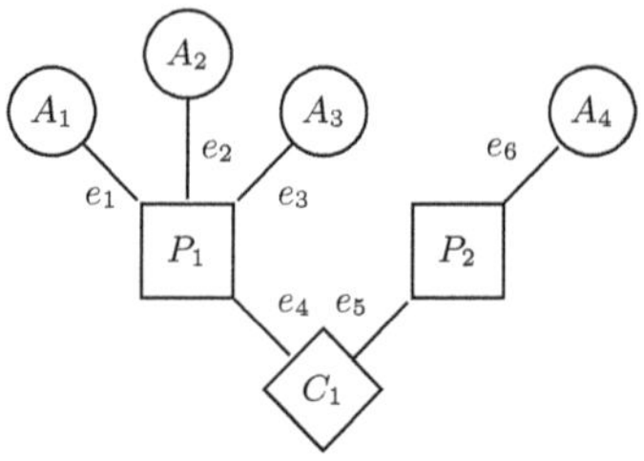

Figure 3: Heterogeneous bibliographic network containing authors (circles), papers (squares), and a conference (diamond).

$$\mathrm{C_{B0}}(e_5) = 2\left[\sum_{s \in \{A_4,P_2\}} \sum_{t \in \{A_1,A_2,A_3,P_1,C_1\}} \frac{\sigma(s,t|e)}{\sigma(s,t)}\right] = 20.$$

The $\mathrm{C_{B0}}(e_4)$ is higher than $\mathrm{C_{B0}}(e_5)$ even if both papers have edges dedicated to the conference. The only difference is the number of corresponding authors of papers P_1 and P_2. The shortest paths from $\{A_1, A_2, A_3\}$ and $\{A_4\}$ to $\{C_1\}$ are the crucial point of the different values. In the case of $\mathrm{C_{B0}}(e_4)$, the flows from three authors, $\{A_1, A_2, A_3\}$, to the conference are counted. In $\mathrm{C_{B0}}(e_5)$, the flow from only one author, $\{A_4\}$, is counted. This shows that a paper written by more authors has a higher value of $\mathrm{C_{B0}}(.)$.

Given the network as illustrated in Figure 3 and initial labels of P_1 and P_2, the label of C_1 can be implied from the labels of P_1 and P_2 under the smoothness assumption. As stated earlier, this research hypothesizes that edges in between communities are less reliable. If $\mathrm{C_{B0}}(e_4)$ and $\mathrm{C_{B0}}(e_5)$ are employed to measure the influence of the labels of P_1 and P_2 over the label of C_1 respectively, then the method tends to assign the initial label of P_2 to C_1 because $\mathrm{C_{B0}}(e_5) < \mathrm{C_{B0}}(e_4)$. This example reveals that a label of a paper written by many authors is less reliable based on the homogeneous betweenness. Obviously, this is not reasonable. Therefore, we propose to ignore flows or the shortest paths originating from irrelevant vertices, which means vertices of non-target types. In summary, one advantage of $\mathrm{C_{B1}}(.)$ over $\mathrm{C_{B0}}(.)$ is that $\mathrm{C_{B1}}(.)$ reduces the influence of irrelevant flows by ignoring the shortest paths originating from authors while considering paper-conference edges in this example.

In this section, two edge betweenness centralities have been introduced, $\mathrm{C_{B0}}(.)$ and $\mathrm{C_{B1}}(.)$. The normalizing function C(.) can be either of them.

3.4 Solving the Optimization Problem

Our optimization method is based on that of GNetMine. However, our cost function is different from theirs, as mentioned in Section 3.3. This section shows the method to optimize our cost function.

We find the set of soft label vectors, $\mathbf{f}_i^c$ for all $i \in \{1, \cdots, t\}$ and $c \in \mathcal{C}$, that optimize J(.) by *block coordinate descent* (BCD) method. It seeks the optimal solution by optimizing only one soft label vector $\mathbf{f}_i^c$ at one time, while keeping the remaining label vectors fixed at their last updated values. The process is repeated until convergence.

First, the local cost function E(.) is transformed into a matrix form. The first term of Eq.(2), can be rewritten as

$$\alpha_i \sum_{p=1}^{n_i} \left(f_{ip}^c - y_{ip}^c\right)^2 = \alpha_i \left(\mathbf{f}_i^c - \mathbf{y}_i^c\right)^\top \left(\mathbf{f}_i^c - \mathbf{y}_i^c\right). \tag{8}$$

The second term of the Eq.(2) can be rewritten as

$$
\begin{aligned}
&\sum_{j=1}^{t} \lambda_{ij} \sum_{p=1}^{n_i}\sum_{q=1}^{n_j} \bar{\mathbf{W}}_{ij,pq} \left(f_{ip}^{c} - f_{jq}^{c}\right)^2 \\
&= \sum_{j=1}^{t} \lambda_{ij} \sum_{p=1}^{n_i}\sum_{q=1}^{n_j} \bar{\mathbf{W}}_{ij,pq} \left({f_{ip}^{c}}^2 + {f_{jq}^{c}}^2 - 2 f_{ip}^{c} f_{jq}^{c}\right) \\
&= \sum_{j=1}^{t} \lambda_{ij} \left(\sum_{p=1}^{n_i}\sum_{q=1}^{n_j} \bar{\mathbf{W}}_{ij,pq} {f_{ip}^{c}}^2 + \sum_{p=1}^{n_i}\sum_{q=1}^{n_j} \bar{\mathbf{W}}_{ij,pq} {f_{jq}^{c}}^2 \right.\\
&\left. - 2 \sum_{p=1}^{n_i}\sum_{q=1}^{n_j} \bar{\mathbf{W}}_{ij,pq} f_{ip}^{c} f_{jq}^{c} \right) \\
&= \sum_{j=1}^{t} \lambda_{ij} \left(\sum_{p=1}^{n_i} f_{ip}^{c} \bar{\mathbf{D}}_{ij,pp} f_{ip}^{c} + \sum_{q=1}^{n_j} f_{jq}^{c} \bar{\mathbf{D}}_{ji,qq} f_{jq}^{c} \right.\\
&\left. - 2 \sum_{p=1}^{n_i}\sum_{q=1}^{n_j} f_{ip}^{c} \bar{\mathbf{W}}_{ij,pq} f_{jq}^{c} \right) \\
&= \sum_{j=1}^{t} \lambda_{ij} \left({\mathbf{f}_i^c}^\top \bar{\mathbf{D}}_{ij} \mathbf{f}_i^c + {\mathbf{f}_j^c}^\top \bar{\mathbf{D}}_{ji} \mathbf{f}_j^c - 2 {\mathbf{f}_i^c}^\top \bar{\mathbf{W}}_{ij} \mathbf{f}_j^c \right), \quad (9)
\end{aligned}
$$

where $\bar{\mathbf{D}}_{ij} \in \mathbb{R}_{\geq 0}^{n_i \times n_i}$ is a diagonal matrix with diagonal elements $\bar{\mathbf{D}}_{ij,pp} = \sum_{q=1}^{n_j} \bar{\mathbf{W}}_{ij,pq}$, for $p \in \{1, \cdots, n_i\}$. Hence, by plugging Eq.(8) and Eq.(9) into Eq.(2), the local cost function can be alternatively defined as

$$
\begin{aligned}
\mathrm{E}(\mathbf{f}_i^c) = &\sum_{j=1}^{t} \lambda_{ij} \left({\mathbf{f}_i^c}^\top \bar{\mathbf{D}}_{ij} \mathbf{f}_i^c + {\mathbf{f}_j^c}^\top \bar{\mathbf{D}}_{ji} \mathbf{f}_j^c - 2 {\mathbf{f}_i^c}^\top \bar{\mathbf{W}}_{ij} \mathbf{f}_j^c \right) \\
&+ \alpha_i \left(\mathbf{f}_i^c - \mathbf{y}_i^c\right)^\top \left(\mathbf{f}_i^c - \mathbf{y}_i^c\right). \quad (10)
\end{aligned}
$$

Let us start by finding one optimal soft label vector while the others are fixed. It can be obtained by setting the first derivative of the local cost function with respect to $\mathbf{f}_i^c$ to zero. The first derivative of E(.) is

$$
\begin{aligned}
&\frac{\partial}{\partial \mathbf{f}_i^c} \left[\sum_{j=1}^{t} \lambda_{ij} \left({\mathbf{f}_i^c}^\top \bar{\mathbf{D}}_{ij} \mathbf{f}_i^c + {\mathbf{f}_j^c}^\top \bar{\mathbf{D}}_{ji} \mathbf{f}_j^c - 2 {\mathbf{f}_i^c}^\top \bar{\mathbf{W}}_{ij} \mathbf{f}_j^c \right) \right.\\
&\left. + \alpha_i \left(\mathbf{f}_i^c - \mathbf{y}_i^c\right)^\top \left(\mathbf{f}_i^c - \mathbf{y}_i^c\right) \right] \\
=&\frac{\partial}{\partial \mathbf{f}_i^c} \left[\sum_{j=1, j\neq i}^{t} \lambda_{ij} \left({\mathbf{f}_i^c}^\top \bar{\mathbf{D}}_{ij} \mathbf{f}_i^c + {\mathbf{f}_j^c}^\top \bar{\mathbf{D}}_{ji} \mathbf{f}_j^c - 2 {\mathbf{f}_i^c}^\top \bar{\mathbf{W}}_{ij} \mathbf{f}_j^c \right) \right.\\
&\left. + \lambda_{ii} \left(2{\mathbf{f}_i^c}^\top \bar{\mathbf{D}}_{ii} \mathbf{f}_i^c - 2 {\mathbf{f}_i^c}^\top \bar{\mathbf{W}}_{ii} \mathbf{f}_i^c \right) + \alpha_i \left(\mathbf{f}_i^c - \mathbf{y}_i^c\right)^\top \left(\mathbf{f}_i^c - \mathbf{y}_i^c\right) \right] \\
= &\sum_{j=1, j\neq i}^{t} \lambda_{ij} \left(2\bar{\mathbf{D}}_{ij}\mathbf{f}_i^c - 2\bar{\mathbf{W}}_{ij}\mathbf{f}_j^c\right) + \lambda_{ii} \left(4\bar{\mathbf{D}}_{ii}\mathbf{f}_i^c - 4\bar{\mathbf{W}}_{ii}\mathbf{f}_i^c\right) \\
&+ \alpha_i \left(2\mathbf{f}_i^c - 2\mathbf{y}_i^c\right) \\
=&2 \left(\sum_{j=1, j\neq i}^{t} \lambda_{ij} \bar{\mathbf{D}}_{ij} + \alpha_i \mathbf{I} + 2\lambda_{ii} \left(\bar{\mathbf{D}}_{ii} - \bar{\mathbf{W}}_{ii}\right) \right) \mathbf{f}_i^c \\
&- 2 \left(\sum_{j=1, j\neq i}^{t} \lambda_{ij} \bar{\mathbf{W}}_{ij} \mathbf{f}_j^c + \alpha_i \mathbf{y}_i^c \right). \quad (11)
\end{aligned}
$$

By setting the first derivative of E(.) with respect to $\mathbf{f}_i^c$, as shown in Eq.(11), to zero, we obtain the optimal $\mathbf{f}_i^c$ that is the minimizer of the local cost function E(.) as

$$
\begin{aligned}
\mathbf{f}_i^{c*} = &\left(\sum_{j=1, j\neq i}^{t} \lambda_{ij} \bar{\mathbf{D}}_{ij} + \alpha_i \mathbf{I} + 2\lambda_{ii} \left(\bar{\mathbf{D}}_{ii} - \bar{\mathbf{W}}_{ii}\right) \right)^{-1} \\
&\left(\sum_{j=1, j\neq i}^{t} \lambda_{ij} \bar{\mathbf{W}}_{ij} \mathbf{f}_j^c + \alpha_i \mathbf{y}_i^c \right). \quad (12)
\end{aligned}
$$

However, the above solution is based on matrix inversion, which is not suitable for a large sparse network because the inverse of a matrix tends to be dense even if the source matrix is sparse. The advantage of a sparse matrix structure cannot be taken. Thus, we present an iterative optimization algorithm that avoids matrix inversion. It is based on the Jacobi iterative method [21]. Given a linear system $\mathbf{Mx} = \mathbf{b}$, the approximate solution at step $k+1$ is

$$
\mathbf{x}_i^{(k+1)} = \frac{1}{\mathbf{M}_{ii}} \left(\mathbf{b}_i - \sum_{j\neq i} \mathbf{M}_{ij} \mathbf{x}_j^{(k)} \right). \quad (13)
$$

Hence, a soft label vector $\mathbf{f}_i^c$ at step $k+1$ is

$$
\begin{aligned}
\mathbf{f}_i^{c(k+1)} = &\left(\sum_{j=1, j\neq i}^{t} \lambda_{ij} \bar{\mathbf{D}}_{ij} + \alpha_i \mathbf{I} + 2\lambda_{ii} \bar{\mathbf{D}}_{ii} \right)^{-1} \\
&\left(\sum_{j=1, j\neq i}^{t} \lambda_{ij} \bar{\mathbf{W}}_{ij} \mathbf{f}_j^{c(k)} + \alpha_i \mathbf{y}_i^c + 2\lambda_{ii} \bar{\mathbf{W}}_{ii} \mathbf{f}_i^{c(k)} \right). \quad (14)
\end{aligned}
$$

Even though Eq.(14) involves matrix inversion, its results are still sparse because the inversion of a diagonal matrix is diagonal as well. The inversion of a diagonal matrix can be easily computed in linear time in accordance with the number of diagonal elements. Algorithm 1 summarizes the iterative optimization algorithm for determining predicted labels of all vertices $v_{ip} \in V$.

3.5 Computational Complexity

Section 3.4 presents an iterative optimization algorithm that aims to seek the optimal soft labels of all vertices. It first starts by initializing soft label vectors $\mathbf{f}_i^c$ at Line 1. Preliminarily, they are initialized to the corresponding initial label vectors $\mathbf{y}_i^c$. The total size of all soft label vectors is $n|C|$, so this step takes $\mathcal{O}(n|C|)$. At Line 2, edge weight matrices are normalized on the basis of their edge betweenness centrality as described in Section 3.3. Assuming centralities are given beforehand, the normalization needs $\mathcal{O}(m)$ since each edge is processed once. In 2008, Brandes introduced an $\mathcal{O}(nm)$ algorithm to compute edge betweenness [4]. It was adapted in this present study. Next, Lines 3-6 create vertex degree matrices $\bar{\mathbf{D}}_{ij}$ derived from the normalized edge weight matrices $\bar{\mathbf{W}}_{ij}$. Basically, the algorithm iterates through all edges, so the time complexity of this step is $\mathcal{O}(m)$. It then computes the first term of Eq.(14). The degree matrices of each vertex type are summed up together. Let us define r_i as the number of neighboring vertex types of a vertex type V_i such that $r_i = |\{j \mid \mathbf{W}_{ij} \in W \wedge \mathbf{W}_{ij} \neq \mathbf{0}\}|$ and $\sum_{i=1}^{t} r_i = 2r$. This line takes $\sum_{i=1}^{t} (n_i r_i + n_i)$ steps.

Algorithm 1: Iterative optimization algorithm

Input : Heterogeneous network $G = (V, E, W)$
Initial label $\mathbf{y}_i^c$, for $i \in \{1, \cdots, t\}$ and $c \in \mathcal{C}$
λ_{ij} and α_i, for $i, j \in \{1, \cdots, t\}$

Output: Predicted label c_{ip}, for $i \in \{1, \cdots, t\}$ and $p \in \{1, \cdots, n_i\}$

1 $\mathbf{f}_i^c \leftarrow \mathbf{y}_i^c$, for $i \in \{1, \cdots, t\}$ and $c \in \mathcal{C}$
2 $\bar{\mathbf{W}}_{ij} \leftarrow$ `EdgeNormalize(`$\mathbf{W}_{ij}$`)`, for $\mathbf{W}_{ij} \in W$
3 $\mathbf{D}_{ij} \leftarrow \mathbf{0}^{n_i \times n_i}$, for $i, j \in \{1, \cdots, t\}$
4 **foreach** $(v_{ip}, v_{jq}) \in E$ **do**
5     $\mathbf{D}_{ij,pp} \leftarrow \mathbf{D}_{ij,pp} + \bar{\mathbf{W}}_{ij,pq}$
6 **end**
7 $\mathbf{M}_i \leftarrow \sum_{j=1, j\neq i}^{t} \lambda_{ij} \bar{\mathbf{D}}_{ij} + \alpha_i \mathbf{I} + 2\lambda_{ii} \bar{\mathbf{D}}_{ii}$, for $i \in \{1, \cdots, t\}$
8 **repeat**
9   **foreach** $c \in \mathcal{C}$ **do**
10   **foreach** $i \in \{1, \cdots, t\}$ **do**
11             $\mathbf{f}_i^c \leftarrow \mathbf{M}_i^{-1} \left(\sum_{j=1, j\neq i}^{t} \lambda_{ij} \bar{\mathbf{W}}_{ij} \mathbf{f}_j^c + \alpha_i \mathbf{y}_i^c + 2\lambda_{ii} \bar{\mathbf{W}}_{ii} \mathbf{f}_i^{c(t)} \right)$
12   **end**
13   **end**
14 **until** *convergence*
15 $c_{ip} \leftarrow \underset{c \in \mathcal{C}}{\arg\max}\, f_{ip}^c$, for $i \in \{1, \cdots, t\}$ and $p \in \{1, \cdots, n_i\}$

Its inequality is

$$\begin{aligned} \sum_{i=1}^{t} (n_i r_i + n_i) &\leq \sum_{i=1}^{t} \left(n_i \sum_{i=1}^{t} r_i \right) + \sum_{i=1}^{t} n_i. \\ &= 2 \sum_{i=1}^{t} (n_i r) + \sum_{i=1}^{t} n_i. \\ &= 2nr + n. \end{aligned}$$

Hence, Line 7 spends $\mathcal{O}(n(r+1))$. It then iteratively optimizes soft label vectors. At Lines 10-12, the soft label vector of a vertex type V_i and a class c is updated. It aggregates the multiplication of edge weights and the current soft label of their endpoints. This operation takes $\mathcal{O}(m_i)$ for each vertex type, in total $\mathcal{O}(m)$. Further, incorporating initial labels and dividing by $\mathbf{M}_i$, which needs $\mathcal{O}(n)$, are conducted. The update procedures are performed for all $c \in \mathcal{C}$ and repeated until convergence. Therefore, the algorithm takes $\mathcal{O}(\tau|C|(n+m))$, where τ is the number of iterations. At Line 15, the final prediction can be determined within $\mathcal{O}(n|C|)$. Finally, the time complexity of the iterative optimization algorithm, presented in Algorithm 1, is $\mathcal{O}(\tau|C|(n+m))$. In our experiment, τ was less than twenty.

4. EXPERIMENTS

This paper proposes to utilize edge betweenness in the edge weight normalization process. Furthermore, two refinements are proposed to make the centrality more suitable for heterogeneous networks. Two questions were raised:

1. Are the two refinements of the edge betweenness really useful?
2. How accurate is the method with the edge betweenness centrality compared with the existing methods?

Two set of experiments were conducted on real-world datasets to answer the questions. Section 4.1 describes the datasets used in this study. Section 4.2 and Section 4.3 reveal evidence to answer the questions.

4.1 Dataset

Heterogeneous Network

We performed experiments on the *four-area* dataset, provided by [10] and [16]. It is a sub-network of the DBLP[1] dataset on four research areas — information retrieval, artificial intelligence, data mining, and database. Hence, there are four possible labels in this dataset. Figure 4 shows the topology of the network derived from this dataset. It contains four types of vertices: *paper*, *author*, *term*, and *conference*. In total, it consists of 36,915 vertices divided into 13,896 papers, 14,216 authors, 8,785 terms, and 18 conferences: SIGIR, WWW, WSDM, CIKM, ECIR, AAAI, ICML, IJCAI, CVPR, KDD, ICDM, PAKDD, SDM, VLDB, EDBT, PODS, ICDE, and SIGMOD. Three kinds of edges exist in the network: author-paper, conference-paper, and term-paper. An author and a paper are connected if and only if the author writes the paper. An edge between a paper and a conference indicates that the paper is published in the conference or journal. The semantic of a relationship between a term and a paper is that the term appears in the title of the paper. In total, the network contains 165,157 edges in the networks. The dataset contains label information of 99 (0.71%) papers, 4049 (28.48%) authors, and 18 (100.00%) conferences.

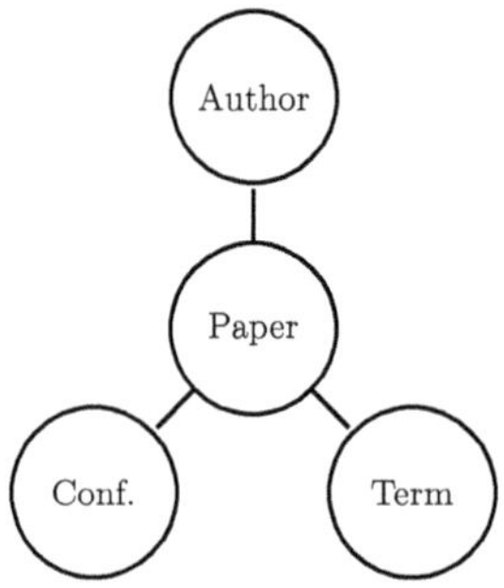

Figure 4: Topology of four-area dataset

Homogeneous Network

In addition, we also studied the effectiveness of methods on three famous homogeneous networks: *Zachary's karate club* [25], *dolphin* [18], and *political blogs* [1]. The Zachary's karate club network represents friendships of 34 members of a karate club at a US university in the 1970s. The dolphin social network represents frequent associations between 62 dolphins in a community living off Doubtful Sound. The political blogs network represents hyperlinks between weblogs regarding US politics, recorded in 2005. The ground-truth labels of all vertices in datasets are available. It is worth conducting experiments on these datasets because they can confirm the effectiveness of methods when edges between the same type of vertices exist. Table 1 summarizes properties of the networks. Figure 5 visualizes the networks where nodes are colored in accordance with ground-truth labels.

[1]http://www.informatik.uni-trier.de/~ley/db/

Table 1: **Properties of political blogs, Zachary's karate club, and dolphin networks.**

Measure	Karate	Dolphin	Political blogs
n	34	62	1,222
m	78	159	16,714
$\lvert\mathcal{C}\rvert$	2	2	2

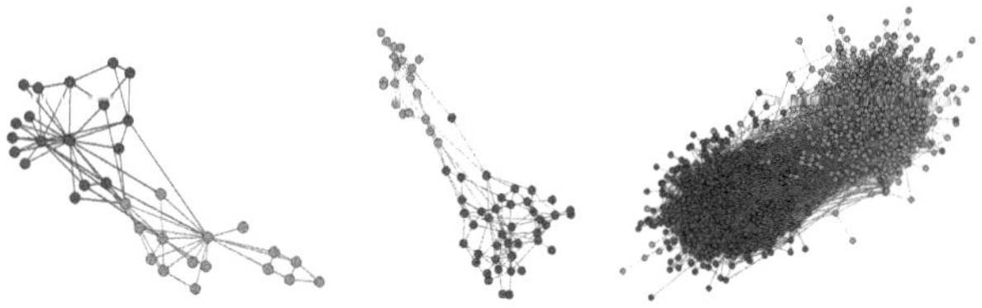

(a) Karate (b) Dolphin (c) Political blogs

Figure 5: Visualization of homogeneous networks used in experiments: Zachary's karate club (a), dolphin (b), and political blogs (c) networks. The colors of vertices indicates their ground-truth labels. The purple edges are inter-community edges. The blue and red edges are intra-community edges.

4.2 Comparison of Edge Betweenness Centralities

Section 3.3 proposed two additional refinements of the edge betweenness. Now, we aim to evaluate their effectiveness via two experiments. First, we compare the capabilities of the centralities C_{B0} and C_{B1} to distinguish intra-community and inter-community edges. It is important to note that inter-community edges connect vertices in different classes together. This capability is crucial because it can prevent labels from erroneously flowing beyond its own class. Second, we evaluate how the centralities can support transductive classifiers to gain higher accuracy.

The first experiment evaluates the proposed centrality which excludes flows from endpoints, C_{B1}, and the conventional centrality, C_{B0}, by using them to rank edges of a network. The inter-community edges are expected to be ranked at the beginning positions of the output. The evaluation metric used in this experiment was the *normalized discounted cumulative gain* (NDCG), proposed by [14]. It is a well-known evaluation metric for information retrieval. It is defined as

$$\mathrm{NDCG} = \frac{\mathrm{DCG}}{\mathrm{IDCG}}, \tag{15}$$

$$\mathrm{DCG} = \sum_{i=1}^{|Q|} \frac{2^{\mathrm{r}(i)} - 1}{\log_2(i+1)},$$

$$\mathrm{IDCG} = \sum_{i=1}^{|R|} \frac{1}{\log_2(i+1)},$$

where $|Q|$ is the size of a ranking result, $|R|$ is the number of inter-community edges, and $\mathrm{r}(i)$ is the relevance score of the ith edge of the result. The relevance score is binary, $\mathrm{r}(i) \in \{0, 1\}$. A relevance score $\mathrm{r}(i)$ is 1 if and only if the ith edge is an inter-community edge, otherwise zero. NDCG ranges from 0.0 to 1.0. NDCG assumes that it is less useful when an inter-community edge is ranked at a lower position of the result. Thus, NDCG penalizes the relevance score logarithmically proportional to the position of the edge. A higher NDCG indicates much better performance. The Zachary's karate club, dolphins, and political blogs networks were used in this experiment because they contain complete label information of vertices. Since the datasets are homogeneous networks, this means that only the property regarding edges' endpoints of C_{B1} was tested. The results are shown in Table 2. They indicate that, by excluding endpoints, the edge betweenness is more likely to assign a high value to inter-community edges that help to prevent erroneous flows. With this property and Eq.(4), normalized weights of inter-community edges tend to be lower than those of intra-community edges.

Table 2: Comparison of NDCG calculated from lists of edges that were sorted according to the proposed centrality C_{B1} which excludes flows from/to endpoints and the conventional homogeneous edge betweenness centralities C_{B0}.

Network	NDCG	
	Excl. endpoints (C_{B1})	Incl. endpoints (C_{B0})
Karate	0.812	0.740
Dolphin	0.804	0.801
Political blogs	0.847	0.820

Next, four variants of edge betweenness were evaluated on the four-area network. The normalizing function of Eq.(4), C(.), is substituted with the following four measures:

Heterogeneous (C_{B1}): $1 + \sum_{s \in V_i \setminus \mathrm{EP}(e)} \sum_{t \in V_j \setminus \mathrm{EP}(e)} \frac{\sigma(s,t|e)}{\sigma(s,t)}$

Heterogeneous incl. endpoints: $1 + \sum_{s \in V_i} \sum_{t \in V_j} \frac{\sigma(s,t|e)}{\sigma(s,t)}$

Homogeneous (C_{B0}): $\sum_{s,t \in V} \frac{\sigma(s,t|e)}{\sigma(s,t)}$

Without normalization: 1.

This experiment evaluated the classification ability of the proposed method with the four normalizing functions on the four-area network. Labeled authors were randomly chosen and added to L. The sizes of L were set to 5%, 10%, 15%, and 20% of authors in the network. The parameters λ_{ij} and α_i were set to 0.2 and 0.1, for $i, j \in \{1, \cdots, 4\}$, respectively, as previous studies [15, 16, 17]. Even though these are not the best parameter settings, but they are effective enough to demonstrate capabilities of centralities. Five independent iterations of the experiment were conducted. We allowed optimization methods to run until L^2 norm of the difference between soft label vectors at the present step and the previous one become less than 0.001.

The accuracies of methods are plotted in Figure 6. The results suggest that the centrality C_{B1} employing our proposed refinements can help the method to achieve a relatively higher accuracy. The method without normalization yields slightly lower accuracy, especially when seed vertices are limited. Thus, from now on, C_{B1} is used as the normalizing function, by plugging it into Eq.(4).

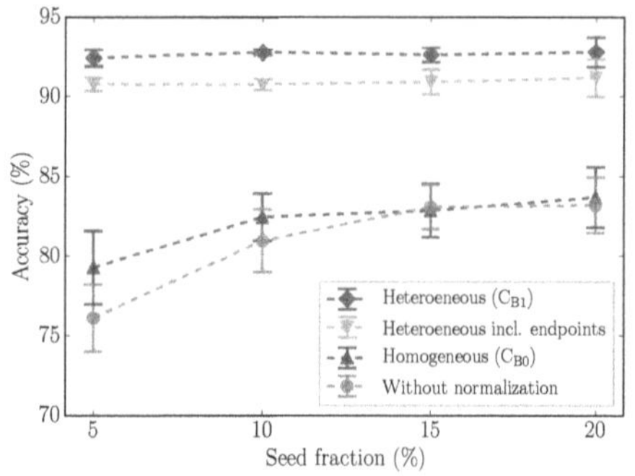

Figure 6: Mean accuracy (± 1 SD) of the proposed method, with four normalizing functions, evaluated on the four-area network where seed vertices are randomly 5%, 10%, 15%, and 20% of authors in the network.

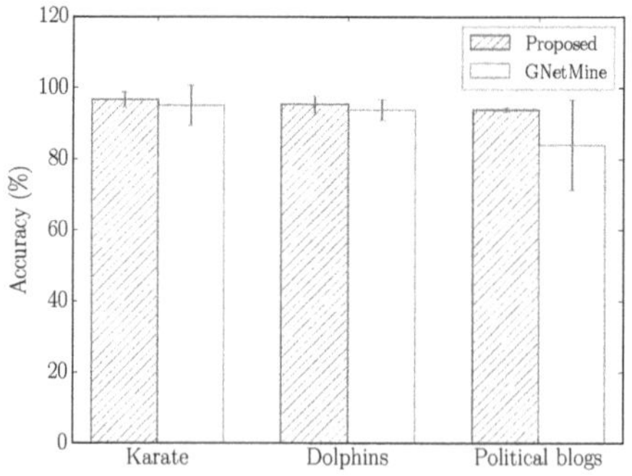

(a) Mean accuracy (± 1 SD)

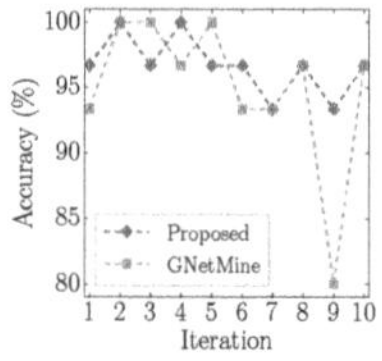

(b) Karate

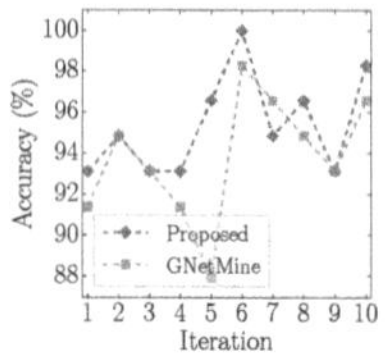

(c) Dolphin

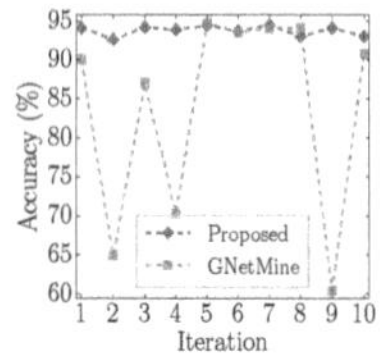

(d) Political blogs

Figure 7: Mean accuracy (± 1 SD) of the proposed method and GNetMine with four seed vertices on three homogeneous networks (a) and the raw accuracy evaluated in each independent iteration of experiments on Zachary's karate club (b) , dolphin (c), and political blogs (d) networks.

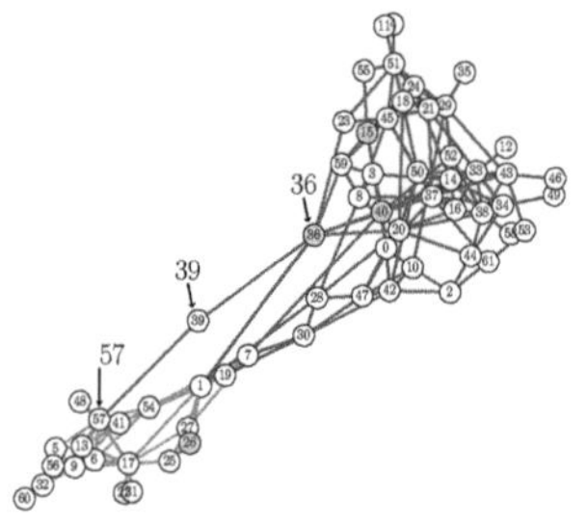

(a) Seed vertices

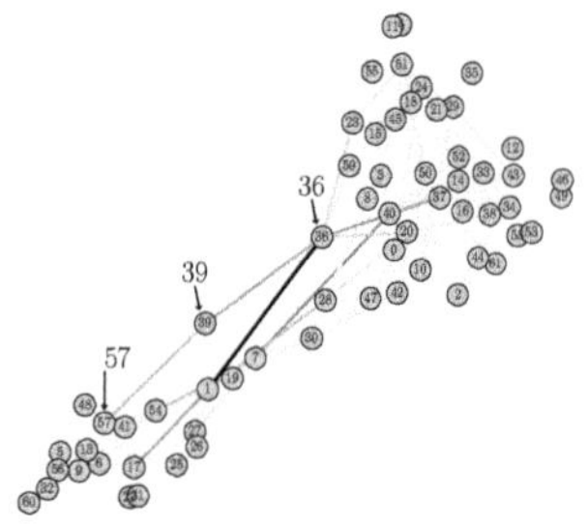

(b) Edge betweenness

Figure 8: Setting of the fifth iteration of experiments on dolphin network, reported in Figure 7(c). (a) The blue and red vertices are seed vertices colored according to their initial labels. The white vertices are unlabeled. The blue and red edges are intra-community edges. The purple edges are inter-community edges. (b) A darker color of an edge shows its higher edge betweenness centrality. The colors of vertices indicate their ground-truth labels.

4.3 Comparison of Methods

We compared the accuracies of the proposed method, using C_{B1}, and two state-of-the-art transductive classifiers on various datasets and settings. The proposed method shares several common hypothesis with GNetMine [16], except the edge weight normalization. Therefore, GNetMine was treated as one of the baselines. Some readers doubt the advantage of generalizing transductive classification to heterogeneous networks. This experiment aims to clarify this point by adding LGC [26], a transductive classifier designed for homogeneous networks, as another baseline system. As in the previous experiment, the parameters λ_i and α_{ij} were set to 0.2 and 0.1 respectively, for all i, j and methods. In all experiments, the label information was the same for every method.

Next, the proposed method and baselines were evaluated on the Zachary's karate club, dolphin, and political blogs networks. Four random vertices were selected and added to L. At least one labeled vertex was guaranteed to be present in each class. The experiment was repeated ten times independently. The networks are homogeneous, hence GNetMine reduces to LGC.

Figure 7(a) compares the accuracies and standard deviations of the proposed method and GNetMine. On average, the proposed method achieves better accuracy. According to the paired one tailed t-test, the differences are statistically significant (p=0.022) in the political blogs network but not in the Zachary's karate club (p=0.150) and dolphin (p=0.054) networks. It is possible to hypothesize that the insignificance is likely to occur in a small network. Figure 7(b), 7(c), and 7(d) present the accuracy obtained in each repetition of experiments on Zachary's karate, dolphin, and political blogs networks, respectively. The detailed results reveal that one important benefit of the proposed method is its stability. The proposed method gains an equivalent level of accuracy in every trial of the experiments but the degree-based methods fails in some repetitions.

Figure 8(a) presents the four seed vertices used in the fifth iteration of the dolphin network experiment reported in Figure 7(c). Figure 8(b) illustrates edge betweenness centralities of edges. A darker line means a higher edge betweenness. Vertex 36 is one of the seed vertices. The blue label could flow into vertex 39. Since vertex 39 is a low degree vertex, based on degree-based normalization, it is highly likely that the blue label can flow further into vertex 57 and its neighbors. In contrast, the proposed method can limit the flow from vertices 39 to 57 because their connection has a relatively high edge betweenness centrality and only a small amount of information flows from vertex 36 to vertex 39. As shown in Figure 9, vertex 57 and its neighbors were incorrectly classified by GNetMine. In contrast, the proposed method can predict their true labels.

The last experiment for this question was done on the four-area dataset. Again, to create the label information,

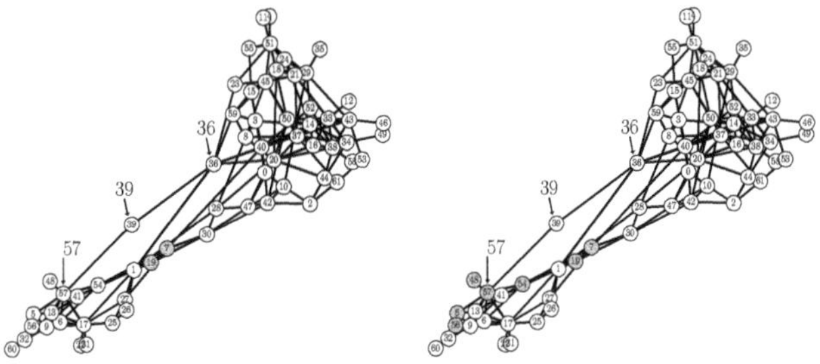

(a) Proposed method (b) GNetMine

Figure 9: Incorrectly predicted vertices, which are orange, of the proposed method (a) and GNetMine (b) in the fifth iteration of the experiment on the dolphin network, reported in Figure 7(c).

Table 3: Properties of four variants of the four-area network

Measure	500A	1000A	5000A	Original
Vertices				
Authors	500	1,000	5,000	14,216
Papers	7,598	9,589	12,998	13,896
Conferences	18	18	18	18
Terms	6,067	7,004	8,453	8,785
Total	14,183	17,611	26,469	36,915
Edges				
Author-Paper	11,530	16,136	30,030	40,491
Term-Paper	59,925	75,798	103,440	110,770
Conf.-Paper	7,598	9,589	12,998	13,896
Total	79,053	101,523	146,468	165,157
Avg. Degree	11.148	11.529	11.067	8.948
Diameter	8	8	8	8

5%, 10%, 15%, and 20% of author vertices were randomly chosen and put into L. In this experiment, five independent repetitions of experiments were conducted as well. Furthermore, the methods were tested on three sub-networks derived from the four-area dataset. The top 500, 1000, and 5000 authors with their corresponding papers, terms, and conferences were extracted. The term top authors means the number of their papers are larger than the others. In the following, the sub-networks will be referred to as 500A, 1000A, and 5000A networks, respectively. Table 3 summarizes these networks and the original network.

The results are shown in Figure 10. They demonstrate that the proposed method significantly outperforms baseline systems on all variants of the four-area network. Figure 10(a), 10(b), and 10(c) shows that the proposed method achieves more than 5 percentage points increase in accuracy from GNetMine when 5% of authors are initially labeled. Table 3 shows the average degrees of vertices in 500A, 1000A, and 5000A networks are higher than eleven. These mean our proposed method is strongly better than GNetMine in dense networks with a few seed vertices. GNetMine yields higher accuracies than LGC. The generalization to heterogeneous networks have a significant advantage in the real-world dataset. The proposed method shows it has great stability as the variance of its accuracy is low, which conforms to the previous results on homogeneous networks.

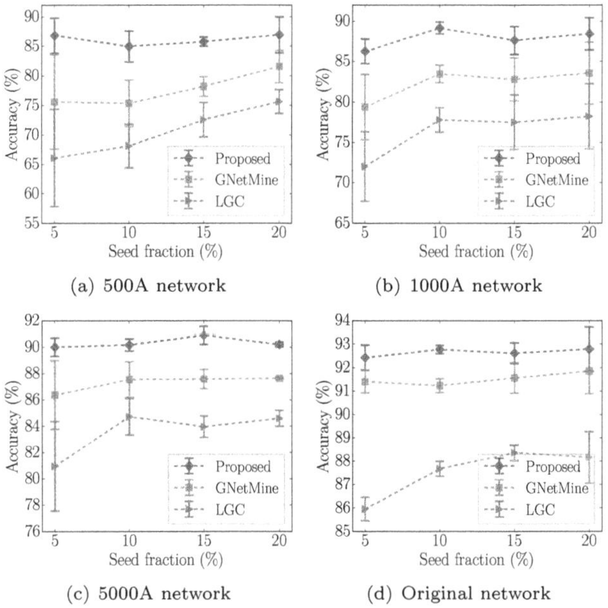

(a) 500A network (b) 1000A network

(c) 5000A network (d) Original network

Figure 10: Mean accuracy (± 1 SD) of the proposed method, GNetMine, and LC on four variants of the four-area network, where seed vertices are randomly 5%, 10%, 15%, and 20% of authors in the network.

5. CONCLUSION

We proposed a novel method for transductive classification on heterogeneous information networks. We have argued that the degree-based edge weight normalization is unsatisfactory when a degree of a vertex cannot be used to imply the reliability of its label. Instead, we proposed a normalization on the basis of edge-betweenness centrality, under the assumption that edges bridging across communities should be considered less reliable. This paper further refined the centrality in two ways. Additional refinements were proposed to make the centrality suitable for heterogeneous networks.

Experimental results have shown that the proposed centrality can distinguish inter-community and intra-community edges effectively. The results revealed that the two refinements have a true benefit on real-world networks. This has played a crucial role in helping the proposed classification method to outperform state-of-the-art methods, GNetMine and LGC. The proposed method gained a lower variance of accuracy over multiple choices of training data.

We studied the betweenness defined under the assumption that flows of information in networks follow the shortest paths. However, another possible assumption is that information flows across random paths rather than the shortest paths. Hence, *random-walk edge betweenness*, proposed by [19], would be worth studying. The main weakness of this study was the computational cost of calculating edge betweenness centrality. Even though it can be computed in $\mathcal{O}(nm)$ with the algorithm introduced by Brandes' algorithm [4], the complexity can be considered impractical in many circumstances. The algorithm needs to be further researched to improve its computational cost, for example, by unitizing a sophisticated approximation method.

6. REFERENCES

[1] L. A. Adamic and N. Glance. The political blogosphere and the 2004 u.s. election: Divided they blog. In *Proceedings of the 3rd International Workshop on Link Discovery*, LinkKDD '05, pages 36–43, New York, NY, USA, 2005. ACM.

[2] S. Baluja, R. Seth, D. Sivakumar, Y. Jing, J. Yagnik, S. Kumar, D. Ravichandran, and M. Aly. Video suggestion and discovery for youtube: taking random walks through the view graph. In *Proceedings of the 17th International Conference on World Wide Web*, pages 895–904. ACM, 2008.

[3] M. Belkin, P. Niyogi, and V. Sindhwani. Manifold regularization: A geometric framework for learning from labeled and unlabeled examples. *Journal of Machine Learning Research*, 7:2399–2434, 2006.

[4] U. Brandes. On variants of shortest-path betweenness centrality and their generic computation. *Social Networks*, 30(2):136–145, May 2008.

[5] O. Chapelle, B. Schölkopf, and A. Zien. *Semi-Supervised Learning*. MIT Press, 2010.

[6] F. R. K. Chung. *Spectral Graph Theory*. American Mathematical Society, 1997.

[7] A. Cuzzocrea, A. Papadimitriou, D. Katsaros, and Y. Manolopoulos. Edge betweenness centrality: A novel algorithm for qos-based topology control over wireless sensor networks. *Journal of Network and Computer Applications*, 35(4):1210–1217, July 2012.

[8] R. Dunn, F. Dudbridge, and C. M. Sanderson. The use of edge-betweenness clustering to investigate biological function in protein interaction networks. *BMC bioinformatics*, 6:39, 2005.

[9] L. C. Freeman. A set of measures of centrality based on betweenness. *Sociometry*, 40(1):35–41, 1977.

[10] J. Gao, F. Liang, W. Fan, Y. Sun, and J. Han. Graph-based consensus maximization among multiple supervised and unsupervised models. In *Advances in Neural Information Processing Systems*, pages 585–593, 2009.

[11] M. Girvan and M. E. J. Newman. Community structure in social and biological networks. *Proceedings of the National Academy of Sciences*, 99(12):7821–7826, 2002.

[12] C. Gong, D. Tao, K. Fu, and J. Yang. Relish: Reliable label inference via smoothness hypothesis. In *Proceedings of the 28th AAAI Conference on Artificial Intelligence*, 2014.

[13] Y. Jacob, L. Denoyer, and P. Gallinari. Learning latent representations of nodes for classifying in heterogeneous social networks. In *Proceedings of the 7th ACM International Conference on Web Search and Data Mining*, WSDM '14, pages 373–382, New York, NY, USA, 2014. ACM.

[14] K. Järvelin and J. Kekäläinen. IR evaluation methods for retrieving highly relevant documents. In *Proceedings of the 23rd Annual International ACM SIGIR Conference on Research and Development in Information Retrieval*, SIGIR '00, pages 41–48, New York, NY, USA, 2000. ACM.

[15] M. Ji, J. Han, and M. Danilevsky. Ranking-based classification of heterogeneous information networks. In *Proceedings of the 17th ACM SIGKDD International Conference on Knowledge discovery and data mining - KDD '11*, page 1298, New York, New York, USA, Aug. 2011. ACM Press.

[16] M. Ji, Y. Sun, M. Danilevsky, J. Han, and J. Gao. Graph regularized transductive classification on heterogeneous information networks. In J. Balcázar, F. Bonchi, A. Gionis, and M. Sebag, editors, *Machine Learning and Knowledge Discovery in Databases SE - 42*, volume 6321 of *Lecture Notes in Computer Science*, pages 570–586. Springer Berlin Heidelberg, 2010.

[17] C. Luo, R. Guan, Z. Wang, and C. Lin. Hetpathmine: A novel transductive classification algorithm on heterogeneous information networks. In M. de Rijke, T. Kenter, A. de Vries, C. Zhai, F. de Jong, K. Radinsky, and K. Hofmann, editors, *Advances in Information Retrieval SE - 18*, volume 8416 of *Lecture Notes in Computer Science*, pages 210–221. Springer International Publishing, 2014.

[18] D. Lusseau, K. Schneider, O. Boisseau, P. Haase, E. Slooten, and S. Dawson. The bottlenose dolphin community of doubtful sound features a large proportion of long-lasting associations. *Behavioral Ecology and Sociobiology*, 54(4):396–405, 2003.

[19] M. E. J. Newman and M. Girvan. Finding and evaluating community structure in networks. *Phys. Rev. E*, 69:026113, Feb 2004.

[20] A. Y. Ng, M. I. Jordan, and Y. Weiss. On spectral clustering: Analysis and an algorithm. In T. G. Dietterich, S. Becker, and Z. Ghahramani, editors, *Advances in Neural Information Processing Systems*, pages 849–856. MIT Press, 2002.

[21] Y. Saad. *Iterative Methods for Sparse Linear Systems*. PWS Publishing Company, Boston, 1st edition, 1996.

[22] Y. Sun, J. Han, X. Yan, P. S. Yu, and T. Wu. Pathsim: Meta path-based top-k similarity search in heterogeneous information networks. In *Proceedings of the VLDB Endowment 2011*, 2011.

[23] M. Szummer and T. Jaakkola. Partially labeled classification with markov random walks. In T. G. Dietterich, S. Becker, and Z. Ghahramani, editors, *Advances in Neural Information Processing Systems 14*, pages 945–952. MIT Press, 2002.

[24] P. P. Talukdar and K. Crammer. New regularized algorithms for transductive learning. In *Proceedings of the European Conference on Machine Learning and Knowledge Discovery in Databases: Part II*, ECML PKDD '09, pages 442–457, Berlin, Heidelberg, 2009. Springer-Verlag.

[25] W. W. Zachary. An information flow model for conflict and fission in small groups. *Journal of Anthropological Research*, 33:452–473, 1977.

[26] D. Zhou, O. Bousquet, T. N. Lal, J. Weston, and B. Schölkopf. Learning with local and global consistency. *Advances in Neural Information Processing Systems*, 16(16):321–328, 2004.

[27] X. Zhu, Z. Ghahramani, and J. Lafferty. Semi-supervised learning using gaussian fields and harmonic functions. In *Proceedings of the 20th International Conference on Machine Learning*, pages 912–919, 2003.

The Troll-Trust Model for Ranking in Signed Networks

Zhaoming Wu
Georgia Institute of Technology
zhaoming@gatech.edu

Charu C. Aggarwal
IBM T. J. Watson Research Center
charu@us.ibm.com

Jimeng Sun
Georgia Institute of Technology
jsun@cc.gatech.edu

ABSTRACT

Signed social networks have become increasingly important in recent years because of the ability to model trust-based relationships in review sites like Slashdot, Epinions, and Wikipedia. As a result, many traditional network mining problems have been re-visited in the context of networks in which signs are associated with the links. Examples of such problems include community detection, link prediction, and low rank approximation. In this paper, we will examine the problem of ranking nodes in signed networks. In particular, we will design a ranking model, which has a clear physical interpretation in terms of the sign of the edges in the network. Specifically, we propose the *Troll-Trust* model that models the probability of trustworthiness of individual data sources as an interpretation for the underlying ranking values. We will show the advantages of this approach over a variety of baselines.

1. INTRODUCTION

Many social network sites, such[1] as Epinions, Slashdot, and Wikipedia, allow users to contribute opinions, feedback, and the ability to indicate their trust or distrust in each other's opinions. Such networks are useful in the context of a wide variety of tasks, such as recommendations, clustering, and classification because they tell us important aspects of the relations between nodes. The trust and distrust relationships in such networks are often represented in the form of *signed networks*. Some examples of such signed networks, are as follows:

1. *Epinions:* Epinions is an online review site, in which users can provide ratings to items. However, users can provide positive and negative ratings not just to items but to other raters. Such positive and negative opinions are represented as directed links between different users [5]. The sign of the link indicates whether the relationship is positive or negative.

[1]http://snap.stanford.edu/data/index.html#signnets

WSDM'16, February 22-25, 2016, San Francisco, CA, USA

DOI: http://dx.doi.org/10.1145/2835776.2835816

2. *Slashdot:* Slashdot is a technology blog, where the users have the option of designating each other as friends or foes. Therefore, friends can be viewed as trusted parties (positive links), whereas foes can be viewed as distrusted parties (negative links).

3. *Wikipedia:* In Wikipedia, users are able to cast positive or negative votes for other admin users. Such votes can be viewed as positive and negative links.

As evident from the discussion above, the vast majority of signed networks arise in the context of trust networks. Such networks are very useful in improving the effectiveness of many applications such as collaborative filtering [7, 19], community detection [4, 11], and link prediction [4, 13, 14, 20]. In many of these applications, human-centric preferences play an important role; therefore, the trust component is relatively important in having an impact on the final results.

An important problem in network analytics is that of ranking nodes based on their reputation. A classical algorithm in this context is known as the *PageRank* method [3]. Ranking has traditionally been used for Web page ranking based on citation mechanisms. *PageRank* is viewed as a measure of reputation (or prestige) of a node in a network because it assumes that only reputable nodes are in-linked to by other nodes. In other words, each in-linking node is a vote of confidence in that node. Furthermore, the prestige of the in-linking node is also accounted for in the *PageRank* equations. However, the traditional *PageRank* equations are based on only the use of positive links. Developing methods for signed versions of *PageRank* is very useful in the context of a variety of applications such as global trust quantification of entities [23].

Over the last few years, a number of methods have been designed for signed network analysis with both positive and negative links [8, 9, 18, 21]. Most of these methods are based on simple modifications of the *PageRank* equations to account for negative weights on the links. However, many of these methods do not have natural interpretations in terms of the reputation values on the nodes. One of the reasons that the *PageRank* algorithm works so effectively is that it can naturally be interpreted in the form of a random surfer model with a clear physical interpretation for the importance of the nodes. While one can heuristically extend these equations with negative values on the links, we will show that the results can sometimes be unintended. In this paper, we will propose a *Troll-Trust* model with clear assumptions on what negative links mean in terms of the trust that users have on one another.

One of the reasons that trustworthy computing has become so important is the open nature of online forums in which users can intentionally post misleading information. Such users are referred to as *trolls*. Troll users might either have malicious intent, profit motives, or simply be inclined to behave in a disruptive way. Such users often have a serious impact on the quality of interaction in online forums. Therefore, the ability to identify users in signed networks based on their trustworthiness is crucial in a myriad of applications. Troll users can often be identified in signed networks, because they often have inbound negative links from other trustworthy users. This is similar to the *PageRank* reputation framework, except that the sign of the link also plays a critical role in reputation determination.

In our model, we use a Bernoulli distribution to characterize each user as either being trustworthy, or being a troll. This is used to construct a probabilistic model in terms of the links between various users. We show the advantages of using such an approach over heuristic extensions of *PageRank*. We also extend the approach to other variations such as personalized *Troll-Trust* ranking model. We show improved results of our techniques over competing methods in the literature.

This paper is organized as follows. The remainder of this section discusses the related work. The motivations of the *Troll-Trust* model are discussed in section 2. The iterative algorithm for the *Troll-Trust* model is illustrated in section 3. Methods for personalized *PageRank* in signed networks are discussed in section 4. The experiments are discussed in section 5. The conclusions are presented in section 6.

1.1 Related Work

Many data mining applications have been designed in the context of a wide variety of social networking applications [1]. In recent years, signed networks have gained increasing attention because of the ability of many social networking sites, such as Epinions, Slashdot, and Wikipedia, to specify trust and distrust relationships between users. Such relationships are useful in discerning between interactions of varying trustworthiness. The use of such networks can be helpful in applications such as collaborative filtering [7, 19], community detection [4, 11], and link prediction [4, 13, 14, 20].

Ranking is a well known problem in the context of unsigned networks [3, 10]. The *PageRank* problem has also been recently explored in the context of signed networks [8, 9, 18, 21]. Methods for finding node bias and prestige are discussed in [16], and this approach is based on the *HITS* algorithm. *PageRank* is useful for assessing the reputation of nodes, and it is also used in other applications such as sign prediction [18, 23]. One of the problems with existing variants of *PageRank* methods is that they heuristically try to modify the *PageRank* equations with the use of negative links. Such heuristic modifications often lose their interpretability, and they do not necessarily reflect the level of trust a given user has in another. In this paper, we will use a model, which is firmly grounded in probabilistic understanding of trust, which is the semantic interpretation in most signed networks. We show that the resulting approach is more robust than the traditional methods for signed *PageRank*.

2. MOTIVATION OF THE TROLL-TRUST MODEL

Before discussing the *Troll-Trust* model in detail, we will first revisit the *PageRank* method, and discuss how it is used in the context of a variety of applications. The traditional *PageRank* model was defined in the context of random surfer model on the Web. The *PageRank* model calculates the probability that a random surfer on the Web visits a given Web page by traversing links outgoing from Web pages in random fashion. In addition, in order to avoid the effect of dead-ends and smooth the ranking values, a restart probability is imposed on nodes. Let $G = (N, A)$ be a directed network with the node set N and the edge set A. Let us assume that the number of nodes in the set N is denoted by n. The nodes are indexed from $1 \ldots n$. The weights of the edges between nodes are stored in an $n \times n$ weight matrix W. Note that an edge weight is non-zero in W only when it is present in A. For traditional networks, all the weights in W are non-negative. In signed networks, however, some of these weights might be negative. The semantic interpretation of the sign in these cases is often one of trust or distrust.

In some signed networks, all weights in W are always drawn from $+1$ or -1, although this is not always the case. In some applications [20], positive or negative weights can be associated with the links, depending on the strength of the interactions. In the traditional random walk model, each node is associated with a probability of visit $\pi(i)$. Furthermore, the transition probability p_{ij} of each edge $(i, j) \in A$ is obtained by dividing each row in W by the sum of the corresponding entries in that row. This can be represented in matrix form as follows. Let D be the diagonal matrix in which the (i, i)th entry is given by the sum of the entries of W in the ith row.

$$D_{ii} = \sum_{j=1}^{n} w_{ij} \tag{1}$$

Then, the *PageRank* transition matrix is given by the following matrix $P = [p_{ij}]$:

$$P = D^{-1}W \tag{2}$$

Then, the *PageRank* equations may be stated in the form of a random surfer having transition probabilities p_{ij}. At each step, the surfer may restart to a random node with probability α. The steady state probability of visit of the random surfer is denoted by $\pi(i)$, and it represents the *PageRank* value. The steady state probability can be related to the transition probabilities by setting $\pi(i)$ to be the probability that the random surfer transitions into node i at a given step:

$$\pi(i) = (1 - \alpha) \cdot \sum_{j=1}^{n} \pi(j) \cdot p_{ji} + \alpha/n \tag{3}$$

Note that the values $\pi(i)$ intuitively represent transition probabilities, and they sum up to 1 over all the different nodes. Larger values of $\pi(i)$ indicate a better reputation for the node.

It is noteworthy that the random surfer model is intuitively interpretable only when the edge weights are non-negative and can be interpreted as transition probabilities. The *PageRank* equations yield stochastic probabilities precisely because of this non-negativity. If one naturally tries to modify the *PageRank* equations with negative weights, it leads to negative ranking values. Unfortunately, this has the impact of making the equations less easily interpretable. In some cases, the resulting reputation values of $\pi(i)$ also become misleading. We will discuss this issue later in this section.

2.1 Problems with Existing Methods

In order to handle the problem of signed networks, a number of possible modifications have been made to the *PageRank* methodology. For example, the work in [9] multiplies the right-hand side of Equation 3 with a heuristic correction factor so that nodes with many incoming negative edges automatically have a lower reputation. The exponential ranking approach [21] uses an exponential variation of the *PageRank* equations in order to model the trust values of nodes. This approach still models the node-specific reputation in a heuristic as a (positive and negative) linear combination of the node-specific trust probabilities. The coefficients of the linear combination correspond to the edge weights. Although the approach provides a *relative* ranking of a heuristic nature, it is often hard to assign an absolute interpretability to the reputation values in terms of how much one should trust a particular user.

Recently, a very simple modification of *PageRank* [18] computes the *PageRank* separately on the positive and negative subgraphs. If the corresponding ranks for the node i are r_i^+ and r_i^-, respectively, then the overall reputation is computed as $r_i^+ - r_i^-$. Unfortunately, this approach does not account for the relative density of the positive and negative links in the network. For example, if a network contains a large number of positive links relative to the negative links, and vice versa, it should affect the reputation values. Unfortunately, the value of $r_i^+ - r_i^-$ is relatively insensitive to the proportion of positive and negative links. For example, if either the positive or the negative links are down-sampled in isolation, it will make only modest differences to the reputation values, as computed by $r_i^+ - r_i^-$. This scenario is intuitively undesirable. When the relative proportion of negative links in a network increases, it is likely that the network contains a larger number of trolls. This should change not only the absolute reputation values, but it should also have an impact on the relative ranking and the nature of the interaction between the various users.

A number of modifications of the *HITS* algorithm are also proposed in [18]. In all these cases, again the basic approach is divide the graph into positive and negative subgraphs to compute the hub and authority scores separately for each subgraph. The authority scores for the positive and negative subgraphs are subtracted from one another to provide the final score. However, this approach has similar issues to the modified *PageRank* method in that it is relatively insensitive to the relative proportion of positive and negative links.

2.2 The Troll-Trust Model

The key of the *Troll-Trust* model is to replace the random surfer model with a new set of probabilities associated with the nodes, which have a clear physical interpretation in terms of the global trustworthiness of the participants. Unlike the random surfer model, in which the steady-state probabilities define random walk probabilities, the probability $\pi(i)$ in this model defines the likelihood that a participant is either trustworthy or a troll. Let E_i be the event that the ith person is trustworthy. Therefore, we have:

$$E_i = \begin{cases} 1 & \text{Person } i \text{ is trustworthy with probability } \pi(i) \\ 0 & \text{Person } i \text{ is a troll with probability } 1 - \pi(i) \end{cases} \tag{4}$$

Therefore, E_i is a Bernoulli random variable with the parameter $\pi(i)$, and our goal is to determine $P(E_i) = \pi(i)$, which gives us a measure of the reputation of individual i. Intuitively, one can also interpret this probability as the likelihood of a user providing misleading information in a trust-centric network where negative links have the semantic interpretation of untrustworthiness. Note that this interpretation of $\pi(i)$ is different from what is normally used in a random surfer model. The default (or *a priori*) value of $\pi(i)$, in a network is set to the global parameter β. Thus, if a network has no positive or negative interactions between users, then the value of $\pi(i)$ for all nodes would be β. The parameter β is useful for settings where the network is very sparse, although its impact is often somewhat limited.

Next, we define the significance of the weights $W = [w_{ij}]$ in the probabilistic modeling process. Intuitively, these weights represents statements of the level to which user i feels that user j is trustworthy. Therefore, we define the event U_{ij} as follows:

$$U_{ij} = \begin{cases} 1 & \text{Person } i \text{ views } j \text{ as trustworthy} \\ 0 & \text{Person } i \text{ views } j \text{ as a troll} \end{cases} \tag{5}$$

Then, we model the probability distribution of the Bernoulli variable U_{ij} as a logistic function of the weights w_{ij}. Large positive values of w_{ij} means that the expected value of U_{ij} should be close to 1. On the other hand, when the weight w_{ij} is negative, the expected value of U_{ij} should be close to 0. In the event that w_{ij} is 0, the expected value of U_{ij} should be β, which is the default value of the trust between any pair of participants. We *model* U_{ij} as Bernoulli random variable whose parameters are defined as logistic function of the weights w_{ij}. Therefore, we have:

$$U_{ij} = \begin{cases} 1 & \text{with probability } \frac{1}{1+e^{-\lambda_0 - \lambda_1 w_{ij}}} \\ 0 & \text{with probability } \frac{1}{1+e^{\lambda_0 + \lambda_1 w_{ij}}} \end{cases} \tag{6}$$

Here λ_0 and λ_1 are user-defined parameters. The value of λ_1 is always set to a nonnegative value. Therefore, increasing the weight w_{ij} also increases the trust probability $P(U_{ij} = 1)$. The value of λ_0 can be derived in terms of the default trustworthiness probability β. Note that when $w_{ij} = 0$, it is necessary for $P(U_{ij} = 1)$ to be β because a zero weight edge corresponds to a neutral opinion and it does not change the default belief of user i in user j. We can use this relationship to derive the value of λ_0 in terms of β. Therefore, we have:

$$P(U_{ij} = 1)_{w_{ij}=0} = \beta = \frac{1}{1 + e^{-\lambda_0 - \lambda_1 (0)}} \tag{7}$$

By simplifying the aforementioned expression, we obtain:

$$\lambda_0 = \ln\left(\frac{\beta}{1-\beta}\right) \tag{8}$$

How can these probability values be used to model the steady-state probability of trustworthiness of an individual? Trust modeling is often used in fact-finding applications. An important point to keep in mind is that if an individual is a troll, it is not necessary that the opposite of their stated facts are always correct. Rather, a lower value of the trust simply lowers the *probability* of their stated facts, included their stated trust in other individuals, to be correct. Therefore, it makes sense to model the reputation of each individual by using the probability of their trustworthiness. In other words, we want to create a model in which the feedback of each individual about other individuals (in terms of the sign and weight of links) is weighted by the probability of their trustworthiness. Just as the *PageRank* model simulates a random walk through the network, the *Troll-Trust* model simulates the following probabilistic process:

Sample a node j selected from the incoming neighbors of a node i, such that the probability of the node j being selected is proportional to its modeled trustworthiness probability $P(E_j = 1)$. Then the trustworthiness probability $P(E_i = 1)$ is modeled as the expected value of $P(U_{ji} = 1)$ over this sampling.

In other words, we use the sampled opinion of the neighbors in a node in order to model its trustworthiness. Furthermore, because the neighbors are weighted by their trust probabilities, this definition is recursive, just like the *PageRank* equations. Therefore, we have the following recursive relationship:

$$P(E_i = 1) = \frac{\sum_{j;(j,i)\in A} P(E_j = 1) \cdot P(U_{ji} = 1)}{\sum_{j;(j,i)\in A} P(E_j = 1)} \quad (9)$$

One can express this relationship directly in terms of the aforementioned variables $\pi(i)$, and the edge weights:

$$\begin{aligned} \pi(i) &= \frac{\sum_{j;(j,i)\in A} \pi(j) \cdot \frac{1}{1+e^{-\lambda_0 - \lambda_1 w_{ji}}}}{\sum_{j:(j,i)\in A} \pi(j)} \\ &= \frac{\sum_{j;(j,i)\in A} \pi(j) \cdot \frac{1}{1+e^{-\ln[\beta/(1-\beta)] - \lambda_1 w_{ji}}}}{\sum_{j;(j,i)\in A} \pi(j)} \end{aligned}$$

Of course, this definition does not yet account for the prior probability β, which is particularly useful in cases where the node i has no incoming nodes, which are also presumably trustworthy. The probability that none of the incoming nodes is trustworthy is given[2] by $\prod_{j:(j,i)\in A}(1 - \pi(j))$. In that case, the trustworthiness of node i is set to the default value β. Therefore, the aforementioned sampling needs to include an additional case in which the trustworthiness of the user i needs to be set to β when the case with probability $\prod_{j:(j,i)\in A}(1-\pi(j))$ occurs. This default scenario can also be viewed as a form of Laplacian smoothing, and it serves a similar goal to the restart step in the *PageRank* algorithm. Therefore, accounting for this default scenario, we need to add the term $\beta \prod_{j:(j,i)\in A}(1 - \pi(j))$ to the numerator, and the term $\prod_{j:(j,i)\in A}(1-\pi(j))$ to the denominator. Therefore, we obtain the following:

$$\pi(i) = \frac{\sum_{j;(j,i)\in A} \frac{\pi(j)}{1+e^{-\ln[\beta/(1-\beta)] - \lambda_1 w_{ji}}} + \beta \prod_{j:(j,i)\in A}(1 - \pi(j))}{\sum_{j;(j,i)\in A} \pi(j) + \prod_{j:(j,i)\in A}(1 - \pi(j))} \quad (10)$$

The aforementioned condition needs to hold for each node $i \in \{1 \ldots n\}$. Furthermore, when the node i has no incoming edges, it is easy to verify that the value of $\pi(i)$ will be set to β by the above equation. The values of β and λ_1 are two user-defined parameters in this algorithm. The selection of these parameters will be described later.

[2]We make the naive assumption that the trustworthiness of nodes is independent of one another.

3. ITERATIVE ALGORITHM

The condition for $\pi(i)$ in the previous section defines a *system* of equations. In this particular case, the system of equation is nonlinear. Unlike *PageRank*, such a nonlinear system of equations is hard to solve in closed form. Such non-linear systems of equations are often solved using iterative methods by starting with an initial set of default values and cycling through the system of equations and updating each value of $\pi(i)$.

Correspondingly, we use an iterative approach to update the probabilities of all the nodes. Let $\pi^t(i)$ be the value of the trust probability $\pi(i)$ of the ith node in the tth iteration.

1. Initialize iteration index $t \Leftarrow 0$.
2. Initialize $\pi^t(i) = \beta$ for each i.
3. For each i update from the probability values in the tth iteration to $(t + 1)$th iteration as follows:

$$\pi^{t+1}(i) \Leftarrow \frac{\sum_{j\in I(i)} \frac{\pi^t(j)}{1+e^{-\ln[\beta/(1-\beta)] - \lambda_1 w_{ji}}} + \beta \prod_{j\in I(i)} (1 - \pi^t(j))}{\sum_{j\in I(i)} \pi^t(j) + \prod_{j\in I(i)} (1 - \pi^t(j))} \quad (11)$$

, where $I(i) = \{j|(j, i) \in A\}$ is an index set.

4. Update $t \Leftarrow t + 1$
5. If converged then report the converged values $\pi^t(1) \ldots \pi^t(n)$ and terminate; else go to step 3

This approach is continued to convergence. In the next section, we will discuss the convergence behavior of this approach.

3.1 Convergence Behavior

We provide the convergence proof of the simplified *Troll-Trust* algorithm. First, we rewrite Eq. 9 in matrix form as follows:

$$\pi^{t+1} = ((A \odot P)^T \pi^t) \oslash (A^T \pi^t)$$

Here, A is the adjacency matrix, and P is a matrix with entries $P_{ij} = \frac{1}{1+\exp\{-\ln \beta/(1-\beta) - \lambda_1 w_{ij}\}}$. $\odot$ and $\oslash$ denotes element-wise multiplication and division respectively. Let us focus on the ith element $\pi^{t+1}(i)$ of the probability vector in the $(t + 1)$th iteration,

$$\pi^{t+1}(i) = \frac{(A_i \odot P_i)^T \pi^t}{A_i^T \pi^t} = \frac{A_{ii} P_{ii} \pi^t(i) + B}{A_{ii} \pi^t(i) + D} \quad (12)$$

Here, A_i and P_i are the ith columns of A and P, respectively. We further denote $B = \sum_{j\neq i} A_{ij} P_{ij} \pi^t(j)$, and $D = \sum_{j\neq i} A_{ij} \pi^t(j)$. Since $A_{ii} \in \{0, 1\}$, $P_{ij} \in (0, 1)$, we immediately have $B < D$ and $\pi^{t+1}(i) < 1, \forall i$, and thus $D \in [0, n - 1)$.

To prove convergence of Eq. 12, we use Banach Fixed Point theorem [2], which we introduce below.

DEFINITION 1. *Let (X, d) be a metric space. Then, a map $T : X \to X$ is called a contraction map on X if there exists $q \in [0, 1)$ such that*

$$d(T(x), T(y)) \leq qd(x, y), \forall\ x, y \text{ in } X$$

THEOREM 1 (BANACH FIXED POINT THEOREM). *Consider a non-empty complete metric space (X, d) with a contraction mapping $T : X \to X$. Then, T admits a unique fixed-point x^* in X (i.e., $T(x^*) = x^*$).*

Furthermore, x^* can be found by using the following approach. We start with an arbitrary element x_0 in X and define a sequence x_n by $x_n = T(x_{n-1})$. Then it can be shown that $x_n \to x^*$.

THEOREM 2. *The* Troll-Trust *algorithm converges to a fixed point.*

PROOF. Let us map the problem within the terminology of the Banach fixed point theorem. Here, in our case $T(x) = \frac{A_{ii}P_{ii}x+B}{A_{ii}x+D}$, and we use the common Euclidean space, with L_2-norm as the associated distance function. The case where $A_{ii} = 0$ (q can be any value in $[0, 1)$) is trivial and we focus on the case where $A_{ii} = 1$, and now $T(x) = \frac{P_{ii}x+B}{x+D}, x \in [0, 1)$

$$T(x) - T(y) = \frac{P_{ii}D - B}{(x + D)(y + D)}(x - y)$$

According to the aforementioned theorem, the convergence proof only requires us to show that

$$q = \frac{|P_{ii}D - B|}{(x + D)(y + D)} < 1$$

. We consider three cases:
Case 0. $P_{ii}D - B = 0$
In this case $q = 0$, which satisfies the condition trivially.
Case 1. $P_{ii}D - B < 0$

$$q = \frac{B - P_{ii}D}{(x + D)(y + D)} < 1 \Leftrightarrow (x + D)(y + D) > B - P_{ii}D$$
$$\Leftarrow D^2 + (x + y + P_{ii} - 1)D + xy > 0\ [D > B] \quad (13)$$

The equation above contains the quadratic function $\varphi(D) = D^2 + (x + y + P_{ii} - 1)D + xy > 0$ with $D \in [0, n - 1)$. Notice when $x + y + P_{ii} - 1 > 0$, the minimum of φ in $[0, n - 1)$ is $\varphi(0) = xy > 0$, and we can choose $P_{ii} = \frac{1}{1+\exp\{-\ln\beta/(1-\beta)-\lambda_1 w_{ii}\}}$ to satisfy such a condition. Therefore, convergence is guaranteed.
Case 2. $P_{ii}D - B > 0$
When $P_{ii}D - B > 0$, similarly, we have

$$q < 1 \Leftrightarrow D^2 + (x + y - P_{ii})D + xy + B > 0 \quad (14)$$

We can now choose P_{ii} so that $(x + y - P_{ii}) > 0$, and thus $\varphi = D^2 + (x+y-P_{ii})D+xy > \varphi(0) = xy > 0$. Since $B \geq 0$, Eq. 14 holds, we also have convergence in Case 2. □

3.2 Selecting the Parameters

An important aspect is the choice of the parameters β and λ_1. Much like *PageRank* this is a heuristic choice. However, one can choose the parameters by using the principle of self consistency with the network structure. The basic idea is to compute the trust values on a network in which around 90% of the links are retained, and the remaining 10% are held out. The computed trust values values are then used to perform sign prediction on the remaining 10% of the links. Various choices of β and λ_1 are tested on these links. After selecting these values of β and λ_1, the approach is then applied to the full data set. A more effective approach for selecting the parameters is to use cross-validation in which the data is divided into various folds and the parameter choices are decided by averaging the performance over various folds.

4. EXTENSIONS TO PERSONALIZED RANKING

In many scenarios, it is desired to determine the personalized ranking values for individuals. For a given user i, one may wish to determine the most similar users to i in the signed network. In other cases, a *subset* of nodes may be selected and it may be desirable to determine the most similar nodes to this subset. For generality, let us consider the case, where it is desired to personalize the ranking with respect to a subset S of nodes. There are two types of personalization which are possible:

- *Weighted personalization:* In this case, prior probabilities are provided for each node in S. These can also be viewed as weights specifying the importance of each node $i_r \in S$. For each node $i_r \in S$, its prior probability is specified as $\beta(i_r)$, as part of the input to the problem. For each node $i_r \notin S$, it is assumed that its prior probability is a small default value of β, which is less than that the prior probabilities of the nodes in S. This case is a very straightforward modification of the global *Troll-Trust* method. Specifically, the prior probabilities in Equation 10 are modified to replace the prior probabilities as follows:

$$\pi(i) = \frac{\sum_{j \in I(i)} \frac{\pi(j)}{1+e^{-\ln[\beta(i)/(1-\beta(i))]-\lambda_1 w_{ji}}} + \beta(i) \prod_{j \in I(i)} (1 - \pi(j))}{\sum_{j \in I(i)} \pi(j) + \prod_{j \in I(i)} (1 - \pi(j))}$$

  Note that $\beta(i)$ is set to a small default value for nodes which are not in S. The iterative update is based on the aforementioned relationship.

- *Hard personalization:* Unlike weighted personalization, it is assumed that the nodes in S are completely trusted, and therefore the values of *both* $\pi(i)$ and $\beta(i)$ are set to 1 for those nodes. Therefore, the Equation 10 is not applied to those nodes, which are in S. For nodes that are not in S, a small default value of β is assumed. For each node i, which is not in S, the following relationship is used to compute $\pi(i)$:

$$\pi(i) = \frac{\sum_{j \in I(i)} \frac{\pi(j)}{1+e^{-\ln[\beta/(1-\beta)]-\lambda_1 w_{ji}}} + \beta \prod_{j \in I(i)} (1 - \pi(j))}{\sum_{j \in I(i)} \pi(j) + \prod_{j \in I(i)} (1 - \pi(j))}$$

The main difference between weighted personalization and hard personalization is the level of trust placed in elements in set S. In the case of hard personalization, it is assumed that the elements of set S are completely trusted, irrespective of how many other users might have pointed to these nodes with negative links. On the other hand, in the case of weighted personalization, even though a prior bias is provided, the final trust probability of these nodes may be different from the prior values. Therefore, the weighted form

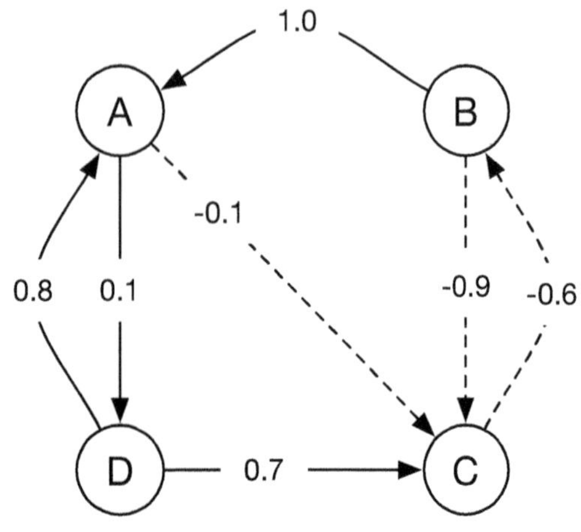

Figure 1: A four-node signed network with 4 positive links and 3 negative (dashed) links. Edge weights are labeled on each edge.

of personalization may be viewed as a softer way of biasing the process.

4.1 Interesting Special Cases and Applications

Personalized ranking has many applications in information search and recommender systems [22, 17]. The *Troll-Trust* model can be applied to various applications such as link prediction problem. It is well known that similar nodes are more likely to form connections [6]. This is the reason that personalized ranking methods were among the earliest methods used for unsigned link prediction [15]. This general principle can also be used in the case of signed networks. Using the same intuition as in the case of unsigned networks, we can make the assumption that an individual node in a signed network is more likely to initiate positive/negative edges to nodes with higher/lower personalized ranking scores with respect to that node. In general, since personalized ranking methods are used in a host of other network-centric applications, such as collective classification, it is conceivable that these methods can also be extended to those cases.

5. EXPERIMENTAL RESULTS

In this section, we will show the effectiveness of the *Troll-Trust* model with respect to baseline methods. We will first use an illustrative example to show that the ranking values obtained from the *Troll-Trust* model are semantically interpretable compared to other straightforward adaptations of ranking algorithms to the signed network scenario. We also apply the approach to an application-centric scenario to show that the underlying ranking approach is more robust. We use three different real datasets from the signed network domain, which are Wikipedia, Slashdot, and Epinions.

5.1 Comparative methods

To study the effectiveness of the *Troll-Trust* algorithm, we compare it to the following baselines. Each of these baselines can be applied to compute global ranking scores for all the nodes in the network:

- *Prestige* [24]

  Prestige is a simple algorithm that considers only positive and negative incoming links. It assumes that a node receiving more positive than negative incoming links is more likely to be trusted.

- *PageRank* [3]

  PageRank was originally designed for unsigned networks. Here, we apply *PageRank* on G^+, the subgraph of a signed network where all the negative links are removed, and positive links are preserved to obtain global trust values.

- *Exponential ranking(Exp)* [21]

  Exponential ranking was designed for ranking nodes in signed networks by heuristically using an exponential variation of the *PageRank* equations to deal with negative links.

- *Modified PageRank(MPR)* [18]

  Modified PageRank applies *PageRank* separately on both G^+, the positive subgraph, and G^-, the negative subgraph. Suppose the corresponding ranks for the node i are r_i^+ and r_i^- respectively. The overall reputation is computed as $r_i^+ - r_i^-$.

- *PageTrust* [9]

  PageTrust is a modified version of *PageRank*, which multiplies the right-hand side of the *PageRank* equation with a heuristic correction factor in an effort to account for negative links.

- *Bias and Prestige*(BAP) [16]

  Bias and Prestige models both bias, which shows the expected weight of an outgoing edge of a node, and prestige, which reflects the expected weight of an incoming edge of a node, recursively in signed networks. The assumption is that the opinions of biased users, even with high prestige, should not be discounted.

- *HITS* [10]

  HITS was originally proposed to analyze the link structure in the *World Wide Web* (*WWW*). To apply *HITS* in signed networks, *HITS* is run separately on both G^+ and G^-. Similar to *Modified PageRank*, the overall authority value is computed as $a_i^+ - a_i^-$, where a_i^+ and a_i^- denote the corresponding authority values for the node i respectively.

5.2 Synthetic Case Study

Before providing the results of ranking algorithms in application-centric scenarios, we provide a synthetic case study on a toy data set, to provide an intuitive understanding of *why* the results from a *Troll-Trust* model may make semantic sense over competing methods. This also explains the later results on why its use in application settings provides more accurate results.

As shown in Figure 1, a signed network is constructed with 4 nodes, 4 positive links, and 3 negative links. The trust/distrust weights on the edges are also indicated. It is intuitively evident that node A is the most trustworthy, given the positive incoming links from other nodes and no negative incoming link. The trustworthiness of node C is more controversial, because it is distrusted by node A and B but partially trusted by node D. We run the *Troll-Trust*

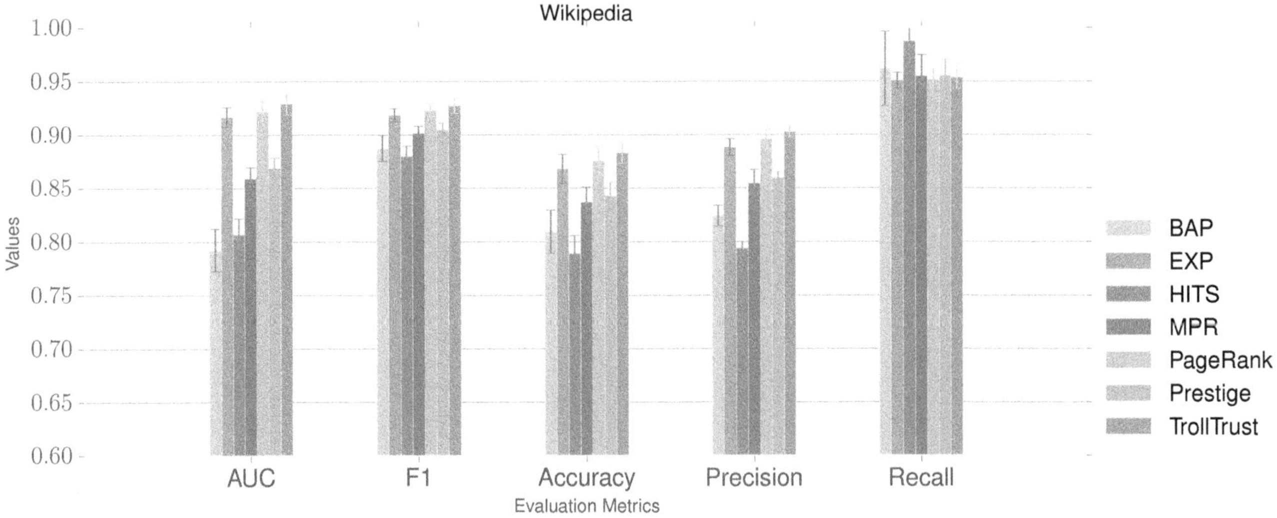

Figure 2: Predictive performance of *Rep* (Eq 15) and *Opt* (Eq 16) based on different ranking algorithms, including *Troll-Trust*, *Exp*, *BAP*, *PageRank*, *Prestige*, *MPR* and *HITS*. Various evaluation measures, such as the *AUC*, *F1 Score*, *Accuracy*, *Precision* and *Recall*, are shown on the Wikipedia network.

Table 1: Global trust values from different models on the signed network in Figure 1

Model	A	B	C	D
Prestige	1.0	0.5	0.3333	1.0
PageRank	0.2025	0.1650	0.5001	0.1324
Exp	0.7074	0.5226	0.4591	0.5168
MPR	0.5687	0.4182	0.5719	0.4412
PageTrust	0.1723	0.1220	0.2154	0.1204
BAP	0.9201	0.4965	0.4568	0.5496
HITS	0.7366	0.4348	0.2473	0.7508
Troll-Trust	0.6708	0.5094	0.4790	0.5168

algorithm together with 8 other baselines on this signed network. The obtained trust values are shown in Table 1. All results are linearly scaled into $[0, 1]$.

It can be observed from Table 1 that some of the baseline algorithms yield poorly interpretable results. *Prestige* is too focused on the number of positive and negative incoming links without taking into account the network structure. *PageRank* on the positive subgraph doesn't take into account negative links at all, therefore node C has the the highest trust value, which is not desirable given the negative links from node A and node B. *PageTrust* tries to incorporate negative links into the *PageRank* model but node C still receives the highest trust value in the modified model. *MPR* and *HITS*, respectively, apply the original *PageRank* and *HITS* separately on the positive and negative subgraph and obtain the difference as the global trust value. However, this type of decomposed approach fails to take the interaction among the two types of links into account.

The results of *BAP*, *Exp* and *Troll-Trust* are more in accordance with intuitive expectations. Although the results of *Exp* and *Troll-Trust* are very similar in this case, further experiments on real datasets will show their difference in prediction tasks.

We should notice that each trust score in the results of the *Troll-Trust* model represents the probability of a node being trustworthy. On the other hand, other baselines, although whose results are able to be scaled into $[0, 1]$, actually lack a probabilistic explanation in their models. Therefore their results are only an intuitive analogy to the trust values from the hidden probabilistic model.

5.3 Data Set Descriptions

We test our proposed work on three real signed network datasets, Epinions, Slashdot and Wikipedia, where each edge is labeled explicitly with either a positive (+1) or a negative (−1) sign. All three datasets are available online.

Table 2: Dataset statistics

Dataset	Node	Edge	+Edge(%)	−Edge(%)
Epinions	131,828	841,372	85.0	15.0
Slashdot	82,144	549,202	77.4	22.6
Wikipedia	10,835	159,388	78.7	21.2

- *Epinions:* Epinions is an online review site, in which users are connected by directed links with positive (+1) or negative (−1) signs. Epinions can be viewed as a directed graph with 131,828 nodes and 841,372 edges, of which 85% are labeled positive.
- *Slashdot:* Slashdot is a technology blog, where the users can tag each other as 'friends' or 'foes'. The 'Friends' tag is indicative of a positive link, whereas the 'foes' tag is indicative of a negative (−1) link. Therefore, Slashdot can represent a signed network with 82,144 nodes and 549,202 edges, of which 77.4% are labeled positive.
- *Wikipedia:* In Wikipedia, users are able to cast supporting or opposing votes for other admin users. Votes are extracted as signed links (+1 for positive votes and −1 for negative votes). This dataset contains 10,835 nodes and 159,388 edges, of which 78.7% are labeled positive.

In all these networks, the proportion of positive links is around 80%. Topological details including the number of nodes, the number of edges, and the proportion of positive

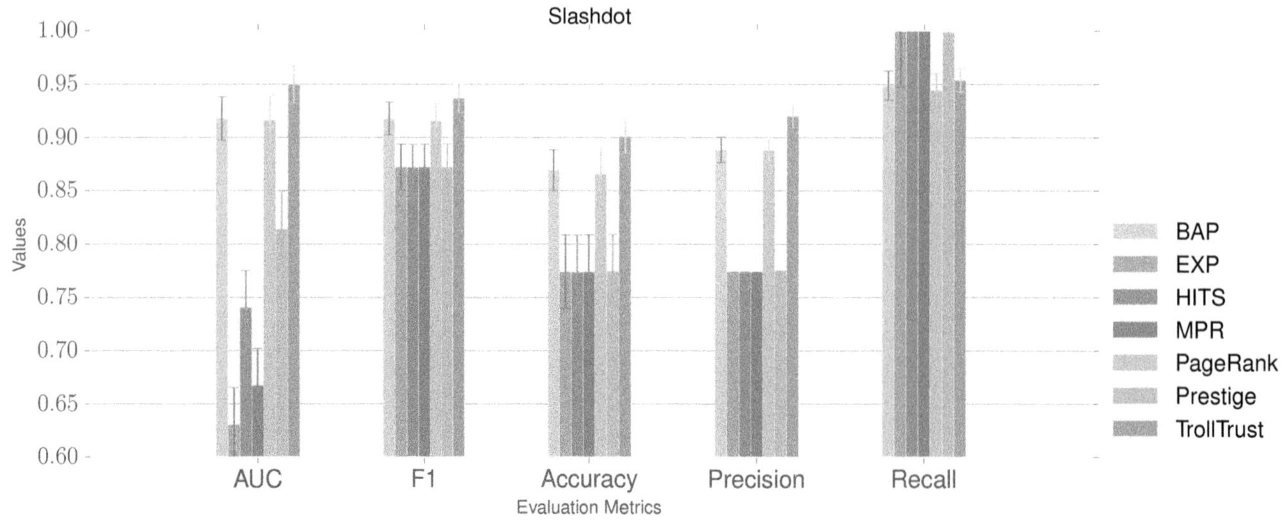

Figure 3: Predictive performance for Slashdot dataset. Other designations are the same as Fig 2

and negative links of all three datasets are summarized in Table 2.

5.4 Testing Methodology

How can we show that one ranking method is better than another? After all, there is no ground-truth availability for the ranks of the nodes in any of the data sets. Therefore, we use an indirect approach, which conforms to the methodology generally used in the literature [18, 21]. The key idea is that the node rankings are often used as a component of various applications, whose effectiveness can be measured more easily. For example, the rank (or trust) of a node is an integral input as a feature to many sign prediction methods. The quality of the latter can be measured easily against a concrete ground-truth. We emphasize that our goal is not to provide new sign prediction methods, but to test the effectiveness of incorporated ranking methods with this indirect approach. Therefore, we will use sign prediction methods to test our approach.

5.4.1 Description of Sign prediction Task

Consider a signed network in which the signs on some edges are not recorded. The sign prediction problem is to predict those hidden signs based on the information obtained from the rest of the network, such as the structure of the network and the signs of other links [13]. To accomplish the prediction task [18], the nodes are ranked in terms of global trust values, which are further used to calculate the *reputation* (*Rep*) and *optimism* (*Opt*) scores. With *Rep* and *Opt* used as features, logistic regression is used as the predictive model. The accuracy is evaluated with the use of measures such as the *Accuracy*, *F1-Score*, *AUC*, *Precision* and *Recall*.

Consider a signed network in which $s(i,j) = \pm 1$ denotes the sign of the edge from from node i to node j. If no edge exists from i to j, then the sign is 0. In the sign prediction problem, we predict the signs of edges for which the sign is unknown.

We adopt the two measures in [18], denoted by *reputation* and *optimism*, as features for sign prediction tasks. Both these features are expressed in terms of ranking scores, and therefore a good performance by the sign prediction task with these features is indicative of a ranking of good quality. The *reputation* feature quantifies the popularity of a node in the network, whereas *optimism* quantifies the pattern of votes a node make in the network. Let $\pi(i)$ denote the global trust score we obtain for node i. Then, the *reputation* (Rep_i) and the *optimism* (Opt_i) features of node i are expressed in terms of $\pi(i)$ (or any other baseline ranking mechanism) as follows:

$$Rep_i = \frac{\sum_{j;(j,i)\in A+} \pi_j - \sum_{j;(j,i)\in A-} \pi_j}{\sum_{j;(j,i)\in A+} \pi_j + \sum_{j;(j,i)\in A-} \pi_j} \tag{15}$$

$$Opt_i = \frac{\sum_{j;(i,j)\in A+} \pi_j - \sum_{j;(i,j)\in A-} \pi_j}{\sum_{j;(i,j)\in A+} \pi_j + \sum_{j;(i,j)\in A-} \pi_j} \tag{16}$$

Here, $A+$ and $A-$ denote the adjacency matrices for the positive and negative subgraphs, respectively. For any given edge, these two features are extracted from its endpoints in order to perform the learning process.

5.5 Evaluation metrics

Next, we briefly introduce our evaluation metrics. In the succeeding discussion, we denote y as the ground truth and $\hat{y}$ as our prediction.

- *Accuracy*

  The accuracy measures the proportion of the successfully predicted instances, which can be biased in the case of unbalanced datasets. Therefore we also use metrics discussed below.

- *Precision and Recall*

  Sign prediction is a binary classification task, and thus we have the following possible outcomes as in Table 3

Table 3: Possible Outcomes in Link Prediction Tasks

Total population	+ Link	− Link
Predicted + Link	True Positive(tp)	False Positive(fp)
Predicted − Link	False Negative(fn)	True Negative(tn)

Based on counts in each categories, precision and recall

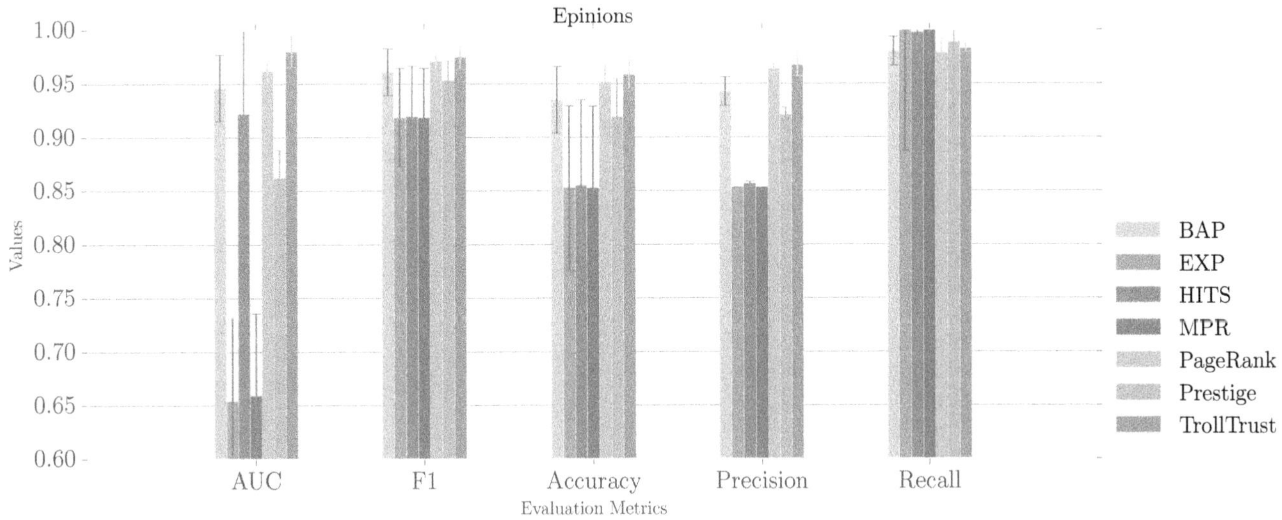

Figure 4: Predictive performance for Epinions dataset. Other designations are the same as Fig 2

is defined as follows:

$$precision = \frac{tp}{tp + fp}$$

$$recall = \frac{tp}{tp + fn}$$

Typically, there is a trade-off between precision and recall.

- *F1-Score*

  To account for the trade-off between precision and recall, we also use F1-Score, the harmonic mean of precision and recall

$$F1 = 2\,\frac{precision \times recall}{precision + recall}$$

  F1-Score falls in the range of $[0, 1]$ and higher value indicates higher predictive power.

- *Area Under ROC Curve (AUC)*

  Another measure accounts for such trade-off is the area under receiver operating characteristics (ROC) curve, which measures the probability that the classifier will rank a randomly chosen positive instance higher than a randomly chosen negative one; a higher AUC would indicate a better predictive performance.

5.6 Experimental setup

For each data set, 10-fold cross-validation is performed to evaluate the predictive model. In each round of cross-validation, for any node i in the signed network G from the dataset, we first run the ranking algorithms to obtain the global trust value $\pi(i)$. Then for any edge $e(u, v)$, four features, Rep_u, Opt_u, Rep_v, Opt_v, are extracted based on $\pi(u)$ and $\pi(v)$ to construct a feature vector. We use logistic regression with $L1$ regularization as the classifier and evaluate the predictive performance by *Accuracy*, *F1-Score*, *AUC*, *Precision* and *Recall*. For clarity, here we use the names of different ranking algorithms to denote different classifiers respectively.

In our *Troll-Trust* model, the parameters are selected via cross-validation on the training data, with the aim of achieving the highest *Accuracy*. As generally assumed, the damping factor in *PageRank* is set to 0.85 and both the initial *Authority* and *Hub* values in *HITS* are set to 1. To guarantee convergence, the μ in *Exp* is set to 1 [21]. In the *PageTrust* algorithm, multiplication of large dense matrices is inevitable, and therefore this algorithm is excluded in our experiments due to the memory limit.

All experiments were conducted on machines with Intel(R) Xeon(R), CPUs @ 2.60GHz and 125GB RAM.

5.7 Results

The predictive performances of the sign prediction methods, based on features derived from different ranking algorithms on Wikipedia, Slashdot and Epinions, are shown in Fig 2, Fig 3 and Fig 4 respectively.

We can observe that on all three datasets our *Troll-Trust* model significantly outperforms other baselines in terms of comprehensive evaluation metrics *AUC*, *F1 Score* and *Accuracy*. High *Recall* scores achieved by baselines indicate that they can be overly aggressive in the prediction task, which yields extremely poor *Precision* scores and mediocre overall performance.

With the *Troll-Trust* model giving the best results, the pattern of the performances of other algorithms seems to vary on different datasets. Surprisingly, we found the unsigned *PageRank* to be reasonably stable on all the datasets, even though it was not the best performer. There can be multiple reasons behind it. First of all, although the information about negative links is completely ignored in *PageRank* algorithm, it is taken into account into the computation of the *Rep* and *Opt* during the feature extraction process. Furthermore, all three datasets are highly imbalanced with about 80% positive links. As a result, the the *PageRank* model is able to perform well on at least the positive parts of the network. Nevertheless, it is still outperformed by the *Troll-Trust* model.

Another model that is relatively stable is *Prestige*, while the results are not desirable, which is expected since it does not differentiate the trustworthiness of the incoming neighbors. The performance of other algorithms including *Exp*, *BAP*, *MPR* and *HITS* fluctuates according to the datasets. The heuristic modifications in these model can account for such instability. Although *Exp* performed well in the case study presented in Section 5.2, it does not perform as well in the sign prediction tasks.

6. CONCLUSIONS AND SUMMARY

This paper presents a *Troll-Trust* model for ranking in signed networks. One of the interesting aspects of the model is that there is a clear semantic interpretation of the ranking values in terms of the trust probabilities. Such a semantic interpretation provides a model which is more clearly rooted in the dynamics of such signed networks. This is also reflected in the fact that our model provides predictions of high quality. We also develop a personalized version of the ranks, which can be used for other applications such as link prediction. Our experimental results show that the *Troll-Trust* model provides more accurate results than competing methods for the sign prediction tasks.

7. ACKNOWLEDGEMENT

Research was sponsored by the Army Research Laboratory and was accomplished under Cooperative Agreement Number W911NF-09-2-0053. The views and conclusions contained in this document are those of the authors and should not be interpreted as representing the official policies, either expressed or implied, of the Army Research Laboratory or the U.S. Government. The U.S. Government is authorized to reproduce and distribute reprints for Government purposes notwithstanding any copyright notation here on.

8. REFERENCES

[1] C. Aggarwal Social network data analytics. *Springer*, 2011.

[2] S. Banach. Sur les opérations dans les ensembles abstraits et leur application aux équations intégrales. *Fund. Math*, 3(1):133–181, 1922.

[3] S. Brin, and L. Page. The anatomy of a large-scale hypertextual Web search engine. *Computer networks and ISDN systems*, 30(1), pp. 107–117, 1998.

[4] K. Y. Chiang, C. J. Hsieh, N. Natarajan, I. S., Dhillon, and A. Tewari. Prediction and clustering in signed networks: a local to global perspective. *The Journal of Machine Learning Research*, 15(1), pp. 1177–1213, 2014.

[5] Ramanthan Guha, Ravi Kumar, Prabhakar Raghavan, and Andrew Tomkins. Propagation of trust and distrust. In *Proceedings of the 13th international conference on World Wide Web*, pages 403–412. ACM, 2004.

[6] W. Cukierski, B. Hamner, and B. Yang. Graph-based features for supervised link prediction. In *International Joint Conference on Neural Networks (IJCNN)*, pp. 1237–1244, 2011.

[7] M. Jamali and M. Ester. TrustWalker: A random-walk model for combining trust-based and item-based recommendation. *ACM KDD Conference*, pp. 397–406, 2009.

[8] S. Kamvar, M. Schlosser, and H. Garcia-Molina. The eigentrust algorithm for reputation management in P2P networks. *World Wide Web Conference*, pp. 640–651, 2003.

[9] C. de Kerchove and P. V. Dooren. The PageTrust algorithm: how to rank web pages when negative links are allowed? *SIAM Conference on Data Mining*, pp. 346–352, 2008.

[10] J. M. Kleinberg, Authoritative Sources in a Hyperlinked Environment, *Journal of the ACM*, 46(5), pp. 604–632, 1999.

[11] J. Kunegis, S. Schmidt, A. Lommatzsch, J. Lerner, E. W. De Luca, and S. Albayrak. Spectral analysis of signed graphs for clustering, prediction and visualization. *SIAM Conference on Data Mining*, 2010.

[12] J. Kunegis, A. Lommatzsch, and C. Bauckhage. The slashdot zoo: mining a social network with negative edges. *World Wide Web Conference*, pp. 741–750, 2009.

[13] J. Leskovec, D. Huttenlocher, and J. Kleinberg. Predicting positive and negative links in online social networks. *World Wide Web Conference*, pp. 641–650, 2010.

[14] J. Leskovec, D. Huttenlocher, and J. Kleinberg. Signed networks in social media. *SIGCHI Conference on Human Factors in Computing Systems*, pp. 1361–1370, 2010.

[15] D. Liben-Nowell and J. Kleinberg. The link-prediction problem for social networks. *Journal of the American society for information science and technology*, 58(7), pp. 1019–1031, 2007.

[16] A. Mishra and A. Bhattacharya. Finding the bias and prestige of nodes in networks based on trust scores. *Proceedings of the 20th international conference on World Wide Web*, pp. 567–576, 2011.

[17] S. Rendle, C. Freudenthaler, Z. Gantner, and L. Schmidt-Thieme. BPR: Bayesian personalized ranking from implicit feedback. In *Uncertainty in Artificial Intelligence (UAI)*, pp. 452–461, 2009.

[18] M. Shahriari and M. Jalili. Ranking nodes in signed social networks, *Social Network Analysis and Mining*, 4:172, 2014.

[19] P. Symeonidis, E. Tiakas, and Y. Manolopoulos. Transitive node similarity for link prediction in social networks with positive and negative links. *ACM Conference on Recommender Systems*, pp. 183–190, 2010.

[20] J. Tang, S. Chang, C. Aggarwal, and H. Liu. Negative link prediction in social media, *WSDM Conference*, 2015.

[21] V. Traag, Y. Nesterov, P. van Dooren. Exponential Ranking: taking into account negative links. *Social Informatics*, 6430, pp. 192–202, 2010.

[22] H. Wang, X. He, M.-W. Chang, Y. Song, R. W. White, and W. Chu. Personalized ranking model adaptation for web search. In *ACM SIGIR Conference*, pp. 323–332, 2013.

[23] T. Zhang, H. Jiang, Z. Bao, and Y. Zhang. Characterization and edge sign prediction in signed networks. *Journal of Industrial and Intelligent Information* Vol, 1(1), 2013.

[24] K. Zolfaghar and A. Aghaie. Mining trust and distrust relationships in social web applications. In *Intelligent Computer Communication and Processing Conference(ICCP)*, pp. 73–80, 2010.

Multileave Gradient Descent for Fast Online Learning to Rank

Anne Schuth[†]
a.g.schuth@uva.nl

Harrie Oosterhuis[†]
harrie.oosterhuis@student.uva.nl

Shimon Whiteson[†]
shimon.whiteson@cs.ox.ac.uk

Maarten de Rijke[†]
derijke@uva.nl

[†] University of Amsterdam, Amsterdam, The Netherlands
[‡] University of Oxford, Oxford, United Kingdom

ABSTRACT

Modern search systems are based on dozens or even hundreds of ranking features. The *dueling bandit gradient descent* (DBGD) algorithm has been shown to effectively learn combinations of these features solely from user interactions. DBGD explores the search space by comparing a possibly improved ranker to the current production ranker. To this end, it uses *interleaved comparison methods*, which can infer with high sensitivity a preference between two rankings based only on interaction data. A limiting factor is that it can compare only to a single exploratory ranker.

We propose an online learning to rank algorithm called *multileave gradient descent* (MGD) that extends DBGD to learn from so-called *multileaved comparison methods* that can compare a set of rankings instead of merely a pair. We show experimentally that MGD allows for better selection of candidates than DBGD without the need for more comparisons involving users. An important implication of our results is that orders of magnitude less user interaction data is required to find good rankers when multileaved comparisons are used within online learning to rank. Hence, fewer users need to be exposed to possibly inferior rankers and our method allows search engines to adapt more quickly to changes in user preferences.

Categories and Subject Descriptors

H.3 [**Information Storage and Retrieval**]: H.3.3 Information Search and Retrieval

Keywords

Information retrieval; Learning to rank; Interleaved comparisons; Multileaved comparisons

1. INTRODUCTION

Modern search engines base their rankings on combinations of dozens or even hundreds of features. *Learning to rank*, i.e., finding an optimal combination of features, is an active area of research.

WSDM 2016, February 22 - 25, 2016, San Francisco, CA, USA.

ACM 978-1-4503-3716-8/16/02 ...$15.00.
DOI: http://dx.doi.org/10.1145/2835776.2835804.

Traditionally, learning was done *offline* by optimizing for performance on a training set consisting of queries and relevance assessments produced by human assessors. However, such datasets are time consuming and expensive to produce. Moreover, these assessments are not always in line with actual user preferences [23]. And since data of users interacting with a search engine are often readily available, research is focussing more on learning *online* instead [10, 13, 22, 31]. Online learning to rank methods optimize combinations of rankers while interacting with users of a search engine. While interacting with the search engine, users leave a trace of interaction data, e.g., query reformulations, mouse movements, and clicks, that can be used to infer preferences. Clicks have proven to be a valuable source of information when interpreted as a preference between either rankings [22] or documents [13]. In particular, when clicks are interpreted using interleaved comparison methods, they can reliably infer preferences between a pair of rankers [4, 13, 14].

Dueling bandit gradient descent (DBGD) [31] is an online learning to rank algorithm that learns from these interleaved comparisons. It uses the inferred preferences to estimate a gradient, which is followed to find a locally optimal ranker. At every learning step, DBGD estimates this gradient with respect to a *single* exploratory ranker and updates its solution if the exploratory ranker seems better. Exploring *more than one* ranker before updating towards a promising one could lead to finding a better ranker using fewer updates. However, when using interleaved comparisons, this would be too costly, since it would require pairwise comparisons involving users between all exploratory rankers. Instead, we propose to learn from comparisons of multiple rankers at once, using a single user interaction. In this way, our proposed method, *multileave gradient descent* (MGD), aims to speed up online learning to rank.

We propose two variants of MGD that differ in how they estimate the gradient. In MGD *winner takes all* (MGD-W), the gradient is estimated using one ranker randomly sampled from those who won the multileaved comparison. In MGD *mean winner* (MGD-M), the gradient is estimated using the mean of all winning rankers.

In this paper, we answer the following research questions.

RQ1 Can MGD learn faster from user feedback (i.e., using fewer clicks) than DBGD does?

RQ2 Does MGD find a better local optimum than DBGD?

RQ3 Which update approach, MGD-W or MGD-M, maximizes learning speed? Which finds a better local optimum?

Our contributions are:

- Two approaches, MGD-W and MGD-M, to using multileaved comparison outcomes in an online learning to rank method.

- Extensive empirical validation of our new methods via experiments on nine learning to rank datasets, showing that MGD-W and MGD-M outperform the state of the art in online learning to rank.

In Section 2 we discuss related work; Section 3 includes a detailed description of interleaving and multileaving methods and of DBGD, which are three elements that play a central role in this paper. In Section 4 we introduce multileave gradient descent. In Section 5 we detail our experimental setup. Section 6 provides both results and their analysis. We conclude in Section 7.

2. RELATED WORK

Related work for this paper comes in two areas. First, there are learning to rank methods in Section 2.1. Particularly important for this paper is the *dueling bandit gradient descent* (DBGD) method, which is therefore described in more detail in Section 3.2. Second, there are evaluation methods in Section 2.2, of which the interleaving and multileaving methods play a crucial role in this paper. Therefore, these are described in more detail in Section 3.1.

2.1 Online learning to rank

Learning to rank comes in online and offline variants. Offline learning to rank methods [19] can be supervised and semi-supervised [29]. Offline learning methods suffer from drawback of requiring labeled datasets, which are expensive to produce and the models learned do not necessarily align with user satisfaction [23].

Our focus is on online learning to rank methods that learn from online evaluation methods, based on users' interactions with IR systems [10, 31], without requiring annotated datasets. One can formulate the online learning to rank for IR problem as a *reinforcement learning* (RL) problem. The problem can be modeled as a contextual bandit problem that assumes that consecutive queries are independent of each other [18, 27]. A crucial difference between typical RL problems and the application to IR is that in the IR scenario the reward cannot directly be observed. Instead, user interactions with an IR system can be interpreted as a biased and noisy preference for either rankings [22] or documents [13].

Many methods for online learning to rank have been proposed. Hofmann et al. [10] explore learning from pairwise document preference while most methods are based on the listwise learning paradigm where preferences between rankers are inferred from clicks. Such pairwise preferences can come from interleaving methods as discussed in Sections 2.2 and 3.1. One influential learning to rank method is *dueling bandit gradient descent* (DBGD) [31], which is extended upon in this paper and therefore explained in more detail in Section 3.2. DBGD implements a stochastic gradient descent method to find the best ranker in an infinite space of rankers. This algorithm has been extended before by Hofmann et al. [11] such that it would reuse historical interaction data and not just live user interactions. Alternative methods are based on the k-armed bandit formulation by [32] and assume a finite space of possible rankers, the best of which needs to be found.

2.2 Evaluation for information retrieval

Evaluation has always been an integral part of information retrieval (IR) research. IR evaluation comes in three flavors: offline, in the form of users studies, and online.

Firstly, there is Cranfield-style evaluation, as introduced by Cleverdon et al. [5], a form of evaluation we refer to as *offline*. This type of evaluation is based on test collections that consist of queries, documents, and relevance assessments of these documents with respect to these queries. Test collections can be used to evaluate systems by computing offline evaluation metrics such as MAP, NDCG, ERR [23]. It forms the basis of most TREC-style evaluation benchmarks [30]. A major advantage of offline evaluation is the repeatability of experiments and the ease of evaluation of many and new rankers. However, relevance assessments are typically produced by trained human judges. This is not only time consuming and expensive, it is also not entirely clear how useful such relevance assessments really are as agreement with actual users' preferences is not necessarily high [23]. Several approaches to address the high costs of producing relevance assessments have been described [3, 24]; even further steps are taken in [1, 2], with proposals for automatically created test collections.

A second form of evaluation is through *user studies*. In this type of studies, users and their interaction behavior are studied in a lab setting [16]. This makes such evaluations even more expensive than offline evaluation, specifically because experiments are not repeatable and do not scale up.

Thirdly, *online evaluation* exploits the interactions of real users with a live search engine [17]. Online evaluation comes in several dominant forms. In *A/B testing* two rankers are shown to two distinct groups of users. For each group, click metrics are computed and the outcomes are compared to determine which ranker is better. *Interleaved comparison methods* [4, 13, 14] have been shown to be highly sensitive, much more so than A/B metrics [4, 22], meaning that less interaction data are required to detect differences between rankers. Interleaved comparison methods take as input two rankings and produce an interleaved result list. The interleaved list is shown to users and interactions with interleaved lists are interpreted so as to determine which of the two input rankers wins the comparison. Several interleaving methods exist. *Balanced interleave* (BI) [15] starts by randomly selecting a ranker to start with. Then, alternating, documents that have not been picked are picked from the two input rankings. BI can result in a preference for a ranker irrespective of where a user clicks. This bias is corrected in *team draft interleave* (TDI) [22], which we discuss in Section 3.1. More recent methods include *document constraints* (DC) [7] and *probabilistic interleave* (PI) [9]. A major advantage of PI is that it can also infer preferences between rankers that were not originally interleaved. This allows one to learn from historical interaction data [11]. However, PI risks showing users poor rankings. This shortcoming was addressed in *optimized interleave* (OI) [21] by restricting the allowed interleavings to only those that are a union of prefixes of the two input rankings.

Recently, interleaving methods have been extended to *multileaving* methods [26] that allow for comparisons of more than two rankers at once. In particular, Schuth et al. [26] extend TDI to *team draft multileave* (TDM) and OI to *optimized multileave* (OM). TDM forms part of our motivation and is discussed in detail in Section 3.1.

Our work is different from the work mentioned above in that our online learning to rank methods are the first to learn from multileaving comparison feedback. So far, online learning to rank methods only learned from pairwise preferences between either documents or rankers. Our methods are the first to learn from n-way preferences between rankers.

3. BACKGROUND

We describe in more detail two types of related work on which our work depends: interleaved and multileaved comparison methods (Section 3.1) and dueling bandit gradient descent (DBGD; Section 3.2).

3.1 Interleaving and multileaving

Interleaved comparison methods are highly sensitive online evaluation methods for information retrieval systems [4, 13, 14]. These methods combine the documents from a pair of rankings into a single document list and present this combined list to the user. The user's interaction with this result list is then used to infer a preference for one of the input rankings. It was shown that, typically, this way of comparing two rankers requires one to two orders of magnitude less data when compared to A/B testing [4]. Multileaved comparison methods [26] allow for more than two rankers to be compared using a similar methodology, reducing the amount of interaction data required even further.

Several interleaving methods have been proposed over the years, see Section 2. We build upon *team draft interleave* (TDI) [22] and an extended version called *team draft multileave* (TDM) [26].

TDI works as follows. When a user enters a query into a search engine, the query is passed to the two rankers to be compared. The rankings these rankers produce are then interleaved in a process analogous to picking teams for a friendly team-sport match. The documents are players and there are two teams representing the two rankers. Each team has a preference ordering over players, corresponding to the ranking over documents. In each round, the teams take turns picking their most preferred, still available player. Which teams chooses first is determined randomly. Selected players are appended to the interleaved list, and the team they are assigned to is recorded.[1] This interleaved list is shown to the user, who may click on some documents in this list. The clicked documents give credit to the team to which they belong. The team, or ranker, that receives the most credit wins the comparison. If n rankers must be compared, an interleaving method such as TDI needs $n \cdot (n-1)$ queries to determine how they all relate to each other.

By contrast, for TDM, a user's query is passed to all n rankers at once. These rankers each produce their rankings, which are integrated into a single ranking using a team selection process similar to that of TDI. However, there now are n teams that take turns.[2] This implies that, in case n is larger than the number of slots in the interleaved list, some teams may not be represented. Inferring which teams win is now done by counting the number of clicked documents for each team. The result is a partial ordering over the n rankers. Thus, only a single query, instead of $n \cdot (n-1)$ queries, is needed to compare all n rankers. Of course, many queries are still needed for a *reliable* comparison, and potentially more so than with TDI. However, it was shown that this tradeoff can be quite favorable for TDM [26]. Note that TDM reduces to TDI for $n = 1$.

3.2 Dueling bandit gradient descent

Dueling bandit gradient descent (DBGD) [31] is an online learning to rank method that learns from user feedback in the form of clicks. In particular, DBGD learns from a *relative* interpretation of this feedback produced by, e.g., TDI (see Section 3.1). DBGD, shown in Algorithm 1, assumes that rankers can be represented by weight vectors, starting of with a randomly initialised weight vector $\mathbf{w}_0^0$, referred to as the *current best ranker*. For each query that is issued, on line 6, an exploratory *candidate ranker* $\mathbf{w}_t^1$ is created by slightly perturbing the weight vector of the current best ranker. Both the current best ranker and the candidate ranker create their rankings of documents for the issued query. These two rankings are interleaved using, e.g., TDI, on line 8. Then, on line 9 this interleaving is shown to the user who issued the query and clicks are observed. The interactions of this user with the interleaving are interpreted by the interleaving method on line 10 to determine who won the comparison. If the candidate won, the weight vector of the current best ranker is updated with an α step towards the weight vector of the candidate ranker. If not, the weight vector is not

Algorithm 1 Dueling Bandit Gradient Descent (DBGD).

1: **Input**: α, δ, $\mathbf{w}_0^0$
2: **for** $t \leftarrow 1..\infty$ **do**
3: $\quad q_t \leftarrow receive\_query(t)$ *// obtain a query from a user*
4: $\quad \mathbf{l}_0 \leftarrow generate\_list(\mathbf{w}_t^0, q_t)$ *// ranking of current best*
5: $\quad \mathbf{u}_t^1 \leftarrow sample\_unit\_vector()$
6: $\quad \mathbf{w}_t^1 \leftarrow \mathbf{w}_t^0 + \delta \mathbf{u}_t^1$ *// create a candidate ranker*
7: $\quad \mathbf{l}_1 \leftarrow generate\_list(\mathbf{w}_t^1, q_t)$ *// exploratory ranking*
8: $\quad \mathbf{m}_t, \mathbf{t}_t \leftarrow TDI\_interleave(\mathbf{l})$ *// interleaving and teams*
9: $\quad \mathbf{c}_t \leftarrow receive\_clicks(\mathbf{m}_t)$ *// show interleaving to the user*
10: $\quad \mathbf{b}_t \leftarrow TDI\_infer(\mathbf{t}_t, \mathbf{c}_t)$ *// set of winning candidates*
11: $\quad$ **if** $\mathbf{w}_t^0 \in \mathbf{b}_t$ **then**
12: $\qquad \mathbf{w}_{t+1}^0 \leftarrow \mathbf{w}_t^0$ *// if current best wins or ties, no update*
13: $\quad$ **else**
14: $\qquad \mathbf{w}_{t+1}^0 \leftarrow \mathbf{w}_t^0 + \alpha \mathbf{u}_t^1$ *// update α step towards candidate*

Algorithm 2 Multileave Gradient Descent (MGD).

1: **Input**: n, α, δ, $\mathbf{w}_0^0$, $update(\mathbf{w}, \alpha, \{\mathbf{b}\}, \{\mathbf{u}\})$
2: **for** $t \leftarrow 1..\infty$ **do**
3: $\quad q_t \leftarrow receive\_query(t)$ *// obtain a query from a user*
4: $\quad \mathbf{l}_0 \leftarrow generate\_list(\mathbf{w}_t^0, q_t)$ *// ranking of current best*
5: $\quad$ **for** $i \leftarrow 1...n$ **do**
6: $\qquad \mathbf{u}_t^i \leftarrow sample\_unit\_vector()$
7: $\qquad \mathbf{w}_t^i \leftarrow \mathbf{w}_t^0 + \delta \mathbf{u}_t^i$ *// create a candidate ranker*
8: $\qquad \mathbf{l}_t^i \leftarrow generate\_list(\mathbf{w}_t^i, q_t)$ *// exploratory ranking*
9: $\quad \mathbf{m}_t, \mathbf{t}_t \leftarrow TDM\_multileave(\mathbf{l}_t)$ *// multileaving and teams*
10: $\quad \mathbf{c}_t \leftarrow receive\_clicks(\mathbf{m}_t)$ *// show multileaving to the user*
11: $\quad \mathbf{b}_t \leftarrow TDM\_infer(\mathbf{t}_t, \mathbf{c}_t)$ *// set of winning candidates*
12: $\quad$ **if** $\mathbf{w}_t^0 \in \mathbf{b}_t$ **then**
13: $\qquad \mathbf{w}_{t+1}^0 \leftarrow \mathbf{w}_t^0$ *// if current best among winners, no update*
14: $\quad$ **else**
15: $\qquad \mathbf{w}_{t+1}^0 \leftarrow update(\mathbf{w}_t^0, \alpha, \mathbf{b}_t, \mathbf{u}_t)$ *// Algorithm 3 or 4*

updated. This process repeats indefinitely, yielding a continuously adaptive system.

4. MULTILEAVE GRADIENT DESCENT

In this section, we propose a new algorithm called *multileave gradient descent* (MGD).

4.1 Extending DBGD with multileaving

MGD is shown in Algorithm 2. As in DBGD, MGD learns from online feedback and uses a *current best ranker*, which is updated based on user feedback. For each query, MGD uses the *current best ranker* to create a ranking. Subsequently, on lines 5 through 8, n exploratory candidate rankers are generated along with their corresponding rankings. Unlike DBGD, which is restricted to a single candidate ranker during comparison, MGD can handle multiple candidate rankers because it uses multileaving, which on line 9 creates a single document list out of the n rankings. After observing user clicks on this ranker, on line 10, a set of rankers that won the comparison is inferred. In our case, TDM is used and thus the set of winners contains the candidate(s) that received the greatest number of clicks. If the *current best ranker* is among the winners, then no candidate is considered to be better and no update is performed. However, if not, the *current best ranker* is updated accordingly on line 15, using one of two update methods described in Section 4.2. In this way, MGD incrementally improves the *current best ranker*.

By comparing multiple candidates at each iteration the probability of finding a better candidate ranker than the current best is expected to increase. Furthermore, adding more rankers to the comparison increases the expected value of the resulting ranker, since the candi-

[1] For documents belonging to a prefix that the two input rankings have in common, no teams are assigned to increase sensitivity [4].
[2] As in TDI, documents belonging to a prefix that is common to all n rankings are not assigned to teams.

Algorithm 3 MGD update function: winner takes all (MGD-W).

Input: $\mathbf{w}, \alpha, \mathbf{b}, \mathbf{u}$ // *in* $\mathbf{b}$ *are only winners*
$\mathbf{b}^j \leftarrow pick\_random\_uniformly(\mathbf{b})$
return $\mathbf{w} + \alpha \mathbf{u}^j$

Algorithm 4 MGD update function: mean winner (MGD-M).

Input: $\mathbf{w}, \alpha, \mathbf{b}, \mathbf{u}$ // *in* $\mathbf{b}$ *are only winners*
return $\mathbf{w} + \alpha \frac{1}{|\mathbf{u}|} \sum_{\mathbf{b}^j \in \mathbf{b}} \mathbf{u}^j$

date rankers will also compete with each other. Correspondingly, the intuition behind MGD is that the use of multileaving improves the learning speed compared to DBGD. It should be noted, though, that the quality of the document list presented to the user may decrease: as MGD is more exploratory than DBGD, i.e., multileaving lets more candidate rankers add documents to the list, thus the *current best ranker* is exploited less than in the DBGD case.

4.2 Multileave approaches to gradient descent

DBGD generates each candidate ranker by sampling a unit sphere uniformly and adding the resulting unit vector to the *current best ranker*. For the MGD approaches in this paper this procedure was repeated n times to create a set of n candidate rankers. However, this approach might have the drawback that it can produce identical or very similar candidate rankers. Thus it is possible that during an iteration identical candidates are compared, potentially compromising the exploratory benefits of using MGB. But since the dimensionality of the feature space is expected to be much greater than the number of candidates, it is most unlikely the set contains similar rankers.

The simple update method of DBGD is only applicable to a single winning candidate ranker. Conversely, MGD requires an approach to infer an update from a winning set of candidate rankers. We introduce two approaches for performing updates: MGD *winner takes all* (MGD-W) and MGD *mean winner* (MGD-M) displayed in Algorithm 3 and 4 respectively. MGD-W picks a random candidate ranker out of the set of winners and performs the DBGD update as if it were the only winner. This has the disadvantage that all other winning candidates are discarded, but it has the advantage that the update is performed towards a candidate that was part of the comparison. MGD-M, on the other hand, takes the mean of the winning candidate rankers and performs the DBGD update as if the mean was the only winner. In contrast with MGD-W, MGD-M uses all the winning candidates in its update. However, the update is performed towards the mean of the winning rankers, thereby assuming that the mean of all winners is preferred over the *current best ranker*, despite the two not having been directly compared. Thus, updates could actually harm the current best ranker. However, this risk also exists for MGD-W since user interaction is expected to contain noise and can result in poor candidate ranker winning a comparison. Note that both methods reduce to DGBD for $n = 1$.

An alternative way of comparing many candidate rankers without having to do many comparisons with users involved, is DBGD with *candidate pre-selection* (CPS) [11]. However, this method reuses historical interaction data which it requires to be generated stochastically using potentially unsafe rankings [21]. MGD is a new way of comparing candidates that does not have this drawback.

5. EXPERIMENTS

In this section, we detail our experiments which are designed to answer the research questions posed in Section 1.[3] We are interested in whether and how our newly introduced algorithm MGD (RQ1) learns faster than DBGD; (RQ2) converges to a better optimum compared to DBGD; and (RQ3) how the two variants MGD-W and MGD-M compare to each other.

[3]All our experimental code is open source and available at `https://bitbucket.org/ilps/lerot` [25].

Table 1: Instantiations of CCM [6] as used in our experiments.

		$P(click = 1\|R)$			$P(stop = 1\|R)$		
Relevance grade R		0	1	2	0	1	2
perfect	(per)	0.0	0.5	1.0	0.0	0.0	0.0
navigational	(nav)	0.05	0.5	0.95	0.2	0.5	0.9
informational	(inf)	0.4	0.7	0.9	0.1	0.3	0.5
almost random	(a.ra)	0.4	0.5	0.6	0.5	0.5	0.5

All our experiments assume a stream of independent queries coming from users interacting with the system we are training. Users are presented with a results list in response to their query and may or may not interact with the list by clicking on one or more documents. The queries come from static datasets (Section 5.1) and the clicks from a click model (Section 5.2). In Section 5.3 we describe the experiments we run. Our evaluation measures are described in Section 5.4.

5.1 Datasets

We use nine learning to rank datasets that are distributed as LETOR 3.0 and 4.0 [20]. The datasets each consist of (1) queries, only represented by their identifier, (2) manual relevance assessments for documents with respect to these queries, and (3) documents represented as feature vectors, again, with respect to each query. Feature vectors consist of 45, 46, or 64 features encoding ranking models such as TF.IDF, BM25, Language Modeling, PageRank, and HITS on different parts of the documents. All the datasets come split into 5 folds, which we use for 5-fold cross validation. Each dataset encodes a search task. Most tasks come from TREC Web Tracks between 2003 and 2008. The only exception is the *OHSUMED* dataset with 106 queries which comes from a query log of the search engine on the MedLine abstract database. *HP2003*, *HP2004*, *NP2003*, and *NP2004* all implement navigational tasks which are homepage finding and named-page finding, respectively; both *TD2003* and *TD2004* implement topic distillation tasks which is an informational task. *HP2003, HP2004, NP2003, NP2004, TD2003* and *TD2004* contain documents from the .GOV collection which was crawled from the .gov domain; each contains between 50 and 150 queries and about 1,000 judged documents per query. The last two datasets, *MQ2007* and *MQ2008*, are more recent and use the .GOV2 collection; they contain more queries, 1700 and 800 respectively, but far fewer assessments per query. *OHSUMED*, *MQ2007*, and *MQ2008* have graded relevance judgments from 0, not relevant, to 2, highly relevant. The other datasets have binary relevance labels with grade 0 for not relevant and grade 2 for relevant.

5.2 Simulating clicks

We use the setup described by Hofmann [8] to simulate user interactions. In their setup, clicks are produced based on a *cascade click model* (CCM) [6]. This model explains behavior of web search users as follows. Users are assumed to start examining results lists from the first document in the list and then work their way down the list. For each document they encounter, users decide whether it warrants a click, which is modeled as $P(click = 1|R)$, a click probability conditioned on the human generated relevance label R. After clicking, the user's information need may either be satisfied or they continue down the rank list. In CCM, this is modeled with $P(stop = 1|R)$, the probability of stopping conditioned on the relevance label R.

In Table 1, we first list the three instantiations of CCM that we use in all our experiments. These three instantiations model a *perfect* user that clicks on all highly relevant and only on relevant documents. Then, a *navigational* instantiation encoding a navigational task where a user is mostly looking for a single highly relevant document. And lastly, an *informational* instantiation that models a user who would typically click on several documents, less dependent on their relevance. These three models have increasing levels of noise, as less and less is determined by the relevance labels of documents. Then, we use the *almost random* instantiation only for some of our experiments to test what happens when feedback becomes extremely noisy. Note that the datasets that only have binary relevance use instantiations for the lowest and highest relevance labels (0 and 2) in Table 1.

5.3 Experimental runs

To evaluate the effect of the number of candidates n that are being contrasted in a multileave experiment, both flavors of multileave gradient descent, MGD-W and MGD-M, are run with $n \in \{1, 2, 6, 9, 20\}$. We included $n = 9$ to capture the case were all documents in the top top $\kappa = 10$ come from different rankers. We write MGD-W-n (MGD-M-n) to indicate settings in which we run MGD-W (MGD-M) with n candidates.

In our experiments we contrast the performance of MGD-W and MGD-M with each other as well as with the DBGD baseline. A run with $n = 1$ is included to verify wether this setting has no significant difference with the baseline. The bulk of our experiments consist of 1,000 iterations (i.e., simulated user impressions) each and is run 25 times on each fold resulting in 125 runs over each dataset. One experiment is run with 100,000 query impressions and the same number of repetitions. In total, our results are based on over 86M simulated query impressions.

The parameters of the MGD algorithm are set according to the current standard for DBGD [31]. Accordingly, the candidates were generated with $\delta = 1$, updates for DBGD were performed with $\alpha = 0.01$, and zeros used for initialization of $\mathbf{w}_0^0$. For MGD we increased the learning rate to $\alpha = 0.03$ by tuning it on *NP2003*, see Section 6.4.2.

5.4 Evaluation

To assess performance, NDCG [12] is computed on held-out data. We use the top $\kappa = 10$ for simulating clicks and computing the NDCG:

$$NDCG = \sum_{i=1}^{\kappa} \frac{2^{rel(\mathbf{r}[i])-1}}{log_2(i+1)} iNDCG^{-1}.$$

This metric calculates the gain over relevance labels $rel(\mathbf{r}[i])$ for each document, which is then normalized by the maximal NDCG possible, the ideal NDCG (iNDCG). *Offline* performance is determined by computing the average NDCG score of the *current best ranker* over a held-out set. Furthermore, since the user experience with MGD may be inferior to the existing DBGD algorithm, *online* performance is also assessed, by computing the cumulative NDCG over the results shown to the user. For online performance, a discount factor of $\gamma = 0.995$ is used [8, 28]. This factor ensures that impressions beyond a horizon of 1,000 impressions have an impact of less than 1%. To verify whether differences are statistically significantly different, a two tailed Student's t-test is used.

6. RESULTS AND ANALYSIS

In this section we present the results of our experiments and answer the research questions posed in Section 1. Furthermore, in Section 6.4, we investigate the effect of n, the number of candidates, and α, the learning rate.

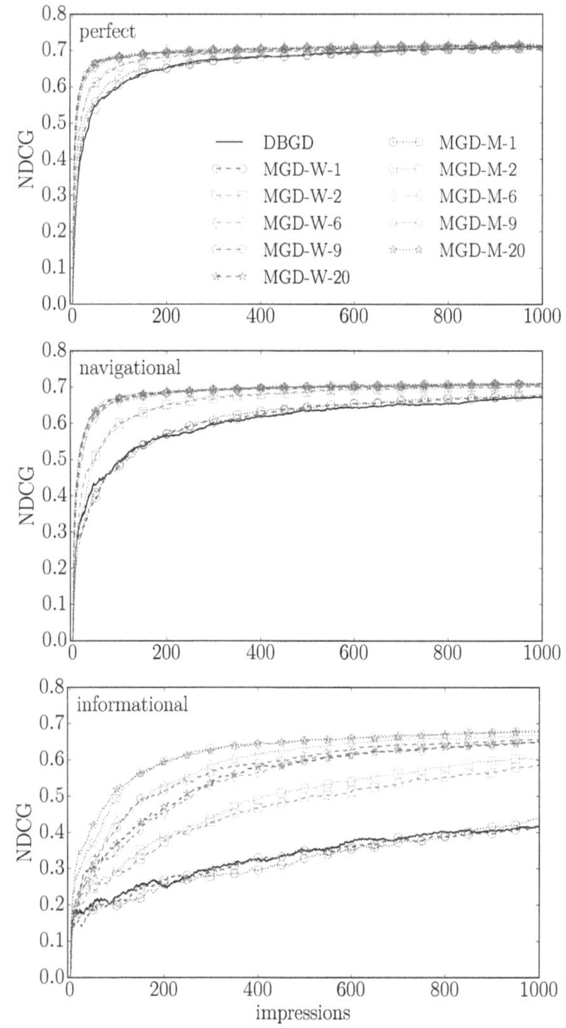

Figure 1: Offline performance (NDCG) on MGD-W and MGD-M with varying number of candidates compared to DBGD on *NP2003* dataset for the *perfect*, *navigational* and *informational* click model.

6.1 Learning speed

We start by answering RQ1: whether MGD learns faster than DBGD. The plots in Figure 1 show how offline performance, measured as NDCG on a held-out fold, increases as the learning methods observe more queries. These plots are based only on queries from *NP2003* and are illustrative of performance on all other datasets. We see that when n, the number of candidates that are being multileaved, increases, offline performance of both MGD-M-n and MGD-W-n improves monotonically. Furthermore, systems with more candidates learn much faster. In the case of *perfect* feedback, there is less of an effect as there is less to gain over an already well performing baseline. But when the noise in user feedback increases, the advantage of MGD over DBGD becomes stronger. Interestingly, for $n = 20$, the MGD methods obtain an NDCG value on *informational* feedback that is close to the converged performance on *perfect* feedback. In other words, the inclusion of more candidates counters the noise introduced by the click model. In Table 2 we see the same effect for all datasets: generally, under *perfect* feedback converged performance does not change much; however, if the feedback is noisier, then the more candidates are added, the

Table 2: Offline score (NDCG) after 1,000 query impressions of each of the algorithms for the 3 instantiations of the CCM (see Table 1). Bold values indicate maximum performance per dataset and click model. Statistically significant improvements (losses) over the DBGD baseline are indicated by △ ($p < 0.05$) and ▲ ($p < 0.01$) (▽ and ▼). We show the standard deviation between brackets.

		HP2003	NP2003	TD2003	HP2004	NP2004	TD2004	MQ2007	MQ2008	OHSUMED
perfect	**DBGD**	0.766 (0.06)	0.710 (0.05)	0.299 (0.09)	0.730 (0.07)	0.715 (0.08)	0.303 (0.03)	0.381 (0.03)	0.476 (0.04)	0.443 (0.05)
	MGD-W-2	0.771 (0.06)	0.705 (0.05)	0.314 (0.08)	0.731 (0.06)	0.726 (0.07)	0.306 (0.03)	0.392 (0.02) ▲	0.480 (0.04)	0.445 (0.05)
	MGD-W-4	0.771 (0.06)	0.712 (0.05)	0.318 (0.08)	0.742 (0.06)	**0.732** (0.07)	0.310 (0.04)	0.396 (0.02) ▲	0.481 (0.04)	**0.447** (0.05)
	MGD-W-6	0.778 (0.06)	0.712 (0.05)	0.314 (0.08)	0.745 (0.06)	0.725 (0.07)	0.308 (0.04)	0.398 (0.02) ▲	0.479 (0.04)	0.444 (0.05)
	MGD-W-9	0.774 (0.06)	0.713 (0.05)	0.314 (0.07)	0.744 (0.06)	0.725 (0.07)	0.311 (0.04)	0.400 (0.02) ▲	0.481 (0.04)	0.430 (0.04) ▽
	MGD-W-20	0.776 (0.06)	0.710 (0.05)	0.314 (0.07)	**0.749** (0.06) △	0.726 (0.07)	0.308 (0.04)	0.396 (0.02) ▲	0.480 (0.04)	0.438 (0.05)
	MGD-M-2	0.771 (0.07)	0.712 (0.05)	0.312 (0.08)	0.743 (0.06)	0.730 (0.08)	0.311 (0.04)	0.392 (0.02) ▲	0.480 (0.04)	0.443 (0.05)
	MGD-M-4	0.777 (0.07)	0.711 (0.05)	0.317 (0.07)	0.742 (0.07)	0.729 (0.07)	0.315 (0.04) ▲	0.400 (0.02) ▲	0.482 (0.04)	**0.447** (0.05)
	MGD-M-6	0.779 (0.06)	**0.716** (0.04)	0.320 (0.07)	0.747 (0.06) △	0.725 (0.07)	0.312 (0.04) △	0.402 (0.02) ▲	0.481 (0.04)	**0.447** (0.05)
	MGD-M-9	**0.780** (0.06)	0.714 (0.05)	**0.322** (0.07) △	0.747 (0.06) △	0.726 (0.07)	0.311 (0.04)	0.406 (0.02) ▲	**0.484** (0.04)	0.437 (0.04)
	MGD-M-20	0.777 (0.06)	0.714 (0.05)	0.321 (0.07) △	0.747 (0.06) △	0.724 (0.08)	**0.316** (0.04) ▲	**0.408** (0.02) ▲	**0.484** (0.04)	0.446 (0.04)
navigational	**DBGD**	0.725 (0.07)	0.672 (0.06)	0.281 (0.09)	0.676 (0.08)	0.693 (0.08)	0.281 (0.03)	0.370 (0.03)	0.460 (0.04)	0.433 (0.06)
	MGD-W-2	0.766 (0.06) ▲	0.702 (0.05) ▲	0.306 (0.09) △	0.732 (0.06) ▲	0.715 (0.08) △	0.303 (0.03) ▲	0.372 (0.03)	0.466 (0.04)	**0.438** (0.05)
	MGD-W-4	0.769 (0.06) ▲	0.708 (0.05) ▲	0.314 (0.08) ▲	0.735 (0.06) ▲	0.720 (0.08) ▲	**0.307** (0.04) ▲	0.380 (0.02) ▲	0.469 (0.04)	0.437 (0.04)
	MGD-W-6	**0.772** (0.06) ▲	0.705 (0.05) ▲	0.312 (0.08) ▲	0.738 (0.06) ▲	0.721 (0.08) ▲	0.304 (0.04) ▲	0.382 (0.02) ▲	0.468 (0.04)	0.431 (0.05)
	MGD-W-9	0.771 (0.06) ▲	0.708 (0.05) ▲	0.304 (0.07) △	0.738 (0.06) ▲	**0.725** (0.08) ▲	0.304 (0.04) ▲	0.388 (0.02) ▲	0.470 (0.04) △	0.431 (0.05)
	MGD-W-20	0.771 (0.06) ▲	0.710 (0.05) ▲	0.314 (0.07) ▲	0.738 (0.06) ▲	0.721 (0.07) ▲	0.304 (0.04) ▲	0.386 (0.03) ▲	0.470 (0.04)	0.432 (0.05)
	MGD-M-2	0.766 (0.06) ▲	0.703 (0.06) ▲	0.302 (0.08)	0.726 (0.06) ▲	0.717 (0.08) △	0.301 (0.04) ▲	0.376 (0.03)	0.467 (0.04)	0.435 (0.05)
	MGD-M-4	0.768 (0.06) ▲	0.705 (0.05) ▲	0.312 (0.08) ▲	0.738 (0.06) ▲	0.721 (0.07) ▲	0.305 (0.04) ▲	0.385 (0.02) ▲	0.468 (0.04)	0.435 (0.04)
	MGD-M-6	**0.772** (0.06) ▲	0.707 (0.05) ▲	0.309 (0.07) ▲	0.736 (0.07) ▲	0.723 (0.08) ▲	0.305 (0.04) ▲	0.387 (0.03) ▲	**0.473** (0.04) ▲	0.437 (0.05)
	MGD-M-9	0.771 (0.06) ▲	0.710 (0.05) ▲	0.317 (0.08) ▲	**0.741** (0.06) ▲	0.724 (0.07) ▲	0.302 (0.04) ▲	**0.391** (0.02) ▲	0.472 (0.04) △	0.436 (0.04)
	MGD-M-20	0.769 (0.06) ▲	**0.711** (0.04) ▲	**0.318** (0.08) ▲	**0.741** (0.06) ▲	0.720 (0.07) ▲	0.306 (0.04) ▲	0.390 (0.02) ▲	0.472 (0.04) △	0.437 (0.05)
informational	**DBGD**	0.460 (0.22)	0.418 (0.19)	0.167 (0.10)	0.401 (0.21)	0.489 (0.19)	0.197 (0.08)	0.323 (0.05)	0.419 (0.05)	0.407 (0.05)
	MGD-W-2	0.677 (0.11) ▲	0.585 (0.13) ▲	0.223 (0.10) ▲	0.625 (0.11) ▲	0.629 (0.11) ▲	0.233 (0.07) ▲	0.338 (0.04) △	0.427 (0.05)	0.418 (0.05)
	MGD-W-4	0.722 (0.07) ▲	0.636 (0.09) ▲	0.253 (0.09) ▲	0.667 (0.10) ▲	0.662 (0.09) ▲	0.258 (0.05) ▲	0.343 (0.04) ▲	0.440 (0.04) ▲	0.422 (0.05) △
	MGD-W-6	0.727 (0.06) ▲	0.652 (0.07) ▲	0.249 (0.09) ▲	0.674 (0.09) ▲	0.669 (0.10) ▲	0.272 (0.04) ▲	0.344 (0.04) ▲	0.441 (0.04) ▲	0.423 (0.05) △
	MGD-W-9	0.727 (0.06) ▲	0.656 (0.07) ▲	0.264 (0.10) ▲	0.679 (0.07) ▲	0.670 (0.09) ▲	0.259 (0.05) ▲	0.339 (0.04) ▲	0.434 (0.04) △	0.418 (0.06)
	MGD-W-20	0.729 (0.06) ▲	0.649 (0.06) ▲	0.252 (0.09) ▲	0.675 (0.09) ▲	0.664 (0.10) ▲	0.260 (0.05) ▲	0.341 (0.04) ▲	0.434 (0.05) △	0.415 (0.05)
	MGD-M-2	0.696 (0.09) ▲	0.606 (0.10) ▲	0.241 (0.09) ▲	0.634 (0.12) ▲	0.645 (0.12) ▲	0.246 (0.07) ▲	0.333 (0.04)	0.430 (0.05)	0.421 (0.05) △
	MGD-M-4	0.736 (0.06) ▲	0.659 (0.07) ▲	0.276 (0.09) ▲	0.685 (0.08) ▲	0.682 (0.09) ▲	0.271 (0.04) ▲	0.350 (0.03) ▲	0.443 (0.04) ▲	0.427 (0.05) ▲
	MGD-M-6	0.742 (0.06) ▲	0.667 (0.06) ▲	0.275 (0.09) ▲	0.692 (0.07) ▲	0.687 (0.09) ▲	0.278 (0.04) ▲	0.351 (0.04) ▲	0.448 (0.04) ▲	0.427 (0.05) ▲
	MGD-M-9	0.745 (0.06) ▲	**0.681** (0.06) ▲	0.283 (0.08) ▲	**0.710** (0.08) ▲	0.698 (0.08) ▲	0.284 (0.04) ▲	**0.361** (0.03) ▲	**0.454** (0.04) ▲	0.425 (0.05) ▲
	MGD-M-20	**0.752** (0.06) ▲	0.677 (0.07) ▲	**0.295** (0.08) ▲	0.703 (0.07) ▲	**0.703** (0.08) ▲	**0.291** (0.04) ▲	0.356 (0.03) ▲	0.452 (0.04) ▲	**0.430** (0.05) ▲

more MGD improves over the baseline. Offline performance for MGD goes up dramatically for noisy feedback compared to the baseline and the standard deviation (between brackets in the table) drops dramatically. This indicates much more stable performance for MGD. As a sanity check, we see in Figure 1 that both MGD-W-1 and MGD-M-1 perform very close to the DBGD baseline. This is to be expected because, besides their learning rates, both methods are algorithmically identical to the baseline for $n = 1$.

Offline performance, however, only tells half the story in an online learning to rank setting. Users are exposed to interleaved and multileaved lists that are used by the systems to infer preferences. Since the quality of these lists may vary, it is critical to measure the impact on users. Note that the quality of these list varies due to a combination of two factors: the quality of the rankers learned so far and the impact of the interleaving or multileaving method. We measure online performance by computing the NDCG score of the lists that users observe and discounting it over time (see Section 5.4). Figure 2 displays the online performance for all systems, again on a single dataset. Just like with offline performance, MGD outperforms DBGD more when the noise in the feedback increases. In fact, Table 3 shows that under *perfect* feedback, online performance for one dataset actually decreases compared to the baseline. This suggests that, for feedback without noise, increasing exploration, which is a direct consequence of adding candidates, is not as helpful for maximizing online performance. In other words, while adding candidates increases offline performance, in the absence of feedback noise it may harm online performance through the introduction of excessive exploration. However, generally, whether there is noise in the click feedback or not, MGD outperforms DBGD. Also for online performance, the standard deviation of MGD is much lower than for DBGD, irrespective of the noise.

Our answer to RQ1 is thus that MGD with increasing numbers of candidates learns increasingly faster than DBGD in terms of offline performance. In terms of online performance, MGD is on par with or outperforms DBGD when feedback has realistic levels of noise.

6.2 Convergence

In this section, we answer RQ2: whether MGD converges to a better optimum than DBGD. To do so, we investigate converged offline performance only. Table 2 shows converged performance after 1,000 query impressions for all the datasets that we consider. Note that for *NP2003* these values correspond to the points on the

Table 3: Online score (discounted cumulative NDCG, see Section 5.4) of each of the algorithms for the 3 instantiations of the CCM (see Table 1). Bold values indicate maximum performance per dataset and click model. Statistically significant improvements (losses) over the DBGD baseline are indicated by △ ($p < 0.05$) and ▲ ($p < 0.01$) (▽ and ▼). We show the standard deviation between brackets.

		HP2003	NP2003	TD2003	HP2004	NP2004	TD2004	MQ2007	MQ2008	OHSUMED
perfect	**DBGD**	95.88 (23.04)	97.79 (7.19)	36.28 (16.18)	97.93 (19.02)	102.92 (8.81)	**42.92** (14.73)	60.11 (4.49)	78.17 (4.54)	70.43 (3.85)
	MGD-W-2	110.77 (5.91) ▲	101.71 (5.87) ▲	41.19 (4.84) ▲	100.92 (6.67)	106.69 (6.17) ▲	38.15 (3.32) ▼	60.49 (3.23)	78.79 (3.97)	72.58 (3.58) ▲
	MGD-W-4	112.96 (5.14) ▲	103.42 (5.94) ▲	42.36 (3.91) ▲	104.44 (5.27) ▲	108.94 (5.48) ▲	38.50 (2.66) ▼	61.33 (3.47) △	78.52 (4.96)	72.73 (3.14) ▲
	MGD-W-6	113.37 (5.13) ▲	104.13 (5.42) ▲	43.00 (3.94) ▲	104.79 (5.46) ▲	110.02 (5.39) ▲	38.13 (2.43) ▼	61.22 (3.30) △	78.76 (4.01)	72.73 (3.48) ▲
	MGD-W-9	114.66 (4.57) ▲	**105.79** (5.88) ▲	43.53 (3.63) ▲	**107.22** (4.80) ▲	110.27 (5.69) ▲	38.39 (2.35) ▼	60.62 (3.42)	78.12 (3.93)	70.32 (3.11)
	MGD-W-20	**116.25** (4.21) ▲	104.96 (5.23) ▲	44.43 (4.19) ▲	106.23 (5.22) ▲	109.94 (5.91) ▲	39.79 (2.42) ▽	60.28 (3.35)	78.07 (3.87)	72.42 (3.58) ▲
	MGD-M-2	111.23 (5.59) ▲	101.42 (6.54) ▲	41.26 (4.37) ▲	101.67 (7.35) △	108.24 (6.08) ▲	37.51 (2.86) ▼	61.43 (3.54) △	79.08 (4.29)	72.74 (4.00) ▲
	MGD-M-4	113.91 (4.86) ▲	103.48 (5.61) ▲	42.64 (4.39) ▲	103.58 (5.62) ▲	109.70 (5.79) ▲	38.39 (2.43) ▼	**61.85** (3.10) ▲	**79.11** (4.41)	**72.84** (3.63) ▲
	MGD-M-6	113.46 (4.66) ▲	104.25 (5.02) ▲	43.22 (3.88) ▲	105.31 (5.16) ▲	109.80 (5.66) ▲	38.68 (2.47) ▼	61.00 (3.06)	78.97 (3.91)	72.78 (3.16) ▲
	MGD-M-9	115.81 (4.21) ▲	105.09 (4.71) ▲	44.02 (4.06) ▲	106.79 (5.36) ▲	**110.88** (5.94) ▲	38.38 (2.11) ▼	60.64 (2.75)	77.88 (3.86)	70.97 (3.12)
	MGD-M-20	115.67 (4.99) ▲	104.75 (4.79) ▲	**44.50** (3.71) ▲	107.05 (4.71) ▲	110.51 (5.69) ▲	40.18 (2.31) ▽	61.57 (3.10) ▲	78.69 (3.73)	72.51 (3.24) ▲
navigational	**DBGD**	78.79 (24.72)	85.83 (13.70)	32.21 (15.15)	80.61 (20.58)	90.92 (13.27)	37.46 (13.46)	58.07 (4.96)	76.04 (5.21)	66.99 (5.71)
	MGD-W-2	105.53 (8.45) ▲	95.55 (8.07) ▲	38.54 (5.71) ▲	92.59 (10.96) ▲	100.96 (9.07) ▲	35.72 (4.74)	59.24 (4.34) △	77.18 (4.95)	71.34 (4.56) ▲
	MGD-W-4	110.07 (6.55) ▲	100.22 (6.74) ▲	41.58 (4.81) ▲	100.37 (7.05) ▲	105.81 (6.72) ▲	37.90 (2.68)	59.57 (4.11) △	78.18 (4.52) ▲	72.00 (3.47) ▲
	MGD-W-6	109.97 (5.47) ▲	101.36 (5.14) ▲	41.66 (4.39) ▲	101.00 (6.46) ▲	107.07 (5.95) ▲	38.21 (3.00)	60.18 (3.28) ▲	77.88 (4.35) ▲	72.62 (3.67) ▲
	MGD-W-9	**113.17** (5.33) ▲	101.71 (5.19) ▲	43.03 (4.53) ▲	102.54 (5.67) ▲	106.63 (6.02) ▲	39.04 (2.86)	**60.71** (3.54) ▲	77.91 (4.49) ▲	72.69 (3.84) ▲
	MGD-W-20	112.18 (4.70) ▲	101.85 (5.68) ▲	42.24 (4.60) ▲	102.82 (5.80) ▲	107.02 (6.20) ▲	39.28 (2.91)	60.55 (3.14) ▲	77.77 (4.34) ▲	72.39 (3.37) ▲
	MGD-M-2	106.27 (8.78) ▲	94.34 (8.44) ▲	39.21 (5.48) ▲	94.70 (9.55) ▲	103.34 (8.49) ▲	36.40 (4.00)	59.65 (4.32) ▲	77.72 (4.73) ▲	71.04 (4.52) ▲
	MGD-M-4	109.44 (6.21) ▲	99.22 (6.87) ▲	41.02 (4.33) ▲	99.01 (7.37) ▲	105.82 (6.92) ▲	38.09 (3.21)	60.25 (3.59) ▲	78.16 (4.53) ▲	72.49 (3.81) ▲
	MGD-M-6	110.70 (5.77) ▲	100.56 (5.54) ▲	42.45 (4.57) ▲	102.04 (6.37) ▲	106.04 (6.51) ▲	38.28 (3.48)	60.31 (3.30) ▲	77.84 (4.89) ▲	**72.79** (3.57) ▲
	MGD-M-9	112.30 (5.35) ▲	**102.95** (5.62) ▲	42.74 (4.55) ▲	**103.96** (6.55) ▲	**107.41** (5.94) ▲	**39.55** (3.08)	60.36 (3.29) ▲	77.89 (3.94) ▲	72.71 (3.97) ▲
	MGD-M-20	111.38 (5.37) ▲	102.23 (5.45) ▲	**43.10** (4.34) ▲	102.88 (5.79) ▲	106.78 (5.16) ▲	38.79 (2.76)	60.21 (3.56) ▲	**78.23** (4.13) ▲	72.53 (3.11) ▲
informational	**DBGD**	48.23 (27.66)	50.42 (19.83)	22.46 (11.82)	43.36 (21.88)	59.58 (22.88)	27.76 (11.89)	55.60 (6.00)	71.94 (5.56)	62.99 (7.22)
	MGD-W-2	72.76 (18.10) ▲	64.09 (18.01) ▲	25.94 (7.55) ▲	62.61 (18.11) ▲	69.48 (16.80) ▲	26.52 (6.26)	55.83 (4.98)	73.33 (5.09) △	66.39 (5.93) ▲
	MGD-W-4	78.49 (16.93) ▲	73.02 (14.67) ▲	29.34 (6.15) ▲	70.73 (14.81) ▲	78.97 (13.16) ▲	28.21 (5.60)	56.04 (4.11)	74.31 (4.93) ▲	67.70 (4.44) ▲
	MGD-W-6	81.96 (14.73) ▲	73.66 (12.21) ▲	30.84 (6.17) ▲	70.90 (12.56) ▲	81.44 (11.32) ▲	29.12 (4.57)	56.24 (4.18)	**74.86** (4.79) ▲	67.75 (4.55) ▲
	MGD-W-9	85.14 (10.63) ▲	77.57 (10.24) ▲	30.26 (5.61) ▲	73.60 (11.66) ▲	82.86 (11.52) ▲	28.45 (4.36)	56.09 (3.61)	73.64 (4.71) △	68.48 (4.52) ▲
	MGD-W-20	84.44 (11.41) ▲	74.65 (9.53) ▲	29.91 (4.96) ▲	69.06 (13.01) ▲	81.78 (10.73) ▲	28.56 (4.28)	56.18 (3.46)	73.09 (4.87)	67.51 (4.63) ▲
	MGD-M-2	70.70 (18.56) ▲	66.03 (18.38) ▲	27.33 (6.76) ▲	61.78 (20.42) ▲	71.30 (18.17) ▲	27.29 (6.20)	56.28 (4.55)	73.35 (5.68) △	67.15 (5.63) ▲
	MGD-M-4	84.38 (14.30) ▲	76.41 (12.63) ▲	28.98 (5.88) ▲	72.82 (14.05) ▲	82.12 (11.01) ▲	28.44 (4.77)	56.58 (4.35)	74.45 (4.87) ▲	**68.75** (4.49) ▲
	MGD-M-6	85.51 (11.36) ▲	76.37 (11.58) ▲	31.55 (6.33) ▲	73.52 (13.17) ▲	83.05 (10.23) ▲	28.59 (4.16)	**56.88** (4.11)	74.26 (5.07) ▲	67.97 (4.47) ▲
	MGD-M-9	**87.84** (8.50) ▲	**81.04** (8.74) ▲	**32.45** (4.90) ▲	75.81 (10.21) ▲	**86.05** (7.79) ▲	**30.21** (3.74) △	55.91 (3.67)	74.50 (4.44) ▲	68.65 (4.51) ▲
	MGD-M-20	86.73 (7.24) ▲	80.99 (7.72) ▲	32.07 (4.23) ▲	**76.72** (9.64) ▲	82.92 (8.21) ▲	29.68 (3.32)	56.57 (3.48)	73.99 (4.61) ▲	68.50 (3.49) ▲

right vertical axis of Figure 1. These graphs are also illustrative for all datasets and show that increasing the number of candidates results in a better converged offline performance. In the case of *perfect* feedback, the effect of the number of candidates is not very strong; for most datasets and algorithms no significant improvement over the baseline is apparent. However, when noise in the feedback increases, and thus when feedback becomes more realistic compared to the *perfect* instantiation, the effect becomes much stronger as more candidates are used. In general, as Table 2 shows, this effect is significant and substantial as soon as more than one candidate is used.

For many datasets, performance of MGD after 1,000 query impressions is almost on par with DBGD trained without noise. However, as Figure 1 and Table 2 show, MGD with enough candidates *always* outperforms DBGD after 1,000 queries.

The graphs in Figure 1 clearly suggest that not all systems converge within 1,000 impressions. For this reason, we ran an additional longer experiment with 100,000 queries with *informational* feedback. Figure 3 shows the results with the same setup as in Figure 1 but over a larger number of queries. The graph shows that even after 100,000 queries DBGD has not converged, and MGD still performs better. Nonetheless, the difference between the algorithms decreases over time, until they converge to a similar level of performance. Thus, both algorithms seem to converge to the same optimum but DBGD requires many more queries than MGD to do so.

Hence, we answer RQ2 as follows: MGD converges to an optimum which is at least as good as the optimum DBGD finds. However, MGD does so much faster, as shown in Section 6.1.

6.3 Comparing outcome interpretations

In this section we answer RQ3: how MGD-W and MGD-M compare to each other. Figure 1, which shows the learning curves of both methods for varying click models, indicates that, in terms of offline performance, there is no substantial difference between MGD-W and MGD-M for the *perfect* and *navigational* click models. However, for the *informational* click model, which has noisier feedback, MGD-M consistently outperforms MGD-W. The same applies to all datasets we considered, see Table 2. In the offline setting, MGD-M is the better approach as it is more capable of handling noise than MGD-W.

In terms of *online* performance, MGD-M also usually outperforms MGD-W, see Figure 2 and Table 3. Again, the effect is

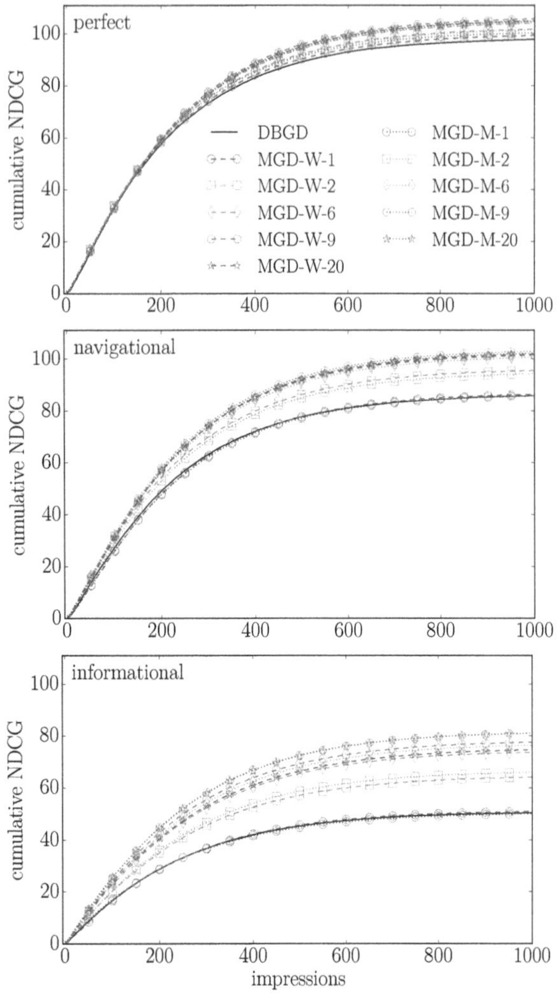

Figure 2: Online performance (discounted cumulative NDCG) on MGD-W and MGD-M with varying number of candidates compared to DBGD on *NP2003* dataset for *perfect*, *navigational* and *informational* click model instantiations.

stronger when there is more noise in the feedback. Generally, MGD-M has lower standard deviation than MGD-W indicating that it is more stable.

Note that the *informational* click model has a high probability to produce multiple clicks because its stop probabilities are low (see Table 1). This typically leads to multiple winners of a TDM comparison, which in turn allows MGD-M to be different from MGD-W. Thus, a potential reason for MGD-M to outperform MGD-W is that the mean of several unit vectors is shorter than a unit vector. As a result, MGD-M updates the current best weight vector with smaller steps. In other words, for DBGD and MGD-W we have that $|w_t^0 - w_{t+1}^0| = \alpha \cdot \delta$, while for MGD-M $|w_t^0 - w_{t+1}^0| \leq \alpha \cdot \delta$.

We tested this hypothesis by normalizing the mean vector to a unit vector before updating using MGD-M, so Algorithm 4 was effectively changed such that $|w_t^0 - w_{t+1}^0| = \alpha \cdot \delta$. The result is depicted in Table 4, where we see how MGD-M with normalized update directions indeed performs slightly worse than MGD-M without normalization for the *informational* click model in terms of offline performance, confirming that some of its advantage indeed comes from the smaller update step. Nonetheless, MGD-M with normalization still either performs on par with or better than MGD-W, so not all of its performance advantage can be attributed to

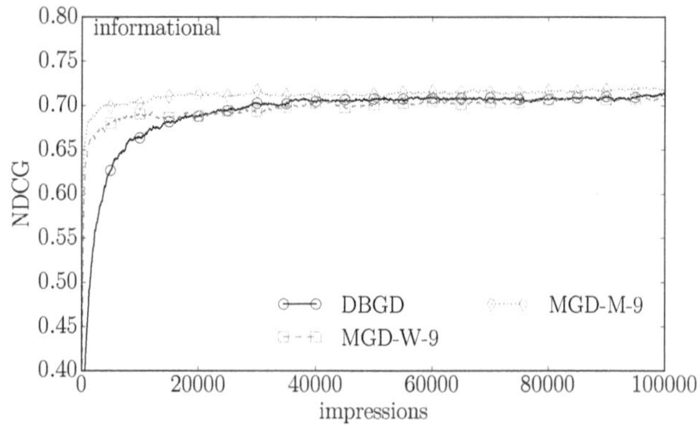

Figure 3: Offline performance (NDCG) on MGD-W and MGD-M with 9 candidates compared to DBGD on *NP2003* dataset an *informational* click model.

Table 4: Performance of MGD-M, MGD-W and normalized MGD-M each with 9 candidates for the three instantiations of the CCM (see Table 1). Run on the *NP2003* dataset; performance evaluated after 1,000 impressions.

		perfect	*navigational*	*informational*
offline	**MGD-W**	0.713 (0.05)	0.708 (0.05)	0.656 (0.07)
	MGD-M	0.714 (0.05)	0.710 (0.05)	0.681 (0.06)
	Norm MGD-M	0.711 (0.04)	0.710 (0.04)	0.667 (0.06)
online	**MGD-W**	105.785 (5.88)	101.708 (5.19)	77.568 (10.24)
	MGD-M	105.087 (4.71)	102.953 (5.62)	81.037 (8.74)
	Norm MGD-M	105.844 (5.21)	102.686 (5.32)	81.676 (9.46)

smaller updates. This implies that the *direction* of the update taken by MGD-M is better than that of MGD-W.

To answer RQ3, while in general both MGD methods outperform DBGD, MGD-M is better at handling high noise levels, making it more effective than MGD-W overall. The advantage of MGD-M over MGD-W comes from both the update direction and a smaller update size.

6.4 Number of candidates and learning rate

In this section, we investigate some remaining questions.

6.4.1 *Number of candidates*

In Section 6.1 we have already discussed the interplay between the amount of noise in the feedback and the optimal number of candidates in MGD. Figure 4 shows the effect of increasing the number of candidates even further to a maximum of 1,000 candidates. Note that as soon as the number of candidate rankers goes beyond the length of the result shown to users, the only effect of increasing it even further is that the probability of including the current best ranker decreases.[4] We see in Figure 4, Table 2 and Table 3 that *both* offline and online performance generally go up when the number of candidates goes up. However, beyond approximately 10 candidates this either stabilizes or fluctuates slightly, depending on the amount of noise in the click model. This matches $\kappa = 10$, the result list length in our experiments. We increase the noise further than we did until now by including results for an *almost random* click model instantiation. Still in Figure 4 (the green curves near the bottom in both plots), we see that the more noise we add, the more MGD benefits from adding candidates.

[4]This is an artifact that stems from the way we generate candidates and the fact that we use TDM as our multileaving method.

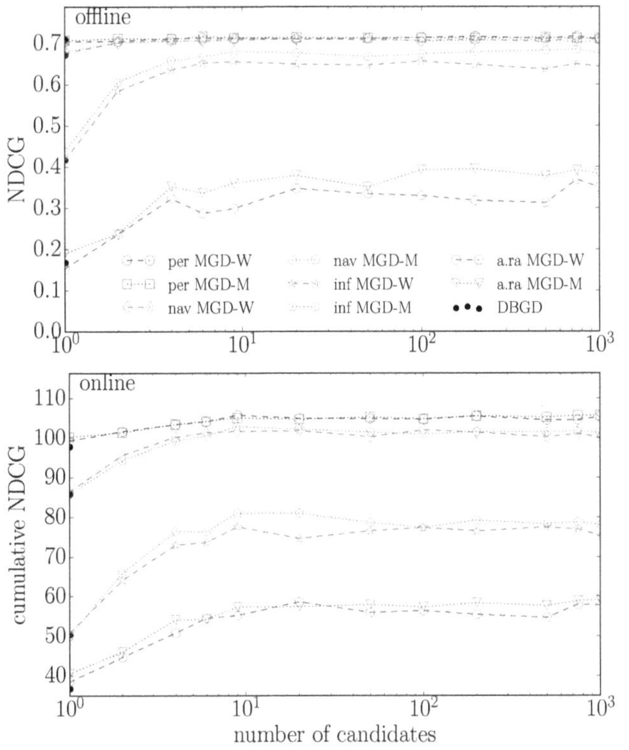

Figure 4: Sweep over the number of candidates in terms of offline and online performance for MGD-M and MGD-W after 1,000 impressions. Performed on *NP2003* using *all four* instantiations of the click model. DBGD is displayed by the black dots on the left axis. Note the log scale on the horizontal axis.

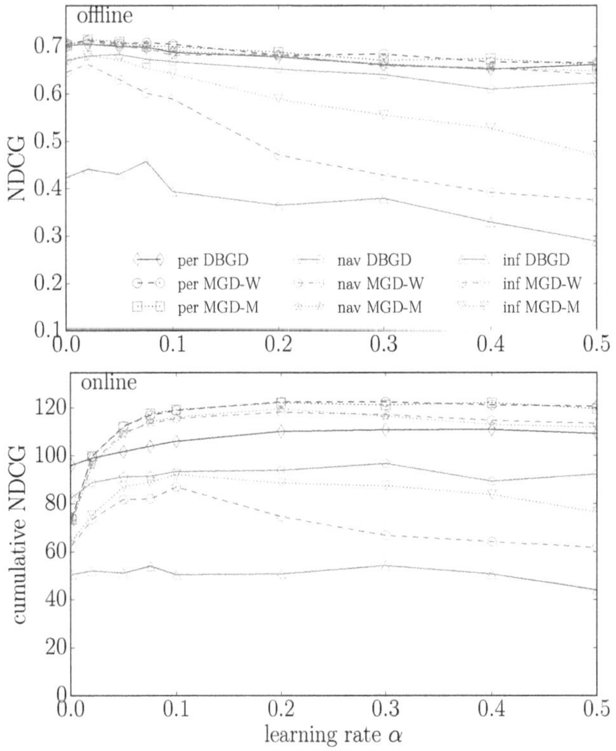

Figure 5: Sweep over learning rate values in terms of offline and online performance after 1,000 impressions for MGD-M and MGD-W with 9 candidates and DBGD. Performed on *NP2003* using three different click models with varying degrees of noise.

In conclusion, both offline and online performance increase with the number of candidates when noise is present, but this effect appears to be limited by the length of the result list shown to users.

6.4.2 Learning rate

Our MGD algorithms are sufficiently different from DBGD to warrant a new investigation of the learning rate α. The results in Section 6.3 suggest that some of MGD-M's superior performance over MGD-W could be explained by the smaller steps this algorithm takes. To further investigate this effect, we vary the learning rate.

Figure 5, which shows a sweep over learning rates, again shows a considerable difference between MGD-M and MGD-W. Furthermore, for most algorithms online performance increases when α goes up while offline performance drops slowly. With a learning rate close to zero, MGD performs notably worse than DBGD because multileaving interferes more with the ranking presented to the user, while the low learning rates prevents it from adapting quickly. Conversely, when the learning rate increases, MGD greatly outperforms DBGD in terms of online performance for all three click models. This illustrates the tradeoff MGD makes: multileaving distorts the ranking shown to the user, but when the learning rate increases it compensates by adapting to the user faster. So, interestingly, also when there is no noise in the feedback, MGD can greatly outperform DBGD if the learning rate is chosen appropriately. Note that, for all our other experiments, we chose a fixed value of $\alpha = 0.03$ for MGD based on these plots. This point denotes a reasonable tradeoff between offline and online performance. This is a different optimum than DBGD and, since DBGD is equal to MGD with a single candidate, it seems the optimal learning rate depends on the number of candidates. Ideally, one would find a learning rate that is optimal for each number of candidates. Doing so would only increase MGD's performance advantage.

In sum, this experiment shows that DBGD and MGD have different optimal learning rates and that MGD can greatly outperform DBGD, both offline and online, when the learning rate is chosen appropriately.

7. CONCLUSION

We proposed an extension of *dueling bandit gradient descent* (DBGD), an online learning to rank method. DBGD is limited to exploring only a single candidate ranker at a time. Where DBGD uses interleaved comparisons to infer *pairwise* preferences, our newly introduced method—*multileave gradient descent* (MGD)—learns from comparisons between a set of rankers to infer n*-way* preferences between n candidate ranker improvements. We proposed two specific ways of using these preferences for updating a current best ranker. The first variant, MGD-W, picks a ranker to update towards at random from among the rankers that win a comparison; the second variant, MGD-M, updates towards the mean of all winners of the comparison.

Our empirical results, based on extensive experiments on nine learning to rank datasets encompassing 86M user interactions, show that either variant dramatically improves over the DBGD baseline. In particular, when the noise in user feedback increases, we find that both MGD-W and MGD-M are capable of learning better rankers much faster than the baseline does. When the number of candidate rankers we consider increases from 1 (as in the baseline), offline performance—measured on held-out data—and online performance—measured on the results shown to users—consistently go up until it converges at around 10 candidate rankers. After 1,000 query impressions with *noisy* feedback, MGD performs almost on par with DBGD trained on feedback *without any noise*. We further show that MGD obtains at least the same converged performance that DBGD ultimately obtains, but that it does so using orders of magnitude less user interaction data. From the two variants we compared, MGD-M performs either equal to, or outperforms MGD-W. The advantage of MGD-M over MGD-W comes from both the update direction and smaller update size.

An important implication of our results is that orders of magnitude less user interaction data is required to find good rankers when multileaved comparisons are used as feedback mechanism for online learning to rank. This results in far fewer users being exposed to inferior rankers and it allows search engines to adapt faster to changes in user preferences.

Our findings give rise to several directions that remain to be explored. Firstly, we sampled candidate rankers randomly uniformly from a unit sphere around the current best ranker. Alternatively, one could consider selecting rankers such that all directions are covered, which may speed up learning even further. Secondly, currently we have two strategies for interpreting multileave comparison outcomes, MGD-M and MGD-W. We could consider an additional strategy that takes a weighted combination of all the compared rankers, potentially even down weighting the directions for loosing candidate rankers. Thirdly, we noticed that often, in particular closer to convergence, many of the compared rankers become very similar. One could consider adapting the multileaving algorithm to not attempt to infer preferences between rankers that produce the same rankings, but rather, consider all these to be the same rankers.

Acknowledgements. This research was partially supported by Amsterdam Data Science, the Dutch national program COMMIT, Elsevier, the European Community's Seventh Framework Programme (FP7/2007-2013) under grant agreement nr 312827 (VOX-Pol), the ESF Research Network Program ELIAS, the HPC Fund, the Royal Dutch Academy of Sciences (KNAW) under the Elite Network Shifts project, the Microsoft Research Ph.D. program, the Netherlands eScience Center under project number 027.012.105, the Netherlands Institute for Sound and Vision, the Netherlands Organisation for Scientific Research (NWO) under project nrs 727.011.005, 612.001.116, HOR-11-10, 640.006.013, 612.066.930, CI-14-25, SH-322-15, the Yahoo! Faculty Research and Engagement Program, and Yandex.

REFERENCES

[1] L. Azzopardi, M. de Rijke, and K. Balog. Building simulated queries for known-item topics: an analysis using six European languages. In *SIGIR '07*. ACM, 2007.

[2] R. Berendsen, M. Tsagkias, W. Weerkamp, and M. de Rijke. Pseudo test collections for training and tuning microblog rankers. In *SIGIR '13*. ACM, 2013.

[3] B. Carterette and J. Allan. Incremental test collections. In *CIKM*. ACM, 2005.

[4] O. Chapelle, T. Joachims, F. Radlinski, and Y. Yue. Large-scale validation and analysis of interleaved search evaluation. *ACM Trans. Inf. Syst.*, 30(1), 2012.

[5] C. W. Cleverdon, J. Mills, and M. Keen. Factors determining the performance of indexing systems. Aslib cranfield project, Cranfield: College of Aeronautics, 1966.

[6] F. Guo, C. Liu, and Y. M. Wang. Efficient multiple-click models in web search. In *WSDM '09*. ACM, 2009.

[7] J. He, C. Zhai, and X. Li. Evaluation of methods for relative comparison of retrieval systems based on clickthroughs. In *CIKM '09*. ACM, 2009.

[8] K. Hofmann. *Fast and Reliably Online Learning to Rank for Information Retrieval*. PhD thesis, U. Amsterdam, 2013.

[9] K. Hofmann, S. Whiteson, and M. de Rijke. A probabilistic method for inferring preferences from clicks. In *CIKM '11*. ACM, 2011.

[10] K. Hofmann, S. Whiteson, and M. de Rijke. Balancing exploration and exploitation in listwise and pairwise online learning to rank for information retrieval. *Information Retrieval*, 16(1), 2012.

[11] K. Hofmann, A. Schuth, S. Whiteson, and M. de Rijke. Reusing historical interaction data for faster online learning to rank for IR. In *WSDM '13*. ACM, 2013.

[12] K. Järvelin and J. Kekäläinen. Cumulated gain-based evaluation of IR techniques. *ACM Trans. Inf. Syst.*, 20(4), 2002.

[13] T. Joachims. Optimizing search engines using clickthrough data. In *KDD '02*. ACM, 2002.

[14] T. Joachims. Evaluating retrieval performance using clickthrough data. In *Text Mining*. Physica/Springer, 2003.

[15] T. Joachims, L. A. Granka, B. Pan, H. Hembrooke, F. Radlinski, and G. Gay. Evaluating the accuracy of implicit feedback from clicks and query reformulations in Web search. *ACM Trans. Inf. Syst.*, 25(2), 2007.

[16] D. Kelly. Methods for evaluating interactive information retrieval systems with users. *Found. & Tr. Inform. Retr.*, 3 (1–2):1–224, 2009.

[17] R. Kohavi, R. Longbotham, D. Sommerfield, and R. M. Henne. Controlled experiments on the web: survey and practical guide. *Data Min. & Knowl. Disc.*, 18(1), 2009.

[18] L. Li, W. Chu, J. Langford, and X. Wang. Unbiased offline evaluation of contextual-bandit-based news article recommendation algorithms. In *WSDM '11*, 2011.

[19] T.-Y. Liu. Learning to rank for information retrieval. *Found. & Tr. Inform. Retr.*, 3(3):225–331, 2009.

[20] T.-Y. Liu, J. Xu, T. Qin, W. Xiong, and H. Li. LETOR: Benchmark dataset for research on learning to rank for information retrieval. In *LR4IR '07*, 2007.

[21] F. Radlinski and N. Craswell. Optimized interleaving for online retrieval evaluation. In *WSDM '13*. ACM, 2013.

[22] F. Radlinski, M. Kurup, and T. Joachims. How does clickthrough data reflect retrieval quality? In *CIKM '08*. ACM, 2008.

[23] M. Sanderson. Test collection based evaluation of information retrieval systems. *Found. & Tr. Inform. Retr.*, 4(4):247–375, 2010.

[24] M. Sanderson and H. Joho. Forming test collections with no system pooling. In *SIGIR '04*. ACM, 2004.

[25] A. Schuth, K. Hofmann, S. Whiteson, and M. de Rijke. Lerot: An online learning to rank framework. In *LivingLab '13*. ACM, 2013.

[26] A. Schuth, F. Sietsma, S. Whiteson, D. Lefortier, and M. de Rijke. Multileaved comparisons for fast online evaluation. In *CIKM '14*, pages 71–80. ACM, Nov. 2014.

[27] A. L. Strehl, C. Mesterharm, M. L. Littman, and H. Hirsh. Experience-efficient learning in associative bandit problems. In *ICML '06*, 2006.

[28] R. Sutton and A. G. Barto. *Reinforcement Learning: An Introduction*. MIT Press, 1998.

[29] M. Szummer and E. Yilmaz. Semi-supervised learning to rank with preference regularization. In *CIKM '11*. ACM, 2011.

[30] E. M. Voorhees and D. K. Harman. *TREC: Experiment and Evaluation in Information Retrieval*. MIT Press, 2005.

[31] Y. Yue and T. Joachims. Interactively optimizing information retrieval systems as a dueling bandits problem. In *ICML '09*, 2009.

[32] Y. Yue, J. Broder, R. Kleinberg, and T. Joachims. The K-armed dueling bandits problem. *J. Comp. and System Sciences*, 78(5), 2009.

AMiner: Toward Understanding Big Scholar Data

Jie Tang
Department of Computer Science and Technology, Tsinghua University
Tsinghua National Laboratory for Information Science and Technology (TNList)
jietang@tsinghua.edu.cn

ABSTRACT

In this talk, I present a novel academic search and mining system, **AMiner**[1], the second generation of the ArnetMiner system [9]. Different from traditional academic search systems that focus on document (paper) search, AMiner aims to provide a systematic modeling approach to gain a deep understanding of the large and heterogeneous networks formed by authors, papers they have published, and venues in which they were published. The system extracts researchers' profiles automatically from the Web [7] and integrates them with published papers after name disambiguation [3]. It has collected a large scholar dataset, with more than 130,000,000 researcher profiles and 100,000,000 papers from multiple publication databases. We have also developed an approach named COSNET [12] to connect AMiner with several professional social networks, such as LinkedIn and VideoLectures, which significantly enriches the scholar metadata. Based on our integrated big scholar data, we devised a unified topic modeling approach to modeling the different entities (authors, papers, venues) simultaneously and providing a topic-level expertise search by leveraging the modeling results [8]. In addition, AMiner offers a set of *researcher-centered* functions, including social influence analysis [5], influence visualization [1], collaboration recommendation [6], relationship mining [4, 10], similarity analysis [11], and community evolution [2]. The system has been in operation since 2006 and has attracted more than 7,000,000 independent IP accesses from over 200 countries/regions.

Categories and Subject Descriptors

H.2.8 [**Database Applications**]: Data Mining

Keywords

Academic search; Recommendation; Integration; Social influence

1. BIOGRAPHY

Jie Tang is an associate professor with the Department of Computer Science and Technology at Tsinghua University, and was also visiting scholar at Cornell University and Hong Kong University of Science and Technology. His interests include social network analysis, data mining, and machine learning. He has published more than 100 journal/conference papers and holds 14 patents. He served as PC Co-Chair of CIKM'16, WSDM'15, ASONAM'15, SocInfo'12, KDD-CUP/Workshop/Local Co-Chair of KDD'11-15, and as the PC member of more than 50 international conferences. He is the founder of AMiner.org (ArnetMiner), which has attracted more than 7 million independent IP accesses from 220 countries/regions in the world. He was honored with the Newton Advanced Scholarship Award, CCF Young Scientist Award, and NSFC Excellent Young Scholar.

[1]http://aminer.org

WSDM'16, February 22–25, 2016, San Francisco, CA, USA.
© 2016 ACM. ISBN 978-1-4503-3716-8/16/02 ...$15.00.
DOI: http://dx.doi.org/10.1145/2835776.2835849.

Acknowledgements. The work is supported by the National High-tech R&D Program (2014AA015103), National Basic Research Program of China (2014CB340506, 2012CB316006), Natural Science Foundation of China (61222212), and a research fund supported by Huawei Inc.

2. REFERENCES

[1] L. Shi, H. Tong, J. Tang, and C. Lin. Vegas: Visual influence graph summarization on citation networks. *IEEE TKDE*, 2015.

[2] Y. Sun, J. Tang, J. Han, C. Chen, and M. Gupta. Co-evolution of multi-typed objects in dynamic star networks. *IEEE TKDE*, 26(12):2942–2955, 2014.

[3] J. Tang, A. Fong, B. Wang, and J. Zhang. A unified probabilistic framework for name disambiguation in digital library. *IEEE TKDE*, 24(6):975–987, 2012.

[4] J. Tang, T. Lou, J. Kleinberg, and S. Wu. Transfer link prediction across heterogeneous social networks. *ACM TOIS*, 2015.

[5] J. Tang, J. Sun, C. Wang, and Z. Yang. Social influence analysis in large-scale networks. In *KDD'09*, pages 807–816, 2009.

[6] J. Tang, S. Wu, J. Sun, and H. Su. Cross-domain collaboration recommendation. In *KDD'12*, pages 1285–1294, 2012.

[7] J. Tang, L. Yao, D. Zhang, and J. Zhang. A combination approach to web user profiling. *ACM TKDD*, 5(1):1–44, 2010.

[8] J. Tang, J. Zhang, R. Jin, Z. Yang, K. Cai, L. Zhang, and Z. Su. Topic level expertise search over heterogeneous networks. *Machine Learning Journal*, 82(2):211–237, 2011.

[9] J. Tang, J. Zhang, L. Yao, J. Li, L. Zhang, and Z. Su. Arnetminer: Extraction and mining of academic social networks. In *KDD'08*, pages 990–998, 2008.

[10] C. Wang, J. Han, Y. Jia, J. Tang, D. Zhang, Y. Yu, and J. Guo. Mining advisor-advisee relationships from research publication networks. In *KDD'10*, pages 203–212, 2010.

[11] J. Zhang, J. Tang, C. Ma, H. Tong, Y. Jing, and J. Li. Panther: Fast top-k similarity search on large networks. In *KDD'15*, pages 1445–1454, 2015.

[12] Y. Zhang, J. Tang, Z. Yang, J. Pei, and P. Yu. Cosnet: Connecting heterogeneous social networks with local and global consistency. In *KDD'15*, pages 1485–1494, 2015.

Serving a Billion Personalized News Feeds

Lars Backstrom
Facebook
Menlo Park, CA, USA
lars@fb.com

ABSTRACT

Feed ranking's goal is to provide perople with over a billion personalized experiences. We strive to provide the most compelling content to each person, personalized to them so that they are most likely to see the content that is most interesting to them.

Similar to a newspaper, putting the right stories above the fold has always been critical to engaging customers and interesting them in the rest of the paper. In feed ranking, we face a similar challenge, but on a grander scale. Each time a person visits, we need to find the best piece of content out of all the available stories and put it at the top of feed where people are most likely to see it. To accomplish this, we do large-scale machine learning to model each person, figure out which friends, pages and topics they care about and pick the stories each particular person is interested in. In addition to the large-scale machine learning problems we work on, another primary area of research is understanding the value we are creating for people and making sure that our objective function is in alignment with what people want.

Keywords
Invited Talk

BIO

I graduated from Cornell as an undergrad in 2004 and with a PhD in 2009. I joined Facebook in the fall of 2009. At Facebook, I first worked on the People You May Know system, trying to find people who users are friends with but not yet connected to on Facebook. This combined machine learning with network science, as we worked to use the graph structure to sort of find missing edges and connect them. Since late 2010, I've been working on News Feed, trying to understand the social graph to find people's closest friends and connect everyone with their friends and family by showing the most relevant content produced by those people in News Feed.

WSDM'16, February 22–25, 2016, San Francisco, CA, USA
ACM 978-1-4503-3716-8/16/02.
http://dx.doi.org/10.1145/2835776.2835848

The Predictive Power of Massive Data about our Fine-Grained Behavior

Foster Provost
Professor of Data Science and Information Systems
Center for Data Science & Stern School of Business
New York University
New York, NY 10012

ABSTRACT

What really is it about "big data" that makes it different from traditional data? In this talk I illustrate one important aspect: massive ultra-fine-grained data on individuals' behaviors holds remarkable predictive power. I examine several applications to marketing-related tasks, showing how machine learning methods can extract the predictive power and how the value of the data "asset" seems different from the value of traditional data used for predictive modeling.

I then dig deeper into explaining the predictions made from massive numbers of fine-grained behaviors by applying a counter-factual framework for explaining model behavior based on treating the individual behaviors as evidence that is combined by the model. This analysis shows that the fine-grained behavior data incorporate various sorts of information that we traditionally have sought to capture by other means. For example, for marketing modeling the behavior data effectively incorporate demographics, psychographics, category interest, and purchase intent.

Finally, I discuss the flip side of the coin: the remarkable predictive power based on fine-grained information on individuals raises new privacy concerns. In particular, I discuss privacy concerns based on inferences drawn about us (in contrast to privacy concerns stemming from violations to data confidentiality). The evidence counterfactual approach used to explain the predictions also can be used to provide online consumers with transparency into the reasons why inferences are drawn about them. In addition, it offers the possibility to design novel solutions such as a privacy-friendly "cloaking device" to inhibit inferences from being drawn based on particular behaviors.

This talk draws on work from several papers [1-11].

BIO

Foster Provost is Professor of Data Science and Information Systems and Andre Meyer Faculty Fellow at New York University's Stern School of Business and Interim Director for NYU's Center for Data Science. He is coauthor of the best-selling book, Data Science for Business. His research focuses on modeling behavior data, modeling (social) network data, crowd-sourcing for data science, aligning data science with application goals, and privacy-friendly methods. His research has won many awards, including the INFORMS Design Science Award and best paper awards at KDD across three decades. He cofounded several companies based on his research, including Dstillery and Integral Ad Science. Foster previously was Editor-in-Chief of the journal Machine Learning. His latest music album, Mean Reversion, is scheduled to be released in 2015.

WSDM'16, February 22–25, 2016, San Francisco, CA, USA
ACM 978-1-4503-3716-8/16/02.
http://dx.doi.org/10.1145/2835776.2835846

REFERENCES

1. Chen, Daizhuo and Fraiberger, Samuel P. and Moakler, Robert and Provost, Foster. "Enhancing Transparency and Control When Drawing Data-Driven Inferences About Individuals" (2015). NYU Working Paper No. 2451/33969. Available at SSRN: http://ssrn.com/abstract=2611542

2. Dalessandro, B., D. Chen, T. Raeder, C. Perlich, M. Han Williams, and F. Provost. 2014. Scalable hands-free transfer learning for online advertising. In *Proceedings of the 20th ACM SIGKDD international conference on Knowledge discovery and data mining* (KDD '14). ACM, New York, NY, USA, 1573-1582.

3. Junqué de Fortuny, E., D. Martens, and F. Provost. "Predictive Modeling with Big Data: Is Bigger Really Better?" *Big Data* 1(4), 215-226, 2013.

4. Junqué de Fortuny, E. M. Stankova, J. Moeyersoms, B. Minnaert, F. Provost, and D. Martens. 2014. Corporate residence fraud detection. In *Proceedings of the 20th ACM SIGKDD international conference on Knowledge discovery*

and data mining (KDD '14). ACM, New York, NY, USA, 1650-1659.

5. Martens, D., F. Provost, J. Clark, E. Junqué de Fortuny. "Mining Fine-Grained Consumer Payment Data to Improve Targeted Marketing." *To appear in MISQ.*

6. Martens, D. and F. Provost. "Explaining Data-Driven Document Classifications." *MIS Quarterly* 38(1), 73-99, 2014.

7. Perlich, C., B. Dalessandro, O. Stitelman, T. Raeder , F. Provost. "Machine learning for targeted display advertising: Transfer learning in action." *Machine Learning* 95(1):103-127, 2014.

8. Provost, F., B. Dalessandro, R. Hook, X. Zhang & A. Murray. Audience Selection for On-line Brand Advertising: Privacy-friendly Social Network Targeting. In *Proceedings of the Fifteenth ACM SIGKDD International Conference on Knowledge Discovery and Data Mining* (KDD-2009).

9. Provost, F., D. Martens, and A. Murray. "Finding Mobile Consumers with a Privacy-Friendly Geo-Similarity Network." *Information Systems Research* 26(2), 243-265, 2015.

10. Raeder, T., O. Stitelman, B. Dalessandro, C. Perlich, and F. Provost. "Design Principles of Massive, Robust Prediction Systems." In *Proceedings of the Eighteenth ACM SIGKDD International Conference on Knowledge Discovery and Data Mining* (KDD 2012).

11. Raeder, T., C. Perlich, B. Dalessandro, O. Stitelman, and F. Provost. "Scalable Supervised Dimensionality Reduction Using Clustering." In *Proceedings of the Nineteenth ACM SIGKDD International Conference on Knowledge Discovery and Data Mining* (KDD 2013).

Information Evolution in Social Networks

Lada A. Adamic
Facebook Inc.
Menlo Park, CA
ladamic@fb.com

Thomas M. Lento
Facebook Inc.
Menlo Park, CA
tlento@fb.com

Eytan Adar
U. Michigan
Ann Arbor, MI
eadar@umich.edu

Pauline C. Ng
Genome Institute of Singapore
Singapore, Singapore
pauline.c.ng@gmail.com

ABSTRACT

Social networks readily transmit information, albeit with less than perfect fidelity. We present a large-scale measurement of this imperfect information copying mechanism by examining the dissemination and evolution of thousands of memes, collectively replicated hundreds of millions of times in the online social network Facebook. The information undergoes an evolutionary process that exhibits several regularities. A meme's mutation rate characterizes the population distribution of its variants, in accordance with the Yule process. Variants further apart in the diffusion cascade have greater edit distance, as would be expected in an iterative, imperfect replication process. Some text sequences can confer a replicative advantage; these sequences are abundant and transfer "laterally" between different memes. Subpopulations of the social network can preferentially transmit a specific variant of a meme if the variant matches their beliefs or culture. Understanding the mechanism driving change in diffusing information has important implications for how we interpret and harness the information that reaches us through our social networks.

1. INTRODUCTION

Richard Dawkins coined the word "meme" to designate ideas or messages that spread and evolve analogously to genes through communication [12]. Determining the extent to which the gene analogy applies to memes has been hampered by the lack of large-scale data containing the evolution histories of many memes, where one can pinpoint when and where information was modified and how the modifications were subsequently diffused. In this study we are able to gather precisely such data, consisting of near-complete traces of thousands of memes, collectively comprising over 460 million individual instances propagated via Facebook. Facebook is an online social network that enables individuals to communicate with their friends. The primary mechanism for this communication are *status updates* which appear in news feeds of friends. A message or idea that is appealing can quickly propagate, as those friends can choose to post the message as their own status update, thus exposing their own friends. In this way Facebook acts as a large petri dish in which memes can mutate and replicate over the substrate of the network of friendship ties. While there are other environments where memes flourish, those memes that do enter Facebook can be examined in detail, uncovering mechanisms previously difficult–or impossible–to study.

Prior studies have either analyzed the overall popularity of memes [11,24,33,35,36,40,41], or examined a small sample of meme variants in detail [2,7,17,25,37,38]. However, neither the large– nor small–scale studies have been been able to formulate a model by which new meme variants arise. This has left a gap in our understanding of the mechanism by which social networks can not only cause information to spread [5,10], but can also cause it to evolve, a mechanism that carries important implications for the fidelity of all socially transmitted information, as well as for specific types of information such as political campaign messages [33]. The extent to which the biological analogy of genetic evolution carries over into the evolution of memes is also unclear. We will use the terminology from genetics in describing the processes memes undergo, but defer evaluation of the biological analogy to the Discussion.

WSDM'16, February 22 - 25, 2016, San Francisco, CA, USA

ISBN 978-1-4503-3716-8/16/02...$15.00

DOI: http://dx.doi.org/10.1145/2835776.2835827

2. DATA

We analyzed de-identified data gathered over a time span of 18 months, from April 2009 to October 2011, during which many memes were propagated as textual status updates on Facebook. This period and medium represents a unique opportunity to study the evolution of memes, one which has not presented itself before or since. To understand how memes mutate naturally as they are transmitted from individual to individual, an environment is needed where individuals can freely both share information with their friends and always have the opportunity to modify the information. Prior to April 2009 character limits on status updates curtailed the length, modifiability and replication ability of memes. However, once the character limit had been increased, allowing one to not only express a complete idea or story, but also add replication instructions, e.g. "copy and paste" or "repost", memes immediately started to flourish. Widely propagated memes would typically carry these instructions because there was yet no "share" functionality, which could at the click of a button exactly replicate the information as one's own update. As a result, memes propagating via a manual copy and paste mechanism can be exact, or they might contain a "mutation", an accidental or intentional modification. Since the notion of a meme was first based on the parallels between genes and ideas, we consider how textual status updates match genes in their structure and mechanics. First, they encode information, whether it is a joke, a warning, or a call to action, in a way that parallels genetic information: a string of characters is "transcribed", allowing for some characters to be added, deleted, or substituted. Second, the replication (accurate or inaccurate) can be performed by anyone exposed to the meme. There are other forms

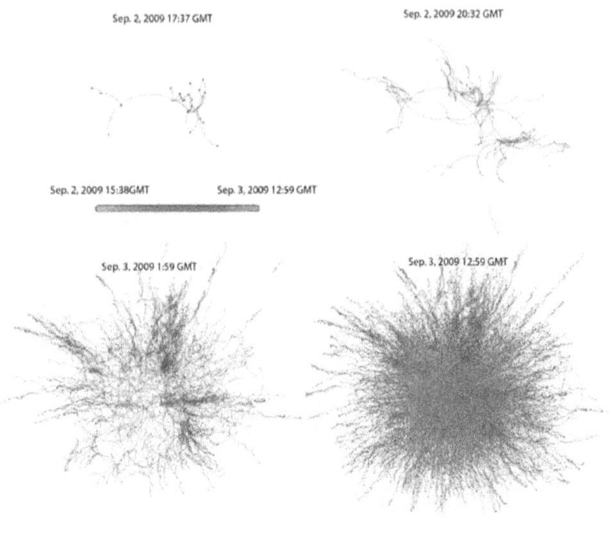

Figure 1: Early diffusion of the "no one should" meme. In a span of two days the meme diffused through many individuals and generated diffusion cascades of non-negligible depth.

in which memes occur in online environments, e.g. photographs or videos. However, the information in these is not as readily analyzed, and they cannot be as easily modified by anyone as spoken or written ideas can. We therefore focus our attention on textual status updates on Facebook to understand how information evolves when anyone can easily modify and retell it.

In order to generate a set of candidate memes, we identified status updates that had at least 100 exact copies. Nearly all such status updates contained replication instructions such as 'copy', 'paste', and 'repost'. The few exceptions included updates generated automatically by Facebook applications and some ubiquitous memes: jokes and "wise" sayings. We therefore narrowed our scope to status updates containing replication terms such as 'copy', 'paste', etc., which included the vast majority of memes propagating via Facebook, but excluded ubiquitous text whose origin would be difficult to discern. Since the replication instructions we searched for were in English, the process captured primarily English language variants of memes.

Prior to clustering the variants into memes, we removed non-alphanumeric characters and converted the remainder to lowercase. Each distinct variant was shingled into overlapping 4-word-grams, creating a term frequency vector from the 4-grams. Sorting the meme variants by month, then by frequency, we created a new cluster, i.e. a meme, if the cosine similarity of the 4-gram vector was below 0.2 to all prior clusters. Otherwise, we added the status update to the cluster it matched most closely and adjusted the term-frequency vector of the matching cluster to incorporate the additional variant. We modified the term frequency vector of existing clusters, or created a new cluster, only if the variant frequency exceeded 100 within a month. In a post-processing step we aggregated clusters whose term vectors had converged to a unigram cosine similarity exceeding 0.4. We then gathered all variants for these 4,087 most significant memes by assigning status updates to them if their cosine similarity exceeded 0.05 using 4-grams and 0.1 using unigrams. The unigram threshold assured that an unrelated status update wasn't erroneously included in a cluster simply for containing a relatively rare substring. The number and size of memes was insensitive to moderate adjustment of thresholds.

99.49% of posts identified as memes were made by individuals, allowing us to potentially trace the meme across the friendship graph. The remainder were made primarily by Facebook pages: group entities which enable one-to-many communication. For each meme, we induce the subgraph of directed friendship connections from people who posted the meme to their friends who posted before. We add edges between the posts of the same meme that are from the same person. We sort edges first by Levenshtein edit distance and then by time elapsed, picking the closest match as the parent in the diffusion tree. The process generates a diffusion forest rather than a tree because some origins are unknown, e.g. if a post has been deleted, or if it was propagated through a page rather than an individual's status update. Picking the textually and temporally closest source gives us a conservative estimate of how much mutation is occurring in a meme.

We define the popularity of a variant to be the number of copies of that variant posted as a Facebook status update, and the popularity of the meme as a whole to be the sum of the popularity of all of its variants. Our sample includes some memes which never proliferated in large numbers, yet nevertheless produced at least one variant with 100 or more instances. This presented a challenge to estimating the distribution of variant popularity, especially for smaller memes of low mutation rates, where very few distinct variants are generated. We therefore appropriately limited ourselves to memes with a sufficient number of observations to yield accurate statistics. To estimate power-law exponents, which require observations over several orders of magnitude, we included memes with upwards of 100,000 variants. To estimate the required number of variants to generate accurate Gini coefficients, we simulated the Yule process and contrasted the asymptotic Gini coefficient for a meme that had evolved for a long time period, with the G during the early evolution of the meme. We found that the two values matched closely once the meme had grown to over 1,000 variants and so set this as the lower bound for the number of variants for the empirical measurements of G.

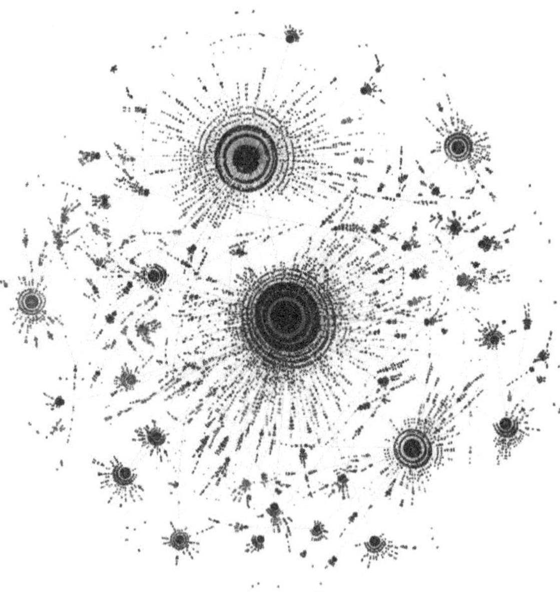

Figure 2: Approximate phylogenetic forest of the "no one should" meme. Each node is a variant, and each edge connects a variant to the most likely ancestor variant. Nodes are colored by timing prompt: rest of the day (blue), next 24 hours (red), or other (purple), showing that mutations in the timing prompt are preserved along the branches of the tree.

2.1 Mapping individuals' political leanings

To understand selection based on political inclinations of individuals in the United States, we used political affiliations specified by individuals in their Facebook profiles. Among active Facebook users in the United States in May of 2012, approximately 17.6% entered a political affiliation in their profiles. Because of the freeform nature of affiliation entry, there is a long tail of political affiliations, and 1.6 million distinct terms used, from *Democratic Party* to *Politics, n: [Poly "many" + tics "blood-sucking parasites"]* . The top 100 designations, listed in Table 1, accounted for 86.6% of all entries. We limited our analysis to those among the top 100 affiliations that could be mapped on a liberal to conservative scale, -2 being very liberal, 0 being moderate or independent, and 2 being very conservative. We excluded responses such as "Other", "I don't care", and "Libertarian (Party)". For example, we labeled the Tea Party as very conservative, and the Green Party as very liberal, the rest are specified in Table 1. These 51 designations comprise 41.2% of all people who had entered something into the political affiliation field on their profiles. Prior to December 2010, the responses were limited to a choice of (Very Liberal, Liberal, Moderate, Conservative, Very Conservative, Apathetic, Libertarian and Other). "Other" remained a popular choice and accounts for fully 41.4% of all responses. "Liberal" and "Democratic Party" accounted for 14.8%, while "Republican Party" and "Conservative" accounted for 15.5%.

Table 1: Most popular political leanings for US users in 2012 mapped on a -2 to 2 Liberal to Conservative scale.

valence	political affiliation specified
-2	Very Liberal, Liberal Democratic Party, Green Party, Peace and Freedom Party, Socialist, Communism, Communist, Socialist Party USA
-1	Democratic Party, Liberal, Barack Obama, Democratic, Democrat, OBAMA, Conservative Democrat, Progressive, Moderate Liberal, Democratic Party of the Virgin Islands, Conservative liberal, Democrata
0	Moderate, Independent, Independence Party of America, Neutral, Independent, Middle of the road, Independent Party, Moderate Party, Centrist
1	Republican Party, Conservative, Conservative Party, Republican, Independent Citizens Movement, Conservatives, Conservative Independent, Rebublican, Reform Party of the United States of America, Liberal conservative, Fiscal Conservative, Moderate conservative, NOBAMA, GOP, Liberal Republican, OBAMA SUCKS!
2	Very Conservative, Tea Party, Constitution Party, Conservative Republicans, Conservative Republican, America First Party

3. RESULTS

3.1 Replication

In this study, we are interested in memes that are replicated when a person copies a piece of text from a friend. As the process of friend copying from friend is repeated, large diffusion cascades may occur as shown in Figure 1. Typically, one replicates the meme by selecting the text of a friend's update, copying it, pasting it into one's own status update box, and sometimes editing the text further before clicking 'post'. However, the abundance of typos in some variants indicates that they were retyped character-by-character as opposed to replicated via a block copy-and-paste action. We define the mutation rate μ as the proportion of copies which introduce new edits as opposed to creating exact replicas. We further link

Table 2: Normalized text of the most common variants of the appreciation meme M1190. The pairwise Levenshtein distances are: $l(n1, n2) = 65, l(n2, n3) = 3, l(n1, n3) = 65, l(n1, f1) = 283, l(n1, c1) = 235, l(c1, f1) = 185, l(c1, c2) = 25$.

rank	copies	variant
n1	71831	somewhere right now a nurse is getting yelled at for being late with pain meds while holding her bladder because she doesn t have time to pee starving because she missed her break being pooped peed bled on and is missing her family while taking care of yours in the minute you took to read this nurses all over the world are saving lives re post this if you are a nurse love a nurse or appreciate one
f2	59352	a firefighter is being yelled at for taking too long to get there while trying desperately to save the life of a total stranger holding his bladder because he didn t have time to pee when the alarm sounded starving because he missed one of his three meals tired because the alarm sounded just as he closed his eyes it s now 4 in the morning and missing his family while taking care of yours re post if you are a firefighter love a firefighter or appreciate a firefighter
c1	26649	somewhere a cop is being yelled at for taking too long to get there trying to save the life of a total stranger holding his bladder because his mdt just went off starving because he missed a meal having to keep a stone face at an accident scene where there s 2 dead kids and now its 4 am and he s missing his family while taking care of yours re post if you are a cop love a cop or appreciate a cop
n2	18068	somewhere right now a nurse is getting yelled at for being late with meds holding their bladder because they don t have time to pee starving because they missed lunch being peed on puked on pooped on bled on and is missing their family while taking care of yours in the minute it took you to read this nurses all over the world are saving lives repost if you are a nurse love a nurse or appreciate a nurse
n3	17954	somewhere right now a nurse is getting yelled at for being late with meds holding their bladder because they don t have time to pee starving because they missed lunch being peed on puked on pooped on bled on and is missing their family while taking care of yours in the minute it took you to read this nurses all over the world are saving lives repost if you are a nurse love a nurse or appreciate nurses
c2	15175	somewhere a cop is being yelled at for taking too long to get there trying to save the life of a total stranger holding his bladder because his mdt just went off starving because he missed a meal having to keep a stone face at an accident scene where there s 2 dead kids and now its 4 am and he s missing his family while taking care of yours re post if you are a cop love a cop or appreciate a cop you all know who you are

each new variant to the variant it was most likely derived from, as described below.

To see concretely how mutation occurs we consider the meme "No one should die because they cannot afford health care and no one should go broke because they get sick. If you agree please post this as your status for the rest of the day." In this form, which emerged early on in the meme's evolution, it was copied over 470,000 times. A variant prepending "thinks that" (which would follow the individual's name), was copied 60,000 times. The third most popular variant inserted "We are only as strong as the weakest among us" in the middle. Some copies changed "the rest of the day" to "the next 24 hours." Figure 2 shows how this particular timing trait

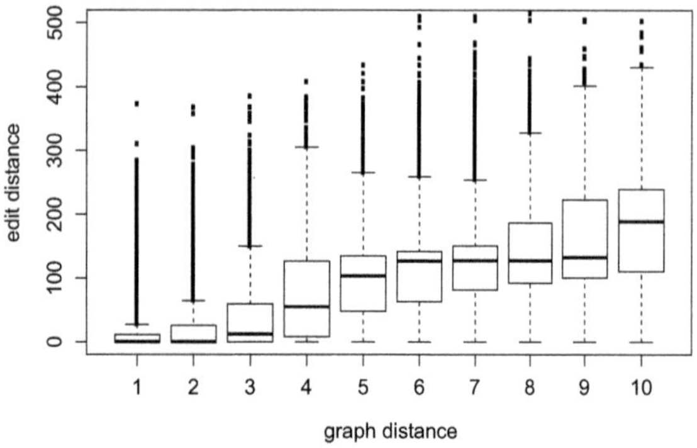

Figure 3: Edit distance from the root typically increases as a node is further down in the copy chain, i.e. the greater the number of hops in the diffusion tree. Here edit distance is shown for a sample of memes where copy chains reached a length of 10 or greater.

is passed down through the genetic lineage. The high number of exact copies is consistent with this meme having a modest and typical mutation rate $\mu = 0.11$. That is, 89% of the copies were exact, while 11% introduced a mutation.

In order to trace the lineage of particular variants, we use the edit distance between the variant an individual posted and the variants previously posted by that person's friends. We define the edit distance as the number of character additions and deletions that must be performed in order to obtain one variant of the meme from another. For example, changing the phrase "thinks that" to "agrees that" creates two variants separated by edit distance 10, since the 5 characters 't h i n k' are deleted and 'a g r e e' are added. Further examples are given in Table 2. As might be expected, there is a compound effect of such mutations over several generations, with edit distance increasing as copy is made from copy is made from copy (Figure 3).

3.2 Population Genetics of Memes

The first striking pattern in the data is the uneven popularity of the variants, shown in Figure 4. For 121 of the 123 largest memes with over 100,000 distinct variants each, a Kolmogorov-Smirnov test confirmed a power-law fit ($D < 0.05$), with maximum likelihood-fitted exponents of 2.01 ± 0.15. Expanding to the 435 memes with an excess of 10,000 variants yielded similar exponents: 1.99 ± 0.21.

Although a variety of processes can produce power laws [4,31], we show that the evolution of memes in an online environment can be modeled by the Yule process [42]. This simple process, previously used to model the number of species per genus, bacterial populations [27] and protein domain family sizes [23,32], contains just two simple components: replication and mutation. The process starts with a single variant of a meme. Each individual instance of the meme has an equal probability of generating a new copy per unit time. The probability of a copy containing a mutation is μ, and we let $r = \frac{\mu}{1-\mu}$ be the ratio between the probability of a mutated and non-mutated copy.

For very large times, the probability that the number of copies of a variant exceeds y is given by [42]:

$$Pr(Y \geq y) = r\frac{\Gamma(1+r)\Gamma(y)}{\Gamma(y+1+r)} \tag{1}$$

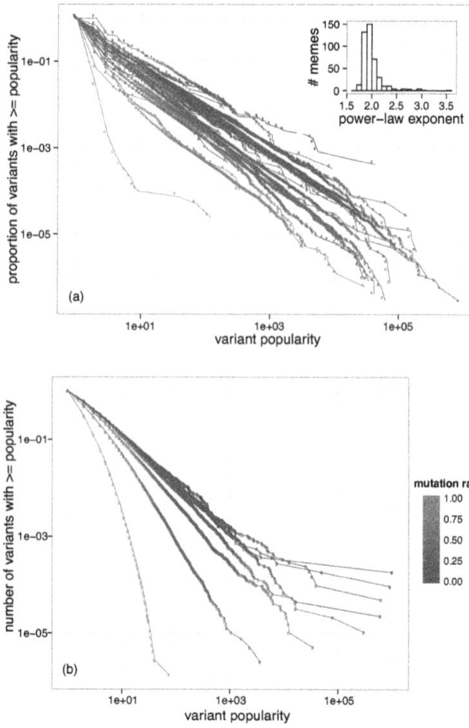

Figure 4: Distributions of variant frequency in (a) a sample of observed memes, (b) a simulated Yule process. The inset shows the distribution of fitted power-law exponents for all memes with $\geq 10,000$ variants.

where Γ is the gamma function. As the mutation rate $\mu \rightarrow 0$, $r \rightarrow 0$. This simplifies to $Pr(Y = y) = \frac{1}{y(y+1)}$, i.e. a power-law distribution with exponent 2. For higher mutation rates, the tail of the distribution, as $y \rightarrow \infty$, is given by

$$Pr(Y \geq y) \sim r\Gamma(1+r)y^{-(1+r)} \tag{2}$$

Thus the Yule model predicts that memes with a low mutation rate will have variants distributed according to a power-law distribution with an exponent close to 2, which is what we observed with our data (Figure 4(a), inset). The Yule model also predicts that memes with a high mutation rate will deviate from a power law because frequent mutation prevents any single variant from achieving an extremely high number of identical copies. Simulations of the Yule model for a range of mutation rates produce variant popularity distributions, shown in Figure 4(b), which bear a close resemblance to the empirically observed distributions in Figure 4(a).

The observed power-law distributions for low mutation rates (and their absence for high mutation rates), make the Yule process a plausible mechanism of variant creation and replication. However, many different mechanisms can produce similar distributions, and we want to validate the model predictions further, even for less popular memes where the data is insufficient to confirm a power-law fit. We use the Gini coefficient G to measure the inequality in variant frequency within a meme and to compare it against the G predicted by the Yule model for μ observed for that meme. $G = 0$ if all variants are equally popular (e.g., if every copy is a mutation), and $G = 1$ if only one variant is present (i.e., $\mu = 0$). If mutation can occur ($\mu > 0$), but none of the mutated variants are able to produce additional copies, then $G = 1 - \mu$. For a power-law distribution where $Pr(Y \geq y) \sim y^{-\alpha}$, $G = \frac{1}{2\alpha - 1}$ [29]. Using Eq. 2, we

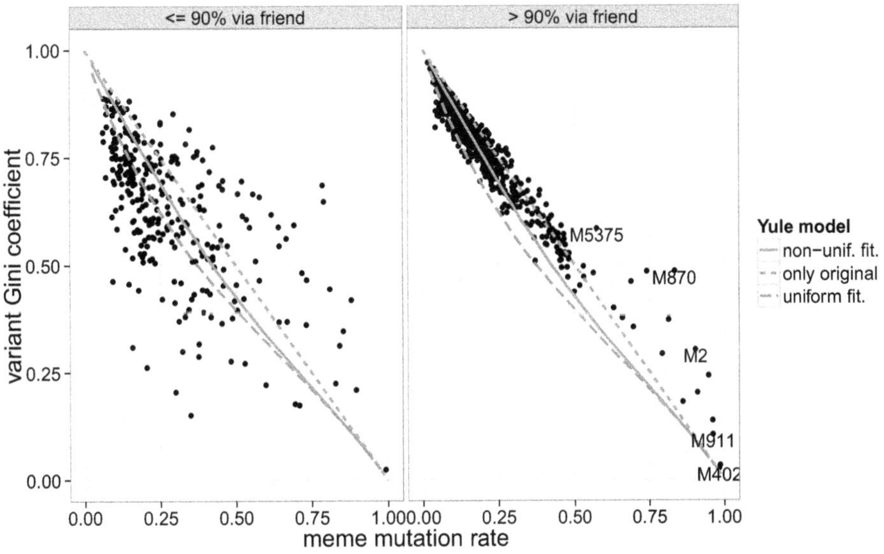

Figure 5: Correspondence between the Gini coefficient G and the mutation rate for memes with over 1000 distinct variants: (a) 287 memes with $\leq$ 90% of instances being posted following a friend's post, and (b) 876 memes with $>$ 90% instances posted after a friend. $1 - \mu$ is the expected relationship if none of the mutations but the original are viable. Two simulations, with uniform and variable fitness, are shown for comparison. The identified memes are: M2 (copy sentence from p. 56 of closest book), M402 (child's birthweight in honor of mother's day), M870 (place of birth), M911 (first concert you attended), M5375 (zodiac sign).

can derive the correspondence $G = \frac{1-\mu}{1+\mu}$, valid for μ close to 0 in the Yule model. This allows us to form a direct prediction from the Yule model of the expected G for a given μ. Since the theoretical prediction holds only for small μ and uniform fitness, we also simulate the Yule process with both uniform and normally distributed variant fitness, to derive relationships between G and μ over the full range $0 < \mu < 1$, as shown in Figure 5.

Empirically, we need to be able to determine whether an individual copy is a mutation or not. We do this by connecting meme instances through the friendship graph. If someone posts a new variant distinct from those previously posted by their friends, the instance is counted as a mutation. If they post an exact copy of one of their friends' previous posts, then it is counted as a copy. Figure 5 shows a close correspondence ($\rho = -0.97$) between the mutation rate and G, for memes with over 1,000 variants and over 90% of instances diffusing through the social network, i.e. having at least 90% of posts occurring after a friend's post. The curves delineate theoretical and simulated predictions while each point represents an entire meme, with the vast majority of memes falling between these two curves. This lends additional support that meme propagation follows the Yule model. Note that the correspondence between mutation rate and Gini coefficient is no coincidence and depends crucially on the ability to measure the mutation rate precisely, as demonstrated by the contrast between Figures 5(a) and (b). If fewer than 50% of a meme's posts follow friends' posts of the same meme, it is likely that meme replication is being driven at least partly outside of the social network. This adds uncertainty to the replication path and μ, reducing the correlation between μ and G significantly ($\rho = -0.60$).

Only a handful of memes appeared to mutate at rates above $\mu > 0.5$. Such rates are remarkably high, with more than one out of every two copies resulting in mutation. Indeed, unlike the vast majority of copy and paste memes which simply instruct the reader to replicate them, memes with what appeared to be very high mutation rates specifically instructed the person transmitting them to modify the text of the meme, typically by adding custom information: M402 and M4416 (see [1] for meme text) asked for the birthweights of one's children, M6265 for oldest friends, and M431 for billboard charts from one's birthday. The replication mechanics of these *customizable* memes are different. Rather than copying the entire text of the meme, a portion of the text is copied, while the remainder can be changed. In order to analogously treat customizable memes one would need to identify and remove the substitutable text, which is beyond the scope of our method.

Even though the replication mechanics are different for customizable memes, one might still be able to make a prediction about the distribution of copies among variants based only on the rate of change of the entire text, including customization. For example, one might assume that the main variant, containing the replication instructions, but no customization, would be the only variant with non-zero fitness and hence multiple copies, since any customization would make the variant irrelevant to the next person copying the text. In that case the prediction would be $G = 1 - \mu$. While several memes fall roughly on this line, customizable memes typically have higher Gini coefficient than expected, meaning that even though these memes prompt the text to be modified, these modifications tend to coincidentally produce the same variant. This is especially pronounced for memes where such coincidences are more likely to happen. For example, M870 asks its host to copy it, and add their place of birth. This gives it a very high mutation rate, but also a high G, related to the power-law distribution of population center sizes [15,34], i.e. individuals are likely to independently generate identical strings even while mutating the meme. The same elevated Gini coefficient due to many identical customizations occurs to a lesser extent in memes asking the host to copy a sentence from a book (M2), list their zodiac sign (M5375), and mention the first concert they attended (M911). On the other hand, the meme asking for children's names and birthweights (M402), has both a μ close to 1, and G close to 0. Therefore, while the Yule model is a good fit for the great majority memes which are ideas evolving "naturally" under low mutation rates, it is not appropriate for the handful of textual games inducing high mutation rates and coincidental copies.

Finally, we examine whether mutation rate affects the successful spread of a meme, but find no overall effect of mutation rate on the total number of copies of the meme ($\rho(N_{meme}, \mu_{meme}) < 0.1$). We further find that meme mutation rates are constant over time ($\rho(t, \mu_t) < 0.04$), and that the most popular variants are just as likely to generate mutated copies as less popular ones (ρ(num mutated copies, popularity) $> .95$), indicating that a meme does not converge to an optimal consensus sequence.

3.3 Mutation characteristics

While the Yule model explains the overall distributions of different variants, a more detailed look reveals several interesting patterns in the mechanics of how new variants are created: where edits occur, whether the length matters, and whether an entire meme or just parts of it are inserted into other memes.

First, there is a non-uniform probability of mutation along the length of the meme (see Figure 6). This is likely in part due to the copy and paste mechanism for replication, where most people copy and paste the text rather than typing it anew. After pasting, they might prepend, append, or modify the text. To identify the locations where text is most likely to be mutated, we segmented each variant into overlapping sequences of 4 words (4-grams). For each 4-gram within the most popular variant of a meme, we computed the proportion of other variants that contained it. On average, a 4-gram occurring in the middle of the most popular variant is preserved in 70.2% of other variants. This falls to 59.3% for the first 4-gram, and 50.3% for the last. Edits at the margins are likely to occur because the selection of text to be copied is incomplete, e.g. it misses the start or end. Similarly, pre/post-paste modifications will be at the beginning/end of the meme, unless the person moves the cursor.

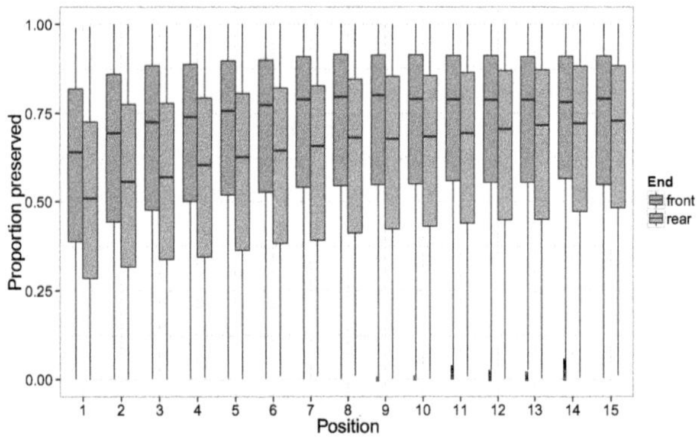

Figure 6: Probability that a segment of a meme is preserved as a function of its location within the most popular variant of that meme.

If memes are being replicated through a simple mouse swipe, one would expect a weak selection pressure for shorter variants, reflective primarily of the additional effort of reading and copying a longer meme. Figure 7 shows just such a weak within-meme selection pressure toward slightly shorter variants. Variants that are too short, and potentially have lost some of the message of the meme, are again not as popular. Consistent with the selection pressure being weak, we observe a high variation both in the average string length between memes (mean length = 356.7 ± 303.95), and length of individual variants within a meme (average within-meme length difference=69.90 ± 195.85).

Many people are exposed to and even participate in replications of several memes. This gives them the opportunity to transfer textual sequences from one meme to another. Just four 4-grams occurred in over 200 memes with a prevalence of between 5 and 95% of the variants. They contained individual words which were initially used to identify memes in the data, but arranged them in a specific way: "put this as your", "copy and paste this", "this as your status", "re[-]post if you". We computed the ratio r_g of the average frequency of all variants containing a given 4-gram against the average frequency of variants of the same meme that do not have the exact 4-gram. For the four most widespread 4-grams, $r_g > 1.4$, meaning that even though all variants contained replication keywords, these *specific* formulations of replication instructions were advantageous.

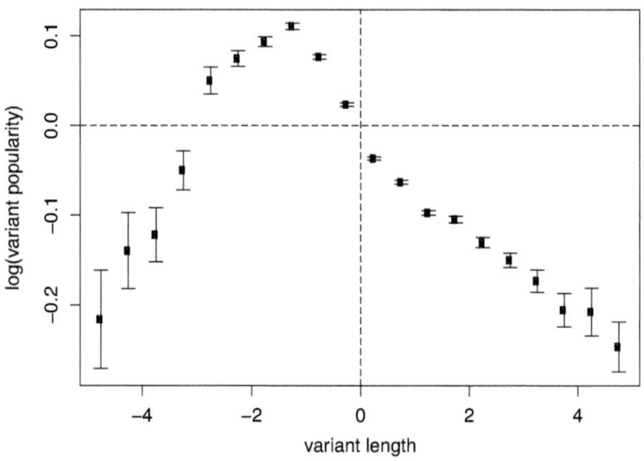

Figure 7: Relative frequency of a variant within a meme as a function of its length relative to other variants.

In Table 3 we list the top 4-grams with the highest r_g and occurring in over 20 memes. As mentioned, although all strings clustered into memes had some substring associated with replication, e.g. "post" or "copy", the most successful variants put these together in clear replication instructions, e.g. "copy and paste", "as your status", "into your status", which can facilitate the meme's expression and transmission [18]. Other successful substrings include encouragement and allusions to competition ("see how many people"), persistence cues ("status for at least"), or conditions that are easy to match or identify with ("if you love your", "if you know someone", "paste if you agree", "proud to be a"). A specific pattern, "of you won't", occurred in prompts such as "95% of you won't copy this, but the 5% who [have a positive attribute] will". 144 memes contained at least one variant matching "won't [...] will". These variants had significantly higher likelihood of being copied, 10.98 copies on average, relative to an average of 7.05 overall. In 102 of the 144 cases the individual who introduced the phrasing into the meme had either used it previously in another meme, or had a friend who had, suggesting that in a large number of cases the substring could have been transferred from one meme to another. On the other hand, some copy errors, occurring in significant numbers, e.g. "ago comment like unlike write", which indicate spurious selection of Facebook boilerplate text below the update, enjoyed only one fourth of the popularity of variants which did not contain them, possibly indicating a notion of *grammatical fitness*. This is further supported by a mild negative correlation between the within-meme relative number of English spelling errors s for a variant and its popularity y ($\rho(s, \log(y)) = -0.133, p < 10^{-15}$).

Sometimes, although infrequently, more than a short substring will be shared between separate memes. This occurs when one

Table 3: 4-grams which conferred replicative advantage on the variants which contained them, within memes where they represented between 5 and 95% of the population.

4 gram	r_g	# memes
plain copy and paste		
please post this as	2.59	23
it as your status	2.23	28
copy and paste and	2.08	20
to copy and paste	2.04	27
this into your status	2.03	29
condition/identification/agreement		
paste if you agree	2.84	25
and paste if you	2.02	35
if you love your	2.00	21
status if you know	1.98	20
your status to show	1.94	28
status to show your	1.92	20
proud to be a	1.79	20
post if you agree	1.79	67
status if you are	1.79	33
if you know someone	1.78	24
other		
see how many people	2.85	25
status for at least	1.99	29

meme mutates so drastically that it becomes a separate meme, but also when memes recombine at later points, such as when two separate memes are copied and pasted together, thereby merging into a single fused meme. One such example is a variant of an anti-bullying meme (M4038A) with over 300,000 copies, which at one point was pasted together with a meme about a sick child (M4038B). The hybrid, containing most of the text of the two original memes, was exactly copied over 10,000 times. Similarly, these fused memes contain both messages of the original meme. The combination might not occur for months after the memes are individually introduced. For example, M954, a chain letter meme [20], was present in fragments since November 2008. The status update character limit imposed at that time did not permit it to be copied entirely, and the fragments posted were likely transferred from copies spreading via email. M26, a similar but distinct chain letter, first appeared in April of 2009. They combined in an awkward copy-and-paste two years later, in October 2011, with over 300 copies made of the combination, including attempts at correcting the copy error in the transition from one meme to the other.

3.4 Adaptation of Memes to Niches

So far we have presented aggregate characteristics of meme evolution. Examining the evolution of a meme in detail can give insight into how a meme adapts to specific niches within the social network environment. Prior work on cultural transmission has examined how language [22] and music [26] evolve in experimental settings. These lacked the social network structure where different variants are adopted by populations having different preferences. The niche can be time or location-specific; A meme asking mothers to describe their childrens' features, in some variants was prepended by "In honor of mother's day" (M4416) and an Amber alert (M246) appeared with the same make of car and license plate but different locations where the child was abducted: Edmonton, KY, Edmonton, Canada, Quebec, "Washington", and sometimes multiple locations simultaneously.

Here we explore in more detail a meme–"No one should die because they can't afford health insurance…"–that initially appeared as a political meme but then its variants evolved to appeal to other demographics, including the opposing political party. The meme goes on to say "no one should go broke because they get sick", which is something President Obama stated in his weekly address on August 14th, 2009, shortly before the meme appeared, and again when addressing the US Congress on healthcare reform on Sept. 9, 2009, when the meme had already taken hold. The meme would appeal primarily to liberals, which we were able to verify by computing the average political leaning for those people in the US who both filled this field out in their profile and posted the meme. Although the most prominent variants of the meme propagated primarily from liberal to liberal, some (humorous) variants appealed across the political spectrum, e.g. "no one should be without a beer because they cannot afford one…". Humor has been noted to play an important role in online discussions [6], and political satire and memes [39]. Other variants, criticizing the bill (e.g., "no one should die because the government is involved with health care…") appealed primarily to conservatives (see Table 4). These secondary variants peaked at different times (see Figure 8).

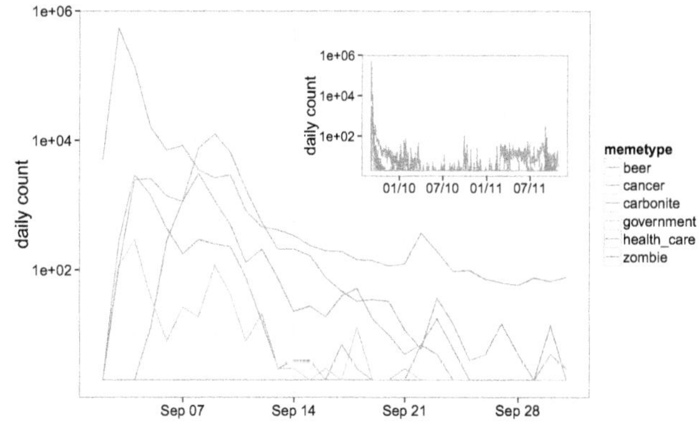

Figure 8: Different variants of the "no one should…" meme (see Table 4) peak in popularity at different times. The inset shows that the meme persisted in low numbers for two years.

Once a person posts a meme, they are unlikely to repost it again. That is, exposure to one variant of a meme usually confers immunity to others. However, a small fraction of people post a meme more than once, sometimes years apart, as they identify that the message is still important. In the case of the "no one should" meme, 4.36% of posts were repeat posts by the same individual. Of those posting the meme a second time with a non-healthcare related variant, 40.4% had posted a healthcare variant previously. Another, more subtle, interaction is that exposure to one variant of a meme can make an individual more susceptible to other variants parodying the original variant. This is evident for the health care meme, where among the 61,979 people posting one of the non-healthcare variants, a full 93.0% had at least one friend who had previously posted a healthcare variant. This collaborative success of memes has also been observed in a population of image memes [11].

3.5 Network diffusion dynamics

Just as different biological species experience population booms and declines, memes experience bursts of activity with different variants being dominant in different periods. Figure 8 shows that the above mentioned variants of a single meme occurred proximately in time, but peaked at different points. Variants of the appreciation meme, listed in Table 2, peaked weeks apart. Simulations of a meme diffusing and mutating according to the Yule

Table 4: Average political bias of individuals sharing variants of the 'no one should' meme (-2: very liberal, +2: very conservative).

keyword	average bias	example
health care	-0.87	die because they cannot afford health care...
carbonite	-0.37	be frozen in carbonite because... they couldn't pay Jabba the Hut
zombie	-0.30	die because of zombies if they cannot afford a shotgun...
cancer	-0.02	have to worry about dying tomorrow but cancer patients do...
wine	0.15	go thirsty because they cannot afford wine...
beer	0.22	be without a beer because they cannot afford one...
government	0.88	die because the government is involved with health care...
Obamacare	0.96	die because Obamacare rations their healthcare...
taxes	0.97	go broke because government taxes and spends...

process in a fixed and evenly mixed population, excluding network topology, can easily reproduce the distributions of variants within a meme (see Figure 4(b)), but not the bursts in popularity of individual variants. The ingredients missing are network diffusion [3,16,35,41], combined with network growth and variable user activity levels [19].

In order to simulate meme diffusion in a realistic, yet tractable network environment, we selected a small country with a large proportion of the population being Facebook users, and over 2 million having 100 or more Facebook friends. We used this actual friendship network within the country for the memes to diffuse over. In the simulation, we infected a single individual with one variant of a meme. The simulation proceeds as follows. Every friend of an infected individual is flagged as having the potential to be infected the next time they log in. Login frequencies vary between users, with each user being assigned a uniform (0,1) random variable (0.1 corresponds to logging in every 10th day on average, 1.0 to logging in every day). Once users log in, they have a probability of becoming infected that decays exponentially with each subsequent login since their first exposure. This is intended to capture both the meme being pushed down further in their Facebook feed, and also the fact that someone who chooses not to post at first exposure is less likely to post at subsequent exposures.

Such a model typically produces a single-peaked distribution in overall meme popularity (see Figure 9(a)), with different variants peaking at different times. The peak widens when individuals join the network while the meme is diffusing, but the distribution is still single-peaked Figure 9(b). Interestingly, at the point at which only several tens of thousands of status updates are posted, 1 million users, constituting over half of the network, are potentially exposed because their friends have posted. This leaves little room for untouched areas of the network that could contribute to secondary peaks.

Finally, when we further modify the simulation such that variants have variable fitness (mean=1, sd=0.5), we observe multiple peaks (see Figure 9(c)). As mentioned, memes' fitness can vary due to the particular sequence they carry and how that message aligns with susceptibilities in the underlying network transmitting them. Variation in fitness can also be due to external factors, e.g. versions of an anti-bullying meme mentioning that it's anti-bullying week, or all similar versions receiving a boost when Facebook altered its feed-ranking algorithm to cluster status updates containing similar text and placed them together near the top of a user's feed. Thus a Yule process incorporating variable fitness, and overlaid on a growing network of variably active nodes, can explain the observed bursty meme variant popularity.

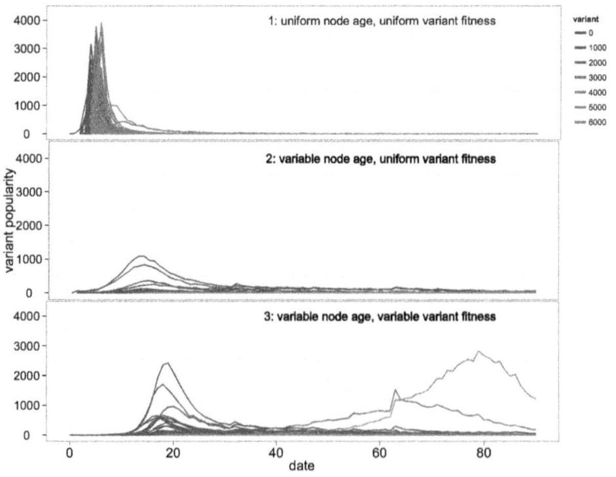

Figure 9: Simulated popularity of variants in a network simulation model, under different conditions.

4. DISCUSSION

There are convenient analogies between the language of genes and biological evolution that are helpful to us in discussing and analyzing memes. At the most basic level, memes contain two key ingredients that are reminiscent of biological populations: replication and mutation [13]. When Richard Dawkins introduced the concept of a meme, he suggested that "memes should be regarded as living structures, not just metaphorically but technically" (Richard Dawkins, Selfish Gene p.192.) In this study, we apply this concept more rigorously to Facebook memes and find similarities between genes and memes. In biology, a gene's genotype is the DNA sequence, and the gene's phenotype is the resulting function that the gene carries out. For textual memes, the string is the information that is being passed, or the 'genotype.' The 'phenotype' is what is expressed by the meme, which can include the meme's message and replication instructions.

We define a meme according to biological terms. A gene is a hereditary unit that is transmitted to offspring. Thus, since the meme is transmitted when copied and pasted, the meme itself can be considered to be a gene. Genotype is the description of variants within the gene. For example, a bacterium with a mutation in the Lac gene that knocks out Lac's gene function is described to have the genotype Lac-. Genotypic variants can be simple text edits that don't change the meme's meaning (e.g. a misspelling), or they can have larger effects such as a change in meaning ("healthcare" versus "beer"). The genotype is a representation of differences, for example, "post for 24 hours" versus "post for a day" are two possible genotypes for a particular meme. The genotype is independent of any effects of the environment and is heritable [9].

Phenotypes are observable characteristics which include morphology and behavior, and are influenced by both environment and genotype. One possible phenotype then, is the expression of the meme itself, because the meme's entity defines its morphology. This is similar to RNA viruses where the genetic information is contained within the RNA (the genotype), but when the RNA is expressed, this becomes a phenotypic trait [9]. Similarly, when a meme is posted (expressed), this becomes a phenotype.

There are many other meme phenotypes; we provide some examples of behavior phenotypes. One behavior phenotype is the average time a meme is posted. This phenotype depends on the meme's genotype (whether the meme says "post for a day"), and the environment (whether people using Facebook follow directions, remember to log in and update, etc.) Another meme phenotype is a meme's appeal to a certain demographic. This will depend on which variant of the meme is being used (whether the genotype is "healthcare" or "taxes"), and how much the intended target audience places importance on the issue being discussed (environment).

In biology, mutations occur randomly and blindly. Most mutations are neutral, but occasionally, some mutations are deleterious or advantageous [21]. Neutral mutations do not affect gene function, deleterious mutations are evolutionarily disadvantageous, while advantageous mutations provide a positive benefit to its carriers. Extending the analogy, neutral edits in memes are minor edits to the string that do not change the meaning of the meme. The Yule process is a neutral model where each meme variant has the same probability of copying itself, and possibly mutating again. Notably, most memes follow the Yule process (Figure 5) which suggests that most meme variants are neutral with respect to the parent's meme. We also find some 'advantageous' mutations that increase the likelihood of a meme being copied (Table 3). There is one critical difference between biology and social media: evolution is a blind process in biology, but in social media, there can be a conscious effort to create mutations that will intentionally spread a meme's presence (i.e. marketing campaigns). We discuss further similarities, as well as some mechanistic differences, pertaining to the more detailed replication mechanism, below.

The first is the slight preference for shorter variants of the same meme, analogous to the observations of bacteria favoring small genomes for fast replication [30]. Both memes and genes are shaped by the same two factors: their length has to be sufficient to encompass information that helps them to replicate, but excessive length slows down replication.

Even more interesting mutation mechanisms also have parallels across both genes and memes. For example, advantageous sequences can occur across multiple memes, likely transferred by a single individual from one meme to another. This process is analogous to lateral gene transfer in bacteria wherein useful genetic code, e.g. plasmids conferring antibiotic resistance, can be transferred through mechanisms other than replication. Yet another example is that of fusion. In genomes, two single genes are combined in a fusion event to create a single functional gene that retains both functionalities of the two single genes [14]. We observed several fusion events between different memes, some giving rise to popular variants.

Some similarities in the replication mechanism might be spurious. For example, mutations of both genes [8] and memes occur preferentially at the boundaries. Many mutations occur at the beginning and end of a gene (untranslated regions) because most of the function is in the middle of the gene and so mutations at the gene boundaries do not affect gene function [8]. Similarly, we observe that meme strings tend to have text edits at the beginning and end of a meme (Figure 6). The same factor could be at play, e.g. even the most common variants frequently start with a non-essential or generic address: "everyone", "attention", and end with words also not essential to the message: "if you agree", "takes a second", "so your fb friends are aware". However, we cannot rule out that the beginnings and ends of memes are simply more vulnerable because of the block copy-and-paste mechanism.

There are several limitations to this study. Narrowly defining the success of a meme to be the number of copies posted, while keeping the analogy of a gene's replicative success, does not account for all of the memes' effect, which might encompass the number of exposures to the meme and the resulting reaction e.g. in the form of likes and comments. Furthermore, while copy-and-paste memes provide an easy means to study unit of transmission needed in memetics, they do not address other mechanisms in cultural evolution, such as the adoption and evolution of norms, which may also hold interesting biological analogies [28].

In summary, we have described how information evolves as it is passed from individual to individual in a social network, sometimes exactly, and sometimes with a modification which produces a new variant. This process is well-described by the Yule model, with the mutation rate predicting the distribution of popularity among variants. Although many variants appear to emerge from neutral drift, there is evidence of some selection, as successful subsequences were found across memes, and individual meme variants were found to match preferences of individuals transmitting them. A clear limitation of the present study is that the information analyzed was of but one type (copy-and-paste memes) and was observed in a single environment. However, this same environment was the first opportunity to study the evolution of information with precision and on a large scale. We believe our findings are likely to be applicable to a range of environments where information diffuses through multiple steps with a potential for modification, and that the observed evolutionary process carries important implications for the reach and fidelity of information diffusing through social networks.

5. ACKNOWLEDGMENTS

We thank Brian Karrer, Eytan Bakshy, Jon Kleinberg, Jure Leskovec, Alex Dow and Mark Newman for comments.

6. REFERENCES

[1] www.ladamic.com/research/data/memetext.html. *Supplementary table: Normalized text of the most common variant of memes*, 2015.

[2] L. Adamic, T. M. Lento, and A. T. Fiore. How you met me. *ICWSM'12*, 2012.

[3] E. Adar and L. Adamic. Tracking information epidemics in blogspace. In *Web Intelligence'05*, pages 207–214. IEEE, 2005.

[4] P. Andriani and B. McKelvey. Perspective-from Gaussian to Paretian thinking: causes and implications of power laws in organizations. *Organization Science*, 20(6):1053–1071, 2009.

[5] E. Bakshy, I. Rosenn, C. Marlow, and L. Adamic. The role of social networks in information diffusion. In *Proc. WWW'12*, pages 519–528. ACM, 2012.

[6] N. K. Baym. The performance of humor in computer-mediated communication. *JCMC*, 1(2):0–0, 1995.

[7] C. H. Bennett, M. Li, and B. Ma. Chain letters and evolutionary histories. *Scientific American*, 288(6):76–81, 2003.

[8] A. Chakravarti et al. Population genetics – making sense out of sequence. *Nature genetics*, 21(Suppl 1):56–60, 1999.

[9] B. Charlesworth and D. Charlesworth. *Elements of evolutionary genetics*. Roberts and Company Publishers Greenwood Village, 2010.

[10] J. Cheng, L. Adamic, P. A. Dow, J. M. Kleinberg, and J. Leskovec. Can cascades be predicted? In *WWW'14*, pages 925–936, 2014.

[11] M. Coscia. Competition and success in the meme pool: a case study on Quickmeme.com. *ICWSM 2013*, 2013.

[12] R. Dawkins. *The selfish gene*. Oxford University Press, USA, 1976.

[13] S. F. Elena and R. E. Lenski. Evolution experiments with microorganisms: the dynamics and genetic bases of adaptation. *Nature Reviews Genetics*, 4(6):457–469, 2003.

[14] A. J. Enright, I. Iliopoulos, N. C. Kyrpides, and C. A. Ouzounis. Protein interaction maps for complete genomes based on gene fusion events. *Nature*, 402(6757):86–90, 1999.

[15] X. Gabaix. Zipf's law for cities: an explanation. *The Quarterly Journal of Economics*, 114(3):739–767, 1999.

[16] M. Girvan, D. S. Callaway, M. E. J. Newman, and S. H. Strogatz. Simple model of epidemics with pathogen mutation. *Phys. Rev. E*, 65:031915, Mar 2002.

[17] C. Heath, C. Bell, and E. Sternberg. Emotional selection in memes: The case of urban legends. *Journal of Personality and Social Psychology*, 81(6):1028, 2001.

[18] F. Heylighen. What makes a meme successful? Selection criteria for cultural evolution. *Proc. 16th Int. Congress on Cybernetics*, 1998.

[19] J. L. Iribarren and E. Moro. Impact of human activity patterns on the dynamics of information diffusion. *Phys. Rev. Lett.*, 103:038702, Jul 2009.

[20] M. D. Kibby. Email forwardables: folklore in the age of the internet. *New Media & Society*, 7(6):770–790, 2005.

[21] M. Kimura. *The neutral theory of molecular evolution*. Cambridge University Press, 1984.

[22] S. Kirby, H. Cornish, and K. Smith. Cumulative cultural evolution in the laboratory: An experimental approach to the origins of structure in human language. *Proceedings of the National Academy of Sciences*, 105(31):10681–10686, 2008.

[23] E. Koonin, Y. Wolf, G. Karev, et al. The structure of the protein universe and genome evolution. *Nature*, 420(6912):218–223, 2002.

[24] J. Leskovec, L. Backstrom, and J. Kleinberg. Meme-tracking and the dynamics of the news cycle. In *KDD'09*, pages 497–506. ACM, 2009.

[25] D. Liben-Nowell and J. Kleinberg. Tracing information flow on a global scale using internet chain-letter data. *PNAS*, 105(12):4633, 2008.

[26] R. M. MacCallum, M. Mauch, A. Burt, and A. M. Leroi. Evolution of music by public choice. *PNAS*, 109(30):12081–12086, 2012.

[27] B. Mandelbrot. A population birth-and-mutation process, I: Explicit distributions for the number of mutants in an old culture of bacteria. *Journal of Applied Probability*, pages 437–444, 1974.

[28] A. Mesoudi, A. Whiten, and K. N. Laland. Towards a unified science of cultural evolution. *Behavioral and Brain Sciences*, 29(04):329–347, 2006.

[29] T. Moothathu. Sampling distributions of Lorenz curve and Gini index of the Pareto distribution. *Sankhyā: The Indian Journal of Statistics, Series B*, pages 247–258, 1985.

[30] N. A. Moran, A. Mira, et al. The process of genome shrinkage in the obligate symbiont Buchnera aphidicola. *Genome Biol*, 2(12):1–0054, 2001.

[31] M. Newman. Power laws, Pareto distributions and Zipf's law. *Contemporary physics*, 46(5):323–351, 2005.

[32] J. Qian, N. Luscombe, and M. Gerstein. Protein family and fold occurrence in genomes: power-law behaviour and evolutionary model. *Journal of Molecular Biology*, 313(4):673–681, 2001.

[33] J. Ratkiewicz, M. Conover, M. Meiss, B. Gonçalves, S. Patil, A. Flammini, and F. Menczer. Truthy: mapping the spread of astroturf in microblog streams. In *WWW'11*, pages 249–252, New York, NY, USA, 2011. ACM.

[34] W. Reed. The Pareto, Zipf and other power laws. *Economics Letters*, 74(1):15–19, 2001.

[35] D. Romero, B. Meeder, and J. Kleinberg. Differences in the mechanics of information diffusion across topics: Idioms, political hashtags, and complex contagion on twitter. In *WWW'11*, pages 695–704. ACM, 2011.

[36] E. Segev, N. A., N. Stolero, and L. Shifman. Families and networks of internet memes: The relationship between cohesiveness, uniqueness, and quiddity concreteness. *JCMC*, 2015.

[37] L. Shifman. An anatomy of a YouTube meme. *New Media & Society*, 2011.

[38] L. Shifman and M. Thelwall. Assessing global diffusion with Web memetics: The spread and evolution of a popular joke. *JASIST*, 60(12):2567–2576, 2009.

[39] P. D. d. Silva and J. L. Garcia. YouTubers as satirists: Humour and remix in online video. *JedDEM*, 4(1):89–114, 2012.

[40] M. Simmons, L. Adamic, and E. Adar. Memes online: Extracted, subtracted, injected, and recollected. *ICWSM 2011*, 2011.

[41] L. Weng, A. Flammini, A. Vespignani, and F. Menczer. Competition among memes in a world with limited attention. *Scientific Reports*, 2, 2012.

[42] G. Yule. A mathematical theory of evolution, based on the conclusions of Dr. JC Willis, FRS. *Philosophical Transactions of the Royal Society of London B: Biological Sciences*, 213(402-410):21–87, 1925.

Nonlinear Laplacian for Digraphs and its Applications to Network Analysis

Yuichi Yoshida
National Institute of Informatics and
Preferred Infrastructure, Inc.
yyoshida@nii.ac.jp

ABSTRACT

In this work, we introduce a new Markov operator associated with a digraph, which we refer to as a nonlinear Laplacian. Unlike previous Laplacians for digraphs, the nonlinear Laplacian does not rely on the stationary distribution of the random walk process and is well defined on digraphs that are not strongly connected. We show that the nonlinear Laplacian has nontrivial eigenvalues and give a Cheeger-like inequality, which relates the conductance of a digraph and the smallest non-zero eigenvalue of its nonlinear Laplacian. Finally, we apply the nonlinear Laplacian to the analysis of real-world networks and obtain encouraging results.

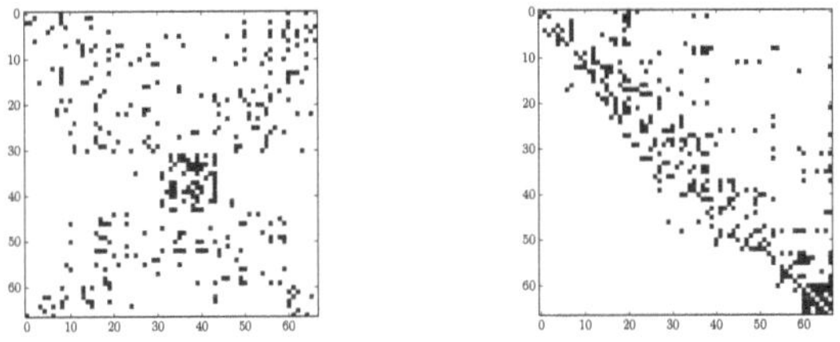

(a) Chung (b) Nonlinear

Figure 1: Adjacency matrix of a real-world network

Categories and Subject Descriptors

E.1 [**Data**]: Data Structures—*Graphs and networks*; G.2.2 [**Discrete Mathematics**]: Graph Theory—*Graph algorithms*

Keywords

Spectral graph theory

1. INTRODUCTION

Spectral graph theory is a versatile tool for analyzing networks. It is used for embedding networks into low-dimensional spaces [27, 36], clustering or partitioning vertices [31], ordering vertices by their importance [9, 32], learning partially labeled networks [21], and analyzing graph theoretic measures [2, 3]. For further details, we refer to surveys [18, 28, 33, 34] and books [15, 17].

The central notion of spectral graph theory is the *Laplacian*, which is a Markov operator associated with an undirected graph. Let $G = (V, E)$ be an undirected graph. Then, the Laplacian L of G is defined as $L = D - A$, where A is the adjacency matrix of G and D is a diagonal matrix with D_{uu} being the degree of u. For some applications, the *normalized Laplacian* $\mathcal{L} = D^{-1/2}LD^{-1/2} = I - D^{-1/2}AD^{-1/2}$ is more useful. Roughly speaking, spectral graph theory consists of relations between graph theoretic measures and the eigenvalues and eigenvectors of a (normalized) Laplacian and their applications.

Many real-world networks are digraphs. Although spectral graph theory is well established for undirected graphs, it cannot be directly applied to digraphs. To overcome this issue, several extensions of (normalized) Laplacians for digraphs have been proposed [13, 24, 37]. However, all these extensions have a common drawback: they reweigh vertices using the stationary distribution π of the random walk process. Hence, they can be defined only for strongly connected digraphs. Moreover, most vertices with a small probability in π are disregarded, which is undesirable in many applications such as ordering and clustering tasks. For example, see Figure 1a for the adjacency matrix of the friendship network in a high school in Illinois [23], where vertices are ordered using Chung's normalized Laplacian [11], which is one of the most studied Laplacians for digraphs. We extracted the largest strongly connected component in the network. Although we can find a tightly connected community in the middle of the adjacency matrix, the rest is rather scattered. This is because that community has a large mass in the stationary distribution, and the ordering of the remaining vertices can be arbitrary.

1.1 Our contributions

In this work, we define a *(normalized) nonlinear Laplacian* for digraphs. As opposed to previous Laplacians for digraphs, our Laplacian does not rely on the stationary distribution of the random walk process. Hence, it can be defined on digraphs that are not strongly connected. Because we do not weigh vertices using the stationary distribution, we obtain more intuitive results in several applications. Further details are provided below.

WSDM'16, February 22–25, 2016, San Francisco, CA, USA.
 ISBN 978-1-4503-3716-8/16/02 ...$15.00.
DOI: http://dx.doi.org/10.1145/2835776.2835785.

Spectral ordering.

In spectral ordering, we order vertices using the second eigenvector of a (normalized) Laplacian. We do not use the first eigenvector because it is trivial and does not have any structural information. Let $G = (V, E)$ be a digraph. If we use Chung's normalized Laplacian, it turns out that its second eigenvector $\boldsymbol{z} \in \mathbb{R}^V$ is the minimizer of

$$\sum_{(u,v)\in E} \left(x_u - x_v\right)^2 \frac{\pi_u}{d_u^+}$$

subject to $\sum x_u^2 \pi_u = 1$, where $\boldsymbol{x} = \{x_u\}_{u\in V}$ is a variable vector, π_u is the probability of staying at $u \in V$ in the stationary distribution, and d_u^+ is the out-degree of $u \in V$. Then, we order the vertices according to the value of z_u. Roughly speaking, the arc (u, v) has the effect of bringing u and v closer, and this effect is strong when the probability π_u is large. This intuitively explains why we obtained Figure 1a.

On the other hand, the second eigenvector $\boldsymbol{z}' \in \mathbb{R}^V$ of a normalized nonlinear Laplacian is the minimizer of

$$\sum_{(u,v)\in E} \left([x_u - x_v]^+\right)^2. \tag{1}$$

subject to $\sum x_u^2 d_u = 1$, where $[a]^+ = \max\{a, 0\}$ and d_u is the degree of $u \in V$, i.e., the sum of the in-degree and out-degree of u. We note that (1) matches the objective function used to compute the second eigenvector of the normalized Laplacian of an undirected graph, except for the existence of $[\cdot]^+$. The term $[x_u - x_v]^+$ respects the direction of the arc $(u, v) \in E$ in the sense that $[x_u - x_v]^+ > 0$ if $x_u > x_v$ and $[x_u - x_v]^+ = 0$ if $x_u \le x_v$. Hence, x_u tends to be smaller than x_v. See Figure 1b for the adjacency matrix where vertices are ordered according to the second eigenvector of the normalized nonlinear Laplacian of the high-school network. The tightly connected community is located in the lower right, and other vertices are ordered so that most arcs are headed from a vertex with a smaller index to that with a larger index. From this figure, we can observe that most arcs in the network respect the global ranking of the vertices.

Spectral clustering.

Another important application of spectral graph theory is clustering. Intuitively speaking, a cluster is a vertex set that has a large number of edges (arcs) within S and only a small number of edges (arcs) leaving S. For undirected graphs, this concept is formalized as the notion of *conductance*, defined as

$$\phi(S) = \frac{\mathrm{cut}(S)}{\min\{\mathrm{vol}(S), \mathrm{vol}(V \setminus S)\}}, \tag{2}$$

where $\mathrm{cut}(S)$ is the number of edges crossing S and $V \setminus S$ and $\mathrm{vol}(S)$ is the sum of the degrees of the vertices in S. There is a beautiful connection between the conductance and the second eigenvalue λ of a normalized Laplacian, which is referred to as Cheeger's inequality [2, 3]:

$$\frac{\lambda}{2} \le \min_{\emptyset \subsetneq S \subsetneq V} \phi(S) \le \sqrt{2\lambda}.$$

Partitioning algorithms based on this connection have been widely used in practice owing to their efficiency and high-quality solutions that they often provide [7, 20]. Recalling that many real-world networks are directed, it is natural to extend Cheeger's inequality to digraphs. Although Chung's normalized Laplacian can be used to show Cheeger-like inequality, it only bounds the conductance with respect to the stationary distribution. Because of this biased notion of conductance, spectral clustering based on Chung's normalized Laplacian may output a set with many arcs leaving it (if those arcs are unimportant for the random walk process).

On the other hand, a normalized nonlinear Laplacian can be used to show a Cheeger-like inequality that bounds a natural extension of the conductance:

$$\phi^+(S) = \frac{\mathrm{cut}^+(S)}{\min\{\mathrm{vol}(S), \mathrm{vol}(V \setminus S)\}},$$

where $\mathrm{cut}^+(S)$ is the number of arcs leaving S and $\mathrm{vol}(S)$ is the sum of the degrees of the vertices in S. Arguably, $\phi^+(S)$ is a more direct extension of the conductance (2) than the one used in [11].

As the name suggests, a (normalized) nonlinear Laplacian is a nonlinear Markov operator, and in general, it is NP-hard to compute its eigenvalues and eigenvectors. To resolve this issue, we use the *heat equation*:

$$\mathrm{d}\boldsymbol{x} = -\mathcal{L}(\boldsymbol{x})\mathrm{d}t,$$

where $\mathcal{L} : \mathbb{R}^V \to \mathbb{R}^V$ is the (normalized) nonlinear Laplacian. We prove that if we initiate a simulation of the heat equation with a vector orthogonal to the trivial first eigenvector, then the solution to the heat equation converges to some nontrivial eigenvector (although it might not be the second one).

We experimentally confirm that our method runs fast and effectively obtains a vector for which the value of (1) is small as well as a set of vertices with a small conductance. Then, we demonstrate through experiments that a nonlinear Laplacian is a useful tool for analyzing structures of real-world directed networks.

Although our results can be easily extended to weighted digraphs, we consider only unweighted digraphs for simplicity.

1.2 Organization

The remainder of this paper is organized as follows. Section 2 reviews related studies. Section 3 introduces the notions used throughout this paper. Section 4 formally defines a nonlinear Laplacian and describes its properties. Section 5 outlines an algorithm for computing the eigenvalues of the nonlinear Laplacian. Section 6 presents the experimental results. Finally, Section 7 summarizes our findings and concludes the paper with a brief discussion on the scope for future work.

2. RELATED WORK

Because spectral graph theory has been applied to many areas, we cannot review them all. See [18, 34] for surveys of spectral clustering and [15, 17, 28, 33] for surveys of other applications. Here, we focus on its application to digraphs.

Let $G = (V, E)$ be a digraph and π be its stationary distribution. Chung [11] defined the Laplacian for a digraph as $L_\pi = \Pi - \frac{\Pi P^T + P\Pi}{2}$, where Π is a diagonal matrix with $\Pi_{uu} = \pi_u$ and $P = AD^{-1}$ is the transition matrix; the normalized Laplacian for a digraph is $\mathcal{L}_\pi = \Pi^{-1/2} L \Pi^{-1/2}$. Then, she showed the following Cheeger-like inequality.

$$\frac{\lambda}{2} \le \min_{\emptyset \subsetneq S \subsetneq V} \phi_\pi(S) \le \sqrt{2\lambda}.$$

Here, λ is the second eigenvalue of the normalized Laplacian $\mathcal{L}_\pi$, and $\phi_\pi(S)$ is the conductance with respect to the random walk process, i.e.,

$$\min_{\emptyset \subsetneq S \subsetneq V} \frac{\mathrm{cut}_\pi(S)}{\min\{\pi(S), \pi(V \setminus S)\}},$$

where $\pi(S) = \sum_{u \in S} \pi_u$ and $\mathrm{cut}_\pi(S) = \sum_{(u,v)\in E} \frac{\pi_u}{d_u}$. Intuitively speaking, $\pi(S)$ is the probability of staying at a vertex in S and $\mathrm{cut}_\pi(S)$ is the probability of passing through an arc leaving S in the random walk process. Chung's Laplacian is also used for the embedding task [11].

Based on Chung's normalized Laplacian, Andersen *et al.* [1] proposed a local clustering algorithm and Gleich [19] proposed a hierarchical spectral graph clustering algorithm, both for digraphs. Zhou *et al.* [37] employed Chung's normalized Laplacian for learning labeled and unlabeled digraphs. Several connections between Chung's normalized Laplacian and graph theoretic measures can be found in [16]

Another version of the Laplacian for digraphs, known as the Diplacian, was proposed in [24]. We note that a stationary distribution is still required to define the Diplacian and that its eigenvalues can be complex numbers because the Diplacian is an asymmetric matrix. A Laplacian for digraphs with positive and negative edge weights has been considered in [8].

Nonlinear variants of Rayleigh quotients were also used to study vertex expansion [20] and hypergraphs [25].

3. PRELIMINARIES

We denote by $\mathbb{R}_+$ the set of non-negative real values. For an integer $k \in \mathbb{N}$, $[k]$ denotes the set $\{1, 2, \ldots, k\}$. For a real value $x \in \mathbb{R}$, $[x]^+$ and $[x]^-$ denote $\max\{x, 0\}$ and $\min\{x, 0\}$, respectively.

A vector is denoted by a bold symbol, such as $\boldsymbol{x}$. Let $\boldsymbol{x} \in \mathbb{R}^V$ be a vector indexed by a finite set V. Then, for $u \in V$, x_u denotes the u-th element of $\boldsymbol{x}$. Let $\boldsymbol{x}^\perp$ denote the subspace orthogonal to $\boldsymbol{x}$. Further, for a subspace $U \leq \mathbb{R}^V$, let $U^\perp$ denote the subspace orthogonal to U, and let Π_U denote the projection operator to U.

Notations for undirected graphs.

Let $G = (V, E)$ be an undirected digraph. The *degree* of a vertex v, denoted by d_v, is the number of edges incident to v. The *volume* of S, $\mathrm{vol}(S)$, is defined as $\sum_{v \in S} d_v$. For a subset $S \subseteq V$, the *boundary* is the set of edges crossing S and $V \setminus S$, i.e., $\partial(S) = \{\{u, v\} \in E \mid u \in S, v \in V \setminus S\}$. We define $\mathrm{cut}(S) = |\partial(S)|$. The *conductance* of S, denoted by $\phi(S)$, is defined as

$$\phi(S) = \frac{\mathrm{cut}(S)}{\min\{\mathrm{vol}(S), \mathrm{vol}(V \setminus S)\}}.$$

The *conductance* of G is $\phi_G = \min_{\emptyset \subsetneq S \subsetneq V} \phi(S)$.

The *adjacency matrix* $A \in \mathbb{R}^{V \times V}$ of G is a matrix such that A_{uv} equals the number of edges between u and v. Let $D \in \mathbb{R}^{V \times V}$ be a matrix such that $D_{uu} = d_u$ for each $u \in V$ and $D_{uv} = 0$ for $u \neq v$. Then, the *transition matrix* of G is $P = AD^{-1}$.

Notations for digraphs.

Let $G = (V, E)$ be a digraph. The *out-degree* d_v^+ and the *in-degree* d_v^- of a vertex v are the number of arcs leaving and entering v, respectively. Then, the *degree* of v is defined as $d_v = d_v^+ + d_v^-$. The *volume* of S, denoted by $\mathrm{vol}(S)$, is defined as $\sum_{v \in S} d_v$. For a subset $S \subseteq V$, the *out-boundary* $\partial^+(S)$ and the *in-boundary* $\partial^-(S)$ are the set of arcs leaving and entering S, respectively. Thus, $\partial^+(S) = \{(u, v) \in E \mid u \in S, v \in V \setminus S\}$ and $\partial^-(S) = \{(u, v) \in E \mid u \in V \setminus S, v \in S\}$. Then, we define $\mathrm{cut}^+(S) = |\partial^+(S)|$ and $\mathrm{cut}^-(S) = |\partial^-(S)|$. The *out-conductance* $\phi^+(S)$ and the *in-conductance* $\phi^-(S)$ of S are defined as

$$\phi^+(S) = \frac{\mathrm{cut}^+(S)}{\min\{\mathrm{vol}(S), \mathrm{vol}(V \setminus S)\}} \quad \text{and}$$

$$\phi^-(S) = \frac{\mathrm{cut}^-(S)}{\min\{\mathrm{vol}(S), \mathrm{vol}(V \setminus S)\}},$$

respectively. Then, we define the *conductance* $\phi(S)$ of S as $\min\{\phi^+(S), \phi^-(S)\}$. Note that

$$\phi(S) = \frac{\min\{\mathrm{cut}^+(S), \mathrm{cut}^+(V \setminus S)\}}{\min\{\mathrm{vol}(S), \mathrm{vol}(V \setminus S)\}} = \min\{\phi^+(S), \phi^+(V \setminus S)\}.$$

The *conductance* of G is $\phi_G = \min_{\emptyset \subsetneq S \subsetneq V} \phi(S)$.

The definitions of the adjacency matrix and transition matrix of a digraph are similar to those of an undirected graph.

3.1 Spectral graph theory for undirected graphs

Now, we review basic facts in spectral graph theory for undirected graphs. We define the *Laplacian* of an undirected graph G as $L_G = D - A$ and the *normalized Laplacian* as $\mathcal{L}_G = I - D^{-1/2} A D^{-1/2}$. The smallest eigenvalue of $\mathcal{L}_G$ is 0, and the corresponding eigenvector is $\boldsymbol{\mu}_G \in \mathbb{R}^V$, where the u-th element of $\boldsymbol{\mu}_G$ is $\sqrt{d_u/\mathrm{vol}(V)}$. Following Cheeger's inequality [2, 3] connects the second-smallest eigenvalue λ_G of $\mathcal{L}_G$ and the conductance ϕ_G:

$$\frac{\lambda_G}{2} \leq \phi_G \leq \sqrt{2\lambda_G}.$$

The *Rayleigh quotient* of a Markov operator $M : \mathbb{R}^V \to \mathbb{R}^V$ is

$$\mathcal{R}_M(\boldsymbol{x}) := \frac{\boldsymbol{x}^T M(\boldsymbol{x})}{\boldsymbol{x}^T \boldsymbol{x}}.$$

The *Rayleigh quotient* $\mathcal{R}_G : \mathbb{R}^V \to \mathbb{R}$ of an undirected graph $G = (V, E)$ is the Rayleigh quotient of the normalized Laplacian $\mathcal{L}_G$, i.e.,

$$\mathcal{R}_G(\boldsymbol{x}) = \mathcal{R}_{\mathcal{L}_G}(\boldsymbol{x}) = \frac{\sum_{(u,v)\in E} \left(x_u/\sqrt{d_u} - x_v/\sqrt{d_v} \right)^2}{\sum_{u \in V} x_u^2}. \quad (3)$$

It is easy to see that $\lambda_G = \inf_{\boldsymbol{x} \in \mathbb{R}^V : \langle \boldsymbol{x}, \boldsymbol{\mu}_G \rangle = 0} \mathcal{R}_G(\boldsymbol{x})$.

4. SPECTRAL THEORY FOR DIGRAPHS

In this section, we develop a spectral theory for digraphs based on the nonlinear Laplacian. We define the nonlinear Laplacian and its normalized version in Section 4.1. Because the normalized nonlinear Laplacian is a nonlinear Markov operator, it is not obvious that it has an eigenvector at all. In Section 4.2, we show that this is the case using the heat equation associated with the normalized nonlinear Laplacian. Finally, Section 4.3 discusses Cheeger's inequality based on the nonlinear normalized Laplacian.

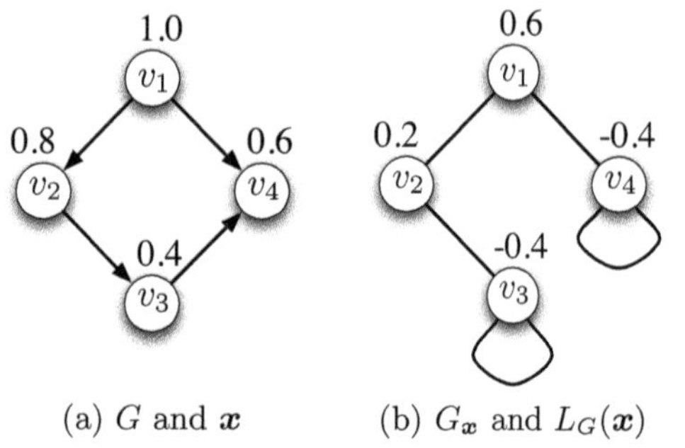

Figure 2: Computation of the nonlinear Laplacian as a Markov operator

4.1 Laplacian operator for digraphs

Now, we define the nonlinear Laplacian:

Definition 4.1 *Let $G = (V, E)$ be a digraph. Given a vector $\boldsymbol{x} \in \mathbb{R}^V$, the nonlinear Laplacian $L_G : \mathbb{R}^V \to \mathbb{R}^V$ computes a vector $L_G(\boldsymbol{x})$ as follows:*

1. *We construct an undirected graph $G_{\boldsymbol{x}}$ on the vertex set V as follows: for each $(u, v) \in E$, we add an edge $\{u, v\}$ if $x_u \geq x_v$, and we add self-loops $\{u, u\}$ and $\{v, v\}$ otherwise.*
2. *Let $L_{G_{\boldsymbol{x}}}$ be the Laplacian of $G_{\boldsymbol{x}}$.*
3. *Then, $L_G(\boldsymbol{x}) = L_{G_{\boldsymbol{x}}}\boldsymbol{x}$.*

Figure 2 shows an example of the computation by the nonlinear Laplacian. Suppose that we have a digraph G and a vector $\boldsymbol{x}$ as shown in Figure 2a. Then, the undirected graph $G_{\boldsymbol{x}}$ and $L_G(\boldsymbol{x})$ will be as shown in Figure 2b. For example, the arc (v_1, v_2) in G is replaced by an edge $\{v_1, v_2\}$ since $x_{v_1} \geq x_{v_2}$, and the arc (v_3, v_4) in G is replaced by two loops $\{v_3, v_3\}$ and $\{v_4, v_4\}$ since $x_{v_3} < x_{v_4}$. Then, $L_G(\boldsymbol{x})$ is computed according to the Laplacian of $G_{\boldsymbol{x}}$. For example, the value of $L_G(\boldsymbol{x})_{v_1}$ is $1.0 \cdot 2 - 0.8 - 0.6 = 0.6$ and the value of $L_G(\boldsymbol{x})_{v_4}$ is $0.6 \cdot 2 - 1.0 - 0.6 = -0.4$. It is instructive to notice that $\boldsymbol{x}^T L_G(\boldsymbol{x}) = \sum_{(u,v)\in E}\left([x_u - x_v]^+\right)^2$.

The normalized nonlinear Laplacian $\mathcal{L}_G : \mathbb{R}^V \to \mathbb{R}^V$ of a digraph G is simply $D^{-1/2}L_G D^{-1/2}$. For ease of understanding, let us define $\mathcal{L}_G$ as a Markov operator:

Definition 4.2 *Let $G = (V, E)$ be a digraph. Given a vector $\boldsymbol{x} \in \mathbb{R}^V$, the normalized nonlinear Laplacian $\mathcal{L}_G : \mathbb{R}^V \to \mathbb{R}^V$ computes a vector $\mathcal{L}_G(\boldsymbol{x})$ as follows:*

1. *We construct an undirected graph $G_{\boldsymbol{x}}$ on the vertex set V as follows: for each $(u, v) \in E$, we add an edge $\{u, v\}$ if $\frac{x_u}{\sqrt{d_u}} \geq \frac{x_v}{\sqrt{d_v}}$, and we add self-loops $\{u, u\}$ and $\{v, v\}$ otherwise.*
2. *Let $\mathcal{L}_{G_{\boldsymbol{x}}}$ be the normalized Laplacian of $G_{\boldsymbol{x}}$.*
3. *Then, $\mathcal{L}_G(\boldsymbol{x}) = \mathcal{L}_{G_{\boldsymbol{x}}}\boldsymbol{x}$.*

In this work, we mainly focus on the normalized nonlinear Laplacian because of its connection to conductance.

We say that a vector $\boldsymbol{z} \in \mathbb{R}^V$ is an *eigenvector* of $\mathcal{L}_G$ if $\mathcal{L}_G(\boldsymbol{z}) = \gamma\boldsymbol{z}$ for some $\gamma \in \mathbb{R}$, and we call γ the *eigenvalue* associated with $\boldsymbol{z}$. We note that the number of eigenvalues of $\mathcal{L}_G$ may be much larger or smaller than n since $\mathcal{L}_G$ is a nonlinear Markov operator. It is easy to see that $\mathcal{L}_G$ has an eigenvalue of 0 associated with the eigenvector $\boldsymbol{\mu}_G$. In the next section, we will show that $\mathcal{L}_G$ has many other eigenvalues. To this end, it is useful to introduce the *Rayleigh quotient* $\mathcal{R}_G : \mathbb{R}^V \to \mathbb{R}$ of a digraph $G = (V, E)$, which is the Rayleigh quotient of the normalized Laplacian $\mathcal{L}_G$.

Lemma 4.3 *We have*

$$\mathcal{R}_G(\boldsymbol{x}) = \frac{\sum_{(u,v)\in E}\left([x_u/\sqrt{d_u} - x_v/\sqrt{d_v}]^+\right)^2}{\sum_{u\in V} x_u^2}.$$

PROOF. Let $G' = (V, E')$ be the undirected graph constructed when computing $\mathcal{L}_G(\boldsymbol{x})$. Recalling (3), we have

$$\boldsymbol{x}^T\mathcal{L}_G(\boldsymbol{x}) = \boldsymbol{x}^T\mathcal{L}_{G'}\boldsymbol{x} = \sum_{\{u,v\}\in E'}\left(\frac{x_u}{\sqrt{d_u}} - \frac{x_v}{\sqrt{d_v}}\right)^2$$

$$= \sum_{\substack{(u,v)\in E:\\ x_u/\sqrt{d_u}\geq x_v/\sqrt{d_v}}}\left(\frac{x_u}{\sqrt{d_u}} - \frac{x_v}{\sqrt{d_v}}\right)^2$$

$$+ \sum_{\substack{(u,v)\in E:\\ x_u/\sqrt{d_u}< x_v/\sqrt{d_v}}}\left(\left(\frac{x_u}{\sqrt{d_u}} - \frac{x_u}{\sqrt{d_u}}\right)^2 + \left(\frac{x_v}{\sqrt{d_v}} - \frac{x_v}{\sqrt{d_v}}\right)^2\right)$$

$$= \sum_{(u,v)\in E}\left(\left[\frac{x_u}{\sqrt{d_u}} - \frac{x_v}{\sqrt{d_v}}\right]^+\right)^2.$$

We have the lemma since $\mathcal{R}_G(\boldsymbol{x}) = \frac{\boldsymbol{x}^T\mathcal{L}_G(\boldsymbol{x})}{\boldsymbol{x}^T\boldsymbol{x}}$. □

4.2 Eigenvalues and heat equation

In this section, we show that $\mathcal{L}_G$ has many eigenvalues besides the trivial one.

Theorem 4.4 *Given a digraph G, for every subspace $U \leq \mathbb{R}^V$ of positive dimension, the operator $\Pi_U\mathcal{L}_G$ has an eigenvector, i.e., there exists a non-zero vector $\boldsymbol{x} \in U$ and $\gamma \in \mathbb{R}_+$ such that*

$$\Pi_U\mathcal{L}_G(\boldsymbol{x}) = \gamma\boldsymbol{x} \quad \text{and} \quad \gamma = \mathcal{R}_U(\boldsymbol{x}),$$

where $\mathcal{R}_U$ is the Rayleigh quotient of the Markov operator $\Pi_U\mathcal{L}_G$.

To prove Theorem 4.4, we consider the following process.

Definition 4.5 (Heat equation in a subspace) *Let $G = (V, E)$ be a digraph and $U \leq \mathbb{R}^V$ be a subspace. We stipulate that the time evolution of $\boldsymbol{x} \in U$ obeys the following equation:*

$$\mathrm{d}\boldsymbol{x} = -\Pi_U\mathcal{L}_G(\boldsymbol{x})\mathrm{d}t, \qquad (4)$$

where Π_U is the projection operator to U. The initial condition is given by a non-zero vector $\boldsymbol{x}_0 \in U$. Let $\boldsymbol{x}_t$ denote $\boldsymbol{x}$ at time $t \in \mathbb{R}_+$.

The process with the normalized Laplacian of an undirected graph is referred to as the heat equation in the literature [12, 22]. We do not write $\frac{\mathrm{d}\boldsymbol{x}}{\mathrm{d}t}$ because $\boldsymbol{x}$ is not differentiable. Note that $\boldsymbol{x}_t$ is non-zero and contained in U for all $t \in \mathbb{R}_+$.

Now, we analyze how $\mathcal{R}_U(\boldsymbol{x})$ changes under the heat equation (4). In what follows, we fix a digraph $G = (V, E)$ and a subspace $U \leq \mathbb{R}^V$ of positive dimension.

Lemma 4.6 *We have*

$$\mathrm{d}\|\boldsymbol{x}\|^2 = -2\mathcal{R}_U(\boldsymbol{x})\|\boldsymbol{x}\|^2\mathrm{d}t.$$

PROOF.

$$\mathrm{d}\|\boldsymbol{x}\|^2 = 2\boldsymbol{x}^T\mathrm{d}\boldsymbol{x} = -2\boldsymbol{x}^T\Pi_U\mathcal{L}_G(\boldsymbol{x})\mathrm{d}t = -2\mathcal{R}_U(\boldsymbol{x})\|\boldsymbol{x}\|^2\mathrm{d}t.$$

□

We define $\overline{\boldsymbol{x}} = \boldsymbol{x}/\|\boldsymbol{x}\|$. Then, we have the following.

Lemma 4.7 *We have*

$$\mathrm{d}\mathcal{R}_U(\boldsymbol{x}) = 2(\mathcal{R}_U(\overline{\boldsymbol{x}})^2 - \|\Pi_U\mathcal{L}_G(\overline{\boldsymbol{x}})\|^2)\mathrm{d}t.$$

PROOF. From Lemma 4.6, we have $\mathrm{d}\|\boldsymbol{x}\| = -\mathcal{R}_U(\boldsymbol{x})\|\boldsymbol{x}\|\mathrm{d}t$. Note that

$$\mathrm{d}\overline{\boldsymbol{x}} = \frac{\|\boldsymbol{x}\|\mathrm{d}\boldsymbol{x} - \boldsymbol{x}\mathrm{d}\|\boldsymbol{x}\|}{\|\boldsymbol{x}\|^2} = \frac{\boldsymbol{x}\mathcal{R}_U(\boldsymbol{x})\|\boldsymbol{x}\| - \Pi_U\mathcal{L}_G(\boldsymbol{x})\|\boldsymbol{x}\|}{\|\boldsymbol{x}\|^2}\mathrm{d}t$$
$$= \Big(\frac{\mathcal{R}_U(\boldsymbol{x})\boldsymbol{x}}{\|\boldsymbol{x}\|} - \frac{\Pi_U\mathcal{L}_G(\boldsymbol{x})}{\|\boldsymbol{x}\|}\Big)\mathrm{d}t = \Big(\mathcal{R}_U(\overline{\boldsymbol{x}})\overline{\boldsymbol{x}} - \Pi_U\mathcal{L}_G(\overline{\boldsymbol{x}})\Big)\mathrm{d}t.$$

Let $\mathcal{L}_t$ be the normalized Laplacian constructed when computing $\mathcal{L}_G(\boldsymbol{x}_t)$. Further, let $\mathcal{Q}(\boldsymbol{x}) = \boldsymbol{x}^T\Pi_U\mathcal{L}_G(\boldsymbol{x})$ and $\mathcal{Q}_t(\boldsymbol{x}) = \boldsymbol{x}^T\Pi_U\mathcal{L}_t\boldsymbol{x}$. Then, we have

$$\mathrm{d}\mathcal{R}_U(\boldsymbol{x}) = \mathrm{d}\mathcal{Q}(\overline{\boldsymbol{x}}) = \mathrm{d}\mathcal{Q}_t(\overline{\boldsymbol{x}}) = \Big(\frac{\mathrm{d}\mathcal{Q}_t(\overline{\boldsymbol{x}})}{\mathrm{d}\overline{\boldsymbol{x}}}\Big)^T\mathrm{d}\overline{\boldsymbol{x}}$$
$$= 2(\Pi_U\mathcal{L}_t\overline{\boldsymbol{x}})^T(\mathcal{R}_U(\overline{\boldsymbol{x}})\overline{\boldsymbol{x}} - \Pi_U\mathcal{L}_G(\overline{\boldsymbol{x}}))\mathrm{d}t$$
$$= 2(\Pi_U\mathcal{L}_G(\overline{\boldsymbol{x}}))^T(\mathcal{R}_U(\overline{\boldsymbol{x}})\overline{\boldsymbol{x}} - \Pi_U\mathcal{L}_G(\overline{\boldsymbol{x}}))\mathrm{d}t$$
$$= 2(\mathcal{R}_U(\overline{\boldsymbol{x}})^2 - \|\Pi_U\mathcal{L}_G(\overline{\boldsymbol{x}})\|^2)\mathrm{d}t.$$

□

Corollary 4.8 *$\mathcal{R}_U(\boldsymbol{x})$ is non-increasing in t.*

PROOF. Note that $\|\Pi_U\mathcal{L}_G(\overline{\boldsymbol{x}})\| \geq \overline{\boldsymbol{x}}^T\Pi_U\mathcal{L}_G(\overline{\boldsymbol{x}}) = \mathcal{R}_U(\overline{\boldsymbol{x}})$. The inequality holds because $\overline{\boldsymbol{x}}$ is a unit vector. From Lemma 4.7, we have $\mathrm{d}\mathcal{R}_U(\boldsymbol{x}) \leq 0$. Since $\mathcal{R}_U$ is a continuous function of t, we have the desired result. □

Theorem 4.9 *Suppose that we initiate a simulation of the heat equation with a non-zero vector $\boldsymbol{x}_0 \in U$. Then, as $t \to \infty$, $\boldsymbol{x}$ and $\mathcal{R}_U(\boldsymbol{x})$ converge to some $\boldsymbol{z} \in \mathbb{R}^V$ and $\gamma \in \mathbb{R}_+$, respectively, such that*

$$\Pi_U\mathcal{L}_G(\boldsymbol{x}) = \gamma\boldsymbol{x} \quad \textit{and} \quad \gamma = \mathcal{R}_U(\boldsymbol{x}).$$

PROOF. Note that $\mathcal{R}_U(\boldsymbol{x})$ is bounded from below by 0 from Lemma 4.3. Since $\mathcal{R}_U(\boldsymbol{x})$ is non-increasing from Corollary 4.8, $\mathcal{R}_U(\boldsymbol{x})$ converges to some non-negative value as $t \to \infty$.

Let γ be the limit. We have $\lim_{t\to\infty}\|\Pi_U\mathcal{L}_G(\overline{\boldsymbol{x}})\|^2 = \gamma^2$ by Lemma 4.7. It follows that $\lim_{t\to\infty}\big(\Pi_U\mathcal{L}_G(\overline{\boldsymbol{x}}) - \gamma\overline{\boldsymbol{x}}\big)^T\Pi_U\mathcal{L}_G(\overline{\boldsymbol{x}}) = 0$. Since $\lim_{t\to\infty}\|\Pi_U\mathcal{L}_G(\overline{\boldsymbol{x}})\| = \gamma$ and $\|\overline{\boldsymbol{x}}\| = 1$, we must have $\lim_{t\to\infty}\Pi_U\mathcal{L}_G(\overline{\boldsymbol{x}}) - \gamma\overline{\boldsymbol{x}} = 0$ or $\lim_{t\to\infty}\Pi_U\mathcal{L}_G(\overline{\boldsymbol{x}}) = 0$. However, the latter implies that $\gamma = 0$. Hence, we have $\lim_{t\to\infty}\Pi_U\mathcal{L}_G(\overline{\boldsymbol{x}}) - \gamma\overline{\boldsymbol{x}} = 0$ in both cases. □

Theorem 4.9 immediately shows the existence of the eigenvalue and eigenvector of $\Pi_U\mathcal{L}_G$, which establishes Theorem 4.4.

Now that $\Pi_U\mathcal{L}_G$ has an eigenvalue and eigenvector for any subspace $U \leq \mathbb{R}^V$ of positive dimension, we define the second eigenvalue λ_G of $\mathcal{L}_G$ as the smallest eigenvalue of $\Pi_{\mu_G^\perp}\mathcal{L}_G$.

Let λ_U be the smallest eigenvalue of $\Pi_U\mathcal{L}_G$. The following lemma is helpful for understanding the relation between the eigenvalues of $\Pi_U\mathcal{L}_G$ and $\mathcal{L}_G$.

Lemma 4.10 *It holds that*

$$\lambda_U = \inf_{\boldsymbol{x}\in U}\mathcal{R}_G(\boldsymbol{x}),$$

where λ_U is the smallest eigenvalue of $\Pi_U\mathcal{L}_G$. In particular,

$$\lambda_G = \inf_{\boldsymbol{x}\in\mu_G^\perp}\mathcal{R}_G(\boldsymbol{x}).$$

PROOF. Let $\boldsymbol{z}$ be the eigenvector of $\Pi_U\mathcal{L}_G$ associated with λ_U. Note that $\boldsymbol{z} \in U$ holds because $\Pi_U\mathcal{L}_G(\boldsymbol{z}) = \lambda_U\boldsymbol{z}$. Then, we have

$$\lambda_U = \inf_{\boldsymbol{x}\in\mathbb{R}^V}\frac{\boldsymbol{x}^T\Pi_U\mathcal{L}_G(\boldsymbol{x})}{\boldsymbol{x}^T\boldsymbol{x}} = \inf_{\boldsymbol{x}\in U}\frac{\boldsymbol{x}^T\Pi_U\mathcal{L}_G(\boldsymbol{x})}{\boldsymbol{x}^T\boldsymbol{x}} = \inf_{\boldsymbol{x}\in U}\mathcal{R}(\boldsymbol{x}).$$

The second claim is immediate. □

4.3 Cheeger's inequality for digraphs

For a digraph G, let λ_G be the second-smallest eigenvalue of $\mathcal{L}_G$. In this section, we show the following Cheeger-like inequality for digraphs.

Theorem 4.11 *Let $G = (V,E)$ be a digraph. Then, we have*

$$\frac{\lambda_G}{2} \leq \phi_G \leq 2\sqrt{\lambda_G}.$$

Given a vector, we can compute a set of vertices with a guarantee on its conductance using the following lemma.

Lemma 4.12 *Let $G = (V,E)$ be a digraph and let $\tilde{\boldsymbol{x}} \in [0,1]^V$. There exists a set $S \subseteq \mathrm{supp}(\tilde{\boldsymbol{x}})$ such that*

$$\frac{\mathrm{cut}^+(S)}{\mathrm{vol}(S)} \leq \frac{\sum_{(u,v)\in E}[\tilde{x}_u - \tilde{x}_v]^+}{\sum_{u\in V} d_u\tilde{x}_u}.$$

Moreover, we can compute such a set S in $O(|V|+|E|)$ time.

PROOF. For $r \in [0,1]$, we define a function $F_r : [0,1] \to \{0,1\}$ as $F_r(x) = 1$ if $x \geq r$ and $F_r(x) = 0$ otherwise. For any $a \in [0,1]$, it is easy to see that $\int_0^1 F_r(a)\mathrm{d}r = a$. Now, observe that if $a - b \geq 0$, then $F_r(a) - F_r(b) \geq 0$ for any $r \in [0,1]$, and if $a - b \leq 0$, then $F_r(a) - F_r(b) \leq 0$ for any $r \in [0,1]$. Therefore,

$$\int_0^1 [F_r(a) - F_r(b)]^+\mathrm{d}r = \Big[\int_0^1 F_r(a)\mathrm{d}r - \int_0^1 F_r(b)\mathrm{d}r\Big]^+$$
$$= [a-b]^+.$$

Hence, we have

$$\frac{\int_0^1\sum_{(u,v)\in E}[F_r(\tilde{x}_u) - F_r(\tilde{x}_v)]^+\mathrm{d}r}{\int_0^1\sum_{u\in V} d_uF_r(\tilde{x}_u)\mathrm{d}r} = \frac{\sum_{(u,v)\in E}[\tilde{x}_u - \tilde{x}_v]^+}{\sum_{u\in V} d_u\tilde{x}_u}.$$

Therefore, there exists $r' \in [0,1]$ such that

$$\frac{\sum_{(u,v)\in E}[F_{r'}(\tilde{x}_u) - F_{r'}(\tilde{x}_v)]^+}{\sum_{u\in V} d_uF_{r'}(\tilde{x}_u)} \leq \frac{\sum_{(u,v)\in E}[\tilde{x}_u - \tilde{x}_v]^+}{\sum_{u\in V} d_u\tilde{x}_u}.$$

Let S denote the support of the vector $F_{r'}(\boldsymbol{x})$. Since $F_{r'}(\cdot)$ is a value in $\{0,1\}$, we have

$$\frac{\sum_{(u,v)\in E}[F_{r'}(\tilde{x}_u)-F_{r'}(\tilde{x}_v)]^+}{\sum_{u\in V} d_u F_{r'}(\tilde{x}_u)} = \frac{\sum_{(u,v)\in E}\mathbb{I}[u\in S\vee v\notin S]}{\sum_{u\in S} d_u} = \frac{\mathrm{cut}^+(S)}{\mathrm{vol}(S)},$$

where $\mathbb{I}[e]$ denotes the indicator of the event e. Therefore, we have

$$\frac{\mathrm{cut}^+(S)}{\mathrm{vol}(S)} \leq \frac{\sum_{(u,v)\in E}[\tilde{x}_u-\tilde{x}_v]^+}{\sum_{u\in V} d_u\tilde{x}_u} \quad \text{and} \quad S\subseteq \mathrm{supp}(\tilde{\boldsymbol{x}}).$$

We can find this set S as follows. First, we sort vertices $v_1,\ldots,v_n$ such that $\tilde{x}_{v_1}\geq\cdots\geq\tilde{x}_{v_n}$. Then, we consider sets of the form $\{v_1,\ldots,v_k\}$ for $k\in[n-1]$ and return the set with the smallest conductance. The running time of this algorithm is $O(|V|+|E|)$. □

Similarly, we can show the following.

Lemma 4.13 *Let $G=(V,E)$ be a digraph and let $\tilde{\boldsymbol{x}}\in[-1,0]^V$. There exists a set $S\subseteq\mathrm{supp}(\tilde{\boldsymbol{x}})$ such that*

$$\frac{\mathrm{cut}^-(S)}{\mathrm{vol}(S)} \leq \frac{\sum_{(u,v)\in E}[\tilde{x}_u-\tilde{x}_v]^+}{-\sum_{u\in V} d_u\tilde{x}_u}.$$

Moreover, we can find such a set S in $O(|V|+|E|)$ time.

Lemma 4.14 *Given a digraph $G=(V,E)$ and a vector $\boldsymbol{x}\in\mathbb{R}^V$ with $\langle\boldsymbol{x},\boldsymbol{\mu}_G\rangle=0$, there exists a set $S\subseteq V$ such that*

$$\phi(S)\leq 2\sqrt{\mathcal{R}_G(\boldsymbol{x})}.$$

Moreover, we can find such a set S in $O(|V|+|E|)$ time.

Proof. Let $\tilde{\boldsymbol{x}}\in\mathbb{R}^V$ be $\tilde{x}_u=x_u/\sqrt{d_u}$ for each $u\in V$. Then, we have $\sum_{u\in V}d_u\tilde{x}_u=\sum_{u\in V}\sqrt{d_u}x_u=\langle\boldsymbol{x},\boldsymbol{\mu}_G\rangle\cdot\sqrt{\mathrm{vol}(V)}=0$. Then, we have by Lemma 4.3,

$$\mathcal{R}_G(\boldsymbol{x}) = \frac{\sum_{(u,v)\in E}\left([\tilde{x}_u-\tilde{x}_v]^+\right)^2}{\sum_{u\in V}d_u\tilde{x}_u^2-\left(\sum_{u\in V}d_u\tilde{x}_u\right)^2/\left(\sum_{u\in V}d_u\right)} = \frac{\sum_{(u,v)\in E}\left([\tilde{x}_u-\tilde{x}_v]^+\right)^2}{\sum_{u,v\in V}d_ud_v\left(\tilde{x}_u-\tilde{x}_v\right)^2/\left(\sum_{u\in V}d_u\right)}.$$

Let $\tilde{\boldsymbol{y}}=\tilde{\boldsymbol{x}}+c\mathbf{1}$ for some appropriate $c\in\mathbb{R}$ such that $\mathrm{vol}(\mathrm{supp}(\tilde{\boldsymbol{y}}^+))\leq\mathrm{vol}(V)/2$ and $\mathrm{vol}(\mathrm{supp}(\tilde{\boldsymbol{y}}^-))\leq\mathrm{vol}(V)/2$ hold. Let $\boldsymbol{y}\in\mathbb{R}^V$ be $y_u=\sqrt{d_u}\tilde{y}_u$ for each $u\in V$. Then, we get $\mathcal{R}_G(\boldsymbol{x})=\mathcal{R}_G(\boldsymbol{y})$.

We have $[a^+]^2+[a^-]^2=a^2$ for any $a\in\mathbb{R}$ and $([a^+-b^+]^+)^2+([a^--b^-]^+)^2\leq([a-b]^+)^2$ for any $a,b\in\mathbb{R}$. Therefore, we have

$$\mathcal{R}_G(\boldsymbol{y}) = \frac{\sum_{(u,v)\in E}\left([\tilde{y}_u-\tilde{y}_v]^+\right)^2}{\sum_{u\in V}d_u\tilde{y}_u^2}$$
$$\geq \frac{\sum_{(u,v)\in E}\left([\tilde{y}_u^+-\tilde{y}_v^+]^+\right)^2+\sum_{(u,v)\in E}\left([\tilde{y}_u^--\tilde{y}_v^-]^+\right)^2}{\sum_{u\in V}d_u(\tilde{y}_u^+)^2+\sum_{u\in V}d_u(\tilde{y}_u^-)^2}$$
$$\geq \min\left\{\frac{\sum_{(u,v)\in E}\left([\tilde{y}_u^+-\tilde{y}_v^+]^+\right)^2}{\sum_{u\in V}d_u(\tilde{y}_u^+)^2},\frac{\sum_{(u,v)\in E}\left([\tilde{y}_u^--\tilde{y}_v^-]^+\right)^2}{\sum_{u\in V}d_u(\tilde{y}_u^-)^2}\right\}.$$

Let $\tilde{\boldsymbol{y}}^*\in\{\tilde{\boldsymbol{y}}^+,\tilde{\boldsymbol{y}}^-\}$ be the vector corresponding to the minimum in the previous inequality. Let σ be 1 if $\tilde{\boldsymbol{y}}^*=\tilde{\boldsymbol{y}}^+$ and -1 if $\tilde{\boldsymbol{y}}^*=\tilde{\boldsymbol{y}}^-$. Then,

$$\sum_{(u,v)\in E}\left[\sigma(\tilde{y}_u^*)^2-\sigma(\tilde{y}_v^*)^2\right]^+$$
$$=\sum_{(u,v)\in E}[\tilde{y}_u^*-\tilde{y}_v^*]^+(|\tilde{y}_u^*|+|\tilde{y}_v^*|)$$
$$\leq\sqrt{\sum_{(u,v)\in E}\left([\tilde{y}_u^*-\tilde{y}_v^*]^+\right)^2}\left(\sqrt{\sum_{(u,v)\in E}(\tilde{y}_u^*)^2}+\sqrt{\sum_{(u,v)\in E}(\tilde{y}_v^*)^2}\right)$$
$$=\sqrt{\sum_{(u,v)\in E}\left([\tilde{y}_u^*-\tilde{y}_v^*]^+\right)^2}\left(\sqrt{\sum_{u\in V}d_u^+(\tilde{y}_u^*)^2}+\sqrt{\sum_{v\in V}d_v^-(\tilde{y}_v^*)^2}\right)$$
$$=2\sqrt{\sum_{(u,v)\in E}\left([\tilde{y}_u^*-\tilde{y}_v^*]^+\right)^2}\sqrt{\sum_{u\in V}d_u(\tilde{y}_u^*)^2}.$$

The inequality uses the Cauchy-Schwarz inequality.

Let $\boldsymbol{y}^*=\boldsymbol{y}^+$ if $\tilde{\boldsymbol{y}}^*=\tilde{\boldsymbol{y}}^+$ and $\boldsymbol{y}^*=\boldsymbol{y}^-$ otherwise. From $\mathcal{R}_G(\boldsymbol{y}^*)\leq\mathcal{R}_G(\boldsymbol{y})=\mathcal{R}_G(\boldsymbol{x})$, we have

$$\frac{\sum_{(u,v)\in E}\left[\sigma(\tilde{y}_u^*)^2-\sigma(\tilde{y}_v^*)^2\right]^+}{\sum_{u\in V}d_u(\tilde{y}_u^*)^2}\leq 2\sqrt{\mathcal{R}_G(\boldsymbol{y}^*)}\leq 2\sqrt{\mathcal{R}_G(\boldsymbol{x})}.$$

With the vector $\sigma(\tilde{\boldsymbol{y}}^*)^2$ (after normalization), we invoke Lemma 4.12 if $\boldsymbol{y}^*=\boldsymbol{y}^+$ and Lemma 4.13 otherwise. Then, we get a set $S\subseteq\mathrm{supp}(\tilde{\boldsymbol{y}}^*)$ with $\mathrm{vol}(S)\leq\mathrm{vol}(\mathrm{supp}(\tilde{\boldsymbol{y}}^*))\leq\mathrm{vol}(V)/2$. Moreover, we have $\mathrm{cut}^+(S)/\mathrm{vol}(S)\leq 2\sqrt{\mathcal{R}_G(\boldsymbol{x})}$ in the former case, and we have $\mathrm{cut}^-(S)/\mathrm{vol}(S)\leq 2\sqrt{\mathcal{R}_G(\boldsymbol{x})}$ in the latter case. In both cases, we have $\phi(S)\leq 2\sqrt{\mathcal{R}_G(\boldsymbol{x})}$. □

Proof of Theorem 4.11. First, we show that $\lambda_G/2\leq\phi_G$. To this end, consider any set $S\subseteq V$ such that $\mathrm{vol}(S)\leq\mathrm{vol}(V\backslash S)$. We consider the following two cases: (i) $\mathrm{cut}^+(S)\leq\mathrm{cut}^-(S)$ and (ii) $\mathrm{cut}^+(S)>\mathrm{cut}^-(S)$.

Suppose the case (i). Let $\tilde{\boldsymbol{x}}\in\mathbb{R}^V$ be the indicator vector of S, and $\tilde{\boldsymbol{y}}$ be the component of $\tilde{\boldsymbol{x}}$ orthogonal to $\boldsymbol{\mu}_G$. Let

$\boldsymbol{y} \in \mathbb{R}^V$ be $y_u = \sqrt{d_u}\tilde{y}_u$. Then from Lemma 4.3,

$$\lambda_G \le \mathcal{R}_G(\boldsymbol{y}) = \frac{\sum_{(u,v)\in E}\left([\tilde{y}_u - \tilde{y}_v]^+\right)^2}{\sum_{u\in V} d_u \tilde{y}_u^2}$$

$$= \frac{\sum_{(u,v)\in E}\left([\tilde{x}_u - \tilde{x}_v]^+\right)^2}{\sum_{u\in V} d_u \tilde{x}_u^2 - \left(\sum_{u\in V} d_u \tilde{x}_u\right)^2 / \left(\sum_{u\in V} d_u\right)}$$

$$= \frac{\mathrm{cut}^+(S)}{\mathrm{vol}(S) - \mathrm{vol}(S)^2/\mathrm{vol}(V)} = \frac{\mathrm{cut}^+(S)/\mathrm{vol}(S)}{1 - \mathrm{vol}(S)/\mathrm{vol}(V)} \le 2\phi(S).$$

The case (ii) can be analyzed analogously. Since the choice of S was arbitrary, we get $\lambda_G/2 \le \phi_G$.

Now, we show that $\phi_G \le 2\sqrt{\lambda_G}$. This is immediate by invoking Lemma 4.14 with the eigenvector $\boldsymbol{z} \in \boldsymbol{\mu}_G^\perp$ corresponding to λ_G and the relation $\lambda_G = \mathcal{R}_G(\boldsymbol{z})$ in Lemma 4.10. □

5. ALGORITHMS FOR COMPUTING EIGENVALUES AND EIGENVECTORS

In this section, we present algorithms for computing the eigenvalues of the normalized nonlinear Laplacian and a set of small conductance.

First, let us consider the problem of computing eigenvalues. As mentioned earlier, computing the eigenvalues of a nonlinear Markov operator is NP-Hard in general. To overcome this issue, we simply simulate the heat equation in the space $\boldsymbol{\mu}_G^\perp$. Let $\boldsymbol{x}$ be its solution. By Theorem 4.9, $\boldsymbol{x}$ converges to some eigenvector $\boldsymbol{z}$ of $\Pi_{\boldsymbol{\mu}_G^\perp}\mathcal{L}_G$. Although $\boldsymbol{z}$ might not be the second eigenvector of $\mathcal{L}_G$, because the heat equation on the undirected graph $G_{\boldsymbol{z}}$ is involved as $t \to \infty$, we can guarantee that $\boldsymbol{z}$ is the second eigenvector of $G_{\boldsymbol{z}}$ [12].

Unfortunately, we cannot simulate the heat equation exactly because the exact form of $\mathcal{L}_G$ can change in infinitesimal time. To deal with this issue, we simulate the heat equation by discretizing time. More specifically, we choose a sufficiently small $\Delta t \in \mathbb{R}$, and in each step, we update $\boldsymbol{x}$ by $\boldsymbol{x} - \Pi_{\mu^\perp}\mathcal{L}(\boldsymbol{x})\Delta t$ and t by $t + \Delta t$. This is exactly the Euler method, which is a numerical procedure for solving ordinary differential equations. Although our heat equation involves a non-differential process, in Section 6, we will experimentally confirm on real-world digraphs that the Rayleigh quotient of the resulting vector is stable under the choice of Δt. This means that we can set Δt to a somewhat large value, thereby reducing the computational costs of the simulation. Clearly, the time complexity of the Euler method is $O(\frac{T}{\Delta t}(|V|+|E|))$.

Although we also implemented the Runge-Kutta method and the Runge-Kutta-Fehlberg method [6] for simulating the heat equation, we did not achieve any improvement over the Euler method. Hence, we omit the details.

Once we have obtained a vector $\boldsymbol{x}$ by simulating the heat equation, by applying Lemma 4.14, we can round it to a set of conductance $O(\sqrt{\mathcal{R}_G(\boldsymbol{x})})$. The details are given in Algorithm 1. Again, the time complexity is $O(\frac{T}{\Delta t}(|V|+|E|))$.

6. EXPERIMENTS

We conducted experiments on a Linux server with an Intel Xeon E5-2690 (2.90 GHz) processor and 256 GB of main memory. All the algorithms were implemented in C# and run using Mono 2.10.8.1. The parameters of the networks used in our experiments are listed in Table 1. The runtimes of Algorithm 1 with $\Delta t = 1$ and $T = 1000$ are also listed. Except for s208_st, we used the largest strongly connected component in each network.

Algorithm 1 Partitioning using the heat equation

Input: A digraph $G = (V, E)$, $\Delta t \in \mathbb{R}_+$, $T \in \mathbb{R}_+$
Output: A set S.
 $\boldsymbol{x}_0 \leftarrow$ an arbitrary vector with $\boldsymbol{x}_0 \in \boldsymbol{\mu}^\perp$.
 while $t \le T$ **do**
  $\boldsymbol{x} = \boldsymbol{x} - \Pi_{\boldsymbol{\mu}_G^\perp}\mathcal{L}_G(\boldsymbol{x})\Delta t$.
  $t = t + \Delta t$.
 $S \leftarrow$ the set obtained by applying Lemma 4.14 to $\boldsymbol{x}$.
 return S.

Table 1: Dataset

Name	n	m	Time
Narragan [30]	30	139	0.16 s
s208_st [29]	122	189	0.04 s
C. elegans [35]	239	1918	1.04 s
Political Blogs [1]	793	15839	2.83 s
US Airports [23]	1402	28032	7.40 s
Enron [23]	9164	761911	65.1 s
Epinions1 [23]	32223	443506	71.4 s

6.1 Computing eigenvalues and eigenvectors

Figure 3 shows the convergence of the Rayleigh quotient $\mathcal{R}_G$ of several networks for different choices of Δt. For each setting, we ran Algorithm 1 five times and obtained the expectation and variance of the results. We can observe that for any choice of Δt, the Rayleigh quotient has a small variance and converges to nearly the same value. This shows the robustness of our algorithm.

Figure 4 plots the convergence of the conductance of the set obtained by Algorithm 1. Again, the conductance is robust under the choice of Δt.

6.2 Spectral embedding

Figure 5 shows the spectral embedding of several networks, where the x-coordinate and y-coordinate of each vertex are set to the values of the second eigenvector and third eigenvector, respectively. We used the normalized nonlinear Laplacian and Chung's normalized Laplacian to obtain the eigenvalues. Because we cannot compute the second and third eigenvectors for the normalized nonlinear Laplacian, we used the vector $\boldsymbol{z}$ orthogonal to $\boldsymbol{\mu}_G$ and the vector $\boldsymbol{z}'$ orthogonal to $\boldsymbol{\mu}_G$ and $\boldsymbol{z}$ obtained by simulating the heat equation with $\Delta t = 1$ and $T = 1000$, in place of the second and third eigenvectors, respectively. The spectral embedding of Narragan (Figure 5a) based on Chung's normalized Laplacian puts a vertex with a large in-degree in the midst of the figure. This is because that vertex has a high probability mass in the stationary distribution, and such a vertex has a significant impact on the Rayleigh quotient associated with Chung's normalized Laplacian. In contrast, the normalized nonlinear Laplacian respects the direction of arcs, and a vertex with a large in-degree tends to be put to the right, as we can see from Figure 5b.

Recall that we cannot define Chung's normalized Laplacian for digraphs that are not strongly connected, and hence,

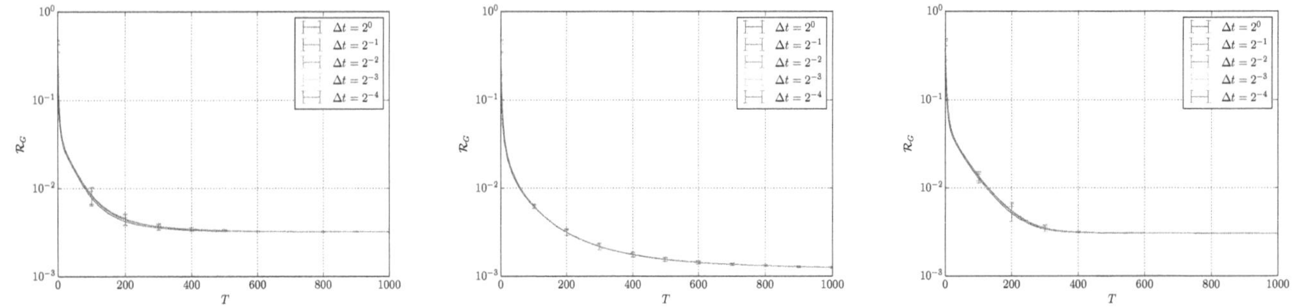

(a) Political Blogs (b) Enron (c) Epinions1

Figure 3: Convergence of $\mathcal{R}_G$

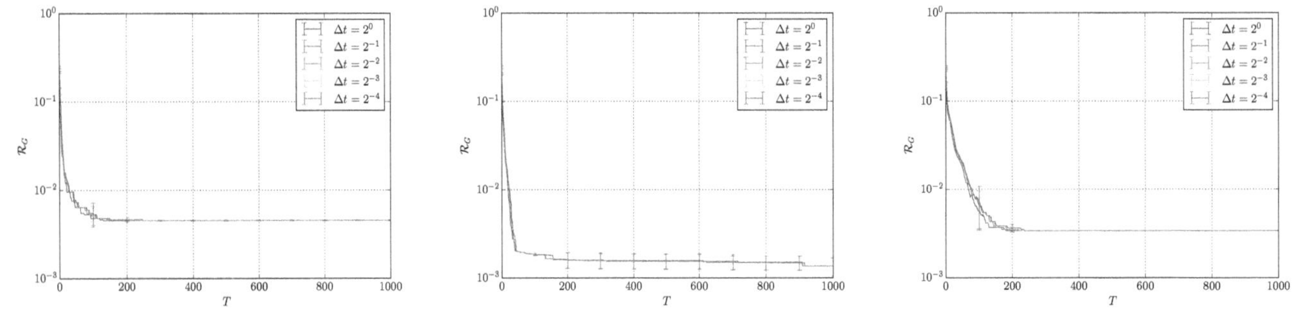

(a) Political Blogs (b) Enron (c) Epinions1

Figure 4: Convergence of ϕ

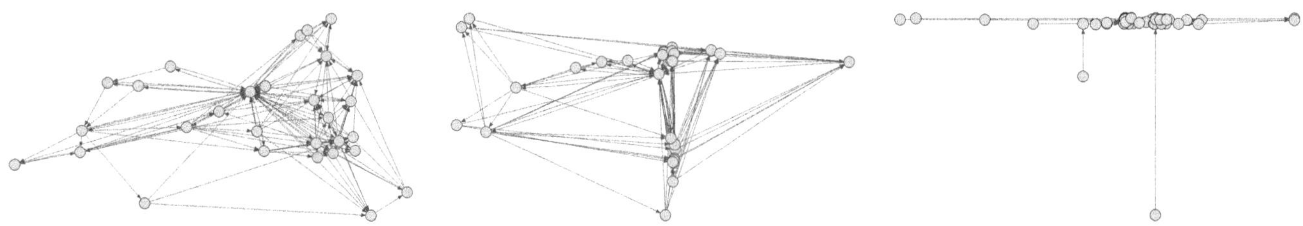

(a) Narragan (Chung) (b) Narragan (Nonlinear) (c) s208_st (Nonlinear)

Figure 5: Embedding based on the eigenvectors

we cannot embed such digraphs using Chung's normalized Laplacian. In contrast, the normalized nonlinear Laplacian is well defined even on digraphs that are not strongly connected. See Figure 5c for an example of embedding a digraph that is not strongly connected using the normalized nonlinear Laplacian. We can observe that the embedding respects the direction of arcs and most arcs head to the right.

6.3 Spectral ordering and conductance

In order to reveal the structures of larger networks, we sorted the vertices of several networks in increasing order of the values of the second eigenvectors of normalized Laplacians. Figure 6 shows the resulting adjacency matrices obtained by the normalized nonlinear Laplacian and Chung's normalized Laplacian. The adjacency matrices obtained by Chung's normalized Laplacian are rather scattered, and we cannot observe any meaningful structure of the networks. In contrast, we can observe from the adjacency matrices constructed by the normalized nonlinear Laplacian that (i) in C. elegans and Political Blogs, most arcs are headed from vertices of lower indices to those of larger indices, which represents the flow of signals or information in the network and (ii) in US Airports, we have two communities that are tightly connected internally and are loosely connected to each other.

This observation can be confirmed quantitatively by using the sweep profile. The *sweep profile* of the vertex ordering $v_1, \ldots, v_n$ is the vector $\phi_1, \ldots, \phi_{n-1}$, where ϕ_i is the conductance of the set $\{v_1, \ldots, v_i\}$. Figure 7 shows the sweep profile of several networks using the second eigenvalues of the normalized nonlinear Laplacian and Chung's normalized

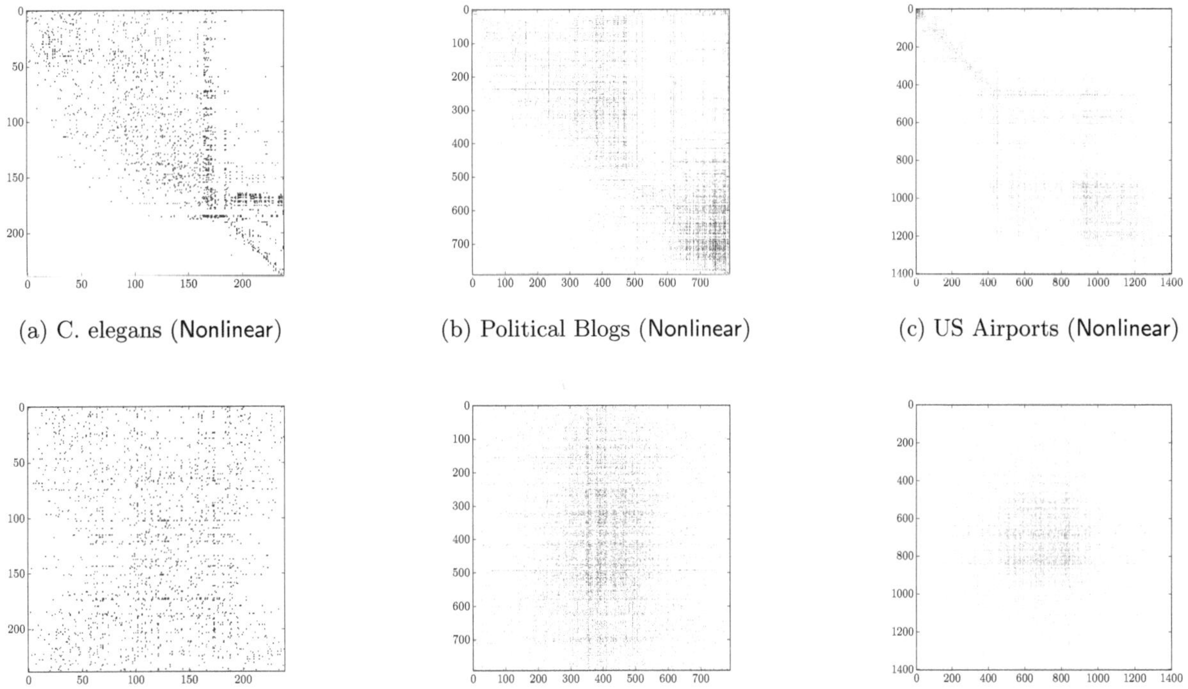

(a) C. elegans (Nonlinear) (b) Political Blogs (Nonlinear) (c) US Airports (Nonlinear)

(d) C. elegans (Chung) (e) Political Blogs (Chung) (f) US Airports (Chung)

Figure 6: Adjacency matrix after sorting vertices according to the second eigenvector

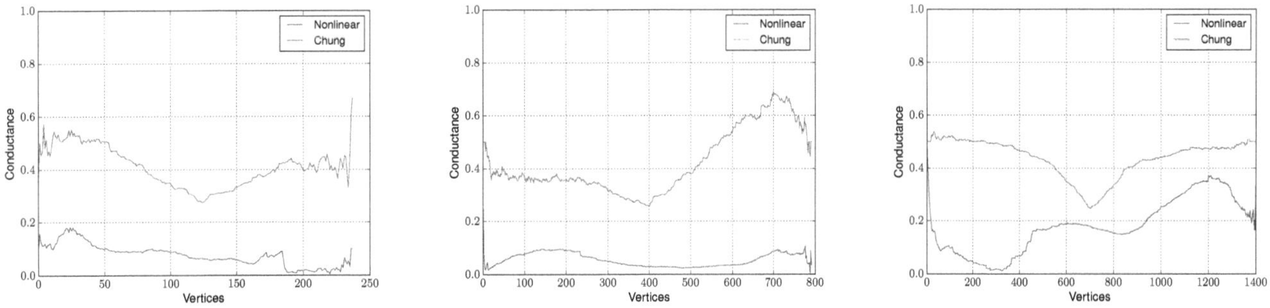

(a) C. elegans (b) Political Blogs (c) US Airports

Figure 7: Conductance obtained by sweeping vertices

Laplacian. The conductances obtained by the normalized nonlinear Laplacian are consistently smaller than those obtained by Chung's normalized Laplacian. The sweep profiles of C. elegans and Political Blogs obtained by the normalized nonlinear Laplacian are small in every position because most arcs in those networks are ordered in the same direction. We can observe that the set of the first 300 vertices in US Airports has a small conductance, which implies that the two communities in US Airports are well separated.

7. CONCLUSIONS

In this paper, we introduced a nonlinear Laplacian for digraphs that does not rely on the stationary distribution. By analyzing the heat equation, we showed several basic properties of the nonlinear Laplacian and presented an algorithm for computing its eigenvalues. In addition, we showed a Cheeger-like inequality that connects the second eigenvalue of the nonlinear Laplacian and the conductance. Finally, we experimentally demonstrated that our method achieves a smaller conductance than previous methods and that the nonlinear Laplacian is a useful tool for analyzing the structures of directed networks.

Potential directions for future work include extending this work to find local communities containing a specified vertex. Although there are several algorithms for finding local communities in an undirected graph, their analysis crucially exploits the linearity of the Laplacians of graphs [4, 13, 14, 22].

Acknowledgment

The author would like to thank A. Louis, Y. Nakatsukasa, and T. Takaguchi for their insightful comments. Y. Y. is supported by JSPS Grant-in-Aid for Young Scientists (B) (No. 26730009), MEXT Grant-in-Aid for Scientific Research on Innovative Areas (No. 24106003), and JST, ERATO, Kawarabayashi Large Graph Project.

8. REFERENCES

[1] L. A. Adamic and N. Glance. The political blogosphere and the 2004 U.S. election: divided they blog. In *LinkKDD*, pages 36–43, 2005.

[2] N. Alon. Eigenvalues and expanders. *Combinatorica*, 6(2):83–96, 1986.

[3] N. Alon and V. D. Milman. λ_1, isoperimetric inequalities for graphs, and superconcentrators. *Journal of Combinatorial Theory, Series B*, 38(1):73–88, 1985.

[4] R. Andersen, F. Chung, and K. Lang. Local graph partitioning using pagerank vectors. In *FOCS*, pages 475–486, 2006.

[5] R. Andersen, F. Chung, and K. Lang. Local partitioning for directed graphs using pagerank. In *WAW*, pages 166–178, 2007.

[6] K. Atkinson, W. Han, and D. E. Stewart. *Numerical Solution of Ordinary Differential Equations*. John Wiley & Sons, 2011.

[7] S. T. Barnard and H. D. Simon. Fast multilevel implementation of recursive spectral bisection for partitioning unstructured problems. *Concurrency: Practice and Experience*, 6(2):101–117, 1994.

[8] F. Bauer. Normalized graph Laplacians for directed graphs. *Linear Algebra and its Applications*, 436(11):4193–4222, 2012.

[9] P. Bonacich. Some unique properties of eigenvector centrality. *Social Networks*, 29(4):555–564, 2007.

[10] M. Chen, Q. Yang, and X. Tang. Directed graph embedding. In *IJCAI*, pages 2707–2712, 2007.

[11] F. Chung. Laplacians and the Cheeger inequality for directed graphs. *Annals of Combinatorics*, 9(1):1–19, 2005.

[12] F. Chung. The heat kernel as the pagerank of a graph. *Proceedings of the National Academy of Sciences*, 104(50):19735–19740, 2007.

[13] F. Chung. Random walks and local cuts in graphs. *Linear Algebra and its Applications*, 423(1):22–32, 2007.

[14] F. Chung. A local graph partitioning algorithm using heat kernel pagerank. *Internet Mathematics*, 6(3):315–330, 2009.

[15] F. R. K. Chung. *Spectral graph theory*. American Mathematical Society, 1997.

[16] F. R. K. Chung. The diameter and Laplacian eigenvalues of directed graphs. *The Electronic Journal of Combinatorics*, 13(1):N4, 2006.

[17] D. Cvetković, P. Rowlinson, and S. Simić. *An introduction to the theory of graph spectra*. Cambridge University Press, 2010.

[18] M. Filippone, F. Camastra, F. Masulli, and S. Rovetta. A survey of kernel and spectral methods for clustering. *Pattern Recognition*, 41(1):176–190, 2008.

[19] D. Gleich. Hierarchical directed spectral graph partitioning. Technical report, Stanford University, 2006.

[20] B. Hendrickson and R. Leland. An improved spectral graph partitioning algorithm for mapping parallel computations. *SIAM Journal on Scientific Computing*, 16(2):452–469, 1995.

[21] T. Joachims. Transductive learning via spectral graph partitioning. *ICML*, pages 290–297, 2003.

[22] K. Kloster and D. F. Gleich. Heat kernel based community detection. In *KDD*, pages 1386–1395, 2014.

[23] J. Kunegis. KONECT - the Koblenz network collection. In *International Web Observatory Workshop*, pages 1343–1350, 2013.

[24] Y. Li and Z.-L. Zhang. Digraph Laplacian and the degree of asymmetry. *Internet Mathematics*, 8(4):381–401, 2012.

[25] A. Louis. Hypergraph Markov operators, eigenvalues and approximation algorithms. In *STOC*, pages 713–722, 2015.

[26] A. Louis, P. Raghavendra, and S. Vempala. The complexity of approximating vertex expansion. In *FOCS*, pages 360–369. IEEE, 2013.

[27] B. Luo, R. C Wilson, and E. R. Hancock. Spectral embedding of graphs. *Pattern Recognition*, 36(10):2213–2230, 2003.

[28] R. Merris. Laplacian matrices of graphs: a survey. *Linear Algebra and its Applications*, 197-198:143–176, 1994.

[29] R. Milo, S. Itzkovitz, N. Kashtan, R. Levitt, S. Shen-Orr, I. Ayzenshtat, M. Sheffer, and U. Alon. Superfamilies of evolved and designed networks. *Science*, 303(5663):1538–1542, 2004.

[30] M. E. Monaco and R. E. Ulanowicz. Comparative ecosystem trophic structure of three US mid-atlantic estuaries. *Marine Ecology Progress Series*, 161:239–254, 1997.

[31] J. Ruan and W. Zhang. An efficient spectral algorithm for network community discovery and its applications to biological and social networks. *ICDM*, pages 643–648, 2007.

[32] B. Ruhnau. Eigenvector-centrality — a node-centrality? *Social Networks*, 22(4):357–365, 2000.

[33] D. A. Spielman. Spectral graph theory and its applications. In *FOCS*, pages 29–38. IEEE, 2007.

[34] U. von Luxburg. A tutorial on spectral clustering. *Statistics and computing*, 17(4):395–416, 2007.

[35] D. J. Watts and S. H. Strogatz. Collective dynamics of 'small-world' networks. *Nature*, 393(6684):440–442, 1998.

[36] S. Yan, D. Xu, B. Zhang, H.-J. Zhang, Q. Yang, and S. Lin. Graph embedding and extensions: A general framework for dimensionality reduction. *IEEE Transactions on Pattern Analysis and Machine Intelligence*, 29(1):40–51, 2006.

[37] D. Zhou, J. Huang, and B. Schölkopf. Learning from labeled and unlabeled data on a directed graph. In *ICML*, pages 1036–1043, 2005.

Querying and Tracking Influencers in Social Streams

Karthik Subbian
University of Minnesota,
Minneapolis, MN 55455.
karthik@cs.umn.edu

Charu C. Aggarwal
IBM TJ Watson Research Ctr,
Yorktown Heights, NY 10598.
charu@us.ibm.com

Jaideep Srivastava
University of Minnesota,
Minneapolis, MN 55455.
srivasta@cs.umn.edu

ABSTRACT

Influence analysis is an important problem in social network analysis due to its impact on viral marketing and targeted advertisements. Most of the existing influence analysis methods determine the influencers in a static network with an influence propagation model based on pre-defined edge propagation probabilities. However, none of these models can be queried to find influencers in both context and time-sensitive fashion from a streaming social data. In this paper, we propose an approach to maintain real-time influence scores of users in a social stream using a topic and time-sensitive approach, while the network and topic is constantly evolving over time. We show that our approach is efficient in terms of online maintenance and effective in terms various types of real-time context- and time-sensitive queries. We evaluate our results on both social and collaborative network data sets.

1. INTRODUCTION

The problem of finding influential actors is important in various domains such as viral marketing [7] and political campaigns. The problem was formally defined by Kempe et al. [15] as an optimization problem over all possible subsets of nodes with cardinality k. Subsequently, a significant amount of work [15, 14, 18, 10, 9, 13] has been done on this area. All these approaches are static in the sense that they work with a fixed model of network structure and edge probabilities. In practice, however, the influence of actors are defined by how their messages are propagated in the social network over time. Such propagation can only be observed from the underlying *social stream*, such as a Twitter feed or the sequence of Facebook activities. This problem setting is highly dynamic because the social stream evolves over time, as different actors initiate messages which are propagated in varying degrees over the network. The influence of an actor is best learned by observing the patterns of message propagations over time, as some actors are more successful than others in initiating new cascades of information flow in the network. The use of such information flows in identifying influencers has recently been recognized [24].

A major disadvantage of existing influence analysis methods is that they do not enable the ability to *query* the influencers in a *context-specific* fashion. Ideally, one would like to be able to use search terms to determine influencers that are specific to a given context. For example, the top influencers for the search term "*Egypt Unrest*" would be very different from that of the search term "*PGA Golf Tour*". The inflexibility of existing methods is, in part, because the existing methods [18, 10, 9, 15] decouple the problem of influence analysis from learning content-centric influence probabilities [11]. Clearly, one cannot learn a new set of relevant edge probabilities every time a query is initiated.

The influencers in a social stream are *time-sensitive* and may rapidly evolve [2], as different external events may lead to changes in the influence patterns over time. For instance, a query such as "*winter boots*" may generally have prominent entities associated with shoe stores as the most influential entities, but an (advertisement) statement from a popular figure in the entertainment industry, such as Justin Bieber, on a specific boot style[1] may change this ordering. Important events can often dynamically change the influencers, and this can only be tracked in a *time-sensitive* and *online fashion* from the underlying activities in the social stream.

We address these issues by considering a more flexible *real-time setting* in this paper, in which we enable the ability to *query* a social stream for various types of *context-sensitive* and *time-sensitive* influencers. Any influence query includes four components, corresponding to (a) influencer set, (b) influenced set, (c) query content such as keywords, and (d) time. The last of these components is often (implicitly) assumed to be the current time, although our framework is flexible enough to provide responses to historical queries as well. The influence score $\mathcal{I}(S_1, S_2, \mathcal{Q}, t)$ represents the aggregate influence score of actor set S_1 on actor set S_2 with respect to content $\mathcal{Q}$ at time t. Most of the queries are resolved by evaluating this score and then ranking it over various possibilities in the argument. One or more of the arguments in $\mathcal{I}(S_1, S_2, \mathcal{Q}, t)$ can be instantiated to a "*" (don't care) in order to enable more general queries in which all possibilities for the matching are considered. For instance, the queries $\mathcal{I}(\text{"David"}, *, \text{"Egypt unrest"}, t)$ and $\mathcal{I}(\text{"John"}, *, \text{"Egypt unrest"}, t)$ can be used to compare the total influence of David and John on the topic "*Egypt unrest*" at time t. Some examples of useful queries that can be resolved with this approach are as follows:

- For a given query context $\mathcal{Q}$, determining the top-k *influencers* at time t can be formulated as: $\max_{X:|X|=k} \mathcal{I}(X, *, \mathcal{Q}, t)$. It is also possible to constrain the query to consider a specific subset Y in the second argument, corresponding to the influenced actors. For example, a winter clothing merchant might decide to consider only those actors whose location profiles correspond to colder regions.

[1]http://money.msn.com/now/post.aspx?post=ea03f857-18c1-414f-97bc-7bc5d0b2ab06

WSDM'16, February 22–25, 2016, San Francisco, CA, USA.
© 2016 ACM. ISBN 978-1-4503-3716-8/16/02...$15.00
DOI: http://dx.doi.org/10.1145/2835776.2835788

- Determining the top-k *influenced* actors at time t, for a given query context $\mathcal{Q}$, can be extremely useful in context-specific subscriptions and in recommending interesting public content to influenced users.
- Influence queries can also be useful in context-sensitive link recommendation, such as finding the top-k influencer-influenced pairs, for a given query context $\mathcal{Q}$.

Influence queries can provide significant business insights into the content, network, and temporal dynamics of the social stream. In addition, dynamic variants of existing problems can be formulated using this querying framework to leverage our approach. For example, the traditional influence maximization problem [15] is that of maximizing the influence of node set X (of size k) for the entire network, for any content, across all time points. In other words, the traditional problem can be formulated as $\max_{X:|X|=k} \mathcal{I}(X,*,*,*)$. An important difference from traditional influence analysis is that these queries are now resolved in a dynamic and data-driven way with the help of the social stream.

1.1 Contributions and Organization

In this paper, we propose an online approach in which we process the incoming social stream objects to create an *incrementally (lazy) updatable data structure of flow paths*. This data structure implicitly tracks all the influence information corresponding to the different content of all users in real-time. This goal is achieved by tracking information flow patterns in a tree-like data structure across various paths of the network in a context- and time-sensitive fashion. This data structure can then be queried in a flexible way to yield a variety of insights that are not normally possible with a traditional influence-based model. It is important to note that our framework provides the ability to *query influencers* for different contexts without any re-computation of influencers from scratch, unlike existing approaches [10, 9, 15].

Our approach is well-suited for applications where the hardware available for execution is limited. To handle such scenarios, we provide an *approximation technique* (based on the available hardware) and show that our approximation is close enough to actual value. We establish a tight lower bound on the accuracy for this purpose. Our approach also has a well-established relationship with *Katz similarity* measure. Finally, we evaluate our approach using social and collaboration data sets and show several interesting case studies and precision-recall experiments for different types of queries. To the best of our knowledge, this is the first *influence querying and tracking* model for *social streams*.

This paper is organized as follows. The remainder of this section discusses the related work. In the next section, we formalize the problem of online influence analysis for social streams. In section 3, we will provide an efficient algorithm for querying and tracking influencers from social streams. Section 4 contains the experimental results. The conclusions and summary are contained in section 5.

1.2 Related Work

The problem of tracking influencers in a network is often treated as an influence maximization problem [15, 14, 18, 10, 9]. The problem of influence maximization is that of finding the top-k nodes such that the average infection spread is maximized under a specific influence propagation model. There are two popular choices for the influence propagation model, which are referred to as the Independent Cascade (IC) and Linear Threshold (LT) [15] models, respectively. In these models, it is assumed that the edge propagation probabilities for the influence propagation model are already provided. Therefore, it is difficult to query these models for a specific context (or content), unless the edge propagation probabilities are learned as a separate problem in its own right [11]. In the dynamic social stream setting, such a model is too inflexible to *simultaneously track the influencers in different contexts, while also adjusting for the evolution in the flow patterns and influencers over time*.

Information flow mining has been recognized as a useful tool for the problem of influence analysis. A number of basic models for influence analysis in social networks are discussed in [15]. Related work on information flow mining and cascades may be found in [16, 18, 19, 22]. The problem of information flow mining and influence analysis has been related in [12, 24]. There are game theoretic [26] and supervised learning models [25] applied for finding influencers. However, these techniques are applicable only for static graphs and not for streaming social data. There are a few topic-specific influence analysis models [5, 8, 21, 27], but they are either not online, or they cannot be queried in a context- and time-sensitive fashion.

There is a surge of recent literature on social streams [3]. As the content of many social networks, such as *Twitter*, are often available only in the form of social streams of user activity. Social streams have been explored in the context of event detection [1, 23], topic-based browsing [6], classification [29], and influence analysis [24]. There have been some attempts to compute influencers in an online setting [17, 30], but these approaches are not context-specific and cannot be queried. There are other interesting works on topic-specific influence maximization [4]. However, our focus is more on a general keyword-based influence querying scheme for streaming scenarios. As we will see later, our approach is related to a flow-based version of the Katz measure [20], a popular centrality measure.

2. REAL-TIME FLOW-BASED INFLUENCE ANALYSIS

In this section, we discuss the necessary notations and the problem definition to introduce the online influence analysis model for social streams. We assume that we have a social stream $\mathcal{S}(t)$ at time t. It should be pointed out that the social stream $\mathcal{S}(t)$ can be used to construct a temporal network $G(t) = (V(t), E(t))$, which is based on all the edges received so far till time t. It is assumed that all edges in the network are directed, which corresponds to the direction of the information flow along an edge in $E(t)$. Each actor $a_i \in V$ performs a number of *content-based actions* such as sending tweets, exchanging messages, or placing wall posts, etc. Because this process occurs simultaneously over the entire set of actors in the social network, the stream of content created by the different actors can be *globally* treated as a *social stream* of text content. We denote the set of all distinct keywords that appear in the social stream by $\mathcal{K} = \{K_1, \ldots, K_m\}$. Each content-token K_i in the stream is associated with the following meta-data:

- The content-token $K_i \in \mathcal{K}$ represents a component of the content created by an actor in the social stream. This could correspond to the actual string of the tweet/post, or only specific parts of the post, such as URL strings, keywords, or hash tags. In the event that the cascade behavior is being observed broadly in the form of topics, rather than re-posts, the string K_i could also simply be one of a set of a topical dictionary of keywords (contained in the tweet). An interesting feature of our approach is that it can be easily applied to an arbitrary subset of content-tokens or even latent topics to facilitate topic-specific influence in the network (Section

3.3). However, for the purpose of this paper we treat $\mathcal{K}$ as the dictionary of content-tokens and each content token (K_i) denotes a unique hashtag or a keyword. We feel such keyword-based treatment allows for better granularity of analysis.

- It is assumed that the content K_i is created by some actor a_j. The value j is an index drawn from the actor set $V(t)$, and it represents the actor who is responsible for the origination of that particular piece of content.
- It is assumed that the content K_i is received by actor $a_l \in V(t)$, and it represents the recipient of that content. This recipient could be an email recipient in an email network, a follower of the tweet sender in *Twitter*, or any other form of communication in a social network.

The continuous flow of such user content through a network is referred to as social stream ($\mathcal{S}$) [24], and it is often the *only observable aspect of the dynamics of a social network.* In many social networks, such as *Twitter*, this form of social stream data is available using a subscription-based access.

2.1 The Flow-based Query Model

We now set up the model for the influence querying problem, and show its relationship to many of the existing methods in the literature. More specifically, we will discuss how the flow paths are used in the context of influencer querying. The intuition behind the flow-based approach is that influencers that are important to a specific content are often the originators of messages or tweets related to that content. The same observation is true about the pairwise influence between nodes. When a particular actor a_i is influential on actor a_j with respect to a particular content set (e.g., keywords), it will lead to a significant amount of flow of the corresponding content set form a_i to a_j and then to a_j's neighbors, through multiple flow paths. Thus, by tracking the flow paths for different keywords, one can perform effective content-centric analysis.

For the purpose of this paper, we assume that a dictionary of keyword $\mathcal{K}$ is available, and all content flow weights are computed in terms of the transmission of messages containing these keywords. The use of keywords, as opposed to segments of text, actually allows for better granularity of analysis, since the content flows can be computed in terms of these keywords, and then aggregated over different flow paths for a particular topic.

First, we define the concept of a valid flow between a pair of nodes a_j and a_k, with respect to a specific content token K_i. Intuitively, this concept represents the transmitting of a keyword K_i along a specific path $a_j = b_1 \dots b_r = a_k$ leading from a_j to a_k, such that each transmission between successive nodes occurs in that order. We formally define this concept as a *valid flow*:

DEFINITION 1 (VALID FLOW). *A valid flow $\mathcal{F}$ of keyword K_i from a_j to a_k is an ordered set of nodes $a_j = b_1 \dots b_s = a_k \in N$, such that the following conditions are satisfied:*

1. *An edge exists between nodes b_r and b_{r+1} in the base network, for all $r = 1 \dots s-1$.*
2. *The node b_{r+1} transmits a message containing the keyword K_i, after a message is transmitted from node b_r containing the same keyword.*

Thus, a flow from node a_j to node a_k, of the keyword K_i is indicative of the influence that node a_j has over node a_k. Note that the flow of a message occurs over a particular duration that corresponds to the elapsed time since the first transmission of message keyword from node a_j. We refer to this as the flow duration:

DEFINITION 2 (FLOW DURATION). *Consider a valid flow $\mathcal{F}$ of keyword K_i from a_j to a_k. Let t_c be the current time, and t_o be the original time at which the keyword was transmitted from node a_j. Then, the flow duration from node a_j to node a_k is equal to $\delta t = t_c - t_o$.*

The notion of flow duration refers to the *latency* of influence response. When the flow duration (δt) is large, the significance of the content flow decays over time in terms of its influence. This is important, especially if the influence scores are to be made temporally sensitive for more effective analysis. Therefore, we assume a decay factor of λ, and assume exponential decay in order to define the *flow weight* of a particular path.

DEFINITION 3 (DECAYED FLOW WEIGHT). *Let δt be the flow duration of a particular flow $\mathcal{F}$ at a current time t_c, and λ be the decay factor. Then, the decayed flow weight is given by $2^{-(\lambda\delta t)}$.*

The flow $\mathcal{F}$ has a half-life of $1/\lambda$, since the weight of a flow reduces by a factor of 2 every $1/\lambda$ time units. Note that the rate at which the information decays is a constant for all users in our model (i.e. λ). More specifically, the rate of decay before and after the message is transmitted by (the last actor) a_k in flow $\mathcal{F}$ is λ. Thus, the decayed flow weight expression, in Definition 3, is independent of the time of transmission of the message by actor a_k. The decayed flow weight can be further used to define the aggregate path flow.

DEFINITION 4 (AGGREGATE PATH FLOW). *The aggregate path flow $\mathcal{A}(\mathcal{P}, K_i, t_c)$ at current time t_c, for keyword K_i along a particular path $\mathcal{P} = \langle a_j, \dots, a_k \rangle$, is the sum of the flow weights on that path for the keyword K_i over all different valid propagation of the keyword from node j to node k along path $\mathcal{P}$.*

Note that the aggregate path flow is caused by repeated flow of a keyword K_i along a particular path. For two flows to be considered distinct, the keywords would need to have been transmitted at a distinct time at the source or destination node in the path, and also satisfy all the valid flow constraints.

This path flow can be aggregated across a set of paths that are specific to a particular source and destination node, to define a pairwise value, as opposed to a path-wise value.

DEFINITION 5 (AGGREGATE PAIRWISE FLOW). *The aggregate pairwise flow $\mathcal{V}(a_j, a_k, K_i, t_c)$ at time t_c for keyword K_i from node a_j to node a_k is equal to sum of the value of the flows on the paths from node a_j to node a_k. Therefore, is S_{jk} be the set of paths from node j to node k, we have:*

$$\mathcal{V}(a_j, a_k, K_i, t_c) = \sum_{\mathcal{P} \in \mathcal{S}_{jk}} \mathcal{A}(\mathcal{P}, K_i, t_c) \tag{1}$$

We now formally introduce the atomic influence function $\mathcal{I}(a_j, a_k, \mathcal{Q}, t)$, which is the influence exerted by node a_j on a_k, for the context $\mathcal{Q}$ (query keywords), at time t. This function can be computed as a sum of the aggregate pairwise flows over all the query keywords $K_i \in Q$. It is important to note that this influence function is asymmetric. In other words, the influence exerted from a_j to a_k can be very different from the influence in the other direction.

DEFINITION 6 (ATOMIC INFLUENCE FUNCTION). *The atomic influence value $\mathcal{I}(a_j, a_k, \mathcal{Q}, t)$ for a node a_j to influence a_k, is defined as the sum of the aggregate pairwise flows over all keywords $K_i \in \mathcal{Q}$ in the data:*

$$\mathcal{I}(a_j, a_k, \mathcal{Q}, t) = \sum_{K_i \in \mathcal{Q}} \mathcal{V}(a_j, a_k, K_i, t) \tag{2}$$

So far, we have explained how the individual content tokens arriving in the social stream $\mathcal{T}$ can be used to model an influence function $\mathcal{I}$, in content, network and time sensitive fashion. It is possible to convert the keywords to other representations in scenarios where it leads to enhanced performance. For example, the content tokens tracked may be URLs or high level topics, while the incoming query may be still a collection of textual tokens. In such cases, a probabilistic latent factor model can be used to compute the association of tracked content tokens to given query tokens. We will revisit this discussion in detail, after we explain a simplified version of the algorithm in the next section.

2.2 General Flow-based Query Processing

The aforementioned computation of the atomic influence function for calculating influence scores in pairwise fashion can be generalized to a wider range of queries easily. An important observation is that the "don't care" conditions, denoted by '*', can be treated as implicit summations. For instance, we have $\mathcal{I}(*, a_k, \mathcal{Q}, t) = \sum_{a_j \in V} \mathcal{I}(a_j, a_k, \mathcal{Q}, t) = \mathcal{I}(V, a_k, \mathcal{Q}, t)$. In this section, we denote the influencer and the influenced as a_j and a_k, respectively. The three main applications of the atomic influence function are as follows:

Influencer Search Queries ($\alpha\,(a_j, \mathcal{Q}, t)$): A typical form of querying is similar to using a search engine. Given a contextual query, $\mathcal{Q} = \{w_1, w_2, ..., w_k\}$, a relevant set of influencers are computed for $\mathcal{Q}$ at the current time t, using the atomic influence function, which is defined as $\alpha(a_j, \mathcal{Q}, t) = \mathcal{I}(a_j, *, \mathcal{Q}, t)/\mathcal{I}(*, *, \mathcal{Q}, t)$. We normalize the scores across all users for the query, before comparing them with each other. We find the top-k (a_j) nodes that have the highest influence scores (using the atomic query $\alpha(a_j, \mathcal{Q}, t)$) and arrange them in the descending order. A user can also query the influencers in a similar way for an earlier time $t' < t$.

Link Prediction Queries ($\beta\,(a_j, a_k, t)$): Social network users tend to connect to the users who influence them highly. Hence, one can use this query to find the top-k users who have the greatest influence on user a_k at current time t. This query is very similar to the link prediction problem where directional (e.g., follower) links are predicted on the basis of context-sensitive influence. Here, the atomic influence function can be defined as $\beta(a_j, a_k, t) = \mathcal{I}(a_j, a_k, *, t)/\mathcal{I}(*, a_k, *, t)$ to find the influence of nodes a_j on a_k across all $K_i \in \mathcal{K}$.

Concept-specific temporal queries ($\gamma\,(Q, [t_1, t_2])$): These queries can be used to find the evolution of influence of a particular concept or phrase across a time horizon $[t1, t2]$ [2]. Here, a concept or phrase (Q) is given, and its influence over a time window is measured and compared. The atomic influence function is computed as $\gamma(Q, [t_1, t_2]) = \mathcal{I}(*, *, Q, t)/\mathcal{I}(*, *, Q, *), t \in [t1, t2]$.

We will discuss these three applications in detail in our experiments section.

2.3 Relationship with Katz Measure

The aforementioned atomic influence function is closely related to the Katz measure [20]. The Katz measure is defined in terms of the weighted sum of the number of all possible paths between a pair of nodes and the weight decays exponentially with the length of the underlying path. Specifically, if $\mathcal{P}_{ij}$ be the set of paths between nodes a_i and a_j, then the Katz measure $K(a_i, a_j)$ is defined as follows:

[2]Here the time interval is discrete, with a specific time granularity days, hours, minutes, etc.

$$K(a_i, a_j) = \sum_{P \in \mathcal{P}_{ij}} \beta^{|P|} \quad (3)$$

Here β is the discount factor on the path length, which in our case is analogous to the flow-based temporal decay factor. This is also analogous to the original definition of the Katz measure, in which longer paths are discounted to a greater degree. Thus, our flow-based approach computes exponentially decayed flow weights across different paths, as a more dynamic, time- and content-sensitive way of measuring the importance of nodes. In an indirect sense, this way of computing node importance can be considered a flow-based analogue to the Katz measure in static networks. Because the Katz measure has been shown to be effective for link recommendation in static networks, it lends greater credence to its use in the flow-based streaming scenario. Of course, the Katz measure is used rarely in static networks because of the complexity of enumerating over a large number of possible paths. The important point to understand is that the flow-based measure *significantly* changes in the importance of different paths in the update process, and can also be more efficiently computed in the streaming scenario, because of the availability of a dynamic update process (see Section 3.2). Most paths in the network are used rarely by the different flows, and therefore the flow-based measure provides a better weighting to the different paths in terms of *user actions*. This skew in the distribution of user behavior across different paths also allows for a more efficient computation of the atomic influence function, as compared to the static case, because of the number of paths with significant flow is much smaller. We will use this intuition later to provide an efficient approximation to our algorithm in Section 3.1.

2.4 Challenges and Intuition

The problem of flow-based online influence analysis is extremely challenging because of its computational and real-time constraints. One major challenge is that the number of possible paths between a pair of nodes are exponential and so are the number of flows. Furthermore, real-time tracking becomes extremely difficult, when the number of paths involved is extremely large.

A salient observation is that while the number of possible flows is large, only a small number of them may be significant enough to be maintained. This fact will be exploited in order to create a pruned approximation of the flow paths. This pruned version can keep approximate track of the different paths in an efficient and dynamic way. We provide an analysis that shows our approximation significantly reduces the complexity of the maintaining all flow paths, while retaining the effectiveness of the querying process.

3. INFLUENCER TRACKING ALGORITHM

In this section, we will present the basic flow-based influencer tracking algorithm. As discussed earlier, a key part of this approach is the aggregation of flow paths together with the relevant weights and updating them *in real-time* as the new social stream object arrives. Therefore, the main focus of this approach is to find an efficient way to keep track of the flow paths. For ease in discussion, we will first describe the algorithm with two simplifying assumptions. The first assumption is that the keyword set $\mathcal{K}$ contains a single keyword K. We dropped the subscript i in K_i, since we are dealing with a single keyword assumption. The second simplifying assumption is to set the decay factor $\lambda = 0$ (no decay), so that path weights essentially correspond to the counts of all the messages received so far. Later, we will describe how to modify the algorithm to the general case. This two-stage exposition eases the understanding of the algorithm. Before discussing the algorithm in detail, we will first introduce the concept of the *flow-path tree* that is an essential data structure for keeping track of the flow paths. Our first description will use a very simple version of the path tree, without any latent factor model (such as topic model), no decay and a single keyword. Later, we will systematically discuss the changes required for each of the increasing levels of complexity.

The flow-path tree $\mathcal{T}$ is a compressed representation of all the flow paths that have been encountered so far. This tree is used in order to keep track of all the information flows in the stream so far. For a set of paths $\mathcal{P} = P_1 \ldots P_n$ with flow weights $w_1 \ldots w_n$, along which a flow of the keyword $\mathcal{K}$ has occurred, the flow-path tree is defined as follows:

DEFINITION 7 (FLOW-PATH TREE). *A flow-path tree $\mathcal{T}$ for a set of paths $\mathcal{P} = \{P_1 \ldots P_n\}$ is defined as follows:*

1. *The root of the tree $\mathcal{T}$ is the null node.*
2. *Each path from the root to a leaf* must *correspond to exactly one path $P_i \in \mathcal{P}$, and a path from the root to an internal node* may *correspond to a path in $\mathcal{P}$.*
3. *The weight associated with a node (other than null node) is equal to the flow weight corresponding to the path from root to that node.*

The flow-path tree is different from frequent pattern tree (fp-tree) in several ways. The most important difference is that fp-tree is a representation for *item sets*, where the order does not matter. While in the flow-path tree the ordering of node matters the most. Hence, in our problem, the strategy of using the most frequent node in the root will not help. Moreover, while constructing the fp-tree each transaction in the database is used to update the counts in the tree. While in our scenario, there is no notion of a transaction and multiple paths that may have influenced a node is extracted from graph $G(t)$ and then updated in the flow-path tree. All nodes that propagated a content w will have their own root node (for content w) in flow-path tree, while in fp-tree transactions with same item w will not necessarily be a root node under *null*.

The overall framework for the influencer tracking algorithm (for a single keyword) is illustrated in Fig. 1. This particular description shows only how the flow paths are updated for the arrival of a message containing a single keyword K. In practice, however, all keywords in a given message will need to be extracted, and multiple updates will need to be performed to the flow tree. Furthermore, this procedure will need to be performed every time a message from a user originates at a given node a_i. The input to the algorithm is the network $G(t)$, the originating node a_i, and the current status of the path tree $\mathcal{T}$.

The basic idea in the algorithm is to trace back all the paths in the network $G(t)$ starting at node a_i, at which the keyword K has appeared in the past. For example, if node a_j has an outgoing edge to node a_i, and has propagated the keyword K before a_i, then the path $\langle a_j, a_i \rangle$ is added to the tree $\mathcal{T}$ if non-existent, and the count is increased by 1. Then, the path $\langle a_j, a_i \rangle$ is added to the candidate list $\mathcal{C}$ for further backtracking. Note that all paths in $\mathcal{C}$ will always end with the node a_i, but not all these paths may be relevant because the keyword K may not have had a flow along the immediate prefix (obtained by removing node a_i) of some of these paths. This relevance can be checked by examining whether the immediate prefix of this path occurs in $\mathcal{T}$. More specifically, for any path $P \in \mathcal{C}$ all nodes in the network $G(t)$, which have incoming edges into the first node in the path P are examined, along with the temporal ordering. For any such node a_k, a new path $a_k \oplus P$ is created by appending a_k to the beginning of the path P. Then, it is checked whether

Algorithm *UpdateFlowPaths*(Originating Node: a_i,
  Network: $G(t)$, Social Stream: $\mathcal{S}$, Flow-Path Tree: $\mathcal{T}$)
begin
  Receive the next message containing keyword K in
  in social stream $\mathcal{S}$ originating at node a_i;
  Create singleton node a_i in tree $\mathcal{T}$ as child of root
   node if it does not already exist;
  $\mathcal{C} = \{a_i\}$; { Candidate paths for expansion }
  Update weight of singleton path containing only
   node a_i in tree $\mathcal{T}$ by 1;
  while $\mathcal{C}$ is not empty
  begin
   Delete the first path P from $\mathcal{C}$ and
    denote the first node of P by a_j;
   for each $a_k \notin P$ in $V(t)$ with an incoming edge to a_j
    if prefix of path $a_k \oplus P$ exists in $\mathcal{T}$ and a_k has
     propagated keyword K prior to a_j
     if the complete path $a_k \oplus P$ exists in $\mathcal{T}$
      Increment weight of last node of path $a_k \oplus P$
      by 1 in $\mathcal{T}$;
     else
      Create last node of P as child for prefix
      of path $a_k \oplus P$ in $\mathcal{T}$ with weight as 1;
     endif
     Add $a_k \oplus P$ to $\mathcal{C}$;
    endif
   endfor
  endwhile
end

Figure 1: Updating the Flow Paths for Single Keyword Simplification

the *prefix of* $a_k \oplus P$ [3] occurs in $\mathcal{T}$. If the prefix does exist, then a new child node of the prefix can be created in $\mathcal{T}$, corresponding to $a_k \oplus P$, if such a child node does not already exist. The count of this child node is incremented by 1. The path $a_k \oplus P$ is added to the candidate set $\mathcal{C}$ for further exploration. Once a path has been explored in $\mathcal{C}$, it is deleted from $\mathcal{C}$. The termination criterion for the algorithm is the case when no more paths in $\mathcal{C}$ remain to be explored. It should be pointed out that while the number of possible paths in the network is exponential, the number of paths relating to a specific keyword is usually much smaller. This number is even smaller in the decay-based scenario discussed later, where very few paths are relevant to a particular keyword at a specific time. Nevertheless, the challenge arises that the tree $\mathcal{T}$ can grow rather large in many scenarios, because the number of children of a node in $\mathcal{T}$ can be as large as the in-degree of the corresponding node in $G(t)$. Since the degrees of nodes may sometimes be large, this can lead to an explosion in the number of nodes in the $\mathcal{T}$. In the next section, we will show how to improve the efficiency of the representation.

3.1 Speeding up by Pruning

Since the flows are skewed across the different paths in the tree, it is possible to use pruning to reduce the tree size and improve the efficiency of representation. Specifically, the tree size can be reduced by pruning out the low frequency leaves in the tree. The overall approach for building the flow-path tree uses an additional pruning phase, in which the low frequency leaves of the tree are removed.

In order to achieve this goal, the number of nodes in the tree always allowed to vary between n and N, where $n = \alpha \cdot N$ for $\alpha \in [0, 1]$. Smaller values of α improves the space complexity, while

[3] Prefix of $a_k \oplus P$ is the path obtained after removing the last node of P.

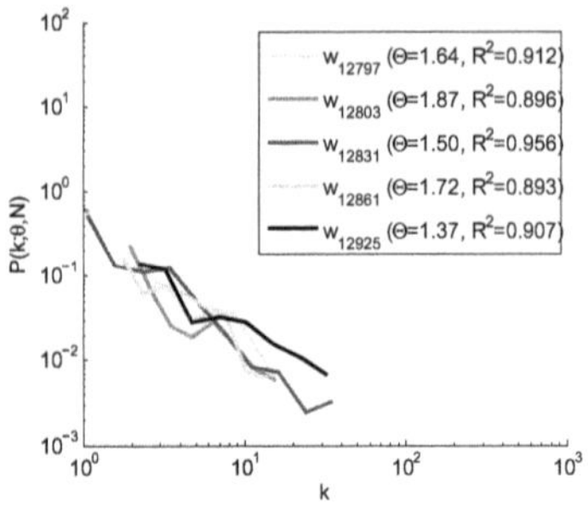

Figure 2: The best-fit estimate of the Zipf parameter θ and corresponding R^2 for few flow-path trees are shown in the legend.

larger values provide better accuracy of estimation. The pruning approach is triggered whenever the total number of leaves in the tree reaches N. The pruning approach sequentially removes the leaves from the tree until the total number of nodes in the tree is equal to $\alpha \cdot N$. A question arises here as to how much of the flow weight is lost by using the pruning approach, since the reduction in the flow weight reduces the accuracy of estimation. We will show that for modestly large values of N, the amount of flow weight lost is very small, in scenarios where the flow weights are skewed. Furthermore, because only the low frequency paths are lost, and the influence scores are mostly relevant to the high frequency paths, the impact of pruning is even lower.

The relative flow weights in a flow-path tree can be approximately modeled to be proportional to the Zipf distribution $1/i^\theta$ for $\theta > 1$. We confirm this by verifying the best fit estimates of the distribution of flow weights for several flow-path trees in our experiments on a real-life (Twitter) data set, described in detail in Section 4. In Fig. 3, we show the flow weight distribution for a few trees in rank versus frequency plots. We see that average R^2 is 0.926 across all flow path trees and the fit was statistically significant at 5% significance level. We now show that the reduction in flow weight, drawn from a Zipf distribution, is typically less than $\log(\alpha \cdot N)/\log(N)$.

THEOREM 1. *Let the flow weights on the N nodes in the tree be distributed according to the Zipf distribution $1/i^\theta$ for $\theta \geq 1$. Then, the total fraction $F(N, \alpha)$ of the flow in the top $n = \alpha \cdot N$ nodes of the tree is at least equal to:*

$$F(N,\alpha) \geq \mathit{log}(n)/\mathit{log}(N) = 1 - \mathit{log}(1/\alpha)/\mathit{log}(N) \quad (4)$$

Proof: The cumulative flow weight $C(n)$ for the top n flows is given by:

$$C(n) = \sum_{i=1}^{n} 1/i^\theta \quad (5)$$

Here, we are trying to determine the value of $C(\alpha N)/C(N)$. The function $C(\alpha N)/C(N)$ is an increasing function of θ for $\alpha < 1$, and $\theta \geq 1$. This is because the derivative of $C(\alpha N)/C(N)$ with respect to θ can be shown to be positive for $\theta \geq 1$. Therefore, the minimum value of the function is achieved at $\theta = 1$. Therefore, we have:

$$F(N,\alpha) \geq \frac{\sum_{i=1}^{n} 1/i}{\sum_{i=1}^{N} 1/i} \quad (6)$$

Note that the value of $\sum_{i=1}^{n} 1/i$ can be asymptotically approximated by $\log(n)$ for large values of n. The result follows. ■

The skew helps significantly in retaining the vast majority of the heavy flows. For example, in a flow tree with 100,000 paths, discarding half the least frequent paths would result in total flow weight reduction of only $1 - \log(50000)/\log(100000) = 0.06$ of the flow weight. Thus, the vast majority of the heavy flows are retained, which are the ones most relevant for the influence analysis process anyway. This suggests that the pruning process can be used to significantly reduce the complexity of the flow-path tree, while retaining the effectiveness of analysis. This is essentially because of the skew in the flows on different paths in the tree.

3.2 Incorporating Decay

A key issue is the incorporation of decay in the computation of flow weights. At first sight, this looks challenging because it would seem that it is required to continuously update the flow weights at each time stamp because of the decay. However, in practice, it is not necessary to update the flow weights for each time-stamp. Rather, it is sufficient to perform the updates in a *lazy fashion*, as described below. This is because of the *multiplicative property* of decay computations.

LEMMA 1 (MULTIPLICATIVE PROPERTY). *Let $\mathcal{A}(\mathcal{P}, K_i, t)$ be the aggregate flow value at the time t for path $\mathcal{P}$ with destination node a_k. Then, if no new message has been transmitted at destination node a_k in the time interval (t_1, t_2), then the flow values at times t_1 and t_2 are related by the following multiplicative rule:*

$$\mathcal{A}(\mathcal{P}, K_i, t_2) = \mathcal{A}(\mathcal{P}, K_i, t_1) \cdot 2^{-\lambda(t_2 - t_1)} \quad (7)$$

The key pre-condition in the aforementioned rule is that no message should have been transmitted at the destination node a_k of the path. This suggests a lazy approach for performing the multiplicative update, in which the decay-based multiplicative update is performed only whenever a message is transmitted at a node, corresponding to which the flow is added. Therefore, for each path, in the flow tree, each node contains the time-stamp information about the last time that the flow value of the corresponding path was updated. This is referred to as the *last path update time-stamp*. Whenever a path in the flow tree is updated, the first step is to apply the multiplicative decay factor to that node, and then add the newly arriving flow value. The newly arriving flow value (which needs to be added to the current flow value of the path in the tree) is computed according to Definition 3, rather than the simple addition of one unit. The *last path update time stamp* of that node is updated to the current time.

The incorporation of decay into the flow analysis process has the additional advantage of reducing the number of updates. Recall that the algorithm in Fig. 1 performs a backtrack starting at the destination node at which the keyword currently appears. When a particular path being examined has a very low aggregate flow value, then it can be pruned from consideration. In other words, the path does not need to be extended backwards in Fig. 1, when its flow value is below a given threshold. Such paths are therefore not added to the candidate list $\mathcal{C}$. Specifically, a threshold ϵ on the flow path value is imposed for pruning purposes.

3.3 Generalizing beyond Keywords

So far, we have constructed the flow-path tree with the use of a single content token. The generalization to full keyword sets can be easily performed by adding an additional level to the flow-path tree. Specifically, this additional top most level corresponds to the choice of keyword being tracked. The first step in this process is to map each keyword to one of these branches. Subsequently, the flow paths in that branch are updated using the approach discussed earlier.

It is sometimes helpful to track the influence of users on latent topics. While our algorithm is designed to create a flow-path tree for each keyword because of its natural connection to query-processing, it can be very well used for latent topics. To compute the influence scores on latent topics, one can use the posterior of each topic given the query keyword, and compute the atomic influence function for the generalized list of latent topics ($\mathcal{Z}$) as shown in (8).

$$\mathcal{I}(j, k, \mathcal{Q}, t_c) = \sum_{z \in \mathcal{Z}} \sum_{K_i \in \mathcal{Q}} p(z|K_i, t_c)\mathcal{V}(j, k, z, t_c) \quad (8)$$

This way one can query the topical influencers using latent topics, rather than explicitly using the content tokens in the post. Thus, the proposed approach is general enough to handle individual content tokens, n-gram phrases, and latent topics. We refer to our algorithm as **QUIS**, which is an acronym for **QU**erying **I**nfluencers in social **S**treams.

4. EXPERIMENTAL RESULTS

In this section, we will first evaluate the quality of influencers produced by the real-time flow-based query model compared to several baselines. Then, we will provide sensitivity and efficiency analysis of our querying framework. We also discuss several user- and concept-specific temporal queries to demonstrate the importance of influence query models in various scenarios.

4.1 Data sets

We evaluate the effectiveness and efficiency in two different data sets, belonging to the social network and research collaboration domains. For the social data set, we used Twitter, and for the collaboration data set we used DBLP.

Twitter Data Set: We used tweets over a period of 37 days from March 25, 2014 to May 1, 2014 (on the 10% feed of *Twitter*) and filtered the stream to contain tweets with one of the following set of hash tags related to the blocked news in Turkey for *Twitter* after the corruption allegations: "#turkey, #twitterblockedinturkey, #direntwitter, #twitterisblockedinturkey, #25martkorkusu, #twittericinsokagacikiyoruz, #youtube blockedinturkey, #erdogan, #1mayis". The resulting data set contained 1,919,294 ($\approx$ 1.9 million) tweets. Each extracted post contained the time stamp, user identifier and its content. We extracted all the unique hash-tags from these postings and treated them as the propagated keywords. This entire stream contained 131,574 unique hash-tags and 293,363 unique users. We constructed the relationship network of these users using the *mentions* between them for the past 10 months until 1st of May, 2014. The resulting network contained 293,363 users and 799,605 edges.

DBLP Data Set: The DBLP data set is publicly available and can be downloaded from arnetminer.org [4] [28]. This data set contained a stream of documents (2,084,055 papers), which were temporally ordered based on the year of publication (until 2011). The relationship network G of authors is constructed using their co-authorship relationship. We excluded all papers that did not have any authors, abstract or year of publication in our stream. We considered the abstract of each paper as the message posted by the authors of the paper. Our keyword set ($\mathcal{K}$) was constructed using uni-, bi- and tri-grams of the words appearing in these abstracts. In order to track the interesting keywords, we used the ratio of fraction of keyword occurrences in a specific topic to the fraction of keyword occurrences in the entire corpus. We extracted 24 topics from the field of computer science in the *Microsoft Academic search* Website and constructed the list of top 10 conferences for each topic. If a paper is published in the selected sample of venues for this topic, then the words in the abstract are counted for that topic. By using this approach, we extracted the top-1000 interesting keywords (uni- to tri-grams) for all the 24 topics and created a model based on them. It resulted in 12,974 interesting words across the entire stream. Our final cleaned data stream contained, 330,000 documents with total of 337,081 distinct authors. We set $N = 10^3$ and $\alpha = 0.5$, for our approach as default values, unless specified otherwise.

[4]http://arnetminer.org/citation

4.2 Baselines

We used some of the most popular baselines used in several other recent influence analysis works [15, 10, 9]. The first baseline is the *PMIA* algorithm discussed in [9]. It is the prefix excluded extension of Maximum Influence Arborescence (PMIA) model. This algorithm takes a network structure with predefined edge probabilities as input. We have used the weighted cascade model proposed in [15] to compute the edge probabilities. Our next baseline algorithm is *DegreeDiscountIC*, which is the degree discount heuristic of [10] developed for the uniform IC model. For the PageRank baseline, we used the power-iteration method to compute the page rank values and the restart probability was set to 0.15. The stopping criteria was set 10^{-7}, which is the difference in the L_1 norm between two successive iterations. We also used the degree and weighted-degree as additional baselines.

4.3 Evaluation Measures

We evaluated the effectiveness of our approach in terms of the quality of the influencers returned by different queries. We compared the top-k influencers returned by our approach against the ground truth of influencers for each query. We used the precision and recall evaluation measures, shown in Equations (9) and (10), respectively, to compare against the baselines. The list of top-k influencers returned by each approach is compared with the list of ground-truth influencers. The precision measures the fraction of users retrieved that are relevant, while recall measures the fraction of relevant users that are successfully retrieved.

$$precision = \frac{|\texttt{relevant} \cap \texttt{retrieved}|}{|\texttt{retrieved}|}, \quad (9)$$

$$recall = \frac{|\texttt{relevant} \cap \texttt{retrieved}|}{|\texttt{relevant}|}. \quad (10)$$

The ground-truth used for the *DBLP* data set was based on the *citation* counts of authors for each topical area, and the venue was used to decide the topic for each paper. Because the influence analysis needed to be performed in a time-sensitive way, the ground-truth was also computed at various time-points. The ground truth for Twitter data set contained the *retweet* counts for each user until a specific time point (based on the time parameter in the query). There were no specific topics in the *Twitter* data set, because the data set was already focused on the Turkey event. The re-tweet counts were counted only for the tweets in our stream.

4.4 Effectiveness Results

We evaluated the quality of the influencers discovered by each approach in comparison with the ground truth. For our approach, we generated the list of top-1000 influencers using the influencer search queries as described in Section 2.2. The precision and recall values were computed by sweeping through the top-1000 influencers (from 1 to 1000) for each method. For Twitter, our query was a set of hashtags related to the Turkey incident: "#turkey, #twit-

Method	DM	NW	ML	CV	HW	SE
QUIS	**0.096**	**0.092**	**0.042**	**0.084**	**0.146**	**0.028**
PMIA	0.022	0.01	0.014	0.055	0.061	0.014
DDIC	0.02	0.012	0.017	0.037	0.089	0.014
PR	0.035	0.018	0.029	0.067	0.114	0.025
DEG	0.012	0.006	0.013	0.026	0.062	0.006
WTDDEG	0.021	0.009	0.013	0.056	0.064	0.013

Table 1: AUC computed for PR plots for six different computer science fields in 2005

Method	DM	NW	ML	CV	HW	SE
QUIS	**0.097**	**0.101**	**0.037**	**0.083**	**0.121**	**0.057**
PMIA	0.019	0.009	0.008	0.045	0.03	0.006
DDIC	0.021	0.015	0.016	0.034	0.078	0.011
PR	0.036	0.016	0.02	0.068	0.099	0.014
DEG	0.016	0.012	0.015	0.028	0.066	0.006
WTDDEG	0.017	0.008	0.007	0.044	0.032	0.006

Table 2: AUC computed for PR plots for various computer science fields in 2011

terblockedinturkey, #direntwitter, #twitterisblockedinturkey, #25-martkorkusu, #twittericinsokagacikiyoruz, # youtubeblockedinturkey, #erdogan, #1mayis". In the context of *DBLP* we evaluated field-specific influencers, because the influencers were different for each field (such as Data Mining, Networking, etc.). In order to construct the query keywords, that were representative of each field, we selected the ten most cited papers and further filtered the 30 most frequent phrases for each field. These phrases form the query for each area. We computed the influencers for 6 different areas corresponding to Data Mining (DM), Networking (NW), Machine Learning (ML), Computer Vision (CV), Hardware (HW), and Software Engineering (SW). Each of the baseline methods required an interaction network with edge weights. In order to make the networks query-specific, we extracted the co-authorship network for the query by selecting the co-authorship relationships in papers that contained at least one of the query words. The edge weights were constructed by counting the number of query words present in the co-authored publications. This value represents the strength of query-specific co-authorship interactions. The top influencers computed from these methods were used to determine the precision and recall.

The precision-recall (PR) curves for the data mining and networking areas, at the beginning of year 2011 and 2005, are shown in Fig. 3(a) and (b), respectively. The precision-recall plot for the *Twitter* data set computed at the beginning of day May 1, 2014 is shown in Fig. 3(c). Due to limited space, we show the area under the curve (a point-wise value) for PR plots for 2005 and 2011 for six different fields in Tables 1 and 2, respectively. The influencers of the Turkey incident were evaluated on May 1 and April 13, 2014. As per the AUC values, our approach provides *the best performance in context-specific queries*. The main reason for the performance of our approach is that we look at path-level interactions of influence, while the propagation model based methods [10, 9] look only at pairwise interactions. Also, the abstraction of all the query information into a single edge-wise probability score is too unstable. This is especially true when the query-words overlap with more than one area. These issues do not affect our approach as we track specific keywords or phrases and use the phrase-level influence to compute a query-specific influence score. This may also be the reason for the inconsistency in baseline performance. For example, while PageRank performs better than the other baselines in DBLP, PMIA does better in Twitter.

Method	May 1, 2014	April 13, 2014
QUIS	**0.141**	**0.125**
PMIA	0.092	0.102
DDIC	0.095	0.101
PR	0.053	0.053
DEG	0.084	0.088
WTDDEG	0.096	0.104

Table 3: AUC computed for PR plots for Turkey incident on *Twitter* at two different time points.

	DBLP		Twitter	
α	mean(Δ_x)	dev(Δ_x)	mean(Δ_x)	dev(Δ_x)
0.25	0.00045	0.0000466	0.08979	0.00585
0.50	0.00031	0.0000355	0.07435	0.00491
0.75	0.00021	0.0000233	0.06101	0.00418
0.95	0.00013	0.0000164	0.05218	0.00378

Table 4: Mean and deviation of Δ_x for DBLP and Twitter data sets computed at 2011 and May 1, 2014 respectively.

4.5 Sensitivity Analysis

The value of α denotes the pruning parameter and ranges from 0 to 1. Larger values of α result in reduced pruning. In order to measure the impact of pruning on effectiveness, we computed the value $\Delta_x(\alpha) = (\mathcal{I}(x,*,*,t) - \mathcal{I}_\alpha(x,*,*,t))/\mathcal{I}(x,*,*,t)$. Here, $\mathcal{I}(x,*,*,t)$ denotes the total influence of user x with no pruning, and $\mathcal{I}_\alpha(x,*,*,t)$ is the total influence computed after pruning with parameter α. Similarly, the quantity $\Delta_w(\alpha) = (\mathcal{I}(*,*,w,t) - \mathcal{I}_\alpha(*,*,w,t))/\ \mathcal{I}(*,*,w,t)$ computes the fractional loss of influence scores per word w. We reported the mean and deviation of Δ_w in Fig. 4, and those of Δ_x in Table 4. As discussed earlier, by *retaining even a small fraction* $\alpha = 0.25$ of the nodes, we are able to provide *an excellent estimate of the total influence* in both data sets.

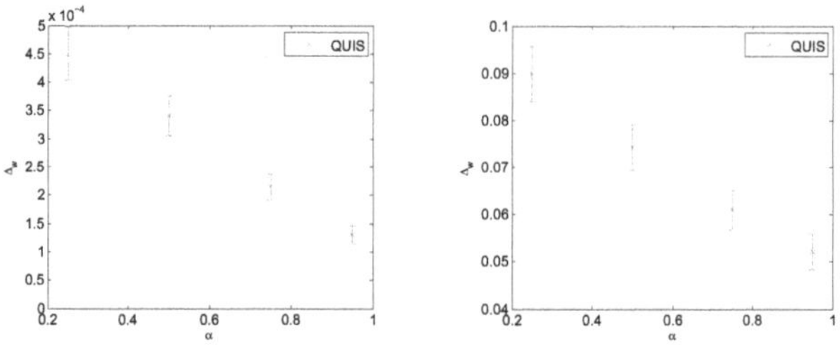

(a) DBLP (2011) (b) Twitter (May 1, 2014)

Figure 4: Mean and deviation of Δ_w for DBLP and Twitter data sets for various α values, computed at the beginning of 2011 and May 1, 2014 respectively.

4.6 Case Study of Context and User-specific Queries

In this section, we show how our framework can be used for querying context and user-specific influence values at different time points. In order to evaluate the context specific queries, we selected the query "frequent itemsets fpgrowth fptree," and we determined the top-3 influencers using our framework for every year from 2000 to 2011. We discuss the top-3 influencers for this keyword in 2000 and 2002, when this query gained traction. In 2000, the top influencers were Philip Yu, Jeffrey Ullman, and Shalom Tsur, because keywords such as fp-growth and fp-tree were not yet recognized. In

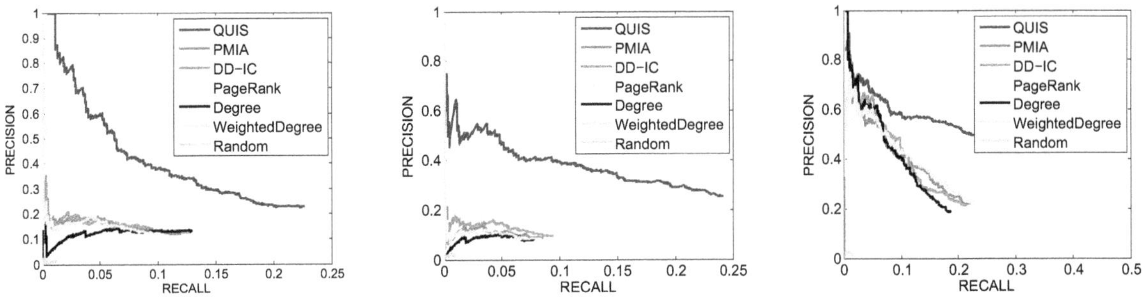

(a) Data mining query (2011) (b) Network query (2005) (c) Twitter Turkey query (1st May 2014)

Figure 3: Precision-Recall (PR) plots for two fields in DBLP and Turkey incident in Twitter data set are shown. The quality of influencers found by each approach is evaluated using the PR plot. Our approach performs consistently better in multiple field-specific queries and at multiple time points.

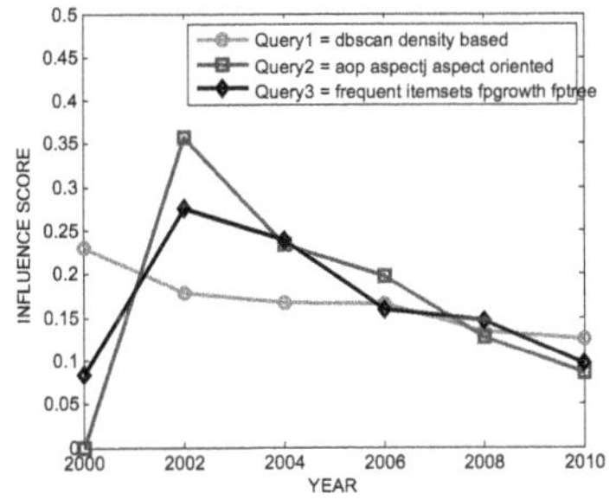

Figure 5: Growth and decay of influence for various concept-based queries.

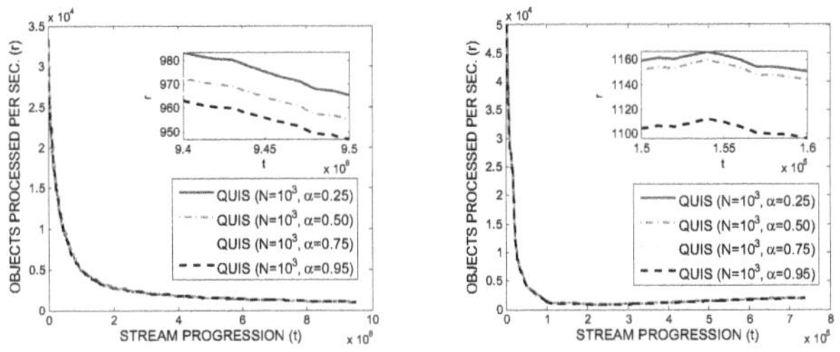

(a) DBLP (b) Twitter

Figure 6: Number of objects processed per second with stream progression. The inset shows the computational reduction level due to pruning.

2002, the most influential individuals were Jiawei Han, Yiwen Yin and Jian Pei. The temporal aspects of influence queries can be used to understand the historical trends of a specific query in terms of its influence. For instance, in the case of the aforementioned query on frequent pattern mining, the influence values change over time, as illustrated in Fig. 5. Such queries can be used to understand the growth and decay of the influence of specific concepts. We refer to these queries as "*concept-specific temporal queries*" in Section 2.2.

One can also use our framework to *query for the most influential keywords for specific individuals*. For example, we queried DBLP for "Jiawei Han" in 2002 and obtained "fpgrowth" as the most influential keyword. However, in 2006 and 2008, the word "skylines" was the most relevant one. For Hans-Peter Kriegel, the keyword "dbscan" was the most influential one in 2000 and 2002. Such user-centered queries can be used to *understand the change in the user-specific behavior over time*.

4.7 Efficiency Analysis

We evaluate the efficiency in terms of the number of objects processed per second in the stream, and the total running time for each query. The variation in the number of objects processed per second versus the number of stream objects processed (i.e., progression of stream) is shown in Fig. 6. The processing rate reduces initially, because the number of objects indexed in the cascades are initially very small, and they gradually increase over time. As the increase in the number of objects stabilizes over time because of pruning, the processing rate stabilizes. The plot also shows the effect of pruning on the running time as well. As the value of α increases, a larger number of objects are retained in the index. Therefore, the approach is slower in this case.

The efficiency can be evaluated in terms of model building and query execution. Model building is incremental, and therefore we report the incremental time taken to build a model for a year for DBLP, and a day for *Twitter*. These time-spans reflect the time-scales at which these respective data sets were analyzed. The query execution time is the total time required to access the influence scores computed at time t from the incrementally updated tree-index, and determine the top-k influencers for the query. For the baselines, the model-building time is the total time taken to extract the context-specific network structure, and the querying time is equal to that required to list the top-k influencers using its approach. There is no straightforward one-to-one comparison of the running time, because our approach is incremental and query-based, for which there is no other (known) baseline. The degree-centrality measures are computed in linear time and can be extremely scalable for large networks. However, the *model-building* time to make them query-sensitive is large. On the other hand, arborescence-based methods such as PMIA are computationally expensive, and their query-time is very high. *Our approach does much better in terms of total time as it maintains the model incrementally*, and the querying process simply sums several influence scores in a linearly scalable way. The running times in Table 5, are in seconds and computed for DBLP in the beginning of 2011, and for the Twitter data sets on May 1, 2014.

5. CONCLUSIONS

The ability to understand the dynamics of influence in a context-specific way is very important in various applications. In this paper, we address this problem by proposing an influence-query framework. By using this framework, one can query for individual in-

	DBLP			Twitter		
Method	Model	Query	Total	Model	Query	Total
QUIS	65.68	0.15	65.83	12.25	0.051	12.30
PMIA	192.31	43.05	235.36	180.47	1959.36	1959.36
DDIC	192.31	1.05	193.36	180.47	2.25	182.72
PR	192.31	0.09	192.40	180.47	0.68	181.15
DEG	192.31	0.01	192.32	180.47	0.50	180.97
WTDDEG	192.31	0.01	192.32	180.47	0.62	181.09

Table 5: Running time (seconds) for various methods.

fluence values, context-specific influence values, or the temporal influence evolution. We enable a streaming and incremental approach, which suits the social stream scenario. Furthermore, we show that the quality of influencers obtained by our approach is superior to those obtained from the baselines. We anticipate that our scheme will enable broader classes of influence functions, which will be helpful in various industrial applications. This will be the focus of our future work.

6. ACKNOWLEDGMENTS

This research was sponsored by the Defense Advanced Research Project Agency (DARPA) agreement number W911NF-12-C-0028, U.S. Army Research Laboratory (ARL) cooperative agreement number W911NF-09-2-0053 and IBM Ph.D. Fellowship. The views and conclusions contained in this document are those of the authors and should not be interpreted as representing the official policies, either expressed or implied, of the DARPA, ARL, or the U.S. Government. The U.S. Government is authorized to reproduce and distribute reprints for Government purposes notwithstanding any copyright notation here on.

7. REFERENCES

[1] C. Aggarwal and K. Subbian. Event detection in social streams. In *SDM*, volume 12, pages 624–635. SIAM, 2012.

[2] C. Aggarwal and K. Subbian. Evolutionary network analysis: A survey. *ACM Computing Surveys (CSUR)*, 47(1):10, 2014.

[3] C. C. Aggarwal. Mining text and social streams: a review. *SIGKDD Explorations*, 15(2):9–19, 2013.

[4] C. Aslay, N. Barbieri, F. Bonchi, and R. A. Baeza-Yates. Online topic-aware influence maximization queries. In *EDBT*, pages 295–306, 2014.

[5] N. Barbieri, F. Bonchi, and G. Manco. Topic-aware social influence propagation models. *Knowledge and information systems*, 37(3):555–584, 2013.

[6] M. S. Bernstein, B. Suh, L. Hong, J. Chen, S. Kairam, and E. H. Chi. Eddi: interactive topic-based browsing of social status streams. In *UIST*, pages 303–312, 2010.

[7] S. Bhagat, A. Goyal, and L. V. Lakshmanan. Maximizing product adoption in social networks. In *WSDM*, pages 603–612, 2012.

[8] B. Bi, Y. Tian, Y. Sismanis, A. Balmin, and J. Cho. Scalable topic-specific influence analysis on microblogs. In *WSDM*, pages 513–522. ACM, 2014.

[9] W. Chen, C. Wang, and Y. Wang. Scalable influence maximization for prevalent viral marketing in large-scale social networks. In *KDD*, pages 1029–1038. ACM, 2010.

[10] W. Chen, Y. Wang, and S. Yang. Efficient influence maximization in social networks. In *KDD*, pages 199–208. ACM, 2009.

[11] A. Goyal, F. Bonchi, and L. V. Lakshmanan. Learning influence probabilities in social networks. In *WSDM*, pages 241–250. ACM, 2010.

[12] A. Goyal, F. Bonchi, and L. V. Lakshmanan. A data-based approach to social influence maximization. *VLDB*, 5(1):73–84, 2011.

[13] A. Goyal, W. Lu, and L. V. Lakshmanan. Celf++: optimizing the greedy algorithm for influence maximization in social networks. In *WWW*, pages 47–48. ACM, 2011.

[14] A. Goyal, W. Lu, and L. V. Lakshmanan. Simpath: An efficient algorithm for influence maximization under the linear threshold model. In *ICDM*, pages 211–220, 2011.

[15] D. Kempe, J. Kleinberg, and É. Tardos. Maximizing the spread of influence through a social network. In *KDD*, pages 137–146. ACM, 2003.

[16] J. Kleinberg. The flow of on-line information in global networks. In *SIGMOD*, pages 1–2. ACM, 2010.

[17] K. Kutzkov, A. Bifet, F. Bonchi, and A. Gionis. Strip: stream learning of influence probabilities. In *KDD*, pages 275–283. ACM, 2013.

[18] J. Leskovec, A. Krause, C. Guestrin, C. Faloutsos, J. VanBriesen, and N. Glance. Cost-effective outbreak detection in networks. In *KDD*, pages 420–429. ACM, 2007.

[19] J. Leskovec, M. McGlohon, C. Faloutsos, N. S. Glance, and M. Hurst. Patterns of cascading behavior in large blog graphs. In *SDM*, volume 7, pages 551–556. SIAM, 2007.

[20] D. Liben-Nowell and J. Kleinberg. The link-prediction problem for social networks. *Jour. of the Amer. soc. for info. sci. and tech.*, 58(7):1019–1031, 2007.

[21] L. Liu, J. Tang, J. Han, M. Jiang, and S. Yang. Mining topic-level influence in heterogeneous networks. In *CIKM*, pages 199–208. ACM, 2010.

[22] B. A. Prakash, D. Chakrabarti, N. C. Valler, M. Faloutsos, and C. Faloutsos. Threshold conditions for arbitrary cascade models on arbitrary networks. *KAIS*, 33(3):549–575, 2012.

[23] A. Ritter, O. Etzioni, S. Clark, et al. Open domain event extraction from twitter. In *KDD*, pages 1104–1112, 2012.

[24] K. Subbian, C. Aggarwal, and J. Srivastava. Content-centric flow mining for influence analysis in social streams. In *CIKM*, pages 841–846. ACM, 2013.

[25] K. Subbian and P. Melville. Supervised rank aggregation for predicting influencers in twitter. In *SocialCom*, pages 661–665. IEEE, 2011.

[26] K. Subbian, D. Sharma, Z. Wen, and J. Srivastava. Social capital: the power of influencers in networks. In *AAMAS*, pages 1243–1244, 2013.

[27] J. Tang, J. Sun, C. Wang, and Z. Yang. Social influence analysis in large-scale networks. In *KDD*, pages 807–816. ACM, 2009.

[28] J. Tang, D. Zhang, and L. Yao. Social network extraction of academic researchers. In *ICDM'07*, pages 292–301, 2007.

[29] M.-H. Tsai, C. Aggarwal, and T. Huang. Towards classification of social streams. In *SIAM Conference on Data Mining*, 2015.

[30] H. Zhuang, Y. Sun, J. Tang, J. Zhang, and X. Sun. Influence maximization in dynamic social networks. In *ICDM*, pages 1313–1318. IEEE, 2013.

Centrality-Aware Link Recommendations

Nikos Parotsidis
Dipartimento di Ingegneria
Civile e Ingegneria Informatica
Università di Roma
"Tor Vergata", Roma, Italy
nikos.parotsidis@uniroma2.it

Evaggelia Pitoura
Department of Computer
Science & Engineering
University of Ioannina
pitoura@cs.uoi.gr

Panayiotis Tsaparas
Department of Computer
Science & Engineering
University of Ioannina
tsap@cs.uoi.gr

ABSTRACT

Link recommendations are critical for both improving the utility and expediting the growth of social networks. Most previous approaches focus on suggesting links that are highly likely to be adopted. In this paper, we add a different perspective to the problem by aiming at recommending links that also improve specific properties of the network. In particular, our goal is to recommend to users links that if adopted would improve the user centrality in the network. Specifically, we introduce the *centrality-aware link recommendation problem* as the problem of recommending to a user u, k links from a pool of recommended links so as to maximize the *expected* decrease of the sum of the shortest path distances of u to all other nodes in the network. We show that the problem is NP-hard, but our optimization function is monotone and sub-modular which guarantees a constant approximation ratio for the greedy algorithm. We present a fast algorithm for computing the expected decrease caused by a set of recommendations which we use as a building block in our algorithms. We provide experimental results that evaluate the performance of our algorithms with respect to both the accuracy of the prediction and the improvement in the centrality of the nodes, and we study the tradeoff between the two.

Categories and Subject Descriptors

H.2.8 [**Database Applications**]: Data mining; E.1 [**Data Structures**]: Graphs and networks

Keywords

Probabilistic Networks, Link Recommendations, Node Centrality, Social Networks

1. INTRODUCTION

Link recommendations constitute an important task in social networks. Recommending to network users connections of potential interest helps them grow their social circle and increases the added value of the social experience. At the same time, link recommendations are beneficial to the network as a whole, since they expedite the network growth, and they increase the overall user engagement. Therefore, substantial research effort has been devoted to producing recommendations of high accuracy [14]. Most previous research on link recommendation focuses on predicting or estimating the likelihood of the connections being adopted by the user. Various approaches have been proposed to this end, based on exploring structural properties of the network, attributes of the users, previous user interactions, or other factors [14, 2, 25].

In this paper, we add a new perspective to the problem by aiming at recommending links that if adopted by the users would lead to networks with the small world property, i.e., short paths between users. This is an important property, since it improves connectivity among the nodes of the network and facilitates and amplifies dynamic processes. For instance, users of professional networks want to be close to other nodes in the network as an indicator of their individual importance. Moreover, the small world phenomenon helps social network users spread their content faster on the network. At the same time, network owners can benefit from small average shortest paths, since this is one of the key properties that helps viral marketing and information diffusion. Therefore, it is in the interest of both the network as a whole, and of the individual users to maintain and strengthen the smaller world phenomenon.

In particular, we assume that we are given as set C of link recommendations for user u along with an estimation of the probability p_e of each link e in C being adopted by u and added to the network. We assume that these recommendations are produced by some existing link recommendation algorithm. Given a number k of links to recommend to u, we want to select k of the links in C so as to increase the "centrality" of u, that is, minimize its shortest path distance to the other nodes in the network. Since depending on p_e, the user may or may not accept a particular link, the addition of the links to the network results in a probabilistic graph, and the decrease in the shortest path lengths is a random variable. Thus, our objective becomes to maximize the *expected* reduction in the shortest path lengths.

There is a natural tradeoff between the accuracy (likelihood to be adopted) and the utility (improvement in centrality) of the link recommendations. Links that connect to "close-by" users are likely to be adopted but do not improve the centrality of the node. Links that link to "far-away" nodes are less likely to be adopted but they result in sig-

WSDM'16, February 22–25, 2016, San Francisco, CA, USA.
© 2016 ACM. ISBN 978-1-4503-3716-8/16/02. . . $15.00
DOI: http://dx.doi.org/10.1145/2835776.2835818

nificant decrease in the distances with the remaining graph. The expected reduction is an objective function that combines naturally the utility and the accuracy of the recommendations. We should note that our goal is not to propose yet another link recommendation algorithm. Instead, we are interested in selecting from the results of an existing link recommendation algorithm a set of links that result in a large reduction in the shortest path distances of a node in expectation. In this way, we combine the likelihood of the link to appear with its effect on the centrality of the node.

Although there has been some previous work on selecting edges to add to a graph so that specific criteria are met, such as minimizing the average all-pair shortest path distances (e.g., [18, 19]), or improving the average closeness centrality of a specific node ([4, 8]), our work is the first to consider the addition of probabilistic edges. We make the following contributions:

- We define the novel problem of Centrality-Aware Link Recommendations, where given a set of link recommendations and their likelihood, we aim to select k recommendations that maximize the reduction of the expected distances of the node to the rest of the graph.
- We show that our problem is NP-hard, but our objective function is monotone and submodular, and as a result the greedy algorithm gives a solution with constant approximation factor. We also propose an efficient algorithm for computing the expected reduction by exploiting the properties of our problem.
- We evaluate our approach experimentally using real datasets and link recommendations produced by two commonly used recommendation algorithms. We compare the efficiency and effectiveness of our algorithms under different settings, and we demonstrate that we can achieve a sizeable reduction in distances with an acceptable sacrifice in prediction accuracy. We also report experimental results that quantify the trade-off between link-prediction accuracy and centrality utility.

The remainder of this paper is structured as follows. In Section 2, we present related work, in Section 3, we provide the formal definition of our problem. Section 4 includes complexity results and Section 5 our algorithms. In Section 6, we present the results of our experimental evaluation. Section 7 concludes the paper.

2. RELATED WORK

The problem of minimizing the average all-pairs shortest path distance via edge addition was previously studied in [18, 19, 17]. Papagelis et al. [18, 17] study the problem of adding k edges, from the set of missing edges of the graph, in order to minimize the average shortest paths in the graph. In [19], we consider a variation of the problem where the set of candidate edges is given as an input, and the goal is to select a subset of k of them. These works do not focus on link recommendations, and they do not consider probabilistic edges.

The idea of promoting graph properties via link recommendations is explored by Li et al. [12], where they re-rank link recommendations in order to promote information diffusion in a social network. Also, Chaoji et al. [3] consider as input a set of recommended links and compute k edges per node that boost content spread in the network. Both these works focus on maximizing diffusion spread. Maximizing the reduction in average network distances poses a different set of challenges.

The average shortest path length is related to the average *closeness centrality* of nodes in the graph. Ishakian et al. [8] study the problem of finding the k edges whose addition to the graph maximizes the centrality of a *specific* target node. The same problem was considered by Crescenzi et al. [4], where they show that the greedy algorithm provides a $(1 - 1/e)$-approximation factor, and that this approximation bound is tight. Sariyüce et al. [21] propose an incremental algorithm to efficiently update the closeness centrality values under changes in network topology. Meyerson and Tagiku [15] study the problem of finding the k edges whose addition minimizes the shortest path distances between all pairs of nodes. They prove that several variations of the problem, including the single source shortest paths, are *NP-hard* and they provide a $O(1)$ approximation algorithm. Tong et al. [22] search for the k edges whose addition will best enable the propagation of information in the network under the SIS model [5]. Lazaridou et al. [10] identify the set of top-k pairs of nodes whose distances are reduced the most as the result of edge additions. None of these works considers the case of probabilistic edges and expected centrality, or link recommendations.

The problem of finding shortest paths in a graph with independent randomly distributed edge lengths is known to be *#P-complete* [23]. Frieze and Grimmett [7] present a formula for computing the exact expected shortest path distance between two nodes, but it requires the knowledge of all the different paths between the two nodes. The enumeration of the paths between two nodes in a network is also known to be *#P-complete* [23]. Frank [6] uses Monte Carlo results to develop a method for computing shortest paths in probabilistic graphs.

There is a significant amount of work on problems over probabilistic graphs. For example, Potamias et al. [20] consider the problem of computing the k nearest neighbors, and Kollios et al. [9] study clustering on probabilistic graphs. However, the problem we study in this paper is novel.

Finally, there is a large body of work on the problem of link recommendations [14, 2, 25]. As mentioned earlier, our goal in this paper is not to introduce a new recommendation algorithm. Instead, we propose selecting from the recommendations of an existing algorithm those links that could improve network properties.

3. PROBLEM FORMULATION

We consider as input to our problem a graph $G = (V, E)$ and a set C of link recommendations for user u along with their probability of being adopted by u. In particular, $C = \{(e, p_e) : e \notin E, p_e \in [0, 1]\}$ consists of a set of candidate edges incident to u not present in G, where each edge $e \in C$ is associated with the probability p_e that e will appear in the network. We assume that the probability p_e of link $e = (u, v)$ is provided by some link recommendation algorithm that estimates p_e based on the structural properties of the graph (e.g., the number of neighbors that u and v have in common), on attribute values of the nodes (e.g., on how similar u and v are, by exploiting homophily), or other factors. We will refer to the edges of the candidate set C as *probabilistic* edges.

Under this setting, we study the problem of identifying the set $S \subseteq C$ of k edges such that the addition of the edges in S to graph G minimizes the *expected* shortest path lengths of node u to all other nodes in G.

Given a subset $S \subseteq C$ of the candidate edges, we use $\widetilde{G}_S$ to denote the *probabilistic* graph that results by adding the set of edges S to the graph G. Let $D_{\widetilde{G}_S}(u,v)$ denote the random variable whose value is the length of the shortest path distance between u and v in the graph $\widetilde{G}_S$. To compute the expectation $E[D_{\widetilde{G}_S}(u,v)]$ we need to consider all possible $2^{|S|}$ graphs that may result by the materialization of the edges in S. Each graph has a specific probability to appear. Given a subset of edges $F \subseteq S$, the probability of exactly these edges appearing in the graph is equal to:

$$P(F) = \prod_{e \in F} p_e \prod_{e \in S \setminus F} (1 - p_e)$$

Now, let $d_G(u,v)$ be the shortest path distance between nodes u and of v in the *deterministic* graph G, and let $G \cup F$ denote the *deterministic* graph that results from the addition of the edges in F to G. Then, the expected shortest path distance between u and v, after the addition of the probabilistic set of edges S to the graph G is equal to:

$$E[D_{\widetilde{G}_S}(u,v)] = \sum_{F \in 2^S} P(F) d_{G \cup F}(u,v) \tag{1}$$

where, 2^S denotes the powerset of the set S.

Let $L_G(u) = \sum_{v \in V} d_G(u,v)$ denote the sum of shortest path lengths of node u to all the nodes in a graph G. This value is directly connected to the centrality of node u; a node with short paths to other nodes is a central node in the graph. We also define $L_{\widetilde{G}_S}(u) = \sum_{v \in V} E[D_{\widetilde{G}_S}(u,v)]$ to be the *expected* sum of shortest path lengths of node u in the probabilistic graph $\widetilde{G}_S$. The addition of any edge in a graph can only reduce the shortest path lengths of u. This allows us to define $R_u(S) = L_G(u) - L_{\widetilde{G}_S}(u)$ to be the expected reduction in the shortest path lengths of u caused by the addition of the probabilistic edge set S to the graph G. We are looking for the set S of size k that maximizes $R_u(S)$, for a given u. We formally define our problem as follows.

PROBLEM 1. [CENTRALITY-AWARE LINK RECOMMENDATIONS (CALR)]. *Given a graph $G = (V, E)$, a user u, a positive integer k, and a candidate set $C = \{(e, p_e) : e \notin E, p_e \in [0, 1]\}$ of probabilistic edges incident to u recommended by a link-recommendation algorithm, select a set $S \subseteq C$ of size k to recommend to u, such that $R_u(S)$ is maximized.*

4. COMPLEXITY ANALYSIS

In this section we study theoretically the CALR problem. First, we give a formula for the efficient computation of the expected reduction in the shortest path length between two nodes. We then show that the CALR problem is NP-hard and we consider approximate solutions.

4.1 Expected single source shortest path length computation

The computation of the expected shortest path length between two nodes in a general probabilistic graph is known to be a #P-complete problem, since it requires the consideration of all possible paths between the two nodes, which, in the general case, may be exponentially many. However, in our setting, where the probabilistic edges are all incident on a single node u, and we are interested in the single source paths from u, we can avoid this computation thanks to the following property.

PROPERTY 4.1. *Given a deterministic graph G, a target node u, and a set of probabilistic edges S all incident on u, any simple path from u to any other node in the probabilistic graph $\widetilde{G}_S$ uses at most one probabilistic edge $e \in S$.*

Given Property 4.1, for a node u, and a target node v, we only need to consider $|S|$ shortest paths between nodes u and v. However, using Equation (1) to compute the expected shortest path length between u and v is still expensive, since it considers all $2^{|S|}$ possible materializations of the probabilistic edges. We now consider a more efficient computation of the shortest path length between node u and a node v.

For a random variable X that takes natural values between 1 and N, the expected value of X can be computed as $E[X] = \sum_{i=1}^{N} P[X \geq i]$. Therefore, we can compute the expected shortest path length between source node u and a node v in the probabilistic graph $\widetilde{G}_S$ as follows.

$$E[D_{\widetilde{G}_S}(u,v)] = \sum_{i=1}^{d_{\max}} P[D_{\widetilde{G}_S}(u,v) \geq i] \tag{2}$$

where $d_{\max} = d_G(u,v)$ is the length of the shortest path between u and v in the deterministic graph G.

To compute the probability $P[D_{\widetilde{G}_S}(u,v) \geq i]$ we need to consider the effect of the addition of each edge to the graph G. We define $C_\ell = \{e \in C : d_{G \cup e}(u,v) = \ell\}$ to be the set of candidate edges such that when added individually to the initial graph G the shortest path between u and v in the *deterministic* graph $G \cup e$ has length ℓ. Note that $C_{d_{\max}}$ is the set of edges whose addition to G does not reduce the shortest path between u and v. Also, for some i, $1 \leq i \leq d_{\max}$, we define $M_i = \bigcup_{1 \leq \ell < i} C_\ell$ to be the set of edges whose addition to the graph G results in shortest path length *strictly less* than i.

Now, consider a set $S \subseteq C$ of candidate edges, and the resulting probabilistic graph $\widetilde{G}_S$. The probability that the distance between u and v in the graph $\widetilde{G}_S$ is at least i is equal to the probability that none of the edges in $S \cap M_i$ appear in the graph. Therefore, we have:

$$P[D_{\widetilde{G}_S}(u,v) \geq i] = \prod_{e \in S \cap M_i} 1 - p_e \tag{3}$$

Combining Equations (2) and (3) we can compute the expected length of the shortest path between source node u and a node v in the probabilistic graph $\widetilde{G}_S$ in polynomial time. We can then compute the expected sum of shortest path lengths $L_{\widetilde{G}_S}(u)$, and the expected reduction $R_u(S)$ in the sum of shortest paths.

We note that Property 4.1, and all the ensuing analysis holds also for directed graphs, since any simple path from the target vertex u to any other vertex uses at most one outgoing probabilistic edge from u. Thus, the algorithms described in Section 5 for undirected graphs can easily be modified to work for the directed case.

4.2 Hardness and Approximation

Our problem contains as a special case the deterministic case where all candidate edges have probability one. This problem is known to be NP-hard [15]. Given that the problem is NP-hard we look for approximation algorithms with provable approximation guarantees. To this end we will show that our optimization function $R_u(S)$ is *monotone* and *submodular*.

Let Ω be a set, and let $f : 2^{\Omega} \rightarrow \mathbb{R}$ denote a set function over Ω. The function f is (increasingly) monotone if for every set $S \subset \Omega$ and every $x \in \Omega \setminus S$ it holds that $f(S) \leq f(S \cup x)$. The function f is submodular, if for every $X, Y \subseteq \Omega$ with $X \subseteq Y$ and every $x \in \Omega$ it holds that $f(X \cup \{x\}) - f(X) \geq f(Y \cup \{x\}) - f(Y)$. It is well known [16] that when maximizing a monotone and submodular set function under cardinality constraints, the simple greedy algorithm that always adds to the set the element with the largest marginal gain has approximation factor $1 - 1/e$ where e is the base of the natural logarithm.

We will now show that our function is monotone and submodular.

LEMMA 4.2 (MONOTONICITY). *The function $R_u(S)$ is increasingly monotone.*

PROOF. Given a set $S \subseteq C$ and an edge $eC \setminus S$, we will prove that $P[D_{\tilde{G}_{S \cup e}}(u,v) \geq i] \leq P[D_{\tilde{G}_S}(u,v) \geq i]$, that is, the probability of having a long path between u and v decreases as we add edges to the set S. Then, from Equation (2) it follows that for every node v, $E[D_{\tilde{G}_{S \cup e}}(u,v)] \leq E[D_{\tilde{G}_S}(u,v)]$, and thus $L_{\tilde{G}_{S \cup e}}(u) \leq L_{\tilde{G}_S}(u)$. Since $L_G(u)$ is constant, it follows that $R_u(S \cup e) \geq R_u(S)$, that is, the function is increasingly monotone.

Without loss of generality assume that $e \in C_\ell$ for some ℓ, $1 \leq \ell \leq d_{\max}$. It follows that $e \in M_i$ for all $i > \ell$. From Equation (3) it follows that $P[D_{\tilde{G}_{S \cup e}}(u,v) \geq i] = P[D_{\tilde{G}_S}(u,v) \geq i]$ for $i \leq \ell$, and $P[D_{\tilde{G}_{S \cup e}}(u,v) \geq i] = (1 - p_e)P[D_{\tilde{G}_S}(u,v) \geq i]$ for $i > \ell$, which proves our claim. □

LEMMA 4.3 (SUBMODULARITY). *The function $R_u(S)$ is submodular.*

PROOF. Similar to before, in order to show that the function $R_u(S)$ is submodular, we will work with the probabilities $P[D_{\tilde{G}_S}(u,v) \geq i]$. In the following, for a fixed pair (u,v), we will use $P_S(i)$ to denote the probability $P[D_{\tilde{G}_S}(u,v) \geq i]$.

Let S and S' be two sets of probabilistic edges such that $S \subseteq S'$, and let e be a candidate edge not in S'. It is not hard to see that in order to prove that $R_u(S \cup e) - R_u(S) \geq R_u(S' \cup e) - R_u(S')$, it suffices to show that for every (u,v), $P_S(i) - P_{S \cup e}(i) \geq P_{S'}(i) - P_{S' \cup e}(i)$, for $1 \leq i \leq d$.

Without loss of generality assume that $e \in C_\ell$ for some ℓ, $1 \leq \ell \leq d_{\max}$. Similar to the previous proof, for $i \leq \ell$, we have that $P_{S \cup e}(i) = P_S(i)$, and $P_{S' \cup e}(i) = P_{S'}(i)$ and thus our claim holds. For $i > \ell$ we have that $P_{S \cup e}(i) = (1 - p_e)P_S(i)$, and therefore $P_S(i) - P_{S \cup e}(i) = p_e P_S(i)$. Similarly, $P_{S'}(i) - P_{S' \cup e}(i) = p_e P_{S'}(i)$. From the monotonicity property we have that $P_S(i) \geq P_{S'}(i)$, and thus our claim holds. □

COROLLARY 4.4. *The greedy algorithm for the CALR problem achieves $(1 - 1/e)$ approximation ratio.*

5. ALGORITHMS

In this section we present algorithms for the CALR problem. We consider the Greedy algorithm and other more efficient heuristics.

Algorithm 1 The *Greedy* algorithm

Input: Graph G, node u, set of probabilistic edges C
Output: Set S of k recommendations to u

1: $S = \emptyset$
2: **for** $1 \leq i \leq k$ **do**
3:   **for** $e \in C$ **do**
4:     Compute $R_u(S \cup e)$
5:   **end for**
6:   $e^* = \arg\max_{e \in C}\{R_u(S \cup e)\}$
7:   $S = S \cup e^*$
8:   $C = C \setminus e^*$
9: **end for**
10: **return** S

Algorithm 2 The ESSSP algorithm

Input: Graph G, node u, set of probabilistic edges S
Output: $L_{\tilde{G}_S}(u)$

Compute $d_G(u,v), \forall v \in V$
Initialize $b_v(\ell) = 1$, $\forall v \in V$, $1 \leq \ell \leq d_G(u,v)$
for $e = (u,x) \in S$ **do**
  Compute $d_G(x,v)$, $\forall v \in V$
  for $v \in V \setminus u$ **do**
    if $d_G(x,v) + 1 < d_G(u,v)$ **then**
      $\ell = d_G(x,v) + 1$
      $b_v(\ell) = b_v(\ell) * (1 - p_e)$
    end if
  end for
end for
$SUM = 0$
for $v \in V \setminus u$ **do**
  $prob = 1$
  for $\ell = 1 ... d_G(u,v) - 1$ **do**
    $prob = prob * b_v(\ell)$
    $SUM = SUM + prob$
  end for
end for
return $L_{\tilde{G}_S}(u) = SUM$

5.1 The Greedy algorithm

The Greedy algorithm builds the solution set S incrementally, starting with the empty set. Given as input the node u and the set of candidate edges C, in each iteration it selects the edge $e^* \in C \setminus S$ whose addition causes the largest reduction in the expected distances of node u. The outline of the algorithm is shown in Algorithm 1.

An important step in the execution of the Greedy algorithm is step 4, where we compute the expected reduction caused by the addition of edge e. This entails the computation of the expected lengths of the shortest paths between u and all nodes in the graph. In the general case this is hard, since it would require considering an exponential number of paths. However, as we have discussed in Section 4 we can compute this quantity efficiently by exploiting the properties of our problem.

We now describe the computation of $L_{\tilde{G}_S}(u)$, the expected length of single-source shortest paths for a node u for a given set S, in detail. For convenience in this computation we use a slight variation of the Equation (3). Namely, given the sets C_ℓ, $1 \leq \ell \leq d_{\max}$, and a set of edges S, let $S_\ell = C_\ell \cap S$.

For some value $1 \leq i \leq d_{\max}$, we have:

$$P[D_{\tilde{G}_S}(u,v) \geq i] = \prod_{\ell=1}^{i-1} 1 - P(S_\ell) \quad (4)$$

where $P(S_\ell) = 1 - \prod_{e \in S_\ell}(1 - p_e)$ is the probability that at least one edge in S_ℓ appears in the graph, and $1 - P(S_\ell)$ is the probability that no edge in S_ℓ appears in the graph.

The Expected Single Source Shortest Path (ESSP) Algorithm (shown in Algorithm 2) proceeds as follows. We first compute all single-source shortest paths from u. We refer to the length of the shortest path between u and another node v, in the initial deterministic graph G, as $d_G(u,v)$. For each node v, we maintain a vector b_v, of size $d_G(u,v)$, where $b_v(\ell)$ contains the probability that there is no edge $e \in S$ whose addition to G results in a shortest path between u and v of length ℓ in the deterministic graph $G \cup e$. For a given v, this value corresponds to the probability $1 - P(S_\ell)$. Given the $b_v(\ell)$ values, for all $v \in V$, $1 \leq \ell \leq d_G(u,v)$, we can apply in turn Equations (4) and (2) to compute the expected shortest path length between u and v as $E[D_{\tilde{G}_S}(u,v)] = \sum_{i=1}^{d_G(u,v)} \prod_{\ell=1}^{i-1} b_v(\ell)$. Summing over all nodes $v \in V$ gives us $L_{\tilde{G}_S}$.

We compute the $b_v(\ell)$ values incrementally. Initially, we set $b_v(\ell) = 1$, for all $v \in V$, $1 \leq i \leq d_G(u,v)$. We then process the edges in S one by one. For each edge $e = (u,x) \in S$, with probability p_e, we compute all single-source shortest paths from x in the deterministic graph G, and we identify the nodes v for which $d_G(x,v) + 1 < d_G(u,v)$, that is, the addition of e created a new shortest path between u and v through node x. In this case, the edge e creates a shorter path between u and v of length $\ell = d_G(x,v) + 1$ with probability p_e. We update the value $b_v(\ell)$ to represent the new correct probability of non existence of an edge whose addition in G creates a shortest path of length ℓ, i.e., $b_v(\ell) = (1 - p_e) \cdot b_v(\ell)$. After processing all edges in S, the vector b_v for node v has values $b_v(\ell) = 1 - P(S_\ell)$.

The ESSSP algorithm has complexity $O(|S|(m+n)+n\delta)$, where m is the number of edges and δ is the diameter of the deterministic graph G, and uses space $O(n\delta)$. The m factor comes from the BFS traversal in step 4. The Greedy algorithm performs $k|C|$ calls of the ESSSP algorithm, where $|S|$ takes values $1, ..., k$, resulting in complexity $O(k^2|C|(m+n)+k|C|n\delta)$. The space complexity of the Greedy algorithm is also $O(n\delta)$.

5.2 Efficient Heuristics

The Greedy algorithm has known approximation guarantees: it computes an $(1 - 1/e)$ approximate solution for the CALR problem. However, since it needs to recompute the expected reduction caused by an edge in each iteration, it is slow, and does not scale well for large networks. We now consider some efficient heuristics, with no provable guarantees, in order to compare the trade-off between efficiency and effectiveness of our methods.

Top Edges: This method assigns to each edge $e \in C$, a score equal to the expected reduction in the shortest paths of u achieved by the addition of edge e to G, i.e., $R_u(e)$. Since we consider every edge independently, we do not need to run Algorithm 2 for computing the expected reduction $R_u(e)$. We can instead compute for each node v where $d_G(u,v) < d_{G \cup e}(u,v)$ the difference $d_G(u,v) - d_{G \cup e}(u,v)$, sum the differences over all such nodes, and multiply by p_e. Computing the values $d_G(u,v)$ and $d_{G \cup e}(u,v)$ can be done easily by performing two BFS traversals, one on the graph G and one on the graph $G \cup e$. Then, the edges are sorted according to their score and the k edges with the greater score are returned. The time complexity of this method is $O(|C|(m+n))$.

Deterministic Greedy Algorithm: This is a variation of the greedy algorithm that ignores the probabilities of the edges. This method also builds the solution set S incrementally, starting with the empty set. In each iteration it selects the edge $(u,v) \in C \setminus S$ that maximizes the reduction $L_{G \cup S}(u) - L_{G \cup S \cup e}(u)$ on the shortest paths of u between the deterministic graphs $G \cup S$ and $G \cup S \cup e$. The edge e with the maximum reduction is added to the solution set S. Computing the reduction caused by an edge can be done with a BFS traversal. Each iteration takes time $O(|C|(m+n))$, which implies a total running time $O(k|C|(m+n))$; the space complexity is linear.

6. EXPERIMENTS

The goals of our experiments are three-fold. First, we address the practical problem of estimating edge probabilities from the scores of a link recommendation algorithm. Then, we focus on the effectiveness of the algorithms and of the CALR approach in general. In particular, we highlight how the CALR approach achieves a balance between the accuracy of the recommendations, and the utility of the network resulting from the successful recommendations. We study and quantify this tradeoff. Finally, we evaluate the efficiency of our algorithms for the CALR problem.

6.1 Baselines

In our experiments we consider all the algorithms that we defined in Section 5. We use *Greedy* to denote the Greedy algorithm, *TopEdges* to denote the algorithm that selects the top-k edges according to their $R_u(e)$ score, and *D-Greedy* to denote the deterministic Greedy algorithm. We also consider the following baselines that do not take into account the effect of the edge addition on the node centrality.

Most probable: In this method we select the k edges with the highest probability. The algorithm simply sorts the edges in the candidate set C according to their probability; ties are resolved arbitrarily. This method corresponds to a traditional link recommendation algorithm. It serves the purpose of understanding the trade-off between prediction accuracy and the decrease in the shortest path distances. We will refer to this method as *MostProb*.

Random: In this method we randomly select k edges from the candidate set C. Note that this is not a completely random selection (as it is used in [13], where the random predictor selects randomly from all non-existent edges), since we select randomly from the set C which already contains links that are relevant to the user. We will refer to this method as *Random*.

6.2 Datasets and Recommendation Algorithms

We use two different datasets in our experiments, each corresponding to a different type of network. Both datasets contain information about the time when each edge was created.

- The *Facebook* dataset [24] consists of a social graph from the Facebook New Orleans network. Nodes rep-

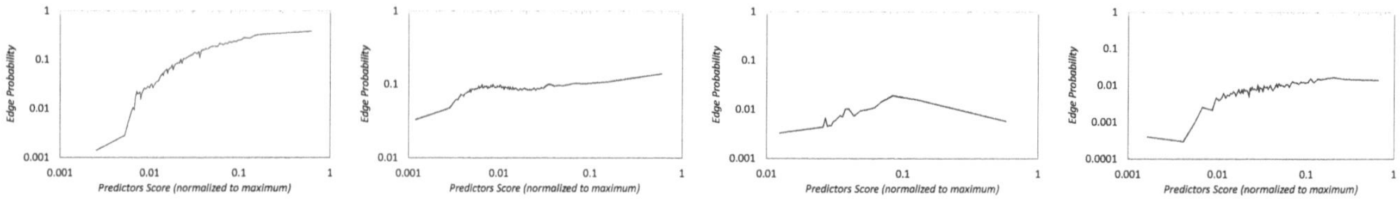

(a) *AA* on *Facebook* (b) *RPR* on *Facebook* (c) *AA* on *DBLP* (d) *RPR* on *DBLP*

Figure 1: Empirical probability function for the normalized scores (log-log scale).

Table 1: Dataset characteristics. $r(AA)$ and $r(RPR)$: number of nodes for which *AdamicAdar* and *RootedPageRank* produce sufficient number of recommendations; F: the number of edges that appeared after the initial instance.

dataset	$\|V\|$	$\|E\|$	$r(AA)$	$r(RPR)$	F
Facebook	53,306	555,763	46,687	53,306	242,929
DBLP	96,516	364,907	47,121	96,515	175,238

resent users, and edges user friendships. The dataset contains the activity of the network from September 2006 until February 2009.

- The *DBLP* dataset[1] [11] consists of a collaboration graph of authors of computer science papers, where an edge between two authors represents a common publication. We consider the *DBLP* graph containing authors and co-authorship relationships between 1990 and 2013.

Our algorithms take as input an initial set of link recommendations where each link is associated with a score that determines the confidence of the algorithm in the prediction. We use two different link recommendation algorithms in our experiments: The *AdamicAdar* (AA) [1] algorithm, and the *RootedPageRank* (RPR) [13] algorithm[2]. For each node u the link recommendation algorithms generate a candidate set C_u, that contains the links with the highest scores. We set $|C_u| = 20$, since in practice the number of recommended links is small and therefore this way we can select diverse, yet relevant, links.

For each dataset we create two graph instances: One consisting of edges up to a specific time, and one consisting of all edges. The first graph instance is given as input to the link recommendation algorithm to produce the candidate link recommendations. We choose the initial instances so as to meet three conditions: (i) the number of nodes is sufficiently large; (ii) there is a significant number of links that appear after the initial instance, and (iii) the link recommendation algorithms can produce a sufficient number of recommendations for many of the nodes in the graph.

For the *Facebook* dataset, the initial instance is the largest connected component of the graph until November 2007. The characteristics of the graph are shown in Table 1. For this instance the *AdamicAdar* method produces at least 20 recommendations for 87.5% of the nodes, while the *RootedPageRank* algorithm provides a sufficient number of recommendations for all nodes. For the *DBLP* dataset, the initial instance is constructed by considering the edges that appeared until the year 2000. To deal with the sparsity of the data, which inhibits the link recommendation algorithms, we iteratively delete the nodes with degree less that 3. The characteristics of the resulting graph are shown in Table 1. For this dataset, the *AdamicAdar* method produces a sufficient number of link recommendation for about half of the nodes, while the *RootedPageRank* produces at least 20 recommendations for all nodes.

We evaluate the prediction accuracy of our methods by considering the new edges that appear in the final instance of the dataset among the nodes that are included in the first instance. For both datasets, the number of edges that appear in the final instance (the last column of the table) is sufficiently large.

6.3 The edge probability function

The link recommendation algorithms provide scores that correspond to the confidence of the algorithms in their recommendation. Intuitively, the higher the score, the more likely the recommendation to be accepted. However, the score itself does not give the probability that the recommendation is successful. We thus need a way to transform these scores into probabilities, as needed by the CALR problem. To this end, we follow the following process. We first normalize the scores by dividing with the maximum score over all predictions, so as to obtain values between 0 and 1. Given an edge with normalized score x, we then apply a function $f(x)$ to shape the edge probability function. We consider four different functions in our experiments: (i) The logarithmic function $f_1(x) = 0.4\log_{10}(x) + 1$; (ii) The linear function $f_2(x) = x$; (iii) The power-law function $f_3(x) = x^3$; (iv) The exponential function $f_4(x) = 2^{10(x-1)}$. Each function yields probabilities with different properties.

We also compute the *empirical probability function* of an edge to appear in the graph given its score. Given all the (normalized) scores for all predictions of the recommendation algorithm, we create an equal-frequency histogram, where each bucket contains $10,000$ scores. We then count the fraction of edges in each bucket that appear in the final instance of the network. This defines the probability of an edge with a score that falls within the bucket range to appear in the graph, yielding a probability function.

We computed the empirical probability function for all network and link recommendation algorithm pairs that we consider. The resulting probability functions (in log-log scale) are shown in Figure 1. No clear and consistent pattern emerges from these plots. The functions in Figure 1.a

[1]KONECT, http://konect.uni-koblenz.de/

[2]In our experiments, we used the implementations in the LPmade software package, available at http://mloss.org/software/view/307/ .

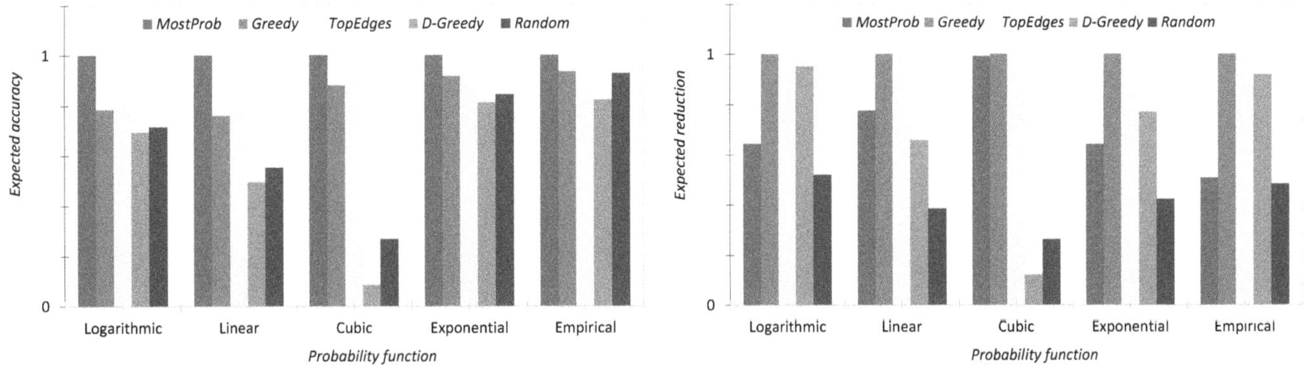

(a) *Expected Accuracy* (b) *Expected Prediction*

Figure 2: Relative performance of the algorithms for different probability functions on the *Facebook* dataset, with *RootedPageRank* recommendations, for $k = 5$.

Table 2: Effectiveness of the methods in terms of the expected reduction $\bar{\mathcal{R}}$ and the expected accuracy $\bar{\mathcal{A}}$.

	Facebook								*DBLP*							
	AdamicAdar				*RootedPageRank*				*AdamicAdar*				*RootedPageRank*			
	$k=2$		$k=5$		$k=2$		$k=5$		$k=2$		$k=5$		$k=2$		$k=5$	
methods	$\bar{\mathcal{A}}$	$\bar{\mathcal{R}}$	$\bar{\mathcal{A}}$	$\bar{\mathcal{R}}$	$\bar{\mathcal{A}}$	$\bar{\mathcal{R}}$	$\bar{\mathcal{A}}$	$\bar{\mathcal{R}}$	$\bar{\mathcal{A}}$	$\bar{\mathcal{R}}$	$\bar{\mathcal{A}}$	$\bar{\mathcal{R}}$	$\bar{\mathcal{A}}$	$\bar{\mathcal{R}}$	$\bar{\mathcal{A}}$	$\bar{\mathcal{R}}$
MostProb	5.485	0.050	4.813	0.107	3.821	0.369	2.904	0.604	11.888	0.102	10.044	0.223	16.265	0.761	13.134	1.223
Greedy	3.986	0.130	3.862	0.213	2.813	0.528	2.207	0.779	7.290	0.383	7.039	0.580	10.476	1.361	8.290	1.925
TopEdges	3.987	0.130	3.861	0.213	2.820	0.528	2.218	0.779	7.293	0.383	7.044	0.580	10.532	1.360	8.344	1.923
D-Greedy	3.639	0.124	3.644	0.209	1.407	0.256	1.437	0.512	6.492	0.369	6.671	0.573	6.160	0.856	6.415	1.562
Random	3.636	0.033	3.624	0.081	1.597	0.122	1.602	0.300	6.871	0.072	6.868	0.178	7.145	0.273	7.154	0.663

and 1.d seem logarithmic, while the function in Figure 1.b looks like a power-law with a small exponent. Surprisingly, in some cases (Figures 1.b and 1.c) the function is not increasingly monotone, meaning that edges with higher scores are assigned lower probabilities.

6.4 Expected Reduction vs Expected Accuracy

In this first set of experiments, we consider an idealized scenario where we assume that the probability functions that map scores to probabilities are perfectly accurate, and we have exact estimates for the probabilities of the links. Our goal is to understand, under this scenario, the relative performance of the different algorithms, and how the different probability functions affect their performance. Note that for this experiment, we do not make use of the second graph instance in order to assess the success of the recommendations. Instead, we assume that edges will appear in the graph with the probability they are assigned.

For a link recommendation algorithm L let $r(L)$ be the set of nodes for which L produces at least 20 recommendations. For a node u, let S_u be the set of links selected by our algorithm, where $|S_u| = k$. We consider $k = 2$ and $k = 5$ link recommendations per user. Given the set S_u, we compute the expected reduction $\mathcal{R}_u(S_u)$ for node u as described in Sections 3 and 4. To make numbers comparable across different nodes and datasets, we normalize the reduction by $L_G(u)$, the sum of shortest paths of node u before the addition of the edges in S_u. Finally, we compute the average reduction $\bar{\mathcal{R}} = \frac{1}{|r(L)|}\sum_{u\in r(L)} \mathcal{R}_u(S_u)/L_G(u)$, over all nodes in consideration.

Furthermore, for each selected set S_u we compute the *expected accuracy* of the selection as $\mathcal{A}_u(S_u) = \frac{1}{k}\sum_{e\in S_u} p_e$, that is, the fraction of the predictions that will appear in expectation. We then compute the average expected accuracy $\bar{\mathcal{A}} = \frac{1}{|r(L)|}\sum_{u\in r(L)} \mathcal{A}_u(S_u)$ by taking the average over all nodes in consideration.

In Figure 2 we see the performance of the different algorithms for the different probability functions for the *Facebook* dataset, when using the *RootedPageRank* recommendation algorithm, for $k = 5$. In this figure, we normalize the accuracy and reduction values by the maximum, so as to study the relative performance of the algorithms. As expected the *Greedy* algorithm achieves the best performance in terms of expected reduction, while the *MostProb* algorithm achieves the top performance in terms of expected accuracy.

The first observation is that *TopEdges*, which is a single iteration of the *Greedy* algorithm, performs essentially the same as *Greedy*. Therefore, we can obtain a significant speedup in the running time of the selection (see Section 6.7), without sacrificing performance. The only case where there is a noticeable difference is in the case of the logarithmic probability function. The logarithmic function is the flattest of the functions we consider, which means that it gives non-negligible probability even to edges with low scores. The *Greedy* algorithm is able to find such edges and improve the expected reduction. However, this results in a small loss in accuracy. Note that, in general, the *TopEdges* method tends to select slightly more probable edges. This is due to the fact that *Greedy* takes into account the interac-

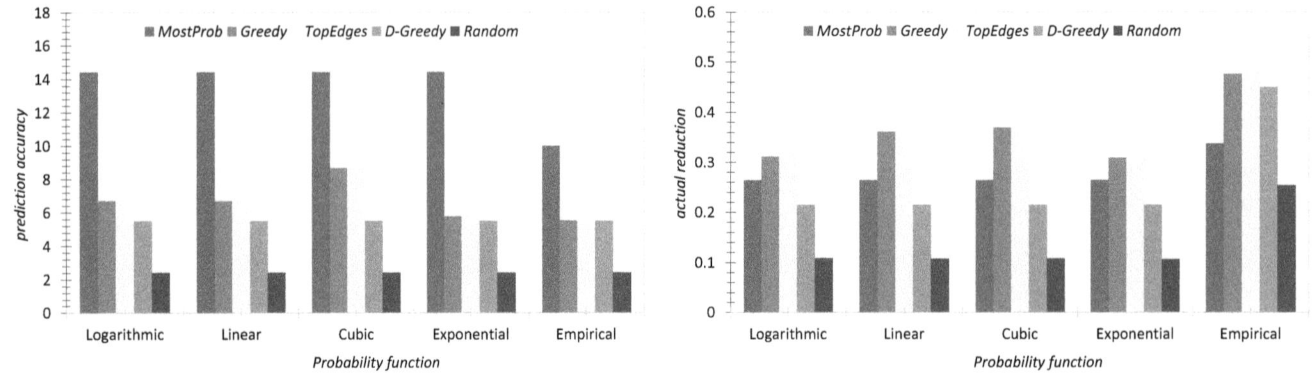

(a) *Prediction Accuracy* (b) *Actual reduction*

Figure 3: Performance of the algorithms for different probability functions on the *Facebook* dataset, with *RootedPageRank* recommendations, for $k = 5$.

Table 3: Prediction accuracy $\widehat{\mathcal{A}}$ and actual reduction $\widehat{\mathcal{R}}$ achieved by all methods.

	Facebook								*DBLP*							
	AdamicAdar				*RootedPageRank*				*AdamicAdar*				*RootedPageRank*			
	$k=2$		$k=5$		$k=2$		$k=5$		$k=2$		$k=5$		$k=2$		$k=5$	
methods	$\widehat{\mathcal{A}}$	$\widehat{\mathcal{R}}$	$\widehat{\mathcal{A}}$	$\widehat{\mathcal{R}}$	$\widehat{\mathcal{A}}$	$\widehat{\mathcal{R}}$	$\widehat{\mathcal{A}}$	$\widehat{\mathcal{R}}$	$\widehat{\mathcal{A}}$	$\widehat{\mathcal{R}}$	$\widehat{\mathcal{A}}$	$\widehat{\mathcal{R}}$	$\widehat{\mathcal{A}}$	$\widehat{\mathcal{R}}$	$\widehat{\mathcal{A}}$	$\widehat{\mathcal{R}}$
MostProb	21.338	0.172	18.142	0.323	16.490	0.264	14.408	0.469	2.309	0.021	1.892	0.044	2.887	0.078	2.191	0.132
Greedy	11.843	0.274	11.095	0.446	8.957	0.370	8.671	0.594	1.777	0.061	1.547	0.099	2.286	0.152	1.786	0.220
TopEdges	11.844	0.274	11.096	0.446	8.957	0.370	8.671	0.594	1.776	0.061	1.543	0.099	2.286	0.152	1.785	0.220
D-Greedy	6.332	0.202	7.418	0.388	4.344	0.215	5.497	0.450	1.325	0.064	1.331	0.100	1.404	0.121	1.381	0.200
Random	1.167	0.076	2.906	0.188	0.972	0.108	2.431	0.263	0.123	0.012	0.314	0.032	0.130	0.029	0.321	0.078

tions between the edges in the selected set, while *TopEdges* considers only the individual effect of each edge.

The second observation is that the *Greedy* and *TopEdges* algorithms achieve performance competitive to the *MostProb* algorithm in terms of accuracy. At worse, they achieve around 80% of the accuracy of the *MostProb* algorithm, while at the same time they achieve 40% more in reduction. Therefore, they can achieve considerable reduction, with a manageable loss in accuracy.

The third observation is that the probability function has a significant effect in the performance of the algorithms. As the function becomes more skewed, the algorithms *Greedy*, *TopEdges*, and *MostProb* become more similar in both metrics. This is due to the fact that the more "steep" functions penalize heavily the small scores. Given that the score values tend to follow a power-law distribution, this results in many edges with very low probabilities. Such edges must cause a very large reduction in order to be selected. As a result all algorithms tend to select edges with high probability, which explains the converging behavior. This is especially pronounced in the cubic probability function, which is the most skewed in our collection.

The above discussion explains also the poor performance of *D-Greedy*. The *D-Greedy* algorithm does not take probabilities into account, and decides based solely on the shortest path reduction. As a result it performs the worst in terms of accuracy (worse than random), indicating that reduction is inversely correlated with prediction probability. Interestingly, *D-Greedy* performs poorly even in terms of the expected reduction in the case of skewed probability functions. This is due to the fact that high reduction edges have very low probabilities, since, in general, the link recommendation algorithms give high scores to links to near-by nodes.

Finally, for the empirical probability function the relative behavior of the algorithms in terms of the expected reduction is similar to that of the logarithmic function. This agrees with our observation in Figure 1.b that the probability function is a power-law with a very small exponent. With respect to the expected accuracy, the *MostProb* algorithm is clearly the best, but all algorithms follow closely. This may be a result of the fact that even for high scores, the probability function never assigns large probabilities. It is also possible that the irregularities of the empirical function affect the results.

Our observations carry over for both datasets, for the different recommendation algorithms, and for different values of k. Table 2 shows detailed results for the linear probability function. The *Greedy* and *TopEdges* achieve considerable increase in the expected reduction compared to the *MostProb*, while sacrificing little in terms of accuracy.

6.5 Prediction accuracy vs actual reduction

In this set of experiments, we assess the recommendations produced by our algorithms in terms of their accuracy in predicting links that will appear in the graph, and the actual reduction they achieve when added to the graph.

Given the initial graph instance G, let F denote the set of edges added to the graph in the later instance. For a set of recommendations S_u selected by our algorithm for node u, the set $F_u = S_u \cap F$ is the subset of the recommendations that u actually accepted. We define the accuracy of

Table 4: Prediction accuracy $\widehat{\mathcal{A}}$ and actual reduction $\widehat{\mathcal{R}}$ achieved by the hybrid k-link recommendation.

		Facebook				*DBLP*					
		AdamicAdar		*RootedPageRank*		*AdamicAdar*		*RootedPageRank*			
MostProb(l)	*TopEdges*(k-l)	$\widehat{\mathcal{A}}$	$\widehat{\mathcal{R}}$	$\widehat{\mathcal{A}}$	$\widehat{\mathcal{R}}$	$\widehat{\mathcal{A}}$	$\widehat{\mathcal{R}}$	$\widehat{\mathcal{A}}$	$\widehat{\mathcal{R}}$	$\widehat{\mathcal{RA}}$	$\widehat{\mathcal{RR}}$
0	5	8.634	0.427	6.695	0.592	1.420	0.102	1.595	0.228	0.000	1.000
1	4	10.637	0.424	8.141	0.580	1.580	0.098	1.810	0.222	0.275	0.938
2	3	12.467	0.416	9.701	0.566	1.697	0.094	1.975	0.214	0.504	0.853
3	2	14.286	0.406	11.201	0.545	1.790	0.087	2.078	0.199	0.693	0.716
4	1	16.110	0.389	12.730	0.513	1.862	0.077	2.142	0.174	0.856	0.502
5	0	18.142	0.323	14.408	0.469	1.892	0.044	2.191	0.132	1.000	0.000

the recommendation set S_u as $\mathcal{A}_u = |F_u|/|S_u|$, that is, the fraction of the recommendations that were accepted by u. We define the *actual* prediction accuracy of our algorithm as $\widehat{\mathcal{A}} = \frac{1}{|r(L)|}\sum_{u\in r(L)} \mathcal{A}(S_u)$, that is, the average prediction accuracy over all the set nodes $r(L)$, for which the original link prediction algorithm L generated sufficient number of recommendations.

Given the set F_u, we define the normalized reduction for node u, as $\mathcal{R}_u = (L_G(u) - L_{G\cup F_u}(u))/L_G(u)$, where $L_{G\cup F_u}(u)$ is the sum of shortest paths from u in the *deterministic* graph $G \cup F_u$. Note that this definition measures the effect of the set F_u in isolation from other edges in F. We define the *actual* reduction of our algorithm as $\widehat{\mathcal{R}} = \frac{1}{|r(L)|}\sum_{u\in r(L)} \mathcal{R}_u$, that is, the average normalized reduction over all nodes in cosideration.

To evaluate our algorithms, we repeat the experiments in Section 6.4, and we measure the actual prediction accuracy $\widehat{\mathcal{A}}$, and the actual reduction $\widehat{\mathcal{R}}$. Figure 3 shows the performance of the different algorithms for different probability functions on the *Facebook* dataset, with link recommendations provided by the *RootedPageRank* algorithm, for $k = 5$. The relative behavior of the algorithms remains consistent with what we observed in Section 6.4. The *MostProb* method achieves the highest accuracy rate (14.4%) and performs better than all the other algorithms by a factor of at least 2. The *Greedy* and *TopEdges* methods are again essentially identical. They outperform the rest of the algorithms in terms of actual reduction, while achieving around 50% of the accuracy of *MostProb*. *D-Greedy* performs the worst in terms of both metrics, but it is now consistently better than random. This indicates that, in real data, edges that cause high reduction have non-negligible probability to appear.

Among the different probability functions, all algorithms achieve the highest reduction for the empirical probability function. This is reasonable, but we should take into account that the empirical function is computed using the data from F. It is surprising that the prediction accuracy of *MostProb* drops for the empirical function. This is due to the non-monotonic behavior of the probability function for this dataset, and to the fact that binning creates ties between the probability values of scores that fall in the same bucket.

Among the remaining functions, the best performance in terms of both prediction accuracy and actual reduction is achieved for the cubic function. Note that the probability function can be used as a "knob" to regulate how much emphasis we put on the score of the edge vs. the reduction it causes in the graph. The experimental results suggest that it is important to use distributions that bias the algorithms towards high probability edges, since these edges also offer high reduction, while retaining high accuracy.

Our observations hold for all datasets, for different recommendation algorithms, and different values of k. Table 3 shows detailed results for the cubic probability function. We observe that *Greedy* obtains a considerable decrease in the shortest paths with an acceptable loss in accuracy.

6.6 Hybrid link recommendations

In this set of experiments, we evaluate a *hybrid* recommendation system that aims to combine high accuracy recommendations with high reduction edge additions. In this hybrid link selection method, given a node u, a set C_u of candidate edges, and a value k, we generate a recommendation set S of size k, by taking the set $S_{MostProb}$ with the $\ell, \ell < k$, most probable edges in C_u, and a set $S_{TopEdges}$ with the top $k-\ell$ edges recommended by the *TopEdges* algorithm from the set $C_u \setminus S_{MostProb}$.

We run experiments with the cubic function for all pairs of datasets and recommendation algorithms, for $k = 5$. Table 4 shows our results in detail, for all $0 \leq \ell \leq k$. There is a clear tradeoff between prediction accuracy and actual reduction. As we recommend more edges from the set of the most probable edges, the prediction accuracy $\widehat{\mathcal{A}}$ increases, while the actual reduction value $\widehat{\mathcal{R}}$ decreases.

To evaluate the performance of the hybrid recommendations for different values of ℓ we also compute the fraction $\widehat{\mathcal{RA}}(\ell) = (\widehat{\mathcal{A}}(\ell) - \widehat{\mathcal{A}}(0))/(\widehat{\mathcal{A}}(5) - \widehat{\mathcal{A}}(0))$, where $\widehat{\mathcal{A}}(\ell)$ is the prediction accuracy for a given value of ℓ. This quantity indicates where the value $\widehat{\mathcal{A}}(\ell)$ lies relatively to the minimum and the maximum value of $\widehat{\mathcal{A}}$. Respectively, for the actual reduction $\widehat{\mathcal{R}}$, we compute the fraction $\widehat{\mathcal{RR}}(\ell) = (\widehat{\mathcal{R}}(\ell) - \widehat{\mathcal{R}}(5))/(\widehat{\mathcal{R}}(0) - \widehat{\mathcal{R}}(5))$. In the last two columns of Table 4 we report the average values of $\widehat{\mathcal{RA}}(\ell)$ and $\widehat{\mathcal{RR}}(\ell)$. For instance, the recommendation for $\ell = 3$, on average, the prediction accuracy increase is equal to the 69.3% of the maximum increase, while the actual reduction is 71.6% of the maximum reduction. We find that the value $\ell = 3$ offers the best tradeoff between accuracy and reduction.

6.7 Efficiency

In our final set of experiments we evaluate the efficiency of our algorithms. All algorithms were implemented in `C++` and compiled using the `g++v.4.6.4` compiler. We report the running times on a GNU/Linux machine, with Ubuntu (SMP): a Intel(R) Xeon(R) CPU server 64-bit NUMA machine with four processors and 16GB of RAM memory. Each

Table 5: Running times (in milliseconds) on the *Facebook* and *DBLP* datasets for $|C| = 20$ and $k = 5$.

	Facebook		*DBLP*	
methods	*AA*	*RPR*	*AA*	*RPR*
Greedy	253	455	109	304
TopEdges	69	99	25	35
D-Greedy	195	313	87	137

processor has 4 cores sharing a 8MB L3 cache, and each core has a 256KB private L2 cache and 2.40GHz speed.

We assess the efficiency of the *Greedy*, *D-Greedy*, and *TopEdges* methods. We exclude the *MostProb* method since it requires just sorting of 20 values. The running times of the algorithms (in milliseconds) are shown in Table 5 for $k = 5$. Clearly, the *Greedy* algorithm is the slowest, with the *D-Greedy* method a close second. The *TopEdges* algorithm performs significantly faster that both, and it always runs in less than 0.1 seconds for all our test cases.

7. CONCLUSIONS

In this paper, we considered the problem of recommending links to network users that are of interest to them, and also improve their centrality in the network. We proposed an efficient greedy algorithm for this task that exploits a fast algorithm for computing the expected reduction caused by the addition of a probabilistic link in a network. Our experiments show that our approach strikes a balance between the prediction accuracy of the recommendations, and their effect on the centrality of the user in the resulting network.

For future work, it would be interesting to extend our proposed solution to consider recommendations that minimize the expected *all-pais* shortest path lengths. This natural extension considers the utility of the network as a whole when recommending edges to a specific user. It would also be interesting to consider recommendations that optimize other criteria beyond shortest paths. Finally, in our work we touched upon the problem of transforming link recommendation scores into probabilities. This is an interesting problem that merits further investigation.

Acknowledgments

This work has been supported by the Marie Curie Reintegration Grant project titled JMUGCS which has received research funding from the European Union.

8. REFERENCES

[1] L. A. Adamic and E. Adar. Friends and neighbors on the web. *Social Networks*, 25(3), 2003.

[2] L. Backstrom and J. Leskovec. Supervised random walks: predicting and recommending links in social networks. In *WSDM*, pages 635–644, 2011.

[3] V. Chaoji, S. Ranu, R. Rastogi, and R. Bhatt. Recommendations to boost content spread in social networks. In *WWW*, pages 529–538, 2012.

[4] P. Crescenzi, G. D' Angelo, L. Severini, and Y. Velaj. Greedily improving our own centrality in a network. In *SEA*, pages 43–55. 2015.

[5] D. Easley and J. Kleinberg. *Networks, Crowds, and Markets: Reasoning About a Highly Connected World.* Cambridge University Press, 2010.

[6] H. Frank. Shortest paths in probabilistic graphs. *Operations Research*, 17(4):583–599, 1969.

[7] A. Frieze and G. Grimmett. The shortest-path problem for graphs with random arc-lengths. *Discrete Applied Mathematics*, 10(1):57 – 77, 1985.

[8] V. Ishakian, D. Erdös, E. Terzi, and A. Bestavros. A framework for the evaluation and management of network centrality. In *SDM*, pages 427–438, 2012.

[9] G. Kollios, M. Potamias, and E. Terzi. Clustering large probabilistic graphs. *IEEE Trans. Knowl. Data Eng.*, 25(2):325–336, 2013.

[10] K. Lazaridou, K. Semertzidis, E. Pitoura, and P. Tsaparas. Identifying converging pairs of nodes on a budget. In *EDBT*, 2015.

[11] M. Ley. The DBLP computer science bibliography: Evolution, research issues, perspectives. In *SPIRE*, 2002.

[12] D. Li, Z. Xu, S. Li, X. Sun, A. Gupta, and K. Sycara. Link recommendation for promoting information diffusion in social networks. In *WWW (Companion Volume)*, 2013.

[13] D. Liben-Nowell and J. Kleinberg. The link-prediction problem for social networks. *Journal of the American Society for Information Science and Technology*, 58(7):1019–1031, 2007.

[14] D. Liben-Nowell and J. M. Kleinberg. The link prediction problem for social networks. In *ACM CIKM*, pages 556–559, 2003.

[15] A. Meyerson and B. Tagiku. Minimizing average shortest path distances via shortcut edge addition. In *APPROX*, pages 272–285, 2009.

[16] G. Nemhauser, L. Wolsey, and M. Fisher. An analysis of the approximations for maximizing submodular set functions. *Mathematical Programming*, pages 265–294, 1978.

[17] M. Papagelis. Refining social graph connectivity via shortcut edge addition. *TKDD*, 10(2):12, 2015.

[18] M. Papagelis, F. Bonchi, and A. Gionis. Suggesting ghost edges for a smaller world. In *CIKM*, pages 2305–2308. ACM, 2011.

[19] N. Parotsidis, E. Pitoura, and P. Tsaparas. Selecting shortcuts for a smaller world. In *SDM*, 2015.

[20] M. Potamias, F. Bonchi, A. Gionis, and G. Kollios. K-nearest neighbors in uncertain graphs. *Proceedings of the VLDB Endowment*, 3(1-2):997–1008, 2010.

[21] A. E. Sariyüce, K. Kaya, E. Saule, and Ü. V. Çatalyürek. Incremental algorithms for network management and analysis based on closeness centrality. *CoRR*, abs/1303.0422, 2013.

[22] H. Tong, B. A. Prakash, T. Eliassi-Rad, M. Faloutsos, and C. Faloutsos. Gelling, and melting, large graphs by edge manipulation. In *CIKM*, pages 245–254, 2012.

[23] L. G. Valiant. The complexity of enumeration and reliability problems. *SIAM Journal on Computing*, 8(3):410–421, 1979.

[24] B. Viswanath, A. Mislove, M. Cha, and K. P. Gummadi. On the evolution of user interaction in facebook. In *WOSN*, pages 37–42, 2009.

[25] Z. Yin, M. Gupta, T. Weninger, and J. Han. A unified framework for link recommendation using random walks. In *ASONAM*, pages 152–159, 2010.

Relational Learning with Social Status Analysis

Liang Wu[†], Xia Hu[‡] and Huan Liu[†]
[†]Computer Science & Engineering, School of CIDSE, Arizona State University, Tempe, AZ, USA
[‡]Department of Computer Science and Engineering, Texas A&M University, College Station, TX, USA
{wuliang, huan.liu}@asu.edu, hu@cse.tamu.edu

ABSTRACT

Relational learning has been proposed to cope with the interdependency among linked instances in social network analysis, which often adopts network connectivity and social media content for prediction. A common assumption in existing relational learning methods is that data instances are equally important. The algorithms developed based on the assumption may be significantly affected by outlier data and thus less robust. In the meantime, it has been well established in social sciences that actors are naturally of different social status in a social network. Motivated by findings from social sciences, in this paper, we investigate whether social status analysis could facilitate relational learning. Particularly, we propose a novel framework RESA to model social status using the network structure. It extracts robust and intrinsic latent social dimensions for social actors, which are further exploited as features for supervised learning models. The proposed method is applicable for real-world relational learning problems where noise exists. Extensive experiments are conducted on datasets obtained from real-world social media platforms. Empirical results demonstrate the effectiveness of RESA and further experiments are conducted to help understand the effects of parameter settings to the proposed model and how local social status works.

Categories and Subject Descriptors

H.2.8 [**Database Management**]: Database applications—*Data Mining*; J.4 [**Social and Behavioral Sciences**]: Sociology

Keywords

Social Dimensions, Social Media, Relational Learning

1. INTRODUCTION

Social media websites have become a popular open platform for people to connect with their friends, express opinions and share feelings. Online user-generated data becomes a key data source for researchers to study scientific and commercial problems [37] which are related to social actors. To better understand online behaviors of social network users, categorization of social network users is fundamental for various tasks. Take stock price prediction [4] as an example, the sentiment dynamics of users in a specific group may indicate corresponding stock prices. Although some social media platforms enable users to categorize themselves by uploading tags, such information is often incomplete and unavailable in real applications, which necessitates the use of relational learning (RL).

RL has become an effective tool for classifying nodes in a network. They leverage network structures as well as attributes of social actors, which often result in improvement over models without considering network structures [11]. Given attributes and social links of social actors, and labels from training examples, RL methods view the prediction as a supervised learning problem over networked data, assuming links between nodes to be indicators of proximity over labels, i.e., social actors with links connected with each other are assumed to have similar labels [20, 21]. However, since social media content is often noisy, RL could be prone to poor performance due to the massive amount of information of low quality. For example, expressions such as 'Coooool' and 'omg!' are confusing, phenomena like 'sarcasm' even reverse the meaning of a word vector [28]. In addition, the proximity assumption of social links does not hold. Random social links are established due to reflexive reciprocity and link farming [12].

Meanwhile, social status has been intensively studied in profiling social actors [13]. As indicated by self-categorization theory, social status influences goals individuals pursue, and further affects the way they pursue [17] and the positive social identity they obtain. The social psychological finding motivates us to investigate the use of social status for relational learning. However, it is challenging to incorporate social status into relational learning. First, social status is difficult to estimate. Although various kinds of algorithms have been proposed to estimate social influence, such methods focus on estimating individual centrality in terms of certain network structure instead of social status. For example, experts in a professional area may have a high social status but fewer friends in a social network, who will be overlooked by existing influence modeling methods. Second, we are lack of an effective way to incorporate social status into RL. Existing work only considers links between

WSDM'16, February 22–25, 2016, San Francisco, CA, USA.
 ISBN 978-1-4503-3716-8/16/02... $15.00
DOI: http://dx.doi.org/10.1145/2835776.2835782

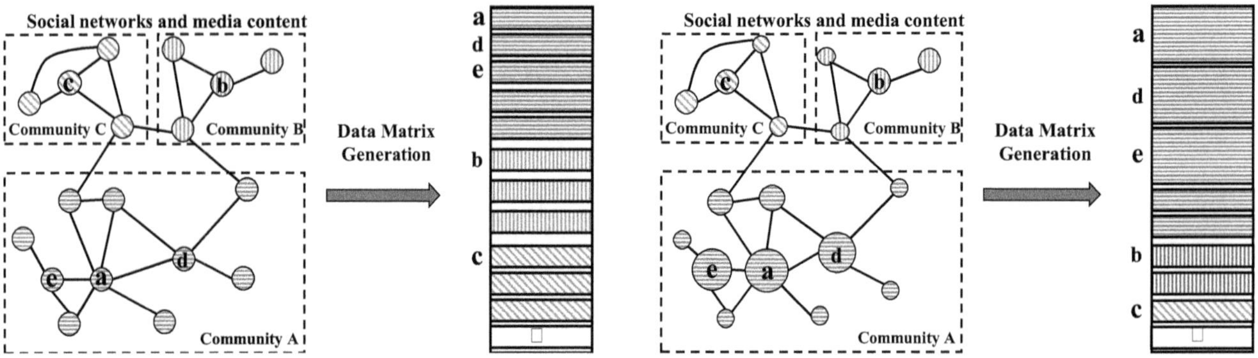

(a) Relational learning with equally weighted users.

(b) Relational learning with users weighted by global importance.

Figure 1: Illustrative examples of relational learning with different kinds of user weights.

nodes as an indicator of homophily, which fails to leverage them to reveal the social status.

In this paper, We propose a novel RElational learning framework based on Social status Analysis (RESA) to better predict labels of linked nodes through selecting influential agents of higher social status. Social status is used for constructing robust social dimensions based on social media content. Supervised models can then be built on the data in the latent social space.

The contribution of this work is threefold:

- We exploit social connections as an indicator of social importance to find influential individuals for RL. The proposed framework is resilient to noisy data through incorporating social status.
- A mathematical model is put forward to leverage social network structures. The model enables the automatic selection of information sources with higher social status and then generates robust social dimensions.
- Extensive experiments are conducted to test the effectiveness of the proposed model. It is demonstrated that network classification with the proposed social dimensions outperforms competitive baselines.

The rest of this paper is organized as follows. In Section 2, we briefly introduce the proposed framework. In Section 3, we investigate incorporating social status into RL. In Section 4, we show empirical evaluation with discussion. Related work is discussed in Section 5. Conclusion and possible future work are presented in Section 6.

2. RESA FRAMEWORK

Social media platforms enable users to label themselves through user profiling and content subscription. Since such labels are often unavailable and may be incomplete, it is of great significance to predict such labels of social actors with limited training information. Rather than merely focus on the network structure [22, 32], we focus on social media content. Since social content is idiosyncratic, informal and casual, we examine how to generate latent social dimensions in the presence of misinformation and noise by incorporating social status. In this section, we will introduce our motivation of the proposed framework and formally formulate the problem and introduce intuitions and the general framework of RESA.

2.1 Motivation

Social actors are multidimensional, which indicates that social status should also be evaluated from different aspects. Existing social influence prediction algorithms often produce a scalar to represent individual status, which overlook individuals with high status but is not universally central. In this work, we reduce social status into two perspectives: global social status and local social status in a specific domain. Next, we describe details of the two aspects.

Figure 1 shows two illustrative examples for incorporating social status into relational learning, where the area of circles and heights of rows in the data matrix indicate the social status. Figure 1(a) illustrates why existing RL methods are prone to low performance without considering social status. Since nodes marked with letters are connected by more people, their information is supposed to be more useful than information generated by others. As shown by the data matrix, without considering it, information generated by important users like Barack Obama are treated the same with anybody else, though their posts are more important.

Figure 1(b) illustrates how social status works for RL. Through upweighting importance of nodes with greater centrality, information from nodes of higher social status are better focused. The problem is that the iterative mutual reinforcement between neighbors of existing centrality measures forces less popular communities to be overwhelmed by the globally influential groups, since communities are of different levels of activeness. As shown in Figure 1(b), although b and c may be less important than d and e, once node a is selected, b and c are more informative. Thus, b and c represent social actors with high social status but are of less centrality. For example, though Barack Obama and Pope Francis are more important globally, it is favorable to select social actors from diverse groups and backgrounds, such as athletes and professors, as well.

In this work, we aim to select social actors with high social status and upweight the content they generate during training. The content is extracted from their posts and social status depends on global centrality and local social influence. Next, we will introduce formulation and general framework of the problem.

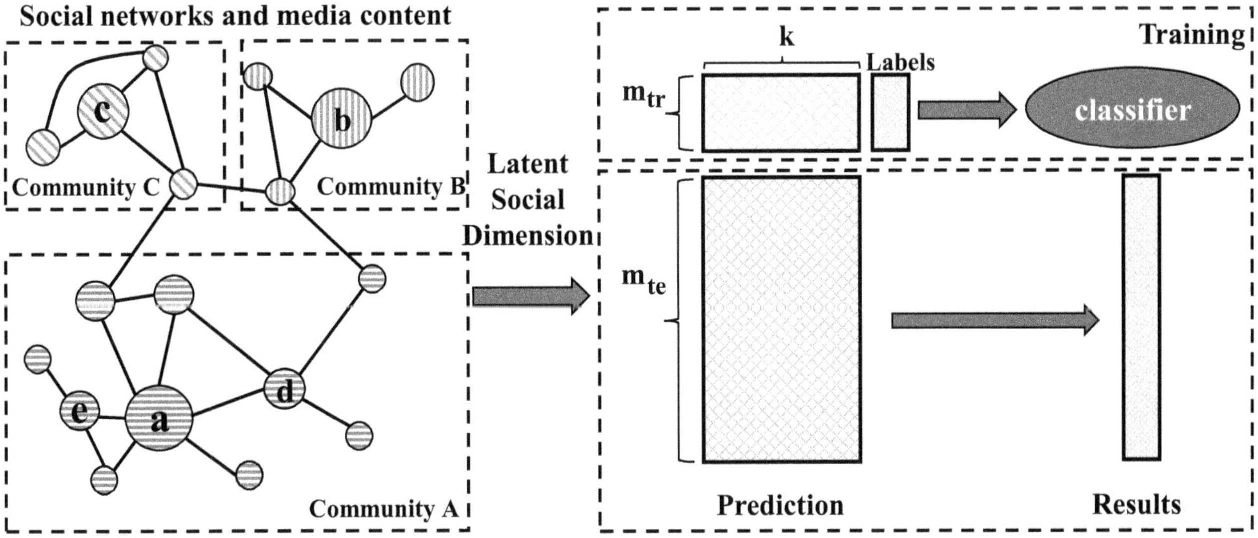

Figure 2: Relational Learning with Social Status Analysis.

2.2 Problem Formulation

Consider $\mathbf{V} \in \mathbb{R}^{n \times m}$ is the attribute matrix, where $\mathbf{V} = (\boldsymbol{v}_1, \boldsymbol{v}_2, \ldots, \boldsymbol{v}_m)$ and each row is represented as $\boldsymbol{v}_i$, which is the attribute vector of user i. The columns may refer to user attributes depending on different websites. $\mathbf{A}$ is the adjacency matrix of the underlying social network dataset with each entry $\mathbf{A}_{ij}$ equaling to one if i follows j and equaling zero otherwise. A label set $\boldsymbol{y}$ represents certain social tags and each user owns one or multiple labels. We aim to predict labels of a user given the network structure and his/her social media content. More formally, the problem is stated as follows:

Input

a user-attribute matrix $\boldsymbol{V}$, an adjacency matrix $\boldsymbol{A}$ and the training information matrix $\boldsymbol{Y}^{tr} = \{0,1\}^{m_{tr} \times t}$, where t is the number of labels and m_{tr} is the number of training instances.

Output

labels of test users, $\boldsymbol{Y}^{te} = \{0,1\}^{m_{te} \times t}$, where m_{te} is the size of testing data.

The social labels can be obtained from different sources in different platforms. For example, Flickr users can join different groups and BlogCatalog users are able to subscribe and add tags for themselves. Such explicit group memberships and interest tags can then be extracted as labels. A user usually joins various groups and subscribes various interest tags.

2.3 General Framework

Latent social dimensions have been proposed to transform user links to intrinsic features for RL [32]. Since interests of an individual are often complex, such social dimensions enable user interests to be better represented. Different from existing RL methods which only regard social links as an indicator of homophily, we view them as an indicator of social status, which represents the weights of a user and its content. For example, if a user has been followed by numerous people and has higher social influence in a social network, his posted content is more probable to be useful and of better quality. Thus, we first adopt linkage analysis algorithms to calculate how important a user is globally. Locally influential nodes are important for modeling structures of social networks. As mentioned in [1], local forceful nodes are important for preventing misinformation during the process of information aggregation. Thus, we further propose to construct social dimensions through leveraging the local social influence as well as global influence using social relations. The detailed procedure of our proposed work is illustrated in Figure 2, which consists of two steps: constructing latent social dimensions and learning a relational classifier.

Dimension Extraction: First, we concentrate on extracting latent dimensions from social media content. Social actors are assumed to be equally weighted by existing methods. As social media content in real world is noisy, information from influential sources should be zoomed in. This inspires us to incorporate a weight into the extraction procedure. The social weights are derived from the network structure. Although global social status is easy to be derived from the network structure, local status is difficult to obtain. In order to highlight more local influencers from small groups and balance contribution from different communities, we introduce a intra-group exclusive sparsity regularizer. It stimulates representative nodes in small groups to be higher weighted. A toy example is depicted in Figure 2, where the area of each circle represents its importance. In our framework, the influencers with high local social status are better focused, meaning that Node b and c are of more importance than e and d.

Relational Classifier Construction: After the social dimensions are generated, social actors are mapped to the new space and represented by latent factors. Supervised learning algorithms, such as regression and classification, can then be employed upon them to enable network classification. The dimension can easily be extended through combining more features generated from other sources, like

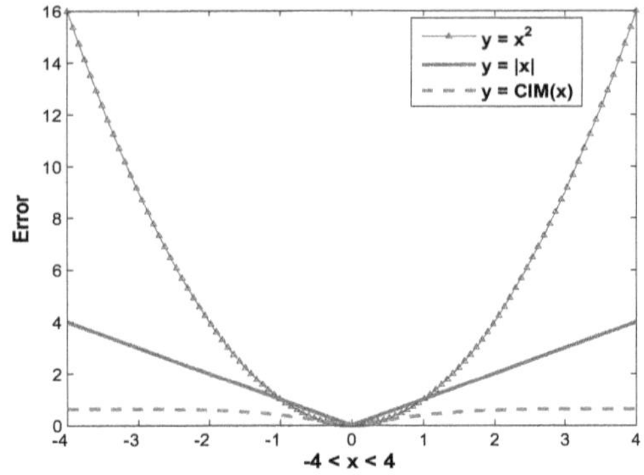

Figure 3: Curves of different cost functions in the range from -1 to 1.

network structure and user profiles. In this work, we only concentrate on the social media content. Since the classifier determines the identity label by learning upon the features, its prediction accuracy is an indicator telling whether the extracted dimensions are informative and descriptive. Due to the scalability and simplicity, we follow [32] and selected one-vs-rest linear SVM for discriminative learning.

3. RELATIONAL LEARNING FRAMEWORK WITH SOCIAL STATUS

In this section, we introduce how we induce latent social dimensions. The resultant latent social dimensions should be informative in the presence of noise. Since how to cope with noisy links has been discussed in previous work [32], we focus on reducing the negative impact of noise through selecting information sources with higher social status. The problem of social dimensions induced from user-generated content is to obtain an optimal low-rank representation $\mathbf{W} \in \mathbb{R}^{m\times k}$ $(k \ll n)$, which best describes the social affiliations. As the social dimension represents the probability an instance is assigned to a cluster, we constrain it to be nonnegative.

3.1 Global Social Status Modeling for Relational Learning

Existing RL methods regard each instance equally weighted, which ignore that social actors are of different social status. Since the degree distribution of real social network subjects to power law and has a heavy tail [2], the equivalence assumption leads the model to be biased by less popular users. Unfortunately, they may even be dominated by the outliers in real world applications. Eq.(1) is a general form of dimension reduction algorithms, and it minimizes the sum of squared reconstruction loss:

$$\min_{\boldsymbol{W},\boldsymbol{H}} \sum_{i}^{m} (\boldsymbol{v}_i - \boldsymbol{w}_i\boldsymbol{H}^T)(\boldsymbol{v}_i - \boldsymbol{w}_i\boldsymbol{H}^T)^T, \tag{1}$$

where $\boldsymbol{V}$ is decomposed into two latent factor $\mathbf{W}$ and $\mathbf{H}$. $\mathbf{H} \in \mathbb{R}^{n\times k}$ $(k \ll n)$ describes associations between features and social affiliations, .

Figure 3 denotes the curve of different cost functions. As shown in the figure, the squared loss increases quadratically when error becomes large. So such models are optimal when the noise $n \sim \mathcal{N}(\mu, \sigma^2)$ and it is small. However, when the noise becomes large, such algorithms are not resilient to outliers. In order to solve the problem, we propose to adopt the global social impact as weights of social actors to select more important information agents for constructing social dimensions. Given the social influence of each user, Eq.(1) can be reformulated as:

$$\begin{aligned} \min_{\boldsymbol{W},\boldsymbol{H}} \quad & \sum_{i=1}^{m} \mathbf{c}_i(\boldsymbol{v}_i - \boldsymbol{w}_i\boldsymbol{H}^T)(\boldsymbol{v}_i - \boldsymbol{w}_i\boldsymbol{H}^T)^T \\ \text{subject to} \quad & \sum_{i=1}^{m} \mathbf{c}_i = 1, \end{aligned} \tag{2}$$

where $\mathbf{c} \in \mathbb{R}^m$ and $\mathbf{c}_i$ is the social impact of user i, the values are positive and sum to 1 for all users. Eq.(2) is a row based normalization based on social impact. Influential nodes will be upweighted and users in the heavy tail will be avoided to dominate the calculation.

Since Eq.(2) is not jointly convex in terms of $\boldsymbol{W}$ and $\boldsymbol{H}$, we solve the problem in an iterative manner. By fixing one variable each time, the objective is convex to the counter part and the optimal solution can be obtained. Motivated by the optimization method proposed in [8], we develop the update rules as follows:

While fixing H, update W:

$$\boldsymbol{W}_{ik} = \boldsymbol{W}_{ik}\frac{(\boldsymbol{C}\otimes\boldsymbol{V}\boldsymbol{H})_{ik}}{(\boldsymbol{C}\otimes(\boldsymbol{W}\boldsymbol{H}^T)\boldsymbol{H})_{ik}}, \tag{3}$$

where $\boldsymbol{c}$ is the global social status and will be discussed in Section 3.4 and $\boldsymbol{C} = \mathbf{c}\mathbf{1}_n^T$. $\otimes$ is Hadamard product and has higher operator precedence over matrix product.

While fixing W, update H:

$$\boldsymbol{H}_{jk} = \boldsymbol{H}_{jk}\frac{((\boldsymbol{C}\otimes\boldsymbol{V})^T\boldsymbol{W})_{jk}}{((\boldsymbol{C}\otimes(\boldsymbol{W}\boldsymbol{H}^T))^T\boldsymbol{W})_{jk}}. \tag{4}$$

3.2 Local Social Status Modeling for Relational Learning

By incorporating the global social status, if there exist some groups with significantly higher influence than the others, the resultant social dimensions will be biased by them. Different kinds of social affiliations are of different popularity. Globally influential groups may contribute redundant information, since users with similar social affiliations tend to have overlapped social attributes. As mentioned earlier, once the most influential social actor is selected, members in the same group become less informative. Our aim is to actively select more various nodes from different groups through upweighting locally influential information sources.

In this section, we use $\boldsymbol{c}$ to represent individual weight for each user. Assume we have a static affiliation matrix $\boldsymbol{S} \in \mathbb{R}^{m\times g}$, where $\boldsymbol{S}_{ij} = 1$ means user i is a member of affiliation j and g is the number of all groups, we introduce the exclusive group LASSO penalty [16], $\ell_{1,2}$-*norm*, to achieve the intra-group sparsity for $\boldsymbol{c}$:

$$\ell_{1,2}(\boldsymbol{c}) = \frac{1}{2}\sum_{j=1}^{g}\Big(\sum_{i,S_{ij}=1}|\boldsymbol{c}_i|\Big)^2. \tag{5}$$

$\ell_{1,2}$-*norm* first sums up over intra-group variables, and imposes an ℓ_2-*norm* to regularize the sum. Its minimization leads to intra-group sparsity. Concretely, it enforces more zero entries to take place in a group. The property is desirable for our assumption since it tends to select locally representative influencers in different groups. By the definition of $\ell_{1,2}$-*norm*, Eq.(5) can be formulated as:

$$\ell_{1,2}(\boldsymbol{c}) = \frac{1}{2}\sum_{i=1}^{g}(\boldsymbol{c}^T\boldsymbol{S}_{*i})^2 \quad (6)$$

$$= \frac{1}{2}\sum_{i=1}^{g}\boldsymbol{c}^T\boldsymbol{S}_{*i}\boldsymbol{S}_{*i}^T\boldsymbol{c} \quad (7)$$

$$= \frac{1}{2}\boldsymbol{c}^T\boldsymbol{S}\boldsymbol{S}^T\boldsymbol{c}, \quad (8)$$

where $\boldsymbol{S}_{*i} \in \mathbb{R}^{m\times 1}$ and denotes the membership of group i. By jointly considering the global and local social status, the objective can be reformulated as:

$$\min_{\mathbf{c},\mathbf{W},\mathbf{H}} \sum_{i}^{m} \mathbf{c}_i(\boldsymbol{v}_i - \boldsymbol{w}_i\boldsymbol{H}^T)(\boldsymbol{V}_i - \boldsymbol{W}_i\boldsymbol{H}^T)^T + \frac{1}{2}\boldsymbol{c}^T\boldsymbol{S}\boldsymbol{S}^T\boldsymbol{c}. \quad (9)$$

For simplicity, we replace $\boldsymbol{S}\boldsymbol{S}^T$ by $\boldsymbol{D} \in \mathbb{R}^{m\times m}$. Each entry $\boldsymbol{D}_{ij}$ denotes the correlation between user i and j in terms of their overlapping affiliations. A large correlation $\boldsymbol{D}_{ij}$ forces user i's weight $\boldsymbol{c}_i$ to be small if $\boldsymbol{c}_j$ has a higher social status. Thus, intra-group sparsity actively selects the most influential people in one group to be upweighted. The resultant $\boldsymbol{c}$ balances the contribution of different social affiliations and avoids being biased by only the top group and their redundant information.

3.3 Optimization

The optimization objective is not jointly convex to $\boldsymbol{W}$, $\boldsymbol{H}$ and $\boldsymbol{c}$. We update them in an iterative manner.

When $\boldsymbol{c}$ is fixed, the optimization has the same form with Eq.(2). Thus, $\boldsymbol{W}$ and $\boldsymbol{H}$ can be updated iteratively as denoted in Eq.(3) and Eq.(4).

When $\boldsymbol{W}$ and $\boldsymbol{H}$ are fixed, the objective function can be reformulated as:

$$\min_{\mathbf{c}} \quad \sum_{i=1}^{m}\boldsymbol{c}_i\boldsymbol{t}_i + \frac{1}{2}\boldsymbol{c}^T\boldsymbol{D}\boldsymbol{c}$$
$$\text{subject to} \quad lb < c_i < ub, \sum_{i=1}^{m}\boldsymbol{c}_i = 1, \quad (10)$$

where $t_i = (\boldsymbol{v}_i - \boldsymbol{w}_i\boldsymbol{H}^T)(\boldsymbol{v}_i - \boldsymbol{w}_i\boldsymbol{H}^T)^T$. Then optimization of Eq.(10) is transformed to a quadratic programming (QP) problem and the solution is similar to that introduced in [6]. Here we adopt two parameters, the upper bound ub and lower bound lb. The two bounds control the maximum and minimum weight of a node correspondingly.

The algorithm to extract social dimensions is summarized in Algorithm 1.

3.4 Discussion

In order to select both globally and locally influential social actors, RESA needs each user's global social influence and the social affiliations as input. In this section, we introduce how we measure the global influence and their affiliations based on network structures. We adopt the individual PageRank centrality to reveal the global social impact and describe a modularity maximization algorithm to discover the community memberships of different users.

The network structure of social network can be exploited to infer the authority of each user. Various algorithms have been proposed to predict the social influence in a social network [39]. Since we focus on leveraging the connectivity to build up robust social dimensions in this work, e directly adopt PageRank (PR) [27] to estimate the celebrity of each user. PR was proposed for web search to infer page importance based on the hyperlink structure and was proven to be useful for finding important people in a social network. Note that other centrality estimation methods can also be incorporated into our framework. In order to discover the social group affiliations, we adopt the modularity maximization approach [32]. The concept of modularity is introduced to measure the community structure of complex networks [7, 25]. It is to measure the deviation of interactions between users from a real social network to a uniform random graph. Here, we denote the social affiliation matrix as $\mathbf{S} \in \mathbb{R}^{m\times g}$. $\mathbf{S}$ and the optimal PageRank scores $\boldsymbol{c} \in \mathbb{R}^{m\times g}$ are then be used by the proposed model in Section 3.2. Note that the proposed framework is independent to the estimation of global social impact and social affiliation and different measures can be used. To choose the best measure is not the main focus of this paper, which remains an important direction of future work.

Algorithm 1 Social Dimension Extraction

Input: The user attribute matrix $\boldsymbol{V} \in \mathbb{R}^{m\times n}$,
the initial latent factors $\boldsymbol{W} \in \mathbb{R}^{m\times k}$ and $\boldsymbol{H} \in \mathbb{R}^{n\times k}$,
the social affiliation matrix $\boldsymbol{S} \in \mathbb{R}^{m\times k}$,
the vector of individual global influence $\boldsymbol{c} \in \mathbb{R}^{m}$,
Output: Social dimension $\boldsymbol{W}$, $\boldsymbol{H}$ and $\boldsymbol{c}$.
Repeat
Calculate $\boldsymbol{C} = \boldsymbol{c}\mathbf{1}_n^T$
Update $\boldsymbol{W}$ by $\boldsymbol{W}_{ik} = \boldsymbol{W}_{ik}\frac{(\boldsymbol{C}\otimes\boldsymbol{V}\boldsymbol{H})_{ik}}{(\boldsymbol{C}\otimes(\boldsymbol{W}\boldsymbol{H}^T)\boldsymbol{H})_{ik}}$;
Update $\boldsymbol{H}$ by $\boldsymbol{H}_{jk} = \boldsymbol{H}_{jk}\frac{((\boldsymbol{C}\otimes\boldsymbol{V})^T\boldsymbol{W})_{jk}}{((\boldsymbol{C}\otimes(\boldsymbol{W}\boldsymbol{H}^T))^T\boldsymbol{W})_{jk}}$;
Update $\boldsymbol{c}$ by Eq.(10);
until Convergence

4. EXPERIMENTS

In this section, we introduce experiment details to validate the effectiveness of the proposed framework. We first introduce our datasets and the methods used for comparison. Then we discuss the performance based on the two datasets. After investigating the sensitivity of RESA when the social dimensionality changes, we further verify how the social constraint works during training. Finally, we examine the effectiveness of RESA on the datasets. Empirical results of RL based on the social dimensions generated by other models are also presented.

4.1 Data Sets

In order to examine how the relational classifier behaves on real world social media websites, two datasets obtained from BlogCatalog[1] and Flickr[2] are adopted in our work. Both of them are publicly available and have been used previous work [32, 34].

Table 1 illustrates some statistics about the two datasets. The users are randomly sampled from the two websites, and various kinds of intrinsic attributes are extracted as features. We adopt the user interest tags in BlogCatalog and explicit

[1]http://www.blogcatalog.com/
[2]http://www.flickr.com/

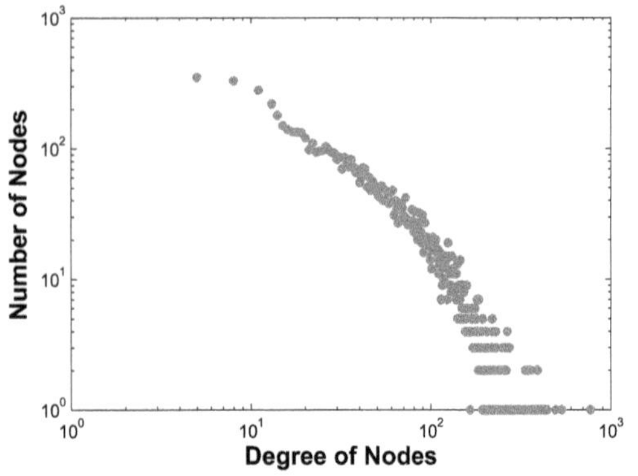

(a) BlocCatalog Dataset.

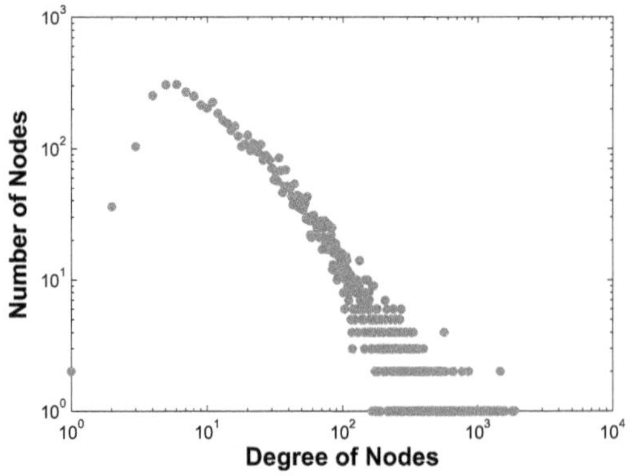

(b) Flickr Dataset.

Figure 4: The degree distribution of nodes in two datasets.

Table 1: The statistics about employed datasets.

	# of Instances	# of Labels	# of features
BlogCatalog	5198	6	8189
Flickr	7575	9	12047

group memberships as identity labels. In order to better understand the distributions, we further explore the degree distribution of them in Figure 4. The x-axis and y-axis are both of log scale. As shown in the figure, the two networks are scale-free [3], meaning that only few nodes are of a high degree and a large portion of users have few connections.

4.2 Baseline Methods and Metrics

We select several representative methods for comparison. As we mainly focus on leveraging social status for building robust RL, more variants are not included. LFM only considers the latent structure of social media content and GNMF incorporates social relations as homophily indicators. CIMNMF is robust to large noise and GSIM is used for validating the global social status.

Latent Factor Model: Latent Factor Model (LFM) has been proven a useful tool for reducing dimensions in real applications. For social media analysis, since the feature often represents the tweeted words and user tags, a negative value is often meaningless and confusing, here we constrain all entries of factors to be nonnegative. Such constraint can reduce the model into Nonnegative Matrix Factorization. We employ the model proposed by Lee and Seung [29], and adopt the multiplicative update rule.

Graph Regularized NMF: To take advantage of the linkage information between users in social network data, another common assumption is users with social links should share a higher similarity in terms of content. In order to compare our model with such intuition, we adopt the Graph Regularized NMF (GNMF) model [5].

Robust NMF: Traditional dimension reduction algorithms suffer from noise due to the cost function they used. For example, one of the most common cost function, ℓ_2-*norm*, which is adopted for reducing dimensions by methods like NMF and Principal Component Analysis (PCA), assumes noise $n \sim \mathcal{N}(\mu, \sigma^2)$ and it is small. But in real applications, the noise are large and impulsive, and sometimes contain large corruptions. As shown in Figure 3, squared loss increases quadratically when its argument becomes large. Various robust cost functions are introduced to solve this problem in areas of signal processing and computer vision. In this work, we adopt Correntropy Induced Metric (CIM) to compare our proposed model with such robust methods. Correntropy was proposed in information theoretic learning [19] to calculate the distance between two random variables, and it was further extended as CIM to process non-Gaussian noise and large corruptions in measuring distance of two vectors. In this work, the CIMNMF model [8] is adopted as a baseline method.

Global Social Impact Model: In order to further investigate the effectiveness of local social status, we also adopted the method introduced in Section 3.1 (GSIM) as a baseline, which only considers global social status.

4.3 Metrics

F_1-measure: To test the prediction accuracy in terms of both precision and recall, we adopted the F_1-measure to evaluate the performance.

Macro-F_1: Since in our methods, there are multiple labels to be predicted. For each task t, F_1^t can be computed. In order to get the overall performance, we first adopt the Macro-averaged F_1-measure as:

$$Macro - F_1 = \frac{1}{|\boldsymbol{T}|}\sum_{t \in \boldsymbol{T}} F_1^t, \tag{11}$$

where $\boldsymbol{T}$ is the set of all identity labels and F_1^t is the F_1-measure of task t.

Micro-F_1: A possible problem of Macro-F_1 is, since the size of different labels varies, the task with fewer instances may be overemphasized. In order to cope with this problem, we adopted Micro-averaged F_1-measure. First, we calculate the micro averaged precision and recall:

$$Micro - precision = \frac{\#TP}{\#TP + \#FP} \tag{12}$$

$$Micro - recall = \frac{\#TP}{\#TP + \#FN}, \tag{13}$$

where #TP is the number of true positives, #FP is the number of false positives and #FN is the number of false negatives. Then Micro-F_1 is the harmonic average of Micro-precision and Micro-recall.

Table 2: The F_1-measure of different methods on BlogCatalog Data with varying training ratio.

	Training Ratio	10%	20%	30%	40%	50%	60%	70%	80%	90%
	LFM	0.6977	0.7074	0.7223	0.7359	0.7425	0.7476	0.7562	0.7581	0.7669
	GNMF	0.7221	0.7352	0.7507	0.7530	0.7546	0.7550	0.7568	0.7627	0.7707
Micro-F_1(%)	CIMNMF	0.7170	0.7280	0.7382	0.7405	0.7476	0.7492	0.7507	0.7508	0.7518
	GSIM	0.6975	0.7143	0.7283	0.7328	0.7382	0.7441	0.7495	0.7499	0.7520
	RESA	**0.7527**	**0.7566**	**0.7630**	**0.7677**	**0.7757**	**0.7760**	**0.7826**	**0.7883**	**0.8103**
	LFM	0.6958	0.7109	0.7206	0.7305	0.7363	0.7397	0.7532	0.7541	0.7632
	GNMF	0.7162	0.7308	0.7476	0.7508	0.7512	0.7537	0.7550	0.7577	0.7695
Macro-F_1(%)	CIMNMF	0.7116	0.7241	0.7349	0.7370	0.7406	0.7412	0.7464	0.7466	0.7481
	GSIM	0.6911	0.7093	0.7252	0.7280	0.7398	0.7406	0.7459	0.7468	0.7474
	RESA	**0.7497**	**0.7525**	**0.7572**	**0.7637**	**0.7710**	**0.7779**	**0.7795**	**0.7809**	**0.8087**

Table 3: The F_1-measure of different methods on Flickr Data with varying training ratio.

	Training Ratio	10%	20%	30%	40%	50%	60%	70%	80%	90%
	LFM	0.5443	0.5622	0.5705	0.5722	0.5746	0.5857	0.5868	0.5939	0.6065
	GNMF	0.5545	0.5588	0.5677	0.5735	0.5761	0.5767	0.5792	0.5811	0.5924
Micro-F_1(%)	CIMNMF	0.3587	0.4084	0.4556	0.4561	0.4808	0.4934	0.5043	0.5173	0.5381
	GSIM	0.5395	0.5584	0.5627	0.5640	0.5646	0.5652	0.5685	0.5709	0.5724
	RESA	**0.5690**	**0.5770**	**0.5967**	**0.6086**	**0.6136**	**0.6169**	**0.6364**	**0.6394**	**0.6444**
	LFM	0.5306	**0.5536**	**0.5673**	**0.5694**	**0.5687**	**0.5792**	**0.5823**	0.5873	0.6053
	GNMF	**0.5512**	0.5521	0.5615	0.5667	0.5682	0.5703	0.5762	0.5761	0.5849
Macro-F_1(%)	CIMNMF	0.3394	0.3658	0.4126	0.4089	0.4494	0.4393	0.4764	0.4908	0.5262
	GSIM	0.5364	0.5500	0.5528	0.5539	0.5560	0.5537	0.5639	0.5608	0.5673
	RESA	0.5170	0.5293	0.5298	0.5366	0.5419	0.5774	0.5777	**0.5894**	**0.6159**

4.4 Experiments on BlogCatalog Data

The performance of different methods on BlogCatalog dataset with varying training ratio, from 10% to 90%, is illustrated in Table 2. For each training ratio, samples are randomly split into training and testing set. We repeat this process 10 times and report the average results. The highest performance under each setting is highlighted in bold face. In terms of both Micro-F_1 and Macro-F_1, our proposed model RESA outperforms the baselines. As shown in the table, the performance of GNMF, which adopts the user graph regularization, is the closest to that of RESA. It implies that the homophily phenomena are observed on this dataset, meaning that users are likely to follow similar people. When less data is used for training, CIMNMF performs better than LFM. But it is outperformed by LFM when more data are used for training. The performance of CIMNMF is also worse than GNMF on both measures. This indicates that the robust methods are not directly applicable to social media analysis. GSIM has the lowest Micro- and Macro-F_1 among all five methods. It shows that using the static global social status leads the model to be biased by certain nodes, which finally resulted in an unfavorable result.

4.5 Experiments on Flickr Data

The performance of different methods on Flickr dataset with varying training ratio, from 10% to 90%, is illustrated in Table 3. In terms of Micro-F_1, the proposed RESA outperforms other methods all the time. Compared with experimental results of BlogCatalog dataset, where GNMF is the runner-up and outperforms other baselines, LFM performs better than GNMF on Flickr dataset. It indicates that their performance varies with different settings and they are not stable enough. Similarly, GSIM does not perform very well, which proves the static and global social impact leads to a biased representation, although introducing locally influential information sources can significantly improve the performance. But since we only use PageRank centrality in our work to induce the global influence, other centrality measures may have different performance. CIMNMF has the worst performance among all methods, and falls behind RESA about 20% to 60% under different settings. This large lag further proves that the CIMNMF method cannot directly be applied to social media dataset.

But the proposed RESA fails to perform the best under some settings when we use Macro-F_1. As depicted in Table 3, though it performs the best under the setting of 80% and 90% training ratio, RESA is outperformed by LFM and GNMF when less portion is used for training. Since LFM is the runner up method under most settings of Micro-F_1, the Macro-F_1 result indicates that LFM, which does not consider any graph structure, is a competitive baseline for generating social dimensions. By both considering the Macro-F_1 and Micro-F_1, a conclusion can be made that RESA fails to identify certain tasks with fewer training instances. But when we increase the training ratio, RESA converges to and outperforms LFM.

4.6 Effectiveness of Social Status

In this section, we plan to test how social status works to facilitate RL. As discussed in Section 3.4, global social status is obtained separately from centrality measures. In Eq.9, global social status is used as prior for $\mathbf{c}$. To test how it contributes to RESA, we propose a variant of RESA, which initializes $\mathbf{c}$ using random values. We named the model as Local Social Influence Model (LSIM). We vary number of training iterations and record results of two models, which are presented in Figure 5. As shown by results of BlogCatalog and Flickr datasets, RESA converges

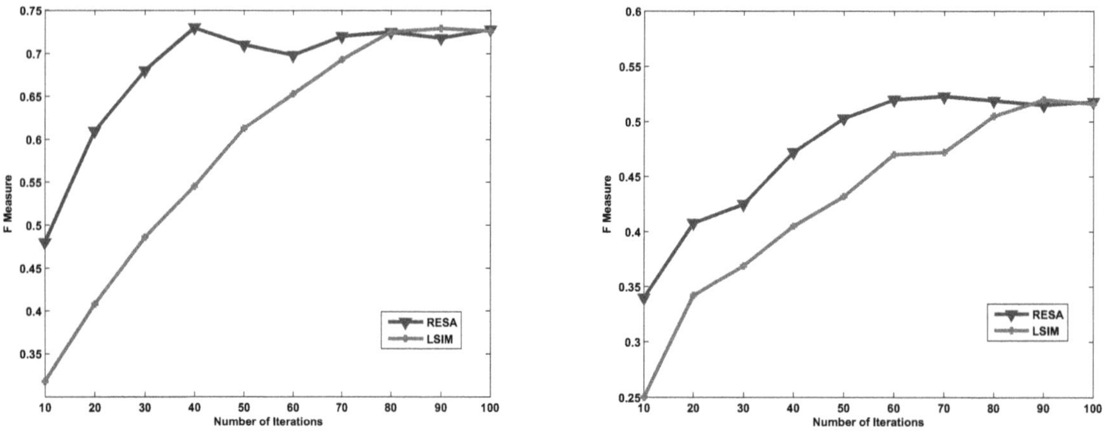

(a) Micro-F_1 on BlogCatalog Data. (b) Micro-F_1 on Flickr Data.

Figure 5: The Micro-F_1 *measure* of *RESA* and *LSIM* .

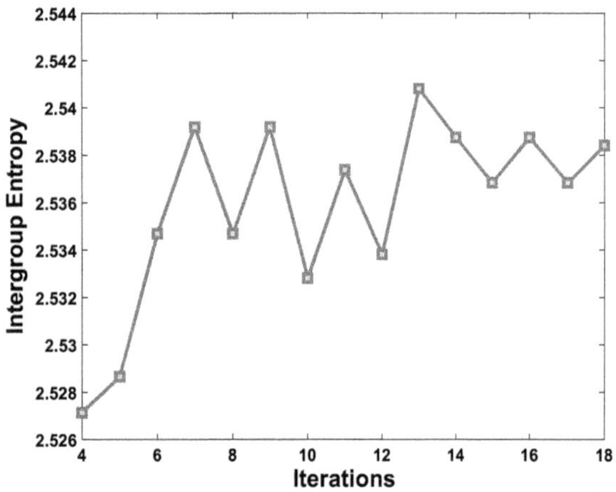

Figure 6: Changes of Inter-group Entropy.

more efficiently than LSIM, meaning that it takes less epochs to obtain the optimal solution. LSIM is able to gradually converges to RESA with more iterations. The result indicates that LSIM can converge to the optimal solution with more iterations and global social status helps the model to converge more efficiently.

Unlike global social impact, which is easily accessible, it is difficult to validate usefulness of local social status. In order to further investigate how the proposed model achieves to capture the local social influence, here we define the inter-group diversity:

$$\boldsymbol{P} = \boldsymbol{S}^T \boldsymbol{c}. \tag{14}$$

The weight of each group can be calculated through collecting weight of instances from the group as in Eq.(14). We treat the group weights as their probabilities and calculate the entropy of the underlying distribution. Thus, the entropy measures the inter-group diversity of group weight distribution. Figure 6 denotes the changes of inter-group entropy. As shown in the figure, the entropy increases with the number of iterations. At first it fluctuates around between 2.535 and 2.540, and finally converges after more iterations. The results indicate that the $\ell_{1,2}$-*norm* is effective in increasing inter-group diversity and thus selecting influencers of high local social status.

4.7 Sensitivity of Latent Dimensionality

In this section, we vary the dimensionality of social dimensions and observe the performance on both datasets. The dimensions are changed in the range of 10 to 100. The corresponding results on BlogCatalog and Flickr data are illustrated in Figure 7. As denoted by the figures, both Micro- and Macro-F_1 increase significantly when the dimensionality is small. The increasing ratio decreases when there are more dimensions and finally converges when k increases to 60 or more. When k increases to 100, the Macro-F_1 on BlogCatalog data and the Micro-F_1 on Flickr data even decrease. The results prove that user behaviors are idiocratic: when there are too few social dimensions, it fails to describe the idiocrasy. But a too large dimensionality is also meaningless, since the extra dimensions are not informative and may worsen the performance.

5. RELATED WORK

Relational learning refers to the learning over relational information between connected instances. Unlike traditional machine learning tasks, the connections made the classical i.i.d. assumption no longer applicable. In order to predict labels of linked instances, various methods have been proposed. Collective inference has been proposed to classify graph nodes based on the network structure [10, 15], where the graph structure of a node is often transformed into its features. The structural features are further fed to a supervised learning framework, which iteratively predicts class labels of unlabeled examples. Such methods are able to achieve a better accuracy through capturing autocorrelation between labels of neighbors.

Besides merely focusing on the relationship between one hub friends, other models are proposed to capture the long-distance autocorrelation [38]. They assume there exist hidden topics, where connections between users and

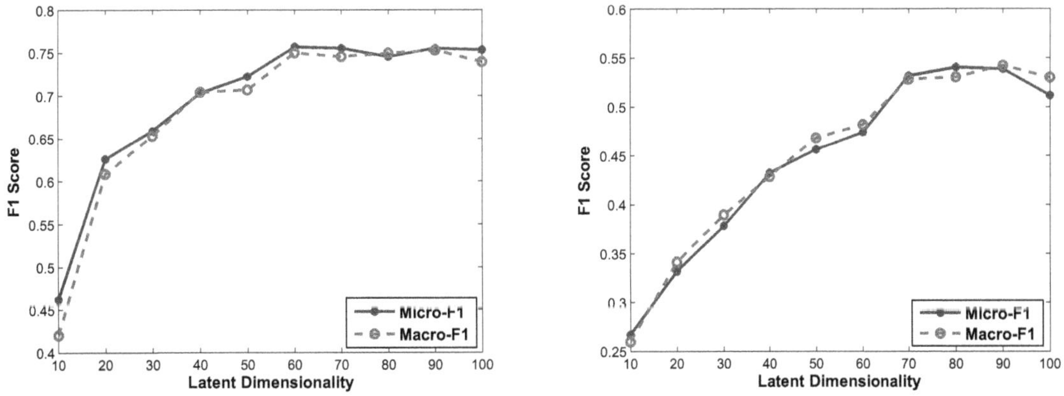

(a) F_1-measure on BlogCatalog Data.

(b) F_1-measure on Flickr Data.

Figure 7: The sensitivity in terms of different varying dimensionality.

social attributes of users are generated according to their group memberships. Such latent memberships are used for learning a supervised model to classify connected nodes. In [24], Neville and Jensen propose to replace the soft clustering with disjoint clusters, and use such cluster memberships as features to infer labels of social actors. The hard clustering manner reduces the computational cost, but it requires each actor to be assigned to one group. The assumption may not hold for real world social networks, since some nodes may not show a clear relationship to any groups. The strong assumption forces these nodes to be assigned randomly and thus bringing in noise.

Learning latent social dimensions based on social connections, attributes and social media content has attracted much attention from both RL [32] and other related classification tasks on social media instances. Since social content is often of high dimensionality and noisy, theses methods solve the problem through learning a low rank representation social actors, which can be regarded as feature extraction. Another more direct way is to select discriminant features based on the latent social affiliations[30]. Since social connections and social media content are often noisy, methods in this stream which assume all nodes are equally weighted are not resilient to outliers. In order to infer user weights from social connections, PageRank [14] and topic propagation [31] have been adopted. A static social weight can reflect how globall influential a node is globally, but learning with such a weight may bias the model with influential groups. Nodes from the same group may introduce too much overlapped information, which is unfavorable. In our work, we use global influence as a prior and actively upweight local influencers from small groups, so as to achieve greater inter-group diversity.

Our work is also related to matrix factorization and sparse machine learning methods. Matrix factorization has been used in various applications such as recommendation [35] and distance metric learning [36] to reduce dimensionality. Sparse learning has been proposed to enforce the data representation to have more zeros. The structures of sparsity include group level [23], tree level [18], differences between features [33] and so on. Most sparse learning algorithms focus on learning a sparse representation for instances [9], while our work aims to select informative instances. Nie et al. propose to select representative instances from the dataset using $\ell_{2,1}$-*norm* [26]. The proposed model is different since we measure how informative a node is based on its social status and the social group it belongs to.

6. CONCLUSION AND FUTURE WORK

The availability of social relations enables RL algorithms to better model and predict data instances in a network environment, where the i.i.d. assumption no longer holds. In this paper, we investigate how to leverage the global and local social influence for RL. To capture global social context, we adopt PageRank centrality to weight the importance of different nodes. To capture the local social influence, we force individuals in a same group to compete with each other, thus obtaining the intra-group sparsity. The inter-group sparsity enable influential nodes in small communities to survive and reduce overlapped information from the top influential groups. With these solutions, we propose a framework RESA to integrate local and global social influence for constructing the latent social dimensions. Experimental results on real-world datasets show that the proposed method outperforms under most settings. We also conduct experiments to further understand how the local social status works.

There are several possible directions remaining to be investigated in the future. First, as new users may join the community and social media content and social relations of existing social actors may evolve overtime, it is challenging to efficiently update the model. In our paper, the exclusive group LASSO forces nodes to be either influencers or non-influential nodes. But in reality, a hierarchy may exist among social actors. Thus, we plan to explore whether different structures are hidden behind social status, and how other kinds of sparse learning methods can help to better model social influences. Third, we will investigate centrality measures other than PageRank on analyzing the social network structure.

7. ACKNOWLEDGEMENTS

This work was supported, in part, by the Office of Naval Research grants N000141410095 and N000141310835.

8. REFERENCES

[1] D. Acemoglu, A. Ozdaglar, and A. ParandehGheibi. Spread of (mis) information in social networks. *Games and Economic Behavior*, 70(2):194–227, 2010.

[2] R. Albert and A.-L. Barabási. Statistical mechanics of complex networks. *Reviews of modern physics*, 74(1):47, 2002.

[3] A.-L. Barabási et al. Scale-free networks: a decade and beyond. *science*, 325(5939):412, 2009.

[4] J. Bollen, H. Mao, and X. Zeng. Twitter mood predicts the stock market. *Journal of Computational Science*, 2(1), 2011.

[5] D. Cai, X. He, J. Han, and T. S. Huang. Graph regularized nonnegative matrix factorization for data representation. *IEEE Transactions on Pattern Analysis and Machine Intelligence.*

[6] J. Currie and D. I. Wilson. Opti: lowering the barrier between open source optimizers and the industrial matlab user. *Foundations of computer-aided process operations*, pages 8–11, 2012.

[7] L. Danon, J. Duch, A. Arenas, and A. Díaz-guilera. Comparing community structure identification. *J. Stat. Mech*, 2005.

[8] L. Du, X. Li, and Y. Shen. Robust nonnegative matrix factorization via half-quadratic minimization. In *ICDM*, pages 201–210, 2012.

[9] L. Du and Y.-D. Shen. Unsupervised feature selection with adaptive structure learning. In *Proceedings of the 21th ACM SIGKDD International Conference on Knowledge Discovery and Data Mining*, pages 209–218. ACM.

[10] H. Eldardiry and J. Neville. An analysis of how ensembles of collective classifiers improve predictions in graphs. In *CIKM*, pages 225–234, 2012.

[11] L. Getoor and B. Taskar. *Introduction to statistical relational learning.* MIT press, 2007.

[12] S. Ghosh and et al. Understanding and combating link farming in the twitter social network. In *Proceedings of the 21st international conference on World Wide Web*, pages 61–70. ACM, 2012.

[13] M. A. Hogg and D. I. Terry. Social identity and self-categorization processes in organizational contexts. *Academy of management review*, 25(1):121–140, 2000.

[14] X. Hu, J. Tang, H. Gao, and H. Liu. Actnet: Active learning for networked texts in microblogging. In *SDM*, pages 306–314. Citeseer, 2013.

[15] D. Jensen, J. Neville, and B. Gallagher. Why collective inference improves relational classification. In *KDD*, pages 593–598. ACM, 2004.

[16] D. Kong, R. Fujimaki, J. Liu, F. Nie, and C. Ding. Exclusive feature learning on arbitrary structures via l1,2-norm. In *NIPS*, pages 1655–1663. 2014.

[17] N. Lin. Social networks and status attainment. *Annual review of sociology*, pages 467–487, 1999.

[18] J. Liu and J. Ye. Moreau-Yosida regularization for grouped tree structure learning. In *NIPS*, pages 1459–1467, 2010.

[19] W. Liu, P. P. Pokharel, and J. C. Príncipe. Correntropy: properties and applications in non-gaussian signal processing. *Signal Processing, IEEE Transactions on*, 55(11):5286–5298, 2007.

[20] Q. Lu and L. Getoor. Link-based classification. In *ICML*, volume 3, pages 496–503, 2003.

[21] S. A. Macskassy and F. Provost. A simple relational classifier. In *MRDM-2003*, page 64. Citeseer.

[22] S. A. Macskassy and F. Provost. Classification in networked data: A toolkit and a univariate case study. *JMLR*, 8:935–983, 2007.

[23] L. Meier, S. Van De Geer, and P. Bühlmann. The group lasso for logistic regression. *Journal of the Royal Statistical Society: Series B (Statistical Methodology)*, 70(1):53–71, 2008.

[24] J. Neville and D. Jensen. Leveraging relational autocorrelation with latent group models. In *4th International Workshop on Multi-relational mining*, pages 49–55. ACM, 2005.

[25] M. Newman. Modularity and community structure in networks. *PNAS*, 103(23):8577âĂŞ8582, 2006.

[26] F. Nie, H. Wang, H. Huang, and C. Ding. Early active learning via robust representation and structured sparsity. In *Proceedings of IJCAI*, pages 1572–1578. AAAI Press, 2013.

[27] L. Page and et al. The pagerank citation ranking: Bringing order to the web. 1999.

[28] A. Rajadesingan, R. Zafarani, and H. Liu. Sarcasm detection on twitter: A behavioral modeling approach. In *WSDM 2015*. ACM, 2015.

[29] D. Seung and L. Lee. Algorithms for non-negative matrix factorization. In *NIPS*, volume 13, pages 556–562, 2011.

[30] J. Tang and H. Liu. Unsupervised feature selection for linked social media data. In *SIGKDD*, 2012.

[31] J. Tang, J. Sun, C. Wang, and Z. Yang. Social influence analysis in large-scale networks. In *KDD*, pages 807–816. ACM, 2009.

[32] L. Tang and H. Liu. Relational learning via latent social dimensions. In *ACM International Conference on Knowledge Discovery and Data Mining*, 2009.

[33] R. Tibshirani, M. Saunders, S. Rosset, J. Zhu, and K. Knight. Sparsity and smoothness via the fused lasso. *Journal of the Royal Statistical Society: Series B (Statistical Methodology)*, 67(1):91–108, 2005.

[34] X. Wang, L. Tang, H. Gao, and H. Liu. Discovering overlapping groups in social media. In *ICDM*, 2010.

[35] L. Wu, A. Chin, G. Xu, L. Du, X. Wang, K. Meng, Y. Guo, and Y. Zhou. Who will follow your shop? exploiting multiple information sources in finding followers. In *DASFAA*, pages 401–415, 2013.

[36] L. Wu, L. Du, B. Liu, G. Xu, Y. Ge, Y. Fu, J. Li, Y. Zhou, and H. Xiong. Heterogeneous metric learning with content-based regularization for software artifact retrieval. In *ICDM*, pages 610–619, 2014.

[37] G. Xu. *Social Media Mining and Social Network Analysis: Emerging Research: Emerging Research.* IGI Global, 2013.

[38] Z. Xu, V. Tresp, S. Yu, and K. Yu. Nonparametric relational learning for social network analysis. In *KDD 2008 Workshop on Social Network Mining and Analysis*, 2008.

[39] R. Zafarani, A. A. Mohammad, and H. Liu. *Social Media Mining: An Introduction.* 2014.

Equality and Social Mobility in Twitter Discussion Groups

Katherine Ellis
Department of Electrical and Computer Engineering
UC San Diego
La Jolla, CA
kellis@ucsd.edu *

Moises Goldszmidt
Samsung Research America (SRA)
Mountain View, CA
moises.goldszmidt@gmail.com

Gert Lanckriet
Department of Electrical and Computer Engineering
UC San Diego
La Jolla, CA
glanckriet@ucsd.edu

Nina Mishra
Computer Science Dept.
Stanford University
Palo Alto, CA
nmishra@gmail.com

Omer Reingold
Samsung Research America (SRA)
Mountain View, CA
omer.reingold@gmail.com

ABSTRACT

Online groups, including chat groups and forums, are becoming important avenues for gathering and exchanging information ranging from troubleshooting devices, to sharing experiences, to finding medical information and advice. Thus, issues about the *health* and *stability* of these groups are of particular interest to both industry and academia. In this paper we conduct a large scale study with the objectives of first, characterizing essential aspects of the interactions between the participants of such groups and second, characterizing how the nature of these interactions relate to the health of the groups. Specifically, we concentrate on Twitter Discussion Groups (TDGs), self-organized groups that meet on Twitter by agreeing on a hashtag, date and time. These groups have repeated, real-time meetings and are a rising phenomenon on Twitter. We examine the interactions in these groups in terms of the *social equality* and *mobility* of the exchange of attention between participants, according to the @mention convention on Twitter. We estimate the health of a group by measuring the retention rate of participants and the change in the number of meetings over time. We find that social equality and mobility are correlated, and that equality and mobility are related to a group's health. In fact, equality and mobility are as predictive of a group's health as some prior characteristics used to predict health of other online groups. Our findings are based on studying 100 thousand sessions of over two thousand discussion groups over the period of June 2012 to June 2013. These finding are not only relevant to stakeholders interested in maintaining these groups, but to researchers and academics interested in understanding the behavior of participants in online discussions. We also find the parallel with findings on the relationship between economic mobility and equality and health indicators in real-world nations striking and thought-provoking.

Categories and Subject Descriptors

I.5 [**Pattern Recognition**]: General

Keywords

Social Networks; Generative Models; Graph Analysis

1. INTRODUCTION

Online groups are of interest to researchers for a variety of reasons. First, there is a wealth of information and expertise on a variety of topics being discussed in online groups. In some cases groups cover solutions on how to deal with technical issues that are otherwise hard to find. Some discussions can also provide a sense of the pulse and sentiment on different socio-political issues. Similarly, information and opinions on books, music and movies are often shared. Second (and the motivation behind our work), these groups provide an incredible new telescope to study the nature of human interaction and behavior, albeit in a particular environment with all the biases inherent to the media (online interactions), at scale. From a pragmatic point of view, stakeholders would like to understand how to keep the groups active and healthy. From a scientific point of view, answers to these questions provide some insight into the nature of human interactions.

Online communities manifest in a number of forms — some examples that have been studied in the literature include Internet Relay Chats [25], Yahoo groups [3] and Ning groups [17]. In this work we focus on Twitter discussion groups (TDGs) [9]. TDGs are synchronized, real-time conversations that occur repeatedly (sometimes periodically), and with sessions usually lasting 1-2 hours. Participants agree on a hashtag, date and time, and then append the hashtag to their tweet so others in the group can follow the conversation at that date and time using the standard Twitter interface. Topics of these groups are numerous and varied. For example, there are support groups for postpartum depression and borderline personality disorder. Other groups enable participants to connect with others with similar hobbies and interests like skiing, photography, movies,

*Work done while Katherine, Moises, Nina, and Omer were at Microsoft Research, Silicon Valley.

WSDM 2016, February 22-25, 2016, San Francisco, CA, USA

http://dx.doi.org/10.1145/2835776.2835814

wines and food. Some of these groups have a moderator (which may change with meetings), some invite medical experts and other personalities, and some are organized around sport team events. The richness of subject matter and popularity of Twitter makes it a compelling social network to study. Additionally, the real-time nature and limited time window of each TDG session is more similar to real-world group meetings than some other online forms of discussions such as forums and message boards.

Our first goal in this paper is to characterize the interactions of participants in a TDG, in terms of the attention exchange through the "@mention" mechanism. In particular, we characterize the interaction between the participants in terms of social *equality* and *mobility*, where the analogous currency is the accumulation and distribution of attention. Mechanistically, participants in Twitter give and receive attention via an "@mention." A user directs a tweet to a specific individual by @mentioning them to strike a conversation, to reply to a question or comment, or by retweeting the content of that user. In all these cases a user is explicitly signaling the importance of the other user and/or the content (s)he has generated. In groups with high equality the attention is divided more evenly between participants. In groups with bigger degrees of social mobility, members are able to move between different levels of attention from session to session. These concepts will be more formally defined in section 5.

Our second goal is to establish the relationship between these social equality and mobility characteristics and the *health* of a TDG. Specifically, we measure group health by the retention rate of participants over time and stability in terms of the number of sessions per period. Intuitively, a group is healthy if many people continue to attend sessions and sessions continue to take place regularly. We take inspiration from the socioeconomics literature where research has demonstrated that countries with more egalitarian income distribution and with better possibilities of economic mobility tend to be healthier [29, 14, 12, 26]. Health in these studies is measured in a variety of ways including life expectancy, infant mortality, and homicide rates.

In this paper we present the results of a large scale study of over two thousand Twitter discussion groups with over 100 thousand sessions. To the best of our knowledge this is the first large scale study to quantify the relationship between social equality and mobility to the health of online groups at scale. The main contributions of our study are:

1. A probabilistic model that captures interaction patterns between users (based on the models introduced in [1]). We establish that each participant in the TDG can be profiled by a probability distribution on three archetypical patterns of interaction. Archetype A is the one that receives the most attention (mentions), archetype B is the one that gives the most attention, and archetype C is the less active. See Section 4 for further discussion and definitions.[1]

2. We establish that mobility and inequality are statistically correlated and we find that (a) there are high degrees of inequality in TDGs (the top 10% gets 40% of the attention) but there are high degrees of mobility (so it is not always the same 10% that receives the bulk of the attention).

3. Higher mobility and lower inequality correlate to and predict healthier groups. In fact, equality and mobility are so powerful that they are as predictive of a group's health as other graph-based statistics used to predict health. We observe similar results even when concentrating on natural subsets of TDGs such as cohesive groups (where there are high levels of interconnectivity between frequent participants).

[1]One may try to measure attention by simply counting the number of @mentions received by a participant (which can lead to definitions of equality and mobility). Such a "first approximation" is limited in that it fails to take into account the source of each @mention (*e.g.*, being mentioned by a central participant may be more indicative that the participant being mentioned is more central too).

2. RELATED WORK

We next describe how our work compares to prior research in machine learning, social networks, and sociology.

Role Identification in Networks.

A variety of techniques aim to discover core and periphery structures in networks. Borgatti and Everett [6] investigate techniques for identifying core and periphery nodes. Subsequent work [23] assigned nodes along a continuous spectrum from those that lie in the heart of a core to those that lie in the outer reaches of the periphery. Other methods core/periphery identification methods include [11, 13].

Another line of work that identifies roles in networks is the Mixed-Membership Stochastic Block model [1]. In this model, each node is modeled by a distribution over k types — these types are defined by a square $k \times k$ matrix indicating the likelihood that type i communicates with type j. One of the benefits of this model is that a user can probabilistically take on every role (as opposed to being assigned exactly one), and it seamlessly weights the importance of each role in the communication. We adapt this model for our setting by using it to identify the different roles of participants in a session (we expand upon this in Section 4). Note that there is extensive literature in the sociology community that describes the functional roles that individuals play in groups [4]. For example, there are task roles (*e.g.*, opinion seeker, evaluator), social and maintenance roles (*e.g.*, supporter, harmonizer) and individual Roles (*e.g.*, aggressor). While these definitions are quite compelling, due to the scale of data that we process we require automated techniques for role identification.

Group Growth.

A large-scale study of 44K Yahoo groups was conducted in [3]. Yahoo groups differ from Twitter discussion groups in that the former are more akin to a forum without predesignated meetings, while the latter are real-time meetings. One interesting discovery made in [3] is that people who eventually become heavily-engaged receive preferential treatment from the first message that they post (see also [16]). This finding may be an early indication that mobility, or ability to reach the core, is signaled in the first communication with a group.

Kairam et al [17] study Ning groups which are more akin to forums where people post content at will and not within predesignated windows of time. The decline of a Twitter discussion group is thus more readily apparent. In contrast, [17] define group death as a group that stops adding new members. In addition, while the object of study is friendship links in the Ning graph, in our work, the object of study is @mention, a finer granularity interaction that can encourage people to remain in the conversation.

Other factors are also known to affect why people join and leave online communities. A person with more friends in a group is more likely to join [18] and the more interconnected their friends are, the more this likelihood increases [2]. This finding may also be viewed as a signal of the importance of mobility in that if a person has many friends already in the core of a group, it may increase their chances of becoming core members. On the opposite side, infrequent communication hampers group responsiveness [19] while excessive communication is perceived as message overload [7, 15].

Twitter Discussion Groups.

The initial discovery of Twitter groups was reported in [10]. In that work, a *group* was also represented as a hashtag, but the definition was more strict. In addition to requiring that the group met in a synchronized window of time, their work also required that meetings occur with predictable regularity, *i.e.*, every t days, and that the group was cohesive in the sense that the people who attended the most meetings communicated with each other. We investigate synchronized and cohesive groups, but drop the requirement that groups meet with strict regularity. Discussion groups were defined in [9], where the goal was to rank chats according to a specified query. This paper focuses on modeling social structure and predicting group health.

Equality and Mobility.

Prior work has investigated the differences between more and less equal societies [22, 20, 28]. For example, countries with more egalitarian income distributions tend to have higher life expectancy rates [27], lower infant mortality rates [29], lower homicide rates [14, 12, 26] and more social mobility [5, 30]. These correlations were discovered at national scales, *e.g.*, the US has very inequitable income differences and also lower life expectancy. While Twitter discussion groups may lack the diversity and intricacies of real-world economies, we can see them as a microcosm of society in which people form relationships, exchange ideas and participate in a community. The economic constructs in these works have inspired us to measure the exchange of attention in Twitter (via the @mention) as a sort of currency. In our work, we ask whether the correlations found at national levels are mirrored in the Twitter equivalents of these measures. (No causal claims are made.)

3. REPRESENTATION OF TWITTER DATA

In this section we describe the process of taking raw tweets and (a) identifying the sessions that constitute discussion groups, (b) representing the exchange of attention amongst the participants in each session using the @mention graph, and (c) modeling archetypical patterns of interaction and participant profiles.

3.1 Identifying TDG sessions

In this study we follow [9] and regard TDGs as self-organized and synchronized group discussions focused on specific topics that use Twitter as a platform to meet with some regularity. Logistically, members agree on a hashtag and a meeting time (*e.g.*, 3pm Pacific Time on Sundays) to discuss a subject of interest. A participant indicates his or her involvement in the discussion by including the designated hashtag in each of their tweets. We call a specific instance, or meeting, of a given group a *session*.

Operationally, we define a session as a two-hour window in which at least 20% of the week's tweets using the hashtag occur within the window [9]. For our study, we restricted our analyses to TDGs that had at least 12 sessions in a 12-month period. In addition, TDGs should contain between 25 and 200 participants [2] in each session and at least 5 participants who attended at least 5 sessions.

Given the above criteria, we conducted a search on the complete corpus of Twitter for a 12 month period (June 2012 - June 2013) and identified a total of 2418 different TDGs consisting of over 113,000 individual sessions. This task required the analysis of petabytes of data which we achieved using the SCOPE language [8] on a large distributed computing cluster.

3.2 Representing sessions

For our analysis, we strip away the semantics and content of the conversation and focus on the structure of interactions by representing each session by an @mention graph. In Twitter, a user explicitly *mentions* another user by appending an "@" symbol to the name of the other user in the text of the tweet (For example, a tweet mentioning user Y will include the text "@Y"). We separate mentions into three types: replies, retweets, and other tweets. When user X replies to a tweet created by user Y, their new tweet will mention user Y. Similarly, when user X retweets (an action similar to forwarding an email) a tweet created by user Y, X's new tweet will mention user Y. In general, the author of a tweet can mention user Y by adding the text "@Y" anywhere in the tweet. In each of these situations, we view user X mentioning user Y as user X giving attention to user Y — either by responding to something user Y said, promoting something user Y said, or specifically naming user Y.

An @mention graph is defined as a graph $\mathcal{G} = (\mathcal{N}, \mathcal{E})$ where the nodes $\mathcal{N}$ are participants in the session and the edges $\mathcal{E}$ are @mentions between participants. For example, if participant X mentions participant Y, there will be an edge from X to Y. If participant X mentions multiple participants, there will be an edge from X to each participant mentioned. In our analyses we differentiate between replies, retweets and other tweets. We decompose the set of edges into $\mathcal{E} = \{\mathcal{E}_{RT}, \mathcal{E}_{Re}, \mathcal{E}_{O}\}$, where $\mathcal{E}_{RT}$ are retweets, $\mathcal{E}_{Re}$ are replies and $\mathcal{E}_{O}$ are all other tweets containing an @mention. In addition, each edge $e \in \mathcal{E}$ has an integer weight corresponding to the number of times the mention occurred during the session. A visualization of the @mention graph for an example TDG session is shown in Figure 1 (a).

4. MODELING SESSIONS

To analyze equality and mobility in terms of attention (@mention) exchanges, we generate a latent model of interactions based on the explicit evidence in the @mention graph. Our model is a generalization of a well known generative probabilistic model called the *mixed membership stochas-*

[2]We focused on groups small enough to allow interactions between participants – too large of a group inhibits real discussion.

Figure 1: The @mention graph and learned model for an example session of the TDG #mtos, "Movie Talk on Sunday".

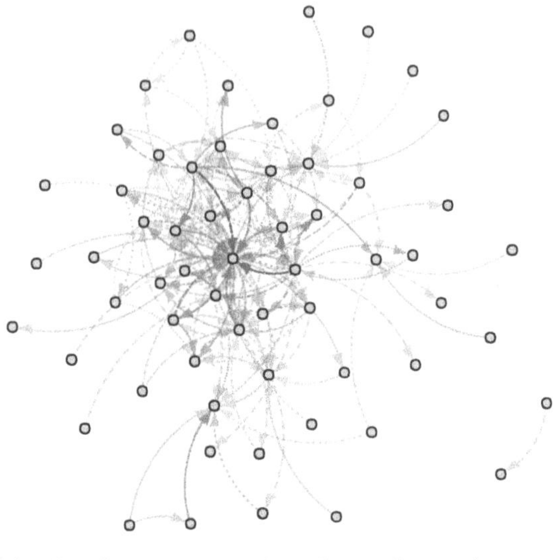

(a) The @mention graph. Green (dashed) edges are retweets, red (dotted) edges are replies, purple (solid) edges are normal @mentions.

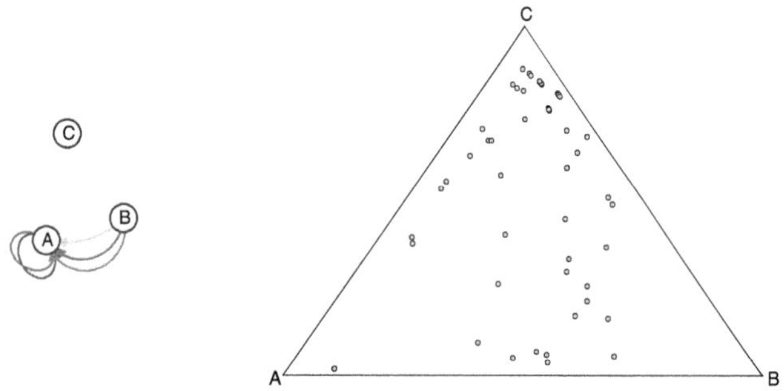

(b) The archetype matrices Λ. (c) The membership vectors π on the simplex.

tic blockmodel [1, 24]. The next few subsections describe the model and its output in the form of a set of roles for the participants in the TDG sessions. These roles form the basis for the characterization of mobility and inequality.

4.1 The interaction model

For modeling the interactions between the participants, given the @mention graph, we extend the generative model in [1] as follows: each participant is characterized by a latent vector π that represents a distribution over the different *roles* that the participant can take in terms of his/her actions (e.g., initiating or receiving an @mention) in the session. We call these roles *archetypes*. In addition, we want to capture (a) the different types of edges that @mention graph exhibits (i.e., replies, retweets and other tweets) and (b) the number of times specific mentions are made. To this end we generalize the model to contain 3 matrices corresponding to the 3 modes of interaction. Each entry in each of one of the matrices Λ_i represents the probability that a participant of archetype X interacts (in a specific way) with a participant of archetype Y. Furthermore, the entries of the matrix contain the intensity parameter of a Poisson distribution, which encodes the expected number of times that the different archetypes interact. Thus the activity in an @mention graph $\mathcal{G} = (\mathcal{N}, \mathcal{E})$ where $\mathcal{E} = \{\mathcal{E}_{RT}, \mathcal{E}_{Re}, \mathcal{E}_O\}$ is modeled according to the following generative process:

- For each node $i \in \mathcal{N}$
  - Draw a K dimensional latent archetype vector: $\pi_i \sim \text{Dirichlet}(\alpha)$
- For each pair of nodes $(i, j) \in \mathcal{N} \times \mathcal{N}$:
  - Draw archetype indicator for the initiator, $z_{i \to j} \sim \text{Multinomial}(\pi_i)$.
  - Draw archetype indicator for the receiver, $z_{i \leftarrow j} \sim \text{Multinomial}(\pi_j)$.
  - For each edge type $\mathcal{E}_m \in \mathcal{E}$:
    * Sample the weight of the edge, $e_{ij,m} \sim \text{Poisson}(z_{i \to j} \Lambda_m z_{i \leftarrow j})$.

where $\Lambda_m(i, j)$ is the Poisson intensity parameter, *i.e.*, the expected number of type m mentions of archetype j by archetype i. Our use of a generative model to uncover the latent roles of the participants, as opposed as for example, counting directed edges in the @mention graph, provides the ability to automatically take into account the importance of the edge in relation to the role of both the participants (nodes) at the extremes of each edge.

4.2 Fitting session models

We used variational message passing [31] in the Infer.NET package [21] to fit the parameters of our model for each TDG session (*i.e.*, the type vector π for each participant and the interaction matrices Λ). Although there are a large number of sessions (>113,000), parallelization was straightforward as we fit a model for each session independently.[3] We used a combination of Dryad/Linq [32] for managing the distributed (parallel) computation of the models on a cluster of 20 servers.

The original model as well as our generalized version has a free parameter: the number of archetypes K. This is a model selection problem, and it is usually resolved using a penalized likelihood approach such as the Bayesian Information Criterion (BIC) [1]. The tension is that if K is too small, we may be unable to express important aspects of the interaction, while if it is too large we may be overfitting. For our analysis, we also need the same K in all models to enable the computation of statistics of groups (across sessions) and to be able to compare and contrast among the different groups.[4] we performed an exploratory analysis over a sample covering over 10% of the total number of sessions. Our observations were that the majority of the models maximized BIC for $K = 3$, and over 75% of the models maximized BIC for $K < 4$. We therefore settled on $K = 3$.We observed in our explorations that increasing K by 1 has the effect of identifying subgroups inside the session rendering two (essentially) indistinguishable archetypes in terms of the mentioning action. Thus, we don't lose any information relevant to our analysis by forcing $K = 3$ in these cases. Similarly, the addition of an archetype in those

[3]Note that fitting a model per TDG (as opposed to by session) would remove traces of the evolution of the archetypes over time.
[4]This need is different, for example, from trying to analyze in more detail the roles of participants in an isolated session.

sessions where BIC was maximized by $K = 2$, forces the split of one archetype into two very similar archetypes in terms of the mentioning action.

4.3 Naming the archetypes

In addition, we must address the identifiability issue in comparing latent models between different sessions and groups. To this end we examined the expected number of mentions for each archetype (according to the Λ matrices), and devised a naming convention in order to match archetypes between sessions. We use the letters A, B, and C to denote the three archetypes. Formally, the expected number of mentions received by archetype k is computed as:

$$E[k \text{ is mentioned}] = \sum_m \sum_{l \neq k} \Pi(l)\Lambda_m(l,k),$$

where $\Pi(l)$ is the prior probability of archetype l, *i.e.*, $\Pi(l) = \frac{1}{N}\sum_{i=1}^{N} \pi_i(l)$. Similarly, the expected number of mentions sent by archetype k is

$$E[k \text{ mentions}] = \sum_m \sum_{l \neq k} \Pi(l)\Lambda_m(k,l).$$

We define A to be the archetype that has the highest expected number of mentions in a session. On average, A displays a significantly higher probability of being mentioned than any other archetype. The two other archetypes are not as well distinguished by their expected number of times being mentioned, but are quite different on average when considering their expected number of times mentioning others. We thus define B to be the archetype with the higher expected number of mentions (among the two remaining). The remaining archetype is named C.

In our data analysis over the 113K sessions, we found that 100% of groups have E[A is mentioned] more than double E[B is mentioned], while 57% of groups had E[B mentions] more than double E[C mentions] and 73% of groups had E[B mentions] at least 50% more than E[C mentions].

4.4 A qualitative look at session models

The sessions models learn abstractions describing prototypical patterns of interaction that are directly interpretable. Figure 1 shows an example session for the TDG "#MTOS" (Movie Talk on Sunday). Each session of Movie Talk on Sunday is centered on a set of movie-related questions. Throughout the session, a host or moderator tweets questions and participants in the chat answer the questions and discuss their answers. In this session of "mtos", there was a guest host who wrote the list of questions. He is introduced at the beginning of the session by the group's founder. Participants often reply to him when answering questions (although answers are often provided using only the hashtag #mtos, without mentioning anyone), and thank him at the end of the session by mentioning him. As participants respond to questions throughout the session, they often retweet answers they agree with, or reply to a user to engage more about an answer they made. In part (b) of Figure 1 the archetypes A, B and C are represented graphically in terms of the probabilities of mentioning other archetypes. We see that the most common modes of interaction are archetype B mentioning archetype A, or archetype A mentioning another archetype A. The most likely type of mention is a reply from B to A. In part (c) the latent profiles π of each participant in the session are visualized on the simplex. The guest host is located at the bottom left corner of the simplex, indicating that he is the most dominant archetype A participant in the session. This is expected, as the host he sends and receives the most attention. Participants along the left edge of the simplex have low weight on archetype B — they may be mentioned frequently but rarely mention others. For example, one participant that falls in this location provided some answers that others agreed with and retweeted. Participants along the right edge of the simplex have low weight on archetype A — they may mention others often but are rarely mentioned. One participant that falls near the middle of this area is a user who often retweeted answers to signify agreement. Notice that the bottom right corner is fairly empty of participants, indicating that in this session, there were no participants who mentioned others often but were never mentioned themselves. This seems to indicate that if you initiate discussion in this community you will receive some attention in exchange.

5. STATISTICS

In order to examine concepts of social mobility and inequality in TDGs, we define a set of statistics based on the session models learned in the previous section.

Equality.

We propose a set of statistics characterizing whether attention is distributed equally amongst participants in the discussion (or to what extent it is concentrated in the hands of the privileged few). The intent is to mirror notions of economic inequality, namely, to what extent the total wealth in a country is controlled by the wealthiest X% of people (commonly "the 1%"). We propose three sets of statistics with the objective of obtaining analogous metrics of inequality over TDG participants. These statistics are computed on the session models described in the previous section and averaged over all the sessions of a TDG.

The first statistic consists of the proportion of the total weight on archetype k that is held by the 10% of participants who have the largest weight on archetype k:

$$\text{Top10}_k = \frac{\sum_{i \in S} \pi_i(k)}{\sum_{i=1}^{N} \pi_i(k)},$$

where $S =$ is the set of $N/10$ participants with largest π_k. Note that as Top10_k approaches 1, more attention is focused on a select few. A small value suggests that attention is spread more evenly.

We explore two other ways to measure disparity in attention. For each archetype, we can first order participants according to their weight on the archetype, and then identify the top fraction of participants required to reach 50% of the weight on the archetype. A third simple set of statistics is the average weight on each archetype. A complete list of inequality statistics can be found in Table 1.

Mobility.

Similarly to inequality, we are interested in characterizing the ability of participants to change their dominant archetype over time. For example, a change in proportion from archetype C to archetype A in the profile of a participant will signal a change in the status of that participant. This also mirrors the notion of mobility in economic terms that characterize ability to move (usually upward) in income over time. Mobility statistics are computed over a sequence of session models, and thus can only be measured for participants that attend multiple sessions. We compute mobility statistics over the set N_a of participants who attended at least five sessions. As with the equality statistics, we explore three sets of measures of mobility.

The first statistic is the average range of participants' weight on a specific archetype, computed as,

$$\text{AvgRange}_k = \frac{1}{N_a}\sum_{i=1}^{N_a} \max_t \pi_{i,t}(k) - \min_t \pi_{i,t}(k).$$

It follows that larger ranges signal greater mobility in participants' archetype over time.

The second statistic is the probability that a given participant will have at least half their membership in a specific archetype (most notably the archetype A),

$$\text{Half}_k = Pr(\pi(k) >= 0.5) = \frac{1}{N_a}\sum_{i=1}^{N_a} \mathbb{I}[\pi_i(k) >= 0.5]$$

Since A is the archetype that receives the most attention, Half_A measures the fraction of participants that receive a lot of attention in at least one session.

The third and final set of statistics encodes the probability of transitioning between archetypes. We construct a state space model over the archetypes and build a Markov chain to describe the probabilities that a participant will transition between archetypes in subsequent sessions. The model has four states: A, B, C and not present. The transition probabilities between each state are calculated by summing the changes between each participant's type from one session to the next (only participants who attended at least 5 meetings were included). Higher between-state transition probabilities indicate higher mobility between archetypes. For example a high $Pr(B \rightarrow A)$ indicates "upward" mobility, as a participant is more likely to move from the less attention-gathering to the more attention-gathering archetype.

Additional Statistics.

In addition to mobility and equality, we consider other statistics derived from the session models. These include the expected number of mentions of each tweet type (reply, retweet, etc.), and the probability of each archetype being mentioned. Details can be found in Table 1. Further, we compute several statistics independently of the models. These include the number of sessions, average size of sessions, clique sizes and other graph-based statistics that have been successfully used in previous work to predict growth and decline of online groups [17]. We will compare these additional statistics to the model-based mobility and equality statistics in upcoming sections.

6. CHARACTERIZING EQUALITY AND MOBILITY IN TDGS

Figure 2 summarizes inequality and mobility statistics for the TDGs we studied. Overall, we found that groups exhibit significant levels of inequality. On average, the top 10% of archetype A held 41% of the weight on archetype A. At the same time we also see that many groups exhibit high levels of mobility. On average, the range of weight on archetype A is 0.3, and in many groups a significantly higher range is observed. In fact, the distribution is highly bimodal.

Figure 2: Distribution of (a) inequality and (b) mobility statistics for all 2418 TDGs. Groups are separated by graph structure into star, fragmented, and other groups.

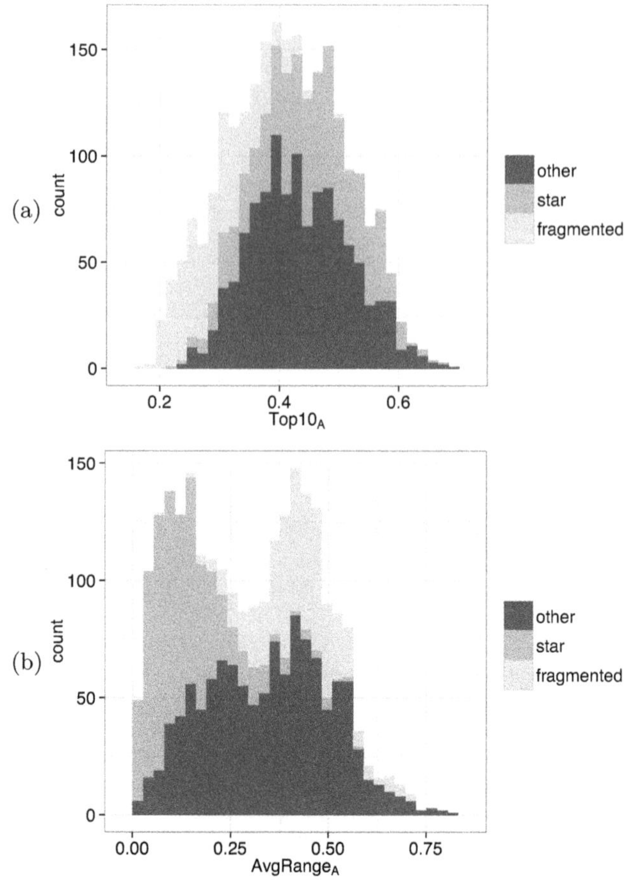

Star and fragmented @mention graphs.

We find that the bimodality in the distribution of mobility across TDGs can be explained by identifying two subtypes of very different structures of @mention graphs. We define star graphs as @mention graphs in which over X% of incoming edges are directed to one or two participants. We define fragmented graphs as @mention graphs in which less than Y% of participants are in the largest connected component. For our analyses we set X to 90% and Y to 75%. With these subclasses of graph structures, the bimodality of the mobility statistic seen in Figure 2 can be explained by grouping TDGs into fragmented and star groups. We see that groups corresponding to star graphs display the highest degree of inequality and the lowest degree of mobility, while the fragmented groups display the opposite characteristics.

We notice that many star graphs correspond to groups that center around a celebrity or a television show. The celebrity might tweet something, and many people retweet or reply to them. Similarly, when the TV show airs, many people will mention the TV show handle in their tweets discussing the show. In these cases the celebrity-like participant commands an unequal share of the attention, and it is very unlikely for any other given participant to move into such a position of power. Conversely, many fragmented graphs correspond to groups that center around a common interest, such as a sports team. For example, when the team plays, many people will tweet to each other about the game, al-

Table 1: List of all statistics.

		Feature name	Description
Model Statistics	Inequality	$\Pi[k]$	Average weight on archetype k
		$Weight50_k$	The fraction of participants required to reach 50% of the weight on archetype k
		$Top10_k$	The proportion of the total weight on archetype k that is held by the top 10% of participants
	Mobility	$AvgRange_k$	The average range of weight on archetype k
		$Half_k$	The probability that a given participant will have at least 0.5 weight on archetype k
		$Pr(k \rightarrow l)$	Probability of transitioning from archetype k to archetype l from one session to the next
		$\mathbb{E}[k$ is mentioned$]$	Expected number of times archetype k is mentioned
		$\mathbb{E}[k$ mentions$]$	Expected number of mentions made by archetype k
		$\mathbb{E}[k$ recevies a mention of type $l]$	Expected number of times archetype k is mentioned with a certain tweet type (retweet, reply or normal)
		$\mathbb{E}[k$ mentions of type $l]$	Expected number of times archetype k mentions with a certain tweet type (retweet, reply or normal)
		Pr(k is mentioned)	Probability that a given tweet mentions archetype k
		Pr(k mentions)	Probability that a given tweet is sent by archetype k
Other Statistics		numSessions	Number of sessions between 25 and 200 participants in the 12 month period we observed
		avgN	Average number of participants in each session
		ratioActiveN	Ratio of the number of participants who attended at least 5 meetings over the average number of participants
		avgAttendance	Average number of meetings participants attended
		density	Average number of tweets per participant
		avgTime	Average number of days between sessions
		stdTime	Standard deviation of the number of days between sessions
		maxClique	Size of the maximal clique
		nClusters	Number of disconnected clusters
		maxCluster	Size of largest cluster
		cliqueRatio	Fraction of participants in the maximal clique
		clusterRatio	Fraction of partcipants in the largest connected cluster
		centralityDegree	Average degree of centrality
		closeness	Average closeness (transitivity)

though there is no central participant leading discussion. In these cases attention can be spread more equally among participants and upward mobility in terms of attention may be more easily achieved. Figure 3 shows a few example @mention graphs belonging to these subtypes.

6.1 Correlation of equality and mobility

We find that mobility and equality in TDGs are not independent. Using $Top10_A$ to represent inequality and $AvgRange_A$ to represent mobility[5], the coefficient of correlation between inequality and mobility is -0.512[6]. This negative correlation between inequality and mobility mirrors the relationship observed in socioeconomic studies — as inequality grows, it becomes more difficult to move between social strata. This relationship is intuitive when considering the "extreme" star and graph structures discussed in Section 6. However, concern that groups with these extreme graph structures may not represent "true discussion" (*i.e.*, groups that are so tightly organized around a central figure have limited interaction) leads us to consider another subtype of group that is more aligned with our traditional notion of a discussion-based community. Toward this end, we define a subtype of TDGs called cohesive groups.

Cohesive groups.

Cohesive TDGs have a solid core of members that interact among themselves and persist between sessions. More specifically, we define a group as "cohesive" if the 5 participants who attended the most sessions (over the course of a year) have at least 4 shared edges in the @mention graph representing every session. These "cohesive" groups capture our idea of a discussion-based group, requiring consistent interaction between several key participants. This cohesion measure has been used previously to identify Twitter groups [10]. When we restrict our analysis to only cohesive TDGs, we find that the inverse relationship between inequality and mobility holds — in fact, it is strengthened. The coefficient of correlation between $Top10_A$ and $AvgRange_A$ is -0.661. Figure 4 graphically displays this relationship. In Section 7, as we investigate how mobility and equality affect group health, we will pay special attention to the cohesive groups.

[5] We chose $Top10_A$ and $AvgRange_A$ as intuitive measures of inequality and mobility; the alternative statistics listed in table 1 show similar correlations.

[6] Correlation for star and fragmented groups is -0.324 and -0.068, respectively.

Figure 3: Examples of @mention graphs of three subtypes of TDGs. "Star" TDGs (a) have one (or two) participant(s) mentioned far more than the rest. "Fragmented" graphs (b) represent discussions with many disjointed participants. "Cohesive" TDGs (c) have a strongly connected main component of participants that persist between multiple sessions.

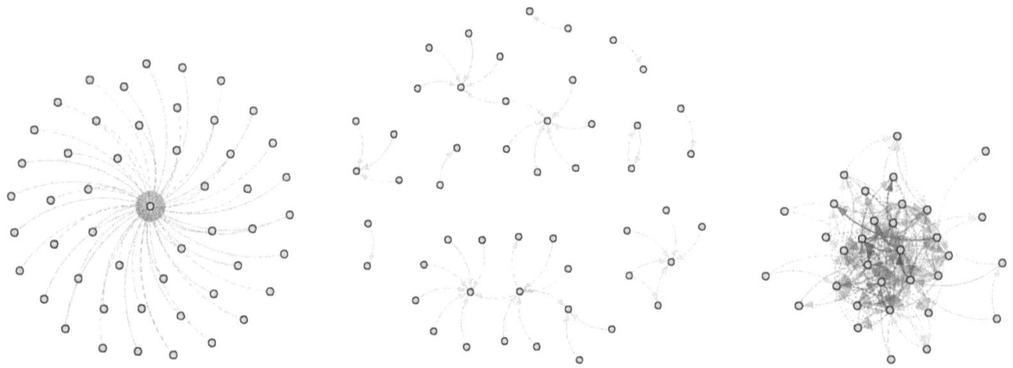

(a) star (b) fragmented (c) cohesive

Figure 4: Inequality and mobility are inversely correlated. For clarity, we show the relationship only for cohesive groups (r = -0.661, MSE = 0.018).

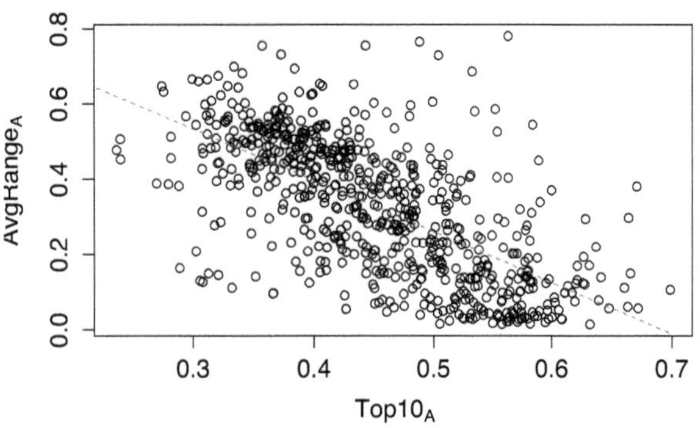

7. GROUP HEALTH

Finally, we study the relationship between the statistics computed in Section 5 and the health of a TDG. We use two measures of health: the stability or decline of the number of sessions of the group over time, and the power of retention of participants. Since this is a complex multivariate problem, we use machine learning and statistical pattern recognition to quantify these associations.

7.1 Session decline

Problem setup.

First, we attempt to use the statistics to actually *forecast* the decline or stability of the TDGs. More specifically, we use statistics computed from one year of data (June 2012 to June 2013) to predict changes in the following six months. We measure the change in the number of sessions between the 6 months from June 2012 to November 2012 and the 6 months from June 2013 to November 2013. We selected these time periods (the same six months of the year) to avoid any confounding seasonality effect (*e.g.*, chats about football going dormant in the springtime). We define two populations: those TDGs that declined by at least 70% in the number of sessions, and an equal number of the most *stable* TDGs (this resulted in 398 stable groups, namely those with less than 5% change). We build a classifier that takes as input the statistics of interest for a TDG (*e.g.*, mobility, inequality) and as output a decision on whether the group will remain *stable* or *decline*. The accuracy of this classifier is a measure of the precision by which one can establish the future change of a TDG just by looking at these computed statistics, and quantifies the predictive power of the statistics for the decline or stability of the TDG.

After benchmarking several classifiers, including random forests and support vector machines, we settled on logistic regression (augmented with L1 and L2 regularization) as the main classifier. The estimation of accuracy is done using 10 fold cross-validation. We gather results using the mobility and equality statistics, as well as some additional statistics we computed from the model (see Section 5. We also compare some statistics that are unrelated to the model — such as the number of sessions of the group, average number of participants, and maximal clique size in the @mention graph. These features correspond to some previously used to predict online group growth in related literature [17]. A full list of statistics is shown in Table 1. It is important to note here that our intention with these experiments is not to build the optimal classifier for precisely forecasting group decline, but to understand the relationships between these statistics (particularly those with meaningful interpretations in terms of social interactions, *i.e.*, mobility and inequality) and group health.

Results.

The results are presented in Table 2. We present classification results for all declining or stable TDGs (N = 796) and also for the subset of cohesive TDGs (N = 260). Despite the fact that forecasting is a very difficult problem, accuracies are still well above the 0.5 baseline.[7]. The accuracy using just the mobility statistics as input to the classifier is between 0.721 and 0.772. Most notably, the mobility statistics alone capture between 96% to 98% of the maximum accuracy (achieved using all the features), and comparable accuracy to the non-model features that have been successfully used in previous work to predict group growth [17]. As we relax the constraints on the definition of a stable TDG from exhibiting a change of 5% to plus/minus 14%, and sim-

[7]The two populations of declining and stable TDGs have an equal number of groups, namely 398.

ilarly we label a TDG as declining when it presents at least a 50% reduction, the accuracy of the forecasting exercise is reduced from 0.72 to 0.63, as this is a very noisy exercise. Yet, we remark that (a) this is still significant (*i.e.*, above the baseline of 0.50 – again equal populations) and (b) the relationships between the different group of statistics remain the same.

Table 2: Accuracy of predicting groups that declined (> 70% decline in number of meetings) vs. those that stayed stable (< 5% change in number of meetings) in the next six months (based on features from the previous year).

	All	Cohesive
Inequality	0.680 (0.052)	0.760 (0.090)
Mobility	0.721 (0.047)	0.772 (0.086)
All model	0.751 (0.064)	0.779 (0.074)
Non-model	0.693 (0.061)	0.772 (0.090)
All	0.754 (0.062)	0.785 (0.070)

Figure 5: Distributions of the mobility statistic measuring the average range of π_A, grouped by declining and stable TDGs.

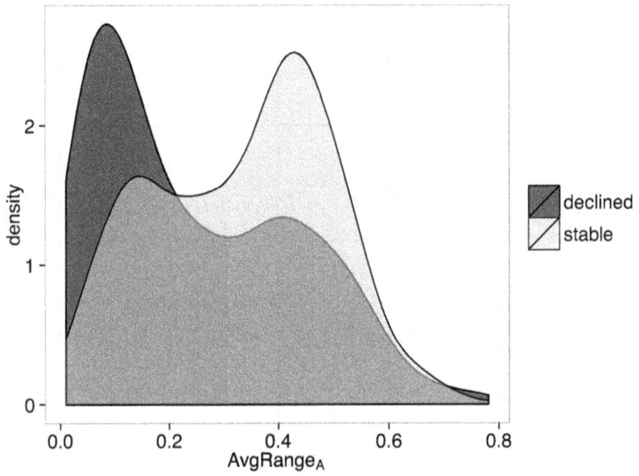

To understand the directionality of the relationship between equality or mobility and decline or stability, we build classifiers based on a single statistic. Using the equality statistic $Top10_A$ (see Table 1) alone, the threshold to classify a chat as "declining" is a value greater than or equal to 0.466 (0.59 accuracy[8]). This indicates that greater inequality in the distribution of attention over the participants in a TDG is associated with greater likelihood of the number of sessions declining in the future. Using the mobility statistics $AvgRange_A$ (see Table 1) alone, the threshold to classify a group as "declining" is a value less than or equal to 0.350 (0.62 accuracy). This indicates that lower mobility over the attention receiving archetype (A) between session to session is associated with greater likelihood of the number of sessions declining in the future. Figure 5 shows the distributions of the mobility statistic $AvgRange_A$ for declining and stable chats. We recall that the direction of these relationships match those found in socioeconomic research, where higher mobility and lower inequality were found to be associated with healthier nations.

[8]Performance was similar for the other features when taken individually. Higher performance with combined features indicates that they capture complementary information.

7.2 Participant retention

Problem Setup.

A second measure of a group's health is the retention rate of its participants, *i.e.*, how likely participants are to return to the group. We quantify the retention rate over 12 months of data as follows: Given that a participant attends a session in the first 10 months, what is the probability that he or she returns to a second session in those 12 months? Similar to the forecasting exercise in the previous section, we study the relationship between the group statistics and the *retention rate* using the accuracy of learned classifiers as a measure of association. We define two populations: the 300 groups that had the lowest retention rate and the 300 groups with highest retention rate. The resulting "low retention" population has retention rates below 12%, and the "high retention" population has retention rates above 42%. As before, we use logistic regression and 10 fold cross-validation to estimate performance.

Results.

Results of the retention rate classification task are presented in Table 3. Again, we show results for all groups (N = 600) and the subset of groups that are cohesive (N = 172). These results show that association between the group statistics and retention rate is even stronger than with decline (part of this is due to the fact that we are no longer predicting the future — retention rate is calculated for only the first 12 months of data). Mobility statistics alone result in accuracies between 0.830 and 0.872 — between 93 and 98 percent of the maximum accuracy. While highest classification accuracy is obtained using a combined set of statistics, comparable performance with the equality and mobility statistics alone indicates the presence of a relationship between these characteristics and the retention rate of a TDG.

Table 3: Classification accuracy distinguishing groups with high retention vs. low retention. 300 groups with lowest retention rate (< 0.12) vs. 300 groups with highest retention rate (> 0.42).

	All	Cohesive
Inequality	0.773 (0.054)	0.814 (0.081)
Mobility	0.834 (0.040)	0.872 (0.059)
All model	0.875 (0.039)	0.895 (0.061)
Non-model	0.800 (0.044)	0.855 (0.051)
All	0.887 (0.037)	0.890 (0.044)

8. CONCLUSIONS

In this paper we have proposed a framework for characterizing the interactions of participants in online discussion groups in terms of social equality and mobility. We have shown that in the context of TDGs, (a) mobility and inequality are statistically correlated, with an inverse relationship that mirrors the socioeconomic literature, and (b) higher mobility and lower inequality correlate to and predict healthier groups. In fact, equality and mobility are as predictive of a group's health as other characteristics of online groups that have been previously used to predict the health of online groups and communities. Such observations may be useful to group moderators or other stakeholders, as a more tangible metric on which to monitor the group.

These results hold even when restricting analysis to cohesive groups, which fit the natural idea of discussion-based communities with recurring members. We find these micro-level analogs in online discussion groups non-obvious and thought-provoking.

In any analysis such as this, some initial assumptions must be made. We chose to use a generative model to uncover latent spheres of attention and intuitive metrics of mobility and inequality, although there are many possible ways of defining these concepts. Future work should investigate how robust these results are to the modeling assumptions and parameter choices made. It would also be interesting to see if our findings hold for other types of online communities. In addition, while our results uncovered interesting correlations and predictive relations, further research is needed to establish causal relationship. In such a case, it could also be fascinating to uncover the social mechanisms in which equality and mobility may contribute to the health of an online community.

This work also spawns other interesting avenues for future research. Other measures of group health may be interesting, including: the quality of the exchanged content or diversity in terms of the demographic characteristics of participants. Also, while we shed some light on the demise of a group, there is much to be understood about their birth. If group formation is itself sparked on Twitter then there may be electronic trails that help us understand the different ways that groups form and there is an opportunity to characterize how the interactions between participants determine this birth. Additionally, our work is based on "machine-perceived" measures of equality and mobility. This gives us the advantage of quantifying at scale the connection to group health. Future work might explore how human-perceived notions of equality or mobility (which can perceive more than changes in the @mention graph) differs from these automatic measures. Finally, the level of attention that different participants receive within a typical session exhibit significant levels of inequality. Yet, over many sessions typical discussion groups display high levels of mobility (it is not the case that the same participants receive the attention). This raises the question of whether online communities (or at least those we examined) are closer to meritocracies than "real-word" communities.

9. REFERENCES

[1] E. M. Airoldi, D. M. Blei, S. E. Fienberg, and E. P. Xing. Mixed membership stochastic blockmodels. In *NIPS*, pages 33–40, 2009.

[2] L. Backstrom, D. Huttenlocher, J. Kleinberg, and X. Lan. Group formation in large social networks: Membership, growth, and evolution. In *KDD*, 2006.

[3] L. Backstrom, R. Kumar, C. Marlow, J. Novak, and A. Tomkins. Preferential behavior in online groups. In *WSDM*, 2008.

[4] K. D. Benne and P. Sheats. Functional roles of group members. *Journal of social issues*, 4(2):41–49, 1948.

[5] J. Blanden, P. Gregg, and S. Machin. Intergenerational mobility in europe and north america. *Report supported by the Sutton Trust, Centre for Economic Performance, London School of Economics*, 2005.

[6] S. P. Borgatti and M. G. Everett. Models of core/periphery structures. *Social networks*, 21(4):375–395, 2000.

[7] B. S. Butler. Membership size, communication activity, and sustainability: A resource-based model of online social structures. *Info. Sys. Research*, 12(4), Dec. 2001.

[8] R. Chaiken, B. Jenkins, P.-Å. Larson, B. Ramsey, D. Shakib, S. Weaver, and J. Zhou. Scope: easy and efficient parallel processing of massive data sets. *Proceedings of the VLDB Endowment*, 1(2):1265–1276, 2008.

[9] J. Cook, A. Das, K. Kenthapadi, and N. Mishra. Ranking twitter discussion groups. In *COSN*, 2014.

[10] J. Cook, K. Kenthapadi, and N. Mishra. Group chats on Twitter. In *WWW*, 2013.

[11] P. Csermely, A. London, L.-Y. Wu, and B. Uzzi. Structure and dynamics of core/periphery networks. *Journal of Complex Networks*, 1(2):93–123, 2013.

[12] P. Fajnzlber, D. Lederman, and N. Loayza. Inequality and violent crime. *JL & Econ.*, 45:1, 2002.

[13] P. Holme. Core-periphery organization of complex networks. *Physical Review E*, 72(4):046111, 2005.

[14] C.-C. Hsieh and M. D. Pugh. Poverty, income inequality, and violent crime: a meta-analysis of recent aggregate data studies. *Criminal Justice Review*, 18(2):182–202, 1993.

[15] Q. Jones, G. Ravid, and S. Rafaeli. Information overload and the message dynamics of online interaction spaces: A theoretical model and empirical exploration. *Info. Sys. Research*, 15(2), 2004.

[16] E. Joyce and R. Kraut. Predicting continued participation in newsgroups. *J. Comput. Mediat. Comm*, 11(3), 2006.

[17] S. R. Kairam, D. J. Wang, and J. Leskovec. The life and death of online groups: Predicting group growth and longevity. In *WSDM*, pages 673–682, 2012.

[18] G. Kossinets and D. J. Watts. Empirical analysis of an evolving social network. *Science*, 311(5757), 2006.

[19] M. L. Markus. Toward a "critical mass" theory of interactive media universal access, interdependence and diffusion. *Communication research*, 14(5), 1987.

[20] M. Marmot and R. Wilkinson. *Social determinants of health.* Oxford University Press, 2005.

[21] T. Minka, J. Winn, J. Guiver, S. Webster, Y. Zaykov, B. Yangel, A. Spengler, and J. Bronskill. Infer.NET 2.6, 2014. Microsoft Research Cambridge. http://research.microsoft.com/infernet.

[22] K. Pickett and R. Wilkinson. *The Spirit Level: Why Greater Equality Makes Societies Stronger.* Bloomsbury Publishing, 2010.

[23] M. P. Rombach, M. A. Porter, J. H. Fowler, and P. J. Mucha. Core-periphery structure in networks. *SIAM Journal on Applied mathematics*, 74(1):167–190, 2014.

[24] M. Shafiei and H. Chipman. Mixed-membership stochastic block-models for transactional networks. In *Data Mining (ICDM), 2010 IEEE 10th International Conference on*, pages 1019–1024, Dec 2010.

[25] C. C. Werry. Internet relay chat. *Computer-mediated communication: Linguistic, social and cross-cultural perspectives*, pages 47–63, 1996.

[26] R. Wilkinson. Why is violence more common where inequality is greater? *Annals of the New York Academy of Sciences*, 1036(1):1–12, 2004.

[27] R. G. Wilkinson. Income distribution and life expectancy. *BMJ: British Medical Journal*, 304(6820):165, 1992.

[28] R. G. Wilkinson. *Unhealthy societies: the afflictions of inequality.* Routledge, 2002.

[29] R. G. Wilkinson and K. E. Pickett. Income inequality and population health: a review and explanation of the evidence. *Social science & medicine*, 62(7):1768–1784, 2006.

[30] R. G. Wilkinson and K. E. Pickett. The problems of relative deprivation: why some societies do better than others. *Social science & medicine*, 65(9):1965–1978, 2007.

[31] J. Winn and C. Bishop. Variational message passing. *Journal of Machine Learning Research*, 6:661–694, 2005.

[32] Y. Yu, M. Isard, D. Fetterly, M. Budiu, U. Erlingsson, P. K. Gunda, and J. Currey. DryadLINQ: A system for general-purpose distributed data-parallel computing using a high-level language. In *OSDI*, 2008.

Learning Distributed Representations of Data in Community Question Answering for Question Retrieval

Kai Zhang *
State Key Laboratory of Software Development Environment
Beihang University, China
zhangkai@buaa.edu.cn

Wei Wu
Microsoft Research
Beijing, China
wuwei@microsoft.com

Fang Wang
State Key Laboratory of Software Development Environment
Beihang University, China
fangwang@buaa.edu.cn

Ming Zhou
Microsoft Research
Beijing, China
mingzhou@microsoft.com

Zhoujun Li
State Key Laboratory of Software Development Environment
Beihang University, China
lizj@buaa.edu.cn

ABSTRACT

We study the problem of question retrieval in community question answering (CQA). The biggest challenge within this task is lexical gaps between questions since similar questions are usually expressed with different but semantically related words. To bridge the gaps, state-of-the-art methods incorporate extra information such as word-to-word translation and categories of questions into the traditional language models. We find that the existing language model based methods can be interpreted using a new framework, that is they represent words and question categories in a vector space and calculate question-question similarities with a linear combination of dot products of the vectors. The problem is that these methods are either heuristic on data representation or difficult to scale up. We propose a principled and efficient approach to learning representations of data in CQA. In our method, we simultaneously learn vectors of words and vectors of question categories by optimizing an objective function naturally derived from the framework. In question retrieval, we incorporate learnt representations into traditional language models in an effective and efficient way. We conduct experiments on large scale data from Yahoo! Answers and Baidu Knows, and compared our method with state-of-the-art methods on two public data sets. Experimental results show that our method can significantly improve on baseline methods for retrieval relevance. On 1 million training data, our method takes less than 50 minutes to learn a model on a single multicore machine, while the translation based language model needs more than 2 days to learn a translation table on the same machine.

*The work was done when the first author was an intern at Microsoft Research Asia.

WSDM 2016, February 22-25, 2016, San Francisco, CA, USA
 ISBN 978-1-4503-3716-8/16/02 ...$15.00.
DOI: http://dx.doi.org/10.1145/2835776.2835786.

Categories and Subject Descriptors

H.3.3 [**Information Storage and Retrieval**]: Information Search and Retrieval—*Retrieval models*

Keywords

community question answering; question retrieval; word vector representation; unsupervised model

1. INTRODUCTION

Community question answering (CQA) portals, like Yahoo! Answers and Baidu Knows, have became popular platforms for people to gain knowledge from others. The knowledge is organized as questions posted by askers and lists of answers provided by answerers. There is also a significant amount of metadata associated with questions and answers. For example, askers choose categories for their questions, and award best answer marks to answerers whose answers are the most informative or satisfying. The data has made CQA portals valuable resources for many tasks like information retrieval, data mining, and question answering, etc.

One fundamental task for leveraging the knowledge in CQA is finding similar questions for new queries (a.k.a. question retrieval). Many studies have been done along this line [10, 26, 5, 24, 4, 29]. The biggest challenge in question retrieval is that users often express similar meanings with different but semantically related words, which generates lexical gaps between similar questions. For example, for the query "what are good foods for a gymnast to eat", there is a similar question "Im a gymnast, what should my meal plan be".The two questions have similar meanings but share very few common words, which prevents traditional retrieval models like BM25 [19], and language models for information retrieval (LMIR) [18, 27] from recognizing their similarity. To bridge the lexical gaps, state-of-the-art methods leverage word-to-word (or phrase-to-phrase) translation probabilities [10, 26] or question categories [5, 4], and expand the traditional language models with semantic matching items.

Existing models, although proposed from different background, can be interpreted by a unified framework. In fact, we find that traditional language models (LMIR) [18, 27] , translation based language models (TRLM) [26], and language models with category smoothing (LMC) [5] match questions in a similar manner, that is they represent words and question categories as elements in a vector space and linearly combine the dot products of the vectors as a similarity function. The advantage of taking this view is that it provides us with a new perspective to understand existing models and inspires us to create new models. From the framework, we find that the key to measuring question similarity is how to represent the data in CQA. Existing models, however, are either heuristic on data representation or difficult to scale up. For example, in LMIR and LMC, words are represented as indices in a vocabulary and similarity of words is ignored entirely. Although in LMC a category vector is considered for matching semantically similar questions, it is still not clear how semantic relations of words are modeled. Translation based language models go beyond the simple word-level matching, and model the semantic relations of words by mapping the word vectors in LMIR to a new vector space with a word-word translation matrix. The models, however, rely heavily on translation probabilities whose estimation needs a cubic time algorithm with respect to the vocabulary size [10], and thus are difficult to scale up. Since existing models suffer from such problems, a natural question arises: whether we can automatically learn representations of words and categories in CQA for question retrieval. The learning approach must appropriately model the relations of words, and be unsupervised and efficient enough to leverage the big data in CQA.

In this paper, we propose learning representations of data in CQA and leveraging the representations for question retrieval. The learning approach is conducted by optimizing an objective naturally derived from the framework. The objective applies a non-linear transformation to the linear combination of dot products of word vectors and question category vectors. In learning, we consider local relatedness of words. A word is only related to a question category and words from a small window in a question or in the associated answers. Our method simultaneously embeds words in questions, words in answers, and question categories into a vector space, which extends the recently proposed continuous bag-of-words (CBOW) architecture [12, 15, 7] for learning distributed representations for words in machine learning. We benefit from the architecture by a negative sampling technique and an optimization algorithm that runs in linear time with respect to number of words in training data and is independent of vocabulary size. The implementation code is published at `https://github.com/ComputerHobbyist/cqa`.

We create a retrieval model by incorporating the representations of data into traditional language models. Specifically, we take category vectors as centroids of clusters, and partition the vocabulary by assigning each word to the cluster of its most similar category. In each cluster, we calculate the similarity of each word and its top N similar words. The similarities are normalized as probabilities. We replace the word-word translation probability in TRLM with the probability calculated using word vectors. The "new" TRLM is further combined with the similarity of a word vector and a category vector as the final retrieval model. The model enjoys many advantages. First, since a word is only related to words from the same category, the category vector can help filter noise in word-word similarity. Second, when calculating word-word similarity, we only care about words in a small cluster. This can greatly enhance model estimation efficiency. Third, since we only keep nearest neighbors for each word, online memory cost only linearly increases with vocabulary size. The new retrieval model can be integrated into a learning to rank system as a feature to improve the performance of the system on question ranking.

We conduct experiments on large scale data from Yahoo! Answers and Baidu Knows, and compare our method with state-of-the-art methods on data sets published at `https://github.com/ComputerHobbyist/cqa`. On 1 million training data, the translation based language model needs nearly 2 days to learn a translation table on a single multicore machine, while on the same machine, our method takes less than 50 minutes to learn a model and significantly improves upon baseline methods of retrieval relevance.

Our contributions in the paper are three-fold: (1) proposal of a unified framework which provides a new perspective for existing retrieval models; (2) proposal of a new embedding based retrieval model; (3) empirical verification of the proposed model on both efficacy and efficiency.

2. RELATED WORK

Together with the flourishing of community question answering (CQA) archives, research on question retrieval in CQA has received much attention. State-of-the-art methods are based on language models [18, 27]. For example, Cao et al. [5, 4] propose a language model with category smoothing in which they estimate a new smoothing item from questions under the same category. Jeon el al. [10] propose learning word-to-word translation probabilities from question-question pairs collected based on similar answers. Xue et al. [26] learn a translation model from question-answer pairs. In this paper, we interpret language model based methods from an embedding perspective, and find that existing models suffer from efficacy and efficiency problems. Inspired by this perspective, we propose an approach that automatically learns the representations of data in an efficient way. The learnt representations are incorporated into LMIR to create a new model that is proven to be more effective in question retrieval through public data sets.

Learning distributed representations for words with neural network architectures has become a hot research topic in recent years [2, 17, 16, 13, 8, 12, 15, 11, 7], and has proven successful on speech recognition, image annotation, machine translation and other NLP tasks [21, 20, 6, 25, 14]. For statistical language modeling, Bengio et al. [2] proposed a neural network language model (NNLM) which simultaneously learns a distributed representation for each word and the probability function for word sequences expressed by the representations. The model obtains better generalization ability from the distributed representations of words, and is proven to be more effective than n-gram language models. To enhance the efficiency of NNLM, Morin et al. [17] introduced a hierarchical softmax method as an approximation of the full softmax in NNLM. Recently, Mikolov et al. [12, 15] have simplified the architecture of NNLM, and proposed continuous bag-of-words (CBOW) and Skip-gram models that can further speed up the learning of word representations. They show that the learning approach is surprisingly good at capturing the semantic relations of words. Le and Mikolov further extend the architectures of CBOW and Skig-gram and learn a paragraph vector to represent variable-length pieces of texts [11]. In this work, we learn distributed representations of data in CQA for question retrieval. Our learning method extends the CBOW architecture by simultaneously embedding words in questions, words in answers, and question categories into a vector space.

Before our work, there have already existed some studies on building deep architectures for searching. For example, Huang et al. [9] propose a deep structured semantic model (DSSM) for matching queries and documents. Shen et al. [22] follow the idea of DSSM and proposed a convolutional latent semantic model (CLSM) to express n-gram level and sentence level contextual structures in matching. The problem of applying DSSM and CLSM to question retrieval in CQA is that both of them need large scale supervision signals for training, which are not easy to obtain in CQA. Contrary to DSSM and CLSM, our model is totally unsupervised, and thus can leverage big data from CQA to learn semantic similarities between questions.

3. PRELIMINARIES

Before presenting the new framework, we first give an overview of state-of-the-art retrieval models in CQA.

3.1 Language Models for Information Retrieval

Recently, language models for information retrieval (LMIR) [18, 27] and their extensions have proven effective for question retrieval in CQA. Formally, given a query question q and a candidate question Q, LMIR calculates the similarity between q and Q by

$$P(q|Q) = \prod_{w\in q} [(1-\lambda)P_{ml}(w|Q) + \lambda P_{ml}(w|C)], \quad (1)$$

where $P_{ml}(w|Q)$ represents the maximum likelihood of a word w estimated from Q, and $P_{ml}(w|C)$ is a smoothing item which is calculated as the maximum likelihood in a large corpus C. The smoothing item avoids zero probability which stems from the words appearing in the query but not in the candidate. $\lambda \in (0,1)$ is a parameter which acts as a trade-off between the likelihood and the smoothing item.

3.2 Language Models with Category Smoothing

In most CQA portals, each question is tagged with one or several categories by askers. The categories can be viewed as explicit topics of questions, and thus can reflect semantic similarities between questions. To leverage question categories, Cao et al. [5] propose a language model with category smoothing (LMC) by expanding LMIR with a new smoothing item estimated from questions under the same category. The underlying idea is that questions under the same category are similar at a topic level. The model of LMC is defined as

$$P(q|Q) = \prod_{w\in q} [(1-\lambda)P_{ml}(w|Q) + \lambda P_{s}(w|Q)], \quad (2)$$

where

$$P_s(w|Q) = (1-\beta)P_{ml}(w|C) + \beta P_{ml}(w|Cat(Q)).$$

Here $\beta \in (0,1)$ is a parameter. $Cat(Q)$ denotes the category of candidate question Q, which is usually a root category or a leaf category in the category hierarchy of a CQA portal. $P_{ml}(w|Cat(Q))$ is the maximal likelihood of word w estimated from $Cat(Q)$. Note that in Equation (2), we do not involve the question classification item as in the work of Cao el al. [5], since the item only sightly improves the model from empirical results [5].

3.3 Translation-based Language Model

Translation based language models (TRLM) [3] leverage word-to-word or phrase-to-phrase translation probabilities estimated from questions and answers to match semantically similar questions. TRLM can be formulated as

$$P(q|Q) = \prod_{w\in q} [(1-\lambda)P_{mx}(w|Q) + \lambda P_{ml}(w|C)], \quad (3)$$

where

$$P_{mx}(w|Q) = (1-\beta)P_{ml}(w|Q) + \beta P_{tr}(w|Q)$$
$$P_{tr}(w|Q) = \sum_{v\in Q} P_{tp}(w|v)P_{ml}(v|Q).$$

Here λ and β are parameters. $P_{tp}(w|v)$ represents the translation probability from word v in candidate question Q to word w in query question q.

Xue, et al. [26] further improved TRLM by introducing an extra answer likelihood item $P_{ml}(w|a)$ estimated from an answer a of question Q. The model can be represented as

$$P(q|Q,a) = \prod_{w\in q} [(1-\lambda)P_{mx}(w|Q,a) + \lambda P_{ml}(w|C)] \quad (4)$$

where

$$P_{mx}(w|Q,a) = \alpha P_{ml}(w|Q) + \beta P_{tr}(w|Q) + \gamma P_{ml}(w|a).$$

Here α, β and γ are parameters satisfying $\alpha+\beta+\gamma=1$. We denote the model in Equation (4) as TAL.

4. A FRAMEWORK FOR RETRIEVAL MODELS IN CQA

In this section, we interpret the existing language model based methods described in Section 3 with a new framework. We find that these models perform question matching in a similar manner, that is they represent words in questions, words in answers, and question categories as vectors in a vector space and calculate question similarity by dot products of the vectors. The framework exposes the essence of question retrieval to us and inspires us to create better retrieval models.

From Equation (1), (2), (3), and (4), we can see that the existing retrieval models can be represented as

$$P(q|Q) = \prod_{w\in q} P(w|Q),$$

where $P(q|Q)$ is the generation probability of a query q from a candidate Q, and $P(w|Q)$ is the generation probability of a word w from Q. Note that in LMC and TAL, Q not only means the question itself, but also contains metadata associated with the question. In LMC, the metadata is the category of Q, while in TAL, it is the answer of Q. We can understand $P(q|Q)$ and $P(w|Q)$ as similarity functions between q and Q, and w and Q, respectively. When performing question matching, all the existing models decompose the question-question similarity to a product of several word-question similarity functions. The difference between them is how they define and estimate the word-question similarity function.

For LMIR, if we define $v_{ohs}(w)$ as the one-hot-spot representation of a word w in which only one element is equal to one indicating the index of w in the vocabulary and all other elements are zero, then $P_{ml}(w|Q)$ in Equation (1) can be re-written as

$$P_{ml}(w|Q) = \frac{1}{L_Q} v_{ohs}(w) \cdot \sum_{w' \in Q} v_{ohs}(w'),$$

where L_Q is the length of Q. Since $P_{ml}(w|C)$ in Equation (1) is independent of Q, we denote it as $b(w)$. Thus, the word-question similarity for LMIR can be expressed as

$$\frac{1-\lambda}{L_Q} v_{ohs}(w) \cdot \sum_{w' \in Q} v_{ohs}(w') + \lambda b(w).$$

For LMC, $P_{ml}(w|Cat(Q))$ in Equation (2) can be re-written as

$$P_{ml}(w|Cat(Q)) = \frac{1}{L_{cat}} v_{ohs}(w) \cdot \sum_{w' \in Cat(Q)} v_{ohs}(w'),$$

where L_{cat} is number of words in $Cat(Q)$. If we understand $\sum_{w' \in Cat(Q)} v_{ohs}(w')$ as a vector representation for category $Cat(Q)$, and denote it as $v(Cat(Q))$, then the word-question similarity function for LMC can be represented as

$$\alpha_1 v_{ohs}(w) \cdot \sum_{w' \in Q} v_{ohs}(w') + \alpha_2 v_{ohs}(w) \cdot v(Cat(Q)) + \alpha_3 b(w),$$

where $\alpha_1 = \frac{1-\lambda}{L_Q}$, $\alpha_2 = \frac{\lambda\beta}{L_{cat}}$, and $\alpha_3 = \lambda(1-\beta)$.

For TRLM and TAL, we denote the translation matrix as $M_{tr} = (P_{tp}(w|v))_{n \times n}$ and the length of answer a as L_a, then $P_{tr}(w|Q)$ in Equation (3) and $P_{ml}(w|a)$ in Equation (4) can be re-written as

$$P_{tr}(w|Q) = \frac{1}{L_Q} [M_{tr}^{\top} v_{ohs}(w)] \cdot \sum_{w' \in Q} v_{ohs}(w')$$

$$P_{ml}(w|a) = \frac{1}{L_a} v_{ohs}(w) \cdot \sum_{w' \in a} v_{ohs}(w').$$

The word-question similarity for TRLM can be represented as

$$[\alpha_1 I + \alpha_2 M_{tr}^{\top}] v_{ohs}(w) \cdot \sum_{w' \in Q} v_{ohs}(w') + \alpha_3 v_{ohs}(w) \cdot \sum_{w' \in a} v_{ohs}(w') + \alpha_4 b(w),$$

where $\alpha_1 = \frac{(1-\lambda)\alpha}{L_Q}$, $\alpha_2 = \frac{(1-\lambda)\beta}{L_Q}$, $\alpha_3 = \frac{(1-\lambda)\gamma}{L_a}$, and $\alpha_4 = \lambda$.

From the analysis above, we find that the existing retrieval models share some common characteristics in calculating word-question similarity: (1) they represent words in questions, words in answers, and question categories as vectors; (2) they calculate dot products of the vectors and linearly combine the dot products. These models, therefore, can be viewed as special cases of the following general framework for question retrieval:

$$f(q, Q) = \prod_{w \in q} g(w, Q) \tag{5}$$

$$g(w, Q) = \alpha_1 A v(w) \cdot \sum_{w' \in Q} v(w') + \alpha_2 v(w) \cdot v(Cat(Q)) + \alpha_3 v(w) \cdot \sum_{w' \in a} v(w') + \alpha_4 b(w). \tag{6}$$

Here, we use $f(q, Q)$ and $g(w, Q)$ to represent general similarity functions for a question pair and a word-question pair, respectively. $v(w)$ and $v(Cat(Q))$ represent vector representations of a word and a question category, respectively. $b(w)$ is an intercept independent of Q. A is a linear transformation which is the identity matrix in LMIR and LMC, and $[\alpha_1 I + \alpha_2 M_{tr}^{\top}]$ in TRLM and TAL. α_1, α_2, α_3, and α_4 are parameters.

The framework gives us some insight on matching questions: the key to calculating question similarity is how to represent data in CQA in a vector space, including words in questions, words in answers, and question categories. For LMIR and LMC, words and categories are represented in a heuristic way. The one-hot-spot representation is simple, but totally ignores the similarity of words. Different words are orthogonal in the vector space. Although there is a category vector in LMC, it is defined as a summation of one-hot-spot representations, and thus does not model the relations of words, either. TRLM and TAL leverage translation matrix M_{tr} and transform the one-hot-spot representation of word $v_{ohs}(w)$ to a new vector. Word similarity is encoded in the new vector. The problem with TRLM and TAL is that the estimation of M_{tr} needs a cubic time algorithm with respect to vocabulary size [10]. Therefore, it is difficult for TRLM and TAL to scale up to very large data.

The problems suffered by existing models motivate us to think of representing data in CQA in a better and more efficient way. In the next section, we will elaborate our method of learning representations for data in CQA and leveraging representations for question retrieval.

5. LEARNING REPRESENTATIONS OF DATA FOR QUESTION RETRIEVAL

Inspired by the framework in Section 4, we propose learning representations of data in CQA. The learning approach optimizes a question similarity function derived from the framework, models local relatedness of words, and can be implemented with an algorithm running in linear time with respect to number of words in training data. With the representations of data, we create a question retrieval by incorporating the representations into LMIR.

5.1 Learning Approach

We derive a question similarity function from Equation (5) and Equation (6). Specifically, we consider the following functions:

$$f(q, Q) = \prod_{w \in q} g(w, Q), \tag{7}$$

$$g(w, Q) = \frac{e^{y(w,Q)}}{\sum_{w' \in V} e^{y(w',Q)}}, \tag{8}$$

$$y(w, Q) = v(w) \cdot \left[\sum_{w' \in Q} v(w') + v(Cat(Q)) + \sum_{w' \in a} v(w') \right], \tag{9}$$

where V represents the vocabulary. From the equations above, we can see that $y(w, Q)$ is a special case of the general word-question similarity function given by Equation (6). Here, we set $\alpha_1 = \alpha_2 = \alpha_3 = 1$, fix $A = I$, and drop the intercept $b(w)$ in Equation (6). We fix A as an identity matrix, because the information of the linear transformation can be encoded in the learning of vectors. The intercept $b(w)$ in the existing models is designed for avoiding zero matching scores due to orthogonality of word vectors. We try to learn a distributed representation that can reflect semantic relations of words. Therefore, we do not have to worry about the issue. In spite of this, one can still consider A and $b(w)$ in learning and see whether they can further improve retrieval performance. We leave this for future work. Differing from existing models, we apply the softmax function (i.e., $e^{y(w,Q)}/\sum_{w' \in V} e^{y(w',Q)}$) to $y(w,Q)$ and transform the linear combination of dot products to a probability distribution.

We expect to learn representations of words and question categories by maximizing the similarity between similar question pairs. The problem is that the learning needs large scale supervision signals indicating the similarity between question pairs which are not easy to obtain. Therefore, we consider maximizing the similarity between a question and itself. Our learning approach can be formulated as

$$\arg\max_{v(w), v(Cat(Q))} \prod_{i=1}^{N} f(Q_i, Q_i) = \prod_{i=1}^{N} \prod_{w \in Q_i} g(w, Q_i), \qquad (10)$$

where $\{Q_i\}_{i=1}^{N}$ represents questions we have collected from CQA. We denote the category and the answer associated with Q_i by $Cat(Q_i)$ and a_i respectively. From the definition of $y(w,Q)$ in Equation (9), we know that by optimizing Equation (10), each word in a question is forced to be similar to every word in the question and every word in the answer. This is not reasonable, since in a question, especially in a long question, words appearing in a long distance are usually less related to each other. For example in a question like "what are good foods for a gymnast to eat", compared to "food", "what" is obviously less related to "gymnast". Since answers are usually much longer than questions, the problem could become more serious. The current definition of $y(w,Q)$ ignores locations of words and thus loses local structures within questions and answers. Besides this problem, in $y(w,Q)$, the category vector $v(Cat(Q))$ is equally weighted with each word vector $v(w')$ (see Equation (9)). Since we take a summation on word vectors, the effect of category vector is easily overwhelmed by the word vectors in learning. To solve these problems, we re-define the objective function in problem (10) by factorizing the probability $g(w,Q_i)$ in Equation (10). Each factor defines a probability distribution on words in which a word w is only similar to the category of Q_i and words in a small window around w in Q_i or a_i. Formally, the new objective function of our learning approach is given by:

$$\prod_{i=1}^{N} \prod_{w \in Q_i} \left[\prod_{j \in pos(w,Q_i)} \hat{g}(w, c(w,Q_i,j)) \prod_{j \in pos(w,a_i)} \hat{g}(w, c(w,a_i,j)) \right]. \qquad (11)$$

$\forall j \in pos(w,Q_i)$,

$$\hat{g}(w, c(w,Q_i,j)) = \frac{e^{\hat{y}(w,c(w,Q_i,j))}}{\sum_{w' \in V} e^{\hat{y}(w',c(w,Q_i,j))}},$$

$$\hat{y}(w, c(w,Q_i,j)) = v(w) \cdot \left[\sum_{l=j-k, l\neq j}^{j+k} v(w_{(Q_i,l)}) + v(Cat(Q_i)) \right], \qquad (12)$$

and $\forall j \in pos(w,a_i)$,

$$\hat{g}(w, c(w,a_i,j)) = \frac{e^{\hat{y}(w,c(w,a_i,j))}}{\sum_{w' \in V} e^{\hat{y}(w',c(w,a_i,j))}},$$

$$\hat{y}(w, c(w,a_i,j)) = v(w) \cdot \left[\sum_{l=j-k, l\neq j}^{j+k} v(w_{(a_i,l)}) + v(Cat(Q_i)) \right]. \qquad (13)$$

In Equation (12) and Equation (13), $w_{(Q_i,l)}$ and $w_{(a_i,l)}$ represent the l-th word in question Q_i and answer a_i respectively. $pos(w,Q_i) = \{j | w_{(Q_i,j)} = w\}$ and $pos(w,a_i) = \{j | w_{(a_i,j)} = w\}$ indicate locations of word w in Q_i and a_i respectively. $c(w,Q_i,j)$ is defined as $\sum_{l=j-k,l\neq j}^{j+k} v(w_{(Q_i,l)}) + v(Cat(Q_i)$ which represents the context of word w in Q_i. $c(w,a_i,j)$ is similarly defined and represents the context of w in a_i. k is the window size. Note that in $\prod_{w \in Q_i}$ of Equation (11) we only enumerate distinct words in Q_i.

If we remove $\prod_{j \in pos(w,a_i)} \hat{g}(w, c(w,a_i,j))$ from Equation (11) and $v(Cat(Q_i))$ from Equation (12), then the learning method becomes

$$\arg\max_{v(w)} \prod_{i=1}^{N} \prod_{w \in Q_i} \prod_{j \in pos(w,Q_i)} \frac{e^{v(w) \cdot \sum_{l=j-k,l\neq j}^{j+k} v(w_{(Q_i,l)})}}{\sum_{w' \in V} e^{v(w') \cdot \sum_{l=j-k,l\neq j}^{j+k} v(w_{(Q_i,l)})}}.$$

This is equivalent to learning word representations using the continuous bag-of-words (CBOW) model [12, 15, 7] on question set $\{Q_i\}_{i=1}^{N}$. Our method extends CBOW by simultaneously embedding question categories and answer words.

Inspired by the connection of our method and CBOW, we consider optimizing the objective (11) by employing the negative sampling technique [12, 15, 7] which has proven both effective and efficient in learning word embeddings. Specifically, we learn the vectors of words and question categories by maximizing the following function:

$$\sum_{i=1}^{N} \sum_{w \in Q_i} [\sum_{j \in pos(w,Q_i)} \bar{g}(w, c(w,Q_i,j)) + \sum_{j \in pos(w,a_i)} \bar{g}(w, c(w,a_i,j))],$$

where

$$\bar{g}(w, c(x)) = \log \sigma(\hat{y}(w,c(x))) + \sum_{w' \in Neg(c(x))} \log[1 - \sigma(\hat{y}(w',c(x)))].$$

Here, $\sigma(x) = 1/(1+e^{-x})$ is the sigmoid function. $\hat{y}(w,c(x))$ is defined by Equation (12) or Equation (13) depending on $c(x) = c(w,Q_i,j)$ or $c(x) = c(w,a_i,j)$. $Neg(c(x))$ represents a set of randomly sampled negative examples for $c(x)$. The optimization problem can be easily solved by stochastic gradient ascent. The gradient of $\bar{g}(w,c(x))$ is given by:

$$\frac{\partial \bar{g}(w,c(x))}{\partial v(Cat(Q))} = \sigma(-\hat{y}(w,c(x)))v(w) - h_{neg}(w,c(x)),$$

$\forall w' \in c(x)$:

$$\frac{\partial \bar{g}(w,c(x))}{\partial v(w')} = \sigma(-\hat{y}(w,c(x)))v(w) - h_{neg}(w,c(x)),$$

where $h_{neg}(w,c(x)) = \sum_{w' \in Neg(c(x))} \sigma(\hat{y}(w',c(x)))v(w')$, $\forall w' \in Neg(c(x))$:

$$\frac{\partial \bar{g}(w,c(x))}{\partial v(w')} = -\sigma(\hat{y}(w',c(x)))c(x),$$

and if w is the target word in $\bar{g}(w, c(x))$:

$$\frac{\partial \bar{g}(w, c(x))}{\partial v(w)} = \sigma(-\hat{y}(w, c(x)))c(x).$$

The training complexity is $O\left(M \times [2k \times D + D \times N_{neg}]\right)$, where M is the number of words in the training data, D is the dimension of vectors, and N_{neg} is the number of negative samples. The implementation code is published at `https://github.com/ComputerHobbyist/cqa`.

5.2 Retrieval Model

We consider creating a retrieval model with the learned representations of words and question categories. One straightforward way is to calculate $f(q, Q)$ and $g(w, Q)$ defined by Equation (7), Equation (8) and Equation (9) using the learned vectors and taking $f(q, Q)$ as a retrieval model. In practice, however, this strategy is infeasible, since there is a normalizer $\sum_{w' \in V} e^{y(w', Q)}$ in the definition of $g(w, Q)$, and for every candidate Q, we have to calculate its similarity with each word in the vocabulary. The time complexity is $O(|V|)$, and is too expensive for online retrieval and ranking. Moreover, from experimental results, we find that $f(q, Q)$ performs badly on measuring question similarity. Therefore, we propose an alternative way to leverage the learned representations for retrieval.

We borrow an idea from translation based language models, and consider incorporating word-word similarity and word-category similarity calculated with the learned vectors into LMIR. Specifically, suppose that there are a total of N_{cat} categories, and for the i-th category c_i, the vector representation is $v(c_i)$. We partition vocabulary V as $\{C_i\}_{i=1}^{N_{cat}}$ with $\{v(c_i)\}_{i=1}^{N_{cat}}$, and the i-th word cluster C_i is defined as $\{w_j \mid cosine\,(v(w_j), v(c_i)) > cosine\,(v(w_j), v(c_k)), \forall k \neq i\}$. In other words, we take the vector of categories as centroid of clusters, and assign each word to the cluster of its most similar category under Cosine similarity. Within each cluster, we find top N similar words for each word with Cosine similarity, and define a word-word similarity function as

$$P_{sim}(w_i|w_j) = \begin{cases} \frac{e^{v(w_i)\cdot v(w_j)}}{\sum_{w' \in Sim(w_j)} e^{v(w')\cdot v(w_j)}} & \text{if } w_i \in Sim(w_j) \\ 0 & \text{otherwise} \end{cases} \tag{14}$$

Here, we use $Sim(w_j)$ to represent the top N similar words of word w_j. $P_{sim}(w_i|w_j)$ can be understand as a translation probability from w_j to w_i. Our idea is that we replace the translation probability $P_{tp}(w_i|w_j)$ in TRLM with $P_{sim}(w_i|w_j)$. The "new" TRLM is further combined with a word-category similarity function defined as

$$s_{cat}(w, c) = \frac{e^{v(w)\cdot v(c)}}{\sum_{w' \in V} e^{v(w')\cdot v(c)}}. \tag{15}$$

Thus, given a query question q and a candidate question Q, our retrieval model is given by

$$P(q|Q) = \prod_{w \in q} \left[(1-\lambda)P_{mx}(w|Q) + \lambda P_s(w|Q)\right], \tag{16}$$

where

$$\begin{aligned} P_{mx}(w|Q) &= (1-\alpha)P_{ml}(w|Q) + \alpha P_{sim}(w|Q), \\ P_s(w|Q) &= (1-\beta)P_{ml}(w|C) + \beta s_{cat}\left(w, Cat(Q)\right), \\ P_{sim}(w|Q) &= \sum_{v \in Q} P_{sim}(w|v)P_{ml}(v|Q). \end{aligned} \tag{17}$$

Table 1: Statistics of the two CQA data sets

	Yahoo	Baidu
Question Number	1,076,425	983,914
Description Number	872,981	552,959
Answer Number	7,567,268	3,768,391
Vocabulary Size	279,353	163,110

Here λ, α and β are parameters, satisfying $\lambda,\ \alpha,\ \beta \in (0, 1)$. We name our retrieval model distributed representation based language model (DRLM).

DRLM has many advantages over translation based language models. First, it extends TRLM by considering category vectors, thus question matching is not only conducted on a word level, but also on a topic level. Second, it is more efficient than TRLM on model estimation. From Section 5.1, we know that the time complexity for learning representations of data is $O\left(M \times [2k \times D + D \times N_{neg}]\right)$. After learning, the time complexity for constructing the retrieval model is $O\left(|V| \times N_{cat} \times D + [\frac{|V|}{N_{cat}}]^2 \times D\right)$[1]. On the other hand, the time complexity for estimating a translation table for TRLM is $O\left(T \times |V|^2\right)$ in which T is the number of question-answer pairs [10]. In general, T is larger than $|V|$ on millions of data in CQA, thus in representing semantic relations of words, TRLM needs a cubic time algorithm with respect to vocabulary size to process data in CQA, while our method only needs to scan the data word by word a few times, and then we get both the representation of words and the representation of categories. Calculating similarity for pairs of words can be slow, but we only have to care about words in a small cluster. Moreover, since the vocabulary is partitioned, the estimation of P_{sim} can be implemented in parallel offline. In practice, we find that the estimation of DRLM is very efficient, and we can conclude that our method is easy to scale up and is capable of leveraging big data in CQA. Finally, word-word translation is calculated within clusters defined by category vectors. Therefore, besides the advantage on efficiency, our model can leverage categories to filter noise in similarity of words.

In DRLM, we only keep similarity of a word with its top N similar words, which makes the translation table very sparse. This strategy can not only further calibrate word similarity, but also keep online memory cost linearly increasing with the vocabulary size.

6. EXPERIMENTS

We conducted experiments to test the performance of the proposed method on question retrieval.

6.1 Experiment Setup

6.1.1 Data Sets

We crawled 1 million questions (a.k.a. question titles) associated with descriptions (a.k.a. question bodies) and answers from Yahoo! Answers and Baidu Knows. Yahoo! Answers and Baidu Knows represent the largest and most popular CQA archives in English and Chinese, respectively. In both Yahoo! Answers and Baidu Knows, there is a hierarchy of category. In Yahoo Answers, there are 26 root categories and 1263 leaf categories, while in Baidu Knows,

[1]In practice, we have observed that words almost uniformly distribute over clusters, and thus the size of each cluster is close to $|V|/N_{cat}$.

there are 14 root categories and 984 leaf categories. Each question in our crawled data has a root category and a leaf category (we ignore the categories on middle layers of the hierarchy). Table 1 gives details on the two data sets. We use the data sets for training models and have published them at `https://github.com/ComputerHobbyist/cqa`.

We test our model on two labeled sets published at `https://github.com/ComputerHobbyist/cqa`. One contains 1,685 English queries and each query has 15 labeled candidate questions. The other one contains 1,140 Chinese queries and each query has 13 labeled candidate questions. In both of the two sets, the candidates are returned by an inline ranking algorithm in Lucene.Net which is an open indexing source. The labels are either 1 or 0, meaning relevant or irrelevant. Note that the two labeled sets are expansions of those used in our previous work [28]. After the work, we further label 262 new English queries and 535 new Chinese queries and combine the newly labeled data with those in [28]. We follow [28] and randomly split each of the two data sets to a validation set and a test set with a ratio 1 : 3. On the validation set, we tune parameters of different models, while on the test set, we evaluate ranking performance of different models. For all English data, we remove stop words and conduct stemming, and for all Chinese data, we conduct Chinese word segmentation.

To evaluate the performance of different models, we follow [28], and employ Mean Average Precision (MAP) [1], Mean Reciprocal Rank (MRR) [23], R-Precision (R-Prec) [5], and precision at position 1 (P@1) as evaluation measures.

6.1.2 Baselines

We take the language model for information retrieval (LMIR) given by Equation (1) as a baseline method. In addition to that, we also consider the following baseline methods:

Language Model with Category Smoothing We implement LMC given by Equation (2). The word distribution under a category in LMC is estimated using the training data. Besides the leaf category smoothing technique used in [5], we also consider root categories of questions, and estimate a root category smoothing item. We denote a language model with leaf category smoothing as LMC_{leaf}, and a language model with root category smoothing as LMC_{root}.

Translation based Language Model We learn word-word translation probabilities from the training data using MGIZA++ [2] which is a multi-thread version of GIZA++. Since in [28], there is a comprehensive comparison between different variants of translation based language models, we select the best ones as baseline methods in this paper. For the English data set, we used $TAL_{Q\&D-AllA}$ in which a question is concatenated with its description as an enriched question, all answers under the question are concatenated as a long document, and the translation table is learned from pairs of the enriched question and the long answer document. For the Chinese data set, we use TAL_{Q-D} in which we learn the translation table from question-description pairs. For reference, we also report the comparison with TAL_{Q-D} and $TAL_{Q\&D-AllA}$ on the English data set and the Chinese data set, respectively.

In our model, we only keep top N similar words for each word in the translation table. To make a fair comparison, we also truncate the translation table in TAL by keeping top N words that can be translated from a word, and denote the models as TAL^{trunc}.

The original TAL in Equation (4) does not take categories into account. Therefore, we linearly combine $P_{mx}(w|Q,a)$ in Equation (4) with the leaf category smoothing item $P_{ml}(w|Cat(Q))$ in Equation (2), and incorporate the category information into TAL. The enriched TAL is denoted as TAL^{cat}.

LDA based Models We compare DRLM with four LDA based models in [28], including $TBLM_{LDA}$, $QATM + TransLM$, $TBLM_{QATM}$, and $TBLM_{SQATM}$ which is our major contribution in [28].

CBOW and Skip-gram We learn word vectors by employing the original CBOW and Skip-gram models with the negative sampling technique and use the learned word vectors to create several retrieval models for comparison. For both English data and Chinese data, we concatenate questions, descriptions, and answers as a document and run the algorithm of CBOW and Skip-gram using the code shared at `https://code.google.com/p/word2vec/`. With the word vectors, we create the following models: (1) we average word vectors in both a query question and a candidate question, and calculate the Cosine similarity of the two vectors. We denote the models as $CBOW_{cos}$ and $Skip_{cos}$; (2) We first find the top N similar words for each word using Cosine similarity, then calculate word-word translation probabilities using P_{sim}. We replace the translation probabilities in TRLM with the new probabilities, and denote the models as $CBOW_{trlm}$ and $Skip_{trlm}$. Note that this is equivalent to implementing our DRLM with word vectors learned using CBOW and Skip-gram. (3) We linearly combine $CBOW_{trlm}$ and $Skip_{trlm}$ with the leaf category smoothing item $P_{ml}(w|Cat(Q))$ in Equation (2) like what we did in TAL^{cat}. We denote the models as $CBOW^{cat}_{trlm}$ and $Skip^{cat}_{trlm}$.

In addition to DRLM, we also implement two simple models for comparison using the vectors learned by the method described in Section 5.1 . First, we average vectors of words in a question as a question vector, calculate Cosine similarity of two question vectors and Cosine similarity for a question vector and a category vector, and linearly combine the two cosine similarity functions. We denote this model as DR_{cos}. Second, we remove word-category similarity (i.e., $s_{cat}(w, Cat(Q))$ in Equation (17) from DRLM. We denote the model as $DRLM_{no-cat}$.

6.1.3 Parameter Tuning

We tune parameters for different models based on their performance on MAP. For LMIR, LMC and TAL, we selected parameters $\{\lambda, \alpha, \beta, \gamma\}$ from {0.1, 0.2, $\cdots$, 0.9}. For CBOW, Skip-gram, and our model, we set the number of negative samples (i.e.,N_{neg}) in {5, 10, 15}, the dimension of vectors (i.e.,D) in {100, 200, 300, 400, 500}, and the window size (i.e., k) in {1, 2, $\cdots$ 7}. In TAL^{trunc} and our model, we set N= 10,000 in the top N words. We tune the combination parameters in DRLM, DR_{cos}, TAL^{cat}, $CBOW_{trlm}$, $Skip_{trlm}$, $CBOW^{cat}_{trlm}$, and $Skip^{cat}_{trlm}$ in the same way as in LMIR, LMC, and TAL.

6.2 Evaluation Results

We run algorithms on a workstation with one Intel Core i7 4785T processor (4 cores). For our method, we use root categories for embedding, and concatenate answers under a

[2] `http://www.kyloo.net/software/doku.php/mgiza:overview`

Table 2: Evaluation results on Yahoo data and Baidu data (1 million)

	Yahoo data				Baidu data			
	MAP	MRR	R-Prec	P@1	MAP	MRR	R-Prec	P@1
$LMIR$	0.758	0.844	0.661	0.759	0.724	0.787	0.610	0.681
LMC_{root}	0.771	0.860	0.684	0.781	0.734	0.806	0.626	0.701
LMC_{leaf}	0.773	0.863	0.685	0.783	0.737	0.805	0.632	0.703
TAL_{Q-D}	0.770	0.856	0.681	0.776	0.735	0.807	0.631	0.704
$TAL_{Q\&D-AllA}$	0.774	0.863	0.687	0.784	0.727	0.794	0.618	0.694
TAL^{cat}	0.776	0.864	0.689	0.788	0.743	0.811	0.638	0.709
TAL^{trunc}	0.777	0.862	0.688	0.785	0.739	0.808	0.636	0.707
$QATM + TransLM$	0.769	0.856	0.683	0.774	0.733	0.804	0.627	0.704
$TBLM_{LDA}$	0.772	0.860	0.683	0.782	0.737	0.804	0.632	0.705
$TBLM_{QATM}$	0.773	0.868	0.686	0.786	0.730	0.799	0.620	0.696
$CBOW_{cos}$	0.719	0.810	0.618	0.710	0.682	0.757	0.556	0.649
$Skip_{cos}$	0.719	0.821	0.614	0.715	0.686	0.765	0.561	0.660
$CBOW_{trlm}$	0.772	0.859	0.686	0.781	0.741	0.812	0.632	0.712
$Skip_{trlm}$	0.773	0.861	0.684	0.785	0.743	0.813	0.633	0.715
$CBOW^{cat}_{trlm}$	0.773	0.863	0.685	0.787	0.745	0.815	0.636	0.718
$Skip^{cat}_{trlm}$	0.775	0.866	0.689	0.792	0.747	0.818	0.642	0.721
DR_{cos}	0.722	0.824	0.624	0.720	0.690	0.771	0.570	0.669
$DRLM_{no-cat}$	0.774	0.861	0.687	0.786	0.745	0.815	0.637	0.719
$TBLM_{SQATM}$	0.780	0.869	0.694	0.793	0.741	0.814	0.640	0.710
$DRLM$	**0.789**	**0.881**	0.701	**0.816**	**0.761**	**0.835**	**0.657**	**0.738**

question as a long answer document. Table 2 lists evaluation results of different models on the two data sets.

From Table 2, we can see that DRLM outperforms all the baseline methods on both Yahoo data and Baidu data, and the improvements, except on R-Prec on Yahoo data over $TBLM_{SQATM}$, are statistically significant over all the baseline methods on all metrics (t-test, p value < 0.05).

DRLM significantly outperforms LMIR and LMC, which demonstrates that the learned representations in DRLM can express semantic relations of words and effectively bridge the lexical gaps in similar questions. It significantly improves upon the CBOW and Skip-gram based methods. Particularly, it is much better than the heuristic combination of embedding based translation models (i.e., $CBOW_{trlm}$ and $Skip_{trlm}$) and the category smoothing item (i.e., $P_{ml}(w|Cat(Q))$. This result indicates that category embedding can reinforce the effect of word embedding, and word-category similarity calculated in the vector space is very useful for identifying the semantic similarities between questions. $DRLM_{no-cat}$ is comparable with $CBOW_{trlm}$ and $Skip_{trlm}$, which further emphasizes the importance of category embedding in our model. DR_{cos} performs much worse than DRLM, which tells us that the trivial method of using the learned representations does not work in retrieval. DRLM outperforms all LDA based models. Particularly, it outperforms $TBLM_{SQATM}$ even though it does not leverage information on answer quality. The results indicate that the embedding approach we proposed is more effective at capturing semantic relations of words and categories. Finally, we find that DRLM is much better than translation based language models on both efficacy and efficiency. Particularly, on efficiency, although we have exploited a multi-threaded tool, it still took us more than 2 days to learn the translation table for TAL. On the other hand, with the same data and on the same machine, our method only needs 9 minutes to finish the learning of data representations and less than 40 minutes to estimate the retrieval model after learning.

LMC_{leaf} is slightly better than LMC_{root}, indicating that word distributions under fine-grained categories are more useful for question retrieval. Truncation on the translation table of TAL only slightly improves performance. We find that many translation probabilities are already zero in the original translation table, as many word pairs scarcely co-occurred in question-answer pairs. Skip-gram based methods are slightly better than CBOW based methods. The result is consistent with the conclusion drawn by Mikolov et al. in [15]. $Skip_{cos}$ and $CBOW_{cos}$ perform badly, indicating that the average of word vectors cannot represent the semantics of questions. The bad performance of DR_{cos} also verified this conclusion.

6.3 Discussions

Experiments on 1 million data have verified the advantages of our method on both efficacy and efficiency. In fact, the high efficiency of DRLM allows us to learn representations with bigger data. Therefore, we collect an extra 9 million questions associated with descriptions and answers from both Yahoo! Answers and Baidu Knows. Together with the 1 million data from before, we have a total of 10 million data for both the Yahoo data set and the Baidu data set. We conduct experiments on the bigger data sets, and study (1) if DRLM is still better than the baseline methods; (2) how the efficacy and efficiency of DRLM change with the growth of data.

In addition to the experiments on the bigger data sets, we use a real example to explain how the learned representations of words and question categories in DRLM help bridge lexical gaps between similar questions. We also compare DRLM with $f(q, Q)$ given by Equation (7), in which $f(q, Q)$ is calculated using vectors learned by the method in Section 5.1.

6.3.1 Comparison of retrieval models on bigger data

Table 3 gives the evaluation results of different models on 10 million data. On such a scale, TAL and $TBLM_{SQATM}$ become infeasible (e.g., taking months to run), therefore, we only compare DRLM with LMIR, the best LMC (i.e., LMC_{leaf}), and the best embedding based baseline (i.e., $Skip^{cat}_{trlm}$). From the table, we can see that (1) after we increase training data, all methods become better; (2) Our method still significantly outperforms all baseline methods on all metrics (t-test, p value < 0.05), which is consistent with the results on the 1 million pieces of data;

6.3.2 Changes of DRLM with the growth of data

Besides comparisons between different models, we also examine how the efficacy and efficiency of DRLM changes with the growth of data. Specifically, we train DRLM on 1 million, 3 million, 5 million, 7 million and 10 million data. Figure 1 shows how the efficacy of DRLM changes with the growth of data. We can see that the upward trend on P@1 is very clear. DRLM becomes better and better on P@1 when training data increases. On other metrics, although the performance of DRLM drops sometimes, the overall trend is similar to that on P@1. Figure 2 shows how the training time changed with the growth of data. We can see that the training time almost linearly increases with training data[3], which demonstrates the scalability of our method. Particularly, on 10 million data, our method only needs 50 minutes to learn the representations of data, and less than 200 minutes to estimate the retrieval model with the representations, which is very efficient.

6.3.3 Case study

We try to explain why DRLM is effective in measuring question similarity with a real example from the test data. For the query "how to cut bicycle shifter cable", there is a relevant candidate "how do I remove cable housing from a shifter on a bike". The two questions express similar meanings with different but semantically related words such as "bike" and "bicycle" and "cut" and "remove". DRLM ranks the candidate in the top position. We check the learned vectors and find that the vectors of "bike" and "bicycle" and the vectors of "cut" and "remove" are grouped into the same clusters. Given "bike" and " remove", the words that correspond to the largest translation probabilities (i.e., $P_{sim}(w_i|w_j)$ in Equation (14)) are "bicycle" and "cut", respectively. Moreover, the category of the candidate is "Sports" and the similarity between the vector of "bicycle" in the query and the vector of "Sports" is very large. Through learning, our method embeds words and categories into a vector space where semantically similar ones are close to each other. Therefore, DRLM can successfully capture the similarity between the query and the candidate even though they share few common words. On the other hand, LMIR fails on this case. It ranks the relevant candidate in a lower position than another irrelevant candidate "how do I find out what type of bicycle cables I need in order to replace them on my bike" due to the more common words shared by the query and the irrelevant candidate.

6.3.4 Comparison of $f(q, Q)$ and DRLM

As we have explained in Section 5, we do not employ $f(q, Q)$ defined by Equation (7) as a retrieval model because the normalizer in $g(w, Q)$ cannot be efficiently calculated. In spite of this, we still want to study if $f(q, Q)$, as a similarity measure of question pairs, is better than DRLM when we calculate $f(q, Q)$ using the vectors learned by the method described in Section 5.1.

Table 4 shows the comparison of the two models. We can see that $f(q, Q)$ is much worse than DRLM. From the

[3]The number of words does not increase as fast as the number of training data.

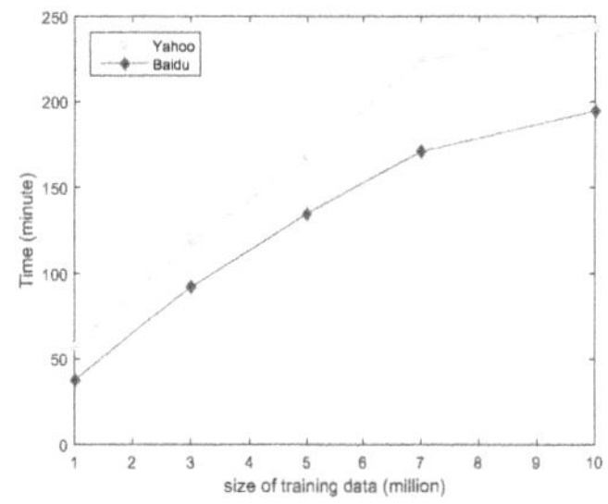

Figure 2: Changes of training time (mins) of DRLM on Yahoo data and Baidu data

results, we can conclude that the retrieval model we propose in Section 5.2 is superior in both efficiency and efficacy on measuring question similarity.

7. CONCLUSION

We propose learning distributed representations of data in CQA and leveraging the representations for question retrieval. The learning approach is inspired by a new framework for existing retrieval models. Our approach simultaneously embeds words and categories of questions into a vector space and models local relatedness of words in learning. We create a retrieval model with the learned representations. Evaluation results on public data sets show that the proposed method can significantly improve upon existing models in terms of both efficacy and efficiency.

8. ACKNOWLEDGEMENT

The work is supported in part by the National Natural Science Foundation of China (Grant Nos. 61170189, 61370126, 61202239), National High Technology Research and Development Program of China under grant (No.2015AA016004), Major Projects of the National Social Science Fund of China under grant (No.14&ZH0036), Science and Technology Innovation Ability Promotion Project of Beijing (PXM2015-014203-000059), the Fund of the State Key Laboratory of Software Development Environment (No. SKLSDE-2015ZX-16), and Microsoft Research Asia Fund (No. FY14-RES-OPP-105).

9. REFERENCES

[1] R. Baeza-Yates and B. Ribeiro-Neto. *Modern Information Retrieval.* Addison-Wesley Longman Publishing Co., Inc., Boston, MA, USA, 1999.

[2] Y. Bengio, R. Ducharme, P. Vincent, and C. Janvin. A neural probabilistic language model. *JMLR '03*, 3:1137–1155, Mar. 2003.

[3] A. Berger, R. Caruana, D. Cohn, D. Freitag, and V. Mittal. Bridging the lexical chasm: statistical approaches to answer-finding. In *SIGIR'00*, pages 192–199, 2000.

[4] X. Cao, G. Cong, B. Cui, and C. S. Jensen. A generalized framework of exploring category information for question retrieval in community question answer archives. In *WWW'10*, pages 201–210, 2010.

[5] X. Cao, G. Cong, B. Cui, C. S. Jensen, and C. Zhang. The use of categorization information in language models for question retrieval. In *CIKM'09*, pages 265–274, 2009.

[6] R. Collobert and J. Weston. A unified architecture for natural language processing: Deep neural networks with multitask learning. In *ICML '08*, pages 160–167, New York, NY, USA, 2008. ACM.

[7] Y. Goldberg and O. Levy. word2vec explained: deriving mikolov et al.'s negative-sampling word-embedding method. *arXiv preprint arXiv:1402.3722*, 2014.

Table 3: Evaluation results on Yahoo data and Baidu data (10 million)

	Yahoo data				Baidu data			
	MAP	MRR	R-Prec	P@1	MAP	MRR	R-Prec	P@1
$LMIR$	0.765	0.850	0.675	0.763	0.740	0.810	0.631	0.707
LMC_{leaf}	0.778	0.868	0.691	0.794	0.747	0.816	0.637	0.718
$Skip^{cat}_{trlm}$	0.782	0.874	0.693	0.802	0.756	0.827	0.654	0.737
$DRLM$	**0.794**	**0.887**	**0.708**	**0.825**	**0.769**	**0.843**	**0.668**	**0.751**

Table 4: Comparison of $f(q, Q)$ and DRLM on 1 million data

	Yahoo data				Baidu data			
	MAP	MRR	R-Prec	P@1	MAP	MRR	R-Prec	P@1
$f(q, Q)$	0.654	0.738	0.554	0.606	0.605	0.667	0.470	0.516
$DRLM$	0.789	0.881	0.701	0.816	0.761	0.835	0.657	0.738

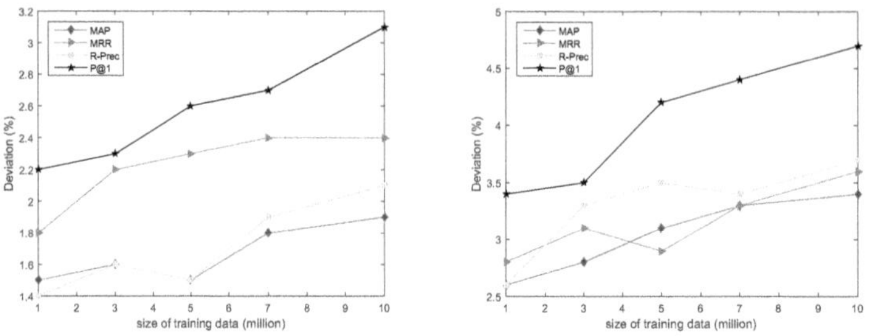

(a) Changes of efficacy of DRLM on Yahoo data (b) Changes of efficacy of DRLM on Baidu data

Figure 1: Changes of efficacy of DRLM on the two data sets. y axis represents the percentage of deviation of DRLM from TAL trained using 1 million data.

[8] E. H. Huang, R. Socher, C. D. Manning, and A. Y. Ng. Improving word representations via global context and multiple word prototypes. In *ACL'12*, pages 873–882, Stroudsburg, PA, USA, 2012. ACL.

[9] P.-S. Huang, X. He, J. Gao, L. Deng, A. Acero, and L. Heck. Learning deep structured semantic models for web search using clickthrough data. In *CIKM '13*, pages 2333–2338, New York, NY, USA, 2013. ACM.

[10] J. Jeon, W. B. Croft, and J. H. Lee. Finding similar questions in large question and answer archives. In *CIKM'05*, pages 84–90, 2005.

[11] Q. Le and T. Mikolov. Distributed representations of sentences and documents. In *ICML '14*, pages 1188–1196, 2014.

[12] T. Mikolov, K. Chen, G. Corrado, and J. Dean. Efficient estimation of word representations in vector space. *CoRR*, abs/1301.3781, 2013.

[13] T. Mikolov, M. KarafiÃąt, L. Burget, J. CernockÃ¡, and S. Khudanpur. Recurrent neural network based language model. In T. Kobayashi, K. Hirose, and S. Nakamura, editors, *INTERSPEECH*, pages 1045–1048. ISCA, 2010.

[14] T. Mikolov, Q. V. Le, and I. Sutskever. Exploiting similarities among languages for machine translation. *CoRR*, abs/1309.4168, 2013.

[15] T. Mikolov, I. Sutskever, K. Chen, G. S. Corrado, and J. Dean. Distributed representations of words and phrases and their compositionality. In *NIPS '13*, pages 3111–3119. Curran Associates, Inc., 2013.

[16] A. Mnih and G. E. Hinton. A scalable hierarchical distributed language model. In *NIPS '09*, pages 1081–1088. Curran Associates, Inc., 2009.

[17] F. Morin and Y. Bengio. Hierarchical probabilistic neural network language model. In R. G. Cowell and Z. Ghahramani, editors, *Proceedings of the Tenth International Workshop on Artificial Intelligence and Statistics*, pages 246–252. Society for Artificial Intelligence and Statistics, 2005.

[18] J. Ponte and W. Croft. A language modeling approach to information retrieval. In *SIGIR' 98*, pages 275–281, 1998.

[19] S. E. Robertson, S. Walker, S. Jones, M. Hancock-Beaulieu, and M. Gatford. Okapi at trec-3. In *TREC*, 1994.

[20] H. Schwenk, D. Dchelotte, and J.-L. Gauvain. Continuous space language models for statistical machine translation. In *COLING-ACL '06*, pages 723–730, Stroudsburg, PA, USA, 2006. ACL.

[21] H. Schwenk and J.-L. Gauvain. Neural network language models for conversational speech recognition. In *International Conference on Speech and Language Processing*, pages 1215–1218, 2004.

[22] Y. Shen, X. He, J. Gao, L. Deng, and G. Mesnil. A latent semantic model with convolutional-pooling structure for information retrieval. In *CIKM '14*, pages 101–110, New York, NY, USA, 2014. ACM.

[23] E. M. Voorhees. The trec-8 question answering track report. In *Proceedings of the 8th Text Retrieval Conference*, pages 77–82, 1999.

[24] K. Wang, Z. Ming, and T.-S. Chua. A syntactic tree matching approach to finding similar questions in community-based qa services. In *SIGIR'09*, pages 187–194, 2009.

[25] J. Weston, S. Bengio, and N. Usunier. Wsabie: Scaling up to large vocabulary image annotation. In *IJCAI'11*, pages 2764–2770. AAAI Press, 2011.

[26] X. Xue, J. Jeon, and W. B. Croft. Retrieval models for question and answer archives. In *SIGIR'08*, pages 475–482, 2008.

[27] C. Zhai and J. Lafferty. A study of smoothing methods for language models applied to information retrieval. *ACM Trans. Inf. Syst.*, 22(2):179–214, 2004.

[28] K. Zhang, W. Wu, H. Wu, Z. Li, and M. Zhou. Question retrieval with high quality answers in community question answering. In *CIKM '14*, pages 371–380, New York, NY, USA, 2014. ACM.

[29] G. Zhou, L. Cai, J. Zhao, and K. Liu. Phrase-based translation model for question retrieval in community question answer archives. In *ACL'11*, pages 653–662, 2011.

Inferring Latent Triggers of Purchases with Consideration of Social Effects and Media Advertisements

Yusuke Tanaka*, Takeshi Kurashima*, Yasuhiro Fujiwara†, Tomoharu Iwata‡, Hiroshi Sawada*
*NTT Service Evolution Laboratories, †NTT Software Innovation Center
‡NTT Communication Science Laboratories
*1-1 Hikari-no-oka, Yokosuka-Shi, Kanagawa, 239-0847 Japan
†3-9-11 Midori-cho, Musashino-shi, Tokyo, 180-8585 Japan
‡2-4 Hikaridai, Seika-Cho, Soraku-gun, Kyoto, 619-0237 Japan
{tanaka.y, kurashima.takeshi, fujiwara.yasuhiro, iwata.tomoharu, sawada.hiroshi}@lab.ntt.co.jp

ABSTRACT

This paper proposes a method for inferring from single-source data the factors that trigger purchases. Here, single-source data are the histories of item purchases and media advertisement views for each individual. We assume a sequence of purchase events to be a stochastic process incorporating the following three factors: (a) user preference, (b) social effects received from other users, and (c) media advertising effects. As our user-purchase model incorporates the latent relationships between users and advertisers, it can infer the latent triggers of purchases. Experiments on real single-source data show that our model can (a) achieve high prediction accuracy for purchases, (b) discover the key information, i.e., popular items, influential users, and influential advertisers, (c) estimate the relative impact of the three factors on purchases, and (d) find user segments according to the estimated factors.

Categories and Subject Descriptors

H.2.8 [**Database Management**]: Database Application—*Data Mining*

Keywords

Single-source data; Purchase behavior; Marked point processes

1. INTRODUCTION

Recent advances in information technology have increased our exposure to information in daily life. Users are exposed to so much information through web browsing, TV watching, and the use of social media, and make decisions (i.e., purchase an item) based on the information. For example, users may purchase items recommended by their friends and may also purchase items promoted by TV advertisements. Marketers are interested in analyzing the impact of such information on purchase behavior, because it provides useful knowledge for optimizing advertising strategies [14] and viral marketing [3, 10].

In order to evaluate the effectiveness of their advertising strategies, marketing research companies continue to collect time-series data of item purchases and advertisement views for each user. Histories of purchase and view events are collected from 'single-sources' (i.e., individual users), so this data is called 'single-source data'. In the field of marketing science, many methods have been proposed for estimating media advertising effects by analyzing single-source data [11, 23, 24]. Most of these methods assume that a user's purchase behavior is triggered by only advertisements. This assumption, however, looks outdated. With the development of the web and social media, it is becoming increasingly important to consider social effects such as recommendations by other users. The previous methods are difficult to accurately evaluate the advertising effects since they ignore social effects.

The purpose of this paper is to estimate the factors that trigger purchases and discover useful knowledge for marketers in single-source data. This is, however, quite challenging to accomplish, mainly because event order and timing do not always show a direct causality. For example, a user watching an ad on TV may not become immediately keen to buy right away. Likewise, a latest recommendation by other users does not always trigger an immediate purchase. Furthermore, a purchase can occur independently of these external factors, i.e., item purchases can be driven by user preference.

In order to effectively detect the causes of purchases, we focus on the strength of relationships between users and advertisers. This is because how strongly an advertiser influences a user depends on the relationship between them. For example, familiar users, such as friends or family, have a stronger impact than strangers. Likewise, a familiar company's ad on TV has a stronger impact on the user' willingness to buy than an unfamiliar company's ad. Given the above, we develop a new probabilistic model for inferring the factors that trigger purchases from single-source data. The model incorporates three factors: (a) user preference, (b) social effects received from other users, and (c) media advertising effects. We model users' willingness to buy over

WSDM'16, February 22–25, 2016, San Francisco, CA, USA.

DOI: http://dx.doi.org/10.1145/2835776.2835789

time by incorporating the latent relationships between users and advertisers. By using efficient Bayesian inference based on the stochastic EM algorithm [5], we can obtain the latent triggers for purchases. Our model can estimate not only media advertising effects but also social effects and user preferences for each purchase event. Therefore, we can also evaluate the relative impact of the three factors on purchases for each user. The estimated impact of advertising is useful for marketers. For example, when marketers want to evaluate advertising strategies for a product that has been sold before, our model can show to what extent the advertisements were responsible for the purchases of the product. In addition, our model can discover users who are likely to be influenced by media advertisement from the estimated latent triggers; we can expect high advertising effectiveness by targeting these users through advertising management. Furthermore, we can find influential users that trigger chain-reaction purchases from the estimated relationships between users; we can expect higher sales by targeting the influential users in viral marketing.

We demonstrate the effectiveness of the proposed model by using real single-source data, the histories of item purchases and TV advertisement views by individuals. We evaluate the validity of our proposed model in terms of its accuracy in predicting purchases. In addition, we show three practical uses of our model by demonstrating that the model can actually extract the useful knowledge to marketers. First, we show that our model can discover key information, i.e., poplar items, influential users and influential advertisers. This knowledge is helpful in optimizing the marketing strategies. Second, we demonstrate that our model can infer the impact of factors that trigger purchases. When marketers want to evaluate their advertising strategies for a product, we can estimate how many purchases were triggered by their advertisements. Third, we show that our model can find user segments based on their consumption behavior. This can suggest better approaches to activating the users.

This paper is organized as follows: Section 2 outlines related work. Section 3 describe the details of the single-source data used. In Section 4, we construct the proposed model with its three factors and present a Bayesian inference procedure to infer the latent triggers for purchases. Section 5 demonstrates the effectiveness of the proposed model by using real single-source data. Finally, we present our conclusions in Section 6.

2. RELATED WORK

Many statistical methods have been studied for analyzing the social effects among users given a social network structure [1, 27]. These methods are often used for viral marketing [3, 10, 15] and ranking influential users [21]. However, in many online social media, it is difficult to directly obtain the strength of relationships between users. Thus, estimating the influences among users from their activities is an important research topic.

Influences among users are often inferred by using information diffusion models, and a number of such models have recently been proposed for inferring the influences between users without prior knowledge (e.g., users' network structure) based on maximum likelihood [8, 13, 16]. A key restrictive assumption in these methods is that a user selects an item only once in the item selection sequence. More flexible models have been proposed [5, 19] based on a point process framework. Point processes [20] are stochastic processes for modeling event occurrence over time. We can use marked point processes [9] to model the occurrence of an augmented event that is the pair of time and another random element (e.g., user). Cascade Poisson process [19] models event sequences of item selection based on marked point processes. Shared cascade Poisson process (SCPP) [5] is an extension of cascade Poisson process. SCPP can infer the latent influences between users in online social communities from the selection sequences of multiple items. SCPP does not consider the media advertising effects, which is important for modeling purchase behavior. The proposed model is an extension of SCPP, and can estimate the effect that each factor has in triggering purchases by simultaneously analyzing not only purchase events but also advertisement view events. Therefore, our model can estimate and evaluate the impact of media advertising. Furthermore, our model can capture the social effects and each user's preference more precisely.

In the field of marketing science, many methods have been proposed for analyzing the impact of media advertising. Most of the methods estimate how effective media advertisements are in triggering purchases in the overall market [11, 23]. These methods, unfortunately, cannot evaluate the advertising effects for each user, and cannot also estimate social effects and user preferences. Based on single-source data, Terui *et al.* [24] proposed a model that can analyze the advertising effects for each user by modeling *advertising stock*: the cumulative effects of media advertising. In online advertising, Rosales *et al.* [17] proposed a model for analyzing the advertiser's attributes (e.g., ad type, campaign, etc.) that can be expected to contribute to users' conversion actions such as adding an item to the shopping cart and making a purchase. However, these methods assume that purchases are triggered only by media advertisements. The proposed model includes three factors. Different from previous methods, our model can estimate the impact of media advertising except for the possible effects of other factors.

A few methods consider both social and advertising effects when estimating the factors that trigger purchases, similar to our method [4, 22]. However, since these models treat social and advertising effects as one factor, they do not evaluate the impact of each factor for each user; these models do not estimate whose recommendation or which advertisement triggered a purchase. Therefore, these models cannot be used for finding, for each user, influential users, estimating user relationships, and inferring the impact of advertising.

3. SINGLE-SOURCE DATA

In this section, we describe the details of **single-source data**, which are the histories of viewing a media (TV, Web) advertisement and purchase behavior over time for each single-source (i.e., individual user). Single-source data are collected by marketing research companies, such as TiVO Research Inc[1] and INTAGE Inc[2], for the purpose of analyzing advertisement effects.

In our experiments, we used individual consumer panel research data (SCI) and INTAGE single source panel data (i-SSP) collected by INTAGE Inc. Note that panels consist of users who agreed to provide detailed information on their

[1]http://www.tivoresearch.com
[2]http://www.intage.co.jp

Table 1: Notations of single-source data.

Symbol	Description
$\boldsymbol{I}$	set of items
$\boldsymbol{U}$	set of users
$\boldsymbol{M}$	set of advertisers
i	item, $i \in \boldsymbol{I}$
u^{p}_{ij}	user of the jth purchase event of item i, $u^{\mathrm{p}}_{ij} \in \boldsymbol{U}$
u^{v}_{ij}	user of the kth view event of item i, $u^{\mathrm{v}}_{ij} \in \boldsymbol{U}$
m_i	advertiser of item i, $m_i \in \boldsymbol{M}$
t^{p}_{ij}	time of the jth purchase event of item i
t^{v}_{ik}	time of the kth view event of TV advertisement of item i
$\boldsymbol{D}$	set of purchase events
$\boldsymbol{C}$	set of view events of TV advertisement
T	observation period
J_i	number of purchase events for item i in $t \in [0, T]$
K_i	number of view events for item i in $t \in [0, T]$

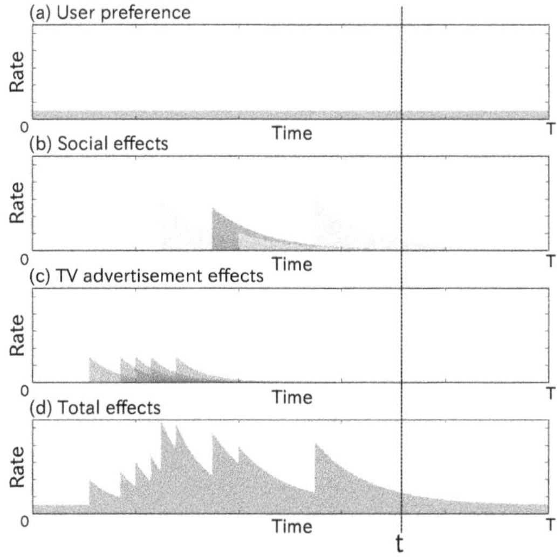

Figure 1: Plot of purchase rate of item i by user u according to our model. (a) Purchase rate based on user preference. (b) Purchase rate based on social effects received from other users. (c) Purchase rate based on TV advertising effects. (d) Purchase rate based on the three factors given the preceding purchase/view events.

behavior over time. SCI records users' purchase histories for daily shopping. On returning from a shopping, users enter their purchase information into an online data collection system. i-SSP records users' view histories for TV advertisements. The view histories are collected automatically using an in-home recording device connected to household television sets.

Suppose that we have a set of purchase events $\boldsymbol{D} = \{\boldsymbol{D}_i\}_{i \in \boldsymbol{I}}$, where $\boldsymbol{I}$ is a set of items. A purchase event sequence of item i consists of J_i events, $\boldsymbol{D}_i = \{(t^{\mathrm{p}}_{ij}, u^{\mathrm{p}}_{ij})\}_{j=1}^{J_i}$, in the time period from 0 to T. $(t^{\mathrm{p}}_{ij}, u^{\mathrm{p}}_{ij})$ is the jth purchase event of item i, which represents that user u^{p}_{ij} purchased item i at time t^{p}_{ij}. Without loss of generality, we assume that events are sorted by their timestamps, $t^{\mathrm{p}}_{ij} \leq t^{\mathrm{p}}_{ij'}$, for $j < j'$. We also have a set of events of viewing TV advertisements $\boldsymbol{C} = \{\boldsymbol{C}_i\}_{i \in \boldsymbol{I}}$. An event sequence of viewing TV advertisements of item i consists of K_i events, $\boldsymbol{C}_i = \{(t^{\mathrm{v}}_{ik}, u^{\mathrm{v}}_{ik})\}_{k=1}^{K_i}$, in the time period from 0 to T. $(t^{\mathrm{v}}_{ik}, u^{\mathrm{v}}_{ik})$ is the kth view events of TV advertisements of item i, which represents that user u^{v}_{ik} viewed a TV advertisement of item i at time t^{v}_{ik}. Similar to purchase data, we can assume that events are sorted by their timestamps, $t^{\mathrm{v}}_{ik} \leq t^{\mathrm{v}}_{ik'}$, for $k < k'$. Note that the set of users $\boldsymbol{U}$ is common between purchases and views. Additionally, each item has information that represents advertiser $m_i \in \boldsymbol{M}$ who promotes item i, where $\boldsymbol{M}$ is a set of advertisers. The notations used in this paper are listed in Table 1.

4. MODEL

4.1 Proposed Model

We propose a new probabilistic model for inferring the latent triggers for purchases from single-source data. In the proposed model, a sequence of purchase events is assumed to be generated from marked point processes [9]. They are stochastic processes for modeling the occurrence of purchase events for each item, where an event represents a pair of time and user (t, u). The marked point processes are governed by a non-negative *purchase rate*, $\lambda_i(t, u)$. $\lambda_i(t, u)$ is the instantaneous probability of user u purchasing item i at time t. We model the purchase rate based on the following three factors: (a) user preference, (b) social effects received from other users, and (c) media advertising effects. First, let $f_i(u)$ be the purchase rate based on user preferences, it represents how strongly user u wants to buy item i. Second, let $g_{(i,t',u')}(t, u)$ be the purchase rate of user u purchasing item i at time t influenced by the event in which user u' purchased item i at time t'. Third, let $h_{(i,t',m_i)}(t, u)$ be the purchase rate of user u purchasing item i at time t influenced by the event that user u viewed a TV advertisement of item i at time t'. Details of each purchase rate are given in the following paragraphs. We have the following assumptions with regard to a user's purchase based on each purchase rate: a user's purchase can be triggered by (a) her/his preferences, (b) preceding purchase events by other users, and (c) preceding view events of TV advertisements. By combining the three factors, we can obtain the purchase rate based on these factors, $\lambda_i(t, u)$, as follows:

$$\lambda_i(t, u) = f_i(u) + \sum_{(t',u') \in \boldsymbol{D}_{it \setminus u}} g_{(i,t',u')}(t, u) + \sum_{(t',u') \in \boldsymbol{C}_{itu}} h_{(i,t',m_i)}(t, u), \tag{1}$$

where $\boldsymbol{D}_{it\setminus u} = \{(t', u') | (t', u') \in \boldsymbol{D}_i \text{ and } t' < t \wedge u' \neq u\}$ is the set of purchase events before time t excluding user u's ones, and $\boldsymbol{C}_{itu} = \{(t', u') | (t', u') \in \boldsymbol{C}_i \text{ and } t' < t \wedge u' = u\}$ is the set of view events of user u before time t.

(a) Purchase rate based on user preferences. We assume that each user has a different preference for each item. As described in Figure 1(a), we also assume that purchase rate based on user preferences is constant in the time period from 0 to T. This non-negative constant rate is called the "background rate" in the point processes framework [20].

The purchase rate at which user u purchases item i based on personal preference is as follows:

$$f_i(u) = \alpha_i \phi_{iu}. \quad (2)$$

Here, $\alpha_i \geq 0$ is the rate at which item i is purchased without being triggered by the preceding events. α_i represents the general popularity of item i; a high popularity suggests many purchases are made without being triggered by other users or TV advertisements. $\phi_{iu} \geq 0$ is the probability that a user who purchases item i is in fact user u, where $\sum_{u \in \boldsymbol{U}} \phi_{iu} = 1$. If user u prefers item i more strongly than other users, ϕ_{iu} becomes large.

(b) Purchase rate based on the social effects received from other users. We assume that a purchase event can be triggered by the preceding purchase events of other users. For example, users are apt to purchase the same item purchased by their friends. We also assume that the influences of other users depend on the user and decays over time. For example, the effects of familiar users, such as friends or family, are larger than those of strangers. Furthermore, this decay over time is a natural assumption because trends evolve or change and is often used when modeling information diffusion processes between users [8, 13, 16]. We model the purchase rate at which user u purchases item i at time t influenced by the event that user u' purchased item i at time t' as follows:

$$g_{(i,t',u')}(t,u) = \begin{cases} \alpha_{u'} \theta_{u'u} e^{-\gamma^{\mathrm{P}}(t-t')} & \text{if } t' < t \\ 0 & \text{otherwise.} \end{cases} \quad (3)$$

Here, $\alpha_{u'} \geq 0$ represents the influence of user u' on other users. The second factor $\theta_{u'u} \geq 0$ represents the strength of the relation from user u' to user u, where $\sum_{u \in \boldsymbol{U} \setminus u'} \theta_{u'u} = 1$. Note that $\boldsymbol{U} \setminus u'$ represents the result of the procedures that exclude user u' from set $\boldsymbol{U}$. The product of these factors, $\alpha_{u'} \theta_{u'u}$, corresponds to the influence from user u' to user u. The third factor $e^{-\gamma^{\mathrm{P}}(t-t')}$ models decay of the influence over time with parameter $\gamma^{\mathrm{P}} \geq 0$. Since an event does not influence on past events, the purchase rate is zero when $t' \geq t$. Figure 1(b) illustrates the temporal dynamics of social effects received from other users, where the colored part represents the social effects of each user.

(c) Purchase rate based on TV advertising effects. We assume that a user's purchases can be triggered by the preceding view events. We also assume that the influences of advertiser depend on the user and decay over time. For example, a familiar company's ad on TV has a stronger effect than those of unfamiliar advertisers. We model the purchase rate that user u purchases item i at time t influenced by the event that user u views an advertisement of item i at time t' as follows:

$$h_{(i,t',m_i)}(t,u) = \begin{cases} \alpha_{m_i} \omega_{m_i u} e^{-\gamma^{\mathrm{V}}(t-t')} & \text{if } t' < t \\ 0 & \text{otherwise.} \end{cases} \quad (4)$$

Note that TV advertising effects are directed from advertiser m_i to user u unlike the effects between users. $\alpha_{m_i} \geq 0$ is the influence of advertiser m_i on the users through TV advertisements. The second factor $\omega_{m_i u} \geq 0$ represents the strength of the relation from advertiser m_i to user u, where $\sum_{u \in \boldsymbol{U}} \omega_{m_i u} = 1$. The product of these factors, $\alpha_{m_i} \omega_{m_i u}$, corresponds to the effects of ads from advertiser m_i to user u. The third factor, $e^{-\gamma^{\mathrm{V}}(t-t')}$, models the decay of the influence over time using parameter $\gamma^{\mathrm{V}} \geq 0$. Advertising effects are often modeled by using an exponential pattern, called *carryover effects*, in marketing science [2, 23]. Figure 1(c) illustrates the temporal dynamics of TV advertising effects.

Table 2: Parameters of the proposed model

Symbol	Description
α_i	popularity of item i, $\alpha_i \geq 0$
α_u	influence of user u, $\alpha_u \geq 0$
α_m	influence of advertiser m, $\alpha_m \geq 0$
ϕ_{iu}	preference of user u to item i $\phi_{iu} \geq 0$, $\sum_{u \in \boldsymbol{U}} \phi_{iu} = 1$
$\theta_{u'u}$	strength of relation from user u' to user u $\theta_{u'u} \geq 0$, $\sum_{u \in \boldsymbol{U} \setminus u'} \theta_{u'u} = 1$
ω_{mu}	strength of relation from advertiser m to user u $\omega_{mu} \geq 0$, $\sum_{u \in \boldsymbol{U}} \omega_{mu} = 1$
$\gamma^{\mathrm{P}}, \gamma^{\mathrm{V}}$	decay parameter, $\gamma^{\mathrm{P}} \geq 0$, $\gamma^{\mathrm{V}} \geq 0$

By substituting (2)-(4) into (1), we can obtain purchase rate based on the three factors whose temporal dynamics are illustrated in Figure 1(d). Parameters of the proposed model are summarized in Table 2: popularity of each item, $\{\alpha_i\}_{i \in \boldsymbol{I}}$, influence of each user, $\{\alpha_u\}_{u \in \boldsymbol{U}}$, influence of each advertiser, $\{\alpha_m\}_{m \in \boldsymbol{M}}$, relationship between users, $\boldsymbol{\Theta} = \{\boldsymbol{\theta}_u\}_{u \in \boldsymbol{U}}$, $\boldsymbol{\theta}_u = \{\theta_{uu'}\}_{u' \in \boldsymbol{U} \setminus u}$, relationship between user and advertiser, $\boldsymbol{\Omega} = \{\boldsymbol{\omega}_m\}_{m \in \boldsymbol{M}}$, $\boldsymbol{\omega}_m = \{\omega_{mu}\}_{u \in \boldsymbol{U}}$, user preferences to items, $\boldsymbol{\Phi} = \{\boldsymbol{\phi}_i\}_{i \in \boldsymbol{I}}$, $\boldsymbol{\phi}_i = \{\phi_{iu}\}_{u \in \boldsymbol{U}}$, and parameters of influence decay over time, $\boldsymbol{\gamma} = \{\gamma^{\mathrm{P}}, \gamma^{\mathrm{V}}\}$.

4.2 Inference

Given purchase events $\boldsymbol{D}$ and view events $\boldsymbol{C}$, we infer the model parameters shown in Table 2. For this, we employ the stochastic EM algorithm, in which newly introduced latent variables $\boldsymbol{Z}$ are sampled in the E-step and model parameter $\boldsymbol{\gamma}$ are optimized in the M-step as described in Section 4.2.1. Other model parameters $\boldsymbol{\alpha} = \{\alpha_l\}_{l \in \boldsymbol{U} \cup \boldsymbol{M} \cup \boldsymbol{I}}$, $\boldsymbol{\Theta}$, $\boldsymbol{\Omega}$, $\boldsymbol{\Phi}$ are integrated out in the stochastic EM algorithm, and their point estimates are obtained as shown in Section 4.2.2.

4.2.1 *Inferring latent triggers via stochastic EM algorithm*

We assume that a set of purchase events $\boldsymbol{D}_i$ is generated from a marked point process with rate $\lambda_i(t,u)$. Given the multiple purchase event sequences $\boldsymbol{D} = \{\boldsymbol{D}_i\}_{i \in \boldsymbol{I}}$, the likelihood function of $\boldsymbol{D}$ is described as follows:

$$P(\boldsymbol{D}|\boldsymbol{C}, \boldsymbol{\alpha}, \boldsymbol{\Theta}, \boldsymbol{\Omega}, \boldsymbol{\Phi}, \boldsymbol{\gamma}) = \prod_{i \in \boldsymbol{I}} \exp\left(-\int_0^T \sum_{u \in \boldsymbol{U}} \lambda_i(t,u) dt\right) \prod_{j=1}^{J_i} \lambda_i(t_{ij}^{\mathrm{P}}, u_{ij}^{\mathrm{P}}), \quad (5)$$

where the exponential factor of (5) represents the probability of no purchase events occurring in the time period from 0 to T. Here, we can analytically calculate the integral as follows:

$$\int_0^T \sum_{u \in \boldsymbol{U}} \lambda_i(t,u) dt = \alpha_i T + \frac{1}{\gamma^{\mathrm{P}}} \sum_{j=1}^{J_i} \alpha_{u_{ij}} \left(1 - e^{-\gamma^{\mathrm{P}}(T - t_{ij}^{\mathrm{P}})}\right) + \frac{\alpha_{m_i}}{\gamma^{\mathrm{V}}} \sum_{k=1}^{K_i} \left(1 - e^{-\gamma^{\mathrm{V}}(T - t_{ik}^{\mathrm{V}})}\right). \quad (6)$$

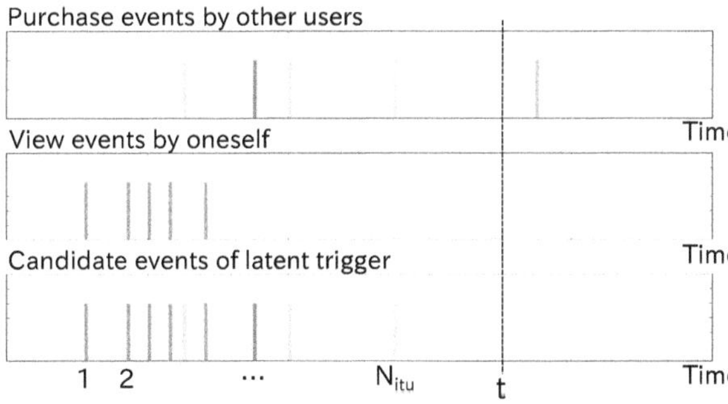

Figure 2: Candidate event set of latent triggers; preceding purchase/view events of item i before time t for user u.

By the superposition theorem of point processes [20], the point processes with the recursive rates, $\lambda_i(t,u)$ (1), can be decomposed into independent point processes with each rate. We use this theorem to simplify the inference without changing the model. We define the candidate set of latent triggers as $\boldsymbol{D}_{it\backslash u} \cup \boldsymbol{C}_{itu}$, which is the set of preceding events of item i before time t. Figure 2 shows the candidate set of latent triggers, where N_{itu} is the number of events in the candidate set. We introduce latent variable $z_{ij} \in \{0,\ldots,N_{itu}\}$ to indicate the index of latent trigger event of the jth event of item i, where $z_{ij}=0$ indicates that the event was triggered by the purchase rate based on user preferences. By using latent variable z, the purchase rate (1) can be written as $\lambda_i(t,u)=\sum_z \lambda_i(t,u,z)$, where the augmented purchase rate is as follows:

$$\lambda_i(t,u,z) = \begin{cases} f_i(u) & \text{if } z=0 \\ g_{(i,t_{iz},d_{iz})}(t,u) & \text{if } z\neq 0 \wedge d_{iz}\in \boldsymbol{U} \\ h_{(i,t_{iz},d_{iz})}(t,u) & \text{if } z\neq 0 \wedge d_{iz}\in \boldsymbol{M}, \end{cases} \quad (7)$$

where $d_{iz} \in \boldsymbol{U}\cup\boldsymbol{M}$ is a dummy variable; $d_{iz}=u_{iz}$ if the event indicated by z_{ij} is a purchase event, and $d_{iz}=m_i$ if the event is a view event.

Combining (5), (6) and (7), we obtain the joint distribution of observed purchase events $\boldsymbol{D}$ and latent variables $\boldsymbol{Z}=\{\{z_{ij}\}_{j=1}^{J_i}\}_{i\in\boldsymbol{I}}$,

$$\begin{aligned} & P(\boldsymbol{D},\boldsymbol{Z}|\boldsymbol{C},\boldsymbol{\alpha},\boldsymbol{\Theta},\boldsymbol{\Omega},\boldsymbol{\Phi},\boldsymbol{\gamma}) \\ & = \prod_{i\in\boldsymbol{I}} \exp\Bigg[\alpha_i T + \frac{1}{\gamma^{\mathrm{P}}}\sum_{j=1}^{J_i}\alpha_{u_{ij}}\left(1-e^{-\gamma^{\mathrm{P}}(T-t^{\mathrm{P}}_{ij})}\right) \\ & + \frac{\alpha_{m_i}}{\gamma^{\mathrm{V}}}\sum_{k=1}^{K_i}\left(1-e^{-\gamma^{\mathrm{V}}(T-t^{\mathrm{V}}_{ik})}\right)\Bigg]\prod_{j=1}^{J_i}\lambda_i(t^{\mathrm{P}}_{ij},u^{\mathrm{P}}_{ij},z_{ij}). \end{aligned} \quad (8)$$

We use the following Dirichlet priors over $\boldsymbol{\theta}_u$, $\boldsymbol{\omega}_m$ and $\boldsymbol{\phi}_i$ as: $P(\boldsymbol{\Theta}) \propto \prod_{u\in\boldsymbol{U}}\prod_{u'\in\boldsymbol{U}\backslash u}\theta_{uu'}^{\beta_1-1}$, $P(\boldsymbol{\Omega}) \propto \prod_{m\in\boldsymbol{M}}\prod_{u\in\boldsymbol{U}}\omega_{mu}^{\beta_2-1}$ and $P(\boldsymbol{\Phi}) \propto \prod_{i\in\boldsymbol{I}}\prod_{u\in\boldsymbol{U}}\phi_{iu}^{\beta_3-1}$. Here, $\boldsymbol{\beta}=\{\beta_1,\beta_2,\beta_3\}$ are hyperparameters, each of which is estimated by using the fixed-point iteration method described in [12]. Furthermore, we use the following Gamma priors over α_l, $l\in\boldsymbol{U}\cup\boldsymbol{M}\cup\boldsymbol{I}$ as: $P(\alpha_l)\propto \alpha_l^{a-1}\exp(-b\alpha_l)$, where a and b are hyperparameters and in this paper we set $a=b=1$, which is equivalent to an exponential distribution with mean of 1. With the help of the conjugacy of the priors, the marginalization can be calculated analytically over the parameters. Integrating out the parameters gives the following marginalized joint distribution:

$$\begin{aligned} & P(\boldsymbol{D},\boldsymbol{Z}|\boldsymbol{C},\boldsymbol{\gamma},\boldsymbol{\beta},a,b) \\ & = \int P(\boldsymbol{D},\boldsymbol{Z}|\boldsymbol{C},\boldsymbol{\alpha},\boldsymbol{\Theta},\boldsymbol{\Omega},\boldsymbol{\Phi},\boldsymbol{\gamma})P(\boldsymbol{\alpha}|a,b)P(\boldsymbol{\Theta}|\beta_1) \\ & \quad \times P(\boldsymbol{\Omega}|\beta_2)P(\boldsymbol{\Phi}|\beta_3)d\boldsymbol{\alpha}d\boldsymbol{\Theta}d\boldsymbol{\Omega}d\boldsymbol{\Phi} \\ & \propto \exp\left(-\sum_{i\in\boldsymbol{I}}\sum_{j:z_{ij}\neq 0}\eta(d_{iz_{ij}})(t^{\mathrm{P}}_{ij}-t_{iz_{ij}})\right) \\ & \times \prod_{u'\in\boldsymbol{U}}\frac{\prod_{u\in\boldsymbol{U}\backslash u'}\Gamma(L_{u'u}+\beta_1)}{\Gamma(L_{u'}+\beta_1(|\boldsymbol{U}|-1))}\prod_{m\in\boldsymbol{M}}\frac{\prod_{u\in\boldsymbol{U}}\Gamma(L_{mu}+\beta_2)}{\Gamma(L_m+\beta_2|\boldsymbol{U}|)} \\ & \times \prod_{i\in\boldsymbol{I}}\frac{\prod_{u\in\boldsymbol{U}}\Gamma(L_{iu}+\beta_3)}{\Gamma(L_i+\beta_3|\boldsymbol{U}|)}\prod_{l\in\boldsymbol{U}\cup\boldsymbol{M}\cup\boldsymbol{I}}\frac{\Gamma(L_l+a)}{(R_l+b)^{L_l+a}}, \end{aligned} \quad (9)$$

where

$$\eta(d_{iz_{ij}}) = \begin{cases} \gamma^{\mathrm{P}} & \text{if } d_{iz_{ij}}\in\boldsymbol{U} \\ \gamma^{\mathrm{V}} & \text{if } d_{iz_{ij}}\in\boldsymbol{M}, \end{cases} \quad (10)$$

and we define the set of only time information for either purchase events or view events as $\{t_{ij},|j=1,\ldots,N_{itu}\}$. Here, $L_{u'u}=\sum_{i\in\boldsymbol{I}}\sum_{j=1}^{J_i}\delta(d_{iz_{ij}},u')\delta(u_{ij},u)$ is the number of events for user u triggered by user u' and $L_{u'}=\sum_{u\in\boldsymbol{U}\backslash u'}L_{u'u}$ is the total number of events triggered by user u', where $\delta(x,y)=1$ if $x=y$, and $\delta(x,y)=0$ otherwise. $L_{mu}=\sum_{i\in\boldsymbol{I}}\sum_{k=1}^{K_i}\delta(d_{iz_{ik}},m)\delta(u_{ik},u)$ is the number of events for user u triggered by advertiser m and $L_m=\sum_{u\in\boldsymbol{U}}L_{mu}$ is the total number of events triggered by advertiser m. Furthermore, $L_{iu}=\sum_{j=1}^{J_i}\delta(u_{ij},u)\delta(z_{ij},0)$ is the number of events in which the user who purchased item i based on preference was in fact user u and $L_i=\sum_{j=1}^{J_i}\delta(z_{ij},0)$ is the number of purchase events of item i triggered by user preferences. Additionally,

$$R_l = \begin{cases} T & \text{if } l\in\boldsymbol{I} \\ \frac{1}{\gamma^{\mathrm{P}}}\sum_{t\in\boldsymbol{D}_l}\left(1-e^{-\gamma^{\mathrm{P}}(T-t)}\right) & \text{if } l\in\boldsymbol{U} \\ \frac{1}{\gamma^{\mathrm{V}}}\sum_{t\in\boldsymbol{C}_l}\left(1-e^{-\gamma^{\mathrm{V}}(T-t)}\right) & \text{if } l\in\boldsymbol{M}, \end{cases} \quad (11)$$

where $\boldsymbol{D}_l$ is a set of timestamps of purchase events of user l. $\boldsymbol{C}_l$ is a set of times when advertiser l broadcast a TV ad, noting that $\boldsymbol{C}_l$ is not the set of times of view events.

Based on (9), we present a stochastic EM algorithm for the inference. In the E-step, a new value for z_{ij} is sampled from the following probability:

$$\begin{aligned} & P(z_{ij}=y|\boldsymbol{D},\boldsymbol{Z}_{\backslash ij},\boldsymbol{C},\boldsymbol{\gamma},\boldsymbol{\beta},a,b) \\ & \quad \propto \frac{P(\boldsymbol{D},\boldsymbol{Z}_{\backslash ij},z_{ij}=y|\boldsymbol{C},\boldsymbol{\gamma},\boldsymbol{\beta},a,b)}{P(\boldsymbol{D}_{\backslash ij},\boldsymbol{Z}_{\backslash ij}|\boldsymbol{C},\boldsymbol{\gamma},\boldsymbol{\beta},a,b)}, \end{aligned} \quad (12)$$

where $y\in\{0,1,\ldots,N_{itu}\}$, subscript $\backslash ij$ represents the procedure that excludes the jth event of item i. Based on the procedure of Gibbs sampling, z_{ij} for all i and j are sampled sequentially.

In the M-step, we estimate the decay parameters $\boldsymbol{\gamma}$ and Dirichlet parameter $\boldsymbol{\beta}$. Given $\boldsymbol{Z}$, updated in the E-step, these parameters are estimated by maximizing the logarithm of the joint likelihood (9). We estimate $\boldsymbol{\gamma}$ and $\boldsymbol{\beta}$ using Newton's method and the fixed point iteration method [12], respectively. By iterating the E-step and M-step until convergence, we can estimate latent variables $\boldsymbol{Z}$, decay parameters $\boldsymbol{\gamma}$ and Dirichlet parameters $\boldsymbol{\beta}$.

4.2.2 Point estimates of integrated out parameters

If we obtain $\boldsymbol{Z}$, $\boldsymbol{\gamma}$ and $\boldsymbol{\beta}$ from the above procedure, we can obtain point estimates of the integrated-out parameters by using maximum posteriori given $\boldsymbol{Z}$. The posteriors for these parameters are given by

$$P(\alpha_l|\boldsymbol{D},\boldsymbol{Z},\boldsymbol{\gamma},a,b) = \text{Gamma}(L_l + a, R_l + b), \quad (13)$$
$$P(\boldsymbol{\theta}_u|\boldsymbol{D},\boldsymbol{Z},\beta_1) = \text{Dirichlet}(L_{u'u} + \beta_1), \quad (14)$$
$$P(\boldsymbol{\omega}_m|\boldsymbol{D},\boldsymbol{Z},\beta_2) = \text{Dirichlet}(L_{mu} + \beta_2), \quad (15)$$
$$P(\boldsymbol{\phi}_i|\boldsymbol{D},\boldsymbol{Z},\beta_3) = \text{Dirichlet}(L_{iu} + \beta_3). \quad (16)$$

The point estimates of the parameters are given by

$$\hat{\alpha}_l = \frac{L_l + a}{R_l + b}, \quad (17)$$

which can be used for finding popular items, influential users, and influential advertisers, and

$$\hat{\theta}_{u'u} = \frac{L_{u'u} + \beta_1}{L_{u'} + \beta_1|\boldsymbol{U} - 1|}, \quad \hat{\omega}_{mu} = \frac{L_{mu} + \beta_2}{L_m + \beta_2|\boldsymbol{M}|}, \quad (18)$$

which can be used for analyzing the relationships between users and advertisers, and

$$\hat{\phi}_{iu} = \frac{L_{iu} + \beta_3}{L_u + \beta_3|\boldsymbol{U}|}, \quad (19)$$

which can be used for analyzing user preferences to items.

5. EXPERIMENTS

In this section, we show the effectiveness of the proposed model by conducting quantitative evaluations on real single-source data in Section 5.1. We also conducted the qualitative evaluations in accordance with the three practical uses by analyzing the estimated model parameters in Section 5.2.

5.1 Quantitative Evaluation

The purpose of this quantitative evaluation is to validate the proposed model in terms of its prediction accuracy. This leads to increase confidence in the knowledge about the purchase behaviors indicated by the estimated parameters of our model. We note that predictive performance is the most commonly used measure for evaluating the appropriateness of a learned model [5, 6].

We used real single-source data that are the histories of purchase and view events of TV advertisements in daily life gathered over 52 weeks (January 1, 2013 – December 31, 2013)[3]. The data sets consist of three categories: Canned Coffee, Beer and Soft Drink. For each data set, we prepared 3 different training and test data splits by changing the test months: August, October and December. For example, if the model was evaluated using purchase events in August as test data, the model was trained using the purchase/view events in the period from January to July as training data. Note that we omitted users who bought less than five items during the training period. In our experiments, each event timestamp is measured in days. Details of the data sets used in our experiments are shown in Table 3.

We compared the proposed model with shared cascade Poisson processes (SCPP) [5]. SCPP considers only social effects in calculating the purchase rate. The social effects are determined from the estimated influences between users. In addition, we compared our model with the homogeneous Poisson process (PP) [20] as a baseline method. PP is a stochastic process for modeling event occurrence with a constant rate. In experiments we used the purchase rate described in (2) for the baseline method; the baseline method assumes that each user makes a decision based only on her/his preferences. The predictive performance is evaluated by the negative logarithm of the likelihood for purchase events (t, u) in the test period, T to T', as follows:

Table 3: Statistics of the data sets

Data Set	Canned Coffee	Beer	Soft Drink
#purchases	51,120	54,830	140,999
#views	102,480	339,331	598,121
#users	743	1,135	2,108
#advertisers	11	7	19
#items	40	36	75

$$L_1 = \sum_{i \in \boldsymbol{I}} \left(-\int_T^{T'} \sum_{u \in \boldsymbol{U}} \lambda_i(t,u)dt \right) \sum_{(t,u) \in \boldsymbol{D}_i^{\text{test}}} \log \lambda_i(t,u), \quad (20)$$

where $\boldsymbol{D}_i^{\text{test}}$ is the test data for item i. When the value of L_1 is small, the predictive performance is high. Figure 3 shows the results for each data set. "Proposed" in the figure indicate the results of our model. In this figure, the X-axis plots test month and the Y-axis plots the negative logarithm of the test likelihood, and the method marked by asterisk (*) achieves the best performance. Figure 3 shows that, regardless of test month, our model matched or bettered the predictive performance of the alternatives. Since the proposed model considers three key factors, it can appropriately predict the user's purchase behavior. SCPP yielded slightly better predictive performance in only one experimental setting (category = Soft Drink, test month = August). However, SCPP cannot estimate the media advertising effects, in which many marketers are interested.

To show the validity of our model, we also compared it with the most commonly used methods for predicting user behavior. Non-negative tensor factorization (NTF) can analyze the temporal patterns of user purchase behavior [18]. This method has been applied and performs well in practical applications such as recommender systems [6]. In experiments, we constructed a three dimensional array, called tensor, which consists of user, item and time. In addition, we compared our model with a multinomial distribution as a baseline method. Since multinomial model predicts the chosen items based only on each user's purchase history, it always suggests the most chosen items in the past. These comparative methods cannot predict when a user will purchase an item, different from PP, SCPP, and our proposed model. Thus we compared our model with multinomial model and NTF in terms of the predictive performance of each user's item selection at the time when she made the decision. We evaluated the predictive performance by the negative logarithm of the likelihood for user u in the test period as follows:

$$L_2 = \sum_{i \in \boldsymbol{I}} \sum_{(t,u) \in \boldsymbol{D}_i^{\text{test}}} \log \bar{\lambda}_i(t,u), \quad (21)$$

[3]We used individual consumer panel research data (SCI) and INTAGE single source panel (i-SSP) collected by INTAGE Inc.

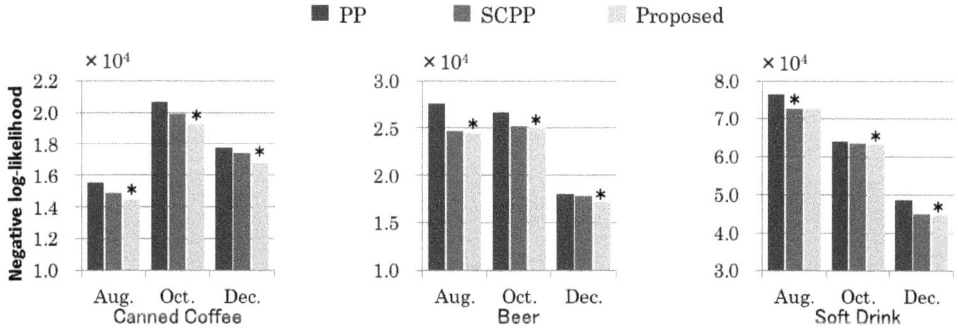

Figure 3: Comparisons of negative logarithm of the likelihood for purchase events (t, u) in the test period.

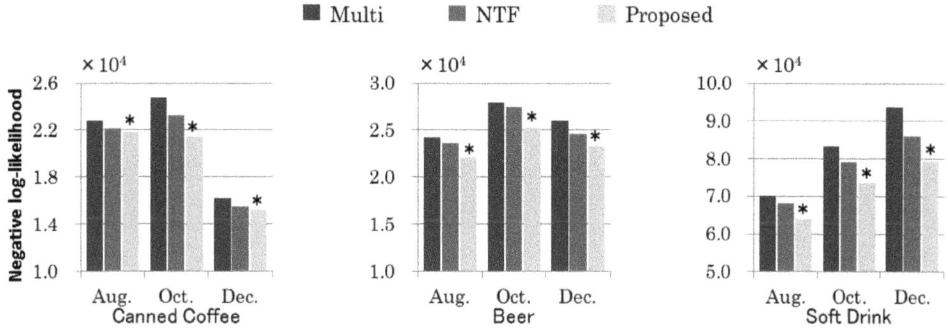

Figure 4: Comparisons of negative logarithm of the likelihood for user u given purchase time t in the test period.

where

$$\bar{\lambda}_i(t,u) = \frac{\lambda_i(t,u)}{\sum_{u' \in U} \lambda_i(t,u')}, \qquad (22)$$

is the rate normalized so that the total summation is 1. L_2 has a small score if predictive performance is high. Figure 4 shows the results. For each data set and test month, the proposed model performed better than the other methods. These results indicate that our model has excellent ability to predict user purchase behavior unlike the most commonly used methods.

5.2 Qualitative Evaluation

The parameters learned by our model provide important insights into consumers' behaviors. In this section, we show three practical uses of our model, and the model can actually extract the useful knowledge to marketers.

Discovering key information. By using the estimated parameters of our model, we can discover the key information, i.e., popular items, influential users, and influential advertisers. Figure 5 shows the values of item popularity $\{\alpha_i\}_{i \in \boldsymbol{I}}$, user influence $\{\alpha_u\}_{u \in \boldsymbol{U}}$, and advertiser influence $\{\alpha_m\}_{m \in \boldsymbol{M}}$ estimated by the proposed model for Canned coffee data set. In this figure, items, users and advertisers are sorted by their parameter values. As shown, a few items, users and advertisers, have large values. This results suggest that a particular set of items is popular in Canned coffee market (Figure 5(a)), a small set of influential users exist in this market (Figure 5(b)), and a few companies have strong impact through their TV advertisements (Figure 5(c)). These results are useful to marketers when they want to optimize marketing strategies. For example, discovering popular items yields an opportunity to reduce advertising costs because these items are likely to be purchased even without social effect or advertising effect. Furthermore, marketers can expect the pervasive benefits by targeting the influential users in viral marketing. When marketers want to determine the optimal allocation of marketing resources, we can suggest that TV advertisements are effective for the influential advertisers identified by our model.

Evaluation of the factors that trigger purchases. By using the posterior distribution of latent variables in (12), we can analyze the relative impact of the three factors that trigger purchases. Algorithm 1 shows the procedure of calculating the strengths of the three factors for jth purchase event of item i. The inputs are the posterior distribution and the set of dummy variables $\{d_{iy}\}_{y=1}^{N_{itu}}$ as described in Section 4.2. E_f, E_g and E_h is the degree of user preferences, social effects, and TV advertising effects, respectively. Note that the sum of E_f, E_g and E_h equals 1. Algorithm 1 calculated the degree of the three factors for each purchase event in the training period (January 1, 2013 – November 30, 2013). Table 4 shows the ratio of the three factors. The ratio of social effects was large for all data sets. This suggest that the influence of other users greatly impacts our purchase behavior in various categories. On the other hand, the ratio of TV advertising effects looks relatively small for all data sets. As described in a previous paper [25], advertising effects can be classified into (a) *direct effect* and (b) *intermediate effect*. Direct effect leads to purchases in the near future, i.e., short term. For example, a user purchases a new product immediately after viewing its TV ad. On the other hand, intermediate effect shapes the users' beliefs and attitudes toward the brand, and so molds purchase intent over the

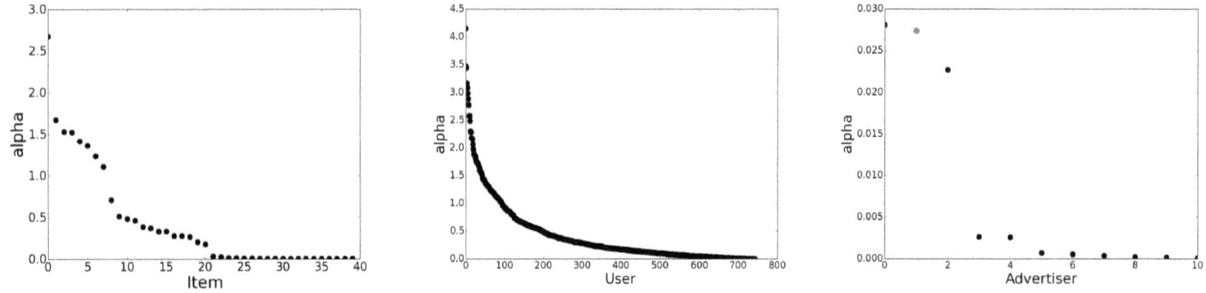

(a) Item popularity $\{\alpha_i\}_{i \in \boldsymbol{I}}$ (b) User influence $\{\alpha_u\}_{u \in \boldsymbol{U}}$ (c) Advertiser influence $\{\alpha_m\}_{m \in \boldsymbol{M}}$

Figure 5: Estimated item popularity (a), user influence (b), and advertiser influence (c) for Canned coffee data set. Items, users, and advertisers are sorted by their parameter values. An advertiser, represented by the red point in Figure (c), is the focus of the evaluation of the factors that trigger purchases.

Algorithm 1 Calculate degree of the three factors for the jth purchase event of item i.

Require: $P(z_{ij}|\boldsymbol{D}, \boldsymbol{Z}_{\setminus ij}, \boldsymbol{C}, \boldsymbol{\gamma}, \boldsymbol{\beta}, a, b)$, $\{d_{iy}\}_{y=1}^{N_{itu}}$

$E_f \leftarrow P(z_{ij} = 0|\boldsymbol{D}, \boldsymbol{Z}_{\setminus ij}, \boldsymbol{C}, \boldsymbol{\gamma}, \boldsymbol{\beta}, a, b)$
$E_g \leftarrow 0$
$E_h \leftarrow 0$
$y \leftarrow 1$
while $y \leq N_{itu}$ **do**
  if $d_{iy} \in \boldsymbol{U}$ **then**
    $E_g \leftarrow E_g + P(z_{ij} = y|\boldsymbol{D}, \boldsymbol{Z}_{\setminus ij}, \boldsymbol{C}, \boldsymbol{\gamma}, \boldsymbol{\beta}, a, b)$
  else
    $E_h \leftarrow E_h + P(z_{ij} = y|\boldsymbol{D}, \boldsymbol{Z}_{\setminus ij}, \boldsymbol{C}, \boldsymbol{\gamma}, \boldsymbol{\beta}, a, b)$
  end if
  $y \leftarrow y + 1$
end while
return E_f, E_g, E_h

long term. For example, exposure to TV ads makes a good impression on users, and leads to purchases in the future. Our model infers the direct advertising effect, not the intermediate effect. In our model, the intermediate effect is absorbed into either user preferences or social effects. Thus, the results in Table 4 indicate the direct (short-term) effect of advertisements.

Next, we focus on an influential advertiser, and analyze the purchase trigger factors. The advertiser indicated by the red point in Figure 5(c) is an influential advertiser in the Canned coffee data set. We focus on this advertiser in the following evaluation, because it actively launched new or renewed products in the training period. Figure 6 shows the estimated degrees of the three trigger factors for the influential advertiser in the Canned coffee data set. Note that we aggregated E_f, E_g and E_h for each purchase event per week, and this figure plots the total number of purchase events per week. The blue, red, and green bars indicate the number of events caused by the factors of user preferences, social effects, and TV advertising, respectively.

As shown in this figure, while the number of events triggered by user preferences did not so change over time, the amount of events caused by social and TV advertising effects changed over time. This suggests the existence of some popular items that sell well based on user preference regardless

Table 4: The ratio of estimated factors (%)

Data Set	Canned Coffee	Beer	Soft Drink
Preferences	8.3	9.6	8.6
Social effects	89.3	89.0	89.8
TV ads effects	2.4	1.4	1.6

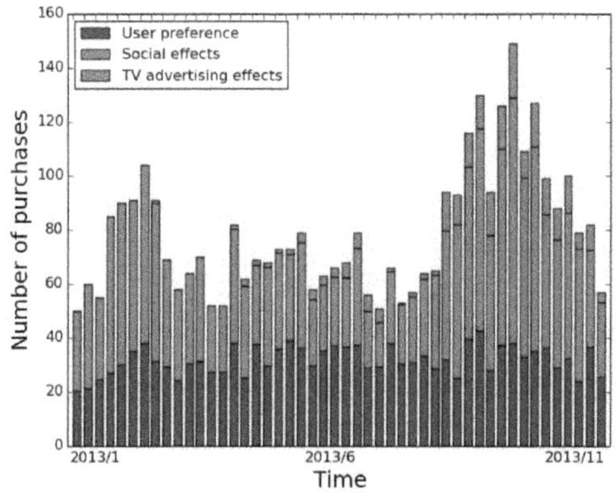

Figure 6: Estimated number of purchases triggered by each factor. This figure plots the total number of purchase events per week. The three colors represent the estimated strengths of the three trigger factors.

of trends or TV advertisements. Furthermore, this result shows that TV ads had relatively large impact in the last quarter of the training period. In autumn and winter (from October to March), some companies offer heated coffee cans and cold coffee cans in warm months (from April to September). New and renewed products are often launched at the changeover points of the product type. Figures 7(a) and (b) show the trigger factors of the renewed products, and Figure 7(c) shows those of new products. These figures show that purchases of renewed products are triggered more often by user preference unlike new products; purchases of new products are triggered more often by social and TV advertising effects. This is because users already have an attitude to the prior-generation products and are willing to buy them regardless of social and TV advertising effects. In addition, the results indicate that advertisements for new products

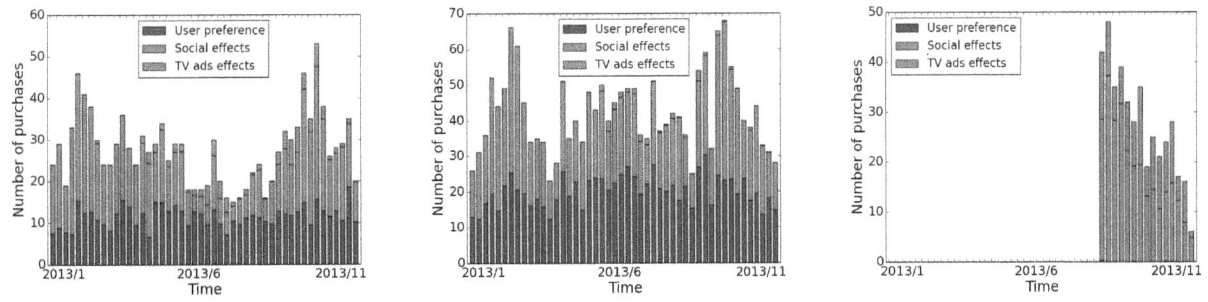

(a) Renewed product 1 (b) Renewed product 2 (c) New product

Figure 7: Estimated amount of purchases triggered by the three factors for new or renewed products.

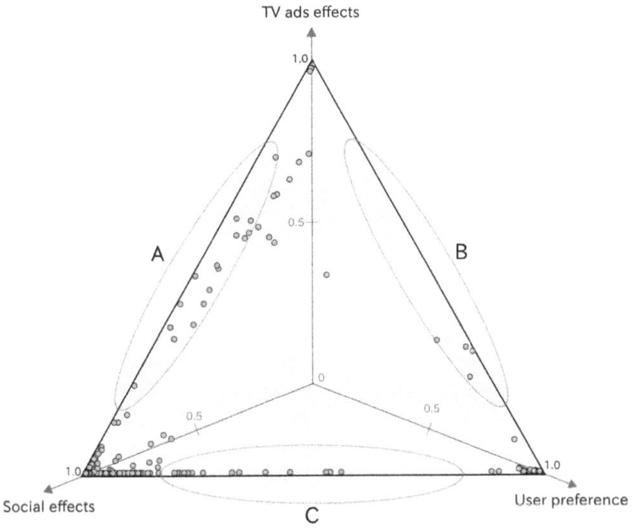

Figure 8: Segmenting users based on estimated latent triggers

leads directly to purchases, while advertisements for existing products (e.g., renewed product) has little influence on purchase behavior. Our evaluation demonstrates that the proposed model can quantitatively evaluate the factors that trigger purchase behavior, a highly useful attribute for marketers. For example, when marketers want to evaluate their advertising strategies for a product, our model can evaluate how many purchases were triggered by the advertisements.

Segmentation of users. For a marketer, user segmentation is an important step in optimizing advertising and recommendation strategies. Our proposed model can characterize each user by her/his type of consumption behavior. Figure 8 plots users on a 2-simplex for Canned coffee data set. In our model, users are characterized in terms of the three factors (e.g., preference, social and TV ads effects). We aggregated E_f, E_g and E_h for each user's purchase events into the three factors, and normalized their sum to 1. Many users occupy a corner of the simplex, and few users lie on the center. The results suggest that many users can be assigned to one of three classes according to the factor that dominates their purchase decisions. This makes it easier for marketers to determine the advertising strategies. Marketers who want to advertise their products effectively should focus on users occupying the top corner of the simplex since they are likely to respond strongly to the advertisements. For the users lying in the left corner, marketers should adopt an indirect approach through the users with which have a strong relationship (e.g., viral marketing) since they are likely to be influenced by other users. Furthermore, users lying in the bottom right corner should be shown favorite products since they are not influenced by the other factors.

The users inside of circle A, B and C in Figure 8 are characterized by any two factors. For example, the users inside circle A in Figure 8 are influenced by both social and TV advertising effects. As shown, there are far fewer users inside circle B than A or C. The result proves that advertisements are ineffective for the user who buys items based on preference. For marketers, the user with high preference score is a highly attractive customer since she/he actively chooses items. The result also shows that marketing strategies based on social effects such as viral marketing are the most effective way of increasing the number of good customers.

6. CONCLUSIONS

This paper proposed a probabilistic model for inferring the latent triggers from single-source data. The model incorporates three factors: (a) user preference, (b) social effects received from other users, and (c) TV advertising effects. Based on marked point process framework, we modeled users' willingness to buy over time through the incorporation of latent relationships between users and advertisers; a clear advance over previous models. By using an efficient Bayesian inference approach based on the stochastic EM algorithm, we can obtain the latent purchase triggers.

We used real single-source data to evaluate the effectiveness of the proposed model. We showed its validity in terms of its prediction accuracy. In addition, we showed three practical uses of our model, and the knowledge useful to marketers that the model can actually extract. First, our model can discover the key information, that is, popular items, influential users, and influential advertisers by using the estimated parameters. Second, our model can estimate the relative impact of each factor in triggering purchases. Experiments showed that when marketers want to evaluate advertising strategies for a product, the proposed model can suggest how many purchases were triggered by their advertisements. Finally, our model can find user segments based on their type of consumption behavior. As we demonstrated, the user segments can suggest better approaches to activating the users.

Our model is not limited to the single-source data used in our experiments, but is widely applicable to any history of user behavior, for example, viewing web advertisements. Our future work includes extending our model to incorporate the effects of seasonal sales [7] and the relations among items [26]. These extensions are expected to improve the model's predictive performance.

7. REFERENCES

[1] E. Bakshy, J. M. Hofman, W. A. Mason, and D. J. Watts. Everyone's an Influencer: Quantifying Influence on Twitter. In *Proceedings of the 4th ACM International Conference on Web Search and Data Mining*, pages 65–74, 2011.

[2] F. M. Bass and D. G. Clarke. Testing Distributed Lag Models of Advertising Effect. *Journal of Marketing Research*, 9(3):298–308, 1972.

[3] P. Domingos. Mining Social Networks for Viral Marketing. *IEEE Intelligent Systems*, 20:80–82, 2005.

[4] A. Ishii, H. Arakaki, N. Matsuda, S. Umemura, T. Urushidani, N. Yamagata, and N. Yoshida. The 'Hit' Phenomenon: A Mathematical Model of Human Dynamics Interactions as A Stochastic Process. *New Journal of Physics*, 14, 2012.

[5] T. Iwata, A. Shah, and Z. Ghahramani. Discovering Latent Influence in Online Social Activities via Shared Cascade Poisson Processes. In *Proceedings of the 19th ACM SIGKDD International Conference on Knowledge Discovery and Data Mining*, pages 266–274, 2013.

[6] A. Karatzoglou, X. Amatriain, L. Baltrunas, and N. Oliver. Multiverse Recommendation: N-Dimensional Tensor Factorization for Context-Aware Collaborative Filtering. In *Proceedings of the 4th ACM Conference on Recommender Systems*, pages 79–86, 2010.

[7] H. Kim, N. Takaya, and H. Sawada. Tracking Temporal Dynamics of Purchase Decisions via Hierarchical Time-Rescaling Model. In *Proceedings of the 23th ACM International Conference on Information and Knowledge Management*, pages 1389–1398, 2014.

[8] T. Kurashima, T. Iwata, N. Takaya, and H. Sawada. Probabilistic Latent Network Visualization: Inferring and Embedding Diffusion Networks. In *Proceedings of the 20th ACM SIGKDD International Conference on Knowledge Discovery and Data Mining*, pages 1236–1245, 2014.

[9] G. Last and A. Brandt. *Marked Point Processes on the Real Line: The Dynamical Approach (Probability and Its Applications).* Springer, 1995.

[10] J. Leskovec, L. A. Adamic, and B. A. Huberman. The Dynamics of Viral Marketing. In *Proceedings of the 7th ACM Conference on Electronic Commerce*, pages 228–237, 2006.

[11] N. Mehta, X. Chen, O. Narasimhan. Informing, Transforming, and Persuading: Disentangling The Multiple Effects of Advertising on Brand Choice Decisions. *Marketing Science*, 27(3):334–355, 2008.

[12] T. Minka. Estimating A Dirichlet Distribution. 2000.

[13] S. A. Myers and J. Leskovec. On The Convexity of Latent Social Network Inference. In *Advances in Neural Information Processing Systems*, pages 1741–1749, 2010.

[14] P. A. Naik, K. Raman, and R. S. Winer. Planning Marketing-Mix Strategies in The Presence of Interaction Effects. *Marketing Science*, 24(1):25–34, 2005.

[15] M. Richardson and P. Domingos. Mining Knowledge-Sharing Sites for Viral Marketing. In *Proceedings of the 8th ACM SIGKDD International Conference on Knowledge Discovery and Data Mining*, pages 61–70, 2002.

[16] M. Gomez-Rodriguez, D. Balduzzi, and B. Scholkopf. Uncovering The Temporal Dynamics of Diffusion Networks. In *Proceedings of the 29th International Conference on Machine Learning*, pages 561–568, 2011.

[17] R. Rosales, H. Cheng, and E. Manavoglu. Post-Click Conversion Modeling and Analysis for Non-Guaranteed Delivery Display Advertising. In *Proceedings of the 5th ACM International Conference on Web Search and Data Mining*, pages 293–302, 2012.

[18] A. Shashua and T. Hazan. Non-Negative Tensor Factorization with Applications to Statistics and Computer Vision. In *Proceedings of the 22th International Conference on Machine Learning*, pages 792–799, 2005.

[19] A. Simma and M. I. Jordan. Modeling Events with Cascades of Poisson Processes. In *Proceedings of the 26th Conference on Uncertainty in Artificial Intelligence*, pages 546–555, 2010.

[20] D. L. Snyder and M. I. Miller. *Random Point Processes in Time and Space*, Springer, 1991.

[21] X. Song, Y. Chi, K. Hino, and B. L. Tseng. Information Flow Modeling Based on Diffusion Rate for Prediction and Ranking. In *Proceedings of the 16th International Conference on World Wide Web*, pages 191–200, 2007.

[22] R. Takahashi, H. Mizuta, N. Abe, R. L. Kennedy, V. J. Jeffs, R. Shah, and R. H. Crites. Collective Response Spike Prediction for Mutually Interacting Consumers. In *IEEE 13th International Conference on Data Mining*, pages 727–736, 2013.

[23] G. J. Tellis, R. K. Chandy, D. Macinnis, and P. Thaivanich. Modeling The Microeffects of Television Advertising: Which Ad Works, When, Where, for How Long, and Why? *Marketing Science*, 24(3):351–366, 2005.

[24] N. Terui, M. Ban, and G. M. Allenby. The Effect of Media Advertising on Brand Consideration and Choice. *Marketing Science*, 30(1):74–91, 2011.

[25] D. Vakratsas and T. Ambler. How Advertising Works: What Do We Really Know? *Journal of Marketing*, 63(1):26–43, 1999.

[26] J. Wang and Y. Zhang. Opportunity Model for E-commerce Recommendation: Right Product; Right Time. In *Proceedings of the 36th International ACM SIGIR Conference on Research and Development in Information Retrieval*, pages 303–312, 2013.

[27] D. J. Watts and P. S. Dodds. Influence, Networks, and Public Opinion Formation. *Journal of Consumer Research*, 34:441–458, 2007.

Towards Modelling Language Innovation Acceptance in Online Social Networks

Daniel Kershaw
Highwire CDT
Lancaster University
d.kershaw1@lancaster.ac.uk

Matthew Rowe
School of Computing and Communications
Lancaster University
m.rowe@lancaster.ac.uk

Patrick Stacey
School of Business and Economics
Loughborough University
p.stacey@lboro.ac.uk

ABSTRACT

Language change and innovation is constant in on-line and off-line communication, and has led to new words entering people's lexicon and even entering modern day dictionaries, with recent additions of *'e-cig'* and *'vape'*. However the manual work required to identify these 'innovations' is both time consuming and subjective. In this work we demonstrate how such innovations in language can be identified across two different OSN's (Online Social Networks) through the operationalisation of known language acceptance models that incorporate relatively simple statistical tests. From grounding our work in language theory, we identified three statistical tests that can be applied - variation in; *frequency*, *form* and *meaning*. Each show different success rates across the two networks (Geo-bound Twitter sample and a sample of Reddit). These tests were also applied to different community levels within the two networks allowing for different innovations to be identified across different community structures over the two networks, for instance: identifying regional variation across Twitter, and variation across groupings of Subreddits, where identified example innovations included *'casualidad'* and *'cym'*.

Categories and Subject Descriptors

H.3.1 [**Information Storage and Retrieval**]: Content Analysis and Indexing—*Linguistic processing*
; H.3.3 [**Information Storage and Retrieval**]: Information Search and Retrieval—*Clustering, Information filtering*

General Terms

Language Change, Language Evolution, OSN, Twitter, Reddit

1. INTRODUCTION

Language is a faculty of human life that people take for granted; it allows for the communication of ideas, thoughts and emotions from one person to another or a group of people. Language is necessary yet fragile in that it is in constant flux through numerous pressures and constraints in usage [8]. Communicating through on-line mediums has become dominant in recent times; this itself adds extra pressure on the language being used to communicate. This pressure ultimately comes from the merging of space and time in the nature of on-line communication, i.e. having to communicate what would have been verbal and visual in-situ cues though written text in a time dependent nature [10]. This has led to an explosion of innovative and evolutionary language use in order to allow the user to communicate effectively though the medium [12].

The various forms of change seen can be referred to as language change / evolution; these are terms that not only draw attention to the difference in the states of a language at two points in time, but also gives an in-depth look at which components within the language have altered and the reasons for these alterations. By separating language change into structural (e.g. grammar and word formation) and non-structural components (e.g. the context that the language is used in) the term allows for the explanation of linguistic variation that cannot be solely explained by the structure of the language itself [5]. Such changes are therefore not so-called "free" variations but may, in fact, be correlated with extra-linguistic social features, such as social class, age, and gender. The fields of machine learning and data mining have used language (written and spoken forms) to develop and enhance many systems. However language is usually treated as a static entity, with a limited acknowledgement of the evolutionary dynamics of language. By treating language as a static entity generalisable systems are produced; however treating it as static incurs technical debt within systems through the need for retraining or modifications [29].

Assessing language evolution poses a number of challenges both from a technical perspective and theoretical perspective due to large numbers of variables that could be classified as 'language evolution', e.g. morphological and syntactic change, and variations within different communities [30]. In this paper we investigate the concept of language change and innovation in on-line social networks; this is done through grounding our work in language innovation acceptance models, together with the use of data mining techniques such as word embedding and statistical tests. To ultimately understand language change we need to examine that change over time, and what factors influence it. However this is itself challenging due to the scale of data being published and the myriad ways that language can evolve and be influenced.

WSDM'16, February 22–25, 2016, San Francisco, CA, USA.

ACM 978-1-4503-3716-8/16/02 ...$15.00.
DOI: http://dx.doi.org/10.1145/2835776.2835784 .

Thus, in this work we propose a large-scale computational model that enables language innovation to be tracked over time. This is done through applying known linguistic acceptance models to aid in the classification of accepted language innovations.
The contributions of our work are as follows:

- **Word innovation acceptance models through computation means**: An approach to the operationalization of accepted linguistical innovation acceptance models from Metcalf and Barnhart [24, 3].
- **Identification of local and global acceptance**: Showing that the computational automation of the models allows for the acceptance of an innovation to be seen within large datasets.
- **Multiple network analysis**: Language innovation and acceptance can be seen through two different datasets showing that innovation and acceptance is dependent on the community.
- **Large Corpus Analysis**: Shows the ability to perform large textual analysis with minimal pre-processing and filtering of the initial dataset; through the development of a open source scalable framework (See Section 9 for data release information)

The impact of this work is not limited to academic fields. Marketers draw on the understanding of consumers whom they are trying to target; the importance of understanding OSN's for marketers has been seen in the implementation and development of a large body of work in understanding and predicting influential users within the network that can aid the dissemination of a message during a campaign. Hence, by understanding how language emerges and changes, one can identify key individuals who contribute to and shape such adoption.

The rest of the paper is structured as follows: Section 2 highlights state-of-the-art work in linguistic innovation detection and diffusion through computational means, along with uses of language as a feature in OSNs. Section 3 describes the linguistic innovation acceptance models that influence the process of this work. Section 4 introduces the OSNs that will be used within this work, along with the models that are developed through the influence of the language innovation models in the previous section, and Section 5 details the challenges in processing such large datasets. Section 6 presents our experiments following the application of our computational framework to identify language acceptance over the Twitter and Reddit datasets. Finally, Section 7 and 8 critiques the methods that have been applied, highlighting whether these have been effective in identifying potential innovation acceptance within the chosen datasets.

2. RELATED WORK

The following section identifies related work across the fields of NLP and Social Media analysis. All of which have seen a growing interest in assessing language change, down in part to the fact that fine-grained data is now available with ease for researchers and that increases in computing power has allowed for vast volumes to be analysed.

Through the use of stochastic sampling computational models [13] have shown that traditional language diffusion models (gravity and wave) can be applied to on-line social media data, showing new terms diffusing over the geographical landscape of the USA. Previous investigations [14] identified correlations between demographic data, geography and language styles; again through computer modelling. Though pre-filtering to identify candidate innovations was performed over the whole dataset, this then meant that words specialised to smaller communities would have been pushed out in favour of innovations in larger communities. Thus the results would have only been valid for potentially dominant communities.

Social factors including age and gender have been shown to have a strong influence on communication styles in on-line discourse; age and gender of a user can be predicted through the use of machine learning systems that have been trained using features such as variation in topics and emoticon usage [28]. Though again there was limited acknowledgement of the communities of practice, and generalisation of the population as a whole.

By assessing the morphological characteristics of word blends introduced in OSNs means that the source words were determined along with the respective definitions of the innovation [7]. Though it is also the change of meaning that heavily influences language evolution, through the use of neural nets and deep learning, large scale semantic changes have also been shown in the Google N-gram corpus and social media datasets [19]. Again both these studies generalised to a whole population, without identifying that the meaning of words is dependent on the community that is using them.

As mentioned it is not only the individual that changes language, but the interactions and roles within a community that influence the change. Social roles of users within OSNs have been studied in earnest (though not looking at language). Through assessing and automatically classifying interaction patterns within Reddit [6], models were able to predict 'answer' roles within Reddit; and showed that user roles transcended multiple communities within the network, meaning that users maintain the same interaction patterns within different communities and potentially different networks. However, this was limited to highly specialist communities that had highly dynamic interactions on specific topics. Again, through the use of topic-specific networks, opinion leaders were identified and assessed for their reach within the network [35] and ignored the dynamics of user roles over time.

As inferred throughout our work, and as the reader will see below, language change and evolution is dependent on the dynamics of the social network. The dynamics of a social network have been shown to highly influence the diffusion and propagation of news and memes through on-line and offline social networks, with the rate of diffusion being a factor of; time, network structure, randomness and numerous other factors. Through time series and feature based classification one is able to identify and predict the success or failure of meme diffusion through a social network, this has been done by identifying communities, and thus the audience size, network structure, and speed of growth [31]. However this only has the ability to detect static meme diffusion, through the use of NLP systems and fuzzy matching, the evolution of news reports and opinions can be seen to propagate through social networks, showing that blog propagation of news events peaks 2hrs after that of main stream news [22]. However, this was not on a word level, and needed the whole article to identify similar content.

There is a vast amount of research that covers aspects of language change and evolution, though each has its limitations - from limited sampling methods, over-simplified assumptions of communities within a network, and limits if using fuzzy matching to detect diffusion. In this paper we investigate, for the first time, how language evolves at both the global level and the community level. We do this through the innovative operationalisation of language acceptance models in a computational framework.

3. LANGUAGE INNOVATION ACCEPTANCE

The following section explains the grounded models from within the field of linguistics and lexicography that form the basis of computational methods developed in Section 4.3. Original studies from within linguistics looked at identifying the variations in pronunciations within New York [20], though recently the ability to access Google's Historic N-Gram dataset research have shown changes in meanings of words over time [19]. With the introduction of on-line communication there has been a multitude of innovation, from shortening '*your*' to '*ur*', combining words, and creating new abbreviations i.e. *bae*; to name a few; which come under the definition of 'innovation' and 'evolution' [10].

However the existence of an innovation does not automatically mean it is 'accepted' into a language: for it to be 'accepted' it must be acknowledged by the community that use the innovation. Thus acceptance of an innovation is defined by a community within the context of the community, ultimately drawing in the dynamics of the community and the agent as the definition of acceptance [9]. This can be related back to structuration theory where the agent and communication between the agent and community is in constant flux, being defined and redefined within each context [16].

One of the aims of linguists and lexicographers is to understand language at a point in time; this can be seen through the existence and modification of dictionaries, however a fundamental issue is how to decide when a word can be added to a dictionary. For this reason a number of models have been developed to aid the decision process; two that are widely cited are Barnhart's VFRGT [3] and Metcalf's FUDGE scale [24]. Both were developed as tools to assess and predict if new innovations introduced into a community would be maintained or lost. However both were developed to be used by lexicographers through a scoring method: hence the scoring was at the discretion of the scorer, and therefore subjective.

Metcalf stated that for a word to be accepted into a language it must first fulfil 5 points that are measured on a scale of 0 to 2, where the higher the total score the higher the probability of the word being accepted into the language:

- (F) Frequency of the word
- (U) Unobtrusiveness of the word - the word should not be used for an exotic reason
- (D) Diversity of users and situations - the variation of situations and users using the innovation
- (G) Generation of other forms and meaning - if the word starts influencing other innovations then those words have an increased chance of *success*
- (E) Endurance of the concept to which the word refers - in reference to historic meanings of the word

Barnhart proposed a similar measure for evaluating new words; again identifying time and frequency as key components, but also including the number of forms that use the word, and number of genres:

- (V) Number of forms, including variation in spelling and/or derived forms
- (F) Frequency of the word
- (R) Number of sources. e.g. newspaper, magazine, books
- (G) Number of genres the word is used within - news, poetry, spoken, blogs
- (T) Time span of the word

Both measures have time and frequency at the core of the acceptance model, though there are variations on other variables. The morphological form of the word is identified in both but for different reasons: Metcalf is concerned with the word being unobtrusive, i.e. *does it look like existing words?*; whereas Barnhart is concerned with the morphology compared to other innovations. Metcarf also identifies user situation as a key component where as Barnhart separates out source and genre.

Models such as the ones mentioned have been used in a number of studies to identify the acceptance of new words. [21] used Metcalf's scale to identify the acceptance of novel Chinese verbs, showing that they have an accuracy of 60% for predicting the acceptance of new novel verbs. One of the limitation of scoring is that it is at the discretion of the scorer, i.e. a lexicographer with intimate knowledge of the language may have have a better understanding and may give different results .

4. METHODS

In the following section we present the methods used to operationlise the theory discussed in Section 3, along with introducing the datasets that experiments were carried out upon. The methods draw prominently from the fields of data mining and NLP, but also due to the size of the data being processed from distributed computing and big data systems also.

4.1 Datasets

For this study two datasets (Twitter and Reddit) were used to investigate language innovation and acceptance. The two networks were initially selected due to their varying network structure and user dynamics. Both OSN's display fast-paced content generation, dynamic user interaction and ease of sampling a large proportion to the whole network due to the networks' public nature.

Twitter is an OSN based around the submission of short (140 chars) messages; either in response to another person's message or to broadcast a message to the followers. Twitter was sampled through the use of the Twitter streaming API;[1] this allowed for automatic delivery of up to 10% of the Twitter fire-hose.

Query strings were applied to the initial set up to limit the sample under certain constraints: a geo-location filter was

[1] `https://api.twitter.com`

applied limiting tweets to be delivered only if they contained origin coordinates from within the UK.

Table 1: Dataset Statistics

Word	Reddit	Twitter
Users	3,108,844	1,696,630
Posts	73,528,954	111,067,539
Communities	22,055	3,052
Words	15,413,783	7,304,896
Innovations	62,414	42,937
Time periods	28 weeks	37 weeks

The second dataset sampled was Reddit. Reddit is an online news and entertainment community, it is self-organised into self-regulating communities called subreddits; these generally have overarching topics such as 'Personal Finance' or 'Conservative'. In response to submitted posts users can submit comments; these comments can either be direct comments on the original post or comment on other comments. There are other features such as voting on posts and comments, though this goes out of the scope of the paper [32].

The reasons for using Reddit are that *a*) the user base is highly active,[2] *b*) the popularity of the site is relatively high [11] (though this is skewed to a younger demographic, much the same way as Twitter) and, *c*) the majority of comments and posts on the site are public .

In previous research the sampling method for Reddit focused on mining the 1000 most recent comments highly active users, thus creating a user focused dataset [26]. For this research a different sampling method was used focusing on getting a representative dataset of active engagement on subreddits. The stream of most recent comments were scraped,[3] leading to the whole set of comments on the given thread to be downloaded (the number of comments per post could range from one, to many thousands).

4.2 Data Groupings

A given dataset can be grouped in to two dimensions: time and community membership. The following section aims to explain how the grouping of the data is performed.

4.2.1 Time Grouping

To group the data by time a function $weekofyear(e)$ returns the week the Tweet or Reddit post was created on, this is based off the creation time of the data point. We define time groupings as deriving a set as follows:

$$E_k = \{e : weekofyear(e) = k, e \in E\} \quad (1)$$

Where k is the number of weeks since the first item collected within each dataset. and E is the set of all entities (Reddit posts or Twitter tweets).

4.2.2 Community Detection

The datasets (Reddit and Twitter) pose two separate challenges due to the nature of the networks; geography bound (Twitter) and interest bound (Reddit); the aim is to associate a post to a community.

For the Reddit dataset community membership of a post was inferred through decomposition of the Reddit graph into *meta-interest communities*. This was performed through the use of backbone network decomposition; by assessing if the edge between two subreddits is statistical significant based on number of users that comment on both subreddits [26]; by applying an α cut of 0.05 for the significance between nodes allowed for the graph to adhere to a power law distribution [26]. The resulting communities of related subreddits were computed through the use of the Louvain community detection algorithm [4]. This resulted in the dataset being broken down into on three community levels; local (the subreddit), regional (collection of subreddits) and global (all subreddits).

As the Twitter dataset was geographically bound from within the UK this meant that Tweets could be clustered through the use of the longitude and latitude associated with each tweet. There are four Geo-location groups within the UK; National, Regional, Post Code District and Post Code, e.g. a tweet from Post Code LA1 would appear in the LA1 set, LA set, which is itself part of the North West set, which is in turn part of the national set. To compute this a kd-tree data structure was implemented in Java that allowed for quick nearest-neighbour look-up [23]; this was used to find the shortest distance between a tweet and the centroid of a postcode.

Comparisons can be taken between the varying community definitions across Reddit and Twitter. One could say that a low-level community defined by a postcode *LA1* could be compared to a subreddit (the lowest community in Reddit), potentially containing a greater convergence on topic and language used; whereas a higher level community could be classed as showing the 'general' patterns that are global understood across all sub communities.

To group data into their relevant communities a function $community(e)$ that returns the set of entities in a community r:

$$E_r = \{e : community(e) = r, e \in E\} \quad (2)$$

Where $e \in E$ is a given entity (Tweet or Reddit post) in the set of entities (E), and R is the set of all possible communities for the given dataset, for which r belongs to.

4.3 Operationalisation

This research aims to operationalise the acceptance models proposed by Metcalf and Barnhart (Section 3) to show the existence of language change within OSN's, thus creating an equivalent computational model that maintains the properties and heuristics proposed in both. Operationalising FUDGE and VFRGT models in a technical sense means identifying a number of variables that are believed to subsume the properties of each heuristic variable proposed in each model. Though some of this work has been been done before; through the use of normalised frequencies or words in a dataset in replace of frequency, the majority of the metrics are novel.

4.3.1 Variation in Frequency

As stated in both FUDGE and VERGH, frequency of innovations is a core indication that the word could have been accepted into language.

Using the relative frequency as a proxy for popularity is becoming a standard analysis in much of linguistic research, this can be seen in trend detection on Twitter [18, 13]. Even though this is simple it can show insights into what is happening within a dataset in a relatively easy manner; however

[2]http://www.reddit.com/about/
[3]http://www.reddit.com/new/

it can potentially be misleading if used as the only form of analysis.

Through the use of variation in frequency we aim to identify a statistically significant change in the frequency of innovations; this will allow for the identification of a potential activation point where innovations have gained the attention/adoption of the population. For this we use a uni-gram language model, for each time period (t). For a given time period (t) the probability of a word (w) being used is proportional to the whole dataset within the same time period.

$$T(w,t) = \frac{|w \in C_t|}{|C_t|} \tag{3}$$

Where C_t is a bag of words at time t, $|C_t|$ is the size of the corpus for time period (t) and $|w \in C_t|$ is the frequency of the word within the same time period.

To apply this to all time periods in the data set we apply the function $T(w,t)$ to each time period t.

$$\tau_w^f = \{T(w,t) : t = [0, ..., n]\} \tag{4}$$

4.3.2 *Diversity of form*

As identified by both Metcalf and Barnhart variation in form of a word is key to acceptance as this shows that the innovation may have entered people's vocabulary and that they feel people will understand concepts conveyed through varying the morphological form of the word. The variation in form can take a number of modes; from dropping a letter, to attaching a prefix or suffix in written communication or variation in tone when conveying the word.

For simplicity of this work variation is assessed as the probability of prefix and suffix addition to an innovation. This allows one to see if there is morphological variation in the term. Two lists of common prefix and suffix were taken from the (OED) Oxford English Dictionary, these included; 'ing', 'homo' and 'hetro'. As with the previous feature we aim to generate a time signal for the probability of prefix (τ_w^P) and suffix (τ_w^S). Where P and S are the list of prefix and suffix respectively:

$$MP(w,t,P) = \frac{\sum_p^P |beginswith(w,p,C_t)|}{|C_t|} \tag{5}$$

And the same is applied for suffixes:

$$MS(w,t,S) = \frac{\sum_s^S |endswith(w,s,C_t)|}{|C_t|} \tag{6}$$

Where MS and MP are functions that take a word w, at a time period t and a list of prefixes P or a list of suffixes respectively S, and produces the probability of prefix or suffix addition. The functions $startswith(w,p)$ and $endwith(w,s)$ are both indicator functions that return a 1 or 0. To then convert this into a time series τ_P^w and τ_S^w one on applies the function to each time period in the dataset, such as:

$$\tau_w^P = \{MP(w,t,P) : t = [0, ..., n]\} \tag{7}$$

and

$$\tau_w^S = \{MS(w,t,S) : t = [0, ..., n]\} \tag{8}$$

4.3.3 *Diversity of meaning*

The final measure aims to combine *generation of other form and meaning* and *endurance of meaning*. As stated in Section 3 for innovations to enter into general usage they cannot be too specific and their meaning has to be diverse but also common. A number of ways have been developed that allow for analysis of how 'similar' the meanings of the words are, including WordNet [25]. This is a large linguistic database which represents the synonyms of words within a graph structure. Such systems like WordNet though cannot be used within this type of research as it requires the innovation to be within the database which by definition an innovation would not be. For this reason we propose a new method that relies on word co-occurrence and embedding of the word within its own dataset.

Recently within the fields of data mining and NLP there has been growing work using neural-net based techniques for learning the vector representations of words; these have been used for a number of tasks such as POS tagging and Machine Translations [34]. [1] proposed `word2vec`, an unsupervised method of learning the embedded dimensions of word vectors by maximising the likelihood that words are predicted from their context and vice versa. The datasets used within the work allows for both time series analysis and clustering of data on community membership, and allows for the assessment of word embeddings across communities and across time periods. We propose that for each time period (t) we apply `word2vec` to each community (c), this then provides the word embedding model ($W2V_t^c$). Then for each innovation we query the model ($W2V_t^c$) for the top 100 'similar' words, and from this the Jaccard Similarity Index (JSI) is computed as the similarity between communities. Through averaging out the similarity measure per time series, we produce a time signal (τ_w^{w2v}) which indicates the evolution of meaning of the word across communities. We define $JSI(A,B)$ as a function that takes 2 sets of words and computes the Jaccard Similarity Score:

$$JSI(A,B) = \frac{|A \cap B|}{|A \cup B|} \tag{9}$$

And $W2V(w_i, 100)$ is defined to return the top-100 vector similar words for a given input word:

$$S_t^{w,r} = function(r, w, t, K) \tag{10}$$

Where $S_t^{w,r}$ is the vector of words (of length K) for the given period (t) for the community (r) for a given word (w). Therefore to compute the average JSI (Jaccard Similarity Index) for a given time period (t) a Cartesian product is taken across all communities (R) with the JSI computed for each combination, and then divided by the number of communities ($|R|$):

$$f(w,t,R) = \frac{\sum_{i,v \in R, i \neq v} JSI(s_t^{w,v}, s_t^{w,i})}{|R|\,(|R|-1)} \tag{11}$$

The aim here is compute values that show a similarity between communities while still showing variation. If the value is near 0 then it could mean that the word is too diverse for general usage (i.e. too colloquial), while a word with a value near 1 would potentially indicate that it is too specific.

To turn this into a time series one would as in the previous methods apply it to each time period in turn:

$$\tau_w^{w2v} = \{f(w,t,R) : t = [0, ..., n]\} \tag{12}$$

4.3.4 Increase/Decrease Classification

The aim of this work is to identify statistically significant changes in the usage of word innovations. The initial presumption taken is that language change (e.g. change in frequency) happens in a monotonic fashion; thus by applying a Spearman's Rank to each words' time series we were able to determine a metric for the increase or decrease in popularity (the resulting distribution was normally distributed). Finally to find innovations that had changed significantly a sample was taken from outside the higher and lower 95% confidence intervals as follows: if a word appeared above the upper confidence interval then it was classified as *increasing* whereas if it appeared beneath the lower confidence interval then it was classified as *decreasing*.

To compute the spearmans value (ρ_w) for each word (w) we take the vector time series τ_w (where τ_w is modified for the given metric computed e.g. τ_w^P indicating the time series for the prefix addition of word w). We define ρ_w as the Spearman's Rank (though again it is modified for the given metric e.g. ρ_w^P for prefix addition) correlation coefficient between the time series vector of the word and t, the ordered vector of weeks since the start of the data collection:

$$\rho_w = SpearmansCorrelation(\tau_w, t) \tag{13}$$

4.3.5 Limitations

The three method proposed though do not cover all the categories proposed through the VFRGT and FUDGE frameworks, this was due to the aim of the research looking into the ability to perform an acceptance mode. The missing categories will be covered in future work such as analysis by genre as we feel the topic requires a more concentrated exploration.

5. COMPUTATIONAL METHODS

The following section describes the computational methods used to implement the metrics on the datasets collected.

5.1 Technical Setup

As with most research analysing social media, the size of the data is a constraining factor. A number of systems were evaluated, such as Hadoop and equivalents, and ultimately Spark [33] was chosen as the processing engine - this allowed for a more interactive interrogation of the data. The specialised tools used throughout our work are as follows:

- TwitterNLP [27]: was used to tokenize tweets with its specialist tokonizer.
- Spark 1.3.1 [33]: allowed for high performance in memory processing of all datasets.

5.2 Pre-Processing

As previously stated the datasets where chosen due to them having different characteristics, for this reason each needs to go through a pre-processing pipeline to allow for analysis using a standardised data format. The initial textual data contained a lot of noise such as hashtags, usernames and HTTP links; through using TwitterNLP's POS tagger [27], we were able to identify tokens such as *hashtags* and *mentions*, which were then removed before the analytic stage. A second level of cleansing was also applied: through using regex long pattern repetitions of the same letter were truncated down to just three characters, e.g. *soooooooo* would be normalised to *soo* (as done in [17]).

The premise of this work was to identify the acceptance of innovations, thus a word must be classified as an innovation or not an innovation. To do this a word was classified as an innovation if it did not appear within the BNC (British National Corpus) [2]. The BNC was chosen to be the baseline for British Language as it is one of the most comprehensive studies of British English Language in recent times, taking its sources not only from books, but also newspapers, written communication and oral discourse transcripts.

Though the datasets have been filtered through cleaning and selection there is still a large proportion of words that could be classified as noise, therefore to *counteract* this potential noise we defined a word as an innovation if it had been used at least 100 times across the whole dataset being considered.

6. EXPERIMENT

The following section will apply the computational methods that have been developed in Section 4.3 to the datasets that have been discussed in Section 4.1.

6.1 Variation in Frequency

Frequency as stated is used as a proxy to determine the popularity of a term over a period of time; by combining this with the mined communities allows for an analysis of different growth and decay of innovations across the networks.

Figure 3 shows the growth and decay of innovation across the two networks on a global level, with noticeable differences are apparent; both are normal though Reddit has a lower variance of 0.00558 compared to 0.083585, and is positively skewed compared to Twitter.

Initially sampling was performed on the global level of the network, with Fig 1 and 4 showing the top and bottom 5 Spearman's Rank for the respective datasets. At this high level of the network, one can state that the innovations growing appear to be highly colloquial and potential originating from on-line games e.g. 'scrims' and 'cooldown'. However when analysing the community structure on the level below (Regions) one can see a number of variations across the UK (Table 2): for instance, in the top-5 innovations for both Wales (North and South) we see terms such as 'bootyfull' (see Figure 7) and 'cyw', these are colloquial but are not derived from the computing gaming community.

Even though words such as 'selfi' appear in the top-5 of 'Greater London' (Table 2) it would appear that when contrasting against its normalised frequencies across other regions (Figure 10) that it is more prevalent in the Channel Islands. However this is due to the Channel Islands having a lower population compared to Greater London, and as a result a new word in the Channel Islands has a greater impact compared to Greater London.

Contrasting the networks and community levels using the distributions and terms sampled one can make a number of informed observations pertaining to the dynamics of the networks. Because Reddit is topic-focused and has a more structured community, this could lead to faster innovation uptakes. This contrasts with Twitter, where community is inferred though geographical locations, and where an innovation is exposed to a larger audience - as a result an innovation could have a higher chance of being rejected, as the nature of conversation has to be more diverse and have a

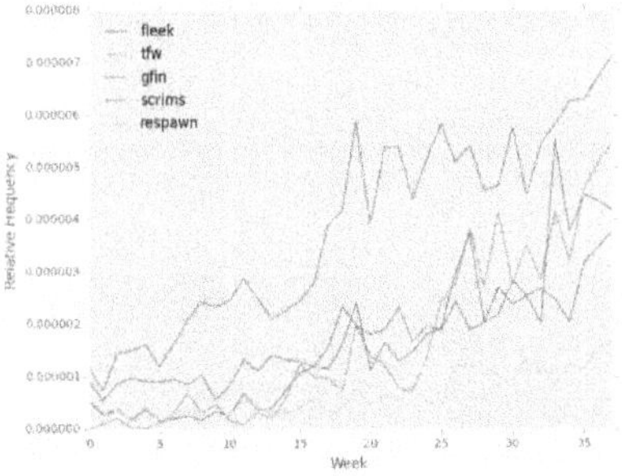

Figure 1: Popularity Increasing - Twitter (Global)

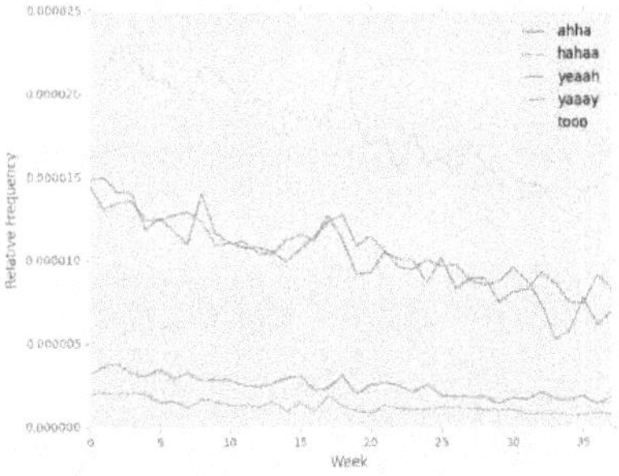

Figure 2: Popularity Decreasing - Twitter (Global)

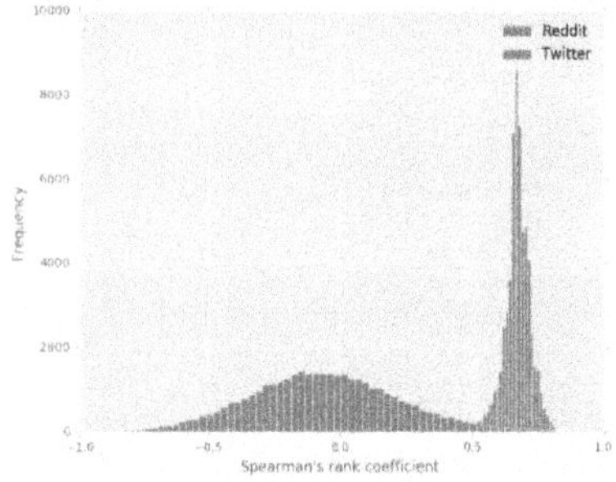

Figure 3: Spearman Rank Distribution - Twitter & Reddit (Global)

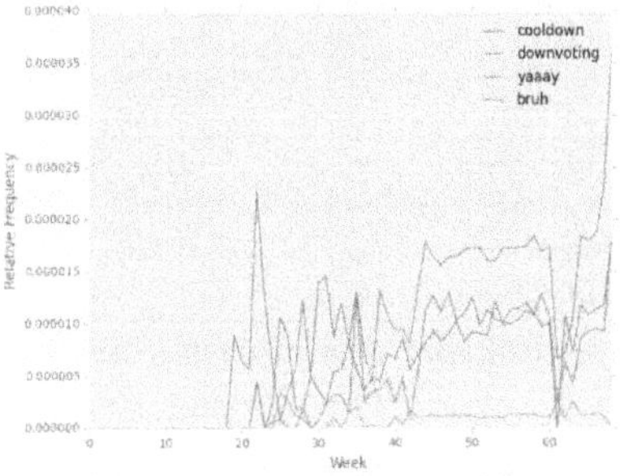

Figure 4: Popularity Increasing - Reddit (Global)

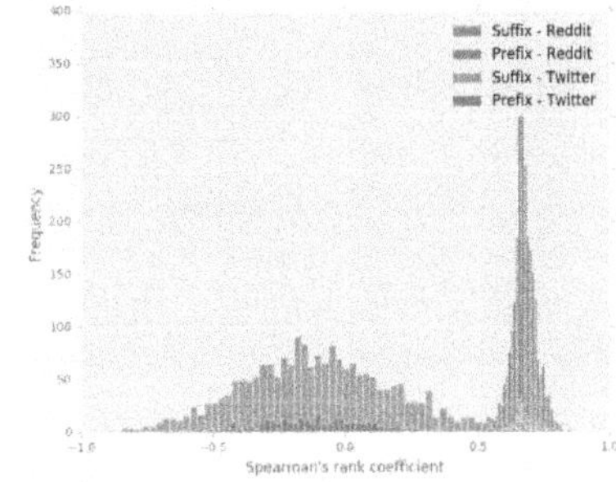

Figure 5: Spearman Rank Dist' (Form Variation) - Twitter & Reddit (Global)

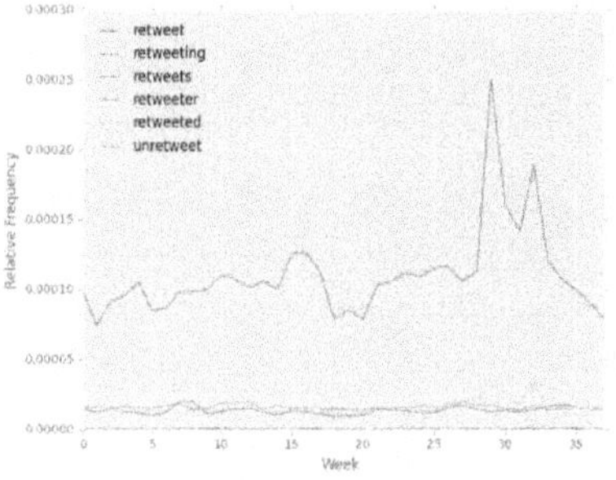

Figure 6: Relative Frequency of form variation of 'retweet' - Twitter (Global)

Table 2: Top 5 innovations per Region (Sample)

Region	Top 5 Words
Channel Islands	mmpressure, cwind, gusthumidity, bisous, capte
Greater London	casualidad, escocs, selfi, trabajando, tambem
Home Counties	cdk, contam, equinix, kaminey, bekah
North West	sitego, ziferblat, alura, dzis, prostu
Northern Ireland	gfin, pentatonix, fcking, mitchs, mphgentle
Scotland (South & Central)	cloudynight, mphrain, cwind, medpace, vuckic
Wales (North)	parklife, inout, torylib, loveshop, cyw (Coming your way)
Wales (South)	lollol, bootyful, gennith, juga, kaspas

more diverse audience. Within the top-5 innovation for regions within the UK from Twitter (Table 2), one can see a large proportion of dubious 'innovations' such as *gusthumidity*, this can be put down to Twitter weather stations being potentially introduced during data collection; these devices tweet out the weather on a frequent bases, thus giving the appearance of an innovation increasing over time.

6.2 Variation in Form

A metric for variation in form was computed through averaging the probability per time series of all the varying forms of a given word. The same sampling method was applied as

Table 3: Twitter (Global) sample increase

Word	P	Definition
fleek	0.940586	"Eyebrows on point","Eyebrows on fleek"
tfw	0.914754	"That Feel When" (Acronym)
scrims	0.869088	"In oonline gaming a scrim is a practice match. A scrim can be any online game, but notable in Counter-strike."
respawn	0.887351	"Also known as spawn, respawn is a gaming term used to describe the action of a coming back to life after being killed."

the previous method where a Spearman's Rank was applied across each time series and then ranked.

Looking at the distribution of the two metrics (prefix and suffix) for Twitter and Reddit (Figure 5) shows the similarity in spread for all innovations, however there is a noticeable difference with suffix addition which has a higher frequency compared to prefix additions. By sampling the 95% confidence interval one is able to see examples of words with varying prefix and suffix addition (see Table 5): some of these innovations are timely such as UKIP (as the dataset was mined during a UK general election), whereas the growth in innovations around the word 'vape' appears to be in line with an increase in the UK population taking up the habit [15].

The majority of innovations though were the addition of 's' to the end of a word (73%) followed by 'ing'. 67% of innovations only had one variation in form, as the number

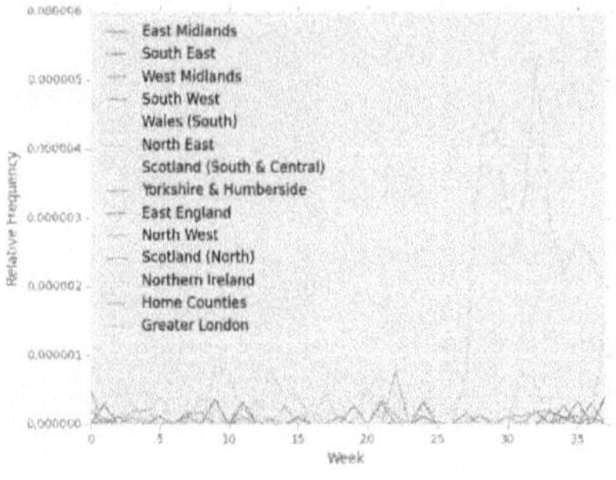

Figure 7: Regional variation in the word 'bootyful'- Twitter (Regional)

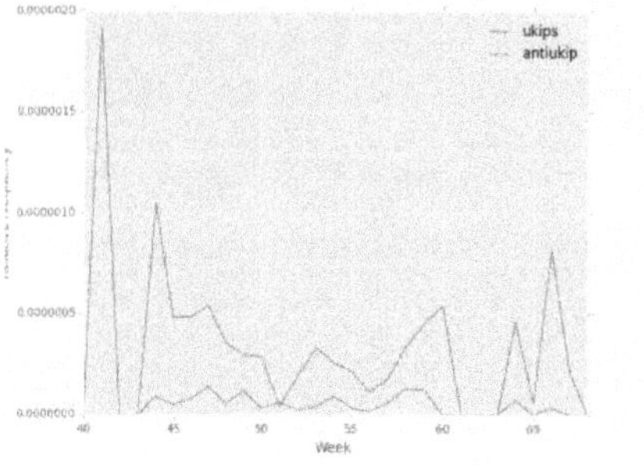

Figure 8: UKIP variation in form - Reddit (Global)

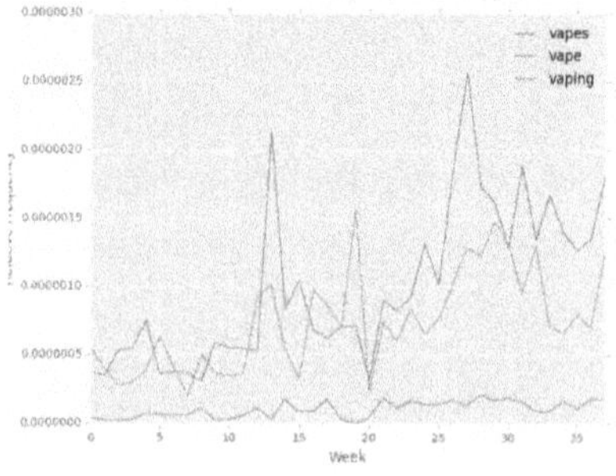

Figure 9: Relative Frequency of form variation of 'vape' - Twitter (Global)

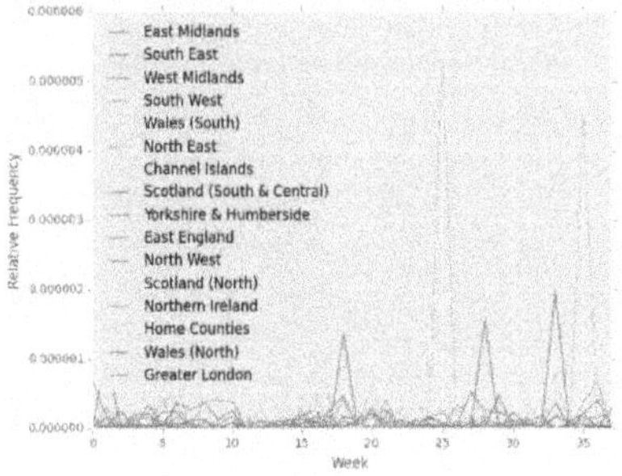

Figure 10: Regional variation in the word 'selfi'- Twitter (Regional)

Table 4: Reddit (Global) sample increase

Word	P	Definition
lamo	0.905310	"Someone possessing the quality of lameness"
bruh	0.869210	"is a variation of the slang term Bro that is often added as an interjection of feigned shock or disappointment"
downvoting	0.826010	"In competitions, the act of voting low other's entries for the purpose of improving oneself's entry"
cooldown	0.818814	"The time required for a spell or action to reset before it can be used again "

of forms increased the innovation appeared to become more specialised such as 'snapchat', 'snapchatted' and 'snapchatting' all referring to the same concept of using the Snapchat app, this trend was also seen for Facebook, and other online/mobile app platforms.

6.3 Variation in Meaning

The final computed feature was variation in meaning, which aimed to assess the coherence in the meaning of a word across the community structure of the two networks. The sampling method for this experiment varied from the previous two; here we assessed the meaning of previously sampled words.

Following initial testing at a week-level of granularity for the time period of each region achieved no results, as each period had insufficient data to learn the embedding. For this

Table 5: Sample of Variation of Form

Network	Word	Example
Twitter	retweet	retweeting, retweets, retweeted, retweeter, unretweet
	vape	valpes
	esport	esports
Reddit	overclock	overclockable, overclocking, overclocker, overclocks, overclocked
	ukip	ukips, antiukip
	facepalm	facepalmes, facepalming, facepalms

reason we modified the time granularity to a month, which allowed for the embedding to be learnt across a greater time period. However even with this modification limited results were achieved again: this ultimately resulted from the sparse words that were sampled from the methods above, where words even though classified as an innovation did not appear across *all* the communities, but when they did they they appeared at a *low* rank and thus the learned embedding, from the `word2vec` function, generated sparse words within the context of the innovation.

This could be seen when assessing the innovation 'fangirl',[4] one would think that this would have a common embedding as can be seen across the Internet, however the embedded dimensions for the innovation in the East Midlands include 'people' and 'swag' where as in East England 'itunes' and 'diesel' potentially words meaning what the areas are 'fangirling' over.

7. DISCUSSION

The following section breaks down the four research contributions of this work and discusses how they have been fulfilled, along with the limitations of each.

We have shown that through relatively straightforward statistical and computational models that one is able to identify and determine the potential acceptance of a word into a 'language'. However, it should be stated that while on a global level it appears to be heavily influenced by the innovation of highly active communities, this could be seen in the predominant growth of gaming terms in the Twitter global analysis. This could come from one of two issues with the analysis: the use of frequency-based methods where a

[4] A female fan, especially one who is obsessive about comics, film, music, or science fiction.

sudden spike in usage highly affects the results, along with uneven community sizes across the datasets e.g. Twitter Greater London has a larger set of words than that of the Channel Islands.

Contrasts between the two networks (Reddit and Twitter) showed some interesting differences. These were highlighted on the regional levels, where Twitter's innovations appeared to be bound be the geo-location (e.g. bootyful), and Reddits' bound by the topic of meta subreddit groups (e.g. cooldown).

It should be noted though that this form of research is only sampling the population on-line, thus is not a real world representation. A representational sample could be achieved through smoothing methods applied to this work, though as language is defined through the community that use the language what is innately being researched is the language of the Internet (Internet Linguistics) and potentially not the language of physical population.

Using Spearman's Rank may not have been the best sampling method for assessing the change in usage of an innovation. It does reveal intriguing insights into innovation growth, however it appeared to favour 'bursty' low-ranking words. Alternate ranking methods could have been used instead of frequency, such as applying a natural rank to each word in a time series, and then performing the experiments over the resulting data, this would have removed some of the 'burstiness' of words as an increase in rank would be linear and not dependent on the size of the corpus (e.g. normalised frequency). However, the measure did not detect innovations that were already present from the beginning of the data collection, only indicating innovations that appeared during the research.

Identification of variation in forms appeared to be successful, as it filtered out words that have only been used once. The produced results appeared to correlate with tacit knowledge of communities on Reddit and events within the UK. However, it may have been better to use a Levenshtein distance measure between words to assess their varying forms, as this would have allowed for a greater detection of none standard usage of the innovation than constraining it to just the use of a fixed list - this will be explored in our future work.

Limited results were achieved for determining a consensus of meaning, this came from the issues of innovations being used sparsely across communities, thus for the majority of regions the word may not have been used means that no embedded meaning could be computed. This could indicate that a word has not reached a global level of acceptance, or that the sampling method as stated before only detects 'bursty' innovations that are too locally used.

8. CONCLUSION

In this work we demonstrated that through the use of relatively simple statistical tests one is able to use known linguistic models to assess language and its change in on-line social networks. We have shown that when the methods are applied to two on-line social networks, they can show variation in innovations usage and persistence; this can be seen in the increase in words such as 'vape' and 'retweet'. We have also shown that these methods can be applied to the individual communities that make up the networks, where we have shown how varying community structure has potentially different language dynamics.

This work has implications further afield than the perceived linguistics and on-line social network analysis, with it having potential value in recommender systems and digital humanities. Further work will look into identifying the dynamics of language innovations within the context of users, along with the influence communities have over language and innovation diffusion.

9. DATA ACCESS STATEMENTS

All data and code created during this research are openly available from Lancaster University data archive at `http://dx.doi.org/10.17635/lancaster/researchdata/46`.

10. ACKNOWLEDGEMENTS

This work is funded by the Digital Economy programme (RCUK Grant EP/G037582/1), which supports the High-Wire Centre for Doctoral Training (`http://highwire.lancs.ac.uk`).

11. REFERENCES

[1] Distributional Semantics Resources for Biomedical Text Processing. pages 1–5, Nov. 2013.

[2] G. Aston and L. Burnard. *The BNC handbook: exploring the British National Corpus with SARA.* Capstone, 1998.

[3] D. K. Barnhart. A Calculus for New Words. 28(1):132–138, 2007.

[4] V. D. Blondel, J.-L. Guillaume, R. Lambiotte, and E. Lefebvre. Fast unfolding of communities in large networks. *Journal of Statistical Mechanics: Theory and Experiment*, physics.soc-ph(10), Oct. 2008.

[5] R. K. Blot. *Language and Social Identity.* Greenwood Publishing Group, Jan. 2003.

[6] C. Buntain and J. Golbeck. Identifying social roles in reddit using network structure. In *WWW Companion '14: Proceedings of the companion publication of the 23rd international conference on World wide web companion.* International World Wide Web Conferences Steering Committee, Apr. 2014.

[7] C. P. Cook. Exploiting Linguistic Knowledge to Infer Properties of Neologisms, 2010.

[8] W. Croft. Mixed languages and acts of identity: An evolutionary approach William Croft. *The mixed language debate: Theoretical and empirical ...*, 2003.

[9] W. Croft. Evolution: Language Use and the Evolution of Languages. *The Language Phenomenon*, (Chapter 5):93–120, 2013.

[10] D. Crystal. *Language and the Internet.* Cambridge University Press, Sept. 2001.

[11] M. Duggan and A. Smith. 6% of online adults are reddit users. *Pew Internet & American Life Project*, 2013.

[12] J. Eisenstein. What to do about bad language on the internet. In *Proceedings of NAACL-HLT*, 2013.

[13] J. Eisenstein, B. O'Connor, N. A. Smith, and E. P. Xing. Mapping the geographical diffusion of new words. *arXiv.org*, page 5268, Oct. 2012.

[14] J. Eisenstein, N. A. Smith, and E. P. Xing. Discovering sociolinguistic associations with structured sparsity. In *HLT '11: Proceedings of the 49th Annual Meeting of the Association for Computational*

Linguistics: Human Language Technologies. Association for Computational Linguistics, June 2011.

[15] S. L. Emery, L. Vera, J. Huang, and G. Szczypka. Wanna know about vaping? Patterns of message exposure, seeking and sharing information about e-cigarettes across media platforms. *Tobacco Control*, 23(Supplement 3):17–25, July 2014.

[16] A. Giddens. *The Giddens Reader.* Stanford University Press, Jan. 1993.

[17] B. Han, P. Cook, and T. Baldwin. Lexical Normalization for Social Media Text. *Acm Transactions on Intelligent Systems and Technology*, 4(1):–27, Jan. 2013.

[18] D. Kershaw, M. Rowe, and P. Stacey. Towards tracking and analysing regional alcohol consumption patterns in the UK through the use of social media. *WebSci*, pages 220–228, 2014.

[19] V. Kulkarni, R. Al-Rfou, B. Perozzi, and S. Skiena. Statistically Significant Detection of Linguistic Change. *arXiv.org*, page 3315, Nov. 2014.

[20] W. Labov. *The social stratification of English in New York city.* Cambridge University Press, 2006.

[21] S. L. Lai and V. T. Ng. Collaborative discovery of Chinese neologisms in social media. In *Systems, Man and Cybernetics (SMC), 2014 IEEE International Conference on*, pages 4107–4112. IEEE, 2014.

[22] J. Leskovec, L. Backstrom, and J. Kleinberg. Meme-tracking and the dynamics of the news cycle. In *KDD '09: Proceedings of the 15th ACM SIGKDD international conference on Knowledge discovery and data mining*, pages 497–506, New York, New York, USA, June 2009. ACM Request Permissions.

[23] S. Maneewongvatana and D. M. Mount. On the Efficiency of Nearest Neighbor Searching with Data Clustered in Lower Dimensions. In *Computational Science — ICCS 2001*, pages 842–851. Springer Berlin Heidelberg, Berlin, Heidelberg, July 2001.

[24] A. A. Metcalf. *Predicting New Words.* The Secrets of Their Success. Houghton Mifflin Harcourt, 2004.

[25] G. A. Miller. WordNet: a lexical database for English. *Communications of the ACM*, 38(11):39–41, Nov. 1995.

[26] R. S. Olson and Z. P. Neal. Navigating the massive world of reddit: Using backbone networks to map user interests in social media. *arXiv.org*, page 3387, Dec. 2013.

[27] O. Owoputi, B. O'Connor, C. Dye, K. Gimpel, N. Schneider, and N. A. Smith. Improved Part-of-Speech Tagging for Online Conversational Text with Word Clusters .

[28] D. Rao, D. Yarowsky, A. Shreevats, and M. Gupta. Classifying latent user attributes in twitter. In *SMUC '10: Proceedings of the 2nd international workshop on Search and mining user-generated contents.* ACM Request Permissions, Oct. 2010.

[29] D. Sculley, G. Holt, D. Golovin, E. Davydov, T. Phillips, D. Ebner, V. Chaudhary, and M. Young. *Machine Learning: The High-Interest Credit Card of Technical Debt.* 2003.

[30] L. Trask. *Language Change.* Routledge, June 2013.

[31] L. Weng and Y.-Y. Ahn. Predicting Successful Memes using Network and Community Structure. *arXiv.org*, page 6199, Mar. 2014.

[32] T. Weninger, X. A. Zhu, and J. Han. An exploration of discussion threads in social news sites: A case study of the Reddit community. In *Advances in Social Networks Analysis and Mining (ASONAM), 2013 IEEE/ACM International Conference on*, pages 579–583, 2013.

[33] M. Zaharia, M. Chowdhury, M. J. Franklin, S. Shenker, and I. Stoica. Spark: Cluster Computing with Working Sets . pages 1–7, May 2010.

[34] X. Zhang and Y. LeCun. Text Understanding from Scratch. *arXiv.org*, page 1710, Feb. 2015.

[35] Y. Zhao, G. Wang, P. S. Yu, S. Liu, and S. Zhang. Inferring social roles and statuses in social networks. In *KDD '13: Proceedings of the 19th ACM SIGKDD international conference on Knowledge discovery and data mining*, page 695, New York, New York, USA, Aug. 2013. ACM Request Permissions.

Discriminative Learning of Infection Models

Nir Rosenfeld
School of Computer Science
The Hebrew University of Jerusalem
nir.rosenfeld@mail.huji.ac.il

Mor Nitzan
Racah Institute of Physics and Faculty of Medicine
The Hebrew University of Jerusalem
mor.nitzan@mail.huji.ac.il

Amir Globerson
School of Computer Science
Tel Aviv University
gamir@post.tau.ac.il

ABSTRACT

Infection and diffusion processes over networks arise in many domains. These introduce many challenging prediction tasks, such as influence estimation, trend prediction, and epidemic source localization. The standard approach to such problems is generative: assume an underlying infection model, learn its parameters, and infer the required output. In order to learn efficiently, the chosen infection models are often simple, and learning is focused on inferring the parameters of the model rather than on optimizing prediction accuracy. Here we argue that for prediction tasks, a discriminative approach is more adequate. We introduce DIMPLE, a novel discriminative learning framework for training classifiers based on dynamic infection models. We show how highly non-linear predictors based on infection models can be "linearized" by considering a larger class of prediction functions. Efficient learning over this class is performed by constructing "infection kernels" based on the outputs of infection models, and can be plugged into any kernel-supporting framework. DIMPLE can be applied to virtually any infection-related prediction task and any infection model for which the desired output can be calculated or simulated. For influence estimation in well-known infection models, we show that the kernel can either be computed in closed form, or reduces to estimating co-influence of seed pairs. We apply DIMPLE to the tasks of influence estimation on synthetic and real data from Digg, and to predicting customer network value in Polly, a viral phone-based development-related service deployed in low-literate communities. Our results show that DIMPLE outperforms strong baselines.

1. INTRODUCTION

Infection processes arise in many different contexts and are very diverse in nature, extending from the spread of diseases, rumors and ideas, to the propagation of information and the adoption of new products. Such processes are often modeled as stochastic processes over networks. In social contexts, the network edges represent the medium over which "infections" occur, such as friendship relations, physical proximity, or communicational links. Infection processes introduce challenging analysis and prediction problems, with many practical applications. Recent years have seen an abundance of work in this domain, including conditions for epidemic outbreaks [30], outbreak detection [23], epidemic source localization [39], optimal immunization strategies [12], influence and trend prediction [7, 10], and influence maximization [9, 19], to name a few.

Our focus in the current work is on predicting various outcomes of diffusion processes. There are many possible outcomes of interest, such as the number of people infected, whether a particular area of a network is infected, or the overall cost of the infection. For such tasks, a straightforward *generative* approach is to assume a simple infection model, estimate its parameters, and infer the desired outputs from the learned model. This approach is appealingly simple, and is indeed used by the majority of works in this domain (e.g. [2, 10, 15, 26, 35, 36]). Nonetheless, such a generative approach has several drawbacks. First, the general hardness of parameter estimation and inference often leads to the a-priori selection of simple infection models, which offer computational benefits, but lack explanatory power.[1] Second, algorithms for learning and inference are usually custom-made for a specific task under a specific infection model, and do not generalize to other tasks and models. Third, if the task at hand is to predict some quantity related to the infection process, learning the model parameters may not be optimal with respect to the prediction task. This is especially true if the assumed model is only a coarse approximation of the true dynamics.

An alternative to the above is to take a *discriminative* approach and train a predictor to maximize the accuracy on the task of interest. While this is generally an effective approach, in infection-related problems it is not clear how to extract informative features, what the proper representation might be, or even what hypothesis classes would contain good predictors. Moreover, different tasks may require different representations, even though they might share the same underlying dynamics.

In this work we introduce DIMPLE (Discriminative Infection Model Prediction and LEarning), a novel discriminative learning framework for general prediction tasks in the domain of infection processes over networks. By introducing

WSDM'16, February 22–25, 2016, San Francisco, CA, USA.

ISBN 978-1-4503-3716-8/16/02...$15.00

DOI: http://dx.doi.org/10.1145/2835776.2835802

[1]For instance, in the *independent cascade model*, the assumed independence between infections leads to decomposable objectives [25, 26], or to tractable combinatorial problems over trees and DAGs [35].

infection kernels, we show how predictors based on generative infection models can be learned discriminatively within standard kernel-supporting methods. DIMPLE fuses the *generative* and *discriminative* approaches: it enjoys the benefits of each, and overcomes several of the aforementioned drawbacks. Specifically, it enjoys the following properties:

Generality: DIMPLE can be used for learning to predict potentially any property related to an infection process. The only requirement is that the property can be calculated, approximated, or estimated (e.g. by simulating the dynamics). This is a relatively weak condition since even complex infection models which are hard to learn are usually straightforward to simulate. DIMPLE can therefore be applied to various tasks such as influence estimation, user activity prediction, epidemic source localization, and others.

Prediction oriented approach: By learning an infection model in a discriminative fashion, we are able to produce predictions with lower error compared to generative methods. Instead of trying to learn the "true" parameters of a simple infection model, we learn an optimal weighting of parameters with respect to the given prediction task.

Convex optimization: Our approach employs a convex optimization problem, and is therefore free of local optima issues, which are sometimes an issue when maximizing likelihood. Specifically, our learner uses a kernel-based Support Vector Regression (SVR) optimizer.

The remainder of the paper is organized as follows. In Sections 2 and 3 we provide the problem definition and solution framework. In sections 4 and 5 we show how to compute infection kernels for both known and general infection models. In Section 6 we review related work on infection models. Section 7 contains experiments on the tasks of influence estimation and predicting customer network value for both synthetic and real data. Conclusions are summarized in Section 8.

2. PROBLEM DEFINITION

Consider a network over which some *infection process* takes place. An infection process can be thought of as any process where the state or action of a node in the network can (potentially) affect the future states or actions of its neighboring nodes. Such processes, although often governed by simple local rules, can give rise to complex, global phenomena.

Given a (possibly partial) history of network states, our task is to predict some property of future outcomes. As a working example in this section we consider the task of *influence estimation*: given a network $G = (V, E)$ and a set of initially infected "seed" nodes $x \subseteq V$, predict the expected number of eventually infected nodes $y \in \mathbb{R}^+$ [19].

We take a probabilistic perspective and assume the process is stochastic in nature, namely that there exists some joint probability distribution $P(x, y)$. In our discriminative setting, we are given a sample set $\{(x^m, y^m)\}_{m=1}^M$ sampled from $P(x, y)$, where x^m and y^m denote a seed and its influence, respectively. Our goal is to learn a low-error prediction function $f : \mathcal{X} \to \mathcal{Y}$, which will generalize well to unseen samples. Formally, we would like f to have a low generalization error $\mathbb{E}_P[\ell(f(x), y)]$ for some loss function $\ell : \mathcal{Y} \times \mathcal{Y} \to \mathbb{R}^+$. Here we set ℓ to be the squared loss, but our method easily applies to the absolute loss, the 0-1 loss, and others.

3. SOLUTION FRAMEWORK - DIMPLE

In regression, where performance is measured by mean squared error (MSE), the learning task is to minimize the expected squared error $\mathbb{E}\left[(f(x) - y)^2\right]$ over functions f in some hypothesis class $\mathcal{F}$. Since the task at hand is predicting outcomes of infection processes, our choice of hypothesis class is inspired by *models* of such processes. For instance, our hypothesis class may contain functions based on different parameterizations of the *independent cascade* model, where each parameterization θ corresponds to a different set of edge infection probabilities $\{\theta_{ij} \in [0, 1]\}_{(i,j)\in E}$.

3.1 Model-Based Regression Functions

When the distribution $P(x, y)$ is known, the predictor minimizing the MSE can be evaluated, and is given by the conditional mean [3], namely the expectation of y given x: $\mathbb{E}_P[y|x]$.[2] Since in general P is unknown, we do not have access to the true conditional mean. However, for any stochastic dynamical infection model parameterized by $\theta \in \Theta$, we can consider the hypothesis class:

$$\mathcal{F}_\Theta = \left\{f \,:\, f(x; \theta) = \mathbb{E}_\theta[y|x]\,,\ \theta \in \Theta\right\} \qquad (1)$$

where the expectation is taken w.r.t. the conditional probability $P(y|x; \theta)$ corresponding to the infection model.

Intuitively our hypothesis class contains the conditional means of all distributions generated by some parametrization of our model; if our model captures the true dynamics, $\mathcal{F}_\Theta$ will contain the true conditional mean.

3.2 Learning

After choosing an infection model, our next step is to learn the optimal regression function $f \in \mathcal{F}_\Theta$, or equivalently, to find the $\theta \in \Theta$ which minimizes the expected loss. In the Empirical Risk Minimization paradigm [42], the goal of minimizing the expected loss is replaced with the goal of minimizing the empirical loss over the training samples. In our case, the learning objective is given by:

$$\min_{\theta\in\Theta} \frac{1}{M} \sum_{m=1}^{M} \left(f(x^m; \theta) - y^m\right)^2, \qquad f(x; \theta) = \mathbb{E}_\theta[y|x] \quad (2)$$

Given the nature of the regression functions we consider, this objective may be hard to optimize since most infection dynamics have a complex, highly non-linear and non-convex dependence on θ. Non-linear effects such as phase transitions and tipping-points are notorious hallmarks of processes resulting from such complex dependencies (e.g., see [11]).

Since $f(x; \theta)$ can be computed or estimated, one alternative for solving Eq. (2) is to apply non-convex optimization techniques such as gradient descent or local-search methods. When θ is high-dimensional, this approach suffers from several drawbacks. First, it often gets stuck in suboptimal local minima, leading to poor performance. Second, it can be computationally costly, since in general the gradient of Eq. (2) cannot be computed analytically and must be estimated empirically. Third, constraining our regression function to a single model may not be expressive enough for prediction tasks where the real dynamics are complex.

In the next section we propose extending $\mathcal{F}_\Theta$ to a *larger* hypothesis class, which contains *linear* predictors and is

[2]For the absolute loss, the optimal prediction is the median of $P(y|x)$, and for the 0-1 loss it is $\text{argmax}_y P(y|x)$ [3].

more expressive. Its linearity allows for efficient optimization, and its expressiveness can benefit accuracy.

3.3 Extending the Hypothesis Class

Consider the following identity:

$$f(x;\theta) = \int_{\Theta} f(x;\theta')\delta_\theta(\theta')d\theta' \quad (3)$$

where $\delta_\theta(\theta') = \delta(\theta' - \theta)$ is the Dirac delta function centered at θ. Thus, the set of functions $\mathcal{F}_\Theta$ is isomorphic to the set of delta functions $\delta_\theta(\theta')$. This of course does not make learning any easier. It will however be worthwhile to now consider *arbitrary functions* $w(\theta')$ rather than just δ functions. Consider the set of functions of the form:

$$g(x;w) = \int_{\Theta} f(x;\theta)w(\theta)d\theta \quad (4)$$

Assuming f and w are square integrable over Θ, we can view g as an inner product over functions in L^2, denoted:

$$g(x;w) = \langle f(x), w\rangle \quad (5)$$

In what follows we will switch from optimizing over functions in $\mathcal{F}_\Theta$ to optimizing over the set of possible $g(x;w)$ functions, namely:

$$\mathcal{G} = \{g : g(x;w) = \langle f(x), w\rangle, \ w \in L^2\} \quad (6)$$

The set $\mathcal{G}$ includes functions which are weighted linear combinations of functions in $\mathcal{F}_\Theta$, with weights given by $w(\theta)$ (see Figure 1). The set $\mathcal{G}$ is more expressive than $\mathcal{F}_\Theta$ in the following sense: if we were allowed to choose $w(\theta') = \delta_\theta(\theta')$ then clearly any function in $\mathcal{F}_\Theta$ would have been in G (due to Eq. (3)). This is not formally the case, since δ are not square integrable. However, we can find a square integrable function w that is arbitrarily close to δ and thus G is a superset of F up to arbitrary precision.

Plugging back into the learning objective and adding regularization produces a convex optimization problem over the space of square-integrable functions $w \in L^2$:

$$\min_{w\in L^2} \frac{1}{M}\sum_{m=1}^{M} \left(\langle f(x^m), w\rangle - y^m\right)^2 + \frac{\lambda}{2}\|w\|_2^2 \quad (7)$$

Although the objective is now convex, it is not clear how the function w can be represented or handled. Luckily, by applying the Representer Theorem [38, 20], a predictor with the optimal weight function w^* can be represented as:

$$g(x;w^*) = \sum_{m=1}^{M} \alpha_m K(x, x^m) \quad (8)$$

for some coefficients α, where $K(\cdot,\cdot)$ is the kernel function:

$$K(x,x') = \langle f(x), f(x')\rangle = \int f(x;\theta)f(x';\theta)d\theta \quad (9)$$

Intuitively, the *infection kernel* $K(x,x')$ measures the similarity in infections between two seeds x, x' over all $\theta \in \Theta$. Given the kernel matrix of the data, the above problem can be solved by standard tools such as SVRs [42]. The difficulty now reduces to computing the kernel matrix, which we address in the following section.

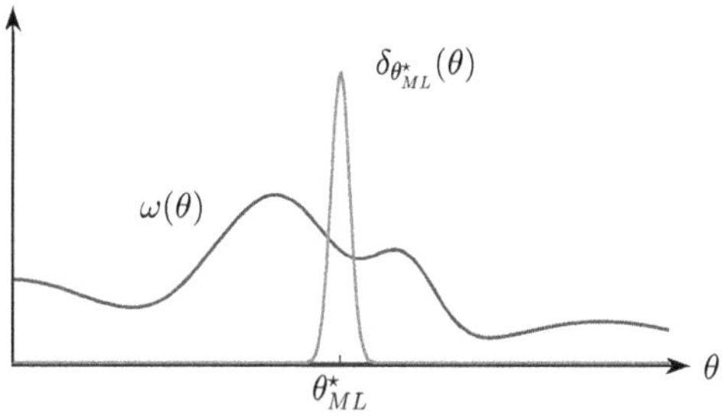

Figure 1: An illustration of learning a single δ_θ over $\mathcal{F}_\Theta$ (such as in maximum likelihood) versus learning a w-weighted mixture of parameters over $\mathcal{G}$.

4. COMPUTING THE KERNEL MATRIX

In order to compute $K(x,x')$, the product $f(x;\theta)f(x';\theta)$ needs to be integrated over the whole range of θ. In general this can be a hard task since θ may be high-dimensional. In Sec. 4.1, 4.2 we show that in some important cases the computational difficulty can be reduced to the complexity of simulating the model. In Sec. 4.3 we discuss other cases where the integral is estimated via sampling.

4.1 Independent Cascade Kernel

One of the most studied infection models is the independent cascade model [13, 19]. In its simplest discrete-time variant, if node i is infected at time t, it attempts to infect each of its uninfected neighbors j independently with probability of success θ_{ij}. If i succeeds in infecting j, j becomes infected at time $t+1$. After its infection attempts, i becomes inactive. In our setting, a network is initialized with a set of infected seed nodes. This triggers a cascade of infections, which carries on until all nodes are infected or until the process dies out.

Calculating the kernel for this process can be significantly simplified by turning to the following equivalent process, introduced in [19]. First, sample each edge $e \in E$ to be *active* with probability θ_e. Then, node i is infected if it is reachable from some node in the seed set $x \subseteq V$ over the graph with active edges $A \subseteq E$. We denote by $P_\theta(A)$ the probability of A being the active edge set under θ.

To see how this formulation allows us to compute the kernel, consider again the task of influence estimation, where the goal is to predict the expected cascade size (or number of ultimately infected nodes) given a set of initially infected seed nodes. In our discriminative setup, given a network G, an example x contains the seed set and a label y is the seed's influence. Hence, our predictor for the influence of seed x is $f(x;\theta) = \mathbb{E}_\theta[r(x,A)]$, where $r(x,A)$ is the number of nodes reachable from x under A. Plugging this into Eq. (9) yields:

$$K(x,x') = \int_{\Theta} \mathbb{E}_\theta[r(x,A)]\,\mathbb{E}_\theta[r(x',A')]\,\mathrm{d}\theta \quad (10)$$

$$= \int_{\Theta}\left(\sum_{A\subseteq E} P_\theta(A)r(x,A)\right)\left(\sum_{A'\subseteq E} P_\theta(A')r(x',A')\right)\mathrm{d}\theta$$

$$= \sum_{A,A'\subseteq E} r(x,A)r(x',A')\int_{\Theta} P_\theta(A)P_\theta(A')\,\mathrm{d}\theta$$

Note that now the integral is only over the distribution of active edge sets. Luckily this integral can be calculated in closed form, as shown next. For simplicity assume a uniform prior $P(\theta)$ over θ. The integral is then equal to a joint distribution Q^{IC} over active edge set pairs (A, A'):

$$Q^{IC}(A, A') = \int_{\Theta} P(A, A', \theta)\, \mathrm{d}\theta = \tag{11}$$

$$= \int_{\Theta} P_\theta(A) P_\theta(A') P(\theta)\, \mathrm{d}\theta \propto \int_{\Theta} P_\theta(A) P_\theta(A')\, \mathrm{d}\theta$$

Since edges are sampled independently as Bernoulli variables, the probability Q^{IC} also factorizes over the edges of the graph, simplifying into:

$$\begin{aligned} Q^{IC}(A, A') &= \prod_{e \in E} \int_{\Theta} P_\theta(A_e) P_\theta(A'_e)\, \mathrm{d}\theta_e \\ &= \prod_{e \in E} \int_{\Theta_e} \theta_e^{A_e} (1-\theta_e)^{1-A_e} \theta_e^{A'_e} (1-\theta_e)^{1-A'_e} d\theta_e \\ &= \prod_{e \in E} Q_e^{IC}(A_e, A'_e) \end{aligned}$$

where $A_e = 1$ if $e \in A$ and 0 otherwise. The integral can then be calculated, resulting in:[3]

$$Q_e^{IC}(A_e, A'_e) = \begin{cases} 1/3 & A_e = A'_e = 1 \\ 1/6 & A_e \neq A'_e \\ 1/3 & A_e = A'_e = 0 \end{cases} \tag{12}$$

for $\Theta_e = [0, 1]$.[4] Hence, the kernel can be written as:

$$\begin{aligned} K(x, x') &\propto \sum_{A, A'} Q^{IC}(A, A') r(x, A) r(x', A') \\ &= \mathbb{E}_{Q^{IC}}\left[r(x, A) r(x', A')\right] \end{aligned} \tag{13}$$

An interesting observation is that under this representation, the infection kernel $K(x, x')$ is in fact the *co-influence* of seeds x, x' under a *bi-dependent cascade model*, where pairs of (dependent) cascades are generated from the joint infection dynamics governed by Q^{IC}. Even though we started out considering influence under *all* of the possible parameterizations θ, our final kernel entries correspond to *co*-influence under a *single* parameterization defined by Q^{IC}.

Although computing influence is known to be #P-hard under the independent cascade (and linear threshold) model [6], it can be efficiently estimated up to arbitrary precision using sampling [8]. Similarly $K(x, x')$ can be estimated by sampling active subgraphs from $Q^{IC}(A, A')$, computing $r(x, A)$ and $r(x', A')$,[5] and averaging.

4.2 Linear Threshold Kernel

Another popular model in the influence literature is the linear threshold model. In its weighted formulation, each node i is associated with a random threshold $\tau_i \sim U(0, 1)$, and each of its neighbors j has weight θ_{ji}, where $\sum_j \theta_{ji} \leq 1$. At each time step, node i becomes infected if the sum of weights of its infected neighbors exceeds τ_i.

The linear threshold model also has an equivalent formulation using sampled active edge sets [19]. First, for each node i we sample either one incoming edge (j, i) with probability θ_{ji}, or no incoming edges with probability $1 - \sum_j \theta_{ji}$. Then, the set of infected nodes are those reachable from some seed node in the active subgraph.

Let $\theta_{\cdot i}$ and $A_{\cdot i}$ be the parameters and active state of all incoming edges of node i, respectively. Since all $\theta_{ji} \in \theta_{\cdot i}$ must sum to no more than one, they are now dependent. Hence, while Eq. (10) still holds, the joint distribution $Q^{LT}(A, A')$ now factorizes only over nodes:

$$\begin{aligned} Q^{LT}(A, A') &\propto \int_{\Theta} P_\theta(A) P_\theta(A')\, \mathrm{d}\theta \\ &= \prod_{i \in V} \int_{\Theta_i} P_\theta(A_{\cdot i}) P_\theta(A'_{\cdot i})\, \mathrm{d}\theta_{\cdot i} \equiv \prod_{i \in V} Q_i^{LT}(A_{\cdot i}, A'_{\cdot i}) \end{aligned} \tag{14}$$

where Θ_i is the d_i-dimensional simplex. This gives us:[3]

$$Q_i^{LT}(A_{\cdot i}, A'_{\cdot i}) = \begin{cases} \frac{2}{(d_i+1)(d_i+2)} & A_{\cdot i} = A'_{\cdot i} \\ \frac{1}{(d_i+1)(d_i+2)} & A_{\cdot i} \neq A'_{\cdot i} \end{cases} \tag{15}$$

To sample from Q^{LT}, for each node i we first sample the event $A_{\cdot i} = A'_{\cdot i}$ with probability $2/3$ and $A_{\cdot i} \neq A'_{\cdot i}$ with probability $1/3$. Then, in the first case we uniformly sample a joint edge (or no edge), and in the second case we uniformly sample different edges (or a single edge in either $A_{\cdot i}$ or $A'_{\cdot i}$).

4.3 General Infection Kernel Computation

In the above two cases we used certain properties of the infection models that facilitated factorization of the kernel integral and its closed form evaluation. For more complex processes such structure may not be available.

Note that in the general case there are two sources of difficulty. First, the regression function $f(x; \theta) = \mathbb{E}_\theta[y|x]$ may be hard to calculate exactly (as in the independent cascade model above). Second, the kernel integral requires integration over a high-dimensional θ space. For the first problem, we assume there exists a black box that yields exact or approximate values of $f(x; \theta)$ (e.g. with simulation as in [19]). For the θ integration problem, we resort to computing the integral numerically using Monte-Carlo integration [27].

To illustrate this approach, assume that θ is integrated over some domain set Θ with finite volume C, and define:

$$h(\theta) = f(x^i; \theta) f(x^j; \theta) \tag{16}$$

We can re-write the integral of Eq. (9) as:

$$K(x^i, x^j) = \int_{\Theta} h(\theta) d\theta = C \int_{\Theta} p(\theta) h(\theta) d\theta \tag{17}$$

where $p(\theta) = 1/C$ is the uniform density over Θ. The right-most term in Eq. (17) is proportional to the expectation of h over $p(\theta)$, and can be estimated empirically:

$$\mathbb{E}_{U(\Theta)}[h(\theta)] \simeq \frac{1}{N} \sum_{k=1}^{N} h(\theta_k), \qquad \theta_k \sim U(\Theta) \quad \forall k \tag{18}$$

Furthermore, the standard error of this estimator decreases asymptotically as $\frac{C\sigma_f}{\sqrt{N}}$ (where σ_f is the standard deviation of f w.r.t. the density p). There exist much more elaborate sampling schemes, with better control for variance (e.g., Quasi-Monte Carlo [24] , Recursive Stratified Sampling [31]), though for our experiments uniform sampling

[3] For details, see the supplementary material.

[4] For $\Theta_e = [a, b]$, the corresponding probabilities are $\frac{b^3-a^3}{3(b-a)}$, $\frac{b^2-a^2}{2(b-a)} - \frac{b^3-a^3}{3(b-a)}$, and $\frac{b^3-a^3}{3(b-a)} - \frac{b^2-a^2}{b-a} + 1$.

[5] The estimation of K can be significantly sped up by approximating $r(x, A)$ using the sketching method of [8].

converged fairly quickly. Finally, we note that the process can be significantly sped up by estimating all entries of f over a single set of sampled θ values (e.g., see [32]).

5. BRANCHING PROCESSES

In this section we discuss a diffusion process that is compatible with the data used in the experiments in Sec. 7.2.

Consider a service that spreads by word-of-mouth (WoM), where new users join the service based on referrals from friends. In such settings, an important task is to predict the future contribution of new users to the spread of the service, as this can serve as a basis for targeted actions. In marketing, customers are evaluated by their *customer lifetime value* (CLV) - the predicted future net profit associated with them. In referral settings, CLV is broken down into a customer's intrinsic value and *network value* - the expected profit attributed to her via WoM referrals [17, 9].

An effective way to measure network value is to allocate credit to existing users for recruiting new members. Given a user who recently joined the service, our task is to predict the future referral credit which will be attributed to her. In our discriminative setup, an example x may include features describing a user i and her initial actions, while the label y will contain the credit allocated to her up to some horizon. Our predictor $f(x;\theta)$ will be the credit expected to be allocated to user i.

By modeling referral recruitments as infections, we can harness the power of infection models to predict future credit. However, both independent cascade and linear threshold models are inadequate for this task since they operate on a given, complete underlying network. In this setting, credit originates from future parts of the network, which are unobserved at sample time.

A suitable choice for modeling infections when the network is latent is a *branching process* [28]. In this model, an infection tree is generated by recursively sampling the number of (infected) children a node in the tree has from some distribution. While a branching processes is usually used to model population growth, as an infection model it can be used to predict referral credit in evolving networks.

In a *multi-level marketing* credit scheme, each time a new user i joins the service, one credit point is recursively distributed along a "recruitment tree". Credit from i's joining is attributed not only to her parent $\pi(i)$, but also to her grandparent, $\pi^2(i)=\pi(\pi(i))$, and so forth. Quantitatively, out of the one credit point due to i's joining, $1/2$ is credited to $\pi(i)$, $(1/2)^2$ is credited to $\pi^2(i)$, $(1/2)^3$ to $\pi^3(i)$, and in general, $\pi^k(i)$ gets $(1/2)^k$ credit points from i. The recursion is bounded by some predetermined depth δ in order to control the bias introduced by the users' time of joining.

Branching processes are natural candidates as infection models for such recursive credit schemes. To apply a branching process to our task, we set the distribution governing the number of children to be a function of the features x and a weight vector θ. For instance, for a geometric distribution, we can set the success probability p to be a scaled sigmoid:

$$p(x;\theta)=\text{sig}(\langle\theta,x\rangle), \qquad \text{sig}\,(z)=\frac{b-a}{1+e^{-z}}+a \tag{19}$$

where $0\leq a<b\leq 1$. The expected number of offsprings $\mu_\ell(x;\theta)$ at each depth ℓ in trees generated by such a process is easy to compute analytically. By setting the root to be $\mu_0(x;\theta)=1$ and using $\mu_1(x;\theta)=\mu(x;\theta)=\frac{1}{p(x;\theta)}-1$, the expected number of nodes at depth ℓ is:

$$\mu_\ell(x;\theta)=\mu_{\ell-1}(x;\theta)\cdot\mu(x;\theta)=\big(\mu(x;\theta)\big)^\ell \tag{20}$$

and the expected credit of user i is therefore:

$$f(x;\theta)=\sum_{\ell=1}^{\delta}\frac{1}{2^\ell}\mu_\ell(x;\theta) \tag{21}$$

When Eq. (19) is unscaled ($b=1$, $a=0$), the resulting kernel can be computed in closed form.[3] It turns out that $0<a,b<1$ leads to more stable kernels, and we thus use Sec. 4.3 for kernel estimation.

6. RELATED WORK

Current methods for solving infection-related tasks over networks typically assume an underlying infection model. The two most common models are the linear threshold model [16] and the independent cascade model [13]. Variations and generalizations of these models have also been studied (e.g. [19, 15, 37]). Various methods have been proposed for learning the parameters of these models from data. In [15], given a social graph and an action log, the infection probabilities over the edges are inferred using different statistical models under the assumption that the infections are independent. Other works use a maximum-likelihood approach for estimating the infection probabilities for various models [2, 36]. In [26], a convex formulation is provided for maximizing the likelihood of the independent cascade model.

Several works aim at inferring a latent underlying network by estimating the edge infection probabilities. These include NetInf [14] which infers network connectivity, and ConNIe [25] and NetRate [35], which infer connectivity and infection rates. The models are learned from sample cascades (who got infected by whom and at what time), and used within a maximum-likelihood approach to infer the model parameters and network structure.

Another class of methods focus on a specific property of the infection process. A main task in the field of diffusion networks concerns the problem of influence maximization, namely, choosing a seed of nodes which, if infected, will result in the largest expected number of overall infected nodes. The authors in [19] show how influence can be maximized efficiently in the linear threshold and independent cascade models. In [10], the authors use a generative approach to learn an influence predictor over a large class of coverage functions, which generalize several infection models.

Several works take a discriminative approach for predicting various infection-related quantities. In [7], the authors extract features out of cascades and use various classifiers to predict whether the final size of a given cascade will be above or below the median. In [41], the authors extract topological, temporal, and content-related features and use linear regression to predict the propagation of information. In [43], the authors suggest a Linear Influence Model for estimating node-specific non-parametric influence functions, which are then used to predict the overall future number of infections. In [1] regression trees are used to investigate and predict the influence of nodes given their attributes and history.

The interplay between generative and discriminative approaches has been studied in several works. In [29] the authors analyze settings in which generative classifiers are expected to outperform discriminative ones and vice versa. However, the generative results were under the assumption that the generative model is correct, which rarely holds. In general, the discriminative framework is well supported via the empirical risk minimization framework of Vapnik [42] and others, which provides sample complexity guarantees for algorithms minimizing empirical classification error.

A very different approach to combine generative and discriminative schemes was suggested in [18]. They use a learned generative model to construct a kernel matrix that measures the "distance" between instances according to the sensitivity of their likelihood to changes in the parameters of the model. In contrast to this, we propose an approach that, like logistic regression, involves full discriminative training while still building on the generative form.

7. EXPERIMENTAL EVALUATION

We evaluate the performance of DIMPLE on the tasks of influence estimation and customer network value prediction, and compare it to standard feature-based regression methods and to relevant generative approaches found in the literature when applicable. Our results show that DIMPLE outperforms other methods in various settings.

7.1 Influence Estimation

We perform experiments on influence estimation on both synthetic and real data. Our synthetic experiments include two different settings, both of which generalize the independent cascade model to more realistic diffusion mechanisms. In our real data experiment we predict the number of votes a Digg[6] article receives given a seed of initial voters.

We compared DIMPLE to baselines of two types: discriminative feature-based regression methods, and prediction based on generative models. For discriminative methods we used Linear Regression with ℓ^2 regularization and Support Vector Regression (SVR) [42] with both a linear (SVR-LIN) and an RBF kernel (SVR-RBF). As features we used structural and topological properties, centrality measures, and statistics computed over the activity log of the infection process (see Table 1). The generative methods we compared to are NetRate [35], InfluLearner [10], and the maximum-likelihood approach for the discrete-time independent cascade model (DIC-ML) suggested in [26].[7] The input to DIMPLE includes samples (x, y), where x contains a seed and y is influence. It is important to note that while all other methods require as input the full cascade data (who was infected, when, and sometimes by whom), DIMPLE requires only the network, the seeds, and the number of infected nodes per cascade.

In all synthetic settings, we used networks generated with R-MAT [4], with parameters that have been shown to generate synthetic networks which mimic real-world networks in several aspects.[8] Using synthetic networks allows us to average over a large set of diverse instances of both networks and dynamics.

7.1.1 *Within-Cascade Dependencies*

Simple infection models often assume that when a node is infected, it attempts to infect each of its neighbors independently. However, this assumption does not hold in many real-world settings. For instance, if a Toronto resident receives an article concerning upcoming events in Toronto, she might be more likely to forward it to her friends who live in Toronto than to friends who live elsewhere. In general, knowing that node i infected a neighbor j which belongs to some group k can affect the probability of i infecting other neighbors in that group.

In such cases, learning the parameters of a simple, independent model may result in poor performance. To demonstrate this, we first generalize the independent cascade model to allow for "group dependencies" and then evaluate different methods for influence estimation under these dynamics.

In our experiment, each node in the network is assigned to one of K groups. When node i is infected, it infects *all* of its neighbors j who are in group k with probability θ_{ik}. Hence, in a single infection attempt, either all neighbors in a certain group are infected, or none are. This introduces within-cascade dependencies. Notice that when each neighbor belongs to a different group, this model is equivalent to the independent cascade model.

Each instance in the experiment was carried out as follows. First, we generated a network of 1,000 nodes, randomly allocated nodes to K groups, and sampled node-group infection probabilities θ_{ik} uniformly from $[0, 0.25]$. Next, we created 500 train and test samples by randomly choosing seeds of five nodes and simulating the group-dependent dynamics. Labels were set by averaging the number of infected nodes over multiple cascades (10 for training, 10,000 for test). We repeated this procedure for multiple networks and sample sets, and for each instance for several values of K.

We compared the performance of DIMPLE to that of other methods, both discriminative and generative.[9] We experimented with two variants of DIMPLE, one with a kernel based on the grouped dynamics (DIMPLE-G), and the other based on the standard independent cascade model (DIMPLE-IC). The grouped-cascade kernel can be computed in a similar fashion to Sec. 4.1 by sampling edges in groups.[3]

As shown in Figure 2 (left), when infections are independent, DIMPLE performs well, though not as well as DIC-ML. However, the performance of DIC-ML and other generative methods deteriorates quickly when dependencies are introduced. Furthermore, while DIMPLE only uses seeds and cascade sizes as input, the generative methods require the infection times of all nodes in each cascade. When there are few groups, the prediction task becomes harder due to the high degree of dependence. While feature based methods and NetRate perform better here than with weak dependencies, DIMPLE retains its advantage. It is interesting to note that the DIMPLE variant with the *independent* kernel performs as well as the group-dependent variant across all values of K, even when the data contains dependencies.

7.1.2 *Between-Cascade Dependencies*

Another assumption in simple infection models is that edge probabilities are constant across cascades, and that cascades are carried out independently of one another. This assumption is not always realistic. For instance, if cascades correspond to different types of content and if users have different contextual preferences, infection probabilities will vary and cascades will become dependent.

[6]http://digg.com

[7]For training SVRs we used LIBSVM [5]. For NetRate and Influlearner we used code provided by the respective authors.

[8]Parameters were set to $[0.5, 0.1; 0.1, 0.3]$. These set the recursive block-wise structure of the network.

[9]We are not aware of any closed-form maximum likelihood estimators for the generalized infection dynamics we discuss.

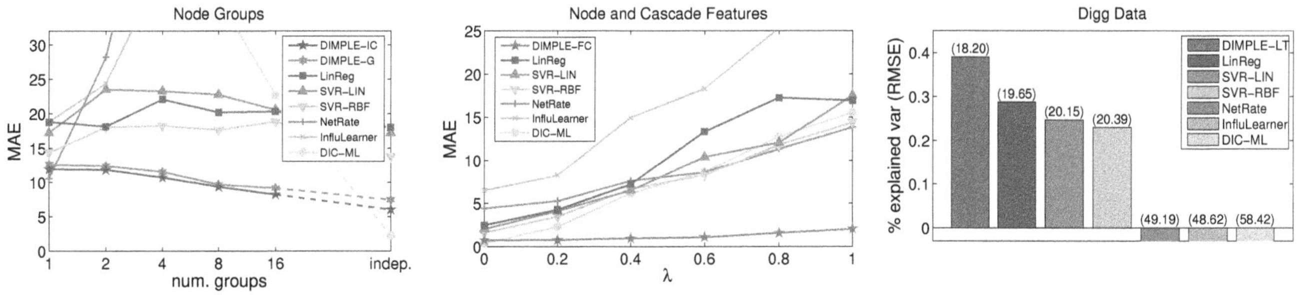

Figure 2: Influence estimation results. Left: An infected node infects either all or none of its neighbors in each group (with enough groups, infections become independent). Middle: As λ grows, infection probabilities increasingly depend on the cascade features (at $\lambda = 0$ they are independent). Right: For Digg, bars show percentage of explained variance (higher is better), and numbers in brackets show RMSE (lower is better).

To explore this setting, we present a generalization of the independent cascade model in which infection probabilities depend on features of nodes and cascades. Given node feature vectors x^i, x^j and a feature vector c describing the contents of a cascade, we set the edge infection probabilities to:

$$p_{ij}^c = \text{sig}\Big((1-\lambda)\sum_k \alpha_k x_k^i x_k^j + \lambda \sum_\ell \beta_\ell c_\ell\Big) \tag{22}$$

where α, β are weight vectors and λ is a scalar interpolating between fully node-defined and fully content-defined infection probabilities. Note that when $\lambda = 0$, this reduces to an independent cascade model. Setting $\lambda > 0$ introduces between-cascade dependencies.

Each instance in the experiment was generated as follows. First, we generated a network of 300 nodes and sampled features and weights for both nodes and cascades uniformly from $[-1, 1]^3$. Next, we created 250 train and test samples by randomly choosing five-node seeds and simulating infections using the standard independent cascade model dynamics with edge probabilities p_{ij}^c for a given λ. Labels were generated as in Sec. 7.1.1. We repeated this procedure for multiple networks and sample sets, over a range of λ values.

We compared the performance of DIMPLE with a feature-based cascade kernel (DIMPLE-FC) to other discriminative and generative methods.[9] DIMPLE was trained by simulating the dynamics over 1,000 randomly drawn values of (α, β, λ). The kernel was constructed from influence estimations over these simulations. Figure 2 (middle) displays the average MAE for a range of λ-s. For $\lambda = 0$, where the dynamics are equivalent to the standard independent cascade model, DIMPLE attains comparable results to DIC-ML which learns the (true in this case) model parameters using an exact maximum-likelihood approach. As λ grows and the cascade features have a higher effect on infection probabilities, the performance of all other methods quickly deteriorates, while DIMPLE maintains a low error.

7.1.3 *Predicting Digg Votes*

Digg is a popular social news-aggregation platform, where users submit links to news articles and vote on articles submitted by fellow users. Digg also facilitates a social network where users can "follow" other users. Followers receive updates on the actions of their followees, such as article submissions and votes; hence, the submission of an article can trigger a cascade of votes across the network. Since users are exposed to articles either by an update from a followee or via an external source, we consider as the seed of an article both the article's submitter and all users who voted on it prior to having any of their followees do so. Our task is to predict the number of votes of an article given its seed.

We use the data provided in [21] which includes the social network as well as all votes and articles that appeared on Digg's front page in June 2009. As we are interested in the network effect of the spread of votes, we focus on votes made before the article was promoted to the front page, and on voters who are members of the social network. Our sample set includes 3,301 articles submitted by 429 distinct users, with 191,880 votes by a total of 3,767 voting users, of which 1,919 acted as seed nodes. We consider articles with at least one vote (other than the submitter's), and edges for which both users co-voted on at least 5 articles. Results are averaged over several 75:25 train-test splits. As can be seen in Figure 2 (right), DIMPLE with a linear threshold kernel (DIMPLE-LT) outperforms all other methods on this task, while generative methods preform worse than predicting the mean.

7.2 Predicting Customer Network Value

In this section we demonstrate the versatility of our approach by applying it to the prediction of customer network value in a unique real-world dataset. Our goal is to predict the amount of credit attributed to users in a referral-based development-related phone service. The characteristics of our data and the goal of our prediction task do not fit standard generative methods. As we show, DIMPLE with a branching-process kernel outperforms other methods.

Data.

Polly [33, 34] is a phone-based system, developed by researchers at Carnegie Mellon University and Lahore University of Management Sciences, whose goal is to provide development-related services to low-literate communities. In its basic form, Polly is a viral voice-based game, where users can record messages and forward funny voice-altered variations of the original message to friends. On top of this entertainment platform, Polly includes a 'payload': when a user interacts with the system, she is offered to listen to targeted development-related content, such as job ads ap-

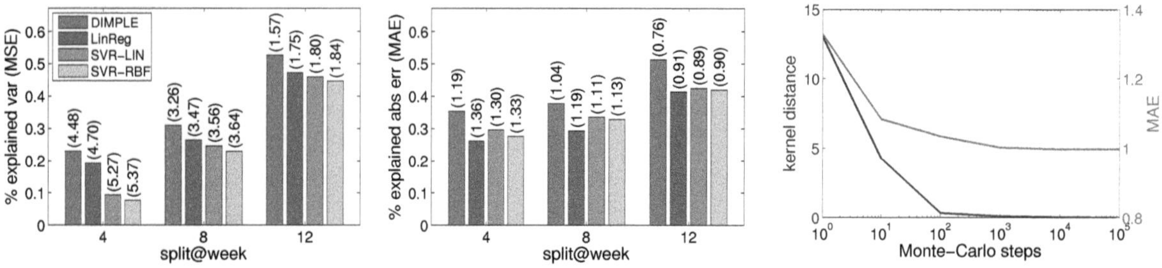

Figure 3: Polly results. Left and middle: MSE and MAE of predicting network value over various train-test splits. Bars show percentage of explained variance or absolute error (higher is better), numbers in brackets show MSE or MAE (lower is better). Right: Convergence of the Monte-Carlo kernel estimation process, showing the ℓ_2 distance between consecutive kernels (lower blue line) and the final MAE (top green line).

propriate for low-skilled workers. A user can then choose to listen to these ads, and also forward them to friends.

In rural areas where Polly was deployed, phone-based cellular services are abundant, but literacy is often scarce. The high unemployment rate is attributed not to a lack of jobs, but rather to a lack of information regarding job opportunities, which is often textual. This signifies the importance of a person-to-person voice-based system as a platform for spreading important content such as job ads. The system exploits the high phone-based connectivity of its users and the active role they take to make job ads widely accessible.

In our experiments, we use data collected from a study carried out with Polly in Pakistan in 2012 [34]. Polly was seeded to five select individuals, which quickly triggered an exponential rise in activity. For our analysis, we used data collected during the first four months following seeding. During this time, Polly has spread to 21,786 users, who engaged in 46,675 interactions. For generality, the only information we use in our experiments is the message log which consists of who sent a message to whom and when.

Prediction task.

One of the main considerations in Polly is the spread of the service to new users. Since Polly relies solely on word-of-mouth, predicting the future contribution of new users to the spread of the service is crucial. A natural way to quantify the contribution of users is to measure their network value using a referral credit scheme like the one described in Sec. 5, where the credit for recruiting a new user is recursively distributed across the edges of a "recruiting tree". Under this setting, our goal is to predict the future credit of new users who performed k interactions with the system up to some time horizon T.

Since the referral process in Polly is infectious in nature, applying methods based on infection processes seems advantageous. However, since the task is to predict infections of latent nodes in an unknown part of the network, standard infection models such as the independent cascade and linear threshold models do not apply here. In contrast, the branching process described in Sec. 5 is a natural choice, as it can describe how a credit tree "grows" from a single node.

We introduce a small variation on the model in Sec. 5. The Polly data contains many users who do not spread the service. We thus consider two types of nodes: *active* nodes which can have offsprings, and *passive* nodes which cannot. At any point in the branching process we assume that the number of active and passive offsprings is geometrically distributed with parameters $p^{\text{act}}(x;\theta_a)$ and $p^{\text{pas}}(x;\theta_p)$, respectively. Denote the corresponding expected values by $\mu^{\text{act}}(x;\theta_a)$ and $\mu^{\text{pas}}(x;\theta_p)$. Then, assuming the process starts with a single active node, the expected overall number of nodes at depth ℓ is:

$$\mu(\ell,x;\theta_a,\theta_p) = \mu_\ell^{\text{act}}(x;\theta_a) + \mu_{\ell-1}^{\text{act}}(x;\theta_a)\mu^{\text{pas}}(x;\theta_p) \quad (23)$$

and the predictor is:

$$f(x;\theta_a,\theta_p) = \sum_{\ell=1}^{\delta} \frac{1}{2^\ell}\mu(\ell,x;\theta_a,\theta_p) \quad (24)$$

To calculate the kernel, we use the approach in Sec. 4.3.

Evaluation details.

In our experiments we created a sample x for each new user at the time she sent her $k = 3^{\text{rd}}$ message, and set the label y to be the credit she accumulated up to $T = 7$ days from sample time, while restricting the depth of credit trees to $\delta = 5$. This resulted in 12,494 samples, with about 500-1,500 samples per week. For each sampled user, we computed a set of features based on the system's log up to that time. We used both topological and activity related features of focal nodes, their parents, and their children (see Table 1).

We split the sample set into a series of training and test sets, with splits taken at one week intervals, and compared DIMPLE to other discriminative methods. Selection of meta-parameters was performed by training on the early part of the train set and validating on the later part, with a split proportional to that of the train and test sets. For the branching process in DIMPLE, we chose the geometric distribution for both active and passive nodes, and used the expected credit (for MSE) and median credit (for MAE) as our predictors. Figure 3 displays the accuracy of DIMPLE and other feature based methods. DIMPLE attains superior performance across all splits. Figure 3 (right) presents the convergence rate of the kernel and the reduction in error as a function of the number of Monte-Carlo steps. As can be seen, the error drops considerably even after as few as 100 steps, and at 1,000 steps the error is very close to that of 100,000.

8. CONCLUSIONS

In this paper we introduced DIMPLE, a discriminative method for learning predictors for dynamic infection processes over networks. Our predictors are inspired by generative processes but are trained to achieve optimal accuracy. The prediction functions are highly non-linear in their original formulation. However, we show that by switching to a larger hypothesis space, the problem is effectively "linearized" and one can use kernel methods for optimization.

Switching to the larger hypothesis space G has an advantage in terms of expressive power, but may run the risk of overfitting. As with any kernel based method, it turns out that generalization is actually not dependent on the dimension of the feature space (which in our case, as in RBF kernels, is infinite since $w(\theta)$ is a function of θ), but rather on the margin with which the data can be separated (e.g., see [40]). As with any other kernel method, whether or not such a large margin exists is problem dependent. The empirical success of DIMPLE in our experiments demonstrates that this is likely to be the case in practice.

Our experiments clearly demonstrate that DIMPLE can be applied to a wide range of tasks and dynamics. In particular, we apply it to the tasks of influence estimation and customer network value prediction.

The method as presented is very general, and is not restricted to infection processes. It can in fact be applied to other tasks involving general dynamic processes over networks, such as link prediction with triadic-closure based network evolution models [22]. We leave this for future work.

Acknowledgments: We would like to thank Jacob Goldenberg and Lev Muchnik for valuable discussions, Roni Rosenfeld for motivation and data, and Elad Eban for inspiration. Mor Nitzan is grateful to the Azrieli Foundation for the award of an Azrieli Fellowship. This work was supported by the Intel Collaborative Research Institute for Computational Intelligence (ICRI-CI), and by the Israel Ministry of Science and Technology - Knowledge Center in Machine Learning and Artificial Intelligence.

	Influence estimation			Network value (Polly)			
	Seed	Seed neighbors	Within-seed	Focal node	First parent	Last parent	Sons (first 3)
outgoing degree	✓	✓	✓	✓	✓	✓	✓
incoming degree	✓	✓	✓	✓	✓	✓	✓
# out neighbors	✓						
# in neighbors	✓						
mean neis.' deg.	✓	✓		✓			
log-betweenness	✓	✓	✓	✓	✓	✓	✓
eigencentrality	✓	✓					
clustering coeff.	✓	✓	✓	✓	✓	✓	✓
distance histogram			✓				
# incoming msgs				✓	✓	✓	✓
# parents				✓			
time of rcvd msgs				✓			
hour of sent msgs				✓			
self-msg indicator				✓			
rank amongst sons				✓			
time of first msg					✓		✓
time of last msg						✓	
time to first msg					✓		
time to last msg						✓	

Table 1: Features used in the experiments. In the influence estimation experiments for each feature we used the mean, min., and max. over all seed nodes.

9. REFERENCES

[1] E. Bakshy, J. M. Hofman, W. A. Mason, and D. J. Watts. Everyone's an influencer: quantifying influence on twitter. In *Proc. of the 4th int. conf. on Web search and data mining*, pages 65–74. ACM, 2011.

[2] E. Bakshy, B. Karrer, and L. A. Adamic. Social influence and the diffusion of user-created content. In *Proc. of the 10th ACM conference on Electronic commerce*, pages 325–334. ACM, 2009.

[3] J. O. Berger. *Statistical decision theory and Bayesian analysis.* Springer, 1985.

[4] D. Chakrabarti, Y. Zhan, and C. Faloutsos. R-mat: A recursive model for graph mining. In *SDM*, volume 4, pages 442–446. SIAM, 2004.

[5] C.-C. Chang and C.-J. Lin. LIBSVM: A library for support vector machines. *ACM Transactions on Intelligent Systems and Technology*, 2:27:1–27:27, 2011.

[6] W. Chen, C. Wang, and Y. Wang. Scalable influence maximization for prevalent viral marketing in large-scale social networks. In *Proc. of the 16th int. conf. on Knowledge discovery and data mining*, pages 1029–1038, 2010.

[7] J. Cheng, L. Adamic, P. A. Dow, J. M. Kleinberg, and J. Leskovec. Can cascades be predicted? In *Proc. of the 23rd int. conf. on World wide web*, pages 925–936, 2014.

[8] E. Cohen, D. Delling, T. Pajor, and R. F. Werneck. Sketch-based influence maximization and computation: Scaling up with guarantees. In *Proc. of the 23rd int. conf. on Conference on Information and Knowledge Management*, pages 629–638, 2014.

[9] P. Domingos and M. Richardson. Mining the network value of customers. In *Proc. of the 7th int. conf. on Knowledge discovery and data mining*, pages 57–66. ACM, 2001.

[10] N. Du, Y. Liang, E. M.-F. Balcan, and G. EDU. Influence function learning in information diffusion networks. In *Proc. of The 31st int. conf. on Machine Learning*, pages 2016–2024, 2014.

[11] V. M. Eguiluz and K. Klemm. Epidemic threshold in structured scale-free networks. *Phys. Rev. Letters*, 89(10):108701, 2002.

[12] G. Giakkoupis, A. Gionis, E. Terzi, and P. Tsaparas. Models and algorithms for network immunization. Technical report, University of Helsinki, 2005.

[13] J. Goldenberg, B. Libai, and E. Muller. Talk of the network: A complex systems look at the underlying process of word-of-mouth. *Marketing letters*, 12(3):211–223, 2001.

[14] M. Gomez Rodriguez, J. Leskovec, and A. Krause. Inferring networks of diffusion and influence. In *Proc.*

of the 16th int. conf. on Knowledge discovery and data mining, pages 1019–1028. ACM, 2010.

[15] A. Goyal, F. Bonchi, and L. V. Lakshmanan. Learning influence probabilities in social networks. In *Proc. of the third ACM int. conf. on Web search and data mining*, pages 241–250. ACM, 2010.

[16] M. Granovetter. Threshold models of collective behavior. *American journal of sociology*, pages 1420–1443, 1978.

[17] J. E. Hogan, K. N. Lemon, and B. Libai. Quantifying the ripple: Word-of-mouth and advertising effectiveness. *Journal of Advertising Research*, 44(03):271–280, 2004.

[18] T. Jaakkola and D. Haussler. Exploiting generative models in discriminative classifiers. In *Advances in Neural Inf. Processing Systems*, pages 487–493, 1998.

[19] D. Kempe, J. Kleinberg, and É. Tardos. Maximizing the spread of influence through a social network. In *Proc. of the 9th int. conf. on Knowledge discovery and data mining*, pages 137–146. ACM, 2003.

[20] G. S. Kimeldorf and G. Wahba. A correspondence between bayesian estimation on stochastic processes and smoothing by splines. *The Annals of Math. Stat.*, pages 495–502, 1970.

[21] K. Lerman and R. Ghosh. Information contagion: An empirical study of the spread of news on digg and twitter social networks. *ICWSM*, 10:90–97, 2010.

[22] J. Leskovec, L. Backstrom, R. Kumar, and A. Tomkins. Microscopic evolution of social networks. In *Proc. of the 14th int. conf. on Knowledge discovery and data mining*, pages 462–470. ACM, 2008.

[23] J. Leskovec, A. Krause, C. Guestrin, C. Faloutsos, J. VanBriesen, and N. Glance. Cost-effective outbreak detection in networks. In *Proc. of the 13th int. conf. on Knowledge discovery and data mining*, pages 420–429. ACM, 2007.

[24] W. J. Morokoff and R. E. Caflisch. Quasi-monte carlo integration. *Journal of computational physics*, 122(2):218–230, 1995.

[25] S. Myers and J. Leskovec. On the convexity of latent social network inference. In *Advances in Neural Inf. Processing Systems*, pages 1741–1749, 2010.

[26] P. Netrapalli and S. Sanghavi. Learning the graph of epidemic cascades. In *ACM SIGMETRICS Performance Evaluation Review*, volume 40, pages 211–222. ACM, 2012.

[27] M. E. Newman, G. T. Barkema, and M. Newman. *Monte Carlo methods in statistical physics*, volume 13. Clarendon Press Oxford, 1999.

[28] P. Ney and A. Joffe. *Branching processes*. Springer, 1978.

[29] A. Y. Ng and M. I. Jordan. On discriminative vs. generative classifiers: A comparison of logistic regression and naive bayes. *Advances in neural inf. processing systems*, 2:841–848, 2002.

[30] R. Pastor-Satorras and A. Vespignani. Epidemic spreading in scale-free networks. *Phys. rev. letters*, 86(14):3200, 2001.

[31] W. H. Press and G. R. Farrar. Recursive stratified sampling for multidimensional monte carlo integration. *Computers in Physics*, 4(2):190–195, 1990.

[32] A. Rahimi and B. Recht. Weighted sums of random kitchen sinks: Replacing minimization with randomization in learning. In *Advances in neural inf. processing systems*, pages 1313–1320, 2009.

[33] A. A. Raza, M. Pervaiz, C. Milo, S. Razaq, G. Alster, J. Sherwani, U. Saif, and R. Rosenfeld. Viral entertainment as a vehicle for disseminating speech-based services to low-literate users. In *Proc. of the Fifth int. conf. on Information and Communication Technologies and Development*, pages 350–359. ACM, 2012.

[34] A. A. Raza, F. Ul Haq, Z. Tariq, M. Pervaiz, S. Razaq, U. Saif, and R. Rosenfeld. Job opportunities through entertainment: Virally spread speech-based services for low-literate users. In *Proc. of the SIGCHI Conference on Human Factors in Computing Systems*, pages 2803–2812. ACM, 2013.

[35] M. G. Rodriguez, D. Balduzzi, and B. Schölkopf. Uncovering the temporal dynamics of diffusion networks. *arXiv preprint arXiv:1105.0697*, 2011.

[36] K. Saito, R. Nakano, and M. Kimura. Prediction of information diffusion probabilities for independent cascade model. In *Knowledge-Based Intelligent Information and Engineering Systems*, pages 67–75. Springer, 2008.

[37] K. Saito, K. Ohara, Y. Yamagishi, M. Kimura, and H. Motoda. Learning diffusion probability based on node attributes in social networks. In *Foundations of Intelligent Systems*, pages 153–162. Springer, 2011.

[38] B. Schölkopf, R. Herbrich, and A. J. Smola. A generalized representer theorem. In *Computational learning theory*, pages 416–426. Springer, 2001.

[39] D. Shah and T. Zaman. Rumors in a network: Who's the culprit? *Information Theory, IEEE Transactions on*, 57(8):5163–5181, 2011.

[40] J. Shawe-Taylor, P. L. Bartlett, R. C. Williamson, and M. Anthony. Structural risk minimization over data-dependent hierarchies. *Information Theory, IEEE Transactions on*, 44(5):1926–1940, 1998.

[41] O. Tsur and A. Rappoport. What's in a hashtag? content based prediction of the spread of ideas in microblogging communities. In *Proc. of the 5th int. conf. on web search and data mining*, pages 643–652, 2012.

[42] V. Vapnik. *The nature of statistical learning theory*. Springer, 2000.

[43] J. Yang and J. Leskovec. Modeling information diffusion in implicit networks. In *10th int. conf. on Data Mining*, pages 599–608. IEEE, 2010.

Representation Learning for Information Diffusion through Social Networks: an Embedded Cascade Model

Simon Bourigault, Sylvain Lamprier, Patrick Gallinari

Sorbonne Universités, UPMC Univ Paris 06, UMR 7606, LIP6, F-75005, Paris, France
CNRS, UMR 7606, LIP6, F-75005, Paris, France

firstname.lastname@lip6.fr

ABSTRACT

In this paper, we focus on information diffusion through social networks. Based on the well-known Independent Cascade model, we embed users of the social network in a latent space to extract more robust diffusion probabilities than those defined by classical graphical learning approaches. Better generalization abilities provided by the use of such a projection space allows our approach to present good performances on various real-world datasets, for both diffusion prediction and influence relationships inference tasks. Additionally, the use of a projection space enables our model to deal with larger social networks.

Keywords

Machine learning; Information diffusion; Representation Learning

1. INTRODUCTION

Over the last 10 years, the sharing of content through Online Social Networks has become a major source of information for many users. Most websites now use social networks APIs that enable users to easily retweet, share, rate, comment, tag or like any piece of information. User actions are a rich source of information for companies and for marketing. They can for example be used as indicators of *popularity* for items or persons and predicting the popularity of information items has been widely studied [20] by analyzing whole *population* statistics. Many problems in domains like information propagation, social network analysis or marketing require a finer grained modeling of diffusion and propagation phenomena, at the scale of *users*. With the development of social resources, an increasing attention has been devoted to this modeling problem. For web and social data, analyzing user interactions for modeling diffusion phenomena presents a series of difficulties:

- Users are often heterogeneous with different behaviors or interests and they interact with each other through various channels at the same time.
- Relationships between users are hard to detect and to characterize. For example, it has been shown that "weak ties" between users who don't often interact with each other are important in the information diffusion process [2], whereas they are difficult to capture.
- Diffusion cascades vary in length considerably in different applications, which makes their dynamics difficult to learn and to predict [10].

The observation of a diffusion process often comes down to collecting interaction traces indicating when people do post or send a piece of information or buy a product. Most often, the process underlying the observations is hidden: one just observes when and where the actions do occur but one does not know why. Modeling the diffusion process then amounts to approximate this mechanism based on the observations. The model can then be used in different tasks relevant for the specific application like predicting who will get infected, inferring the diffusion structure, detecting influential users, etc. The purpose of this paper is to develop a diffusion model by learning from observations. For this, we will focus on the well-known Independent Cascade model (IC) which defines an iterative process of diffusion in a network. In this context, the problem of modeling diffusion comes down to learning probability distributions characterizing the hidden influence relationships between users, in order to discover the main communication channels of the network. Learning diffusion distributions in IC from observation data has been initiated in the mid 2000 [18, 34] and since that several variants have been proposed as described in section 2. The models that we consider here perform the following hypothesis: infection[1] is binary, the diffusion network is unknown, influence relationships do not depend on the propagated content (while this could be easily incorporated in our model), infection probabilities between users do not vary in time.

In existing cascade models, diffusion probabilities are learned using non parametric or parametric formulations of the distributions defined on the edges of a diffusion graph. We develop here an alternative approach based on representation learning techniques. Instead of learning probabilities on a discrete structure corresponding to a diffusion

WSDM'16, February 22–25, 2016, San Francisco, CA, USA.

ISBN 978-1-4503-3716-8/16/02...$15.00

DOI: http://dx.doi.org/10.1145/2835776.2835817

[1]Throughout this paper, we indifferently talk about infection or contamination to denote the fact that the propagated content has reached a given user of the network.

graph, we model the diffusion space as a continuous latent space where relative positions of users are used to define their content transmission likelihood. We follow the general scheme defined in [34] for learning IC distributions and propose a diffusion model based on users embeddings in a latent projection space. This model presents better generalization abilities with a lower memory cost. Our contributions are summarized below.

- We propose a new model for learning diffusion probabilities from diffusion episode observations. Its novelty consists of mapping the observation episodes onto a continuous latent space. The probabilities will be inferred from the relative positions of the users in this space. This model presents several advantages: 1. it allows us to learn directly from the observed data without making hypothesis about an underlying network which is very often only partially known. 2. this non parametric formulation allows to adjust the model complexity to the dynamics of the observed data so that the model offers a better control over generalization ability. 3. the model allows us capturing dependencies between probabilities which are not considered with other IC models. 4. the computational memory requirements are greatly reduced w.r.t. discrete based diffusion models, which allows us to consider more complex interaction schemes.
- We develop an algorithm based on a stochastic gradient approach which is well suited to handle large observation sets.
- We evaluate the algorithm on two tasks: contamination prediction in order to retrieve the eventually infected users and influence relationships inference, and compare it with the baseline IC model of [34] and with two state of the art models.

The paper is organized as follows. Section 2 presents background and motivations for the proposed approach. Section 3 defines the notations used throughout the paper and describes the diffusion model. Section 4 presents evaluation of the model on real datasets for the two tasks of infection prediction and link prediction.Finally, Section 5 concludes our works and gives some insights into possible future works.

2. MOTIVATIONS AND RELATED WORKS

While the study of diffusion phenomena firstly emerged in epidemiology and social science contexts, the development of social networks opened an unprecedented era for new related research directions. Most of the proposed iterative models of diffusion are based on two fundamental models (that can be unified on the same framework [21]) : the Independent Cascade (IC) [13] model and the Linear Threshold (LT) [16] model. Both model a user-to-user contamination process : while IC models the spread of diffusion as cascades of infections over the network, LT determines infections of users according to thresholds of the influence pressure incoming from the neighborhood of each user (assuming influence additivity). We focus in this paper on IC-like formalisms, or more generaly on cascade-based approaches which appear well fitted to reproduce realistic diffusion dynamics [20]. While the parameters of these models (transmission probabilities) initially needed to be set manually, Gruhl et al. [18] developed a first attempt to automatically learn diffusion probabilities from observations. A few years later, in a seminal paper, [34] proposed the learning methodology we extend in this article. It corresponds to a clear improvement w.r.t. [18], since it replaced an "exactly one influencer" assumption by a more realistic "at least one influencer" one. From there, IC has served as a basis for many variants and extensions of cascades-based approaches. Several of these variants consider different ways for dealing with users' infection timestamps [32, 33, 14, 12], others focus on the inclusion of context information in the original IC model [35, 38, 19, 22, 36].

Cascade based models classically make the assumption that the diffused content transits from users to users in the social network following explicit links in the graph[34, 39, 14, 37]. This is inherited from historical models of diffusion and is not adapted to many internet situations. For example, it is often the case that a user does not cite his source (blogs, tweet) and in this case there is no indication of who infected him. The social network is generally not a closed world and users may get their information from many different channels - again there is no way to go back to the source or to know how long it took for propagating the information. In other domains like in marketing, one can track the actions of a customer, but one does not know who influenced him. To summarize, even though the links of a network may sometimes correspond to useful information, they are often not representative of the real diffusion channels of a social network [39, 28]. In addition to the above examples, note that the social graph captured on an online social network (friends, followers, subscriptions...) is often incomplete, irrelevant [37] or sometimes unknown (for privacy reasons for instance). Cascade models can be used when there is no a priori graph structure, simply by considering a complete graph linking or by considering an interaction graph including all possible transmissions observed in a training set [2]. Either one of the two solutions has been used in several works like [28, 15, 14]. Note that [15] and [29] also proposed methods for efficiently selecting relevant edges from the complete graph of users.

However, considering complete graph structures (or rather dense interaction graphs) appears intractable for many datasets: the number of parameters of IC is $\mathcal{O}(d \times |\mathcal{U}|)$, with $|\mathcal{U}|$ the number of users in the network and d its average degree. Its memory complexity very quickly grows with the size of the network. By transposing the problem in a continuous space, our model skips this limitation of discrete formulations. Compression abilities offered by the representation learning field help to cope with such complexity.

Besides, the diffusion dynamics are usually influenced by many factors that are difficult to model a priori. Classical cascade models have difficulties to reproduce them. Social graphs are indeed known to possess lots of properties that distinguish them from random graphs (power-law node degrees, low diameter, etc...) [27]. One important and well-known property of social networks is that they contain *communities*, which can roughly be defined as groups of "similar" users. Recently, [3] showed that when dealing with information diffusion, communities do not only refer to users who interact with *each other* (usually called cohesive

[2]Relation u, v is considered only if there exists at least one diffusion episode in the training set where u is infected before v.

communities), but also to users who interact with the *same other groups of users* (usually referred to as 2-mode communities). These two types of communities were later studied in [40, 31]. These works tell us two important things about information diffusion :

- If there is diffusion between users a and b in a network, and diffusion between b and c, then user a is more likely to diffuse content to c. This is due to the presence of *cohesive* communities.
- If there is diffusion between a and c, diffusion between b and c, and between a and d, then b is more likely to diffuse content to d. This is due to the presence of *2-mode* communities [40].

In classical cascade models, any sets of probabilities can be defined on links, without any regularization constraints on the extracted diffusion network. Besides leading to overfitting issues, this can lead to unrealistic communication structures (especially when no prior information is given about the social structure of the considered network). On another hand, thanks to geometric constraints on continuous spaces, projecting users in a continuous representation space naturally allows one to capture such social regularities, which cannot be represented in discrete models without additional assumptions about the underlying network. Figure 1 depicts our proposal, which thus consists in moving from a classical influence graph paradigm to an influence continuous space one for the modelization of diffusion dynamics in social networks.

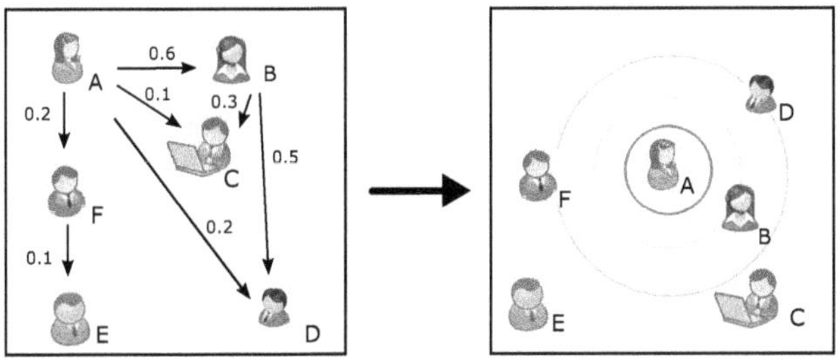

Figure 1: From an influence graph to a continuous influence space. On the left, values associated to edges represent influence probabilities between users. On the right, these influence probabilities are functions of the relative positions of two users. Circles represent equi-probability levels for the diffusion from user A to other users.

Learning representation has been a growing topic recently with applications in many domains [4]. It has been used to learn complex relationships between items like for example in [5]. Since diffusion episodes are essentially temporal series of binary events, learning from sequences is also relevant to the topic of this paper. Representation learning has been used in a series of applications involving sequences or more generally dynamic data. A probabilistic model has been recently proposed in [9] for playlist prediction, where the use of a latent space prevents from having to learn transition probabilities for every single possible pair of songs. While close, our problem differs from this work on the fact that diffusion cascades spread as tree structures, not straight sequences, with possibly simultaneous infections. In our case, influence causalities are hidden: any of the previously infected users can be the source of a given observed new infection. Recently, the idea to use embeddings to predict sequences of elements was also developed in language models such as *W*ord2Vec [26]. Here, embeddings reflect the syntactic and semantic structures of the data sequences (e.g. sentences). Once again, using an embedding is a way to add a regularization over words representations : two words with similar meanings tend to be projected close to each other, and will thus be predicted in a similar context. Recurrent neural networks, which build fixed size embeddings from sequences, have also been used with success in applications like speech recognition [17] or more recently for translation [11].

At last, user embeddings for diffusion tasks have been employed in [6], where infected users are projected near the infection source, the distance reflecting their respective rank of infection. However the goal was different. This model did not attempted to model the diffusion dynamics, but only to determine final infections knowing a unique source of diffusion.

3. EMBEDDINGS FOR DIFFUSION

3.1 Notations

Traditionally, information diffusion on networks is observed as a set $\mathcal{D}$ of "diffusion episodes" $\mathcal{D} = (D_1, D_2, \ldots, D_n)$. A diffusion episode D is a set of timestamped user actions related to the same piece of information. It can correspond, for instance, to a set of users who "liked" a specific YouTube video, posted a given url, replied to a given message, etc... It describes to whom and *when* an item spreads through the network, but not *how* diffusion happens: Contrary to cascade structures, the information of who infected who is unknown in such observed inputs. Cascade models usually perform assumptions on this latent factor to build their influence graphs [34].

Given a social network composed of a set of N users[3] $\mathcal{U} = (u_1, ..., u_N)$, a diffusion episode D is then defined as a set of infected users associated with their timestamps of infection: $D = \{(u, t^D(u)) | u \in \mathcal{U} \wedge t^D(u) < \infty\}$, where $t^D : \mathcal{U} \rightarrow \mathbb{R}^+$ gives infection timestamps for users infected by the diffusion in concern, or ∞ for non infected ones. Timestamps returned by t^D are relative timestamps given the one of the first infected user (i.e., the source of diffusion, for which t^D is 0). In the following, we note $D(t)$ the set of users who have been infected by diffusion D before timestamp t: $D(t) = \{u \in \mathcal{U} | t^D(u) < t\}$. Symmetrically, we note $\bar{D}(t)$ the set of users who have not been infected before t. $D(\infty)$ is the set of all eventually infected users.

3.2 Diffusion Model

As stated above, we build upon the well-known Independent Cascade Model. We propose to embed it in a continuous space to capture regularities between diffusion relationships of the network and to lighten the memory cost of the model. Based on the relative positions of users, the model allows one to simulate diffusion processes that comply to the observed dynamics.

IC follows an iterative process for simulating cascades of diffusion, where, at each iteration, each newly infected user u gets a unique chance to infect other users v of the network

[3]We talk about users throughout the paper, but the results remain valid for any other kinds of nodes.

with some probability $P_{u,v}$. Here, we consider a slightly modified version of IC, as done in [25], where diffusion between users is assumed to follow uniform delay distributions rather than occurring in successive discrete time-steps. In real life, diffusion indeed occur in continuous time, not discrete. Moreover, [23] recently showed that letting time delay considerations aside when learning transmission probabilities from real-world social data allows one to obtain more robust models since not disturbed by usually noisy infection timestamps. Therefore, as advised in this paper, we only consider partial orders of infections rather than exact infection timestamps to build our model of diffusion.

In our model, the probability for a user to be infected by a diffusion process D thus depends on all previously infected users in D. Given a set of potentially influential users $I \subseteq \mathcal{U}$ (i.e. a set of previously infected users), the probability $P(v|I)$ to observe the infection of a user $v \in \mathcal{U} \setminus I$ knowing this set is therefore defined as:

$$P(v|I) = 1 - \prod_{u \in I}(1 - P_{u,v}) \tag{1}$$

where $P_{u,v}$ stands for the probability of transmission from user u to user v. $P(v|I)$ then corresponds to the probability that at least one user from I succeeded in transmitting content to v. While in IC an individual transmission probability $P_{u,v}$ is estimated for every pair of users (u, v), we propose to use a function of the users latent representation $f : \mathbb{R}^d \times \mathbb{R}^d \to [0, 1]$, where d is the size of the latent space:

$$P_{u,v} = f(z_u, \omega_v) \tag{2}$$

where $z_u \in \mathbb{R}^d$ is the representation of user u as a sender of a content, while $\omega_v \in \mathbb{R}^d$ is the representation of user v as a receiver of the diffused content. Then, two sets of parameters $Z = (z_u)_{u\in\mathcal{U}}$ and $\Omega = (\omega_u)_{u\in\mathcal{U}}$ are defined to embed the users, one used for the "source" users and the other for "target" ones, to allow the representation of oriented diffusion networks (diffusion relationships are not symmetric in most of networks).

Different choices are possible for f. We performed different tests and came out with the following function that has been used throughout all the experiments in this paper. Since the contagion probabilities are independent one from the other, the only formal requirement is that f gives a value in $[0, 1]$, so that it can be interpreted as a probability.

$$f(z_u, \omega_v) = \frac{1}{1 + exp(z_u^{(0)} + \omega_v^{(0)} + \sum\limits_{i=1}^{d-1} (z_u^{(i)} - \omega_v^{(i)})^2)} \tag{3}$$

where $x^{(i)}$ stands for the i-th component of the vector x. It defines a transmission probability that decreases as the distance between the sender u and the receiver v in the latent space increases. The use of a sigmoid function presents the great advantage of returning a real value in $[0, 1]$ which thus can act as a consistent probability that can directly be used as an influence probability $P_{u,v}$ in our model. Moreover, this function is smoothed at its bounds, which allows variations to have a greater impact for some critical levels which correspond to distances between users between which influence is uncertain. Slight variations of extreme (low or high) values must indeed have less impact on the model probabilities since such values usually concern obvious influences (at least after a sufficient number of learning iterations). Note that we add biases $z_u^{(0)}$ and $\omega_v^{(0)}$ that act as priors on the general tendency to infect other users for u and to become infected for v. These parameters allow the model to get more degrees of freedom, by determining specific functions of probability computations according to who are the users in concern: the same distance between embeddings of two users z_u and ω_v does not lead to the same probability according to who is the sender u and who is the receiver v.

3.3 Learning Algorithm

We follow [34], or more exactly [23] for its time-relaxed version, in the derivation of the likelihood. Considering the set of all pairwise transmission probabilities $\mathcal{P} = \{P_{u,v} | (u, v) \in \mathcal{U}^2\}$, the probability of observing a specific diffusion episode is (if we let time considerations aside and focus on partial orders of infection as advised in [23]):

$$P(D) = \prod_{v \in D(\infty)} P_v^D \prod_{v \in \bar{D}(\infty)} (1 - P_v^D) \tag{4}$$

where $P_v^D = P(v|D(t^D(v)))$ is the probability of observing user v knowing previously infected users in D. Also, it is possible to consider the following log-likelihood for all diffusion episodes from the training set $\mathcal{D}$:

$$\mathcal{L}(\mathcal{P}; \mathcal{D}) = \sum_{D \in \mathcal{D}} \Big(\sum_{v \in D(\infty)} log(P_v^D) + \sum_{v \in \bar{D}(\infty)} log(1 - P_v^D)\Big) \tag{5}$$

Due to the formulation of the probability P_v^D (equation 1), this log-likelihood is very difficult to maximize directly. However, following the learning methodology described in [34], an Expectation-Maximization (EM) algorithm can be defined to solve this optimization problem. This algorithm considers the following expectation function $\mathcal{Q}(\mathcal{P}|\hat{\mathcal{P}})$:

$$\mathcal{Q}(\mathcal{P}|\hat{\mathcal{P}}) = \sum_{D \in \mathcal{D}} \left(\Phi^D(\mathcal{P}|\hat{\mathcal{P}}) + \sum_{v \in \bar{D}(\infty)} \sum_{u \in D(\infty)} log(1 - P_{u,v}) \right) \tag{6}$$

where $\Phi^D(\mathcal{P}|\hat{\mathcal{P}})$ corresponds to the expected value, for a given diffusion episode D, of the first term of the log likelihood function, which stands for the log likelihood w.r.t. infected users only. It is computed with respect to the conditional distribution of success of diffusion between users under the current estimate of probabilities $\hat{\mathcal{P}}$. Knowing that a user v is infected with an estimated probability $\hat{P_v^D}$ (which is computed via formula 1 with estimated transmission probabilities $\hat{P_{u,v}}$), the conditional probability that the diffusion from a given previously infected user u succeeded is given by $\frac{\hat{P_{u,v}}}{\hat{P_v^D}}$. Considering success and fail cases for each possible transmission of content implies the following expectation term:

$$\Phi^D(\mathcal{P}|\hat{\mathcal{P}}) = \sum_{v \in D(\infty)} \sum_{u \in D(t^D(v))} \frac{\hat{P_{u,v}}}{\hat{P_v^D}} \log(P_{u,v}) + (1 - \frac{\hat{P_{u,v}}}{\hat{P_v^D}}) \log(1 - P_{u,v}) \tag{7}$$

Note that, with transmission probabilities depending on relative positions in a continuous space rather than being set independently for each pair of considered users, the likelihood maximization problem detailed above cannot be decomposed into some independent convex optimization subproblems. Our optimization problem is not convex, however, using stochastic gradient procedures, it is possible to define an efficient learning process which converges to effective local maxima when the number of dimensions is well fitted (a number of $d = 25$ dimensions appears as a good trade-off as observed in section 4).

The pseudo-code of the learning process of our model is given by algorithm 1. It corresponds to an extension of the EM algorithm used in [34], adapted to our non parametric model of the transmission probabilities $\mathcal{P} = \{P_{u,v} | (u,v) \in \mathcal{U}^2\}$. By considering $P_{u,v} = f(z_u, \omega_v)$ for each pair of users (u,v) as proposed in equation 2, the aim is to find optimal parameters Z and Ω that maximize the likelihood given by equation 5. We use a stochastic gradient ascent process to learn parameters sets Z^* and Ω^*. At each iteration, the process:

1. Line 8: Samples a diffusion episode D from $\mathcal{D}$;

2. Line 9: Samples a user v to consider from $\bar{D}(1)$ (the initial users of the diffusion episode are not considered since their infection cannot be explained by any previously infected user);

3. Lines 11 to 18: If v is infected in the diffusion episode D, computes the current estimates $\hat{P_v^D}$ and $\hat{P_{u,v}}$ for all users u infected before v in D. This is done by considering formula 1 and 2 with the current values z_u and ω_v.

4. Lines 19 to 29: Uses a gradient ascent step to update the values of Z and Ω. This update step aims at increasing the value of $\mathcal{Q}(\mathcal{P}|\hat{\mathcal{P}})$ (see equation 6). If the user v is infected in D, the update step involves a derivation of $\Phi^D(\mathcal{P}|\hat{\mathcal{P}})$ (lines 22 to 25). Otherwise, it involves a derivation of $log(1 - P_{u,v})$ (lines 25 to 28). The learning rate ϵ used in our experiments is 10^{-4}.

5. Lines 31 to 38: Tests the convergence of the learning every $freq$ iterations. After having computed all the pairwise transmission probabilities $\mathcal{P}$ using embeddings parameters Z and Ω, the algorithm computes the global log-likelihood by using formula 5. If this log-likelihood has not increased since the last computation, the learning process stops and returns current Z and Ω parameters. In our experiments this convergence test is performed every 1000000 iterations.

Note that, due to our sampling process (lines 8 and 9), every pair (u,v) is not associated with episodes from $\mathcal{D}$ in the same proportion as in formula 6. Without any correction, it would induce a biased learning process where pairs occurring in small episodes would be over-considered compared to their weight in formula 6. Therefore, lines 1 and 10 aim at computing a correction for this sampling related bias. According to our sampling process, the probability to consider the set of transmission probabilities to a given user v for a given episode D equals:

$$\frac{1}{|\mathcal{D}| \times |\bar{D}(1)|}$$

Now, we would like each transmission probability occurrence in formula 6 to be considered uniformly, thus following the

Algorithm 1: Stochastic Learning of Embedded IC

Input:
$\mathcal{U}$: the set of Users; $\mathcal{D}$: the set of Diffusion Episodes;
d: the number of dimensions of the projection space;
ϵ: the learning step;
$freq$: the frequency of stop tests;
Output:
$Z = \{\forall u \in \mathcal{U} : z_u \in \mathbb{R}^d\}$ the sender embeddings ;
$\Omega = \{\forall u \in \mathcal{U} : \omega_u \in \mathbb{R}^d\}$ the receiver embeddings ;

1 $nbProbas \leftarrow \sum_{D \in \mathcal{D}} \sum_{u \in D(\infty)} |\bar{D}(t^D(u)+1)|$;
2 **for** $u \in \mathcal{U}$ **do**
3 $\quad z_u \leftarrow$ Random values in $[-1,1]^d$;
4 $\quad \omega_u \leftarrow$ Random values in $[-1,1]^d$;
5 **end**
6 $oldL \leftarrow -\infty$; $it \leftarrow 0$;
7 **while** $true$ **do**
8 $\quad$ Sample $D \in \mathcal{D}$;
9 $\quad$ Sample $v \in \bar{D}(1)$;
10 $\quad \alpha \leftarrow \frac{|\mathcal{D}| \times |\bar{D}(1)|}{nbProbas}$;
11 $\quad$ **if** $t^D(v) < \infty$ **then**
12 $\quad\quad \hat{P_v^D} \leftarrow 1$;
13 $\quad\quad$ **for** $u \in D(t^D(v))$ **do**
14 $\quad\quad\quad \hat{P_{u,v}} = f(z_u, \omega_v)$;
15 $\quad\quad\quad \hat{P_v^D} \leftarrow \hat{P_v^D} \times (1 - \hat{P_{u,v}})$;
16 $\quad\quad$ **end**
17 $\quad\quad \hat{P_v^D} \leftarrow 1 - \hat{P_v^D}$;
18 $\quad$ **end**
19 $\quad$ **for** $u \in D(t^D(v))$ **do**
20 $\quad\quad \xi_u^+ \leftarrow \frac{\partial \log f(z_u, \omega_v)}{\partial z_u}$;
$\quad\quad \xi_u^- \leftarrow \frac{\partial \log(1 - f(z_u, \omega_v))}{\partial z_u}$;
21 $\quad\quad \xi_v^+ \leftarrow \frac{\partial \log f(z_u, \omega_v)}{\partial \omega_v}$;
$\quad\quad \xi_v^- \leftarrow \frac{\partial \log(1 - f(z_u, \omega_v))}{\partial \omega_v}$;
22 $\quad\quad$ **if** $t^D(v) < \infty$ **then**
23 $\quad\quad\quad z_u \leftarrow z_u + \alpha \times \epsilon \times (\frac{\hat{P_{u,v}}}{\hat{P_v^D}} \xi_u^+ + (1 - \frac{\hat{P_{u,v}}}{\hat{P_v^D}}) \xi_u^-)$;
24 $\quad\quad\quad \omega_v \leftarrow \omega_v + \alpha \times \epsilon \times (\frac{\hat{P_{u,v}}}{\hat{P_v^D}} \xi_v^+ + (1 - \frac{\hat{P_{u,v}}}{\hat{P_v^D}}) \xi_v^-)$;
25 $\quad\quad$ **else**
26 $\quad\quad\quad z_u \leftarrow z_u + \alpha \times \epsilon \times \xi_u^-$;
27 $\quad\quad\quad \omega_v \leftarrow \omega_v + \alpha \times \epsilon \times \xi_v^-$;
28 $\quad\quad$ **end**
29 $\quad$ **end**
30 $\quad it \leftarrow it + 1$;
31 $\quad$ **if** it mod $freq = 0$ **then**
32 $\quad\quad \mathcal{P} \leftarrow \{P_{u,v} | (u,v) \in \mathcal{U}^2 \wedge P_{u,v} = f(z_u, \omega_v)\}$;
33 $\quad\quad L \leftarrow$ Computation of the global log-likelihood using formula 5 with probabilities in $\mathcal{P}$;
34 $\quad\quad$ **if** $L \leq oldL$ **then**
35 $\quad\quad\quad$ **return** (Z, Ω);
36 $\quad\quad$ **end**
37 $\quad\quad oldL \leftarrow L$;
38 $\quad$ **end**
39 **end**

probability:

$$\frac{1}{\sum\limits_{D \in \mathcal{D}} \sum\limits_{u \in D(\infty)} |\bar{D}(t^D(u)+1)|}$$

whose denominator is computed as *nbProbas* (line 1) in the algorithm. This corresponds to the sum of counts of considered probabilities in each episode D (the total number of considered probabilities in formula 6). Then, to correct the sampling related bias, we compute (line 10):

$$\alpha = \frac{|\mathcal{D}| \times |\ \bar{D}(1)\ |}{\sum\limits_{D \in \mathcal{D}} \sum\limits_{u \in D(\infty)} |\bar{D}(t^D(u)+1)|}$$

Finally α is used in gradient updates (lines 22 to 28) to re-adjust the importance of the samples in the log-likelihood to maximize.

4. EXPERIMENTS

4.1 Datasets

Various datasets extracted from the Web have been used for our experiments. These datasets can be divided in two categories : User-Item and User-User datasets.

User-Item Datasets

These datasets essentially consist of triplets of the form : *(user,item,timestamp)*. Each triplet indicates that a given user interacted with some information item at a known time, either by liking it, commenting it, clicking it or sharing it. Each item corresponds to a diffused content, which infects every user who interacted with it. The "source" users are the ones who first interacted with it[4].

Digg is a collaborative news portal on which users can post links to *stories* (articles, blog posts, videos...). Other users can then "digg" these stories if they like it. Stories appear on the front page of Digg based on the amount of "diggs" they have received. We used the Digg stream API to collect the *complete* Digg history (every single story posted, all diggs, and all comments) during a one month time window.

Lastfm is a music streaming website. We used the data collected in [8], which is the complete history of users and songs over one year.

Irvine This dataset was presented in [30]. It contains users posts to forums from an online students community at the University of California, Irvine. Each forum is considered to represent an information item.

Twitter We monitored the tweets of a set of about 5000 active Twitter users during 2 weeks, while the 2012 US Presidential Campaign. We then consider each hashtag to represent one information item spreading in the network.

[4]Note that for these datasets, there does not exist any explicit known graph. In such cases, it is therefore particulary useful to get approaches able to extract influence channels without any external information other than the infection data.

User-User Datasets

In these datasets, only user-user interactions are observed. Users post blog or microblog messages. We use the procedure described in [14] to build the data. Each message can contain a link to another message posted by another user. We consider each set of linked messages to be a diffusion episode gathering users who wrote those messages.

ICWSM The International AAAI Conference on Weblogs and Social Media 2009 published a corpus containing 44 millions of blog posts collected over a 1-year period [7]. We consider each blog to be a "user" in the social network and diffusion episodes are composed of sets of posts which are linked to each other by citations: each connected component of the posts graph is an episode.

Memetracker The memetracker dataset described in [24] contains millions of blog posts and news articles. Each website or blog stands as a user, and we use the phrase clusters extracted by [24] to trace the flow of information.

Online Social Networks datasets tend to be very noisy. To limit the effect of noise, we filter users to only keep a fraction of the most active ones. We also limit the learning set to a relatively small number of diffusion episodes. Limiting the number of learning cascades is necessary to keep classical models (IC, CTIC, NetRate) tractable. It also makes the learning data sparser, which is a more realistic setup, and will help us to observe the generalization ability of our approach.

As explained in section 3.2, we do *not* consider social graphs of the networks to learn the models, since they often turn out to be either irrelevant or are simply unknown in real-life applications. All of the tested models that require a graph are therefore learned on the "co-participation" graph: we created link a link (u, v) if and only if there is at least one diffusion episode D that contains both u and v and $t^D(u) < t^D(v)$.

Table 1 gives some statistics about the datasets. This table reports numbers of users and episodes considered in our experiments. It also reports the average length of diffusion episodes, as well as the co-participation graph number of links and density (i.e. $\frac{\text{nbLinks}}{(\text{nbUsers} \times (\text{nbUsers}-1)}$).

4.2 Baselines

The following state-of-the-art models are considered in our experiments:

- **IC**: the classic independent cascade model our works grounds in. As done for our model, we consider a relaxed version of IC with uniform delays of infection, since it greatly better fits real-world social data and leads to obtain much better results for the tasks set in our experiments. Weights are learned as defined in [34].

- **Netrate**: as *IC*, *Netrate* [14] is a cascade model which defines influence probability distributions on the network to model information propagation. It considers time-dependent distributions instead of static probabilities as in IC or in our model: parametric time-dependent distributions are learned to best fit with

Table 1: Some statistics about our real datasets

Corpus	Users	Links	Density	Train Episodes	Test Episodes	Avg episode size
Irvine	847	74871	0.1	433	49	14.6
Icwsm	2270	4775	0.001	19027	1000	2.22
Memetracker	498	229073	0.9	10000	1000	2.17
Digg	3295	689416	0.06	17000	1000	2.43
Twitter	2841	884832	0.09	10000	1000	20.5
LastFm	986	708159	0.72	10000	1000	7.25

observed infection timestamps. Note that we only report here results obtained with the *exponential* version of the *NetRate* model, as other distribution laws proposed in [14] (i.e., *power* and *rayleigh* laws) lead us to similar results.

- **CTIC**: As defined in [32], *CTIC* is a continuous-time version of the *IC* model. As *NetRate*, it uses exponential distributions to model delays of diffusion between users, but rather than a single parameter for each relationship, delays and influence factors are considered as separated parameters, which leads to more freedom w.r.t. to observed diffusion tendencies. Delays and influence parameters are learned conjointly by an EM-like algorithm.

We then describe two sets of experiments used to evaluate the model. The first one is the prediction of infected users and the second one is the prediction of diffusion relationships between users.

4.3 Diffusion Prediction

As true communication probabilities are unknown in the case of real-world social networks, our model cannot be assessed by considering a divergence measure between inferred probabilities $\mathcal{P}$ and a ground truth $\mathcal{P}^*$. We therefore propose to consider a related task of diffusion prediction in which we try to retrieve the set of eventually infected users $D(\infty)$, given a set of initiators $D(1)$.

For all models, training is performed on a training set by maximizing a likelihood. This allows to learn the model parameters (diffusion probabilities in IC, probability distribution parameter values in Netrate and CTIC, representations in our model). All the models are generative so that once a model is trained, it can be used for prediction tasks on a test set. The diffusion prediction task however requires the use of Monte-Carlo simulations to estimate infections probabilities knowing source users of infections. Starting from a seed set of users, each model is run iteratively for each simulation, with successive infections occurring according to the learned diffusion laws. Statistics (e.g. performance measures) can then be computed on the test set. Reported results obtained are averages over 1000 simulations for each diffusion episode of the test set.

Models are evaluated by considering various evaluation measures:

- MSE: predicted probabilities are compared with the actual values of infections for each users (0 or 1) using a mean-squared-error measure;
- LogLikelihood: the average log-likelihood $\mathcal{L}(\mathcal{P};\mathcal{D})$ for all diffusion episodes from the testing set, while rescaling all probabilities in $[10^{-5}, 1-10^{-5}]$ to avoid $log(0)$ problems;
- MAP: the classical mean average precision measure computed over rankings of users in decreasing order of their infection probability;
- F1: the classical F1 measure, with precision and recall scores adapted for the evaluation of predicted diffusions:

$$p = \frac{\sum_{u\in\mathcal{D}(\infty)} P_u^{\mathcal{D}}}{\sum_{u\in\mathcal{U}} P_u^{\mathcal{D}}} \qquad r = \frac{\sum_{u\in\mathcal{D}(\infty)} P_u^{\mathcal{D}}}{|\mathcal{D}(\infty)|}$$

$$F1 = \frac{2*p.r}{p+r}$$

Before comparing our model to state of the art models presented above, we first consider the impact of the number of dimensions of the projection space on the processing time required for the learning step to converge (see algorithm 1 for details about the stop criterion) and the effectiveness of the model to predict test episodes. We report here experiments performed on the Digg dataset, but similar observations can be done on other ones. Figure 2 plots results obtained on a Intel(R) Core(TM) i7 CPU 950@3.07GHz according to different numbers of dimensions of the projection space, on a logarithmic scale. From this, we can note that the processing time of the learning (CPU time given in seconds) increases logarithmically with regards to the number of dimensions, while very few increase of effectiveness (in term of log-likelihood on the test episodes) is observed with numbers of dimensions greater than 25. In the following, we therefore set the number of dimensions of the projection space to $d = 25$, which appears as a good trade-off between processing time and model accuracy.

Table 2 presents average effectiveness results obtained by the different experimented approaches on the various datasets described above, in term of their ability to predict test episodes according to measures of MSE, log-likelihood, MAP and F1 described above. This table highlights results that are significantly better than IC with a exponent star. Best results obtained for a corpus and a given measure are given in bold. The first thing that should be noted is that our model performs *at least as well* as all other experimented models for all datasets. It obtains the best result in almost all cells, except the MAP for Irvine and F1 for Digg for which it obtains a slightly lower score than some other models but without observing a significant difference with them. Relatively low results obtained by CTIC and NetRate can be explained by the fact that, as recently shown in [23], no delay regularities can be observed in the data and that taking them into account disturb the extraction of transmission probabilities. The superior results obtained by our model show that this approach has been able to successfully embed the probabilities $P_{u,v}$ in a latent space. This performance is obtained with a much lower number of parameters

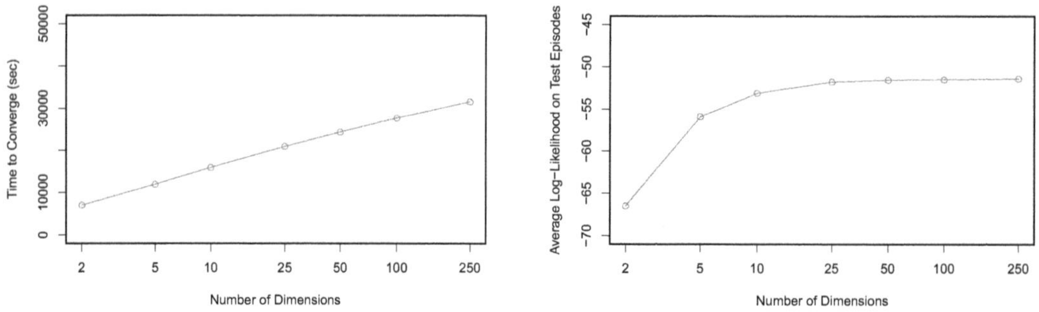

Figure 2: Time (in seconds) for the learning step to converge and average log-likelihood results obtained on test episodes, according to different numbers of dimensions of the projection space, on a logarithmic scale. Results obtained on the Digg dataset.

Corpus	Model	MSE	LogLikelihood	MAP	F1	nbParams
Irvine	IC	15,31	-960,5	0,079	0,020	74871
	NetRate	15,42	-892,13	0,078	0,019	74871
	CTIC	15,29	-771,42*	**0,080**	0,020	149742
	Embedded IC	**14,53***	**-532,5***	0,079	**0,025***	42350
ICWSM	IC	0,2	-8,3	0,77	**0,651**	4775
	NetRate	0,23	-9,01	0,72	0,357	4775
	CTIC	0,22	-8,46	0,76	0,482	9550
	Embedded IC	**0,19**	**-6,14***	**0,78**	**0,651**	113500
MemeTracker	IC	32,62	-795,85	0,22	0,0585	229073
	NetRate	34,55	-850,48	0,17	0,0442	229073
	CTIC	33,27	-802,52	0,22	0,0551	458146
	Embedded IC	**32,15**	**-791,3**	**0,23**	**0,0632***	24900
Digg	IC	2,1	-69,5	0,411	**0,201**	689416
	NetRate	1,95	-64,01*	0,409	0,199	689416
	CTIC	1,92*	-64,18*	0,413	**0,201**	1378832
	Embedded IC	**1,79***	**-51,75***	**0,434***	0,198	164750
Twitter	IC	6,70	-412,75	0,047	0,012	884832
	NetRate	6,91	-428,78	0,039	0,011	884832
	CTIC	6,72	-401,56	0,049	0,012	1769664
	Embedded IC	**5,47***	**-223,15***	**0,056***	**0,013**	142050
LastFM	IC	12,13	-409,5	0,132	0,026	708159
	NetRate	13,91	-413,02	0,112	0,022	708159
	CTIC	12,12	-409,3	0,128	0,025	1416318
	Embedded IC	**11,62***	**-405**	**0,151***	**0,027**	49300

Table 2: Results obtained on real-world datasets. Values with a star are significantly better than IC ones (95% student t-test). Values in bold correspond to the best results obtained for the experiment in concern.

than for all other approaches (except on Icwsm, which owns a very low density as observed in table 1), as shown in the rightmost column. We can see that all measures behave differently. This is linked to datasets properties:

- The MSE of Embedded IC is significantly better on the User-items datasets: Irvine, Digg, and LastFM. On these datasets, diffusion is actually difficult to detect : one user's liking the same item as another one does not necessarily means that one *influenced* the other. These two users may just happen to have similar centers of interest [1]. It is difficult to learn a IC model in this context. Thanks to its latent space, our Embedded IC is able to identify diffusion links between users, which leads to a better MSE. See subsection 4.4 for additional results about this property of Embedded IC.

- The Log-Likelihood of our model is better on the Irvine, Icwsm, Digg and Twitter datasets. These datasets happen to have something in common: they have a much lower co-participation graph density (table 1). This means that the IC model can only learn a very small amount of transmission probabilities, and is unable to predict diffusion between the majority of users pairs. Our Embedded IC, however, can infer diffusion probabilities for *all* user pairs.

- Finally, Embedded IC achieves a higher MAP on the Digg, Twitter and LastFM datasets. These websites also have a specific property in common: they behave more like "information portals". When a user arrives on Digg or LastFM, the first thing he finds is a list of popular items, a list of new items, and some recommendations based on his browsing history. User-to-User interactions are much less important. On Twitter, the User-to-User interactions are very important, but there also is a "Trending Topics" sections. This means that on those websites, diffusion happens on a more "global" scale: the more popular an information is, the more likely it is to infect new users. This phenomenon is better captured by our embedded approach, where each user has at least a small chance to infect *any* other one.

Overall, these results highlight various advantages of our approach over IC: less parameters to learn, better generalization and the ability to model different types diffusion. But they also show us that diffusion remains a complex phenomenon, that can take a lot of different forms. All the datasets we collected are quite different in term of size and density. On top of that, each one has its own mechanism of diffusion (retweets, messages threads, word-of-mouth...). This explains why all the models behave differently on each dataset and why we needed several measures to captures several properties. The problem of Information Diffusion Prediction is not only hard, it also appears to be very specific to the website to which one wishes to apply it.

4.4 Influence Relationships Detection

For a second evaluation, we applied the models for a task of detection of interactions from diffusion episodes. This allows us to better analyze the ability of our approach to identify important diffusion channels between users. Given a population and a set of diffusion episodes over this population, the goal is to find which influence relationships are the most likely to exist between users. This task has been extensively studied (see [14, 15] and references therein).

We used the Memetracker dataset for this experiment, which was used for a similar task by [14]. We extract an actual ground truth set of links E: for each post of website v containing a hyperlink to website u, we put a link (u, v) in E. It is important to note that the existence of a link (u, v) means that we *actually observed* a specific piece of information going from u to v.

For each pair of users (u, v), the learned probability of transmission $P_{u,v}$ is interpreted as the probability for a link to exist between them. We sort the probabilities obtained by the models in descending order, then plot a Precision-Recall curve to evaluate results.

Results are presented in figure 3 as Precision/ Recall curves. It can be observed that our Embedded IC model clearly outperforms all the other models on this task. This illustrates the ability of our approach to infer links that are not present in the training set and to identify important ones. Discrete cascade models will always learn a transmission rate of 0 on links (u, v) such that no diffusion episode in the training set contains user u then user v. Such relationship may however exist in the actual graph, and our model is able to retrieve some of them. Most importantly, like we said above, ground truth links are the ones on which we observed actual information diffusion. We can therefore be sure that those links are influence links, and not just homophily relations [1].

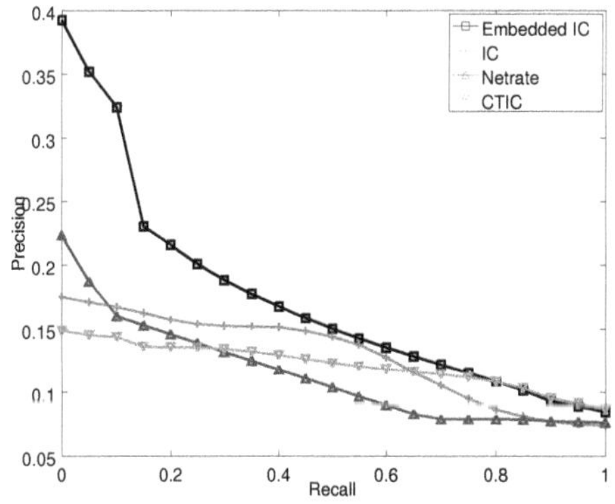

Figure 3: Recall-Precision of link prediction on the Memetracker Dataset.

5. CONCLUSION

In this paper, we have presented an embedded version of the Independent Cascade Model to predict information diffusion in Online Social Networks. Based on observations of the community structures in social network, we proposed to project users of a social network in a latent space, and then to use the distances between them to compute the probabilities of transmission.

We have performed experiments on a large collection of datasets. Results show that we are able to correctly embed users to reach usually better, else at least the same, performance levels as IC, while learning less parameters.

Future works will focus on several possibilities of extension. The most obvious one would be to use the *type* or the *content* of diffusing information to refine our prediction. In our setting, this comes down to learn a content-dependent metric between users representations in our projection space. Finally, the stochastic algorithm we presented could be adapted to an online context, to give a "live" prediction of diffusion as infections are observed.

6. ACKNOWLEDGMENTS

This work has been partially supported by the REQUEST project (projet Investissement d'avenir, 2014-2017), the LOCUST project (ANR, 2015-2018) and the project ARESOS from the CNRS program MASTODONS.

7. REFERENCES

[1] A. Anagnostopoulos, R. Kumar, and M. Mahdian. Influence and correlation in social networks. In *KDD'08*, pages 7–15. ACM, 2008.

[2] E. Bakshy, I. Rosenn, C. Marlow, and L. Adamic. The role of social networks in information diffusion. In *WWW'12*, pages 519–528. ACM, 2012.

[3] N. Barbieri, F. Bonchi, and G. Manco. Cascade-based community detection. In *WSDM '13*, pages 33–42, New York, NY, USA, 2013. ACM.

[4] Y. Bengio, A. C. Courville, and P. Vincent. Representation learning: A review and new perspectives. *IEEE Trans. Pattern Anal. Mach. Intell.*, 35(8):1798–1828, 2013.

[5] A. Bordes, N. Usunier, A. García-Durán, J. Weston, and O. Yakhnenko. Translating embeddings for modeling multi-relational data. In *NIPS'13*, pages 2787–2795, 2013.

[6] S. Bourigault, C. Lagnier, S. Lamprier, L. Denoyer, and P. Gallinari. Learning social network embeddings for predicting information diffusion. In *WSDM '14*, pages 393–402, New York, NY, USA, 2014. ACM.

[7] K. Burton, A. Java, and I. Soboroff. The icwsm 2009 spinn3r dataset. In *ICWSM'09*, May 2009.

[8] O. Celma. *Music Recommendation and Discovery in the Long Tail.* Springer, 2010.

[9] S. Chen, J. L. Moore, D. Turnbull, and T. Joachims. Playlist prediction via metric embedding. In *KDD'12*, pages 714–722. ACM, 2012.

[10] J. Cheng, L. Adamic, P. A. Dow, J. M. Kleinberg, and J. Leskovec. Can cascades be predicted? In *WWW'14*, pages 925–936, New York, NY, USA, 2014. ACM.

[11] K. Cho, B. van Merrienboer, Ç. Gülçehre, D. Bahdanau, F. Bougares, H. Schwenk, and Y. Bengio. Learning phrase representations using RNN encoder-decoder for statistical machine translation. In *EMNLP'14*, pages 1724–1734, 2014.

[12] N. Du, L. Song, M. Yuan, and A. J. Smola. Learning networks of heterogeneous influence. In *NIPS'12*, pages 2780–2788. Curran Associates, Inc., 2012.

[13] J. Goldenberg, B. Libai, and E. Muller. Talk of the network: A complex systems look at the underlying process of word-of-mouth. *Marketing letters*, 12(3):211–223, 2001.

[14] M. Gomez-Rodriguez, D. Balduzzi, and B. Schölkopf. Uncovering the temporal dynamics of diffusion networks. In *ICML-11*, pages 561–568. ACM, 2011.

[15] M. Gomez Rodriguez, J. Leskovec, and A. Krause. Inferring networks of diffusion and influence. In *KDD '10*, New York, NY, USA, 2010. ACM.

[16] M. Granovetter. Threshold Models of Collective Behavior. *American Journal of Sociology*, 83(6):1420–1143, 1978.

[17] A. Graves, A. Mohamed, and G. E. Hinton. Speech recognition with deep recurrent neural networks. In *ICASSP'13*, pages 6645–6649, 2013.

[18] D. Gruhl, R. Guha, D. Liben-Nowell, and A. Tomkins. Information diffusion through blogspace. In *WWW '04*, pages 491–501, New York, NY, USA, 2004. ACM.

[19] A. Guille and H. Hacid. A predictive model for the temporal dynamics of information diffusion in online social networks. In *WWW '12 Companion*. ACM, 2012.

[20] A. Guille, H. Hacid, C. Favre, and D. A. Zighed. Information diffusion in online social networks: A survey. *SIGMOD Rec.*, 42(2):17–28, July 2013.

[21] D. Kempe, J. Kleinberg, and E. Tardos. Maximizing the spread of influence through a social network. In *KDD '03*, pages 137–146. ACM, 2003.

[22] C. Lagnier, L. Denoyer, E. Gaussier, and P. Gallinari. Predicting information diffusion in social networks using content and user's profiles. In *ECIR '13*, 2013.

[23] S. Lamprier, S. Bourigault, and P. Gallinari. Extracting diffusion channels from real-world social data: a delay-agnostic learning of transmission probabilities. In *ASONAM'15*, pages 178–185. IEEE Computer Society, 2015.

[24] J. Leskovec, L. Backstrom, and J. Kleinberg. Meme-tracking and the dynamics of the news cycle. In *KDD '09*, pages 497–506, NY, USA, 2009. ACM.

[25] M. Mathioudakis, F. Bonchi, C. Castillo, A. Gionis, and A. Ukkonen. Sparsification of influence networks. In *KDD '11*, pages 529–537, NY, USA, 2011. ACM.

[26] T. Mikolov, I. Sutskever, K. Chen, G. S. Corrado, and J. Dean. Distributed representations of words and phrases and their compositionality. In *NIPS'13*, pages 3111–3119. Curran Associates, Inc., 2013.

[27] A. Mislove, M. Marcon, K. P. Gummadi, P. Druschel, and B. Bhattacharjee. Measurement and analysis of online social networks. In *IMC '07*, pages 29–42, New York, NY, USA, 2007. ACM.

[28] A. Najar, L. Denoyer, and P. Gallinari. Predicting information diffusion on social networks with partial knowledge. In *WWW '12 Companion*, pages 1197–1204, New York, NY, USA, 2012. ACM.

[29] P. Netrapalli and S. Sanghavi. Learning the graph of epidemic cascades. *SIGMETRICS Perform. Eval. Rev.*, 40(1):211–222, June 2012.

[30] T. Opsahl and P. Panzarasa. Clustering in weighted networks. *Social networks*, 31(2):155–163, 2009.

[31] M. Sachan, A. Dubey, S. Srivastava, E. P. Xing, and E. Hovy. Spatial compactness meets topical consistency: Jointly modeling links and content for community detection. In *WSDM '14*, pages 503–512, New York, NY, USA, 2014. ACM.

[32] K. Saito, M. Kimura, K. Ohara, and H. Motoda. Learning continuous-time information diffusion model for social behavioral data analysis. In *ACML '09*, pages 322–337, Berlin, Heidelberg, 2009. Springer-Verlag.

[33] K. Saito, M. Kimura, K. Ohara, and H. Motoda. Generative models of information diffusion with asynchronous timedelay. *Journal of Machine Learning Research - Proceedings Track*, 13:193–208, 2010.

[34] K. Saito, R. Nakano, and M. Kimura. Prediction of information diffusion probabilities for independent cascade model. In *KES '08*, pages 67–75. Springer-Verlag, 2008.

[35] K. Saito, K. Ohara, Y. Yamagishi, M. Kimura, and H. Motoda. Learning diffusion probability based on node attributes in social networks. In M. Kryszkiewicz, H. Rybinski, A. Skowron, and Z. W. Ras, editors, *ISMIS*, volume 6804 of *LNCS*, pages 153–162. Springer, 2011.

[36] H. Su, A. Gionis, and J. Rousu. Structured prediction of network response. In *ICML'14*, pages 442–450. JMLR Workshop and Conference Proceedings, 2014.

[37] G. Ver Steeg and A. Galstyan. Information-theoretic measures of influence based on content dynamics. In *WSDM'13*, pages 3–12, New York, NY, USA, 2013. ACM.

[38] L. Wang, S. Ermon, and J. E. Hopcroft. Feature-enhanced probabilistic models for diffusion network inference. In *ECML PKDD'12*, pages 499–514. Springer-Verlag, 2012.

[39] J. Yang and J. Leskovec. Modeling information diffusion in implicit networks. In ICDM'10, pages 599–608, Washington, DC, USA, 2010. IEEE Computer Society.

[40] J. Yang, J. McAuley, and J. Leskovec. Detecting cohesive and 2-mode communities indirected and undirected networks. In *WSDM '14*, pages 323–332, New York, NY, USA, 2014. ACM.

Ensemble Models for Data-driven Prediction of Malware Infections

Chanhyun Kang[†], Noseong Park[†], B. Aditya Prakash[*], Edoardo Serra[+], and V. S. Subrahmanian[†]
[*]Department of Computer Science, Virginia Tech., Blacksburg
[†]Department of Computer Science and UMIACS, University of Maryland, College Park
[+]Department of Computer Science, Boise State University, Boise
{chanhyun, npark}@cs.umd.edu, badityap@cs.vt.edu, edoardoserra@boisestate.edu, vs@umiacs.umd.edu

ABSTRACT

Given a history of detected malware attacks, can we predict the number of malware infections in a country? Can we do this for different malware and countries? This is an important question which has numerous implications for cyber security, right from designing better anti-virus software, to designing and implementing targeted patches to more accurately measuring the economic impact of breaches. This problem is compounded by the fact that, as externals, we can only detect a fraction of actual malware infections.

In this paper we address this problem using data from Symantec covering more than *1.4 million hosts* and 50 malware spread across 2 years and multiple countries. We first carefully design domain-based features from both malware and machine-hosts perspectives. Secondly, inspired by epidemiological and information diffusion models, we design a novel temporal non-linear model for malware spread and detection. Finally we present ESM, an ensemble-based approach which combines both these methods to construct a more accurate algorithm. Using extensive experiments spanning multiple malware and countries, we show that ESM can effectively predict malware infection ratios over time (both the actual number and trend) upto 4 times better compared to several baselines on various metrics. Furthermore, ESM's performance is stable and robust even when the number of *detected* infections is low.

Keywords

cyber security; malware attacks; prediction model; information diffusion; anti-virus;

1. INTRODUCTION

The goal of this paper is to develop methods to predict the percentage of hosts in a given population (we use country in our experiments) that will be infected by a particular piece of malware, given some historical data about the malware and the hosts, but with no information whatsoever on how the hosts are connected together. This is made even more challenging by the fact that not all truly infected machines are actually detected to be infected (by say using some anti-virus software). This problem is an important one with immediate applications in web and cyber security. For example, a better prediction of the number of infections in a country will enable anti-virus companies and security firms to better deploy patches and safety measures to counter threats.

In order to achieve this, we make several contributions. First, we define a very novel set of features that are related to the ability of hosts to detect malware and patch vulnerabilities. In order to achieve this, we present a novel host-malware bipartite graph and a bi-fix-point algorithm to compute these features. These lead to a feature-based prediction model (FBP). Then, building upon the well-known SIR-model of disease spread, we develop an epidemiologically-inspired predictive model called DIPS in which each host is either in a detected, infected, patched, or susceptible state. We define the model and show how to learn the parameters of the model in a data-driven way. We also define a variant of DIPS called DIPS-EXP. The outputs of these models, as well as outputs of past work on predicting epidemic spreads, are then fed into three different ensemble models: ESM_0, $\text{ESM}_1$and FBP^{+}_{Funnel}. We study the relative predictive accuracies of all of these models. On split-sample 10-fold cross validation tests, ESM_0 provides the best performance, significantly outperforming past work by large margins, irrespective of whether we use root mean squared error (RMSE), normalized RMSE (NRMSE), or Pearson Correlation Coefficient (PCC) as our measure. All the experiments use large-scale extensive real-data from Symantec's Worldwide Intelligence Network Environment (WINE) data set.

The paper is organized as follows. We describe our dataset and set-up in the next section. Section 3 describes statistical features we develop for our task and the feature based prediction model (FBP). In Section 4, we propose a novel non-linear time-series model (DIPS). The ensemble models (ESM) to combine two suggested models (FBP and DIPS) is described in Section 5. In Section 6 we present our empirical data analysis including the prediction task. We review related work in Section 7, and we discuss the implications of our results in Section 8.

2. DATASET AND SET-UP

Symantec's WINE data is collected from real-world hosts running Symantec anti-virus software. Users of Symantec's product line have a choice of opting-in to report telemetry

WSDM'16, February 22–25, 2016, San Francisco, CA, USA.
© 2016 ACM. ISBN 978-1-4503-3716-8/16/02...$15.00
DOI: http://dx.doi.org/10.1145/2835776.2835834

about the security events[1] (e.g. executable file downloads, virus detection) that occur on their hosts. The WINE dataset contains information about the hosts, files of the hosts and malware recognized on a file of a host.

We selected the 100 most frequently detected malware from the WINE data and extracted infection information about hosts infected by these malware using the following records. *Anti-virus telemetry.* Anti-virus (AV) telemetry records detection history of known malware over hosts. From each record, we extracted the detection time and the hash (MD5 and SHA2) of the malicious file detected. Each record indicates that the anti-virus has blocked an attack that may have resulted in an infection.
Binary reputation. The binary reputation data records all binary executable files – benign or malicious – that were downloaded/copied on end-hosts worldwide. From each record, we extracted the creation time of the malicious file in the host (infection time) and the country where the host was when the file was infected.

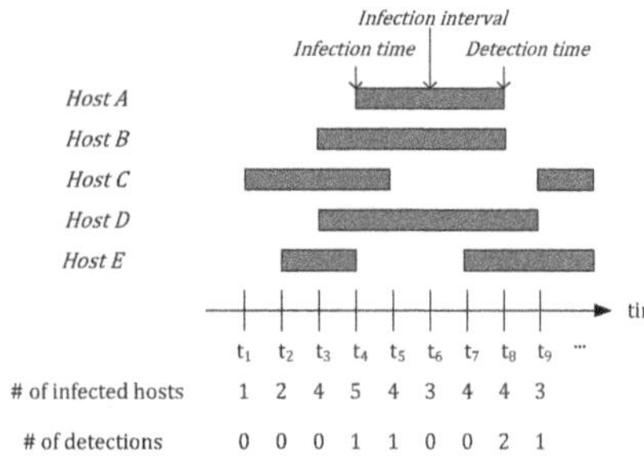

Figure 1: Examples of infections/infection intervals

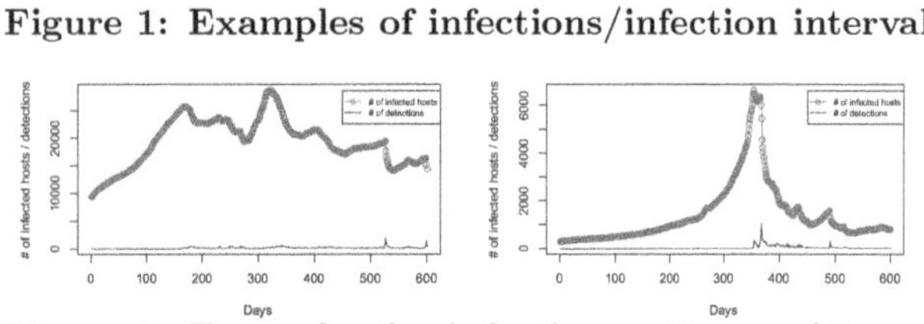

Figure 2: Examples for infection patterns of 2 malware in the US in our dataset. Number of infected hosts (bold red) and number of detection (blue) vs time (in days). Note that the number of detection are a fraction of the number of infected hosts and that both time-series are highly non-linear.

We note that an infection interval is the period from the infection time to the detection time of a malware in a host (See Figure 1). When the length of the infection interval is larger than 0, we call it an infection.[2] The number of infections over the 100 most frequently detected malware during 640 days was 3,170,669 (for the US alone, it was 989,263). The infection patterns are very different (See Figure 2). We adopt the following approach to address this problem: (a) we first carefully define and extract novel domain-based features from the WINE datasets including measures of hosts' detection ability and incompetence — we call this feature-based prediction (FBP) ; (b) we then construct a novel non-linear temporal model called DIPS (Detected, Infected, Patched, and Susceptible) based on epidemiological principles, and then (c) utilize sound regression methods to link both the features as well as the epidemiology-based models to the *dependent* variable (the number of malware infections). Because the inputs of FBP as well as multiple DIPS variants and FUNNEL[19] are themselves predictors that feed into yet another predictor, our overall framework is an ensemble prediction method.

[1]The events included in WINE are representative of events that Symantec observes around the world [23].

[2]If the anti-virus software blocked a file containing a malware immediately when the files appeared, then the detection record is not an infection in our framework.

3. FEATURE-BASED PREDICTION (FBP)

In a very dynamic environment like malware infections and patching, it is not possible to predict infection patterns solely based on infection trends. Some amount of domain knowledge has to be incorporated (for example, when the number of detected infections are small). Hence as a first step, we build a feature-based prediction model (FBP), where given past history we extract meaningful features of hosts and malware. Essentially these features encode the defending abilities of hosts and infection properties of the malware as relative scores.

Next, we describe the domain-based features we constructed for our analysis in more detail. We define $\mathcal{H}$ and $\mathcal{M}$ as the set of hosts and the set of malware, respectively. For each host $h \in \mathcal{H}$, $\mathcal{F}(h)$ denotes the set of files of h. For $f \in \mathcal{F}(h)$, t_f^h is the time stamp representing the time when f appears on h. For each host $h \in \mathcal{H}$, the malware detection set $dH(h)$ of h is a set of tuples of the form (f, m, t) where $f \in \mathcal{F}(h)$, $m \in \mathcal{M}$ and t is the time stamp when the file f infected by the malware m is discovered on the host h. By using the malware detection sets for each host, we define the set of host detection $dM(m)$ of the malware m as $dM(m) = \{(f, h, t) | h \in \mathcal{H}, f \in \mathcal{F}(h), (f, m, t) \in dH(h)\}$.

Vulnerabilities: Let V be the set of all vulnerabilities. Given a malware $m \in \mathcal{M}$ the set $Vu(m)$ is the set of all vulnerabilities used by this malware. For each vulnerability $v \in V$, two time stamps are important [5]:

- **Anti-virus signatures released.** Once the vulnerability is disclosed, anti-virus vendors release new signatures for ongoing attacks and created heuristic detection for the exploit. After this point, the attacks can be detected on end-hosts with updated A/V signatures. We denote this as t_v^s. We can retrieve this information from Symantec website or the National Vulnerabilities Database (NVD)[3] maintained by NIST (National Institute of Standards and Technology of the US Government).

- **Patch released.** On the disclosure date, or shortly afterward, the software vendor releases a patch for the vulnerability. After this point, the hosts that have applied the patch are no longer susceptible to the exploit. We denote this as t_v^p. This information is readily available from NVD.

3.1 Incompetence

Given a host $h \in \mathcal{H}$ and a tuple $(f, m, t) \in dH(h)$, we define two classes of features: hosts' incompetence in detecting malware and incompetence in patching (*DI* and *PI*, respectively). For each, we consider an absolute case and a relative case (i.e *ADI*, *API*, *RDI* and *RPI*). These four measures measure the incompetence of a host in detecting and patching the malware m associated with file f. The

[3]https://nvd.nist.gov/

only difference between the relative case and absolute case is that the absolute case does not consider the time t_v^s for each vulnerability v contained in a malware.

$$
\begin{aligned}
ADI(h,f,m,t) = &\ t - t_f^h \\
RDI(h,f,m,t) = &\ \max_{v\in Vu(m)} \max(0, t - \max(t_v^s, t_f^h)) \\
API(h,m) = &\ (\max_{(f,m,t)\in dH(h)} t) - (\min_{(f,m,t)\in dH(h)} t_f^h) \\
RPI(h,m) = &\ \max_{v\in Vu(m)} \max(0, (\max_{(f,m,t)\in dH(h)} t \\
&\ - \max(t_v^p, (\min_{(f,m,t)\in dH(h)} t_f^h))))
\end{aligned}
$$

For instance, absolute detection incompetence, $ADI(h,f,m,t)$ of host h w.r.t. a file f of malware m and the time t when f was detected by host h is simply $(t - t_f^h)$, i.e. the time that passed from the detection time to the time of original infection. The relative detection incompetence $RDI(h,f,m,t)$ looks at all possible vulnerabilities v that malware m exploits. For each such vulnerability, it looks at the time elapsed between when the file f was detected by host h and when either the file infected the host or when an updated anti-virus signature could have detected it. The longer this time gap, the more incompetent the host. The absolute and relative (API, RPI) patching incompetence are similarly defined.

Estimation by using only the WINE *datasets.* The relative detection and patch incompetence formulas can be rewritten as:

$$
\begin{aligned}
RDI(h,f,m,t,) &= \max(0, t - \max((\min_{v\in Vu(m)} t_v^s), t_f^h))) \\
RPI(h,m) &= \max(0, (\max_{(f,m,t)\in dH(h)} t - \\
&\quad \max((\min_{v\in Vu(m)} t_v^p), (\min_{(f,m,t)\in dH(h)} t_f^h))))
\end{aligned}
$$

For a malware m, $t^s(m) = \min_{v\in Vu(m)} t_v^s$ denotes the earliest time at which a host downloaded an anti-virus signature for the vulnerability (we call this "time signature"), showing that it might have become aware of the malware, and $t^p(m) = \min_{v\in Vu(m)} t_v^p$ denotes the earliest time the host applied a patch for a vulnerability for malware m (we call this "patch signature"). Both these quantities are recorded by WINE. Then, the two measures becomes the following:

$$
\begin{aligned}
RDI(h,f,m,t,) = &\ \max(0, t - \max(t^s(m), t_f^h)) \\
RPI(h,m) = &\ \max(0, (\max_{(f,m,t)\in dH(h)} t) - \\
&\ \max(t^p(m), (\min_{(f,m,t)\in dH(h)} t_f^h))))
\end{aligned}
$$

A possible way to estimate time signature and patch signature of a malware in WINE is:

$$
\begin{aligned}
t^s(m) = &\ \min_{v\in Vu(m)} t_f^m \\
\approx &\ \min_{h\in\mathcal{H},(f,m,t)\in dH(h)} t \\
t^p(m) = &\ \min_{v\in Vu(m)} t_v^p \\
\approx &\ \min_{h\in\mathcal{H},(,m',t')\in dH(h)} \max_{(f,m,t)\in dH(h)} t
\end{aligned}
$$

Average Incompetence. Average/relative detection/patching incompetence of a host h can be defined by aggregation.

$$
\begin{aligned}
AADI(h) &= \frac{\sum_{(f,m,t)\in dH(h)} ADI(h,f,m,t)}{|dH(h)|} \\
ARDI(h) &= \frac{\sum_{(f,m,t)\in dH(h)} RDI(h,f,m,t)}{|dH(h)|} \\
AAPI(h) &= \frac{\sum_{m\in\{m'|(,m',)\in dH(h)\}} API(h,m)}{|\{m'|(,m',)\in dH(h)\}|} \\
ARPI(h) &= \frac{\sum_{m\in\{m'|(,m',)\in dH(h)\}} RPI(h,m)}{|\{m'|(,m',)\in dH(h)\}|}
\end{aligned}
$$

For instance, average patch incompetence (AAPI) is obtained by adding up the average patch incompetence of the host w.r.t. all malware files that it patched, and dividing this by the number of such malware files associated with that host.

3.2 Features on Bipartite Host-Malware (HM) Graphs

Given a training set of historical WINE data, we can derive a bipartite graph whose vertices are hosts and malware, respectively. An edge links a host and malware if the training data shows that the malware has infected the host. Edges can be weighted with quantities like ADI, RDI, API, and RPI as defined earlier in this section.

We now define some novel features using HM-graphs. The absolute detection ability (ADA) of a host h captures the host's ability to detect malware, while the absolute detection hardness (ADH) of a malware m captures the difficulty in detecting that malware. Clearly, these two quantities are closely intertwined. We define them below in a mutually recursive manner.

$$
\begin{aligned}
ADA(h) &= \textstyle\sum_{(f,m,t)\in dH(h)} w_{12}(h,f,m,t)\cdot ADH(m) \\
ADH(m) &= \textstyle\sum_{(f,h,t)\in dM(m)} w_{21}(m,f,h,t)\cdot ADA(h)
\end{aligned}
$$

where $h \in \mathcal{H}, m \in \mathcal{M}$ and

$$
\begin{aligned}
w_{12}(h,f,m,t) &= \frac{\frac{1}{ADI(h,f,m,t)}}{\sum_{(f',h',t')\in dM(m)} \frac{1}{ADI(h',f',m,t')}} \\
w_{21}(m,f,h,t) &= \frac{ADI(h,f,m,t)}{\sum_{(f',m',t')\in dH(h)} ADI(h,f',m',t')}
\end{aligned}
$$

By way of explanation, consider the definition of $ADA(h)$. To do this, we look at every (f,m,t) triple in the training set. If h can detect m, then the harder m is to detect (captured by $ADH(m)$ in the formula), the better h's detection abilities are. Thus, when considering a specific (f,m,t) triple, the definition of $ADA(h)$ multiplies $ADH(m)$ by a quantity w_{12} which is the relative competence (inverse of absolute detection incompetence $ADI(h,f,m,t)$). A similar rationale applies to the definition of ADH. As in the previous section, we can define relative variants, RDA, RDH as well.

$$
\begin{aligned}
RDA(h) &= \textstyle\sum_{(f,m,t)\in dH(h)} w_{12}(h,f,m,t) * RDH(m) \\
RDH(m) &= \textstyle\sum_{(f,h,t)\in dM(m)} w_{21}(m,f,h,t) * RDA(h)
\end{aligned}
$$

where $h \in \mathcal{H}, m \in \mathcal{M}$ and

$$
\begin{aligned}
w_{12}(h,f,m,t) &= \frac{\frac{1}{RDI(h,f,m,t)}}{\sum_{(f',h',t')\in dM(m)} \frac{1}{RDI(h',f',m,t')}} \\
w_{21}(m,f,h,t) &= \frac{RDI(h,f,m,t)}{\sum_{(f',m',t')\in dH(h)} RDI(h,f',m',t')}
\end{aligned}
$$

3.2.1 Fix-point Computation and Convergence Result

As ADA, ADH are mutually recursively defined, one may wonder if they are well-defined. We show below, an iterative fix-point computation procedures that describes how this may be achieved. We now define the iterations ADA^i, ADH^i as follows. Let $ADA^0(h) = \frac{1}{|\mathcal{H}|}$, $ADH^0(m) = \frac{1}{|\mathcal{M}|}$ for $h \in \mathcal{H}, m \in \mathcal{M}$,then for iteration $i > 0$,

$$
\begin{aligned}
ADA^i(h) &= \textstyle\sum_{(f,m,t)\in dH(h)} w_{12}(h,f,m,t) * ADH^{i-1}(m) \\
ADH^i(m) &= \textstyle\sum_{(f,h,t)\in dM(m)} w_{21}(m,f,h,t) * ADA^{i-1}(h)
\end{aligned}
$$

We can capture the above computations as a bi-fix-point algorithm, Algorithm 1 that maintains two lists ADA, ADH. The entry $ADA(h)$ specifies the value of the ADA quantity computed thus far - similarly for the entry $ADH(m)$. These two lists are manipulated. We assume the existence of an equivalence relation $\equiv$ on ADA and ADH lists, telling us when two ADA lists and two ADH lists are essentially the same. For instance, we can decide that ADA lists ℓ_1, ℓ_2 are similar whenever a measure of distance, such as cosine distance or Jaccard distance, between the two vectors is below a threshold.

Algorithm 1: BiFixpoint

Input : $\mathcal{H}, \mathcal{M}, T$ (*T is a training set *)
Output: ADA, ADH
forall $h \in \mathcal{H}$, $ADA(h) \leftarrow \frac{1}{|\mathcal{H}|}$ (* initialize *)
forall $m \in \mathcal{M}$, $ADH(m) \leftarrow \frac{1}{|\mathcal{M}|}$
change $\leftarrow$ true;
while *change* **do**
  $ADA'(h) \leftarrow \sum_{(f,m,t)\in dH(h)} w_{12}(h,f,m,t) * ADH(m)$
  $ADH(m) \leftarrow \sum_{(f,h,t)\in dM(m)} w_{21}(m,f,h,t) * ADA(h)$
  if $ADA' \sim ADA$ *and* $ADH' \equiv ADH$ **then**
    change $\leftarrow$ false
  else
    $ADA \leftarrow ADA'$ and $ADH \leftarrow ADH'$
  end
end
return ADA, ADH

The following result shows that this algorithm is guaranteed to converge.

THEOREM 1. *For any sets $(\mathcal{H}, \mathcal{M}, T)$, $BiFixpoint(\mathcal{H}, \mathcal{M}, T)$ is guaranteed to converge and the returned solution is unique.*

PROOF. The recursive equations describing RDA and RDH have the same structure of those of a bipartite Markov Chain where the first partition is the set of hosts $\mathcal{H}$ and the second is the set of malware $\mathcal{M}$. In fact we can rewrite the equations in the following way $RDA(h) = \sum_{m\in\{m'|(,m',)\in dH(h)\}} p_{12}(h,m) * RDH(m)$ and $RDH(m) = \sum_{h\in\{f|(,h,)\in dM(m)\}} p_{21}(m,h) * RDA(h)$ where $p_{12}(h,m) = \sum_{(f,m,t)\in dH(h)} w_{12}(h,f,m,t)$ and $p_{21}(m,h) = \sum_{(f,h,t)\in dM(m)} w_{21}(m,f,h,t)$. Because of the definition of the weights w_{12} and w_{21}, it follows that for each $m \in \mathcal{M}$, $\sum_{h\in\{h'|(,h',)\in dM(m)\}} p_{12}(h,m) = 1$ and for each $h \in \mathcal{H}$, $\sum_{m\in\{m'|(,m',)\in dH(h)\}} p_{21}(m,h) = 1$. In addition both the $p_{1,2}(h,m)$ (with $m \in \mathcal{M}$ and $h \in \{h'|(,h',) \in dM(m)\}$) and $p_{2,1}(m,h)$ (with $h \in \mathcal{H}$ and $m \in \{m'|(,m',) \in dH(h)\}$) are greater than zero. Moreover, by construction, if we have an edge (h,m) also the edge (m,h) exists, both with value (probability) greater than zero. The last statement implies that for each pair of nodes (a,b) in each connected components in this Markov chain the probability to reach a from b (and vice versa) after a finite number of steps is greater than zero. This implies that, for each connect component, the associate transition matrix is regular, it follows that the $BiFixpoint(\mathcal{H}, \mathcal{M}, T)$ algorithm converges and the returned solution is unique. □

3.3 Patch Ability

Exactly analogous to the measures defined above, we can define two patch abilities: absolute and relative. The absolute patch ability (APA) and absolute patch hardness (APH) are defined in the following way:

$$\begin{aligned} APA(h) &= \textstyle\sum_{m\in\{m'|(,m',)\in dH(h)\}} w_{12}(h,m) \cdot APH(m) \\ APH(m) &= \textstyle\sum_{h\in\{h'|(,h',)\in dM(m)\}} w_{21}(m,h) \cdot APA(h) \end{aligned}$$

where $h \in \mathcal{H}$, $m \in \mathcal{M}$, and

$$\begin{aligned} w_{12}(h,m) &= \frac{\frac{1}{API(h,m)}}{\sum_{h''\in\{h'|(,h',)\in dM(m)\}} \frac{1}{API(h'',m)}} \\ w_{21}(m,h) &= \frac{API(h,m)}{\sum_{m''\in\{m'|(,m',)\in dH(h)\}} API(h,m'')} \end{aligned}$$

The relative patch ability (APA) and relative patch hardness (APH) are defined in the following way:

$$\begin{aligned} RPA(h) &= \textstyle\sum_{m\in\{m'|(,m',)\in dH(h)\}} w_{12}(h,m) * RPH(m) \\ RPH(m) &= \textstyle\sum_{h\in\{h'|(,h',)\in dM(m)\}} w_{21}(m,h) * RPA(h) \end{aligned}$$

where $h \in \mathcal{H}$, $m \in \mathcal{M}$ and

$$\begin{aligned} w_{12}(h,m) &= \frac{\frac{1}{RPI(h,m)}}{\sum_{h''\in\{h'|(,h',)\in dM(m)\}} \frac{1}{RPI(h'',m)}} \\ w_{21}(m,h) &= \frac{RPI(h,m)}{\sum_{m''\in\{m'|(,m',)\in dH(h)\}} RPI(h,m'')} \end{aligned}$$

In order to compute the patch ability we can use the $BiFixpoint(\mathcal{H}, \mathcal{M}, T)$ algorithm with opportune modifications according the specific equations. By following the same proof methodology of Theorem 1, is possible to prove that the resulting algorithm converge and the returned solution is unique.

3.4 Collaborative Features

Let H be a set of all hosts and H' be a subset of H. We use a memory based collaborative filtering approach to produce features whose meaning is close to the number of malware infections in a specific set of hosts H', i.e. all the hosts of a specific country. The basic intuition under this collaborative filtering is that if host h is infected by malware m and host h' similar to h, then h' could also be infected by m. We assume the existence of a function $sim : H \times H \to [0,1]$ that similarity between hosts. Given a host $h \in H'$, the percentage of infected hosts in H (weighted by the similarity) by malware m is

$$infected(h,m) = \frac{\sum_{h'\in H, \exists(,m,)\in dH(h')} sim(h,h')}{|H|} \quad (1)$$

where $\exists(,m,) \in dH(h')$ is used to check if h is infected by m. Intuitively $infected(h,m)$ estimates the possibility that the host will be infected by m. In fact, the greater the percentage of hosts similar to h infected by m, the greater is the possibility (or probability) that h will be infected by m. Since we want to predict the expected number of infected hosts in H', our resulting variable is the following:

$$\sum_{h\in H'} infected(h,m)$$

If we assume that $infected(h,m)$ is a correct estimation of the probability that the host h will be infected by m, the value $\sum_{h\in H'} infected(h,m)$ estimates the expected number of infected host in H'. Since H can be huge (millions of hosts), we consider a reduced subset $\tilde{H}$ obtained by uniformly sampling H, and then we replace H in Eq 1 by $\tilde{H}$.

Similarity Measures. We define different notions of similarity – each of these notions yields a different feature estimating the expected number of infected hosts. The definitions below show some examples.

$$sim1(h,h') = 1 - |ADA(h) - ADA(h')|$$

$$sim2(h,h') = 1 - |RDA(h) - RDA(h')|$$

$$sim3(h,h') = 1 - |APA(h) - APA(h')|$$

$$sim4(h,h') = 1 - |RPA(h) - RPA(h')|$$

$$sim5(h,h') = 1 - \sqrt{\frac{(ADA(h)-ADA(h'))^2 + (APA(h)-APA(h'))^2}{2}}$$

$$sim6(h,h') = 1 - \sqrt{\frac{(ADA(h)-RDA(h'))^2 + (RPA(h)-RPA(h'))^2}{2}}$$

3.5 The FBP Model

The FBP Model is a general framework to predict the ratio of hosts infected by malware m in country c with a given regression method r such as GPR (Gaussian Process Regression), Elastic Net, Ridge, Lasso, and etc. The dependent and independent variables for the regression method are following:

Dependent variable. The dependent variable for each country -malware pair (c, m) is the percentage of hosts in country c infected by malware m.

Independent variables (features). For each country-malware pair (c, m), we compute $ADI, API, RDI, RPI, AADI, ARDI, AAPI, ARPI, ADA, RDA, APA$ and RPA of hosts in country c, APH and RPH of malware m and the *collaborative variables* of the hosts in c with the 6 similarity measures. Other features are the percentages of the hosts which were not detected for m in countries which are economically similar to country c.[4] Two measures, Human Development Index (HDI) and Per Capita GDP PPP of countries are used to determine the similar countries. The features are computed for each day d with respect to four different time intervals from 0, $d-60$, $d-30$, $d-10$ to d day.

Nearest Neighbors (additional feature selection) To make the learned model more robust, we also take features of the $k-$nearest neighbors. For a given country-malware pair (c,m) and similarity measure S, we find the k *most similar* country-malware pair(s) P_k to (c,m) with respect to the past infection pattern. We then use the features of P_k as well (in addition to those of (c,m)) for predicting. Various existing techniques can be used for measuring similarity between two time-series e.g. Dynamic Time Warping (DTW), Euclidean distance etc.

4. TIME-SERIES MODEL BASED PREDICTION (DIPS)

In this section we propose a novel non-linear time-series model called DIPS (short for Detected, Infected, Patched, Susceptible) which is a variant of the SIR model of disease spread tailored for malware. Typical infection patterns (see Figure 2) are highly non-linear. Hence intuitively linear approaches are ill-suited to this task. Malware spread has multiple similarities to information diffusion and epidemiology (indeed, some of the earliest papers on this topic try to model it as a disease). Inspired by these models, DIPS adapts a recent model [19] to handle malware infections. The most challenging part is to deal with difference in the *detected* and *actual* infections. We assume that in the training dataset we have the true (as well as the detected) number of infections but in the test dataset, we are only given the number of actual detections.

4.1 Model Parameters

Similar to fundamental models like the Susceptible-Infected-Recovered (SIR) 'mumps-like' model, our model assumes that the machine population can be in one of the following states:

- *Susceptible:* In this state, a machine is not patched and hence is vulnerable to an attack by a particular malware.
- *Infected:* In this state, the machine is now infected, and spreads the malware by infecting other susceptible hosts.
- *Detected:* In this state, we have detected that the machine is infected (by say an anti-virus software running on the machine). Note that not all infected machines may be detected as infected.
- *Patched:* As the name suggests, in this state the machine is patched, and cannot get infected.

We temporally track the number of hosts in each of these states. In addition, we assume we have a variable $DET(t)$ which is the true number of detection at time t.

[4]We define that country C and C' are similar w.r.t. measure T when $|T(C) - T(C')|/(T(C) + (T(C')) * 0.5 \leq p$ where $p = \{3\%, 6\%, 9\%, 12\%, 15\%, 18\%\}$.

4.2 The DIPS Model

We are now ready to describe the DIPS model. There are a total of N potential susceptible hosts for the malware (one may also assume that there is an inflow of additional hosts at every time tick). Each host starts out in the Susceptible state. From the susceptible state, a host may move into the Patched state (at the rate of $\theta(t)$) or the Infected state. We assume each infected host may infect a susceptible host at a certain rate (called $\beta(t)$), which is also periodic and dictated by users' habitual behavior. An infected host may move into the Detected state upon detection, after which the host may become susceptible again (if it is not patched), or be patched (at the rate of $\delta(t)$) and never get infected again — these transitions are shown in Figure 3.

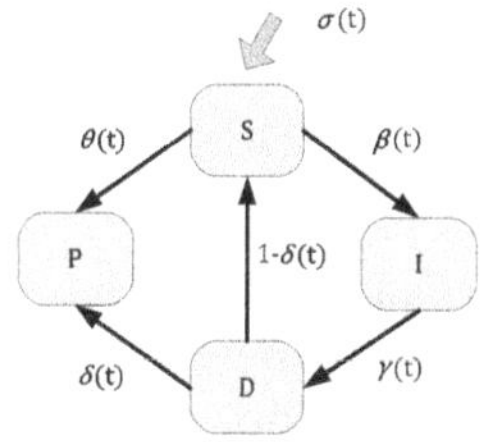

Figure 3: DIPS model. D, I, P and S are the Detected, Infected state, Patched and Susceptible states

Infection Rate $\beta(t)$: This is the rate at which an infected host infects susceptible machines. We assume $\beta(t)$ has the following form:

$$\beta(t) = \beta_0(1 + P_a \cos(\frac{2\pi}{P_p}(t + P_S))) \quad where,$$

- β_0: is the infection rate by users' (who are using the hosts) habitual behavior averaged over days
- P_p: stands for the period of a cycle. Infection data, like information diffusion data, and epidemiological data, typically shows obvious periodicity (like weekly) which we want to capture.
- P_a: represents the amplitude of the fluctuation.
- P_S: represents the phase shift in the cycle.

Patching rates $\delta(t)$ and $\theta(t)$: As mentioned above, we assume that susceptible hosts get patched at the same rate $\theta(t)$ and hosts in the detected state get patched at rate $\delta(t)$. More formally:

$$\begin{aligned} \theta(t) = &\quad 0\ (t < t_p) \quad or \quad \theta_0\ (t \geq t_p) \\ \delta(t) = &\quad 0\ (t < t_p, t_d) \quad or \quad \delta_0\ (t \geq t_p, t_d) \end{aligned}$$

where t_p is the start time of the patching and t_d is the first detection time.

Error rate $\gamma(t)$*:* This captures the fact that the number of true detections $DET(t)$ may not exactly match the number of detection in our model (i.e. the number of hosts in the $D(t)$ state).

Finally, putting everything together, the DIPS model can be expressed using the following differential equations:

$$
\begin{aligned}
S(t+1) &= S(t) - \beta(t)S(t)I(t) + (1-\delta(t))D(t) - \theta(t)S(t) \\
I(t+1) &= I(t) + \beta(t)S(t)I(t) - \gamma_0 DET(t) \\
D(t+1) &= \gamma_0 DET(t) \\
P(t+1) &= P(t) + \delta(t)D(t) + \theta(t)S(t) \qquad (2)
\end{aligned}
$$

Intuitively, $S(t), I(t), D(t), P(t)$ capture the number of hosts in a susceptible, infected, detected, and patched state, respectively.

The DIPS*-exp model.*

We have another variant of the DIPS model, called DIPS-exp where we have an inflow of additional susceptible hosts at every time-tick ($\sigma(t)$). All the equations in Equation 2 remain the same, except for the equation defining $S(t+1)$ which changes to:

$$S(t+1) = S(t) - \beta(t)S(t)I(t) + (1-\delta(t))D(t) - \theta(t)S(t) + \sigma(t)$$

4.3 Model Learning

The parameters of the DIPS model $\Theta = \{N, \beta_0, P_a, P_S, \gamma_0, t_p, \theta_0, \delta_0\}$ (DIPS-exp additionally has a parameter of σ_0) need to be learned. Given two real time-sequences, $I_{true}(t)$ and $D_{true}(t)$, of the number of actual infections and detection (resp.) at time-tick t, we find the parameters which optimize the following equation:

$$\Theta^* = \arg\min_{\Theta} \sum_t (I_{true}(t) - I_{\Theta}(t))^2.$$

The learning algorithm is given in Algorithm 2. Basically, there are two phases to learn the parameters. The first step is to adjust the initial parameters to fit them on overall infection time-sequences ($I^{sum}_{true}(t)$ and $D^{sum}_{true}(t)$) and fix parameter t_p,θ_0, P_a and P_S. The learning order of the parameters is $N \to \beta_0 \to \gamma_0(\to \sigma_0) \to t_p \to \delta_0 \to \theta_0 \to P_a \to P_S$[5]. The second step is to fit the learned parameters on the specific infection pattern of country c for malware m. Here, we only update the following parameters: $N \to \beta_0 \to \gamma_0(\to \sigma_0) \to \delta_0$. The $LearnParameters(\Theta, I(t), D(t), flag)$ is the function to update the given parameter values Θ applying parameter $p \in \Theta \leftarrow \arg\min_p \sum_t (I(t) - I_{\Theta}(t))^2$ and to return the updated parameters, Θ' and the error, $\sum_t (I(t) - I_{\Theta'}(t))^2$. The flag represents the learning order of each step (if $flag = 1$, the first step, else the second step). Initially, $S(0) = N - D(0) - I(0), P(0) = 0, D(0) = DET(0)$, and $I(0) = I_{true}(0)$. We leverage the Levenberg-Marquardt (LM) algorithm [16] for each *argmin* in *LearnParameters*.

Algorithm 2: DIPS learning algorithm

Input : country c, malware m and $X(m) = \{(c', I_{true}(t), D_{true}(t)) | c' \in Countries, I_{true}(t)$ and $D_{true}(t)$ for c' and $m\}$
Output: $\Theta = \{N, \beta_0, P_a, P_S, \gamma_0, t_p, \theta_0, \delta_0, (\sigma_0)\}$
$\Theta \leftarrow \{N', \beta'_0, P'_a, P'_S, \gamma'_0, t'_p, \theta'_0, \delta'_0, (\sigma'_0)\}$ `// Assign default parameter values`
$I^{sum}_{true}(t), D^{sum}_{true}(t) \leftarrow \sum_{c' \in Countries, (c', I(t), D(t)) \in X(m)} I(t), D(t)$ `// Sum of # of infections/detection over countries w.r.t. each time`
$err \leftarrow infinite, err' \leftarrow 0, \Theta' \leftarrow \Theta$
while $err > err'$ **do**
  `// Learn all parameters`
  $< err', \Theta' > \leftarrow LearnParameters(\Theta', I^{sum}_{true}(t), D^{sum}_{true}(t), 1)$
  if $err > err'$ **then**
    $\Theta \leftarrow \Theta'$, $err \leftarrow err'$
    $err' \leftarrow 0$
  end
end
Let $(c', I_{true}(t), D_{true}(t)) \in X(m)$ where c' equals c
$\Theta' \leftarrow \Theta$, $err' \leftarrow 0$
while $err > err'$ **do**
  `// Learn` $N, \beta_0, \gamma_0(\sigma_0), \delta_0$ `only`
  $< err', \Theta' > \leftarrow LearnParameters(\Theta', I_{true}(t), D_{true}(t), 0)$
  if $err > err'$ **then**
    $\Theta \leftarrow \Theta'$, $err \leftarrow err'$
    $err' \leftarrow 0$
  end
end
return Θ

5. ENSEMBLE MODELS (ESM)

We have suggested three models: feature based prediction (FBP), and time-series model based prediction (DIPS and DIPS-exp). We now propose ensemble models, ESM which combine both of them to improve performance. We add the expected number of infections we get from the DIPS and DIPS-exp models as features for our feature prediction model. We do not use the *learned* parameters Θ^* of DIPS directly as features. This is because DIPS is highly non-linear; to take advantage of it, we use the *output* of DIPS instead.

To summarize, we extract all the features, add the output of DIPS as additional features, and then use a regression model to perform prediction. We used a variety of models like logistic regression and Gaussian process regression.

6. EMPIRICAL ANALYSES

In this section, we empirically analyze the performance of the proposed prediction methods. Specifically, we study three questions:

- Q1: Can we predict the number of hosts in a country that are infected by a malware?
- Q2: How does predictive accuracy change with the number of infections?
- Q3: Does the prediction performance of the models depend on the number of hosts monitored?

Experiment setting. We focused on top 50 most infectious malware in the 100 malware infection data extracted from WINE, and the top 40 countries (by GDP), leading to 2000 (50x40) country-malware pairs. This data includes over 1.45M unique hosts and 2.99M infections. The number of reported hosts varies from just 634 (Iran) to 554,969 (United States). We ran the experiment over 541 days from 60th to 600th day among total 640 days. Because infection data is not complete for the head and the tail periods, we eliminated the first 60 and last 40 days of the 640-day data set.

Performance metrics. We checked RMSE (root mean squared error), NRMSE (normalized RMSE), and Pearson correlation coefficient (PCC) to evaluate performance. $NRMSE$

[5]The order affects the prediction performance a lot.

$= RMSE\ /(max(X) - min(X))$, where X is a set of ground true infection ratios of each malware-country pair over all days. Due to space constraints, we focus on NRMSE[6].

Train/Test Split. Each prediction model was trained in the first l days (on the features defined earlier) and tested for the remaining days. We used 80% of the data for training and the rest for validation.

Prediction models. We tested 7 different prediction models, FUNNEL [19][7], FBP, DIPS, DIPS-EXP, two different ESM models (ESM_0 and ESM_1) and FBP^{+}_{Funnel}[8]. FUNNEL is a recently proposed time-series model which has been used to predict large scale disease patterns (and like DIPS, it too is based on epidemiological models like SEIR). However, intuitively, FUNNEL is too tailored to model disease trends (like taking into account strong seasonality and locality) and not malware attacks. For example, it does not distinguish between detected and patched states, and its parameters are not suitable to represent malware infection. ESM_0 refers to ESM using FBP with the expected values of the two DIPS models as additional features for each pair. ESM_1 uses FBP with FUNNEL and DIPS models. To estimate the performance of ESM more precisely, we also tested FBP^{+}_{Funnel} which uses FBP with only FUNNEL (but without DIPS).

For FBP, we tested various regression methods such as GPR (Gaussian Process Regression), Elastic Net, Ridge, Lasso, and etc with k more country-malware pairs whose infection patterns are similar with each country-malware. We tested with $k \in \{0, 1, 2\}$. The similarity was measured by Dynamic Time Wrapping (DTW). For FBP, DTW showed best performance in our testing among several similarity measures, such as Euclidean distance, average correlation coefficient, DTW and etc. In testing with 2000 (country,malware) pairs, FBP showed the best performance with GPR and $k = 2$ w.r.t. the average RMSE and NRMSE. The average correlation coefficients were similar for all. We did not consider $k > 2$ because the performance improvement from $k = 1$ to $k = 2$ was very trivial. In the following experiment sections, we fix k = 2 and GPR for FBP and the FBP setting was used for ESM_0, ESM_1 and FBP^{+}_{Funnel} also.

6.1 Performance over all countries and malware

Answering Q1 with overall performance. The overall performance of the prediction models is shown in Table 1. FBP is clearly better than FUNNEL with respect to all four measures, showing that the features defined in Section 3 are useful to predict infection patterns generally. Also, DIPS shows good prediction performance. The average MAE*, RMSE and NRMSE are 25%, 30% and 73% respectively of FUNNEL. Moreover the average correlation coefficient is more than 6 times that of FUNNEL. ESM models (FBP+DIPS) shows significant performance improvement from FBP and the best performance with respect to NRMSE. DIPS models show slightly better prediction performance w.r.t. MAE*, RMSE and Correlation coefficient than ESM_0 and ESM_1. We can also confirm that FBP^{+}_{Funnel} (FBP with FUNNEL only) and

Model	MAE*	RMSE	NRMSE	C.C.
FBP	73.74	0.00170	0.179	0.12
FUNNEL	127.83	0.00269	0.226	0.08
DIPS	32.36	0.00083	0.165	0.50
DIPS-EXP	36.56	0.00096	0.223	0.48
ESM_0	39.41	0.00115	0.150	0.31
ESM_1	41.84	0.00118	0.151	0.31
FBP^{+}_{Funnel}	79.01	0.00189	0.179	0.19

Table 1: Average of MAE, RMSE, NRMSE and Correlation coefficient over 2000 pairs in testing period. Training ratio is 0.8. The MAE* values were computed with |# of ground true infected hosts - the expected # of infected hosts|. Others were based on the infection ratio of each country.

ESM_1 (ESM_0 with FUNNEL) do not show clear improvement from FBP and ESM_0. This suggests that DIPS significantly improves upon the predictive accuracy of past work. In any case we wish to point out that FUNNEL was designed and intended for disease patterns and not malware spread.

More detailed analysis: Performance of the prediction models for each country-malware pair is shown in Figure 4. DIPS models show many cases having very high correlation coefficient and very low NRMSE. But there are some cases having very high NRMSE when the correlation coefficient is very low. On the other hand, NRMSE of FBP is relatively low even when the correlation coefficient is pretty low. Interestingly, ESM models have the both strength of FBP and *DIPS*. To analyze the performance more, kernel density estimations are shown in Figure 5. As you see in Figure 5 (a), the density of ESM models and DIPS models are high in very high correlation coefficient values. In Figure 5 (b), the density of DIPS models and ESM models are really high with very low NRMSE values. But DIPS models have very long tail having very high NRMSE values.

Answering Q2. We define the infectiousness level as the average number of infected hosts over all days. Precisely, $ln(1 + Avg.\#\ infected\ hosts\ over\ days)$, here 1 is added as a default because $Avg.\#\ infected\ hosts\ over\ days$ could be less than 1. In Figure 6, we projected values of correlation coefficients and NRMSE over the infectiousness level w.r.t. each country-malware pair in order to check how each model works in different infectiousness levels. Each dot corresponds to a certain country-malware pair — the infectiousness level varies a lot. In terms of correlation coefficient, DIPS shows the best performance across all infectiousness levels especially with very high values in highly infectiousness levels, and ESM_0 follows after it. Switching the perspective to NRMSE more interestingly, DIPS still shows very good performance in general but some glitches in relatively lower infectiousness levels. This shows the performance of DIPS may be less robust when the number of infections is low. On the other hand, NRMSE of FBP is still low in the situation. This means the two models are very complementary to each other. So, ESM models show very stable and reliable performance regardless of infectiousness levels for both measures. Shortly, FUNNEL doesn't show any good performance even in highly infectiousness levels.

6.2 Performance for certain countries

Answering Q3. The number of reported hosts over countries in our data is very different. Figure 7 shows the performance of the models according to each country. The order

[6]The other two measures provide similar results.

[7]The code was downloaded from http://www.cs.kumamoto-u.ac.jp/~yasuko/software.html

[8]The source code for the models suggested in this paper are available at http://www.umiacs.umd.edu/research/CDIG/projects/CCAFE.html

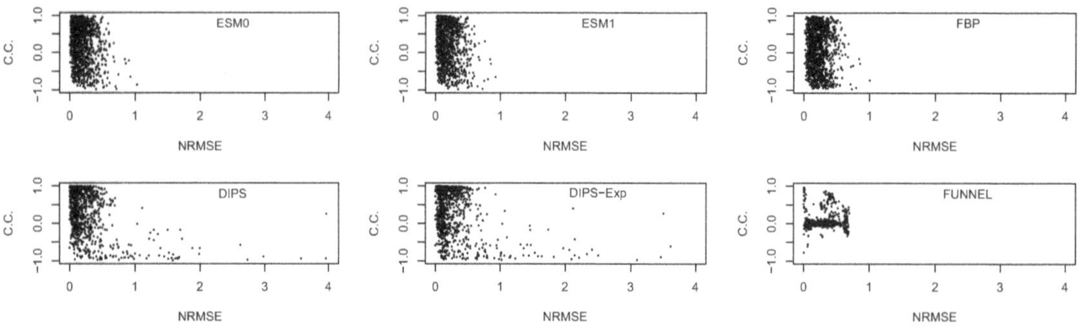

Figure 4: Scatter plot for NRMSE and Correlation coefficient over 2000 pairs. Each point represents the performance for each country-malware pair.

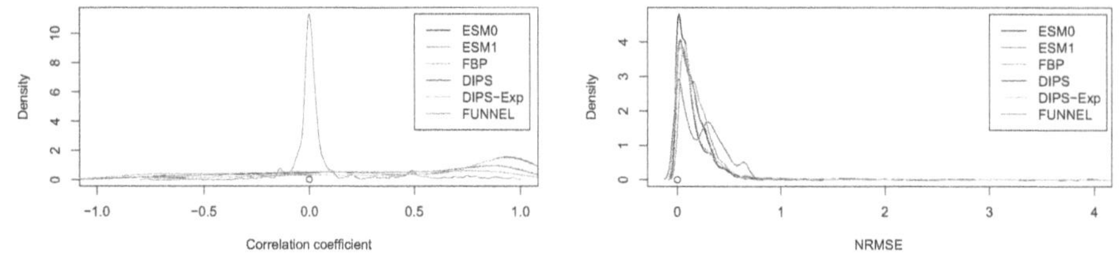

(a) Correlation coefficients (b) NRMSE

Figure 5: Kernel Density of (a) Correlation coefficient and (b) NRMSE over 2000 pairs

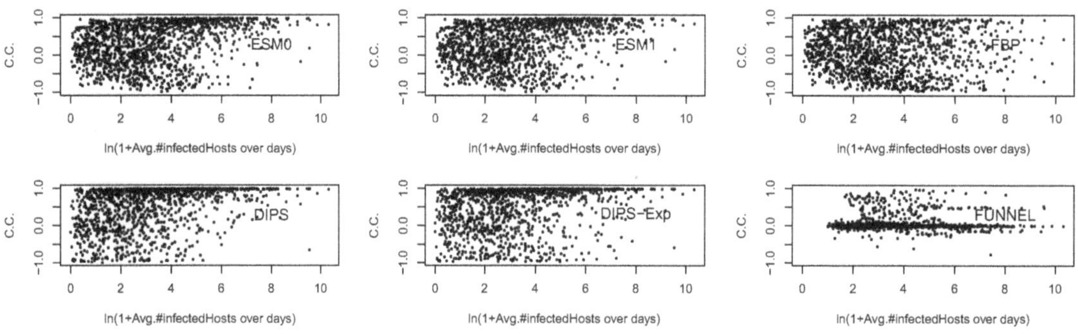

(a) Correlation coefficient

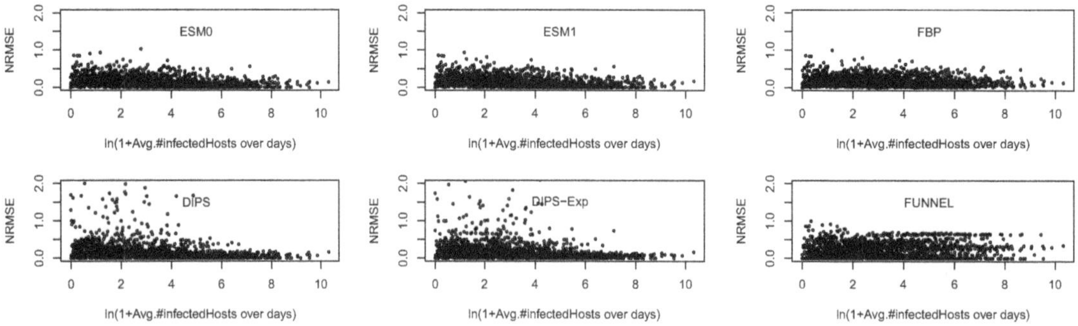

(b) NRMSE

Figure 6: (a) Correlation coefficient and (b) NRMSE by ln(1+ Avg.# infected hosts over all days)

of countries from left to right is the descending order w.r.t. the number of hosts in each country. DIPS models show good correlation coefficients. ESM models show stable and good performance for NRMSE over countries whose number of monitored hosts are very different. The overall prediction performance of DIPS and ESM do not depend on the size of monitored hosts except the cases when the number of monitored hosts are really small relatively. But for the countries having really small number of hosts, such as Nigeria (704) and Iran (634), the models show slightly worse correlation coefficient.

6.3 Summary of experiments

ESM and DIPS have low prediction errors and relatively high correlation coefficient values on average over all 2000

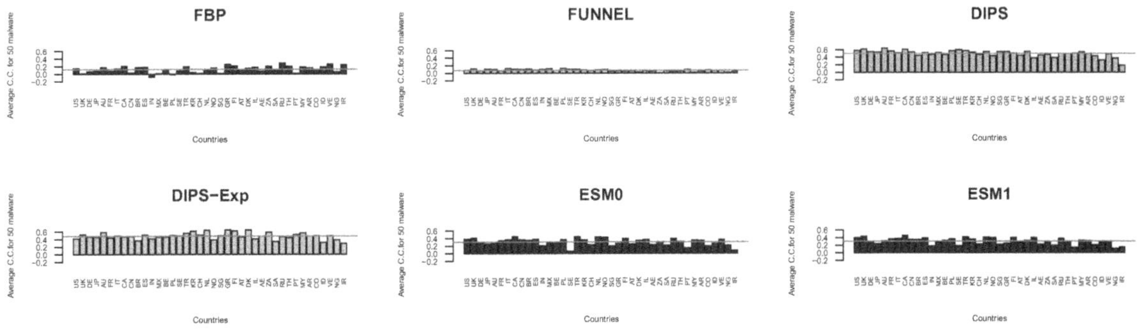

(a) *Correlation*

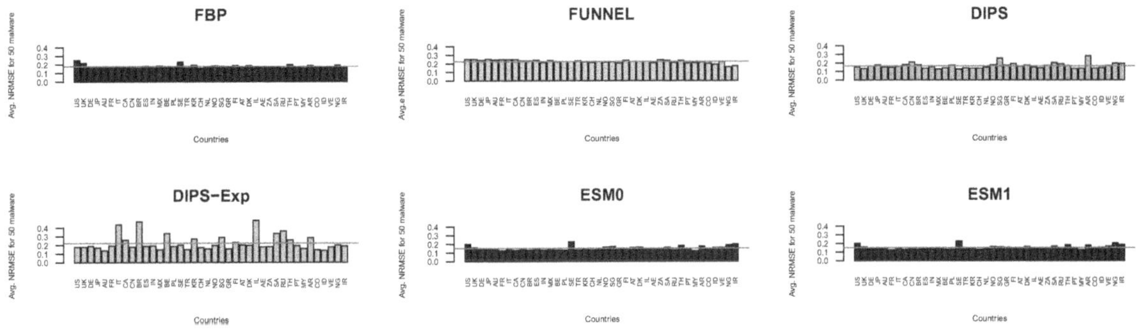

(b) *NRMSE*

Figure 7: (a) Correlation coefficient and (b) NRMSE by each country. The order from left to right is the descending order by the number of hosts over countries. Each red line is the average over countries.

(country,malware) pairs. Both models have better prediction performance for the country-malware pairs having more infected hosts. For the cases having lower infectious levels, DIPS was not reliable and sometimes yielded very large errors. Interestingly, in the lower infectious levels, DIPS and FBP showed complementary performance. So, the combination of two techniques, ESM showed good and very stable performance for almost all cases except the very small number cases where DIPS was originally the best.

7. RELATED WORK

We considered related work in cyber-security, data mining and epidemiology. Much research has tried to model malware propagation. In July 2001, the Code Red worm infected 359,000 hosts on the Internet in less than 14 hours [22]. Code Red achieved this by probing random IP addresses (using different seeds for its pseudo-random number generator) and infecting all hosts vulnerable to an IIS exploit. Staniford et. al. [26, 25] analyzed the Code Red worm traces and proposed an analytic model for its propagation. They also argue that optimization like hit-list scanning, permutation scanning can allow a worm to saturate 95% of vulnerable hosts on the Internet in less than 2 seconds. Such techniques were subsequently employed by worms released in the wild, such as the Slammer worm [21] (infected 90% of all vulnerable hosts within 10 minutes) and the Witty worm [28]. Gkantsidis et al. study the dissemination of software patches through the Windows Update service and find that approximately 80% of hosts request a patch within a day after it is released; the number of hosts drops by an order of magnitude during the second day, and is further reduced by factor of 2 in day three [8]. Additionally, [27] [15] [17] conducted measurement studies into routing instability in Broder Gateway Protocol (BGP) routers caused by catastrophic events, such as worm outbreaks or power outages. Other recent research also includes using machine learning methods like belief propagation on the file-machine graph [6] to infer files' reputations (say malicious or benign). Papalexakis et. al. [23] propose the SharkFin and GeoSplit models of spatio-temporal propagation of malware based on an analysis of the WINE data. Their system models only the total volume of malware attacks as a whole over time using a simplified model. In contrast, in this paper we model the *magnitude* of malware attacks *per machine* in context of the *machine usage* and using many more sophisticated variables. Remotely related work also comes from the area of information diffusion. Information diffusion is the phenomena in which an action or idea becomes widely adopted due to the influence of others, typically, neighbors in some network [4, 9, 10]. There are a lot of dynamic process on graphs, all of which are related to virus propagation like blogs cascades [1, 14, 11] and information cascades [18].

Finally our DIPS model is inspired by epidemiological models. The canonical textbooks and surveys discussing fundamental epidemiological models like SIS and SIR include [12, 2]. Much work has gone into finding epidemic thresholds (minimum virulence of a virus which results in an epidemic) for a variety of networks [3, 20, 2, 13, 7, 24].

8. CONCLUSIONS

In this paper, we studied the problem of predicting the volume of actual malware infections in a country given past data. This is a challenging problem because we can only detect a fraction of malware infections. There are many potential benefits of accurately predicting malware volume, which can have implications for better anti-virus software, and targeted patching. Using Symantec's extensive malware database in WINE, we investigated the infection patterns of 50 malware in more than 1.4 million hosts spread over two years in several countries. We present ESM, an ensemble based approach which carefully leverages well-designed domain-specific features (FBP) and a novel non-linear time-series model DIPS which incorporates detection and infections seamlessly. We show that our approach gives robust and stable predictions, even in case of low volume of infections, across all the countries over several metrics (correlation coefficients and NRMSE).

Acknowledgments: This paper is based on work partially supported by the Maryland Procurement Office under Contract No. H98230-14-C-0137, by the NEH under Grant No. HG-229283-15, by ORNL under Task Order 4000143330, by the VT College of Engineering, and a Facebook faculty gift.

We thank Symantec for providing access to the WINE platform. Other researchers may reproduce and verify our results by analyzing the reference data set we recorded in WINE (WINE-2013-001) after signing a research agreement with Symantec.

9. REFERENCES

[1] E. Adar and L. A. Adamic. Tracking information epidemics in blogspace. *Web Intelligence*, pages 207–214, 2005.

[2] R. M. Anderson and R. M. May. *Infectious Diseases of Humans*. Oxford University Press, 1991.

[3] N. Bailey. *The Mathematical Theory of Infectious Diseases and its Applications*. Griffin, London, 1975.

[4] S. Bikhchandani, D. Hirshleifer, and I. Welch. A theory of fads, fashion, custom, and cultural change in informational cascades. *Journal of Political Economy*, 100(5):992–1026, October 1992.

[5] L. Bilge and T. Dumitras. Before we knew it: an empirical study of zero-day attacks in the real world. In *ACM Conference on Computer and Communications Security*, pages 833–844, 2012.

[6] D. H. P. Chau, C. Nachenberg, J. Wilhelm, A. Wright, and C. Faloutsos. Polonium : Tera-scale graph mining for malware detection. In *SDM*, Mesa, AZ, April 2011.

[7] A. Ganesh, L. Massoulie, and D. Towsley. The effect of network topology in spread of epidemics. *IEEE INFOCOM*, 2005.

[8] C. Gkantsidis, T. Karagiannis, and M. Vojnovic. Planet scale software updates. In *SIGCOMM*, pages 423–434, 2006.

[9] J. Goldenberg, B. Libai, and E. Muller. Talk of the network: A complex systems look at the underlying process of word-of-mouth. *Marketing Letters*, 2001.

[10] M. Granovetter. Threshold models of collective behavior. *Am. Journal of Sociology*, 83(6):1420–1443, 1978.

[11] D. Gruhl, R. Guha, D. Liben-Nowell, and A. Tomkins. Information diffusion through blogspace. In *WWW '04*, 2004.

[12] H. W. Hethcote. The mathematics of infectious diseases. *SIAM Review*, 42, 2000.

[13] J. O. Kephart and S. R. White. Measuring and modeling computer virus prevalence. *IEEE Computer Society Symposium on Research in Security and Privacy*, 1993.

[14] R. Kumar, J. Novak, P. Raghavan, and A. Tomkins. On the bursty evolution of blogspace. In *WWW '03: Proceedings of the 12th international conference on World Wide Web*, pages 568–576, New York, NY, USA, 2003. ACM Press.

[15] M. Lad, X. Zhao, B. Zhang, D. Massey, and L. Zhang. Analysis of BGP Update Burst During Slammer Attack. In *The 5th International Workshop on Distributed Computing*, Dec 2005.

[16] K. Levenberg. A method for the solution of certain non-linear problems in least squares. *Quarterly Journal of Applied Mathmatics*, II(2):164–168, 1944.

[17] J. Li, Z. Wu, and E. Purpus. CAM04-5: Toward Understanding the Behavior of BGP During Large-Scale Power Outages. *GLOBECOM '06. IEEE*, pages 1–5, Nov. 2006.

[18] Y. Matsubara, Y. Sakurai, B. A. Prakash, L. Li, and C. Faloutsos. Rise and fall patterns of information diffusion: model and implications. In *Proceedings of the 18th ACM SIGKDD international conference on Knowledge discovery and data mining*, KDD '12, pages 6–14, 2012.

[19] Y. Matsubara, Y. Sakurai, W. G. Van-Panhuis, and C. Faloutsos. Funnel: automatic mining of spatially coevolving epidemics. In *KDD*, pages 105–114, 2014.

[20] A. G. McKendrick. Applications of mathematics to medical problems. In *Proceedings of Edin. Math. Society*, volume 44, pages 98–130, 1925.

[21] D. Moore, V. Paxson, S. Savage, C. Shannon, S. Staniford, and N. Weaver. Inside the Slammer worm. *Security & Privacy, IEEE*, 1(4):33–39, 2003.

[22] D. Moore, C. Shannon, and K. C. Claffy. Code-red: a case study on the spread and victims of an internet worm. In *Internet Measurement Workshop*, pages 273–284, 2002.

[23] E. E. Papalexakis, T. Dumitras, D. H. Chau, B. A. Prakash, and C. Faloutsos. Spatio-temporal mining of software adoption & penetration. In *2013 IEEE/ACM International Conference on Advances in Social Networks Analysis and Mining*, 2013.

[24] B. A. Prakash, D. Chakrabarti, M. Faloutsos, N. Valler, and C. Faloutsos. Threshold conditions for arbitrary cascade models on arbitrary networks. In *ICDM*, 2011.

[25] S. Staniford, D. Moore, V. Paxson, and N. Weaver. The top speed of flash worms. In *WORM*, pages 33–42, 2004.

[26] S. Staniford, V. Paxson, and N. Weaver. How to 0wn the internet in your spare time. In *Proceedings of the 11th USENIX Security Symposium*, pages 149–167, Berkeley, CA, USA, 2002. USENIX Association.

[27] L. Wang, X. Zhao, D. Pei, R. Bush, D. Massey, A. Mankin, S. Wu, and L. Zhang. Observation and Analysis of BGP Behavior under Stress. In *IMW*, 2002.

[28] N. Weaver and D. Ellis. Reflections on Witty: Analyzing the attacker. *;login: The USENIX Magazine*, 29(3):34–37, June 2004.

WSDM Cup 2016 – Entity Ranking Challenge

Alex D. Wade
Microsoft Research
One Microsoft Way
Redmond, WA USA
awade@microsoft.com

Kuansan Wang
Microsoft Research
One Microsoft Way
Redmond, WA USA
kuansanw@microsoft.com

Yizhou Sun
Northeastern University
360 Huntington Avenue
Boston, MA USA
yi.sun@neu.edu

Antonio Gulli
Elsevier B.V.
Radarweg 29, 1043 NX
Amsterdam The Netherlands
a.gulli@elsevier.com

ABSTRACT
In this paper, we describe the WSDM Cup entity ranking challenge held in conjunction with the 2016 Web Search and Data Mining conference (WSDM 2016). Participants in the challenge were provided access to the Microsoft Academic Graph (MAG), a large heterogeneous graph of academic entities, and were invited to calculate the query-independent importance of each publication in the graph. Submissions for the challenge were open from August through November 2015, and a public leaderboard displayed teams' progress against a set of training judgements. Final evaluations were performed against a separate, withheld portion of the evaluation judgements. The top eight performing teams were then invited to submit papers to the WSDM Cup workshop, held at the WSDM 2016 conference.

Keywords
Heterogeneous graphs; Microsoft Academic; Microsoft Academic Graph

1. INTRODUCTION
The recent explosive growth of data recording our daily online activities are often manifested as heterogeneous graphs, ranging from Facebook's Open Graph that records our social and communication activities to the graphs gathered by major search engine companies that represent a snapshot of our collective knowledge. As demonstrated in many web search and data mining applications (e.g., [1] [2] [3]), a critical element to make the best use of the data is the ability to assess the relative importance of the nodes in these networks.

The sphere of scholarly research outputs and related entities can similarly be manifested as a heterogeneous graph. In assessing and ranking scholarly entities, citation metrics have long reigned as the primary means of measuring relative impact and importance. In the 1950's Eugene Garfield established the Journal Impact Factor (JIF) [4] to aide librarians in evaluating which journal subscriptions to preserve in the face of rising subscription costs and static library budgets. A decade ago, Jorge Hirsch created the h-index, a scholar-centric metric based on the distribution of one's publications to the number of citations received, in order to quantify "the cumulative impact and relevance of an individual's scientific research output" [5]. And indeed for individual publications themselves, many academic discovery services today rely upon cumulative citation counts as a key ranking feature.

However, the overall reliance upon citation metrics is not without disadvantages, including, but not limited to the notion that individual citations may carry uneven weights or semantic meanings [6], and that citation metrics inherently take years to emerge following the publication of the paper being cited. The drawbacks are well known, and the Weighted PageRank [7] and the emerging alt-metrics movement [8] are examples of responses to these limitations.

2. DATA
In 2015, Microsoft Research released a static snapshot of the Microsoft Academic Graph (MAG), a large heterogeneous graph comprised of publications, authors, venues (e.g., journals or conferences), organizations, and the fields of study [9] in order to enable the community to jointly work on a modern, principled and scalable way for measuring scholarly impacts and influences. The relationships and the inherent heterogeneity of objects in this graph provide new opportunities to evaluate and rank objects. For instance, the relative importance of new publications that have yet to receive any citations might be inferred from the venues, authors, or author affiliations of the publications.

The Microsoft Academic Graph used in this challenge contains approximately 140 million publication records, 650 million citation relationships, 40 million authors, 3.5 million institutions, 60,000 journals and conference "venues" and 55,000 fields of study. As a reference, a static rank score based on the PageRank algorithm [10] was provided as a part of the MAG data for papers. This data was made available as a series of text files on Azure blob storage, and could be downloaded or copied to a personal Azure account for use in the project. Challenge participants were asked to use the 2015-08-20 version of the MAG for development.

3. CHALLENGE TASK
The stated goal of the 2016 WSDM Cup challenge was to advance the start-of-the-art of data mining algorithms in quantifying the importance of nodes in a heterogeneous graph. For the purpose of the challenge, the importance is defined in the context of search, i.e., the participants were asked to compute the query-independent

WSDM'16, February 22-25, 2016, San Francisco, CA, USA
ACM 978-1-4503-3716-8/16/02.
http://dx.doi.org/10.1145/2835776.2855119

static ranks for the graph. To make the task more manageable, the challenge focused on the publications in the MAG, even though the algorithms may be applicable to authors, venues and other types of nodes as well. More specifically, the participants were asked to assign a single numerical value to each paper, with a larger value representing a more important paper. Participants were also encouraged to utilize any additional public information that is not already included in the MAG (e.g., information about best paper or test-of-time awards and other honors, abstract and full text body of each paper).

4. EVALUATION

The evaluation used Pairwise Correctness as the metric to evaluate the submitted entries. The challenge organizers employed scholars of good academic standing with extensive experience serving on conference program committees or journal review boards in the field of Computer Science to perform pairwise judgments on publications. These judges were presented with pairs of articles they have previously cited or read, and asked to make a binary assessment on which article from each pair has or is likely to have more impact on their fields of study. These judgements were divided into two sets, the first used to calculate the score on the Leaderboard during the development phase. The second set was withheld as the evaluation data, and was used to calculate the final results.

The eight participant teams whose entries had the highest pairwise correctness scores were invited to the 2016 WSDM Cup workshop. and qualified for a "bonus" round of evaluation where the result from each qualifying team will replace the static rank of an existing web search engine and be deployed as online experiments. For this portion, the Challenge effectively evaluates the entries in their abilities to predict the ranking order the search engine users prefer.

5. RESULTS

Over 30 teams actively submitted results for evaluation. Of these, 19 teams performed better than PageRank.

Table 1. Final scores for top eight teams (plus *PageRank*)

Score	Team Name	Institutions
0.684	NTU_Pseudo-Tripartite	National Taiwan University National Chengchi University
0.676	Eigenfactor	University of Washington
0.671	ufmglatin	U Federal de Minas Gerais
0.664	NTU_WeightedPR	Academica Sinica National Taiwan University
0.659	bletchleypark	Open University Mendeley
0.656	teambuaa	Beihang University
0.651	sapirank	Sapienza University of Rome
0.642	NTU_Ensemble	Academica Sinica National Taiwan University National Chengchi Univeristy
0.618	*PageRank*	*n/a*

The winning team was NTU_Pseudo_Tripartite, made up of Ming-Han Feng, Kuan-Hou Chan, and Huan-Yuan Chen of National Taiwan University, and Ming-Feng Tsai of National Chengchi University, Taiwan.

The top eight teams were subsequently invited to re-submit ranking results based on an updated instance of the MAG data (version 2015-11-06) to be used in a special 'bonus round' online evaluation. The results of this online evaluation will be presented at the 2016 WSDM Cup workshop, to be held in conjunction with the WSDM Conference in February 2016. Table 1 contains the top eight team scores based on the final evaluations, as well as the PageRank performance over the same evaluation judgements.

6. REFERENCES

[1] Aral, S., and Walker, D. 2012. Identifying influential and susceptible members of social networks, *Science*, pp. 337-341, 2012. http://doi.org/10.1126/science.1215842

[2] Wang, Y., Cong, G., Song, G., and Xie, K. 2010. Community-based greedy algorithm for mining top-k influential nodes in mobile social network, in *Proceedings of the 16th ACM SIGKDD international conference on knowledge discovery and data mining*. http:// doi.org/10.1145/1835804.1835935

[3] Sun, Y., Yu, Y. and Han, J. 2009. Ranking-based clustering of heterogeneous information networks with star network schema, in *Proceedings of the 15th ACM SIGKDD international conference on knowledge discovery and data mining*. http://doi.org/10.1145/1557019.1557107

[4] Garfield, E. 2006. The history and meaning of the journal impact factor, *Journal of American Medical Association*, vol. 295, no. 1. http://doi.org/ 10.1001/jama.295.1.90

[5] Hirsch, J. E. 2005. An index to quantify an individual's scientific research output, *Proceedings of the National Academy of Sciences*, vol. 102, no. 46, pp. 16596-16572. http://doi.org/10.1073/pnas.0507655102

[6] Sinha, A., Shen, Z., Song, Y., Ma, H., Eide, D., Hsu, B., Wang, K. 2015. An Overview of Microsoft Academic Service (MAS) and Applications. In *Proceedings of the 24th International Conference on World Wide Web (WWW '15)*. http://research.microsoft.com/apps/pubs/default.aspx?id=246609

[7] Yan, E. and Ding, Y. 2010. Measuring scholarly impact in heterogeneous networks," in *Proceedings of the 73rd ASIST annual meeting*, Pittsburgh PA. http://doi.org/10.1002/meet.14504701033

[8] Priem, J., Groth, P., and Taraborelli, D. 2012. The Altmetric collection, *PLOS ONE*, vol. 7, no. 11. http://doi.org/10.1371/journal.pone.0048753

[9] Microsoft Academic Graph. In http://aka.ms/academicgraph, November 2015.

[10] Brin, S., Page, L, Motwani, R., Winograd, T. 1999. The PageRank Citation Ranking: Bringing Order to the Web. Technical Report. Stanford InfoLab. http://ilpubs.stanford.edu:8090/422/

Dynamic Collective Entity Representations for Entity Ranking

David Graus
University of Amsterdam
d.p.graus@uva.nl

Manos Tsagkias
904Labs
manos@904labs.com

Wouter Weerkamp
904Labs
wouter@904labs.com

Edgar Meij
Yahoo Labs
emeij@yahoo-inc.com

Maarten de Rijke
University of Amsterdam
derijke@uva.nl

ABSTRACT

Entity ranking, i.e., successfully positioning a relevant entity at the top of the ranking for a given query, is inherently difficult due to the potential mismatch between the entity's description in a knowledge base, and the way people refer to the entity when searching for it. To counter this issue we propose a method for constructing dynamic collective entity representations. We collect entity descriptions from a variety of sources and combine them into a single entity representation by learning to weight the content from different sources that are associated with an entity for optimal retrieval effectiveness. Our method is able to add new descriptions in real time and learn the best representation as time evolves so as to capture the dynamics of how people search entities. Incorporating dynamic description sources into dynamic collective entity representations improves retrieval effectiveness by 7% over a state-of-the-art learning to rank baseline. Periodic retraining of the ranker enables higher ranking effectiveness for dynamic collective entity representations.

Keywords

Entity ranking; Content representation

1. INTRODUCTION

Many queries issued to general web search engines are related to entities [20]. Entity ranking, where the goal is to position a relevant entity at the top of the ranking for a given query, is therefore becoming an ever more important task [4, 5, 10–12]. In this paper we focus on the scenario in which a searcher enters a query that can be satisfied by returning an entity from a knowledge base (e.g., Wikipedia). Note that this is not the same task as entity linking, where the goal is to identify to which entities a searcher refers in her query.

Entity ranking is inherently difficult due to the potential mismatch between the entity's description in a knowledge base and the way people refer to the same entity when searching for it. When we look at how entities are described, two aspects, context and time, are of particular interest and pose challenges to any solution to entity ranking. Here we explain both aspects.

WSDM 2016, February 22 – 25, 2016, San Francisco, CA, USA

ISBN 978-1-4503-3716-8/16/02...$15.00
DOI: http://dx.doi.org/10.1145/2835776.2835819

Context dependency: Consider the entity `Germany`. A history student could expect this entity to show up when searching for entities related to World War II. In contrast, a sports fan searching for World Cup 2014 soccer results is also expecting to find the same entity. The challenge then becomes how to capture these different contexts for one single entity.

Time dependency: Entities are not static in how they are perceived. Consider `Ferguson, Missouri`, which had a fairly standard city description before the shooting of Michael Brown happened in August 2014. After this event, the entity description of Ferguson changed substantially, reflecting people's interest in the event, its aftermath and impact on the city.

We propose a method that addresses both challenges raised above. First, we use the collective intelligence as offered by a wide range of entity "description sources" (e.g., tweets and tags that mention entities), and we combine these into a "collective entity representation," i.e., a representation that encapsulates different ways of how people refer to or talk about the entity. Consider the example in Figure 1 in which a tweet offers a very different way to refer to the entity `Anthropornis` than the original knowledge base description does. Second, our method takes care of the time dependency by incorporating dynamic entity description sources, which in turn affect the entity descriptions in near real time. Dynamics is part of our method in two ways: (i) we leverage dynamic description sources to expand entity representations, and (ii) we learn how to combine the different entity descriptions for optimal retrieval at specific time intervals. The resulting *dynamic collective entity representations* capture both the different contexts of an entity and its changes over time. We refer to the collection of descriptions from different sources that are associated with an entity as the entity's *representation*. Our method is meant to construct the optimal representation for retrieval, by assigning weights to the descriptions from different sources.

Collecting terms associated with documents and adding them to the document (document expansion) is in itself not a novel idea. Previous work has shown that it improves retrieval effectiveness in a variety of retrieval tasks; see Section 2. However, while information retrieval on the open web is inherently dynamic, document expansion for search has mainly been studied in static, context-independent settings, in which expansion terms from one source are aggregated and added to the collection before indexing [21, 26, 27, 39]. In contrast, our method leverages different dynamic description sources (e.g, queries, social media, web pages), and in this way uses collective intelligence to bridge the gap between the

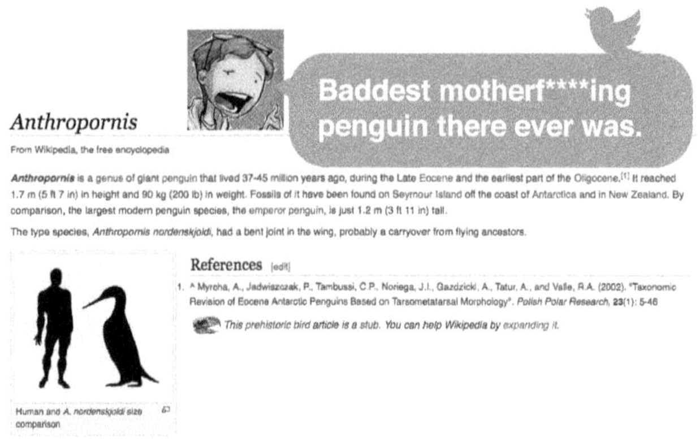

Figure 1: Entity description of `Anthropornis` in Wikipedia and a tweet with an alternative description of the same entity.

terms used in a knowledge base's entity descriptions and the terms that people use to refer to entities.

To achieve this, we represent entities as fielded documents [24], where each field contains content that comes from a single description source. In a dynamic setting such as our entity ranking setting, where new entity descriptions come in as a stream, learning weights for the various fields in batch is not optimal. Ideally, the ranker continuously updates its ranking model to successfully rank the entities and incorporate newly incoming descriptions. Hence, constructing a dynamic entity representation for optimal retrieval effectiveness boils down to dynamically learning to optimally weight the entity's fields that hold content from the different description sources. To this end we exploit implicit user feedback (i.e., clicks) to retrain our model and continually adjust the weights associated to the entity's fields, much like online learning to rank [16].

Our dynamic collective entity representations generate one additional challenge, which is related to the heterogeneity that exists among entities and among description sources. Popular head entities are likely to receive a larger number of external descriptions than tail entities. At the same time the description sources differ along several dimensions (e.g., volume, quality, novelty). Given this heterogeneity, linearly combining retrieval scores (as is commonly done in structured retrieval models) proves to be suboptimal. We therefore extend our method to include features that enable the ranker to distinguish between different types of entities and stages of entity representations.

We address these three research questions:

RQ1 Does entity ranking effectiveness increase by using dynamic collective entity representations? We compare a baseline entity ranking method based on the information in the knowledge base only to our method that incorporates additional description sources (web anchors, queries, tags, and tweets).

RQ2 Does entity ranking effectiveness increase when employing additional field and entity importance features? We answer this question by incorporating field and entity importance features to our knowledge base-only baseline ranker and our proposed method, and compare their performance.

RQ3 Does entity ranking effectiveness increase when we continuously learn the optimal way to combine the content from different description sources? We compare a static entity ranking baseline that is trained once at the start, to our proposed method that is retrained at regular intervals.

The main contribution of this paper is a novel approach to constructing dynamic collective entity representations, which takes into account the temporal and contextual dependencies of entity descriptions. We show that dynamic collective entity representations better capture how people search for entities than their original knowledge base descriptions. In addition, we show how field importance features better inform the ranker, thus increasing retrieval effectiveness. Furthermore, we show how continuously updating the ranker enables higher ranking effectiveness. Finally, we perform extensive analyses of our results and show that incorporating dynamic signals into the dynamic collective entity representation enables a better matching of users' queries to entities.

2. RELATED WORK

Related work comes in three flavors: entity ranking, document expansion and fielded or structured information retrieval.

2.1 Entity ranking

Recent years have shown an increase in entity ranking research. Main causes for this were the introductions of the INEX Entity Ranking track [10–12] and the TREC Entity track [4, 5]. Exploiting content and structure of knowledge bases is common practice in entity ranking, for example by including anchor texts and inter-entity links [33], category structure [3, 32], entity types [18], or internal link structure [38]. More recently, researchers have also started to focus on using query logs for entity ranking. Billerbeck et al. [8] use query logs of a web search engine to build click and sessions graphs and walk the graph to answer entity queries. Mottin et al. [29] use query logs to train an entity ranking system using different sets of features. Unlike us, the authors assume a static setting (i.e., no online learning) and do not take into account external sources for entity representation. Hong et al. [17] follow a similar line of thought and enrich their knowledge base using linked web pages and queries from a query log. Again, the authors assume a static setting in which web pages and queries are added to the knowledge base before any ranking experiments are performed. One of the few initial attempts to bring in time in entity ranking is a position paper by Balog and Nørvåg [2], who propose temporally-aware entity retrieval, in which temporal information from knowledge bases is required.

2.2 Document expansion

Singhal and Pereira [34] are one of the first to use document expansion in a (speech) retrieval setting, motivated by the vocabulary mismatch introduced by errors made by automatic speech transcription. Ever since, using external sources for expanding document representations has been a popular approach to improve retrieval effectiveness. In particular, it was shown that anchors can improve ad-hoc web search [14, 26, 39, 40].

Kemp and Ramamohanarao [19] state that document transformation using search history, i.e., adding queries that lead to the document to be clicked, brings documents closer to queries and hence improves retrieval effectiveness. Similarly, Xue et al. [41] study the use of click-through data by adding queries to clicked document representations. In this case, the click-through data includes a score that is derived from the number of clicks the query yields for a single document. Gao et al. [15] follow a similar approach, but add smoothing to click-through data to counter sparsity issues. Amitay et al. [1] study the effectiveness of query reformulations for document expansion by appending all queries in a reformulation session to the top-k returned documents for the last query. Scholer et al. [32] propose a method to either add additional terms from associated queries to documents or replace the original content with these associated queries, all with the goal of providing more accurate document representations.

Looking at other sources for expansion, Bao et al. [6] improve web search using social annotations (tags). They use the annotations both as additional content as well as popularity measure. Lee and Croft [21] explore the use of social anchors (i.e., content of social media posts linking to a document) to improve ad hoc search. Noll and Meinel [30] investigate of a variety of "metadata" sources, including anchors, social annotations, and search queries. They show that social annotations are concise references to entities and outperform anchors in several retrieval tasks. Efron et al. [13] show that document expansion can be beneficial when searching for very short documents (tweets).

2.3 Fielded retrieval

A common approach to incorporate the document expansions into a document is to create fielded documents [31, 42]. Based on fielded documents, a variety of retrieval methods have been proposed. Robertson et al. [31] introduce BM25F, the fielded version of BM25, which linearly combines query term frequencies over different field types. Broder et al. [9] propose an extension to BM25F, taking into account term dependencies. Svore and Burges [35] use a machine learning approach for learning BM25 over multiple fields, the original document fields (e.g., title and body) and so-called "popularity" fields (e.g., anchors, query-clicks). Macdonald et al. [24] compare the linear combination of term frequencies before computing retrieval scores to directly using retrieval scores in the learning to rank setting and show that it is hard to determine a clear winner.

What sets our work apart from the aforementioned work is that we deal with dynamic fields with continually changing content, and study continually adapting entity representations and rankers. Our method is required to reweigh fields continuously to reflect changes in the fields' content. Continually (re-)tuning parameters of fielded retrieval methods such as BM25F when documents in the index change is exceedingly expensive, rendering these methods unsuitable for this scenario.

3. DYNAMIC COLLECTIVE ENTITY REPRESENTATIONS

3.1 Problem statement

The problem of entity ranking is: given a query q and a knowledge base KB populated with entities $e \in E$, find the best matching e that satisfies q. Both e and q are represented in some (individual or joint) feature space that captures a range of dimensions, which characterize them individually (e.g., content, quality) and jointly (e.g., relationships through click logs).

The problem itself is a standard information retrieval problem, where the system needs to bridge the gap between the vocabulary used in queries and documents. This is a long-standing but still open problem that has been tackled from many perspectives. One is to design better similarity functions, another is to develop methods for enhancing the feature spaces. Our method shares characteristics with both perspectives, as we will now explain.

3.2 Approach

Our approach to the entity ranking problem consists of two interleaved steps. First, we use external description sources (described in §3.3) to expand entity representations and reduce the vocabulary gap between queries and entities. We do so by representing entities as fielded documents, where each field corresponds to content that comes from one description source. Second, we train a classification-based entity ranker, that employs different types of features to learn to weight and combine the content from each field of the entity for optimal retrieval (§3.4).

External description sources may continually update and change the content in the entity's fields, through user feedback (i.e., clicks) following an issued query, or when users generate content on external description sources that is linked to a KB entity (e.g., Twitter, Delicious). Consequently, the feature values that represent the entities change, which may invalidate previously learned optimal feature weights and asks for continuously updating the ranking model.

Table 1: Summary of the nine description sources we consider: Knowledge Base entity descriptions (KB), KB anchors, KB redirects, KB category titles, KB inter-hyperlinks, queries, web anchors, tweets, and tags from Delicious.

Data source	Size	Period	Affected entities
Static expansion sources			
KB	4,898,356	August 2014	–
KB anchors	15,485,915	August 2014	4,361,608
KB redirects	6,256,912	August 2014	N/A
KB categories	1,100,723	August 2014	N/A
KB inter-links	28,825,849	August 2014	4,322,703
Dynamic expansion sources			
Queries	47,002	May 2006	18,724
Web anchors	9,818,004	2012	876,063
Twitter	52,631	2011–2014	38,269
Delicious	4,429,692	2003–2011	289,015

3.3 Description sources

To construct dynamic collective entity representations we use two types of description sources: (i) a knowledge base (KB) from which we extract the initial entity representations, and (ii) a set of external description sources that we use to expand the aforementioned entity representation.

We differentiate between external description sources that are non-timestamped (*static*) and ones that are timestamped (*dynamic*). Non-timestamped sources are those where no time information is available, and sources that are not inherently dynamic, e.g., web archives and aggregates over archives like web anchors. Timestamped external description sources are sources whose content is associated with a timestamp, and where the nature of the source is inherently dynamic or time-dependent, e.g., tweets or query logs. We describe each type of external description source below, the number of total descriptions, and affected entities, and we provide a summary in Table 1.

Knowledge base. The knowledge base that we use as our initial index of entities, and which we use to construct the initial entity representations, is a snapshot of Wikipedia from August 3, 2014 with 14,753,852 pages. We filter out non-entity pages ("special" pages such as category, file, and discussion pages), yielding 4,898,356 unique entities.

Static description sources.

Knowledge base. Knowledge base entities have rich metadata that can be leveraged for improving retrieval [3, 32, 33]. We consider four types of metadata to construct the KB entity representations: (i) anchor text of inter-knowledge base hyperlinks, (ii) redirects, (iii) category titles, and (iv) titles of entities that are linked from and to each entity. Editorial conventions and Wikipedia's quality control ensures these expansions to be of high quality.

Web anchors. Moving away from the knowledge base itself, the web provides rich information on how people refer to entities leading to tangible improvements in retrieval [39]. We extract anchor texts of links to Wikipedia pages from the Google Wikilinks corpus.[1] We collect 9,818,004 anchor texts for 876,063 entities. Web anchors differ from KB anchors as they can be of lower quality (due to absence of editorial conventions) but also of much larger volume. While in theory web anchors could be associated with timestamps, in a typical scenario they are aggregated over large archives, where extracting timestamps for diverse web-pages is non-trivial.

Dynamic description sources.

Twitter. Mishne and Lin [27] show how leveraging terms from tweets that do not exist in the pages linked to from tweets can improve retrieval effectiveness of those pages. We follow a similar approach and mine all English tweets that contain links to Wikipedia pages that represent the entities in our KB. These are extracted from an archive of Twitter's sample stream, spanning four years (2011–2014), resulting in 52,631 tweets for 38,269 entities.

Delicious. Social tags are concise references to entities and have shown to outperform anchors in several retrieval tasks [30]. We extract tags associated with Wikipedia pages from SocialBM0311[2] resulting in 4,429,692 timestamped tags for 289,015 entities.

Queries. We use a publicly available query log from MSN sampled between May 1 and May 31, 2006, consisting of 15M queries and their metadata: timestamps and URLs of clicked documents. We keep only queries that result in clicks on Wikipedia pages that exist in our snapshot of Wikipedia, resulting in 47,002 queries associated with 18,724 uniquely clicked entities. We hold out 30% of the queries for development (e.g., parameter tuning, feature engineering; 14,101 queries) and use 70% (32,901 queries) for testing. Our use of queries is twofold: (i) queries are used as input to evaluate the performance of our system, and also (ii) as external description source, to expand the entity description with the terms from a query that yield a click on an entity. While this dual role of queries may promote head entities that are often searched, we note that "headness" of entities differs across description sources, and even tail entities may benefit from external descriptions (as illustrated by the `Anthropornis` example in Fig. 1).

3.4 Adaptive entity ranking

The second step in our method is to employ a supervised entity ranker that learns to weight the fields that hold content from the different description sources for optimal retrieval effectiveness. Two challenges arise in constructing collective dynamic entity representations.

Heterogeneity. External description sources exhibit different dynamics in terms of volume and quality of content [22], and differences in number and type of entities to which they link (see, e.g., Table 1). This heterogeneity causes issues both within entities, since different description sources contribute different amounts and types of content to the entity's fields, and between entities, since popular entities may receive overall more content from external description sources than tail entities.

Dynamicness. Dynamic external description sources cause the entity's descriptions to change in near real-time. Consequently, a static ranking model cannot capture the evolving and continually changing index that follows from our dynamic scenario, hence we employ an adaptive ranking model that is continuously updated.

[1] https://code.google.com/p/wiki-links/

[2] http://www.zubiaga.org/datasets/socialbm0311/

4. MODEL

In the following section we describe our supervised ranking approach, by first explaining the entity representation, the set of features we employ for learning an optimal representation for retrieval, and finally the supervised method.

4.1 Entity Representation

To deal with dynamic entity representations, which are composed of content from different external description sources, we model entities as fielded documents:

$$e = \{\overline{f}^e_{title}, \overline{f}^e_{text}, \overline{f}^e_{anchors}, \ldots, \overline{f}^e_{query}\}. \quad (1)$$

Where $\overline{f}^e$ corresponds to the field term vector that represents e's content from a single source (denoted in subscript). We refer to this collection of field term vectors as the entity's *representation*.

The fields with content from dynamic description sources may change over time. We refer to the process of adding an external description source's term vector to the entity's corresponding field term vector as an *update*. To model these dynamically changing fields, we discretize time (i.e., $T = \{t_1, t_2, t_3, \ldots, t_n\}$), and define *updating* fields as:

$$\overline{f}^e_{query}(t_i) = \overline{f}^e_{query}(t_{i-1}) + \begin{cases} \overline{q}, & \text{if } e_{clicked} \\ 0, & \text{otherwise} \end{cases} \quad (2)$$

$$\overline{f}^e_{tweets}(t_i) = \overline{f}^e_{tweets}(t_{i-1}) + \overline{tweet}_e \quad (3)$$

$$\overline{f}^e_{tags}(t_i) = \overline{f}^e_{tags}(t_{i-1}) + \overline{tag}_e. \quad (4)$$

In equation 2, $\overline{q}$ represents the term vector of query q that is summed element-wise to e's query field term vector ($\overline{f}^e_{query}$) at time t_i, if e is clicked by a user that issues q. In equation 3, $\overline{tweet}_e$ represents the field term vector of a tweet that contains a link to the Wikipedia page of e, which also gets added element-wise to the corresponding field ($\overline{f}^e_{tweets}$). Finally, in equation 4, $\overline{tag}_e$ is the term vector of a tag that a user assigns to the Wikipedia page of e.

To estimate e's relevance to a query q given the above-described representation one could e.g., linearly combine retrieval scores between q's term vector $\overline{q}$ and each $\overline{f} \in e$. However, due to the heterogeneity that exists both between the different fields that make up the entity representation, and between different entities (described in §3.4), linearly combining similarity scores may be suboptimal [31], and hence we employ a supervised single-field weighting model [24]. Here, each field's contribution towards the final score is individually weighted, through learned field weights from implicit user feedback.

4.2 Features

To learn the optimal entity representation for retrieval, we employ three types of features that express field and entity importance: first, *field similarity* features are computed per field and boil down to query–field similarity scores. Next, *field importance* features, likewise computed per field aim to inform the ranker of the status of the field at that point in time (i.e., to favor fields with more and novel content). Finally, we employ *entity importance* features, which operate on the entity level and aim to favor recently updated entities.

4.2.1 Field similarity

The first set of features model the similarity between a query and a field, which we denote as ϕ_{sim}. For query–field similarity, we compute TF×IDF cosine similarity. We define

$$\phi_{sim}(q, \overline{f}, t_i) = \sum_{w \in q} n(w, \overline{f}(t_i)) \cdot \log \frac{|C^{t_i}|}{|\{\overline{f}(t_i) \in C^{t_i} : w \in \overline{f}(t_i)\}|}, \tag{5}$$

where w corresponds to a query term, $n(w, \overline{f}(t_i))$ is the frequency of term w in field f at time t_i. C^{t_i} is the collection of fields at time t_i, and $|\cdot|$ indicates set cardinality. More elaborate similarity functions can be used, e.g., BM25(F), however, we choose a parameterless similarity function that requires no tuning. This allows us to directly compare the contribution of the different expansion fields without having additional factors play a role, such as length normalization parameters, which affect different fields in non-trivial ways.

4.2.2 *Field importance*

The next set of features is also computed per field, ϕ_p is meant to capture a field's *importance* at time t_i:

$$\phi_p(\overline{f}(t_i), e) = S(\overline{f}(t_i), e). \tag{6}$$

We instantiate four different field importance features. First, we consider two ways to compute a field's length, either in terms (7) or in characters (8):

$$\phi_{p_1}(\overline{f}(t_i), e) = |\overline{f}(t_i)| \tag{7}$$

$$\phi_{p_2}(\overline{f}(t_i), e) = \sum_{w \in \overline{f}(t_i)} |w| \tag{8}$$

The third field importance scoring function captures a field's novelty at time t_i, to favor fields that have been updated with previously unseen, newly associated terms to the entity (i.e., terms that were not in the original entity representation at t_0):

$$\phi_{p_3}(\overline{f}(t_i), e) = |\{w \in \overline{f}(t_i) : w \notin \overline{f}(t_0)\}|. \tag{9}$$

The fourth field importance scoring function expresses whether a field has undergone an update at time t_i:

$$\phi_{p_4}(\overline{f}, t_i, e) = \sum_{j=0}^{i} += \begin{cases} 1, & \text{if } update(\overline{f}(t_j)) \\ 0, & \text{otherwise,} \end{cases} \tag{10}$$

where $update(\overline{f}(t_j))$ is a Boolean function indicating whether field f was updated at time j, i.e., we sum from t_0 through t_i and accumulate updates to the fields.

4.2.3 *Entity importance*

The feature ϕ_I models the entity's importance. We compute the time since the entity last received an update to favor recently updated entities:

$$\phi_I(e, t_i) = t_i - \max_{\overline{f} \in e} time_{\overline{f}}, \tag{11}$$

Here, t_i is the current time, and $time_{\overline{f}}$ is the update time of field $\overline{f}$. $\max_{\overline{f}}$ corresponds to the timestamp of the entity's field that was most recently updated.

4.3 Machine learning

Given the features explained in the previous section, we employ a supervised ranker to learn the optimal feature weights for retrieval;

$$\Omega = (\omega_e, \omega_{\overline{f}_{title}}, \omega_{p1_{title}}, \omega_{p2_{title}}, \ldots, \omega_{\overline{f}_{text}}, \omega_{p1_{text}}, \ldots)$$

Here, Ω corresponds to the weight vector, which is composed of individual weights (ω) for each of the field features (similarity and importance) and the entity importance feature.

To find the optimal Ω, we train a classification-based re-ranking model, and learn from user interactions (i.e., clicks). The model employs the features detailed in the previous section, and the classification's confidence score is used as a ranking signal. As input, the ranker receives a feature vector (x), extracted for each entity-query pair. The associated label y is positive (1) for the entities that were clicked by a user who issued query q. We define x as

$$x = \{\phi_{sim_1}, \phi_{p1_1}, \phi_{p2_1}, \phi_{p3_1}, \phi_{p4_1}, \ldots, \phi_{sim_{|e|}}, \phi_{p1_{|e|}}, \phi_{p2_{|e|}}, \phi_{p3_{|e|}}, \phi_{p4_{|e|}}, \phi_I\} \tag{12}$$

Where $|e|$ corresponds to the number of fields that make up the entity representation ($\overline{f} \in e$).

See Algorithm 1 for an overview of our machine learning method in pseudo-code. As input, our supervised classifier is given a set of $\langle q, e, L\rangle$-tuples (see l.4). These tuples consist of a query (q), a candidate entity (e), and a (binary) label (L): positive (1) or negative (0). Given an incoming query, we first perform top-k retrieval (see §5.2 for details) to yield our initial set of candidate entities: $\mathcal{E}_{candidate}$ (l.8). For each entity, we extract the features which are detailed in Section 4.2 (l.12) and have the classification-based ranker R output a confidence score for e belonging to the positive class, which is used to rank the candidate entities (l.13). Labels are acquired through user interactions, i.e., entities that are in the set of candidate entities and clicked after issuing a query are labeled as positive instances (l.16–22), used to retrain R (l.24). Finally, after each query, we allow entities to be updated by dynamic description sources: tweets and tags (l.26), we provide more details in §5.1.

Algorithm 1 Pseudo-algorithm for learning optimal Ω^T.

Require: Ranker R, Knowledge Base KB, Entities $\mathcal{E}$

1: $\mathcal{E} \longleftarrow \{e_1, e_2, \ldots, e_{|KB|}\}$
2: $e \longleftarrow \{\overline{f}_{title}, \overline{f}_{anchors}, \ldots, \overline{f}_{text}\}$
3:
4: $\mathcal{L} = \{\langle q_1, e_1, \{0,1\}\rangle, \langle q_1, e_2, \{0,1\}\rangle, \ldots, \langle q_n, e_m, \{0,1\}\rangle\}$
5: $R \longleftarrow$ Train($\mathcal{L}$)
6:
7: **while** q **do**
8:     $\mathcal{E}_{candidate} \longleftarrow$ Top-k retrieval(q)
9:     $\mathcal{E}_{ranked} \longleftarrow []$
10:
11:     **for** $e \in \mathcal{E}_{candidate}$ **do**
12:         $\phi_e \longleftarrow$ Extract features(e)
13:         $\mathcal{E}_{ranked} \longleftarrow$ Classify(R, ϕ_e)
14:     **end for**
15:
16:     $e_{clicked} \longleftarrow$ Observe click($q, \mathcal{E}$)
17:     **if** $e_{clicked} \in \mathcal{E}_{candidate}$ **then**
18:         $\mathcal{L} \longleftarrow \mathcal{L} \cup \{\langle q, e_{clicked}, 1\rangle\}$
19:         $e_{clicked} \longleftarrow e_{clicked} \cup \{text_q\}$
20:     **else**
21:         $\mathcal{L} \longleftarrow \mathcal{L} \cup \{\langle q, e_{clicked}, 0\rangle\}$
22:     **end if**
23:
24:     $R \longleftarrow$ Train($\mathcal{L}$)
25:     **for** $e \in \mathcal{E}$ **do**
26:         $e \longleftarrow e \cup \{\overline{f}_{e,tweet_1}, \overline{f}_{e,tag_1}, \ldots, \overline{f}_{e,tweet_i}, \overline{f}_{e,tag_j}\}$
27:     **end for**
28: **end while**

5. EXPERIMENTAL SETUP

In this section we start by describing our experiments and how they allow us to answer the research questions raised in Section 1, and then, we present our machine learning setting and describe our evaluation methodology.

Experiment 1. To answer our first research question, *does entity ranking effectiveness increase using dynamic collective entity representations?*, we compare our proposed dynamic collective entity ranking method to a baseline that only incorporates KB fields for entity ranking: KBER (Knowledge Base Entity Representations). We restrict both the baseline and our Dynamic Collective Entity Representation (DCER) method to the set of field similarity features (§4.2.1), which we denote as KBER_{sim} and DCER_{sim}. This allows us to provide clear insights into the contribution of the fields' content in ranking effectiveness. In addition, we perform an ablation study and compare the similarity-baseline to several approaches that incorporate content from a single external description source (denoted KB+source_{sim}).

Experiment 2. We address RQ2, *does entity ranking effectiveness increase when employing field and entity features*, by comparing the KBER_{sim} baseline that only incorporates field similarity features, to the KBER baseline that incorporates the entity and field importance features, and to our DCER method.

Experiment 3. Finally, to answer our third research question, *does entity ranking effectiveness increase when we continuously learn the optimal entity representations?* We compare our proposed entity ranking system DCER to its non-adaptive counterpart (DCER_{na}), that we do not periodically retrain. Contrasting the performance of this non-adaptive system with our adaptive system allows us to tease apart the effects of adding more training data, and the effect of the additional content that comes from dynamic external description sources. Here too, we include an ablation study, and compare to non-adaptive approaches that incorporate content from a single external description source (denoted KB+source_{na}).

Baselines. Due to our focus on dynamic entity representations and adaptive rankers, running our method on datasets from seemingly related evaluation campaigns such as those in TREC and INEX is not feasible. We are constrained by the size of datasets, i.e., we need datasets that are sufficiently large (thousands of queries) and time-stamped, which excludes the aforementioned evaluation campaigns, and hence direct comparison to results obtained there. Furthermore, employing existing fielded retrieval methods such as BM25F as baselines is not feasible either, as they are exceedingly expensive to retrain online, as discussed in Section 2.

For these reasons we consider the following supervised baselines in our experiments; KBER_{sim} is an online learning classification-based entity ranker, that employs field similarity features on entity representations composed of KB description sources (i.e., title, text, categories, anchors, redirects and links fields). KBER is the same baseline system, extended with the full set of features (described in §4.2). Finally, DCER_{na} is a non-adaptive baseline: it incorporates all external description sources, and all features as our proposed DCER method, but does not periodically retrain.

5.1 Data alignment

In our experiments we update the fields that jointly represent an entity with external descriptions that come in a streaming manner, from a range of heterogeneous external description sources. This assumes that all data sources run in parallel in terms of time. In a real-world setting this assumption may not always hold as systems need to integrate historical data sources that span different time periods and are of different size for bootstrapping. We simulate this scenario by choosing data sources that do not originate from the same time period nor span the same amount of time (see also Table 1). To remedy this, we introduce a method for time-aligning all data sources (which range from 2009 to 2014) to the timeline of the query log (which dates from 2006). We apply a *source-time* transformation to mitigate the dependence of content popularity on time and when it was created [36, 37]. Each query is treated as a time unit, and we distribute the expansions from the different sources over the queries, as opposed to obeying the misaligned timestamps from the query log and expansion sources.

To illustrate: given n queries and a total of k items for a given expansion source, after each query we update the entity representations with $\frac{n}{k}$ expansions of that particular expansion source. In our dataset we have 32,901 queries, 52,631 tweets, and 4,429,692 tags. After each query we distribute 1 query, 2 tweets, and 135 tags over the entities in the index. Mapping real time to source time evenly spreads the content of each data source within the timespan of the query log. This smooths out bursts but retains the same distribution of content over entities (in terms of, e.g., entity popularity). The diminishing effect on burstiness is desirable in the case of misaligned corpora, as bursts are informative of news events, which would not co-occur in the different data sources. Although our re-aligned corpora cannot match the quality of real parallel corpora, our method offers a robust lower bound to understand the utility of collective dynamic entity representations of our method. We reiterate that the goal of this paper is to study the effect of dynamic entity representations, and adapting rankers, not to leverage temporal features.

5.2 Machine learning

We apply machine learning for learning how to weight the different fields that make up an entity representation for optimal retrieval effectiveness. In response to a query, we first generate an initial set of candidate entities by retrieving the top-k entities to limit the required computational resources for extracting all features for all documents in the collection [23]. Our top-k retrieval method involves ranking all entities using our similarity function (described in §4.2.1), where we collapse the fielded entity representation into a single document.[3] We choose Random Forests as our machine learning algorithm because it has proven robust in a range of diverse tasks (e.g., [28]), and can produce confidence scores that we employ as ranking signal. In our experiments, we set the number of trees to 500 and the number of features each decision tree considers for the best split to $\sqrt{|\Omega|}$.

5.3 Evaluation

For evaluating our method's adaptivity and performance over time, we create a set of incremental time-based train/test splits as in [7]. We first split the query log into K chunks of size N: $\{C_1, C_2, C_3, \ldots, C_K\}$. We then allocate the first chunk (C_1) for training the classifier and start iteratively evaluating each succeeding query. Once the second chunk of queries (C_2) has been evaluated, we expand the training set with it and retrain the classifier. We then continue evaluating the next chunk of queries (C_3). This procedure is repeated, continually expanding the training set and retraining the classifier with N queries (we set N=500 in our experiments). In this scenario, users' clicks are treated as ground truth and the classifier's goal is to rank clicked entities at position 1. We do not distinguish between clicks (e.g., satisfied clicks and non-

[3] We set $k = 20$ as it has shown a fair tradeoff between high recall (80.1% on our development set) and low computational expense.

Table 2: **Performance of field similarity-based entity ranking methods using KB entity representations ($\texttt{KBER}_{sim}$) and dynamic collective entity representations ($\texttt{DCER}_{sim}$) in terms of MAP and P@1. Significance tested against $\texttt{KBER}_{sim}$. Oracle marks upper bound performance given our top-k scenario.**

Run	MAP	P@1
KBER_{sim}	0.5579	0.4967
DCER_{sim}	**0.5971**▲	**0.5573**▲
Oracle	0.6653	0.6653

satisfied clicks), and we leave more advanced user models, e.g., which incorporate skips, as future work.

To show the robustness of our method we apply five-fold cross-validation over each run, i.e., we generate five alternatively ordered query logs by shuffling the queries. We keep the order of the dynamic description sources fixed to avoid conflating the effect of queries' order with that of the description sources.

Since we are interested in how our method behaves over time, we plot the MAP at each query over the five-folds, as opposed to averaging the scores over all chunks across folds (as in [7]) and losing this temporal dimension. In addition to reporting MAP, we report on P@1, as there is only a single relevant entity per query in our experimental setup. We test for statistical significance using a two-tailed paired t-test. Significant differences are marked ▲ for $\alpha = 0.01$.

6. RESULTS AND ANALYSIS

We report on the experimental results for each of our three experiments, in turn, and provide an analysis of the results to better understand the behavior of our method.

6.1 Dynamic collective entity representations

In our first experiment, we explore the impact of the description sources we use for constructing dynamic collective entity representations. We compare the $\texttt{KBER}_{sim}$ baseline, which incorporates field similarity on KB descriptions, to our $\texttt{DCER}_{sim}$ method, which incorporates field similarity features on all description sources (web anchors, tweets, tags, and queries). Table 2 shows the performance in terms of MAP and P@1 of the baseline ($\texttt{KBER}_{sim}$) and $\texttt{DCER}_{sim}$ after observing all queries in our dataset. We include an oracle run as a performance upper bound given our top-k retrieval scenario.

The results show that the dynamic collective entity representations manage to significantly outperform the KB entity representations for both metrics, and that $\texttt{DCER}_{sim}$ presents the correct entity at the top of the ranking for over 55% of the queries.

Next, we look into the impact on performance of individual description sources for our dynamic collective entity representations. We add each source individually to the $\texttt{KBER}_{sim}$ baseline. Figure 2 shows how each individual description source contributes to more effective ranking, with `KB+tags` narrowly outperforming `KB+web` as the best single source. Combining all sources into one, yields the best results, outperforming `KB+tags` by more than 3%. We observe that after about 18,000 queries, `KB+tags` overtakes the (static) `KB+web` method, suggesting that newly incoming tags yield higher ranking effectiveness. All runs show an upward trend and seem to level out around the 30,000th query. This pattern is seen across ranking methods, which indicates that the upward trend can be attributed to the addition of more training data (queries).

Table 3 lists the results of all methods along with the improvement rate (relative improvement when going from 10,000 to all queries). The runs that incorporate dynamic description sources (i.e., `KB+tags`, `KB+tweets`, and `KB+queries`) show the highest relative improvements (at 6.4%, 6.1% and 6.9% respectively). Interestingly, for P@1, the `KB+queries` method yields a substantial relative improvement (+8.9%), indicating that the added queries provide a strong signal for ranking the clicked entities at the top.

The comparatively lower learning rates of methods that incorporate only static description sources ($\texttt{KBER}_{sim}$ and `KB+web` yield relative improvements of +5.8% and +5.5%, respectively), suggest that the entity content from dynamic description sources effectively contributes to higher ranking performance as the entity representations change and the ranker is able to reach a new optimum. $\texttt{DCER}_{sim}$, the method that incorporates all available description sources, shows a comparatively lower relative improvement, which is likely due to it hitting a ceiling, and not much relative improvement can be gained.

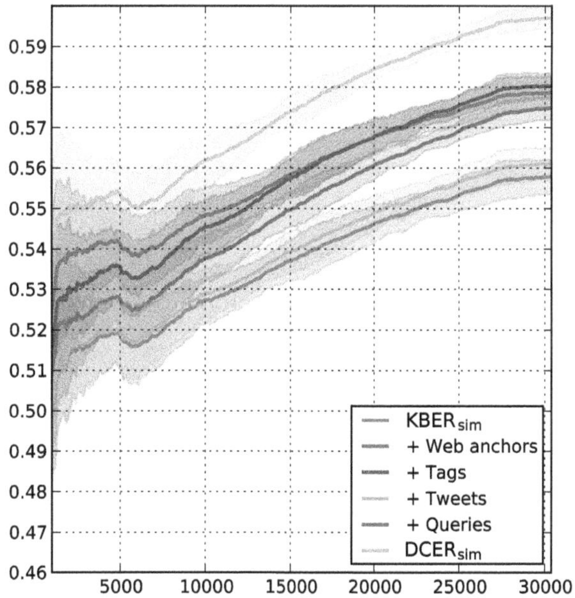

Figure 2: Impact on performance of individual description sources. MAP on the y-axis, number of queries on the x-axis. The line represents MAP, averaged over 5-folds. Standard deviation is shown as a shade around the line. This plot is best viewed in color.

Table 3: Comparison of relative improvement between runs with different field similarity features. We report on MAP and P@1 at query 10,000 and the last query. Rate corresponds to the percentage of improvement between the 10,000th and final query. Significance tested against $\texttt{KBER}_{sim}$.

Run	MAP (10k)	MAP (end)	Rate	P@1 (10k)	P@1 (end)	Rate
KBER_{sim}	0.5274	0.5579	+5.8%	0.4648	0.4967	+6.9%
KB+Web_{sim}	0.5485	0.5787▲	+5.5%	0.4965	0.5282▲	+6.4%
KB+Tags_{sim}	0.5455	0.5804▲	+6.4%	0.4930	0.5317▲	+7.8%
KB+Tweets_{sim}	0.5290	0.5612▲	+6.1%	0.4673	0.5021▲	+7.5%
KB+Queries_{sim}	0.5379	0.5750▲	**+6.9%**	0.4813	0.5242▲	**+8.9%**
DCER_{sim}	0.5620	**0.5971**▲	+6.2%	0.5178	**0.5573**▲	+7.6%

6.1.1 Feature weights over time

A unique property in our scenario is that, over time, more training data is added to the system, and more descriptions from dynamic sources come in, both of which are expected to improve system's performance. To better understand our system's behavior, we look into the learned feature weights for both a static system and our dynamic one at each retraining interval. Figure 3 shows the weights for six static fields (categories, title, anchors, links, text, redirects) and three dynamic fields (queries, tweets, tags).

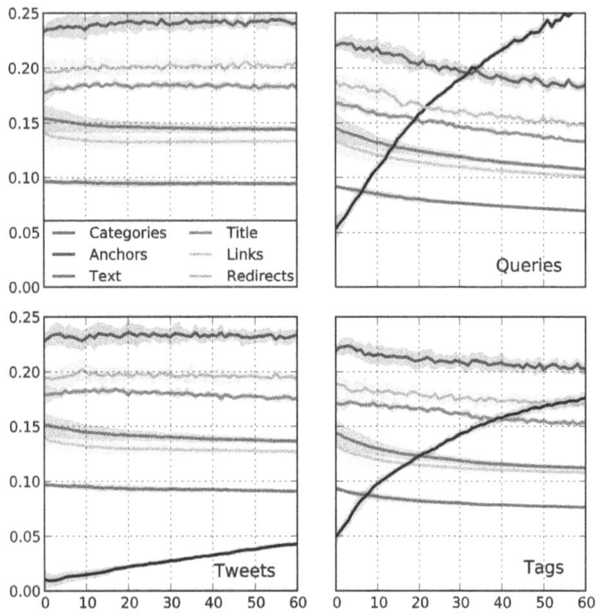

Figure 3: Feature weights over time: y-axis shows (relative) feature weights, x-axis shows each chunk of 500 queries where the ranker is retrained. Starting from top left in a clock-wise direction we show the following runs: KBER$_{sim}$ (baseline), KB+Queries, KB+Tags, KB+Tweets. The black line shows the dynamic description source's weight. This plot is best viewed in color.

The KBER$_{sim}$ baseline shows little change in the feature weights as more training data is added. The anchors' weight increases slightly, while the text and categories fields' weights steadily decline over time. The latter two features show a steadily decreasing standard deviation, indicating that the ranker becomes more confident in the assigned weights.

For KB+queries it is apparent that the queries field weight increases substantially as both the ranking method receives more training data and the entity representations receive more content from the queries description source. At the same time, anchors, redirects, and title field weights, which were assigned consistently high weights in KBER$_{sim}$, seem to pay for the increase of the importance of queries. Text, category, and links show similar patterns to the baseline run; steadily declining weights, converging in terms of a decreasing standard deviation.

The KB+tags run shows a similar pattern as KB+queries: we observe an increase over time of the weight assigned to the field that holds content from the tag description source, at the cost of original KB fields, resulting in improved ranking effectiveness. Looking at KB+tweets, however, we observe a different pattern. The tweets field starts out with a very low weight, and although the weight steadily increases, it remains low. The ranker here, too, becomes more confident on this source's weight, with the standard deviation dissolving over time. Looking at the higher performance of KB+tweets in comparison to the KBER$_{sim}$ baseline, together with the field's weight increasing over time, we can conclude that the tweets that are added to the entity representations over time provide added value.

6.2 Modeling field importance

In our second experiment, we turn to the contribution of the additional field and entity importance features. Table 4 lists the results of the best performing run with only field similarity features (DCER$_{sim}$), the KBER baseline that incorporates the full set of features, and our proposed DCER method which likewise incorporates the full set of features.

Table 4: Comparison of relative improvement between the KBER baseline with field importance features for KB fields, and our DCER method with these features for all fields. We also show the best performing run without field and entity importance features. Significance tested against KBER.

Run	MAP (10k)	MAP (end)	Rate	P@1 (10k)	P@1 (end)	Rate
Oracle	–	0.6653	–	–	0.6653	–
DCER$_{sim}$	0.5620	0.5971	+6.2%	0.5178	0.5573	+7.6%
KBER	0.5853	0.6129	+4.7%	0.5559	0.5831	+4.9%
DCER	0.5923	**0.6200**$^\blacktriangle$	+4.7%	0.5655	**0.5925**$^\blacktriangle$	+4.8%

The results show that modeling field and entity importance significantly improves effectiveness of both the KBER$_{sim}$ baseline and the DCER$_{sim}$ runs. After running through the entire dataset, the performance of DCER approaches that of the oracle run which also explains why the differences between the two approaches here is rather small: we are very close to the maximum achievable score.

Figure 4 shows the performance of the two approaches over time. The pattern is similar to the one in Section 6.1: both lines show a steady increase, while DCER maintains to be the best performing.

6.3 Ranker adaptivity

In our third experiment, we compare our adaptive ranker (DCER), which is continuously retrained, to a non-adaptive baseline (DCER$_{na}$), which is only trained once at the start and is not retrained.

Table 5: Comparing relative improvement between runs with and without an adaptive ranker. Statistical significance tested against their non-adaptive counterparts.

Run	Adaptive	MAP	P@1
KBER$_{na}$	no	0.5198	0.4392
KBER	yes	0.5579$^\blacktriangle$	0.4967$^\blacktriangle$
DCER$_{na}$	no	0.5872	0.5408
DCER	yes	**0.5971**$^\blacktriangle$	**0.5573**$^\blacktriangle$

Results in Table 5 show that incrementally re-training the ranker is beneficial to entity ranking effectiveness. For both KBER and DCER we see a substantial improvement when moving from one single batch training to continuously retraining the ranker. To better understand this behavior, we plot in Figure 5 the performance of all runs we consider over time and at the same time; Table 6 provides the detailed scores. Broadly speaking we observe similar patterns between adaptive and non-adaptive methods, and we identify three interesting points. First, for the non-adaptive methods, the absolute performance is substantially lower across the board. Second,

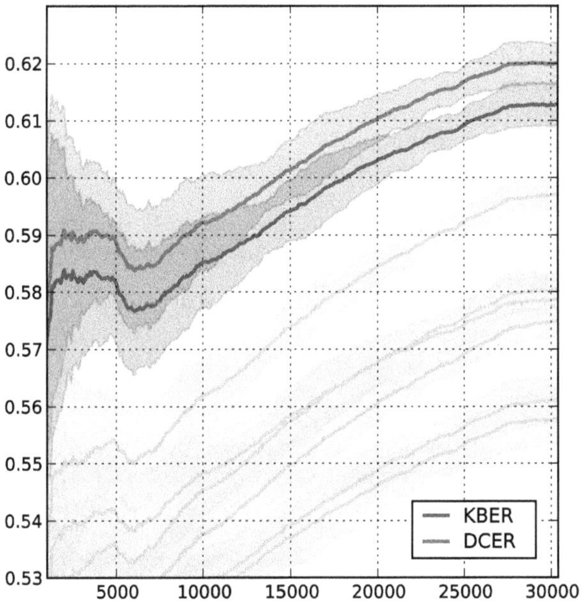

Figure 4: Runs with field similarity, field importance, and entity importance features. MAP on the y-axis, number of queries on the x-axis. The line represents MAP, averaged over 5-folds. Standard deviation is shown as a shade around the line. This plot is best viewed in color.

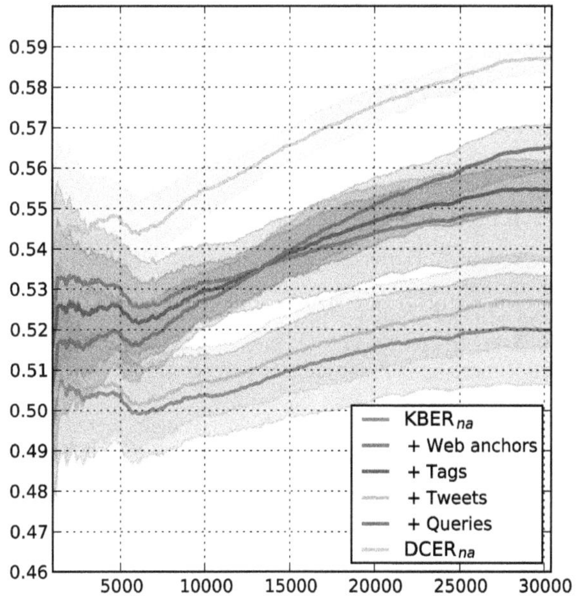

Figure 5: Individual description sources with nonadaptive ranker. MAP on the y-axis, number of queries on the x-axis. The line represents MAP, averaged over 5-folds. Standard deviation is shown as a shade around the line. This plot is best viewed in color.

for the adaptive methods, the standard deviation (as shown in Figures 2 and 5) is substantially lower, which indicates that retraining increases the ranking method's confidence in optimally combining the different descriptions for the entity representation. Third, the learning rates in the adaptive setting are substantially higher, reaffirming our observation that learning a single global feature weight vector is not optimal.

Table 6: Comparing relative improvement between non-adaptive runs. Significance tested against KBER$_{na}$.

Run	MAP (10k)	MAP (end)	Rate	P@1 (10k)	P@1 (end)	Rate
KBER$_{na}$	0.5040	0.5198	+3.1%	0.4286	0.4392	+2.5%
KB+Web$_{na}$	0.5318	0.5493▲	+3.3%	0.4698	0.4829▲	+2.8%
KB+Tags$_{na}$	0.5298	0.5546▲	+4.7%	0.4671	0.4904▲	+5.0%
KB+Tweets$_{na}$	0.5074	0.5269▲	+3.8%	0.4334	0.4490▲	+3.6%
KB+Queries$_{na}$	0.5275	0.5650▲	**+7.1%**	0.4659	0.5090▲	+9.2%
DCER$_{na}$	0.5548	**0.5872**▲	+5.8%	0.5063	0.5408▲	+6.8%

Table 6 shows that the difference in learning rates between methods that only incorporate static description sources (`KBER`, `KB+web`) and methods that incorporate dynamic sources is pronounced, in particular for the tags and queries sources. This indicates that even with fixed feature weights, the content that comes in from the dynamic description sources yields an improvement in entity ranking effectiveness. Finally, the methods that only incorporate static description sources also show lower learning rates than their adaptive counterparts, which indicates that retraining and adapting feature weights is desirable even with static entity representations.

7. CONCLUSIONS

In this paper we have presented a method for constructing dynamic collective entity representations by leveraging collective intelligence to improve entity ranking. Our results demonstrate that incorporating dynamic description sources into dynamic collective entity representations enables a better matching of users' queries to entities. Furthermore, we show how continuously updating the ranker leads to improved ranking effectiveness in dynamic collective entity representations.

Our study of the impact of dynamic collective entity representations was performed in a controlled scenario, where we collect and leverage different data sources. One restriction of working with these freely available resources is that it proves hard to find aligned and sizeable datasets. In particular, the temporal misalignment between different corpora prevents the analysis of temporal patterns that may span across sources (e.g., queries and tweets showing similar activity around entities when news events unfold). In part, these restrictions can be circumvented, e.g., increasing the (comparatively) low number of tweets by enriching them through e.g., entity linking methods [25], where entities identified in tweets could be expanded. Additional challenges and opportunities may arise when increasing the scale of the data collections. Opportunities may lie in exploiting session or user information for more effective use of user interaction signals. Challenges include so-called "swamping" [31] or "document vector saturation" [19], i.e., entity drift that is more prone to happen when the size of the data collections increase.

Acknowledgments. This research was supported by Amsterdam Data Science, the Dutch national program COMMIT, Elsevier, the European Community's Seventh Framework Programme (FP7/2007-2013) under grant agreement nr 312827 (VOX-Pol), the ESF Research Network Program ELIAS, the Royal Dutch Academy of Sciences (KNAW) under the Elite Network Shifts project, the Microsoft Research Ph.D. program, the Netherlands eScience Center under project nr 027.012.105, the Netherlands Institute for Sound and Vision, the Netherlands Organisation for Scientific Research (NWO) under project nrs 727.011.005, 612.001.116, HOR-11-10, 640.006.013, 612.066.930, CI-14-25, SH-322-15, 652.002.001, the Yahoo Faculty Research and Engagement Program, and Yandex. All content represents the opinion of the authors, which is not necessarily shared or endorsed by their respective employers and/or sponsors.

REFERENCES

[1] E. Amitay, A. Darlow, D. Konopnicki, and U. Weiss. Queries as anchors: selection by association. In *HYPERTEXT '05*, pages 193–201, 2005.

[2] K. Balog and K. Nørvåg. On the use of semantic knowledge bases for temporally-aware entity retrieval. In *Proceedings of ESAIR '12*, pages 1–2, 2012.

[3] K. Balog, M. Bron, and M. de Rijke. Category-based query modeling for entity search. In *ECIR '10*, pages 319–331, 2010.

[4] K. Balog, A. de Vries, P. Serdyukov, P. Thomas, and T. Westerveld. Overview of the TREC 2009 entity track. In *TREC '09*, 2010.

[5] K. Balog, P. Serdyukov, and A. de Vries. Overview of the TREC 2010 entity track. In *TREC '10*, 2011.

[6] S. Bao, G. Xue, X. Wu, Y. Yu, B. Fei, and Z. Su. Optimizing web search using social annotations. In *WWW '07*, pages 501–510, 2007.

[7] R. Bekkerman, A. McCallum, and G. Huang. Automatic categorization of email into folders: Benchmark experiments on Enron and SRI corpora. *Center for Intelligent Information Retrieval, Technical Report IR*, 418, 2004.

[8] B. Billerbeck, G. Demartini, C. Firan, T. Iofciu, and R. Krestel. Ranking entities using web search query logs. In *ECDL '10*, pages 273–281, 2010.

[9] A. Broder, E. Gabrilovich, V. Josifovski, G. Mavromatis, D. Metzler, and J. Wang. Exploiting site-level information to improve web search. In *CIKM '10*, pages 1393–1396, 2010.

[10] A. de Vries, A.-M. Vercoustre, J. A. Thom, N. Craswell, and M. Lalmas. Overview of the INEX 2007 entity ranking track. In *INEX '07*, pages 245–251, 2008.

[11] G. Demartini, A. de Vries, T. Iofciu, and J. Zhu. Overview of the INEX 2008 entity ranking track. In *INEX '08*, pages 243–252, 2009.

[12] G. Demartini, T. Iofciu, and A. de Vries. Overview of the INEX 2009 entity ranking track. In *INEX '09*, pages 254–264, 2010.

[13] M. Efron, P. Organisciak, and K. Fenlon. Improving retrieval of short texts through document expansion. In *SIGIR '12*, pages 911–920, 2012.

[14] N. Eiron and K. S. McCurley. Analysis of anchor text for web search. In *SIGIR '03*, pages 459–460, 2003.

[15] J. Gao, W. Yuan, X. Li, K. Deng, and J.-Y. Nie. Smoothing clickthrough data for web search ranking. In *SIGIR '09*, pages 355–362, 2009.

[16] K. Hofmann, S. Whiteson, and M. de Rijke. A probabilistic method for inferring preferences from clicks. In *CIKM '11*, pages 249–258, 2011.

[17] K. Hong, P. Pei, Y.-Y. Wang, and D. Hakkani-Tur. Entity ranking for descriptive queries. In *SLT '14*, 2014.

[18] R. Kaptein, P. Serdyukov, A. de Vries, and J. Kamps. Entity ranking using wikipedia as a pivot. In *CIKM '10*, pages 69–78, 2010.

[19] C. Kemp and K. Ramamohanarao. Long-term learning for web search engines. In *PKDD '02*, pages 263–274, 2002.

[20] R. Kumar and A. Tomkins. A characterization of online browsing behavior. In *WWW '10*, pages 561–570, 2010.

[21] C.-J. Lee and W. B. Croft. Incorporating social anchors for ad hoc retrieval. In *OAIR '13*, pages 181–188, 2013.

[22] F. Li, M. L. Lee, and W. Hsu. Entity profiling with varying source reliabilities. In *KDD '14*, pages 1146–1155, 2014.

[23] T.-Y. Liu. Learning to rank for information retrieval. *FnTIR*, 3(3):225–331, 2009.

[24] C. Macdonald, R. L. Santos, I. Ounis, and B. He. About learning models with multiple query-dependent features. *ACM TOIS*, 31(3):11:1–11:39, 2013.

[25] E. Meij, W. Weerkamp, and M. de Rijke. Adding semantics to microblog posts. In *WSDM '12*, pages 563–572, 2012.

[26] D. Metzler, J. Novak, H. Cui, and S. Reddy. Building enriched document representations using aggregated anchor text. In *SIGIR '09*, pages 219–226, 2009.

[27] G. Mishne and J. Lin. Twanchor text: A preliminary study of the value of tweets as anchor text. In *SIGIR '12*, pages 1159–1160, 2012.

[28] A. Mohan, Z. Chen, and K. Q. Weinberger. Web-search ranking with initialized gradient boosted regression trees. *JMLR Workshop and Conference Proceedings*, 14:77–89, 2011.

[29] D. Mottin, T. Palpanas, and Y. Velegrakis. Entity ranking using click-log information. *Intelligent Data Analysis*, 17(5): 837–856, 2013.

[30] M. Noll and C. Meinel. The metadata triumvirate: Social annotations, anchor texts and search queries. In *International Conference on Web Intelligence and Intelligent Agent Technology (WI-IAT '08)*, pages 640–647, 2008.

[31] S. Robertson, H. Zaragoza, and M. Taylor. Simple bm25 extension to multiple weighted fields. In *CIKM '04*, pages 42–49, 2004.

[32] F. Scholer, H. E. Williams, and A. Turpin. Query association surrogates for web search: Research articles. *JASIST*, 55(7): 637–650, 2004.

[33] W. Shen, J. Wang, and J. Han. Entity linking with a knowledge base: Issues, techniques, and solutions. *TKDE*, 27(2):443–460, 2014.

[34] A. Singhal and F. Pereira. Document expansion for speech retrieval. In *SIGIR '99*, pages 34–41, 1999.

[35] K. M. Svore and C. J. Burges. A machine learning approach for improved bm25 retrieval. In *CIKM '09*, pages 1811–1814, 2009.

[36] G. Szabo and B. A. Huberman. Predicting the popularity of online content. *CACM*, 53(8):80–88, 2010.

[37] M. Tsagkias, W. Weerkamp, and M. de Rijke. News comments: Exploring, modeling, and online prediction. In *ECIR '10*, pages 191–203, 2010.

[38] A.-M. Vercoustre, J. A. Thom, and J. Pehcevski. Entity ranking in wikipedia. In *SAC '08*, pages 1101–1106, 2008.

[39] T. Westerveld, W. Kraaij, and D. Hiemstra. Retrieving web pages using content, links, urls and anchors. In *TREC '01*, 2001.

[40] M. Wu, D. Hawking, A. Turpin, and F. Scholer. Using anchor text for homepage and topic distillation search tasks. *JASIST*, 63(6):1235–1255, 2012.

[41] G.-R. Xue, H.-J. Zeng, Z. Chen, Y. Yu, W.-Y. Ma, W. Xi, and W. Fan. Optimizing web search using web click-through data. In *CIKM '04*, pages 118–126, 2004.

[42] H. Zaragoza, N. Craswell, M. Taylor, S. Saria, and S. Robertson. Microsoft Cambridge at TREC-13: Web and hard tracks. In *TREC '04*, 2004.

Relationship Queries on Extended Knowledge Graphs

Mohamed Yahya[1], Denilson Barbosa[2], Klaus Berberich[1], Qiuyue Wang[3], Gerhard Weikum[1]
[1]Max-Planck Institute for Informatics [2]University of Alberta [3]Renmin University of China
{myahya, kberberi, weikum}@mpi-inf.mpg.de
denilson@ualberta.ca qiuyuew@ruc.edu.cn

ABSTRACT

Entity search over text corpora is not geared for relationship queries where answers are tuples of related entities and where a query often requires joining cues from multiple documents. With large knowledge graphs, structured querying on their relational facts is an alternative, but often suffers from poor recall because of mismatches between user queries and the knowledge graph or because of weakly populated relations.

This paper presents the TriniT search engine for querying and ranking on extended knowledge graphs that combine relational facts with textual web contents. Our query language is designed on the paradigm of SPO triple patterns, but is more expressive, supporting textual phrases for each of the SPO arguments. We present a model for automatic query relaxation to compensate for mismatches between the data and a user's query. Query answers – tuples of entities – are ranked by a statistical language model. We present experiments with different benchmarks, including complex relationship queries, over a combination of the Yago knowledge graph and the entity-annotated ClueWeb'09 corpus.

Keywords

Relationship Queries; Extended Knowledge Graphs; Query Relaxation

1. INTRODUCTION

1.1 Motivation and Problem

Searching for entities and associated properties has received much attention for both web contents and enterprise documents. Examples are queries for "musicians who contributed to movie soundtracks" or "companies that acquired Internet startups". IR-centric approaches typically associate entities with statistical language models in order to match and rank entity mentions and surrounding phrases in text corpora [3]. Semantic-Web-style approaches, on the other hand, rather tap structured knowledge graphs (KGs) such as Freebase or Linked Open Data (LOD) collections such as combinations of DBpedia, Yago, and MusicBrainz, and use SPARQL queries to retrieve relevant RDF triples [16].

Neither of these paradigms provides good support for *relationship queries* that connect multiple entities in a specific way and *return tuples of connected entities*. Consider, for example, the task of finding songs that appear in movies and returning a list of ⟨song, movie⟩ pairs. This cannot be fully expressed by IR-centric entity search which is bound to return spurious results where a movie is merely mentioned in the textual proximity of a song (e.g., "My Way" and the film "The Man with the Golden Arm" in a Frank Sinatra biography). On the other hand, the SPARQL language supports expressive and precise queries over RDF graphs of entity-relationship triples, but its results are limited by the properties (i.e., relation types, binary predicates) and facts (i.e., relation instances, predicate arguments) that the underlying KG or LOD collection contains. So none of the established paradigms can adequately cope with relationship queries.

Examples: In principle, the above example could be formulated by the following SPARQL query:

```
SELECT ?s ?m WHERE {
  ?s type song .  ?m type movie .  ?s musicInFilm ?m }
```

where `?s` and `?m` are variables and the second line contains three triple patterns over the subject-predicate-object (SPO) triples of the underlying KG. The query should return bindings for song-movie pairs that are in the desired relationship. However, this works only if the KG does indeed offer the predicate *musicInFilm* and that predicate is sufficiently well populated. If the KG instead contained predicates *filmHasSoundtrack* of type *movie* × *album* and *albumContainsSong* of type *album* × *song*, the user would need to formulate a very different query and non-expert users would typically fail to get this right. Even if the user succeeded in posing the best query formulation, the answers would be limited by the facts of the KG, while the web or social media could potentially hold many additional answers.

Similar cases arise in domains like business or sports, for example, when searching for "South-American football players and European championships that they have won" (with answers such as Lionel Messi and the UEFA Champions League). Here one challenge that users would struggle with is to properly formulate the two-hop join query with triple patterns `?p type player . ?p playedFor ?t . ?t won ?c . ?t type footballClub` as KGs associate championships with teams, not players. IR-style entity search would be more convenient for users, but loses precision and would be mis-

WSDM'16, February 22–25, 2016, San Francisco, CA, USA.

ISBN 978-1-4503-3716-8/16/02...$15.00
DOI: http://dx.doi.org/10.1145/2835776.2835795

led by co-occuring players and teams who were opponents in final matches.

Problem Statement: The above information needs are examples of *relationship queries*, which we define here as SPARQL-like SPO queries with two or more distinct variables joined by one or more relationships. Such queries typically have two or more variables in their projection list (the `SELECT` clause). This is in contrast to entity search queries where there is a single variable in the query, whose bindings are the query result. The problem addressed in this work is how to express and process *relationship queries* over both *structured KGs and unstructured text/web corpora*. We emphasize the coexistence and combination of KG and text, as they complement each other in terms of potential answers.

Although we cast this problem into a structured query language like SPARQL (and will extend this language), it should be noted that users such as analysts or journalists need a less formal UI. Our methods can provide a form-filling UI, which is user-friendly yet allows to generate (extended) SPARQL queries. Natural-language question answering (QA) [19] and the translation of questions into queries [7, 13, 35] would be a suitable UI as well.

1.2 Approach and Contribution

We developed a comprehensive system, TriniT (for "Triples & Text"), to address the problem of relationship queries. TriniT builds on three insights and novel contributions.

First, we extend a KG by running Open Information Extraction (OIE) techniques [24] on a large Web corpus and capturing triples of textual expressions along with their surrounding contexts. By means of Named Entity Disambiguation (NED) techniques [17], we obtain a combined dataset with structured facts and text triples as first-class citizens. Prior work [9–11] has looked into the interplay of KG and text corpora, but limited this to either using distant knowledge for enhancing text search or using textual witnesses for fact statistics in the KG.

Second, for querying the extended KG, XKG for short, we extend the SPARQL notion of triple patterns to allow each of the SPO components to be a URI denoting entities, classes or predicates, or a typed literal (e.g., dates), or a textual phrase. Note that the W3C standard for SPARQL requires S and P to be URI's and O to be a URI or a literal. By supporting text in each of the SPO positions, we can formulate queries that tap into both structured and textual triples simultaneously. For example, we can find more song-movie pairs, beyond what the KG offers, by the triple pattern `?s "appeared in" ?m` (in conjunction with other triple patterns). Prior work on extending SPARQL with text predicates [11] has treated text as annotations of entire SPO facts, typically based on keyphrases that are associated with the S and O entities, and advocated SPO+text (SPOX) quad patterns. On many queries, this loses precision as the system cannot distinguish anymore if the X component specifically refers to S, P, or O.

Third, despite the additional convenience of using text for SPO components, the potential mismatch between the user's vocabulary and the names and phrases in the KG and XKG still makes proper query formulation a difficult task. To overcome this obstacle, TriniT provides a framework for query relaxation rules, and algorithms to automatically apply rules to generate relaxed queries that yield higher recall. For example, a user-provided triple pattern `?p won ?c` for the (football player, championship) example query can be automatically rewritten into a text-based pattern `?p "has won" ?c` (which can find more matches in the text corpus with entity linkage to the KG) or into the more elaborate and appropriate patterns `?p playedFor ?t . ?t won ?c`. The answer-ranking model of TriniT considers the potential target drift of such relaxations, and computes overall rankings for the results of different rewritings. Prior work on query relaxation for RDF and XML data [1, 11, 12] was restricted to simple structural rewritings like replacing a predicate by a variable or lexical rewritings like replacing a class with a super-class.

The novel contributions of this work can be summarized as follows:

- an extension of SPARQL triple patterns supporting expressive search over extended KGs in a convenient manner, along with a judiciously designed answer-ranking model;
- a framework and algorithms for relaxation rules that support the automatic rewriting of user queries to improve recall while preserving the query focus;
- experiments with complex relationship queries over the combination of the YAGO knowledge graph and the ClubWeb'09 corpus, demonstrating the viability and benefits of our model and methods.

2. DATA MODEL AND QUERY LANGUAGE

2.1 Extended Knowledge Graphs

In the standard setting of an RDF-based knowledge graph (KG), we have two sets of objects: i) *resources* R encoded as URI's for entities, classes, or predicates (called properties in RDF), and ii) *literals* L for values like numbers, dates, etc. Predicates $P \subseteq R$ are a special kind of resource used to create facts that describe resources.

Definition 1 (Knowledge Graph (KG)). *A knowledge graph (KG) is a set of triples from* $(R \times R \times R) \cup (R \times R \times L)$.

The three components of a triple are called the *subject*, *predicate*, and *object*, or SPO for short. When O is a resource, like an entity or class, the triple captures a relationship (e.g., someone's spouse or membership in a semantic class); when O is a literal, the triple expresses an attribute value for an entity (e.g., someone's birthdate or salary). A predicate can be seen as a binary relation, whose arguments are the subject and object. Alternatively, the subject and object can be seen as vertices connected by an edge labeled with the predicate.

However big a KG could be, it is bound to provide incomplete knowledge, as there is always additional detail and finesse that could be found in additional text sources. The goal of extending a KG is to account for missing entities, classes, predicates, or facts. To do this, we combine the KG with one or more textual corpora annotated with entities and predicates, some of which may already exist in the KG whereas others are missing so far. The triples are extracted from text by information extraction (IE) techniques, and become additional knowledge which can be used to bridge the gap between the information needs of users and the KG. More specifically, we use Open IE methods like [24] to extract triples that consist of two noun phrases (for S and O) that are connected by a noun phrase, verb phrase, or a preposition (for P). We additionally employ methods for

Named Entity Disambiguation (NED) like [17] to map the two noun phrases into entities registered in the KG. This process is prone to error, but can be tuned to favor precision over recall. In our experimental studies, the IE and NED error rates are low, and their benefit clearly outweighs the errors.

As an example, suppose that the original KG contains the triples in the left column of Table 1 (for simplicity we use names for entities, classes, and predicates rather than URI's which would be required by the official RDF standard).

Additionally, assume that Open IE has identified further triples shown in the right column of Table 1 where some of the SPO components are mere text phrases as they could not be mapped to any entity, class, or predicate in the KG. The union of all these triples forms the extended knowledge graph, XKG for short. For an XKG we do no longer refer to resources and literals, but instead collectively call all of these simply tokens C.

Definition 2 (Extended Knowledge Graph (XKG)). *An extended knowledge graph (XKG) is a bag of triples over tokens; that is, triples are from* $C \times C \times C$.

The XKG being treated as a bag of triples takes into account that the IE process can produce the same triple many times from different documents. We exploit this kind of redundancy – not present in the original pure KG – in our ranking model.

2.2 Triple Pattern Queries

We now define the triple pattern query language for querying XKGs. Let V be an infinite set of variables, distinct from tokens, and always prefixed with a question mark.

Definition 3 (Triple Pattern and its Results). *A triple pattern q is a triple from $V \cup C \times V \cup C \times V \cup C$. The results of a triple pattern are triples t from the XKG such that the tokens in q that are not variables are matched by t. For the variables in q, the corresponding tokens in t are called bindings.*

Examples of triple patterns are: `?x usedIn KillBill` (with a predicate and an entity as tokens) and `?x` *"appears in" "Kill Bill Vol 1"* (with two phrases as tokens).

Definition 4 (Query). *A query $Q = \{q_1, ...q_n\}$ is a set of triple patterns q_i and a projection list $P(Q)$ of variables (typically with variables occurring in multiple q_i, forming join predicates). We require the join graph that is constituted by the q_i as vertices and edges between them whenever two of the triple patterns share a variable, to be a connected graph (to avoid computing Cartesian products). $P(Q)$ is a (usually proper) subset of the variables in Q, defining the output structure (typically entity tuples).*

Relationship queries are those containing at least two distinct variables, requiring one or more relationships to join them. In such queries, the projection list typically contains two or more variables ($|P(Q)| \geq 2$), in which case answers are proper tuples. This is in contrast with traditional entity search which have a single variable, hence $|P(Q)| = 1$.

Definition 5 (Query Answer). *For query Q, an answer (a) is a mapping of the variables in Q to tokens in C. Applying an answer (a) to a triple pattern $q_i \in Q$ results in the triple t_i, we denote this by $a(q_i) = t_i$. The restriction of a query answer to bindings of variables in $P(Q)$ is called a projected answer, denoted a_P.*

Example query 1: Finding movies with British songs could be expressed as:

```
SELECT ?s ?m WHERE {
   ?s type song .  ?m type movie .  ?s usedIn ?m .
   ?s performedBy ?x .  ?x bornIn UK }
```

Note that the KG in Table 1 alone would have no results to this query, whereas the XKG yields the desired result (`WalterMitty, SpaceOddity`). Alternatively to the triple pattern `?a` *"born"* `UK`, we could specify the condition `?a ?p` *"British"*. Neither of these is easy to formulate by a user who does not know the XKG data really well.

Example query 2: Finding movies with American songs and their singers requires both elaborate use of long paths in the XKG (i.e., join chains) and the use of text-based triples in the XKG:

```
SELECT ?m ?s ?x WHERE {
   ?s type song .  ?m type movie .
   ?m hasSoundtrack ?a .  ?a contains ?s .
   ?s performedBy ?x .  ?x ?p "American" }
```

Again, formulating such a sophisticated query is awfully hard for a user who does not know details of the underlying XKG. We will see in Section 3 that such sophisticated queries can be generated by automatically rewriting a simpler user query based on query relaxation rules.

3. QUERY RELAXATION

Query formulations by a user may fail to return the expected answer(s), either because the user has insufficient understanding of the predicates, classes, and entities in the XKG, or because no answer can completely satisfy all conditions in the query.

Our solution to the above problems is *query relaxation*, where one or more parts of the query are automatically rewritten in order to compute answers that are likely to satisfy an information need but cannot be obtained by the original query. We first define our framework for query relaxation, and then discuss specific choices of relaxation rules.

Definition 6 (Relaxation Rule). *Given a query $Q = \{q_1, ..., q_n\}$, a relaxation rule is a triple $r = (\mathbf{q}, \mathbf{q}', w)$, where $\mathbf{q} \subseteq Q$ and is non-empty, $\mathbf{q}'$ is a set of triple patterns, and $w \in [0, 1]$ is a relaxation weight that captures the closeness between $\mathbf{q}$ and $\mathbf{q}'$.*

Definition 7 (Relaxation Rule Application, Relaxed Query). *Given a query Q and a relaxation rule $r = (\mathbf{q} \subseteq Q, \mathbf{q}', w)$, the application of r to Q results in query $Q' = r(Q) = (Q \setminus \mathbf{q}) \cup \mathbf{q}'$ with $P(Q') = P(Q)$.*

Given a query Q and a sequence of relaxation rules $\mathbf{r} = (r_1, ..., r_m)$, a relaxed query is a query $Q' = r_m(...r_1(Q))$.

Rationale: As an example, reconsider the example queries of Section 2. The user may issue the seemingly perfect query:

```
SELECT ?s ?m WHERE {
  ?s type song .  ?m type movie .  ?s usedIn ?m .
  ?s performedBy ?x .  ?x bornIn UK }
```

to retrieve British songs in movies. However, this may not return any results at all. To retrieve good candidates, we could drop an entire triple pattern from the query such as the one about birth in the UK, or we can relax overly restrictive predicates like `bornIn` by a textual token like *"born"* or even by a variable that can be matched by any predicate or token. Likewise, if the specified entity token `UK`

KG Triples			XKG Triples		
S	P	O	S	P	O
BangBang	type	song	DavidBowie	*"born and lives in"*	UK
SpaceOddity	type	song	DavidBowie	won	*"best British singer"*
KillBill	type	movie	BangBang	*"by"*	NancySinatra
WalterMitty	type	movie	*"Sinatra's daughter"*	bornIn	USA
SpaceOddity	usedIn	WalterMitty	NancySinatra	*"an"*	*"American singer"*
SpaceOddity	performedBy	DavidBowie	*"Lonely Shepherd"*	*"appears in"*	KillBill
KillBill	hasSoundtrack	KillBillAlbum	*"Lonely Shepherd"*	performedBy	*"Zamfir"*
KillBillAlbum	contains	BangBang	*"Zamfir"*	bornIn	Romania

Table 1: Example triples in KG (left) and additional samples in XKG (right).

is not directly matched in the XKG, we could generate semantically related tokens like *"British"*, *"English"*, *"Scottish"*, *"from London"*, etc. All these variants can be automatically generated in our relaxation framework.

Obviously, some relaxations drift away from the original user request. For example, *"Scottish"* or *"from London"* seem to be less focused in approximating the original UK than *"British"* – so their relaxation weights should be lower than the weight for *"British"*. Of course, replacing UK by a variable would be an even stronger relaxation and should have an even lower weight.

The order in which relaxations are applied results in different queries. In Section 4 we discuss our query ranking and processing schemes. The two are designed to incrementally explore relaxations only if they can contribute to producing the top-k-scoring answers. This approach avoids explicit enumeration of all possible relaxations of a query, which can be prohibitively expensive.

Relaxations in TriniT: TriniT provides interfaces for users to implement their own relaxations. In this work we consider two concrete forms of relaxation that are relevant to the benchmarks we consider: structural relaxations and predicate paraphrasing. Structural relaxations result in replacing a triple pattern by a set of triple patterns that conceptually denote a path. We apply this to spatial predicates that connect an entity with a location (e.g. from `(?x bornIn UK)` to `(?x bornIn ?y . ?y locatedIn UK)`). We define an operator that instantiates such rules based on the query. Such rules can also be automatically mined from the XKG using the method of [14].

Predicate paraphrasing is the most important type of relaxation we consider in this work. We generate paraphrases for XKG predicates using the XKG itself. For each predicate (e.g., `graduatedFrom`), we generate paraphrases (e.g., *"went to"*) and inverse paraphrases (e.g., *"alumnus"*) by considering the overlap between predicate arguments in the XKG. Given two predicates (incl. textual ones), p_1 and p_2, where $args(p_i) = \{(s,o),(s,p_i,o) \in XKG\}$ (i.e., subject-object pairs co-occurring with p_i), the weight assigned to the relaxation $r = (\{?x\ p_1\ ?y\}, \{?x\ p_2\ ?y\}, w)$ is:

$$w = \frac{|\, args(p_1) \cap args(p_2)\,|}{|\, args(p_2)\,|}.$$

Inverse paraphrases are generated and weighted in the same manner as above, by matching the XKG with an inverted version of itself, where the subject and object components of a triple are switched. In our experiments, we do not consider paraphrases that are stop words, as these consistently hurt results. Table 2 shows examples of paraphrases and inverse paraphrases (indicated by the $^{-1}$ superscript) for both KG and textual relations extracted from our XKG.

Predicate	Paraphrase
graduatedFrom	*"graduated from"*
graduatedFrom	*"went to"*
graduatedFrom	*"alumnus"* $^{-1}$
"performed by"	*"recorded by"*
"performed by"	*"singer"*
"performed by"	*"performance of"* $^{-1}$

Table 2: Example predicate paraphrases

Approaches such as [15] can also be utilized to obtain more paraphrases.

4. ANSWER RANKING AND QUERY PROCESSING

The scoring model of TriniT is based on a statistical language model (LM) for triple patterns, the basic building blocks of a query. For composing the triples from different sub-queries into overall answers, we judiciously aggregate the scores of the retrieved triples. Upfront, it is not obvious how to do this in a principled and efficiently implementable manner. Our setting with joins, queries over many variables, and bindings for multiple variables in the projected output is very different from established language models for entity search [2]. Also, by treating triples obtained from OpenIE as first-class citizens instead of using text to contextualize triples, it differs from existing language models [11, 12] for ranking and relaxation in knowledge graphs.

Answers for Single Triple Patterns: In analogy to the traditional IR setting, we can view a triple pattern as a document which generates individual triples. In this generative setting, we define a language model for each such triple pattern using a mixture model as follows:

$$P(t \mid q_i) = \lambda \frac{\#t}{|q_i|} + (1-\lambda)\frac{\#t}{|XKG|},$$

where $\#t$ denotes the number of occurrences of triple t in the XKG, $|q_i|$ is the total number of triples matching q_i in the XKG. Likewise, $|XKG|$ is the total size (i.e., number of triples) of the XKG and λ is a tunable parameter between 0 and 1. The first term is defined to be non-zero only if t matches q_i. The above defines a proper probability distribution: for each q_i, summing up over all triples in the XKG will always give us 1.

There are some subtle differences between this setting and the traditional IR setting. Smoothing with a background model (the XKG in our case) serves two purposes in traditional IR, namely to avoid zero probabilities and to attain an *idf*-like effect [38]. In our setting, since we only consider triples t that match the triple pattern q_i, zero probabilities are not an issue. Further, a relative weighting of triple patterns, corresponding to the *idf*-like effect, is already obtained by considering triple-pattern selectivities $|q_i|$, that is, how many matching triples exist. For our mixture model, the parameter λ thus controls whether the probabilities $P(t|q_i)$ are only based on the number of occurrences of t (for $\lambda = 0$) or also consider triple-pattern selectivities (for $\lambda > 0$), resulting in a relative weighting of triple patterns in the query.

Answers for Entire Queries: With answer scores defined for single triple patterns, we compute the score of a complete answer a for a composite query Q as follows:

$$score(a, Q) = \prod_{q_i} P(a(q_i)|q_i),$$

where $a(q_i) = t$ is the XKG triple resulting from the application of answer a to q_i.

Multiple answers can produce the same projected answer a_P, which is the result the user is interested in. For example, in a query with variables for movies, songs, and artists, if the final output is required to be pairs of merely movies and artists, the songs are "projected away", and we may obtain duplicates of the same movie-artist pair.

Thus, for each binding of the projection variables we need to define how to aggregate the scores of the individual results (with bindings for all three variables) for the whole group of duplicates. While summing up scores seems a natural choice, it incurs two problems: i) inflating the score of answers with frequently occurring entities (e.g., artists with many songs in many movies), and ii) forcing the query processing to retrieve all duplicates for each projected answer as they contribute to the scoring. Especially the second point would be critical from an efficiency perspective and rule out early pruning when scanning posting lists during query processing. Therefore, we opt to use the maximum score for each group rather than the sum over all duplicates, and define the score of a projected answer of a query as

$$score(a_P, Q) = \max_{a:a_P \subseteq a} score(a, Q).$$

Scoring with Query Relaxation: We finally extend our scoring model to account for query relaxation. Starting with a user-provided query, Q, we relax it in one or more steps by applying a sequence of relaxation operators $r_1, ..., r_n$ to obtain $Q' = r_n(...r_1(Q))$. Each relaxation operator r_l carries a relaxation weight $w_l \in [0, 1]$ which reflects how much a relaxed query drifts away from the previous query.

The score of an answer obtained from a relaxation is defined as:

$$score(a, Q, Q') = \prod_{l=1}^{n} w_l \times score(a, Q').$$

Intuitively, the score of a with respect to Q' is attenuated to reflect the divergence of Q' from the original query Q. For the special case where $n = 0$, i.e. $Q' = Q$, with no relaxation operators invoked, $score(a, Q, Q') = score(a, Q)$.

Because it is possible to generate the same answer through multiple distinct relaxations, we define the score of an answer with respect to the original query and the space of all possible relaxations $\mathbf{r}$ as:

$$score(a, Q, \mathbf{r}) = \max_{\substack{Q'=r_n(...r_1(Q)),\\ r_l \in \mathbf{r}}} score(a, Q, Q').$$

Here, an answer is assigned the maximum score it can obtain from any of the possible relaxations of the query (including the original query). The rationale for this design decision is analogous to the above score aggregation over duplicates when variables are projected away and in line with [31]: we want to avoid unduly inflating the influence of seeing the same answer many times in different contexts and allow for early pruning in query processing.

Finally, the score of a projected answer in a setting with relaxation is defined as:

$$score(a_P, Q, \mathbf{r}) = \max_{a:a_P \subseteq a} score(a, Q, \mathbf{r})$$

Query Processing in TriniT is a natural fit for the top-k paradigm [20] where the goal is to produce the best k answers with the highest scores while accessing as little of the data as possible. Our implementation uses *inverted indexes* to retrieve matching triples in decreasing order of their probability $P(t|q_i)$ from the XKG. This score monotonicity ensures that the algorithm can maintain result candidates in a priority queue with upper bounds for their final scores, and apply a threshold test for early termination. Our query processor applies the *incremental merge* algorithm [31] to automatically invoke relaxations judiciously and combine answers for a triple pattern and its relaxations.

5. EXPERIMENTAL EVALUATION

We report on an experimental evaluation that demonstrates the effectiveness of TriniT and provides insights into answering relationship-centric queries. We make our results publicly available (http://mpii.de/yago-naga/TriniT).

5.1 Methods

We compare two different configurations of TriniT with three natural state-of-the-art baselines. Figure 1(c) shows an example query for each system. The first TriniT configuration (TriniT-Relax) processes queries without considering relaxations. We contrast this to TriniT+Relax where TriniT has access to relaxations that it can automatically invoke as needed during query processing.

The first baseline we consider (ES) is based on the work by Balog et al. [2] for entity search. Here, an entity is represented by two fields containing the semantic types it belongs to and a textual description. We use Model 4, which is most effective one that allows us to enforce type constraints that are crucial for good results. The ES approach cannot return tuples in response to relationship queries, so we formulate queries to ask about a single entity (a single variable).

The second baseline (ERS) is that by Li et al. [23] for entity-relationship search. Here, queries are evaluated over an entity-annotated corpus. The score of a match of a query condition (a textual description of a typed variable or textual relation connecting two such variables) depends on the proximity of phrases in the condition and variable bindings.

Finally, we compare TriniT with SPOX(SPO+teXt), an extended version of the approach by Elbassuoni et al. [11]. Each SPO triple pattern in the KG is associated with textual keywords, which are an aggregation of keywords associated with the S and O components of the triple. For example, the triple `RusselCrowe actedIn ABeautifulMind` would be associated with the set of keywords {*'john', 'nash', 'true', 'story', 'princeton', 'australia'* ...}. On the query side, SPO triple patterns can optionally come with teXtual conditions that specify constraints which cannot be expressed in structured SPO

[ALGOL-JohnBackus-TuringAward]

(a)

"Programming languages invented by a Turing Award winner."

(b)

TriniT:

```
SELECT ?x ?y WHERE {?x type programming_language .
 ?y type person .  ?y "invented" ?x .
 ?y won TuringAward}
```

ES:

```
type:(programming_language) text:(programming language
invented by a turing award winner)
```

ERS:

```
SELECT ?x ?y FROM programming_language ?x, person ?y
WHERE ?x:["won", "turing award"] AND ?x,?y:["invented"]}
```

SPOX:

```
SELECT ?x ?y WHERE {?x type programming_language .
 ?y type person .  ?x ?r ?y ["invented"] .
 ?y won TuringAward}
```

(c)

Figure 1: Query generation & formulation example

form over the KG. For example, the SPOX pattern `?x actedIn ?y['true story']` is used to for actors in a movie based on a true story. During query answering, the SPO parts of the query are first matched against the KG, and the answers are subsequently ranked using language models that consider witness counts of KG triples as well teXtual keyword conditions with their frequencies. The original SPOX approach includes a form of relaxation in which entities or relations in a query are replaced by variables. We improve on this by moving these entities or relations to the X component of a triple instead of completely discarding them. This way they can still influence the final ranking of answers. We report results from this improved approach. We do not consider [12] as a baseline since relaxations here are performed by replacing KG entities and relations with other KG relations, which almost always results in semantic drift, as KGs rarely contain redundancy.

5.2 Benchmarks

Existing entity-search queries tend not to be relationship-centric. A contribution of this work is a new set of 70 inherently relationship-centric information needs, referred to as COMPLEX queries here (e.g., *"Programming languages invented by people who won the Turing Award."*). We next describe how these queries were generated. A query was constructed starting from a *chain* of entities (e.g., `[ALGOL-JohnBackus-TuringAward]`) where some become part of the query and others serve as an answer. These chains are automatically sampled from domains within the XKG, where a domain is the set of entities that fall within a specified set of semantic types. The domains we consider are cinema, music, books, sports, computing, and military conflicts. The cinema domain, for example, includes entities of the types `actor`, `show`, `director`, `award`, and `producer`. Within each domain, we iteratively sample entities starting from a pivot entity to form a chain. The first pivot entity (`ALGOL` in our example) is sampled non-uniformly based on a popularity prior from the domain. Next, we find the 20 entities in the domain that have the highest coherence with the current pivot by the Wikipedia-link measure of Milne & Witten [25]. We then sample these entities non-uniformly, based on the number of XKG facts connecting them to the pivot to choose the next pivot. This process is repeated to obtain chains of size 2-4 (determined randomly). A human annotator then constructs a question from the chain asking for the first entity while containing multiple unknowns corresponding to other entities in the chain. An annotator can discard a chain if she thinks no interesting question can be generated from it. Figure 1(a) shows an example of a chain, and (b) shows the corresponding question formulated by the human annotator. While the question is constructed by considering a single chain, it can have many answers. In the example of Figure 1, `(Pascal,NiklausWirth)` and `(Smalltalk,AlanKay)` are two possible answers among several others.

We additionally ran experiments with two benchmarks from previous work. The first, ESQ, is a set of 485 entity-centric queries compiled by Balog & Neumayer [4]. We remove from this dataset SemSearch ES and INEX LD queries as they do not fit our setting. SemSearch ES contains queries such as *"YMCA Tampa"* and *"nokia e73"*, which refer to a specific entity with no relations at all. INEX LD, is highly keyword centric (e.g. *"allegedly caused World War I"*) with a very noisy gold standard (e.g. `Aerial_bombing_of_cities` is considered a relevant entity for the above query). This leaves us with 255 queries from which we remove 37 involving aggregation (e.g., *"movies with eight or more Academy Awards"*) as these are beyond the capability of all the systems in this experiment, leaving us with 218 queries. Unlike our COMPLEX queries, ESQ queries ask for individual entities rather than tuples, and are usually expressed in the form of a type (e.g., *"EU countries"*) or a type with a description that contains a single relation (e.g., *"movies directed by Francis Ford Coppola"*).

The other benchmark from prior work, which we call ERQ, is constructed by Li et al. [23] and consists of 28 queries. 22 of the queries in this dataset are similar to the ones in ESQ, with 6 only asking for pairs of entities.

System Input Generation: TriniT and each of the three baselines described in Section 5.1 expects a specific form of query as shown in Figure 1(c). In the first step, an information need in the form of a question (Figure 1(b)) is shown to a human annotator who is asked to translate it into a proto-query. In the second step, the proto-query is used to automatically create queries for the four systems using a set of rules described below. The annotator, after being shown four examples of question-to-proto-query translation, is presented with the UI shown in Figure 2. Here, each row provides SPO fields for specifying SPO triple patterns. Each field provides auto-completion functionality for KG entities (S and O) and predicates (P). The annotator is asked to express the given question in SPO form, and is instructed to use the auto-completion suggestions when appropriate, or resort to textual tokens if necessary.

For ES, the type field is filled with the type associated with the first variable in the proto-query, and the text of the question is used in the text field. For ERS and SPOX, variable type-constraints are maintained. ERS cannot deal with KG entities and relations in the query (it only returns entity tuples as results), so they are mapped to their textual form. SPOX can only deal with entities and relations in the S and P components, respectively, but not textual tokens. To accommodate this, we extend an SPO triple pattern in the proto-query with an X component and move the S/O textual component there – note that this is not the

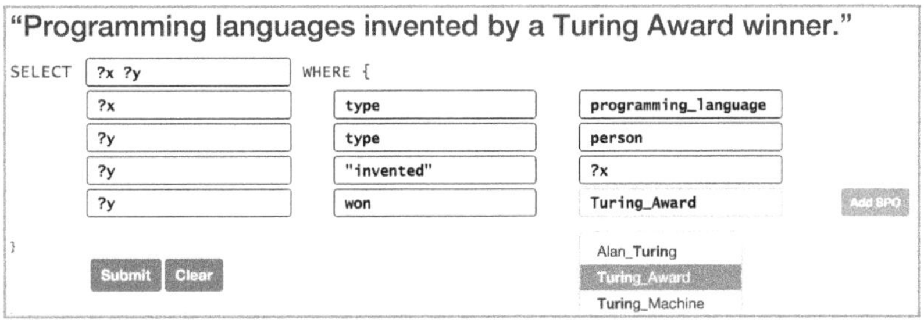

Figure 2: Proto-query interface, with input for the question in Figure 1(a).

same as SPOX relaxation described above, which is part of query processing. In real life, we envision a system used by professionals such as journalists and researchers willing to invest some learning effort in exchange for the more expressive querying they get in return from the different types of queries, with support from appropriate UIs.

5.3 Data

We finally describe the data we use for TriniT and the various baselines we consider. We note that we run our own implementations of the baselines on a scale larger than what was previously reported.

We use as our KG Yago2s, whose predicates connect entities from Wikipedia to other entities (e.g. `TomHanks actedIn ForrestGump`), literals (e.g. `TomHanks birthDate 1956-7-9`), or semantic types (e.g. `TomHanks type actor`), with a total of 48M triples (44M class assignments, and 4.4M relations and attributes).

As a text corpus, we use the FACC1 dataset, which annotates text spans in the ClueWeb'09 corpus with entities linked to Wikipedia entities (via Freebase) with a precision and recall estimated to be 80-85% and 70-85%.

For TriniT, we construct the XKG by combining the KG described above with the result of a simple yet effective open information extraction scheme over the annotated ClueWeb corpus as follows. We look for pairs of entity annotations in the same sentence separated by a string of at most 50 characters, and create a triple where the two entities are the subject and object, and the separating string is the relation connecting them. In this way we obtain 392M extractions, resulting in 65M unique triples. For predicate paraphrases, we run the predicate paraphrasing scheme described in Section 3 on top of the XKG to generate 172M pairs of scored predicate paraphrases like those in Table 2.

We use the annotated ClueWeb corpus for ERS as we did for TriniT. In addition, ERS takes type associations from our KG, ensuring ERS has data comparable to that used by TriniT. We attempted to evaluate the three benchmarks on the ERS online demo. However, it contained only a subset of the entities and types needed to answer COMPLEX and ES queries, preventing a fair comparison with other systems. For SPOX, we use our the annotated ClueWeb corpus to associate keywords with entities and subsequently KG triples. To do this we find all words that occur in the same sentence as an entity and keep those with a positive association (using normalized PMI) with the entity. SPOX uses the same KG as TriniT, Yago2s.

In ES we use an entity's Wikipedia page to populate its textual description, in line with [2]. We tried to extend this by adding to this field sentences from the annotated ClueWeb corpus that mention the entity. However, this resulted in worse retrieval effectiveness. We populate the semantic type field for an entity from the types it is associated with in the KG.

	ESQ (218)			
	P@5	MAP	NDCG	R
ES	0.183	0.138	0.211	0.093
ERS	0.182	0.150	0.232	0.119
SPOX	**0.249**	**0.218**	**0.336**$^{\triangle}$	**0.188**
TriniT-Relax	0.158	0.140	0.192	0.093
TriniT+Relax	0.218	0.190	0.287	0.156

	ERQ (28)			
	P@5	MAP	NDCG	R
ES	0.492	0.388	0.489	0.236
ERS	0.408	0.353	0.387	0.177
SPOX	0.577	0.561	0.580	0.248
TriniT-Relax	0.467	0.448	0.502	0.174
TriniT+Relax	**0.637**	**0.614**	**0.692**	**0.267**

	COMPLEX (70)			
	P@5	MAP	NDCG	R
ES	0.132	0.104	0.172	0.115
ERS	0.249	0.243	0.322	0.234
SPOX	0.243	0.237	0.250	0.134
TriniT-Relax	0.370	0.360	0.419	0.258
TriniT+Relax	**0.603**$^{\triangle}$	**0.594**$^{\triangle}$	**0.775**$^{\triangle}$	**0.613**$^{\triangle}$

Table 3: Experimental results.

5.4 Results and Analysis

Table 3 shows our experimental results. Following earlier work, we use precision@5, NDCG (with binary relevance), MAP, and recall as quality measures. For queries with an empty results list, we define all measures to be 0.

For ESQ queries, we use the gold standard provided with the benchmark. For ERQ and COMPLEX no gold standard is given, so we crowdsource relevance judgments and determine the relevance of an answer by majority vote of three judges. Note that since the XKG contains noise, human annotators were instructed to base their judgments on the real world rather than on the XKG. Inter-annotator agreement was measured using Fleiss' kappa to be 0.837 indicating almost perfect agreement. In all cases we use binary relevance.

ERQ and COMPLEX queries do not easily lend themselves to computing the complete set of relevant results, with queries such as *“NBA teams married to actresses, and the teams they play for”* (COMPLEX) or *“people born in Spain”* (ERQ). To compute NDCG and recall, we use pooling from the various systems to create a golden standard. Since ES returns single entities and not tuples, we project all answers on the same dimension as the one used for the ES query and compute the golden standard over that dimension.

$^{\triangle}$Significant improvement (two-tailed paired t-test, $p < 0.01$).

I- "Spouses of actors who graduated from an Ivy League university."

Query: `SELECT ?x ?y ?z WHERE { ?x type person . ?y type actor . ?z type university . ?y graduatedFrom ?z . ?x marriedTo ?y . ?z "member of" IvyLeague }`

XKG: `ChristopherReeve graduatedFrom JuilliardSchool`
`ChristopherReeve "went to" CornellUniversity`

Relaxations: `(?w graduatedFrom ?z)→(?w "went to" ?z): 0.066`

Relevant answers:
-TriniT-Relax: ϕ
-TriniT+Relax:
`{(DanaReeve, ChristopherReeve, CornellUniversity)}`

II-"Lieutenant governors of the province where Ottawa is located."

Query: `SELECT ?x ?y WHERE {?x type province . ?y type person . Ottawa locatedIn ?y . ?x "lieutenant governor of" ?y }`

XKG: `Ottawa locatedIn NationalCapitalRegion`
`NationalCapitalRegion locatedIn Ontario`
`Ontario "lieutenant governor" DavidOnley`
`HilaryWeston "lieutenant governor of" Ontario`

Relaxations:
`(?w locatedIn ?z)→(?w locatedIn ?u . ?u locatedIn ?z): 1.0`
`(?w locatedIn ?z) → (?w "part of" ?z): 0.073`
`(?w "lieutenant governor of" ?z)→ (?z "lieutenant governor" ?w): 0.259`

Relevant answers:
-TriniT-Relax: ϕ
-TriniT+Relax:
`{(DavidOnley, Ontario), (HilaryWeston, Ontario)}`

Figure 3: Anecdotal examples of results

Figure 3 gives illustrative examples from our COMPLEX queries set. We discuss the results by benchmark next.

ESQ Queries: Here SPOX outperforms all systems. On these non-relationship centric queries, SPOX boils down to an improved version of ES. If a query can be formulated in a structured manner, then this tends to be reflected in SPOX query formulations, resulting in SPO only queries, without the X components. When this is not possible, most of the query conditions end up in the X component of a type-constraint triple pattern either by formulation or through the improved SPOX relaxation scheme we described above.

TriniT is penalized against SPOX on queries that can be satisfactorily answered with keywords without the need to establish crisp relationships, as TriniT requires. For example, the query *"Nordic authors known for children's literature"* is reduced in the SPOX model to `?x type author[`*'nordic children's literature'*`]`. Here, looking at the co-occurrences of an author and the keywords suffices to return good answers. On the other hand, the SPO query formulation used for TriniT, with P set to *"known for"*, could not find matches in the XKG, even with relaxation. This result demonstrates that keyword based querying is an effective paradigm for a certain class of queries. Once we move to more relationship-centric queries below, we start observing the advantage of TriniT's approach.

We can already observe the advantages of relaxation at this stage. For example, on a simple query asking for *"Italian Nobel winners"*, the TriniT query uses the KG predicate `won`. While this looks reasonable, the KG only lists winners of specific Nobel prizes (e.g., `NobelPrizeInLiterature`). Only by relaxing `won` to the inverse textual predicate, *"winner"*, is the TriniT query able to return the correct answers from triples like `(NobelPrize "winner" EnricoFermi)`.

It is also interesting to observe the relatively close performance of ES and ERS. For most ESQ queries, ERS will reduce to ES, with a type constraint and a set of keywords describing the target entity, but with different scoring schemes.

ERQ Queries vary in how relationship-centric they are. The majority of ERQ queries (22/28) ask about a single entity, not a tuple, requiring no joins. The rest, while they ask for a tuple, can all conceivably be answered from an individual document describing a relevant entity. ERQ queries like *"films starring Robert de Niro, and their directors"* and *"Novels and their Academy Award winning film adaptations"* issued to the ES system in search for movies/novels, respectively, return satisfactory results. TriniT, when answering such questions is able to return tuples with an explanation of the precise relations that hold between the various entities in a tuple (either those part of the user's query, or matched through relaxation).

Seemingly simple ERQ queries which ask for a list of individual entities, not tuples, can be easily mishandled due to a lack of relation awareness. Results from ES and ERS for the query *"football players who were FIFA Player of the Year"* include the entities `DavidBeckham` and `ThierryHenry`, both of whom were runners-up for the award, but never actually received it. TriniT is able to handle this query correctly.

For this class of queries SPOX starts to suffer when the desired relationships connecting two variables are either not sufficiently populated or unavailable in the KG.

COMPLEX Queries are the most interesting: they require combining factual knowledge from multiple sources and establishing the existence of the relation specified in the query. TriniT with relaxations significantly outperforms all other systems on this dataset. Figure 3(I) helps understand why. It would be rare to find documents where keyword matching would correctly answer this query. Even then, we cannot expect to obtain a complete list of results. This query is inherently relationship-centric, best fit for TriniT. The original TriniT query contains one textual XKG predicate *"member of"*, as no KG relation covers it. However, the KG relation `graduatedFrom` lacks sufficient coverage, as the fact `(ChristopherReeve graduatedFrom CornellUniversity)` is missing. The XKG compensates for this through the textual relation *"went to"* (see Table 2), which is exploited by an automatically-invoked relaxation to facilitate the return of the relevant answer shown. For ES, this query, like most others in the benchmark, is too challenging: the evidence needed to answer is multiple hops away from a relevant entity. As in earlier examples, ERS can be brittle when establishing the existence of a relation in the query is critical for answering it. ERS scores entities in an answer based on their proximity to each other and to query terms expressing relations that must hold. This can be detrimental due to the complexities of natural language: e.g., *"private and public universities including Ivy League members, MIT, VanderbiltUniversity, SwarthmoreCollege , CalBerkeley..."* is incorrectly taken as evidence of `SwarthmoreCol-`

lege's membership in the IvyLeague. Figure 3(II) shows an example of a COMPLEX query where multiple relaxations are triggered, including a structural relaxation of the spatial locatedIn predicate, a predicate paraphrase and inverse paraphrase. On this query, SPOX fails as it contains no relation connecting a pair of entities that can serve as correct bindings of ?x and ?y, both of which have to be projected to the user. In this case, SPOX's relaxation scheme is not helpful. Here, ERS turns out to be more effective than SPOX as it relies on a less rigid scheme for answering queries.

5.5 Discussion

On relationship-centric queries, TriniT+Relax outperforms the baselines by a clear margin. This is most pronounced for the COMPLEX benchmark with relationship-centric queries – the very point that paper aims to address. Here the gains are high in all metrics.

It is also important to understand the limitations of TriniT and why it fails on some queries. Simpler entity queries can often be answered satisfactorily using traditional keyword-based approaches, as we have seen for SPOX over ESQ. Here, TriniT's relationship-centric approach is crucial only when keyword matches are misleading and crisp relations must be established. For TriniT+Relax, we observe that losses are mostly due to incorrect XKG facts and semantic drift in the relaxations. Such incorrect facts arise from incorrect entity annotations, or shortcomings in the extraction scheme. Generally, incorrect facts matching a triple pattern are less frequent than correct ones, which also means that the answers obtained through these have smaller weights. This is usually a problem for queries with a small number of expected correct answers, where the correct answers rank highest, and incorrect ones are at the bottom of the list.

The second source of incorrect answers is relaxations that drift from the original query intention. Again, this is mostly an issue in queries where few correct answers are expected compared to the number of answers actually returned, and can often be pruned away by observing a sudden drop in answer scores. This is why the scoring scheme presented in Section 4 uses *max* rather than *sum* for score aggregation.

6. RELATED WORK

Entity Search: Methods for entity search over large text corpora have been greatly advanced; [3] gives an overview. In these models, queries are keywords and return ranked lists of individual entities. Some methods use knowledge bases for feature expansion [9], but stick to the same query-and-answer model. One of the currently best methods is [2], which is based on entity language models and harnesses entity categories (i.e., semantic types) for ranking and for restricting answers to the desired type – so it can, for example, ensure that a query returns only songs, not movies, albums, or singers. However, the model is still limited to computing a list of single entities. So there is no way of returning tuples of entities, such as song-movie pairs, as answers. We included the method of [2] as a baseline in our experiments.

Query Relaxation: In IR, the classic case for query relaxation is query expansion for keyword queries [34] or recommendations for query reformulation [8]. Some work along these lines has explored the use of thesauri or knowledge bases, to generate semantically related terms for a given query. For structured data, generating relaxed queries has been explored for relational data (e.g., [26,39]) and for RDF data [11,12]. For tree-structured XML data, structural relaxation techniques have been developed, such as rewriting an XPath child condition into a descendant condition (e.g., [1]) or using semantic-relatedness-based relaxations for content terms in XPath queries (e.g., [32]). None of these is suitable for the combination of graph-structured data and text corpora.

Search on Knowledge Graphs: There is ample work on querying RDF databases and Linked-Open-Data with SPARQL [16]. However, this is exact-match querying on structured data emphasizing efficiency and scale while disregarding ranking or relaxation. Keyword-based graph search has also been extensively studied for relational databases [37]. These include ranking, but are limited to structured data and do not consider full documents attached to graph nodes. The most notable works on ranking SPARQL query answers are [11, 22], using statistical language models and supporting entity-tuple answers. Our approach is largely inspired by these models. However, this prior work has limited support for keywords attached to triples and does not extend to our XKG setting with text-based triples derived from large corpora. The same limitation holds for work on graph query languages (e.g., [36]). Finally, there are methods for telegraphic text queries over structured KGs (e.g., [28]), but they do not extend to the more demanding case of XKG.

Question Answering: Natural-language question answering (QA) is traditionally based on passage retrieval and statistical learning over unstructured text corpora. Even the ground-breaking IBM Watson system has made only limited use of structured data for special cases [19]. Recently, new approaches to QA have developed methods for translating user questions into structured queries that can be evaluated on KGs and Linked Data [7,13,30,33,35]. This line of research does not consider the combination of text and triples in an XKG, though.

Querying Entity-Annotated Text: Searching and exploring text corpora that are annotated with entities and/or linked to a KG has been addressed in various projects, most notably the Broccoli system [5,6], ERQ [23], and STICS [18]. Albeit not based on SPARQL, these are very expressive and powerful search engines. However, except for ERQ (see below) they do not provide any non-trivial ranking of results – which is crucial for XKG.

The work of [21,29] addresses telegraphic text queries over XKG-like combinations of text and data. The approach here is to jointly learn the segmentation and entity interpretation of the input query (in text form) and the ranking of candidate results. There is no notion of structured queries, though, and the more advanced queries that our model allows are beyond the scope of that prior work. Most importantly, queries that need to test for multiple relationships and return tuples of entities are not supported.

Closest to our approach is the ERQ system [23]. This work integrated text conditions into a structured query language with typed variables for both entities and entity pairs (i.e., relationships). Albeit primarily addressing richer entity-relationship search over Wikipedia, this method could be applied to XKG. We therefore include it as a baseline in our experimental studies.

7. CONCLUSION

Knowledge workers like journalists or analysts need query functionality that goes beyond the established line of entity search. This paper has addressed these needs by developing a powerful query language and a search engine, TriniT, for *relationship queries*, tapping the combination of knowledge graphs and web corpora to compute answers. For ease of use, TriniT starts with SPO-structured triple patterns that users can easily generate by a form-based UI, but allows also text phrases in each of the SPO components. Then, TriniT automatically and incrementally relaxes the query by rewriting rules for higher recall. Experiments with advanced queries over an extended knowledge graph of web-scale size demonstrate the viability of our approach and its benefits over prior work.

Acknowledgment. Qiuyue Wang is supported by the National Natural Science Foundation of China (Grant no. 61202331, 61532010).

8. REFERENCES

[1] S. Amer-Yahia, N. Koudas, A. Marian, D. Srivastava, D. Toman: Structure and Content Scoring for XML. VLDB 2005.

[2] K. Balog, M. Bron, M. de Rijke: Query Modeling for Entity Search Based on Terms, Categories, and Examples. TOIS 29(4), 2011.

[3] K. Balog, Y. Fang, M. de Rijke, P. Serdyukov, L. Si: Expertise Retrieval. Foundations and Trends in Information Retrieval 6(2-3), 2012.

[4] K. Balog, R. Neumayer: A Test Collection for Entity Search in DBpedia. SIGIR 2013.

[5] H. Bast, A. Chitea, F. M. Suchanek, I. Weber: ESTER: Efficient Search on Text, Entities, and Relations. SIGIR 2007.

[6] H. Bast, F. Bäurle, B. Buchhold, E. Haußmann: Semantic Full-text Search with Broccoli. SIGIR 2014.

[7] J. Berant, A. Chou, R. Frostig, P. Liang: Semantic Parsing on Freebase from Question-Answer Pairs. EMNLP 2013.

[8] P. Boldi, F. Bonchi, C. Castillo, S. Vigna: Query Reformulation Mining: Models, Patterns, and Applications. Information Retrieval 14(3), 2010.

[9] J. Dalton, L. Dietz, J. Allan: Entity Query Feature Expansion Using Knowledge Base Links. SIGIR 2014.

[10] B. B. Dalvi, E. Minkov, P. P. Talukdar, W. W. Cohen: Automatic Gloss Finding for a Knowledge Base using Ontological Constraints. WSDM 2015.

[11] S. Elbassuoni, M. Ramanath, R. Schenkel, M. Sydow, G. Weikum: Language-model-based Ranking for Queries on RDF-graphs. CIKM 2009.

[12] S. Elbassuoni, M. Ramanath, G. Weikum: Query Relaxation for Entity-Relationship Search. ESWC 2011.

[13] A. Fader, L. Zettlemoyer, O. Etzioni: Open Question Answering over Curated and Extracted Knowledge Bases. KDD 2014.

[14] L. A. Galárraga, C. Teflioudi, K. Hose, F. M. Suchanek: AMIE: Association Rule Mining under Incomplete Evidence in Ontological Knowledge Bases. WWW 2013.

[15] E. Gabrilovich, C. Markovitch: Computing Semantic Relatedness using Wikipedia-Based Explicit Semantic Analysis. IJCAI 2007.

[16] T. Heath, C. Bizer: Linked Data: Evolving the Web into a Global Data Space. Morgan & Claypool 2011.

[17] J. Hoffart et al.: Robust Disambiguation of Named Entities in Text. EMNLP 2011.

[18] J. Hoffart, D. Milchevski, G. Weikum: STICS: Searching with Strings, Things, and Cats. SIGIR 2014.

[19] IBM Journal of Research and Development 56(3), Special Issue on "This is Watson", 2012.

[20] I. F. Ilyas, G. Beskales, M. A. Soliman: A Survey of Top-k Query Processing Techniques in Relational Database Systems. Computing Surveys 40(4), 2008.

[21] M. Joshi, U. Sawant S. Chakrabarti: Knowledge Graph and Corpus Driven Segmentation and Answer Inference for Telegraphic Entity-seeking Queries. EMNLP 2014.

[22] G. Kasneci, F. M. Suchanek, G. Ifrim, M. Ramanath, G. Weikum: NAGA: Searching and Ranking Knowledge. ICDE 2008.

[23] X. Li, C. Li, C. Yu: Entity-Relationship Queries over Wikipedia. TIST 3(4), 2012.

[24] Mausam, M. Schmitz, S. Soderland, R. Bart, O. Etzioni: Open Language Learning for Information Extraction. EMNLP-CoNLL 2012.

[25] D. Milne, I.H. Witten: An Effective, Low-Cost Measure of Semantic Relatedness Obtained from Wikipedia Links. WIKIAI 2008.

[26] D. Mottin, A. Marascu, S. Basu Roy, G. Das, T. Palpanas, Y. Velegrakis: A Probabilistic Optimization Framework for the Empty-Answer Problem. PVLDB 6(14), 2013.

[27] Z. Nie, Y. Ma, S. Shi, J. Wen, W. Ma: Web Object Retrieval. WWW 2007.

[28] J. Pound, A. K. Hudek, I. F. Ilyas, G. E. Weddell: Interpreting Keyword Queries over Web Knowledge Bases. CIKM 2012.

[29] U. Sawant, S. Chakrabarti: Learning Joint Query Interpretation and Response Ranking. WWW 2013.

[30] S. Shekarpour, A.-C. N. Ngomo, S. Auer: Question Answering on Interlinked Data. WWW 2013.

[31] M. Theobald, R. Schenkel, G. Weikum:: Efficient and Self-tuning Incremental Query Expansion for Top-k Query Processing. SIGIR 2005.

[32] M. Theobald, H. Bast, D. Majumdar, R. Schenkel, G. Weikum: TopX: Efficient and Versatile Top-k Query Processing for Semistructured Data. VLDB J. 17(1), 2008.

[33] C. Unger et al.: Template-based Question Answering over RDF Data. WWW 2012.

[34] J. Xu, W. B. Croft: Query Expansion Using Local and Global Document Analysis. SIGIR 1996.

[35] M. Yahya, K. Berberich, S. Elbassuoni, M. Ramanath, V. Tresp, G. Weikum: Natural Language Questions for the Web of Data. EMNLP-CoNLL 2012.

[36] S. Yang, Y. Wu, H. Sun, X. Yan: Schemaless and Structureless Graph Querying. PVLDB 7(7), 2014.

[37] J. X. Yu, L. Qin, L. Chang: Keyword Search in Databases. Morgan & Claypool 2009.

[38] C. Zhai, J. Lafferty: A Study of Smoothing Methods for Language Models Applied to Information Retrieval. TOIS 22(2), 2004.

[39] X. Zhou, J. Gaugaz, W. Balke, W. Nejdl: Query Relaxation using Malleable Schemas. SIGMOD 2007.

Improving Website Hyperlink Structure Using Server Logs

Ashwin Paranjape*
Stanford University
ashwinp@cs.stanford.edu

Robert West*
Stanford University
west@cs.stanford.edu

Leila Zia
Wikimedia Foundation
leila@wikimedia.org

Jure Leskovec
Stanford University
jure@cs.stanford.edu

ABSTRACT

Good websites should be easy to navigate via hyperlinks, yet maintaining a high-quality link structure is difficult. Identifying pairs of pages that should be linked may be hard for human editors, especially if the site is large and changes frequently. Further, given a set of useful link candidates, the task of incorporating them into the site can be expensive, since it typically involves humans editing pages. In the light of these challenges, it is desirable to develop data-driven methods for automating the link placement task. Here we develop an approach for automatically finding useful hyperlinks to add to a website. We show that passively collected server logs, beyond telling us which existing links are useful, also contain implicit signals indicating which nonexistent links would be useful if they were to be introduced. We leverage these signals to model the future usefulness of yet nonexistent links. Based on our model, we define the problem of link placement under budget constraints and propose an efficient algorithm for solving it. We demonstrate the effectiveness of our approach by evaluating it on Wikipedia, a large website for which we have access to both server logs (used for finding useful new links) and the complete revision history (containing a ground truth of new links). As our method is based exclusively on standard server logs, it may also be applied to any other website, as we show with the example of the biomedical research site Simtk.

1. INTRODUCTION

Websites are networks of interlinked pages, and a good website makes it easy and intuitive for users to navigate its content. One way of making navigation intuitive and content discoverable is to provide carefully placed hyperlinks. Consider for instance Wikipedia, the free encyclopedia that anyone can edit. The links that connect articles are essential for presenting concepts in their appropriate context, for letting users find the information they are looking for, and for providing an element of serendipity by giving users the chance to explore new topics they happen to come across without intentionally searching for them.

Unfortunately, maintaining website navigability can be difficult and cumbersome, especially if the site is large and changes frequently [7, 21]. For example, about 7,000 new pages are created on Wikipedia every day [35]. As a result, there is an urgent need to keep the site's link structure up to date, which in return requires much manual effort and does not scale as the website grows, even with thousands of volunteer editors as in the case of Wikipedia. Neither is the problem limited to Wikipedia; on the contrary, it may be even more pressing on other sites, which are often maintained by a single webmaster. Thus, it is important to provide automatic methods to help maintain and improve website hyperlink structure.

Considering the importance of links, it is not surprising that the problems of finding missing links and predicting which links will form in the future have been studied previously [17, 19, 22, 32]. Prior methods typically cast improving website hyperlink structure simply as an instance of a link prediction problem in a given network; *i.e.*, they extrapolate information from existing links in order to predict the missing ones. These approaches are often based on the intuition that two pages should be connected if they have many neighbors in common, a notion that may be quantified by the plain number of common neighbors, the Jaccard coefficient of sets of neighbors, and other variations [1, 17].

However, simply considering the existence of a link on a website is not all that matters. Networks in general, and hyperlink graphs in particular, often have traffic flowing over their links, and a link is of little use if it is never traversed. For example, in the English Wikipedia, of all the 800,000 links added to the site in February 2015, the majority (66%) were not clicked even a single time in March 2015, and among the rest, most links were clicked only very rarely. For instance, only 1% of links added in February were used more than 100 times in all of March (Fig. 1). Consequently, even if we could perfectly mimic Wikipedia editors (who would *a priori* seem to provide a reasonable gold standard for links to add), the suggested links would likely have little impact on website navigation.

Furthermore, missing-link prediction systems can suggest a large number of links to be inserted into a website. But before links can be incorporated, they typically need to be examined by a human, for several reasons. First, not all sites provide an interface that lets content be changed programmatically. Second, even when such an interface is available, determining where in the source page to place a suggested link may be hard, since it requires finding, or introducing, a phrase that may serve as anchor text [19]. And third, even when identifying anchor text automatically is possible, human verification and approval might still be required in order to ensure that the recommended link is indeed correct and appropriate. Since the addition of links by humans is a slow and expensive process, presenting the complete ranking of all suggested links to editors is unlikely to be useful. Instead, a practical system should choose a well composed subset of candidate links of manageable size.

*AP and RW contributed equally, RW as a Wikimedia Research Fellow.

WSDM'16, February 22–25, 2016, San Francisco, CA, USA.

ACM ISBN 978-1-4503-3716-8/16/02

DOI: http://dx.doi.org/10.1145/2835776.2835832

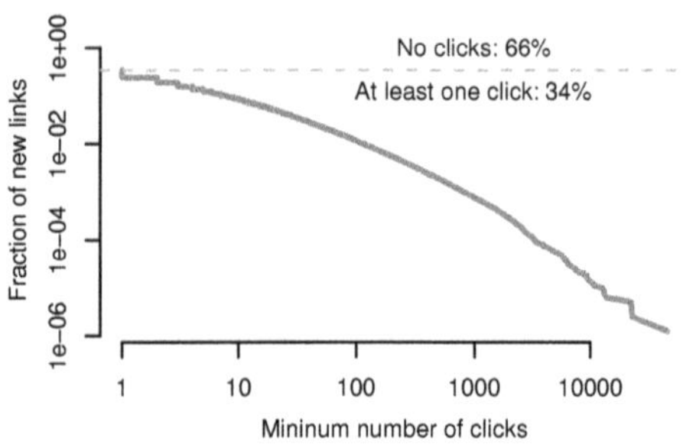

Figure 1: Complementary cumulative distribution function of the number of clicks received in March 2015 by links introduced in the English Wikipedia in February 2015.

Thus, what is needed is an automatic approach to improving website hyperlink structure that accounts for website navigation patterns and suggests a limited number of highly relevant links based on the way they will impact the website's navigability.

Present work. Here we develop an automatic approach for suggesting missing but potentially highly used hyperlinks for a given website. Our approach is language- and website-independent and is based on using access logs as collected by practically all web servers. Such logs record users' natural browsing behavior, and we show that server logs contain strong signals not only about which existing links are presently used, but also about how heavily currently nonexistent links would be used if they were to be added to the site. We build models of human browsing behavior, anchored in empirical evidence from log data, that allow us to predict the usage of any potentially introduced hyperlink (s,t) in terms of its *clickthrough rate, i.e.*, the probability of being chosen by users visiting page s. The models are based on the following intuition: Consider a page s not linked to another page t. A large fraction of users visiting s and later on, via an indirect path, t, suggests that they might have taken a direct shortcut from s to t had the shortcut existed. Even though one could hope to detect such events by parsing the logs, our approach is even more general. One of our models is able to estimate the fraction of people who would take a shortcut (s,t) only based on the pairwise page transition matrix. That is, we are able to estimate navigation probabilities over longer paths by combining information about individual link transitions.

The second important aspect of our solution is that we only suggest a small number of the top K most useful links, where K is a 'link budget' constraint. Consider a naïve approach that first ranks all candidate links by their probability of being used and then simply returns the top K. An extreme outcome would be for all K links to be placed in a single page s. This is problematic because it seems *a priori* more desirable to connect a large number of pages reasonably well with other pages than to connect a single page extremely well. This intuition is confirmed by the empirical observation that the expected number of clicks users take from a given page s is limited and not very sensitive to the addition of new links out of s. Thus we conclude that inserting yet another out-link to s after some good ones have already been added to it achieves less benefit than adding an out-link to some other page s' first. This diminishing-returns property, besides accurately mirroring human behavior, leads to an optimization procedure that does not over-optimize on single source pages but instead spreads good links across many pages.

We demonstrate and evaluate our approach on two very different websites: the full English Wikipedia and Simtk, a small community of biomedical researchers. For both websites we utilize complete web server logs collected over a period of several months and demonstrate that our models of human browsing behavior are accurate and lead to the discovery of highly relevant and useful hyperlinks. Having full access to the logs of Wikipedia, one of the highest-traffic websites in the world, is particularly beneficial, as it allows us to perform a unique analysis of human web-browsing behavior. Our results on Simtk show that our method is general and applies well beyond Wikipedia.

The following are the main contributions of this paper:

- We introduce the link placement problem under budget constraints, and design objective functions anchored in empirically observed human behavior and exposing an intuitive diminishing-returns property. We also provide an efficient algorithm for optimizing these objectives (Sec. 2).
- We identify signals in the logs that can indicate the usage of a future link before it is introduced, and we operationalize these signals in simple but effective methods for finding promising new links and estimating their future clickthrough rates (Sec. 3).
- We characterize the usage and impact of newly added links by analyzing human navigation traces mined from Wikipedia's server logs (Sec. 5).

2. THE LINK PLACEMENT PROBLEM

First we introduce the *link placement problem under budget constraints*. In this context, the budget refers to a maximum allowable number of links that may be suggested by an algorithm. As mentioned in the introduction, realistic systems frequently require a human in the loop for verifying that the links proposed by the algorithm are indeed of value and for inserting them. As we need to avoid overwhelming the human editors with more suggestions than they can respond to, we need to carefully select our suggestions.

Formally, the task is to select a set A of suggested links of a given maximum size K, where the quality of the chosen set A is determined by an *objective function* f:

$$\text{maximize} \quad f(A) \tag{1}$$

$$\text{subject to} \quad |A| \leq K. \tag{2}$$

In principle, any set function $f: 2^V \to \mathbb{R}$ may be plugged in (where V is the set of pages on the site, and 2^V is the set of all subsets of V), but the practical usefulness of our system relies vitally on a sensible definition of f. In particular, f should be based on a reasonable model of human browsing behavior and should score link sets for which the model predicts many clicks above link sets for which it predicts fewer clicks.

In the following we introduce two simplified models of human browsing behavior and propose three objective functions f based on these models. Then, we show that two of these objectives have the useful property of diminishing returns and discuss the implications thereof. Finally, we show that all three objectives can be maximized exactly by a simple and efficient greedy algorithm.

2.1 Browsing models and objective functions

We first define notation, then formulate two web-browsing models, and finally design three objective functions based on the models.

Notation. We model hyperlink networks as directed graphs $G = (V,E)$, with *pages* as nodes and *hyperlinks* as edges. We refer to the endpoints of a link (s,t) as *source* and *target*, respectively. Unlinked pairs of nodes are considered potential *link candidates*. We denote the overall number of views of a page s by N_s. When users are in s, they have a choice to either stop or follow out-links of s. To simplify notation, we model stopping as a link click to a special sink page $\varnothing \notin E$ that is taken to be linked from every other page. Further, N_{st} counts the transitions from s to t via direct clicks of the link (s,t). Finally, a central quantity in this research is the *click-through rate* p_{st} of a link (s,t). It measures the fraction of times users click to page t, given that they are currently on page s:

$$p_{st} = N_{st}/N_s. \quad (3)$$

The *stopping probability* is given by $p_{s\varnothing}$. Note that, since in reality users may click several links from the same source page, p_{st} is generally not a distribution over t given s.

Next we define two models of human web-browsing behavior.

Multi-tab browsing model. This model captures a scenario where the user may follow several links from the same page s, *e.g.*, by opening them in multiple browser tabs. We make the simplifying assumption that, given s, the user decides for each link (s,t) independently (with probability p_{st}) if he wants to follow it.

Single-tab browsing model. This is a Markov chain model where the user is assumed to follow exactly one link from each visited page s. This corresponds to a user who never opens more than a single tab, as might be common on mobile devices such as phones. The probability of choosing the link (s,t) is proportional to p_{st}.

Based on these browsing models, we now define objective functions that model the value provided by the newly inserted links A. Note that the objectives reason about the clickthrough rates p_{st} of links A that do not exist yet, so in practice p_{st} is not directly available but must be estimated from data. We address this task in Sec. 3.

Link-centric multi-tab objective. To capture the value of the newly inserted links A, this first objective assumes the multi-tab browsing model. The objective computes the expected number of new-link clicks from page s as $\sum_{t:(s,t)\in A} p_{st}$ and aggregates this quantity across all pages s:

$$f_1(A) = \sum_s w_s \sum_{t:(s,t)\in A} p_{st}. \quad (4)$$

If we choose $w_s = N_s$ then $f_1(A)$ measures the expected number of clicks received by all new links A jointly when s is weighted according to its empirical page-view count. In practice, however, page-view counts tend to follow heavy-tailed distributions such as power laws [2], so a few top pages would attract a disproportional amount of weight. We mitigate this problem by using $w_s = \log N_s$, *i.e.*, by weighting s by the order of magnitude of its raw count.

Page-centric multi-tab objective. Our second objective also assumes the multi-tab browsing model. However, instead of measuring the total expected number of clicks on all new links A (as done by f_1), this objective measures the expected number of source pages on which at least one new link is clicked (hence, we term this objective *page-centric,* whereas f_1 is link-centric):

$$f_2(A) = \sum_s w_s \left(1 - \prod_{t:(s,t)\in A} 1 - p_{st}\right). \quad (5)$$

Here, the product specifies the probability of no new link being clicked from s, and one minus that quantity yields the probability of clicking at least one new link from s. As before, we use $w_s = \log N_s$.

Single-tab objective. Unlike f_1 and f_2, our third objective is based on the single-tab browsing model. It captures the number of page views upon which the one chosen link is one of the new links A:

$$f_3(A) = \sum_s w_s \frac{\sum_{t:(s,t)\in A} p_{st}}{\sum_{t:(s,t)\in A} p_{st} + \sum_{t:(s,t)\in E} p_{st}}. \quad (6)$$

The purpose of the denominator is to renormalize the independent probabilities of all links—old and new—to sum to 1, so p_{st} becomes a distribution over t given s. Again, we use $w_s = \log N_s$.

2.2 Diminishing returns

Next, we note that all of the above objective functions are monotone, and that f_2 and f_3 have a useful diminishing-returns property.

Monotonicity means that adding one more new link to the solution A will never decrease the objective value. It holds for all three objectives (we omit the proof for brevity):

$$f(A \cup \{(s,t)\}) - f(A) \geq 0. \quad (7)$$

The difference $f(A \cup \{(s,t)\}) - f(A)$ is called the *marginal gain* of (s,t) with respect to A.

The next observation is that, under the link-centric multi-tab objective f_1, marginal gains never change: regardless of which links are already present in the network, we will always have

$$f_1(A \cup \{(s,t)\}) - f_1(A) = w_s p_{st}. \quad (8)$$

This means that f_1 assumes that the solution quality can be increased indefinitely by adding more and more links to the same source page s. However, we will see later (Sec. 5.2) that this may not be the case in practice: adding a large number of links to the same source page s does not automatically have a large effect on the total number of clicks made from s.

This discrepancy with reality is mitigated by the more complex objectives f_2 and f_3. In the page-centric multi-tab objective f_2, further increasing the probability of at least one new link being taken becomes ever more difficult as more links are added. This way, f_2 discourages adding too many links to the same source page.

The same is true for the single-tab objective f_3: since the click probabilities of all links from s—old and new—are required to sum to 1 here, it becomes ever harder for a link to obtain a fixed portion of the total probability mass of 1 as the page is becoming increasingly crowded with strong competitors.

More precisely, all three objective functions f have the *submodularity* property (proof omitted for brevity):

$$f(B \cup \{(s,t)\}) - f(B) \leq f(A \cup \{(s,t)\}) - f(A), \quad \text{for } A \subseteq B, \quad (9)$$

but while it holds with equality for f_1 (Eq. 8), this is not true for f_2 and f_3. When marginal gains decrease as the solution grows, we speak of *diminishing returns.*

To see the practical benefits of diminishing returns, consider two source pages s and u, with s being vastly more popular than u, *i.e.*, $w_s \gg w_u$. Without diminishing returns (under objective f_1), the marginal gains of candidates from s will nearly always dominate those of candidates from u (*i.e.*, $w_s p_{st} \gg w_u p_{uv}$ for most (s,t) and (u,v)), so u would not even be considered before s has been fully saturated with links. With diminishing returns, on the contrary, s would gradually become a less preferred source for new links. In other words, there is a trade-off between the popularity of s on the one hand (if s is frequently visited then links that are added to it get more exposure and are therefore more frequently used), and its 'crowdedness' with good links, on the other.

As a side note we observe that, when measuring 'crowdedness', f_2 only considers the newly added links A, whereas f_3 also takes the pre-existing links E into account. In our evaluation (Sec. 6.1.3), we will see that the latter amplifies the effect of diminishing returns.

2.3 Algorithm for maximizing the objectives

We now show how to efficiently maximize the three objective functions. We first state two key observations that hold for all three

Algorithm 1 Greedy marginal-gain link placement

Input: Hyperlink graph $G = (V, E)$; source-page weights w_s; clickthrough rates p_{st}; budget K; objective f
Output: Set A of links that maximizes $f(A)$ subject to $|A| \leq K$
1: $Q \leftarrow$ new priority queue
2: **for** $s \in V$ **do**
3: $\quad \Sigma_E \leftarrow \sum_{(s,t)\in E} p_{st}$ *// sum of p_{st} values of old links from s*
4: $\quad \Sigma \leftarrow 0$ *// sum of new p_{st} values seen so far for s*
5: $\quad \Pi \leftarrow 1$ *// product of new $(1 - p_{st})$ values seen so far for s*
6: $\quad C \leftarrow 0$ *// current objective value for s*
7: $\quad$ **for** $t \in V$ in decreasing order of p_{st} **do**
8: $\quad\quad \Sigma \leftarrow \Sigma + p_{st}$
9: $\quad\quad \Pi \leftarrow \Pi \cdot (1 - p_{st})$
10: $\quad\quad$ **if** $f = f_1$ **then** $C' \leftarrow w_s \cdot \Sigma$
11: $\quad\quad$ **else if** $f = f_2$ **then** $C' \leftarrow w_s \cdot (1 - \Pi)$
12: $\quad\quad$ **else if** $f = f_3$ **then** $C' \leftarrow w_s \cdot \Sigma / (\Sigma + \Sigma_E)$
13: $\quad\quad$ Insert (s, t) into Q with the marginal gain $C' - C$ as value
14: $\quad\quad C \leftarrow C'$
15: $\quad$ **end for**
16: **end for**
17: $A \leftarrow$ top K elements of Q

objectives and then describe an algorithm that builds on these observations to find a globally optimal solution:

1. For a single source page s, the optimal solution is given by the top K pairs (s,t) with respect to p_{st}.
2. Sources are 'independent': the contribution of links from s to the objective does not change when adding links to sources other than s. This follows from Eq. 4–6, by noting that only links from s appear in the expressions inside the outer sums.

These observations imply that the following simple, greedy algorithm always produces an optimal solution[1] (pseudocode is listed in Algorithm 1). The algorithm processes the data source by source. For a given source s, we first obtain the optimal solution for s alone by sorting all (s,t) with respect to p_{st} (line 7; *cf.* observation 1). Next, we iterate over the sorted list and compute the marginal gains of all candidates (s,t) from s (lines 7–15). As marginal gains are computed, they are stored in a global priority queue (line 13); once computed, they need not be updated any more (*cf.* observation 2). Finally, we return the top K from the priority queue (line 17).

3. ESTIMATING CLICKTHROUGH RATES

In our above exposition of the link placement problem, we assumed we are given a clickthrough rate p_{st} for each link candidate (s,t). However, in practice these values are undefined before the link is introduced. Therefore, we need to estimate what the clickthrough rate for each nonexistent link would be in the hypothetical case that the link were to be inserted into the site.

Here we propose four ways in which historical web server logs can be used for estimating p_{st} for a nonexistent link (s,t). Later (Sec. 6.1.1) we evaluate the resulting predictors empirically.

Method 1: Search proportion. What we require are indicators of users' need to transition from s to t before the direct link (s,t) exists. Many websites provide a search box on every page, and thus one way of reaching t from s without taking a direct click is to 'teleport' into t by using the search box. Therefore, if many users search for t from s we may interpret this as signaling the need to go from s to t, a need that would also be met by a direct link. Based on this intuition, we estimate p_{st} as the *search proportion* of (s,t), defined as the number of times t was reached from s via search, divided by the total number N_s of visits to s.

[1]For maximizing general submodular functions (Eq. 9), a greedy algorithm gives a $(1 - 1/e)$-approximation [20]. But in our case, observation 2 makes greedy optimal: our problem is equivalent to finding a maximum-weight basis of a uniform matroid of rank K with marginal gains as weights; the greedy algorithm is guaranteed to find an optimal solution in this setting [10].

Algorithm 2 Power iteration for estimating path proportions from pairwise transitions probabilities

Input: Target node t, pairwise transition matrix P with $P_{st} = p_{st}$
Output: Vector Q_t of estimated path proportions for all source pages when the target page is t
$Q_t \leftarrow (0, \ldots, 0)^T$
$Q_{tt} \leftarrow 1$
$Q'_t \leftarrow (0, \ldots, 0)^T$ *// used for storing the previous value of Q_t*
while $\|Q_t - Q'_t\| > \varepsilon$ **do**
$\quad Q'_t \leftarrow Q_t$
$\quad Q_t \leftarrow PQ_t$ *// recursive case of Eq. 10*
$\quad Q_{tt} \leftarrow 1$ *// base case of Eq. 10*
end while

Method 2: Path proportion. Besides search, another way of reaching t from s without a direct link is by navigating on an indirect path. Thus, we may estimate p_{st} as the *path proportion* of (s,t), defined as N^*_{st}/N_s, where N^*_{st} is the observed number of navigation paths from s to t. In other words, path proportion measures the average number of paths to t, conditioned on first seeing s.

Method 3: Path-and-search proportion. Last, we may also combine the above two metrics. We may interpret search queries as a special type of page view, and the paths from s to t via search may then be considered indirect paths, too. Summing search proportion and path proportion, then, gives rise to yet another predictor of p_{st}. We refer to this joint measure as the *path-and-search proportion*.

Method 4: Random-walk model. The measures introduced above require access to rather granular data: in order to mine keyword searches and indirect navigation paths, one needs access to complete server logs. Processing large log datasets may, however, be computationally difficult. Further, complete logs often contain personally identifiable information, and privacy concerns may thus make it difficult for researchers and analysts to obtain unrestricted log access. For these reasons, it is desirable to develop clickthrough rate estimation methods that manage to make reasonable predictions based on more restricted data. For instance, although the Wikipedia log data used in this paper is not publicly available, a powerful dataset derived from it, the matrix of pairwise transition counts between all English Wikipedia articles, was recently published by the Wikimedia Foundation [34]. We now describe an algorithm for estimating path proportions solely based on the *pairwise* transition counts for those links that already exist.

As defined above, the path proportion measures the expected number of paths to t on a navigation trace starting from s; we denote this quantity as Q_{st} here. For a random walker navigating the network according to the empirically measured transitions probabilities, the following recursive equation holds:

$$Q_{st} = \begin{cases} 1 & \text{if } s = t, \\ \sum_u p_{su} Q_{ut} & \text{otherwise.} \end{cases} \tag{10}$$

The base case states that the expected number of paths to t from t itself is 1 (*i.e.*, the random walker is assumed to terminate a path as soon as t is reached). The recursive case defines that, if the random walker has not reached t yet, he might do so later on, when continuing the walk according to the empirical clickthrough rates.

Solving the random-walk equation. The random-walk equation (Eq. 10) can be solved by power iteration. Pseudocode is listed as Algorithm 2. Let Q_t be the vector containing as its elements the estimates Q_{st} for all pages s and the fixed target t. Initially, Q_t has entries of zero for all pages with the exception of $Q_{tt} = 1$, as per the base case of Eq. 10 (lines 1–2). We then keep multiplying Q_t with the matrix of pairwise transition probabilities, as per the recursive case of Eq. 10 (line 6), resetting Q_{tt} to 1 after every step (line 7). Since this reset step depends on the target t, the algorithm needs to be run separately for each t we are interested in.

The algorithm is guaranteed to converge to a fixed point under the condition that $\sum_s p_{st} < 1$ for all t (proof omitted for conciseness), which is empirically the case in our data.

4. DATASETS AND LOG PROCESSING

In this section we describe the structure and processing of web server logs. We also discuss the properties of the two websites we work with, Wikipedia and Simtk.

4.1 From logs to trees

Log format. Web server log files contain one entry per HTTP request, specifying *inter alia:* timestamp, requested URL, referer URL, HTTP response status, user agent information, client IP address, and proxy server information via the HTTP X-Forwarded-For header. Since users are not uniquely identifiable by IP addresses (*e.g.*, several clients might reside behind the same proxy server, whose IP address would then be logged), we create an approximate user ID by computing an MD5 digest of the concatenation of IP address, proxy information, and user agent. Common bots and crawlers are discarded on the basis of the user agent string.

From logs to trees. Our goal is to analyze the traces users take on the hyperlink network of a given website. However, the logs do not represent these traces explicitly, so we first need to reconstruct them from the raw sequence of page requests.

We start by grouping requests by user ID and sorting them by time. If a page t was requested by clicking a link on another page s, the URL of s is recorded in the referer field of the request for t. The idea, then, is to reassemble the original traces from the sequence of page requests by joining requests on the URL and referer fields while preserving the temporal order. Since several clicks can be made from the same page, *e.g.*, by opening multiple browser tabs, the navigation traces thus extracted are generally trees.

While straightforward in principle, this method is unfortunately unable to reconstruct the original trees perfectly. Ambiguities arise when the page listed in the referer field of t was visited several times previously by the same user. In this situation, linking t to all its potential predecessors results in a directed acyclic graph (DAG) rather than a tree. Transforming such a DAG into a tree requires a heuristic approach. We proceed by attaching a request for t with referer s to the *most recent* request for s by the same user. If the referer field is empty or contains a URL from an external website, the request for t becomes the root of a new tree.

Not only is this greedy strategy intuitive, since it seems more likely that the user continued from the most recent event, rather than resumed an older one; it also comes with a global optimality guarantee. More precisely, we observe that in a DAG G with edge weights w, attaching each internal node v to its minimum-weight parent $\arg\min_u w_{uv}$ yields a minimum spanning tree of G. We follow this approach with time differences as edge weights. Hence, the trees produced by our heuristic are the best possible trees under the objective of minimizing the sum (or mean) of all time differences spanned by the referer edges.

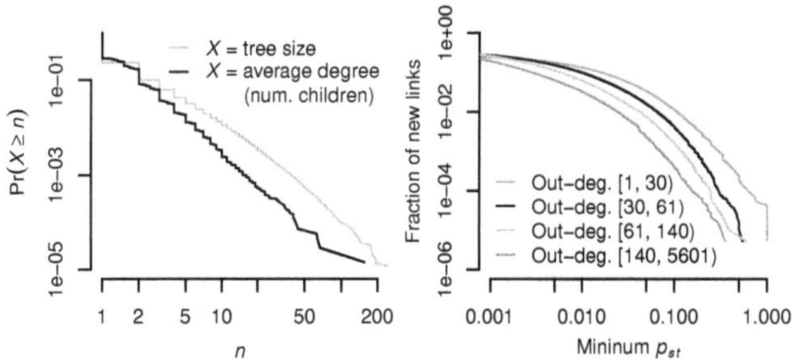

(a) Tree properties (b) New-link usage

Figure 2: Wikipedia dataset statistics. (a) CCDF of size and average degree of navigation trees. (b) CCDF of clickthrough rate for various source-page out-degrees. (Log–log scales.)

Mining search events. When counting keyword searches, we consider both site-internal search (*e.g.*, from the Wikipedia search box) and site-external search from general engines such as Google, Yahoo, and Bing. Mining internal search is straightforward, since all search actions are usually fully represented in the logs. An external search from s for t is defined to have occurred if t has a search engine as referer, if s was the temporally closest previous page view by the user, and if s occurred at most 5 minutes before t.

4.2 Wikipedia data

Link graph. The Wikipedia link graph is defined by nodes representing articles in the main namespace, and edges representing the hyperlinks used in the bodies of articles. Furthermore, we use the English Wikipedia's publicly available full revision history (spanning all undeleted revisions from 2001 through April 3, 2015) to determine when links were added or removed.

Server logs. We have access to Wikimedia's full server logs, containing all HTTP requests to Wikimedia projects. We consider only requests made to the desktop version of the English Wikipedia. The log files we analyze comprise 3 months of data, from January through March 2015. For each month we extracted around 3 billion navigation trees. Fig. 2(a) summarizes structural characteristics of trees by plotting the complementary cumulative distribution functions (CCDF) of the tree size (number of page views) and of the average degree (number of children) of non-leaf page views per tree. We observe that trees tend to be small: 77% of trees consist of a single page view; 13%, of two page views; and 10%, of three or more page views. Average degrees also follow a heavy-tailed distribution. Most trees are linear chains of all degree-one nodes, but page views with larger numbers of children are still quite frequent; *e.g.*, 6% (44 million per month) of all trees with at least two page views have an average degree of 3 or more.

4.3 Simtk data

Our second log dataset stems from Simtk.org, a website where biomedical researchers share code and information about their projects. We analyze logs from June 2013 through February 2015.

Contrasting Simtk and Wikipedia, we note that the Simtk dataset is orders of magnitude smaller than the Wikipedia dataset, in terms of both pages and page views, at hundreds, rather than millions, of pages, and tens of millions, rather than tens of billions, of page

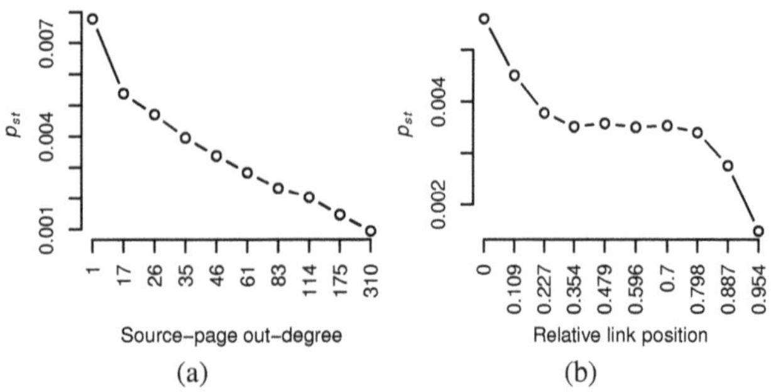

Figure 3: Clickthrough rate as function of (a) source-page out-degree and (b) relative position of link in wiki markup of source page (0 is top; 1 is bottom). Lower bin boundaries on x-axis.

views. Simtk's hyperlink structure is also significantly less dense than Wikipedia's. On the one hand, this means that there is much improvement to be made by a method such as ours; on the other hand, it also means that the navigation traces mined from the logs are less rich than for Wikipedia. Therefore, instead of extracting trees, we extract *sessions,* defined here as sequences of page views with idle times of no more than one hour [13] between consecutive events. Further, to be consistent, we compute path proportions (Sec. 3) by tallying up how often s occurred before t in the same session, rather than on a path in the same tree.

5. EVALUATION: EFFECTS OF NEW LINKS

The goal of this section is to investigate the effects of adding new links and assess some of the assumptions we made when formulating the link placement problem (Sec. 2). In particular, we answer the following questions: First, how much click volume do new links receive? Second, are several new links placed in the same source page independent of each other, or do they compete for clicks?

To answer these questions, we consider the around 800,000 links (s,t) added to the English Wikipedia in February 2015 and study all traces involving s in the months of January and March 2015.

5.1 Usage of new links

In the introduction we have already alluded to the fact that new links tend to be rarely used, to the extent that 66% of the links added in February were not used even a single time in March, and only 1% were used more than 100 times (Fig. 1).

While Fig. 1 plots absolute numbers, Fig. 2(b) shows the complementary cumulative distribution function (CCDF) of the clickthrough rate p_{st}, stratified by the out-degree of the source page s. We observe that, depending on source-page out-degree, between 3% and 13% of new links achieve over 1% clickthrough, with higher values for lower-degree source pages. This finding is confirmed by Fig. 3(a), which plots the clickthrough rate p_{st} against source-page out-degree and shows a strong negative trend.

Finally, Fig. 3(b) confirms the fact that the popularity of a link is also correlated with its position in the source page [16], with links appearing close to the top of the page achieving a clickthrough rate about 1.6 times as high as that of links appearing in the center, and about 3.7 times as high as that of links appearing at the bottom.

5.2 Competition between links

Traces are generally trees, not chains (Sec. 4.1). While in chains, p_{st} would form a distribution over t given s, *i.e.*, $\sum_t p_{st} = 1$, this is not necessary in trees, where several next pages may be opened from the same page s, such that, in the most extreme case (when all $p_{st} = 1$), $\sum_t p_{st}$ may equal the out-degree of s.

In the multi-tab browsing model with its independence assumption (Sec. 2.1), we would see no competition between links; the larger the out-degree of s, the larger the expected number of clicks from s for fixed p_{st}. In its pure form, this model seems unlikely to be true, since it would imply a reader scanning the entire page, evaluating every link option separately, and choosing to click it with its probability p_{st}. In a less extreme form, however, it is well conceivable that adding many good links to a page s might significantly increase the number of links a given user chooses to follow from s.

In Sec. 5.1 we already saw that links from pages of higher out-degree tend to have lower individual clickthrough rates, which may serve as a first sign of competition, or interaction, between links. As our link placement method is allowed to propose only a limited number of links, the question of interaction between links is of crucial importance. Next we investigate this question more carefully.

First we define the *navigational degree* d_s of s to be the total number of transitions out of s, divided by the total number of times s was seen as an internal node of a tree, *i.e.*, without stopping there:

$$d_s = \frac{\sum_{t \neq \varnothing} N_{st}}{N_s - N_{s\varnothing}}. \tag{11}$$

In other words, the navigational degree of s is simply the average number of transitions users make out of s, given that they do not stop in s. We also define the *structural degree,* or *out-degree,* of s to be the number of pages s links to.

Next, we examine the relation of the structural degree of s with (1) the probability of stopping at s and (2) the navigational degree of s, across a large and diverse set of pages s.

Fig. 4(a), which has been computed from the transition counts for 300,000 articles in January 2015, shows that stopping is less likely on pages of larger structural degree, with a median stopping probability of 89% for pages with less than 10 out-links, and 76% for pages with at least 288 out-links. Additionally, given that users do not stop in s, they make more clicks on average when s offers more links to follow (median 1.00 for less than 10 out-links *vs.* 1.38 for 288 or more out-links; Fig. 4(b)).

These effects could be explained by two hypotheses. It is possible that (i) simply adding more links to a page also makes it more likely that more links are taken; or (ii) structural degree may be correlated with latent factors such as 'interestingness' or 'topical complexity': a more complex topic s will have more connections (*i.e.*, links) to other topics that might be relevant for understanding s; this would lead to more clicks from s to those topics, but not simply because more link options are present but because of inherent properties of the topic of s.

To decide which hypothesis is true, we need to control for these inherent properties of s. We do so by tracking the same s through time and observing whether changes in structural degree are correlated with changes in navigational degree for fixed s as well. In particular, we consider two snapshots of Wikipedia, one from January 1, 2015, and the other from March 1, 2015. We take these snapshots as the approximate states of Wikipedia in the months of January and March, respectively. Then, we compute structural and navigational degrees, as well as stopping probabilities, based exclusively on the links present in these snapshots, obtaining two separate values for each quantity, one for January and one for March. For a fixed page s, the difference between the March and January values now captures the effect of adding or removing links from s on the stopping probability and the navigational degree of s.

Fig. 4(c) and 4(d) show that this effect is minuscule, thus lending support to hypothesis ii from above: as structural degree grows or shrinks, both stopping probability (Fig. 4(c)) and navigational degree (Fig. 4(d)) vary only slightly, even for drastic changes in

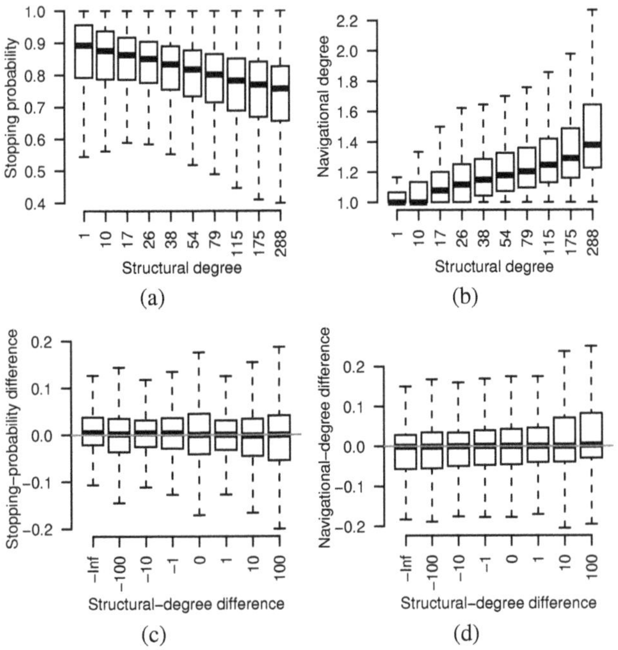

Figure 4: Across different source pages, structural degree is (a) negatively correlated with stopping probability, and (b) positively correlated with navigational degree. When fixing the source page, however, structural degree has only a small effect on (c) stopping probability and (d) navigational degree. The *y*-axes in (c) and (d) are relative with respect to the values from January. Lower bin boundaries on *x*-axes. Boxes show quartiles; whiskers show the full range without outliers.

link structure; *e.g.*, when 100 links or more are added, the median relative increase in navigational degree is still only 0.3%, and when 100 links are deleted, the median relative decrease is only 0.1%.

This is not to say that adding links has no effect at all, but this effect stems from extreme, rather than typical, values, as indicated by the upward (downward) shift of interquartile ranges (Fig. 4(d)) as links are added (removed).

In a nutshell, simply adding more links does not increase the overall number of clicks taken from a page. Instead, links compete with each other for user attention. This observation has important implications for user modeling and hence for budget-constrained link placement algorithms: one should avoid spending too much of one's budget on the same source page, since this will not increase click volume indefinitely; rather, one should spread high-clickthrough links across many different source pages.

These findings justify, *post hoc,* the diminishing-returns properties of the objective functions f_2 and f_3 (Sec. 2.2).

6. EVALUATION: LINK PLACEMENT

Next we demonstrate the universality of our approach by evaluating it on two very different websites, Wikipedia and Simtk.

6.1 Wikipedia

The analysis of results for Wikipedia is divided into three parts. First, we show that the estimation methods from Sec. 3 are suited for predicting the clickthrough rates of new links. Since the evaluation set of added links is known only after the fact, a practically useful system must have the additional ability to identify such links on its own before they are introduced. Therefore, we then check whether a large predicted p_{st} value indeed also means that the link is worthy of addition. Last, we investigate the behavior of our algorithm for link placement under budget constraints.

	Mean absolute err.	Pearson corr.	Spearman corr.
Path prop.	**0.0057** (±0.0003)	0.58 (±0.12)	**0.64** (±0.01)
Search prop.	0.0070 (±0.0004)	0.49 (±0.22)	0.17 (±0.02)
P&S prop.	**0.0057** (±0.0003)	**0.61** (±0.13)	**0.64** (±0.01)
Rand. walks	0.0060 (±0.0004)	0.53 (±0.13)	0.59 (±0.02)
Mean baseln.	0.0072 (±0.0004)	0.20 (±0.06)	0.34 (±0.02)

Table 1: Comparison of clickthrough rate estimation methods on Wikipedia, with bootstrapped 95% confidence intervals.

We also developed a graphical user interface that makes it easy to add missing links to Wikipedia: users are shown our suggestions and accept or decline them with the simple click of a button [24].

6.1.1 *Estimating clickthrough rates*

As described in Sec. 5, we have identified 800,000 links that were added to the English Wikipedia in February 2015. Here we evaluate how well we can predict the clickthrough rates p_{st} of these links in March 2015 from log data of January 2015, *i.e.*, before the link was added. In particular, we compare five different methods (Sec. 3):

1. search proportion,
2. path proportion,
3. the combined path-and-search proportion,
4. random walks, and
5. a mean baseline.

The mean baseline makes the same prediction for all candidates originating in the same source page *s*, namely the average clickthrough rate of all out-links of *s* that already exist.

Table 1 evaluates the results using three different metrics: mean absolute error, Pearson correlation, and Spearman rank correlation. The table shows that across all metrics path proportion and path-and-search proportion perform best. Further, it is encouraging to see that the random-walk–based predictor, which only requires the pairwise transition matrix, is not lagging behind by much. Also, recall from Fig. 3(a) that p_{st} is to a large part determined by source-page out-degree. This is why the mean baseline performs quite well (mean absolute error of 0.72%, *vs.* 0.57% achieved by the best-performing method) even though it predicts the same value for all links from the same page (but see the next section for when the baseline fails). For a graphical perspective on the relation between predicted and ground-truth values, we refer to Fig. 5(a) and 5(b).

6.1.2 *Predicting link addition*

Our models for clickthrough prediction reason about the hypothetical scenario that a link (s,t) is added to the site. In the previous subsection we showed that the models manage to predict the future usage of a link fairly well for the subset of links that were actually added. But, as stated above, this set is not known when the predictors are deployed in practice.

Intuitively, a large predicted clickthrough rate p_{st} should also imply that (s,t) is a useful link and should thus be added. Here we test whether this is actually the case by evaluating whether our high-ranking predictions using the January data correspond to links that were added to Wikipedia in February.

For this task, we need a ground-truth set of positive and negative examples. We require a non-negligible number of positive examples for which our methods can potentially predict a high p_{st} value. Since our methods are based mainly on path and search counts, we therefore consider all links added in February with at least 10 indirect paths or searches in January; call this set *L*. Since in reality

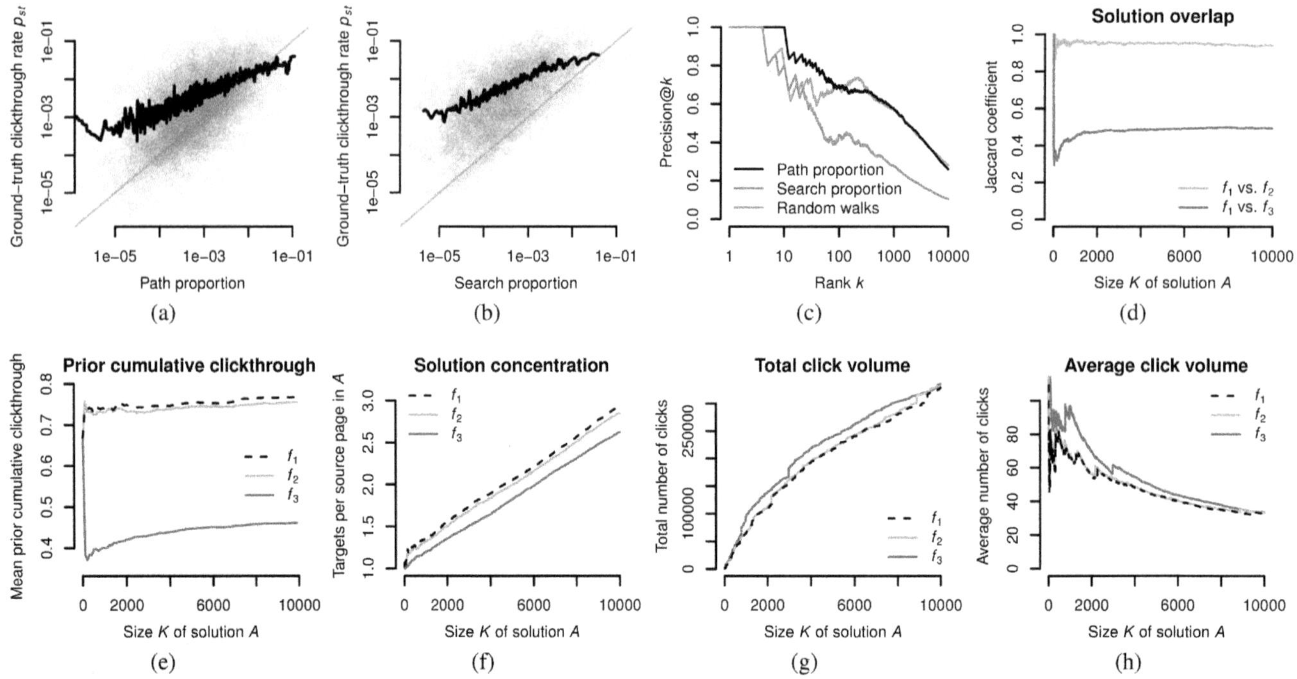

Figure 5: Wikipedia results. (a) Path proportion *vs.* clickthrough rate. (b) Search proportion *vs.* clickthrough rate (log–log; black lines correspond to gray dots kernel-smoothed on linear scales). (c) Precision at k on link prediction task (Sec. 6.1.2; logarithmic x-axis); path-and-search proportion nearly identical to path proportion and thus not shown. (d–h) Results of budget-constrained link placement for objectives of Eq. 4–6 (Sec. 6.1.3); 'prior cumulative clickthrough' refers to second term in denominator of Eq. 6.

most page pairs are never linked, we also need to add a large number of negative examples to the test set. We do so by including all out-links of the sources, and in-links of the targets, appearing in L. Using this approach, we obtain a set of about 38 million link candidates, of which 9,000 are positive examples. The aforementioned threshold criterion is met by 7,000 positive, and 104,000 negative, examples. Therefore, while there is a fair number of positive examples with many indirect paths and searches, they are vastly outnumbered by negative examples with that same property; this ensures that retrieving the positive examples remains challenging for our methods (*e.g.*, returning all links meeting the threshold criterion in random order yields a precision of only 6%).

Given this labeled dataset, we evaluate the precision at k of the candidate ranking induced by the predicted p_{st} values. The results, plotted in Fig. 5(c), indicate that our methods are well suited for predicting link addition. Precision stays high for a large set of top predictions: of the top 10,000 predictions induced by the path-proportion and random-walk measures, about 25% are positive examples; among the top 2,000 predictions, as many as 50% are positive. As before, random walks perform nearly as well as the more data-intensive path proportion, and better than search proportion.

Note that the mean baseline, which performed surprisingly well on the clickthrough rate prediction task (Sec. 6.1.1), does not appear in the plot. The reason is that it fails entirely on this task, producing only two relevant links among its top 10,000 predictions. We conclude that it is easy to give a good p_{st} estimate when it is known which links will be added. However, predicting whether a link should be added in the first place is much harder.

6.1.3 *Link placement under budget constraints*

The above evaluations concerned the quality of predicted p_{st} values. Now we rely on those values being accurate and combine them in our budget-constrained link placement algorithm (Sec. 2.3). We use the p_{st} values from the path-proportion method.

First, we consider how similar the solutions produced by the different objective functions are. For this purpose, Fig. 5(d)) plots the Jaccard coefficients between the solutions of f_1 and f_2 (orange) and between the solutions of f_1 and f_3 (blue) as functions of the solution size K. We observe that f_1 and f_2 produce nearly identical solutions. The reason is that clickthrough rates p_{st} are generally very small, which entails that Eq. 4 and 5 become very similar (formally, this can be shown by a Taylor expansion around 0). Objective f_3, on the contrary, yields rather different solutions; it tends to favor source pages with fewer pre-existing high-clickthrough links (due to the second term in the denominator of Eq. 6; Fig. 5(e)) and attempts to spread links more evenly over all source pages (Fig. 5(f)). In other words, f_3 offers a stronger diminishing-returns effect: the marginal value of more links decays faster when some good links have already been added to the same source page.

Next, we aim to assess the impact of our suggestions on real Wikipedia users. Recall that we suggest links based on server logs from January 2015. We quantify the impact of our suggestions in terms of the total number of clicks they received in March 2015 (contributed by links added by editors after January). Fig. 5(g), which plots the total March click volume as a function of the solution size K, shows that (according to f_3) the top 1,000 links received 95,000 clicks in total in March 2015, and the top 10,000 received 336,000 clicks. Recalling that two-thirds of all links added by humans receive no click at all (Fig. 1), this clearly demonstrates the importance of the links we suggest. Fig. 5(h) displays the average number of clicks per suggested link as a function of K. The decreasing shape of the curves implies that higher-ranked suggestions received more clicks, as desired. Finally, comparing the three objectives, we observe that f_3 fares best on the Wikipedia dataset: its suggestions attract most clicks (Fig. 5(g) and 5(h)), while also being spread more evenly across source pages (Fig. 5(f)).

These results show that the links we suggest fill a real user need. Our system recommends useful links before they would normally

	Mean absolute err.	Pearson corr.	Spearman corr.
Path prop.	0.020 (±0.003)	**0.41** (±0.10)	**0.50** (±0.09)
Mean baseln.	**0.013** (±0.003)	−0.01 (±0.11)	−0.27 (±0.10)

Table 3: Performance of path-proportion clickthrough estimation on Simtk, with bootstrapped 95% confidence intervals.

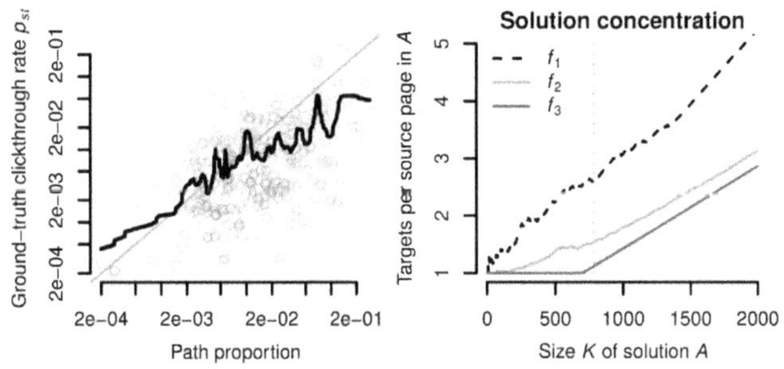

(a) (b)

Figure 6: Simtk results. (a) Path proportion *vs.* clickthrough rate (black line corresponds to gray dots kernel-smoothed on linear scales). (b) Solution concentration of budget-constrained link placement; dotted vertical line: number of distinct pages.

be added by editors, and it recommends additional links that we may assume would also be clicked frequently if they were added.

Table 2 illustrates our results by listing the top link suggestions.

6.2 Simtk

It is important to show that our method is general, as it relies on no features specific to Wikipedia. Therefore, we conclude our evaluation with a brief discussion of the results obtained on the second, smaller dataset from Simtk.

For evaluating our approach, we need to have a ground-truth set of new links alongside their addition dates. Unlike for Wikipedia, no complete revision history is available for Simtk, but we can nonetheless assemble a ground truth by exploiting a specific event in the site's history: after 6 months of log data, a sidebar with links to related pages was added to all pages. These links were determined by a recommender system once and did not change for 6 months. Our task is to predict these links' clickthrough rates p_{st} for the 6 months after, based on log data from the 6 months before.

The results on the p_{st} prediction task are summarized in Table 3; we compare path proportion to the mean baseline (*cf.* Sec. 6.1.1). At first glance, when considering only mean absolute error, it might seem as though the former were outperformed by the latter. But upon closer inspection, we realize that this is simply because the baseline predicts very small values throughout, which tend to be close to the ground-truth values, but cannot discriminate between good and bad candidates, as signified by the negative correlation coefficients. Path proportion, on the contrary, does reasonably well, at Pearson (Spearman) correlation coefficients of 0.41 (0.50). This correlation can be observed graphically in Fig. 6(a).

Last, we analyze the solutions of our budget-constrained link placement algorithm. Our first observation is that the two multi-tab objectives f_1 and f_2 differ much more on Simtk than on Wikipedia (with Jaccard coefficients between 40% and 60%, compared to over 90%), which shows that the page-centric multi-tab objective f_2 is not redundant but adds a distinct option to the repertoire.

We also observe that the value of the single-tab objective f_3 saturates after inserting around as many links as there are pages (750). The reason is that only very few links were available and clicked before the related-link sidebar was added, so the second term in the denominator of Eq. 6 is typically much smaller than the first term and the numerator; with the first link added to s, the ratio in Eq. 6 becomes close to 1, and the contribution of s to f_3 close to its possible maximum w_s. Thereafter, the objective experiences extreme diminishing returns for s. Fig. 6(b) confirms that f_3 starts by inserting one link into each of the around 750 pages.

We conclude that with few pre-existing links, the page-centric multi-tab objective f_2 might be better suited than the single-tab objective f_3, as it provides a more balanced trade-off between the number of links per source page and predicted clickthrough rates.

7. DISCUSSION AND RELATED WORK

There is a rich literature on the task of link prediction and recommendation, so rather than trying to be exhaustive, we refer the reader to the excellent survey by Liben-Nowell and Kleinberg [17] and to some prior methods for the specific case of Wikipedia [11, 19, 22, 32], as it is also our main evaluation dataset. The important point to make is that most prior methods base their predictions on the static structure of the network, whereas we focus on how users interact with this static structure by browsing and searching on it.

Among the few link recommendation methods that take usage data into account are those by Grecu [12] and West *et al.* [31]. They leverage data collected through a human-computation game in which users navigate from a given start to a given target page on Wikipedia, thereby producing traces that may be used to recommend new 'shortcut' links from pages along the path to the target page. Although these approaches are simple and work well, they are limited by the requirement that the user's navigation target be explicitly known. Eliciting this information is practically difficult and, worse, may even be fundamentally impossible: often users do not have any target in mind, *e.g.*, during exploratory search [18] or when browsing the Web for fun or distraction. Our approach alleviates this problem, as it does not rely on a known navigation target, but rather works on passively collected server logs.

Web server logs capture user needs and behavior in real time, so another clear advantage of our log-based approach is the timeliness of the results it produces. This is illustrated by Table 2, where most suggestions refer to current events, films, music, and books.

Our random-walk model (Sec. 3) builds on a long tradition of Markovian web navigation models [6, 8, 27]. Among other things, Markov chains have been used to predict users' next clicks [6, 26] as well as their ultimate navigation targets [30]. Our model might be improved by using a higher-order Markov model, based on work by Chierichetti *et al.* [5], who found that human browsing is around 10% more predictable when considering longer contexts.

Further literature on human navigation includes information foraging [4, 23, 25, 30], decentralized network search [14, 15, 29], and the analysis of click trails from search result pages [3, 9, 33].

In the present work we assume that frequent indirect paths between two pages indicate that a direct link would be useful. While this is confirmed by the data (Fig. 5(a)), research has shown that users sometimes deliberately choose indirect routes [28], which may offer additional value [33]. Detecting automatically in the logs when this is the case would be an interesting research problem.

Our method is universal in the sense that it uses only data logged by any commodity web server software, without requiring access to other data, such as the content of pages in the network. We demonstrate this generality by applying our method on two rather different websites without modification. While this is a strength of our approach, it would nonetheless be interesting to explore if the accuracy of our link clickthrough model could be improved by using machine learning to combine our current estimators, based on path counts, search counts, and random walks, with domain-specific elements such as the textual or hypertextual content of pages.

(a) Page-centric multi-tab objective f_2

	Source	Target
*	ITunes Originals – Red Hot Chili Peppers	Road Trippin' Through Time
*	Internat. Handball Federation	2015 World Men's Handball Champ.
	Baby, It's OK!	Olivia (singer)
	Payback (2014)	Royal Rumble (2015)
*	Nordend	Category:Mountains of the Alps
*	Gran Hotel	Grand Hotel (TV series)
*	Edmund Ironside	Edward the Elder
*	Jacob Aaron Estes	The Details (film)
	Confed. of African Football	2015 Africa Cup of Nations
	Live Rare Remix Box	Road Trippin' Through Time

(b) Single-tab objective f_3

	Source	Target
*	ITunes Originals – Red Hot Chili Peppers	Road Trippin' Through Time
*	Gran Hotel	Grand Hotel (TV series)
*	Tithe: A Modern Faerie Tale	Ironside: A Modern Faery's Tale
*	Nordend	Category:Mountains of the Alps
*	Jacob Aaron Estes	The Details (film)
	Blame It on the Night	Blame (Calvin Harris song)
*	Internat. Handball Federation	2015 World Men's Handball Champ.
*	The Choice (novel)	Benjamin Walker (actor)
	Payback (2014)	Royal Rumble (2015)
*	Just Dave Van Ronk	No Dirty Names

Table 2: Top 10 link suggestions of Algorithm 1 using objectives f_2 and f_3. Clickthrough rates p_{st} estimated via path proportion (Sec. 3). Objective f_1 (not shown) yields same result as f_2 but includes an additional link for source page *Baby, It's OK!*, demonstrating effect of diminishing returns on f_2. Asterisks mark links added by editors after prediction time, independently of our predictions.

A further route forward would be to extend our method to other types of networks that people navigate. For instance, citation networks, knowledge graphs, and some online social networks could all be amenable to our approach. Finally, it would be worthwhile to explore how our methods could be extended to not only identify links inside a given website but to also links between different sites.

In summary, our paper makes contributions to the rich line of work on improving the connectivity of the Web. We hope that future work will draw on our insights to increase the usability of websites as well as the Web as a whole.

Acknowledgments. This research has been supported in part by NSF IIS-1016909, IIS-1149837, IIS-1159679, CNS-1010921, NIH R01GM107340, Boeing, Facebook, Volkswagen, Yahoo, SDSI, and Wikimedia Foundation. Robert West acknowledges support by a Stanford Graduate Fellowship.

8. REFERENCES

[1] L. Adamic and E. Adar. Friends and neighbors on the Web. *Social Networks*, 25(3):211–230, 2003.

[2] E. Adar, J. Teevan, and S. T. Dumais. Large scale analysis of Web revisitation patterns. In *CHI*, 2008.

[3] M. Bilenko and R. White. Mining the search trails of surfing crowds: Identifying relevant websites from user activity. In *WWW*, 2008.

[4] E. H. Chi, P. Pirolli, K. Chen, and J. Pitkow. Using information scent to model user information needs and actions and the Web. In *CHI*, 2001.

[5] F. Chierichetti, R. Kumar, P. Raghavan, and T. Sarlos. Are Web users really Markovian? In *WWW*, 2012.

[6] B. D. Davison. Learning Web request patterns. In *Web Dynamics*. Springer, 2004.

[7] P. Devanbu, Y.-F. Chen, E. Gansner, H. Müller, and J. Martin. Chime: Customizable hyperlink insertion and maintenance engine for software engineering environments. In *ICSE*, 1999.

[8] D. Downey, S. Dumais, and E. Horvitz. Models of searching and browsing: Languages, studies, and application. In *IJCAI*, 2007.

[9] D. Downey, S. Dumais, D. Liebling, and E. Horvitz. Understanding the relationship between searchers' queries and information goals. In *CIKM*, 2008.

[10] J. Edmonds. Matroids and the greedy algorithm. *Mathematical Programming*, 1(1):127–136, 1971.

[11] S. Fissaha Adafre and M. de Rijke. Discovering missing links in Wikipedia. In *LinkKDD*, 2005.

[12] M. Grecu. Navigability in information networks. Master's thesis, ETH Zürich, 2014.

[13] A. Halfaker, O. Keyes, D. Kluver, J. Thebault-Spieker, T. Nguyen, K. Shores, A. Uduwage, and M. Warncke-Wang. User session identification based on strong regularities in inter-activity time. In *WWW*, 2015.

[14] D. Helic, M. Strohmaier, M. Granitzer, and R. Scherer. Models of human navigation in information networks based on decentralized search. In *HT*, 2013.

[15] J. Kleinberg. The small-world phenomenon: An algorithmic perspective. In *STOC*, 2000.

[16] D. Lamprecht, D. Helic, and M. Strohmaier. Quo vadis? On the effects of Wikipedia's policies on navigation. In *Wiki-ICWSM*, 2015.

[17] D. Liben-Nowell and J. Kleinberg. The link-prediction problem for social networks. *JASIST*, 58(7):1019–1031, 2007.

[18] G. Marchionini. Exploratory search: From finding to understanding. *Communications of the ACM*, 49(4):41–46, 2006.

[19] D. Milne and I. H. Witten. Learning to link with Wikipedia. In *CIKM*, 2008.

[20] G. L. Nemhauser, L. A. Wolsey, and M. L. Fisher. An analysis of approximations for maximizing submodular set functions – I. *Mathematical Programming*, 14(1):265–294, 1978.

[21] C. Nentwich, L. Capra, W. Emmerich, and A. Finkelstein. Xlinkit: A consistency checking and smart link generation service. *TOIT*, 2(2):151–185, 2002.

[22] T. Noraset, C. Bhagavatula, and D. Downey. Adding high-precision links to Wikipedia. In *EMNLP*, 2014.

[23] C. Olston and E. H. Chi. ScentTrails: Integrating browsing and searching on the Web. *TCHI*, 10(3):177–197, 2003.

[24] A. Paranjape, R. West, and L. Zia. Project website, 2015. `https://meta.wikimedia.org/wiki/Research:Improving_link_coverage` (accessed Dec. 10, 2015).

[25] P. Pirolli. *Information foraging theory: Adaptive interaction with information*. Oxford University Press, 2007.

[26] R. R. Sarukkai. Link prediction and path analysis using Markov chains. *Computer Networks*, 33(1):377–386, 2000.

[27] P. Singer, D. Helic, A. Hotho, and M. Strohmaier. HypTrails: A Bayesian approach for comparing hypotheses about human trails on the Web. In *WWW*, 2015.

[28] J. Teevan, C. Alvarado, M. S. Ackerman, and D. R. Karger. The perfect search engine is not enough: A study of orienteering behavior in directed search. In *CHI*, 2004.

[29] C. Trattner, D. Helic, P. Singer, and M. Strohmaier. Exploring the differences and similarities between hierarchical decentralized search and human navigation in information networks. In *i-KNOW*, 2012.

[30] R. West and J. Leskovec. Human wayfinding in information networks. In *WWW*, 2012.

[31] R. West, A. Paranjape, and J. Leskovec. Mining missing hyperlinks from human navigation traces: A case study of Wikipedia. In *WWW*, 2015.

[32] R. West, D. Precup, and J. Pineau. Completing Wikipedia's hyperlink structure through dimensionality reduction. In *CIKM*, 2009.

[33] R. White and J. Huang. Assessing the scenic route: Measuring the value of search trails in Web logs. In *SIGIR*, 2010.

[34] E. Wulczyn and D. Taraborelli. Wikipedia Clickstream. Website, 2015. `http://dx.doi.org/10.6084/m9.figshare.1305770` (accessed July 16, 2015).

[35] E. Zachte. Wikipedia statistics. Website, 2015. `https://stats.wikimedia.org/EN/TablesWikipediaZZ.htm` (accessed July 16, 2015).

Long-tail Vocabulary Dictionary Extraction from the Web

Zhe Chen
University of Michigan
Ann Arbor, MI 48109-2121
chenzhe@umich.edu

Michael Cafarella
University of Michigan
Ann Arbor, MI 48109-2121
michjc@umich.edu

H. V. Jagadish
University of Michigan
Ann Arbor, MI 48109-2121
jag@umich.edu

ABSTRACT

A *dictionary* — a set of instances belonging to the same conceptual class — is central to information extraction and is a useful primitive for many applications, including query log analysis and document categorization. Considerable work has focused on generating accurate dictionaries given a few example seeds, but methods to date cannot obtain long-tail (rare) items with high accuracy and recall.

In this paper, we develop a novel method to construct high-quality dictionaries, especially for long-tail vocabularies, using just a few user-provided seeds for each topic. Our algorithm obtains *long-tail* (*i.e.*, rare) items by building and executing high-quality webpage-specific extractors. We use webpage-specific structural and textual information to build more accurate per-page extractors in order to detect the long-tail items from a single webpage. These webpage-specific extractors are obtained via a co-training procedure using distantly-supervised training data. By aggregating the page-specific dictionaries of many webpages, LYRETAIL is able to output a high-quality comprehensive dictionary.

Our experiments demonstrate that in long-tail vocabulary settings, we obtained a 17.3% improvement on mean average precision for the dictionary generation process, and a 30.7% improvement on F1 for the page-specific extraction, when compared to previous state-of-the-art methods.

Categories and Subject Descriptors

H.2.8 [**Database Management**]: Database applications-Data Mining

Keywords

Set expansion; information extraction; long-tail dictionary

1. INTRODUCTION

In information extraction (IE), a *dictionary* (also known as gazetteers) refers to a set of instances belonging to the same conceptual class; for example, a camera brand dictionary contains "Canon", "Nikon" and so on. Dictionaries are extremely useful in many IE tasks. For example, many information extraction systems use dictionaries along with a set of textual features to extract entities (e.g. Person, Organization,.png Location) and relationships between entities (e.g. Person's birth date or phone number) [17, 25]. Moreover, dictionaries are a useful primitive for many real-life applications. For example, commercial engines such as Google and Yahoo!, use dictionaries for query analysis, document categorization, and ad matching [22]. The quality and coverage of the dictionaries is essential to the success of those applications [25].

Building dictionaries is an important task, and considerable work has been done to develop automated techniques that can build a dictionary from only a few user-provided seeds [27, 14]. For instance, a user can collect many popular camera brand names by giving seeds such as "Canon" and "Nikon". These approaches are largely frequency-based: they require a candidate to be observed on multiple webpages before the system can decide whether the candidate is a true dictionary item; as a result, these approaches often cannot accurately extract items that appear infrequently. However, many topics contain *long-tail* items that appear very infrequently. These are highly valuable for downstream applications [9]. For example, there are hundreds of camera brands, including the less-known "Aigo" and "Acer"; and thousands of colors, including "Amaranth Pink" and "Bazaar".

In this paper, we propose a novel approach for constructing high-quality dictionaries with only a few user-given seeds, especially for long-tail vocabularies (*i.e.*, dictionaries that contain long-tail items). We observe that many long-tail items only appear on a small number of webpages. Unlike previous efforts, our approach is not a frequency-driven approach that requires items to appear on many webpages. Instead, we leverage the webpage's structural and textual information to conduct more accurate extraction on each single webpage, thus making it possible to detect long-tail items that appear rarely.

Building high-quality page-specific extractors is challenging. For example, Figure 1 shows two example webpages with extractable dictionary items for camera manufacturers. Their formatting is entirely different: Figure 1 (a) uses multiple HTML lists, and Figure 1 (b) uses HTML tables. To obtain all the camera manufacturers, simply extracting the entire list or table is not sufficient: the items are divided into many sublists which contain both in-set and related out-of-set items (*e.g.*, the tripod manufacturer "Gitzo").

Furthermore, obtaining training data for page-level extractors is difficult. The user only provides a few seeds; it

WSDM'16, February 22–25, 2016, San Francisco, CA, USA.

DOI: http://dx.doi.org/10.1145/2835776.2835778.

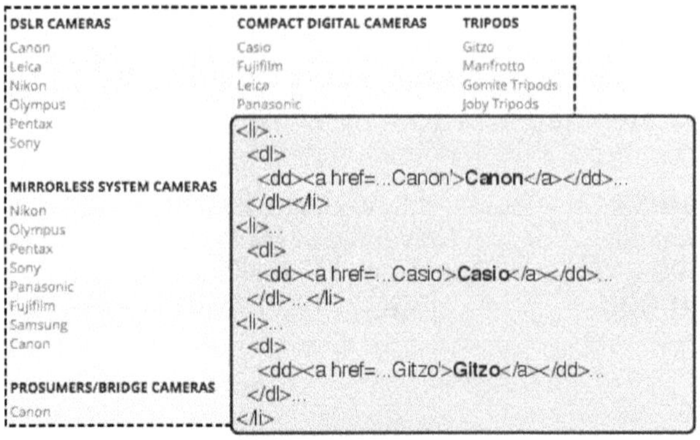

(a) From valuebasket.com

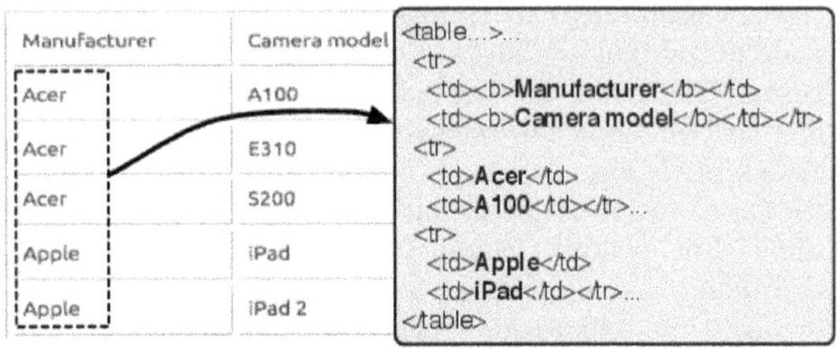

(b) From forensic.belkasoft.com

Figure 1: A list of camera manufacturers from two websites, with corresponding HTML source code.

is not practical to ask a user for labeled examples for each page. We can use distant supervision techniques to build per-page training examples [30]. Positive examples are often easy to obtain: we can employ an existing set expansion technique to obtain an *initial dictionary* to serve as positive training examples. But, obtaining negative training data is especially difficult in our application. One simple way is to select candidates that are on the webpage but not present in the initial dictionary. However, because the initial dictionary is likely not complete, the randomly selected entity could be a true dictionary entity that has simply not yet been extracted. Finding candidates that are in an off-topic existing knowledge base (KB) to produce negative training examples [32] is also not applicable, because it is hard to find an entry for a great number of the entities on the webpages due to the poor coverage of these existing KBs [11].

Finally, sequence information is essential for a high-quality page-specific extractor. For example in Figure 1, camera manufacturers (*e.g.* "Canon", "Leica") and out-of-set items (*e.g.* "Gitzo", "Manfrotto") are sequentially correlated. However, training an extractor with sequential features is challenging: it is impractical to ask humans for fully labeled sequential training examples, and partially labeled sequence data is not sufficient to train an accurate sequential model.

To tackle these challenges, we develop an extraction system LYRETAIL. Using only a few user-given seeds, LYRETAIL builds a unique extraction model that produces a high-quality page-specific dictionary (PSD) for each input webpage automatically. By aggregating the PSDs of many webpages retrieved from the web, LYRETAIL can compute a high-quality comprehensive dictionary (CD) as the result.

Our contribution mainly lies in two parts: First, LYRETAIL generates training data for building high-quality page-specific extractors automatically: a form of distant supervision. In particular, it uses the co-occurrence information from our large-scale crawled web lists dataset to obtain negative examples; our key insight is that negative examples often co-occur with entities that do not belong to the initial dictionary. For example, "Gitzo" is a negative example, as none of its cooccurrence partners (*e.g.*, "Manfrotto") belong to the initial dictionary generated by a few camera band seed examples. Second, we propose a co-training framework that can incorporate sequential features to jointly infer a high-quality dictionary on each single webpage. We leverage the output from the extractor built on web lists to train a semi-supervised conditional random field (CRF) as the resulting page-specific extractor. As a result, we are able to build high-quality page-specific extractors on each webpage; these are often able to distinguish infrequently-observed true extractions from incorrect ones. These results are then aggregated into high-quality long-tail dictionaries.

There is an additional problem we face when exploiting page-specific extraction: the intended target page-specific dictionary (PSD) is sometimes ambiguous given only a few seeds. For example, if a user provides examples of "Atlanta Braves", she could have intended a dictionary of Major League Baseball (MLB) teams or a dictionary of all U.S. sports teams. Fortunately, we can address this problem by building training data at different *granularities*, each of which yields a different PSD. For example, when we include "Brooklyn Nets" as a negative example, we would build a page extractor for the MLB teams; otherwise we would extract all the U.S. sports teams. This method is a convenient side effect of our architecture.

Contributions and Outline — In this paper, we study the problem of building a high-quality dictionary extraction system, especially in long-tail vocabulary settings. Our contributions include:

- LYRETAIL's software architecture, which builds and applies many page-specific extractors to obtain high precision and recall on long-tail items (Section 2).
- A framework and algorithms for distant supervision and training of the page-specific extractors. Our framework allows us to build a customized joint-inference extractor for each of many hundreds of pages, while requiring just three explicit seeds from the user (Section 3 and 4). By combining the outputs of multiple page-specific extractors, we can produce high-precision and high-recall dictionaries. (Section 5).
- A comprehensive evaluation, which shows that in long-tail vocabulary settings, LYRETAIL has obtained 17.3% improvement on mean averaged precision for the dictionary generation process and 30.7% improvement on F1 for the page-specific extraction, comparing to the state-of-the-art methods (Section 6).

We also cover related work in Section 7, and finally conclude with Section 8.

2. SYSTEM OVERVIEW

In this section, we present the system framework of LYRETAIL, as shown in Figure 2. Overall, LYRETAIL supports the ***dictionary generation*** process: it takes in seeds and generates a high-quality comprehensive dictionary (CD) as the output. LYRETAIL consists of three stages, as follows:

1. Webpages Fetcher — First, the seeds are used to ***fetch webpages***. To find webpages that are useful for the page-specific extraction tasks, we use an existing search engine to

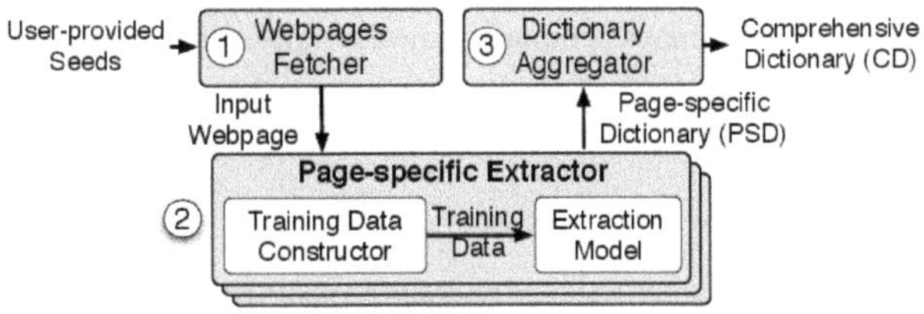

Figure 2: The framework of LYRETAIL.

retrieve the top-k webpages to serve as the input webpages. We simply concatenate all the seeds as the search query. For example, if the seeds are {canon, nikon}, we formulate the disjunctive search query as "canon nikon". We discuss the input webpages in detail in Section 2.1.

2. Page-specific Extractor — Second, the page-specific extractor attempts to build a high-quality extractor model for each single input webpage. LYRETAIL constructs a set of resources for the PSD automatically: training examples and webpage-parameterized features. In particular, the training examples (both positive and negative examples) are generated from an initial dictionary produced using an existing set expansion method SEAL [27]. By generating different sets of training examples, we can subtly change the page-specific extractor to produce PSDs at different "granularities". We discuss this idea further in Section 4.2.

3. Dictionary Aggregator — After obtaining a PSD on each single webpage, the dictionary aggregator merges the PSDs from many webpages and produces the unified high-quality comprehensive dictionary (CD) as the output.

We experimented with making LYRETAIL an iterative process, like other past extraction systems [1, 4, 28]: the CD of each round of execution can be used as a newer initial dictionary for the next round. In practice, we do not run LYRETAIL iteratively, as the performance improvement after the 1st round is not significant (as we discuss in Section 6.4).

2.1 Data Sources for Page-specific Extractor

The page-specific extractor uses two data sources: the input webpages provide the dictionary entity candidates for extraction, and the web lists are used to generate distantly-supervised training data.

Input Webpage — An input webpage is our raw source for target dictionary entities. Thus, we construct a unique *page-specific extractor* for each input webpages, in order to detect the *true* dictionary items as the PSD.

The webpages are generated by a search engine from the user-given seeds and have a variety of formatting styles, as shown in Figure 1. Because in this work we do not focus on text segmentation, our crawler uses a handful of rules to retain only "structure-segmented" pages, in which the candidate entities are already segmented by the HTML structure. We treat each leaf HTML element in a webpage as a candidate for the PSD.

LYRETAIL is currently designed to handle a particular kind of stylized text: those with recurrent patterns. In Figure 1, "Canon" and "Gitzo" are in a recurrent pattern (though only "Canon" is a correct camera brand extraction). We use the positive examples to find all the dictionary entities on a webpage. For each such entity, we define its *xpath pattern* to be the list of tags of all the nodes along a path to the root in the HTML DOM tree. Since the initial dictionary is often a high-precision but small dictionary, we assume a xpath pattern is a recurrent pattern if it contains at least one dictionary entity found by the initial dictionary. Thus, we identify all the recurrent-pattern entities $\mathbf{x} = \{x_1, ..., x_n\}$ on the webpage and use these as candidates for extraction by the page-specific extractor. There may be more than one recurrent pattern on a webpage.

Web Lists — To generate resources for the page-specific extractor, we use data from a large number of web-crawled HTML lists. We obtained HTML lists from the ClueWeb09 crawl[1], using the regular expression "$\langle ul(.*?)\langle/ul\rangle$", where each $\langle li\rangle$ item represents a list item. The web lists data can be very noisy. There are many non-entity elements (such as hyperlinks) in lists. Thus, we used the following heuristics to filter the noisy lists: we only keep lists with more than four items; we remove an item if its string length is above a predefined threshold or it contains more than five tokens. We also de-duplicate the crawled lists by their Internet domains: if a list appears in one domain many times, we only count it once. In the end, we obtained 83 million web HTML lists, then used a 9 million sample of this dataset (due to efficiency issues) as our web lists dataset.

3. PAGE-SPECIFIC EXTRACTION

In this section, we introduce LYRETAIL's page-specific extractor. We formulate the page-specific extraction problem as a classification task. Let $\mathbf{s} = \{s_1, ..., s_m\}$ be the set of m seeds, and $\mathbf{x}$ be the candidates for the PSD on this input webpage. Each entity $x \in \mathbf{x}$ takes a label $l(x) \in \{\mathsf{true}, \mathsf{false}\}$, representing whether x is a *true* dictionary entity or not. Therefore, the page-specific extractor's task is to assign a label to each $x \in \mathbf{x}$ such that $\{x|l(x) = \mathsf{true}\}$ represents the extracted PSD.

Now we introduce our two distinct feature sets and distantly-supervised training examples to construct the page-specific extraction model.

3.1 Two Distinct Sets of Features

We are able to derive two distinct sets of features: *web list features* from the web lists dataset, and *webpage-parameterized features* from the target extraction webpage.

3.1.1 Web List Features

We are able to define a set of features on the web lists dataset, as some of the lists are more likely to contain positive or negative instances. We formally define the *web list features* as $\mathbf{f_d} = \{f_{d_i}(x)\}$, where each $f_{d_i}(x) \in \mathbf{f_d}$ is a boolean function represents whether an entity x belongs to a unique list L_i from the web lists dataset. The raw number of the web list features could be large, but we remove any feature that assigns the same value to all entities, then employ feature selection methods [13] to pick the top-k features.

3.1.2 Webpage-parameterized Features

For each webpage, we synthesize a large number of *webpage-parameterized features* without direct human knowledge of the page. These features are not written by hand and do not embody direct human knowledge of each webpage. However, they are also not the same as traditional "domain-independent" features which are fixed for a large set of webpages. Instead, the feature set differs from webpage to web-

[1] http://lemurproject.org/clueweb09.php

No.	Features
1	Current element's HTML tag
2	Current element's HTML attributes
3	Previous item's HTML tag
4	Previous item's HTML attributes
5	Next item's HTML tag
6	Next item's HTML attributes
7	Parent item's HTML tag
8	Parent item's HTML attributes
9	Preceding word
10	Following word

Table 1: The HTML structural property features.

page. These webpage-parameterized features are feasible because we are able to generate webpage-specific training data.

We parse the HTML code and construct *two* families of features for each dictionary candidate x on a webpage, *entity features* and *sequential dependency*, as follows:

Entity Features — The *entity features* describe the properties associated with each entity x, and they contain *three* categories of properties. The first category describes entities' HTML *structural properties*, as shown in Table 1. They operate on each entity $x \in \mathbf{x}$. Each feature serves as a boolean function, representing whether the entity has this property. For example, "Canon" in Figure 1 generates the structural property features, including whether the current element's tag is "$\langle a \rangle$" (Feature 1).

The *xpath properties* are boolean functions for each entity $x \in \mathbf{x}$ based on its xpath. The xpath for each entity consists of a set of HTML elements along the path to the root in the HTML DOM tree. For each xpath, we use all the xpath elements with tag information to generate the xpath property feature space. For example, the xpath "/html/table[2]" (*i.e.*, the second "table" HTML element under "html") has the *elements* "html" and "table[2]", where "table" is the *tag* of the element "table[2]". The xpath "/html/table[2]" generates xpath features, including whether "table[2]" is the depth-2 xpath element, and whether "table" is the depth-2 xpath tag.

Finally, we created three *textual properties*: whether the current element contains letters; whether the current element contains numbers; and whether the current element contains punctuations.

In the end, we merge all the features mentioned above but remove a feature if it assigns the same value to all the entities, yielding the entity features $\mathbf{f_k} = \{f_k(x, l)\}$. The resulting number of the webpage-parameterized features is often small, and we give more details in Section 6.2.

Sequential Dependency — The *sequential dependency* characterizes the sequential pattern of adjacent entities. If we consider all the elements as a sequence according to its appearance in textual order, labels for adjacent elements may follow transition patterns. This observation can be incorporated as linear-chain pairwise transition features $\mathbf{f'_k} = \{f'_k(x_i, l_i, x_{i+1}, l_{i+1})\}$.

3.2 Training Data Construction

Training data is a critical need for our page-specific extractor. Direct human supervision is too expensive, so we use a distant supervision based method to generate training data. Figure 3 shows the training examples of the webpage entities and the desired output. Now we discuss how to generate the positive and negative training data.

As mentioned earlier, our training examples are generated using the low-precision, high-recall web lists data presented in Section 2.1. The web lists data is of a large scale and contains a broader range of entities than existing knowledge bases (*e.g.*, Freebase). The key insight (observed in [14]) is that in web lists, entities belonging to the same set tend to co-occur frequently, and entities that are not members of the same set are less likely to co-occur.

Webpage Entities	Training Example	Desired Output
Canon	True	True
Leica	Unknown	True
Nikon	True	True
Olympus	True	True
Pentax	Unknown	True
Gitzo	False	False
Manfrotto	Unknown	False

Figure 3: An example of the training data and the desired output for a part of entities in Figure 1 (a).

Positive Examples — *Positive examples* are derived from both a *low-recall* but *high-precision* initial dictionary $\mathbf{d}$ and the web lists data.

First, for each entity $x \in \mathbf{x}$, we test whether x is contained in $\mathbf{d}$. If $x \in \mathbf{d}$, then x is a positive instance; otherwise it is not. We generate the initial dictionary $\mathbf{d}$ using an existing set expansion technique (*e.g.*, SEAL [27]). For example, given seeds "Canon" and "Nikon", we can use SEAL to produce a ranked list of popular camera brand names as $\mathbf{d}$.

In addition, if an entity co-occurs often with the entities in the initial dictionary $\mathbf{d}$, it should also be a positive instance. We use the *initial dictionary similarity* (IDSim) to characterize the similarity between an entity x and the initial dictionary $\mathbf{d}$ as follows:

$$IDSim(x, \mathbf{d}) = \frac{1}{|\mathbf{d}|} \sum_{e \in \mathbf{d}} Sim(x, e) \tag{1}$$

where $Sim(x, e) = \frac{|LS_i \cap LS_j|}{|LS_i \cup LS_j|}$, ($LS_i$ and LS_j represent the set of lists that contain the entity e_i and e_j, respectively). It represents how frequently two entities co-occur in one list [14]. If $IDSim(x, \mathbf{d}) \geq \lambda_p$, we know that the entity x is relatively likely to co-occur with entities in $\mathbf{d}$ and x is a positive instance; otherwise it is not.

In summary, for each $x \in \mathbf{x}$, if $x \in \mathbf{d}$ or $IDSim(x, \mathbf{d}) \geq \lambda_p$, x is a positive instance; otherwise it is not. In practice we chose $\lambda_p = 0.01$.

Negative Examples — Negative examples are essential in constructing an effective extraction model, but finding them automatically in our application is not straightforward. The key insight is that if an entity strongly co-occurs only with entities excluded by the initial dictionary, we have some evidence this entity is a negative example. For example, in Figure 1, we might observe that "Gitzo" often co-occurs with "Manfrotto" and so on but rarely with an entity in the initial dictionary; thus, we believe "Gitzo" is a negative example.

We choose the negative training example based on the following two properties. First we use the initial dictionary similarity (IDSim) to determine if the testing entity x is relatively unlikely to co-occur with entities in the initial dictionary $\mathbf{d}$: if $IDSim(x, \mathbf{d}) \leq \lambda_d$ (where λ_d is a predefined threshold), we know that the co-occurrence between x and the entities in $\mathbf{d}$ is unlikely.

Second, we ensure an entity must have a certain level of popularity in the web lists, to ensure we have enough evidence to label it as negative. We define an entity x's *popularity* using its frequency, $freq(x)$. Thus, if $freq(x) \geq \lambda_f$, where λ_f is a pre-defined threshold, we assume x is popular; otherwise, it is not.

In summary, we assume an entity $x \in \mathbf{x}$ is a negative example if $IDSim(x, \mathbf{d}) \leq \lambda_d$ and $freq(x) \geq \lambda_f$, where λ_f and λ_d are two predefined thresholds.[2] We also call λ_d the *negative example threshold.* In practice, we set $\lambda_f = 50$ but vary the value of λ_d to produce negative training examples at different granularities. The resulting negative training sets can further be used to produce page-specific dictionaries at different granularities. We discuss this dictionary granularity problem in Section 4.2.

4. IMPLEMENTING PAGE-SPECIFIC EXTRACTORS

A conventional way to construct the page-specific extractor is to simply combine the two sets of features mentioned in Section 3.1 and build a single classifier that labels candidate dictionary items as "in-dictionary" or not. However, in our setting the two feature sets are derived from two distinct data sources, one from the web lists data and one from the input webpage; in similar situations, past researchers have had success with *co-training methods.* These methods train multiple distinct classifiers to maximize their mutual agreement in order to improve learning performance [31]. We pursue a similar strategy (and show in Section 6 that we can thereby beat the conventional approach).

Thus, we develop two distinct classifiers defined on two distinct sets of features: the ***list extractor*** E_{list} defined on the web lists features and the ***webpage extractor*** E_{page} defined on the webpage-parameterized features.

The ***list extractor*** E_{list} is a non-page-specific classifier. Let $\mathbf{x} = \{x\}$ be the set of candidates for the PSD on the input webpage. Let $\mathbf{l} = \{l(x)\}$ be the corresponding labels for each $x \in \mathbf{x}$, where each $l(x) \in \{\mathsf{true}, \mathsf{false}\}$ represents whether the entity x is a *true* dictionary entity or not. The probability distribution of the classifier E_{list} is defined as:

$$P_{list}(\mathbf{l} \mid \mathbf{x}) = \frac{1}{Z} \exp\left(\sum_x \mathbf{w_d f_d}\right)$$

where $\mathbf{f_d}$ are the web list features mentioned in Section 3.1.1, $\mathbf{w_d}$ are associated weights, and Z is a normalization factor.

Similarly, the ***webpage extractor*** E_{page} is page-specific and uses a conditional random field defined on the PSD candidates $\mathbf{x}$. The joint distribution of the classifier E_{page} is:

$$P_{page}(\mathbf{l} \mid \mathbf{x}) = \frac{1}{Z'} \exp\left(\sum_x (\mathbf{w_k f_k} + \mathbf{w_{k'} f_{k'}})\right)$$

where $\mathbf{f_k}$ and $\mathbf{f_{k'}}$ are the webpage-parameterized features mentioned in Section 3.1.2, $\mathbf{w_k}$ and $\mathbf{w_{k'}}$ are associated weights, and Z' is a normalization factor.

4.1 Combining Two Extractors

To combine the two classifiers is not straightforward. The *list extractor* may fail to distinguish items that are lacking information in the web lists: while the web lists is of a large scale, for some extremely rare entities, it is possible that we find *no* information in the web lists. On the other hand, the *webpage extractor* is able to produce expressive features for all testing dictionary candidates, but it requires further information: we are not able to train an accurate CRF with only partial labels of the sequence data.

Thus, we propose a co-training method that trains the two classifiers so as to encourage consensus decisions. As shown in Algorithm 1, we utilize the *list extractor* to construct an accurate *webpage extractor.* Let E_{list} be the *list extractor,* and E_{page} be the *webpage extractor.* Let $D = \{\mathbf{x_0}, \mathbf{l_0}\}$ be the automatically generated training data as discussed in Section 3.2. We first train the *list extractor* E_{list} using the training data D, and measure E_{list}'s mean accuracy of prediction on $\mathbf{x_0}$ with respect to $\mathbf{l_0}$. If the accuracy score is fairly accurate and above a predefined threshold θ_a, we obtain E_{list}'s predicted probability distribution on $\mathbf{x_0}$ as the *prior distribution* P_{list}; otherwise we use the default *prior distribution* $P_{default}$.[3]

Algorithm 1 Co-training Algorithm

1: Train E_{list} on D
2: $mscore = mean\_accuracy(E_{list}(\mathbf{x_0}), \mathbf{y_0})$
3: $P_{default} = \{p(x = l | x \in \mathbf{x_0}) = p_l^l(1 - p_l)^{1-l}\}$
4: $P_{list} = (mscore > \theta_a)?E_{list}(\mathbf{x}); P_{default}$
5: Train E_{page} by optimizing Equation 2
6: Return $E_{page}(\mathbf{x})$

To estimate the parameters for the *webpage extractor* E_{page}, we utilize a semi-supervised conditional random field framework [20] that ensures E_{page} produces a similar probability distribution to E_{list}. We estimate the unknown parameters $\mathbf{w} = \{\mathbf{w_k}, \mathbf{w_k'}\}$ by maximizing the likelihood of the objective function $P_{page}(\mathbf{l} \mid \mathbf{x})$, based on the training data $D' = \{\mathbf{x}, E_{list}(\mathbf{x})\}$. The goal is to maximize the regularized log likelihood, as follows:

$$\max_{\mathbf{w}} \sum_x \mathbf{w_k f_k} + \sum_x \mathbf{w_k' f_k'} - logZ(\mathbf{w_{k,k'}}) \\ -\lambda D(P_k || P_{list}) - \frac{\sum_k w^2}{2\sigma^2} \quad (2)$$

where $\frac{\sum_k w_k^2}{2\sigma^2}$ is a common choice of regularization to avoid overfitting, based on the Euclidean norm of $\mathbf{w}$ and on a regularization parameter $\frac{1}{2\sigma^2}$.

After obtaining the values for $\mathbf{w} = \{\mathbf{w_k}, \mathbf{w_k'}\}$, we infer the most likely assignment for each variable $x \in \mathbf{x}$ by employing a dynamic programming algorithm (*i.e.*, Viterbi) [19, 20].

4.2 Webpage Dictionary Granularity

With just a few user-given seeds, the extraction target may be ambiguous. For example, given seeds "Atlanta Braves" and "Chicago Cubs", it is not clear what is the ideal PSD: the user may intend to get all the MLB teams or all of the U.S. sports teams. It worth noting that the granularity issue only applies to certain categories; not all the dictionary categories have the ambiguous granularity. For example, the seeds "Amaranth Pink" and "Red" can be used to indicate a dictionary of color in a straightforward way.

We can address this PSD ambiguity problem by manipulating the negative example threshold λ_d. Consider the seeds "Atlanta Braves" and "Chicago Cubs" in relation to entities "Brooklyn Nets" and "Football". If a user intends to extract MLB teams, both "Brooklyn Nets" and "Football" should be negative examples; if a user intends to extract all U.S. sports teams, "Football" should be a negative ex-

[2] We also used heuristics to filter out "obviously bad" candidates as negative examples. *E.g.*, we remove items that were extremely long in either character length or token length.

[3] In practice we simply set $\theta_a = 0.8$, $p_l = 0.95$

Algorithm 2 PSDGranularities

Input: a set of negative example thresholds $\{\lambda_d\}$, a webpage wp
Output: PSDs of granularities G

1: $G = []$
2: **for** each λ_d in $\{\lambda_d\}$ **do**
3: Get positive training data $\{x_{pos}\}$
4: Get negative training data $\{x_{neg}\}$ using λ_d
5: Train page-specific extractor E using $\{x_{pos}\}$ and $\{x_{neg}\}$
6: Apply E on webpage wp and extract a PSD g.
7: $G \leftarrow G \cup g$
8: **end for**

ample while "Brooklyn Nets" should not be. If "Brooklyn Nets" has a higher IDSim than "Football", we are able to construct different training sets by varying λ_d. By using a tighter threshold we can obtain a training set that is tailored for just MLB teams; by using a looser threshold we can obtain a training set that admits all the sports teams on the page. We demonstrate the PSD granularities with two examples in Section 6.2.

5. DICTIONARY AGGREGATOR

In this section, we present the algorithm of LYRETAIL's *dictionary aggregator.* The dictionary aggregator merges PSDs from a set of input webpages and produces a high-quality CD as the output. Similar to SEAL, we employ the *lazy walk process* technique [27] to merge PSDs. The goal of this method is to formulate a quality score for each unique entity in PSDs, and the score represents the similarity between the entity and items in the initial dictionary.

The *lazy walk process* technique is defined on a random walk graph. To construct the random walk graph, we create a node for each webpage and a node for each unique entity in PSDs. An edge exists between a webpage node and an entity node if the entity appears on the webpage.

Our transition process is similar to SEAL [27]. To transit from a source node x, one randomly picks an adjacent node y with a uniform distribution proportional to the degree of node x. More specifically, $p(y|x) = \frac{1}{degree\ of\ x}$. At each step, there is also some probability α of staying at x. Putting everything together, the probability of reaching any node z from x is computed recursively as follows: $P(z|x) = \alpha I(x = z) + (1-\alpha)\sum_y P(y|x)P(z|y)$, where $I(x = z)$ is a binary function that returns 1 if node x and node z are the same, 0 otherwise. We used SEAL's setting for this lazy walk process (*e.g.*, choosing $\alpha = 0.5$), except for the starting source nodes.

To capture the similarity of an entity to items in the initial dictionary $\mathbf{d}$, we define the starting source nodes as a probability distribution $\mathbf{p_0}$ over a set of entity nodes $\mathbf{n_s}$ in the graph s.t. for each $n \in \mathbf{n_s}$, $n \in \mathbf{d}$. Recall that $\mathbf{d}$ is a ranked list and its top m entities are the seeds. It is intuitive that an entity ranked higher in $\mathbf{d}$ should have a higher probability in $\mathbf{p_0}$ than one ranked lower. We use a power-law distribution to characterize this property. Let β be the decay ratio and $0 < \beta < 1$ (in practice we chose $\beta = 0.9$). Let σ is a normalization factor to ensure the sum of $\mathbf{p_0}$ to be 1. The initial distribution $\mathbf{p_0}$ is defined as follows: for $d_i \in \mathbf{d}$ where i represents d_i's rank in $\mathbf{d}$, $p_0(d_i) = \frac{1}{\sigma}$ if $i \le m$, and $p_0(d_i) = \frac{\beta^{k-i}}{\sigma}$ if $i > m$; for $e \notin \mathbf{d}$, $p_0(e) = 0$.

Category	Seed Examples
	Common Vocabulary Dictionaries
country	nepal, hungary, burkina faso
mlb-team	chicago white sox, san francisco giants, pittsburgh pirates
nba-team	new york knicks, charlotte bobcats, san antonio spurs
nfl-team	philadelphia eagles, cleveland browns, san diego chargers
us-president	andrew jackson, john quincy adams, thomas jefferson
us-state	delaware, virginia, michigan
	Long-tail Vocabulary Dictionaries
disease	alopecia, cold sore, scabies
mattress	sealy, serta, simmons
camera	fujifilm, minolta, huawei
cmu-building	resnik house, fraternity quadrangle, mellon institute
color	metal navy, windsor tan, rose quartz

Table 2: Three seed examples of 11 dictionary categories for the page-specific extraction evaluation.

6. EXPERIMENTS

In this section, we evaluate and demonstrate that LYRETAIL is able to produce high-quality dictionaries especially in long-tail vocabulary settings. First, we measure the performance of the page-specific extraction and also demonstrate that it can produce page-specific dictionaries (PSDs) at different granularities. Second, we evaluate the quality of the comprehensive dictionary (CD) emitted by the LYRETAIL dictionary generation process. Finally we test LYRETAIL's system configuration by trying different parameter settings.

6.1 Experiment Setup

To evaluate our system, we have collected 11 dictionary categories, as shown in Table 2. They are cmu-building, country, disease, mlb-team, nba-team, nfl-team, us-president, us-state, camera-marker, color, and mattress-maker. These categories are chosen based on previous work [14, 27]. We use cmu-building, mattress, camera, disease and color to illustrate long-tail vocabularies (*i.e.*, dictionaries that contain long-tail entities); we use the remaining 6 categories to illustrate common vocabularies that contain only popular entities. We selected three random seeds from each of the 11 categories as follows: for the first eight categories, we randomly sample from the dictionary instances collected from [26]; for camera and color, we randomly selected three seeds from Wikipedia;[4] for mattress, the seeds were randomly selected from a manually collected dictionary.

LYRETAIL uses a mix of code from several languages and projects. The core LYRETAIL code is in Python. We used an existing HTML parsing tool, BeautifulSoup, to obtain all the elements from an HTML webpage. Our page-specific extractor was implemented based on the Mallet Java library.[5] We also use the Python scikit-learn library for its logistic regression method.[6]

6.2 Page-specific Extractor

In this section, we evaluate the performance of the *page-specific extractor.* We also show the result of extracting PSDs at multiple granularities.

We prepared the data sources as follows. We followed the seed selection process described in Section 6.1; the three randomly selected seeds for each category are shown in Table 2. For each category, we sent the three seeds to Google and obtained top-100 webpages as the input webpages. We

[4] http://en.wikipedia.org/wiki/List_of_digital_camera_brands
http://en.wikipedia.org/wiki/List_of_colors
[5] Mallet: http://mallet.cs.umass.edu
[6] scikit-learn: http://scikit-learn.org/

Method	Feature	Training Data	Model
List-rand	Section 3.1.1	Random	Classification
List-basic	Section 3.1.1	Section 3.2	Classification
LT-basic	Section 3.1.1 and 3.1.2	Section 3.2	Classification
LYRETAIL	Section 3.1.1 and 3.1.2	Section 3.2	Section 4

Table 3: Methods for the lesion study.

skipped webpages that cannot be downloaded and those that did not satisfy the recurrent pattern criteria mentioned in Section 2.1. Also, we only kept webpages containing more than three dictionary instances as the evaluation set. In the end, we kept 444 webpages (56.4% of the total) for all the categories. We then asked human experts to identify all of the correct dictionary entities on a webpage for each of the 11 categories. For long-tail (common) vocabulary settings, We produced an average number of 57.3 (55.1) unique training examples among 177.7 (72.8) entities with 8.4 (8.6) webpage-parameterized features and the top-10 web list features for each page-specific extractor.[7]

Methods — We compared the following methods:

- Seal uses the wrapper of SEAL [27] to obtain the PSD.[8]
- SealDict uses SEAL [27] to first generate a dictionary (from multiple pages), then constructs the PSD as the intersection between the SEAL dictionary and entities on a target webpage.
- Lyretail is our proposed page-specific extractor as described in Section 4.

In addition we compare Lyretail with the following three methods to study the influence of each component in the LYRETAIL framework. The detailed configurations of the three methods can also be found in Table 3. We used logistic regression classification for all three basic methods. We also tried other classification methods (*e.g.*, SVM and decision tree), which performed comparably or worse.

- List-rand is a logistic regression classifier based on the web lists features. It randomly selects negative examples from the entities on the webpage excluded by the positive examples.
- List-basic is a logistic regression classifier based on the web lists features. It uses our distant supervised training data as described in Section 3.2.
- LT-basic is a basic version of our page-specific extractor: it is a logistic regression classifier using both the webpage-parameterized and web lists features.

We report the averaged per-page F1 score for each category, and we tried a set of settings for the above 5 methods: For SealDict, we vary the dictionary size from 10 to 2000 and report the best F1 score. For List-rand, we randomly selected the negative examples for 10 times and report the averaged per-page F1. For List-basic, LT-basic and Lyretail, we obtained the top 20 items using SEAL as the initial dictionary, and tested 7 settings from 0 to 0.01 for the negative example threshold and chose the best per-page F1 score.[9]

[7]We have tried different feature selection methods [13] for the web lists features to obtain the top-k features according to F1, accuracy, or Chi-Squared. The differences are not significant.

[8]SEAL's code: `https://github.com/TeamCohen/SEAL`.

[9]We choose the top 20 items produced by SEAL as the initial dictionary to maintain a high-precision though low-recall set. The averaged precision of the initial dictionary is 0.999 for common vocabularies and 0.746 for long-tail vocabularies by randomly picking seeds from the ground-truth for 10 rounds.

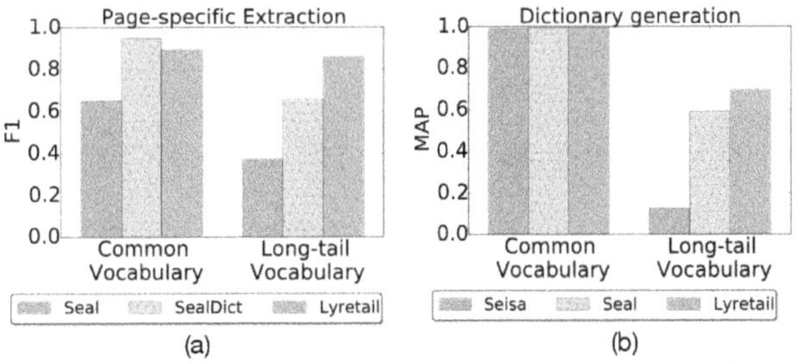

Figure 4: The summarized performance on LYRETAIL's page-specific extraction and dictionary generation on common and long-tail vocabulary settings.

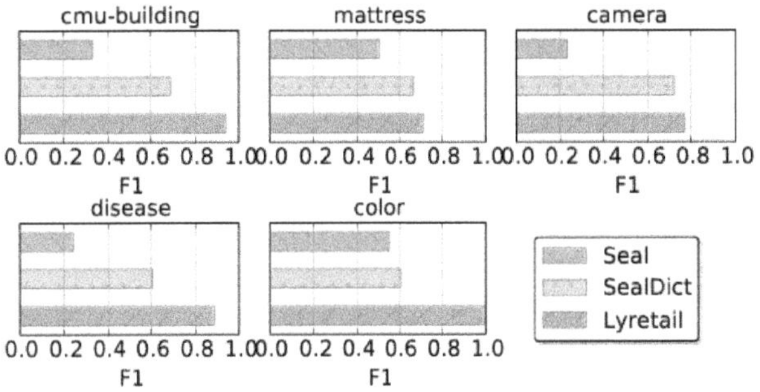

Figure 5: The F1 performance of the page-specific extractors in long-tail vocabulary categories. We compare LYRETAIL with simple methods based on the previous work SEAL.

Performance — We now compare Lyretail with Seal and SealDict, simple methods based on SEAL. Figure 4 (a) shows the average F1 performance for LYRETAIL's page-specific extraction on common and long-tail vocabularies. As shown in the Figure, we can see that Lyretail (with an average F1 of 0.892) is able to produce high-precision, high-recall PSDs in almost all the categories. Moreover, we achieved comparable performance in the common vocabulary settings and obtained 30.7% improvement in the long-tail vocabulary settings. It demonstrates that LYRETAIL is able to construct high-quality page-specific extractors that can obtain even infrequently-observed dictionary entities.

Figure 5 shows the detail results for the averaged F1 of the three methods on the five long-tail vocabulary categories. SealDict (with average precision of 0.827 and recall of 0.569) loses to Lyretail because SealDict uses the dictionaries generated by SEAL, thus failing to recognize some out-of-set items on webpages. We noticed that many extraction errors of SealDict is due to failing to detect infrequent observed dictionary items. (Which itself is sometimes due to expression diversity for certain items. For example, "New York Yankees" can also be written as "NY Yankees". For the six common vocabulary categories (*e.g.*, mlb-team and us-states), our system always beats Seal, but loses slightly to SealDict. The reason is that LYRETAIL attempts to infer *true* dictionary entities based on a small initial dictionary of size 20, while SealDict uses an already high-quality dictionary to find any matching dictionary entities on the webpage.

Lesion Study — We now examine which components of LYRETAIL are the most influential, by comparing Lyretail with three basic versions of the page-specific extractor: List-rand, List-basic and LT-basic. Figure 6 shows the F1 performance of the four methods in long-tail vocabulary settings: Lyretail is better than the other three methods. For the six

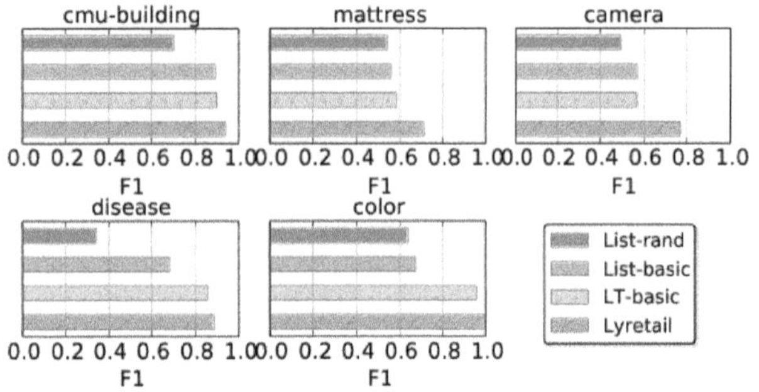

Figure 6: The F1 performance of the page-specific extractors in long-tail vocabulary categories. We compare LYRETAIL with two baseline methods.

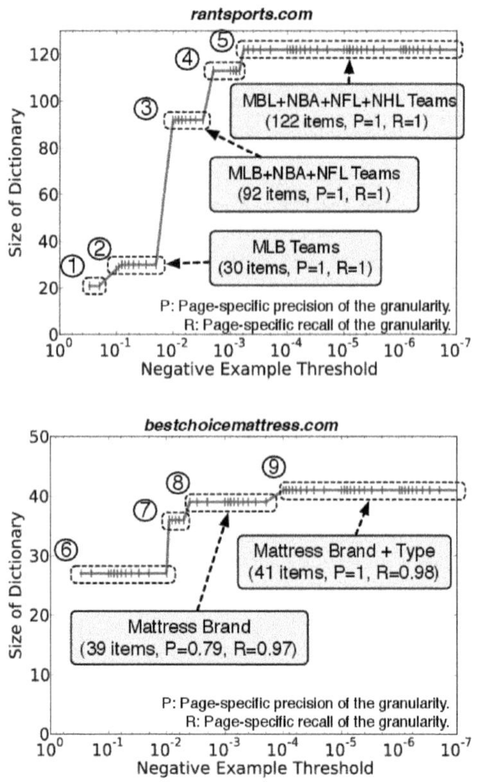

Figure 7: The granularities of the dictionary produced from two websites by trying a set of negative example thresholds.

common vocabulary settings, all four methods perform similarly. It demonstrates that our mechanism of training data generation and co-training framework is effective for building a high-quality page-specific extractor.

Granularity — We now demonstrate our page-specific extractor is able to produce different granularities of the PSD, by varying the negative example threshold from 0 to 0.3.

Figure 7 shows the dictionary sizes under each setting of the negative example thresholds on two webpages, rantsport.com and bestchoicemattress.com. As shown in the Figure, we identified five semantically meaningful plateaus out of nine granularities, and measured the page-specific precision and recall for each identified granularity. For example, the granularity at the 2nd plateau is identified to be MLB teams, with page-specific precision and recall both equal to 1. It indicates that at this granularity, we correctly obtained all the available MLB teams on rantsport.com.

By varying the negative example threshold, we observe that the plateaus exist in almost every webpage, though not all the granularities generated are semantically meaningful.

In summary, the page-specific extractor is able to produce a high-quality dictionary per webpage, especially in long-tail vocabulary settings. Also, it is able to present meaningful dictionary granularities.

6.3 Lyretail Dictionary Generation

To evaluate LYRETAIL's ability to generate CDs, we again selected three random seeds for each of the 11 dictionary categories. We followed the seed selection process as descried in Section 6.1, and we fetched top-100 webpages for each set of seeds from Google. We repeated this seed selection and webpage fetching process 10 times and report the averaged precision for top-k results.[10] We removed the seeds if none of the methods can produce any results (as was the case for 2 seed selections for cmu-building and 1 seed selection for color). For each instance in the top-k result, we asked human experts to determine whether it belongs to the dictionary.

Methods — We compared the following methods:

- Seal, a previous set expansion algorithm [27].
- Seisa, another previous set expansion algorithm [14].
- Lyretail, our proposed system.

We also compare Lyretail with List-rand, List-basic, and LT-basic for a lesion study. List-rand, List-basic, and LT-basic are all built on the LYRETAIL framework but use the List-rand, List-basic, and LT-basic page-specific extractor, respectively.

We report the averaged precision for top-k results over 10 times, and we set up the above five methods as follows: For Seal, we directly used its code from Github. It is not possible to compare to Seisa directly, because their original web list dataset is not available; we reimplemented the Seisa's algorithm on our web crawled HTML lists. For List-basic, LT-basic, and Lyretail, we obtained the top 20 items using SEAL as the initial dictionary, and set the negative example threshold to be 1e-6.

Performance — We now compare Lyretail with the two previous techniques, Seal and Seisa. Figure 4 (b) shows the mean averaged precision (MAP) for LYRETAIL's dictionary generation on common and long-tail vocabularies. As shown in the Figure, we can see that in common vocabulary settings, Lyretail matches Seal and Seisa; in long-tail vocabulary, Lyretail substantially outperforms those other methods by 17.3%. It demonstrates that LYRETAIL is able to construct high-quality dictionaries in both common and long-tail vocabulary settings.

Figure 8 shows the detailed results for the precision of the top-k results of the three methods on the five long-tail vocabulary categories. For the other six categories (*e.g.*, mlb-team and us-states), there is not much difference among the three methods. These are relatively small vocabularies, and existing methods largely do well at them. LYRETAIL is able to match the previous systems' performance.

Lesion Study — We now examine which components of LYRETAIL are the most influential, by comparing Lyretail with the three baselines, List-rand, List-basic and LT-basic.

[10] We do not use the actual recall because it is usually difficult to enumerate the universe of instances for every category.

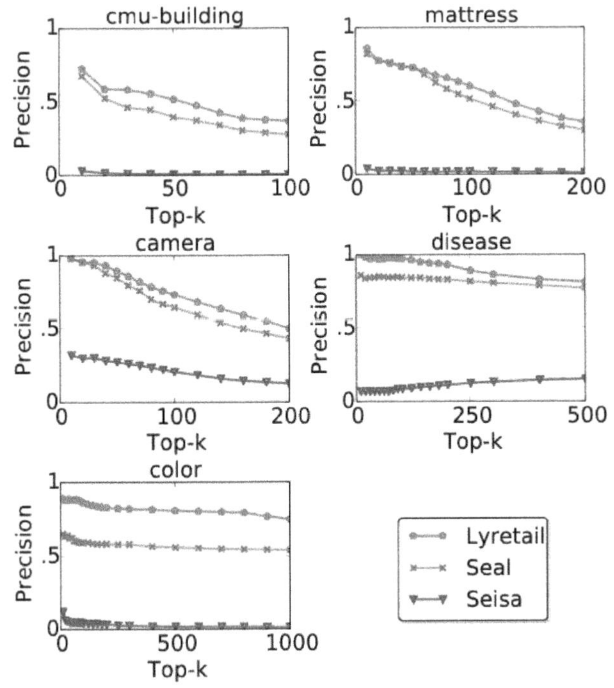

Figure 8: The precision of the top-k dictionary. We compare LYRETAIL with two previous methods.

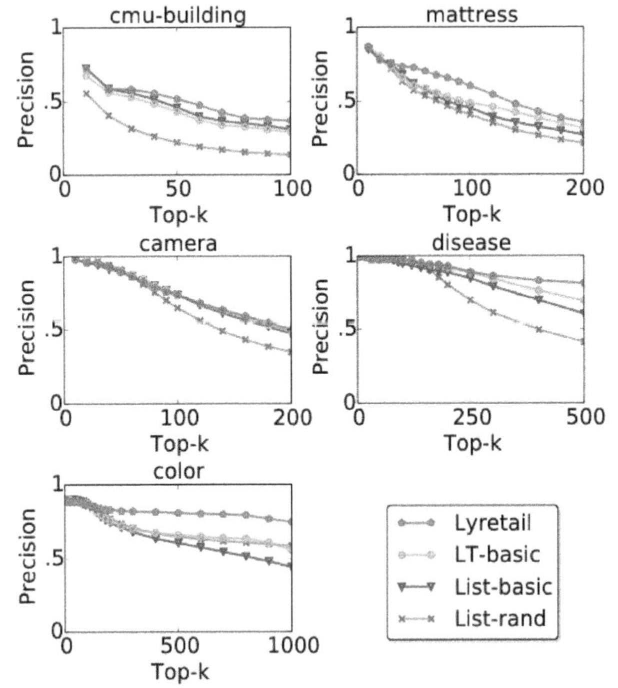

Figure 9: The precision of the top-k dictionary. We compare LYRETAIL with two baseline methods.

Figure 9 shows the precision of the top-k results for the four methods in long-tail vocabulary settings: Lyretail outperforms the three baselines. For the other six common vocabulary settings, all four methods perform similarly. Again, it demonstrates that Lyretail's good results are primarily due to our training data and extractor construction mechanism.

In summary, we have demonstrated that LYRETAIL is able to generate high-quality dictionaries. Especially in long-tail settings, LYRETAIL has obtained 17.3% improvement on mean averaged precision (MAP) for the dictionary generation process and 30.7% improvement on F1 for page-specific extraction, comparing to the state-of-the-art methods.

6.4 System Configuration

In this section, we evaluate the influence of three factors that influence the quality of CD for LYRETAIL: the number of iterations, the negative example threshold, and the initial dictionary size. We used the same setting as in Section 6.3.

Iterative Process – First we evaluate the influence of LYRETAIL's iterative framework on the dictionary quality. We used the same setting as in Section 6.3 (initial dictionary size of 20 and negative example threshold of 1e-6), but emit dictionaries of 5 iterations. The performance increases slightly when we do multiple rounds of iterations, but the differences of precision for top-k results are not huge at less than 0.05. During the iterations, the initial dictionary is the only changed input, and it indicates that the changes on the 20 initial dictionary entities are not huge enough to influence the performance significantly.

Negative Example Threshold — We tried a set of settings for the negative example threshold λ_d from 0 to 0.1 on all categories. We observed that a lower λ_d — perhaps unsurprisingly — tends to lead to a lower precision for highly-ranked values of k, but higher recall later. In most of the cases, the differences are not huge at less than 0.1, But the precision can drop significantly in categories such as camera and color. For example, the top-100 precision dropped by 0.2 by changing λ_d from 0.005 to 0.1 in camera. However, the differences of the precision are not significant at less than 0.1 when we varying λ_d between 0 and 1e-5.

Initial Dictionary Size — To evaluate the influence of the initial dictionary size on the dictionary quality. We tried a set of settings for the initial dictionary size from 10 to 500 on all categories, and measured the precision of the top-k results. We observe that the performance tends to be better when we use a high-precision initial dictionary of a larger size. But, the differences of the precision on top-k results are not huge at less than 0.1, with the exception of color, where the precision of the top-1000 results increases by 0.12 when changing the initial dictionary size from 10 to 20.

6.5 Limitations

LYRETAIL relies on web lists information to produce high-quality training examples. If we were to apply the system to obscure topics for which there is no web lists support — consider technical categories from intranet pages, such as industry-specific chemical compounds — LYRETAIL would likely be ineffective. In such cases, manual training examples or other intranet-derived domain knowledge base might need to be provided in order to produce more accurate results.

7. RELATED WORK

The goal of LYRETAIL is similar that of research into ***set expansion***, including SEAL [27, 28, 29, 24] and SEISA [14]. SEAL uses a simple pattern matching (*i.e.*, suffixes and prefix-based extractors) method to obtain candidate entities from many webpages, then employs a graph-based random walk to rank candidates entities according to their closeness to the seeds on the graph. As a result, the method is able to accurately identify frequently mentioned items but fail to detect infrequently mentioned long-tail items. SEISA is an iterative algorithm to aggregate dictionaries using the co-occurrence frequency between each pairwise dictionary item in the web HTML lists dataset and Microsoft query logs. The method relies entirely on the co-occurrence frequency information, and thus also tends to ignore infrequently-observed entities. Rong *et al.* [24] focuses on distinguishing multi-faceted clusters of the expanded entities by fusing ego-networks and existed ontology. In contrast, we build high-quality page-specific extractors to better identify long-tail dictionary items.

The series of work on ***wrapper induction*** [10, 18, 7] can be used for page-specific extraction, but these methods are rule-based and are inapplicable to produce high-quality page-level webpage extractors in our cases. More recently, Dalvi *et al.* [8] proposed the framework for wrapper induction on large scale data, and Pasupat and Liang [23] developed page-specific models to extract entities of a find-grained category. However both methods require a decent amount of training data while we at most have a few seeds.

Our page-specific extractor is similar to ***co-training*** work [3, 6, 5, 16], which exploits conditionally-independent features to improve classification performance. Unlike past work, our page-specific extractors contain sequential properties and it is not practical to train it with only partial labeled data.

Our page-specific extractor uses a ***distant supervision*** based method. Distant supervision based method has been widely used on entity and relationship extraction from the web [2, 12, 21, 32], and these work derive training examples from predefined heuristics or from existing KBs. However, those approaches are not practical in our case: heuristics cannot capture the semantics of the entities; and in the existing KBs, it is hard to find an entry for a great number of the entities on the webpages due the KBs' poor coverage [11]. Instead we uses a noisy but large-scale web list dataset to derive the negative training data. Hoffmann, *et al.* [15] also uses web HTML lists but their goal is to learn semantic lexicons in order to expand the training data.

8. CONCLUSIONS AND FUTURE WORK

In this paper, we have demonstrated that LYRETAIL is able to generate high-quality dictionaries: as good as previous work in the case of small vocabularies, and substantially better than previous work in large vocabulary settings. In the future we aim to improve LYRETAIL by exploiting the dictionary information in novel ways, such as new search engines that combine data search with some elements of data integration systems.

9. ACKNOWLEDGMENTS

The authors are grateful for feedback from Michael Anderson, Dolan Antenucci, Matthew Burgess, Yongjoo Park, Fei Xu and reviewers for their useful comments. This work was supported by National Science Foundation grant IIS-1054913 as well as gifts from Google and Yahoo!

10. REFERENCES

[1] E. Agichtein and L. Gravano. Snowball: Extracting relations from large plain-text collections. In *Proceedings of the Fifth ACM Conference on Digital Libraries*, pages 85–94, 2000.

[2] M. Banko, M. J. Cafarella, S. Soderland, M. Broadhead, and O. Etzioni. Open information extraction from the web. In *Proceedings of the 20th International Joint Conference on Artifical Intelligence*, pages 2670–2676, 2007.

[3] A. Blum and T. Mitchell. Combining labeled and unlabeled data with co-training. In *Annual conference on Computational learning theory*, pages 92–100. ACM, 1998.

[4] S. Brin. Extracting patterns and relations from the world wide web. In *WebDB*, pages 172–183, 1999.

[5] N. V. Chawla and G. I. Karakoulas. Learning from labeled and unlabeled data: An empirical study across techniques and domains. *J. Artif. Intell. Res.*, 23:331–366, 2005.

[6] M. Collins and Y. Singer. Unsupervised models for named entity classification. In *Proceedings of the joint SIGDAT conference on empirical methods in natural language processing and very large corpora*, pages 100–110, 1999.

[7] V. Crescenzi, G. Mecca, and P. Merialdo. Roadrunner: Towards automatic data extraction from large web sites. In *VLDB*, pages 109–118, 2001.

[8] N. Dalvi, R. Kumar, and M. Soliman. Automatic wrappers for large scale web extraction. *VLDB*, 4(4):219–230, 2011.

[9] N. Dalvi, A. Machanavajjhala, and B. Pang. An analysis of structured data on the web. *VLDB*, 5(7):680–691, 2012.

[10] A. Doan, A. Y. Halevy, and Z. G. Ives. *Principles of Data Integration*. Morgan Kaufmann, 2012.

[11] X. L. Dong, E. Gabrilovich, G. Heitz, W. Horn, and N. Lao. Knowledge vault: A web-scale approach to probabilistic knowledge fusion. In *KDD*, 2014.

[12] O. Etzioni, M. Cafarella, D. Downey, A.-M. Popescu, T. Shaked, S. Soderland, D. S. Weld, and A. Yates. Unsupervised named-entity extraction from the web: An experimental study. *ARTIFICIAL INTELLIGENCE*, 165:91–134, 2005.

[13] G. Forman. An extensive empirical study of feature selection metrics for text classification. *The Journal of machine learning research*, 3:1289–1305, 2003.

[14] Y. He and D. Xin. Seisa: Set expansion by iterative similarity aggregation. In *WWW*, pages 427–436, 2011.

[15] R. Hoffmann, C. Zhang, and D. S. Weld. Learning 5000 relational extractors. In *ACL*, pages 286–295, 2010.

[16] R. Jones. *Learning to extract entities from labeled and unlabeled text*. PhD thesis, University of Utah, 2005.

[17] R. Krishnamurthy, Y. Li, S. Raghavan, F. Reiss, S. Vaithyanathan, and H. Zhu. Systemt: A system for declarative information extraction. *SIGMOD*, 37(4):7–13, 2009.

[18] N. Kushmerick, D. S. Weld, and R. Doorenbos. Wrapper induction for information extraction. In *IJCAI*, 1997.

[19] J. Lafferty, A. McCallum, and F. Pereira. Conditional random fields: Probabilistic models for segmenting and labeling sequence data. In *ICML*, pages 282–289, 2001.

[20] G. S. Mann and A. McCallum. Generalized expectation criteria for semi-supervised learning with weakly labeled data. *J. Mach. Learn. Res.*, 11:955–984, Mar. 2010.

[21] M. Mintz, S. Bills, R. Snow, and D. Jurafsky. Distant supervision for relation extraction without labeled data. In *ACL*, pages 1003–1011, 2009.

[22] P. Pantel, E. Crestan, A. Borkovsky, A.-M. Popescu, and V. Vyas. Web-scale distributional similarity and entity set expansion. In *EMNLP*, pages 938–947, 2009.

[23] P. Pasupat and P. Liang. Zero-shot entity extraction from web pages. In *ACL*, 2014.

[24] X. Rong, Z. Chen, Q. Mei, and E. Adar. Egoset: Exploiting word ego-networks and user-generated ontology for multifaceted set expansion. *WSDM*, 2016.

[25] S. Roy, L. Chiticariu, V. Feldman, F. R. Reiss, and H. Zhu. Provenance-based dictionary refinement in information extraction. In *SIGMOD*, pages 457–468, 2013.

[26] R. C. Wang. *Language-Independent Class Instance Extraction Using the Web*. PhD thesis, Carnegie Mellon University, 2009.

[27] R. C. Wang and W. W. Cohen. Language-independent set expansion of named entities using the web. In *ICDM '07*, pages 342–350, 2007.

[28] R. C. Wang and W. W. Cohen. Iterative set expansion of named entities using the web. In *ICDM*, pages 1091–1096, 2008.

[29] R. C. Wang and W. W. Cohen. Character-level analysis of semi-structured documents for set expansion. In *EMNLP*, pages 1503–1512, 2009.

[30] F. Wu and D. S. Weld. Autonomously semantifying wikipedia. In *CIKM*, pages 41–50, 2007.

[31] C. Xu, D. Tao, and C. Xu. A survey on multi-view learning. *CoRR*, abs/1304.5634, 2013.

[32] W. Xu, R. Hoffmann, L. Zhao, and R. Grishman. Filling knowledge base gaps for distant supervision of relation extraction. In *ACL*, 2013.

Semantic Documents Relatedness using Concept Graph Representation

Yuan Ni
IBM Research, China
niyuan@cn.ibm.com

Qiong Kai Xu
IBM Research, China
xuqkai@cn.ibm.com

Feng Cao
IBM Research, China
caofeng@cn.ibm.com

Yosi Mass
IBM Research, Haifa
yosimass@il.ibm.com

Dafna Sheinwald
IBM Research, Haifa
dafna@il.ibm.com

Hui Jia Zhu
IBM Research, China
zhuhuij@cn.ibm.com

Shao Sheng Cao
Xidian University
shelsoncao@gmail.com

ABSTRACT

We deal with the problem of document representation for the task of measuring semantic relatedness between documents. A document is represented as a compact *concept graph* where nodes represent concepts extracted from the document through references to entities in a knowledge base such as DBpedia. Edges represent the semantic and structural relationships among the concepts. Several methods are presented to measure the strength of those relationships. Concepts are weighted through the concept graph using closeness centrality measure which reflects their relevance to the aspects of the document. A novel similarity measure between two concept graphs is presented. The similarity measure first represents concepts as continuous vectors by means of neural networks. Second, the continuous vectors are used to accumulate pairwise similarity between pairs of concepts while considering their assigned weights. We evaluate our method on a standard benchmark for document similarity. Our method outperforms state-of-the-art methods including ESA (Explicit Semantic Annotation) while our concept graphs are much smaller than the concept vectors generated by ESA. Moreover, we show that by combining our concept graph with ESA, we obtain an even further improvement.

Categories and Subject Descriptors

H.3.1 [**Information Storage and Retrieval**]: Content Analysis and Indexing; I.2.4 [**Artificial Intelligence**]: Semantic Networks; I.2.7 [**Artificial Intelligence**]: Text Analysis

WSDM'16, February 22–25, 2016, San Francisco, CA, USA.

ACM 978-1-4503-3716-8/16/02 ...$15.00.
DOI: http://dx.doi.org/10.1145/2835776.2835801 .

General Terms

Algorithms, Performance

Keywords

Document Representation, Document Semantic Similarity, DBpedia, Graph Model, Neural Network

1. INTRODUCTION

Semantic relatedness, or similarity between documents plays an important role in many textual applications such as information retrieval, document classification and clustering, question answering and more. Measurement of semantic relatedness comprises two constituents: an effective representation of documents, and a similarity measure between documents in terms of their respective representations.

Most document representations map the documents to vectors of a fixed length, aiming to map semantically related documents to close vectors in the vector space. The simplest representation of these is the *bag-of-words*, where a document is represented as a vector of frequencies organized with respect to a vocabulary of words. Component i of the vector reflects the frequency, in the represented document, of the i-th word of the vocabulary. Bag-of-words only represents the syntax of the words and their frequencies. It does not address multiple meanings of same word or synonymy of words. It also totally ignores the order of the words in the document.

Latent topic models, such as *Latent Semantic Analysis* [5], *Latent Dirichlet Allocation* [2], or *Word2Vec* [11], map words and documents to vectors whose components represent latent topics. The (configurable) length of those vectors is much smaller than with bag-of-words. The effectiveness of this representation for indication of semantic relatedness of documents was experimentally verified. The latent topics, however, are hard to interpret, they are not as intuitive as the components of the bag-of-words vectors.

The growing popularity of Semantic Web, Wikipedia, DBpedia and other universal knowledge bases, brought a new type of representing vectors, where the i-th component reflects the relative weight, or relevance of the i-th concept of the knowledge base in the represented document. Thus, the length of these concept vectors equals the number of concepts in the knowledge base, which could be in the millions. Nevertheless, the simple correspondence between components and concepts makes these vectors intuitive, easier for human interpretation. Gabrilovich and Markovitch initiated this direction with their ESA [7].

The representations and similarity measurements described above have some shortcomings. The bag-of-words model lacks reflection of the semantics of the text. The topic models (both latent and explicit) do not consider the structure and relationships among the topics or concepts used for the representation.

In this paper we propose a novel document representation and a measurement of similarity, that combine the advantages of them all. Specifically, our method i) uses topic models that are based on explicit concepts ii) considers the relationships among the concepts and iii) uses neural network based methods to represent concepts (as opposed to words) as continuous vectors.

For document representation we build a graph whose nodes are explicit concepts from a knowledge base. Similarly to Schuhmacher and Ponzetto [16], we extract the concepts directly from the document text using a mention detection tool such as SpotLight [4] or TagME [6]. However, there are several differences from [16]. First, we observe that some concepts may be closely related to the main aspects of the document while others may drift. Consider, for example, the text segment:

The ***study*** *shows an increase in* ***forced abortions, female infanticide***

Where concepts **study**, **forced abortions** and **female infanticide** are detected. Obviously, concept **study** is not as relevant to the text's aspect as the other two concepts.

Thus we assign weights to nodes in the graph as described below, while [16] only assigns weights to edges in the graph. The second major difference from [16] is that our similarity measure exploits the assigned weights with an extension of Word2Vec [11] to represent concepts as continuous vectors, while the similarity in [11] is based on Graph Edit Distance that considers only transitions between nodes in the graph.

To capture the relative importance, or weight, of the detected concepts, we arrange them as nodes in a *concept graph*, and use the knowledge base to assign weights to edges between each pair of concepts. We consider different types of relationships and structural links among the concepts and their environment in the knowledge base. Similarly to [9], we argue that concepts with higher coherence are more important to the aspects of the document. To evaluate the coherence of each concept with other concepts, we use the concept's level of centrality, which measures its closeness, through the weighted edges of the concept graph, to the rest of the concepts. We take the concept's centrality level to be its weight in the concept graph.

To evaluate semantic relatedness between two documents, we measure the similarity between their concept graphs as the weighted sum of contributions from all pairs of nodes, one from each graph, of their pairwise similarity. The weights are the weights of the nodes in their respective concept graphs. We suggest several pairwise similarity measures, one of which is a novel measure, for which we propose *Concept2Vec* that expands upon Word2Vec [11] to represent a concept as a continuous vector of 200 dimensions.

We evaluate our document representation and similarity measures on LP50 [10], a standard benchmark for document similarity. We show that our method outperforms the state-of-art method ESA, while our concept graphs are much smaller than the concept vectors generated by ESA. Moreover, we show that by combining our concept graph with ESA, we exceed each method separately, thus outperforming all other known systems.

To summarize, our contributions are the following:

- We propose a document representation as a concept graph whose nodes and edges are weighted. In its weighted edges, the concept graph reflects the strength of relationships among concepts and their environment. We propose several methods to weight the edges, and propose the centrality measure to assign weights to the nodes, which indicate the importance of the different concepts to the aspects of the document.
- We propose Concept2Vec for representing concepts as continuous vectors using neural networks that extend Word2Vec from words to concepts.
- We propose a measure of similarity between concept graphs.
- We evaluate our method on a document similarity benchmark and show that it outperforms other methods. We conduct extensive experiments to verify the effectiveness of each of the components of our method.

The rest of the paper is organized as follows. Section 2 presents related work. Section 3 provides an overview of our methods. Section 4 describes the detailed techniques to build the concept graph and in Section 5 we describe how we assign weights to the concepts in the concept graph. Section 6 introduces the Concept2Vec and the similarity measure between two concept graphs. Section 7 evaluates experimental results and we conclude our paper in Section 8.

2. RELATED WORK

One of the first, plain representations introduced is the *bag-of-words*, where the document is represented by the multiset (bag) of the words making up its text. This gives rise to the *Vector Space Model* (VSM) [15], where all documents are represented as vectors of same number of components, being the size of the underlying word vocabulary. Component i of the vector representing document d reflects the frequency of the i-th vocabulary word in d. By VSM, semantically related documents are represented by close vectors, or points, in the vector space. Specifically, similarity between documents is measured by the angle (or the cosine of the angle) between their representing vectors. Optional tunings of the vector's entries, like *idf* weighting, or normalization by document length, are often used, having been shown to enhance accuracy of indication of semantic similarity. Bag-of-words does not address polysemy (the same word can have multiple meanings) and synonymy (two words can represent the same concept), and it totally ignores the order of the words in the document. It is thus weak in reflecting an overall semantic meaning of the document. Subsequent, more intricate variations of VSM [18][14] aim at alleviating this problem through employing an extended vocabulary of pairs of words, or even larger sets, building on the distributional hypothesis by which words that occur in similar contexts tend to have similar meanings.

Also building on same hypothesis, latent topic models such as *Latent Semantic Analysis* (LSA) [5], *Latent Dirichlet Allocation* (LDA) [2], or *Word2Vec* [11], establish associations between words, or terms that occur in similar contexts, associations that are extracted from example corpora. The methods differ in the way they derive these associations from the example data, ranging from mathematical operations on matrices formed from the bag-of-words vectors, to neural networks, but similar in the expression of the derived associations through the representation of words and documents as (continuous) vectors, of a much lower (configurable) dimension than the original bag-of-words vectors, such that vectors representing semantically similar words or documents are close to one another in the vector space, as can be measured by the cosine distance between them. Latent topic models circumvent synonymy since they map the documents into a vector space of (latent) topics instead of using words. These latent topics, however, are hard to interpret, they are not as intuitive as the original bag-of-words vectors.

With the proliferation of Semantic Web, Wikipedia, DBpedia and other universal knowledge bases, which are continually expanded by the general crowd, and abundantly referenced as a source of high dimensional space of fine grained natural concepts, a new form of vector representation evolved, which reflects the knowledge base concepts that are relevant to the represented document. The semantic meanings of a document, as expressed through these concepts, is easier for human interpretation. *Explicit Semantic Analysis* (ESA) by Gabrilovich and Markovitch [7] was pioneering in this direction, expressing of the meaning of any text in terms of a weighted vector of Wikipedia concepts. Wikipedia contains an article for each of its concepts, whose title is that concept. ESA quantifies the strength of association $assoc(w, c)$ of word w with concept c as the TFIDF weight of word w in the Wikipedia article titled c. The strength of association $assoc(T, c)$ of text T with Wikipedia concept c is defined as the sum, over the words $\{w_i\}$ of T, of $assoc(w_i, c)$ multiplied by the TFIDF weight of w_i in T. These $assoc(T, c)$ values, organized in a vector whose length is the number of Wikipedia concepts (a few millions), form the ESA representation of T. The Wikipedia concepts that make up the ESA representation have explicit semantic meanings, and are intuitive for human understanding, as opposed to the obscure topics of the above latent topic models. Similarly to the previous methods, semantic relatedness of documents is measured by the cosine of the angle between their respective concept vectors.

While ESA totally ignores Wikipedia's wikilinks, which are its inter-article links, Yeh et al. [19] employ a random walk on the Wikipedia graph, whose nodes are Wikipedia's articles, or concepts, and edges – its wikilinks. The walk starts with a distribution of mass over the nodes, a distribution derived from the given text, either as the end result of ESA on the given text, or through detection of mentions of Wikipedia concepts in the text, by existing or especially developed tools. The stationary distribution converged to by the random walk yields the representation of the text as a vector whose length equals the number of Wikipedia articles. Semantic relatedness between two texts is computed as with ESA - by the cosine similarity of their concept vector representations.

Unlike ESA that uses a large number of concepts, methods like Schuhmacher and Ponzetto [16] only reference a small number of DBPedia concepts, relying, instead, on their explored inter-relatedness. Given a text, mentions of DBPedia concepts within it are first identified using existing tools, such as SpotLight [4] or TagME [6]. A graph is then generated whose nodes are the identified concepts, and the concepts which are connected to them through a semantic relation found in DBpedia, and whose edges are these applied DBpedia semantic relations. The edges are further weighted using information theoretic measures, independent of the given text, aiming to capture the degree of associativity between the concepts connected by each edge. Semantic relatedness between two documents is measured by a tailored variation of the graph edit distance (GED) between their respective graph representations, a variation which only considers distance between nodes. Node distance, in turn, is computed along the paths of DBpedia's semantic relations, weighted as suggested above. For similarity between documents, the nodes themselves are not weighted, namely, a pair of nodes (one from each graph) contributes the distance between them to the total edit distance, without any notion of weight, or significance to the analyzed text, of each node relative to the other nodes in its graph. In contrast, we assign weights to nodes based on their importance in the text and our similarity measure combines the weights with an extension of Word2Vec [11] for concepts' representation.

Huang et al [9] continue a line of works that represent a document using a bag of words and concepts. They define several features that capture concept centrality. Some of their features consider the local concept centrality of concepts among other concepts in the same document. For document similarity they define other features that consider the relative concept centrality of concepts in one document with respect to concepts in the other document. Altogether, a total of 17 features are specified. They use machine learning to learn the weights of the features. Our method uses a similar notion of centrality, although slightly different in the details, and fewer features. We believe that our results can improve with additional features, and with tuning per subject domain.

3. OVERVIEW

In this section, we overview our concept graph and its generation from a given document. Techniques are specified in detail in section 4.2.

The key idea of document representation by a concept graph is to link the concepts in the document text to entities of a knowledge base, and to explore the structural and semantic information among them in the knowledge base, to create a graph for these entities. Based on the observation that the core aspects of a document should be a set of closely related concepts, we measure the centrality, over the graph, of each concept to obtain its weight.

Figure 1 depicts the architecture of our method. First, given the input document, we use an existing mention detection tool such as Spotlight [4] or TagMe [6] to detect the mentions in the document text. A mention is a term/phrase in the text that corresponds to a defined concept in the knowledge base. In this paper, we use DBpedia as our knowledge base. The English version of DBpedia 2014 comprises 4.58 million concepts, each corresponds to a Wikipedia article. These are annotated with 583 million facts. Given

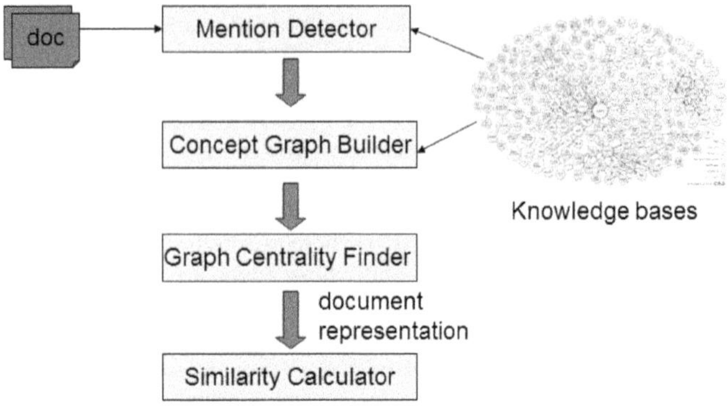

Figure 1: Architecture of our method

the following document text, for example, the tool will detect four mentions and their corresponding concepts (shown in brackets).

Gambling [http://dbpedia.org/resource/Gambling] *increases* ***aggregate demand*** [http://dbpedia.org/resource/Aggregate_demand] *for* ***goods and services*** [http://dbpedia.org/resource/Goods_and_Services] *in the* ***economy*** [http://dbpedia.org/resource/Economy]

The nodes of the concept graph are the detected concepts in the given document. We measure the strength of association between each pair of concepts, based, as follows, on their features and their relationship in the knowledge base. Any pair of concepts with a non-zero association between them is connected by an edge in the concept graph, whose weight is taken to be the strength of that association. The inter-concept association is calculated as a combination of three types of associations, each reflecting the extent of similarity, or relatedness of the concepts in the scope of one feature:

- Context association: relative frequency of occurrence of both concepts in same contexts.
- Category association: how close the concepts are in the knowledge base taxonomy of categories
- Structure association: the related structural information from the knowledge base

Once the edges are determined, the centrality of each node in the concept graph is computed, and set to be the weight of the node.

Finally we define several measures of similarity between two concept graphs which aim to reflect the semantic relatedness of the documents they represent.

4. CONCEPT GRAPH GENERATION

We start with a brief background of the DBpedia knowledge base and continue to a detailed description of the generation of our concept graph.

4.1 DBpedia Data

As aforementioned, our method relies on the semantic association and structural relationship from a knowledge base. We choose DBpedia [1] as our knowledge base due to its large coverage and variety of relationship types on both ontology level and instance level. The proposed approach, however, could also be applied to other knowledge base such as YAGO [8] or Freebase.

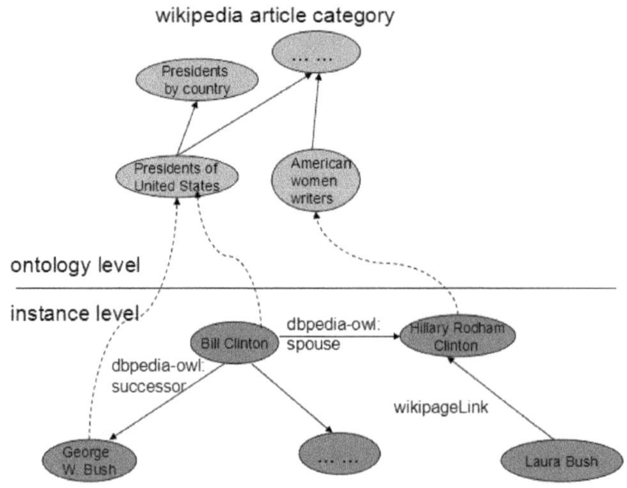

Figure 2: Referenced DBpedia Data

DBpedia is a crowd-sourced community effort to extract structured information from Wikipedia and make this information available on the Web. Every Wikipedia page has a corresponding concept in the DBpeida knowledge base. DBpedia is provided as a collection of files, or datasets, each with a specific type of data. Figure 2 shows the part of DBpedia data that we reference in this paper, that comprises instance level data and ontology level data. For the instance level data, we use the Wikipedia pagelinks dataset, that was created from the internal links between Wikipedia articles, and the mapping based infobox dataset, which is a clean version of the Wikipedia infoboxes, that together describe 4.58 million concepts and the relationship among them. We use the former dataset to measure context association between concepts, and the latter, which specifies relations like, e.g., relationship `dbpedia-owl:spouse` between concept `Bill Clinton` and concept `Hillary Rodham Clinton` – to measure structural association between concepts. For the ontology level data, we use the article categories dataset from DBpedia to provide the classification information for each instance and we use the taxonomy of categories dataset to measure the category association between concepts. The reason to use the article category dataset is that it has quite a large coverage and is constantly evolving.

4.2 Concept Graph Builder

Given a document, we first extract its concepts by employing a mention detection tool. The extracted concepts form the nodes of the concept graph. The edges of the graph represent the relationships between the concepts as derived from DBPedia, through the three kinds of association between concepts: context association, category association and structure association. In the following subsections, we describe how we measure the extent of these associations.

4.2.1 Context Association

Context association between two concepts reflects how often both concepts share contexts. In Wikipedia, we take shared contexts to be shared incoming links, i.e., pages that point to both concepts. A large number of shared incoming links indicates a high context association. Given two concept m_1 and m_2 we use the metric from [12] to measure their context associations. Let M_1 and M_2 denote the respective sets of incoming links to m_1 and m_2, then

$$ctxt(m_1, m_2) = 1 - \frac{\log(\max(|M_1|, |M_2|)) - \log(|M_1 \cap M_2|)}{\log|W| - \log(\min(|M_1|, |M_2|))} \quad (1)$$

where $|W|$ is the total number of concepts in the knowledge base.

4.2.2 Category Association

As mentioned in Section 4.1, DBpedia provides with category information for each concept, and a taxonomy of categories. Categories are intended to group together pages on similar subjects. Hence, if two concepts belong to the same Wikipedia category, they are associated with the same topic. Through the Wikipedia taxonomy of categories, We measure similarity of categories to evaluate the level of category association between concepts. Given two concepts m_1 and m_2, let $C_1 = \{c_{11}, c_{12}, \ldots, c_{1p}\}$, and $C_2 = \{c_{21}, c_{22}, \ldots, c_{2q}\}$ denote the respective sets of categories that m_1 and m_2 belong to. We measure the category association between these two concepts by first finding the pairwise similarity between any two individual categories c_{1i} and c_{2j}, and then combining the pairwise category similarities between all pairs of categories one from C_1 and the other from C_2, to form the groupwise similarity between C_1 and C_2, which is set to be the level of category association between the given two concepts. Next we define three workable pairwise similarity measures, and their combination into groupwise similarity.

Pairwise category similarity. Several works [13, 17] proposed to calculate the similarity of two categories in a taxonomy based on the specificity, or the information content of the categories. First, the information content score $IC(c)$ is computed for each node c in the taxonomy. Then given two nodes c_i and c_j in the taxonomy, let $MSCA(c_i, c_j)$ denote the common ancestor of c_i and c_j with highest information content, then the pairwise similarity of c_i and c_j is computed as follows.

$$pairwise(c_i, c_j) = \frac{IC(MSCA(c_i, c_j))}{IC(c_i) + IC(c_j)}$$

Different metrics are proposed to measure the information content of a node in the taxonomy [13]. The idea is that the more specific the node is in the taxonomy, the higher is its information content. In general, those metrics are either intrinsic or extrinsic. An intrinsic metric considers only the topological properties of the taxonomic backbone, whereas an extrinsic metric [13] also considers the instances that belong to each category in the taxonomy. In this paper, we try two intrinsic and one extrinsic metrics.

The first intrinsic metric uses the depth of the category in the taxonomy, i.e., its specificity, as its information content. Formally,

$$IC_{depth}(c) = \frac{\log(\max(depth(c)))}{\log(max\_depth)}$$

where max_depth denotes the maximum depth of the taxonomy. Note that the IC_{depth} assumes that the given taxonomy is a DAG (Directed Acyclic Graph). However, the taxonomy of Wikipedia categories does contain cycles. Moreover, the set of Wikipedia categories contains a large number of "Administrative" categories which define the status or stage of the pages, ignoring any semantic information about the page, and thus should not be considered in our metrics. In Appendix A we describe how we cleaned the taxonomy from cycles and administrative categories.

The second intrinsic metric considers the number of descendants of a category in the taxonomy to measure its information content. A large number of descendants indicates generality, or lower specificity. The descendants based information content of a category c is defined as

$$IC_{desc}(c) = 1 - \frac{\log(|D(c)|)}{\log(|C|)}$$

where $D(c)$ denotes the set of descendants of category c and C – the set of all categories in the taxonomy.

Extrinsic metrics consider also the number of instances that belong to a category. A large number of instances indicates a general, less specific category. For example, category `American` has a larger number of instances than category `Presidents of United States`. Formally,

$$IC_{inst}(c) = 1 - \frac{\log(I(D(c)))}{\log(I(C))}$$

where $I(D(c))$ denotes the number of instances that belong to category c or its descendants, and $I(C)$ denotes the total number of instances in DBPedia.

In Section 7, we compare these metrics experimentally.

Groupwise category similarity. Given two concepts m_1 and m_2 and their categories $C_1 = \{c_{11}, c_{12}, \ldots, c_{1p}\}$ and $C_2 = \{c_{21}, c_{22}, \ldots, c_{2q}\}$, for each $c_{1i} \in C_1$, find $best(c_{1i})$ which is the maximal pairwise similarity between c_{1i} and any category c_{2k} in C_2. Similarly, find $best(c_{2j})$ for each $c_{2j} \in C_2$. Groupwise similarity denoted by $cat(C_1, C_2)$) is defined as the average best similarity over all pairs,

$$cat(C_1, C_2) = 0.5 * \frac{\sum_{i=1}^{p} best(c_{1i})}{p} + 0.5 * \frac{\sum_{j=1}^{q} best(c_{2j})}{q} \quad (2)$$

4.2.3 Structure Association

Wikipedia infoboxes contain information about concepts and their various types of relationships, thus inducing a structural graph, $G(V, E)$, over the concepts, whose edges $e \in E$ are labeled by predicates $pred(e)$ that indicate the type of the relationship. We define the weight of an edge e to be

$$w(e) = \log(|pred(e)|)/\log(|E|)$$

where $|pred(e)|$ is the frequency of $pred(e)$ in E. Our intuition is that frequent predicates represent a general, less significant relationship. We thus define the structure association between two concepts m_1, and m_2, as the inverse of the sum of the weights of the edges $e_1, e_2, \ldots, e_k$ of the shortest path from m_1 to m_2:

$$struct(m_1, m_2) = \frac{1}{\sum_1^k w(e_k)} \quad (3)$$

To find the shortest path between m_1 and m_2, we use bi-directional breadth first search, and we set a threshold k to constraint the number of steps to guarantee performance. If we find no path within k steps, we set $struct(m_1, m_2) = 0$.

5. ASSIGNING WEIGHTS TO CONCEPTS

In the concept graph we generate for a given document, we assign weights to the concepts to reflect their relevance to the aspects of the document. We use two weight assignment methods: a global method that is based on the strength of the semantic relationships among the concepts, and a local method that is based on content similarity between the Wikipedia page of the concept and the given document.

5.1 Concept Graph based Weights

In graph theory and network analysis, centrality measurement is used to identify the most important nodes within a graph/network, the most influential persons in a social network, key infrastructure nodes in the Internet and more. According to different criteria of "importance" which suit different purposes, different graph properties of a node are considered for the evaluation of its centrality [3]. The most popular properties are: (1) degree, or number of ties that the node has, as high degree indicates popularity in the network, (2) closeness, or the inverse of the sum of the node's distances (length of shortest path) to all other nodes in the network, and (3) betweenness, or the number of shortest paths, between any two other nodes, that go through the node, as a node of high betweenness is critical to establish the short connections for other nodes in the network.

The set of concepts to represent the aspects of the document should be closely related, close to one another in the concept graph. We thus chose to measure centrality, or importance of a node, through its closeness property. Instead of using the shortest path between two concepts as in the traditional method, we define the distance between two nodes as the inverse of the weight of the edge between them in the concept graph. Let m_1 and m_2 be two concepts in the concept graph. We define

$$dist(m_1, m_2) = \frac{1}{\lambda_1 \cdot ctxt(m_1, m_2) + \lambda_2 \cdot cat(m_1, m_2) + \lambda_3 \cdot struct(m_1, m_2)} \quad (4)$$

where λ_i are wieght parameters of the three types of associations.

Subsequently, we define the closeness based centrality of a concept m as

$$centrality(m) = \frac{1}{|V|} * \sum_{m_j \in V} \frac{1}{dist(m, m_j)} \quad (5)$$

where V is the set of concepts in the concept graph.

5.2 Content based Weights

Complementing the global centrality measure for scoring a node in the concept graph is a local measure, being the similarity between the Wikipedia page that represents the concept and the document itself. We apply IR methods to measure this similarity, specifically, we use the simple tf-idf measure of document similarity. Formally, the content-based score of a concept m with respect to document d is defined as

$$content(m) = \frac{\vec{m} * \vec{d}}{\| \vec{m} \| * \| \vec{d} \|} \quad (6)$$

where $\vec{m}$ and $\vec{d}$ are the bag-of-words vector representations of m and d respectively.

We use the content-based weights of concepts for two purposes. First, we combine them with the centrality based weights. Second, we use them to filter out concepts that may be erroneously detected by the mention detection tool. Such errors may happen due to wrong disambiguation of concepts when mapping them to the knowledge base. A low content similarity of a concept is an indication that the concept is not related to the document. Therefore we remove concepts that have a content similarity lower than some threshold. For the remaining concepts we combine their centrality and content weights using a linear combination.

6. SEMANTIC RELATEDNESS OF DOCUMENTS

Given two documents, D_1 and D_2, we generate both respective concept graphs, and weight their nodes, as described in Sections 4 and 5, and turn to compute the semantic relatedness between these documents in terms of features of our concept graphs.

6.1 Pairwise Concept Similarity

A simple pairwise concept similarity is based on [12] which considers the shared incoming links in the knowledge base. We call it the Wikilink pairwise similarity, and use Eq. (1) to measure it.

We present another, novel pairwise similarity measure between two concepts that uses a neural network to represent concepts as continuous vectors.

6.1.1 Concept2Vector representation

We expand upon the Skip-Gram model by Mikolov et al. [11] to represent concepts as continuous vectors. We refer to our method as *Concept2Vector*. We first describe how we train the model and then how we use it for similarity.

Data Corpus preparation. To train a model for representing concepts as vectors, we need a data corpus that provides the context of each concept. We exploit the Wikipedia internal links for that. An internal link in a Wikipedia page (referred to as *wikilink*) comprises a reference (hyperlink) to another Wikipedia article and an optional surface form that represents the referenced article. Since each Wikipedia article corresponds to a concept in DBpedia, we consider each wikilink as a reference to a DBpedia concept. We preprocessed all wikipedia pages, replacing the surface form in each wikilink by the title of the referenced article. If the referenced article redirects to another page then we replace the surface form by the title of the target page. Consider, for example, the wikilink with a surface form `Oxford University` that references the page `University_of_Oxford`, and assume that the concept `Phi_Beta_Kappa` redirects to `Phi_Beta_Kappa_Society`. Then the text

"He is an alumnus of `Georgetown University`, where he was a member of `Kappa Kappa Psi` and `Phi Beta Kappa` and earned a `Rhodes Scholarship` to attend the `Oxford University`"

is replaced by

"He is an alumnus of `Georgetown_University`, where he was a member of `Kappa_Kappa_Psi` and `Phi_Beta_ Kapp a_Society` and earned a `Rhodes_Scholarship` to attend the `University_of_Oxford`"

After pre-processing, each page in Wikipedia contains original words (that do not appear as part of a wikilink) and the concepts, each treated as one term.

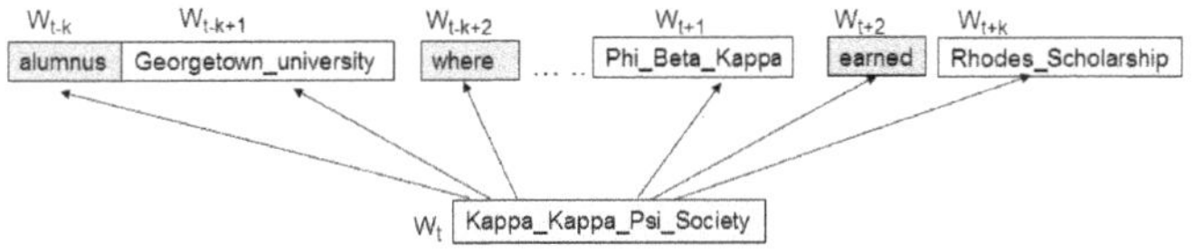

Figure 3: The Training Example for the Sentence

Model Usage. Based on Mikolov [11], Skip-Gram model is better for infrequent-terms representation. Since the occurrence of links in Wikipedia is sparse we choose the Skip-Gram model. The Skip-Gram model aims to maximize the probability of current term based on its surrounding terms. The parameters we used to train the model is as follows, window size = 10, sub-sampling = $1e-3$, cutoff min-count = 0. Figure 3 shows a model structure for the above text.

After the training, we obtain a vector for each term which could be either a word or a concept. All vectors have the same length, we took it to be 200. The model generates the vectors for 4.27 millions concepts in total. Compared with the total 4.58 millions concepts in DBpedia, the coverage of the concepts is 93.2%, which covers most of useful concepts already. The vector representation could be further improved by completing more Wikipeida links. It is observed that if a concept appears multiple times in a Wikipedia article, usually the Wikipedia link is only added for the first occurrence. Then we could try to add more links by using the exact matching in the same article. If a phrase in the following part of a Wikipedia article matches an explicit Wikipedia link, then we could add a new Wikipedia link on the phrase. In this way, more Wikipedia links could be generated, then we could obtain better and more complete context of a concept. Thus, the quality of the vectors could be improved.

The pairwise similarity between two concepts, m_1 and m_2, is defined as the cosine similarity between their respective Concept2Vector representations, $\vec{m_1}$ and $\vec{m_2}$:

$$Concept2VecSim(m_1, m_2) = \frac{\vec{m_1} * \vec{m_2}}{\|\vec{m_1}\| * \|\vec{m_2}\|} \quad (7)$$

We can also take the pairwise similarity to be a linear combination of the above, as described in the experiments section, Section 7.

6.2 Document Similarity

We extend the groupwise similarity measure of 4.2.2 by incorporating weights into the equation. Let $\{m_{1i}\}_{i=1}^{p}$ be the concepts in the concept graph of D_1 and $\{m_{2j}\}_{j=1}^{q}$ the concepts in the concept graph of D_2. Let $\{w_{1i}\}_{i=1}^{p}$ and $\{w_{2j}\}_{j=1}^{q}$ be their respective weights. We define the semantic relatedness between D_1 and D_2 as:

$$ConceptGraphSim(D_1, D_2) =$$
$$0.5 * \frac{\sum_1^p w_{1i} * best(m_{1i})}{\sum_1^p w_{1i}} + 0.5 * \frac{\sum_1^q w_{2j} * best(m_{2j})}{\sum_1^q w_{2j}} \quad (8)$$

where $best(m_{1i})$ ($best(m_{2j})$ respectively) is the best pairwise similarity for m_{1i} (m_{2j} respectively) over all concepts in $\{m_{2j}\}_{j=1}^{q}$ ($\{m_{1i}\}_{i=1}^{p}$ respectively).

To derive the final similarity score of two documents we combine the ConceptGraphSim with ESA [7] scores using a linear combination.

The above two similarity measures are quite different from each other. First, the ConceptGraphSim uses a small number of concepts detected directly from the document while ESA uses a large vector of concepts that are supposed to indirectly represent the document. Second, the ConceptGraphSim uses a unique aggregation of the pairwise similarities between pairs of concepts while ESA uses a cosine similarity between two concept vectors. It should be noted that the pairwise similarities of ConceptGraphSim between each pair of concepts uses a cosine-similarity between their continuous vector representations. Thus the ConceptGraphSim comprises both a pairwise similarity and cosine similarity.

7. PERFORMANCE STUDY

To verify the effectiveness of our method we conduct comprehensive experiments to verify the contribution of different parameters for the generation of the concept graph and for its application to document similarity. Our results show that the proposed concept graph captures the essential aspects of the document content and it outperforms other methods for semantic similarity of documents.

7.1 Experimental Testbed

Data Sets. We use the LP50 [10] dataset for evaluating our document semantic similarity. LP50 consists of 50 news articles from the Australian Broadcasting Corporation (ABC). The documents are of varying length, from 51 to 126 words and they cover a number of broad topics. Each pair of documents was judged by 8 to 12 different annotators, who rated the pairs on a scale of 1 to 5, where 1 indicates "highly unrelated" and 5 – "highly related". The final rate of each pair was taken as the average over all its judgments. The result is 1225 pairs with 67 distinct relatedness scores.

Evaluation metric. Similar to [10, 7, 16] we use the Pearson linear correlation to measure the agreement with the human judgments.

Experimental Setup. We make use of the TagMe [6] as our mention detection tool. As described in section 6.1.1 we processed Wikipedia to generate the Concept2Vector model. We generated vectors for 3 million words and for 4 million concepts. The vector for each term has 200 dimensions. We set the threshold for filtering our concepts with a low content similarity (section 5.2) to 0.001. We test a variety of configurations of our method. The various parameters and their values are shown in Table 1 with a reference in brackets to the section where they are described. To evaluate each parameter separately we fix the other parameters and vary that parameter. The values in bold are the default values that we fix when evaluating a specific parameter.

As we show in the rest of this section, the best results were achieved using a simple linear combination of all described parameters. Specifically for assigning weights to edges in the concept graph of a document, the best results were achieved when using a linear combination of ctxt (Eq. 1), cat (Eq. 2) and struct (Eq. 3) similarity between two concepts. For assigning weights to concepts in the concept graph, the best result was achieved when using a linear combination of the centrality based weights (Eq. 5) and content based weights (Eq. 6). For the pairwise similarity between a pair of concepts, the best result was obtained by a linear combination of Concept2VecSim (i.e the Cosine similarity between the vector representations of the two concepts) and the ctxt based

Table 1: Configuration Parameters

Parameter	Symbol	Value
Category association (4.2.2)	IC	**depth**, desc, inst
Concept Graph Centrality(5.1)	Dist	ctxt, cat, struct, **ctxt+cat+struct**
Concept weights (5)	Weight	none, centrality, content, **centrality + content**
Pairwise Concept similarity (6.1)	conceptSim	ctxt, Concept2VecSim, **ctxt + Concept2VecSim**
Document similarity (6.2)	documentSim	**ConceptGraphSim**, ESA, ConceptGraphSim + ESA

similarity (Eq. 1). Finally we show that for the overall document similarity, a linear combination of our ConceptGraphSim method with ESA yields the best results. We leave it for future work to learn the parameters automatically.

All the experiments were conducted on a 2.8GHz Intel Core machine with 8GB main memory running Windows 7, and all our algorithms are implemented in Java.

7.2 Compare to state-of-the-art

We compare the best configuration of our method (using the bold values of each parameter in Table 1) to the following state-of-art methods in document similarity measurement, i.e. Latent Semantic Analysis (LSA) [5], Explicit Semantic Analysis (ESA) [7], graph model (GED) [16], WikiWalk [19], and ConceptLearned [9]. Table 2 shows the results. Our method combined with ESA, termed `ConceptGraphSim + ESA` achieved 0.786 Pearson correlation which outperformed all other methods except ConceptLearned [9] which achieved 0.808. We should note that ConceptLearned [9] uses a relatively large number of 17 features compared with our system. Moreover, their weights are learned and tested using k-fold cross validation on the same dataset, thus it might be overfitted to the LP50 benchmark. Our method is not domain specific. Moreover, we believe that we could further improve our performance on that dataset by combining more features and learning their weights, but we leave it for future work.

Among the other methods, ESA achieved 0.72 Pearson correlation. The method `ESA Implemented` is our implementation of ESA where we index the Wikipedia documents into a Lucene[1] index. To generate the ESA concepts vector for a given document, we use the document content as a query to the Lucene index with a BM25 similarity model. Similar to [19] we take the top-625 results as the ESA concepts. We got some improvement 0.727 when we add to the generated query, pairs of terms from the document content in a sliding window of size 7. Our method without ESA, termed `ConceptGraphSim` achieves 0.745 correlation (p-value $= 2.02E - 217$).

In general, both our method and ESA use a set of weighted concepts to represent the document. Yet, there are several differences between the two. First, ESA uses a large number of concepts while we use only the concepts that are detected in the document. On average we use about 20 concepts for each document while ESA uses 625 concepts (lower numbers achieved worse performance for ESA). Second, ESA uses just a cosine similarity between two vectors while we explore all pairwise similarity between pairs of concepts and take the best matching combination.

[1] http://lucene.apache.org/

Table 2: Comparison with Existing Methods on the LP50 dataset

Parameter	Pearson correlation
LSA [5]	0.60
GED [16]	0.63
ESA paper [7]	0.720
ESA implemented	0.727
ConceptGraphSim	0.745
WikiWalk + ESA [19]	0.772
ConceptGraphSim + ESA	0.786
ConceptsLearned [9]	0.808

Our hypothesis is that the two methods (ConceptGraphSim and ESA) complement each other since each uses a different set of concepts and a different similarity measure. We tried therefore to combine the two methods using a linear combination. This follows the work of WikiWalk [19] that also builds on top of ESA. They use personalized PageRank on all Wikipedia pages where the personalized teleport vector uses the ESA weights on concepts detected in the document. As can be seen in Table 2, our method combined with ESA achieve a higher correlation than WikiWalk with ESA. It should be noted that WikiWalk report that their ESA implementation achieved correlation of 0.766 so their improvement over ESA is quite negligible. Moreover, the WikiWalk implementation for document similarity requires to run a personalized PageRank for each document which is quite inefficient compared with our derivation of weights.

Next we report the parameter tuning of the different configurations of our method. Please be noticed that the performance is reported without the combination with ESA.

7.3 Effect of Concept Weight Strategies

As discussed in Section 5, we provide two strategies to assign weights to the concepts in the concept graph. The first strategy, termed `centrality`, is based on the closeness centrality of concepts in the concept graph (Eq. 4). The second strategy, termed `content` is based on cosine similarity between the bag-of-words vectors of the document and the Wikipedia page that represents the concept (Eq. 6). Furthermore, for the centrality based weights we presented three different methods (termed ctxt, cat and struct) to measure the similarity between pair of concepts. Table 3 shows the effect of the different weighting strategies on the final results when fixing all other parameters to their default values.

For the centrality weights (Eq. 4) we try some simple linear combinations of the three association methods, namely ctxt (Eq. 1), cat (Eq. 2) and struct (Eq. 3) . We try using the ctxt level only (setting $\lambda_1 = 1$, $\lambda_2 = 0$ and $\lambda_3 = 0$), combining the ctxt with struct (setting $\lambda_1 = 1$, $\lambda_2 = 0$ and $\lambda_3 = 1$) and combining the three kinds of associations together. We can see that for the centrality weights, the best correlation reaches 0.683 when using the three association methods together. We tried also several weighted combination for the centrality weights with different values of the $\lambda_1, \lambda_2, \lambda_3$ but we got similar results.

Table 3: Effect of Centrality Metrics and Concept Weight Strategies

Weight,Dist		Pearson Correlation
Concept Association for Centrality	ctxt	0.663
	ctxt+struct	0.672
	ctxt+cat+struct	0.683
Concept Weights	none	0.655
	centrality	0.683
	content	0.736
	centrality + content	0.745

Table 4: Effect of Pairwise Concept Similarity

conceptSim	Pearson Correlation
ctxt	0.725
Concept2VecSim	0.732
ctxt+Concept2VecSim	0.745

For the concept weights parameter, we see that the baseline method which uses uniform weights (line that corresponds to "none" in the table) got correlation of only 0.655. The content-based weights achieve a correlation of 0.736 which is better than the correlation of 0.683 by the centrality-based weights. It should be mentioned that the content-based weights are similar to the weights used in ESA. Still we show that by combining the centrality weights derived from the concept graph with the content-based weights we get an improved correlation of 0.745 compared to each method separately.

7.4 Effect of Pairwise Concept Similarity

Table 4 shows the results for varying the Pairwise concept similarity scorers while fixing all other parameters to their default values. Our proposed Concept2VecSim method which exploits the neural network representation of concepts (Eq. 7) achieves correlation of 0.732 which is better than the wikilinks based similarity, termed `ctxt`, (Eq. 1). In addition, the Concept2VecSim is more efficient than the wikilinks based similarity since it uses a cosine-similarity between the continuous vectors of the two concepts which are of size 200. In comparison, the ctxt similarity intersects two sets of incoming links which could have a larger number of elements.

Similar to the phenomena presented in the previous section, the combination of several methods achieves better results than each method separately. We can see that using a simple linear combination of ctxt with Concept2VecSim method yields a correlation of 0.745 which is better than the correlation of the two similarity measures separately.

7.5 Effect of IC Metrics for Category level Association

Table 5 summarizes results of experiments with different IC (Information Content) metrics for calculating category level association, as discussed in Section 4.2. We can see that the three methods achieve quite similar results.

Table 5: Effect of IC on Category Level Association

Parameter	Pearson Correlation
depth	0.745
desc	0.745
inst	0.746

8. CONCLUSIONS

We presented `concept graph` for representing a document using its detected concepts. The concept graph utilizes DBPedia to explore relationships among the detected concepts and weighs the concepts according to their closeness centrality to reflect their relevance to the aspects of the document. We then presented a novel similarity measure `ConceptGraphSim` between two documents by comparing their concept graphs. The similarity measure first represents concepts as continuous vectors using neural network and then combines pairwise similarity between pairs of concepts using their continuous vector representations and their assigned weights. Our ConceptGraphSim combined with ESA achieved Pearson correlation of 0.786 on the LP50 dataset which outperformed other methods, except one system [9] that achieved a better Pearson correlation of 0.808. We believe that by adding more features as they did we can improve our results. We further believe that the combination of concept based centrality with neural networks as we demonstrated in our system, has a high potential that can be further exploited to achieve better results.

We conducted an extensive evaluation on the various parameters of our method. We show that by combining several weighting methods and several pairwise concept similarity measures we improve over each method separately. For example we show that the best strategy to assign weights to concepts is achieved by combining their centrality-based weights with content-based weights. Similarly, we show that combining the pairwise similarity between continuous vector representations of concepts with a pairwise similarity that considers associated context, improves over each method separately.

For future work, we plan to add more features and to improve the quality of the concept graph representation by either improving the accuracy of the mention detection tool or enriching the concept graph with additional related concepts from the knowledge base.

9. REFERENCES

[1] C. Bizer, J. Lehmann, G. Kobilarov, S. Auer, C. Becker, R. Cyganiak, and S. Hellmann. Dbpedia – a crystallization point for the web of data. *Web Semantics*, 2009.

[2] D. M. Blei, A. Y. Ng, and M. I. Jordan. Latent dirichlet allocation. *Journal of Machine Learning Research (JMLR)*, 2003.

[3] S. P. Borgatti. Centrality and network flow. *Social Networks 27*, 2005.

[4] J. Daiber, M. Jakob, C. Hokamp, and P. N. Mendes. Improving efficiency and accuracy in multilingual entity extraction. In *Proceedings of the 9th International Conference on Semantic Systems (I-Semantics)*, 2013.

[5] S. Deerwester, S. T. Dumais, G. W. Furnas, T. K. Landauer, and R. Harshman. Indexing by latent semantic analysis. *Journal of the American Society for Information Science*, 1990.

[6] P. Ferragina and U. Scaiella. Fast and accurate annotation of short texts with wikipedia pages. *IEEE Software 29(1)*, 2012.
[7] E. Gabrilovich and S. Markovitch. Computing semantic relatedness using wikipedia-based explicit semantic analysis. In *Proceedings of the 20th International Joint Conference on Artificial Intelligence*, 2007.
[8] J. Hoffart, F. M. Suchanek, K. Berberich, and G. Weikum. Yago2: A spatially and temporally enhanced knowledge base from wikipedia. *Artificial Intelligence*, 2013.
[9] L. Huang, D. Milne, E. Frank, and I. H. Witten. Learning a concept-based document similarity measure. *Journal of the Association for Information Science and Technology*, 2012.
[10] M. D. Lee, B. Pincombe, and M. Welsh. An empirical evaluation of models of text document similarity. In *Proceedings of Annual Conference of the Cognitive Science Society (CogSci)*, 2005.
[11] T. Mikolov, K. Chen, G. Corrado, and J. Dean. Efficient estimation of word representations in vector space. In *Proceeding of the International Conference on Learning Representation (ICLR) Workshop*, 2013.
[12] D. Milne and I. H. Witten. An effective, low cost measure of semantic relatedness obtained from wikipedia links. In *Proceedings of AAAI Workshop on Wikipedia and Artificial Intelligence*, 2008.
[13] P. Resnik. Using information content to evaluate semantic similarity in a taxonomy. In *Proceedings of the 14th International Joint Conference on Artificial Intelligence*, 1995.
[14] G. Salton. *The SMART Retrieval System: Experiments in Automatic Document Processing.* Prentice - Hall, Upper Saddle River, NJ, USA, 1971.
[15] G. Salton, A. Wong, and C. S. Yang. A vector space model for automatic indexing. *Commun. ACM*, 1975.
[16] M. Schuhmacher and S. P. Ponzetto. Knowledge-based graph document modeling. In *Proceedings of the ACM International Conference on Web Search and Data Mining (WSDM)*, 2014.
[17] N. Seco, T. Veale, and J. Hayes. An intrinsic information content metric for semantic similarity in wordnet. In *Proceedings of 16th European Conference on Artificial Intelligence*, 2004.
[18] P. D. Turney and P. Pantel. From frequency to meaning: Vector space models of semantics. *Artificial Intelligence Research*, 2010.
[19] E. Yeh, D. Ramage, C. D. Manning, E. Agirre, and A. Soroa. Wikiwalk: Random walks on wikipedia for semantic relatedness. In *Proceedings of the 2009 Workshop on Graph-based Methods for Natural Language Processing*, 2009.

APPENDIX

A. CLEANING WIKIPEDIA TAXONOMY

In Section 4.2.2, we mentioned that the computation of similarity between Wikipedia categories through the taxonomy of categories is based on the assumption that the taxonomy is acyclic. The taxonomy is defined in the Wikipedia category dataset of DBpedia by the skos:broader relationship specified between category pages. The taxonomy is the implied directed graph, whose nodes are the categories, and a directed edge leads from node c_1 to node c_2 for each pair of categories c_1 and c_2 such that c_2 is specified as skos:broader in the page of c_1. Namely, an edge leads from a category to a broader, more general category. That directed graph is supposed to be acyclic, inducing a global hierarchical taxonomy of categories. However, as Wikipedia categories are defined and assigned in the hierarchy by humans, cycles are unavoidable. For example, the cycle shown in Figure 4 is implied by the skos:broader relations found in DBpedia pages of categories.

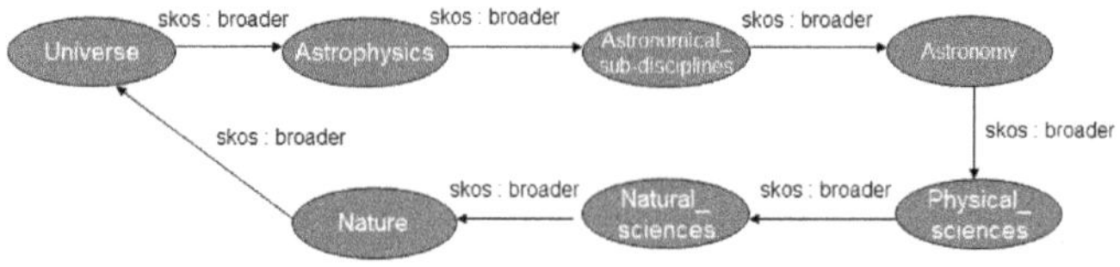

Figure 4: A Cycle in Wikipedia Category Hierarchy

We thus conducted a preprocessing step to remove edges from the category hierarchy to make it acyclic. Detecting a cycle, we removed an edge from it, which was selected by the following heuristic. For each node v in the cycle, we count the number, $desc(v)$, of its descendants in the taxonomy, which are the nodes from each of which a directed path leads to v, a path which does not visit any node on the cycle but v. Now, since every edge $e = (s_e, t_e)$ leads from a category s_e to a broader category t_e, we expect $desc(t_e)$ to exceed $desc(s_e)$. Our heuristic is thus to remove an edge $e = (s_e, t_e)$ where $desc(t_e) < desc(s_e)$. If multiple edges satisfy this requirement, we remove the one with largest difference $desc(s_e) - desc(t_e)$. Based on this heuristic, we have removed 2523 edges in total, leaving 1824523 edges in place.

Another issue mentioned in Section 4.2.2 is that the set of Wikipedia categories also contains the administrative categories which are intended for use by editors or by automated tools, based on features of the current state of articles. For example, the concept Albert Einstein belongs to the category Articles with unsourced statements. These administrative categories hinder the evaluation of category level association, since two concepts that belong to the same administrative category do not have semantic similarity. There is no explicit indication of an administrative category, and we tried to identify them through their being subcategories of *Category : Wikipedia_administration*. However, we could not simply remove a whole subgraph, since it may include many topic bearing categories. Wikipedia maintains some naming conventions for editors to assign the title on each Wikipedia page. Relying on these, we propose the following three conditions on the category name, aka label, each of which implies an administrative categories. i) The label begins with WikiProjects, Wikipedia, or Articles, e.g., `Category:Articles_needing_translation_from_French_Wikipedia` ii) The label ends with stubs, templates, e.g., `Category:England_RL_templates` iii) The label contains missing, cleanup, unknown, pages, e.g., `Category:Year_of_death_missing`

Employing the above conditions, we identified and removed 62509 administrative categories, leaving 798962 categories in place.

EgoSet: Exploiting Word Ego-networks and User-generated Ontology for Multifaceted Set Expansion

Xin Rong[1], Zhe Chen[2], Qiaozhu Mei[1,2], Eytan Adar[1,2]
[1]School of Information, [2]Computer Science and Engineering
University of Michigan
Ann Arbor, MI
{ronxin,chenzhe,qmei,eadar}@umich.edu

ABSTRACT

A key challenge of entity set expansion is that multifaceted input seeds can lead to significant incoherence in the result set. In this paper, we present a novel solution to handling multifaceted seeds by combining existing user-generated ontologies with a novel word-similarity metric based on skip-grams. By blending the two resources we are able to produce sparse word ego-networks that are centered on the seed terms and are able to capture semantic equivalence among words. We demonstrate that the resulting networks possess internally-coherent clusters, which can be exploited to provide non-overlapping expansions, in order to reflect different semantic classes of the seeds. Empirical evaluation against state-of-the-art baselines shows that our solution, *EgoSet*, is able to not only capture multiple facets in the input query, but also generate expansions for each facet with higher precision.

CCS Concepts

•Computing methodologies → Information extraction; Semantic networks; •Information systems → *Clustering; Web mining; Information retrieval;*

Keywords

Web Mining; Information Extraction; Entity Set Expansion

1. INTRODUCTION

Entity set expansion is useful for a number of applications, including question answering [27], query suggestion [6], consumer vocabulary construction [29], and knowledge extraction [22]. For example, given *lincoln*, *nixon*, and *obama* as seeds, one might expect a set expander to find all American presidents. Formally, entity set expansion is defined as finding a set of "sibling" entities given one or a few examples, such that the entities and the seeds belong to the same semantic class [35].

The task of set expansion can be challenging if the input seeds fall into multiple semantic classes. If the seeds are multifaceted, the result set will often contain suggestions pulled from multiple senses. For example, given the term *orange* as the seed, a set expansion algorithm may produce a combination of colors (e.g., *red, green, blue*) and fruits (e.g., *peach, grape, lemon*). Some senses may also be significantly less popular than others. For example, *atlanta* may most commonly be of the class *cities in Georgia, US* but it also fits within *Olympic host cities*. Providing multiple input seeds may help orient the algorithm (e.g., *atlanta* AND *barcelona* would make the *Olympic* class more likely). Even if multiple seeds are provided, the results can still be ambiguous, as different classes can have a large number of overlapping members. Having multiple seeds as input may help narrow down the semantics, but multi-seed queries can still possess multifacetedness. For example, *lemon*, *lime*, *olive*, and *orange* all belong to *names of colors* and *names of fruits*, which makes disambiguation potentially challenging.

In reality, users or upstream applications cannot always provide an accurate list of seeds that narrows the search space down to one semantic class. Instead of relying on a univocal set of seeds, we aim to provide an entity set expansion algorithm that automatically organizes the expanded entities into multiple facets, which correspond to the most common senses of the seeds.

User-generated ontologies, such as those found in Wikipedia, represent one possible route forward. For example, a simple algorithm would find all categories for input seeds and then return grouped matches that are siblings within each category. However, such user-generated ontologies, due to its nature of human categorization, often have problems such as mixing multiple concepts in one category, or containing noise in certain categories [10].

An alternative approach is to "learn" sibling relationships among entities directly from a large corpus. Distributional similarity is one way to do this. Distributional similarity measures word relatedness with the assumption that similar words appear in similar contexts [18]. Such similarity metrics can facilitate set expansion by finding relevant terms [33, 30] and optimizing the internal coherence of the result entity set [12]. However, for multifaceted seeds, distributional similarity may not naturally group the related terms into distinct semantic classes, even if the coverage of sibling terms increases with sufficient data.

In order to find desired groupings for multifaceted seeds, we utilize a word-network representation. Specifically, we treat words that are distributionally similar to the seed (the ego) as nodes and use the pairwise similarity between those words to create weighted edges, thereby forming an "ego-network." This representation is useful for our task because ego-networks for multifacted seeds often display modular community structure, where each community contains possible set-expansions for a particular semantic facet of the seed. Figure 1 shows an example ego-network of the term *beijing*, where two distinct clusters exist and can be used for expansions toward different semantic classes. To increase the accuracy of

WSDM'16, February 22–25, 2016, San Francisco, CA, USA.

ISBN 978-1-4503-3716-8/16/02...$15.00

DOI: http://dx.doi.org/10.1145/2835776.2835808

Figure 1: Ego-network of *beijing* with three communities: major cities in China (upper left), provinces in China (lower left), and Olympic host cities (right).

the extracted sibling terms, we use a set of skip-gram features that impose strong positional constraints on the context, and we find that appropriate filtering and sampling on such a feature set can more precisely recover sibling relations and thus result in ego-networks with even better modular structure. However, a limitation of such a refined distributional similarity metric is that it favors popular terms and under-performs for long-tail terms in certain domains, such as musical records and movie titles.

To create a system that performs well in all domains, we fuse the ego-network model with user-created ontologies into a new system: EgoSet. EgoSet uses the ego-network to find the initial clusters for a seed, and aligns those clusters with user-created ontologies. These clusters are "purified" by this process to generate set-expansions that are not only structurally aligned with the seed's facets but also of high precision.

The most significant contributions of this work are: (1) addressing the problem of multifaceted set-expansion through the construction of the ego-networks using novel skip-gram features and (2) the unsupervised integration of the ego-networks and mined ontologies to create comprehensive and internally coherent entity sets. To evaluate the EgoSet system, we created a new evaluation dataset of single- and multi-seed queries (all multifaceted). Empirical evaluation shows that our system outperforms state-of-the-art baselines in terms of the coverage on different semantic classes, as well as the precision in each individual cluster.

2. USER-CREATED ONTOLOGIES

Ontologies are a natural resource for set expansion. Wikipedia, for example, contains various curated lists suitable for ontology construction, including category tags, lists and tables in the articles, and *List-of* pages. Qualitatively, we have found the List-of pages to have the right combination of being prevalent and relatively "clean". To obtain this data, we crawled all English Wikipedia pages titled "List of . . . ", and obtained 187,017 pages (collected on March 12, 2015). If the page contained tables, we treated each table column as a sublist, and obtained 1,124,708 sublists. We kept the 38,078 lists and sublists with at least 5 entities. The remainder were considered as too short and thus discarded. The retained lists became our working ontology.

Table 1 shows the titles of several Wikipedia lists that cover the entity *apple*. Despite their relative high quality, Wikipedia lists

List Title	Size
List of English words of Anglo-Saxon origin	1046
List of record labels	627
List of defunct automobile manufacturers	513
List of multinational corporations	85
List of plants in the Bible	41
List of most valuable crops and live-stocks	29
List of the largest IT companies	9
List of loanwords in Malayalam	5
...	...

Table 1: Eight example Wikipedia lists (of 99) containing *apple*.

may not be the "ultimate" results of set expansion due to: (1) some groups of lists contain overlapping topics, such as *List of laptop brands and manufacturers* and *List of computer hardware manufacturers*; (2) many lists mix two or more concepts together and thus result in incoherent clusters, such as *List of most valuable crops and live-stocks*, which mixes fruit with vegetables and animals; (3) many lists cover topics that are too rare or obscure, such as *List of loanwords in Malayalam*.

These issues motivate an interesting question: how do we generate internally-coherent clusters that provide a comprehensive coverage of the "common senses" of the input seeds? While there are existing studies that tackle this problem by using topic modeling [1, 38], their performance is usually not satisfactory. An important reason is that the co-occurrence relationship between entities learned from these list ontologies do not correlate well with their similarity relations in real text. While user-created ontologies may combine entities together in various interesting ways, text data most truthfully reflect our common sense about entity relations. Our preference is thus to first identify relevant clusters based on text, and only then refine those with the user-generated ontologies.

3. EGOSET

In this section, we introduce our proposed EgoSet system. As depicted in Figure 2, the system contains both indexing and querying elements.

3.1 Feature Extraction

To extract sibling relations from text, distributional similarity is frequently employed [23, 30, 37]. There are multiple possible feature definitions for distributional similarity. Given a term T_0 in a sentence, one can define a context window W around T_0, and extract features from W. Common features include unigrams (e.g., T_1), n-grams (e.g., T_1T_2), and skip-grams (e.g., "T_{-1} __ T_1", where T_0 is replaced with a placeholder). We use skip-grams instead of unigrams or n-grams because skip-grams impose stronger positional constraints on where contextual words may appear with regard to the target term. Otherwise, we risk finding relevant concepts (e.g., *apple* vs. *ipad*) rather than truly sibling entities (*apple* vs. *microsoft*). In addition to distributional similarity, we could also use patterns (e.g., "w_1, *such as* w_2, w_3, *and* w_4") to find sibling entities, but as Shi et al. [30] indicate, patterns tend to introduce more noise than distributional similarity as the corpus scales up.

In practice, we find that using a combination of skip-grams of varying lengths can lead to even better performance than a single length setting. Figure 2(a) illustrates the skip-gram features we extract from each context window. For target term T_0, six different features are extracted. For example, skip-gram S_2 = "$T_{-2}\,T_{-1}$ __ T_1".

Note that our skip-gram feature set should not be confused with

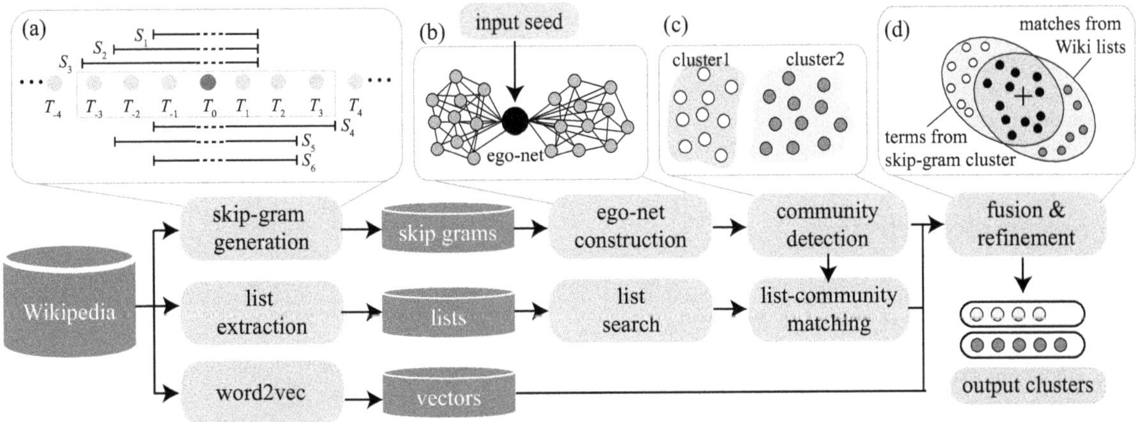

Figure 2: The end-to-end system pipeline showing the indexing of ego-networks and serving of a single-seed query.

the skip-gram model in word2vec, which is a well known word embedding toolkit [20]. In the skip-gram model of word2vec, given an input word, the training objective function measures how well the neural network model predicts every single token in the skip-gram surrounding that input word. The sequential order of the tokens in that skip-gram is ignored as the objective function takes the average of the prediction error for each token [28]. In contrast, we treat each skip-gram S_i as an integral unit, which leads to much sparser feature space but much tighter semantic constraints.

After feature extraction, many existing approaches assign feature weights using point-wise mutual information (PMI) [8] for each skip-gram s and word w:

$$f_{w,s} = \log \frac{X_{w,s}}{\sum_{w'} X_{w',s} \cdot \sum_{s'} X_{w,s'}} \quad (1)$$

where $X_{w,s}$ is the co-occurrence count between w and s. This weighting strategy tends to promote rare skip-grams. Given our large feature space, this strategy is not particularly helpful. We find that many extracted features can be discarded and a sample of the remaining features is sufficient for extracting sibling relations. This can be better understood in the context of a bipartite network.

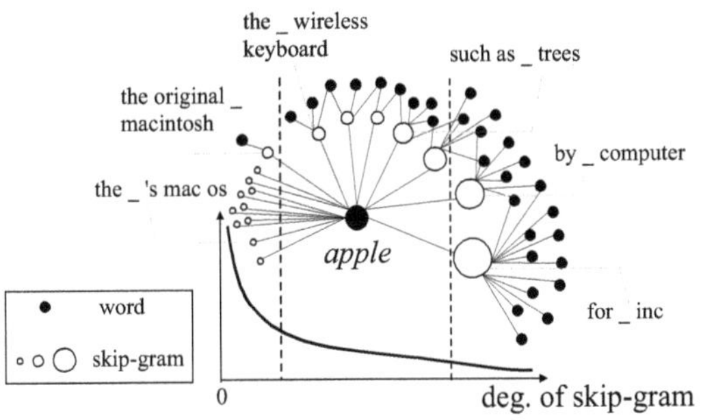

Figure 3: Bipartite network of words and skip-grams in the neighborhood of *apple* and the degree distribution of skip-grams.

Figure 3 illustrates the neighborhood of *apple* in a bipartite network of words and skip-grams. From left to right, the degree of skip-grams increases, and so changes their importance in capturing sibling terms. By inspecting example skip-grams connected to the seed word, it can be seen that skip-grams on the left end of the distribution are not particularly useful in connecting the seed word to the others. For example, "*the* __*'s mac os*" only captures the uniqueness of *apple* instead of the commonality it shares with its peers. In practice, we find that most sibling relations are effectively recovered by skip-grams with 5–50 neighbors. For example, "*the* __ *wireless keyboard*" falls in this range, and is useful for linking terms of electronic companies together. In comparison, a more frequent skip-gram, "*for* __", may be less precise in finding siblings, as it mixes a lot of companies together. We have found that we can discard skip-grams with fewer than 5 neighbors, or more than 2,500, without seriously impacting performance.

After this filtering process, we assign weight for each skip-gram s and word w using:

$$f_{w,s} = \log(1 + X_{w,s})[\log |W| - \log(\sum_{w} X_{w,s})] \quad (2)$$

where $X_{w,s}$ is the co-occurrence count between w and s, and $|W|$ is the total number of words in the vocabulary. This weight assignment is equivalent to tf-idf if we consider each w as a "document", and each s as a "term." In practice, we find this weight function to work better than PMI.

Even with strict filtering, each word may still have a large number of skip-grams. To further improve computational efficiency, we reduce the dimensionality of the feature space by sampling 300 skip-grams per word using weighted minhash [14], which is an algorithm that randomly samples elements from sets and still preserve weighted Jaccard similarity between any pair of sets:

$$J(w_1, w_2) = \frac{\sum_k \min(f_{w_1,s_k}, f_{w_2,s_k})}{\sum_k \max(f_{w_1,k}, f_{w_2,s_k})} \quad (3)$$

where f_{w,s_k} is the weight of the kth skip-gram for word w.

3.2 Ego-network Construction

After executing the above process each word has a skip-gram vector. These can be used to construct an ego-network (e.g., Figure 1) which can then be utilized to perform clustering analysis and find semantic classes. For each word w, we find 250 nearest neighbors, which will become the nodes of the ego-network. For each pair of terms we compute a similarity score using weighted Jaccard similarity as defined in Eq. (3). If any pair of words, w_i and w_j, have a similarity score higher than a threshold (e.g., 0.05), then a link is created between them. The reasons for building ego-networks, instead of a giant network of the entire vocabulary are twofold: (1) ego-networks are more convenient for indexing and serving in run-time; and (2) the filtering and sampling of features in the previous step make the feature space sparse enough for efficiently finding nearest neighbors and constructing ego-networks.

Note that if multiple seeds are given as input, we may still construct an "ego-network" by finding the nearest neighbors that have the closest mean distances to the seeds.

3.3 Ego-community Detection

Community detection is conducted by first removing the "ego" (the seed) from the ego-network (see Figure 2 (c)). The seed, naturally, belongs to every community and the edges from the ego may confuse the algorithm. Experimenting with a number of community detection algorithms [16], we find that Louvain [3] balances efficiency with good performance across many networks. Louvain is a hierarchical clustering algorithm that starts by assigning a different community to each node, followed by greedily aggregating communities to optimize the modularity of the network partition until the modularity cannot be further improved, and the "optimal" number of communities is thus identified.

Figure 1 shows the ego-network of *beijing* and its nearest neighbors. After removing *beijing*, the ego/seed, from the network, we can obtain two distinct clusters (without even having to apply community detection; simply checking connected components suffices for this case). By increasing the number of nearest neighbors, we can identify other clusters, such as Chinese provinces, which *beijing* should also belong to. Since our skip-gram extraction strategy produces much sparser a feature set than existing methods, the resulted ego-networks from our method tend to possess better community structure. We provide an empirical evaluation comparing the quality of the ego-network clusters created using different methods in Section 4.

3.4 Fusing Ego-communities and Ontologies

As explained in Section 1, distributional similarity and ontologies should be used jointly to compensate each other's disadvantages. In order to achieve this, for each cluster in the ego-network, we find Wikipedia lists that "match" the content of the cluster by checking if the Jaccard index between the list and the cluster is above a threshold (e.g., $\theta_1 = 0.75$). Then the elements of both the matched lists and the cluster are all pooled together as candidates, and an ensemble model is employed to decide which candidates should remain (Figure 2(d)).

Assuming there are N candidates, then for each candidate w_O, the ensemble model takes into account the mean distance from w_O to all other candidates, $\bar{d}_{w_O} = \frac{1}{N}\sum_{w_i} f(w_O, w_i)$, where f is one of three different distance/similarity metrics: (1) Hamming distance of Wikipedia list memberships; (2) weighted Jaccard similarity of the skip-gram vectors; and (3) Cosine similarity of the word embedding vectors learned by word2vec [20] on the same corpus. For each metric f, a binary decision is made as to whether w_O should be removed from the cluster, based on w_O's percentile in the distribution of $\bar{d}_w$ among all w's (the threshold is empirically determined). Then we take the "majority vote" of those three metrics to finally decide whether to remove w_O. The reason of introducing word embedding vectors is to further improve the reliability of the ensemble model. As evidenced in Section 4, using just Wiki lists and skip-gram vectors can achieve comparable performance.

By employing the ensemble model, we aim to improve precision by pulling outliers from the word cluster as well as to improve recall by adding missing elements from the lists. We call this process "fusion" or cluster purification.

Figure 4 illustrates the distributions of $\bar{d}_w$ under three similarity metrics for the candidate terms corresponding to the "company" cluster of the seed word *apple*. Each dot in the figure corresponds to a candidate term w. The y-axes are the values of $\bar{d}_w$, and the x-axes are the percentiles of w in the distribution of $\bar{d}_w$. In each distribution, from left to right, there can be seen multiple "drops", which separate "good" terms from relatively "worse" terms. The right-most detectable drop in each distribution is marked with a dashed line, which corresponds to empirically determined threshold for distinguishing outliers. While different metrics generally agree on what terms are ranked the highest, they usually differ as to what terms get rejected. In this particular case, several non-IT companies are identified as outliers and removed, including *nestle*, *boeing*, and *starbucks* (*mysql* is also deleted as an outlier). On the contrary, *oracle* is rejected under only one metric, and is thus "saved." Without this step of outlier removal, some of the spurious terms might get a high ranking because of one of the distance metrics and thus may harm the precision of the final result.

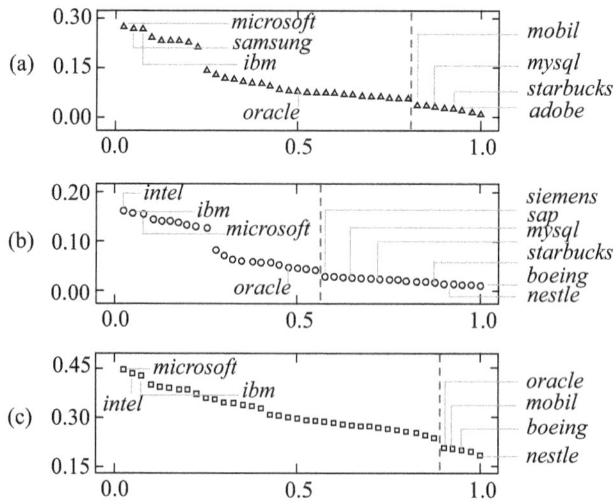

Figure 4: Distribution of $\bar{d}_w$ for candidates in the "company" cluster of *apple* using similarity metrics based on: (a) Wikipedia Lists, (b) skip-gram vectors, (c) word2vec

After purification, all remaining members in the cluster are ranked by a linear combination of $\bar{d}_w$'s under the three similarity metrics. Therefore, for each cluster, we obtain a ranked list of entities. And overall we obtain a list of ranked lists as result.

3.5 Post-processing

The result of the previous step needs to go through additional post-processing, mainly because of three issues: (1) there may be duplicate clusters, because different clusters may have been matched against the same Wikipedia list and, after purification, there may be pairs of clusters that contain highly similar members; (2) there may exist off-topic clusters, because the matched Wikipedia lists may not capture the topic implied in the seed entities; (3) there may be some clusters that are too small due to data sparsity or the existence of noise in the source data. We adopt the following solutions to solve these problems.

To address the first issue (duplicate clusters), we perform deduplication as follows. For each pair of cluster (c_i, c_j) (note that the elements in the cluster are already ranked by $\bar{d}_w$), define $V_m(c_i, c_j)$ as the number of overlapping elements between the top m elements of c_i and the top m elements of c_j. Then, if any of the conditions below is satisfied, we drop one of (c_i, c_j) that has a lower coherence score $\Gamma(c)$ than the other:

- $V_5(c_i, c_j) \geqslant 3$;
- $V_{10}(c_i, c_j) \geqslant 5$;
- $V_\infty(c_i, c_j) \geqslant \min(0.3 \times \min(|c_i|, |c_j|), 10)$,

where $|c|$ is the size of the cluster c, and the coherence score of a cluster is defined as the average of pair distance,

$$\Gamma(c) = \frac{1}{|c|^2} \sum_{w_i, w_j \in c} f(w_i, w_j). \quad (4)$$

This deduplication strategy gives high-ranking elements in each cluster higher priorities, which are most important to the perceived quality of the expansion results.

To address the second issue (off-topic clusters), we examine if all of the seed terms are present in the purified cluster.[1] If any seed term is missing, it is a good indication that the matched Wikipedia lists may have led to a semantic drift away from the topics of the seeds, and thus the cluster should be eliminated.

Finally, for the third issue (tiny clusters), we simply remove clusters whose size is smaller than 5. After these post-processing steps, the retained list of ranked lists are returned as the final result.

3.6 Summary

Algorithm 1 summarizes the entire process of serving a set expansion query. Note that the process of creating ego-networks is not included. In the algorithm, θ_1 and θ_2 are parameters used for determining cut-off thresholds. The tuning of these parameters will be discussed in Section 4.4.

Data: $Q = \{q\}$: input seed(s)
$W = \{w\}$: collection of entities (the vocabulary)
$\mathbf{E} = \{E_w\}$: collection of skip-gram-based ego-nets
$L_{wk} = \{l\}$: collection of Wikipedia lists
f_{wk}, f_{ego}, f_{w2v}: three similarity metrics (Section 3.4)
Result: $C = \{c\}$: output clusters
start
$E_Q \leftarrow \cup_{q \in Q} E_q$, obtain "ego-net" of all seeds
$C \leftarrow$ community detection on network E_Q
for *every cluster* $c \in C$ **do**
  $L_c \leftarrow \{l \in L_{wk}, \text{Jaccard}(l, c) > \theta_1\}$, match lists;
  $W_c \leftarrow \{w \in E_Q\} \cup \{w \in l, l \in L_c\}$, all candidates;
  for $f \in \{f_{wk}, f_{ego}, f_{w2v}\}$ **do**
    for $w \in W_c$ **do**
      $\bar{d}_w = \frac{1}{N} \sum_{w' \in W_c} f(w, w')$;
    end
    $D_f \sim N(\mu, \sigma^2) \leftarrow$ distribution of $\bar{d}_w$ for $w \in W_c$;
    $\xi_f \leftarrow \mu - \sigma\theta_2$, cut-off threshold;
    $\tau_{w,f} \leftarrow \mathbb{1}(\bar{d}_w > \xi_f)$, cut-off decision for $w \in W_c$;
  end
  $c \leftarrow \{w \in c; \text{if} \sum_{f \in \{f_{wk}, f_{ego}, f_{w2v}\}} \tau_{w,f} \geqslant 2\}$;
end
$C \leftarrow$ Dedupe(C), see Section 3.5;
$C \leftarrow$ Drop $c \in C$ if $q \notin c, \forall q \in Q$;
$C \leftarrow$ Drop $c \in C$ if $|c| \leqslant 5$.

Algorithm 1: Entire process of serving a set expansion query.

Multi-seed queries: According to Algorithm 1, it can be seen that multi-seed queries are handled in a very similar fashion to single-seed queries. The differences are: (1) instead of deriving an ego-net of a single seed, we merge the ego-nets of all seeds together into a larger "ego-net"; (2) wherever we need to evaluate the similarity of a candidate entity to the "seed", we replace the "seed" with the centroid of all seeds in the corresponding distance space.

[1]Although the seed terms are removed prior to ego-community detection, they can be added back during list matching.

4. EXPERIMENTS AND RESULTS

We conducted three types of evaluations on EgoSet. First, we use a data-driven approach to create a ground-truth dataset, which includes queries and the corresponding expected classes. This dataset is good for testing how well the system captures the common senses of a query and how precise the returned ranked lists are. Second, we have humans to label all the classes and instances returned by the system given selected queries in order to study its precision. Third, we conduct case studies on selected multiseed multifaceted queries to understand the quality of each individual similarity metric and their interactions.

Data: We retrieved the English Wikipedia 2014 full text (56 million articles, 1.2 billion words). We selected the top 50,000 most frequent n-grams ($n \leqslant 5$) as our core vocabulary (excluding the top-50 as stop words). All text is lower-cased and tokenized using the Stanford Tokenizer.[2]

4.1 Queries and Ground Truth

We created a query set by sampling multifaceted terms from the core vocabulary. To determine the degree to which a term is multifaceted, we look up the term in Wikipedia and examine whether there is a disambiguation page for it and, if so, how many different senses the term possesses. We sampled 50 unigrams with varying degree of multifacetedness. These queries cover a wide variety of topics, such as locations, companies, celebrities, and food. Then we attempted to follow a similar procedure as [38] to manually determine the ground-truth categories for each query. However, we found it to be infeasible to determine a really "comprehensive" or "standard" list of categories per query. Instead, we looked at a minimum of 50 instances of usage in the Wikipedia corpus and Google News[3] search results for each query word, and created a list of *minimally required semantic classes* (MRSC) based on its most popular senses. For example, the MRSCs of *apple* include *Fruit* and *Famous IT Companies*. To avoid bias, we did not look at Wikipedia lists during this process. We found 89 distinct MRSCs, with 5.1 MRSCs per query on average (the median is 4), while allowing different queries to share the same MRSCs.[4]

Note that we did not use existing ground-truth datasets because no existing dataset specifically targets multifaceted entity set expansion, especially for multi-seed multifaceted queries.

Type	Count	Examples
1-seed	50	apple, green, mercury, python, ...
2-seed	50	copper+gold, gnu+squirrel, beaver+elk, ...
3-seed	30	franklin+hamilton+newton, artemis+poseidon+apollo, ...
4-seed	20	orange+lemon+lime+olive, orchid+rose+violet+lavender, ...

Table 2: Summary of queries

Since we also want to test multi-seed multifaceted queries, we looked at the overlap between some pairs or even groups of categories, which enables us to generate multi-seed queries as well.

[2]http://nlp.stanford.edu/software/tokenizer.shtml.
[3]https://news.google.com/
[4]Our dataset is available at http://bit.ly/egoset-data.

Such multi-seed queries are generated by randomly sampling from the common members of all pairs of MRSCs that are overlapping, such as *Colors* and *Fruit*, and then sampling from the overlapping entities. We created 100 multi-seed queries, including 50 two-seed queries, 30 three-seed queries, and 20 four-seed queries. Table 2 shows a summary of the query set with several examples.

4.2 Evaluation of Ego-communities

We compare the quality of the word clusters obtained from the ego-networks based on skip-gram similarity metrics against a state-of-the-art word embedding model, as well as clusters obtained using non-network methods. We use only single-seed queries for this experiment in order to focus on the quality of the ego-communities with the simplest setting. For each query, 150 nearest neighbors are retrieved, and different clustering or community detection methods are used to obtain the clusters, which are then compared to the ground-truth MRSCs. Although MRSCs cannot be considered as having a comprehensive coverage on all possible clusters, they can serve to judge the relative quality of different similarity metrics.

4.2.1 *Metrics*

For each cluster set $C = c_1, c_2, \ldots, c_K$ and the corresponding MRSC set $R = r_1, r_2, \ldots, r_M$, three metrics from [9] are adopted in evaluating the quality of clusters, including

- Cluster Purity: measures the average accuracy of word assignment in the clusters. With N defined as the total number of nearest neighbors: $\text{purity}(C, R) = \frac{1}{N}\sum_k \max_m |c_k \cap r_m|$
- Normalized Mutual Information (NMI): similar to purity, adding penalization to C if it contains too many clusters. $\text{NMI}(C, R) = \frac{I(C,R)}{[H(C)+H(R)]/2}$, where $I(C, R) = \sum_k \sum_m \frac{|c_k \cap r_m|}{N}$, and $H(C) = -\sum_k \frac{|c_k|}{N} \log \frac{|c_k|}{N}$.
- Rand Index (RI): defined as the accuracy of predicting whether a pair of words should belong to the same cluster for all of the $\frac{N(N-1)}{2}$ pairs of words.

Note that some of the details are adjusted from [9] to accommodate our experiment setting.

4.2.2 *Baselines*

The following approaches are compared:

- **word2vec**: the embedding vectors learned using word2vec [20, 21].[5] We used the "skip-gram" model[6], set vector dimension to be 500, window size 8, and used 5 negative samples per update and 5 iterations through the entire Wikipedia corpus. For clustering, k-means with $k = 5$ is used;
- **word2vec-net**: ego-networks built using the above vectors with Cosine similarity;
- **EgoSet-SG**: our skip-gram vectors, used for both k-means and ego-networks.

For both word representations, Louvain [3] is used for community detection on ego-networks. The number of communities is determined by finding the partition with maximum modularity.

4.2.3 *Results*

Table 3 shows the evaluation results. It can be seen that our proposed similarity metrics consistently outperform word2vec under three different metrics. In addition, for the same set of nearest neighbors, network-based community detection tends to outperform k-means, especially under NMI, although it is not directly comparable as the number of clusters for k-means is predetermined. In short, this result indicates that while both metrics are applied to the same corpus, skip-gram-based methods may better facilitate the recovery of distinct clusters in ego-networks than word embeddings learned by word2vec.

Representation	Clustering	Purity	NMI	RI
word2vec	k-means	0.168	0.260	0.236
word2vec-net	Louvain	0.166	0.394	0.220
EgoSet-SG	k-means	**0.213**	0.404	0.432
	Louvain	0.210	**0.460**	**0.484**

Table 3: Evaluation of nearest neighbor clusters

4.3 End-to-end Evaluation

Our second set of experiments evaluate the performance of the end-to-end pipeline for multifaceted queries. We explain the input/output, metrics, and baselines, before presenting the results.

4.3.1 *Input and Output*

The input for each test case is a query, which can be either a single seed or multiple seeds (see Table 2). The output is a set of clusters. Each cluster is a ranked list of entities. The entities in the output are drawn from a vocabulary of 50,000 popular entities in Wikipedia. See Section 4.6 for a discussion about long-tail entities.

4.3.2 *Metric*

Because the output of multifaceted set expansion is a list of ranked lists, we customize a common ranking metric, mean average precision (MAP), for our evaluations. For a set of queries Q, we define mean-MAP (MMAP) as

$$\text{MMAP}_k = \frac{1}{Q}\sum_{q=1}^{Q} \frac{1}{M_q}\sum_{m=1}^{M_q} \text{AP}_k(C_{qi^*}; R_{qm}) \quad (5)$$

where M_q is the number of MRSCs for q; R_{qm} is the m-th MRSC for q; $\text{AP}_k(c, r)$ is the conventional average precision at k given a ranked list c and an unordered ground-truth set r; and C_{qi^*} is the output cluster that best matches R_{qm} among all clusters generated for q (using Jaccard).

This metric not only captures the internal-coherence of the clusters, but also possesses two important characteristics: (1) it captures how comprehensively the result set covers MRSCs. If an output C fails to capture one of the MRSCs, it will be penalized with a low precision score, since for each MRSC a best matching C_{qi^*} will be selected regardless; (2) it allows the output set to include additional topics, which is important because we cannot guarantee that our MRSC sets cover all possible senses of the input seeds.

The precision values for each baseline is calculated as follows: for each query, for each cluster in the ground truth, we find the cluster among output clusters that have the biggest Jaccard similarity. Then we calculate the precision@k values by comparing this cluster against the ground truth cluster. The precision scores are averaged across all ground-truth clusters of the query, then averaged across all queries, resulting in mean average precision@k (MAP@K). Given the event that the output cluster generates fewer clusters than the ground truth (e.g. the baseline SEAL can only generate one cluster), then the same output cluster will be matched towards multiple ground-truth clusters, which inherently penalizes its precision. Since we cannot guarantee that our ground-truth clusters comprehensively cover all senses of a query, we do not penalize any cluster outside the matched clusters.

[5] https://code.google.com/p/word2vec/.

[6] Not to be confused with our proposed skip-gram feature set. The word2vec toolkit does not have positional contraints on individual tokens within a skip-gram.

		1 seed			2 seeds			3 seeds			4 seeds		
		p@5	p@10	p@20	p@5	p@10	p@20	p@5	p@10	p@20	p@5	p@10	p@20
baseline	SEAL	-	-	-	0.208	0.169	0.138	0.368	0.312	0.269	0.393	0.342	0.298
	NeedleSeek	0.432	0.372	0.325	-	-	-	-	-	-	-	-	-
single	WikiList	0.369	0.331	0.292	0.313	0.295	0.250	0.401	0.340	0.284	0.379	0.366	0.325
	word2vec	0.360	0.296	0.249	0.317	0.271	0.219	0.389	0.313	0.247	0.431	0.373	0.320
fusion	EgoSet-SG & WikiList	0.465	0.413	0.358	0.357	0.316	0.272	0.366	0.325	0.280	0.447	0.374	0.329
	word2vec & WikiList	0.390	0.331	0.289	0.334	0.313	0.222	0.373	0.303	0.240	0.352	0.333	0.308
	EgoSet-ALL	**0.490**	**0.427**	**0.372**	**0.369**	**0.323**	**0.274**	**0.432**	**0.370**	**0.313**	**0.453**	**0.399**	**0.356**

Table 4: End-to-end performance evaluation.

4.3.3 *Baselines*

We perform comparison across the following baselines.

- **SEAL:** Set Expander for Any Language [35, 36]. The published implementation was used with default settings.[7] We only managed to execute multi-seed queries using SEAL, and acquired a single ranked list per query.
- **NeedleSeek:** Web semantic mining prototype by Microsoft Research [38, 30].[8] Semantic maps were retrieved for each single-seed query using an API provided by the authors.
- **WikiList:** Wikipedia lists only. For each input query q, we find its 200 nearest neighbors using Hamming distance of list memberships. Then an ego-network is built using pairwise distance of its neighbors, and community detection (Louvain) is performed to acquire clusters. Cluster members are ranked towards each cluster centroid.
- **word2vec:** Same as **word2vec-net** in Section 4.2.
- **fusion models:** set expansion pipelines with two or three sources. **EgoSet-SG** represents our skip-gram feature set. **EgoSet-ALL** is the method that fuses all three sources (see Section 3.4).

4.3.4 *Results*

Table 4 contains three separate groups of results, including queries of single seeds, double seeds, and three or more seeds. Three major observations can be made: (1) Between single-source methods, **WikiList** consistently outperforms **word2vec**; (2) Fusion-based methods consistently outperform single-source methods; (3) The complete **EgoSet-ALL** method outperforms two-source fusion methods (**EgoSet-SG & WikiList** and **word2vec & WikiList**).

These observations support that our ensemble solution can indeed effectively purify the clusters generated by skip-grams. Note that although the precision numbers reported here may seem lower than those in other state-of-the-art work (e.g., [34]), they may not reflect the actual perceived quality of the results. This is because our evaluation metric, MMAP_k, takes into account the coverage of semantic classes, and automatically penalizes situations where there lacks sense coverage for a given query.

4.4 Parameter Analysis

The parameters in our proposed pipeline fall into two categories. The first category is associated with corpus processing and ego-network construction. Here we list a set of parameters that directly influence the quality of ego-networks:

- range of skip-gram lengths (e.g., 3–5 tokens): longer skip-grams may capture more semantics of the entity, but will lead to a sparser feature space;
- maximum degree of a skip-gram in a word-feature bipartite network (e.g., 2500): a larger value means more skip-grams will be considered with the risk of creating more spurious links between words and poorer efficiency;
- number of min-hash dimensions used for sampling skip-grams (e.g, 300): a larger value means better preservation of the "true" word similarity value, at the cost of computation efficiency. This parameter is analogous to the vector dimension in word2vec;
- number of nearest neighbors to index in an ego-network (e.g., 250): a larger value improves the long-tail performance, at the cost of computational efficiency.

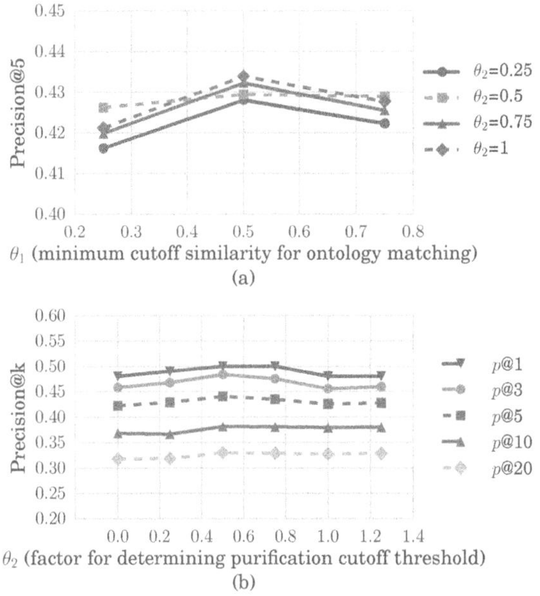

Figure 5: Parameter analysis for fusing ego-network communities with ontologies.

The second category of parameters are associated with the process of fusing ego-communities with ontologies (Section 3.4). As can be seen in Algorithm 1, there are two important parameters (θ_1 and θ_2):

- θ_1, minimum cut-off Jaccard similarity for matching ontology lists (e.g., 0.75): a larger value means more strict selection of ontology lists;
- θ_2, a factor for determining the cut-off threshold in purification (see Algorithm 1): a larger value means more aggressive cut-offs in the purification process.

Figure 5 shows the influence of the relevant parameters on the system performance. According to Figure 5(a), the strictness of matching ontology lists plays an important role, and requires proper trade-off between two extremes. A proper value of θ_1 should be set

[7] https://github.com/TeamCohen/SEAL.
[8] http://needleseek.msra.cn/

Multi-seed Query	Identified Ego-clusters	Top Skip-gram
brown white	Cluster 1: brown white green williams roberts johnson jackson smith evans jones ... (popular English last names)	kenneth ___ ,
	Cluster 2: white red blue black yellow brown green purple light_blue ... (colors)	colors are ___ and
beijing shanghai	Cluster 1: tianjin guangzhou shanghai shenzhen chongqing beijing wuhan chengdu dalian shenyang ... (major Chinese cities)	in ___ , china .
	Cluster 2: liaoning heilongjiang hebei tianjin shanghai jilin inner_mongolia shanxi beijing hunan ... (Chinese province-level administrative regions)	of ___ , china .
beaver elk	Cluster 1: coyote moose elk cougar beaver bison opossum marten wolverine fisher ... (animals)	deer , ___ ,
	Cluster 2: westmoreland schuylkill fayette crawford beaver elk greene fulton chester ... (counties in Pennsylvania)	in ___ county , pennsylvania

Table 5: Case study of multi-seed multifacted queries

between 0.5 and 0.75. According to Figure 5(b), the quality of the result is not very sensitive to the selection of θ_2. This is because in the actual implementation each type of similarity metrics (i.e., f_{WikiList}, f_{EgoSet}, and f_{word2vec}) also has a flat minimum cutoff threshold, which is independent of θ_2.

Note that word2vec also has a number of tunable parameters, which will not be discussed here.

4.5 Case Study

Table 5 presents three case studies for multi-seed expansion. In all cases, the algorithm succeeds in finding at least two facets of the query. On the right column is a top weighted skip-gram identified for each cluster. This gives us an idea how skip-grams capture the commonality of words and coercing them into a cluster. Note that all phrases (e.g., "light blue" or "inner mongolia") are converted unigrams by concatenating their tokens during pre-processing.

4.6 Discussions

There are several details that are worth discussing:

Number of semantic classes: The number of semantic classes returned by EgoSet is automatically determined. There are two factors: (1) the community detection algorithm (Louvain) returns a partition of the graph with the number of communities that yields the best modularity; (2) in post-processing, if two clusters are too similar (Jaccard index greater than a threshold), they will be merged, which will reduce the number of classes (see Section 3.5).

Scalability: Our proposed pipeline is highly scalable. Although the candidate entities are drawn from a large vocabulary, we only need to keep in memory the ego-networks, i.e., the nodes and links related to the nearest neighbors of the seed words (hence the name "EgoSet"). We experimented with ego-network construction of large n-gram vocabularies: by using Map-Reduce on a moderate cluster (70 cores), the process of extracting features and indexing nearest neighbors can be finished within 5 hours for a vocabulary of 1 million n-grams. After this pre-processing step, during serving time, we only need to look up input seeds in a nearest-neighbor index, without having to iterate through every word in the vocabulary. In addition, similar to [11], most of the computation carried out in the pipeline can be done using sparse matrices, which may further improve the overall efficiency.

Interplay of three similarity metrics: We exploit three different similarity metrics in our system, including skip-gram-based similarity, ontology-based similarity, and word-embedding-based metric. While there is a great amount of commonality in terms of what is captured by the three metrics, they all have their own distinct characteristics: our proposed skip-gram-based similarity metric is great for producing networks with good community structure and performs especially well on geolocation terms (e.g., Figure 1), but it tends to under-perform in some domains, such as movie titles and musical records. In contrast, Wikipedia lists, although quite noisy, provide good coverage on almost every domain, and thus can compensate the skip-gram-based metric to improve recall. Moreover, embedding vectors produced by word2vec has similar characteristics to our skip-gram-based metric, but its performance on multifaceted queries is not as satisfactory. Due to reasons explained in Section 3.1, word2vec-generated embeddings tend to mix non-sibling entities together (e.g., *apple* and *ipad*), which makes it difficult to generate high-quality clusters in word ego-networks. This difference is also shown in Table 3. However, through proper fusing techniques, such as our proposed ensemble model, these three metrics can facilitate each other and lead to improvement of set expansion performance.

Long-tail terms: We intentionally distinguish our work from previous work that focuses on optimizing the performance of long-tail expansion, and thus we do not particularly attempt to address the coverage of long-tail terms in the expansion results (we do care about supporting long-tail queries, which is why we develop the ensemble model). Since there is already plenty of existing work that optimizes the precision and recall given an unambiguous set of seeds, some of which can achieve near-perfect performance (e.g., [24]), we choose to instead focus our study on addressing the ambiguity that exist among many entity set expansion queries. We aim to make the top 5 to 20 ranked entities in each result cluster good enough, so that one can potentially supply the result of our system to downstream expansion algorithms that specialize in long-tail expansions to achieve overall good performance.

Handling n-grams: We treat n-grams as unigrams by concatenating the tokens. This is done by using Mikolov's word2phrase tool published alongside word2vec [20].

Choice and availability of ontologies: The Wikipedia lists used in our pipeline may be replaced with other similar ontologies. When an existing ontology is not readily available, an automatically created ontology (e.g., using techniques of [33]) may be used instead. We do not yet know how well our proposed method works in such scenarios. We leave these topics for future work.

Future work: It would be interesting to conduct a theoretical analysis in order to explain the characteristics of skip-gram-based distributional similarity metric, and how it improves local ego-community structure for multifaceted seeds. Another potential improvement is to integrate more sources of information into the system, including co-occurrence between entities in the Web corpus, Web tables and lists, as well as Wikipedia categories. In addition, our reviewers raised several important points which we could not address within the scope of this paper and would leave as future work, including: (1) building a system pipeline that handles a mixture of both "single-faceted" and multifaceted queries; (2) evaluating the system against a collection of queries in which multiple terms possess one single common sense but each of the term itself is multifaceted; and (3) developing a simpler or more elegant solution with fewer components or without having to rely on a number of different data sources.

5. RELATED WORK

The problem of completing an entity set given a few seeds has attracted a great amount of research effort. Google Sets was among the earliest work that supported open-domain set expansion [32]. It used proprietary algorithms and is no longer publicly accessible. Ghahramani and Heller [11] formulate the same task as a Bayesian inference problem, where they develop a probabilistic model that tests whether a candidate entity belongs to some unknown cluster that contains the input seeds. Their model exploits the co-occurrence relations between entities in documents, and is shown to have achieved comparable performance to Google Sets. Wang and Cohen [35, 36] propose the *SEAL* system, which submits input seeds as queries to a search engine, and mines the top-ranked webpages using a graph-based ranking model to obtain a ranked list of entities as result. The graphs constructed in SEAL contain heterogeneous sets of nodes, including documents, entities, and wrappers (prefixes and suffixes close to named entities in HTML documents). SEAL effectively leverages the analogous patterns observed around sibling entities in HTML pages, and is shown to outperform Google Sets. In more recent work, Pantel et al. [24] build a highly scalable set expansion pipeline with MapReduce; He and Xin [12] design an iterative similarity aggregation process; and Wang et al. [34] achieves near-perfect precision for completing a set of named entities with not only a few input seeds, but also an explicitly specified label (in natural language) for the intended entity set. Chen et al. [7] improve performance on long-tail term expansions by leveraging "page-specific" extractors built in a supervised fashion. While these approaches perform well for expanding a well-defined semantic class, they are not designed for handling multifaceted seeds. In real usage, the user or upstream applications of an entity set expander may not always be able to provide a clear and unambiguous set of seeds, and the capability of handling multifacetedness in input seeds is important. In comparison to these studies, our work has community detection algorithms embedded in the pipeline with proper post-processing, and can thus correctly handle multifaceted seeds by returning multiple semantic classes as results.

There are also existing techniques that can handle multifaceted seeds for set expansion. These techniques usually involve a batch process that mines the Web to automatically create semantic classes and acquire their corresponding member instances [1, 9, 25, 26, 30, 31, 33, 37]. The core to these techniques include two aspects: (1) mining hyponym (*is-a*) relations between an entity and a class label, for which contextual patterns (e.g., Hearst patterns [13]) are often used; (2) mining sibling relations among entities, which can be achieved by using contextual patterns and distributional similarity on a text corpus [25, 30, 33], or leveraging structural clues in Web tables and lists [9], or a combination of both unstructured and structured data [26, 31]. Compared to these techniques, our pipeline does not stop at the batch process: we introduce effective post-processing techniques that are specially designed to accommodate individual sets of input seeds, especially multifaceted ones.

Perhaps the most relevant work to ours is by Zhang et al. [38]. The authors address multifaceted queries by using topic modeling to refine raw semantic classes for a specific multifaceted query. We show that our method outperforms theirs on multifaceted queries, and can handle multi-seed queries whereas theirs cannot. In addition, Kong and Allan [15] also target multifacetedness of queries but are aimed at finding relevant entities instead of strict siblings of the query. To the best of knowledge, our work is the first to provide a rigorous evaluation against multi-seed multifaceted seeds for entity set expansion.

Recent advances in neural embedding models provide alternative solutions to finding semantic classes, such as [2, 17]. The neural embedding model proposed in these studies are trained with syntactic contexts rather than windows of words. They use a dependency parser to parse the text and contextual words are taken from the proximity of the target word on a parse tree. Syntactic relations between the words are also used to construct the context. As a result, such models can have the effect of grouping words that share similar semantic roles or even semantic classes. Our proposed method may be benefited by the strict sibling entity relations recovered in such dependency-based embedding models.

More generally, our work is also related to word sense disambiguation [5, 4], sense discovery [23], and clustering [18, 19].

6. CONCLUSIONS

We discovered that multifaceted terms possess highly modular ego-community structure in their word ego-networks. To exploit such a nice property for multifaceted set expansion, we designed novel skip-gram features to enhance such modular structure, and proposed the EgoSet pipeline to fuse ego-communities with user-created ontologies, as well as word embeddings, through an ensemble model. As result, we are able to provide accurate entity set expansion for multifaceted seeds through a simple procedure that outperforms state-of-the-art baselines. By only indexing and serving with ego-networks, our proposed pipeline is also efficient enough to support Web-scale set expansion tasks.

Acknowledgments

This work is partially supported by the National Science Foundation under grant numbers IIS-1054199 and CCF-1048168. We thank our reviewers for very helpful comments and suggestions.

References

[1] Ramnath Balasubramanyan, Bhavana Dalvi, and William W Cohen. From topic models to semi-supervised learning: Biasing mixed-membership models to exploit topic-indicative features in entity clustering. In *MLKDD*, 2013.

[2] Mohit Bansal, Kevin Gimpel, and Karen Livescu. Tailoring continuous word representations for dependency parsing. In *ACL*, 2014.

[3] Vincent D Blondel, Jean-Loup Guillaume, Renaud Lambiotte, and Etienne Lefebvre. Fast unfolding of communities in large networks. *Journal of Statistical Mechanics: Theory and Experiment*, 2008.

[4] Jordan L Boyd-Graber, David M Blei, and Xiaojin Zhu. A topic model for word sense disambiguation. In *EMNLP-CoNLL*, 2007.

[5] Junfu Cai, Wee Sun Lee, and Yee Whye Teh. Improving word sense disambiguation using topic features. In *EMNLP-CoNLL*, 2007.

[6] Huanhuan Cao, Daxin Jiang, Jian Pei, Qi He, Zhen Liao, Enhong Chen, and Hang Li. Context-aware query suggestion by mining click-through and session data. In *KDD*, 2008.

[7] Zhe Chen, Michael Cafarella, and H. V. Jagadish. Long-tail vocabulary dictionary extraction from the web. In *WSDM*, 2016.

[8] Kenneth Ward Church and Patrick Hanks. Word association norms, mutual information, and lexicography. *Computational linguistics*, 16(1):22–29, 1990.

[9] Bhavana Bharat Dalvi, William W Cohen, and Jamie Callan. Websets: Extracting sets of entities from the web using unsupervised information extraction. In *WSDM*, 2012.

[10] Xin Luna Dong, Evgeniy Gabrilovich, Geremy Heitz, Wilko Horn, and Ni Lao. Knowledge vault: A web-scale approach to probabilistic knowledge fusion. In *KDD*, 2014.

[11] Zoubin Ghahramani and Katherine Heller. Bayesian sets. In *NIPS*, 2005.

[12] Yeye He and Dong Xin. Seisa: set expansion by iterative similarity aggregation. In *WWW*, 2011.

[13] Marti A Hearst. Automatic acquisition of hyponyms from large text corpora. In *Computational linguistics*, 1992.

[14] Sergey Ioffe. Improved consistent sampling, weighted minhash and l1 sketching. In *ICDM*, 2010.

[15] Weize Kong and James Allan. Extracting query facets from search results. In *SIGIR*, 2013.

[16] Andrea Lancichinetti and Santo Fortunato. Community detection algorithms: a comparative analysis. *Physical review E*, 80, 2009.

[17] Omer Levy and Yoav Goldberg. Dependency-based word embeddings. In *ACL*, 2014.

[18] Dekang Lin. Automatic retrieval and clustering of similar words. In *ACL*, 1998.

[19] Dekang Lin and Xiaoyun Wu. Phrase clustering for discriminative learning. In *ACL*, 2009.

[20] Tomas Mikolov, Kai Chen, Greg Corrado, and Jeffrey Dean. Efficient estimation of word representations in vector space. *arXiv preprint arXiv:1301.3781*, 2013.

[21] Tomas Mikolov, Ilya Sutskever, Kai Chen, Greg S Corrado, and Jeff Dean. Distributed representations of words and phrases and their compositionality. In *NIPS*, 2013.

[22] Marie-Francine Moens, Juanzi Li, and Tat-Seng Chua. Knowledge extraction from wikis/bbs/blogs/news web sites. In *Mining User Generated Content*, 2015.

[23] Patrick Pantel and Dekang Lin. Discovering word senses from text. In *KDD*, 2002.

[24] Patrick Pantel, Eric Crestan, Arkady Borkovsky, Ana-Maria Popescu, and Vishnu Vyas. Web-scale distributional similarity and entity set expansion. In *EMNLP*, 2009.

[25] Marius Pasca. Acquisition of categorized named entities for web search. In *CIKM*, 2004.

[26] Marius Pasca. Open-domain fine-grained class extraction from web search queries. In *EMNLP*, 2013.

[27] John Prager. Question answering using constraint satisfaction. In *ACL*, 2004.

[28] Xin Rong. word2vec parameter learning explained. *arXiv preprint arXiv:1411.2738*, 2014.

[29] Abeed Sarker and Graciela Gonzalez. Portable automatic text classification for adverse drug reaction detection via multi-corpus training. *Journal of Biomedical Informatics*, 2014.

[30] Shuming Shi, Huibin Zhang, Xiaojie Yuan, and Ji-Rong Wen. Corpus-based semantic class mining: distributional vs. pattern-based approaches. In *Computational Linguistics*, 2010.

[31] Partha Pratim Talukdar, Joseph Reisinger, Marius Paşca, Deepak Ravichandran, Rahul Bhagat, and Fernando Pereira. Weakly-supervised acquisition of labeled class instances using graph random walks. In *EMNLP*, 2008.

[32] Simon Tong and Jeff Dean. System and methods for automatically creating lists, March 25 2008. US Patent 7,350,187.

[33] Benjamin Van Durme and Marius Pasca. Finding cars, goddesses and enzymes: Parametrizable acquisition of labeled instances for open-domain information extraction. In *AAAI*, 2008.

[34] Chi Wang, Kaushik Chakrabarti, Yeye He, Kris Ganjam, Zhimin Chen, and Philip A Bernstein. Concept expansion using web tables. In *WWW*, 2015.

[35] Richard C Wang and William W Cohen. Language-independent set expansion of named entities using the web. In *ICDM*, 2007.

[36] Richard C Wang and William W Cohen. Iterative set expansion of named entities using the web. In *ICDM*, 2008.

[37] Seon Yang and Youngjoong Ko. Extracting comparative entities and predicates from texts using comparative type classification. In *ACL*, 2011.

[38] Huibin Zhang, Mingjie Zhu, Shuming Shi, and Ji-Rong Wen. Employing topic models for pattern-based semantic class discovery. In *ACL*, 2009.

Extracting Search Query Patterns via the Pairwise Coupled Topic Model

Takuya Konishi[†§] takuya-ko@nii.ac.jp
Takuya Ohwa[†§] takuyaohwa@nii.ac.jp
Sumio Fujita[‡] sufujita@yahoo-corp.jp
Kazushi Ikeda[*] kazushi@is.naist.jp
Kohei Hayashi[†§] kohei-h@nii.ac.jp

[†]National Institute of Informatics [§]JST, ERATO, Kawarabayashi Large Graph Project
[‡]Yahoo Japan Corporation [*]Nara Institute of Science and Technology

ABSTRACT

A fundamental yet new challenge in information retrieval is the identification of patterns behind search queries. For example, the query "NY restaurant" and "boston hotel" shares the common pattern "`LOCATION SERVICE`". However, because of the diversity of real queries, existing approaches require data preprocessing by humans or specifying the target query domains, which hinders their applicability.

We propose a probabilistic topic model that assumes that each term (e.g., "NY") has a topic (`LOCATION`). The key idea is that we consider topic co-occurrence in a query rather than a topic sequence, which significantly reduces computational cost yet enables us to acquire coherent topics without the preprocessing. Using two real query datasets, we demonstrate that the obtained topics are intelligible by humans, and are highly accurate in keyword prediction and query generation tasks.

Keywords

Search queries; Query intent analysis; Topic model

1. INTRODUCTION

When people want to find new information on the Internet, they commonly use search engines. Users interact with search engines by queries, and their intents and personal backgrounds are expected to be preserved in query logs.

Extracting the low-dimensional hidden structures behind search queries is an essential task to obtain user information. This is motivated by our intuition that, while real queries are diverse and unorganized and the number of possible queries are nearly infinite, most real queries fall into a combination of a few terms from multiple categories. For example, the query "NY restaurant" consists of two terms "NY" and "restaurant". Clearly, "NY" indicates `LOCATION` and "restaurant" specifies the type of `SERVICE`. If we know such *is-a* relationships, we can infer that the user wants to use `SERVICE` and s/he lives in/will go to `LOCATION` in the near future. Such knowledge provides a rich interpretation about user needs and is beneficial for better search experiences in related applications. Query recommendation in Internet advertising is a typical example [2, 15]. For advertising clients, extracted query patterns can be used to suggest cost-effective queries, i.e., less-known and having low advertising rate but expected to have the same advertising performance as hot keywords. Furthermore, interpretable query patterns are potentially applicable to predicting click through rate [11], profiling users [9], improving search results [17], and query expansion [21].

The identification of such categories and *is-a* relationships has emerged as a new area in information retrieval (IR). This is referred to as query templates [1] and several approaches has been proposed to solve this task [1, 8, 14]. Although such approaches have demonstrated the usefulness of query templates for real applications, they have several limitations. First, they need the specification of target domain beforehand [1, 14], i.e., we must collect queries that are related to a certain theme, such as automobiles, travels, and movies. This preprocessing reduces the number of queries and the diversity drastically. However, it loses the generality and much useful information, such as cross-domain knowledge. Another issue is that the need for human assistance [8]. While humans can identify the term-category relationships with high accuracy, its expensive resource cost and low throughput hampers the applicability to large-scale query logs. In addition, due to the expensive computational cost, the number of the category (K) is considerably restricted to be small such as $K \simeq 6$.

Topic models [3, 4, 22] are alternatives to solve the query template task. Topic models learn the relationships between a term and a category as a *topic* from a large number of documents (i.e., queries) in an unsupervised manner. Desirably, topic models are feasible with $K \geq 100$ categories. However, they typically assume that each document contains many terms and are not suitable for query logs, which are extremely sparse [3, 4]. In addition, there is no straightforward way to incorporate information from a sequence of topics. For example, a topic sequence (`LOCATION`, `SERVICE`) appears frequently in real queries, but (`SERVICE`, `SERVICE`) is very rare. Exploiting such correlation information will further improve the performance.

To address the above issues, we propose the pairwise coupled topic model (PCTM)—a probabilistic topic model for

WSDM'16, February 22–25, 2016, San Francisco, CA, USA.

ACM ISBN 978-1-4503-3716-8/16/02.
DOI: http://dx.doi.org/10.1145/2835776.2835794.

query logs. The PCTM approximates the co-occurrence information over queries by topic pairs, which significantly enriches the model and overcomes the brevity and sparseness of queries. On the basis of the approximation, we derive a fully-Bayesian inference algorithm with collapsed Gibbs sampling, which handles queries as a collection of term pairs and significantly reduces computational cost from $O(K^M)$ to $O(M^2K^2)$ where M is the length of a query. In the PCTM, M is essentially very small and we can manage sufficient sizes of K as $K \simeq 100$. Moreover, by exploiting the sparsity of the topic correlation, we develop an efficient computation technique for the collapsed Gibbs sampling.

Our contributions are summarized as follows.

Versatility: The PCTM can handle queries of any domains, and it is not necessary to specify them. In addition, the PCTM does not require human assistance.

Extracting sparse cross-domain relation: The PCTM estimates topic co-occurrence as a sparse covariance matrix, which gives us cross-domain knowledge as an interpretable network of topics.

Computational Efficiency: Our computational trick reduces the sampling cost from $O(K^2)$ to $O(K)$ with almost no expense.

Our study primarily focuses on extracting the structures that commonly appear among search queries, rather than adapting specific information retrieval tasks. Thus, we evaluate the PCTM with respect to the following three fundamental viewpoints: the coherence of estimated topics, the accuracy of keyword prediction where the model infer a term given other terms in the query, and the ability of query generation. These abilities are key in many applications. For example, coherent topics help practitioners to understand the results of specific IR tasks in a deeper way. Keyword prediction is used for query suggestion and spelling correction. Generating natural queries is necessary for query recommendation in Internet advertising.

2. MODELING QUERY LOGS

2.1 Problem Definition

Given a set of queries, we would like to obtain the following knowledge: (a) a set of distinct categories of terms used in query logs, (b) *is-a* relationships between the categories and terms, and (c) a mapping from a query to query pattern represented by a sequence of the categories. Let us explain the detail by using an example. Suppose we have the query, "chicago hotel cheapest" where "chicago", "hotel", and "cheapest" are instances of the categories `LOCATION`, `SERVICE`, and `CONDITION` respectively. Such categories are related to many other terms, e.g., `LOCATION` is associated with a variety of terms that indicate the names of places. Note that a term can possibly belong to multiple categories, e.g., "chicago" may be associated with a `MOVIE` category in other queries. With such many-to-many relationships, the query pattern is recovered as a sequence of categories (`LOCATION`, `SERVICE`, `CONDITION`).

We notice that it is difficult to obtain the category information from any other external resources in advance (e.g., dictionaries and thesauruses) because the concepts defined by external resources do not always correspond to desirable categories that reflect the actual query activities. For example, both "houston" and "miami" are names of places; however, queries containing "houston" and queries containing "miami" could be very different in terms of user intent and personal backgrounds. The former is in a residential area, and would likely be used with `DAILYLIFE` keywords, such as "houston apartment" or "houston job". In contrast, the latter is in a resort area and would likely be used with `TRAVEL` keywords, such as "miami hotel" or "miami restaurant". Treating these two terms as the same category loses such query-specific information.

2.2 Naive Query Model

To obtain knowledge from query logs, we consider a simple probabilistic model of a query based on a topic model. Suppose we have an M-long query $\boldsymbol{q} = (w_1, \ldots, w_M)$ where each term $w_m \in \{1, \ldots, V\}$ has a latent topic $z_m \in \{1, \ldots, K\}$ and these terms are conditionally independent given the topics. Under this assumption, the joint probability of $\boldsymbol{q}$ and $\boldsymbol{z} = (z_1, \ldots, z_M)$ is expressed as follows:

$$p(\boldsymbol{q}, \boldsymbol{z}) = p(\boldsymbol{z})p(\boldsymbol{q}|\boldsymbol{z}) = p(z_1, \ldots, z_M) \prod_{w_m \in \boldsymbol{q}} p(w_m|z_m). \quad (1)$$

This formulation satisfies the requirements mentioned in Section 2.1: (a) categories (i.e., topics) are represented as the latent variables $\boldsymbol{z}$, (b) *is-a* relationships between w_m and z_m are represented as term distribution $p(w_m|z_m)$ that indicates the probability of term occurrences given a topic, and (c) a sequence of the categories is represented as a topic sequence $(z_1, \ldots, z_M)$, and $p(z_1, \ldots, z_M)$ is the distribution that indicates the probability of the occurrences of the topic sequence. Note that representing *is-a* relationships by the term distribution enables that one term can be associated with multiple topics.

Without loss of generality, model (1) is rewritten as a product of the multinomial distribution for terms and the tensor-variate multinomial distribution for a topic sequence as follows:

$$p(\boldsymbol{q}, \boldsymbol{z}) = \pi_{z_1,\ldots,z_M} \prod_{w_m \in \boldsymbol{q}} \phi_{w_m,z_m}. \quad (2)$$

ϕ_{w_m,z_m} denotes the probability of the term w_m given topic z_m, and $\pi_{z_1,\ldots,z_M}$ denotes the probability of the topic sequence $(z_1, \ldots, z_M)$; thus, $\pi_{z_1,\ldots,z_M}$ can be considered as an M-th order tensor having K^M elements, which represent the probabilities of all possible sequences of topics $z_1, \ldots, z_M$.

Model (2) is general and flexible; however, it requires huge computational cost in parameter estimation. Bayesian inference needs to marginalize the latent variables $\boldsymbol{z}$, which is equivalent to computing a summation of all possible values of $\pi_{z_1,\ldots,z_M}$ in Eq. (2) and this requires $O(K^M)$ computation. Even though query length M is relatively small compared to that of normal documents, practically M could be more than 10 in real query logs and it would easily make parameter estimation computationally infeasible.

3. PCTM: PAIRWISE COUPLED TOPIC MODEL

As discussed above, the main computational cost of model (2) arises from the full dependency of $p(z_1, \ldots, z_M)$. In this section, we consider relaxation of this assumption.

3.1 Pairwise Decomposition of Topics

Our key idea is that, in most queries, the full dependency of a topic sequence is sufficiently approximated by a collection of pairwise relationships among topics. For example, let us reconsider query "chicago hotel cheapest". Here, we can recognize that "chicago" is used as LOCATION rather than MOVIE because it is jointly used with "hotel". Similarly, "hotel cheapest" sufficiently determines the context of both "hotel" and "cheapest". Therefore, in this example, two term pairs "chicago hotel" and "hotel cheapest" are sufficient to estimate the intent of this query.

By following this observation, we assume that $p(z_1, \dots, z_M)$ is decomposed as the product of the second-order tensors with respect to z. For example, if $M = 3$, the joint probability of topics is written as:

$$p(z_1, z_2, z_3) \propto (\Psi(z_1, z_2)\Psi(z_1, z_3)\Psi(z_2, z_3))^{\frac{1}{2}}, \qquad (3)$$

where $\Psi(\cdot, \cdot)$ is a potential function representing a pairwise interaction of topics. Note that we introduce exponential weight $\frac{1}{M-1} = \frac{1}{2}$ for later convenience. While a general potential function takes unnormalized and unconstrained real values, we suppose the each potential indicates the probabilities of the occurrence of topic pairs. In spite of such definition, Eq. (3) requires normalizing constant because of dependencies between potentials. Eq. (3) can be generalized as follows:

$$p(z_1, \dots, z_M) \propto \left(\prod_{(i,j) \in B_M} \Psi(z_i, z_j) \right)^{\frac{1}{M-1}}, \qquad (4)$$

where B_M is the set of all possible pair indices in an M-long sequence, i.e., $|B_M| = {}_MC_2 = M(M-1)/2$. Substituting decomposition (4) into model (1) yields:

$$p(\boldsymbol{q}, \boldsymbol{z}) \propto \prod_{w_m \in \boldsymbol{q}} p(w_m|z_m) \left(\prod_{(i,j) \in B_M} \Psi(z_i, z_j) \right)^{\frac{1}{M-1}}$$

$$\propto \left(\prod_{(i,j) \in B_M} p(w_i|z_i)p(w_j|z_j)\Psi(z_i, z_j) \right)^{\frac{1}{M-1}}. \qquad (5)$$

Interestingly, Eq. (5) implies that pairwise decomposition of topics (3) allows us to deal with the entire model as the product of the sub model with respect to term pairs (w_i, w_j) and topic pairs (z_i, z_j) for $(i, j) \in B_M$.

3.2 Modeling Terms and Topic Pairs

Model (5) yet has an issue of the computational cost. The parameters of the potentials depend on the normalizing constant, which requires $O(K^M)$ computation.

To avoid this, we decompose queries into term pairs and directly model the term pairs. We introduce new variables: $\boldsymbol{b} = \{b_i\}_{i=1}^{|B_M|} = \{(w_{i,1}, w_{i,2})\}_{i=1}^{|B_M|}$ denotes all possible term pairs in an M-long query and $\boldsymbol{x} = \{x_i\}_{i=1}^{|B_M|} = \{(z_{i,1}, z_{i,2})\}_{i=1}^{|B_M|}$ denotes the corresponding topic pairs. Differently from Eq. (5), all the term and topic pairs are defined as different variables. The new model is then described as

$$p(\boldsymbol{b}, \boldsymbol{x}) = \prod_{i=1}^{|B_M|} p(b_i|x_i)p(x_i), \qquad (6)$$

where $p(b_i|x_i) = p(w_{i,1}|z_{i,1})p(w_{i,2}|z_{i,2}) = \phi_{w_{i,1},z_{i,1}}\phi_{w_{i,2},z_{i,2}}$,

$p(x_i) = p(z_{i,1}, z_{i,2}) = \psi_{z_{i,1},z_{i,2}}$.

$p(x_i)$ is the $K \times K$ matrix-variate multinomial distribution where the parameter $\psi_{\cdot,\cdot}$ represents the probability of topic co-occurrence, i.e., the covariance of topics. As in Eq. (1), this model satisfies requirements (a) and (b) described in Section 2.2. We will discuss (c) in Section 3.4.

Compared to model (5), model (6) drastically reduces the computational cost. Since all latent variables are independent in $p(\boldsymbol{b}, \boldsymbol{x})$, we can separately take the marginalization with respect to topic pairs, which reduces computational cost from the topic sequence $O(K^M)$ to the sum of topic pairs $O(M^2K^2)$.

On the basis of model (6), we construct the PCTM for the set of queries. Suppose we have $N \geq M$ term pairs obtained by decomposing M queries.[1] Let $B = \{b_i\}_{i=1}^N = \{(w_{i,1}, w_{i,2})\}_{i=1}^N$ denote the term pairs and $X = \{x_i\}_{i=1}^N = \{(z_{i,1}, z_{i,2})\}_{i=1}^N$ denote the corresponding topic pairs. By introducing the Dirichlet prior distributions $p(\boldsymbol{\phi}_k|\beta) \equiv \mathrm{Dir}(\boldsymbol{\phi}_k|\beta\mathbb{1})$ $(k = 1, \dots, K)$ and $p(\boldsymbol{\psi}|\gamma) \equiv \mathrm{Dir}(\boldsymbol{\psi}|\gamma\mathbb{1})$, the joint distribution of the PCTM is given as

$$p(B, X, \boldsymbol{\phi}, \boldsymbol{\psi}|\beta, \gamma) = \prod_{i=1}^N p(b_i|x_i, \boldsymbol{\phi})p(x_i|\boldsymbol{\psi}) \prod_{k=1}^K p(\boldsymbol{\phi}_k|\beta)p(\boldsymbol{\psi}|\gamma)$$

$$= \prod_{i=1}^N p(w_{i,1}|z_{i,1}, \boldsymbol{\phi})p(w_{i,2}|z_{i,2}, \boldsymbol{\phi})p(x_i|\boldsymbol{\psi}) \prod_{k=1}^K p(\boldsymbol{\phi}_k|\beta)p(\boldsymbol{\psi}|\gamma), \qquad (7)$$

where $\boldsymbol{\phi} = \{\boldsymbol{\phi}_k\}_{k=1}^K$.

3.3 Inference Algorithm

We infer the parameters by collapsed Gibbs sampling that enable Bayesian inference, which is more robust and effective for avoiding overfitting than point estimation by e.g. the EM algorithm. The joint distribution after marginalizing out $\boldsymbol{\phi}$ and $\boldsymbol{\psi}$ is given as:

$$p(B, X|\beta, \gamma) = \int p(B|X, \boldsymbol{\phi})p(\boldsymbol{\phi}|\beta)d\boldsymbol{\phi} \int p(X|\boldsymbol{\psi})p(\boldsymbol{\psi}|\gamma)d\boldsymbol{\psi}$$

$$= \left(\frac{\Gamma(V\beta)}{\Gamma(\beta)^V} \right)^K \prod_{k=1}^K \frac{\prod_{v=1}^V \Gamma(n_{v|k} + \beta)}{\Gamma(n_{\cdot|k} + V\beta)}$$

$$\frac{\Gamma(K^2\gamma)}{\Gamma(\gamma)^{K^2}} \frac{\prod_{k=1}^K \prod_{l=1}^K \Gamma(n_{k,l} + \gamma)}{\Gamma(N + K^2\gamma)}, \qquad (8)$$

where $\Gamma(\cdot)$ is the gamma function, $n_{v|k} = \sum_{i=1}^N \mathbb{I}_v[w_{i,1}]\mathbb{I}_k[z_{i,1}] + \mathbb{I}_v[w_{i,2}]\mathbb{I}_k[z_{i,2}]$, $n_{\cdot|k} = \sum_{v=1}^V n_{v|k}$, and $n_{k,l} = \sum_{i=1}^N \mathbb{I}_k[z_{i,1}]\mathbb{I}_l[z_{i,2}]$ ($\mathbb{I}_a[b]$ is an indicator function that takes 1 when $a = b$). Note that the marginalization has the closed-form solution as in Eq. (8) because of the inconsistency of the topics introduced in Eq. (6). This makes expensive sampling of $\boldsymbol{\phi}$ and $\boldsymbol{\psi}$ unnecessary, whereas original model (5) requires.

Samples of X are obtained by the following conditional distribution:

$$p(x_i = (k, l)|B^{-i}, b_i = (w_{i,1}, w_{i,2}), X^{-i})$$

$$\propto \begin{cases} (n_{k,l}^{-i} + \gamma) \frac{(n_{w_{i,1}|k}^{-i}+\beta)(n_{w_{i,2}|l}^{-i}+\beta)}{(n_{\cdot|k}^{-i}+V\beta)(n_{\cdot|l}^{-i}+V\beta)} & (k \neq l) \\ (n_{k,k}^{-i} + \gamma) \frac{(n_{w_{i,1}|k}^{-i}+\beta)(n_{w_{i,2}|k}^{-i}+\beta)}{(n_{\cdot|k}^{-i}+1+V\beta)(n_{\cdot|k}^{-i}+V\beta)} & (k = l) \end{cases}, \qquad (9)$$

[1] Hereafter, we ignore single-term queries so that each query contains two terms or more. We also assume that a query does not include the same terms; thus, we eliminate duplicate terms, e.g., we convert "NY NY restaurant" to "NY restaurant".

Algorithm 1 Collapsed Gibbs sampling for the PCTM

for all term pairs i =1... N **do**
  for all topic pairs (k, l) =(1,1)... (K, K) **do**
    Compute the probability $p(x_i = (k,l)|B, X^{-i})$
  end for
  Sample the topic pair x_i
end for

where the notation $-i$ indicates the set of variables or the counts excluding the variable at the ith position. We compute Eq. (9) for all term pairs as summarized in Algorithm 1.

The mechanism of learning topics with the PCTM may not intuitive. While other topic models (e.g., latent Dirichlet allocation (LDA) [4]) learn topics by term co-occurrence, the PCTM does not use this information explicitly in the modeling level. However, the PCTM does use this information during inference. This is why the PCTM can learn coherent topics. By following Algorithm 1, let us explain this with a simple example. Suppose we observe a term pair b_1=("chicago", "hotel") as a first data query. Since $n_{w|k}$ and $n_{k,l}$ are initialized randomly, the topics of "chicago" and "hotel" are sampled randomly. Let "chicago" and "hotel" be assigned to topic 1 and topic 2 respectively. These assignments increase $n_{\text{chicago}|\text{topic1}}$, $n_{\text{hotel}|\text{topic2}}$, and $n_{\text{topic1},\text{topic2}}$. Next, suppose we observe a term pair b_2=("ny", "hotel"). Here, "hotel" will be assigned to topic 2 because $n_{\text{hotel}|\text{topic2}}$ is higher. Now, "ny" will be assigned to topic 1 because, while $n_{\text{ny}|\text{topic1}}$ and $n_{\text{ny}|\text{topic2}}$ are still random, $n_{\text{topic1},\text{topic2}}$ is higher. In this example, although "chicago" and "ny" are never co-occurred in b_1 and b_2, they are assigned to the same topic 1.

We estimate the integrated ϕ and ψ as follows:

$$\hat{\phi}_{v,k} = \frac{n_{v|k} + \beta}{n_{\cdot|k} + V\beta} \quad \text{and} \quad \hat{\psi}_{k,l} = \frac{n_{k,l} + \gamma}{N + K^2\gamma}, \tag{10}$$

where $n_{v|k}$, $n_{\cdot|k}$ and $n_{k,l}$ are computed by the obtained samples of topic pairs from Algorithm 1.

3.4 Recovering Topic Sequences with Topic Inconsistency

As mentioned, changing formulation from Eq. (5) to Eq. (6) improves computational complexity. However, Eq. (6) looses information about queries, and it causes the *topic inconsistency* problem. Given a query "chicago hotel cheapest", consider two term pairs b_1 = ("chicago","hotel") and b_2 = ("chicago","cheapest"). In Eq. (5), $z_{1,1}$ and $z_{2,1}$ are treated as the same variable. However, in Eq. (6), they are different variables, and the estimated topics can be different. This problem becomes an obstacle for satisfying the requirement (c) of Section 2.1.

To avoid this, we consider an approximate way to recover the most probable topic sequence. Consider an M-long query $\boldsymbol{q} = (w_1, \ldots, w_M)$ with a topic sequence $\boldsymbol{z} = (z_1, \ldots, z_M)$. In the PCTM, the posterior of the topic pair x_i given the term pair b_i and the estimated parameters $\hat{\phi}$ and $\hat{\psi}$ is written as follows:

$$p(x_i|b_i, \hat{\phi}, \hat{\psi})_{kl} = \frac{\hat{\psi}_{k,l}\hat{\phi}_{w_{i,1},k}\hat{\phi}_{w_{i,2},l}}{\sum_{k'=1}^{K}\sum_{l'=1}^{K}\hat{\psi}_{k',l'}\hat{\phi}_{w_{i,1},k'}\hat{\phi}_{w_{i,2},l'}}. \tag{11}$$

By combining with Bayes' rule, we approximate the posterior of the topic sequence by the following Markov chain:

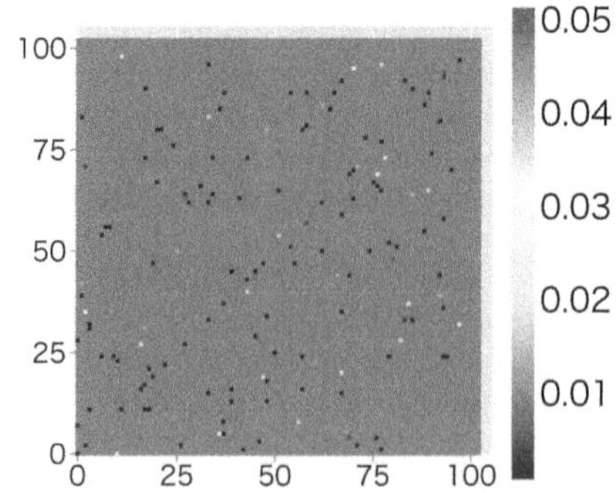

Figure 1: Estimated $\hat{\psi}$ from the AOL dataset (see Section 5 for more details)

$$\begin{aligned} &p(\boldsymbol{z}|\boldsymbol{q}) \\ &\approx p(z_1, z_2|\boldsymbol{q})p(z_3|z_2, \boldsymbol{q})p(z_4|z_3, \boldsymbol{q}) \ldots p(z_M|z_{M-1}, \boldsymbol{q}) \\ &\approx p(x_1|b_1)p(x_{2|1}|b_2)p(x_{3|2}|b_3) \ldots p(x_{M-1|M-2}|b_{M-1}) \end{aligned} \tag{12}$$

where

$$p(x_{i|i-1}|b_i)_{kl} = \frac{p(x_i|b_i)_{kl}}{p(z_{i,1}|b_i)_l} = \frac{p(x_i|b_i)_{kl}}{\sum_k p(x_i|b_i)_{kl}} \tag{13}$$

denotes the conditional posterior of $z_{i,2}$ given $z_{i,1}$. The last line of Eq. (12) enables us to compute the most probable sequence of topics by forward algorithms, such as the Viterbi algorithm [18].

3.5 Speeding-up Gibbs Sampling

Collapsed Gibbs sampling (Algorithm 1) requires $O(K^2)$ computations to check the probabilities of each topic pair, and the total complexity amounts to $O(NK^2)$. While this is significantly better than that of the naive model (1), the K^2 term is sometimes problematic when K is large.

Surprisingly, by exploiting the property of query logs, we can reduce the $O(K^2)$ computation to $O(K)$. The key assumption is that, in a query, a topic co-occurs with only a few specific topics. For example, a topic `SERVICE` co-occurs frequently with `LOCATION`, but rarely with other topics such as `MOVIE`, `ELECTRONICS` and `TOY`. Moreover, if the number of frequently co-occurred topics is $O(1)$ for each topic, the total number of meaningful topic pairs is bounded by $O(K)$. In such case, estimated $\hat{\psi}$ is supposed to be very sparse. In fact, as demonstrated in Figure 1, we observe that this assumption is fairly reasonable for real query logs.

On the basis of the above property, we propose a fast sampling algorithm that skips unnecessary probability computations in the collapsed Gibbs sampling,[2] which we refer to as *conditioned sampling*. First, we define that topic pair (k, l) is *active* if $n_{k,l} > 0$ in current samples; otherwise *inactive* (i.e., $n_{k,l} = 0$). Then, we consider to divide topic pairs into the two sets S and $\bar{S}$; S is the set of a few active topic pairs having high probability, and $\bar{S}$ is the set of many other inactive topic pairs having low probability. Let μ denote the total probability of the active topic pairs.

Now we consider to sample x_i from Eq. (9). For each topic pair x_i, we flip a biased coin such that $p(\text{head}) = \mu$. If it comes up heads (tails), we sample x_i by computing Eq. (9) among only S ($\bar{S}$). In most cases, x_i is sampled

[2]Similar techniques are used in [23].

Algorithm 2 Conditioned sampling for the PCTM

```
for all term pairs i =1...N do
  Compute the probability μ
  Choose S or S̄ according to μ
  if Select S then
    for all active topic pairs (k, l) in S do
      Compute the probability p(x_i = (k, l)|B, X^{-i})
    end for
    Sample the topic pair x_i
  else
    for all inactive topic pairs (k, l) in S̄ do
      Compute the probability p(x_i = (k, l)|B, X^{-i})
    end for
    Sample the topic pair x_i
  end if
end for
```

from S because μ is larger than $1-\mu$. In addition, sampling from S is more tractable than the exact sampling because we compute Eq. (9) for only a few active topic pairs. Conversely, sampling from $\bar{S}$ requires $O(K^2)$; however because $1-\mu$ is sufficiently small, this procedure rarely occurs. Taken together, the average time complexity per x_i is $O(\mu|S| + (1-\mu)(K^2-|S|))$. Here we assume two conditions: (i) $|S| = O(K)$, which we discussed above, and (ii) $1-\mu = O(1/K)$. Under these conditions, $\mu|S| = O(K)$ and $(1-\mu)(K^2-|S|) = O(K)$, and the total complexity is reduced to $O(K)$. Whole the procedures are summarized as in Algorithm 2. Now we check the validity of condition (ii). Substituting zero into all the counts such as $n_{k,l}^{-i}$ in Eq. (9) yields $p(x_i = (k,l)|B, X^{-i}) \propto \gamma$ (we ignore $1/V^2$ because it is constant), which implies that $1-\mu$ has $O(K^2\gamma)$ probability. Because its normalizer is approximately given by $N + K^2\gamma$ (see the update equation of $\hat{\psi}$ (10)), $1-\mu = O(1/K)$ unless $N > K^3\gamma$. Here, we empirically found that the PCTM with the small γ such as $O(1/K^2)$ performs well. Instead, as long as using such small γ, the condition is relaxed to $N > K$, which is obviously satisfied.

Note that, if we know the true value of $\mu = \sum_i \sum_{(k,l)\in S} p(x_i = (k,l)|B, X^{-i})$, the obtained samples from the above procedure are exactly the same as the original sampler. However, the computation of μ requires the summation of Eq. (9), taking $O(NK^2)$. Therefore, as an approximation, we use the following probability:

$$\mu = \sum_{(k,l)\in S} p(x_i = (k,l)|X^{-i}) = \frac{N-1+|S|\gamma}{N-1+K^2\gamma}, \qquad (14)$$

which we can compute in constant time. Note that Eq. (14) is the total probability of the active topic pairs with assuming that B is generated by the model, instead of the observed B. Therefore, it may have a small deviation from the true μ; however, we empirically confirmed that the obtained samples have almost the same quality as the exact ones (Section 5.6).

4. RELATED WORK

4.1 Topic Models for Search Logs

Topic models have been widely used for modeling search log datasets with different motivations. One motivation has been to improve search results based on search log histories [5, 9, 17]. For example, Harvey *et al.* proposed a topic model that incorporates search engine users for user profiling to improve personalized searches [9]. Other researchers have explored topic models for traditional search log tasks, such as predicting click-through rates [11, 12]. Jiang *et al.* proposed a topic model for some information included in search logs, such as URLs and timestamps [11]. Search logs are valuable sources of information for obtaining web-based knowledges. Xu *et al.* proposed a topic model for named entity mining with an efficient semi-supervised learning algorithm [20].

As in the above models, topic models have been used for modeling search log datasets that contain not only queries and other information, such as users, time stamps, URLs, and click-through logs. On the other hand, we focus on modeling the queries themselves. In our setting, we require only raw queries, which extends the range of application.

4.2 Query Templates

Query template methods have been explored to obtain query patterns [1, 8, 14]. Agarwal *et al.* advocated concepts of query templates and proposed a probabilistic inference framework for mining templates based on tripartite graphs among queries, websites, and templates [1]. Han *et al.* studied a human-assisted method for analyzing query templates that incorporates crowdsourcing for query interpretation [8].

Pandey and Punera proposed a probabilistic generative model for queries and query templates [14]. In that model, templates are defined as a topic sequence without duplication, which is not an actual topic assignment for each term. Given a template per query, the model generates the number of terms assigned to the topics included in the template with the Poisson distribution and assigns the topics for each term. For example, the query "toyota 2002 seat cover" is assumed to have a template (`BRAND`, `YEAR`, `PARTS`) and is generated by the topic assignments (`BRAND`, `YEAR`, `PARTS`, `PARTS`), that is, the model generates "toyota" from `BRAND`, "2002" from `YEAR`, and "seat" and "cover" from `PARTS`.

Although these methods have been demonstrated to extract meaningful query patterns, they only dealt with queries in a particular domain. This restriction improves the quality of query templates for that domain; however, it must perform preprocessing to limit target domains by using such as query classification. For example, one proposed method [1] assumes that *is-a* relationships in a domain are given *a priori* using other methods, such as named entity mining, and they only focused on query pattern extraction. Another proposed model [14] does not employ assumptions about domains; however, it also requires domain limitation due to the computational cost that arises from the dependencies among topics. Compared to those methods, we tackle a more challenging task, i.e., extraction of category and query patterns simultaneously without domain limitation and other preprocessing methods.

4.3 Relation to Other Topic Models

The PCTM is related to other topic models, including LDA [4], the most popular topic model. We can apply LDA to query logs by considering a single query as a document; however the performance may not be good due to the following reasons. First, although LDA assumes that a topic assigned to a term is drawn from a document-specific topic

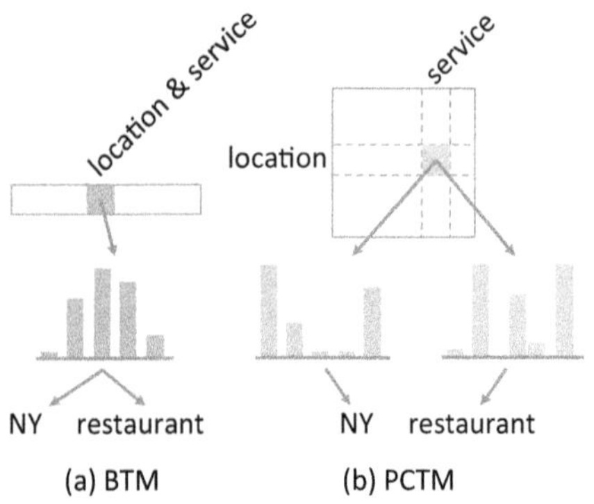

Figure 2: Generative processes of (a) BTM and (b) PCTM

distribution, short texts such as queries have no more than a few terms in a document. This would cause the sparsity problem, i.e., LDA suffers from the lack of information for each query in estimating the topic distribution [22]. Moreover, if a dataset contains D documents, LDA has a parameter of size $D \times K$, and since D is normally very large in query logs, we must consider memory usage for parameter inference carefully. In contrast, the PCTM has only one distribution that generates topic pairs over the dataset. This avoids the sparsity problem, and the topic pair distribution is represented by a K^2 matrix, which does not depend on the number of documents. In the parameter inference, LDA requires $O(K)$ computation to check the probability of a single term. Therefore, if the average length of documents is L, the total time complexity is $O(DLK)$.

Yan *et al.* proposed the biterm topic model (BTM) [22]. While the BTM and PCTM can be considered topic models for term pairs, the key difference is that the BTM assumes that a term pair shares the same topic. This assumption leads a great success of the BTM in application to short texts because term pairs in general short texts would rarely take completely different topics. However this assumption is not suitable for modeling queries because a query consists of multiple terms having a variety of topics.

To clarify this difference, we illustrate the generative processes of the BTM and PCTM in Figure 2. Recall the example "NY restaurant" mentioned in Section 1. The BTM assigns the same topic for every two terms. Thus, because the location names and service names, such as "NY" and "restaurant", frequently appear in the same queries, the BTM estimates them as an integrated topic of `SERVICE` and `LOCATION`. Such mixing of topics is not desirable in terms of the interpretability. In contrast, the PCTM assigns a topic *pair* for every two terms. This allows to learn `SERVICE` and `LOCATION` as different topics.

The correlated topic model (CTM) has been proposed to extract topics and their correlations from documents [3]. The CTM assumes the logistic normal distribution to model the correlation and was shown to be successful meaningful topic correlation from the academic journal dataset. However, since the CTM also models topic distribution for each document, it would suffer from the sparsity problem as discussed in LDA. Moreover, while a variational inference algorithm has been proposed, there is no analytical solution and it requires to perform the conjugate gradient method for the parameter inference, which uses huge amount of memory space.

Note that the PCTM has the same structure as the product space mixture model (PMM) [10]. Compared to the PMM, we provide the following three contributions: we associate the PMM with a fully-dependent topic model (2), we demonstrate applicability to query log modeling, and we formulate a fully-Bayesian framework and derive an efficient inference algorithm with collapsed Gibbs sampling rather than an annealed EM algorithm [10].

Table 1: Summary of the query log datasets where D is the number of documents, V is the number of terms in the vocabulary, and M is the number of terms in a query.

	D	V	Average M	Language
Yahoo	996K	15K	2.31	Japanese
AOL	583K	14K	2.77	English

5. EXPERIMENTS

5.1 Setting

We prepared two real query logs: AOL and Yahoo! Japan datasets. The AOL dataset consists of approximately 20 million queries [16]. The Yahoo! Japan dataset consists of approximately 600 million queries sampled from one week search logs. In our experiments, we examined the abilities of the PCTM for typical queries. To conduct such experiments, we performed the following preprocessing. We eliminated queries from the datasets that included low frequency terms or stop words. We then performed random sampling to reduce the data size. This preprocessing extracted typical queries randomly; while the domains of queries were still diverse. In addition, for the AOL dataset, we performed stemming with the Porter's algorithm[3]. Table 1 summarizes the preprocessed datasets.

Throughout the experiments, we compared the PCTM with the LDA and BTM. As explained in Section 4.3, LDA handles a query as a document. Note that we also attempted to evaluate the CTM with an R implementation[4]; however, this did not work in our experimental environment[5] due to memory overflow. All models were inferred with collapsed Gibbs sampling. We iterated 1,000 samples for the LDA and BTM, and 500 samples for the PCTM. We obtained the last sample in a Markov chain and made use of this sample to estimate parameters, which was required in some experiments. In all experiments and the models, the number of topics was fixed to 100, and β, which is a common hyperparameter, was fixed to 0.1. [6] Since α of LDA is a sensitive parameter [19], we assumed an asymmetric prior and estimated by using Minka's fixed point iteration [13]. For α of the BTM and γ of the PCTM, we assumed a symmetric prior and used fixed values; we set α of the BTM to $\frac{50}{K}$ and γ of the PCTM to $\frac{50}{K^2}$ [22]. [7]

[3]http://tartarus.org/martin/PorterStemmer/

[4]http://cran.r-project.org/web/packages/topicmodels/index.html

[5]CPU:Intel Corei7-3770 3.40GHz, Memory:16GB RAM

[6]For the LDA and BTM, we follow the notation of hyperparameters from [7] and [22], respectively.

[7]While we did not estimate α of the BTM and γ of the

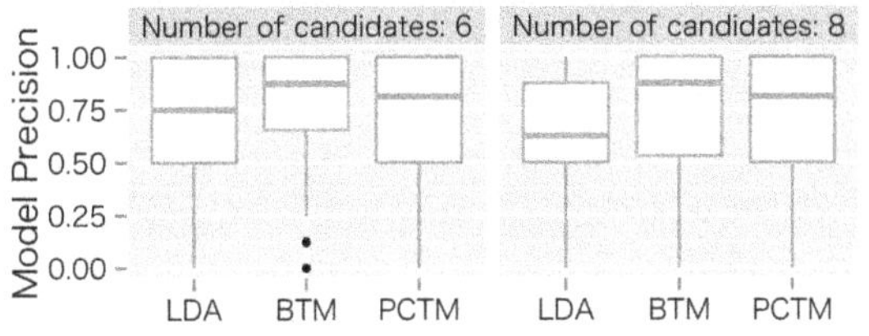

Figure 3: Results of the word intrusion task. Each panel shows the results for the number of displayed terms.

5.2 Human Evaluation of Topic Quality

In our first experiment, we investigated the interpretability of estimated topics for humans, i.e., how natural and meaningful topics are compared to human knowledge. We conducted three evaluation tasks via crowdsourcing: word intrusion and topic intrusion tasks proposed in [6], and query selection task, which we explain in detail in the following subsections. In these experiments, we used the Yahoo! dataset, and the tasks were performed through using the Yahoo! Japan crowdsourcing service. All jobs contained ten tasks and were assigned to eight different workers [6].

5.2.1 *Word Intrusion*

The word intrusion task evaluated the cohesion of a group of terms belonging to the same topic. In this task, several terms that belong to the same topic, except for one term (an intruder), were displayed and, a crowdworker attempted to locate the intruder. The intruder was selected randomly at low probability in the topic, but at high probability in another topic. The other displayed terms were selected with high probability in the topic. Therefore, if the topic was significantly cohesive, the intruder was clearly isolated from the other terms, and the crowdworker could find the intruder easily. We performed this task by varying the number of displayed terms (6 and 8). We used 50 topics, from which a large number of terms were assigned in the last samples of the inference. Performance was measured according to the precision of intruders detection. We compute the fraction of intruder detection by 8 workers for each topic.

The results are shown in Figure 3. At first glance, we see that LDA looks worse than the BTM and PCTM. In fact, there was significant difference[8] between LDA and the BTM, while the difference was not detected between LDA and the PCTM. Although the PCTM was slightly worse than the BTM, the difference was not significant. We discuss the reason why the performances of the BTM and PCTM are nearly the same in Section 6.

5.2.2 *Topic Intrusion*

The topic intrusion task examined how relevant topics were assigned to queries. For each task, we displayed a query and four topics such that three of the topics were the most relevant to the query but the remaining topic was chosen randomly from the top-10 most irrelevant topics. Then, similar to the word intrusion task, a crowdworker attempted to identify the irrelevant topic. Each topic was represented as T terms having the top-T highest probability in the topic. We

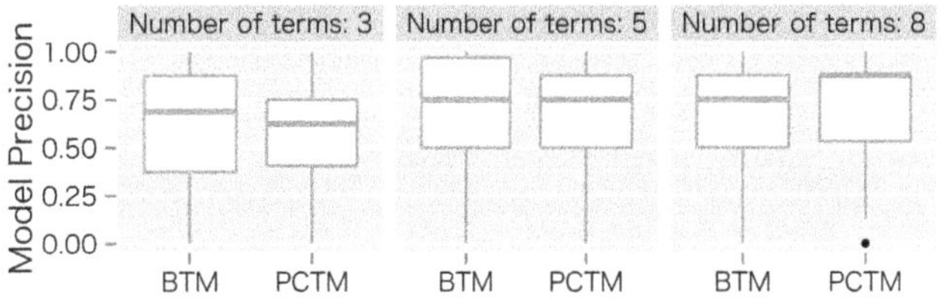

Figure 4: Results of the topic intrusion task

performed this task with varying T (3, 5, and 8). Note that as the number of displayed terms increased, topics became more identifiable. We used 50 queries in total, which were chosen randomly from the dataset. As the same manner of the word intrusion task, we evaluated the performance by the precision. Note that we excluded LDA from this experiment because the estimated topic distributions were very sparse; thus, we could not select three relevant topics.

For the BTM and PCTM, to collect relevant topics for a given query, we estimate topic probability of the query by taking the average of the topic probability of the term pairs. In the BTM, the probability of topic z_q in an M-long query q is expressed as follows:

$$p(z_q|q)_k = \frac{2}{M(M-1)} \sum_{b_i \in B(q)} p(z_i|b_i)_k, \tag{15}$$

where $B(q)$ is the set of term pairs in q and $p(z_i|b_i)_k$ is the posterior probability of topic $z_i = k$ given term pair b_i, which can be estimated in the same manner as Eq. (11). For the PCTM, we first compute the probability of topic pair x_q in query q:

$$p(x_q|q)_{kl} = \frac{2}{M(M-1)} \sum_{b_i \in B(q)} p(x_i|b_i)_{kl}, \tag{16}$$

where $p(x_i|b_i)_{kl}$ is given by Eq. (11). To obtain the probability of individual topic z_q, we then compute the following probability:

$$p(z_q|q)_k = \frac{1}{2} \sum_{l=1}^{K} p(x_q|q)_{kl} + p(x_q|q)_{lk}, \tag{17}$$

i.e., we take the average for each element and its diagonal element and marginalize out topic l.

The results are shown in Figure 4. We observe that there was no significant difference[8] between the BTM and PCTM; however, the performances of the PCTM tends to increase as the number of displayed terms increases. This is in contrast to the BTM, in which performance does not change with respect to the number of displayed terms. This implies that the PCTM obtained more coherent topics; thus, crowdworkers could use the increased terms as meaningful information effectively.

5.2.3 *Query Selection*

The query selection task evaluates how topic models recover a user intent as a query pattern. In each task, we display an actual (target) query and three groups of artificial queries, which are respectively generated by LDA, the BTM, and the PCTM. We let crowdworkers infer the search intent of the target query and then select a group having the most number of queries that have the same intent. For example, we consider a target query as "NY restaurant" in which the intent is assumed to be (`LOCATION SERVICE`). If a

PCTM, these prior effects will be relatively less than that of LDA because topic (topic pair) distribution is shared among all the latent variables.

[8] In terms of the one side paired t-test with 95% confidence.

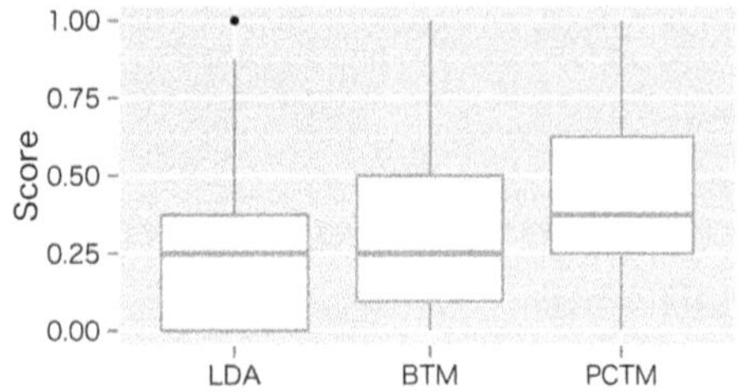

Figure 5: Results of the query selection task

crowdworker infer the intent correctly, a group consisting of (LOCATION SERVICE)-queries, such as "chicago lottery" and "florida hotel", should be selected.

We randomly selected 300 2-long queries from the training dataset and used as the target queries. For these 2-long target queries, we estimated the topic pair which takes maximum posterior probability at the end of the inference. For each model, we fixed the length of generated queries to 2 and selected by the following procedure. Given the estimated topic pair in a target query, we compute the posterior probability of 2-long queries, i.e., term pairs. For the PCTM, we computed the probability of term pair $b = (w_1, w_2)$ given topic pair $x = (z_1, z_2)$ and the estimated parameter $\hat{\phi}$ as follows:

$$p(b = (w_1, w_2)|x = (z_1, z_2), \hat{\phi}) = \hat{\phi}_{w_1,z_1}\hat{\phi}_{w_2,z_2}. \qquad (18)$$

The BTM and LDA computed the probabilities in the same manner. Finally, we used the top-5 term pairs taking the most high probability as the displayed queries. We measured the score which is the fraction of the selected by 8 workers for each target query.

The results are shown in Figure 5. The PCTM was significant better[8] than the BTM and LDA. This means that the PCTM could obtain topic pairs where the intents are closer to ones interpreted by humans than the others.

5.3 Keyword Prediction

In this experiment, we evaluated performance in terms of keyword prediction, i.e., given several terms as a part of a query, we attempted to predict the term that a user will input next. From the whole dataset, we randomly selected 10% of the queries and picked one term for each query as test data. We repeated this procedure 10 times and created training and testing datasets. We randomly initialized the latent variables for each trial. Then, after learning the parameters with the training dataset, we calculated the perplexity for each dataset using the last 100 samples for prediction.

While LDA can perform this experiment simply without modifications, the BTM and PCTM could not. Therefore, we computed the predictive probability for a single term rather than for a term pair. We computed this by assuming that the positions of missing terms in the test queries were known in advance, and that the set of term pairs preserved the missing positions. We regarded missing terms as latent variables in the models and performed collapsed Gibbs sampling on these variables in the parameter inference. The sample of the jth term in the ith term pair was obtained by following the conditional distribution in the PCTM:

$$p(w_{i,j} = v|B^{-i,j}, X^{-i}, x_i = (k,l)) = \frac{n^{-i}_{w_{i,j}|k} + \beta}{n^{-i}_{\cdot|k} + V\beta}, \qquad (19)$$

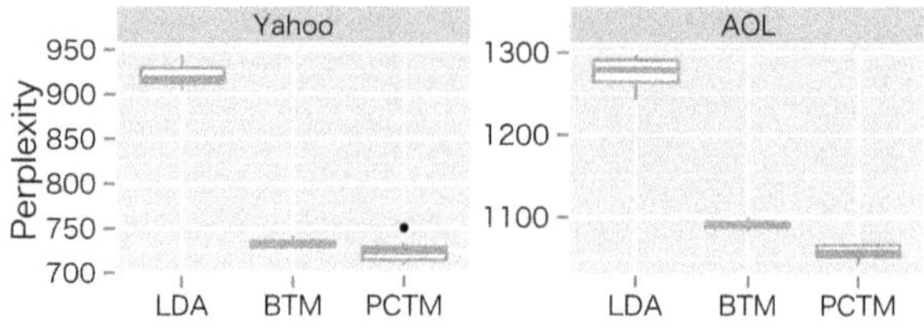

Figure 6: Results of the keyword prediction task. Lower perplexity indicates the better performance.

where $B^{-i,j}$ denotes that the set of term pairs excluding only $w_{i,j}$. The samples of the BTM were obtained in the same manner. After parameter inference, the predictive probability of missing term $w_{i,j}$ was calculated by Eq. (19). We then took the average of the terms, which was contained in separate term pairs but was identical in a query.[9]

The results are shown in Figure 6. For both datasets, the PCTM outperformed the BTM. Indeed, the PCTM was significantly better[8] than the BTM in both datasets.

5.4 Query Generation

In this experiment, we investigated the ability of the topic models as query generators, which is important for query recommendation application in Internet advertising. To evaluate the performance, we learned each model by using training data and computed the top-10,000 most frequent 2-long queries. Then, we measured AUC against the test queries, which we randomly selected another 100,000 2-long queries[10]. In addition, we investigated the total number of generated queries detected in the test data. Note that, while we also performed query generation in the query selection task (Section 5.2.3), the evaluation criterion is different in terms of that the query selection takes the user intent into account; this experiment purely evaluate how the topic models can generate natural queries, regardless of the user intents. We computed the probability of term pair $b = (w_1, w_2)$ whose topic pair is marginalized out as follows:

$$p(b = (w_1, w_2)|\hat{\phi}, \hat{\psi}) = \sum_{z_1}\sum_{z_2} \hat{\phi}_{w_1,z_1}\hat{\phi}_{w_2,z_2}\hat{\psi}_{z_1,z_2}. \qquad (20)$$

The probabilities of the BTM and LDA are computed in the same way as the PCTM. Note that we computed the document specific parameters of LDA from estimated $\boldsymbol{\alpha}$.

The results are shown in Table 2. The AUC of the PCTM was higher than the BTM and LDA in both datasets. This result implies that the occurrence probability of a query computed by the PCTM reflects the occurrence of the real query logs. Moreover, the PCTM detected the most queries from test data in both datasets. The result indicates the PCTM has more natural generative process for real query logs than the BTM and LDA.

5.5 Estimated Topics and Topic Co-occurrences

Here, we compare the obtained topics as a qualitative evaluation using the AOL dataset. We show the LOCATION

[9]Compared to the training dataset of LDA, that of the BTM and PCTM includes the position information about the missing terms. Since LDA does not require such information in the traditional way to compute the perplexity, we did not perform the sampling of the missing terms for LDA.

[10]We allowed the test data to include queries consisting of duplicate terms, such as "NY NY" and "restaurant restaurant".

Table 2: **Results of AUC and the total number of detected queries in the query generation task**

AUC	Yahoo	AOL
LDA	0.5743	0.5634
BTM	0.5729	0.6080
PCTM	0.6021	0.6144

Total num.	Yahoo	AOL
LDA	645	632
BTM	2,173	1,437
PCTM	3,196	1,880

Table 3: Estimated topics about location

	Top 20 terms
LDA	lottery state universe florida lotto california ny texas unit ohio map michigan job pa georgia result nj illinois virginia service
BTM	san la vegas diego hotel francisco antonio casino california nevada jose nv mission citi cabo reno valley mexico grand lo
PCTM	florida ny texas san nj ohio chicago nc virginia nyc houston fl va pa lo orlando michigan angel la california

topic in Table 3; for each model, we selected a topic such that the most number of terms related to locations in the top-20 topic terms were used. The result shows that the PCTM obtained the most cohesive topic that only contains the terms related to location, while the BTM and LDA topics are corrupted by some non-geographical terms, such as "lottery" and "hotel". This is a reasonable result for LDA because it counts the topic probability for every document, (i.e., query) and a document is extremely short; thus, terms appearing in the same query were likely to be assigned to the same topic. A similar interpretation holds for the BTM. As described in Section 4.3, the BTM mitigates the brevity problem of queries and assumes that term pairs must be assigned to the same topic, which causes contamination of "not-geographical-but-jointly-used" terms, such as "hotel".

Figure 1 shows $\hat{\psi}$, which represents the relationships among topics, i.e., $\hat{\psi}_{kl}$ indicates the probability of how often topics k and l are jointly used in term pairs. Note that in Figure 1 the elements are shown in gray where $n_{k,l}$ in Eq. (10) takes 0, which shows that $\hat{\psi}$ is actually very sparse. This indicates that each topic co-occurs with only a few other topics. This result agrees with common sense; people possibly search "NY hotel" but not "lottery hotel".

An unique advantage of the PCTM compared to the LDA and BTM is that we obtain the relationship among topics as $\hat{\psi}$. Figure 7 represents relationships among "public" topics, which we see that topic 3 represents public facilities and is associated with topics about location (topic 4), public service (topic 0), and job (topic 1). We clearly observe that the PCTM could obtain the network of topics that is very reasonable to our general knowledge. This is a surprising result because the PCTM is a fully unsupervised approach and we did not use any human resources.

5.6 Scalability

In this experiment, we compared the methods with various K as 30, 50, and 100 by using the AOL dataset. First, we checked $|S|$, the size of S, in exact and conditioned sampling. Figure 8 describes the changes of the size in 500 iterations for each setting. We see that, the sizes of both sampling

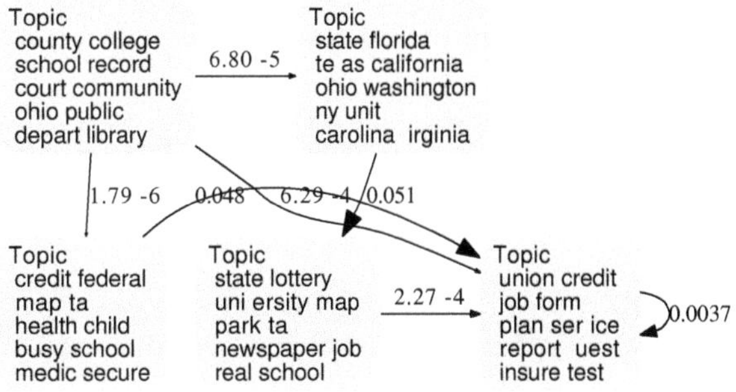

Figure 7: A subgraph of topic relationships estimated by the PCTM. We put an edge between the topics if the corresponding entry of $\hat{\psi}$ has larger probability than $\frac{\gamma}{N+K^2\gamma}$. For each topic, the top-10 terms are displayed. For each edge, we show the value of $\hat{\psi}$ and the larger value indicates the strong connectivity.

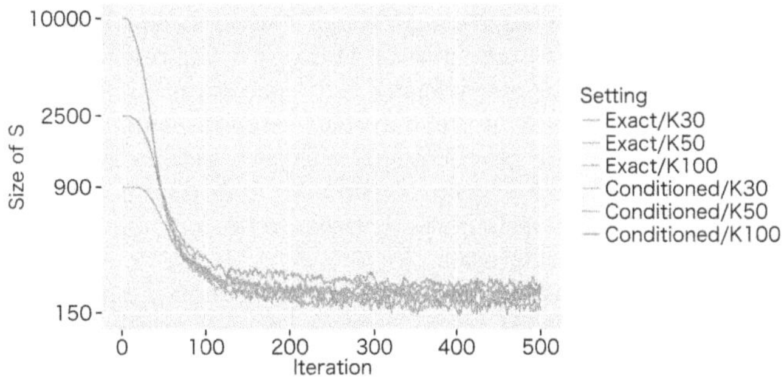

Figure 8: Transitions of the size of S

behaved in surprisingly similar ways. Another interesting observation is that, all the sizes were fluctuated between about 150 and 200, i.e., $|S| = O(1)$ and it suffices condition (i) in Section 3.5.

Next, we evaluated how conditioned sampling reduces the actual runtime. We compared all the models in addition to the PCTM with conditioned sampling. Note that we fixed all the elements of $\boldsymbol{\alpha}$ in LDA to $50/K$ for fair comparisons. The results are shown in Table 4. As expected, LDA, the BTM, and the PCTM with the conditioned sampler run in $O(K)$ time, whereas the normal PCTM required $O(K^2)$.

Finally, we compared exact and conditioned sampling by the keyword prediction task in Section 5.3. The results are shown in Table 5, telling us that conditioned sampling keeps the same performance as exact sampling.

6. CONCLUSION AND DISCUSSION

We have proposed a new probabilistic topic model for query logs. The PCTM can capture topic co-occurrences in a query, which make topics more coherent without limiting the target domain of queries. For model learning, we derived a fully-Bayesian inference algorithm with the efficient computational trick for the collapsed Gibbs sampler. We have examined three types of experiments, i.e., crowdsourcing, keyword prediction, and query generation tasks.

We discuss four concerns of the PCTM for future improvements.

Firstly, sometimes the PCTM learns overlapped topics,

Table 4: Comparisons of the runtime (in minutes)

	$K = 30$	$K = 50$	$K = 100$
LDA	5.02	7.2	14.31
BTM	8.12	12.84	24.57
PCTM (Exact)	239.79	657.80	2621.02
PCTM (Conditioned)	104.82	153.56	276.50

Table 5: Perplexity of exact and conditioned sampling

	$K = 30$	$K = 50$	$K = 100$
Exact	1451.14	1242.66	1057.96
Conditioned	1450.16	1240.03	1054.38

i.e., the topics having almost the same term distributions. This is caused by the flexibility of the PCTM. Further regularization to remove such redundancy is an important future work of the PCTM.

Secondly, the number of latent variables increases quadratically with query length. Although this situation is fairly better than the approximation of Eq. (5) where the number is the same as query length but the computational cost grows exponentially, it still may cause scaling issues for very long queries. One practical option is just eliminating such long queries before learning the model. This does not affect to the performance significantly because the long queries are quite rare in real datasets.

Thirdly, we discuss that the PCTM did not significantly outperform the BTM in the word and topic intrusion tasks. While the PCTM can obtain separated topic representation as described in Section 4.3, we found that this property did not seem to contribute to the improvement in the both tasks. For example, in the word intrusion task, even though we displayed "hotel" and "florida" included in the integrated topic `LOCATION & SERVICE` estimated by the BTM, crowdworkers possibly infer that these terms are associated with each other more than the other intruder term, because people frequently use location and service names in web search. Conversely, in the query selection task, the PCTM significantly outperformed the BTM because this task requires the separability of topics for what crowdworkers can recognize query intents. In contrast to the word and topic intrusion tasks, the PCTM significantly outperformed the LDA and BTM with respect to keyword prediction, which is a similar characteristic to the CTM; The CTM may select an intruder from highly correlated topics in word intrusion. This results in degenerating the performance because the intruder from the correlated topic confuses crowdworkers [6]. The PCTM seems to have the same problem since it incorporates such correlations between topics.

Fourthly, although the conditioned sampler of the PCTM significantly reduces the computational cost, the runtime is still slower than LDA and the BTM. The main reason is S, the set of active topic pairs, is too large in the initial state. In fact, when $K = 100$, 74% of the runtime was for first 100 iterations. This implies some good initialization for topic pairs may reduce the runtime significantly. For example, the topic distributions obtained by LDA can be useful for the initialization.

Acknowledgments

We thank Naomi Sasaya, Nobuyuki Shimizu, Yoshiko Takeuchi, and Shinichi Tsuzaki for providing helpful comments and organizing the crowdsourcing tasks. KI was supported by MEXT Kakenhi 15H01620. KH was supported by MEXT Kakenhi 15K16055.

7. REFERENCES

[1] G. Agarwal, G. Kabra, and K. C.-C. Chang. Towards rich query interpretation: Walking back and forth for mining query templates. In *WWW*, 2010.

[2] R. Agrawal, A. Gupta, Y. Prabhu, and M. Varma. Multi-label learning with millions of labels: Recommending advertiser bid phrases for web pages. In *WWW*, 2013.

[3] D. M. Blei and J. D. Lafferty. A correlated topic model of science. *The Annals of Applied Statistics*, 1(1):17–35, 2007.

[4] D. M. Blei, A. Y. Ng, and M. I. Jordan. Latent Dirichlet allocation. *JMLR*, 3:993–1022, 2003.

[5] M. J. Carman, F. Crestani, M. Harvey, and M. Baillie. Towards query log based personalization using topic models. In *CIKM*, 2010.

[6] J. Chang, J. Boyd-Graber, C. Wang, S. Gerrish, and D. M. Blei. Reading tea leaves: How humans interpret topic models. In *NIPS*, 2009.

[7] T. L. Griffiths and M. Steyvers. Finding scientific topics. *PNAS*, 101:5228–5235, 2004.

[8] J. Han, J. Fan, and L. Zhou. Crowdsourcing-assisted query structure interpretation. In *IJCAI*, 2013.

[9] M. Harvey, F. Crestani, and M. J. Carman. Building user profiles from topic models for personalised search. In *CIKM*, 2013.

[10] T. Hofmann and J. Puzicha. Statistical models for co-occurrence data. Technical report, Massachusetts Institute of Technology Artificial Intelligence Laboratory, 1998.

[11] D. Jiang, K. W. T. Leung, W. Ng, and H. Li. Beyond click graph: Topic modeling for search engine query log analysis. In *DASFAA*, 2013.

[12] D. Jiang and W. Ng. Mining web search topics with diverse spatiotemporal patterns. In *SIGIR*, 2013.

[13] T. P. Minka. Estimating a Dirichlet distribution. Technical report, Microsoft, 2000.

[14] S. Pandey and K. Punera. Unsupervised extraction of template structure in web search queries. In *WWW*, 2012.

[15] S. Pandey, K. Punera, M. Fontoura, and V. Josifovski. Estimating advertisability of tail queries for sponsored search. In *SIGIR*, 2010.

[16] G. Pass, A. Chowdhury, and C. Torgeson. A picture of search. In *Proceedings of the 1st International Conference on Scalable Information Systems*, 2006.

[17] W. Song, Y. Zhang, T. Liu, and S. Li. Bridging topic modeling and personalized search. In *COLING*, 2010.

[18] A. Viterbi. Error bounds for convolutional codes and an asymptotically optimum decoding algorithm. *IEEE Transactions on Information Theory*, 13(2):260–269, 2006.

[19] H. M. Wallach, D. Mimno, and A. McCallum. Rethinking LDA: Why priors matter. In *NIPS*, 2009.

[20] G. Xu, S.-H. Yang, and H. Li. Named entity mining from click-through data using weakly supervised latent Dirichlet allocation. In *SIGKDD*, 2009.

[21] J. Xu and W. B. Croft. Query expansion using local and global document analysis. In *SIGIR*, 1996.

[22] X. Yan, J. Guo, Y. Lan, and X. Cheng. A biterm topic model for short texts. In *WWW*, 2013.

[23] L. Yao, D. Mimno, and A. McCallum. Efficient methods for topic model inference on streaming document collections. In *SIGKDD*, 2009.

The Past and Future of Systems for Current Events

Mor Naaman
Jacobs Institute
Cornell Tech
New York, NY
mor@jacobs.cornell.edu

ABSTRACT

People share in social media an overwhelming amount of content from real-world events. These events range from major global events like an uprising or an earthquake, to local events and emergencies such as a fire or a parade; from media events like the Oscar's, to events that enjoy little media coverage such as a conference or a music concert. This shared media represents an important part of our society, culture and history. At the same time, this social media content is still fragmented across services, hard to find, and difficult to consume and understand.

We have worked since 2008, in both research and startup settings, to tackle key challenges in making social media information about events accessible and usable. These challenges include detecting new events in a stream of content (e.g. [1]), identifying content related to events (e.g., [2]) and organizing event content to be presented in a ways that get *better* when new content is added (e.g., [3]). A core useful concept for all these challenges is *Attention Rank*: how to computationally model the human attention reflected in real-time social media content. (This work was supported in part by National Science Foundation grants Number 1446374 and 1444493).

Several recent commercial services (Twitter, Instagram and even Snapchat) attempt to better present "moments" and other trending events. Still, I argue that there are no current systems that provide a coherent summary or narrative representation of event content from social media at scale using automated or semi-automated tools. My own startup that addressed this very problem moved away from it despite initial success.

There are several open challenges before we can reliably provide precise and engaging narratives for all the world's stories. One such key challenge is developing flexible systems that intelligently apply a combination of machines and humans to create appropriate narratives for events of any type and size. Social media – a mirror and record of our humanity – is now rapidly expanding to include real-time mobile video and even virtual reality. The work to make sense of all this information is far from complete.

WSDM'16 Feb 22-25, 2016, San Francisco, CA, USA.

ACM ISBN 978-1-4503-3716-8/16/02.

DOI: http://dx.doi.org/10.1145/2835776.2835850

Categories and Subject Descriptors

H.4 [**Information Systems Applications**]: Miscellaneous

Keywords

social media, events, information organization, startup

Bio

Mor Naaman is an associate professor of Information Science at the Jacobs Institute at Cornell Tech, where he is the founder of the Connective Media hub, and leads a research group focused on social technologies. His research applies multidisciplinary methods to 1) gain a better understanding of people and their use of social tech; 2) extract insights about people, technology and society from social media and other sources of social data, and 3) develop new social technologies as well as novel tools to make social data more accessible and usable in various settings.

Previously, Mor was on the faculty at Rutgers SC&I, led a research team at Yahoo! Research Berkeley, received a Ph.D. in Computer Science from the Stanford InfoLab, and played professional basketball for Hapoel Tel Aviv. He is a recipient of a NSF Early Faculty CAREER Award, corporate research awards and grants from companies like Google and AOL, and multiple best paper awards. Find out more about Mor at http://mornaaman.com.

1. REFERENCES

[1] H. Becker, M. Naaman, and L. Gravano. Beyond trending topics: Real-world event identification on twitter. In *ICWSM 2011*.

[2] H. Becker, M. Naaman, and L. Gravano. Learning similarity metrics for event identification in social media. In *WSDM 2010*.

[3] R. Schwartz, M. Naaman, and R. Teodoro. Editorial algorithms: Using social media to discover and report local news. In *ICWSM 2015*.

Barbara Made the News: Mining the Behavior of Crowds for Time-Aware Learning to Rank

Flávio Martins* flaviomartins@acm.org

João Magalhães* jm.magalhaes@fct.unl.pt

Jamie Callan† callan@cs.cmu.edu

*NOVA LINCS, Department of Computer Science
Faculty of Science and Technology
Universidade NOVA de Lisboa
2829-516 Caparica, Portugal

†Language Technologies Institute
Carnegie Mellon University
5000 Forbes Avenue
Pittsburgh, PA 15213, USA

ABSTRACT

In Twitter, and other microblogging services, the generation of new content by the crowd is often biased towards immediacy: *what is happening now.* Prompted by the propagation of commentary and information through multiple mediums, users on the Web interact with and produce new posts about newsworthy topics and give rise to trending topics. This paper proposes to leverage on the behavioral dynamics of users to estimate the most relevant time periods for a topic. Our hypothesis stems from the fact that when a real-world event occurs it usually has *peak times* on the Web: a higher volume of *tweets*, new visits and edits to related Wikipedia articles, and news published about the event.

In this paper, we propose a novel time-aware ranking model that leverages on multiple sources of crowd signals. Our approach builds on two major novelties. First, a unifying approach that given query q, mines and represents temporal evidence from multiple sources of crowd signals. This allows us to predict the temporal relevance of documents for query q. Second, a principled retrieval model that integrates temporal signals in a learning to rank framework, to rank results according to the predicted temporal relevance. Evaluation on the TREC 2013 and 2014 Microblog track datasets demonstrates that the proposed model achieves a relative improvement of 13.2% over lexical retrieval models and 6.2% over a learning to rank baseline.

Categories and Subject Descriptors

H.3.3 [**Information Storage and Retrieval**]: Information Search and Retrieval—*Search process; Retrieval models*

Keywords

Microblog search; Twitter; Social media; Learning to Rank; Time-aware ranking models; Temporal Information Retrieval

WSDM'16, February 22–25, 2016, San Francisco, CA, USA.

DOI: http://dx.doi.org/10.1145/2835776.2835825

1. INTRODUCTION

A networked world and the pervasiveness of Internet access enables the rapid adoption of new online communication mediums. People are increasingly sharing new information via microblogging services and other similar social media services. Events are discussed in real-time, thus search became a pressing demand from Web users in general.

Standard search techniques, such as retrieval schemes based on language modeling have proven to be very effective in Web documents. However, standard text retrieval functions have under-performed in the ranking of microblog posts, because *tweets* are short and highly biased by real-world events. Previous research in time-aware ranking explored the assumption that more recent documents are more relevant [15]. Later models revised this assumption in line with what is observed in Twitter and other real-time document collections: for time-sensitive queries, documents tend to cluster temporally [8, 9]. Most prior work gather temporal information from a single source, typically either the corpus itself (e.g., Twitter) or Wikipedia (e.g., in the form of edits or views). These strategies assume that all important events will have an impact on Twitter or Wikipedia, and that the temporal signal available from Twitter or Wikipedia will be clear and unambiguous, however that is not always the case.

We depart from previous approaches, by observing that events have an impact not only on Twitter but also in other Web domains such as news, clicks, query logs, etc. Our approach is based on the intuition that discussions about an event (and therefore relevant documents) are more likely to occur around the same time periods across multiple social-media services. Thus, it is reasonable to assume that it would be advantageous to expand these methods to further integrate external sources, to offer more context to the *tweets* as well as to the users' queries intent. Temporal queries may not exhibit temporal patterns of user search behavior in query logs or even in the temporal density of an initial set of retrieved documents, but still contain underlying temporal information needs. In this context, we aim at refining the temporal relevance density function of a time-sensitive query by using multiple external Web sources.

This approach brings a series of novel contributions: (1) the mining of crowd signals from different Web sources (e.g., news, Wikipedia articles, and Twitter) to detect relevant time periods, and (2) a unifying method to generate temporal features that can be used for multiple time-aware tasks, and (3) a time-aware ranking model based on learning to rank.

Evaluation on the TREC 2013 and TREC 2014 Microblog Track datasets has shown that the proposed retrieval model outperforms state-of-the-art methods. More specifically, we found that most queries benefited from at least a second source of temporal information.

This paper is organized as follows: in section 2 we briefly analyze an event that motivates the proposed method; in section 3 we present the related work; section 4 details the mining of temporal crowd signals; the ranking framework is formalized in section 5 where we detail ranking with multiple temporal features; evaluation is presented in section 6; and a more fine-grained discussion of results in section 7.

2. BARBARA MADE THE NEWS

On February 2013 it was revealed that Barbara Walters, a well-known figure in the U.S. television, got chicken pox. This real-world event sparked multiple processes on the Web, such as the propagation of news articles about the event, commentary on Twitter and an increased interest in the article page for "Barbara Walters" on Wikipedia. Often, these signals can be mined as the event unfolds and for some Web sources can also be mined retrospectively. In Figure 1 we dissect how multiple Web sources can show signals related to the crowd behavior in reaction to this newsworthy event.

When searching Twitter for "Barbara Walters, chicken pox", we cannot make out from the visualization of *Twitter* (the distribution of initially retrieved documents) any of the time periods that are actually relevant (the distribution of relevant tweets). Having found no useful temporal evidence using only the collection (i.e., Twitter Feedback) we turn our attention to extra external sources that can help disambiguate the days that are temporally relevant to this query.

The *Wikipedia views* signal chart for this topic shows the volume of page views per-day of the "Barbara Walters" article on Wikipedia. We see that the biggest spike was dominated by March 4, and in the following days the interest in the page decreases. This actually corresponds to the highest volume day in the ground-truth, albeit with about a day of lag.

Turning our attention to *News* sources we are able to spot three (3) main time periods that are good candidates to better model temporal relevance. The first peak corresponds to a news article with alarming news about *chicken pox* mentioning *Barbara Walters*, which accompanied the discussion of the topic on Twitter, the second peak corresponds to the propagation of news that Barbara Walters is recovering and the third peak is related to the news of her return to the U.S. television talk show "The View" on ABC.

To verify the relevance of each time period evidenced by each source, we can examine the volume of relevant tweets per day on Twitter using the list of relevant documents (Qrels), Figure 1b. The key insight from this comparison is that two temporal sources have useful information providing different, but relevant information. This analysis hints that mining multiple sources of evidence to detect when events are *happening* can be more robust than using only a single source of evidence (i.e., the corpus).

The rationale supporting our research hypothesis calls for a method that overcomes this problem by disambiguating the relevant time periods using multiple sources of evidence: internal and external, to improve retrieval in time-sensitive scenarios such as search on Twitter. Our approach is to mine useful temporal features to propose a novel time-aware ranking method with multiple temporal sources (RMTS).

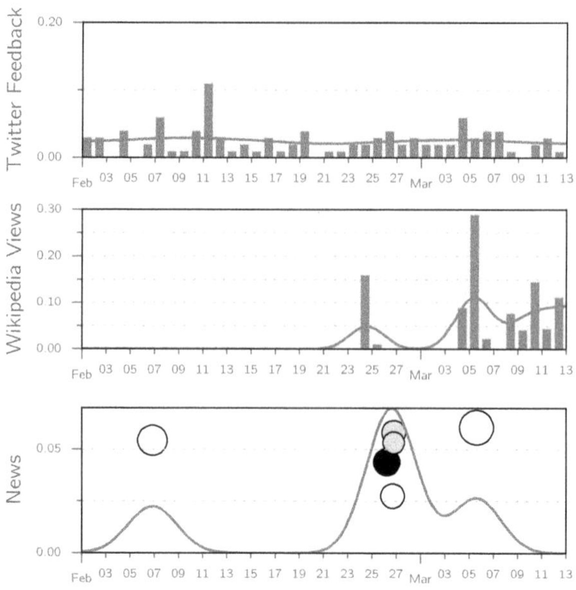

(a) Temporal evidence from multiple Web sources.

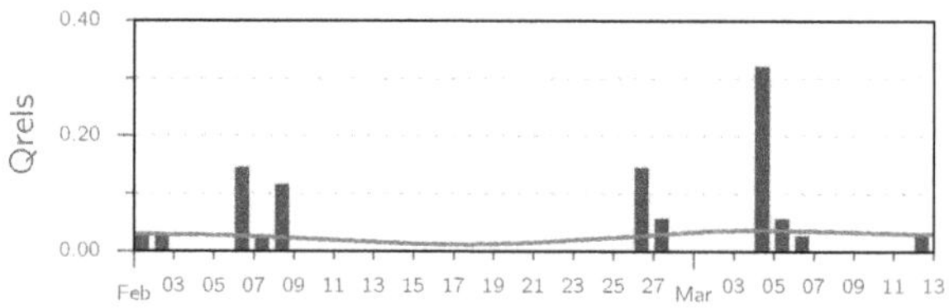

(b) Temporal distribution of relevant tweets (qrels).

Figure 1: Results for query "Barbara Walters, chicken pox" on different sources. The histograms indicate the volume of data for each source per day. In the News source, each circle corresponds to a matching news article, its size is proportional to the Jaccard index between the query and the news headline. Its color indicates the news site (Reuters – gray, Associated Press – black and USA Today – white). The curves depict a smoothed estimate.

3. BACKGROUND AND RELATED WORK

One of the main issues in microblogs is the quality of the posts themselves. Removing duplicates (i.e. *retweets*), *tweets* written in unwanted target languages, and spam improves the ranking performance [14]. Some techniques [16] estimate the *tweet's* quality using textual features such as the presence of emoticons, slang and unknown vocabulary, following prior research on blog post retrieval [26]. More elaborate approaches [7, 27] measure the influence of authors instead, using features such as the number of followers and the number of *retweets* to estimate the author's credibility.

Another main issue is the temporal relevance of the microblog posts. Previous research [25] has revealed that people search Twitter to find temporally relevant information, monitor popular trends, discover breaking news and follow events. Therefore, it is imperative that the design of search tools for social media incorporates the time dimension.

Existing works on time-aware ranking can be classified according to two main notions of relevance with respect to time [18]: 1) recency-based ranking, and 2) time-dependent ranking. Recency-based ranking usually improves scoring in social media and microblogs. Most topics searched by users on Twitter seem to imply a real-time information need [25], therefore recency ranking methods can be useful in social media search. Recency can be easily integrated into text retrieval with the time-based language model method proposed by Li and Croft [15], an extension to the standard query-likelihood model [20, 30]. The use of *recency priors* to promote recently published documents proposed by Li and Croft [15] assumes that in production systems, documents published closer to the time of the query are more relevant to the query. Given the document D timestamp T_D, they propose to model $P(D)$ in the query-likelihood model via the exponential distribution, $P(D) = \lambda e^{-\lambda(T_C - T_D)}$, where $\lambda \geq 0$ is the decay rate parameter of the exponential distribution and T_C is the most recent date in the collection. In the microblog search scenario Efron and Golovchinsky [8] found that $\lambda = 0.01$ provided the best average performance. This is a simple approach that usually outperforms the standard query-likelihood model.

However, Jones and Diaz [11] notes that queries that favor recency are just a subset of the time-sensitive queries. Dakka et al. [6] identified the need to find the important time periods for time-sensitive queries and to integrate this temporal relevance in the ranking model. Their ranking model explicitly divides documents into its lexical and temporal evidences: W_D, the words in the document and T_D, the document's timestamp, leading to $P(D|Q) \sim P(W_D|Q)P(T_D|Q)P(W_D)P(T_D)$. Dakka et al. [6] proposes techniques to estimate the $P(T_D|Q)$ from histograms, however the calculation of the histogram bins is linked to many parameters.

Additionally, a few time-based pseudo-relevance feedback methods were proposed for retrieval in time-sensitive collections. Whiting et al. [28] combines pseudo-relevant document term distribution and temporal collection evidence using a variant of PageRank over a weighted graph that models the temporal correlation between n-grams. Another approach by Peetz et al. [19] leverages on the temporal distribution of the pseudo-relevant documents themselves. For each query, bursty time periods are identified and then documents from these periods are selected for feedback. The query model is updated with new terms sampled from the higher quality documents selected.

Efron et al. [9] proposed a general and principled retrieval model for microblog search with temporal feedback. Their approach models the temporal density of a query $f(t|q)$ with a kernel density estimate, with all the advantages brought by this method: the natural smoothness of the resulting function and a fully automated way to estimate the model variables (bandwidth selection is data-driven, i.e: a function of the initial rank). This estimated temporal relevance is then employed to rerank documents with a log-linear model.

In contrast to previous work, we propose to use multiple external Web sources to robustly identify the relevant time periods for each query, instead of relying only on the temporal distribution of pseudo-relevant documents. Our method also accounts for the underestimation of the density at the boundaries, which can negatively affect queries with relevant documents near temporal extremes (e.g., query-time).

There are several previous works employing feature-based methods and machine learning for ranking with temporal features. Dai et al. [5] propose to run each query against a set of rankers, which are weighted based on the temporal profile of a query, and therefore minimize the risk of degraded performance due to misclassifying the query in terms of recency intent. Recent time-dependent ranking approaches have resorted to learning to rank techniques that exploit non-temporal and temporal features [4, 12].

4. TEMPORAL CROWD SIGNALS

The starting point of our hypothesis is that many real-world events originate a burst of simultaneous Web activity in multiple, possibly heterogeneous, data sources. The analysis of multiple temporal evidences is a powerful tool that can allow us to stitch together information from these sources [3]. The first step towards a solution requires the design of a unified representation of temporal signals extracted from several different sources.

4.1 A Unified Representation of Temporal Crowd Signals

Considering a set $S \in \{s_1, s_2, \ldots, s_k, \ldots\}$ of information sources that reflect a real-world event, our goal is to discover the relevance of a timestamp for a particular query. In other words, we wish to infer a function

$$f_{s_k}(q_a, t_b) \in [0, 1] \tag{1}$$

for each source s_k, to compute a relevance correlation score for the query q_a at instant t_b (this will be formalized as document d_b timestamp). To devise the f_{s_k} functions, we need to mine the behavior of the crowds on each source to discover signals that are related to the query at hand. In our framework, a signal corresponds to any user activity that is registered by the information source, e.g., a Wikipedia page view, a tweet, or the publication of a news article. Once we discover these signals, their timestamps and relevance to the query are collected into two sets:

$$T^{s_k} = \{t_1^{s_k}, t_2^{s_k}, \ldots, t_n^{s_k}\} \quad W^{s_k} = \{w_1^{s_k}, w_2^{s_k}, \ldots, w_n^{s_k}\} \tag{2}$$

Each pair $(t_i^{s_k}, w_i^{s_k})$ fully characterizes a temporal signal – it saves the signal i timestamp and its importance to the query that originated the mining process.

For each source of temporal signals s_k and its set of (mined) timestamps $T^{s_k} = \{t_1^{s_k}, t_2^{s_k}, \ldots, t_n^{s_k}\}$ we propose to use the same unified representation. For each document d_b we would like to find $P(r|t_{d_b}, q_a, s_k)$, the probability of relevance of its timestamp t_{d_b} according to source s_k and given query q_a. The estimation of the joint distribution $f_{s_k}(q_a, t)$ over the time span of the corpus is key. The probability density function $f_{s_k}(t_{d_b}|q_a)$ is approximated by a kernel density estimation which is advantageous due to the natural smoothness of the resulting function:

$$\hat{f_{s_k}}(t) = \frac{1}{nh} \sum_{i=0}^{n} w_i^{s_k} K\left(\frac{t - t_i^{s_k}}{h}\right) \tag{3}$$

where $t_i^{s_k}$ are the timestamps mined from a source s_k, the kernel function $K(z)$ corresponds to the Gaussian kernel $\mathcal{N}(z, 0)$, and the optimal bandwidth h can be estimated by a data-driven method such as Silverman's rule-of-thumb $h^* \approxeq 1.06\,\hat{\sigma}\,n^{-1/5}$. Finally, the vector $\{w_1^{s_k}, w_2^{s_k}, \ldots, w_n^{s_k}\}$, of non-negative weights on the $t_i^{s_k}$'s timestamps, weights each timestamp by its importance (e.g., to a query).

4.2 Temporal Signals from Multiple Sources

Most microblog queries are temporally spiky, following live events related to breaking news, celebrities, other entities and events, periodic queries, e.g., TV shows, and ongoing events. Our approach is volume-based and we assume as a starting point that topics bursting on Twitter are correlated with News and a higher volume of page views and edits for relevant Wikipedia pages.

To extract temporal crowd signals that are relevant to the search query, one needs to design source-specific methods that filter candidate signals and compute their relevance to the search query. This is the process that we discuss next.

4.2.1 News

Our system indexes the news headlines produced by multiple news sources incrementally. We select a small number of high signal-to-noise ratio sources of News: the Associated Press (AP), BBC's UK and World (BBC), Reuters and USA Today. We used an automatic rule-based extraction method to extract explicit non-relative temporal expressions [23] to detect the publication date of the news articles. A per-site timezone was set manually to adjust the site's time offsets.

For a given query q_a, we focus on finding a set of news headlines matching the search query, therefore we first retrieve a set of candidate headlines $H = \{h_1, h_2, \ldots, h_n\}$ from our index using a standard retrieval method. The temporal signals of the news source s_h are represented by the set $T^{s_h} = \{t_1^{s_h}, t_2^{s_h}, \ldots, t_n^{s_h}\}$ of headline timestamps.

The timestamp of each headline $t_i^{s_h}$ should be weighted according to its relevance to the query. Therefore, we measure the similarity of each headline to the query using the Jaccard similarity coefficient because usually in both headlines and queries $TF_i = 1$. This choice also avoids overweighting headlines with repeated words. The Jaccard index of Jaccard similarity coefficient of two sets of words A and B is given by $J(A, B) = \frac{|A \cap B|}{|A \cup B|}$. Thus, the weight $w_i^{s_h}$ of each timestamp $t_i^{s_h}$ is computed as the Jaccard similarity coefficient $J(q_a, h_i)$.

4.2.2 Wikipedia

To find a Wikipedia article relevant to the query q_a, our system searches for article titles on Wikipedia using their API. The first 10 candidate page titles returned are ranked using the Jaccard similarity coefficient and the most similar page title is selected. We hypothesize that users searching on Twitter and on the Web using text queries do so using similar queries and we try to model this behavior. Following this rationale we posit that, especially in the case of page views, if we don't find the article that best matches the query we should still get some feedback from alternative articles, because users are also likely to have interacted with them when searching the Web for information about a topic that is trending on Twitter.

Wikipedia page views. To obtain page view statistics of Wikipedia articles we use a public API[1] that provides histograms of counts binned by day (we will refer to this source as s_v). For our temporal signal extraction we fetch data from 1 December 2012 up until the time of the query, therefore the temporal signals for a query can go up to 4 months of data. To eliminate noise we normalize the frequencies using the mean of article view counts per day and obtain a normalized set of view counts per-day $W^{s_v} = \{w_1^{s_v}, w_2^{s_v}, \ldots, w_n^{s_v}\}$.

[1] http://stats.grok.se/

Finally, the temporal signals extracted from page views are represented as $T^{s_v} = \{t_1^{s_v}, t_2^{s_v}, \ldots, t_n^{s_v}\}$. In this case there is one timestamp per-day over the past months. To minimize error, we set the timestamp to midnight.

Wikipedia page edits. In the case of Wikipedia page edits, source s_e, we fetch the latest revisions before the time of the query of the Wikipedia article selected, via the Special:Export[2] feature on Wikipedia. We process the XML response and calculate the changes between each consecutive pairs of revisions in sequence and filter out article changes signed-off by known automatic Wikipedia Bots[3].

For the purposes of processing this temporal signal we use $TF(q, e)$, the term-frequency of terms in the query matching the text added in an edit e. This approach aims to restrict the edits, and hence the timestamps to the ones we find a stronger evidence of relatedness. Following this intuition, we treat terms in the Wikipedia article title as stop words for the calculation of $TF(q, e)$ (e.g., for page "Barbara Walters" changes matching only "Barbara" and/or "Walters" are not counted). The temporal signals extracted from page edits is given by $T^{s_e} = \{t_1^{s_e}, t_2^{s_e}, \ldots, t_n^{s_e}\}$. The weight $w_i^{s_e}$ of each timestamp is computed as the $\sum_j TF_j(q_a, e)$, the number of terms shared by the query and the edit.

4.2.3 Twitter

The crowd signals from Twitter, source s_t, are essential to assess the time periods that are more relevant to a query. Recent works on time-aware ranking for *tweet* search [6, 9] look at the ranked list of Tweets produced by a standard retrieval model and their timestamps for temporal feedback. These methods are rooted in the assumption that a search query will originate two distinct distributions, a lexical one and temporal one, that must be integrated into a single rank. The way we mine temporal crowd signals from Twitter is inspired by this family of approaches. The set of temporal signals are extracted from tweets retrieved with query q_a – the temporal signals $T^{s_t} = \{t_1^{s_t}, t_2^{s_t}, \ldots, t_n^{s_t}\}$ collect the tweets' timestamps. The weight $w_i^{s_t}$ of each timestamp is obtained according to the score computed with the query-likelihood retrieval model, i.e. $w_i^{s_t} = P(q_a|d_b)/\sum_{j=1}^{n} P(q_a|d_j)$

5. RANKING FRAMEWORK

Our search model follows a learning to rank (LTR) framework that integrates text features, domain specific features (e.g. number of hashtags) and temporal features extracted from crowd behaviors. In this section, we will first discuss the learning to rank model, followed by the description of a comprehensive set of non-temporal features, and will then address the computation of the model parameters.

5.1 Ranking with Multiple Temporal Signals

Typical LTR models consider a diverse set of features from the corpus. In this paper we integrate the features into a linear model, where the retrieval score of document d_b for a given query q_a is given by

$$LTR(q_a, d_b) = \sum_i \alpha_i f_{l_i}(q_a, d_b) + \sum_j \beta_j f_{c_j}(d_b) \quad (4)$$

The set of lexical features, f_{l_i} covers several text statistics and retrieval scores. Learning to rank literature has also

[2] https://en.wikipedia.org/wiki/Special:Export
[3] https://en.wikipedia.org/wiki/Wikipedia:Bots

extensively shown that non-lexical features f_{c_j}, such as clicks and number followers, are essential to capture the relevance of a document.

In the previous section, we saw how temporal evidence can be mined from data generated by the crowds. Table 2 summarizes the set of temporal feature signals. We proposed a unified view of how temporal signals from the crowds can be represented in a common way. Following this reasoning, we are now ready to plug-in multiple temporal evidence into the initial retrieval model, by extending it to support the time dimension:

$$RMTS(q_a, t_{d_b}, d_b) = \sum_i \alpha_i f_{l_i}(q_a, d_b) + \sum_j \beta_j f_{c_j}(d_b) + \sum_k \gamma_k f_{s_k}(q_a, t_{d_b}) \quad (5)$$

where t_{d_b} is the timestamp of document d_b , f_{s_k} returns the likelihood that day t_{d_b} is relevant to the query q_a under the distribution of the crowd source s_k. The crowd source s_k indexes one of the temporal sources described in the previous section. The coefficients α_i, β_j and γ_k correspond to the feature weights.

The RMTS model (Ranking with Multiple Temporal Signals) is composed of three independent parts that capture different statistics of the information domain. This model is a well grounded method that generalizes the integration of multiple temporal evidences into a single unified retrieval model. At this point, it becomes clear the divide between previous work, relying entirely in the corpus timestamps, and the proposed approach that looks at the crowd behaviors outside the corpus to better estimate the temporal relevance of the query. The factorization of crowd temporal information into a rich set of temporal signals, provides a more robust way to disambiguate the relevant days for each search query.

5.2 Non-temporal features

The non-temporal features in Table 1 include text-similarity scores computed over the tweet-text corpus and domain specific features such as the number of hastags in the tweet-text or the number of followers of the tweet's author.

The first set of features consider popular retrieval baselines that have proven to be effective in many scenarios, including temporal search with specific additions to address the temporal dimension. BM25 is our first text retrieval features, one of the most popular text retrieval models. In the language modeling approach [20, 30] to retrieval, a language model is created for each document and the ranking is based on the probability of generating the query. The language model with Dirichlet smoothing [30] is the third text feature baseline - it is also the baseline model in TREC Microblog.

In the Twitter domain, we found that rare words are actually critical for particular queries. To address this phenomena, we isolated the Inverse Document Frequency (IDF) as a separate feature and not just embedded in other models such as BM25. This way, we allow the LTR framework to best weight the importance of rare words. The length of the tweet is the last text-based feature.

Besides text-based features, Table 1 also includes a commonly used microblog-specific features computed over the contents of the tweets' text and users' metrics. This set of features captures the number of mentions, number of followers, number of URLs among other microblog-specific features.

Feature name	Feature description
BM25	Okapi BM25 score for tweet-text.
LM.Dir	Language modeling score for tweet-text.
IDF	Sum of term IDF in tweet-text.
Length	Tweet-text length.
NumURLs	Number of URLs in tweet-text.
HasURLs	True if tweet-text contains URLs.
NumHashtags	Number of Hashtags in tweet-text.
HasHashtags	True if tweet-text contains Hashtags.
NumMentions	Number of Mentions in tweet-text.
HasMentions	True if tweet-text contains Mentions.
isReply	True if tweet-text is a reply.
NumStatuses	Number of user's statuses.
NumFollowers	Number of user's followers.

Table 1: Non-temporal ranking features used by Coordinate Ascent in the RMTS method and other methods based on learning to rank.

Feature name	Feature description
Recency (**R**)	Recency prior [15].
Twitter Feedback (**TF**)	Temporal feedback [9].
Wikipedia Views (**WV**)	Wikipedia article page views.
Wikipedia Edits (**WE**)	Wikipedia article page edits.
News	News headlines.

Table 2: Temporal ranking features used by Coordinate Ascent in the RMTS methods. All the features (except for Recency) are produced using kernel density estimation of time series extracted from: the initially retrieved timeline, Wikipedia and News.

5.3 Computing the Model Coefficients

First, we turn our attention to the problem of correctly estimating the density of individual temporal sources. The temporal histograms of the different sources are quite heterogeneous, indicating different trends and densities across the timeline. Thus, it also required us to revise the standard KDE method and include boundary correction methods [31].

Second, we address the computation of the model coefficients (α_i, β_j and γ_k) weighting the contribution of its corresponding feature (temporal or non-temporal) to the final score. To estimate the values of the coefficients we first observed how these sources of temporal signals are related. A real-world event initiates a series of social-media content that users exchange and access sequentially, for example, a news article may trigger a series of Wikipedia page views and the posting of several *tweets*. This cascade effect suggests that temporal sources might cover the event timeline sequentially. Following this reasoning, we computed the coefficients with coordinate ascent to optimize the MAP retrieval measure.

Coordinate ascent [17] is a learning to rank method that is often used to optimize a retrieval metric directly. A recent work uses it to rank microblog posts using quality features [2] and it has been shown to obtain higher performance compared to other learning to rank methods on Twitter datasets [29]. On each iteration, the coordinate ascent algorithm moves towards the optimal solution along one coordinate at a time.

In other words, each coefficient is updated individually while all the others are fixed. This process is repeated until convergence and using several random starts to avoid local minima.

5.4 Query dependent rankers

In the current formalization, we assume that all external sources are equally relevant to every query, i.e. the γ_k coefficient is constant for every query. A deeper inspection of the queries quickly reveals that some queries are more temporal than others. Thus, based on the crowd temporal signals, we grouped queries into temporal vs non-temporal and trained two different LTR models for each group of queries. This procedure further expands the temporal reasoning towards the query analsys. Our assumption is that a query is classified as being temporal if the news sources returns news matching the query. Otherwise, the query is classified as being atemporal. This distinction enables us to train two models: the first model with temporal features and a second model without such features. Now, at query time, the system can decide to use the RMTS model (Eq. (5)) or the LTR model (Eq. (4)) that has no temporal features.

6. EVALUATION

This section presents the evaluation of the methods described in the previous sections on the TREC microblog search test-bed. In the TREC microblog ad-hoc search task, the user wishes to find the most recent and relevant posts. The task can be summarized as: at time t, find *tweets* about topic q. Therefore, systems should favor highly informative *tweets* relevant to the query topic that were published before the query time. Our experiments delve into the problem of reranking *tweets* sampled using a standard retrieval method i.e., query-likelihood taking into account temporal crowd signals from different sources.

6.1 Datasets and Protocol

TREC datasets. The experiments were performed with the Tweets2013 corpus using the query topics of the TREC 2013 and TREC 2014 editions of the Microblog track. The Tweets2013 corpus was created for the TREC 2013 edition and is much larger (240 million *tweets*) than Tweets2011 (16 million *tweets*) used in TREC 2011 and TREC 2012. The corpus was created by crawling the public stream sample via the Twitter streaming API over a period spanning from 1 February, 2013 - 31 March, 2013 (inclusive). The TREC Microblog queries are mainly queries about entities and events. NIST provided relevance judgments over 60 topics for TREC 2013 and 55 topics for TREC 2014 on a three-point scale of "informativeness": not relevant, relevant and highly relevant.

Filtering Duplicates and Languages. In the test collection used, *retweets* are considered not relevant because they are seen as duplicate documents. Therefore, we filtered *Twitter-style retweets* using the tweet metadata available and we also filter out *RT-style retweets* that start with *RT*.

Assessors evaluated only relevant *tweets* written in English, therefore we use a language filter to remove *tweets* in other languages. To build this filter we used the language detection library ldig[4] with a trained model for 19 languages.

Sources. The sources of temporal evidence are the corpus (Twitter), Wikipedia page views and edits, BBC, USA Today, CNN and Associated Press news articles.

Protocol. To allow the comparability to previous and future work with the same datasets we do training on the TREC 2013 topics and test on the TREC 2014 topics. For learning to rank we used Coordinate Ascent set to optimize mean average precision (MAP) using 20% of the training data for validation. In our experiments we follow TREC and report the MAP and P30 results. Statistical significance of effectiveness differences are determined using two-sided paired t-tests following the recommendations by Sakai [22].

6.2 Baselines

The first baseline is the **BM25** [21] retrieval function parametrized with $k_1 = 1.2$ and $b = 0.75$. The second, is the **IDF** retrieval function isolated, which has advantages for *tweets* retrieval. It favors rare words, a common trait in microblogs, was also included in the experiments as a second baseline. The third baseline is the query likelihood retrieval model with Dirichlet prior smoothing [30] with $\mu = 2500$, which we will refer to as the **LM.Dir** model. Both baselines are useful for comparison purposes. There are two temporal ranking baselines: **Recency** [15] and **KDE(score)** [9], a state-of-the-art temporal feedback method. Finally, the strongest baseline **LTR** is a learning to rank model with the full set of non-temporal features listed in Table 1.

6.3 Results

Using the described setup we performed an evaluation of these temporal ranking methods and present the results in Table 3. All methods evaluated use no future evidence, relying only on information that is pre-indexed and that can be processed at query time.

Retrieval performance over all queries. First, we compare the performance of standard text retrieval baselines over the full set of queries (All). The IDF ranking function provides higher performance than the others in MAP and P30. The intuition for this result is that term-frequency is not very important for ranking short texts, and therefore both BM25 and LM.Dir can hurt the retrieval performance by over-weighting term-frequency. This also surfaces more spam documents with repeated words for these models.

Second, both temporal ranking baselines outperform text retrieval baselines. The KDE(score) method outperforms Recency with a MAP result of 0.4455 (Recency with 0.4297). These two baselines use only the collection as a single source of temporal relevance evidence.

Finally, learning to rank with multiple temporal features delivered the best results. The proposed method RMTS, which combines temporal evidences of the collection with several additional sources of temporal signals from the Web, obtains the best results in MAP as well as P30 outperforming the state-of-the-art methods. We annotated Table 3 with symbols denoting the statistically significance level ($p < 0.01$ or $p < 0.05$) of differences in effectiveness with respect to the stronger baselines: LTR and KDE(score) methods.

RMTS produced statistically significant improvements for MAP and P30. MAP improved 0.0281 over LTR using non-temporal features. This corresponds to a relative improvement of 6.2%. We follow the recommendations of Sakai [22] to report the results and statistical significance tests. According to a two-sided paired t-test for the difference in MAP $\bar{d} = 0.0281$ (with the unbiased estimate of the population variance $V = 0.0020$), RMTS statistically significantly outperforms the LTR model ($t(54) = 4.67$, $p < 0.000020$,

[4]http://github.com/shuyo/ldig

	Temporal		Atemporal		T+A		All	
Method	MAP	P30	MAP	P30	MAP	P30	MAP	P30
				Text retrieval baselines				
BM25 [ ]	0.4054	0.6202	0.4319	0.6392	0.4136	0.6261	0.4136	0.6261
IDF	0.4275	0.6561	0.4360	0.6235	0.4301	0.6461	0.4301	0.6461
LM.Dir [ ]	0.4331	0.6491	0.4112	0.6020	0.4264	0.6345	0.4264	0.6345
				Temporal ranking baselines				
Recency [ ]	0.4429	0.6667	0.4152	0.6196	0.4343	0.6521	0.4297	0.6552
KDE(score) [ ]	0.4621	0.6711	0.4030	0.5961	0.4438	0.6479	0.4455	0.6509
				Learning to rank models				
LTR (Eq. (4))	0.4688	0.6991	0.4308	0.6216	0.4571	0.6751	0.4528	0.6703
RMTS (Eq. (5))	$0.5011^{\ddagger⁑}$	$0.7254^{\ddagger}$	0.4422	0.6353	$\mathbf{0.4829}^{\ddagger⁑}$	$0.6976^{\ddagger *}$	$\mathbf{0.4809}^{\ddagger⁑}$	$0.6939^{\ddagger *}$

Table 3: Temporal ranking methods results. Symbols † and * stand for a $p < 0.05$ statistical significant improvement over KDE(score) and LTR respectively (‡ and $^⁑$ for $p < 0.01$).

$ES_{pairedt} = 0.64$, 95% CI $[0.0161, 0.0400]$). Additionally, according to a two-sided paired t-test for the difference in MAP $\bar{d} = 0.0355$ (with the unbiased estimate of the population variance $V = 0.0049$), RMTS statistically significantly outperforms KDE(score) ($t(54) = 3.73$, $p < 0.000468$, $ES_{pairedt} = 0.51$, 95% CI $[0.0165, 0.0544]$).

Most surprisingly, P30 achieved a very competitive result that is in the same range as the top runs of TREC Microblog 2014. Considering that the top TREC systems use more elaborate techniques such as lexical pseudo-relevance feedback (PRF) and Ensemble methods, this result becomes an important takeaway message: temporal signals from the crowds provide key information for microblog search. According to a two-sided paired t-test for the difference in P30 means $\bar{d} = 0.0236$ (with the unbiased estimate of the population variance $V = 0.0049$), RMTS statistically significantly outperforms LTR ($t(54) = 2.48$, $p < 0.0164$, $ES_{pairedt} = 0.34$, 95% CI $[0.0047, 0.0426]$). Additionally, according to a two-sided paired t-test for the difference in P30 means $\bar{d} = 0.0430$ (with the unbiased estimate of the population variance $V = 0.0117$), RMTS statistically significantly outperforms KDE(score) ($t(54) = 2.92$, $p < 0.005126$, $ES_{pairedt} = 0.40$, 95% CI $[0.0137, 0.0723]$).

Temporal Query Performance Prediction. TREC query topics consist of both temporal and nontemporal queries, therefore it could be advantageous to classify the query as to selectively use the temporal crowd signals or not. Automatically using temporal features for ranking can lead to performance degradation and lower retrieval effectiveness if the query is non-temporal. Despite the low number of training queries (only 60) we discriminate the TREC 2013 queries into two classes using a simple strategy: we trained a temporal model with the 32 queries that have news articles and a second non-temporal model with 28 queries that do not have news articles. TREC 2014 queries were used for testing and were split into 38 temporal queries and 17 atemporal queries – results are shown in Table 3.

Results showed that this improved results over LTR (T+A column in Table 3): the MAP result of 0.4829 was the best result in all experiments. According to a two-sided paired t-test for the difference in means $\bar{d} = 0.0258$ (with the unbiased estimate of the population variance $V = 0.0038$), RMTS(T+A) statistically significantly outperforms LTR(T+A) ($t(54) = 3.09$, $p < 0.0031$, $ES_{pairedt} = 0.42$, 95% CI $[0.0092, 0.0424]$).

In the atemporal set of queries, Recency [ ] and KDE(score) [ ] proved to be more vulnerable to the temporal evidence when the query is not temporal. This is probably due to the fact that both models always assume the query to be temporal, relying exclusively on the single source of temporal evidence that they have. Thus, query temporal classification in microblog search is a promising, yet difficult, research direction that can further improve time-aware ranking models.

7. DISCUSSION

In this section we provide a discussion of the results in three parts. First, a per-feature and per-query analysis of the RMTS ranking model. Second, we examine the contributions of the individual sources to the final ranking. Finally, we examine the robustness of RMTS to missing sources.

7.1 Per-feature and per-query analysis

In general temporal ranking methods have a tendency to improve the overall performance of a system at the cost of degrading the performance of a number of other queries. In Figure 2 we present the per-query differences in Avg. Prec. relative to the LTR system to analyse the cumulative gains in performance of each feature across the set of test queries. We found that the proposed method can indeed improve over the LTR in most queries (36 out of 55). Only a few queries lose performance when using multiple sources. This is an indication that some sources were incorrectly selected or provided low quality temporal evidence. Such effect has been widely recognized in temporal query performance prediction work. In these experiments, we decided not to filter sources, and instead use all sources for every query to best understand their role in the final retrieval model.

The use of *recency priors* improves the Avg. Prec. of many queries that are more recency biased, however not all temporal queries favor recency, therefore the performance of those is degraded with this method. It is clear that some queries are not temporal: the *recency priors* and the temporal feedback models could not improve the rank of LTR in 29 and 26 queries respectively (from a total of 55 test queries).

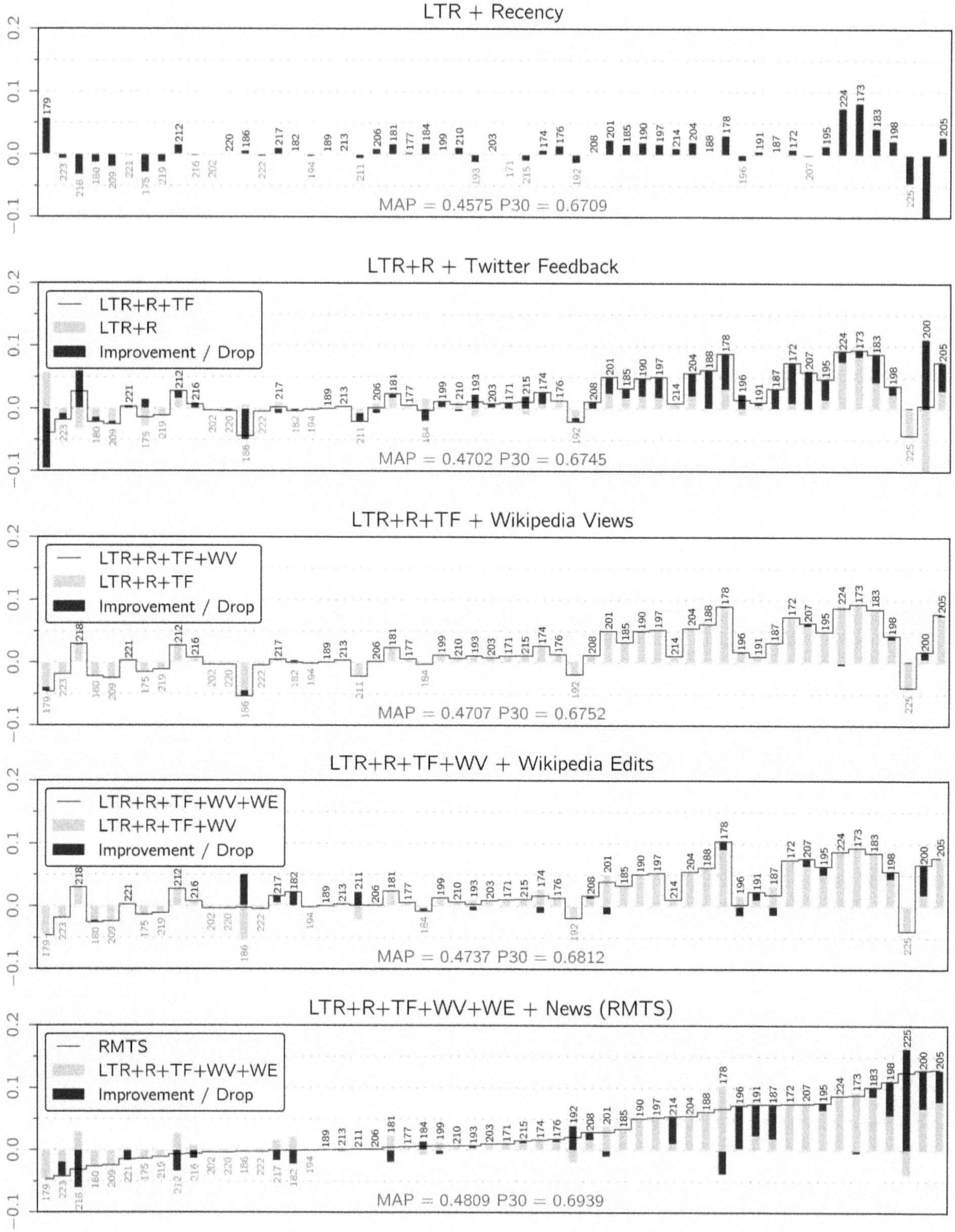

Figure 2: Per-feature retrieval results of the RMTS model: graphs show AP relative improvements over LTR by adding each temporal feature incrementally to the LTR model. Each graph illustrates the per-query results, where bars are labeled with the TREC topic number. Topic labels appear above/below if the performance improved/dropped relative to LTR.

Our model RMTS could not improve on 17 queries. While the difference is on only ~10% of the total queries, our interpretation is that the queries are not all temporal. This is further confirmed by looking at the query topics. Topic MB223 ("dog off leash") for instance seems to be a non-temporal query that does not improve with temporal ranking. In this case, every temporal source introduced noise and Avg. Prec. dropped almost 0.05. Of note, the queries MB179 ("care of Iditarod dogs") that improves with the recency feature and Topic MB212 ("Kate Middleton maternity wear") that improves with Recency and Twitter Feedback, but their initial gains are inverted in the final model.

In the third graph it appears that the Wikipedia Views feature does not contribute much to ranking. However, the reason is that the learned weight for this feature was found to be low in the complete RMTS model. As seen in Table 4 the Wikipedia Views feature improved results when used independently. Moreover, it seems that withholding the WV feature improves the results slightly in terms of MAP but not P30 (see Table 5).

Finally, we also note that not all queries used the full range of external sources. For some queries it was not possible to find relevant news articles or select a Wikipedia article to provide useful evidence in the time-span of the corpus.

7.2 Contributions of Individual Sources

The use of multiple temporal crowd signals calls for a deeper analysis of the contributions that each source makes to the final rank. In this experiment we examine the contribution of each temporal source to the improvement in MAP over the LTR model. By looking at the results on Table 4, we can observe that relative improvements in MAP with each individual temporal signal are in the range of +2.67% to +4.51%, reaching +6.02% with RMTS. The temporal crowd signals that offer the most balanced MAP and P30 improvements are the News sources and Wikipedia edits.

The best improvement in MAP is obtained with the Twitter Feedback feature and the best improvement in P30 is obtained by the Wikipedia Edits feature. However, we observe that no source is particularly more effective than others across both retrieval metrics. This further evidences the stability of the proposed method. In summary, all f_{s_k} signals have a positive impact in the scores, but when combined as a whole, they outperform all other models with a MAP of 0.4809 and P30 of 0.6939. Actually, this is in line with our hypothesis: each temporal signal f_{s_k} can provide different relevant time periods.

7.3 Robustness to Missing Sources

To further examine the robustness of the proposed method we studied the impact that a missing temporal source would cause in the final rank. This is a quite practical aspect in a real production system, where a temporal source might be temporarily unavailable. Table 5 presents the MAP and P30 results. There are two key facts arising from this table: the first one is related to the influence of the News temporal signals, and the second one concerns the low drop in MAP performance caused by missing any other temporal source. In general MAP results are only slightly affected by each individual missing source – in the worst case, the MAP drops 2.74% when withholding the News. We consider this to be an excellent measure of the robustness to faulty temporal sources. Moreover, this further hints that multiple sources can provide complementary temporal signals. On the one hand, the most important fact we take from these results is that the News is a key source of temporal signals. On the other hand, the News feature is a group of news sources and not a single news source (e.g. AP). Thus, the drop in the number of temporal information with its removal could be considered greater compared with the other features.

Method	MAP	P30
LTR	0.4528	0.6703
LTR_{+R}	+2.67%*	+1.36%
LTR_{+TF}	+4.51%‡	+0.54%
LTR_{+WV}	+2.67%*	+1.00%
LTR_{+WE}	+2.78%*	+2.16%
LTR_{+News}	+3.05%‡	+1.72%
RMTS	+6.21%‡	+3.52%*

Table 4: Contributions of individual temporal sources to the ranking. Figures are relative improvement over non-temporal baseline. Symbol * stands for a $p < 0.05$ statistical significant improvement over LTR (‡ for $p < 0.01$).

Method	MAP	P30
RMTS	0.4809	0.6939
$RMTS_{-R}$	−0.94%*	−1.66%*
$RMTS_{-TF}$	−1.31%	−1.12%
$RMTS_{-WV}$	+0.48%	−0.95%
$RMTS_{-WE}$	−1.10%*	−0.76%
$RMTS_{-News}$	−2.74%*	−1.90%*

Table 5: Ranking robustness to missing sources. Symbol * stands for a $p < 0.05$ statistical significant difference compared to the RMTS model with all the temporal features (‡ for $p < 0.01$).

8. CONCLUSIONS AND FUTURE WORK

This paper proposed the RMTS framework that mines the behavior of the crowds for temporal signals. This new time-aware ranking method integrates lexical, domain and temporal evidences from multiple Web sources to rank microblog posts. It explores the signals from: Wikipedia (through page views and page edit history), news articles, and Twitter feedback to estimate the temporal relevance of search topics.

Retrieval precision. We evaluated our system using the experimental setup used in the evaluation campaigns for microblog search at TREC 2013 and TREC 2014. Experiments confirmed our hypothesis: the proposed approach offered a relative improvement of 13.2% over BM25 and the Language Model with Dirichlet smoothing and 6.2% over a strong learning to rank baseline with several lexical and domain features. Both improvements were statistically significant.

RMTS is less biased. A key advantage of the proposed RMTS model is its robustness and stability: the improvement over the LTR model (non-temporal features) could not be pin-pointed to a single source of temporal evidence, moreover, the retrieval model is tolerant to faulty temporal sources.

Unified representation of temporal signals. The proposed framework offers a principled methodology for mining and representing temporal signals from multiple crowds. It allows predicting temporal relevance from heterogeneous pairs of timestamps and weights mined from very diverse sources.

Effective use of Wikipedia temporal signals. The behavior dynamics of Wikipedia users is an effective source of temporal evidence for time-aware ranking. Previous works exploit article views statistics [3] and edit history [10, 24] for detecting events and entities related to the events, however to the best of our knowledge this is the first work that explores the use of multiple external sources for time-aware ranking.

There are two main challenges that we wish to further explore. News sources are a relatively easy resource to crawl, therefore the next steps could delve into the scaling of the number of news sources crawled to obtain better coverage of topics and other advantages. However, new research questions arise: for a query q *which news sources should be selected?* and, *how to weight them for each query?* The second challenge is related to the query performance prediction. Temporal query classification is a difficult task as reported by a recent work by Kanhabua et al. [13], where they studied the problem of detecting event-related queries in Web search streams (query logs). This is the second open problem that we will address as future work.

9. REFERENCES

[1] M. Bendersky, D. Metzler, and W. B. Croft. Effective query formulation with multiple information sources. In *Proceedings of WSDM '12*, 2012, 443–452.

[2] J. Choi, W. B. Croft, and J. Y. Kim. Quality models for microblog retrieval. In *Proceedings of CIKM '12*, 2012, 1834–1838.

[3] M. Ciglan and K. Nørvåg. WikiPop: Personalized event detection system based on wikipedia page view statistics. In *Proceedings of CIKM '10*, 2010, 1931–1932.

[4] M. Costa, F. Couto, and M. Silva. Learning temporal-dependent ranking models. In *Proceedings of SIGIR '14*, 2014, 757–766.

[5] N. Dai, M. Shokouhi, and B. D. Davison. Learning to rank for freshness and relevance. In *Proceedings of SIGIR '11*, 2011, 95–104.

[6] W. Dakka, L. Gravano, and P. Ipeirotis. Answering general time-sensitive queries. *IEEE Trans. Knowl. Data Eng.*, 24(2):220–235, 2012.

[7] M. Efron. Information search and retrieval in microblogs. *J. Am. Soc. Inf. Sci. Technol.*, 62(6):996–1008, 2011.

[8] M. Efron and G. Golovchinsky. Estimation methods for ranking recent information. In *Proceedings of SIGIR '11*, 2011, 495–504.

[9] M. Efron, J. Lin, J. He, and A. de Vries. Temporal feedback for tweet search with non-parametric density estimation. In *Proceedings of SIGIR '14*, 2014, 33–42.

[10] M. Georgescu, N. Kanhabua, D. Krause, W. Nejdl, and S. Siersdorfer. Extracting event-related information from article updates in wikipedia. In *Proceedings of ECIR'13*, 2013, 254–266.

[11] R. Jones and F. Diaz. Temporal profiles of queries. *ACM Trans Inf Syst*, 25(3), 2007.

[12] N. Kanhabua and K. Nørvåg. Learning to rank search results for time-sensitive queries. In *Proceedings of CIKM '12*, 2012, 2463–2466.

[13] N. Kanhabua, T. Ngoc Nguyen, and W. Nejdl. Learning to detect event-related queries for web search. In *Proceedings of WWW '15 Companion*, 2015, 1339–1344.

[14] Y. Kim, R. Yeniterzi, and J. Callan. Overcoming vocabulary limitations in twitter microblogs. In *Proceedings of TREC 2012*, 2012.

[15] X. Li and W. B. Croft. Time-based language models. In *Proceedings of CIKM '03*, 2003, 469–475.

[16] K. Massoudi, M. Tsagkias, M. de Rijke, and W. Weerkamp. Incorporating query expansion and quality indicators in searching microblog posts. In *Proceedings of ECIR'11*, 2011, 362–367.

[17] D. Metzler and W. B. Croft. Linear feature-based models for information retrieval. *Inf Retrieval*, 10(3):257–274, 2007.

[18] R. B. Nattiya Kanhabua and K. Nørvåg. Temporal information retrieval. *Found. Trends® Inf. Retr.*, 9(2): 91–208, 2015.

[19] M.-H. Peetz, E. Meij, and M. de Rijke. Using temporal bursts for query modeling. *Inf Retrieval*, 1–35, 2013.

[20] J. M. Ponte and W. B. Croft. A language modeling approach to information retrieval. In *Proceedings of SIGIR '98*, 1998, 275–281.

[21] S. E. Robertson, S. Walker, S. Jones, M. Hancock-Beaulieu, and M. Gatford. Okapi at TREC-3. In *Proceedings of TREC 1994*, 1994.

[22] T. Sakai. Statistical reform in information retrieval? *SIGIR Forum*, 48(1):3–12, 2014.

[23] F. Schilder and C. Habel. Temporal information extraction for temporal question answering. In *New Directions in Question Answering*, 2003, 35–44.

[24] T. Steiner, S. van Hooland, and E. Summers. MJ no more: Using concurrent wikipedia edit spikes with social network plausibility checks for breaking news detection. In *Proceedings of WWW '13 Companion*, 2013, 791–794.

[25] J. Teevan, D. Ramage, and M. R. Morris. #TwitterSearch: A comparison of microblog search and web search. In *Proceedings of WSDM '11*, 2011, 35–44.

[26] W. Weerkamp and M. de Rijke. Credibility-inspired ranking for blog post retrieval. *Inf Retrieval*, 15(3-4): 243–277, 2012.

[27] J. Weng, E.-P. Lim, J. Jiang, and Q. He. TwitterRank: Finding topic-sensitive influential twitterers. In *Proceedings of WSDM '10*, 2010, 261–270.

[28] S. Whiting, I. A. Klampanos, and J. M. Jose. Temporal pseudo-relevance feedback in microblog retrieval. In *Advances in Information Retrieval*, number 7224 in Lecture Notes in Computer Science. 2012.

[29] T. Xu, D. W. Oard, and P. McNamee. HLTCOE at TREC 2014: Microblog and clinical decision support. In *Proceedings of The Twenty-Third Text REtrieval Conference, TREC 2014, Gaithersburg, Maryland, USA, November 19-21, 2014*, 2014.

[30] C. Zhai and J. Lafferty. A study of smoothing methods for language models applied to information retrieval. *ACM Trans Inf Syst*, 22(2):179–214, 2004.

[31] J. Ćwik and J. Mielniczuk. Data-dependent bandwidth choice for a grade density kernel estimate. *Statistics & Probability Letters*, 16(5):397 – 405, 1993.

Wiggins: Detecting Valuable Information in Dynamic Networks Using Limited Resources

Ahmad Mahmoody
Dept. of Computer Science
Brown University
Providence, RI, USA
ahmad@cs.brown.edu

Matteo Riondato
Two Sigma Investments
New York City, NY, USA
matteo@twosigma.com

Eli Upfal
Dept. of Computer Science
Brown University
Providence, RI, USA
eli@cs.brown.edu

"Have you found it, Wiggins?"
[Sherlock Holmes in *A Study in Scarlet*]

ABSTRACT

Detecting new information and events in a dynamic network by probing individual nodes has many practical applications: discovering new webpages, analyzing influence properties in network, and detecting failure propagation in electronic circuits or infections in public drinkable water systems. In practice, it is infeasible for anyone but the owner of the network (if existent) to monitor all nodes at all times. In this work we study the constrained setting when the observer can only probe a small set of nodes at each time step to check whether new pieces of information (items) have reached those nodes.

We formally define the problem through an infinite time generating process that places new items in subsets of nodes according to an unknown probability distribution. Items have an exponentially decaying *novelty*, modeling their decreasing value. The observer uses a *probing schedule* (i.e., a probability distribution over the set of nodes) to choose, at each time step, a small set of nodes to check for new items. The goal is to compute a schedule that minimizes the average novelty of undetected items. We present an algorithm, WIGGINS, to compute the optimal schedule through convex optimization, and then show how it can be adapted when the parameters of the problem must be learned or change over time. We also present a scalable variant of WIGGINS for the MapReduce framework. The results of our experimental evaluation on real social networks demonstrate the practicality of our approach.

Categories and Subject Descriptors

G.2.2 [**Discrete Mathematics**]: Graph Theory—*Graph algorithms*; H.2.8 [**Database Management**]: Database Applications—*Data mining*

Keywords

Information diffusion; Rumor catching; Social networks

WSDM 2016, February 22–25, 2016, San Francisco, CA, USA

ISBN 978-1-4503-3716-8/16/02...$15.00
DOI: http://dx.doi.org/10.1145/2835776.2835830 .

1. INTRODUCTION

Many applications require the detection of events in a network as soon as they happen or shortly thereafter, as the value of the information obtained by detecting the events decays rapidly as time passes. For example, an emerging trend in algorithmic stock trading is the use of automatic search through the Web and social networks for pieces of information that can be used in trading decisions before they appear in the more popular news sites [10, 14, 24, 28]. Similarly, intelligence, business and politics analysts are scanning online sources for new information or rumors. While new items are often reblogged, retweeted, and posted on a number of sites, it is sufficient to find an item once, as fast as possible, before it loses its relevance or freshness. There is no benefit in seeing multiple copies of the same news item or rumor. This is also the case when monitoring for intrusions, infections, or defects in, respectively, a computer network, a public water system, or a large electronic circuit.

Monitoring for new events or information is a fundamental search and detection problem in a distributed data setting, not limited to social networks or graph analysis. In this setting, the data is distributed among a large number of nodes, and new items appear in individual nodes (for example, as the products of processing the data available locally at the node), and may propagate (being copied) to neighboring nodes on a physical or a virtual network. The goal is to detect at least one copy of each new item as soon as possible. The search application can access any node in the system, but it can only *probe* (i.e., check for new items on) a few nodes at a time. To minimize the time to find new items, the search application needs to optimize the schedule of probing nodes, taking into account (i) the distribution of copies of items among the nodes (to choose which nodes to probe), and (ii) the decay of the items' *novelty* (or relevance/freshness) over time (to focus the search on most relevant items). The main challenge is how to devise a good probing schedule in the absence of prior knowledge about the generation and distribution of items in the network.

Contributions. In this work we study the novel problem of computing an optimal node probing schedule for detecting new items in a network under resource scarceness, i.e., when only a few nodes can be probed at a time. Our contributions to the study of this problem are as follows:

- We formalize a generic process that describes the creation and distribution of information in a network, and define the computational task of learning this process by probing the nodes in the network according to a schedule. The process and task are parametrized by the resource limitations of the observer and the decay rate of the novelty of items. We introduce a *cost* measure to compare different schedules: the cost of a schedule is the limit of the average expected novelty of uncaught items at each time step. On the basis of these concepts, we formally define the *Optimal Probing Schedule Problem*, which requires to find the schedule with minimum cost.

- We conduct a theoretical study of the cost of a schedule, showing that it can *be computed explicitly* and that it is a *convex function* over the space of schedules. We then introduce WIGGINS,[1] an algorithm to compute the optimal schedule by solving a constrained convex optimization problem through the use of an iterative method based on Lagrange multipliers.
- We discuss variants of WIGGINS for the realistic situation where the parameters of the process needs to be learned or can change over time. We show how to compute a schedule which is (probabilistically) guaranteed to have a cost very close to the optimal by only observing the generating process for a limited amount of time. We also present a MapReduce adaptation of WIGGINS to handle very large networks.
- Finally, we conduct an extensive experimental evaluation of WIGGINS and its variants, comparing the performances of the schedules it computes with natural baselines, and showing how it performs extremely well in practice on real social networks when using well-established models for generating new items (e.g., the independence cascade model [17]).

To the best of our knowledge, the problem we study is novel and we are the first to devise an algorithm to compute an optimal schedule, both when the generating process parameters are known and when they need to be learned.

Paper Organization. In Sect. 2 we give the fundamental definitions, and formally introduce the settings and the problem. We discuss related works in Sect. 3. In Sect. 4 we describe our algorithm WIGGINS and its variants. The results of our experimental evaluation are presented in Sect. 5. We conclude by outlining directions for future work in Sect. 6.

2. PROBLEM DEFINITION

In this section we formally introduce the problem and define our goal.

Let $G = (V, E)$ be a graph with $|V| = n$ nodes. W.l.o.g. we let $V = [n]$. Let $\mathcal{F} \subseteq 2^V$ be a collection of subsets of V, i.e., a collection of sets of nodes. Let π be a function from $\mathcal{F}$ to $[0, 1]$ (not necessarily a probability distribution). We model the generation and diffusion of information in the network by defining a *generating process* $\Gamma = (\mathcal{F}, \pi)$. Γ is a infinite discrete-time process which, at each time step t, generates a collection of sets $\mathcal{I}_t \subseteq \mathcal{F}$ such that each set $S \in \mathcal{F}$ is included in $\mathcal{I}_t$ with probability $\pi(S)$, independent of t and of other sets generated at time $t' \leq t$. For any t and any $S \in \mathcal{I}_t$, the ordered pair (t, S) represents an *item* - a piece of information that was generated at time t and reached *instantaneously* the nodes in S. We choose to model the diffusion process as instantaneous because this abstraction accurately models the view of an outside *resource-limited observer* that does not have the resources to monitor simultaneously all the nodes in the network at the fine time granularity needed to observe the different stages of the diffusion process.

Probing and schedule. The observer can only monitor the network by *probing* nodes. Formally, by *probing a node* $v \in V$ *at time* t, we mean obtaining the set $I(t, v)$ of items (t', S) such that $t' \leq t$ and $v \in S$:[2]

$$I(t,v) := \{(t', S) \ : \ t' \leq t, S \in \mathcal{I}_{t'}, v \in S\} \ .$$

Let U_t be the union of the sets $\mathcal{I}_{t'}$ generated by Γ at any time $t' \leq t$, and so $I(t, v) \subseteq U_t$.

We model the *resource limitedness of the observer* through a constant, user-specified, parameter $c \in \mathbb{N}$, representing the maximum number of nodes that can be probed at any time, where probing a node v returns the value $I(t, v)$.

The observer chooses the c nodes to probe by following a schedule. In this work we focus on *memoryless* schedules, i.e., the choice of nodes to probe at time t is independent from the choice of nodes probed at any time $t' < t$. More precisely, a *probing c-schedule* p is a probability distribution on V. At each time t, the observer chooses a set P_t of c nodes to probe, such that P_t is obtained through *random sampling of V without replacement according to* p, independently from $P_{t'}$ from $t' < t$. Memoryless schedules are simple, easy to store, and fast to implement.

Caught items, uncaught items, and novelty. We say that an item (t', S) is *caught at time* $t \geq t'$ iff

1. a node $v \in S$ is probed at time t; and
2. no node in S was probed in the interval $[t', t-1]$.

Let C_t be the set of items caught by the observer at any time $t' \leq t$. We have $C_t \subseteq U_t$. Let $N_t = U_t \setminus C_t$ be the *set of uncaught items at time* t, i.e., items that were generated at any time $t' \leq t$ and have not been caught yet at time t. For any item $(t', S) \in N_t$, we define the *θ-novelty of* (t', S) *at time* t as

$$\mathsf{f}_\theta(t, t', S) := \theta^{t-t'},$$

where $\theta \in (0, 1)$ is a user-specified parameter modeling how fast the value of an item decreases with time if uncaught. Intuitively, pieces of information (e.g., rumors) have high value if caught almost as soon as they have appeared in the network, but their value decreases fast (i.e., exponentially) as more time passes before being caught, to the point of having no value in the limit.

Load of the system and cost of a schedule. The set N_t of uncaught items at time t imposes a *θ-load,* $L_\theta(t)$, *on the graph at time* t, defined as the sum of the θ-novelty at time t of the items in N_t:

$$L_\theta(t) := \sum_{(t',S)\in N_t} \mathsf{f}_\theta(t, t', S) \ .$$

The quantity $L_\theta(t)$ is a random variable, depending both on Γ and on the probing schedule p, and as such it has an expectation $\mathbb{E}[L_\theta(t)]$ w.r.t. all the randomness in the system.

[1]In the Sherlock Holmes novel *A study in scarlet* by A. Conan Doyle, Wiggins is the leader of the "Baker Street Irregulars", a band of street urchins employed by Holmes as intelligence agents.

[2]The set S appears in the notation for an item only for clarity of presentation: we are *not* assuming that when we probe a node and find an item (t, S) we obtain information about S.

The θ-*cost of a schedule* p is defined as the limit, for $t \to \infty$, of the average expected load of the system:

$$\mathsf{cost}_\theta(\mathsf{p}) := \lim_{t\to\infty} \frac{1}{t} \sum_{t' \le t} \mathbb{E}[L_\theta(t)]$$

$$= \lim_{t\to\infty} \frac{1}{t} \sum_{t' \le t} \mathbb{E}\left[\sum_{(t'',S)\in N_{t'}} \mathsf{f}_\theta(t', t'', S) \right] .$$

Intuitively, the load at each time indicates the amount of novelty we did not catch at that time, and the cost function measures the average of such loss over time. The limit above always exists (Lemma 1).

We now have all the necessary ingredients to formally define the problem of interest in this work.

Problem definition. Let $G = (V, E)$ be a graph and $\Gamma = (\mathcal{F}, \pi)$ be a generating process on G. Let $c \in \mathbb{N}$ and $\theta \in (0, 1)$. The (θ, c)-*Optimal Probing Schedule Problem* ((θ, c)-OPSP) requires to find the *optimal c-schedule* p^*, i.e., the schedule with *minimum* θ-cost over the set S_c of c-schedules:

$$\mathsf{p}^* = \arg\min_{\mathsf{p}} \{\mathsf{cost}_\theta(\mathsf{p}), \mathsf{p} \in \mathsf{S}_c\} .$$

Thus, the goal is to design a c-schedule that discovers the maximum number of items weighted by their novelty value (which correspond to those generated most recently). The parameter θ controls how fast the novelty of an item decays, and influences the choices of a schedule. When θ is closed to 0, items are relevant only for a few steps and the schedule must focus on the most recently generated items, catching them as soon as they are generated (or at most shortly thereafter). At the other extreme ($\theta \approx 1$), an optimal schedule must maximizes the total number of discovered items, as their novelty decays very slowly.

Viewing the items as "information" disseminated in the network, an ideal schedule assigns higher probing probability to nodes that act as *information hubs*, i.e., nodes that receive a large number of items. Thus, an optimal schedule p^*, identifies information hubs among the nodes. This task (finding information hubs) can be seen as the complement of the *influence maximization problem* [17, 18]. In the influence maximization problem we look for a set of nodes that *generate* information that reach most nodes. In the information hubs problem, we are interested in a set of nodes that *receive* the most of information, thus the most informative nodes for an observer.

In the following sections, we may drop the specification of the parameters from θ-novelty, θ-cost, θ-load, and c-schedule, and from their respective notation, as the parameters will be clear from the context.

3. RELATED WORK

The novel problem we focus on in this work generalizes and complements a number of problems studied in the literature.

The "Battle of Water Sensor Network" challenge [31] motivated a number of works on *outbreak detection*: the goal is to optimally place static or moving sensors in water networks to detect contamination [13, 20, 25]. The optimization can be done w.r.t. a number of objectives, such as maximizing the probability of detection, minimizing the detection time, or minimizing the size of the subnetwork affected by the phenomena [25]. A related work [1] considered sensors that are sent along fixed paths in the network with the goal of gathering sufficient information to locate possible contaminations. Early detection of contagious outbreaks by monitoring the neighborhood (friends) of a randomly chosen node (individual) was studied by Christakis and Fowler [7]. Krause et al. [21] present efficient schedules for minimizing energy consumption in battery operated sensors, while other works analyzed distributed solutions with limited communication capacities and costs [11, 19, 22]. In contrast, our work is geared to detection in huge but virtual networks such as the Web or social networks embedded in the Internet, where it is possible to "sense" or probe (almost) any node at approximately the same cost. Still only a restricted number of nodes can be probed at each steps but the optimization of the probing sequence is over a much larger domain, and the goal is to identify the outbreaks (items) regardless of their size and solely by considering their interest value.

Our methods complement the work on *Emerging Topic Detection* where the goal is to identify emerging topics in a social network, assuming full access to the stream of all postings. Providers, such as Twitter or Facebook, have an immediate access to all tweets or postings as they are submitted to their servers [4, 27]. Outside observers need an efficient mechanism to monitor changes, such as the methods developed in this work.

Web-crawling is another research area that study how to obtain the most recent snapshots of the web. However, it differs from our model in two key points: our model allows items to propagate their copies, and they will be caught if any of their copies is discovered (where snapshots of a webpage belong to that page only), and all the generated items should be discovered (not just the recent ones) [8, 34].

The goal of the News and Feed Aggregation problem is to capture updates in news websites (e.g. by RSS feeds) [3, 15, 30, 32]. Our model differs from that setting in that we consider copies of the same news in different web sites as equivalent and therefore are only interested in discovering one of the copies.

4. THE WIGGINS ALGORITHM

In this section we present the algorithm WIGGINS (and its variants) for solving the Optimal Probing Schedule Problem (θ, c)-OPSP for generating process $\Gamma = (\mathcal{F}, \pi)$ on a graph $G = (V, E)$.

We start by assuming that we have complete knowledge of Γ, i.e., we know $\mathcal{F}$ and π. This strong assumption allows us to study the theoretical properties of the cost function and motivates the design of our algorithm, WIGGINS, to compute an optimal schedule. We then remove the assumption and show how we can extend WIGGINS to only use a collection of observations from Γ. Then we discuss how to recalibrate our algorithms when the parameters of the process (e.g., π or $\mathcal{F}$) change over time. Finally, we show an algorithm for the MapReduce framework that allows us to scale to large networks.

4.1 Computing the Optimal Schedule

We first conduct a theoretical analysis of the cost function cost_θ, and then use the results to develop WIGGINS, our algorithm to compute the optimal c-schedule (i.e., solve the (θ, c)-OPSP).

4.1.1 Analysis of the cost function

Assume for now that we know Γ, i.e., we have complete knowledge of $\mathcal{F}$ and π. Under this assumption, we can exactly compute the θ-cost of a c-schedule.

LEMMA 1. *Let* $\mathsf{p} = (\mathsf{p}_1, \ldots, \mathsf{p}_n)$ *be a c-schedule. Then*

$$\mathsf{cost}_\theta(\mathsf{p}) := \lim_{t\to\infty} \frac{1}{t} \sum_{t'=0}^{t} \mathbb{E}[L_\theta(t')] = \sum_{S\in\mathcal{F}} \frac{\pi(S)}{1-\theta(1-\mathsf{p}(S))^c}, \quad (1)$$

where $\mathsf{p}(S) = \sum_{v\in S} \mathsf{p}_v$.

PROOF. Let t be a time step, and consider the quantity $\mathbb{E}[L_\theta(t)]$. By definition we have

$$\mathbb{E}[L_\theta(t)] = \mathbb{E}\left[\sum_{(t',S)\in N_t} \mathsf{f}_\theta(t,t',S)\right] = \mathbb{E}\left[\sum_{(t',S)\in N_t} \theta^{t-t'}\right],$$

where N_t is the set of uncaught items at time t. Let now, for any $t' \leq t$, $N_{t,t'} \subseteq N_t$ be the set of uncaught items in the form (t', S). Then we can write

$$\mathbb{E}[L_\theta(t)] = \mathbb{E}\left[\sum_{t'=0}^{t} \sum_{(t',S)\in N_{t,t'}} \theta^{t-t'}\right].$$

Define now, for each $S \in \mathcal{F}$, the random variable $X_{S,t',t}$ which takes the value $\theta^{t-t'}$ if $(t', S) \in N_{t,t'}$, and 0 otherwise. Using the linearity of expectation, we can write:

$$\mathbb{E}[L_\theta(t)] = \sum_{S\in\mathcal{F}} \sum_{t'=0}^{t} \mathbb{E}[X_S, t', t]$$

$$= \sum_{S\in\mathcal{F}} \sum_{t'=0}^{t} \theta^{t-t'} \Pr(X_{S,t,t'} = \theta^{t-t'}). \quad (2)$$

The r.v. $X_{S,t,t'}$ takes value $\theta^{t-t'}$ if and only if the following two events E_1 and E_2 both take place:

- E_1: the set $S \in F$ belongs to $\mathcal{I}_{t'}$, i.e., is generated by Γ at time t';
- E_2: the item (t', S) is uncaught at time t. This is equivalent to say that no node $v \in S$ was probed in the time interval $[t', t]$.

We have $\Pr(E_1) = \pi(S)$, and

$$\Pr(E_2) = (1-\mathsf{p}(S))^{c(t-t')}.$$

The events E_1 and E_2 are independent, as the process of probing the nodes is independent from the process of generating items, therefore, we have

$$\Pr(X_{S,t,t'} = \theta^{t-t'}) = \Pr(E_1)\Pr(E_2) = \pi(S)(1-\mathsf{p}(S))^{c(t-t')}.$$

We can plug this quantity in the rightmost term of (2) and write

$$\lim_{t\to\infty} \mathbb{E}[L_\theta(t)] = \lim_{t\to\infty} \sum_{S\in\mathcal{F}} \sum_{t'=0}^{t} \theta^{t-t'} \pi(S)(1-\mathsf{p}(S))^{c(t-t')}$$

$$= \lim_{t\to\infty} \sum_{S\in\mathcal{F}} \pi(S) \sum_{t'=0}^{t} (\theta(1-\mathsf{p}(S))^c)^t$$

$$= \sum_{S\in\mathcal{F}} \frac{\pi(S)}{1-\theta(1-\mathsf{p}(S))^c}, \quad (3)$$

where we used the fact that $\theta(1-\mathsf{p}(S))^c < 1$. We just showed that the sequence $(\mathbb{E}[L_\theta(t)])_{t\in\mathbb{N}}$ converges as $t \to \infty$. Therefore, its Cesàro mean, i.e., $\lim_{t\to\infty} \frac{1}{t}\sum_{t'=0}^{t} \mathbb{E}[L_\theta(t)]$, equals to its limit [12, Sect. 5.4] and we have

$$\mathsf{cost}_\theta(\mathsf{p}) = \lim_{t\to\infty} \frac{1}{t} \sum_{t'=0}^{t} \mathbb{E}[L_\theta(t)] = \lim_{t\to\infty} \mathbb{E}[L_\theta(t)]$$

$$= \sum_{S\in\mathcal{F}} \frac{\pi(S)}{1-\theta(1-\mathsf{p}(S))^c}.$$

□

We now show that $\mathsf{cost}_\theta(\mathsf{p})$, as expressed by the r.h.s. of (1) is a convex function over its domain S_c, the set of all possible c-schedules. We then use this result to show how to compute an optimal schedule.

THEOREM 1. *The cost function* $\mathsf{cost}_\theta(\mathsf{p})$ *is a convex function over* S_c.

PROOF. For any $S \in \mathcal{F}$, let

$$f_S(\mathsf{p}) = \frac{1}{1-\theta(1-\mathsf{p}(S))^c}.$$

The function $\mathsf{cost}_\theta(\mathsf{p})$ is a linear combination of $f_S(\mathsf{p})$'s with positive coefficients. Hence to show that $\mathsf{cost}_\theta(\mathsf{p})$ is convex it is sufficient to show that, for any $S \in \mathcal{F}$, $f_S(\mathsf{p})$ is convex.

We start by showing that $g_S(\mathsf{p}) = \theta(1-\mathsf{p}(S))^c$ is convex. This is due to the fact that its Hessian matrix is positive semidefinite [2]:

$$\frac{\partial}{\partial \mathsf{p}_i \partial \mathsf{p}_j} g_S(\mathsf{p}) = \begin{cases} \theta c(c-1)(1-\mathsf{p}(S))^{c-2} & i,j \in S \\ 0 & \text{otherwise} \end{cases}$$

Let $\mathbf{v}_S$ be a $n \times 1$ vector in $\mathbb{R}^n$ such that its i-th coordinate is $\left[c(c-1)(1-\mathsf{p}(S))^{c-2}\right]^{1/2}$ if $i \in S$, and 0 otherwise. We can write the Hessian matrix of g_S as

$$\nabla^2 g_S = V_S * V_S^{\mathsf{T}},$$

and thus, $\nabla^2 g_S$ is positive semidefinite matrix and g is convex. From here, we have that $1 - g_S$ is a *concave* function. Since $f_S(\mathsf{p}) = \frac{1}{1-g_S(\mathsf{p})}$ and the function $h(x) = \frac{1}{x}$ is convex and non-increasing, then f_S is a convex function. □

If for every $v \in V$, $S = \{v\}$ belongs to $\mathcal{F}$, then the function g_S in the above proof is *strictly* convex, and so is f_S.

We then have the following corollary of Thm. 1.

COROLLARY 1. *Any schedule* p *with locally minimum cost is an optimal schedule (i.e., it has global minimum cost). Furthermore, if for every* $v \in V$, $\{v\}$ *belongs to* $\mathcal{F}$, *the optimal schedule is* unique.

4.1.2 The Algorithm

Corollary 1 implies that one can compute an optimal c–schedule p^* (i.e., solve the (θ, c)-OPSP) by solving the unconstrained minimization of cost_θ over the set S_c of all c-schedules, or equivalently by solving the following constrained minimization problem on $\mathbb{R}^n$:

$$\begin{array}{lrcll} \min\limits_{\mathsf{p}\in\mathbb{R}^n} & \mathsf{cost}_\theta(\mathsf{p}) & & & \\ & \sum_{i=1}^{n} \mathsf{p}_i & = & 1 & \\ & \mathsf{p}_i & \geq & 0 & \forall i \in \{1,\ldots,n\} \end{array} \quad (4)$$

Since the function cost_θ is convex and the constraints are linear, the optimal solution can, theoretically, be found efficiently [2]. In practice though, available convex optimization problem solvers can not scale well with the number n of variables, especially when n is in the millions as is the case for modern graphs like online social networks or the Web. Hence we developed WIGGINS, an iterative method based on *Lagrange multipliers* [2, Sect. 5.1], which can scale efficiently and can be adapted to the MapReduce framework of computation [9], as we show in Sect. 4.4. While we can not prove that this iterative method always converges, we can prove (Thm. 2) that (i) if at any iteration the algorithm examines an optimal schedule, then it will reach convergence at the next iteration, and (ii) if it converges to a schedule, that schedule is optimal. In Sect. 5 we show our experimental results illustrating the convergence of WIGGINS in different cases.

WIGGINS takes as inputs the collection $\mathcal{F}$, the function π, and the parameters c and θ, and outputs a schedule p which, if convergence (defined in the following) has been reached, is the optimal schedule. It starts from a uniform schedule $\mathsf{p}^{(0)}$, i.e., $\mathsf{p}_i^{(0)} = 1/n$ for all $1 \le i \le n$, and iteratively refines it until convergence (or until a user-specified maximum number of iterations have been performed). At iteration $j \ge 1$, we compute, for each value i, $1 \le i \le n$, the function

$$W_i(\mathsf{p}^{(j-1)}) := \sum_{\substack{S\in\mathcal{F}\\ \text{s.t. } i\in S}} \frac{\theta c\pi(S)(1-\mathsf{p}^{(j-1)}(S))^{c-1}}{(1-\theta(1-\mathsf{p}^{(j-1)}(S))^c)^2} \qquad (5)$$

and then set

$$\mathsf{p}_i^{(j)} = \frac{\mathsf{p}_i^{(j-1)} W_i(\mathsf{p}^{(j-1)})}{\sum_{z=1}^n \mathsf{p}_z^{(j-1)} W_z(\mathsf{p}^{(j-1)})} \ .$$

The algorithm then checks whether $\mathsf{p}^{(j)} = \mathsf{p}^{(j-1)}$. If so, then we reached convergence and we can return $\mathsf{p}^{(j)}$ in output, otherwise we perform iteration $j+1$. The pseudocode for WIGGINS is in Algorithm 1. The following theorem shows the correctness of the algorithm in case of convergence.

THEOREM 2. *We have that:*

1. *if at any iteration j the schedule $\mathsf{p}^{(j)}$ is optimal, then* WIGGINS *reaches convergence at iteration $j+1$; and*
2. *if* WIGGINS *reaches convergence, then the returned schedule p is optimal.*

PROOF. From the method of the Lagrange multipliers [2, Sect. 5.1], we have that, if a schedule p is optimal, then there exists a value $\lambda \in \mathbb{R}$ such that p and λ form a solution to the following system of $n+1$ equations in $n+1$ unknowns:

$$\nabla[\mathsf{cost}_\theta(\mathsf{p}) + \lambda(\mathsf{p}_1 + \ldots + \mathsf{p}_n - 1)] = 0, \qquad (6)$$

where the gradient on the l.h.s. is taken w.r.t. (the components of) p and to λ (i.e., has $n+1$ components).

For $1 \le i \le n$, the i-th equation induced by (6) is

$$\frac{\partial}{\partial \mathsf{p}_i}\mathsf{cost}_\theta(\mathsf{p}) + \lambda = 0,$$

or, equivalently,

$$\sum_{\substack{S\in\mathcal{F}\\ \text{s.t.} i\in S}} \frac{\theta c\pi(S)(1-\mathsf{p}(S))^{c-1}}{(1-\theta(1-\mathsf{p}(S))^c)^2} = \lambda \ . \qquad (7)$$

The term on the l.h.s. is exactly $W_i(\mathsf{p})$. The $(n+1)$-th equation of the system (6) (i.e., the one involving the partial derivative w.r.t. λ) is

$$\sum_{z=1}^n \mathsf{p}_z = 1 \ . \qquad (8)$$

Consider now the first claim of the theorem, and assume that we are at iteration j such that j is the minimum iteration index for which the schedule $\mathsf{p}^{(j)}$ computed at the end of iteration j is optimal. Then, for any i, $1 \le i \le n$, we have

$$W_i(\mathsf{p}^{(j)}) = \lambda$$

because $\mathsf{p}^{(j)}$ is optimal and hence all identities in the form of (7) must be true. For the same reason, (8) must also hold for $\mathsf{p}^{(j)}$. Hence, for any $1 \le i \le n$, we can write the value $\mathsf{p}_i^{(j+1)}$ computed at the end of iteration $j+1$ as

$$\mathsf{p}_i^{(j+1)} = \frac{\mathsf{p}_i^{(j)} W_i(\mathsf{p}^{(j)})}{\sum_{z=1}^n \mathsf{p}_z^{(j)} W_z(\mathsf{p}^{(j)})} = \frac{\mathsf{p}_i^{(j)}\lambda}{1\cdot\lambda} = \mathsf{p}_i^{(j)},$$

which means that we reached convergence and WIGGINS will return $\mathsf{p}^{(j+1)}$, which is optimal.

Consider the second claim of the theorem, and let j be the first iteration for which $\mathsf{p}^{(j)} = \mathsf{p}^{(j-1)}$. Then we have, for any $1 \le i \le n$,

$$\mathsf{p}_i^{(j)} = \frac{\mathsf{p}_i^{(j-1)} W_i(\mathsf{p}^{(j-1)})}{\sum_{z=1}^n \mathsf{p}_z^{(j-1)} W_z(\mathsf{p}^{(j-1)})} = \mathsf{p}_i^{(j-1)} \ .$$

This implies

$$W_i(\mathsf{p}^{(j-1)}) = \sum_{z=1}^n \mathsf{p}_z^{(j-1)} W_z(\mathsf{p}^{(j-1)}) \qquad (9)$$

and the r.h.s. does not depend on i, and so neither does $W_i(\mathsf{p}^{(j-1)})$. Hence we have $W_1(\mathsf{p}^{(j-1)}) = \cdots = W_n(\mathsf{p}^{(j-1)})$ and can rewrite (9) as

$$W_i(\mathsf{p}^{(j-1)}) = \sum_{z=1}^n \mathsf{p}_z^{(j-1)} W_i(\mathsf{p}^{(j-1)}),$$

which implies that the identity (8) holds for $\mathsf{p}^{(j-1)}$. Moreover, if we set

$$\lambda = W_1(\mathsf{p}^{(j-1)})$$

we have that all the identities in the form of (7) hold. Then, $\mathsf{p}^{(j-1)}$ and λ form a solution to the system (6), which implies that $\mathsf{p}^{(j-1)}$ is optimal and so must be $\mathsf{p}^{(j)}$, the returned schedule, as it is equal to $\mathsf{p}^{(j-1)}$ because WIGGINS reached convergence. □

4.2 Approximation through Sampling

We now remove the assumption, not realistic in practice, of knowing the generating process Γ exactly through $\mathcal{F}$ and π. Instead, we observe the process using, for a limited time interval, a schedule that iterates over all nodes (or a schedule that selects each node with uniform probability), until we have observed, for each time step t in a limited time interval $[a,b]$, the set $\mathcal{I}_t$ generated by Γ, and therefore we have access to a collection

$$\mathcal{I} = \{\mathcal{I}_a, \mathcal{I}_{a+1}, \ldots, \mathcal{I}_b\}. \qquad (10)$$

Algorithm 1: WIGGINS

input : $\mathcal{F}$, π, c, θ, and maximum number T of iterations
output: A c-schedule p (with globally minimum θ-cost, in case of convergence)

1 **for** $i \leftarrow 1$ **to** n **do**
2     $\mathsf{p}_i \leftarrow 1/n$
3 **end**
4 **for** $j \leftarrow 1$ **to** T **do**
5   **for** $i \leftarrow 1$ **to** n **do**
6         $W_i \leftarrow 0$
7   **end**
8   **for** $S \in \mathcal{F}$ **do**
9   **for** $i \in S$ **do**
10             $W_i \leftarrow W_i + \frac{\theta c \pi(S)(1-\mathsf{p}(S))^{c-1}}{(1-\theta(1-\mathsf{p}(S))^c)^2}$
11   **end**
12   **end**
13     $\mathsf{p}^{\text{old}} \leftarrow \mathsf{p}$
14   **for** $i \leftarrow 1$ **to** n **do**
15         $\mathsf{p}_i \leftarrow \frac{\mathsf{p}_i^{\text{old}} \cdot W_i}{\sum_i \mathsf{p}_i^{\text{old}} \cdot W_i}$
16   **end**
17   **if** $\mathsf{p}^{\text{old}} = \mathsf{p}$ **then** // test for convergence
18   **break**
19   **end**
20 **end**
21 **return** p

We refer to $\mathcal{I}$ as a *sample gathered in the time interval* $[a, b]$. We show that a schedule computed with respect to a sample $\mathcal{I}$ taken during an interval of $\ell(\mathcal{I}) = b - a = O(\varepsilon^{-2} \log n)$ steps has cost which is within a multiplicative factor $\varepsilon \in [0, 1]$ of the optimal schedule. We then adapt WIGGINS to optimize with respect to such sample.

We start by defining the cost of a schedule w.r.t. to a sample $\mathcal{I}$.

DEFINITION 1. *Suppose* p *is a c-schedule and* $\mathcal{I}$ *is as in Equation* (10), *with* $\ell(\mathcal{I}) = b - a$. *The* θ*-cost of* p *w.r.t. to* $\mathcal{I}$ *denoted by* $\mathsf{cost}_\theta(\mathsf{p}, \mathcal{I})$ *is defined as*

$$\mathsf{cost}_\theta(\mathsf{p}, \mathcal{I}) := \frac{1}{\ell(\mathcal{I})} \sum_{S \in \mathcal{I}} \frac{1}{1 - \theta(1 - \mathsf{p}(S))^c} .$$

For $1 \leq i \leq n$, define now the functions

$$W_i(\mathsf{p}, \mathcal{I}) = \frac{1}{\ell(\mathcal{I})} \sum_{S \in \mathcal{I} : i \in S} \frac{\theta c (1 - \mathsf{p}(S))^{c-1}}{(1 - \theta(1 - \mathsf{p}(S))^c)^2} .$$

We can then define a variant of WIGGINS, which we call WIGGINS-APX. The differences from WIGGINS are:

1. the loop on line 8 in Alg. 1 is only over the sets that appear in at least one $\mathcal{I}_j \in \mathcal{I}$.
2. WIGGINS-APX uses the values $W_i(\mathsf{p}, \mathcal{I})$ (defined above) instead of $W_i(\mathsf{p})$ (line 10 in Alg. 1);

If WIGGINS-APX reaches convergence, it returns a schedule with the minimum cost w.r.t. the sample $\mathcal{I}$. More formally, by following the same steps as in the proof of Thm. 2, we can prove the following result about WIGGINS-APX.

LEMMA 2. *We have that:*

1. *if at any iteration* j *the schedule* $\mathsf{p}^{(j)}$ *has minimum cost w.r.t.* $\mathcal{I}$, *then* WIGGINS-APX *reaches convergence at iteration* $j + 1$; *and*
2. *if* WIGGINS-APX *reaches convergence, then the returned schedule* p *has minimum cost w.r.t.* $\mathcal{I}$.

Let $\ell(\mathcal{I})$ denote the length of the time interval during which $\mathcal{I}$ was collected. For a c-schedule p, $\mathsf{cost}_\theta(\mathsf{p}, \mathcal{I})$ is an approximation of $\mathsf{cost}_\theta(\mathsf{p})$, and intuitively the larger $\ell(\mathcal{I})$, the better the approximation.

We now show that, if $\ell(\mathcal{I})$ is large enough, then, with high probability (i.e., with probability at least $1 - 1/n^r$ for some constant r), the schedule p returned by WIGGINS-APX in case of convergence has a cost $\mathsf{cost}_\theta(\mathsf{p})$ that is close to the cost $\mathsf{cost}_\theta(\mathsf{p}^*)$ of an optimal schedule p^*.

THEOREM 3. *Let* r *be a positive integer, and let* $\mathcal{I}$ *be a sample gathered during a time interval of length*

$$\ell(\mathcal{I}) \geq \frac{3(r \ln(n) + \ln(4))}{\varepsilon^2(1 - \theta)} . \tag{11}$$

Let p^* *be an optimal schedule, i.e., a schedule with minimum cost. If* WIGGINS-APX *converges, then the returned schedule* p *is such that*

$$\mathsf{cost}_\theta(\mathsf{p}^*) \leq \mathsf{cost}_\theta(\mathsf{p}) \leq \frac{1 + \varepsilon}{1 - \varepsilon} \mathsf{cost}_\theta(\mathsf{p}^*) .$$

To prove Thm. 3, we need the following technical lemma.

LEMMA 3. *Let* p *be a c-schedule and* $\mathcal{I}$ *be a sample gathered during a time interval of length*

$$\ell(\mathcal{I}) \geq \frac{3(r \ln(n) + \ln(2))}{\varepsilon^2(1 - \theta)}, \tag{12}$$

where r *is any natural number. Then, for every schedule* p *we have*

$$\Pr(|\mathsf{cost}_\theta(\mathsf{p}, \mathcal{I}) - \mathsf{cost}_\theta(\mathsf{p})| \geq \varepsilon \cdot \mathsf{cost}_\theta(\mathsf{p})) < \frac{1}{n^r} .$$

PROOF. For any $S \in \mathcal{F}$, let X_S be a random variable which is $\frac{1}{1-\theta(1-\mathsf{p}(S))^c}$ with probability $\pi(S)$, and zero otherwise. Since $\mathsf{p}(S) \in [0, 1]$, we have

$$1 \leq X_S \leq \frac{1}{1 - \theta} .$$

If we let $X = \sum_{S \in \mathcal{F}} X_S$, then

$$\mathsf{cost}_\theta(\mathsf{p}) = \mathbb{E}[X] = \sum_{S \in \mathcal{F}} \mathbb{E}[X_S] \geq \sum_{S \in \mathcal{F}} \pi(S) . \tag{13}$$

Let $Z = \sum_{S \in \mathcal{F}} \pi(S)$. Then we have

$$Z \leq X \leq \frac{Z}{1 - \theta} .$$

Let X_S^i be the i-th draw of X_S, during the time interval $\mathcal{I}$ it was sampled from, and define $X^i = \sum_{S \in \mathcal{F}} X_S^i$. We have

$$\mathsf{cost}_\theta(\mathsf{p}, \mathcal{I}) = \frac{1}{\ell(\mathcal{I})} \sum_i X^i .$$

Let now

$$\mu = \frac{\ell(\mathcal{I})(1 - \theta)}{Z} \mathsf{cost}_\theta(\mathsf{p}) .$$

By using the Chernoff bound for Binomial random variables [29, Corol. 4.6], we have

$$\Pr\left(|\mathsf{cost}_\theta(\mathsf{p},\mathcal{I})-\mathsf{cost}_\theta(\mathsf{p})|\geq\varepsilon\mathsf{cost}_\theta(\mathsf{p})\right)$$
$$=\Pr\left(\left|\sum_i X^i-\ell(\mathcal{I})\mathsf{cost}_\theta(\mathsf{p})\right|\geq\varepsilon\ell(\mathcal{I})\mathsf{cost}_\theta(\mathsf{p})\right)$$
$$=\Pr\left(\left|\frac{1-\theta}{Z}\sum_i X^i-\mu\right|\geq\varepsilon\mu\right)\leq 2\exp\left(-\frac{\varepsilon^2\mu}{3}\right)$$
$$\leq 2\exp\left(-\frac{\varepsilon^2\ell(\mathcal{I})(1-\theta)\mathsf{cost}_\theta(\mathsf{p})}{3Z}\right)\leq 2\exp\left(-\frac{\varepsilon^2\ell(\mathcal{I})(1-\theta)}{3}\right),$$

where the last inequality follows from the rightmost inequality in (13). The thesis follows from our choice of $\ell(\mathcal{I})$. □

We can now prove Thm. 3.

PROOF OF THM. 3. The leftmost inequality is immediate, so we focus on the one on the right. For our choice of $\ell(\mathcal{I})$ we have, through the union bound, that, with probability at least $1-1/n^r$, at the same time:

$$\begin{aligned}(1-\varepsilon)\mathsf{cost}_\theta(\mathsf{p})\leq\mathsf{cost}_\theta(\mathsf{p},\mathcal{I})&\leq(1+\varepsilon)\mathsf{cost}_\theta(\mathsf{p}),\text{ and}\\(1-\varepsilon)\mathsf{cost}_\theta(\mathsf{p}^*)\leq\mathsf{cost}_\theta(\mathsf{p}^*,\mathcal{I})&\leq(1+\varepsilon)\mathsf{cost}_\theta(\mathsf{p}^*)\end{aligned}\quad(14)$$

Since we assumed that WIGGINS-APX reached convergence when computing p, then Thm. 3 holds, and p is a schedule with minimum cost w.r.t. $\mathcal{I}$. In particular, it must be

$$\mathsf{cost}_\theta(\mathsf{p},\mathcal{I})\leq\mathsf{cost}_\theta(\mathsf{p}^*,\mathcal{I})\ .$$

From this and (14), We then have

$$(1-\varepsilon)\mathsf{cost}_\theta(\mathsf{p})\leq\mathsf{cost}_\theta(\mathsf{p},\mathcal{I})\leq\mathsf{cost}_\theta(\mathsf{p}^*,\mathcal{I})\leq(1+\varepsilon)\mathsf{cost}_\theta(\mathsf{p}^*)$$

and by comparing the leftmost and the rightmost terms we get the thesis. □

4.3 Dynamic Settings

In this section we discuss how to handle changes in the parameters $\mathcal{F}$ and π as the (unknown) generating process Γ evolves over time. The idea is to maintain an estimation $\tilde{\pi}(S)$ of $\pi(S)$ for each set $S\in\mathcal{F}$ that we discover in the probing process, together with the last time t such that an item (t,S) has been generated (and caught at a time $t'>t$). If we have not caught an item in the form (t'',S) in an interval significantly longer than $1/\tilde{\pi}(S)$, then we assume that the parameters of Γ changed. Hence, we trigger the collection of a new sample and compute a new schedule as described in Sect. 4.2.

Note that when we adapt our schedule to the new environment (using the most recent sample) the system converges to its stable setting exponentially (in θ) fast. Suppose L items have been generated since we detected the change in the parameters until we adapt the new schedule. These items, if not caught, loose their novelty exponentially fast, since after t steps their novelty is at most $L\theta^t$ and decreases exponentially. In our experiments (Sect. 5) we provide different examples that illustrate how the load of the generating process becomes stable after the algorithm adapts itself to the changes of parameters.

4.4 Scaling up with MapReduce

In this section, we discuss how to adapt WIGGINS-APX to the MapReduce framework [9]. We denote the resulting algorithm as WIGGINS-MR.

In MapReduce, algorithms work in *rounds*. At each round, first a function map is executed independently (and therefore potentially massively in parallel) on each element of the input, and a number of (or zero) key-value pairs of the form (k,v) are emitted. Then, in the second part of the round, the emitted pairs are partitioned by key and elements with the same key are sent to the same machine (called the *reducer* for that key), where a function reduce is applied to the whole set of received pairs, to emit the final output.

Each iteration of WIGGINS-APX is spread over two rounds of WIGGINS-MR. At each round, we assume that the current schedule p is available to all machines (this is done in practice through a distributed cache). In the first round, we compute the values p_iW_i, $1\leq i\leq n$, in the second round these values are summed to get the normalization factor, and in the third round the schedule p is updated. The input in the first round are the sets $S\in\mathcal{I}$. The function $\mathsf{map}_1(S)$ outputs, a key-value pair (i,v_S) for each $i\in S$, with

$$v_S=\frac{\theta c(1-\mathsf{p}(S))^{c-1}}{\ell(\mathcal{I})(1-\theta(1-\mathsf{p}(S))^c)^2}\ .$$

The reducer for the key i receives the pairs (i,v_S) for each $S\in\mathcal{I}$ such that $i\in S$, and aggregates them to output the pair (i,g_i), with

$$g_i=\mathsf{p}_i\sum v_S=\mathsf{p}_iW_i\ .$$

The set of pairs (i,g_i), $1\leq i\leq n$ constitutes the input to the next round. Each input pair is sent to the same reducer,[3] which computes the value

$$g=\sum_{i=1}^n g_i=\sum_{i=1}^n\mathsf{p}_iW_i$$

and uses it to obtain the new values $\mathsf{p}_i=g_i/g$, for $1\leq i\leq n$. The reducer then outputs (i,p_i). At this point, the new schedule is distributed to all machines again and a new iteration can start.

The same results we had for the quality of the final schedule computed by WIGGINS-APX in case of convergence carry over to WIGGINS-MR.

5. EXPERIMENTAL RESULTS

In this section we present the results of our experimental evaluation of WIGGINS-APX.

Goals. First, we show that for a given sample $\mathcal{I}$, WIGGINS-APX converges quickly to a schedule p^* that minimizes $\mathsf{cost}_\theta(\mathsf{p},\mathcal{I})$ (see Thm. 2). In particular, our experiments illustrate that the sequence $\mathsf{cost}_\theta(\mathsf{p}^{(1)},\mathcal{I}),\mathsf{cost}_\theta(\mathsf{p}^{(2)},\mathcal{I}),\ldots$ is descending and converges after few iterations. Next, we compare the output schedule of WIGGINS-APX to four other schedules: (i) uniform schedules, (ii) proportional to out-degrees, (iii) proportional to in-degrees, and (iv) proportional to *undirected* degrees, i.e., the number of incident edges. Specifically, we compute the costs of these schedules according to a sample $\mathcal{I}$ that satisfies the condition in Lemma 3 and compare them. Then, we consider a specific example for which we know the *unique* optimal schedule, and show that for larger samples WIGGINS-APX outputs a schedule closer to the optimal. Finally, we demonstrate how our method can adapt itself to the changes in the network parameters.

[3]This step can be made more scalable through *combiners*, an advanced MapReduce feature.

Datasets	#nodes	#edges	$(\|V_{1K}\|, \|V_{500}\|, \|V_{100}\|)$	gen. rate
Enron-Email	36692	367662	(9,23,517)	7.22
Brightkite	58228	428156	(2,7,399)	4.54
web-Notredame	325729	1497134	(43,80,1619)	24.49
web-Google	875713	5105039	(134,180,3546)	57.86

Table 1: The datasets, corresponding statistics, and the rate of generating new items at each step.

Environment and Datasets. We implemented WIGGINS-APX in C++. The implementation of WIGGINS-APX never loads the entire sample to the main memory, which makes it very practical when using large samples. The experiments were run on a Opteron 6282 SE CPU (2.6 GHz) with 12GB of RAM. We tested our method on graphs from the SNAP repository[4] (see Table 1 for details). We always consider the graphs to be directed, replacing undirected edges with two directed ones.

Generating process. The generating process $\Gamma = (\mathcal{F}, \pi)$ we use in our experiments (except those in Sect. 5.1.1) simulates an *Independent-Cascade (IC) model* [17]. Since explicitly computing $\pi(S)$ in this case does not seem possible, we simulate the creation of items according to this model as follows. At each time t, items are generated in two phases: a "creation" phase and a "diffusion" phase. In the creation phase, we simulate the creation of "rumors" at the nodes: we flip a biased coin for each node in the graph, where the bias depends on the out-degree of the node. We assume a partition of the nodes into classes based on their out-degrees, and, we assign the same head probability for the biased coins of nodes in the same class, as shown in Table 2. In Table 1, for each dataset we report the size of the classes and the expected number of flipped coins with outcome head at each time (rightmost column). Let now v be a node whose coin

Class	Nodes in class	Bias
V_{1K}	$\{i \in V \,:\, \mathsf{deg}^+(i) \geq 1000\}$	0.1
V_{500}	$\{i \in V \,:\, 500 \leq \mathsf{deg}^+(i) < 1000\}$	0.05
V_{100}	$\{i \in V \,:\, 100 \leq \mathsf{deg}^+(i) < 500\}$	0.01
V_0	$\{i \in V \,:\, \mathsf{deg}^+(i) < 100\}$	0.0

Table 2: Classes and bias for the generating process.

had outcome head in the most recent flip. In the "diffusion" phase we simulate the spreading of the "rumor" originating at v through network according to the IC model, as follows. For each directed edge $e = u \to w$ we fix a probability p_e that a rumor that reached u is propagated through this edge to node w (as in IC model), and events for different rumors and different edges are independent. Following the literature [5, 6, 16, 17, 33], we use $p_{u \to w} = \frac{1}{\mathsf{deg}^-(w)}$. If we denote with S the final set of nodes that the rumor created at v reached during the (simulated) diffusion process (which always terminates), we have that through this process we generated an item (t, S), without the need to explicitly define $\pi(S)$.

5.1 Efficiency and Accuracy

In Sect. 4.1 we showed that when a run of WIGGINS-APX converges (according to a sample $\mathcal{I}$) the computed c-schedule is optimal with respect to the sample $\mathcal{I}$ (Lemma 2).

[4] **http://snap.stanford.edu**

In our first experiment, we measure the rate of convergence and the execution time of WIGGINS-APX. We fix $\epsilon = 0.1$, $\theta = 0.75$, and consider $c \in \{1, 3, 5\}$. For each dataset, we use a sample $\mathcal{I}$ that satisfies (12), and run WIGGINS-APX for 30 iterations. Denote the schedule computed at round i by p^i. As shown in Figure 1, the sequence of cost values of the schedules p^i's, $\mathsf{cost}_\theta(\mathsf{p}^i, \mathcal{I})$, converges extremely fast after few iterations.

Datasets	$\|\mathcal{I}\|$	avg. item size	avg. iter. time (sec)
Enron-Email	97309	12941.33	204.59
Brightkite	63652	17491.08	144.35
web-Notredame	393348	183.75	10.24
web-Google	998038	704.74	121.88

Table 3: Sample size, average size of items in the sample, and the running time of each iteration in WIGGINS-APX (for $c = 1$).

For each graph, the size of the sample $\mathcal{I}$, the average size of sets in $\mathcal{I}$, and the average time of each iteration is given in Table 3. Note that the running time of each iteration is a function of both sample size and sizes of the sets (informed-sets) inside the sample.

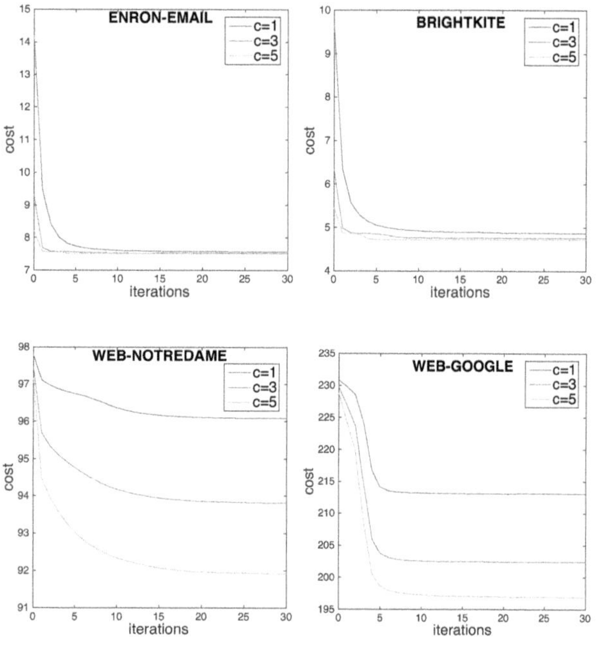

Figure 1: The cost of intermediate c-schedules at iterations of WIGGINS-APX according to $\mathcal{I}$.

Next, we extract the 1-schedules output by WIGGINS-APX, and compare its cost to four other natural schedules: **unif**, **outdeg**, **indeg**, and **totdeg** that probe each node, respectively, uniformly, proportional to its out-degree, proportional to its in-degree, and proportional to the number of incident edges. Note that for undirected graphs **outdeg**, **indeg**, and **totdeg** are essentially the same schedule.

To have a fair comparison among the costs of these schedules and WIGGINS-APX, we calculate their costs according to 10 independent samples, $\mathcal{I}_1, \ldots, \mathcal{I}_{10}$ that satisfy (12), and compute the average. The results are shown in Table 4, and show that WIGGINS-APX outperforms the other four schedules.

Dataset	WIGGINS-APX	uniform	outdeg	indeg	totdeg
Enron-Email	7.55	14.16	9.21	9.21	9.21
Brightkite	4.85	9.64	6.14	6.14	6.14
web-Notredame	96.10	97.78	97.37	97.43	97.40
web-Google	213.15	230.88	230.48	230.47	230.47

Table 4: Comparing the costs of 5 different 1-schedules.

5.1.1 *A Test on Convergence to Optimal Schedule*

Here, we further investigate the convergence of WIGGINS-APX, using an example graph and process for which we know the *unique* optimal schedule. We study how close the WIGGINS-APX output is to the optimal schedule when (i) we start from different initial schedules, p^0, or (ii) we use samples $\mathcal{I}$'s obtained during time intervals of different lengths.

Suppose $G = (V, E)$ is the complete graph where $V = [n]$. Let $\Gamma = (\mathcal{F}, \pi)$ for $\mathcal{F} = \{S \in 2^{[n]} \mid 1 \leq |S| \leq 2\}$, and $\pi(S) = \frac{1}{|\mathcal{F}|}$. It is easy to see that $\mathsf{cost}_\theta(\mathsf{p})$ is a symmetric function, and thus, the uniform schedule is optimal. Moreover, by Corollary 1 the uniform schedule is the only optimal schedule, since $\{v\} \in \mathcal{F}$ for every $v \in V$. Furthermore, we let $\theta = 0.99$ to increase the sample complexity (as in Lemma 3) and make it harder to learn the uniform/optimal schedule.

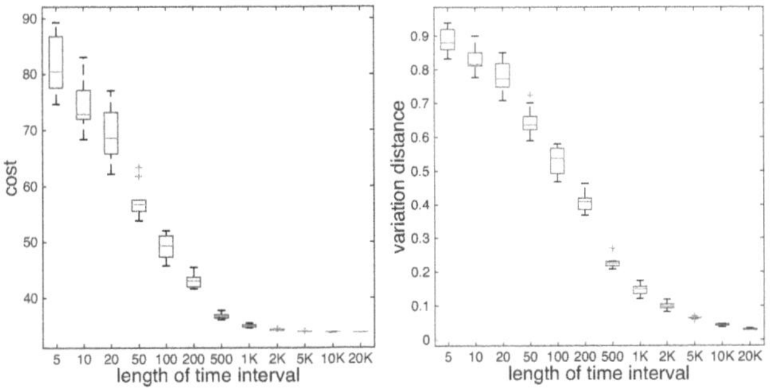

Figure 2: The cost of WIGGINS-APX outputs and their variation distance to the optimal schedule: The top and bottom edge of each box are the 25th and 75th percentiles respectively , and the median (50th percentile) is shown by a red line segment. The + symbols denote outliers, i.e., points larger than $q_3 + 1.5(q_3 - q_1)$ or smaller than $q_1 - 1.5(q_3 - q_1)$, where q_1 and q_3 are the 25th and 75th percentiles, respectively. The whiskers extend to the most extreme data points that are not outliers.

In our experiments we run the WIGGINS-APX algorithm, using (i) different *random* initial schedules, and (ii) samples $\mathcal{I}$ obtained from time intervals of different lengths. For each sample, we run WIGGINS-APX 10 times with 10 different random initial schedules, and compute the **exact** cost of each schedule, and its variation distance to the uniform schedule. Our results are plotted in Figure 2, and as shown, by increasing the sample size (using longer time intervals of sampling) the output schedules gets very close to the uniform schedule (the variance gets smaller and smaller).

5.2 Dynamic Settings

In this section, we present experimental results that show how our algorithm can adapt itself to the new situation. The experiment is illustrated in Fig. 3. For each graph, we start by following an optimal 1-schedule in the graph. At the beginning of each "gray" time interval, the labels of the nodes are permuted randomly, to impose great disruptions in the system. Following that, at the beginning of each "green" time interval our algorithm starts gathering samples of Γ. Then, WIGGINS-APX computes the schedule for the new sample, using 50 rounds of iterations, and starts probing. The length of each colored time interval is $R = \frac{3(\log(n)+\log(2))}{\epsilon^2(1-\theta)}$, for $\epsilon = 0.5$ and $\theta = 0.75$, motivated by Theorem 3.

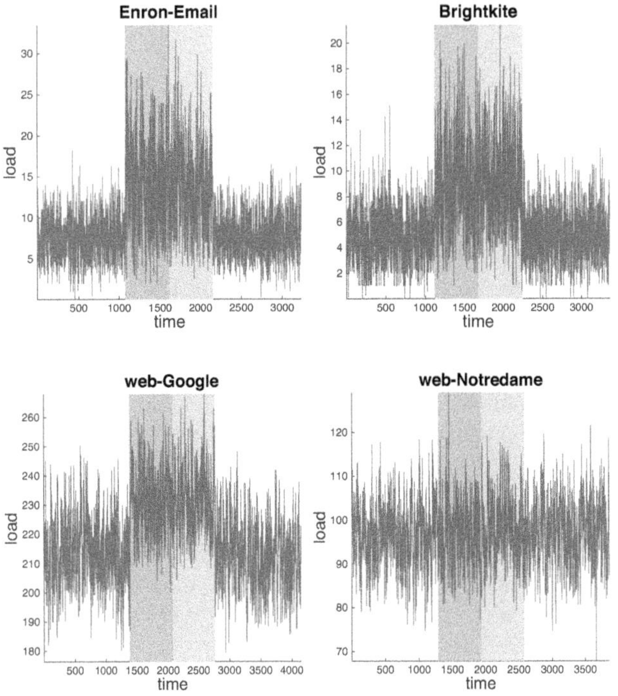

Figure 3: Perturbation, Sampling, and Adapting (For details see Section 5.2).

Since the cost function is defined asymptotically (and explains the asymptotic behavior of the system in response to a schedule), in Figure 3 we plot the load of the system $L_\theta(t)$ over the time (blue), and the *average* load in the normal and perturbed time intervals (red). Based on this experiment, and as shown in Figure 3, after adapting to the new schedule, the effect of the disruption caused by the perturbation disappears immediately. Note that when the difference between the optimal cost and any other schedule is small (like web-Notredame), the jump in the load will be small (e.g., as shown in Figure 1 and Table 4, the cost of the initial schedule for web-Notredame is very close the optimal cost, obtained after 30 iteration).

6. CONCLUSIONS

We formulate and study the (θ, c)-Optimal Probing Schedule Problem, which requires to find the best probing schedule that allows an observer to find most pieces of information recently generated by a process Γ, by probing a limited number of nodes at each time step.

We design and analyze an algorithm, WIGGINS, that can solve the problem optimally if the parameters of the process Γ are known, and then design a variant that computes a high-quality approximation of the optimum schedule when only a sample of the process is available. We also show that WIGGINS can be adapted to the MapReduce framework of computation, which allows us to scale up to networks with million of nodes. The results of experimental evaluation on a variety of graphs and generating processes show that WIGGINS and its variants are very effective in practice.

Interesting directions for future work include generalizing the problem to allow for non-memoryless schedules and different novelty functions.

7. ACKNOWLEDGEMENTS

This work was supported by NSF grant IIS-1247581.

8. REFERENCES

[1] M. Agumbe Suresh, R. Stoleru, R. Denton, E. Zechman, and B. Shihada. Towards optimal event detection and localization in acyclic flow networks. ICDCN'12, 2012.

[2] S. Boyd and L. Vandenberghe. *Convex optimization.* Cambridge university press, 2004.

[3] L. Bright, A. Gal, and L. Raschid. Adaptive pull-based policies for wide area data delivery. *ACM TODS*, 31(2):631–671, 2006.

[4] M. Cataldi, L. Di Caro, and C. Schifanella. Emerging topic detection on Twitter based on temporal and social terms evaluation. MDMKDD'10, 2010.

[5] W. Chen, Y. Wang, and S. Yang. Efficient influence maximization in social networks. KDD'09, 2009.

[6] W. Chen, C. Wang, and Y. Wang. Scalable influence maximization for prevalent viral marketing in large-scale social networks. KDD'10, 2010.

[7] N. A. Christakis and J. H. Fowler. Social network sensors for early detection of contagious outbreaks. *PLoS ONE*, 5(9):e12948, 2010.

[8] A. Dasgupta, A. Ghosh, R. Kumar, C. Olston, S. Pandey, and A. Tomkins. The discoverability of the web. WWW'07, 2007.

[9] J. Dean and S. Ghemawat. MapReduce: simplified data processing on large clusters. *CACM*, 51(1): 107–113, 2008.

[10] A. Delaney. *The Growing Role of News in Trading Automation*, Oct. 2009. `http://www.machinereadablenews.com/images/dl/Machine_Readable_News_and_Algorithmic_Trading.pdf`.

[11] D. Golovin, M. Faulkner, and A. Krause. Online distributed sensor selection. IPSN'10, 2010.

[12] G. H. Hardy. *Divergent series*, volume 334. Am. Math. Soc., 1991.

[13] W. Hart and R. Murray. Review of sensor placement strategies for contamination warning systems in drinking water distribution systems. *J. Water Resources Planning and Manag.*, 136(6):611–619, 2010. doi: 10.1061/(ASCE)WR.1943-5452.0000081.

[14] B. Hope. How computers trawl a sea of data for stock picks. *The Wall Street Journal*, Apr. 1st 2015.

[15] R. Horincar, B. Amann, and T. Artières. Online refresh strategies for content based feed aggregation. *World Wide Web*, 1–35, 2014.

[16] K. Jung, W. Heo, and W. Chen. IRIE: Scalable and robust influence maximization in social networks. *arXiv:1111.4795*, 2011.

[17] D. Kempe, J. Kleinberg, and E. Tardos. Maximizing the spread of influence through a social network. KDD'03, 2003.

[18] D. Kempe, J. Kleinberg, and E. Tardos. Influential nodes in a diffusion model for social networks. ICALP'05, 2005.

[19] A. Krause and C. Guestrin. Submodularity and its applications in optimized information gathering. *ACM TIST*, 2(4):32:1–32:20, 2011.

[20] A. Krause, J. Leskovec, C. Guestrin, J. VanBriesen, and C. Faloutsos. Efficient sensor placement optimization for securing large water distribution networks. *J. Water Resources Planning and Manag.*, 134(6):516–526, 2008.

[21] A. Krause, R. Rajagopal, A. Gupta, and C. Guestrin. Simultaneous placement and scheduling of sensors. IPSN'09, 2009.

[22] A. Krause, C. Guestrin, A. Gupta, and J. Kleinberg. Robust sensor placements at informative and communication-efficient locations. *ACM TSN*, 7(4): 31:1–31:33, 2011.

[23] C. J. Kuhlman, G. Tuli, S. Swarup, M. V. Marathe, and S. S. Ravi. Blocking simple and complex contagion by edge removal. ICDM'13, 2013.

[24] N. L. Latar. The robot journalist in the age of social physics: The end of human journalism? In *The New World of Transitioned Media*, 65–80. Springer, 2015.

[25] J. Leskovec, A. Krause, C. Guestrin, C. Faloutsos, J. M. VanBriesen, and N. S. Glance. Cost-effective outbreak detection in networks. KDD'07, 2007.

[26] A. Li and L. Tang. The complexity and approximability of minimum contamination problems. TAMC'11, 2001.

[27] M. Mathioudakis and N. Koudas. Twittermonitor: Trend detection over the Twitter stream. SIGMOD'10, 2010.

[28] W. McKinney. *Structured Data Challenges in Finance and Statistics*, 2011. `http://www.slideshare.net/wesm/structured-data-challenges-in-finance-and-statistics`.

[29] M. Mitzenmacher and E. Upfal. *Probability and Computing: Randomized Algorithms and Probabilistic Analysis.* Cambridge University Press, 2005.

[30] M. Oita and P. Senellart. Deriving dynamics of web pages: A survey. TWAW'11, 2011.

[31] A. Ostfeld et al. The battle of the water sensor networks (BWSN): A design challenge for engineers and algorithms. *J. Water Resources Planning and Manag.*, 134(6):556–568, 2008.

[32] K. C. Sia, J. Cho, and H.-K. Cho. Efficient monitoring algorithm for fast news alerts. *Knowledge and Data Engineering, IEEE Transactions on*, 19(7): 950–961, 2007.

[33] Y. Tang, X. Xiao, and Y. Shi. Influence maximization: Near-optimal time complexity meets practical efficiency. *arXiv:1404.0900*, 2014.

[34] J. L. Wolf, M. S. Squillante, P. Yu, J. Sethuraman, and L. Ozsen. Optimal crawling strategies for web search engines. WWW'02, 2002.

Understanding Offline Political Systems by Mining Online Political Data

David Lazer
Northeastern University
177 Huntington Ave
Boston, MA 02115
d.lazer@neu.edu

Oren Tsur
Northeastern U. & Harvard U.
177 Huntington Ave
Boston, MA 02115
orentsur@seas.harvard.edu

Tina Eliassi-Rad
Rutgers University
110 Frelinghuysen Road
Piscataway, NJ 08854
tina@eliassi.org

ABSTRACT

"Man is by nature a political animal", as asserted by Aristotle. This political nature manifests itself in the data we produce and the traces we leave online. In this tutorial, we address a number of fundamental issues regarding mining of political data: What types of data could be considered political? What can we learn from such data? Can we use the data for prediction of political changes, *etc*? How can these prediction tasks be done efficiently? Can we use online socio-political data in order to get a better understanding of our political systems and of recent political changes? What are the pitfalls and inherent shortcomings of using online data for political analysis? In recent years, with the abundance of data, these questions, among others, have gained importance, especially in light of the global political turmoil and the upcoming 2016 US presidential election. We introduce relevant political science theory, describe the challenges within the framework of computational social science and present state of the art approaches bridging social network analysis, graph mining, and natural language processing.

Categories and Subject Descriptors

H.2.8 [**Database Applications**]: Data mining; E.1 [**Data Structures**]: Graphs and networks

Keywords

Computational social science, political data, social and information networks, graph mining

1. INTRODUCTION

Mining of online socio-political data can revolutionize our understanding of socio-political systems. However, there exists an unfortunate gap between scholars in computer science and political/social sciences. This gap is manifested in the failure of both computer and political scientists to predict political events such as the (magnitude of the) Arab spring, the rise of ISIL (a.k.a. ISIS), and the recent Russia-Ukraine crisis, just to name a few. Computer scientists are often unaware of (or at best agnostic to) relevant social and political theories, which can lead to asking the wrong research questions and drawing erroneous socio-political conclusions. Political/social scientists have deep knowledge of the socio-political theories and fundamental insights on complex socio-political systems, but they often lack the modeling and algorithmic expertise for learning and mining from massive amounts of data. This disparity can lead to using naive (inadequate) methods, setting up experiments incorrectly, misinterpreting empirical results, and misprediction of the existence or magnitude of major events. The goal of this tutorial is to bridge the aforementioned gap by covering the relevant socio-political theories and the state-of-art algorithms in natural language processing, social network analysis, and graph mining. We demonstrate the great potential in this interdisciplinary collaboration by showcasing several success stories.

WSDM'16, February 22–25, 2016, San Francisco, CA, USA

ACM ISBN 978-1-4503-3716-8/16/02.
DOI: http://dx.doi.org/10.1145/2835776.2855112

2. TUTORIAL DESCRIPTION

The tutorial is divided into three sections (one section per hour). In the first hour, we present socio-political theories that have been used successfully in computational social science studies. In the second hour, we overview state-of-the art algorithms in mining socio-political networks. In the third (and last) hour, we discuss recent algorithmic successes that utilize both natural language processing and social network analysis.

First hour: Socio-political theories. We introduce computational social science, focusing on political science. We cover the following four areas:

- Socio-political theory
- Empirical political science
- Demographic modeling and its challenges
- The importance of networks in analysis of socio-political data

Second hour: Mining socio-political networks. We give an overview of the state-of-the-art algorithms for learning and mining from socio-political network data. We cover the following areas:

- Community detection
- Role discovery

- Event prediction (covering both causal and passive predictions)
- Transfer learning

Third hour: Mining form and content. We discuss the connection between form (i.e., network topology) and content (i.e., language) in an influence maximization setting, bridging the gap between network analysis and natural language processing, focusing on the following methods:

- Topic models
- Word embeddings
- Time series analysis

Throughout the tutorial, we highlight success stories from collaborations between computer scientists and political/social scientists.

3. TUTORIAL SLIDES AND RESOURCES

The tutorial slides and list of resources are available at the following URL: *https://sites.google.com/site/orentsur/wsdm_2016_tutorial_political_mining*. The list of resources include select publications on the following topics:

- "Polling" by social media analysis
- Political polarization in social media
- Demographics of social media users
- Sentiment analysis and opinion mining
- Using machine learning for political analysis
- Analysis of and prediction based on political texts
- Prediction of global events
- Community detection
- Role discovery
- Transfer learning
- Time-series analysis

In addition, the aforementioned URL has links to datasets and publicly available software.

4. INTENDED AUDIENCE AND PREREQUISITE

The intended audience are researchers and practitioners who want to learn about algorithms and applications of mining online socio-political data, supported by political science theory. There are no prerequisites. Our emphasis will be on the intuition behind all the formal concepts and tools.

5. TUTORS' BIOGRAPHIES

- **David Lazer** is Distinguished Professor of Political Science and Computer Science at Northeastern University. He is one of the leading figures in computational social science. Educated in political science at the University of Michigan, he began his career at the Harvard Kennedy School. He subsequently accepted a position at Northeastern to establish the Lazer Lab on computational social science. His research focuses on the nexus of network science, computational social science, and collaborative intelligence. He is the founder of the citizen science website Volunteer Science and the political visualization website VisPolics. His research has been published in such journals as Science, PNAS, the American Political Science Review, Organization Science, and the Administrative Science Quarterly, and has received extensive coverage in the media, including the New York Times, NPR, the Washington Post, the Wall Street Journal, and CBS Evening News.
- **Oren Tsur** is a postdoctoral fellow at the Center for Network Science at Northeastern University and is affiliated with Harvard's School for Engineering and Applied Science (SEAS) and Harvard's Institute for Quantitative Social Science (IQSS). He earned his Ph.D. in Computer Science from the Hebrew University focusing on sentiment analysis and content based information diffusion. He currently combines natural language processing and network analysis in order to model and predict complex social dynamics. His work was published in both the NLP and the web/data science communities. Oren was invited to present his work in various research institutes as well as in industry leaders such as Yahoo, Microsoft and IBM. He co-organized the workshop on NLP and Social Dynamics at ACL 2014.
- **Tina Eliassi-Rad** is an Associate Professor of Computer Science at Rutgers University. She earned her Ph.D. in Computer Sciences (with a minor in Mathematical Statistics) at the University of Wisconsin-Madison. Tina's current research lays at the intersection of graph mining, network science, and computational social science. Within data mining and machine learning, her research has been applied to the World-Wide Web, text corpora, large-scale scientific simulation data, complex networks, and cyber situational awareness. She has published over 60 peer-reviewed papers (including a best paper runner-up award at ICDM 2009 and a best interdisciplinary paper award at CIKM 2012); and has given over 100 invited presentations. In 2010, she received an Outstanding Mentor Award from the US DOE Office of Science.

6. ACKNOWLEDGEMENTS

For Lazer and Tsur, this work was supported in part by NSF CMMI-1125095, by IARPA via Department of Interior National Business Center (DoI/NBC) contract D12PC00285, and by ARO Grant No. 00003934. For Eliassi-Rad, this work was supported in part by NSF CNS-1314603 and by DTRA HDTRA1-10-1-0120.

Click Models for Web Search and their Applications to IR

WSDM 2016 Tutorial

Aleksandr Chuklin
Google Switzerland &
University of Amsterdam
Zürich, Switzerland
a.chuklin@uva.nl

Ilya Markov
University of Amsterdam
Amsterdam, The Netherlands
i.markov@uva.nl

Maarten de Rijke
University of Amsterdam
Amsterdam, The Netherlands
derijke@uva.nl

ABSTRACT

In this tutorial we give an overview of click models for web search. We show how the framework of probabilistic graphical models helps to explain user behavior, build new evaluation metrics and perform simulations. The tutorial discusses foundational aspects alongside experimental details and applications, with live demos and discussions of publicly available resources.

Keywords

Click models; web search

1. INTRODUCTION

Click models, probabilistic models of the behavior of search engine users, have been studied extensively by the information retrieval community during the last decade.

A good body of work has been published on click models over the past five to ten years. Importantly, the area continues to be an active one, with new models aimed at describing and/or predicting behavioral data being proposed at each of the main information retrieval conferences (SIGIR, WSDM, WWW, CIKM) over the past few years. There is also a fair number of publications that *use* click models presented in the main information retrieval conferences as well as ACM journals such as TOIS. All this indicates that there is a substantial and continued level of interest in the topic.

Indeed, we now have a handful of basic click models, inference methods, evaluation principles and applications for click models, that form the building blocks of ongoing research efforts in the area. The time is right to organize and present this material to a broad audience of interested information retrieval researchers, whether junior or senior. Many of the click models available today have been proposed by different industrial and academic research groups—one of the key aims of our proposed tutorial is to bring these together and offer a unified perspective. To achieve this, we describe the basic click models, inference methods and evaluation principles. We supplement this with an account of available datasets and packages plus a live demo based on these. We also present click model applications accompanied by examples.

WSDM 2016 February 22-25, 2016, San Francisco, CA, USA

ACM ISBN 978-1-4503-3716-8/16/02.

DOI: http://dx.doi.org/10.1145/2835776.2855113

We expect the tutorial to be useful for both researchers and practitioners that either want to develop new click models, use them in their own research in other areas or apply the models described here to improve actual search systems.

2. OBJECTIVES

A large body of research on click models has been developed. This research has improved our understanding of user behavior in web search and facilitated the usage of click models in various search-related tasks. Current studies use a broad range of notations and terminology, perform experiments using different and mostly proprietary datasets, do not detail the model inference procedures used and, thus, do not provide a general systematic view on the research area. This, in turn, slows down the development and hinders the application of click models. The goal of this tutorial is to bring together current efforts in the area, summarize the research performed so far and give a holistic view on existing click models for web search. More specifically, the aims of this tutorial are the following:

1. Describe existing click models in a unified way, i.e., using common notation and terminology, so that different models can easily be related to each other.

2. Compare commonly used click models, discuss their advantages and limitations and provide a set of recommendations on their usage.

3. Provide ready-to-use formulas and implementations of existing click models and detail general inference procedures to facilitate the development of new ones.

4. Give an overview of existing datasets and tools for working with click models and develop new ones.

5. Provide an overview of click model applications and directions for future development of click models.

Our target audience consists of researchers and developers in information retrieval who are interested in formally capturing user interactions with search engine result pages, whether for ranking purposes, to simulate user behavior in a lab setting, or simply to gain deeper insights in user behavior and interaction data. The tutorial will be useful as an overview for anyone starting research work in the area as well as for practitioners seeking concrete recipes.

The tutorial aims to provide a map of an increasingly rich landscape of click models. By the end of the half-day tutorial, attendees should be familiar with the basic definitions and intuitions of what we consider to be the core models, with inference tasks for these models, and with uses of these models. While our presentation is necessarily formal in places, we make a serious effort to relate the models, the inference procedures and the applications back to the core information retrieval task and to web search data by including a fair number of examples. We hope that this supplies attendees who are new to the area with effective means to start using click models in their own research.

3. DETAILED SCHEDULE

The tutorial is organized in two blocks of 1.5 hrs.

Block 1 (1.5 hours)

1. Introduction, historical notes, aims.
2. Basic click models

   Here, we describe basic click models for web search, starting with the simplest random click model and arriving to the more sophisticated DCM, DBN and UBM models [1, 3, 4]. We discuss models' assumptions, observed and hidden random variables, models' parameters and relations between parameters and random variables. We also demonstrate how to infer click probabilities (either full or conditional) and simulate the users' clicks.
3. Click model parameter estimation (training)

   We describe the process of training click model parameters from past click observations. We review two main parameter estimation techniques, namely maximum likelihood estimation (MLE) and the expectation-maximization algorithm (EM). We then give several examples of MLE and EM parameter estimation for existing click models to support the theory.
4. Click model evaluation

   We discuss different ways to evaluate click models and to compare them to each other. We start with traditional approaches, such as log-likelihood/perplexity evaluation and click-through rate prediction, and then discuss more application-oriented evaluation methods like NDCG evaluation.

Block 2 (1.5 hours)

5. Data and tools

   Here, we discuss publicly available datasets for experimenting with click models. We also describe open-source software packages and libraries that facilitate working with click models.
6. Live Demo

   During the live demo we compare the click models, discussed during the first block, using the presented evaluation methods. We also discuss the differences between parameter estimation techniques from the practical point of view (e.g., learned parameters, learning time). The demo uses an open source package maintained by Markov[1] as well as samples from interaction data shared by Yandex.[2]
7. Advanced click models

   Here we present a brief overview of main development directions of click models and discuss most prominent members of each class. We discuss models' assumptions and main applications.
8. Click model applications

   In this part, we discuss different applications for modern click models in different areas such as ranking, evaluation or user simulation. We augment the theoretical discussion with the practical demonstrations of some of the applications.
9. Recap and discussion

4. TYPE OF SUPPORT MATERIALS TO BE SUPPLIED TO ATTENDEES

- The authors' version of the book on click models [2]
- Copy of the slides
- Code and data samples to follow live demos and for offline experimentation

We also maintain a web site with all resources related to this tutorial at http://clickmodels.weebly.com.

Acknowledgements

The tutorial is partially based on research that was supported by Amsterdam Data Science, the Dutch national program COMMIT, Elsevier, the European Community's Seventh Framework Programme (FP7/2007-2013) under grant agreement nr 312827 (VOX-Pol), the ESF Research Network Program ELIAS, the Royal Dutch Academy of Sciences (KNAW) under the Elite Network Shifts project, the Microsoft Research Ph.D. program, the Netherlands eScience Center under project number 027.012.105, the Netherlands Institute for Sound and Vision, the Netherlands Organisation for Scientific Research (NWO) under project nrs 727.011.005, 612.001.116, HOR-11-10, 640.006.013, 612.066.930, CI-14-25, SH-322-15, 652.002.-001, the Yahoo Faculty Research and Engagement Program, and Yandex. All content represents the opinion of the authors, which is not necessarily shared or endorsed by their respective employers and/or sponsors.

REFERENCES

[1] O. Chapelle and Y. Zhang. A dynamic bayesian network click model for web search ranking. In *WWW*, pages 1–10, 2009.

[2] A. Chuklin, I. Markov, and M. de Rijke. *Click Models for Web Search*. Morgan & Claypool, 2015.

[3] G. E. Dupret and B. Piwowarski. A user browsing model to predict search engine click data from past observations. In *SIGIR*, pages 331–338, 2008.

[4] F. Guo, C. Liu, and Y. M. Wang. Efficient multiple-click models in web search. In *WSDM*, pages 124–131, 2009.

[1] https://github.com/markovi/PyClick
[2] http://imat-relpred.yandex.ru/en/datasets

Query Understanding for Search on All Devices at WSDM 2016

Amit Goyal
Yahoo Labs
goyal@yahoo-inc.com

Jianfeng Gao
Microsoft Research
jfgao@microsoft.com

Hongbo Deng, Yi Chang
Yahoo Labs
{hbdeng,yichang}@yahoo-inc.com

It is our great pleasure to welcome you to the QRUMS 2016, the workshop on Query Understanding for Search on All Devices, held as part of the WSDM 2016 conference in San Francisco, USA.

Theme and Purpose of the workshop:

Query understanding has become a crucial component for today's search engines. It is important to improve query understanding as query formulation is the way through which users express their search intent to a search engine. With the ubiquitousness of mobile devices, it is even more important to better understand user intent as typing on mobile is hard and time consuming. This workshop focuses on query understanding for mobile search with a motivation of reducing user efforts in formulating queries and getting their expected search results quickly.

One of the most important problem in query understanding is Query auto-completion (QAC). QAC is the first service through which users interact with a search engine to input their search intent. QAC has to provide and update their suggestion lists based on each new character typed by the user in the search box. Returned suggestion lists are ranked based on different relevance models, such as most popular completion (based on historical frequency counts from query logs) [1], time-based (giving more weight to breaking news or recent popular queries) [10, 12, 11], location-based [9], context-sensitive (based on user's context) [1, 5], personalized (based on user's profile) [9], click modeling (based on user's past clicks) [6], user-QAC interactions [8, 4], adaptive query auto-completion [13]. QAC becomes even more important as the focus shifts from desktop search to mobile search. On mobile, due to small typing keyboard, it is even more important to exploit all user and its context information available on mobile to provide the user better search suggestions.

On query understanding and QAC: there is also a need of personalized and context models, especially for name queries. For example, a user may talk to his smart phone, "forward an email to Bill". This implicitly triggers the query understanding engine to map "Bill" to a specific person in his/her address book. In such a case, contextual information, such as the content of the email to be forwarded and the user's recent communication patterns (i.e., how frequently she talks/emails to different Bill's), is instrumental. Similarly, if a user chooses to key in a person name, the engine should be able to suggest the full name based on the prefix the user types, e.g., "J" → "John" or "Jianfeng". The studies on how to improve personalized and contextual model for query auto-completion/understanding are crucial to improve user experience (especially for mobiles). Yet, there is not much research in the academic world.

Another important problem in query processing for mobile search is spelling correction [3, 2, 7]. Due to a small typing keyboard, users are more prone to make spelling mistakes. Spelling mistakes made on mobile can be a lot different than made on desktop, hence it is an interesting, important, and challenging problem to explore. We encourage researchers (especially those from industry labs) to explore the use of search logs to mine spelling correction patterns. For example, [3] reports a new speller that uses a set of large-scale translation and language models that capture millions of spelling correction patterns learned from search logs.

Objectives: This workshop is dedicated to presentations and discussions on query understanding for mobile search. The workshop will bring together researchers from information retrieval, web mining, natural language processing, and machine learning, who are working on or interested in this area. It will provide a forum for the researchers to identify the issues and the challenges, to share their latest research results, to express a diverse range of opinions about this topic, and to discuss future directions. We believe that this workshop will become an important milestone in the advancement of query understanding for mobile search.

Review Process: The call for papers solicited submissions in the area of query understanding . Themes of interests were diverse and spanned query recommendation, query categorization, spelling correction, query reformulation, and QAC. Each submission was reviewed by at least three Program Committee members and final decisions were made by the workshop chairs. PC members include many experts in the field. We are grateful to all of them for their thorough and insightful reviews.

Program: In this year's workshop, we are delighted to have several invited talks as part of the workshop. Milad Shokouhi from Microsoft Research, Michael Bendersky from Google Research will give the invited talks.

We hope that you will find this workshop interesting and thought-provoking and that the workshop will provide you

WSDM'16, February 22–25, 2016, San Francisco, CA, USA.
ACM 978-1-4503-3716-8/16/02.
http://dx.doi.org/10.1145/2835776.2855115.

with a valuable opportunity to share ideas with other researchers and practitioners from institutions around the world.

1. REFERENCES

[1] Z. Bar-Yossef and N. Kraus. Context-sensitive query auto-completion. In *Proceedings of the International Conference on World Wide Web (WWW)*, pages 107–116. ACM, 2011.

[2] H. Duan and B.-J. P. Hsu. Online spelling correction for query completion. In *Proceedings of the 20th International Conference on World Wide Web*, WWW '11, pages 117–126. ACM, 2011.

[3] J. Gao, X. Li, D. Micol, C. Quirk, and X. Sun. A large scale ranker-based system for search query spelling correction. In *Proceedings of the 23rd International Conference on Computational Linguistics*, COLING '10, pages 358–366. Association for Computational Linguistics, 2010.

[4] K. Hofmann, B. Mitra, F. Radlinski, and M. Shokouhi. An eye-tracking study of user interactions with query auto completion. In *Proceedings of the 23rd ACM International Conference on Conference on Information and Knowledge Management*, CIKM '14, pages 549–558. ACM, 2014.

[5] W. Kong, R. Li, J. Luo, A. Zhang, Y. Chang, and J. Allan. Predicting search intent based on pre-search context. In *Proceedings of the 38th International ACM SIGIR Conference on Research and Development in Information Retrieval*, pages 503–512, 2015.

[6] Y. Li, A. Dong, H. Wang, H. Deng, Y. Chang, and C. Zhai. A two-dimensional click model for query auto-completion. In *Proceedings of the ACM International Conference on Research and Development in Information Retrieval (SIGIR)*, pages 455–464. ACM, 2014.

[7] Y. Li, H. Duan, and C. Zhai. A generalized hidden markov model with discriminative training for query spelling correction. In *Proceedings of the 35th International ACM SIGIR Conference on Research and Development in Information Retrieval*, SIGIR '12, pages 611–620. ACM, 2012.

[8] B. Mitra, M. Shokouhi, F. Radlinski, and K. Hofmann. On user interactions with query auto-completion. In *Proceedings of the ACM International Conference on Research and Development in Information Retrieval (SIGIR)*, pages 1055–1058. ACM, 2014.

[9] M. Shokouhi. Learning to personalize query auto-completion. In *Proceedings of the ACM International Conference on Research and Development in Information Retrieval (SIGIR)*, pages 103–112. ACM, 2013.

[10] M. Shokouhi and K. Radinsky. Time-sensitive query auto-completion. In *Proceedings of the ACM International Conference on Research and Development in Information Retrieval (SIGIR)*, pages 601–610. ACM, 2012.

[11] S. Whiting and J. M. Jose. Recent and robust query auto-completion. In *Proceedings of the International Conference on World Wide Web (WWW)*, pages 971–982. International World Wide Web Conferences Steering Committee, 2014.

[12] S. Whiting, J. McMinn, and J. M. Jose. Exploring real-time temporal query auto-completion. In *DIR*, pages 12–15, 2013.

[13] A. Zhang, A. Goyal, W. Kong, H. Deng, A. Dong, Y. Chang, C. A. Gunter, and J. Han. adaqac: Adaptive query auto-completion via implicit negative feedback. In *Proceedings of the 38th International ACM SIGIR Conference on Research and Development in Information Retrieval*, SIGIR '15, pages 143–152. ACM, 2015.

TargetAd 2016: Int'l Workshop on Ad Targeting at Scale

Mihajlo Grbovic
Yahoo Labs
Sunnyvale, CA
mihajlo@yahoo-inc.com

Nemanja Djuric
Yahoo Labs
Sunnyvale, CA
nemanja@yahoo-inc.com

Vladan Radosavljevic
Yahoo Labs
Sunnyvale, CA
vladan@yahoo-inc.com

ABSTRACT

The 2nd International Workshop on Ad Targeting at Scale will be held in San Francisco, California, USA on February 22nd, 2016, co-located with the 9th ACM International Conference on Web Search and Data Mining (WSDM). The main objective of the workshop is to address the challenges of ad targeting in web-scale settings. The workshop brings together interdisciplinary researchers in computational advertising, recommender systems, personalization, and related areas, to share, exchange, learn, and develop preliminary results, new concepts, ideas, principles, and methodologies on applying data mining technologies to ad targeting. We have constructed an exciting program of eight refereed papers and several invited talks that will help us better understand the future of ad targeting.

Keywords

Computational advertising; ad targeting; audience modeling

1. INTRODUCTION

Personalization of online content has become an important feature for many internet services. It has been defined as "the ability to proactively tailor products and product purchasing experiences to tastes of individual consumers based upon their personal and preference information" [1], which may lead to improved user experience and directly translate into financial gains for online businesses [2]. In addition, personalization fosters stronger bond between users and companies, and can help in increasing user loyalty and retention [3]. For these reasons it has been recognized as an important strategic goal of major internet companies [4, 5], and is a focus of significant research efforts. Personalized content has already become an integral part of many popular online services, a trend likely to continue in the future.

We consider content personalization from the viewpoint of targeted advertising [6], an increasingly important aspect of online businesses. In recent years, targeted advertising has become one of the largest and most lucrative advertising channels. Despite the fact that traditional offline advertising still accounts for the majority of overall advertising expenditures [13], future potential of this burgeoning field is clearly exemplified by reported ad revenue of over 49 billion dollars in 2014 in the US alone, combined with a remarkable growth of around 20% on a yearly basis [12]. The size and importance of the online advertising, as well as the interesting open questions that the scale and variety of the targeting tasks bring, has drawn attention of many researchers from both industry and academia, resulting in a number of novel methods, improvements, and workshops dedicated to the flourishing field [7, 8, 9]. In order to maintain and improve upon this positive trend, researchers in academia and industry alike are faced with numerous algorithmic, theoretical, and practical challenges that need immediate attention. This was one of the main motivating factors that prompted us to organize the TargetAd workshop.

WSDM'16, February 22–25, 2016, San Francisco, CA, USA.

ACM ISBN 978-1-4503-3716-8/16/02.
DOI: **http://dx.doi.org/10.1145/2835776.2855116**

2. OBJECTIVE

The objective of the workshop is to bring together interdisciplinary practitioners and researchers from both industrial and academic research labs in order to discuss the state-of-the-art research, as well as future directions in the field of ad targeting in the era of Big Data. We expect the workshop to foster and grow stronger a community of researchers interested in this diverse area, and yield future collaborations and exchanges.

3. TOPICS OF INTEREST

Due to a large diversity of the internet medium, targeted advertising has evolved to encompass many different outlets for the advertisers interested in reaching their target audiences. These include behavioral targeting [9, 14] (where users are targeted based on their general browsing behavior), sponsored search advertising [11, 16] (where ads are targeted towards issued search queries), advertising in social networks [10], e-mail retargeting [15] (targeting users based on their e-mail interaction patterns), site retargeting, video advertising, and app install advertising, to name a few.

The TargetAd workshop provides a forum for researchers from all these areas to share information, challenges, and latest results from latest investigations into this diverse set of applications. The topics of the workshop include, but are not limited to the following:

- Machine learning-based ad targeting;
- Ad targeting in social networks;
- Ad targeting on mobile devices;
- Recommender systems;
- Pay-per-install targeting strategies;
- Machine learning in sponsored search;
- Contextual advertising;
- Large-scale user modeling for ad targeting;

- Data-driven methods for interest targeting;
- Privacy-preserving targeting;
- Behavioral targeting;
- Post-conversion feature attribution;
- Click-conversion modeling in display advertising;
- Machine learning for bidding strategies;
- Content categorization for ad targeting;
- Experience with deployed systems.

4. ORGANIZERS

The TargetAd workshop is organized by a team of researchers with several years of industry experience in the ad targeting field, and builds upon successful event previously organized at the 24th International World Wide Web Conference (WWW 2015). The list of the organizers is presented below:

- Mihajlo Grbovic (Yahoo Labs, USA);
- Nemanja Djuric (Yahoo Labs, USA);
- Vladan Radosavljevic (Yahoo Labs, USA).

5. WORKSHOP PROGRAM

The program will be presented in form of a half-day workshop, with several invited talks from the leading researchers. The list of confirmed speakers includes Shuang Yang, AI and Data Science Lead at Operator, who will talk about large-scale ad targeting and mobile advertising at Operator, and other leaders in the domain.

Additionally, after reviewing a number of high-quality submissions, the PC members have accepted eight research papers on a diverse set of topics, including video advertising, anomaly detection in ad platforms, preserving privacy in advertising, app-install predictions, location-based advertising, personalized search in e-commerce, and novel forms of user representations for ad targeting. The full list of paper is given bellow:

- Bowen Zhou and Shahriar Shariat (Turn Inc.), "Finding Needle in a Million Metrics: Anomaly Detection in a Large-scale Computational Advertising Platform";
- Yukihiro Tagami, Hayato Kobayashi, Shingo Ono, and Akira Tajima (Yahoo Japan), "Distributed Representations of Web Browsing Sequences for Ad Targeting";
- Ratko Orlandic (Yahoo Inc.), "Sponsored Video Advertising: Filling the Void between Online and TV Advertising";
- Chih-Ya Shen (Research Center for Information Technology Innovation, Academia Sinica) et al., "On Spatial-Aware Viral Marketing for Location-based Advertisements";
- Ian Nathan Anggono (University of New South Wales), Hamed Haddadi (Queen Mary University of London), and Mohamed Ali Kaafar (Data61), "Preserving Privacy in Geo-Targeted Advertising";
- Zhen Xia, Musen Wen, Liang Wang, Qiang Ma, Datong Chen, and Peiji Chen (Yahoo Inc.), "Building a Bi-directed Recommendation System for Mobile Users and App-install Ad Campaigns";
- Brendan Kitts (PrecisionDemand), Garrett Badeau (Adap.tv), Davood Shamsi (AOL Platforms), and Rob Luenberger (AOL Platforms), "Demographic Prediction of Web Requests from Labeled Aggregate Data";
- Yi-An Chen (Yahoo Taiwan) et al., "Toward Personalized Product Search for eCommerce Sites: A Case Study in Yahoo! Taiwan".

Acknowledgements

Putting together TargetAd 2016 was a team effort. We would like to thank the speakers and the authors for providing the content of this year's program. We are also very grateful to the members of the Program Committee, who worked diligently in reviewing papers and providing constructive feedback for the authors.

6. REFERENCES

[1] R. K. Chellappa and R. G. Sin. Personalization versus privacy: An empirical examination of the online consumer's dilemma. *Information Technology and Management*, 6(2-3):181–202, 2005.

[2] D. Riecken. Personalized views of personalization. *Communications of the ACM*, 43(8):27–28, 2000.

[3] J. Alba, J. Lynch, B. Weitz, C. Janiszewski, R. Lutz, A. Sawyer, and S. Wood. Interactive home shopping: consumer, retailer, and manufacturer incentives to participate in electronic marketplaces. *The Journal of Marketing*, pages 38–53, 1997.

[4] U. Manber, A. Patel, and J. Robison. Experience with personalization on Yahoo! *Communications of the ACM*, 43(8):35, 2000.

[5] A. S. Das, M. Datar, A. Garg, and S. Rajaram. Google news personalization: Scalable online collaborative filtering. In *WWW*, pages 271–280. ACM, 2007.

[6] D. Essex. Matchmaker, matchmaker. *Communications of the ACM*, 52(5):16–17, 2009.

[7] M. Aly, A. Hatch, V. Josifovski, and V. K. Narayanan. Web-scale user modeling for targeting. *WWW*, 2012.

[8] S. Pandey, M. Aly, A. Bagherjeiran, A. Hatch, P. Ciccolo, A. Ratnaparkhi, and M. Zinkevich. Learning to target: what works for behavioral targeting. *CIKM*, 2011.

[9] Chen, Ye, Dmitry Pavlov, and John F. Canny Large-scale behavioral targeting. In *ACM SIGKDD*, 2009.

[10] Grbovic, M., Radosavljevic, V., Djuric, N., Bhamidipati, N., and Nagarajan, A. Gender and Interest Targeting for Sponsored Post Advertising at Tumblr. In *ACM SIGKDD*, pages 1819–1828, 2015.

[11] Grbovic, M., Djuric, N., Radosavljevic, V., Silvestri, F., and Bhamidipati, N. Context-and content-aware embeddings for query rewriting in sponsored search. In *ACM SIGIR*, pages 383–392, 2015.

[12] A. K. Jain, L. Hong, and S. Pankanti. Iab internet advertising revenue report: 2014 results. Technical report, Interactive Advertising Bureau, 2014.

[13] PwC. Global entertainment and media outlook: 2014-2018. Technical report, 2014.

[14] N. Djuric, V. Radosavljevic, M. Grbovic, and N. Bhamidipati. Hidden conditional random fields with deep user embeddings for ad targeting. In *ICDM*, pp. 779–784, 2014.

[15] M. Grbovic, V. Radosavljevic, N. Djuric, N. Bhamidipati, J. Savla, V. Bhagwan, and D. Sharp E-commerce in Your Inbox: Product Recommendations at Scale. In *ACM SIGKDD*, pp. 1809–1818, 2015.

[16] B. J. Jansen and T. Mullen. Sponsored search: An overview of the concept, history, and technology. *International Journal of Electronic Business*, 6(2):114–131, 2008.

WSDM 2016 Workshop on the Ethics of Online Experimentation

Solon Barocas
Princeton
sbarocas@princeton.edu

Fernando Diaz
Microsoft
fdiaz@microsoft.com

1. OVERVIEW AND MOTIVATION

Online experimentation is now a core and near-constant part of the operation of a production online service, such as a web search engine or social media service. These are large-scale experiments that involve research subjects often numbering in the hundreds of thousands and wide-ranging, computer-automated variations in experimental treatment. In some cases, the results of online experiments may be of use internally to optimize system performance (for example, a test may be conducted to help make web page layout decisions). In other cases, the results may be of academic interest (for example, an experiment may be conducted to test a hypothesis about human behavior). Because of their rapid deployment and broad impact, online experimentation systems provide an extremely valuable tool for scientists and engineers.

Despite this statistical power, in some situations, an online experiment can raise difficult ethical questions. One only needs to revisit the conversations resulting from the Facebook emotional contagion experiment to understand that some experiments may, at the very least, warrant careful review before being conducted. Since this episode, scholarship published mainly in the qualitative research and information law communities indicates that this may not be an isolated incident. Ethical and legal problems probably arise in other online experiments, published or not. As experimentation platforms and users become easily accessible, scientists and practitioners may increasingly put the well-being and trust of end users at risk.

In light of these concerns, organizations often review online experiments before they are actually conducted. In production settings, the review process might vary with respect to formality or standards across companies and even groups within companies. When intended or used for academic publication, experiments or data may have undergone inconsistent review processes, some implementing academic-style institutional review boards and others none at all. Although there is a suggestion that service providers are concerned about the wellbeing of end users, the community does not yet have a framework for "best practices" when it comes to reviewing online experiments, be they for internal or external consumption.

WSDM'16, February 22–25, 2016, San Francisco, CA, USA.
ACM ISBN 978-1-4503-3716-8/16/02..
DOI: http://dx.doi.org/10.1145/2835776.2855117

This workshop aims to draw together researchers from inside and outside of the computer science community in order to present and discuss ethical issues involved in these new experimentation systems. Because these conversations have already been happening separately in several different communities, a dialog such as that proposed by this workshop should provide a clearer understanding for both communities about the issues involved. Unlike the related forums in Section 4, the proposed workshop provides an opportunity for practitioners, who are likely to be attending WSDM, to discuss these issues in depth with peers from disciplines outside of the computer science community. This is especially important as online experimentation begins to draw the attention of policymakers and regulators.

2. SCOPE

We will encourage participation by individuals from the following communities:

- practitioners who run online experimentation in production systems (e.g. web search, computational advertising, news recommendation)
- researchers (both inside and outside companies) involved in the emerging field of computational social science,
- critical commentators from more qualitative traditions in the social sciences, particularly communications and sociology
- scholars of information law and policy
- experts in research ethics

We believe that the first two communities will be well-represented at WSDM, which has traditionally been a venue attracting participation from those in academia and industry who work on large-scale experimentation systems. We also believe that the convenient location of San Francisco will help attract participation from individuals outside of the computer science community, particularly those who work on legal or policy issues at major companies located in the Bay Area.

The types of topics being addressed in this workshop include:

- case studies of ethical issues confronted by or overlooked in planning and executing an online experiment
- comparison between production experiments for internal insights and industrial research for academic publication

- collaboration between academic and industry researchers and the blurring of the line between scholarship and business operations
- existing experiment review processes (e.g. streamlining for rapid development settings), including oversight, accountability, and enforcement mechanisms
- incentive structures that impact whether experiments move ahead or undergo sufficient ethical review
- applicability of established research ethics principles and procedures (e.g., informed consent at scale)
- conditions or aspects of an experiment that act as triggers for ethical review (or exempt the experiment from review)
- ethical issues in online experimentation that do not qualify as human subject research
- formal regulations imposed from outside (e.g., professional societies' policies, industry-wide self-regulatory programs, and law)

3. OBJECTIVES

For computer scientists, we believe that this workshop will promote a new area of research into the design of algorithms or best practices for considering ethics during experimentation, be it for academic or industrial ends. Along these lines, we also hope to have impact on training in data science and machine learning as it relates to ethics. For practitioners, we believe that these discussions may result in more consistent best practices across companies when it comes to ethics and trust from users. This may take the form of employee training or, in some cases, more standardized review processes.

For those outside of the computer science community, we hope that a closer dialog with practitioners will result in more nuanced policy recommendations. A better understanding of the scope and nature of online experimentation–and how it differs from earlier, offline versions of experiments–will be crucial to the development of appropriate and effective policy. Direct contact with practitioners will allow those working on ethics and policy to recognize where existing normative principles, regulatory frameworks, and institutional procedures work well in guiding online experiments and where they need to be revisited or rethought.

4. RELATED WORKSHOPS

The Workshop on Fairness, Accountability, and Transparency in Machine Learning[1], run at NIP 2014 and ICML 2015, brought together computer scientists, legal scholars, advocates, and policymakers to discuss how normative concerns should constrain the practical application of machine learning, but also how these concerns might lend themselves to novel computational solutions.

The Workshop on Ethics for Studying Sociotechnical Systems in a Big Data World[2], run at CSCW 2015, focused on academic research conducted using large (social) data.

When Companies Study Their Customers: The Changing Face of Science, Research, and Ethics[3], run by the Silicon Flatirons Center for Law, Technology, and Entrepreneurship at the University of Colorado and the Tech Policy Lab at the University of Washington, explored the legal and policy questions posed by research conducted by companies.

[1]http://www.fatml.org/

[2]https://cscwethics2015.wordpress.com/

[3]http://www.silicon-flatirons.org/events.php?id=1556

The Workshop on Designing Ethical Review Processes for Big Data Research[4], run by the Future of Privacy Forum, will focus on the legal questions around large-scale online experimentation.

The Workshop on the Ethics of Online Experimentation pushes these existing conversations forward by fostering productive exchange between those directly involved in designing and conducting online experiments and those who have thought through their implications.

5. ORGANIZERS

Solon Barocas is a Postdoctoral Research Associate at the Center for Information Technology Policy at Princeton University. He completed his doctorate in the department of Media, Culture, and Communication at New York University, where he remains an affiliate of the Information Law Institute. Dr. Barocas also works with the Data & Society Research Institute and serves on its National Science Foundation-funded Council for Big Data, Ethics, and Society. His research focuses on emerging computational techniques for data analysis–particularly those based on machine learning–and explores the ethical and epistemological issues that they raise. His recent work exploring the ways that machine learning can give rise to unintentional discrimination won the It won the Best Paper Award at the 2014 Privacy Law Scholars Conference. He has worked with the Intel Science & Technology Center for Social Computing under its Algorithmic Living research theme, the Berkman Center for Internet and Society at Harvard University on the Global Network Initiative, the Center for Global Communication Studies at the University of Pennsylvania on NGOs as information intermediaries, and the Stern School of Business at New York University on its Social Impact program. He has co-organized conferences on Governing Algorithms (NYU 2013) and Web Privacy and Transparency (Princeton University 2014), and started and continues to run a traveling workshop on Fairness, Accountability, and Transparency in Machine Learning (NIPS 2014 and ICML 2015).

Fernando Diaz is a senior researcher at Microsoft Research and a founding member of the MSR-NYC lab. Prior to joining Microsoft, Fernando was a senior scientist at Yahoo Research. His primary research interest is formal information retrieval models and his research experience includes distributed information retrieval approaches to web search, interaction logging and modeling, interactive and faceted retrieval, mining of temporal patterns from news and query logs, cross-lingual information retrieval, graph-based retrieval methods, and synthesizing information from multiple corpora. He received degrees in Computer Science and Political Science, both from the University of Michigan, and a Ph.D. from the University of Massachusetts Amherst. His work on federation won the best paper awards at the WSDM 2009, SIGIR 2009, and ECIR 2011 conferences. His work on crisis informatics has received awards at SIGIR 2011 and ISCRAM 2013. He is a co-organizer of the Temporal Summarization track and Web track at TREC 2013-2015 and WSDM 2014. He is also co-organized workshops on Social Media During Crisis (SIGIR 2011, WWW 2015), Time-Aware Information Access (SIGIR 2012-2014), and Reproducibility of Results (SIGIR 2015).

[4]http://www.futureofprivacy.org/2015/08/26/call-for-papers-beyond-irbs/

Second Workshop on Search and Exploration of X-Rated Information (SEXI'16)

WSDM Workshop Summary

Vanessa Murdock
Microsoft
vanmur@microsoft.com

Charles L.A. Clarke
Waterloo University
claclark@plg.uwaterloo.ca

Jaap Kamps
University of Amsterdam
kamps@uva.nl

Jussi Karlgren
Gavagai & KTH Stockholm
jussi@kth.se

ABSTRACT

Adult content is pervasive on the web, has been a driving factor in the adoption of the Internet medium, and is responsible for a significant fraction of traffic and revenues, yet rarely attracts attention in research. The research questions surrounding adult content access behaviors are unique, and interesting and valuable research in this area can be done ethically. WSDM 2016 features a half day workshop on *Search and Exploration of X-Rated Information* (SEXI) for information access tasks related to adult content. While the scope of the workshop remains broad, special attention is devoted to the privacy and security issues surrounding adult content by inviting keynote speakers with extensive experience on these topics. The recent release of the personal data belonging to customers of the adult dating site Ashley Madison provides a timely context for the focus on privacy and security.

Categories and Subject Descriptors: H.3.30 [**Information Storage and Retrieval**]: General

Keywords: Adult content; Privacy and security; Research ethics; Research practice

1. INTRODUCTION

The second workshop on *Search and Exploration of X-Rated Information* (SEXI) for information access tasks related specifically to adult content was held at WSDM'16 in San Francisco, building on the success of the first workshop at WSDM'13 [5, 6]. The WSDM'13 workshop was the first of this kind that has been presented in the web mining and information retrieval communities, and for WSDM 2016 we proposed a second workshop that brings these issues to the fore. We intend an open and respectful discussion of issues about adult information access, which will illuminate the areas in which adult information access, and user-generated adult content differ from standard information access, and standard user-generated content. We seek to define a set of research areas which represent ethical and legal opportunities to explore the research questions surrounding adult content. Special care is given to ensure that no adult content is actually presented at the workshop, and that the discussion remains respectful and professional, and at the same time fun. While the scope of the workshop remains broad, the workshop has special theme: privacy and security issues surrounding adult content.

The recent release of the personal data belonging to customers of the adult dating site Ashley Madison provides a timely context for the focus on privacy and security [1] The data collected by adult sites, derived from both visitors to the site and providers of content, is arguably more sensitive than other commercial data, because of the controversial nature of the sites themselves.

Adult content is pervasive on the web, has been a driving factor in the adoption of the Internet medium, and is responsible for a significant fraction of traffic and revenues, yet rarely attracts attention in research [1, 2]. The scientific community has spent considerable energy studying user-generated content and information access on the web, to the exclusion of adult content. This is understandable, as the topic is distasteful to some, and requires special legal and ethical considerations when asking employees, contractors and students to analyze and process the data. Furthermore, methods that work for other types of information access behavior are assumed to work for all types of content, including adult content.

We argue that this is an incorrect assumption. In fact, even core concepts such as relevance and diversity, which are fundamental to any application involving information seeking and access, are defined differently for adult content. Adult queries frequently fall outside of the taxonomy of queries (informational, transactional, navigational) that applies to standard web queries. Users searching for adult content frequently have an entertainment need, rather than an information need. Thus, because of the nature of the content, the user may be more satisfied with multiple similar images, than with a set of search results that capture different meanings of the query terms. Furthermore, understanding that a user is searching for a term in an adult context often disambiguates the term.

For example, consider the query "bikini." In a non-adult context, the user might be querying about a ham and cheese sandwich, or may be interested in viewing catalog photos of bikinis to purchase, or perhaps would like images of the Bikini Islands. Since the search engine cannot be sure, one strategy is to represent multiple senses of the query in the results presented to the user. In an adult context, images of catalog photos, sandwiches and islands will be more than an annoyance. Images of people wearing bikinis, although repetitive and not representing a diverse sense of the query term, is what the user is expecting.

[1]http://www.wired.com/2015/08/happened-hackers-posted-stolen-ashley-madison-data/ visited December 2015

WSDM 2016 February 22-25, 2016, San Francisco, CA, USA
ACM ISBN 978-1-4503-3716-8/16/02.
DOI: http://dx.doi.org/10.1145/2835776.2855118

Equal in importance to serving adult content in the best possible way, is the issue of avoiding serving adult content to those who are not looking for it. Many innocuous terms (such as "snake," "cougar," "swimsuit") have adult connotations. Understanding when a person uploading content is uploading adult content is important. Often the only information available to determine the adultness of an image or video are the vague tags the user applies. Complicating the interpretation of the tags is that adult content may be described euphemistically with ordinary nouns that reflect a particular visual imagery. Similarly, when a person issues a query, it is not always clear whether they are searching for adult content, and it is extremely important for the search engine to understand this before serving adult content to a person who is not expecting it.

2. OPEN QUESTIONS

The workshop seeks a greater understanding of the particular issues in accessing adult content, especially user-generated adult content on the web. The discussion is limited to adult content that is legal, although topics such as identifying online predators, child pornography, or human trafficking are within of the scope.

The focus of the workshop on privacy and security issues surrounding adult content, was chosen in order to put this area of research on the agenda, and explore the basic research questions that should be addressed in the field, the types of data needed for research, and and the barriers to doing research this area. Due to the lack of attention to this area of research there are many open questions. These questions include:

Classification Even researchers and search applications not interested in adult content will have to deal with it in order to avoid it—presenting adult content to innocuous searchers is clearly a massive failure both for the individual searcher as well as for the reputation of the service. What are automatic methods for identifying adult content, in particular adult user-generated content? How can we identify adult content in video, images, and text? What is the best way to identify adult query intent, and deal with ambiguous requests? What are the appropriate ad placement strategies in adult content?

Access Access to adult content seems to require a different approach than the ubiquitous navigation search—with searchers exhibiting an exploratory information seeking behavior, characterized by a diverse set of relevance criteria. How should adult content be ranked? How should search, exploration, and recommendation be balanced? How does searching adult content relate to search on adult chat sites and social networks? Is there a benefit to personalizing adult content?

Evaluation Given the distinct nature of adult content and the diverse relevance criteria, appropriate evaluation is crucial. What is a relevant result, and what are suitable metrics for relevance? Is adult content a recall-oriented, or precision-oriented task? What is the right level of evaluation—individual requests or whole search sessions? What is similarity and diversity in adult content? How important is the avoidance of failure, relative to success? Are searchers for adult content more tolerant of non-relevant results?

Ethics What are the ethical issues in working with adult content in an academic environment? What are the ethical implications for the search industry, given that it partly facilitates the online adult industry? How can adult material be made available so as to promote responsible behavior through the whole chain from production to consumption? Is adult user-generated content more ethical than professionally produced media?

Security and Privacy Adult content is one of the primary vehicles for malware on the internet. In addition, as many adult content sites collect personally identifying data (such as user names and credit card numbers), particular care must be taken to protect the data collected from visitors to the sites, as well as content providers. While users of these sites are not typically doing anything illegal, they provide an enticing target to thieves because of the controversial nature of the industry. In addition, as the adult entertainment industry moves toward content generated by private citizens, and away from large commercial producers, the potential for harm to private citizens producing the content increases.

The workshop aims to define a set of research areas, to elucidate the special issues surrounding the access of user-generated adult content. A set of best-practices for working with this data in an academic environment was discussed, and a research agenda for the near future was proposed. Special care is taken to select and moderate the program to present the information in a respectful and scientific manner.

3. FORMAT AND PROGRAM

The workshop is planned to feature two keynote speakers, the first keynote addressing the technical engineering challenges of given access to, or avoiding, adult content on the Web, and the second keynote addressing the social aspects of online adult content.

Accepted papers include Largillier et al. [3], who investigate the efficient filtering of adult web content, aiming to prevent surfacing this content in the wrong context. Mattmann et al. [4] study detecting human trafficking based on crawling ads related to them, revealing invaluable cues for law enforcement and governmental organizations to identify victims and intervene to aid them.

Short presentations by participants are also planned, along with a closing panel. A full report of the workshop will appear in the June 2016 issue of SIGIR Forum.

REFERENCES

[1] L. Azzopardi. Searching for unlawful carnal knowledge. In N. J. Belkin, C. L. A. Clarke, N. Gao, J. Kamps, and J. Karlgren, editors, *Proceedings of the SIGIR'11 Workshop on "entertain me" : Supporting Complex Search Tasks*, pages 17–18. ACM Press, 2011.

[2] A. C. Halavais. Small pornographies. *SIGGROUP Bulletin*, 25(2):19–22, 2005. URL http://doi.acm.org/10.1145/1067721.1067725.

[3] T. Largillier, G. Peyronnet, and S. Peyronnet. Efficient filtering of adult content using textual information. In Murdock et al. [7], pages 9–15.

[4] C. Mattmann, G. Yang, H. Manjunatha, T. G. N, A. J. Zhou, J. Luo, and L. J. McGibbney. Multimedia metadata-based forensics in human trafficking web data. In Murdock et al. [7], pages 16–20.

[5] V. Murdock, C. L. A. Clarke, J. Kamps, and J. Karlgren. Report on the workshop on search and exploration of x-rated information (SEXI 2013). *SIGIR Forum*, 47(1):31–37, June 2013. http://dx.doi.org/10.1145/2433396.2433507.

[6] V. Murdock, C. L. A. Clarke, J. Kamps, and J. Karlgren, editors. *SEXI'13: Proceedings of the WSDM'13 Workshop on Search and Exploration of X-rated Information*, 2013. ACM Press.

[7] V. Murdock, C. L. A. Clarke, J. Kamps, and J. Karlgren, editors. *SEXI'16: Proceedings of the WSDM'16 Workshop on Search and Exploration of X-rated Information*, 2016. ACM Press.

Mining Complaints to Improve a Product: a Study about Problem Phrase Extraction from User Reviews

Elena Tutubalina
Big Data and Textual Analysis Lab
Higher Institute of Information Technologies and Information Systems
Kazan Federal University, Kazan, 420008, Russia
elvtutubalina@kpfu.ru

ABSTRACT

The rapidly growing availability of user reviews has become an important resource for companies to detect customer dissatisfaction from textual opinions. There have been few recent studies conducted on business-related opinion tasks to extract more refined opinions about a product's quality problems or technical failures. The focus of this study is the extraction of problem phrases, mentioned in user reviews about products. We explore main opinion mining tasks to determine whether given text from reviews contains a mention of a problem. We formulate research questions and propose knowledge-based methods and probabilistic models to classify users' phrases and extract latent problem indicators, aspects and related sentiments from online reviews.

Keywords

opinion mining; user reviews; problem phrase extraction

1. PROBLEM PHRASE EXTRACTION

At the present time much work has been focused on opinion mining tasks, which is useful for customers and including sentiment classification of negative and positive texts, extraction of products' features and overall ratings from reviews. An important task has received less attention – *problem phrase extraction*, that is, extraction of information about products' failures and missing functionality, which is related to companies' requirements or developers' activities and causes customer dissatisfaction with products.

During the last decades, consumer products have grown in complexity, and consumer dissatisfaction has been increasingly caused by usability problems, in addition to problems with technical failures. While companies resolve bugs and errors with technical support services, the existence of the 'No-Fault Found' phenomenon was discovered in recent studies, also called *soft usability problems*. Moreover, consumers with complaints could also reproduce negative word-of-mouth publicity through social media sites. Therefore, this scenario illustrates the importance of the described task.

WSDM 2016 February 22-25, 2016, San Francisco, CA, USA

ACM ISBN 978-1-4503-3716-8/16/02.
DOI: http://dx.doi.org/10.1145/2835776.2855080

The main research problem of this thesis is to investigate the content of user reviews with the aims of examining various causes of customer complaints about technical and non-technical problems: *How to discover, model and classify refined information from user opinions in order to improve a product quality and user satisfaction of a product.* The research problem consists of five specific research questions. We start by analyzing user reviews from the companies' perspective: ***RQ1:*** *How do we define a problem with a product and detect problem phrases without a loss of quality after switching the product domain?* [1]. We extract an associated vocabulary of opinion words (problem indicators) for each type of problem and develop knowledge-based methods. Next, we go through classification errors: ***RQ2:*** *How does the performance of the proposed classification methods depend on company-specific product targets, which affect customer satisfaction?* [2]. Classification results are presented on datasets with reviews about electronics, cars, home tools, and baby products. Then we employ probabilistic modeling techniques to extract problem targets mentioned in user reviews, and to detect problem indicators in texts: ***RQ3:*** *How do we discover both problem words and product targets from a collection of reviews?* [3]. The model contains two latent distributions over topical aspects and over indicators separately. We use domain-independent knowledge about problem phrases to set the model's priors. Finally, we plan to explore how characteristics of an app with review's sentiment influences the type of feedback: ***RQ4-RQ5:*** *What is the impact of sentiment as topic-specific information about user opinions? How do we automatically detect differences in the distribution of problems for price groups of products and demographic groups of customers?* We plan to add hidden and observed variables into the proposed model.

Acknowledgments This work was supported by Russian Science Foundation (Project no. 15-11-10019). Thanks to the ACM SIGIR for a Student Travel Grant.

References

[1] V. Ivanov and E. Tutubalina. Clause-based approach to extracting problem phrases from user reviews of products. In *Analysis of Images, Social Networks and Texts*, pages 229–236. Springer, 2014.

[2] E. Tutubalina. Dependency-based problem phrase extraction from user reviews of products. In *Text, Speech, and Dialogue*, pages 199–206. Springer, 2015.

[3] E. Tutubalina. Target-based topic model for problem phrase extraction. In *Advances in Information Retrieval*, pages 271–277. Springer, 2015.

Web-scale Multimedia Search for Internet Video Content

Lu Jiang*
School of Computer Science
Carnegie Mellon University
Pittsburgh, PA 15213
lujiang@cs.cmu.edu

ABSTRACT

The Internet has been witnessing an explosion of video content. According to a Cisco study, video content is estimated to account for 80% of all the entire world's internet traffic by 2019. Video data are becoming one of the most valuable sources to assess information and knowledge. However, existing video search solutions are still based on text matching (*text-to-text* search), and could fail for the huge volumes of videos that have little relevant metadata or no metadata at all. The need for large-scale and intelligent video search, which bridges the gap between the user's information need and the video content, seems to be urgent.

In this thesis, we propose an accurate, efficient and scalable search method for video content. As opposed to text matching, the proposed method relies on automatic video content understanding, and allows for intelligent and flexible search paradigms over the video content, including *text-to-video* and *text&video-to-video* search. Fig. 1 illustrates an example. Suppose our goal is to search the videos about birthday party. In traditional *text-to-text* queries, we have to search the keywords in the user-generated metadata (titles or descriptions). In a *text-to-video* query, however, we might look for visual clues in the video content such as "cake", "gift" and "kids", audio clues like "birthday song" and "cheering sound", or visible text like "happy birthday". See Fig. 1(a). *Text-to-video* queries are flexible and can be further refined by Boolean and temporal operators. After watching the retrieved videos, the user may select a few interesting videos to find more relevant videos like these. This can be achieved by issuing a *text&video-to-video* query which adds the selected video examples to the query. See Fig. 1(b).

The proposed method provides a new dimension of looking at content-based video search, from finding a simple concept like "puppy" to searching a complex incident like "a scene in urban area where people running away after an explosion". To achieve this ambitious goal, we propose several novel methods focusing on accuracy, efficiency and scalability in the novel search paradigm. First, we introduce a novel self-paced curriculum learning theory that allows for training more accurate semantic concepts. Second, we propose a novel and scalable approach to index semantic concepts that can significantly improve the search efficiency with minimum accuracy loss. Third, we design a novel video reranking algorithm that can boost accuracy for video retrieval.

The extensive experiments demonstrate that the proposed methods are able to surpass state-of-the-art accuracy on multiple datasets. In addition, our method can efficiently scale up the search to hundreds of millions videos, and only takes about 0.2 second to search a semantic query on a collection of 100 million videos, 1 second to process a hybrid query over 1 million videos. Based on the proposed methods, we implement E-Lamp Lite, the first of its kind large-scale semantic search engine for Internet videos. According to National Institute of Standards and Technology (NIST), it achieved the best accuracy in the TRECVID Multimedia Event Detection (MED) 2013, 2014 and 2015, the most representative task for content-based video search. To the best of our knowledge, E-Lamp Lite is the first content-based semantic search engine that is capable of indexing and searching a collection of 100 million videos.

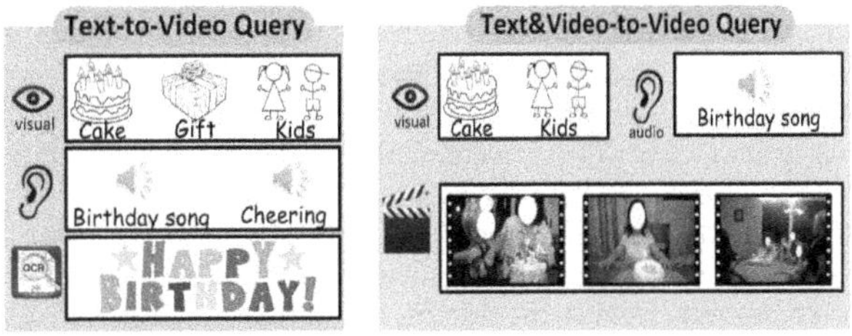

(a) text-to-video (b) text&video-to-video

Figure 1: Proposed queries on "birthday party".

Categories and Subject Descriptors

H.3.1 [**Information Storage and Retrieval**]: Content Analysis and Indexing; H.3.3 [**Information Search and Retrieval**]: Search process; I.2.10 [**Vision and Scene Understanding**]: Video analysis

Keywords

Big Data; Web Search; Video Content Search; Content-based Retrieval; Multimedia Event Detection

*This work was partially supported by the Intelligence Advanced Research Projects Activity (IARPA) via Department of Interior National Business Center contract number D11PC20068.

WSDM 2016 February 22-25, 2016, San Francisco, CA, USA

ACM ISBN 978-1-4503-3716-8/16/02.
DOI: http://dx.doi.org/10.1145/2835776.2855081

Affective Computing of Image Emotion Perceptions

Sicheng Zhao

School of Computer Science and Technology
Harbin Institute of Technology, Harbin, China
schzhao@gmail.com

Images can convey rich semantics and evoke strong emotions in viewers. The research of my PhD thesis focuses on image emotion computing (IEC), which aims to predict the emotion perceptions of given images. The development of IEC is greatly constrained by two main challenges: affective gap and subjective evaluation [5]. Previous works mainly focused on finding features that can express emotions better to bridge the affective gap, such as elements-of-art based features [2] and shape features [1].

Based on the emotion representation models, including categorical emotion states (CES) and dimensional emotion space (DES) [5], three different tasks are traditionally performed on IEC: affective image classification, regression and retrieval. The state-of-the-art methods on the three above tasks are image-centric, focusing on the dominant emotions for the majority of viewers.

For my PhD thesis, I plan to answer the following questions: 1. Compared to the low-level elements-of-art based features, can we find some higher level features that are more interpretable and have stronger link to emotions? 2. Are the emotions that are evoked in viewers by an image subjective and different? If they are, how can we tackle the user-centric emotion prediction? 3. For image-centric emotion computing, can we predict the emotion distribution instead of the dominant emotion category?

1. The artistic elements must be carefully arranged and orchestrated into meaningful regions and images to describe specific semantics and emotions. The rules, tools or guidelines of arranging and orchestrating the elements-of-art in an artwork are known as the principles-of-art, which consider various artistic aspects, including *balance*, *emphasis*, *harmony*, *variety*, *gradation*, *movement*, *rhythm*, and *proportion* [5]. We systematically study and formulize the former 6 artistic principles, explaining the concepts and translating these concepts into mathematical formulae.

2. The images in Abstract dataset [2] were labeled by 14 people on average. 81% images are assigned with 5 to 8 emotions. So the perceived emotions of different viewers may vary. To further demonstrate this observation, we set up a large-scale dataset, named Image-Emotion-Social-Net dataset, with over 1 million images downloaded from Flickr. To get the personalized emotion labels, firstly we use traditional lexicon-based methods as in [4] to obtain the text segmentation results of the title, tags and descriptions from uploaders for expected emotions and the comments from viewers for actual emotions. Then we compute the average value of valence, arousal and dominance of the segmentation results as ground truth for dimensional emotion representation based on recently published VAD norms of 13,915 English lemmas [3]. After refinement, we obtain 1,434,080 emotion labels on 1,012,901 images uploaded by 11,347 users and commented by 106,688 users.

WSDM 2016 February 22-25, 2016, San Francisco, CA, USA

ACM ISBN 978-1-4503-3716-8/16/02.

DOI: http://dx.doi.org/10.1145/2835776.2855082

From the statistics, we can conclude that the emotions that are evoked in viewers by an image are subjective and different. Therefore, predicting the personalized emotion perceptions for each viewer is more reasonable and important. In such cases, the emotion prediction tasks become user-centric. Intuitively, four types of factors can influence the emotion perception: visual content, social context, temporal evolution, and location influence. We initially propose rolling multi-task hypergraph learning to jointly combine these factors for personalized emotion perception prediction [8].

3. By the statistical analysis on the images viewed by a large population, we observe that though subjective and different, the personalized emotion perceptions follow certain distributions. Predicting the emotion probability distribution instead of a single dominant emotion for an image is accordant with the subjective evaluation, which reveals the difference of emotional reactions between users. Generally, the distribution prediction task can be formulized as a regression problem. For different emotion representation models, the distribution prediction varies slightly [7, 6].

For CES, the task aims to predict the discrete probability of different emotion categories, the sum of which equals to 1. We propose to use shared sparse learning to predict the discrete probability distribute of image emotion [7]. For DES, the task usually transfers to predict the parameters of specified continuous probability distribution, the form of which should be firstly decided, such as Gaussian distribution [6].

This work was supported by the NSFC (61472103, 61133003).

1. REFERENCES

[1] X. Lu, P. Suryanarayan, R. B. Adams Jr, J. Li, M. G. Newman, and J. Z. Wang. On shape and the computability of emotions. In *ACM MM*, 2012.

[2] J. Machajdik and A. Hanbury. Affective image classification using features inspired by psychology and art theory. In *ACM MM*, 2010.

[3] A. B. Warriner, V. Kuperman, and M. Brysbaert. Norms of valence, arousal, and dominance for 13,915 english lemmas. *Behavior Research Methods*, 45(4):1191–1207, 2013.

[4] Y. Yang, J. Jia, S. Zhang, B. Wu, Q. Chen, J. Li, C. Xing, and J. Tang. How do your friends on social media disclose your emotions? In *AAAI*, 2014.

[5] S. Zhao, Y. Gao, X. Jiang, H. Yao, T.-S. Chua, and X. Sun. Exploring principles-of-art features for image emotion recognition. In *ACM MM*, 2014.

[6] S. Zhao, H. Yao, and X. Jiang. Predicting continuous probability distribution of image emotions in valence-arousal space. In *ACM MM*, 2015.

[7] S. Zhao, H. Yao, X. Jiang, and X. Sun. Predicting discrete probability distribution of image emotions. In *IEEE ICIP*, 2015.

[8] S. Zhao, H. Yao, W. Xie, and X. Jiang. User-centric affective computing of image emotion perceptions. In *AAAI*, 2016.

Event Search and Analytics

Detecting Events in Semantically Annotated Corpora for Search & Analytics

Dhruv Gupta
Max Planck Institute for Informatics, Saarbrücken, Germany
Saarbrücken Graduate School of Computer Science, Saarbrücken, Germany
dhgupta@mpi-inf.mpg.de

CCS Concepts
•**Information systems→Information systems applications; Data mining; Information extraction;**

Keywords
Information Retrieval; Text Analytics; Text Summarization; Semantic Annotations; Diversity & Novelty; Semantic Search

ABSTRACT

Information retrieval systems have largely relied on word statistics in text corpora to satisfy information needs of users by retrieving documents with high relevance for a given keyword query. In my PhD research I hypothesize that information needs of users can be satisfied to a greater extent by using *events* as means of navigation in text corpora. An event, in my context is an act performed by certain actor(s) at a specific location during a specific time interval. With the availability of tools that can provide us with accurate semantic annotations in form of named entities, geographic locations, and temporal expressions; we can leverage growing number of knowledge resources such as Wikipedia and ontologies such as Freebase [1] to understand natural language text and mine important events. Formally we can state the central hypothesis as follows:

> **Central Hypothesis** Given text corpora with semantic annotations; traditional information retrieval models can be improved by utilizing knowledge about *events* and using *events* as proxies for information needs.

Consider the text [1] below. Having semantic annotations in this text we can now devise algorithms that can deduce that the event is that of Usain Bolt winning Olympic competition in Beijing, China.

> ... Beijing$^{\langle Geo:(39.55,116.23)\rangle}$ where Bolt $^{\langle Wiki:Usain\_Bolt\rangle}$ announced himself to the world with two Olympic golds and two world records in 2008$^{\langle Time:[01-01-2008,31-12-2008]\rangle}$ ...

[1] http://www.bbc.com/sport/0/athletics/34032366

WSDM 2016 February 22-25, 2016, San Francisco, CA, USA

ACM ISBN 978-1-4503-3716-8/16/02.
DOI: http://dx.doi.org/10.1145/2835776.2855083

Research Objectives. Given text corpora with semantic annotations, I describe three important research problems: *i.* identifying important events; *ii.* using events for retrieval tasks; and *iii.* using events for analytics.

Identifying Important Events. *Events* are the proposed building blocks for further text analysis. Given semantically annotated text corpora, the objective shall be to report important events given a multidimensional query consisting either of keywords, time, geographical location or named entities. For example, given keyword query `summer olympics`; the reported events will be the various summer Olympics with their location, time interval, participating named entities, and keywords describing the events.

Diversifying and Summarizing Search Results are retrieval tasks that try to address the information need underlying an ambiguous query at different levels of textual granularity. I propose to use the mined set of *events* as information intents. This will allow for automatic creation of *event timelines* or *entity biographies.*

Semantic Search and Analytics. The mined set of *events* can further be utilized for search and analytics. The objective would to first model the mined set of events as a *data cube* (see Figure 1) and subsequently provide *data cube operations* [2]: roll, slice, dice, drill up, and drill down.

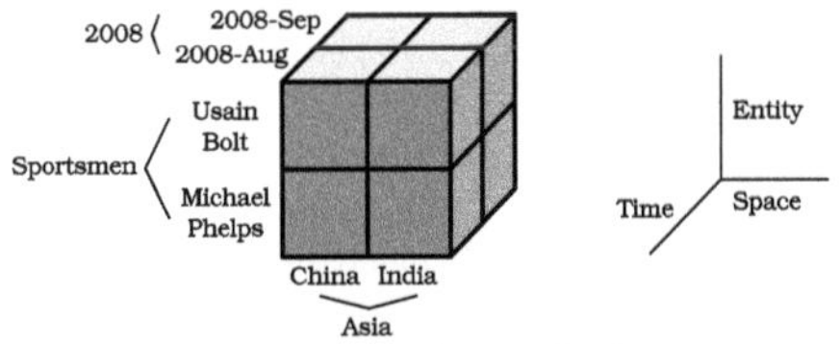

Figure 1: Example data cube for events

Conclusion. In this abstract I laid out an outline of the research work that I envisage to carry out for my PhD dissertation. The research in its culmination shall provide us methods to computationally extract world history as sequence of temporally ordered events and portray future events to take place from semantically annotated corpora. The research would also provide ways to perform semantic search and large scale event analytics on these annotated corpora.

REFERENCES

[1] Bollacker K. et al. Freebase: A collaboratively created graph database for structuring human knowledge. SIGMOD'08.

[2] Han J. et al. *Data Mining: Concepts and Techniques.* Morgan Kaufmann Publishers Inc., 3rd edition, 2011.

[3] Gupta D. *Event Search and Analytics.* WSDM'16 Doctoral Consortium.

Understanding Diffusion Processes: Inference and Theory

Xinran He
University of Southern California
Los Angeles, CA ,United States
xinranhe@usc.edu

ABSTRACT

With increasing popularity of social media and social networks sites, analyzing the social networks offers great potential to shed light on human social structure and provides great marketing opportunities. Usually, social network analysis starts with extracting or learning the social network and the associated parameters. Contrary to other analytical tasks, this step is highly non-trivial due to amorphous nature of social ties and the challenges of noisy and incomplete observations. My research focuses on improving accuracy in inferring the network as well as analyzing the consequences when the extracted network is noisy or erroneous. To be more precise, I propose to study the following two questions with a special focus on analyzing diffusion behaviors: (1) How to utilize special properties of social networks to improve accuracy of the extracted network under noisy and missing data; (2) How to characterize the impact of noise in the inferred network and carry out robust analysis and optimization.

Usually the first step towards social influence analysis is to infer the diffusion network. Assuming a probabilistic model of influence and a model of how the timing of individuals' adoption decisions correlates, one can use these data to estimate the strengths of influence between pairs of individuals. However, existing approaches for Network Inference rely on the common assumption that the observations used to train the models are complete, while missing observations are commonplace in practice due to time or technical limitations in data collection. Therefore, I propose to study the impact of incomplete observations and design efficient method to compensate for noise or incompleteness in observed data. I propose to exploit the fact that social networks have more specific structure than arbitrary graphs. A joint estimation of the graph generation model and the actual network structure is likely to significantly improve the estimation accuracy. Moreover, incorporating the content information of the cascade also has potential to improve the inference accuracy. Therefore, I propose to combine the Correlated Topic Model [1] and Hawkes Process [5, 4, 6] into a unified model to utilize content information [2].

Due to noise or missing data in the observations, even in the best case, one would expect that the inferred network structure and link strengths will only be an approximation to the truth; in other words, noise in the data will be pervasive for inferred social networks. I propose to focus on the algorithmic question of *Influence Maximization* [3] in the context of noisy social network data. More specifically, I propose to consider the following questions: Given an instance of an Influence Model, with level of mis-estimation: (1) Decide whether the objective function on this instance varies smoothly with perturbations to the parameters. (2) If the dependence is smooth, how to find a robustly near-optimal solution.

WSDM 2016 February 22-25, 2016, San Francisco, CA, USA

ACM ISBN 978-1-4503-3716-8/16/02.

DOI: http://dx.doi.org/10.1145/2835776.2855084

Categories and Subject Descriptors

[**Human-centered computing**]: Social networks

Keywords

Diffusion process, Network Inference, Influence Maximization, Social network analysis

1. REFERENCES

[1] D. Blei and J. Lafferty. Correlated topic models. In *Proc. 18th Advances in Neural Information Processing Systems*, pages 147–152, 2006.

[2] X. He, T. Rekatsinas, J. Foulds, L. Getoor, and Y. Liu. Hawkestopic: A joint model for network inference and topic modeling from text-based cascades. In *Proc. 32nd Intl. Conf. on Machine Learning*, 2015.

[3] D. Kempe, J. Kleinberg, and E. Tardos. Maximizing the spread of influence in a social network. In *Proc. 9th Intl. Conf. on Knowledge Discovery and Data Mining*, pages 137–146, 2003.

[4] S. W. Linderman and R. P. Adams. Discovering latent network structure in point process data. In *Proc. 31st Intl. Conf. on Machine Learning*, 2014.

[5] S.-H. Yang and H. Zha. Mixture of mutually exciting processes for viral diffusion. In *Proc. 30th Intl. Conf. on Machine Learning*, 2013.

[6] K. Zhou, H. Zha, and L. Song. Learning social infectivity in sparse low-rank network using multi-dimensional hawkes processes. In *Proc. 30th Intl. Conf. on Machine Learning*, 2013.

E-commerce Product Recommendation by Personalized Promotion and Total Surplus Maximization

Qi Zhao
University of California, Santa Cruz
1506 High St., Santa Cruz, 95060, CA, USA
qzhao2@ucsc.edu

ABSTRACT

Existing recommendation algorithms treat recommendation problem as rating prediction and the recommendation quality is measured by RMSE or other similar metrics. However, we argued that when it comes to E-commerce product recommendation, recommendation is more than rating prediction by realizing the fact price plays a critical role in recommendation result. In this work, we propose to build E-commerce product recommender systems based on fundamental economic notions. We first proposed an incentive compatible method that can effectively elicit consumer's willingness-to-pay in a typical E-commerce setting and in a further step, we formalize the recommendation problem as maximizing total surplus. We validated the proposed WTP elicitation algorithm through crowd sourcing and the results demonstrated that the proposed approach can achieve higher seller profit by personalizing promotion. We also proposed a total surplus maximization (TSM) based recommendation framework. We specified TSM by three of the most representative settings - e-commerce where the product quantity can be viewed as infinity, P2P lending where the resource is bounded and freelancer marketing where the resource (job) can be assigned to one freelancer. The experimental results of the corresponding datasets shows that TSM exceeds existing approach in terms of total surplus.

Keywords

E-commerce; recommendation; economics; surplus maximization; personalized promotion

1. RECOMMENDATION BY PERSONALIZED PROMOTION

We proposed to elicit consumer's WTP in E-commerce setting and conduct personalized promotion to improve seller's profit. Our proposed approach comprises two major ingredients BDM auction - which guarantees to be incentive compatible and lottery - which helps collect data at lowest cost.

WSDM 2016 February 22-25, 2016, San Francisco, CA, USA

ACM ISBN 978-1-4503-3716-8/16/02...$15.00

DOI: http://dx.doi.org/10.1145/2835776.2855085

Our experiment setting includes a full-fledged E-commerce product search system similar to Amazon. The system hosts real skin care products from Amazon. The experimental subjects are hired from Amazon Mechanical Turk. Each subject is instructed to go through multiple steps - BDM training (screening unqualified subjects), selecting favorite products, ranking and bidding. Linear regression models are trained on the collected bidding data. Given any user-product pair, optimal pricing is sought by maximizing the expected seller profit. The proposed approach is evaluated against several baseline algorithms using RMSE and seller profit as metrics. The experimental results suggest that the proposed approach significantly outperforms baseline algorithms. Please refer to [1] for details.

2. RECOMMENDATION BY TOTAL SURPLUS MAXIMIZATION

We proposed to treating the recommendation problem as matching producer and consumer so that the total surplus will be maximized. This is motivated by the fact that the perceived value of the same product vary across individuals. Hence, the total surplus of selling the same products to different consumers might be different. We argued that it is important for recommender systems to consider the benefits of both consumers and producers. As a result, total surplus maximization is a sensible optimizing objective to achieve this goal.

We proposed a TSM based recommendation framework that can easily specified for various applications such as E-commerce product recommendation, P2P lending and freelancer marketing. In particular, the personalized utility and product quantity constraint can be easily specified according to application. We showed that each specification can be treated as a standard constrained optimization problem. We evaluated the proposed framework on real datasets from E-commerce, P2P lending and freelancer marketing and the results suggest that our approach yields much higher total surplus that standard collaborative filtering based techniques.

3. REFERENCES

[1] Q. Zhao, Y. Zhang, D. Friedman, and F. Tan. E-commerce recommendation with personalized promotion. In *Proceedings of the 9th ACM Conference on Recommender Systems*, pages 219–226. ACM, 2015.

Detecting Social Media Icebergs by Their Tips: Rumors, Persuasion Campaigns, and Information Needs

Zhe Zhao
Department of EECS
University of Michigan
zhezhao@umich.edu

ABSTRACT

Online activities of more than one billion social media users all over the world form a resourceful ocean of data. Many social media mining techniques try to explore this ocean and extract different types of resources. In this thesis, we present a framework that can detect different types of meaningful social media phenomena. They usually can be viewed as a group of online activities from many social media users with a common or similar objective, such as spreading of rumors, bursting information needs on events and products, or asking for support of an action. These different types of social media phenomena are relatively rare but can be very influential.

Detecting them is challenging according to its characteristics. Each phenomenon contains a collection of activities that usually take variety of forms. Taking the spreading of rumor in social media as an example, one rumor may be spread in different forms of statements and expressions. And it can be very hard to distinguish them from statements from trustful sources. Existing work of detecting different types of social media phenomena usually adopts classifiers trained on features of a single activity or cluster of activities [1]. However, the features from single activity are not sufficient for many detection tasks. And the features from cluster of activities will not be significant until that cluster becomes large enough, which cannot be used in early stage detection .

In this thesis, we propose to detect meaningful social media phenomena by signal user behaviors observed at an early stage. Just like spotting icebergs in the ocean by their tips, in our case, the tip of a social media iceberg is a small proportion of activities that exist only in social media icebergs. And they can be found even at the early stage. Therefore, we design our detection framework to first detect these specific signal activities. Then we will use them to understand the characteristic of the entire collection of activities from social media phenomena . What we learned can be used to train accurate classifiers to identify whether a collection of activities containing signal activities is a target social media phenomenon or not. This framework is generic and can be applied on detecting many different types of collective activities in social media. We apply our framework on detecting three types of meaningful social media phenomena, i.e., emerging information needs, trending rumors, and persuasion campaigns.

To detect emerging information needs, we train a classifier to detect user asking question behaviors as signals. We analyze all the questions detected by this classifier and extract keywords from their content to identify emerging information needs. We find out that as signal activities, the questions being asked are substantially different from other types of activities. The keywords extracted from those questions have a considerable power of predicting the trends of Google queries[2].

In our work of detecting trending rumors[3], we find that when there is a rumor, even though most posts do not raise questions about it, there may be a few that do. These questions suspecting whether a piece of information is true or not can help us identify controversial and unconfirmed statements, such as social media rumors. Therefore, we adopt this type enquiry activities as signal to detect rumors. Experiment results show that our rumor detection approach can detect social media rumors at early stage effectively and efficiently.

At last, we propose to apply and improve our framework to detect another very important type of social media phenomena, i.e., persuasion campaigns. We will first study and provide a formal definition of social media persuasion campaigns. Then we will implement our detection framework and experiment it with different signal activities. We also propose to develop an algorithm to discover activities opposing the detected persuasion campaigns. We will conduct experiments on Twitter to check the effectiveness and efficiency of our method.

WSDM 2016 February 22-25, 2016, San Francisco, CA, USA

ACM ISBN 978-1-4503-3716-8/16/02.

DOI: http://dx.doi.org/10.1145/2835776.2855086

Categories and Subject Descriptors

H.3.3 [**Information Search and Retrieval**]: Text Mining

Keywords

Social Media Phenomena, Early Detection, Signal Activities

1. REFERENCES

[1] S. Kong, Q. Mei, L. Feng, F. Ye, and Z. Zhao. Predicting bursts and popularity of hashtags in real-time. In *Proceedings of the 37th international ACM SIGIR conference on Research & development in information retrieval*, pages 927–930. ACM, 2014.

[2] Z. Zhao and Q. Mei. Questions about questions: An empirical analysis of information needs on twitter. In *WWW*, pages 1545–1556, 2013.

[3] Z. Zhao, P. Resnick, and Q. Mei. Enquiring minds: Early detection of rumors in social media from enquiry posts. In *WWW*, pages 1395–1405, 2015.

User Modeling in Large Social Networks

Yuxiao Dong
Department of Computer Science and Engineering
Interdisciplinary Center for Network Science and Applications (iCeNSA)
University of Notre Dame, Notre Dame, IN 46556
ydong1@nd.edu

ABSTRACT

This proposal aims to harness the power of data, social, and network sciences to model user behavior in social networks. Specifically, we focus on individual users and investigate the interplay between their behavior and subsequently emergent social phenomena. Work in this proposal unveils the significant social strategies that are used by people to satisfy their social needs. We apply computational methods to address user modeling problems, including demographic inference, link recommendation, and social impact prediction. The proposed research work can be translated into applications in large social systems, such as mobile communication, online social media, and academic collaboration.

Keywords

user behavior; social impact; computational social science

1. INTRODUCTION

The interactions between individuals form the structural backbone of human societies, which manifest as networks. In a network sense, individuals matter in the ways in which their connections activate the emergence of new phenomena at larger, societal levels. In this proposal, we focus on modeling the various ways that different users are embedded in and interact within a network.

As the emergence of online social networking sites in the first years of the 21st century, social network data has been explosively explored and studied. Essentially, a cornucopia of scientific advances, such as link prediction [9], influence maximization [8], community detection [7], and diffusion processes [10], have been and are being achieved by researchers from diverse communities. Indeed, social network research has developed itself as an interdisciplinary field, which attracts attention and simultaneously benefits from a variety of disciplines, such as data mining, sociology, physics, business and so on.

In this proposal, we aim to harness the power of social, data, and network sciences to model user behavior in social networks from multiple dimensions. Work on sociodemogrpahic modeling [5, 3] discovers that during the active dating period, younger users are active in broadening social connections with males and females alike, while after reaching 35 years of age people tend to keep small, closed, and same-gender social circles. We also propose a data science model *WhoAmI* that demonstrates a greater than 80% potential predictability for inferring users' gender from phone call behavior and 73% for users' age from text messaging interactions. Work on modeling link formation [6, 4] studies the problem of link prediction in coupled networks, where we have the structure information of one source network and the interactions between this network and another target network, and aim to predict the missing links in the target network. We present a computational framework *CoupledLP* that is able to help a mobile operator achieve an accuracy of 80% for uncovering the top links of its competitor's network. Work on modeling social impact [1, 2] finds that in academic social networks, a researcher's authority on the publication topic and the venue in which a paper is published are crucial factors to the increase of his or her h-index, while the topic popularity and the co-authors' h-indices are of surprisingly little relevance. By leveraging relevant factors, we can predict whether a newly (previously) published paper will contribute to an author's future h-index with an F_1 score of 0.77 (0.99). To this end, modeling users in social networks offers the potential to understand the principles that underpin our highly connected world—from individuals, to communities, to societies.

Acknowledgments. The Ph.D. study is supported in part by the Army Research Laboratory under Cooperative Agreement Number W911NF-09-2-0053, the U.S. Air Force Office of Scientific Research (AFOSR) and the Defense Advanced Research Projects Agency (DARPA) grant #FA9550-12-1-0405, and the National Science Foundation (NSF) Grants BCS-1229450 and IIS-1447795.

2. REFERENCES

[1] Y. Dong, R. A. Johnson, and N. V. Chawla. Will this paper increase your h-index? scientific impact prediction. In *WSDM '15*, pages 149–158, 2015.
[2] Y. Dong, R. A. Johnson, Y. Yang, and N. V. Chawla. Collaboration signatures reveal scientific impact. In *ASONAM '15*, pages 480–487, 2015.
[3] Y. Dong, J. Tang, T. Lou, B. Wu, and N. V. Chawla. How long will she call me? distribution, social theory and duration prediction. In *Machine Learning and Knowledge Discovery in Databases*, pages 16–31. Springer, 2013.
[4] Y. Dong, J. Tang, S. Wu, J. Tian, N. V. Chawla, J. Rao, and H. Cao. Link prediction and recommendation across heterogeneous social networks. In *ICDM'12*, pages 181–190, 2012.
[5] Y. Dong, Y. Yang, J. Tang, Y. Yang, and N. V. Chawla. Inferring user demographics and social strategies in mobile social networks. In *KDD'14*, pages 15–24, 2014.
[6] Y. Dong, J. Zhang, J. Tang, N. V. Chawla, and B. Wang. Coupledlp: Link prediction in coupled networks. In *KDD '15*, pages 199–208, 2015.
[7] M. Girvan and M. E. J. Newman. Community structure in social and biological networks. *PNAS*, 99(12):7821–7826, 2002.
[8] D. Kempe, J. Kleinberg, and E. Tardos. Maximizing the spread of influence through a social network. In *KDD'03*, pages 137–146, 2003.
[9] D. Liben-Nowell and J. Kleinberg. The link prediction problem for social networks. In *CIKM '03*, pages 556–559, 2003.
[10] R. Pastor-Satorras and A. Vespignani. Epidemic spreading in scale-free networks. *Physical review letters*, 86(14):3200, 2001.

WSDM 2016 February 22-25, 2016, San Francisco, CA, USA

ACM ISBN 978-1-4503-3716-8/16/02.
DOI: http://dx.doi.org/10.1145/2835776.2855087

Feature Generation and Selection on the Heterogeneous Graph for Music Recommendation

Chun Guo
School of Informatics and Computing
Indiana University Bloomington
Bloomington, IN, USA, 47405
chunguo@indiana.edu

ABSTRACT

In the past decade, online music streaming services (MSS), e.g. Pandora and Spotify, experienced exponential growth. The sheer volume of music collection makes music recommendation increasingly important and the related algorithms are well-documented. In prior studies, most algorithms employed content-based model (CBM) and/or collaborative filtering (CF) [3]. The former one focuses on acoustic/signal features extracted from audio content, and the latter one investigates music rating and user listening history. Actually, MSS generated user data present significant heterogeneity. Taking user-music relationship as an example, *comment*, *bookmark*, and *listening history* may potentially contribute to music recommendation in very different ways. Furthermore, user and music can be implicitly related via more complex relationships, e.g., *user-play-artist-perform-music*. From this viewpoint, user-user, music-music or user-music relationship can be much more complex than the classical CF approach assumes.

For these reasons, we model music metadata and MSS generated user data in the form of a heterogeneous graph, where 6 different types of nodes interact through 16 types of relationships. We can propose many recommendation hypotheses based on the ways users and songs are connected on this graph, in the form of meta paths. The recommendation problem, then, becomes a (supervised) random walk problem on the heterogeneous graph [2]. Unlike previous heterogeneous graph mining studies, the constructed heterogeneous graph in our case is more complex, and manually formulated meta-path based hypotheses cannot guarantee good performance. In the pilot study [2], we proposed to automatically extract all the potential meta paths within a given length on the heterogeneous graph scheme, evaluate their recommendation performance on the training data, and build a learning to rank model with the best ones. Results show that the new method can significantly enhance the recommendation performance.

However, there are two problems with this approach: 1. including the individually best performing meta paths in the learning to rank model neglects the dependency between features; 2. it is very time consuming to calculate graph based features. Traditional feature selection methods would only work if all feature values are readily available, which would make this recommendation approach highly inefficient. In this proposal, we attempt to address these two problems by adapting the feature selection for ranking method (FSR) proposed by Geng, Liu, Qin, and Li [1]. This feature selection method developed specifically for learning to rank tasks evaluates features based on their importance when used alone, and their similarity between each other. Applying this method on the whole set of meta-path based features would be very costly. Alternatively, we use it on sub meta paths that are shared components of multiple full meta paths. We start from sub meta paths of length=1 and only the ones selected by FSR have the chance to grow to sub meta paths of length=2. Then we repeat this process until the selected sub meta paths grow to full ones. During each step, we drop some meta paths because they contain unselected sub meta paths. Finally, we will derive a subset of the original meta paths and save time by extracting values for fewer features. In our preliminary experiment, the proposed method outperforms the original FSR algorithm in both efficiency and effectiveness.

Keywords

Music Recommendation, Meta-Path, Feature Selection

1. REFERENCES

[1] X. Geng, T.-Y. Liu, T. Qin, and H. Li. Feature selection for ranking. In *Proceedings of the 30th Annual International ACM SIGIR Conference on Research and Development in Information Retrieval*, SIGIR '07, pages 407–414, New York, NY, USA, 2007. ACM.

[2] C. Guo and X. Liu. Automatic feature generation on heterogeneous graph for music recommendation. In *Proceedings of the 38th International ACM SIGIR Conference on Research and Development in Information Retrieval*, SIGIR '15, pages 807–810, New York, NY, USA, 2015. ACM.

[3] Y. Song, S. Dixon, and M. Pearce. A survey of music recommendation systems and future perspectives. In *Proceedings of the 9th International Symposium on Computer Music Modeling and Retrieval*, CMMR '12, pages 395–410, 2012.

WSDM 2016 February 22-25, 2016, San Francisco, CA, USA

ACM ISBN 978-1-4503-3716-8/16/02.
DOI: http://dx.doi.org/10.1145/2835776.2855088

Temporal Formation and Evolution of Online Communities

Hossein Fani
Faculty of Computer Science, University of New Brunswick, NB, Canada
Laboratory for Systems, Software and Semantics (LS^3), Ryerson University, ON, Canada
hosseinfani@gmail.com

ABSTRACT

Prediction of users' behaviour, interests, and influence are of interest within the realm of online social networks due to the wide range of applications, such as personalized recommendations and marketing campaigns. However, the proposed approaches are not always scalable to a large number of users and huge amount of content generated by them. Community-level studies are introduced to help facilitate scalability, among others, highlighting the main properties of the network at a higher collective macro level.

The state-of-the-art community detection methods mainly focused on identification of online communities and possible impacts or influence relationships from several aspects, e.g. communities of users that are formed based on shared relationships and topological similarities, or communities that consist of users that share similar content. However, there are not much existing research work studying detection of communities that simultaneously share topical and temporal similarities. For example, users who contribute to the topic '*Julian Assange Allegations by Swedish Prosecutors*' might show their inclination with a week time delay due to their interest priority. The community of users who are interested in the topic *this week* could be different from those who become interested in the *following week*. In our proposed method we identify user communities that have similar temporal dispositions according to their topics of interest. To this end, we apply multivariate time series analysis to measure the inter-user similarity. The proposed approach will be able to identify the following types of communities: *i)* the community of users who are only interested in a given topic and in a same time period; therefore, supporting topic-driven community detection. *ii)* the communities of users who are interested in a same topic but in different time periods; hence, supporting temporality in the community detection process.

Furthermore, the existing studies have not explored the *causation* relationship between the communities, named inter-community causation, i.e. a community, the *cause*, makes other community, the *effect*, happen. Causation provides systematic explanation as to why communities are formed and helps to predict future communities. For example, a community around the topic '*Julian Assange and the WikiLeaks*' gives rise to intense discussions around topics such as 'Internet Censorship' and '*Blocking Wikileaks*' in the online social networks and cause a new corresponding communities. Since causality is a temporally asymmetric relation, i.e., the cause *precedes* the effect, we employ Granger concept of causality, G-causality for short, to incorporates precedence through time series. Assuming no hypothesis about the data, Granger's method sits in complete harmony with our community detection model and forms a coherent framework besides its simplicity, robustness, extendability. Our final G-causality-based model will be a weighted directed acyclic graph (DAG) of communities. In this graph, the edge direction represent the cause to effect relationship of its adjacent communities. Figure 1 shows two samples of causation patterns amongst communities.

To sum up, we address two main questions in this research proposal: *i)* how can communities with similar topical and temporal behaviours be identified, and *ii)* how can causation relation between different online communities be detected and modeled. We model users' behaviour towards topics of interest through multivariate time series to identify like-minded communities. Further, we use Granger's concept of causality to infer causation between detected communities from corresponding users' time series. We evaluate the proposed approach empirically on a dataset of tweets. We assess the performance of the proposed community detection methods with the state of the art and verify the causal model through its prediction accuracy.

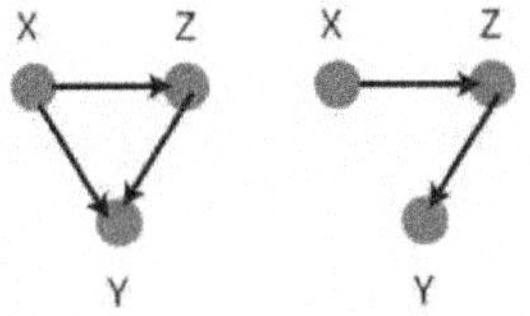

Figure 1: Two possible causation triads

WSDM 2016 February 22-25, 2016, San Francisco, CA, USA

ACM ISBN 978-1-4503-3716-8/16/02.

DOI: http://dx.doi.org/10.1145/2835776.2855089

Mining the Web for Intelligent Problem Solving for Programmers

Xin Rong
School of Information
University of Michigan
Ann Arbor, MI, 48109
ronxin@umich.edu

ABSTRACT

Programming can be hard to learn and master. Novice programmers often find themselves struggling with terminology, concepts, or different solutions to the same problem with little clue on how to choose the best one. Professional programmers often spend a considerable amount of time learning to use third-party libraries, APIs, or an unfamiliar piece of code. Although programmers can turn to search engines or question-and-answer websites for help, the problem solving process can often take multiple iterations and can be time-consuming. An integrated system that can recognize a programmer's difficulties and provide contextualized solutions is thus desirable, as it may significantly reduce the amount of manual effort required in the loop of troubleshooting.

Ideally, a programmer should be able to interact with such an intelligent system using natural language, in a way similar to how they document code or communicate with peers. However, using automatic natural language processing techniques to address programming questions is very difficult, mainly due to the following reasons: (1) the terms and common expressions vary greatly across different domains and individual programmers, making it difficult to associate relevant concepts together; (2) the solution to the user's trouble in programming often requires multiple steps or different resources, which requires deep understanding of the relations or dependencies of the possible solutions, as well as the user's personal capability of handling those solutions; (3) the documents in the training data usually include a mixture of general-domain expressions with mentions of variables, functions, and classes, as well as source code, making low-level text processing difficult; (4) the evaluation of the system generally requires skilled experts to provide ground truth, which is expensive and often unreliable.

We address the above difficulties and build an intelligent programming helper system by mining the massive data available online related to programming, including question-and-answer websites, tutorials, blogs, and code repositories. In specific, the study involves three important components. First, we use information extraction techniques to extract common programming tasks, issues, and solutions from the Web data, and establish connections between these extracted elements by leveraging their discrete or distributed representations (e.g., using neural embedding models). Such techniques have been shown to be useful in helping general users solve problems that require interactions with a complex computer software application through the interface of natural language [2, 1]. Second, we study how to handle complicated problems that require multiple steps to solve. The existing troubleshooting instances documented online are collectively modeled as a heterogeneous network, on which the random walk paths can be exploited to recommend solutions [3]. Third, we study how to personalize the problem-solving process for users with varying levels of skills and background knowledge. In particular, each user's past adoptions of technologies and the adoption behavior in his/her social community can be jointly leveraged to provide the appropriate recommendations of technologies and may even promote innovations (e.g., new algorithms) in the process [4]. Collectively, these three components form an integral solution to computer-assisted problem solving for programmers driven by big data, and may have impact on various different domains, including information extraction, language modeling, natural language understanding, automatic problem solving, and social network analysis.

WSDM 2016 February 22-25, 2016, San Francisco, CA, USA

ACM ISBN 978-1-4503-3716-8/16/02.

DOI: http://dx.doi.org/10.1145/2835776.2855091

CCS Concepts

•Information systems → Data mining; •Software and its engineering → *Software development techniques;*

Keywords

Software Engineering; Language Modeling; Human-computer Interaction

References

[1] Eytan Adar, Mira Dontcheva, and Gierad Laput. Commandspace: Modeling the relationships between tasks, descriptions and features. In *User interface software and technology*, pages 167–176. ACM, 2014.

[2] Adam Fourney, Richard Mann, and Michael Terry. Query-feature graphs: bridging user vocabulary and system functionality. In *User interface software and technology*, pages 207–216. ACM, 2011.

[3] Ni Lao, Tom Mitchell, and William W Cohen. Random walk inference and learning in a large scale knowledge base. In *EMNLP*, pages 529–539. Association for Computational Linguistics, 2011.

[4] Xin Rong and Qiaozhu Mei. Diffusion of innovations revisited: from social network to innovation network. In *CIKM*, pages 499–508. ACM, 2013.

Optimizing Search Interactions within Professional Social Networks

Nikita Spirin
Department of Computer Science, University of Illinois at Urbana-Champaign
Thomas M. Siebel Center for Computer Science, 201 N Goodwin Ave, Urbana, IL 61801, USA
spirin2@illinois.edu

ABSTRACT

To help users cope with the scale and influx of new information, professional social networks (PSNs) provide a search functionality. However, most of the search engines within PSNs today only support keyword queries and basic faceted search capabilities overlooking serendipitous network exploration and search for relationships between entities. This results in siloed information and a limited search space. My thesis is that we must redesign all major elements of a search user interface, such as input, control, and informational, to enable more effective search interactions within PSNs. I will introduce new insights and algorithms supporting the thesis.

Keywords

Search User Interaction; Query Log Analysis; Online Social Network; Job Search; Entity Search; Snippet; Filtering

Categories and Subject Descriptors

H.3.3 [**Information Search and Retrieval**]: Information filtering, Retrieval models, Search process, Selection process

1. KEY CONTRIBUTIONS

A large scale analysis of Facebook Graph Search (FBGS) query logs [3]. I examined how search behavior differs for different query types, how it changes for users from various demographic groups, and how it depends on the graph distance between a searcher and a person to be searched. The analysis revealed new findings and suggested many design implications: users search more for friends using NEQs and for non-friends using SQs, which shows their complementary roles in enabling effective PSN search; structured query (SQ) usage behavior has a wider variation across different demographics, and, hence, it makes sense to direct search personalization efforts on SQs. The crux of this work is that users do benefit from more control and highly interactive query suggestions — they engage in a new type of search behavior (exploratory search for non-friends).

WSDM 2016 February 22-25, 2016, San Francisco, CA, USA

ACM ISBN 978-1-4503-3716-8/16/02.

DOI: http://dx.doi.org/10.1145/2835776.2855092

An algorithm for relevance-aware search results filtering [2], which improves the quality of search results sorted by an attribute value (e.g. likes, date, salary). It is based on the dynamic programming, directly optimizes a given search quality metric, and, therefore, theoretically optimal. According to the experiments, it does outperform all baselines and lead to 2-4% increase in search quality.

An algorithm for snippets generation for job search. It allows to generate informative snippets that contain the key information (resp. and req. for a job) right on a SERP and help users make clicks mostly on relevant results. Plus, it helps optimize content for mobile devices and avoid irregularities of job postings coming from multiple websites by converting them into a standardized structured representation. The algorithm leverages the power of big data to minimize supervision required for model training, and, hence, could be easily deployed internationally. Basedon a series of offline and online experiments: (1) the algorithm achieves high extraction accuracy (86% precision at 94% coverage for English [1] and 97% precision at 100% coverage by a highly-tuned enterprise-grade model for Russian); (2) structured snippets improve the majority of user-centric search quality metrics (e.g. apply rate conditioned on click is 13% and total applies 1.6% up; number of short clicks by 5.5% down).

A user study analyzing the effectiveness of *delta*-snippets for entity search. The common belief is that query-biased snippets are the most effective. However, it is not necessarily the case for entity search since there is less need to duplicate the information from a query in a snippet (all results exactly match the query). By reasoning from basic principles, I introduce the concept of *delta*-snippet, which shows information complementary to the query and more effectively uses a screen space (esp. on mobile), and investigate it via a user study. I examine how users interact with *delta*-snippets and how it changes users' productivity.

2. REFERENCES

[1] N. Spirin and K. Karahalios. Unsupervised approach to generate informative structured snippets for job search engines. WWW '13.

[2] N. Spirin, M. Kuznetsov, J. Kiseleva, Y. Spirin, and P. Izhutov. Relevance-aware filtering of tuples sorted by an attribute value via direct optimization of search quality metrics. SIGIR'15.

[3] N. V. Spirin, J. He, M. Develin, K. G. Karahalios, and M. Boucher. People search within an online social network: Large scale analysis of facebook graph search query logs. CIKM '14.

Author Index

www.ingramcontent.com/pod-product-compliance
Ingram Content Group UK Ltd.
Pitfield, Milton Keynes, MK11 3LW, UK
UKHW051420290926
15471UKWH00009B/1699

9 781450 344999